The International THESAURUS of QUOTATIONS

Revised and Updated

Compiled by
Eugene Ehrlich and Marshall DeBruhl

HarperPerennial
A Division of HarperCollinsPublishers

HarperCollins books may be purchased for educational, business or sales promotional use. For information, please write: Special Markets Department, HarperCollins Publishers, Inc., 10 East 53rd Street, New York, NY 10022.

First edition compiled by Rhoda Thomas Tripp.

SECOND EDITION

Designed by C. Linda Dingler

ISBN 0-06-273373-7

---

00 ❖/RRD 10 9 8 7 6

Contents

Publisher's Preface v

How to Use the Indexes vii

International Thesaurus of Quotations 1

Index of Authors and Sources 781

Index of Key Words 817

Index of Categories 993

Publisher's Preface

Over a century ago Peter Mark Roget invented a method of classifying words by meaning and called the collection that he made a "thesaurus." His book quickly proved to be the most precise and useful compendium of synonyms ever devised. Frequently revised to keep pace with a changing language, it has long held a place beside the dictionary as a basic tool for speakers and writers.

In *The International Thesaurus of Quotations*, we have tried to create a book that performs with quotations the same service that *Roget's International Thesaurus* performs with words and phrases. This new reference book, originally compiled at our request by Mrs. Tripp, and now revised and updated by Eugene Ehrlich and Marshall DeBruhl, is primarily intended for those who want to use quotations, rather than simply to read them or recall them to mind. Like its model, it is for persons who have an idea and who are looking for the means to express it exactly and effectively. Although its indexes offer the key to finding half-remembered quotations, it is particularly designed for a generation that seldom memorizes literary passages. Its users will very likely turn to it less often to recall a familiar saying than to find fresh words that eloquently express and enlarge ideas of their own.

In order to make the contents of this book readily accessible to that purpose, we have adopted the basic principles of Roget's *Thesaurus*. Certain features of his classification scheme, however, are not suited to the cataloguing of quotations. An alphabetical arrangement of subject headings, for example, provides readier access to quotations than any adaptation that we might have made of Roget's synopsis of categories. At the same time, we have found it advantageous to remain faithful to those qualities of Roget's book which, in our estimation, account for the effectiveness with which it achieves its objectives. These qualities are comprehensiveness, timeliness, and precision, which together add up to utility.

The criterion of utility demanded that we make our thesaurus of quotations as much a practical tool as Roget's *Thesaurus*. Since both books are primarily intended for the convenience of speakers and writers, we had to decide at the outset what kinds of quotations would be most used today in writing and formal speech. Almost any quotation might, of course, find some occasion for use, but a book intended for quick and frequent reference must be kept to a handy size. It was evident that, although comprehensiveness was to be one of our goals, we must find a stricter definition for it than mere inclusiveness.

Examination of the larger standard anthologies was helpful in showing us that we could well do without whole classes of material, such as slogans, titles of books and songs, and old saws. Much more reluctantly we decided to eliminate phrases in favor of quotations in complete sentences. Although this decision was dictated mainly by consideration of space, we felt that familiar phrases, however colorful or apt, quickly degenerate into clichés that tend to ossify speech rather than enliven it. Omitting phrases enabled us to include sixteen thousand quotations, each of which makes a complete, though concise, statement of a point of view about some aspect of life.

Another characteristic of utility that we hoped to achieve in this book was timeliness, in its broad sense of relevance to the concerns of present-day users. Our thesaurus, if it were to be useful to a wide range of speakers and writers in a generation preoccupied with the present moment, would have to give full attention to its own age without being obsessed by it. More than a third of the quotations in this book come from our own century. Many of the book's most contemporary-sounding observations were, however, made by men of other centuries, some as far back as the time of Solon. Scores of penetrating and pungent comments have been gathered from figures who are represented in most anthologies only by pious sentiments. Nevertheless, piety has its spokesmen here, as does every shade of opinion on philosophical, political, and social topics. And we have retained the thousands of familiar quotations that have something to say to our time.

In keeping with the global awareness of the reading public today, we have included quotations, both old and new, from the literatures of many countries. Where up-to-date translations were not available, we asked translators to supply them. In addition to quotations, there are proverbs from many peoples, some not previously represented in standard books of quotations.

An important aspect of timeliness in a modern

book of quotations is, simply, time. Because time is a scarce and highly valued commodity among today's readers and audiences, writers and speakers must perforce be sparing in the demands that they make upon it. Lengthy quotations, therefore, are not in favor, and we have included none in this thesaurus. There are very few that exceed fifty words in length, and most are considerably shorter. In order to insure, however, that users of the quotations can check them if they wish against their original context, we have given a full citation of the source in every case where that source could be discovered.

The third characteristic of utility in which we hoped to match Roget's *Thesaurus* was precision. The key to the success of the Roget system is the exactness with which it classified words by subject. Since our thesaurus is intended primarily to aid those who in searching for quotations can best find them through subject categories, it was essential that we classify each quotation strictly by its meaning. This seemed an obvious aim for any collection of quotations arranged by subject, but investigation of other topically arranged anthologies showed us that their quotations were often included under subject headings that reflected key words rather than the meanings of the quotations as a whole. (For example, the well-known proverb "In the country of the blind the one-eyed man is king" is usually placed under the heading Blindness, though the proverb is obviously not concerned with physical affliction.) We tried to avoid this pitfall by examining the basic sense of each quotation apart from its apparent subject matter, which is often quite different. Many of the greatest sayings, however, do not have absolute meanings. They owe their universality to their ambiguity, their capacity to hold different meanings for different people and ages. Inevitably, users of this thesaurus will quarrel with our decisions in categorizing certain quotations. We hope that the profusion of cross-references we have made between categories will enable them to find every quotation that bears any relation to a given subject. The indexes of key words and authors should lead users to familiar quotations.

A word should be said about our solution to the problem of quotations that have more than one source. The origin of most proverbs is, by their nature, untraceable. We have generally cited the earliest sources of which we are aware, but we have not hesitated to choose later versions of the same ideas when they seemed more felicitously worded. We followed this same practice with sayings attributed to individuals.

As we have said, our intention has been to construct a reference book for speakers and writers that would worthily complement *Roget's International Thesaurus*. In so doing we have deliberately focused our attention on a somewhat strictly defined goal. Happily, the acute perceptions and lively words of thoughtful and witty men and women have a life of their own that refuses to be confined by lexicographic theories. We hope that users of this book will find it as helpful as we have tried to make it. We would be disappointed, however, if they could not take equal satisfaction in browsing through its pages for the casual pleasures they will find there.

Mrs. Tripp was aided by the persons listed below in gathering, indexing, and classifying the quotations for the first edition of this book. We extend our thanks to them. In most instances where translators are not specified, French translations are by Miss Holder or Mrs. Hatvary, Latin translations by Miss Vaughan.

Geraldyne Addison
Ernestine Samuels Austen
Joan Cenedella
Arlene Donly
George Flynn
Michael Gelber
Zachary Goodyear
Maureen Grice
Roy Harris
Bertha Hatvary
Walter Hayward
Maryse Holder
Gloria Jordan
Geraldine Koepke
Margaret Miner
Samuel Mitnick
Robert Nero
Charles North
Gail Quinn
Michael Rose
Richard Schlesinger
Sharon Schlesinger
William Schwartz
Susan Simon
Victoria Simons
William Stern
Anne Vaughan
Lewis Warsh

James B. Simpson's *Contemporary Quotations*, published by the Thomas Y. Crowell Company in 1964, was used as a source for some of the quotations dated 1950 and later.

How to Use the Indexes

If you have an idea and want a quotation that expresses it, you can find the quotation through any of these methods:

The Index of Authors and Sources This index lists persons quoted in this book. For example, if you want to find a quote by Eugene O'Neill, look up his name to find the categories in which his quotations can be found.

The Index of Key Words If you only half recall a saying, you can find the whole quotation by looking up one of its important words in the key word index. For example, if you are trying to locate "Man's loneliness is but his fear of life" but can only remember "loneliness," find "loneliness" in the key word index and scan the short versions of quotations until you find what you want. Then refer to the text for the full quotation.

The Index of Categories Here you will find an overview of all the subjects listed in the text, along with cross-references. If you look up "respectability," for example, you will find the number of a category that lists quotations referring to respectability (category 809) and a cross-reference to "propriety" (category 749).

Numbers after index entries refer to categories and paragraphs in the main section of this book, not to page numbers. The part of the number before the decimal point refers to the category in which the quotation you are looking up is found. The part of the number after the decimal point refers to the paragraph within the category. One of the entries in the Index of Authors and Sources, for example, you see:

Angelou, Maya (1928–). American writer, musician, teacher. 221.3; 422.2; 775.2; 927.1; 978.5; 987.1; 992.2

This means that you will find the first quotation by Maya Angelou in third paragraph of category 221—the last one is in the second paragraph of category 992.

A

1. ABILITY

See also 311. EXCELLENCE; 962. TALENT; 1037. VOCATIONS

1. Natural abilities are like natural plants, that need pruning by study; and studies themselves do give forth directions too much at large, except they be bounded in by experience.

FRANCIS BACON, "OF STUDIES," *ESSAYS* (1625)

2. We may complain and cavil at the anarchy which is the amateur's natural element, but in soberness we must agree that if the amateur did not exist it would be necessary to invent him.

JACQUES BARZUN, "THE INDISPENSABLE AMATEUR," *CRITICAL QUESTIONS* (1982)

3. As many languages as he has, as many friends, as many arts and trades, so many times is he a man.

EMERSON, "CULTURE," *THE CONDUCT OF LIFE* (1860)

4. Everyone must row with the oars he has.

ENGLISH PROVERB

5. The same man cannot well be skilled / in everything; each has his special excellence.

EURIPIDES, *RHESUS* (C. 455–441 B.C.), TR. RICHMOND LATTIMORE

6. In a world as empirical as ours, a youngster who does not know what he is good *at* will not be sure what he is good *for*.

EDGAR Z. FRIEDENBERG, "EMOTIONAL DEVELOPMENT IN ADOLESCENCE," *THE VANISHING ADOLESCENT* (1959)

7. 'Tis skill, not strength, that governs a ship.

THOMAS FULLER, M.D., *GNOMOLOGIA* (1732), 5116

8. Most do violence to their natural aptitude, and thus attain superiority in nothing.

BALTASAR GRACIÁN, *THE ART OF WORLDLY WISDOM* (1647), 24, TR. JOSEPH JACOBS

9. Skill and confidence are an unconquered army.

GEORGE HERBERT, *JACULA PRUDENTUM* (1651)

10. One should stick to the sort of thing for which one was made; / I tried to be an herbalist, / Whereas I should keep to the butcher's trade.

LA FONTAINE, "THE HORSE AND THE WOLF," *FABLES* (1668–94), TR. MARIANNE MOORE

11. It is easier to appear worthy of positions that we have not got, than of those that we have.

LA ROCHEFOUCAULD, *MAXIMS* (1665), TR. KENNETH PRATT

12. Our vanity desires that what we do best should be considered what is hardest for us.

NIETZSCHE, *BEYOND GOOD AND EVIL* (1886), 143, TR. WALTER KAUFMANN

13. Skills vary with the man. We must tread a straight path and strive by that which is born in us.

PINDAR, *ODES* (5TH C. B.C.). NEMEA 1, TR. RICHMOND LATTIMORE

2. ABSENCE

See also 673. PARTING

1. The heart may think it knows better: the senses know that absence blots people out. We have really no absent friends.

ELIZABETH BOWEN, *THE DEATH OF THE HEART* (1938), 2.2

2. Our hours in love have wings; in absence crutches.

COLLEY CIBBER, *XERXES* (1699), 4.3

3. It takes time for the absent to assume their true shape in our thoughts. After death they take on a firmer outline and then cease to change.

COLETTE, "THE CAPTAIN," *EARTHLY PARADISE* (1966), 1, ED. ROBERT PHELPS

4. How great love is, presence best trial makes, / But absence tries how long this love will be.

JOHN DONNE, "VALEDICTION: OF THE BOOK," *SONGS AND SONNETS* (1633)

5. Those who are absent are always wrong.

ENGLISH PROVERB

6. Absence sharpens love, presence strengthens it.

THOMAS FULLER, M.D., *GNOMOLOGIA* (1732), 755

7. When you part from your friend, you grieve not; / For that which you love most in him may be clearer

in his absence, as the mountain to the climber is clearer from the plain.

KAHLIL GIBRAN, "ON FRIENDSHIP," *THE PROPHET* (1923)

8. Sometimes, when one person is missing, the whole world seems depopulated.

LAMARTINE, *PREMIÈRES MÉDITATIONS POÉTIQUES* (1820), I

9. Absence lessens ordinary passions and augments great ones, as the wind blows out a candle and makes a fire blaze.

LA ROCHEFOUCAULD, *MAXIMS* (1665), TR. KENNETH PRATT

10. Absences are a good influence in love and keep it bright and delicate.

ROBERT LOUIS STEVENSON, TITLE ESSAY, I, *VIRGINIBUS PUERISQUE* (1881)

11. Greater things are believed of those who are absent.

TACITUS, *HISTORIES* (A.D. 104–109), 2.83

12. Absence makes the heart grow frozen, not fonder.

JUDITH VIORST, *NECESSARY LOSSES* (1986)

ABSTINENCE

See 865.SELF-DENIAL

3. THE ABSURD

See also 4. ABSURDITY; 30. ALIENATION; 317. EXISTENTIALISM; 573. MEANING

1. If life must not be taken too seriously—then so neither must death.

SAMUEL BUTLER, (D. 1902), "DEATH," *NOTE-BOOKS* (1912)

2. The absurd is essentially a divorce. It lies in neither of the elements compared; it is born of their confrontation.

ALBERT CAMUS, *THE MYTH OF SISYPHUS* (1955), TR. JUSTIN O'BRIEN

3. In a world where everything is ridiculous, nothing can be ridiculed. You cannot unmask a mask.

G. K. CHESTERTON, "ON THE COMIC SPIRIT," *GENERALLY SPEAKING* (1928)

4. Life is a jest, and all things show it; / I thought so once, but now I know it.

JOHN GAY, "MY OWN EPITAPH," *FABLES* (1727–38)

5. Unextinguished laughter shakes the skies.

HOMER, *ILIAD* (9TH C. B.C.), 1.771, TR. ALEXANDER POPE

6. Life has to be given a meaning because of the obvious fact that it has no meaning.

HENRY MILLER, "CREATIVE DEATH," *THE WISDOM OF THE HEART* (1941)

7. Man's "progress" is but a gradual discovery that his questions have no meaning.

SAINT-EXUPÉRY, *THE WISDOM OF THE SANDS* (1948), 39, TR. STUART GILBERT

8. The more absurd life is, the more insupportable death is.

JEAN-PAUL SARTRE, *THE WORDS* (1964), I

9. God made everything out of the void, but the void shows through.

PAUL VALÉRY, *MAUVAISES PENSÉES ET AUTRES* (1941)

4. ABSURDITY

See also 3. THE ABSURD; 820. RIDICULE

1. At any streetcorner the feeling of absurdity can strike any man in the face. As it is, in its distressing nudity, in its light without effulgence, it is elusive.

ALBERT CAMUS, *THE MYTH OF SISYPHUS* (1955), TR. JUSTIN O'BRIEN

2. There is no idea, no fact, which could not be vulgarized and presented in a ludicrous light.

DOSTOYEVSKY, "MR. —BOV AND THE QUESTION OF ART," *POLNOYE SOBRANIYE SOCHINYENI (COMPLETE COLLECTED WORKS,* 1895), V. 9

3. The privilege of absurdity; to which no living creature is subject but man only.

THOMAS HOBBES, *LEVIATHAN* (1651), 1.5

4. There is but one step from the sublime to the ridiculous.

NAPOLEON I, AFTER THE RETREAT FROM RUSSIA, DECEMBER 1812

5. Life is full of infinite absurdities, which, strangely enough, do not even need to appear plausible, since they are true.

LUIGI PIRANDELLO, *SIX CHARACTERS IN SEARCH OF AN AUTHOR* (1921), I, TR. EDWARD STORER

6. Look for the ridiculous in everything and you will find it.

JULES RENARD, *JOURNAL,* FEBRUARY 1890, TR.-ED. LOUISE BOGAN AND ELIZABETH ROGET

7. No one is laughable who laughs at himself.

SENECA, *DE CONSTANTIA SAPIENTIS* (1ST C.)

ACCIDENT

See 116. CHANCE

ACCOMPLISHMENT

See 1. ABILITY; 6. ACHIEVEMENT

5. ACCUSATION

See also 206. CRITICISM; 515. JUDGING OTHERS; 905. SLANDER

1. Accusing is proving, where Malice and Force sit judges.

THOMAS FULLER, M.D., *GNOMOLOGIA* (1732), 758

2. Even doubtful accusations leave a stain behind them.

THOMAS FULLER, M.D., *GNOMOLOGIA* (1732), 1395

3. It is honorable to be accused by those who deserve to be accused.

LATIN PROVERB

6. ACHIEVEMENT

See also 33. AMBITION; 55. ASPIRATION; 945. SUCCESS

1. It is not the going out of port, but the coming in, that determines the success of a voyage.

HENRY WARD BEECHER, *PROVERBS FROM PLYMOUTH PULPIT* (1887)

2. By their fruits ye shall know them.

BIBLE, MATTHEW 7:20

3. Achievement, n. The death of endeavor and the birth of disgust.

AMBROSE BIERCE, *THE DEVIL'S DICTIONARY* (1881–1911)

4. To know a man, observe how he wins his object, rather than how he loses it; for when we fail our pride supports us, when we succeed, it betrays us.

CHARLES CALEB COLTON, *LACON* (1825), 1.265

5. The house praises the carpenter.

EMERSON, *JOURNALS*, 1836

6. The reward of a thing well done is to have done it.

EMERSON, "NEW ENGLAND REFORMERS," *ESSAYS: SECOND SERIES* (1844)

7. If you tell [count] every step, you will make a long journey of it.

THOMAS FULLER, M.D., *GNOMOLOGIA* (1732), 2793

8. Students who don't want to get anywhere are sure to get somewhere.

GÜNTER GRASS, *LOCAL ANAESTHETIC* (1970)

9. Back of every achievement is a proud wife and a surprised mother-in-law.

BROOKS HAYS, *NEW YORK HERALD TRIBUNE*, DEC. 2, 1961

10. When you feel how depressingly / slowly you climb, / it's well to remember that / Things Take Time.

PIET HEIN, "T.T.T.," *GROOKS* (1966)

11. A man dies still if he has done nothing, as one who has done much.

HOMER, *ILIAD* (9TH C. B.C.), 9.320, TR. RICHMOND LATTIMORE

12. Thou shalt ever joy at eventide if thou spend the day fruitfully.

THOMAS À KEMPIS, *THE IMITATION OF CHRIST* (1426), 1.25

13. The heights by great men reached and kept / Were not attained by sudden flight, / But they, while their companions slept, / Were toiling upward in the night.

LONGFELLOW, "THE LADDER OF SAINT AUGUSTINE" (1858), 10

14. His enemies said he [Robert Kennedy] was consumed with selfish ambition, a ruthless opportunist exploiting his brother's legend. But he was too passionate and too vulnerable ever to be the cool and confident operator his brother was.

JACK NEWFIELD, *ROBERT KENNEDY* (1969)

15. Since it is not granted us to live long, let us transmit to posterity some memorial that we have at least lived.

PLINY THE YOUNGER, *LETTERS* (C. 97–110), 3.7, TR. WILLIAM MELMOTH AND W. M. L. HUTCHINSON

16. Mighty rivers can easily be leaped at their source.

PUBLILIUS SYRUS, *MORAL SAYINGS* (1ST C. B.C.), 442, TR. DARIUS LYMAN

17. Let the end try the man.

SHAKESPEARE, *2 HENRY IV* (1597–98), 2.2.50

18. Down the stairs and up Fifth Avenue. Hippety-hop, I'm a Bunny!

GLORIA STEINEM, "I WAS A PLAYBOY BUNNY," *OUTRAGEOUS ACTS AND EVERYDAY REBELLIONS* (1983)

19. The awareness of the ambiguity of one's highest achievements (as well as one's deepest failures) is a definite symptom of maturity.

PAUL TILLICH, *TIME*, MAY 17, 1963

20. To achieve great things we must live as though we were never going to die.

VAUVENARGUES, *REFLECTIONS AND MAXIMS* (1746), 142, TR. F. G. STEVENS

7. ACQUAINTANCES

See also 152. COMPANY; 365. FRIENDSHIP

1. Acquaintance, n. A person whom we know well enough to borrow from, but not well enough to lend to.

AMBROSE BIERCE, *THE DEVIL'S DICTIONARY* (1881–1911)

2. How casually and unobservedly we make all our most valued acquaintances.

EMERSON, *JOURNALS*, 1833

3. There is a scarcity of friendship, but not of friends.

THOMAS FULLER, M.D., *GNOMOLOGIA* (1732), 4880

4. If a man does not make new acquaintance as he advances through life, he will soon find himself left alone.

SAMUEL JOHNSON, QUOTED IN BOSWELL'S *LIFE OF SAMUEL JOHNSON*, APRIL 1775

5. What causes us to like new acquaintances is not so much weariness of our old ones, or the pleasure of change, as disgust at not being sufficiently admired by those who know us too well, and the hope of being admired more by those who do not know so much about us.

LA ROCHEFOUCAULD, *MAXIMS* (1665), TR. KENNETH PRATT

6. Chance acquaintances are sometimes the most memorable, for brief friendships have such definite starting and stopping points that they take on a quality of art, of a *whole* thing, which cannot be broken or spoiled.

WILLIAM SAROYAN, *CHANCE MEETINGS* (1978)

8. ACQUISITION

See also 403. GREED; 602. MONEY; 716. POSSESSION; 746. PROPERTY

1. Seek not proud riches, but such as thou mayest get justly, use soberly, distribute cheerfully, and leave contentedly.

FRANCIS BACON, "OF RICHES," *ESSAYS* (1625)

2. Hand, n. A singular instrument worn at the end of a human arm and commonly thrust into somebody's pocket.

AMBROSE BIERCE, *THE DEVIL'S DICTIONARY* (1881–1911)

3. It is easy to get everything you want, provided you first learn to do without the things you can not get.

ELBERT HUBBARD, *THE NOTE BOOK* (1927)

4. I glory / More in the cunning purchase of my wealth / Than in the glad possession.

BEN JONSON, *VOLPONE* (1605), I.I

5. With the catching end the pleasures of the chase.

ABRAHAM LINCOLN, SPEECH, JAN. 27, 1838

6. The collector walks with blinders on; he sees nothing but the prize. In fact, the acquisitive instinct is incompatible with true appreciation of beauty.

ANNE MORROW LINDBERGH, "A FEW SHELLS," *GIFT FROM THE SEA* (1955)

7. In the race for money some men may come first, but man comes last.

MARYA MANNES, IN *LIFE*, JUNE 12, 1964

8. An end to our getting is the only end to our losses.

PUBLILIUS SYRUS, *MORAL SAYINGS* (1ST C. B.C.), 661, TR. DARIUS LYMAN

9. [I]t is among the less privileged groups relatively new to leisure and consumption that the zest for possessions retains something of its pristine energy.

DAVID RIESMAN, *ABUNDANCE FOR WHAT?* (1964)

10. How could there be any question of acquiring or possessing, when the one thing needful for a man is to *become*—to *be* at last, and to die in the fullness of his being.

SAINT-EXUPÉRY, *THE WISDOM OF THE SANDS* (1948), 38, TR. STUART GILBERT

11. Accursed greed for gold, / To what dost thou not drive the heart of man?

VERGIL, *AENEID* (30-19 B.C.), 3.56, TR. T. H. DELABERE-MAY

9. ACTION

See also 10. ACTIVITY; 227. DEEDS; 504. INVOLVEMENT; 974. THEORY

1. In the arena of human life the honours and rewards fall to those who show their good qualities in action.

ARISTOTLE, *NICOMACHEAN ETHICS* (4TH C. B.C.), I.8, TR. J. A. K. THOMSON

2. A thought which does not result in an action is nothing much, and an action which does not proceed from a thought is nothing at all.

GEORGES BERNANOS, "FRANCE BEFORE THE WORLD OF TOMORROW," *THE LAST ESSAYS OF GEORGES BERNANOS* (1955), TR. JOAN AND BARRY ULANOV

3. Only the action that is moved by love for the good at hand has the hope of being responsible and generous.

WENDELL BERRY, "STANDING BY WORDS," *STANDING BY WORDS* (1983)

4. Action should culminate in wisdom.

BHAGAVADGITA, 4, TR. P. LAL

5. Unreal is action without discipline, charity without sympathy, ritual without devotion.

BHAGAVADGITA, 17, TR. P. LAL

6. It's all right to hesitate if you then go ahead.

BERTOLT BRECHT, PROLOGUE, *THE GOOD WOMAN OF SETZUAN* (1938–40), TR. BENTLEY AND APELMAN

7. ..."Men of action," whose minds are too busy with the day's work to see beyond it. They are essential men, we cannot do without them, and yet we must not allow all our vision to be bound by the limitations of "men of action."

PEARL S. BUCK, *WHAT AMERICA MEANS TO ME* (1943), 4

8. Think'st thou existence doth depend on time? / It doth; but actions are our epochs.

BYRON, *MANFRED* (1817), 2.1

9. He that has done nothing has known nothing.

THOMAS CARLYLE, "CORN-LAW RHYMES" (1832)

10. Once turn to practice, error and truth will no longer consort together.

THOMAS CARLYLE, "CORN-LAW RHYMES" (1832)

11. There can be no acting or doing of any kind, till it be recognized that there is a thing to be done; the thing once recognized, doing in a thousand shapes becomes possible.

THOMAS CARLYLE, *CHARTISM* (1839), 6

12. In action, be primitive; in foresight, a strategist.

RENÉ CHAR, *LEAVES OF HYPNOS*, 72, IN *HYPNOS WAKING* (1956), TR. JACKSON MATHEWS AND OTHERS

13. A man's most open actions have a secret side to them.

JOSEPH CONRAD, *UNDER WESTERN EYES* (1911), 1.2

14. One starts an action / Simply because one must do *something*.

T. S. ELIOT, *THE ELDER STATESMAN* (1958), 2

15. Begin and proceed on a settled and not-to-be-shaken conviction that but little is permitted to any man to do or to know, and if he complies with the first grand laws, he shall do well.

EMERSON, *JOURNALS*, 1832

16. No matter how much faculty of idle seeing a man has, the step from knowing to doing is rarely taken.

EMERSON, "POWER," *THE CONDUCT OF LIFE* (1860)

17. People who know how to act are never preachers.

EMERSON, *JOURNALS*, 1844

18. The materials of action are variable, but the use we make of them should be constant.

EPICTETUS, *DISCOURSES* (2ND C.), 2.5, TR. THOMAS W. HIGGINSON

19. Most men are in a coma when they are at rest and mad when they act.

EPICURUS, "VATICAN SAYINGS" (3RD C. B.C.), 11, IN *LETTERS, PRINCIPAL DOCTRINES, AND VATICAN SAYINGS*,, TR. RUSSEL M. GEER

20. Action is the proper fruit of knowledge.

THOMAS FULLER, M.D., *GNOMOLOGIA* (1732), 760

21. Can it be that action is active resignation? Something is trying to develop; it moves ever so slightly, and there comes your man of action and bashes in the hothouse windows.

GÜNTER GRASS, *LOCAL ANAESTHETIC* (1970)

22. Act quickly, think slowly.

GREEK PROVERB

23. In our era, the road to holiness necessarily passes through the world of action.

DAG HAMMARSKJÖLD, "1955," *MARKINGS* (1964), TR. LEIF SJOBERG AND W. H. AUDEN

24. Life is made up of constant calls to action, and we seldom have time for more than hastily contrived answers.

LEARNED HAND, SPEECH, NEW YORK CITY, JAN. 27, 1952

25. A life of action and danger moderates the dread of death. It not only gives us fortitude to bear pain, but teaches us at every step the precarious tenure on which we hold our present being.

WILLIAM HAZLITT, "ON THE FEAR OF DEATH," *TABLE TALK* (1821–22)

26. To dispose a soul to action we must upset its equilibrium.

ERIC HOFFER, *THE ORDEAL OF CHANGE* (1964), 5

27. Action will remove the doubt that theory cannot solve.

TEHYI HSIEH, *CHINESE EPIGRAMS INSIDE OUT AND PROVERBS* (1948), 1

28. The great end of life is not knowledge but action.

THOMAS HENRY HUXLEY, "TECHNICAL EDUCATION" (1877)

29. Act only on that maxim whereby you can at the same time will that it should become a universal law.

IMMANUEL KANT, *CRITIQUE OF PRACTICAL REASON* (1788)

30. Action [is] the great business of mankind, and the whole matter about which all laws are conversant.

JOHN LOCKE, *AN ESSAY CONCERNING HUMAN UNDERSTANDING* (1690), 2.22.10

31. Lust and force are the source of all our actions; lust causes voluntary actions, force involuntary ones.

PASCAL, *PENSÉES* (1670), 334, TR. W. F. TROTTER

32. The test of any man lies in action.

PINDAR, *ODES* (5TH C. B.C.), OLYMPIA 4, TR. RICHMOND LATTIMORE

33. We cannot withdraw our cards from the game. Were we as silent and as mute as stones, our very passivity would be an act.

JEAN-PAUL SARTRE, "PRÉSENTATION DES TEMPS MODERNES," *SITUATIONS* (1947–49), V. 2

34. I myself must mix with action, lest I wither by despair.

LORD TENNYSON, "LOCKSLEY HALL" (1842)

35. From the moment of birth we are immersed in action, and can only fitfully guide it by taking thought.

ALFRED NORTH WHITEHEAD, *SCIENCE AND THE MODERN WORLD* (1925), 12

10. ACTIVITY

See also 9. ACTION; 163. COMPULSIVENESS; 411. HASTE; 446. IDLENESS; 504. INVOLVEMENT; 533. LEISURE; 812. RESTLESSNESS

1. The quality of a life is determined by its activities.

ARISTOTLE, *NICOMACHEAN ETHICS* (4TH C. B.C.), 1.10, TR. J. A. K. THOMSON

2. Renunciation and activity both liberate, / but to work is better than to renounce.

BHAGAVADGITA, 5, TR. P. LAL

3. It is better to wear out than to rust out.

RICHARD CUMBERLAND, QUOTED IN GEORGE HORNE'S *SERMON ON THE DUTY OF CONTENDING FOR THE TRUTH* (1730–92)

4. The worshipper of energy is too physically energetic to see that he cannot explore certain higher fields until he is still.

CLARENCE DAY, *THIS SIMIAN WORLD* (1920), 5

5. The most active lives have so much routine as to preclude progress almost equally with the most inactive.

EMERSON, *JOURNALS,* 1833

6. He that is everywhere is nowhere.

THOMAS FULLER, M.D., *GNOMOLOGIA* (1732), 2176

7. The majority prove their worth by keeping busy. A busy life is the nearest thing to a purposeful life.

ERIC HOFFER, *THE ORDEAL OF CHANGE* (1964), 5

8. If you want work well done, select a busy man: the other kind has no time.

ELBERT HUBBARD, *THE NOTE BOOK* (1927)

9. Determine never to be idle. No person will have occasion to complain of the want of time who never loses any. It is wonderful how much may be done if we are always doing.

THOMAS JEFFERSON, LETTER TO MARTHA JEFFERSON, MAY 5, 1787

10. There is no kind of idleness by which we are so easily seduced as that which dignifies itself by the appearance of business.

SAMUEL JOHNSON, *THE IDLER* (1758–60), 48

11. Travel, trouble, music, art, / A kiss, a frock, a rhyme,— / I never said they feed my heart, / But still, they pass my time.

DOROTHY PARKER, "FAUTE DE MIEUX," *ENOUGH ROPE* (1926), 2

12. Our nature consists in motion; complete rest is death.

PASCAL, *PENSÉES* (1670), 129, TR. W. F. TROTTER

13. Men need some kind of external activity, because they are inactive within.

SCHOPENHAUER, "FURTHER PSYCHOLOGICAL OBSERVATIONS," *PARERGA AND PARALIPOMENA* (1851), TR. T. BAILEY SAUNDERS

14. Every one has time if he likes. Business runs after nobody: people cling to it of their own free will and think that to be busy is a proof of happiness.

SENECA, *LETTERS TO LUCILIUS* (1ST C.), 106.1, TR. E. PHILLIPS BARKER

15. Better to be eaten to death with a rust than to be scoured to nothing with perpetual motion.

SHAKESPEARE, *2 HENRY IV* (1597–98), 1.2.245

16. Where most of us end up there is no knowing, but the hellbent get where they are going.

JAMES THURBER, "THE WOLF WHO WENT PLACES," *FURTHER FABLES FOR OUR TIME* (1956)

17. Let me say to you now that to do nothing at all is the most difficult thing in the world, the most difficult and the most intellectual.

OSCAR WILDE, *THE ARTIST AS CRITIC: THE CRITICAL WRITINGS OF OSCAR WILDE*, RICHARD ELLMANN, ED. (1969)

11. ACTORS

See also 59. AUDIENCE; 144. COMEDIANS; 972. THEATER

1. For an actress to be a success she must have the face of Venus, the brains of Minerva, the grace of Terpsichore, the memory of Macaulay, the figure of Juno, and the hide of a rhinoceros.

ETHEL BARRYMORE, QUOTED IN GEORGE JEAN NATHAN'S *THE THEATRE IN THE FIFTIES* (1953)

2. What is it in the actor, the stage, that casts so powerful a spell on the young imagination?

JOYCE CARY, *EXCEPT THE LORD* (1953)

3. The movie actor, like the sacred king of primitive tribes, is a god in captivity.

ALEXANDER CHASE, *PERSPECTIVES* (1966)

4. One of the grave dangers inherent in the various stages of any theatrical career—whether it be budding, quiescent or diminishing—is the advice of friends.

MOSS HART, *ACT ONE* (1959)

5. Players, Sir! I look on them as no better than creatures set upon tables and joint stools to make faces and produce laughter, like dancing dogs.

SAMUEL JOHNSON, QUOTED IN BOSWELL'S *LIFE OF SAMUEL JOHNSON*, 1775

6. An actor can remember his briefest notice well into senescence and long after he has forgotten his phone number and where he lives.

JEAN KERR, "ONE HALF OF TWO ON THE AISLE," *PLEASE DON'T EAT THE DAISIES* (1957)

7. By the time an actor knows how to act any sort of part he is often too old to act any but a few.

W. SOMERSET MAUGHAM, *THE SUMMING UP* (1938), 31

8. O, it offends me to the soul to hear a robustious periwig-pated fellow tear a passion to tatters, to very rags, to split the ears of the groundlings.

SHAKESPEARE, *HAMLET* (1600), 3.2.9

9. Every actor in his heart believes everything bad that's printed about him.

ORSON WELLES, NEWS REPORTS, JAN. 13, 1956

ADAPTATION

See 12. ADJUSTMENT

12. ADJUSTMENT

See also 171. CONFORMITY; 637. NORMALITY

1. It is not necessarily those lands which are the most fertile or most favoured in climate that seem to me the happiest, but those in which a long struggle of adaptation between man and his environment has brought out the best qualities of both.

T. S. ELIOT, "AFTER STRANGE GODS" (1934)

2. The best / Thing we can do is to make wherever we're lost in / Look as much like home as we can.

CHRISTOPHER FRY, *THE LADY'S NOT FOR BURNING* (1949), 3

3. Every new adjustment is a crisis in self-esteem.

ERIC HOFFER, *THE ORDEAL OF CHANGE* (1963)

4. We are all sentenced to capital punishment for the crime of living, and though the condemned cell of our earthly existence is but a narrow and bare dwelling-place, we have adjusted ourselves to it, and made it tolerably comfortable for the little while we are to be confined in it.

OLIVER WENDELL HOLMES, SR., *OVER THE TEACUPS* (1891), 2

5. All conditioning aims at that: making people like their inescapable social destiny.

ALDOUS HUXLEY, *BRAVE NEW WORLD* (1932)

6. Ours must be the first age whose great goal, on a nonmaterial plane, is not fulfillment but adjustment; and perhaps just such a goal has served as maladjustment's weapon.

LOUIS KRONENBERGER, *COMPANY MANNERS* (1954), 1.4

7. Adjustment, that synonym for conformity that comes more easily to the modern tongue, is the theme of our swan song, the piper's tune to which we dance on the brink of the abyss, the siren's melody that destroys our senses and paralyzes our wills.

ROBERT LINDER, TITLE ESSAY, *MUST YOU CONFORM?* (1956)

8. I dance to the tune that is played.

SPANISH PROVERB

9. There are no conditions to which a man cannot become accustomed, especially if he sees that all those around him live in the same way.

LEO TOLSTOY, *ANNA KARENINA* (1873–76), 7.13

10. Adapt or perish, now as ever, is Nature's inexorable imperative.

H. G. WELLS, *MIND AT THE END OF ITS TETHER* (1946), 19

13. ADMINISTRATION

See also 315. EXECUTIVES

1. The worst kind of management seeks a single optimum, a one-scale index of efficiency, like the mindless scales of 1 to 10 for grading a woman's beauty or one to four stars for a movie's appeal.

JAMES FALLOWS, *NATIONAL DEFENSE* (1981)

2. An administration, like a machine, does not create. It carries on.

SAINT-EXUPÉRY, *FLIGHT TO ARRAS* (1942), 10, TR. LEWIS GALANTIÈRE

3. Bad administration, to be sure, can destroy good policy; but good administration can never save bad policy.

ADLAI STEVENSON, SPEECH, LOS ANGELES, SEPT. 11, 1952

14. ADMIRATION

See also 49. APPROVAL; 353. FOLLOWING; 426. HONORS; 712. POPULARITY; 808. RESPECT; 1068. WORSHIP

1. Admiration is a very short-lived passion that immediately decays upon growing familiar with its object, unless it be still fed with fresh discoveries, and kept alive by a new perpetual succession of miracles rising up to its view.

JOSEPH ADDISON, *THE SPECTATOR* (1711–12), 256

2. Admiration involves a glorious obliquity of vision.

MAX BEERBOHM, "SOME DAMNABLE ERRORS ABOUT CHRISTMAS," *A CHRISTMAS GARLAND* (1895)

3. Admiration, n. Our polite recognition of another's resemblance to ourselves.

AMBROSE BIERCE, *THE DEVIL'S DICTIONARY* (1881–1911)

4. The capacity to admire others is not my most fully developed trait.

HENRY KISSINGER, *WHITE HOUSE YEARS* (1979)

5. Always we like those who admire us, but we do not always like those whom we admire.

LA ROCHEFOUCAULD, *MAXIMS* (1665), TR. KENNETH PRATT

6. Fools admire, but men of sense approve.

ALEXANDER POPE, *AN ESSAY ON CRITICISM* (1711), 2.190

7. We admire people to the extent that we cannot explain what they do, and the word "admire" then means "marvel at."

B.F. SKINNER, *BEYOND FREEDOM AND DIGNITY* (1971)

ADOLESCENCE

See 1071. YOUTH

ADULTERY

See 472. INFIDELITY

15. ADVANTAGE

See also 153. COMPARISON; 154. COMPENSATION; 549. LOSERS

1. A guardian angel comes when you are very young, and gives you special dispensation. From what? From the world. Yours might be luck. Mine is money.

JANE BOWLES, *TWO SERIOUS LADIES* (1943)

2. It's them as take advantage that get advantage i' this world.

GEORGE ELIOT, *ADAM BEDE* (1859), 32

3. Every advantage has its tax.

EMERSON, "COMPENSATION," *ESSAYS: FIRST SERIES* (1841)

4. He that has one eye is a prince among those that have none.

THOMAS FULLER, M.D., *GNOMOLOGIA* (1732), 2137

5. Against great advantages in another, there are no means of defending ourselves except love.

GOETHE, *ELECTIVE AFFINITIES* (1809), 23

6. Fortune turns everything to the advantage of those she favours.

LA ROCHEFOUCAULD, *MAXIMS* (1665), TR. KENNETH PRATT

7. The concessions of the privileged to the unprivileged are seldom brought about by any better motive than the power of the unprivileged to extort them.

JOHN STUART MILL, *THE SUBJUGATION OF WOMEN* (1869), 3

8. Generally speaking, the less privileged groups in democratic society, as they become aware of their interests and their political power, will be found to press for ever more state intervention in practically all fields.

GUNNAR MYRDAL, *BEYOND THE WELFARE STATE* (1960)

9. When Fortune is on our side, popular favor bears her company.

PUBLILIUS SYRUS, *MORAL SAYINGS* (1ST. C. B.C.), 275, TR. DARIUS LYMAN

16. ADVENTURE

See also 216. DANGER; 313. EXCITEMENT

1. An adventure is only an inconvenience rightly considered. An inconvenience is only an adventure wrongly considered.

G. K. CHESTERTON, "ON RUNNING AFTER ONE'S HAT," *ALL THINGS CONSIDERED* (1908)

2. We pay for security with boredom, for adventure with bother.

PETER DE VRIES, *COMFORT ME WITH APPLES* (1956)

3. It is only in adventure that some people succeed in knowing themselves—in finding themselves.

ANDRÉ GIDE, *JOURNALS,* OCT. 26, 1924, TR. JUSTIN O'BRIEN

4. Give me the storm and tempest of thought and action, rather than the dead calm of ignorance and faith!

ROBERT C. INGERSOLL, *THE GODS* (1872)

5. Life is either a daring adventure or nothing. To keep our faces toward change and behave like free spirits in the presence of fate is strength undefeatable.

HELEN KELLER, *LET US HAVE FAITH* (1940)

6. What people speak of as adventure is something nobody in his right mind would seek out, and it becomes romantic only when one is safely at home.

LOUIS L'AMOUR, *EDUCATION OF A WANDERING MAN* (1989)

7. There are two kinds of adventurers: those who go truly hoping to find adventure and those who go secretly hoping they won't.

WILLIAM LEAST HEAT MOON, *BLUE HIGHWAYS* (1982)

8. They sicken of the calm, who know the storm.

DOROTHY PARKER, "FAIR WEATHER," *SUNSET GUN* (1928)

9. A life without adventure is likely to be unsatisfying, but a life in which adventure is allowed to take whatever form it will is sure to be short.

BERTRAND RUSSELL, "SOCIAL COHESION AND HUMAN NATURE," *AUTHORITY AND THE INDIVIDUAL* (1949)

10. If we didn't live venturously, plucking the wild goat by the beard, and trembling over precipices, we should never be depressed, I've no doubt; but already should be faded, fatalistic and aged.

VIRGINIA WOOLF, *A WRITER'S DIARY,* MAY 26, 1924

17. ADVERSITY

See also 153. COMPARISON; 154. COMPENSATION; 157. COMPLAINT; 180. CONSOLATIONS; 228. DEFEAT; 245. DIFFICULTY; 287. ENDURANCE; 329. FAILURE; 549. LOSERS; 550. LOSS; 751. PROSPERITY AND ADVERSITY; 946. SUFFERING

1. Misfortune / wandering the same track lights now upon one / and now upon another.

AESCHYLUS, *PROMETHEUS BOUND* (C. 478 B.C.), TR. DAVID GRENE

2. Better be wise by the misfortunes of others than by your own.

AESOP, "THE LION, THE ASS AND THE FOX HUNTING," *FABLES* (6TH C. B.C.), TR. THOMAS JAMES

3. A high heart ought to bear calamities and not flee them, since in bearing them appears the grandeur of the mind and in fleeing them the cowardice of the heart.

PIETRO ARETINO, LETTER TO THE KING OF FRANCE, APRIL 24, 1525, TR. SAMUEL PUTNAM

4. The beauty of the soul shines out when a man bears with composure one heavy mischance after another, not because he does not feel them, but because he is a man of high and heroic temper.

ARISTOTLE, *NICOMACHEAN ETHICS* (4TH C. B.C.), I.10, TR. J. A. K. THOMSON

5. Calamity is man's true touchstone.

BEAUMONT AND FLETCHER, *FOUR PLAYS IN ONE: THE TRIUMPH OF HONOUR* (1647), I

8. He that fashions calamity for his neighbor, the instrument of his wounding is in his own hand.

BERECHIAH BEN NATRONAI HA-NAKDAN, *FABLES OF A JEWISH AESOP* (1967)

7. Man is born unto trouble, as the sparks fly upward.

BIBLE, JOB 5:7

8. Calamity, n. ... Calamities are of two kinds: misfortune to ourselves, and good fortune to others.

AMBROSE BIERCE, *THE DEVIL'S DICTIONARY* (1881–1911)

9. To be unable to bear an ill is itself a great ill.

BION, (2ND C. B.C.?), QUOTED IN DIOGENES LAERTIUS' *LIVES AND OPINIONS OF EMINENT PHILOSOPHERS* (3RD C. A.D.), TR. R. D. HICKS

10. If there is a possibility of several things going wrong, the one that will cause the most damage will be the one to go wrong.

ARTHUR BLOCH, "MURPHOLOGY," *MURPHY'S LAW* (1979)

11. When working on a project, if you put away a tool that you're certain you're finished with, you will need it instantly.

ARTHUR BLOCH, "LAW OF ANNOYANCE," *MURPHY'S LAW* (1979)

12. In every kind of adversity, the bitterest part of a man's affliction is to remember that he once was happy.

BOETHIUS, *THE CONSOLATION OF PHILOSOPHY* (A.D. 524), 2

13. Welcome each rebuff / That turns earth's smoothness rough, / Each sting that bids nor sit nor stand but go!

ROBERT BROWNING, "RABBI BEN EZRA," *DRAMATIS PERSONAE* (1864), 6

14. Public calamity is a mighty leveller.

EDMUND BURKE, SPEECH, "ON CONCILIATION WITH THE AMERICAN COLONIES," MARCH 22, 1775

15. Adversity, if a man is set down to it by degrees, is more supportable with equanimity by most people than any great prosperity arrived at in a single lifetime.

SAMUEL BUTLER, (D. 1902), *THE WAY OF ALL FLESH* (1903), 5

16. Adversity is the first path to Truth.

BYRON, *DON JUAN* (1819–24), 12.50

17. There are three modes of bearing the ills of life: by indifference, by philosophy, and by religion.

CHARLES CALEB COLTON, *LACON* (1825), 1.95

18. He that has never suffered extreme adversity, knows not the full extent of his own depravation.

CHARLES CALEB COLTON, *LACON* (1825), 1.19

19. An earthquake achieves what the law promises but does not in practice maintain—the equality of all men.

IGNAZIO SILONE, "WHY I BECAME A SOCIALIST," IN *THE GOD THAT FAILED* (1949), ED. RICHARD CROSSMAN

20. He deposes Doom / Who hath suffered him—.

EMILY DICKINSON, POEM (C. 1862)

21. They say that if you get bored enough with calamity you can learn to laugh.

LAWRENCE DURRELL, *MONSIEUR* (1974)

22. The memory of man is as old as misfortune.

LAWRENCE DURRELL, *BALTHAZAR* (1958), 4.12

23. Every calamity is a spur and valuable hint.

EMERSON, "FATE," *THE CONDUCT OF LIFE* (1860)

24. Misfortunes when asleep are not to be awakened.

ENGLISH PROVERB

25. The misfortune of the wise is better than the prosperity of the fool.

EPICURUS, (3RD C. B.C.), QUOTED IN DIOGENES LAERTIUS' *LIVES AND OPINIONS OF EMINENT PHILOSOPHERS* (3RD C. A.D.), TR. R. D. HICKS

26. Disaster appears, to crush / one man now, but afterward another.

EURIPIDES, *ALCESTIS* (438 B.C.), TR. RICHMOND LATTIMORE

27. Human misery must somewhere have a stop: / there is no wind that always blows a storm.

EURIPIDES, *HERACLES* (C. 422 B.C.), TR. WILLIAM ARROWSMITH

28. Ignorance of one's misfortunes is clear gain.

EURIPIDES, *ANTIOPE* (C. 408 B.C.), 204, TR. M. H. MORGAN

29. In misfortune, what friend remains a friend?

EURIPIDES, *HERACLES* (C. 422 B.C.), TR. WILLIAM ARROWSMITH

30. If the roof caves in and the tenants are sitting in the debris, they will laugh like hell. They will endure any hardship as long as it means trouble for the landlord.

HARRY GOLDEN, "THE LANDLORD," *ONLY IN AMERICA* (1958)

31. For more than fifty years, the Western world has haunted itself with rumors of its own death.

MICHAEL HARRINGTON, *THE ACCIDENTAL CENTURY* (1966)

32. Greater dooms win greater destinies.

HERACLITUS, *FRAGMENTS* (C. 500 B.C.), 70, TR. PHILIP WHEELWRIGHT

33. No man can smile in the face of adversity and mean it.

EDGAR WATSON HOWE, *COUNTRY TOWN SAYINGS* (1911)

34. If the Chrysler crisis had come up during a Republican administration, the company would have gone down the tubes before you could say Herbert Hoover.

LEE IACOCCA, *IACOCCA: AN AUTOBIOGRAPHY* (1984) WITH WILLIAM NOVAK

35. If a man talks of his misfortunes there is something in them that is not disagreeable to him; for where there is nothing but pure misery there never is any recourse to the mention of it.

SAMUEL JOHNSON, QUOTED IN BOSWELL'S *LIFE OF SAMUEL JOHNSON*, 1780

36. He knows not his own strength that hath not met adversity.

Ben Jonson, "Explorata," *Timber* (1640)

37. There is no man in this world without some manner of tribulation or anguish, though he be king or pope.

Thomas à Kempis, *The Imitation of Christ* (1426), 1.22

38. Philosophy triumphs easily over past evils and future evils; but present evils triumph over it.

La Rochefoucauld, *Maxims* (1665)

39. People don't ever seem to realize that doing what's right's no guarantee against misfortune.

William McFee, *Casuals of the Sea* (1916), 2.1.6

40. The world is quickly bored by the recital of misfortune, and willingly avoids the sight of distress.

W. Somerset Maugham, *The Moon and Sixpence* (1919), 16

41. The oldest and best known evil was ever more supportable than one that was new and untried.

Montaigne, "Of vanity," *Essays* (1580–88), tr. Charles Cotton and W. C. Hazlitt

42. The only incurable troubles of the rich are the troubles that money can't cure, / Which is a kind of trouble that is even more troublesome if you are poor.

Ogden Nash, "The Terrible People," *Versus from 1929 On* (1959)

43. [Robert] Kennedy identified with people, not data, or institutions, or theories. Poverty was a specific black face for him, not a manila folder full of statistics.

Jack Newfield, *Robert Kennedy* (1969)

44. That which does not kill me makes me stronger.

Nietzsche, "Maxims and Missiles," 8, *Twilight of the Idols* (1888), tr. Anthony M. Ludovici

45. The drowning man is not troubled by rain.

Persian Proverb

46. With man, most of his misfortunes are occasioned by man.

Pliny the Elder, *Natural History* (1st. c.), 7.5, tr. J. Bostock and H. T. Riley

47. I never knew any man in my life who could not bear another's misfortunes perfectly like a Christian.

Alexander Pope, *Thoughts on Various Subjects* (1727)

48. Learn to see in another's calamity the ills which you should avoid.

Publilius Syrus, *Moral Sayings* (1st. c. b.c.), 120, tr. Darius Lyman

49. To be brave in misfortune is to be worthy of manhood; to be wise in misfortune is to conquer fate.

Agnes Repplier, "Strayed Sympathies," *Under Dispute* (1924)

50. Fire is the test of gold; adversity, of strong men.

Seneca, *On Providence* (1st c.), 5.9

51. Light troubles speak; the weighty are struck dumb.

Seneca, *Hippolytus* (1st c.), 607, tr. Frank Justus Miller

52. Misery acquaints a man with strange bedfellows.

Shakespeare, *The Tempest* (1611–12), 2.2.43

53. Sweet are the uses of adversity, / Which, like the toad, ugly and venomous, / Wears yet a precious jewel in his head.

Shakespeare, *As You Like It* (1599–1600), 2.1.12

54. The worst is not / So long as we can say "This is the worst."

Shakespeare, *King Lear* (1605–06), 4.1.27

55. It is a painful thing / To look at your own trouble and know / That you yourself and no one else has made it.

Sophocles, *Ajax* (c. 447 b.c.), tr. John Moore

56. One's own escape from troubles makes one glad; / but bringing friends to trouble is hard grief.

Sophocles, *Antigone* (442–41 b.c.), tr. Elizabeth Wyckoff

57. God gives almonds to those who have no teeth.

Spanish Proverb

58. By trying we can easily learn to endure adversity. Another man's, I mean.

Mark Twain, "Pudd'nhead Wilson's New Calendar," *Following the Equator* (1897), 2.3

59. Adversity in immunological doses has its uses; more than that crushes.

John Updike, "On One's Own Oeuvre," *Hugging the Shore* (1983)

60. Trouble will come soon enough, and when he does come receive him as pleasantly as possible. Like the tax-collector, he is a disagreeable chap to have in

one's house, but the more amiably you greet him the sooner he will go away.

ARTEMUS WARD, "HUNTING TROUBLE," *ARTEMUS WARD IN LONDON* (1872)

61. When you are down and out, something always turns up—and it is usually the noses of your friends.

ORSON WELLES, *THE NEW YORK TIMES*, APRIL 1, 1962

18. ADVERTISING

See also 104. BUSINESS AND COMMERCE; 105. BUYING AND SELLING; 745. PROPAGANDA; 760. PUBLICITY

1. The advertisements in a newspaper are more full of knowledge in respect to what is going on in a state or community than the editorial columns are.

HENRY WARD BEECHER, *PROVERBS FROM PLYMOUTH PULPIT* (1887)

2. The deeper problems connected with advertising come less from the unscrupulousness of our "deceivers" than from our pleasure in being deceived, less from the desire to seduce than from the desire to be seduced.

DANIEL J. BOORSTIN, *THE IMAGE* (1962), 5.3

3. There, in the window of a freshly painted clapboard building, just off the road, a bewitching and seductive red neon sign spoke to him in a universal tongue: COCA-COLA, it announced, COCA-COLA, and he went faint with gastric epiphany.

T. CORAGHESSON BOYLE, *EAST IS EAST* (1990)

4. "Back in the days when American billboard advertising was in flower [said Hemingway], there were two slogans that I always rated above all others: the old Cremo Cigar ad that proclaimed, Spit Is a Horrid Word—but Worse on the end of Your Cigar, and Drink Schlitz in Brown Bottles and Avoid that Skunk Taste. You don't get creative writing like that any more."

A.E. HOTCHNER, *PAPA HEMINGWAY* (1966)

5. Advertisements are now so numerous that they are very negligently perused, and it is therefore become necessary to gain attention by magnificence of promises, and by eloquences sometimes sublime and sometimes pathetic.

SAMUEL JOHNSON, *THE IDLER* (1758–60), 40

6. Promise, large promise, is the soul of an advertisement.

SAMUEL JOHNSON, *THE IDLER* (1758–60), 41

7. [The advertiser] is the overrewarded court jester and court pander at the democratic court.

JOSEPH WOOD KRUTCH, "PERMISSIVE EXPLOITATION," *HUMAN NATURE AND THE HUMAN CONDITION* (1959)

8. What is a self-image? Who started talking about one? I rather fancy it was Madison Avenue.

MADELEINE L'ENGLE, *A CIRCLE OF QUIET* (1972)

9. The modern Little Red Riding Hood, reared on singing commercials, has no objection to being eaten by the wolf.

MARSHALL MCLUHAN, "BOOK OF THE HOUR," *THE MECHANICAL BRIDE* (1951)

10. The [broadcast] commercial is the invention of a profoundly Christian nation—it proceeds to sell something in which it does not altogether believe, and it interrupts the mood.

NORMAN MAILER, *CANNIBALS AND CHRISTIANS* (1967)

11. I think that I shall never see / A billboard lovely as a tree. / Indeed, unless the billboards fall / I'll never see a tree at all.

OGDEN NASH, "SONG OF THE OPEN ROAD," *VERSES FROM 1929 ON* (1959)

12. Advertising in the final analysis should be news. If it is not news it is worthless.

ADOLPH S. OCHS, *THE NEW YORK TIMES MAGAZINE*, MARCH 9, 1958

13. The people who flood our living-rooms with a smorgasbord of commercial messages about fetid breath, moist underarms and troubled intestines know this: an appropriate time, place and manner to sell a product is any that sells the product.

GEORGE F. WILL, "PRIVACY IN THE REPUBLIC OF APPETITES," *THE PURSUIT OF HAPPINESS AND OTHER SOBERING THOUGHTS* (1978)

19. ADVICE

1. There is nothing which we receive with so much reluctance as advice.

JOSEPH ADDISON, *THE SPECTATOR* (1711–12), 512

2. It is an easy thing for one whose foot / is on the outside of calamity / to give advice and to rebuke the sufferer.

AESCHYLUS, *PROMETHEUS BOUND* (C. 478 B.C.), TR. DAVID GRENE

3. Distrust interested advice.

AESOP, "THE FOX WITHOUT A TAIL," *FABLES* (6TH C. B.C.), TR. JOSEPH JACOBS

4. Never trust the advice of a man in difficulties.

Aesop, "The Fox and the Goat," *Fables* (6th c. b.c.?), tr. Joseph Jacobs

5. The light that a man receiveth by counsel from another is drier and purer than that which cometh from his own understanding and judgment, which is ever infused and drenched in his affections and customs.

Francis Bacon, "Of Friendship," *Essays* (1625)

6. In the multitude of counsellors there is safety.

Bible, Proverbs 11:14 and 24:6

7. Advice, n. The smallest current coin.

Ambrose Bierce, *The Devil's Dictionary* (1881–1911)

8. Who cannot give good counsel? 'Tis cheap, it costs them nothing.

Robert Burton, *The Anatomy of Melancholy* (1621), 2.2.3

9. We ask advice, but we mean approbation.

Charles Caleb Colton, *Lacon* (1825), 1.190

10. We are all wise for other people, none for himself.

Emerson, *Journals,* 1834

11. Do people conform to the instructions of us old ones? Each thinks he must know best about himself, and thus many are lost entirely.

Goethe, quoted in Johann Peter Eckermann's *Conversations with Goethe,* Sept. 18, 1823

12. "If a man is going to leave one wife to marry another, it's better if he divorces the first before he marries the second."

Joseph Heller, *Good as Gold* (1979)

13. The advice of the elders to young men is very apt to be as unreal as a list of the hundred best books.

Oliver Wendell Holmes, Sr., speech, Boston, Jan. 8, 1897

14. It is not often that any man can have so much knowledge of another, as is necessary to make instruction useful.

Samuel Johnson, *The Rambler* (1750–52), 87

15. The toad beneath the harrow knows / Exactly where each tooth-point goes; / The butterfly upon the road / Preaches contentment to that toad.

Rudyard Kipling, "Pagett, M.P." *Departmental Ditties* (1886)

16. We may give advice, but we cannot inspire conduct.

La Rochefoucauld, *Maxims* (1665)

17. You will always find some Eskimos ready to instruct the Congolese on how to cope with heat waves.

Stanislaw Lec, *Unkempt Thoughts* (1962), tr. Jacek Galazka

18. I do hope that you will someday learn (1) not to get into trouble with the authorities; (2) not to have fights with the other boys.

Louise Bennett Lord, from letter to young son, quoted in James Lord's *Six Exceptional Women* (1994)

19. This is the gist of what I know: / Give advice and buy a foe.

Phyllis McGinley, "A Garland of Precepts," *The Love Letters of Phyllis McGinley* (1954)

20. I wish you would give up the idea of Spain.

Maxwell Perkins, Letter to Ernest Hemingway, in *Editor to Author: The Letters of Maxwell Perkins* (1950). ed. John Hall Wheelock

21. Where's the man who counsel can bestow, / Still pleased to teach, and yet not proud to know?

Alexander Pope, *An Essay on Criticism* (1711), 3.72

22. We are so happy to advise others that occasionally we even do it in their interest.

Jules Renard, *Journal* (1887–1910)

23. It is wrong to follow the advice of an adversary; nevertheless it is right to hear it, that you may do the contrary; and this is the essence of good policy.

Sa'di, *Gulistan* (1258), 8.18, tr. James Ross

24. Friendly counsel cuts off many foes.

Shakespeare, *1 Henry VI* (1591–92), 3.1. 184

25. "If a lady comes up to you and tells you that your dear mama is lying in a faint on the pavement round the corner, don't you believe her, don't have anything to do with her, do not go with her into the cab. It is the White Slave Traffic."

Stevie Smith, "Syler's Green," in *Me Again* (1981)

26. In giving advice seek to help, not to please, your friend.

Solon, (7th–6th c. b.c.), quoted in Diogenes Laertius' *Lives and Opinions of Eminent Philosophers* (3rd c. a.d.), tr. R. D. Hicks

27. It can be no dishonor / to learn from others when they speak good sense.

SOPHOCLES, *ANTIGONE* (442–41 B.C.), TR. ELIZABETH WYCKOFF

28. No enemy is worse than bad advice.

SOPHOCLES, *ELECTRA* (C. 418–14 B.C.), TR. DAVID GRENE

29. I have lived some thirty years on this planet, and I have yet to hear the first syllable of valuable or even earnest advice from my seniors.

THOREAU, "ECONOMY," *WALDEN* (1854)

30. The counsels of old age give light without heat, like the sun in winter.

VAUVENARGUES, *REFLECTIONS AND MAXIMS* (1746), 159

31. It is always a silly thing to give advice, but to give good advice is absolutely fatal.

OSCAR WILDE, *THE ARTIST AS CRITIC: THE CRITICAL WRITINGS OF OSCAR WILDE*. ED. RICHARD ELLMANN(1969)

20. AESTHETICS

See also 53. ART AND ARTISTS; 72. BEAUTY; 207. CRITICISM, PROFESSIONAL; 614. MUSIC; 708. POETRY AND POETS; 1069. WRITING AND WRITERS

1. Pleasure is by no means an infallible critical guide, but it is the least fallible.

W. H. AUDEN, "READING," *THE DYER'S HAND* (1962)

2. The eye is the painter and the ear the singer.

EMERSON, *JOURNALS*, 1836

3. Pay attention only to the form; emotion will come spontaneously to inhabit it. A perfect dwelling always finds an inhabitant.

ANDRÉ GIDE, "PORTRAITS AND APHORISMS," *PRETEXTS* (1903), TR. ANGELO P. BERTOCCI AND OTHERS

4. Aesthetics is for the artist like ornithology is for the birds.

BARNETT NEWMAN, QUOTED IN "SPEAKING OF BOOKS," *THE NEW YORK TIMES BOOK REVIEW*, FEB. 18, 1968

5. Tomes of aesthetic criticism hang on a few moments of real delight and intuition.

GEORGE SANTAYANA, *THE LIFE OF REASON: REASON IN ART* (1905–06), 10

6. Is it the obligation of great art to be continually interesting? I think not.

SUSAN SONTAG, "MICHEL LEIRIS' *MANHOOD*," *AGAINST INTERPRETATION* (1966)

7. Ethics, like natural selection, make existence possible. Aesthetics, like sexual selection, make life lovely and wonderful, fill it with new forms, and give it progress, and variety and change.

OSCAR WILDE, "THE CRITIC AS ARTIST," *INTENTIONS* (1891)

AFFECTATION

See 45. APPEARANCE; 732. PRETENSION

21. AFFECTION

See also 22. AFFINITY; 284. EMOTIONS; 365. FRIENDSHIP; 551. LOVE

1. Most people would rather get than give affection.

ARISTOTLE, *NICOMACHEAN ETHICS* (4TH C. B.C.), 8.8, TR. J. A. K. THOMSON

2. We are uneasy with an affectionate man, for we are positive he wants something of us, particularly our love.

EDWARD DAHLBERG, "ON LOVE AND FRIENDSHIP," *REASONS OF THE HEART* (1965)

3. Most affections are habits or duties we lack the courage to end.

HENRY DE MONTHERLANT, *QUEEN AFTER DEATH* (1942), 2.3

4. The affections cannot keep their youth any more than men.

EMERSON, *JOURNALS*, 1831

5. One must not be mean with affections; what is spent of the funds is renewed in the spending itself. Left untouched for too long, they diminish imperceptibly or the lock gets rusty; they are there all right but one cannot make use of them.

SIGMUND FREUD, LETTER TO MARTHA BERNAYS, AUG. 18, 1882

6. Whatever pretext we may give for our affections, often it is only interest and vanity which cause them.

LA ROCHEFOUCAULD, *MAXIMS* (1665), TR. KENNETH PRATT

7. Talk not of wasted affection, affection never was wasted; / If it enrich not the heart of another, its waters, returning / Back to their springs, like the rain, shall fill them full of refreshment; / That which the fountain sends forth returns again to the fountain.

LONGFELLOW, *EVANGELINE* (1847), 2.1

8. Affection is created by habit, community of interests, convenience and the desire of companionship. It is a comfort rather than an exhilaration.

W. SOMERSET MAUGHAM, *THE SUMMING UP* (1938), 77

9. A mixture of admiration and pity is one of the surest recipes for affection.

André Maurois, *Ariel* (1923)

10. Human nature is so constructed that it gives affection most readily to those who seem least to demand it.

Bertrand Russell, *The Conquest of Happiness* (1930), 12

11. Praise is well, compliment is well, but affection—that is the last and final and most precious reward that any man can win, whether by character or achievement.

Mark Twain, "When in Doubt, Tell the Truth," *Speeches* (1923), ed. A. B. Paine

22. AFFINITY

See also 57. Association

1. There can be little liking where there is no likeness.

Aesop, "The Collier and the Fuller," *Fables* (6th c. b.c.?), tr. Thomas James

2. It is a great bond to dislike the same things.

George Santayana, Letter to Bertrand Russell (1911)

3. The profoundest affinities are those most readily felt.

George Santayana, *The Life of Reason: Reason and Society* (1905–06), 1

4. When elderly invalids meet with fellow-victims of their own ailments, then at last real conversation begins, and life is delicious.

Logan Pearsall Smith, *Afterthoughts* (1931), 2

23. AFRICAN-AMERICANS

See also 85. Blacks

1. The African race is an india-rubber ball: the harder you dash it to the ground, the higher it will rise.

African Proverb

AFTERLIFE

See 414. Heaven; 416. Hell; 454. Immortality

24. AFTERTHOUGHT

1. Second thoughts are ever wiser.

Euripides, *Hippolytus* (428 b.c.), 436, tr. M. H. Morgan

2. Afterthought makes the first resolve a liar.

Sophocles, *Antigone* (442–41 b.c.), tr. Elizabeth Wyckoff

AGE

See 298. Era; 586. Middle Age; 653. Old Age; 1071. Youth

25. AGENTS

See also 104. Business and Commerce; 105. Buying and Selling

1. The last I heard of the young man in question, he was trying to eke out a miserable existence as a book agent while he was looking about for a position somewhere with the Government as a janitor or for some other equally humble occupation.

Booker T. Washington, *My Larger Education* (1911)

AGGRAVATION

See 508. Irritations

26. AGGRESSION

See also 155. Competition; 357. Force; 859. Self-Assertion; 1032. Violence; 1042. War

1. At worst, is not this an unjust world, full of nothing but beasts of prey, four-footed or two-footed?

Thomas Carlyle, "Count Cagliostro" (1833)

2. If there is no evidence that sport lowers aggression, at the same time it should be said that there is also no evidence that sport is motivated by aggression.

Erich Fromm, *The Anatomy of Human Destructiveness* (1973)

3. Attack is the reaction. I never think I have hit hard unless it rebounds.

Samuel Johnson, quoted in Boswell's *Life of Samuel Johnson,* April 2, 1775

4. No absolute is going to make the lion lie down with the lamb: unless the lamb is inside.

D. H. Lawrence, *The Later D. H. Lawrence* (1952)

5. It is unfair to blame man too fiercely for being pugnacious; he learned the habit from Nature.

Christopher Morley, *Inward Ho!* (1923), 8

6. To knock a thing down, especially if it is cocked at an arrogant angle, is a deep delight to the blood.

George Santayana, *The Life of Reason: Reason in Society* (1905–06), 3

7. The extent to which human aggression exemplifies innate tendencies is not clear.

B.F. Skinner, *Beyond Freedom and Dignity* (1971)

8. The curse of modern times is the preponderance of male hormones in places where they can do long-term damage. Even if we're not talking about wars between nations or assaults on nature, there's still that aggressiveness that keeps us apart from each other and the problems we need to be working on.

Robert James Waller, *The Bridges of Madison County* (1992)

AGNOSTICISM

See 265. Doubt, Religious; 904. Skepticism; 1004. Unbelief

27. AGREEMENT

See also 46. Appeasement; 51. Argument; 162. Compromise; 167. Conciliation; 252. Discord; 772. Quarreling; 994. Treaties

1. It is by universal misunderstanding that all agree. For if, by ill luck, people understood each other, they would never agree.

Charles Baudelaire, *Intimate Journals* (1887), 99, tr. Christopher Isherwood

2. Minds do not act together in public; they simply stick together; and when their private activities are resumed, they fly apart again.

Frank Moore Colby, "Simple Simon," *The Colby Essays* (1926), v. 1

3. We are more inclined to hate one another for points on which we differ, than to love one another for points on which we agree.

Charles Caleb Colton, *Lacon* (1825), 2.127

4. Insofar as it represents a genuine reconciliation of differences, a consensus is a fine thing; insofar as it represents a concealment of differences, it is a miscarriage of democratic procedure.

J. William Fulbright, speech, U.S. Senate, Oct. 22, 1965

5. Men ... are not agreed about any one thing, not even that heaven is over our heads.

Montaigne, "Apology for Raimond de Sebonde," *Essays* (1580–88), tr. Charles Cotton and W. C. Hazlitt

6. Nobody agrees with anybody else anyhow, but adults conceal / it and infants show it.

Ogden Nash, "Birdies, Don't Make Me Laugh," *Verses from 1929 On* (1959)

7. Agreement is made more precious by disagreement.

Publilius Syrus, *Moral Sayings* (1st c. b.c.), 151

8. Friends are generally of the same sex, for when men and women agree, it is only in their conclusions; their reasons are always different.

George Santayana, *The Life of Reason: Reason in Society* (1905–06), 6

AGRICULTURE

See 337. Farms and Farming

AID

See 56. Assistance

AIM

See 286. Ends; 771. Purpose

28. AIRPLANES

See also 991. Transportation

1. Lovers of air travel find it exhilarating to hang poised between the illusion of immortality and the fact of death.

Alexander Chase, *Perspectives* (1966)

2. I wonder if politicians know less about the land, now that they campaign by air.

André Dubus, "Railroad Sketches," *Broken Vessels* (1991)

3. Every time we hit an air pocket and the plane dropped about five hundred feet (leaving my stomach in my mouth) I vowed to give up sex, bacon, and air travel if I ever made it back to *terra firma* in one piece.

Erica Jong, *Fear of Flying* (1973)

4. For all professional pilots there exists a kind of guild, without charter and without by-laws. It demands no requirements for inclusion save an understanding of the wind, the compass, the rudder, and fair fellowship.

Beryl Markham, *West With the Night* (1942)

5. There is not much to say about most airplane journeys. Anything remarkable must be disastrous, so you define a good flight by negatives: you didn't get hijacked, you didn't crash, you didn't throw up, you weren't late, you weren't nauseated by the food.

Paul Theroux, *The Old Patagonian Express* (1979)

29. AIR POLLUTION

1. I durst not laugh, for fear of opening my lips and receiving the bad air.

SHAKESPEARE, *JULIUS CAESAR* (1599–1600), 1.2.250

30. ALIENATION

See also 3. THE ABSURD; 219. DEADNESS, SPIRITUAL; 290. ENNUI; 300. ESCAPE; 466. INDIFFERENCE; 915. SOLITUDE

1. When one realizes that his life is worthless he either commits suicide or travels.

EDWARD DAHLBERG, "ON FUTILITY," *REASONS OF THE HEART* (1965)

2. The man who regards his own life and that of his fellow-creatures as meaningless is not merely unfortunate but almost disqualified for life.

EINSTEIN, "THE MEANING OF LIFE," *THE WORLD AS I SEE IT* (1934), TR. ALAN HARRIS

3. I am an invisible man. No, I am not a spook like those who haunted Edgar Allan Poe; nor am I one of your Hollywood-movie ectoplasms.

RALPH ELLISON, *THE INVISIBLE MAN* (1952)

4. Everything intercepts us from ourselves.

EMERSON, *JOURNALS,* 1833

5. The torture of being the unseen object, and the constantly observed subject.

LEROI JONES, *THE SYSTEM OF DANTE'S HELL* (1963)

6. As this is the simple truth—that to live is to feel oneself lost—he who accepts it has already begun to find himself, to be on firm ground.

JOSÉ ORTEGA Y GASSET, *THE REVOLT OF THE MASSES* (1930), 14

7. Peace dies when the framework is ripped apart. When there is no longer a place that is yours in the world. When you know no longer where your friend is to be found.

SAINT-EXUPÉRY, *FLIGHT TO ARRAS* (1942), 13, TR. LEWIS GALANTIÈRE

31. ALOOFNESS

See also 142. COLDNESS; 983. TOGETHERNESS

1. Retirement accords with the tone of my mind: / I will not descend to a world I despise.

BYRON, "LINES," *HOURS OF IDLENESS* (1806), 1

2. A man's profundity may keep him from opening on a first interview, and his caution on a second; but I should suspect his emptiness if he carried on his reserve to a third.

CHARLES CALEB COLTON, *LACON* (1825), 2.81

3. To spare oneself from grief at all cost can be achieved only at the price of total detachment, which excludes the ability to experience happiness.

ERICH FROMM, *MAN FOR HIMSELF* (1947), 4

4. By keeping men off, you keep them on.

JOHN GAY, *THE BEGGAR'S OPERA* (1728), 1.8, AIR 9

5. Reserve is an artificial quality that is developed in most of us but as the result of innumerable rebuffs.

W. SOMERSET MAUGHAM, *THE SUMMING UP* (1938), 19

6. The main motive for "non-attachment" is a desire to escape from the pain of living, and above all from love, which, sexual or non-sexual, is hard work.

GEORGE ORWELL, "REFLECTIONS ON GHANDI," *SHOOTING AN ELEPHANT* (1950)

7. If a man makes me keep my distance, the comfort is, he keeps his at the same time.

JONATHAN SWIFT, *THOUGHTS ON VARIOUS SUBJECTS* (1711)

8. For an impenetrable shield, stand inside yourself.

THOREAU, *JOURNAL,* JUNE 27, 1840

32. ALTERNATION

1. What's my turn today may be thine tomorrow.

THOMAS FULLER, M.D., *GNOMOLOGIA* (1732), 5513

ALTRUISM

See 433. HUMANITARIANISM

33. AMBITION

See also 6. ACHIEVEMENT; 55. ASPIRATION; 291. ENTERPRISE; 945. SUCCESS

1. A man's worth is no greater than the worth of his ambitions.

MARCUS AURELIUS, *MEDITATIONS* (2ND C.), 7.3, TR. MAXWELL STANIFORTH

2. What shall it profit a man, if he shall gain the whole world, and lose his own soul?

BIBLE, MARK 8:36

3. No bird soars too high, if he soars with his own wings.

WILLIAM BLAKE, "PROVERBS OF HELL," *THE MARRIAGE OF HEAVEN AND HELL* (1790)

4. If you take big paces you leave big spaces.

Burmese Proverbs (1962), 100, ed. Hla Pe

5. He who would rise in the world should veil his ambition with the forms of humanity.

Chinese Proverb

6. All ambitions are lawful except those which climb upward on the miseries or credulities of mankind.

Joseph Conrad, "A Familiar Preface," *A Personal Record* (1912)

7. Who never climbed high never fell low.

Thomas Fuller, M.D., *Gnomologia* (1732), 5713

8. The true way is the middle one, halfway between deserving a place and pushing oneself into it.

Baltasar Gracián, *The Art of Worldly Wisdom* (1647), 199, tr. Joseph Jacobs

9. Nothing arouses ambition so much in the heart as the trumpet-clang of another's fame.

Baltasar Gracián, *The Art of Worldly Wisdom* (1647), 75, tr. Joseph Jacobs

10. Nothing is so common-place as to wish to be remarkable.

Oliver Wendell Holmes, Sr., *The Autocrat of the Breakfast Table* (1858), 12

11. Ambition is only vanity ennobled.

Jerome K. Jerome, "On Vanity and Vanities," *The Idle Thoughts of an Idle Fellow* (1889)

12. Ambition makes more trusty slaves than need.

Ben Jonson, *Sejanus His Fall* (1603), 1.1

13. A slave has but one master; an ambitious man has as many masters as there are people who may be useful in bettering his position.

La Bruyére, *Characters* (1688), 8.70, tr. Henri Van Laun

14. Ambition does not see the earth she treads on: the rock and the herbage are of one substance to her.

Walter Savage Landor, "Tiberius and Vipsania," *Imaginary Conversations* (1824–53)

15. We often pass from love to ambition, but we hardly ever return from ambition to love.

La Rochefoucauld, *Maxims* (1665), tr. Kenneth Pratt

16. An upstart is a sparrow eager to be betrothed to a hornbill.

Malay Proverb

17. Be wise; / Soar not too high to fall; but stoop to rise.

Philip Massinger, *The Duke of Milan* (1620), 1.2

18. People Who Do Things exceed my endurance; / God, for a man that solicits insurance!

Dorothy Parker, "Bohemia," *Sunset Gun* (1928)

19. All sins have their origin in a sense of inferiority, otherwise called ambition.

Cesare Pavese, *The Burning Brand* (1961)

20. The tallest trees are most in the power of the winds, and ambitious men of the blasts of fortune.

William Penn, *Some Fruits of Solitude* (1693), 2.97

21. There is a mortal breed most full of futility. / In contempt of what is at hand, they strain into the future, / hunting impossibilities on the wings of ineffectual hopes.

Pindar, *Odes* (5th c. b.c.), Pythia 3, tr. Richmond Lattimore

22. He is much to be dreaded who stands in dread of poverty.

Publilius Syrus, *Moral Sayings* (1st c. b.c.), 933, tr. Darius Lyman

23. Ambition often puts men upon doing the meanest offices; so climbing is performed in the same posture with creeping.

Jonathan Swift, *Thoughts on Various Subjects* (1711)

24. In private enterprises men may advance or recede, whereas they who aim at empire have no alternative between the highest success and utter downfall.

Tacitus, *Histories* (a.d. 104–109), 2.74, tr. Alfred J. Church and William J. Brodribb

25. This is the posture of fortune's slave: one foot in the gravy, one foot in the grave.

James Thurber, "The Mouse and the Money," *Further Fables for Our Time* (1956)

26. The greatest evil which fortune can inflict on men is to endow them with small talents and great ambition.

Vauvenargues, *Reflections and Maxims* (1746), 562, tr. F. G. Stevens

AMBIVALENCE

See 170. Conflict, Inner

34. AMERICA AND AMERICANS

See also 106. California; 107. Canada; 421. Hollywood; 628. New England; 632. New York; 1044. Washington, D.C.

1. It is a sad fact about our culture that a poet can earn much more money writing or talking about his art than he can by practicing it.

W. H. AUDEN, FOREWORD, *THE DYER'S HAND* (1962)

2. The making of an American begins at that point where he himself rejects all other ties, any other history, and himself adopts the vesture of his adopted land.

JAMES BALDWIN, "MANY THOUSANDS GONE" (1951), *NOTES OF A NATIVE SON* (1955)

3. I think I was lucky to be exposed to American life when both the United States and I were young and full of stupendous illusions.

LUIGI BARZINI, *O AMERICA* (1977)

4. Americans (as seen from a distance) were known to get things done, ruthlessly, meticulously, quickly, against all obstacles.

LUIGI BARZINI, *O AMERICA* (1977)

5. In those years the adjective "American," added to any noun, indicated something naturally excellent, a drastic improved version of a dreary Old World article, or a diabolically new invention.

LUIGI BARZINI, *O AMERICA* (1977)

6. [M]any Americans preferred to live in a consoling world of their own creation, just as many of them preferred the synthetic, the make-believe, the man-made products, to those of God, in other words the imitation chemical vanilla.

LUIGI BARZINI, *O AMERICA* (1977)

7. American muse, whose strong and diverse heart / So many men have tried to understand / But only made it smaller with their art, / Because you are as various as your land.

STEPHEN VINCENT BENÉT, "INVOCATION," *JOHN BROWN'S BODY* (1928)

8. This nation's impulse is toward the future, and tradition seems more of a shackle to it than an inspiration.

ALLAN BLOOM, *THE CLOSING OF THE AMERICAN MIND* (1987)

9. Never have people been more the masters of their environment. Yet never has a people felt more deceived and disappointed. For never has a people expected so much more than the world could offer.

DANIEL J. BOORSTIN, INTRODUCTION TO *THE IMAGE* (1962)

10. [Americans] expect to eat and stay thin, to be constantly on the move and ever more neighborly ... to revere God and be God.

DANIEL J. BOORSTIN, *NEWSWEEK*, FEB. 26, 1962

11. He knew them. Americans. They killed each other over dinner, shot one another for sport, mugged old ladies in the street. Help like that he didn't need.

T. CORAGHESSON BOYLE, *EAST IS EAST* (1990)

12. We are not a nation, but a union, a confederacy of equal and sovereign states.

JOHN C. CALHOUN, LETTER TO OLIVER DYER, JAN. 1, 1849

13. There is a rowdy strain in American life, living close to the surface but running very deep. Like an ape behind a mask, it can display itself suddenly with terrifying effect.

BRUCE CATTON, *THIS HALLOWED GROUND* (1956)

14. There is nothing the matter with Americans except their ideals. The real American is all right; it is the ideal American who is all wrong.

G. K. CHESTERTON, QUOTED IN *THE NEW YORK TIMES*, FEB. 1, 1931

15. Americans think of themselves collectively as a huge rescue squad on twenty-four-hour call to any spot on the globe where dispute and conflict may erupt.

ELDRIDGE CLEAVER, "RALLYING ROUND THE FLAG," *SOUL ON ICE* (1968)

16. It has always been cited as an irrepressible symptom of America's vitality that her people, in fair times and foul, believe in themselves and their institutions.

ALISTAIR COOKE, "PUT NOT YOUR TRUST IN PRINCES...," *AMERICA OBSERVED: FROM THE 1940S TO THE 1980S* (1988)

17. If an American were condemned to confine his activity to his own affairs, he would be robbed of one half of his existence.

ALEXIS DE TOCQUEVILLE, *DEMOCRACY IN AMERICA* (1835–39), 1.14

18. And I am quite serious when I say that I do not believe there are, on the whole earth besides, so many intensified bores as in these United States.

CHARLES DICKENS, LETTER TO JOHN FORSTER (1842) *THE SELECTED LETTERS OF CHARLES DICKENS*. ED. F.W. DUPEE, 1960

19. I think it impossible, utterly impossible, for any Englishman to live here [in America], and be happy.

CHARLES DICKENS, LETTER TO JOHN FORSTER (1842) *THE SELECTED LETTERS OF CHARLES DICKENS*. ED. F.W. DUPEE, 1960

20. We Americans are tempted to distinguish ourselves from other current and former inhabitants of this planet by assuming that we are ruled by "progress."

MICHAEL DORRIS, "MICE," *PAPER TRAIL* (1994)

21. Little of beauty has America given the world save the rude grandeur God himself stamped on her bosom; the human spirit in this new world has expressed itself in vigor and ingenuity rather than in beauty.

W. E. B. Du Bois, *The Souls of Black Folk* (1903), 14

22. Behold [America], th' land iv freedom, where ivry man's as good as ivry other man, on'y th' other man don't know it.

Finley Peter Dunne, "The New York Custom House," *Mr. Dooley's Opinions* (1901)

23. Whatever America hopes to bring to pass in the world must first come to pass in the heart of America.

Dwight D. Eisenhower, Inaugural Address, Jan. 20, 1953

24. The Yankee is one who, if he once gets his teeth set on a thing, all creation can't make him let go.

Emerson, *Journals,* 1842

25. In America nature is autocratic, saying, "I am not arguing, I am telling you."

Erik H. Erikson, *Childhood and Society* (1950), 8

26. A rigid America is also weak and vulnerable, because it sacrifices its unique strength: the energy of people who think they can always make something new of their lives.

James Fallows, *More Like Us* (1989), 6

27. America is so vast that almost everything said about it is likely to be true, and the opposite is probably equally true.

James T. Farrell, introduction to H. L. Mencken's *Prejudices: A Selection* (1958)

28. "I'm glad I'm American," she said. "Here in Italy I feel that everybody's dead. Carthaginians and old Romans and Moorish pirates and medieval princes with poisoned rings.

F. Scott Fitzgerald, *The Crack-Up* (1945)

29. There was even a recurrent idea in America about an education that would leave out history and the past, that should be a sort of equipment for aerial adventure, weighed down by none of the stowaways of inheritance or tradition.

F. Scott Fitzgerald, *The Crack-Up* (1945)

30. So much of learning to be an American is learning not to let your individuality become a nuisance.

Edgar Z. Friedenberg, "The Impact of the School," *The Vanishing Adolescent* (1959)

31. In the modern world, we Americans are the old inhabitants. We first had political freedom, high industrial production, an economy of abundance.

Paul Goodman, *Growing Up Absurd* (1960), 7.2

32. The organization of American society is an interlocking system of semi-monopolies notoriously venal, an electorate notoriously unenlightened, misled by mass media notoriously phony.

Paul Goodman, *The Community of Scholars* (1962)

33. There is a familiar America. It is celebrated in speeches and advertised on television and in the magazines. It has the highest mass standard of living the world has ever known.

Michael Harrington, *The Other America* (1963)

34. Our affluent [American] society contains those of talent and insight who are driven to prefer poverty, to choose it, rather than to submit to the desolation of an empty abundance.

Michael Harrington, *The Other America* (1962), 5.1

35. Thou, O my country, hast thy foolish ways, / Too apt to purr at every stranger's praise!

Oliver Wendell Holmes, Sr., "An After-Dinner Poem" (1843)

36. I tremble for my country when I reflect that God is just.

Thomas Jefferson, *Notes on the State of Virginia* (1784–85), 18

37. I look forward to a great future for America—a future in which our country will match its military strength with our moral restraint, its wealth with our wisdom, its power with our purpose.

John F. Kennedy, address, Amherst College, Mass. Oct. 26, 1963

38. The American Way is so restlessly creative as to be essentially destructive; the American Way is to carry common sense itself almost to the point of madness.

Louis Kronenberger, "Last Thoughts," *Company Manners* (1954)

39. The typical American believes that no necessity of the soul is free and that there are precious few, if any, which cannot be bought.

Joseph Wood Krutch, "The European Visitor," *If You Don't Mind My Saying So* (1964)

40. America is a passionate idea or it is nothing. America is a human brotherhood or it is a chaos.

Max Lerner, "The United States as Exclusive Hotel," *Actions and Passions* (1949)

41. If destruction be our lot we must ourselves be its author and finisher. As a nation of free men we must live through all time, or die by suicide.

ABRAHAM LINCOLN, SPEECH, SPRINGFIELD, ILL., JAN. 27, 1838

42. America, which has the most glorious present still existing in the world today, hardly stops to enjoy it, in her insatiable appetite for the future.

ANNE MORROW LINDBERGH, "THE BEACH AT MY BACK," *GIFT FROM THE SEA* (1955)

43. This is America, / This vast, confused beauty, / This staring, restless speed of loveliness, / Mighty, overwhelming, crude, of all forms, / Making grandeur out of profusion, / Afraid of no incongruities, / Sublime in its audacity, / Bizarre breaker of moulds.

AMY LOWELL, "THE CONGRESSIONAL LIBERTY," *WHAT'S O'CLOCK* (1925)

44. The American character looks always as if it had just had a rather bad haircut, which gives it, in our eyes at any rate, a greater humanity than the European, which even among its beggars has an all too professional air.

MARY MCCARTHY, "AMERICA THE BEAUTIFUL: THE HUMANIST IN THE BATHTUB," *ON THE CONTRARY* (1961)

45. The happy ending is our national belief.

MARY MCCARTHY, "AMERICA THE BEAUTIFUL: THE HUMANIST IN THE BATHTUB," *ON THE CONTRARY* (1961)

46. We are a nation of twenty million bathrooms, with a humanist in every tub.

MARY MCCARTHY, "AMERICA THE BEAUTIFUL: THE HUMANIST IN THE BATHTUB," *ON THE CONTRARY* (1961)

47. American youth attributes much more importance to arriving at driver's-license age than at voting age.

MARSHALL MCLUHAN, *UNDERSTANDING MEDIA* (1964), 22

48. If American men are obsessed with money, American women are obsessed with weight. The men talk of gain, the women talk of loss, and I do not know which talk is the more boring.

MARYA MANNES, *MORE IN ANGER* (1958), 1.3

49. Americans seem sometimes to believe that if you are a thinker you must be a frowning bore, because thinking is so damn serious.

JACQUES MARITAIN, *REFLECTIONS ON AMERICA* (1958), 15

50. The American people, taking one with another, constitute the most timorous, sniveling, poltroonish, ignominious mob of serfs and goose-steppers ever gathered under one flag in Christendom since the end of the Middle Ages.

H. L. MENCKEN, *PREJUDICES: THIRD SERIES* (1922), 1

51. I have never been able to look upon America as young and vital but rather as prematurely old, as a fruit which rotted before it had a chance to ripen.

HENRY MILLER, "DR. SOUCHON: SURGEON-PAINTER," *THE AIR-CONDITIONED NIGHTMARE* (1945)

52. It isn't the oceans which cut us off from the world—it's the American way of looking at things.

HENRY MILLER, "LETTER TO LAFAYETTE," *THE AIR-CONDITIONED NIGHTMARE* (1945)

53. To an American, land is solidity, goodness, and hope. American history is about land.

WILLIAM LEAST HEAT MOON, QUOTING A NORTH CAROLINIAN, IN *BLUE HIGHWAYS* (1982)

54. America is still a government of the naïve, for the naïve, and by the naïve. He who does not know this, nor relish it, has no inkling of the nature of his country.

CHRISTOPHER MORLEY, *INWARD HO!* (1923), 5

55. When at peace they [Americans] are reluctant to think of the possibility of war. When at war they concentrate solely on winning the war, as if it were a grim football match, and refuse to worry about the peace which is the goal of war.

PHILIP E. MOSELY, "TECHNIQUES OF NEGOTIATION," *NEGOTIATING WITH THE RUSSIANS* (1951)

56. America is the longest argument in the world.

BILL MOYERS, BROADCAST ON PUBLIC BROADCASTING SYSTEM

57. The pursuit of happiness, which American citizens are obliged to undertake, tends to involve them in trying to perpetuate the moods, tastes and aptitudes of youth.

MALCOLM MUGGERIDGE, "WOMEN OF AMERICA," *THE MOST OF MALCOLM MUGGERIDGE* (1966)

58. Safety razors make it hard to grow beards in America: America would be a better place if there were a few bearded, savage, terrible old men.

LEWIS MUMFORD, *FINDINGS AND KEEPINGS. ANALECTS FOR AN AUTOBIOGRAPHY* (1957)

59. We must always remember that America is a great nation today not because of what government did for people but because of what people did for themselves and for one another.

RICHARD M. NIXON, *BEYOND PEACE* (1994)

60. America is still a frontier country of wide open spaces. Our closeness to nature is one reason why our problem is not repression but regression; our notorious violence is the constant eruption of primitiveness, of anarchic individualism.

CAMILLE PAGLIA, SEX, ART, AND AMERICAN CULTURE (1992)

61. The American: a titan enamored of progress, a fanatical giant who worships "getting things done" but never asks himself what he is doing nor why he is doing it.

OCTAVIO PAZ, "NIHILISM AND DIALECTICS," *ALTERNATING CURRENT* (1973)

62. I loved the audacity of that American principle which says, When life gets tainted or goes stale, junk it! Leave it behind! Go West!

JONATHAN RABAN, *OLD GLORY* (1982)

63. In America, a nation that believes it transcends history, each generation can be a world of its own.

RICHARD REEVES, *TIME* MAGAZINE, NOV. 22, 1993

64. If we ever pass out as a great nation we ought to put on our tombstone "America died from a delusion that she had moral leadership."

WILL ROGERS, *THE AUTOBIOGRAPHY OF WILL ROGERS* (1949), 16

65. Self-help and self-control are the essence of the American tradition.

FRANKLIN D. ROOSEVELT, STATE OF THE UNION MESSAGE, JAN. 3, 1934

66. I sometimes think that the saving grace of America lies in the fact that the overwhelming majority of Americans are possessed of two great qualities—a sense of humor and a sense of proportion.

FRANKLIN D. ROOSEVELT, ADDRESS, SAVANNAH, GA., NOV. 18, 1933

67. From the very beginning our people have markedly combined practical capacity for affairs with power of devotion to an ideal. The lack of either quality would have rendered the other of small value.

THEODORE ROOSEVELT, SPEECH, PHILADELPHIA, NOV. 22, 1902

68. America is the greatest of opportunities and the worst of influences.

GEORGE SANTAYANA, *THE LAST PURITAN* (1935), 14

69. America has a way of inventing tradition each morning and erasing the past by nightfall, and the hold of ancient custom is endangered by a thousand cicumstances.

ISRAEL SHENKER, *COAT OF MANY COLORS* (1985)

70. It's complicated, being an American, / Having the money and the bad conscience, both at the same time.

LOUIS SIMPSON, "ON THE LAWN AT THE VILLA," *SELECTED POEMS* (1965)

71. The patriots are those who love America enough to see her as a model to mankind.

ADLAI STEVENSON, "THE HARD KIND OF PATRIOTISM," *HARPER'S MAGAZINE,* JULY 1963

72. With the supermarket as our temple and the singing commercial as our litany, are we likely to fire the world with an irresistible vision of America's exalted purpose and inspiring way of life?

ADLAI STEVENSON, *WALL STREET JOURNAL,* JUNE 1, 1960

73. We [America] are a nation that has always gone in for the loud laugh, the wow, the belly laugh and the dozen other labels for the roll-'em-in-the-aisles gagerissimo.

JAMES THURBER, "THE QUALITY OF MIRTH," *THE NEW YORK TIMES,* FEB. 21, 1960

74. America is a large, friendly dog in a very small room. Every time it wags its tail, it knocks over a chair.

ARNOLD TOYNBEE, NEWS SUMMARIES, JULY 14, 1954

75. There isn't a single human characteristic that can be safely labeled as "American."

MARK TWAIN, "WHAT PAUL BOURGET THINKS OF US" (1895)

76. We Americans worship the almighty dollar! Well, it is a worthier god than Heredity Privilege.

MARK TWAIN, *NOTE-BOOK* (1935)

77. We [Americans] are the lavishest and showiest and most luxury-loving people on the earth; and at our masthead we fly one true and honest symbol, the gaudiest flag the world has ever seen.

MARK TWAIN, "DIPLOMATIC PAY AND CLOTHES" (1899)

78. It is ironic that a nation that has never experienced a coup d'état should be so obsessed with the idea of conspiracy.

GORE VIDAL, *REFLECTIONS UPON A SINKING SHIP* (1969)

79. The American vice is explanation.

GORE VIDAL, "RICH KIDS," *THE SECOND AMERICAN REVOLUTION AND OTHER ESSAYS* (1982)

80. [His] mentality was one that had been remarked upon as being peculiarly American since the nation had been born—the restless, erratic insight and imagination of a gadgeteer.

KURT VONNEGUT, *PLAYER PIANO* (1952)

81. Whatever else an American believes or disbelieves about himself, he is absolutely sure he has a sense of humor.

E. B. WHITE, "SOME REMARKS ON HUMOR," *THE SECOND TREE FROM THE CORNER* (1954)

82. America is now liberty-conscious. In a single generation it has progressed from being toothbrush-conscious, to being air-minded, to being liberty-conscious.

E.B. WHITE, *ONE MAN'S MEAT* (1944)

83. The South is the land of the sustained sibilant. Everywhere, for the appreciative visitor, the letter "s" insinuates itself in the scene: in the sound of sea and sand, in the singing shell, in the heat of sun and sky, in the sultriness of the gentle hours, in the siesta, in the stir of birds and insects.

E.B. WHITE, "THE RING OF TIME," IN *THE ART OF THE PERSONAL ESSAY* (1994), ED. PHILLIP LOPATE

84. It is possible to believe in progress as a fact without believing in progress as an ethical principle; but in the catechism of many Americans, the one goes with the other.

NORBERT WIENER, *THE HUMAN USE OF HUMAN BEINGS* (1954), 2

85. In America the President reigns for four years, and Journalism governs for ever and ever.

OSCAR WILDE, *THE SOUL OF MAN UNDER SOCIALISM* (1891)

86. The youth of America is their oldest tradition.

OSCAR WILDE, *A WOMAN OF NO IMPORTANCE* (1893), 1

87. America was established not to create wealth but to realize a vision, to realize an ideal—to discover and maintain liberty among men.

WOODROW WILSON, ADDRESS, CHICAGO, FEB. 12, 1912

88. Just what is it that America stands for? If she stands for one thing more than another it is for the sovereignty of self-governing people.

WOODROW WILSON, SPEECH, PITTSBURGH, PA., JAN. 29, 1916

89. We [Americans] have a great ardor for gain; but we have a deep passion for the rights of man.

WOODROW WILSON, SPEECH, NEW YORK, DEC. 6, 1911

90. The thing that impresses me most about America is the way parents obey their children.

DUKE OF WINDSOR, *LOOK*, MARCH 5, 1957

AMUSEMENT

See 292. ENTERTAINMENT; 436. HUMOR; 526. LAUGHTER

35. ANALOGY

See also 524. LANGUAGE

1. Though analogy is often misleading, it is the least misleading thing we have.

SAMUEL BUTLER, (D. 1902), "LORD, WHAT IS MAN?" *NOTE-BOOKS* (1912)

2. Analogies, it is true, decide nothing, but they can make one feel more at home.

SIGMUND FREUD, "THE DISSECTION OF THE PSYCHICAL PERSONALITY," *NEW INTRODUCTORY LECTURES ON PSYCHOANALYSIS* (1933), TR. JAMES STRACHEY

3. Metaphors are not to be trifled with. A single metaphor can give birth to love.

MILAN KUNDERA, *THE UNBEARABLE LIGHTNESS OF BEING* (1984)

4. The metaphor is perhaps one of man's most fruitful potentialities. Its efficacy verges on magic, and it seems a tool for creation which God forgot inside one of His creatures when He made him.

JOSÉ ORTEGA Y GASSET, *THE DEHUMANIZATION OF ART* (1925)

5. All perception of truth is the detection of an analogy.

THOREAU, *JOURNAL*, SEPT. 5, 1851

36. ANARCHY

See also 395. GOVERNMENT; 913. SOCIETY

1. Anarchy is the stepping stone to absolute power.

NAPOLEON I, *MAXIMS* (1804–15)

37. ANCESTRY

See also 83. BIRTH; 308. EVOLUTION

1. There are many kinds of conceit, but the chief one is to let people know what a very ancient and gifted family one descends from.

BENVENUTO CELLINI, *AUTOBIOGRAPHY* (1558–66), TR. GEORGE BULL

2. To forget one's ancestors is to be a brook without a source, a tree without a root.

CHINESE PROVERB

3. High birth is a poor dish at table.

ITALIAN PROVERB

4. People who can comfort the dead can also chase after them to hurt them further—a reverse ancestor worship.

MAXINE HONG KINGSTON, *THE WOMAN WARRIOR* (1976)

5. Birth is nothing without virtue, and we have no claim to share in the glory of our ancestors unless we strive to resemble them.

MOLIÈRE, *DON JUAN* (1665), 4.2, TR. JOHN WOOD

6. Good birth is a fine thing, but the merit is our ancestors'.

PLUTARCH, "THE EDUCATION OF CHILDREN," *MORALIA* (C. A.D. 100), TR. MOSES HADAS

7. Pride thyself on what virtue thou hast, and not on thy parentage.

SA'DI, *GULISTAN* (1258), 8.60, TR. JAMES ROSS

8. A man who prides himself on his ancestry is like the potato plant, the best part of which is under ground.

SPANISH PROVERB

9. Each has his own tree of ancestors, but at the top of all sits Probably Arboreal.

ROBERT LOUIS STEVENSON, *MEMORIES AND PORTRAITS* (1887), 6

38. ANGELS

See also 414. HEAVEN

1. An angel is a spiritual being, created by God without a body, for the service of Christendom and the Church.

MARTIN LUTHER, *TABLE TALK* (1569), 569

2. It is not known precisely where angels dwell—whether in the air, the void, or the planets. It has not been God's pleasure that we should be informed of their abode.

VOLTAIRE, "ANGELS," *PHILOSOPHICAL DICTIONARY* (1764)

3. He did not believe in angels with soft faces and bright wings, but he believed in the dark spirits that hovered over the heads of lonely men.

THOMAS WOLFE, *LOOK HOMEWARD, ANGEL* (1929)

39. ANGER

See also 212. CURSING; 467. INDIGNATION; 968. TEMPER, BAD

1. Anger represents a certain power, when a great mind, prevented from executing its own generous desires, is moved by it.

PIETRO ARETINO, LETTER TO GIROLAMO QUIRINI, NOV. 21, 1537, TR. SAMUEL PUTNAM

2. It is easy to fly into a passion—anybody can do that—but to be angry with the right person to the right extent and at the right time and with the right object and in the right way—that is not easy, and it is not everyone who can do it.

ARISTOTLE, *NICOMACHEAN ETHICS* (4TH C. B.C.), 2.9, TR. J. A. K. THOMSON

3. No man is angry that feels not himself hurt.

FRANCIS BACON, "OF ANGER," *ESSAYS* (1625)

4. A man that does not know how to be angry does not know how to be good.

HENRY WARD BEECHER, *PROVERBS FROM PLYMOUTH PULPIT* (1887)

5. He that is slow to anger is better than the mighty; and he that ruleth his spirit than he that taketh a city.

BIBLE, PROVERBS 16:32

6. Let not the sun go down upon your wrath.

BIBLE, EPHESIANS 4:26

7. The tigers of wrath are wiser than the horses of instruction.

WILLIAM BLAKE, "PROVERBS OF HELL," *THE MARRIAGE OF HEAVEN AND HELL* (1790)

8. A background of wrath, which can be stirred up to the murderous infernal pitch, does lie in every man.

THOMAS CARLYLE, "TWO HUNDRED AND FIFTY YEARS AGO" (1850)

9. I know of no more disagreeable situation than to be left feeling generally angry without anybody in particular to be angry at.

FRANK MOORE COLBY, "THE LITERATURE OF MALICIOUS EXPOSURE," *THE COLBY ESSAYS* (1926), V. 1

10. Many people lose their tempers merely from seeing you keep yours.

FRANK MOORE COLBY, "TRIALS OF AN ENCYCLOPEDIST," *THE COLBY ESSAYS* (1926), V. 1

11. Life is thorny; and youth is vain; / And to be wroth with one we love / Doth work like madness in the brain.

SAMUEL TAYLOR COLERIDGE, *CHRISTABEL* (1816), 2.410

12. Anger is one of the sinews of the soul; he that wants [lacks] it hath a maimed mind.

THOMAS FULLER, D.D., "OF ANGER," *THE HOLY STATE AND THE PROFANE STATE* (1642)

13. Anger as soon as fed is dead— / 'Tis starving makes it fat—.

EMILY DICKINSON, POEM (C. 1881)

14. A sharp-tempered woman, or, for that matter, a man, / Is easier to deal with than the clever type / Who holds her tongue.

EURIPIDES, *MEDEA* (431 B.C.), TR. REX WARNER

15. When do you really get enraged? When you have a neighbor who never lets you feel at home.

THOMAS L. FRIEDMAN, *NEW YORK TIMES*, SEPT. 5, 1993

16. Anger may be foolish and absurd, and one may be irritated when in the wrong; but a man never feels outraged unless in some respect he is at bottom right.

VICTOR HUGO, "FANTINE," *LES MISÉRABLES* (1862), 2.7, TR. CHARLES E. WILBOUR

17. In times of great stress or adversity, it's always best to keep busy, to plow your anger and your energy into something positive.

LEE IACOCCA, *IACOCCA: AN AUTOBIOGRAPHY* (1984) WITH WILLIAM NOVAK

18. Usually when people are sad, they don't do anything. They just cry over their condition. But when they get angry, they bring about a change.

MALCOLM X, *MALCOLM X SPEAKS* (1965), 9

19. He who doesn't know anger doesn't know anything. He doesn't know the immediate.

HENRI MICHAUX, *SELECTED WRITINGS* (1952), TR. RICHARD ELLMAN

20. How often, being moved under a false cause, if the person offending makes a good defense and presents us with a just excuse, are we angry against truth and innocence itself?

MONTAIGNE, "OF ANGER," *ESSAYS* (1580–88), TR. CHARLES COTTON AND W. C. HAZLITT

21. Nothing on earth consumes a man more quickly than the passion of resentment.

NIETZSCHE, *ECCE HOMO* (1888), TR. ANTHONY M. LUDOVICI

22. Always shun whatever may make you angry.

PUBLILIUS SYRUS, *MORAL SAYINGS* (1ST C. B.C.), 879, TR. DARIUS LYMAN

23. Anger would inflict punishment on another; meanwhile, it tortures itself.

PUBLILIUS SYRUS, *MORAL SAYINGS* (1ST C. B.C.), 1009, TR. DARIUS LYMAN

24. The bare recollection of anger kindles anger.

PUBLILIUS SYRUS, *MORAL SAYINGS* (1ST C. B.C.), 125, TR. DARIUS LYMAN

25. The brain may devise laws for the blood, but a hot temper leaps o'er a cold decree.

SHAKESPEARE, *THE MERCHANT OF VENICE* (1596–97), 1.2.19

26. There is no old age for a man's anger, / Only death.

SOPHOCLES, *OEDIPUS AT COLONUS* (401 B.C.), TR. ROBERT FITZGERALD

27. In the souls of the people the grapes of wrath are filling and growing heavy, growing heavy for the vintage.

JOHN STEINBECK, *THE GRAPES OF WRATH* (1939)

28. When angry, count four; when very angry, swear.

MARK TWAIN, "PUDD'NHEAD WILSON'S CALENDAR," *PUDD'NHEAD WILSON* (1894), 10

40. ANGLO-SAXONS

1. An Anglo-Saxon, Hinnissy, is a German that's forgot who was his parents.

FINLEY PETER DUNNE, "ON THE ANGLO-SAXON," *MR. DOOLEY IN PEACE AND IN WAR* (1898)

41. ANIMALS

See also 82. BIRDS; 347. FISH; 481. INSECTS; 486. INSTINCT

1. Is it not wonderful, that the love of the [animal] parent should be so violent while it lasts and that it should last no longer than is necessary for the preservation of the young?

JOSEPH ADDISON, *THE SPECTATOR* (1711–12), 120

2. If man in a time of need seeks deeper knowledge concerning himself, then he must explore those animal horizons from which we have made our quick little march.

ROBERT ARDREY, *AFRICAN GENESIS* (1961)

3. The Llama is a woolly sort of fleecy hairy goat, / With an indolent expression and an undulating throat / Like an unsuccessful literary man.

HILAIRE BELLOC, "THE LLAMA," *MORE BEASTS FOR WORSE CHILDREN* (1897)

4. The great pleasure of a dog is that you may make a fool of yourself with him and not only will he not scold you, but he will make a fool of himself too.

SAMUEL BUTLER, (D. 1902), "HIGGLEDY-PIGGLEDY," *NOTE-BOOKS* (1912)

5. Everyone's pet is the most outstanding. This begets mutual blindness.

JEAN COCTEAU, *DIARY OF AN UNKNOWN* (1952; 1988), TR. JESSE BROWNER

6. If one is of the masculine gender, a poodle is the insignia of one's deviation.

MART CROWLEY, *THE BOYS IN THE BAND* (1968)

7. Dogs have more love than integrity. They've been true to us, yes, but they haven't been true to themselves.

CLARENCE DAY, *THIS SIMIAN WORLD* (1920), 7

8. Elephants suffer from too much patience. Their exhibitions of it may seem superb,—such power and such restraint, combined, are noble,—but a quality carried to excess defeats itself.

CLARENCE DAY, *THIS SIMIAN WORLD* (1920), 7

9. Animals are such agreeable friends—they ask no questions, they pass no criticisms.

GEORGE ELIOT, "MR. GILFIL'S LOVE-STORY," *SCENES OF CLERICAL LIFE* (1857), 7

10. The Rum Tum Tugger is a terrible bore:/When you let him in, then he wants to be out;/He's always on the wrong side of every door,/And as soon as he's at home, then he'd like to get about.

T.S. ELIOT, "THE RUM TUM TUGGER," *OLD POSSUM'S BOOK OF PRACTICAL CATS* (1939)

11. The Latin proverb, *homo homini lupus*—man is a wolf to man—... is a libel on the wolf, which is a gentle animal with other wolves.

GEOFFREY GORER, *THE NEW YORK TIMES MAGAZINE*, Nov. 27, 1966

12. One must remember that both wild things and men are animals, but wild things are not people.

HELEN HOOVER, "THE RESIDENT BIRDS," *THE LONG-SHADOWED FOREST* (1963)

13. A dog gets lonesome just like a human. He wants to associate with other dogs, but when they take him out, the poor dog is on a leash and cannot run around.

LANGSTON HUGHES, *SIMPLE SPEAKS HIS MIND* (1950)

14. We have enslaved the rest of the animal creation, and have treated our distant cousins in fur and feathers so badly that beyond doubt, if they were able to formulate a religion, they would depict the Devil in human form.

WILLIAM RALPH INGE, "THE IDEA OF PROGRESS," *OUTSPOKEN ESSAYS: SECOND SERIES* (1922)

15. Cats are rather delicate creatures and they are subject to a good many different ailments, but I never heard of one who suffered from insomnia.

JOSEPH WOOD KRUTCH, "FEBRUARY," *THE TWELVE SEASONS* (1949)

16. Cats seem to go on the principle that it never does any harm to ask for what you want.

JOSPEH WOOD KRUTCH, "FEBRUARY," *THE TWELVE SEASONS* (1949)

17. Man can be defined, if one wishes, as a languagized mammal.

CHARLTON LAIRD, *THE MIRACLE OF LANGUAGE* (1953)

18. There is no faith which has never yet been broken, except that of a truly faithful dog.

KONRAD Z. LORENZ, *KING SOLOMON'S RING* (1952), 10, TR. MARJORIE KERR WILSON

19. It is a deep-lying patriarchal instinct in the dog which leads him—at least in the more manly, outdoor breeds—to recognize and honor in the man of the house and head of the family his absolute master and overlord, protector of the hearth; and to find in the relation of vassalage to him the basis and value of his own existence, whereas his attitude toward the rest of the family is much more independent.

THOMAS MANN, "A MAN AND HIS DOG" (1918)

20. On the Continent stray cats are judged individually on their merit—some are loved, some are only respected; in England they are universally worshipped as in ancient Egypt.

GEORGE MIKES, *HOW TO BE AN ALIEN* (1946)

21. If you're going to make such an unholy fuss about dogs you should have stayed in England, where they feed the dogs steak and let people in the slums die of starvation.

JESSICA MITFORD, *DAUGHTERS AND REBELS* (1960)

22. Which of us has not been stunned by the beauty of an animal's skin or its flexibility in motion?

MARIANNE MOORE, "OF BEASTS AND JEWELS," *THE COMPLETE PROSE OF MARIANNE MOORE* (1986)

23. A dog's best friend is his illiteracy.

OGDEN NASH, TITLE POEM, *THE PRIVATE DINING ROOM* (1953)

24. The trouble with a kitten is / That / Eventually it becomes a / Cat.

Ogden Nash, "The Kitten," *Verses from 1929 On* (1959)

25. A real dog, beloved and therefore pampered by his mistress, is a lamentable spectacle. He suffers from fatty degeneration of his moral being.

Agnes Repplier, "The Idolatrous Dog," *Under Dispute* (1924)

26. Our dogs will love and admire the meanest of us, and feed our colossal vanity with their uncritical homage.

Agnes Repplier, "The Idolatrous Dog," *Under Dispute* (1924)

27. There is nothing like a man for bringing out the animal in an animal.

Roger Rosenblatt, "Experimental Animals," *The Man in the Water* (1994)

28. A dog will never forget the crumb thou gavest him, though thou mayst afterwards throw a hundred stones at his head.

Sa'di, *Gulistan* (1258), 8.99, tr. James Ross

29. There is one respect in which brutes show real wisdom when compared with us—I mean their quiet, placid enjoyment of the present moment.

Schopenhauer, "On the Sufferings of the World," *Parerga and Paralipomena* (1851), tr. T. Bailey Saunders

30. O happy dogs of England/Bark well at errand boys/If you lived anywhere else/You would not be allowed to make such an infernal noise.

Stevie Smith, "Syler's Green," in *Me Again* (1981)

31. Charley is a mind-reading dog. There have been many trips in his lifetime, and often he has to be left at home. He knows we are going long before the suitcase has come out, and he paces and worries and whines and goes into a state of mild hysteria, old as he is.

John Steinbeck, *Travels with Charley* (1962)

32. I need a dog pretty badly. I dreamed of dogs last night. They sat in a circle and looked at me and I wanted all of them.

John Steinbeck, *Steinbeck: A Life in Letters,* eds. Elaine Steinbeck and Robert Wallsten, (1975)

33. To escort a cat abroad on a leash is against the nature of a cat, and to permit it to venture forth for exercise unattended into a night of new dangers is against the nature of the owner.

Adlai Stevenson, *Cat Catalog* (1976)

34. Dogs live with man as courtiers round a monarch, steeped in the flattery of his notice and enriched with sinecures. To push their favor in this world of pickings and caresses is, perhaps, the business of their lives; and their joys may lie outside.

Robert Louis Stevenson, "The Character of Dogs" (1883)

35. Those who wish to pet and baby wild animals, "love" them. But those who respect their natures and wish to let them live normal lives, love them more.

Edwin Way Teale, "April 28," *Circle of the Seasons* (1953)

36. Cats are a standing rebuke to behavioral scientists wanting to know how the minds of animals work. The mind of a cat is an unscrutable mystery.

Lewis Thomas, "Clever Animals," *Late Night Thoughts on Listening to Mahler's Ninth Symphony* (1983)

37. My favorite animal is the mule. He has more horse sense than a horse. He knows when to stop eating—and he knows when to stop working.

Harry S Truman, *Mr. Citizen* (1960)

38. Of all God's creatures there is only one that cannot be made the slave of the lash. That one is the cat. If man could be crossed with the cat it would improve man, but it would deteriorate the cat.

Mark Twain, *Notebook* (1935)

39. The cat is never vulgar.

Car Van Vechten, *Cat Catalog* (1976)

40. The dog was created specially for children. He is the god of frolic.

Henry Beecher Ward, *Proverbs from Plymouth Pulpit* (1887)

41. Let dogs delight to bark and bite, / For God hath made them so; / Let bears and lions growl and fight, / For 'tis their nature too.

Isaac Watts, *Divine Songs for Children* (1720), 16

42. They say a reasonable amount o' fleas is good fer a dog—keeps him from broodin' over *bein'* a dog, mebbe.

Edward Noyes Westcott, *David Harum* (1898), 32

43. The cow crunching with depressed head surpasses any statue, / And a mouse is miracle enough to stagger sextillions of infidels.

Walt Whitman, "Song of Myself," *Leaves of Grass* (1855–92)

44. The best thing about animals is that they don't talk much.

THORTON WILDER, *THE SKIN OF OUR TEETH* (1942), 1

ANSWER

See 480. INQUIRY

ANTICIPATION

See 318. EXPECTATION; 1040. WAITING

42. ANTIQUITY

See also 136. CLASSICS; 402. GREECE, ANCIENT; 419. HISTORY AND HISTORIANS; 676. PAST; 986. TRADITION

1. An archeologist is the best husband any woman can have: the older she gets, the more interested he is in her.

AGATHA CHRISTIE, NEWS REPORTS, MARCH 9, 1954

2. If we look backwards to antiquity, it should be as those that are winning a race.

CHARLES CALEB COLTON, *LACON* (1825), 2.148

3. When eras die, their legacies / Are left to strange police. / Professors in New England guard / The glory that was Greece.

CLARENCE DAY, "THOUGHTS ON DEATHS," *THOUGHTS WITHOUT WORDS* (1928)

4. Antiquity was perhaps created to provide professors with their bread and butter.

JULES DE GONCOURT, *JOURNAL*, JAN. 6, 1866

5. I never fail to be moved by knowing that the ground on which I walk is layered with the past—with achievement and strife and the repeated passions and conflicts of the human creature, always changing, always the same. Generations passing like grass.

EVA HOFFMAN., *EXIT INTO HISTORY* (1993)

6. Had the Greeks held novelty in such disdain as we, what work of ancient date would now exist?

HORACE, *EPISTLES* (20-C. 8 B.C.), 2.1

7. Antiquity is full of the praises of another antiquity still more remote.

VOLTAIRE, "ANCIENTS AND MODERNS," *PHILOSOPHICAL DICTIONARY* (1764)

ANTS

See 481. INSECTS

43. ANXIETY

See also 343. FEAR; 482. INSECURITY; 868. SELF-DOUBT

1. The thing that used to worry him most was the fact that people always used to ask him what he was looking so worried about.

DOUGLAS ADAMS, *THE HITCHHIKER'S GUIDE TO THE GALAXY* (1979)

2. We poison our lives with fear of burglary and shipwreck and, ask anyone, the house is never burgled and the ship never goes down.

JEAN ANOUILH, *THE REHEARSAL* (1950), 2, TR. LUCIENNE HILL

3. Jealousy and anger shorten life, and anxiety brings on old age too soon.

APOCRYPHA, ECCLESIASTICUS 30:24

4. As a rule, what is out of sight disturbs men's minds more seriously than what they see.

JULIUS CAESAR, *GALLIC WAR* (58–52 B.C.), TR. H. J. EDWARDS

5. Our imagination and reasoning powers facilitate anxiety; the anxious feeling is precipitated not by an absolute impending threat—such as the worry about an examination, a speech, travel—but rather by the symbolic and often unconscious representations.

WILLARD GAYLIN, *FEELINGS: OUR VITAL SIGNS* (1979)

6. Fine worries, like fine wines, are at their best only after they have been properly mellowed.

DAN GREENBURG WITH MARCIA JACOBS, *HOW TO MAKE YOURSELF MISERABLE* (1966)

7. How much pain have cost us the evils which have never happened.

THOMAS JEFFERSON, LETTER TO THOMAS JEFFERSON SMITH, FEB. 21, 1825

8. This is, I think, very much the Age of Anxiety, the age of the neurosis, because along with so much that weighs on our minds there is perhaps even more that grates on our nerves.

LOUIS KRONENBERGER, "THE SPIRIT OF THE AGE," *COMPANY MANNERS* (1954)

9. Fear, born of the stern matron Responsibility, sits on one's shoulders like some heavy imp of darkness, and one is preoccupied and, possibly, cantankerous.

WILLIAM MCFEE, "THE CRUSADERS," *HARBOURS OF MEMORY* (1921)

10. Now anxiety is the mark of spiritual insecurity. It is the fruit of unanswered questions. But questions cannot go unanswered unless they first be asked.

THOMAS MERTON, *NO MAN IS AN ISLAND* (1955)

11. Grief has limits, whereas apprehension has none. For we grieve only for what we know has happened, but we fear all that possibly may happen.

PLINY THE YOUNGER, *LETTERS* (C. 97–110), 8.17, TR. WILLIAM MELMOTH AND W. M. L. HUTCHINSON

12. Without anxiety life would have very little savor.

MAY SARTON, "TUESDAY, JANUARY 7TH," *THE HOUSE BY THE SEA: A JOURNAL* (1977)

13. We are more often frightened than hurt: our troubles spring more often from fancy than reality.

SENECA, *LETTERS TO LUCILIUS* (1ST C.), 13, TR. E. PHILLIPS BARKER

14. Tenterhooks are the upholstery of the anxious seat.

ROBERT SHERWOOD, NEWS REPORTS, NOV. 15, 1955

15. Anxiety and conscience are a powerful pair of dynamos. Between them, they have ensured that I shall work hard, but they cannot ensure that one shall work at anything worthwhile.

ARNOLD J. TOYNBEE, "WHY AND HOW I WORK," *SATURDAY REVIEW*, APRIL 5, 1969

16. My apprehensions come in crowds; / I dread the rustling of the grass; / The very shadows of the clouds / Have power to shake me as they pass: / I question things and do not find / One that will answer to my mind; / And all the world appears unkind.

WILLIAM WORDSWORTH, "THE AFFLICTION OF MARGARET—" (1804), 10

17. Worries go down better with soup than without.

YIDDISH PROVERBS (1949), ED. HANAN J. AYALTI

APATHY

See 219. DEADNESS, SPIRITUAL; 466. INDIFFERENCE

44. APOLOGY

See also 792. REGRET

1. Apologies only account for that which they do not alter.

BENJAMIN DISRAELI, SPEECH, JULY 28, 1871

2. Apology is only egotism wrong side out.

OLIVER WENDELL HOLMES, SR., *THE PROFESSOR AT THE BREAKFAST TABLE* (1860), 6

3. "Excuse me, pray." Without that excuse I would not have known there was anything amiss.

PASCAL, *PENSÉES* (1670), 58, TR. W. F. TROTTER

45. APPEARANCE

See also 54. ARTIFICIALITY; 192. COSMETICS; 267. DRESS; 338. FASHION; 407. HAIR; 444. IDENTITY; 732. PRETENSION; 825. ROLE-PLAYING

1. Outside show is a poor substitute for inner worth.

AESOP, "THE FOX AND THE MASK," *FABLES* (6TH C. B.C.?), TR. JOSEPH JACOBS

2. She wears a "slip" beneath this dress but the materials of both are so thin that her dark sweated nipples are stuck to them and show through, and it is at her nipples, mainly, that the men keep looking.

JAMES AGEE, *LET US NOW PRAISE FAMOUS MEN* (1941)

3. The Lord seeth not as man seeth; for man looketh on the outward appearance, but the Lord looketh on the heart.

BIBLE, 1 SAMUEL 16:7

4. Alice Malloy had dark, stringy hair, and even her husband, who loved her more than he knew, was sometimes reminded by her lean face of a tenement doorway on a rainy day, for her countenance was long, vacant, and weakly lighted, a passage for the gentle transports and miseries of the poor.

JOHN CHEEVER, "O CITY OF BROKEN DREAMS," *THE STORIES OF JOHN CHEEVER* (1980)

5. Fine words and an insinuating appearance are seldom associated with true virtue.

CONFUCIUS, *ANALECTS* (6TH C. B.C.), 1.3, TR. JAMES LEGGE

6. Always scorn appearances and you always may.

EMERSON, "SELF-RELIANCE," *ESSAYS: FIRST SERIES* (1841)

7. They are not all saints who use holy water.

ENGLISH PROVERB

8. 'Tis not the habit that makes the monk.

THOMAS FULLER, M.D., *GNOMOLOGIA* (1732), 5104

9. A good presence is letters of recommendation.

THOMAS FULLER, M.D., *GNOMOLOGIA* (1732), 170

10. Things are seldom what they seem, / Skim milk masquerades as cream.

W. S. GILBERT, *H. M. S. PINAFORE* (1878), 2

11. What is not seen is as if it was not. Even the Right does not receive proper consideration if it does not seem right.

Baltasar Gracián, *The Art of Worldly Wisdom* (1647), 130, tr. Joseph Jacobs

12. I have often caught sight of myself, my spine humped over, defining my hollowness, my head too heavy for my body, swinging like the oversized blossom of some cruelly bred plant; admiration for the world spread for the world to see on my gullible face—unlike my other face with the sour look of a starved peasant.

Maureen Howard, *Bridgeport Bus* (1965)

13. Personal appearance is looking the best you can for the money.

Virginia Cary Hudson, *O Ye Jigs & Juleps!* (1962)

14. Most men wear their belts low here, there being so many outstanding bellies, some big enough to have names of their own and be formally introduced.

Garrison Keillor, *Lake Wobegon Days* (1985)

15. [Chinese] Women looked like great sea snails—the corded wood, babies, and laundry they carried were the whorls on their backs.

Maxine Hong Kingston, *The Woman Warrior* (1976)

16. We love good looks rather than what is practical, / Though good looks may prove destructive.

La Fontaine, "The Stag and His Reflection," *Fables* (1668–94), tr. Marianne Moore

17. A man, in order to establish himself in the world, does everything he can to appear established there.

La Rochefoucauld, *Maxims* (1665), tr. Kenneth Pratt

18. Be content to seem what you really are.

Martial, *Epigrams* (A.D. 86), 10.83

19. It is easy to be beautiful; it is difficult to appear so.

Frank O'Hara, title poem, *Meditations in an Emergency* (1967)

20. He might have just been in a play that closed in Philadelphia. He might have been with a law firm.

J.D. Salinger, "Just Before the War with the Eskimos," in *Nine Stories by J.D. Salinger* (1953)

21. It is only shallow people who do not judge by appearances. The true mystery of the world is the visible, not the invisible.

Oscar Wilde, *The Picture of Dorian Gray* (1891), 2

46. APPEASEMENT

See also 27. Agreement; 162. Compromise; 167. Conciliation; 994. Treaties

1. Yield to all and you will soon have nothing to yield.

Aesop, "The Man and His Two Wives," *Fables* (6th c. B.C.?), tr. Joseph Jacobs

2. An appeaser is one who feeds a crocodile—hoping it will eat him last.

Sir Winston Churchill, *Reader's Digest,* December 1954

3. If once you have paid him the Danegeld / You never get rid of the Dane.

Rudyard Kipling, "Dane-Geld" (1910)

4. No man can tame a tiger into a kitten by stroking it. There can be no appeasement with ruthlessness. There can be no reasoning with an incendiary bomb.

Franklin D. Roosevelt, Fireside Chat, Dec. 29, 1940

5. A really great people, proud and high-spirited, would face all the disasters of war rather than purchase that base prosperity which is bought at the price of national honor.

Theodore Roosevelt, speech, Harvard University, Feb. 23, 1907

6. No man can sit down and withhold his hands from the warfare against wrong and get peace from his acquiescence.

Woodrow Wilson, address, Denver, Colo., May 7, 1911

APPETITE

See 238. Desires; 403. Greed; 437. Hunger; 494. Intemperance; 970. Temperance

47. APPRECIATION

See also 48. Appreciation, Lack of; 49. Approval; 399. Gratitude; 722. Praise; 1026. Value

1. Do not expect to be acknowledged for what you are, much less for what you would be; since no one can well measure a great man but upon the bier.

Walter Savage Landor, "Lucullus and Caesar" *Imaginary Conversations* (1824–53)

48. APPRECIATION, LACK OF

See also 47. Appreciation; 475. Ingratitude

1. Neither cast ye pearls before swine, lest they trample them under their feet, and turn again and rend you.

Bible, Matthew 7:6

2. Futility: playing a harp before a buffalo.

BURMESE PROVERBS (1962), 28, ED. HLA PE

3. It is folly to sing twice to a deaf man.

ENGLISH PROVERB

4. What is the voice of song, when the world lacks the ear of taste?

NATHANIEL HAWTHORNE, "CANTERBURY PILGRIMS," *THE SNOW IMAGE* (1851)

5. Hay is more acceptable to an ass than gold.

LATIN PROVERB

6. A frog would leap from a throne of gold into a puddle.

PUBLILIUS SYRUS, *MORAL SAYINGS* (1ST C. B.C.), 821, TR. DARIUS LYMAN

APPROPRIATENESS

See 949. SUITABILITY

49. APPROVAL

See also 14. ADMIRATION; 47. APPRECIATION; 474. INGRATIATION; 712. POPULARITY; 722. PRAISE

1. The simulated approval and affection with which parents and teachers are often urged to solve behavior problems are counterfeit. So are flattery, backslapping, and many other ways of "winning friends."

B.F. SKINNER, *BEYOND FREEDOM AND DIGNITY* (1971)

2. Women fear endangering men's approval so much, we don't even wait for them to say no. Or else we protect them, even if it means saying no to ourselves.

GLORIA STEINEM, "CAMPAIGNING," *OUTRAGEOUS ACTS AND EVERYDAY REBELLIONS* (1983)

APRIL

See 854. SEASONS

APTITUDE

See 1. ABILITY; 376. GENIUS; 962. TALENT

50. ARCHITECTURE

See also 53. ART AND ARTISTS; 237. DESIGN; 430. HOUSES

1. Architecture is inhabited sculpture.

CONSTANTIN BRANCUSI, QUOTED IN IGOR STRAVINSKY'S *THEMES AND EPISODES* (1966)

2. By early 1943, the Pentagon was complete—a building big enough to house forty thousand people and all their accoutrements, the largest building in the world, conceived, funded, designed and constructed in a little more than a year. And on the day it was finished, it was already too small.

DAVID BRINKLEY, *WASHINGTON GOES TO WAR* (1988)

3. We shape our buildings: thereafter they shape us.

SIR WINSTON CHURCHILL, *TIME*, SEPT. 12, 1960

4. The brevity of human life gives a melancholy to the profession of the architect.

EMERSON, *JOURNALS*, 1842

5. Light, God's eldest daughter, is a principal beauty in a building.

THOMAS FULLER, D.D., "OF BUILDING," *THE HOLY STATE AND THE PROFANE STATE* (1642)

6. The job of the architect becomes more difficult in this secular age. Where once he had a god to extol, he now has humans like himself; where once he had "he," he now has "she" and "they."

NIKKI GIOVANNI, "ARCHITECTURE," *RACISM 101* (1994)

7. I call architecture "petrified music." Really there is something in this; the tone of mind produced by architecture approaches the effect of music.

GOETHE, QUOTED IN JOHANN PETER ECKERMANN'S *CONVERSATIONS WITH GOETHE*, MARCH 23, 1829

8. No building was safe from the furniture, the pictures, the human beings that it would presently contain.

GRAHAM GREENE, A BURNT-OUT CASE (1960)

9. An arch never sleeps.

HINDUSTANI PROVERB

10. The Golden Arches of McDonald's rise, glorious across the landscape, contempo-monolithic, simple in concept as Stonehenge if we could but see it.

MAUREEN HOWARD, *FACTS OF LIFE* (1978)

11. The genius of architecture seems to have shed its maledictions over this land.

THOMAS JEFFERSON, *NOTES ON THE STATE OF VIRGINIA* (1784–85), 15

12. Even the West has known the architecture of empty space, whose object, for thousands of years, has been less to construct divine houses, than to create sacred places, to seize upon mystery and to immerse man in it—whether by raising the cyclopean pedestal that surrounds him with stars, or by hollowing out the sanctuary that wraps him in haunted night.

ANDRÉ MALRAUX, "THE METAMORPHOSIS OF THE GODS," (1953), TR. WILLARD TRASK

13. Of all forms of visible otherworldliness, it seems to me, the Gothic is at once the most logical and the most beautiful. It reaches up magnificently—and a good half of it is palpably useless.

H. L. Mencken, "The New Architecture," *The American Mercury*, February 1931

14. Architecture is either the prophecy of an unformed society or the tomb of a finished one.

Lewis Mumford, *Findings and Keepings. Analects for an Autobiography* (1975)

15. If the design of the building be originally bad, the only virtue it can ever possess will be signs of antiquity.

John Ruskin, *Modern Painters* (1843–60), v. 1, 2.1.7.26

16. No architecture is so haughty as that which is simple.

John Ruskin, *The Stones of Venice* (1851–53), v. 2, 6.78

17. No person who is not a great sculptor or painter can be an architect. If he is not a sculptor or painter, he can only be a builder.

John Ruskin, *Lectures on Architecture and Painting* (1853), no. 61

18. When we build, let us think that we build for ever.

John Ruskin, *The Seven Lamps of Architecture* (1849), 5

19. Lovely promise and quick ruin are seen nowhere better than in Gothic architecture.

George Santayana, "Avila," *Persons and Places: The Background of My Life* (1944)

20. Architecture is the art of organizing a mob of craftsmen. This, the original meaning of the word, expresses an essential fact...the conceptions of an architect must be worked out by other hands and other minds than his own.

Geoffrey Scott, *The Architecture of Humanism* (1914), 2

21. The art of architecture studies not structure in itself, but the effect of structure on the human spirit.

Geoffrey Scott, *The Architecture of Humanism* (1914), 4

22. I am sometimes visited by the heretical thought that there is no such thing as good and bad architecture, any more than there is good and bad nature. It is all in where you stand at the time.

John Updike, "Can Architecture Be Criticized?" *Odd Jobs* (1991)

23. Rattling the bones is not architecture. Less is only more where more is no good.

Frank Lloyd Wright, "The Language of Organic Architecture," *The Future of Architecture* (1953)

51. ARGUMENT

See also 252. Discord; 258. Dissent; 656. Opinion; 690. Persuasion; 772. Quarreling; 785. Reason

1. There is nothing that a New-Englander so nearly worships as an argument.

Henry Ward Beecher, *Proverbs from Plymouth Pulpit* (1887)

2. Positive, adj. Mistaken at the top of one's voice.

Ambrose Bierce, *The Devil's Dictionary* (1881–1911)

3. When an argument is over, how many weighty reasons does a man recollect which his heat and violence made him utterly forget?

Eustace Budgell, in *The Spectator* (1711–12), 197

4. It is not he who gains the exact point in dispute who scores most in controversy, but he who has shown the most forbearance and the better temper.

Samuel Butler, (d. 1902), "Reconciliation," *Note-Books* (1912)

5. Somebody has to have the last word. If not, every argument could be opposed by another and we'd never be done with it.

Albert Camus, *The Fall* (1956)

6. If you would convince others, seem open to conviction yourself.

Lord Chesterfield, *Letters to His Son*, Feb. 22, 1748

7. A majority is always the best repartee.

Benjamin Disraeli, *Tancred* (1847), 14

8. In a philosophical dispute, he gains most who is defeated, since he learns most.

Epicurus, "Vatican Sayings" (3rd c. b.c.), 74, in *Letters, Principal Doctrines, and Vatican Sayings*,, tr. Russel M. Geer

9. Argument seldom convinces anyone contrary to his inclinations.

Thomas Fuller, M.D., *Gnomologia* (1732), 812

10. One may be confuted and yet not convinced.

Thomas Fuller, M.D., *Gnomologia* (1732), 3771

11. The best way I know of to win an argument is to start by being in the right.

Lord Hailsham, *The New York Times*, Oct. 16, 1960

12. If in argument we can make a man angry with us, we have drawn him from his vantage ground and overcome him.

Walter Savage Landor, "Marcus Tullius and Quinctus Cicero," *Imaginary Conversations* (1824–53)

13. Anyone who in discussion relies upon authority uses, not his understanding, but rather his memory.

Leonardo Da Vinci, *Notebooks* (c. 1500), tr. Jean Paul Richter

14. In arguing of the shadow, we forgo the substance.

John Lily, *Euphues: The Anatomy of Wit* (1579)

15. When we wish to correct with advantage, and to show another that he errs, we must notice from what side he views the matter, for on that side it is usually true.

Pascal, *Pensées* (1670), 9, tr. W. F. Trotter

16. A disputant no more cares for the truth than the sportsman for the hare.

Alexander Pope, *Thoughts on Various Subjects* (1727)

17. True disputants are like true sportsmen; their whole delight is in the pursuit.

alexander Pope, *Thoughts on Various Subjects* (1727)

18. The most savage controversies are those about matters as to which there is no good evidence either way.

Bertrand Russell, "An Outline of Intellectual Rubbish," *Unpopular Essays* (1950)

19. The partisan, when he is engaged in a dispute, cares nothing about the rights of the question, but is anxious only to convince his hearers of his own assertions.

Socrates, in Plato's *Phaedo* (4th-3rd c. b.c.), tr. Benjamin Jowett

20. Arguments only confirm people in their own opinions.

Booth Tarkington, *Looking Forward to the Great Adventure* (1926)

21. It is difficult to be emphatic when no one is emphatic on the other side.

Charles Dudley Warner, "Thirteenth Week," *My Summer in a Garden* (1871)

22. Arguments are to be avoided; they are always vulgar and often convincing.

Oscar Wilde, *The Importance of Being Earnest* (1895), 2

52. ARISTOCRACY

See also 135. Class; 587. Middle Class; 682. The People; 780. Rank; 913. Society

1. There is a natural aristocracy among men. The grounds of this are virtue and talent.

Thomas Jefferson, letter to John Adams, Oct. 28, 1813

2. High people, Sir, are the best; take a hundred ladies of quality, you'll find them better wives, better mothers, more willing to sacrifice their own pleasures to their children, than a hundred other women.

Samuel Johnson, quoted in Boswell's *Life of Samuel Johnson,* May 14, 1778

3. Where position is felt to be a birthright, generosity is possible (though not guaranteed); flexibility is not inhibited by a commitment to perpetual success.

Henry A. Kissinger, *American Foreign Policy* (1969)

4. There is no stronger craving in the world than that of the rich for titles, except that of the titled for riches.

Hesketh Pearson, *The Marrying Americans* (1961)

ARITHMETIC

See 570. Mathematics

ARMS

See 229. Defense; 588. The Military; 641. Nuclear Power; 1042. War; 1049. Weapons

ARMY

See 588. The Military

53. ART AND ARTISTS

See also 20. Aesthetics; 50. Architecture; 201. Creation and Creativity; 237. Design; 614. Music; 666. Painting; 972. Theater; 1069. Writing and Writers

1. Art is in love with luck, and luck with art.

Agathon, quoted in Aristotle's *Nicomachean Ethics* (4th c. b.c.), 6.4, tr. J. A. K. Thomson

2. True art selects and paraphrases, but seldom gives a verbatim translation.

Thomas Bailey Aldrich, "Leaves from a Notebook," *Ponkapog Papers* (1903)

3. There is no comfort in adversity / More sweet than Art affords. The studious mind / Poising in medita-

tion, there is fixed, / And sails beyond its troubles unperceiving.

AMPHIS, (4TH C. B.C.)

4. Life is very nice, but it lacks form. It's the aim of art to give it some.

JEAN ANOUILH, *THE REHEARSAL* (1950), 1.2, TR. LUCIENNE HILL

5. The business of every art is to bring something into existence, and the practice of an art involves the study of how to bring into existence something which is capable of having such an existence and has its efficient cause in the maker and not in itself.

ARISTOTLE, *NICOMACHEAN ETHICS* (4TH C. B.C.), 6.4, TR. J. A. K. THOMSON

6. Nobody is fully alive who cannot apply to art as much discrimination and appreciation as he applies to the work by which he earns his living.

BROOKS ATKINSON, "MARCH 12," *ONCE AROUND THE SUN* (1951)

7. All art is a kind of confession, more or less oblique. All artists, if they are to survive, are forced, at last, to tell the whole story, to vomit the anguish up.

JAMES BALDWIN, "THE NORTHERN PROTESTANT," *NOBODY KNOWS MY NAME* (1961)

8. Art distills sensation and embodies it with enhanced meaning in memorable form—or else it is not art.

JACQUES BARZUN, *THE HOUSE OF INTELLECT* (1959), 6

9. As a matter of history great developments in art have often been remarkably separate from religious motivation and use.

RUTH BENEDICT, *PATTERNS OF CULTURE* (1934)

10. I wonder whether art has a higher function than to make me feel, appreciate, and enjoy natural objects for their art value?

BERNARD BERENSON, *TIME*, APRIL 25, 1955

11. The artist is the most interesting of all phenomena, for he represents creativity, the definition of man.

ALLAN BLOOM, *THE CLOSING OF THE AMERICAN MIND* (1987)

12. What is more natural in a democratic age than that we should begin to measure the stature of a work of art—especially of a painting—by how widely and how well it is reproduced?

DANIEL J. BOORSTIN, *THE IMAGE* (1962), 4.1

13. Art is meant to disturb. Science reassures.

GEORGES BRAQUE, *PENSÉES SUR L'ART*

14. Perhaps art is simply an organism's reaction against its retentive limitations.

JOSEPH BRODSKY, *WATERMARK* (1992)

15. The artist has never been a dictator, since he understands better than anybody else the variations in human personality.

HEYWOOD BROUN, "BRING ON THE ARTIST," *NEW YORK WORLD TELEGRAM*, JAN. 19, 1933

16. One may do whate'er one likes / In Art: the only thing is, to make sure / That one does like it.

ROBERT BROWNING, "NOON," *PIPPA PASSES* (1841)

17. What critics often ask for is the impossible, though this may be a salutary means of extending the borders of art.

ANTHONY BURGESS, *YOU'VE HAD YOUR TIME* (1990)

18. Every man's work, whether it be literature or music or pictures or architecture or anything else, is always a portrait of himself, and the more he tries to conceal himself the more clearly will his character appear in spite of him.

SAMUEL BUTLER, (D. 1902), *THE WAY OF ALL FLESH* (1903), 14

19. The youth of an art is, like the youth of anything else, its most interesting period.

SAMUEL BUTLER, (D. 1902), "A PAINTER'S VIEWS ON PAINTING," *NOTE-BOOKS* (1912)

20. An artist conscientiously moves in a direction which for some good reason he takes, putting one work in front of the other with the hope he'll arrive before death overtakes him.

JOHN CAGE, "ERIK SATIE," *SILENCE* (1961)

21. After all, perhaps the greatness of art lies in the perpetual tension between beauty and pain, the love of men and the madness of creation, unbearable solitude and the exhausting crowd, rejection and consent.

ALBERT CAMUS, "THE ARTIST AND HIS TIME," *RESISTANCE, REBELLION, AND DEATH* (C. 1950)

22. I know with certainty that a man's work is nothing but the long journey to recover, through the detours of art, the two or three simple and great images which first gained access to his heart.

ALBERT CAMUS, *THE NEW YORK TIMES*, JAN. 24, 1960

23. One who desires nothing, hopes for nothing, and fears nothing cannot be an artist.

ANTON CHEKHOV, LETTER TO ALEXEY S. SUVORIN (1892)

24. The dignity of the artist lies in his duty of keeping awake the sense of wonder in the world. In this long

vigil he often has to vary his methods of stimulation; but in this long vigil he is also himself striving against a continual tendency to sleep.

G. K. Chesterton, "On Maltreating Words," *Generally Speaking* (1928)

25. An artist carries on throughout his life a mysterious, uninterrupted conversation with his public.

Maurice Chevalier, *Holiday,* September 1956

26. Without tradition, art is a flock of sheep without a shepherd. Without innovation, it is a corpse.

Sir Winston Churchill, *Time,* May 11, 1953

27. An artist cannot speak about his art any more than a plant can discuss horticulture.

Jean Cocteau, *Newsweek,* May 16, 1955

28. The true work of art is the one which the seventh wave of genius throws up the beach where the undertow of time cannot drag it back.

Cyril Connolly, *The Unquiet Grave* (1945), 3

29. An artist is a man of action, whether he creates a personality, invents an expedient, or finds the issue of a complicated situation.

Joseph Conrad, *The Mirror of the Sea* (1906), 9

30. The artist's morality lies in the force and truth of his description.

Jules Barbey D'Aurevilly, introduction to *Une vieille maîtresse* (1851)

31. The artistic impulse seems not to wish to produce finished work. It certainly deserts us half-way, after the idea is born; and if we go on, art is labor.

Clarence Day, *This Simian World* (1920), 6

32. The attitude that nature is chaotic and that the artist puts order into it is a very absurd point of view, I think. All that we can hope for is to put some order into ourselves.

Willem De Kooning, in *trans/formation,* 1951

33. Every major work of art is a transgression, but the artist is not necessarily, by nature, a transgressor.

E.L. Doctorow, "Theodore Dreiser: Book One and Book Two," *Jack London, Hemingway, and the Constitution* (1993)

34. For us artists there waits the joyous compromise through art with all that wounded or defeated us in daily life.

Lawrence Durrell, *Justine* (1957), 1

35. Life, the raw material, is only lived *in potentia* until the artist deploys it in his work.

Lawrence Durrell, *Justine* (1957), 1

36. The artist's work constitutes the only satisfactory relationship he can have with his fellow men since he seeks his real friends among the dead and the unborn.

Lawrence Durrell, *Mountolive* (1959), 1

37. Every master knows that the material teaches the artist.

Ilya Ehrenburg, "What I Have Learned," *Saturday Review,* Sept. 30, 1967

38. There is no progress in art.

Ilya Ehrenburg, "What I Have Learned," *Saturday Review,* Sept. 30, 1967

39. It has been said that great art is the night thought of man. It may emerge without warning from the soundless depths of the unconscious, just as supernovas may blaze up suddenly in the farther reaches of void space.

Loren Eiseley, "The Hidden Teacher," *The Star Thrower* (1978)

40. No generation is interested in art in quite the same way as any other; each generation, like each individual, brings to the contemplation of art its own categories of appreciation, makes its own demands upon art, and has its own uses for art.

T. S. Eliot, "The Use of Poetry and the Use of Criticism" (1933)

41. No poet, no artist of any art, has his complete meaning alone. His significance, his appreciation is the appreciation of his relation to the dead poets and artists.

T. S. Eliot, "Tradition and the Individual Talent" (1919)

42. But it's hard to talk about art. Maybe there should be a law against it, some First Amendment gag order like crying fire in a crowded theater.

Stanley Elkin, "Some Overrated Masterpieces," *The Best American Essays* (1992)

43. Every artist writes his own autobiography.

Havelock Ellis, *The New Spirit* (1890)

44. Life is as the sea, art a ship in which man conquers life's crushing formlessness, reducing it to a course, a series of swells, tides and wind currents inscribed on a chart.

Ralph Ellison, *Shadow & Act* (1964)

45. Art is a jealous mistress.

EMERSON, "WEALTH," *THE CONDUCT OF LIFE* (1860)

46. It depends little on the object, much on the mood, in art.

EMERSON, *JOURNALS,* 1836

47. Picture and sculpture are the celebrations and festivities of form.

EMERSON, "ART," *ESSAYS: FIRST SERIES* (1841)

48. By artist I mean of course everyone who has tried to create something which was not here before him, with no other tools and material than the uncommerciable ones of the human spirit.

WILLIAM FAULKNER, ADDRESS, NEW YORK CITY, JAN. 25, 1955

49. The aim of every artist is to arrest motion, which is life, by artificial means and hold it fixed so that a hundred years later, when a stranger looks at it, it moves again since it is life.

WILLIAM FAULKNER, INTERVIEW, *WRITERS AT WORK: FIRST SERIES* (1958)

50. Great art is the contempt of a great man for small art.

F. SCOTT FITZGERALD, *THE CRACK-UP* (1945)

51. To make us feel small in the right way is a function of art; men can only make us feel small in the wrong way.

E. M. FORSTER, "A BOOK THAT INFLUENCED ME," *TWO CHEERS FOR DEMOCRACY* (1951)

52. In art, as in love, instinct is enough.

ANATOLE FRANCE, *LE JARDIN D'EPICURE* (1895)

53. Art helps nature, and experience art.

THOMAS FULLER, M.D., *GNOMOLOGIA* (1732), 814

54. The artist cannot get along without a public; and when the public is absent, what does he do? He invents it, and turning his back on his age, he looks toward the future for what the present denies.

ANDRÉ GIDE, "THE IMPORTANCE OF THE PUBLIC," *PRETEXTS* (1903), TR. ANGELO P. BERTOCCI AND OTHERS

55. The work of art is a part of nature seen through a temperament.

ANDRÉ GIDE, "THE LIMITS OF ART," *PRETEXTS* (1903), TR. ANGELO P. BERTOCCI AND OTHERS

56. The work of art is the exaggeration of an idea.

ANDRÉ GIDE, *JOURNALS* (1896), TR. JUSTIN O'BRIEN

57. There is no better deliverance from the world than through art; and a man can form no surer bond with it than through art.

GOETHE, *ELECTIVE AFFINITIES* (1809), 23

58. The fact that all of us die anyway (the rumor turns out to be true) is a mere detail in the celestial glow of imagination. The artist's eyes destroy death.

HERBERT GOLD, "CALIFORNIA NATION—EUREKA! I FOUND THE WATER," *BOHEMIA* (1993)

59. Nature scarcely ever gives us the very best; for that we must have recourse to art.

BALTASAR GRACIÁN, *THE ART OF WORLDLY WISDOM* (1647), 12, TR. JOSEPH JACOBS

60. I believe in the power of great art to transcend geographical boundaries, political differences and even the restrictions of time.

ARMAND HAMMER, *HAMMER* (1987), WITH NEIL LYNDON

61. Nobody, I think, ought to read poetry, or look at pictures or statues, who cannot find a great deal more in them than the poet or artist has actually expressed.

NATHANIEL HAWTHORNE, *THE MARBLE FAUN* (1860), 41

62. Wonder at the first sight of works of art may be the effect of ignorance and novelty; but real admiration and permanent delight in them are the growth of taste and knowledge.

WILLIAM HAZLITT, "ON THE PLEASURE OF PAINTING," *TABLE TALK* (1821–22)

63. Bullfighting is the only art in which the artist is in danger of death and in which the degree of brilliance in the performance is left to the fighter's honor.

ERNEST HEMINGWAY, *DEATH IN THE AFTERNOON* (1932)

64. The genuine artist is as much a dissatisfied person as the revolutionary, yet how diametrically opposed are the products each distills from his dissatisfaction.

ERIC HOFFER, *THE PASSIONATE STATE OF MIND* (1954), 17

65. Art and science create a balance to material life and enlarge the world of living experience. Art leads to a more profound concept of life, because art itself is a profound expression of feeling.

HANS HOFMANN, *SEARCH FOR THE REAL* (1967)

66. If you would have me weep, you must first of all feel grief yourself.

HORACE, *ARS POETICA* (13–8 B.C.)

67. He is the true enchanter, whose spell operates, not upon the senses, but upon the imagination and the heart.

WASHINGTON IRVING, "STRATFORD ON AVON," *THE SKETCH BOOK OF GEOFFREY CRAYON, GENT.* (1819–20)

68. The moment you cheat for the sake of beauty, you know you're an artist.

MAX JACOB, *ART POÉTIQUE* (1922)

69. The first prerogative of an artist in any medium is to make a fool of himself.

PAULINE KAEL, "IS THERE A CURE FOR FILM CRITICISM?" *I LOST IT AT THE MOVIES* (1965)

70. Art changes all the time, but it never "improves." It may go down, or up, but it never improves as technology and medicine improve.

ALFRED KAZIN, "ART ON TRIAL," *HARPER'S MAGAZINE*, OCTOBER 1967

71. If art is to nourish the roots of our culture, society must set the artist free to follow his vision wherever it takes him.

JOHN F. KENNEDY, ADDRESS, AMHERST COLLEGE, AMHERST, MASS., OCT. 26, 1963

72. We must never forget that art is not a form of propaganda; it is a form of truth.

JOHN F. KENNEDY, ADDRESS, AMHERST COLLEGE, AMHERST, MASS., OCT. 26, 1963

73. Art does not reproduce the visible; rather, it makes visible.

PAUL KLEE, *THE INWARD VISION* (1959)

74. The more minimal the art, the more maximum the explanation.

HILTON KRAMER, QUOTED IN MARILYN BENDER'S *THE BEAUTIFUL PEOPLE* (1967)

75. Art, for most Americans, is a very queer fish—it can't be reasoned with, it can't be bribed, it can't be doped out or duplicated; above all, it can't be cashed in on.

LOUIS KRONENBERGER, *COMPANY MANNERS* (1954), 1.1

76. The language of art is powerful to those who understand it, and puzzling to those who do not. What we do know is that here was the modern human mind at work, spinning symbolism and abstraction in a way that only *Homo sapiens* is capable of doing.

RICHARD LEAKEY, *THE ORIGIN OF HUMANKIND* (1994)

77. Democracy has no place in the arts; the word democracy, as it is presently misused, is a euphemism for deterioration.

WALTER LEGGE AND ELISABETH SCHWARZKOPF, *ON AND OFF THE RECORD: A MEMOIR OF WALTER LEGGE* (1982)

78. Art enlarges experience by admitting us to the inner life of others.

WALTER LIPPMANN, "THE GOLDEN RULE AND AFTER," *A PREFACE TO POLITICS* (1914)

79. The artist in his teens who is happy is a charlatan. Life comes bursting in all around us too suddenly, too crudely, too cruelly, for happiness.

WILLIAM MCFEE, "DEDICATION," *HARBOURS OF MEMORY* (1921)

80. With the pride of the artist, you must blow against the walls of every power that exists, the small trumpet of your defiance.

NORMAN MAILER, *THE DEER PARK* (1955), 28

81. The only domain where the divine is visible is that of art, whatever name we choose to call it.

ANDRÉ MALRAUX, *LES MÉTAMORPHOSES DES DIEUX* (1957), 2.1

82. There is a way of being an artist that goes so deep and is so much a matter of origins and destinies that no longing seems to it sweeter and more worth knowing than longing after the bliss of the commonplace.

THOMAS MANN, "TONIO KRÖGER" (1903), *DEATH IN VENICE*,, TR. H. T. LOWE-PORTER

83. Thought that can merge wholly into feeling, feeling that can merge wholly into thought—these are the artist's highest joy.

THOMAS MANN, TITLE STORY (1913), *DEATH IN VENICE*,, TR. H. T. LOWE-PORTER

84. An art is only great and significant if it is one that all may enjoy. The art of a clique is but a plaything.

W. SOMERSET MAUGHAM, *THE SUMMING UP* (1938), 76

85. Art should be appreciated with passion and violence, not with a tepid, deprecating elegance that fears the censoriousness of a common room.

W. SOMERSET MAUGHAM, *THE SUMMING UP* (1938), 24

86. The grandeur of man lies in song, not in thought.

FRANÇOIS MAURIAC, "THE POET'S PRIDE," *SECOND THOUGHTS* (1961), TR. ADRIENNE FOULKE

87. I already have a wife, who is too much for me; one who keeps me unceasingly struggling on. It is my art, and my works are my children.

MICHELANGELO BUONARROTI, *COMPLETE POEMS AND SELECTED LETTERS OF MICHELANGELO* (1963), TR. CREIGHTON GILBERT

88. No one has mastery/Before he is at the end/Of his art and his life.

MICHELANGELO BUONARROTI, *COMPLETE POEMS AND SELECTED LETTERS OF MICHELANGELO* (1963), TR. CREIGHTON GILBERT

89. Art teaches nothing, except the significance of life.

HENRY MILLER, "REFLECTIONS ON WRITING," *THE WISDOM OF THE HEART* (1941)

90. I feel that America is essentially against the artist, that the enemy of America is the artist, because he stands for individuality and creativeness, and that's *un*-American somehow.

HENRY MILLER, INTERVIEW, *WRITERS AT WORK: SECOND SERIES* (1963)

91. When we think we don't like art it is because it is artificial art.

MARIANNE MOORE, "ONE TIMES ONE," *THE COMPLETE PROSE OF MARIANNE MOORE* (1986)

92. Every work of art is an abstraction from time; it denies the reality of change and decay and death.

LEWIS MUMFORD, *FINDINGS AND KEEPINGS. ANALECTS FOR AN AUTOBIOGRAPHY* (1975)

93. Every artist is an unhappy lover. And unhappy lovers want to tell their story.

IRIS MURDOCH, *THE BLACK PRINCE* (1973)

94. To speak of morals in art is to speak of legislature in sex. Art is the sex of the imagination.

GEORGE JEAN NATHAN, "ART," *AMERICAN MERCURY*, JULY 1926

95. Art is essentially the affirmation, the blessing, and the deification of existence.

NIETZSCHE, *THE WILL TO POWER* (1888), 821, TR. ANTHONY M. LUDOVICI

96. Art raises its head where creeds relax.

NIETZSCHE, *HUMAN, ALL TOO HUMAN* (1878), 150, TR. HELEN ZIMMERN

97. Just as our historical beginnings are utterly mysterious—why are we born? why when and as we are?—so too are the beginnings of works of art and of "artists."

JOYCE CAROL OATES, "BEGINNINGS," *(WOMAN) WRITER: OCCASIONS AND OPPORTUNITIES* (1988)

98. The trend toward pure art betrays not arrogance, as is often thought, but modesty. Art that has rid itself of human pathos is a thing without consequence—just art with no other pretenses.

JOSÉ ORTEGA Y GASSET, *THE DEHUMANIZATION OF ART* (1925)

99. Were art to redeem man, it could do so only by saving him from the seriousness of life and restoring him to an unexpected boyishness.

JOSÉ ORTEGA Y GASSET, *THE DEHUMANIZATION OF ART* (1925)

100. Being an artist means ceasing to take seriously that very serious person we are when we are not an artist.

JOSÉ ORTEGA Y GASSET, *THE DEHUMANIZATION OF ART* (1925)

101. All art constantly aspires towards the condition of music.

WALTER PATER, "GIORGIONE," *STUDIES IN THE HISTORY OF THE RENAISSANCE* (1873)

102. Art comes to you proposing frankly to give nothing but the highest quality to your moments as they pass.

WALTER PATER, "CONCLUSION," *STUDIES IN THE HISTORY OF THE RENAISSANCE* (1873)

103. Art is what remains of religion: the dance above the yawning abyss.

OCTAVIO PAZ, "NIHILISM AND DIALECTICS," *ALTERNATING CURRENT* (1973)

104. The classical artist can be recognized by his sincerity, the romantic by his laborious insincerity.

CHARLES PÉGUY, PREFACE TO JEAN HUGUES' *LA GRÈVE*

105. Art is a lie that makes us realize the truth.

PABLO PICASSO, *QUOTE*, SEPT. 21, 1958

106. As to the artists, do we not know that he only of them whom love inspires has the light of fame?—he whom love touches not walks in darkness.

PLATO, *THE SYMPOSIUM* (4TH C. B.C.), TR. BENJAMIN JOWETT

107. The death of every art form seems imminent at least once in every century; but while the very funeral arrangements go forward, some child is born who is Michelangelo, Picasso, Yeats.

REYNOLDS PRICE (1987), *A COMMON ROOM 1954–1987* (1987)

108. Ods life! must one swear to the truth of a song?

MATTHEW PRIOR, "A BETTER ANSWER" (1718)

109. I believe that all true art is classic, but the dictates of the mind rarely permit of its being recognized as such when it first appears.

MARCEL PROUST, *LETTERS OF MARCEL PROUST* (1949). TR.-ED. MINA CURTISS

110. Less disappointing than life is, great works of art do not begin by giving us all their best.

MARCEL PROUST, *REMEMBRANCE OF THINGS PAST: WITHIN A BUDDING GROVE* (1913–27), TR. C. K. SCOTT-MONCRIEFF

111. Thanks to art, instead of seeing one world, our own, we see it multiplied and as many original artists as there are, so many worlds are at our disposal.

MARCEL PROUST, *REMEMBRANCE OF THINGS PAST: THE PAST RECAPTURED* (1913–27), TR. STEPHEN HUDSON

112. Art is never didactic, does not take kindly to facts, is helpless to grapple with theories, and is killed outright by a sermon.

AGNES REPPLIER, "FICTION IN THE PULPIT," *POINTS OF VIEW* (1891)

113. Most events are inexpressible, taking place in a realm which no word has ever entered, and more inexpressible than all else are works of art, mysterious existences, the life of which, while ours passes away, endures.

RAINER MARIA RILKE, *LETTERS TO A YOUNG POET,* FEB. 17, 1903, TR. M. D. HERTER NORTON

114. Art is a by-product of an honest and successful attempt to do something well.

ANDREW A. ROONEY, "MOVIES," *PIECES OF MY MIND* (1984)

115. An artist doesn't necessarily have deeper feelings than other people, but he can express these feelings. He is like everyone else—only more so! He speaks with a Formal Sigh.

NED ROREM, "FOUR QUESTIONS ANSWERED," *MUSIC FROM INSIDE OUT* (1967)

116. Artists—by definition innocent—don't steal. But they do borrow without giving back.

NED ROREM, "ANATOMY OF TWO SONGS," *MUSIC FROM INSIDE OUT* (1967)

117. An artist should be well read in the best books, and thoroughly high bred, both in heart and bearing. In a word, he should be fit for the best society, *and should keep out of it*.

JOHN RUSKIN, *THE STONES OF VENICE* (1851–53), V. 3, 2.13

118. Fine art is that in which the hand, the head, and the heart of man go together.

JOHN RUSKIN, *THE TWO PATHS* (1859), 2

119. Great art is precisely that which never was, nor will be taught, it is preeminently and finally the expression of the spirits of great men.

JOHN RUSKIN, *MODERN PAINTERS* (1843–60), V. 3, 4.3.28

120. To follow art for the sake of being a great man, and therefore to cast about continually for some means of achieving position or attracting admiration, is the surest way of ending in total extinction.

JOHN RUSKIN, *MODERN PAINTERS* (1843–60), V. 3, 4.3.3

121. We must not subject him who creates to the desires of the multitude. It is, rather, his creation that must become the multitude's desire.

SAINT-EXUPÉRY, *THE WISDOM OF THE SANDS* (1948), 23, TR. STUART GILBERT

122. Art is the response to the demand for entertainment, for the stimulation of our senses and imagination, and truth enters into it only as it subserves these ends.

GEORGE SANTAYANA, *THE SENSE OF BEAUTY* (1896), 2

123. Art, like life, should be free, since both are experimental.

GEORGE SANTAYANA, *THE LIFE OF REASON: REASON IN ART* (1905–06), 9

124. The man who would emancipate art from discipline and reason is trying to elude rationality, not merely in art, but in all existence.

GEORGE SANTAYANA, *THE LIFE OF REASON: REASON IN ART* (1905–06), 9

125. The arts must study their occasions; they must stand modestly aside until they can slip in fitly into the interstices of life.

GEORGE SANTAYANA, *THE SENSE OF BEAUTY* (1896), 2

126. Every artist is *in* everything he creates, and indeed if the truth is told, every person is *in* his life, *in* his work, whatever his work may be, and this is visible in his face, figure, stance, movement, and totality.

WILLIAM SAROYAN, *SONS COME & GO, MOTHERS HANG IN FOREVER* (1979)

127. Art is the right hand of nature. The latter only gave us being, but the former made us men.

SCHILLER, *FIESCO* (1783), 2.17

128. The artist is the child of his time; but woe to him if he is also its disciple, or even its favorite.

SCHILLER, *ON THE AESTHETIC EDUCATION OF MAN* (1795), 9, TR. REGINALD SNELL

129. Art almost always has its ingredient of impudence, its flouting of established authority, so that it may substitute its own authority and its own enlightenment.

BEN SHAHN, "ARTISTS IN COLLEGES," *THE SHAPE OF CONTENT* (1957)

130. The true artist will let his wife starve, his children go barefoot, his mother drudge for his living at seventy, sooner than work at anything but his art.

GEORGE BERNARD SHAW, *MAN AND SUPERMAN* (1903), 1

131. Without art, the crudeness of reality would make the world unbearable.

George Bernard Shaw, *Back to Methuselah* (1921), 5

132. You use a glass mirror to see your face: you use works of art to see your soul.

George Bernard Shaw, *Back to Methuselah* (1921), 5

133. Poets, not otherwise than philosophers, painters, sculptors, and musicians, are, in one sense, the creators, and, in another, the creations, of their age.

Shelley, preface, *Prometheus Unbound* (1818–19)

134. Art postulates communion, and the artist has an imperative need to make others share the joy which he experiences himself.

Igor Stravinsky, *An Autobiography* (1936), 10

135. The artist is the lover of Nature, therefore he is her slave and her master.

Rabindranath Tagore, *Stray Birds* (1916), 85

136. Most of the faint intimations of immortality of which we are occasionally aware would seem to arise out of Art or the materials of Art.

James Thurber, *Collecting Himself* (1989)

137. What marks the artist is his power to shape the material of pain we all have.

Lionel Trilling, "Art and Neurosis," *The Liberal Imagination* (1950)

138. Art imitates Nature in this: not to dare is to dwindle.

John Updike, "Beerbohm and Others," *Assorted Prose* (1965)

139. Art is like baby shoes. When you coat them with gold, they can no longer be worn.

John Updike, "Alphonse Peintre," *Assorted Prose* (1965)

140. The refusal to rest content, the willingness to risk excess on behalf of one's obsessions, is what distinguishes artists from entertainers, and what makes some artists adventurers on behalf of us all.

John Updike, "Franny and Zooey," *Assorted Prose* (1965)

141. The creation of a work of art, like an act of love, is our one small "yes" at the center of a vast "no."

Gore Vidal, *Rocking the Boat* (1962)

142. The good artist, like the wise man, addresses himself to life and invests with his private vision the deeds and thoughts of men.

Gore Vidal, *Rocking the Boat* (1962)

143. To open up the new, to look back on the old may bring forth like discoveries in the practice of art.

Eudora Welty, "The House of Willa Cather," *The Eye of the Story* (1978)

144. Fertilisation of the soul is the reason for the necessity of art.

Alfred North Whitehead, *Science and the Modern World* (1925), 13

145. If art [is] to have a special train, the critic must keep some seats reserved on it.

Oscar Wilde, *The Artist as Critic: The Critical Writings of Oscar Wilde* (1969) ed. Richard Ellmann

146. It is through Art, and through Art only, that we can realize our perfection; and through Art, and Art only, that we can shield ourselves from the sordid perils of actual existence.

Oscar Wilde, *The Artist as Critic: The Critical Writings of Oscar Wilde* (1969) ed. Richard Ellmann

147. The final revelation is that Lying, the telling of beautiful untrue things, is the proper aim of Art.

Oscar Wilde, *The Artist as Critic: The Critical Writings of Oscar Wilde* (1969) ed. Richard Ellmann

148. All art is at once surface and symbol. Those who go beneath the surface do so at their peril.

Oscar Wilde, preface, *The Picture of Dorian Gray* (1891)

149. Good artists exist simply in what they make, and consequently are perfectly uninteresting in what they are.

Oscar Wilde, *The Picture of Dorian Gray* (1891), 4

150. No great artist ever sees things as they really are. If he did he would cease to be an artist.

Oscar Wilde, "The Decay of Lying," *Intentions* (1891)

151. To reveal art and conceal the artist is art's aim.

Oscar Wilde, preface, *The Picture of Dorian Gray* (1891)

152. This is the artist, then—life's hungry man, the glutton of eternity, beauty's miser, glory's slave.

Thomas Wolfe, *Of Time and the River* (1935), 62

153. If you ask me what I came to do in this world, I, an artist, I will answer you: "I am here to live out loud."

Émile Zola, *Mes haines* (1866)

54. ARTIFICIALITY

See also 45. Appearance; 60. Authenticity; 732. Pretension; 951. Superficiality

1. Ours is the age of substitutes: instead of language, we have jargon; instead of principles, slogans; and, instead of genuine ideas, Bright ideas.

ERIC BENTLEY, *THE DRAMATIC EVENT* (1954)

2. To know only artificial night is as absurd and evil as to know only artificial day.

HENRY BESTON, "NIGHT ON THE GREAT BEACH," *THE OUTERMOST HOUSE* (1928)

3. Natural beauty is essentially temporary and sad; hence the impression of obscene mockery which artificial flowers give us.

JOHN UPDIKE, "RHYMING MAX," *ASSORTED PROSE* (1965)

4. A cynic might suggest as the motto of modern life this simple legend—"Just as good as the real."

CHARLES DUDLEY WARNER, "FIRST STUDY," *BACKLOG STUDIES* (1873)

5. The first duty in life is to be as artificial as possible. What the second duty is no one has yet discovered.

OSCAR WILDE, "PHRASES AND PHILOSOPHIES FOR THE USE OF THE YOUNG" (1891)

ASCETICISM

See 865. SELF-DENIAL

55. ASPIRATION

See also 6. ACHIEVEMENT; 33. AMBITION; 945. SUCCESS

1. What you are must always displease you, if you would attain to that which you are not.

ST. AUGUSTINE, *SERMONS* (5TH C.), 150

2. Ah, but a man's reach should exceed his grasp, / Or what's a heaven for?

ROBERT BROWNING, "ANDREA DEL SARTO," *MEN AND WOMEN* (1855)

3. If you aspire to the highest place, it is no disgrace to stop at the second, or even the third, place.

CICERO, *ON ORATORY* (55 B.C.)

4. Every man believes that he has a greater possibility.

EMERSON, "CIRCLES," *ESSAYS: FIRST SERIES* (1841)

5. First, say to yourself what you would be; and then do what you have to do.

EPICTETUS, *DISCOURSES* (2ND C.), 3.23, TR. THOMAS W. HIGGINSON

6. Slight not what's near through aiming at what's far.

EURIPIDES, *RHESUS* (C. 455–41 B.C.), 482, TR. M. H. MORGAN

7. Just as a cautious businessman avoids tying up all his capital in one concern, so, perhaps, worldly wisdom will advise us not to look for the whole of our satisfaction from a single aspiration.

SIGMUND FREUD, *CIVILIZATION AND ITS DISCONTENTS* (1930), 2, TR. JAMES STRACHEY

8. I drink the wine of aspiration and the drug of illusion. Thus I am never dull.

JOHN GALSWORTHY, *THE WINE HORN MOUNTAIN*

9. People are always neglecting something they can do in trying to do something they can't do.

EDGAR WATSON HOWE, *COUNTRY TOWN SAYINGS* (1911)

10. He who stands on tiptoe does not stand firm.

LAO TZU, *THE CHARACTER OF TAO* (6TH. C. B.C.), 24, TR. LIN YUTANG

11. If you would hit the mark, you must aim a little above it; / Every arrow that flies feels the attraction of earth.

LONGFELLOW, "ELEGIAC VERSE" (1881)

12. Life is a petty thing unless it is moved by the indomitable urge to extend its boundaries. Only in proportion as we are desirous of living more do we really live.

JOSÉ ORTEGA Y GASSET, *THE DEHUMANIZATION OF ART* (1925)

13. The American dream. Those three short, simple words encompass the hopes and aspirations of all the peoples on earth. The words are not only short and simple. They are also fragile.

ROSS PEROT, *UNITED WE STAND: HOW WE CAN TAKE BACK OUR COUNTRY* (1992)

14. May God grant me love for that which has splendor; / but in this time of my life let me strive for attainable things.

PINDAR, *ODES* (5TH C. B.C.), PYTHIA 11, TR. RICHMOND LATTIMORE

15. He who bears in his heart a cathedral to be built is already victorious. He who seeks to become sexton of a finished cathedral is already defeated.

SAINT-EXUPÉRY, *FLIGHT TO ARRAS* (1942), 22, TR. LEWIS GALANTIÈRE

16. The clash between the aspirations of the people for a better life and the insistence of their rulers on building a powerful state, regardless of human sacrifice, runs through the whole of Russian history.

HARRISON E. SALISBURY, *RUSSIA* (1965)

17. 'Tis but a base, ignoble mind / That mounts no higher than a bird can soar.

SHAKESPEARE, *2 HENRY VI* (1590–91), 2.1

18. An aspiration is a joy for ever, a possession as solid as a landed estate, a fortune which we can never exhaust and which gives us year by year a revenue of pleasurable activity.

ROBERT LOUIS STEVENSON, "EL DORADO," *VIRGINIBUS PUERISQUE* (1881)

19. It is only the fools who keep straining at high C all their lives.

CHARLES DUDLEY WARNER, "THIRD STUDY," *BACKLOG STUDIES* (1873)

20. We are all in the gutter, but some of us are looking at the stars.

OSCAR WILDE, *LADY WINDERMERE'S FAN* (1892), 3

21. Too low they build, who build beneath the stars.

EDWARD YOUNG, *NIGHT THOUGHTS* (1742–46), 8.215

ASSERTION

See 859. SELF-ASSERTION

56. ASSISTANCE

See also 120. CHARITY; 235. DEPENDENCE; 384. GIFTS AND GIVING; 433. HUMANITARIANISM; 887. SERVICE; 1023. USEFULNESS

1. If the sailors become too numerous, the ship sinks.

ARABIC PROVERB

2. It is hideous and coarse to assume that we can do something for others—and it is vile not to endeavor to do it.

EDWARD DAHLBERG, *BECAUSE I WAS FLESH* (1963)

3. The aid we can give each other is only incidental, lateral, and sympathetic.

EMERSON, *JOURNALS,* 1836

4. It is not necessary to light a candle to the sun.

ENGLISH PROVERB

5. Often we can help each other most by leaving each other alone; at other times we need the hand-grasp and the word of cheer.

ELBERT HUBBARD, *THE NOTE BOOK* (1927)

6. With so many roosters crowing, the sun never comes up.

ITALIAN PROVERB

7. We are doubly willing to jump into the water after some one who has fallen in, if there are people present who have not the courage to do so.

NIETZSCHE, *HUMAN, ALL TOO HUMAN* (1878), 325, TR. HELEN ZIMMERN

8. At bottom, and just in the deepest and most important things, we are unutterably alone, and for one person to be able to advise or even help another, a lot must happen, a lot must go well, a whole constellation of things must come right in order once to succeed.

RAINER MARIA RILKE, *LETTERS TO A YOUNG POET,* APRIL 5, 1903, TR. M. D. HERTER NORTON

9. 'Tis not enough to help the feeble up, / But to support him after.

SHAKESPEARE, *TIMON OF ATHENS* (1607–08), 1.1.107

10. The bird thinks it is an act of kindness to give the fish a lift in the air.

RABINDRANATH TAGORE, *STRAY BIRDS* (1916), 123

11. Knowing sorrow well, I learn the way to succor the distressed.

VERGIL, *AENEID* (30–19 B.C.), 1.630, TR. T. H. DELABERE-MAY

57. ASSOCIATION

See also 22. AFFINITY; 152. COMPANY; 333. FAMILIARITY; 804. REPUTATION

1. The strong and the weak cannot keep company.

AESOP, "THE TWO POTS," *FABLES* (6TH C. B.C.?), TR. JOSEPH JACOBS

2. Whoever touches pitch will be defiled.

APOCRYPHA, ECCLESIASTICUS 13:1

3. A wise man associating with the vicious becomes an idiot; a dog traveling with good men becomes a rational being.

ARABIC PROVERB

4. Can a man take fire in his bosom, and his clothes not be burned?

BIBLE, PROVERBS 6:27

5. A man is known by the company he organizes.

AMBROSE BIERCE, "SAW," *THE DEVIL'S DICTIONARY* (1881–1911)

6. Tell me thy company, and I'll tell thee what thou art.

CERVANTES, *DON QUIXOTE* (1605–15), 2.3.23, TR. PETER MOTTEUX AND JOHN OZELL

7. Bad company is as instructive as debauchery: one is indemnified for the loss of innocence by the loss of prejudice.

DENIS DIDEROT, *RAMEAU'S NEPHEW* (1762), TR. JACQUES BARZUN AND RALPH H. BOWEN

8. The sun visits cesspools without being defiled.

DIOGENES THE CYNIC, (4TH C. B.C.), QUOTED IN DIOGENES LAERTIUS' *LIVES AND OPINIONS OF EMINENT PHILOSOPHERS* (3RD C. A.D.), TR. R. D. HICKS

9. Every man is like the company he is wont to keep.

EURIPIDES, *PHOENIX* (C. 425 B.C.), 809, TR. M. H. MORGAN

10. Better fare hard with good men than feast it with bad.

THOMAS FULLER, M.D., *GNOMOLOGIA* (1732), 893

11. He that lies down with dogs shall rise up with fleas.

LATIN PROVERB

12. The lion is ashamed, it's true, when he / Hunts with the fox:—of foxes, not of guile.

GOTTHOLD EPHRAIM LESSING, *NATHAN THE WISE* (1779), 3.5, TR. BAYARD QUINCY MORGAN

13. By associating with good and evil persons a man acquires the virtues and vices which they possess, even as the wind blowing over different places takes along good and bad odours.

PANCHATANTRA (C. 5TH C.), 1, TR. FRANKLIN EDGERTON

14. If you live with a cripple, you will learn to limp.

PLUTARCH, "THE EDUCATION OF CHILDREN," *MORALIA* (C. A.D. 100), TR. MOSES HADAS

15. To take refuge with an inferior is to betray one's self.

PUBLILIUS SYRUS, *MORAL SAYINGS* (1ST C. B.C.), 667, TR. DARIUS LYMAN

16. Court the society of a superior, and make much of the opportunity; for in the company of an equal thy good fortune must decline.

SA'DI, *GULISTAN* (1258), 6.2, TR. JAMES ROSS

17. Let me have men about me that are fat, / Sleek-headed men, and such as sleep-a-nights. / Yond Cassius has a lean and hungry look. / He thinks too much. Such men are dangerous.

SHAKESPEARE, *JULIUS CAESAR* (1599–1600), 1.2.192

18. It is better to weep with wise men than to laugh with fools.

SPANISH PROVERB

19. Satan's friendship reaches to the prison door.

TURKISH PROVERB

ASSURANCE

See 115. CERTAINTY; 860. SELF-CONFIDENCE

ASTRONOMY

See 415. THE HEAVENS; 849. SCIENCE

ATHEISM

See 1004. UNBELIEF

ATOM

See 641. NUCLEAR POWER

58. ATTITUDE

See also 689. PERSPECTIVE

1. If you look at life one way, there is always cause for alarm.

ELIZABETH BOWEN, *THE DEATH OF THE HEART* (1938), 3.6

2. There is no object on earth which cannot be looked at from a cosmic point of view.

DOSTOYEVSKY, "CRITICAL ARTICLES: INTRODUCTION," *POLNOYE SOBRANIYE SOCHINYENI* (*COMPLETE COLLECTED WORKS*, 1895), V. 9

3. There are no ugly loves nor handsome prisons.

BENJAMIN FRANKLIN, *POOR RICHARD'S ALMANACK* (1732–57)

4. It is the disposition of the thought that altereth the nature of the thing.

JOHN LYLY, *EUPHUES: THE ANATOMY OF WIT* (1579)

5. All seems infected that the infected spy, / As all looks yellow to the jaundiced eye.

ALEXANDER POPE, *AN ESSAY ON CRITICISM* (1711), 2.358

6. The eye of the master fattens the steed.

SPANISH PROVERB

AUDACITY

See 92. BOLDNESS

59. AUDIENCE

See also 11. ACTORS; 650. OBSERVATION; 972. THEATER

1. Actors should be overheard, not listened to, and the audience is fifty percent of the performance.

SHIRLEY BOOTH, NEWS SUMMARIES, DEC. 13, 1954

2. If one talks to more than four people, it is an audience; and one cannot really think or exchange thoughts with an audience.

ANNE MORROW LINDBERGH, "THE PAPER AND STRING OF LIFE," *NORTH TO THE ORIENT* (1935)

3. The audience is a very curious animal. It is shrewd rather than intelligent. Its mental capacity is less than that of its most intellectual members.

W. SOMERSET MAUGHAM, *THE SUMMING UP* (1938), 36

4. The audience is not the least important actor in the play and if it will not do its allotted share the play falls to pieces.

W. SOMERSET MAUGHAM, *THE SUMMING UP* (1938), 36

5. It's the admirer and the watcher who provoke us to all the insanities we commit.

SENECA, *LETTERS TO LUCILIUS* (1ST C.), 94.71, TR. E. PHILLIPS BARKER

6. An audience is an abstraction; it has no taste. It must depend on the only person who has (pardon, should have), the conductor.

IGOR STRAVINSKY, *CONVERSATIONS WITH IGOR STRAVINSKY* (1959)

7. To have great poets, there must be great audiences too.

WALT WHITMAN, "VENTURES ON AN OLD THEME," *NOTES LEFT OVER* (1881)

60. AUTHENTICITY

See also 54. ARTIFICIALITY

1. Men often applaud an imitation and hiss the real thing.

AESOP, "THE BUFFOON AND THE COUNTRYMAN," *FABLES* (6TH C. B.C.?), TR. JOSEPH JACOBS

2. The authentic is almost never found by being pursued; but there is no missing it when you are in its presence.

EVA HOFFMAN., *EXIT INTO HISTORY* (1993)

61. AUTHORITY

See also 531. LEADERSHIP; 644. OBEDIENCE; 719. POWER; 831. RULERS

1. No one can estimate the power of authority among poor and uneducated people in a world whose problems confuse even the wisest.

JOYCE CARY, *EXCEPT THE LORD* (1953)

2. Authority, as he knows it, is always dangerous, selfish, inexplicable. It looks after its own mysterious affairs in a dark privacy. It never explains.

JOYCE CARY, *MISTER JOHNSON* (1939)

3. If your heart is quite set upon a crown, make and put on one of roses, for it will make the prettier appearance.

EPICTETUS, *DISCOURSES* (2ND C.), 1.19, TR. THOMAS W. HIGGINSON

4. Authority is never without hate.

EURIPIDES, *ION* (C. 421–408 B.C.), TR. RONALD F. WILLETTS

5. New faces / Have more authority than accustomed ones.

EURIPIDES, *ANDROMACHE* (C. 426 B.C.), TR. JOHN F. NIMS

6. Lawful and settled authority is very seldom resisted when it is well employed.

SAMUEL JOHNSON, *THE RAMBLER* (1750–52), 50

7. Authority has every reason to fear the skeptic, for authority can rarely survive in the face of doubt.

ROBERT LINDNER, "EDUCATION FOR MATURITY," *MUST YOU CONFORM?* (1956)

8. Most men, after a little freedom, have preferred authority with the consoling assurances and the economy of effort which it brings.

WALTER LIPPMANN, *A PREFACE TO MORALS* (1929), 1.1.3

9. Jurisdiction is not given for the sake of the judge, but for that of the litigant.

PASCAL, *PENSÉES* (1670), 878, TR. W. F. TROTTER

10. Man, proud man, / Drest in a little brief authority, / Most ignorant of what he's most assured.

SHAKESPEARE, *MEASURE FOR MEASURE* (1604–05), 2.2.117

AUTHORS

See 1069. WRITING AND WRITERS

62. AUTOBIOGRAPHY

See also 81. BIOGRAPHY

1. I've always had a sneaking fondness for Martin Van Buren. He wrote his autobiography, you know, and never once mentioned his wife. Now that's what I call a man's man.

CLEVELAND AMORY, "YOUR GOVERNMENT," *THE TROUBLE WITH NOWADAYS* (1979)

2. When writing of oneself one should show no mercy. Yet why at the first attempt to discover one's

own truth does all inner strength seem to melt away in floods of self-pity and tenderness and rising tears?

GEORGES BERNANOS, *THE DIARY OF A COUNTRY PRIEST* (1936), 1, TR. PAMELA MORRIS

3. In reviewing my life, in tracing its course, I fill my cell with the pleasure of being what for want of a trifle I failed to be, recapturing, so that I may hurl myself into them as into dark pits, those moments when I strayed through the trap-ridden compartments of a subterranean sky.

JEAN GENET, *OUR LADY OF THE FLOWERS* (1949)

4. Autobiography is now as common as adultery, and hardly less reprehensible.

JOHN GRIGG, *SUNDAY TIMES*, LONDON, FEB. 28, 1962

5. The *Sonnets* [of Shakespeare] have the fascination of an autobiography, without its clarity. It is like reading an important document in a cave by the light of matches which keep blowing out.

GILBERT HIGHET, *THE POWERS OF POETRY* (1960)

6. "Reader, I am myself the subject of my book; you would be unreasonable to spend your leisure on so frivolous and so vain a matter."

BERNARD MALAMUD, *DUBIN'S LIVES* (1979)

7. When you put down the good things you ought to have done, and leave out the bad ones you did do—well, that's Memoirs.

WILL ROGERS, *THE AUTOBIOGRAPHY OF WILL ROGERS* (1949), 16

8. To start writing about your life is, from one standpoint, to stop living it. You must avoid adventures today so as to make time for registering those of yesterday.

NED ROREM, "RANDOM NOTES FROM A DIARY," *MUSIC FROM INSIDE OUT* (1967)

9. One senses, in all autobiography, a straining toward perfection, perfection of a kind that connects the individual with a cosmic pattern which, because it is perfect in itself, verifies that individual's own potential perfection.

ROGER ROSENBLATT, "BLACK AUTOBIOGRAPHY," *THE MAN IN THE WATER* (1994)

10. What pursuit is more elegant than that of collecting the ignominies of our nature and transfixing them for show, each on the bright pin of a polished phrase?

LOGAN PEARSALL SMITH, *AFTERTHOUGHTS* (1931), 6

11. I always say, keep a diary and someday it'll keep you.

MAE WEST, IN *EVERY DAY'S A HOLIDAY* (1937)

63. AUTOMATION

See also 966. TECHNOLOGY

1. The danger of the past was that men became slaves. The danger of the future is that men may become robots.

ERICH FROMM, *THE SANE SOCIETY* (1955), 9

64. AUTOMOBILES

See also 991. TRANSPORTATION

1. Except the American woman, nothing interests the eye of American man more than the automobile, or seems so important to him as an object of esthetic appreciation.

A. H. BARR, JR., ON DISPLAYING "POP ART" THAT INCORPORATED PIECES OF OLD AUTOMOBILES, 1963

2. After all, what is a pedestrian? He is a man who has two cars—one being driven by his wife, the other by one of his children.

ROBERT BRADBURY, *THE NEW YORK TIMES*, SEPT. 5, 1962

3. The automobile has not merely taken over the street, it has dissolved the living tissue of the city. Its appetite for space is absolutely insatiable; moving and parked, it devours urban land, leaving the buildings as mere islands of habitable space in a sea of dangerous and ugly traffic.

JAMES MARSTON FITCH, *THE NEW YORK TIMES*, MAY 1, 1960

4. To George F. Babbitt, as to most prosperous citizens of Zenith, his motor car was poetry and tragedy, love and heroism. The office was his pirate ship but the car his perilous excursion ashore.

SINCLAIR LEWIS, *BABBITT* (1922)

5. Driving a car [in Florence, Italy], you are in danger of killing; walking or standing, of being killed.

MARY MCCARTHY, *THE STONES OF FLORENCE* (1959)

6. The car has become a secular sanctuary for the individual, his shrine to the self, his mobile Walden Pond.

EDWARD MCDONAGH, *TIME*, MAY 10, 1963

7. The car has become an article of dress without which we feel uncertain, unclad, and incomplete.

MARSHALL MCLUHAN, *UNDERSTANDING MEDIA* (1964), 22

8. People on horses look better than they are. People in cars look worse than they are.

MARYA MANNES, *MORE IN ANGER* (1958), 1.4

9. Our national flower is the concrete cloverleaf.

LEWIS MUMFORD, *QUOTE*, OCT. 8, 1961

10. Beneath this slab / John Brown is stowed. / He watched the ads, / And not the road.

OGDEN NASH, "LATHER AS YOU GO," *GOOD INTENTIONS* (1943)

11. The thought was instantly smashed from my head by the noise of what sounded like an intercontinental bronchial hemorrhage, as the stock cars took off from their starting positions and went roaring around the stadium.

JONATHAN RABAN, *OLD GLORY* (1981)

12. [D]rivers in a traffic jam, frustrated by each other's presence, are not the most amiable of men.

DAVID RIESMAN, *ABUNDANCE FOR WHAT?* (1964)

13. A man today never feels so alive as when he is hurtling from one point to another on the azimuth.

JEAN SHEPHERD, "I HEAR AMERICA SINGING: OR -LEAVES OF GRASS' REVISITED," *THE FERRARI IN THE BEDROOM* (1972)

14. If you want to take a couple of weeks off and do something that you will never forget, that trip up the Alaskan Highway will do until they run excursion capsules to the Moon.

JEAN SHEPHERD, "ONE DAY THE FOG LIFTED—," *THE FERRARI IN THE BEDROOM* (1972)

15. Everything in life is somewhere else, and you get there in a car.

E. B. WHITE, "FRO-JOY," *ONE MAN'S MEAT* (1944)

16. As hand-to-hand combat has gradually disappeared from our civilization, even in wartime, and competition has become more and more sophisticated and abstract, Americans have turned to the automobile to satisfy their love of direct aggression.

TOM WOLFE, *THE KANDY-KOLORED TANGERINE-FLAKE STREAMLINE BABY* (1965)

AUTONOMY

See 867. SELF-DETERMINATION; 880. SELF-SUFFICIENCY

AUTUMN

See 854. SEASONS

AVARICE

See 403. GREED

AWARENESS

See 175. CONSCIOUSNESS; 883. SENSIBILITY

B

65. BABIES

See also 123. CHILDREN

1. John did not remember very clearly the first time she had gone, to have Roy; folks said that he had cried and carried on the whole time his mother was away; he remembered only enough to be afraid every time her belly began to swell, knowing that each time the swelling began it would not end until she was taken from him, to come back with a stranger.

James Baldwin, *Go Tell It on the Mountain* (1953)

2. The human baby, the human being, is a mosaic of animal and angel.

Jacob Bronowski, *The Ascent of Man* (1973)

3. They [babies] are so small and so helpless that they contribute vastly to a comforting glow in the ego of the grown-up.

Heywood Broun, "Holding a Baby," in *Fifty Great Essays* (1964)

4. There are one hundred and fifty-two distinctly different ways of holding a baby—and all are right.

Heywood Broun, "Holding a Baby," *Seeing Things at Night* (1921)

5. Tender are a mother's dreams, / But her babe's not what he seems. / See him plotting in his mind / To grow up some other kind.

Clarence Day, "Thoughts on Peculiar Dawns," *Thoughts Without Words* (1928)

6. Every baby born into the world is a finer one than the last.

Charles Dickens, *Nicholas Nickleby* (1838–39), 36

7. Infancy conforms to nobody; all conform to it.

Emerson, "Self-Reliance," *Essays: First Series* (1841)

8. A baby is an angel whose wings decrease as his legs increase.

French Proverb

9. Once upon a time and a very good time it was there was a moocow coming down along the road and this moocow that was down along the road met a nicens little boy named baby tuckoo....

James Joyce, *Portrait of the Artist as a Young Man* (1916)

10. There lay the little miracle among the pillows: so well formed, so encompassed, as it were, with the harmony of sweet proportions, with little hands that even then, though so much tinier, were beautiful as now; with wide-open eyes blue as the sky and brighter than the sunshine—and almost in that very second he felt himself captured and held fast.

Thomas Mann, "Disorder and Early Sorrow" (1925)

11. All babies look like Winston Churchill.

Edward R. Murrow, Television broadcast, *Person to Person*

12. Adam and Eve had many advantages, but the principal one was that they escaped teething.

Mark Twain, "Pudd'nhead Wilson's Calendar," *Pudd'nhead Wilson* (1894), 4

66. BACHELORS

1. It is a truth universally acknowledged, that a single man in possession of a good fortune, must be in want of a wife.

Jane Austen, *Pride and Prejudice* (1813), 1

2. I would be married, but I'd have no wife, / I would be married to a single life.

Richard Crashaw, "On Marriage," *The Delights of the Muses* (1646)

3. There is no character in the comedy of human life more difficult to play well than that of an old bachelor.

Washington Irving, "Bachelors," *Bracebridge Hall* (1822)

4. Marriage has many pains, but celibacy has no pleasures.

Samuel Johnson, *Rasselas* (1759), 26

5. The great sculptors and architects who stamped the outward city [Florence, Italy] with its permanent image or style—Brunelleschi, Donatello, Michelangelo—were all bachelors. Monks, soldier-saints, prophets, hermits were the city's heroes.

Mary McCarthy, *The Stones of Florence* (1959)

6. The bachelor's admired freedom is often a yoke, for the freer a man is to himself the greater slave he often is to the whims of others.

GEORGE JEAN NATHAN, *THE BACHELOR LIFE* (1941)

7. The fear of women is the basis of good health.

SPANISH PROVERB

8. Bachelor's fare: bread and cheese and kisses.

JONATHAN SWIFT, *POLITE CONVERSATION* (1738), I

9. He was himself a homeless bachelor with a past, much in debt, and nothing gave more pleasure than to envy his friends their wives and comforts and to speak of them intimately and disparagingly.

DYLAN THOMAS, *PORTRAIT OF THE ARTIST AS A YOUNG DOG* (1940)

10. He's such an old bachelor that the way he cleans out his fireplace is to carry the ashes through the house, shovel-load at a time, and dump 'em out through the front door.

EUDORA WELTY, *LOSING BATTLES* (1970)

67. BACKGROUND

See also 294. ENVIRONMENT

1. The background reveals the true being and state of being of the man or thing. If I do not possess the background, I make the man transparent, the thing transparent.

JUAN RAMÓN JIMÉNEZ, "JOSÉ MARTÍ," *SELECTED WRITINGS* (1957), TR. H. R. HAYS

BAD

See 307. EVIL; 1055. WICKEDNESS; 1070. WRONGDOING

BAD TEMPER

See 968. TEMPER, BAD

68. BANALITY

See also 95. BORES

1. The banalities of a great man pass for wit.

ALEXANDER CHASE, *PERSPECTIVES* (1966)

2. American bankers believe in the personal touch; the teller conveys a sense that he happens to be there accidentally and he is overjoyed at the lucky chance of the encounter.

GRAHAM GREENE (1958), *OUR MAN IN HAVANA*

3. In modern life nothing produces such an effect as a good platitude. It makes the whole world kin.

OSCAR WILDE, *AN IDEAL HUSBAND* (1895), I

69. BANKING

See also 104. BUSINESS AND COMMERCE

1. [T]he turn of the century was the age of the banker, so much so that the leading bankers of the day had become legendary figures in the public imagination—vast, overshadowing behemoths whose colossal power seemed to reach everywhere.

DORIS KEARNS GOODWIN, *THE FITZGERALDS AND THE KENNEDYS* (1987)

2. Put not your trust in money, but put your money in trust.

OLIVER WENDELL HOLMES, SR., *THE AUTOCRAT OF THE BREAKFAST TABLE* (1858), 2

3. A bank is a place that will lend you money if you can prove that you don't need it.

BOB HOPE, QUOTED IN ALAN HARRINGTON'S "THE TYRANNY OF FORMS," *LIFE IN THE CRYSTAL PALACE* (1959)

4. The short-term international capital market is shrunken and erratic, and cannot be relied upon to cushion the effects of tendencies to disequilibrium in the balance of payments.

GUNNAR MYRDAL, *BEYOND THE WELFARE STATE* (1960)

70. BARBARISM

See also 133. CIVILIZATION

1. To most people a savage nation is wan that doesn't wear oncomf'rtable clothes.

FINLEY PETER DUNNE, "CASUAL OBSERVATIONS," *MR. DOOLEY'S PHILOSOPHY* (1990)

2. Savagery is necessary every four or five hundred years in order to bring the world back to life. Otherwise the world would die of civilization.

EDMOND AND JULES DE GONCOURT, *JOURNAL*, SEPT. 3, 1855, TR. ROBERT BALDICK

3. Men have been barbarians much longer than they have been civilized. They are only precariously civilized, and within us there is the propensity, persistent as the force of gravity, to revert under stress and strain, under neglect or temptation, to our first natures.

WALTER LIPPMANN, *THE PUBLIC PHILOSOPHY* (1955), 7.5

4. Since barbarism has its pleasures it naturally has its apologists.

George Santayana, *The Life of Reason: Reason in Society* (1905–06), 3

5. The existence of the soldier, next to capital punishment, is the most grievous vestige of barbarism which survives among men.

Alfred De Vigny, *Servitude et grandeur militaires* (1835), 1.2

71. BASEBALL

See also 929. Sports

1. Baseball, it is said, is only a game. True. And the Grand Canyon is only a hole in Arizona. Not all holes, or games, are created equal.

George F. Will, *Men At Work: The Craft of Baseball* (1990)

BASHFULNESS

See 980. Timidity

BATHING

See 137. Cleanliness

72. BEAUTY

See also 121. Charm; 192. Cosmetics; 396. Grace; 1003. Ugliness

1. Beauty is one of the rare things that do not lead to doubt of God.

Jean Anouilh, *Becket* (1959), 1

2. Beauty, real beauty, is something very grave. If there is a God, He must be partly that.

Jean Anouilh, *The Rehearsal* (1950), 2, tr. Lucienne Hill

3. Things are beautiful if you love them.

Jean Anouilh, *Mademoiselle Colombe* (1950), 2.2, tr. Louis Kronenberger

4. Personal beauty requires that one should be tall; little people may have charm and elegance, but beauty—no.

Aristotle, *Nicomachean Ethics* (4th c. b.c.), 4.3, tr. J. A. K. Thomson

5. Beauty is a greater recommendation than any letter of introduction.

Aristotle (4th c. b.c.), quoted in Diogenes Laertius' *Lives and Opinions of Eminent Philosophers* (3rd c.), tr. R. D. Hicks

6. Anything in any way beautiful derives its beauty from itself, and asks nothing beyond itself. Praise is no part of it, for nothing is made worse or better by praise.

Marcus Aurelius, *Meditations* (2nd c.), 4.20, tr. Maxwell Staniforth

7. She was as unmistakably American as the pink two-cent Washington postage stamp, as the Stars and Stripes, definitely more American in my eyes than the frizzy-haired big-bosomed dolls who won the title of Miss America each year at Atlantic City.

Luigi Barzini, *O America* (1977)

8. Beauty, n. The power by which a woman charms a lover and terrifies a husband.

Ambrose Bierce, *The Devil's Dictionary* (1881–1911)

9. Beauty is unbearable, drives us to despair, offering us for a minute the glimpse of an eternity that we should like to stretch out over the whole of time.

Albert Camus, *Notebooks 1935–1942* (1962), 1, tr. Philip Thody

10. There is in true beauty, as in courage, somewhat which narrow souls cannot dare to admire.

William Congreve, *The Old Bachelor* (1693), 4.4

11. It's only skin deep and it's transitory too. It's terribly transitory. I mean, how long does it last—thirty or forty or fifty years at the most—depending on how well you take care of yourself.

Mart Crowley, *The Boys in the Band* (1968)

12. Beauty—be not caused—It Is— / Chase it, and it ceases— / Chase it not, and it abides—.

Emily Dickinson, poem (c. 1862)

13. Unless all ages and races of men have been deluded by the same mass hypnotist (who?), there seems to be such a thing as beauty, a grace wholly gratuitous.

Annie Dillard, "Heaven and Earth in Jest," *Pilgrim at Tinker Creek* (1974)

14. Any extraordinary degree of beauty in man or woman involves a moral charm.

Emerson, "Worship," *The Conduct of Life* (1860)

15. Beauty without expression tires.

Emerson, "Beauty," *The Conduct of Life* (1860)

16. If eyes were made for seeing, / Then Beauty is its own excuse for being.

Emerson, "The Rhodora," *May Day and Other Pieces* (1867)

17. The beautiful rests on the foundations of the necessary.

EMERSON, "THE POET," *ESSAYS: SECOND SERIES* (1844)

18. Things are pretty, graceful, rich, elegant, handsome, but, until they speak to the imagination, not yet beautiful.

EMERSON, "BEAUTY," *THE CONDUCT OF LIFE* (1860)

19. We fly to Beauty as an asylum from the terrors of finite nature.

EMERSON, *JOURNALS*, 1836

20. Oh, what a vileness human beauty is, / corroding, corrupting everything it touches!

EURIPIDES, *ORESTES* (408 B.C.), TR. WILLIAM ARROWSMITH

21. The young prince in velvet gathered in lovely domesticity around the queen amid the hush of rich draperies may presently grow up to be Pedro the Cruel or Charles the Mad, but the moment of beauty was there.

F. SCOTT FITZGERALD, *THE CRACK-UP* (1945)

22. Beauty is a primeval phenomenon, which itself never makes its appearance, but the reflection of which is visible in a thousand different utterances of the creative mind, and is as various as nature herself.

GOETHE, QUOTED IN JOHANN PETER ECKERMANN'S *CONVERSATIONS WITH GOETHE*, APRIL 18, 1827

23. She was built with curves like the hull of a racing yacht, and you missed none of it with that wool jersey.

ERNEST HEMINGWAY, *THE SUN ALSO RISES* (1926)

24. I do not want no pretty woman. First thing you know, you fall in love with her—then you got to kill somebody about her. She'll make you so jealous, you'll bust!

LANGSTON HUGHES, *SIMPLE SPEAKS HIS MIND* (1950)

25. She who is born a beauty is born betrothed.

ITALIAN PROVERB

26. A thing of beauty is a joy for ever: / Its loveliness increases; it will never / Pass into nothingness.

KEATS, *ENDYMION* (1817), 1.1

27. Beauty is truth, truth beauty,—that is all / Ye know on earth, and all ye need to know.

KEATS, "ODE ON A GRECIAN URN" (1819)

28. He was the mightiest of Puritans no less than of philistines who first insisted that beauty is only skin deep.

LOUIS KRONENBERGER, *COMPANY MANNERS* (1954), 1.1

29. Beauty hath no true glass, except it be / In the sweet privacy of loving eyes.

JAMES RUSSELL LOWELL, "A CHIPPEWA LEGEND" (1843)

30. And his heart was stirred, it felt a father's kindness: such an emotion as the possessor of beauty can inspire in one who has offered himself up in spirit to create beauty.

THOMAS MANN, *DEATH IN VENICE* (1911)

31. beauty gets the best of it / in this world.

DON MARQUIS, "UNJUST," *ARCHY AND MEHITABEL* (1927)

32. Beauty is an ecstasy; it is as simple as hunger. There is really nothing to be said about it.

W. SOMERSET MAUGHAM, *CAKES AND ALE* (1930), 11

33. Beauty in all things—no, we cannot hope for that; but some place set apart for it.

EDNA ST. VINCENT MILLAY, "INVOCATION TO THE MUSES," *MAKE BRIGHT THE ARROWS* (1940)

34. Beauty is Nature's coin, must not be hoarded, / But must be current, and the good thereof / Consists in mutual and partaken bliss.

MILTON, *COMUS* (1634), 739

35. Beauty, though injurious, hath strange power, / After offence returning, to regain / Love once possessed.

MILTON, *SAMSON AGONISTES* (1671), 1003

36. Beauty is everlasting / and dust is for a time.

MARIANNE MOORE, "IN DISTRUST OF MERITS," *COLLECTED POEMS* (1951)

37. Truth is the strong compost in which beauty may sometimes germinate.

CHRISTOPHER MORLEY, *INWARD HO!* (1923), 2

38. Judgment of beauty can err, what with the wine and the dark.

OVID, *THE ART OF LOVE* (C. A.D. 8), 1, TR. ROLFE HUMPHRIES

39. Take the advice of light when you're looking at linens or jewels; / Looking at faces or forms, take the advice of the day.

OVID, *THE ART OF LOVE* (C. A.D. 8), 1, TR. ROLFE HUMPHRIES

40. 'Tis not a lip or eye we beauty call, / But the joint force and full result of all.

ALEXANDER POPE, *AN ESSAY ON CRITICISM* (1711), 2.45

41. A five-year old is in a pretty good position to assess who is beautiful and who is not. Removed

from the confusions of sexuality, he or she can judge a face as a face.

Roger Rosenblatt, "The Late Afternoon," *The Man in the Water* (1994)

42. Beauty deprived of its proper foils and adjuncts ceases to be enjoyed as beauty, just as light deprived of all shadow ceases to be enjoyed as light.

John Ruskin, *Modern Painters* (1843–60), v. 3, 4.3.14

43. Remember that the most beautiful things in the world are the most useless: peacocks and lilies, for instance.

John Ruskin, *The Stones of Venice* (1851–53), v. 1, 2.17

44. A little beauty is preferable to much wealth.

Sa'di, *Gulistan* (1258), 3.28, tr. James Ross

45. All beauties are to be honored, but only one embraced.

George Santayana, "No. 302 Beacon Street," *Persons and Places: The Background of My Life* (1944)

46. To keep beauty in its place is to make all things beautiful.

George Santayana, *The Life of Reason: Reason in Art* (1905–06), 9

47. Outstanding beauty, like outstanding gifts of any kind, tends to get in the way of normal emotional development, and thus of that particular success in life which we call happiness.

Milton R. Sapirstein, *Paradoxes of Everyday Life* (1955), 4

48. Beauty itself doth of itself persuade / The eyes of men without an orator.

Shakespeare, *The Rape of Lucrece* (1594), 29

49. Beauty provoketh thieves sooner than gold.

Shakespeare, *As You Like It* (1599–1600), 1.3.112

50. Bleak factory buildings and billboard-cluttered avenues look as beautiful, through the camera's eye, as churches and pastoral landscapes.

Susan Sontag, *On Photography* (1977)

51. Beauty is nothing other than the promise of happiness.

Stendhal, *On Love* (1822), 17

52. Beauty is not immortal. In a day / Blossom and June and rapture pass away.

Arthur Stringer, "A Fragile Thing Is Beauty."

53. Beauty is truth's smile / when she beholds her own face / in a perfect mirror.

Rabindranath Tagore, *Fireflies* (1928)

54. O Beauty, find thyself in love, not in the flattery of thy mirror.

Rabindranath Tagore, *Stray Birds* (1916), 28

55. Beauty more than bitterness / Makes the heart break.

Sara Teasdale, "Vignettes Overseas," *Rivers to the Sea* (1915)

56. Look for a lovely thing and you will find it, / It is not far— / It never will be far.

Sara Teasdale, "Night," *Stars To-night* (1930)

57. Spend all you have for loveliness, / Buy it and never count the cost; / For one white singing hour of peace / Count many a year of strife well lost, / And for a breath of ecstasy / Give all you have been, or could be.

Sara Teasdale, "Barter," *Love Songs* (1917)

58. And is there any moral shut / Within the bosom of the rose?

Lord Tennyson, "Moral," *The Day-Dream* (1835)

59. Loveliness / Needs not the foreign aid of ornament, / But is when unadorned adorned the most.

James Thomson, "Autumn," *The Seasons* (1726–30), 204

60. Such is beauty ever,—neither here nor there, now nor then,—neither in Rome nor in Athens, but wherever there is a soul to admire.

Thoreau, *Journal*, Jan. 21, 1838

61. Ask a toad what is beauty ...; he will answer that it is a female with two great round eyes coming out of her little head, a large flat mouth, a yellow belly and a brown back.

Voltaire, "Beauty," *Philosophical Dictionary* (1764)

62. It is not sufficient to see and to know the beauty of a work. We must feel and be affected by it.

Voltaire, "Taste," *Philosophical Dictionary* (1764)

63. They are the elect to whom beautiful things mean only Beauty.

Oscar Wilde, preface, *The Picture of Dorian Gray* (1891)

64. Nothing lasts except beauty—and I shall create that.

Thomas Wolfe, *Thomas Wolfe's Letters to His Mother* (1943)

73. BED

See also 605. MORNING; 633. NIGHT; 906. SLEEP

1. The fate of the worm refutes the pretended ethical teaching of the proverb, which assumes to illustrate the advantage of early rising and does so by showing how extremely dangerous it is.

THOMAS BAILEY ALDRICH, "ASIDES: WRITERS AND TALKERS," *PONKAPOG PAPERS* (1903)

2. When I lie down, I say, When shall I arise, and the night be gone? and I am full of tossings to and fro unto the dawning of the day.

BIBLE, JOB 7:4

3. Bed is a bundle of paradoxes: we go to it with reluctance, yet we quit it with regret.

CHARLES CALEB COLTON, *LACON* (1825), 2.262

4. I used to lie for hours staring into the dark of the sleeping house, feeling the loneliness that only the sleepless know when the queer feeling comes that it is the sleeping who are alive and that those awake are disembodied ghosts.

LOREN EISELEY, "ENDURE THE NIGHT," IN *FIFTY FAMOUS ESSAYS* (1964)

5. He that riseth late must trot all day.

BENJAMIN FRANKLIN, *POOR RICHARD'S ALMANACK* (1732–57)

6. As a seasoned insomniac, I knew sometimes the way to beat sleeplessness was to outwit it: to pretend you didn't *care* about sleeping. Then sometimes sleep became piqued, like a rejected lover, and crept up to try to seduce you.

ERICA JONG, *FEAR OF FLYING* (1973)

7. The average, healthy, well-adjusted adult gets up at seven-thirty in the morning feeling just plain terrible.

JEAN KERR, "WHERE DID YOU PUT THE ASPIRIN?" *PLEASE DON'T EAT THE DAISIES* (1957)

8. Was it for this I uttered prayers, / And sobbed and cursed and kicked the stairs, / That now, domestic as a plate, / I should retire at half-past eight?

EDNA ST. VINCENT MILLAY, "GROWN-UP," *A FEW FIGS FROM THISTLES* (1920)

9. 'Tis very warm weather when one's in bed.

JONATHAN SWIFT, *JOURNAL TO STELLA,* NOV. 8, 1710

10. A man's bed is his cradle, but a woman's is often her rack.

JAMES THURBER, "THE CHIPMUNK AND HIS MATE," *FURTHER FABLES FOR OUR TIME* (1956)

BEES

See 481. INSECTS

74. BEGGARS

See also 384. GIFTS AND GIVING; 718. POVERTY

1. A beggar woman who stands soliciting in front of Palazzo Strozzi, when offered alms a second time in the same day, absently, by another Florentine, refuses: "No. You gave me before."

MARY MCCARTHY, *THE STONES OF FLORENCE* (1959)

2. The poor man commands respect; the beggar must always excite anger.

NAPOLEON I, *MAXIMS* (1804–15)

3. Beggars should be abolished entirely! Verily, it is annoying to give to them and it is annoying not to give to them.

NIETZSCHE, "ON THE PITYING," *THUS SPOKE ZARATHUSTRA* (1883–92), 2, TR. WALTER KAUFMANN

75. BEGINNING

See also 76. BEGINNING AND ENDING; 285. ENDING

1. A journey of a thousand miles must begin with a single step.

CHINESE PROVERB

2. The merit belongs to the beginner should his successor do even better.

EGYPTIAN PROVERB

3. The great majority of men are bundles of beginnings.

EMERSON, *JOURNALS,* 1828

4. It is better to begin in the evening than not at all.

ENGLISH PROVERB

5. Once begun, / A task is easy; half the work is done.

HORACE, *EPISTLES* (20-C. 8 B.C.), 1.2

6. The births of all things are weak and tender, and therefore we should have our eyes intent on beginnings.

MONTAIGNE, "OF MANAGING THE WILL," *ESSAYS* (1580–88), TR. W. C. HAZLITT

76. BEGINNING AND ENDING

See also 75. BEGINNING; 285. ENDING

1. Men perish because they cannot join the beginning with the end.

ALCMAEON (C. 500 B.C.), QUOTED IN PHILIP WHEELWRIGHT'S *HERACLITUS*

2. Better is the end of a thing than the beginning thereof.

BIBLE, ECCLESIASTES 7:8

3. It is easy to see the beginnings of things, and harder to see the ends.

JOAN DIDION, "GOODBYE TO ALL THAT," IN *THE ART OF THE PERSONAL ESSAY* (1994), ED. PHILLIP LOPATE

4. A good beginning makes a good ending.

ENGLISH PROVERB

5. You begin well in nothing except you end well.

THOMAS FULLER, M.D., *GNOMOLOGIA* (1732), 5863

6. Life never presents us with anything which may not be looked upon as a fresh starting point, no less than as a termination.

ANDRÉ GIDE, *THE COUNTERFEITERS* (1925), 3.13, TR. DOROTHY BUSSY

7. Do, and have done. The former is far the easiest.

AUGUSTUS WILLIAM HARE, *GUESSES AT TRUTH* (1827)

8. Great is the art of beginning, but greater the art is of ending.

LONGFELLOW, "ELEGIAC VERSE" (1881)

9. Every exit is an entry somewhere else.

TOM STOPPARD, *ROSENCRANTZ & GUILDENSTERN ARE DEAD* (1967)

77. BEHAVIOR

See also 213. CUSTOM; 563. MANNERS; 604. MORALITY

1. She's entirely devoid of the affected squawk and squeals and shiverings which ruin most girls—and the consequent vacuum is not filled by hot air, but by unobstreperous intelligence, tinged with a charming limeadish sarcasm.

JAMES AGEE, *LETTERS OF JAMES AGEE TO FATHER FLYE* (1962)

2. What truly leads the evolutionary procession, in other words, is behavior.

ROBERT ARDREY, *THE TERRITORIAL IMPERATIVE* (1966)

3. Conduct is three-fourths of our life and its largest concern.

MATTHEW ARNOLD, *LITERATURE AND DOGMA* (1873), 1

4. The Italian way of life cannot be considered a success except by temporary visitors. It solves no problems. It makes them worse.

LUIGI BARZINI, *THE ITALIANS* (1964)

5. Man is not committed in detail by his biological constitution to any particular variety of behavior.

RUTH BENEDICT, *PATTERNS OF CULTURE* (1934)

6. Behavior, n. Conduct, as determined, not by principle, but by breeding.

AMBROSE BIERCE, *THE DEVIL'S DICTIONARY* (1881–1911)

7. A foul-mouthed oaf, a drunken laborer lying in a drain, a beaten wife with blackened eyes and torn clothes, cannot be made romantic to a child who sees how other children suffer from bad-tempered parents, from drunken fathers to termagant mothers.

JOYCE CARY, *EXCEPT THE LORD* (1953)

8. In great matters, men behave as they are expected to; in little ones, as they would naturally.

CHAMFORT, *MAXIMES ET PENSÉES* (1805), 52

9. A beautiful behavior is better than a beautiful form; it gives a higher pleasure than statues or pictures; it is the finest of the fine arts.

EMERSON, "MANNERS," *ESSAYS: SECOND SERIES* (1844)

10. Men in all societies possess the biological equipment to remove their hats or shoes, but it is the birth within a particular culture that decides that a Jew will keep his hat and shoes on in his place of worship, a Mohammedan will take off his shoes, and a Christian will keep his shoes on but remove his hat.

PETER FARB, *MAN'S RISE TO CIVILIZATION* (1968)

11. [M]an can be conditioned to behave in almost every desired way; but only "almost."

ERICH FROMM, *THE ANATOMY OF HUMAN DESTRUCTIVENESS* (1973)

12. Behavior is a mirror in which every one displays his own image.

GOETHE, *ELECTIVE AFFINITIES* (1809), 23

13. There are jus times when you can't let the right thing stand in yo way.

WINSTON GROOM, *FORREST GUMP* (1986)

14. A man's behavior is the index of the man, and his discourse is the index of his understanding.

ALI IBN-AB-TALIB, *SENTENCES* (7TH C.), 7, TR. SIMON OCKLEY

15. When, in the present world, men behave well, that is no doubt sometimes because they are creatures of habit as well as, sometimes, because they are reasonable.

JOSEPH WOOD KRUTCH, "IGNOBLE UTOPIAS," *THE MEASURE OF MAN* (1954)

16. We live everything as it comes, without warning, like an actor going on cold.

MILAN KUNDERA, *THE UNBEARABLE LIGHTNESS OF BEING* (1984)

17. Then George F. Babbitt did a dismaying thing. He wiped his face in the guest towel!

SINCLAIR LEWIS, *BABBITT* (1922)

18. He was deferential, ingratiating, concerned for your pleasure, like a waiter with a tray of French pastry in his hand.

MARY MCCARTHY, *THE COMPANY SHE KEEPS* (1942)

19. It's one thing for a man not to know, not to have learned; it's another not to be able to live by what one does know.

BERNARD MALAMUD, *DUBIN'S LIVES* (1979)

20. The only way to enjoy the fun of catching people behaving disgustingly is to have children. One has to keep having them, however, because it is incorrect to correct grown people, even if you have grown them yourself.

JUDITH MARTIN, *MISS MANNERS' GUIDE TO EXCRUCIATINGLY CORRECT BEHAVIOR* (1979)

21. The conduct of our lives is the true mirror of our doctrine.

MONTAIGNE, "OF THE EDUCATION OF CHILDREN," *ESSAYS* (1580–88), TR. W. C. HAZLITT

22. Right conduct can never, except by some rare accident, be prompted by ignorance or hindered by knowledge.

BERTRAND RUSSELL, "THE TABOO ON SEX KNOWLEDGE," *MARRIAGE AND MORALS* (1929)

23. Fine conduct is always spontaneous.

SENECA, *LETTERS TO LUCILIUS* (1ST C.), 66.16, TR. E. PHILLIPS BARKER

24. Yasha spent his Sabbath talking and smoking cigarettes among musicians. To the earnest moralists who attempted to get him to change his ways, he would always answer: "When were you in heaven, and what did God look like?"

ISAAC BASHEVIS SINGER, *THE MAGICIAN OF LUBLIN* (1960)

25. Unable to understand how or why the person we see behaves as he does, we attribute his behavior to a person we cannot see, whose behavior we cannot explain either but about whom we are not inclined to ask questions.

B.F. SKINNER, *BEYOND FREEDOM AND DIGNITY* (1971)

26. It is in our collective behavior that we are most mysterious.

LEWIS THOMAS, "COMPUTERS," *THE LIVES OF A CELL* (1974)

27. Our behavior toward each other is the strangest, most unpredictable, and almost entirely unaccountable of all the phenomena with which we are obliged to live.

LEWIS THOMAS, "MAKING SCIENCE WORK," *LATE NIGHT THOUGHTS ON LISTENING TO MAHLER'S NINTH SYMPHONY* (1983)

BEING

See 316. EXISTENCE

78. BELIEF

See also 202. CREDULITY; 265. DOUBT, RELIGIOUS; 330. FAITH; 904. SKEPTICISM; 954. SUPERSTITION; 1004. UNBELIEF; 1005. UNCERTAINTY

1. When you want to believe in something you also have to believe in everything that's necessary for believing in it.

UGO BETTI, *STRUGGLE TILL DAWN* (1949), 2, TR. G. H. MCWILLIAM

2. Everything possible to be believed is an image of truth.

WILLIAM BLAKE, *THE MARRIAGE OF HEAVEN AND HELL* (1790)

3. He does not believe that does not live according to his belief.

THOMAS FULLER, M.D., *GNOMOLOGIA* (1732), 1838

4. The belief that becomes truth for me ... is that which allows me the best use of my strength, the best means of putting my virtues into action.

ANDRÉ GIDE, *THE COUNTERFEITERS* (1925), 2.4, TR. DOROTHY BUSSY

5. Through fear of resembling one another, through horror at having to submit, through uncertainty as well, through skepticism and complexity, there is a multitude of individual little beliefs for the triumph of strange little individuals.

ANDRÉ GIDE, "CONCERNING INFLUENCE IN LITERATURE," *PRETEXTS* (1903)

6. We are so constituted that we believe the most incredible things; and, once they are engraved upon the memory, woe to him who would endeavor to erase them.

GOETHE, *THE SORROWS OF YOUNG WERTHER* (1774), 1, AUG. 15, 1771, TR. VICTOR LANGE

7. We believe what we want to believe, what we like to believe, what suits our prejudices and fuels our passions.

SYDNEY J. HARRIS, "LIES ARE NOT EASILY PUT TO REST," *CLEARING THE GROUND* (1986)

8. Loving is half of believing.

VICTOR HUGO, *LES CHANTS DU CRÉPUSCULE* (1835), 38

9. Believe that life *is* worth living, and your belief will help create the fact.

WILLIAM JAMES, "IS LIFE WORTH LIVING?" *THE WILL TO BELIEVE* (1896)

10. If you build it [a ballpark], he will come.

W.P. KINSELLA, *SHOELESS JOE* (1982)

11. First there is a time when we believe everything without reasons, then for a little while we believe with discrimination, then we believe nothing whatever, and then we believe everything again—and, moreover, give reasons why we believe everything.

GEORG CHRISTOPH LICHTENBERG, *APHORISMS* (1764–99), TR. J. P. STERN

12. Under all that we think, lives all we believe, like the ultimate veil of our spirits.

ANTONIO MACHADO, *JAUN DE MAIRENA* (1943), 33, TR. BEN BELITT

13. Nothing is so firmly believed, as what we least know.

MONTAIGNE, "THAT A MAN IS SOBERLY TO JUDGE OF THE DIVINE ORDINANCES," *ESSAYS* (1580–88), TR. W. C. HAZLITT

14. Convictions are more dangerous enemies of truth than lies.

NIETZSCHE, *HUMAN, ALL TOO HUMAN* (1878), 483, TR. HELEN ZIMMERN

15. It is natural for the mind to believe, and for the will to love; so that, for want of true objects, they must attach themselves to false.

PASCAL, *PENSÉES* (1670), 81, TR. W. F. TROTTER

16. It is desire that engenders belief and if we fail as a rule to take this into account, it is because most of the desires that create beliefs end ... only with our own life.

MARCEL PROUST, *REMEMBRANCE OF THINGS PAST: THE SWEET CHEAT GONE* (1913–27), TR. C. K. SCOTT-MONCRIEFF

17. Man makes holy what he believes as he makes beautiful what he loves.

ERNEST RENAN, "LA TENTATION DU CHRIST," *ETUDES D'HISTOIRE RELIGIEUSE* (1857)

18. Man is a credulous animal, and must believe *something;* in the absence of good grounds for belief, he will be satisfied with bad ones.

BERTRAND RUSSELL, "AN OUTLINE OF INTELLECTUAL RUBBISH," *UNPOPULAR ESSAYS* (1950)

19. The fact that an opinion has been widely held is no evidence whatever that it is not utterly absurd; indeed in view of the silliness of the majority of mankind, a widespread belief is more likely to be foolish than sensible.

BERTRAND RUSSELL, "CHRISTIAN ETHICS," *MARRIAGE AND MORALS* (1929)

20. Much of human history can, I think, be described as a gradual and sometimes painful liberation from provincialism, the emerging awareness that there is more to the world than was generally believed by our ancestors.

CARL SAGAN, *BROCA'S BRAIN: REFLECTIONS ON THE ROMANCE OF SCIENCE* (1979)

21. Of what worth are convictions that bring not suffering?

SAINT-EXUPÉRY, *THE WISDOM OF THE SANDS* (1948), 29, TR. STUART GILBERT

22. There is only one position for an artist anywhere: and that is, upright.

DYLAN THOMAS, *QUITE EARLY ONE MORNING* (1954)

23. That which has been believed by everyone, always and everywhere, has every chance of being false.

PAUL VALÉRY, *TEL QUEL I* (1943)

24. Man can believe the impossible, but man can never believe the improbable.

OSCAR WILDE, "THE DECAY OF LYING," *INTENTIONS* (1891)

25. For I believe in harbors at the end.

THOMAS WOLFE, *LOOK HOMEWARD, ANGEL* (1929)

BENEVOLENCE

See 433. HUMANITARIANISM; 519. KINDNESS

79. BETRAYAL

See also 993. TREASON

1. They talk of a man betraying his country, his friends, his sweetheart. There must be a moral bond first. All a man can betray is his conscience.

JOSEPH CONRAD, *UNDER WESTERN EYES* (1911), 1.2

2. If I had to choose between betraying my country and betraying my friend, I hope I should have the guts to betray my country.

E. M. Forster, "What I Believe," *Two Cheers for Democracy* (1951)

3. There's a bad odor about a man who's been betrayed.

Maureen Howard, *Before My Time* (1974)

4. Though those that are betrayed / Do feel the treason sharply, yet the traitor / Stands in worse case of woe.

Shakespeare, *Cymbeline* (1609–10), 3.4.87

80. BIBLE

1. Thy word is a lamp unto my feet, and a light unto my path.

Bible, Psalms 119:105

2. Those who talk of the Bible as a "monument of English prose" are merely admiring it as a monument over the grave of Christianity.

T. S. Eliot, "Religion and Literature" (1935)

3. It's a pity people pick and choose what they learn from the Bible.

Graham Greene, A Burnt-Out Case (1960)

4. The English Bible—a book which if everything else in our language should perish, would alone suffice to show the whole extent of its beauty and power.

Thomas Babington Macaulay, "On John Dryden" (1828)

5. It was subtle of God to learn Greek when he wished to become an author—and not to learn it better.

Nietzsche, *Beyond Good and Evil* (1886), 121, tr. Walter Kaufmann

6. The Scripture in time of disputes is like an open town in time of war, which serves indifferently the occasions of both parties.

Alexander Pope, *Thoughts on Various Subjects* (1727)

7. We pick out a text here and there to make it serve our turn; whereas, if we take it all together, and considered what went before and what followed after, we should find it meant no such thing.

John Selden, "The Scriptures," *Table Talk* (1689)

8. In the Bible, fate was often presented as the handmaiden of morality: sin was succeeded by misfortune, righteousness by prosperity, with reward and punishment instrumental in persuading man to obey divine commandments.

Israel Shenker, *Coat of Many Colors* (1985)

9. The Christian's Bible is a drug store. Its contents remain the same, but the medical practice changes.

Mark Twain, "Bible Teaching and Religious Practice" (1923)

BIGOTRY

See 264. Dogmatism; 335. Fanaticism; 500. Intolerance; 726. Prejudices

81. BIOGRAPHY

See also 62. Autobiography; 93. Books and Reading; 1069. Writing and Writers

1. In writing biography, fact and fiction shouldn't be mixed. And if they are, the fiction parts should be printed in red ink, the fact parts in black ink.

Catherine Drinker Bowen, *Publishers' Weekly*, March 24, 1958

2. After a person dies, his biographers feel free to give him a glittering list of intimate friends. Anecdotes are so much tastier spiced with expensive names.

Louise Brooks, "The Other Face of W. C. Fields," *Lulu in Hollywood* (1982)

3. A well-written Life is almost as rare as a well-spent one.

Thomas Carlyle, "Richter," *Edinburgh Review* (1827)

4. How inexpressibly comfortable to know our fellow-creature; to see into him, understand his goings-forth, decipher the whole heart of his mystery: nay, not only to see into him, but even to see out of him, to view the world altogether as he views it.

Thomas Carlyle, "Biography" (1832)

5. Read no history: nothing but biography, for that is life without theory.

Benjamin Disraeli, *Contarini Fleming* (1844), 1.23

6. Nobody can write the life of a man but those who have eaten and drunk and lived in social intercourse with him.

Samuel Johnson, quoted in Boswell's *Life of Samuel Johnson*, March 31, 1772

7. No one had written a good long life of Schubert. He had lived long in music and short in life.

Bernard Malamud, *Dubin's Lives* (1979)

8. What I fear is not being forgotten after my death, but, rather, not being enough forgotten. As we were saying, it is not our books that survive, but our poor lives that linger in the histories.

François Mauriac, interview, *Writers at Work: First Series* (1958)

9. Biographies are but the clothes and buttons of the man—the biography of the man himself cannot be written.

Mark Twain, *Autobiography* (1924), v. 1

10. Every great man has his disciples, and it is usually Judas who writes the biography.

Oscar Wilde, *The Artist as Critic: The Critical Writings of Oscar Wilde* (1969) ed. Richard Ellmann

82. BIRDS

1. Nothing wholly admirable ever happens in this country except the migration of birds.

Brooks Atkinson, "March 23," *Once Around the Sun* (1951)

2. The owl, that bird of onomatopoetic name, is a repetitious question wrapped in feathery insulation especially for Winter delivery.

Hal Borland, "Questioner—December 27," *Sundial of the Seasons* (1964)

3. That's the wise thrush; he sings each song twice over, / Lest you should think he never could recapture / The first fine careless rapture!

Robert Browning, "Home-thoughts, from Abroad," *Dramatic Romances and Lyrics* (1845), 2

4. No ladder needs the bird but skies / To situate its wings, / Nor any leader's grim baton / Arraigns it as it sings.

Emily Dickinson, poem (1883?)

5. If you lie down in a village square hoping to capture a sea gull, you could stay there your whole life without succeeding. But a hundred miles from shore it's different. Sea gulls have a highly developed instinct for self-preservation on land but at sea they're very cocky.

Gabriel García Márquez, *The Story of a Shipwrecked Sailor* (1986)

6. Cheerfulness is proper to the cock, which rejoices over every little thing, and crows with varied and lively movements.

Leonardo Da Vinci, *Notebooks* (c. 1500), tr. Jean Paul Richter

7. He clasps the crag with crooked hands; / Close to the sun in lonely lands, / Ringed with the azure world, he stands. / The wrinkled sea beneath him crawls; / He watches from his mountain walls, / And like a thunderbolt he falls.

Lord Tennyson, "The Eagle" (1851)

83. BIRTH

See also 37. Ancestry; 75. Beginning; 221. Death; 539. Life

1. The best thing for a man to do is to be born and, being born, to die at once.

Pietro Aretino, letter to Pietro Trivisano dai Crocicchieri, Dec. 18, 1537, tr. Samuel Putnam

2. We brought nothing into this world, and it is certain we can carry nothing out.

Bible, 1 Timothy 6:7

3. The egg it is the source of all. / 'Tis everyone's ancestral hall. / The bravest chief that ever fought, / The lowest thief that e'er was caught, / The harlot's lip, the maiden's leg, / They each and all came from an egg.

Clarence Day, "Thoughts on Peculiar Dawns," *Thoughts Without Words* (1928)

4. There is nothing like a start, and being born, however pessimistic one may become in later years, is undeniably a start.

William McFee, "Lost Adventures," *Harbours of Memory* (1921)

5. One must mourn not the death of men, but their birth.

Montesquieu, *Lettres persanes* (1721), 40

6. The hour which gives us life begins to take it away.

Seneca, *Hercules Furens* (1st c.), 1.874

7. Our birth is nothing but our death begun.

Edward Young, *Night Thoughts* (1742–46), 5.718

84. BIRTH CONTROL

See also 713. Population; 802. Reproduction

1. A small family is soon provided for.

English Proverb

2. No woman can call herself free who does not own and control her body. No woman can call herself free until she can choose consciously whether she will or will not be a mother.

Margaret Sanger, *Parade*, Dec. 1, 1963

3. At Vatican Council II, one dissenting Roman Catholic theologian declared: "Yes, the Bible says 'Be fruitful and multiply,' but that was when the population was two per square world."

ISRAEL SHENKER, *COAT OF MANY COLORS* (1985)

4. The pills were ethical because they didn't interfere with a person's ability to reproduce, which would have been unnatural and immoral. All the pills did was take every bit of pleasure out of sex.

KURT VONNEGUT, *WELCOME TO THE MONKEY HOUSE* (1970)

85. BLACKS

See also 23. AFRICAN-AMERICAN; 591. MINORITIES; 775. RACIAL PREJUDICE; 1054. WHITES

1. An American Negro, however deep his sympathies, or however bright his rage, ceases to be simply a black man when he faces a black man from Africa.

JAMES BALDWIN, "ALAS, POOR RICHARD," IN *THE ART OF THE PERSONAL ESSAY* (1994), ED. PHILLIP LOPATE

2. It is only in his music, which Americans are able to admire because a protective sentimentality limits their understanding of it, that the Negro in America has been able to tell his story.

JAMES BALDWIN, "MANY THOUSANDS GONE" (1951), *NOTES OF A NATIVE SON* (1955)

3. Our dehumanization of the Negro then is indivisible from our dehumanization of ourselves; the loss of our own identity is the price we pay for our annulment of his.

JAMES BALDWIN, "MANY THOUSANDS GONE" (1951), *NOTES OF A NATIVE SON* (1955)

4. The Negro is superior to the white race. If the latter do not forget their pride of race and color, and amalgamate with the purer and richer blood of the blacks, they will die out and wither away in unprolific skinniness.

HENRY WARD BEECHER, SPEECH, NEW YORK CITY, 1866

5. It is not healthy when a nation lives within a nation, as colored Americans are living inside America. A nation cannot live confident of its tomorrow if its refugees are among its own citizens.

PEARL S. BUCK, *WHAT AMERICA MEANS TO ME* (1943), 1

6. The Negro revolt is not aimed at winning friends but at winning freedom, not interpersonal warmth but institutional justice.

HARVEY COX, *THE SECULAR CITY* (1966), 6

7. Having despised us, it is not strange that Americans should seek to render us despicable; having enslaved us, it is natural that they should strive to prove us unfit for freedom; having denounced us as indolent, it is not strange that they should cripple our enterprises.

FREDERICK DOUGLASS, *PROCEEDINGS OF THE COLORED NATIONAL CONVENTION,* ROCHESTER, NEW YORK, JULY 6–8, 1853

8. Just being a Negro doesn't qualify you to understand the race situation any more than being sick makes you an expert on medicine.

DICK GREGORY, "...AND THEY DIDN'T EVEN HAVE WHAT I WANTED," *NIGGER* (1964)

9. To be a Negro is to participate in a culture of poverty and fear that goes far deeper than any law for or against discrimination.

MICHAEL HARRINGTON, *THE OTHER AMERICA* (1962), 4

10. If you are black the only roads into the mainland of American life are through subservience, cowardice, and loss of manhood. These are the white man's roads.

LE ROI JONES, "BLACK IS A COUNTRY," *HOME* (1966)

11. It is a measure of the Negro's circumstance that, in America, the smallest things usually take him so very long, and that, by the time he wins them, they are no longer little things: they are miracles.

MURRAY KEMPTON, "GEORGE," *PART OF OUR TIME* (1955)

12. Only in the case of the Negro has the melting pot failed to bring a minority into the full stream of American life.

JOHN F. KENNEDY, *A NATION OF IMMIGRANTS* (1958)

13. We will not be satisfied until justice rolls down like waters and righteousness like a mighty stream.

MARTIN LUTHER KING, JR., SPEECH, WASHINGTON, D.C., JUNE 15, 1963

14. A young white boy's badness is simply the overflowing of young animal spirits; the black boy's badness is badness, pure and simple.

LETTER FROM A NEGRO MOTHER, *THE INDEPENDENT,* SEPT. 18, 1902

15. The black man continues on his way. He plods wearily no longer—he is striding freedom road with the knowledge that if he hasn't got the world in a jug, at least he has the stopper in his hand.

ADAM CLAYTON POWELL, "BLACK POWER: A FORM OF GODLY POWER," *KEEP THE FAITH, BABY!* (1967)

16. Treat us like men, and there is no danger but we will all live in peace and happiness together. For we are not like you, hard hearted, unmerciful, and unforgiving. What a happy country this will be, if the whites will listen.

DAVID WALKER, *WALKER'S APPEAL* (SEPT. 28, 1829)

BLAME

See 206. CRITICISM; 405. GUILT; 803. REPROOF; 847. SCAPEGOAT

BLASPHEMY

See 441. ICONOCLASM; 506. IRREVERENCE; 957. SWEARING

86. BLINDNESS, PHYSICAL

See also 882. SENSES; 897. SIGHT

1. Blindness has not been for me a total misfortune; it should not be seen in a pathetic way. It should be seen as a way of life: one of the styles of living.

JORGE LUIS BORGES, "BLINDNESS," IN *THE ART OF THE PERSONAL ESSAY* (1994), ED. PHILLIP LOPATE

2. There is a budding morrow in midnight; / There is a triple sight in blindness keen.

KEATS, "TO HOMER" (1818)

3. As they say of the blind, / Sounds are the things I see.

SOPHOCLES, *OEDIPUS AT COLONUS* (401 B.C.), TR. ROBERT FITZGERALD

87. BLINDNESS, SPIRITUAL

See also 483. INSENSITIVITY; 683. PERCEPTION; 1007. UNDERSTANDING; 1035. VISION

1. They are ill discoverers that think there is no land, when they see nothing but sea.

FRANCIS BACON, *THE ADVANCEMENT OF LEARNING* (1605), 2.7.5

2. People who shut their eyes to reality simply invite their own destruction, and anyone who insists on remaining in a state of innocence long after that innocence is dead turns himself into a monster.

JAMES BALDWIN, "STRANGER IN THE VILLAGE" (1953), *NOTES OF A NATIVE SON* (1955)

3. It is we that are blind, not Fortune.

SIR THOMAS BROWNE, *RELIGIO MEDICI* (1642), 1

4. He has the greatest blind side who thinks he has none.

DUTCH PROVERB

5. There are none so blind as they that won't see.

ENGLISH PROVERB

6. Most people do not take heed of the things they encounter, nor do they grasp them even when they have learned about them, although they suppose they do.

HERACLITUS, *FRAGMENTS* (C. 500 B.C.), 57, TR. PHILIP WHEELWRIGHT

7. He does not weep who does not see.

VICTOR HUGO, "JEAN VALJEAN," *LES MISÉRABLES* (1862), 1.16, TR. CHARLES E. WILBOUR

8. We run carelessly to the precipice, after we have put something before us to prevent us seeing it.

PASCAL, *PENSÉES* (1670), 183, TR. W. F. TROTTER

9. A blind man who sees is better than a seeing man who is blind.

PERSIAN PROVERB

88. BLUNDER

See also 299. ERROR

1. Half of our mistakes in life arise from feeling where we ought to think, and thinking where we ought to feel.

JOHN CHURTON COLLINS, (1848–1908), APHORISM

2. He who is shipwrecked the second time cannot lay the blame on Neptune.

ENGLISH PROVERB

3. It is worse than a crime: it is a blunder.

JOSEPH FOUCHÉ, COMMENT ON THE EXECUTION OF THE DUC D'ENGHIEN, MARCH 21, 1804, TR. TALLEYRAND

4. A stumble may prevent a fall.

THOMAS FULLER, M.D., *GNOMOLOGIA* (1732), 424

5. I hate all bungling like sin, but most of all bungling in state affairs, which produces nothing but mischief to thousands and millions.

GOETHE, QUOTED IN JOHANN PETER ECKERMANN'S *CONVERSATIONS WITH GOETHE,* MARCH 1832

6. Great blunders are often made, like large ropes, of a multitude of fibres.

VICTOR HUGO, "COSETTE," *LES MISÉRABLES* (1862), 5.10, TR. CHARLES E. WILBOUR

7. Mistakes are a part of life; you can't avoid them. All you can hope is that they won't be too expensive and that you don't make the same mistake twice.

LEE IACOCCA, *IACOCCA: AN AUTOBIOGRAPHY* (1984) WITH WILLIAM NOVAK

8. It's not the tragedies that kill us, it's the messes.

Dorothy Parker, interview, *Writers at Work: First Series* (1958)

9. The pain others give passes away in their later kindness, but that of our own blunders, especially when they hurt our vanity, never passes away.

William Butler Yeats, *Dramatis Personae* (1896–1902)

10. Better to trip with the feet than with the tongue.

Zeno of Citium (c. 300 B.C.),, quoted in Diogenes Laertius' *Lives and Opinions of Eminent Philosophers* (3rd c. A.D.), tr. R. D. Hicks

BLUSHING

See 893. Shame

89. BOASTING

See also 166. Conceit

1. He who killeth a lion when absent feareth a mouse when present.

English Proverb

2. You must stir it and stump it, / And blow your own trumpet, / Or trust me, you haven't a chance.

W. S. Gilbert, *Ruddigore* (1887), 1

3. Nothing ought more to humiliate men who have merited great praise than the care they still take to boast of little things.

La Rochefoucauld, *Maxims* (1665), tr. Kenneth Pratt

BOATS

See 895. Ships and Boats

90. BODY

See also 413. Health; 589. Mind and Body

1. Poor body, time and the long years were the first tailors to teach you the merciful use of clothes! Though some scold to-day because you are too much seen, to my mind, you are not seen fully enough or often enough when you are beautiful.

Henry Beston, "The Year at High Tide," *The Outermost House* (1928)

2. The dear, stupid body is as easily satisfied as a spaniel.

Annie Dillard, "Total Eclipse," *Teaching a Stone to Talk* (1982)

3. Only death reveals what a nothing the body of man is.

Juvenal, *Satires* (c. 100), 10.172, tr. Hubert Creekmore

4. Body am I entirely, and nothing else; and soul is only a word for something about the body.

Nietzsche, "On the Despisers of the Body," *Thus Spoke Zarathustra* (1883–92), tr. Walter Kaufmann

5. The abdomen is the reason why man does not easily take himself for a god.

Nietzsche, *Beyond Good and Evil* (1886), 141, tr. Walter Kaufmann

6. Though it be disfigured by many defects, to whom is his own body not dear?

Panchatantra (c. 5th c.), 1, tr. Franklin Edgerton

7. What is more important in life than our bodies or in the world than what we look like?

George Santayana, "My Sister Susana," *Persons and Places: The Background of My Life* (1944)

8. He will be the slave of many masters who is his body's slave.

Seneca, *Letters to Lucilius* (1st c.), 14.1, tr. E. Phillips Barker

9. Gwilym was a tall young man aged nearly twenty, with a thin stick of a body and spade-shaped face. You could dig the garden with him.

Dylan Thomas, *Portrait of the Artist as a Young Dog* (1940)

10. If any thing is sacred the human body is sacred.

Walt Whitman, *I Sing the Body Electric* (1855–81), 8

BODY AND SOUL

See 589. Mind and Body

91. BOHEMIANS

See also 171. Conformity; 468. Individualism

1. The importance of the Beats is twofold: first, they act out a critique of the organized system that everybody in some sense agrees with. But second—and more important in the long run—they are a kind of major pilot study of the use of leisure in an economy of abundance.

Paul Goodman, *Growing Up Absurd* (1960), 9.1

2. Bohemia is nothing more than the little country in which you do not live. If you try to obtain citizenship in it, at once the court and retinue pack the royal archives and treasure and move away beyond the hills.

O. Henry, "The Country of Elusion," *The Trimmed Lamp* (1907)

3. It is not difficult to be unconventional in the eyes of the world when your unconventionality is but the convention of your set.

W. SOMERSET MAUGHAM, *THE MOON AND SIXPENCE* (1919), 14

4. In almost any society, I think, the quality of the nonconformists is likely to be just as good as and no better than that of the conformists.

MARGARET MEAD, *REDBOOK*, JANUARY 1961

5. Bohemia and all its works are vanished out of America; or, more exactly, bohemia has migrated to the middle class, and is alive and well in condo and suburb.

CYNTHIA OZICK, "THE FUNCTION OF THE SMALL PRESS," *METAPHOR & MEMORY* (1989)

92. BOLDNESS

See also 26. AGGRESSION; 195. COURAGE; 859. SELF-ASSERTION; 980. TIMIDITY

1. Tact in audacity is knowing how far you can go without going too far.

JEAN COCTEAU, "LE COQ ET L'ARLEQUIN," *LE RAPPEL À L'ORDRE* (1926)

2. Boldness, without the rules of propriety, becomes insubordination.

CONFUCIUS, *ANALECTS* (6TH C. B.C.), 8.2, TR. JAMES LEGGE

3. The people I respect most behave as if they were immortal and as if society was eternal.

E. M. FORSTER, "WHAT I BELIEVE," *TWO CHEERS FOR DEMOCRACY* (1951)

4. A decent boldness ever meets with friends.

HOMER, *ODYSSEY* (9TH C. B.C.), 7.67, TR. ALEXANDER POPE

5. It is the bold man who every time does best, at home or abroad.

HOMER, *ODYSSEY* (9TH C. B.C.), 7, TR. E. V. RIEU

6. Unless you enter the tiger's den you cannot take the cubs.

JAPANESE PROVERB

7. In difficult situations when hope seems feeble, the boldest plans are safest.

LIVY, *AB URBE CONDITA* (C. 29 B.C.), 25.28

8. The best mask for demoralization is daring.

LUCAN, *ON THE CIVIL WAR* (1ST C.), TR. ROBERT GRAVES

9. When the mouse laughs at the cat, there is a hole nearby.

NIGERIAN PROVERB

10. Audacity augments courage; hesitation, fear.

PUBLILIUS SYRUS, *MORAL SAYINGS* (1ST C. B.C.), 63, TR. DARIUS LYMAN

11. Yield not thy neck / To fortune's yoke, but let thy dauntless mind / Still ride in triumph over all mischance.

SHAKESPEARE, *3 HENRY VI* (1590–91), 3.3.16

12. Be bold, but not too bold. Have courage, but not too much.

FAY WELDON, *REMEMBER ME* (1976)

BOMB, ATOM

See 641. NUCLEAR POWER

93. BOOKS AND READING

See also 62. AUTOBIOGRAPHY; 81. BIOGRAPHY; 136. CLASSICS; 244. DICTIONARIES; 344. FICTION; 538. LIBRARIES; 545. LITERATURE; 1064. WORDS; 1069. WRITING AND WRITERS

1. A man is known by the company his mind keeps.

THOMAS BAILEY ALDRICH, "LEAVES FROM A NOTEBOOK," *PONKAPOG PAPERS* (1903)

2. Some books are undeservedly forgotten; none are undeservedly remembered.

W. H. AUDEN, "READING," *THE DYER'S HAND* (1962)

3. Books will speak plain when counselors blanch.

FRANCIS BACON, "OF COUNSEL," *ESSAYS* (1625)

4. Some books are to be tasted, others to be swallowed, and some few to be chewed and digested.

FRANCIS BACON, "OF STUDIES," *ESSAYS* (1625)

5. A book is good company. It is full of conversation without loquacity. It comes to your longing with full instruction, but pursues you never.

HENRY WARD BEECHER, *PROVERBS FROM PLYMOUTH PULPIT* (1887)

6. Of all the ways of acquiring books, writing them oneself is regarded as the most praiseworthy method.

WALTER BENJAMIN, "UNPACKING MY LIBRARY," IN *THE ART OF THE PERSONAL ESSAY* (1994), ED. PHILLIP LOPATE

7. Of making many books there is no end; and much study is a weariness of the flesh.

BIBLE, ECCLESIASTES 12:12

8. Best-sellerism is the star system of the book world. A "best seller" is a celebrity among books. It is a book

known primarily (sometimes exclusively) for its well-knownness.

Daniel J. Boorstin, *The Image* (1962), 4.8

9. Books succeed, / And lives fail.

Elizabeth Barrett Browning, *Aurora Leigh* (1856), 7.705

10. The possession of a book becomes a substitute for reading it.

Anthony Burgess, "The Book Is Not for Reading," *The New York Times Book Review,* Dec. 4, 1966

11. How much there is in books that one does not want to know, that it would be a mere weariness and burden to the spirit to know.

John Burroughs, *Indoor Studies* (1889)

12. In books lies the soul of the whole past time.

Thomas Carlyle, *On Heroes, Hero-Worship and the Heroic in History* (1841), 5

13. "What is the use of a book," thought Alice, "without pictures or conversations?"

Lewis Carroll, *Alice's Adventures in Wonderland* (1865), 1

14. Most of today's books have an air of having been written in one day from books read the night before.

Chamfort, *Maximes et pensées* (1805), 6

15. What is responsible for the success of many works is the rapport between the mediocrity of the author's ideas and the mediocrity of the public's.

Chamfort, *Maximes et pensées* (1805), 6

16. When one can read, can penetrate the enchanted realm of books, why write?

Colette, "The Footwarmer," *Earthly Paradise* (1966), 1

17. Many books require no thought from those who read them, and for a very simple reason—they made no such demand upon those who wrote them.

Charles Caleb Colton, *Lacon* (1825), 2.248

18. Some read to think—these are rare; some to write, these are common; and some read to talk, and these form the great majority.

Charles Caleb Colton, *Lacon* (1825), 1.554

19. While thought exists, words are alive and literature becomes an escape, not from, but into living.

Cyril Connolly, *The Unquiet Grave* (1945), 3

20. The man who reads only for improvement is beyond the hope of much improvement before he begins.

Jonathan Daniels, *Three Presidents and Their Books,* (1956)

21. The reading of all good books is like conversation with the finest men of past centuries.

Descartes, *Discourse on Method* (1639), 1

22. A precious—mouldering pleasure—'tis— / To meet an Antique Book— / In just the Dress his Century wore— / A privilege—I think—.

Emily Dickinson, poem (c. 1862)

23. Reading, to most people, means an ashamed way of killing time disguised under a dignified name.

Ernest Dimnet, *The Art of Thinking* (1928), 3.8

24. A book is not harmless merely because no one is consciously offended by it.

T. S. Eliot, "Religion and Literature" (1935)

25. Books take their place according to their specific gravity as surely as potatoes in a tub.

Emerson, *Journals,* 1834

26. I should as soon think of swimming across Charles River, when I wish to go to Boston, as of reading all my books in originals, when I have them rendered for me in my mother tongue.

Emerson, "In Praise of Books," *The Conduct of Life* (1860)

27. We are too civil to books. For a few golden sentences we will turn over and actually read a volume of four or five hundred pages.

Emerson, *Journals,* 1841

28. What can we see, read, acquire, but ourselves. Take the book, my friend, and read your eyes out, you will never find there what I find.

Emerson, *Journals,* 1832

29. A wicked book is the wickeder because it cannot repent.

English Proverb

30. I suggest that the only books that influence us are those for which we are ready, and which have gone a little farther down our particular path than we have yet got ourselves.

E. M. Forster, "A Book That Influenced Me," *Two Cheers for Democracy* (1951)

31. [P]eople in a novel can be understood completely by the reader, if the novelist can be understood completely by the reader, if the novelist wishes; their inner as well as their outer life can be exposed.

E.M. Forster, "People," *Aspects of the Novel* (1927)

32. Learning hath gained most by those books by which the printers have lost.

Thomas Fuller, D.D., "Of Books," *The Holy State and the Profane State* (1642)

33. To read a writer is for me not merely to get an idea of what he says, but to go off with him, and travel in his company.

André Gide, "Third Imaginary Interview," *Pretexts* (1903)

34. I know every book of mine by its scent, and I have but to put my nose between the pages to be reminded of all sorts of things.

George Gissing, "Spring," *The Private Papers of Henry Ryecroft* (1903)

35. What a convenient and delightful world is this world of books!—if you bring to it not the obligations of the student, or look upon it as an opiate for idleness, but enter it rather with the enthusiasm of the adventurer!

David Grayson, *Adventures in Contentment* (1907), 12

36. Books give not wisdom where was none before, / But where some is, there reading makes it more.

Sir John Harington, *Epigrams* (1615), 1.2

37. The book-worm wraps himself up in his web of verbal generalities, and sees only the glimmering shadows of things reflected from the minds of others.

William Hazlitt, "On the Ignorance of the Learned," *Table Talk* (1821–22)

38. We decided that we would teach reading because the kids couldn't read well, and because you had to be able to read in America in order to be equal.

James Herndon, *How to Survive in Your Native Land* (1971)

39. What refuge is there for the victim who is oppressed with the feeling that there are a thousand new books he ought to read, while life is only long enough for him to attempt to read a hundred?

Oliver Wendell Holmes, Sr., *Over the Teacups* (1891), 7

40. Good readers make much out of little.

Irving Howe, "How Are Characters Conceived?" *A Critic's Notebook* (1994)

41. A book on cheap paper does not convince. It is not prized, it is like a wheezy doctor with pigtail tobacco breath, who needs a manicure.

Elbert Hubbard, *The Philistine* (1895–1915)

42. [S]ometimes I wish the public were equally aware of the men of our race in the cultural fields. You, for instance, have you ever bought a book by a Negro writer?

Langston Hughes, *Simple Speaks His Mind* (1950)

43. A bad book is as much of a labour to write as a good one; it comes as sincerely from the author's soul.

Aldous Huxley, *Point Counter Point* (1928), 13

44. A man ought to read just as inclination leads him, for what he reads as a task will do him little good.

Samuel Johnson, quoted in Boswell's *Life of Samuel Johnson*, July 14, 1763

45. One of the amusements of idleness is reading without the fatigue of close attention; and the world, therefore, swarms with writers whose wish is not to be studied, but to be read.

Samuel Johnson, *The Idler* (1758–60), 31

46. We find little in a book but what we put there. But in great books, the mind finds room to put many things.

Joseph Joubert, *Pensées* (1842), 22.98, tr. Katharine Lyttelton

47. There is as much trickery required to grow rich by a stupid book as there is folly in buying it.

La Bruyère, *Characters* (1688), 1.46, tr. Henri Van Laun

48. I love to lose myself in other men's minds. When I am not walking, I am reading; I cannot sit and think. Books think for me.

Charles Lamb, "Detached Thoughts on Books and Reading," *Last Essays of Elia* (1833)

49. In some respects the better a book is, the less it demands from binding.

Charles Lamb, "Detached Thoughts on Books and Reading," *Last Essays of Elia* (1833)

50. For one who reads, there is no limit to the number of lives that may be lived, for fiction, biography, and history offer an inexhaustible number of lives in many parts of the world, in all periods of time.

Louis L'Amour, *Education of a Wandering Man* (1989)

51. What is reading but silent conversation?

Walter Savage Landor, "Aristoteles and Callisthenes," *Imaginary Conversations* (1824–53)

52. I have decided that the trouble with print is, it never changes its mind.

Ursula K. Le Guin, "Introductory Note," *Dancing at the Edge of the World* (1989)

53. A book is a mirror: if an ass peers into it, you can't expect an apostle to look out.

GEORG CHRISTOPH LICHTENBERG, *APHORISMS* (1764–99), TR. J. P. STERN

54. To read means to borrow; to create out of one's readings is paying off one's debts.

GEORG CHRISTOPH LICHTENBERG, *APHORISMS* (1764–99), TR. H. HATFIELD

55. Reading furnishes the mind only with materials of knowledge; it is thinking makes what we read ours.

JOHN LOCKE, *OF THE CONDUCT OF THE UNDERSTANDING* (1706), 20

56. Endless volumes, larger, fatter, / Prove man's intellectual climb, / But in essence it's a matter / Just of having lots of time.

"ENDLESS VOLUMES," EDITORIAL, *THE LONDON TIMES LITERARY SUPPLEMENT,* DEC. 28, 1967

57. There are favorable hours for reading a book, as for writing it.

LONGFELLOW, "TABLE-TALK," *DRIFTWOOD* (1857)

58. All books are either dreams or swords.

AMY LOWELL, "SWORD BLADES AND POPPY SEEDS," *SWORD BLADES AND POPPY SEEDS* (1914)

59. Never had he lost himself in a book as one does when that single work seems the most important in the world; unique, a little, all-embracing universe, into which one plunges and submerges oneself in order to draw nourishment out of every syllable.

THOMAS MANN, "THE BLOOD OF THE WALSUNGS" (1905)

60. Make him [the reader] laugh and he will think you a trivial fellow, but bore him in the right way and your reputation is assured.

W. SOMERSET MAUGHAM, *THE GENTLEMAN IN THE PARLOUR* (1930)

61. The only important thing in a book is the meaning it has for you.

W. SOMERSET MAUGHAM, *THE SUMMING UP* (1938), 26

62. Books are not absolutely dead things, but do contain a potency of life in them to be as active as that soul was whose progeny they are; nay they do preserve as in a vial the purest efficacy and extraction of that living intellect that bred them.

MILTON, *TRACTATE OF EDUCATION* (1644)

63. Who kills a man kills a reasonable creature, God's image; but he who destroys a good book kills reason itself.

MILTON, *AREOPAGITICA* (1644)

64. Every abridgement of a good book is a stupid abridgement.

MONTAIGNE, "OF THE ART OF CONFERENCE," *ESSAYS* (1580–88)

65. He that I am reading seems always to have the most force.

MONTAIGNE, "APOLOGY FOR RAIMOND DE SEBONDE," *ESSAYS* (1580–88), TR. W. C. HAZLITT

66. I seek in the reading of books, only to please myself, by an honest diversion.

MONTAIGNE, "OF BOOKS," *ESSAYS* (1580–88), TR. W. C. HAZLITT

67. I have never known any distress that an hour's reading did not relieve.

MONTESQUIEU, *PENSÉES DIVERSES* (1899)

68. A book is made better by good readers and clearer by good opponents.

NIETZSCHE, *MISCELLANEOUS MAXIMS AND OPINIONS* (1879), 2153, TR. PAUL V. COHN

69. Books for all the world are always foul-smelling books: the smell of small people clings to them.

NIETZSCHE, *BEYOND GOOD AND EVIL* (1886), 30, TR. WALTER KAUFMANN

70. When we read too fast or too slowly, we understand nothing.

PASCAL, *PENSÉES* (1670), 69, TR. W. F. TROTTER

71. I do not think anyone can read War and Peace too much. I read it six times....

MAXWELL PERKINS, *EDITOR TO AUTHOR: THE LETTERS OF MAXWELL PERKINS* (1950). ED. JOHN HALL WHEELOCK

72. It is a sad book [Cry, the Beloved Country], but that is as it should be. So was the Iliad and so is the Bible.

MAXWELL PERKINS, *EDITOR TO AUTHOR: THE LETTERS OF MAXWELL PERKINS* (1950). LETTER TO ALAN PATON. ED. JOHN HALL WHEELOCK

73. How many good books suffer neglect through the inefficiency of their beginnings!

EDGAR ALLAN POE, *MARGINALIA* (1844–49), 1

74. Reading is the scourge of childhood because, in a sense, it creates adulthood.

NEIL POSTMAN, "WHEN THERE WERE NO CHILDREN," *THE DISAPPEARANCE OF CHILDHOOD* (1982)

75. No man understands a deep book until he has seen and lived at least part of its contents.

EZRA POUND, *THE ABC OF READING* (1934)

76. There is no reason why the same man should like the same books at eighteen and forty-eight.

EZRA POUND, *THE ABC OF READING* (1934), 8

77. They like my books better in England than in France; a translation would be very successful there.

MARCEL PROUST, *LETTERS OF MARCEL PROUST* (1949), TR. MINA CURTISS

78. There may be no more pleasing picture in the world than that of a child peering into a book—the past and the future entrancing each other.

ROGER ROSENBLATT, "WOULD YOU MIND IF I BORROWED THIS BOOK?" *THE MAN IN THE WATER* (1994)

79. All books are divisible into two classes: the books of the hour, and the books of all time.

JOHN RUSKIN, *SESAME AND LILIES* (1865), 1.8

80. It is impossible to read in America, except on a train, because of the telephone. Everyone has a telephone, and it rings all day and most of the night.

BERTRAND RUSSELL, *IMPRESSIONS OF AMERICA* (1924)

81. People say that life is the thing, but I prefer reading.

LOGAN PEARSALL SMITH, *AFTERTHOUGHTS* (1931), 6

82. A best-seller is the gilded tomb of a mediocre talent.

LOGAN PEARSALL SMITH, *AFTERTHOUGHTS* (1931), 5

83. No furniture so charming as books.

SYDNEY SMITH, QUOTED IN LADY S. HOLLAND'S *MEMOIR* (1855), V. 1.9

84. I have lost all sense of home, having moved about so much. It means to me now—only that place were the books are kept.

JOHN STEINBECK, *STEINBECK: A LIFE IN LETTERS,* EDS. ELAINE STEINBECK AND ROBERT WALLSTEN (1975)

85. Hard-covered books break up friendships. You loan a hard-covered book to a friend and when he doesn't return it you get mad at him. It makes you mean and petty. But twenty-five-cent books are different.

JOHN STEINBECK, NEWS SUMMARIES, APRIL 25, 1954

86. In anything fit to be called by the name of reading, the process itself should be absorbing and voluptuous; we should gloat over a book, be rapt clean out of ourselves.

ROBERT LOUIS STEVENSON, "A GOSSIP ON ROMANCE" (1882)

87. A great book should leave you with many experiences, and slightly exhausted at the end. You live several lives while reading it.

WILLIAM STYRON, INTERVIEW, *WRITERS AT WORK: FIRST SERIES* (1958)

88. Books, like proverbs, receive their chief value from the stamp and esteem of ages through which they have passed.

SIR WILLIAM TEMPLE, "OF ANCIENT AND MODERN LEARNING," *MISCELLANEA* (1692), V. 2

89. In the best travel books the word *alone* is implied on every exciting page, as subtle and ineradicable as a watermark.

PAUL THEROUX, *THE OLD PATAGONIAN EXPRESS* (1979)

90. Books must be read as deliberately and reservedly as they are written.

THOREAU, "READING," *WALDEN* (1854)

91. How many a man has dated a new era in his life from the reading of a book!

THOREAU, "READING," *WALDEN* (1854)

92. Books are the treasured wealth of the world and the fit inheritance of generations and nations.

THOREAU, "READING," *WALDEN* (1854)

93. Books, the oldest and the best, stand naturally and rightfully on the shelves of every cottage.... Their authors are a natural and irresistible aristocracy in every society, and, more than kings and emperors, exert an influence on mankind.

THOREAU, "READING," *WALDEN* (1854)

94. Why should we leave it to Harper & Brothers and Redding & Co. to select our reading?

THOREAU, "READING," *WALDEN* (1854)

95. It is with books as with men—a very small number play a great part; the rest are lost in the multitude.

VOLTAIRE, "BOOKS," *PHILOSOPHICAL DICTIONARY* (1764)

96. Have you any right to read, especially novels, until you have exhausted the best part of the day in some employment that is called practical?

CHARLES DUDLEY WARNER, "FIRST STUDY," *BACKLOG STUDIES* (1873)

97. There is no such thing as a moral or an immoral book. Books are well written, or badly written. That is all.

Oscar Wilde, preface, *The Picture of Dorian Gray* (1891)

98. Second-hand books are wild books, homeless books; they have come together in vast flocks of variegated feather, and have a charm which the domesticated volumes of the library lack.

Virginia Woolf, "Street Haunting," in *The Art of the Personal Essay* (1994), ed. Phillip Lopate

94. BOREDOM

See also 95. Bores; 270. Dullness; 290. Ennui

1. Passions are less mischievous than boredom, for passions tend to diminish, boredom to increase.

Jules Barbey D'Aurevilly, *Une vieille maîtresse* (1851), 2

2. Society is now one polished horde, / Formed of two mighty tribes, the *Bores* and *Bored*.

Byron, *Don Juan* (1819–24), 13.95

3. Boredom dismantles the mind, renders it superficial, out at the seams, saps it from within and dislocates it.

E.M. Cioran, "Some Blind Alleys: A Letter," in *The Art of the Personal Essay* (1994), ed. Phillip Lopate

4. One must choose in life between boredom and torment.

Mme De Staël, letter to Claude Rochet, 1800

5. Boredom is not an end product, is comparatively rather an early stage in life and art. You've got to go by or past or through boredom, as through a filter, before the clear product emerges.

F. Scott Fitzgerald, *The Crack-Up* (1945)

6. Man is the only animal that can be bored.

Erich Fromm, *The Sane Society* (1955), 3

7. A nap, my friend, is a brief period of sleep which overtakes superannuated persons when they endeavour to entertain unwelcome visitors or to listen to scientific lectures.

George Bernard Shaw, *Back to Methuselah* (1921), 4.1

8. One can be bored until boredom becomes the most sublime of all emotions.

Logan Pearsall Smith, *Afterthoughts* (1931), 4

9. Boredom: the desire for desires.

Leo Tolstoy, *Anna Karenina* (1873–76), 5.8

95. BORES

See also 68. Banality; 94. Boredom; 270. Dullness

1. The man who suspects his own tediousness is yet to be born.

Thomas Bailey Aldrich, "Leaves from a Notebook," *Ponkapog Papers* (1903)

2. Bore, n. A person who talks when you wish him to listen.

Ambrose Bierce, *The Devil's Dictionary* (1881–1911)

3. Each man reserves to himself alone the right of being tedious.

Emerson, *Journals*, 1843

4. It is the peculiarity of the bore that he is the last person to find himself out.

Oliver Wendell Holmes, Sr., *Over the Teacups* (1891), 4

5. If the best company is that which we leave feeling most satisfied with ourselves, it follows that it is the company we leave most bored.

Giacomo Leopardi, *Pensieri* (1834–37), 21, tr. William Fense Weaver

6. What things are sure this side of paradise: / Death, taxes, and the counsel of the bore. / Though we outwit the tithe, make death our friend, / Bores we have with us even to the end.

Phyllis McGinley, "A Choice of Weapons," *The Love Letters of Phyllis McGinley* (1954)

7. A healthy male adult bore consumes each year one and a half times his own weight in other people's patience.

John Updike, "Confessions of a Wild Bore," *Assorted Prose* (1965)

8. The secret of being a bore is to tell everything.

Voltaire, *Sept discours en vers sur l'homme* (1738), 2

96. BORROWING AND LENDING

See also 222. Debt; 647. Obligation

1. A borrowed cloak does not keep one warm.

Arabic Proverb

2. The borrower is servant to the lender.

Bible, Proverbs 22:7

3. One must be strict even in little things.

James Boswell, *Journal of a Tour Through the Courts of Germany* (1764)

4. The human species, according to the best theory I can form of it, is composed of two distinct races, the men who borrow, and the men who lend.

CHARLES LAMB, "THE TWO RACES OF MEN," *ESSAYS OF ELIA* (1823)

5. Neither a borrower nor a lender be; For loan oft loses both itself and friend.

SHAKESPEARE, *HAMLET* (1600), 1.3.75

6. The person whom you favoured with a loan, if he be a good man, will think himself in your debt after he has paid you.

RICHARD STEELE, *THE SPECTATOR* (1711–12), 346

7. Have a horse of your own and you may borrow another's.

WELSH PROVERB

BOURGEOISIE

See 587. MIDDLE CLASS

97. BOYS

See also 123. CHILDREN; 916. SONS; 1071. YOUTH

1. Boys naturally look on all force as an enemy.

HENRY ADAMS, *THE EDUCATION OF HENRY ADAMS* (1907), 1

2. A boy is a piece of existence quite separate from all things else, and deserves separate chapters in the natural history of men.

HENRY WARD BEECHER, *PROVERBS FROM PLYMOUTH PULPIT* (1887)

3. A lazy boy and a warm bed are difficult to part.

DANISH PROVERB

4. I have pretty large experience of boys, and you're a bad set of fellows.

CHARLES DICKENS, *GREAT EXPECTATIONS* (1860–1861)

5. A boy becomes an adult three years before his parents think he does, and about two years after he thinks he does.

GENERAL LEWIS B. HERSHEY, NEWS SUMMARIES, DEC. 31, 1951

6. Boys are capital fellows in their own way, among their mates; but they are unwholesome companions for grown people.

CHARLES LAMB, "THE OLD AND THE NEW SCHOOLMASTER," *ESSAYS OF ELIA* (1823)

7. It was the smile of a boy at his own birthday party, the lad who is both humbled and wondrously elated by the realization that he is in a room full of people who are happy, abnormally happy, one might say, to see him alive and in their presence.

TOM WOLFE, *THE BONFIRE OF THE VANITIES* (1987)

BRAVERY

See 195. COURAGE

BREEDING

See 37. ANCESTRY; 391. GOOD BREEDING; 802. REPRODUCTION

98. BREVITY

See also 923. SPEAKING

1. Let thy speech be short, comprehending much in few words.

APOCRYPHA, ECCLESIASTICUS 32:8

2. Least said is soonest disavowed.

AMBROSE BIERCE, "SAW," *THE DEVIL'S DICTIONARY* (1881–1911)

3. Brevity is very good, / When we are, or are not understood.

SAMUEL BUTLER (D. 1680), *HUDIBRAS* (1663), 1.1

4. Men are born with two eyes, but with one tongue, in order that they should see twice as much as they say.

CHARLES CALEB COLTON, *LACON* (1825), 1.112

5. When I struggle to be terse, I end by being obscure.

HORACE, *ARS POETICA* (13–8 B.C.)

6. Half a brain is enough for him who says little.

ITALIAN PROVERB

7. To be brief is almost a condition of being inspired.

GEORGE SANTAYANA, *LITTLE ESSAYS* (1920), 57

8. Men of few words are the best men.

SHAKESPEARE, *HENRY V* (1598–99), 3.2.40

9. All pleasantry should be short; and it might even be as well were the serious short also.

VOLTAIRE, "PRIOR, BUTLER, AND SWIFT," *PHILOSOPHICAL DICTIONARY* (1764)

99. BRIBERY

See also 191. CORRUPTION; 971. TEMPTATION

1. Many a man has been dined out of his religion, and his politics, and his manhood, almost.

HENRY WARD BEECHER, *PROVERBS FROM PLYMOUTH PULPIT* (1887)

2. They say the gods themselves / Are moved by gifts, and gold does more with men than words.

EURIPIDES, *MEDEA* (431 B.C.), TR. REX WARNER

3. A friend that you buy with presents will be bought from you.

THOMAS FULLER, M.D., *GNOMOLOGIA* (1732), 121

4. He that bringeth a present findeth the door open.

THOMAS FULLER, M.D., *GNOMOLOGIA* (1732), 2052

BROAD-MINDEDNESS

See 984. TOLERANCE

100. BROTHERHOOD

See also 151. COMMUNITY; 498. INTERNATIONAL RELATIONS; 626. NEIGHBORS; 1016. UNITY

1. Have we not all one father? hath not one God created us?

BIBLE, MALACHI 2:10

2. While there is a lower class I am in it, while there is a criminal element I am of it; while there is a soul in prison, I am not free.

EUGENE V. DEBS, SPEECH, CLEVELAND, OHIO, SEPT. 9, 1917

3. There is the sky, which is all men's together, there / is the world to live in, fill with houses of our own / nor hold another's, nor tear it from his hands by force.

EURIPIDES, *HELEN* (412 B.C.), TR. RICHMOND LATTIMORE

4. I ought not to fear to survive my own people so long as there are men in the world; for there are always some whom one can love.

ANATOLE FRANCE, *THE CRIME OF SYLVESTRE BONNARD* (1881), 2, TR. LAFCADIO HEARN

5. It is easy enough to be friendly to one's friends. But to befriend the one who regards himself as your enemy is the quintessence of true religion. The other is mere business.

MOHANDAS K. GANDHI, *NON-VIOLENCE IN PEACE AND WAR* (1948), 2.248

6. My country is the world; my countrymen are mankind.

WILLIAM LLOYD GARRISON, PROSPECTUS FOR *THE LIBERATOR* (1803)

7. A low capacity for getting along with those near us often goes hand in hand with a high receptivity to the idea of the brotherhood of men.

ERIC HOFFER, *THE ORDEAL OF CHANGE* (1964), 11

8. A man may have strong humanitarian and democratic principles; but if he happens to have been brought up as a bath-taking, shirt-changing lover of fresh air, he will have to overcome certain physical repugnances before he can bring himself to put those principles into practice.

ALDOUS HUXLEY, *JESTING PILATE* (1926), 1

9. As man increases his knowledge of the heavens, why should he fear the unknown on earth? As man draws nearer to the stars, why should he not also draw nearer to his neighbor?

LYNDON B. JOHNSON, NEWS CONFERENCE, JOHNSON CITY, TEXAS, AUG. 29, 1965

10. Our most basic common link is that we all inhabit this planet. We all breathe the same air. We all cherish our children's future. And we are all mortal.

JOHN F. KENNEDY, ADDRESS, THE AMERICAN UNIVERSITY, WASHINGTON, D.C., JUNE 10, 1963

11. The supreme reality of our time is our indivisibility as children of God and the common vulnerability of this planet.

JOHN F. KENNEDY, ADDRESS TO IRISH PARLIAMENT, DUBLIN, JUNE 28, 1963

12. We seek not the worldwide victory of one nation or system but a worldwide victory of men.

JOHN F. KENNEDY, STATE OF THE UNION MESSAGE, JAN. 14, 1963

13. There is neither East nor West, Border, nor Breed, nor Birth, / When two strong men stand face to face, though they come from the ends of the earth!

RUDYARD KIPLING, "THE BALLAD OF EAST AND WEST" (1899)

14. Every experience proves that the real problem of our existence lies in the fact that we ought to love one another, but do not.

REINHOLD NIEBUHR, *CHRISTIAN REALISM AND POLITICAL PROBLEMS* (1953), 8

15. Those who love not their fellow-beings live unfruitful lives, and prepare for their old age a miserable grave.

SHELLEY, PREFACE, *ALASTOR* (1815)

16. The universal brotherhood of man is our most precious possession, what there is of it.

MARK TWAIN, "PUDD'NHEAD WILSON'S NEW CALENDAR," *FOLLOWING THE EQUATOR* (1897), 1.27

17. Our true nationality is mankind.

H. G. WELLS, *THE OUTLINE OF HISTORY* (1920, 1921), 40.1

18. A "fraternity" is the antithesis of *fraternity.* The first (that is, the order of organization) is predicated on the idea of exclusion; the second (that is, the abstract thing) is based on a feeling of total equality.

E. B. WHITE, "INTIMATIONS," *ONE MAN'S MEAT* (1944)

BROTHERS

See 334. FAMILY

101. BUDGET

See also 223. DEBT, NATIONAL; 277. ECONOMICS; 964. TAXES

1. As quickly as you start spending federal money in large amounts, it looks like free money.

DWIGHT D. EISENHOWER, FEB. 9, 1955

2. The Federal Government is the people and the budget is a reflection of their need.

JOHN F. KENNEDY, ADDRESS, AMERICAN SOCIETY OF NEWSPAPER EDITORS, WASHINGTON, D.C., APRIL 19, 1963

3. The budget is a mythical bean bag. Congress votes mythical beans into it, and then tries to reach in and pull real beans out.

WILL ROGERS, *THE AUTOBIOGRAPHY OF WILL ROGERS* (1949), 18

4. In general, the art of government consists in taking as much money as possible from one part of the citizens to give to the other.

VOLTAIRE, "MONEY," *PHILOSOPHICAL DICTIONARY* (1764)

BUGS

See 481. INSECTS

102. BUREAUCRACY

See also 932. STATISTICS

1. Large organization is loose organization. Nay, it would be almost as true to say that organization is always disorganization.

G. K. CHESTERTON, "THE BLUFF OF THE BIG SHOPS," *OUTLINE OF SANITY* (1926)

2. "Up or out" greatly magnified the careerist emphasis on holding a position rather than doing a job.

JAMES FALLOWS, *NATIONAL DEFENSE* (1981)

3. There is nothing wrong with the United States that a dose of smaller and less intrusive government will not cure.

MILTON FRIEDMAN & ROSE FRIEDMAN, *TYRANNY OF THE STATUS QUO* (1984)

4. Government defines the physical aspects of man by means of The Printed Form, so that for every man in the flesh there is an exactly corresponding man on paper.

JEAN GIRAUDOUX, *THE ENCHANTED* (1933), 3, ADAPTED BY MAURICE VALENCY

5. His chief hate was Washington bureaucracy; second to that, liberals; then cops.

JACK KEROUAC, *ON THE ROAD* (1957)

6. It's all papers and forms, the entire Civil Service is like a fortress made of papers, forms and red tape.

ALEXANDER OSTROVSKY

7. I guess this is why I hate governments, all governments. It is always the rule, the fine print, carried out by fine-print men. There's nothing to fight, no wall to hammer with frustrated fists.

JOHN STEINBECK, *TRAVELS WITH CHARLEY* (1962)

8. There is something about a bureaucrat that does not like a poem.

GORE VIDAL, *REFLECTIONS UPON A SINKING SHIP* (1969)

103. BURIAL

See also 221. DEATH; 367. FUNERALS; 610. MOURNING

1. The graveyard is about fifty by a hundred yards inside a wire fence. There are almost no trees in it: a lemon verbena and a small magnolia; it is all red clay and very few weeds.

JAMES AGEE, *LET US NOW PRAISE FAMOUS MEN* (1941)

2. Nature is honest, we aren't; we embalm our dead.

UGO BETTI, *GOAT ISLAND* (1946), 2, 3

3. Epitaph, n. An inscription on a tomb, showing that virtues acquired by death have a retroactive effect.

AMBROSE BIERCE, *THE DEVIL'S DICTIONARY* (1881–1911)

4. It makes small difference to the dead, if they / are buried in the tokens of luxury. All this / is an empty glorification left for those who live.

EURIPIDES, *THE TROJAN WOMEN* (415 B.C.), TR. RICHMOND LATTIMORE

5. The marble keeps merely a cold and sad memory of a man who would else be forgotten. No man who needs a monument ever ought to have one.

NATHANIEL HAWTHORNE, *ENGLISH NOTE-BOOKS,* NOV. 12, 1857

6. Ritual disposal of the dead speaks clearly of an awareness of death, and thus an awareness of self.

RICHARD LEAKEY, *THE ORIGIN OF HUMANKIND* (1994)

7. They were together now in the vault under the tombstone; their ashes were, with the remains of those of their children who were not buried elsewhere, although all their names were incised on the stone.

Bernard Malamud, *Dubin's Lives* (1979)

8. A cemetery saddens us because it is the only place of the world in which we do not meet our dead again.

François Mauriac, "All Souls' Day," *Cain, Where Is Your Brother?* (1962)

9. Heap not on this mound / Roses that she loved so well; / Why bewilder her with roses, / That she cannot see or smell?

Edna St. Vincent Millay, "Epitaph," *Second April* (1921)

10. There would be a black, six-foot-deep gap hacked in the hard ground. That shadow would marry this shadow, and the peculiar, yellowish soil of our locality seal the wound in the whiteness, and yet another snowfall erase the traces of newness in Joan's grave.

Sylvia Plath, *The Bell Jar* (1963)

104. BUSINESS AND COMMERCE

See also 18. Advertising; 25. Agents; 69. Banking; 105. Buying and Selling; 108. Capitalism; 277. Economics; 315. Executives; 489. Insurance; 503. Investment; 738. Profiteering

1. The customer is always right! John Wanamaker must be turning in his grave. If you're a customer today, you're an intruder.

Cleveland Amory, "The Servant Problem," *The Trouble with Nowadays* (1979)

2. Live together like brothers and do business like strangers.

Arabic Proverb

3. Time is the measure of business.

Francis Bacon, "Of Dispatch," *Essays* (1625)

4. For the merchant, even honesty is a financial speculation.

Charles Baudelaire, *Intimate Journals* (1887), 97, tr. Christopher Isherwood

5. No matter who reigns, the merchant reigns.

Henry Ward Beecher, *Proverbs from Plymouth Pulpit* (1887)

6. The commerce of the world is conducted by the strong, and usually it operates against the weak.

Henry Ward Beecher, *Proverbs from Plymouth Pulpit* (1887)

7. Corporation, n. An ingenious device for obtaining individual profit without individual responsibility.

Ambrose Bierce, *The Devil's Dictionary* (1881–1911)

8. Dispatch is the soul of business, and nothing contributes more to Dispatch than Method.

Lord Chesterfield, *Letters to His Son*, Feb. 5, 1750

9. The business of America is business.

Calvin Coolidge, address, Society of Newspaper Editors, Jan. 17, 1925

10. Keep thy shop, and thy shop will keep thee.

English Proverb

11. The customer is an object to be manipulated, not a concrete person whose aims the businessman is interested to satisfy.

Erich Fromm, *Escape from Freedom* (1941), 4

12. The riskiness of modern corporate life is in fact the harmless conceit of the modern corporate executive, and it is vigorously proclaimed. Precisely because he lives an orderly and careful life the executive is moved to identify himself with the dashing entrepreneur of economic literature.

John Kenneth Galbraith, *The Affluent Society* (1958)

13. Production only fills a void that it has itself created.

John Kenneth Galbraith, *The Affluent Society* (1958), 11.1

14. It is difficult but not impossible to conduct strictly honest business. What is true is that honesty is incompatible with the amassing of a large fortune.

Mohandas K. Gandhi, *Non-Violence in Peace and War* (1948), 2.127

15. Everything which is properly *business* we must keep carefully separate from *life*. Business requires earnestness and method; life must have a freer handling.

Goethe, *Elective Affinities* (1809), 4

16. Honour sinks where commerce long prevails.

Oliver Goldsmith, *The Traveller* (1765), 91

17. American society has tried so hard and so ably to defend the practice and theory of production for

profit and not primarily for use that now it has succeeded in making its jobs and products profitable and useless.

PAUL GOODMAN, *GROWING UP ABSURD* (1960), 1.1

18. In the end, all business operations can be reduced to three words: people, product, and profits.

LEE IACOCCA, *IACOCCA: AN AUTOBIOGRAPHY* (1984) WITH WILLIAM NOVAK

19. Merchants have no country. The mere spot they stand on does not constitute so strong an attachment as that from which they draw their gains.

THOMAS JEFFERSON, LETTER TO HORATIO G. SPAFFORD, MARCH 17, 1814

20. What need had the businessman to scribble or philosophize when he dominated the imagination of his time and the frantic materialism that was his principle of existence had become the haunting central figure in contemporary life?

ALFRED KAZIN, *ON NATIVE GROUNDS* (1942)

21. Ours is not so much an age of vulgarity as of vulgarization; everything is tampered with or touched up, or adulterated or watered down, in an effort to make it palatable, in an effort to make it pay.

LOUIS KRONENBERGER, "THE SPIRIT OF THE AGE," *COMPANY MANNERS* (1954)

22. A corporation is an artificial being, invisible, intangible, and existing only in contemplation of law.

JOHN MARSHALL, *TRUSTEES OF DARTMOUTH COLLEGE V. WOODWARD* (1819)

23. It takes no more actual sagacity to carry on the everyday hawking and haggling of the world, or to ladle out its normal doses of bad medicine and worse law, than it takes to operate a taxicab or fry a pan of fish.

H. L. MENCKEN, "THE FEMININE MIND," *IN DEFENSE OF WOMEN* (1922)

24. By putting business before every other manifestation of life, our mechanical and financial civilization has forgotten the chief business of life: namely, growth, reproduction, development. It pays infinite attention to the incubator—and it forgets the egg!

LEWIS MUMFORD, *FINDINGS AND KEEPINGS. ANALECTS FOR AN AUTOBIOGRAPHY* (1975)

25. A man in business must put up many affronts if he loves his own quiet.

WILLIAM PENN, *SOME FRUITS OF SOLITUDE* (1693), 1.182

26. A man who is always ready to believe what is told him will never do well, especially a businessman.

PETRONIUS, *SATYRICON* (1ST C.), TR. M. HESELTINE

27. If you can build a business up big enough, it's respectable.

WILL ROGERS, *THE AUTOBIOGRAPHY OF WILL ROGERS* (1949), 13

28. There are two fools in every market: one asks too little, one asks too much.

RUSSIAN PROVERB

29. People of the same trade seldom meet together, even for merriment and diversion, but the conversation ends in a conspiracy against the public, or in some contrivance to raise prices.

ADAM SMITH, *THE WEALTH OF NATIONS* (1776), 1.10

30. You never expected justice from a company, did you? They have neither a soul to lose, nor a body to kick.

SYDNEY SMITH, QUOTED IN LADY S. HOLLAND'S *MEMOIR* (1855), V. 1.11

31. Perpetual devotion to what a man calls his business, is only to be sustained by perpetual neglect of many other things.

ROBERT LOUIS STEVENSON, "AN APOLOGY FOR IDLERS," *VIRGINIBUS PUERISQUE* (1881)

32. In democracies, nothing is more great or more brilliant than commerce: it attracts the attention of the public, and fills the imagination of the multitude; all energetic passions are directed towards it.

ALEXIS DE TOCQUEVILLE, *DEMOCRACY IN AMERICA* (1835–39), 2.2.19

33. To ensure that no one gained an advantage over anyone else, commercial law [in the 14th century] prohibited innovation in tools or techniques, underselling below a fixed price, working late by artificial light, employing extra apprentices or wife and underage children, and advertising of wares or praising them to the detriment of others.

BARBARA W. TUCHMAN, *A DISTANT MIRROR* (1978)

34. The bonus is really one of the great give-aways in business enterprise. It is the annual salve applied to the conscience of the rich and the wounds of the poor.

E. B. WHITE, "CONTROL," *ONE MAN'S MEAT* (1944)

35. What is good for the country is good for General Motors, and vice versa.

CHARLES E. WILSON, NEWS REPORTS, JAN. 23, 1953

36. Big business is not dangerous because it is big, but because its bigness is an unwholesome inflation created by privileges and exemptions which it ought not to enjoy.

WOODROW WILSON, ACCEPTANCE SPEECH, DEMOCRATIC NATIONAL CONVENTION, JULY 7, 1912

37. The world is too much with us; late and soon, / Getting and spending, we lay waste our powers: / Little we see in Nature that is ours; / We have given our hearts away, a sordid boon!

WILLIAM WORDSWORTH, "THE WORLD IS TOO MUCH WITH US" (1807)

BUSYNESS

See 10. ACTIVITY

105. BUYING AND SELLING

See also 8. ACQUISITION; 18. ADVERTISING; 25. AGENTS; 104. BUSINESS AND COMMERCE; 108. CAPITALISM; 746. PROPERTY

1. Men go shopping just as men go out fishing or hunting, to see how large a fish may be caught with the smallest hook.

HENRY WARD BEECHER, *PROVERBS FROM PLYMOUTH PULPIT* (1887)

2. A false balance is abomination to the Lord: but a just weight is his delight.

BIBLE, PROVERBS 11:1

3. Auctioneer, n. The man who proclaims with a hammer that he has picked a pocket with his tongue.

AMBROSE BIERCE, *THE DEVIL'S DICTIONARY* (1881–1911)

4. A man without a smiling face must not open a shop.

CHINESE PROVERB

5. He that speaks ill of the mare will buy her.

BENJAMIN FRANKLIN, *POOR RICHARD'S ALMANACK* (1732–57)

6. Man does not only sell commodities, he sells himself and feels himself to be a commodity.

ERICH FROMM, *ESCAPE FROM FREEDOM* (1941), 4

7. He who findeth fault meaneth to buy.

THOMAS FULLER, M.D., *GNOMOLOGIA* (1732), 2383

8. The urge to consume is fathered by the value system which emphasizes the ability of the society to produce.

JOHN KENNETH GALBRAITH, *THE AFFLUENT SOCIETY* (1958), 11.2

9. Try novelties for salesman's bait, / For novelty wins everyone.

GOETHE, "MARTHA'S GARDEN," *FAUST: PART I* (1808), TR. PHILIP WAYNE

10. Looking at bargains from a purely commercial point of view, someone is always cheated, but looked at with the simple eye both seller and buyer always win.

DAVID GRAYSON, *ADVENTURES IN CONTENTMENT* (1907), 2

11. Pleasing ware is half sold.

GEORGE HERBERT, *JACULA PRUDENTUM* (1651)

12. When a man is trying to sell you something, don't imagine he is that polite all the time.

EDGAR WATSON HOWE, *COUNTRY TOWN SAYINGS* (1911)

13. He would sell even his share of the sun.

ITALIAN PROVERB

14. Never buy what you do not want because it is cheap; it will be dear to you.

THOMAS JEFFERSON, LETTER TO THOMAS JEFFERSON SMITH, FEB. 21, 1825

15. Ours is the country where, in order to sell your product, you don't so much point out its merits as you first work like hell to sell yourself.

LOUIS KRONENBERGER, *COMPANY MANNERS* (1954), 3.3

16. If you don't want prosperity to falter, then Buy, Buy, Buy—on credit, of course. In other words, the surest way of bringing on a rainy day is to prepare for it.

JOSEPH WOOD KRUTCH, "THE TWENTIETH CENTURY: DAWN OR TWILIGHT?" *HUMAN NATURE AND THE HUMAN CONDITION* (1959)

17. "Scorn not the common man," says the age of abundance. "He may have no soul; his personality may be exactly the same as his neighbor's; and he may not produce anything worth having. But thank God, he consumes."

JOSEPH WOOD KRUTCH, "THE CONDITION CALLED PROSPERITY," *HUMAN NATURE AND THE HUMAN CONDITION* (1959)

18. His name was George F. Babbitt. He was forty-six years old now, in April, 1920, and he made nothing in particular, neither butter nor shoes nor poetry, but he was nimble in the calling of selling houses for more than people could afford to pay.

SINCLAIR LEWIS, *BABBITT* (1922)

19. Production goes up and up because high pressure advertising and salesmanship constantly create new

needs that must be satisfied: this is *Admass*—a consumer's race with donkeys chasing an electric carrot.

J. B. PRIESTLEY, "THE WRITER IN A CHANGING SOCIETY," *THOUGHTS IN THE WILDERNESS* (1957)

20. Today the future occupation of all moppets is to be skilled consumers.

DAVID RIESMAN, "A JURY OF THEIR PEERS," *THE LONELY CROWD* (1950)

21. Cheat me in price, but not in the goods I purchase.

SPANISH PROVERB

22. Forgive us for frantic buying and selling; for advertising the unnecessary and coveting the extravagant, and calling it good business when it is not good for you.

UNITED PRESBYTERIAN CHURCH, *LITANY FOR HOLY COMMUNION* (1968)

23. Conspicuous consumption of valuable goods is a means of reputability to the gentleman of leisure.

THORSTEIN VEBLEN, *THE THEORY OF THE LEISURE CLASS* (1899), 4

24. When I call on a client, I come by cab, and I am sleek and clean and foursquare. I carry myself as though I've made a quiet killing on the stock market, and have come to call more as a public service than anything else.

KURT VONNEGUT, *WELCOME TO THE MONKEY HOUSE* (1970)

C

CALAMITY

See 17. ADVERSITY

106. CALIFORNIA

1. California, that advance post of our civilisation, with its huge aircraft factories, TV and film studios, automobile way of life..., its flavourless cosmopolitanism, its charlatan philosophies and religions, its lack of anything old and well-tried, rooted in tradition and character.

J. B. PRIESTLEY, "THEY COME FROM INNER SOURCE SPACE," *THOUGHTS IN THE WILDERNESS* (1957)

2. From time to time the continent shifts, and everything that isn't fastened down slides into Southern California.

FRANK LLOYD WRIGHT, TELEVISION INTERVIEW

CALMNESS

See 160. COMPOSURE; 989. TRANQUILITY

CALUMNY

See 905. SLANDER

107. CANADA

1. Geography has made us [America and Canada] neighbors. History has made us friends. Economics has made us partners. And necessity has made us allies. Those whom nature hath so joined together, let no man put asunder.

JOHN F. KENNEDY, ADDRESS TO CANADIAN PARLIAMENT, OTTAWA, MAY 17, 1961

CANDOR

See 362. FRANKNESS

108. CAPITALISM

See also 104. BUSINESS AND COMMERCE; 105. BUYING AND SELLING; 716. POSSESSION; 738. PROFITEERING; 746. PROPERTY

1. There is a good deal of solemn cant about the common interests of capital and labor. As matters stand, their only common interest is that of cutting each other's throat.

BROOKS ATKINSON, "SEPTEMBER 7," *ONCE AROUND THE SUN* (1951)

2. In the market economy the price that is offered is counted upon to produce the result that is sought.

JOHN KENNETH GALBRAITH, *THE NEW INDUSTRIAL STATE* (1967)

3. One beats the bush, another catches the bird.

GERMAN PROVERB

4. Capitalism is moving toward its end massively, imperceptibly, like a glacier. Its decadence is cold, not hot.

MICHAEL HARRINGTON, *THE ACCIDENTAL CENTURY* (1966)

5. To talk of capitalism as an economic system is the first step away from fatalism.

MICHAEL HARRINGTON, *THE ACCIDENTAL CENTURY* (1966)

6. [C]apitalist man was accomplishing moral and political virtue as well as observing economic reason when he vigorously pursued his personal gain.

MICHAEL HARRINGTON, *THE ACCIDENTAL CENTURY* (1966)

7. The cement in our whole democracy today is the worker who makes $15 an hour. He's the guy who will buy a house and a car and a refrigerator. He's the oil in the engine.

LEE IACOCCA, *IACOCCA: AN AUTOBIOGRAPHY* (1984) WITH WILLIAM NOVAK

8. Bearing all this in mind, we see that there is no Russian national understanding which would permit the early establishment in Russia of anything resembling the private enterprise system as we know it.

GEORGE F. KENNAN, *AMERICAN DIPLOMACY 1900–1950* (1951)

9. If you mean by capitalism the God-given right of a few big corporations to make all the decisions that will affect millions of workers and consumers and to exclude everyone else from discussing and examining those decisions, then the unions are threatening capitalism.

MAX LERNER, "A LOOK AT THE BOOKS AND A SHARE OF THE PIE," *ACTIONS AND PASSIONS* (1949)

10. Landlords, like all other men, love to reap where they never sowed.

KARL MARX, "FIRST MANUSCRIPT" (1884), *EARLY WRITINGS*, ED. T. B. BOTTOMORE

11. A businessman is someone who buys at ten and is happy to get out at twelve. The other kind of man buys at ten, sees it rise to eighteen and does nothing. He is waiting for it to rise to twenty. When it drops to two he waits for it to get back to ten.

V.S. NAIPAUL, *A BEND IN THE RIVER* (1979)

12. Thanks to our free-enterprise system and phenomenal advances in marketing, we now stand on the threshold of an era when the American palate, stimulated by delicacies formerly reserved only for a Maecenas, will one day hold aloft a gustatory torch for the entire world.

S.J. PERELMAN, *THE RISING GORGE* (1961)

13. The great dynamic success of capitalism had given us a powerful weapon in our battle against Communism—*money*.

RONALD REAGAN, *AN AMERICAN LIFE* (1990)

14. Everyone who lives in an industrialized society is obliged gradually to give up the past, but in certain countries, such as the United States and Japan, the break with the past has been particularly traumatic.

SUSAN SONTAG, *ON PHOTOGRAPHY* (1977)

15. No economic activity was more irrepressible [in the 14th century] than the investment and lending at interest of money; it was the basis for the rise of the Western capitalist economy and the building of private fortunes—and it was based on the sin of usury.

BARBARA W. TUCHMAN, *A DISTANT MIRROR* (1978)

16. The trouble with the profit system has always been that it was highly unprofitable to most people.

E. B. WHITE, "CONTROL," *ONE MAN'S MEAT* (1944)

CAPITAL PUNISHMENT

See 767. PUNISHMENT, CAPITAL

109. CAPTIVITY

See also 735. PRISON; 889. SERVITUDE

1. The guns on the walls that surround the prison accurately, though unwittingly, index the true character of the penitentiary in our day.

EUGENE V. DEBS, *WALLS AND BARS* (1927)

2. Fetters of gold are still fetters, and silken cords pinch.

ENGLISH PROVERB

3. A cat pent up becomes a lion.

ITALIAN PROVERB

4. If men and women are in chains, anywhere in the world, then freedom is endangered everywhere.

JOHN F. KENNEDY, CAMPAIGN STATEMENT, WASHINGTON, D.C., PULASKI DAY, OCT. 2, 1960

5. I don't want the cheese, I just want to get out of the trap.

LATIN AMERICAN PROVERB

6. Familiarize yourself with the chains of bondage and you prepare your own limbs to wear them.

ABRAHAM LINCOLN, SPEECH, EDWARDSVILLE, ILL., SEPT. 11, 1858

7. A deer with a chain of gold, if she escape, will run off to the forest to eat grass.

MALAY PROVERB

8. Man is born free; and everywhere he is in chains.

ROUSSEAU, *THE SOCIAL CONTRACT* (1762), 1.1, TR. G. D. H. COLE

CARD-PLAYING

See 369. GAMBLING

CAREFULNESS

See 112. CAUTIOUSNESS; 728. PREPAREDNESS; 755. PRUDENCE

CATHOLICISM

See 125. CHRISTIANITY

CATS

See 41. ANIMALS

110. CAUSE AND EFFECT

See also 116. CHANCE; 176. CONSEQUENCES; 240. DESTINY; 815. RETRIBUTION

1. A bird does not fly because it has wings; it has wings because it flies.

ROBERT ARDREY, *THE TERRITORIAL IMPERATIVE* (1966)

2. Take away the cause, and the effect ceases; what the eye ne'er sees, the heart ne'er rues.

CERVANTES, *DON QUIXOTE* (1605–15), 2.4.67, TR. JOHN OZELL

3. Shallow men believe in luck.... Strong men believe in cause and effect.

EMERSON, "WORSHIP," *THE CONDUCT OF LIFE* (1860)

4. The secret of the world is the tie between person and event. Person makes event and event person.

EMERSON, "FATE," *THE CONDUCT OF LIFE* (1860)

5. Nothing comes from nothing.

LUCRETIUS, *ON THE NATURE OF THINGS* (1ST C. B.C.), 1

6. Every why hath a wherefore.

SHAKESPEARE, *THE COMEDY OF ERRORS* (1592–93), 2.2.45

7. Our least deed, like the young of the land crab, wends its way to the sea of cause and effect as soon as born, and makes a drop there to eternity.

THOREAU, *JOURNAL*, MARCH 14, 1838

8. There's no limit to how complicated things can get, on account of one thing always leading to another.

E. B. WHITE, TITLE CHAPTER, *QUO VADIMUS?* (1939)

111. CAUSES

See also 445. IDEOLOGY; 568. MASS MOVEMENTS; 674. PARTISANSHIP

1. Obstinacy in a bad cause is but constancy in a good.

SIR THOMAS BROWNE, *RELIGIO MEDICI* (1642), 1

2. When great causes are on the move in the world, stirring all men's souls, drawing them from their firesides, casting aside comfort, wealth and the pursuit of happiness in response to impulses at once awe-striking and irresistible, we learn that we are spirits, not animals.

SIR WINSTON CHURCHILL, RADIO BROADCAST, JUNE 16, 1941

3. If a cause be good, the most violent attack of its enemies will not injure it so much as an injudicious defense of it by its friends.

CHARLES CALEB COLTON, *LACON* (1825), 1.475

4. A just cause is not ruined by a few mistakes.

DOSTOYEVSKY, "CRITICAL ARTICLES: INTRODUCTION," *POLNOYE SOBRANIYE SOCHINYENI* (*COMPLETE COLLECTED WORKS*, 1895), V. 9

5. The best cause requires a good pleader.

DUTCH PROVERB

6. Those whose cause is just will never lack / good arguments.

EURIPIDES, *HECUBA* (C. 425 B.C.), TR. WILLIAM ARROWSMITH

7. A good cause and a good tongue: and yet money must carry it.

THOMAS FULLER M.D., *GNOMOLOGIA* (1732), 139

8. Truth never damages a cause that is just.

MOHANDAS K. GANDHI, *NON-VIOLENCE IN PEACE AND WAR* (1948), 2.162

9. Faith in a holy cause is to a considerable extent a substitute for the lost faith in ourselves.

ERIC HOFFER, *THE TRUE BELIEVER* (1951), 1.2.8

10. We can be satisfied with moderate confidence in ourselves and with a moderately good opinion of ourselves, but the faith we have in a holy cause has to be extravagant and uncompromising.

ERIC HOFFER, *THE ORDEAL OF CHANGE* (1964), 1

11. It is characteristic of all movements and crusades that the psychopathic element rises to the top.

ROBERT LINDNER, "POLITICAL CREED AND CHARACTER," *MUST YOU CONFORM?* (1956)

12. Henceforward, I shout to the heavens, I shall deliver no more lectures on behalf of good causes: I am the good cause that denies the need for such lectures. Avaunt, importuning world! Back to my cell.

LEWIS MUMFORD, *FINDINGS AND KEEPINGS. ANALECTS FOR AN AUTOBIOGRAPHY* (1975)

13. In a just cause the weak will beat the strong.

SOPHOCLES, *OEDIPUS AT COLONUS* (401 B.C.), TR. ROBERT FITZGERALD

112. CAUTIOUSNESS

See also 755. PRUDENCE

1. He that observeth the wind shall not sow; and he that regardeth the clouds shall not reap.

BIBLE, ECCLESIASTES 11:4

2. When a man feels the difficulty of doing, can he be other than cautious and slow in speaking?

CONFUCIUS, *ANALECTS* (6TH C. B.C.), 12.3, TR. JAMES LEGGE

3. He that will not sail till all dangers are over must never put to sea.

THOMAS FULLER, M.D., *GNOMOLOGIA* (1732), 2353

4. Avoiding danger is no safer in the long run than outright exposure. The fearful are caught as often as the bold.

HELEN KELLER, *LET US HAVE FAITH* (1940)

5. The torment of precautions often exceeds the dangers to be avoided. It is sometimes better to abandon one's self to destiny.

NAPOLEON I, *MAXIMS* (1804–15)

6. Measure a thousand times and cut once.

TURKISH PROVERB

7. The awful thing about most people is their caution—the crawling, abject bird-in-a-hand theory.

THOMAS WOLFE, *THOMAS WOLFE'S LETTERS TO HIS MOTHER* (1943)

CELEBRITY

See 332. FAME

CELIBACY

See 122. CHASTITY; 601. MONASTICISM

113. CENSORSHIP

See also 731. PRESS, FREEDOM OF THE; 823. RIGHTS

1. As we see censorship it is a stupid giant traffic policeman answering "Yes" to "Am I my brother's copper?" He guards a one-way street and his semaphore has four signs, all marked "STOP."

FRANKLIN P. ADAMS, *NODS AND BECKS* (1944)

2. We are willing enough to praise freedom when she is safely tucked away in the past and cannot be a nuisance. In the present, amidst dangers whose outcome we cannot foresee, we get nervous about her, and admit censorship.

E. M. FORSTER, "THE TERCENTENARY OF THE - AREOPAGITICA,'" *TWO CHEERS FOR DEMOCRACY* (1951)

3. Where there is official censorship it is a sign that speech is serious. Where there is none, it is pretty certain that the official spokesmen have all the loudspeakers.

PAUL GOODMAN, *GROWING UP ABSURD* (1960), 2.2

4. Persons who undertake to pry into, or cleanse out all the filth of a common sewer, either cannot have very nice noses, or will soon lose them.

WILLIAM HAZLITT, "ON THE CLERICAL CHARACTER," *POLITICAL ESSAYS* (1819)

5. No government ought to be without censors; and where the press is free, no one ever will.

THOMAS JEFFERSON, LETTER TO GEORGE WASHINGTON, SEPT. 9, 1792

6. Men in earnest have no time to waste / In patching fig-leaves for the naked truth.

JAMES RUSSELL LOWELL, "A GLANCE BEHIND THE CURTAIN" (1843)

7. We'll open in Boston and stay there two weeks. Maybe they'll make us cut out some of the dirty stuff, but we can put it back in for New York.

JOHN O'HARA, *THE INSTRUMENT* (1967)

8. Censorship may be useful for the preservation of morality, but can never be so for its restoration.

ROUSSEAU, *THE SOCIAL CONTRACT* (1762), 4.7, TR. G. D. H. COLE

9. Assassination is the extreme form of censorship.

GEORGE BERNARD SHAW, *THE REJECTED STATEMENT,* 1

CENSURE

See 206. CRITICISM; 803. REPROOF

114. CEREMONY

See also 197. COURTESY; 563. MANNERS; 749. PROPRIETY

1. Ritualism, n. A Dutch Garden of God where He may walk in rectilinear freedom, keeping off the grass.

AMBROSE BIERCE, *THE DEVIL'S DICTIONARY* (1881–1911)

2. Feasts must be solemn and rare, or else they cease to be feasts.

ALDOUS HUXLEY, *DO WHAT YOU WILL* (1929)

3. It is superstition to put one's hope in formalities; but it is pride to be unwilling to submit to them.

PASCAL, *PENSÉES* (1670), 249, TR. W. F. TROTTER

115. CERTAINTY

See also 264. DOGMATISM; 856. SECURITY; 1005. UNCERTAINTY

1. Oh! let us never, never doubt / What nobody is sure about!

HILAIRE BELLOC, "THE MICROBE," *MORE BEASTS FOR WORSE CHILDREN* (1897)

2. Life is the art of drawing sufficient conclusions from insufficient premises.

SAMUEL BUTLER (D.1902), "LORD, WHAT IS MAN?" *NOTE-BOOKS* (1912)

3. There is one thing certain, namely, that we can have nothing certain; therefore it is not certain that we can have nothing certain.

SAMUEL BUTLER (D. 1902), "FIRST PRINCIPLES," *NOTE-BOOKS* (1912)

4. I try not to guess.

JOSEPH CAMPBELL, *THE POWER OF MYTH* (1988)

5. To have his path made clear for him is the aspiration of every human being in our beclouded and tempestuous existence.

JOSEPH CONRAD, *THE MIRROR OF THE SEA* (1906), 27

6. Certainty generally is illusion, and repose is not the destiny of man.

OLIVER WENDELL HOLMES, JR., SPEECH, BOSTON UNIVERSITY SCHOOL OF LAW, JAN. 8, 1897

7. A reasonable probability is the only certainty.

EDGAR WATSON HOWE, *COUNTRY TOWN SAYINGS* (1911)

8. Every area of trouble gives out a ray of hope, and the one unchangeable certainty is that nothing is certain or unchangeable.

JOHN F. KENNEDY, STATE OF THE UNION MESSAGE, JAN. 11, 1962

9. There is only one thing about which I am certain, and this is that there is very little about which one can be certain.

W. SOMERSET MAUGHAM, *THE SUMMING UP* (1938), 5

10. It is the dull man who is always sure, and the sure man who is always dull. The more a man dreams, the less he believes.

H. L. MENCKEN, *PREJUDICES: SECOND SERIES* (1920), 1

11. There is many a slip 'twixt the cup and the lip.

PALLADAS (FL. A.D. 400), IN *THE GREEK ANTHOLOGY* (7TH C. B.C.–10TH C. A.D.), 10.32

12. Certainties are arrived at only on foot.

ANTONIO PORCHIA, *VOCES* (1968), TR. W. S. MERWIN

13. In a universe of ambiguity, this kind of certainty comes only once, and never again, no matter how many lifetimes you live.

ROBERT JAMES WALLER, *THE BRIDGES OF MADISON COUNTY* (1992)

116. CHANCE

See also 129. CIRCUMSTANCE; 340. FATE; 360. FORTUNE

1. Accident counts for much in companionship as in marriage.

HENRY ADAMS, *THE EDUCATION OF HENRY ADAMS* (1907), 4

2. Life is full of chances and changes, and the most prosperous of men may in the evening of his days meet with great misfortunes.

ARISTOTLE, *NICOMACHEAN ETHICS* (4TH C. B.C.), 1.9, TR. J. A. K. THOMSON

3. They, believe me, who await / No gifts from chance, have conquered fate.

MATTHEW ARNOLD, "RESIGNATION," *THE STRAYED REVELLER, AND OTHER POEMS* (1849)

4. They who lose today may win tomorrow.

CERVANTES, *DON QUIXOTE* (1605–15), 1.1.7, TR. JOHN OZELL

5. It is not Justice the servant of men, but accident, hazard, Fortune—the ally of patient Time—that holds an even and scrupulous balance.

JOSEPH CONRAD, *LORD JIM* (1900), 34

6. We are ruled by chance but never have enough patience to accept its despotism.

EDWARD DAHLBERG, "ON FUTILITY," *REASONS OF THE HEART* (1965)

7. Enjoy yourself, drink, call the life you live today / your own, but only that, the rest belongs to chance.

EURIPIDES, *ALCESTIS* (438 B.C.), TR. RICHMOND LATTIMORE

8. There is an ambush everywhere from the army of accidents; therefore the rider of life runs with loosened reins.

HĀFIZ, GHAZALS FROM THE *DIVAN* (14TH C.), 84, TR. JUSTIN HUNTLY MCCARTHY

9. Chance and chance alone has a message for us. Everything that occurs because of necessity, everything expected, repeated day in and day out, is mute.

MILAN KUNDERA, *THE UNBEARABLE LIGHTNESS OF BEING* (1984)

10. Fortune and humour govern the world.

LA ROCHEFOUCAULD, *MAXIMS* (1665), TR. KENNETH PRATT

11. Chance gives rise to thoughts, and chance removes them; no art can keep or acquire them.

PASCAL, *PENSÉES* (1670), 370, TR. W. F. TROTTER

12. Chance favors the prepared mind.

LOUIS PASTEUR, QUOTED IN *DICTIONARY OF SCIENTIFIC BIOGRAPHY*, ED. CHARLES C. GILLESPIE

13. If I'd gotten the job I wanted at Montgomery Ward, I suppose I would never have left Illinois.

RONALD REAGAN, *AN AMERICAN LIFE* (1990)

14. What the reason of the ant laboriously drags into a heap, the wind of accident will collect in one breath.

SCHILLER, *FIESCO* (1783), 2.4

15. Every possession and every happiness is but lent by chance for an uncertain time, and may therefore be demanded back the next hour.

SCHOPENHAUER, *THE WORLD AS WILL AND IDEA* (1819), 1

16. Chance makes a football of man's life.

SENECA, *LETTERS TO LUCILIUS* (1ST C.), 16.5, TR. E. PHILLIPS BARKER

17. Why should man fear since chance is all in all / for him, and he can clearly foreknow nothing? / Best to live lightly, as one can, unthinkingly.

SOPHOCLES, *OEDIPUS THE KING* (C. 430 B.C.), TR. DAVID GRENE

18. On Friday noon, July the twentieth, 1714, the finest bridge in all Peru broke and precipitated five travelers into the gulf below.

THORNTON WILDER, *THE BRIDGE OF SAN LUIS REY* (1927)

117. CHANGE

See also 118. CHANGELESSNESS; 179. CONSISTENCY; 350. FLEXIBILITY; 464. INCONSISTENCY; 479. INNOVATION; 640. NOVELTY; 654. OPEN-MINDEDNESS; 741. PROGRESS; 800. REPETITION; 990. TRANSIENCE

1. For what wears out the life of mortal men? / 'Tis that from change to change their being rolls; / 'Tis that repeated shocks, again, again, / Exhaust the energy of strongest souls / And numb the elastic powers.

MATTHEW ARNOLD, "THE SCHOLAR-GIPSY," *POEMS* (1853)

2. The absurd man is he who never changes.

AUGUSTE BARTHÉLÉMY, *MA JUSTIFICATION* (1830–31)

3. Great cultural changes begin in affectation and end in routine.

JACQUES BARZUN, *THE HOUSE OF INTELLECT* (1959)

4. Weep not that the world changes—did it keep / A stable, changeless state, 'twere cause indeed to weep.

WILLIAM CULLEN BRYANT, "MUTATION" (1824)

5. The interval between the decay of the old and the formation and the establishment of the new, constitutes a period of transition, which must always necessarily be one of uncertainty, confusion, error, and wild and fierce fanaticism.

JOHN C. CALHOUN, *A DISQUISITION ON GOVERNMENT* (1850)

6. To remain young one must change. The perpetual campus hero is not a young man but an old boy.

ALEXANDER CHASE, *PERSPECTIVES* (1966)

7. Change as change is mere flux and lapse; it insults intelligence. Genuinely to know is to grasp a permanent end that realizes itself through changes.

JOHN DEWEY, "THE INFLUENCE OF DARWINISM ON PHILOSOPHY" (1909)

8. Life is not a static thing. The only people who do not change their minds are incompetents in asylums, who can't, and those in cemeteries.

SEN. EVERETT M. DIRKSEN, PRESS CONFERENCE, WASHINGTON, D.C., JAN. 1, 1965

9. In the life of one man, never / The same time returns.

T. S. ELIOT, *MURDER IN THE CATHEDRAL* (1935), 1

10. We cannot remain consistent with the world save by growing inconsistent with our past selves.

HAVELOCK ELLIS, PREFACE, *THE DANCE OF LIFE* (1923)

11. All is change; all yields its place and goes.

EURIPIDES, *HERACLES* (C. 422 B.C.), TR. WILLIAM ARROWSMITH

12. There is something in the pang of change / More than the heart can bear, / Unhappiness remembering happiness.

EURIPIDES, *IPHIGENIA IN TAURIS* (C. 414–12 B.C.), TR. WITTER BYNNER

13. Language does not stand still. Surprisingly, despite this knowledge, most speakers are fearful of change.

PETER FARB, *WORD PLAY* (1973)

14. All changes, even the most longed for, have their melancholy; for what we leave behind us is a part of ourselves; we must die to one life before we can enter into another!

ANATOLE FRANCE, *THE CRIME OF SYLVESTRE BONNARD* (1881), 2, TR. LAFCADIO HEARN

15. Through loyalty to the past, our mind refuses to realize that tomorrow's joy is possible only if today's makes way for it; that each wave owes the beauty of its line only to the withdrawal of the preceding one.

ANDRÉ GIDE, *JOURNALS*, 1928, TR. JUSTIN O'BRIEN

16. Just as nature abhors a vacuum, humans resist change. Change will occur; vacuums will be filled.

NIKKI GIOVANNI, "EARTHLINGS: THE FUTURE TRADITION," *RACISM 101* (1994)

17. We accept the verdict of the past until the need for change cries out loudly enough to force upon us a choice between the comforts of further inertia and the irksomeness of action.

LEARNED HAND, ADDRESS, SUPREME JUDICIAL COURT OF MASSACHUSETTS, NOV. 21, 1942

18. You cannot step twice into the same river, for other waters are continually flowing in.

HERACLITUS, *FRAGMENTS* (C. 500 B.C.), 21, TR. PHILIP WHEELWRIGHT

19. Nothing is permanent but change.

HERACLITUS (FL. C. 500 B.C.), QUOTED IN DIOGENES LAERTIUS' *LIVES AND OPINIONS OF EMINENT PHILOSOPHERS* (3RD C. A.D.)

20. Even in slight things the experience of the new is rarely without some stirring of foreboding.

ERIC HOFFER, *THE ORDEAL OF CHANGE* (1964), 1

21. There is a certain relief in change, even though it be from bad to worse.

WASHINGTON IRVING, "TO THE READER," *TALES OF A TRAVELLER* (1824)

22. The more things change, the more they remain the same.

ALPHONSE KARR, *LES GUÊPES,* JANUARY 1849

23. Change is the law of life. And those who look only to the past or the present are certain to miss the future.

JOHN F. KENNEDY, ADDRESS, FRANKFURT, WEST GERMANY, JUNE 25, 1963

24. Progress is a nice word. But change is its motivator. And change has its enemies.

ROBERT F. KENNEDY, "FEDERAL POWER AND LOCAL POVERTY," *THE PURSUIT OF JUSTICE* (1964)

25. For young people today things move so *fast* there is no problem of adjustment. Before you can adjust to A, B has appeared leading C by the hand, and with D in the distance.

LOUIS KRONENBERGER, "REFLECTIONS AND COMPLAINTS OF LATE MIDDLE AGE," *THE CART AND THE HORSE* (1964), 3

26. Whenever a thing changes and quits its proper limits, this change is at once the death of that which was before.

LUCRETIUS, *ON THE NATURE OF THINGS* (1ST C. B.C.), 3, TR. H. A. J. MUNRO

27. On the old highway maps of America, the main routes were red and the back roads blue. Now even the colors are changing.

WILLIAM LEAST HEAT MOON, *BLUE HIGHWAYS* (1982)

28. The greatest of the changes that science has brought is the acuity of change; the greatest novelty the extent of novelty.

J. ROBERT OPPENHEIMER, "THE SCIENCES AND MAN'S COMMUNITY," LECTURE, 1953

29. Continuity in everything is unpleasant. Cold is agreeable, that we may get warm.

PASCAL, *PENSÉES* (1670), 355, TR. W. F. TROTTER

30. Time, in the turning-over of days, works change for better or worse.

PINDAR, *ODES* (5TH C. B.C.), ISTHMIA 3, TR. RICHMOND LATTIMORE

31. "Change" is scientific, "progress" is ethical; change is indubitable, whereas progress is a matter of controversy.

BERTRAND RUSSELL, "PHILOSOPHY AND POLITICS," *UNPOPULAR ESSAYS* (1950)

32. When old words die out on the tongue, new melodies break forth from the heart; and where the old tracks are lost, new country is revealed with its wonders.

RABINDRANATH TAGORE, *GITANJALI* (1912), 37

33. The old order changeth yielding place to new, / And God fulfills himself in many ways, / Lest one good custom should corrupt the world.

LORD TENNYSON, "THE PASSING OF ARTHUR," *IDYLLS OF THE KING* (1869)

34. In every age of well-marked transition there is the pattern of habitual dumb practice and emotion which is passing, and there is oncoming a new complex of habit.

ALFRED NORTH WHITEHEAD, *ADVENTURES OF IDEAS* (1933), 1

35. There is a time for departure even when there's no certain place to go.

TENNESSEE WILLIAMS, *CAMINO REAL* (1953), 8

118. CHANGELESSNESS

See also 117. CHANGE

1. Wood may remain ten years in the water, but it will never become a crocodile.

CONGOLESE PROVERB

2. It is a long lane that has no turning.

ENGLISH PROVERB

3. Happiness is never really so welcome as changelessness.

GRAHAM GREENE, *THE HEART OF THE MATTER* (1948), 3.3

4. [S]o many social changes are as irreversible as the reaction when sodium is thrown into water.

GUNNAR MYRDAL, *BEYOND THE WELFARE STATE* (1960)

5. Everything that has been is eternal: the sea will wash it up again.

NIETZSCHE, *THE WILL TO POWER* (1888), 1065, TR. ANTHONY M. LUDOVICI

6. There is an aura of changelessness to sport. There is the flux of competition, but it occurs within the ordering confinement of clear rules.

GEORGE F. WILL, *MEN AT WORK: THE CRAFT OF BASEBALL* (1990)

7. Me this unchartered freedom tires; / I feel the weight of chance-desires: / My hopes no more must change their name, / I long for a repose that ever is the same.

WILLIAM WORDSWORTH, "ODE TO DUTY" (1805)

CHAOS

See 257. DISORDER

119. CHARACTER

See also 444. IDENTITY; 491. INTEGRITY; 687. PERSONALITY

1. Character is tested by true sentiments more than by conduct. A man is seldom better than his word.

LORD ACTON, POSTSCRIPT, LETTER TO MANDELL CREIGHTON, APRIL 5, 1887

2. He had fallen into the usual masculine blunder of mixing up smartness of intelligence with strength of character.

HENRY ADAMS, *DEMOCRACY: AN AMERICAN NOVEL* (1880)

3. In necessary things, unity; in doubtful things, liberty; in all things, charity.

RICHARD BAXTER (1615–1691), MOTTO

4. Happiness is not the end of life: character is.

HENRY WARD BEECHER, *LIFE THOUGHTS* (1858)

5. As he thinketh in his heart, so is he.

BIBLE, PROVERBS 23:7

6. The more peculiarly his own a man's character is, the better it fits him.

CICERO, *DE OFFICIIS* (44 B.C.), 1.31.113

7. I know sage, wormwood, and hyssop, but I can't smell character unless it stinks.

EDWARD DAHLBERG, "ON HUMAN NATURE," *REASONS OF THE HEART* (1965)

8. Men are what their mothers made them.

EMERSON, "FATE," *THE CONDUCT OF LIFE* (1860)

9. Nature magically suits the man to his fortunes, by making these the fruit of his character.

EMERSON, "FATE," *THE CONDUCT OF LIFE* (1860)

10. People seem not to see that their opinion of the world is also a confession of character.

EMERSON, "WORSHIP," *THE CONDUCT OF LIFE* (1860)

11. As if they were our own handiwork, we place a high value on our characters.

EPICURUS, "VATICAN SAYINGS" (3RD C. B.C.), 15, IN *LETTERS, PRINCIPAL DOCTRINES, AND VATICAN SAYINGS,* TR. RUSSEL M. GEER

12. Old age and sickness bring out the essential characteristics of a man.

FELIX FRANKFURTER, *FELIX FRANKFURTER REMINISCES* (1960), 2

13. Fortitude is the capacity to say "no" when the world wants to hear "yes."

ERICH FROMM, *THE REVOLUTION OF HOPE* (1968)

14. Genius is formed in quiet, character in the stream of human life.

GOETHE, *TORQUATO TASSO* (1790), 1.2

15. A man's character is his guardian divinity.

HERACLITUS, *FRAGMENTS* (C. 500 B.C.), 69, TR. PHILIP WHEELWRIGHT

16. Character cannot be developed in ease and quiet. Only through experience of trial and suffering can the soul be strengthened, vision cleared, ambition inspired, and success achieved.

HELEN KELLER, *HELEN KELLER'S JOURNAL* (1938)

17. Between ourselves and our real natures we interpose that wax figure of idealizations and selections which we call our character.

WALTER LIPPMANN, "SOME NECESSARY ICONOCLASM," *A PREFACE TO POLITICS* (1914)

18. Talking in a soft modest voice, he [Barry Goldwater] radiated at this moment the skinny boy-

ish sincerity of a fellow who wears glasses but is determined nevertheless to have a good time. It was not unreminiscent of Arthur Miller: that same mixture of vast solemnity and unspoiled boyhood, a sort of shucks and aw shit in the voice.

Norman Mailer, *Cannibals and Christians* (1967)

19. If you talked or laughed in church, told lies, had impure thoughts or conversations, you were bad; if you obeyed your parents or guardians, went to confession and communion regularly, said prayers for the dead, you were good.

Mary McCarthy, *The Company She Keeps* (1942)

20. Listen to a man's words and look at the pupil of his eye. How can a man conceal his character?

Mencius, *Works* (4th–3rd c. b.c.), 4, tr. Charles A. Wong

21. No man can climb out beyond the limitations of his own character.

John Morley, "Robespierre," *Critical Miscellanies* (1871–1908)

22. The ultimate test of a nation's character is not how it responds to adversity in war but how it meets the challenge of peace.

Richard M. Nixon, *Beyond Peace* (1994)

23. When the character's right, looks are a greater delight.

Ovid, *The Art of Beauty* (c. a.d. 8), tr. Rolfe Humphries

24. Character is much easier kept than recovered.

Thomas Paine, *The American Crisis* (1776–83), 13

25. Character is inured habit.

Plutarch, "The Education of Children," *Moralia* (c. a.d. 100), tr. Moses Hadas

26. His own character is the arbiter of every one's fortune.

Publilius Syrus, *Moral Sayings* (1st c. b.c.), 283, tr. Darius Lyman

27. Not on the stage alone, in the world also, a man's real character comes out best in his asides.

Alexander Smith, "William Dunbar," *Dreamthorp* (1863)

28. No one is ignorant that our character and turn of mind are intimately connected with the water-closet.

Voltaire, "Slow Bellies," *Philosophical Dictionary* (1764)

29. [Pres. Lyndon] Johnson was a middle-aged man of smalltown America, both a Westerner and a Southerner, and except where politics had demonstrably forced his growth—as on the question of civil rights—he functioned like most men, as a product of his background.

Tom Wicker, *JFK and LBJ* (1968)

30. A career in flying was like climbing one of those ancient Babylonian pyramids made up of a dizzy progression of steps and ledges, a ziggurat, a pyramid extraordinarily high and steep; and the idea was to prove at every foot of the way up that pyramid that you were one of the elected and anointed ones who had *the right stuff* and could move higher and higher and even—ultimately, God willing, one day—that you might be able to join that special few at the very top, that elite who had the capacity to bring tears to men's eyes, the very Brotherhood of the Right Stuff itself.

Tom Wolfe, *The Right Stuff* (1979)

31. Character begins to form at the first pinch of anxiety about ourselves.

Yevgeny Yevtushenko, "There's Something I Often Notice: (To M. Roshchin)," *The New Russian Poets: 1953 to 1966* (1966), tr. George Reavey

120. CHARITY

See also 384. Gifts and Giving; 433. Humanitarianism; 519. Kindness; 551. Love; 984. Tolerance

1. They were also very bountiful, especially the ladies. They were always raising money to buy skinny chickens for people who lived in tenements or organizing private schools that often went bankrupt.

John Cheever, *The Falconer* (1977)

2. Did universal charity prevail, earth would be a heaven, and hell a fable.

Charles Caleb Colton, *Lacon* (1825), 1.160

3. He that has no charity deserves no mercy.

English Proverb

4. Would we hold liberty, we must have charity—charity to others, charity to ourselves, crawling up from the moist ovens of a steaming world, still carrying the passional equipment of our ferocious ancestors, emerging from black superstition amid carnage and atrocity to our perilous present.

Learned Hand, *The Spirit of Liberty* (1959)

5. Charity in the theatre usually begins and ends with people who have a play opening the week following one's own. Their unlikely benevolence is not so much a purity of heart as the knowledge that they face a fir-

ing line with rifles aimed in exactly the same direction.

MOSS HART, *ACT ONE* (1959)

6. To think ill of mankind, and not wish ill to them, is perhaps the highest wisdom and virtue.

WILLIAM HAZLITT, *CHARACTERISTICS* (1823), 241

7. I as little fear that God will damn a man that has charity, as I hope that the priests can save one who has not.

ALEXANDER POPE, *THOUGHTS ON VARIOUS SUBJECTS* (1727)

8. In faith and hope the world will disagree, / But all mankind's concern is charity.

ALEXANDER POPE, *AN ESSAY ON MAN* (1733–34), 3.303

9. The robbed that smiles steals something from the thief.

SHAKESPEARE, *OTHELLO* (1604–05), 1.3.208

10. The silver ore of pure charity is an expensive article in the catalogue of a man's good qualities.

RICHARD BRINSLEY SHERIDAN, *THE SCHOOL FOR SCANDAL* (1777), 5.2

11. Charity and personal force are the only investments worth anything.

WALT WHITMAN, "SONG OF PRUDENCE," *LEAVES OF GRASS* (1855–92)

121. CHARM

1. Charm: that quality in others of making us more satisfied with ourselves.

HENRI FRÉDÉRIC AMIEL, *JOURNAL* (1882–84)

2. It's [charm] a sort of bloom on a woman. If you have it, you don't need to have anything else; and if you don't have it, it doesn't much matter what else you have.

J. M. BARRIE, *WHAT EVERY WOMAN KNOWS* (1908), 1

3. Charm is a glow within a woman that casts a most becoming light on others.

JOHN MASON BROWN, *VOGUE*, NOV. 15, 1956

4. Charming people live up to the very edge of their charm, and behave just as outrageously as the world will let them.

LOGAN PEARSALL SMITH, *AFTERTHOUGHTS* (1931), 3

5. A beauty is a woman you notice; a charmer is one who notices you.

ADLAI STEVENSON, *THE STEVENSON WIT* (1966)

6. All charming people, I fancy, are spoiled. It is the secret of their attraction.

OSCAR WILDE, *THE PORTRAIT OF MR. W. H.* (1901)

7. It's absurd to divide people into good and bad. People are either charming or tedious.

OSCAR WILDE, *LADY WINDERMERE'S FAN* (1892)

122. CHASTITY

See also 601. MONASTICISM; 770. PURITY; 865. SELF-DENIAL

1. Give me chastity and continence, but not just now.

ST. AUGUSTINE, *CONFESSIONS* (5TH C.), 8.7

2. The essence of chastity is not the suppression of lust, but the total orientation of one's life towards a goal.

DIETRICH BONHOEFFER, "MISCELLANEOUS THOUGHTS," *LETTERS AND PAPERS FROM PRISON* (1953), TR. EBERHARD BETHGE

3. Be warm, but pure; be amorous, but be chaste.

BYRON, *ENGLISH BARDS AND SCOTCH REVIEWERS* (1809)

4. Chastity is not chastity in an old man, but a disability to be unchaste.

JOHN DONNE, *SERMONS*, NO. 5, 1619

5. Chastity more rarely follows fear, or a resolution, or a vow, than it is the mere effect of lack of appetite and, sometimes even, of distaste.

ANDRÉ GIDE, *JOURNALS*, MARCH 12, 1938, TR. JUSTIN O'BRIEN

6. Too chaste an adolescence makes for a dissolute old age. It is doubtless easier to give up something one has known than something one imagines.

ANDRÉ GIDE, *JOURNALS*, JAN. 21, 1929, TR. JUSTIN O'BRIEN

7. A woman's chastity consists, like an onion, of a series of coats.

NATHANIEL HAWTHORNE, *JOURNALS*, MARCH 16, 1854

8. I will find you twenty lascivious turtles ere one chaste man.

SHAKESPEARE, *THE MERRY WIVES OF WINDSOR* (1597), 2.1.82

9. If you cannot be chaste, be cautious.

SPANISH PROVERB

10. The only chaste woman is the one who has not been asked.

SPANISH PROVERB

11. To gain victory over the flesh was the purpose of fasting and celibacy, which denied the pleasures of this world for the sake of reward in the next.

BARBARA W. TUCHMAN, *A DISTANT MIRROR* (1978)

CHEERFULNESS

See 392. GOOD NATURE

123. CHILDREN

See also 65. BABIES; 97. BOYS; 218. DAUGHTERS; 334. FAMILY; 385. GIRLS; 670. PARENTHOOD; 916. SONS

1. Blessed be childhood, which brings down something of heaven into the midst of our rough earthliness.

HENRI FRÉDÉRIC AMIEL, *JOURNAL*, JAN. 26, 1868, TR. MRS. HUMPHRY WARD

2. The life of children, as much as that of intemperate men, is wholly governed by their desires.

ARISTOTLE, *NICOMACHEAN ETHICS* (4TH C. B.C.), 3.12, TR. J. A. K. THOMSON

3. Notice, for example, that people who talk about "the joys of childhood" are always adults. Only an adult, utterly remote from the reality of childhood, could suppose it is time of "joys."

RUSSELL BAKER , *THE NEW YORK TIMES*, APRIL 1, 1994

4. Children have never been very good at listening to their elders, but they have never failed to imitate them.

JAMES BALDWIN, "FIFTH AVENUE, UPTOWN," *NOBODY KNOWS MY NAME* (1961)

5. That energy which makes a child hard to manage is the energy which afterward makes him a manager of life.

HENRY WARD BEECHER, *PROVERBS FROM PLYMOUTH PULPIT* (1887)

6. Children tend to be rather better observers of adults' characters than adults are of children's, because children are so dependent on adults that it is very much in their interest to discover the weaknesses of their elders.

ALLAN BLOOM, *THE CLOSING OF THE AMERICAN MIND* (1987)

7. Childish fantasy, like the sheath over the bud, not only protects but curbs the terrible budding spirit, protects not only innocence from the world, but the world from the power of innocence.

ELIZABETH BOWEN, *THE DEATH OF THE HEART* (1938), 3.5

8. There is no end to the violations committed by children on children, quietly talking alone.

ELIZABETH BOWEN, *THE HOUSE IN PARIS* (1935), 1.2

9. Boys like romantic tales; but babies like realistic tales—because they find them romantic.

G. K. CHESTERTON, "THE LOGIC OF ELFLAND," *ORTHODOXY* (1908)

10. Who takes the child by the hand, takes the mother by the heart.

DANISH PROVERB

11. In the little world in which children have their existence, whosoever brings them up, there is nothing so finely perceived and so finely felt, as injustice.

CHARLES DICKENS, *GREAT EXPECTATIONS* (1860–1861)

12. It may be only small injustice that the child can be exposed to; but the child is small, and its world is small, and its rocking-horse stands as many hands high, according to scale, as a big-boned Irish hunter.

CHARLES DICKENS, *GREAT EXPECTATIONS* (1860–1861)

13. As soon as a child has left the room his strewn toys become affecting.

EMERSON, *JOURNALS*, 1839

14. There never was child so lovely but his mother was glad to get him asleep.

EMERSON, *JOURNALS*, 1836

15. We find delight in the beauty and happiness of children that makes the heart too big for the body.

EMERSON, "ILLUSIONS," *THE CONDUCT OF LIFE* (1860)

16. Children are poor men's riches.

ENGLISH PROVERB

17. No child is capable of speech until he has heard other human beings speak, and even two infants reared together cannot develop a language from scratch.

PETER FARB, *WORD PLAY* (1973)

18. "Well, I guess the children have left for school by this time—I might as well go home."

F. SCOTT FITZGERALD, LETTER OF RING LARDNER TO F. SCOTT FITZGERALD, IN *THE CRACK-UP* (1945)

19. It is difficult for young people to live things down. We will tolerate vice, grand larceny and the quieter forms of murder in our contemporaries....but our children's friends must show a blank service record.

F. SCOTT FITZGERALD, *THE CRACK-UP* (1945)

20. That child whose mother has never smiled upon him is worthy neither of the table of the gods nor the couch of the goddesses.

ANATOLE FRANCE, *THE CRIME OF SYLVESTRE BONNARD* (1881), 1, TR. LAFCADIO HEARN

21. Children are completely egoistic; they feel their needs intensely and strive ruthlessly to satisfy them.

SIGMUND FREUD, "DREAMS OF THE DEATH OF BELOVED PERSONS," *THE INTERPRETATION OF DREAMS* (1899), TR. JAMES STRACHEY

22. Your children are not your children. / They are the sons and daughters of Life's longing for itself.

KAHLIL GIBRAN, "ON CHILDREN," *THE PROPHET* (1923)

23. Who knows whether there may not be a moment in childhood when the world changes forever, like making a face when the clock strikes?

GRAHAM GREENE, *OUR MAN IN HAVANA* (1958)

24. Childhood is a short season.

HELEN HAYES, "CARRIAGE TRADE," *LOVING LIFE* (1987), WITH MARION GLASSEROW GLADNEY

25. There had always been kids in school who were smart—that is, the school said they were smart, they could be shown to have been smart at some time in their lives on the school's own tests—but who did not do well in school, who got bad grades and who were a pain in the ass.

JAMES HERNDON, *HOW TO SURVIVE IN YOUR NATIVE LAND* (1971)

26. If you want to honor me, give some young boy or girl who's coming along trying to create arts and write and compose and sing and act and paint and dance and make something out of the beauties of the Negro race—give that child some help.

LANGSTON HUGHES, *SIMPLE SPEAKS HIS MIND* (1950)

27. A little girl without a doll is almost as unfortunate and quite as impossible as a woman without children.

VICTOR HUGO, "COSETTE," *LES MISÉRABLES* (1862), 3.8, TR. CHARLES E. WILBOUR

28. Children are remarkable for their intelligence and ardor, for their curiosity, their intolerance of shams, the clarity and ruthlessness of their vision.

ALDOUS HUXLEY, "VULGARITY IN LITERATURE," *MUSIC AT NIGHT* (1931)

29. I'm still not sure what is meant by good fortune and success. I know fame and power are for the birds. But then life suddenly comes into focus for me. And, ah, there stand my kids.

LEE IACOCCA, *TALKING STRAIGHT* (1988), WITH SONNY KLEINFELD

30. Children need models rather than critics.

JOSEPH JOUBERT, *PENSÉES* (1842), 18.1, TR. KATHARINE LYTTELTON

31. Children are the true connoisseurs. What's precious to them has no price—only value.

BEL KAUFMAN, TELEVISION INTERVIEW, 1967

32. Children, of course, don't understand at first that they are being cheated. They come to school with a degree of faith and optimism, and they often seem to thrive during the first few years. It is sometimes not until the third grade that their teachers start to see the warning signs of failure. By the fourth grade many children see it too.

JONATHAN KOZOL, *SAVAGE INEQUALITIES* (1991)

33. A child's nature is too serious a thing to admit of its being regarded as a mere appendage to another being.

CHARLES LAMB, "A BACHELOR'S COMPLAINT OF THE BEHAVIOUR OF MARRIED PEOPLE," *ESSAYS OF ELIA* (1823)

34. Thou, straggler into loving arms, / Young climber up of knees, / When I forget thy thousand ways, / Then life and all shall cease.

MARY LAMB, "PARENTAL RECOLLECTIONS," *POETRY FOR CHILDREN* (1809)

35. A torn jacket is soon mended; but hard words bruise the heart of a child.

LONGFELLOW, "TABLE-TALK," *DRIFTWOOD* (1857)

36. Children are God's apostles, day by day / Sent forth to preach of love, and hope, and peace.

JAMES RUSSELL LOWELL, "ON THE DEATH OF A FRIEND'S CHILD" (1844)

37. Children were strangers you loved because you could love. If they gave back love when they were grown you were ahead of the game.

BERNARD MALAMUD, *DUBIN'S LIVES* (1979)

38. Childhood is the kingdom where nobody dies.

EDNA ST. VINCENT MILLAY, "CHILDHOOD IS THE KINGDOM WHERE NOBODY DIES," *WINE FROM THESE GRAPES* (1934)

39. We find ourselves more taken with the running up and down, the games, and puerile simplicities of our children, than we do, afterward, with their most

complete actions; as if we had loved them for our sport, like monkeys, and not as men.

MONTAIGNE, "OF THE AFFECTIONS OF FATHERS TO THEIR CHILDREN," *ESSAYS* (1580–88), TR. W. C. HAZLITT

40. The bottomless bitter misery of childhood: how little even now it is understood. Probably no adult misery can be compared with a child's despair.

IRIS MURDOCH, *A WORD CHILD* (1975)

41. No one, at any rate no English writer, has written better about childhood than Dickens. In spite of all the knowledge that has accumulated since, in spite of the fact that children are now comparatively sanely treated, no novelist has shown the same power of entering into the child's point of view.

GEORGE ORWELL, "CHARLES DICKENS," *A COLLECTION OF ESSAYS* (1954)

42. Children notice things first, people later.

WALKER PERCY, "UNCLE WILL'S HOUSE," *SIGNPOSTS IN A STRANGE LAND* (1991)

43. Children are the living messages we send to a time we will not see.

NEIL POSTMAN, "INTRODUCTION," *THE DISAPPEARANCE OF CHILDHOOD* (1982)

44. Children pick up words as pigeons peas / And utter them again as God shall please.

JOHN RAY, *ENGLISH PROVERBS* (1670)

45. Children are entitled to their otherness, as anyone is; and when we reach them, as we sometimes do, it is generally on a point of sheer delight, to us so astonishing, but to them so natural.

ALASTAIR REID, *PLACES, POEMS, PREOCCUPATIONS* (1963)

46. Slum kids die slowly, their lives eroded at so languid a pace that even they would have trouble tracing the disintegration. To the children of war death explodes like a car bomb.

ROGER ROSENBLATT, "CAMBODIA," *THE MAN IN THE WATER* (1994)

47. Give a little love to a child, and you get a great deal back.

JOHN RUSKIN, *THE CROWN OF WILD OLIVE* (1866), 2

48. Children, after being limbs of Satan in traditional theology and mystically illuminated angels in the minds of educational reformers, have reverted to being little devils—not theological demons inspired by the Evil One, but scientific Freudian abominations inspired by the Unconscious.

BERTRAND RUSSELL, "THE VIRTUE OF THE OPPRESSED," *UNPOPULAR ESSAYS* (1950)

49. A child is not frightened at the thought of being patiently transmuted into an old man.

SAINT-EXUPÉRY, *FLIGHT TO ARRAS* (1942), 4, TR. LEWIS GALANTIÈRE

50. If you really want to hear about it, the first thing you'll probably want to know is where I was born, and what my lousy childhood was like, and how my parents were occupied and all before they had me, and all that David Copperfield kind of crap, but I don't feel like going into it.

J. D. SALINGER, *THE CATCHER IN THE RYE* (1951)

51. Children are natural mythologists: they beg to be told tales, and love not only to invent but to enact falsehoods.

GEORGE SANTAYANA, *DIALOGUES IN LIMBO* (1925), 5

52. A child hasn't a grown-up person's appetite for affection. A little of it goes a long way with them; and they like a good imitation of it better than the real thing, as every nurse knows.

GEORGE BERNARD SHAW, *GETTING MARRIED* (1911)

53. God's greatest blessing is children. The only problem is that you have to support them. It's a problem, not a disadvantage.

ISRAEL SHENKER, *COAT OF MANY COLORS* (1985)

54. Children are the anchors that hold a mother to life.

SOPHOCLES, *PHAEDRA* (C. 435–29 B.C.), TR. M. H. MORGAN

55. Perhaps a child who is fussed over gets a feeling of destiny, he thinks he is in the world for something important and it gives him drive and confidence.

BENJAMIN SPOCK, *NEW YORK SUNDAY NEWS*, MAY 11, 1958

56. A child should always say what's true, / And speak when he is spoken to, / And behave mannerly at table: / At least as far as he is able.

ROBERT LOUIS STEVENSON, "WHOLE DUTY OF CHILDREN," *A CHILD'S GARDEN OF VERSES* (1885)

57. Life's aspirations come / in the guise of children.

RABINDRANATH TAGORE, *FIREFLIES* (1928)

58. If men do not keep on speaking terms with children, they cease to be men, and become merely machines for eating and for earning money.

JOHN UPDIKE, "A FOREWORD FOR YOUNGER READERS," *ASSORTED PROSE* (1965)

59. The difference between a childhood and a boyhood must be this: our childhood is what we alone

have had; our boyhood is what any boy in our environment would have had.

John Updike, "Environment," *Assorted Prose* (1965)

60. Children begin by loving their parents. After a time they judge them. Rarely, if ever, do they forgive them.

Oscar Wilde, *A Woman of No Importance* (1893), 2

61. All children find chaos congenial. Any unruliness, even by nature, advances the child's program of subverting authority.

George F. Will, "Ideological Storms," *Suddenly: The American Idea Abroad and At Home, 1986–1990* (1990)

62. A simple Child, / That lightly draws its breath, / And feels its life in every limb, / What should it know of death?

William Wordsworth, "We Are Seven" (1798)

63. As far as rearing children goes, the basic idea I try to keep in mind is that a child is a person. Just because they happen to be a little shorter than you doesn't mean they are dumber than you.

Frank Zappa, *The Real Frank Zappa Book* (1989), with Peter Occhiogrosso

124. CHOICE

See also 725. Preference; 1056. Will

1. You choose, you live the consequences. Every yes, no, maybe, creates the school you call your personal experience.

Richard Bach, *Running from Safety* (1994)

2. Alternatives, and particularly desirable alternatives, grow only on imaginary trees.

Saul Bellow, *Dangling Man* (1944)

3. What man wants is simply *independent* choice, whatever that independence may cost and wherever it may lead.

Dostoyevsky, *Notes from Underground* (1864), 1.7, tr. Constance Garnett

4. As a man thinketh so is he, and as a man chooseth so is he.

Emerson, "Spiritual Laws," *Essays: First Series* (1841)

5. It is your own conviction which compels you; that is, choice compels choice.

Epictetus, *Discourses* (2nd c.), 1.17, tr. Thomas W. Higginson

6. Because we are intelligent creatures—meaning that we are freed from instinctive and patterned behavior to a degree unparalleled in the animal kingdom—we are capable of, and dependent on, using rational choice to decide our futures.

Willard Gaylin, *Feelings: Our Vital Signs* (1979)

7. Some of necessity go astray, because for them there is no such thing as a right path.

Thomas Mann, "Tonio Kröger" (1903), *Death in Venice*,, tr. H. T. Lowe-Porter

8. It is this struggle that has caused one Russian ruler after another to put guns before butter, to build steel mills instead of fine new apartment houses, to invest in physics laboratories rather than swimming pools, to dig new canals instead of building public parks, to manufacture heavy tanks rather than sports cars.

Harrison E. Salisbury, *Russia* (1965)

CHRIST

See 511. Jesus

125. CHRISTIANITY

See also 80. Bible; 126. Church; 138. Clergy; 330. Faith; 511. Jesus; 565. Martyrs and Martyrdom; 596. Missionaries; 601. Monasticism; 769. Puritans and Puritanism; 797. Religion; 835. Sabbath; 836. Sacrament; 840. Saints and Sainthood; 841. Salvation

1. The glory of Christianity is to conquer by forgiveness.

William Blake, "To the Deists," *Jerusalem* (1804–20)

2. Christians have burnt each other, quite persuaded / That all the Apostles would have done as they did.

Byron, *Don Juan* (1819–24), 1.83

3. Those of us who were brought up as Christians and who have lost our faith have retained the Christian sense of sin without the saving belief in redemption. This poisons our thought and so paralyses us in action.

Cyril Connolly, *The Unquiet Grave* (1945), 1

4. Christ beats his drum, but he does not press men; Christ is served with voluntaries.

John Donne, *Sermons*, No. 39, 1626

5. By the irresistible maturing of the general mind, the Christian traditions have lost their hold.

Emerson, "Worship," *The Conduct of Life* (1860)

6. Every stoic was a stoic; but in Christendom where is the Christian?

Emerson, "Self-Reliance," *Essays: First Series* (1841)

7. Instead of making Christianity a vehicle of truth, you make truth only a horse for Christianity.

EMERSON, *JOURNALS*, 1832

8. It is curious that Christianity, which is idealism, is sturdily defended by the brokers, and steadily attacked by the idealists.

EMERSON, *JOURNALS*, 1853

9. No one is without Christianity, if we agree on what we mean by the word. It is every individual's individual code of behavior by means of which he makes himself a better human being than his nature wants to be, if he followed his nature only.

WILLIAM FAULKNER, INTERVIEW, *WRITERS AT WORK: FIRST SERIES* (1958)

10. Christianity, above all, consoles; but there are naturally happy souls who do not need consolation. Consequently Christianity begins by making such souls unhappy, for otherwise it would have no power over them.

ANDRÉ GIDE, *JOURNALS*, OCT. 10, 1893, TR. JUSTIN O'BRIEN

11. The difficulty comes from this, that Christianity (Christian orthodoxy) is exclusive and that belief in *its* truth excludes belief in any other truth. It does not absorb; it repulses.

ANDRÉ GIDE, *JOURNALS*, JUNE 14, 1926, TR. JUSTIN O'BRIEN

12. Almost every sect of Christianity is a perversion of its essence, to accommodate it to the prejudices of the world.

WILLIAM HAZLITT, "ON THE CAUSES OF METHODISM," *THE ROUND TABLE* (1817)

13. The Papacy is not other than the Ghost of the deceased Roman Empire, sitting crowned upon the grave thereof.

THOMAS HOBBES, *LEVIATHAN* (1651), 4.47

14. The Catholic Church with its foreshortened American history and tangled puritanical roots was as inviolate to my mother and father as it was to the last-ditch aristocrats of Evelyn Waugh.

MAUREEN HOWARD, *FACTS OF LIFE* (1978)

15. Christianity supplies a Hell for the people who disagree with you and a Heaven for your friends.

ELBERT HUBBARD, *THE NOTE BOOK* (1927)

16. The Christian religion not only was at first attended with miracles, but even at this day cannot be believed by any reasonable person without one.

DAVID HUME, *ON MIRACLES*, 2

17. No man is a Christian who cheats his fellows, perverts the truth, or speaks of a "clean bomb," yet he will be the first to make public his faith in God.

MARYA MANNES, *MORE IN ANGER* (1958), 4.6

18. The chief contribution of Protestantism to human thought is its massive proof that God is a bore.

H. L. MENCKEN, *MINORITY REPORT* (1956), 309

19. 'Tis faith alone that vividly and certainly comprehends the deep mysteries of our religion.

MONTAIGNE, "APOLOGY FOR RAIMOND DE SEBONDE," *ESSAYS* (1580–88), TR. W. C. HAZLITT

20. No kingdom has ever suffered as many civil wars as Christ's.

MONTESQUIEU, *LETTRES PERSANES* (1721), 29

21. Christianity in particular should be dubbed a great treasure-chamber of ingenious consolations, such a store of refreshing, soothing, deadening drugs has it accumulated within itself.

NIETZSCHE, *THE GENEALOGY OF MORALS* (1887), 3.17, TR. HORACE B. SAMUEL

22. The Catholic must adopt the decision handed down to him; the Protestant must learn to decide for himself.

ROUSSEAU, *LES CONFESSIONS* (1766–70)

23. The true Christian is in all countries a pilgrim and a stranger.

GEORGE SANTAYANA, *WINDS OF DOCTRINE* (1913)

24. If a Jew is fascinated by Christians it is not because of their virtues, which he values little, but because they represent anonymity, humanity without race.

JEAN-PAUL SARTRE, *ANTI-SEMITE AND JEW* (1948)

25. Christianity in the suburb is cheerful. The church is a centre of social activity and those who go to church need never be lonely.

STEVIE SMITH, "A LONDON SUBURB," IN *ME AGAIN* (1981)

CHRISTMAS

See 420. HOLIDAYS

126. CHURCH

See also 125. CHRISTIANITY; 127. CHURCH AND STATE; 128. CHURCHGOING; 138. CLERGY; 565.

MARTYRS AND MARTYRDOM; 596. MISSIONARIES; 601. MONASTICISM; 724. PREACHING AND PREACHERS; 797. RELIGION; 836. SACRAMENT; 840. SAINTS AND SAINTHOOD

1. I have no objections to churches so long as they do not interfere with God's work.

BROOKS ATKINSON, "NOVEMBER 10," *ONCE AROUND THE SUN* (1951)

2. Except the Lord build the house, they labour in vain that build it.

BIBLE, PSALMS 127:1

3. A temple is a landscape of the soul.

JOSEPH CAMPBELL, *THE POWER OF MYTH* (1988)

4. The real ecumenical crisis today is not between Catholics and Protestants but between traditional and experimental forms of church life.

HARVEY COX, *THE SECULAR CITY* (1966), 7

5. Why do people in churches seem like cheerful, brainless tourists on a packaged tour of the Absolute?

ANNIE DILLARD, "AN EXPEDITION TO THE POLE," *TEACHING A STONE TO TALK* (1982)

6. God builds his temple in the heart on the ruins of churches and religions.

EMERSON, "WORSHIP," *THE CONDUCT OF LIFE* (1860)

7. If I should go out of church whenever I hear a false sentiment, I could never stay there five minutes.

EMERSON, *JOURNALS,* 1841

8. He who is near the Church is often far from God.

FRENCH PROVERB

9. In the visible church the true Christians are invisible.

GERMAN PROVERB

10. My own mind is my own church.

THOMAS PAINE, *THE AGE OF REASON* (1794, 1796), I

11. While God waits for His temple to be built of love, / men bring stones.

RABINDRANATH TAGORE, *FIREFLIES* (1928)

12. The Church [in the 14th century] gave ceremony and dignity to lives that had little of either. It was the source of beauty and art to which all had some access and which many helped to create.

BARBARA W. TUCHMAN, *A DISTANT MIRROR* (1978)

13. The chiefest sanctity of a temple is that it is a place to which men go to weep in common.

MIGUEL DE UNAMUNO, "THE MAN OF FLESH AND BONE," *TRAGIC SENSE OF LIFE* (1913), TR. J. E. CRAWFORD FLITCH

14. The itch of disputation will prove the scab of the Church.

SIR HENRY WOTTON, *PANEGYRIC OF KING CHARLES* (1649)

127. CHURCH AND STATE

See also 126. CHURCH; 930. STATE

1. Render to Caesar the things that are Caesar's, and to God the things that are God's.

BIBLE, MARK 12:17

2. All religions united with government are more or less inimical to liberty. All separated from government are compatible with liberty.

HENRY CLAY, SPEECH, U.S. HOUSE OF REPRESENTATIVES, MARCH 24, 1818

3. In all ages, hypocrites, called priests, have put crowns upon the heads of thieves, called kings.

ROBERT G. INGERSOLL, *PROSE-POEMS AND SELECTIONS* (1884)

4. The church must be reminded that it is not the master or the servant of the state, but rather the conscience of the state.

MARTIN LUTHER KING, JR., *STRENGTH TO LOVE* (1963), 6.3

5. Two orders of mankind are the enemies of church and state; the king without clemency, and the holy man without learning.

SA'DI, *GULISTAN* (1258), 8.20, TR. JAMES ROSS

128. CHURCHGOING

See also 126. CHURCH; 724. PREACHING AND PREACHERS

1. How beautiful to have the church always open, so that every tired wayfaring man may come in and be soothed by all that art can suggest of a better world when he is weary with this.

EMERSON, *JOURNALS,* 1833

2. The idea of God ends in a paltry Methodist meeting-house.

EMERSON, *JOURNALS,* 1850

3. No temple can still the personal griefs and strifes in the breasts of its visitors.

MARGARET FULLER, *SUMMER ON THE LAKES* (1844), I

4. Many come to bring their clothes to church rather than themselves.

THOMAS FULLER, M.D., *GNOMOLOGIA* (1732), 3342

5. The eleven o'clock hour on Sunday is the most segregated hour in American life.

JAMES A. PIKE, *U.S. NEWS & WORLD REPORT*, MAY 16, 1960

6. Our hymn-books resound with a melodious cursing of God and enduring Him forever.

THOREAU, "ECONOMY," *WALDEN* (1854)

7. One of the advantages of pure congregational singing is that you can join in the singing whether you have a voice or not. The disadvantage is, that your neighbor can do the same.

CHARLES DUDLEY WARNER, "SEVENTH STUDY," *BACKLOG STUDIES* (1873)

CINEMA

See 611. MOVIES

129. CIRCUMSTANCE

See also 116. CHANCE; 305. EVENTS; 624. NECESSITY

1. It is futile to rail at circumstances / For they are indifferent. He shall fare well / Who confronts circumstances aright.

ANONYMOUS QUOTATION IN PLUTARCH'S "CONTENTMENT", *MORALIA* (C. A.D. 100), TR. MOSES HADAS

2. Man is not the creature of circumstances. Circumstances are the creatures of men.

BENJAMIN DISRAELI, *VIVIAN GREY* (1826–27), 6.7

3. None of us can help the things life has done to us. They're done before you realize it, and once they're done they make you do other things until at last everything comes between you and what you'd like to be, and you've lost your true self forever.

EUGENE O'NEILL, *LONG DAY'S JOURNEY INTO NIGHT* (1956), 2.1

4. If all our happiness is bound up entirely in our personal circumstances it is difficult not to demand of life more than it has to give.

BERTRAND RUSSELL, *THE CONQUEST OF HAPPINESS* (1930), 10

5. The people who get on in this world are the people who get up and look for the circumstances they want, and, if they can't find them, make them.

GEORGE BERNARD SHAW, *MRS. WARREN'S PROFESSION* (1898), 2

6. What a man is depends on his character; but what he does, and what we think of what he does, depends on his circumstances.

GEORGE BERNARD SHAW, PREFACE, *MAJOR BARBARA* (1905)

7. I make the most of all that comes, / And the least of all that goes.

SARA TEASDALE, "THE PHILOSOPHER"

130. CIRCUS

1. Circus, n. A place where horses, ponies and elephants are permitted to see men, women and children acting the fool.

AMBROSE BIERCE, *THE DEVIL'S DICTIONARY* (1881–1911)

2. The circus comes as close to being the world in microcosm as anything I know; in a way, it puts all the rest of show business in the shade.

E.B. WHITE, "THE RING OF TIME," IN *THE ART OF THE PERSONAL ESSAY* (1994), ED. PHILLIP LOPATE

131. CITIES

See also 194. THE COUNTRY; 546. LONDON; 632. NEW YORK; 671. PARIS; 944. SUBURBS; 1029. VENICE; 1044. WASHINGTON, D.C.

1. New Orleans is stirring, rattling, and sliding faintly in its fragrance and in the enormous richness of its lust; taxis are still parked along Dauphine Street and the breastlike, floral air is itchy with the stilletos and embroiderings above black blood drumthroes of an eloquent cracked indiscoverable cornet, which exists only in the imagination and somewhere in the past, in the broken heart of Louis Armstrong; yet even in that small portion which is the infested genitals of that city, never free, neither of desire nor of waking pain, there are the qualities of the tender desolations of profoundest night.

JAMES AGEE, *LET US NOW PRAISE FAMOUS MEN* (1941)

2. A great city is not to be confounded with a populous one.

ARISTOTLE, *POLITICS* (4TH C. B.C.), 7.4, TR. BENJAMIN JOWETT

3. A very populous city can rarely, if ever, be well governed.

ARISTOTLE, *POLITICS* (4TH C. B.C.), 7.4, TR. BENJAMIN JOWETT

4. A ghetto can be improved in one way only: out of existence.

JAMES BALDWIN, "FIFTH AVENUE, UPTOWN," *NOBODY KNOWS MY NAME* (1961)

5. A quiet city is a contradiction in terms. It is a thing uncanny, spectral.

MAX BEERBOHM, "ADVERTISEMENTS," *MAINLY ON THE AIR* (1946)

6. The silence of a shut park does not sound like country silence: it is tense and confined.

ELIZABETH BOWEN, *THE DEATH OF THE HEART* (1938), 1.6

7. If a large city can, after intense intellectual efforts, choose for its mayor a man who merely will not steal from it, we consider it a triumph of the suffrage.

FRANK MOORE COLBY, "ON SEEING TEN BAD PLAYS," *THE COLBY ESSAYS* (1926), V. 1

8. In great cities men are more callous both to the happiness and the misery of others, than in the country; for they are constantly in the habit of seeing both extremes.

CHARLES CALEB COLTON, *LACON* (1825), 2.94

9. If you would be known, and not know, vegetate in a village; if you would know, and not be known, live in a city.

CHARLES CALEB COLTON, *LACON* (1825), 1.334

10. No city should be too large for a man to walk out of in a morning.

CYRIL CONNOLLY, *THE UNQUIET GRAVE* (1945), 1

11. God the first garden made, and the first city Cain.

ABRAHAM COWLEY, "THE GARDEN" (1666)

12. The real illness of the American city today, and especially of the deprived groups within it, is voicelessness.

HARVEY COX, *THE SECULAR CITY* (1966), 6

13. Cities degrade us by magnifying trifles.

EMERSON, "CULTURE," *THE CONDUCT OF LIFE* (1860)

14. What is the city in which we sit here, but an aggregate of incongruous materials, which have obeyed the will of some man?

EMERSON, "FATE," *THE CONDUCT OF LIFE* (1860)

15. 'Tis the men, not the houses, that make the city.

THOMAS FULLER, M.D., *GNOMOLOGIA* (1732), 5121

16. Parks are but pavement disguised with a growth of grass.

GEORGE GISSING, "SPRING," *THE PRIVATE PAPERS OF HENRY RYECROFT* (1903)

17. What we get in the city is not life, but what someone else tells us about life.

DAVID GRAYSON, *ADVENTURES IN CONTENTMENT* (1907), 13

18. In the Big City a man will disappear with the suddenness and completeness of the flame of a candle that is blown out.

O. HENRY, "THE SLEUTHS," *SIXES AND SEVENS* (1911)

19. Cities produce ferocious men, because they produce corrupt men; the mountains, the forest, and the sea, render men savage; they develop the fierce, but yet do not destroy the human.

VICTOR HUGO, "FANTINE," *LES MISÉRABLES* (1862), 2.6, TR. CHARLES E. WILBOUR

20. Great cities are not like towns, only larger. They differ from towns and suburbs in basic ways, and one of these is that cities are, by definition, full of strangers.

JANE JACOBS, *THE DEATH AND LIFE OF GREAT AMERICAN CITIES* (1961), 1.2

21. The urban man is an uprooted tree, he can put out leaves, flowers and grow fruit but what a nostalgia his leaf, flower, and fruit will always have for mother earth!

JUAN RAMÓN JIMÉNEZ, "ARISTOCRACY AND DEMOCRACY," *SELECTED WRITINGS* (1957), TR. H. R. HAYS

22. A neighborhood is where, when you go out of it, you get beat up.

MURRAY KEMPTON, QUOTING PUERTO RICAN LABOR OFFICE WORKER, "GROUP DYNAMICS," *AMERICA COMES OF MIDDLE AGE* (1963)

23. Peace and freedom walk together. In too many of our cities today, the peace is not secure because freedom is incomplete.

JOHN F. KENNEDY, COMMENCEMENT ADDRESS, AMERICAN UNIVERSITY, WASHINGTON, D.C., JUNE 10, 1963

24. We will neglect our cities to our peril, for in neglecting them we neglect the nation.

JOHN F. KENNEDY, MESSAGE TO U.S. CONGRESS, JAN. 30, 1962

25. I swore I'd be in Chicago tomorrow, and made sure of that, taking a bus to Chicago, spending most of my money, and didn't give a damn, just as long as I'd be in Chicago tomorrow.

JACK KEROUAC, *ON THE ROAD* (1957)

26. East St. Louis—which the local press refers to as "an inner city without an outer city"—has some of the sickest children in America. Of 66 cities in Illinois, East St. Louis ranks first in fetal death, first in premature birth, and third in infant health.

JONATHAN KOZOL, *SAVAGE INEQUALITIES* (1991)

27. The sweetest souls, like the sweetest flowers, soon canker in cities, and no purity is rarer there than the purity of delight.

WALTER SAVAGE LANDOR, "LA FONTAINE AND DE LA ROCHEFOUCAULT," *IMAGINARY CONVERSATIONS* (1824–53)

28. Any city may have one period of magnificence, like Boston or New Orleans or San Francisco, but it takes a real one to keep renewing itself until the past is perennially forgotten.

A.J. LIEBLING, "APOLOGY FOR BREATHING," *BACK WHERE I CAME FROM* (1938)

29. I have an affection for a great city. I feel safe in the neighborhood of man, and enjoy the sweet security of streets.

LONGFELLOW, "THE GREAT METROPOLIS," *DRIFTWOOD* (1857)

30. To say the least, a town life makes one more tolerant and liberal in one's judgment of others.

LONGFELLOW, *HYPERION* (1839), 2.10

31. The city is squalid and sinister, / With the silver-barred street in the midst, / Slow-moving, / A river leading nowhere.

AMY LOWELL, "A LONDON THOROUGHFARE. 2 A.M.," *SWORD BLADES AND POPPY SEEDS* (1914)

32. Florence is a manly town, and the cities of art that appeal to the current sensibility are feminine, like Venice and Siena.

MARY MCCARTHY, *THE STONES OF FLORENCE* (1959)

33. Those who know Florence [Italy] a little often compare it to Boston. It is full of banks, loan agencies, and insurance companies, of shops selling place mats and doilies and tool-leather desk sets.

MARY MCCARTHY, *THE STONES OF FLORENCE* (1959)

34. Santa Barbara people are conservative—not like in L.A., where everybody wears rhinestones on their glasses to show that they own an airplane factory.

S.J. PERELMAN, *THE RISING GORGE* (1961)

35. No wonder the streets had seemed so empty. The city [Minneapolis] had gone somewhere else and cunningly hidden itself inside its own façade.

JONATHAN RABAN, *OLD GLORY* (1981)

36. The city has always been an embodiment of hope and a source of feeling guilt; a dream pursued, and found vain, wanting, and destructive.

JONATHAN RABAN, *SOFT CITY* (1974)

37. To the newcomer who has not learned its language, a large city is a chaos of details, a vast Woolworths store of differently colored, simlarly priced objects.

JONATHAN RABAN, *SOFT CITY* (1974)

38. [O]ne of the things people are fleeing when they leave the city is the need either to reject people who are less well educated than themselves, or to accept them with all that implies for their children's education and future placement in the society.

DAVID RIESMAN, *ABUNDANCE FOR WHAT?* (1964)

39. What is the city but the people?

SHAKESPEARE, *CORIOLANUS* (1607–08), 3.1. 199

40. The city man, in his neon-and-mazda glare, knows nothing of nature's midnight. His electric lamps surround him with synthetic sunshine. They push back the dark. They defend him from the realities of the age-old night.

EDWIN WAY TEALE, *NORTH WITH THE SPRING* (1951), 15

41. The thing generally raised on city land is taxes.

CHARLES DUDLEY WARNER, "SIXTEENTH WEEK," *MY SUMMER IN A GARDEN* (1871)

42. There is practically no sense that is not violated every time we return from the country or the sea to Paris or London or New York.

EVELYN WAUGH, "CITIES OF THE FUTURE," *THE OBSERVER*, AUG. 11, 1929

43. Commuters give the city its tidal restlessness; natives give it solidity and continuity; but the settlers give it passion.

E. B. WHITE, "HERE IS NEW YORK," *HOLIDAY*, APRIL 1949

44. A great city is that which has the greatest men and women.

WALT WHITMAN, "SONG OF THE BROAD-AXE," 4, *LEAVES OF GRASS* (1855–92)

45. Las Vegas takes what in other American towns is but a quixotic inflammation of the senses for some poor salary mule in the brief interval between the flagstone rambler and the automatic elevator downtown and magnifies it, foliates it, embellishes it into an institution.

TOM WOLFE, *THE KANDY-KOLORED TANGERINE-FLAKE STREAMLINE BABY* (1965)

46. Oh, blank confusion! true epitome / Of what the mighty City is herself, / To thousands upon thousands of her sons, / Living amid the same perpetual whirl / Of trivial objects, melted and reduced / To one identity.

WILLIAM WORDSWORTH, *THE PRELUDE* (1799–1805), 7

132. CITIZENS

See also 395. GOVERNMENT; 930. STATE; 1038. VOTING

1. It is not always the same thing to be a good man and a good citizen.

ARISTOTLE, *NICOMACHEAN ETHICS* (4TH C. B.C.), 5.2, TR. J. A. K. THOMSON

2. Man exists for his own sake and not to add a laborer to the State.

EMERSON, *JOURNALS*, 1839

3. Those self-important fathers of their country / Think they're above the people. Why they're nothing! / The citizen is infinitely wiser.

EURIPIDES, *ANDROMACHE* (C. 426 B.C.), TR. JOHN F. NIMS

4. To educate the masses politically is to make the totality of the nation a reality to each citizen. It is to make the history of the nation part of the personal experience of each of its citizens.

FRANTZ FANON, "THE PITFALLS OF NATIONAL CONSCIOUSNESS," *THE WRETCHED OF THE EARTH* (1961), TR. CONSTANCE FARRINGTON

5. Every President of the United States since Harry Truman has proclaimed that it is the duty of the citizen to consume.

MICHAEL HARRINGTON, *THE ACCIDENTAL CENTURY* (1966)

6. In America there must be only citizens, not divided by grade, first and second, but citizens, east, west, north, and south.

JOHN F. KENNEDY, CAMPAIGN ADDRESS, NATIONAL CONFERENCE ON CONSTITUTIONAL RIGHTS AND AMERICAN FREEDOM, NEW YORK CITY, OCT. 12, 1960

7. Our whole system of government is based on "We the people," but if we the people don't pay attention to what's going on, we have no right to bellyache or squawk when things go wrong.

RONALD REAGAN, *AN AMERICAN LIFE* (1990)

8. The first requisite of a good citizen in this republic of ours is that he shall be able and willing to pull his weight.

THEODORE ROOSEVELT, ADDRESS, NEW YORK CITY, NOV. 11, 1902

9. Every subject's duty is the King's, but every subject's soul is his own.

SHAKESPEARE, *HENRY V* (1598–99), 4.1.185

10. All the citizens of a state cannot be equally powerful, but they may be equally free.

VOLTAIRE, "GOVERNMENT," *PHILOSOPHICAL DICTIONARY* (1764)

11. Citizenship *is* man's basic right for it is nothing less than the right to have rights. Remove this priceless possession and there remains a stateless person, disgraced and degraded in the eyes of his countrymen.

CHIEF JUSTICE EARL WARREN, DISSENT, *PEREZ V. BROWNELL* (1958)

12. Whatever makes men good Christians, makes them good citizens.

DANIEL WEBSTER, SPEECH, PLYMOUTH, MASS., DEC. 22, 1820

133. CIVILIZATION

See also 70. BARBARISM; 210. CULTURE; 741. PROGRESS; 913. SOCIETY

1. Civilization is the lamb's skin in which barbarism masquerades.

THOMAS BAILEY ALDRICH, "LEAVES FROM A NOTEBOOK," *PONKAPOG PAPERS* (1903)

2. The crimes of extreme civilization are probably worse than those of extreme barbarism, because of their refinement, the corruption they presuppose, and their superior degree of intellectuality.

JULES BARBEY D'AUREVILLY, "LA VENGEANCE D'UNE FEMME," *LES DIABOLIQUES* (1874)

3. Western civilization, because of fortuitous historical circumstances, has spread itself more widely than any other local group that has so far been known.

RUTH BENEDICT, *PATTERNS OF CULTURE* (1934)

4. A good civilization spreads over us freely like a tree, varying and yielding because it is alive. A bad civilization stands up and sticks out above us like an umbrella—artificial, mathematical in shape; not merely universal, but uniform.

G. K. CHESTERTON, "CHEESE," *ALARMS AND DISCURSIONS* (1910)

5. The true savage is a slave, and is always talking about what he must do; the true civilised man is a free man, and is always talking about what he may do.

G. K. CHESTERTON, "HUMANITARIANISM AND STRENGTH," *ALL THINGS CONSIDERED* (1908)

6. Civilization is an active deposit which is formed by the combustion of the Present with the Past. Neither

in countries without a Present nor in those without a Past is it to be discovered.

CYRIL CONNOLLY, *THE UNQUIET GRAVE* (1945), 2

7. The civilization of one epoch becomes the manure of the next.

CYRIL CONNOLLY, *THE UNQUIET GRAVE* (1945), 2

8. Increased means and increased leisure are the two civilisers of man.

BENJAMIN DISRAELI, "CONSERVATIVE PRINCIPLES," SPEECH, APRIL 3, 1872

9. Th' fav'rite pastime iv civilized man is croolty to other civilized man.

FINLEY PETER DUNNE, "CORPORAL PUNISHMENT," *DISSERTATIONS BY MR. DOOLEY* (1906)

10. The true test of civilization is, not the census, nor the size of cities, nor the crops—no, but the kind of man the country turns out.

EMERSON, "CIVILIZATION," *SOCIETY AND SOLITUDE* (1870)

11. Reading, writing, teaching, learning, are all activities aimed at introducing civilizations to each other.

CARLOS FUENTES, "HOW I STARTED TO WRITE," IN *THE ART OF THE PERSONAL ESSAY* (1994), ED. PHILLIP LOPATE

12. The civilized man is a larger mind but a more imperfect nature than the savage.

MARGARET FULLER, *SUMMER ON THE LAKES* (1844), 6

13. The model of modern Western civilization is the virus: the pure bit of information, which turns its environment into endless reproductions of itself.

URSULA K. LE GUIN, "TEXT, SILENCE, PERFORMANCE," *DANCING AT THE EDGE OF THE WORLD* (1989)

14. The social moulds civilization fits us into have no more relation to our actual shapes than the conventional shapes of the constellations have to real star patterns.

THOMAS HARDY, *JUDE THE OBSCURE* (1895), 4.1

15. Civilizations die from philosophical calm, irony, and the sense of fair play quite as surely as they die of debauchery.

JOSEPH WOOD KRUTCH, "THE PARADOX OF HUMANISM," *THE MODERN TEMPER* (1929)

16. Civilization could not exist until there was written language, because without written language no generation could bequeath to succeeding generations anything but its simpler findings.

CHARLTON LAIRD, *THE MIRACLE OF LANGUAGE* (1953)

17. In the dust where we have buried the silent races and their abominations we have buried so much of the delicate magic of life.

D. H. LAWRENCE, QUOTED IN STEWART L. UDALL'S *THE QUIET CRISIS* (1963), 1

18. Human history, if you read it right, is the record of the efforts to tame Father. Next to striking of fire and the discovery of the wheel, the greatest triumph of what we call civilization was the domestication of the human male.

MAX LERNER, "THE REVOLT OF THE AMERICAN FATHER," *THE UNFINISHED COUNTRY* (1959), 2

19. As civilization advances, man grows unconscious of the primitive elements of life; he is separated from them by his perfection of material techniques.

CHARLES A. LINDBERGH, "THE PRIMITIVE PASSING," *AUTOBIOGRAPHY OF VALUES* (1978)

20. The sense of a long last night over civilization is back again; it has perhaps not been here so intensely in thirty years, not since the Nazis were prospering, but it is coming back.

NORMAN MAILER, *CANNIBALS AND CHRISTIANS* (1967)

21. Why build these cities glorious / If man unbuilded goes? / In vain we build the world, unless / The builder also grows.

EDWIN MARKHAM, "MAN-MAKING" (1920)

22. Civilization does everything for the mind and favors it entirely at the expense of the body.

NAPOLEON I, *MAXIMS* (1804–15)

23. You can't say civilization dont advance,... for in every war they kill you a new way.

WILL ROGERS, *THE AUTOBIOGRAPHY OF WILL ROGERS* (1949), 14

24. The passage from the state of nature to the civil state produces a very remarkable change in man, by substituting justice for instinct in his conduct.

ROUSSEAU, *THE SOCIAL CONTRACT* (1762), 1.8, TR. G. D. H. COLE

25. Civilization is the making of civil persons.

JOHN RUSKIN, *THE CROWN OF WILD OLIVE* (1866)

26. Every advance in civilization has been denounced as unnatural while it was recent.

BERTRAND RUSSELL, "AN OUTLINE OF INTELLECTUAL RUBBISH," *UNPOPULAR ESSAYS* (1950)

27. The more we realize our minuteness and our impotence in the face of cosmic forces, the more

astonishing becomes what human beings have achieved.

Bertrand Russell, *New Hopes for a Changing World* (1951)

28. Civilization is a movement and not a condition, a voyage and not a harbor.

Arnold Toynbee, *Reader's Digest,* October 1958

29. Soap and education are not as sudden as a massacre, but they are more deadly in the long run.

Mark Twain, "The Facts Concerning the Recent Resignation," *Sketches New and Old* (1900)

30. Nature is rarely allowed to enter the sacred portals of civilized society.

Hendrik Willem Van Loon, *Multiple Man* (1928)

31. The darkest secret of this country, I am afraid, is that too many of its citizens imagine that they belong to a much higher civilization somewhere else.

Kurt Vonnegut, *Bluebeard* (1987)

32. What will remain of a civilization that reverences a man above all the poets because he can make a cheap automobile at$500 each?

Thomas Wolfe, *Thomas Wolfe's Letters to His Mother* (1943)

33. A few suits of clothes, some money in the bank, and a new kind of fear constitute the main differences between the average American today and the hairy men with clubs who accompanied Attila to the city of Rome.

Philip Wylie, *Generation of Vipers* (1942), 1

CIVIL RIGHTS

See 823. Rights

134. CLARITY

1. What is conceived well is expressed clearly, / And the words to say it with arrive with ease.

Nicolas Boileau, *L'Art poétique* (1674), 1

2. The language of the law must not be foreign to the ears of those who are to obey it.

Learned Hand, *The Spirit of Liberty* (1959)

3. Every man speaks and writes with intent to be understood; and it can seldom happen but he that understands himself might convey his notions to another, if, content to be understood, he did not seek to be admired.

Samuel Johnson, *The Idler* (1758–60), 36

4. Language is in decline. Not only has eloquence departed but simple, direct speech as well, though pomposity and banality have not.

Edwin Newman, *Strictly Speaking* (1974)

5. A matter that becomes clear ceases to concern us.

Nietzsche, *Beyond Good and Evil* (1886), 80, tr. Walter Kaufmann

6. Modern English, especially written English, is full of bad habits which spread by imitation and which can be avoided if one is willing to take the necessary trouble.

George Orwell, "Politics and the English Language," *A Collection of Essays* (1954)

7. Clarity is the politeness of the man of letters.

Jules Renard, *Journal,* 1892

8. There is a poignancy in all things clear, / In the stare of the deer, in the ring of a hammer in the morning. / Seeing a bucket of perfectly lucid water / We fall to imagining prodigious honesties.

Richard Wilbur, "Clearness," *Ceremony* (1950)

135. CLASS

See also 52. Aristocracy; 233. Democracy; 297. Equality; 587. Middle Class; 682. The People; 780. Rank; 910. Snobbery; 913. Society; 933. Status

1. I was told that the Privileged and the People formed two nations.

Benjamin Disraeli, *Sybil* (1845), 4.8

2. [T]he thing about living in a village at the foot of a mountain is that the world for you becomes, without thinking about it, self-contained. People are of two kinds, really: from the Valley, and from Elsewhere.

Henry Louis Gates, Jr., "Up the Hill," *Colored People* (1994)

3. While its [Harvard's] undergraduate life was still controlled [in 1908–1912] by a select group of rich and fashionable families whose sons merely arrived when they were due to fill the places that had been waiting for them from the day they were born, it was, at the same time, opening its doors to a more cosmopolitan student population and beginning to take the first tentative steps toward mitigating the evils of a pyramidal social system that concentrated all its social honors upon the rich and the wellborn.

Doris Kearns Goodwin, *The Fitzgeralds and the Kennedys* (1987)

4. In class society everyone lives as a member of a particular class, and every kind of thinking, without exception, is stamped with the brand of a class.

Mao Tse-Tung, *Quotations from Chairman Mao Tse-tung* (1966), 2

5. Socially, I never belonged to any class, rich or poor. To the rich I was poor, and to the poor I was poor pretending to be like the rich.

John O'Hara, *The Instrument* (1967)

6. Planning ahead is a measure of class. The rich and even the middle class plan for future generations, but the poor can plan ahead only a few weeks or days.

Gloria Steinem, "The Time Factor," *Outrageous Acts and Everyday Rebellions* (1983)

7. The diminution of the reality of class, however socially desirable in many respects, seems to have the practical effect of diminishing our ability to see people in their difference and specialness.

Lionel Trilling, "Art and Fortune," *The Liberal Imagination* (1950)

136. CLASSICS

See also 42. Antiquity; 93. Books and Reading; 986. Tradition

1. Speak of the moderns without contempt and of the ancients without idolatry; judge them all by their merits, but not by their age.

Lord Chesterfield, *Letters to His Son,* Feb. 22, 1748

2. A great classic means a man whom one can praise without having read.

G. K. Chesterton, "Tom Jones and Morality," *All Things Considered* (1908)

3. [L]iterature begins with the possible model of experience, and what it produces is the literary model we call the classic.

Northrop Frye, *The Educated Imagination* (1964)

4. The praise of ancient authors proceeds not from the reverence of the dead, but from the competition and mutual envy of the living.

Thomas Hobbes, "A Review and Conclusion," *Leviathan* (1651)

5. What a sense of security in an old book which Time has criticized for us!

James Russell Lowell, "Library of Old Authors," *Literary Essays* (1864–90)

6. In Art, the public accept what has been, because they cannot alter it, not because they appreciate it. They swallow their classics whole, and never taste them.

Oscar Wilde, *The Soul of Man Under Socialism* (1891)

137. CLEANLINESS

See also 248. Dirtiness; 413. Health

1. Cleanliness is not next to godliness nowadays, for cleanliness is made an essential and godliness is regarded as an offence.

G. K. Chesterton, "On Lying in Bed," *Tremendous Trifles* (1909)

2. The graveyards are full of women whose houses were so spotless you could eat off the floor. Remember the second wife always has a maid.

Heloise Cruse, *Saturday Evening Post,* March 2, 1963

3. People who wash much have a high mind about it, and talk down to those who wash little.

Emerson, *Journals,* 1847

4. Hygiene is the corruption of medicine by morality.

H. L. Mencken, *Prejudices: Third Series* (1922), 14

5. Man and other civilized animals are the only creatures that ever become dirty.

John Muir, *A Thousand-Mile Walk to the Gulf* (1916), 5

6. I test my bath before I sit, / And I'm always moved to wonderment / That what chills the finger not a bit / Is so frigid upon the fundament.

Ogden Nash, "Samson Agonistes," *Good Intentions* (1943)

7. What separates two people most profoundly is a different sense and degree of cleanliness.

Nietzsche, *Beyond Good and Evil* (1886), 271, tr. Walter Kaufmann

138. CLERGY

See also 125. Christianity; 126. Church; 596. Missionaries; 601. Monasticism; 724. Preaching and Preachers

1. The clergyman is expected to be a kind of human Sunday.

Samuel Butler (d. 1902), *The Way of All Flesh* (1903), 26

2. Clergy are men as well as other folks.

Henry Fielding, *Joseph Andrews* (1742), 2.6

3. A broad hat does not always cover a venerable head.

Thomas Fuller, M.D., *Gnomologia* (1732), 26

4. In times of death and famine, reason is on the side of the priests—who have their own kind of logic which cries for miracles and, on occasion, invents them.

JEAN GIRAUDOUX, *JUDITH* (1931), 1, TR. JOHN K. SAVACOOL

5. Priests are no more necessary to religion than politicians to patriotism.

JOHN HAYNES HOLMES, *THE SENSIBLE MAN'S VIEW OF RELIGION* (1933)

6. I have always considered a clergyman as the father of a larger family than he is able to maintain.

SAMUEL JOHNSON, QUOTED IN BOSWELL'S *LIFE OF SAMUEL JOHNSON*, APRIL 1778

7. Hood an ass with reverend purple, / So you can hide his two ambitious ears, / And he shall pass for a cathedral doctor.

BEN JONSON, *VOLPONE* (1605), 1.2

8. The clergy would have us believe them against our own reason, as the woman would have her husband against his own eyes.

JOHN SELDEN, "CLERGY," *TABLE TALK* (1689)

9. The clergy [in the 14th century] on the whole were probably no more lecherous or greedy or untrustworthy than other men, but because they were supposed to be better or nearer to God than other men, their failings attracted more attention.

BARBARA W. TUCHMAN, *A DISTANT MIRROR* (1978)

139. CLEVERNESS

See also 200. CRAFTINESS; 493. INTELLIGENCE; 943. SUBTLETY; 1061. WIT

1. It is a / profitable thing, if one is wise, to seem foolish.

AESCHYLUS, *PROMETHEUS BOUND* (C. 478 B.C.), TR. DAVID GRENE

2. Sharp men, like sharp needles, break easy, though they pierce quick.

HENRY WARD BEECHER, *PROVERBS FROM PLYMOUTH PULPIT* (1887)

3. All clever men are birds of prey.

ENGLISH PROVERB

4. The bold are helpless without cleverness.

EURIPIDES, *HELEN* (412 B.C.), TR. RICHMOND LATTIMORE

5. It is not strength, but art, obtains the prize, / And to be swift is less than to be wise.

HOMER, *ILIAD* (9TH C. B.C.), 23.383, TR. ALEXANDER POPE

6. The desire of appearing clever often prevents our becoming so.

LA ROCHEFOUCAULD, *MAXIMS* (1665), TR. KENNETH PRATT

7. Here's a good rule of thumb: / Too clever is dumb.

OGDEN NASH, "REFLECTION ON INGENUITY," *VERSES FROM 1929 ON* (1959)

8. The devil can cite Scripture for his purpose.

SHAKESPEARE, *THE MERCHANT OF VENICE* (1596–97), 1.3.99

140. CLIMATE

See also 950. SUN; 1050. WEATHER

1. What men call gallantry, and gods adultery, / Is much more common where the climate's sultry.

BYRON, *DON JUAN* (1819–24), 1.63

2. In all countries where nature does the most, man does the least.

CHARLES CALEB COLTON, *LACON* (1825), 1.67

3. Growing up in the English countryside seemed an interminable process. Freezing winter gave way to frosty spring, which in turn merged into chilly summer—but nothing ever, ever happened.

JESSICA MITFORD, *DAUGHTERS AND REBELS* (1960)

CLIQUES

See 910. SNOBBERY

CLOTHING

See 267. DRESS; 338. FASHION

141. COFFEE

1. Coffee should be black as Hell, strong as death, and sweet as love.

TURKISH PROVERB

142. COLDNESS

See also 31. ALOOFNESS

1. The cold in clime are cold in blood, / Their love can scarce deserve the name.

BYRON, *THE GIAOUR* (1813)

2. Are you then unable to recognize a sob unless it has the same sound as yours?

ANDRÉ GIDE, *JOURNALS*, 1922, TR. JUSTIN O'BRIEN

3. Men of cold passions have quick eyes.

NATHANIEL HAWTHORNE, *JOURNALS*, 1837

4. Every heart has its secret sorrows which the world knows not, and oftentimes we call a man cold, when he is only sad.

LONGFELLOW, *HYPERION* (1839), 3.4

5. What makes people hard-hearted is this, that each man has, or fancies he has, as much as he can bear in his own troubles.

SCHOPENHAUER, "FURTHER PSYCHOLOGICAL OBSERVATIONS," *PARERGA AND PARALIPOMENA* (1851), TR. T. BAILEY SAUNDERS

COLONIALISM

See 458. IMPERIALISM

143. COLOR

1. Colors speak all languages.

JOSEPH ADDISON, *THE SPECTATOR* (1711–12), 416

2. Grey is a colour that always seems on the eve of changing to some other colour.

G. K. CHESTERTON, "THE GLORY OF GREY," *ALARMS AND DISCURSIONS* (1910)

3. The purest and most thoughtful minds are those which love colour the most.

JOHN RUSKIN, *THE STONES OF VENICE* (1851–53), V. 2, 5.30

4. I think it pisses God off if you walk by the color purple in a field somewhere and don't notice it.

ALICE WALKER, *THE COLOR PURPLE* (1982)

144. COMEDIANS

See also 145. COMEDY; 292. ENTERTAINMENT; 436. HUMOR

1. All that the comedian has to show for his years of work and aggravation is the echo of forgotten laughter.

FRED ALLEN, *TREADMILL TO OBLIVION* (1954)

2. Who are a little wise, the best fools be.

JOHN DONNE, "THE TRIPLE FOOL," *SONGS AND SONNETS* (1633)

3. The test of a real comedian is whether you laugh at him before he opens his mouth.

GEORGE JEAN NATHAN, "TEST OF A COMEDIAN," *AMERICAN MERCURY*, SEPTEMBER 1929

4. All comedians are people who really deeply consider the human experience not only a dirty trick perpetrated by a totally meaningless procedure of accidents, but an unbearable ordeal every day, which can be made tolerable only by mockery in one form or another.

WILLIAM SAROYAN, *CHANCE MEETINGS* (1978)

145. COMEDY

See also 144. COMEDIANS; 292. ENTERTAINMENT; 436. HUMOR; 844. SATIRE; 972. THEATER; 987. TRAGEDY; 1061. WIT

1. Like dreams, farces show the disguised fulfillment of repressed wishes.

ERIC BENTLEY, "THE PSYCHOLOGY OF FARCE," INTRODUCTION TO *LET'S GET A DIVORCE AND OTHER PLAYS* (1958)

2. All tragedies are finished by a death, / All comedies are ended by a marriage.

BYRON, *DON JUAN* (1819–24), 3.9

3. It is very difficult to be wholly joyous or wholly sad on this earth. The comic, when it is human, soon takes upon itself the face of pain.

JOSEPH CONRAD, "A FAMILIAR PREFACE," *A PERSONAL RECORD* (1912)

4. Comedy is an escape, not from the truth but from despair; a narrow escape into faith.

CHRISTOPHER FRY, *TIME*, NOV. 20, 1950

5. Comedy naturally wears itself out—destroys the very food on which it lives; and by constantly and successfully exposing the follies and weaknesses of mankind to ridicule, in the end leaves itself nothing worth laughing at.

WILLIAM HAZLITT, "ON MODERN COMEDY," *THE ROUND TABLE* (1817)

6. Comedy speaks for civilization; farce bears an ill-concealed, sometimes unconcealed animus against civilization. Often against civility too.

IRVING HOWE, "FARCE AND FICTION," *A CRITIC'S NOTEBOOK* (1994)

7. Comedy appeals to the collective mind of the audience and this grows fatigued; while farce appeals to a more robust organ, their collective belly.

W. SOMERSET MAUGHAM, *THE SUMMING UP* (1938), 39

8. We couldn't live without comedy.

SEAN O'CASEY, "THE POWER OF LAUGHTER: WEAPON AGAINST EVIL," *FIFTY FAMOUS ESSAYS* (1964)

9. Comedy springs from the ludicrous; but the ludicrous is stuck in the muck of reality, resolutely hostile to what is impossible.

CYNTHIA OZICK, "CULTURAL IMPERSONATION," *ART & ARDOR* (1983)

10. The people you like when you meet them and while you know them, and the people you remember fondly, are invariably people who have a sense of *comedy*, not just a sense of humor.

WILLIAM SAROYAN, *CHANCE MEETINGS* (1978)

11. When comedy fails, seriousness begins to leak back in.

SUSAN SONTAG, "GOING TO THEATER, ETC.," *AGAINST INTERPRETATION* (1966)

12. Comedy has ceased to be a challenge to the mental processes. It has become a therapy of relaxation, a kind of tranquilizing drug.

JAMES THURBER, "MAGICAL LADY," *LANTERNS AND LANCES* (1961)

13. The only rules comedy can tolerate are those of taste, and the only limitations those of libel.

JAMES THURBER, "THE DUCHESS AND THE BUGS," *LANTERNS AND LANCES* (1961)

COMMAND

See 61. AUTHORITY; 531. LEADERSHIP

COMMERCE

See 104. BUSINESS AND COMMERCE; 105. BUYING AND SELLING; 738. PROFITEERING

146. COMMITMENT

See also 111. CAUSES; 504. INVOLVEMENT

1. To act is to be committed, and to be committed is to be in danger.

JAMES BALDWIN, "MY DUNGEON SHOOK," *THE FIRE NEXT TIME* (1962)

2. The beauty of a strong, lasting commitment is often best understood by a man incapable of it.

MURRAY KEMPTON, "O'ER MOOR AND FEN," *PART OF OUR TIME* (1955)

3. The need for devotion to something outside ourselves is even more profound than the need for companionship. If we are not to go to pieces or wither away, we all must have some purpose in life; for no man can live for himself alone.

ROSS PARMENTER, "THE DOCTOR AND THE CLEANING WOMAN," *THE PLANT IN MY WINDOW* (1949)

147. COMMITTEES

See also 579. MEETINGS

1. A committee is a group that keeps the minutes and loses hours.

MILTON BERLE, NEWS SUMMARIES, JULY 1, 1954

2. We always carry out by committee anything in which any one of us alone would be too reasonable to persist.

FRANK MOORE COLBY, "SUBSIDIZING AUTHORS," *THE COLBY ESSAYS* (1926), V. 1

3. What is a committee? A group of the unwilling, picked from the unfit, to do the unnecessary.

RICHARD HARKNESS, *NEW YORK HERALD TRIBUNE*, JUNE 15, 1960

COMMON MAN

See 682. THE PEOPLE

148. COMMON SENSE

See also 720. PRACTICALITY; 755. PRUDENCE

1. Common sense is the most fairly distributed thing in the world, for each one thinks he is so well-endowed with it that even those who are hardest to satisfy in all other matters are not in the habit of desiring more of it than they already have.

DESCARTES, *DISCOURSE ON METHOD* (1639), I

2. Common sense is as rare as genius.

EMERSON, "EXPERIENCE," *ESSAYS: SECOND SERIES* (1844)

3. Nothing astonishes men so much as common sense and plain dealing.

EMERSON, "ART," *ESSAYS: FIRST SERIES* (1841)

4. Poverty, Frost, Famine, Rain, Disease, are the beadles and guardsmen that hold us to Common Sense.

EMERSON, *JOURNALS*, 1836

5. The best prophet is common sense, our native wit.

EURIPIDES, *HELEN* (412 B.C.), TR. RICHMOND LATTIMORE

6. Fine sense and exalted sense are not half so useful as common sense.

ALEXANDER POPE, *THOUGHTS ON VARIOUS SUBJECTS* (1727)

7. A man of great common sense and good taste—meaning thereby a man without originality or moral courage.

GEORGE BERNARD SHAW, "NOTES: JULIUS CAESAR," *CAESAR AND CLEOPATRA* (1906)

8. Why level downward to our dullest perception always, and praise that as common sense? The commonest sense is the sense of men asleep, which they express by snoring.

THOREAU, "CONCLUSION," *WALDEN* (1854)

9. Most people die of a sort of creeping common sense, and discover when it is too late that the only things one never regrets are one's mistakes.

OSCAR WILDE, *THE PICTURE OF DORIAN GRAY* (1891), 3

149. COMMUNICATION

See also 134. Clarity; 188. Conversation; 648. Obscurantism; 923. Speaking; 1069. Writing and Writers

1. You cannot speak of ocean to a well-frog,—the creature of a narrower sphere. You cannot speak of ice to a summer insect,—the creature of a season.

Chuang Tzu, "Autumn Floods" (4th–3rd c. b.c.), tr. Herbert A. Giles

2. Much unhappiness has come into the world because of bewilderment and things left unsaid.

Dostoyevsky, "Critical Articles: Introduction," *Polnoye Sobraniye Sochinyeni* (*Complete Collected Works,* 1895), v. 9

3. Use what language you will, you can never say anything but what you are.

Emerson, "Worship," *The Conduct of Life* (1860)

4. When the eyes say one thing, and the tongue another, a practised man relies on the language of the first.

Emerson, "Behavior," *The Conduct of Life* (1860)

5. Gestures and facial expressions do indeed communicate, as anyone can prove by turning off the sound on a television set and asking watchers to characterize the speakers from the picture alone.

Peter Farb, *Word Play* (1973)

6. [A]n inability to communicate has little to do with international friction—as is seen in the special ferocity of wars fought between people who speak the same language.

Peter Farb, *Word Play* (1973)

7. When younger, I thought one of the particulars of being "Homo sapiens" was to communicate. I have not learned not to, though I am cautious when I try.

Nikki Giovanni, "I Plant Geraniums," *Racism 101* (1994)

8. The dumbness in the eyes of animals is more touching than the speech of men, but the dumbness in the speech of men is more agonizing than the eyes of animals.

Hindustani Proverb

9. Communication is not to be confused with communications, Ed Murrow would say.

Alexander Kendrick, *Prime Time* (1969)

10. Every word that falls from the mouth is a coin lost. Silently they gave and accepted food with both hands.

Maxine Hong Kingston, *The Woman Warrior* (1976)

11. It is easier to communicate with spirits than for one university department to communicate with another.

G. Wilson Knight, *Neglected Powers* (1971)

12. Good communication is stimulating as black coffee, and just as hard to sleep after.

Anne Morrow Lindbergh, "Argonauta," *Gift from the Sea* (1955)

13. We seek pitifully to convey to others the treasures of our heart, but they have not the power to accept them, and so we go lonely, side by side but not together, unable to know our fellows and unknown by them.

W. Somerset Maugham, *The Moon and Sixpence* (1919), 41

14. Not communicating saves energy; it keeps people from worrying about things they cannot do anything about; and it eliminates an enormous amount of useless talk.

Edwin Newman, *Strictly Speaking* (1974)

15. Mass communication communicates massively: its language lacks precise articulation and avoids demanding terms; it argues for the kind of behavior in life which will make a "good program": ethic equals showbiz.

Frederic Raphael, "The Language of Television," in *The State of the Language* (1980) ed. by Leonard Michaels and Christopher Ricks

16. I distrust the incommunicable; it is the source of all violence.

Jean-Paul Sartre, *What Is Literature* (1950), tr. Bernard Frechtman

17. The articulate voice is more distracting than mere noise.

Seneca, *Letters to Lucilius* (1st c.), 56, tr. E. Phillips Barker

1. Communication is a continual balancing act, juggling the conflicting needs for intimacy and independence.

Deborah Tannen, *You Just Don't Understand* (1990)

18. Precision of communication is important, more important than ever, in our era of hair-trigger balances, when a false, or misunderstood word may create as much disaster as a sudden thoughtless act.

James Thurber, "Friends, Romans, Countrymen, Lend Me Your Ear Muffs," *Lanterns and Lances* (1961)

COMMUNICATIONS

See 576. Media

150. COMMUNISM

See also 395. GOVERNMENT; 894. SHARING; 912. SOCIALISM

1. In dealing with the Communists, remember that in their mind what is secret is serious, and what is public is merely propaganda.

CHARLES E. BOHLEN, QUOTED BY JAMES RESTON IN *THE NEW YORK TIMES,* JAN. 2, 1966

2. There is not one single social or economic principle or concept in the philosophy of the Russian Bolshevik which has not been realized, carried into action, and enshrined in immutable laws a million years ago by the white ant.

SIR WINSTON CHURCHILL, "POLITICS," *THE CHURCHILL WIT* (1965), ED. BILL ADLER

3. One strength of the communist system of the East is that it has some of the character of a religion and inspires the emotions of a religion.

EINSTEIN, *OUT OF MY LATER LIFE* (1950), 31

4. What is a communist? One who hath yearnings / For equal division of unequal earnings.

EBENEZER ELLIOTT, "EPIGRAM," *POETICAL WORKS* (1840)

5. Communists have committed great crimes, but at least they have not stood aside, like an established society, and been indifferent. I would rather have blood on my hands than water like Pilate.

GRAHAM GREENE, *THE COMEDIANS* (1966)

6. People I meet today, especially journalists who interview me, are astonished to hear that Lenin told me, in effect, that Communism was not working and that the Revolution needed American capital and technical aid.

ARMAND HAMMER, *HAMMER* (1987), WITH NEIL LYNDON

7. Communism was overthrown by life, by thought, by dignity.

VÁCLAV HAVEL, "POLITICS, MORALITY, AND CIVILITY," *SUMMER MEDITATIONS* (1992), TR. PAUL WILSON

8. As an organized political group, the Communists have done nothing to damage our society a fraction as much as what their enemies have done in the name of defending us against subversion.

MURRAY KEMPTON, "WHAT HARVEY DID," *AMERICA COMES OF MIDDLE AGE* (1963)

9. The Communists offer one precious, fatal boon: they take away the sense of sin.

MURRAY KEMPTON, "THE SHELTERED LIFE," *PART OF OUR TIME* (1955)

10. Communism has sometimes succeeded as a scavenger, but never as a leader. It has never come to power in any country that was not disrupted by war or internal corruption or both.

JOHN F. KENNEDY, ADDRESS, NORTH ATLANTIC TREATY ORGANIZATION HEADQUARTERS, NAPLES, ITALY, JULY 3, 1963

11. "You and I can make a mistake. Not the [Communist] Party. The Party, comrade, is more than you and I and a thousand others like you and I."

ARTHUR KOESTLER, *DARKNESS AT NOON* (1940)

12. We should not wonder at the success of communism, for so much of its success is rather that of religion.

ROBERT LINDNER, "POLITICAL CREED AND CHARACTER," *MUST YOU CONFORM?* (1956)

13. We Communists are like seeds and the people are like the soil. Wherever we go, we must unite with the people, take root and blossom among them.

MAO TSE-TUNG, *QUOTATIONS FROM CHAIRMAN MAO TSE-TUNG* (1966), 28

14. The objection to a Communist always resolves itself into the fact that he is not a gentleman.

H. L. MENCKEN, *MINORITY REPORT* (1956), 15

15. The color of communism was not red but gray.

RICHARD M. NIXON, *BEYOND PEACE* (1994)

16. Communism is like Prohibition, it's a good idea but it won't work.

WILL ROGERS, *THE AUTOBIOGRAPHY OF WILL ROGERS* (1949), 12

17. Cow of many—well milked and badly fed.

SPANISH PROVERB

18. Communism is the corruption of a dream of justice.

ADLAI STEVENSON, SPEECH, URBANA, ILL., 1951

151. COMMUNITY

See also 100. BROTHERHOOD; 983. TOGETHERNESS; 1016. UNITY

1. What is not good for the swarm is not good for the bee.

MARCUS AURELIUS, *MEDITATIONS* (2ND C.), 6.54, TR. MORRIS HICKEY MORGAN

2. The life history of the individual is first and foremost an accommodation to the patterns and standards traditionally handed down in his community.

RUTH BENEDICT, *PATTERNS OF CULTURE* (1934)

3. Rain does not fall on one roof alone.

Cameroonian Proverb

4. When the head aches, all the members partake of the pain.

Cervantes, *Don Quixote* (1605–15), 2.3.2, tr. John Ozell

5. No man is an island, entire of itself; every man is a piece of the continent.

John Donne, *Devotions* (1624), 17

6. Life is lived in common, but not in community.

Michael Harrington, *The Other America* (1962), 7.4

7. Your own safety is at stake when your neighbor's wall is ablaze.

Horace, *Epistles* (20–c. 8 B.C.), 1.18

8. In the city one clings to nostalgic and unreal signs of community, takes forced refuge in codes, badges and coteries; the city's life, of surfaces and locomotion, usually seems too dangerous and demanding to live through with any confidence.

Jonathan Raban, *Soft City* (1974)

9. Mankind has become so much one family that we cannot insure our own prosperity except by insuring that of everyone else. If you wish to be happy yourself, you must resign yourself to seeing others also happy.

Bertrand Russell, "The Science to Save Us from Science," *The New York Times Magazine*, March 19, 1950

10. I am a part of all that I have met.

Lord Tennyson, "Ulysses" (1842)

152. COMPANY

See also 7. Acquaintances; 57. Association; 365. Friendship; 428. Hospitality; 496. Interestingness; 794. Relationships, Human; 914. Society, Polite; 983. Togetherness

1. He who must needs have company, must needs have sometimes bad company.

Sir Thomas Browne, *Christian Morals* (1716), 3

2. The social, friendly, honest man, / Whate'er he be, / 'Tis he fulfils great Nature's plan, / And none but he!

Robert Burns, "Epistle to John Lapraik No. 2" (1786)

3. We do not mind our not arriving anywhere nearly so much as our not having any company on the way.

Frank Moore Colby, "Thinking It Through in Haste," *The Margin of Hesitation* (1921)

4. What is the odds so long as the fire of soul is kindled at the taper of conviviality, and the wing of friendship never moults a feather?

Charles Dickens, *The Old Curiosity Shop* (1840), 2

5. How many times go we to comedies, to masques, to places of great and noble resort, nay even to church only to see the company?

John Donne, *Sermons*, No. 16, 1622

6. No man can have society upon his own terms. If he seek it, he must serve it too.

Emerson, *Journals*, 1833

7. To be social is to be forgiving.

Robert Frost, "The Star-Splitter," *New Hampshire* (1923)

8. I live in the crowd of jollity, not so much to enjoy company as to shun myself.

Samuel Johnson, *Rasselas* (1759), 16

9. No man is much pleased with a companion who does not increase, in some respect, his fondness of himself.

Samuel Johnson, *The Rambler* (1750–52), 104

10. In general, American social life constitutes an evasion of talking to people. Most Americans don't, in any vital sense, get together; they only do things together.

Louis Kronenberger, *Company Manners* (1954)

11. While you are alone you are entirely your own master and if you have one companion you are but half your own, and the less so in proportion to the indiscretion of his behavior.

Leonardo Da Vinci, *Notebooks* (c. 1500), tr. Jean Paul Richter

12. Man loves company even if only that of a small burning candle.

Georg Christoph Lichtenberg, *Aphorisms* (1764–99), tr. H. Hatfield

13. "Love or perish" we are told and we tell ourselves. The phrase is true enough so long as we do not interpret it as "Mingle or be a failure."

Phyllis McGinley, "A Lost Privilege," *The Province of the Heart* (1959)

14. An ancient father says that a dog we know is better company than a man whose language we do not understand.

Montaigne, "Of liars," *Essays* (1580–88), tr. W. C. Hazlitt

15. At the heart of our friendly or purely social relations, there lurks a hostility momentarily cured but recurring by fits and starts.

MARCEL PROUST, *REMEMBRANCE OF THINGS PAST: CITIES OF THE PLAIN* (1913–27), TR. C. K. SCOTT-MONCRIEFF

16. An agreeable companion on a journey is as good as a carriage.

PUBLILIUS SYRUS, *MORAL SAYINGS* (1ST C. B.C.), 143, TR. DARIUS LYMAN

17. Society in shipwreck is a comfort to all.

PUBLILIUS SYRUS, *MORAL SAYINGS* (1ST C. B.C.), 144, TR. DARIUS LYMAN

18. To have the universe bear one company would be a great consolation in death.

PUBLILIUS SYRUS, *MORAL SAYINGS* (1ST C. B.C.), 894, TR. DARIUS LYMAN

19. Society is no comfort / To one not sociable.

SHAKESPEARE, *CYMBELINE* (1609–10), 4.2.12

20. The American has dwindled into an Odd Fellow,—one who may be known by the development of his organ of gregariousness.

THOREAU, *CIVIL DISOBEDIENCE* (1849)

21. What men call social virtues, good fellowship, is commonly but the virtue of pigs in a litter, which lie close together to keep each other warm.

THOREAU, *JOURNAL*, OCT. 23, 1851

22. I had three chairs in my house; one for solitude, two for friendship, three for society.

THOREAU, "VISITORS," *WALDEN* (1854)

23. It is surprising how many great men and women a small house will contain.

THOREAU, "VISITORS," *WALDEN* (1854)

24. Good company and good discourse are the very sinews of virtue.

IZAAK WALTON, *THE COMPLEAT ANGLER* (1653), 1.2

153. COMPARISON

See also 15. ADVANTAGE; 17. ADVERSITY; 154. COMPENSATION; 180. CONSOLATIONS; 187. CONTRAST; 795. RELATIVENESS

1. Comparison, more than reality, makes men happy or wretched.

THOMAS FULLER, M.D., *GNOMOLOGIA* (1732), 1133

2. Instead of comparing our lot with that of those who are more fortunate than we are, we should compare it with the lot of the great majority of our fellow men. It then appears that we are among the privileged.

HELEN KELLER, *WE BEREAVED* (1929)

3. I murmured because I had no shoes, until I met a man who had no feet.

PERSIAN PROVERB

4. The man with toothache thinks everyone happy whose teeth are sound. The poverty stricken man makes the same mistake about the rich man.

GEORGE BERNARD SHAW, "MAXIMS FOR REVOLUTIONISTS," *MAN AND SUPERMAN* (1903)

COMPASSION

See 583. MERCY; 698. PITY

154. COMPENSATION

See also 15. ADVANTAGE; 153. COMPARISON; 180. CONSOLATIONS; 751. PROSPERITY AND ADVERSITY

1. Every sweet hath its sour; every evil its good.

EMERSON, "COMPENSATION," *ESSAYS: FIRST SERIES* (1841)

155. COMPETITION

See also 26. AGGRESSION; 33. AMBITION

1. Competitions are for horses, not artists.

BÉLA BARTÓK, *SATURDAY REVIEW,* AUG. 25, 1962

2. It is in the blood of genius to love play for its own sake, and whether one uses one's skill on thrones or women, swords or pens, gold or fame, the game's the thing.

GELETT BURGESS, "APRIL ESSAYS," *THE ROMANCE OF THE COMMONPLACE* (1916)

3. One barber shaves not so close but another finds work.

ENGLISH PROVERB

4. When two souls compose a single song, / The muse fans / Livid wrath before long.

EURIPIDES, *ANDROMACHE* (C. 426 B.C.), TR. JOHN F. NIMS

5. He may well win the race that runs by himself.

BENJAMIN FRANKLIN, *POOR RICHARD'S ALMANACK* (1732–57)

6. Potter is potter's enemy, and craftsman is craftsman's / rival; tramp is jealous of tramp, and singer of singer.

HESIOD, *WORKS AND DAYS* (8TH C. B.C.), 25, TR. RICHMOND LATTIMORE

7. A country's competitiveness starts not on the factory floor or in the engineering lab. It starts in the classroom.

Lee Iacocca, *Talking Straight* (1988), with Sonny Kleinfeld

8. Man is a gaming animal. He must be always trying to get the better in something or other.

Charles Lamb, "Mrs. Battle's Opinions on Whist," *Essays of Elia* (1823)

9. Man has risen so far above all other species that he competes in ways unique in nature. He fights by means of complicated weapons; he fights for ends remote in time.

Charles A. Lindbergh, "The Reefs of Biak," *Autobiography of Values* (1978)

10. A horse never runs so fast as when he has other horses to catch up and outpace.

Ovid, *The Art of Love* (c. a.d. 8), 3, tr. J. Lewis May

11. We learn not for life but for the debating-room.

Seneca, *Letters to Lucilius* (1st c.), 106.12, tr. E. Phillips Barker

12. Do as adversaries do in law—/ Strive mightily, but eat and drink as friends.

Shakespeare, *The Taming of the Shrew* (1593–94), 1.2.278

156. COMPLACENCY

See also 166. Conceit; 733. Pride; 909. Smugness

1. Comfort, n. A state of mind produced by contemplation of a neighbor's uneasiness.

Ambrose Bierce, *The Devil's Dictionary* (1881–1911)

2. The seat of perfect contentment is in the head; for every individual is thoroughly satisfied with his own proportion of brains.

Charles Caleb Colton, *Lacon* (1825), 1.163

3. If happiness in self-content is placed, / The wise are wretched, and fools only blessed.

William Congreve, *The Double-Dealer* (1694), 3.3

4. The man who thinks his wife, his baby, his house, his horse, his dog, and himself severally unequalled, is almost sure to be a good-humored person, though liable to be tedious at times.

Oliver Wendell Holmes, Sr., *The Autocrat of the Breakfast Table* (1858), 1

5. Most human beings have an almost infinite capacity for taking things for granted.

Aldous Huxley, "Variations on a Philosopher," *Themes and Variations* (1950)

6. The form most contradictory to human life that can appear among the human species is the "self-satisfied man."

José Ortega y Gasset, *The Revolt of the Masses* (1930), 11

7. Complacency is the enemy of study. We cannot really learn anything until we rid ourselves of complacency.

Mao Tse-Tung, *Quotations from Chairman Mao Tse-Tung* (1966), 33

8. The path is smooth that leadeth on to danger.

Shakespeare, *Venus and Adonis* (1593), 788

157. COMPLAINT

1. To make wail and lament for one's ill fortune, when one will win a tear from the audience, is well worthwhile.

Aeschylus, *Prometheus Bound* (c. 478 b.c.), tr. David Grene

2. The dogs bark, but the caravan moves on.

Arabic Proverb

3. There's a billboard in a little farm town in the Midwest that says: IF YOU COMPLAIN ABOUT FARMERS, DON'T TALK WITH YOUR MOUTH FULL.

Lee Iacocca, *Talking Straight* (1988), with Sonny Kleinfeld

4. When people cease to complain, they cease to think.

Napoleon I, *Maxims* (1804–15)

5. He that falls by himself never cries.

Turkish Proverb

COMPLETION

See 285. Ending

158. COMPLIANCE

See also 690. Persuasion

1. He that complies against his will, / Is of his own opinion still.

Samuel Butler (d. 1680), *Hudibras* (1663), 3.3

2. Much compliance, much craft.

THOMAS FULLER, M.D., *GNOMOLOGIA* (1732), 3479

159. COMPLIMENTS

See also 349. FLATTERY

1. Compliments cost nothing, yet many pay dear for them.

GERMAN PROVERB

2. A compliment is something like a kiss through a veil.

VICTOR HUGO, "SAINT DENIS," *LES MISÉRABLES* (1862), 8.1, TR. CHARLES E. WILBOUR

3. When you cannot get a compliment in any other way pay yourself one.

MARK TWAIN, *NOTEBOOK* (1935)

4. Ah, now-a-days we are all of us so hard up, that the only pleasant things to pay are compliments. They're the only things we *can* pay.

OSCAR WILDE, *LADY WINDERMERE'S FAN* (1892), 1

COMPOSERS

See 614. MUSIC

160. COMPOSURE

See also 989. TRANQUILITY

1. To bear all naked truths, / And to envisage circumstance, all calm, / That is the top of sovereignty.

KEATS, "HYPERION" (1820), 2

2. Everyone knows that in most people's estimation, to do anything cooly is to do it genteelly.

HERMAN MELVILLE, *MOBY-DICK* (1851), 5

3. He is a first-rate collector who can, upon all occasions, collect his wits.

GEORGE DENNISON PRENTICE, *PRENTICEANA* (1860)

4. Nothing is so aggravating as calmness. There is something positively brutal about the good temper of most modern men.

OSCAR WILDE, *A WOMAN OF NO IMPORTANCE* (1893), 2

161. COMPREHENSION

See also 1007. UNDERSTANDING

1. It takes a long time to understand nothing

EDWARD DAHLBERG, "ON WISDOM AND FOLLY," *REASONS OF THE HEART* (1965)

162. COMPROMISE

See also 27. AGREEMENT; 46. APPEASEMENT; 167. CONCILIATION; 994. TREATIES

1. Compromise, n. Such an adjustment of conflicting interests as gives each adversary the satisfaction of thinking he has got what he ought not to have, and is deprived of nothing except what was justly his due.

AMBROSE BIERCE, *THE DEVIL'S DICTIONARY* (1881–1911)

2. All government,—indeed, every human benefit and enjoyment, every virtue and every prudent act,—is founded on compromise and barter.

EDMUND BURKE, SPEECH, "ON CONCILIATION WITH THE AMERICAN COLONIES," MARCH 22, 1775

3. If one could recover the uncompromising spirit of one's youth, one's greatest indignation would be for what one has become.

ANDRÉ GIDE, *THE COUNTERFEITERS* (1925), 1.18, TR. DOROTHY BUSSY

4. A lean compromise is better than a fat lawsuit.

GEORGE HERBERT, *JACULA PRUDENTUM* (1651)

5. It is better to lose the saddle than the horse.

ITALIAN PROVERB

6. Some of my colleagues who are criticized today for lack of forthright principles—or who are looked upon with scorn as compromising "politicians"—are simply engaged in the fine art of conciliating, balancing and interpreting the forces and factions of public opinion, an art essential to keeping our nation united and enabling our Government to function.

JOHN F. KENNEDY, *PROFILES IN COURAGE* (1956)

7. If you cannot catch a bird of paradise, better take a wet hen.

NIKITA KHRUSHCHEV, QUOTED IN *TIME*, JAN. 6, 1958

8. The important point was that whatever errors America had made [in Vietnam] "we are so powerful [according to Secretary Kissinger] that Hanoi is simply unable to defeat us militarily" and must therefore eventually be forced to compromise.

WILLIAM SHAWCROSS, *SIDESHOW* (1979)

163. COMPULSIVENESS

See also 10. ACTIVITY; 627. NEUROSIS; 651. OBSESSION

1. They must needs go whom the Devil drives.

CERVANTES, *DON QUIXOTE* (1605–15), 1.4.4, TR. JOHN OZELL

164. COMPUTERS

1. Computer users soon learn that the miraculous powers of personal computers are based on avoidance of error.

ROBERT BURCHFIELD, *UNLOCKING THE ENGLISH LANGUAGE*

165. CONCEALMENT

See also 200. CRAFTINESS; 440. HYPOCRISY

1. Do not reveal your thoughts to everyone, lest you drive away your good luck.

APOCRYPHA ECCLESIASTICUS 8:19

2. The power of hiding ourselves from one another is mercifully given, for men are wild beasts, and would devour one another but for this protection.

HENRY WARD BEECHER, *PROVERBS FROM PLYMOUTH PULPIT* (1887)

3. There is nothing that gives more assurance than a mask.

COLETTE, "LITERARY APPRENTICESHIP: -CLAUDINE,'" *EARTHLY PARADISE* (1966), 2

4. It is most absurdly said, in popular language, of any man, that he is disguised in liquor; for, on the contrary, most men are disguised by sobriety.

THOMAS DE QUINCEY, *CONFESSIONS OF AN ENGLISH OPIUM-EATER* (1821–56)

5. He who conceals his disease cannot expect to be cured.

ETHIOPIAN PROVERB

6. From your confessor, lawyer and physician, / Hide not your case on no condition.

SIR JOHN HARINGTON, *THE METAMORPHOSIS OF AJAX* (1596), 98

7. No man, for any considerable period, can wear one face to himself, and another to the multitude, without finally getting bewildered as to which may be the true.

NATHANIEL HAWTHORNE, *THE SCARLET LETTER* (1850), 20

8. Our greatest pretenses are built up not to hide the evil and the ugly in us, but our emptiness. The hardest thing to hide is something that is not there.

ERIC HOFFER, *THE PASSIONATE STATE OF MIND* (1954), 217

9. A man had rather have a hundred lies told of him than one truth which he does not wish should be told.

SAMUEL JOHNSON, QUOTED IN BOSWELL'S *LIFE OF SAMUEL JOHNSON,* APRIL 15, 1773

10. Customary use of artifice is the sign of a small mind, and it almost always happens that he who uses it to cover one spot uncovers himself in another.

LA ROCHEFOUCAULD, *MAXIMS* (1665), TR. KENNETH PRATT

11. We are so accustomed to disguise ourselves to others, that in the end we become disguised to ourselves.

LA ROCHEFOUCAULD, *MAXIMS* (1665), TR. KENNETH PRATT

12. The surest way of concealing from others the boundaries of one's own knowledge is not to overstep them.

GIACOMO LEOPARDI, *PENSIERI* (1834–37), 86, TR. WILLIAM FENSE WEAVER

13. Talking about oneself can also be a means to conceal oneself.

NIETZSCHE, *BEYOND GOOD AND EVIL* (1886), 169, TR. WALTER KAUFMANN

14. Woe to him who doesn't know how to wear his mask, be he king or Pope!

LUIGI PIRANDELLO, *HENRY IV* (1922), I, TR. EDWARD STORER

15. The bad are frequently good enough to let you see how bad they are, but the good as frequently endeavor to get between you and themselves.

THOREAU, *JOURNAL* DEC. 2, 1851

16. Everyone is a moon and has a dark side which he never shows to anybody.

MARK TWAIN, *NOTEBOOK* (1935)

17. A mask tells us more than a face.

OSCAR WILDE, "PEN, PENCIL AND POISON," *INTENTIONS* (1891)

166. CONCEIT

See also 89. BOASTING; 156. COMPLACENCY; 435. HUMILITY; 733. PRIDE; 876. SELF-LOVE; 1027. VANITY

1. The smaller the mind the greater the conceit.

AESOP, "THE GNAT AND THE BULL," *FABLES* (6TH C. B.C.?), TR. THOMAS JAMES

2. Why do men seek honour? Surely in order to confirm the favourable opinion they have formed of themselves.

ARISTOTLE, *NICOMACHEAN ETHICS* (4TH C. B.C.), I.5, TR. J. A. K. THOMSON

3. To say that a man is vain means merely that he is pleased with the effect he produces on other people. A conceited man is satisfied with the effect he produces on himself.

MAX BEERBOHM, "QUIA IMPERFECTUM," *AND EVEN NOW* (1920)

4. There has never been a poet or orator who thought another better than himself.

CICERO, *AD ATTICUM* (1ST C. B.C.), 14

5. Those who know the least of others think the highest of themselves.

CHARLES CALEB COLTON, *LACON* (1825), 1.443

6. I've never any pity for conceited people, because I think they carry their comfort about with them.

GEORGE ELIOT, *THE MILL ON THE FLOSS* (1860), 5.4

7. What is the first business of philosophy? To part with self-conceit. For it is impossible for any one to begin to learn what he thinks that he already knows.

EPICTETUS, *DISCOURSES* (2ND C.), 2.17, TR. THOMAS W. HIGGINSON

8. Conceit is vanity driven from all other shifts, and forced to appeal to itself for admiration.

WILLIAM HAZLITT, *CHARACTERISTICS* (1823), 110

9. Whenever Nature leaves a hole in a person's mind, she generally plasters it over with a thick coat of self-conceit.

LONGFELLOW, "INTELLECT," *THE BLANK-BOOK OF A COUNTRY SCHOOLMASTER* (1857)

10. The bigger a man's head, the worse his headache.

PERSIAN PROVERB

11. Every person thinks his own intellect perfect, and his own child handsome.

SA'DI, *GULISTAN* (1258), 8.31, TR. JAMES ROSS

CONCENTRATION

See 903. SINGLE-MINDEDNESS

167. CONCILIATION

See also 46. APPEASEMENT; 162. COMPROMISE; 994. TREATIES

1. A soft answer turneth away wrath.

BIBLE, PROVERBS 15:1

2. Blessed are the peacemakers, / For they have freed themselves from sinful wrath.

DANTE, "PURGATORIO," 17, *THE DIVINE COMEDY* (C. 1300–21), TR. LAWRENCE GRANT WHITE

3. Be swift to hear, slow to speak, slow to wrath.

BIBLE, JAMES 1:19

4. Blessed are the peacemakers: for they shall be called the children of God.

BIBLE, MATTHEW 5:9

5. Your If is the only peacemaker. Much virtue in If.

SHAKESPEARE, *AS YOU LIKE IT* (1599–1600), 5.4.107

6. It behooves a prudent person to make trial of everything before arms.

TERENCE, *THE EUNUCH* (161 B.C.), 4.7.19, TR. HENRY THOMAS RILEY

CONDOLENCE

See 960. SYMPATHY

CONDUCT

See 77. BEHAVIOR

168. CONFESSION

1. We acknowledge our faults in order to repair by our sincerity the damage they have done us in the eyes of others.

LA ROCHEFOUCAULD, *MAXIMS* (1665), TR. KENNETH PRATT

2. The moment had come for her to tell her husband. By this single, cathartic act, she would, she believed, rid herself of the doubts and anxieties that beset her.

MARY MCCARTHY, *THE COMPANY SHE KEEPS* (1942)

3. The confession of one man humbles all.

ANTONIO PORCHIA, *VOCES* (1968), TR. W. S. MERWIN

4. Confession of our faults is the next thing to innocence.

PUBLILIUS SYRUS, *MORAL SAYINGS* (1ST C. B.C.), 1060, TR. DARIUS LYMAN

5. It is not the criminal things which are hardest to confess, but the ridiculous and shameful.

ROUSSEAU, *CONFESSIONS* (1766–70), 1.1

CONFIDENCE

See 115. CERTAINTY; 664. OVERCONFIDENCE; 855. SECRETS; 860. SELF-CONFIDENCE

169. CONFIDENCES

See also 855. SECRETS

1. No receipt [recipe] openeth the heart, but a true friend, to whom you may impart griefs, joys, fears, hopes, suspicions, counsels, and whatsoever lieth upon the heart to oppress it.

FRANCIS BACON, "OF FRIENDSHIP," *ESSAYS* (1625)

2. We rarely confide in those who are better than we are.

ALBERT CAMUS, *THE FALL* (1956)

3. Shyness has laws: you can only give yourself, tragically, to those who least understand.

LAWRENCE DURRELL, *JUSTINE* (1957), 2

4. It is so much easier to tell intimate things in the dark.

WILLIAM MCFEE, *CASUALS OF THE SEA* (1916), 1.1.4

5. If thou tellest the sorrows of thy heart, let it be to him in whose countenance thou mayst be assured of prompt consolation.

SA'DI, *GULISTAN* (1258), 3.13, TR. JAMES ROSS

6. A healthy ear can stand hearing sick words.

SENEGALESE PROVERB

7. To whom you tell your secrets, to him you resign your liberty.

SPANISH PROVERB

170. CONFLICT, INNER

See also 497. INTERESTS, DIVIDED; 691. PERVERSENESS

1. I hate and love. You ask, perhaps, how that can be? / I know not, but I feel the agony.

CATULLUS, *POEMS* (1ST C. B.C.), 85, TR. GILBERT HIGHET

2. We are sure to be losers when we quarrel with ourselves; it is a civil war, and in all such contentions, triumphs are defeats.

CHARLES CALEB COLTON, *LACON* (1825), 1.439

3. What man knows is everywhere at war with what he wants.

JOSEPH WOOD KRUTCH, "THE GENESIS OF A MOOD," *THE MODERN TEMPER* (1929)

171. CONFORMITY

See also 12. ADJUSTMENT; 91. BOHEMIANS; 468. INDIVIDUALISM; 637. NORMALITY; 933. STATUS; 935. STEREOTYPES

1. Abnormal, adj. Not conforming to standard. In matters of thought and conduct, to be independent is to be abnormal, to be abnormal is to be detested.

AMBROSE BIERCE, *THE DEVIL'S DICTIONARY* (1881–1911)

2. It may well be that a society's greatest madness seems normal to itself.

ALLAN BLOOM, "MUSIC," *THE CLOSING OF THE AMERICAN MIND* (1987)

3. Conformity is the ape of harmony.

EMERSON, *JOURNALS*, 1840

4. The great majority of men grow up and grow old in seeming and following.

EMERSON, *JOURNALS*, 1841

5. No man on earth is truly free, / All are slaves of money or necessity. / Public opinion or fear of prosecution / forces each one, against his conscience, to conform.

EURIPIDES, *HECUBA* (C. 425 B.C.), TR. WILLIAM ARROWSMITH

6. People are always talking about originality, but what do they mean? As soon as we are born, the world begins to work upon us, and this goes on to the end.

GOETHE, QUOTED IN JOHANN PETER ECKERMANN'S *CONVERSATIONS WITH GOETHE*, MAY 12, 1825

7. Conformity is inevitable when folks huddle together in rebellion.

HERBERT GOLD, "PROTOCOLS OF THE ELDERS OF BOHEMIA," *BOHEMIA* (1993)

8. Try not to beat back the current, yet be not drowned in its waters; / Speak with the speech of the world, think with the thoughts of the few.

JOHN HAY, "DISTICHS" (1871?), 17

9. Success, recognition, and conformity are the bywords of the modern world where everyone seems to crave the anesthetizing security of being identified with the majority.

MARTIN LUTHER KING, JR., *STRENGTH TO LOVE* (1963), 2

10. One of the saddest things about conformity is the ghastly sort of non-conformity it breeds: the noisy protesting, the aggressive rebelliousness, the rigid counterfetishism.

LOUIS KRONENBERGER, *COMPANY MANNERS* (1954), 3.3

11. Conformity, humility, acceptance—with these coins we are to pay our fares to paradise.

ROBERT LINDNER, TITLE ESSAY, *MUST YOU CONFORM?* (1956)

12. How protean are the devices available to human intelligence when it lends itself to the persistence of the conformist error.

ROBERT LINDNER, "HOMOSEXUALITY AND THE CONTEMPORARY SCENE," *MUST YOU CONFORM?* (1956)

13. Trumpet in a herd of elephants; / Crow in the company of cocks; / Bleat in a flock of goats.

MALAY PROVERB

14. No reason makes it right / To shun accepted ways from stubborn spite; / And we may better join the

foolish crowd / Than cling to wisdom, lonely though unbowed.

Molière, *The School for Husbands* (1661), 1.2, tr. Donald M. Frame

15. Men are created different; they lose their social freedom and their individual autonomy in seeking to become like each other.

David Riesman, "Autonomy and Utopia," *The Lonely Crowd* (1950)

16. "Queuemania" is an ailment that afflicts people with a compulsive urge to line up behind someone or something, even a lamp-post.

Thomas P. Ronan, *The New York Times,* Aug. 23, 1955

17. We're all getting lashed to the great wheel of uniformity.

Robert James Waller, *The Bridges of Madison County* (1992)

18. We are half ruined by conformity, but we should be wholly ruined without it.

Charles Dudley Warner, "Eighteenth Week," *My Summer in a Garden* (1871)

19. We arrange our lives—even the best and boldest men and women that exist, just as much as the most limited—with reference to what society conventionally rules and makes right.

Walt Whitman, "Ventures, on an Old Theme," *Notes Left Over* (1881)

CONFUSION

See 257. Disorder

172. CONGRESS

See also 395. Government; 711. Politics and Politicians; 761. Public Office

1. Of representative assemblies may not this good be said: That contending parties in a country do thereby ascertain one another's strength? They fight there, since fight they must, by petition, parliamentary eloquence, not by sword, bayonet and bursts of military cannon.

Thomas Carlyle, *Chartism* (1839), 8

2. Congress—these, for the most part, illiterate hacks whose fancy vests are spotted with gravy, and whose speeches, hypocritical, unctuous, and slovenly, are spotted also with the gravy of political patronage.

Mary McCarthy, "America the Beautiful: The Humanist in the Bathtub," *On the Contrary* (1961)

3. Large legislative bodies resolve themselves into coteries, and coteries into jealousies.

Napoleon I, *Maxims* (1804–15)

4. It is the duty of the President to propose and it is the privilege of the Congress to dispose.

Franklin D. Roosevelt, press conference, July 23, 1937

5. It could probably be shown by facts and figures that there is no distinctly native American criminal class except Congress.

Mark Twain, "Pudd'nhead Wilson's New Calendar," *Following the Equator* (1897), 1.8

173. CONQUEST

See also 945. Success; 1042. War

1. When you have gained a victory, do not push it too far; 'tis sufficient to let the company and your adversary see 'tis in your power but that you are too generous to make use of it.

Eustace Budgell, in *The Spectator* (1711–12), 197

2. The problems of victory are more agreeable than those of defeat, but they are no less difficult.

Sir Winston Churchill, speech, House of Commons, Nov. 11, 1942

3. He that has gone so far as to cut the claws of the lion, will not feel himself quite secure until he has also drawn his teeth.

Charles Caleb Colton, *Lacon* (1825), 1.43

4. A conqueror is like a cannonball. He cannot stop of his own accord. He must go on until he runs down or hits something.

Leonard Cooper, *Many Roads to Moscow* (1968)

5. The god of Victory is said to be one-handed, but Peace gives victory to both sides.

Emerson, *Journals,* 1867

6. Dead men have no victory.

Euripides, *The Phoenician Women* (c. 411–409 B.C.), tr. Elizabeth Wyckoff

7. All victories breed hate, and that over your superior is foolish or fatal.

Baltasar Gracián, *The Art of Worldly Wisdom* (1647), 7, tr. Joseph Jacobs

8. 'Tis man's to fight, but Heaven's to give success.

Homer, *Iliad* (9th c. B.C.), 6.427, tr. Alexander Pope

9. In human history a moral victory is always a disaster, for it debauches and degrades both the victor and the vanquished.

H. L. Mencken, "The Calamity of Appomattox," *The American Mercury,* September 1930

10. Triumph cannot help being cruel.

José Ortega y Gasset, *Notes on the Novel* (1925)

11. There is no pain in the wound received in the moment of victory.

Publilius Syrus, *Moral Sayings* (1st c. B.C.), 1077, tr. Darius Lyman

12. The right of conquest has no foundation other than the right of the strongest.

Rousseau, *The Social Contract* (1762), 1.4, tr. G. D. H. Cole

13. You win the victory when you yield to friends.

Sophocles, *Ajax* (c. 447 B.C.), tr. John Moore

14. Minds are conquered not by arms, but by love and magnanimity.

Spinoza, *Ethics* (1677), 4, tr. Andrew Boyle

15. War will of itself discover and lay open the hidden and rankling wounds of the victorious party.

Tacitus, *Histories* (A.D. 104–109), 2.77, tr. William J. Brodribb

16. To conquer with arms is to make only a temporary conquest; to conquer the world by earning its esteem is to make a permanent conquest.

Woodrow Wilson, address to Congress, Nov. 11, 1918

174. CONSCIENCE

See also 405. Guilt; 604. Morality; 822. Right; 1070. Wrongdoing

1. Conscience is the frame of character, and love is the covering for it.

Henry Ward Beecher, *Proverbs from Plymouth Pulpit* (1887)

2. Conscience is thoroughly well-bred and soon leaves off talking to those who do not wish to hear it.

Samuel Butler (d. 1902), *Note-Books* (1912)

3. In many walks of life, a conscience is a more expensive encumbrance than a wife or a carriage.

Thomas De Quincey, "Preliminary Confessions," *Confessions of an English Opium-Eater* (1821–56)

4. Nothing but man of all invenomed things / Doth work upon itself, with inborne stings.

John Donne, "Elegy on the Lady Marckham" (1609)

5. God has delegated himself to a million deputies.

Emerson, "Worship," *The Conduct of Life* (1860)

6. A guilty conscience needs no accuser.

English Proverb

7. The fact that human conscience remains partially infantile throughout life is the core of human tragedy.

Erik H. Erikson, *Childhood and Society* (1950), 7

8. There is one thing alone / that stands the brunt of life throughout its course, / a quiet conscience.

Euripides, *Hippolytus* (428 B.C.), tr. David Grene

9. A good conscience is the best divinity.

Thomas Fuller, M.D., *Gnomologia* (1732), 141

10. Conscience is a just but a weak judge. Weakness leaves it powerless to execute its judgment.

Kahlil Gibran, "A Story of a Friend," *Thoughts and Meditations* (1960), tr. Anthony R. Ferris

11. Conscience is a coward, and those faults it has not strength enough to prevent it seldom has justice enough to accuse.

Oliver Goldsmith, *The Vicar of Wakefield* (1766), 13

12. Perhaps, if we don't always have a conscious conscience, we have a subliminal one, from which the memory of past wrongs is not so easily erased.

Eva Hoffman, *Exit Into History* (1993)

13. If we cannot be powerful and happy and prey on others, we invent conscience and prey on ourselves.

Elbert Hubbard, *The Philistine* (1895–1915)

14. Welcome, O life! I go to encounter for the millionth time the reality of experience and to forge in the smithy of my soul the uncreated conscience of my race.

James Joyce, *Portrait of the Artist as a Young Man* (1916)

15. History is *a priori* amoral; it has no conscience.

Arthur Koestler, *Darkness at Noon* (1940)

16. To sell oneself for thirty pieces of silver is an honest transaction; but to sell oneself to one's own conscience is to abandon mankind.

Arthur Koestler, *Darkness at Noon* (1940)

17. Our conscience is not the vessel of eternal verities. It grows with our social life, and a new social condition means a radical change in conscience.

Walter Lippmann, "Some Necessary Iconoclasm," *A Preface to Politics* (1914)

18. A state of conscience is higher than a state of innocence.

THOMAS MANN, IN *I BELIEVE* (1939), ED. CLIFTON FADIMAN

19. Conscience is the guardian in the individual of the rules which the community has evolved for its own preservation.

W. SOMERSET MAUGHAM, *THE MOON AND SIXPENCE* (1919), 14

20. Every authentic artist is engaged in this creating of the conscience of the race, even though he or she may be unaware of the fact.

ROLLO MAY, *THE COURAGE TO CREATE* (1975)

21. Conscience is the inner voice which warns us that someone may be looking.

H. L. MENCKEN, "SENTENTIAE," *A BOOK OF BURLESQUES* (1920)

22. The laws of conscience, which we pretend to be derived from nature, proceed from custom.

MONTAIGNE, "OF CUSTOM," *ESSAYS* (1580–88), TR. W. C. HAZLITT

23. There is only one way to achieve happiness on this terrestrial ball, / And that is to have either a clear conscience, or none at all.

OGDEN NASH, "INTER-OFFICE MEMORANDUM," *I'M A STRANGER HERE MYSELF* (1938)

24. It is only because man believes himself to be free, not because he is free, that he experiences remorse and pricks of conscience.

NIETZSCHE, *HUMAN, ALL TOO HUMAN* (1878), 39, TR. HELEN ZIMMERN

25. The bite of conscience teaches men to bite.

NIETZSCHE, "ON THE PITYING," *THUS SPOKE ZARATHUSTRA* (1883–92), 2, TR. WALTER KAUFMANN

26. An evil conscience is often quiet, but never secure.

PUBLILIUS SYRUS, *MORAL SAYINGS* (1ST C. B.C.), 1084, TR. DARIUS LYMAN

27. Even when there is no law, there is conscience.

PUBLILIUS SYRUS, *MORAL SAYINGS* (1ST C. B.C.), 237, TR. DARIUS LYMAN

28. The strongest feelings assigned to the conscience are not moral feelings at all; they express merely physical antipathies.

GEORGE SANTAYANA, *THE LIFE OF REASON: REASON IN SCIENCE* (1905–06), 9

29. A peace above all earthly dignities, / A still and quiet conscience.

SHAKESPEARE, *HENRY VIII* (1612–13), 3.2.379

30. Conscience does make cowards of us all.

SHAKESPEARE, *HAMLET* (1600), 3.1.83

31. My conscience hath a thousand several tongues, / And every tongue brings in a several tale, / And every tale condemns me for a villain.

SHAKESPEARE, *RICHARD III* (1592–93), 5.3.194

32. Trust that man in nothing who has not a conscience in everything.

LAURENCE STERNE, *SERMONS* (1760–69), 27

33. The more estimable the offender, the greater the torment.

VOLTAIRE, *SÉMIRAMIS* (1748), 5.8

34. Conscience and cowardice are really the same things. Conscience is the trade name of the firm.

OSCAR WILDE, *THE PICTURE OF DORIAN GRAY* (1891), 1

175. CONSCIOUSNESS

See also 883. SENSIBILITY; 1006. UNCONSCIOUSNESS

1. A sub-clerk in the post office is the equal of a conqueror if consciousness is common to them.

ALBERT CAMUS, "THE ABSURD MAN," *THE MYTH OF SISYPHUS* (1942), TR. JUSTIN O'BRIEN

2. I do not know the man so bold / He dare in lonely Place / That awful stranger Consciousness / Deliberately face—.

EMILY DICKINSON, POEM (C. 1874)

3. To be too conscious is an illness—a real thoroughgoing illness.

DOSTOYEVSKY, *NOTES FROM UNDERGROUND* (1864), 1.2, TR. CONSTANCE GARNETT

4. There are many who feel consciously hopeful and unconsciously hopeless, and there are few for whom it is the other way around.

ERICH FROMM, *THE REVOLUTION OF HOPE* (1968)

5. Whatever diverts the mind from itself may help.

BERNARD MALAMUD, *DUBIN'S LIVES* (1979)

6. The ultimate gift of conscious life is a sense of the mystery that encompasses it.

LEWIS MUMFORD, "ORIENTATION TO LIFE," *THE CONDUCT OF LIFE* (1951)

176. CONSEQUENCES

See also 110. CAUSE AND EFFECT; 340. FATE; 507. IRREVOCABLENESS; 815. RETRIBUTION

1. Quite often good things have hurtful consequences. There are instances of men who have been ruined by their money or killed by their courage.

ARISTOTLE, *NICOMACHEAN ETHICS* (4TH C. B.C.), 1.3, TR. J. A. K. THOMSON

2. How great a matter a little fire kindleth!

BIBLE, JAMES 3:5

3. A mighty flame followeth a tiny spark.

DANTE, "PARADISO," 1, *THE DIVINE COMEDY* (C. 1300–21), TR. P. H. WICKSTEED

4. The sower may mistake and sow his peas crookedly: the peas make no mistake, but come up and show his line.

EMERSON, *JOURNALS,* 1843

5. A bad beginning makes a bad ending.

EURIPIDES, *AEOLUS* (C. 423 B.C.), 32, TR. M. H. MORGAN

6. Everything we do has a result. But that which is right and prudent does not always lead to good, nor the contrary to what is bad.

GOETHE, QUOTED IN JOHANN PETER ECKERMANN'S *CONVERSATIONS WITH GOETHE,* DEC. 25, 1825

7. Logical consequences are the scarecrows of fools and the beacons of wise men.

THOMAS HENRY HUXLEY, "ANIMAL AUTOMATISM" (1874)

8. The consequences of our actions take hold of us quite indifferent to our claim that meanwhile we have "improved."

NIETZSCHE, *BEYOND GOOD AND EVIL* (1886), 179, TR. WALTER KAUFMANN

9. In each action we must look beyond the action at our past, present, and future state, and at others whom it affects, and see the relations of all those things. And then we shall be very cautious.

PASCAL, *PENSÉES* (1670), 505, TR. W. F. TROTTER

177. CONSERVATION

See also 29. AIR POLLUTION; 294. ENVIRONMENT; 995. TREES

1. Do no dishonour to the earth lest you dishonour the spirit of man.

HENRY BESTON, "ORION RISES ON THE DUNES," *THE OUTERMOST HOUSE* (1928)

2. The world to-day is sick to its thin blood for lack of elemental things, for fire before the hands, for water welling from the earth, for air, for dear earth itself underfoot.

HENRY BESTON, "THE BEACH," *THE OUTERMOST HOUSE* (1928)

3. It is good to realize that, if love and peace can prevail on earth, and if we can teach our children to honor nature's gifts, the joys and beauties of the outdoors will be here forever.

JIMMY CARTER, *AN OUTDOOR JOURNAL: ADVENTURES AND REFLECTIONS* (1988)

4. We lose the forest for the trees, forgetting, even so far as we think at all, that we are trustees for those who come after us, squandering the patrimony which we have received.

LEARNED HAND, *THE SPIRIT OF LIBERTY* (1959)

5. The earth we abuse and the living things we kill will, in the end, take their revenge; for in exploiting their presence we are diminishing our future.

MARYA MANNES, *MORE IN ANGER* (1958), 1.5

6. The nation that destroys its soil destroys itself.

FRANKLIN D. ROOSEVELT, LETTER TO THE GOVERNORS URGING UNIFORM SOIL CONSERVATION LAWS, FEB. 26, 1937

7. Everything is perfect coming from the hands of the Creator; everything degenerates in the hands of man.

ROUSSEAU, *ÉMILE* (1762), 1

8. The long fight to save wild beauty represents democracy at its best. It requires citizens to practice the hardest of virtues—self-restraint.

EDWIN WAY TEALE, "FEBRUARY 2," *CIRCLE OF THE SEASONS* (1953)

9. The more we get out of the world the less we leave, and in the long run we shall have to pay our debts at a time that may be very inconvenient for our own survival.

NORBERT WIENER, *THE HUMAN USE OF HUMAN BEINGS* (1954), 2

178. CONSERVATISM

See also 536. LIBERALISM; 710. POLITICAL PARTIES; 776. RADICALISM

1. When a nation's young men are conservative, its funeral bell is already rung.

HENRY WARD BEECHER, *PROVERBS FROM PLYMOUTH PULPIT* (1887)

2. Conservative, n. A statesman who is enamored of existing evils, as distinguished from the Liberal, who wishes to replace them with others.

AMBROSE BIERCE, *THE DEVIL'S DICTIONARY* (1881–1911)

3. A conservative government is an organised hypocrisy.

BENJAMIN DISRAELI, SPEECH, "AGRICULTURAL DISTRESS," MARCH 17, 1845

4. The philosophical conservative is someone willing to pay the price of other people's suffering for his principles.

E.L. DOCTOROW, "RONALD REAGAN," *JACK LONDON, HEMINGWAY, AND THE CONSTITUTION* (1993)

5. All conservatives are such from personal defects. They have been effeminated by position or nature ... and can only, like invalids, act on the defensive.

EMERSON, "FATE," *THE CONDUCT OF LIFE* (1860)

6. Conservatism, ever more timorous and narrow, disgusts the children, and drives them for a mouthful of fresh air into radicalism.

EMERSON, "POWER," *THE CONDUCT OF LIFE* (1860)

7. In the conventional wisdom of conservatives, the modern search for security is regularly billed as the greatest single threat to economic progress.

JOHN KENNETH GALBRAITH, *THE AFFLUENT SOCIETY* (1958)

8. The conservatives nearly always tolerate the demagogue while he is destroying liberals.

HARRY GOLDEN, *ONLY IN AMERICA* (1958)

9. A man who is determined never to move out of the beaten road cannot lose his way.

WILLIAM HAZLITT, "CHARACTER OF THE LATE MR. PITT," *THE ROUND TABLE* (1817)

10. [T]o the reactionary ear every whispered criticism of the elite classes has always sounded like the opening shot of an uprising.

RICHARD HOFSTADTER, *THE AMERICAN POLITICAL TRADITION* (1948)

11. A mellowing rigorist is always a much pleasanter object to contemplate than a tightening liberal, as a cold day warming up to 32° Fahrenheit is much more agreeable than a warm one chilling down to the same temperature.

OLIVER WENDELL HOLMES, SR., *THE POET AT THE BREAKFAST TABLE* (1872), 1

12. Orthodoxy: That peculiar condition where the patient can neither eliminate an old idea nor absorb a new one.

ELBERT HUBBARD, *THE NOTE BOOK* (1927)

13. No matter how I'm doing financially, the Depression has never disappeared from my consciousness. To this day, I hate waste. When neckties went from narrow to wide, I kept all my old ones until the style went back to narrow.

LEE IACOCCA, *IACOCCA: AN AUTOBIOGRAPHY* (1984) WITH WILLIAM NOVAK

14. The sickly, weakly, timid man fears the people, and is a Tory by nature.

THOMAS JEFFERSON, LETTER TO LAFAYETTE, NOV. 4, 1823

15. The [Barry] Goldwater movement excited the depths because the apocalypse was brought more near, and like millions of other whites, I had been leading a life which was a trifle too pointless and a trifle too full of guilt and my gullet was close to nausea with the empty promises of an empty liberal center.

NORMAN MAILER, *CANNIBALS AND CHRISTIANS* (1967)

16. Ribbons a-flutter and orchids a-tremble, / Yearly the vigilant Daughters assemble, / Affirming in fervid and firm resolutions / Their permanent veto on all revolutions.

MARYA MANNES, "D. A. R. WANTS ATOMS-FOR-PEACE PROJECT ABANDONED," *SUBVERSE: RHYMES FOR OUR TIMES* (1959)

17. All reactionaries are paper tigers.

MAO TSE-TUNG, *QUOTATIONS FROM CHAIRMAN MAO TSE-TUNG* (1966), 6

18. [W]e have become a conservative country, despite our worldwide reputation for seeking novelty, in that we are unable to envisage alternative futures for ourselves.

DAVID RIESMAN, *ABUNDANCE FOR WHAT?* (1964)

19. A conservative is a man with two perfectly good legs who, however, has never learned to walk forward.

FRANKLIN D. ROOSEVELT, RADIO ADDRESS, OCT. 26, 1939

20. A reactionary is a somnambulist walking backwards.

FRANKLIN D. ROOSEVELT, RADIO ADDRESS, OCT. 26, 1939

21. The radical invents the views. When he has worn them out the conservative adopts them.

MARK TWAIN, *NOTEBOOK* (1935)

22. The only reactionaries are those who find themselves at home in the present.

MIGUEL DE UNAMUNO, "DON QUIXOTE TODAY," *TRAGIC SENSE OF LIFE* (1913), TR. J. E. CRAWFORD FLITCH

179. CONSISTENCY

See also 117. CHANGE; 464. INCONSISTENCY

1. A foolish consistency is the hobgoblin of little minds, adored by little statesmen and philosophers and divines.

EMERSON, "SELF-RELIANCE," *ESSAYS: FIRST SERIES* (1841)

2. The consistent thinker, the consistently moral man, is either a walking mummy or else, if he has not succeeded in stifling all his vitality, a fanatical monomaniac.

ALDOUS HUXLEY, *DO WHAT YOU WILL* (1929)

3. It is not best to swap horses while crossing the river.

ABRAHAM LINCOLN, REPLY TO THE NATIONAL UNION LEAGUE, JUNE 9, 1864

4. All sudden and violent changes, whatever their causes or character, must tend to decrease the respect for *status quo* as a natural order of things.

GUNNAR MYRDAL, *BEYOND THE WELFARE STATE* (1960)

5. To hold the same views at forty as we held at twenty is to have been stupefied for a score of years and to take rank, not as a prophet, but as an unteachable brat, well birched and none the wiser.

ROBERT LOUIS STEVENSON, "CRABBED AGE AND YOUTH," *VIRGINIBUS PUERISQUE* (1881)

6. There are those who would misteach us that to stick in a rut is consistency—and a virtue, and that to climb out of the rut is inconsistency—and a vice.

MARK TWAIN, "CONSISTENCY" (1923)

180. CONSOLATIONS

See also 17. ADVERSITY; 154. COMPENSATION; 798. REMEDIES

1. Perhaps the greatest consolation of the oppressed is to consider themselves superior to their tyrants.

JULIEN GREEN, *ADRIENNE MESURAT* (1927), 1.9

2. The kind of solace that arises from having company in misery is spiteful.

SENECA, *AD MARCIAM DE CONSOLATIONE* (1ST C.)

3. There is nothing so bitter that a patient mind cannot find some solace for it.

SENECA, "ON PEACE OF MIND," *MORAL ESSAYS* (1ST C.), 10

4. Many a green isle needs must be / In the deep wide sea of Misery, / Or the mariner, worn and wan, / Never thus could voyage on.

SHELLEY, "LINES WRITTEN AMONG THE EUGANEAN HILLS" (1818)

181. CONSTANCY AND INCONSTANCY

See also 491. INTEGRITY; 472. INFIDELITY; 556. LOYALTY

1. We should measure affection, not like youngsters by the ardor of its passion, but by its strength and constancy.

CICERO, *DE OFFICIIS* (44 B.C.), 1.15.47

2. One man; two loves. No good ever comes of that.

EURIPIDES, *ANDROMACHE* (C. 426 B.C.), TR. JOHN F. NIMS

3. Only the person who has faith in himself is able to be faithful to others.

ERICH FROMM, *THE ART OF LOVING* (1956), 4

4. To be capable of steady friendship or lasting love, are the two greatest proofs, not only of goodness of heart, but of strength of mind.

WILLIAM HAZLITT, *CHARACTERISTICS* (1823), 235

5. It is as foolish to make experiments upon the constancy of a friend, as upon the chastity of a wife.

SAMUEL JOHNSON, QUOTED IN BOSWELL'S *LIFE OF SAMUEL JOHNSON*, SEPT. 9, 1779

6. Constancy in love is a perpetual inconstancy, which makes the heart attach itself successively to all the qualities of the person we love, giving preference now to one and presently to another.

LA ROCHEFOUCAULD, *MAXIMS* (1665), TR. KENNETH PRATT

7. There are two sorts of constancy in love; the one comes from the constant discovery in our beloved of new grounds for love, and the other comes from making it a point of honour to be constant.

LA ROCHEFOUCAULD, *MAXIMS* (1665), TR. KENNETH PRATT

8. The violence we do to ourselves in order to remain faithful to the one we love is hardly better than an act of infidelity.

LA ROCHEFOUCAULD, *MAXIMS* (1665)

9. The heart grows weary after a little / Of what it loved for a little while.

EDNA ST. VINCENT MILLAY, "THREE SONGS FROM 'THE LAMP AND THE BELL,'" 2, *THE HARP-WEAVER* (1923)

10. He wears his faith but as the fashion of his hat.

SHAKESPEARE, *MUCH ADO ABOUT NOTHING* (1598–99), 1.1.75

11. O heaven, were man / But constant, he were perfect!

SHAKESPEARE, *THE TWO GENTLEMEN OF VERONA* (1594–95), 5.4.110

12. Men's minds are given to change in hate and friendship.

SOPHOCLES, *AJAX* (C. 447 B.C.), TR. JOHN MOORE

13. Out upon it, I have loved / Three whole days together; / And am like to love three more, / If it prove fair weather.

SIR JOHN SUCKLING, "A POEM WITH THE ANSWER," *FRAGMENTA AUREA* (1646)

14. There is nothing in this world constant but inconstancy.

JONATHAN SWIFT, *A CRITICAL ESSAY UPON THE FACULTIES OF THE MIND* (1707)

15. Faithfulness is to the emotional life what consistency is to the life of the intellect—simply a confession of failures.

OSCAR WILDE, *THE PICTURE OF DORIAN GRAY* (1891), 4

182. CONSTITUTIONS

See also 395. GOVERNMENT

1. The Constitution of the United States is a law for rulers and people, equally in war and peace, and covers with the shield of its protection all classes of men, at all times, and under all circumstances.

JUSTICE DAVID DAVIS, *EX PARTE MILLIGAN* (1866)

2. The voice of the Constitution is the inescapably solemn self-consciousness of the people giving the law unto themselves.

E.L. DOCTOROW, "A CITIZEN READS THE CONSTITUTION," *JACK LONDON, HEMINGWAY, AND THE CONSTITUTION* (1993)

3. One stands, in fact, in awe of the Constitution of the United States, though it is an idea and not quite a reality.

NIKKI GIOVANNI, "ARCHITECTURE," *RACISM 101* (1994)

4. The fathers who contrived and passed the Consititution were wise in their generation; as time passes, we come more and more to realize their powers of divination.

LEARNED HAND, *THE SPIRIT OF LIBERTY* (1959)

5. Some men look at constitutions with sanctimonious reverence, and deem them like the ark of the covenant, too sacred to be touched.

THOMAS JEFFERSON, LETTER TO SAMUEL KERCHEVAL, JULY 12, 1816

6. Though written constitutions may be violated in moments of passion or delusion, yet they furnish a text to which those who are watchful may again rally and recall the people; they fix too for the people the principles of their political creed.

THOMAS JEFFERSON, LETTER TO JOSEPH PRIESTLEY, JUNE 19, 1802

7. The Constitution is more than literature, but as literature, it is primarily a work of the imagination. It imagined a country: fantastic. More fantastic still, it imagined a country full of people imagining themselves.

ROGER ROSENBLATT, "WORDS ON PIECES OF PAPER," *THE MAN IN THE WATER* (1994)

8. Constitutions are checks upon the hasty action of the majority. They are the self-imposed restraints of a whole people upon a majority of them to secure sober action and a respect for the rights of the minority.

WILLIAM HOWARD TAFT, VETO OF ARIZONA ENABLING ACT, AUG. 22, 1911

CONSUMERS

See 105. BUYING AND SELLING

183. CONTEMPLATION

See also 723. PRAYER; 875. SELF-KNOWLEDGE; 927. SPIRITUALITY

1. Nowhere can man find a quieter or more untroubled retreat than in his own soul.

MARCUS AURELIUS, *MEDITATIONS* (2ND C.), 4.3, TR. MAXWELL STANIFORTH

2. I neglect God and his angles for the noise of a fly, for the rattling of a coach, for the whining of a door.

JOHN DONNE, *SERMONS,* No. 80, 1626

3. If thou may not continually gather thyself together, do it some time at least once a day, morning or evening.

THOMAS À KEMPIS, *THE IMITATION OF CHRIST* (1426), 1.19

184. CONTEMPORANEOUSNESS

See also 298. ERA; 374. GENERATIONS; 599. MODERNITY

1. If you lack the power to demoralize yourself along with the age, to go as low and as far, do not complain of being misunderstood by it.

E.M. CIORAN, "SOME BLIND ALLEYS: A LETTER," IN *THE ART OF THE PERSONAL ESSAY* (1994), ED. PHILLIP LOPATE

2. The men who come on the stage at one period are all found to be related to each other. Certain ideas are in the air.

EMERSON, "FATE," *THE CONDUCT OF LIFE* (1860)

3. Let me stand in my age with all its waters flowing round me. If they sometimes subdue, they must finally upbear me, for I seek the universal—and that must be the best.

MARGARET FULLER, *SUMMER ON THE LAKES* (1844), 5

4. Woe to these people who have no appetite for the very dish that their age serves up.

ANDRÉ GIDE, "SECOND IMAGINARY INTERVIEW," *PRETEXTS* (1903)

5. Men are more like the time they live in than they are like their fathers.

ALI IBN-ABI-TALIB, *SENTENCES* (7TH C.), 79, TR. SIMON OCKLEY

6. A man lives not only his personal life, as an individual, but also, consciously or unconsciously, the life of his epoch and his contemporaries.

THOMAS MANN, *THE MAGIC MOUNTAIN* (1924), 2.2, TR. H. T. LOWE-PORTER

7. The man who thinks only of his own generation is born for few.

SENECA, *LETTERS TO LUCILIUS* (1ST C.), 79.17, TR. E. PHILLIPS BARKER

8. All our affirmations are mere matters of chronology; and even our bad taste is nothing more than the bad taste of the age we live in.

LOGAN PEARSALL SMITH, *AFTERTHOUGHTS* (1931), 5

9. A man is wise with the wisdom of his time only, and ignorant with its ignorance. Observe how the greatest minds yield in some degree to the superstitions of their age.

THOREAU, *JOURNAL*, JAN. 31, 1853

10. We are obliged to place ourselves on the level of our age before we can rise above it.

VOLTAIRE, "BUFFOONERY," *PHILOSOPHICAL DICTIONARY* (1764)

185. CONTEMPT

See also 920. SOUR GRAPES

1. There is no fate that cannot be surmounted by scorn.

ALBERT CAMUS, TITLE ESSAY, *THE MYTH OF SISYPHUS* (1942), TR. JUSTIN O'BRIEN

2. Men more quickly learn and more gladly recall what they deride than what they approve and esteem.

HORACE, *EPISTLES* (20–C. 8 B.C.), 2.1

3. There is no being so poor and so contemptible, who does not think there is somebody still poorer, and still more contemptible.

SAMUEL JOHNSON, QUOTED IN BOSWELL'S *LIFE OF SAMUEL JOHNSON*, FEB. 15, 1766

4. If he dropped a pun or a platitude into the conversation, it was just as if he had dropped a plate—there would be a moment of frozen silence, then the talk would go on as before.

MARY MCCARTHY, *THE COMPANY SHE KEEPS* (1942)

5. Moral contempt is a far greater indignity and insult than any kind of crime.

NIETZSCHE, *THE WILL TO POWER* (1888), 740, TR. ANTHONY M. LUDOVICI

6. The great despisers are the great reverers.

NIETZSCHE, "ON THE HIGHER MAN," *THUS SPOKE ZARATHUSTRA* (1883–92), 4, TR. WALTER KAUFMANN

7. Who can refute a sneer?

WILLIAM PALLEY, *PRINCIPLES OF MORAL AND POLITICAL PHILOSOPHY* (1785), V, 2, 5.9

8. Silence is the most perfect expression of scorn.

GEORGE BERNARD SHAW, *BACK TO METHUSELAH* (1921), 5

9. Everything can be borne except contempt.

VOLTAIRE, "PHILOSOPHER," *PHILOSOPHICAL DICTIONARY* (1764)

186. CONTENTMENT

See also 156. COMPLACENCY; 251. DISCONTENT; 409. HAPPINESS; 701. PLAIN LIVING; 845. SATISFACTION; 989. TRANQUILITY

1. Be content with your lot; one cannot be first in everything.

AESOP, "THE PEACOCK AND JUNO," *FABLES* (6TH C. B.C.?), TR. JOSEPH JACOBS

2. I have learned, in whatsoever state I am, therewith to be content

BIBLE, PHILIPPIANS 4:11

3. Content may dwell in all stations. To be low, but above contempt, may be high enough to be happy.

SIR THOMAS BROWNE, *CHRISTIAN MORALS* (1716), 1

4. If you would know contentment, let your deeds be few.

DEMOCRITUS, (5TH–4TH C. B.C.), QUOTED IN MARCUS AURELIUS' *MEDITATIONS* (2ND C. A.D.), 4.24

5. Do not spoil what you have by desiring what you have not; but remember that what you now have was once among the things only hoped for.

EPICURUS, "VATICAN SAYINGS" (3RD C. B.C.), 35, IN *LETTERS, PRINCIPAL DOCTRINES, AND VATICAN SAYINGS*, TR. RUSSEL M. GEER

6. That man is happiest / who lives from day to day and asks no more, / garnering the simple goodness of a life.

EURIPIDES, *HECUBA* (C. 425 B.C.), TR. WILLIAM ARROWSMITH

7. Better a little fire to warm us than a great one to burn us.

THOMAS FULLER, M.D., *GNOMOLOGIA* (1732), 865

8. Fat hens lay few eggs.

GERMAN PROVERB

9. Oh, don't the days seem lank and long, / When all goes right and nothing goes wrong / And isn't your life extremely flat / With nothing whatever to grumble at!

W. S. GILBERT, *PRINCESS IDA* (1884), 3

10. Nothing will content him who is not content with a little.

GREEK PROVERB

11. Let me say this: bein a idiot is no box of chocolates.

WINSTON GROOM, *FORREST GUMP* (1986)

12. Be content with what thou hast received, and smooth thy frowning forehead, for the door of choice is not open either to thee or me.

HĀFIZ, GHAZALS FROM THE *DIVAN* (14TH C.), 12, TR. JUSTIN HUNTLY MCCARTHY

13. He is poor who does not feel content.

JAPANESE PROVERB

14. If you are foolish enough to be contented, don't show it, but grumble with the rest.

JEROME K. JEROME, "ON GETTING ON IN THE WORLD," *THE IDLE THOUGHTS OF AN IDLE FELLOW* (1889)

15. He who is contented is rich.

LAO TZU, *THE CHARACTER OF TAO* (6TH C. B.C.), 33, TR. LIN YUTANG

16. Contentment is a warm sty for the eaters and sleepers.

EUGENE O'NEILL, *MARCO MILLIONS* (1928), 2.2

17. All fortune belongs to him who has a contented mind. Is not the whole earth covered with leather for him whose feet are encased in shoes?

PANCHATANTRA (C. 5TH C.), 2, TR. FRANKLIN EDGERTON

18. If we have youth, beauty, blessed gifts, strength, if we find fame, fortune, favor, fulfillment, it is easy to be nice, to turn a warm heart to the world.

OLIVER SACKS, *A LEG TO STAND ON* (1984)

19. If thou covetest riches, ask not but for contentment, which is an immense treasure.

SA'DI, *GULISTAN* (1258), 2.27, TR. JAMES ROSS

20. My crown is called content; / A crown it is that seldom kings enjoy.

SHAKESPEARE, *3 HENRY VI* (1590–91), 3.1.64

21. Poor and content is rich, and rich enough.

SHAKESPEARE, *OTHELLO* (1604–05), 3.3.172

22. Good friends, good books and a sleepy conscience: this is the ideal life.

MARK TWAIN, *NOTEBOOK (1935)*

23. Well-being is attained by little and little, and nevertheless it is no little thing itself.

ZENO OF CITIUM (C. 300 B.C.), QUOTED IN DIOGENES LAERTIUS' *LIVES AND OPINIONS OF EMINENT PHILOSOPHERS* (3RD C. A.D.), TR. R. D. HICKS

CONTRADICTION

See 464. INCONSISTENCY

187. CONTRAST

See also 153. COMPARISON

1. 'Tis Opposites—entice— / Deformed Men—ponder Grace— / Bright fires—the Blanketless— / The Lost—Day's face— / The Blind—esteem it be / Enough Estate—to see—.

EMILY DICKINSON, POEM (C. 1862)

2. We are so made that we can derive intense enjoyment only from a contrast and very little from a state of things.

SIGMUND FREUD, *CIVILIZATION AND ITS DISCONTENTS* (1930), 2, TR. JAMES STRACHEY

3. It is by disease that health is pleasant; by evil that good is pleasant; by hunger, satiety; by weariness, rest.

HERACLITUS, *FRAGMENTS* (C. 500 B.C.), 99, TR. PHILIP WHEELWRIGHT

4. Sleep, riches, and health, to be truly enjoyed, must be interrupted.

Jean Paul Richter, *Flower, Fruit, and Thorn* (1796–97), 8

CONTROVERSY

See 51. Argument; 252. Discord; 772. Quarreling

CONVALESCENCE

See 896. Sickness

188. CONVERSATION

See also 149. Communication; 543. Listening; 923. Speaking

1. Good-nature is more agreeable in conversation than wit, and gives a certain air to the countenance which is more amiable than beauty.

Joseph Addison, *The Spectator* (1711–12), 169

2. For parlor use the vague generality is a life-saver.

George Ade, "The Wise Piker," *Forty Modern Fables* (1901)

3. Conversation, n. A fair for the display of the minor mental commodities, each exhibitor being too intent upon the arrangement of his own wares to observe those of his neighbor.

Ambrose Bierce, *The Devil's Dictionary* (1881–1911)

4. A conversation is a dialogue, not a monologue. That's why there are so few good conversations: due to scarcity, two intelligent talkers seldom meet.

Truman Capote, *Music for Chameleons* (1980)

5. No discussion between two persons can be of any use, until each knows clearly what it is that the other asserts.

Lewis Carroll, *The Letters of Lewis Carroll*, ed. Morton N. Cohen (1979)

6. Too much agreement kills a chat.

Eldridge Cleaver, "A Day in Folsom Prison," *Soul on Ice* (1968)

7. Talk ought always to run obliquely, not nose to nose with no chance of mental escape.

Frank Moore Colby, "Simple Simon," *The Colby Essays* (1926), v. 1

8. Private, accidental, confidential conversation breeds thought. Clubs produce oftener words.

Emerson, *Journals*, 1836

9. The art of conversation, or the qualification for a good companion, is a certain self-control, which now holds the subject, now lets it go, with a respect for the emergencies of the moment.

Emerson, *Journals* 1854

10. The best of life is conversation, and the greatest success is confidence, or perfect understanding between sincere people.

Emerson, "Behavior," *The Conduct of Life* (1860)

11. Speakers who have grown up in the American community unconsciously know its rules about taking turns in conversations—in the same way that they know the rules of grammar and the rules about appropriate speech in various situations.

Peter Farb, *Word Play* (1973)

12. Very strong personalities must confine themselves in mutual conversation to very gentle subjects.

F. Scott Fitzgerald, *The Crack-Up* (1945)

13. He divides conversation into two categories: when you speak, and when you listen to yourself speak.

John Fowles, *Daniel Martin* (1977)

14. Reading makes a full man, meditation a profound man, discourse a clear man.

Benjamin Franklin, *Poor Richard's Almanack* (1732–57)

15. Never speak of yourself to others; make them talk about themselves instead: therein lies the whole art of pleasing. Everyone knows it and everyone forgets it.

Edmond and Jules de Goncourt, *Idées et sensations* (1866)

16. If to talk to oneself when alone is folly, it must be doubly unwise to listen to oneself in the presence of others.

Baltasar Gracián, *The Art of Worldly Wisdom* (1647), 141, tr. Joseph Jacobs

17. A person who talks with equal vivacity on every subject, excites no interest in any. Repose is as necessary in conversation as in a picture.

William Hazlitt, *Characteristics* (1823)

18. The art of conversation is the art of hearing as well as of being heard.

William Hazlitt, "On the Conversation of Authors," *The Plain Speaker* (1826)

19. That is the happiest conversation where there is no competition, no vanity, but a calm quiet interchange of sentiments.

SAMUEL JOHNSON, QUOTED IN BOSWELL'S *LIFE OF SAMUEL JOHNSON*, APRIL 14, 1775

20. Conversation is not a search after knowledge, but an endeavour at effect.

KEATS, LETTER TO BENJAMIN ROBERT HAYDON, MAY 10–11, 1817

21. The success of conversation consists less in being witty than in bringing out wit in others; the man who leaves after talking with you, pleased with himself and his own wit, is perfectly pleased with you.

LA BRUYÈRE, *CHARACTERS* (1688), 5.16

22. Confidence contributes more to conversation than wit.

LA ROCHEFOUCAULD, *MAXIMS* (1665), TR. KENNETH PRATT

23. To listen closely and reply well is the highest perfection we are able to attain in the art of conversation.

LA ROCHEFOUCAULD, *MAXIMS* (1665), TR. KENNETH PRATT

24. Do you know that conversation is one of the greatest pleasures in life? But it wants leisure.

W. SOMERSET MAUGHAM, "THE FALL OF EDWARD BARNARD," *THE TREMBLING OF A LEAF* (1921)

25. We do not talk—we bludgeon one another with facts and theories gleaned from cursory readings of newspapers, magazines and digests.

HENRY MILLER, "THE SHADOWS," *THE AIR-CONDITIONED NIGHTMARE* (1945)

26. For table-talk, I prefer the pleasant and witty before the learned and the grave; in bed, beauty before goodness.

MONTAIGNE, "OF FRIENDSHIP," *ESSAYS* (1580–88), TR. W. C. HAZLITT

27. True conversation is an interpenetration of worlds, a genuine intercourse of souls, which doesn't have to be self-consciously profound but does have to touch matters of concern to the soul.

THOMAS MOORE, *SOUL MATES* (1994)

28. I withheld a riposte that would have seared him if I had been able to think of it, and followed him into the office.

S.J. PERELMAN, *THE RISING GORGE* (1961)

29. The more the pleasures of the body fade away, the greater to me is the pleasure and charm of conversation.

PLATO, *THE REPUBLIC* (4TH C. B.C.), 1, TR. BENJAMIN JOWETT

30. Wit in conversation is only a readiness of thought and a facility of expression, or (in the midwives' phrase) a quick conception, and an easy delivery.

ALEXANDER POPE, *THOUGHTS ON VARIOUS SUBJECTS* (1727)

31. In a conversation, keep in mind that you're more interested in what you have to say than anyone else is.

ANDREW A. ROONEY, "A PENNY SAVED IS A WASTE OF TIME," *PIECES OF MY MIND* (1984)

32. Whoever interrupts the conversation of others to make a display of his fund of knowledge, makes notorious his own stock of ignorance.

SA'DI, *GULISTAN* (1258), 8.95, TR. JAMES ROSS

33. It is a secret known but to few, yet of no small use in the conduct of life, that when you fall into a man's conversation, the first thing you should consider is, whether he has a greater inclination to hear you, or that you should hear him.

RICHARD STEELE, *THE SPECTATOR* (1711–12), 49

34. It is an impertinent and unreasonable fault in conversation for one man to take up all the discourse.

RICHARD STEELE, *THE SPECTATOR* (1711–12), 428

35. It is a wonderful thing that so many, and they not reckoned absurd, shall entertain those with whom they converse by giving them the history of their pains and aches and imagine such narrations their quota of conversation.

RICHARD STEELE, *THE SPECTATOR* (1711–12),100

36. Is there anything more terrible than a "call"? It affords an occasion for the exchange of the most threadbare commonplaces. Calls and the theatre are the two great centers for the propagation of platitudes.

MIGUEL DE UNAMUNO, *ESSAYS AND SOLILOQUIES* (1924), TR. J. E. CRAWFORD FLITCH

37. The necessity of saying something, the embarrassment produced by the consciousness of having nothing to say, and the desire to exhibit ability, are three things sufficient to render even a great man ridiculous.

VOLTAIRE, "SOCIETY OF LONDON, AND ACADEMIES," *PHILOSOPHICAL DICTIONARY* (1764)

38. That talk must be very well in hand and under great headway, that an anecdote thrown in front of will not pitch off the track and wreck.

CHARLES DUDLEY WARNER, "THIRD STUDY," *BACKLOG STUDIES* (1873)

189. COOKS AND COOKING

See also 274. EATING; 355. FOOD

1. The discovery of a new dish does more for the happiness of mankind than the discovery of a star.

ANTHELME BRILLAT-SAVARIN, *PHYSIOLOGIE DU GOÛT* (1825), 9

2. Cookery has become an art, a noble science; cooks are gentlemen.

ROBERT BURTON, *THE ANATOMY OF MELANCHOLY* (1621), 1.2.2.2

3. God sends meat and the Devil sends cooks.

ENGLISH PROVERB

4. Cooking is like love. It should be entered into with abandon or not at all.

HARRIET VAN HORNE, *VOGUE,* OCT. 15, 1956

5. A good cook is the peculiar gift of the gods. He must be a perfect creature from the brain to the palate, from the palate to the finger's end.

WALTER SAVAGE LANDOR, "ANACREON AND POLYCRATES," *IMAGINARY CONVERSATIONS* (1824–53)

6. Somewhere lives a bad Cajun cook, just as somewhere must live one last ivory-billed woodpecker. For me, I don't expect ever to encounter either one.

WILLIAM LEAST HEAT MOON, *BLUE HIGHWAYS* (1982)

7. Bad cooks—and the utter lack of reason in the kitchen—have delayed human development longest and impaired it most.

NIETZSCHE, *BEYOND GOOD AND EVIL* (1886), 234, TR. WALTER KAUFMANN

8. Let onions lurk within the bowl / And, scarce-suspected, animate the whole

SYDNEY SMITH, "RECIPE FOR SALAD," QUOTED IN LADY S. HOLLAND'S *MEMOIR* (1855), V. 1.11

9. A good cook is a certain slow poisoner, if you are not temperate.

VOLTAIRE, "POISONINGS," *PHILOSOPHICAL DICTIONARY* (1764)

10. The vision of milk and honey, it comes and goes. But the odor of cooking goes on forever.

E.B. WHITE, *ONE MAN'S MEAT* (1944)

COOLNESS

See 142. COLDNESS; 160. COMPOSURE

190. COOPERATION

See also 1016. UNITY

1. Winning wars, after all, is the ultimate test not of the quality of single men but of their capacity to work together and accept common sacrifices.

LUIGI BARZINI, *THE ITALIANS* (1964)

2. Every smallest step of modern industry depends upon a cooperation whose maintenance and regulation is the very stuff of law.

LEARNED HAND, *THE SPIRIT OF LIBERTY* (1959)

COQUETRY

See 351. FLIRTATION

191. CORRUPTION

See also 99. BRIBERY; 307. EVIL; 900. SIN; 934. STEALING; 971. TEMPTATION; 1055. WICKEDNESS

1. If the camel once get his nose in the tent, his body will soon follow.

ARABIC PROVERB

2. Where God hath a temple, the Devil will have a chapel.

ROBERT BURTON, *THE ANATOMY OF MELANCHOLY* (1621), 3.4.1.1

3. Corruption is like a ball of snow: whence once set a-rolling it must increase.

CHARLES CALEB COLTON, *LACON* (1825), 2.6

4. Countries are like fruit-the worms are always inside.

JEAN GIRAUDOUX, *SIEGFRIED* (1928), 1, TR. PETER H. JUDD

5. The scandalous question that hangs over modern government and excites perpetual outrage is about political money and what it buys. What exactly do these contributors get in return for the hundreds of thousands, even millions of dollars they funnel to the politicians?

WILLIAM GREIDER, *WHO WILL TELL THE PEOPLE?* (1992)

6. Public money is like holy water; everyone helps himself to it.

ITALIAN PROVERB

7. No man is worthy of unlimited reliance—his treason, at best, only waits for sufficient temptation.

H. L. MENCKEN, "THE SKEPTIC," *THE SMART SET,* MAY 1919

8. The corruption of the age is made up by the particular contribution of every individual man; some contribute treachery, others injustice, irreligion, tyranny, avarice, cruelty, according to their power.

MONTAIGNE, "OF VANITY," *ESSAYS* (1580–88), TR. W. C. HAZLITT

9. The corruption of every government begins nearly always with that of principles.

MONTESQUIEU, *L'ESPRIT DES LOIS* (1748), 1

10. There is something in corruption which, like a jaundiced eye, transfers the color of itself to the object it looks upon, and sees everything stained and impure.

THOMAS PAINE, *THE AMERICAN CRISIS* (1776–83), 6

11. Corruption wins not more than honesty.

SHAKESPEARE, *HENRY VIII* (1612–13), 3.2.444

12. Lilies that fester smell far worse than weeds.

SHAKESPEARE, *SONNETS* (1609), 94.14

13. There is no odor so bad as that which arises from goodness tainted.

THOREAU, "ECONOMY," *WALDEN* (1854)

14. The first gold star a child gets in school for the mere performance of a needful task is its first lesson in graft.

PHILIP WYLIE, *GENERATION OF VIPERS* (1942), 7

192. COSMETICS

See also 326. FACE; 685. PERFUME

1. Most women are not so young as they are painted.

MAX BEERBOHM, "IN DEFENSE OF COSMETICS" (1922)

2. God hath given you one face, and you make yourselves another.

SHAKESPEARE, *HAMLET* (1600), 3.1.149

193. COSMOPOLITANISM

See also 498. INTERNATIONAL RELATIONS; 917. SOPHISTICATION

1. I am a citizen of the world.

DIOGENES THE CYNIC (4TH C. B.C.), QUOTED IN DIOGENES LAERTIUS' *LIVES AND OPINIONS OF EMINENT PHILOSOPHERS* (3RD C. A.D.), TR. R. D. HICKS

2. To be really cosmopolitan, a man must be at home even in his own country.

THOMAS WENTWORTH HIGGINSON, "HENRY JAMES," *SHORT STUDIES OF AMERICAN AUTHORS* (1906)

3. A man's feet must be planted in his country, but his eyes should survey the world.

GEORGE SANTAYANA, *THE LIFE OF REASON: REASON IN SOCIETY* (1905–06), 7

4. That man's the best cosmopolite / Who loves his native country best.

LORD TENNYSON, "HANDS ALL ROUND" (1885)

COST

See 1026. VALUE

COUNSEL

See 19. ADVICE

194. THE COUNTRY

See also 131. CITIES; 337. FARMS AND FARMING; 352. FLOWERS; 371. GARDENING; 944. SUBURBS

1. To sit in the shade on a fine day and look upon verdure is the most perfect refreshment.

JANE AUSTEN, *MANSFIELD PARK* (1814), 9

2. It is only in the country that we can get to know a person or a book.

CYRIL CONNOLLY, *THE UNQUIET GRAVE* (1945), 3

3. I want a horse and plough,/Chickens too,/Just one cow,/With a wistful moo.

NOËL COWARD, "WORLD WEARY," *THIS YEAR OF GRACE* (1928)

4. God made the country, and man made the town.

WILLIAM COWPER, "THE SOFA," *THE TASK* (1785), 749

5. Nor rural sights alone, but rural sounds, / Exhilarate the spirit, and restore / The tone of languid Nature.

WILLIAM COWPER, "THE SOFA," *THE TASK* (1785), 182

6. The city has a face, the country a soul.

JACQUES DE LACRETELLE, "LES PAYSAGES HÉRITÉS," *IDÉES DANS UN CHAPEAU* (1946)

7. The lowest and vilest alleys of London do not present a more dreadful record of sin than does the smiling and beautiful countryside.

SIR ARTHUR CONAN DOYLE, "COPPER BEECHES," *THE ADVENTURES OF SHERLOCK HOLMES* (1891)

8. I lived in solitude in the country and noticed how the monotony of a quiet life stimulates the creative mind.

EINSTEIN, *OUT OF MY LATER YEARS* (1950), 24

9. A man's soul may be buried and perish under a dungheap or in a furrow of the field, just as well as under a pile of money.

NATHANIEL HAWTHORNE, *JOURNALS*, JUNE 1, 1841

10. The good thing about the country is ... that we don't have there any bad weather at all—only a number of different kinds of good.

JOSEPH WOOD KRUTCH, "JUNE," *THE TWELVE SEASONS* (1949)

11. A man must be of a very quiet and happy nature, who can long endure the country; and, moreover, very well contented with his own insignificant person.

LONGFELLOW, *HYPERION* (1839), 2.10

12. Why one day in the country / Is worth a month in town; / Is worth a day and a year / Of the dusty, musty, lag-last fashion / That days drone elsewhere.

CHRISTINA ROSSETTI, "SUMMER" (1862)

13. I have no relish for the country; it is a kind of healthy grave.

SYDNEY SMITH, LETTER TO MISS G. HARCOURT, 1838

14. The country has its charms—cheapness for one.

ROBERT SMITH SURTEES, *HILLINGDON HILL* (1845), 5

195. COURAGE

See also 92. BOLDNESS; 199. COWARDICE; 239. DESPAIR; 343. FEAR; 940. STRENGTH; 980. TIMIDITY

1. It is easy to be brave from a safe distance.

AESOP, "THE WOLF AND THE KID," *FABLES* (6TH C. B.C.?), TR. JOSEPH JACOBS

2. Until the day of his death, no man can be sure of his courage.

JEAN ANOUILH, *BECKET* (1959), 1

3. All bravery stands upon comparisons.

FRANCIS BACON, "OF VAIN-GLORY," *ESSAYS* (1625)

4. Courage is the thing. All goes if courage goes.

J. M. BARRIE, RECTORIAL ADDRESS, ST. ANDREW'S, MAY 3, 1922

5. It is a brave act of valour to contemn [despise] death; but where life is more terrible than death, it is then the truest valour to dare to live.

SIR THOMAS BROWNE, *RELIGIO MEDICI* (1642), 1

6. Valour lies just half way between rashness and cowheartedness.

CERVANTES, *DON QUIXOTE* (1605–15), 2.3.4, TR. JOHN OZELL

7. The paradox of courage is that a man must be a little careless of his life even in order to keep it.

G. K. CHESTERTON, "THE METHUSELAHITE," *ALL THINGS CONSIDERED* (1908)

8. Between cowardice and despair, valour is gendred.

JOHN DONNE, *PARADOXES, PROBLEMS, AND ESSAYS* (1633), 3

9. None but the brave deserves the fair.

JOHN DRYDEN, "ALEXANDER'S FEAST" (1687), 15

10. Every man has his own courage, and is betrayed because he seeks in himself the courage of other persons.

EMERSON, *JOURNALS*, 1847

11. A coward turns away but a brave man's choice / Is danger.

EURIPIDES, *IPHIGENIA IN TAURIS* (C. 414–12 B.C.), TR. WITTER BYNNER

12. This is courage in a man: / to bear unflinchingly what heaven sends.

EURIPIDES, *HERACLES* (C. 422 B.C.), TR. WILLIAM ARROWSMITH

13. Without justice, courage is weak.

BENJAMIN FRANKLIN, *POOR RICHARD'S ALMANACK* (1732–57)

14. Life only demands from you the strength you possess. Only one feat is possible—not to have run away.

DAG HAMMARSKJÖLD, "1925–1930," *MARKINGS* (1964), TR. W. H. AUDEN

15. People with courage and character always seem sinister to the rest.

HERMANN HESSE, *DEMIAN* (1919), 2, TR. MICHAEL LEBECK

16. A nation which has forgotten the quality of courage which in the past has been brought to public life is not as likely to insist upon or reward that quality in its chosen leaders today—and in fact we have forgotten.

JOHN F. KENNEDY, *PROFILES IN COURAGE* (1956)

17. Love of fame, fear of disgrace, schemes for advancement, desire to make life comfortable and pleasant, and the urge to humiliate others are often at the root of the valour men hold in such high esteem.

LA ROCHEFOUCAULD, *MAXIMS* (1665)

18. No one can answer for his courage when he has never been in danger.

LA ROCHEFOUCAULD, *MAXIMS* (1665), TR. KENNETH PRATT

19. Perfect valour consists in doing without witnesses that which we would be capable of doing before everyone.

La Rochefoucauld, *Maxims* (1665), tr. Kenneth Pratt

20. Hidden valor is as bad as cowardice.

Latin Proverb

21. There are few men who know how to go to their deaths with dignity, and often they are not those whom one would expect.

Primo Levi, *Survival in Auschwitz* (1959)

22. Tough guys don't dance. You had better believe it.

Norman Mailer, *Tough Guys Don't Dance* (1984)

23. His [Gen. Douglas MacArthur's] twenty-two medals—thirteen of them for heroism—probably exceeded those of any other figure in American history. He seemed to seek death on battlefields.

William Manchester, *American Caesar* (1978)

24. Courage is not a virtue or value among other personal values like love or fidelity. It is the foundation that underlies and gives reality to all other virtues and personal values.

Rollo May, *The Courage to Create* (1975)

25. Courage is like love; it must have hope for nourishment.

Napoleon I, *Maxims* (1804–15)

26. Everyone becomes brave when he observes one who despairs.

Nietzsche, "The Welcome," *Thus Spoke Zarathustra* (1883–92), 4, tr. Walter Kaufmann

27. Courage is a kind of salvation.

Plato, *The Republic* (4th c. B.C.), 4, tr. Benjamin Jowett

28. That man is not truly brave who is afraid either to seem to be, or to be, when it suits him, a coward.

Edgar Allan Poe, *Marginalia* (1844–49), 8

29. That is at bottom the only courage demanded of us: to have courage for the most strange, the most singular and the most inexplicable that we may encounter.

Rainer Maria Rilke, *Letters to a Young Poet,* Aug. 12, 1904, tr. M. D. Herter Norton

30. Courage does not always march to airs blown by a bugle: is not always wrought out of the fabric ostentation wears.

Frances Rodman, "For a Six-Year-Old," *The New York Times,* May 13, 1961

31. Valor is a gift. Those having it never know for sure whether they have it till the test comes. And those having it in one test never know for sure if they will have it when the next test comes.

Carl Sandburg, news reports, Dec. 14, 1954

32. Life without the courage for death is slavery.

Seneca, *Letters to Lucilius* (1st c.), 77.15, tr. E. Phillips Barker

33. Sometimes even to live is an act of courage.

Seneca, *Letters to Lucilius* (1st c.), 78.3, tr. E. Phillips Barker

34. Courage mounteth with occasion.

Shakespeare, *King John* (1596–97), 2.1.82

35. It is courage, courage, courage, that raises the blood of life to crimson splendor.

George Bernard Shaw, *Back to Methuselah* (1921), 1.2

36. They are surely to be esteemed the bravest spirits who, having the clearest sense of both the pains and pleasures of life, do not on that account shrink from danger.

Thucydides, *The Peloponnesian War* (c. 400 B.C.), 2.40, tr. Benjamin Jowett

37. If wisdom in government eludes us, perhaps courage could substitute—the moral courage to terminate mistakes.

Barbara W. Tuchman, "If Mao Had Come to Washington in 1945," *Notes From China* (1972)

38. Courage is resistance to fear, mastery of fear-not absence of fear. Except a creature be part coward it is not a compliment to say it is brave.

Mark Twain, "Pudd'nhead Wilson's Calendar," *Pudd'nhead Wilson* (1894), 12

196. COURT, ROYAL

See also 520. Kings; 829. Royalty

1. The two maxims of any great man at court are, always to keep his countenance, and never to keep his word.

Jonathan Swift, *Thoughts on Various Subjects* (1711)

COURT OF LAW

See 517. Justice; 528. Law and Lawyers

197. COURTESY

See also 114. Ceremony; 378. Gentleman; 391. Good Breeding; 563. Manners; 749. Propriety; 830. Rudeness

1. Politeness, n. The most acceptable hypocrisy.

Ambrose Bierce, *The Devil's Dictionary* (1881–1911)

2. Courtesy is the due of man to man; not of suit-of-clothes to suit-of-clothes.

Thomas Carlyle, "Corn-Law Rhymes" (1832)

3. It is wise to apply the oil of refined politeness to the mechanism of friendship.

Colette, "The Pure and the Impure," *Earthly Paradise* (1966), 5

4. Many of our newly smart would rather be found murdering their children than being kind to their parents. They would prefer to be damned for rudeness than to be snickered at for courtesy.

Irwin Edman, "How to Be Sweet Though Sophisticated," in *Fifty Great Essays* (1964)

5. We must be as courteous to a man as we are to a picture, which we are willing to give the advantage of a good light.

Emerson, "Behavior," *The Conduct of Life* (1860)

6. All doors open to courtesy.

Thomas Fuller, M.D., *Gnomologia* (1732), 512

7. There is a courtesy of the heart. It is akin to love. Out of it arises the purest courtesy in the outward behavior.

Goethe, *Elective Affinities* (1809), 23

8. Courtesy is the politic witchery of great personages.

Baltasar Gracián,, *The Art of Worldly Wisdom* (1647), 40, tr. Joseph Jacobs

9. In truth, politeness is artificial good humor, it covers the natural want of it, and ends by rendering habitual a substitute nearly equivalent to the real virtue.

Thomas Jefferson, letter to Thomas Jefferson Randolph, Nov. 24, 1808

10. There can be no defence like elaborate courtesy.

E. V. Lucas, *Reading, Writing, and Remembering* (1932)

11. The knowledge of courtesy and good manners is a very necessary study. It is, like grace and beauty, that which begets liking and an inclination to love one another at the first sight.

Montaigne, "The ceremony of the interview of princes," *Essays* (1580–88), tr. W. C. Hazlitt

12. Politeness is to human nature what warmth is to wax.

Schopenhauer, "The Wisdom of Life," *Parerga and Paralipomena* (1851)

13. The greater man the greater courtesy.

Lord Tennyson, "The Last Tournament," *Idylls of the King* (1871)

198. COURTSHIP

See also 351. Flirtation; 551. Love; 564. Marriage; 826. Romance; 857. Seduction

1. Those marriages generally abound most with love and constancy that are preceded by a long courtship. The passion should strike root and gather strength before marriage be grafted on it.

Joseph Addison, *The Spectator* (1711–12), 261

2. A man running after a hat is not half so ridiculous as a man running after a wife.

G.K. Chesterton, "On Running After One's Hat," in *The Art of the Personal Essay* (1994), ed. Phillip Lopate

3. If you cannot inspire a woman with love of you, fill her above the brim with love of herself—all that runs over will be yours.

Charles Caleb Colton, *Lacon* (1825), 2.89

4. Courtship to marriage is as a very witty prologue to a very dull play.

William Congreve, *The Old Bachelor* (1693), 5.4

5. Either you have a rival or you don't. If you have one, you must please in order to be preferred to him, and if you don't you must still please—in order to avoid having one.

Pierre Choderlos De Laclos, Letter 152, *Les Liaisons dangereuses* (1782)

6. Let men tremble to win the hand of woman, unless thy win along with it the utmost passion of her heart!

Nathaniel Hawthorne, *The Scarlet Letter* (1850), 15

7. Do not let any sweet-talking woman beguile your good sense / with the fascinations of her shape. It's your barn she's after.

Hesiod, *Works and Days* (8th c. b.c.), 373, tr. Richmond Lattimore

8. A woman might as well propose: her husband will claim she did.

Edgar Watson Howe, *Country Town Sayings* (1911)

9. Men are always doomed to be duped, not so much by the arts of the [other] sex as by their own imaginations. They are always wooing goddesses, and marrying mere mortals.

WASHINGTON IRVING, "WIVES," *BRACEBRIDGE HALL* (1822)

10. In England the boy pats his adored one on the back and says softly, "I don't object, you know." If he is quite mad with passion, he may add: "I rather fancy you, in fact."

GEORGE MIKES, *HOW TO BE AN ALIEN* (1946)

11. When once the young heart of a maiden is stolen, / The maiden herself will steal after it soon.

THOMAS MOORE, "OMENS," *IRISH MELODIES* (1807–35)

12. Sexual behavior in our species goes through three characteristic phases: pair formation, precopulatory activity, and copulation, usually but not always in that order. The pair-formation stage, usually referred to as courtship, is remarkably prolonged by animal standards.

DESMOND MORRIS, *THE NAKED APE* (1967)

13. I flee who chases me, and chase who flees me.

OVID, *THE LOVES* (C. A.D. 8), 2.19, TR. J. LEWIS MAY

14. This swift business / I must uneasy make, lest too light winning / Make the prize light.

SHAKESPEARE, *THE TEMPEST* (1611–12), 1.2.450

199. COWARDICE

See also 195. COURAGE; 300. ESCAPE; 304. EVASION; 343. FEAR; 980. TIMIDITY

1. There was no room in God's army for the coward heart, no crown awaiting him who put mother or father, sister or brother, sweetheart or friend above God's will. Let the church cry amen to this!

JAMES BALDWIN, *GO TELL IT ON THE MOUNTAIN* (1953)

2. Cowards never use their might, / But against such as will not fight.

SAMUEL BUTLER (D. 1680), *HUDIBRAS* (1663), 1.3

3. That cowardice is incorrigible which the love of power cannot overcome.

CHARLES CALEB COLTON, *LACON* (1825), 1.44

4. No man gains credit for his cowardly courtesies.

EMERSON, *JOURNALS*, 1832

5. Many would be cowards if they had courage enough.

THOMAS FULLER, M.D., *GNOMOLOGIA* (1732), 3366

6. Between two cowards, he has the advantage who first detects the other.

ITALIAN PROVERB

7. The most mortifying infirmity in human nature, to feel in ourselves, or to contemplate in another, is, perhaps, cowardice.

CHARLES LAMB, "STAGE ILLUSION," *LAST ESSAYS OF ELIA* (1833)

8. Perfect courage and utter cowardice are two extremes which rarely occur.

LA ROCHEFOUCAULD, *MAXIMS* (1655), TR. KENNETH PRATT

9. Let us be wary of ready-made ideas about cowardice and courage: the same burden weighs infinitely more heavily on some shoulders than on others.

FRANÇOIS MAURIAC, "SOLITUDE DURING THE WAR," *SECOND THOUGHTS* (1961), TR. ADRIENNE FOULKE

10. Cowards die many times before their deaths; / The valiant never taste of death but once.

SHAKESPEARE, *JULIUS CAESAR* (1599–1600), 2.2.32

11. The human race is a race of cowards: and I am not only marching in that procession but carrying a banner.

MARK TWAIN, "REFLECTIONS ON BEING THE DELIGHT OF GOD," *MARK TWAIN IN ERUPTION* (1940), ED. BERNARD DE VOTO

200. CRAFTINESS

See also 139. CLEVERNESS; 165. CONCEALMENT; 943. SUBTLETY

1. With foxes we must play the fox.

THOMAS FULLER, M.D., *GNOMOLOGIA* (1732), 5797

2. Every man wishes to be wise, and they who cannot be wise are almost always cunning.

SAMUEL JOHNSON, *THE IDLER* (1758–60), 92

3. A man has made great progress in cunning when he does not seem too clever to others.

LA BRUYÈRE, *CHARACTERS* (1688), 8.85

4. There is great ability in knowing how to conceal one's ability.

LA ROCHEFOUCAULD, *MAXIMS* (1665)

5. If men are only shrewd enough, they may even serve kings, eat poison, and dally with women.

PANCHATANTRA (C. 5TH C.), 1, TR. FRANKLIN EDGERTON

6. The fox knows many tricks, but the hedgehog's one trick is the best of all.

ATTRIBUTED BY ZENOBIUS TO PIGRES, *MARGITES* (6TH C. B.C.?)

7. He can best avoid a snare who knows how to set one.

PUBLILIUS SYRUS, *MORAL SAYINGS* (1ST C. B.C.), 573, TR. DARIUS LYMAN

201. CREATION AND CREATIVITY

See also 53. ART AND ARTISTS; 241. DESTRUCTION; 485. INSPIRATION; 708. POETRY AND POETS; 872. SELF-EXPRESSION; 1069. WRITING AND WRITERS

1. The saving grace of all really great gifts is that the persons who bear their burden remain superior to what they have done, at least as long as the source of creativity is alive.

HANNAH ARENDT, "ACTION," *THE HUMAN CONDITION* (1958)

2. The noblest works and foundations have proceeded from childless men, which have sought to express the images of their minds, where those of their bodies have failed.

FRANCIS BACON, "OF PARENTS AND CHILDREN," *ESSAYS* (1625)

3. The creative person is both more primitive and more cultivated, more destructive, a lot madder and a lot saner, than the average person.

FRANK BARRON, *THINK,* NOVEMBER–DECEMBER 1962

4. The history of creation is but a succession of battles between amateurs of genius—inspired heretics—and orthodox professionals.

JACQUES BARZUN, "THE INDISPENSABLE AMATEUR," *CRITICAL QUESTIONS* (1982)

5. In the end, like the Almighty Himself, we make everything in our image, for want of a more reliable model; our artifacts tell more about ourselves than our confessions.

JOSEPH BRODSKY, *WATERMARK* (1992)

6. God was satisfied with his own work, and that is fatal.

SAMUEL BUTLER (D. 1902), *NOTE-BOOKS* (1912)

7. For good and evil, man is a free creative spirit. This produces the very queer world we live in, a world in continous creation and therefore continuous change and insecurity.

JOYCE CARY, INTERVIEW, *WRITERS AT WORK: FIRST SERIES* (1958)

8. What was any art but a mold in which to imprison for a moment the shining elusive element which is life itself—life hurrying past us and running away, too strong to stop, too sweet to lose.

WILLA CATHER, *THE SONG OF THE LARK* (1915)

9. Every production must resemble its author.

CERVANTES, AUTHOR'S PREFACE, *DON QUIXOTE* (1605–15), TR. JOHN OZELL

10. With the offspring of genius, the law of parturition is reversed: the throes are in the conception, the pleasure in the birth.

CHARLES CALEB COLTON, *LACON* (1825), 2.17

11. Our inventions mirror our secret wishes.

LAWRENCE DURRELL, *MOUNTOLIVE* (1959), 7

12. Nature is a rag merchant, who works up every shred and ort and end into new creations.

EMERSON, "CONSIDERATIONS BY THE WAY," *THE CONDUCT OF LIFE* (1860)

13. Creative minds always have been known to survive any kind of bad training.

ANNA FREUD, 1968 ANNUAL FREUD LECTURE TO NEW YORK PSYCHOANALYTIC SOCIETY

14. Man unites himself with the world in the process of creation.

ERICH FROMM, *THE ART OF LOVING* (1956), 2

15. Man's main task in life is to give birth to himself.

ERICK FROMM, *MAN FOR HIMSELF* (1947), 4

16. The would-bees take their honey from the flowers of creation.

HERBERT GOLD, "UPPER BOHEMIA IN AMERICA," *BOHEMIA* (1993)

17. All men are creative but few are artists.

PAUL GOODMAN, *GROWING UP ABSURD* (1960), 9.3

18. Had Shakespeare listened to the news of Duncan's death in a tavern or heard the knocking on his own bedroom door after he had finished the writing of *Macbeth?*

GRAHAM GREENE (1958), *OUR MAN IN HAVANA*

19. The most gifted members of the human species are at their creative best when they cannot have their way.

ERIC HOFFER, *THE ORDEAL OF CHANGE* (1964), 6

20. Man, like Deity, creates in his own image.

ELBERT HUBBARD, *THE NOTE BOOK* (1927)

21. Human salvation lies in the hands of the creatively maladjusted.

MARTIN LUTHER KING, JR., *STRENGTH TO LOVE* (1963), 2.3

22. I like the fact that in ancient Chinese art the great painters always included a deliberate flaw in their work: human creation is never perfect.

MADELEINE L'ENGLE, *A CIRCLE OF QUIET* (1972)

23. Let a human being throw the energies of his soul into the making of something, and the instinct of workmanship will take care of his honesty.

WALTER LIPPMANN, "THE CHANGING FOCUS," *A PREFACE TO POLITICS* (1914)

24. I see the creative accomplishments of which highly gifted humans are capable as special cases of the universal creative process, that game played by everyone against everyone else, from which wells up all that has never been before.

KONRAD LORENZ, *THE WANING OF HUMANENESS* (1983), TR. ROBERT WARREN KICKER

25. I *believe* that both art and the human striving for cognitive comprehension are manifest forms of the grand game in which nothing more is stipulated than the game's rules; both art and actively solicited perceptions are but special cases of the recurring creative act to which we owe our existence.

KONRAD LORENZ, *THE WANING OF HUMANENESS* (1983), TR. ROBERT WARREN KICKER, 3

26. In creating, the only hard thing's to begin; / A grass blade's no easier to make than an oak.

JAMES RUSSELL LOWELL, *A FABLE FOR CRITICS* (1848)

27. Generalization is necessary to the advancement of knowledge; but particularity is indispensable to the creations of the imagination.

THOMAS BABINGTON MACAULAY, "MILTON" (1825)

28. One must die to life in order to be utterly a creator.

THOMAS MANN, "TONIO KRÖGER" (1903), *DEATH IN VENICE*, TR. H. T. LOWE-PORTER

29. The artist produces for the liberation of his soul. It is his nature to create as it is the nature of water to run down hill.

W. SOMERSET MAUGHAM, *THE SUMMING UP* (1938), 49

30. Creativity is not merely the innocent spontaneity of our youth and childhood; it must also be married to the passion of the adult human being, which is a passion to live beyond one's death.

ROLLO MAY, *THE COURAGE TO CREATE* (1975)

31. What Kierkegaard said about love is also true of creativity: every person must start at the beginning.

ROLLO MAY, *THE COURAGE TO CREATE* (1975)

32. We live at a time when man believes himself fabulously capable of creation, but he does not know what to create.

JOSÉ ORTEGA Y GASSET, *THE REVOLT OF THE MASSES* (1930), 4

33. In life it is more necessary to lose than to gain. A seed will only germinate if it dies.

BORIS PASTERNAK, *I REMEMBER* (1959)

34. I will work out the divinity that is busy within my mind / and tend the means that are mine.

PINDAR, *ODES* (5TH C. B.C.), PYTHIA 3, TR. RICHMOND LATTIMORE

35. He who does not know how to create should not know.

ANTONIO PORCHIA, *VOCES* (1968), TR. W. S. MERWIN

36. Creativity is a by-product of hard work. If I never have another really new idea, it won't matter.

ANDREW A. ROONEY, "PREFACE," *PIECES OF MY MIND* (1984)

37. The artist finds a greater pleasure in painting than in having completed the picture.

SENECA, *LETTERS TO LUCILIUS* (1ST C.), 9.7, TR. E. PHILLIPS BARKER

38. If I bind the future I bind my will. If I bind my will I strangle creation.

GEORGE BERNARD SHAW, *BACK TO METHUSELAH* (1921), 1.1

39. A creative artist works on his next composition because he was not satisfied with his previous one.

DMITRI SHOSTAKOVICH, *THE NEW YORK TIMES*, OCT. 25, 1959

40. Three hours of writing require twenty hours of preparation. Luckily I have learned to dream about the work, which saves me some working time.

JOHN STEINBECK, *STEINBECK: A LIFE IN LETTERS*. EDS. ELAINE STEINBECK AND ROBERT WALLSTEN (1975)

41. In order to create there must be a dynamic force, and what force is more potent than love?

IGOR STRAVINSKY, *AN AUTOBIOGRAPHY* (1936), 5

42. There is a great gulf between the really creative person and normal people. The totally creative person does not have the rest of his life in proper proportion.

CAITLIN THOMAS, *CAITLIN* (1986), WITH GEORGE TREMLETT

43. The art of creation / is older than the art of killing.

ANDREY VOZNESENSKY, "POEM WITH A FOOTNOTE," *THE NEW YORK TIMES BOOK REVIEW*, MAY 19, 1967

44. The market kills more artistic passion than anything else.

Robert James Waller, *The Bridges of Madison County* (1992)

45. Shakespeare might have met Rosencrantz and Guildenstern in the white streets of London, or seen the serving-men of rival houses bite their thumbs at each other in the open square: but Hamlet came out of his soul, and Romeo out of his passion.

Oscar Wilde, *The Artist as Critic: The Critical Writings of Oscar Wilde* (1969), ed. Richard Ellmann

46. The imagination imitates. It is the critical spirit that creates.

Oscar Wilde, *Intentions* (1891)

202. CREDULITY

See also 78. Belief; 618. Naïveté; 955. Surprise; 1063. Wonder

1. People everywhere enjoy believing things that they know are not true. It spares them the ordeal of thinking for themselves and taking responsibility for what they know.

Brooks Atkinson, "February 2," *Once Around the Sun* (1951)

2. The most imaginative people are the most credulous, for to them everything is possible.

Alexander Chase, *Perspectives* (1966)

3. Precisely in proportion to our own intellectual weakness will be our credulity as to those mysterious powers assumed by others.

Charles Caleb Colton, *Lacon* (1825), 2.86

4. Our credulity is greatest concerning the things we know least about. And since we know least about ourselves, we are ready to believe all that is said about us. Hence the mysterious power of both flattery and calumny.

Eric Hoffer, *The Passionate State of Mind* (1955)

5. Each believes easily what he fears and what he desires.

La Fontaine, "The Wolf and the Fox," *Fables* (1668–94)

6. Credulity is the man's weakness, but the child's strength.

Charles Lamb, "Witches, and Other Night-Fears," *Essays of Elia* (1823)

7. There is no crime in the cynical American calendar more humiliating than to be a sucker.

Max Lerner, "How Grateful Should Europe Be?" *Actions and Passions* (1949)

8. People can be induced to swallow anything, provided it is sufficiently seasoned with praise.

Molière, *The Miser* (1668), 1, tr. John Wood

203. CREEDS

See also 264. Dogmatism; 330. Faith; 445. Ideology; 797. Religion

1. There lies at the back of every creed something terrible and hard for which the worshipper may one day be required to suffer.

E. M. Forster, "What I Believe," *Two Cheers for Democracy* (1951)

2. It is only in the lonely emergencies of life that our creed is tested: then routine maxims fail, and we fall back on our gods.

William James, "The Sentiment of Rationality," *The Will to Believe* (1896)

3. There is no doctrine will do good where nature is wanting.

Ben Jonson, "Of the Diversity of Wits," *Timber* (1640)

4. I know that a creed is the shell of a lie.

Amy Lowell, "Evelyn Ray," *What's O'Clock* (1925)

204. CRIME

See also 307. Evil; 448. Illegality; 518. Killing; 900. Sin; 934. Stealing; 1030. Vice; 1070. Wrongdoing

1. Expulsion and genocide, though both are international offenses, must remain distinct; the former is an offense against fellow-nations, whereas the latter is an attack upon human diversity as such, that is, upon a characteristic of the "human status" without which the very words "mankind" or "humanity" would be devoid of meaning.

Hannah Arendt, *Eichmann in Jerusalem* (1963)

2. There exists among the intolerably degraded the perverse and powerful desire to force into the arena of the actual those fantastic crimes of which they have been accused, achieving their vengeance and their own destruction through making the nightmare real.

James Baldwin, "Many Thousands Gone" (1951), *Notes of a Native Son* (1955)

3. If the people would but analyze the human equation of a prison they might better account for the crimes that are visited upon them in cities, towns, and hamlets, ofttimes by men who graduated with an education and equipment for just that sort of retributive service from some penal institution.

Eugene V. Debs, *Walls and Bars* (1927)

4. The great thieves lead away the little thief.

Diogenes The Cynic (4th c. B.C.), quoted in Diogenes Laertius' *Lives and Opinions of Eminent Philosophers* (3rd c. A.D.), tr. R. D. Hicks

5. The chief problem in any community cursed with crime is not the punishment of the criminals, but the preventing of the young from being trained to crime.

W. E. B. Du Bois, *The Souls of Black Folk* (1903), 9

6. The more featureless and commonplace a crime is, the more difficult it is to bring it home.

Sir Arthur Conan Doyle, "The Boscombe Valley Mystery," *The Adventures of Sherlock Holmes* (1891)

7. Commit a crime, and the earth is made of glass. There is no such thing as concealment.

Emerson, "Compensation," *Essays: First Series* (1841)

8. Juvenile delinquency serves many purposes, including that of providing sadistic adults with fantasies suited to their special tastes.

Edgar Z. Friedenberg, "The Impact of the School," *The Vanishing Adolescent* (1959)

9. He who holds the ladder is as bad as the thief.

German Proverb

10. When a felon's not engaged in his employment, / Or maturing his felonious little plans, / His capacity for innocent enjoyment / Is just as great as any honest man's.

W. S. Gilbert, *The Pirates of Penzance* (1879), 2

11. it takes all sorts of / people to make an / underworld.

Don Marquis, "mehitabel again," *Archy's Life of Mehitabel* (1933)

12. Collective crimes incriminate no one.

Napoleon I, *Maxims* (1804–15)

13. [I]n rural areas the majority of the victims of violent crime know their assailants (indeed, are probably married to them); in cities, the killer and the mugger come out of the anonymous dark, their faces unrecognized, their motives obscure.

Jonathan Raban, *Soft City* (1974)

14. Great crimes come never singly; they are linked / To sins that went before.

Racine, *Phaedra* (1677), 4, tr. Robert Henderson

15. Most men only commit great crimes because of their scruples about petty ones.

Cardinal de Retz, *Mémoires* (1718)

16. Crime is a logical extension of the sort of behavior that is often considered perfectly respectable in legitimate business.

Robert Rice, *The Business of Crime* (1956)

17. Successful and fortunate crime is called virtue.

Seneca, *Hercules Furens* (1st c.), 255

18. Between the acting of a dreadful thing / And the first motion, all the interim is / Like a phantasma or a hideous dream. / The genius and the mortal instruments / Are then in council, and the state of man, / Like to a little kingdom, suffers then / The nature of an insurrection.

Shakespeare, *Julius Caesar* (1599–1600), 2.1.63

19. Fear succeeds crime—it is its punishment.

Voltaire, *Sémiramis* (1748), 5.1

20. The faculties for getting into jail seem to be ample. We want more organizations for keeping people out.

Charles Dudley Warner, "Eighth Study," *Backlog Studies* (1873)

21. The criminal is not alone when he returns to the scene of the crime; he is joined there by his victim, and both are driven by the same curiosity: to relive that moment which stamped past and future for each.

Elie Wiesel, *Legends of Our Times* (1968)

205. CRISES

See also 17. Adversity

1. No blare of trumpets announces a modern crisis. In these matter-of-fact times, a telephone call will do.

Elie Abel, *The Missile Crisis* (1966)

2. I can still hear my mother wailing over some new kitchen crisis, "Oh God," and my father answering cozily from the silo, "Were you calling me, dear?"

Peter De Vries, *Comfort Me With Apples* (1956)

3. We learn geology the morning after the earthquake.

Emerson, "Considerations by the Way," *The Conduct of Life* (1860)

4. Great crises produce great men and great deeds of courage.

JOHN F. KENNEDY, *PROFILES IN COURAGE* (1956)

5. When written in Chinese, the word "crisis" is composed of two characters—one represents danger and the other represents opportunity.

JOHN F. KENNEDY, ADDRESS, UNITED NEGRO COLLEGE FUND CONVOCATION, INDIANAPOLIS, IND., APRIL 12, 1959

6. I don't see America as a mainland, but as a sea, a big ocean. Sometimes a storm arises, a formidable current develops, and it seems it will engulf everything. Wait a moment, another current will appear and bring the first one to naught.

JACQUES MARITAIN, *REFLECTIONS ON AMERICA* (1958), 4

7. Nationwide thinking, nationwide planning and nationwide action are the three great essentials to prevent nationwide crises for future generations to struggle through.

FRANKLIN D. ROOSEVELT, SPEECH, NEW YORK CITY, APRIL 25, 1936

206. CRITICISM

See also 5. ACCUSATION; 207. CRITICISM, PROFESSIONAL; 342. FAULTS; 515. JUDGING OTHERS; 803. REPROOF; 863. SELF-CRITICISM

1. The blow of a whip raises a welt, but a blow of the tongue crushes bones.

APOCRYPHA, ECCLESIASTICUS 28:17

2. No man can tell another his faults so as to benefit him, unless he loves him.

HENRY WARD BEECHER, *PROVERBS FROM PLYMOUTH PULPIT* (1887)

3. Judge not, that ye be not judged.

BIBLE, MATTHEW 7:1

4. Wherein thou judgest another, thou condemnest thyself.

BIBLE, ROMANS 2:1

5. If a man is devout, we accuse him of hypocrisy; if he is not, of impiety; if he is humble, we look on his humility as a weakness; if he is generous, we call his courage pride.

LOUIS BOURDALOUE, "SUR LE JUGEMENT TÉMÉRAIRE" (1822–26)

6. I do not resent criticism, even when, for the sake of emphasis, it parts for the time with reality.

SIR WINSTON CHURCHILL, SPEECH, HOUSE OF COMMONS, JAN. 22, 1941

7. Never join with your friend when he abuses his horse or his wife, unless the one is about to be sold, and the other to be buried.

CHARLES CALEB COLTON, *LACON* (1825), 1.376

8. It is much easier to be critical than to be correct.

BENJAMIN DISRAELI, SPEECH, JAN. 24, 1860

9. Criticism should not be querulous and wasting, all knife and root-puller, but guiding, instructive, inspiring, a south wind, not an east wind.

EMERSON, *JOURNALS*, 1847

10. It is easier to discover a deficiency in individuals, in states, and in Providence, than to see their real import and value.

HEGEL, INTRODUCTION TO *PHILOSOPHY OF HISTORY* (1832), TR. JOHN SIBREE

11. There is so much good in the worst of us, / And so much bad in the best of us, / That it hardly behooves any of us / To talk about the rest of us.

ATTRIBUTED TO EDWARD WALLIS HOCH, (1849–1925)

12. You may scold a carpenter who has made you a bad table, though you cannot make a table. It is not your trade to make tables.

SAMUEL JOHNSON, QUOTED IN BOSWELL'S *LIFE OF SAMUEL JOHNSON*, JUNE 15, 1763

13. Men are ready to suffer anything from others or from heaven itself, provided that, when it comes to words, they are untouched.

GIACOMO LEOPARDI, *PENSIERI* (1834–37), 1, TR. WILLIAM FENSE WEAVER

14. I have never found, in a long experience of politics, that criticism is ever inhibited by ignorance.

HAROLD MACMILLAN, *WALL STREET JOURNAL*, AUG. 13, 1963

15. People ask you for criticism, but they only want praise.

W. SOMERSET MAUGHAM, *OF HUMAN BONDAGE* (1915), 50

16. The greater one's love for a person the less room for flattery. The proof of true love is to be unsparing in criticism.

MOLIÈRE, *THE MISANTHROPE* (1666), 2, TR. JOHN WOOD

17. We every day and every hour say things of another that we might more properly say of ourselves, could we but apply our observations to our own concerns.

MONTAIGNE, "OF THE AFFECTIONS OF FATHERS TO THEIR CHILDREN," *ESSAYS* (1580–88), TR. W. C. HAZLITT

18. I don't care how unkind the things people say about me so / long as they don't say them to my face.

OGDEN NASH, "HUSH, HERE THEY COME," *VERSES FROM 1929 ON* (1959)

19. They have a right to censure that have a heart to help.

WILLIAM PENN, *SOME FRUITS OF SOLITUDE* (1693), 1.46

20. It is folly to censure him whom all the world adores.

PUBLILIUS SYRUS, *MORAL SAYINGS* (1ST C. B.C.), TR. DARIUS LYMAN

21. Next to the joy of the egotist is the joy of the detractor.

AGNES REPPLIER, "WRITING AN AUTOBIOGRAPHY," *UNDER DISPUTE* (1924)

22. Many a man will have the courage to die gallantly, but will not have the courage to say, or even to think, that the cause for which he is asked to die is an unworthy one. Obloquy is, to most men, more painful than death.

BERTRAND RUSSELL, "AN OUTLINE OF INTELLECTUAL RUBBISH," *UNPOPULAR ESSAYS* (1950)

23. Expose not the secret failings of mankind, otherwise you must verily bring scandal upon them and distrust upon yourself.

SA'DI, *GULISTAN* (1258), 8.41, TR. JAMES ROSS

24. Take each man's censure, but reserve thy judgment.

SHAKESPEARE, *HAMLET* (1600), 1.3.69

25. Censure is the tax a man pays to the public for being eminent.

JONATHAN SWIFT, *THOUGHTS ON VARIOUS SUBJECTS* (1711)

26. I am sorry to think that you do not get a man's most effective criticism until you provoke him.

THOREAU, *JOURNAL*, MARCH 15, 1854

207. CRITICISM, PROFESSIONAL

See also 20. AESTHETICS

1. They who are to be judges must also be performers.

ARISTOTLE, *POLITICS* (4TH C. B.C.), 8.6, TR. BENJAMIN JOWETT

2. There should be a dash of the amateur in criticism. For the amateur is a man of enthusiasm who has not settled down and is not habit-bound.

BROOKS ATKINSON, "JULY 8," *ONCE AROUND THE SUN* (1951)

3. One cannot review a bad book without showing off.

W. H. AUDEN, "READING," *THE DYER'S HAND* (1962)

4. Critics are like brushers of noblemen's clothes.

FRANCIS BACON, *APOTHEGMS* (1625), 64

5. The critic who justly admires all kinds of things simultaneously cannot love any one of them.

MAX BEERBOHM, "GEORGE MOORE," *MAINLY ON THE AIR* (1946)

6. A good writer is not *per se* a good book critic. No more than a good drunk is automatically a good bartender.

JIM BISHOP, *NEW YORK JOURNAL-AMERICAN*, NOV. 26, 1957

7. Posterity is as likely to be wrong as anybody else.

HEYWOOD BROUN, "THE LAST REVIEW," *SITTING ON THE WORLD* (1924)

8. 'Tis strange the mind, that very fiery particle, / Should let itself be snuffed out by an article.

BYRON, *DON JUAN* (1819–24), 11.60

9. A man must serve his time to every trade / Save Censure—Critics all are ready made.

BYRON, *ENGLISH BARDS AND SCOTCH REVIEWERS* (1809)

10. As soon / Seek roses in December—ice in June; / Hope constancy in wind, or corn in chaff, / Believe a woman or an epitaph, / Or any other thing that's false, before / You trust in Critics.

BYRON, *ENGLISH BARDS AND SCOTCH REVIEWERS* (1809)

11. Only paper flowers are afraid of the rain. We are not afraid of the noble rain of criticism because with it will flourish the magnificent garden of music.

KONSTANTIN DANKEVICH, *THE NEW YORK TIMES*, NOV. 19, 1959

12. Criticism is easy, art is difficult.

PHILIPPE DESTOUCHES, *LE GLORIEUX* (1732), 2.5

13. You know who critics are?—the men who have failed in literature and art.

BENJAMIN DISRAELI, *LOTHAIR* (1870), 28

14. Do any newspaper commentators really write with the fear that their opinions will be read twenty-five, fifty, and a hundred years hence and be compared with the verdicts of later generations? If so, they have absurd and childish notions. Most opinions printed in a newspaper are for a glance at the breakfast table and then the wastebasket.

OLIN DOWNES, *OLIN DOWNES ON MUSIC* (1957), ED. IRENE DOWNES

15. A critic is a lug-worm in the liver of literature.

LAWRENCE DURRELL, *MONSIEUR* (1974)

16. Every nation, every race, has not only its own creative, but its own critical turn of mind; and is even more oblivious of the shortcomings and limitations of its critical habits than of those of its creative genius.

T. S. ELIOT, "TRADITION AND THE INDIVIDUAL TALENT" (1919)

17. No man can be criticised but by a greater than he. Do not, then, read the reviews.

EMERSON, *JOURNALS*, 1842

18. Taking to pieces is the trade of those who cannot construct.

EMERSON, *JOURNALS*, 1858

19. Now, in reality, the world have paid too great a compliment to critics, and have imagined them men of much greater profundity than they really are.

HENRY FIELDING, *TOM JONES* (1749), 5.1

20. A man is a critic when he cannot be an artist, in the same way that a man becomes an informer when he cannot be a soldier.

FLAUBERT, *CORRESPONDENCE, À LOUISE COLET*, OCTOBER 1846

21. A critic has no right to the narrowness which is the frequent prerogative of the creative artist.

E.M. FORSTER, *ASPECTS OF THE NOVEL* (1927)

22. Although the novel exercises the rights of a created object, criticism has not those rights, and too many little mansions in English fiction have been acclaimed to their own detriment as important edifices.

E.M. FORSTER, "INTRODUCTORY," *ASPECTS OF THE NOVEL* (1927)

23. A good critic is the man who describes his adventures among masterpieces.

ANATOLE FRANCE, PREFACE TO *LA VIE LITTÉRAIRE* (1883–92), 1

24. The real connoisseurs in art are those who make people accept as beautiful something everybody used to consider ugly, by revealing and resuscitating the beauty in it.

JULES DE GONCOURT, *JOURNAL*, JUNE 30, 1881, TR. ROBERT BALDICK

25. The Stones that Critics hurl with Harsh Intent / A Man may use to build his Monument.

ARTHUR GUITERMAN, *A POET'S PROVERBS* (1924)

26. When a man says he sees nothing in a book, he very often means that he does not see himself in it: which, if it is not a comedy or a satire, is likely enough.

AUGUSTUS WILLIAM HARE, *GUESSES AT TRUTH* (1827)

27. What the mulberry leaf is to the silkworm, the author's book, treatise, essay, poem, is to the critical larvae that feed upon it. It furnishes them with food and clothing.

OLIVER WENDELL HOLMES, SR., *OVER THE TEACUPS* (1891), 2

28. The slanders of the pen pierce to the heart; they rankle longest in the noblest spirits; they dwell ever present in the mind and render it morbidly sensitive to the most trifling collision.

WASHINGTON IRVING, "ENGLISH WRITERS ON AMERICA," *THE SKETCH BOOK OF GEOFFREY CRAYON, GENT* (1819–20)

29. Criticism is a study by which men grow important and formidable at a very small expense.

SAMUEL JOHNSON, "DICK MINIM," *THE IDLER*, JUNE 9, 1759

30. He who first praises a book becomingly is next in merit to the author.

WALTER SAVAGE LANDOR, "ALFIERI AND SALOMON," *IMAGINARY CONVERSATIONS* (1824–53)

31. [C]onfusion of reporting with art criticism is materially responsible for the unholy division the young century set up between great art and the concert industry.

PAUL HENRY LANG, "THE DECLINE OF THE WEST?" *MUSIC IN WESTERN CIVILIZATION* (1941)

32. Nature fits all her children with something to do, / He who would write and can't write can surely review.

JAMES RUSSELL LOWELL, *A FABLE FOR CRITICS* (1848)

33. A good critic is the sorcerer who makes some hidden spring gush forth unexpectedly under our feet.

FRANÇOIS MAURIAC, "A CRITIQUE OF CRITICISM," *SECOND THOUGHTS* (1961), TR. ADRIENNE FOULKE

34. The critic, to interpret his artist, even to understand his artist, must be able to get into the mind of his artist; he must feel and comprehend the vast pressure of the creative passion.

H. L. MENCKEN, *PREJUDICES: FIRST SERIES* (1919), 1

35. There is no fate more distressing for an artist than to have to show himself off before fools, to see

his work exposed to the criticism of the vulgar and ignorant.

MOLIÈRE, *THE WOULD-BE GENTLEMAN* (1670), 2, TR. JOHN WOOD

36. There is no reward so delightful, no pleasure so exquisite, as having one's work known and acclaimed by those whose applause confers honour.

MOLIÈRE, *THE WOULD-BE GENTLEMAN* (1670), 1, TR. JOHN WOOD

37. Every place swarms with commentaries; of authors there is great scarcity.

MONTAIGNE, "OF EXPERIENCE," *ESSAYS* (1580–88), TR. W. C. HAZLITT

38. There is more ado to interpret interpretations than to interpret things, and more books upon books than upon any other subject; we do nothing but comment upon one another.

MONTAIGNE, "OF EXPERIENCE," *ESSAYS* (1580–88), TR. W. C. HAZLITT

39. Scarcely any literature is so entirely unprofitable as the so-called criticism that overlays a pity text with a windy sermon.

JOHN MORLEY, "EMERSON," *CRITICAL MISCELLANIES* (1871–1908)

40. Criticism is the windows and chandeliers of art: it illuminates the enveloping darkness in which art might otherwise rest only vaguely discernible, and perhaps altogether unseen.

GEORGE JEAN NATHAN, *THE CRITIC AND THE DRAMA* (1922), 1

41. Insects sting, not from malice, but because they want to live. It is the same with critics—they desire our blood, not our pain.

NIETZSCHE, *MISCELLANEOUS MAXIMS AND OPINIONS* (1879), 164, TR. PAUL V. COHN

42. Let such teach others who themselves excel, / And censure freely who have written well.

ALEXANDER POPE, *AN ESSAY ON CRITICISM* (1711), 1.15

43. Some judge of authors' names, not works, and then / Nor praise nor blame the writings, but the men.

ALEXANDER POPE, *AN ESSAY ON CRITICISM* (1711), 2.212

44. Works of art are of an infinite loneliness and with nothing so little to be reached as with criticism.

RAINER MARIA RILKE, *LETTERS TO A YOUNG POET*, APRIL 23, 1903, TR. M. D. HERTER NORTON

45. To substitute judgments of fact for judgments of value, is a sign of pedantic and borrowed criticism.

GEORGE SANTAYANA, *THE SENSE OF BEAUTY* (1896), 2

46. With an artist no sane man quarrels, any more than with the colour of a child's eyes.

GEORGE SANTAYANA, *THE LIFE OF REASON: REASON IN ART* (1905–06), 9

47. If certain Critics were as clearsighted as they are malignant, how great would be the benefit to be derived from their writings!

SHELLEY, PREFACE, *THE REVOLT OF ISLAM* (1817)

48. Interpretation, based on the highly dubious theory that a work of art is composed of items of content, violates art. It makes art into an article for use, for arrangement into a mental scheme of categories.

SUSAN SONTAG, *AGAINST INTERPRETATION* (1961)

49. In a culture whose already classical dilemma is the hypertrophy of the intellect at the expense of energy and sensual capability, interpretation is the revenge of the intellect upon art.

SUSAN SONTAG, TITLE ESSAY, *AGAINST INTERPRETATION* (1961)

50. He that can carp in the most eloquent or acute manner at the weakness of the human mind is held by his fellows as almost divine.

SPINOZA, *ETHICS* (1677), 3, TR. ANDREW BOYLE

51. I notice that a number of reviewers (what lice they are) complain that I deal particularly in the subnormal and the psychopathic. If said critics would inspect their neighbors within one block, they would find that I deal with the normal and the ordinary.

JOHN STEINBECK, *STEINBECK: A LIFE IN LETTERS*. EDS. ELAINE STEINBECK AND ROBERT WALLSTEN (1975)

52. Of all the cants which are canted in this canting world, though the cant of hypocrites may be the worst, the cant of criticism is the most tormenting.

LAURENCE STERNE, *TRISTRAM SHANDY* (1759–67), 3.12

53. It is my conviction that the public always shows itself more honest in its spontaneity than do those who officially set themselves up as judges of works of art.

IGOR STRAVINSKY, *POETICS OF MUSIC* (1947), 4

54. If the men of wit and genius would resolve never to complain in their works of critics and detractors, the next age would not know that they ever had any.

JONATHAN SWIFT, *THOUGHTS ON VARIOUS SUBJECTS* (1711)

55. A critic is a man who knows the way but can't drive the car.

KENNETH TYNAN, *THE NEW YORK TIMES MAGAZINE,* JAN. 9, 1966

56. Despite the warnings of other times, the impetuous and the confident continue their indiscriminate cultivation of weeds at the expense of occasional flowers.

GORE VIDAL, *ROCKING THE BOAT* (1962)

57. [A]rtists reproduce themselves or each other, with wearisome iteration. But criticism is always moving on, and the critic is always developing.

OSCAR WILDE, *THE ARTIST AS CRITIC: THE CRITICAL WRITINGS OF OSCAR WILDE* (1969) ED. RICHARD ELLMANN

58. When critics disagree, the artist is in accord with himself.

OSCAR WILDE, PREFACE, *THE PICTURE OF DORIAN GRAY* (1891)

59. Has anybody ever seen a dramatic critic in the daytime? Of course not. They come out after dark, up to no good.

P. G. WODEHOUSE, *NEW YORK MIRROR,* MAY 27, 1955

208. CROWDS

See also 597. MOB; 713. POPULATION

1. A man has his distinctive personal scent which his wife, his children and his dog can recognize. A crowd has a generalized stink. The public is odorless.

W. H. AUDEN, "THE POET AND THE CITY," *THE DYER'S HAND* (1962)

2. Observe any meetings of people, and you will always find their eagerness and impetuosity rise or fall in proportion to their numbers.

LORD CHESTERFIELD, *LETTERS TO HIS SON,* SEPT. 13, 1748

3. I do not believe that any human being is fundamentally happier for being finally lost in a crowd, even if it is called a crowd of comrades.

G. K. CHESTERTON, "ABOUT THE WORKERS," *AS I WAS SAYING* (1936)

4. As crowds increase we build our forts of inattention, and the more we talk the easier it is to mean little and listen not at all.

FRANK MOORE COLBY, "SIMPLE SIMON," *THE COLBY ESSAYS* (1926), V. I

5. Away with this hurrah of masses, and let us have the considerate vote of single men.

EMERSON, "CONSIDERATIONS BY THE WAY," *THE CONDUCT OF LIFE* (1860)

6. In the crowd, herd, or gang, it is a mass-mind that operates—which is to say, a mind without subtlety, a mind without compassion, a mind, finally, uncivilized.

ROBERT LINDNER, "THE MUTINY OF THE YOUNG," *MUST YOU CONFORM?* (1956)

7. Nothing is so uncertain or unpredictable as the feelings of a crowd.

LIVY, *AB URBE CONDITA* (C. 29 B.C.), 31.34

8. Under crowded conditions the friendly social interactions between members of a group become reduced, and the destructive and aggressive patterns show a marked rise in frequency and intensity.

DESMOND MORRIS, *THE NAKED APE* (1967)

9. The state fair sprawled across a hillside and a valley, and at first glance it did indeed look like a city under occupation by an army of rampaging Goths.

JONATHAN RABAN, *OLD GLORY* (1981)

10. I would rather sit on a pumpkin and have it all to myself than be crowded on a velvet cushion.

THOREAU, "ECONOMY," *WALDEN* (1854)

209. CRUELTY

See also 838. SADISM; 1018. UNKINDNESS

1. Man is subject to innumerable pains and sorrows by the very condition of humanity, and yet, as if nature had not sown evils enough in life, we are continually adding grief to grief and aggravating the common calamity by our cruel treatment of one another.

JOSEPH ADDISON, *THE SPECTATOR* (1711–12), 169

2. Cruelty ever proceeds from a vile mind, and often from a cowardly heart.

LODOVICO ARIOSTO, *ORLANDO FURIOSO* (1516), 36, NOTES, TR. SIR JOHN HARINGTON

3. When men are inhuman, take care not to feel towards them as they do towards other humans.

MARCUS AURELIUS, *MEDITATIONS* (2ND C.), 7.65, TR. MAXWELL STANIFORTH

4. Man's inhumanity to man / Makes countless thousands mourn.

ROBERT BURNS, "MAN WAS MADE TO MOURN" (1786)

5. Cruelty is, perhaps, the worst kind of sin. Intellectual cruelty is certainly the worst kind of cruelty.

G. K. CHESTERTON, "CONCEIT AND CARICATURE," *ALL THINGS CONSIDERED* (1908)

6. Children know how to be cruel, and the cruelty of their elders is the surest residue of the malaise the young feel toward things strange, things other, things that reveal our own ignorance or insufficiency.

Carlos Fuentes, "How I Started to Write," in *The Art of the Personal Essay* (1994), ed. Phillip Lopate

7. Cruelty is the law pervading all nature and society; and we can't get out of it if we would.

Thomas Hardy, *Jude the Obscure* (1895), 5.8

8. The theatre breeds its own kind of cruelty, and its sadism takes on a keener edge since it can be enjoyed under the innocent guise of critical judgment.

Moss Hart, *Act One* (1959)

9. Pity is not natural to man. Children always are cruel. Savages are always cruel.

Samuel Johnson, quoted in Boswell's *Life of Samuel Johnson,* July 20, 1763

10. Today there's more fellowship among snakes than among mankind. / Wild beasts spare those with similar markings.

Juvenal, *Satires* (c. 100), 15.159, tr. Hubert Creekmore

11. Is cruelty a moral judgment if it is fundamental to forms of life? Who is man to say that the workings of nature, and therefore of the divine plan of which he himself is part, are cruel?

Charles A. Lindbergh, "The Primitive Passing," *Autobiography of Values* (1978)

12. Nature has, herself, I fear, imprinted in man a kind of instinct to inhumanity.

Montaigne, "Of cruelty," *Essays* (1580–88), tr. W. C. Hazlitt

13. Man is the cruelest animal. At tragedies, bullfights, and crucifixions he has so far felt best on earth; and when he invented hell for himself, behold, that was his heaven on earth.

Nietzsche, "The Convalescent," *Thus Spoke Zarathustra* (1883–92), 3, tr. Walter Kaufmann

14. Opinions which justify cruelty are inspired by cruel impulses.

Bertrand Russell, "Ideas That Have Harmed Mankind," *Unpopular Essays* (1950)

15. There is in man a specific lust for cruelty which infects even his passion of pity and makes it savage.

George Bernard Shaw, "Preface on Doctors: The Scientific Investigation of Cruelty," *The Doctor's Dilemma* (1913)

16. Man is worse than an animal when he is an animal.

Rabindranath Tagore, *Stray Birds* (1916), 248

17. The vast majority of the race, whether savage or civilized, are secretly kind-hearted and shrink from inflicting pain, but in the presence of the aggressive and pitiless minority they don't dare to assert themselves.

Mark Twain, *The Mysterious Stranger* (1916)

210. CULTURE

See also 133. Civilization; 487. Institutions; 913. Society

1. Culture, the acquainting ourselves with the best that has been known and said in the world, and thus with the history of the human spirit.

Matthew Arnold, preface, *Literature and Dogma* (1873)

2. Culture, with its processes and functions, is a subject upon which we need all the enlightenment we can achieve, and there is no direction in which we can seek with greater reward than in the facts of preliterate societies.

Ruth Benedict, *Patterns of Culture* (1934)

3. What really binds men together is their culture, the ideas and the standards they have in common.

Ruth Benedict, *Patterns of Culture* (1934)

4. Culture as art is the peak expression of man's creativity, his capacity to break out of nature's narrow bounds, and hence out of the degrading interpretation of man in modern natural and political science.

Allan Bloom, "Culture," *The Closing of the American Mind* (1987)

5. Culture is the one thing that we cannot deliberately aim at. It is the product of a variety of more or less harmonious activities, each pursued for its own sake.

T. S. Eliot, *Notes Towards the Definition of Culture* (1948)

6. A cheerful, intelligent face is the end of culture.

Emerson, "Culture," *The Conduct of Life* (1860)

7. A cultivated man, wise to know and bold to perform, is the end to which nature works.

Emerson, "Power," *The Conduct of Life* (1860)

8. Culture opens the sense of beauty.

Emerson, "Culture." *The Conduct of Life* (1860)

9. Culture has never the translucidity of custom; it abhors all simplification. In its essence it is opposed to custom, for custom is always the deterioration of culture.

FRANTZ FANON, "ON NATIONAL CULTURE," *THE WRETCHED OF THE EARTH* (1961), TR. CONSTANCE FARRINGTON

10. If you're anxious for to shine in the high aesthetic line as a man of culture rare, / You must get up all the germs of the transcendental terms, and plant them everywhere.

W. S. GILBERT, *PATIENCE* (1881), 1

11. Man is born a barbarian, and only raises himself above the beast by culture.

BALTASAR GRACIÁN, *THE ART OF WORLDLY WISDOM* (1647), 87, TR. JOSEPH JACOBS

12. Human life is reduced to real suffering, to hell, only when two ages, two cultures and religions overlap.

HERMANN HESSE, PREFACE TO *DER STEPPENWOLF* (1927), TR. REV. WALTER SORELL

13. Of the significant and pleasurable experiences of life only the simplest are open indiscriminately to all. The rest cannot be had except by those who have undergone a suitable training.

ALDOUS HUXLEY, "BELIEFS," *ENDS AND MEANS* (1937)

14. Educated people do indeed speak the same languages; cultivated ones need not speak at all.

LOUIS KRONENBERGER, "OVERTURE," *THE CART AND THE HORSE* (1964), 1

15. Prig and philistine, Ph.D. and C.P.A., despot of English 218c and big shot of the Kiwanis Club—how much, at bottom, they both hate Art, and how hard it is to know which of them hates it the more.

LOUIS KRONENBERGER, *COMPANY MANNERS* (1954), 1.4

16. Culture is perishing in overproduction, in an avalanche of words, in the madness of quantity.

MILAN KUNDERA, *THE UNBEARABLE LIGHTNESS OF BEING* (1984)

17. Humans become human through intense learning not just of survival skills but of customs and social mores, kinship and social laws—that is, culture.

RICHARD LEAKEY, *THE ORIGIN OF HUMANKIND* (1994)

18. The value of culture is its effect on character. It avails nothing unless it ennobles and strengthens that. Its use is for life. Its aim is not beauty but goodness.

W. SOMERSET MAUGHAM, *THE SUMMING UP* (1938), 24

19. Learning is nothing without cultivated manners, but when the two are combined in a woman, you have one of the most exquisite products of civilization.

ANDRÉ MAUROIS, *ARIEL* (1924), 16, TR. ELLA D'ARCY

20. Culture itself is neither education nor law-making: it is an atmosphere and a heritage.

H. L. MENCKEN, *MINORITY REPORT* (1956), 360

21. In the Anthropology Club, as I understood it, you were permitted, if not required, to despise only one thing, and that was your own culture, that of the West.

CHARLES PORTIS, *GRINGOS* (1991)

22. [T]he situation of the factory worker today is reminiscent in certain respects of that of the nineteenth-century capitalist whose wife dragged him reluctantly toward "culture" and away from his "materialistic" preoccupations.

DAVID RIESMAN, *ABUNDANCE FOR WHAT?* (1964)

23. A culture must be reasonably stable, but it must also change, and it will presumably be strongest if it can avoid excessive respect for tradition and fear of novelty on the one hand and excessively rapid change on the other.

B.F. SKINNER, *BEYOND FREEDOM AND DIGNITY* (1971), 8

24. Culture is an instrument wielded by professors to manufacture professors, who when their turn comes will manufacture professors.

SIMONE WEIL, *THE NEED FOR ROOTS* (1949)

25. Business men who are busy the whole day and immediately go to bed after supper, snoring like cows, are not likely to contribute anything to culture.

LIN YUTANG, "ON CONVERSATION," *THE IMPORTANCE OF LIVING* (1937)

CURES

See 798. REMEDIES

211. CURIOSITY

See also 480. INQUIRY

1. One shouldn't be too inquisitive in life / Either about God's secrets or one's wife.

CHAUCER, "WORDS BETWEEN THE HOST AND THE MILLER," *THE CANTERBURY TALES* (C. 1387–1400), TR. NEVILL COGHILL

2. Creatures whose mainspring is curiosity will enjoy the accumulating of facts, far more than the pausing at times to reflect on those facts.

CLARENCE DAY, *THIS SIMIAN WORLD* (1920), 9

3. Only that mind draws me which I cannot read.

EMERSON, *JOURNALS*, 1847

4. We are all like Scheherazade's husband, in that we want to know what happens next.

E.M. FORSTER, "INTRODUCTORY," *ASPECTS OF THE NOVEL* (1927)

5. Enquire not what boils in another's pot.

THOMAS FULLER, M.D., *GNOMOLOGIA* (1732), 1373

6. Eminence interested her far less than decadence; she understood that her readers felt an obscure, understandable pleasure reading about degradation but resented, in a perfectly human way, too long a tenure by the Famous in the pinnacles of success.

DORIS GRUMBACH, *THE MISSING PERSON* (1981)

7. Curiosity is one of the permanent and certain characteristics of a vigorous intellect.

SAMUEL JOHNSON, *THE RAMBLER* (1750–52), 103

8. There are various sorts of curiosity; one is from interest, which makes us desire to know that which may be useful to us; and the other, from pride which comes from the wish to know what others are ignorant of.

LA ROCHEFOUCAULD, *MAXIMS* (1665), TR. KENNETH PRATT

9. Glory and curiosity are the two scourges of the soul; the last prompts us to thrust our noses into everything, the other forbids us to leave anything doubtful and undecided.

MONTAIGNE, "THAT IT IS FOLLY TO MEASURE TRUTH AND ERROR BY OUR OWN CAPACITY," *ESSAYS* (1580–88), TR. W. C. HAZLITT

10. I am often amazed at how much more capability and enthusiasm for science there is among elementary school youngsters than among college students.

CARL SAGAN, *BROCA'S BRAIN: REFLECTIONS ON THE ROMANCE OF SCIENCE* (1979)

11. He that breaks a thing to find out what it is has left the path of wisdom.

J. R. R. TOLKIEN, *THE FELLOWSHIP OF THE RING* (1954), 2.2

212. CURSING

See also 957. SWEARING

1. A thousand curses never tore a shirt.

ARABIC PROVERB

213. CUSTOM

See also 77. BEHAVIOR; 406. HABIT; 986. TRADITION

1. Since custom is the principal magistrate of man's life, let men by all means endeavor to obtain good customs.

FRANCIS BACON, "OF CUSTOM AND EDUCATION," *ESSAYS* (1625)

2. Customs represent the experience of mankind.

HENRY WARD BEECHER, *PROVERBS FROM PLYMOUTH PULPIT* (1887)

3. Custom reconciles us to everything.

EDMUND BURKE, *A PHILOSOPHICAL INQUIRY INTO THE ORIGIN OF OUR IDEAS OF THE SUBLIME AND BEAUTIFUL* (1756), 18

4. Innumerable are the illusions and legerdemain-tricks of custom: but of all of these, perhaps the cleverest is her knack of persuading us that the miraculous, by simple repetition, ceases to be miraculous.

THOMAS CARLYLE, *SARTOR RESARTUS* (1833–34), 3.4

5. Custom looks to things that are past, and fashion to things that are present, but both of them are somewhat blind as to things that are to come.

CHARLES CALEB COLTON, *LACON* (1825), 1.547

6. Custom is the guide of the ignorant.

ENGLISH PROVERB

7. At every moment of his life the Shoshone must be careful to observe the complicated folkways of his group, to do reverence to superhuman powers, to remember the courtesies and obligations of family, to pay homage to certain sacred plants, or to avoid particular places.

PETER FARB, *MAN'S RISE TO CIVILIZATION* (1968)

8. Despite the theories traditionally taught in high-school social studies, the truth is: the more primitive the society, the more leisured its way of life.

PETER FARB, *MAN'S RISE TO CIVILIZATION* (1968)

9. What men call civilization is the condition of present customs; what they call barbarism, the condition of past ones.

ANATOLE FRANCE, *SUR LA PIERRE BLANCHE* (1903), 4

10. Custom makes all things easy.

THOMAS FULLER, M.D., *GNOMOLOGIA* (1732), 1225

11. Most of the things we do, we do for no better reason than that our fathers have done them or our

neighbors do them, and the same is true of a larger part than what we suspect of what we think.

Oliver Wendell Holmes, Jr., speech, Boston, Jan. 8, 1897

12. Old custom is hard to break and scarce any man will be led otherwise than seemeth good unto himself.

Thomas à Kempis, *The Imitation of Christ* (1426), 1.14

13. There is no conceivable human action which custom has not at one time justified and at another condemned.

Joseph Wood Krutch, "The Genesis of a Mood," *The Modern Temper* (1929)

14. What humanity abhors, custom reconciles and recommends to us.

John Locke, *Some Thoughts Concerning Education* (1693), 116

15. You must not refuse any additional cups of tea under the following circumstances: if it is hot; if it is cold; if you are tired; if anybody thinks that you might be tired; if you are nervous; if you are gay; before you go out; if you are out; if you have just returned home; if you feel like it; if you do not feel like it; if you have had no tea for some time; if you have just had a cup.

George Mikes, *How to Be an Alien* (1946)

16. Customs are made for customary circumstances, and customary characters.

John Stuart Mill, *On Liberty* (1859), 3

17. He who does anything because it is the custom, makes no choice.

John Stuart Mill, *On Liberty* (1859), 3

18. Custom is a second nature, and no less powerful.

Montaigne, "Of managing the will," *Essays* (1580–88), tr. W. C. Hazlitt

19. There is nothing so extreme that is not allowed by the custom of some nation or other.

Montaigne, "Apology for Raimond de Sebonde," *Essays* (1580–88), tr. W. C. Hazlitt

20. When one wants to change manners and customs, one should not do so by changing the laws.

Montesquieu, *L'Esprit des lois* (1748), 19.16

21. There are a lot of people who must have the table laid in the usual fashion or they will not enjoy the dinner.

Christopher Morley, *Inward Ho!* (1923), 9

22. Custom creates the whole of equity, for the simple reason that it is accepted.

Pascal, *Pensées* (1670), 294, tr. W. F. Trotter

23. Custom determines what is agreeable.

Pascal, *Pensées* (1670), 309, tr. W. F. Trotter

24. We are more sensible of what is done against custom than against nature.

Plutarch, "Of Eating Flesh," *Moralia* (c. a.d. 100)

25. The universality of a custom is pledge of its worth.

Agnes Repplier, "The Pilgrim's Staff," *Compromises* (1904)

26. There is nothing sacred about convention: there is nothing sacred about primitive passions or whims; but the fact that a convention exists indicates that a way of living has been devised capable of maintaining itself.

George Santayana, *Persons and Places: The Middle Span* (1945), 3

27. How many things, both just and unjust, are sanctioned by custom!

Terence, *The Self-Tormentor* (163 b.c.), 4.7.11, tr. Henry Thomas Riley

28. Often a quite assified remark becomes sanctified by use and petrified by custom; it is then a permanency, its term of activity a geologic period.

Mark Twain, "Does the Race of Man Love a Lord?" *North American Review*, April 1902

214. CYNICISM

1. Life—the way it really is—is a battle not between Bad and Good, but between Bad and Worse.

Joseph Brodsky, *Watermark* (1992)

2. A cynic is not merely one who reads bitter lessons from the past; he is one who is prematurely disappointed in the future.

Sydney J. Harris, *On the Contrary* (1962), 7

3. The cynics in life are the people who are always trying to do things for people who don't want things done for them.

Marianne Moore, "Pym," *The Complete Prose of Marianne Moore* (1986)

4. It is only the cynicism that is born of success that is penetrating and valid.

George Jean Nathan, "Cynicism," *Monks Are Monks* (1929)

5. What is a cynic? A man who knows the price of everything, and the value of nothing.

Oscar Wilde, *Lady Windermere's Fan* (1892), 3

D

215. DANCING

1. A good education is usually harmful to a dancer. A good calf is better than a good head.

AGNES DE MILLE, NEWS SUMMARIES, FEB. 1, 1954

2. Dancing is the loftiest, the most moving, the most beautiful of the arts, because it is no mere translation or abstraction from life; it is life itself.

HAVELOCK ELLIS, *THE DANCE OF LIFE* (1923), 2

3. To urgent unknown music she danced for them, danced against them. Her strong small body became a force: the sequence of leaps, back falls, contractions, spun from her endlessly, like magic scarves.

MAUREEN HOWARD, *FACTS OF LIFE* (1978)

4. Dance is the only art of which we ourselves are the stuff of which it is made.

TED SHAWN, *TIME,* JULY 25, 1955

216. DANGER

See also 16. ADVENTURE; 92. BOLDNESS; 195. COURAGE; 313. EXCITEMENT; 976. THREAT

1. Who will pity a snake charmer bitten by a serpent, or any who go near wild beasts?

APOCRYPHA, ECCLESIASTICUS 12:13

2. Perils commonly ask to be paid in pleasures.

FRANCIS BACON, "OF LOVE," *ESSAYS* (1625)

3. Dangers, by being despised, grow great.

EDMUND BURKE, SPEECH, "ON THE PETITION OF THE UNITARIANS," 1792

4. Mystery magnifies danger as the fog the sun.

CHARLES CALEB COLTON, *LACON* (1825), 1.359

5. However well organized the foundations of life may be, life must always be full of risks.

HAVELOCK ELLIS, *ON LIFE AND SEX: ESSAYS OF LOVE AND VIRTUE* (1937), 1

6. The wise man in the storm prays God, not for safety from danger, but for deliverance from fear.

EMERSON, *JOURNALS,* 1833

7. Danger and delight grow on one stalk.

ENGLISH PROVERB

8. A man who has been in danger / When he comes out of it forgets his fears, / And sometimes he forgets his promises.

EURIPIDES, *IPHIGENIA IN TAURIS* (C. 414–12 B.C.), TR. WITTER BYNNER

9. Danger past, God is forgotten.

THOMAS FULLER, M.D, *GNOMOLOGIA* (1732), 1234

10. In comradeship is danger countered best.

GOETHE, "ON THE LOWER PENEUS," *FAUST: PART II* (1832), TR. PHILIP WAYNE

11. Great perils have this beauty, that they bring to light the fraternity of strangers.

VICTOR HUGO, "SAINT DENIS," *LES MISÉRABLES* (1862), 12.4, TR. CHARLES E. WILBOUR

12. Any danger spot is tenable if men—brave men—will make it so.

JOHN F. KENNEDY, ADDRESS TO THE NATION, JULY 25, 1961

13. It is pleasurable, when winds disturb the waves of a great sea, to gaze out from land upon the great trials of another.

LUCRETIUS, *ON THE NATURE OF THINGS* (1ST C. B.C.), 2

14. To be alive at all involves some risk.

HAROLD MACMILLAN, QUOTED IN *THE NEW YORK TIMES,* DEC. 30, 1959

15. So long as money can answer, it were wrong in any business to put the life in danger.

SA'DI, *GULISTAN* (1258), 8.15, TR. JAMES ROSS

16. Everything is sweetened by risk.

ALEXANDER SMITH, "OF DEATH AND THE FEAR OF DYING," *DREAMTHORP* (1863)

17. When tremendous dangers are involved, no one can be blamed for looking to his own interest.

THUCYDIDES, *THE PELOPONNESIAN WAR* (C. 400 B.C.), 1.6, TR. REX WARNER

217. DARKNESS

See also 633. NIGHT

1. The best way to live is by not knowing what will happen to you at the end of the day, when the sun goes down and the supper is to be cooked.

DONALD BARTHELME, "THE EDUCATIONAL EXPERIENCE," *AMATEURS* (1976)

2. Once man understands that he is caught up in a blind energy, he transcends it. There is light in the darkness.

MICHAEL HARRINGTON, *THE ACCIDENTAL CENTURY* (1966)

3. There is in the darkness a unity, if you will, that cannot be achieved in any other environment, a blending of self with what the self perceives, and exquisite mystical experience.

BERNARD MALAMUD, *THE NATURAL* (1952)

4. The world grows bigger as the light leaves it. There are no boundaries and no landmarks. The trees and the rocks and the anthills begin to disappear, one by one, whisked away under the magical cloak of evening.

BERYL MARKHAM, *WEST WITH THE NIGHT* (1942)

5. In darkness one may be / ashamed of what one does, without the shame of disgrace.

SOPHOCLES, *THE WOMEN OF TRACHIS* (C. 413 B.C.), TR. MICHAEL JAMESON

6. It was that hour of dusk when the streetlights and headlights come on but make little difference.

TOM WOLFE, *THE BONFIRE OF THE VANITIES* (1987)

218. DAUGHTERS

See also 385. GIRLS; 670. PARENTHOOD

1. To an old father, nothing is more sweet / Than a daughter. Boys are more spirited, but their ways / Are not so tender.

EURIPIDES, *THE SUPPLIANT WOMEN* (C. 421 B.C.), TR. FRANK W. JONES

2. An Irish-American virgin at the age of thirty, she took care of her senile father until he died, and then her cancer-ridden mother until her death.

DORIS GRUMBACH, *THE MISSING PERSON* (1981)

3. When I go home my mother and I play a cannibal game; we eat each other over the years, tender morsel by morsel until there is nothing left but dry bone and wig. She is winning—needless to say she has had so much more experience.

MAUREEN HOWARD, *BRIDGEPORT BUS* (1965)

4. The dread ballet classes of former years had been an ordeal—all the little daughters of doctors and dentists, *socialites* from Fairfield in squirrel coats and Tyrolean skirts, the heiress of a girdle empire escorted by a black maid.

MAUREEN HOWARD, *FACTS OF LIFE* (1978)

5. I sometimes have the feeling that her entire life was merely a continuation of her mother's, much as the course of a ball on the billiard table is merely the continuation of the player's arm movement.

MILAN KUNDERA, *THE UNBEARABLE LIGHTNESS OF BEING* (1984)

6. Trust not your daughter's minds / By what you see them act.

SHAKESPEARE, *OTHELLO* (1604–05), 1.1.171

7. A fluent tongue is the only thing a mother don't like her daughter to resemble her in.

RICHARD BRINSLEY SHERIDAN, *ST. PATRICK'S DAY* (1775), 1.2

8. He who has daughters is always a shepherd.

SPANISH PROVERB

9. The Mother weeps / At that white funeral of the single life, / Her maiden daughter's marriage; and her tears / Are half of pleasure, half of pain.

LORD TENNYSON, "TO H.R.H. PRINCESS BEATRICE" (1843)

DAWN

See 605. MORNING

DAYDREAMS

See 336. FANTASY

219. DEADNESS, SPIRITUAL

See also 30. ALIENATION; 466. INDIFFERENCE; 504. INVOLVEMENT

1. Shame on the soul, to falter on the road of life while the body still perseveres.

MARCUS AURELIUS, *MEDITATIONS* (2ND C.), 6.29, TR. MAXWELL STANIFORTH

2. It's extraordinary how we go through life with eyes half shut, with dull ears, with dormant thoughts. Perhaps it's just as well; and it may be that it is this very dullness that makes life to the incalculable majority so supportable and so welcome.

JOSEPH CONRAD, *LORD JIM* (1900), 13

3. It takes so many years / To learn that one is dead.

T. S. ELIOT, *THE FAMILY REUNION* (1939), 2.3

4. Most persons have died before they expire—died to all earthly longings, so that the last breath is only, as it were, the locking of the door of the already deserted mansion.

Oliver Wendell Holmes, Sr., *The Professor at the Breakfast Table* (1860), 11

5. It is nothing to die; it is frightful not to live.

Victor Hugo, "Jean Valjean," *Les Misérables* (1862), 9.5, tr. Charles E. Wilbour

6. The only true infidelity is for a live man to vote himself dead.

Herman Melville, *Mardi and a Voyage Thither* (1849), 13

7. To live a life half dead, a living death.

Milton, *Samson Agonistes* (1671), 100

8. To fear love is to fear life, and those who fear life are already three parts dead.

Bertrand Russell, "Sex and Individual Well-Being," *Marriage and Morals* (1929)

9. The worst evil of all is to leave the ranks of the living before one dies.

Seneca, "On Peace of Mind," *Morals Essays* (1st c.), tr. Aubrey Stewart

220. DEAFNESS

1. None so deaf as he that will not hear.

Thomas Fuller, M.D., *Gnomologia* (1732), 3657

221. DEATH

See also 83. Birth; 103. Burial; 302. Eternity; 367. Funerals; 454. Immortality; 539. Life; 541. Life and Death; 606. Mortality; 610. Mourning; 767. Punishment, Capital; 948. Suicide

1. Pain lays not its touch / Upon a corpse.

Aeschylus, *Fragments* (525–456 B.C.), 250, tr. Edward H. Plumptre

2. The descent to Hades is much the same from whatever place we start.

Anaxagoras, (6th c. B.C.), quoted in Diogenes Laertius' *Lives and Opinions of Eminent Philosophers* (3rd c. A.D.), tr. R. D. Hicks

3. I answer the heroic question "Death, where is thy sting?" with "It is here in my heart and mind and memories."

Maya Angelou, "Death and the Legacy," *Wouldn't Take Nothing for My Journey Now* (1993)

4. Death cancels everything but truth.

Anonymous

5. Death has to be waiting at the end of the ride before you truly see the earth, and feel your heart, and love the world.

Jean Anouilh, *The Lark* (1955), 2, adapted by Lillian Hellman

6. Do not rejoice over anyone's death; remember that we all must die.

Apocrypha, Ecclesiasticus 7:7

7. Hardest of deaths to a mortal / Is the death he sees ahead.

Bacchylides, *Croesus* (5th c. B.C.), 3.15

8. It is as natural to die as to be born.

Francis Bacon, "Of Death," *Essays* (1625)

9. Men fear death, as children fear to go in the dark; and as that natural fear in children is increased with tales, so is the other.

Francis Bacon, "Of Death," *Essays* (1625)

10. Unless a writer is extremely old when he dies, in which case he has probably become a neglected institution, his death must always seem untimely.

James Baldwin, "Alas, Poor Richard," in *The Art of the Personal Essay* (1994), ed. Phillip Lopate

11. To him, perpetual thought of death was a sin. Drive your cart and your plow over the bones of the dead.

Saul Bellow, *Herzog* (1964)

12. Dust thou art, and unto dust shalt thou return.

Bible, Genesis 3:19

13. We must needs die, and are as water spilt on the ground, which cannot be gathered up again.

Bible, 2 Samuel 14:14

14. Even at our birth, death does but stand aside a little. And every day he looks towards us and muses somewhat to himself whether that day or the next he will draw nigh.

Robert Bolt, *A Man for All Seasons* (1962), 2

15. Death is the supreme festival on the road to freedom.

Dietrich Bonhoeffer, "Miscellaneous Thoughts," *Letters and Papers from Prison* (1953), tr. Eberhard Bethge

16. Perhaps the best proof of the Almighty's existence is that we never know when we are to die.

JOSEPH BRODSKY, *WATERMARK* (1992)

17. Though it be in the power of the weakest arm to take away life, it is not in the strongest to deprive us of death.

SIR THOMAS BROWNE, *RELIGIO MEDICI* (1642), 1

18. We all labour against our own cure, for death is the cure of all diseases.

SIR THOMAS BROWNE, *RELIGIO MEDICI* (1642), 2

19. Sustained and soothed / By an unfaltering trust, approach thy grave, / Like one who wraps the drapery of his couch / About him, and lies down to pleasant dreams.

WILLIAM CULLEN BRYANT, "THANATOPSIS" (1811)

20. To die is to leave off dying and do the thing once for all.

SAMUEL BUTLER (D. 1902), *NOTE-BOOKS* (1912)

21. To die completely, a person must not only forget but be forgotten, and he who is not forgotten is not dead.

SAMUEL BUTLER (D. 1902), "DEATH," *NOTE-BOOKS* (1912)

22. Death, so called, is a thing which makes men weep, / And yet a third of Life is passed in sleep.

BYRON, *DON JUAN* (1819–24), 14.3

23. What is this Death?—a quiet of the heart? / The whole of that of which we are a part?

BYRON, "A FRAGMENT" (1816)

24. Men are convinced of your arguments, your sincerity, and the seriousness of your efforts only by your death.

ALBERT CAMUS, *THE FALL* (1956)

25. The dead are all holy, even they that were base and wicked while alive. Their baseness and wickedness was not they, was but the heavy and unmanageable environment that lay round them.

THOMAS CARLYLE, "BIOGRAPHY" (1832)

26. Death is always sad, I suppose, to us who look forward to it: I expect it will seem very different when we can look back upon it.

LEWIS CARROLL, *THE LETTERS OF LEWIS CARROLL*, ED. MORTON N. COHEN (1979)

27. I shall not die of a cold. I shall die of having lived.

WILLA CATHER, *DEATH COMES FOR THE ARCHBISHOP* (1927)

28. The fear of death is for all of us everywhere, but for the great intelligence of the opium eater it is beautifully narrowed into the crux of drugs.

JOHN CHEEVER, *THE FALCONER* (1977)

29. Death does not blow a trumpet.

DANISH PROVERB

30. There is only one way to be prepared for death: to be sated. In the soul, in the heart, in the spirit, in the flesh. To the brim.

HENRY DE MONTHERLANT, "EXPLICIT MYSTERIUM," *MORS ET VITA* (1932)

31. Death is the supple Suitor / That wins at last— / It is a stealthy Wooing / Conducted first / By pallid innuendoes / And dim approach / But brave at last with Bugles.

EMILY DICKINSON, POEM (C. 1878)

32. The distance that the dead have gone / Does not at first appear— / Their coming back seems possible / For many an ardent year.

EMILY DICKINSON, *POEMS* (C. 1862–86)

33. We never know we go when we are going— / We jest and shut the Door— / Fate—following—behind us bolts it— / And we accost no more—.

EMILY DICKINSON, POEM (C. 1881)

34. You'll find it—when you try to die— / The Easier to let go— / For recollecting such as went— / You could not spare—you know.

EMILY DICKINSON, POEM (C. 1862)

35. Any man's death diminishes me, because I am involved in mankind; and therefore never send to know for whom the bell tolls; it tolls for thee.

JOHN DONNE, *DEVOTIONS* (1624), 17

36. God himself took a day to rest in, and a good man's grave is his Sabbath.

JOHN DONNE, *SERMONS*, NO. 12, 1622

37. All human things are subject to decay, / And when fate summons, monarchs must obey.

JOHN DRYDEN, *MAC FLECKNOE* (1682), 11.1

38. Death in itself is nothing; but we fear / To be we know not what, we know not where.

JOHN DRYDEN, *AURENGZEBE* (1676), 4.1

39. I have seen the eternal Footman hold my coat, and snicker.

T. S. ELIOT, "THE LOVE SONG OF J. ALFRED PRUFROCK" (1915)

40. Our fear of death is like our fear that summer will be short, but when we have had our swing of pleasure, our fill of fruit, and our swelter of heat, we say we have had our day.

EMERSON, *JOURNALS*, 1855

41. Death always comes too early or too late.

ENGLISH PROVERB

42. Why, do you not know, then, that the origin of all human evils, and of baseness, and cowardice, is not death, but rather the fear of death?

EPICTETUS, *DISCOURSES* (2ND C.), 3.26, TR. THOMAS W. HIGGINSON

43. Death, the most dreaded of evils, is therefore of no concern to us; for while we exist death is not present, and when death is present we no longer exist.

EPICURUS, LETTER TO MENOECEUS (3RD C. B.C.), IN *LETTERS, PRINCIPAL DOCTRINES, AND VATICAN SAYINGS*, TR. RUSSEL M. GEER

44. It is possible to provide security against other ills, but as far as death is concerned, we men all live in a city without walls.

EPICURUS, "VATICAN SAYINGS" (3RD C. B.C.), 36, IN *LETTERS, PRINCIPAL DOCTRINES, AND VATICAN SAYINGS*, TR. RUSSEL M. GEER

45. Your life feels different on you, once you greet death and understand your heart's position.

LOUISE ERDRICH, "LOVE MEDICINE," *LOVE MEDICINE* (1984)

46. To die with glory, if one has to die at all, / is still, I think, pain for the dier.

EURIPIDES, *RHESUS* (C. 455–441 B.C.), TR. RICHMOND LATTIMORE

47. What good can come from meeting death with tears?... If a man / Is sorry for himself, he doubles death.

EURIPIDES, *IPHIGENIA IN TAURIS* (C. 414–12 B.C.), TR. WITTER BYNNER

48. What greater pain could mortals have than this: / To see their children dead before their eyes?

EURIPIDES, *THE SUPPLIANT WOMEN* (C. 421 B.C.), TR. FRANK W. JONES

49. It hath often been said, that it is not death, but dying, which is terrible.

HENRY FIELDING, *AMELIA* (1751), 3.4

50. Death is never sweet, not even if it is suffered for the highest ideal.

ERICH FROMM, *ESCAPE FROM FREEDOM* (1941), 7

51. To die is poignantly bitter, but the idea of having to die without having lived is unbearable.

ERICH FROMM, *MAN FOR HIMSELF* (1947), 4

52. The nearest friends can go / With anyone to death, comes so far short / They might as well not try to go at all.

ROBERT FROST, "HOME BURIAL," *NORTH OF BOSTON* (1914)

53. Death surprises us in the midst of our hopes.

THOMAS FULLER, M.D., *GNOMOLOGIA* (1732), 1254

54. He hath lived ill that knows not how to die well.

THOMAS FULLER, M.D., *GNOMOLOGIA* (1732), 1890

55. Is life a boon? / If so, it must befall / That Death, whene'er he call, / Must call too soon.

W. S. GILBERT, *THE YEOMAN OF THE GUARD* (1888), 1

56. Death holds no horrors. It is simply the ultimate horror of life.

JEAN GIRAUDOUX, *THE ENCHANTED* (1933), 2, ADAPTED BY MAURICE VALENCY

57. Death is the next step after the pension—it's perpetual retirement without pay.

JEAN GIRAUDOUX, *THE ENCHANTED* (1933), 3, ADAPTED BY MAURICE VALENCY

58. Few are wholly dead: / Blow on a dead man's embers / And a live flame will start.

ROBERT GRAVES, "TO BRING THE DEAD TO LIFE," *COLLECTED POEMS* (1961)

59. Death borders upon our birth, and our cradle stands in the grave.

JOSEPH HALL, *EPISTLES* (1608), 3.2

60. Do not seek death. Death will find you. But seek the road which makes death a fulfillment.

DAG HAMMARSKJÖLD, "1957," *MARKINGS* (1964), TR. W. H. AUDEN

61. In the last stages of a final illness, we need only the absence of pain and the presence of family.

HELEN HAYES, "A STOP ALONG THE WAY," *LOVING LIFE* (1987), WITH MARION GLASSEROW GLADNEY

62. Our repugnance to death increases in proportion to our consciousness of having lived in vain.

WILLIAM HAZLITT, "ON THE LOVE OF LIFE," *THE ROUND TABLE* (1817)

63. There was a time when we were not: this gives us no concern—why then should it trouble us that a time will come when we shall cease to be?

WILLIAM HAZLITT, "ON THE FEAR OF DEATH," *TABLE TALK* (1821–22)

64. We dread life's termination as the close, not of enjoyment, but of hope.

WILLIAM HAZLITT, "ON THE LOVE OF LIFE," *THE ROUND TABLE* (1817)

65. "I'm going to die," she said; then waited and said, "I hate it."

ERNEST HEMINGWAY, *A FAREWELL TO ARMS* (1929)

66. To die is to go into the Collective Unconscious, to lose oneself in order to be transformed into form, pure form.

HERMANN HESSE, QUOTED IN MIGUEL SERRANO'S *C. G. JUNG AND HERMANN HESSE* (1966), TR. FRANK MACSHANE

67. Man is the only animal that contemplates death, and also the only animal that shows any sign of doubt of its finality.

WILLIAM ERNEST HOCKING, *THE MEANING OF IMMORTALITY IN HUMAN EXPERIENCE* (1957)

68. Death has but one terror, that it has no tomorrow.

ERIC HOFFER, *THE PASSIONATE STATE OF MIND* (1954), 206

69. There is need for some kind of make-believe in order to face death unflinchingly. To our real, naked selves there is not a thing on earth or in heaven worth dying for.

ERIC HOFFER, *THE TRUE BELIEVER* (1951), 3.13.47

70. Death's dark way / Must needs be trodden once, however we pause.

HORACE, *ODES* (23-C. 15 B.C.), 1.28

71. One thing is sure, there are just two respectable ways to die. One is of old age, and the other is by accident.

ELBERT HUBBARD, *THE PHILISTINE* (1895–1915)

72. A belief in hell and the knowledge that every ambition is doomed to frustration at the hands of a skeleton have never prevented the majority of human beings from behaving as though death were no more than an unfounded rumor, and survival a thing beyond the bounds of possibility.

ALDOUS HUXLEY, "VARIATIONS ON A BAROQUE TOMB," *THEMES AND VARIATIONS* (1950)

73. Our last garment is made without pockets.

ITALIAN PROVERB

74. For dying, you always have time.

JEWISH PROVERB , *A TREASURY OF JEWISH FOLKLORE* (1948)

75. A year after Hemingway died on the front page, Faulkner went off after a binge, as if dying was nobody's business but his own.

ALFRED KAZIN, *BRIGHT BOOK OF LIFE* (1973)

76. The end of all is death and man's life passeth away suddenly as a shadow.

THOMAS À KEMPIS, *THE IMITATION OF CHRIST* (1426), 1.23

77. Dust into Dust, and under Dust to lie, / Sans Wine, sans Song, sans Singer, and—sans End!

OMAR KHAYYÁM, *RUBÁIYÁT* (11TH–12TH C.), TR. EDWARD FITZGERALD, 4TH ED., 24

78. Strange, is it not? that of the myriads who / Before us passed the door of Darkness through, / Not one returns to tell us of the Road, / Which to discover we must travel too.

OMAR KHAYYÁM, *RUBÁIYÁT* (11TH–12TH C.), TR. EDWARD FITZGERALD, 4TH ED., 64

79. Those most like the dead are those most loath to die.

LA FONTAINE, "DEATH AND THE DYING," *FABLES* (1688–94), TR. MARIANNE MOORE

80. Neither the sun nor death can be looked at steadily.

LA ROCHEFOUCAULD, *MAXIMS* (1665), TR. KENNETH PRATT

81. Without death there would be no awareness of life, and the recurring selection and renewal that has caused life's progress would be ended.

CHARLES A. LINDBERGH, "THE PRIMITIVE PASSING," *AUTOBIOGRAPHY OF VALUES* (1978)

82. Not all the preaching since Adam / Has made Death other than Death.

JAMES RUSSELL LOWELL, "AFTER THE BURIAL," *UNDER THE WILLOWS AND OTHER POEMS* (1868)

83. You may complete as many generations as you please during your life; none the less will that everlasting death await you.

LUCRETIUS, *ON THE NATURE OF THINGS* (1ST C. B.C.), 3, TR. H. A. J. MUNRO

84. What once was cuddled must learn to kiss/The cold worm's mouth. That's all the mystery.

ARCHIBALD MACLEISH, *JB* (1957)

85. It is death that is the guide of our life, and our life has no goal but death.

MAURICE MAETERLINCK, "THE PRE-DESTINED," *THE TREASURE OF THE HUMBLE* (1896), TR. ALFRED SUTRO

86. In every death is a celebration; in every ecstasy, one little death.

NORMAN MAILER, *HARLOT'S GHOST* (1991)

87. Flowers and buds fall, and the old and ripe fall.

MALAY PROVERB

88. A man's dying is more the survivors' affair than his own.

THOMAS MANN, *THE MAGIC MOUNTAIN* (1924), 6.8, TR. H. T. LOWE-PORTER

89. One cannot live with the dead; either we die with them or we make them live again. Or else we forget them.

LOUIS MARTIN-CHAUFFIER, *L'HOMME ET LA BÊTE* (1947), 1

90. The grave's a fine and private place, / But none, I think, do there embrace.

ANDREW MARVELL, "TO HIS COY MISTRESS" (1650)

91. Death hath a thousand doors to let out life.

PHILIP MASSINGER, *A VERY WOMAN* (1655), 5.4

92. So take care of your life and take notice and be observant, for the number of widows is always far greater than the number of widowers.

MICHELANGELO BUONARROTI, *COMPLETE POEMS AND SELECTED LETTERS OF MICHELANGELO* (1963), TR. CREIGHTON GILBERT

93. Blessed be Death, that cuts in marble / What would have sunk to dust!

EDNA ST. VINCENT MILLAY, "KEEN," *THE HARP-WEAVER* (1923)

94. Even Rome cannot grant us a dispensation from death.

MOLIÈRE, *L'ETOURDI* (1665), 2.4

95. God is favorable to those whom he makes to die by degrees; 'tis the only benefit of old age. The last death will be so much the less painful: it will kill but a quarter of a man or but half a one at most.

MONTAIGNE, "OF EXPERIENCE," *ESSAYS* (1580–88), TR. W. C. HAZLITT

96. The perpetual work of your life is but to lay the foundation of death.

MONTAIGNE, "THAT TO STUDY PHILOSOPHY IS TO LEARN TO DIE," *ESSAYS* (1580–88), TR. W. C. HAZLITT

97. A death is the most terrible of facts.

IRIS MURDOCH, *A WORD CHILD* (1975)

98. One should die proudly when it is no longer possible to live proudly.

NIETZSCHE, "SKIRMISHES IN A WAR WITH THE AGE," 36, *TWILIGHT OF THE IDOLS* (1888), TR. ANTHONY M. LUDOVICI

99. One should part from life as Odysseus parted from Nausicaa—blessing it rather than in love with it.

NIETZSCHE, *BEYOND GOOD AND EVIL* (1886), 96, TR. WALTER KAUFMANN

100. It costs me never a stab nor squirm / To tread by chance upon a worm. / "Aha, my little dear," I say, / "Your clan will pay me back one day."

DOROTHY PARKER, "THOUGHT FOR A SUNSHINY MORNING," *SUNSET GUN* (1928)

101. All I know is that I must soon die, but what I know least is this very death which I cannot escape.

PASCAL, *PENSÉES* (1670), 194, TR. W. F. TROTTER

102. The last act is tragic, however happy all the rest of the play is; at the last a little earth is thrown upon our head, and that is the end for ever.

PASCAL, *PENSÁES* (1670), 210, TR. W. F. TROTTER

103. Death is a camel that lies down at every door.

PERSIAN PROVERB

104. Rich man and poor move side by side toward the limit / of death.

PINDAR, *ODES* (5TH C. B.C.), NEMEA 7, TR. RICHMOND LATTIMORE

105. As men, we are all equal in the presence of death.

PUBLILIUS SYRUS, *MORAL SAYINGS* (1ST C. B.C.), 1, TR. DARIUS LYMAN

106. One of the very important things that have to be learned around the time dying becomes a real prospect is to recognize those occasions when we have been useful in the world.

ROGER ROSENBLATT, LEWIS THOMAS, QUOTED BY ROGER ROSENBLATT IN "LEWIS THOMAS ON THE ART OF DYING," *THE MAN IN THE WATER* (1994)

107. He who has gone, so we but cherish his memory, abides with us, more potent, nay, more present, than the living man.

SAINT-EXUPÉRY, *THE WISDOM OF THE SANDS* (1948), 2, TR. STUART GILBERT

108. [I]f Death stepped miraculously through the glass and came in after you, in all probability you just

got up and went along with him, ferociously but quietly.

J.D. SALINGER, *RAISE HIGH THE ROOF BEAM, CARPENTERS* (1963)

109. Death either destroys or unhusks us. If it means liberation, better things await us when our burden's gone: if destruction, nothing at all awaits us; blessings and curses are abolished.

SENECA, *LETTERS TO LUCILIUS* (1ST C.), 24.18, TR. E. PHILLIPS BARKER

110. Death takes us piecemeal, not at a gulp.

SENECA, *LETTERS TO LUCILIUS* (1ST C.), 120.18, TR. E. PHILLIPS BARKER

111. There is nothing after death, and death itself is nothing.

SENECA, *THE TROJAN WOMEN* (1ST C.), 397, TR. FRANK JUSTUS MILLER

112. He that dies pays all debts.

SHAKESPEARE, *THE TEMPEST* (1611–12), 3.2.140

113. Men must endure / Their going hence, even as their coming hither.

SHAKESPEARE, *KING LEAR* (1605–06), 5.2.9

114. The sense of death is most in apprehension, / And the poor beetle that we tread upon, / In corporal sufferance finds a pang as great / As when a giant dies.

SHAKESPEARE, *MEASURE FOR MEASURE* (1604–05), 3.1.78

115. The tongues of dying men / Enforce attention like deep harmony.

SHAKESPEARE, *RICHARD II* (1595–96), 2.1.5

116. This fell sergeant, Death, / Is strict in his arrest.

SHAKESPEARE, *HAMLET* (1600), 5.2.347

117. Life levels all men: death reveals the eminent.

GEORGE BERNARD SHAW, "MAXIMS FOR REVOLUTIONISTS," *MAN AND SUPERMAN* (1903)

118. It is a modest creed, and yet / Pleasant if one considers it, / To own that death itself must be, / Like all the rest, a mockery.

SHELLEY, "THE SENSITIVE PLANT" (1820)

119. When the lamp is shattered / The light in the dust lies dead— / When the cloud is scattered / The rainbow's glory is shed. / When the lute is broken, / Sweet tones are remembered not; / When the lips have spoken, / Loved accents are soon forgot.

SHELLEY, "WHEN THE LAMP IS SHATTERED" (1822), 1

120. How little room / Do we take up in death, that, living, know / No bounds!

JAMES SHIRLEY, *THE WEDDING* (1626), 4.4

121. Death takes away the commonplace of life.

ALEXANDER SMITH, "OF DEATH AND THE FEAR OF DYING," *DREAMTHORP* (1863)

122. Nobody knows, in fact, what death is, nor whether to man it is not perchance the greatest of all blessings; yet people fear it as if they surely knew it to be the worst of evils.

SOCRATES, IN PLATO'S *APOLOGY* (4TH C. B.C.), TR. LANE COOPER

123. Even the bold will fly when they see Death / drawing in close enough to end their life.

SOPHOCLES, *ANTIGONE* (442–41 B.C.), TR. ELIZABETH WYCKOFF

124. For the dead there are no more toils.

SOPHOCLES, *THE WOMEN OF TRACHIS* (C. 413 B.C.), TR. MICHAEL JAMESON

125. Death, when it approaches, ought not to take one by surprise. It should be part of the full expectancy of life. Without an ever-present sense of death life is insipid.

MURIEL SPARK, *MEMENTO MORI* (1959)

126. Death is a convention, a certification to the end of pain, something for the vital statistics book, not binding upon anyone but the keepers of graveyard records.

WALLACE STEGNER, "LETTER, MUCH TOO LATE," *WHEN THE BLUEBIRD SINGS IN THE LEMONADE SPRINGS* (1992)

127. Death is not anything ... death is not ... It's the absence of presence, nothing more ... the endless time of never coming back ... a gap you can't see, and when the wind blows through it, it makes no sound.

TOM STOPPARD, *ROSENCRANTZ & GUILDENSTERN ARE DEAD* (1967), 3

128. There is no God found stronger than death; and death is a sleep.

ALGERNON CHARLES SWINBURNE, "HYMN TO PROSERPINE," *POEMS AND BALLADS: FIRST SERIES* (1866)

129. Old men must die, or the world would grow mouldy, would only breed the past again.

LORD TENNYSON, PROLOGUE, *BECKET* (1884)

130. When we are dead / Rugs are no richer than a quick-thorn bed.

THEOGNIS, (6TH C. B.C.)

131. Do not go gentle into that good night, / Old age should burn and rave at close of day; / Rage, rage against the dying of the light.

DYLAN THOMAS, "DO NOT GO GENTLE INTO THAT GOOD NIGHT," *COLLECTED POEMS* (1953)

132. In the depth of the anxiety of having to die is the anxiety of being eternally forgotten.

PAUL TILLICH, *THE ETERNAL NOW* (1963), 1.2.3

133. Death is like a fisherman who catches fish in his net and leaves them for a while in the water; the fish is still swimming but the net is around him, and the fisherman will draw him up—when he thinks fit.

IVAN TURGENEV, *ON THE EVE* (1860), 35, TR. CONSTANCE GARNETT

134. Let us endeavour so to live that when we come to die even the undertaker will be sorry.

MARK TWAIN, "PUDD'NHEAD WILSON'S CALENDAR," *PUDD'NHEAD WILSON* (1894), 6

135. The world so quickly readjusts itself after any loss, that the return of the departed would nearly always throw it, even the circle most interested, into confusion.

CHARLES DUDLEY WARNER, "NINTH STUDY," *BACKLOG STUDIES* (1873)

136. Every death even the cruellest death / drowns in the total indifference of Nature / Nature herself would watch unmoved / if we destroyed the entire human race.

PETER WEISS, *MARAT/SADE* (1964), 1.12, TR. ADRIAN MITCHELL

137. To die is different from what any one supposed, and luckier.

WALT WHITMAN, "SONG OF MYSELF," *LEAVES OF GRASS* (1855–92)

138. Stretched out on a plank of wood amid a multitude of blood-covered corpses, fear frozen in his eyes, a mask of suffering on the bearded, stricken mask that was his face, my father gave back his soul at Buchenwald.

ELIE WIESEL, *LEGENDS OF OUR TIMES* (1968)

139. I hate people who say they have no fear of death. They are liars, and fools, and hypocrites.

THOMAS WOLFE, *THOMAS WOLFE'S LETTERS TO HIS MOTHER* (1943)

140. It was, he thought, the strong good medicine of death.

THOMAS WOLFE, *LOOK HOMEWARD, ANGEL* (1929)

141. The last voyage, the longest, the best.

THOMAS WOLFE, *LOOK HOMEWARD, ANGEL* (1929)

142. There is only one thing that a brave and honest man—a gentleman—should be afraid of. And that is death. He should carry the fear of death forever in his heart—for that ends all his glory, and he should use it as a spur to ride his life across the barriers.

THOMAS WOLFE, *THOMAS WOLFE'S LETTERS TO HIS MOTHER* (1943)

143. Edgar Allan Poe!—*Poe!*—the ruin of the dissolute—in the Bronx—*the Bronx!* The meaningless whirl, the unbridled flesh, the obliteration of home and hearth!—and, waiting in the last room, the Red Death.

TOM WOLFE, *THE BONFIRE OF THE VANITIES* (1987)

DEBATE

See 51. ARGUMENT

DEBAUCHERY

See 739. PROFLIGACY

222. DEBT

See also 96. BORROWING AND LENDING; 101. BUDGET; 223. DEBT, NATIONAL; 647. OBLIGATION

1. Interest works night and day, in fair weather and in foul. It gnaws at a man's substance with invisible teeth.

HENRY WARD BEECHER, *PROVERBS FROM PLYMOUTH PULPIT* (1887)

2. There are but two ways of paying debt: increase of industry in raising income, increase of thrift in laying out.

THOMAS CARLYLE, "GOVERNMENT," *PAST AND PRESENT* (1843)

3. It is hard to pay for bread that has been eaten.

DANISH PROVERB

4. Say nothing of my debts unless you mean to pay them.

ENGLISH PROVERB

5. Creditors are a superstitious sect, great observers of set days and times.

BENJAMIN FRANKLIN, *POOR RICHARD'S ALMANACK* (1732–57)

6. A poor man's debt makes a great noise.

THOMAS FULLER, M.D., *GNOMOLOGIA* (1732), 355

7. The first of the month falls every month, too, North or South. And them white folks who sends bills never forgets to send them—the phone bill, the furniture bill, the water bill, the gas bill, insurance, house rent.

LANGSTON HUGHES, *SIMPLE SPEAKS HIS MIND* (1950)

8. A creditor is worse than a master; for a master owns only your person, a creditor owns your dignity and can belabour that.

VICTOR HUGO, "MARIUS," *LES MISÉRABLES* (1862), 5.2, TR. CHARLES E. WILBOUR

9. If thy debtor be honest and capable, thou hast thy money again, if not with increase, with praise; if he prove insolvent, don't ruin him to get that which it will not ruin thee to lose, for thou art but a steward.

WILLIAM PENN, *SOME FRUITS OF SOLITUDE* (1693), 1.48

10. A small loan makes a debtor; a great one, an enemy.

PUBLILIUS SYRUS, *MORAL SAYINGS* (1ST C. B.C.), 12, TR. DARIUS LYMAN

11. Words pay no debts.

SHAKESPEARE, *TROILUS AND CRESSIDA* (1601–02), 3.2.58

223. DEBT, NATIONAL

See also 101. BUDGET

1. A national debt, if it is not excessive, will be to us a national blessing.

ALEXANDER HAMILTON, LETTER TO ROBERT MORRIS, APRIL 30, 1781

2. No nation ought to be without a debt. A national debt is a national bond; and when it bears no interest, is in no case a grievance.

THOMAS PAINE, "OF THE PRESENT ABILITY OF AMERICA," *COMMON SENSE* (1776)

3. The debt is like a crazy aunt we keep down in the basement. All the neighbors know she's there, but nobody wants to talk about her.

ROSS PEROT, *UNITED WE STAND: HOW WE CAN TAKE BACK OUR COUNTRY* (1992)

4. Our national debt after all is an internal debt owed not only *by* the nation but *to* the nation. If our children have to pay interest on it they will pay that interest to *themselves*.

FRANKLIN D. ROOSEVELT, SPEECH BEFORE THE AMERICAN RETAIL FOUNDATION, WASHINGTON, MAY 22, 1939

DECADENCE

See 191. CORRUPTION; 226. DECLINE; 557. LUXURY

DECEIT

See 224. DECEPTION

DECENCY

See 749. PROPRIETY

224. DECEPTION

See also 165. CONCEALMENT; 331. FALSEHOOD; 440. HYPOCRISY; 864. SELF-DECEPTION

1. Dishonesty is the raw material not of quacks only, but also in great part of dupes.

THOMAS CARLYLE, "COUNT CAGLIOSTRO" (1833)

2. Without some dissimulation no business can be carried on at all.

LORD CHESTERFIELD, *LETTERS TO HIS SON,* MAY 22, 1749

3. There are some frauds so well conducted that it would be stupidity not to be deceived by them.

CHARLES CALEB COLTON, *LACON* (1825), 1.96

4. No mask like open truth to cover lies, / As to go naked is the best disguise.

WILLIAM CONGREVE, *LOVE FOR LOVE* (1695), 5.4

5. A clean glove often hides a dirty hand.

ENGLISH PROVERB

6. Man is practised in disguise; / He cheats the most discerning eyes.

JOHN GAY, INTRODUCTION TO *FABLES* (1727–38)

7. Who will not be deceived must have as many eyes as hairs on his head.

GERMAN PROVERB

8. Deceive not thy physician, confessor, nor lawyer.

GEORGE HERBERT, *JACULA PRUDENTUM* (1651)

9. We are never so easily deceived as when we imagine we are deceiving others.

LA ROCHEFOUCAULD, *MAXIMS* (1665), TR. KENNETH PRATT

10. What renders us so bitter against those who trick us is that they believe themselves to be more clever than we are.

LA ROCHEFOUCAULD, *MAXIMS* (1665), TR. KENNETH PRATT

11. It is vain to find fault with those arts of deceiving wherein men find pleasure to be deceived.

John Locke, *An Essay Concerning Human Understanding* (1690), 3.11.34

12. W[ith] extramarital courtship, the deception was prolonged where it had been ephemeral, necessary where it had been frivolous, conspiratorial where it had been lonely.

Mary McCarthy, *The Company She Keeps* (1942)

13. The more skillful the performance of false cheer, the more pleasing the effect is upon one's public and on that private audience to whom one owes even more.

Judith Martin, "Unpleasant Facts of Life," *Miss Manners' Guide to Excruciatingly Correct Behavior* (1979)

14. Whoever has even once become notorious by base fraud, even if he speaks the truth, gains no belief.

Phaedrus, *Fables* (1st c.), 1.10.1, tr. H. T. Riley

15. If any man thinks to swindle / God, he is wrong.

Pindar, *Odes* (5th c. b.c.), Olympia 1, tr. Richmond Lattimore

16. It is more tolerable to be refused than deceived.

Publilius Syrus, *Moral Sayings* (1st c. b.c.), 836, tr. Darius Lyman

17. The fraud delights my soul, and if he is big and clever and conceals his fraudulence for years, I am all the more impressed and entertained by his achievement.

William Saroyan, "The Actor in the Street," *Sons Come & Go, Mothers Hang In Forever* (1979)

18. I like not fair terms and a villain's mind.

Shakespeare, *The Merchant of Venice* (1596–97), 1.3.180

19. One may smile, and smile, and be a villain. X

Shakespeare, *Hamlet* (1600), 1.5.108

20. The words of the double-tongued are as if they were harmless, but they reach even to the inner part of the bowels. Praise be to the Lord, who distinguishes our cause and delivers us from the unjust and deceitful man.

Muriel Spark, *The Ballad of Peckham Rye* (1960)

21. You can fool too many of the people too much of the time.

James Thurber, "The Owl Who Was God," *The Thurber Carnival* (1945)

22. Hatred of dishonesty generally arises from fear of being deceived.

Vauve-Nargues, *Reflections and Maxims* (1746), 523, tr. F. G. Stevens

23. People always overdo the matter when they attempt deception.

Charles Dudley Warner, "Tenth Week," *My Summer in a Garden* (1871)

24. If such people ask news of me,—be silent, or say that I am dead. Let me be dead to them as they are dead to me.

Thomas Wolfe, *Thomas Wolfe's Letters to His Mother* (1943)

225. DECISION

See also 24. Afterthought; 465. Indecision; 807. Resolution

1. To be always ready a man must be able to cut a knot, for everything cannot be untied.

Henri Frédéric Amiel, *Journal,* June 16, 1851, tr. Mrs. Humphry Ward

2. Decide, v.i. To succumb to the preponderance of one set of influences over another set.

Ambrose Bierce, *The Devil's Dictionary* (1881–1911)

3. It is the characteristic excellence of the strong man that he can bring momentous issues to the fore and make a decision about them. The weak are always forced to decide between alternatives they have not chosen themselves.

Dietrich Bonhoeffer, "Miscellaneous Thoughts," *Letters and Papers from Prison* (1953), tr. Eberhard Bethge

4. Drug misuse is not a disease, it is a decision, like the decision to step out in front of a moving car. You would call that not a decision but an error in judgment. When a bunch of people begin to do it, it is a social error, a life-style.

Philip K. Dick, *A Scanner Darkly* (1977)

5. Once a change of direction has begun, even though it's the wrong one, it still tends to clothe itself as thoroughly in the appurtenances of rightness as if it had been a natural all along.

F. Scott Fitzgerald, *The Crack-Up* (1945)

6. In whatever arena of life one may meet the challenge of courage, whatever may be the sacrifices he faces if he follows his conscience—the loss of his friends, his fortune, his contentment, even the

esteem of his fellow men—each man must decide for himself the course he will follow.

JOHN F. KENNEDY, *PROFILES IN COURAGE* (1956)

7. Nothing is more difficult, and therefore more precious, than to be able to decide.

NAPOLEON I, *MAXIMS* (1804–15)

8. It is always thus, impelled by a state of mind which is destined not to last, that we make our irrevocable decisions.

MARCEL PROUST, *REMEMBRANCE OF THINGS PAST: WITHIN A BUDDING GROVE* (1913–27), TR. C. K. SCOTT-MONCRIEFF

9. Many women feel it is natural to consult with their partners at every turn, while many men automatically make more decisions without consulting their partners.

DEBORAH TANNEN, *YOU JUST DON'T UNDERSTAND* (1990)

10. "I never made a decision in my life that wasn't one hundred per cent selfish."

JOHN UPDIKE, *THE CENTAUR* (1963)

226. DECLINE

See also 329. FAILURE; 653. OLD AGE

1. There is not a more unhappy being than a superannuated idol.

JOSEPH ADDISON, *THE SPECTATOR* (1711–12), 73

2. Statesmen and beauties are very rarely sensible of the gradations of their decay.

LORD CHESTERFIELD, *LETTERS TO HIS SON*, FEB. 26, 1754

3. He should be envied / Who when his strength is spent lays down his life. / Old age reserves a melancholy fate / For noble souls before their life is done.

CORNEILLE, *LE CID* (1636), 2.8, TR. PAUL LANDIS

4. The various aspects of decadence cannot be turned into functions of the economy and neither can they be grasped without relating them to this dynamic part of contemporary life.

MICHAEL HARRINGTON, *THE ACCIDENTAL CENTURY* (1966)

5. The passing years steal from us one thing after another.

HORACE, *EPISTLES* (20-C. 8 B.C.), 2.2

6. As favour and riches forsake a man, we discover in him the foolishness they concealed, and which no one perceived before.

LA BRUYÈRE, *CHARACTERS* (1688), 6.4, TR. HENRI VAN LAUN

7. How many worthy men have we known to survive their own reputation, who have seen and suffered the honor and glory most justly acquired in their youth, extinguished in their own presence?

MONTAIGNE, "OF GLORY," *ESSAYS* (1580–88), TR. W. C. HAZLITT

8. The Wine of Life keeps oozing drop by drop, / The Leaves of Life keep falling one by one.

OMAR KHAYYÁM, *RUBÁIYÁT* (11TH–12TH C.), TR. EDWARD FITZGERALD, 4TH ED., 8

9. When the snake is old, the frog will tease him.

PERSIAN PROVERB

10. Apples taste sweetest when they're going.

SENECA, *LETTERS TO LUCILIUS* (1ST C.), 12.4, TR. E. PHILLIPS BARKER

11. Men shut their doors against a setting sun.

SHAKESPEARE, *TIMON OF ATHENS* (1607–08), 1.2.150

12. The wolf loses his teeth, but not his inclinations.

SPANISH PROVERB

13. Like our shadows, / Our wishes lengthen as our sun declines.

EDWARD YOUNG, *NIGHT THOUGHTS* (1742–46), 5.627

227. DEEDS

See also 9. ACTION; 176. CONSEQUENCES; 388. GOLDEN RULE; 393. GOODNESS; 433. HUMANITARIANISM; 887. SERVICE; 888. SERVICES; 1070. WRONGDOING

1. We become just by performing just actions, temperate by performing temperate actions, brave by performing brave actions.

ARISTOTLE, *NICOMACHEAN ETHICS* (4TH C. B.C.), 2.1, TR. J. A. K. THOMSON

2. A man makes no noise over a good deed, but passes on to another as a vine to bear grapes again in season.

MARCUS AURELIUS, *MEDITATIONS* (2ND C.), 5.16, TR. MORRIS HICKEY MORGAN

3. Anything that is worth doing has been done frequently. Things hitherto undone should be given, I suspect, a wide berth.

MAX BEERBOHM, "FROM BLOOMSBURY TO BAYSWATER," *MAINLY ON THE AIR* (1946)

4. Whatsoever thy hand findeth to do, do it with thy might.

BIBLE, ECCLESIASTES 9:10

5. Great actions are not always true sons / Of great and mighty resolutions.

SAMUEL BUTLER (D. 1680), *HUDIBRAS* (1663), 1.1

6. Urgent necessity prompts many to do things, at the very thoughts of which they perhaps would start at other times.

CERVANTES, *DON QUIXOTE* (1605–15), 1.3.9, TR. JOHN OZELL

7. Time often serves to justify a deed / Which seems at first unjustifiable.

CORNEILLE, *LE CID* (1636), 5.7, TR. PAUL LANDIS

8. Our deeds determine us, as much as we determine our deeds.

GEORGE ELIOT, *ADAM BEDE* (1859), 29

9. What I must do is all that concerns me, not what the people think.

EMERSON, "SELF-RELIANCE," *ESSAYS: FIRST SERIES* (1841)

10. A man is not good or bad for one action.

THOMAS FULLER, M.D., *GNOMOLOGIA* (1732), 280

11. The most decisive actions of our life—I mean those that are most likely to decide the whole course of our future—are, more often than not, unconsidered.

ANDRÉ GIDE, *THE COUNTERFEITERS* (1925), 3.16, TR. DOROTHY BUSSY

12. The greatest pleasure I know is to do a good action by stealth, and to have it found out by accident.

CHARLES LAMB, "THE ATHENAEUM," JAN. 4, 1834

13. Though men pride themselves on their great actions, often they are not the result of any great design but of chance.

LA ROCHEFOUCAULD, *MAXIMS* (1665), TR. KENNETH PRATT

14. All the beautiful sentiments in the world weigh less than a single lovely action.

JAMES RUSSELL LOWELL, *ROUSSEAU AND THE SENTIMENTALISTS* (1870)

15. Is it really so difficult to tell a good action from a bad one? I think one usually knows right away or a moment afterward, in a horrid flash of regret.

MARY MCCARTHY, "MY CONFESSION," *ON THE CONTRARY* (1961)

16. To treat of human actions is to deal wholly with second causes.

HERMAN MELVILLE, SUPPLEMENT TO *BATTLEPIECES AND ASPECTS OF THE WAR* (1866)

17. Men are all alike in their promises. It is only in their deeds that they differ.

MOLIÈRE, *THE MISER* (1668), 1, TR. JOHN WOOD

18. Saying is one thing and doing is another; we are to consider the sermon and the preacher distinctly and apart.

MONTAIGNE, "OF ANGER," *ESSAYS* (1580–88), TR. W. C. HAZLITT

19. The majority of men are more capable of great actions than of good ones.

MONTESQUIEU, *VARIÉTÉS*

20. One will seldom go wrong if one attributes extreme actions to vanity, average ones to habit, and petty ones to fear.

NIETZSCHE, *HUMAN, ALL TOO HUMAN* (1878), 74, TR. HELEN ZIMMERN

21. Whatever is done for love always occurs beyond good and evil.

NIETZSCHE, *BEYOND GOOD AND EVIL* (1886), 153, TR. WALTER KAUFMANN

22. Noble deeds are most estimable when hidden.

PASCAL, *PENSÉES* (1670), 159, TR. W. F. TROTTER

23. Not always actions show the man; we find / Who does a kindness is not therefore kind.

ALEXANDER POPE, *MORAL ESSAYS* (1731–35), 1.109

24. The stellar universe is not so difficult of comprehension as the real actions of other people.

MARCEL PROUST, *REMEMBRANCE OF THINGS PAST: THE CAPTIVE* (1913–27), TR. C. K. SCOTT-MONCRIEFF

25. It is no profit to have learned well, if you neglect to do well.

PUBLILIUS SYRUS, *MORAL SAYINGS* (1ST C. B.C.), 1043, TR. DARIUS LYMAN

26. Not all of those to whom we do good love us, neither do all those to whom we do evil hate us.

JOSEPH ROUX, *MEDITATIONS OF A PARISH PRIEST* (1886), 9.41, TR. ISABEL F. HAPGOOD

27. The profit on a good action is to have done it.

SENECA, *LETTERS TO LUCILIUS* (1ST C.), 81.20, TR. E. PHILLIPS BARKER

28. Only the actions of the just / Smell sweet, and blossom in their dust.

JAMES SHIRLEY, *THE CONTENTION OF AJAX AND ULYSSES* (1659), 1.3

29. Ugly deeds are taught by ugly deeds.

SOPHOCLES, *ELECTRA* (C. 418–14 B.C.), TR. DAVID GRENE

30. Every great action is extreme when it is undertaken. Only after it has been accomplished does it seem possible to those creatures of more common stuff.

STENDHAL, *THE RED AND THE BLACK* (1830), 2.11

31. What old people say you cannot do, you try and find that you can. Old deeds for old people, and new deeds for new.

THOREAU, "ECONOMY," *WALDEN* (1854)

32. Each little thing that we do passes into the great machine of life which may grind our virtues to powder and make them worthless, or transform our sins into elements of a new civilisation, more marvelous and more splendid than any that has gone before.

OSCAR WILDE, "THE CRITIC AS ARTIST," *INTENTIONS* (1891)

228. DEFEAT

See also 17. ADVERSITY; 173. CONQUEST; 329. FAILURE

1. Defeat is a school in which truth always grows strong.

HENRY WARD BEECHER, *PROVERBS FROM PLYMOUTH PULPIT* (1887)

2. Who, apart / From ourselves, can see any difference between / Our victories and our defeats?

CHRISTOPHER FRY, *THOR, WITH ANGELS* (1948)

3. After a couple of days and after a hundred coffees and a thousand cigarettes and a million words and quite a few lunchtime beers we were able to agree that we didn't know nothing.

JAMES HERNDON, *HOW TO SURVIVE IN YOUR NATIVE LAND* (1971)

4. [Japanese Emperor Hirohito, broadcasting a declaration of surrender in 1945:] "After pondering deeply the general trends of the world and the actual conditions obtaining in Our Empire today, We have decided to effect a settlement of the present situation by resorting to an extraordinary measure."

JOHN HERSEY, *HIROSHIMA* (1946)

5. There are defeats more triumphant than victories.

MONTAIGNE, "OF CANNIBALS," *ESSAYS* (1580–88), TR. W. C. HAZLITT

6. The light of the one weak lamp in a rusty circle fell across the brickheaps and the broken wood and the dust that had been houses once, where the small and hardly known and never-to-be-forgotten people of the dirty town had lived and loved and died and, always, lost.

DYLAN THOMAS, *PORTRAIT OF THE ARTIST AS A YOUNG DOG* (1940)

229. DEFENSE

See also 856. SECURITY; 956. SURVIVAL

1. It may well be that we shall by a process of sublime irony have reached a state in this story where safety will be the sturdy child of terror, and survival the twin brother of annihilation.

SIR WINSTON CHURCHILL, SPEECH, HOUSE OF COMMONS, MARCH 1, 1955

2. No nation ever had an army large enough to guarantee it against attack in time of peace or insure it victory in time of war.

CALVIN COOLIDGE, ADDRESS, OCT. 6, 1925

3. Be as beneficent as the sun or the sea, but if your rights as a rational being are trenched on, die on the first inch of your territory.

EMERSON, *JOURNALS*, 1832

4. It is not widely known that, ever since the end of the Korean War, the United States has spent essentially the same amount of money on defense, in real terms, every single year.

JAMES FALLOWS, *NATIONAL DEFENSE* (1981)

5. The guns and the bombs, the rockets and the warships, are all symbols of human failure. They are necessary symbols. They protect what we cherish. But they are witness to human folly.

LYNDON B. JOHNSON, ADDRESS, THE JOHNS HOPKINS UNIVERSITY, APRIL 7, 1965

6. Diplomacy and defense are not substitutes for one another. Either alone would fail.

JOHN F. KENNEDY, ADDRESS, UNIVERSITY OF WASHINGTON, SEATTLE, NOV. 16, 1961

7. It is an unfortunate fact that we can secure peace only by preparing for war.

JOHN F. KENNEDY, CAMPAIGN ADDRESS, SEATTLE, WASH., SEPT. 6, 1960

8. Stretch a bow to the very full, / And you will wish you had stopped in time.

LAO TZU, *THE CHARACTER OF TAO* (6TH C. B.C.), 9, TR. LIN YUTANG

9. It is not the armed forces which can protect our democracy. It is the moral strength of democracy

which alone can give any meaning to the efforts at military security.

MAX LERNER, "THE NEGROES AND THE DRAFT," *ACTIONS AND PASSIONS* (1949)

10. The price of eternal vigilance is indifference.

MARSHALL MCLUHAN, *UNDERSTANDING MEDIA* (1964), 2

11. Isn't the best defense always a good attack?

OVID, *THE LOVES* (C. A.D. 8), 1.7, TR. ROLFE HUMPHRIES

12. Peace with a cudgel in hand is war.

PORTUGUESE PROVERB

13. The core of our defense is the faith we have in the institutions we defend.

FRANKLIN D. ROOSEVELT, SPEECH, DAYTON, OHIO, OCT. 12, 1940

14. The arms race is based on an optimistic view of technology and a pessimistic view of man. It assumes there is no limit to the ingenuity of science and no limit to the deviltry of human beings.

I. F. STONE, "NIXON AND THE ARMS RACE," *THE NEW YORK REVIEW OF BOOKS,* MARCH 27, 1969

15. To be prepared for war is one of the most effectual means of preserving peace.

GEORGE WASHINGTON, SPEECH TO BOTH HOUSES OF CONGRESS, JAN. 8, 1790

DEFERENCE

See 808. RESPECT

230. DEFINITION

See also 134. CLARITY; 244. DICTIONARIES; 1064. WORDS

1. A definition is the enclosing a wilderness of idea within a wall of words.

SAMUEL BUTLER (D. 1902), "HIGGLEDY-PIGGLEDY," *NOTE BOOKS* (1912)

2. Define, define, well-educated infant.

SHAKESPEARE, *LOVE'S LABOUR'S LOST* (1594–95), 1.2.99

231. DELAY

See also 465. INDECISION; 727. PREMATURENESS; 765. PUNCTUALITY; 907. SLOWNESS; 979. TIMELINESS

1. Delay always breeds danger and to protract a great design is often to ruin it.

CERVANTES, *DON QUIXOTE* (1605–15), 1.4.2, TR. JOHN OZELL

2. Defer not till to-morrow to be wise, / To-morrow's sun to thee may never rise.

WILLIAM CONGREVE, *LETTER TO COBHAM*

3. We are always getting ready to live, but never living.

EMERSON, *JOURNALS,* 1834

4. One of these days is none of these days.

ENGLISH PROVERB

5. There is a time when the word "eventually" has the soothing effect of a promise, and a time when the word evokes in us bitterness and scorn.

ERIC HOFFER, *THE PASSIONATE STATE OF MIND* (1954), 163

6. Delay is preferable to error.

THOMAS JEFFERSON, LETTER TO GEORGE WASHINGTON, MAY 16, 1792

7. procrastination is the / art of keeping up with yesterday.

DON MARQUIS, "CERTAIN MAXIMS OF ARCHY," *ARCHY AND MEHITABEL* (1927)

8. Life, as it is called, is for most of us one long postponement.

HENRY MILLER, "THE ENORMOUS WOMB," *THE WISDOM OF THE HEART* (1941)

9. You put things off and then one morning you wake up and say—today I will change the oil in my truck.

CHARLES PORTIS, *GRINGOS* (1991)

10. It isn't working that's so hard, it's getting ready to work.

ANDREW A. ROONEY, "PROCRASTINATION," *PIECES OF MY MIND* (1984)

11. By-and-by is easily said.

SHAKESPEARE, *HAMLET* (1600), 3.2.404

12. Procrastination is the thief of time.

EDWARD YOUNG, *NIGHT THOUGHTS* (1742–46), 1.393

232. DEMAGOGUERY

See also 568. MASS MOVEMENTS; 711. POLITICS AND POLITICIANS; 763. PUBLIC SPEAKING

1. Where the laws are not supreme, there demagogues spring up.

ARISTOTLE, *POLITICS* (4TH C. B.C.), 4.4, TR. BENJAMIN JOWETT

2. Primitive, simplistic anti-Communism is all too often used as a common denominator for diverse

efforts to perpetuate one's own power in a democratic system, convert opinions into dogma, and kill off all opposition, even silent.

EUGENE KOGON, "LESSONS FOR TOMORROW," *THE PATH TO DICTATORSHIP 1918–1933* (1966)

233. DEMOCRACY

See also 135. CLASS; 297. EQUALITY; 363. FREEDOM; 395. GOVERNMENT; 537. LIBERTY; 591. MINORITIES; 913. SOCIETY; 1038. VOTING

1. The masses are the material of democracy, but its form—that is to say, the laws which express the general reason, justice, and utility—can only be rightly shaped by wisdom, which is by no means a universal property.

HENRI FRÉDÉRIC AMIEL, *JOURNAL* FEB. 16, 1874, TR. MRS. HUMPHRY WARD

2. Democracy is the form of government in which the free are rulers.

ARISTOTLE, *POLITICS* (4TH C. B.C.), 4.4, TR. BENJAMIN JOWETT

3. If liberty and equality, as is thought by some, are chiefly to be found in democracy, they will be best attained when all persons alike share in the government to the utmost.

ARISTOTLE, *POLITICS* (4TH C. B.C.), 4.4, TR. BENJAMIN JOWETT

4. Democracy means government by discussion but it is only effective if you can stop people talking.

CLEMENT ATTLEE, *ANATOMY OF BRITAIN* (1962)

5. The real democratic American idea is, not that every man shall be on a level with every other man, but that every man shall have liberty to be what God made him, without hindrance.

HENRY WARD BEECHER, *PROVERBS FROM PLYMOUTH PULPIT* (1887)

6. All men are capable of reason. That is the fundamental principle of democracy. Because everybody's mind is capable of true knowledge, you don't have to have a special authority, or a special revelation telling you that this is the way things should be.

JOSEPH CAMPBELL, *THE POWER OF MYTH* (1988)

7. It's characteristic of democracy that majority rule is understood as being effective not only in politics but also in thinking. In thinking, of course, the majority is always wrong.

JOSEPH CAMPBELL, *THE POWER OF MYTH* (1988)

8. In a democracy the general good is furthered only when the special interests of competing minorities accidentally coincide—or cancel each other out.

ALEXANDER CHASE, *PERSPECTIVES* (1966)

9. It has been said that Democracy is the worst form of government except all those other forms that have been tried from time to time.

SIR WINSTON CHURCHILL, SPEECH, HOUSE OF COMMONS, NOVEMBER 1947

10. Democracy is the name we give to the people each time we need them.

ROBERT DE FLERS, *L'HABIT VERT* (1912), 1.2

11. Democratic institutions generally give men a lofty notion of their country and themselves.

ALEXIS DE TOCQUEVILLE, *DEMOCRACY IN AMERICA* (1835–39), 2.3.3

12. When the people rule, they must be rendered happy, or they will overturn the state.

ALEXIS DE TOCQUEVILLE, *DEMOCRACY IN AMERICA* (1835–39), 1.17

13. Democratic nations care but little for what has been, but they are haunted by visions of what will be.

ALEXIS DE TOCQUEVILLE, *DEMOCRACY IN AMERICA* (1835–39), 2.1.17

14. The most may err as grossly as the few.

JOHN DRYDEN, *ABSALOM AND ACHITOPHEL* (1681), 1.782

15. The evils of popular government appear greater than they are; there is compensation for them in the spirit and energy it awakens.

EMERSON, "POWER," *CONDUCT OF LIFE* (1860)

16. Two Cheers for Democracy: one because it admits variety and two because it permits criticism. Two cheers are quite enough: there is no occasion to give three.

E. M. FORSTER, "WHAT I BELIEVE," *TWO CHEERS FOR DEMOCRACY* (1951)

17. My notion of democracy is that under it the weakest should have the same opportunity as the strongest. This can never happen except through non-violence.

MOHANDAS K. GANDHI, *NON-VIOLENCE IN PEACE AND WAR* (1948), 1.269

18. You cannot possibly have a broader basis for any government than that which includes all the people, with all their rights in their hands, and with an equal power to maintain their rights.

WILLIAM LLOYD GARRISON, *LIFE* (1885–89), V. 4

19. Bipartisan democracy presupposes the individual, whose welfare is identical with that of the community in which he lives, the absence of coherent social classes, a basic uniformity of interest throughout.

LEARNED HAND, *THE SPIRIT OF LIBERTY* (1959)

20. Even though counting heads is not an ideal way to govern, at least it is better than breaking them.

LEARNED HAND, SPEECH, FEDERAL BAR ASSOCIATION, MARCH 8, 1932

21. Every government degenerates when trusted to the rulers of the people alone. The people themselves therefore are its only safe depositories.

THOMAS JEFFERSON, *NOTES ON THE STATE OF VIRGINIA* (1784–85), 14

22. I know no safe depository of the ultimate powers of the society but the people themselves; and if we think them not enlightened enough to exercise their control with a wholesome discretion, the remedy is not to take it from them, but to inform their discretion by education.

THOMAS JEFFERSON, LETTER TO WILLIAM C. JARVIS, SEPT. 28, 1820

23. Modesty and reverence are no less virtues of freemen than the democratic feeling which will submit neither to arrogance nor to servility.

OLIVER WENDELL HOLMES JR., SPEECH, HARVARD LAW SCHOOL ASSOCIATION, NOV. 5, 1886

24. Democracy is the superior form of government, because it is based on a respect for man as a reasonable being.

JOHN F. KENNEDY, *WHY ENGLAND SLEPT* (1940)

25. Self-government requires qualities of self-denial and restraint.

JOHN F. KENNEDY, CAMPAIGN ADDRESS, WASHINGTON, D.C., SEPT. 20, 1960

26. The grand paradox of our society is this: we magnify man's rights but we minimize his capacities.

JOSEPH WOOD KRUTCH, "THE FUNCTION OF DISCOURSE," *THE MEASURE OF MAN* (1954)

27. Because democratic institutions do not renew themselves as effortlessly as flowering trees, they demand the ceaseless tinkering of people who possess both the courage and the honesty to admit their mistakes and accept responsibility for even the most inglorious acts.

LEWIS LAPHAM, *IMPERIAL MASQUERADE* (1990)

28. The faith in reason insists that the poverty of democracy offers a greater hope for mankind than the prosperity that attaches itself to aristocracy or despotism.

LEWIS LAPHAM, *IMPERIAL MASQUERADE* (1990)

29. A democracy is a state which recognizes the subjection of the minority to the majority, that is, an organization for the systematic use of violence by one class against the other, by one part of the population against another.

LENIN, *THE STATE AND THE REVOLUTION* (1917)

30. The taste of democracy becomes a bitter taste when the fullness of democracy is denied.

MAX LERNER, "THE NEGROES AND THE DRAFT," *ACTIONS AND PASSIONS* (1949)

31. On the whole, with scandalous exceptions, Democracy has given the ordinary worker more dignity than he ever had.

SINCLAIR LEWIS, *IT CAN'T HAPPEN HERE* (1935)

32. This country, with its institutions, belongs to the people who inhabit it. Whenever they shall grow weary of the existing government, they can exercise their constitutional right of amending it, or their revolutionary right to dismember or overthrow it.

ABRAHAM LINCOLN, FIRST INAUGURAL ADDRESS, MARCH 4, 1861

33. No amount of charters, direct primaries, or short ballots will make a democracy out of an illiterate people.

WALTER LIPPMANN, "REVOLUTION AND CULTURE," *A PREFACE TO POLITICS* (1914)

34. This is one of the paradoxes of the democratic movement—that it loves a crowd and fears the individuals who compose it—that the religion of humanity should have no faith in human beings.

WALTER LIPPMANN, "ROUTINEER AND INVENTOR," *A PREFACE TO POLITICS* (1914)

35. "The consent of the governed" is more than a safeguard against ignorant tyrants: it is an insurance against benevolent despots as well.

WALTER LIPPMANN, "THE GOLDEN RULE AND AFTER," *A PREFACE TO POLITICS* (1914)

36. The tragedy of modern democracies is that they have not yet succeeded in effecting democracy.

JACQUES MARITAIN, "LA TRAGÉDIE DE LA DÉMOCRATIE," *CHRISTIANISME ET DÉMOCRATIE* (1940)

37. Democracy is the theory that the common people know what they want, and deserve to get it good and hard.

H. L. MENCKEN, "SENTENTIAE," *A BOOK OF BURLESQUES* (1920)

38. What democracy needs most of all is a party that will separate the good that is in it theoretically from the evils that beset it practically, and then try to erect that good into a workable system.

H. L. MENCKEN, "A GLANCE AHEAD," *NOTES ON DEMOCRACY* (1926)

39. The blind lead the blind. It's the democratic way.

HENRY MILLER, "WITH EDGAR VARÈSE IN THE GOBI DESERT," *THE AIR-CONDITIONED NIGHTMARE* (1945)

40. Democracy represents the disbelief in all great men and in all élite societies: everybody is everybody's equal.

NIETZSCHE, *THE WILL TO POWER* (1888), 752, TR. ANTHONY M. LUDOVICI

41. The majority is the best way, because it is visible, and has strength to make itself obeyed. Yet it is the opinion of the least able.

PASCAL, *PENSÉES* (1670), 877, TR. W. F. TROTTER

42. Let the people think they govern and they will be governed.

WILLIAM PENN, *SOME FRUITS OF SOLITUDE* (1693), 1.337

43. One voice is tiny, and alone it cannot be heard above the din of politics as usual. The people's voice, when it cries as one, is a great roar.

ROSS PEROT, *UNITED WE STAND: HOW WE CAN TAKE BACK OUR COUNTRY* (1992)

44. The republic which sinks to sleep, trusting to constitutions and machinery, to politicians and statesmen, for the safety of its liberties, never will have any.

WENDELL PHILLIPS, QUOTED IN *THE AMERICAN POLITICAL TRADITION*, ED. RICHARD HOFSTADTER (1948)

45. Democracy ... is a charming form of government, full of variety and disorder, and dispensing a sort of equality to equals and unequals alike.

PLATO, *THE REPUBLIC* (4TH C. B.C.), 8, TR. BENJAMIN JOWETT

46. One of the evils of democracy is, you have to put up with the man you elect whether you want him or not.

WILL ROGERS, *THE AUTOBIOGRAPHY OF WILL ROGERS* (1949), 17

47. Democracy, the practice of self-government, is a covenant among free men to respect the rights and liberties of their fellows.

FRANKLIN D. ROOSEVELT, STATE OF THE UNION MESSAGE, JAN. 4, 1939

48. Democracy is not a static thing. It is an everlasting march.

FRANKLIN D. ROOSEVELT, SPEECH, LOS ANGELES, OCT. 1, 1935

49. Were there a people of gods, their government would be democratic. So perfect a government is not for men.

ROUSSEAU, *THE SOCIAL CONTRACT* (1762), 3.5, TR. G. D. H. COLE

50. Democracy substitutes election by the incompetent many for appointment by the corrupt few.

GEORGE BERNARD SHAW, "MAXIMS FOR REVOLUTIONISTS," *MAN AND SUPERMAN* (1903)

51. If Despotism failed only for want of a capable benevolent despot, what chance has Democracy, which requires a whole population of capable voters.

GEORGE BERNARD SHAW, "EPISTLE DEDICATORY," *MAN AND SUPERMAN* (1903)

52. Self-criticism is the secret weapon of democracy, and candor and confession are good for the political soul.

ADLAI STEVENSON, ADDRESS, DEMOCRATIC NATIONAL CONVENTION, JULY 21, 1952

53. The essence of a republican government is not command. It is consent.

ADLAI STEVENSON, SPEECH, SPRINGFIELD, ILL., AUG. 14, 1952

54. We are called a democracy, for the administration is in the hands of the many and not of the few.

THUCYDIDES, *THE PELOPONNESIAN WAR* (C. 400 B.C.), 2.37, TR. BENJAMIN JOWETT

55. No government is perfect. One of the chief virtues of a democracy, however, is that its defects are always visible and under democratic processes can be pointed out and corrected.

HARRY S TRUMAN, ADDRESS TO CONGRESS (1947)

56. A President and his wise men can only propose; but Congress disposes. It is when President and Congress agree that American history marches forward.

THEODORE WHITE, *IN SEARCH OF HISTORY* (1978)

57. That a peasant may become king does not render the kingdom democratic.

WOODROW WILSON, ADDRESS, CHATTANOOGA, TENN., AUG. 31, 1910

58. The world must be made safe for democracy. Its peace must be planted on the tested foundations of political liberty.

WOODROW WILSON, ADDRESS TO CONGRESS, APRIL 2, 1917

DEMOCRATS

See 710. POLITICAL PARTIES

234. DENTISTS

1. Dentist, n. A prestidigitator who, putting metal into your mouth, pulls coins out of your pocket.

AMBROSE BIERCE, *THE DEVIL'S DICTIONARY* (1881–1911)

2. Actually I only wanted to have my tartar removed, though I had my suspicions: He's sure to find something. They always find something.

GÜNTER GRASS, *LOCAL ANAESTHETIC* (1970)

3. The hands of the clock pointed to one-thirty the other day, and my own, more flaccid than vermicelli, dangled inertly beside the dental chair as Dr. Yankwich shoved aside his drill, fired alternate round of compressed air and raspberry shrub down my throat, and straightened up. "There—wasn't it a breeze?" he asked gaily.

S.J. PERELMAN, *THE RISING GORGE* (1961)

4. Dentistry is more impressive in town—what the rural man calls cleaning the teeth is called "prophylaxis" in New York.

E.B. WHITE, *ONE MAN'S MEAT* (1944)

235. DEPENDENCE

See also 56. ASSISTANCE; 880. SELF-SUFFICIENCY

1. Nothing is more desirable than to be released from an affliction, but nothing is more frightening than to be divested of a crutch.

JAMES BALDWIN, INTRODUCTION, *NOBODY KNOWS MY NAME* (1961)

2. Hegel held that the two sexes were of necessity different, the one being active and the other passive, and of course the female would be the passive one.

SIMONE DE BEAUVOIR, *THE SECOND SEX* (1953)

3. To be obliged to beg our daily happiness from others bespeaks a more lamentable poverty than that of him who begs his daily bread.

CHARLES CALEB COLTON, *LACON* (1825), 1.445

4. There is not a soul who does not have to beg alms of another, either a smile, a handshake, or a fond eye.

EDWARD DAHLBERG, "ON LOVE AND FRIENDSHIP," *REASONS OF THE HEART* (1965)

5. We often have to put up with most from those on whom we most depend.

BALTASAR GRACIÁN, *THE ART OF WORLDLY WISDOM* (1647), 159, TR. JOSEPH JACOBS

6. Life for most of us is full of steep stairs to go puffing up and, later, of shaky stairs to totter down; and very early in the history of stairs must have come the invention of banisters.

LOUIS KRONENBERGER, "UNBRAVE NEW WORLD," *THE CART AND THE HORSE* (1964), 2

7. To depend on one's own child is blindness in one eye; to depend on a stranger, blindness in both eyes.

MALAY PROVERB

8. He who is being carried does not realize how far the town is.

NIGERIAN PROVERB

9. Independence? That's middle class blasphemy. We are all dependent on one another, every soul of us on earth.

GEORGE BERNARD SHAW, *PYGMALION* (1913), 5

10. [T]he desire for freedom and independence becomes more of an issue for many men in relationships, whereas interdependence and connection become more of an issue for many women.

DEBORAH TANNEN, *YOU JUST DON'T UNDERSTAND* (1990)

236. DEPRIVATION

See also 550. LOSS; 625. NEED; 718. POVERTY

1. Unlike the American President's chronic problem of finding ways to give away the country's permanent economic surplus, [Soviet Premier Nikita] Khrushchev's was the problem of rationing permanent scarcity.

ELIE ABEL, *THE MISSILE CRISIS* (1966)

2. Where can one find a profounder desolation than in the poor child who has lost its mother?

JOYCE CARY, *EXCEPT THE LORD* (1953)

237. DESIGN

See also 53. ART AND ARTISTS

1. Are you pro- or anti-macassar?

PETER DE VRIES, *I HEAR AMERICA SWINGING* (1976)

2. Always design a thing by considering it in its next larger context—a chair in a room, a room in a house, a house in an environment, an environment in a city plan.

ELIEL SAARINEN, *TIME*, JULY 2, 1956

238. DESIRES

See also 366. FRUSTRATION; 675. PASSION; 845. SATISFACTION

1. The desire for imaginary benefits often involves the loss of present blessings.

AESOP, "THE KITES AND THE SWANS," *FABLES* (6TH C. B.C.?), TR. GEORGE FYLER TOWNSEND

2. We would often be sorry if our wishes were gratified.

AESOP, "THE OLD MAN AND DEATH," *FABLES* (6TH C. B.C.?), TR. JOSEPH JACOBS

3. Make us, not fly to dreams, but moderate desire.

MATTHEW ARNOLD, *EMPEDOCLES ON ETNA* (1852), 1.2

4. Men have a thousand desires to a bushel of choices.

HENRY WARD BEECHER, *PROVERBS FROM PLYMOUTH PULPIT* (1887)

5. Great desire obtains little.

BURMESE PROVERBS (1962), 466, ED. HLA PE

6. Mankind, why do ye set your hearts on things / That, of necessity, may not be shared?

DANTE, "PURGATORIO," 14, *THE DIVINE COMEDY* (C. 1300–21), TR. LAWRENCE GRANT WHITE

7. Longing, the hope for fulfillment, is the one unwavering passion of the world's commerce.

E.L. DOCTOROW, "THEODORE DREISER: BOOK ONE AND BOOK TWO," *JACK LONDON, HEMINGWAY, AND THE CONSTITUTION* (1993)

8. What the eye sees not, the heart craves not.

DUTCH PROVERB

9. Those desires that do not bring pain if they are not satisfied are not necessary; and they are easily thrust aside whenever to satisfy them appears difficult or likely to cause injury.

EPICURUS, "PRINCIPAL DOCTRINES" (3RD C. B.C.), 26, IN *LETTERS, PRINCIPAL DOCTRINES, AND VATICAN SAYINGS*, TR. RUSSEL M. GEER

10. If you desire many things, many things will seem but a few.

BENJAMIN FRANKLIN, *POOR RICHARD'S ALMANACK* (1732–57)

11. Modern man lives under the illusion that he knows what he wants, while he actually wants what he is supposed to want.

ERICH FROMM, *ESCAPE FROM FREEDOM* (1941), 7

12. Our desires, once realized, haunt us again less readily.

MARGARET FULLER, *SUMMER ON THE LAKES* (1844), 1

13. There are mornings when all men experience with fatigue a flush of tenderness that makes them horny.

JEAN GENET, *OUR LADY OF THE FLOWERS* (1949)

14. Other people's appetites easily appear excessive when one doesn't share them.

ANDRÉ GIDE, *THE COUNTERFEITERS* (1925), 3.1, TR. DOROTHY BUSSY

15. We are never further from our wishes than when we imagine that we possess what we have desired.

GOETHE, *ELECTIVE AFFINITIES* (1809), 23

16. Catastrophe and desire are linked in our lives as the moon is linked to that reflected light from the sun which enables the eye to see it.

HERBERT GOLD, "THE MAGIC WILL," *THE MAGIC WILL* (1971)

17. How few are our real wants! and how easy is it to satisfy them! Our imaginary ones are boundless and insatiable.

AUGUSTUS WILLIAM HARE, *GUESSES AT TRUTH* (1827)

18. A strong passion for any object will ensure success, for the desire of the end will point out the means.

WILLIAM HAZLITT, "ON MANNER," *THE ROUND TABLE* (1817)

19. The wretched are in this respect fortunate, that they have the strongest yearnings after happiness; and to desire is in some sense to enjoy.

WILLIAM HAZLITT, *CHARACTERISTICS* (1823)

20. It is hard to fight against impulsive desire; whatever it wants it will buy at the cost of the soul.

HERACLITUS, *FRAGMENTS* (C. 500 B.C.), 51, TR. PHILIP WHEELWRIGHT

21. It would not be better if things happened to men just as they wish.

Heraclitus, *Fragments* (c. 500 B.C.), 52, tr. Philip Wheelwright

22. Often, the thing we pursue most passionately is but a substitute for the one thing we really want and cannot have.

Eric Hoffer, *The Passionate State of Mind* (1954), 3

23. We are less dissatisfied when we lack many things than when we seem to lack but one thing.

Eric Hoffer, *The True Believer* (1951), 2.5.23

24. Life is a progress from want to want, not from enjoyment to enjoyment.

Samuel Johnson, quoted in Boswell's *Life of Samuel Johnson,* May 1776

25. Some desire is necessary to keep life in motion, and he whose real wants are supplied must admit those of fancy.

Samuel Johnson, *Rasselas* (1759), 8

26. There are certain people who so ardently and passionately desire a thing, that from dread of losing it they leave nothing undone to make them lose it.

La Bruyère, *Characters* (1688), 4.61, tr. Henri Van Laun

27. It is very much easier to extinguish a first desire than to satisfy those which follow it.

La Rochefoucauld, *Maxims* (1665), tr. Kenneth Pratt

28. Man is a mixture of desires that extend beyond his knowledge and often result in action conflicting with rationality.

Charles A. Lindbergh, "Atlantis," *Autobiography of Values* (1978)

29. It is impossible to abolish either with a law or an axe the desires of men.

Walter Lippmann, "The Taboo," *A Preface to Politics* (1914)

30. Granting our wish one of Fate's saddest jokes is!

James Russell Lowell, "Two Scenes from the Life of Blondel, Autumn, 1863," *Under the Willows and Other Poems* (1868), 2.2

31. Desire projected itself visually: his fancy, not quite yet lulled since morning, imaged the marvels and terrors of the manifold earth.

Thomas Mann, *Death in Venice* (1911)

32. In real life wishing, divorced from willing, is sterile and begets nothing.

Cynthia Ozick, "Morgan and Maurice: A Fairy Tale," *Art & Ardor* (1983)

33. The ordinary life of men is like that of the saints. They all seek their satisfaction, and differ only in the object in which they place it; they call those their enemies who hinder them.

Pascal, *Pensées* (1670), 642, tr. W. F. Trotter

34. We do not succeed in changing things according to our desire, but gradually our desire changes.

Marcel Proust, *Remembrance of Things Past: The Sweet Cheat Gone* (1913–27), tr. C. K. Scott-Moncrieff

35. I look at what I have not and think myself unhappy; others look at what I have and think me happy.

Joseph Roux, *Meditations of a Parish Priest* (1886), 5.38, tr. Isabel F. Hapgood

36. The superiority of the distant over the present is only due to the mass and variety of the pleasures that can be suggested, compared with the poverty of those that can at any time be felt.

George Santayana, *Little Essays* (1920), 97, ed. Logan Pearsall Smith

37. It seems to me that the most universal revolutionary wish now or ever is a wish for heaven, a wish by a human being to be honored by angels for something other than beauty or usefulness.

Kurt Vonnegut, "The Sexual Revolution," *Palm Sunday* (1981)

239. DESPAIR

See also 195. Courage; 253. Discouragement; 427. Hope

1. You may not know it, but at the far end of despair, there is a white clearing where one is almost happy.

Jean Anouilh, *Restless Heart* (1934), 3, tr. Lucienne Hill

2. There's something so showy about desperation, it takes hard wits to see it's a grandiose form of funk.

Elizabeth Bowen, *The Death of the Heart* (1938), 3.6

3. Try the Lamentations of Jeremiah. They always pick me up.

Peter De Vries, Letter to Paul Theroux, quoted in *The New York Times* (1993)

4. Safe Despair it is that raves— / Agony is frugal. / Puts itself severe away / For its own perusal.

EMILY DICKINSON, POEM (C. 1873)

5. In despair there are the most intense enjoyments, especially when one is very acutely conscious of the hopelessness of one's position.

DOSTOYEVSKY, *NOTES FROM UNDERGROUND* (1864), 1.2, TR. CONSTANCE GARNETT

6. In a real dark night of the soul it is always three o'clock in the morning, day after day.

F. SCOTT FITZGERALD, "THE CRACK-UP," *THE CRACK-UP* (1945)

7. Despair is the price one pays for setting onself an impossible aim.

GRAHAM GREENE, *THE HEART OF THE MATTER* (1948), 2.4

8. When water covers the head, a hundred fathoms are as one.

PERSIAN PROVERB

9. If clearness about things produces a fundamental despair, a fundamental despair in turn produces a remarkable clearness or even playfulness about ordinary matters.

GEORGE SANTAYANA, "MY MOTHER," *PERSONS AND PLACES: THE BACKGROUND OF MY LIFE* (1944)

10. I was much further out than you thought / And not waving but drowning.

STEVIE SMITH, "NOT WAVING BUT DROWNING," *SELECTED POEMS* (1964)

11. The mass of men lead lives of quiet desperation. What is called resignation is confirmed desperation. From the desperate city you go into the desperate country, and have to console yourself with the bravery of minks and muskrats.

THOREAU, "ECONOMY," *WALDEN* (1854)

12. Lord save us all from old age and broken health and a hope tree that has lost the faculty of putting out blossoms.

MARK TWAIN, LETTER TO JOE T. GOODMAN, APRIL 1891

DESPOTISM

See 1002. TYRANNY

240. DESTINY

See also 340. FATE; 360. FORTUNE; 624. NECESSITY

1. How true it is that our destinies are decided by nothings and that a small imprudence helped by some insignificant accident, as an acorn is fertilized by a drop of rain, may raise the trees on which perhaps we and others shall be crucified.

HENRI FRÉDÉRIC AMIEL, *JOURNAL*, APRIL 9, 1856, TR. MRS. HUMPHRY WARD

2. Love nothing but that which comes to you woven in the pattern of your destiny. For what could more aptly fit your needs?

MARCUS AURELIUS, *MEDITATIONS* (2ND C.), 7.57, TR. MAXWELL STANIFORTH

3. Destiny, n. A tyrant's authority for crime and a fool's excuse for failure.

AMBROSE BIERCE, *THE DEVIL'S DICTIONARY* (1881–1911)

4. [B]eneath everything else, North and West, there ran a profound, unvoiced, almost subconscious conviction that the [American] nation was going to go on growing—in size, in power, in everything a man could think of—and in that belief there was a might and a fury that would take form instantly at the moment of shock.

BRUCE CATTON, *THIS HALLOWED GROUND* (1956)

5. It is a mistake to look too far ahead. Only one link of the chain of destiny can be handled at a time.

SIR WINSTON CHURCHILL, SPEECH, HOUSE OF COMMONS, FEB. 27, 1945

6. If thou follow thy star, thou canst not fail of glorious heaven.

DANTE, "PURGATORIO," 3, *THE DIVINE COMEDY* (C. 1300–21), TR. CHARLES ELIOT NORTON

7. How easy 'tis, when Destiny proves kind, / With full-spread sails to run before the wind!

JOHN DRYDEN, *ASTRAEA REDUX* (1660), 11.63

8. It seems that great minds a hundred years ago saw what would happen today or tomorrow, while we to whom it is happening blind ourselves in order not to be disturbed in our daily routine.

ERICH FROMM, *THE REVOLUTION OF HOPE* (1968)

9. [Destiny] is simply the relentless logic of each day we live.

JEAN GIRAUDOUX, *TIGER AT THE GATES* (1935), 1, TR. CHRISTOPHER FRY

10. Destiny grants us our wishes, but in its own way, in order to give us something beyond our wishes.

GOETHE, *ELECTIVE AFFINITIES* (1809), 28

11. We are not permitted to choose the frame of our destiny. But what we put into it is ours.

Dag Hammarskjöld, "1945–1949: Towards new shores—?" *Markings* (1964), tr. W. H. Auden

12. It's a good thing God doesn't let you look a year or two into the future, or you might be sorely tempted to shoot yourself.

Lee Iacocca, *Iacocca: An Autobiography* (1984) with William Novak

13. Thy lot or portion of life is seeking after thee; therefore be at rest from seeking after it.

Ali Ibn-Abi-Talib (7th c.), quoted in Emerson's "Self-Reliance," *Essays: First Series*

14. Our destiny rules over us, even when we are not yet aware of it; it is the future that makes laws for our to-day.

Nietzsche, *Human, All Too Human* (1878), tr. Helen Zimmern

15. 'Tis all a Chequer-board of Nights and Days / Where Destiny with Men for Pieces plays: / Hither and thither moves, and mates, and slays, / And one by one back in the Closet lays.

Omar Khayyám, *Rubáiyát* (11th–12th c.), tr. Edward FitzGerald, 1st ed., 49

16. Everything comes gradually and at its appointed hour.

Ovid, *The Art of Love* (c. A.D. 8), 1, tr. J. Lewis May

17. Where destiny blunders, human prudence will not avail.

Publilius Syrus, *Moral Sayings* (1st c. B.C.), 943, tr. Darius Lyman

18. There's a divinity that shapes our ends, / Rough-hew them how we will.

Shakespeare, *Hamlet* (1600), 5.2.10

19. Whatever God has brought about / Is to be borne with courage.

Sophocles, *Oedipus at Colonus* (401 B.C.), tr. Robert Fitzgerald

241. DESTRUCTION

See also 441. Iconoclasm; 1032. Violence

1. A missile is a missile. It makes no great difference whether you are killed by a missile fired from the Soviet Union or from Cuba.

Elie Abel, *The Missile Crisis* (1966)

2. When one builds and another tears down, what do they gain but toil?

Apocrypha, Ecclesiasticus 34:23

3. All destruction, by violent revolution or however it be, is but new creation on a wider scale.

Thomas Carlyle, *On Heroes, Hero-Worship and the Heroic in History* (1841), 4

4. One minute gives invention to destroy; / What to rebuild, will a whole age employ.

William Congreve, *The Double-Dealer* (1694), 1.3

5. There is nothing we value and hunt and cultivate and strive to draw to us, but in some hour we turn and rend it.

Emerson, *Journals*, 1836

6. According to the Office of Technology Assessment, 3 Minuteman missiles and 7 Poseidon missiles could destroy 73 percent of oil-refining capacity in the Soviet Union.

James Fallows, *National Defense* (1981)

7. To be able to destroy with good conscience, to be able to behave badly and call your bad behavior "righteous indignation"—this is the height of psychological luxury, the most delicious of moral treats.

Aldous Huxley, *Crome Yellow* (1921)

8. The impulse to mar and to destroy is as ancient and almost as nearly universal as the impulse to create. The one is an easier way than the other of demonstrating power.

Joseph Wood Krutch, *The Best of Two Worlds* (1950)

9. It is not science that has destroyed the world, despite all the gloomy forebodings of the earlier prophets. It is man who has destroyed man.

Max Lerner, "The Human Heart and the Human Will," *Actions and Passions* (1949)

10. Let not him who is houseless pull down the house of another, but let him work diligently and build one for himself, thus by his example assuring that his own shall be safe from violence when built.

Abraham Lincoln, reply to the New York Workingmen's Association, March 21, 1864

11. The Earth has killed itself. It is black, petrified, wizened, poisoned, burst; insanity has blown it rotten; and no creatures at all, joyful, despairing, cruel, kind, dumb, afire, loving, dull, shortly and brutishly hunt their days down like enemies on that corrupted face.

Dylan Thomas, *Quite Early One Morning* (1954)

DEVELOPMENT

See 404. Growth and Development; 571. Maturity

242. DEVIL

See also 387. God; 416. Hell

1. It's a sort of curious phenomenon that God is somehow not quite as nice as the devil; the devil doesn't punish you for behaving well, but God punishes you for behaving badly.

Jacob Bronowski, *Magic, Science, and Civilization* (1978)

2. An apology for the Devil: It must be remembered that we have only heard one side of the case. God has written all the books.

Samuel Butler (d. 1902), "Higgledy Piggledy," *Note Books* (1912)

3. In the desert, an old monk had once advised a traveler, the voices of God and the Devil are scarcely distinguishable.

Loren Eiseley, "The Star Thrower," *The Star Thrower* (1978)

4. One is always wrong to open a conversation with the devil, for, however he goes about it, he always insists upon having the last word.

André Gide, *Journals,* 1917, tr. Justin O'Brien

5. Why should the Devil have all the good tunes?

Ascribed to Rowland Hill, (1795–1879)

6. The devil is merely a fallen angel, and when God lost Satan he lost one of his best lieutenants.

Walter Lippmann, "The Red Herring," *A Preface to Politics* (1914)

7. Sometimes / The Devil is a gentleman.

Shelley, "Peter Bell the Third" (1819), 2.2

8. God seeks comrades and claims love, / the Devil seeks slaves and claims obedience.

Rabindranath Tagore, *Fireflies* (1928)

9. A person [Satan] who has during all time maintained the imposing position of spiritual head of four-fifths of the human race, and political head of the whole of it, must be granted the possession of executive abilities of the loftiest order.

Mark Twain, "Concerning the Jews," *Harper's Magazine,* September 1899

10. We may not pay Satan reverence, for that would be indiscreet, but we can at least respect his talents.

Mark Twain, "Concerning the Jews," *Harper's Magazine,* September 1899

DEVOTION

See 1068. Worship

243. DIAGNOSIS

See also 798. Remedies

1. A disease known is half cured.

Thomas Fuller, M.D., *Gnomologia* (1732), 75

DICTATORSHIP

See 1002. Tyranny

244. DICTIONARIES

See also 230. Definition; 1064. Words

1. [L]exicography is a chastening as well as an illuminating and fascinating art.

Robert Burchfield, *Unlocking the English Language* (1989)

2. Neither is a dictionary a bad book to read. There is no cant in it, no excess of explanation, and it is full of suggestion,—the raw material of possible poems and histories.

Emerson, "In Praise of Books," *The Conduct of Life* (1860)

3. The dictionary is a closed system in which someone interested in the meaning of a word can go around and around and end up exactly where he started, simply because words are defined in terms of other words, and these, in turn, are defined in terms of still other words.

Peter Farb, *Word Play* (1973)

4. When I feel inclined to read poetry I take down my Dictionary. The poetry of words is quite as beautiful as that of sentences. The author may arrange the gems effectively, but their shape and lustre have been given by the attrition of ages.

Oliver Wendell Holmes, Sr., "The Autocrat's Autobiography," *The Autocrat of the Breakfast Table* (1858), 1

5. Lexicographer: a writer of dictionaries, a harmless drudge.

Samuel Johnson, quoted in Boswell's *Life of Samuel Johnson,* 1755

6. Of course, one dictionary is as good as another to most people, who use them for spellers and bet-settlers and accessories to crossword puzzles and Scrabble games.

Kurt Vonnegut, *Welcome to the Monkey House* (1970)

245. DIFFICULTY

See also 17. Adversity; 157. Complaint; 281. Effort; 327. Facility; 585. Method; 686. Perseverance

1. It is hard to keep a secret, to employ leisure well, and to be able to bear an injury.

Chilon, (6th c. B.C.), quoted in Diogenes Laertius' *Lives and Opinions of Eminent Philosophers* (3rd c. A.D.), tr. R. D. Hicks

2. A smooth sea never made a skillful mariner.

English Proverb

3. Every path has its puddle.

English Proverb

4. Difficulties are things that show what men are.

Epictetus, *Discourses* (2nd c.), 1.24, tr. Thomas W. Higginson

5. All things are difficult before they are easy.

Thomas Fuller, M.D., *Gnomologia* (1732), 560

6. Nothing is easy to the unwilling.

Thomas Fuller, M.D., *Gnomologia* (1732), 3663

7. Many things difficult to design prove easy to performance.

Samuel Johnson, *Rasselas* (1759), 13

8. If at times our actions seem to make life difficult for others, it is only because history has made life difficult for us all.

John F. Kennedy, State of the Union Message, Jan. 14, 1963

9. I walk firmer and more secure up hill than down.

Montaigne, "Of the education of children," *Essays* (1580–88), tr. W. C. Hazlitt

10. In the difficult are the friendly forces, the hands that work on us.

Rainer Maria Rilke, *Letters* (1892–1910; 1910–26), tr. M. D. Herter Norton

246. DIGNITY

1. What is dignity without honesty?

Cicero, *Ad Atticum* (1st c. B.C.), 7

2. Let not a man guard his dignity, but let his dignity guard him.

Emerson, *Journals*, 1836

3. The only kind of dignity which is genuine is that which is not diminished by the indifference of others.

Dag Hammarskjöld, "1955," *Markings* (1964), tr. Leif Sjoberg and W. H. Auden

4. Dignity is a matter which concerns only mankind.

Livy, *Ab Urbe Condita* (c. 29 B.C.), 6.41

5. What could be more essential in a pluralistic society like ours than that every citizen see dignity in every other human being everywhere?

Kurt Vonnegut, "William Ellery Channing," *Palm Sunday* (1970)

DILIGENCE

See 281. Effort

247. DIPLOMATS AND DIPLOMACY

See also 498. International Relations; 994. Treaties

1. The ambassadors of peace shall weep bitterly.

Bible, Isaiah 33:7

2. Consul, n. In American politics, a person who having failed to secure an office from the people is given one by the Administration on condition that he leave the country.

Ambrose Bierce, *The Devil's Dictionary* (1881–1911)

3. Diplomats are useful only in fair weather. As soon as it rains they drown in every drop.

Charles de Gaulle, *Newsweek*, Oct. 1, 1962

4. There are three species of creatures who when they seem coming are going, / When they seem going they come: Diplomats, women, and crabs.

John Hay, "Distichs" (1871?), 2

5. Lofty words cannot construct an alliance or maintain it; only concrete deeds can do that.

John F. Kennedy, address, Frankfurt, West Germany, June 25, 1963

6. A diplomat should be yielding and supple as a liana that can be bent but not broken.

Malay Proverb

7. Diplomacy is the police in grand costume.

Napoleon I, *Maxims* (1804–15)

8. Foreign relations are like human relations. They are endless. The solution of one problem usually leads to another.

JAMES RESTON, *SKETCHES IN THE SAND* (1967)

9. The only real diplomacy ever performed by a diplomat is in deceiving their own people after their dumbness has got them into a war.

WILL ROGERS, *THE AUTOBIOGRAPHY OF WILL ROGERS* (1949), 16

10. My advice to any diplomat who wants to have a good press is to have two or three kids and a dog.

CARL ROWAN, *NEW YORKER*, DEC. 7, 1963

11. Diplomacy is the lowest form of politeness because it misquotes the greatest number of people. A nation, like an individual, if it has anything to say, should simply say it.

E. B. WHITE, "COMPOST," *ONE MAN'S MEAT* (1944)

12. An ambassador is an honest man sent to lie abroad for the commonwealth.

SIR HENRY WOTTON, WITTICISM WRITTEN IN THE AUTOGRAPH ALBUM OF CHRISTOPHER FLECKMORE (1604), PUBLISHED IN *RELIQUIAE WOTTONIANAE* (1651)

248. DIRTINESS

See also 137. CLEANLINESS

1. Mud-pies gratify one of our first and best instincts. So long as we are dirty, we are pure.

CHARLES DUDLEY WARNER, "PRELIMINARY," *MY SUMMER IN A GARDEN* (1871)

DISADVANTAGE

See 15. ADVANTAGE; 549. LOSERS

DISAGREEMENT

See 27. AGREEMENT; 258. DISSENT; 658. OPPOSITION

249. DISAPPOINTMENT

See also 254. DISILLUSIONMENT; 318. EXPECTATION; 920. SOUR GRAPES

1. Disappointment tears the bearable film of life.

ELIZABETH BOWEN, *THE HOUSE IN PARIS* (1935), 2.1

2. A good salad may be the prologue to a bad supper.

THOMAS FULLER, M.D., *GNOMOLOGIA* (1732), 174

DISASTER

See 17. ADVERSITY

DISCIPLES

See 353. FOLLOWING

250. DISCIPLINE

See also 470. INDULGENCE; 766. PUNISHMENT; 862. SELF-CONTROL; 988. TRAINING

1. He who requires much from himself and little from others, will keep himself from being the object of resentment.

CONFUCIUS, *ANALECTS* (6TH C. B,C.), 15.14, TR. JAMES LEGGE

2. Do not consider painful what is good for you.

EURIPIDES, *MEDEA* (431 B.C.), TR. REX WARNER

3. When gentle persuasion [of children] falls on deaf ears, we resort to ridicule and rebuke. Then we return to threats and punishment. This is the *modus operandi* of a mutual frustration society.

HAIM G. GINOTT, *BETWEEN PARENT & TEENAGER* (1969)

4. Perfect discipline requires recognition of infallibility. Infallibility requires the observance of discipline.

GEORGE F. KENNAN, *AMERICAN DIPLOMACY 1900–1950* (1951)

5. If men live decently it is because / discipline saves their very lives for them.

SOPHOCLES, *ANTIGONE* (442–41 B.C.), TR. ELIZABETH WYCKOFF

251. DISCONTENT

See also 186. CONTENTMENT; 1011. UNHAPPINESS

1. He that is discontented in one place will seldom be happy in another.

AESOP, "THE ASS AND HIS MASTERS," *FABLES* (6TH C. B.C.?), TR. THOMAS JAMES

2. What a miserable thing life is: you're living in clover, only the clover isn't good enough.

BERTOLT BRECHT, *JUNGLE OF CITIES* (1924), 5, TR. ANSELM HOLLO

3. Man is fond of counting his troubles, but he does not count his joys. If he counted them up as he ought to, he would see that every lot has enough happiness provided for it.

DOSTOYEVSKY, *NOTES FROM UNDERGROUND* (1864), 2.4, TR. CONSTANCE GARNETT

4. To have a grievance is to have a purpose in life.

ERIC HOFFER, *THE PASSIONATE STATE OF MIND* (1954), 166

5. When you are in Rome you long to be in the country, and when you are in the country you praise the distant town to the skies.

Horace, *Satires* (35–30 B.C.), 2.7

6. It is a flaw / In happiness, to see beyond our bourn,— / It forces us in summer skies to mourn, / It spoils the singing of the nightingale.

Keats, "Epistle to John Hamilton Reynolds" (1818)

7. Wealth ... and poverty: the one is the parent of luxury and indolence, and the other of meanness and viciousness, and both of discontent.

Plato, *The Republic* (4th c. B.C.), 4, tr. Benjamin Jowett

8. Discontent is the first step in the progress of a man or a nation.

Oscar Wilde, *A Woman of No Importance* (1893), 2

252. DISCORD

See also 27. Agreement; 51. Argument; 258. Dissent; 345. Fighting; 658. Opposition; 772. Quarreling; 1042. War

1. He who incites to strife is worse than he who takes part in it.

Aesop, "The Trumpeter Taken Prisoner," *Fables* (6th c. B.C.?), tr. Thomas James

2. It is a difficult matter for man to realize the extreme importance of social discriminations which seem outwardly insignificant but which produce in woman moral and intellectual effects so profound that they appear to spring from her original nature.

Simone de Beauvoir, *The Second Sex* (1953)

3. Where no wood is, there the fire goeth out: so where there is no tale-bearer, the strife ceaseth.

Bible, Proverbs 26:20

4. All men who reflect on controversial matters should be free from hatred, friendship, anger, and pity.

Julius Caesar, quoted in Sallust's *Conspiracy of Catiline* (1st c. B.C.), 51

5. Wars of opinion, as they have been the most destructive, are also the most disgraceful of conflicts, being appeals from right to might and from argument to artillery.

Charles Caleb Colton, *Lacon* (1825), 1.534

6. When a man induces his wife to turn suspicious thoughts against her own father, then that is surely cause enough for resentment.

Kazuo Ishiguro, *An Artist of the Floating World* (1986)

7. The ultimate measure of a man is not where he stands in moments of comfort and convenience, but where he stands at times of challenge and controversy.

Martin Luther King, Jr, *Strength to Love* (1963), 3.2

8. The unity of freedom has never relied on uniformity of opinion.

John F. Kennedy, State of the Union Message, Jan. 14, 1963

9. Discord gives a relish for concord.

Publilius Syrus, *Moral Sayings* (1st c. B.C.), 198, tr. Darius Lyman

10. What sets men at variance is but the treachery of language, for always they desire the same things.

Saint-Exupéry, *The Wisdom of the Sands* (1948), 17, tr. Stuart Gilbert

11. Civil dissension is a viperous worm / That gnaws the bowels of the commonwealth.

Shakespeare, *1 Henry VI* (1591–92), 3.1.72

253. DISCOURAGEMENT

See also 239. Despair

1. Go home. Go West. Go back where you came from. Why did you ever leave Ohio?

Betty Comden and Adolph Green, *Wonderful Town* (1953)

2. Trouble has no necessary connection with discouragement—discouragement has a germ of its own, as different from trouble as arthritis is different from a stiff joint.

F. Scott Fitzgerald, "The Crack-Up," *The Crack-Up* (1945)

DISCOVERY

See 479. Innovation

DISCRETION

See 755. Prudence

DISHONESTY

See 191. Corruption; 224. Deception; 331. Falsehood; 934. Stealing

254. DISILLUSIONMENT

See also 249. DISAPPOINTMENT

1. Not merely the idols fell, but also the habit of faith.

HENRY ADAMS, *THE EDUCATION OF HENRY ADAMS* (1918)

2. The proof that a philosopher does not know what he is talking about is apt to sadden his followers before it reacts on himself.

HENRY ADAMS, *THE EDUCATION OF HENRY ADAMS* (1918)

3. Disillusion can become itself an illusion / If we rest in it.

T. S. ELIOT, *THE COCKTAIL PARTY* (1949), 2

4. Once I thought that Lake Forest was the most glamorous place in the world. Maybe it was.

F. SCOTT FITZGERALD, *THE CRACK-UP* (1945)

5. The flowers of life are but illusions. How many fade away and leave no trace; how few yield any fruit; and the fruit itself, how rarely does it ripen!

GOETHE, *THE SORROWS OF YOUNG WERTHER* (1774), 1, AUG. 30, 1771, TR. VICTOR LANGE

6. Our bitterest wine is always drained from crushed ideals.

ARTHUR STRINGER, *THE DEVASTATOR* (1944)

7. The youth gets together his materials to build a bridge to the moon, or, perchance, a palace or temple on the earth, and, at length, the middle-aged man concludes to build a woodshed with them.

THOREAU, *JOURNAL*, JULY 14, 1852

8. Hope is the only good thing that disillusion respects.

VAUVENARGUES, *REFLECTIONS AND MAXIMS* (1746), 690, TR. F. G. STEVENS

255. DISLIKE

See also 288. ENEMIES; 301. ESTRANGEMENT; 412. HATRED; 594. MISANTHROPY

1. Rejection is a form of self-assertion. You have only to look back upon yourself as a person who hates this or that to discover what it is that you secretly love.

GEORGE SANTAYANA, "MY FATHER," *PERSONS AND PLACES: THE BACKGROUND OF MY LIFE* (1944)

256. DISOBEDIENCE

See also 644. OBEDIENCE; 786. REBELLION

1. Disobedience, the rarest and most courageous of virtues, is seldom distinguished from neglect, the laziest and commonest of the vices.

GEORGE BERNARD SHAW, "MAXIMS FOR REVOLUTIONISTS," *MAN AND SUPERMAN* (1903)

2. Disobedience, in the eyes of any one who has read history, is man's original virtue. It is through disobedience that progress has been made, through disobedience and through rebellion.

OSCAR WILDE, *THE SOUL OF MAN UNDER SOCIALISM* (1891)

257. DISORDER

See also 661. ORDER

1. Chaos often breeds life, when order breeds habit.

HENRY ADAMS, *THE EDUCATION OF HENRY ADAMS* (1918), 16

2. I came, I saw, I was confused.

BREYTEN BREYTENBACH, *RETURN TO PARADISE* (1993)

3. Chaos, if it does not harden into a pattern of disorder, may be more fruitful than a regularity too easily accepted and a success too easily achieved.

LEWIS MUMFORD, *FINDINGS AND KEEPINGS. ANALECTS FOR AN AUTOBIOGRAPHY* (1975)

4. We're all muddlers. The thing is to see is when one's got to stop muddling.

IRIS MURDOCH, *A WORD CHILD* (1975)

5. Man spends a great deal of time making order out of chaos, yet insists that the emotions be disordered. I order my emotions: I am insane.

NATHANAEL WEST , *THE DREAM LIFE OF BALSO SNELL* (1931)

DISPOSITION

See 392. GOOD NATURE; 968. TEMPER, BAD; 969. TEMPERAMENT

DISPUTE

See 51. ARGUMENT; 772. QUARRELING

258. DISSENT

See also 51. ARGUMENT; 252. DISCORD; 256. DISOBEDIENCE; 364. FREE SPEECH; 658. OPPOSITION; 731. PRESS, FREEDOM OF THE; 753. PROTEST; 772. QUARRELING; 786. REBELLION; 819. REVOLUTION; 1032. VIOLENCE

1. We owe almost all our knowledge not to those who have agreed, but to those who have differed.

CHARLES CALEB COLTON, *LACON* (1825), 2.121

2. Assent—and you are sane— / Demure—you're straightway dangerous— / And handled with a Chain—.

EMILY DICKINSON, POEM (C. 1862)

3. Dissent and dissenters have no monopoly on freedom. They must tolerate opposition. They must accept dissent from their dissent.

ABE FORTAS, *CONCERNING DISSENT AND CIVIL DISOBEDIENCE* (1968)

4. If a community decides that some conduct is prejudicial to itself, and so decides by numbers sufficient to impose its will upon dissenters, I know of no principle which can stay its hand.

LEARNED HAND, *THE SPIRIT OF LIBERTY* (1959)

5. They that approve a private opinion, call it opinion; but they that mislike it, heresy, and yet heresy signifies no more than private opinion.

THOMAS HOBBES, *LEVIATHAN* (1651), 1.11

6. A heresy can spring only from a system that is in full vigor.

ERIC HOFFER, *THE ORDEAL OF CHANGE* (1964), 5

7. Freedom to differ is not limited to things that do not matter much. That would be a mere shadow of freedom. The test of its substance is the right to differ as to things that touch the heart of the existing order.

JUSTICE ROBERT JACKSON, *WEST VIRGINIA STATE BOARD. V. BARNETTE* (1943)

8. It is more often from pride than from defective understanding that people oppose established opinions: they find the best places taken in the good party and are reluctant to accept inferior ones.

LA ROCHEFOUCAULD, *MAXIMS* (1665), TR. KENNETH PRATT

9. In religion, it is not the sycophants or those who cling most faithfully to the status quo who are ultimately praised. It is the insurgents.

ROLLO MAY, *THE COURAGE TO CREATE* (1975)

10. In a dead religion there are no more heresies.

ANDRÉ SUARÈS, *PÉGUY* (1912), 4

11. Say, Not so, and you will outcircle the philosophers.

THOREAU, *JOURNAL,* JUNE 26, 1840

12. Discussion in America means dissent.

JAMES THURBER, "THE DUCHESS AND THE BUGS," *LANTERNS AND LANCES* (1961)

259. DISTRUST

See also 79. BETRAYAL; 997. TRUST

1. He who is too much afraid of being duped has lost the power of being magnanimous.

HENRI FRÉDÉRIC AMIEL, *JOURNAL,* DEC. 26, 1868, TR. MRS. HUMPHRY WARD

2. Suspicion is a thing very few people can entertain without letting the hypothesis turn, in their minds, into fact.

DAVID CORT, *SOCIAL ASTONISHMENTS* (1963)

3. What loneliness is more lonely than distrust?

GEORGE ELIOT, *MIDDLEMARCH* (1871–72), 5.44

4. At the gate which suspicion enters, love goes out.

THOMAS FULLER, M.D., *GNOMOLOGIA* (1732), 828

5. I had rather take my chance that some traitors will escape detection than spread abroad a spirit of general suspicion and distrust, which accepts rumor and gossip in place of undismayed and unintimidated inquiry.

LEARNED HAND, SPEECH, NEW YORK STATE UNIVERSITY, OCT. 24, 1952

6. It is a matter of regret that many low, mean suspicions turn out to be well founded.

EDGAR WATSON HOWE, *VENTURES IN COMMON SENSE* (1919), 32.28

7. When you grow suspicious of a person and begin a system of espionage upon him, your punishment will be that you will find your suspicions true.

ELBERT HUBBARD, *THE NOTE BOOK* (1927)

8. It is more shameful to mistrust one's friends than to be deceived by them.

LA ROCHEFOUCAULD, *MAXIMS* (1665), TR. KENNETH PRATT

9. Our distrust justifies the deceit of others.

LA ROCHEFOUCAULD, *MAXIMS* (1665), TR. KENNETH PRATT

10. Made wary by impostors, men look for something wrong even in the righteous.

PANCHATANTRA (C. 5TH C.), 1, TR. FRANKLIN EDGERTON

11. Trust in God, but tie your camel.

PERSIAN PROVERB

12. The most mistrustful are often the greatest dupes.

CARDINAL DE RETZ, *MÉMOIRES* (1718)

13. I hold it cowardice / To rest mistrustful where a noble heart / Hath pawned an open hand in sign of love.

SHAKESPEARE, *3 HENRY VI* (1590–91), 4.2.7

14. O father Abram, what these Christians are, / Whose own hard dealing teaches them suspect / The thoughts of others!

SHAKESPEARE, *THE MERCHANT OF VENICE* (1596–97), 1.3.161

15. I fear the Greeks even when they bring gifts.

VERGIL, *AENEID* (30–19 B.C.), 2.49

16. We have to distrust each other. It is our only defense against betrayal.

TENNESSEE WILLIAMS, *CAMINO REAL* (1953), 10

260. DIVERSITY

See also 469. INDIVIDUALITY; 1014. UNIQUENESS; 1016. UNITY

1. Them which is of other naturs thinks different.

CHARLES DICKENS, *MARTIN CHUZZLEWIT* (1844), 19

2. There are no elements so diverse that they cannot be joined in the heart of a man.

JEAN GIRAUDOUX, *SIEGFRIED* (1928), 4, TR. PETER H. JUDD

3. There never were, in the world, two opinions alike, no more than two hairs, or two grains; the most universal quality is diversity.

MONTAIGNE, "OF THE RESEMBLANCE OF CHILDREN TO THEIR FATHERS," *ESSAYS* (1580–88), TR. W. C. HAZLITT

DIVIDED INTERESTS

See 170. CONFLICT, INNER; 497. INTERESTS, DIVIDED

DIVINE REVELATION

See 816. REVELATION, DIVINE

261. DIVINITY

See also 387. GOD; 432. HUMANISM

1. There is surely a piece of divinity in us, something that was before the elements, and owes no homage unto the sun.

SIR THOMAS BROWNE, *RELIGIO MEDICI* (1642), 2

2. Earth's crammed with heaven, / And every common bush afire with God.

ELIZABETH BARRETT BROWNING, *AURORA LEIGH* (1856), 7.821

3. The mystery of a person, indeed, is ever divine to him that has a sense for the godlike.

THOMAS CARLYLE, *SARTOR RESARTUS* (1833–34), 2.4

4. If we meet no gods, it is because we harbor none. If there is grandeur in you, you will find grandeur in porters and sweeps.

EMERSON, "WORSHIP," *THE CONDUCT OF LIFE* (1860)

5. With man more and more ubiquitous, with nature transformed from a mysterious given into a product of the human will, divinity is in crisis.

MICHAEL HARRINGTON, *THE ACCIDENTAL CENTURY* (1966)

6. What is divine escapes men's notice because of their incredulity.

HERACLITUS, *FRAGMENTS* (C. 500 B.C.), 63, TR. PHILIP WHEELWRIGHT

7. Man is God by his faculty for thought.

LAMARTINE, PREMIÈRE PRÉFACE, *LES PREMIÈRES MÉDITATIONS* (1820)

8. My deeply held belief is that if a god of anything like the traditional sort exists, our curiosity and intelligence are provided by such a god.

CARL SAGAN, *BROCA'S BRAIN: REFLECTIONS ON THE ROMANCE OF SCIENCE* (1979)

262. DIVORCE

See also 564. MARRIAGE

1. I have heard earnest American sociologists say that American children have a *right* to the divorce experience as an enriching element of an advanced civilisation.

ANTHONY BURGESS, *YOU'VE HAD YOUR TIME* (1990)

2. The only solid and lasting peace between a man and his wife is, doubtless, a separation.

LORD CHESTERFIELD, *LETTERS TO HIS SON,* SEPT. 1, 1763

3. Our marriage is dead, when the pleasure is fled: / 'Twas pleasure first made it an oath.

JOHN DRYDEN, *SONGS* (1673), 25.7

4. Better a tooth out than always aching.

THOMAS FULLER, M.D., *GNOMOLOGIA* (1732), 869

5. There are four minds in the bed of a divorced man who marries a divorced woman.

HAGGADAH, *PALESTINIAN TALMUD* (4TH C.)

6. Amoebas, once they have themselves well pulled in two, go their ways—they practice divorce, but no remarriage.

CHARLTON LAIRD, *THE MIRACLE OF LANGUAGE* (1953)

7. Alimony—The ransom that the happy pay to the devil.

H. L. MENCKEN, "SENTENTIAE," *A BOOK OF BURLESQUES* (1920)

8. A [Jewish] woman could not divorce her husband, but she could petition for divorce, and the religious courts could force him to grant the divorce on grounds of impotence, denial of conjugal rights, or unreasonable restriction of her freedom—for example, preventing her from attending funerals or wedding parties.

ISRAEL SHENKER, *COAT OF MANY COLORS* (1985)

9. Divorce is probably of nearly the same date as marriage. I believe, however, that marriage is some weeks more ancient.

VOLTAIRE, "DIVORCE," *PHILOSOPHICAL DICTIONARY* (1764)

263. DOCTORS

See also 234. DENTISTS; 577. MEDICINE; 757. PSYCHIATRY

1. Keep away from physicians. It is all probing and guessing and pretending with them. They leave it to Nature to cure in her own time, but they take the credit. As well as very fat fees.

ANTHONY BURGESS, "1592–1599," *NOTHING LIKE THE SUN* (1964), 8

2. A patient in th' hands iv a doctor is like a hero in th' hands iv a story writer. He's goin' to suffer a good dale, but he's goin' to come out all right in th' end.

FINLEY PETER DUNNE, "GOING TO SEE THE DOCTOR," *MR. DOOLEY ON MAKING A WILL* (1919)

3. The best surgeon is he that hath been hacked himself.

ENGLISH PROVERB

4. Every physician almost hath his favourite disease.

HENRY FIELDING, *TOM JONES* (1749), 2.9

5. God heals, and the doctor takes the fees.

BENJAMIN FRANKLIN, *POOR RICHARD'S ALMANACK* (1732–57)

6. Yesterday Dr Marcus went to see the statue of / Zeus. / Though Zeus, / & though marble, / We're burying the statue today.

GREEK ANTHOLOGY (7TH C. B.C.–10TH C. A.D.), 11.113, TR. DUDLEY FITTS

7. Doctors cut, burn, and torture the sick, and then demand of them an undeserved fee for such services.

HERACLITUS, *FRAGMENTS* (C. 500 B.C.), 107, TR. PHILIP WHEELWRIGHT

8. As long as men are liable to die and are desirous to live, a physician will be made fun of, but he will be well paid.

LA BRUYÈRE, *CHARACTERS* (1688), 14.65, TR. HENRI VAN LAUN

9. There's a sort of decency among the dead, a remarkable discretion: you never find them making any complaint against the doctor who killed them!

MOLIÈRE, *A DOCTOR IN SPITE OF HIMSELF* (1666), 3, TR. JOHN WOOD

10. Who ever saw one physician approve of another's prescription, without taking something away, or adding something to it?

MONTAIGNE, "OF THE RESEMBLANCE OF CHILDREN TO THEIR FATHERS," *ESSAYS* (1580–88), TR. W. C. HAZLITT

11. A physician can sometimes parry the scythe of death, but has no power over the sand in the hourglass.

HESTER LYNCH PIOZZI, LETTER TO FANNY BURNEY, NOV. 12, 1781

12. Only a fool will make a doctor his heir.

RUSSIAN PROVERB

13. There is among doctors, in acute hospitals at least, a presumption of stupidity in their patients.

OLIVER SACKS, *A LEG TO STAND ON* (1984)

14. Let no one suppose that the words doctor and patient can disguise from the parties the fact that they are employer and employee.

GEORGE BERNARD SHAW, "PREFACE ON DOCTORS: THE FUTURE OF PRIVATE PRACTICE," *THE DOCTOR'S DILEMMA* (1913)

15. There is no better surgeon than one with many scars.

SPANISH PROVERB

16. What do I want in a doctor? Perhaps more than anything else—a friend with special knowledge.

JOHN STEINBECK, *STEINBECK: A LIFE IN LETTERS* (1975), EDS. ELAINE STEINBECK AND ROBERT WALLSTEN

17. There are worse occupations in this world than feeling a woman's pulse.

LAURENCE STERNE, "THE PULSE," *A SENTIMENTAL JOURNEY* (1768)

18. The best doctors in the world are Doctor Diet, Doctor Quiet, and Doctor Merryman.

Jonathan Swift, *Polite Conversation* (1738), 2

19. To preserve a man alive in the midst of so many chances and hostilities, is as great a miracle as to create him.

Jeremy Taylor, *The Rule and Exercise of Holy Dying* (1651), 1

20. Men who are occupied in the restoration of health to other men, by the joint exertion of skill and humanity, are above all the great of the earth. They even partake of divinity, since to preserve and renew is almost as noble as to create.

Voltaire, "Physicians," *Philosophical Dictionary* (1764)

21. Physicians are like kings— / They brook no contradiction.

John Webster, *The Duchess of Malfi* (c. 1613), 5.2

DOCTRINE

See 973. THEOLOGY

264. DOGMATISM

See also 115. Certainty; 203. Creeds; 335. Fanaticism; 445. Ideology; 500. Intolerance; 620. Narrowness; 726. Prejudices; 879. Self-Righteousness

1. Bigot, n. One who is obstinately and zealously attached to an opinion that you do not entertain.

Ambrose Bierce, *The Devil's Dictionary* (1881–1911)

2. The man who never alters his opinion is like standing water, and breeds reptiles of the mind.

William Blake, "A Memorable Fancy," *The Marriage of Heaven and Hell* (1790)

3. It is in the uncompromisingness with which dogma is held and not in the dogma or want of dogma that the danger lies.

Samuel Butler (d. 1902), *The Way of All Flesh* (1903), 68

4. There are two kinds of people in the world: the conscious dogmatists and the unconscious dogmatists. I have always found myself that the unconscious dogmatists were by far the most dogmatic.

G. K. Chesterton, "On Europe and Asia," *Generally Speaking* (1928)

5. We call a man a bigot or a slave of dogma because he is a thinker who has thought thoroughly and to a definite end.

G. K. Chesterton, "The Error of Impartiality," *All Things Considered* (1908)

6. Religion is as effectually destroyed by bigotry as by indifference.

Emerson, *Journals*, 1831

7. We are least open to precise knowledge concerning the things we are most vehement about.

Eric Hoffer, *The Passionate State of Mind* (1954), 60

8. No man should dogmatize except on the subject of theology. Here he can take his stand, and by throwing the burden of proof on the opposition, he is invincible. We have to die to find out whether he is right.

Elbert Hubbard, *The Note Book* (1927)

9. Profound ignorance makes a man dogmatic. The man who knows nothing thinks he is teaching others what he has just learned himself; the man who knows a great deal can't imagine that what he is saying is not common knowledge, and speaks more indifferently.

La Bruyère, *Characters* (1688), 5.76

10. How strange it is to see with how much passion / People see things only in their own fashion!

Molière, *The School for Wives* (1662), 1.2, tr. Donald M. Frame

11. It is those people who know that they are right because some outside or higher power conveys the conviction to them who do the great damage in the world.

Maxwell Perkins, *Editor to Author: The Letters of Maxwell Perkins* (1950), ed. John Hall Wheelock

12. When people are fanatically dedicated to political or religious faiths or any other kinds of dogmas or goals, it's always because these dogmas or goals are in doubt.

Robert M. Pirsig, *Zen and the Art of Motorcycle Maintenance* (1974)

13. I am Sir Oracle, / And when I ope my lips, let no dog bark!

Shakespeare, *The Merchant of Venice* (1596–97), 1.1.93

14. The most positive men are the most credulous.

Jonathan Swift, *Thoughts on Various Subjects* (1711)

15. Bigotry tries to keep truth safe in its hand / with a grip that kills it.

Rabindranath Tagore, *Fireflies* (1928)

DOGS

See 41. ANIMALS

DOUBT

See 265. DOUBT, RELIGIOUS; 904. SKEPTICISM; 1005. UNCERTAINTY

265. DOUBT, RELIGIOUS

See also 330. FAITH; 904. SKEPTICISM; 1004. UNBELIEF; 1005. UNCERTAINTY

1. Do we, holding that the gods exist, / deceive ourselves with unsubstantial dreams / and lies, while random careless chance and change / alone control the world?

EURIPIDES, *HECUBA* (C. 425 B.C.), TR. WILLIAM ARROWSMITH

2. Wilt Thou not take the doubt of Thy children whom the time commands to try all things in the place of the unquestioning faith of earlier generations?

OLIVER WENDELL HOLMES, SR., *THE POET AT THE BREAKFAST TABLE* (1872), 7

3. Question with boldness even the existence of a God; because, if there be one, he must more approve of the homage of reason, than that of blindfolded fear.

THOMAS JEFFERSON, LETTER TO PETER CARR, AUG. 10, 1787

4. Ten thousand difficulties do not make one doubt.

JOHN HENRY NEWMAN, *APOLOGIA PRO VITA SUA* (1864)

5. O Lord, if there is a Lord, save my soul, if I have a soul.

ERNEST RENAN, *PRIÈRE D'UN SCEPTIQUE*

6. I am afraid I shall not find Him [God]: but I shall still look for Him, if He exists. He may be appreciative of my efforts.

JULES RENARD, *JOURNAL*, SEPTEMBER 1903, ED. AND TR., TR. ELIZABETH ROGET

7. Doubt is part of all religion. All the religious thinkers were doubters.

ISAAC BASHEVIS SINGER, *THE NEW YORK TIMES*, DEC. 3, 1978

8. There lives more faith in honest doubt, / Believe me, than in half the creeds.

LORD TENNYSON, "IN MEMORIAM A. H. H." (1850), 96

9. A faith which does not doubt is a dead faith.

MIGUEL DE UNAMUNO, *THE AGONY OF CHRISTIANITY* (1925)

10. In the present age doubt has become immune to faith and faith has dissociated itself from doubt.

GABRIEL VAHANIAN, *THE DEATH OF GOD* (1962), 1

11. People were always asking for good sound proofs; doubt springs eternal in the human breast, even in countries where the Inquisition can read your very thoughts in your eyes.

THORNTON WILDER, *THE BRIDGE OF SAN LUIS REY* (1927)

DRAMA

See 972. THEATER

266. DREAMS

See also 442. IDEALISM; 449. ILLUSION; 336. FANTASY; 906. SLEEP

1. In our dreams (writes Coleridge) images represent the sensations we think they cause; we do not feel horror because we are threatened by a sphinx; we dream of a sphinx in order to explain the horror we feel.

JORGE LUIS BORGES, "PARABLES," IN *FIFTY GREAT ESSAYS* (1964)

2. But a man who doesn't dream is like a man who doesn't sweat. He stores up a lot of poison.

TRUMAN CAPOTE, *THE GRASS HARP* (1951)

3. Dreaming permits each and every one of us to be quietly and safely insane every night of our lives.

WILLIAM DEMENT, *NEWSWEEK*, NOV. 30, 1959

4. Judge of your natural character by what you do in your dreams.

EMERSON, *JOURNALS*, 1833

5. The net of the sleeper catches fish.

GREEK PROVERB

6. I still got dreams like anybody else, an ever so often, I am thinkin about how things might of been.

WINSTON GROOM, *FORREST GUMP* (1986)

7. We are not hypocrites in our sleep.

WILLIAM HAZLITT, "ON DREAMS," *THE PLAIN SPEAKER* (1826)

8. We often forget our dreams so speedily: if we cannot catch them as they are passing out at the door, we never set eyes on them again.

WILLIAM HAZLITT, "ON DREAMS," *THE PLAIN SPEAKER* (1826)

9. The waking have one world in common; sleepers have each a private world of his own.

HERACLITUS, *FRAGMENTS* (C. 500 B.C.), 15, TR. PHILIP WHEELWRIGHT

10. Dreaming is not merely an act of communication (or coded communication, if you like); it is also an aesthetic activity, a game of the imagination, a game that is a value in itself.

MILAN KUNDERA, *THE UNBEARABLE LIGHTNESS OF BEING* (1984)

11. She entered his dreams sane and left mad. She began with words of love and ended with sounds that frightened him.

BERNARD MALAMUD, *DUBIN'S LIVES* (1979)

12. Dreams are faithful interpreters of our inclinations; but there is art required to sort and understand them.

MONTAIGNE, "OF EXPERIENCE," *ESSAYS* (1580–88), TR. W. C. HAZLITT

13. Do you want to know what I most regret about my youth? That I didn't dream more boldly and demand of myself more impossible things; for all one does in maturity is to carve in granite or porphyry the soap bubble one blew in youth! Oh to have dreamed harder!

LEWIS MUMFORD, *FINDINGS AND KEEPINGS. ANALECTS FOR AN AUTOBIOGRAPHY* (1975)

14. Just let them come, visit, like birds.

IRIS MURDOCH., *THE SACRED AND PROFANE LOVE MACHINE* (1974)

15. In bed my real love has always been the sleep that rescued me by allowing me to dream.

LUIGI PIRANDELLO, *THE RULES OF THE GAME* (1918), 2, TR. WILLIAM MURRAY

16. Everywhere about the house in my dream, the sand was endlessly blowing, burying the print of the coyote and lizard, rattling in the vibora weed, driftng close to the ground like barren snow so that the whole earth seemed to be moving, a restless gray ghost of itself trying to find those lusty prairie breasts, fertile as a woman and flowing with milk and wild honey, that used to be.

CONRAD RICHTER, *THE SEA OF GRASS* (1937)

17. There is a prodigious selfishness in dreams: they live perfectly deaf and invulnerable amid the cries of the real world.

GEORGE SANTAYANA, *THE LIFE OF REASON: REASON IN COMMON SENSE* (1905–06), 10

18. I talk of dreams; / Which are the children of an idle brain, / Begot of nothing but vain fantasy.

SHAKESPEARE, *ROMEO AND JULIET* (1594–95), 1.4.96

19. Whatever doesn't really happen is dreamed at night. It happens to one if it doesn't happen to another, tomorrow if not today, or a century hence if not next year.

ISAAC BASHEVIS SINGER, "GIMPEL THE FOOL" (1953)

20. In the drowsy dark cave of the mind / dreams build their nest with fragments / dropped from day's caravan.

RABINDRANATH TAGORE, *FIREFLIES* (1928)

21. Dreams are true while they last, and do we not live in dreams?

LORD TENNYSON, "THE HIGHER PANTHEISM" (1869)

22. The old dreams were good dreams; they didn't work out, but I'm glad I had them.

ROBERT JAMES WALLER, *THE BRIDGES OF MADISON COUNTY* (1992)

23. Action is limited and relative. Unlimited and absolute is the vision of him who sits at ease and watches, who walks in loneliness and dreams.

OSCAR WILDE, *THE ARTIST AS CRITIC: THE CRITICAL WRITINGS OF OSCAR WILDE*, RICHARD ELLMANN, ED. (1969)

267. DRESS

See also 45. APPEARANCE; 338. FASHION; 642. NUDITY

1. She is dressed to feel dangerous, perfumed to exude suggestions of nights in Babylon, and painted to drive men insane. How can she possibly avoid facing up to the terrible chasm between dream and reality when, in this musky state of mind, she must sit at a formica bar and squeeze mustard out of a plastic bottle?

RUSSELL BAKER, "ALL DOWNHILL FROM BABYLON," *ALL THINGS CONSIDERED* (1962)

2. Clothes and manners do not make the man; but, when he is made, they greatly improve his appearance.

HENRY WARD BEECHER, *PROVERBS FROM PLYMOUTH PULPIT* (1887)

3. From the cradle to the coffin underwear comes first.

BERTOLT BRECHT, *THE THREEPENNY OPERA* (1928), 2.2, TR. ERIC BENTLEY

4. Probably every new and eagerly expected garment ever put on since clothes came in, fell a trifle short of the wearer's expectation.

CHARLES DICKENS, *GREAT EXPECTATIONS* (1860–1861)

5. Any man may be in good spirits and good temper when he's well dressed. There an't much credit in that.

CHARLES DICKENS, *MARTIN CHUZZLEWIT* (1844), 5

6. *We* know, Mr. Weller—we, who are men of the world—that a good uniform must work its way with the women, sooner or later.

CHARLES DICKENS, *PICKWICK PAPERS* (1836–37), 7

7. Know, first, who you are; and then adorn yourself accordingly.

EPICTETUS, *DISCOURSES* (2ND C.), 3.1, TR. THOMAS W. HIGGINSON

8. That so-called feminine ardor for clothes shopping had been flagging for some time. Between 1980 and 1986, at the same time that women were buying more houses, cars, restaurant dinners, and health care services, they were buying fewer pieces of clothing—from dresses to underwear.

SUSAN FALUDI, *BACKLASH* (1991)

9. Women dress well in countries where they undress often.

FRENCH SAYING

10. A man with a good coat upon his back meets with a better reception than he who has a bad one.

SAMUEL JOHNSON, QUOTED IN BOSWELL'S *LIFE OF SAMUEL JOHNSON* JULY 20, 1763

11. Fine clothes are good only as they supply the want of other means of procuring respect.

SAMUEL JOHNSON, QUOTED IN BOSWELL'S *LIFE OF SAMUEL JOHNSON* MARCH 27, 1776

12. Camouflage is a game we all like to play, but our secrets are as surely revealed by what we want to seem to be as by what we want to conceal.

RUSSELL LYNES, "THE TRUTH ABOUT STATUS," *ARCHITECTURAL DIGEST* (1977)

13. In clothes as well as speech, the man of sense / Will shun all these extremes that give offense, / Dress unaffectedly, and, without haste, / Follow the changes in the current taste.

MOLIÈRE, *THE SCHOOL FOR HUSBANDS* (1661), 1.2, TR. DONALD M. FRAME

14. A man becomes the creature of his uniform.

NAPOLEON I, *MAXIMS* (1804–15)

15. A lady wants to be dressed exactly like everybody else but she gets pretty up- / set if she sees anybody else dressed exactly like / her.

OGDEN NASH, "THOUGHTS THOUGHT ON AN AVENUE," *MARRIAGE LINES* (1964)

16. The most loyal and faithful woman indulges her imagination in a hypothetical liaison whenever she dons a new street frock for the first time.

GEORGE JEAN NATHAN, "GENERAL CONCLUSIONS ABOUT THE COARSE SEX," *THE THEATRE, THE DRAMA, THE GIRLS* (1921)

17. Contentment preserves one even from catching a cold. Has a woman who knew she was well-dressed ever caught cold?

NIETZSCHE, "MAXIMS AND MISSILES," 25, *TWILIGHT OF THE IDOLS* (1888), TR. ANTHONY M. LUDOVICI

18. Where's the man could ease a heart / Like a satin gown?

DOROTHY PARKER, "THE SATIN DRESS," *ENOUGH ROPE* (1926), 1

19. A procession of sinuous long-stemmed beauties wound its way to the footlights attired in peasant costumes, large sections of which evidently had been lost in shipment from France.

S.J. PERELMAN, *THE RISING GORGE* (1961)

20. The problem of what to wear gave me pause; ordinarily, I prefer black tie for these sentimental occasions, as a cummerbund flattens the belly, but lacking at for the moment—the cummerbund, not the belly—I compromised on a vest, and flicked a bath towel over my shoes.

S.J. PERELMAN, *THE RISING GORGE* (1961)

21. Here, if one didn't have a family one was at least supposed to be a delegate to a visiting convention, with a lapel badge and a light hound's-tooth suit to prove it.

JONATHAN RABAN, *OLD GLORY* (1981)

22. She was wearing a canary-yellow two-piece bathing suit, one piece of which she would not actually be needing for another nine or ten years.

J.D. SALINGER, "A PERFECT DAY FOR BANANAFISH," IN *NINE STORIES BY J.D. SALINGER* (1953)

23. Costly thy habit as thy purse can buy, / But not expressed in fancy; rich, not gaudy.

SHAKESPEARE, *HAMLET* (1600), 1.3.70

24. The apparel oft proclaims the man.

SHAKESPEARE, *HAMLET* (1600), 1.3.72

25. To call a fashion wearable is the kiss of death. No new fashion worth its salt is ever wearable.

EUGENIA SHEPPARD, *NEW YORK HERALD TRIBUNE*, JAN. 13, 1960

26. A man cannot dress, but his ideas get clothed at the same time.

LAURENCE STERNE, *TRISTRAM SHANDY* (1759–67), 9.13

27. No one knows how ungentlemanly he can look, until he has seen himself in a shocking bad hat.

ROBERT SMITH SURTEES, *MR. FACEY ROMFORD'S HOUNDS* (1865), 9

28. Beware of all enterprises that require new clothes, and not rather a new wearer of clothes.

THOREAU, "ECONOMY," *WALDEN* (1854)

29. She's adorned / Amply that in her husband's eye looks lovely.

JOHN TOBIN, *THE HONEYMOON* (1805), 3.4

30. [T]hose running tights the young women wear now, so they look like spacewomen, raspberry red and electric green so tight they show every muscle right into the crack between the buttocks, what is the point of them? Display. Young animals need to display.

JOHN UPDIKE, *RABBIT AT REST* (1990)

31. Let me be dressed fine as I will, / Flies, worms, and flowers, exceed me still.

ISAAC WATTS, *DIVINE SONGS FOR CHILDREN* (1720), 22

32. With an evening coat and a white tie, anybody, even a stockbroker, can gain a reputation for being civilized.

OSCAR WILDE, *THE PICTURE OF DORIAN GRAY* (1891)

268. DRINKING

1. Bronze is the mirror of the form; wine, of the heart.

AESCHYLUS, *FRAGMENTS* (525–456 B.C.), 384, TR. M. H. MORGAN

2. The vine bears three kinds of grapes: the first of pleasure, the next of intoxication, and the third of disgust.

ANACHARSIS (C. 600 B.C.), QUOTED IN DIOGENES LAERTIUS' *LIVES AND OPINIONS OF EMINENT PHILOSOPHERS* (3RD. C. A.D.), TR. R. D. HICKS

3. When the cock is drunk, he forgets about the hawk.

ASHANTI PROVERB

4. I'd read somewhere that nine out of ten adults in Alaska had a drinking problem. I could believe it. Snow, ice, sleet, wind, the dark night of the soul: what else were you supposed to do?

T. CORAGHESSON BOYLE, "THE HAT," *IF THE RIVER WAS WHISKEY* (1989)

5. Man, being reasonable, must get drunk; / The best of Life is but intoxication.

BYRON, *DON JUAN* (1819–24), 2.179

6. [D]rink, in those days, was an evil inconceivable in ours. The fearful uncertainty of life, unemployment, the appalling squalor of slums, drove millions of the weaker nerve to drink.

JOYCE CARY, *EXCEPT THE LORD* (1953)

7. Drink moderately, for drunkenness neither keeps a secret, nor observes a promise.

CERVANTES, *DON QUIXOTE* (1605–15), 2.4.43, TR. JOHN OZELL

8. Under a bad cloak there is often a good drinker.

CERVANTES, *DON QUIXOTE* (1605–15), 2.3.33

9. Wine, to a gifted bard, / Is a mount that merrily races; / From watered wits / No good has ever grown.

CRATINUS (6TH–5TH C. B.C., QUOTED BY NICAENETUS (FL. 280 B.C.)

10. What the sober man has in his heart, the drunken man has on his lips.

DANISH PROVERB

11. Intemperance is the only vulgarity.

EMERSON, *JOURNALS* 1841

12. The secret of drunkenness is, that it insulates us in thought, whilst it unites us in feeling.

EMERSON, *JOURNALS* 1857

13. It's the wise man who stays home when he's drunk.

EURIPIDES, *THE CYCLOPS* (C. 425 B.C.), TR. WILLIAM ARROWSMITH

14. It is only the first bottle that is expensive.

FRENCH PROVERB

15. There are more old drunkards than old doctors.

FRENCH PROVERB

16. Bacchus hath drowned more men than Neptune.

THOMAS FULLER, M.D., *GNOMOLOGIA* (1732), 830

17. From wine what sudden friendship springs!

JOHN GAY, "THE SQUIRE AND HIS CUR," *FABLES* (1727–38)

18. Brandy is lead in the morning, silver at noon, gold at night.

GERMAN PROVERB

19. I fear the man who drinks water / And so remembers this morning what the rest of us said last night.

GREEK ANTHOLOGY (7TH C. B.C.–10TH C. A.D.), 11.31, TR. DUDLEY FITTS

20. Wine is like rain: when it falls on the mire it but makes it the fouler, / But when it strikes the good soil wakes it to beauty and bloom.

JOHN HAY, "DISTICHS" (1871?), 7

21. Although it is better to hide our ignorance, this is hard to do when we relax over wine.

HERACLITUS, *FRAGMENTS* (C. 500 B.C.), 53, TR. PHILIP WHEELWRIGHT

22. Drink not the third glass, which thou canst not tame, / When once it is within thee.

GEORGE HERBERT, "THE CHURCH PORCH," 5, *THE TEMPLE* (1633)

23. Wine can of their wits the wise beguile, / Make the sage frolic, and the serious smile.

HOMER, *ODYSSEY* (9TH C. B.C.), 14.520, TR. ALEXANDER POPE

24. What does drunkenness not accomplish? It unlocks secrets, confirms our hopes, urges the indolent into battle, lifts the burden from anxious minds, teaches new arts.

HORACE, *EPISTLES* (20-C. 8 B.C.), 1.5.16

25. Who, after wine, talks of war's hardships or of poverty?

HORACE, *ODES* (23 B.C.), 1.18.5

26. Malt does more than Milton can, / To justify God's ways to man.

A. E. HOUSMAN, *A SHROPSHIRE LAD* (1896), 62

27. "Drink took to me," said Simple. "Whiskey just naturally likes me but beer likes me better."

LANGSTON HUGHES, *SIMPLE SPEAKS HIS MIND* (1950)

28. God made only water, but man made wine.

VICTOR HUGO, "LA FÊTE CHEZ THÉRÈSE," *LES CONTEMPLATIONS* (1856)

29. We drink one another's healths and spoil our own.

JEROME K. JEROME, "ON EATING AND DRINKING," *THE IDLE THOUGHTS OF AN IDLE FELLOW* (1889)

30. Claret is the liquor for boys; port for men; but he who aspires to be a hero must drink brandy.

SAMUEL JOHNSON, QUOTED IN BOSWELL'S *LIFE OF SAMUEL JOHNSON*, APRIL 7, 1779

31. Wine gives a man nothing. It neither gives him knowledge nor wit; it only animates a man, and enables him to bring out what a dread of the company has repressed.

SAMUEL JOHNSON, QUOTED IN BOSWELL'S *LIFE OF SAMUEL JOHNSON*, APRIL 28, 1778

32. Wine is only sweet to happy men.

KEATS, "TO—[FANNY BRAWNE]" (1819)

33. The drinking man is never less himself than during his sober intervals.

CHARLES LAMB, "CONFESSIONS OF A DRUNKARD," *LAST ESSAYS OF ELIA* (1833)

34. Long quaffing maketh a short life.

JOHN LYLY, *EUPHUES: THE ANATOMY OF WIT* (1579)

35. an old stomach / reforms more whiskey drinkers / than a new resolve.

DON MARQUIS, "ARCHY ON THIS AND THAT," *ARCHY DOES HIS PART* (1935)

36. Drink to-day, and drown all sorrow; / You shall perhaps not do it to-morrow.

MASSINGER, *THE BLOODY BROTHER* (C. 1616), 2.2

37. He that will to bed go sober / Falls with leaf still in October.

MASSINGER, *THE BLOODY BROTHER* (C. 1616), 2.2

38. Candy / Is dandy / But liquor / Is quicker.

OGDEN NASH, "REFLECTIONS ON ICE-BREAKING," *VERSES FROM 1929 ON* (1959)

39. Drink! for you know not whence you came, nor why: / Drink! for you know not why you go, nor where.

OMAR KHAYYÁM, *RUBÁIYÁT* (11TH–12TH C.), TR. EDWARD FITZGERALD, 4TH ED., 74

40. I wonder often what the Vintners buy / One half so precious as the stuff they sell.

OMAR KHAYYÁM, *RUBÁIYÁT* (11TH–12TH C.), TR. EDWARD FITZGERALD, 4TH ED., 95

41. When there is plenty of wine, sorrow and worry take wing.

OVID, *THE ART OF LOVE* (C. A.D. 8), 1, TR. ROLFE HUMPHRIES

42. Too much and too little wine. Give him none, he cannot find truth; give him too much, the same.

PASCAL, *PENSÉES* (1670), 71, TR. W. F. TROTTER

43. There are two reasons for drinking: one is, when you are thirsty, to cure it; the other, when you are not thirsty, to prevent it.

THOMAS LOVE PEACOCK, *MELINCOURT* (1817), 16

44. In wine there is truth.

PLINY THE ELDER, *NATURAL HISTORY* (1ST C.), 14.141, TR. H. T. RILEY

45. To dispute with a drunkard is to debate with an empty house.

PUBLILIUS SYRUS, *MORAL SAYINGS* (1ST C. B.C.), 4, TR. DARIUS LYMAN

46. Drunkenness doesn't create vices, but it brings them to the fore.

SENECA, *LETTERS TO LUCILIUS* (1ST C.), 83.20, TR. E. PHILLIPS BARKER

47. Good wine is a good familiar creature if it be well used.

SHAKESPEARE, *OTHELLO* (1604–05), 2.3.313

48. Lechery, sir, it [drink] provokes, and unprovokes: it provokes the desire, but it takes away the performance.

SHAKESPEARE, *MACBETH* (1605–06), 2.3.32

49. O God, that men should put an enemy in their mouths to steal away their brains! that we should with joy, pleasance, revel, and applause transform ourselves into beasts!

SHAKESPEARE, *OTHELLO* (1604–05), 2.3.291

50. A bumper of good liquor / Will end a contest quicker / Than justice, judge, or vicar.

RICHARD BRINSLEY SHERIDAN, *THE DUENNA* (1775), 2.3

51. For a bad night, a mattress of wine.

SPANISH PROVERB

52. I liked the taste of beer, its live, white lather, its brass-bright depths, the sudden world through the wet-brown walls of the glass, the tilted rush to the lips and the slow swallowing down to the lapping belly, the salt on the tongue, the foam at the corners.

DYLAN THOMAS, *PORTRAIT OF THE ARTIST AS A YOUNG DOG* (1940)

53. Water taken in moderation cannot hurt anybody.

MARK TWAIN, *NOTEBOOK* (1935)

54. What marriage is to morality, a properly conducted licensed liquor traffic is to sobriety.

MARK TWAIN, *NOTEBOOK* (1935)

55. Over the bottle many a friend is found.

YIDDISH PROVERBS (1949)

DRUDGERY

See 1065. WORK

269. DRUGS

1. A drug for everything is madness. Legal or not, prescribed or not, over-counter under-counter bought for blood on street-corners—every pill separates us from knowing our own completion and from being taught by what's true.

RICHARD BACH, *RUNNING FROM SAFETY* (1994)

2. Opiate, n. An unlocked door in the prison of Identity. It leads into the jail yard.

AMBROSE BIERCE, *THE DEVIL'S DICTIONARY* (1881–1911)

3. Only the opium eater truly understands the pain of death.

JOHN CHEEVER, *THE FALCONER* (1977)

4. The spirit of the world, the great calm presence of the creator, comes not forth to the sorceries of opium or of wine.

EMERSON, "THE POET," *ESSAYS: SECOND SERIES* (1844)

5. The vaporish cocaine loosens the contours of their lives and sets their bodies adrift, and so they are untouchable.

JEAN GENET, *OUR LADY OF THE FLOWERS* (1949)

6. Drugs are nihilistic: they undermine all values and radically overturn all our ideas about good and evil, what is just and what is unjust, what is permitted and what is forbidden.

OCTAVIO PAZ, "GRACE, ASCETICISM, MERITS," *ALTERNATING CURRENT* (1973)

7. He had been gambling and drinking and eating now and again at the buffet tables the casinos keep heaped with food day and night, but mostly hopping himself up with good old amphetamine, cooling himself down with meprobamate, then hooking down more alcohol, until now, after sixty hours, he was slipping into the symptoms of toxic schizophrenia.

TOM WOLFE, *THE KANDY-KOLORED TANGERINE-FLAKE STREAMLINE BABY* (1965)

DRUNKENNESS

See 268. DRINKING

270. DULLNESS

See also 94. BOREDOM; 95. BORES; 447. IGNORANCE; 941. STUPIDITY

1. I have never met an author who admitted that people did not buy his book because it was dull.

W. SOMERSET MAUGHAM, *THE SUMMING UP* (1938), 46

2. Dullness is the coming of age of seriousness.

OSCAR WILDE, "PHRASES AND PHILOSOPHIES FOR THE USE OF THE YOUNG" (1891)

271. DUTY

See also 647. OBLIGATION; 810. RESPONSIBILITY

1. Rich men are to bear the infirmities of the poor. Wise men are to bear the mistakes of the ignorant.

HENRY WARD BEECHER, *PROVERBS FROM PLYMOUTH PULPIT* (1887)

2. Nobody is bound by any obligation unless it has first been freely accepted.

UGO BETTI, *THE FUGITIVE* (1953), 3, TR. G. H. MCWILLIAM

3. In practice it is seldom very hard to do one's duty when one knows what it is, but it is sometimes exceedingly difficult to find this out.

SAMUEL BUTLER (D. 1902), "FIRST PRINCIPLES," *NOTE BOOKS* (1912)

4. Do your duty, and leave the rest to the gods.

CORNEILLE, *HORACE* (1640), 2.8

5. must's a schoolroom in the month of may

E. E. CUMMINGS, "NOTHING FALSE AND POSSIBLE IS LOVE," *100 SELECTED POEMS* (1959)

6. You will always find those who think they know what is your duty better than you know it.

EMERSON, "SELF-RELIANCE," *ESSAYS: FIRST SERIES* (1841)

7. Duty largely consists of pretending that the trivial is critical.

JOHN FOWLES, *THE MAGUS* (1965), 18

8. What, then, is your duty? What the day demands.

GOETHE, *SPRÜCHE IN PROSA,* 3.151

9. The last pleasure in life is the sense of discharging our duty.

WILLIAM HAZLITT, *CHARACTERISTICS* (1823), 409

10. The burning conviction that we have a holy duty toward others is often a way of attaching our drowning selves to a passing raft.

ERIC HOFFER, *THE TRUE BELIEVER* (1951), 1.2.11

11. When habit has strengthened our sense of duties, they leave us no time for other things; but when young we neglect them and this gives us time for anything.

THOMAS JEFFERSON, LETTER TO ABIGAIL ADAMS, AUG. 22, 1813

12. Without duty, life is soft and boneless; it cannot hold itself together.

JOSEPH JOUBERT, *PENSÉES* (1842), 8.52, TR. KATHARINE LYTTELTON

13. What is the use of such terrible diligence as many tire themselves out with, if they always postpone their exchange of smiles with Beauty and Joy to cling to irksome duties and relations?

HELEN KELLER, *MY RELIGION* (1927)

14. God obligeth no man to more than he hath given him ability to perform.

KORAN (6TH AND 7TH C.), 65

15. Whilst weakness and timidity keep us to our duty, virtue has often all the honour for it.

LA ROCHEFOUCAULD, *MAXIMS* (1665), TR. KENNETH PRATT

16. The cradle is rocked but the baby is pinched.

MALAY PROVERB

17. Duty then is the sublimest word in our language. Do your duty in all things. You cannot do more. You should never wish to do less.

ROBERT E. LEE (1807–70), INSCRIPTION BENEATH HIS BUST IN THE HALL OF FAME FOR GREAT AMERICANS, NEW YORK UNIVERSITY

18. When Duty comes a-knocking at your gate, / Welcome him in; for if you bid him wait, / He will depart only to come once more / And bring seven other duties to your door.

EDWIN MARKHAM, "DUTY" (1922)

19. If a sense of duty tortures a man, it also enables him to achieve prodigies.

H. L. MENCKEN, *PREJUDICES: FIRST SERIES* (1919)

20. A sahib has got to act like a sahib; he has got to appear resolute, to know his own mind and do definite things.

GEORGE ORWELL, "SHOOTING AN ELEPHANT," *A COLLECTION OF ESSAYS* (1954)

21. To an honest man, it is an honor to have remembered his duty.

PLAUTUS, *THE THREE-PENNY DAY* (C. 194 B.C.), 3.2

22. Conscientious men are, almost everywhere, less encouraged than tolerated.

JOSEPH ROUX, *MEDITATIONS OF A PARISH PRIEST* (1886), 4.80, TR. ISABEL F. HAPGOOD

23. There is no growth except in the fulfillment of obligations.

SAINT-EXUPÉRY, *FLIGHT OF ARRAS* (1942), 20, TR. LEWIS GALANTIÈRE

24. Alas! When duty grows thy law, enjoyment fades away.

SCHILLER, "THE PLAYING BOY" (1795)

25. The words of Mercury are harsh after the songs of Apollo.

SHAKESPEARE, *LOVE'S LABOUR'S LOST* (1594–95), 5.2.40

26. When a stupid man is doing something he is ashamed of, he always declares that it is his duty.

GEORGE BERNARD SHAW, *CAESAR AND CLEOPATRA* (1906), 3

27. There is no duty we so much underrate as the duty of being happy.

ROBERT LOUIS STEVENSON, "AN APOLOGY FOR IDLERS," *VIRGINIBUS PUERISQUE* (1881)

28. If you are chosen town clerk, forsooth, you cannot go to Tierra del Fuego this summer; but you may go to the land of infernal fire nevertheless.

THOREAU, "CONCLUSION," *WALDEN* (1854)

29. The paths of glory at least lead to the Grave, but the paths of duty may not get you Anywhere.

JAMES THURBER, "THE PATIENT BLOODHOUND," *FABLES OF OUR TIME* (1943)

30. There's life alone in duty done, / And rest alone in striving.

JOHN GREENLEAF WHITTIER, "THE DROVERS" (1847)

31. Duty is what one expects from others, it is not what one does one's self.

OSCAR WILDE, *A WOMAN OF NO IMPORTANCE* (1893), 2

E

EARNESTNESS

See 886. SERIOUSNESS

272. EARTH

See also 177. CONSERVATION; 415. THE HEAVENS; 623. NATURE; 1067. WORLD

1. Touch the earth, love the earth, honour the earth, her plains, her valleys, her hills, and her seas; rest your spirit in her solitary places.

HENRY BESTON, "ORION RISES ON THE DUNES," *THE OUTERMOST HOUSE* (1928)

2. Earth being so good, would Heaven seem best?

ROBERT BROWNING, "THE LAST RIDE TOGETHER," *MEN AND WOMEN* (1855), 9

3. Earth, with her thousand voices, praises God.

SAMUEL TAYLOR COLERIDGE, "HYMN BEFORE SUNRISE" (1802)

4. Let me enjoy the earth no less / Because the all-enacting Might / That fashioned forth its loveliness / Had other aims than my delight.

THOMAS HARDY, "LET ME ENJOY," *TIME'S LAUGHINGSTOCKS AND OTHER VERSES* (1909)

5. The earth is given as a common stock for man to labor and live on.

THOMAS JEFFERSON, LETTER TO JAMES MADISON, 1785

EASE

See 327. FACILITY; 533. LEISURE

273. EAST AND WEST

See also 498. INTERNATIONAL RELATIONS

1. It was the East that should have sent us missionaries.

JEAN COCTEAU, *DIARY OF AN UNKNOWN* (1952; 1988), TR. JESSE BROWNER

2. The West can teach the East how to get a living, but the East must eventually be asked to show the West how to live.

TEHYI HSIEH, *CHINESE EPIGRAMS INSIDE OUT AND PROVERBS* (1948), 588

EASTER

See 420. HOLIDAYS

274. EATING

See also 189. COOKS AND COOKING; 355. FOOD; 403. GREED; 437. HUNGER; 645. OBESITY; 981. TIPPING; 1028. VEGETARIANISM

1. Every man should eat and drink, and enjoy the good of all his labour, it is the gift of God.

BIBLE ECCLESIASTES 3:13

2. Tell me what you eat and I will tell you who you are.

ANTHELME BRILLATAVARIN, *PHYSIOLOGIE DU GOÛT* (1825), 4

3. A full gut supports moral precepts.

BURMESE PROVERBS (1962), 109

4. Man is the only animal that can remain on friendly terms with the victims he intends to eat until he eats them.

SAMUEL BUTLER (D. 1902), "MIND AND MATTER," *NOTE-BOOKS* (1912)

5. That all-softening, overpowering knell, / The Tocsin of the Soul—the dinner-bell.

BYRON, *DON JUAN* (1819–24), 5.49

6. Dinner is to a day what dessert is to dinner.

MICHAEL DORRIS, "THE QUEST FOR PIE," *PAPER TRAIL* (1994)

7. Spread the table and contention will cease.

ENGLISH PROVERB

8. The glutton digs his grave with his teeth.

ENGLISH PROVERB

9. When a man's stomach is full it makes no difference whether he is rich or poor.

EURIPIDES, *ELECTRA* (413 B.C.), TR. EMILY TOWNSEND VERMEULE

10. A good meal ought to begin with hunger.

FRENCH PROVERB

11. I have known many meat eaters to be far more non-violent than vegetarians.

MOHANDAS K. GANDHI, *NON-VIOLENCE IN PEACE AND WAR* (1948), 1.323

12. A gourmet is just a glutton with brains.

PHILLIP W. HABERMAN, JR., "HOW TO BE A CALORIE CHISELER," *VOGUE*, JAN. 15, 1961

13. Life, within doors, has few pleasanter prospects than a neatly arranged and well-provisioned breakfast-table.

NATHANIEL HAWTHORNE, *THE HOUSE OF THE SEVEN GABLES* (1851), 7

14. "We can't eat straight hamburger in a Renaissance *palazzo* on the Grand Canal," Ernest [Hemingway] said. "The caviar will take the curse off it."

A.E. HOTCHNER, *PAPA HEMINGWAY* (1966)

15. Where the guests at a gathering are well-acquainted, they eat 20 per cent more than they otherwise would.

EDGAR WATSON HOWE, *COUNTRY TOWN SAYINGS* (1911)

16. This morning I paid seventy cents for two little old dried-up slivers of bacon and one cockeyed egg. It took me till noon to get my appetite back.

LANGSTON HUGHES, *SIMPLE SPEAKS HIS MIND* (1950)

17. A man may be a pessimistic determinist before lunch and an optimistic believer in the will's freedom after it.

ALDOUS HUXLEY, "PASCAL," *DO WHAT YOU WILL* (1929)

18. The whole of nature, as has been said, is a conjugation of the verb to eat, in the active and passive.

WILLIAM RALPH INGE, "CONFESSIO FIDEI," *OUTSPOKEN ESSAYS: SECOND SERIES* (1922)

19. A man seldom thinks with more earnestness of anything than he does of his dinner.

SAMUEL JOHNSON, QUOTED BY HESTER LYNCH PIOZZI IN *ANECDOTES OF SAMUEL JOHNSON* (1786)

20. A man is in general better pleased when he has a good dinner upon his table, than when his wife talks Greek.

SAMUEL JOHNSON, QUOTED IN BIRKBECK HILL'S *JOHNSONIAN MISCELLANIES* (1897), V. 2

21. I hate a man who swallows [his food], affecting not to know what he is eating. I suspect his taste in higher matters.

CHARLES LAMB, "GRACE BEFORE MEAT," *ESSAYS OF ELIA* (1823)

22. He that eateth well, drinketh well; he that drinketh well, sleepeth well; he that sleepeth well, sinneth not; he that sinneth not goeth straight through Purgatory to Paradise.

WILLIAM LITHGOW, *RARE ADVENTURES* (1614)

23. The art of dining well is no slight art, the pleasure not a slight pleasure.

MONTAIGNE, "OF EXPERIENCE," *ESSAYS* (1580–88), TR. W. C. HAZLITT

24. Strange to see how a good dinner and feasting reconciles everybody.

SAMUEL PEPYS, *DIARY*, NOV. 9, 1665

25. As one who achieved the symmetry of a Humphrey Bogart and the grace of a jaguar purely on pastry, I have no truck with lettuce, cabbage and similar chlorophyll.

S.J. PERELMAN, *THE MOST OF S.J. PERELMAN* (1958)

26. There is nothing to which men, while they have food and drink, cannot reconcile themselves.

GEORGE SANTAYANA, *INTERPRETATIONS OF POETRY AND RELIGION* (1900)

27. Serenely full, the epicure would say, / Fate cannot harm me, I have dined today.

SYDNEY SMITH, QUOTED IN LADY S. HOLLAND'S *MEMOIR* (1855), V. 1.11

28. Seeing is deceiving. It's eating that's believing.

JAMES THURBER, *FURTHER FABLES FOR OUR TIME* (1956)

29. As I ramble through life, whatever be my goal, I will unfortunately always keep my eye upon the doughnut and not upon the whole.

WENDY WASSERSTEIN, "TO LIVE AND DIET," *BACHELOR GIRLS* (1990)

30. One cannot think well, love well, sleep well, if one has not dined well.

VIRGINIA WOOLF, *A ROOM OF ONE'S OWN* (1929), 1

275. EAVESDROPPING

1. Listeners ne'er hear good of themselves.

JOHN RAY, *ENGLISH PROVERBS* (1670)

276. ECCENTRICITY

See also 469. INDIVIDUALITY; 662. ORIGINALITY

1. They [eccentrics] are explosive mixtures. Some of them are as sensitive as those fulminates which can be detonated by a falling leaf.

GILBERT HIGHET, *THE ART OF TEACHING* (1950)

2. Once I knew a dumb girl in the office at the zipper factory who filled in all the four letter words of the easy home-town puzzle. *S H I T* she wrote when she could not guess the answer.

MAUREEN HOWARD, *BRIDGEPORT BUS* (1965)

3. We might define an eccentric as a man who is a law unto himself, and a crank as one who, having determined what the law is, insists on laying it down to others.

LOUIS KRONENBERGER, *COMPANY MANNERS* (1954), 3.3

4. Eccentricity has always abounded when and where strength of character has abounded; and the amount of eccentricity in a society has generally been proportional to the amount of genius, mental vigor, and moral courage which it contained.

JOHN STUART MILL, *ON LIBERTY* (1859), 3

5. More cranks take up unfashionable errors than unfashionable truths.

BERTRAND RUSSELL, "AN OUTLINE OF INTELLECTUAL RUBBISH," *UNPOPULAR ESSAYS* (1950)

6. Life in the [London] suburb is richer at the lower levels. At these levels the people are not self-conscious at all, they are at liberty to be as eccentric as they please, they do not know that they are eccentric.

STEVIE SMITH, "A LONDON SUBURB," IN *ME AGAIN* (1981)

277. ECONOMICS

See also 101. BUDGET; 104. BUSINESS AND COMMERCE; 964. TAXES

1. The fully planned economy, so far from being unpopular, is warmly regarded by those who know it best.

JOHN KENNETH GALBRAITH, *THE NEW INDUSTRIAL STATE* (1967)

2. I don't think you can spend yourself rich.

GEORGE HUMPHREY, NEWS SUMMARIES, JAN. 28, 1957

3. Bad times are indelible. They stay with you forever.

LEE IACOCCA, *IACOCCA: AN AUTOBIOGRAPHY* (1984) WITH WILLIAM NOVAK

4. I do not believe that Washington should do for the people what they can do for themselves through local and private effort.

JOHN F. KENNEDY, CAMPAIGN ADDRESS, ASSOCIATED BUSINESS PUBLICATIONS CONFERENCE, NEW YORK CITY, OCT. 12, 1960

5. the high cost of / living isnt so bad if you / dont have to pay for it.

DON MARQUIS, "THE MERRY FLEA," *ARCHY AND MEHITABEL* (1927)

6. In most circles, the idea of economic planning has been in disrepute most of the time and, particularly in America, has almost carried connotations of intellectual and moral perversion and even political subversion.

GUNNAR MYRDAL, *BEYOND THE WELFARE STATE* (1960)

7. In the United States, and to only slightly lesser degree in all the other rich and economically progressive Western countries, public debate has at all times been dominated by the adherents of a "free" economy.

GUNNAR MYRDAL, *BEYOND THE WELFARE STATE* (1960)

8. Economists are about as useful as astrologers in predicting the future (and, like astrologers, they never let failure on one occasion diminish certitude on the next).

ARTHUR SCHLESINGER, JR., *THE NEW YORK TIMES* (APRIL 15, 1993)

ECONOMY

See 277. ECONOMICS; 977. THRIFT

278. ECSTASY

See also 409. HAPPINESS; 616. MYSTICISM

1. Take all away from me, but leave me Ecstasy, / And I am richer then than all my Fellow Men—.

EMILY DICKINSON, POEM (C. 1885)

2. At the climax, you were lit up with a quiet ecstasy, which enveloped your blessed body in a supernatural nimbus, like a cloak that you pierced with your head and feet.

JEAN GENET, *OUR LADY OF THE FLOWERS* (1949)

3. *Ecstasy* is the accurate term for the intensity of consciousness that occurs in the creative act.

ROLLO MAY, *THE COURAGE TO CREATE* (1975)

EDITORS AND EDITING

See 764. PUBLISHING

279. EDUCATION

See also 522. KNOWLEDGE; 532. LEARNING; 570. MATHEMATICS; 848. SCHOLARS AND SCHOLARSHIP; 965. TEACHING; 988. TRAINING

1. Nothing in education is so astonishing as the amount of ignorance it accumulates in the form of inert facts.

HENRY ADAMS, *THE EDUCATION OF HENRY ADAMS* (1907), 25

EDUCATION

2. Education makes a greater difference between man and man than nature has made between man and brute.

JOHN ADAMS, LETTER TO ABIGAIL ADAMS, OCT. 29, 1776

3. In my day the schools taught two things, love of country and penmanship—now they don't teach either.

CLEVELAND AMORY, "WHY YOURS TRULY WAS THE ONLY ONE TO CARRY THE SPEAR," *THE TROUBLE WITH NOWADAYS* (1979

4. Education is an ornament in prosperity and a refuge in adversity.

ARISTOTLE, (4TH C. B.C.), QUOTED IN DIOGENES LAERTIUS' *LIVES AND OPINIONS OF EMINENT PHILOSOPHERS* (3RD C. A.D.), TR. R. D. HICKS

5. The roots of education are bitter, but the fruit is sweet.

ARISTOTLE, (4TH C. B.C.), QUOTED IN DIOGENES LAERTIUS' *LIVES AND OPINIONS OF EMINENT PHILOSOPHERS* (3RD C. A.D.), TR. R. D. HICKS

6. It takes most men five years to recover from a college education, and to learn that poetry is as vital to thinking as knowledge.

BROOKS ATKINSON, "AUGUST 31," *ONCE AROUND THE SUN* (1951)

7. The important thing is the educational experience itself—how to survive it.

DONALD BARTHELME, "THE EDUCATIONAL EXPERIENCE," *AMATEURS* (1976)

8. Education, n. That which discloses to the wise and disguises from the foolish their lack of understanding.

AMBROSE BIERCE, *THE DEVIL'S DICTIONARY* (1881–1911)

9. An education, other than purely professional or technical, can even seem to be an impediment.

ALLAN BLOOM, *THE CLOSING OF THE AMERICAN MIND* (1987)

10. Education is the movement from darkness to light.

ALLAN BLOOM, *THE CLOSING OF THE AMERICAN MIND* (1987)

11. The importance of these [college] years for an American cannot be overestimated. They are civilization's only chance to get to him.

ALLAN BLOOM, *THE CLOSING OF THE AMERICAN MIND* (1987)

12. Education makes a people easy to lead, but difficult to drive; easy to govern, but impossible to enslave.

LORD BROUGHAM, SPEECH, HOUSE OF COMMONS, JAN. 29, 1828

13. There's a new tribunal now / Higher than God's—the educated man's!

ROBERT BROWNING,, "THE POPE," *THE RING AND THE BOOK* (1868–69)

14. While my friends were discussing Pearl Harbor as the country's problem, I took it personally. It dawned on me that the Japanese attack could be my ticket out of high school.

ART BUCHWALD, *LEAVING HOME: A MEMOIR* (1993)

15. The grand result of schooling is a mind with just vision to discern, with free force to do: the grand schoolmaster is Practice.

THOMAS CARLYLE, "CORN-LAW RHYMES" (1832)

16. By nature all men are alike, but by education widely different.

CHINESE PROVERB

17. The educational process has no end beyond itself; it is its own end.

JOHN DEWEY, *DEMOCRACY AND EDUCATION* (1916)

18. The function of the university is not simply to teach bread-winning, or to furnish teachers for the public schools or to be a centre of polite society; it is, above all, to be the organ of that fine adjustment between real life and the growing knowledge of life, an adjustment which forms the secret of civilization.

W. E. B. DU BOIS, *THE SOULS OF BLACK FOLK* (1903), 5

19. How is it that little children are so intelligent and men so stupid? It must be education that does it.

ALEXANDRE DUMAS FILS, QUOTED IN L. TREICH'S *L'ESPRIT D'ALEXANDRE DUMAS*

20. Knowledge has outstripped character development, and the young today are given an education rather than an upbringing.

ILYA EHRENBURG, "WHAT I HAVE LEARNED," *SATURDAY REVIEW,* SEPT. 30, 1967

21. Meek young men grow up in colleges and believe it is their duty to accept the views which books have given, and grow up slaves.

EMERSON, *JOURNALS,* 1836

22. The things taught in colleges and schools are not an education, but the means of education.

EMERSON, *JOURNALS,* 1831

23. We are shut up in schools and college recitation rooms for ten or fifteen years, and come out at last with a bellyful of words and do not know a thing.

EMERSON, *JOURNALS,* 1839

24. What we do not call education is more precious than that which we call so.

EMERSON, "SPIRITUAL LAWS," *ESSAYS: FIRST SERIES* (1841)

25. Only the educated are free.

EPICTETUS, *DISCOURSES* (2ND C.), 2.1

26. Whoso neglects learning in his youth, loses the past and is dead for the future.

EURIPIDES, *PHRIXUS* (C. 412 B.C.), 927, TR. M. H. MORGAN

27. An education which does not cultivate the will is an education that depraves the mind.

ANATOLE FRANCE, *THE CRIME OF SYLVESTRE BONNARD* (1881), 2, TR. LAFCADIO HEARN

28. The atmosphere [in the school lunchroom] is not quite that of a prison, because the students are permitted to talk quietly, under the frowning scrutiny of teachers standing around on duty, during their meal—they are not supposed to talk while standing in line, though this rule is only sporadically enforced.

EDGAR Z. FRIEDENBERG, *COMING OF AGE IN AMERICA* (1963)

29. Education is the ability to listen to almost anything without losing your temper or your self-confidence.

ROBERT FROST, *READER'S DIGEST,* APRIL 1960

30. Learning makes a man fit company for himself.

THOMAS FULLER, M.D., *GNOMOLOGIA* (1732), 3163

31. Laws and rules of conduct are for the state of childhood; education is an emancipation.

ANDRÉ GIDE, *JOURNALS*, 1894, TR. JUSTIN O'BRIEN

32. Educational progress is a national concern; education is a private one.

NIKKI GIOVANNI, "CAMPUS RACISM 101," *RACISM 101* (1994)

33. Education makes us more stupid than the brutes. A thousand voices call to us on every hand, but our ears are stopped with wisdom.

JEAN GIRAUDOUX, *THE ENCHANTED* (1933), 2, ADAPTED BY MAURICE VALENCY

34. They teach in academies far too many things, and far too much that is useless.

GOETHE, QUOTED IN JOHANN PETER ECKERMANN'S *CONVERSATIONS WITH GOETHE,* FEB. 24, 1824

35. The philosophic aim of education must be to get each one out of his isolated class and into the one humanity.

PAUL GOODMAN, *COMPULSORY MIS-EDUCATION* (1964)

36. There *is* only one curriculum, no matter what the method of education: what is basic and universal in human experience and practice, the underlying structure of culture.

PAUL GOODMAN, *GROWING UP ABSURD* (1960), 4.6

37. It is better to be able neither to read nor write than to be able to do nothing else.

WILLIAM HAZLITT, "ON THE IGNORANCE OF THE LEARNED," *TABLE TALK* (1821–22)

38. That which any one has been long learning unwillingly, he unlearns with proportionable eagerness and haste.

WILLIAM HAZLITT, "ON PERSONAL CHARACTER," *THE PLAIN SPEAKER* (1826)

39. Much learning does not teach understanding.

HERACLITUS, *FRAGMENTS* (C. 500 B.C.), 6, TR. PHILIP WHEELWRIGHT

40. Cafeteria-style education, combined with the unwillingness of our schools to place demands on students, has resulted in a steady diminishment of commonly shared information between generations and between young people themselves.

E.D. HIRSCH, JR., *CULTURAL LITERACY* (1987)

41. The achievement of high universal literacy is the key to all other fundamental improvements in American education.

E.D. HIRSCH, JR., *CULTURAL LITERACY* (1987)

42. The main part of intellectual education is not the acquisition of facts but learning how to make facts live.

OLIVER WENDELL HOLMES, JR., SPEECH, HARVARD LAW SCHOOL ASSOCIATION, NOV. 5, 1886

43. The schools of the country are its future in miniature.

TEHYI HSIEH, *CHINESE EPIGRAMS INSIDE OUT AND PROVERBS* (1948), 22

44. That man, I think, has had a liberal education, who has been so trained in youth that his body is the ready servant of his will.

THOMAS HENRY HUXLEY, "A LIBERAL EDUCATION" (1868)

45. The aim of education is the knowledge not of facts but of values.

WILLIAM RALPH INGE, IN "THE CHURCH IN THE WORLD," OCTOBER, 1932

46. Colleges are places where pebbles are polished and diamonds are dimmed.

ROBERT G. INGERSOLL, *PROSE-POEMS AND SELECTIONS* (1884)

47. State a moral case to a ploughman and a professor. The former will decide it as well, and often better than the latter, because he has not been led astray by artificial rules.

Thomas Jefferson, letter to Peter Carr, Aug. 10, 1787

48. The goal of education is the advancement of knowledge and the dissemination of truth.

John F. Kennedy, address, Harvard University, Cambridge, Mass., 1956

49. I find the three major administrative problems on a campus are sex for the students, athletics for the alumni, and parking for the faculty.

Clark Kerr, *Time,* Nov. 17, 1958

50. The White House, in advancing the agenda for a [school] "choice" plan, rests its faith on market mechanisms. What reason have the black and very poor to lend their credence to a market system that has proved so obdurate and so resistant to their pleas at every turn?

Jonathan Kozol, *Savage Inequalities* (1991)

51. No one can "get" an education, for of necessity education is a continuing process.

Louis L'Amour, *Education of a Wandering Man* (1989)

52. A single conversation across the table with a wise man is better than ten years' mere study of books.

Longfellow, *Hyperion* (1839), 1.7

53. The world no doubt is the best or most serviceable schoolmaster; but the world's curriculum does not include Latin and Greek.

E. V. Lucas, *Reading, Writing, and Remembering* (1932), 3

54. Education then, beyond all other devices of human origin, is a great equalizer of the conditions of men,—the balance wheel of the social machinery.

Horace Mann, report as Secretary of Massachusetts State Board of Education, 1848

55. A good deal of education consists of unlearning—the breaking of bad habits as with a tennis serve.

Mary McCarthy, *How I Grew* (1987)

56. Education in a technological world of replaceable and expendable parts is neuter.

Marshall McLuhan, "Co-Education," *The Mechanical Bride* (1951)

57. School days, I believe, are the unhappiest in the whole span of human existence. They are full of dull, unintelligible tasks, new and unpleasant ordinances, brutal violations of common sense and common decency.

H. L. Mencken, "Travail," *The Baltimore Evening Sun,* Oct. 8, 1928

58. Human nature is not a machine to be built after a model, and set to do exactly the work prescribed for it, but a tree, which requires to grow and develop itself on all sides, according to the tendency of the inward forces which make it a living thing.

John Stuart Mill, *On Liberty* (1859), 3

59. Oh, children, growing up to be / Adventurers into sophistry, / Forbear, forbear to be of those / That read the rood to learn the rose.

Edna St. Vincent Millay, untitled poem, *Mine the Harvest* (1954)

60. The aim of the college, for the individual student, is to eliminate the need in his life for the college; the task is to help him become a self-educating man.

C. Wright Mills, "Mass Society and Liberal Education," *Power, Politics and People* (1963)

61. Once you have the cap and gown all you need do is open your mouth. Whatever nonsense you talk becomes wisdom and all the rubbish, good sense.

Molière, *The Imaginary Invalid* (1673), 3, tr. John Wood

62. A man must always study, but he must not always go to school: what a contemptible thing is an old abecedarian!

Montaigne, "All things have their season," *Essays* (1580–88), tr. C. Hazlitt

63. We only labor to stuff the memory, and leave the conscience and the understanding unfurnished and void.

Montaigne, "Of pedantry," *Essays* (1580–88), tr. W. C. Hazlitt

64. Higher education is booming in the United States; the Gross National Mind is mounting along with the Gross National Product.

Malcolm Muggeridge, "The Gross National Mind," *The Most of Malcolm Muggeridge* (1966)

65. Education produces natural intuitions, and natural intuitions are erased by education.

Pascal, *Pensées* (1670), 95, tr. W. F. Trotter

66. Knowledge which is acquired under compulsion obtains no hold on the mind.

Plato, *The Republic* (4th c. b.c.), 7, tr. Benjamin Jowett

67. The direction in which education starts a man, will determine his future life.

PLATO, *THE REPUBLIC* (4TH C. B.C.), 4, TR. BENJAMIN JOWETT

68. Nature without learning is blind, learning apart from nature is fractional, and practice in the absence of both is aimless.

PLUTARCH, "THE EDUCATION OF CHILDREN," *MORALIA* (C. A.D. 100), TR. MOSES HADAS

69. It is only the ignorant who despise education.

PUBLILIUS SYRUS, *MORAL SAYINGS* (1ST C. B.C.), 571, TR. DARIUS LYMAN

70. [O]ur society offers little in the way of reeducation for those who have been torn away from their traditional culture and suddenly exposed to all the blandishments of mass culture—even the churches which follow the hillbillies to the city often make use of the same "hard sell" that the advertisers and politicians do.

DAVID RIESMAN, *ABUNDANCE FOR WHAT?* (1964)

71. The vine that has been made to bear fruit in the spring, withers and dies before autumn.

ROUSSEAU, *ÉMILE* (1762), 4

72. Education, properly understood, is that which teaches discernment.

JOSEPH ROUX, *MEDITATIONS OF A PARISH PRIEST* (1886), 7.7, TR. ISABEL F. HAPGOOD

73. Education is the leading human souls to what is best, and making what is best out of them; and these two objects are always attainable together, and by the same means; the training which makes men happiest in themselves also makes them most serviceable to others.

JOHN RUSKIN, *THE STONES OF VENICE* (1851–53), 3

74. Education, which was at first made universal in order that all might be able to read and write, has been found capable of serving quite other purposes. By instilling nonsense it unifies populations and generates collective enthusiasm.

BERTRAND RUSSELL, "AN OUTLINE OF INTELLECTUAL RUBBISH," *UNPOPULAR ESSAYS* (1950)

75. The great difficulty in education is to get experience out of ideas.

GEORGE SANTAYANA, *THE LIFE OF REASON: REASON IN COMMON SENSE* (1905–06)

76. To observe people in conflict is a necessary part of a child's education. It helps him to understand and accept his own occasional hostilities and to realize that differing opinions need not imply an absence of love.

MILTON R. SAPIRSTEIN, *PARADOXES OF EVERYDAY LIFE* (1955)

77. Education, like neurosis, begins at home.

MILTON R. SAPIRSTEIN, *PARADOXES OF EVERYDAY LIFE* (1955), 2

78. What we call education and culture is for the most part nothing but the substitution of reading for experience, of literature for life, of the obsolete fictitious for the contemporary real.

GEORGE BERNARD SHAW, "EPISTLE DEDICATORY," *MAN AND SUPERMAN* (1903)

79. Was putting a man on the moon actually easier than improving education in our public schools?

B.F. SKINNER, *BEYOND FREEDOM AND DIGNITY* (1971)

80. We need to unlearn some of our respect for education, since it has undermined our respect for ourselves.

GLORIA STEINEM, *REVOLUTION FROM WITHIN* (1992)

81. What does education often do? It makes a straight-cut ditch of a free, meandering brook.

THOREAU, *JOURNAL*, 1850

82. Education consists mainly in what we have unlearned.

MARK TWAIN, *NOTEBOOK* (1935)

83. In the first place God made idiots. This was for practice. Then he made school boards.

MARK TWAIN, "PUDD'NHEAD WILSON'S NEW CALENDAR," *FOLLOWING THE EQUATOR* (1897), 2.25

84. So they provided jails called schools, equipped with tortures called an education.

JOHN UPDIKE, *THE CENTAUR* (1963)

85. Education—whether its object be children or adults, individuals or an entire people—consists in creating motives.

SIMONE WEIL, *THE NEED FOR ROOTS* (1952), TR. ARTHUR WILLS

86. Children have a natural antipathy to books—handicraft should be the basis of education. Boys and girls should be taught to use their hands to make something, and they would be less apt to destroy and be mischievous.

OSCAR WILDE, *THE ARTIST AS CRITIC: THE CRITICAL WRITINGS OF OSCAR WILDE* (1969) ED. RICHARD ELLMANN

87. If you meet at dinner a man who has spent his life in educating himself...you rise from table richer, and conscious that a high ideal has for a moment touched and sanctifed your days. But oh! to sit next a man who spent his life in trying to educate others! What a dreadful experience that is! How appalling is that ignorance which is the inevitable result of the fatal habit of imparting opinions!

OSCAR WILDE, *THE ARTIST AS CRITIC: THE CRITICAL WRITINGS OF OSCAR WILDE* (1969) ED. RICHARD ELLMANN

88. [E]verybody who is incapable of learning has taken to teaching—that is really what our enthusiasm for education has come to.

OSCAR WILDE, *THE ARTIST AS CRITIC: THE CRITICAL WRITINGS OF OSCAR WILDE* (1969) ED. RICHARD ELLMANN

89. Genius lasts longer than Beauty. That accounts for the fact that we all take such pains to overeducate ourselves.

OSCAR WILDE, *THE PICTURE OF DORIAN GRAY* (1891), 1

EFFECT

See 110. CAUSE AND EFFECT

280. EFFICIENCY

See also 585. METHOD

1. A new broom is good for three days.

ITALIAN PROVERB

281. EFFORT

See also 245. DIFFICULTY; 291. ENTERPRISE; 686. PERSEVERANCE; 1065. WORK

1. They that sow in tears shall reap in joy.

BIBLE, PSALMS 126:5

2. By labor fire is got out of a stone.

DUTCH PROVERB

3. Elbow-grease is the best polish.

ENGLISH PROVERB

4. Nothing is got without pain but dirt and long nails.

ENGLISH PROVERB

5. Much effort, much prosperity.

EURIPIDES, *THE SUPPLIANT WOMEN* (C. 421 B.C.), TR. FRANK W. JONES

6. Try first thyself, and after call in God; / For to the worker God himself lends aid.

EURIPIDES, *HIPPOLYTUS* (428 B.C.), 435, TR. M. H. MORGAN

7. Care and diligence bring luck.

THOMAS FULLER, M.D., *GNOMOLOGIA* (1732), 1057

8. To win one's joy through struggle is better than to yield to melancholy.

ANDRÉ GIDE, *JOURNALS*, MAY 12, 1927, TR. JUSTIN O'BRIEN

9. Life can be difficult for kids born with a gold spoon in their mouth, because they never really get to find out if they're able to work hard and make it on their own.

LEE IACOCCA, *TALKING STRAIGHT* (1988), WITH SONNY KLEINFELD

10. Few things are impossible to diligence and skill.

SAMUEL JOHNSON, *RASSELAS* (1759), 12

11. Despite the success cult, men are most deeply moved not by the reaching of the goal but by the grandness of effort involved in getting there—or failing to get there.

MAX LERNER, "MAN'S BELIEF IN HIMSELF," *THE UNFINISHED COUNTRY* (1959), 5

12. Effort is only effort when it begins to hurt.

JOSÉ ORTEGA Y GASSET, "IN SEARCH OF GOETHE FROM WITHIN, LETTER TO A GERMAN," *PARTISAN REVIEW*, DECEMBER 1949, TR. WILLIAM R. TRASK

13. The struggle alone pleases us, not the victory.

PASCAL, *PENSÉES* (1670), 135, TR. W. F. TROTTER

14. No one knows what he can do till he tries.

PUBLILIUS SYRUS, *MORAL SAYINGS* (1ST C. B.C.), 786, TR. DARIUS LYMAN

15. Nothing can come of nothing.

SHAKESPEARE, *KING LEAR* (1605–06), 1.1.91

16. To travel hopefully is a better thing than to arrive, and the true success is to labor.

ROBERT LOUIS STEVENSON, "EL DORADO," *VIRGINIBUS PUERISQUE* (1881)

EGOTISM

See 873. SELF-IMPORTANCE

ELECTIONS

See 1038. VOTING

282. ELEGANCE

See also 338. FASHION; 942. STYLE; 963. TASTE

1. It seems to me that invisibility is the required provision of elegance. Elegance ceases to exist when it is noticed.

JEAN COCTEAU, *DIARY OF AN UNKNOWN* (1952; 1988), TR. JESSE BROWNER

2. The famous Florentine elegance, which attracts tourists to the shops on Via Tornabuoni and Via della Vigna Nuova, is characterized by austerity of line, simplicity, economy of effect.

MARY MCCARTHY, *THE STONES OF FLORENCE* (1959)

3. Elegance is good taste *plus* a dash of daring.

CARMEL SNOW, *THE WORLD OF CARMEL SNOW* (1962)

4. The only real elegance is in the mind; if you've got that, the rest really comes from it.

DIANA VREELAND, *NEWSWEEK*, DEC. 10, 1962

283. ELOQUENCE

See also 690. PERSUASION; 763. PUBLIC SPEAKING; 923. SPEAKING

1. Everything that steel achieves in war can be won in politics by eloquence.

DEMETRIUS (4TH–3RD C. B.C.), QUOTED IN DIOGENES LAERTIUS' *LIVES AND OPINIONS OF EMINENT PHILOSOPHERS* (3RD C. A.D.), TR. R. D. HICKS

2. The eloquent man is he who is no beautiful speaker, but who is inwardly and desperately drunk with a certain belief.

EMERSON, *JOURNALS*, 1845

3. He that has no silver in his purse should have silver on his tongue.

THOMAS FULLER, M.D., *GNOMOLOGIA* (1732), 2149

4. There is no more sovereign eloquence than the truth in indignation.

VICTOR HUGO, "MARIUS," *LES MISÉRABLES* (1862), 4.1, TR. CHARLES E. WILBOUR

5. Eloquence lies as much in the tone of the voice, in the eyes, and in the speaker's manner, as in his choice of words.

LA ROCHEFOUCAULD, *MAXIMS* (1665),, TR. KENNETH PRATT

6. True eloquence consists in saying all that should be said, and that only.

LA ROCHEFOUCAULD, *MAXIMS* (1665), TR. KENNETH PRATT

7. Today it is not the classroom nor the classics which are the models of eloquence, but the ad agencies.

MARSHALL MCLUHAN, "PLAIN TALK," *THE MECHANICAL BRIDE* (1951)

8. [William F. Buckley [Jr.] does not speak so much as exhale, but he exhales polysyllabically, and the results are remarkable.

EDWIN NEWMAN, *STRICTLY SPEAKING* (1974)

9. Continuous eloquence wearies.

PASCAL, *PENSÉES* (1670), 355, TR. W. F. TROTTER

10. A thing said walks in immortality / if it has been said well.

PINDAR, *ODES* (5TH C. B.C.), ISTHMIA 4, TR. RICHMOND LATTIMORE

EMBARRASSMENT

See 893. SHAME

EMINENCE

See 332. FAME; 386. GLORY; 945. SUCCESS

284. EMOTIONS

See also 21. AFFECTION; 170. CONFLICT, INNER; 412. HATRED; 551. LOVE; 675. PASSION; 883. SENSIBILITY; 969. TEMPERAMENT

1. A man's heart changes his countenance, either for good or for evil.

APOCRYPHA, ECCLESIASTICUS 13:25

2. We are adhering to life now with our last muscle—the heart.

DJUNA BARNES, *NIGHTWOOD* (1937)

3. No emotion, any more than a wave, can long retain its own individual form.

HENRY WARD BEECHER, *PROVERBS FROM PLYMOUTH PULPIT* (1887)

4. Men live but by intervals of reason under the sovereignty of humour [caprice] and passion.

SIR THOMAS BROWNE, *A LETTER TO A FRIEND* (1690)

5. We have hearts within, / Warm, live, improvident, indecent hearts.

ELIZABETH BARRETT BROWNING, *AURORA LEIGH* (1856), 3.461

6. Where the heart lies, let the brain lie also.

ROBERT BROWNING, "ONE WORD MORE," *MEN AND WOMEN* (1855), 1

7. Great feelings take with them their own universe, splendid or abject. They light up with their passion an exclusive world in which they recognize their climate.

ALBERT CAMUS, *THE MYTH OF SISYPHUS* (1955), TR. JUSTIN O'BRIEN

8. Man is, and was always, a block-head and dullard; much readier to feel and digest, than to think and consider.

THOMAS CARLYLE, *SARTOR RESARTUS* (1833–34), 1.8

9. Men, as well as women, are much oftener led by their hearts than by their understandings.

LORD CHESTERFIELD, *LETTERS TO HIS SON*, JUNE 21, 1748

10. The heart has such an influence over the understanding that it is worth while to engage it in our interest.

LORD CHESTERFIELD, *LETTERS TO HIS SON*, MARCH 9, 1748

11. It is as healthy to enjoy sentiment as to enjoy jam.

G. K. CHESTERTON, "ON SENTIMENT," *GENERALLY SPEAKING* (1928)

12. The English are loth to express their feelings, but in my stall in the choir I could feel the pent-up, passionate emotion, and also the fear of the congregation, not of death or wounds or material loss, but of defeat and the final ruin of Britain.

SIR WINSTON CHURCHILL, *THEIR FINEST HOUR* (1949)

13. Let my heart be wise. / It is the gods' best gift.

EURIPIDES, *MEDEA* (431 B.C.), TR. REX WARNER

14. The emotions may be endless. The more we express them, the more we may have to express.

E. M. FORSTER, "NOTES ON THE ENGLISH CHARACTER," *ABINGER HARVEST* (1936)

15. The heart errs like the head; its errors are not any the less fatal, and we have more trouble getting free of them because of their sweetness.

ANATOLE FRANCE, *LITTLE PIERRE* (1918), 5

16. Feelings are the fine instruments which shape decision-making in an animal cursed and blessed with intelligence, and the freedom which is its corollary. They are signals directing us toward goodness, safety, pleasure, and group survival.

WILLARD GAYLIN, *FEELINGS: OUR VITAL SIGNS* (1979)

17. The important thing is being capable of emotions, but to experience only *one's own* would be a sorry limitation.

ANDRÉ GIDE, *JOURNALS*, MAY 12, 1892, TR. JUSTIN O'BRIEN

18. All the knowledge I possess everyone else can acquire, but my heart is all my own.

GOETHE, *THE SORROWS OF YOUNG WERTHER* (1774), 2, MAY 9, 1772, TR. VICTOR LANGE

19. Every person's feelings have a front-door and a side-door by which they may be entered.

OLIVER WENDELL HOLMES, SR., *THE AUTOCRAT OF THE BREAKFAST TABLE* (1858), 6

20. Blossoms are scattered by the wind and the wind cares nothing, but the blossoms of the heart no wind can touch.

YOSHIDA KENKŌ, "THE INEVITABLE WAY," *THE HARVEST OF LEISURE* (*TSURE-ZURE GUSA*, C. 1330–35), TR. RYUKICHI KURATA

21. The head does not know how to play the part of the heart for long.

LA ROCHEFOUCAULD, *MAXIMS* (1665), TR. KENNETH PRATT

22. The human heart is like a ship on a stormy sea driven about by winds blowing from all four corners of heaven.

MARTIN LUTHER, PREFACE TO HIS TRANSLATION OF THE *PSALMS* (1534)

23. Time cools, time clarifies; no mood can be maintained quite unaltered through the course of hours.

THOMAS MANN, *THE MAGIC MOUNTAIN* (1924), 7.9, TR. H. T. LOWE-PORTER

24. Pity me that the heart is slow to learn / What the swift mind beholds at every turn.

EDNA ST. VINCENT MILLAY, *SONNETS* (1941), 29

25. One ought to hold on to one's heart; for if one lets it go, one soon loses control of the head too.

NIETZSCHE, "ON THE PITYING," *THUS SPOKE ZARATHUSTRA* (1883–92), 2, TR. WALTER KAUFMANN

26. One of the effects of safe and civilized life is an immense oversensitiveness which makes all the primary emotions seem somewhat disgusting.

GEORGE ORWELL, "LOOKING BACK ON THE SPANISH WAR" (1943)

27. The heart has its reasons which reason does not know.

PASCAL, *PENSÉES* (1670), 277

28. In a full heart there is room for everything, and in an empty heart there is room for nothing.

ANTONIO PORCHIA, *VOCES* (1968), TR. W. S. MERWIN

29. All emotions are pure which gather you and lift you up; that emotion is impure which seizes only *one* side of your being and so distorts you.

RAINER MARIA RILKE, *LETTERS TO A YOUNG POET*, NOV. 4, 1904, TR. M. D. HERTER NORTON

30. Nothing vivifies, and nothing kills, like the emotions.

JOSEPH ROUX, *MEDITATIONS OF A PARISH PRIEST* (1886), 5.2, TR. ISABEL F. HAPGOOD

31. Reason guides but a small part of man, and that the least interesting. The rest obeys feeling, true or false, and passion, good or bad.

JOSEPH ROUX, *MEDITATIONS OF A PARISH PRIEST* (1886), 4.95, TR. ISABEL F. HAPGOOD

32. Whatever makes an impression on the heart seems lovely in the eye.

SA'DI, *GULISTAN* (1258), 5.1, TR. JAMES ROSS

33. It is only with the heart that one can see rightly; what is essential is invisible to the eye.

SAINT-EXUPÉRY, *THE LITTLE PRINCE* (1943), 21, TR. KATHERINE WOODS

34. Emotion is primarily about nothing, and much of it remains about nothing to the end.

GEORGE SANTAYANA, *THE LIFE OF REASON: REASON IN ART* (1905–06), 4

35. The heart is forever inexperienced.

THOREAU, "RUMORS FROM AN AEOLIAN HARP," *A WEEK ON THE CONCORD AND MERRIMACK RIVERS* (1849)

36. Emotion has taught mankind to reason.

VAUVENARGUES, *REFLECTIONS AND MAXIMS* (1746), 154, TR. F. G. STEVENS

37. The secret of life is never to have an emotion that is unbecoming.

OSCAR WILDE, *A WOMAN OF NO IMPORTANCE* (1893), 3

EMPATHY

See 960. SYMPATHY; 1008. UNDERSTANDING OTHERS

EMULATION

See 451. IMITATION

ENDEAVOR

See 281. EFFORT

285. ENDING

See also 75. BEGINNING; 76. BEGINNING AND ENDING; 286. ENDS; 574. MEANS AND ENDS

1. Very, very slowly, the dwarf remnants of what was once our mighty sun will cool and dim, until it embarks on its final metamorphosis, gradually solidifying into a crystal of extraordinary rigidity. Eventually it will fade out completely, merging quietly into the blackness of space.

PAUL DAVIES, *THE LAST THREE MINUTES* (1994)

2. It was not clear how it would end. In nineteenth-century novels, they get married. In twentieth-century novels, they get divorced. Can you have an ending in which they do neither?

ERICA JONG, *FEAR OF FLYING* (1973)

3. When she got a letter from him that had been dictated to his stenographer, she knew that his splurge was over.

MARY MCCARTHY, *THE COMPANY SHE KEEPS* (1942)

4. God alone can finish.

JOHN RUSKIN, *MODERN PAINTERS* (1843–60), V. 3, 4.9.4

286. ENDS

See also 285. ENDING; 574. MEANS AND ENDS; 608. MOTIVES; 771. PURPOSE

1. Whatsoever thou takest in hand, remember the end, and thou shalt never do amiss.

APOCRYPHA, ECCLESIASTICUS 7:36

2. Men achieve a certain greatness unawares, when working to another aim.

EMERSON, "CONSIDERATIONS BY THE WAY," *THE CONDUCT OF LIFE* (1860)

3. The question should be, is it worth trying to do, not can it be done?

ALLARD LOWENSTEIN, *THE NEW YORK TIMES BOOK REVIEW*, NOV. 7, 1993

4. What is there more of in the world than anything else? Ends.

CARL SANDBURG, *THE PEOPLE, YES* (1936)

287. ENDURANCE

See also 677. PATIENCE; 686. PERSEVERANCE; 806. RESIGNATION; 937. STOICISM; 956. SURVIVAL

1. To bear is to conquer our fate.

THOMAS CAMPBELL, "ON VISITING A SCENE IN ARGYLESHIRE"

2. The man who sticks it out against his fate / shows spirit, but the spirit of a fool.

EURIPIDES, *HERACLES* (C. 422 B.C.), TR. WILLIAM ARROWSMITH

3. 'Tis as manlike to bear extremities as godlike to forgive.

JOHN FORD, *'TIS PITY SHE'S A WHORE* (1633), 4.3

4. To endure what is unendurable is true endurance.
JAPANESE PROVERB

5. Sorrow and silence are strong, and patient endurance is godlike.
LONGFELLOW, *EVANGELINE* (1847), 2.1

6. Endurance is the crowning quality, / And patience all the passion of great hearts.
JAMES RUSSELL LOWELL, "COLUMBUS" (1844)

7. To bear lightly the neck's yoke / brings strength; but kicking / against the goads is the way / of failure.
PINDAR, *ODES* (5TH C. B.C.), PYTHIA 2, TR. RICHMOND LATTIMORE

8. Many can brook the weather that love not the wind.
SHAKESPEARE, *LOVE'S LABOUR'S LOST* (1594–95), 4.2.34

9. We may be masters of our every lot / By bearing it.
VERGIL, *AENEID* (30–19 B.C.), 5.710, TR. T. H. DELABERE-MAY

288. ENEMIES

See also 301. ESTRANGEMENT; 412. HATRED; 476. INJURY; 665. PACIFISM; 817. REVENGE

1. Enemies' promises were made to be broken.
AESOP, "THE NURSE AND THE WOLF," *FABLES* (6TH C. B.C.?), TR. JOSEPH JACOBS

2. You will only injure yourself if you take notice of despicable enemies.
AESOP, "THE BALD MAN AND THE FLY," *FABLES* (6TH C. B.C.?), TR. JOSEPH JACOBS

3. Pay attention to your enemies, for they are the first to discover your mistakes.
ANTISTHENES (5TH–4TH C. B.C.), QUOTED IN DIOGENES LAERTIUS' *LIVES AND OPINIONS OF EMINENT PHILOSOPHERS* (3RD C. A.D.), TR. R. D. HICKS

4. If thine enemy hunger, feed him; if he thirst, give him drink: for in so doing thou shalt heap coals of fire on his head.
BIBLE, PROVERBS 25:21 AND ROMANS 12:20

5. You shall judge of a man by his foes as well as by his friends.
JOSEPH CONRAD, *LORD JIM* (1900), 34

6. There's nothing like the sight / Of an old enemy down on his luck.
EURIPIDES, *HERAKLEIDAI* (C. 429–27 B.C.), TR. RALPH GLADSTONE

7. Your worst enemy / Becomes your best friend, once he's underground.
EURIPIDES, *HERAKLEIDAI* (C. 429–27 B.C.), TR. RALPH GLADSTONE

8. There is no little enemy.
FRENCH PROVERB

9. If we are bound to forgive an enemy, we are not bound to trust him.
THOMAS FULLER, M.D., *GNOMOLOGIA* (1732), 2728

10. A wise man gets more use from his enemies than a fool from his friends.
BALTASAR GRACIÁN, *THE ART OF WORDLY WISDOM* (1647), 84, TR. JOSEPH JACOBS

11. Invite your friend to dinner; have nothing to do with your enemy.
HESIOD, *WORKS AND DAYS* (8TH C. B.C.), 342, TR. RICHMOND LATTIMORE

12. It is your enemies who keep you straight. For real use one active, sneering enemy is worth two ordinary friends.
EDGAR WATSON HOWE, *COUNTRY TOWN SAYINGS* (1911)

13. He who has a thousand friends has not a friend to spare, / And he who has one enemy shall meet him everywhere.
ALI IBN-ABI-TALIB (7TH C.), QUOTED IN EMERSON'S *CONDUCT OF LIFE*, 7

14. One must know one's enemy as he is, not as one, for whatever motives, wishes him to be.
EUGENE KOGON, "LESSONS FOR TOMORROW," *THE PATH TO DICTATORSHIP 1918–1933* (1966)

15. Our enemies approach nearer to truth in their judgments of us than we do ourselves.
LA ROCHEFOUCAULD, *MAXIMS* (1665), TR. KENNETH PRATT

16. If we could read the secret history of our enemies, we should find in each man's life sorrow and suffering enough to disarm all hostility.
LONGFELLOW, "TABLE-TALK," *DRIFTWOOD* (1857)

17. Shun an angry man for a moment—your enemy forever.
PUBLILIUS SYRUS, *MORAL SAYINGS* (1ST C. B.C.) 396, TR. DARIUS LYMAN

18. There is no safety in regaining the favor of an enemy.
PUBLILIUS SYRUS, *MORAL SAYINGS* (1ST C. B.C.), 174, TR. DARIUS LYMAN

19. If you have an enemy, do not requite him evil with good, for that would put him to shame. Rather prove that he did you some good.

NIETZSCHE, "ON THE ADDER'S BITE," *THUS SPOKE ZARATHUSTRA* (1883–92), 1, TR. WALTER KAUFMANN

20. Whenever thy hand can reach it, tear out thy foe's brain, for such an opportunity washes anger from the mind.

SA'DI, *GULISTAN* (1258), 3.28, TR. JAMES ROSS

21. He makes no friend who never made a foe.

LORD TENNYSON, "LANCELOT AND ELAINE," *IDYLLS OF THE KING* (1859)

22. Be thine enemy an ant, see in him an elephant.

TURKISH PROVERB

23. It is curious how often one prefers his enemies to his friends.

GORE VIDAL, REFLECTIONS UPON A SINKING SHIP (1969)

24. One of the most time-consuming things is to have an enemy.

E.B. WHITE, "A REPORT IN JANUARY," *ESSAYS OF E. B. WHITE* (1977)

ENERGY

See 281. EFFORT; 1036. VITALITY

289. ENGLAND AND ENGLISHMEN

See also 546. LONDON

1. The English may not like music, but they absolutely love the noise it makes.

SIR THOMAS BEECHAM, *NEW YORK HERALD TRIBUNE*, MARCH 9, 1961

2. It is a part of English hypocrisy—or English reserve—that, whilst we are fluent enough in grumbling about small inconveniences, we insist on making light of any great difficulties or griefs that may beset us.

MAX BEERBOHM, "BOOKS WITHIN BOOKS," *AND EVEN NOW* (1920)

3. The English have a scornful insular way / Of calling the French light.

ELIZABETH BARRETT BROWNING, *AURORA LEIGH* (1856), 6.1

4. The English winter—ending in July, / To recommence in August.

BYRON, *DON JUAN* (1819–24), 13.42

5. The maxim of the British people is "Business as usual."

SIR WINSTON CHURCHILL, SPEECH, GUILDHALL, NOV. 9, 1914

6. English life is nothing but a huge masquerade ball in which the participants contrive to conceal their feelings, their addresses, their hobbies, their incomes, their decorations, their sorrows, their talents, their achievements, and even their names.

PIERRE DANINOS, *THE SECRET OF MAJOR THOMPSON* (1957), TR. DON CORTES

7. "If animals had a Pope," Major Thompson said to me, "their Vatican would be in London. And if by some dire submarine cataclysm that noble vessel, Great Britain, were to be shipwrecked and start to founder, believe me, there would surely be somebody in Westminster to cry from the top of the Tower: "Dogs first!"

PIERRE DANINOS, *THE SECRET OF MAJOR THOMPSON* (1957), TR. DON CORTES

8. One of the marked superiorities the English enjoy over other peoples is their ability to imbue the foreigner with a crippling inferiority complex the moment he sets foot on British soil.

PIERRE DANINOS, *THE SECRET OF MAJOR THOMPSON* (1957), TR. DON CORTES

9. "It is in bad taste," is the most formidable word an Englishman can pronounce.

EMERSON, *JOURNALS*, 1839

10. Englishmen must have an island.

F. SCOTT FITZGERALD, *THE CRACK-UP* (1945)

11. It is not that the Englishman can't feel—it is that he is afraid to feel. He has been taught at his public school that feeling is bad form. He must not express great joy or sorrow, or even open his mouth too wide when he talks—his pipe might fall out if he did.

E. M. FORSTER, "NOTES ON THE ENGLISH CHARACTER," *ABINGER HARVEST* (1936)

12. In the end it may well be that Britain will be honored by the historians more for the way she disposed of an empire than for the way in which she acquired it.

DAVID ORMSBY GORE, *THE NEW YORK TIMES*, OCT. 28, 1962

13. The Englishman walks before the law like a trained horse in the circus. He has the sense of legality in his bones, in his muscles.

MAXIM GORKY, *ENEMIES* (1906), 1

14. The difference between the vanity of a Frenchman and an Englishman seems to be this: the one thinks everything right that is French, the other thinks everything wrong that is not English.

WILLIAM HAZLITT, *CHARACTERISTICS* (1823), 334

15. The Englishman is too apt to neglect the present good in preparing against the possible evil.

WASHINGTON IRVING, "ENGLISH AND FRENCH CHARACTER," *WOLFERT'S ROOST* (1855)

16. An Englishman is never so natural as when he's holding his tongue.

HENRY JAMES, *THE PORTRAIT OF A LADY* (1881), 10

17. I knew I was in England by the smell.

ERICA JONG, *FEAR OF FLYING* (1973)

18. It is good to be on your guard against an Englishman who speaks French perfectly; he is very likely to be a card-sharper or an attaché in the diplomatic service.

W. SOMERSET MAUGHAM, *THE SUMMING UP* (1938), 29

19. An Englishman never takes his collar off when he is writing. How can you expect him to show you his soul?

WILLIAM MCFEE, "REVIEWING BOOKS," *HARBOURS OF MEMORY* (1921)

20. One matter Englishmen don't think in the least funny is their happy consciousness of possessing a deep sense of humor.

MARSHALL MCLUHAN, "THE BALLET LUCE," *THE MECHANICAL BRIDE* (1951)

21. The Englishman, be it noted, seldom resorts to violence; when he is sufficiently goaded he simply opens up, like the oyster, and devours his adversary.

HENRY MILLER, "RAIMU," *THE WISDOM OF THE HEART* (1941)

22. Humor is practically the only thing about which the English are utterly serious.

MALCOLM MUGGERIDGE, "TREAD SOFTLY FOR YOU TREAD ON MY JOKES," *THE MOST OF MALCOLM MUGGERIDGE* (1966)

23. If you ask any ordinary reader which of Dickens's proletarian characters he can remember, the three he is almost certain to mention are Bill Sykes, Sam Weller and Mrs. Gamp. A burglar, a valet and a drunken midwife—not exactly a representative cross-section of the English working class.

GEORGE ORWELL, "CHARLES DICKENS," *A COLLECTION OF ESSAYS* (1954)

24. In its attitude towards Dickens the English public has always been a little like the elephant which feels a blow with a walking-stick as a delightful tickling.

GEORGE ORWELL, "CHARLES DICKENS," *A COLLECTION OF ESSAYS* (1954)

25. But Lord! To see the absurd nature of Englishmen that cannot forbear laughing and jeering at everything that looks strange.

SAMUEL PEPYS, *DIARY,* NOV. 27, 1662

26. Curious race, the English. Once they warm up, there's no telling what they'll do for you.

S.J. PERELMAN, *THE RISING GORGE* (1961)

27. England is the paradise of individuality, eccentricity, heresy, anomalies, hobbies, and humours.

GEORGE SANTAYANA, "THE BRITISH CHARACTER," *SOLILOQUIES IN ENGLAND* (1922)

28. An Englishman thinks he is moral when he is only uncomfortable.

GEORGE BERNARD SHAW, *MAN AND SUPERMAN* (1930), 3

29. Go anywhere in England, where there are natural, wholesome, contented, and really nice English people; and what do you always find? That the stables are the real centre of the household.

GEORGE BERNARD SHAW, *HEARTBREAK HOUSE* (1920), 1

30. There is nothing so bad or so good that you will not find Englishmen doing it; but you will never find an Englishman in the wrong. He does everything on principle.

GEORGE BERNARD SHAW, *THE MAN OF DESTINY* (1907)

31. In England the rich own the poor and the men own the women.

TOM STOPPARD, *TRAVESTIES* (1974)

32. You are the slaves of laws. The French are slaves of men.

VOLTAIRE, IN CONVERSATION WITH JAMES BOSWELL, *BOSWELL ON THE GRAND TOUR: GERMANY AND SWITZERLAND* (1928)

33. The way to ensure summer in England is to have it framed and glazed in a comfortable room.

HORACE WALPOLE, LETTER TO WILLIAM COLE, MAY 28, 1774

34. Why is it, do you suppose, that an Englishman is unhappy until he has explained America?

E.B. WHITE, "RIPOSTE," *ESSAYS OF E. B. WHITE* (1977)

35. They [the English] have a special word, "civil," for what is elsewhere merely ordinary politeness.

EDMUND WILSON, *THE FORTIES* (1983)

36. I travelled among unknown men, / In lands beyond the sea; / Nor, England! did I know till then / What love I bore to thee.

WILLIAM WORDSWORTH, "I TRAVELLED AMONG UNKNOWN MEN" (1801)

ENGLISH

See 289. ENGLAND AND ENGLISHMEN; 524. LANGUAGE

ENJOYMENT

See 704. PLEASURE

290. ENNUI

See also 30. ALIENATION; 94. BOREDOM

1. Ennui has made more gamblers than avarice, more drunkards than thirst, and perhaps as many suicides as despair.

CHARLES CALEB COLTON, *LACON* (1825), 1.259

2. The flesh is sad, alas, and I've read all the books.

STÉPHANE MALLARMÉ, "BRISE MARINE," *POÉSIES COMPLÈTES* (1887)

ENOUGH

See 947. SUFFICIENCY

291. ENTERPRISE

See also 33. AMBITION; 281. EFFORT; 657. OPPORTUNITY; 880. SELF-SUFFICIENCY

1. None will improve your lot / If you yourselves do not.

BERTOLT BRECHT, *ROUNDHEADS AND PEAKHEADS* (1933), 3, TR. N. GOOLD-VERSCHOYLE

2. Neither a wise man nor a brave man lies down on the tracks of history to wait for the train of the future to run over him.

DWIGHT D. EISENHOWER, CAMPAIGN SPEECH, *TIME,* OCT. 6, 1952

3. On the neck of the young man sparkles no gem so gracious as enterprise.

HĀFIZ, QUOTED BY EMERSON IN "POWER," *THE CONDUCT OF LIFE* (1860)

4. The passion to get ahead is sometimes born of the fear lest we be left behind.

ERIC HOFFER, *THE PASSIONATE STATE OF MIND* (1954), 257

5. Nothing will ever be attempted, if all possible objections must be first overcome.

SAMUEL JOHNSON, *RASSELAS* (1759), 6

6. Go and wake up your luck.

PERSIAN PROVERB

292. ENTERTAINMENT

See also 130. CIRCUS; 144. COMEDIANS; 145. COMEDY; 576. MEDIA; 614. MUSIC; 703. PLAY; 972. THEATER

1. For what do we live, but to make sport for our neighbours, and laugh at them in our turn?

JANE AUSTEN, *PRIDE AND PREJUDICE* (1813), 57

2. The mass production of distraction is now as much a part of the American way of life as the mass production of automobiles.

C. WRIGHT MILLS, "THE UNITY OF WORK AND LEISURE," *POWER, POLITICS AND PEOPLE* (1963)

3. Mass entertainment in America has been dominated for a long time by the mode of documentary realism.

DAVID RIESMAN, *ABUNDANCE FOR WHAT?* (1964)

293. ENTHUSIASM

See also 335. FANATICISM; 513. JOIE DE VIVRE; 928. SPONTANEITY; 1036. VITALITY; 1073. ZEAL

1. He too serves a certain purpose who only stands and cheers.

HENRY ADAMS, *THE EDUCATION OF HENRY ADAMS* (1907), 24

2. In things pertaining to enthusiasm, no man is sane who does not know how to be insane on proper occasions.

HENRY WARD BEECHER, *PROVERBS FROM PLYMOUTH PULPIT* (1887)

3. Enthusiasm, n. A distemper of youth, curable by small doses of repentance in connection with outward applications of experience.

AMBROSE BIERCE, *THE DEVIL'S DICTIONARY* (1881–1911)

4. You can't sweep other people off their feet, if you can't be swept off your own.

CLARENCE DAY, "A WILD POLISH HERO," *THE CROW'S NEST* (1921)

5. Nothing great was ever achieved without enthusiasm.

EMERSON, "CIRCLES," *ESSAYS: FIRST SERIES* (1841)

6. [A] decline of exuberance is just barely noticeable in America, making itself felt particularly among the most highly educated and the well-to-do in a loss of appetite for work and perhaps even for leisure.

DAVID RIESMAN, *ABUNDANCE FOR WHAT?* (1964)

7. We are all experiments in enthusiasms, narrow and preordained.

KURT VONNEGUT, "CHILDREN," *PALM SUNDAY* (1981)

294. ENVIRONMENT

See also 67. BACKGROUND; 177. CONSERVATION; 370. GARBAGE

1. When the Pleiades and the wind in the grass are no longer a part of the human spirit, a part of very flesh and bone, man becomes, as it were, a kind of cosmic outlaw, having neither the completeness and integrity of the animal nor the birthright of a true humanity.

HENRY BESTON, FOREWORD TO *THE OUTERMOST HOUSE* (1928)

2. The environment does not determine man's culture; it merely sets the outer limits and at the same time offers opportunities.

PETER FARB, *MAN'S RISE TO CIVILIZATION* (1968)

3. We are all passengers aboard one ship, the Earth, and we must not allow it to be wrecked. There will be no second Noah's Ark.

MIKHAIL GORBACHEV, *PERESTROIKA* (1987)

4. In remaking the world in the likeness of a steam-heated, air-conditioned metropolis of apartment buildings we have violated one of our essential attributes—our kinship with nature.

ROSS PARMENTER, "INWARD SIGN," *THE PLANT IN MY WINDOW* (1949)

5. A grateful environment is a substitute for happiness. It can quicken us from without as a fixed hope and affection, or the consciousness of a right life, can quicken us from within.

GEORGE SANTAYANA, *THE SENSE OF BEAUTY* (1896), 26

6. Overcrowding can be corrected only by inducing people not to crowd, and the environment will continue to deteriorate until polluting practices are abandoned.

B.F. SKINNER, *BEYOND FREEDOM AND DIGNITY* (1971)

7. Man is messy, but any creature that can create space vehicles can probably cope.

GEORGE F. WILL, "THE POLITICAL ECHO OF ECOPHOBIA," *SUDDENLY: THE AMERICAN IDEA ABROAD AND AT HOME, 1986–1990* (1990)

295. ENVY

See also 561. MALICE

1. In few men is it part of nature to respect / a friend's prosperity without begrudging him.

AESCHYLUS, *AGAMEMNON* (458 B.C.), TR. RICHMOND LATTIMORE

2. As iron is eaten away by rust, so the envious are consumed by their own passion.

ANTISTHENES (5TH–4TH C. B.C.), QUOTED IN DIOGENES LAERTIUS' *LIVES AND OPINIONS OF EMINENT PHILOSOPHERS* (3RD C. A.D.), TR. R. D. HICKS

3. He that cannot possibly mend his own case will do what he can to impair another's.

FRANCIS BACON, "OF ENVY," *ESSAYS* (1625)

4. Let age, not envy, draw wrinkles on thy cheeks.

SIR THOMAS BROWNE, *A LETTER TO A FRIEND* (1690)

5. For one man who sincerely pities our misfortunes, there are a thousand who sincerely hate our success.

CHARLES CALEB COLTON, *LACON* (1825), 1.507

6. If envy were a fever, all the world would be ill.

DANISH PROVERB

7. Envy is everywhere. / Who is without envy? And most people / Are unaware or unashamed of being envious.

T. S. ELIOT, *THE ELDER STATESMAN* (1958), I

8. Envy is the tax which all distinction must pay.

EMERSON, *JOURNALS,* 1824

9. It is only at the tree loaded with fruit that the people throw stones.

FRENCH PROVERB

10. Nothing sharpens sight like envy.

THOMAS FULLER, M.D., *GNOMOLOGIA* (1732), 3674

11. Envy's a sharper spur than pay.

JOHN GAY, "THE ELEPHANT AND THE BOOKSELLER," *FABLES* (1727–38)

12. The envious die not once, but as oft as the envied win applause.

BALTASAR GRACIÁN, *THE ART OF WORLDLY WISDOM* (1647), 162, TR. JOSEPH JACOBS

13. How much better a thing it is to be envied than to be pitied.

HERODOTUS, *THE HISTORIES* (5TH C. B.C.), 3.52, TR. A. D. GODLEY

14. All envy is proportionate to desire; we are uneasy at the attainments of another, according as we think

our own happiness would be advanced by the addition of that which he withholds from us.

Samuel Johnson, *The Rambler* (1750–52), 17

15. Envy is more irreconcilable than hatred.

La Rochefoucauld, *Maxims* (1665), tr. Kenneth Pratt

16. Envy is destroyed by true friendship, as coquetry by true love.

La Rochefoucauld, *Maxims* (1665), tr. Kenneth Pratt

17. Our envy always lasts much longer than the happiness of those we envy.

La Rochefoucauld, *Maxims* (1665), tr. Kenneth Pratt

18. Those who speak against the great do not usually speak from morality, but from envy.

Walter Savage Landor, "Diogenes and Plato," *Imaginary Conversations* (1824–53)

19. Even success softens not the heart of the envious.

Pindar, *Odes* (5th c. B.C.), Pythia 2, tr. Richmond Lattimore

20. Our nature holds so much envy and malice that our pleasure in our own advantages is not so great as our distress at others'.

Plutarch, "Contentment," *Moralia* (c. A.D. 100), tr. Moses Hadas

21. Envy ... is one form of a vice, partly moral, partly intellectual, which consists in seeing things never in themselves but only in their relations.

Bertrand Russell, *The Conquest of Happiness* (1930), 6

22. There is not a passion so strongly rooted in the human heart as envy.

Richard Brinsley Sheridan, *The Critic* (1779), 1.1

23. Man will do many things to get himself loved; he will do all things to get himself envied.

Mark Twain, "Pudd'nhead Wilson's New Calendar," *Following the Equator* (1897), 1.21

24. I can endure my own despair, / But not another's hope.

William Walsh, "Song: Of All the Torments" (1692?)

296. EPIGRAMS

See also 572. Maxims; 773. Quotations

1. What is an epigram? A dwarfish whole, / Its body brevity, and wit its soul.

Samuel Taylor Coleridge, "An Epigram" (1802)

EPOCH

See 298. Era

297. EQUALITY

See also 135. Class; 233. Democracy; 471. Inequality; 823. Rights

1. Equality consists in the same treatment of similar persons.

Aristotle, *Politics* (4th c. B.C.) 7.14, tr. Benjamin Jowett

2. The democrats think that as they are equal they ought to be equal in all things.

Aristotle, *Politics* (4th c. B.C.) 5.1, tr. Benjamin Jowett

3. Intellect has nothing to do with equality except to respect it as a sublime convention.

Jacques Barzun, *The House of Intellect* (1959)

4. Woman has always been man's dependent, if not his slave; the two sexes have never shaped the world in equality. And even today woman is heavily handicapped, though her situation is beginning to change.

Simone de Beauvoir, *The Second Sex* (1953)

5. Although the Jeffersonian Law ("All men are created equal") is the first article of the American faith, the facts of American life have demonstrated for some time now that it is an irksome faith to live by.

Alistair Cooke, "The Coronation of Miss Oklahoma," *America Observed: From the 1940s to the 1980s* (1988)

6. In place of equal respect, the nation offered women the Miss America beauty pageant, established in 1920—the same year women won the vote.

Susan Faludi, *Backlash* (1991)

7. [A]s women began to challenge their own internalized views of a woman's proper place, their desire and demand for equal status and free choice began to grow exponentially.

Susan Faludi, *Backlash* (1991)

8. Naked I came into the world, naked I shall go out of it! And a very good thing too, for it reminds me that I am naked under my shirt, whatever its colour.

E. M. Forster, "What I Believe," *Two Cheers for Democracy* (1951)

9. Just as modern mass production requires the standardization of commodities, so the social process requires standardization of man, and this standardization is called equality.

Erich Fromm, *The Art of Loving* (1956), 2

10. There can be no truer principle than this—that every individual of the community at large has an equal right to the protection of government.

ALEXANDER HAMILTON, ADDRESS, CONSTITUTIONAL CONVENTION, JUNE 29, 1787

11. When all candles be out, all cats be grey.

JOHN HEYWOOD, *PROVERBS* (1546), 1.5

12. We clamor for equality chiefly in matters in which we ourselves cannot hope to obtain excellence.

ERIC HOFFER, *THE PASSIONATE STATE OF MIND* (1954), 198

13. The man who insists he is as good as anybody, believes he is better.

EDGAR WATSON HOWE, *COUNTRY TOWN SAYINGS* (1911)

14. We hold these truths to be self-evident, that all men are created equal, that they are endowed by their creator with certain unalienable Rights, that among these are Life, Liberty and the pursuit of happiness.

THOMAS JEFFERSON, *DECLARATION OF INDEPENDENCE,* JULY 4, 1776

15. It is better that some should be unhappy than that none should be happy, which would be the case in a general state of equality.

SAMUEL JOHNSON, QUOTED IN BOSWELL'S *LIFE OF SAMUEL JOHNSON,* APRIL 7, 1776

16. It is the American vice, the democratic disease which expresses its tyranny by reducing everything unique to the level of the herd.

HENRY MILLER, "RAIMU," *THE WISDOM OF THE HEART* (1941)

17. Weariness is the shortest path to equality and fraternity—and finally liberty is bestowed by sleep.

NIETZSCHE, *THE WANDERER AND HIS SHADOW* (1880), 263, TR. PAUL V. COHN

18. Where there are no distinctions there can be no superiority; perfect equality affords no temptation.

THOMAS PAINE, "THOUGHTS ON THE PRESENT STATE OF AMERICAN AFFAIRS," *COMMON SENSE* (1776)

19. Even though a god, I have learned to obey the times.

PALLADAS (FL. A.D. 400), "ON A STATUE OF HERACLES," IN *THE GREEK ANTHOLOGY* (7TH C. B.C.–10TH C. A.D.), 9.441

20. Unless man is committed to the belief that all of mankind are his brothers, then he labors in vain and hypocritically in the vineyards of equality.

ADAM CLAYTON POWELL, "BLACK POWER: A FORM OF GODLY POWER," *KEEP THE FAITH, BABY!* (1967)

21. The Lord so constituted everybody that no matter what color you are you require the same amount of nourishment.

WILL ROGERS, *THE AUTOBIOGRAPHY OF WILL ROGERS* (1949), 12

22. Inside the polling booth every American man and woman stands as the equal of every other American man and woman. There they have no superiors. There they have no masters save their own minds and consciences.

FRANKLIN D. ROOSEVELT, SPEECH, WORCESTER, MASS., OCT. 21, 1936

23. In America everybody is of opinion that he has no social superiors, since all men are equal, but he does not admit that he has no social inferiors.

BERTRAND RUSSELL, "IDEAS THAT HAVE HARMED MANKIND," *UNPOPULAR ESSAYS* (1950)

24. When none but the wealthy had watches, they were almost all very good ones: few are now made which are worth much, but everybody has one in his pocket.

ALEXIS DE TOCQUEVILLE, *DEMOCRACY IN AMERICA* (1835–39), 2.1.11

25. The principle of equality does not destroy the imagination, but lowers its flight to the level of the earth.

ALEXIS DE TOCQUEVILLE, *DEMOCRACY IN AMERICA* (1835–39), 2.3.11

298. ERA

See also 184. CONTEMPORANEOUSNESS; 374. GENERATIONS; 599. MODERNITY; 641. NUCLEAR POWER; 676. PAST; 1001. TWENTIETH CENTURY

1. In every age "the good old days" were a myth. No one ever thought they were good at the time. For every age has consisted of crises that seemed intolerable to the people who lived through them.

BROOKS ATKINSON, "FEBRUARY 8," *ONCE AROUND THE SUN* (1951)

2. Every age has its pleasures, its style of wit, and its own ways.

NICOLAS BOILEAU, *L'ART POÉTIQUE* (1674), 3.374

3. 'Tis hard to find a whole age to imitate, or what century to propose for example.

SIR THOMAS BROWNE, *CHRISTIAN MORALS* (1716), 3

4. Every age, / Through being beheld too close, is ill-discerned / By those who have not lived past it.

ELIZABETH BARRETT BROWNING, *AURORA LEIGH* (1856), 5.167

5. The "good old times"—all times when old are good— / Are gone.

BYRON, *THE AGE OF BRONZE* (1823)

6. How strange it is that we of the present day are constantly praising that past age which our fathers abused, and as constantly abusing that present age, which our children will praise.

CHARLES CALEB COLTON, *LACON* (1825), 2.101

7. The "times," "the age," what is that, but a few profound persons and a few active persons who epitomize the times?

EMERSON, "FATE," *THE CONDUCT OF LIFE* (1860)

8. Time is a strange thing. It is a whimsical tyrant, which in every century has a different face for all that one says and does.

GOETHE, QUOTED IN JOHANN PETER ECKERMANN'S *CONVERSATIONS WITH GOETHE*, FEB. 25, 1824

9. Every age thinks its battle the most important of all.

HEINRICH HEINE, "DON'T LAUGH, LATER READER ...," *HEINRICH HEINE, WORKS OF PROSE* (1943), TR. E. B. ASHTON

10. If it is the great delusion of moralists to suppose that all previous ages were less sinful than their own, then it is the great delusion of intellectuals to suppose that all previous ages were less sick.

LOUIS KRONENBERGER, "THE SPIRIT OF THE AGE," *COMPANY MANNERS* (1954)

11. In history as it comes to be written, there is usually some Spirit of the Age which historians can define, but the shape of things is seldom so clear to those who live them. To most thoughtful men it has generally seemed that theirs was an Age of Confusion.

JOSEPH WOOD KRUTCH, "THE LOSS OF CONFIDENCE," *THE MEASURE OF MAN* (1954)

12. Every age has a keyhole to which its eye is pasted.

MARY MCCARTHY, "MY CONFESSION," *ON THE CONTRARY* (1961)

13. At each epoch of history the world was in a hopeless state, and at each epoch of history the world muddled through; at each epoch the world was lost, and at each epoch it was saved.

JACQUES MARITAIN, *REFLECTIONS ON AMERICA* (1958), 19.4

14. All thoughts are always ready, potentially if not actually. Each age selects and assimilates the philosophy that is most apt for its wants.

JOHN MORLEY, "EMERSON," *CRITICAL MISCELLANIES* (1871–1908)

15. These are the times that try men's souls.

THOMAS PAINE, *THE AMERICAN CRISIS* (1776–83), 1

16. Every epoch, under names more or less specious, has deified its peculiar errors.

SHELLEY, *A DEFENCE OF POETRY* (1821)

17. The altar cloth of one aeon is the doormat of the next.

MARK TWAIN, *NOTEBOOK* (1935)

18. Each age has its choice of the death it will die.

CHARLES DUDLEY WARNER, "SECOND STUDY," *BACKLOG STUDIES* (1873)

19. Every epoch has its character determined by the way its population re-act to the material events which they encounter.

ALFRED NORTH WHITEHEAD, *ADVENTURES IN IDEAS* (1933), 6

20. We live in the age of the overworked and the undereducated.

OSCAR WILDE, *THE ARTIST AS CRITIC: CRITICAL WRITINGS OF OSCAR WILDE*, ED. RICHARD ELLMAN(1969)

299. ERROR

See also 88. BLUNDER; 331. FALSEHOOD; 457. IMPERFECTION; 464. INCONSISTENCY; 684. PERFECTION; 999. TRUTH AND FALSEHOOD

1. The errors of young men are the ruin of business, but the errors of aged men amount to this, that more might have been done, or sooner.

FRANCIS BACON, "OF YOUTH AND AGE," *ESSAYS* (1625)

2. The Errors of a Wise Man make your Rule / Rather than the Perfections of a Fool.

WILLIAM BLAKE, "ENGLISH ENCOURAGEMENT OF ART: CROMEK'S OPINIONS PUT INTO RHYME" (1808–11)

3. Truth, crushed to earth, shall rise again; / The eternal years of God are hers; / But Error, wounded, writhes in pain, / And dies among his worshippers.

WILLIAM CULLEN BRYANT, "THE BATTLE-FIELD" (1837)

4. Every great mistake has a halfway moment, a split second when it can be recalled and perhaps remedied.

PEARL S. BUCK, *WHAT AMERICA MEANS TO ME* (1943), 10

5. Computer-users soon learn that the miraculous powers of personal computers are based on avoidance of error.

ROBERT BURCHFIELD, *UNLOCKING THE ENGLISH LANGUAGE* (1989)

6. I do not mind lying, but I hate inaccuracy.

SAMUEL BUTLER (D. 1902), "TRUTH AND CONVENIENCE," *NOTE-BOOKS* (1912)

7. There is no such source of error as the pursuit of absolute truth.

SAMUEL BUTLER (D. 1902), "TRUTH AND CONVENIENCE," *NOTE-BOOKS* (1912)

8. When everyone is wrong, everyone is right.

PIERRE-CLAUDE NIVELLE DE LA CHAUSSÉE, *LA GOUVERNANTE* (1744), 1.3

9. Any man can make mistakes, but only an idiot persists in his error.

CICERO, *PHILIPPICS* (44–43 B.C.), 6

10. Truth is a good dog; but beware of barking too close to the heels of an error, lest you get your brains kicked out.

SAMUEL TAYLOR COLERIDGE, *TABLE TALK,* JUNE 7, 1830

11. Ignorance is a blank sheet, on which we may write; but error is a scribbled one, on which we must first erase.

CHARLES CALEB COLTON, *LACON* (1825), 1.1

12. Who has enough credit in this world to pay for his mistakes?

EDWARD DAHLBERG, "ON WISDOM AND FOLLY," *REASONS OF THE HEART* (1965)

13. This is a hard and precarious world, where every mistake and infirmity must be paid for in full.

CLARENCE DAY, *THIS SIMIAN WORLD* (1920), 19

14. No doubt about it: error is the rule, truth is the accident of error.

GEORGES DUHAMEL, "AVANT-PROPOS," *LE NOTAIRE DU HAVRE* (1933)

15. He who is wrong fights against himself.

EGYPTIAN PROVERB

16. People seldom learn from the mistakes of others—not because they deny the value of the past, but because they are faced with new problems.

ILYA EHRENBURG, "WHAT I HAVE LEARNED," *SATURDAY REVIEW,* SEPT. 30 1967

17. Man must strive, and striving he must err.

GOETHE, "PROLOGUE IN HEAVEN," *FAUST: PART I* (1808), TR. PHILIP WAYNE

18. The greatest mistake you can make in life is to be continually fearing you will make one.

ELBERT HUBBARD, *THE NOTE BOOK* (1927)

19. If you own up to your mistakes, you don't suffer as much. But that's a tough lesson to learn.

LEE IACOCCA, *TALKING STRAIGHT* (1988), WITH SONNY KLEINFELD

20. Error of opinion may be tolerated where reason is left free to combat it.

THOMAS JEFFERSON, FIRST INAUGURAL ADDRESS, MARCH 4, 1801

21. [E]very error has its consequences and venges itself unto the seventh generation.

ARTHUR KOESTLER, *DARKNESS AT NOON* (1940)

22. All men are liable to error; and most men are, in many points, by passion or interest, under temptation to it.

JOHN LOCKE, *AN ESSAY CONCERNING HUMAN UNDERSTANDING* (1690), 4.20.17

23. It is one thing to show a man that he is in error, and another to put him in possession of truth.

JOHN LOCKE, *AN ESSAY CONCERNING HUMAN UNDERSTANDING* (1690), 4.7.11

24. Were half the power that fills the world with terror, / Were half the wealth bestowed on camps and courts, / Given to redeem the human mind from error, / There were no need of arsenals or forts.

LONGFELLOW, "THE ARSENAL AT SPRINGFIELD" (1845)

25. The errors of great men are venerable because they are more fruitful than the truths of little men.

NIETZSCHE, "FRAGMENT OF A CRITIQUE OF SCHOPENHAUER" (1867), IN *THE PORTABLE NIETZSCHE,* TR. WALTER KAUFMANN

26. The most powerful cause of error is the war existing between the senses and reason.

PASCAL, *PENSÉES* (1670), 82, TR. W. F. TROTTER

27. The man who can own up to his error is greater than he who merely knows how to avoid making it.

CARDINAL DE RETZ, *MÉMOIRES* (1718)

28. We are more conscious that a person is in the wrong when the wrong concerns ourselves.

JOSEPH ROUX, *MEDITATIONS OF A PARISH PRIEST* (1886), 4.25, TR. ISABEL F. HAPGOOD

29. Truth lies within a little and certain compass, but error is immense.

HENRY ST. JOHN, *REFLECTIONS UPON EXILE* (1716)

30. A life spent in making mistakes is not only more honorable but more useful than a life spent doing nothing.

GEORGE BERNARD SHAW, "PREFACE ON DOCTORS: THE TECHNICAL PROBLEM," *THE DOCTOR'S DILEMMA* (1913)

31. A man should never be ashamed to own he has been in the wrong, which is but saying, in other words, that he is wiser today than he was yesterday.

JONATHAN SWIFT, *THOUGHTS ON VARIOUS SUBJECTS* (1711)

32. Who can deny that all men are violent lovers of truth, when we see them so positive in their errors, which they will maintain out of their zeal to truth, although they contradict themselves every day of their lives?

JONATHAN SWIFT, *THOUGHTS ON VARIOUS SUBJECTS* (1711)

33. All erroneous ideas would perish of their own accord if given clear expression.

VAUVENARGUES, *REFLECTIONS AND MAXIMS* (1746), 6, TR. F. G. STEVENS

34. Error flies from mouth to mouth, from pen to pen, and to destroy it takes ages.

VOLTAIRE, "ASSASSIN," *PHILOSOPHICAL DICTIONARY* (1764)

35. Love truth, but pardon error.

VOLTAIRE, *SEPT DISCOURS EN VERS SUR L'HOMME* (1738), 3

36. The progress of rivers to the ocean is not so rapid as that of man to error.

VOLTAIRE, "RIVERS," *PHILOSOPHICAL DICTIONARY* (1764)

37. Why do you necessarily have to be wrong just because a few million people think you are?

FRANK ZAPPA, *THE REAL FRANK ZAPPA BOOK* (1989), WITH PETER OCCHIOGROSSO

300. ESCAPE

See also 199. COWARDICE; 304. EVASION; 343. FEAR; 449. ILLUSION

1. Oh that I had wings like a dove! for then would I fly away, and be at rest.

BIBLE, PSALMS 55:6

2. Those that fly, may fight again, / Which he can never do that's slain. / Hence timely running's no mean part / Of conduct, in the martial art.

SAMUEL BUTLER (D. 1680), *HUDIBRAS* (1663), 3.3

3. We must be very careful not to assign to this deliverance [Dunkirk] the attributes of a victory. Wars are not won by evacuations.

SIR WINSTON CHURCHILL, *THEIR FINEST HOUR* (1949)

4. The efforts which we make to escape from our destiny only serve to lead us into it.

EMERSON, "FATE," *THE CONDUCT OF LIFE* (1860)

5. The man does better who runs from disaster than he who is caught by it.

HOMER, *ILIAD* (9TH C. B.C.), 14.81, TR. RICHMOND LATTIMORE

6. A man trying to escape never thinks himself sufficiently concealed.

VICTOR HUGO, "COSETTE," *LES MISÉRABLES* (1862), 5.6, TR. CHARLES E. WILBOUR

7. There is no need of spurs when the horse is running away.

PUBLILIUS SYRUS, *MORAL SAYINGS* (1ST C. B.C.), 216, TR. DARIUS LYMAN

8. Flight is lawful, when one flies from tyrants.

RACINE, *PHAEDRA* (1677), 5, TR. ROBERT HENDERSON

9. It is always fair sailing, when you escape evil.

SOPHOCLES, *PHILOCTETES* (409 B.C.), TR. DAVID GRENE

10. He who flees will fight again.

TERTULLIAN, *DE FUGA IN PERSECUTIONE* (3RD C.), 10

ESTABLISHMENT

See 487. INSTITUTIONS

ESTEEM

See 722. PRAISE; 808. RESPECT; 871. SELF-ESTEEM

301. ESTRANGEMENT

See also 255. DISLIKE; 552. LOVE, LOSS OF

1. At best, the renewal of broken relations is a nervous matter.

HENRY ADAMS, *THE EDUCATION OF HENRY ADAMS* (1907), 16

2. A broken friendship may be soldered, but will never be sound.

THOMAS FULLER, M.D., *GNOMOLOGIA* (1732), 27

3. The surest sign of the estrangement of the opinions of two persons is when they both say something ironical to each other and neither of them feels the irony.

NIETZSCHE, *HUMAN, ALL TOO HUMAN* (1878), 331, TR. HELEN ZIMMERN

302. ETERNITY

See also 454. IMMORTALITY; 978. TIME; 990. TRANSIENCE

1. Eternity is a terrible thought. I mean, where's it going to end?

TOM STOPPARD, *ROSENCRANTZ & GUILDENSTERN ARE DEAD* (1967), 2

ETHICS

See 604. MORALITY

ETIQUETTE

See 563. MANNERS

303. EUROPE

1. Europe has what we do not have yet, a sense of the mysterious and inexorable limits of life, a sense, in a word, of tragedy. And we [Americans] have what they sorely need: a sense of life's possibilities.

JAMES BALDWIN, "THE DISCOVERY OF WHAT IT MEANS TO BE AN AMERICAN," *NOBODY KNOWS MY NAME* (1961)

2. We go to Europe to be Americanized.

EMERSON, "CULTURE," *THE CONDUCT OF LIFE* (1860)

3. He was fairly happy, except that, like many people living in Europe, he would rather have been in America, and he had discovered writing.

ERNEST HEMINGWAY, *THE SUN ALSO RISES* (1926)

4. If it was Europe that gave us on the coast some idea of our history, it was Europe, I feel, that also introduced us to the lie.

V.S. NAIPAUL, *A BEND IN THE RIVER* (1979)

5. The great mistake about Europe is taking the countries seriously and letting them quarrel and drop bombs on one another.

EDMUND WILSON, *THE FORTIES* (1983)

304. EVASION

See also 300. ESCAPE; 783. REALISM

1. It is the wise man's part / to leave in darkness everything that is ugly.

EURIPIDES, *HIPPOLYTUS* (428 B.C.), TR. DAVID GRENE

2. Many people today don't want honest answers insofar as honest means unpleasant or disturbing. They want a soft answer that turneth away anxiety.

LOUIS KRONENBERGER, "UNBRAVE NEW WORLD," *THE CART AND THE HORSE* (1964), 2

3. Who shrinks from knowledge of his calamities but aggravates his fear; troubles half seen do torture all the more.

SENECA, *AGAMEMNON* (1ST C.), 419, TR. FRANK JUSTUS MILLER

305. EVENTS

See also 129. CIRCUMSTANCE

1. Often do the spirits / Of great events stride on before the events, / And in today already walks tomorrow.

SAMUEL TAYLOR COLERIDGE, *WALLENSTEIN* (1800), 1.5.1

2. People to whom nothing has ever happened / Cannot understand the unimportance of events.

T. S. ELIOT, *THE FAMILY REUNION* (1939), 1.1

3. The soul contains the event that shall befall it, for the event is only the actualization of its thoughts; and what we pray to ourselves for is always granted.

EMERSON, *THE CONDUCT OF LIFE* (1860)

4. The enemy of the conventional wisdom is not ideas but the march of events.

JOHN KENNETH GALBRAITH, *THE AFFLUENT SOCIETY* (1958), 2.4

5. There are no events so disastrous that adroit men do not draw some advantage from them, nor any so fortunate that the imprudent cannot turn to their own prejudice.

LA ROCHEFOUCAULD, *MAXIMS* (1665), TR. KENNETH PRATT

6. Nothing befalls us that is not of the nature of ourselves. There comes no adventure but wears to our soul the shape of our everyday thoughts.

MAURICE MAETERLINCK, *WISDOM AND DESTINY* (1898), 10, TR. ALFRED SUTRO

7. How something important happens is the business of historians and newspapers, the effect it has is the business of philosophers and writers and especially poets.

KARL SHAPIRO, *REPORTS OF MY DEATH* (1990)

8. The great events of one's life often leave one unmoved: they pass out of consciousness, and, when one thinks of them, become unreal. Even the scarlet flowers of passion seem to grow in the same meadow as the poppies of oblivion. But the little things, the things of no moment, remain with us.

OSCAR WILDE, *THE ARTIST AS CRITIC: THE CRITICAL WRITINGS OF OSCAR WILDE* (1969) ED. RICHARD ELLMANN

306. EVIDENCE

See also 715. PORTENT; 744. PROOF

1. By a small sample we may judge of the whole piece.

CERVANTES, *DON QUIXOTE* (1605–15), 1.1.4, TR. JOHN OZELL

2. Some circumstantial evidence is very strong, as when you find a trout in the milk.

THOREAU, *JOURNAL*, NOV. 11, 1850

307. EVIL

See also 191. CORRUPTION; 204. CRIME; 389. THE GOOD; 390. GOOD AND EVIL; 393. GOODNESS; 900. SIN; 1055. WICKEDNESS; 1070. WRONGDOING

1. Destroy the seed of evil, or it will grow up to your ruin.

AESOP, "THE SWALLOW AND THE OTHER BIRDS," *FABLES* (6TH C. B.C.?), TR. JOSEPH JACOBS

2. No notice is taken of a little evil, but when it increases it strikes the eye.

ARISTOTLE, *POLITICS* (4TH C. B.C.), 6.4, TR. BENJAMIN JOWETT

3. Some men wish evil and accomplish it / But most men, when they work in that machine, / Just let it happen somewhere in the wheels. / The fault is no decisive, villainous knife / But the dull saw that is the routine mind.

STEPHEN VINCENT BENÉT, *JOHN BROWN'S BODY* (1928), 5

4. Sufficient unto the day is the evil thereof.

BIBLE, MATTHEW 6:34

5. Those who would extirpate evil from the world know little of human nature. As well might punch be palatable without souring as existence agreeable without care.

JAMES BOSWELL, *LONDON JOURNAL*, JULY 5, 1763

6. If men were basically evil, who would bother to improve the world instead of giving it up as a bad job at the outset?

VAN WYCK BROOKS, *FROM A WRITER'S NOTEBOOK* (1958)

7. There is this of good in real evils; they deliver us, while they last, from the petty despotism of all that were imaginary.

CHARLES CALEB COLTON, *LACON* (1825), 2.219

8. All evils are equal when they are extreme.

CORNEILLE, *HORACE* (1640), 1.3

9. God may still be in His Heaven, but there is more than sufficient evidence that all is not right with the world.

IRWIN EDMAN, "HOW TO BE SWEET THOUGH SOPHISTICATED," *ADAM, THE BABY, AND THE MAN FROM MARS* (1929)

10. Every evil to which we do not succumb is a benefactor.

EMERSON, "COMPENSATION," *ESSAYS: FIRST SERIES* (1841)

11. Good is a good doctor, but Bad is sometimes a better.

EMERSON, "CONSIDERATIONS BY THE WAY," *THE CONDUCT OF LIFE* (1860)

12. Evil enters like a needle and spreads like an oak tree.

ETHIOPIAN PROVERB

13. Evil men by their own nature cannot ever prosper.

EURIPIDES, *ION* (C. 421–408 B.C.), TR. RONALD F. WILLETTS

14. Some men have a necessity to be mean, as if they were exercising a faculty which they had to practically neglect since early childhood.

F. SCOTT FITZGERALD, *THE CRACK-UP* (1945)

15. The Devil gets up to the belfry by the vicar's skirts.

THOMAS FULLER, M.D., *GNOMOLOGIA* (1732), 4476

16. Must I do all the evil I can before I learn to shun it? Is it not enough to know the evil to shun it? If not, we should be sincere enough to admit that we love evil too well to give it up.

MOHANDAS K. GANDHI, *NON-VIOLENCE IN PEACE AND WAR* (1948), 2.74

17. There are two infinities in this world: God up above, and down below, human baseness.

JULES DE GONCOURT, *JOURNAL*, NOV. 23, 1862, TR. ROBERT BALDICK

18. He who does evil that good may come, pays a toll to the devil to let him into heaven.

AUGUSTUS WILLIAM HARE, *GUESSES AT TRUTH* (1827)

19. The man who does evil to another does evil to himself, / and the evil counsel is most evil for him who counsels it.

HESIOD, *WORKS AND DAYS* (8TH C. B.C.), 265, TR. RICHMOND LATTIMORE

20. It is by its promise of a sense of power that evil often attracts the weak.

ERIC HOFFER, *THE PASSIONATE STATE OF MIND* (1954), 91

21. What we most want to ask of our Maker is an unfolding of the divine purpose in putting human beings into conditions in which such numbers of them would be sure to go wrong.

OLIVER WENDELL HOLMES SR., *OVER THE TEACUPS* (1891), 10

22. He who passively accepts evil is as much involved in it as he who helps to perpetrate it. He who accepts evil without protesting against it is really cooperating with it.

MARTIN LUTHER KING, JR., *STRIDE TOWARD FREEDOM* (1958)

23. When evil acts in the world it always manages to find instruments who believe that what they do is not evil but honorable.

MAX LERNER, "THE CASE OF THE WOLF WHISTLE," *THE UNFINISHED COUNTRY* (1959), 4

24. When you choose the lesser of two evils, always remember that it is still an evil.

MAX LERNER, "POLITICS AND THE CONNECTIVE TISSUE," *ACTIONS AND PASSIONS* (1949)

25. It is the evil that lies in ourselves that is ever least tolerant of the evil that dwells within others.

MAURICE MAETERLINCK, *WISDOM AND DESTINY* (1898), 108, TR. ALFRED SUTRO

26. There is no explanation for evil. It must be looked upon as a necessary part of the order of the universe. To ignore it is childish; to bewail it senseless.

W. SOMERSET MAUGHAM, *THE SUMMING UP* (1938), 73

27. Evil alone has oil for every wheel.

EDNA ST. VINCENT MILLAY, UNTITLED POEM, *MINE THE HARVEST* (1954)

28. The great epochs of our life come when we gain the courage to rechristen our evil as what is best in us.

NIETZSCHE, *BEYOND GOOD AND EVIL* (1886), 116, TR. WALTER KAUFMANN

29. Submit to the present evil, lest a greater one befall you.

PHAEDRUS, *FABLES* (1ST C.), 1.2.31, TR. H. T. RILEY

30. Six well-spent years will pay off all the evil you have committed.

JEAN-JACQUES ROUSSEAU, IN CONVERSATION WITH JAMES BOSWELL., *BOSWELL ON THE GRAND TOUR: GERMANY AND SWITZERLAND* (1928)

31. If you expect the wise man to be as angry as the baseness of crimes requires, then he must not only be angry but go insane.

SENECA, *ON ANGER* (1ST C.)

32. Shall I tell you what the real evil is? To cringe to the things that are called evils, to surrender to them our freedom, in defiance of which we ought to face any suffering.

SENECA, *LETTERS TO LUCILIUS* (1ST C.), 85.28, TR. E. PHILLIPS BARKER

33. Men's evil manners live in brass; their virtues / We write in water.

SHAKESPEARE, *HENRY VIII* (1612–13), 4.2.45

34. There is some soul of goodness in things evil, / Would men observingly distil it out.

SHAKESPEARE, *HENRY V* (1598–99), 4.1.4

35. Between two evils, I always pick the one I never tried before.

MAE WEST, IN *KLONDIKE ANNIE* (1936)

308. EVOLUTION

See also 37. ANCESTRY; 741. PROGRESS

1. What could not be denied was that in vast segments of the animal world natural selection of the most qualified individuals took place not by competition for females but by competition for space.

ROBERT ARDREY, *AFRICAN GENESIS* (1961)

2. Natural selection deals ruthlessly with any population, bird or beaver, which fails to solve the problems of its environment with all those resources, learned or unlearned, which may be at its disposal.

ROBERT ARDREY, *THE TERRITORIAL IMPERATIVE* (1966)

3. The preoccupation with the choice of a mate both by male and female I regard as a continuing echo of the major selective force by which we have evolved.

JACOB BRONOWSKI, *THE ASCENT OF MAN* (1973)

4. From the war of nature, from famine and death, the most exalted object which we are capable of conceiving, namely, the production of the higher animals, directly follows.

CHARLES DARWIN, "CONCLUSION," *THE ORIGIN OF SPECIES* (1859)

5. As to modesty and decency, if we are simians we have done well, considering: but if we are something else—fallen angels—we have indeed fallen far.

CLARENCE DAY, *THIS SIMIAN WORLD* (1920), 13

6. Evolution loves death more than it loves you or me. This is easy to write, easy to read, and hard to believe.

ANNIE DILLARD, "FECUNDITY," *PILGRIM AT TINKER CREEK* (1974)

7. It's more comfortable to feel that we're a slight improvement on a monkey thin such a fallin' off fr'm th' angels.

Finley Peter Dunne, "On the Descent of Man," *Mr. Dooley On Making a Will* (1919)

8. When the theory of evolution destroyed the picture of God as the supreme Creator, confidence in God as the all-powerful Father of man fell with it, although many were able to combine a belief in God with the acceptance of the Darwinian theory.

Erich Fromm, *The Anatomy of Human Destructiveness* (1973)

9. Darwinian Man, though well-behaved, / At best is only a monkey shaved!

W. S. Gilbert, *Princess Ida* (1884), 2

10. It is an error to imagine that evolution signifies a constant tendency to increased perfection. That process undoubtedly involves a constant remodeling of the organism in adaptation to new conditions; but it depends on the nature of those conditions whether the direction of the modifications effected shall be upward or downward.

Thomas Henry Huxley, *The Struggle for Existence in Human Society* (1888)

11. [N]atural selection operates according to immediate cirumstances and not toward a long-term goal. *Homo sapiens* did eventually evolve as a descendant of the first humans, but there was nothing inevitable about it.

Richard Leakey, *The Origin of Humankind* (1994)

12. The individual is at the apex of his species' past, at the entrance to its future.

Charles A. Lindbergh, "Out of Eden," *Autobiography of Values* (1978)

13. Every mutation through a new combination of genetic factors that provides the organism with a new opportunity for coming to terms with the conditions of its environment signifies no more and no less than that *new information about this environment* has got into that organic system. *Adaptation is essentially a cognitive process.*

Konrad Lorenz, *The Waning of Humaneness* (1983), tr. Robert Warren Kicker, 3

14. Natural selection does not give any preference at all to anything that, in the long run, could be advantageous for the species but blindly rewards everything that, momentarily, affords greater procreative success.

Konrad Lorenz, *The Waning of Humaneness* (1983), tr. Robert Warren Kicker, 3

15. We are the first species to have taken our evolution into our own hands.

Carl Sagan, *Broca's Brain: Reflections on the Romance of Science* (1979)

16. The tide of evolution carries everything before it, thoughts no less than bodies, and persons no less than nations.

George Santayana, *Little Essays* (1920), 44

17. A person's genetic endowment, a product of the evolution of the species, is said to explain part of the workings of his mind and his personal history the rest.

B.F. Skinner, *Beyond Freedom and Dignity* (1971)

18. I believe that our Heavenly Father invented man because he was disappointed in the monkey.

Mark Twain, *Mark Twain in Eruption* (1940)

309. EXAGGERATION

1. It is only a short step from exaggerating what we can find in the world to exaggerating our power to remake the world.

Daniel J. Boorstin, *The Image: A Guide to Pseudo-Events in America* (1961)

2. The temptation to vivify the tale and make it walk abroad on its own legs is hard to deny.

Gelett Burgess, "Sub Rosa," *The Romance of the Commonplace* (1916)

3. Exaggeration is a prodigality of the judgment which shows the narrowness of one's knowledge or one's taste.

Baltasar Gracián, *The Art of Worldly Wisdom* (1647), 41, tr. Joseph Jacobs

4. A tendency to exaggeration was a Roman trait.

Edith Hamilton, *Mythology* (1940)

5. To exaggerate is to weaken.

Jean-François de la Harpe, *Mélanie* (1770), 1.1

6. Vice-President Ford, possibly preparing for higher duties, assessed Kissinger's part in the Syrian-Israeli troop disengagement as "the great diplomatic triumph of this century or perhaps any other."

Edwin Newman, *Strictly Speaking* (1974)

7. Exaggeration, the inseparable companion of greatness.

Voltaire, "Solomon," *Philosophical Dictionary* (1764)

310. EXAMPLE

1. Example is the best precept.

Aesop, "The Two Crabs," *Fables* (6th c. b.c.?), tr. Joseph Jacobs

2. The crab instructs its young, "Walk straight ahead—like me."

HINDUSTANI PROVERB

3. We need someone, I say, on whom our character may mould itself: you'll never make the crooked straight without a ruler.

SENECA, *LETTERS TO LUCILIUS* (1ST C.), 11.10, TR. E. PHILLIPS BARKER

4. Few things are harder to put up with than the annoyance of a good example.

MARK TWAIN, "PUDD'NHEAD WILSON'S CALENDAR," *PUDD'NHEAD WILSON* (1894), 19

311. EXCELLENCE

See also 1. ABILITY; 376. GENIUS; 584. MERIT; 952. SUPERIORITY; 962. TALENT; 1037. VOCATIONS

1. What is well done is done soon enough.

SEIGNEUR DU BARTAS, *DIVINE WEEKES AND WORKES* (1578), 1.1

2. Anyone who has achieved excellence in any form knows that it comes as a result of ceaseless concentration.

LOUISE BROOKS, "THE OTHER FACE OF W. C. FIELDS," *LULU IN HOLLYWOOD* (1982)

3. Human excellence means nothing / Unless it works with the consent of God.

EURIPIDES, *THE SUPPLIANT WOMEN* (C. 421 B.C.), TR. FRANK W. JONES

4. There is none who cannot teach somebody something, and there is none so excellent but he is excelled.

BALTASAR GRACIÁN, *THE ART OF WORLDLY WISDOM* (1647), 195, TR. JOSEPH JACOBS

5. Either dance well or quit the ballroom.

GREEK PROVERB

6. Men of genius do not excel in any profession because they labour in it, but they labour in it because they excel.

WILLIAM HAZLITT, *CHARACTERISTICS* (1823), 416

7. One shining quality lends a lustre to another, or hides some glaring defect.

WILLIAM HAZLITT, *CHARACTERISTICS* (1823), 162

8. It is not sufficiently considered in the hour of exultation, that all human excellence is comparative; that no man performs much but in proportion to what others accomplish, or to the time and opportunities which have been allowed him.

SAMUEL JOHNSON, *THE RAMBLER* (1750–52), 127

9. The heart of man does not tolerate an absence of the excellent and supreme.

JOSÉ ORTEGA Y GASSET, "PRELIMINARY MEDITATION," *MEDITATIONS ON QUIXOTE* (1914)

10. We measure the excellency of other men by some excellency we conceive to be in ourselves.

JOHN SELDEN, "MEASURE OF THINGS," *TABLE TALK* (1689)

11. Life's like a play: it's not the length, but the excellence of the acting that matters.

SENECA, *LETTERS TO LUCILIUS* (1ST C.), 77.20, TR. E. PHILLIPS BARKER

312. EXCESS

See also 309. EXAGGERATION; 324. EXTRAVAGANCE; 403. GREED; 470. INDULGENCE; 494. INTEMPERANCE; 557. LUXURY; 598. MODERATION; 947. SUFFICIENCY; 970. TEMPERANCE

1. The road of excess leads to the palace of wisdom.

WILLIAM BLAKE, "PROVERBS OF HELL," *THE MARRIAGE OF HEAVEN AND HELL* (1790)

2. To go beyond is as wrong as to fall short.

CONFUCIUS, *ANALECTS* (6TH C. B.C.), 11.15, TR. JAMES LEGGE

3. The best of things, beyond their measure, cloy.

HOMER, *ILIAD* (9TH C. B.C.), 13.795, TR. ALEXANDER POPE

4. The dinosaur's eloquent lesson is that if some bigness is good, an overabundance of bigness is not necessarily better.

ERIC JOHNSTON, *QUOTE*, FEB. 23, 1958

5. Too much work and too much energy kill a man just as effectively as too much assorted vice or too much drink.

RUDYARD KIPLING, "THROWN AWAY," *PLAIN TALES FROM THE HILLS* (1888)

6. Excess on occasion is exhilarating. It prevents moderation from acquiring the deadening effect of a habit.

W. SOMERSET MAUGHAM, *THE SUMMING UP* (1938), 15

7. It's just as unpleasant to get more than you bargain for as to get less.

GEORGE BERNARD SHAW, *GETTING MARRIED* (1911)

8. Excesses accomplish nothing. Disorder immediately defeats itself.

Woodrow Wilson, address to Congress, Nov. 11, 1918

313. EXCITEMENT

See also 16. Adventure; 216. Danger

1. People's sympathies seem generally to be with the fire so long as no one is in danger of being burned.

Samuel Butler (d. 1902), "Written Sketches," *Note-Books* (1912)

314. EXCUSES

See also 322. Explanation; 342. Faults; 782. Rationalization

1. With the help of an "if" you might put Paris into a bottle.

French Proverb

2. One unable to dance blames the unevenness of the floor.

Malay Proverb

315. EXECUTIVES

See also 13. Administration

1. What is worth doing is worth the trouble of asking somebody to do it.

Ambrose Bierce, "Saw," *The Devil's Dictionary* (1881–1911)

2. Some men owe most of their greatness to the ability of detecting in those they destine for their tools the exact quality of strength that matters for their work.

Joseph Conrad, *Lord Jim* (1900), 42

3. If you make believe that ten guys in pin-striped suits are back in a kindergarten class playing with building blocks, you'll get a rough picture of what life in a corporation is like.

Lee Iacocca, *Talking Straight* (1988), with Sonny Kleinfeld

4. A decision is the action an executive must take when he has information so incomplete that the answer does not suggest itself.

Arthur William Radford, *Time,* Feb. 25, 1957

5. Nothing is impossible for the man who doesn't have to do it himself.

A. H. Weiler, in a privately circulated memorandum of *The New York Times*

EXILE

See 423. Homeland

316. EXISTENCE

See also 317. Existentialism; 444. Identity; 539. Life

1. Why does one exist? That's not my problem. One does exist. The thing to do is to take no notice but go at it on the run and to keep on going right on until you die.

Simone de Beauvoir, *Les Belles Images* (1966), tr. Patrick O'Brian (1968)

2. As long as any man exists, there is some need of him; let him fight for his own.

Emerson, "Nominalist and Realist," *Essays: Second Series* (1844)

3. Man is the only animal for whom his own existence is a problem which he has to solve.

Erich Fromm, *Man for Himself* (1947), 3

4. The individual who has to justify his existence by his own efforts is in eternal bondage to himself.

Eric Hoffer, *The Ordeal of Change* (1964), 5

5. Every life is its own excuse for being.

Elbert Hubbard, *The Note Book* (1927)

6. An atom tossed in a chaos made / Of yeasting worlds, which bubble and foam. / Whence have I come? / What would be home? / I hear no answer. I am afraid!

Amy Lowell, "The Last Quarter of the Moon," *Sword Blades and Poppy Seeds* (1914)

7. We have two lives, Roy, the life we learn with and the life we live with after that.

Bernard Malamud, *The Natural* (1952)

8. We spend our lives talking about this mystery: our life.

Jules Renard, *Journal,* April 1894, tr. Elizabeth Roget

9. A sanctity hangs about the sources of our being, whether physical, social, or imaginary.

George Santayana, *The Life of Reason: Reason in Society* (1905–06), 7

10. That I exist is a perpetual surprise which is life.

Rabindranath Tagore, *Stray Birds* (1916), 22

11. Being is the great explainer.

Thoreau, *Journal,* Feb. 26, 1841

317. EXISTENTIALISM

See also 3. The Absurd; 316. Existence

1 Throughout the nineteenth century, there was a conservative existentialism which protested against the rationalization of life in a machine society.

Michael Harrington, *The Accidental Century* (1966)

2. Man is nothing else but what he makes of himself. Such is the first principle of existentialism.

Jean-Paul Sartre, *Existentialism* (1947)

3. Existentialism is possible only in a world where God is dead or a luxury, and where Christianity is dead.

Gabriel Vahanian, *The Death of God* (1962), 9

318. EXPECTATION

See also 249. Disappointment; 368. Future; 427. Hope; 1040. Waiting

1. Nothing is so good as it seems beforehand.

George Eliot, *Silas Marner* (1861)

2. You come to the United States not knowing what to expect. Then all your worst prejudices are confirmed.

John Fowles, *Daniel Martin* (1977)

3. The hours we pass with happy prospects in view are more pleasing than those crowned with fruition.

Oliver Goldsmith, *The Hermit* (1764), 10

4. The best part of our lives we pass in counting on what is to come.

William Hazlitt, "On Novelty and Familiarity," *The Plain Speaker* (1826)

5. Lighten grief with hopes of a brighter morrow; / Temper joy, in fear of a change of fortune.

Horace, *Odes* (23-c. 15 B.C.), 2.10

6. If pleasures are greatest in anticipation, just remember that this is also true of trouble.

Elbert Hubbard, *The Note Book* (1927)

7. It seems to be the fate of man to seek all his consolations in futurity. The time present is seldom able to fill desire or imagination with immediate enjoyment, and we are forced to supply its deficiencies by recollection or anticipation.

Samuel Johnson, *The Rambler* (1750–52), 203

8. As I walked purposefully down Kilindini Road, past the rows of Indian shops full of brummagem—the ivory knickknacks, fly whisks, and musical chamber pots that called up nostalgic memoirs of Sixth Avenue—my nerves tingled with exultation.

S.J. Perelman, *The Rising Gorge* (1961)

9. Blessed is he who expects nothing, for he shall never be disappointed.

Alexander Pope, letter to John Gay, Oct. 6, 1727

10. Even if it is to be, what end do you serve by running to meet distress?

Seneca, *Letters to Lucilius* (1st c.), 13, tr. E. Phillips Barker

11. Oft expectation fails and most oft there / Where most it promises, and oft it hits / Where hope is coldest and despair most fits.

Shakespeare, *All's Well That Ends Well* (1602–03), 2.1.145

12. 'Tis expectation makes a blessing dear; / Heaven were not heaven if we knew what it were.

Sir John Suckling, "Against Fruition," *Fragmenta Aurea* (1646), 4

319. EXPEDIENCY

See also 574. Means and Ends

1. In practice, such trifles as contradictions in principle are easily set aside; the faculty of ignoring them makes the practical man.

Henry Adams, *The Education of Henry Adams* (1907), 3

2. Philanthropic and religious bodies do not commonly make their executive officers out of s aints.

Emerson, "Power," *The Conduct of Life* (1860)

3. We do what we must, and call it by the best names.

Emerson, "Considerations by the Way," *The Conduct of Life* (1860)

4. a certain / alloy of expediency improves the / gold of morality and makes / it wear all the longer.

Don Marquis, "clarence the ghost," *Archy and Mehitabel* (1927)

5. Policy sits above conscience.

Shakespeare, *Timon of Athens* (1607–08), 3.2.94

6. In every sort of danger there are various ways of winning through, if one is ready to do and say anything whatever.

Socrates, in Plato's *Apology* (4th c. B.C.), tr. Lane Cooper

7. Custom adapts itself to expediency.

TACITUS, *ANNALS* (A.D. 115–117?), 12.6, TR. ALFRED J. CHURCH AND WILLIAM J. BRODRIBB

320. EXPENDABILITY

See also 1012. UNIMPORTANCE

1. A man overboard, a mouth the less.

DUTCH PROVERB

2. In the world I fill up a place, which may be better supplied when I have made it empty.

SHAKESPEARE, *AS YOU LIKE IT* (1599–1600), 1.2.203

321. EXPERIENCE

See also 504. INVOLVEMENT; 532. LEARNING; 539. LIFE; 917. SOPHISTICATION

1. We cannot appreciate the art of any age without first acquiring an equivalent of the experience it depicts.

JACQUES BARZUN, "ROMANTICISM: DEFINITION OF AN AGE," *CRITICAL QUESTIONS* (1982)

2. Experience isn't interesting until it begins to repeat itself—in fact, till it does that, it hardly *is* experience.

ELIZABETH BOWEN, *THE DEATH OF THE HEART* (1938), 1.1

3. We do but learn to-day what our better advanced judgements will unteach us tomorrow.

SIR THOMAS BROWNE, *RELIGIO MEDICI* (1642), 2

4. You cannot create experience. You must undergo it.

ALBERT CAMUS, *NOTEBOOKS 1935–1942* (1962), 1, TR. PHILIP THODY

5. The authentic insight and experience of any human soul, were it but insight and experience in hewing of wood and drawing of water, is real knowledge, a real possession and acquirement.

THOMAS CARLYLE, "CORN-LAW RHYMES" (1832)

6. The knowledge of the world is only to be acquired in the world, and not in a closet.

LORD CHESTERFIELD, *LETTERS TO HIS SON,* OCT. 4, 1746

7. When you have really exhausted an experience you always reverence and love it.

G. K. CHESTERTON, "THE CONTENTED MAP," *A MISCELLANY OF MEN* (1912)

8. Experience is a comb which nature gives us when we are bald.

CHINESE PROVERB

9. To most men, experience is like the stern lights of a ship, which illumine only the track it has passed.

SAMUEL TAYLOR COLERIDGE, *TABLE TALK* (1835)

10. No one over thirty-five is worth meeting who has not something to teach us,—something more than we could learn ourselves, from a book.

CYRIL CONNOLLY, *THE UNQUIET GRAVE* (1945), 1

11. Life is a succession of lessons enforced by immediate reward, or, oftener, by immediate chastisement.

ERNEST DIMNET, *THE ART OF THINKING* (1928), 2.6

12. Experience is the only teacher, and we get his lesson indifferently in any school.

EMERSON, *JOURNALS,* 1845

13. Life is a succession of lessons which must be lived to be understood.

EMERSON, "ILLUSIONS," *THE CONDUCT OF LIFE* (1860)

14. Only the wearer knows where the shoe pinches.

ENGLISH PROVERB

15. Experience, travel— / These are an education in themselves.

EURIPIDES, *ANDROMACHE* (C. 426 B.C.), TR. JOHN F. NIMS

16. Scalded cats fear even cold water.

THOMAS FULLER, M.D., *GNOMOLOGIA* (1732), 4075

17. He who has once burnt his mouth always blows his soup.

GERMAN PROVERB

18. Secondhand experience breaks down a block from the car lot.

URSULA K. LE GUIN, "BRYN MAWR COMMENCEMENT ADDRESS," *DANCING AT THE EDGE OF THE WORLD* (1989)

19. You know more of a road by having travelled it than by all the conjectures and descriptions in the world.

WILLIAM HAZLITT, "ON THE CONDUCT OF LIFE," *LITERARY REMAINS* (1836)

20. I have but one lamp by which my feet are guided, and that is the lamp of experience. I know of no way of judging of the future but by the past.

PATRICK HENRY, SPEECH, VIRGINIA CONVENTION, MARCH 23, 1775

21. The fool knows after he's suffered.

HESIOD, *WORKS AND DAYS* (8TH C. B.C.), 218, TR. RICHMOND LATTIMORE.

22. Experience is not what happens to you; it is what you do with what happens to you.

Aldous Huxley, *Reader's Digest,* March 1956

23. From their own experience or from the recorded experience of others (history), men learn only what their passions and their metaphysical prejudices allow them to learn.

Aldous Huxley, *Collected Essays* (1959)

24. A man should have the fine point of his soul taken off to become fit for this world.

Keats, letter to John Hamilton Reynolds, Nov. 22, 1817

25. Many people know so little about what is beyond their short range of experience. They look within themselves—and find nothing! Therefore they conclude that there is nothing outside themselves, either.

Helen Keller, *The World I Live In* (1908)

26. We arrive at the various stages of life quite as novices.

La Rochefoucauld, *Maxims* (1665), tr. Kenneth Pratt

27. Experience does not err; only your judgments err by expecting from her what is not in her power.

Leonardo Da Vinci, *Notebooks* (c. 1500), tr. Jean Paul Richter

28. He who neglects to drink of the spring of experience is likely to die of thirst in the desert of ignorance.

Ling Po, epigram

29. No man's knowledge here can go beyond his experience.

John Locke, *An Essay Concerning Human Understanding* (1690), 2.1.19

30. One thorn of experience is worth a whole wilderness of warning.

James Russell Lowell, "Shakespeare Once More," *Among My Books* (1870)

31. The finest edge is made with the blunt whetstone.

John Lyly, *Euphues: The Anatomy of Wit* (1579)

32. No one can shed light on vices he does not have or afflictions he has never experienced.

Antonio Machado, *Juan de Mairena* (1943), 13, tr. Ben Belitt

33. If your train's on the wrong track every station you come to is the wrong station.

Bernard Malamud, *Dubin's Lives* (1979)

34. The past exudes legend: one can't make pure clay of time's mud.

Bernard Malamud, *Dubin's Lives* (1979)

35. Not sense data or atoms or electrons or packets of energy, but purposes, interests, and meanings, constitute the underlying facts of human experience.

Lewis Mumford, "Orientation to Life," *The Conduct of Life* (1951)

36. The burnt child, urged by rankling ire, / Can hardly wait to get back at the fire.

Ogden Nash, "Experience to Let," *I'm a Stranger Here Myself* (1938)

37. A strong and well-constituted man digests his experiences (deeds and misdeeds) just as he digests his meats, even when he has some tough morsels to swallow.

Nietzsche, *The Genealogy of Morals* (1887), 3.16, tr. Horace B. Samuel

38. Men use a new lesson or experience later on as a ploughshare or perhaps also as a weapon; women at once make it into an ornament.

Nietzsche, *Miscellaneous Maxims and Opinions* (1879), 290, tr. Paul V. Cohn

39. When one has finished building one's house, one suddenly realizes that in the process one has learned something that one really needed to know in the worst way—before one began.

Nietzsche, *Beyond Good and Evil* (1886), 277, tr. Walter Kaufmann

40. Nothing has happened to you unless you make much of it.

Menander (4th–3rd c. b.c.), quoted in Plutarch's "Contentment," *Moralia* (c. a.d. 100), tr. Moses Hadas

41. No man alive can say, This shall not happen to me.

Menander (4th–3rd c. b.c.), quoted in Plutarch's "Contentment," *Moralia* (c. a.d. 100), tr. Moses Hadas

42. Why the need, rising in some very nearly to the level of compulsion, to verify experience by way of language?—to scrupulously record and preserve the very passing of Time?

Joyce Carol Oates, *(Woman) Writer: Occasions and Opportunities* (1988)

43. He who has been bitten by a snake fears a piece of string.

Persian Proverb

44. What is experience? A poor little hut constructed from the ruins of the palace of gold and marble called our illusions.

Joseph Roux, *Meditations of a Parish Priest* (1886), 4.15, tr. Isabel F. Hapgood

45. Experience seems to most of us to lead to conclusions, but empiricism has sworn never to draw them.

George Santayana, *Character and Opinion in the United States* (1921), 3

46. Everything happens to everybody sooner or later if there is time enough.

George Bernard Shaw, *Back to Methuselah* (1921), 4

47. Men are wise in proportion, not to their experience, but to their capacity for experience.

George Bernard Shaw, "Maxims for Revolutionists," *Man and Superman* (1903)

48. If we shake hands with icy fingers, it is because we have burnt them so horribly before.

Logan Pearsall Smith, *Afterthoughts* (1931), 2

49. He who was first an acolyte, and afterwards an abbot or curate, knows what the boys do behind the altar.

Spanish Proverb

50. Doubtless the world is quite right in a million ways; but you have to be kicked about a little to convince you of the fact.

Robert Louis Stevenson, "Crabbed Age and Youth," *Virginibus Puerisque* (1881)

51. It is strange how often a heart must be broken / Before the years can make it wise.

Sara Teasdale, "Dust," *Flame and Shadow* (1920)

52. Others' follies teach us not / Nor much their wisdom teaches; / And most, of sterling worth, is what / Our own experience preaches.

Lord Tennyson, "Will Waterproof's Lyrical Monologue" (1842)

53. There's nothing in the world so unfair as a man who has no experience of life; he thinks nothing is done right except what he's doing himself.

Terence, *The Brothers* (160 b.c.), tr. William A. Oldfather

54. Experience is in the fingers and head. The heart is inexperienced.

Thoreau, *Journal,* April 3, 1841

55. The difference between ancients and moderns is that the ancients asked what have we experienced, and moderns asked what can we experience.

Alfred North Whitehead, *Adventures in Ideas* (1933), 15

56. Experience is the name everyone gives to their mistakes.

Oscar Wilde, *Lady Windermere's Fan* (1892), 3

57. To regret one's own experiences is to arrest one's own development. To deny one's own experiences is to put a lie into the lips of one's life. It is no less than a denial of the soul.

Oscar Wilde, *De Profundis* (1905)

EXPERTS

See 924. Specialists

322. EXPLANATION

See also 314. Excuses; 782. Rationalization

1. There is no waste of time in life like that of making explanations.

Benjamin Disraeli, speech, "University Education Bill (Ireland)," March 11, 1873

2. Never explain. Your friends do not need it and your enemies will not believe you anyway.

Elbert Hubbard, *The Note Book* (1927)

323. EXPLOITATION

See 549. Losers

324. EXTRAVAGANCE

See also 312. Excess; 557. Luxury; 598. Moderation; 977. Thrift

1. We deny that it is fun to be saving. It is fun to be prodigal. Go to the butterfly, thou parsimonious sluggard; consider her ways and get wise.

Franklin P. Adams, *Nods and Becks* (1944)

2. Dry happiness is like dry bread. We eat, but we do not dine. I wish for the superfluous, for the useless, for the extravagant, for the too much, for that which is not good for anything.

Victor Hugo, "Jean Valjean," *Les Misérables* (1862), 5.6, tr. Charles E. Wilbour

EXTREMISM

See 335. Fanaticism

325. EYES

See also 326. FACE; 882. SENSES; 897. SIGHT; 925. SPECTACLES

1. The eyes indicate the antiquity of the soul.

EMERSON, "BEHAVIOR," *THE CONDUCT OF LIFE* (1860)

2. The eyes have one language everywhere.

GEORGE HERBERT, *JACULA PRUDENTUM* (1651)

3. I dislike an eye that twinkles like a star. Those only are beautiful which, like the planets, have a steady, lambent light, are luminous, but not sparkling.

LONGFELLOW, *HYPERION* (1839), 3.4

F

326. FACE

See also 149. COMMUNICATION; 192. COSMETICS; 325. EYES; 882. SENSES

1. There are mystically in our faces certain characters which carry in them the motto of our souls, wherein he that cannot read A,B,C may read our natures.

SIR THOMAS BROWNE, *RELIGIO MEDICI* (1642), 2

2. There is a case for keeping wrinkles. They are the long-service stripes earned in the hard campaign of life.

DAILY MAIL, LONDON, EDITORIAL, "IN PRAISE OF WRINKLES," JAN. 20, 1961

3. A man finds room in the few square inches of his face for the traits of all his ancestors; for the expression of all his history, and his wants.

EMERSON, "BEHAVIOR," *THE CONDUCT OF LIFE* (1860)

4. Not only does beauty fade, but it leaves a record upon the face as to what became of it.

ELBERT HUBBARD, *THE NOTE BOOK* (1927)

5. The features of our face are hardly more than gestures which have become permanent.

MARCEL PROUST, *REMEMBRANCE OF THINGS PAST: WITHIN A BUDDING GROVE* (1913–27), TR. C. K. SCOTT-MONCRIEFF

6. There are quantities of human beings, but there are many more faces, for each person has several.

RAINER MARIA RILKE, *THE NOTEBOOKS OF MALTE LAURIDS BRIGGE* (1910), TR. M. D. HERTER NORTON

7. A lovely face is the solace of wounded hearts and the key of locked-up gates.

SA'DI, *GULISTAN* (1258), 3.28, TR. JAMES ROSS

327. FACILITY

See also 245. DIFFICULTY

1. He who accounts all things easy will have many difficulties.

LAO TZU, *THE SIMPLE WAY* (6TH C. B.C.)

2. For easy things, that may be got at will, / Most sorts of men do set but little store.

EDMUND SPENSER, *AMORETTI* (1595), 51

328. FACTS

See also 784. REALITY; 932. STATISTICS; 974. THEORY

1. You can't make the Duchess of Windsor into Rebecca of Sunnybrook Farm. The facts of life are very stubborn things.

CLEVELAND AMORY, NEWS REPORTS, OCT. 6, 1955

2. Conclusive facts are inseparable from inconclusive except by a head that already understands and knows.

THOMAS CARLYLE, *CHARTISM* (1839), 2

3. Facts are the images of history, just as images are the facts of fiction.

E.L. DOCTOROW, "FALSE DOCUMENTS," *JACK LONDON, HEMINGWAY, AND THE CONSTITUTION* (1993)

4. The grand aim of all science is to cover the greatest number of empirical facts by logical deduction from the smallest number of hypotheses or axioms.

EINSTEIN, *LIFE*, JAN. 9, 1950

5. If a man will kick a fact out of the window, when he comes back he finds it again in the chimney corner.

EMERSON, *JOURNALS*, 1842

6. The chief value of the new fact, is to enhance the great and constant fact of life.

EMERSON, "THE POET," *ESSAYS: SECOND SERIES* (1844)

7. Time dissipates to shining ether the solid angularity of facts.

EMERSON, "HISTORY," *ESSAYS: FIRST SERIES* (1841)

8. A wise man recognizes the convenience of a general statement, but he bows to the authority of a particular fact.

OLIVER WENDELL HOLMES, SR., *THE POET AT THE BREAKFAST TABLE* (1872), 10

9. All generous minds have a horror of what are commonly called "facts." They are the brute beasts of the intellectual domain.

OLIVER WENDELL HOLMES, SR., *THE AUTOCRAT OF THE BREAKFAST TABLE* (1858), 1

10. Though we face the facts of sex we are more reluctant than ever to face the fact of death or the crueler facts of life, either biological or social.

JOSEPH WOOD KRUTCH, TITLE ESSAY, 1, *IF YOU DON'T MIND MY SAYING SO* (1964)

11. A fact is like a sack which won't stand up when it is empty. In order that it may stand up, one has to put into it the reason and sentiment which have caused it to exist.

LUIGI PIRANDELLO, *SIX CHARACTERS IN SEARCH OF AN AUTHOR* (1921), 1, TR. EDWARD STORER

12. The facts are to blame, my friend. We are all imprisoned by facts: I was born, I exist.

LUIGI PIRANDELLO, *THE RULES OF THE GAME* (1918), 1, TR. WILLIAM MURRAY

13. When you have duly arrayed your "facts" in logical order, lo, it is like an oil-lamp that you have made, filled and trimmed, but which sheds no light unless first you light it.

SAINT-EXUPÉRY, *THE WISDOM OF THE SANDS* (1948), 43, TR. STUART GILBERT

14. Consciousness of a fact is not knowing it: if it were, the fish would know more of the sea than the geographers and the naturalists.

GEORGE BERNARD SHAW, *BACK TO METHUSELAH* (1921), 4.1

15. You will find that the truth is often unpopular and the contest between agreeable fancy and disagreeable fact is unequal. For, in the vernacular, we Americans are suckers for good news.

ADLAI STEVENSON, COMMENCEMENT ADDRESS, MICHIGAN STATE UNIVERSITY, JUNE 8, 1958

16. It is the spirit of the age to believe that any fact, no matter how suspect, is superior to any imaginative exercise, no matter how true.

GORE VIDAL, "FRENCH LETTERS: THEORIES OF THE NEW NOVEL," *ENCOUNTER*, DECEMBER 1967

329. FAILURE

See also 17. ADVERSITY; 226. DECLINE; 228. DEFEAT; 549. LOSERS; 550. LOSS; 945. SUCCESS

1. [W]hat frightened him, and kept him more than ever on his knees, was the knowledge that, once having fallen, nothing would be easier than to fall again. Having possessed Esther, the carnal man awoke, seeing the possibility of conquest everywhere.

JAMES BALDWIN, *GO TELL IT ON THE MOUNTAIN* (1953)

2. The young think that failure is the Siberian end of the line, banishment from all the living, and tend to do what I then did—which was to hide.

JAMES BALDWIN, "ALAS, POOR RICHARD," IN *THE ART OF THE PERSONAL ESSAY* (1994), ED. PHILLIP LOPATE

3. Woe to him that is alone when he falleth; for he hath not another to help him up.

BIBLE, ECCLESIASTES 4:10

4. The tragedy of life is not that man loses but that he almost wins.

HEYWOOD BROUN, "SPORT FOR ART'S SAKE," *PIECES OF HATE, AND OTHER ENTHUSIASMS* (1922)

5. Fail I alone, in words and deeds?/ Why, all men strive and who succeeds?

ROBERT BROWNING, "THE LAST RIDE TOGETHER," *MEN AND WOMEN* (1855), 5

6. All men that are ruined, are ruined on the side of their natural propensities.

EDMUND BURKE, *LETTERS ON A REGICIDE PEACE* (1795–97), 1

7. Doing is overrated, and success undesirable, but the bitterness of failure even more so.

CYRIL CONNOLLY, *THE UNQUIET GRAVE* (1945), 4

8. O human race! Born to ascend on wings, / Why do ye fall at such a little wind?

DANTE, "PURGATORIO," 12, *THE DIVINE COMEDY* (C. 1300–21), TR. LAWRENCE GRANT WHITE

9. Nothing more aggravates ill success than the near approach to good.

HENRY FIELDING, *TOM JONES* (1749), 13.2

10. One is always more vexed at losing a game of any sort by a single hole or ace, than if one has never had a chance of winning it.

WILLIAM HAZLITT, "ON GREAT AND LITTLE THINGS," *LITERARY REMAINS* (1836)

11. In the long run, failure was the only thing that worked predictably. All else was accidental.

JOSEPH HELLER, *GOOD AS GOLD* (1979)

12. There is no loneliness greater than the loneliness of a failure. The failure is a stranger in his own house.

ERIC HOFFER, *THE PASSIONATE STATE OF MIND* (1954), 223

13. The line between failure and success is so fine that we scarcely know when we pass it: so fine that we are often on the line and do not know it.

ELBERT HUBBARD, *THE NOTE BOOK* (1927)

14. There is no failure except in no longer trying.

Elbert Hubbard, *The Note Book* (1927)

15. There is the greatest practical benefit in making a few failures early in life.

Thomas Henry Huxley, "On Medical Education" (1870)

16. There is not a fiercer hell than the failure in a great object.

Keats, preface, *Endymion* (1818)

17. We are neurotically haunted today by the imminence, and by the ignominy, of failure. We know at how frightening a cost one *succeeds*: to fail is something too awful to think about.

Louis Kronenberger, "Our Unhappy Happy Endings," *The Cart and the Horse* (1964), 2

18. Men fall from great fortune because of the same shortcomings that led to their rise.

La Bruyère, *Characters* (1688), 8.34

19. We may stop ourselves when going up, never when coming down.

Napoleon I, *Maxims* (1804–15)

20. Though not constitutionally averse to the crackle of greenbacks, I learned many years ago—twenty-eight, in fact—that of all the roads to insolvency open to my profession, entanglement in a revue is the shortest.

S.J. Perelman, *The Rising Gorge* (1961)

21. Flops are a part of life's menu and I've never been a girl to miss out on any of the courses.

Rosalind Russell, *New York Herald Tribune,* April 11, 1957

22. I would prefer even to fail with honor than win by cheating.

Sophocles, *Philoctetes* (409 B.C.), tr. David Grene

23. All men are mortal, and therefore all men are losers; our profoundest loyalty goes out to the failed.

John Updike, "The Boston Red Sox, as of 1986," *Odd Jobs* (1991)

24. We women adore failures. They lean on us.

Oscar Wilde, *A Woman of No Importance* (1893), 1

25. He that lies on the ground cannot fall.

Yiddish Proverbs (1949)

330. FAITH

See also 78. Belief; 203. Creeds; 265. Doubt, Religious; 904. Skepticism; 1004. Unbelief

1. The relation of faith between subject and object is unique in every case. Hundreds may believe, but each has to believe by himself.

W. H. Auden, "Genius and Apostle," *The Dyer's Hand* (1962)

2. Faith is to believe what you do not yet see; the reward for this faith is to see what you believe.

St. Augustine, *Sermons* (5th c.), 43

3. A man consists of the faith that is in him. Whatever his faith is, he is.

Bhagavadgita, 17, tr. Christopher Isherwood

4. Faith is the substance of things hoped for, the evidence of things not seen.

Bible, Hebrews 11:1

5. Faith without works is dead.

Bible, James 2:26

6. He's a Blockhead who wants a proof of what he can't Perceive, / And he's a Fool who tries to make such a Blockhead believe.

William Blake, "To Flaxman" (1808–11)

7. To believe only possibilities is not faith, but mere philosophy.

Sir Thomas Browne, *Religio Medici* (1642), 1

8. What is faith but a kind of betting or a speculation after all?

Samuel Butler (d. 1902), *Note-Books* (1912)

9. You can do very little with faith, but you can do nothing without it.

Samuel Butler (d. 1902), "Rebelliousness," *Note-Books* (1912)

10. Faith—is the Pierless Bridge / Supporting what We see / Unto the Scene that We do not—.

Emily Dickinson, poem (c. 1864)

11. A believer, a mind whose faith is consciousness, is never disturbed because other persons do not yet see the fact which he sees.

Emerson, *Journals,* 1836

12. I thought how we might have to yell to be heard by Higher Power, but that's not saying it's not *there*. And that is faith for you. It's belief even when the gods don't deliver.

Louise Erdrich, "Love Medicine," *Love Medicine* (1984)

13. The care of God for us is a great thing, / if a man believe it at heart: / it plucks the burden of sorrow from him.

Euripides, *Hippolytus* (428 B.C.), tr. David Grene

14. Faith, to my mind, is a stiffening process, a sort of mental starch, which ought to be applied as sparingly as possible.

E. M. Forster, "What I Believe," *Two Cheers for Democracy* (1951)

15. Faith is not a weak form of belief or knowledge; it is not faith in this or that; faith is the conviction about the not yet proven, the knowledge of the real possibility, the awareness of pregnancy.

Erich Fromm, *The Revolution of Hope* (1968)

16. If you have abandoned one faith, do not abandon all faith. There is always an alternative to the faith we lose. Or is it the same faith under another mask?

Graham Greene, *The Comedians* (1966)

17. A faith that sets bounds to itself, that will believe so much and no more, that will trust thus far and no further, is none.

Augustus William Hare, *Guesses at Truth* (1827)

18. If your faith is opposed to experience, to human learning and investigation, it is not worth the breath used in giving it expression.

Edgar Watson Howe, *Ventures in Common Sense* (1919), 3.7

19. Faith is a living and unshakeable confidence, a belief in the grace of God so assured that a man would die a thousand deaths for its sake.

Martin Luther, preface to his translation of St. Paul's epistle to the Romans (1522)

20. He [Gen. Douglas MacArthur] never went to church, but he read the Bible every day and regarded himself as one of the world's two great defenders of Christendom. (The other was the pope.)

William Manchester, *American Caesar* (1978)

21. Faith, like a jackal, feeds among the tombs, and even from these dead doubts she gathers her most vital hope.

Herman Melville, *Moby-Dick* (1851), 7

22. The terrors of truth and dart of death / To faith alike are vain.

Herman Melville, "The Conflict of Convictions," *Battlepieces and Aspects of the War* (1866)

23. Faith may be defined briefly as an illogical belief in the occurrence of the improbable.

H. L. Mencken, *Prejudices: Third Series* (1922), 14

24. The most satisfying and ecstatic faith is almost purely agnostic. It trusts absolutely without professing to know at all.

H. L. Mencken, "Quid Est Veritas?" *Damn! A Book of Calumny* (1918)

25. Not Truth, but Faith, it is / That keeps the world alive.

Edna St. Vincent Millay, "Interim," *Renascence* (1917)

26. And what is faith, love, virtue unassayed / Alone, without exterior help sustained?

Milton, *Paradise Lost* (1667), 9.335

27. Let none henceforth seek needless cause to approve / The faith they owe; when earnestly they seek / Such proof, conclude, they then begin to fail.

Milton, *Paradise Lost* (1667), 9.1140

28. Faith, fanatic Faith, once wedded fast / To some dear falsehood, hugs it to the last.

Thomas Moore, "The Veiled Prophet of Khorassan," *Lalla Rookh* (1817)

29. Faith embraces many truths which seem to contradict each other.

Pascal, *Pensées* (1670), 861, tr. W. F. Trotter

30. It is your own assent to yourself, and the constant voice of your own reason, and not of others, that should make you believe.

Pascal, *Pensées* (1670), 260, tr. W. F. Trotter

31. Faith means that a man should regard any disaster simply as a fate-determined blow which must be endured.

Anwar el-Sadat, *In Search of Identity* (1977)

32. Proofs are the last thing looked for by a truly religious mind which feels the imaginative fitness of its faith.

George Santayana, *Interpretations of Poetry and Religion* (1900)

33. Hope looks for unqualified success; but Faith counts certainly on failure, and takes honorable defeat to be a form of victory.

Robert Louis Stevenson, title essay, 2, *Virginibus Puertisque* (1881)

34. Faith speaks when hope dissembles: / Faith lives when hope dies dead.

ALGERNON CHARLES SWINBURNE, "JACOBITE SONG," *ASTROPHEL AND OTHER POEMS* (1894)

35. Cleave ever to the sunnier side of doubt, / And cling to Faith beyond the forms of Faith.

LORD TENNYSON, "THE ANCIENT SAGE" (1885)

36. Faith embraces itself and the doubt about itself.

PAUL TILLICH, *THE NEW YORK TIMES,* MAY 5, 1963

37. Faith is believing what you know ain't so.

MARK TWAIN, "PUDD'NHEAD WILSON'S NEW CALENDAR," *FOLLOWING THE EQUATOR* (1897), 1.12

38. Faith is, before all and above all, wishing God may exist.

MIGUEL DE UNAMUNO, "FAITH, HOPE, AND CHARITY," *TRAGIC SENSE OF LIFE* (1913), TR. J. E. CRAWFORD FLITCH

39. Faith consists in believing not what seems true, but what seems false to our understanding.

VOLTAIRE, "FAITH," *PHILOSOPHICAL DICTIONARY* (1764)

FAITHFULNESS

See 181. CONSTANCY AND INCONSTANCY; 472. INFIDELITY

FALL

See 854. SEASONS

FALLING

See 329. FAILURE

331. FALSEHOOD

See also 224. DECEPTION; 558. LYING; 864. SELF-DECEPTION; 999. TRUTH AND FALSEHOOD; 998. TRUTH; 1000. TRUTHFULNESS

1. Man can certainly keep on lying (and does so), but he cannot make truth falsehood.

KARL BARTH, QUOTED IN HIS OBITUARY, *THE NEW YORK TIMES,* DEC. 11, 1968

332. FAME

See also 353. FOLLOWING; 386. GLORY; 418. HEROES AND HEROISM; 426. HONORS; 584. MERIT; 649. OBSCURITY; 804. REPUTATION; 1068. WORSHIP

1. No public character has ever stood the revelation of private utterance and correspondence.

LORD ACTON, POSTSCRIPT, LETTER TO MANDELL CREIGHTON, APRIL 5, 1887

2. If men of eminence are exposed to censure on one hand, they are as much liable to flattery on the other. If they receive reproaches which are not due to them, they likewise receive praises which they do not deserve.

JOSEPH ADDISON, *THE SPECTATOR* (1711–12), 101

3. A celebrity is a person who works hard all his life to become known, then wears dark glasses to avoid being recognized.

FRED ALLEN, *TREADMILL TO OBLIVION* (1954)

4. Fame is like a river, that beareth up things light and swollen, and drowns things weighty and solid.

FRANCIS BACON, "OF CEREMONIES AND RESPECTS," *ESSAYS* (1625)

5. You canna expect to be baith grand and comfortable.

J. M. BARRIE, *THE LITTLE MINISTER* (1891), 10

6. Men prominent in life are mostly hard to converse with. They lack small-talk, and at the same time one doesn't like to confront them with their own great themes.

MAX BEERBOHM, "T. FENNING DODWORTH," *MAINLY ON THE AIR* (1946)

7. A sign of a celebrity is often that his name is worth more than his services.

DANIEL J. BOORSTIN, *THE IMAGE* (1962), 5.4

8. Celebrity: the advantage of being known by those who don't know you.

CHAMFORT, *MAXIMES ET PENSÉES* (1805), 1

9. There are many paths to the top of the mountain, but the view is always the same.

CHINESE PROVERB

10. Celebrity: I picture myself as a marble bust with legs to run everywhere.

JEAN COCTEAU, "DES BEAUX-ARTS CONSIDÉRÉS COMME UN ASSASSINAT," *ESSAI DE CRITIQUE INDIRECTE* (1932)

11. A man's renown is like the hue of grass, / Which comes and goes.

DANTE, "PURGATORIO," 11, *THE DIVINE COMEDY* (C. 1300–21), TR. LAWRENCE GRANT WHITE

12. Fame is a bee. / It has a song—/ It has a sting—/ Ah, too, it has a wing.

EMILY DICKINSON, *POEMS* (C. 1862–86)

13. How dreary—to be—Somebody! / How public—like a Frog— / To tell your name—the livelong June—/ To an admiring Bog!

Emily Dickinson, poem (c. 1861)

14. Fame sometimes hath created something of nothing.

Thomas Fuller, M.D., "Of Fame," *The Holy State and the Profane State* (1642)

15. All fame is dangerous: good bringeth envy; bad, shame.

Thomas Fuller, M.D., *Gnomologia* (1732), 513

16. Your first realization when you become an important person is that all day and all night, whatever the circumstances, people want to hear you talk about yourself.

Gabriel García Márquez, *The Story of a Shipwrecked Sailor* (1986)

17. For a good man fame is always a problem.

Graham Greene, *A Burnt-Out Case* (1960)

18. We imagine that the admiration of the works of celebrated men has become common, because the admiration of their names has become so.

William Hazlitt, "Why the Arts Are Not Progressive," *Round Table* (1817)

19. Fame usually comes to those who are thinking about something else.

Oliver Wendell Holmes, Sr., *The Autocrat of the Breakfast Table* (1858), 12

20. How vain, without the merit, is the name.

Homer, *Iliad* (9th c. b.c.), 17.158, tr. Alexander Pope

21. Men have a solicitude about fame; and the greater share they have of it, the more afraid they are of losing it.

Samuel Johnson, quoted in Boswell's *Life of Samuel Johnson*, July 21, 1763

22. On any morning these days whole segments of the population wake up to find themselves famous, while, to keep matters shipshape, whole contingents of celebrities wake up to find themselves forgotten.

Louis Kronenberger, "The Spirit of the Age," *Company Manners* (1954)

23. The boy who hankers after fame has no idea what fame is. The thing that gives our every move its meaning is always totally unknown to us.

Milan Kundera, *The Unbearable Lightness of Being* (1984)

24. There is no business in this world so troublesome as the pursuit of fame: life is over before you have hardly begun your work.

La Bruyère, *Characters* (1688), 2.9, tr. Henri Van Laun

25. Actors, politicians, and writers—all of us are but creatures of the hour. Long-lasting fame comes to but few.

Louis L'Amour, *Education of a Wandering Man* (1989)

26. I think there's a danger in overexposure. Just think what happened to Lady Godiva—she became a chocolate.

Kenneth Jay Lane, *The New York Times*, Dec. 13, 1993

27. The renown of great men should always be measured by the means which they have used to acquire it.

La Rochefoucauld, *Maxims* (1665), tr. Kenneth Pratt

28. When I hear a man applauded by the mob I always feel a pang of pity for him. All he has to do to be hissed is to live long enough.

H. L. Mencken, *Minority Report* (1956), 351

29. We are all clever enough at envying a famous man while he is yet alive, and at praising him when he is dead.

Mimnermus, extant fragment (7th c. b.c.)

30. The dispersing and scattering our names into many mouths, we call making them more great.

Montaigne, "Of glory," *Essays* (1580–88), tr. W. C. Hazlitt

31. We are more solicitous that men speak of us, than how they speak.

Montaigne, "Of glory," *Essays* (1580–88), tr. W. C. Hazlitt.

32. There are few people living who are not flattered by the request for an autograph, and it may be taken as axiomatic that when they do not want this signature of yours they do not want you.

Gerald Moore, *Am I Too Loud? A Musical Autobiography* (1962)

33. Put a rogue in the limelight and he will act like an honest man.

Napoleon I, *Maxims* (1804–15)

34. Fame's carapace does not allow for easy breathing.

Joyce Carol Oates, "Pseudonymous Selves," *(Woman) Writer: Occasions and Opportunities* (1988)

35. A very quiet and tasteful way to be famous is to have a famous relative. Then you can not only be nothing, you can do nothing, too.

P.J. O'Rourke, *Modern Manners* (1988)

36. False is the praise which says that men's eminence comes from their noble qualities; for the people of this world as a rule do not care about a man's true nature.

Panchatantra (c. 5th c.), 1, tr. Franklin Edgerton

37. The charm of fame is so great that we like every object to which it is attached, even death.

Pascal, *Pensées* (1670), 158, tr. W. F. Trotter

38. Unblemished let me live, or die unknown; / O grant an honest fame, or grant me none!

Alexander Pope, *The Temple of Fame* (1711), 523

39. Would you be known by everybody? Then you know nobody.

Publilius Syrus, *Moral Sayings* (1st c. B.C.), 979, tr. Darius Lyman

40. Fame, that public destruction of one in process of becoming, into whose building-ground the mob breaks, displacing his stones.

Rainer Maria Rilke, *The Notebooks of Malte Laurids Brigge* (1910), tr. M. D. Herter Norton

41. He lives in fame that died in virtue's cause.

Shakespeare, *Titus Andronicus* (1592–93), 1.1.390

42. Fame is but an inscription on a grave, and glory the melancholy blazon on a coffin lid.

Alexander Smith, "On the Writing of Essays," *Dreamthorp* (1863)

43. People before the public live an imagined life in the thought of others, and flourish or feel faint as their self outside themselves grows bright or dwindles in that mirror.

Logan Pearsall Smith, *Afterthoughts* (1931), 3

44. Fame has also this great drawback, that if we pursue it we must direct our lives in such a way as to please the fancy of men, avoiding what they dislike and seeking what is pleasing to them.

Spinoza, *On the Correction of the Understanding* (1677), 1, tr. Andrew Boyle

45. A plague on eminence! I hardly dare cross the street any more without a convoy, and I am stared at wherever I go like an idiot member of a royal family or an animal in a zoo; and zoo animals have been known to die from stares.

Igor Stravinsky, "Stravinsky on the Musical Scene and Other Matters," *The New York Review of Books* (May 12, 1966)

46. Blessed is he whose fame does not outshine his truth.

Rabindranath Tagore, *Stray Birds* (1916), 295

47. There is no faster way of destroying a man, or mocking his ideas, than making him fashionable.

Paul Theroux, *The Old Patagonian Express* (1979)

48. He who seeks fame by the practice of virtue asks only for what he deserves.

Vauvenargues, *Reflections and Maxims* (1746), 295, tr. F. G. Stevens

49. If you wish to obtain a great name or to found an establishment, be completely mad; but be sure that your madness corresponds with the turn and temper of your age.

Voltaire, "Ignatius Loyola," *Philosophical Dictionary* (1764)

50. The modern world is not given to uncritical admiration. It expects its idols to have feet of clay, and can be reasonably sure that press and camera will report their exact dimensions.

Barbara Ward, *Saturday Review,* Sept. 30, 1961

51. A guy at the bar, well-dressed, came up behind Cassius [Muhammad Ali] and touched him lightly at about the level of the sixth rib and went back to the bar and told his girl, "That's Cassius Clay. I just touched him, no kidding."

Tom Wolfe, *The Kandy-Kolored Tangerine-Flake Streamline Baby* (1965)

333. FAMILIARITY

See also 499. Intimacy; 612. The Mundane

1. Familiarity breeds contentment.

George Ade, "The Uplift That Moved Sideways," *Hand-Made Fables* (1920)

2. When we know exactly all a man's views and how he comes to speak and act so and so, we lose any respect for him, though we may love and admire him.

James Boswell, *London Journal,* Feb. 3, 1763

3. That song is best esteemed with which our ears are most acquainted.

William Byrd, preface to *Psalmes, Songs, and Sonnets* (1611)

4. Every ship is a romantic object, except that we sail in.

EMERSON, "EXPERIENCE," *ESSAYS: SECOND SERIES* (1844)

5. The hues of the opal, the light of the diamond, are not to be seen if the eye is too near.

EMERSON, "FRIENDSHIP," *ESSAYS: FIRST SERIES* (1841)

6. Though familiarity may not breed contempt, it takes off the edge of admiration.

WILLIAM HAZLITT, *CHARACTERISTICS* (1823), 2

7. Where's the cheek that doth not fade, / Too much gazed at?

KEATS, "FANCY" (1818)

8. Great men lose somewhat of their greatness by being near us; ordinary men gain much.

WALTER SAVAGE LANDOR, "AESCHINES AND PHOCION," *IMAGINARY CONVERSATIONS* (1824–53)

9. Though the familiar use of things about us take off our wonder, yet it cures not our ignorance.

JOHN LOCKE, *AN ESSAY CONCERNING HUMAN UNDERSTANDING* (1690), 3.6.9

10. Sweets grown common lose their dear delight.

SHAKESPEARE, *SONNETS* (1609), 102.12

11. Familiar acts are beautiful through love.

SHELLEY, *PROMETHEUS UNBOUND* (1818–19), 4

12. Familiarity breeds contempt—and children.

MARK TWAIN, *NOTEBOOK* (1935)

13. Familiarity is the thing—the sense of belonging. It grants exemption from all evil, all shabbiness.

E.B. WHITE, "HOME-COMING," *ESSAYS OF E. B. WHITE* (1977)

334. FAMILY

See also 37. ANCESTRY; 65. BABIES; 123. CHILDREN; 218. DAUGHTERS; 422. HOME; 564. MARRIAGE; 670. PARENTHOOD; 796. RELATIVES; 916. SONS

1. Of those that are drawn away, each is drawn elsewhere toward another: once more a man and a woman, in a loneliness they are not liable at that time to notice, are tightened together upon a bed: and another family has begun.

JAMES AGEE, *LET US NOW PRAISE FAMOUS MEN* (1941)

2. When brothers agree, no fortress is so strong as their common life.

ANTISTHENES (5TH–4TH C. B.C.), QUOTED IN DIOGENES LAERTIUS' *LIVES AND OPINIONS OF EMINENT PHILOSOPHERS* (3RD C. A.D.), TR. R. D. HICKS

3. Cruel is the strife of brothers.

ARISTOTLE, *POLITICS* (4TH C. B.C.), 7.7, TR. BENJAMIN JOWETT

4. The family is the association established by nature for the supply of man's everyday wants.

ARISTOTLE, *POLITICS* (4TH C. B.C.), 1.2, TR. BENJAMIN JOWETT

5. He that hath wife and children hath given hostages to fortune; for they are impediments to great enterprises, either of virtue or mischief.

FRANCIS BACON, "OF MARRIAGE AND SINGLE LIFE," *ESSAYS* (1625)

6. I think the family is the place where the most ridiculous and least respectable things in the world go on.

UGO BETTI, *THE INQUIRY* (1944–45), 1.8

7. I believe that more unhappiness comes from this source than from any other—I mean from the attempt to prolong family connections unduly and to make people hang together artificially who would never naturally do so.

SAMUEL BUTLER (D. 1902), "ELEMENTARY MORALITY," *NOTE-BOOKS* (1912)

8. The family is the test of freedom; because the family is the only thing that the free man makes for himself and by himself.

G. K. CHESTERTON, "DRAMATIC UNITIES," *FANCIES VERSUS FADS* (1923)

9. The parents' age must be remembered, both for joy and anxiety.

CONFUCIUS, *ANALECTS* (6TH C. B.C.), 4.21, TR. WINBERG CHAI

10. Accidents will happen in the best-regulated families.

CHARLES DICKENS, *DAVID COPPERFIELD* (1849–50), 28

11. As states subsist in part by keeping their weaknesses from being known, so is it the quiet of families to have their chancery and their parliament within doors, and to compose and determine all emergent differences there.

JOHN DONNE, *SERMONS,* NO. 32, 1625

12. There's no vocabulary / For love within a family, love that's lived in / But not looked at, love within the light of which / All else is seen, the love within which / All other love finds speech. / This love is silent.

T. S. ELIOT, *THE ELDER STATESMAN* (1958), 2

13. Family quarrels are bitter things. They don't go by any rules. They're not like aches or wounds; they're more like splits in the skin that won't heal because there's not enough material.

F. Scott Fitzgerald, *The Crack-Up* (1945)

14. Families break up when people take hints you don't intend and miss hints you do intend.

Robert Frost, interview, *Writers at Work: Second Series.* (1963)

15. Perhaps no American family—with the possible exception of the Adams family—has had a more vivid and powerful impact on the life of their times. But the Kennedy tale—the spiral compound of glory, achievement, degradation and almost mythical tragedy—exerts a fascination upon us that goes beyond their public achievements.

Doris Kearns Goodwin, *The Fitzgeralds and the Kennedys* (1987)

16. There is nothing like tasting the grit of fear for rediscovering that the umbilical cord is made of piano wire.

Moss Hart, *Act One* (1959)

17. Natural affection is a prejudice: for though we have cause to love our nearest connections better than others, we have no reason to think them better than others.

William Hazlitt, "On Prejudice," *Sketches and Essays* (1839)

18. When you deal with your brother, be pleasant, but get a witness.

Hesiod, *Works and Days* (8th c. b.c.), 371, tr. Richmond Lattimore

19. If he hadn't been my father I would have loved the spectacle he created—one performance following quickly upon another—like a versatile old vaudevillian with his audience (wife and children) in the palm of his hand.

Maureen Howard, *Facts of Life* (1978)

20. The only rock I know that stays steady, the only institution I know that works, is the family.

Lee Iacocca, *Talking Straight* (1988), with Sonny Kleinfeld

21. A man's women folk, whatever their outward show of respect for his merit and authority, always regard him secretly as an ass, and with something akin to pity.

H. L. Mencken, "The Feminine Mind," *In Defense of Women* (1922)

22. There is little less trouble in governing a private family than a whole kingdom.

Montaigne, "Of solitude," *Essays* (1580–88), tr. W. C. Hazlitt

23. The family the soul wants is a felt network of relationship, an evocation of a certain kind of interconnection that grounds, roots, and nestles.

Thomas Moore, *Soul Mates* (1994)

24. One would be in less danger / From the wiles of the stranger / If one's own kin and kith / Were more fun to be with.

Ogden Nash, "Family Court," *Verses From 1929 On* (1959)

25. Rich parents are famous both for miserliness and astonishing longevity. And, when they finally do die, you'll find they've left their estate in inviolate trust to the golden retrievers.

P.J. O'Rourke, *Modern Manners* (1988)

26. A family is but too often a commonwealth of malignants.

Alexander Pope, *Thoughts on Various Subjects* (1717)

27. Bringing up a family should be an adventure, not an anxious discipline in which everybody is constantly graded for performance.

Milton R. Sapirstein, *Paradoxes of Everyday Life* (1955), 3

28. An ounce of blood is worth more than a pound of friendship.

Spanish Proverb

29. Between brothers, two witnesses and a notary.

Spanish Proverb

30. Happy or unhappy, families are all mysterious.

Gloria Steinem, "Ruth's Song," *Outrageous Acts and Everyday Rebellions* (1983)

31. Sacred family!... The supposed home of all the virtues, where innocent children are tortured into their first falsehoods, where wills are broken by parental tyranny, and self-respect smothered by crowded, jostling egos.

August Strindberg, *The Son of a Servant* (1886)

32. The Family! Home of all social evils, a charitable institution for indolent women, a prison workshop for the slaving breadwinner, and a hell for children.

August Strindberg, *The Son of a Servant* (1886)

33. He that loves not his wife and children, feeds a lioness at home and broods a nest of sorrows.

JEREMY TAYLOR, "MARRIED LOVE," *SERMONS* (1651–53)

34. Happy families are all alike; every unhappy family is unhappy in its own way.

LEO TOLSTOY, *ANNA KARENINA* (1873–76), 1.1, TR. CONSTANCE GARNETT

35. [T]he family in the West is finished.... its origin was economic, not biological.... the odd group of strangers that make up every family no longer have any reason to live together, to suffer from one another's jagged edges.

GORE VIDAL, *ROCKING THE BOAT* (1962)

36. Being a grownup means assuming responsibility for yourself, for your children, and—here's the big curve—for your parents.

WENDY WASSERSTEIN, "MODERN MATURITY," *BACHELOR GIRLS* (1990)

37. Father raised his glass one last time and we repeated after him: "Next year in Jerusalem." None of us could know that this was our last Passover meal as a family.

ELIE WIESEL, *LEGENDS OF OUR TIMES* (1968)

38. There is something sad and terrifying about big families.

THOMAS WOLFE, *THOMAS WOLFE'S LETTERS TO HIS MOTHER* (1943)

335. FANATICISM

See also 264. DOGMATISM; 293. ENTHUSIASM; 500. INTOLERANCE; 726. PREJUDICES; 1073. ZEAL

1. A fanatic is one who can't change his mind and won't change the subject.

SIR WINSTON CHURCHILL, QUOTED IN *THE NEW YORK TIMES,* JULY 5, 1954

2. He that rides his hobby gently must always give way to him that rides his hobby hard.

EMERSON, *JOURNALS,* 1832

3. There is no strong performance without a little fanaticism in the performer.

EMERSON, *JOURNALS,* 1859

4. Political extremism involves two prime ingredients: an excessively simple diagnosis of the world's ills and a conviction that there are identifiable villains back of it all.

JOHN W. GARDNER, *NO EASY VICTORIES* (1968), 2

5. I would remind you that extremism in the defense of liberty is no vice. And let me remind you also that moderation in the pursuit of justice is no virtue.

BARRY GOLDWATER, ACCEPTANCE SPEECH, REPUBLICAN NATIONAL CONVENTION, JULY 16, 1964

6. The less justified a man is in claiming excellence for his own self, the more ready is he to claim all excellence for his nation, his religion, his race or his holy cause.

ERIC HOFFER, *THE TRUE BELIEVER* (1951), 1.2.9

7. If there is anything more dangerous to the life of the mind than having no independent commitment to ideas, it is having an excess of commitment to some special and constricting idea.

RICHARD HOFSTADTER, *ANTI-INTELLECTUALISM IN AMERICAN LIFE* (1963), 1.2

8. At least two thirds of our miseries spring from human stupidity, human malice and those great motivators and justifiers of malice and stupidity, idealism, dogmatism and proselytizing zeal on behalf of religious or political idols.

ALDOUS HUXLEY, *TOMORROW AND TOMORROW AND TOMORROW* (1956)

9. Fanatics have their dreams, where-with they weave / A paradise for a sect.

KEATS, "THE FALL OF HYPERION" (1819), 1

10. What is objectionable, what is dangerous about extremists is not that they are extreme, but that they are intolerant. The evil is not what they say about their cause, but what they say about their opponents.

ROBERT F. KENNEDY, "EXTREMISM, LEFT AND RIGHT," *THE PURSUIT OF JUSTICE* (1964)

11. There is no arguing with the pretenders to a divine knowledge and to a divine mission. They are possessed with the sin of pride, they have yielded to the perennial temptation.

WALTER LIPPMANN, *THE PUBLIC PHILOSOPHY* (1955), 7.5

12. The true inquisitor is a creature of policy, not a man of blood by taste.

JOHN MORLEY, "ROBESPIERRE," *CRITICAL MISCELLANIES* (1871–1908)

13. There is no place in a fanatic's head where reason can enter.

NAPOLEON I, *MAXIMS* (1804–15)

14. When you've got a Chautauqua in your head, it's extremely hard not to inflict it on innocent people.

ROBERT M. PIRSIG, *ZEN AND THE ART OF MOTORCYCLE MAINTENANCE* (1974)

15. Belief in a Divine mission is one of the many forms of certainty that have afflicted the human race.

Bertrand Russell, "Ideas That Have Harmed Mankind," *Unpopular Essays* (1950)

16. Fanaticism consists in redoubling your effort when you have forgotten your aim.

George Santayana, introduction, *The Life of Reason: Reason in Common Sense* (1905–06)

17. There is nobody as enslaved as the fanatic, the person in whom one impulse, one value, has assumed ascendency over all others.

Milton R. Sapirstein, *Paradoxes of Everyday Life* (1955), 8

18. An infallible method of making fanatics is to persuade before you instruct.

Voltaire, "Oracles," *Philosophical Dictionary* (1764)

336. FANTASY

See also 266. Dreams; 383. Ghosts; 449. Illusion; 450. Imagination; 818. Reverie

1. To believe in one's dreams is to spend all of one's life asleep.

Chinese Proverb

2. Dreams are the subtle Dower / That make us rich an Hour— / Then fling us poor / Out of the purple door.

Emily Dickinson, poem (c. 1876)

3. Few have greater riches than the joy / That comes to us in visions, / In dreams which nobody can take away.

Euripides, *Iphigenia in Tauris* (c. 414–12 B.C.), tr. Witter Bynner

4. Only the dreamer shall understand realities, though in truth his dreaming must be not out of proportion to his waking.

Margaret Fuller, *Summer on the Lakes* (1844), 5

5. He who passes not his days in the realm of dreams is the slave of the days.

Kahlil Gibran, "The Goddess of Fantasy," *Thoughts and Meditations* (1960), tr. Anthony R. Ferris

6. We do not really feel grateful toward those who make our dreams come true; they ruin our dreams.

Eric Hoffer, *The Passionate State of Mind* (1954), 232

7. A fantasy can be equivalent to a paradise and if the fantasy passes, better yet, because eternal paradise would be very boring.

Juan Ramón Jiménez, "To Burn Completely," *Selected Writings* (1957), tr. H. R. Hays

8. No man will be found in whose mind airy notions do not sometime tyrannize, and force him to hope or fear beyond the limits of sober probability.

Samuel Johnson, *Rasselas* (1759), 44

9. Ever let the Fancy roam, / Pleasure never is at home.

Keats, "Fancy" (1818)

10. Where all is but dream, reasoning and arguments are of no use, truth and knowledge nothing.

John Locke, *An Essay Concerning Human Understanding* (1690), 4.2.14

11. Round about what is, lies a whole mysterious world of might be, a psychological romance of possibilities and things that do not happen.

Longfellow, "Table-Talk," *Driftwood* (1857)

12. Safe upon the solid rock the ugly houses stand: / Come and see my shining palace built upon the sand!

Edna St. Vincent Millay, "Second Fig," *A Few Figs from Thistles* (1921)

13. The lie of a pipe dream is what gives life to the whole misbegotten mad lot of us, drunk or sober.

Eugene O'Neill, *The Iceman Cometh* (1946), 1

14. A dreamer lives forever, / And a toiler dies in a day.

John Boyle O'Reilly, "The Cry of the Dreamer," *Works* (1891)

15. A dream is always simmering below the conventional surface of speech and reflection.

George Santayana, *The Life of Reason: Reason in Common Sense* (1905–06), 2

16. The dreamer can know no truth, not even about his dream, except by awaking out of it.

George Santayana, *Dialogues in Limbo* (1925), 2

17. Our truest life is when we are in dreams awake.

Thoreau, "The Inward Morning," *A Week on the Concord and Merrimack Rivers* (1849)

18. If you have built castles in the air, your work need not be lost; that is where they should be. Now put the foundations under them.

Thoreau, "Conclusion," *Walden* (1854)

19. If ambitious fantasies make people blush, and sexual fantasies make people blush and feel guilty, fantasies of violence and death may make people blush and feel guilty—and frightened too.

JUDITH VIORST, *NECESSARY LOSSES* (1986)

20. Fantasy is no good unless the seed it springs from is a truth, a truth about human beings.

EUDORA WELTY, "FAIRY TALE OF THE NATCHEZ TRACE," *THE EYE OF THE STORY* (1978)

21. It is in our idleness, in our dreams, that the submerged truth sometimes comes to the top.

VIRGINIA WOOLF, *A ROOM OF ONE'S OWN* (1929), 2

22. Life moves out of a red flare of dreams / Into a common light of common hours, / Until old age brings the red flare again.

WILLIAM BUTLER YEATS, *THE LAND OF HEART'S DESIRE* (1894)

337. FARMS AND FARMING

1. The largest single step in the ascent of man is the change from nomad to village agriculture.

JACOB BRONOWSKI, *THE ASCENT OF MAN* (1973)

2. Burn down your cities and leave our farms, and your cities will spring up again as if by magic; but destroy our farms and the grass will grow in the streets of every city in the country.

WILLIAM JENNINGS BRYAN, "CROSS OF GOLD" SPEECH, JULY 8, 1896

3. It is thus with farming: if you do one thing late, you will be late in all your work.

CATO THE ELDER, *DE AGRI CULTURA* (2ND C. B.C.)

4. Farming looks mighty easy when your plow is a pencil, and you're a thousand miles from the corn field.

DWIGHT D. EISENHOWER, ADDRESS, PEORIA, ILL., SEPT. 25, 1956

5. Remote though your farm may be, / It's something to be the lord of one green lizard—and free.

JUVENAL, *SATIRES* (C. 100), 3.230, TR. HUBERT CREEKMORE

6. It makes but little difference whether you are committed to a farm or the county jail.

THOREAU, "WHERE I LIVED, AND WHAT I LIVED FOR," *WALDEN* (1854)

7. Blessed be agriculture! if one does not have too much of it.

CHARLES DUDLEY WARNER, "PRELIMINARY," *MY SUMMER IN A GARDEN* (1871)

8. There is life in the ground: it goes into the seeds; and it also, when it is stirred up, goes into the man who stirs it.

CHARLES DUDLEY WARNER, "PRELIMINARY," *MY SUMMER IN A GARDEN* (1871)

9. When tillage begins, other arts follow. The farmers therefore are the founders of human civilization.

DANIEL WEBSTER, REMARKS ON AGRICULTURE, JAN. 13, 1840

10. A good farmer is nothing more nor less than a handy man with a sense of humus.

E. B. WHITE, "THE PRACTICAL FARMER," *ONE MAN'S MEAT* (1944)

338. FASHION

See also 45. APPEARANCE; 267. DRESS; 282. ELEGANCE; 407. HAIR; 640. NOVELTY

1. Nothing is thought rare / Which is not new, and followed; yet we know / That what was worn some twenty years ago / Comes into grace again.

BEAUMONT AND FLETCHER, PROLOGUE TO *THE NOBLE GENTLEMAN* (1647), 4

2. Fashion, which elevates the bad to the level of the good, subsequently turns its back on bad and good alike.

ERIC BENTLEY, INTRODUCTION TO *NAKED MASKS: FIVE PLAYS BY LUIGI PIRANDELLO* (1952)

3. Fashion, n. A despot whom the wise ridicule and obey.

AMBROSE BIERCE, *THE DEVIL'S DICTIONARY* (1881–1911)

4. Women thrive on novelty and are easy meat for the commerce of fashion. Men prefer old pipes and torn jackets.

ANTHONY BURGESS, *YOU'VE HAD YOUR TIME* (1990)

5. He is only fantastical that is not in fashion.

ROBERT BURTON, *THE ANATOMY OF MELANCHOLY* (1621), 3.2.2.3

6. Fashion is made to become unfashionable.

COCO CHANEL, *LIFE*, AUG. 19, 1957

7. There's never a new fashion but it's old.

CHAUCER, "THE KNIGHT'S TALE," *THE CANTERBURY TALES* (C. 1387–1400), TR. NEVILL COGHILL

8. If you are not in fashion, you are nobody.

LORD CHESTERFIELD, *LETTERS TO HIS SON*, APRIL 30, 1750

9. One had as good be out of the world, as out of the fashion.

COLLEY CIBBER, *LOVE'S LAST SHIFT* (1696), 2

10. Art produces ugly things which frequently become beautiful with time. Fashion, on the other hand, produces beautiful things which always become ugly with time.

JEAN COCTEAU, *NEW YORK WORLD-TELEGRAM & SUN,* AUG. 21, 1960

11. [Fashion's] smile has given wit to dullness and grace to deformity, and has brought everything into vogue, by turns, but virtue.

CHARLES CALEB COLTON, *LACON* (1825), 1.547

12. Ladies of Fashion starve their happiness to feed their vanity, and their love to feed their pride.

CHARLES CALEB COLTON, *LACON* (1825), 2.217

13. Women who had discovered pants, low-heeled shoes, and loose sweaters during World War II were reluctant to give them up in peacetime.

SUSAN FALUDI, *BACKLASH* (1991)

14. The present fashion is always handsome.

THOMAS FULLER, M.D., *GNOMOLOGIA* (1732), 4718

15. Even knowledge has to be in the fashion, and where it is not, it is wise to affect ignorance.

BALTASAR GRACIÁN, *THE ART OF WORLDLY WISDOM* (1647), 120, TR. JOSEPH JACOBS

16. Fashion is the abortive issue of vain ostentation and exclusive egotism: it is haughty, trifling, affected, servile, despotic, mean and ambitious, precise and fantastical, all in a breath—tied to no rule, and bound to conform to every whim of the minute.

WILLIAM HAZLITT, "ON FASHION," *SKETCHES AND ESSAYS* (1839)

17. The fear of becoming a "has been" keeps some people from becoming anything.

ERIC HOFFER, *THE PASSIONATE STATE OF MIND* (1954), 231

18. Fashion is only the attempt to realize Art in living forms and social intercourse.

OLIVER WENDELL HOLMES, SR., *THE PROFESSOR AT THE BREAKFAST TABLE* (1860), 6

19. The greater part of mankind judge of men only by their fashionableness or their fortune.

LA ROCHEFOUCAULD, *MAXIMS* (1665), TR. KENNETH PRATT

20. Fashion is more powerful than any tyrant.

LATIN PROVERB

21. Fashion condemns us to many follies; the greatest is to make oneself its slave.

NAPOLEON I, *MAXIMS* (1804–15)

22. I cannot keep track of all the vagaries of fashion, / Every day, so it seems, brings in a different style.

OVID, *THE ART OF LOVE* (C. A.D. 8), 3, TR. ROLFE HUMPHRIES

23. Be not the first by whom the new are tried, / Nor yet the last to lay the old aside.

ALEXANDER POPE, *AN ESSAY ON CRITICISM* (1711), 2.133

24. New customs, / Though they be never so ridiculous / (Nay, let 'em be unmanly), yet are followed.

SHAKESPEARE, *HENRY VIII* (1612–13), 1.2.2

25. The fashion wears out more apparel than the man.

SHAKESPEARE, *MUCH ADO ABOUT NOTHING* (1598–99), 3.3.148

26. Fashions, after all, are only induced epidemics.

GEORGE BERNARD SHAW, "PREFACE ON DOCTORS: FASHIONS AND EPIDEMICS," *THE DOCTOR'S DILEMMA* (1913)

27. Every generation laughs at the old fashions, but follows religiously the new.

THOREAU, *WALDEN* (1854), 1

28. It is fancy rather than taste which produces so many new fashions.

VOLTAIRE, "TASTE," *PHILOSOPHICAL DICTIONARY* (1764)

339. FASTIDIOUSNESS

1. It is not only a troublesome but slavish to be nice [fastidious].

WILLIAM PENN, *SOME FRUITS OF SOLITUDE* (1693), 2.136

2. A nice man is a man of nasty ideas.

JONATHAN SWIFT, *THOUGHTS OF VARIOUS SUBJECTS* (1711)

340. FATE

See also 116. CHANCE; 240. DESTINY; 360. FORTUNE; 624. NECESSITY; 754. PROVIDENCE; 937. STOICISM

1. These struggling tides of life that seem / In wayward, aimless course to tend, / Are eddies of the mighty stream / That rolls to its appointed end.

WILLIAM CULLEN BRYANT, "THE CROWDED STREET" (1843)

2. Whatsoe'er we perpetrate, / We do but row, we are steered by fate.

SAMUEL BUTLER (D. 1680), *HUDIBRAS* (1663), 1.1

3. [M]en see things late, and it may be that at times an evil fate drives them on.

BRUCE CATTON, *THIS HALLOWED GROUND* (1956)

4. I do not believe in a fate that falls on men however they act; but I do believe in a fate that falls on them unless they act.

G. K. CHESTERTON, "ON HOLLAND," *GENERALLY SPEAKING* (1928)

5. Superiority to Fate / Is difficult to gain / 'Tis not conferred of Any / But possible to earn.

EMILY DICKINSON, POEM (C. 1866)

6. Whatever limits us, we call Fate.

EMERSON, "FATE," *THE CONDUCT OF LIFE* (1860)

7. Necessity is harsh. / Fate has no reprieve.

EURIPIDES, *HECUBA* (C. 425 B.C.), TR. WILLIAM ARROWSMITH

8. Failure or success seem to have been allotted to men by their stars. But they retain the power of wriggling, of fighting with their star or against it, and in the whole universe the only really interesting movement is this wriggle.

E. M. FORSTER, "OUR DIVERSIONS," *ABINGER HARVEST* (1936)

9. See how the Fates their gifts allot, / For A is happy—B is not. / Yet B is worthy, I dare say, / Of more prosperity than A.

W. S. GILBERT, *THE MIKADO* (1885), 2

10. Even-handed fate / Hath but one law for small and great: / That ample urn holds all men's names.

HORACE, *ODES* (23–C. 15 B.C.), 3.1

11. Perhaps the most majestic feature of our whole existence is that while our intelligences are powerful enough to penetrate deeply into the evolution of this quite incredible Universe, we still have not the smallest clue to our own fate.

FRED HOYLE, "THE EXPANDING UNIVERSE," *THE NATURE OF THE UNIVERSE* (1950)

12. As you go through life, there are thousands of little forks in the road, and there are a few really big forks—those moments of reckoning, moments of truth.

LEE IACOCCA, *IACOCCA: AN AUTOBIOGRAPHY* (1984) WITH WILLIAM NOVAK

13. If fate means you to lose, give him a good fight anyhow.

WILLIAM MCFEE, *CASUALS OF THE SEA* (1916), 2.1.2

14. Fate has to do with events in history that are the summary and unintended results of innumerable decisions of innumerable men.

C. WRIGHT MILLS, "CULTURE AND POLITICS," *POWER, POLITICS AND PEOPLE* (1963)

15. The Moving Finger writes; and, having writ, / Moves on: nor all your Piety nor Wit / Shall lure it back to cancel half a Line, / Nor all your Tears wash out a Word of it.

OMAR KHAYYÁM, *RUBÁIYÁT* (11TH–12TH C.), TR. EDWARD FITZGERALD, 4TH ED., 71

16. Fate was dealing from the bottom of the deck.

S.J. PERELMAN, *THE RISING GORGE* (1961)

17. Fate leads the willing, and drags along the reluctant.

SENECA, *LETTERS TO LUCILIUS* (1ST C.)

18. What fates impose, that men must needs abide; / It boots not to resist both wind and tide.

SHAKESPEARE, *3 HENRY VI* (1590–91), 4.3.58

19. There is no armour against fate; / Death lays his icy hands on kings.

JAMES SHIRLEY, *THE CONTENTION OF AJAX AND ULYSSES* (1659), 3

20. Fate has terrible power. / You cannot escape it by wealth or war. / No fort will keep it out, no ships outrun it.

SOPHOCLES, *ANTIGONE* (442–41 B.C.), TR. ELIZABETH WYCKOFF

21. Luck or tragedy, some people get runs. Then of course there are those who divide it even, good and bad, but we never hear of them. Such a life doesn't demand attention. Only the people who get the good or bad runs.

JOHN STEINBECK, *STEINBECK: A LIFE IN LETTERS* (1975), EDS. ELAINE STEINBECK AND ROBERT WALLSTEN

FATHERS

See 670. PARENTHOOD

341. FATIGUE

1. Life is one long process of getting tired.

SAMUEL BUTLER (D. 1902), "LORD, WHAT IS MAN?" *NOTE-BOOKS* (1912)

2. In the morning a man walks with his whole body; in the evening, only with his legs.

EMERSON, *JOURNALS*, 1836

3. The feeling of sleepiness when you are not in bed, and can't get there, is the meanest feeling in the world.

EDGAR WATSON HOWE, *COUNTRY TOWN SAYINGS* (1911)

4. The strongest have their moments of fatigue.

NIETZSCHE, *THE WILL TO POWER* (1888), TR. ANTHONY M. LUDOVICI

FATNESS

See 645. OBESITY

342. FAULTS

See also 168. CONFESSION; 206. CRITICISM; 314. EXCUSES; 354. FOLLY; 457. IMPERFECTION; 542. LIMITATIONS; 684. PERFECTION; 803. REPROOF; 1047. WEAKNESS

1. It is easier to confess a defect than to claim a quality.

MAX BEERBOHM, "HOSTS AND GUESTS," *AND EVEN NOW* (1920)

2. The greatest of faults, I should say, is to be conscious of none.

THOMAS CARLYLE, *ON HEROES, HERO-WORSHIP AND THE HEROIC IN HISTORY* (1841), 2

3. The real fault is to have faults and not to amend them.

CONFUCIUS, *ANALECTS* (6TH C. B.C.), 15.29, TR. WINBERG CHAI

4. I have no confidence in a man whose faults you cannot see.

EDWARD DAHLBERG, "ON HUMAN NATURE," *REASONS OF THE HEART* (1965)

5. Our faults are not seen, / But past us; neither felt, but only in / The punishment.

JOHN DONNE, "ODE: OF OUR SENSE OF SIN," *DIVINE POEMS* (1607)

6. A man must thank his defects, and stand in some terror of his talents.

EMERSON, "FATE," *THE CONDUCT OF LIFE* (1860)

7. He is lifeless that is faultless.

ENGLISH PROVERB

8. Rich men's faults are covered with money and physicians' with earth.

ENGLISH PROVERB

9. Worse / than a true evil is it to bear the burden of faults that are not truly yours.

EURIPIDES, *HELEN* (412 B.C.), TR. RICHMOND LATTIMORE

10. A benevolent man should allow a few faults in himself, to keep his friends in countenance.

BENJAMIN FRANKLIN, *AUTOBIOGRAPHY* (1791), 1

11. Those see nothing but faults that seek for nothing else.

THOMAS FULLER, M.D., *GNOMOLOGIA* (1732), 5021

12. Certain defects are necessary for the existence of individuality.

GOETHE, *ELECTIVE AFFINITIES* (1809), 22

13. People will allow their faults to be shown them; they will let themselves be punished for them; they will patiently endure many things because of them; they only become impatient when they have to lay them aside.

GOETHE, *ELECTIVE AFFINITIES* (1809), 22

14. It is well that there is no one without a fault; for he would not have a friend in the world.

WILLIAM HAZLITT, *CHARACTERISTICS* (1823)

15. It is too bad how thoughtlessly we set up harsh and unkind rules against ourselves. No one is born without faults. That man is best who has fewest.

HORACE, *SATIRES* (35–30 B.C.), 1.3

16. Gladly we desire to make other men perfect but we will not amend our own fault.

THOMAS À KEMPIS, *THE IMITATION OF CHRIST* (1426), 1.16

17. There exists scarcely any man so accomplished, or so necessary to his own family, but he has some failing which will diminish their regret at his loss.

LA BRUYÈRE, *CHARACTERS* (1688), 2.35, TR. HENRI VAN LAUN

18. If we had no faults, we would not take so much pleasure in noticing them in others.

LA ROCHEFOUCAULD, *MAXIMS* (1665)

19. We only admit to minor faults to persuade ourselves that we have no major ones.

LA ROCHEFOUCAULD, *MAXIMS* (1665)

20. We have scarcely any faults which are not more pardonable than the shifts we make to hide them.

LA ROCHEFOUCAULD, *MAXIMS* (1665), TR. KENNETH PRATT

21. The defects of human nature afford us opportunities of exercising our philosophy, the best employment of our virtues. If all men were righteous, all hearts true and frank and loyal, what use would our virtues be?

MOLIÈRE, *THE MISANTHROPE* (1666), 5, TR. JOHN WOOD

22. Our shortcomings are the eyes with which we see the ideal.

NIETZSCHE, *MISCELLANEOUS MAXIMS AND OPINIONS* (1879), 86, TR. PAUL V. COHN

23. Truly it is an evil to be full of faults; but it is a still greater evil to be full of them, and to be unwilling to recognize them.

PASCAL, *PENSÉES* (1670), 100, TR. W. F. TROTTER

24. Whoe'er he be / That tells my faults, I hate him mortally.

ALEXANDER POPE, *PROLOGUE TO THE WIFE OF BATH'S TALE* (C. 1709)

25. Whoever is aware of his own failing will not find fault with the failings of other men.

SA'DI, *GULISTAN* (1258), 5.19, TR. JAMES ROSS

26. Whatever folly men commit, be their shortcomings or their vices what they may, let us exercise forbearance; remember that when these faults appear in others it is our follies and vices that we behold.

SCHOPENHAUER, "ON THE SUFFERINGS OF THE WORLD," *PARERGA AND PARALIPOMENA* (1851), TR. T. BAILEY SAUNDERS

27. They say best men are moulded out of faults, / And, for the most, become much more the better / For being a little bad.

SHAKESPEARE, *MEASURE FOR MEASURE* (1604–05), 5.1.444

28. More faults are often committed while we are trying to oblige than while we are giving offense.

TACITUS, *ANNALS* (A.D. 115–117?), 15.21, TR. WILLIAM J. BRODRIBB

29. The faultfinder will find faults even in paradise.

THOREAU, "CONCLUSION," *WALDEN* (1854)

30. Our failings sometimes bind us to one another as closely as could virtue itself.

VAUVENARGUES, *REFLECTIONS AND MAXIMS* (1746), 176, TR. F. G. STEVENS

31. Misfortunes one can endure—they come from outside, they are accidents. But to suffer for one's own faults—ah! there is the sting of life.

OSCAR WILDE, *LADY WINDERMERE'S FAN* (1892), 1

32. None of us can stand other people having the same faults as ourselves.

OSCAR WILDE, *THE PICTURE OF DORIAN GRAY* (1891), 1

FAVORS

See 888. SERVICES

343. FEAR

See also 43. ANXIETY; 195. COURAGE; 199. COWARDICE; 300. ESCAPE; 304. EVASION; 980. TIMIDITY

1. "Don't Panic." It's the first helpful or intelligible thing anybody's said to me all day.

DOUGLAS ADAMS, *THE HITCHHIKER'S GUIDE TO THE GALAXY* (1979)

2. Fear is stronger than arms.

AESCHYLUS, *SEVEN AGAINST THEBES* (468–67 B.C.), TR. DAVID GRENE

3. There are times when fear is good. / It must keep its watchful place / at the heart's controls. There is / advantage in the wisdom won from pain.

AESCHYLUS, *THE EUMENIDES* (458 B.C.), TR. RICHMOND LATTIMORE

4. God! Is there anything uglier than a frightened man!

JEAN ANOUILH, *ANTIGONE* (1942), TR. LEWIS GALANTIÈRE

5. Sex is a sideshow in the world of the animal, for the dominant color of that world is fear.

ROBERT ARDREY, *AFRICAN GENESIS* (1961)

6. The meaning I picked, the one that changed my life: *Overcome fear, behold wonder*.

RICHARD BACH, *RUNNING FROM SAFETY* (1994)

7. It all goes back to those German existentialists who tell you how good dread is for you, how it saves you from distraction and gives you your freedom and makes you authentic. God is no more. But Death is.

SAUL BELLOW, *HERZOG* (1964)

8. Behind everything we feel, there is always a sense of fear.

UGO BETTI, *STRUGGLE TILL DAWN* (1949), 1, TR. G. H. MCWILLIAM

9. No passion so effectually robs the mind of all its powers of acting and reasoning as fear.

EDMUND BURKE, *A PHILOSOPHICAL INQUIRY INTO THE ORIGIN OF OUR IDEAS OF THE SUBLIME AND BEAUTIFUL* (1756), 2.2

10. Fear is sharp-sighted, and can see things under ground, and much more in the skies.

CERVANTES, *DON QUIXOTE* (1605–15), 1.3.6, TR. JOHN OZELL

11. How does one kill fear, I wonder? How do you shoot a spectre through the heart, slash off its spectral head, take it by its spectral throat?

JOSEPH CONRAD, *LORD JIM* (1900), 33

12. I suddenly remember something I've been told about fear. That amid a hail of machine gun fire you notice the existence of your skin.

MARGUERITE DURAS, *THE WAR: A MEMOIR* (1986), TR. BARBARA BRAY

13. Fear is an instructor of great sagacity and the herald of all revolutions.

EMERSON, "COMPENSATION," *ESSAYS: FIRST SERIES* (1841)

14. It is not death or pain that is to be dreaded, but the fear of pain or death.

EPICTETUS, *DISCOURSES* (2ND C.), 2.1, TR. THOMAS W. HIGGINSON

15. Any device whatever by which one frees himself from the fear of others is a natural good.

EPICURUS, "PRINCIPAL DOCTRINES" (3RD C. B.C.), 6, IN *LETTERS, PRINCIPAL DOCTRINES, AND VATICAN SAYINGS*, TR. RUSSEL M. GEER

16. He that fears you present will hate you absent.

THOMAS FULLER, M.D., *GNOMOLOGIA* (1732), 2101

17. After seven days at sea, thirst is a feeling unto itself; it's a deep pain in the throat, in the sternum, and especially beneath the clavicles. And it's also the fear of suffocating.

GABRIEL GARCÍA MÁRQUEZ, *THE STORY OF A SHIPWRECKED SAILOR* (1986)

18. A child understands fear, and the hurt and hate it brings.

NADINE GORDIMER, "MY FATHER LEAVES HOME," *JUMP AND OTHER STORIES* (1991)

19. A good scare is worth more to a man than good advice.

EDGAR WATSON HOWE, *COUNTRY TOWN SAYINGS* (1911)

20. God is good, there is no devil but fear.

ELBERT HUBBARD, *THE NOTE BOOK* (1927)

21. One has fear in front of a goat, in back of a mule, and on every side of a fool.

JEWISH PROVERB, *A TREASURY OF JEWISH FOLKLORE* (1948)

22. Evil is uncertain in the same degree as good, and for the reason that we ought not to hope too securely, we ought not to fear with too much dejection.

SAMUEL JOHNSON, *THE RAMBLER* (1750–52), 30

23. O! / How vain and vile a passion is this fear! / What base uncomely things it makes men do.

BEN JONSON, *SEJANUS HIS FALL* (1603), 5.6

24. Just as courage imperils life, fear protects it.

LEONARDO DA VINCI, *NOTEBOOKS* (C. 1500), TR. JEAN PAUL RICHTER

25. What we fear comes to pass more speedily than what we hope.

PUBLILIUS SYRUS, *MORAL SAYINGS* (1ST C. B.C.), 805, TR. DARIUS LYMAN

26. Of all the passions, fear weakens judgment most.

CARDINAL DE RETZ, *MÉMOIRES* (1718)

27. The only thing we have to fear is fear itself—nameless, unreasoning, unjustified terror which paralyzes needed efforts to convert retreat into advance.

FRANKLIN D. ROOSEVELT, FIRST INAUGURAL ADDRESS, MARCH 4, 1933

28. Fear is the main source of superstition, and one of the main sources of cruelty.

BERTRAND RUSSELL, "AN OUTLINE OF INTELLECTUAL RUBBISH," *UNPOPULAR ESSAYS* (1950)

29. Neither a man nor a crowd nor a nation can be trusted to act humanely or to think sanely under the influence of a great fear.

BERTRAND RUSSELL, "AN OUTLINE OF INTELLECTUAL RUBBISH," *UNPOPULAR ESSAYS* (1950)

30. Fear is, I believe, a most effective tool in destroying the soul of an individual—and the soul of a people.

ANWAR EL-SADAT, "THE SECOND REVOLUTION," *IN SEARCH OF IDENTITY* (1977)

31. Were the diver to think on the jaws of the shark he would never lay hands on the precious pearl.

SA'DI, *GULISTAN* (1258), 3.28, TR. JAMES ROSS

32. He who fears from near at hand often fears less.

SENECA, *THE TROJAN WOMEN* (1ST C.), 516

33. Where fear is, happiness is not.

SENECA, *LETTERS TO LUCILIUS* (1ST C.), 74.5, TR. E. PHILLIPS BARKER

34. Present fears / Are less than horrible imaginings.

SHAKESPEARE, *MACBETH* (1605–06), 1.3.137

35. Fear betrays unworthy souls.

VERGIL, *AENEID* (30–19 B.C.), 4.13

36. Fear could never make virtue.

VOLTAIRE, "SOCRATES," *PHILOSOPHICAL DICTIONARY* (1764)

FICTION

37. The terror of society, which is the basis of morals, the terror of God, which is the secret of religion—these are the two things that govern us.

OSCAR WILDE, *THE PICTURE OF DORIAN GRAY* (1891), 2

FEBRUARY

See 854. SEASONS

FEELINGS

See 284. EMOTIONS

FELLOWSHIP

See 152. COMPANY

344. FICTION

See also 938. STORYTELLING; 1069. WRITING AND WRITERS

1. The practice of fiction can be dangerous: it puts ideas into the head of the world.

ANTHONY BURGESS, *YOU'VE HAD YOUR TIME* (1990)

2. What, in fact, is a novel but a universe in which action is endowed with form, where final words are pronounced, where people possess one another completely, and where life assumes the aspect of destiny?

ALBERT CAMUS, "REBELLION AND THE NOVEL," *THE REBEL* (1951), TR. ANTHONY BOWER

3. What is a novel if not a conviction of our fellow-men's existence strong enough to take upon itself a form of imagined life clearer than reality and whose accumulated verisimilitude of selected episodes puts to shame the pride of documentary history?

JOSEPH CONRAD, *A PERSONAL RECORD* (1912), I

4. Science fiction writers, I am sorry to say, really do not know anything.

PHILIP K. DICK, *I HOPE I SHALL ARRIVE SOON* (1985)

5. A novel is a printed circuit through which flows the force of a reader's own life.

E.L. DOCTOROW, "FALSE DOCUMENTS," *JACK LONDON, HEMINGWAY, AND THE CONSTITUTION* (1993)

6. It may be that the most avid readers of new fiction in America today are film producers, an indication of the trouble we're in.

E.L. DOCTOROW, "THE BELIEFS OF WRITERS," *JACK LONDON, HEMINGWAY, AND THE CONSTITUTION* (1993)

7. I have always known that writing fiction had little effect on the world; that if it did, young men would not have gone to war after *The Iliad*.

ANDRÉ DUBUS, "AFTER TWENTY YEARS," *BROKEN VESSELS* (1991)

8. Good fiction is made of that which is real, and reality is difficult to come by.

RALPH ELLISON, *SHADOW & ACT* (1964)

9. Don't make a novel to establish a principle of political economy. You will spoil both.

EMERSON, *JOURNALS*, 1857

10. I can find my biography in every fable that I read.

EMERSON, *JOURNALS*, 1866

11. The love of novels is the preference of sentiment to the senses.

EMERSON, *JOURNALS*, 1831

12. The final test for a novel will be our affection for it, as it is the test of our friends, and of anything else which we cannot define.

E. M. FORSTER, "INTRODUCTORY," *ASPECTS OF THE NOVEL* (1927)

13. A novel is based on evidence, + or -x, the unknown quantity being the temperament of the novelist, and the unknown quantity always modifies the effect of the evidence, and sometimes transforms it entirely.

E.M. FORSTER, "PEOPLE," *ASPECTS OF THE NOVEL* (1927)

14. [I]t is the function of the novelist to reveal the hidden life at its source: to tell us more about Queen Victoria than could be known, and thus to produce a character who is not the Queen Victoria of history.

E.M. FORSTER, "PEOPLE," *ASPECTS OF THE NOVEL* (1927)

15. Against the sustained tick of a watch, fiction takes the measure of a life, a season, a look exchanged, the turning point, desire as brief as a dream, the grief and terror that after childhood we cease to express.

MAVIS GALLANT, "WHAT IS STYLE?" *PARIS NOTEBOOKS* (1986)

16. History is a novel which did take place; a novel is history that could take place.

JULES DE GONCOURT, *IDÉES ET SENSATIONS* (1866)

17. The subject of a novel is not the plot. Who remembers what happened to Lucien de Rebempré in the end?

GRAHAM GREENE, *A BURNT-OUT CASE* (1960)

18. He wrote a novel, and it was not really such a bad novel as the critics later called it, although it was a very poor novel.

ERNEST HEMINGWAY, *THE SUN ALSO RISES* (1926)

19. Journalism allows its readers to witness history; fiction gives its readers an opportunity to live it.

JOHN HERSEY, *TIME,* MARCH 13, 1950

20. The novelist screws up his courage in order to invest another two or three years in another attempt to float a boat of original design upon an invented ocean.

EDWARD HOAGLAND, "BEING BETWEEN BOOKS," *THE TUGMAN'S PASSAGE* (1982)

21. Readers of novels are a strange folk, upon whose probable or even possible tastes no wise book-maker would ever venture to bet.

E. V. LUCAS, *READING, WRITING, AND REMEMBERING* (1932), 14

22. Just as the painter thinks with his brush and paints the novelist thinks with his story.

W. SOMERSET MAUGHAM, *THE SUMMING UP* (1938), 5

23. A novel is what you call something that won't sell if you call it poems or short stories.

WALKER PERCY, "THE STATE OF THE NOVEL: DYING ART OR NEW SCIENCE?" *SIGNPOSTS IN A STRANGE LAND* (1991)

24. When the characters are really alive before their author, the latter does nothing but follow them in their action, in their words, in the situations which they suggest to him.

LUIGI PIRANDELLO, *SIX CHARACTERS IN SEARCH OF AN AUTHOR* (1921), 3, TR. EDWARD STORER

25. Ours is the first generation that has grown up with science-fiction ideas.

CARL SAGAN, *BROCA'S BRAIN: REFLECTIONS ON THE ROMANCE OF SCIENCE* (1979)

26. Fiction is to the grown man what play is to the child; it is there that he changes the atmosphere and tenor of his life.

ROBERT LOUIS STEVENSON, "A GOSSIP ON ROMANCE" (1882)

27. Novels are sweets. All people with healthy literary appetites love them—almost all women; a vast number of clever, hardheaded men.

WILLIAM MAKEPEACE THACKERAY, "ON A LAZY, IDLE BOY," *THE ROUNDABOUT PAPERS* (1863)

28. Fiction is nothing less than the subtlest instrument for self-examination and self-display that Mankind has invented yet.

JOHN UPDIKE, "THE IMPORTANCE OF FICTION," *ODD JOBS* (1991)

29. Novels, except as aids to masturbation, play no part in contemporary life.

GORE VIDAL, *ROCKING THE BOAT* (1962)

30. History is the recital of facts represented as true. Fable, on the other hand, is the recital of facts represented as fiction.

VOLTAIRE, "HISTORY," *PHILOSOPHICAL DICTIONARY* (1764)

31. Plots are no more exhausted than men are. Every man is a new creation, and combinations are simply endless.

CHARLES DUDLEY WARNER, "SIXTH STUDY," *BACKLOG STUDIES* (1873)

32. All fiction for me is a kind of magic and trickery—a confidence trick, trying to make people believe something is true that isn't.

ANGUS WILSON, INTERVIEW, *WRITERS AT WORK: FIRST SERIES* (1958)

33. Fiction is like a spider's web, attached ever so slightly perhaps, but still attached to life at all four corners.

VIRGINIA WOOLF, *A ROOM OF ONE'S OWN* (1929), 3

345. FIGHTING

See also 252. DISCORD; 772. QUARRELING; 1042. WAR

1. People seem to fight about things very unsuitable for fighting. They make a frightful noise in support of very quiet things. They knock each other about in the name of very fragile things.

G. K. CHESTERTON, "ON CHANGES IN TASTE," *GENERALLY SPEAKING* (1928)

2. What counts is not necessarily the size of the dog in the fight—it's the size of the fight in the dog.

DWIGHT D. EISENHOWER, ADDRESS TO REPUBLICAN NATIONAL COMMITTEE, JAN. 31, 1958

3. Never contend with a man who has nothing to lose.

BALTASAR GRACIÁN, *THE ART OF WORLDY WISDOM* (1647), 172, TR. JOSEPH JACOBS

4. There are not fifty ways of fighting, there is only one: to be the conqueror.

ANDRÉ MALRAUX, *L'ESPOIR* (1937), 2.2.12

5. To love life for some men is to love fighting, for fighting, and not love, is seen as man's deepest passion.

JOYCE CAROL OATES, "FIVE PREFACES," *(WOMAN) WRITER: OCCASIONS AND OPPORTUNITIES* (1988)

6. In a fight the rich man tries to save his face, the poor man his coat.

RUSSIAN PROVERB

7. To fight is a radical instinct; if men have nothing else to fight over they will fight over words, fancies, or women, or they will fight because they dislike each other's looks, or because they have met walking in opposite directions.

GEORGE SANTAYANA, *THE LIFE OF REASON: REASON IN SOCIETY* (1905–06), 3

FINISHING

See 285. ENDING

346. FIRE

1. Fire, as we have learned to our cost, has an insatiable hunger to be fed. It is a nonliving force that can even locomote itself.

LOREN EISELEY, "THE LAST NEANDERTHAL," *THE STAR THROWER* (1978)

2. Fire is the most tolerable third party.

THOREAU, *JOURNAL,* JAN. 2, 1853

347. FISH

See also 348. FISHING

1. Fish die belly-upward and rise to the surface; it is their way of falling.

ANDRÉ GIDE, *JOURNALS,* MAY 18, 1930, TR. JUSTIN O'BRIEN

348. FISHING

See also 347. FISH

1. Overwork, n. A dangerous disorder affecting high public functionaries who want to go fishing.

AMBROSE BIERCE, *THE DEVIL'S DICTIONARY* (1881–1911)

2. The gods do not deduct from man's allotted span the hours spent in fishing.

BABYLONIAN PROVERB, OFTEN QUOTED BY HERBERT HOOVER

3. Corned-beef sandwiches were good enough for him, but for the catfish he'd bought at least a pound of filet steak.

JONATHAN RABAN, *OLD GLORY* (1982)

4. Angling may be said to be so like the mathematics that it can never be fully learnt.

IZAAK WALTON, "EPISTLE TO THE READER," *THE COMPLEAT ANGLER* (1653)

FLAG

See 678. PATRIOTISM

349. FLATTERY

See also 159. COMPLIMENTS

1. There is no food more satiating than milk and honey; and just as such foods produce disgust for the palate, so perfumed and gallant words make our ears belch.

PIETRO ARETINO, LETTER TO GIANFRANCESCO POCOPANNO, NOV. 24, 1537, TR. SAMUEL PUTNAM

2. Mountains of gold would not seduce some men, yet flattery would break them down.

HENRY WARD BEECHER, *PROVERBS FROM PLYMOUTH PULPIT* (1887)

3. Flattery is a juggler, and no kin unto sincerity.

SIR THOMAS BROWNE, *CHRISTIAN MORALS* (1716), 1

4. Some indeed there are who profess to despise all flattery, but even these are nevertheless to be flattered, by being told that they do despise it.

CHARLES CALEB COLTON, *LACON* (1825), 1.444

5. We must be careful how we flatter fools too little, or wise men too much, for the flatterer must act the very reverse of the physician, and administer the strongest dose only to the weakest patient.

CHARLES CALEB COLTON, *LACON* (1825), 2.198

6. If a man is vain, flatter. If timid, flatter. If boastful, flatter. In all history, too much flattery never lost a gentleman.

KATHRYN CRAVENS, *PURSUIT OF GENTLEMEN* (1952)

7. We love flattery, even though we are not deceived by it, because it shows that we are of importance enough to be courted.

EMERSON, "GIFTS," *ESSAYS: SECOND SERIES* (1844)

8. Flattery sits in the parlour when plain dealing is kicked out of doors.

THOMAS FULLER, M.D., *GNOMOLOGIA* (1732), 1552

9. Roughness may turn one's humour, but flattery one's stomach.

THOMAS FULLER, M.D., *GNOMOLOGIA* (1732), 4061

10. Flattery is a challenge. The proper turning away from it, undercutting, diminishing it without offense

or vehemence, is a social grace sweeter even than the swift determination to keep ahead in the race of hospitality.

Elizabeth Hardwick, "Timon of Paris," *Bartleby in Manhattan* (1983)

11. Flattery pleases very generally. In the first place, the flatterer may think what he says to be true; but, in the second place, whether he thinks so or not, he certainly thinks those whom he flatters of consequence enough to be flattered.

Samuel Johnson, quoted in Boswell's *Life of Samuel Johnson,* April 11, 1775

12. It is necessary to the success of flattery, that it be accommodated to particular circumstances or characters, and enter the heart on that side where the passions are ready to receive it.

Samuel Johnson, *The Rambler* (1750–52), 106

13. Of all wild beasts preserve me from a tyrant; / And of all tame, a flatterer.

Ben Jonson, *Sejanus His Fall* (1603), 1.1

14. Learn that every flatterer / Lives at the flattered listener's cost.

La Fontaine, "The Fox and the Crow," *Fables* (1668–94), tr. Marianne Moore

15. We imagine sometimes that we hate flattery, but it is only the manner of flattering which we hate.

La Rochefoucauld, *Maxims* (1665), tr. Kenneth Pratt

16. [T]here is no other way of guarding oneself against flattery than by letting men understand that they will not offend you by speaking the truth; but when everyone can tell you the truth, you lose their respect.

Niccolo Machiavelli, *The Prince* (1517)

17. The world is grown so full of dissimulation and compliment, that men's words are hardly any signification of their thoughts.

Richard Steele, *The Spectator* (1711–12), 103

18. Flattery is all right—if you don't inhale.

Adlai Stevenson, speech, Feb. 1, 1961

19. Love of flattery, in most men, proceeds from the mean opinion they have of themselves; in women, from the contrary.

Jonathan Swift, *Thoughts on Various Subjects* (1711)

20. We despise no source that can pay us a pleasing attention.

Mark Twain, "Does the Race of Man Love a Lord?" *North American Review,* April 1902

350. FLEXIBILITY

See also 117. Change; 652. Obstinacy; 654. Open-Mindedness; 656. Opinion

1. The hearts of the great can be changed.

Homer, *Iliad* (9th c. b.c.), 15.203, tr. Richmond Lattimore

2. My opinion is a view I hold until—well-until I find out something that changes it.

Luigi Pirandello, *Each in His Own Way* (1924), 1, tr. Arthur Livingston

FLIES

See 481. Insects

FLIGHT

See 28. Airplanes; 300. Escape

351. FLIRTATION

See also 198. Courtship; 551. Love; 742. Promiscuity; 857. Seduction

1. Life is not long enough for a coquette to play all her tricks in.

Joseph Addison, *The Spectator* (1711–12), 89

2. Some of these teen-aged innocent angels were consummate experts in the diabolical arts of keeping a boy, or a number of boys at the same time, in a frenzied state of hopeful uncertainty.

Luigi Barzini, *O America* (1977)

3. She who trifles with all / Is less likely to fall / Than she who but trifles with one.

John Gay, "The Coquet Mother and the Coquet Daughter" (1727)

4. When you see a woman who can go nowhere without a staff of admirers, it is not so much because they think she is beautiful, it is because she has told them they are handsome.

Jean Giraudoux, *The Apollo of Bellac* (1942), adapted by Maurice Valency

5. He who wins a thousand common hearts is entitled to some renown; but he who keeps undisputed sway over the heart of a coquette is indeed a hero.

Washington Irving, "The Legend of Sleepy Hollow," *The Sketch Book of Geoffrey Crayon, Gent.* (1819–20)

6. Love's greatest miracle is the curing of coquetry.

La Rochefoucauld, *Maxims* (1665), tr. Kenneth Pratt

7. Ah, Dubin, you meet a pretty girl on the road and are braced to hop on a horse in pursuit of youth.

BERNARD MALAMUD, *DUBIN'S LIVES* (1979)

8. Flirtation is merely an expression of considered desire coupled with an admission of its impracticability.

MARYA MANNES, "A PLEA FOR FLIRTATION," *BUT WILL IT SELL?* (1955–64)

9. One must cease letting oneself be eaten when one tastes best: that is known to those who want to be loved long.

NIETZSCHE, "ON FREE DEATH," *THUS SPOKE ZARATHUSTRA* (1883–92), 1, TR. WALTER KAUFMANN

10. Venus favors the bold.

OVID, *THE ART OF LOVE* (C. A.D. 8), 1, TR. ROLFE HUMPHRIES

11. Whether a pretty woman grants or withholds her favours, she always likes to be asked for them.

OVID, *THE ART OF LOVE* (C. A.D. 8), 1, TR. J. LEWIS MAY

352. FLOWERS

1. Without the gift of flowers and the infinite diversity of their fruits, man and bird, if they had continued to exist at all, would be today unrecognizable.

LOREN EISELEY, "HOW FLOWERS CHANGED THE WORLD," *THE STAR THROWER* (1978)

2. The flower is the poetry of reproduction. It is an example of the eternal seductiveness of life.

JEAN GIRAUDOUX, *THE ENCHANTED* (1933), 1, ADAPTED BY MAURICE VALENCY

3. There is that in the glance of a flower which may at times control the greatest of creation's braggart lords.

JOHN MUIR, *A THOUSAND-MILE WALK TO THE GULF* (1916), 5

4. A flowerless room is a soulless room, to my way of thinking; but even one solitary little vase of a living flower may redeem it.

VITA SACKVILLE-WEST, *VITA SACKVILLE-WEST'S GARDEN BOOK* (1983)

5. To me the meanest flower that blows can give / Thoughts that do often lie too deep for tears.

WILLIAM WORDSWORTH, "ODE: INTIMATIONS OF IMMORTALITY FROM RECOLLECTIONS OF EARLY CHILDHOOD" (1803), 11

FOG

See 1050. WEATHER

353. FOLLOWING

See also 14. ADMIRATION; 531. LEADERSHIP; 568. MASS MOVEMENTS; 1068. WORSHIP

1. Having disciples is in the end like having children, only not with love but with self-love preeminent.

LOUIS KRONENBERGER, "REFLECTIONS AND COMPLAINTS OF LATE MIDDLE AGE," *THE CART AND THE HORSE* (1964), 3

2. Every master has but one disciple, and that one becomes unfaithful to him, for he too is destined for mastership.

NIETZSCHE, *MIXED OPINIONS AND MAXIMS* (1879), 357, IN *THE PORTABLE NIETZSCHE*, TR. WALTER KAUFMANN

3. The followers of a great man often put their eyes out, so that they may be the better able to sing his praise.

NIETZSCHE, *MISCELLANEOUS MAXIMS AND OPINIONS* (1879), 390, TR. PAUL V. COHN

354. FOLLY

See also 342. FAULTS; 356. FOOLS; 781. RASHNESS; 941. STUPIDITY

1. The folly of one man is the fortune of another.

FRANCIS BACON, "OF FORTUNE," *ESSAYS* (1625)

2. If others had not been foolish, we should be so.

WILLIAM BLAKE, "PROVERBS OF HELL," *THE MARRIAGE OF HEAVEN AND HELL* (1790)

3. Folly loves the martyrdom of Fame.

BYRON, "MONODY ON THE DEATH OF R. B. SHERIDAN" (1816)

4. If we're not foolish young, we're foolish old.

CHAUCER, "THE KNIGHT'S TALE," *THE CANTERBURY TALES* (C. 1387–1400), TR. NEVILL COGHILL

5. It is folly to drown on dry land.

ENGLISH PROVERB

6. Wisdom at times is found in folly.

HORACE, *ODES* (23–C. 15 B.C.), 4.12

7. Folly pursues us at all periods of our lives. If someone seems wise it is only because his follies are proportionate to his age and fortune.

LA ROCHEFOUCAULD, *MAXIMS* (1665), TR. KENNETH PRATT

8. He who lives without folly is not so wise as he believes.

LA ROCHEFOUCAULD, *MAXIMS* (1665), TR. KENNETH PRATT

9. The folly which we might have ourselves committed is the one which we are least ready to pardon in another.

JOSEPH ROUX, *MEDITATIONS OF A PARISH PRIEST* (1886), 4.84, TR. ISABEL F. HAPGOOD

10. Folly is perennial and yet the human race has survived.

BERTRAND RUSSELL, "AN OUTLINE OF INTELLECTUAL RUBBISH," *UNPOPULAR ESSAYS* (1950)

11. Tell him to be a fool every so often / and to have no shame over having been a fool / yet learning something over every folly.

CARL SANDBURG, *THE PEOPLE, YES* (1936)

12. A way foolishness has of revenging itself is to excommunicate the world.

GEORGE SANTAYANA, *THE LIFE OF REASON: REASON IN ART* (1905–06), 9

13. Do you think that the things people make fools of themselves about are any less real and true than the things they behave sensibly about?

GEORGE BERNARD SHAW, *CANDIDA* (1903), 1

14. What is life but a series of inspired follies? The difficulty is to find them to do.

GEORGE BERNARD SHAW, *PYGMALION* (1913), 2

15. If you think my acts are foolishness / the foolishness may be in a fool's eye.

SOPHOCLES, *ANTIGONE* (442–41 B.C.), TR. ELIZABETH WYCKOFF

16. Give me the young man who has brains enough to make a fool of himself!

ROBERT LOUIS STEVENSON, "CRABBED AGE AND YOUTH," *VIRGINIBUS PUERISQUE* (1881)

17. Those who realize their folly are not true fools.

CHAUNG TZU, *WORKS* (4TH–3RD C. B.C.), 20.2, TR. LIN YUTANG

18. What use is wisdom when folly reigns?

YIDDISH PROVERBS (1949)

355. FOOD

See also 189. COOKS AND COOKING; 274. EATING; 437. HUNGER; 1028. VEGETARIANISM

1. Some people Franz knew once visited the Turkish restaurant and reported to him that the food was quite good and the decor, in general, surprisingly attractive, and that for a *foreign* place, they stressed the "foreign," it was remarkably clean and the service quite up to standards, not what you might expect from the Turks.

WALTER ABISH, *HOW GERMAN IS IT* (1979)

2. They eat the dainty food of famous chefs with the same pleasure with which they devour gross peasant dishes, mostly composed of garlic and tomatoes, or fisherman's octopus and shrimps, fried in heavily scented olive oil on a little deserted beach.

LUIGI BARZINI, *THE ITALIANS* (1964)

3. Public and private food in America has become eatable, here and there extremely good. Only the fried potatoes go on unchanged, as deadly as before.

LUIGI BARZINI, *O AMERICA* (1977)

4. I doubt whether the world holds for any one a more soul-stirring surprise than the first adventure with ice-cream.

HEYWOOD BROUN, "HOLDING A BABY," *SEEING THINGS AT NIGHT* (1921)

5. The Chanukah buckwheat cake or *latke* is much thicker and smaller [than the pancake served in American restaurants] and does not deserve its name unless, when served, it is fairly dripping with fat. It would be futile to attempt a description of it here, for the glories of a successful Chanukah *latke* defy the resources of the richest of Gentile languages.

ABRAHAM CAHAN, *GRANDMA NEVER LIVED IN AMERICA* (1985), ED. MOSES RISCHIN

6. "Women alone always order sole. It means something."

JOHN DOS PASSOS, *MOST LIKELY TO SUCCEED* (1954)

7. Cheese—milk's leap toward immortality.

CLIFTON FADIMAN, *ANY NUMBER CAN PLAY* (1957)

8. Talk of joy: there may be things better than beef stew and baked potatoes and home-made bread—there may be.

DAVID GRAYSON, *ADVENTURES IN CONTENTMENT* (1907), 6

9. A cucumber should be well sliced, and dressed with pepper and vinegar, and then thrown out as good for nothing.

SAMUEL JOHNSON, QUOTED IN BOSWELL'S *JOURNAL OF A TOUR TO THE HEBRIDES WITH SAMUEL JOHNSON,* OCT. 5, 1773

10. "You know," she said, "there's a recipe for macaroni and cheese I've always been meaning to try. It's the one where you boil up about three pounds of macaroni, and then you grate cheese on it. It only takes about three minutes."

GARRISON KEILLOR, *LAKE WOBEGON DAYS* (1985)

11. At one of the "typical" restaurants [in Florence, Italy], recommended by the big hotels, the waiters, who are a family, treat the clients like interlopers, feigning not to notice their presence, bawling orders sarcastically to the kitchen, banging down the dishes, spitting on the floor.

MARY MCCARTHY, *THE STONES OF FLORENCE* (1959)

12. It is surely no mere coincidence that the land of the emancipated and enthroned woman is also the land of canned soup, of canned pork and beans, of whole meals in cans, and of everything else ready made.

H.L. MENCKEN, "THE FEMININE MIND," IN *FIFTY FAMOUS ESSAYS* (1964)

13. The meal, of course, was ghastly—fried plaice smothered in cream sauce, the usual Brussels sprouts boiled beyond cognizance, and a soggy plum tart as fibrous as corrugated paper.

S.J. PERELMAN, *THE RISING GORGE* (1961)

14. Their [the waiters'] eyes sparkled and their pencils flew as she proceeded to eviscerate my wallet—pâté, Whitstable oysters, a sole, filet mignon, and a favorite salad of the Nizam of Hyderabad made of shredded five-pound notes.

S.J. PERELMAN, *THE RISING GORGE* (1961)

15. His [Prince Norodom Sihanouk's] table was one of the best in town, often laden with gooseberries and guinea fowl.... He had nine chefs "because I am a gourmet. They prepare me Cambodian food, French food, Chinese food, anything you want."

WILLIAM SHAWCROSS, *SIDESHOW* (1979)

16. It's impossible to get a recognizable sandwich in the vicinity of this court or an unadorned piece of meat or fish. Order a tuna on rye, and no doubt it'll be topped with melted cheese and a maraschino cherry.

DIANA TRILLING, *MRS. HARRIS: THE DEATH OF THE SCARSDALE DOCTOR* (1981)

17. Happy is said to be the family which can eat onions together. They are, for the time being, separate from the world, and have a harmony of aspiration.

CHARLES DUDLEY WARNER, "EIGHTEENTH WEEK," *MY SUMMER IN A GARDEN* (1871)

18. Our lives are not in the lap of the gods, but in the lap of our cooks.

LIN YUTANG, "ON FOOD AND MEDICINE," *THE IMPORTANCE OF LIVING* (1937)

356. FOOLS

See also 354. FOLLY; 781. RASHNESS; 941. STUPIDITY

1. A prosperous fool is a grievous burden.

AESCHYLUS, *FRAGMENTS* (525–456 B.C.), 383, TR. M. H. MORGAN

2. Fine clothes may disguise, but foolish words will disclose a fool.

AESOP, "THE ASS IN THE LION'S SKIN," *FABLES* (6TH C. B.C.?), TR. JOSEPH JACOBS

3. Weep for the dead, for he lacks the light; and weep for the fool, for he lacks intelligence; weep less bitterly for the dead, for he has attained rest; but the life of the fool is worse than death.

APOCRYPHA, ECCLESIASTICUS 22:11

4. Answer a fool according to his folly.

BIBLE, PROVERBS 26:5

5. Even a fool, when he holdeth his peace, is counted wise.

BIBLE, PROVERBS 17:28

6. The Fool shall not enter into Heaven let him be ever so Holy.

WILLIAM BLAKE, *A VISION OF THE LAST JUDGMENT* (1810)

7. A wise man may be duped as well as a fool; but the fool publishes the triumph of the deceiver.

CHARLES CALEB COLTON, *LACON* (1825), 1.96

8. There is no need to fasten a bell to a fool.

DANISH PROVERB

9. A fool's head never whitens.

ENGLISH PROVERB

10. Talk sense to a fool / and he calls you foolish.

EURIPIDES, *THE BACCHAE* (C. 405 B.C.), TR. WILLIAM ARROWSMITH

11. Wise men ... learn by others' harms, fools scarcely by their own.

BENJAMIN FRANKLIN, "THE WAY TO WEALTH" (JULY 7, 1757)

12. 'Tis wisdom sometimes to seem a fool.

THOMAS FULLER, M.D., *GNOMOLOGIA* (1732), 5125

13. Every man hath a fool in his sleeve.

THOMAS FULLER, M.D., *GNOMOLOGIA* (1732), 1424

14. If the fools do not control the world, it isn't because they are not in the majority.

EDGAR WATSON HOWE, *COUNTRY TOWN SAYINGS* (1911)

15. The fool is not the man who merely does foolish things. The fool is the man who does not know enough to cash in on his foolishness.

ELBERT HUBBARD, *THE NOTE BOOK* (1927)

16. The silliest woman can manage a clever man; but it needs a very clever woman to manage a fool.

RUDYARD KIPLING, "THREE AND—AN EXTRA," *PLAIN TALES FROM THE HILLS* (1888)

17. A learned fool is sillier than an ignorant one.

MOLIÈRE, *LES FEMMES SAVANTES* (1672), 4.3

18. The fool has one great advantage over a man of sense—he is always satisfied with himself.

NAPOLEON I, *MAXIMS* (1804–15)

19. Fools rush in where angels fear to tread.

ALEXANDER POPE, *AN ESSAY ON CRITICISM* (1711), 3.66

20. To never see a fool you lock yourself in your room and smash the looking-glass.

CARL SANDBURG, *THE PEOPLE, YES* (1936)

21. Always the dulness of the fool is the whetstone of the wits.

SHAKESPEARE, *AS YOU LIKE IT* (1599–1600), 1.2.58

22. How ill white hairs become a fool and jester!

SHAKESPEARE, *2 HENRY IV* (1597–98), 5.5.52

23. Let us be thankful for the fools. But for them the rest of us could not succeed.

MARK TWAIN, "PUDD'NHEAD WILSON'S NEW CALENDAR," *FOLLOWING THE EQUATOR* (1897), 1.28

24. If every fool wore a crown, we should all be kings.

WELSH PROVERB

357. FORCE

See also 26. AGGRESSION; 158. COMPLIANCE; 379. GENTLENESS; 665. PACIFISM; 719. POWER; 801. REPRESSION; 940. STRENGTH; 1032. VIOLENCE

1. Let the sword decide after stratagem has failed.

ARABIC PROVERB

2. Forcible ways make not an end of evil, but leave hatred and malice behind them.

SIR THOMAS BROWNE, *CHRISTIAN MORALS* (1716), 3

3. The use of force alone is temporary. It may subdue for a moment, but it does not remove the necessity of subduing again: and a nation is not governed which is perpetually to be conquered.

EDMUND BURKE, SPEECH, "ON CONCILIATION WITH THE AMERICAN COLONIES," MARCH 22, 1775

4. Where might is master, justice is servant.

GERMAN PROVERB

5. The one means that wins the easiest victory over reason: terror and force.

ADOLF HITLER, *MEIN KAMPF* (1924), 1.2

6. Force without reason falls of its own weight.

HORACE, *ODES* (23–C. 15 B.C.), 3.4

7. When a fact can be demonstrated, force is unnecessary; when it cannot be demonstrated, force is infamous.

ROBERT G. INGERSOLL, *PROSE-POEMS AND SELECTIONS* (1884)

8. Force works on servile natures, not the free.

BEN JONSON, *EVERY MAN IN HIS HUMOUR* (1598), 1.2

9. When one by force subdues men, they do not submit to him in heart. They submit because their strength is not adequate to resist.

MENCIUS, *WORKS* (4TH–3RD C. B.C.), 4, TR. CHARLES A. WONG

10. Who overcomes / By force, hath overcome but half his foe.

MILTON, *PARADISE LOST* (1667), 1.648

11. There is no real force without justice.

NAPOLEON I, *MAXIMS* (1804–15)

12. Justice without force is impotent, force without justice is tyranny.... Not being able to make what is just strong, we make what was strong just.

PASCAL, *PENSÉES* (1670), 298

13. Do not expect justice where might is right.

PHAEDRUS, "THE COW, THE GOAT, THE SHEEP AND THE LION," *FABLES* (1ST C.), TR. THOMAS JAMES

14. Where there is no might right loses itself.

PORTUGUESE PROVERB

15. Against naked force the only possible defense is naked force. The aggressor makes the rules for such a war; the defenders have no alternative but matching destruction with more destruction, slaughter with greater slaughter.

FRANKLIN D. ROOSEVELT, MESSAGE TO YOUNG DEMOCRATS CONVENTION, LOUISVILLE, KY., AUG. 21, 1941

16. Not hammer-strokes, but dance of the water sings the pebbles into perfection.

RABINDRANATH TAGORE, *STRAY BIRDS* (1916), 126

17. The Soviet Union could not exist without the image of the empire. The image of the empire could not exist without the image of force. The USSR ended the moment the first hammer pounded the Berlin Wall.

BORIS YELTSIN, *THE STRUGGLE FOR RUSSIA* (1994), TR. CATHERINE A. FITZPATRICK

358. FOREIGNERS AND FOREIGNNESS

1. At twelve noon/The natives swoon/ And no further work is done/ But mad dogs and Englishmen/Go out in the midday sun.

NOËL COWARD, "MAD DOGS AND ENGLISHMEN" (1938)

2. Everything foreign is respected, partly because it comes from afar, partly because it is ready made and perfect.

BALTASAR GRACIÁN, *THE ART OF WORLDLY WISDOM* (1647), 198, TR. JOSEPH JACOBS

3. Admiration for ourselves and our institutions is too often measured by our contempt and dislike for foreigners.

WILLIAM RALPH INGE, "PATRIOTISM," *OUTSPOKEN ESSAYS: FIRST SERIES* (1919)

4. America shudders at anything alien, and when it wants to shut its mind against any man's ideas it calls him a foreigner.

MAX LERNER, "AMERICA IN THE SUNLIGHT," *ACTIONS AND PASSIONS* (1949)

5. Man is not man, but a wolf, to those he does not know.

PLAUTUS, *THE COMEDY OF ASSES* (3RD C. B.C.)

6. Ants and savages put strangers to death.

BERTRAND RUSSELL, "THE FUNCTIONS OF A TEACHER," *UNPOPULAR ESSAYS* (1950)

7. The tears of strangers are only water.

RUSSIAN PROVERB

8. He will deal harshly by a stranger who has not been himself often a traveller and stranger.

SA'DI, *GULISTAN* (1258), 3.28, TR. JAMES ROSS

9. The stranger has no friend, unless it be a stranger.

SA'DI, *GULISTAN* (1258), 3.28, TR. JAMES ROSS

10. Man, by definition, is born a stranger: coming from nowhere, he is thrust into an alien world which existed before him—a world which didn't need him. And which will survive him.

ELIE WIESEL, "THE STRANGER IN THE BIBLE," *FROM THE KINGDOM OF MEMORY* (1990)

FOREIGN RELATIONS

See 498. INTERNATIONAL RELATIONS

359. FORGIVENESS

See also 583. MERCY

1. Be ye kind one to another, tender-hearted, forgiving one another, even as God for Christ's sake hath forgiven you.

BIBLE, EPHESIANS 4:32

2. Forgive us our debts, as we forgive our debtors.

BIBLE, MATTHEW 6:12

3. It is easier to forgive an enemy than to forgive a friend.

WILLIAM BLAKE, "WHAT GOD IS," *JERUSALEM* (1804–20)

4. Forgiveness to the injured does belong; / For they ne'er pardon who have done the wrong.

JOHN DRYDEN, *THE CONQUEST OF GRANADA* (1670–71), 2.1.2

5. Reason to rule but mercy to forgive: / The first is law, the last prerogative.

JOHN DRYDEN, *THE HIND AND THE PANTHER* (1687), 1.261

6. Forgotten is forgiven.

F. SCOTT FITZGERALD, "NOTE-BOOKS," *THE CRACK-UP* (1945)

7. Forgiveness is the answer to the child's dream of a miracle by which what is broken is made whole again, what is soiled is again made clean.

DAG HAMMARSKJÖLD, "1956," *MARKINGS* (1964), TR. W. H. AUDEN

8. The offender never pardons.

GEORGE HERBERT, *JACULA PRUDENTUM* (1651)

9. The ineffable joy of forgiving and being forgiven forms an ecstasy that might well arouse the envy of the gods.

ELBERT HUBBARD, *THE NOTE BOOK* (1927)

10. In Lake Wobegon, we don't forget mistakes.

GARRISON KEILLOR, *LAKE WOBEGON DAYS* (1985)

11. The United States grants the favors of the second, third, or fifty-seventh chance, and its citizens remain free to invent for themselves whatever character draws a crowd or pays the rent.

LEWIS LAPHAM, *IMPERIAL MASQUERADE* (1990)

12. Did man e'er live / Saw priest or woman yet forgive?

JAMES RUSSELL LOWELL, "VILLA FRANCE, 1859," *UNDER THE WILLOWS AND OTHER POEMS* (1868)

13. If there is something to pardon in everything, there is also something to condemn.

NIETZSCHE, *THE WILL TO POWER* (1888), TR. ANTHONY M. LUDOVICI

14. To err is human, to forgive divine.

ALEXANDER POPE, *AN ESSAY ON CRITICISM* (1711), 2.325

15. Forgiving presupposes remembering.

PAUL TILLICH, *THE ETERNAL NOW* (1963), 1.2.2

16. What power has love but forgiveness? / In other words / by its intervention / what has been done / can be undone. / What good is it otherwise?

WILLIAM CARLOS WILLIAMS, "ASPHODEL, THAT GREENY FLOWER," *PICTURES FROM BRUEGHEL* (1962), 3

17. The practice of forgiveness is our most important contribution to the healing of the world.

MARIANNE WILLIAMSON, "MIRACLES," *A RETURN TO LOVE* (1992)

FORM

See 661. ORDER

360. FORTUNE

See also 15. ADVANTAGE; 116. CHANCE; 549. LOSERS; 751. PROSPERITY AND ADVERSITY; 1048. WEALTH

1. Fortune is like the market, where many times, if you can stay a little, the price will fall.

FRANCIS BACON, "OF DELAY," *ESSAYS* (1625)

2. Good luck needs no explanation.

SHIRLEY TEMPLE BLACK, *CHILD STAR* (1988)

3. Who has good luck is good, / Who has bad luck is bad.

BERTOLT BRECHT, *THE EXCEPTION AND THE RULE* (1937), 6, TR. ERIC BENTLEY

4. Let everyone witness how many different cards fortune has up her sleeve when she wants to ruin a man.

BENVENUTO CELLINI, *AUTOBIOGRAPHY* (1558–66), TR. GEORGE BULL

5. Heaven's help is better than early rising.

CERVANTES, *DON QUIXOTE* (1605–15), 2.4.34, TR. JOHN OZELL

6. Good fortune leads one to the highest glory, / But to renounce it calls for equal courage.

CORNEILLE, *CINNA* (1639), 2.1, TR. PAUL LANDIS

7. Luck is not chance— / It's Toil— / Fortune's expensive smile / Is earned—.

EMILY DICKINSON, POEM (C. 1875)

8. To believe in luck, if it were not a solecism so to use the word *believe,* is skepticism.

EMERSON, *JOURNALS,* 1841

9. Don't envy men / Because they seem to have a run of luck, / Since luck's a nine day's wonder. Wait their end.

EURIPIDES, *HERAKLEIDAI* (C. 429–27 B.C.), TR. RALPH GLADSTONE

10. Fortune always will confer an aura / Of worth, unworthily; and in this world / The lucky person passes for a genius.

EURIPIDES, *HERAKLEIDAI* (C. 429–27 B.C.), TR. RALPH GLADSTONE

11. None can hold fortune still and make it last.

EURIPIDES, *HELEN* (412 B.C.), TR. RICHMOND LATTIMORE

12. The man who glories in his luck / May be overthrown by destiny.

EURIPIDES, *THE SUPPLIANT WOMEN* (C. 421 B.C.), TR. FRANK W. JONES

13. There is in the worst of fortune the best of chances for a happy change.

EURIPIDES, *IPHIGENIA IN TAURIS* (C. 414–12 B.C.), 721, TR. M. H. MORGAN

14. Nothing is as obnoxious as other people's luck.

F. SCOTT FITZGERALD, *THE LETTERS OF F. SCOTT FITZGERALD* (1963), ED. ANDREW TURNBULL

15. Fortune pays you sometimes for the intensity of her favors by the shortness of their duration. She soon tires of carrying any one long on her shoulders.

BALTASAR GRACIÁN, *THE ART OF WORLDLY WISDOM* (1647), 28, TR. JOSEPH JACOBS

16. When you find Fortune favorable, stride boldly forward, for she favors the bold, and being a woman, the young.

BALTASAR GRACIÁN, *THE ART OF WORLDLY WISDOM* (1647), 26, TR. JOSEPH JACOBS

17. Some folk want their luck buttered.

THOMAS HARDY, *THE MAYOR OF CASTERBRIDGE* (1886), 13

18. Fortune, men say, doth give too much to many, / But yet she never gave enough to any.

SIR JOHN HARINGTON, "OF FORTUNE," *EPIGRAMS* (1615)

19. Ah Fortune, what god is more cruel to us than thou! How thou delightest ever to make sport of human life!

HORACE, *SATIRES* (35–30 B.C.), 2.7

20. Have but luck, and you will have the rest; be fortunate, and you will be thought great.

VICTOR HUGO, "FANTINE," *LES MISÉRABLES* (1862), 1.12, TR. CHARLES E. WILBOUR

21. Very few live by choice. Every man is placed in his present condition by causes which acted without his foresight, and with which he did not always willingly cooperate; and therefore you will rarely meet one who does not think the lot of his neighbor better than his own.

SAMUEL JOHNSON, *RASSELAS* (1759), 16

22. Fortune, thou hadst no deity, if men / Had wisdom.

BEN JONSON, *SEJANUS HIS FALL* (1603), 5.10

23. Ill fortune never crushed that man whom good fortune deceived not.

BEN JONSON, "EXPLORATA," *TIMBER* (1640)

24. Fortunate persons hardly ever amend their ways: they always imagine that they are in the right when fortune upholds their bad conduct.

LA ROCHEFOUCAULD, *MAXIMS* (1665), TR. KENNETH PRATT

25. Fortune never appears so blind as to those to whom she does no good.

LA ROCHEFOUCAULD, *MAXIMS* (1665), TR. KENNETH PRATT

26. When Fortune comes, seize her in front with a sure hand, because behind she is bald.

LEONARDO DA VINCI, *NOTEBOOKS* (C. 1500), TR. JEAN PAUL RICHTER

27. What men call luck / Is the prerogative of valiant souls, / The fealty life pays its rightful kings.

JAMES RUSSELL LOWELL, "A GLANCE BEHIND THE CURTAIN" (1843)

28. When a man is a favorite of Fortune she never takes him unawares, and, however astonishing her favors may be, she finds him ready.

NAPOLEON I, *MAXIMS* (1804–15)

29. Fortune makes a fool of him whom she favors too much.

PUBLILIUS SYRUS, *MORAL SAYINGS* (1ST C. B.C.), 271, TR. DARIUS LYMAN

30. It is more easy to get a favor from fortune than to keep it.

PUBLILIUS SYRUS, *MORAL SAYINGS* (1ST C. B.C.), 282, TR. DARIUS LYMAN

31. When Fortune flatters, she does it to betray.

PUBLILIUS SYRUS, *MORAL SAYINGS* (1ST C. B.C.), 277, TR. DARIUS LYMAN

32. Fortune's not content with knocking a man down; she sends him spinning head over heels, crash upon crash.

SENECA, *LETTERS TO LUCILIUS* (1ST C.), 8.5, TR. E. PHILLIPS BARKER

33. Luck never made a man wise.

SENECA, *LETTERS TO LUCILIUS* (1ST C.), 76.6, TR. E. PHILLIPS BARKER

34. Fortune brings in some boats that are not steered.

SHAKESPEARE, *CYMBELINE* (1609–10), 4.3.46

35. Fortune is not on the side of the faint-hearted.

SOPHOCLES, *PHAEDRA* (C. 435–29 B.C.), TR. M. H. MORGAN

36. Look how men live, always precariously / balanced between good and bad fortune.

SOPHOCLES, *PHILOCTETES* (409 B.C.), TR. DAVID GRENE

37. The power of fortune is confessed only by the miserable, for the happy impute all their success to prudence or merit.

JONATHAN SWIFT, *THOUGHTS ON VARIOUS SUBJECTS* (1711)

38. Fortune favors the brave.

TERENCE, *PHORMIO* (161 B.C.), TR. WILLIAM A. OLDFATHER

39. Fortune sides with him who dares.

VERGIL, *AENEID* (30–19 B.C.), 10.284, TR. T. H. DELABERE-MAY

40. 'Tis better to be fortunate than wise.

JOHN WEBSTER, *THE WHITE DEVIL* (1612), 5.6

41. Fortune's a right whore: / If she give ought, she deals it in small parcels, / That she may take away all at one swoop.

JOHN WEBSTER, *THE WHITE DEVIL* (1612), 1.1

42. Luck is not something you can mention in the presence of self-made men.

E. B. White, "Control," *One Man's Meat* (1944)

361. FRANCE AND FRENCHMEN

See also 671. Paris

1. In the past the French came to Germany less with the desire to understand it than with a zealous desire to interpret, to analyze it dispassionately, something for which their training at the Ecole Normale Supérieure or the Ecole des Hautes Etudes and the French language superbly equipped them to do.

Walter Abish, *How German Is It* (1979)

2. Everything ends this way in France—everything. Weddings, christenings, duels, burials, swindlings, diplomatic affairs—everything is a pretext for a good dinner.

Jean Anouilh, *Cécile* (1949), tr. Arthur Klein

3. Political thought in France is either nostalgic or utopian.

Raymond Aron, *The Opium of the Intellectual* (1957)

4. How can you be expected to govern a country that has two hundred and forty-six kinds of cheese?

Charles de Gaulle, *Newsweek,* Oct 1, 1962

5. There's a French story that tells how God created the world, and there was no place perfect on it, so he created France. And then he looked at it and said, "This is too good for humanity," so he created Frenchmen to live in it.

James Jones, Interview, *Time* magazine, June 17, 1974

6. The Frenchman is first and foremost a *man.* He is likeable often just because of his weaknesses, which are always thoroughly human, even if despicable.

Henry Miller, "Raimu," *The Wisdom of the Heart* (1941)

7. Who can help loving the land that has taught us / Six hundred and eighty-five ways to dress eggs?

Thomas Moore, *The Fudge Family in Paris* (1818), 8.64

8. The French, for example, are a contemptible nation.

Jean-Jacques Rousseau, in conversation with James Boswell, *Boswell on the Grand Tour: Germany and Switzerland* (1928)

9. The French complain of everything, and always.

Napoleon I, *Maxims* (1804–15)

10. The French are highly individualistic and ungovernable and the extraordinary thing is that, although they project great leaders about once a century, those leaders rule effectively but bequeath chaos.

C. L. Sulzberger, editorial, *The New York Times,* April 30, 1969

11. A French traveler with a sore throat is a wonderful thing to behold, but it takes more than tonsillitis to prevent a Frenchman from boasting.

Paul Theroux, *The Old Patagonian Express* (1979)

12. France has neither winter nor summer nor morals—apart from these drawbacks it is a fine country.

Mark Twain, *Notebook* (1935)

13. In France every man is either an anvil or a hammer; he is a beater or must be beaten.

Voltaire, in conversation with James Boswell, *Boswell on the Grand Tour: Germany and Switzerland* (1928)

14. The Revolution's most important result was Napoleon, whose most important result (as France learned in 1871, and again in 1914, and again in 1940) was the invention of Germany.

George F. Will, "1789's Echo in Iron," *Suddenly: The American Idea Abroad and At Home, 1986–1990* (1990)

362. FRANKNESS

See also 425. Honesty; 901. Sincerity; 1000. Truthfulness

1. Of all plagues, good Heaven, thy wrath can send, / Save, save, oh save me from the candid friend!

George Canning, *New Morality* (1798), 36.207

2. Straightforwardness, without the rules of propriety, becomes rudeness.

Confucius, *Analects* (6th c. b.c.), 8.2, tr. James Legge

3. Plain dealing is a jewel, but they that wear it are out of fashion.

Thomas Fuller, M.D., *Gnomologia* (1732), 3878

4. Praise, of course, is best: plain speech breeds hate. / But ah the Attic honey / Of telling a man exactly what you think of him!

Greek Anthology (7th c. b.c.–10th c. a.d.), 11.340, tr. Dudley Fitts

5. Honesty and wisdom are such a delightful pastime, at another person's expense!

Nathaniel Hawthorne, *The Blithedale Romance* (1852), 16

6. Lies kill love, it's been said. Well, what about frankness, then.

Abel Hermant, *Éloge du mensonge* (1925)

7. It is the weak and confused who worship the pseudosimplicities of brutal directness.

Marshall McLuhan, "The Tough as Narcissus," *The Mechanical Bride* (1951)

8. One open way of speaking introduces another open way of speaking, and draws out discoveries, like wine and love.

Montaigne, "Of profit and honesty," *Essays* (1580–88), tr. W. C. Hazlitt

9. Not every sheer truth / is the better for showing her face. Silence also / many times is the wisest thing for a man to have in his mind.

Pindar, *Odes* (5th c. B.C.), Nemea 5, tr. Richmond Lattimore

10. All faults may be forgiven of him who has perfect candor.

Walt Whitman, preface to *Leaves of Grass* (1855)

11. All cruel people describe themselves as paragons of frankness.

Tennessee Williams, *The Milk Train Doesn't Stop Here Anymore* (1963), 1

FRAUD

See 224. Deception

363. FREEDOM

See also 109. Captivity; 363. Free Speech; 537. Liberty; 823. Rights; 880. Self-Sufficiency; 889. Servitude

1. Better starve free than be a fat slave.

Aesop, "The Dog and the Wolf," *Fables* (6th c. B.C.?), tr. Joseph Jacobs

2. Freedom is not something that anybody can be given; freedom is something people take and people are as free as they want to be.

James Baldwin, "Notes for a Hypothetical Novel," *Nobody Knows My Name* (1961)

3. The misfortune which befalls man from his once having been a child is that his liberty was at first concealed from him, and all his life he will retain the nostalgia for a time when he was ignorant of its exigencies.

Simone de Beauvoir, *Pour une morale de l'ambiguïté* (1947), 2

4. Said a fervent young lady of Hammels,/ "I object to humanity's trammels!/I want to be free!/Like a bird!/Like a bee!/Oh, why am I classed with the mammals?"

Morris Bishop, "Limmericks Long After Lear," *A Subtreasury of American Humor* (1941)

5. Thinking of the future, establishing aims for oneself, having preferences—all this presupposes a belief in freedom, even if one occasionally ascertains that one doesn't feel it.

Albert Camus, *The Myth of Sisyphus* (1955), tr. Justin O'Brien

6. Freedom suppressed and again regained bites with keener fangs than freedom never endangered.

Cicero, *De Officiis* (44 B.C.), 2.7.24

7. Freedom is one of the principal goals of human endeavor, but the best use man can make of his freedom is to place limitations upon it.

Edwin Grant Conklin, "Science and the Faith of the Modern," *Scribner's Magazine*, 1925

8. Freedom has a thousand charms to show, / That slaves, howe'er contented, never know.

William Cowper, *Table Talk* (1782), 260

9. I only ask to be free. The butterflies are free.

Charles Dickens, *Bleak House* (1852), 6

10. Everything that is really great and inspiring is created by the individual who can labor in freedom.

Einstein, *Out of My Later Years* (1950), 7

11. A part of Fate is the freedom of man. Forever wells up the impulse of choosing and acting in his soul.

Emerson, "Fate," *The Conduct of Life* (1860)

12. If you cannot be free, be as free as you can.

Emerson, *Journals*, 1836

13. Though we love goodness and not stealing, yet also we love freedom and not preaching.

Emerson, *Journals*, 1842

14. Wild liberty breeds iron conscience; natures with great impulses have great resources, and return from far.

Emerson, "Power," *The Conduct of Life* (1860)

15. What is it that every man seeks? To be secure, to be happy, to do what he pleases without restraint and without compulsion.

Epictetus, *Discourses* (2nd c.), 4.1, tr. Thomas W. Higginson

16. Freedom is the greatest fruit of self-sufficiency.

EPICURUS, "VATICAN SAYINGS" (3RD C. B.C.), 77, IN *LETTERS, PRINCIPAL DOCTRINES, AND VATICAN SAYINGS*, TR. RUSSEL M. GEER

17. The American feels so rich in his opportunities for free expression that he often no longer knows what he is free from. Neither does he know where he is not free; he does not recognize his native autocrats when he sees them.

ERIK H. ERIKSON, *CHILDHOOD AND SOCIETY* (1950), 8

18. Whilst we strive / To live most free, we're caught in our own toils.

JOHN FORD, *THE LOVER'S MELANCHOLY* (1629), 1.3

19. The combination of economic and political *freedom* produced a golden age in both Great Britain and the United States in the nineteenth century.

MILTON FRIEDMAN & ROSE FRIEDMAN, *FREE TO CHOOSE* (1980)

20. The moment the slave resolves that he will no longer be a slave, his fetters fall. He frees himself and shows the way to others. Freedom and slavery are mental states.

MOHANDAS K. GANDHI, *NON-VIOLENCE IN PEACE AND WAR* (1948), 2.10

21. To know how to free oneself is nothing; the arduous thing is to know what to do with one's freedom.

ANDRÉ GIDE, *THE IMMORALIST* (1902), 1.1, TR. DOROTHY BUSSY

22. He only earns his freedom and existence who daily conquers them anew.

GOETHE, *FAUST* (1832), 2

23. We prate of freedom; we are in deadly fear of life.

LEARNED HAND, SPEECH, HARVARD LAW SCHOOL, MARCH 20, 1930

24. Liberty is the only true riches: of all the rest we are at once the masters and the slaves.

WILLIAM HAZLITT, "COMMONPLACES," *THE ROUND TABLE* (1817), 2

25. The history of the world is none other than the progress of the consciousness of freedom.

HEGEL, INTRODUCTION TO *PHILOSOPHY OF HISTORY* (1832), TR. JOHN SIBREE

26. There can be no real freedom without the freedom to fail.

ERIC HOFFER, *THE ORDEAL OF CHANGE* (1964), 12

27. Unless a man has the talents to make something of himself, freedom is an irksome burden.

ERIC HOFFER, *THE TRUE BELIEVER* (1951), 2.5.26

28. Freedom is the supreme good—freedom from self-imposed limitation.

ELBERT HUBBARD, *THE NOTE BOOK* (1927)

29. It is better to die on your feet than to live on your knees.

DOLORES IBARRURI, SPEECH IN PARIS, SEPT. 3. 1936

30. A man is either free or he is not. There cannot be any apprenticeship for freedom.

LE ROI JONES, "TOKENISM: 300 YEARS FOR FIVE CENTS," *HOME* (1966)

31. The most powerful single force in the world today is neither Communism nor capitalism, neither the H-bomb nor the guided missile—it is man's eternal desire to be free and independent.

JOHN F. KENNEDY, ADDRESS, WASHINGTON, D.C., JULY 2, 1957

32. Freedom is a very great reality. But it means, above all things, freedom from lies.

D. H. LAWRENCE, *PORNOGRAPHY AND OBSCENITY* (1930)

33. Man is a masterpiece of creation, if only because no amount of determinism can prevent him from believing that he acts as a free being.

GEORG CHRISTOPH LICHTENBERG, *APHORISMS* (1764–99), TR. J. P. STERN

34. Real freedom lies in wildness, not in civilization.

CHARLES A. LINDBERGH, "LIFE STREAM," *AUTOBIOGRAPHY OF VALUES* (1978)

35. True freedom is to share / All the chains our brothers wear, / And, with heart and hand, to be / Earnest to make others free!

JAMES RUSSELL LOWELL, "STANZAS ON FREEDOM" (1843), 3

36. You can't separate peace from freedom because no one can be at peace unless he has his freedom.

MALCOLM X, *MALCOLM X SPEAKS* (1965), 12

37. The dagger plunged in the name of Freedom is plunged into the breast of Freedom.

JOSÉ MARTÍ, *GRANOS DE ORO: PENSAMIENTOS SELECCIONADOS EN LAS OBRAS DE JOSÉ MARTÍ* (1942)

38. The liberty of the individual must be thus far limited: he must not make himself a nuisance to other people.

JOHN STUART MILL, *ON LIBERTY* (1859), 3

39. Let us forget such words, and all they mean, / as Hatred, Bitterness and Rancor, Greed, / Intolerance, Bigotry; let us renew / our faith and pledge to Man, his right to be / Himself, and free.

EDNA ST. VINCENT MILLAY, "POEM AND PRAYER FOR AN INVADING ARMY," *MAKE BRIGHT THE ARROWS* (1940)

40. Freedom is the will to be responsible to ourselves.

NIETZSCHE, "SKIRMISHES IN A WAR WITH THE AGE," 36, *TWILIGHT OF THE IDOLS* (1888), TR. ANTHONY M. LUDOVICI

41. Why do men carry guns and build prison camps, when the nurturing earth is made for freedom?

CYNTHIA OZICK, "THE SISTER MELONS OF J. M. COETZEE," *METAPHOR & MEMORY* (1989)

42. True individual freedom cannot exist without economic security and independence. People who are hungry and out of a job are the stuff of which dictatorships are made.

FRANKLIN D. ROOSEVELT, MESSAGE TO CONGRESS, JAN. 11, 1944

43. Freedom is baffling: / men having it often / know not they have it / till it is gone and / they no longer have it.

CARL SANDBURG, "FREEDOM IS A HABIT," *COMPLETE POEMS* (1950)

44. Freedom can't be bought for nothing. If you hold her precious, you must hold all else of little worth.

SENECA, *LETTERS TO LUCILIUS* (1ST C.), 104.34, TR. E. PHILLIPS BARKER

45. When a prisoner sees the door of his dungeon open, he dashes for it without stopping to think where he shall get his dinner outside.

GEORGE BERNARD SHAW, PREFACE TO *BACK TO METHUSELAH* (1921)

46. The very opposite of freedom is cliché, and nothing is less free, more inert with convention and hollow brutality, than a row of four-letter words.

GEORGE STEINER, "NIGHT WORDS," *LANGUAGE AND SILENCE* (1967)

47. We have confused the free with the free and easy.

ADLAI STEVENSON, *PUTTING FIRST THINGS FIRST* (1960)

48. Emancipation from the bondage of the soil / is no freedom for the tree.

RABINDRANATH TAGORE, *FIREFLIES* (1928)

49. As long as possible live free and uncommitted. It makes but little difference whether you are committed to a farm or the county jail.

THOREAU, "WHERE I LIVED, AND WHAT I LIVED FOR," *WALDEN* (1854)

50. If God exists, how can we lay claim to freedom, since He is its beginning and its end?

ELIE WIESEL, *THE GATES OF THE FOREST* (1966), TR. FRANCES FRENAYE

51. It is by his freedom that a man knows himself, by his sovereignty over his own life that a man measures himself.

ELIE WIESEL, "WHAT REALLY MAKES US FREE?" *FROM THE KINGDOM OF MEMORY* (1990)

FREEDOM OF THE PRESS

See 731. PRESS, FREEDOM OF THE

364. FREE SPEECH

See also 258. DISSENT; 364. FREEDOM; 537. LIBERTY; 630. NEWSPAPERS; 731. PRESS, FREEDOM OF THE; 764. PUBLISHING

1. I prefer a little free speech to no free speech at all; but how many have free speech or the chance or the mind for it; and is not free speech here as elsewhere clamped down on in ratio of its freedom and danger?

JAMES AGEE, *LETTERS OF JAMES AGEE TO FATHER FLYE* (1962)

2. Freedom of speech means that you shall not do something to people either for the views they have, or the views they express, or the words they speak or write.

HUGO BLACK, *ONE MAN'S STAND FOR FREEDOM* (1963)

3. Free speech is about as good a cause as the world has ever known. But, like the poor, it is always with us and gets shoved aside in favor of things which seem at some given moment more vital.

HEYWOOD BROUN, "THE MIRACLE OF DEBS," *NEW YORK WORLD*, OCT. 23, 1926

4. The very aim and end of our institutions is just this: that we may think what we like and say what we think.

OLIVER WENDELL HOLMES, SR., *THE PROFESSOR AT THE BREAKFAST TABLE* (1860), 5

5. The right to be heard does not automatically include the right to be taken seriously.

HUBERT H. HUMPHREY, SPEECH TO NATIONAL STUDENT ASSOCIATION, MADISON, WIS., AUG. 23, 1965

6. If all mankind, minus one, were of one opinion, and only one person were of the contrary opinion, mankind would be no more justified in silencing that one person, than he, if he had the power, would be justified in silencing mankind.

John Stuart Mill, *On Liberty* (1859), 2

7. The sound of tireless voices is the price we pay for the right to hear the music of our own opinions.

Adlai Stevenson, speech, New York City, Aug. 28, 1952

FREE WILL

See 363. Freedom; 867. Self-Determination

FRIENDLINESS

See 152. Company

365. FRIENDSHIP

See also 7. Acquaintances; 57. Association; 152. Company; 169. Confidences; 181. Constancy and Inconstancy; 301. Estrangement; 499. Intimacy; 547. Loneliness; 742. Promiscuity; 794. Relationships, Human; 915. Solitude

1. Friends are born, not made.

Henry Adams, *The Education of Henry Adams* (1907), 7

2. Friendship needs a certain parallelism of life, a community of thought, a rivalry of aim.

Henry Adams, *The Education of Henry Adams* (1907), 20

3. One friend in a lifetime is much; two are many; three are hardly possible.

Henry Adams, *The Education of Henry Adams* (1907), 20

4. A doubtful friend is worse than a certain enemy. Let a man be one thing or the other, and we then know how to meet him.

Aesop, "The Hound and the Hare," *Fables* (6th c. b.c.?), tr. Thomas James

5. A new friend is like new wine; when it has aged you will drink it with pleasure.

Apocrypha, Ecclesiasticus 9:10

6. Forsake not an old friend, for a new one does not compare with him.

Apocrypha, Ecclesiasticus 9:10

7. I keep my friends as misers do their treasure, because, of all the things granted us by wisdom, none is greater or better than friendship.

Pietro Aretino, letter to Giovanni Pollastra, July 7, 1537, tr. Samuel Putnam

8. Between friends there is no need of justice.

Aristotle, *Nicomachean Ethics* (4th c. b.c.), 8.1, tr. J. A. K. Thomson

9. My best friend is the man who in wishing me well wishes it for my sake.

Aristotle, *Nicomachean Ethics* (4th c. b.c.), 9.8, tr. J. A. K. Thomson

10. Wishing to be friends is quick work, but friendship is a slow-ripening fruit.

Aristotle, *Nicomachean Ethics* (4th c. b.c.), 8.3, tr. J. A. K. Thomson

11. Friendship is a single soul dwelling in two bodies.

Aristotle (4th c. b.c.), quoted in Diogenes Laertius' *Lives and Opinions of Eminent Philosophers* (3rd c. a.d.), tr. R. D. Hicks

12. Business, you know, may bring money, but friendship hardly ever does.

Jane Austen, *Emma* (1816), 34

13. There is little friendship in the world, and least of all between equals.

Francis Bacon, "Of Followers and Friends," *Essays* (1625)

14. This communicating of a man's self to his friend works two contrary effects; for it redoubleth joys, and cutteth griefs in half.

Francis Bacon, "Of Friendship," *Essays* (1625)

15. There's nothing worth the wear of winning, / But laughter and the love of friends.

Hilaire Belloc, "Dedicatory Ode," *Verses* (1910)

16. Love your friends as if they would some day hate you.

Bias (6th c. b.c.), quoted in Diogenes Laertius' *Lives and Opinions of Eminent Philosophers* (3rd c. a.d.), tr. R. D. Hicks

17. Faithful are the wounds of a friend; but the kisses of an enemy are deceitful.

Bible, Proverbs 27:6

18. A companion loves some agreeable qualities which a man may possess, but a friend loves the man himself.

James Boswell, *London Journal,* July 7, 1763

19. Friendship is a strong and habitual inclination in two persons to promote the good and happiness of one another.

Eustace Budgell, in *The Spectator* (1711–12), 385

20. Old friends, we say, are best, when some sudden disillusionment shakes our faith in a new comrade.

Gelett Burgess, "Old Friends and New," *The Romance of the Commonplace* (1916)

21. Friendship is like money, easier made than kept.

Samuel Butler (d. 1902), *Note-Books* (1912)

22. Friendship is Love without his wings!

Byron, "L'Amitié est L'Amour Sans Ailes" (1806)

23. Don't believe your friends when they ask you to be honest with them. All they really want is to be maintained in the good opinion they have of themselves.

Albert Camus, *The Fall* (1956)

24. A man must eat a peck of salt with his friend before he knows him.

Cervantes, *Don Quixote* (1605–15), 1.3.1, tr. John Ozell

25. Love with its paraphernalia of sexuality, jealousy, nostalgia and exaltation was easier to reognize than friendship, which seemed to have (excepting athletic equipment) no paraphernalia at all.

John Cheever, *Bullet Park* (1960)

26. It is not, as somebody once wrote, the smell of corn bread that calls us back from death; it is the lights and signs of love and friendship.

John Cheever, "The Housebreaker of Shady Hill," *The Stories of John Cheever* (1978)

27. Friendship makes prosperity more brilliant, and lightens adversity by dividing and sharing it.

Cicero, *De Amicitia* (44 B.C.)

28. My only politics have been friendship.

Jean Cocteau, *Diary of an Unknown* (1952; 1988), tr. Jesse Browner

29. The preservation of friendship is seen as opportunism. You are required to be in one camp or the other. You are enjoined to cut your heartstrings if they extend across the barricade.

Jean Cocteau, *Diary of an Unknown* (1952; 1988), tr. Jesse Browner

30. What a delight it is to make friends with someone you have despised!

Colette, "Sido and I," *Earthly Paradise* (1966), 1

31. The firmest friendships have been formed in mutual adversity, as iron is most strongly united by the fiercest flame.

Charles Caleb Colton, *Lacon* (1825), 1.365

32. The real friendships among men are so rare that when they occur they are famous.

Clarence Day, *This Simian World* (1920), 6

33. Friendships begin with liking or gratitude—roots that can be pulled up.

George Eliot, *Daniel Deronda* (1874–76), 4.32

34. A friend may well be reckoned the masterpiece of nature.

Emerson, "Friendship" *Essays: First Series* (1841)

35. Every man passes his life in the search after friendship.

Emerson, "Friendship," *Essays: First Series* (1841)

36. It is one of the blessings of old friends that you can afford to be stupid with them.

Emerson, *Journals,* 1836

37. The only way to have a friend is to be one.

Emerson, "Friendship," *Essays: First Series* (1841)

38. We do not so much need the help of our friends as the confidence of their help in need.

Epicurus, "Vatican Sayings" (3rd c. B.C.), 34, in *Letters, Principal Doctrines, and Vatican Sayings,* tr. Russel M. Geer

39. Friends show their love / in times of trouble, not in happiness.

Euripides, *Orestes* (408 B.C.), tr. William Arrowsmith

40. I loathe a friend whose gratitude grows old, / a friend who takes his friend's prosperity / but will not voyage with him in his grief.

Euripides, *Heracles* (c. 422 B.C.), tr. William Arrowsmith

41. I would / Prefer as friend a good man ignorant / Than one more clever who is evil too.

Euripides, *Ion* (c. 421–408 B.C.), tr. Ronald F. Willetts

42. One loyal friend is worth ten thousand relatives.

Euripides, *Orestes* (408 B.C.), tr. William Arrowsmith

43. Real friendship is shown in times of trouble; / prosperity is full of friends.

Euripides, *Hecuba* (c. 425 B.C.), tr. William Arrowsmith

44. It is in the thirties that we want friends.In the forties we know they won't save us any more than love did.

F. Scott Fitzgerald, *The Crack-Up* (1945)

45. Few are the friends of a man's self, most those of his circumstances.

Baltasar Gracián, *The Art of Worldly Wisdom* (1647), 156, tr. Joseph Jacobs

46. Friendship multiplies the good of life and divides the evil. 'Tis the sole remedy against misfortune, the very ventilation of the soul.

Baltasar Gracián, *The Art of Worldly Wisdom* (1647), 158, tr. Joseph Jacobs

47. Friends provoked become the bitterest of enemies.

Baltasar Gracián, *The Art of Worldly Wisdom* (1647), 257, tr. Joseph Jacobs

48. Have friends. 'Tis a second existence.

Baltasar Gracián, *The Art of Worldly Wisdom* (1647), 111, tr. Joseph Jacobs

49. No real friendship is ever made without an initial clashing which discloses the metal of each to each.

David Grayson, *Adventures in Contentment* (1907), 2

50. Nobody who is afraid of laughing, and heartily too, at his friend, can be said to have a true and thorough love for him.

Augustus William Hare, *Guesses at Truth* (1827)

51. Make all good men your well-wishers, and then, in the years' steady sifting, / Some of them turn into friends. Friends are the sunshine of life.

John Hay, "Distichs" (1871?), 18

52. True friendship is self-love at second-hand.

William Hazlitt, "On the Spirit of Obligations," *The Plain Speaker* (1826)

53. We often choose a friend as we do a mistress—for no particular excellence in themselves, but merely from some circumstance that flatters our self-love.

William Hazlitt, *Characteristics* (1823), 58

54. Women made such swell friends. Awfully swell. In the first place, you had to be in love with a woman to have a bsais of friendship.

Ernest Hemingway, *The Sun Also Rises* (1926)

55. Neither make thy friend equal to a brother; but if thou shalt have made him so, be not the first to do him wrong.

Hesiod, *Works and Days* (8th c. b.c.), 707, tr. J. Banks

56. One cannot help using his early friends as the seaman uses the log, to mark his progress.

Oliver Wendell Holmes, Sr., *The Autocrat of the Breakfast Table* (1858), 4

57. A sympathetic friend can be quite as dear as a brother.

Homer, *Odyssey* (9th c. b.c.), 8, tr. E. V. Rieu

58. Your friend is the man who knows all about you, and still likes you.

Elbert Hubbard, *The Note Book* (1927)

59. My father always used to say that when you die, if you've got five real friends, you've had a great life.

Lee Iacocca, *Iacocca: An Autobiography* (1984) with William Novak

60. That man travels the longest journey that undertakes it in search of a sincere friend.

Ali Ibn-Abi-Talib, *Sentences* (7th c.), 160, tr. Simon Ockley

61. Friends are to be feared, not so much for what they make us do as for what they keep us from doing.

Henrik Ibsen, quoted in André Gide's *Journals*, 1917, tr. Justin O'Brien

62. Friendship is seldom lasting but between equals, or where the superiority on one side is reduced by some equivalent advantage on the other.

Samuel Johnson, *The Rambler* (1750–52), 64

63. That friendship may be at once fond and lasting, there must not only be equal virtue on each part, but virtue of the same kind; not only the same end must be proposed, but the same means must be approved by both.

Samuel Johnson, *The Rambler* (1750–52), 64

64. When my friends are one-eyed, I look at them in profile.

Joseph Joubert, *Pensées* (1842) titre préliminaire

65. Let us make clear that we will never turn our back on our steadfast friends in Israel, whose adherence to the democratic way must be admired by all friends of freedom.

John F. Kennedy, *The Strategy of Peace* (1960)

66. A true friend is the greatest of all blessings, and that which we take the least care of all to acquire.

La Rochefoucauld, *Maxims* (1665), tr. Kenneth Pratt

67. Friendship is only a reciprocal conciliation of interests, and an exchange of good offices; it is a species of commerce out of which self-love always expects to gain something.

La Rochefoucauld, *Maxims* (1665)

68. However rare true love may be, it is less so than true friendship.

La Rochefoucauld, *Maxims* (1665), tr. Kenneth Pratt

69. We do not regret the loss of our friends by reasons of their merit, but because of our needs and for the good opinion that we believed them to have held of us.

La Rochefoucauld, *Maxims* (1665), tr. Kenneth Pratt

70. You can date the evolving life of a mind, like the age of a tree, by the rings of friendship formed by the expanding central trunk.

Mary McCarthy, *How I Grew* (1987)

71. It's no good trying to keep up old friendships. It's painful for both sides. The fact is, one grows out of people, and the only thing is to face it.

W. Somerset Maugham, *Cakes and Ale* (1930), 1

72. We know our friends by their defects rather than by their merits.

W. Somerset Maugham, *The Summing Up* (1938), 57

73. A man of active and resilient mind outwears his friendships just as certainly as he outwears his love affairs, his politics and his epistemology.

H. L. Mencken, *Prejudices: Third Series* (1922), 14

74. If a man should importune me to give a reason why I loved him, I find it could no otherwise be expressed, than by making answer: because it was he, because it was I.

Montaigne, "Of friendship," *Essays* (1580–88), tr. W. C. Hazlitt

75. Friendship is a contract in which we render small services in expectation of big ones.

Montesquieu, *Pensées et jugements* (1899)

76. Love demands infinitely less than friendship.

George Jean Nathan, "Attitude toward Love and Marriage," *The Autobiography of an Attitude* (1925)

77. A friend should be a master at guessing and keeping still.

Nietzsche, "On the Friend," *Thus Spoke Zarathustra* (1883–92), 1, tr. Walter Kaufmann

78. Women can form a friendship with a man very well; but to preserve it—to that end a slight physical antipathy must probably help.

Nietzsche, *Human, All Too Human* (1878), 390, in *The Portable Nietzsche*, tr. Walter Kaufmann

79. Hold a true friend with both your hands.

Nigerian Proverb

80. Love is rarer than genius itself. And friendship is rarer than love.

Charles Péguy, "The Search for Truth," *Basic Verities* (1943), tr. Julian Green

81. Sooner or later you've heard all your best friends have to say. Then comes the tolerance of real love.

Ned Rorem, "Random Notes from a Diary," *Music from Inside Out* (1967)

82. God save me from my friends—I can protect myself from my enemies.

Proverb, common in many languages

83. Friendship either finds or makes equals.

Publilius Syrus, *Moral Sayings* (1st c. B.C.), 32, tr. Darius Lyman

84. The friendship that can come to an end, never really began.

Publilius Syrus, *Moral Sayings* (1st c. B.C.), 719, tr. Darius Lyman

85. We die as often as we lose a friend.

Publilius Syrus, *Moral Sayings* (1st c. B.C.), 323, tr. Darius Lyman

86. Friendship admits of difference of character, as love does that of sex.

Joseph Roux, *Meditations of a Parish Priest* (1886), 9.24, tr. Isabel F. Hapgood

87. To like and dislike the same things, this is what makes a solid friendship.

Sallust, *Conspiracy of Catiline* (1st c. B.C.), 20

88. It is characteristic of spontaneous friendship to take on first, without enquiry and almost at first sight, the unseen doings and unspoken sentiments of our friends; the parts known give us evidence enough that the unknown parts cannot be much amiss.

George Santayana, *Persons and Places: My Host the World* (1953), 6

89. To cement a new friendship, especially between foreigners or persons of a different social world, a spark with which both were secretly charged must fly from person to person, and cut across the accidents of place and time.

George Santayana, *Persons and Places: The Middle Span* (1945), 2

90. No enemy is so annoying as one who was a friend, or still is a friend, and there are many more of these than one would suspect.

William Saroyan, *Chance Meetings* (1978)

91. A friend should bear his friend's infirmities.

SHAKESPEARE, *JULIUS CAESAR* (1599–1600), 4.3.86

92. Friendship is constant in all other things / Save in the office and affairs of love.

SHAKESPEARE, *MUCH ADO ABOUT NOTHING* (1598–99), 2.1.182

93. We need new friends; some of us are cannibals who have eaten their old friends up; others must have ever-renewed audiences before whom to re-enact the ideal version of their lives.

LOGAN PEARSALL SMITH, *AFTERTHOUGHTS* (1931), 3

94. I only asked my friends to be friendly and polite,/I found them indifferent and censorious;/The one I left to silence, the other to reproach:/God send me over all such friends victorious.

STEVIE SMITH, "TWO FRIENDS," IN *ME AGAIN* (1981)

95. I cannot love a friend whose love is words.

SOPHOCLES, *ANTIGONE* (442–41 B.C.), TR. ELIZABETH WYCKOFF

96. To throw away / an honest friend is, as it were, to throw / your life away.

SOPHOCLES, *OEDIPUS THE KING* (C. 430 B.C.), TR. DAVID GRENE

97. I am a hoarder of two things: documents and trusted friends.

MURIEL SPARK, "INTRODUCTION," *CURRICULUM VITAE* (1992)

98. I'm back with my own kind of people here now, the bums and drinkers and no goods and it is a fine thing.

JOHN STEINBECK, *STEINBECK: A LIFE IN LETTERS* (1975), EDS. ELAINE STEINBECK AND ROBERT WALLSTEN

99. A man cannot be said to succeed in this life who does not satisfy one friend.

THOREAU, *JOURNAL*, FEB. 19, 1857

100. In paradoxical fashion she had always been a woman who easily made friends and yet was friendless.

DIANA TRILLING, *MRS. HARRIS: THE DEATH OF THE SCARSDALE DOCTOR* (1981)

101. The proper office of a friend is to side with you when you are in the wrong. Nearly anybody will side with you when you are in the right.

MARK TWAIN, *NOTEBOOK* (1935)

102. Friendship is the marriage of the soul, and this marriage is liable to divorce.

VOLTAIRE, "FRIENDSHIP," *PHILOSOPHICAL DICTIONARY* (1764)

103. Friendship marks a life even more deeply than love. Love risks degenerating into obsession, friendship is never anything but sharing.

ELIE WIESEL, *THE GATES OF THE FOREST* (1966), TR. FRANCES FRENAYE

104. You cannot be friends upon any other terms than upon the terms of equality.

WOODROW WILSON, SPEECH, OCT. 27, 1913

FRUGALITY

See 701. PLAIN LIVING; 977. THRIFT

366. FRUSTRATION

See also 238. DESIRES; 427. HOPE; 459. IMPOTENCE; 1010. UNFULFILLMENT

1. Not to get what you have set your heart on is almost as bad as getting nothing at all.

ARISTOTLE, *NICOMACHEAN ETHICS* (4TH C. B.C.), 9.1, TR. J. A. K. THOMSON

2. The worst things: / To be in bed and sleep not, / To want for one who comes not, / To try to please and please not.

EGYPTIAN PROVERB

3. I suppose she only wanted what she couldn't have. Well, people were that way.

ERNEST HEMINGWAY, *THE SUN ALSO RISES* (1926)

4. By the time I reach the hotel, my frustration is such that I compensate with a Gargantuan tea of watercress sandwiches, rock buns, and pastry that utterly ruin my digestion. It makes for a stimulating afternoon.

S.J. PERELMAN, *THE RISING GORGE* (1961)

5. If women are often frustrated because men do not respond to their troubles by offering matching troubles, men are often frustrated because women do.

DEBORAH TANNEN, *YOU JUST DON'T UNDERSTAND* (1990)

FULFILLMENT

See 504. INVOLVEMENT; 717. POTENTIAL; 1010. UNFULFILLMENT

367. FUNERALS

See also 103. BURIAL; 221. DEATH; 610. MOURNING

1. People ask me what makes a good funeral, and I tell them the most important thing is your man in the casket. If you have a man of substance in there, you have the makings of a first-class funeral.

Cleveland Amory, "These Damnable Religious Changes," *The Trouble with Nowadays* (1979)

2. Spare me the whispering, crowded room, / The friends who come and gape and go, / The ceremonious air of gloom— / All, which makes death a hideous show.

Matthew Arnold, "A Wish" (1867)

3. Funeral, n. A pageant whereby we attest our respect for the dead by enriching the undertaker, and strengthen our grief by an expenditure that deepens our groans and doubles our tears.

Ambrose Bierce, *The Devil's Dictionary* (1881–1911)

4. [F]uneral expenses are the curse of the poor everywhere on earth, they are wasteful and unnecessary, they are the price of foolish ostentation and a display that is less an evidence of grief than a vulgar travesty of those pompous obsequies where no grief is.

Joyce Cary, *Except the Lord* (1953)

5. As soon as she opened the [funeral parlor] door, she was in the hands of a gloved and obsequious usher, ready to sympathize with a grief more profound and sedate than any grief of hers would ever be.

John Cheever, "The Hartleys," *The Stories of John Cheever* (1980)

6. The chief mourner does not always attend the funeral.

Emerson, *Journals,* 1832

7. No American is prepared to attend his own funeral without the services of highly skilled cosmeticians. Part of the American dream, after all, is to live long and die young.

Edgar Z. Friedenberg, "Adult Imagery and Feeling," *The Vanishing Adolescent* (1959)

8. After sixty years the stern sentence of the burial service seems to have a meaning that one did not notice in former years. There begins to be something personal about it.

Oliver Wendell Holmes, Sr., *Over the Teacups* (1891), 2

9. The pomp of funerals has more regard to the vanity of the living than the honour of the dead.

La Rochefoucauld, *Maxims* (1665), tr. Kenneth Pratt

10. One ought to go to a funeral instead of to church when one feels the need of being uplifted. People have on good black clothes, and they take off their hats and look at the coffin, and behave serious and reverent, and nobody dares to make a bad joke.

Thomas Mann, *The Magic Mountain* (1924), 4.3, tr. H. T. Lowe-Porter

11. We simply rob ourselves when we make presents to the dead.

Publilius Syrus, *Moral Sayings* (1st c. b.c.), 1034, tr. Darius Lyman

12. The eulogist spoke charmingly, without a trace of sadness, almost as though he were preparing to present the corpse in the casket with a large check rather than to usher it on to the crematorium.

Philip Roth, *The Counterlife* (1987)

13. The only way to have a funeral is to invite everyone who ever knew the person and just wait for the accident to happen—somebody who comes in out of the blue and says the truth. Everything else is table manners.

Philip Roth, *The Counterlife* (1987)

14. A funeral isn't for the dead. You'll simply be a stage set for a kind of festival maybe. And besides, you won't even be there.

John Steinbeck, *Steinbeck: A Life in Letters* (1975), Eds. Elaine Steinbeck and Robert Wallsten

15. Funerals are pretty compared to death.

Tennessee Williams, *A Streetcar Named Desire* (1947), 1

368. FUTURE

See also 240. Destiny; 318. Expectation; 676. Past; 729. Present

1. The future / you shall know when it has come; before then, forget it.

Aeschylus, *Agamemnon* (458 b.c.), tr. Richmond Lattimore

2. Never let the future disturb you. You will meet it, if you have to, with the same weapons of reason which today arm you against the present.

Marcus Aurelius, *Meditations* (2nd c.), 7.8, tr. Maxwell Staniforth

3. The future is like heaven—everyone exalts it but no one wants to go there now.

James Baldwin, "A Fly in Buttermilk," *Nobody Knows My Name* (1961)

4. We steal if we touch tomorrow. It is God's.

HENRY WARD BEECHER, *PROVERBS FROM PLYMOUTH PULPIT* (1887)

5. Future, n. That period of time in which our affairs prosper, our friends are true and our happiness is assured.

AMBROSE BIERCE, *THE DEVIL'S DICTIONARY* (1881–1911)

6. You can never plan the future by the past.

EDMUND BURKE, *LETTER TO A MEMBER OF THE NATIONAL ASSEMBLY* (1791)

7. Tomorrow lurks in us, the latency to be all that was not achieved before.

LOREN EISELEY, "MAN AGAINST THE UNIVERSE," *THE STAR THROWER* (1978)

8. If a man carefully examine his thoughts he will be surprised to find how much he lives in the future. His well-being is always ahead. Such a creature is probably immortal.

EMERSON, *JOURNALS,* 1827

9. Remember that the future is neither ours nor wholly not ours, so that we may neither count on it as sure to come nor abandon hope of it as certain not to be.

EPICURUS, LETTER TO MENOECEUS (3RD C. B.C.), IN *LETTERS, PRINCIPAL DOCTRINES, AND VATICAN SAYINGS,* TR. RUSSEL M. GEER

10. The man least dependent upon the morrow goes to meet the morrow most cheerfully.

EPICURUS (3RD. C. B.C.), QUOTED IN PLUTARCH'S "CONTENTMENT," *MORALIA* (C. A.D. 100), TR. MOSES HADAS

11. What we look for does not come to pass; / God finds a way for what none foresaw.

EURIPIDES, *ALCESTIS* (438 B.C.), TR. RICHMOND LATTIMORE

12. He that fears not the future may enjoy the present.

THOMAS FULLER, M.D., *GNOMOLOGIA* (1732), 2100

13. Only mothers can think of the future—because they give birth to it in their children.

MAXIM GORKY, *VASSA ZHELEZNOVA* (1910), TR. ALEXANDER BAKSHY

14. The future may be an enemy. Time can turn happy days and nights into nothing.

ELIZABETH HARDWICK, "WIVES AND MISTRESSES," *BARTLEBY IN MANHATTAN* (1983)

15. A preoccupation with the future not only prevents us from seeing the present as it is but often prompts us to rearrange the past.

ERIC HOFFER, *THE PASSIONATE STATE OF MIND* (1954), 75

16. The only way to predict the future is to have power to shape the future.

ERIC HOFFER, *THE PASSIONATE STATE OF MIND* (1954), 78

17. There is nothing like dream to create the future. Utopia to-day, flesh and blood tomorrow.

VICTOR HUGO, "MARIUS," *LES MISÉRABLES* (1862), 4.1, TR. CHARLES E. WILBOUR

18. Yesterday is not ours to recover, but tomorrow is ours to win or to lose.

LYNDON B. JOHNSON, ADDRESS TO THE NATION, NOV. 28, 1963

19. The most prevalent opinion among our so confused contemporaries seems to be that tomorrow will be wonderful—that is, unless it is indescribably terrible, or unless indeed there just isn't any.

JOSEPH WOOD KRUTCH, "THE TWENTIETH CENTURY: DAWN OR TWILIGHT?" *HUMAN NATURE AND THE HUMAN CONDITION* (1959)

20. Morning comes whether you set the alarm or not.

URSULA K. LE GUIN, "SCIENCE FICTION AND THE FUTURE," *DANCING AT THE EDGE OF THE WORLD* (1989)

21. Life is an irreversible process and for that reason its future can never be a repetition of the past.

WALTER LIPPMANN, "REVOLUTION AND CULTURE," *A PREFACE TO POLITICS* (1914)

22. Do we not all spend the greater part of our lives under the shadow of an event that has not yet come to pass?

MAURICE MAETERLINCK, "THE PRE-DESTINED," *THE TREASURE OF THE HUMBLE* (1896), TR. ALFRED SUTRO

23. We are never present with, but always beyond ourselves; fear, desire, hope, still push us on toward the future.

MONTAIGNE, "THAT OUR AFFECTIONS CARRY THEMSELVES BEYOND US," *ESSAYS* (1580–88), TR. W. C. HAZLITT

24. People live for the morrow, because the day-after-to-morrow is doubtful.

NIETZSCHE, *THE WILL TO POWER* (1888), TR. ANTHONY M. LUDOVICI

25. It is the great past, not the dizzy present, that is the best door to the future.

CAMILLE PAGLIA, *SEX, ART, AND AMERICAN CULTURE* (1992)

26. I believe the future is only the past again, entered through another gate.

SIR ARTHUR WING PINERO, *THE SECOND MRS. TANQUERAY* (1893), 4

27. The future struggles that it may not become the past.

Publilius Syrus, *Moral Sayings* (1st c. B.C.), 290, tr. Darius Lyman

28. The future enters into us in order to transform itself in us long before it happens.

Rainer Maria Rilke, *Letters to a Young Poet,* Aug. 12, 1904, tr. M. D. Herter Norton

29. No one can be certain where a nation which spans two continents, whose history begins in the faint traces of early civilization, a nation now struggling to find a new and valid philosophy of existence, will be propelled by the transcendental forces of the nuclear age.

Harrison E. Salisbury, *Russia* (1965)

30. O that a man might know / The end of this day's business ere it come!

Shakespeare, *Julius Caesar* (1599–1600), 5.1.122

31. We know what we are, but know not what we may be.

Shakespeare, *Hamlet* (1600), 4.5.42

32. What men have seen they know; / But what shall come hereafter / No man before the event can see, / Nor what end waits for him.

Sophocles, *Ajax* (c. 447 B.C.), tr. John Moore

33. The future has waited long enough; if we do not grasp it, other hands, grasping hard and bloody, will.

Adlai Stevenson, quoted in Murray Kempton's *America Comes of Middle Age* (1963)

34. The future is too interesting and dangerous to be entrusted to any predictable, reliable agency. We need all the fallibility we can get. Most of all, we need to preserve the absolute unpredictability and total improbability of our connected minds.

Lewis Thomas, "Computers," *The Lives of a Cell* (1974)

35. [H]e was like a man who stands upon a hill above the town he has left, yet does not say "The town is near," but turns his eyes upon the distant soaring ranges.

Thomas Wolfe, *Look Homeward, Angel* (1929)

G

369. GAMBLING

1. Whoever plays deep must necessarily lose his money or his character.

LORD CHESTERFIELD, *LETTERS TO HIS GODSON* (1773)

2. The best throw of the dice is to throw them away.

ENGLISH PROVERB

3. Gambling is the great leveller. All men are equal—at cards.

NIKOLAI GOGOL, *GAMBLERS* (1842)

4. True luck consists not in holding the best of the cards at the table: / Luckiest he who knows just when to rise and go home.

JOHN HAY, "DISTICHS" (1871?), 15

5. I am sorry I have not learnt to play at cards. It is very useful in life: it generates kindness and consolidates society.

SAMUEL JOHNSON, QUOTED IN BOSWELL'S *JOURNAL OF A TOUR TO THE HEBRIDES WITH SAMUEL JOHNSON,* NOV. 21, 1773

6. Cards are war, in disguise of a sport.

CHARLES LAMB, "MRS. BATTLE'S OPINIONS ON WHIST," *ESSAYS OF ELIA* (1823)

7. Adventure upon all the tickets in the lottery, and you lose for certain; and the greater the number of your tickets the nearer you approach to this certainty.

ADAM SMITH, *THE WEALTH OF NATIONS* (1776), 1.10

GAMES

See 369. GAMBLING; 703. PLAY; 929. SPORTS

370. GARBAGE

1. One thing about pioneers that you don't hear mentioned is that they are invariably, by their nature, mess-makers. They go forging ahead, seeing only their noble, distant goal, and never notice any of the crud and debris they leave behind them.

ROBERT M. PIRSIG, *ZEN AND THE ART OF MOTORCYCLE MAINTENANCE* (1974)

371. GARDENING

1. A weed is no more than a flower in disguise, / Which is seen through at once, if love give a man eyes.

JAMES RUSSELL LOWELL, *A FABLE FOR CRITICS* (1848)

2. The only solution is to plow everything under and live on pie.

S.J. PERELMAN, *THE MOST OF S.J. PERELMAN* (1958)

3. There is always something else to do. A gardener should have nine times as many lives as a cat.

VITA SACKVILLE-WEST, *VITA SACKVILLE-WEST'S GARDEN BOOK* (1983)

4. Successful gardening is not necessarily a question of wealth. it is a question of love, taste, and knowledge.

VITA SACKVILLE-WEST, *VITA SACKVILLE-WEST'S GARDEN BOOK* (1983)

5. I like muddling things up; and if a herb looks nice in a border, then why not grow it there? Why not grow anything anywhere so long as it looks right where it is? That is, surely, the art of gardening.

VITA SACKVILLE-WEST, *VITA SACKVILLE-WEST'S GARDEN BOOK* (1983)

6. To own a bit of ground, to scratch it with a hoe, to plant seeds, and watch their renewal of life,—this is the commonest delight of the race, the most satisfactory thing a man can do.

CHARLES DUDLEY WARNER, "PRELIMINARY," *MY SUMMER IN A GARDEN* (1871)

372. GAUCHERIE

See also 396. GRACE

1. God may forgive sins, but awkwardness has no forgiveness in heaven or earth.

EMERSON, TITLE ESSAY, *SOCIETY AND SOLITUDE* (1876)

2. It is a great misfortune not to possess sufficient wit to speak well, nor sufficient judgment to keep silent.

LA BRUYÈRE, *CHARACTERS* (1688), 5.18

373. GENERALIZATION

1. All generalizations are false, including this one.

ALEXANDER CHASE, *PERSPECTIVES* (1966)

2. The cause of all human evils is the not being able to apply general principles to special cases.

EPICTETUS, *DISCOURSES* (2ND C.), 4.1, TR. THOMAS W. HIGGINSON

3. Intellectual generalities are always interesting, but generalities in morals mean absolutely nothing.

OSCAR WILDE, *A WOMAN OF NO IMPORTANCE* (1893), 2

374. GENERATIONS

See also 184. CONTEMPORANEOUSNESS; 298. ERA

1. It is always self-defeating to pretend to the style of a generation younger than your own; it simply erases your own experience in history.

RENATA ADLER, "WHAT'S SO FUNNY?" *THE NEW YORK TIMES,* JULY 7, 1968

2. [O]f all things I find most unbearable is the injustice of one generation to another.

JOYCE CARY, *TO BE A PILGRIM* (1942)

3. Amongst democratic nations, each new generation is a new people.

ALEXIS DE TOCQUEVILLE, *DEMOCRACY IN AMERICA* (1834–39), 2.1.13

4. There was a succession of technological floods, and each new generation looked back to its youth like Father Noah.

MICHAEL HARRINGTON, *THE ACCIDENTAL CENTURY* (1966)

5. It is mere childishness to expect men to believe as their fathers did; that is, if they have any minds of their own. The world is a whole generation older and wiser than when the father was of his son's age.

OLIVER WENDELL HOLMES, SR., *OVER THE TEACUPS* (1891), 10

6. Like leaves on trees the race of man is found,— / Now green in youth, now withering on the ground; / Another race the following spring supplies: / They fall successive, and successive rise.

HOMER, *ILIAD* (9TH C. B.C.), 6.181, TR. ALEXANDER POPE

7. Each generation takes a special pleasure in removing the household gods of its parents from their pedestals, and consigning them to the cupboard.

WILLIAM RALPH INGE, "THE VICTORIAN AGE," *OUTSPOKEN ESSAYS: SECOND SERIES* (1922)

8. Every old man complains of the growing depravity of the world, of the petulance and insolence of the rising generation.

SAMUEL JOHNSON, *THE RAMBLER* (1750–52), 50

9. We have to hate our immediate predecessors to get free of their authority.

D. H. LAWRENCE, QUOTED IN HENRY MILLER'S "CREATIVE DEATH," *THE WISDOM OF THE HEART* (1941)

10. Our strife pertains to ourselves—to the passing generations of men—and it can without convulsion be hushed forever with the passing of one generation.

ABRAHAM LINCOLN, MESSAGE TO CONGRESS, DEC. 1, 1862

11. In a brief space the generations of living beings are changed and like runners pass on the torches of life.

LUCRETIUS, *ON THE NATURE OF THINGS* (1ST C. B.C.), 2

12. Every generation revolts against its fathers and makes friends with its grandfathers.

LEWIS MUMFORD, *THE BROWN DECADES* (1931)

13. Every age and generation must be as free to act for itself in all cases as the ages and generations which preceded it. The vanity and presumption of governing beyond the grave is the most ridiculous and insolent of all tyrannies.

THOMAS PAINE, *THE RIGHTS OF MAN* (1791), 1

14. We think our fathers fools, so wise we grow; / Our wiser sons, no doubt, will think us so.

ALEXANDER POPE, *AN ESSAY ON CRITICISM* (1711), 2.237

15. It is not new for the older generation to bewail the indolence of the young, and there is a tendency for the latter to maintain much of the older ethic screened by a new semantics and an altered ideology.

DAVID RIESMAN, *ABUNDANCE FOR WHAT?* (1964)

16. Nothing so dates a man as to decry the younger generation.

ADLAI STEVENSON, SPEECH, UNIVERSITY OF WISCONSIN, MADISON, OCT. 8, 1952

17. It is one of nature's ways that we often feel closer to distant generations than to the generation immediately preceding us.

IGOR STRAVINSKY, *CONVERSATIONS WITH IGOR STRAVINSKY* (1959)

18. Within your own generation—the same songs, the same wars, the same attitudes toward those wars, the same rules and radio shows in the air—you can gauge the possibilities and impossibilities. With a

person of another generation, you are treading water, playing with fire.

John Updike, *Rabbit at Rest* (1990)

375. GENEROSITY

See also 56. Assistance; 384. Gifts and Giving; 433. Humanitarianism; 525. Largeness; 888. Services; 1021. Unselfishness

1. Cast thy bread upon the waters: for thou shalt find it after many days.

Bible, Ecclesiastes 11:1

2. If a man is prodigal, he cannot be truly generous.

James Boswell, *London Journal,* Feb. 9, 1763

3. If riches increase, let thy mind hold pace with them; and think it not enough to be liberal, but munificent.

Sir Thomas Browne, *A Letter to a Friend* (1690)

4. Generosity is the flower of justice.

Nathaniel Hawthorne, *American Note-Books,* Dec. 19, 1850

5. Of all virtues, magnanimity is the rarest. There are a hundred persons of merit for one who willingly acknowledges it in another.

William Hazlitt, *Characteristics* (1823), 1

6. The hand of liberality is stronger than the arm of power.

Sa'di, *Gulistan* (1258), 2.48, tr. James Ross

7. Generosity gives assistance, rather than advice.

Vauvenargues, *Reflections and Maxims* (1746), 491, tr. F. G. Stevens

8. Magnanimity will not consider the prudence of its motives.

Vauvenargues, *Reflections and Maxims* (1746), 130, tr. F. G. Stevens

376. GENIUS

See also 311. Excellence; 377. Genius vs. Talent; 401. Greatness; 952. Superiority

1. Genius is sorrow's child.

John Adams, letter to Benjamin Waterhouse, May 21, 1821

2. No great genius has ever been without some madness.

Aristotle (4th c. b.c.), quoted in Seneca's "On Peace of Mind," *Moral Essays* (1st c. a.d.)

3. Geniuses are the luckiest of mortals because what they must do is the same as what they most want to do.

W. H. Auden, foreword to Dag Hammarskjöld's *Markings* (1964)

4. Genius is but a greater aptitude for patience.

Attributed to Georges Buffon

5. Discretion is deadly to genius; ruinous to talent.

E.M. Cioran, "Some Blind Alleys: A Letter," in *The Art of the Personal Essay* (1994), ed. Phillip Lopate

6. Never imitate the eccentricities of genius, but toil after it in its truer flights. They are not so easy to follow, but they lead to higher regions.

Charles Dickens, *The Selected Letters of Charles Dickens,* ed. F.W. Dupee (1960)

7. Too often we forget that genius, too, depends upon the data within its reach, that even Archimedes could not have devised Edison's inventions.

Ernest Dimnet, *The Art of Thinking* (1928), 4

8. Patience is a necessary ingredient of genius.

Benjamin Disraeli, *Contarini Fleming* (1832), 4.5

9. Sensibility alters from generation to generation in everybody, whether we will or no; but expression is only altered by a man of genius.

T. S. Eliot, introductory essay (1930) to Samuel Johnson's *London: A Poem and The Vanity of Human Wishes*

10. Genius always finds itself a century too early.

Emerson, *Journals,* 1840

11. Genius seems to consist merely in trueness of sight, in using such words as show that the man was an eye-witness, and not a repeater of what was told.

Emerson, *Journals,* 1834

12. The young man reveres men of genius, because, to speak truly, they are more himself than he is.

Emerson, "The Poet," *Essays: Second Series* (1844)

13. Genius is the ability to put into effect what is in your mind.

F. Scott Fitzgerald, "The Note-Books," *The Crack-Up* (1945)

14. Genius goes around the world in its youth incessantly apologizing for having large feet. What wonder that later in life it should be inclined to raise those feet too swiftly to fools and bores.

F. Scott Fitzgerald, "The Note-Books," *The Crack-Up* (1945)

15. He whose genius appears deepest and truest excels his fellows in nothing save the knack of expression; he throws out occasionally a lucky hint at truths of which every human soul is profoundly though unutterably conscious.

Nathaniel Hawthorne, "The Procession of Life," *Mosses from an Old Manse* (1846)

16. Genius is a native to the soil where it grows—is fed by the air, and warmed by the sun; and is not a hothouse plant or an exotic.

William Hazlitt, "Commonplaces," *The Round Table* (1817), 27

17. The definition of genius is that it acts unconsciously; and those who have produced immortal works have done so without knowing how or why.

William Hazlitt, "Whether Genius Is Conscious of Its Powers?" *The Plain Speaker* (1826)

18. A person of genius should marry a person of character. Genius does not herd with genius.

Oliver Wendell Holmes, Sr., *The Professor at the Breakfast Table* (1860), 11

19. The true genius is a mind of large general powers, accidentally determined to some particular direction.

Samuel Johnson, *Lives of the Poets: Cowley* (1779–81)

20. Everyone is a genius at least once a year. The real geniuses simply have their bright ideas closer together.

Georg Christoph Lichtenberg, *Aphorisms* (1764–99), tr. H. Hatfield

21. Towering genius disdains a beaten path. It seeks regions hitherto unexplored.

Abraham Lincoln, speech, Springfield, Ill., Jan. 27, 1838

22. Genius can only breathe freely in an *atmosphere* of freedom.

John Stuart Mill, *On Liberty* (1859), 3

23. The genius—in work and in deed—is necessarily a squanderer: the fact that he spends himself constitutes his greatness.

Nietzsche, "Skirmishes in a War with the Age," 44, *Twilight of the Idols* (1888), tr. Anthony M. Ludovici

24. There are two types of genius: one which above all begets and wants to beget, and another which prefers being fertilized and giving birth.

Nietzsche, *Beyond Good and Evil* (1886), 248, tr. Walter Kaufmann

25. Better beware of notions like genius and inspiration; they are a sort of magic wand and should be used sparingly by anybody who wants to see things clearly.

José Ortega y Gasset, *Notes on the Novel* (1925)

26. Men of genius are far more abundant than is supposed. In fact, to appreciate thoroughly the work of what we call genius, is to possess all the genius by which the work was produced.

Edgar Allan Poe, *Marginalia* (1844–49), 3

27. The true genius shudders at incompleteness—and usually prefers silence to saying the something which is not every thing that should be said.

Edgar Allan Poe, *Marginalia* (1844–49), 9

28. The concept of genius as akin to madness has been carefully fostered by the inferiority complex of the public.

Ezra Pound, *The ABC of Reading* (1934), 8

29. We should like to have some towering geniuses, to reveal us to ourselves in colour and fire, but of course they would have to fit into the pattern of our society and be able to take orders from sound administrative types.

J. B. Priestley, "Candles Burning Low," *Thoughts in the Wilderness* (1957)

30. Genius has never been accepted without a measure of condonement.

Seneca, *Letters to Lucilius* (1st c.), 114.12, tr. E. Phillips Barker

31. The deep waters of time will flow over us: only a few men of genius will lift a head above the surface, and though doomed eventually to pass into the same silence, will fight against oblivion and for a long time hold their own.

Seneca, *Letters to Lucilius* (1st c.), 21.5, tr. E. Phillips Barker

32. It takes a lot of time to be a genius, you have to sit around so much doing nothing, really doing nothing.

Gertrude Stein, *Everybody's Autobiography* (1937)

33. When a true genius appears in the world, you may know him by this sign, that the dunces are all in confederacy against him.

Jonathan Swift, *Thoughts on Various Subjects* (1711)

34. The persecution of genius fosters its influence.

Tacitus, *Annals* (A.D. 115–117?), 4.35, tr. William J. Brodribb

35. You cannot create genius. All you can do is nurture it.

NINETTE DE VALOIS, *TIME*, SEPT. 26, 1960

36. We wish genius and morality were affectionate companions, but it is a fact that they are often bitter enemies. They don't necessarily coalesce any more than oil and water do.

ARTEMUS WARD, "MORALITY AND GENIUS," *ARTEMUS WARD IN LONDON* (1872)

37. Genius is more often found in a cracked pot than in a whole one.

E. B. WHITE, "LIME," *ONE MAN'S MEAT* (1944)

38. The public is wonderfully tolerant. It forgives everything except genius.

OSCAR WILDE, "THE CRITIC AS ARTIST," *INTENTIONS* (1891)

377. GENIUS VS. TALENT

See also 376. GENIUS

1. To do easily what is difficult for others is the mark of talent. To do what is impossible for talent is the mark of genius.

HENRI FRÉDÉRIC AMIEL, *JOURNAL*, DEC. 17, 1856, TR. MRS. HUMPHRY WARD

2. Coffee is good for talent, but genius wants prayer.

EMERSON, *JOURNALS*, 1841

3. The difference between Talent and Genius is, that Talent says things which he has never heard but once, and Genius things which he has never heard.

EMERSON, *JOURNALS*, 1843

4. Talent is a very common family trait; genius belongs rather to individuals—just as you find one giant or one dwarf in a family, but rarely a whole brood of either.

OLIVER WENDELL HOLMES, SR., "IRIS, HER BOOK," *THE PROFESSOR AT THE BREAKFAST TABLE* (1860)

5. The world is always ready to receive talent with open arms. Very often it does not know what to do with genius.

OLIVER WENDELL HOLMES, SR., "IRIS, HER BOOK," *THE PROFESSOR AT THE BREAKFAST TABLE* (1860)

6. Talent is often to be envied, and genius very commonly to be pitied. It stands twice the chance of the other of dying in a hospital, in jail, in debt, in bad repute.

OLIVER WENDELL HOLMES, SR., "IRIS, HER BOOK," *THE PROFESSOR AT THE BREAKFAST TABLE* (1860)

7. Talent is that which is in a man's power; genius is that in whose power a man is.

JAMES RUSSELL LOWELL, *ROUSSEAU AND THE SENTIMENTALISTS* (1870)

GENTILITY

See 391. GOOD BREEDING; 809. RESPECTABILITY

378. GENTLEMAN

See also 197. COURTESY; 391. GOOD BREEDING; 563. MANNERS

1. To a gentleman, a gentleman—someone who dies without ever pronouncing the word—is a man who climbs Everest, never mentions it to a soul, and listens politely to Pochet's account of how in 1937 in spite of his sciatica, he conquered the Puy de Dôme.

PIERRE DANINOS, *THE SECRET OF MAJOR THOMPSON* (1957), TR. DON CORTES

2. Repose and cheerfulness are the badge of the gentleman,—repose in energy.

EMERSON, "CULTURE," *THE CONDUCT OF LIFE* (1860)

3. To be a gentleman is to be oneself, all of a seam, on camera and off.

MURRAY KEMPTON, "THE PARTY'S OVER," *AMERICA COMES OF MIDDLE AGE* (1963)

4. It is almost a definition of a gentleman to say he is one who never inflicts pain.

JOHN HENRY NEWMAN, *THE IDEA OF A UNIVERSITY* (1853–58), 1.8.10

5. Anyone can be heroic from time to time, but a gentleman is something you have to be all the time. Which isn't easy.

LUIGI PIRANDELLO, *THE PLEASURE OF HONESTY* (1917), 1, TR. WILLIAM MURRAY

6. The gentle minde by gentle deeds is knowne.

EDMUND SPENSER, *THE FAERIE QUEENE* (1596), 6.3.1

379. GENTLENESS

See also 357. FORCE; 519. KINDNESS

1. Fair and softly goes far.

CERVANTES, *DON QUIXOTE* (1605–15), 1.3.2, TR. PETER MOTTEUX AND JOHN OZELL

2. The cat in gloves catches no mice.

ENGLISH PROVERB

380. GEOGRAPHY

See also 140. CLIMATE

1. I remember as a child reading or hearing the words "The Great Divide" and being stunned by the glorious sound, a proper sound for the granite backbone of a continent. I saw in my mind escarpments rising into the clouds, a kind of natural Great Wall of China.

JOHN STEINBECK, *TRAVELS WITH CHARLEY* (1962)

381. GERMANY AND GERMANS

1. Is it possible for anyone in Germany, nowadays, to raise his right hand, for whatever the reason, and not be flooded by the memory of a dream to end all dreams?

WALTER ABISH, *HOW GERMAN IS IT* (1979)

2. We Germans fear God, but nothing else in the world.

OTTO VON BISMARCK, SPEECH IN THE REICHSTAG, FEB. 6, 1888

3. The work of bestial degradation, begun by the victorious Germans, had been carried to its conclusion by the Germans in defeat.

PRIMO LEVI, *SURVIVAL IN AUSCHWITZ* (1959)

4. Whenever the literary German dives into a sentence, that is the last you are going to see of him till he emerges on the other side of his Atlantic with his verb in his mouth.

MARK TWAIN, *A CONNECTICUT YANKEE IN KING ARTHUR'S COURT* (1889), 22

5. The great virtues of the German people have created more evils than idleness ever did vices.

PAUL VALÉRY, "LA CRISE DE L'ESPRIT, 1RE LETTRE," *VARIÉTÉ* (1924–44) V. 1

382. GERMS

1. Microbes is a vigitable, an' ivry man is like a conservatory full iv these potted plants.

FINLEY PETER DUNNE, "CHRISTIAN SCIENCE," *MR. DOOLEY'S OPINIONS* (1901)

383. GHOSTS

See also 449. ILLUSION; 336. FANTASY; 953. SUPERNATURAL

1. Ghost, n. The outward and visible sign of an inward fear.

AMBROSE BIERCE, *THE DEVIL'S DICTIONARY* (1881–1911)

2. I'm inclined to think we are all ghosts—every one of us. It's not just what we inherit from our mothers and fathers that haunts us. It's all kinds of old defunct theories, all sorts of old defunct beliefs, and things like that.

HENRIK IBSEN, *GHOSTS* (1881)

384. GIFTS AND GIVING

See also 74. BEGGARS; 375. GENEROSITY; 433. HUMANITARIANISM; 519. KINDNESS; 595. MISERS; 647. OBLIGATION; 787. RECEIVING; 888. SERVICES; 894. SHARING; 936. STINGINESS

1. To give and then not feel that one has given is the very best of all ways of giving.

MAX BEERBOHM, "HOSTS AND GUESTS," *AND EVEN NOW* (1920)

2. Every good gift and every perfect gift is from above.

BIBLE, JAMES 1:17

3. It is more blessed to give than to receive.

BIBLE, ACTS 20:35

4. Riches may enable us to confer favours, but to confer them with propriety and grace requires a something that riches cannot give.

CHARLES CALEB COLTON, *LACON* (1825), 1.455

5. How painful to give a gift to any person of sensibility, or of equality! It is next worst to receiving one.

EMERSON, *JOURNALS*, 1836

6. The only gift is a portion of thyself.

EMERSON, "GIFTS," *ESSAYS: SECOND SERIES* (1844)

7. We do not quite forgive a giver. The hand that feeds us is in some danger of being bitten.

EMERSON, "GIFTS," *ESSAYS: SECOND SERIES* (1844)

8. There is no benefit in the gifts of a bad man.

EURIPIDES, *MEDEA* (431 B.C.), TR. REX WARNER

9. A gift, with a kind countenance, is a double present.

THOMAS FULLER, M.D., *GNOMOLOGIA* (1732), 131

10. That is the bitterness of a gift, that it deprives us of our liberty.

THOMAS FULLER, M.D., *GNOMOLOGIA* (1732), 4359

11. Avarice hoards itself poor; charity gives itself rich.

GERMAN PROVERB

12. It is well to give when asked, but it is better to give unasked, through understanding.

KAHLIL GIBRAN, "ON GIVING," *THE PROPHET* (1923)

13. We probably have a greater love for those we support than those who support us. Our vanity carries more weight than our self-interest.

Eric Hoffer, *The Passionate State of Mind* (1954), 202

14. What with your friend you nobly share, / At least you rescue from your heir.

Horace, *Odes* (23–c. 15 B.C.), 4.7

15. Bounty always receives part of its value from the manner in which it is bestowed.

Samuel Johnson, letter to the earl of Bute, July 20, 1762, quoted in Boswell's *Life of Samuel Johnson*

16. Let him that desires to see others happy, make haste to give while his gift can be enjoyed, and remember that every moment of delay takes away something from the value of his benefaction.

Samuel Johnson, *The Idler* (1758–60), 43

17. Presents, I often say, endear absents.

Charles Lamb, "A Dissertation upon Roast Pig," *Essays of Elia* (1823)

18. Some people have a knack of putting upon you gifts of no real value, to engage you to substantial gratitude. We thank them for nothing.

Charles Lamb, "Popular Fallacies, ii," *Last Essays of Elia* (1833)

19. We are better pleased to see those on whom we confer benefits than those from whom we receive them.

La Rochefoucauld, *Maxims* (1665), tr. Kenneth Pratt

20. He gives only the worthless gold / Who gives from a sense of duty.

James Russell Lowell, "The Vision of Sir Launfal" (1848), 1.6

21. Gifts are like hooks.

Martial, *Epigrams* (A.D. 86), 5.18, tr. Walter C. A. Kerr

22. The heart and hand of those who always mete out become callous from always meting out.

Nietzsche, "The Night Song," *Thus Spoke Zarathustra* (1883–92), 2, tr. Walter Kaufmann

23. This is what is hardest: to close the open hand because one loves.

Nietzsche, "The Child with the Mirror," *Thus Spoke Zarathustra* (1883–92), 2, tr. Walter Kaufmann

24. Presents, believe me, seduce both men and gods.

Ovid, *The Art of Love* (c. A.D. 8), 3, tr. J. Lewis May

25. A gift in season is a double favor to the needy.

Publilius Syrus, *Moral Sayings* (1st c. B.C.), 90, tr. Darius Lyman

26. The spirit in which a thing is given determines that in which the debt is acknowledged; it's the intention, not the face-value of the gift, that's weighed.

Seneca, *Letters to Lucilius* (1st c.), 81.6, tr. E. Phillips Barker

27. Rich gifts wax poor when givers prove unkind.

Shakespeare, *Hamlet* (1600), 3.1.101

28. You pay a great deal too dear for what's given freely.

Shakespeare, *The Winter's Tale* (1610–11), 1.1.18

29. An enemy's gift is ruinous and no gift.

Sophocles, *Ajax* (c. 447 B.C.), tr. John Moore

30. Leave out my name from the gift / if it be a burden, / but keep my song.

Rabindranath Tagore, *Fireflies* (1928)

31. Man discovers his own wealth / when God comes to ask gifts of him.

Rabindranath Tagore, *Fireflies* (1928)

32. Surely great loving-kindness yet may go / With a little gift: all's dear that comes from friends.

Theocritus, *Idyll* 28 (3rd c. B.C.)

33. When I give I give myself.

Walt Whitman, "Song of Myself," 40, *Leaves of Grass* (1855–92)

34. Give all thou canst; high Heaven rejects the lore / Of nicely-calculated less or more.

William Wordsworth, "Inside of King's College Chapel Cambridge" (1821)

385. GIRLS

See also 1071. Youth

1. Most of them [girls] were as unaware of their breathtaking beauty as wild animals; they seemed as tranquil and unself-conscious as deer in a forest, but who chewed gum instead of grass.

Luigi Barzini, *O America* (1977)

2. I cannot even pretend to feel as much interest in boys as in girls.

Lewis Carroll, *The Letters of Lewis Carroll*, ed. Morton N. Cohen, (1979)

3. There is no need to waste pity on young girls who are having their moments of disillusionment,

for in another moment they will recover their illusion.

COLETTE, "WEDDING DAY," *EARTHLY PARADISE* (1966), 2

4. A lot of young girls together is a romantic secret thing like the first sight of wild ducks at dawn.

F. SCOTT FITZGERALD, *THE CRACK-UP* (1945)

5. Dear to the heart of a girl is her own beauty and charm.

OVID, *THE ART OF BEAUTY* (C. A.D. 8), TR. ROLFE HUMPHRIES

6. She was a girl who for a ringing phone dropped exactly nothing. She looked as if her phone had been ringing continually ever since she had reached puberty.

J.D. SALINGER, "A PERFECT DAY FOR BANANAFISH," IN *NINE STORIES BY J.D. SALINGER* (1953)

GIVING

See 384. GIFTS AND GIVING

GLASSES

See 925. SPECTACLES

386. GLORY

See also 332. FAME; 426. HONORS; 722. PRAISE; 804. REPUTATION

1. It may be a fire—tomorrow it will be ashes.

ARABIC PROVERB

2. Achilles exists only by the grace of Homer. Take away the art of writing from this world and you will probably take away its glory.

CHATEAUBRIAND, PRÉFACE, *LES NATCHEZ* (1826)

3. We are all motivated by a keen desire for praise, and the better a man is, the more he is inspired by glory. The very philosophers themselves, even in those books which they write on contempt of glory, inscribe their names.

CICERO, *PRO ARCHIA* (62 B.C.)

4. Humility must always be the portion of any man who receives acclaim earned in the blood of his followers and the sacrifices of his friends.

DWIGHT D. EISENHOWER, ADDRESS, LONDON, JUNE 12, 1945

5. When glory comes, memory departs.

FRENCH PROVERB

6. The paths of glory lead but to the grave.

THOMAS GRAY, "ELEGY WRITTEN IN A COUNTRY CHURCHYARD," (1742?–50), 9

7. Glory is largely a theatrical concept. There is no striving for glory without a vivid awareness of an audience.

ERIC HOFFER, *THE TRUE BELIEVER* (1951), 3.13.47

8. Do we want laurels for ourselves most, / Or most that no one else shall have any?

AMY LOWELL, "LA RONDE DU DIABLE," *WHAT'S O'CLOCK* (1925)

9. To the ashes of the dead glory comes too late.

MARTIAL, *EPIGRAMS* (A.D. 86), 1.25, TR. WALTER C. A. KERR

10. Glory and repose are things that cannot possibly inhabit in one and the same place.

MONTAIGNE, "OF SOLITUDE," *ESSAYS* (1580–88), TR. W. C. HAZLITT

11. The shortest way to arrive at glory would be to do that for conscience which we do for glory.

MONTAIGNE, "OF REPENTANCE," *ESSAYS* (1580–88), TR. W. C. HAZLITT

12. Glory ought to be the consequence, not the motive of our actions.

PLINY THE YOUNGER, *LETTERS* (C. 97–110), 1.8, TR. W. M. L. HUTCHISON

13. One crowded hour of glorious life / Is worth an age without a name.

SIR WALTER SCOTT, *OLD MORTALITY* (1816), 34

14. Glory is like a circle in the water, / Which never ceaseth to enlarge itself / Till by broad spreading it disperse to naught.

SHAKESPEARE, *1 HENRY VI* (1591–92), 1.2. 133

15. Avoid shame, but do not seek glory,—nothing so expensive as glory.

SYDNEY SMITH, QUOTED IN LADY S. HOLLAND'S *MEMOIR* (1855), V.1.4

16. The nearest way to glory—a short cut, as it were—is to strive to be what you wish to be thought to be.

SOCRATES (5TH–4TH C. B.C.), QUOTED IN CICERO'S *DE OFFICIIS* (44 B.C.), 2.12.43, TR. WALTER MILLER

17. The desire of glory is the last infirmity cast off even by the wise.

TACITUS, *HISTORIES* (A.D. 104–109), 4.6, TR. WILLIAM J. BRODRIBB

18. Glories, like glow-worms, afar off shine bright, / But looked to near, have neither heat nor light.

JOHN WEBSTER, *THE DUCHESS OF MALFI* (C. 1613), 4.2

GLUTTONY

See 274. EATING; 403. GREED

GOALS

See 286. ENDS; 771. PURPOSE

387. GOD

See also 242. DEVIL; 261. DIVINITY; 754. PROVIDENCE; 797. RELIGION; 816. REVELATION, DIVINE; 973. THEOLOGY; 1019. THE UNKNOWN

1. The power that holds the sky's majesty wins our worship.

AESCHYLUS, *THE LIBATION BEARERS* (458 B.C.), TR. RICHMOND LATTIMORE

2. Every man thinks God is on his side. The rich and powerful know He is.

JEAN ANOUILH, *THE LARK* (1955), 1, ADAPTED BY LILLIAN HELLMAN

3. You cannot plumb the depths of the human heart, nor find out what a man is thinking; how do you expect to search out God, who made all these things, and find out his mind or comprehend his thoughts?

APOCRYPHA, JUDITH 8:14

4. We, peopling the void air, / Make Gods to whom to impute / The ills we ought to bear; / With God and Fate to rail at, suffering easily.

MATTHEW ARNOLD, *EMPEDOCLES ON ETNA* (1852), 1.2

5. Canst thou by searching find out God?

BIBLE, JOB 11:7

6. God is our refuge and strength, a very present help in trouble.

BIBLE, PSALMS 46:1

7. If I ascend up into heaven, thou [God] art there: if I make my bed in hell, behold, thou art there.

BIBLE, PSALMS 139:8

8. We should find God in what we do know, not in what we don't; not in outstanding problems, but in those we have already solved.

DIETRICH BONHOEFFER, *LETTERS AND PAPERS FROM PRISON,* MAY 25, 1944, TR. EBERHARD BETHGE

9. God is the Celebrity-Author of the World's Best Seller. We have made God into the biggest celebrity of all, to contain our own emptiness.

DANIEL J. BOORSTIN, *THE IMAGE* (1962), 5

10. I always adhered to the idea that God is time, or at least that His spirit is.

JOSEPH BRODSKY, *WATERMARK* (1992)

11. God is the perfect poet, / Who in his person acts his own creations.

ROBERT BROWNING, *PARACELSUS* (1835), 2

12. God is seen God / In the star, in the stone, in the flesh, in the soul and the clod.

ROBERT BROWNING, "SAUL," *MEN AND WOMEN* (1855), 17

13. God without the devil is dead, being alone.

SAMUEL BUTLER (D. 1902), "ELEMENTARY MORALITY," *NOTE-BOOKS* (1912)

14. God's merits are so transcendent that it is not surprising his faults should be in reasonable proportion.

SAMUEL BUTLER (D. 1902), "REBELLIOUSNESS," *NOTE-BOOKS* (1912)

15. Theist and Atheist: The fight between them is as to whether God shall be called God or shall have some other name.

SAMUEL BUTLER (D. 1902), "REBELLIOUSNESS," *NOTE-BOOKS* (1912)

16. Out of chaos God made a world, and out of high passions comes a people.

BYRON, *SELECTED LETTERS AND JOURNALS* (1982), ED. LESLIE A. MARCHAND

17. The mind of man, cleansed of secondary and merely temporal concerns, beholds with the radiance of a cleansed mirror a reflection of the rational mind of God.

JOSEPH CAMPBELL, *THE POWER OF MYTH* (1988)

18. Any god who can invent hell is no candidate for the Salvation Army.

JOSEPH CAMPBELL, *THE POWER OF MYTH* (1988)

19. When God hands you a gift, he also hands you a whip; and the whip is intended solely for self-flagellation.

TRUMAN CAPOTE, *MUSIC FOR CHAMELEONS* (1980)

20. Is there no God, then, but at best an absentee God, sitting idle, ever since the first Sabbath, at the outside of his Universe?

THOMAS CARLYLE, *SARTOR RESARTUS* (1833–34), 2.7

21. Man appoints, and God disappoints.

CERVANTES, *DON QUIXOTE* (1605–15), 2.4.55, TR. JOHN OZELL

22. Though God's attributes are equal, yet his mercy is more attractive and pleasing in our eyes than his justice.

CERVANTES, *DON QUIXOTE* (1605–15), 2.4.42, TR. JOHN OZELL

23. God is for men and religion for women.

JOSEPH CONRAD, *NOSTROMO* (1904)

24. God is indeed a jealous God— / He cannot bear to see / That we had rather not with Him / But with each other play.

EMILY DICKINSON, *POEMS* (C. 1862–86)

25. If every gnat that flies were an archangel, all that could but tell me that there is a God; and the poorest worm that creeps tells me that.

JOHN DONNE, *SERMONS,* NO. 57, 1628

26. Do not speak of God much. After a very little conversation on the highest nature, thought deserts us and we run into formalism.

EMERSON, *JOURNALS,* 1836

27. God is our name for the last generalization to which we can arrive.

EMERSON, *JOURNALS,* 1836

28. Heaven always bears some proportion to earth. The god of the cannibal will be a cannibal, of the crusaders a crusader, and of the merchants a merchant.

EMERSON, "WORSHIP," *THE CONDUCT OF LIFE* (1860)

29. The only money of God is God. He pays never with any thing less, or any thing else.

EMERSON, "FRIENDSHIP," *ESSAYS: FIRST SERIES* (1841)

30. If god is truly god, he is perfect, / lacking nothing.

EURIPIDES, *HERACLES* (C. 422 B.C.), TR. WILLIAM ARROWSMITH

31. The way of God is complex, he is hard / for us to predict. He moves the pieces and they come / somehow into a kind of order.

EURIPIDES, *HELEN* (412 B.C.), TR. RICHMOND LATTIMORE

32. I have never wished there was a God to call on— I have often wished there was a God to thank.

F. SCOTT FITZGERALD, *THE CRACK-UP* (1945)

33. Most of the time, God speaks in a whisper.

JEAN GRASSO FITZPATRICK, *SOMETHING MORE* (1991)

34. The skirts of the gods / Drag in our mud. We feel the touch / And take it to be a kiss.

CHRISTOPHER FRY, *THOR, WITH ANGELS* (1948)

35. God lies ahead. I convince myself and constantly repeat to myself that: He depends on us. It is through us that God is achieved.

ANDRÉ GIDE, *JOURNALS,* 1947, TR. JUSTIN O'BRIEN

36. I believe in the gods. Or rather I believe that I believe in the gods. But I don't believe that they are great brooding presences watching over us; I believe they are completely absent-minded.

JEAN GIRAUDOUX, *ELECTRA* (1937), 1, TR. PETER H. JUDD

37. The First Cause worked automatically like a somnambulist, and not reflectively like a sage.

THOMAS HARDY, *JUDE THE OBSCURE* (1895), 6.3

38. God is day and night, winter and summer, war and peace, satiety and want.

HERACLITUS, *FRAGMENTS* (C. 500 B.C.), 121, TR. PHILIP WHEELWRIGHT

39. If any man obeys the gods, they listen to him also.

HOMER, *ILIAD* (9TH C. B.C.), 1.218, TR. RICHMOND LATTIMORE

40. To see so much misery everywhere, I suspect that God is not rich. He keeps up appearances, it is true, but I feel the pinch. He gives a revolution as a merchant, whose credit is low, gives a ball.

VICTOR HUGO, "SAINT DENIS," *LES MISÉRABLES* (1862), 12.2, TR. CHARLES E. WILBOUR

41. An honest God is the noblest work of man.

ROBERT G. INGERSOLL, *THE GODS* (1872)

42. Before the world was made, when it was only darkness and mist and waters, God was well aware of Lake Wobegon, my family, our house, and He had me all sketched out down to what size my feet would be (big), which bike I would ride (Schwinn), and the five ears of corn I'd eat for supper that night.

GARRISON KEILLOR, *LAKE WOBEGON DAYS* (1985)

43. It strikes me as somewhat odd that the people who use God's name most frequently, both in life and in literature, usually don't believe in him.

MADELEINE L'ENGLE, *A CIRCLE OF QUIET* (1972)

44. God is what man finds that is divine in himself. God is the best way man can behave in the ordinary occasions of life, and the farthest point to which man can stretch himself.

MAX LERNER, "SEEKERS AND LOSERS," *THE UNFINISHED COUNTRY* (1959), 5

45. 'Tis heaven alone that is given away, / 'Tis only God may be had for the asking.

JAMES RUSSELL LOWELL, PRELUDE TO PART I, "THE VISION OF SIR LAUNFAL" (1848)

46. God is the immemorial refuge of the incompetent, the helpless, the miserable. They find not only sanctuary in His arms, but also a kind of superiority, soothing to their macerated egos; He will set them above their betters.

H. L. MENCKEN, *MINORITY REPORT* (1956), 35

47. It takes a long while for a naturally trustful person to reconcile himself to the idea that after all God will not help him.

H. L. MENCKEN, *MINORITY REPORT* (1956), 194

48. Just are the ways of God, / And justifiable to men; / Unless there be who think not God at all.

MILTON, *SAMSON AGONISTES* (1671), 293

49. Only this I know, / That one celestial father gives to all.

MILTON, *PARADISE LOST* (1667), 5.402

50. If triangles had a god, he would have three sides.

MONTESQUIEU, *LETTRES PERSANES* (1721), 59

51. The heart is a mystery—not a puzzle that can't be solved, but a mystery in the religious sense: unfathomable, beyond manipulation, showing traces of the finger of God.

THOMAS MOORE, *SOUL MATES* (1994)

52. God is a thought that makes crooked all that is straight.

NIETZSCHE, "UPON THE BLESSED ISLES," *THUS SPOKE ZARATHUSTRA* (1883–92), 2, TR. WALTER KAUFMANN

53. If there were only one religion, God would indeed be manifest.

PASCAL, *PENSÉES* (1670), 584, TR. W. F. TROTTER

54. It is the heart which experiences God, and not the reason.

PASCAL, *PENSÉES* (1670), 278, TR. W. F. TROTTER

55. Let us weigh the gain and the loss, in wagering that God is. Consider these alternatives: if you win, you win all; if you lose, you lose nothing. Do not hesitate, then, to wager that He is.

PASCAL, *PENSÉES* (1670), 233

56. It is fear that first brought gods into the world.

PETRONIUS, *SATYRICON* (1ST C.)

57. One on God's side is a majority.

WENDELL PHILLIPS, SPEECH, NOV. 1, 1859

58. It is God that accomplishes all term to hopes, / God, who overtakes the flying eagle, outpasses the dolphin / in the sea; who bends under his strength the man with thoughts too high.

PINDAR, *ODES* (5TH C. B.C.), PYTHIA 2, TR. RICHMOND LATTIMORE

59. God, he whom everyone knows, by name.

JULES RENARD, *JOURNAL*, APRIL 1894, TR. ELIZABETH ROGET

60. Nothing can be lower or more wholly instrumental than the substance and cause of all things.

GEORGE SANTAYANA, *LITTLE ESSAYS* (1920), 26

61. But who can speak to God, or rather who *can't*? The question is, who can get an answer?

WILLIAM SAROYAN, *CHANCE MEETINGS* (1978)

62. Respectable society believed in God in order to avoid having to speak about him.

JEAN-PAUL SARTRE, *THE WORDS* (1964), 1

63. We have been born under a monarchy; to obey God is freedom.

SENECA, "ON A HAPPY LIFE," *MORAL SAYINGS* (1ST C.), TR. AUBREY STEWART

64. As flies to wanton boys are we to the gods. / They kill us for their sport.

SHAKESPEARE, *KING LEAR* (1605–06), 4.1.36

65. It was God who dictated what man should believe and do, leaving man the freedom to accept or scoff, to obey or disregard.

ISRAEL SHENKER, *COAT OF MANY COLORS* (1985)

66. Who created all this? Yasha would ask himself. Was it the sun? If so, then perhaps the sun was God. Yasha had read in some holy book that Abraham had worshiped the sun before accepting the existence of Jehovah.

ISAAC BASHEVIS SINGER, *THE MAGICIAN OF LUBLIN* (1960)

67. Our love for God is tested by the question of whether we seek Him or His gifts.

RALPH W. SOCKMAN, INTERVIEW WITH JAMES B. SIMPSON, 1961

68. God is the indwelling and not the transient cause of all things.

SPINOZA, *ETHICS* (1677), 1, TR. ANDREW BOYLE

69. Your idol is shattered in the dust to prove that God's dust is greater than your idol.

RABINDRANATH TAGORE, *STRAY BIRDS* (1916), 51

70. Closer is He than breathing, and nearer than hands and feet.

LORD TENNYSON, "THE HIGHER PANTHEISM" (1869)

71. There is strife between God's ways and human ways; damned by you, we are absolved by God.

TERTULLIAN, *APOLOGY* (3RD C.), 50

72. Short arm needs man to reach to Heaven, / So ready is Heaven to stoop to him.

FRANCIS THOMPSON, "GRACE OF THE WAY" (1897)

73. If God were not a necessary Being of Himself, He might seem to be made for the use and benefit of men.

JOHN TILLOTSON, *SERMONS* (1695–1704), 93

74. We need God, not in order to understand the *why,* but in order to feel and sustain the ultimate *wherefore,* to give a meaning to the Universe.

MIGUEL DE UNAMUNO, "LOVE, SUFFERING, PITY, AND PERSONALITY," *TRAGIC SENSE OF LIFE* (1913), TR. J. E. CRAWFORD FLITCH

75. If God created us in his own image, we have more than reciprocated.

VOLTAIRE, *LE SOTTISIER,* 32

76. If God did not exist, he would have to be invented.

VOLTAIRE, *À L'AUTEUR DU LIVRE DES TROIS IMPOSTEURS* (1769)

77. Any God I ever felt in church I brought in with me. And I think all the other folks did too. They come to church to *share* God, not find God.

ALICE WALKER, *THE COLOR PURPLE* (1982)

78. No reason can be given for the nature of God, because that nature is the ground of rationality.

ALFRED NORTH WHITEHEAD, *SCIENCE AND THE MODERN WORLD* (1925) 11

79. Almost, I am tempted to say, I will believe in God, yes, in spite of the church and the ministers.

THOMAS WOLFE, *THOMAS WOLFE'S LETTERS TO HIS MOTHER* (1943)

80. A God all mercy is a God unjust.

EDWARD YOUNG, *NIGHT THOUGHTS* (1742–46)

GOLDEN AGE

See 298. ERA

388. GOLDEN RULE

See also 227. DEEDS

1. All things whatsoever ye would that men should do to you, do ye even so to them: for this is the law and the prophets.

BIBLE, MATTHEW 7:12

2. What you do not want done to yourself, do not do to others.

CONFUCIUS, *ANALECTS* (6TH C. B.C.), 15.23, TR. JAMES LEGGE

3. Do not do unto others as you would that they should do unto you. Their tastes may not be the same.

GEORGE BERNARD SHAW, "MAXIMS FOR REVOLUTIONS," *MAN AND SUPERMAN* (1903)

4. Do unto the other feller the way he'd like to do unto you an' do it fust.

EDWARD NOYES WESTCOTT, *DAVID HARUM* (1898), 20

GOLF

See 929. SPORTS

389. THE GOOD

See also 307. EVIL; 390. GOOD AND EVIL; 393. GOODNESS; 822. RIGHT

1. Whatever befalls in accordance with nature should be accounted good.

CICERO, *DE SENECTUTE* (44 B.C.), 19.71

2. We know the good, we apprehend it clearly. / But we can't bring it to achievement.

EURIPIDES, *HIPPOLYTUS* (428 B.C.), TR. DAVID GRENE

3. We look for good on earth and cannot recognize it / when met.

EURIPIDES, *ELECTRA* (413 B.C.), TR. EMILY TOWNSEND VERMEULE

4. Nothing is good for everyone, but only relatively to some people.

ANDRÉ GIDE, *THE COUNTERFEITERS* (1925), 2.4, TR. DOROTHY BUSSY

5. Good things, when short, are twice as good.

BALTASAR GRACIÁN, *THE ART OF WORLDLY WISDOM* (1647), 105, TR. JOSEPH JACOBS

6. The good things of life are not to be had singly, but come to us with a mixture; like a schoolboy's holiday, with a task affixed to the tail of it.

Charles Lamb, "Popular Fallacies, 13," *Last Essays of Elia* (1833)

7. We must take the good with the bad; / For the good when it's good, is so very good / That the bad when it's bad can't be bad!

Molière, second intermission of *The Imaginary Invalid* (1673), tr. Mildred Marmur

8. The good is, like nature, an immense landscape in which man advances through centuries of exploration.

José Ortega y Gasset, "To the Reader," *Meditations on Quixote* (1914)

9. It is good to be tired and wearied by the vain search after the true good, that we may stretch out our arms to the Redeemer.

Pascal, *Pensées* (1670), 422, tr. W. F. Trotter

10. Men always love what is good or what they find good; it is in judging what is good that they go wrong.

Rousseau, *The Social Contract* (1762), 4.7, tr. G. D. H. Cole

11. Our will is always for our own good, but we do not always see what that is.

Rousseau, *The Social Contract* (1762), 2.3, tr. G. D. H. Cole

12. Happiness is not best achieved by those who seek it directly; and it would seem that the same is true of the good.

Bertrand Russell, title essay, *Mysticism and Logic* (1917)

13. There is nothing either good or bad but thinking makes it so.

Shakespeare, *Hamlet* (1600), 2.2.255

14. Everyone places his good where he can and has as much of it as he can, in his own way.

Voltaire, "Good," *Philosophical Dictionary* (1764)

390. GOOD AND EVIL

See also 307. Evil; 389. The Good; 393. Goodness

1. It's wiser being good than bad; / It's safer being meek than fierce: / It's fitter being sane than mad.

Robert Browning, "Apparent Failure," *Dramatis Personae* (1864), 7

2. White shall not neutralize the black, nor good / Compensate bad in man, absolve him so: / Life's business being just the terrible choice.

Robert Browning, "The Pope," *The Ring and the Book* (1868–69)

3. The meaning of good and bad, of better and worse, is simply helping or hurting.

Emerson, *Journals,* 1836

4. People forget the good, because the bad has more punch.

Louise Erdrich, "Mindemoya," *The Bingo Palace* (1994)

5. Good and bad may not be dissevered; / There is, as there should be, a commingling.

Euripides, quoted in Plutarch's "Contentment," *Moralia* (c. a.d. 100), tr. Moses Hadas

6. Even as the holy and the righteous cannot rise beyond the highest which is in each one of you, so the wicked and the weak cannot fall lower than the lowest which is in you also.

Kahlil Gibran, "On Crime and Punishment," *The Prophet* (1923)

7. Nothing is good for him for whom nothing is bad.

Baltasar Gracián, *The Art of Worldly Wisdom* (1647), 250, tr. Joseph Jacobs

8. There is no such thing in man's nature as a settled and full resolve either for good or evil, except at the very moment of execution.

Nathaniel Hawthorne, "Fancy's Show Box," *Twice-Told Tales* (1837)

9. Jove weighs affairs of earth in dubious scales, / And the good suffers while the bad prevails.

Homer, *Odyssey* (9th c. b.c.), 6.229, tr. Alexander Pope

10. Almost all the moral good which is left among us is the apparent effect of physical evil.

Samuel Johnson, *The Idler* (1758–60), 89

11. We often do good in order to accomplish evil with impunity.

La Rochefoucauld, *Maxims* (1665), tr. Kenneth Pratt

12. Evil can be condoned only if in the beyond it is compensated by good and God himself needs immortality to vindicate his ways to man.

W. Somerset Maugham, *The Summing Up* (1938), 70

13. Life in itself is neither good nor evil; it is the scene of good or evil, as you make it.

MONTAIGNE, "THAT TO STUDY PHILOSOPHY IS TO LEARN TO DIE," *ESSAYS* (1580–88), TR. W. C. HAZLITT

14. The common people, on the whole, are still living in the world of absolute good and evil from which the intellectuals have long since escaped.

GEORGE ORWELL, "RAFFLES AND MISS BLANDISH," *A COLLECTION OF ESSAYS* (1954)

15. One should seek for the salutary in the unpleasant; if it is there, it is after all nectar. One should seek for the deceitful in the pleasant; if it is there, it is after all poison.

PANCHATANTRA (C. 5TH C.), 1, TR. FRANKLIN EDGERTON

16. The omission of good is no less reprehensible than the commission of evil.

PLUTARCH, "CONTENTMENT," *MORALIA* (C. A.D. 100), TR. MOSES HADAS

17. Saints cannot arise where there have been no warriors, nor philosophers where a prying beast does not remain hidden in the depths.

GEORGE SANTAYANA, *THE LIFE OF REASON: REASON IN SCIENCE* (1905–06), 9

18. The apprehension of the good / Gives but the greater feeling to the worse.

SHAKESPEARE, *RICHARD II* (1595–96), 1.3.300

19. The evil that men do lives after them; / The good is oft interred with their bones.

SHAKESPEARE, *JULIUS CAESAR* (1599–1600), 3.2.81

20. A good thing which prevents us from enjoying a greater good is in truth an evil.

SPINOZA, *ETHICS* (1677), 4, TR. ANDREW BOYLE

21. Good and evil ... are not what vulgar opinion accounts them; many who seem to be struggling with adversity are happy; many, amid great affluence, are utterly miserable.

TACITUS, *ANNALS* (A.D. 115–117?), 6.22, TR. WILLIAM J. BRODRIBB

22. O, yet we trust that somehow good / Will be the final goal of ill.

LORD TENNYSON, "IN MEMORIAM A. H. H." (1850), 54

23. The character of human life, like the character of the human condition, like the character of all life, is "ambiguity": the inseparable mixture of good and evil, the true and false, the creative and destructive forces—both individual and social.

PAUL TILLICH, *TIME,* MAY 17, 1963

24. The question of good and evil remains in irremediable chaos for those who seek to fathom it in reality. It is a mere mental sport to the disputants, who are captives that play with their chains.

VOLTAIRE, "OPTIMISM," *PHILOSOPHICAL DICTIONARY* (1764)

391. GOOD BREEDING

See also 197. COURTESY; 378. GENTLEMAN; 563. MANNERS; 749. PROPRIETY

1. There is no society or conversation to be kept up in the world without good-nature, or something which must bear its appearance and supply its place. For this reason mankind have been forced to invent a kind of artificial humanity, which is what we express by the word Good-Breeding.

JOSEPH ADDISON, *THE SPECTATOR* (1711–12), 169

2. It is good breeding alone that can prepossess people in your favor at first sight, more time being necessary to discover greater talents.

LORD CHESTERFIELD, *LETTERS TO HIS SON,* C. 1741

3. The scholar without good breeding is a pedant; the philosopher, a cynic.

LORD CHESTERFIELD, *LETTERS TO HIS SON,* OCT. 9, 1747

4. Good breeding, a union of kindness and independence.

EMERSON, "MANNERS," *ESSAYS: SECOND SERIES* (1844)

5. The whole essence of true gentle-breeding (one does not like to say gentility) lies in the wish and the art to be agreeable. Good-breeding is surface-Christianity.

OLIVER WENDELL HOLMES, SR., *THE PROFESSOR AT THE BREAKFAST TABLE* (1860), 6

6. Call me uxorious, spoony, passion's plaything, but let a woman signify her whim by so much as a nod and, by George, I'll climb the highest mountain, swim the deepest ocean to gratify it.

S.J. PERELMAN, *THE RISING GORGE* (1961)

7. The test of a man or woman's breeding is how they behave in a quarrel.

GEORGE BERNARD SHAW, *THE PHILANDERER* (1893), 4

8. Good breeding consists in concealing how much we think of ourselves and how little we think of ourselves and how little we think of other persons.

MARK TWAIN, *NOTEBOOK* (1935)

392. GOOD NATURE

See also 968. TEMPER, BAD

1. I have always preferred cheerfulness to mirth. The latter I consider as an act, the former as an habit of mind. Mirth is short and transient, cheerfulness fixed and permanent.

JOSEPH ADDISON, *THE SPECTATOR* (1711–12), 381

2. Good nature is worth more than knowledge, more than money, more than honor, to the persons who possess it.

HENRY WARD BEECHER, *PROVERBS FROM PLYMOUTH PULPIT* (1887)

3. The teeth are smiling, but is the heart?

CONGOLESE PROVERB

4. Of cheerfulness, or a good temper—the more it is spent, the more of it remains.

EMERSON, "CONSIDERATIONS BY THE WAY," *THE CONDUCT OF LIFE* (1860)

5. The best part of health is fine disposition.

EMERSON, "CONSIDERATIONS BY THE WAY," *THE CONDUCT OF LIFE* (1860)

6. Good-fellowship, unflagging, is the prime requisite for success in our society, and the man or woman who smiles only for reasons of humor or pleasure is a deviate.

MARYA MANNES, *MORE IN ANGER* (1958), 1.2

7. A good disposition is a virtue in itself, and it is lasting; the burden of the years cannot depress it, and love that is founded on it endures to the end.

OVID, *THE ART OF BEAUTY* (C. A.D. 8), TR. J. LEWIS MAY

8. A good-natured man has the whole world to be happy out of.

ALEXANDER POPE, *THOUGHTS ON VARIOUS SUBJECTS* (1727)

9. Good-humor is a philosophic state of mind; it seems to say to Nature that we take her no more seriously than she takes us.

ERNEST RENAN, *FEUILLÈS DÉTACHÉES* (C. 1880)

10. Mutual good humour is a dress we ought to appear in wherever we meet, and we should make no mention of what concerns our selves, without it be of matters wherein our friends ought to rejoice.

RICHARD STEELE, *THE SPECTATOR* (1711–12), 100

11. Few are qualified to shine in company, but it is in most men's power to be agreeable.

JONATHAN SWIFT, *THOUGHTS ON VARIOUS SUBJECTS* (1711)

393. GOODNESS

See also 191. CORRUPTION; 227. DEEDS; 307. EVIL; 389. THE GOOD; 390. GOOD AND EVIL; 433. HUMANITARIANISM; 604. MORALITY; 697. PIETY; 822. RIGHT; 1033. VIRTUE

1. [G]oodness that comes out of hiding and assumes a public role is no longer good, but corrupt in its own terms and will carry its own corruption wherever it goes.

HANNAH ARENDT, "THE PUBLIC AND THE PRIVATE REALM," *THE HUMAN CONDITION* (1958)

2. It is easy to perform a good action, but not easy to acquire a settled habit of performing such actions.

ARISTOTLE, *NICOMACHEAN ETHICS* (4TH C. B.C.), 5.9, TR. J. A. K. THOMSON

3. Goodness is easier to recognize than to define.

W. H. AUDEN, IN *I BELIEVE* (1939)

4. Live not as though there were a thousand years ahead of you. Fate is at your elbow; make yourself good while life and power are still yours.

MARCUS AURELIUS, *MEDITATIONS* (2ND C.), 4.17, TR. MAXWELL STANIFORTH

5. Waste no more time arguing what a good man should be. Be one.

MARCUS AURELIUS, *MEDITATIONS* (2ND C.), 10.16, TR. MAXWELL STANIFORTH

6. Good men are not those who now and then do a good act, but men who join one good act to another.

HENRY WARD BEECHER, *PROVERBS FROM PLYMOUTH PULPIT* (1887)

7. Be not overcome of evil, but overcome evil with good.

BIBLE, ROMANS 12:21

8. No one can be good for long if goodness is not in demand.

BERTOLT BRECHT, *THE GOOD WOMAN OF SETZUAN* (1938–40), 1-A, TR. MAJA APELMAN

9. May the good God pardon all good men.

ELIZABETH BARRETT BROWNING, *AURORA LEIGH* (1856), 4.506

10. The only fault's with time; / All men become good creatures: but so slow!

ROBERT BROWNING, *LURIA* (1846), 5

11. Goodness often blossoms like roses on very rickety trellis-work, and beauty can grow out of nonsense.

HUBERT BUTLER, "AUNT HARRIET," IN *THE ART OF THE PERSONAL ESSAY* (1994), ED. PHILLIP LOPATE

12. They're only truly great who are truly good.

GEORGE CHAPMAN, *REVENGE FOR HONOUR* (1654), 5.2

13. Good is not good, unless / A thousand it possess, / But doth waste with greediness.

JOHN DONNE, "CONFINED LOVE," *SONGS AND SONNETS* (1633)

14. Every actual State is corrupt. Good men must not obey the laws too well.

EMERSON, "POLITICS," *ESSAYS: SECOND SERIES* (1844)

15. Goodness that preaches undoes itself.

EMERSON, *JOURNALS,* 1836

16. It is very hard to be simple enough to be good.

EMERSON, *JOURNALS,* 1836

17. Seek not good from without: seek it within yourselves, or you will never find it.

EPICTETUS, *DISCOURSES* (2ND C.), 3.24, TR. THOMAS W. HIGGINSON

18. A good man has more hope in his death than a wicked man in his life.

THOMAS FULLER, M.D., *GNOMOLOGIA* (1732), 159

19. Jail doesn't teach anyone to do good, nor Siberia, but a man—yes! A man can teach another man to do good—believe me!

MAXIM GORKY, *THE LOWER DEPTHS* (1903), 3, TR. ALEXANDER BAKSHY

20. Goodness is uneventful. It does not flash, it glows.

DAVID GRAYSON, *ADVENTURES IN CONTENTMENT* (1907), 11

21. It is a hard thing for a man / to be righteous, if the unrighteous man is to have the greater right.

HESIOD, *WORKS AND DAYS* (8TH C. B.C.), 271, TR. RICHMOND LATTIMORE

22. All men are good when free from passion, interest, or error.

EUGENIO MARÍA DE HOSTOS, "HOMBRES E IDEAS," *OBRAS* (1939–54), 14

23. To make one good action succeed another, is the perfection of goodness.

ALI IBN-ABI-TALIB, *SENTENCES* (7TH C.), 75, TR. SIMON OCKLEY

24. As I know more of mankind I expect less of them, and am ready now to call a man a good man upon easier terms than I was formerly.

SAMUEL JOHNSON, QUOTED IN BOSWELL'S *LIFE OF SAMUEL JOHNSON,* SEPTEMBER 1783

25. Good men are the stars, the planets of the ages wherein they live, and illustrate the times.

BEN JONSON, "EXPLORATA," *TIMBER* (1640)

26. Be good, sweet maid, and let who will be clever.

CHARLES KINGSLEY, "A FAREWELL."

27. Goodness does not more certainly make men happy than happiness makes them good.

WALTER SAVAGE LANDOR, "LORD BROOKE AND SIR PHILIP SIDNEY," *IMAGINARY CONVERSATIONS* (1824–53)

28. Nobody deserves to be praised for his goodness if he has not the power to be wicked. All other goodness is often only weakness and impotence of the will.

LA ROCHEFOUCAULD, *MAXIMS* (1665), TR. KENNETH PRATT

29. It's easier to swoon in pious dreams / Than do good actions.

GOTTHOLD EPHRAIM LESSING, *NATHAN THE WISE* (1779), 1.3, TR. BAYARD QUINCY MORGAN

30. It is from reason that justice springs, but goodness is born of wisdom.

MAURICE MAETERLINCK, *WISDOM AND DESTINY* (1898), 29, TR. ALFRED SUTRO

31. Loving-kindness is the better part of goodness. It lends grace to the sterner qualities of which this consists.

W. SOMERSET MAUGHAM, *THE SUMMING UP* (1938), 77

32. Good, the more / Communicated, more abundant grows.

MILTON, *PARADISE LOST* (1667), 5.71

33. Goodness thinks no ill / Where no ill seems.

MILTON, *PARADISE LOST* (1667), 3.668

34. There is no man so good, who, were he to submit all his thoughts and actions to the laws, would not deserve hanging ten times in his life.

MONTAIGNE, "OF VANITY," *ESSAYS* (1580–88), TR. W. C. HAZLITT

35. To become a good man, one must have faithful friends, or outright enemies.

NAPOLEON I, *MAXIMS* (1804–15)

36. Whatever harm the evil may do, the harm done by the good is the most harmful harm.

NIETZSCHE, "ON OLD AND NEW TABLETS," *THUS SPOKE ZARATHUSTRA* (1883–92), 3, TR. WALTER KAUFMANN

37. Do good by stealth, and blush to find it fame.

ALEXANDER POPE, *EPILOGUE TO THE SATIRES* (1738), 1.136

38. It is his nature, not his standing, that makes the good man.

PUBLILIUS SYRUS, *MORAL SAYINGS* (1ST C. B.C.), 977 , TR. DARIUS LYMAN

39. A good man will never suspect his friends of shady actions: this is part of his goodness. A good man will never be suspected by the public of using his goodness to screen villains: this is part of his utility.

BERTRAND RUSSELL, "THE HARM THAT GOOD MEN DO," *FIFTY FAMOUS ESSAYS* (1964)

40. The good life, as I conceive it, is a happy life. I do not mean that if you are good you will be happy; I mean that if you are happy you will be good.

BERTRAND RUSSELL, *NEW HOPES FOR A CHANGING WORLD* (1951)

41. Be thou good thyself, and let people speak evil of thee; it is better than to be wicked, and that they should consider thee as good.

SA'DI, *GULISTAN* (1258), 2.22, TR. JAMES ROSS

42. Yes, the idiot is indeed the good man, but only because he doesn't know any better.

WILLIAM SAROYAN, "WHAT IT'S ALL ABOUT," *SONS COME & GO, MOTHERS HANG IN FOREVER* (1979)

43. Good people are good because they've come to wisdom through failure.

WILLIAM SAROYAN, *NEW YORK JOURNAL-AMERICAN,* AUG. 23, 1961

44. If to do were as easy as to know what were good to do, chapels had been churches, and poor men's cottages princes' palaces.

SHAKESPEARE, *THE MERCHANT OF VENICE* (1596–97), 1.2.13

45. Living or dead, to a good man there can come no evil.

SOCRATES, IN PLATO'S *APOLOGY* (4TH C. B.C.), TR. LANE COOPER

46. A good man's pedigree is little hunted up.

SPANISH PROVERB

47. Goodness is the only investment that never fails.

THOREAU, "HIGHER LAWS," *WALDEN* (1854)

48. To be good is noble; but to show others how to be good is nobler and no trouble.

MARK TWAIN, "PUDD'NHEAD WILSON'S NEW CALENDAR," *FOLLOWING THE EQUATOR* (1897), 1

49. I am afraid that good people do a great deal of harm in this world. Certainly the greatest harm they do is that they make badness of such extraordinary importance.

OSCAR WILDE, *LADY WINDERMERE'S FAN* (1892); 1

394. GOSSIP

See also 575. MEDDLING; 693. PETTINESS; 833. RUMORS; 846. SCANDAL; 905. SLANDER

1. He that repeateth a matter separateth very friends.

BIBLE, PROVERBS 17:9

2. Out of some little thing, too free a tongue / Can make an outrageous wrangle.

EURIPIDES, *ANDROMACHE* (C. 426 B.C.), TR. JOHN F. NIMS

3. He's my friend that speaks well of me behind my back.

THOMAS FULLER, M.D., *GNOMOLOGIA* (1732), 2465

4. The best loved man or maid in the town would perish with anguish / Could they hear all that their friends say in the course of a day.

JOHN HAY, "DISTICHS" (1871?), 14

5. To create an unfavourable impression, it is not necessary that certain things should be true, but that they have been said.

WILLIAM HAZLITT, *CHARACTERISTICS* (1823)

6. Gossip is an evil thing by nature, she's a light weight to lift up, / oh very easy, but heavy to carry, and hard to put down again.

HESIOD, *WORKS AND DAYS* (8TH C. B.C.), 761, TR. RICHMOND LATTIMORE

7. Men have always detested women's gossip because they suspect the truth: their meaurements are being taken and compared.

ERICA JONG, *FEAR OF FLYING* (1973)

8. Someone who gossips well has a reputation for being good company or even a wit, never for being a gossip.

LOUIS KRONENBERGER, *COMPANY MANNERS* (1954), 3.1

9. Another good thing about gossip is that it is within / everybody's reach, / And it is much more interesting than any / other form of speech.

OGDEN NASH, "I HAVE IT ON GOOD AUTHORITY," *I'M A STRANGER HERE MYSELF* (1938)

10. Count not him among your friends who will retail your privacies to the world.

PUBLILIUS SYRUS, *MORAL SAYINGS* (1ST C. B.C.), 1038, TR. DARIUS LYMAN

11. Gossip needs no carriage.
RUSSIAN PROVERB

12. Whoever gossips to you will gossip about you.
SPANISH PROVERB

13. There is only one thing in the world worse than being talked about, and that is not being talked about.
OSCAR WILDE, *THE PICTURE OF DORIAN GRAY* (1891), 1

395. GOVERNMENT

See also 36. ANARCHY; 101. BUDGET; 102. BUREAUCRACY; 108. CAPITALISM; 132. CITIZENS; 150. COMMUNISM; 172. CONGRESS; 233. DEMOCRACY; 520. KINGS; 682. THE PEOPLE; 730. PRESIDENCY; 831. RULERS; 912. SOCIALISM; 913. SOCIETY; 930. STATE; 931. STATESMEN AND STATESMANSHIP; 964. TAXES; 985. TOTALITARIANISM; 1038. VOTING

1. As the happiness of the people is the sole end of government, so the consent of the people is the only foundation of it.
JOHN ADAMS, PROCLAMATION (1774)

2. The divine science of government is the science of social happiness, and the blessings of society depend entirely on the constitutions of government.
JOHN ADAMS, *THOUGHTS ON GOVERNMENT* (1776)

3. The essence of a free government consists in an effectual control of rivalries.
JOHN ADAMS, *DISCOURSES ON DAVILA* (1789), 4

4. That rule is the better which is exercised over better subjects.
ARISTOTLE, *POLITICS* (4TH C. B.C.), 1.5, TR. BENJAMIN JOWETT

5. You talk about capitalism and communism and all that sort of thing, but the important thing is the struggle everybody is engaged in to get better living conditions, and they are not interested too much in the form of government.
BERNARD M. BARUCH, IN A PRESS CONFERENCE IN NEW YORK CITY, AUG. 18, 1964

6. It is for men to choose whether they will govern themselves or be governed.
HENRY WARD BEECHER, *PROVERBS FROM PLYMOUTH PULPIT* (1887)

7. The worst thing in this world, next to anarchy, is government.
HENRY WARD BEECHER, *PROVERBS FROM PLYMOUTH PULPIT* (1887)

8. Administration, n. An ingenious abstraction in politics, designed to receive the kicks and cuffs due to the premier or president.
AMBROSE BIERCE, *THE DEVIL'S DICTIONARY* (1881–1911)

9. Government is a contrivance of human wisdom to provide for human wants.
EDMUND BURKE, *REFLECTIONS ON THE REVOLUTION IN FRANCE* (1790)

10. In the long-run every government is the exact symbol of its people, with their wisdom and unwisdom.
THOMAS CARLYLE, *PAST AND PRESENT* (1843), 4.4

11. Government is a contrivance of human wisdom to provide for human wants.
JIMMY CARTER, INAUGURAL ADDRESS AS GOVERNOR OF GEORGIA, JAN. 12, 1971, COLLECTED IN *A GOVERNMENT AS GOOD AS ITS PEOPLE* (1977)

12. The proper function of a government is to make it easy for people to do good and difficult for them to do evil.
JIMMY CARTER, INAUGURAL ADDRESS AS GOVERNOR OF GEORGIA, JAN. 12, 1971, COLLECTED IN *A GOVERNMENT AS GOOD AS ITS PEOPLE* (1977)

13. Government is a trust, and the officers of the government are trustees; and both the trust and the trustees are created for the benefit of the people.
HENRY CLAY, SPEECH, LEXINGTON, KY., MAY 16, 1829

14. The requisites of government are that there be sufficiency of food, sufficiency of military equipment, and the confidence of the people in their ruler.
CONFUCIUS, *ANALECTS* (6TH C. B.C.), 12.7, TR. JAMES LEGGE

15. Nations it may be have fashioned their Governments, but the Governments have paid them back in the same coin.
JOSEPH CONRAD, *UNDER WESTERN EYES* (1911), 1.1

16. Every time the government attempts to handle our affairs, it costs more and the results are worse than if we had handled them ourselves.
BENJAMIN CONSTANT, *COURS DE POLITIQUE CONSTITUTIONNELLE* (1818–20)

17. Every central government worships uniformity: uniformity relieves it from inquiry into an infinity of details, which must be attended to if rules have to be adapted to different men, instead of indiscriminately subjecting all men to the same rule.
ALEXIS DE TOCQUEVILLE, *DEMOCRACY IN AMERICA* (1835–39), 2.4.3

18. In a healthy nation there is a kind of dramatic balance between the will of the people and the government, which prevents its degeneration into tyranny.

EINSTEIN, *OUT OF MY LATER LIFE* (1950), 27

19. Only one in command: that's the way in the home / And the way in the state when it must find / Measures best for mankind.

EURIPIDES, *ANDROMACHE* (C. 426 B.C.), TR. JOHN F. NIMS

20. Those who govern, having much business on their hands, do not generally like to take the trouble of considering and carrying into execution new projects. The best public measures are therefore seldom adopted from previous wisdom, but forced by the occasion.

BENJAMIN FRANKLIN, *AUTOBIOGRAPHY* (1791), 2

21. The view that government's role is to serve as an umpire to prevent individuals from coercing one another was replaced by the view that government's role is to serve as a parent charged with the duty of coercing someone to aid others.

MILTON FRIEDMAN & ROSE FRIEDMAN, *FREE TO CHOOSE* (1980)

22. Religious factions will go on imposing their will on others unless the decent people connected to them recognize that religion has no place in public policy.

BARRY GOLDWATER, IN A SPEECH (1981)

23. Even to observe neutrality you must have a strong government.

ALEXANDER HAMILTON, ADDRESS, CONSTITUTIONAL CONVENTION, JUNE 29, 1787

24. No matter how noble the objectives of a government, if it blurs decency and kindness, cheapens human life, and breeds ill will and suspicion—it is an evil government.

ERIC HOFFER, *THE PASSIONATE STATE OF MIND* (1954), 147

25. Chaos and ineptitude are anti-human; but so too is a superlatively efficient government, equipped with all the products of a highly developed technology.

ALDOUS HUXLEY, *TOMORROW AND TOMORROW AND TOMORROW* (1956)

26. If the perpetual oscillation of nations between anarchy and despotism is to be replaced by the steady march of self-restraining freedom, it will be because men will gradually bring themselves to deal with political, as they now deal with scientific questions.

THOMAS HENRY HUXLEY, "SCIENCE AND CULTURE" (1880)

27. A good government remains the greatest of human blessings, and no nation has ever enjoyed it.

WILLIAM RALPH INGE, "THE STATE, VISIBLE AND INVISIBLE," *OUTSPOKEN ESSAYS: SECOND SERIES* (1922)

28. There are no necessary evils in government. Its evils exist only in its abuses.

ANDREW JACKSON, VETO OF THE BANK BILL, JULY 10, 1832

29. The only orthodox object of the institution of government is to secure the greatest degree of happiness possible to the general mass of those associated under it.

THOMAS JEFFERSON, LETTER TO F. A. VAN DER KEMP, MARCH 22, 1812

30. A compassionate government keeps faith with the trust of the people and cherishes the future of their children. Through compassion for the plight of one individual, government fulfills its purpose as the servant of all the people.

LYNDON B. JOHNSON, *MY HOPE FOR AMERICA* (1964)

31. I would not give half a guinea to live under one form of government rather than another. It is of no moment to the happiness of an individual.

SAMUEL JOHNSON, QUOTED IN BOSWELL'S *LIFE OF SAMUEL JOHNSON,* MARCH 31, 1772

32. Forms of government are forged mainly in the fire of practice, not in the vacuum of theory. They respond to national character and to national realities.

GEORGE F. KENNAN, *AMERICAN DIPLOMACY 1900–1950* (1951)

33. Any system of government will work when everything is going well. It's the system that functions in the pinches that survives.

JOHN F. KENNEDY, *WHY ENGLAND SLEPT* (1940)

34. The basis of effective government is public confidence.

JOHN F. KENNEDY, MESSAGE TO CONGRESS ON ETHICAL CONDUCT IN GOVERNMENT, APRIL 27, 1961

35. It is safe to assert that no government proper ever had a provision in its organic law for its own termination.

ABRAHAM LINCOLN, FIRST INAUGURAL ADDRESS, MARCH 4, 1861

36. No man is good enough to govern another man without that other's consent.

Abraham Lincoln, speech, Oct. 16, 1854

37. It is perfectly true that that government is best which governs least. It is equally true that that government is best which provides most.

Walter Lippmann, "The Red Herring," *A Preface to Politics* (1914)

38. Popular government has not yet been proved to guarantee, always and everywhere, good government.

Walter Lippmann, *The Public Philosophy* (1955), 1.2

39. The invisible government [bosses] is malign. But the evil doesn't come from the fact that it plays horse with the Newtonian theory of the constitution. What is dangerous about it is that we do not see it, cannot use it, and are compelled to submit to it.

Walter Lippmann, "Routineer and Inventor," *A Preface to Politics* (1914)

40. no form of government / matters nearly as much / as the spirit and intelligence / brought to the administration / of any form of government.

Don Marquis, "archy's newest deal," *Archy Does His Part* (1935)

41. It must be that to govern a nation you need a specific talent and that this may very well exist without general ability.

W. Somerset Maugham, *The Summing Up* (1938), 1

42. Virtue alone is not sufficient for the exercise of government; laws alone cannot carry themselves into practice.

Mencius, *Works* (4th–3rd c. b.c.), 4, tr. Charles A. Wong

43. It is very easy to accuse a government of imperfection, for all mortal things are full of it.

Montaigne, "Of presumption," *Essays* (1580–88), tr. W. C. Hazlitt

44. The art of governing consists in not letting men grow old in their jobs.

Napoleon I, *Maxims* (1804–15)

45. Governments arise either out of the people or over the people.

Thomas Paine, *The Rights of Man* (1791), 1

46. Society is produced by our wants and government by our wickedness.

Thomas Paine, "On the Origin and Design of Government," *Common Sense* (1776)

47. Society in every state is a blessing, but government, even in its best state, is but a necessary evil; in its worst state an intolerable one.

Thomas Paine, "On the Origin and Design of Government," *Common Sense* (1776)

48. The guilt of a government is the crime of a whole country.

Thomas Paine, *The American Crisis* (1776–83), 12

49. Governments exist to protect the rights of minorities. The loved and the rich need no protection: they have many friends and few enemies.

Wendell Phillips, speech, Boston, Dec. 21, 1860

50. I have always thought of government as a kind of organism with an insatiable appetite for money, whose natural state is to grow forever unless you do something to starve it.

Ronald Reagan, *An American Life* (1990)

51. Nothing is as dangerous for the state as those who would govern kingdoms with maxims found in books.

Cardinal Richelieu, *Political Testament* (1687), 1.8

52. It is the purpose of the government to see that not only the legitimate interests of the few are protected but that the welfare and rights of the many are conserved.

Franklin D. Roosevelt, speech, Portland, Ore., Sept. 21, 1932

53. The body politic, as well as the human body, begins to die as soon as it is born, and carries in itself the causes of its destruction.

Rousseau, *The Social Contract* (1762), 3.11, tr. G. D. H. Cole

54. Government and co-operation are in all things the laws of life; anarchy and competition the laws of death.

John Ruskin, *Unto This Last* (1862), 3.54

55. In our complex world, there cannot be fruitful initiative without government, but unfortunately there can be government without initiative.

Bertrand Russell, "Control and Initiative," *Authority and the Individual* (1949)

56. A permissive government is a government that leaves control to other sources.

B.F. Skinner, *Beyond Freedom and Dignity* (1971)

57. Government is at best but an expedient; but most governments are usually, and all governments are sometimes, inexpedient.

Thoreau, *Civil Disobedience* (1849)

58. History is replete with proofs, from Cato the Elder to Kennedy the Younger, that if you scratch a statesman you find an actor, but it is becoming harder and harder, in our time, to tell government from show business.

JAMES THURBER, "HOW TO TELL GOVERNMENT FROM SHOW BUSINESS," *COLLECTING HIMSELF* (1989)

59. The pleasure of governing must certainly be exquisite, if we may judge from the vast numbers who are eager to be concerned with it.

VOLTAIRE, "GOVERNMENT," *PHILOSOPHICAL DICTIONARY* (1764)

60. Governments are best classified by considering who are the "somebodies" they are in fact endeavoring to satisfy.

ALFRED NORTH WHITEHEAD, *ADVENTURES IN IDEAS* (1933), 4

61. Man is about the same, in the main, whether with despotism, or whether with freedom.

WALT WHITMAN, "DEMOCRACY IN THE NEW WORLD," *NOTES LEFT OVER* (1881)

62. Government expands to absorb revenue and then some.

TOM WICKER, QUOTED BY HAROLD FABER IN *THE NEW YORK TIMES MAGAZINE,* MARCH 17, 1968

63. No government has ever been beneficent when the attitude of government was that it was taking care of the people. The only freedom consists in the people taking care of the government.

WOODROW WILSON, ADDRESS, SEPT. 4, 1912

64. The firm basis of government is justice, not pity.

WOODROW WILSON, INAUGURAL ADDRESS, MARCH 4, 1912

396. GRACE

See also 372. GAUCHERIE

1. Those graces which from their presumed facility encourage all to attempt an imitation of them, are usually the most inimitable.

CHARLES CALEB COLTON, *LACON* (1825), 1.584

2. Without grace beauty is an unbaited hook.

FRENCH PROVERB

3. Grace is the absence of everything that indicates pain or difficulty, hesitation or incongruity.

WILLIAM HAZLITT, "ON BEAUTY," *THE ROUND TABLE* (1817)

4. If we cannot be decent, let us endeavor to be graceful. If we can't be moral, at least we can avoid being vulgar.

LANGDON MITCHELL, *THE NEW YORK IDEA* (1907), 2

397. GRAFFITI

1. A white wall is the fool's paper.

FRENCH PROVERB

398. GRAMMAR

See also 524. LANGUAGE; 1064. WORDS

1. Grammar, n. A system of pitfalls thoughtfully prepared for the feet of the self-made man, along the path by which he advances to distinction.

AMBROSE BIERCE, *THE DEVIL'S DICTIONARY* (1881–1911)

2. I believe it is imperative to see modern English grammar as a rich and diverse linguistic system deposited on our [England's] shores 1,500 years ago, and left with us *unweakened,* though substantially changed by the social and political events of the intervening period.

ROBERT BURCHFIELD, *UNLOCKING THE ENGLISH LANGUAGE* (1989)

3. The adjective is the banana peel of the parts of speech.

CLIFTON FADIMAN, *READER'S DIGEST,* SEPTEMBER 1956

4. [N]ative speakers of a language know intuitively whether a sentence is grammatical or not. They usually cannot specify exactly what is wrong, and very possibly they make the same mistakes in their own speech, but they know—unconsciously, not as a set of rules they learned in school—when a sentence is incorrect.

PETER FARB, *WORD PLAY* (1973)

5. Quite naturally, scholars assumed that Latin grammar was not merely Latin grammar, but that it was grammar itself. They borrowed it and made the most of it.

CHARLTON LAIRD, *THE MIRACLE OF LANGUAGE* (1953)

6. [G]rammar is not a set of rules; it is something inherent in the language, and language cannot exist without it. It can be discovered, but not invented.

CHARLTON LAIRD, *THE MIRACLE OF LANGUAGE* (1953)

7. [T]he truth seems to be that they [teachers of grammar] were victims of a mighty hoax, one of those

true belly-rumbling impostures which a workaday world can but seldom afford.

CHARLTON LAIRD, *THE MIRACLE OF LANGUAGE* (1953)

8. It is well to remember that grammar is common speech formulated.

W. SOMERSET MAUGHAM, *THE SUMMING UP* (1938), 13

9. The speaker does not feel the *grammatical* rules he is said to apply in composing sentences, and men spoke grammatically for thousands of years before anyone knew there were rules.

B.F. SKINNER, *BEYOND FREEDOM AND DIGNITY* (1971)

10. Damn the subjunctive. It brings all our writers to shame.

MARK TWAIN, *NOTEBOOK* (1935)

11. A writer who can't write in a grammerly manner better shut up shop.

ARTEMUS WARD, "SCIENCE AND NATURAL HISTORY," *ARTEMUS WARD IN LONDON* (1872)

12. English usage is sometimes more than mere taste, judgment, and education—sometimes it's sheer luck, like getting across a street.

E. B. WHITE, "SHOP TALK," *THE SECOND TREE FROM THE CORNER* (1954)

399. GRATITUDE

See also 47. APPRECIATION; 475. INGRATITUDE; 647. OBLIGATION

1. God give you pardon from gratitude / and other mild forms of servitude.

ROBERT CREELEY, "SONG," *FOR LOVE* (1962)

2. Gratefulness is the poor man's payment.

ENGLISH PROVERB

3. Revenge is profitable, gratitude is expensive.

EDWARD GIBBON, *DECLINE AND FALL OF THE ROMAN EMPIRE* (1776), 11

4. In the majority of men gratitude is only a veiled desire of receiving greater benefaction.

LA ROCHEFOUCAULD, *MAXIMS* (1665), TR. KENNETH PRATT

5. We seldom find people ungrateful so long as we are in a position to be beneficial.

LA ROCHEFOUCAULD, *MAXIMS* (1665), TR. KENNETH PRATT

6. A child shows gratitude the way a woman/Shows she likes a pretty dress—/Puts it on and takes it off again—

ARCHIBALD MACLEISH, *JB* (1957)

7. Gratitude is the most exquisite form of courtesy.

JACQUES MARITAIN, *REFLECTIONS ON AMERICA* (1958), 17

8. A grateful mind / By owing owes not, but still pays, at once / Indebted and discharged.

MILTON, *PARADISE LOST* (1667), 4.55

9. Evermore thanks, the exchequer of the poor.

SHAKESPEARE, *RICHARD II* (1595–96), 2.3.65

10. Bees sip honey from flowers and hum their thanks when they leave. / The gaudy butterfly is sure that the flowers owe thanks to him.

RABINDRANATH TAGORE, *STRAY BIRDS* (1916), 127

11. Gratitude is a debt which usually goes on accumulating like blackmail; the more you pay, the more is exacted.

MARK TWAIN, *AUTOBIOGRAPHY* (1924), V. 1

12. For all that you have done, I am ever mindful. How can you doubt that I ever forgot it—but don't remind me of it too much at this time.

THOMAS WOLFE, *THOMAS WOLFE'S LETTERS TO HIS MOTHER* (1943)

400. GREAT AND SMALL

See also 401. GREATNESS; 649. OBSCURITY; 908. SMALLNESS; 1012. UNIMPORTANCE

1. You may share the labours of the great, but you will not share the spoil.

AESOP, "THE LION'S SHARE," *FABLES* (6TH C. B.C.?), TR. JOSEPH JACOBS

2. When the house of a great one collapses / Many little ones are slain.

BERTOLT BRECHT, *THE CAUCASIAN CHALK CIRCLE* (1944–45), 1.1, TR. MAJA APELMAN

3. We find great things are made of little things, / And little things go lessening till at last / Comes God behind them.

ROBERT BROWNING, "MR. SLUDGE, -THE MEDIUM,'" *DRAMATIS PERSONAE* (1864)

4. No man is so tall that he need never stretch and none so small that he need never stoop.

DANISH PROVERB

5. A great man stands on God. A small man stands on a great man.

EMERSON, *JOURNALS*, 1839

6. The privilege and pleasure / That we treasure beyond measure / Is to run on little errands for the Ministers of State.

W. S. GILBERT, *THE GONDOLIERS* (1889), 2

7. From the height from which the great look down on the world all the rest of mankind seem equal.

WILLIAM HAZLITT, "COMMONPLACES," *THE ROUND TABLE* (1817), 23

8. Great men too often have greater faults than little men can find room for.

WALTER SAVAGE LANDOR, "DIOGENES AND PLATO," *IMAGINARY CONVERSATIONS* (1824–53.)

9. However big the whale may be, the tiny harpoon can rob him of life.

MALAY PROVERB

10. The great man is too often all of a piece; it is the little man that is a bundle of contradictory elements. He is inexhaustible. You never come to the end of the surprises he has in store for you.

W. SOMERSET MAUGHAM, *THE SUMMING UP* (1938), 2

11. The herd seek out the great, not for their sake but for their influence; and the great welcome them out of vanity or need.

NAPOLEON I, *MAXIMS* (1804–15)

12. I will be small in small things, great among great.

PINDAR, *ODES* (5TH C. B.C.), PYTHIA 3, TR. RICHMOND LATTIMORE

401. GREATNESS

See also 400. GREAT AND SMALL; 418. HEROES AND HEROISM; 525. LARGENESS; 649. OBSCURITY; 1012. UNIMPORTANCE

1. Men in great places are thrice servants: servants of the sovereign or state, servants of fame, and servants of business.

FRANCIS BACON, "OF GREAT PLACE," *ESSAYS* (1625)

2. Great men are but life-sized. Most of them, indeed, are rather short.

MAX BEERBOHM, "A POINT TO BE REMEMBERED BY VERY EMINENT MEN," *AND EVEN NOW* (1920)

3. He is greatest who is most often in men's good thoughts.

SAMUEL BUTLER (D. 1902), "HIGGLEDY-PIGGLEDY," *NOTE-BOOKS* (1912)

4. Men worship the shows of great men; the most disbelieve that there is any reality of great men to worship.

THOMAS CARLYLE, *ON HEROES, HERO-WORSHIP AND THE HEROIC IN HISTORY* (1841), 3

5. The loftiest towers rise from the ground.

CHINESE PROVERB

6. Greatness and goodness are not means, but ends.

SAMUEL TAYLOR COLERIDGE, "THE GOOD GREAT MAN" (1802)

7. Great men, like comets, are eccentric in their courses, and formed to do extensive good by modes unintelligible to vulgar minds.

CHARLES CALEB COLTON, *LACON* (1825), 1.252

8. Great offices will have great talents.

WILLIAM COWPER, "THE WINTER EVENING," *THE TASK* (1785), 788

9. The greatest spirits are capable of the greatest vices as well as of the greatest virtues.

DESCARTES, *DISCOURSE ON METHOD* (1639) 1

10. Desire of greatness is a godlike sin.

JOHN DRYDEN, *ABSALOM AND ACHITOPHEL* (1681), 1.372

11. Let him be great, and love shall follow him.

EMERSON, "SPIRITUAL LAWS," *ESSAYS: FIRST SERIES* (1841)

12. The measure of a master is his success in bringing all men round to his opinion twenty years later.

EMERSON, "CULTURE," *THE CONDUCT OF LIFE* (1860)

13. To be great is to be misunderstood.

EMERSON, "SELF RELIANCE," *ESSAYS: FIRST SERIES* (1941)

14. When nature removes a great man, people explore the horizon for a successor; but none comes, and none will. His class is extinguished with him. In some other and quite different field, the next man will appear.

EMERSON, "USES OF GREAT MEN," *REPRESENTATIVE MEN* (1850)

15. No great thing is created suddenly.

EPICTETUS, *DISCOURSES* (2ND C.), 1.15, TR. THOMAS W. HIGGINSON

16. Greatness brings no profit to people. / God indeed, when in anger, brings / greater ruin to great men's houses.

EURIPIDES, *MEDEA* (431 B.C.), TR. REX WARNER

17. I distrust Great Men. They produce a desert of uniformity around them and often a pool of blood too, and I always feel a little man's pleasure when they come a cropper.

E. M. Forster, "What I Believe," *Two Cheers for Democracy* (1951)

18. All great expression, which on a superficial survey seems so easy as well as so simple, furnishes after a while, to the faithful observer, its own standard by which to appreciate it.

Margaret Fuller, *Summer on the Lakes* (1844), 1

19. All greatness affects different minds, each in "its own particular kind," and the variations of testimony mark the truth of feeling.

Margaret Fuller, *Summer on the Lakes* (1844), 1

20. Great and good are seldom the same man.

Thomas Fuller, M.D., *Gnomologia* (1732), 1752

21. The privilege of the great is to see catastrophes from a terrace.

Jean Giraudoux, *Tiger at the Gates* (1935), 2.13

22. To make an epoch in the world, two conditions are manifestly essential—a good head and a great inheritance.

Goethe, quoted in Johann Peter Eckermann's *Conversations with Goethe,* May 2, 1824

23. Few great men could pass Personnel.

Paul Goodman, *Growing Up Absurd* (1960), 7.6

24. Great men have to be lifted upon the shoulders of the whole world, in order to conceive their great ideas, or perform their great deeds.

Nathaniel Hawthorne, *Journals,* May 7, 1850

25. He who comes up to his own idea of greatness must always have had a very low standard of it in his mind.

William Hazlitt, "Whether Genius Is Conscious of Its Powers?" *The Plain Speaker* (1826)

26. No man is truly great who is great only in his lifetime. The test of greatness is the page of history.

William Hazlitt, "The Indian Jugglers," *Table Talk* (1821–22)

27. No really great man ever thought himself so.

William Hazlitt, "Whether Genius Is Conscious of Its Powers?" *The Plain Speaker* (1826)

28. A great man's greatest good luck is to die at the right time.

Eric Hoffer, *The Passionate State of Mind* (1954), 276

29. A great man represents a great ganglion in the nerves of society, or, to vary the figure, a strategic point in the campaign of history, and part of his greatness consists in his being *there*.

Oliver Wendell Holmes, Jr., speech on John Marshall, Feb. 4, 1901

30. To know the great men dead is compensation for having to live with the mediocre.

Elbert Hubbard, *The Note Book* (1927)

31. No man was ever great by imitation.

Samuel Johnson, *Rasselas* (1759), 10

32. He ne'er is crowned / With immortality, who fears to follow / Where airy voices lead.

Keats, *Endymion* (1817), 2

33. I would sooner fail than not be among the greatest.

Keats, letter to James Augustus Hessey, Oct. 8, 1818

34. To be a great man it is necessary to know how to profit by the whole of our good fortune.

La Rochefoucauld, *Maxims* (1665), tr. Kenneth Pratt

35. Great men too make mistakes, and many among them do it so often that one is almost tempted to call them little men.

Georg Christoph Lichtenberg, *Aphorisms* (1764–99), tr. J. P. Stern

36. Lives of great men all remind us / We can make our lives sublime, / And, departing, leave behind us / Footprints on the sands of time.

Longfellow, "A Psalm of Life" (1839), 7

37. Every great man inevitably resents a partner in greatness.

Lucan, *On the Civil War* (1st c.), tr. Robert Graves

38. Though a tree grow ever so high, the falling leaves return to the root.

Malay Proverb

39. Men are like the stars: some generate their own light while others reflect the brilliance they receive.

José Martí, *Granos de oro: pensamientos seleccionados en las Obras de José Martí* (1942)

40. Because a man can write great works he is none the less a man.

W. Somerset Maugham, *The Summing Up* (1938), 16

41. Conceit and presumption have not been any more fatal to the world, than the waste which comes

of great men failing in their hearts to recognise how great they are.

JOHN MORLEY, "BYRON," *CRITICAL MISCELLANIES* (1871–1908)

42. In a narrow sphere great men are blunderers.

NAPOLEON I, *MAXIMS* (1804–15)

43. It is the privilege of greatness to confer intense happiness with insignificant gifts.

NIETZSCHE, *HUMAN, ALL TOO HUMAN* (1878), 496, TR. HELEN ZIMMERN

44. A great man does not lose his self-possession when he is afflicted; the ocean is not made muddy by the falling in of its banks.

PANCHATANTRA (C. 5TH C.), 1, TR. FRANKLIN EDGERTON

45. Do not despise the bottom rungs in the ascent to greatness.

PUBLILIUS SYRUS, *MORAL SAYINGS* (1ST C. B.C.), 579

46. Greatness is not the effect of which inspiration is the cause. We are all inspired, but we are all not great.

NED ROREM, "FOUR QUESTIONS ANSWERED," *MUSIC FROM INSIDE OUT* (1967)

47. All great books contain boring portions, and all great lives have contained uninteresting stretches.

BERTRAND RUSSELL, *THE CONQUEST OF HAPPINESS* (1930), 4

48. A great man need not be virtuous, nor his opinions right, but he must have a firm mind, a distinctive luminous character.

GEORGE SANTAYANA, *WINDS OF DOCTRINE* (1913)

49. The loftiest edifices need the deepest foundations.

GEORGE SANTAYANA, *THE LIFE OF REASON: REASON IN SOCIETY* (1905–06), 1

50. Some are born great, some achieve greatness, and some have greatness thrust upon 'em.

SHAKESPEARE, *TWELFTH NIGHT* (1599–1600), 2.5.157

51. They that stand high have many blasts to shake them.

SHAKESPEARE, *RICHARD III* (1592–93), 1.3.259

52. Great men hallow a whole people, and lift up all who live in their time.

SYDNEY SMITH, QUOTED IN LADY S. HOLLAND'S *MEMOIR* (1855), V. 1.7

53. You achieve stature only by being good enough to deserve it, by forcing even the contemptuous and indifferent to pay attention, and to acknowledge that human relations and human emotions are of inexhaustible interest wherever they occur.

WALLACE STEGNER, "COMING OF AGE: THE END OF THE BEGINNING," *WHEN THE BLUEBIRD SINGS IN THE LEMONADE SPRINGS* (1992)

54. Nothing is likely about masterpieces, least of all whether there will be any.

IGOR STRAVINSKY, *CONVERSATIONS WITH IGOR STRAVINSKY* (1959)

55. Great men have all been formed either before academies or independent of them.

VOLTAIRE, "SOCIETY OF LONDON, AND ACADEMIES," *PHILOSOPHICAL DICTIONARY* (1764)

56. There are only two sorts of greatness: true greatness, which is of a spiritual order, and the old, old lie of world conquest. Conquest is an ersatz greatness.

SIMONE WEIL, *THE NEED FOR ROOTS* (1952), TR. ARTHUR WILLS

57. A man is not as big as his belief in himself; he is as big as the number of persons who believe in him.

WOODROW WILSON, SPEECH, OCT. 3, 1912

58. Masterpieces are not single and solitary births; they are the outcome of many years of thinking in common, of thinking by the body of the people, so that the experience of the mass is behind the single voice.

VIRGINIA WOOLF, *A ROOM OF ONE'S OWN* (1929), 4

59. None think the great unhappy but the great.

EDWARD YOUNG, *LOVE OF FAME* (1728), 1.238

402. GREECE, ANCIENT

See also 42. ANTIQUITY

1. The spirit of Greece, passing through and ascending above the world, hath so animated universal nature, that the very rocks and woods, the very torrents and wilds burst forth with it.

WALTER SAVAGE LANDOR, "SCIPIO, POLYBIUS, AND PANAETIUS," *IMAGINARY CONVERSATIONS* (1824–53)

2. We [Greeks] are lovers of the beautiful, yet simple in our tastes, and we cultivate the mind without loss of manliness.

THUCYDIDES, *THE PELOPONNESIAN WAR* (C. 400 B.C.), 2.40, TR. BENJAMIN JOWETT

403. GREED

See also 8. ACQUISITION; 312. EXCESS; 595. MISERS

1. It is not greedy to enjoy a good dinner, any more than it is greedy to enjoy a good concert. But I do think there is something greedy about trying to enjoy the dinner and the concert at the same time.

G. K. CHESTERTON, "ON PLEASURE-SEEKING," *GENERALLY SPEAKING* (1928)

2. The avarice of the miser may be termed the grand sepulchre of all his other passions, as they successively decay.

CHARLES CALEB COLTON, *LACON* (1825), 1.24

3. Avarice is a fine, absorbin' passion, an' manny an ol' fellow is as happy with his arm around his bank account as he was sleigh ridin' with his first girl.

FINLEY PETER DUNNE, "ON OLD AGE," *MR. DOOLEY ON MAKING A WILL* (1919)

4. Want is a growing giant whom the coat of Have was never large enough to cover.

EMERSON, "WEALTH," *THE CONDUCT OF LIFE* (1860)

5. When all other sins are old, avarice is still young.

FRENCH PROVERB

6. He is not poor that hath not much, but he that craves much.

THOMAS FULLER, M.D., *GNOMOLOGIA* (1732), 1937

7. If your desires be endless, your cares and fears will be so too.

THOMAS FULLER, M.D., *GNOMOLOGIA* (1732), 2803

8. Riches have made more covetous men than covetousness hath made rich men.

THOMAS FULLER, M.D., *GNOMOLOGIA* (1732), 4044

9. Nothing in the world is so incontinent as a man's accursed appetite.

HOMER, *ODYSSEY* (9TH C. B.C.), 7, TR. E. V. RIEU

10. Care clings to wealth: the thirst for more / Grows as our fortunes grow.

HORACE, *ODES* (23–C. 15 B.C.), 3.16

11. A covetous man's penny is a stone.

ALI IBN-ABI-TALIB, *SENTENCES* (7TH C.), 8, TR. SIMON OCKLEY

12. Extreme avarice misapprehends itself almost always; there is no passion which more often misses its aim, nor upon which the present has so much influence to the prejudice of the future.

LA ROCHEFOUCAULD, *MAXIMS* (1665), TR. KENNETH PRATT

13. Avarice is a cursed vice: offer a man enough gold, and he will part with his own small hoard of food, however great his hunger.

LUCAN, *ON THE CIVIL WAR* (1ST C.), TR. ROBERT GRAVES

14. People who are greedy have extraordinary capacities for waste—they must, they take in too much.

NORMAN MAILER, *MIAMI AND THE SIEGE OF CHICAGO* (1968), 2.2

15. The covetous man fares worse with his passion than the poor, and the jealous man than the cuckold.

MONTAIGNE, "OF PRESUMPTION," *ESSAYS* (1580–88), TR. W. C. HAZLITT

16. I could not possibly count the gold-digging ruses of women, / Not if I had ten mouths, not if I had ten tongues.

OVID, *THE ART OF LOVE* (C. A.D. 8), 1, TR. ROLFE HUMPHRIES

17. Though avarice will prevent a man from being necessitously poor, it generally makes him too timorous to be wealthy.

THOMAS PAINE, "OF MONARCHY AND HEREDITARY SUCCESSION," *COMMON SENSE* (1776)

18. To hazard much to get much has more of avarice than wisdom.

WILLIAM PENN, *SOME FRUITS OF SOLITUDE* (1693), 1.247

19. Avarice is as destitute of what it has, as poverty of what it has not.

PUBLILIUS SYRUS, *MORAL SAYINGS* (1ST C. B.C.), 1079, TR. DARIUS LYMAN

20. For greed all nature is too little.

SENECA, *HERCULES OETAEUS* (1ST C.), 631, TR. FRANK JUSTUS MILLER

21. Greed's worst point is its ingratitude.

SENECA, *LETTERS TO LUCILIUS* (1ST C.), 73.3, TR. E. PHILLIPS BARKER

22. Though statisticians in our time have never kept the score, Man wants a great deal here below and Woman even more.

JAMES THURBER, "THE GODFATHER AND HIS GODCHILD," *FURTHER FABLES FOR OUR TIME* (1956)

23. Men hate the individual whom they call avaricious only because nothing can be gained from him.

VOLTAIRE, "AVARICE," *PHILOSOPHICAL DICTIONARY* (1764)

GRIEF

See 918. SORROW

GROUP

See 152. COMPANY; 208. CROWDS; 597. MOB

404. GROWTH AND DEVELOPMENT

See also 452. IMMATURITY; 532. LEARNING; 571. MATURITY; 654. OPEN-MINDEDNESS; 717. POTENTIAL; 988. TRAINING

1. I know the most important faculty to develop is one for hard, continuous and varied work and living; but the difference between knowing this and doing anything consistent about it is often abysmal.

JAMES AGEE, *LETTERS OF JAMES AGEE TO FATHER FLYE* (1962)

2. Some people are molded by their admirations, others by their hostilities.

ELIZABETH BOWEN, *THE DEATH OF THE HEART* (1938), 2.2

3. The child is not a prisoner of its inheritance; it holds its inheritance as a new creation which its future actions will unfold.

JACOB BRONOWSKI, *THE ASCENT OF MAN* (1973)

4. Growth itself contains the germ of happiness.

PEARL S. BUCK, "TO THE YOUNG," *TO MY DAUGHTERS, WITH LOVE* (1967)

5. Every one should keep a mental wastepaper basket and the older he grows the more things he will consign to it—torn up to irrecoverable tatters.

SAMUEL BUTLER (D. 1902), "HIGGLEDY-PIGGLEDY," *NOTE-BOOKS* (1912)

6. The strongest principle of growth lies in human choice.

GEORGE ELIOT, *DANIEL DERONDA* (1874–76), 6.42

7. A man's growth is seen in the successive choirs of his friends.

EMERSON, "CIRCLES," *ESSAYS: FIRST SERIES* (1841)

8. In some ways, spiritual growth resembles a game of leapfrog. As soon as we've got past one puzzling question, we discover we're faced with another.

JEAN GRASSO FITZPATRICK, *SOMETHING MORE* (1991)

9. The most important influence on a child is the character of its parents, rather than this or that single event.

ERICH FROMM, *THE ANATOMY OF HUMAN DESTRUCTIVENESS* (1973)

10. Man always dies before he is fully born.

ERICH FROMM, *MAN FOR HIMSELF* (1947), 3

11. Man, the most complicated of the animals, has a relatively short gestation period. Beyond that, he will be born, unlike most mammals, in a ridiculously helpless state.

WILLARD GAYLIN, *FEELINGS: OUR VITAL SIGNS* (1979)

12. A road that does not lead to other roads always has to be retraced, unless the traveller chooses to rust at the end of it.

TEHYI HSIEH, *CHINESE EPIGRAMS INSIDE OUT AND PROVERBS* (1948), 144

13. A child-like man is not a man whose development has been arrested; on the contrary, he is a man who has given himself a chance of continuing to develop long after most adults have muffled themselves in the cocoon of middle-aged habit and convention.

ALDOUS HUXLEY, "VULGARITY IN LITERATURE," *MUSIC AT NIGHT* (1931)

14. Whatever is formed for long duration arrives slowly to its maturity.

SAMUEL JOHNSON, *THE RAMBLER* (1750–52), 169

15. [A]s every parent knows, children go through an adolescent growth spurt, during which they put on inches at an alarming rate. Humans are unique in this respect: most mammalian species, including apes, progress almost directly from infancy to adulthood.

RICHARD LEAKEY, *THE ORIGIN OF HUMANKIND* (1994)

16. Just as we outgrow a pair of trousers, we outgrow acquaintances, libraries, principles, etc., at times before they're worn out and at times—and this is the worst of all—before we have new ones.

GEORG CHRISTOPH LICHTENBERG, *APHORISMS* (1764–99), TR. H. HATFIELD

17. All growth is a leap in the dark, a spontaneous, unpremeditated act without benefit of experience.

HENRY MILLER, "THE ABSOLUTE COLLECTIVE," *THE WISDOM OF THE HEART* (1941)

18. The great golden goal of every childhood—being a Grownup—seemed impossibly far away. There were for us no intermediate goals to fill the great, dull gap; no graduation from one stage of education to the next; no adolescent "first parties" to look forward to.

JESSICA MITFORD, *DAUGHTERS AND REBELS* (1960)

19. Growth is the only evidence of life.

JOHN HENRY NEWMAN, *APOLOGIA PRO VITA SUA* (1864)

20. One must be thrust out of a finished cycle in life, and that leap [is] the most difficult to make—to part with one's faith, one's love, when one would prefer to renew the faith and recreate the passion.

ANAÏS NIN, *THE DIARY OF ANAÏS NIN*, NOVEMBER 1932

21. Stretch your foot to the length of your blanket.

PERSIAN PROVERB

22. Not to go back is somewhat to advance, / And men must walk, at least, before they dance.

ALEXANDER POPE, *EPILOGUE TO THE SATIRES* (1738), 1.1.53

23. Some people seem as if they can never have been children, and others seem as if they could never be anything else.

GEORGE DENNISON PRENTICE, *PRENTICEANA* (1860)

24. There is no fruit which is not bitter before it is ripe.

PUBLILIUS SYRUS, *MORAL SAYINGS* (1ST C. B.C.), 561, TR. DARIUS LYMAN

25. Life is cut to allow for growth ... one may vigorously put on weight before one fills it out entirely.

RAINER MARIA RILKE, LETTER TO ALFRED WALTHER VON HEYMEL, OCT. 12, 1941, IN *WARTIME LETTERS*, TR. M. D. HERTER NORTON

26. No single event can awaken within us a stranger totally unknown to us. To live is to be slowly born.

SAINT-EXUPÉRY, *FLIGHT TO ARRAS* (1942), 8, TR. LEWIS GALANTIÈRE

27. Manhood and sagacity ripen of themselves; it suffices not to repress or distort them.

GEORGE SANTAYANA, *CHARACTER AND OPINION IN THE UNITED STATES* (1921), 2

28. Every man's road in life is marked by the graves of his personal likings.

ALEXANDER SMITH, "ON THE IMPORTANCE OF A MAN TO HIMSELF," *DREAMTHORP* (1863)

29. There is a time in our life when we need to strut our stuff and groove on grandiosity, when we need to be viewed as remarkable and rare, when we need to exhibit ourself in front of a mirror that reflects our self-admiration, when we need a parent to function as that mirror.

JUDITH VIORST, *NECESSARY LOSSES* (1986)

30. The Child is father of the Man.

WILLIAM WORDSWORTH, "MY HEART LEAPS UP WHEN I BEHOLD" (1802)

GUESTS

See 428. HOSPITALITY

405. GUILT

See also 174. CONSCIENCE; 847. SCAPEGOAT; 893. SHAME

1. Where all are guilty, no one is; confessions of collective guilt are the best possible safeguard against the discovery of culprits, and the very magnitude of the crime the best excuse for doing nothing.

HANNAH ARENDT, *ON VIOLENCE* (1969)

2. The wicked flee when no man pursueth; but the righteous are bold as a lion.

BIBLE, PROVERBS 28:1

3. There may be responsible persons, but there are no guilty ones.

ALBERT CAMUS, "THE ABSURD MAN," *THE MYTH OF SISYPHUS* (1942), TR. JUSTIN O'BRIEN

4. We are all exceptional cases.... Each man insists on being innocent, even if it means accusing the whole human race, and heaven.

ALBERT CAMUS, *THE FALL* (1956)

5. The guilty think all talk is of themselves.

CHAUCER, "THE CANON'S YEOMAN'S PROLOGUE," *THE CANTERBURY TALES* (C. 1387–1400), TR. NEVILL COGHILL

6. Guilt is ever at a loss, and confusion waits upon it; when innocence and bold truth are always ready for expression.

WILLIAM CONGREVE, *THE DOUBLE-DEALER* (1694), 4.5

7. Guilt always hurries towards its complement, punishment: only there does its satisfaction lie.

LAWRENCE DURRELL, *JUSTINE* (1957), 3

8. He declares himself guilty who justifies himself before accusation.

THOMAS FULLER, M.D., *GNOMOLOGIA* (1732), 1833

9. Where guilt is, rage and courage doth abound.

BEN JONSON, *SEJANUS HIS FALL* (1602), 2.2

10. This is his first punishment, that by the verdict of his own heart no guilty man is acquitted.

JUVENAL, *SATIRES* (C. 100), 13.2

11. There is a sort of man who pays no attention to his good actions, but is tormented by his bad ones. This is the type that most often writes about himself.

W. SOMERSET MAUGHAM, *THE SUMMING UP* (1938), 4

12. Each of us when he appears before his fellows is clothed in a certain dignity. But every man knows what unconfessable things pass within the secrecy of his own heart.

Luigi Pirandello, *Six Characters in Search of an Author* (1921), 1, tr. Edward Storer

13. How unhappy is he who cannot forgive himself.

Publilius Syrus, *Moral Sayings* (1st c. b.c.), 729, tr. Darius Lyman

14. It is only too easy to compel a sensitive human being to feel guilty about anything.

Morton Irving Seiden, *The Paradox of Hate: A Study in Ritual Murder* (1967), 13

15. So full of artless jealousy is guilt / It spills itself in fearing to be spilt.

Shakespeare, *Hamlet* (1600), 4.5.19

16. Suspicion always haunts the guilty mind; / The thief doth fear each bush an officer.

Shakespeare, *3 Henry VI* (1590–91), 5.4.11

17. To deny all is to confess all.

Spanish Proverb

18. I have never smuggled anything in my life. Why, then, do I feel an uneasy sense of guilt on approaching a customs barrier?

John Steinbeck, *Travels with Charley* (1962)

19. Nothing more unqualifies a man to act with prudence than a misfortune that is attended with shame and guilt.

Jonathan Swift, *Thoughts on Various Subjects* (1711)

H

406. HABIT

See also 213. CUSTOM; 828. ROUTINE

1. To learn new habits is everything, for it is to reach the substance of life. Life is but a tissue of habits.

HENRI FRÉDÉRIC AMIEL, *JOURNAL,* DEC. 30, 1850, TR. MRS. HUMPHRY WARD

2. Habit is a great deadener.

SAMUEL BECKETT, *WAITING FOR GODOT* (1956)

3. Habit, n. A shackle for the free.

AMBROSE BIERCE, *THE DEVIL'S DICTIONARY* (1881–1911)

4. Habit will reconcile us to everything but change.

CHARLES CALEB COLTON, *LACON* (1825), 1.558

5. The evolution from happiness to habit is one of death's best weapons.

JULIO CORTÁZAR, *THE WINNERS* (1960), 14, TR. ELAINE KERRIGAN

6. Man like every other animal is by nature indolent. If nothing spurs him on, then he will hardly think, and will behave from habit like an automaton.

EINSTEIN, *OUT OF MY LATER YEARS* (1950), 24

7. Habit, my friend, is practice long pursued, / That at the last becomes the man himself.

EVENUS (5TH C. B.C.), QUOTED IN ARISTOTLE'S *NICOMACHEAN ETHICS* (4TH C. B.C.), 7.10, TR. J. A. K. THOMSON

8. It is unpleasant to miss even the most trifling thing to which we have been accustomed.

GOETHE, *ELECTIVE AFFINITIES* (1809), 17

9. Wise living consists perhaps less in acquiring good habits than in acquiring as few habits as possible.

ERIC HOFFER, *THE PASSIONATE STATE OF MIND* (1954), 265

10. In twenty-three years of married life, Mrs. Babbitt had seen the paper before her husband just sixty-seven times.

SINCLAIR LEWIS, *BABBITT* (1922)

11. Habituation is a falling asleep or fatiguing of the sense of time; which explains why young years pass slowly, while later life flings itself faster and faster upon its course.

THOMAS MANN, *THE MAGIC MOUNTAIN* (1924), 4.2, TR. H. T. LOWE-PORTER

12. Habit creates the appearance of justice; progress has no greater enemy than habit.

JOSÉ MARTÍ, *GRANOS DE ORO: PENSAMIENTOS SELECCIONADOS EN LAS OBRAS DE JOSÉ MARTÍ* (1942)

13. Ill habits gather by unseen degrees,— / As brooks make rivers, rivers run to seas.

OVID, *METAMORPHOSES* (C. A.D. 8) 15.155, TR. JOHN DRYDEN

14. It is not in novelty but in habit that we find the greatest pleasure.

RAYMOND RADIGUET, *LE DIABLE AU CORPS* (1923)

15. Habit is stronger than reason.

GEORGE SANTAYANA, *INTERPRETATIONS OF POETRY AND RELIGION* (1900)

16. Laws are never as effective as habits.

ADLAI STEVENSON, SPEECH, NEW YORK CITY, AUG. 28, 1952

17. Habit is habit, and not to be flung out of the window by any man, but coaxed downstairs a step at a time.

MARK TWAIN, "PUDD'NHEAD WILSON'S CALENDAR," *PUDD'NHEAD WILSON* (1894), 6

407. HAIR

1. There is not so variable a thing in nature as a lady's headdress: within my own memory I have known it rise and fall above thirty degrees.

JOSEPH ADDISON, *THE SPECTATOR* (1711–12), 98

2. 'Tis not the beard that makes the philosopher.

THOMAS FULLER, M.D., *GNOMOLOGIA* (1732), 5102

3. In the same instant, as I straightened up, giddy with the effort of extricating a mullein from the cucumbers, I realized that the spiny coiffure was in actuality a home permanent and the bulging expanse of gingham below it the rest of Mrs. Kozlich, our current cleaning woman.

S.J. PERELMAN, *THE RISING GORGE* (1961)

4. Two young ladies, in toreador pants and mohair sweaters, whose swirling coiffures looked as though they had been squeezed from an icing gun, had ranged themselves at the fountain.

S.J. PERELMAN, *THE RISING GORGE* (1961)

5. Fair tresses man's imperial race insnare, / And beauty draws us with a single hair.

ALEXANDER POPE, *THE RAPE OF THE LOCK* (1712), 2.27

6. He needed a haircut—especially at the nape of the neck—the worst way, as only a small boy with an almost full-grown head and a reedlike neck can need one.

J.D. SALINGER, "TEDDY," IN *NINE STORIES BY J.D. SALINGER* (1953)

7. [M]y moustache, however sparse, was all mine; it hadn't been put on with spirit gum. I felt it reassuringly with my fingers as I hurried back to school.

J.D. SALINGER, "DE DAUMIER-SMITH'S BLUE PERIOD," IN *NINE STORIES BY J.D. SALINGER* (1953)

408. HANDSHAKE

1. I hate the giving of the hand unless the whole man accompanies it.

EMERSON, *JOURNALS,* 1839

2. A firm, hearty handshake gives a good first impression, and you'll never be forgiven if you don't live up to it.

P.J. O'ROURKE, *MODERN MANNERS* (1988)

409. HAPPINESS

See also 186. CONTENTMENT; 278. ECSTASY; 704. PLEASURE; 750. PROSPERITY; 1011. UNHAPPINESS

1. True happiness is of a retired nature, and an enemy to pomp and noise; it arises, in the first place, from the enjoyment of one's self, and, in the next, from the friendship and conversation of a few select companions.

JOSEPH ADDISON, *THE SPECTATOR* (1711–12), 15

2. Gladness of heart is the life of man, and the rejoicing of a man is length of days.

APOCRYPHA, ECCLESIASTICUS 30:22

3. Different men seek after happiness in different ways and by different means, and so make for themselves different modes of life and forms of government.

ARISTOTLE, *POLITICS* (4TH C. B.C.), 7.8, TR. BENJAMIN JOWETT

4. Happiness depends upon ourselves.

ARISTOTLE, *NICOMACHEAN ETHICS* (4TH C. B.C.), 1.9, TR. J. A. K. THOMSON

5. Happiness is an expression of the soul in considered actions.

ARISTOTLE, *NICOMACHEAN ETHICS* (4TH C. B.C.), 1.8, TR. J. A. K. THOMSON

6. Indeed, man wishes to be happy even when he so lives as to make happiness impossible.

ST. AUGUSTINE, *THE CITY OF GOD* (426), 14

7. A man's happiness,—to do the things proper to man.

MARCUS AURELIUS, *MEDITATIONS* (2ND C.), 8.26, TR. MORRIS HICKEY MORGAN

8. Happy men are grave. They carry their happiness cautiously, as they would a glass filled to the brim which the slightest movement could cause to spill over, or break.

JULES BARBEY D'AUREVILLY, "LE BONHEUR DANS LE CRIME," *LES DIABOLIQUES* (1874)

9. In this world, full often, our joys are only the tender shadows which our sorrows cast.

HENRY WARD BEECHER, *PROVERBS FROM PLYMOUTH PULPIT* (1887)

10. The greatest happiness of the greatest number is the foundation of morals and legislation.

JEREMY BENTHAM, "ELOGIA," *COMMONPLACE BOOKS* (1781–85)

11. When we are not rich enough to be able to purchase happiness, we must not approach too near and gaze on it in shop windows.

TRISTAN BERNARD, *LE DANSEUR INCONNU* (1907)

12. The bird of paradise alights only upon the hand that does not grasp.

JOHN BERRY, *FLIGHT OF WHITE CROWS* (1961)

13. He that is of a merry heart hath a continual feast.

BIBLE PROVERBS 15:15

14. Happiness, n. An agreeable sensation arising from contemplating the misery of another.

AMBROSE BIERCE, *THE DEVIL'S DICTIONARY* (1881–1911)

15. He who binds to himself a joy / Does the winged life destroy; / But he who kisses the joy as it flies / Lives in eternity's sun rise.

WILLIAM BLAKE, "ETERNITY" (1793–99)

16. Whose happiness is so firmly established that he has no quarrel from any side with his estate of life?

BOETHIUS, *THE CONSOLATION OF PHILOSOPHY* (A.D. 524), 2, TR. W. V. COOPER

17. The right to happiness is fundamental: / Men live so little time and die alone.

BERTOLT BRECHT, *THE THREEPENNY OPERA* (1928), 1.3, TR. ERIC BENTLEY

18. All who joy would win / Must share it,— Happiness was born a Twin.

BYRON, *DON JUAN* (1819–24), 2.172

19. One moment may with bliss repay / Unnumbered hours of pain.

THOMAS CAMPBELL, "THE RITTER BANN" (1824)

20. To be happy, we must not be too concerned with others.

ALBERT CAMUS, *THE FALL* (1956)

21. You are forgiven for your happiness and your successes only if you generously consent to share them.

ALBERT CAMUS, *THE FALL* (1956)

22. [H]appiness, to be dissolved into something complete and great.

WILLA CATHER, *MY ANTONIA* (1918)

23. It seldom happens that any felicity comes so pure as not to be tempered and allayed by some mixture of sorrow.

CERVANTES, *DON QUIXOTE* (1605–15), 1.4.14, TR. JOHN OZELL

24. Happiness is like a sunbeam, which the least shadow intercepts.

CHINESE PROVERB

25. Happiness, that grand mistress of the ceremonies in the dance of life, impels us through all its mazes and meanderings, but leads none of us by the same route.

CHARLES CALEB COLTON, *LACON* (1825), 2.109

26. Happiness lies in the fulfillment of the spirit through the body.

CYRIL CONNOLLY, *THE UNQUIET GRAVE* (1945), 1

27. Happiness depends, as Nature shows, / Less on exterior things than most suppose.

WILLIAM COWPER, *TABLE TALK* (1782), 246

28. Illusory joy is often worth more than genuine sorrow.

DESCARTES, *TRAITÉ DES PASSIONS DE L'ÂME* (1650)

29. Eden is that old-fashioned House / We dwell in every day / Without suspecting our abode / Until we drive away.

EMILY DICKINSON, *POEMS* (C. 1862–86)

30. True joy is the earnest which we have of heaven, it is the treasure of the soul, and therefore should be laid in a safe place, and nothing in this world is safe to place it in.

JOHN DONNE, *SERMONS,* NO. 28, (1624–25?)

31. Happiness does not lie in happiness, but in the achievement of it.

DOSTOYEVSKY, *A DIARY OF A WRITER* (1876), 3, JANUARY

32. Present joys are more to flesh and blood, / Than a dull prospect of a distant good.

JOHN DRYDEN, *THE HIND AND THE PANTHER* (1687), II.1658

33. To fill the hour,—that is happiness; to fill the hour, and leave no crevice for a repentance or an approval.

EMERSON, "EXPERIENCE," *ESSAYS: SECOND SERIES* (1844)

34. It is impossible to live a pleasant life without living wisely and well and justly, and it is impossible to live wisely and well and justly without living pleasantly.

EPICURUS (3RD C. B.C.), QUOTED IN DIOGENES LAERTIUS' *LIVES AND OPINIONS OF EMINENT PHILOSOPHERS* (3RD C. A.D.), TR. R. D. HICKS

35. Happiness is brief. / It will not stay. / God batters at its sails.

EURIPIDES, *ORESTES* (408 B.C.), TR. WILLIAM ARROWSMITH

36. Of mortals there is no one who is happy. / If wealth flows in upon one, one may be perhaps / Luckier than one's neighbor, but still not happy.

EURIPIDES, *MEDEA* (431 B.C.), TR. REX WARNER

37. These kind of hair-breadth missings of happiness look like the insults of Fortune.

HENRY FIELDING, *TOM JONES* (1749), 13.2

38. A great obstacle to happiness is to anticipate too great a happiness.

FONTENELLE, *DU BONHEUR* (1687)

39. Human felicity is produced not so much by great pieces of good fortune that seldom happen as by little advantages that occur every day.

BENJAMIN FRANKLIN, *AUTOBIOGRAPHY* (1791), 2

40. What we call happiness in the strictest sense comes from the (preferably sudden) satisfaction of needs which have been dammed up to a high degree.

Sigmund Freud, *Civilization and Its Discontents* (1930), 2, tr. James Strachey

41. Modern man's happiness consists in the thrill of looking at the shop windows, and in buying all that he can afford to buy, either for cash or on installments.

Erich Fromm, *The Art of Loving* (1956), 1

42. Happiness makes up in height for what it lacks in length.

Robert Frost, poem title (1942)

43. He is happy that knoweth not himself to be otherwise.

Thomas Fuller, M.D., *Gnomologia* (1732), 1918

44. No man can be happy without a friend, nor be sure of his friend till he is unhappy.

Thomas Fuller, M.D., *Gnomologia* (1732), 3593

45. Your joy is your sorrow unmasked. / And the selfsame well from which your laughter rises was oftentimes filled with your tears.

Kahlil Gibran, "On Joy and Sorrow," *The Prophet* (1923)

46. Nothing is more fatal to happiness than the remembrance of happiness.

André Gide, *The Immoralist* (1902), 1.8, tr. Dorothy Bussy

47. I have the happiness of the passing moment, and what more can mortal ask?

George Gissing, "Spring," *The Private Papers of Henry Ryecroft* (1903)

48. [Happiness] always looks small while you hold it in your hands, but let it go, and you learn at once how big and precious it is.

Maxim Gorky, *The Zykovs* (1914), 4

49. The search for happiness is one of the chief sources of unhappiness.

Eric Hoffer, *The Passionate State of Mind* (1954), 280

50. One can bear grief, but it takes two to be glad.

Elbert Hubbard, *The Note Book* (1927)

51. Universal happiness keeps the wheels steadily turning; truth and beauty can't.

Aldous Huxley, *Brave New World* (1932)

52. It is neither wealth nor splendor, but tranquility and occupation, which give happiness.

Thomas Jefferson, letter to Mrs. A. S. Marks, 17

53. A peasant and a philosopher may be equally satisfied, but not equally happy. Happiness consists in the multiplicity of agreeable consciousness.

Samuel Johnson, quoted in Boswell's *Life of Samuel Johnson*, February 1766

54. Happiness is enjoyed only in proportion as it is known; and such is the state or folly of man, that it is known only by experience of its contrary.

Samuel Johnson, *The Adventurer* (1753), 67

55. We are long before we are convinced that happiness is never to be found, and each believes it possessed by others, to keep alive the hope of obtaining it for himself.

Samuel Johnson, *Rasselas* (1759), 16

56. Happiness is composed of misfortunes avoided.

Alphonse Karr, *Les Guêpes,* January 1842

57. No matter how dull, or how mean, or how wise a man is, he feels that happiness is his indisputable right.

Helen Keller, *Optimism* (1903), 1

58. When one door of happiness closes, another opens; but often we look so long at the closed door that we do not see the one which has been opened for us.

Helen Keller, *We Bereaved* (1929)

59. Happiness is in the taste, and not in the things.

La Rochefoucauld, *Maxims* (1665), tr. Kenneth Pratt

60. We are never so happy nor so unhappy as we imagine.

La Rochefoucauld, *Maxims* (1665), tr. Kenneth Pratt

61. When you jump for joy, beware that no one moves the ground from beneath your feet.

Stanislaw Lec, *Unkempt Thoughts* (1962), tr. Jacek Galazka

62. I am happy and content because I think I am.

Alain-René Lesage, *Histoire de Gil Blas de Santillane* (1715–35), 7.7

63. I was thinking that surgeons had to be the happiest people on earth. To cut people up and get paid for it—that's happiness, I told myself.

Norman Mailer, *Tough Guys Don't Dance* (1984)

64. it is better to be happy / for a moment / and be burned up with beauty / than to live a long time / and be bored all the while.

Don Marquis, "the lesson of the moth," *Archy and Mehitabel* (1927)

65. A happiness that is sought for ourselves alone can never be found: for a happiness that is diminished by not being shared is not big enough to make us happy.

Thomas Merton, *No Man Is an Island* (1955)

66. Ask yourself whether you are happy, and you cease to be so.

John Stuart Mill, *Autobiography* (1873), 2

67. Unquestionably, it is possible to do without happiness; it is done involuntarily by nineteen-twentieths of mankind.

John Stuart Mill, *Utilitarianism* (1863), 2

68. That thou art happy, owe to God; / That thou continuest such, owe to thyself, / That is, to thy obedience.

Milton, *Paradise Lost* (1667), 5.520

69. One cannot but mistrust a prospect of felicity: one must enjoy it before one can believe in it.

Molière, *Tartuffe* (1664), 4, tr. John Wood

70. There is some shadow of delight and delicacy which smiles upon and flatters us even in the very lap of melancholy.

Montaigne, "That we taste nothing pure," *Essays* (1580–88), tr. W. C. Hazlitt

71. Happiness, I think, lies on the surface...when one plunges under the surface all the buoyant things disappear, and the farther down one gets the more cold and dark it seems: and the more oppressive space feels.

Lewis Mumford, *Findings and Keepings. Analects for an Autobiography* (1975)

72. We should consider every day lost on which we have not danced at least once. And we should call every truth false which was not accompanied by at least one laugh.

Nietzsche, "On Old and New Tablets," *Thus Spoke Zarathustra* (1883–92), 3, tr. Walter Kaufmann

73. There are many roads / to happiness, if the gods assent.

Pindar, *Odes* (5th c. b.c.), Olympia 8, tr. Richmond Lattimore

74. When [man] is happy, he takes his happiness as it comes and doesn't analyze it, just as if happiness were his right.

Luigi Pirandello, *Six Characters in Search of an Author* (1921), 3, tr. Edward Storer

75. Man's real life is happy, chiefly because he is ever expecting that it soon will be so.

Edgar Allan Poe, *Marginalia* (1844–49), 2

76. No man is happy who does not think himself so.

Publilius Syrus, *Moral Sayings* (1st c. b.c.), 584, tr. Darius Lyman

77. The happy man is not he who seems thus to others, but who seems thus to himself.

Publilius Syrus, *Moral Sayings* (1st c. b.c.), 1010, tr. Darius Lyman

78. It is not enough to be happy, it is also necessary that others not be.

Jules Renard, *Journal* (1887–1910)

79. Happiness is indeed a Eurydice, vanishing as soon as gazed upon. It can exist only in *acceptance,* and succumbs as soon as it is laid claim to.

Denis De Rougemont, *Love in the Western World* (1939), 7.4, tr. Montgomery Belgion

80. The happiest is he who suffers the least pain; the most miserable, he who enjoys the least pleasure.

Rousseau, *Émile* (1762), 2

81. The happiness which is lacking makes one think even the happiness one has unbearable.

Joseph Roux, *Meditations of a Parish Priest* (1886), 5.37, tr. Isabel F. Hapgood

82. Italy, and the spring and first love all together should suffice to make the gloomiest person happy.

Bertrand Russell, *The Autobiography of Bertrand Russell: 1872–1914 (1967)*

83. Man needs, for his happiness, not only the enjoyment of this or that, but hope and enterprise and change.

Bertrand Russell, "Philosophy and Politics," *Unpopular Essays* (1950)

84. The fact is always obvious much too late, but the most singular difference between happiness and joy is that happiness is a solid and joy a liquid.

J.D. Salinger, "De Daumier-Smith's Blue Period," in *Nine Stories by J.D. Salinger* (1953)

85. A string of excited, fugitive, miscellaneous pleasures is not happiness; happiness resides in imagina-

tive reflection and judgment, when the *picture* of one's life, or of human life, as it truly has been or is, satisfies the will, and is gladly accepted.

George Santayana, *Persons and Places: The Middle Span* (1945), 1

86. The greatest happiness you can have is knowing that you do not necessarily require happiness.

William Saroyan, news summaries, Dec. 16, 1957

87. Happiness of any given life is to be measured, not by its joys and pleasures, but by the extent to which it has been free from suffering—from positive evil.

Schopenhauer, "On the Sufferings of the World," *Parerga and Paralipomena* (1851), tr. T. Bailey Saunders

88. Unhappy is the man, though he rule the world, who doesn't consider himself supremely blest.

Seneca, *Letters to Lucilius* (1st c.), 9.21, tr. E. Phillips Barker

89. A merry heart goes all the day, / Your sad tires in a mile-a.

Shakespeare, *The Winter's Tale* (1610–11), 4.3.134

90. How bitter a thing it is to look into happiness through another man's eyes!

Shakespeare, *As You Like It* (1599–1600), 5.2.47

91. Silence is the perfectest herald of joy. I were but little happy if I could say how much.

Shakespeare, *Much Ado About Nothing* (1598–99), 2.1.316

92. We have no more right to consume happiness without producing it than to consume wealth without producing it.

George Bernard Shaw, *Candida* (1903), 1

93. It is God's giving if we laugh or weep.

Sophocles, *Ajax* (c. 447 b.c.), tr. John Moore

94. Our happiness depends / on wisdom all the way.

Sophocles, *Antigone* (442–41 b.c.), tr. Elizabeth Wyckoff

95. We live in an ascending scale when we live happily, one thing leading to another in an endless series.

Robert Louis Stevenson, "El Dorado," *Virginibus Puerisque* (1881)

96. I find my joy of living in the fierce and ruthless battles of life, and my pleasure comes from learning something.

August Strindberg, preface to *Miss Julie* (1888)

97. So long as we can lose any happiness, we possess some.

Booth Tarkington, *Looking Forward to the Great Adventure* (1926)

98. Those undeserved joys which come uncalled and make us more pleased than grateful are they that sing.

Thoreau, *Journal*, Feb. 28, 1842

99. A wise man sings his joy in the closet of his heart.

Tibullus, *Elegies* (1st c. b.c.), 3.19, tr. Hubert Creekmore

100. Every man's happiness is built on the unhappiness of another.

Ivan Turgenev, *On the Eve* (1860), 33, tr. Constance Garnett

101. There are people who can do all fine and heroic things but one—keep from telling their happiness to the unhappy.

Mark Twain, *Notebook* (1935)

102. When I was a child people simply looked about them and were moderately happy; today they peer beyond the seven seas, bury themselves waist deep in tidings, and by and large what they see and hear makes them unutterably sad.

E.B. White, *One Man's Meat* (1944)

HARM

See 476. Injury

410. HARMONY

See also 661. Order; 748. Proportion

1. How much finer things are in composition than alone.

Emerson, *Journals*, 1833

2. The hidden harmony is better than the obvious.

Heraclitus, *Fragments* (c. 500 b.c.), 116, tr. Philip Wheelwright

3. Harmony would lose its attractiveness if it did not have a background of discord.

Tehyi Hsieh, *Chinese Epigrams Inside Out and Proverbs* (1948), 292

4. It is indeed from the experience of beauty and happiness, from the occasional harmony between our nature and our environment, that we draw our conception of the divine life.

George Santayana, introduction, *The Sense of Beauty* (1896)

411. HASTE

See also 10. ACTIVITY; 456. IMPATIENCE; 907. SLOWNESS; 926. SPEED

1. We can outrun the wind and the storm, but we cannot outrun the demon of Hurry.

JOHN BURROUGHS, *INDOOR STUDIES* (1889)

2. Ther n' is no werkman whatever he be / That may both werken wel and hastily.

CHAUCER, "THE MERCHANT'S TALE," *THE CANTERBURY TALES* (1387–1400), 585, ED. THOMAS TYRWHITT

3. Whoever is in a hurry shows that the thing he is about is too big for him.

LORD CHESTERFIELD, *LETTERS TO HIS SON,* AUG. 10, 1749

4. One of the great disadvantages of hurry is that it takes such a long time.

G. K. CHESTERTON, "THE CASE FOR THE EPHEMERAL," *ALL THINGS CONSIDERED* (1908)

5. Desire to have things done quickly prevents their being done thoroughly.

CONFUCIUS, *ANALECTS* (6TH C. B.C.), 13.17, TR. JAMES LEGGE

6. Do nothing hastily but catching of fleas.

THOMAS FULLER, M.D., *GNOMOLOGIA* (1732), 1309

7. People in a hurry cannot think, cannot grow, nor can they decay. They are preserved in a state of perpetual puerility.

ERIC HOFFER, *THE PASSIONATE STATE OF MIND* (1954), 172

8. The greatest assassin of life is haste, the desire to reach things before the right time which means overreaching them.

JUAN RAMÓN JIMÉNEZ, "HEROIC REASON," *SELECTED WRITINGS* (1957), TR. H. R. HAYS

9. Along with being forever on the move, one is forever in a hurry, leaving things inadvertently behind—friend or fishing tackle, old raincoat or old allegiance.

LOUIS KRONENBERGER, "REFLECTIONS AND COMPLAINTS OF LATE MIDDLE AGE," *THE CART AND THE HORSE* (1964), 3

10. When you want to hurry something, that means you no longer care about it and want to get on to other things.

ROBERT M. PIRSIG, *ZEN AND THE ART OF MOTORCYCLE MAINTENANCE* (1974)

11. Nothing can be done at once hastily and prudently.

PUBLILIUS SYRUS, *MORAL SAYINGS* (1ST C. B.C.), 557, TR. DARIUS LYMAN

12. Whatever is produced in haste goes hastily to waste.

SA'DI, *GULISTAN* (1258), 8.36, TR. JAMES ROSS

13. Too swift arrives as tardy as too slow.

SHAKESPEARE, *ROMEO AND JULIET* (1594–95), 2.6.15

14. Wisely, and slow. They stumble that run fast.

SHAKESPEARE, *ROMEO AND JULIET* (1594–95), 2.3.94

412. HATRED

See also 255. DISLIKE; 288. ENEMIES; 551. LOVE; 554. LOVE AND HATE; 594. MISANTHROPY

1. Hatred, which could destroy so much, never failed to destroy the man who hated and this was an immutable law.

JAMES BALDWIN, "NOTES OF A NATIVE SON," IN *THE ART OF THE PERSONAL ESSAY* (1994), ED. PHILLIP LOPATE

2. All mourning fears its end and thinks with terror of the day when its pain will subside. In the same way, hate fears above all to be delivered of itself. Once more, it grips its tail between its teeth.

HERVÉ BAZIN, *LA MORT DU PETIT CHEVAL,* 19

3. Even hatred of vileness / Distorts a man's features.

BERTOLT BRECHT, "TO POSTERITY" (1938), TR. MICHAEL HAMBURGER

4. Now Hatred is by far the longest pleasure; / Men love in haste, but they detest at leisure.

BYRON, *DON JUAN* (1819–24), 13.6

5. Pity is a thing often avowed, seldom felt; hatred is a thing often felt, seldom avowed.

CHARLES CALEB COLTON, *LACON* (1825), 1.478

6. Hate is the consequence of fear; we fear something before we hate it; a child who fears noises becomes a man who hates noise.

CYRIL CONNOLLY, *THE UNQUIET GRAVE* (1945), 3

7. The fires of hate, compressed within the heart, / Burn fiercer and will break at last in flame.

CORNEILLE, *LE CID* (1636), 2.3, TR. PAUL LANDIS

8. People who speak the same language can hate one another as easily as can people who speak unrelated languages.

PETER FARB, *WORD PLAY* (1973)

9. Pure good soon grows insipid, wants variety and spirit. Pain is a bitter-sweet, which never surfeits. Love turns, with a little indulgence, to indifference or disgust; hatred alone is immortal.

WILLIAM HAZLITT, "ON THE PLEASURE OF HATING," *THE PLAIN SPEAKER* (1826)

10. The pleasure of hating, like a poisonous mineral, eats into the heart of religion, and turns it to rankling spleen and bigotry; it makes patriotism an excuse for carrying fire, pestilence, and famine into other lands: it leaves to virtue nothing but the spirit of censoriousness.

WILLIAM HAZLITT, "ON THE PLEASURE OF HATING," *THE PLAIN SPEAKER* (1826)

11. To wrong those we hate is to add fuel to our hatred. Conversely, to treat an enemy with magnanimity is to blunt our hatred for him.

ERIC HOFFER, *THE TRUE BELIEVER* (1951), 3.14.70

12. Hatred is so lasting and stubborn, that reconciliation on a sickbed certainly forebodes death.

LA BRUYÈRE, *CHARACTERS* (1688), 11.108, TR. HENRI VAN LAUN

13. To put more faith in lies and hate / Than truth and love is the true atheism.

JAMES RUSSELL LOWELL, "SONNET 17" (1842)

14. Hatred is a feeling which leads to the extinction of values.

JOSÉ ORTEGA Y GASSET, "TO THE READER," *MEDITATIONS ON QUIXOTE* (1914)

15. He whose anger is due to a cause will surely be appeased when the cause is removed. But if his mind harbours groundless hate, how shall another appease him?

PANCHATANTRA (C. 5TH C.), I, TR. FRANKLIN EDGERTON

16. All men naturally hate one another. They employ lust as far as possible in the service of the public weal. But this is only a pretence and a false image of love; for at bottom it is only hate.

PASCAL, *PENSÉES* (1670), 451, TR. W. F. TROTTER

17. Maybe there are times when an honest hatred serves us better than love corrupted by sentimentality, meretriciousness, sententiousness, cuteness.

WALKER PERCY, "THE STATE OF THE NOVEL: DYING ART OR NEW SCIENCE?" *SIGNPOSTS IN A STRANGE LAND* (1991)

18. Great hatred can be concealed in the countenance, and much in a kiss.

PUBLILIUS SYRUS, *MORAL SAYINGS* (1ST C. B.C.), 1036, TR. DARIUS LYMAN

19. The human heart as modern civilization has made it is more prone to hatred than to friendship. And it is prone to hatred because it is dissatisfied.

BERTRAND RUSSELL, *THE CONQUEST OF HAPPINESS* (1930), 6

20. To the eye of enmity virtue appears the ugliest blemish.

SA'DI, *GULISTAN* (1258), 4.1, TR. JAMES ROSS

21. It is enough that one man hate another for hate to gain, little by little, all mankind.

JEAN-PAUL SARTRE, *THE DEVIL AND THE GOOD LORD* (1951), I, THIRD TABLEAU, SCENE 6

22. Hatred is the coward's revenge for being intimidated.

GEORGE BERNARD SHAW, *MAJOR BARBARA* (1905), 3

23. Enmity is catching.

MURIEL SPARK, *MEMENTO MORI* (1959)

24. You want to hate somebody, if you can, just to keep your powers of discrimination bright, and to save yourself from becoming a mere mush of good-nature.

CHARLES DUDLEY WARNER, "NINTH STUDY," *BACKLOG STUDIES* (1873)

HAVES AND HAVE NOTS

See 15. ADVANTAGE; 549. LOSERS; 1011. UNHAPPINESS

413. HEALTH

See also 90. BODY; 137. CLEANLINESS; 577. MEDICINE; 589. MIND AND BODY; 696. PHYSICAL FITNESS; 842. SANITY; 896. SICKNESS

1. The trouble about always trying to preserve the health of the body is that it is so difficult to do without destroying the health of the mind.

G. K. CHESTERTON, "ON THE CLASSICS," *COME TO THINK OF IT* (1930)

2. The sense of wellbeing! It's often with us / When we are young, but then it's not noticed; / And by the time one has grown to consciousness / It comes less often.

T. S. ELIOT, *THE ELDER STATESMAN* (1958), 2

3. The first wealth is health.

EMERSON, "POWER," *THE CONDUCT OF LIFE* (1860)

4. Sickness is felt, but health not at all.

THOMAS FULLER, M.D., *GNOMOLOGIA* (1732), 4160

5. If you mean to keep as well as possible, the less you think about your health the better.

OLIVER WENDELL HOLMES, SR., *OVER THE TEACUPS* (1891), 8

6. We should pray for a sane mind in a sound body.

JUVENAL, *SATIRES* (C. 100), 10.356

7. Preserving the health by too severe a rule is a wearisome malady.

LA ROCHEFOUCAULD, *MAXIMS* (1665), TR. KENNETH PRATT

8. A sound mind in a sound body, is a short but full description of a happy state in this world.

JOHN LOCKE, *SOME THOUGHTS CONCERNING EDUCATION* (1693), 1

9. Life is not living, but living in health.

MARTIAL, *EPIGRAMS* (A.D. 86), 6.70, TR. WALTER C. A. KERR

10. Health is a precious thing, and the only one, in truth, meriting that a man should lay out, not only his time, sweat, labor and goods, but also his life itself to obtain it.

MONTAIGNE, "OF THE RESEMBLANCE OF CHILDREN TO THEIR FATHERS," *ESSAYS* (1580–88), TR. W. C. HAZLITT

11. We are not sensible of the most perfect health, as we are of the least sickness.

MONTAIGNE, "APOLOGY FOR RAIMOND DE SEBONDE," *ESSAYS* (1580–88), TR. W. C. HAZLITT

12. What some call health, if purchased by perpetual anxiety about diet, isn't much better than tedious disease.

GEORGE DENNISON PRENTICE, *PRENTICEANA* (1860)

13. The wish for healing has ever been the half of health.

SENECA, *HIPPOLYTUS* (1ST C.), 249, TR. FRANK JUSTUS MILLER

14. Use your health, even to the point of wearing it out. That is what it is for. Spend all you have before you die; and do not outlive yourself.

GEORGE BERNARD SHAW, "PREFACE ON DOCTORS: THE LATEST THEORIES," *THE DOCTOR'S DILEMMA* (1913)

15. Everyone who is born holds dual citizenship, in the kingdom of the well and in the kingdom of the sick.

SUSAN SONTAG, *ILLNESS AS METAPHOR* (1978)

16. Since we cannot promise our selves constant health, let us endeavour at such temper as may be our best support in the decay of it.

RICHARD STEELE, *THE SPECTATOR* (1711–12), 143

17. When we are well, we all have good advice for those who are ill.

TERENCE, *THE WOMAN OF ANDROS* (166 B.C.)

18. It is a distortion, with something profoundly disloyal about it, to picture the human being as a teetering, fallible contraption, always needing, watching and patching, always on the verge of flapping to pieces.

LEWIS THOMAS, "YOUR VERY GOOD HEALTH," *THE LIVES OF A CELL* (1974)

19. Health is the vital principle of bliss, / And exercise of health.

JAMES THOMSON, *THE CASTLE OF INDOLENCE* (1748), 2.57

20. Look to your health; and if you have it, praise God, and value it next to a good conscience; for health is the second blessing that we mortals are capable of; a blessing that money cannot buy.

IZAAK WALTON, *THE COMPLEAT ANGLER* (1653), 1.21

21. I think the anti-smoking business is a yuppie invention—an extension of the concept that "we'll always be young, rich, and healthy."

FRANK ZAPPA, *THE REAL FRANK ZAPPA BOOK* (1989), WITH PETER OCCHIOGROSSO

HEART

See 284. EMOTIONS

414. HEAVEN

See also 38. ANGELS; 416. HELL

1. This world cannot explain its own difficulties without the assistance of another.

CHARLES CALEB COLTON, *LACON* (1825), 1.540

2. Heaven is large, and affords space for all modes of love and fortitude.

EMERSON, "SPIRITUAL LAWS," *ESSAYS: FIRST SERIES* (1841)

3. Modern man, if he dared to be articulate about his concept of heaven, would describe a vision which would look like the biggest department store in the world, showing new things and gadgets, and himself having plenty of money with which to buy them.

ERICH FROMM, *THE SANE SOCIETY* (1955), 5

4. Those who have had none of the cares of this life to harass and disturb them, have been obliged to have recourse to the hopes and fears of the next to vary the prospect before them.

WILLIAM HAZLITT, "ON A SUN-DIAL," *SKETCHES AND ESSAYS* (1839)

5. The Christian idea of a perfect heaven that is something other than a non-existence is a contradiction in terms.

Aldous Huxley, "Wordsworth in the Tropics," in *Fifty Famous Essays* (1964)

6. "This must be heaven," he says. "No. It's Iowa," I reply automatically.

W.P. Kinsella, *Shoeless Joe* (1982)

7. Do not ask God the way to heaven; he will show you the hardest way.

Stanislaw Lec, *Unkempt Thoughts* (1962), tr. Jacek Galazka

8. Paradise is a center whither the souls of all men are proceeding, each sect in its particular road.

Napoleon I, *Maxims* (1804–15)

9. And that inverted Bowl they call the Sky, / Whereunder crawling cooped we live and die, / Lift not your hands to It for help—for it / As impotently moves as you or I

Omar Khayyám, *Rubáiyát* (11th–12th c.), tr. Edward FitzGerald, 4th ed., 72

10. Heaven is equally distant everywhere.

Petronius, *Satyricon* (1st c.), tr. William Burnaby

11. Believe in something for another World, but dont be too set on what it is, and then you wont start out that life with a disappointment.

Will Rogers, *The Autobiography of Will Rogers* (1949), 16

12. Men have feverishly conceived a heaven only to find it insipid, and a hell to find it ridiculous.

George Santayana, *The Life of Reason: Reason in Art* (1905–06), 9

13. What they do in heaven we are ignorant of; what they do not we are told expressly, that they neither marry, nor are given in marriage.

Jonathan Swift, *Thoughts on Various Subjects* (1711)

14. Heaven is under our feet as well as over our heads.

Thoreau, "The Pond in Winter," *Walden* (1854)

15. This life soon be over, I say. Heaven last all ways.

Alice Walker, *The Color Purple* (1982)

16. All we know / Of what they do above, / Is that they happy are, and that they love.

Edmund Waller, "Upon the Death of My Lady Rich" (1645)

17. Heaven-gates are not so highly arched / As princes' palaces; they that enter there / Must go upon their knees.

John Webster, *The Duchess of Malfi* (c. 1613), 4.2

415. THE HEAVENS

See also 272. Earth; 603. Moon; 921. Space; 950. Sun; 1017. Universe

1. Apparently, a great deal of dark, unseen material exists, whose gravitational pull is responsible for the motions of the stars and galaxies that we see.

John D. Barrow, *The Origin of the Universe* (1994)

2. The heavens declare the glory of God; and the firmament showeth his handiwork.

Bible, Psalms 19:1

3. The heavens call to you, and circle around you, displaying to you their eternal splendours, and your eye gazes only to earth.

Dante, "Purgatorio," 14, *The Divine Comedy* (c. 1300–21), tr. P. H. Wicksteed

4. Many billions of years will elapse before the smallest, youngest stars complete their nuclear burning and shrink into white dwarfs. But with slow, agonizing finality perpetual night will surely fall.

Paul Davies, *The Last Three Minutes* (1994)

5. Overhead the sanctities of the stars shine forevermore,... pouring satire on the pompous business of the day which they close, and making the generations of men show slight and evanescent.

Emerson, *Journals,* 1836

6. At times the whole sky was ringed in shooting points and puckers of light gathering and falling, pulsing, fading, rhythmical as breathing. All of a piece. As if the sky were a pattern of nerves and our thought and memories traveled across it. As if the sky were one gigantic memory for us all.

Louise Erdrich, "The World's Greatest Fishermen," *Love Medicine* (1984)

7. They cannot scare me with their empty spaces / Between stars—on stars where no human race is. / I have it in me so much nearer home / To scare myself with my own desert places.

Robert Frost, "Desert Places," *A Further Range* (1936)

8. Comets are the nearest thing to nothing that anything can be and still be something.

National Geographic Society, press release, March 31, 1955

9. Before the days of Kepler the heavens declared the glory of the Lord.

George Santayana, *The Sense of Beauty* (1896)

10. It is easier to accept the message of the stars than the message of the salt desert. The stars speak of man's insignificance in the long eternity of time; the desert speaks of his insignificance right now.

Edwin Way Teale, *Autumn Across America* (1956), 19

HEDONISM

See 704. Pleasure; 706. Pleasure-Seeking

416. HELL

See also 242. Devil; 414. Heaven

1. There ain't no fans nor no rest and, brother, there ain't no Cokes in hell.

Anonymous North Carolina preacher, quoted in Wilma Dykeman, *The French Broad* (1955)

2. For when will we civilized beings become really serious? said Kierkegaard. Only when we have known hell through and through. Without this, hedonism and frivolity will diffuse hell through all our days.

Saul Bellow, *Herzog* (1964)

3. Hell, madame, is to love no longer.

Georges Bernanos, *The Diary of a Country Priest* (1936), 2

4. Hell has three gates: lust, anger, and greed.

Bhagavadgita, 16, tr. P. Lal

5. Believing in Hell must distort every judgement on this life.

Cyril Connolly, *The Unquiet Grave* (1945), 1

6. What is hell? Hell is oneself, / Hell is alone, the other figures in it / Merely projections.

T. S. Eliot, *The Cocktail Party* (1949), 1.3

7. Hell is the bloodcurdling mansion of time, in whose profoundest circle Satan himself waits, winding a gargantuan watch in his hand.

Antonio Machado, *Juan de Mairena* (1943), 7, tr. Ben Belitt

8. Which way I fly is hell; myself am hell; / And in the lowest deep a lower deep / Still threatening to devour me opens wide, / To which the hell I suffer seems a heaven.

Milton, *Paradise Lost* (1667), 4.75

9. The merit of Mahomet is that he founded a religion without an inferno.

Napoleon I, *Maxims* (1804–15)

10. To work hard, to live hard, to die hard, and then to go to hell after all would be too damned hard.

Carl Sandburg, *The People, Yes* (1936)

11. Hell is a city much like London— / A populous and smoky city.

Shelley, "Peter Bell the Third" (1819), 3.1

12. There is a dreadful Hell, / And everlasting pains; / There sinners must with devils dwell / In darkness, fire, and chains.

Isaac Watts, *Divine Songs for Children* (1720), 11

HELPING

See 56. Assistance; 120. Charity; 384. Gifts and Giving; 433. Humanitarianism

417. HEREDITY

See also 670. Parenthood; 802. Reproduction

1. That which comes of a cat will catch mice.

English Proverb

2. Deep in the cavern of the infant's breast / The father's nature lurks, and lives anew.

Horace, *Odes* (23–c. 15 B.C.), 4.4

3. With him for a sire and her for a dam, / What should I be but just what I am?

Edna St. Vincent Millay, "The Singing-Woman from the Wood's Edge," *A Few Figs from Thistles* (1920)

4. The whelp of a wolf must prove a wolf at last, notwithstanding he may be brought up by a man.

Sa'di, *Gulistan* (1258), 1.4, tr. James Ross

HERESY

See 258. Dissent

418. HEROES AND HEROISM

See also 332. Fame; 386. Glory; 401. Greatness

1. Heroes are very human, most of them; very easily touched by praise.

Max Beerbohm, "A Point to Be Remembered by Very Eminent Men," *And Even Now* (1920)

2. The hero was distinguished by his achievement; the celebrity by his image or trademark. The hero

created himself; the celebrity is created by the media. The hero was a big man; the celebrity is a big name.

DANIEL J. BOORSTIN, *THE IMAGE* (1962), 2.4

3. A hero is someone who has given his or her life to something bigger than oneself.

JOSEPH CAMPBELL, *THE POWER OF MYTH* (1988), ED. BETTY SUE FLOWERS

4. The last act in the biography of the hero is that of the death or departure.

JOSEPH CAMPBELL, *THE HERO WITH A THOUSAND FACES* (1949)

5. This, to me, is the ultimately heroic trait of ordinary people; they say *no* to the tyrant and they calmly take the consequences of this resistance.

PHILIP K. DICK, *I HOPE I SHALL ARRIVE SOON* (1985)

6. The contemporary hero, the mythical pattern in the imitation of whom we would live, remains as yet undefined. We have no hero; what is more to the point, we suspect hero worship.

IRWIN EDMAN, "HOW TO BE SWEET THOUGH SOPHISTICATED," IN *FIFTY GREAT ESSAYS* (1964)

7. Every hero becomes a bore at last.

EMERSON, "USES OF GREAT MEN," *REPRESENTATIVE MEN* (1850)

8. The hero is suffered to be himself.

EMERSON, "BEHAVIOR," *THE CONDUCT OF LIFE* (1860)

9. Show me a hero and I will write you a tragedy.

F. SCOTT FITZGERALD, "THE NOTE-BOOKS," *THE CRACK-UP* (1945)

10. An efficiency-regime cannot be run without a few heroes stuck about it to carry off the dullness—much as plums have to be put into a bad pudding to make it palatable.

E. M. FORSTER, "WHAT I BELIEVE," *TWO CHEERS FOR DEMOCRACY* (1951)

11. The human passions transform man from a mere thing into a hero, into a being that in spite of tremendous handicaps tries to make sense of life.

ERICH FROMM, *THE ANATOMY OF HUMAN DESTRUCTIVENESS* (1973)

12. In war-time a man is called a hero. It doesn't make him any braver, and he runs for his life. But at least it's a hero who is running away.

JEAN GIRAUDOUX, *TIGER AT THE GATES* (1935), I, TR. CHRISTOPHER FRY

13. A hero cannot be a hero unless in an heroic world.

NATHANIEL HAWTHORNE, *JOURNALS*, MAY 7, 1850

14. Heroism does not require spiritual maturity.

ABEL HERMANT, *XAVIER OU LES ENTRETIENS SUR LA GRAMMAIRE FRANÇAISE* (1923), I

15. From the time I read my first Hemingway work, *The Sun Also Rises*, as a student at Soldan High School in St. Louis, I was struck with an affliction common to my generation: Hemingway Awe.

A.E. HOTCHNER, *PAPA HEMINGWAY* (1966)

16. The heroic man does not pose; he leaves that for the man who wishes to be thought heroic.

ELBERT HUBBARD, *THE NOTE BOOK* (1927)

17. Life, misfortunes, isolation, abandonment, poverty, are battlefields which have their heroes; obscure heroes, sometimes greater than the illustrious heroes.

VICTOR HUGO, "MARIUS," *LES MISÉRABLES* (1862), 5.1, TR. CHARLES E. WILBOUR

18. Heroes don't need to talk about what they did.

W.P. KINSELLA, *SHOELESS JOE* (1982)

19. However great the advantages given us by nature, it is not she alone, but fortune with her, which makes heroes.

LA ROCHEFOUCAULD, *MAXIMS* (1665), TR. KENNETH PRATT

20. We moderns do not believe in demigods, but our smallest hero we expect to feel and act as a demigod.

GOTTHOLD EPHRAIM LESSING, *LAOCOÖN* (1766), 4, TR. W. A. STEEL

21. Without heroes we're all plain people and don't know how far we can go.

BERNARD MALAMUD, *THE NATURAL* (1952)

22. His [Gen. Douglas MacArthur's] own heroes were Lincoln and Washington, and in some ways he resembled them.

WILLIAM MANCHESTER, *AMERICAN CAESAR* (1978)

23. No hero to me is the man who, by easy shedding of his blood, purchases fame: my hero is he who, without death, can win praise.

MARTIAL, *EPIGRAMS* (A.D. 86), 1.8, TR. WALTER C. A. KERR

24. The chief business of the nation, as a nation, is the setting up of heroes, mainly bogus.

H. L. MENCKEN, *PREJUDICES: THIRD SERIES* (1922), I

25. "Are there any heroes in the Bible?" he asked. "Was Moses a hero?"

JUDGE JACOB MISHLER, QUOTED IN *SENATOR POTHOLE* (1994), BY LEONARD LURIE

26. When it comes to the pinch, human beings are heroic. Women face childbed and the scrubbing brush, revolutionaries keep their mouths shut in the torture chamber, battleships go down with their guns still firing when their decks are awash.

GEORGE ORWELL, "THE ART OF DONALD MCGILL," *A COLLECTION OF ESSAYS* (1954)

27. The epic disappeared along with the age of personal heroism; there can be no epic with artillery.

ERNEST RENAN, "PROBABILITIÉS," *DIALOGUES ET FRAGMENTS PHILOSOPHIQUES* (1876)

28. [T]here has been a change in heroes within the working-class community.

DAVID RIESMAN, *ABUNDANCE FOR WHAT?* (1964)

29. This thing of being a hero, about the main thing to do is to know when to die. Prolonged life has ruined more men than it ever made.

WILL ROGERS, *THE AUTOBIOGRAPHY OF WILL ROGERS* (1949), 13

30. A hero is a man who does what he can.

ROMAIN ROLLAND, "L'ADOLESCENT," *JEAN CHRISTOPHE* (1904–12), 3

31. Better not be a hero than work oneself up into heroism by shouting lies.

GEORGE SANTAYANA, *DIALOGUES IN LIMBO* (1925), 2

32. Every hero is a Samson. The strong man succumbs to the intrigues of the weak and the many; and if in the end he loses all patience he crushes both them and himself.

SCHOPENHAUER, "A FEW PARABLES," *PARERGA AND PARALIPOMENA* (1851), TR. T. BAILEY SAUNDERS

33. It doesn't take a hero to order men into battle. It takes a hero to be one of those men who go into battle.

H. NORMAN SCHWARZKOPF, INTERVIEW, MARCH 15, 1991, QUOTED IN *IT DOESN'T TAKE A HERO* (1992), WRITTEN WITH PETER PETRE

34. The savage bows down to idols of wood and stone; the civilized man to idols of flesh and blood.

GEORGE BERNARD SHAW, "MAXIMS FOR REVOLUTIONISTS," *MAN AND SUPERMAN* (1903)

35. For the company of the great is good company as Shakespeare understood it, as Plutarch understood it. The past remains the source from which example and precept can still be drawn.

C.V. WEDGWOOD, *HISTORY AND HOPE* (1987)

36. We have more to learn today from the spectacle of a great man at a great moment than from any number of monographs on ancient wage levels.

C.V. WEDGWOOD, *HISTORY AND HOPE* (1987)

HESITATION

See 231. DELAY; 465. INDECISION

HIDING

See 165. CONCEALMENT

419. HISTORY AND HISTORIANS

See also 298. ERA; 676. PAST; 986. TRADITION

1. History provides neither compensation for suffering nor penalties for wrong.

LORD ACTON, POSTSCRIPT, LETTER TO MANDELL CREIGHTON, APRIL 5, 1887

2. History is a tangled skein that one may take up at any point, and break when one has unravelled enough.

HENRY ADAMS, *THE EDUCATION OF HENRY ADAMS* (1907), 20

3. The historian must not try to know what is truth, if he values his honesty; for, if he cares for his truths, he is certain to falsify his facts.

HENRY ADAMS, *THE EDUCATION OF HENRY ADAMS* (1907), 31

4. The only lesson history has taught us is that man has not yet learned anything from history.

ANONYMOUS

5. More history's made by secret handshakes than by battles, bills, and proclamations.

JOHN BARTH, *THE SOT-WEED FACTOR* (1960), 2.1

6. History, n. An account mostly false, of events mostly unimportant, which are brought about by rulers mostly knaves, and soldiers mostly fools.

AMBROSE BIERCE, *THE DEVIL'S DICTIONARY* (1881–1911)

7. What makes a good writer of history is a guy who is suspicious. Suspicion marks the real difference between the man who wants to write honest history and the one who'd rather write a good story.

JIM BISHOP, *THE NEW YORK TIMES*, FEB. 5, 1955

8. We are like ignorant shepherds living on a site where great civilizations once flourished.

ALLAN BLOOM, *THE CLOSING OF THE AMERICAN MIND* (1987)

9. We need history, not to tell us what happened or to explain the past, but to make the past alive so that it can explain us and make a future possible.

ALLAN BLOOM, *THE CLOSING OF THE AMERICAN MIND* (1987)

10. History is largely concerned with arranging good entrances for people; and later exits not always quite so good.

HEYWOOD BROUN, "SPORT FOR ART'S SAKE," *PIECES OF HATE, AND OTHER ENTHUSIASMS* (1922)

11. The history of the world is the record of the weakness, frailty and death of public opinion.

SAMUEL BUTLER (D. 1902), "PICTURES AND BOOKS," *NOTE-BOOKS* (1912)

12. History is the essence of innumerable biographies.

THOMAS CARLYLE, "ON HISTORY" (1830)

13. The disadvantage of men not knowing the past is that they do not know the present. History is a hill or high point of vantage, from which alone men see the town in which they live or the age in which they are living.

G. K. CHESTERTON, "ON ST. GEORGE REVIVIFIED," *ALL I SURVEY* (1933)

14. To be ignorant of what occurred before you were born is to remain always a child. For what is the worth of human life, unless it is woven into the life of our ancestors by the records of history?

CICERO, *ORATOR* (46 B.C.)

15. The more we know of History, the less shall we esteem the subjects of it, and to despise our species is the price we must too often pay for our knowledge of it.

CHARLES CALEB COLTON, *LACON* (1825), 2.157

16. All over the world today, not just in the totalitarian countries, assiduous functionaries in Ministries of Truth are clubbing history dumb and rendering language insensible.

E.L. DOCTOROW, "ORWELL'S *1984*," *JACK LONDON, HEMINGWAY, AND THE CONSTITUTION* (1993)

17. A nation writes its history in the image of its ideal.

ABBA EBAN, *MY PEOPLE* (1968)

18. The history of free men is never really written by chance but by choice—their choice.

DWIGHT D. EISENHOWER, ADDRESS, PITTSBURGH, PA., OCT. 9, 1956

19. The historical sense involves a perception, not only of the pastness of the past, but of its presence.

T. S. ELIOT, "TRADITION AND THE INDIVIDUAL TALENT" (1919)

20. History is the action and reaction of these two, nature and thought—two boys pushing each other on the curbstone of the pavement.

EMERSON, "FATE," *THE CONDUCT OF LIFE* (1860)

21. There is no history; only biography.

EMERSON, *JOURNALS,* 1839

22. It is pleasant to be transferred from an office where one is afraid of a sergeant-major into an office where one can intimidate generals, and perhaps this is why History is so attractive to the more timid among us. We can recover self-confidence by snubbing the dead.

E. M. FORSTER, "THE CONSOLATIONS OF HISTORY," *ABINGER HARVEST* (1936)

23. All that is observable in a man—that is to say his actions and such of his spiritual existence as can be deduced from his actions—falls into the domain of history.

E.M. FORSTER, "PEOPLE," *ASPECTS OF THE NOVEL* (1927)

24. Historians relate not so much what is done as what they would have believed.

BENJAMIN FRANKLIN, *POOR RICHARD'S ALMANACK* (1732–57)

25. History never looks like history when you are living through it. It always looks confusing and messy, and it always feels uncomfortable.

JOHN W. GARDNER, *NO EASY VICTORIES* (1968), 27

26. There are only two great currents in the history of mankind: the baseness which makes conservatives and the envy which makes revolutionaries.

JULES DE GONCOURT, *JOURNAL,* JULY 12, 1867, TR. ROBERT BALDICK

27. People, human beings with all their creative diversity, are the makers of history.

MIKHAIL GORBACHEV, *PERESTROIKA* (1987)

28. History repeats itself, but in such cunning disguise that we never detect the resemblance until the damage is done.

SYDNEY J. HARRIS, "IF HE'S NOT GUILTY, WHY IS HE IN COURT?" *CLEARING THE GROUND* (1986)

29. Peoples and governments never have learned anything from history, or acted on principles deduced from it.

HEGEL, INTRODUCTION TO *PHILOSOPHY OF HISTORY* (1832), TR. JOHN SIBREE

30. The game of history is usually played by the best and the worst over the heads of the majority in the middle.

ERIC HOFFER, *THE TRUE BELIEVER* (1951), 2.4.18

31. That men do not learn very much from the lessons of history is the most important of all the lessons that history has to teach.

ALDOUS HUXLEY, *COLLECTED ESSAYS* (1959)

32. History knows no scruples and no hesitation. Inert and unerring, she flows towards her goal. At every bend in her course she leaves the mud which she carries and the corpses of the drowned.

ARTHUR KOESTLER, *DARKNESS AT NOON* (1940)

33. Truth is a totality, the sum of many overlapping partial images. History, on the other hand, sacrifices totality in the interest of continuity.

EDMUND LEACH, "BRAIN-TWISTER," *NEW YORK REVIEW OF BOOKS*, OCT. 12, 1967

34. For everything is history: What was said yesterday is history, what was said a minute ago is history. But, above all, one is led to misjudge the present, because only the study of historical development permits the weighing and evaluation of the interrelationships among the components of the present-day society.

CLAUDE LÉVI-STRAUSS, *STRUCTURAL ANTHROPOLOGY* (1963)

35. The mark of the historic is the nonchalance with which it picks up an individual and deposits him in a trend, like a house playfully moved in a tornado.

MARY MCCARTHY, "MY CONFESSION," *ON THE CONTRARY* (1961)

36. The history of the world is the history of a privileged few.

HENRY MILLER, *SUNDAY AFTER THE WAR* (1944)

37. The middle sort of historians, of which the most part are, they spoil all; they will chew our meat for us.

MONTAIGNE, "OF BOOKS," *ESSAYS* (1580–88), TR. W. C. HAZLITT

38. Every fact and every work exercises a fresh persuasion over every age and every new species of man. History always enunciates new truths.

NIETZSCHE, *THE WILL TO POWER* (1888), 974, TR. ANTHONY M. LUDOVICI

39. We have need of history in its entirety, not to fall back into it, but to see if we can escape from it.

JOSÉ ORTEGA Y GASSET, *THE REVOLT OF THE MASSES* (1930), 10

40. It is impossible to write ancient history because we lack source materials, and impossible to write modern history because we have far too many.

CHARLES PÉGUY, *CLIO* (1917)

41. There is no history of mankind, there are only many histories of all kinds of aspects of human life. And one of these is the history of political power. This is elevated into the history of the world.

SIR KARL R. POPPER, *THE OPEN SOCIETY AND ITS ENEMIES* (1950)

42. The talent of historians lies in their creating a true ensemble out of facts which are but half-true.

ERNEST RENAN, PREFACE TO 13TH EDITION OF *LA VIE DE JÉSUS* (1863)

43. History was part of the baggage we threw overboard when we launched ourselves into the New World.

WALLACE STEGNER, "THE SENSE OF PLACE," *WHEN THE BLUEBIRD SINGS IN THE LEMONADE SPRINGS* (1992)

44. We can chart our future clearly and wisely only when we know the path which has led to the present.

ADLAI STEVENSON, SPEECH, RICHMOND, VA., SEPT. 20, 1952

45. Wherever men have lived there is a story to be told, and it depends chiefly on the story-teller or historian whether that is interesting or not.

THOREAU, *JOURNAL*, MARCH 18, 1860

46. The very ink with which all history is written is merely fluid prejudice.

MARK TWAIN, "PUDD'NHEAD WILSON'S NEW CALENDAR," *FOLLOWING THE EQUATOR* (1897), 2.33

47. History justifies whatever we want it to. It teaches absolutely nothing, for it contains everything and gives examples of everything.

PAUL VALÉRY, "DE L'HISTOIRE," *REGARDS SUR LE MONDE ACTUEL* (1931)

48. World events are the work of individuals whose motives are often frivolous, even casual.

GORE VIDAL, *ROCKING THE BOAT* (1962)

49. Regrets are idle; yet history is one long regret. Everything might have turned out so differently!

CHARLES DUDLEY WARNER, "EIGHTEENTH WEEK," *MY SUMMER IN A GARDEN* (1871)

50. History is all explained by geography.

Robert Penn Warren, interview, *Writers at Work: First Series* (1958)

51. It should be the historian's business not to belittle but to illuminate the greatness of man's spirit.

C.V. Wedgwood, *History and Hope* (1987)

52. [G]ood writing is almost the concomitant of good history. Literature and history were joined long since by the powers which shaped the human brain; we cannot put them asunder.

C.V. Wedgwood, *History and Hope* (1987)

53. Human history becomes more and more a race between education and catastrophe.

H. G. Wells, *The Outline of History* (1920, 1921), 40.4

54. As soon as histories are properly told there is no more need of romances.

Walt Whitman, preface to *Leaves of Grass* (1855–92)

55. History is spread across this country as evenly as honey on toast.

George F. Will, "Dayton's Mundane Machines and Your Taxes," *Suddenly: The American Idea Abroad and At Home, 1986–1990* (1990)

56. Our history is every human history; a black and gory business, with more scoundrels than wise men at the lead, and more louts than both put together to cheer and follow.

Philip Wylie, *Generation of Vipers* (1942), 7

57. All the old history was written for the amusement of the ruling classes. The lower classes couldn't read, and their rulers didn't care about remembering what happened to them.

Frank Zappa, quoting his father, in *The Real Frank Zappa Book* (1989), with Peter Occhiogrosso

420. HOLIDAYS

See also 631. The New Year; 667. Parades

1. The irony of Christmas is always upon the poor in heart; the mystery of the solstice is always upon the rest of us.

John Cheever, *The Falconer* (1977)

2. [Thanksgiving] as founded be th' Puritans to give thanks f'r bein' presarved fr'm th' Indyans, an' we keep it to give thanks we are presarved fr'm th' Puritans.

Finley Peter Dunne, "Thanksgiving," *Mr. Dooley's Opinions* (1901)

3. How many observe Christ's birthday! How few, his precepts! O! 'tis easier to keep holidays than commandments.

Benjamin Franklin, *Poor Richard's Almanack* (1732–57)

4. Holidays / Have no pity

Eugenio Montale, "Eastbourne," *Selected Poems* (1965), tr. G. S. Fraser

5. People can't concentrate properly on blowing other / people to pieces properly if their minds are poisoned / by thoughts suitable to the twenty-fifth of De- / cember.

Ogden Nash, "Merry Christmas, Nearly Everybody!" *I'm a Stranger Here Myself* (1938)

6. Labor Day symbolizes our determination to achieve an economic freedom for the average man which will give his political freedom reality.

Franklin D. Roosevelt, Fireside Chat, Sept. 6, 1936

7. If all the year were playing holidays, / To sport would be as tedious as to work.

Shakespeare, *I Henry IV* (1597–98), 1.2.228

8. *April 1.* This is the day upon which we are reminded of what we are on the other three hundred and sixty-four.

Mark Twain, "Pudd'nhead Wilson's Calendar," *Pudd'nhead Wilson* (1894), 21

9. I shall manage to eat somewhere and get full—even if at a restaurant—but, God knows, I am still young enough to have a horror of Christmas by myself.

Thomas Wolfe, *Thomas Wolfe's Letters to His Mother* (1943)

421. HOLLYWOOD

See also 611. Movies

1. Conditions in the [movie] industry somehow propose the paradox: "We brought you here for your individuality but while you're here we insist that you do everything to conceal it."

F. Scott Fitzgerald, *The Letters of F. Scott Fitzgerald* (1963), ed. Andrew Turnbull

2. It [Hollywood] is, for example, such a slack soft place—even its pleasure lacking the fierceness of Provence—that withdrawal is practically a condition of safety.

F. Scott Fitzgerald, *The Letters of F. Scott Fitzgerald* (1963), ed. Andrew Turnbull

3. Mother loathed the all-black B movies Hollywood made for the "colored" audience, where the stereotypes were broader and more offensive to her, and where the musical interludes did no justice to real talent, she said, but trivialized it.

GAYLE PEMBERTON, "DO HE HAVE YOUR NUMBER, MR. JEFFREY?" IN *THE ART OF THE PERSONAL ESSAY* (1994), ED. PHILLIP LOPATE

4. In Hollywood, as I've often said, if you don't sing or dance, you end up as an after-dinner speaker.

RONALD REAGAN, *AN AMERICAN LIFE* (1990)

5. He's got an option on the Six-Day War, for a musical. Yul Brynner is already as good as signed to star as Dayan.

PHILIP ROTH, *ZUCKERMAN UNBOUND* (L981)

422. HOME

See also 334. FAMILY; 423. HOMELAND; 428. HOSPITALITY; 430. HOUSES

1. Be it ever so humble, there's no place like home for wearing what you like.

GEORGE ADE, "THE GOOD FAIRY OF THE EIGHTH WARD," *FORTY MODERN FABLES* (1901)

2. The ache for home lives in all of us, the safe place where we can go as we are and not be questioned.

MAYA ANGELOU, *ALL GOD'S CHILDREN NEED TRAVELING SHOES* (1986)

3. Whoever makes home seem to the young dearer and more happy, is a public benefactor.

HENRY WARD BEECHER, *PROVERBS FROM PLYMOUTH PULPIT* (1887)

4. You are a king by your own fire-side, as much as any monarch in his throne.

CERVANTES, AUTHOR'S PREFACE, *DON QUIXOTE* (1605–15), TR. JOHN OZELL

5. It is a most miserable thing to feel ashamed of home.

CHARLES DICKENS, *GREAT EXPECTATIONS* (1860–1861)

6. In love of home, the love of country has its rise.

CHARLES DICKENS, *THE OLD CURIOSITY SHOP* (1840), 38

7. Where Thou art—that—is Home.

EMILY DICKINSON, POEM (C. 1863)

8. Every roof is agreeable to the eye, until it is lifted; then we find tragedy and moaning women, and hard-eyed husbands.

EMERSON, "EXPERIENCE," *ESSAYS: SECOND SERIES* (1844)

9. Let a man behave in his own house as a guest.

EMERSON, *JOURNALS,* 1836

10. The ornament of a house is the friends who frequent it.

EMERSON, "DOMESTIC LIFE," *SOCIETY AND SOLITUDE* (1870)

11. Home is the place where, when you have to go there, / They have to take you in.

ROBERT FROST, "THE DEATH OF THE HIRED MAN," *NORTH OF BOSTON* (1914)

12. The most fortunate of men, / Be he a king or commoner, is he / Whose welfare is assured in his own home.

GOETHE, *IPHIGENIA IN TAURIS* (1787), I, TR. CHARLES E. PASSAGE

13. Daughter am I in my mother's house, / But mistress in my own.

RUDYARD KIPLING, "OUR LADY OF THE SNOWS" (1897)

14. In fact there was but one thing wrong with the Babbitt house: It was not a home.

SINCLAIR LEWIS, *BABBITT* (1922)

15. Stay, stay at home, my heart, and rest; / Homekeeping hearts are happiest.

LONGFELLOW, "SONG" (1877)

16. A home is not a mere transient shelter: its essence lies in its permanence, in its capacity for accretion and solidification, in its quality of representing, in all its details, the personalities of the people who live in it.

H. L. MENCKEN, *PREJUDICES: FIFTH SERIES* (1926), II

17. The dog is a lion in his own house.

PERSIAN PROVERB

18. Happy the man whose wish and care / A few paternal acres bound, / Content to breathe his native air, / In his own ground.

ALEXANDER POPE, *ODE ON SOLITUDE* (1699), I

19. Plasticity loves new moulds because it can fill them, but for a man of sluggish mind and bad manners there is decidedly no place like home.

GEORGE SANTAYANA, *THE LIFE OF REASON: REASON IN SOCIETY* (1905–06), 6

20. 'Tis ever common / That men are merriest when they are from home.

SHAKESPEARE, *HENRY V* (1598–99), I.2.271

21. There are people who were born to stay home rather than follow the beckonings of their imagination: the Emma Bovarys and Anna Kareninas of this world.

DIANA TRILLING, *MRS. HARRIS: THE DEATH OF THE SCARSDALE DOCTOR* (1981)

22. Everybody's always talking about people breaking into houses ... but there are more people in the world who want to break out of houses.

THORNTON WILDER, *THE MATCHMAKER* (1955), 4

423. HOMELAND

See also 678. PATRIOTISM

1. Each blade of grass has its spot on earth whence it draws its life, its strength; and so is man rooted to the land from which he draws his faith together with his life.

JOSEPH CONRAD, *LORD JIM* (1900), 21

2. There is no sorrow above / The loss of a native land.

EURIPIDES, *MEDEA* (431 B.C.), TR. REX WARNER

3. I, for one, know of no sweeter sight for a man's eyes than his own country.

HOMER, *ODYSSEY* (9TH C. B.C.), 9, TR. E. V. RIEU

4. Every man has a lurking wish to appear considerable in his native place.

SAMUEL JOHNSON, QUOTED IN BOSWELL'S *LIFE OF SAMUEL JOHNSON*, JULY 17, 1771

5. Being in a foreign country means walking a tightrope high above the ground without the net afforded a person by the country where he has his family, colleagues, and friends, and where he can easily say what he has to say in a language he has known from childhood.

MILAN KUNDERA, *THE UNBEARABLE LIGHTNESS OF BEING* (1984)

6. It is right to prefer our own country to all others, because we are children and citizens before we can be travellers or philosophers.

GEORGE SANTAYANA, *THE LIFE OF REASON: REASON IN RELIGION* (1905–06), 10

7. Breathes there the man, with soul so dead, / Who never to himself hath said, / This is my own, my native land!

SIR WALTER SCOTT, *THE LAY OF THE LAST MINSTREL* (1805), 6.1

8. The only place where I felt at home, on familiar ground, was the Jewish cemetery. And yet I had never set foot in it before. Children had been forbidden to enter.

ELIE WIESEL, *LEGENDS OF OUR TIMES* (1968)

424. HOMOSEXUALITY

1. Homosexuality is a sickness, just as are baby-rape or wanting to become head of General Motors.

ELDRIDGE CLEAVER, "NOTES ON A NATIVE SON," *SOUL ON ICE* (1968)

2. In spring a young man's fancy turns to a fancy young man.

MART CROWLEY, *THE BOYS IN THE BAND* (1986)

3. Fairies: Nature's attempt to get rid of soft boys by sterilizing them.

F. SCOTT FITZGERALD, "THE NOTE-BOOKS," *THE CRACK-UP* (1945)

4. Sex explains it all. The Colonel's Lady and Judy O'Grady are Lesbians under their skin.

ERNEST HEMINGWAY, *THE SUN ALSO RISES* (1926)

5. Charlie had that defensive contempt for homosexuals which people often have when their own sexuality is an embarrassment to them.

ERICA JONG, *FEAR OF FLYING* (1973)

6. On his best days, the recognizable gay person is treated as a harmless freak, enjoying all the respect accorded to the Bearded Fat Lady at the circus.

MARSHALL KIRK AND HUNTER MADSEN, *AFTER THE BALL: HOW AMERICA WILL CONQUER ITS FEAR AND HATRED OF GAYS IN THE 90S* (1989)

7. There is probably no sensitive heterosexual alive who is not preoccupied with his latent homosexuality.

NORMAN MAILER, "THE HOMOSEXUAL VILLAIN," *ADVERTISEMENTS FOR MYSELF* (1959)

8. There is nothing biologically unusual about a homosexual act of pseudocopulation. Many species indulge in this, under a variety of circumstances.

DESMOND MORRIS, *THE NAKED APE* (1967)

9. Actually there is no such thing as a homosexual person, any more than there is such a thing as a heterosexual person. The words are adjectives describing sexual acts, not people. Those sexual acts are entirely natural; if they were not, no one would perform them.

GORE VIDAL, *THE SECOND AMERICAN REVOLUTION AND OTHER ESSAYS* (1982)

10. Many human beings enjoy sexual relations with their own sex; many don't; many respond to both.

This plurality is part of our nature and not worth fretting about.

GORE VIDAL, *THE SECOND AMERICAN REVOLUTION AND OTHER ESSAYS* (1982)

425. HONESTY

See also 331. FALSEHOOD; 362. FRANKNESS; 491. INTEGRITY; 901. SINCERITY; 1000. TRUTHFULNESS

1. An honest man's word is as good as his bond.

CERVANTES, *DON QUIXOTE* (1605–15), 2.4.34, TR. JOHN OZELL

2. Who cannot open an honest mind / No friend will he be of mine.

EURIPIDES, *MEDEA* (431 B.C.), TR. REX WARNER

3. No such thing as a man willing to be honest—that would be like a blind man willing to see.

F. SCOTT FITZGERALD, "THE NOTE-BOOKS," *THE CRACK-UP* (1945)

4. He that resolves to deal with none but honest men must leave off dealing.

THOMAS FULLER, M.D. *GNOMOLOGIA* (1732), 2267

5. There is no well-defined boundary line between honesty and dishonesty. The frontiers of one blend with the outside limits of the other, and he who attempts to tread this dangerous ground may be sometimes in the one domain and sometimes in the other.

O. HENRY, "BEXAR SCRIP NO. 2692," *ROLLING STONES* (1912)

6. I have no idea what the mind of a lowlife scoundrel is like, but I know what the mind of an honest man is like: it is terrifying.

ABEL HERMANT, *LE BOURGEOIS* (1906), 4

7. Honesty is largely a matter of information, of knowing that dishonesty is a mistake. Principle is not as powerful in keeping people straight as a policeman.

EDGAR WATSON HOWE, *VENTURES IN COMMON SENSE* (1919), 16.10

8. Honesty's praised, then left to freeze.

JUVENAL, *SATIRES* (C. 100), 1.75, TR. HUBERT CREEKMORE

9. A show of a certain amount of honesty is in any profession or business the surest way of growing rich.

LA BRUYÈRE, *CHARACTERS* (1688), 6.44, TR. HENRI VAN LAUN

10. The surest way to remain poor is to be an honest man.

NAPOLEON I, *MAXIMS* (1804–15)

11.The life of an honest man must be a perpetual infidelity.

CHARLES PÉGUY, "THE SEARCH FOR TRUTH," *BASIC VERITIES* (1943), TR. JULIAN GREEN

12. Honesty is for the most part less profitable than dishonesty.

PLATO, *THE REPUBLIC* (4TH C. B.C.), 2, TR. BENJAMIN JOWETT

13. An honest man's the noblest work of God.

ALEXANDER POPE, *AN ESSAY ON MAN* (1733–34), 4.247

14. God looks at the clean hands, not the full ones.

PUBLILIUS SYRUS, *MORAL SAYINGS* (1ST C. B.C.), 715, TR. DARIUS LYMAN

15. To make your children capable of honesty is the beginning of education.

JOHN RUSKIN, *TIME AND TIDE* (1867), 8

16. We are all jellyfish, too pitiful and too afraid of being disliked to be honest.

MAY SARTON, "MONDAY, JANUARY 19TH," *THE HOUSE BY THE SEA: A JOURNAL* (1977)

17. No legacy is so rich as honesty.

SHAKESPEARE, *ALL'S WELL THAT ENDS WELL* (1602–03), 3.5.13

18. I hope I shall always possess firmness and virtue enough to maintain what I consider the most enviable of all titles, the character of an "Honest Man."

GEORGE WASHINGTON (1732–1799), MAXIM

19. I would say that today, dishonesty is the rule, and honesty the exception. It could be, statistically, that more people are honest than dishonest, but the few that really control things are not honest, and that tips the balance.

FRANK ZAPPA, *THE REAL FRANK ZAPPA BOOK* (1989), WITH PETER OCCHIOGROSSO

HONOR

See 491. INTEGRITY

426. HONORS

See also 332. FAME; 386. GLORY

1. A prophet is not without honour, save in his own country.

BIBLE, MATTHEW 13:57

2. A medal glitters, but it also casts a shadow.

Sir Winston Churchill, speech, House of Commons, March 22, 1944

3. The honor paid to a wise man is a great good for those who honor him.

Epicurus, "Vatican Sayings" (3rd c. B.C.), 32, in *Letters, Principal Doctrines, and Vatican Sayings,* tr. Russel M. Geer

4. High honors are sweet / To a man's heart, but ever / They stand close to the brink of grief.

Euripides, *Iphigenia in Aulis* (c. 405 B.C.), tr. Charles R. Walker

5. [D]on't come giving me, who's old enough to die and too near blind to create anything any more anyhow, a great big banquet that *you* eat up in honor of your *own* stomachs as much as in honor of me—who's toothless and can't eat.

Langston Hughes, *Simple Speaks His Mind* (1950)

6. Great honours are great burdens, but on whom / They are cast with envy, he doth bear two loads.

Ben Jonson, *Catiline His Conspiracy* (1611), 3.1

7. Great power, which incites / Great envy, hurls some men to destruction; they are drowned / In a long, splendid stream of honors.

Juvenal, *Satires* (c. 100), 10.56, tr. Hubert Creekmore

8. My slumber broken and my doublet torn, / I find the laurel also bears a thorn.

Walter Savage Landor, "Lately Our Poets" (1863)

9. Let a prize lower my position, if it causes me to be read; that I prefer immediately to all the honors.

Marcel Proust, *Letters of Marcel Proust* (1949), tr.-ed. Mina Curtiss

10. It is sure that those are most desirous of honour or glory who cry out loudest of its abuse and the vanity of the world.

Spinoza, *Ethics* (1677), 5, tr. Andrew Boyle

427. HOPE

See also 239. Despair; 318. Expectation; 1040. Waiting

1. Hope is a waking dream.

Aristotle (4th c. B.C.), quoted in Diogenes Laertius' *Lives and Opinions of Eminent Philosophers* (3rd c. A.D.), tr. R. D. Hicks

2. Hope is a risk that must be run.

Georges Bernanos, "Why Freedom?" *The Last Essays of Georges Bernanos* (1955), tr. Barry Ulanov

3. Hope deferred maketh the heart sick.

Bible, Proverbs 13:12

4. Hope is a prodigal young heir, and Experience is his banker.

Charles Caleb Colton, *Lacon* (1825), 1.108

5. Hope is a strange invention— / A Patent of the Heart— / In unremitting action / Yet never wearing out—.

Emily Dickinson, poem (c. 1877)

6. The reason of idleness and of crime is the deferring of our hopes.

Emerson, "Nominalist and Realist," *Essays: Second Series* (1844)

7. Ten thousand men possess ten thousand hopes. / —A few bear fruit in happiness; the others go awry.

Euripides, *The Bacchae* (c. 405 B.C.), tr. William Arrowsmith

8. He that lives upon hope will die fasting.

Benjamin Franklin, "The Way to Wealth" (July 7, 1757)

9. He fishes on who catches one.

French Proverb

10. To hope means to be ready at every moment for that which is not yet born, and yet not become desperate if there is no birth in our lifetime.

Erich Fromm, *The Revolution of Hope* (1968)

11. If it were not for hopes, the heart would break.

Thomas Fuller, M.D., *Gnomologia* (1732), 2689

12. There are situations in which hope and fear run together, in which they mutually destroy one another, and lose themselves in a dull indifference.

Goethe, *Elective Affinities* (1809), 22

13. Hope is a great falsifier of truth.

Baltasar Gracián, *The Art of Worldly Wisdom* (1647), 19, tr. Joseph Jacobs

14. In the time of trouble avert not thy face from hope, for the soft marrow abideth in the hard bone.

Hāfiz, ghazals from the *Divan* (14th c.), 107, tr. Justin Huntly McCarthy

15. Death is the greatest evil, because it cuts off hope.

William Hazlitt, *Characteristics* (1823), 35

16. It is natural to man to indulge in the illusion of hope. We are apt to shut our eyes against a painful

truth, and listen to the song of that siren, till she transforms us into beasts.

PATRICK HENRY, SPEECH, VIRGINIA CONVENTION, MARCH 23, 1775

17. It is the around-the-corner brand of hope that prompts people to action, while the distant hope acts as an opiate.

ERIC HOFFER, *THE ORDEAL OF CHANGE* (1964), 10

18. The short span of life forbids us to take on far-reaching hopes.

HORACE, *ODES* (23–C. 15 B.C., 1.4

19. There is nothing so well known as that we should not expect something for nothing—but we all do and call it Hope.

EDGAR WATSON HOWE, *COUNTRY TOWN SAYINGS* (1911)

20. Hope is necessary in every condition. The miseries of poverty, sickness, of captivity, would, without this comfort, be insupportable.

SAMUEL JOHNSON, *THE RAMBLER* (1750–52), 67

21. Hope, deceitful as it is, serves at least to lead us to the end of our lives by an agreeable route.

LA ROCHEFOUCAULD, *MAXIMS* (1665), TR. KENNETH PRATT

22. Hope has as many lives as a cat or a king.

LONGFELLOW, *HYPERION* (1839), 3.9

23. the only way boss / to keep hope in the world / is to keep changing its / population frequently.

DON MARQUIS, "ARCHY AND THE OLD UN," *ARCHY'S LIFE OF MEHITABEL* (1933)

24. Oh, what a valiant faculty is hope,
that in a mortal subject, and in a moment,
makes nothing of usurping infinity, immensity,
eternity, and of supplying its master's indigence,
at its pleasure, with all things he can imagine or desire!

MONTAIGNE, "OF NAMES," *ESSAYS* (1580–88), TR. W. C. HAZLITT

25. Hope in reality is the worst of all evils, because it prolongs the torments of man.

NIETZSCHE, *HUMAN, ALL TOO HUMAN* (1878), 71, TR. HELEN ZIMMERN

26. Strong hope is a much greater stimulant of life than any single realised joy could be.

NIETZSCHE, *THE ANTICHRIST* (1888), 23, TR. ANTHONY M. LUDOVICI

27. Never give out while there is hope; but hope not beyond reason, for that shows more desire than judgment.

WILLIAM PENN, *SOME FRUITS OF SOLITUDE* (1693), 1.235

28. Just as dumb creatures are snared by food, human beings would not be caught unless they had a nibble of hope.

PETRONIUS, *SATYRICON* (1ST C.), TR. M. HESELTINE

29. Hope springs eternal in the human breast: / Man never is, but always to be blest.

ALEXANDER POPE, *AN ESSAY ON MAN* (1733–34), 1.95

30. At first we hope too much, later on, not enough.

JOSEPH ROUX, *MEDITATIONS OF A PARISH PRIEST* (1886), 5.8, TR. ISABEL F. HAPGOOD

31. Extreme hopes are born of extreme misery.

BERTRAND RUSSELL, "THE FUTURE OF MANKIND," *UNPOPULAR ESSAYS* (1950)

32. Hope is an echo, hope ties itself yonder, yonder.

CARL SANDBURG, *THE PEOPLE, YES* (1936)

33. Hope is brightest when it dawns from fears.

SIR WALTER SCOTT, *THE LADY OF THE LAKE* (1810), 4.1

34. The miserable have no other medicine / But only hope.

SHAKESPEARE, *MEASURE FOR MEASURE* (1604–05), 3.1.2

35. True hope is swift and flies with swallow's wings; / Kings it makes gods, and meaner creatures kings.

SHAKESPEARE, *RICHARD III* (1592–93), 5.2.23

36. If Winter comes, can Spring be far behind?

SHELLEY, "ODE TO THE WEST WIND" (1819), 5

37. Hope deceives more men than cunning does.

VAUVENARGUES, *REFLECTIONS AND MAXIMS* (1746), 569

38. Hope should no more be a virtue than fear; we fear and we hope, according to what is promised or threatened us.

VOLTAIRE, "VIRTUE," *PHILOSOPHICAL DICTIONARY* (1764)

HORSEMANSHIP

See 821. RIDING

HORSE-RACING

See 929. SPORTS

428. HOSPITALITY

See also 358. FOREIGNERS AND FOREIGNNESS

1. What is there / more kindly than the feeling between host and guest?

AESCHYLUS, *THE LIBATION BEARERS* (458 B.C.), TR. RICHMOND LATTIMORE

2. The lamp was no longer giving any light beyond its own daylighted chimney, and Mrs. Gudger put it out. Even now, with the hot load of the breakfast inside me, I was stiff with cold and was not yet well awake.

JAMES AGEE, *LET US NOW PRAISE FAMOUS MEN* (1941)

3. It is nothing won to admit men with an open door, and to receive them with a shut and reserved countenance.

FRANCIS BACON, "CIVIL KNOWLEDGE," *THE ADVANCEMENT OF LEARNING* (1605), 3

4. The hospitable instinct is not wholly altruistic. There is pride and egoism mixed up with it.

MAX BEERBOHM, "HOSTS AND GUESTS," *AND EVEN NOW* (1920)

5. When hospitality becomes an art, it loses its very soul.

MAX BEERBOHM, "HOSTS AND GUESTS," *AND EVEN NOW* (1920)

6. Withdraw thy foot from they neighbor's house; lest he be weary of thee, and so hate thee.

BIBLE, PROVERBS 25:17

7. Seven days is the length of a guest's life.

BURMESE PROVERBS (1962), 444

8. A house may draw visitors, but it is the possessor alone that can detain them.

CHARLES CALEB COLTON, *LACON* (1825), 1.30

9. Fish and guests smell at three days old.

DANISH PROVERB

10. Happy the man who never puts on a face,
but receives every visitor with that countenance he has on.

EMERSON, *JOURNALS,* 1833

11. My evening visitors, if they cannot see the clock should find the time in my face.

EMERSON, *JOURNALS,* 1842

12. Welcome is the best cheer.

THOMAS FULLER, M.D., *GNOMOLOGIA* (1732), 5470

13. It is equally offensive to speed a guest who would like to stay and to detain one who is anxious to leave.

HOMER, *ODYSSEY* (9TH C. B.C.), 15, TR. E. V. RIEU

14. To be an ideal guest, stay at home.

EDGAR WATSON HOWE, *COUNTRY TOWN SAYINGS* (1911)

15. I will gladly lecture for fifty dollars, but I'll not be a guest for less than a hundred.

ELBERT HUBBARD, *THE PHILISTINE* (1895–1915)

16. Not many sounds in life, and I include all urban and all rural sounds, exceed in interest a knock at the door.

CHARLES LAMB, "VALENTINE'S DAY," *ESSAYS OF ELIA* (1823)

17. A guest sees more in an hour than the host in a year.

POLISH PROVERB

18. Unbidden guests / Are often welcomest when they are gone.

SHAKESPEARE, *I HENRY VI* (1591–92), 2.2.55

HOSPITALS

See 896. SICKNESS

429. HOTELS

1. It was a dark place, with malodorous chambers, miserable food, and a lobby ceiling decorated with as much gilt and gesso as the Vatican chapels.

JOHN CHEEVER, "O CITY OF BROKEN DREAMS," *THE STORIES OF JOHN CHEEVER* (1980)

2. The Milky Way, the hotel where I was scheduled to stay in Las Vegas and whose floor show Fauntleroy was currently headlining, was the town's newest—a vast, foolish beehive of plate glass rearing fifteen stories above the sagebrush, so ruthlessly air-conditioned that I was wheezing like an accordion by the time I unpacked.

S.J. PERELMAN, *THE RISING GORGE* (1961)

3. All saints can do miracles, but few of them can keep a hotel.

MARK TWAIN, *NOTEBOOK* (1935)

430. HOUSES

See also 50. ARCHITECTURE; 422. HOME; 746. PROPERTY

1. A man builds a fine house; and now he has a master, and a task for life; he is to furnish, watch, show it, and keep it in repair the rest of his days.

EMERSON, "WORKS AND DAYS," *SOCIETY AND SOLITUDE* (1870)

2. The worst of a modern stylish mansion is, that it has no place for ghosts.

OLIVER WENDELL HOLMES, SR., *THE POET AT THE BREAKFAST TABLE* (1872), 1

3. Small rooms or dwellings discipline the mind, large ones weaken it.

LEONARDO DA VINCI, *NOTEBOOKS* (C. 1500), TR. JEAN PAUL RICHTER

4. Though the house was not large it had, like all houses in Floral Heights, an altogether royal bathroom of porcelain and glazed tile and metal sleek as silver.

SINCLAIR LEWIS, *BABBITT* (1922)

5. Mexican homes as a rule are closed off to the world by high blank walls of yellowish masonry, topped with broken glass to discourage *escaladores*, or climbing burglars. The gardens and fountains and other delights are hidden, as in an Arab city.

CHARLES PORTIS, *GRINGOS* (1991)

6. The surroundings householders crave are glorified autobiographies ghost-written by willing architects and interior designers who, like their clients, want to show off.

T. H. ROBSJOHN-GIBBINGS, "ROBSJOHN-GIBBINGS NAMES THE BIGGEST BORE," *TOWN AND COUNTRY*, JANUARY 1961

7. A man's house is his stage. Others walk on to play their bit parts. Now and again a soliloquy, a birth, an adultery.

KARL SHAPIRO, *THE BOURGEOIS POET* (1964), 1.29

8. Our houses are such unwieldy property that we are often imprisoned rather than housed in them.

THOREAU, "ECONOMY," *WALDEN* (1854)

9. At a certain season of our life we are accustomed to consider every spot as the possible site of a house.

THOREAU, "WHERE I LIVED, AND WHAT I LIVED FOR," *WALDEN* (1854)

431. HUMAN NATURE

See also 486. INSTINCT; 562. MANKIND

1. Human nature must not be altered in order to have a problem-free world. Man is not just a problem-solving being, as behaviorists would wish us to believe, but a problem-recognizing and -accepting being.

ALLAN BLOOM, *THE CLOSING OF THE AMERICAN MIND* (1987)

2. Human nature is the same everywhere; the modes only are different.

LORD CHESTERFIELD, *LETTERS TO HIS GODSON*, 1773

3. Never can custom conquer nature, for she is ever unconquered.

CICERO, *TUSCULANAE DISPUTATIONS* (44 B.C.), 5.27.78

4. It's a burden to us even to be human beings—men with our own real body and blood; we are ashamed of it, we think it a disgrace and try to contrive to be some sort of impossible generalized man.

DOSTOYEVSKY, *NOTES FROM UNDERGROUND* (1864), 2.10, TR. CONSTANCE GARNETT

5. Even the most sadistic and destructive man is human, as human as the saint.

ERICH FROMM, *THE ANATOMY OF HUMAN DESTRUCTIVENESS* (1973)

6. Could we perfect human nature, we might also expect a perfect state of things.

GOETHE, QUOTED IN JOHANN PETER ECKERMANN'S *CONVERSATIONS WITH GOETHE*, FEB. 25, 1824

7. If mankind is naturally good, he is sure going against his nature more and more of the time. It sounds like a bad joke: the paranoids are after us.

HERBERT GOLD, "LET'S KILL THE FIRST RED-HAIRED MAN WE SEE...," *THE MAGIC WILL* (1971)

8. It is to the credit of human nature, that, except where its selfishness is brought into play, it loves more readily than it hates.

NATHANIEL HAWTHORNE, *THE SCARLET LETTER* (1850), 13

9. The perfect joys of heaven do not satisfy the cravings of nature.

WILLIAM HAZLITT, "ON THE LITERARY CHARACTER," *THE ROUND TABLE* (1817)

10. If human nature eventually is going to take the place of nature everywhere, those of us who have been naturalists will have to transpose the faith in nature which is inherent in the profession to a faith in man—if necessary, man alone in the world.

EDWARD HOAGLAND, "THE RIDGE-SLOPE FOX AND THE KNIFE THROWER," *THE TUGMAN'S PASSAGE* (1982)

11. Drive Nature from your door with a pitchfork, and she will return again and again.

HORACE, *EPISTLES* (20–C. 8 B.C.), 1.10

12. The thief and the murderer follow nature just as much as the philanthropist.

THOMAS HENRY HUXLEY, "EVOLUTION AND ETHICS" (1893)

13. Scenery is fine—but human nature is finer.

KEATS, LETTER TO BENJAMIN BAILEY, MARCH 13, 1818

14. Whenever man forgets that man is an animal, the result is always to make him less humane.

JOSEPH WOOD KRUTCH, "MARCH," *THE TWELVE SEASONS* (1949)

15. Before Man made us citizens, great Nature made us men.

JAMES RUSSELL LOWELL, "ON THE CAPTURE OF FUGITIVE SLAVES NEAR WASHINGTON" (1845), 2

16. [T]he essence of being human is that, in the brief moment we exist on this spinning planet, we can love some persons and some things, in spite of the fact that time and death will ultimately claim us all.

ROLLO MAY, *THE COURAGE TO CREATE* (1975)

17. That a thing is unnatural ... is no argument for its being blamable; since the most criminal actions are, to a being like man, not more unnatural than most of the virtues.

JOHN STUART MILL, "NATURE," *THREE ESSAYS ON RELIGION* (1874)

18. It disturbs me no more to find men base, unjust, or selfish than to see apes mischievous, wolves savage, or the vulture ravenous for its prey.

MOLIÈRE, *THE MISANTHROPE* (1666), 1, TR. JOHN WOOD

19. To be natural means to dare to be as immoral as Nature is.

NIETZSCHE, *THE WILL TO POWER* (1888), TR. ANTHONY M. LUDOVICI

20. The essence of being human is that one does not seek perfection.

GEORGE ORWELL, "REFLECTIONS ON GANDHI," *SHOOTING AN ELEPHANT* (1950)

21. The dictum that human nature cannot be changed is one of those tiresome platitudes that conceal from the ignorant the depths of their own ignorance.

BERTRAND RUSSELL, "IDEAS WHICH HAVE BECOME OBSOLETE," *NEW HOPES FOR A CHANGING WORLD* (1951)

22. What does reason demand of a man? A very easy thing—to live in accord with his own nature.

SENECA, *LETTERS TO LUCILIUS* (1ST C.), 41, TR. E. PHILLIPS BARKER

23. Nature her custom holds, / Let shame say what it will.

SHAKESPEARE, *HAMLET* (1600), 4.7.189

24. One touch of nature makes the whole world kin.

SHAKESPEARE, *TROILUS AND CRESIDA* (1601–02), 3.3.175

25. All is disgust when one leaves his own nature / and does things that misfit it.

SOPHOCLES, *PHILOCTETES* (409 B.C.), TR. DAVID GRENE

26. It is usually the case with most men that their nature is so constituted that they pity those who fare badly and envy those who fare well.

SPINOZA, *ETHICS* (1677), 3, TR. ANDREW BOYLE

27. The human being says that the beast in him has been aroused, when what he actually means is that the human being in him has been aroused.

JAMES THURBER, "THE TROUBLE WITH MAN IS MAN," *LANTERNS AND LANCES* (1961)

28. Nature has always had more power than education.

VOLTAIRE, *VIE DE MOLIÈRE* (1739)

29. Just because we think we're so wonderful doesn't mean we really are. We could be really terrible animals and just never admit it because it would hurt so much.

KURT VONNEGUT, *HOCUS POCUS* (1990)

432. HUMANISM

See also 261. DIVINITY

1. What the world needs is not redemption from sin but redemption from hunger and oppression; it has no need to pin its hopes upon Heaven, it has everything to hope for from this earth.

FRIEDRICH DÜRRENMATT, *THE MARRIAGE OF MR. MISSISSIPPI* (1952), 1, TR. MICHAEL BULLOCK

2. Humanism is not alive and well in Texas. Different colors and types of Texans do not like one another, nor do they pretend to.

MOLLY IVINS, *MOLLY IVINS CAN'T SAY THAT, CAN SHE?* (1991)

3. From the failure of the humanist tradition to participate fully or to act decisively, civilizations may perhaps crumble or perish at the hands of barbarians. But unless the humanist tradition itself in some form survives, there can really be no civilization at all.

LOUIS KRONENBERGER, *COMPANY MANNERS* (1954), 1.1

4. When men can no longer be theists, they must, if they are civilized, become humanists.

WALTER LIPPMANN, *A PREFACE TO MORALS* (1929), 1.7.7

5. In all humanism there is an element of weakness, which in some circumstances may be its ruin, connected with its contempt of fanaticism, its patience, its love of scepticism; in short, its natural goodness.

THOMAS MANN, "EUROPE, BEWARE," *THE THOMAS MANN READER* (1950), TR. H. T. LOWE-PORTER

433. HUMANITARIANISM

See also 56. Assistance; 74. Beggars; 120. Charity; 227. Deeds; 384. Gifts and Giving; 393. Goodness; 594. Misanthropy; 790. Reform; 887. Service; 1021. Unselfishness

1. Do not give, as many rich men do, like a hen that lays her egg and then cackles.

Henry Ward Beecher, *Proverbs from Plymouth Pulpit* (1887)

2. Inasmuch as ye have done it unto one of the least of these my brethren, ye have done it unto me.

Bible, Matthew 25:40

3. Let us not be weary in well doing: for in due season we shall reap, if we faint not.

Bible, Galatians 6:9

4. When thou doest alms, let not thy left hand know what thy right doeth.

Bible, Matthew 6:3

5. Too many have dispensed with generosity to practice charity.

Albert Camus, *The Fall* (1956)

6. Social work is a band-aid on the festering wounds of society.

Alexander Chase, *Perspectives* (1966)

7. It is better to light a candle than to curse the darkness.

Chinese Proverb, Motto of the Christophers

8. A man of humanity is one who, in seeking to establish himself, finds a foothold for others and who, desiring attainment for himself, helps others to attain.

Confucius, *Analects* (6th c. b.c.), 6.28, tr. Winberg Chai

9. If I am virtuous and worthy, for whom should I not maintain a proper concern?

Confucius, *Analects* (6th c. b.c.), 19.3, tr. Winberg Chai

10. Isn't it better to have men being ungrateful than to miss a chance to do good?

Denis Diderot, *Discours sur la poésie dramatique* (1773–78)

11. The rich have no more of the kingdom of heaven than they have purchased of the poor by their alms.

John Donne, *Sermons,* No. 59, 1628

12. In abstract love of humanity one almost always only loves oneself.

Dostoyevsky, *The Idiot* (1868), 3.10, tr. David Magarshack

13. Human rights are universal and indivisible. Human freedom is also indivisible: if it is denied to anyone in the world, it is therefore denied, indirectly, to all people. This is why we cannot remain silent in the face of evil or violence; silence merely encourages them.

Václav Havel, "The Task of Independence," *Summer Meditations* (1992), tr. Paul Wilson

14. By Jove the stranger and the poor are sent, / And what to those we give, to Jove is lent.

Homer, *Odyssey* (9th c. b.c.), 6.247, tr. Alexander Pope

15. That action is best which procures the greatest happiness for the greatest numbers.

Francis Hutcheson, *Inquiry Concerning Moral Good and Evil* (1720), 3

16. A decent provision for the poor is the true test of civilization.

Samuel Johnson, quoted in Boswell's *Life of Samuel Johnson,* 1770

17. Men that talk of their own benefits are not believed to talk of them because they have done them, but to have done them because they might talk of them.

Ben Jonson, "Explorata," *Timber* (1640)

18. Philanthropy is commendable, but it must not cause the philanthropist to overlook the circumstances of economic injustice which make philanthropy necessary.

Martin Luther King, Jr., *Strength to Love* (1963), 3.2

19. A large part of altruism, even when it is perfectly honest, is grounded upon the fact that it is uncomfortable to have unhappy people about one.

H. L. Mencken, *Prejudices: Fourth Series* (1924), 11

20. High-toned humanitarians constantly overestimate the sufferings of those they sympathize with.

H. L. Mencken, *Minority Report* (1956), 226

21. It is not enough to do good; one must do it in the right way.

John Morley, *On Compromise* (1874)

22. If all alms were given only from pity, all beggars would have starved long ago.

Nietzsche, *The Wanderer and His Shadow* (1880), 239, in *The Portable Nietzsche*, tr. Walter Kaufmann

23. The humanitarian wishes to be a prime mover in the lives of others. He cannot admit either the divine or the natural order, by which men have the power to help themselves. The humanitarian puts himself in the place of God.

ISABEL PATERSON, *THE GOD OF THE MACHINE* (1943)

24. The place to improve the world is first in one's own heart and head and hands, and then work outward from there.

ROBERT M. PIRSIG, *ZEN AND THE ART OF MOTORCYCLE MAINTENANCE* (1974)

25. Human altruism which is not egoism, is sterile.

MARCEL PROUST, *REMEMBRANCE OF THINGS PAST: THE PAST RECAPTURED* (1913–27), TR. STEPHEN HUDSON

26. Do good even to the wicked; it is as well to shut a dog's mouth with a crumb.

SA'DI, *GULISTAN* (1258), 1.33, TR. JAMES ROSS

27. The dignity of the individual demands that he be not reduced to vassalage by the largesse of others.

SAINT-EXUPÉRY, *FLIGHT TO ARRAS* (1942), 23, TR. LEWIS GALANTIÈRE

28. How far that little candle throws his beams! / So shines a good deed in a naughty world.

SHAKESPEARE, *THE MERCHANT OF VENICE* (1596–97), 5.1.90

29. He who is too busy doing good finds no time to be good.

RABINDRANATH TAGORE, *STRAY BIRDS* (1916), 184

30. He who wants to do good knocks at the gate; he who loves finds the gate open.

RABINDRANATH TAGORE, *STRAY BIRDS* (1916), 83

31. Altruism has always been one of biology's deep mysteries. Why should any animal, off on its own, specified and labeled by all sorts of signals as its individual self, choose to give up its life in aid of someone else?

LEWIS THOMAS, "ALTRUISM," *LATE NIGHT THOUGHTS ON LISTENING TO MAHLER'S NINTH SYMPHONY* (1983)

32. Philanthropy is almost the only virtue which is sufficiently appreciated by mankind.

THOREAU, *WALDEN* (1854), 1

434. HUMILIATION

See also 820. RIDICULE; 893. SHAME

1. Writing humor in my column isn't as dangerous as performing it. If I fail in front of a live audience, the humiliation is as great as anything a human being can suffer.

ART BUCHWALD, *LEAVING HOME: A MEMOIR* (1993)

2. Imagine now a man who is deprived of everyone he loves, and at the same time of his house, his habits, his clothes, in short, of everything he possesses: he will be a hollow man, reduced to suffering and needs, forgetful of dignity and restraint, for he who loses all often loses himself.

PRIMO LEVI, *SURVIVAL IN AUSCHWITZ* (1959)

3. It is a bitter dose to be taught obedience after you have learned to rule.

PUBLILIUS SYRUS, *MORAL SAYINGS* (1ST C. B.C.), 1019, TR. DARIUS LYMAN

4. Better a quiet death than a public misfortune.

SPANISH PROVERB

435. HUMILITY

See also 166. CONCEIT; 600. MODESTY; 733. PRIDE

1. He never labored so hard to learn a language as he did to hold his tongue and it affected him for life. The habit of reticence—of talking without meaning—is never effaced.

HENRY ADAMS, *THE EDUCATION OF HENRY ADAMS* (1918)

2. Meekness, n. Uncommon patience in planning a revenge that is worth while.

AMBROSE BIERCE, *THE DEVIL'S DICTIONARY* (1881–1911)

3. The eagle never lost so much time as when he submitted to learn of the crow.

WILLIAM BLAKE, "PROVERBS OF HELL," *THE MARRIAGE OF HEAVEN AND HELL* (1790)

4. They are proud in humility; proud in that they are not proud.

ROBERT BURTON, *THE ANATOMY OF MELANCHOLY* (1621), 1.2.3.14

5. Humility has its origin in an awareness of unworthiness, and sometimes too in a dazzled awareness of saintliness.

COLETTE, "LADY OF LETTERS," *EARTHLY PARADISE* (1966), 4, ED. ROBERT PHELPS

6. Nothing is beneath you if it is in the direction of your life.

EMERSON, "WEALTH," *THE CONDUCT OF LIFE* (1860)

7. Humility is a quality for which I have only a limited admiration. In many phases of life it is a great

mistake and degenerates into defensiveness or hypocrisy.

E.M. Forster, "Prophecy," *Aspects of the Novel* (1927)

8. Humility is just as much the opposite of self-abasement as it is of self-exaltation.

Dag Hammarskjöld, "1959," *Markings* (1964), tr. W. H. Auden

9. Humility is not renunciation of pride but the substitution of one pride for another.

Eric Hoffer, *The Passionate State of Mind* (1954), 212

10. Humility is the first of the virtues—for other people.

Oliver Wendell Holmes Sr., *The Professor at the Breakfast Table* (1860), 5

11. Meekness is the mask of malice.

Robert G. Ingersoll, *Prose-Poems and Selections* (1884)

12. Humility is often only feigned submission which people use to render others submissive. It is a subterfuge of pride which lowers itself in order to rise.

La Rochefoucauld, *Maxims* (1665), tr. Kenneth Pratt

13. Plenty of people wish to become devout, but no one wishes to be humble.

La Rochefoucauld, *Maxims* (1665), tr. Kenneth Pratt

14. A man who has humility will have acquired in the last reaches of his beliefs the saving doubt of his own certainty.

Walter Lippmann, *The Public Philosophy* (1955), 10.4

15. One may be humble out of pride.

Montaigne, "Of presumption," *Essays* (1580–88), tr. W. C. Hazlitt

16. He that humbleth himself wishes to be exalted.

Nietzsche, *Human, All Too Human* (1878), 87, tr. Helen Zimmern

17. Humility has the toughest hide.

Nietzsche, "The Stillest Hour," *Thus Spoke Zarathustra* (1883–92), 2, tr. Walter Kaufmann

18. There must be feelings of humility, not from nature, but from penitence, not to rest in them, but to go on to greatness.

Pascal, *Pensées* (1670), 524, tr. W. F. Trotter

19. Who builds a church to God and not to fame, / Will never mark the marble with his name.

Alexander Pope, *Moral Essays* (1731–35), 3.285

20. Humility neither falls far, nor heavily.

Publilius Syrus, *Moral Sayings* (1st c. b.c.), 334, tr. Darius Lyman

21. The first test of a truly great man is his humility.

John Ruskin, *Modern Painters* (1843–60), v. 3, 4.16.24

22. The sons of Adam are formed from dust; if not humble as the dust, they fall short of being men.

Sa'di, *Gulistan* (1258), 2.42, tr. James Ross

23. Humility is a virtue all preach, none practice, and yet everybody is content to hear.

John Selden, "Humility," *Table Talk* (1689)

24. Fundamentalists are less concerned to be systematic and rational than to be humble and faithful, accepting God's commandments because they come from God, not because they proceed from common sense or sophisticated reason.

Israel Shenker, *Coat of Many Colors* (1985)

25. Those who are believed to be most abject and humble are usually most ambitious and envious.

Spinoza, *Ethics* (1677), 3, tr. Andrew Boyle

26. We come nearest to the great when we are great in humility.

Rabindranath Tagore, *Stray Birds* (1916), 57

27. Do not seek so anxiously to be developed, to subject yourself to many influences to be played on; it is all dissipation. Humility like darkness reveals the heavenly lights.

Thoreau, "Conclusion," *Walden* (1854)

436. HUMOR

See also 144. Comedians; 145. Comedy; 526. Laughter; 768. Puns; 820. Ridicule; 881. Sense and Nonsense; 886. Seriousness; 1061. Wit

1. Clumsy jesting is no joke.

Aesop, "The Ass and the Lapdog," *Fables* (6th c. b.c.?), tr. Joseph Jacobs

2. Men will let you abuse them if only you will make them laugh.

Henry Ward Beecher, *Proverbs from Plymouth Pulpit* (1887)

3. Humor is falling downstairs if you do it while in the act of warning your wife not to.

Kenneth Bird, news summaries, May 3, 1954

4. People ask what I am really trying to do with humor. The answer is, "I'm getting even."

ART BUCHWALD, *LEAVING HOME: A MEMOIR* (1993)

5. When once you have got hold of a vulgar joke, you may be certain that you have got hold of a subtle and spiritual idea.

G. K. CHESTERTON, "COCKNEYS AND THEIR JOKES," *ALL THINGS CONSIDERED* (1908)

6. Men will confess to treason, murder, arson, false teeth, or a wig. How many of them will own up to a lack of humor?

FRANK MOORE COLBY, "SATIRE AND TEETH," *THE COLBY ESSAYS* (1926), V. 1

7. A difference of taste in jokes is a great strain on the affections.

GEORGE ELIOT, *DANIEL DERONDA* (1874–76), 2.15

8. The writer's Queen Victoria is his public, and he would do well to keep a bust of the old Queen on his desk with the legend "We are not amused" hanging from it.

H.W. FOWLER, *A DICTIONARY OF MODERN ENGLISH USAGE* (1926)

9. Better lose a jest than a friend.

THOMAS FULLER, M.D., *GNOMOLOGIA* (1732), 915

10. Humor is an affirmation of dignity, a declaration of man's superiority to all that befalls him.

ROMAIN GARY, *PROMISE AT DAWN* (1961)

11. A sharp sense of the ironic can be the equivalent of the faith that moves mountains. Far more quicky than reason or logic, irony can penetrate rage and puncture self-pity.

MOSS HART, *ACT ONE* (1959)

12. There's nothing like a gleam of humor to reassure you that a fellow human being is ticking inside a strange face.

EVA HOFFMAN, *EXIT INTO HISTORY* (1993)

13. A jest often decides matters of importance more effectually and happily than seriousness.

HORACE, *SATIRES* (35–30 B.C.), 1.10

14. As for George Bush of Kennebunkport, Maine—personally I think he's further evidence that the Great Scriptwriter in the Sky has an overdeveloped sense of irony.

MOLLY IVINS, *MOLLY IVINS CAN'T SAY THAT, CAN SHE?* (1991)

15. Of all the griefs that harass the distressed, / Sure the most bitter is a scornful jest.

SAMUEL JOHNSON, *LONDON* (1738)

16. Humor simultaneously wounds and heals, indicts and pardons, diminishes and enlarges; it constitutes inner growth at the expense of outer gain, and those who possess and honestly practice it make themselves more through a willingness to make themselves less.

LOUIS KRONENBERGER, *COMPANY MANNERS* (1954), 3.2

17. The teller of a mirthful tale has latitude allowed him. We are content with less than absolute truth.

CHARLES LAMB, "STAGE ILLUSION," *LAST ESSAYS OF ELIA* (1833)

18. The humorist has a good eye for the humbug; he does not always recognize the saint.

W. SOMERSET MAUGHAM, *THE SUMMING UP* (1938), 20

19. Good taste and humor are a contradiction in terms, like a chaste whore.

MALCOLM MUGGERIDGE, *TIME,* SEPT. 14, 1953

20. Oh Lord, give us a sense of humor with courage to manifest it forth, so that we may laugh to shame the pomps, the vanities, the sense of self-importance of the Big Fellows that the world sometimes sends among us, and who try to take our peace away.

SEAN O'CASEY, "THE POWER OF LAUGHTER," *THE GREEN CROW* (1956)

21. Nothing seems too high or low for the humorist; he is above honor, above faith, preserving sense in religion and sanity in life.

SEAN O'CASEY, "THE POWER OF LAUGHTER: WEAPON AGAINST EVIL," *FIFTY FAMOUS ESSAYS* (1964)

22. A dirty joke is not, of course, a serious attack on morality, but it is a sort of mental rebellion, a momentary wish that things were otherwise.

GEORGE ORWELL, "THE ART OF DONALD MCGILL," *A COLLECTION OF ESSAYS* (1954)

23. Humor to me, Heaven help me, takes in many things. There must be courage; there must be no awe. There must be criticism, for humor, to my mind, is encapsulated in criticism.

DOROTHY PARKER, INTRODUCTION, *THE MOST OF S.J. PERELMAN* (1958)

24. Gentle Dulness ever loves a joke.

ALEXANDER POPE, *THE DUNCIAD* (1743), 2.34

25. The profoundly humorous writers are humorous because they are responsive to the hopeless, uncouth concatenations of life.

V. S. PRITCHETT, "THE MINOR DOSTOYEVSKY," *THE LIVING NOVEL & LATER APPRECIATIONS* (1964)

26. Everything is funny as long as it is happening to somebody else.

WILL ROGERS, "WARNING TO JOKERS: LAY OFF THE PRINCE," *THE ILLITERATE DIGEST* (1942)

27. Fun is a good thing but only when it spoils nothing better.

GEORGE SANTAYANA, "THE COMIC," *THE SENSE OF BEAUTY* (1896)

28. A jest's prosperity lies in the ear / Of him that hears it, never in the tongue / Of him that makes it.

SHAKESPEARE, *LOVE'S LABOUR'S LOST* (1594–95), 5.2.70

29. For every ten jokes, thou hast got an hundred enemies.

LAURENCE STERNE, *TRISTRAM SHANDY* (1759–67), 1.12

30. A truly comic, invented world must live *at the same time* as the world *we* live in.

DYLAN THOMAS, *QUITE EARLY ONE MORNING* (1954)

31. "Do you serve women at this bar?" "No," says the barman, "you've got to bring your own."

DYLAN THOMAS, *QUITE EARLY ONE MORNING* (1954)

32. The things we laugh at are awful while they are going on, but get funny when we look back. And other people laugh because they've been through it too. The closest thing to humor is tragedy.

JAMES THURBER, "SPEAKING OF HUMOR...," *COLLECTING HIMSELF* (1989)

33. Humor is emotional chaos remembered in tranquility.

JAMES THURBER, *NEW YORK POST*, FEB. 29, 1960

34. The secret source of humor is not joy but sorrow. There is no humor in heaven.

MARK TWAIN, "PUDD'NHEAD WILSON'S NEW CALENDAR," *FOLLOWING THE EQUATOR* (1897), 1.10

35. Pleasantry is never good on serious points, because it always regards subjects in that point of view in which it is not the purpose to consider them.

VOLTAIRE, "STYLE," *PHILOSOPHICAL DICTIONARY* (1764)

36. Anyone who is considered funny will tell you, sometimes without your even asking, that deep inside they are very serious, neurotic, introspective people.

WENDY WASSERSTEIN, "JEAN HARLOW'S WEDDING NIGHT," *BACHELOR GIRLS* (1990)

37. The world likes humor, but it treats it patronizingly. It decorates its serious artists with laurel, and its wags with Brussels sprouts.

E. B. WHITE, "SOME REMARKS ON HUMOR," *THE SECOND TREE FROM THE CORNER* (1954)

38. Humour is the first of the gifts to perish in a foreign tongue.

VIRGINIA WOOLF, "ON NOT KNOWING GREEK," *THE COMMON READER: FIRST SERIES* (1925)

437. HUNGER

See also 274. EATING

1. Appetite, n. An instinct thoughtfully implanted by Providence as a solution to the labor question.

AMBROSE BIERCE, *THE DEVIL'S DICTIONARY* (1881–1911)

2. There's no sauce in the world like hunger.

CERVANTES, *DON QUIXOTE* (1605–15), 2.3.5, TR. JOHN OZELL

3. All's good in a famine.

THOMAS FULLER, M.D., *GNOMOLOGIA* (1732), 545

4. If people are hungry, ill-clad, unsheltered or diseased, nothing is so important as to remedy their condition.

JOHN KENNETH GALBRAITH, *THE NEW INDUSTRIAL STATE* (1967)

5. No hungry man who is also sober can be persuaded to use his last dollar for anything but food.

JOHN KENNETH GALBRAITH, *THE NEW INDUSTRIAL STATE* (1967)

6. Hunger can explain many acts. It can be said that all vile acts are done to satisfy hunger.

MAXIM GORKY, *ENEMIES* (1906), 1

7. Love and business and family and religion and art and patriotism are nothing but shadows of words when a man's starving.

O. HENRY, "CUPID À LA CARTE," *HEART OF THE WEST* (1907)

8. Hunger also changes the world—when eating can't be a habit, then neither can seeing.

MAXINE HONG KINGSTON, *THE WOMAN WARRIOR* (1976)

9. A hungry stomach has no ears.

La Fontaine, "The Kite and the Nightingale," *Fables* (1668–94)

10. It has been well said that a hungry man is more interested in four sandwiches than four freedoms.

Henry Cabot Lodge, Jr., news reports, March 29, 1955

11. Hunger is the teacher of the arts and the bestower of invention.

Persius, prologue to the *Satires* (1st c.), 10

12. The belly is ungrateful—it always forgets we already gave it something.

Russian Proverb

13. To him who is stinted of food a boiled turnip will relish like a roast fowl.

Sa'di, *Gulistan* (1258), 3.19, tr. James Ross

14. Everyone I have ever known very well has been concerned that I would eventually starve. Probably I shall. It isn't important enough to me to be an obsession.

John Steinbeck, *Steinbeck: A Life in Letters,* eds. Elaine Steinbeck and Robert Wallsten (1975)

15. I have starved and it isn't nearly as bad as is generally supposed. Four days and a half was my longest stretch. Maybe there are pains that come later. Personally I think terror is the painful part of starvation.

John Steinbeck, *Steinbeck: A Life in Letters,* eds. Elaine Steinbeck and Robert Wallsten (1975)

438. HUNTING

1. There was never any question about the morality of hunting, but neither was there any acceptance of killing for the sake of a trophy.

Jimmy Carter, *An Outdoor Journal: Adventures and Reflections* (1988)

2. The creatures that want to live a life of their own, we call wild. If wild, then no matter how harmless, we treat them as outlaws, and those of us who are specially well brought up shoot them for fun.

Clarence Day, *This Simian World* (1920), 7

3. There is a passion for hunting something deeply implanted in the human breast.

Charles Dickens, *Oliver Twist* (1837–39), 10

4. It is very strange, and very melancholy, that the paucity of human pleasures should persuade us ever to call hunting one of them.

Samuel Johnson, quoted in Birkbeck Hill's *Johnsonian Miscellanies* (1897), v. 1

5. The English country gentleman galloping after a fox—the unspeakable in full pursuit of the uneatable.

Oscar Wilde, *A Woman of No Importance* (1893), 1

HURRY

See 411. Haste; 926. Speed

439. HYPOCHONDRIA

See 896. Sickness

440. HYPOCRISY

See also 224. Deception; 688. Personality, Dual; 901. Sincerity

1. Many among men are they who set high / the show of honor, yet break justice.

Aeschylus, *Agamemnon* (458 B.C.), tr. Richmond Lattimore

2. We are always making God our accomplice, that so we may legalize our own iniquities. Every successful massacre is consecrated by a Te Deum, and the clergy have never been wanting in benedictions for any victorious enormity.

Henri Frédéric Amiel, *Journal,* Oct. 6, 1866, tr. Mrs. Humphry Ward

3. Occident, n. The part of the world lying west (or east) of the Orient. It is largely inhabited by Christians, a powerful subtribe of the Hypocrites, whose principal industries are murder and cheating, which they are pleased to call "war" and "commerce." These, also, are the principal industries of the Orient.

Ambrose Bierce, *The Devil's Dictionary* (1881–1911)

4. Of lies, false modesty is the most decent.

Chamfort, *Maximes et pensées* (1805), 1

5. It is easier to pretend to be what you are not than to hide what you really are; but he that can accomplish both has little to learn in hypocrisy.

Charles Caleb Colton, *Lacon* (1825), 1.315

6. The hater of property and of government takes care to have his warranty deed recorded; and the book written against fame and learning has the author's name on the title-page.

Emerson, *Journals,* 1857

7. Often a noble face hides filthy ways.

EURIPIDES, *ELECTRA* (413 B.C.), TR. EMILY TOWNSEND VERMEULE

8. The true hypocrite is the one who ceases to perceive his deception, the one who lies with sincerity.

ANDRÉ GIDE, *JOURNAL OF "THE COUNTERFEITERS,"* SECOND NOTEBOOK, AUGUST 1921, TR. JUSTIN O'BRIEN

9. I detest that man, who / hides one thing in the depths of his heart, and speaks forth another.

HOMER, *ILIAD* (9TH C. B.C.), 9.312, TR. RICHMOND LATTIMORE

10. Most people have seen worse things in private than they pretend to be shocked at in public.

EDGAR WATSON HOWE, *COUNTRY TOWN SAYINGS* (1911)

11. It is not uncommon to charge the difference between promise and performance, between profession and reality, upon deep design and studied deceit; but the truth is, that there is very little hypocrisy in the world.

SAMUEL JOHNSON, *THE IDLER* (1758–60), 27

12. Spread yourself upon his bosom publicly, whose heart you would eat in private.

BEN JONSON, *EVERY MAN OUT OF HIS HUMOUR* (1599), 3.1

13. Hypocrisy is the homage which vice pays to virtue.

LA ROCHEFOUCAULD, *MAXIMS* (1665), TR. KENNETH PRATT

14. In the mouths of many men soft words are like roses that soldiers put into the muzzles of their muskets on holidays.

LONGFELLOW, "TABLE-TALK," *DRIFTWOOD* (1857)

15. Hypocrisy is a fashionable vice, and all fashionable vices pass for virtues.

MOLIÈRE, *DON JUAN* (1665), 5.2, TR. DONALD M. FRAME

16. The hypocrite who always plays one and the same part ceases at last to be a hypocrite.

NIETZSCHE, *HUMAN, ALL TOO HUMAN* (1878), 51, TR. HELEN ZIMMERN

17. That character in conversation which commonly passes for agreeable is made up of civility and falsehood.

ALEXANDER POPE, *THOUGHTS ON VARIOUS SUBJECTS* (1727)

18. To show an unfelt sorrow is an office / Which the false man does easy.

SHAKESPEARE, *MACBETH* (1605–06), 2.3.142

19. With devotion's visage / And pious action we do sugar o'er / The devil himself.

SHAKESPEARE, *HAMLET* (1600), 3.1.47

20. Hypocrisy in anything whatever may deceive the cleverest and most penetrating man, but the least wide-awake of children recognizes it, and is revolted by it, however ingeniously it may be disguised.

LEO TOLSTOY, *ANNA KARENINA* (1873–76), 3.9, TR. CONSTANCE GARNETT

21. Men use thought only as authority for their injustice, and employ speech only to conceal their thoughts.

VOLTAIRE, DIALOGUE 14, "LE CHAPON ET LA POULARDE" (1763), 14

22. He who lives more lives than one / More deaths than one must die.

OSCAR WILDE, *THE BALLAD OF READING GAOL* (1898), 3.37

I

441. ICONOCLASM

See also 241. DESTRUCTION; 506. IRREVERENCE; 819. REVOLUTION; 986. TRADITION

1. These, if ever, are the brave free days of destroyed landmarks, while the ingenious minds are busy inventing the forms of the new beacons which, it is consoling to think, will be set up presently in the old places.

JOSEPH CONRAD, *A PERSONAL RECORD* (1912), 5

2. Rough work, iconoclasm,—but the only way to get at truth.

OLIVER WENDELL HOLMES, SR., *THE PROFESSOR AT THE BREAKFAST TABLE* (1860), 5

3. We must not roughly smash other people's idols because we know, or think we know, that they are of cheap human manufacture.

OLIVER WENDELL HOLMES, SR., *THE POET AT THE BREAKFAST TABLE* (1872), 11

4. When smashing monuments, save the pedestals—they always come in handy.

STANISLAW LEC, *UNKEMPT THOUGHTS* (1962), TR. JACEK GALAZKA

442. IDEALISM

See also 254. DISILLUSIONMENT; 445. IDEOLOGY; 790. REFORM; 1025. UTOPIA

1. Idealism springs from deep feelings, but feelings are nothing without the formulated idea that keeps them whole.

JACQUES BARZUN, *THE HOUSE OF INTELLECT* (1959), 6

2. Our bodies can be mobilized by law and police and men with guns, if necessary—but where shall we find that which will make us believe in what we must do, so that we can fight through to victory?

PEARL S. BUCK, *WHAT AMERICA MEANS TO ME* (1943), 5

3. If two or three persons should come with a high spiritual aim and with great powers, the world would fall into their hands like a ripe peach.

EMERSON, *JOURNALS*, 1844

4. Never look down to test the ground before taking your next step: only he who keeps his eye fixed on the far horizon will find his right road.

DAG HAMMARSKJÖLD, "1925–1930," *MARKINGS* (1964), TR. W. H. AUDEN

5. All men are prepared to accomplish the incredible if their ideals are threatened.

HERMANN HESSE, *DEMIAN* (1919), 7, TR. MICHAEL LEBECK

6. Idealism is the noble toga that political gentlemen drape over their will to power.

ALDOUS HUXLEY, *NEW YORK HERALD TRIBUNE*, NOV. 25, 1963

7. Don't use that foreign word "ideals." We have that excellent native word "lies."

HENRIK IBSEN, *THE WILD DUCK* (1884), 5

8. Ideals are an imaginative understanding of that which is desirable in that which is possible.

WALTER LIPPMANN, *A PREFACE TO MORALS* (1929), 3.12.7

9. God, when he makes the prophet, does not unmake the man.

JOHN LOCKE, QUOTED IN EMERSON'S *REPRESENTATIVE MEN: SWEDENBORG* (1850)

10. An idealist is one who, on noticing that a rose smells better than a cabbage, concludes that it will also make better soup.

H. L. MENCKEN, "SENTENTIAE," *A BOOK OF BURLESQUES* (1920)

11. It is not materialism that is the chief curse of the world, as pastors teach, but idealism. Men get into trouble by taking their visions and hallucinations too seriously.

H. L. MENCKEN, *MINORITY REPORT* (1956), 305

12. The idealist is incorrigible: if he be thrown out of his Heaven, he makes himself a suitable ideal out of Hell.

NIETZSCHE, *MISCELLANEOUS MAXIMS AND OPINIONS* (1879), 23, TR. PAUL V. COHN

13. The visionary denies the truth to himself, the liar only to others.

NIETZSCHE, *MISCELLANEOUS MAXIMS AND OPINIONS* (1879), 6, TR. PAUL V. COHN

14. It is only in marriage with the world that our ideals can bear fruit: divorced from it, they remain barren.

BERTRAND RUSSELL, TITLE ESSAY, *MYSTICISM AND LOGIC* (1917)

15. It seems to be the fate of idealists to obtain what they have struggled for in a form which destroys their ideals.

BERTRAND RUSSELL, "THE LIBERATION OF WOMEN," *MARRIAGE AND MORALS* (1929)

16. The toe of the star-gazer is often stubbed.

RUSSIAN PROVERB

17. A man gazing on the stars is proverbially at the mercy of the puddles in the road.

ALEXANDER SMITH, "MEN OF LETTERS," *DREAMTHORP* (1863)

443. IDEAS

See also 656. OPINION; 975. THOUGHT

1. Nothing is more dangerous than an idea, when it is the only idea we have.

ALAIN, *LIBRES-PROPOS* (1908–14)

2. Every man with an idea has at least two or three followers.

BROOKS ATKINSON, "JANUARY 2," *ONCE AROUND THE SUN* (1951)

3. Defeat is a fact and victory can be a fact. If the idea is good, it will survive defeat, it may even survive the victory.

STEPHEN VINCENT BENÉT, *JOHN BROWN'S BODY* (1928), 2

4. Hang ideas! They are tramps, vagabonds, knocking at the back-door of your mind, each taking a little of your substance, each carrying away some crumb of that belief in a few simple notions you must cling to if you want to live decently and would like to die easy!

JOSEPH CONRAD, *LORD JIM* (1900), 5

5. Old ideas give way slowly; for they are more than abstract logical forms and categories. They are habits, predispositions, deeply ingrained attitudes of aversion and preference.

JOHN DEWEY, "THE INFLUENCE OF DARWINISM ON PHILOSOPHY" (1909)

6. Black are the brooding clouds and troubled the deep waters, when the Sea of Thought, first heaving from a calm, gives up its Dead.

CHARLES DICKENS, "THIRD QUARTER," *THE CHIMES* (1844)

7. Ideas are fatal to caste.

E. M. FORSTER, *A PASSAGE TO INDIA* (1924), 1.7

8. The only sure weapon against bad ideas is better ideas.

WHITNEY GRISWOLD, *THE NEW YORK TIMES*, FEB. 24, 1959

9. Any new formula which suddenly emerges in our consciousness has its roots in long trains of thought; it is virtually old when it first makes its appearance among the recognized growths of our intellect.

OLIVER WENDELL HOLMES, SR., *THE AUTOCRAT OF THE BREAKFAST TABLE* (1858), 2

10. There never was an idea started that woke up men out of their stupid indifference but its originator was spoken of as a crank.

OLIVER WENDELL HOLMES, SR., *OVER THE TEACUPS* (1891), 7

11. Ideas are born, they struggle, triumph, change, and they are transformed; but is there a dead idea which in the end does not live on, transformed into a broader and clearer goal?

EUGENIO MARÍA DE HOSTOS, "HOMBRES E IDEAS," *OBRAS* (1939–54), 14

12. To say that an idea is fashionable is to say, I think, that it has been adulterated to a point where it is hardly an idea at all.

MURRAY KEMPTON, "THE DAY OF THE LOCUST," *PART OF OUR TIME* (1955)

13. A man may die, nations may rise and fall, but an idea lives on. Ideas have endurance without death.

JOHN F. KENNEDY, ADDRESS, GREENVILLE, N. C., FEB. 8, 1963

14. The thinker dies, but his thoughts are beyond the reach of destruction. Men are mortal; but ideas are immortal.

WALTER LIPPMANN, *A PREFACE TO MORALS* (1929), 1.3.2

15. Just as our eyes need light in order to see, our minds need ideas in order to conceive.

NICOLAS MALEBRANCHE, *RECHERCHE DE LA VÉRITÉ* (1674–75), 6

16. If you are possessed by an idea, you find it expressed everywhere, you even *smell* it.

THOMAS MANN, "TONIO KRÖGER" (1903), *DEATH IN VENICE*, TR. H. T. LOWE-PORTER

17. A single idea, if it is right, saves us the labor of an infinity of experiences.

JACQUES MARITAIN, *REFLECTIONS ON AMERICA* (1958), 12

18. The ideas he put forward, familiar enough when clothed in their usual phraseology, emerged in his writing in a state of undress that had them look exciting and almost new, just as a woman whom one has known for years is always something of a surprise without her clothes on.

MARY MCCARTHY, *THE COMPANY SHE KEEPS* (1942)

19. A young man must let his ideas grow, not be continually rooting them up to see how they are getting on.

WILLIAM MCFEE, "THE IDEA," *HARBOURS OF MEMORY* (1921)

20. One has to be a lowbrow, a bit of a murderer, to be a politician, ready and willing to see people sacrificed, slaughtered, for the sake of an idea, whether a good one or a bad one.

HENRY MILLER, INTERVIEW, *WRITERS AT WORK: SECOND SERIES* (1963)

21. Great ideas are not charitable.

HENRY DE MONTHERLANT, *LE MAÎTRE DE SANTIAGO* (1947), 1.4

22. Beware thoughts that come in the night. They aren't turned properly; they come in askew, free of sense and restriction, deriving from the most remote of sources.

WILLIAM LEAST HEAT MOON, *BLUE HIGHWAYS* (1982)

23. It is one thing to study historically the ideas which have influenced our predecessors, and another thing to seek in them an influence fruitful for ourselves.

JOHN MORLEY, "CARLYLE," *CRITICAL MISCELLANIES* (1871–1908)

24. The chief enemy of peace is the spirit of unreason itself: an inability to conceive alternatives, an unwillingness to reconsider old prejudices, to part with ideological obsessions, to entertain new ideas or to improve new plans.

LEWIS MUMFORD, *IN THE NAME OF SANITY* (1954)

25. Those for whom words have lost their value are likely to find that ideas have also lost their value.

EDWIN NEWMAN, *STRICTLY SPEAKING* (1974)

26. You cannot put a rope around the neck of an idea; you cannot put an idea up against a barrack-square wall and riddle it with bullets; you cannot confine it in the strongest prison cell that your slaves could ever build.

SEAN O'CASEY, *DEATH OF THOMAS ASHE* (1918), 4

27. The secret of living is to find a pivot, the pivot of a concept on which you can make your stand.

LUIGI PIRANDELLO, *THE RULES OF THE GAME* (1918), 1, TR. WILLIAM MURRAY

28. In the life of a nation, few ideas are more dangerous than good solutions to the wrong problems.

ROBERT B. REICH, *THE WORK OF NATIONS* (1991)

29. New ideas are one of the most overrated concepts of our time. Most of the important ideas that we live with aren't new at all.

ANDREW A. ROONEY, "PREFACE," *PIECES OF MY MIND* (1984)

30. General and abstract ideas are the source of the greatest errors of mankind.

ROUSSEAU, *ÉMILE* (1762), 4

31. Man is a fighting animal; his thoughts are his banners, and it is a failure of nerve in him if they are only thoughts.

GEORGE SANTAYANA, *DIALOGUES IN LIMBO* (1925), 2

32. The creative phase of an idea coincides with the period during which it insists, cantankerously, on its boundaries, on what makes it different; but an idea becomes false and impotent when it seeks reconciliation, at cut-rate prices, with other ideas.

SUSAN SONTAG, "PIETY WITHOUT CONTENT," *AGAINST INTERPRETATION* (1966)

33. Every action is an idea before it is an action, and perhaps a feeling before it is an idea, and every idea rests upon other ideas that have preceded it in time.

WALLACE STEGNER, "A CAPSULE HISTORY OF CONSERVATION," *WHEN THE BLUEBIRD SINGS IN THE LEMONADE SPRINGS* (1992)

34. If an idea cannot move on its own, pushing it doesn't help; best to let it lie there.

LEWIS THOMAS, "ON VARIOUS WORDS," *THE LIVES OF A CELL* (1974)

35. The slowness of one section of the world about adopting the valuable ideas of another section of it is a curious thing and unaccountable.

MARK TWAIN, "SOME NATIONAL STUPIDITIES" (1923)

36. An idea does not pass from one language to another without change.

MIGUEL DE UNAMUNO, PREFACE, *TRAGIC SENSE OF LIFE* (1913), TR. J. E. CRAWFORD FLITCH

37. No man can establish title to an idea—at the most he can only claim possession. The stream of thought that irrigates the mind of each of us is a confluent of the intellectual river that drains the whole of the living universe.

MAURICE VALENCY, INTRODUCTION TO *JEAN GIRAUDOUX: FOUR PLAYS* (1958)

38. Human life is driven forward by its dim apprehension of notions too general for its existing language.

ALFRED NORTH WHITEHEAD, *ADVENTURES IN IDEAS* (1933), 2

39. All great ideas are dangerous.

OSCAR WILDE, *DE PROFUNDIS* (1905)

444. IDENTITY

See also 45. APPEARANCE; 119. CHARACTER; 316. EXISTENCE; 469. INDIVIDUALITY; 593. MIRRORS; 619. NAMES; 688. PERSONALITY, DUAL; 858. SELF; 875. SELF-KNOWLEDGE

1. He that is neither one thing nor the other has no friends.

AESOP, "THE BAT, THE BIRDS, AND THE BEASTS," *FABLES* (6TH C. B.C.?), TR. JOSEPH JACOBS

2. Resolve to be thyself: and know, that he / Who finds himself, loses his misery.

MATTHEW ARNOLD, "SELF-DEPENDENCE" (1852)

3. To its own impulse every creature stirs; / Live by thy light, and earth will live by hers!

MATTHEW ARNOLD, "RELIGIOUS ISOLATION," *THE STRAYED REVELLER, AND OTHER POEMS* (1849)

4. A strong sense of identity gives man an idea he can do no wrong; too little accomplishes the same.

DJUNA BARNES, *NIGHTWOOD* (1937)

5. Some things are as they are regardless of what they were.

JOHN D. BARROW, *THE ORIGIN OF THE UNIVERSE* (1994)

6. We wander but in the end there is always a certain peace in being what one is, in being that completely. The condemned man has that joy.

UGO BETTI, *GOAT ISLAND* (1946), 3.2

7. Can the Ethiopian change his skin, or the leopard his spots?

BIBLE, JEREMIAH 13:23

8. To be nobody-but-myself—in a world which is doing its best, night and day, to make you everybody else—means to fight the hardest battle which any human being can fight, and never stop fighting.

E. E. CUMMINGS, QUOTED IN CHARLES NORMAN'S *THE MAGIC-MAKER* (1958)

9. The search for a personal identity is the life task of a teenager.

HAIM G. GINOTT, *BETWEEN PARENT & TEENAGER* (1969)

10. You are, when all is done—just what you are.

GOETHE, "FAUST'S STUDY," *FAUST: PART I* (1808), TR. PHILIP WAYNE

11. Be what you are. This is the first step toward becoming better than you are.

JULIUS CHARLES HARE AND AUGUSTUS WILLIAM HARE, *GUESSES AT TRUTH* (1827)

12. It is thus with most of us; we are what other people say we are. We know ourselves chiefly by hearsay.

ERIC HOFFER, *THE PASSIONATE STATE OF MIND* (1954), 129

13. To say a thing simply: I am my history, but the story of my life is always guarded, self-conscious. It is finally the only story we give to someone we love.

MAUREEN HOWARD, *BEFORE MY TIME* (1974)

14. I'd really love to meet the guy I'm supposed to be. I'd hire him in a second.

LEE IACOCCA, *TALKING STRAIGHT* (1988), WITH SONNY KLEINFELD

15. What thou art, that thou art; that God knoweth thee to be and thou canst be said to be no greater.

THOMAS À KEMPIS, *THE IMITATION OF CHRIST* (1426), 2.6

16. You see in others who you are.

BERNARD MALAMUD, *DUBIN'S LIVES* (1979)

17. While you cannot resolve what you are, at last you will be nothing.

MARTIAL, *EPIGRAMS* (A.D. 86), 2.64, TR. WALTER C. A. KERR

18. [Philosophy] forms us for ourselves, not for others; to be, not to seem.

MONTAIGNE, "OF THE RESEMBLANCE OF CHILDREN TO THEIR FATHERS," *ESSAYS* (1580–88), TR. W. C. HAZLITT

19. Not one of us can lie or pretend. We're all fixed in good faith in a certain concept of ourselves.

LUIGI PIRANDELLO, *HENRY IV* (1922), 1, TR. EDWARD STORER

20. It matters not what you are thought to be, but what you are.

PUBLILIUS SYRUS, *MORAL SAYINGS* (1ST C. B.C.), 785, TR. DARIUS LYMAN

21. We only become what we are by the radical and deep-seated refusal of that which others have made of us.

JEAN-PAUL SARTRE, PREFACE TO FRANTZ FANON'S *THE WRETCHED OF THE EARTH* (1961), TR. CONSTANCE FARRINGTON

22. Rose is a rose is a rose is a rose.

GERTRUDE STEIN, "SACRED EMILY," *GEOGRAPHY AND PLAYS* (1922)

23. I read the landscape to help me through, to know what's come before me there, to find my footing in time.

DEBORAH TALL, "HERE," *FROM WHERE WE STAND* (1993)

24. The extent and condition of our property, and our choice of style in dwelling, create a powerful emblem of our identity and status.

DEBORAH TALL, "DWELLING," *FROM WHERE WE STAND* (1993)

25. There is no ache more / Deadly than the striving to be oneself.

YEVGENIY VINOKUROV, "I," *THE NEW RUSSIAN POETS: 1953 TO 1966* (1966), TR. GEORGE REAVEY

26. At every single moment of one's life one is what one is going to be no less than what one has been.

OSCAR WILDE, *DE PROFUNDIS* (1905)

27. Men can starve from a lack of self-realization as much as they can from a lack of bread.

RICHARD WRIGHT, *NATIVE SON* (1940), 3

445. IDEOLOGY

See also 111. CAUSES; 203. CREEDS; 264. DOGMATISM; 443. IDEAS; 568. MASS MOVEMENTS

1. All truly historical peoples have an idea they must realize, and when they have sufficiently exploited it at home, they export it, in a certain way, by war; they make it tour the world.

VICTOR COUSIN, *COURS DE PHILOSOPHIE MODERNE* (1841–46)

2. Ideology is a specious way of relating to the world. It offers human beings the illusion of an identity, of dignity, and of morality while making it easier for them to part with them.

VÁCLAV HAVEL, "THE POWER OF THE POWERLESS," *OPEN LETTERS: SELECTED WRITINGS 1965–1990* (1991) SELECTED AND EDITED BY PAUL WILSON

3. We are now again in an epoch of wars of religion, but a religion is now called an "ideology.".

BERTRAND RUSSELL, "PHILOSOPHY AND POLITICS," *UNPOPULAR ESSAYS* (1950)

4. [I]deology is the sterner face of myth and we're a myth-making people.

DIANA TRILLING, *MRS. HARRIS: THE DEATH OF THE SCARSDALE DOCTOR* (1981)

5. Ideology is not the product of thought; it is the habit or the ritual of showing respect for certain formulas to which, for various reasons having to do with emotional safety, we have very strong ties of whose meaning and consequences in actuality we have no clear understanding.

LIONEL TRILLING, "THE MEANING OF A LITERARY IDEA," *THE LIBERAL IMAGINATION* (1950)

446. IDLENESS

See also 10. ACTIVITY; 530. LAZINESS; 533. LEISURE; 811. REST; 813. RETIREMENT

1. This wasted time I have found by constant experience to be as indispensable as sleep. It cannot be employed in reading, nor even in thinking upon any serious subject. It must be wasted on trifles—doing nothing. The string of the bow must be slackened, and the bow itself laid aside.

JOHN ADAMS, *DIARY*

2. Consider the lilies of the field, how they grow; they toil not, neither do they spin: And yet I say unto you, That even Solomon in all his glory was not arrayed like one of these.

BIBLE, MATTHEW 6:28–29

3. Expect poison from the standing water.

WILLIAM BLAKE, "PROVERBS OF HELL," *THE MARRIAGE OF HEAVEN AND HELL* (1790)

4. It is because artists do not practise, patrons do not patronize, crowds do not assemble to reverently worship the great work of Doing Nothing, that the world has lost its philosophy and even failed to invent a new religion.

G. K. CHESTERTON, "ON LEISURE," *GENERALLY SPEAKING* (1928)

5. Absence of occupation is not rest, / A mind quite vacant is a mind distressed.

WILLIAM COWPER, *RETIREMENT* (1782), 623

6. But sometimes I think that idlers seem to be a special class for whom nothing can be planned, plead as one will with them—their only contribution to the human family is to warm a seat at the common table.

F. SCOTT FITZGERALD, *THE LETTERS OF F. SCOTT FITZGERALD* (1963), ED. ANDREW TURNBULL

7. Idleness and pride tax with a heavier hand than kings and parliaments.

BENJAMIN FRANKLIN, LETTER ON THE STAMP ACT, JULY 1, 1765

8. Idleness is a mother. She has a son, robbery, and a daughter, hunger.

VICTOR HUGO, "SAINT DENIS," *LES MISÉRABLES* (1862), 7.1, TR. CHARLES E. WILBOUR

9. No man is so methodical as a complete idler, and none so scrupulous in measuring out his time as he whose time is worth nothing.

WASHINGTON IRVING, "MY FRENCH NEIGHBOR," *WOLFERT'S ROOST* (1855)

10. Idleness, like kisses, to be sweet must be stolen.

JEROME K. JEROME, "ON BEING IDLE," *THE IDLE THOUGHTS OF AN IDLE FELLOW* (1889)

11. If you are idle, be not solitary; if you are solitary, be not idle.

SAMUEL JOHNSON, LETTER TO JAMES BOSWELL, OCT. 27, 1779, QUOTED IN BOSWELL'S *LIFE OF SAMUEL JOHNSON*

12. Love is born of idleness and, once born, by idleness is fostered.

OVID, *LOVE'S CURE* (C. A.D. 8), TR. J. LEWIS MAY

13. If a soldier or labourer complain of the hardship of his lot, set him to do nothing.

PASCAL, *PENSÉES* (1670), 130, TR. W. F. TROTTER

14. I think periods of browsing during which no occupation is imposed from without are important in youth because they give time for the formation of these apparently fugitive but really vital impressions.

BERTRAND RUSSELL, *THE AUTOBIOGRAPHY OF BERTRAND RUSSELL: 1872–1914* (1967)

15. A faculty for idleness implies a catholic appetite and a strong sense of personal identity.

ROBERT LOUIS STEVENSON, "AN APOLOGY FOR IDLERS," *VIRGINIBUS PUERISQUE* (1881)

16. It is better to have loafed and lost than never to have loafed at all.

JAMES THURBER, "THE COURTSHIP OF ARTHUR AND AL," *FABLES FOR OUR TIME* (1943)

17. The devil tempts all other men, but idle men tempt the devil.

TURKISH PROVERB

18. To do nothing at all is the most difficult thing in the world, the most difficult and the most intellectual.

OSCAR WILDE, "THE CRITIC AS ARTIST," *INTENTIONS* (1891)

19. Idleness was a sin not against the self or against God but against Mammon and Pierce & Pierce.

TOM WOLFE, *THE BONFIRE OF THE VANITIES* (1987)

IDOLATRY

See 1068. WORSHIP

447. IGNORANCE

See also 270. DULLNESS; 522. KNOWLEDGE; 618. NAÏVETÉ; 941. STUPIDITY

1. Ignorance is the womb of monsters.

HENRY WARD BEECHER, *PROVERBS FROM PLYMOUTH PULPIT* (1887)

2. Wisdom is prevented by ignorance, and delusion is the result.

BHAGAVADGITA, 5, TR. P. LAL

3. If the blind lead the blind, both shall fall into the ditch.

BIBLE, MATTHEW 15:14

4. Ignorance is always ready to admire itself, / Procure yourself critical friends.

NICOLAS BOILEAU, *L'ART POÉTIQUE* (1674), 1

5. Ignorance is not innocence but sin.

ROBERT BROWNING, *THE INN ALBUM* (1875), 5

6. An ignorant man is insignificant and contemptible; nobody cares for his company, and he can just be said to live, and that is all.

LORD CHESTERFIELD, *LETTERS TO HIS SON*, 1739

7. The whole family of pride and ignorance are incestuous, and mutually beget each other.

CHARLES CALEB COLTON, *LACON* (1825), 1.443

8. all ignorance toboggans into know / and trudges up to ignorance again.

E. E. CUMMINGS, "ALL IGNORANCE TOBOGGANS INTO KNOW," *100 SELECTED POEMS* (1959)

9. To be conscious that you are ignorance is a great step to knowledge.

BENJAMIN DISRAELI, *SYBIL* (1845), 5

10. The length of sky is just about the size of my ignorance. Pure and wide.

LOUISE ERDRICH, "SAINT MARIE," *LOVE MEDICINE* (1984)

11. Ignorance and incuriosity are two very soft pillows.

FRENCH PROVERB

12. He that knows least commonly presumes most.

THOMAS FULLER, M.D., *GNOMOLOGIA* (1732), 2208

13. He that knows little often repeats it.

THOMAS FULLER, M.D., *GNOMOLOGIA* (1732), 2209

14. Better an empty purse than an empty head.

GERMAN PROVERB

15. Where ignorance is bliss, / 'Tis folly to be wise.

THOMAS GRAY, "ON A DISTANT PROSPECT OF ETON COLLEGE" (1747), 10

16. I believe that much of the maladjustment in our societies is caused, not by malevolence and corruption, but simply by ignorance.

GILBERT HIGHET, *THE ART OF TEACHING* (1950)

17. Far more crucial than what we know or do not know is what we do not want to know.

ERIC HOFFER, *THE PASSIONATE STATE OF MIND* (1954), 58

18. Ignorance is preferable to error; and he is less remote from the truth who believes nothing, than he who believes what is wrong.

THOMAS JEFFERSON, *NOTES ON THE STATE OF VIRGINIA* (1784–85), 6

19. Nothing in all the world is more dangerous than sincere ignorance and conscientious stupidity.

MARTIN LUTHER KING JR., *STRENGTH TO LOVE* (1963), 4.3

20. Only one who has learned much can fully appreciate his ignorance.

LOUIS L'AMOUR, *EDUCATION OF A WANDERING MAN* (1989)

21. He that had never seen a river, imagined the first he met with to be the sea.

MONTAIGNE, "THAT IT IS FOLLY TO MEASURE TRUTH AND ERROR BY OUR OWN CAPACITY," *ESSAYS* (1580–88), TR. W. C. HAZLITT

22. He who would be cured of ignorance must confess it.

MONTAIGNE, "OF CRIPPLES," *ESSAYS* (1580–88)

23. Genuine victories, the sole conquests yielding no remorse, are those gained over ignorance.

NAPOLEON I, *MAXIMS* (1804–15)

24. It is admirable to consider how many millions of people come into, and go out of, the world, ignorant of themselves and of the world they have lived in.

WILLIAM PENN, *SOME FRUITS OF SOLITUDE* (1693), 1.1

25. Ignorance, if recognized, is often more fruitful than the appearance of knowledge.

WALKER PERCY, "IS A THEORY OF MAN POSSIBLE?" *SIGNPOSTS IN A STRANGE LAND* (1991)

26. From ignorance our comfort flows, / The only wretched are the wise.

MATTHEW PRIOR, "TO THE HON. CHARLES MONTAGUE" (1692), 9

27. Better to be ignorant of a matter than half know it.

PUBLILIUS SYRUS, *MORAL SAYINGS* (1ST C. B.C.), 865, TR. DARIUS LYMAN

28. Nothing is so good for an ignorant man as silence, and if he knew this he would no longer be ignorant.

SA'DI, *GULISTAN* (1258), 8.38, TR. JAMES ROSS

29. Uncultivated minds are not full of wild flowers, like uncultivated fields. Villainous weeds grow in them and they are the haunt of toads.

LOGAN PEARSALL SMITH, *AFTERTHOUGHTS* (1931), 3

30. Blind and naked Ignorance / Delivers brawling judgments, unashamed, / On all things all day long.

LORD TENNYSON, "MERLIN AND VIVIEN," *IDYLLS OF THE KING* (1859)

31. There is that indescribable freshness and unconsciousness about an illiterate person that humbles and mocks the power of the noblest expressive genius.

WALT WHITMAN, PREFACE TO *LEAVES OF GRASS* (1855)

448. ILLEGALITY

See also 204. CRIME; 900. SIN

1. Stolen waters are sweet, and bread eaten in secret is pleasant.

BIBLE, PROVERBS 9:17

ILLNESS

See 896. SICKNESS

449. ILLUSION

See also 266. Dreams; 300. Escape; 383. Ghosts; 617. Myth; 336. Fantasy; 784. Reality

1. Beware lest you lose the substance by grasping at the shadow.

Aesop, "The Dog and the Shadow," *Fables* (6th c. b.c.?), tr. Joseph Jacobs

2. It is always some illusion that creates disillusion, especially in the young, for whom the only alternative to perfection is cynicism.

Jacques Barzun, *Teacher in America* (1944)

3. We [Americans] suffer primarily not from our vices or our weaknesses, but from our illusions. We are haunted, not by reality, but by those images we have put in place of reality.

Daniel J. Boorstin, introduction to *The Image* (1962)

4. Illusions are art, for the feeling person, and it is by art that we live, if we do.

Elizabeth Bowen, *The Death of the Heart* (1938), 1.7

5. Time strips our illusions of their hue, / And one by one in turn, some grand mistake / Casts off its bright skin yearly like the snake.

Byron, *Don Juan* (1819–24), 5.21

6. We must select the illusion which appeals to our temperament, and embrace it with passion, if we want to be happy.

Cyril Connolly, *The Unquiet Grave* (1945), 3

7. A man that is born falls into a dream like a man who falls into the sea. If he tries to climb out into the air as inexperienced people endeavour to do, he drowns.

Joseph Conrad, *Lord Jim* (1900), 20

8. Every age is fed on illusions, lest men should renounce life early and the human race come to an end.

Joseph Conrad, *Victory* (1915), 2.3

9. We wake from one dream into another dream.

Emerson, "Illusions," *The Conduct of Life* (1860)

10. Life is the art of being well deceived; and in order that the deception may succeed it must be habitual and uninterrupted.

William Hazlitt, "On Pedantry," *The Round Table* (1817)

11. Rob the average man of his life-illusion and you rob him of his happiness at one stroke.

Henrik Ibsen, *The Wild Duck* (1884), 5

12. Somewhere along the line I knew there'd be girls, visions, everything; somewhere along the line the pearl would be handed to me.

Jack Kerouac, *On the Road* (1957)

13. The most important part of our lives—our sensations, emotions, desires, and aspirations—takes place in a universe of illusions which science can attenuate or destroy, but which it is powerless to enrich.

Joseph Wood Krutch, "The Disillusion with the Laboratory," *The Modern Temper* (1929)

14. Man has always sacrificed truth to his vanity, comfort and advantage. He lives not by truth but by make-believe.

W. Somerset Maugham, *The Summing Up* (1938), 75

15. Our experience is composed rather of illusions lost than of wisdom acquired.

Joseph Roux, *Meditations of a Parish Priest* (1886), 4.28, tr. Isabel F. Hapgood

450. IMAGINATION

See also 590. Mind; 336. Fantasy; 818. Reverie

1. Imagination, n. A warehouse of facts, with poet and liar in joint ownership.

Ambrose Bierce, *The Devil's Dictionary* (1881–1911)

2. A popular cliché in philosophy says that science is pure analysis or reductionism, like taking the rainbow to pieces; and art is pure synthesis, putting the rainbow together. This is not so. All imagination begins by analyzing nature.

Jacob Bronowski, *The Ascent of Man* (1973)

3. Imagination is like a lofty building reared to meet the sky—fancy is a balloon that soars at the wind's will.

Gelett Burgess, "Where Is Fancy Bred?" *The Romance of the Commonplace* (1916)

4. People can die of mere imagination.

Chaucer, "The Miller's Tale," *The Canterbury Tales* (c. 1387–1400), tr. Nevill Coghill

5. Fairyland is nothing but the sunny country of common sense.

G. K. Chesterton, "The Logic of Elfland," *Orthodoxy* (1908)

6. Imagination = nostalgia for the past, the absent; it is the liquid solution in which art develops the snapshots of reality.

Cyril Connolly, *The Unquiet Grave* (1945), 2

7. Only in men's imagination does every truth find an effective and undeniable existence. Imagination, not invention, is the supreme master of art as of life.

JOSEPH CONRAD, *A PERSONAL RECORD* (1912), 1

8. Imagination, that dost so abstract us / That we are not aware, not even when / A thousand trumpets sound about our ears!

DANTE, "PURGATORIO," 17, *THE DIVINE COMEDY* (C. 1300–21), TR. LAWRENCE GRANT WHITE

9. The Possible's slow fuse is lit / By the Imagination.

EMILY DICKINSON, *POEMS* (C. 1862–86)

10. The necessity of loyalty between friends, the responsibility that the strong owe the infirm, the illusion of ill-gotten gain, the rewards of hard work, honesty, and trust—these are enduring truths glimpsed and judged first through the imagination, first through art.

MICHAEL DORRIS, "MICE," *PAPER TRAIL* (1994)

11. I imagine, therefore I belong and am free.

LAWRENCE DURRELL, *JUSTINE* (1957), 2

12. The imagination and the senses cannot be gratified at the same time.

EMERSON, "BEAUTY," *THE CONDUCT OF LIFE* (1860)

13. There are no days in life so memorable as those which vibrated to some stroke of the imagination.

EMERSON, "BEAUTY," *THE CONDUCT OF LIFE* (1860)

14. In the world of the imagination, anything goes that's imaginatively possible, but nothing really happens.

NORTHROP FRYE, *THE EDUCATED IMAGINATION* (1964)

15. Men endowed with a wild imagination should have, in addition, the great poetic faculty of denying our universe and its values so that they may act upon it with sovereign ease.

JEAN GENET, *OUR LADY OF THE FLOWERS* (1949)

16. Imagination is not something apart and hermetic, not a way of leaving reality behind; it is a way of engaging reality.

IRVING HOWE, "CHARACTERS: ARE THEY LIKE PEOPLE?" *A CRITIC'S NOTEBOOK* (1994)

17. Were it not for imagination a man would be as happy in the arms of a chambermaid as of a duchess.

SAMUEL JOHNSON, QUOTED IN BOSWELL'S *LIFE OF SAMUEL JOHNSON,* MAY 9, 1778

18. Almost any man may like the spider spin from his own inwards his own airy citadel.

KEATS, LETTER TO JOHN HAMILTON REYNOLDS, FEB. 19, 1818

19. Heard melodies are sweet, but those unheard / Are sweeter.

KEATS, "ODE ON A GRECIAN URN" (1819)

20. The problems of the world cannot possibly be solved by skeptics or cynics whose horizons are limited by the obvious realities. We need men who can dream of things that never were.

JOHN F. KENNEDY, ADDRESS, DUBLIN, IRELAND, JUNE 28, 1963

21. Imagination is the mad boarder.

NICOLAS MALEBRANCHE, PREFACE TO *RECHERCHE DE LA VÉRITÉ* (1674–75)

22. Imagination grows by exercise and contrary to common belief is more powerful in the mature than in the young.

W. SOMERSET MAUGHAM, *THE SUMMING UP* (1938), 43

23. Only imagination that towers can reproduce evanescence and render rigidity flexible.

MARIANNE MOORE, "OF BEASTS AND JEWELS," *THE COMPLETE PROSE OF MARIANNE MOORE* (1986)

24. The eyes are not responsible when the mind does the seeing.

PUBLILIUS SYRUS, *MORAL SAYINGS* (1ST C. B.C.), 562, TR. DARIUS LYMAN

25. That which we know is but little; that which we have a presentiment of is immense; it is in this direction that the poet outruns the learned man.

JOSEPH ROUX, *MEDITATIONS OF A PARISH PRIEST* (1886), 1.17, TR. ISABEL F. HAPGOOD

26. I have imagination, and nothing that is real is alien to me.

GEORGE SANTAYANA, *LITTLE ESSAYS* (1920), 42

27. Such tricks hath strong imagination, / That, if it would but apprehend some joy, / It comprehends some bringer of that joy; / Or in the night, imagining some fear, / How easy is a bush supposed a bear!

SHAKESPEARE, *A MIDSUMMER NIGHT'S DREAM* (1595–96), 5.1.18

28. The capacity for imaginative reflex, for moral risk in any human being, is not limitless; on the contrary, it can be rapidly absorbed by fictions, and thus the

cry in the poem may come to sound louder, more urgent, more real than the cry in the street outside.

George Steiner, *Language and Silence* (1967)

29. You can't depend on your judgment when your imagination is out of focus.

Mark Twain, *Notebook* (1935)

30. Imagination is more robust in proportion as reasoning power is weak.

Giambattista Vico, *The New Science* (1725–44), 1.2

31. Woe to the man / who tries to stretch the imagination of man / He shall be mocked he shall be scourged / by the blinkered guardians of morality.

Peter Weiss, *Marat/Sade* (1964), 1.26, tr. Adrian Mitchell

32. Society often forgives the criminal; it never forgives the dreamer.

Oscar Wilde, "The Critic as Artist," *Intentions* (1891)

33. The instant / trivial as it is / is all we have / unless—unless / things the imagination feeds upon, / the scent of the rose, / startle us anew.

William Carlos Williams, "Shadows," *Pictures from Brueghel* (1962)

451. IMITATION

See also 700. Plagiarism; 732. Pretension

1. To refrain from imitation is the best revenge.

Marcus Aurelius, *Meditations* (2nd c.), 6.6, tr. Maxwell Staniforth

2. We are, in truth, more than half what we are by imitation.

Lord Chesterfield, *Letters to His Son,* Jan. 18, 1750

3. Imitation is the sincerest flattery.

Charles Caleb Colton, *Lacon* (1825)

4. The sense of inferiority inherent in the act of imitation breeds resentment. The impulse of the imitators is to overcome the model they imitate.

Eric Hoffer, *The Ordeal of Change* (1964), 4

5. When people are free to do as they please, they usually imitate each other.

Eric Hoffer, *The Passionate State of Mind* (1955)

6. No living person is sunk so low as not to be imitated by somebody.

William James, "The Gospel of Relaxation," *Talks to Teachers and to Students* (1899)

7. The crow that mimics a cormorant gets drowned.

Japanese Proverb

8. Almost all absurdity of conduct arises from the imitation of those whom we cannot resemble.

Samuel Johnson, *The Rambler* (1750–52), 135

9. When the bad imitate the good, there is no knowing what mischief is intended.

Publilius Syrus, *Moral Sayings* (1st c. b.c.), 551, tr. Darius Lyman

10. We all begin life as parasites within the mother, and writers begin their existence imitatively, within the body of letters.

John Updike, *Beerbohm and Others, Assorted Prose* (1965)

11. Universities are filled with poets and novelists conducting demure and careful lives in imitation of Eliot and Forster and those others who (through what seems to be have been discretion) made it.

Gore Vidal, *Rocking the Boat* (1962)

452. IMMATURITY

See also 404. Growth and Development; 571. Maturity

1. We are like thistle-down blown about by the wind—up and down, here and there—but not one in a thousand ever getting beyond seed-hood.

Samuel Butler (d. 1902), "Lord, What Is Man?" *Note-Books* (1912)

2. The wisest man is just a boy / who grieves that he's grown up.

Vincenzo Cardarelli, "Adolescent," *Poesie* (1943)

3. There are cases in which the blade springs, but the plant does not go on to flower. There are cases where it flowers, but no fruit is subsequently produced.

Confucius, *Analects* (6th c. b.c.), 9.21, tr. James Legge

4. How many really capable men are children more than once during the day!

Napoleon I, *Maxims* (1804–15)

5. How shall one who is so weak in his childhood become really strong when he grows older? We only change our fancies.

Pascal, *Pensées* (1670), 88, tr. W. F. Trotter

453. IMMIGRATION

1. A nation, like a tree, does not thrive well till it is engraffed with a foreign stock.

Emerson, *Journals,* 1823

2. In novels and autobiographies, the first positive move that the immigrant makes towards assimilation is to buy himself a suit of city clothes.

Jonathan Raban, *Soft City* (1974)

IMMORALITY

See 307. Evil; 604. Morality; 1030. Vice; 1055. Wickedness; 1070. Wrongdoing

454. IMMORTALITY

See also 302. Eternity; 606. Mortality

1. "Immortals are what you wanted," said Thor in a low, quiet voice. "Immortals are what you got."

Douglas Adams, *The Long Dark Tea-Time of the Soul* (1988)

2. The one thing we fear most is the one thing that is not possible: We cannot die, we cannot be destroyed.

Richard Bach, *Running from Safety* (1994)

3. Immortality makes sense only when the individual soul can be thought of as merging into a great collective mush of sainthood. If we take anything with us into the next world, it is not what survives in the memories of our relicts.

Anthony Burgess, *You've Had Your Time* (1990)

4. It has been said that the immortality of the soul is a "grand peut-être"—but it is still a grand one. Everybody clings to it—the stupidest, and dullest, and wickedest of human bipeds is still persuaded that he is immortal.

Byron, "Ravenna Journal," *Lord Byron, Selected Letters and Journals* (1982), ed. Leslie A. Marchand

5. To live in hearts we leave / Is not to die.

Thomas Campbell, "Hallowed Ground" (1825)

6. Should this my firm persuasion of the soul's immortality prove to be a mere delusion, it is at least a pleasing delusion, and I will cherish it to my latest breath.

Cicero, *De Senectute* (44 B.C.)

7. I love the earth too much to contemplate a life apart from it, although I believe in that life.

André Dubus, "On Charon's Wharf," *Broken Vessels* (1991)

8. Let him who believes in immortality enjoy his happiness in silence; he has no reason to give himself airs about it.

Goethe, quoted in Johann Peter Eckermann's *Conversations with Goethe,* Feb. 25, 1824

9. All our efforts to attain immortality—by statesmanship, by conquest, by science or the arts—are equally vain in the long run, because the long run is longer than any of us can imagine.

Sydney J. Harris, "Real Achievements Lie in the Present," *Clearing the Ground* (1986)

10. Our Creator would never have made such lovely days, and have given us the deep hearts to enjoy them, unless we were meant to be immortal.

Nathaniel Hawthorne, "The Old Manse," *Mosses from an Old Manse* (1846)

11. To occupy an inch of dusty shelf—to have the title of their works read now and then in a future age by some drowsy churchman or casual straggler, and in another age to be lost, even to remembrance. Such is the amount of boasted immortality.

Washington Irving, "The Mutability of Literature," *The Sketch Book of Geoffrey Crayon, Gent.* (1819–20)

12. If life were eternal all interest and anticipation would vanish. It is uncertainty which lends its fascination.

Yoshida Kenkō, "Man the Ephemera," *The Harvest of Leisure* (*Tsure-Zure Gusa,* c. 1330–35), tr. Ryukichi Kurata

13. Immortality is a condition fairly difficult to come by, though the longing for it is in one way or another almost universal and considered by some, therefore, to be beneath one's dignity.

James Lord, *Six Exceptional Women* (1994)

14. I have good hope that there is something after death.

Plato, *Phaedo* (4th–3rd c. B.C.), tr. Lane Cooper

15. The mortal nature is seeking as far as is possible to be everlasting and immortal: and this is only to be attained by generation, because the new is always left in the place of the old.

Plato, *The Symposium* (4th c. B.C.), tr. Benjamin Jowett

16. Man's life is short; and therefore an honorable death is his immortality.

Publilius Syrus, *Moral Sayings* (1st c. B.C.), 1087, tr. Darius Lyman

17. If you question any candid person who is no longer young, he is very likely to tell you that, having tasted life in this world, he has no wish to begin again as a "new boy" in another.

BERTRAND RUSSELL, "IDEAS THAT HAVE HARMED MANKIND," *UNPOPULAR ESSAYS* (1950)

18. All the doctrines that have flourished in the world about immortality have hardly affected men's natural sentiment in the face of death.

GEORGE SANTAYANA, *THE LIFE OF REASON: REASON IN RELIGION* (1905–06), 4

19. Death is the veil which those who live call life: / They sleep, and it is lifted.

SHELLEY, *PROMETHEUS UNBOUND* (1818–19), 3.3

20. We feel and know that we are eternal.

SPINOZA, *ETHICS* (1677), 5, TR. ANDREW BOYLE

21. Thou madest man, he knows not why, / He thinks he was not made to die.

LORD TENNYSON, "IN MEMORIAM A. H. H." (1850)

22. All men think all men mortal but themselves.

EDWARD YOUNG, *NIGHT THOUGHTS* (1742–46), 1.424

455. IMPARTIALITY

See also 517. JUSTICE; 674. PARTISANSHIP

1. What people call impartiality may simply mean indifference, and what people call partiality may simply mean mental activity.

G. K. CHESTERTON, "THE ERROR OF IMPARTIALITY," *ALL THINGS CONSIDERED* (1908)

2. He is not good himself who speaks well of everybody alike.

THOMAS FULLER, M.D., *GNOMOLOGIA* (1732), 1935

3. The tree casts its shade upon all, even upon the woodcutter.

HINDUSTANI PROVERB

4. He who treats his friends and enemies alike, has neither love nor justice.

ROBERT G. INGERSOLL, *PROSE-POEMS AND SELECTIONS* (1884)

5. In the beginning, before the arrival of the white men, I had considered myself neutral. I had wanted neither side to win, neither the army nor the rebels. As it turned out, both sides lost.

V.S. NAIPAUL, *A BEND IN THE RIVER* (1979)

6. "Pity for all" would be hardness and tyranny toward *you,* my dear neighbor.

NIETZSCHE, *BEYOND GOOD AND EVIL* (1886), 82, TR. WALTER KAUFMANN

7. A friend to everybody and to nobody is the same thing.

SPANISH PROVERB

456. IMPATIENCE

See also 411. HASTE; 677. PATIENCE; 812. RESTLESSNESS; 1040. WAITING

1. We're in such a hurry most of the time we never get a chance to talk. The result is a kind of endless day-to-day shallowness, a monotony that leaves a person wondering years later where all the time went and sorry that it's all gone.

ROBERT M. PIRSIG, *ZEN AND THE ART OF MOTORCYCLE MAINTENANCE* (1974)

457. IMPERFECTION

See also 299. ERROR; 342. FAULTS; 542. LIMITATIONS; 684. PERFECTION

1. The perfect human being is uninteresting—the Buddha who leaves the world, you know. It is the imperfections of life that are lovable.

JOSEPH CAMPBELL, *THE POWER OF MYTH* (1988)

2. The best brewer sometimes makes bad beer.

GERMAN PROVERB

3. What day is so festal it fails to reveal some theft?

JUVENAL, *SATIRES* (C. 100), 13.23, TR. HUBERT CREEKMORE

4. All things are literally better, lovelier, and more beloved for the imperfections which have been divinely appointed, that the law of human life may be effort, and the law of human judgment, mercy.

JOHN RUSKIN, *THE STONES OF VENICE* (1851–53), V. 2, 6.25

5. People are crying up the rich and variegated plumage of the peacock, and he is himself blushing at the sight of his ugly feet.

SA'DI, *GULISTAN* (1258), 2.8, TR. JAMES ROSS

6. The habit of looking for beauty in everything makes us notice the shortcomings of things; our sense, hungry for complete satisfaction, misses the perfection it demands.

GEORGE SANTAYANA, *THE SENSE OF BEAUTY* (1896), 30

7. The Fates, like an absent-minded printer, seldom allow a single line to stand perfect and unmarred.

George Santayana, *The Life of Reason: Reason in Society* (1905–06), 1

8. O me! for why is all around us here / As if some lesser god had made the world, / But had not force to shape it as he would?

Lord Tennyson, "The Passing of Arthur," *Idylls of the King* (1859–85), 13

9. The visible imperfections of hand-wrought goods, being honorific, are accounted marks of superiority in point of beauty, or serviceability, or both.

Thorstein Veblen, *The Theory of the Leisure Class* (1899), 6

10. There is no deformity / But saves us from a dream.

William Butler Yeats, "The Phases of the Moon," *The Wild Swans at Coole* (1919)

458. IMPERIALISM

See also 1002. Tyranny

1. It is natural anywhere that people like their own kind, but it is not necessarily natural that their fondness for their own kind should lead them to the subjection of whole groups of other people not like them.

Pearl S. Buck, *What America Means to Me* (1943), 2

2. In imperialism nothing fails like success. If the conqueror oppresses his subjects, they will become fanatical patriots, and sooner or later have their revenge; if he treats them well, and "governs them for their good," they will multiply faster than their rulers, till they claim their independence.

William Ralph Inge, "Patriotism," *Outspoken Essays: First Series* (1919)

3. In the eyes of empire builders men are not men, but instruments.

Napoleon I, *Maxims* (1804–15)

4. Imperialism as he [Kipling] sees it is a sort of forcible evangelising.

George Orwell, "Rudyard Kipling," *A Collection of Essays* (1954)

5. Shall we go on conferring our Civilization upon the peoples that sit in darkness, or shall we give those poor things a rest?

Mark Twain, "To the Person Sitting in the Darkness" (1901)

IMPERMANENCE

See 117. Change; 990. Transience

IMPIETY

See 441. Iconoclasm; 506. Irreverence

IMPORTANCE

See 873. Self-Importance

459. IMPOTENCE

See also 366. Frustration; 719. Power; 1047. Weakness

1. The worst pain a man can have is to know much and be impotent to act.

Herodotus, *The Histories* (5th c. b.c.), 9.16, tr. Aubrey de Sélincourt

2. The realization that he was utterly powerless was like the blow of a sledgehammer, yet it was curiously calming as well.

Milan Kundera, *The Unbearable Lightness of Being* (1984)

3. We look for some reward of our endeavors and are disappointed; not success, not happiness, not even peace of conscience, crowns our ineffectual efforts to do well. Our frailties are invincible, our virtues barren; the battle goes sore against us to the going down of the sun.

Robert Louis Stevenson, "Pulvis et Umbra" (1888)

4. Asks the Possible of the Impossible, "Where is your dwelling-place?" / "In the dreams of the Impotent," comes the answer.

Rabindranath Tagore, *Stray Birds* (1916), 129

5. But what am I? / An infant crying in the night; / An infant crying for the light, / And with no language but a cry.

Lord Tennyson, "In Memoriam A. H. H." (1850), 54

6. Our thought has been "Let every man look out for himself, let every generation look out for itself," while we reared giant machinery which made it impossible that any but those who stood at the levers of control should have a chance to look out for themselves.

Woodrow Wilson, first Inaugural Address, March 4, 1913

460. IMPROVEMENT

See also 717. Potential; 790. Reform; 807. Resolution

IMPULSIVENESS

1. Improvement makes straight roads; but the crooked roads without improvement are roads of genius.

WILLIAM BLAKE, "PROVERBS OF HELL," *THE MARRIAGE OF HEAVEN AND HELL* (1790)

2. Old houses mended, / Cost little less than new, before they're ended.

COLLEY CIBBER, PROLOGUE TO *THE DOUBLE GALLANT* (1707)

3. Every man contemplates an angel in his future self.

EMERSON, *JOURNALS*, 1829

4. Have therefore first zeal to better thyself and then mayst thou have zeal to thy neighbour.

THOMAS À KEMPIS, *THE IMITATION OF CHRIST* (1426), 2.3

5. Happy are they that hear their detractions and can put them to mending.

SHAKESPEARE, *MUCH ADO ABOUT NOTHING* (1598–99), 2.3.237

6. Poets lose half the praise they should have got, / Could it be known what they discreetly blot.

EDMUND WALLER, "UPON THE EARL OF ROSCOMMON'S TRANSLATION OF HORACE" (1680)

7. Half a man's life is devoted to what he calls improvements, yet the original had some quality which is lost in the process.

E.B. WHITE, *ONE MAN'S MEAT* (1944)

IMPROVISATION

See 928. SPONTANEITY

461. IMPULSIVENESS

See also 928. SPONTANEITY; 1053. WHIM

1. If you believed more in life you would fling yourselves less to the moment.

NIETZSCHE, "ON THE PREACHERS OF DEATH," *THUS SPOKE ZARATHUSTRA* (1883–92), 1, TR. WALTER KAUFMANN

462. INADEQUACY

See also 463. INCOMPETENCE; 542. LIMITATIONS

1. That is a bad bridge which is shorter than the stream.

GERMAN PROVERB

463. INCOMPETENCE

See also 462. INADEQUACY

1. A bad workman quarrels with the man who calls him that.

AMBROSE BIERCE, "SAW," *THE DEVIL'S DICTIONARY* (1881–1911)

2. The worse the carpenter, the more the chips.

DUTCH PROVERB

3. A bad workman never gets a good tool.

THOMAS FULLER, M.D., *GNOMOLOGIA* (1732), 5

4. O thrice unhappy home / Whose master doesn't know the difference between a watt and an ohm!

OGDEN NASH, "UP FROM THE WHEELBARROW," *I'M A STRANGER HERE MYSELF* (1938)

INCOMPLETION

See 285. ENDING

464. INCONSISTENCY

See also 117. CHANGE; 179. CONSISTENCY; 691. PERVERSENESS

1. When the man you like switches from what he said a year ago, or four years ago, he is a broadminded person who has courage enough to change his mind with changing conditions. When a man you don't like does it, he is a liar who has broken his promises.

FRANKLIN P. ADAMS, *NODS AND BECKS* (1944)

2. I wish to say what I think and feel today, with the proviso that tomorrow perhaps I shall contradict it all.

EMERSON, *JOURNALS* 1839

3. Speak what you think today in words as hard as cannon balls, and tomorrow speak what tomorrow thinks in hard words again, though it contradict everything you said today.

EMERSON, "SELF-RELIANCE," *ESSAYS: FIRST SERIES* (1841)

4. People who honestly mean to be true really contradict themselves much more rarely than those who try to be "consistent."

OLIVER WENDELL HOLMES, SR., *THE PROFESSOR AT THE BREAKFAST TABLE* (1860), 2

5. For a Russian to be chivalrous with an American is a spiritual impossibility, a conradiction in terms.

KURT VONNEGUT, *WELCOME TO THE MONKEY HOUSE* (1970)

6. Do I contradict myself? / Very well then I contradict myself, / (I am large, I contain multitudes).

WALT WHITMAN, "SONG OF MYSELF," 51, *LEAVES OF GRASS* (1855–92)

INCONSTANCY

See 181. CONSTANCY AND INCONSTANCY; 472. INFIDELITY

465. INDECISION

See also 225. DECISION; 231. DELAY; 771. PURPOSE; 1005. UNCERTAINTY

1. Half the failures in life arise from pulling in one's horse as he is leaping.

AUGUSTUS WILLIAM HARE, *GUESSES AT TRUTH* (1827)

2. There is no more miserable human being than one in whom nothing is habitual but indecision.

WILLIAM JAMES, *THE PRINCIPLES OF PSYCHOLOGY* (1892), 10

3. Indecision is like the stepchild: if he doesn't wash his hands, he is called dirty; if he does, he is wasting the water.

MADAGASCAN PROVERB

4. No wind serves him who addresses his voyage to no certain port.

MONTAIGNE, "OF THE INCONSTANCY OF OUR ACTIONS," *ESSAYS* (1580–88), TR. W. C. HAZLITT

5. It is human nature to stand in the middle of a thing.

MARIANNE MOORE, "A GRAVE," *COLLECTED POEMS* (1951)

6. He who hesitates is sometimes saved.

JAMES THURBER, "THE GLASS IN THE FIELD," *THE THURBER CARNIVAL* (1945)

INDEPENDENCE

See 363. FREEDOM; 537. LIBERTY; 880. SELF-SUFFICIENCY

466. INDIFFERENCE

See also 30. ALIENATION; 219. DEADNESS, SPIRITUAL

1. O, if thou car'st not whom I love / Alas, thou lov'st not me.

JOHN DONNE, "A HYMN TO CHRIST, AT THE AUTHOR'S LAST GOING INTO GERMANY," *DIVINE POEMS* (1607)

2. He injures a fair lady that beholds her not.

THOMAS FULLER, M.D., *GNOMOLOGIA* (1732), 1904

3. Nothing is more conducive to peace of mind than not having any opinion at all.

GEORG CHRISTOPH LICHTENBERG, *APHORISMS* (1764–99), TR. J. P. STERN

4. I know I am but summer to your heart, / And not the full four seasons of the year.

EDNA ST. VINCENT MILLAY, "TWO SEASONS."

5. To try may be to die, but not to care is never to be born.

WILLIAM REDFIELD, "ONE MIGHT HAVE PLAYED HAMLET, THE OTHER DID," *THE NEW YORK TIMES*, JAN. 15, 1968

6. The worst sin towards our fellow creatures is not to hate them, but to be indifferent to them; that's the essence of inhumanity.

GEORGE BERNARD SHAW, *THE DEVIL'S DISCIPLE* (1897), 2

7. I have learned the guilt of indifference. The opposite of love is not hate but indifference.

ELIE WIESEL, "BITBURG," *FROM THE KINGDOM OF MEMORY* (1990)

467. INDIGNATION

See also 39. ANGER

1. A good indignation brings out all one's powers.

EMERSON, *JOURNALS*, 1841

2. There is perhaps no phenomenon which contains so much destructive feeling as "moral indignation," which permits envy or hate to be acted out under the guise of virtue.

ERICH FROMM, *MAN FOR HIMSELF* (1947), 4

3. Indignation does no good unless it is backed with a club of sufficient size to awe the opposition.

EDGAR WATSON HOWE, *VENTURES IN COMMON SENSE* (1919), 32.9

INDISCRIMINATENESS

See 742. PROMISCUITY

468. INDIVIDUALISM

See also 91. BOHEMIANS; 171. CONFORMITY; 444. IDENTITY; 469. INDIVIDUALITY

1. The function of the society is to cultivate the individual. It is not the function of the individual to support society.

JOSEPH CAMPBELL, *THE POWER OF MYTH* (1988), ED. BETTY SUE FLOWERS

2. Let those who would affect singularity with success first determine to be very virtuous, and they will be sure to be very singular.

CHARLES CALEB COLTON, *LACON* (1825), 1.460

3. The experience of recent years—slowing growth and declining productivity—raises a doubt whether private ingenuity can continue to overcome the deadening effects of government control.

MILTON FRIEDMAN & ROSE FRIEDMAN, *FREE TO CHOOSE* (1980)

4. We are not on the way to greater individualism, but are becoming an increasingly manipulated mass civilization.

ERICH FROMM, *THE REVOLUTION OF HOPE* (1968)

5. [H]ow can can one defend the sober virtues of Protestant individualism by disaffiliating from the world?

MICHAEL HARRINGTON, *THE ACCIDENTAL CENTURY* (1966)

6. Individualism is rather like innocence; there must be something unconscious about it.

LOUIS KRONENBERGER, *COMPANY MANNERS* (1954), 3.3

7. True individualists tend to be quite unobservant; it is the snob, the would-be sophisticate, the frightened conformist, who keeps a fascinated or worried eye on what is in the wind.

LOUIS KRONENBERGER, *COMPANY MANNERS* (1954), 3.3

8. Non-conformism is the major, perhaps the only, sin of our time.

ROBERT LINDNER, "HOMOSEXUALITY AND THE CONTEMPORARY SCENE," *MUST YOU CONFORM?* (1956)

9. The man who walks alone is soon trailed by the F.B.I.

WRIGHT MORRIS, *A BILL OF RITES, A BILL OF WRONGS, A BILL OF GOODS* (1967), 7

10. American individualism, much celebrated and cherished, has developed without its essential corrective, which is belonging.

WALLACE STEGNER, "LIVING DRY," *WHEN THE BLUEBIRD SINGS IN THE LEMONADE SPRINGS* (1992)

11. Individualism and mobility are at the core of American identity.

DEBORAH TALL, "DWELLING," *FROM WHERE WE STAND* (1993)

12. If a man does not keep pace with his companions, perhaps it is because he hears a different drummer. Let him step to the music he hears, however measured or far away.

THOREAU, "CONCLUSION," *WALDEN* (1854)

13. Art is the most intense mode of individualism that the world has known.

OSCAR WILDE, *THE SOUL OF MAN UNDER SOCIALISM* (1891)

469. INDIVIDUALITY

See also 260. DIVERSITY; 276. ECCENTRICITY; 444. IDENTITY; 468. INDIVIDUALISM; 662. ORIGINALITY; 858. SELF; 1014. UNIQUENESS

1. The absolutely banal—my sense of my own uniqueness.

W. H. AUDEN, "HIC ET ILLE," *THE DYER'S HAND* (1962)

2. Meeting people unlike oneself does not enlarge one's outlook; it only confirms one's idea that one is unique.

ELIZABETH BOWEN, *THE HOUSE IN PARIS* (1935), 2.3

3. Every individual strives to grow and exclude and to exclude and grow, to the extremities of the universe, and to impose the law of its being on every other creature.

EMERSON, "USES OF GREAT MEN," *REPRESENTATIVE MEN* (1850)

4. We fancy men are individuals; so are pumpkins; but every pumpkin in the field goes through every point of pumpkin history.

EMERSON, "NOMINALIST AND REALIST," *ESSAYS: SECOND SERIES* (1844)

5. Singularity is dangerous in everything.

FÉNELON, *LES AVENTURES DE TÉLÉMAQUE, FILS D'ULYSSE* (1699), 19

6. Anybody who is any good is different from anybody else.

FELIX FRANKFURTER, *FELIX FRANKFURTER REMINISCES* (1960), 2

7. Men are born equal but they are also born different.

ERICH FROMM, *ESCAPE FROM FREEDOM* (1941), 7

8. Man is more interesting than men. God made him and not them in his image. Each one is more precious than all.

ANDRÉ GIDE, *JOURNALS*, 1896, TR. JUSTIN O'BRIEN

9. The individual man tries to escape the race. And as soon as he ceases to represent the race, he represents man.

ANDRÉ GIDE, *JOURNALS*, 1896, TR. JUSTIN O'BRIEN

10. Every one must form himself as a particular being, seeking, however, to attain that general idea of which all mankind are constituents.

GOETHE, QUOTED IN JOHANN PETER ECKERMANN'S *CONVERSATIONS WITH GOETHE*, APRIL 20, 1825

11. If individuality has no play, society does not advance; if individuality breaks out of all bounds, society perishes.

THOMAS HENRY HUXLEY, "ADMINISTRATIVE NIHILISM" (1871)

12. The man whom God wills to slay in the struggle of life He first individualizes.

HENRIK IBSEN, *BRAND* (1866), 5

13. Though all men be made of one metal, yet they be not cast all in one mold.

JOHN LYLY, *EUPHUES: THE ANATOMY OF WIT* (1579)

14. Others can give you a name or a number, but they can never tell you who you really are. That is something you yourself can only discover from within.

THOMAS MERTON, *NO MAN IS AN ISLAND* (1955)

15. When two do the same thing, it is not the same thing after all.

PUBLILIUS SYRUS, *MORAL SAYINGS* (1ST C. B.C.), 338, TR. DARIUS LYMAN

16. To damage the sovereignty of the individual is to replace a community inspired by love, benevolence, and beauty by another based solely on power.

ANWAR EL-SADAT, *IN SEARCH OF IDENTITY* (1977)

17. The flower you single out is a rejection of all other flowers; nevertheless, only on these terms is it beautiful.

SAINT-EXUPÉRY, *THE WISDOM OF THE SANDS* (1948), 6, TR. STUART GILBERT

18. You have to go the rounds from individual to individual in order to gather the totality of the race.

SCHILLER, *ON THE AESTHETIC EDUCATION OF MAN* (1795), 6, TR. REGINALD SNELL

19. As many men, so many minds; every one his own way.

TERENCE, *PHORMIO* (161 B.C.), 2.4.14, TR. HENRY THOMAS RILEY

20. None but himself can be his parallel.

LEWIS THEOBALD, *THE DOUBLE FALSEHOOD* (1727)

470. INDULGENCE

See also 250. DISCIPLINE; 312. EXCESS; 534. LENIENCY

1. If we had to tolerate in others all that we permit in ourselves, life would become completely unbearable.

GEORGES COURTELINE, *LA PHILOSOPHIE DE G. COURTELINE* (1917)

2. Indulgences, not fulfillment, is what the world / Permits us.

CHRISTOPHER FRY, *A PHOENIX TOO FREQUENT* (1950)

3. Excessive indulgence to others, especially to children is in fact only self-indulgence under an alias.

AUGUSTUS WILLIAM HARE, *GUESSES AT TRUTH* (1827)

4. O, give it up, old chap! Sleep it off!

JAMES JOYCE, *A PORTRAIT OF THE ARTIST AS A YOUNG MAN* (1916)

5. A curious and eager soul was imprisoned in all this lard, but by dint of never refusing himself a pheasant or a goose or his daily procession of Roman wines, he was his own bitter jailer.

THORNTON WILDER, *THE BRIDGE OF SAN LUIS REY* (1927)

6. One didn't really believe till one saw it demonstrated that giving oneself up completely to art, to emotion, to enjoyment, without planning for the future or counting the cost, produced dreadful disabilities and bankruptcies later.

EDMUND WILSON, *THE FORTIES* (1983), ED. LEON EDEL

471. INEQUALITY

See also 297. EQUALITY

1. Whatever may be the general endeavor of a community to render its members equal and alike, the personal pride of individuals will always seek to rise above the line, and to form somewhere an inequality to their own advantage.

ALEXIS DE TOCQUEVILLE, *DEMOCRACY IN AMERICA* (1835–39), 2.3.13

2. Couldn't we even argue that it is because men are unequal that they have that much more need to be brothers?

CHARLES DU BOS, *JOURNAL*, FEB. 27, 1918

3. We are all Adam's children, but silk makes the difference.

THOMAS FULLER, M.D., *GNOMOLOGIA* (1732), 5425

472. INFIDELITY

See also 181. CONSTANCY AND INCONSTANCY; 742. PROMISCUITY

1. It is the fear of middle-age in the young, of old-age in the middle-aged, which is the prime cause of infidelity, that infallible rejuvenator.

CYRIL CONNOLLY, *THE UNQUIET GRAVE* (1945), 2

2. When cheated, wife or husband feels the same.

EURIPIDES, *ANDROMACHE* (C. 426 B.C.), TR. JOHN F. NIMS

3. Where there's marriage without love, / there will be love without marriage.

BENJAMIN FRANKLIN, *POOR RICHARD'S ALMANACK* (1732–57)

4. Inconstancy no sin will prove / If we consider that we love / But the same beauty in another face, / Like the same body in another place.

EDWARD HERBERT, "INCONSTANCY" (C. 1610)

5. In twenty-three years of married life he had peered uneasily at every graceful ankle, every soft shoulder; in thought he had treasured them; but not once had he hazarded respectability by adventuring.

SINCLAIR LEWIS, *BABBITT* (1922)

6. Wives invariably flourish when deserted; ... it is the deserting male, the reckless idealist rushing about the world seeking a non-existent felicity, who often ends in disaster.

WILLIAM MCFEE, "KNIGHTS AND TURCOPOLIERS," *HARBOURS OF MEMORY* (1921)

7. Adultery is the application of democracy to love.

H. L. MENCKEN, "SENTENTIAE," *A BOOK OF BURLESQUES* (1920)

8. 'Tis sweet to think, that, where'er we rove, / We are sure to find something blissful and dear, / And that, when we're far from the lips we love, / We've but to make love to the lips we are near.

THOMAS MOORE, "'TIS SWEET TO THINK," *IRISH MELODIES* (1807–35)

9. To aggravate matters, a protegée of the composer's, a 55-dollar-a-week soprano with whom he had dallied in good faith, was loudly demanding a featured spot in the show, on pain of divulging the escapade to her husband.

S.J. PERELMAN, *THE RISING GORGE* (1961)

10. The fickleness of the women I love is only equalled by the infernal constancy of the women who love me.

GEORGE BERNARD SHAW, *THE PHILANDERER* (1893), 4

11. Next to Elka lay a man's form. Another in my place would have made an uproar, and enough noise to rouse the whole town, but the thought occurred to me that I might wake the child.

ISAAC BASHEVIS SINGER, "GIMPEL THE FOOL," TR. SAUL BELLOW, *PARTISAN REVIEW* (1953)

12. No woman is capable of being beautiful who is not incapable of being false.

RICHARD STEELE, *THE SPECTATOR* (1711–12), 33

13. No man worth having is true to his wife, or can be true to his wife, or ever was, or ever will be so.

SIR JOHN VANBRUGH, *THE RELAPSE* (1697), 3.2

14. Adultery is an evil only inasmuch as it is a theft; but we do not steal that which is given to us.

VOLTAIRE, "ADULTERY," *PHILOSOPHICAL DICTIONARY* (1764)

15. Those who are faithful know only the trivial side of love; it is the faithless who know love's tragedies.

OSCAR WILDE, *THE PICTURE OF DORIAN GRAY* (1891), 1

16. Young men want to be faithful, and are not; old men want to be faithless, and cannot.

OSCAR WILDE, *THE PICTURE OF DORIAN GRAY* (1891), 2

473. INFLUENCE

1. Evil communications corrupt good manners.

BIBLE, 1 CORINTHIANS 15:33

2. People exercise an unconscious selection in being influenced.

T. S. ELIOT, "RELIGION AND LITERATURE" (1935)

3. Our chief want in life is somebody who shall make us do what we can.

EMERSON, "CONSIDERATIONS BY THE WAY," *THE CONDUCT OF LIFE* (1860)

4. The best effect of fine persons is felt after we have left their presence.

EMERSON, *JOURNALS*, 1839

5. No one is a light unto himself, not even the sun.

ANTONIO PORCHIA, *VOCES* (1968), TR. W. S. MERWIN

6. Of all the pulpits from which human voice is ever sent forth, there is none from which it reaches so far as from the grave.

JOHN RUSKIN, *THE SEVEN LAMPS OF ARCHITECTURE* (1849), 6.9

7. Half our standards come from our first masters, and the other half from our first loves.

GEORGE SANTAYANA, *THE LIFE OF REASON: REASON IN ART* (1905–06), 10

8. Every hair makes its shadow on the ground.

SPANISH PROVERB

474. INGRATIATION

See also 49. APPROVAL; 712. POPULARITY

1. Please all, and you will please none.

AESOP, "THE MAN, THE BOY, AND THE DONKEY," *FABLES* (6TH C. B.C.?), TR. JOSEPH JACOBS

2. How I like to be liked, and what I do to be liked!

CHARLES LAMB, LETTER TO DOROTHY WORDSWORTH, JAN. 8, 1821

3. Take here the grand secret—if not of pleasing all, yet of displeasing none—court mediocrity, avoid originality, and sacrifice to fashion.

JOHANN KASPAR LAVATER, *APHORISMS ON MAN* (1788)

4. Now and then, this look of commendation would rest particularly on you; whenever this happened, it was as if, in his delight, he had reached over and squeezed you.

MARY MCCARTHY, *THE COMPANY SHE KEEPS* (1942)

5. It is in vain to hope to please all alike. Let a man stand with his face in what direction he will, he must necessarily turn his back on one half of the world.

GEORGE DENNISON PRENTICE, *PRENTICEANA* (1860)

6. Words calculated to catch everyone may catch no one.

ADLAI STEVENSON, ADDRESS, DEMOCRATIC NATIONAL CONVENTION, CHICAGO, JULY 21, 1952

475. INGRATITUDE

See also 399. GRATITUDE; 647. OBLIGATION

1. Wan raison people ar-re not grateful is because they're proud iv thimsilves an' they niver feel they get half what they desarve. Another raison is they know ye've had all th' fun ye're entitled to whin ye do annything f'r annybody.

FINLEY PETER DUNNE, "GRATITUDE," *OBSERVATIONS BY MR. DOOLEY* (1902)

2. A wretched child / Is he who does not return his parents' care.

EURIPIDES, *THE SUPPLIANT WOMEN* (C. 421 B.C.), TR. FRANK W. JONES

3. Men are slower to recognize blessings than evils.

LIVY, *AB URBE CONDITA* (C. 29 B.C.), 30.21

4. Eaten bread is forgotten.

THOMAS FULLER, M.D., *GNOMOLOGIA* (1732), 1358

5. There are far fewer ungrateful men than we believe, for there are far fewer generous men than we think.

SAINT-ÉVREMOND, *SUR LES INGRATS* (1705)

6. Blow, blow, thou winter wind, / Thou are not so unkind / As man's ingratitude.

SHAKESPEARE, *AS YOU LIKE IT* (1599–1600), 2.7.174

7. How sharper than a serpent's tooth it is / To have a thankless child!

SHAKESPEARE, *KING LEAR* (1605–06), 1.4.310

8. If you pick up a starving dog and make him prosperous, he will not bite you. This is the principal difference between a dog and a man.

MARK TWAIN, "PUDD'NHEAD WILSON'S CALENDAR," *PUDD'NHEAD WILSON* (1894), 16

INHERITANCE

See 1058. WILLS AND INHERITANCE

INITIATIVE

See 291. ENTERPRISE

476. INJURY

See also 288. ENEMIES; 477. INJUSTICE; 488. INSULT; 665. PACIFISM; 789. RECOMPENSE; 817. REVENGE; 866. SELF-DESTRUCTION; 946. SUFFERING

1. Injuries may be forgiven, but not forgotten.

AESOP, "THE MAN AND THE SERPENT," *FABLES* (6TH C. B.C.?), TR. JOSEPH JACOBS

2. Reject your sense of injury and the injury itself disappears.

MARCUS AURELIUS, *MEDITATIONS* (2ND C.), 4.7, TR. MAXWELL STANIFORTH

3. Wounds cannot be cured without searching.

FRANCIS BACON, "OF EXPENSE," *ESSAYS* (1625)

4. An injury is much sooner forgotten than an insult.

LORD CHESTERFIELD, *LETTERS TO HIS SON*, OCT. 9, 1746

5. I will not be revenged, and this I owe to my enemy; but I will remember, and this I owe to myself.

CHARLES CALEB COLTON, *LACON* (1825), 1.35

6. Men are apt to offend ('tis true) where they find most goodness to forgive.

WILLIAM CONGREVE, *THE OLD BACHELOR* (1693), 4.4

7. He that does you a very ill turn will never forgive you.

ENGLISH PROVERB

8. 'Tis better to suffer wrong than do it.

THOMAS FULLER, M.D., *GNOMOLOGIA* (1732), 5068

9. Forgetting of a wrong is a mild revenge.

THOMAS FULLER, M.D., *GNOMOLOGIA* (1732), 1592

10. Everyone suffers wrongs for which there is no remedy.

EDGAR WATSON HOWE, *COUNTRY TOWN SAYINGS* (1911)

11. Who offends writes on sand, who is offended on marble.

ITALIAN PROVERB

12. He threatens many that hath injured one.

BEN JONSON, *SEJANUS HIS FALL* (1603), 2.3

13. Wounds heal and become scars. But scars grow with us.

STANISLAW LEC, *UNKEMPT THOUGHTS* (1962), TR. JACEK GALAZKA

14. Nothing may help or heal / While Amor incensed remembers wrong.

HERMAN MELVILLE, "AFTER THE PLEASURE PARTY," *JOHN MARR AND OTHER SAILORS* (1888)

15. It is far pleasanter to injure and afterwards beg forgiveness than to be injured and grant forgiveness. He who does the former gives evidence of power and afterwards of kindness of character.

NIETZSCHE, *HUMAN, ALL TOO HUMAN* (1878), 348, TR. HELEN ZIMMERN

16. A brave man thinks no one his superior who does him an injury; for he has it then in his power to make himself superior to the other by forgiving it.

ALEXANDER POPE, *THOUGHTS ON VARIOUS SUBJECTS* (1727)

17. That which deceives us and does us harm also undeceives us and does us good.

JOSEPH ROUX, *MEDITATIONS OF A PARISH PRIEST* (1886), 5.53, TR. ISABEL F. HAPGOOD

18. Those whom men have injured they despise.

SENECA, *ON ANGER* (1ST C.)

19. Since I wronged you, I have never liked you.

SPANISH PROVERB

20. It belongs to human nature to hate those you have injured.

TACITUS, *AGRICOLA* (C. A.D. 98), 42

21. He that wrongs his friend / Wrongs himself more, and ever bears about / A silent court of justice in his breast, / Himself the judge and jury, and himself / The prisoner at the bar, ever condemned.

LORD TENNYSON, "AYLMER'S FIELD" (1864)

477. INJUSTICE

See also 476. INJURY; 517. JUSTICE; 534. LENIENCY; 790. REFORM

1. Justice is my being allowed to do whatever I like. Injustice is whatever prevents my doing so.

SAMUEL BUTLER (D. 1902), *NOTE-BOOKS* (1912)

2. It is the feeling of injustice that is insupportable to all men.

THOMAS CARLYLE, *CHARTISM* (1839), 1

3. No man at bottom means injustice; it is always for some obscure distorted image of a right that he contends: an obscure image diffracted, exaggerated, in the wonderfulest way, by natural dimness and selfishness; getting tenfold more diffracted by exasperation of contest, till at length it become all but irrecognisable.

THOMAS CARLYLE, *CHARTISM* (1839), 1

4. We must believe in the gods no longer if injustice is to prevail over justice.

EURIPIDES, *ELECTRA* (413 B.C.), TR. JOHN MCLEAN

5. A grievance is most poignant when almost redressed.

ERIC HOFFER, *THE TRUE BELIEVER* (1951), 2.5.22

6. Injustice, swift, erect, and unconfined, / Sweeps the wide earth, and tramples o'er mankind.

HOMER, *ILIAD* (9TH C. B.C.), 9.628, TR. ALEXANDER POPE

7. Abuse a man unjustly, and you will make friends for him.

EDGAR WATSON HOWE, *COUNTRY TOWN SAYINGS* (1911)

8. Nothing is absolutely unjust. There is no real equity, no total grandeur, no pure vice, no absolute crime.

JULIEN OFFROY DE LA METTRIE, "DISCOURS PRÉLIMINAIRE," *OEUVRES PHILOSOPHIQUES* (1754)

9. An unrectified case of injustice has a terrible way of lingering, restlessly, in the social atmosphere like an unfinished equation.

MARY MCCARTHY, "MY CONFESSION," IN *THE ART OF THE PERSONAL ESSAY* (1994), ED. PHILLIP LOPATE

10. Anybody who has ever tried to rectify an injustice or set a record straight comes to feel that he is going mad.

MARY MCCARTHY, "MY CONFESSION," IN *THE ART OF THE PERSONAL ESSAY* (1994), ED. PHILLIP LOPATE

11. There is no social evil, no form of injustice whether of the feudal or the capitalist order which has not been sanctified in some way or other by religious sentiment and thereby rendered more impervious to change.

REINHOLD NIEBUHR, *CHRISTIAN REALISM AND POLITICAL PROBLEMS* (1953), 8

12. Injustice all around is justice.

PERSIAN PROVERB

13. Mankind censure injustice, fearing that they may be victims of it and not because they shrink from committing it.

PLATO, *THE REPUBLIC* (4TH C. B.C.), 1, TR. BENJAMIN JOWETT

14. When innocence trembles, it condemns the judge.

PUBLILIUS SYRUS, *MORAL SAYINGS* (1ST C. B.C.), 944, TR. DARIUS LYMAN

15. Normally a grand jury will indict a ham sandwich if a prosecutor asks it to.

CHARLES S. ROBB, QUOTED IN *THE NEW YORK TIMES*, JAN. 14, 1993

16. Injustice in this world is not something comparative; the wrong is deep, clear, and absolute in each private fate.

GEORGE SANTAYANA, *LITTLE ESSAYS* (1920), 71

478. INNOCENCE

See also 618. NAÏVETÉ; 770. PURITY; 899. SIMPLICITY

1. 'Tis e'er the lot of the innocent in the world, to fly to the wolf for succor from the lion.

JOHN BARTH, *THE SOT-WEED FACTOR* (1960), 3.11

2. Innocence dwells with Wisdom, but never with Ignorance.

WILLIAM BLAKE, ANNOTATIONS, *THE FOUR ZOAS* (C. 1795–1804)

3. The courage of children and beasts is a function of innocence.

ANNIE DILLARD, "THE PRESENT," *PILGRIM AT TINKER CREEK* (1974)

4. Those who are incapable of committing great crimes do not readily suspect them in others.

LA ROCHEFOUCAULD, *MAXIMS* (1665), TR. KENNETH PRATT

5. The great man is he who does not lose his child's-heart.

MENCIUS, *WORKS* (4TH–3RD C. B.C.), 4, TR. CHARLES A. WONG

6. It is innocence that is full and experience that is empty. It is innocence that wins and experience that loses.

CHARLES PÉGUY, "INNOCENCE AND EXPERIENCE," *BASIC VERITIES* (1943), TR. JULIAN GREEN

7. He's armed without that's innocent within.

ALEXANDER POPE, *EPILOGUE TO THE SATIRES* (1738), 1.1.94

8. If you would live innocently, seek solitude.

PUBLILIUS SYRUS, *MORAL SAYINGS* (1ST C. B.C.), 1078, TR. DARIUS LYMAN

9. Whoever blushes is already guilty; true innocence is ashamed of nothing.

ROUSSEAU, *ÉMILE* (1762), 4

10. Thrice happy state again to be / The trustful infant on the knee, / Who lets his rosy fingers play / About his mother's neck, and knows / Nothing beyond his mother's eyes!

LORD TENNYSON, "SUPPOSED CONFESSIONS" (1830)

11. Through our own recovered innocence we discern the innocence of our neighbors.

THOREAU, "SPRING," *WALDEN* (1854)

479. INNOVATION

See also 117. CHANGE; 502. INVENTION; 640. NOVELTY

1. Time is the greatest innovator.

FRANCIS BACON, "OF INNOVATIONS," *ESSAYS* (1625)

2. Who in Europe could have thought of the disappearing bed, a bed during the night, a handsome wardrobe during the day? Where else [than in the United States] could the rocking chair have been invented, in which a man could move and sit still at the same time?

LUIGI BARZINI, *O AMERICA* (1977)

3. We ought not to be over-anxious to encourage innovation in cases of doubtful improvement, for an old system must ever have two advantages over a new one; it is established, and it is understood.

CHARLES CALEB COLTON, *LACON* (1825), 1.521

4. Inventors and men of genius have almost always been regarded as fools at the beginning (and very often at the end) of their careers.

DOSTOYEVSKY, *THE IDIOT* (1868), 3.1, TR. DAVID MAGARSHACK

5. One doesn't discover new lands without consenting to lose sight of the shore for a very long time.

ANDRÉ GIDE, *THE COUNTERFEITERS* (1925), 3.15, TR. DOROTHY BUSSY

6. We are more ready to try the untried when what we do is inconsequential. Hence the remarkable fact that many inventions had their birth as toys.

ERIC HOFFER, *THE ORDEAL OF CHANGE* (1964), 14

7. Great scientific discoveries have been made by men seeking to verify quite erroneous theories about the nature of things.

ALDOUS HUXLEY, "WORDSWORTH IN THE TROPICS," IN *FIFTY FAMOUS ESSAYS* (1964)

8. The new always carries with it the sense of violation, of sacrilege. What is dead is sacred; what is new, that is, *different,* is evil, dangerous, or subversive.

HENRY MILLER, "WITH EDGAR VARÈSE IN THE GOBI DESERT," *THE AIR-CONDITIONED NIGHTMARE* (1945)

9. Discovery follows discovery, each both raising and answering questions, each ending a long search, and each providing the new instruments for a new search.

J. ROBERT OPPENHEIMER, "PROSPECTS IN THE ARTS AND SCIENCES," *FIFTY GREAT ESSAYS* (1964)

10. Let no one say that I have said nothing new; the arrangement of the subject is new.

PASCAL, *PENSÉES* (1670), 22, TR. W. F. TROTTER

11. We have entered, almost without noticing, an age of exploration and discovery unparalleled since the Renaissance.

CARL SAGAN, *BROCA'S BRAIN: REFLECTIONS ON THE ROMANCE OF SCIENCE* (1979)

12. The vitality of a new movement in art or letters can be pretty accurately gauged by the fury it arouses.

LOGAN PEARSALL SMITH, *AFTERTHOUGHTS* (1931), 5

13. The rude beginnings of every art acquire a greater celebrity than the art in perfection; he who first played the fiddle was looked upon as a demigod.

VOLTAIRE, "AMPLIFICATION," *PHILOSOPHICAL DICTIONARY* (1764)

480. INQUIRY

See also 211. CURIOSITY

1. You don't want a million answers as much as you want a few forever questions. The questions are diamonds you hold in the light. Study a lifetime and you see different colors from the same jewel.

RICHARD BACH, *RUNNING FROM SAFETY* (1994)

2. A sudden, bold, and unexpected question doth many times surprise a man and lay him open.

FRANCIS BACON, "OF CUNNING," *ESSAYS* (1625)

3. He who asks questions cannot avoid the answers.

CAMEROONIAN PROVERB

4. Examinations are formidable even to the best prepared, for the greatest fool may ask more than the wisest man can answer.

CHARLES CALEB COLTON, *LACON* (1825), 1.322

5. Better ask twice than lose your way once.

DANISH PROVERB

6. Many a profound genius, I suppose, who fills the world with fame of his exploding renowned errors, is yet every day posed [baffled] by trivial questions at his own supper-table.

EMERSON, *JOURNALS,* 1832

7. The sun shines and warms and lights us and we have no curiosity to know why this is so; but we ask the reason of all evil, of pain, and hunger, and mosquitoes and silly people.

EMERSON, *JOURNALS,* 1830

8. I know of no inquiry which the impulses of man suggests that is forbidden to the resolution of man to pursue.

MARGARET FULLER, *SUMMER ON THE LAKES* (1844), 5

9. 'Tis not every question that deserves an answer.

THOMAS FULLER, M.D., *GNOMOLOGIA* (1732), 5094

10. The questions that are beyond the reach of economics—the beauty, dignity, pleasure and durability of life—may be inconvenient but they are important.

JOHN KENNETH GALBRAITH, *THE NEW INDUSTRIAL STATE* (1967)

11. To question a wise man is the beginning of wisdom.

GERMAN PROVERB

12. Questions show the mind's range, and answers its subtlety.

JOSEPH JOUBERT, *PENSÉES* (1842), 3.21, TR. KATHARINE LYTTELTON

13. I keep six honest serving-men / (They taught me all I knew); / Their names are What and Why and When / And How and Where and Who.

RUDYARD KIPLING, "THE ELEPHANT'S CHILD," *JUST-SO STORIES* (1902)

14. [T]he intellectual treatment of any datum, any experience, any subject, is determined by the nature of our questions, and only carried out in the answers.

SUSANNE K. LANGER, *PHILOSOPHY IN A NEW KEY* (1942)

15. There is frequently more to be learned from the unexpected questions of a child than the discourses of men, who talk in a road, according to the notions they have borrowed and the prejudices of their education.

JOHN LOCKE, *SOME THOUGHTS CONCERNING EDUCATION* (1693), 120

16. The great pleasure of ignorance is the pleasure of asking questions. The man who has lost this pleasure or exchanged it for the pleasure of dogma, which is the pleasure of answering, is already beginning to stiffen.

ROBERT LYND, "THE PLEASURES OF IGNORANCE," IN *I WAS JUST THINKING* (1959)

17. There aren't any embarrassing questions—just embarrassing answers.

CARL ROWAN, *NEW YORKER*, DEC. 7, 1963

18. All inquiries carry with them some element of risk.

CARL SAGAN, *BROCA'S BRAIN: REFLECTIONS ON THE ROMANCE OF SCIENCE* (1979)

INSANITY

See 559. MADNESS

481. INSECTS

1. The Spider as an Artist / Has never been employed— / Though his surpassing Merit / Is freely certified.

EMILY DICKINSON, POEM (C. 1873)

2. Where's the state beneath the firmament / That doth excel the bees for government?

SEIGNEUR DU BARTAS, *DIVINE WEEKES AND WORKES* (1578), 1.5.1

3. Two-legged creatures we are supposed to love as well as we love ourselves. The four-legged, also, can come to seem pretty important. But six legs are too many from the human standpoint.

JOSEPH WOOD KRUTCH, "AUGUST," *THE TWELVE SEASONS* (1949)

4. insects have / their own point / of view about / civilization / a man / thinks he amounts / to a great deal / but to a / flea or a / mosquito a / human being is / merely something / good to eat.

DON MARQUIS, "CERTAIN MAXIMS OF ARCHY," *ARCHY AND MEHITABEL* (1927)

5. Is there a polity better ordered, the offices better distributed, and more inviolably observed and maintained, than that of bees?

MONTAIGNE, "APOLOGY FOR RAIMOND DE SEBONDE," *ESSAYS* (1580–88), TR. W. C. HAZLITT

6. God in His wisdom made the fly / And then forgot to tell us why.

OGDEN NASH, "THE FLY," *GOOD INTENTIONS* (1943)

7. Crickets, ticks, gnats, chiggers...grass bugs, rotten-timber bugs, leaf bugs, water bugs...everything with six legs and wings and stings was whirring or whining or chirruping.

JONATHAN RABAN, *OLD GLORY* (1982)

8. The fly ought to be used as the symbol of impertinence and audacity; for whilst all other animals shun man more than anything else, and run away even before he comes near them, the fly lights upon his very nose.

SCHOPENHAUER, "A FEW PARABLES," *PARERGA AND PARALIPOMENA* (1851), TR. T. BAILEY SAUNDERS

482. INSECURITY

See also 43. ANXIETY; 856. SECURITY; 868. SELF-DOUBT; 1005. UNCERTAINTY

1. Is not man himself the most unsettled of all the creatures of the earth? What is this trembling sensation that is intensified with each ascending step in the natural order?

UGO BETTI, *THE FUGITIVE* (1953), 3, TR. G. H. MCWILLIAM

2. Suspense—is Hostiler than Death— / Death—tho'soever Broad, / Is just Death, and cannot increase— / Suspense—does not conclude—.

EMILY DICKINSON, POEM (C. 1863)

3. What can we take on trust / in this uncertain life? Happiness, greatness, / pride—nothing is secure, nothing keeps.

EURIPIDES, *HECUBA* (C. 425 B.C.), TR. WILLIAM ARROWSMITH

4. How can a man learn navigation / Where there's no rudder?

CHRISTOPHER FRY, *A SLEEP OF PRISONERS* (1951)

5. Many teenagers are tormented by terrors they deem private and personal. They do not know that their anxieties and doubts are universal.

HAIM G. GINOTT, *BETWEEN PARENT & TEENAGER* (1969)

6. We are reassured almost as foolishly as we are alarmed; human nature is so constituted.

VICTOR HUGO, "SAINT DENIS," *LES MISÉRABLES* (1862), 15.1, TR. CHARLES E. WILBOUR

7. The mind leaps, and leaps perhaps with a sort of elation, through the immensities of space, but the spirit, frightened and cold, longs to have once more above its head the inverted bowl beyond which may lie whatever paradise its desires may create.

JOSEPH WOOD KRUTCH, "THE GENESIS OF A MOOD," *THE MODERN TEMPER* (1929)

483. INSENSITIVITY

See also 87. BLINDNESS, SPIRITUAL; 883. SENSIBILITY

1. But we, we have no sense of direction; impetus / Is all we have; we do not proceed, we only / Roll down the mountain, / Like disbalanced boulders, crushing before us many / Delicate springing things, whose plan it was to grow.

EDNA ST. VINCENT MILLAY, UNTITLED POEM, *MAKE BRIGHT THE ARROWS* (1940)

2. O, what men dare do! what men may do! what men daily do, not knowing what they do!

SHAKESPEARE, *MUCH ADO ABOUT NOTHING* (1598–99), 4.1.19

INSIGHT

See 501. INTUITION; 1007. UNDERSTANDING; 1008. UNDERSTANDING OTHERS

INSIGNIFICANCE

See 1012. UNIMPORTANCE

484. INSINCERITY

See also 440. HYPOCRISY; 732. PRETENSION; 901. SINCERITY

1. A false friend and a shadow attend only while the sun shines.

BENJAMIN FRANKLIN, *POOR RICHARD'S ALMANACK* (1732–57)

2. The most exhausting thing in life, I have discovered, is being insincere.

ANNE MORROW LINDBERGH, "CHANNELLED WHELK," *GIFT FROM THE SEA* (1955)

3. What people call insincerity is simply a method by which we can multiply our personalities.

OSCAR WILDE, *THE ARTIST AS CRITIC: CRITICAL WRITINGS OF OSCAR WILDE*, ED. RICHARD ELLMANN (1969)

4. Is insincerity such a terrible thing? I think not. It is merely a method by which we can multiply our personalities.

OSCAR WILDE, *THE PICTURE OF DORIAN GRAY* (1891), 11

INSOMNIA

See 73. BED

485. INSPIRATION

See also 201. CREATION AND CREATIVITY

1. My holy of holies is the human body, health, intelligence, talent, inspiration, love, and absolute freedom—freedom from violence and falsehood, no matter how the last two manifest themselves.

ANTON CHEKHOV, LETTER (1888)

2. Commonsense is the wick of the candle.

EMERSON, *JOURNALS*, 1845

3. There is no wide road which leads to the Muses.

PROPERTIUS, *ELEGIES* (C. 28–C. 16 B.C.), 3.1.14

4. I do not remember—that is the point—the first impulse that pumped and shoved most of the earlier poems along, and they are still too near me, with their vehement beat-pounding black and green rhythms like those of a very young policeman exploding, for me to see the written evidence of it.

DYLAN THOMAS, *QUITE EARLY ONE MORNING* (1954)

486. INSTINCT

See also 431. HUMAN NATURE

1. Trust the instinct to the end, though you can render no reason.

EMERSON, "INTELLECT," *ESSAYS: FIRST SERIES* (1841)

2. When blended with sexuality, the death instinct is transformed into more harmless impulses expressed in sadism or masochism.

ERICH FROMM, *THE ANATOMY OF HUMAN DESTRUCTIVENESS* (1973)

3. Be a good animal, true to your animal instincts.

D. H. LAWRENCE, *THE WHITE PEACOCK* (1911), 2.2

4. When I watch species other than my own, their instinct's wisdom is what most impresses and disturbs me.

Charles A. Lindbergh, "Life Stream," *Autobiography of Values* (1978)

5. Well-bred instinct meets reason halfway.

George Santayana, *The Life of Reason: Reason in Society* (1905–06), 1

487. INSTITUTIONS

See also 102. Bureaucracy

1. The history of institutions is often a history of deception and illusions; for their virtue depends on the ideas that produce and on the spirit that preserves them, and the form may remain unaltered when the substance has passed away.

Lord Acton, "The History of Freedom in Antiquity," address, 1877

2. The test of every religious, political, or educational system, is the man which it forms. If a system injures the intelligence it is bad. If it injures the character it is vicious, if it injures the conscience it is criminal.

Henri Frédéric Amiel, *Journal*, June 17, 1852, tr. Mrs. Humphry Ward

3. Individualities may form communities, but it is institutions alone that can create a nation.

Benjamin Disraeli, speech, Manchester, 1866

4. The test of political institutions is the condition of the country whose future they regulate.

Benjamin Disraeli, speech, "Conservative Principles," April 3, 1872

5. An institution is the lengthened shadow of one man.

Emerson, "Self-Reliance," *Essays: First Series* (1841)

6. We do not make a world of our own, but fall into institutions already made, and have to accommodate ourselves to them to be useful at all.

Emerson, *Journals*, 1832

7. Every institution not only carries within it the seeds of its own dissolution, but prepares the way for its most hated rival.

William Ralph Inge, "The Victorian Age," *Outspoken Essays: Second Series* (1922)

8. Wise and prudent men—intelligent conservatives—have long known that in a changing world worthy institutions can be conserved only by adjusting them to the changing time.

Franklin D. Roosevelt, speech, Syracuse, N.Y., Sept. 29, 1936

9. Catastrophes come when some dominant institution, swollen like a soap-bubble and still standing without foundations, suddenly crumbles at the touch of what may seem a word or an idea, but is really some stronger material force.

George Santayana, *Persons and Places: The Middle Span* (1945), 8

10. The more rational an institution is the less it suffers by making concessions to others.

George Santayana, *The Life of Reason: Reason in Science* (1905–06), 9

488. INSULT

See also 476. Injury; 830. Rudeness

1. No one can be as calculatedly rude as the British, which amazes Americans, who do not understand studied insult and can only offer abuse as a substitute.

Paul Gallico, *The New York Times*, Jan. 14, 1962

2. A wise man is superior to any insults which can be put upon him, and the best reply to unseemly behavior is patience and moderation.

Molière, *The Would-be Gentleman* (1670), 2, tr. John Wood

489. INSURANCE

1. When the praying does no good, insurance does help.

Bertolt Brecht, *The Mother* (1932), 11, tr. Lee Baxandall

2. 'Tis said that persons living on annuities / Are longer lived than others.

Byron, *Don Juan* (1819–24), 2.65

3. Buy an annuity cheap, and make your life interesting to yourself and everybody else that watches the speculation.

Charles Dickens, *Martin Chuzzlewit* (1844), 18

490. THE INTANGIBLE

See also 927. Spirituality

1. Clocks ar-re habichool liars, an' so ar-re scales. As soon as annything gets good enough to weigh ye can't weigh it.

Finley Peter Dunne, "Things Spiritual," *Mr. Dooley Says* (1910)

491. INTEGRITY

See also 119. CHARACTER; 181. CONSTANCY AND INCONSTANCY; 425. HONESTY; 556. LOYALTY; 604. MORALITY; 635. NOBILITY; 734. PRINCIPLE; 901. SINCERITY; 940. STRENGTH; 1033. VIRTUE

1. Let us be true: this is the highest maxim of art and of life, the secret of eloquence and of virtue, and of all moral authority.

HENRI FRÉDÉRIC AMIEL, *JOURNAL,* DEC. 17, 1854, TR. MRS. HUMPHRY WARD

2. A man who permits his honor to be taken, permits his life to be taken.

PIETRO ARETINO, LETTER TO GIAMBATTISTA CASTALDO, MARCH 25, 1537, TR. SAMUEL PUTNAM

3. He that is faithful in that which is least is faithful also in much; and he that is unjust in the least is unjust also in much.

BIBLE, LUKE 16:10

4. Honor is like a steep island without a shore: one cannot return once one is outside.

NICOLAS BOILEAU, *SATIRES* (1666), 10

5. The test of a government is not how popular it is with the powerful and privileged few but how honestly and fairly it deals with the many who must depend on it.

JIMMY CARTER, INAUGURAL ADDRESS AS GOVERNOR OF GEORGIA, JAN. 12, 1971, COLLECTED IN *A GOVERNMENT AS GOOD AS ITS PEOPLE* (1977)

6. Nothing so completely baffles one who is full of trick and duplicity himself, than straightforward and simple integrity in another.

CHARLES CALEB COLTON, *LACON* (1825), 2.140

7. Morality regulates the acts of man as a private individual; honor, his acts as a public man.

ESTEBAN ECHEVERRÍA, *DOGMA SOCIALISTA*

8. Honour, / How much we fight with weakness to preserve thee!

JOHN FORD, *THE BROKEN HEART* (1633), 2.3

9. Would that the simple maxim, that honesty is the best policy, might be laid to heart; that a sense of the true aim of life might elevate the tone of politics and trade till public and private honor became identical.

MARGARET FULLER, *SUMMER ON THE LAKES* (1844), 4

10. Men of integrity, by their very existence, rekindle the belief that as a people we can live above the level of moral squalor. We need that belief; a cynical community is a corrupt community.

JOHN W. GARDNER, "THE AIMS OF A FREE PEOPLE," *EXCELLENCE* (1961)

11. Where there are no men, strive thou to be a man.

HAGGADAH, *PALESTINIAN TALMUD* (4TH C.)

12. Wisdom and virtue are like the two wheels of a cart.

JAPANESE PROVERB

13. Hold it the greatest wrong to prefer life to honor and for the sake of life to lose the reason for living.

JUVENAL, *SATIRES* (C. 100), 8.83

14. To be individually righteous is the first of all duties, come what may to one's self, to one's country, to society, and to civilization itself.

JOSEPH WOOD KRUTCH, TITLE ESSAY, 6, *IF YOU DON'T MIND MY SAYING SO* (1964)

15. Integrity, like humility, is a quality which vanishes the moment we are conscious of it in ourselves. We see it only in others.

MADELEINE L'ENGLE, *A CIRCLE OF QUIET* (1972)

16. He has honor if he holds himself to an ideal of conduct though it is inconvenient, unprofitable, or dangerous to do so.

WALTER LIPPMANN, *A PREFACE TO MORALS* (1929), 3.11.3

17. I could not love thee, dear, so much, / Loved I not honour more.

RICHARD LOVELACE, "TO LUCASTA, ON GOING TO THE WARS" (1649), 3

18. As political commentator Mark Shields observed, the moral high ground is a place where [Senator Alfonse] D'Amato is "subject to nosebleeds."

LEONARD LURIE, *SENATOR POTHOLE* (1994)

19. Bill Clinton's willingness to "play the game" when raising money in Arkansas for his election campaign suggests an insensitivity to conflict-of-interest rules.

LEONARD LURIE, *SENATOR POTHOLE* (1994)

20. You cannot throw words like heroism and sacrifice and nobility and honor away without abandoning the qualities they express.

MARYA MANNES, *MORE IN ANGER* (1958), 3.2

21. The courage of all one really knows comes but late in life.

NIETZSCHE, *THE WILL TO POWER* (1888), TR. ANTHONY M. LUDOVICI

22. Honour and shame from no condition rise; / Act well your part, there all the honour lies.

ALEXANDER POPE, *AN ESSAY ON MAN* (1733–34), 4.193

23. Without money, honor is a malady.

RACINE, *LES PLAIDEURS* (1668), 1.1

24. Honour travels in a strait so narrow / Where one but goes abreast.

SHAKESPEARE, *TROILUS AND CRESSIDA* (1601–02), 3.3.154

25. Rightly to be great / Is not to stir without great argument, / But greatly to find quarrel in a straw / When honour's at the stake.

SHAKESPEARE, *HAMLET* (1600), 4.4.53

26. This above all: to thine own self be true, / And it must follow, as the night the day, / Thou canst not then be false to any man.

SHAKESPEARE, *HAMLET* (1600), 1.3.78

27. The truth is, hardly any of us have ethical energy enough for more than one really inflexible point of honor.

GEORGE BERNARD SHAW, "PREFACE ON DOCTORS: THE PSYCHOLOGY OF SELF-RESPECT IN SURGEONS," *THE DOCTOR'S DILEMMA* (1913)

28. It is an endless and frivolous pursuit to act by any other rule than the care of satisfying our own minds in what we do.

RICHARD STEELE, *THE SPECTATOR* (1711–12), 4

29. Even honor and virtue make enemies, condemning, as they do, their opposites by too close a contrast.

TACITUS, *ANNALS* (A.D.115–117?), 4.33, TR. WILLIAM J. BRODRIBB

30. Integrity can be neither lost nor concealed nor faked nor quenched nor artificially come by nor outlived, nor, I believe, in the long run denied.

EUDORA WELTY, "MUST THE NOVELIST CRUSADE?" *THE EYE OF THE STORY* (1978)

31. When faith is lost, when honor dies, / The man is dead.

JOHN GREENLEAF WHITTIER, "ICHABOD" (1850), 8

32. How happy is he born and taught, / That serveth not another's will; / Whose armour is his honest thought, / And simple truth his utmost skill.

SIR HENRY WOTTON, "THE CHARACTER OF A HAPPY LIFE" (1651), 1

492. INTELLECTUALS AND INTELLECTUALISM

See also 493. INTELLIGENCE; 590. MIND

1. It is always the task of the intellectual to "think otherwise." This is not just a perverse idiosyncrasy. It is an absolutely essential feature of a society.

HARVEY COX, *THE SECULAR CITY* (1966), 10

2. Only those who know the supremacy of the intellectual life—the life which has a seed of ennobling thought and purpose within it—can understand the grief of one who falls from that serene activity into the absorbing soul wasting struggle with worldly annoyances.

GEORGE ELIOT, *MIDDLEMARCH* (1871–72), 73

3. A man known to us only as a celebrity in politics or in trade, gains largely in our esteem if we discover that he has some intellectual taste or skill.

EMERSON, "CULTURE," *THE CONDUCT OF LIFE* (1860)

4. Intellectualism, though by no means confined to doubters, is often the sole piety of the skeptic.

RICHARD HOFSTADTER, *ANTI-INTELLECTUALISM IN AMERICAN LIFE* (1963), 1.2

5. The intellectual is *engagé*—he is pledged, committed, enlisted. What everyone else is willing to admit, namely that ideas and abstractions are of signal importance in human life, he imperatively feels.

RICHARD HOFSTADTER, *ANTI-INTELLECTUALISM IN AMERICAN LIFE* (1963), 1.2

6. The intellectual is constantly betrayed by his vanity. God-like, he blandly assumes that he can express everything in words; whereas the things one loves, lives, and dies for are not, in the last analysis, completely expressible in words.

ANNE MORROW LINDBERGH, *THE WAVE OF THE FUTURE* (1940)

7. On the heights it is warmer than people in the valley suppose, especially in winter. The thinker recognizes the full import of this simile.

NIETZSCHE, *MISCELLANEOUS MAXIMS AND OPINIONS* (1879), 335, TR. PAUL V. COHN

8. England is perhaps the only great country whose intellectuals are ashamed of their own nationality.

GEORGE ORWELL, "ENGLAND YOUR ENGLAND," *A COLLECTION OF ESSAYS* (1954)

9. The intellectual is, quite simply, a human being who has a pencil in his or her hand when reading a book.

George Steiner, "The Uncommon Reader," (1978) Lecture at Bennington College

10. Analysis destroys wholes. Some things, magic things, are meant to stay whole. If you look at their pieces, they go away.

Robert James Waller, *The Bridges of Madison County* (1992)

11. Intellectuals, generally, no longer take jazz seriously.

Tom Wolfe, *The Kandy-Kolored Tangerine-Flake Streamline Baby* (1965)

12. Ironically, rock and roll, or whatever you want to call what the hysterical disc jockeys play, is very much in vogue now among intellectuals in New York and Paris and London.

Tom Wolfe, *The Kandy-Kolored Tangerine-Flake Streamline Baby* (1965)

493. INTELLIGENCE

See also 139. Cleverness; 590. Mind; 785. Reason; 941. Stupidity; 1007. Understanding; 1060. Wisdom

1. A girl's brain is mysterious, but only in a superficial way—a way very exasperating to me.

James Agee, *Letters of James Agee to Father Flye* (1962)

2. If a man is intelligent and Fascist, he is not honest. If he is honest and Fascist, he is not intelligent.

Luigi Barzini, *O America* (1977)

3. Intelligence is characterized by a natural incomprehension of life.

Henri Bergson, *L'Évolution créatrice* (1907)

4. There must be something unique about man because otherwise, evidently, the ducks would be lecturing about Konrad Lorenz, and the rats would be writing papers about B.F. Skinner.

Jacob Bronowski, *The Ascent of Man* (1973)

5. Intelligence in chains loses in lucidity what it gains in intensity.

Albert Camus, "Absolute Negation," *The Rebel* (1951), tr. Anthony Bower

6. A superior man may be made to go to the well, but he cannot be made to go down into it. He may be imposed upon, but he cannot be fooled.

Confucius, *Analects* (6th c. B.C.), 6.24, tr. James Legge

7. It is not enough to have a good mind; the main thing is to use it well.

Descartes, *Discourse on Method* (1639), i

8. To the dull mind all nature is leaden. To the illumined mind the whole world burns and sparkles with light.

Emerson, *Journals,* 1831

9. We pay / a high price for being intelligent. Wisdom hurts.

Euripides, *Electra* (413 B.C.), tr. Emily Townsend Vermeule

10. The test of a first-rate intelligence is the ability to hold two opposed ideas in the mind at the same time, and still retain the ability to function.

F. Scott Fitzgerald, "The Crack-Up," *The Crack-Up* (1945)

11. The French equate intelligence with rational discourse, the Russians with intense soul-searching. For the Mexican, intelligence is inseparable from maliciousness.

Carlos Fuentes, "How I Started to Write," in *The Art of the Personal Essay* (1994), ed. Phillip Lopate

12. One good head is better than a hundred strong hands.

Thomas Fuller, M.D., *Gnomologia* (1732), 3753

13. Generally among intelligent people are found nothing but paralytics and among men of action nothing but fools.

André Gide, "Portraits and Aphorisms," *Pretexts* (1903), tr. others

14. The greatest intelligence is precisely the one that suffers most from its own limitations.

André Gide, *The Counterfeiters* (1925), 3.7, tr. Dorothy Bussy

15. Little-minded people's thoughts move in such small circles that five minutes' conversation gives you an arc long enough to determine their whole curve. An arc in the movement of a large intellect does not sensibly differ from a straight line.

Oliver Wendell Holmes, Sr., *The Autocrat of the Breakfast Table* (1858), i

16. If his IQ slips any lower, we'll have to water him twice a day.

Molly Ivins, *Molly Ivins Can't Say That, Can She?* (1991)

17. An honest heart being the first blessing, a knowing head is the second.

THOMAS JEFFERSON, LETTER TO PETER CARR, AUG. 19, 1785

18. The true, strong, and sound mind is the mind that can embrace equally great things and small.

SAMUEL JOHNSON, QUOTED IN BOSWELL'S *LIFE OF SAMUEL JOHNSON*, APRIL 29, 1778

19. Everyone speaks well of his heart, but no one dares to say it of his head.

LA ROCHEFOUCAULD, *MAXIMS* (1665), TR. KENNETH PRATT

20. The sign of an intelligent people is their ability to control emotions by the application of reason.

MARYA MANNES, *MORE IN ANGER* (1958), 3.1

21. What men, in their egotism, constantly mistake for a deficiency of intelligence in women is merely an incapacity for mastering that mass of small intellectual tricks, that complex of petty knowledges, that collection of cerebral rubberstamps, which constitute the chief mental equipment of the average male.

H.L. MENCKEN, "THE FEMININE MIND," IN *FIFTY FAMOUS ESSAYS* (1964)

22. 'Tis the sharpness of our mind that gives the edge to our pains and pleasures.

MONTAIGNE, "THAT THE RELISH OF GOOD AND EVIL DEPENDS IN A GREAT MEASURE UPON THE OPINION WE HAVE OF THEM," *ESSAYS* (1580–88), TR. W. C. HAZLITT

23. One can do everything with the intellect—that is what makes one so proud of it—except understand another human being.

LEWIS MUMFORD, *FINDINGS AND KEEPINGS. ANALECTS FOR AN AUTOBIOGRAPHY* (1975)

24. If the human intellect functions, it is actually in order to solve the problems which the man's inner destiny sets it.

JOSÉ ORTEGA Y GASSET, "IN SEARCH OF GOETHE FROM WITHIN, LETTER TO A GERMAN," *PARTISAN REVIEW*, DECEMBER 1949, TR. WILLARD R. TRASK

25. The greater intellect one has, the more originality one finds in men. Ordinary persons find no difference between men.

PASCAL, *PENSÉES* (1670), 7, TR. W. F. TROTTER

26. Intellect, without firmness, is craft and chicanery; and firmness, without intellect, perverseness and obstinacy.

SA'DI, *GULISTAN* (1258), 8.65, TR. JAMES ROSS

27. There is nothing inhuman about an intelligent machine; it is indeed an expression of those superb intellectual capabilities that only human beings, of all the creatures on our planet, now possess.

CARL SAGAN, *BROCA'S BRAIN: REFLECTIONS ON THE ROMANCE OF SCIENCE* (1979)

28. Intelligence is quickness in seeing things as they are.

GEORGE SANTAYANA, *LITTLE ESSAYS* (1920), 62

29. A good mind possesses a kingdom.

SENECA, *THYESTES* (1ST C.), 380

30. It's not a man's great frame / Or breadth of shoulders makes his manhood count: / A man of sense has always the advantage.

SOPHOCLES, *AJAX* (C. 447 B.C.), TR. JOHN MOORE

31. With respect to wit, I learned that there was not much difference between the half and the whole.

THOREAU, "VISITORS," *WALDEN* (1854)

32. Many complain of their looks, but none of their brains.

YIDDISH PROVERBS (1949)

494. INTEMPERANCE

See also 268. DRINKING; 312. EXCESS; 739. PROFLIGACY; 970. TEMPERANCE

1. The impulses of an incontinent man carry him in the opposite direction from that towards which he was aiming.

ARISTOTLE, *NICOMACHEAN ETHICS* (4TH C. B.C.), 1.13, TR. J. A. K. THOMSON

2. Debauchee, n. One who has so earnestly pursued pleasure that he has had the misfortune to overtake it.

AMBROSE BIERCE, *THE DEVIL'S DICTIONARY* (1881–1911)

3. If the things that produce the pleasures of the dissolute were able to drive away from their minds their fears about what is above them and about death and pain, and to teach them the limit of desires, we would have no reason to find fault with the dissolute.

EPICURUS, "PRINCIPAL DOCTRINES" (3RD C. B.C.), 10, IN *LETTERS, PRINCIPAL DOCTRINES, AND VATICAN SAYINGS*, TR. RUSSEL M. GEER

4. Since the creation of the world there has been no tyrant like Intemperance, and no slaves so cruelly treated as his.

WILLIAM LLOYD GARRISON, *LIFE* (1885–89), V. 1

5. Intemperance is the plague of sensuality, and temperance is not its bane but its seasoning.

MONTAIGNE, "OF EXPERIENCE," *ESSAYS* (1580–88)

6. When a man has been intemperate so long that shame no longer paints a blush upon his cheek, his liquor generally does it instead.

George Dennison Prentice, *Prenticeana* (1860)

INTENTION

See 771. Purpose

495. INTEREST

See also 874. Selfishness

1. Men are not against you; they are merely for themselves.

Gene Fowler, *Skyline* (1961)

2. Every man's affairs, however little, are important to himself.

Samuel Johnson, letter to the earl of Bute, Nov. 3, 1762, quoted in Boswell's *Life of Samuel Johnson*

3. Principles do not mainly influence even the principled; we talk on principle, but we act on interest.

Walter Savage Landor, "Banos and Alpuente," *Imaginary Conversations* (1824–54)

4. Interest speaks all sorts of tongues, and plays all sorts of parts, even that of disinterestedness.

La Rochefoucauld, *Maxims* (1665)

5. Do not confuse your vested interests with ethics. Do not identify the enemies of your privilege with the enemies of humanity.

Max Lerner, "Politics and the Connective Tissue," *Actions and Passions* (1949)

6. A man will fight harder for his interests than his rights.

Napoleon I, *Maxims* (1804–15)

7. The truth is that no horizon is especially interesting by itself, by virtue of its peculiar content, and that any horizon, wide or narrow, brilliant or dull, varied or monotonous, may possess an interest of its own which merely requires a vital adjustment to be discovered.

José Ortega y Gasset, "Notes on the Novel," *The Dehumanization of Art* (1925)

8. It is common to forget a man and slight him if his good will cannot help you.

Plautus, *The Captives* (3rd c. b.c.)

9. A world of vested interests is not a world which welcomes the disruptive force of candour.

Agnes Repplier, "Are Americans Timid?" *Under Dispute* (1924)

496. INTERESTINGNESS

1. A man who can be entertaining for a full day will be in his grave by night-fall.

Edward Dahlberg, "On Time and Death," *Reasons of the Heart* (1965)

2. If men would avoid that general language and general manner in which they strive to hide all that is peculiar, and would say only what was uppermost in their own minds, after their own individual manner, every man would be interesting.

Emerson, *Journals*, 1827

3. The fascinating necessarily tends to call a certain attention to itself; the interesting need not. An evening spent with a fascinating person leaves vivid memories; one spent with interesting people has merely a sort of bouquet.

Louis Kronenberger, *Company Manners* (1954), 3.1

4. The test of interesting people is that subject matter doesn't matter.

Louis Kronenberger, *Company Manners* (1954), 3.1

497. INTERESTS, DIVIDED

See also 170. Conflict, Inner

1. No man can serve two masters: for either he will hate the one, and love the other; or else he will hold to the one, and despise the other.

Bible, Matthew 6:24

2. The perplexity of life arises from there being too many interesting things in it for us to be interested properly in any of them.

G. K. Chesterton, "The Secret of a Train," *Tremendous Trifles* (1909)

3. He who serves two masters has to lie to one.

Portuguese Proverb

4. Those who set out to serve both God and Mammon soon discover that there is no God.

Logan Pearsall Smith, *Afterthoughts* (1931), 3

498. INTERNATIONAL RELATIONS

See also 100. Brotherhood; 193. Cosmopolitanism; 247. Diplomats and Diplomacy; 273. East and West; 458. Imperialism; 622. Nationalism; 994. Treaties; 1015. United Nations

1. Alliance, n. In international politics, the union of two thieves who have their hands so deeply inserted

in each other's pocket that they cannot separately plunder a third.

AMBROSE BIERCE, *THE DEVIL'S DICTIONARY* (1881–1911)

2. An ally need not own the land he helps.

EURIPIDES, *ION* (C. 421–408 B.C.), TR. RONALD F. WILLETTS

3. Conferences at the top level are always courteous. Name-calling is left to the foreign ministers.

W. AVERELL HARRIMAN, NEWS SUMMARIES, AUG. 1, 1955

4. Bismarck's genius, as well as his great flaw, was the same as that of another outstanding nineteenth-century politician of the German-speaking world, Prince Clemens Metternich. Both men were artificers, able to hold off the future by building a fragile present out of pieces of the past.

ROBERT D. KAPLAN, *BALKAN GHOSTS* (1993)

5. Above all, it behooves us to repress, and if possible to extinguish once and for all, our inveterate tendency to judge others by the extent to which they contrive to be like ourselves.

GEORGE F. KENNAN, *AMERICAN DIPLOMACY 1900–1950* (1951)

6. We shall be judged more by what we do at home than what we preach abroad.

JOHN F. KENNEDY, STATE OF THE UNION MESSAGE, JAN. 14, 1963

7. World peace, like community peace, does not require that each man love his neighbor—it requires only that they live together with mutual tolerance, submitting their disputes to a just and peaceful settlement.

JOHN F. KENNEDY, COMMENCEMENT ADDRESS, AMERICAN UNIVERSITY, WASHINGTON, D.C., JUNE 10, 1963

8. Countries do not assume burdens because it is fair, only because it is necessary.

HENRY A. KISSINGER, *AMERICAN FOREIGN POLICY* (1969)

9. In relations with many domestically weak countries, a radio transmitter can be a more effective form of pressure than a squadron of B-52s.

HENRY A. KISSINGER, *AMERICAN FOREIGN POLICY* (1969)

10. The greatest need of the contemporary international system is an agreed concept of order.

HENRY A. KISSINGER, *AMERICAN FOREIGN POLICY* (1969)

11. Some of the more fatuous flag-waving Americans are in danger of forgetting that you can't extract gratitude as you would extract a tooth; that unless friendship is freely given, it means nothing and less than nothing.

MAX LERNER, "HOW GRATEFUL SHOULD EUROPE BE?" *ACTIONS AND PASSIONS* (1949)

12. Amity itself can only be maintained by reciprocal respect, and true friends are punctilious equals.

HERMAN MELVILLE, SUPPLEMENT TO *BATTLEPIECES AND ASPECTS OF THE WAR* (1866)

13. That expression "positive neutrality" is a contradiction in terms. There can be no more positive neutrality than there can be a vegetarian tiger.

V. K. KRISHNA MENON, *THE NEW YORK TIMES,* OCT. 18, 1960

14. International incidents should not govern foreign policy, but foreign policy, incidents.

NAPOLEON I, *MAXIMS* (1804–15)

15. The friendships of nations, built on common interests, cannot survive the mutability of those interests.

AGNES REPPLIER, "ALLIES," *UNDER DISPUTE* (1924)

16. International crises have their advantages. They frighten the weak but stir and inspire the strong.

JAMES RESTON, *SKETCHES IN THE SAND* (1967)

17. This is the devilish thing about foreign affairs: they are foreign and will not always conform to our whim.

JAMES RESTON, *THE NEW YORK TIMES,* DEC. 16, 1964

18. More than an end to war, we want an end to the beginning of all wars—yes, an end to this brutal, inhuman and thoroughly impractical method of settling the differences between governments.

FRANKLIN D. ROOSEVELT, MESSAGE FOR JEFFERSON DAY, APRIL 13, 1945

19. I asked Tom if countries always apologized when they had done wrong, and he says: "Yes; the little ones does."

MARK TWAIN, *TOM SAWYER ABROAD* (1894)

20. Interest does not tie nations together; it sometimes separates them. But sympathy and understanding does unite them.

WOODROW WILSON, SPEECH, OCT. 27, 1913

21. There must be, not a balance of power, but a community of power; not organized rivalries, but an organized peace.

WOODROW WILSON, ADDRESS TO U.S. SENATE, JAN. 22, 1917

499. INTIMACY

See also 57. Association; 333. Familiarity; 983. Togetherness

1. If ever a man and his wife, or a man and his mistress, who pass nights as well as days together, absolutely lay aside all good-breeding, their intimacy will soon degenerate into a coarse familiarity, infallibly productive of contempt or disgust.

Lord Chesterfield, *Letters to His Son*, Nov. 3, 1749

2. All couples must bear the strain of getting acquainted, having been, up to then, merely intimate.

Peter De Vries, *Comfort Me With Apples* (1956)

3. A man knows his companion in a long journey and a little inn.

Thomas Fuller, M.D., *Gnomologia* (1732), 284

4. No stranger can get a great many notes of torture out of a human soul; it takes one that knows it well,—parent, child, brother, sister, intimate.

Oliver Wendell Holmes, Sr., *The Autocrat of the Breakfast Table* (1858), 6

5. When married people don't get on they can separate, but if they're not married it's impossible. It's a tie that only death can sever.

W. Somerset Maugham, *The Circle* (1921), 3

6. Intimacy requires courage because risk is inescapable. We cannot know at the outset how the relationship will affect us.

Rollo May, *The Courage to Create* (1975)

7. Intimacy begins with oneself. It does no good to try to find intimacy with friends, lovers and family if you are starting out from alienation and division within yourself.

Thomas Moore, *Soul Mates* (1994)

8. The female covers her breasts, and then proceeds to redefine their shape with a brassiere. This sexual signaling device may be padded or inflatable, so that it not only reinstates the concealed shape, but also enlarges it, imitating in this way the breast swelling that occurs during sexual arousal.

Desmond Morris, *The Naked Ape* (1967)

9. The human soul is not framed for continued proximity, and the result of this enforced neighbourhood is often an appalling loneliness for which the rules of the game forbid assuagement.

Iris Murdoch, *The Black Prince* (1973)

10. After the meal, the couple retired to their bedroom. Man and wife don't usually lie together in the daytime, but when he went outside to close the shutters, she did not protest. As soon as he put his arm around her she was aroused, like an adolescent—since a woman who has not been pregnant, remains virginal forever.

Isaac Bashevis Singer, *The Magician of Lublin* (1960)

11. Though all humans need both intimacy and independence, women tend to focus on the first and men on the second. It is as if their lifeblood ran in different directions.

Deborah Tannen, *You Just Don't Understand* (1990)

12. Our daily existence requires both closeness and distance, the wholeness of self, the wholeness of intimacy.

Judith Viorst, *Necessary Losses* (1986)

13. Hillary lies sleepless in her bed. It's spooky in here, she thinks, and she turns on the ceiling light to supplement the night light. Jonathon whickers in his sleep, and reminds her of his guinea pig.

Fay Weldon, *Remember Me* (1976)

INTIMIDATION

See 343. Fear; 357. Force; 976. Threat

500. INTOLERANCE

See also 264. Dogmatism; 335. Fanaticism; 620. Narrowness; 726. Prejudices; 775. Racial Prejudice; 984. Tolerance

1. He has the courage of his conviction and the intolerance of his courage. He is opposed to the death penalty for murder, but he would willingly have anyone electrocuted who disagreed with him on the subject.

Thomas Bailey Aldrich, "Leaves from a Notebook," *Ponkapog Papers* (1903)

2. Traditional Anglo-Saxon intolerance is a local and temporal culture trait like any other.

Ruth Benedict, *Patterns of Culture* (1934)

3. They [the police] learned something from them Harlem riots. They used to beat your head right in public, but now they only beat it after they get you down to the station house.

Langston Hughes, *Simple Speaks His Mind* (1950)

INTROSPECTION

See 758. Psychoanalysis; 875. Self-Knowledge

501. INTUITION

See also 284. EMOTIONS; 683. PERCEPTION; 883. SENSIBILITY

1. It is the heart always that sees, before the head can see.

THOMAS CARLYLE, *CHARTISM* (1839), 5

2. Women, as most susceptible, are the best index of the coming hour.

EMERSON, "FATE," *THE CONDUCT OF LIFE* (1860)

3. Intuition attracts those who wish to be spiritual without any bother, because it promises a heaven where the intuitions of others can be ignored.

E. M. FORSTER, "ROGER FRY," *ABINGER HARVEST* (1936)

502. INVENTION

See also 201. CREATION AND CREATIVITY; 479. INNOVATION; 966. TECHNOLOGY

1. An invention or new combination can be successful only if all if the elements necessary for the recombination are present in the culture.

PETER FARB, *MAN'S RISE TO CIVILIZATION* (1968)

2. I thought of the nameless inventor of the bathtub. I was somehow sure it was a woman. And was the inventor of the bathtub plug a man?

ERICA JONG, *FEAR OF FLYING* (1973)

3. Laws of nature are human *inventions*, like ghosts. Laws of logic, or mathematics are also human inventions, like ghosts. The whole blessed thing is a human invention, including the idea that it *isn't* a human invention.

ROBERT M. PIRSIG, *ZEN AND THE ART OF MOTORCYCLE MAINTENANCE* (1974)

4. Name the greatest of all the inventors. Accident.

MARK TWAIN, *NOTEBOOK* (1935)

5. It must be confessed that the inventors of the mechanical arts have been much more useful to men than the inventors of syllogisms.

VOLTAIRE, "PHILOSOPHY," *PHILOSOPHICAL DICTIONARY* (1764)

503. INVESTMENT

See also 104. BUSINESS AND COMMERCE

1. If a little does not go, much cash will not come.

CHINESE PROVERB

2. 'Tis sweet to know that stocks will stand / When we with daisies lie, / That commerce will continue, / And trades as briskly fly.

EMILY DICKINSON, *POEMS* (C. 1862–86)

3. 'Tis money that begets money.

THOMAS FULLER, M.D., *GNOMOLOGIA* (1732), 5091

4. There is nothing like the ticker tape except a woman—nothing that promises, hour after hour, day after day, such sudden developments; nothing that disappoints so often or occasionally fulfills with such unbelievable, passionate magnificence.

WALTER KNOWLETON GUTMAN, *CORONET,* MARCH 1960

5. Speculation is the romance of trade, and casts contempt upon all its sober realities. It renders the stock-jobber a magician, and the exchange a region of enchantment.

WASHINGTON IRVING, "A TIME OF UNEXAMPLED PROSPERITY," *WOLFERT'S ROOST* (1855)

6. Let Wall Street have a nightmare and the whole country has to help get them back in bed again.

WILL ROGERS, *THE AUTOBIOGRAPHY OF WILL ROGERS* (1949), 14

7. On Wall Street, he and a few others—how many?—three hundred, four hundred, five hundred?—had become precisely that...Masters of the Universe. There was...no limit whatsoever!

TOM WOLFE, *THE BONFIRE OF THE VANITIES* (1987)

504. INVOLVEMENT

See also 10. ACTIVITY; 146. COMMITMENT; 219. DEADNESS, SPIRITUAL; 321. EXPERIENCE; 513. JOIE DE VIVRE

1. To say yes, you have to sweat and roll up your sleeves and plunge both hands into life up to the elbows. It is easy to say no, even if saying no means death.

JEAN ANOUILH, *ANTIGONE* (1942), TR. LEWIS GALANTIÈRE

2. Is it so small a thing / To have enjoyed the sun, / To have lived in the spring, / To have loved, to have thought, to have done?

MATTHEW ARNOLD, *EMPEDOCLES ON ETNA* (1852), 1.2

3. Say "Yes" to the seedlings and a giant forest cleaves the sky. Say "Yes" to the universe and the planets become your neighbors. Say "Yes" to dreams of love and freedom. It is the password to utopia.

BROOKS ATKINSON, "MARCH 19," *ONCE AROUND THE SUN* (1951)

4. Do not fear death so much, but rather the inadequate life.

BERTOLT BRECHT, *THE MOTHER* (1932), 11, TR. LEE BAXANDALL

5. Let the fruition of things bless the possession of them, and take no satisfaction in dying but living rich.

SIR THOMAS BROWNE, *A LETTER TO A FRIEND* (1690)

6. The civilized are those who get more out of life than the uncivilized, and for this the uncivilized have not forgiven them.

CYRIL CONNOLLY, *THE UNQUIET GRAVE* (1945), 2

7. Be a football to Time and Chance, the more kicks, the better, so that you inspect the whole game and know its utmost law.

EMERSON, *JOURNALS,* 1836

8. To finish the moment, to find the journey's end in every step of the road, to live the greatest number of good hours, in wisdom.

EMERSON, "EXPERIENCE," *ESSAYS: SECOND SERIES* (1844)

9. The kind of relatedness to the world may be noble or trivial, but even being related to the basest kind of pattern is immensely preferable to being alone.

ERICH FROMM, *ESCAPE FROM FREEDOM* (1941), 1

10. It is by losing himself in the objective, in inquiry, creation, and craft, that a man becomes something.

PAUL GOODMAN, *THE COMMUNITY OF SCHOLARS* (1962)

11. The joy of life is to put out one's power in some natural and useful or harmless way. There is no other. And the real misery is not to do this.

OLIVER WENDELL HOLMES, JR., SPEECH, BOSTON BAR ASSOCIATION, MARCH 7, 1900

12. Life without absorbing occupation is hell—joy consists in forgetting life.

ELBERT HUBBARD, *THE NOTE BOOK* (1927)

13. Live all you can; it's a mistake not to. It doesn't so much matter what you do in particular, so long as you have your life. If you haven't had that, what have you had?

HENRY JAMES, *THE AMBASSADORS* (1903), 11

14. There is certainly no greater happiness than to be able to look back on a life usefully and virtuously employed, to trace our own progress in existence, by such tokens as excite neither shame nor sorrow.

SAMUEL JOHNSON, *THE RAMBLER* (1750–52), 41

15. A man is an island in the only sense that matters, not an easy way to be. We live in mystery, a cosmos of separate lonely bodies, men, insects, stars. It is all a loneliness and men know it best.

BERNARD MALAMUD, *DUBIN'S LIVES* (1979)

16. The moment one is on the side of life "peace and security" drop out of consciousness. The only peace, the only security, is in fulfillment.

HENRY MILLER, "THE ABSOLUTE COLLECTIVE," *THE WISDOM OF THE HEART* (1941)

17. My trade and art is to live.

MONTAIGNE, "USE MAKES PERFECT," *ESSAYS* (1580–88), TR. W. C. HAZLITT

18. To do all that one is able to do, is to be a man; to do all that one would like to do, is to be a god.

NAPOLEON I, *MAXIMS* (1804–15)

19. Better be left by twenty dears / Than lie in a loveless bed; / Better a loaf that's wet with tears, / Than cold, unsalted bread.

DOROTHY PARKER, "THE WHISTLING GIRL," *SUNSET GUN* (1928)

20. Love, children, and work are the great sources of fertilizing contact between the individual and the rest of the world.

BERTRAND RUSSELL, "THE PLACE OF LOVE IN HUMAN LIFE," *MARRIAGE AND MORALS* (1929)

21. The notion of looking on at life has always been hateful to me. What am I if I am not a participant? In order to be, I must participate.

SAINT-EXUPÉRY, *FLIGHT TO ARRAS* (1942), 20, TR. LEWIS GALANTIÈRE

22. Life finds its wealth by the claims of the world, and its worth by the claims of love.

RABINDRANATH TAGORE, *STRAY BIRDS* (1916), 33

23. However mean your life is, meet it and live it; do not shun it and call it hard names. It is not so bad as you are.

THOREAU, "CONCLUSION," *WALDEN* (1854)

24. It is easier to stay out than get out.

MARK TWAIN, "PUDD'NHEAD WILSON'S NEW CALENDAR," *FOLLOWING THE EQUATOR* (1897), 1.18

505. IRELAND AND IRISHMEN

1. As a consequence [of a closed economic circle], in 1912 there was not a single Irishman who sat on a single board of a major Boston bank.

DORIS KEARNS GOODWIN, *THE FITZGERALDS AND THE KENNEDYS* (1987)

2. The Irish are a fair people; they never speak well of one another.

SAMUEL JOHNSON, QUOTED IN BOSWELL'S *LIFE OF SAMUEL JOHNSON,* FEBRUARY 1775

IRONY

See 436. HUMOR

IRRATIONALITY

See 1020. UNREASON

506. IRREVERENCE

See also 441. ICONOCLASM; 1068. WORSHIP

1. Impiety, n. Your irreverence toward my deity.

AMBROSE BIERCE, *THE DEVIL'S DICTIONARY* (1881–1911)

2. Beware of the community in which blasphemy does not exist: underneath, atheism runs rampant.

ANTONIO MACHADO, *JUAN DE MAIRENA* (1943), I, TR. BEN BELITT

3. All great truths begin as blasphemies.

GEORGE BERNARD SHAW, *ANNAJANSKA* (1919)

4. Irreverence is the champion of liberty and its only sure defense.

MARK TWAIN, *NOTEBOOK* (1935)

507. IRREVOCABLENESS

See also 176. CONSEQUENCES; 340. FATE; 624. NECESSITY; 676. PAST; 806. RESIGNATION

1. What's said is said and goes upon its way, / Like it or not, repent it as you may.

CHAUCER, "THE MANCIPLE'S TALE," *THE CANTERBURY TALES* (C. 1387–1400), TR. NEVILL COGHILL

2. Of this I am quite sure, that if we open a quarrel between the past and the present, we shall find we have lost the future.

SIR WINSTON CHURCHILL, SPEECH, HOUSE OF COMMONS, JUNE 18, 1940

3. The book of Nature is the book of Fate. She turns the gigantic pages—leaf after leaf—never re-turning one.

EMERSON, "FATE," *THE CONDUCT OF LIFE* (1860)

4. What is done, is done: / Spend not the time in tears, but seek for justice.

JOHN FORD, *'TIS PITY SHE'S A WHORE* (1633), 3.9

5. A word and a stone let go cannot be called back.

THOMAS FULLER, M.D., *GNOMOLOGIA* (1732), 485

6. Time flies, and what is past is done.

GOETHE, "MARTHA'S GARDEN," *FAUST: PART I* (1808), TR. PHILIP WAYNE

7. The mill cannot grind with water that's past.

GEORGE HERBERT, *JACULA PRUDENTUM* (1651)

8. What's gone and what's past help / Should be past grief.

SHAKESPEARE, *THE WINTER'S TALE* (1630–11), 3.2.223

9. Of all sad words of tongue or pen, / The saddest are these: "It might have been!"

JOHN GREENLEAF WHITTIER, "MAUD MULLER" (1854), 53

508. IRRITATIONS

1. Men often bear little grievances with less courage than they do large misfortunes.

AESOP, "THE ASS AND THE FROGS," *FABLES* (6TH C. B.C.?), TR. GEORGE FYLER TOWNSEND

2. To great evils we submit; we resent little provocations.

WILLIAM HAZLITT, "ON GREAT AND LITTLE THINGS," *LITERARY REMAINS* (1836)

3. The mass of men live lives of quiet exasperation.

PHYLLIS MCGINLEY, "PIPELINE AND SINKER," *THE PROVINCE OF THE HEART* (1959)

4. too many creatures / both insects and humans / estimate their own value / by the amount of minor irritation / they are able to cause / to greater personalities than themselves.

DON MARQUIS, "PRIDE," *ARCHY DOES HIS PART* (1935)

ISOLATION

See 30. ALIENATION; 31. ALOOFNESS; 915. SOLITUDE

509. ITALY AND ITALIANS

See also 1029. VENICE

1. Italians have discovered America for the Americans; taught poetry, statesmanship, and the ruses of trade to the English; military art to the Germans; cuisine to the French; acting and ballet dancing to the Russians; and music to everybody.

LUIGI BARZINI, *THE ITALIANS* (1964)

2. There were always stupendous (and jealously guarded) beauties in Italy, Sienese Madonnas or

Botticelli Venuses who were greeted with hushed silence and by the turning of men's heads when they walked down a busy street.

LUIGI BARZINI, *O AMERICA* (1977)

3. I think the Romans must have aggravated one another very much, with their noses. Perhaps, they became the restless people they were, in consequence.

CHARLES DICKENS, *GREAT EXPECTATIONS* (1860–1861)

4. Florence she found perfectly sweet, Naples a dream, but very whiffy. In Rome one had simply to sit still and feel.

E.M. FORSTER, *WHERE ANGELS FEAR TO TREAD* (1920)

5. A man who has not been in Italy is always conscious of an inferiority.

SAMUEL JOHNSON, QUOTED IN BOSWELL'S *LIFE OF SAMUEL JOHNSON,* APRIL 11, 1776

ITCH

See 852. SCRATCHING

J

JANUARY
See 854. SEASONS

510. JEALOUSY

See also 295. ENVY

1. Jealousy is that pain which a man feels from the apprehension that he is not equally beloved by the person whom he entirely loves.

JOSEPH ADDISON, *THE SPECTATOR* (1711–12), 170

2. A jealous ear hears all things.

APOCRYPHA, WISDOM OF SOLOMON 1:10

3. Love is strong as death; jealousy is cruel as the grave.

BIBLE, SONG OF SOLOMON 8:6

4. Jealousy is beautiful only on a young and ardent face. After the first wrinkles, trust must return.

ALFRED CAPUS, *LES PASSAGÈRES* (1906), 1.4

5. Jealousy is not at all low, but it catches us humbled and bowed down, at first sight.

COLETTE, "THE PURE AND THE IMPURE," *EARTHLY PARADISE* (1966), 5

6. Jealousy's a proof of love, / But 'tis a weak and unavailing medicine; / It puts out the disease and makes it show, / But has no power to cure.

JOHN DRYDEN, *ALL FOR LOVE* (1678), 4

7. It is not love that is blind, but jealousy.

LAWRENCE DURRELL, *JUSTINE* (1957), 3

8. Jealousy: that dragon which slays love under the pretense of keeping it alive.

HAVELOCK ELLIS, *ON LIFE AND SEX: ESSAYS OF LOVE AND VIRTUE* (1937), 1

9. Jealousy, which serves the struggle for survival, can deteriorate into the envy which draws defeat even from victory.

WILLARD GAYLIN, *FEELINGS: OUR VITAL SIGNS* (1979)

10. Where there is no jealousy there is no love.

GERMAN PROVERB

11. In jealousy there is more of self-love than love.

LA ROCHEFOUCAULD, *MAXIMS* (1665), TR. KENNETH PRATT

12. Jealousy feeds upon suspicion, and it turns into fury or it ends as soon as we pass from suspicion to certainty.

LA ROCHEFOUCAULD, *MAXIMS* (1665)

13. Jealousy is always born with love, but does not always die with it.

LA ROCHEFOUCAULD, *MAXIMS* (1665), TR. KENNETH PRATT

14. Jealousy is the greatest of all evils, and the one which arouses the least pity in the person who causes it.

LA ROCHEFOUCAULD, *MAXIMS* (1665), TR. KENNETH PRATT

15. Love that is fed by jealousy dies hard.

OVID, *LOVE'S CURE* (C. A.D. 8), TR. J. LEWIS MAY

16. The jealous are troublesome to others, but a torment to themselves.

WILLIAM PENN, *SOME FRUITS OF SOLITUDE* (1693), 2.190

17. To jealousy, nothing is more frightful than laughter.

FRANÇOISE SAGAN, *LA CHAMADE* (1966)

18. Trifles light as air / Are to the jealous confirmations strong / As proofs of holy writ.

SHAKESPEARE, *OTHELLO* (1604–05), 3.3.322

19. Whoever had known sexual jealousy, that most destructive of emotions—and this would be so for men no less than women—had known madness and had now to know sympathy for someone who had been carried by jealousy this one terrible step too far, to murder.

DIANA TRILLING, *MRS. HARRIS: THE DEATH OF THE SCARSDALE DOCTOR* (1981)

511. JESUS

1. [W]e had from childhood not only the experience of love and truth common to all family life, but the idea of them embodied in the person of Jesus, a picture always present to our imagination as well as our feelings.

JOYCE CARY, *EXCEPT THE LORD* (1953)

2. [Jesus], a man who was completely innocent, offered himself as a sacrifice for the good of others, including his enemies, and became the ransom of the world. It was a perfect act.

MOHANDAS K. GANDHI, *NON-VIOLENCE IN PEACE AND WAR* (1948), 2.166

3. Jesus did not make a speech or preach a sermon, as we should understand it. By uttering half in speech and half in song the phrases over whose compressed wisdom and memorable form he had labored for long years, he taught his people and the world.

GILBERT HIGHET, *THE ART OF TEACHING* (1950)

4. Well, when Christ comes back this time, I hope He comes back *mad* His own self. I hope He drives the Jim Crowers out of their high places, every living last one of them from Washington to Texas.

LANGSTON HUGHES, *SIMPLE SPEAKS HIS MIND* (1950)

5. Thou hast conquered, O pale Galilean; the world has grown grey from thy breath.

ALGERNON CHARLES SWINBURNE, "HYMN TO PROSERPINE," *POEMS AND BALLADS: FIRST SERIES* (1866)

512. JEWS

1. "I never even realized I was Jewish until I was practically grown up. Or rather, I used to feel that everybody in the world was Jewish, which amounts to the same thing."

JOSEPH HELLER, *GOOD AS GOLD* (1979)

2. From the beginning, the Christian was the theorizing Jew; consequently, the Jew is the practical Christian.

KARL MARX, "THE CAPACITY OF THE PRESENT-DAY JEWS AND CHRISTIANS TO BECOME FREE" (1884), *EARLY WRITINGS*

3. A Jewish man with parents alive is a fifteen-year-old boy, and will remain a fifteen-year-old boy till they die.

PHILIP ROTH, *PORTNOY'S COMPLAINT* (1969)

4. I am a Jew. Hath not a Jew eyes? Hath not a Jew hands, organs, dimensions, senses, affections, passions?

SHAKESPEARE, *THE MERCHANT OF VENICE* (1596–97), 3.1.61

5. The Jews generally give value. They make you pay; but they deliver the goods. In my experience the men who want something for nothing are invariably Christians.

GEORGE BERNARD SHAW, *SAINT JOAN* (1923), 4

6. Embracing and rejecting tradition, bound and liberated by faith, torn between obscurantism and reason, self-assured and self-critical, they were a kaleidoscope of fragments, positions held and abandoned, images formed and shattered, God-fearing Jew, God-denying Jew, passionate and indifferent, hero and villain, yea-sayer, nay-sayer.

ISRAEL SHENKER, *COAT OF MANY COLORS* (1985)

7. Jews are a singular confusion—difficult to define, awkward to describe, impossible to understand. All the virtues, all the vices, every pleasure, every pain—nothing is spared them.

ISRAEL SHENKER, *COAT OF MANY COLORS* (1985)

8. My father was the Jewish half of the family, yet it was my mother who taught me to have pride in that tradition.

GLORIA STEINEM, "RUTH'S SONG," *OUTRAGEOUS ACTS AND EVERYDAY REBELLIONS* (1983)

9. The Jew has his anchorage not in place but in time, in his highly developed sense of history as personal context. Six thousand years of self-awareness are a homeland.

GEORGE STEINER, "A KIND OF SURVIVOR," *LANGUAGE AND SILENCE* (1967)

10. The distinction that Jews have themselves always made between Jews of German origin and Jews of East European origin is as stringent as that between Boston Brahmin and Boston lace-curtain Irish, though much finer.

DIANA TRILLING, *MRS. HARRIS: THE DEATH OF THE SCARSDALE DOCTOR* (1981)

11. That the Jews were unholy was a belief so ingrained by the Church [by the 14th century] that the most devout persons were the harshest in their antipathy, none more so than St. Louis.

BARBARA W. TUCHMAN, *A DISTANT MIRROR* (1978)

12. The impact of the holocaust on believers as well as unbelievers, on Jews as well as Christians, has not yet been evaluated. Not deeply, not enough.

ELIE WIESEL, *LEGENDS OF OUR TIMES* (1968)

513. JOIE DE VIVRE

See also 293. ENTHUSIASM; 504. INVOLVEMENT; 704. PLEASURE; 1036. VITALITY

1. Exuberance is Beauty.

WILLIAM BLAKE, "PROVERBS OF HELL," *THE MARRIAGE OF HEAVEN AND HELL* (1790)

2. Zest is the secret of all beauty. There is no beauty that is attractive without zest.

CHRISTIAN DIOR, *LADIES' HOME JOURNAL*, APRIL 1956

3. Let us live while we live.

PHILIP DODDRIDGE, QUOTED IN JOB ORTON'S *LIFE OF DODDRIDGE* (1764)

4. Exuberance is better than taste.

FLAUBERT, *SENTIMENTAL EDUCATION* (1869), 4, TR. ROBERT BALDICK

5. Live thy life as it were spoil and pluck the joys that fly.

MARTIAL, *EPIGRAMS* (A.D. 86), 7.47, TR. WALTER C. A. KERR

6. The gayety of life, like the beauty and the moral worth of life, is a saving grace, which to ignore is folly, and to destroy is crime. There is no more than we need,—there is barely enough to go round.

AGNES REPPLIER, "THE GAYETY OF LIFE," *COMPROMISES* (1904)

7. What hunger is in relation to food, zest is in relation to life.

BERTRAND RUSSELL, *THE CONQUEST OF HAPPINESS* (1930), 10

JOKES

See 436. HUMOR; 1061. WIT

JOURNALISM

See 629. NEWS; 630. NEWSPAPERS

JOY

See 278. ECSTASY; 409. HAPPINESS; 704. PLEASURE

514. JUDGES

See also 517. JUSTICE; 528. LAW AND LAWYERS

1. That judges of important causes should hold office for life is a disputable thing, for the mind grows old as well as the body.

ARISTOTLE, *POLITICS* (4TH C. B.C.), 2.9, TR. BENJAMIN JOWETT

2. Judges must beware of hard constructions and strained inferences, for there is no worse torture than the torture of laws.

FRANCIS BACON, "OF JUDICATURE," *ESSAYS* (1625)

3. Take all the robes of all the good judges that have ever lived on the face of the earth, and they would not be large enough to cover the iniquity of one corrupt judge.

HENRY WARD BEECHER, *PROVERBS FROM PLYMOUTH PULPIT* (1887)

4. To an incompetent judge I must not lie, but I may be silent; to a competent I must answer.

JOHN DONNE, *SERMONS*, NO. 67, (1630)

5. Conservative political opinion in America cleaves to the tradition of the judge as passive interpreter, believing that his absolute loyalty to authoritative law is the price of his immunity from political pressure and of the security of his tenure.

LEARNED HAND, *THE SPIRIT OF LIBERTY* (1959)

6. The profession of the law of which he [a judge] is a part is charged with the articulation and final incidence of the successive efforts towards justice; it must feel the circulation of the communal blood or it will wither and drop off, a useless member.

LEARNED HAND, *THE SPIRIT OF LIBERTY* (1959)

7. Judges commonly are elderly men, and are more likely to hate at sight any analysis to which they are not accustomed, and which disturbs repose of mind, than to fall in love with novelties.

OLIVER WENDELL HOLMES, JR., ADDRESS, NEW YORK STATE BAR ASSOCIATION, JAN. 17, 1899

8. The judge should not be young; he should have learned to know evil, not from his own soul, but from late and long observation of the nature of evil in others.

PLATO, *THE REPUBLIC* (4TH C. B.C.), 3, TR. BENJAMIN JOWETT

9. He who the sword of heaven will bear / Should be as holy as severe.

SHAKESPEARE, *MEASURE FOR MEASURE* (1604–05), 3.2.275

10. The worthy administrators of justice are like a cat set to take care of a cheese, lest it should be gnawed by the mice. One bite of the cat does more damage to the cheese than twenty mice can do.

VOLTAIRE, "ALLEGORY," *PHILOSOPHICAL DICTIONARY* (1764)

515. JUDGING OTHERS

See also 206. CRITICISM; 663. OTHERS

1. Every man is entitled to be valued by his best moment.

EMERSON, "BEAUTY," *THE CONDUCT OF LIFE* (1860)

2. [W]hile we allow the inhabitants of imaginary remote corners the authenticity of savages or suffer-

ers, we rarely suppose them to possess the authenticity of complex, sophisticated perceptions.

EVA HOFFMAN, *EXIT INTO HISTORY* (1993)

3. To judge a man means nothing more than to ask: What content does he give to the form of humanity? What concept should we have of humanity if he were its only representative?

WILHELM VON HUMBOLDT, *ÜBER DEN GEIST DER MENSCHHEIT* (1797)

4. Our natural egoism leads us to judge people by their relations to ourselves. We want them to be certain things to us, and for us that is what they are; because the rest of them is no good to us, we ignore it.

W. SOMERSET MAUGHAM, *THE SUMMING UP* (1938), 20

5. When we come to judge others it is not by ourselves as we really are that we judge them, but by an image that we have formed of ourselves from which we have left out everything that offends our vanity or would discredit us in the eyes of the world.

W. SOMERSET MAUGHAM, *THE SUMMING UP* (1938), 16

6. Do not judge, and you will never be mistaken.

ROUSSEAU, *ÉMILE* (1762), 3

7. I do not judge men by anything they can do. Their greatest deed is the impression they make on me.

THOREAU, *JOURNAL*, FEB. 18, 1841

516. JUDGMENT

See also 455. IMPARTIALITY

1. So long as the judge is happy.

ARABIC PROVERB

2. Nothing, it appears to me, is of greater value in a man than the power of judgment; and the man who has it may be compared to a chest filled with books, for he is the son of nature and the father of art.

PIETRO ARETINO, LETTER TO FAUSTO LONGIANO, DEC. 17, 1537, TR. SAMUEL PUTNAM

3. For all right judgment of any man or thing it is useful, nay, essential, to see his good qualities before pronouncing on his bad.

THOMAS CARLYLE, "GOETHE," *EDINBURGH REVIEW*, 1828

4. In judgement be ye not too confident, / Even as a man who will appraise his corn / When standing in a field, ere it is ripe.

DANTE, "PARADISO," 13, *THE DIVINE COMEDY* (C. 1300–21), TR. LAWRENCE GRANT WHITE

5. Rightness of judgment is bitterness to the heart.

EURIPIDES, *HIPPOLYTUS* (428 B.C.), TR. DAVID GRENE

6. In order to judge properly, one must get away somewhat from what one is judging, after having loved it.

ANDRÉ GIDE, "PORTRAITS AND APHORISMS," *PRETEXTS* (1903), TR. OTHERS

7. Familiarity confounds all traits of distinction: interest and prejudice take away the power of judging.

WILLIAM HAZLITT, "ON THE KNOWLEDGE OF CHARACTER," *TABLE TALK* (1821–22)

8. A mistake in judgment isn't fatal, but too much anxiety about judgment is.

PAULINE KAEL, "ZEITGEIST AND POLTERGEIST," *I LOST IT AT THE MOVIES* (1965)

9. Such as every man is inwardly so he judgeth outwardly.

THOMAS À KEMPIS, *THE IMITATION OF CHRIST* (1426), 2.4

10. Everyone complains of his memory, but no one complains of his judgment.

LA ROCHEFOUCAULD, *MAXIMS* (1665), TR. KENNETH PRATT

11. He that judges without informing himself to the utmost that he is capable, cannot acquit himself of judging amiss.

JOHN LOCKE, *AN ESSAY CONCERNING HUMAN UNDERSTANDING* (1690), 2.21

12. The ultimate cynicism is to suspend judgment so that you are not judged.

MARYA MANNES, "INTRODUCING MYSELF," *MORE IN ANGER* (1958)

13. The judgment is an utensil proper for all subjects, and will have an oar in everything.

MONTAIGNE, "OF DEMOCRITUS AND HERACLITUS," *ESSAYS* (1580–88), TR. W. C. HAZLITT

14. We easily enough confess in others an advantage of courage, strength, experience, activity, and beauty; but an advantage in judgment we yield to none.

MONTAIGNE, "OF PRESUMPTION," *ESSAYS* (1580–88), TR. W. C. HAZLITT

15. We praise or blame as one or the other affords more opportunity for exhibiting our power of judgement.

NIETZSCHE, *HUMAN, ALL TOO HUMAN* (1878), 86, TR. HELEN ZIMMERN

16. 'Tis with our judgements as our watches, none / Go just alike, yet each believes his own.

ALEXANDER POPE, *AN ESSAY ON CRITICISM* (1711), 1.9

17. A hasty judgment is a first step to recantation.

PUBLILIUS SYRUS, *MORAL SAYINGS* (1ST C. B.C.), 8, TR. DARIUS LYMAN

18. It is one thing to lack a heart and another to possess eyes and a just imagination.

GEORGE SANTAYANA, *THE LIFE OF REASON: REASON IN RELIGION* (1905–06), 10

19. Reason wishes that the judgment it gives be just; anger wishes that the judgment it has given seem to be just.

SENECA, *ON ANGER* (1ST C.)

20. Men, generally going with the stream, seldom judge for themselves, and purity of taste is almost as rare as talent.

VOLTAIRE, "AMPLIFICATION," *PHILOSOPHICAL DICTIONARY* (1764)

517. JUSTICE

See also 455. IMPARTIALITY; 477. INJUSTICE; 514. JUDGES; 534. LENIENCY

1. All virtue is summed up in dealing justly.

ARISTOTLE, *NICOMACHEAN ETHICS* (4TH C. B.C.), 5.1, TR. J. A. K. THOMSON

2. Somehow, our sense of justice never turns in its sleep till long after the sense of injustice in others has been thoroughly aroused.

MAX BEERBOHM, "SERVANTS," *AND EVEN NOW* (1920)

3. It's perfectly obvious that somebody's responsible and somebody's innocent. Otherwise it [justice] makes no sense at all.

UGO BETTI, *LANDSCAPE* (1936), 3, TR. G. H. MCWILLIAM

4. [W]hen a woman gets the idea of justice, there's no teaching her any sense.

JOYCE CARY, *THE HORSE'S MOUTH* (1944)

5. There is a difference between justice and consideration in one's relations to one's fellow men. It is the function of justice not to do wrong to one's fellow men; of considerateness, not to wound their feelings.

CICERO, *DE OFFICIIS* (44 B.C.), 1.28.99

6. The victim to too severe a law is considered as a martyr rather than a criminal.

CHARLES CALEB COLTON, *LACON* (1825), 2.139

7. Men are too unstable to be just; they are crabbed because they have not passed water at the usual time, or testy because they have not been stroked or praised.

EDWARD DAHLBERG, *THE SORROWS OF PRIAPUS* (1957)

8. Many have justice in their hearts, but slowly it is let fly, for it comes not without council to the bow.

DANTE, "PURGATORIO," 6, *THE DIVINE COMEDY* (C. 1300–21), TR. P. H. WICKSTEED

9. Justice is always violent to the party offending, for every man is innocent in his own eyes.

DANIEL DEFOE, *THE SHORTEST WAY WITH THE DISSENTERS* (1702)

10. How can justice fall victim, ever, to what is right?

PHILIP K. DICK, *A SCANNER DARKLY* (1977)

11. I tell ye Hogan's r-right whin he says: "Justice is blind." Blind she is, an' deef an' dumb an' has a wooden leg!

FINLEY PETER DUNNE, "CROSS-EXAMINATIONS," *MR. DOOLEY'S OPINIONS* (1901)

12. In this counthry [America] a man is presoomed to be guilty ontil he's proved guilty an' afther that he's presoomed to be innocent.

FINLEY PETER DUNNE, "ON CRIMINAL TRIALS," *MR. DOOLEY ON MAKING A WILL* (1919)

13. There is no such thing as justice in the abstract; it is merely a compact between men.

EPICURUS, "PRINCIPAL DOCTRINES" (3RD C. B.C.), 33, IN *LETTERS, PRINCIPAL DOCTRINES, AND VATICAN SAYINGS*, TR. RUSSEL M. GEER

14. Keep alive the light of justice, / And much that men say in blame will pass you by.

EURIPIDES, *THE SUPPLIANT WOMEN* (C. 421 B.C.), TR. FRANK W. JONES

15. If we could just figure out how to have more fun at it, maybe more of us would join the ranks of those who seek after justice and mercy.

ROBERT FULGHUM, *IT WAS ON FIRE WHEN I LAY DOWN ON IT* (1989)

16. Justice will not condemn even the Devil himself wrongfully.

THOMAS FULLER, M.D., *GNOMOLOGIA* (1732), 3116

17. Rigid justice is the greatest injustice.

THOMAS FULLER, M.D., *GNOMOLOGIA* (1732), 4055

18. A great deal may be done by severity, more by love, but most by clear discernment and impartial justice.

GOETHE, QUOTED IN JOHANN PETER ECKERMANN'S *CONVERSATIONS WITH GOETHE,* MARCH 22, 1825

19. If a man destroy the eye of another man, they shall destroy his eye.

HAMMURABI, *CODE* (C. 2030 B.C.)

20. Our common law is the stock instance of a combination of custom and its successive adaptations.

LEARNED HAND, *THE SPIRIT OF LIBERTY* (1959)

21. [W]ith the appearance of the modern working class, driven to economic and political organization by the necessities of daily life, a social force had come into being that would be impelled toward the theory and practice of justice.

MICHAEL HARRINGTON, *THE ACCIDENTAL CENTURY* (1966)

22. If you study the history and records of the world you must admit that the source of justice was the fear of injustice.

HORACE, *SATIRES* (35–30 B.C.), 1.3

23. When you cannot be just through virtue, be so through pride.

EUGENIO MARÍA DE HOSTOS, "HOMBRES E IDEAS," *OBRAS* (1939–54), 14

24. Justice should remove the bandage from her eyes long enough to distinguish between the vicious and the unfortunate.

ROBERT G. INGERSOLL, *PROSE-POEMS AND SELECTIONS* (1884)

25. Every one loves justice in the affairs of another.

ITALIAN PROVERB

26. Justice is the right of the weakest.

JOSEPH JOUBERT, *PENSÉES* (1842), 15.17

27. Justice delayed is democracy denied.

ROBERT F. KENNEDY, "TO SECURE THESE RIGHTS," *THE PURSUIT OF JUSTICE* (1964)

28. Justice is the very last thing of all wherewith the universe concerns itself. It is equilibrium that absorbs its attention.

MAURICE MAETERLINCK, *WISDOM AND DESTINY* (1898), 79, TR. ALFRED SUTRO

29. Injustice is relatively easy to bear; what stings is justice.

H. L. MENCKEN, *PREJUDICES: THIRD SERIES* (1922), 3

30. For one crime which is expiated in prison ten thousand are committed thoughtlessly by those who condemn.

HENRY MILLER, "THE SOUL OF ANAESTHESIA," *THE AIR-CONDITIONED NIGHTMARE* (1945)

31. Even the laws of justice themselves cannot subsist without mixture of injustice.

MONTAIGNE, "THAT WE TASTE NOTHING PURE," *ESSAYS* (1580–88), TR. W. C. HAZLITT

32. In matters of government, justice means force as well as virtue.

NAPOLEON I, *MAXIMS* (1804–15)

33. Social justice and compassion are compatible with an intelligent respect for private enterprise and law and order.

CAMILLE PAGLIA, *SEX, ART, AND AMERICAN CULTURE* (1992)

34. We see neither justice nor injustice which does not change its nature with change in climate. Three degrees of latitude reverse all jurisprudence; a meridian decides the truth.

PASCAL, *PENSÉES* (1670), 294, TR. W. F. TROTTER

35. Everywhere there is one principle of justice, which is the interest of the stronger.

PLATO, *THE REPUBLIC* (4TH C. B.C.), I, TR. BENJAMIN JOWETT

36. No one should be judge in his own cause.

PUBLILIUS SYRUS, *MORAL SAYINGS* (1ST C. B.C.), 545, TR. DARIUS LYMAN

37. The judge is condemned when the criminal is acquitted.

PUBLILIUS SYRUS, *MORAL SAYINGS* (1ST C. B.C.), 407, TR. DARIUS LYMAN

38. Extreme justice is often unjust.

RACINE, *THE THEBAID* (1664), 4.3

39. There is a justice, but we do not always see it. Discreet, smiling, it is there, at one side, a little behind injustice, which makes a big noise.

JULES RENARD, *JOURNAL*, DECEMBER 1906, TR. ELIZABETH ROGET

40. It is impossible to be just if one is not generous.

JOSEPH ROUX, *MEDITATIONS OF A PARISH PRIEST* (1886), 4.109, TR. ISABEL F. HAPGOOD

41. We love justice greatly, and just men but little.

JOSEPH ROUX, *MEDITATIONS OF A PARISH PRIEST* (1886), 4.10, TR. ISABEL F. HAPGOOD

42. The jury, passing on the prisoner's life, / May in the sworn twelve have a thief or two / Guiltier than him they try.

SHAKESPEARE, *MEASURE FOR MEASURE* (1604–05), 2.1.19

43. Use every man after his desert, and who should scape whipping?

SHAKESPEARE, *HAMLET* (1600), 2.2.555

44. Justice is impartiality. Only strangers are impartial.

GEORGE BERNARD SHAW, *BACK TO METHUSELAH* (1921), 3

45. Be just before you're generous.

RICHARD BRINSLEY SHERIDAN, *THE SCHOOL FOR SCANDAL* (1777), 4.1

46. A man who deals in fairness with his own, / he can make manifest justice in the state.

SOPHOCLES, *ANTIGONE* (442–41 B.C.), TR. ELIZABETH WYCKOFF

47. If they are just, they are better than clever.

SOPHOCLES, *PHILOCTETES* (409 B.C.), TR. DAVID GRENE

48. There are times when even justice brings harm with it.

SOPHOCLES, *ELECTRA* (C. 418–14 B.C.), TR. DAVID GRENE

49. At best—which is to say, even where our knowledge of a case comes to us only through courtroom evidence—it is difficult for the legal process to keep us at a sanitizing distance from crimes of passion.

DIANA TRILLING, *MRS. HARRIS: THE DEATH OF THE SCARSDALE DOCTOR* (1981)

50. It is better to risk saving a guilty man than to condemn an innocent one.

VOLTAIRE, *ZADIG* (1747), 6

51. Justice is the great interest of man on earth.

DANIEL WEBSTER, ON MR. JUSTICE STORY, SEPT. 12, 1845

52. No man can be just who is not free.

WOODROW WILSON, ACCEPTANCE SPEECH, DEMOCRATIC NATIONAL CONVENTION, JULY 7, 1912

JUVENILE DELINQUENCY

See 204. CRIME

K

518. KILLING

See also 1032. VIOLENCE; 1042. WAR

1. The worst thing that can be said of the most powerful is that they can take your life; but the same thing can be said of the most weak.

CHARLES CALEB COLTON, *LACON* (1825), 1.456

2. Assassination has never changed the history of the world.

BENJAMIN DISRAELI, SPEECH, MAY 1865

3. Every premeditated murder is always governed by a preparatory ceremonial and is always followed by a propitiatory ceremonial. The meaning of both eludes the murderer's mind.

JEAN GENET, *OUR LADY OF THE FLOWERS* (1949)

4. What can you do by killing? Nothing. You kill one dog, the master buys another—that's all there is to it.

MAXIM GORKY, *ENEMIES* (1906), 2

5. [Lincoln, answering friends who advised him to seek protection against assassination:] "If they kill me the next man will be just as bad for them. In a country like this, where our habits are simple, and must be, assassination is always possible, and will come if they are determined upon it."

WILLIAM H. HERNDON, *HERNDON'S LIFE OF LINCOLN* (1888)

6. Whom man kills, him God restoreth to life.

VICTOR HUGO, "FANTINE," *LES MISÉRABLES* (1862), 1.4, TR. CHARLES E. WILBOUR

7. What does the earth look like in the places where people commit atrocities? Is there a bad smell, a genius loci, something about the landscape that might incriminate?

ROBERT D. KAPLAN, *BALKAN GHOSTS* (1993)

8. The overfaithful sword returns the user / His heart's desire at price of his heart's blood.

RUDYARD KIPLING, "THE PRO-CONSULS (LORD MILNER)" (1905)

9. Must we kill to prevent there being any wicked? This is to make both parties wicked instead of one.

PASCAL, *PENSÉES* (1670), 910, TR. W. F. TROTTER

10. One kills a man, one is an assassin; one kills millions, one is a conqueror; one kills everybody, one is a god.

JEAN ROSTAND, *PENSÉES D'UN BIOLOGISTE* (1939)

11. A sword never kills anybody; it's a tool in the killer's hand.

SENECA, *LETTERS TO LUCILIUS* (1ST C.), 87.30, TR. E. PHILLIPS BARKER

12. It hath the primal eldest curse upon't, A brother's murder!

SHAKESPEARE, *HAMLET* (1600), 3.3.37

13. There is no sure foundation set on blood, / No certain life achieved by others' death.

SHAKESPEARE, *KING JOHN* (1596–97), 4.2.104

14. He who bears the brand of Cain shall rule the earth.

GEORGE BERNARD SHAW, *BACK TO METHUSELAH* (1921), 1.2

15. It is long and hard and painful to create life: it is short and easy to steal the life others have made.

GEORGE BERNARD SHAW, *BACK TO METHUSELAH* (1921), 1.2

16. No humane being, past the thoughtless age of boyhood, will wantonly murder any creature which holds its life by the same tenure that he does.

THOREAU, "HIGHER LAWS," *WALDEN* (1854)

17. It is forbidden to kill; therefore all murderers are punished who kill not in large companies, and to the sound of trumpets.

VOLTAIRE, "RIGHTS," *PHILOSOPHICAL DICTIONARY* (1764)

519. KINDNESS

See also 120. CHARITY; 379. GENTLENESS; 384. GIFTS AND GIVING; 1018. UNKINDNESS

1. There is no sickness worse / for me than words that to be kind must lie.

Aeschylus, *Prometheus Bound* (c. 478 B.C.), tr. David Grene

2. The unfortunate need people who will be kind to them; the prosperous need people to be kind to.

Aristotle, *Nicomachean Ethics* (4th c. B.C.), 9.9, tr. J. A. K. Thomson

3. Kindness, n. A brief preface to ten volumes of exaction.

Ambrose Bierce, *The Devil's Dictionary* (1881–1911)

4. The drying up a single tear has more / Of honest fame, than shedding seas of gore.

Byron, *Don Juan* (1819–24), 8.3

5. Kindness acts / Not always as you think; a hated hand / Renders it odious.

Corneille, *Cinna* (1639), 1.2, tr. Paul Landis

6. By Chivalries as tiny, / A Blossom, or a Book, / The seeds of smiles are planted— / Which Blossom in the dark.

Emily Dickinson, poem (c. 1858)

7. There is no beautifier of complexion, or form, or behavior, like the wish to scatter joy and not pain around us.

Emerson, "Behavior," *The Conduct of Life* (1860)

8. Unseasonable kindness gets no thanks.

Thomas Fuller, M.D., *Gnomologia* (1732), 5407

9. True kindness presupposes the faculty of imagining as one's own the suffering and joys of others.

André Gide, "Portraits and Aphorisms," *Pretexts* (1903), tr. others

10. Kindness can become its own motive. We are made kind by being kind.

Eric Hoffer, *The Passionate State of Mind* (1954), 123

11. Always set a high value on spontaneous kindness. He whose inclination prompts him to cultivate your friendship of his own accord, will love you more than one whom you have been at pains to attach to you.

Samuel Johnson, quoted in Boswell's *Life of Samuel Johnson,* c. May 1781

12. Nature, in giving tears to man, confessed that he / Had a tender heart; this is our noblest quality.

Juvenal, *Satires* (c. 100), 15.132, tr. Hubert Creekmore

13. He greeted us with that extra degree of kindness and hospitality which I had noticed in so many Americans; it always gave me the uncomfortable feeling that, no matter how long I lived among them, I should never quite be able to rise to their level of genuine cordiality with strangers.

Jessica Mitford, *Daughters and Rebels* (1960)

14. Do not ask me to be kind; just ask me to act as though I were.

Jules Renard, *Journal,* April 1898, tr. lizabeth Roget

15. Human kindness has never weakened the stamina or softened the fiber of a free people. A nation does not have to be cruel to be tough.

Franklin D. Roosevelt, radio address, Oct. 13, 1940

16. Give nobody's heart pain so long as thou canst avoid it, for one sigh may set a whole world into a flame.

Sa'di, *Gulistan* (1258), 1.26, tr. James Ross

17. Kindness it is that brings forth kindness always.

Sophocles, *Ajax* (c. 447 B.C.), tr. John Moore

18. One who knows how to show and to accept kindness / will be a friend better than any possession.

Sophocles, *Philoctetes* (409 B.C.), tr. David Grene

19. Men are cruel, but Man is kind.

Rabindranath Tagore, *Stray Birds* (1916), 219

20. Kind hearts are more than coronets, / And simple faith than Norman blood.

Lord Tennyson, *Lady Clara Vere de Vere* (1833), 7

21. Benevolence is the characteristic element of humanity, and the great exercise of it is in loving relatives.

Tze-Sze, *The Doctrine of the Mean* (5th c. B.C.), 20.5, tr. James Legge

22. That best portion of a good man's life, / His little, nameless, unremembered acts / Of kindness and of love.

William Wordsworth, "Lines Composed a Few Miles Above Tintern Abbey" (1798)

520. KINGS

See also 196. Court, Royal; 395. Government; 829. Royalty; 831. Rulers

1. Fear created gods; audacity created kings.

Prosper Jolyot Crébillon, *Xerxès* (1714), 1.1

2. In a few years there will be only five kings in the world—the King of England and the four kings in a pack of cards.

King Farouk I Of Egypt, *Life,* April 10, 1950

3. It is no bad thing to be a king—to see one's house enriched and one's authority enhanced.

Homer, *Odyssey* (9th c. b.c.), 1, tr. E. V. Rieu

4. A monarch frequently represents his subjects better than an elected assembly; and if he is a good judge of character he is likely to have more capable and loyal advisers.

William Ralph Inge, "Our Present Discontents," *Outspoken Essays: First Series* (1919)

5. What are kings, when regiment is gone, / But perfect shadows in a sunshine day?

Christopher Marlowe, *Edward II* (c. 1593), 5.1

6. A king can stand people's fighting but he can't last long if people start thinking.

Will Rogers, *The Autobiography of Will Rogers* (1949), 8

7. Kings stand more in need of the company of the intelligent than the intelligent do of the society of kings.

Sa'di, *Gulistan* (1258), 8.6, tr. James Ross

8. A king is he who has laid fear aside and the base longings of an evil heart; whom ambition unrestrained and the fickle favor of the reckless mob move not.

Seneca, *Thyestes* (1st c.), 348, tr. Frank Justus Miller

9. The foremost art of kings is the power to endure hatred.

Seneca, *Hercules Furens* (1st c.), 353

10. Not all the water in the rough rude sea / Can wash the balm off from an anointed king.

Shakespeare, *King Richard II* (1595–96), 3.2.54

11. Kings are like stars—they rise and set, they have / The worship of the world, but no repose.

Shelley, *Hellas* (1821)

12. [O]ne advantage of a monarchy is that a monarchy does not suffer the effects of having great clots of white Christians moping around simply because they aren't the king or queen.

Calvin Trillin, "Growing Up to Be President," *Uncivil Liberties* (1982)

13. All kings is mostly rapscallions.

Mark Twain, *The Adventures of Huckleberry Finn* (1884), 1

521. KISSING

1. [T]hose quite useless articles called "kisses."

Lewis Carroll, *The Letters of Lewis Carroll,* ed. Morton N. Cohen (1979)

2. kisses are a better fate / than wisdom.

e. e. cummings, "since feeling is first," *100 Selected Poems* (1959)

3. We turned on one another deep, drowned gazes, and exchanged a kiss that reduced my bones to rubber and my brain to gruel.

Peter De Vries, *Comfort Me With Apples* (1956)

4. "Kiss me. Again. Once more." Commands to be obeyed when issued by a woman.

Lawrence Durrell, *Monsieur* (1974)

5. The kiss originated when the first male reptile licked the first female reptile, implying in a subtle, complimentary way that she was as succulent as the small reptile he had for dinner the night before.

F. Scott Fitzgerald, "The Note-Books," *The Crack-Up* (1945)

6. I kissed her hard and held her tight and tried to open her lips; they were closed tight.

Ernest Hemingway, *A Farewell to Arms* (1929)

7. Kissing don't last: cookery do!

George Meredith, *The Ordeal of Richard Feverel* (1859), 28

8. A kiss can be a comma, a question mark or an exclamation point. That's basic spelling that every woman ought to know.

Mistinguett, *Theatre Arts,* December 1955

9. A kiss, when all is said, what is it? / An oath that's given closer than before; / A promise more precise; the sealing of / Confessions that till then were barely breathed; / A rosy dot placed on the i in loving.

Edmond Rostand, *Cyrano de Bergerac* (1897), 3.10, tr. Charles Renauld

10. Though I know he loves me, / Tonight my heart is sad; / His kiss was not so wonderful / As all the dreams I had.

Sara Teasdale, "The Kiss," *Helen of Troy* (1911)

11. Without stopping to be sorry for her head he crammed kisses in her mouth, and she wound her

arms up around his own drenched head and returned him kiss for kiss.

EUDORA WELTY, *LOSING BATTLES* (1970)

522. KNOWLEDGE

See also 447. IGNORANCE; 532. LEARNING; 848. SCHOLARS AND SCHOLARSHIP; 1007. UNDERSTANDING; 1019. THE UNKNOWN

1. Knowledge is power.

FRANCIS BACON, "DE HAERESIBUS," *MEDITATIONES SACRAE* (1597)

2. The acquisition of knowledge always involves the revelation of ignorance—almost *is* the revelation of ignorance.

WENDELL BERRY, "PEOPLE, LAND, AND COMMUNITY," *STANDING BY WORDS* (1983)

3. Many men are stored full of unused knowledge. Like loaded guns that are never fired off, or military magazines in times of peace, they are stuffed with useless ammunition.

HENRY WARD BEECHER, *PROVERBS FROM PLYMOUTH PULPIT* (1887)

4. The raft of knowledge ferries the worst sinner to safety.

BHAGAVADGITA, 4, TR. P. LAL

5. He that increaseth knowledge increaseth sorrow.

BIBLE, ECCLESIASTES 1:18

6. The paradox of knowledge is not confined to the small, atomic scale; on the contrary, it is as cogent on the scale of man, and even of the stars.

JACOB BRONOWSKI, *THE ASCENT OF MAN* (1973)

7. Knowledge is a comfortable and necessary retreat and shelter for us in an advanced age; and if we do not plant it while young, it will give us no shade when we grow old.

LORD CHESTERFIELD, *LETTERS TO HIS SON,* DEC. 11, 1747

8. To know a little of anything gives neither satisfaction nor credit, but often brings disgrace or ridicule.

LORD CHESTERFIELD, *LETTERS TO HIS SON,* OCT. 4, 1746

9. Knowledge is two-fold, and consists not only in an affirmation of what is true, but in the negation of that which is false.

CHARLES CALEB COLTON, *LACON* (1825), 1.181

10. Learning without thought is labour lost; thought without learning is perilous.

CONFUCIUS, *ANALECTS* (6TH C. B.C.), 2.15, TR. JAMES LEGGE

11. When you know a thing, to hold that you know it, and when you do not know a thing, to allow that you do not know it: this is knowledge.

CONFUCIUS, *ANALECTS* (6TH C. B.C.), 2.17, TR. JAMES LEGGE

12. Knowledge is power. Unfortunate dupes of this saying will keep on reading, ambitiously, till they have stunned their native initiative, and made their thoughts weak.

CLARENCE DAY, *THIS SIMIAN WORLD* (1920), 9

13. It is knowledge that influences and equalizes the social condition of man; that gives to all, however different their political position, passions which are in common, and enjoyments which are universal.

BENJAMIN DISRAELI, SPEECH, "THE VALUE OF LITERATURE TO MEN OF BUSINESS," OCT. 23, 1844

14. There is no subject so old that something new cannot be said about it.

DOSTOYEVSKY, *A DIARY OF A WRITER* (1876), 3, JULY–AUGUST

15. A man should keep his little brain attic stocked with all the furniture that he is likely to use, and the rest he can put away in the lumber-room of his library, where he can get it if he wants it.

SIR ARTHUR CONAN DOYLE, "FIVE ORANGE PIPS," *THE ADVENTURES OF SHERLOCK HOLMES* (1891)

16. If I cannot brag of knowing something, then I brag of not knowing it.

EMERSON, *JOURNALS,* 1866

17. If you would know what nobody knows, read what everybody reads, just one year afterwards.

EMERSON, *JOURNALS,* 1834

18. Why / do we make so much of knowledge, struggle so hard / to get some little skill not worth the effort?

EURIPIDES, *HECUBA* (C. 425 B.C.), TR. WILLIAM ARROWSMITH

19. To be proud of knowledge is to be blind with light.

BENJAMIN FRANKLIN, *POOR RICHARD'S ALMANACK* (1732–57)

20. 'Tis not knowing much, but what is useful, that makes a wise man.

THOMAS FULLER, M.D., *GNOMOLOGIA* (1732), 5097

21. Books and newspapers assume a "common reader," that is, a person who knows the things known by other literate persons in the culture. Obviously, such assumptions are never identical from writer to writer, but they show a remarkable consistency.

E.D. Hirsch, Jr., *Cultural Literacy* (1987)

22. To be master of any branch of knowledge, you must master those which lie next to it; and thus to know anything you must know all.

Oliver Wendell Holmes, Jr., lecture, Harvard University, Feb. 17, 1886

23. Knowledge and timber shouldn't be much used till they are seasoned.

Oliver Wendell Holmes, Sr., *The Autocrat of the Breakfast Table* (1858), 6

24. If a little knowledge is dangerous, where is the man who has so much as to be out of danger?

Thomas Henry Huxley, "On Elemental Instruction in Physiology" (1877)

25. The fruit of the tree of knowledge always drives man from some paradise or other; and even the paradise of fools is not an unpleasant abode while it is habitable.

William Ralph Inge, "The Idea of Progress," *Outspoken Essays: Second Series* (1922)

26. A desire of knowledge is the natural feeling of mankind; and every human being, whose mind is not debauched, will be willing to give all that he has to get knowledge.

Samuel Johnson, quoted in Boswell's *Life of Samuel Johnson,* July 30, 1763

27. All knowledge is of itself of some value. There is nothing so minute or inconsiderable, that I would not rather know it than not.

Samuel Johnson, quoted in Boswell's *Life of Samuel Johnson,* April 10, 1775

28. Knowledge is of two kinds: we know a subject ourselves, or we know where we can find information upon it.

Samuel Johnson, quoted in Boswell's *Life of Samuel Johnson,* April 18, 1775

29. Man is not weak, knowledge is more than equivalent to force. The master of mechanics laughs at strength.

Samuel Johnson, *Rasselas* (1759), 13

30. An extensive knowledge is needful to thinking people—it takes away the heat and fever; and helps, by widening speculation, to ease the burden of the mystery.

Keats, letter to John Hamilton Reynolds, May 3, 1818

31. Forasmuch as many people study more to have knowledge than to live well therefore ofttimes they err and bring forth little fruit or none.

Thomas à Kempis, *The Imitation of Christ* (1426), 1.3

32. Liberty without learning is always in peril, and learning without liberty is always in vain.

John F. Kennedy, address, Vanderbilt University, Nashville, Tenn., May 18, 1963

33. Knowledge is like money: to be of value it must circulate, and in circulating it can increase in quantity and, hopefully, in value.

Louis L'Amour, *Education of a Wandering Man* (1989)

34. To know things well, we must know them in detail; but as that is almost endless, our knowledge is always superficial and imperfect.

La Rochefoucauld, *Maxims* (1665), tr. Kenneth Pratt

35. Learning acquired in youth arrests the evil of old age; and if you understand that old age has wisdom for its food, you will so conduct yourself in youth that your old age will not lack for nourishment.

Leonardo Da Vinci, *Notebooks* (c. 1500), tr. Jean Paul Richter

36. Every step by which men add to their knowledge and skills is a step also by which they can control other men.

Max Lerner, "Manipulating Life," in the *New York Post,* Jan. 24, 1968

37. It is an anomaly that information, the one thing most necessary to our survival as choosers of our own way, should be a commodity subject to the same merchandising rules as chewing gum.

A.J. Liebling, *The Press* (1961)

38. A reading-machine, always wound up and going, / He mastered whatever was not worth the knowing.

James Russell Lowell, *A Fable for Critics* (1848)

39. There is no more merit in being able to attach a correct description to a picture than in being able to find out what is wrong with a stalled motorcar. In each case it is special knowledge.

W. Somerset Maugham, *The Summing Up* (1938), 24

40. In expanding the field of knowledge we but increase the horizon of ignorance.

Henry Miller, "The Wisdom of the Heart," *The Wisdom of the Heart* (1941)

41. Sin, guilt, neurosis—they are one and the same, the fruit of the tree of knowledge.

Henry Miller, "Creative Death," *The Wisdom of the Heart* (1941)

42. The first and wisest of them all professed / To know this only, that he nothing knew.

Milton, *Paradise Regained* (1671), 4.293

43. Without knowledge, life is no more than the shadow of death.

Molière, *The Would-be Gentleman* (1670), 2, tr. John Wood

44. Such is the constitution of the human mind, that any kind of knowledge, if it be really such, is its own reward.

John Henry Newman, *The Idea of a University* (1853–58), 1.5.2

45. Wisdom sets bounds even to knowledge.

Nietzsche, "Maxims and Missiles," 5, *Twilight of the Idols* (1888), tr. Anthony M. Ludovici

46. Knowledge is the true organ of sight, not the eyes.

Panchatantra (c. 5th c.), 2, tr. Franklin Edgerton

47. Learning, the destroyer of arrogance, begets arrogance in fools; even as light, that illumines the eye, makes owls blind.

Panchatantra (c. 5th c.), 1, tr. Franklin Edgerton

48. Since we cannot be universal and know all that is to be known of everything, we ought to know a little about everything.

Pascal, *Pensées* (1670), 37, tr. W. F. Trotter

49. Most people affirm pleasure to be the good, but the finer sort of wits say it is knowledge.

Plato, *The Republic* (4th c. b.c.), 6, tr. Benjamin Jowett

50. All knowledge that is divorced from justice must be called cunning.

Plato (5th–4th c. b.c.), quoted in Cicero's *De Officiis* (44 b.c.), 1.19.62, tr. Walter Miller

51. A little learning is a dangerous thing; / Drink deep, or taste not the Pierian spring: / There shallow draughts intoxicate the brain, / And drinking largely sobers us again.

Alexander Pope, *An Essay on Criticism* (1711), 2.15

52. What harm in getting knowledge even from a sot, a pot, a fool, a mitten, or an old slipper?

Rabelais, *Gargantua and Pantagruel* (1532–64), 3

53. Knowledge—that is, education in its true sense—is our best protection against unreasoning prejudice and panic-making fear, whether engendered by special interest, illiberal minorities, or panic-stricken leaders.

Franklin D. Roosevelt, speech, Boston, Oct. 31, 1932

54. Seeing is believing and believing is knowing and knowing beats unknowing and the unknown.

Philip Roth, *Zuckerman Unbound* (1981)

55. Whoever acquires knowledge and does not practise it resembles him who ploughs his land and leaves it unsown.

Sa'di, *Gulistan* (1258), 8.42, tr. James Ross

56. Learning is but an adjunct to ourself, / And where we are our learning likewise is.

Shakespeare, *Love's Labour's Lost* (1594–95), 4.3.314

57. The right to know is like the right to live. It is fundamental and unconditional in its assumption that knowledge, like life, is a desirable thing.

George Bernard Shaw, "Preface on Doctors: The Flaw in the Argument," *The Doctor's Dilemma* (1913)

58. The desire of knowledge, like the thirst of riches, increases ever with the acquisition of it.

Laurence Sterne, *Tristram Shandy* (1759–67), 2.3

59. If we value the pursuit of knowledge, we must be free to follow wherever that search may lead us. The free mind is no barking dog, to be tethered on a ten-foot chain.

Adlai Stevenson, speech, University of Wisconsin, Madison, Oct. 8, 1952

60. So much has already been written about everything that you can't find out anything about it.

James Thurber, "The New Vocabularianism," *Lanterns and Lances* (1961)

61. That knowledge which stops at what it does not know, is the highest knowledge.

Chuang Tzu, "The Music of Heaven and Earth" (4th–3rd c. b.c.), tr. Herbert A. Giles

62. I don't know nothing, I think. And glad of it.

ALICE WALKER, *THE COLOR PURPLE* (1982)

63. Knowledge is the only fountain both of the love and the principles of human liberty.

DANIEL WEBSTER, ON COMPLETION OF THE BUNKER HILL MONUMENT, BOSTON, MASS., JUNE 17, 1843

64. Knowledge, in truth, is the great sun in the firmament. Life and power are scattered with all its beams.

DANIEL WEBSTER, ADDRESS ON LAYING THE CORNERSTONE OF THE BUNKER HILL MONUMENT, BOSTON, MASS., JUNE 17, 1825

65. General knowledge may have to be slight or even amateurish knowledge, but it is none the less useful, and we discourage it at our peril.

C.V. WEDGWOOD, *HISTORY AND HOPE* (1987)

66. To live effectively is to live with adequate information.

NORBERT WIENER, *THE HUMAN USE OF HUMAN BEINGS* (1954), 1

67. Education is an admirable thing, but it is well to remember from time to time that nothing that is worth knowing can be taught.

OSCAR WILDE, "THE CRITIC AS ARTIST," *INTENTIONS* (1891)

68. I am still of the opinion that only two topics can be of the least interest to a serious and studious mind—sex and the dead.

WILLIAM BUTLER YEATS, LETTER TO OLIVIA SHAKESPEAR, OCTOBER 1927

69. Information is not knowledge, knowledge is not wisdom, wisdom is not truth, truth is not beauty, beauty is not love, love is not music. Music is the best.

FRANK ZAPPA, FROM *JOE'S GARAGE*, 1979, QUOTED IN *THE REAL FRANK ZAPPA BOOK* (1989), WITH PETER OCCHIOGROSSO

L

LABOR

See 1013. UNIONS; 1065. WORK

LABOR DAY

See 420. HOLIDAYS

LACK

See 236. DEPRIVATION; 625. NEED

LAND

See 337. FARMS AND FARMING; 746. PROPERTY

523. LADY

1. A lady's imagination is very rapid; it jumps from admiration to love, from love to matrimony in a moment.

JANE AUSTEN, *PRIDE AND PREJUDICE* (1813), 6

524. LANGUAGE

See also 35. ANALOGY; 134. CLARITY; 230. DEFINITION; 398. GRAMMAR; 923. SPEAKING; 942. STYLE; 1064. WORDS; 1069. WRITING AND WRITERS

1. Dialect tempered with slang is an admirable medium of communication between persons who have nothing to say and persons who would not care for anything properly said.

THOMAS BAILEY ALDRICH, "LEAVES FROM A NOTEBOOK," *PONKAPOG PAPERS* (1903)

2. Animal language is a contagious expression of mood effecting communication between social partners.

ROBERT ARDREY, *AFRICAN GENESIS* (1961)

3. The varieties of spoken American could not be counted, and most of them were incomprehensible to me, used as I was to the clean-cut pronunciation of Italian.

LUIGI BARZINI, *O AMERICA* (1977)

4. A great deal of Roosevelt's almost magical talent for persuading and manipulating the American people lay in his ability to state his thoughts in simple, homely phrases, in the language of the working neighborhood where visitors sat in the kitchen, with puppies frolicking under the stove, husbands wearing working clothes and wives their one-dollar house-dresses.

DAVID BRINKLEY, *WASHINGTON GOES TO WAR* (1988)

5. I am sure that the two main forms of English, American English and British English, separated geographically from the beginning and severed politically since 1776, are continuing to move apart, and that existing elements of linguistic dissimilarity between them will intensify as time goes on, notwithstanding the power of the cinema, TV, *Time Magazine*, and other two-way gluing and fuelling devices.

ROBERT BURCHFIELD, *UNLOCKING THE ENGLISH LANGUAGE* (1989)

6. In 1776, at the point of severance, except for an infusion of words from east coast Indian languages, the English language of North America was not in any radical way dissimilar from that of what the American settlers called the mother country.

ROBERT BURCHFIELD, *UNLOCKING THE ENGLISH LANGUAGE* (1989)

7. The language of [Doctor] Johnson and Mrs [Hester Lynch] Thrale, and that of their adult contemporaries, was the stately language of the time, polished, stylish, unordinary, even in the intimate pages of their diaries, and the regime of instruction was severe and practical.

ROBERT BURCHFIELD, *UNLOCKING THE ENGLISH LANGUAGE* (1989)

8. If language be not in accordance with the truth of things, affairs cannot be carried on to success.

CONFUCIUS, *ANALECTS* (6TH C. B.C.), 13.5, TR. JAMES LEGGE

9. To a teacher of language there comes a time when the world is but a place of many words and man appears a mere talking animal not much more wonderful than a parrot.

JOSEPH CONRAD, PROLOGUE TO PART I, *UNDER WESTERN EYES* (1911)

10. Correct English is the slang of prigs who write history and essays. And the strongest slang of all is the slang of poets.

GEORGE ELIOT, *MIDDLEMARCH* (1871–72), 2

11. Poetry should help, not only to refine the language of the time, but to prevent it from changing too rapidly.

T. S. ELIOT, "MILTON" (1947)

12. Language is the archives of history.

EMERSON, "THE POET," *ESSAYS: SECOND SERIES* (1844)

13. A sentence begins quite simply, then it undulates and expands, parentheses intervene like quick-set hedges, the flowers of comparison bloom, and three fields off, like a wounded partridge, crouches the principal verb, making one wonder as one picks it up, poor little thing, whether after all it was worth such a tramp, so many guns, and such expensive dogs, and what, after all, is its relation to the main subject, potted so gaily half a page back, and proving finally to have been in the accusative case.

E.M. FORSTER, "PROUST," *ABINGER HARVEST* (1936)

14. How did language develop? In much the same way as an economic order develops through the market—out of the voluntary interaction of individuals, in this case seeking to trade ideas or information or gossip rather than goods and services with one another.

MILTON FRIEDMAN & ROSE FRIEDMAN, *FREE TO CHOOSE* (1980)

15. Wherever illiteracy is a problem, it's as fundamental a problem as getting enough to eat or a place to sleep.

NORTHROP FRYE, *THE EDUCATED IMAGINATION* (1964)

16. The language of Mexicans springs from abysmal extremes of power and impotence, domination and resentment.

CARLOS FUENTES, "HOW I STARTED TO WRITE," IN *THE ART OF THE PERSONAL ESSAY* (1994), ED. PHILLIP LOPATE

17. Russian is a very deceptive language, because it looks easy at first: it's like setting out for a gentle stroll and realizing that you've committed yourself to scaling Himalayan peaks.

ARMAND HAMMER, *HAMMER* (1987), WITH NEIL LYNDON

18. Language,—human language,—after all is but little better than the croak and cackle of fowls, and other utterances of brute nature,—sometimes not so adequate.

NATHANIEL HAWTHORNE, *AMERICAN NOTE-BOOKS,* JULY 14, 1850

19. Language, if it throws a veil over our ideas, adds a softness and refinement to them, like that which the atmosphere gives to naked objects.

WILLIAM HAZLITT, "ON CLASSICAL EDUCATION," *THE ROUND TABLE* (1817)

20. Language is by its very nature a communal thing; that is, it expresses never the exact thing but a compromise—that which is common to you, me and everybody.

THOMAS ERNEST HULME, "ROMANTICISM AND CLASSICISM," *SPECULATIONS* (1923)

21. I am always sorry when any language is lost, because languages are the pedigree of nations.

SAMUEL JOHNSON, QUOTED IN BOSWELL'S *JOURNAL OF A TOUR TO THE HEBRIDES WITH SAMUEL JOHNSON,* SEPT. 18, 1773

22. If language is intimately related to being human, then when we study language we are, to a remarkable degree, studying human nature.

CHARLTON LAIRD, *THE MIRACLE OF LANGUAGE* (1953)

23. Language is a living thing. It must survive in men's minds and on their tongues if it survives at all.

CHARLTON LAIRD, *THE MIRACLE OF LANGUAGE* (1953)

24. You and I who read and write books have very little effect upon language. We may think about it, write about it, and read about it, but it goes on without us, or in spite of us.

CHARLTON LAIRD, *THE MIRACLE OF LANGUAGE* (1953)

25. Next in criminality to him who violates the laws of his country, is he who violates the language.

WALTER SAVAGE LANDOR, "ARCHDEACON HARE AND WALTER LANDOR," *IMAGINARY CONVERSATIONS* (1824–53)

26. [I]t seems inconceivable that a species of human could possess fully modern language and not be fully modern in all other ways, too. For this reason, the evolution of language is widely judged to be the culminating event in the emergence of humanity as we know it today.

RICHARD LEAKEY, *THE ORIGIN OF HUMANKIND* (1994)

27. [S]poken language clearly differentiates *Homo sapiens* from all other creatures. None but humankind produces a complex spoken language, a medium for communication and a medium for introspective reflection.

RICHARD LEAKEY, *THE ORIGIN OF HUMANKIND* (1994)

28. The only living language is the language in which we think and have our being.

ANTONIO MACHADO, *JUAN DE MAIRENA* (1943), 30, TR. BEN BELITT

29. Slang is a poor-man's poetry.

JOHN MOORE, *YOU ENGLISH WORDS* (1962)

30. Language, as we know, is full of illogicalities.

GUNNAR MYRDAL, *BEYOND THE WELFARE STATE* (1960)

31. Will America be the death of English? I'm glad I asked me that. My well-thought-out mature judgment is that it will.

EDWIN NEWMAN, *STRICTLY SPEAKING* (1974)

32. But if thought corrupts language, language can also corrupt thought. A bad usage can spread by tradition and imitation, even among people who should and do know better.

GEORGE ORWELL, "POLITICS AND THE ENGLISH LANGUAGE," *A COLLECTION OF ESSAYS* (1954)

33. Most people who bother with the matter at all would admit that the English language is in a bad way, but it is generally assumed that we cannot by conscious action do anything about it.

GEORGE ORWELL, "POLITICS AND THE ENGLISH LANGUAGE," *A COLLECTION OF ESSAYS* (1954)

34. The great enemy of clear language is insincerity. When there is a gap between one's real and one's declared aims, one turns as it were instinctively to long words and exhausted idioms, like a cuttlefish squirting out ink.

GEORGE ORWELL, "POLITICS AND THE ENGLISH LANGUAGE," *SHOOTING AN ELEPHANT* (1950)

35. Language lies outside of society because it is its foundation; but it also lies within society because that is the only place where it exists and the only place where it develops.

OCTAVIO PAZ, "THE VERBAL PACT AND CORRESPONDENCE," *ALTERNATING CURRENT* (1973)

36. The sum of human wisdom is not contained in any one language, and no single language is CAPABLE of expressing all forms and degrees of human comprehension.

EZRA POUND, *THE ABC OF READING* (1934), 1.3

37. To grasp the meaning of the world of today we use a language created to express the world of yesterday. The life of the past seems to us nearer our true natures, but only for the reason that it is nearer our language.

SAINT-EXUPÉRY, *WIND, SAND, AND STARS* (1939), 3, TR. LEWIS GALANTIÈRE

38. Slang is a language that rolls up its sleeves, spits on its hands and goes to work.

CARL SANDBURG, *THE NEW YORK TIMES,* FEB. 13, 1959

39. It were as wise to cast a violet into a crucible that you might discover the formal principle of its colour and odour, as seek to transfuse from one language into another the creations of a poet.

SHELLEY, *A DEFENCE OF POETRY* (1821)

40. Yiddish has a down-to-earth quality that makes it remote from high-flown rhetoric, and it has a catch-as-catch-can charm derived from its stunning variety—of syntax, spelling, pronunciation, and vocabulary—from region to region.

ISRAEL SHENKER, *COAT OF MANY COLORS* (1985)

41. The pressure on language to deteriorate does not come merely from below, from the "democratic" levelers. It comes also from above, from the fancy jargonmongers, idle game players, fashionable coteries for second-rate intellectuals.

JOHN SIMON, "THE CORRUPTION OF ENGLISH," IN *THE STATE OF THE LANGUAGE* (1980) EDS. LEONARD MICHAELS AND CHRISTOPHER RICKS

42. The alphabet was a great invention, which enabled men to store and to learn with little effort what others had learned the hard way—that is, to learn from books rather than from direct, possibly painful, contact with the real world.

B.F. SKINNER, *BEYOND FREEDOM AND DIGNITY* (1971)

43. *Battered women* is a phrase that uncovered major, long-hidden violence. It helps us to face the fact that, statistically speaking, the most dangerous place for a woman is in her own home, not in the streets.

GLORIA STEINEM, "WORDS AND CHANGE," *OUTRAGEOUS ACTS AND EVERYDAY REBELLIONS* (1983)

44. It begins to look, more and more disturbingly, as if the gift of language is the single human trait that marks us all genetically, setting us apart from all the rest of life.

LEWIS THOMAS, "SOCIAL TALK," *THE LIVES OF A CELL* (1974)

45. Where shall we look for standard English, but to the words of a standard man?

THOREAU, "SUNDAY," *A WEEK ON THE CONCORD AND MERRIMACK RIVERS* (1849)

46. Ours is a precarious language, as every writer knows, in which the merest shadow line often separates affirmation from negation, sense from nonsense, and one sex from the other.

JAMES THURBER, "SUCH A PHRASE AS DRIFTS THROUGH DREAMS," *LANTERNS AND LANCES* (1961)

47. English orthography satisfies all the requirements of the canons of reputability under the law of conspicuous waste. It is archaic, cumbrous, and ineffective; its acquisition consumes much time and effort; failure to acquire it is easy of detection.

THORSTEIN VEBLEN, *THE THEORY OF THE LEISURE CLASS* (1899), 14

48. Remember that, however patient your study, you will never in adult life learn any language perfectly; the best you can hope for is to be a bore.

EVELYN WAUGH, "THE TOURIST'S MANUAL," *VOGUE* MAGAZINE, JULY 1935

49. The only thing that it is advisable to know in any language is the numerals; and even there, you can do a lot with the fingers.

EVELYN WAUGH, "THE TOURIST'S MANUAL," *VOGUE* MAGAZINE, JULY 1935

50. A child, when it begins to speak, learns what it is that it knows.

JOHN HALL WHEELOCK, "A TRUE POEM IS A WAY OF KNOWING," *WHAT IS POETRY?* (1963)

525. LARGENESS

See also 375. GENEROSITY; 401. GREATNESS; 908. SMALLNESS

1. Grains of rice counted— / Can any one so spend life? / Be spacious and wise.

AMY LOWELL, "THE ANNIVERSARY" *WHAT'S O'CLOCK* (1925)

526. LAUGHTER

See also 292. ENTERTAINMENT; 436. HUMOR; 527. LAUGHTER AND TEARS; 820. RIDICULE; 1052. WEEPING; 1061. WIT

1. The greatest enemy of authority, therefore, is contempt, and the surest way to undermine it is laughter.

HANNAH ARENDT, *ON VIOLENCE* (1969)

2. [O]f all the countless folk who have lived before our time on this planet not one is known in history or in legend as having died of laughter.

MAX BEERBOHM, "LAUGHTER," IN *THE ART OF THE PERSONAL ESSAY* (1994), ED. PHILLIP LOPATE

3. Even in laughter the heart is sorrowful; and the end of mirth is heaviness.

BIBLE, PROVERBS 14:13

4. No man who has once heartily and wholly laughed can be altogether irreclaimably bad.

THOMAS CARLYLE, *SARTOR RESARTUS* (1833–34), 1.4

5. The man who cannot laugh is not only fit for treasons, stratagems, and spoils; but his whole life is already a treason and a stratagem.

THOMAS CARLYLE, *SARTOR RESARTUS* (1833–34), 1.4

6. [W]hile the laughter of joy is in full harmony with our deeper life, the laughter of amusement should be kept apart from it. The danger is too great of thus learning to look at solemn things in a spirit of mockery, and to seek in them opportunities for exercising wit.

LEWIS CARROLL, *THE LETTERS OF LEWIS CARROLL*, ED. MORTON N. COHEN (1979)

7. The most wasted day is that in which we have not laughed.

CHAMFORT, *MAXIMES ET PENSÉES* (1805), 1

8. Mirth is the Mail of Anguish.

EMILY DICKINSON, POEM (C. 1860)

9. One can know a man from his laugh, and if you like a man's laugh before you know anything of him, you may confidently say that he is a good man.

DOSTOYEVSKY, *THE HOUSE OF THE DEAD* (1862), 1.3, TR. CONSTANCE GARNETT

10. A human being should beware how he laughs, for then he shows all his faults.

EMERSON, *JOURNALS*, 1836

11. He is not laughed at that laughs at himself first.

THOMAS FULLER, M.D., *GNOMOLOGIA* (1732), 1936

12. There is nothing in which people more betray their character than in what they laugh at.

GOETHE, *ELECTIVE AFFINITIES* (1809), 22

13. If one were required to increase the dramatic seriousness of his face in relation to the seriousness of the problems he had to confront, he would quickly petrify and become his own statue.

VÁCLAV HAVEL, *DISTURBING THE PEACE* (1990)

14. Sudden glory is the passion which maketh those grimaces called laughter.

THOMAS HOBBES, *LEVIATHAN* (1651), 1.6

15. Wouldn't a laugh serve us better than to battle it out with our mortal souls?

MAUREEN HOWARD, *BEFORE MY TIME* (1974)

16. Pain is deeper than all thought; laughter is higher than all pain.

ELBERT HUBBARD, *THE PHILISTINE* (1895–1915)

17. Anything awful makes me laugh. I misbehaved once at a funeral.

CHARLES LAMB, LETTER TO ROBERT SOUTHEY, AUG. 9, 1815

18. You are not angry with people when you laugh at them. Humour teaches tolerance.

W. SOMERSET MAUGHAM, *THE SUMMING UP* (1938), 20

19. A laugh's the wisest, easiest answer to all that's queer.

HERMAN MELVILLE, *MOBY-DICK* (1851), 39

20. One horse-laugh is worth ten thousand syllogisms. It is not only more effective; it is also vastly more intelligent.

H. L. MENCKEN, *PREJUDICES: FOURTH SERIES* (1924), 7

21. He who laughs best to-day, will also laugh last.

NIETZSCHE, "MAXIMS AND MISSILES," 43, *TWILIGHT OF THE IDOLS* (1888), TR. ANTHONY M. LUDOVICI

22. In laughter all that is evil comes together, but is pronounced holy and absolved by its own bliss.

NIETZSCHE, "THE SEVEN SEALS," *THUS SPOKE ZARATHUSTRA* (1883–92), 3, TR. WALTER KAUFMANN

23. Not by warth does one kill but by laughter.

NIETZSCHE, "ON READING AND WRITING," *THUS SPOKE ZARATHUSTRA* (1883–92), 1, TR. WALTER KAUFMANN

24. A laugh is the loud echo of a sigh; a sigh the faint echo of a laugh.

SEAN O'CASEY, "THE POWER OF LAUGHTER," *THE GREEN CROW* (1956)

25. Laughter is wine for the soul—laughter soft, or loud and deep, tinged through with seriousness.

SEAN O'CASEY, "THE POWER OF LAUGHTER: WEAPON AGAINST EVIL," *FIFTY FAMOUS ESSAYS* (1964)

26. Laughter tends to mock the pompous and the pretentious; all man's boastful gadding about, all his pretty pomps, his hoary customs, his wornout creeds, changing the glitter of them into the dullest hue of lead.

SEAN O'CASEY, "THE POWER OF LAUGHTER: WEAPON AGAINST EVIL," *FIFTY FAMOUS ESSAYS* (1964)

27. One inch of joy surmounts of grief a span, / Because to laugh is proper to the man.

RABELAIS, "TO THE READER," *GARGANTUA AND PANTAGRUEL* (1532–64), 1

28. We are in the world to laugh. In purgatory or in hell we shall no longer be able to do so. And in heaven it would not be proper.

JULES RENARD, *JOURNAL*, JUNE 1907, TR. ELIZABETH ROGET

29. What monstrous absurdities and paradoxes have resisted whole batteries of serious arguments, and then crumbled swiftly into dust before the ringing death-knell of a laugh!

AGNES REPPLIER, "A PLEA FOR HUMOR," *POINTS OF VIEW* (1891)

30. Our sincerest laughter / With some pain is fraught: / Our sweetest songs are those that tell of saddest thought.

SHELLEY, "TO A SKYLARK" (1820)

31. Laughter is not at all a bad beginning for a friendship, and it is far the best ending for one.

OSCAR WILDE, *THE PICTURE OF DORIAN GRAY* (1891), 1

527. LAUGHTER AND TEARS

See also 526. LAUGHTER; 1052. WEEPING

1. Excess of sorrow laughs. Excess of joy weeps.

WILLIAM BLAKE, "PROVERBS OF HELL," *THE MARRIAGE OF HEAVEN AND HELL* (1790)

2. And if I laugh at any mortal thing, / 'Tis that I may not weep.

BYRON, *DON JUAN* (1819–24), 4.4

3. We are the only creatures that both laugh and weep. I think it's because we are the only creatures that see the difference between the way things are and the way they might be.

ROBERT FULGHUM, *IT WAS ON FIRE WHEN I LAY DOWN ON IT* (1989)

4. Those who weep recover more quickly than those who smile.

JEAN GIRAUDOUX, *AMPHITRYON 38* (1929), 1, TR. PETER H. JUDD

5. The mad also laugh, or is that what Freud and the others discovered perhaps, that *only* the mad laugh?

WILLIAM SAROYAN, "HOMAGE TO AL NIDEVAR," *SONS COME & GO, MOTHERS HANG IN FOREVER* (1979)

6. The laughter of man is more terrible than his tears, and takes more forms—hollow, heartless, mirthless, maniacal.

JAMES THURBER, "ON THE BRINK OF WAS," *COLLECTING HIMSELF* (1989)

7. We laugh and laugh. Then cry and cry— / Then feebler laugh, Then die.

MARK TWAIN, *NOTEBOOK* (1935)

8. Do you know what laughter is? I'll tell you. It's God's mistake. When God made man in order to bend him to his wishes he carelessly gave him the gift of laughter.

ELIE WIESEL, *THE GATES OF THE FOREST* (1966), TR. FRANCES FRENAYE

9. Laugh, and the world laughs with you; / Weep, and you weep alone; / For the sad old earth must borrow its mirth, / But has trouble enough of its own.

ELLA WHEELER WILCOX, "SOLITUDE," *COLLECTED POEMS* (1917)

528. LAW AND LAWYERS

See also 477. INJUSTICE; 514. JUDGES; 517. JUSTICE; 529. LAW AND ORDER; 534. LENIENCY

1. Wrong must not win by technicalities.

AESCHYLUS, *THE EUMENIDES* (458 B.C.), TR. RICHMOND LATTIMORE

2. God works a wonder now and then, He thought a lawyer was an honest man.

ANONYMOUS, *QUAINT EPITAPHS* (1898)

3. Nobody has a more sacred obligation to obey the law than those who make the law.

JEAN ANOUILH, *ANTIGONE* (1942), TR. LEWIS GALANTIÈRE

4. Good laws, if they are not obeyed, do not constitute good government.

ARISTOTLE, *POLITICS* (4TH C. B.C.), 4.8, TR. BENJAMIN JOWETT

5. Whereas the law is passionless, passion must ever sway the heart of man.

ARISTOTLE, *POLITICS* (4TH C. B.C.), 3.15, TR. BENJAMIN JOWETT

6. It usually takes a hundred years to make a law, and then, after it has done its work, it usually takes a hundred years to get rid of it.

HENRY WARD BEECHER, *PROVERBS FROM PLYMOUTH PULPIT* (1887)

7. Riches without law are more dangerous than in poverty without law.

HENRY WARD BEECHER, *PROVERBS FROM PLYMOUTH PULPIT* (1887)

8. The law is good, if a man use it lawfully.

BIBLE, 1 TIMOTHY 1:8

9. Litigant, n. A person about to give up his skin for the hope of retaining his bones.

AMBROSE BIERCE, *THE DEVIL'S DICTIONARY* (1881–1911)

10. A legal broom's a moral chimney-sweeper, / And that's the reason he himself's so dirty.

BYRON, *DON JUAN* (1819–24), 10.15

11. All bad precedents began as justifiable measures.

JULIUS CAESAR, QUOTED IN SALLUST'S *CONSPIRACY OF CATILINE* (1ST C. B.C.), 51

12. Laws that only threaten, and are not kept, become like the log that was given to the frogs to be their king, which they feared at first, but soon scorned and trampled on.

CERVANTES, *DON QUIXOTE* (1605–15), 2.4.51, TR. JOHN OZELL

13. The science of legislation is like that of medicine in one respect: that it is far more easy to point out what will do harm than what will do good.

CHARLES CALEB COLTON, *LACON* (1825), 1.529

14. Lawyers and painters can soon change white to black.

DANISH PROVERB

15. If there were no bad people there would be no good lawyers.

CHARLES DICKENS, *THE OLD CURIOSITY SHOP* (1840), 56

16. Anyone who takes it upon himself, on his private authority, to break a bad law, thereby authorizes everyone else to break the good ones.

DENIS DIDEROT, *SUPPLEMENT TO BOUGAINVILLE'S "VOYAGE"* (1796)

17. Our statute is a currency which we stamp with our own portrait.

EMERSON, "POLITICS," *ESSAYS: SECOND SERIES* (1844)

18. People say law but they mean wealth.

EMERSON, *JOURNALS,* 1841

19. A just cause needs no interpreting. / It carries its own case. But the unjust argument / since it is sick, needs clever medicine.

EURIPIDES, *THE PHOENICIAN WOMEN* (C. 411–409 B.C.), TR. ELIZABETH WYCKOFF

20. Give a wise man an honest brief to plead / and his eloquence is no remarkable achievement.

EURIPIDES, *THE BACCHAE* (C. 405 B.C.), TR. WILLIAM ARROWSMITH

21. If there isn't a law, there will be.

HAROLD FABER, *THE NEW YORK TIMES MAGAZINE,* MARCH 17, 1968

22. The story of man is the history, first, of the acceptance and imposition of restraints necessary to permit communal life; and second, of the emancipation of the individual within that system of necessary restraints.

ABE FORTAS, *CONCERNING DISSENT AND CIVIL DISOBEDIENCE* (1968)

23. Fragile as reason is and limited as law is as the institutionalized medium of reason, that's all we have standing between us and the tyranny of mere will and the cruelty of unbridled, undisciplined feeling.

FELIX FRANKFURTER, *FELIX FRANKFURTER REMINISCES* (1960), 19

24. God works wonders now and then: / Behold! a lawyer, an honest man!

BENJAMIN FRANKLIN, *POOR RICHARD'S ALMANACK* (1732–57)

25. Laws too gentle are seldom obeyed; too severe, seldom executed.

BENJAMIN FRANKLIN, *POOR RICHARD'S ALMANACK* (1732–57)

26. Law cannot persuade where it cannot punish.

THOMAS FULLER, M.D., *GNOMOLOGIA* (1732), 3148

27. The more laws, the more offenders.

THOMAS FULLER, M.D., *GNOMOLOGIA* (1732), 4663

28. The law is what it is—a majestic edifice, sheltering all of us, each stone of which rests on another.

JOHN GALSWORTHY, *JUSTICE* (1910), 2

29. An unjust law is itself a species of violence. Arrest for its breach is more so.

MOHANDAS K. GANDHI, *NON-VIOLENCE IN PEACE AND WAR* (1948), 2.150

30. The more laws, the less justice.

GERMAN PROVERB

31. There's no better way of exercising the imagination than the study of law. No poet ever interpreted nature as freely as a lawyer interprets truth.

JEAN GIRAUDOUX, *TIGER AT THE GATES* (1935), 2, TR. CHRISTOPHER FRY

32. Laws grind the poor, and rich men rule the law.

OLIVER GOLDSMITH, *THE TRAVELLER* (1765), 386

33. Every new time will give its law.

MAXIM GORKY, *THE LOWER DEPTHS* (1903), 4, TR. ALEXANDER BAKSHY

34. Laws are to govern all alike—those opposed as well as those who favor them. I know of no method to repeal of bad or obnoxious laws so effective as their stringent execution.

ULYSSES S. GRANT, FIRST INAUGURAL ADDRESS, MARCH 4, 1869

35. The lawyer must either learn to live more capaciously or be content to find himself continuously less trusted, more circumscribed, till he becomes hardly more important than a minor administrator, confined to a monotonous round of record and routine, without dignity, inspiration, or respect.

LEARNED HAND, *THE SPIRIT OF LIBERTY* (1959)

36. There is something monstrous in commands couched in invented and unfamiliar language; an alien master is the worst of all. The language of the law must not be foreign to the ears of those who are to obey it.

LEARNED HAND, SPEECH, WASHINGTON, D.C., MAY 11, 1929

37. The people should fight for their law as for their city wall.

HERACLITUS, *FRAGMENTS* (C. 500 B.C.), 82, TR. PHILIP WHEELWRIGHT

38. Those who are too lazy and comfortable to think for themselves and be their own judges obey the laws. Others sense their own laws within them.

HERMANN HESSE, *DEMIAN* (1919), 3, TR. MICHAEL LEBECK

39. The law is the witness and external deposit of our moral life. Its history is the history of the moral development of the race.

OLIVER WENDELL HOLMES, JR., SPEECH, BOSTON, JAN. 8, 1897

40. There are not enough jails, not enough policemen, not enough courts to enforce a law not supported by the people.

HUBERT H. HUMPHREY, SPEECH, WILLIAMSBURG, VA., MAY 1, 1965

41. In the old days, if a neighbor's apples fell into your yard, you worked it out over the back fence or picked them up and made pies. Today, you sue.

LEE IACOCCA, *TALKING STRAIGHT* (1988), WITH SONNY KLEINFELD

42. Laws and institutions must go hand in hand with the progress of the human mind.

THOMAS JEFFERSON, LETTER TO SAMUEL KERCHEVAL, JULY 12, 1816

43. The law is the last result of human wisdom acting upon human experience for the benefit of the public.

SAMUEL JOHNSON, QUOTED IN HESTER LYNCH PIOZZI'S *ANECDOTES OF SAMUEL JOHNSON* (1786)

44. Our nation is founded on the principle that observance of the law is the eternal safeguard of liberty and defiance of the law is the surest road to tyranny.

JOHN F. KENNEDY, TELEVISION ADDRESS APPEALING FOR PEACEFUL COMPLIANCE WITH FEDERAL COURT ORDER ADMITTING JAMES MEREDITH TO UNIVERSITY OF MISSISSIPPI, SEPT. 30, 1962

45. Morality cannot be legislated, but behavior can be regulated. Judicial decrees may not change the heart, but they can restrain the heartless.

MARTIN LUTHER KING JR., *STRENGTH TO LOVE* (1963), 3.3

46. Many laws as certainly make bad men, as bad men make many laws.

WALTER SAVAGE LANDOR, "DIOGENES AND PLATO," *IMAGINARY CONVERSATIONS* (1824–53)

47. Ignore what a man desires and you ignore the very source of his power; run against the grain of a nation's genius and see where you get with your laws.

WALTER LIPPMANN, "THE MAKING OF CREEDS," *A PREFACE TO POLITICS* (1914)

48. No law is quite appropriate for all.

LIVY, *AB URBE CONDITA* (C. 29 B.C.), 34.3

49. Wherever law ends, tyranny begins.

JOHN LOCKE, *TWO TREATISES ON GOVERNMENT* (1690), 2

50. Useless laws weaken necessary ones.

MONTESQUIEU, *L'ESPRIT DES LOIS* (1748), 14

51. Law was once introduced without reason, and has become reasonable.

PASCAL, *PENSÉES* (1670), 294, TR. W. F. TROTTER

52. The best use of good laws is to teach men to trample bad laws under their feet.

WENDELL PHILLIPS, SPEECH, APRIL 12, 1852

53. Law is experience developed by reason and applied continually to further experience.

ROSCOE POUND, *CHRISTIAN SCIENCE MONITOR*, APRIL 24, 1963

54. [T]here is evidence that young men in the big law firms, although they still work harder than most of their clients, do not glory in putting in night work and weekend hours as they once did.

DAVID RIESMAN, *ABUNDANCE FOR WHAT?* (1964)

55. No man is above the law and no man is below it; nor do we ask any man's permission when we ask him to obey it.

THEODORE ROOSEVELT, ADDRESS, JANUARY 1904

56. Good laws lead to the making of better ones; bad ones bring about worse.

ROUSSEAU, *THE SOCIAL CONTRACT* (1762), 3.15, TR. G. D. H. COLE

57. Government can easily exist without law, but law cannot exist without government.

BERTRAND RUSSELL, "IDEAS THAT HAVE HELPED MANKIND," *UNPOPULAR ESSAYS* (1950)

58. If human values were relative, all laws—whether those based on revealed religions or those devised by man—would become meaningless.

ANWAR EL-SADAT, *IN SEARCH OF IDENTITY* (1977)

59. Certain laws have not been written, but they are more fixed than all the written laws.

SENECA THE ELDER, *CONTROVERSIAE* (1ST C. A.D.), 1

60. In law, what plea so tainted and corrupt / But, being seasoned with a gracious voice, / Obscures the show of evil.

SHAKESPEARE, *THE MERCHANT OF VENICE* (1596–97), 3.2.75

61. We must not make a scarecrow of the law, / Setting it up to fear the birds of prey, / And let it keep one shape till custom make it / Their perch, and not their terror.

SHAKESPEARE, *MEASURE FOR MEASURE* (1604–05), 2.1.1

62. Lawyers love paper. They eat, sleep and dream paper. They turn paper into gold, and their files are colorful and their language neoclassical and calligraphically bewigged.

KARL SHAPIRO, *REPORTS OF MY DEATH* (1990)

63. Laws are like spider's webs which, if anything small falls into them they ensnare it, but large things break through and escape.

SOLON (7TH–6TH C. B.C.), QUOTED IN DIOGENES LAERTIUS' *LIVES AND OPINIONS OF EMINENT PHILOSOPHERS* (3RD C. A.D.), TR. R. D. HICKS

64. Rigorous law is often rigorous injustice.

TERENCE, *THE SELF-TORMENTOR* (163 B.C.), 4.5.48, TR. HENRY THOMAS RILEY

65. The lawyer's truth is not Truth, but consistency or a consistent expediency.

THOREAU, *CIVIL DISOBEDIENCE* (1849)

66. The man for whom law exists—the man of forms, the conservative—is a tame man.

THOREAU, *JOURNAL,* MARCH 30, 1851

67. It never occurred to any Enlightenment figure in the eighteenth century that law was not preferable to man.

GORE VIDAL, *THE SECOND AMERICAN REVOLUTION AND OTHER ESSAYS* (1982)

68. Let all the laws be clear, uniform, and precise; to interpret laws is almost always to corrupt them.

VOLTAIRE, *PHILOSOPHICAL DICTIONARY* (1764)

69. The opinion of all lawyers, the unanimous cry of the nation, and the good of the state, are in themselves a law.

VOLTAIRE, "PRIVILEGE—PRIVILEGED CASES," *PHILOSOPHICAL DICTIONARY* (1764)

70. It ain't no sin if you crack a few laws now and then, just so long as you don't break any.

MAE WEST, IN *EVERY DAY'S A HOLIDAY* (1937)

71. The world is shocked, or amused, by the sight of saintly old people hindering in the name of morality the removal of obvious brutalities from a legal system.

ALFRED NORTH WHITEHEAD, *ADVENTURES IN IDEAS* (1933), 20

72. The profession I chose was politics; the profession I entered was law. I entered the one because I thought it would lead to the other.

WOODROW WILSON, QUOTED IN RICHARD HOFSTADTER, *THE AMERICAN POLITICAL TRADITION* (1948)

529. LAW AND ORDER

See also 528. LAW AND LAWYERS; 661. ORDER; 709. POLICE

1. Society cannot exist unless a controlling power upon will and appetite be placed somewhere, and the less of it there is within, the more of it there must be without.

EDMUND BURKE, QUOTED IN LEWIS LAPHAM, *IMPERIAL MASQUERADE* (1990)

2. The call for "law and order" (rather than for life and structure) and for stricter punishment of criminals, as well as the obsession with violence and destruction among some "revolutionaries," are only further instances of the powerful attraction of necrophilia in the contemporary world.

ERICH FROMM, *THE ANATOMY OF HUMAN DESTRUCTIVENESS* (1973)

530. LAZINESS

See also 446. IDLENESS

1. Flee laziness, which, while it produces an immediate delight, ends in the sorrow of repentance. And know that nature without exercise is a seed shut up in the pod, and art without practice is nothing.

PIETRO ARETINO, LETTER TO ANTONIO GALLO, AUG. 6, 1537, TR. SAMUEL PUTNAM

2. Go to the ant, thou sluggard; consider her ways and be wise: / Which having no guide, overseer, or ruler, / Provideth her meat in the summer, and gathereth her food in the harvest.

BIBLE, PROVERBS 6:6–8

3. Laziness travels so slowly that poverty soon overtakes him.

BENJAMIN FRANKLIN, "THE WAY TO WEALTH" (JULY 7, 1757), I

4. Indolence is a delightful but distressing state: we must be doing something to be happy.

WILLIAM HAZLITT, "ON THE PLEASURE OF PAINTING," *TABLE TALK* (1821–22)

5. Don't yield to that alluring witch, Laziness, or else be prepared to surrender all that you have won in your better moments.

HORACE, *SATIRES* (35–30 B.C.), 2.3

6. It is the just doom of laziness and gluttony to be inactive without ease and drowsy without tranquility.

SAMUEL JOHNSON, *THE ADVENTURER* (1753), 39

7. Failure is not our only punishment for laziness: there is also the success of others.

JULES RENARD, *JOURNAL,* JANUARY 1898, TR. ELIZABETH ROGET

531. LEADERSHIP

See also 61. AUTHORITY; 315. EXECUTIVES; 353. FOLLOWING; 644. OBEDIENCE; 831. RULERS

1. He who has never learned to obey cannot be a good commander.

ARISTOTLE, *POLITICS* (4TH C. B.C.), 3.4, TR. BENJAMIN JOWETT

2. The man who commands efficiently must have obeyed others in the past, and the man who obeys dutifully is worthy of being some day a commander.

CICERO, *DE LEGIBUS* (C. 52 B.C.), 3.2.5

3. The superior man is easy to serve and difficult to please.

CONFUCIUS, *ANALECTS* (6TH C. B.C.), 13.25, TR. JAMES LEGGE

4. Men are of no importance. What counts is who commands.

CHARLES DE GAULLE, QUOTED IN *THE NEW YORK TIMES MAGAZINE*, MAY 12, 1968

5. There are men, who, by their sympathetic attractions, carry nations with them, and lead the activity of the human race.

EMERSON, "POWER," *THE CONDUCT OF LIFE* (1860)

6. For the most part our leaders are merely following out in front; they do but marshal us the way that we are going.

BERGEN EVANS, *THE SPOOR OF SPOOKS AND OTHER NONSENSE* (1954)

7. If you command wisely, you'll be obeyed cheerfully.

THOMAS FULLER, M.D., *GNOMOLOGIA* (1732), 2746

8. The leader, mingling with the vulgar host, / Is in the common mass of matter lost.

HOMER, *ODYSSEY* (9TH C. B.C.), 4.397, TR. ALEXANDER POPE

9. The final test of a leader is that he leaves behind him in other men the conviction and the will to carry on.

WALTER LIPPMANN, "ROOSEVELT HAS GONE," *NEW YORK HERALD TRIBUNE*, APRIL 14, 1945

10. [O]ne longs for the presence of a leader like Lincoln, who openly admitted his doubts and as openly preserved his commitment.

ROLLO MAY, *THE COURAGE TO CREATE* (1975)

11. The real leader has no need to lead—he is content to point the way.

HENRY MILLER, "THE WISDOM OF THE HEART," *THE WISDOM OF THE HEART* (1941)

12. A leader is a dealer in hope.

NAPOLEON I, *MAXIMS* (1804–15)

13. The inevitable end of multiple chiefs is that they fade and disappear for lack of unity.

NAPOLEON I, *MAXIMS* (1804–15)

14. To do great things is difficult; but to command great things is more difficult.

NIETZSCHE, "THE STILLEST HOUR," *THUS SPOKE ZARATHUSTRA* (1883–92), 2, TR. WALTER KAUFMANN

15. Any one can hold the helm when the sea is calm.

PUBLILIUS SYRUS, *MORAL SAYINGS* (1ST C. B.C.), 358, TR. DARIUS LYMAN

16. The leader must know, must know that he knows, and must be able to make it abundantly clear to those about him that he knows.

CLARENCE B. RANDALL, *MAKING GOOD IN MANAGEMENT* (1964)

17. A chief is a man who assumes responsibility. He says, "I was beaten." He does not say, "My men were beaten." Thus speaks a real man.

SAINT-EXUPÉRY, *FLIGHT TO ARRAS* (1942), 23, TR. LEWIS GALANTIÈRE

18. We cannot all be masters, nor all masters / Cannot be truly followed.

SHAKESPEARE, *OTHELLO* (1604–05), 1.1.43

19. What a man dislikes in his superiors, let him not display in the treatment of his inferiors.

TSANG SIN, *THE GREAT LEARNING* (5TH C. B.C.), 10.2, TR. JAMES LEGGE

20. What you cannot enforce, / Do not command.

SOPHOCLES, *OEDIPUS AT COLONUS* (401 B.C.), TR. ROBERT FITZGERALD

21. Clearly no one knows what leadership has gone undiscovered in women of all races, and in black and other minority men.

GLORIA STEINEM, "CAMPAIGNING," *OUTRAGEOUS ACTS AND EVERYDAY REBELLIONS* (1983)

22. Those who try to lead the people can only do so by following the mob. It is through the voice of one crying in the wilderness that the ways of the gods must be prepared.

OSCAR WILDE, *THE ARTIST AS CRITIC: CRITICAL WRITINGS OF OSCAR WILDE*, ED. RICHARD ELLMANN (1969)

532. LEARNING

See also 279. EDUCATION; 321. EXPERIENCE; 404. GROWTH AND DEVELOPMENT; 522. KNOWLEDGE; 721. PRACTICE; 848. SCHOLARS AND SCHOLARSHIP

1. To learn is a natural pleasure, not confined to philosophers, but common to all men.

ARISTOTLE, *POETICS* (4TH C. B.C.), 1.5, TR. THOMAS TWINING

2. Never believe on faith, / see for yourself! / What you yourself don't learn / you don't know.

BERTOLT BRECHT, *THE MOTHER* (1932), 6, TR. LEE BAXANDALL

3. The great poem and the deep theorem are new to every reader, and yet are his own experiences, because he himself recreates them.

JACOB BRONOWSKI, "THE CREATIVE MIND," *SCIENCE AND HUMAN VALUES* (1956)

4. Learn as though you would never be able to master it; hold it as though you would be in fear of losing it.

CONFUCIUS, *ANALECTS* (6TH C. B.C.), 8.17, TR. WINBERG CHAI

5. We think we learn from teachers, and we sometimes do. But the teachers are not always to be found in school or in great laboratories. Sometimes what we learn depends upon our own powers of insight.

LOREN EISELEY, "THE HIDDEN TEACHER," *THE STAR THROWER* (1978)

6. Everywhere, we learn only from those whom we love.

GOETHE, QUOTED IN JOHANN PETER ECKERMANN'S *CONVERSATIONS WITH GOETHE*, MAY 12, 1825

7. Make your friends your teachers and mingle the pleasures of conversation with the advantages of instruction.

BALTASAR GRACIÁN, *THE ART OF WORLDLY WISDOM* (1647), 11, TR. JOSEPH JACOBS

8. [T]oday in America vast concourses of youth are flocking to our colleges, eager for something, just what they do not know.

LEARNED HAND, *THE SPIRIT OF LIBERTY* (1959)

9. Learning is its own exceeding great reward.

WILLIAM HAZLITT, "ON OLD ENGLISH WRITERS AND SPEAKERS," *THE PLAIN SPEAKER* (1826)

10. Humans like history, like to know why things start and end, like to have reasons for it, and the school never has any reasons.

JAMES HERNDON, *HOW TO SURVIVE IN YOUR NATIVE LAND* (1971)

11. Wherever there are beginners and experts, old and young, there is some kind of learning going on, and some sort of teaching. We are all pupils and we are all teachers.

GILBERT HIGHET, *THE ART OF TEACHING* (1950)

12. Just as eating against one's will is injurious to health, so study without a liking for it spoils the memory, and it retains nothing it takes in.

LEONARDO DA VINCI, *NOTEBOOKS* (C. 1500), TR. JEAN PAUL RICHTER

13. As turning the logs will make a dull fire burn, so change of studies a dull brain.

LONGFELLOW, "TABLE-TALK," *DRIFTWOOD* (1857)

14. A man has no ears for that to which experience has given him no access.

NIETZSCHE, *ECCE HOMO* (1888), TR. ANTHONY M. LUDOVICI

15. Within seconds her tongue thawed out and began whirring like a dental drill. She knew as if it were the Koran everything Mr. Hemingway had written—better than he did himself, she hazarded archly.

S.J. PERELMAN, *THE RISING GORGE* (1961)

16. Trees and fields tell me nothing; men are my teachers.

PLATO, *PHAEDRUS* (4TH C. B.C.)

17. Freedom to learn is the first necessity of guaranteeing that man himself shall be self-reliant enough to be free.

FRANKLIN D. ROOSEVELT, SPEECH, NEW YORK CITY, JUNE 30, 1938

18. The learning of books that you do not make your own wisdom is money in the hands of another in time of need.

SANSKRIT PROVERB

19. You have learnt something. That always feels at first as if you had lost something.

GEORGE BERNARD SHAW, *MAJOR BARBARA* (1905), 3

20. A man, though wise, should never be ashamed / of learning more, and must unbend his mind.

SOPHOCLES, *ANTIGONE* (442–41 B.C.), TR. ELIZABETH WYCKOFF

21. I have learned throughout my life as a composer chiefly through my mistakes and pursuits of false assumptions, not by my exposure to founts of wisdom and knowledge.

IGOR STRAVINSKY, "CONTINGENCIES," *THEMES AND EPISODES* (1966)

22. To be fond of learning is to be near to knowledge.

TZE-SZE, *THE DOCTRINE OF THE MEAN* (5TH C. B.C.), 20.10, TR. JAMES LEGGE

23. The Jewish tradition of learning—*is* learning. Adam chose knowledge instead of immortality.

Elie Wiesel, "Inside a Library," *From the Kingdom of Memory* (1990)

LEGACY

See 1058. Wills and Inheritance

533. LEISURE

See also 10. Activity; 446. Idleness; 703. Play; 811. Rest; 813. Retirement

1. There can be no high civilization where there is not ample leisure.

Henry Ward Beecher, *Proverbs from Plymouth Pulpit* (1887)

2. When a man's busy, why leisure / Strikes him as wonderful pleasure: / 'Faith, and at leisure once is he? / Straightway he wants to be busy.

Robert Browning, "The Glove," *Dramatic Romances and Lyrics* (1845)

3. What is this life if, full of care, / We have no time to stand and stare?

W. H. Davies, "Leisure," *Songs of Joy* (1911)

4. Friendship requires more time than poor busy men can usually command.

Emerson, "Behavior," *The Conduct of Life* (1860)

5. It takes application, a fine sense of value, and a powerful community-spirit for a people to have serious leisure, and this has not been the genius of the Americans.

Paul Goodman, *Growing Up Absurd* (1960), 1.8

6. To be at ease is better than to be at business. Nothing really belongs to us but time, which even he has who has nothing else.

Baltasar Gracián, *The Art of Worldly Wisdom* (1647), 247, tr. Joseph Jacobs

7. Leisure is one of the three greatest rewards of being a teacher. It is, unfortunately, the privilege which teachers most often misuse.

Gilbert Highet, *The Art of Teaching* (1950)

8. [Leave] all the afternoon for exercise and recreation, which are as necessary as reading. I will rather say more necessary, because health is worth more than learning.

Thomas Jefferson, Letter to John Garland Jefferson. June 11, 1790

9. Leisure and curiosity might soon make great advances in useful knowledge, were they not diverted by minute emulation and laborious trifles.

Samuel Johnson, *The Rambler* (1750–52), 177

10. Leisure was the *sine qua non* of the full Renaissance. The feudal nobility, having lost its martial function, sought diversion all over Europe in cultivated pastimes: sonneteering, the lute, games and acrostics, travel, gentlemanly studies and sports, hunting and hawking, treated as arts.

Mary McCarthy, *Venice Observed* (1956)

11. Lie down and listen to the crabgrass grow, / The faucet leak, and learn to leave them so.

Marya Mannes, "Controverse," *But Will It Sell?* (1955–64)

12. Without leisure there can be neither art nor science nor fine conversation, nor any ceremonious performance of the offices of love and friendship.

Lewis Mumford, *Findings and Keepings. Analects for an Autobiography* (1975)

13. In preindustrial cultures leisure is scarcely a burden or a "problem" because it is built into the ritual and ground plan of life for which people are conditioned in childhood; often they possess a relatively timeless attitude toward events.

David Riesman, *Abundance for What?* (1964)

14. For many—job-ridden, family-ridden, chronically worried and anxious—it was the first real leisure, the first vacation they [convalescents] had ever had—the first time they had ever had time to think—or feel.

Oliver Sacks, *A Leg to Stand On* (1984)

15. Freedom from worries and surcease from strain are illusions that always inhabit the distance.

Edwin Way Teale, "April 3," *Circle of the Seasons* (1953)

16. In itself and in its consequences the life of leisure is beautiful and ennobling in all civilised men's eyes.

Thorstein Veblen, *The Theory of the Leisure Class* (1899), 3

LENDING

See 96. Borrowing and Lending

534. LENIENCY

See also 470. Indulgence; 477. Injustice; 517. Justice; 583. Mercy; 766. Punishment; 890. Severity

1. Pardon one offence, and you encourage the commission of many.

Publilius Syrus, *Moral Sayings* (1st c. b.c.), 750, tr. Darius Lyman

2. Whoever has his foe at his mercy, and does not kill him, is his own enemy.

Sa'di, *Gulistan* (1258), 8.56, tr. James Ross

535. LETTERS

1. The mail on the doormat consisted of the usual things: a rude letter threatening to take away his American Express card, an invitation to apply for an American Express card, and a few bills of the more hysterical and unrealistic type.

Douglas Adams, *The Long Dark Tea-Time of the Soul* (1988)

2. Sir, more than kisses, letters mingle souls; / For, thus friends absent speak.

John Donne, "To Sir Henry Wotton" (1633)

3. We lay aside letters never to read them again, and at last we destroy them out of discretion, and so disappears the most beautiful, the most immediate breath of life, irrecoverably for ourselves and for others.

Goethe, *Elective Affinities* (1809), 27

4. A woman seldom writes her mind but in her postscript.

Richard Steele, *The Spectator* (1711–12), 79

5. Those who are absent, by its means become present; it [mail] is the consolation of life.

Voltaire, "Post," *Philosophical Dictionary* (1764)

536. LIBERALISM

See also 178. Conservatism; 710. Political Parties; 776. Radicalism

1. It may be that just as tonality recurs in music and realism in painting, so the idea of liberalism recurs in politics—though each time in a different vein.

Eva Hoffman, *Exit Into History* (1993)

2. It is no accident that the Victorian age, the heyday of conventionalism, was the cultural bloom of economic liberalism.

Gunnar Myrdal, *Beyond the Welfare State* (1960)

3. A Liberal is a man who uses his legs and his hands at the behest—at the command—of his head.

Franklin D. Roosevelt, radio address, Oct. 26, 1939

4. The essence of the Liberal outlook lies not in *what* opinions are held, but in *how* they are held: instead of being held dogmatically, they are held tentatively, and with a consciousness that new evidence may at any moment lead to their abandonment.

Bertrand Russell, "Philosophy and Politics," *Unpopular Essays* (1950)

LIBERALITY

See 375. Generosity

LIBERTINISM

See 739. Profligacy

537. LIBERTY

See also 109. Captivity; 233. Democracy; 363. Freedom; 823. Rights; 889. Servitude

1. Liberty is not a means to a higher political end. It is itself the highest political end.

Lord Acton, address, "The History of Freedom in Antiquity," Feb. 26, 1877

2. Liberty, next to religion, has been the motive of good deeds and the common pretext of crime.

Lord Acton, address, "The History of Freedom in Antiquity," Feb. 26, 1877

3. Despotism accomplishes great things illegally; liberty doesn't even go to the trouble of accomplishing small things legally.

Balzac, *La Peau de chagrin* (1831), 1

4. Liberty is the soul's right to breath, and, when it can not take a long breath, laws are girdled too tight.

Henry Ward Beecher, *Proverbs from Plymouth Pulpit* (1887)

5. Liberty, n. One of Imagination's most precious possessions.

Ambrose Bierce, *The Devil's Dictionary* (1881–1911)

6. Freedom of the mind requires not only, or not even especially, the absence of legal constraints but the presence of alternative thoughts.

Allan Bloom, "From Socrates' *Apology* to Heidegger's *Rektoratsrede*," *The Closing of the American Mind* (1987)

7. None who have always been free can understand the terrible fascinating power of the hope of freedom to those who are not free.

Pearl S. Buck, *What America Means to Me* (1943), 4

8. Hereditary Bondsmen! know ye not / Who would be free themselves must strike the blow?

BYRON, *CHILDE HAROLD'S PILGRIMAGE* (1812–18), 2.76

9. Liberty may be of no more use / Than stirring up the flame of civil wars; / Then, by disorder fatal to the world, / One wants no king, the other wants no equal.

CORNEILLE, *CINNA* (1639), 2.1, TR. PAUL LANDIS

10. Eternal vigilance is the price of liberty.

JOHN PHILPOT CURRAN, SPEECH ON THE RIGHT OF ELECTION OF THE LORD MAYOR OF DUBLIN, JULY 10, 1790

11. The hungry and the homeless don't care about liberty any more than they care about cultural heritage. To pretend that they do care is cant.

E. M. FORSTER, "LIBERTY IN ENGLAND," *ABINGER HARVEST* (1936)

12. Lean liberty is better than fat slavery.

THOMAS FULLER, M.D., *GNOMOLOGIA* (1732), 3158

13. The cause of liberty becomes a mockery if the price to be paid is the wholesale destruction of those who are to enjoy liberty.

MOHANDAS K. GANDHI, *NON-VIOLENCE IN PEACE AND WAR* (1948), 1.272

14. Liberty is so much latitude as the powerful choose to accord to the weak.

LEARNED HAND, SPEECH, UNIVERSITY OF PENNSYLVANIA LAW SCHOOL, JUNE 1930

15. The spirit of liberty is the spirit which is not too sure it is right.

LEARNED HAND, SPEECH, NEW YORK CITY, MAY 21, 1944

16. Is life so dear or peace so sweet, as to be purchased at the price of chains and slavery? Forbid it, Almighty God! I know not what course others may take, but as for me, give me liberty or give me death!

PATRICK HENRY, SPEECH, VIRGINIA CONVENTION, MARCH 23, 1775

17. If the world knew how to use freedom without abusing it, tyranny would not exist.

TEHYI HSIEH, *CHINESE EPIGRAMS INSIDE OUT AND PROVERBS* (1948), 293

18. Liberation is not deliverance.

VICTOR HUGO, "FANTINE," *LES MISÉRABLES* (1862), 2.9, TR. CHARLES E. WILBOUR

19. Our democracy must demonstrate that it is still prepared to contend patiently, as well as with insight and passion, for the cause of human freedom in Asia, the Middle East, Africa, and Latin America.

JOHN F. KENNEDY, *THE STRATEGY OF PEACE* (1960)

20. We stand for freedom. That is our conviction for ourselves; that is our only commitment to others.

JOHN F. KENNEDY, MESSAGE TO CONGRESS, MAY 25, 1961

21. The shepherd drives the wolf from the sheep's throat, for which the sheep thanks the shepherd as his liberator, while the wolf denounces him for the same act, as the destroyer of liberty, especially as the sheep was a black one.

ABRAHAM LINCOLN, SPEECH, BALTIMORE, APRIL 18, 1864

22. Martyred many times must be / Who would keep his country free.

EDNA ST. VINCENT MILLAY, "TO THE MAID OF ORLEANS," *MAKE BRIGHT THE ARROWS* (1940)

23. Liberty is the right to do what the laws permit.

MONTESQUIEU, *L'ESPRIT DES LOIS* (1748), 11.3

24. The word liberty has often served for the destruction of the substance of liberty.

JOSÉ MARÍA LUIS MORA, *OBRAS SUELTAS*, V. 2, P. 78

25. In order that a people may be free, it is necessary that the governed be sages, and those who govern, gods.

NAPOLEON I, *MAXIMS* (1804–15)

26. People demand freedom only when they have no power.

NIETZSCHE, *THE WILL TO POWER* (1888), 784, TR. ANTHONY M. LUDOVICI

27. He that would make his own liberty secure must guard even his enemy from oppression.

THOMAS PAINE, *DISSERTATION ON FIRST PRINCIPLES OF GOVERNMENT* (1795)

28. Those who expect to reap the blessings of freedom must, like men, undergo the fatigue of supporting it.

THOMAS PAINE, *THE AMERICAN CRISIS* (1776–83), 4

29. Tyranny is always better organized than freedom.

CHARLES PÉGUY, "WAR AND PEACE," *BASIC VERITIES* (1943), TR. JULIAN GREEN

30. Whether in chains or in laurels, liberty knows nothing but victories.

WENDELL PHILLIPS, SPEECH, NOV. 1, 1859

31. A Country can get more real joy out of just Hollering for their Freedom than they can if they get it.

WILL ROGERS, *THE AUTOBIOGRAPHY OF WILL ROGERS* (1949), 17

32. Liberty don't work as good in practice as it does in Speech.

Will Rogers, *There's Not a Bathing Suit in Russia* (1927), 5

33. Oh liberty, what crimes are committed in your name!

Attributed to Madame Roland, last words before her execution, Nov. 8, 1793

34. Our government is based on the belief that a people can be both strong and free, that civilized men need no restraint but that imposed by themselves against abuse of freedom.

Franklin D. Roosevelt, address, Harvard University, Cambridge, Mass., Sept. 18, 1936

35. In the truest sense freedom cannot be bestowed, it must be achieved.

Franklin D. Roosevelt, greeting on 74th anniversary of the Emancipation Proclamation, Sept. 16, 1936

36. To renounce liberty is to renounce being a man, to surrender the rights of humanity and even its duties.

Rousseau, *The Social Contract* (1762), 1.4, tr. G. D. H. Cole

37. Too little liberty brings stagnation, and too much brings chaos.

Bertrand Russell, "The Role of Individuality," *Authority and the Individual* (1949)

38. Liberty plucks justice by the nose; / The baby beats the nurse, and quite athwart / Goes all decorum.

Shakespeare, *Measure for Measure* (1604–05), 1.3.29

39. Liberty means responsibility. That is why most men dread it.

George Bernard Shaw, "Maxims for Revolutionists," *Man and Superman* (1903)

40. A nation has character only when it is free.

Mme De Staël, *De la littérature* (1800), 1.5

41. It is a worthy thing to fight for one's freedom; it is another sight finer to fight for another man's.

Mark Twain, letter to the Reverend Joseph Twichell, 1898

42. It is by the goodness of God that in our country we have those three unspeakably precious things: freedom of speech, freedom of conscience, and the prudence never to practice either of them.

Mark Twain, "Pudd'nhead Wilson's New Calendar," *Following the Equator* (1897), 1.20

43. It must be admitted that liberty is the hardest test that one can inflict on a people. To know how to be free is not given equally to all men and all nations.

Paul Valéry, "On the Subject of Dictatorship," *Reflections on the World Today* (1931), tr. Francis Scarfe

44. The true charter of liberty is independence, maintained by force.

Voltaire, "Venice. And, Incidentally, of Liberty," *Philosophical Dictionary* (1764)

45. Liberty exists in proportion to wholesome restraint.

Daniel Webster, speech at the Charleston Bar Dinner, May 10, 1847

46. Liberty is never out of bounds or off limits; it spreads wherever it can capture the imagination of men.

E. B. White, "Letter from the West," *The Points of My Compass* (1960)

47. When liberty's position is challenged, artists and writers are the ones who first take up the sword.

E.B. White, *One Man's Meat* (1944)

48. The shallow consider liberty a release from all law, from every constraint. The wise see in it, on the contrary, the potent Law of Laws.

Walt Whitman, "Freedom," *Notes Left Over* (1881)

49. Liberty is its own reward.

Woodrow Wilson, address, Sept. 12, 1912

50. Liberty does not consist in mere general declarations of the rights of men. It consists in the translation of those declarations into definite action.

Woodrow Wilson, speech, Philadelphia, July 4, 1914

51. The history of liberty is a history of limitation of government power, not the increase of it.

Woodrow Wilson, address, New York City, Sept. 9, 1912

52. You cannot tear up ancient rootages and safely plant the tree of liberty in soil that is not native to it.

Woodrow Wilson, speech, Sept. 25, 1912

53. When we demand liberty of a person as a constitutional right, we are taking away from the officials their liberty to chop off people's heads.

Lin Yutang, "Freedom of Speech," *With Love and Irony* (1934–40)

538. LIBRARIES

See also 93. Books and Reading

LIFE

1. He loved this street [42nd Street], not for the people or the shops but for the stone lions that guarded the great main building of the Public Library, a building filled with books and unimaginably vast, and which he had never yet dared to enter.

JAMES BALDWIN, *GO TELL IT ON THE MOUNTAIN* (1953)

2. I myself spent hours in the Columbia library as intimidated and embarrassed as a famished gourmet invited to a dream restaurant where every dish from all the world's cuisines, past and present, was available on request.

LUIGI BARZINI, *O AMERICA* (1977)

3. But what can a man see of a library being one day in it?

JAMES BOSWELL, *BOSWELL ON THE GRAND TOUR: GERMANY AND SWITZERLAND* (1928; 1953)

4. The true university of these days is a collection of books.

THOMAS CARLYLE, *ON HEROES, HERO-WORSHIP AND THE HEROIC IN HISTORY* (1841), 5

5. A man's library is a sort of harem.

EMERSON, "IN PRAISE OF BOOKS," *THE CONDUCT OF LIFE* (1860)

6. No place affords a more striking conviction of the vanity of human hopes, than a public library.

SAMUEL JOHNSON, *THE RAMBLER* (1750–52), 106

7. Borrowers of books—those mutilators of collections, spoilers of the symmetry of shelves, and creators of odd volumes.

CHARLES LAMB, "THE TWO RACES OF MEN," *ESSAYS OF ELIA* (1823)

LIES

See 331. FALSEHOOD

539. LIFE

See also 3. THE ABSURD; 83. BIRTH; 221. DEATH; 316. EXISTENCE; 504. INVOLVEMENT; 540. LIFE, STAGES OF; 541. LIFE AND DEATH; 548. LONGEVITY; 573. MEANING; 606. MORTALITY; 990. TRANSIENCE; 1019. THE UNKNOWN; 1067. WORLD

1. Life is a wonderful thing to talk about, or to read about in history books—but it is terrible when one has to live it.

JEAN ANOUILH, *TIME REMEMBERED* (1939), 2.1, TR. PATRICIA MOYES

2. Life is a toy made of glass; it appears to be of inestimable price, but in reality it is very cheap.

PIETRO ARETINO, TER TO BERNARDO TASSO, SEPT. 26, 1537, TR. SAMUEL PUTNAM

3. Men cling to life even at the cost of enduring great misfortune.

ARISTOTLE, *POLITICS* (4TH C. B.C.), 3.6, TR. BENJAMIN JOWETT

4. Life is seldom as unendurable as, to judge by the facts, it logically ought to be.

BROOKS ATKINSON, "DECEMBER 22," *ONCE AROUND THE SUN* (1951)

5. Deem not life a thing of consequence. For look at the yawning void of the future, and at that other limitless space, the past.

MARCUS AURELIUS, *MEDITATIONS* (2ND C.), 4.50, TR. MORRIS HICKEY MORGAN

6. The art of living is more like wrestling than dancing.

MARCUS AURELIUS, *MEDITATIONS* (2ND C.), 7.61, TR. MORRIS HICKEY MORGAN

7. The life of every man is a diary in which he means to write one story, and writes another; and his humblest hour is when he compares the volume as it is with what he vowed to make it.

J. M. BARRIE, *THE LITTLE MINISTER* (1891), 1

8. A living dog is better than a dead lion.

BIBLE, ECCLESIASTES 9:4

9. Sometimes when a man gets older he has a revelation and wants awfully bad to get back to the place where he left his life, but he can't get to that place—not often.

JANE BOWLES, "PLAIN PLEASURES," *THE COLLECTED WORKS OF JANE BOWLES* (1966)

10. The farther a man follows the rainbow, the harder it is for him to get back to the life which he left starving like an old dog.

JANE BOWLES, "PLAIN PLEASURES," *THE COLLECTED WORKS OF JANE BOWLES* (1966)

11. How good is man's life, the mere living! how fit to employ / All the heart and the soul and the senses forever in joy!

ROBERT BROWNING, "SAUL," *MEN AND WOMEN* (1855), 9

12. I count life just a stuff / To try the soul's strength on.

ROBERT BROWNING, "IN A BALCONY," *MEN AND WOMEN* (1855)

13. We mortals cross the ocean of this world / Each in his average cabin of a life; / The best's not big, the worst yields elbowroom.

ROBERT BROWNING, "BISHOP BLOUGRAM'S APOLOGY," *MEN AND WOMEN* (1855), 99

14. Life is not so much a riddle to be read as a Gordian knot that will get cut sooner or later.

SAMUEL BUTLER (D. 1902), "LORD, WHAT IS MAN?" *NOTE-BOOKS* (1912)

15. To live is like to love—all reason is against it, and all healthy instinct for it.

SAMUEL BUTLER (D. 1902), "HIGGLEDY-PIGGLEDY," *NOTE-BOOKS* (1912)

16. We are involved in a life that passes understanding and our highest business is our daily life.

JOHN CAGE, "WHERE ARE WE GOING? AND WHAT ARE WE DOING?" *SILENCE* (1961)

17. In living and in seeing other men, the heart must break or become as bronze.

CHAMFORT, *CARACTÈRES ET ANECDOTES* (1771), 164

18. Life is fleeting—and therefore endurable.

ALEXANDER CHASE, *PERSPECTIVES* (1966)

19. Life is a maze in which we take the wrong turning before we have learnt to walk.

CYRIL CONNOLLY, *THE UNQUIET GRAVE* (1945), 1

20. There are men here and there to whom the whole of life is like an after-dinner hour with a cigar; easy, pleasant, empty, perhaps enlivened by some fable of strife to be forgotten before the end is told.

JOSEPH CONRAD, *LORD JIM* (1900), 5

21. Life is an incurable disease.

ABRAHAM COWLEY, "TO DR. SCARBOROUGH" (1656), 6

22. Man pines to live but cannot endure the days of his life.

EDWARD DAHLBERG, *THE SORROWS OF PRIAPUS* (1957)

23. Our life seems cursed to be a wiggle merely, and a wandering without end.

ANNIE DILLARD, "SOJOURNER," *TEACHING A STONE TO TALK* (1982)

24. Our life is a faint tracing on the surface of mystery, like the idle, curved tunnels of leaf miners on the face of a leaf.

ANNIE DILLARD, "HEAVEN AND EARTH IN JEST," *PILGRIM AT TINKER CREEK* (1974)

25. We live half our waking lives and all of our sleeping lives in some private, useless, and insensible waters we never mention or recall.

ANNIE DILLARD, "TOTAL ECLIPSE," *TEACHING A STONE TO TALK* (1982)

26. When I consider life, 'tis all a cheat. / Yet fooled with hope, men favour the deceit.

JOHN DRYDEN, *AURENGZEBE* (1676), 4.1

27. A minute to smile and an hour to weep in, / A pint of joy to a peck of trouble, / And never a laugh but the moans come double; / And that is life!

PAUL LAURENCE DUNBAR, "LIFE," *THE COMPLETE POEMS* (1962)

28. Life, unlike the inanimate, will take the long way round to circumvent barrenness. A kind of desperate will resides even in a root.

LOREN EISELEY, "THE LAST NEANDERTHAL," *THE STAR THROWER* (1978)

29. Birth, and copulation, and death. / That's all the facts when you come to brass tacks.

T. S. ELIOT, "FRAGMENT OF AN AGON," *SWEENEY AGONISTES* (1926)

30. It has always been difficult for man to realize that his life is all an art. It has been more difficult to conceive it so than to act it so.

HAVELOCK ELLIS, *THE DANCE OF LIFE* (1923), 1

31. Life only avails, not the having lived.

EMERSON, "SELF-RELIANCE," *ESSAYS: FIRST SERIES* (1841)

32. We do not live an equal life, but one of contrasts and patchwork; now a little joy, then a sorrow, now a sin, then a generous or brave action.

EMERSON, *JOURNALS*, 1845

33. We all got holes in our lives. Nobody dies in a perfect garment.

LOUISE ERDRICH, "INSULATION," *THE BINGO PALACE* (1994)

34. Alas!—but why Alas? / It is the lot of mortality we experience.

EURIPIDES (5TH C. B.C.), QUOTED IN PLUTARCH'S "CONTENTMENT," *MORALIA* (C. A.D. 100), TR. MOSES HADAS

35. Life is a short affair; / We should try to make it smooth, and free from strife.

EURIPIDES, *THE SUPPLIANT WOMEN* (C. 421 B.C.), TR. FRANK W. JONES

36. Irony and pity are two good counselors: one, in smiling, makes life pleasurable; the other, who cries, makes it sacred.

ANATOLE FRANCE, *LE JARDIN D'ÉPICURE* (1895)

37. Life is half spent before one knows what life is.

FRENCH PROVERB

38. Life is like an onion, which one peels crying.

FRENCH PROVERB

39. There is only one meaning of life: the act of living itself.

ERICH FROMM, *ESCAPE FROM FREEDOM* (1941), 7

40. Making a living and making a life that's worthwhile are not the same thing. Living *the* good life and living *a* good life are not the same thing.

ROBERT FULGHUM, *IT WAS ON FIRE WHEN I LAY DOWN ON IT* (1989)

41. We are born crying, live complaining, and die disappointed.

THOMAS FULLER, M.D., *GNOMOLOGIA* (1732), 5427

42. All lives are interesting; no one life is more interesting than another. Its fascination depends on how much is revealed, and in what manner.

MAVIS GALLANT, "PAUL LÉAUTAUD, 1872–1956," *PARIS NOTEBOOKS* (1986)

43. Life's a pudding full of plums.

W. S. GILBERT, *THE GONDOLIERS* (1889), I

44. Life's perhaps the only riddle / That we shrink from giving up.

W. S. GILBERT, *THE GONDOLIERS* (1889), I

45. Life is a process where people mix and match, fall apart and come back together.

NIKKI GIOVANNI, "THE SIXTIES," *RACISM 101* (1994)

46. We prate of freedom; we are in deadly fear of life, as much of our own American scene betrays.

LEARNED HAND, *THE SPIRIT OF LIBERTY* (1959)

47. A just conception of life is too large a thing to grasp during the short interval of passing through it.

THOMAS HARDY, *A PAIR OF BLUE EYES* (1873), 19

48. Life is made up of marble and mud.

NATHANIEL HAWTHORNE, *THE HOUSE OF THE SEVEN GABLES* (1851), 2

49. Life is a continued struggle to be what we are not, and to do what we cannot.

WILLIAM HAZLITT, "DISAPPOINTMENT," *LECTURES ON THE DRAMATIC LITERATURE OF THE AGE OF ELIZABETH* (1820)

50. The art of life is to know how to enjoy a little and to endure much.

WILLIAM HAZLITT, "COMMONPLACES," *THE ROUND TABLE* (1817), I

51. Life has a value only when it has something valuable as its object.

HEGEL, INTRODUCTION TO *PHILOSOPHY OF HISTORY* (1832), TR. JOHN SIBREE

52. I'd like to know / what this whole show / is all about / before it's out.

PIET HEIN, "I'D LIKE—," *GROOKS* (1966)

53. Life is made up of sobs, sniffles, and smiles, with sniffles predominating.

O. HENRY, "THE GIFT OF THE MAGI," *THE FOUR MILLION* (1906)

54. There is a saying that no man has tasted the full flavor of life until he has known poverty, love, and war.

O. HENRY, "THE COMPLETE LIFE OF JOHN HOPKINS," *THE VOICE OF THE CITY* (1908)

55. Life is an end in itself, and the only question as to whether it is worth living is whether you have enough of it.

OLIVER WENDELL HOLMES, JR, SPEECH, BOSTON BAR ASSOCIATION, MARCH 7, 1900

56. Life is a fatal complaint, and an eminently contagious one.

OLIVER WENDELL HOLMES, SR., *THE POET AT THE BREAKFAST TABLE* (1872), 12

57. So long as we do not blow our brains out, we have decided life is worth living.

EDGAR WATSON HOWE, *VENTURES IN COMMON SENSE* (1919), 32.23

58. The best way to prepare for life is to begin to live.

ELBERT HUBBARD, *THE NOTE BOOK* (1927)

59. Life is simply one damned thing after another.

ASCRIBED TO ELBERT HUBBARD (1856–1915)

60. The earth belongs to the living, not to the dead.

THOMAS JEFFERSON, LETTER TO JOHN W. EPPES, JUNE 24, 1813

61. I do not cut my life up into days but my days into lives, each day, each hour, an entire life.

JUAN RAMÓN JIMÉNEZ, "HEROIC REASON," *SELECTED WRITINGS* (1957), TR. H. R. HAYS

62. Life is a pill which none of us can bear to swallow without gilding.

SAMUEL JOHNSON, QUOTED IN HESTER LYNCH PIOZZI'S *ANECDOTES OF SAMUEL JOHNSON* (1786)

63. A man's life of any worth is a continual allegory—and very few eyes can see the mystery of his life—a life like the scriptures, figurative.

KEATS, LETTER TO GEORGE AND GEORGIANA KEATS, FEB. 14–MAY 3, 1819

64. Thank you, God, for this good life and forgive us if we do not love it enough.

GARRISON KEILLOR, *LEAVING HOME* (1987)

65. For men must work and women must weep, / And the sooner it's over, the sooner to sleep.

CHARLES KINGSLEY, "THE THREE FISHERS."

66. There is no easy path leading out of life, and few are the easy ones that lie within it.

WALTER SAVAGE LANDOR, "EPICURUS, LEONTION, AND TERNISSA," *IMAGINARY CONVERSATIONS* (1824–53)

67. The essence of life, I concluded, did not lie in the material. It penetrated, but was not bound to, the physical world of science.

CHARLES A. LINDBERGH, "OUT OF EDEN," *AUTOBIOGRAPHY OF VALUES* (1978)

68. Life for the European is a career; for the American, it is a hazard.

MARY MCCARTHY, "AMERICA THE BEAUTIFUL: THE HUMANIST IN THE BATHTUB," *ON THE CONTRARY* (1961)

69. Prufrock had measured out his life with measuring spoons; Dubin, in books resurrecting the lives of others.

BERNARD MALAMUD, *DUBIN'S LIVES* (1979)

70. No man is quick enough to enjoy life.

MARTIAL, *EPIGRAMS* (A.D. 86), 2.90, TR. WALTER C. A. KERR

71. The life force is vigorous. The delight that accompanies it counter-balances all the pains and hardships that confront men. It makes life worth living.

W. SOMERSET MAUGHAM, *THE SUMMING UP* (1938), 73

72. The basic fact about human existence is not that it is a tragedy, but that it is a bore. It is not so much a war as an endless standing in line.

H. L. MENCKEN, *PREJUDICES: SIXTH SERIES* (1927), 3

73. No matter how ruined man and his world may seem to be, and no matter how terrible man's despair may become, as long as he continues to be a man his very humanity continues to tell him that life has a meaning.

THOMAS MERTON, *NO MAN IS AN ISLAND* (1955)

74. It is not true that life is one damn thing after another—it's one damn thing over and over.

EDNA ST. VINCENT MILLAY, *LETTERS OF EDNA ST. VINCENT MILLAY* (1952), ED. A. R. MACDOUGAL

75. The aim of life is to live, and to live means to be aware, joyously, drunkenly, serenely, divinely aware.

HENRY MILLER, "CREATIVE DEATH," *THE WISDOM OF THE HEART* (1941)

76. Nor love thy life, nor hate; but what thou liv'st / Live well; how long or short permit to Heaven.

MILTON, *PARADISE LOST* (1667), 11.553

77. Of all human foibles love of living is the most powerful.

MOLIÈRE, *LOVE'S THE BEST DOCTOR* (1665), 3, TR. JOHN WOOD

78. The great business of life is to be, to do, to do without, and to depart.

JOHN MORLEY, ADDRESS ON APHORISMS, EDINBURGH, 1887

79. Life is the only art that we are required to practice without preparation, and without being allowed the preliminary trials, the failures and botches, that are essential for the training of a mere beginner.

LEWIS MUMFORD, "THE WAY AND THE LIFE," *THE CONDUCT OF LIFE* (1951)

80. Life is strewn with so many dangers, and can be the source of so many misfortunes, that death is not the greatest of them.

NAPOLEON I, *MAXIMS* (1804–15)

81. Life is not having been told that the man has just waxed the floor.

OGDEN NASH, "YOU AND ME AND P. B. SHELLEY," *GOOD INTENTIONS* (1943)

82. We love life, not because we are used to living but because we are used to loving.

NIETZSCHE, "ON READING AND WRITING," *THUS SPOKE ZARATHUSTRA* (1883–92), 1, TR. WALTER KAUFMANN

83. Our lives are merely strange dark interludes in the electric display of God the Father.

EUGENE O'NEILL, *STRANGE INTERLUDE* (1928), 9

84. Life is the external text, the burning bush by the edge of the path from which God speaks.

JOSÉ ORTEGA Y GASSET, "PRELIMINARY MEDITATION," *MEDITATIONS ON QUIXOTE* (1914)

85. In order to master the unruly torrent of life the learned man meditates, the poet quivers, and the political hero erects the fortress of his will.

JOSÉ ORTEGA Y GASSET, "PRELIMINARY MEDITATION," *MEDITATIONS ON QUIXOTE* (1914)

86. I notice no "interplay of life and art." Life is that which—pressingly, persistently, unfailingly, imperially—interrupts.

CYNTHIA OZICK, "PEAR TREE AND POLAR BEAR: A WORD ON LIFE AND ART," *METAPHOR & MEMORY* (1989)

87. Between us and heaven or hell there is only life, which is the frailest thing in the world.

PASCAL, *PENSÉES* (1670), 213, TR. W. F. TROTTER

88. We never live, but we hope to live; and, as we are always preparing to be happy, it is inevitable we should never be so.

PASCAL, *PENSÉES* (1670), 172, TR. W. F. TROTTER

89. The art of living is the art of knowing how to believe lies.

CESARE PAVESE, *THE BURNING BRAND* (1961)

90. Every true man, sir, who is a little above the level of the beasts and plants does not live for the sake of living, without knowing how to live; but he lives so as to give a meaning and a value of his own to life.

LUIGI PIRANDELLO, *SIX CHARACTERS IN SEARCH OF AN AUTHOR* (1921), 3, TR. EDWARD STORER

91. Life is little more than a loan shark: it exacts a very high rate of interest for the few pleasures it concedes.

LUIGI PIRANDELLO, *THE PLEASURE OF HONESTY* (1917), 1, TR. WILLIAM MURRAY

92. One lives in the hope of becoming a memory.

ANTONIO PORCHIA, *VOCES* (1968), TR. W. S. MERWIN

93. Life is short, but its ills make it seem long.

PUBLILIUS SYRUS, *MORAL SAYINGS* (1ST C. B.C.), 124, TR. DARIUS LYMAN

94. Fate loves to invent patterns and designs. Its difficulty lies in complexity. But life itself is difficult because of its simplicity. It has only a few things of a grandeur not fit for us.

RAINER MARIA RILKE, *THE NOTEBOOKS OF MALTE LAURIDS BRIGGE* (1910), TR. M. D. HERTER NORTON

95. "Does the road wind up-hill all the way?" / "Yes, to the very end." / "Will the day's journey take the whole long day?" / "From morn to night, my friend."

CHRISTINA ROSSETTI, "UP-HILL" (1861)

96. From the first moment of life, men ought to begin learning to deserve to live.

ROUSSEAU, *A DISCOURSE ON POLITICAL ECONOMY* (1758), TR. G. D. H. COLE

97. There is no wealth but life.

JOHN RUSKIN, *UNTO THIS LAST* (1862), 4.77

98. Real life is, to most men, a long second-best, a perpetual compromise between the ideal and the possible.

BERTRAND RUSSELL, "THE STUDY OF MATHEMATICS," *MYSTICISM AND LOGIC* (1917)

99. Life has a meaning only if one barters it day by day for something other than itself.

SAINT-EXUPÉRY, *THE WISDOM OF THE SANDS* (1948), 5, TR. STUART GILBERT

100. It is the acme of life to understand life.

GEORGE SANTAYANA, *LITTLE ESSAYS* (1920), 57

101. There is no cure for birth and death save to enjoy the interval.

GEORGE SANTAYANA, "WAR SHRINES," *SOLILOQUIES IN ENGLAND* (1922)

102. It is only in the microscope that our life looks so big. It is an indivisible point, drawn out and magnified by the powerful lenses of Time and Space.

SCHOPENHAUER, "THE VANITY OF EXISTENCE," *PARERGA AND PARALIPOMENA* (1851), TR. T. BAILEY SAUNDERS

103. Life is a task to be done. It is a fine thing to say *defunctus est;* it means that the man has done his task.

SCHOPENHAUER, "ON THE SUFFERINGS OF THE WORLD," *PARERGA AND PARALIPOMENA* (1851), TR. T. BAILEY SAUNDERS

104. The scenes of our life are like pictures done in rough mosaic. Looked at close, they produce no effect. There is nothing beautiful to be found in them, unless you stand some distance off.

SCHOPENHAUER, "THE VANITY OF EXISTENCE," *PARERGA AND PARALIPOMENA* (1851), TR. T. BAILEY SAUNDERS

105. It is more fitting for a man to laugh at life than to lament over it.

Seneca, "On Peace of Mind," *Moral Essays* (1st c.)

106. Life's neither a good nor an evil: it's a field for good and evil.

Seneca, *Letters to Lucilius* (1st c.), 99.12, tr. E. Phillips Barker

107. Nothing is so false as human life, nothing so treacherous. God knows no one would have accepted it as a gift, if it had not been given without our knowledge.

Seneca, *Ad Marciam de Consolatione* (1st c.)

108. Life is as tedious as a twice-told tale / Vexing the dull ear of a drowsy man.

Shakespeare, *King John* (1596–97), 3.4.108

109. Life's but a walking shadow, a poor player, / That struts and frets his hour upon the stage / And then is heard no more. It is a tale / Told y an idiot, full of sound and fury, / Signifying nothing.

Shakespeare, *Macbeth* (1605–06), 5.5.24

110. The time of life is short! / To spend that shortness basely were too long.

Shakespeare, *1 Henry IV* (1597–98), 5.2.82

111. The web of our life is of a mingled yarn, good and ill together.

Shakespeare, *All's Well That Ends Well* (1602–03), 4.3.83

112. Life is too short for men to take it seriously.

George Bernard Shaw, *Back to Methuselah* (1921), 2

113. Living well and beautifully and justly are all one thing.

Socrates, in Plato's *Crito* (4th c. b.c.), tr. Lane Cooper

114. What most counts is not to live, but to live aright.

Socrates, in Plato's *Crito* (4th c. b.c.), tr. Lane Cooper

115. You cannot know a man's life before the man / has died, then only can you call it good or bad.

Sophocles, *The Women of Trachis* (c. 413 b.c.), tr. Michael Jameson

116. The life we all live is amateurish and accidental; it begins in accident and proceeds by trial and error toward dubious ends.

Wallace Stegner, "The Law of Nature and the Dream of Man," *When the Bluebird Sings in the Lemonade Springs* (1992)

117. As wise women and men in every culture tell us: The art of life is not controlling what happens to us, but *using* what happens to us.

Gloria Steinem, *Revolution from Within* (1992)

118. What is the life of man! Is it not to shift from side to side?—from sorrow to sorrow?—to button up one cause of vexation!—and unbutton another!

Laurence Sterne, *Tristram Shandy* (1759–67), 4.31

119. Everyday life is a stimulating mixture of order and haphazardry. The sun rises and sets on schedule but the wind bloweth where it listeth.

Robert Louis Stevenson, "Pan's Pipes," *Virginibus Puerisque* (1881)

120. Life is a tragedy wherein we sit as spectators for a while and then act our part in it.

Jonathan Swift, *Thoughts on Various Subjects* (1711)

121. Life, like a child, laughs, shaking its rattle of death as it runs.

Rabindranath Tagore, *Lover's Gift* (1918), 42

122. Life is given to us, we earn it by giving it.

Rabindranath Tagore, *Stray Birds* (1916), 56

123. Better a thousand times even a swiftly fading, ephemeral moment of life than the epoch-long unconsciousness of the stone.

Edwin Way Teale, *Autumn Across America* (1956), 8

124. Life is a frail moth flying / Caught in the web of the years that pass.

Sara Teasdale, "Come," *Rivers to the Sea* (1915)

125. Now at last I have come to see what life is, / Nothing is ever ended, everything only begun, / And the brave victories that seem so splendid / Are never really won.

Sara Teasdale, "At Midnight," *Flame and Shadow* (1920)

126. Children, who play life, discern its true law and relations more clearly than men, who fail to live it worthily, but who think that they are wiser by experience, that is, by failure.

Thoreau, "Where I Lived, and What I Lived For," *Walden* (1854)

127. Each person is born to one possession which outvalues all his others—his last breath.

Mark Twain, "Pudd'nhead Wilson's New Calendar," *Following the Equator* (1897), 2.6

128. The shortness of life cannot dissuade us from its pleasures, nor console us for its pains.

Vauvenargues, *Reflections and Maxims* (1746), 324, tr. F. G. Stevens

129. What is a great life if not a youthful idea executed by the man of mature years?

Alfred de Vigny, *Cinq-Mars* (1826), 20

130. Life is the saddest thing there is, next to death.

Edith Wharton, *A Backward Glance* (1934)

131. Life has a way of overgrowing its achievements as well as its ruins.

Edith Wharton, "The Spark," *Old New York* (1924)

132. Whoever is not in his coffin and the dark grave let him know he has enough.

Walt Whitman, "The Sleepers," 2, *Leaves of Grass* (1855–92)

133. Life imitates art far more than art imitates life.

Oscar Wilde, "The Decay of Lying," *Intentions* (1891)

134. Life is not governed by will or intention. Life is a question of nerves, and fibers, and slowly built-up cells in which thought hides itself and passion has its dreams.

Oscar Wilde, *The Picture of Dorian Gray* (1891), 19

540. LIFE, STAGES OF

See also 539. Life; 571. Maturity; 653. Old Age; 1071. Youth; 1072. Youth and Age

1. Life is a child playing around your feet, a tool you hold firmly in your grip, a bench you sit down upon in the evening, in your garden.

Jean Anouilh, *Antigone* (1942), tr. Lewis Galantière

2. In the morning, we carry the world like Atlas; at noon, we stoop and bend beneath it; and at night, it crushes us flat to the ground.

Henry Ward Beecher, *Proverbs from Plymouth Pulpit* (1887)

3. Man arrives as a novice at each age of his life.

Chamfort, *Caractères et anecdotes* (1771), 576

4. Every stage of human life, except the last, is marked out by certain and defined limits; old age alone has no precise and determinate boundary.

Cicero, *De Senectute* (44 B.C.)

5. Youth is a blunder; manhood a struggle; old age a regret.

Benjamin Disraeli, *Coningsby* (1844), 3.1

6. I am older now, and sleep less, and have seen most of what there is to see and am not very much impressed any more, I suppose, by anything.

Loren Eiseley, "The Bird and the Machine," *The Star Thrower* (1978)

7. There are but three events which concern men: birth, life, and death. They are unconscious of their birth, they suffer when they die, and they neglect to live.

La Bruyère, *Characters* (1688), 11.48, tr. Henri Van Laun

8. In the morn of life we are alert, we are heated in its noon, and only in its decline do we repose.

Walter Savage Landor, "Menander and Epicurus," *Imaginary Conversations* (1824–53)

9. The four stages of man are infancy, childhood, adolescence and obsolescence.

Art Linkletter, *A Child's Garden of Misinformation* (1965), 8

10. Completed, most lives were alike in stages of living—joys, celebrations, crises, illusions, losses, sorrows.

Bernard Malamud, *Dubin's Lives* (1979)

11. As an infant, man is wrapped in his mother's womb; grown up, he is wrapped in custom; dead, he is wrapped in earth.

Malay Proverb

12. For the complete life, the perfect pattern includes old age as well as youth and maturity.

W. Somerset Maugham, *The Summing Up* (1938), 73

13. Life is a disease; and the only difference between one man and another is the stage of the disease at which he lives.

George Bernard Shaw, *Back to Methuselah* (1921), 2

14. As I get older, my childhood self becomes more accessible to me, but selectively, in images as stylized and suspect as moments remembered from a novel read years ago.

John Updike, "Five Days in Finland at the Age of Fifty-Five," *Odd Jobs* (1991)

15. The golden years of my life are slipping by on stealthy feet at nightfall; there is a footprint in the dark, a bell strikes twelve, and the flying year is gone.

THOMAS WOLFE, *THOMAS WOLFE'S LETTERS TO HIS MOTHER* (1943)

541. LIFE AND DEATH

See also 221. DEATH; 539. LIFE

1. Thus my life is a flight and I lose everything and everything belongs to oblivion.

JORGE LUIS BORGES, "PARABLES," IN *FIFTY GREAT ESSAYS* (1964)

2. If a man know not life which he hath seen, how shall he know death, which he hath not seen?

SAMUEL BUTLER (D. 1902), "DEATH," *NOTE-BOOKS* (1912)

3. What is called a reason for living is also an excellent reason for dying.

ALBERT CAMUS, "AN ABSURD REASONING," *THE MYTH OF SISYPHUS* (1942), TR. JUSTIN O'BRIEN

4. Whatever lives is granted breath / But by the grace and sufferance of Death.

COUNTEE CULLEN, "SONG DIALOGUE," *ON THESE I STAND* (1947)

5. I think that the dying pray at the last not "please," but "thank you," as a guest thanks his host at the door.

ANNIE DILLARD, "THE WATERS OF SEPARATION," *PILGRIM AT TINKER CREEK* (1974)

6. All our life is but a going out to the place of execution, to death.

JOHN DONNE, *SERMONS,* NO. 4, 1619

7. The art of living well and the art of dying well are one.

EPICURUS, LETTER TO MENOECEUS (3RD C. B.C.), IN *LETTERS, PRINCIPAL DOCTRINES, AND VATICAN SAYINGS,*, TR. RUSSEL M. GEER

8. Healthy children will not fear life if their elders have integrity enough not to fear death.

ERIK H. ERIKSON, *CHILDHOOD AND SOCIETY* (1950), 7

9. Death is what men want when the anguish of living / is more than they can bear.

EURIPIDES, *HECUBA* (C. 425 B.C.), TR. WILLIAM ARROWSMITH

10. It is better that we live ever so / Miserably than die in glory.

EURIPIDES, *IPHIGENIA IN AULIS* (C. 405 B.C.), TR. CHARLES R. WALKER

11. Our final experience, like our first, is conjectural. We move between two darknesses.

E. M. FORSTER, "PEOPLE," *ASPECTS OF THE NOVEL* (1927)

12. The whole life of instinct serves the one end of bringing about death.

SIGMUND FREUD, *BEYOND THE PLEASURE PRINCIPLE* (1920), TR. C. J. M. HUBBACK

13. People seek a new orientation, a new philosophy, one which is centered on the priorities of life—physically and spiritually—and not on the priorities of death.

ERICH FROMM, *THE REVOLUTION OF HOPE* (1968)

14. [M]obilizing the love of life is the only force that can defeat the love for the dead.

ERICH FROMM, *THE ANATOMY OF HUMAN DESTRUCTIVENESS* (1973)

15. A good life fears not life nor death.

THOMAS FULLER, M.D., *GNOMOLOGIA* (1732), 157

16. Dying is as natural as living.

THOMAS FULLER, M.D., *GNOMOLOGIA* (1732), 1348

17. I'm not afraid of death. It's the stake one puts up in order to play the game of life.

JEAN GIRAUDOUX, *AMPHITRYON 38* (1929), 2, TR. PETER H. JUDD

18. Grieve not; though the journey of life be bitter, and the end unseen, there is no road which does not lead to an end.

HĀFIZ, GHAZALS FROM THE *DIVAN* (14TH C.), 18, TR. JUSTIN HUNTLY MCCARTHY

19. Some people seem to think that death is the only reality in life. Others, happier and rightlier minded, see and feel that life is the true reality in death.

JULIUS CHARLES HARE AND AUGUSTUS WILLIAM HARE, *GUESSES AT TRUTH* (1827)

20. The most rational cure after all for the inordinate fear of death is to set a just value on life.

WILLIAM HAZLITT, "ON THE FEAR OF DEATH," *TABLE TALK* (1821–22)

21. "Every man's life ends the same way," Ernest [Hemingway] had said, "and it is only the details of how he lived and how he died that distinguish one man from another."

A.E. HOTCHNER, *PAPA HEMINGWAY* (1966)

22. It matters not how a man dies but how he lives. The act of dying is not of importance, it lasts so short a time.

SAMUEL JOHNSON, QUOTED IN BOSWELL'S *LIFE OF SAMUEL JOHNSON*, OCT. 26, 1769

23. Life and death appear more certainly ours than whatsoever else: and yet hardly can that be called ours, which comes without our knowledge, and goes without it.

WALTER SAVAGE LANDOR, "MARCUS TULLIUS AND QUINCTUS CICERO," *IMAGINARY CONVERSATIONS* (1824–53)

24. Our life is made by the death of others.

LEONARDO DA VINCI, *NOTEBOOKS* (C. 1500), TR. JEAN PAUL RICHTER

25. In the attempt to defeat death man has been inevitably obliged to defeat life, for the two are inextricably related. Life moves on to death, and to deny one is to deny the other.

HENRY MILLER, "CREATIVE DEATH," *THE WISDOM OF THE HEART* (1941)

26. Long life, and short, are by death made all one; for there is no long, nor short, to things that are no more.

MONTAIGNE, "THAT TO STUDY PHILOSOPHY IS TO LEARN TO DIE," *ESSAYS* (1580–88), TR. W. C. HAZLITT

27. Who that hath ever been / Could bear to be no more? / Yet who would tread again the scene / He trod through life before?

JAMES MONTGOMERY, *THE FALLING LEAF* (1825)

28. Life is a great surprise. I do not see why death should not be an even greater one.

VLADIMIR NABOKOV, "COMMENTARY," *PALE FIRE* (1962), 549

29. In the midst of life we are in death.

THE ORDER FOR THE BURIAL OF THE DEAD, *THE BOOK OF COMMON PRAYER* (1928)

30. One wants to live, of course, indeed one only stays alive by virtue of the fear of death.

GEORGE ORWELL, "HOW THE POOR DIE," *SHOOTING AN ELEPHANT* (1950)

31. The whole motley confusion of acts, omissions, regrets and hopes which is the life of each one of us finds in death, not meaning or explanation, but an end.

OCTAVIO PAZ, *THE LABYRINTH OF SOLITUDE* (1950)

32. Death then, being the way and condition of life, we cannot love to live if we cannot bear to die.

WILLIAM PENN, *SOME FRUITS OF SOLITUDE* (1693), 1.505

33. Death is but an instant, life a long torment.

BERNARD JOSEPH SAURIN, *BEVERLEI* (1768), 5.5

34. One must take all one's life to learn how to live, and, what will perhaps make you wonder more, one must take all one's life to learn how to die.

SENECA, *ON THE SHORTNESS OF LIFE* (1ST C.)

35. We are wrong in looking forward to death: in great measure it's past already.

SENECA, *LETTERS TO LUCILIUS* (1ST C.), 1.2, TR. E. PHILLIPS BARKER

36. You will die not because you're ill, but because you're alive.

SENECA, *LETTERS TO LUCILIUS* (1ST C.), 78.6, TR. E. PHILLIPS BARKER

37. The weariest and most loathed worldly life / That age, ache, penury, and imprisonment / Can lay on nature is a paradise / To what we fear of death.

SHAKESPEARE, *MEASURE FOR MEASURE* (1604–05), 3.1.129

38. Life does not cease to be funny when people die any more than it ceases to be serious when people laugh.

GEORGE BERNARD SHAW, *THE DOCTOR'S DILEMMA* (1913), 5

39. Death's stamp gives value to the coin of life; making it possible to buy with life what is truly precious.

RABINDRANATH TAGORE, *STRAY BIRDS* (1916), 99

40. Oh Death where is thy sting! It has none. But life has.

MARK TWAIN, *NOTEBOOK* (1935)

41. Pity is for the living, envy is for the dead.

MARK TWAIN, "PUDD'NHEAD WILSON'S NEW CALENDAR," *FOLLOWING THE EQUATOR* (1897), 1.19

42. Whoever has lived long enough to find out what life is, knows how deep a debt of gratitude we owe to Adam, the first great benefactor of our race. He brought death into the world.

MARK TWAIN, "PUDD'NHEAD WILSON'S CALENDAR," *PUDD'NHEAD WILSON* (1894), 3

43. Science says: "We must live," and seeks the means of prolonging, increasing, facilitating and amplifying life, of making it tolerable and acceptable; wisdom says: "We must die," and seeks how to make us die well.

MIGUEL DE UNAMUNO, "ARBITRARY REFLECTIONS," *ESSAYS AND SOLILOQUIES* (1924), TR. J. E. CRAWFORD FLITCH

44. Death is one moment, and life is so many of them.

TENNESSEE WILLIAMS, *THE MILK TRAIN DOESN'T STOP HERE ANYMORE* (1963), 5

LIKING

See 21. AFFECTION; 22. AFFINITY; 725. PREFERENCE

542. LIMITATIONS

See also 342. FAULTS; 452. IMMATURITY; 457. IMPERFECTION; 462. INADEQUACY; 1047. WEAKNESS

1. Each of us has a day, more or less sad, more or less distant, when he has to accept, finally, the fact that he is a man.

JEAN ANOUILH, *ANTIGONE* (1942)

2. The humorous man recognizes that absolute purity, absolute justice, absolute logic and perfection are beyond human achievement and that men have been able to live happily for thousands of years in a state of genial frailty.

BROOKS ATKINSON, "APRIL 4," *ONCE AROUND THE SUN* (1951)

3. Who ever is adequate? We all create situations each other can't live up to, then break our hearts at them because they don't.

ELIZABETH BOWEN, *THE DEATH OF THE HEART* (1938), 3.1

4. Men cease to interest us when we find their limitations.

EMERSON, "CIRCLES," *ESSAYS: FIRST SERIES* (1841)

5. I am not eternity, but a man; a part of the whole, as an hour is of the day.

EPICTETUS, *DISCOURSES* (2ND C.), 2.5, TR. THOMAS W. HIGGINSON

6. Our accepting what we are must always inhibit our being what we ought to be.

JOHN FOWLES, *THE MAGUS* (1965), 27

7. A good marksman may miss.

THOMAS FULLER, M.D., *GNOMOLOGIA* (1732), 163

8. The thing I am most aware of is my limits. And this is natural; for I never, or almost never, occupy the middle of my cage; my whole being surges toward the bars.

ANDRÉ GIDE, *JOURNALS,* AUG. 4, 1930, TR. JUSTIN O'BRIEN

9. We expect more of ourselves than we have any right to, in virtue of our endowments.

OLIVER WENDELL HOLMES, SR., *OVER THE TEACUPS* (1891), 12

10. We cannot all hope to combine the pleasing qualities of good looks, brains, and eloquence.

HOMER, *ODYSSEY* (9TH C. B.C.), 8, TR. E. V. RIEU

11. It is of great use to the sailor to know the length of his line, though he cannot with it fathom all the depths of the ocean.

JOHN LOCKE, *AN ESSAY CONCERNING HUMAN UNDERSTANDING* (1690), 1.1.6

12. O my soul, do not aspire to immortal life, but exhaust the limits of the possible.

PINDAR, *ODES* (5TH C. B.C.), PYTHIA 3.61

13. Knowledge of what is possible is the beginning of happiness.

GEORGE SANTAYANA, *LITTLE ESSAYS* (1920), 105

14. Perhaps nobody ever accomplishes all that he feels lies in him to do; but nearly every one who tries his powers touches the walls of his being occasionally, and learns about how far to attempt to spring.

CHARLES DUDLEY WARNER, "THIRD STUDY," *BACKLOG STUDIES* (1873)

LIQUOR

See 268. DRINKING

543. LISTENING

See also 188. CONVERSATION; 275. EAVESDROPPING; 923. SPEAKING

1. I'm glad I understand that while language is a gift, listening is a responsibility.

NIKKI GIOVANNI, "GRIOTS," *RACISM 101* (1994)

2. To listen acutely is to be powerless, even if you sit on a throne.

CYNTHIA OZICK, "ITALO CALVINO: BRINGING STORIES TO THEIR SENSES," *METAPHOR & MEMORY* (1989)

3. A man who listens because he has nothing to say can hardly be a source of inspiration. The only listening that counts is that of the talker who alternately absorbs and expresses ideas.

AGNES REPPLIER, "THE LUXURY OF CONVERSATION," *COMPROMISES* (1904)

4. Give every man thine ear, but few thy voice.

SHAKESPEARE, *HAMLET* (1600), 1.3.68

5. The reason why we have two ears and only one mouth is that we may listen the more and talk the less.

ZENO OF CITIUM (C. 300 B.C.), QUOTED IN DIOGENES LAERTIUS' *LIVES AND OPINIONS OF EMINENT PHILOSOPHERS* (3RD C. A.D.), TR. R. D. HICKS

544. LITERALNESS

1. The letter killeth, but the spirit giveth life.

BIBLE, 2 CORINTHIANS 3:6

545. LITERATURE

See also 93. BOOKS AND READING; 1069. WRITING AND WRITERS

1. With both agents and publishers hungry for best-sellers, literature will have to end up as a cottage industry.

ANTHONY BURGESS, *YOU'VE HAD YOUR TIME* (1990)

2. There are only two or three human stories, and they go on repeating themselves as fiercely as if they had never happened before.

WILLA CATHER, *O PIONEERS!* (1913)

3. The unusual is only found in a very small percentage, except in literary creations, and that is exactly what makes literature.

JULIO CORTÁZAR, *THE WINNERS* (1960), 31, TR. ELAINE KERRIGAN

4. Shakespeare wouldn't have been any good if he'd stayed in Stratford. He had to go to London to be bathed in the full current of the Renaissance.

JOHN DOS PASSOS, *MOST LIKELY TO SUCCEED* (1954)

5. For the twenty million Americans who are hungry tonight, for the homeless freezing tonight, literature is as useless as a knowledge of astronomy.

ANDRÉ DUBUS, "AFTER TWENTY YEARS," *BROKEN VESSELS* (1991)

6. The "greatness" of literature cannot be determined solely by literary standards though we must remember that whether it is literature or not can be determined only by literary standards.

T. S. ELIOT, "RELIGION AND LITERATURE" (1935)

7. The two basic stories of all times are Cinderella and Jack the Giant Killer—the charm of women and the courage of men.

F. SCOTT FITZGERALD, *THE CRACK-UP* (1945)

8. What is so wonderful about great literature is that it transforms the man who reads it towards the condition of the man who wrote, and brings to birth in us also the creative impulse.

E. M. FORSTER, "ANONYMITY: AN ENQUIRY," *TWO CHEERS FOR DEMOCRACY* (1951)

9. A person who knows nothing about literature may be an ignoramus, but many people don't mind being that.

NORTHROP FRYE, *THE EDUCATED IMAGINATION* (1964)

10. The simple point is that literature belongs to the world man constructs, not to the world he sees; to his home, not his environment.

NORTHROP FRYE, *THE EDUCATED IMAGINATION* (1964)

11. Like every other form of art, literature is no more and nothing less than a matter of life and death. The only question worth asking about a story—or a poem, or a piece of sculpture, or a new concert hall—is, "Is it dead or alive?"

MAVIS GALLANT, "WHAT IS STYLE?" *PARIS NOTEBOOKS* (1986)

12. Reality is not an inspiration for literature. At its best, literature is an inspiration for reality.

ROMAIN GARY, *NEW YORK HERALD TRIBUNE*, JAN. 13, 1960

13. It is with noble sentiments that bad literature gets written.

ANDRÉ GIDE, *JOURNAL*, SEPT. 2, 1940

14. The attempt to devote oneself to literature alone is a most deceptive thing, and that often, paradoxically, is literature that suffers for it.

VÁCLAV HAVEL, *DISTURBING THE PEACE* (1990)

15. The message of guidance that neither politics nor philosophy nor religion now seems able to provide, we look for in modern literature.

IRVING HOWE, "LUIGI PIRANDELLO," *CELEBRATIONS AND ATTACKS* (1979)

16. Literature flourishes best when it is half a trade and half an art.

WILLIAM RALPH INGE, "THE VICTORIAN AGE," *OUTSPOKEN ESSAYS: SECOND SERIES* (1922)

17. The literary world is made up of little confederacies, each looking upon its own members as the lights of the universe; and considering all others as mere transient meteors, doomed soon to fall and be forgotten, while its own luminaries are to shine steadily on to immortality.

WASHINGTON IRVING, "LITERARY LIFE," *TALES OF A TRAVELLER* (1824)

18. The land of literature is a fairy land to those who view it at a distance, but, like all other landscapes, the charm fades on a nearer approach, and the thorns and briars become visible.

WASHINGTON IRVING, "NOTORIETY," *TALES OF A TRAVELLER* (1824)

19. Modern American literature was born in protest, born in rebellion, born out of the sense of loss and indirection which was imposed upon the new generations out of the realization that the old formal culture—the "New England idea"—could no longer serve.

ALFRED KAZIN, *ON NATIVE GROUNDS* (1942)

20. Socrates wrote nothing. Christ wrote nothing.

IRIS MURDOCH, *THE SACRED AND PROFANE LOVE MACHINE* (1974)

21. The existence of good bad literature—the fact that one can be amused or excited or even moved by a book that one's intellect simply refuses to take seriously—is a reminder that art is not the same thing as cerebration.

GEORGE ORWELL, "GOOD BAD BOOKS," *SHOOTING AN ELEPHANT* (1950)

22. The literary sensibility is geared to the timeless, that is, to the now only as an avenue by which all time can be reached.

JOHN SIMON, "SHOULD ALBEE HAVE SAID 'NO THANKS'?" *THE NEW YORK TIMES,* AUG. 20, 1967

23. I refuse to see literature as amusement, as a game. I think that you ought not to approach literature without a moral responsibility for every word you write.

ALEKSANDR SOLZHENITSYN, *THE NEW YORKER,* FEB. 14, 1994

24. Literature usually begets literature.

SUSAN SONTAG, "MICHEL LEIRIS' *MANHOOD,*" *AGAINST INTERPRETATION* (1961)

25. Perversity is the muse of modern literature.

SUSAN SONTAG, "CAMUS' NOTEBOOKS," *AGAINST INTERPRETATION* (1961)

26. The story [Henny-Penny] has the best opening in all literature—"The sky is falling," cried Henny-Penny, "and a piece of it fell on my tail."

JOHN STEINBECK, *STEINBECK: A LIFE IN LETTERS,* EDS. ELAINE STEINBECK AND ROBERT WALLSTEN (1975)

27. No human being ever spoke of scenery for above two minutes at a time, which makes me suspect that we hear too much of it in literature.

ROBERT LOUIS STEVENSON, "TALK AND TALKERS" (1882), I

28. Literature is the human activity that takes the fullest and most precise account of variousness, possibility, complexity, and difficulty.

LIONEL TRILLING, PREFACE, *THE LIBERAL IMAGINATION* (1950)

29. It is reasonable to assume that, by and large, what is not read now will not be read, ever. It is also reasonable to assume that practically nothing that is read now will be read later.

GORE VIDAL, *THE SECOND AMERICAN REVOLUTION AND OTHER ESSAYS* (1982)

30. There must always be some pretentiousness about literature, or else no one would take its pains or endure its disappointments.

GLENWAY WESCOTT, "THE MORAL OF SCOTT FITZGERALD," *THE NEW REPUBLIC,* FEB. 12, 1941

LOAN

See 96. BORROWING AND LENDING; 222. DEBT

LOGIC

See 785. REASON

546. LONDON

See also 289. ENGLAND AND ENGLISHMEN

1. We Britons had at that time particularly settled that it was treasonable to doubt our having and our being the best of everything; otherwise, while I was scared by the immensity of London, I think I might have had some faint doubts whether it was not rather ugly, crooked, narrow, and dirty.

CHARLES DICKENS, *GREAT EXPECTATIONS* (1860–1861)

2. London, that great cesspool into which all the loungers of the Empire are irresistibly drained.

SIR ARTHUR CONAN DOYLE, *A STUDY IN SCARLET* (1887)

3. When a man is tired of London, he is tired of life; for there is in London all that life can afford.

SAMUEL JOHNSON, QUOTED IN BOSWELL'S *LIFE OF SAMUEL JOHNSON,* SEPT. 20, 1777

4. I opened the door—what a freedom was this, for in the hospital there was no liberty to come and go—and stood, for a minute, in the soft air, savoring its fineness and the sweet smell of woods, and seeing in the distance the nightglow of London, city of cities, my mother.

OLIVER SACKS, *A LEG TO STAND ON* (1984)

547. LONELINESS

See also 915. SOLITUDE

1. No one would choose a friendless existence on condition of having all the other things in the world.

Aristotle, *Nicomachean Ethics* (4th c. B.C.), 8.1, tr. J. A. K. Thomson

2. Who knows what true loneliness is—not the conventional word but the naked terror? To the lonely themselves it wears a mask. The most miserable outcast hugs some memory or some illusion.

Joseph Conrad, *Under Western Eyes* (1911), 1.2

3. Our loneliness makes us avid column readers these days.

Edward Hoagland, "What I Think, What I Am," *The Tugman's Passage* (1982)

4. Whom the heart of man shuts out, / Sometimes the heart of God takes in, / And fences them all round about / With silence mid the world's loud din.

James Russell Lowell, "The Forlorn" (1842)

5. The most I ever did for you was to outlive you. / But that is much.

Edna St. Vincent Millay, untitled poem, *Make Bright the Arrows* (1940)

6. In solitude the lonely man is eaten up by himself, among crowds by the many.

Nietzsche, *Miscellaneous Maxims and Opinions* (1879), 348, tr. Paul V. Cohn

7. The lonely one offers his hand too quickly to whomever he encounters.

Nietzsche, "On the Way of the Creator," *Thus Spoke Zarathustra* (1883–92), 1, tr. Walter Kaufmann

8. Man's loneliness is but his fear of life.

Eugene O'Neill, *Lazarus Laughed* (1927), 3.2

9. Loneliness is bred of a mind that has grown earthbound.

Saint-Exupéry, *The Wisdom of the Sands* (1948), 79, tr. Stuart Gilbert

10. The body is a house of many windows: there we all sit, showing ourselves and crying on the passers-by to come and love us.

Robert Louis Stevenson, title essay, 4, *Virginibus Puerisque* (1881)

11. She had figured out that the most pervasive American disease was loneliness, and that even people at the top often suffered from it, and that they could be surprisingly responsive to attractive strangers who were friendly.

Kurt Vonnegut, *Bluebeard* (1987)

12. What should young people do with their lives today? Many things, obviously. But the most daring thing is to create stable communities in which the terrible disease of loneliness can be cured.

Kurt Vonnegut, "Thoughts of a Free Thinker," *Palm Sunday* (1981)

548. LONGEVITY

See also 653. Old Age

1. Often a man who is very old in years has nothing beyond his age by which he can prove that he has lived a long time.

Athenodorus (1st c. B.C.), quoted in Seneca's "On Peace of Mind," *Moral Essays* (1st c. A.D.), tr. Aubrey Stewart

2. The longest-lived and the shortest-lived man, when they come to die, lose one and the same thing.

Marcus Aurelius, *Meditations* (2nd c.), 2.14, tr. Morris Hickey Morgan

3. 'Tis very certain the desire of life / Prolongs it.

Byron, *Don Juan* (1819–24), 2.64

4. Ask who wants to live to be a hundred, and the answer is the person who is ninety-nine.

Betty Comden, *Break the Other Leg* (1994)

5. Measurement of life should be proportioned rather to the intensity of the experience than to its actual length.

Thomas Hardy, *A Pair of Blue Eyes* (1873), 27

6. Life protracted is protracted woe.

Samuel Johnson, *The Vanity of Human Wishes* (1749)

7. It is vanity to desire a long life and to take no heed of a good life.

Thomas à Kempis, *The Imitation of Christ* (1426), 1.1

8. The wise man lives as long as he ought, not so long as he can.

Montaigne, "A custom of the Isle of Cea," *Essays* (1580–88), tr. W. C. Hazlitt

9. The man who has lived the longest is not he who has spent the greatest number of years, but he who has had the greatest sensibility of life.

Rousseau, *Émile* (1762), 1

10. Nothing can be meaner than the anxiety to live on, to live on anyhow and in any shape.

George Santayana, *Winds of Doctrine* (1913)

11. The only President who clearly died of overwork was Polk, and that was a long time ago. Hoover, who

worked intensely and humorlessly as President, lived for more than thirty years after the White House; Truman, who worked intensely and gaily, lived for twenty.

ARTHUR M. SCHLESINGER, JR., *THE IMPERIAL PRESIDENCY* (1973)

12. Not a soul takes thought how well he may live—only how long: yet a good life might be everybody's, a long one can be nobody's.

SENECA, *LETTERS TO LUCILIUS* (1ST C.), 22.17, TR. E. PHILLIPS BARKER

13. Every man desires to live long, but no man would be old.

JONATHAN SWIFT, *THOUGHTS ON VARIOUS SUBJECTS* (1711)

14. They live ill who expect to live always.

PUBLILIUS SYRUS, *MORAL SAYINGS* (1ST C. B.C.), 457, TR. DARIUS LYMAN

549. LOSERS

See also 15. ADVANTAGE; 17. ADVERSITY; 329. FAILURE

1. In a game, just losing is almost as satisfying as just winning.... In life the loser's score is always zero.

W. H. AUDEN, "POSTSCRIPT: THE FRIVOLOUS AND THE EARNEST," *THE DYER'S HAND* (1962)

2. It takes a genius to whine appealingly.

F. SCOTT FITZGERALD, *THE LETTERS OF F. SCOTT FITZGERALD* (1963), ED. ANDREW TURNBULL

3. If a man once fall, all will tread upon him.

THOMAS FULLER, M.D., *GNOMOLOGIA* (1732), 2662

4. Some people are so fond of ill-luck that they run half-way to meet it.

DOUGLAS JERROLD, "MEETING TROUBLES HALF-WAY," *WIT AND OPINIONS OF DOUGLAS JERROLD* (1859)

5. Nobody ever chooses the already unfortunate as objects of his loyal friendship.

LUCAN, *ON THE CIVIL WAR* (1ST C.), TR. ROBERT GRAVES

6. All his life he [Robert Kennedy] had been schooled that nothing was worse than to finish second. But crushing fears are no longer so crushing once they are experienced.

JACK NEWFIELD, *ROBERT KENNEDY* (1969)

7. When the world has once begun to use us ill, it afterwards continues the same treatment with less scruple or ceremony, as men do to a whore.

JONATHAN SWIFT, *THOUGHTS ON VARIOUS SUBJECTS* (1711)

550. LOSS

See also 17. ADVERSITY; 236. DEPRIVATION; 329. FAILURE; 552. LOVE, LOSS OF; 639. NOSTALGIA

1. Loss is nothing else but change, and change is Nature's delight.

MARCUS AURELIUS, *MEDITATIONS* (2ND C.), 9.35, TR. MAXWELL STANIFORTH

2. It is the image in the mind that binds us to our lost treasures, but it is the loss that shapes the image.

COLETTE, "LITERARY APPRENTICESHIP: -CLAUDINE,'" *EARTHLY PARADISE* (1966), 2

3. You must lose a fly to catch a trout.

GEORGE HERBERT, *JACULA PRUDENTUM* (1651)

4. A good man should and must / Sit rather down with loss than rise unjust.

BEN JONSON, *SEJANUS HIS FALL* (1603), 4.3

5. Alack our life, so beautiful to see, / With how much ease life losest, in a day, / What many years with pain and toil amassed!

PETRARCH, "LAURA DEAD," *CANZONIERE* (1360), 229

6. There are occasions when it is undoubtedly better to incur loss than to make gain.

PLAUTUS, *THE CAPTIVES* (3RD C. B.C.), 2.2.77, TR. HENRY THOMAS RILEY

7. The loss which is unknown is no loss at all.

PUBLILIUS SYRUS, *MORAL SAYINGS* (1ST C. B.C.), 38, TR. DARIUS LYMAN

8. Whatever you can lose, reckon of no account.

PUBLILIUS SYRUS, *MORAL SAYINGS* (1ST C. B.C.), 191, TR. DARIUS LYMAN

9. He that is robbed, not wanting what is stol'n, / Let him not know't, and he's not robbed at all.

SHAKESPEARE, *OTHELLO* (1604–05), 3.3.342

10. We begin life with loss. We are cast from the womb without an apartment, a charge plate, a job or a car. We are sucking, sobbing, clinging, helpless babies.

JUDITH VIORST, *NECESSARY LOSSES* (1986)

11. No man can lose what he never had.

IZAAK WALTON, *THE COMPLEAT ANGLER* (1653), 1.5

551. LOVE

See also 21. AFFECTION; 22. AFFINITY; 120. CHARITY; 181. CONSTANCY AND INCONSTANCY; 198. COURTSHIP; 284. EMOTIONS; 351.

LOVE

FLIRTATION; 499. INTIMACY; 510. JEALOUSY; 521. KISSING; 552. LOVE, LOSS OF; 553. LOVE, UNREQUITED; 554. LOVE AND HATE; 555. LOVERS; 675. PASSION; 826. ROMANCE; 857. SEDUCTION; 892. SEX

1. It [love] is a disease to be born with patience, like any nervous complaint, and to be treated with counter-irritants.

HENRY ADAMS, *DEMOCRACY: AN AMERICAN NOVEL* (1880)

2. You say that love is nonsense.... I tell you it is no such thing. For weeks and months it is a steady physical pain, an ache about the heart, never leaving one, by night or by day; a long strain on one's nerves like toothache or rheumatism, not intolerable at any one instant, but exhausting by its steady drain on the strength.

HENRY ADAMS, *DEMOCRACY: AN AMERICAN NOVEL* (1880)

3. Love is, above all, the gift of oneself.

JEAN ANOUILH, *ARDÈLE* (1948), 2, TR. LUCIENNE HILL

4. Among those whom I like or admire, I can find no common denominator, but among those whom I love, I can: all of them make me laugh.

W. H. AUDEN, "NOTES ON THE COMIC," *THE DYER'S HAND* (1962)

5. It is impossible to love and be wise.

FRANCIS BACON, "OF LOVE," *ESSAYS* (1625)

6. Many waters cannot quench love, neither can floods drown it.

BIBLE, SONG OF SOLOMON 8:7

7. There is no fear in love; but perfect love casteth out fear.

BIBLE, 1 JOHN 4:18

8. Who would give a law to lovers? / Love is unto itself a higher law.

BOETHIUS, *THE CONSOLATION OF PHILOSOPHY* (A.D. 524), 3

9. To fall in love is to create a religion that has a fallible god.

JORGE LUIS BORGES, "THE MEETING IN A DREAM," *OTHER INQUISITIONS* (1952), TR. R. L. SIMMS

10. There is only one way to be happy by means of the heart—to have none.

PAUL BOURGET, *LA PHYSIOLOGIE DE L'AMOUR MODERNE* (1890)

11. When you love someone all your saved-up wishes start coming out.

ELIZABETH BOWEN, *THE DEATH OF THE HEART* (1938), 1.9

12. On the whole, love comes with the speed of light; separation, with that of sound.

JOSEPH BRODSKY, *WATERMARK* (1992)

13. Whoso loves / Believes the impossible.

ELIZABETH BARRETT BROWNING, *AURORA LEIGH* (1856), 5.409

14. O Lyric Love, half angel and half bird, / And all a wonder and a wild desire.

ROBERT BROWNING, *THE RING AND THE BOOK* (1868–69), 1

15. Eternal Love doth keep / In his complacent arms, the earth, the air, the deep.

WILLIAM CULLEN BRYANT, "THE AGES" (1821)

16. Love dies only when growth stops.

PEARL S. BUCK, "WHAT SHALL I TELL MY DAUGHTER," *TO MY DAUGHTERS, WITH LOVE* (1967)

17. The more violent the love, the more violent the anger.

BURMESE PROVERBS (1962), 453

18. 'Tis sweet to know there is an eye will mark / Our coming, and look brighter when we come.

BYRON, *DON JUAN* (1819–24), 1.123

19. Then fly betimes, for only they / Conquer Love that run away.

THOMAS CAREW, "CONQUEST BY FLIGHT," *POEMS* (1640)

20. I had come at last and my heart was beating again strongly to a heart that could not know despair because it forgot itself in the duty of its love.

JOYCE CARY, *EXCEPT THE LORD* (1953)

21. Love is Nature's second sun.

GEORGE CHAPMAN, *ALL FOOLS* (C. 1599), 1.1

22. Love is the admiration and cherishing of the amiable qualities of the beloved person, upon the condition of yourself being the object of their action.

SAMUEL TAYLOR COLERIDGE, *TABLE TALK,* JUNE 24, 1827

23. Sympathy constitutes friendship; but in love there is a sort of antipathy, or opposing passion. Each strives to be the other, and both together make up one whole.

SAMUEL TAYLOR COLERIDGE, *TABLE TALK,* SEPT. 27, 1830

24. All thoughts, all passions, all delights, / Whatever stirs this mortal frame, / All are ministers of Love, / And feed his sacred flame.

SAMUEL TAYLOR COLERIDGE, "LOVE" (1799)

25. Friendship often ends in love; but love in friendship—never.

CHARLES CALEB COLTON, *LACON* (1825), 2.83

26. To love a thing means wanting it to live.

CONFUCIUS, *ANALECTS* (6TH C. B.C.), 12.10, TR. WINBERG CHAI

27. If there's delight in love, 'tis when I see / That heart which others bleed for, bleed for me.

WILLIAM CONGREVE, *THE WAY OF THE WORLD* (1700), 3.12

28. Words are the weak support of cold indifference; love has no language to be heard.

WILLIAM CONGREVE, *THE DOUBLE-DEALER* (1694), 4.5

29. Love is a tyrant sparing none.

CORNEILLE, *LE CID* (1636), 1.2, TR. PAUL LANDIS

30. Love lives on hope, and dies when hope is dead; / It is a flame which sinks for lack of fuel.

CORNEILLE, *LE CID* (1636), 1.2, TR. PAUL LANDIS

31. Love alone / is the true seed of every merit in you, / and of all acts for which you must atone.

DANTE, "PURGATORIO," 17, *THE DIVINE COMEDY* (1300–21), TR. JOHN CIARDI

32. No man may be so cursed by priest or pope / but what the Eternal Love may still return / while any thread of green lives on in hope.

DANTE, "PURGATORIO," 3, *THE DIVINE COMEDY* (C. 1300–21), TR. JOHN CIARDI

33. Pleasure of love lasts but a moment, / Pain of love lasts a lifetime.

JEAN PIERRE CLARIS DE FLORIAN, *CÉLESTINE* (1842)

34. Behold this little Bane— / The Boon of all alive— / As common as it is unknown / The name of it is Love.

EMILY DICKINSON, POEM (C. 1878)

35. Love is done when Love's begun, / Sages say, / But have Sages known?

EMILY DICKINSON, POEM (C. 1880)

36. Unable are the Loved to die / For Love is Immortality.

EMILY DICKINSON, POEM (C. 1864)

37. Love, with very young people, is a heartless business. We drink at that age from thirst, or to get drunk; it is only later in life that we occupy ourselves with the individuality of our wine.

ISAK DINESEN, "THE OLD CHEVALIER," *SEVEN GOTHIC TALES* (1934)

38. Being got it [love] is a treasure sweet, / Which to defend, is harder than to get: / And ought not be profaned on either part, / For though 'tis got by chance, 'tis kept by art.

JOHN DONNE, ELEGY 17, "THE EXPOSTULATION" (1635)

39. I am two fools, I know, for loving, and for saying so.

JOHN DONNE, "THE TRIPLE FOOL," *SONGS AND SONNETS* (1633)

40. Love all love of other sights controls, / And makes one little room an everywhere.

JOHN DONNE, "THE GOOD-MORROW" (1633)

41. Love built on beauty, soon as beauty, dies.

JOHN DONNE, ELEGY 2, "THE ANAGRAM" (1635)

42. Love is a growing, or full constant light; / And his first minute, after noon, is night.

JOHN DONNE, "A LECTURE UPON THE SHADOW," *SONGS AND SONNETS* (1633)

43. Love, all alike, no season knows, nor clime, / Nor hours, age, months, which are the rags of time.

JOHN DONNE, "THE SUN RISING," *SONGS AND SONNETS* (1633)

44. Without outward declarations, who can conclude an inward love?

JOHN DONNE, *SERMONS,* NO. 21, 1623

45. Love transforms: it simultaneously makes us larger and limits our possibilities. It changes our history even as it breaks a new path through the present.

MICHAEL DORRIS, "THE POWER OF LOVE," *PAPER TRAIL* (1994)

46. In order to love simply, it is necessary to know how to show love.

DOSTOYEVSKY, "BOOKISHNESS AND LITERACY," *POLNOYE SOBRANIYE SOCHINYENI* (*COMPLETE COLLECTED WORKS,* 1895), V. 9

47. With love one can live even without happiness.

DOSTOYEVSKY, *NOTES FROM UNDERGROUND* (1864), 2.4, TR. CONSTANCE GARNETT

48. Heaven be thanked, we live in such an age, / When no man dies for love, but on the stage.

JOHN DRYDEN, EPILOGUE TO *MITHRIDATES* (1678)

49. Love reckons hours for months, and days for years; / And every little absence is an age.

JOHN DRYDEN, *AMPHITRYON* (1690), 3.1

50. Pains of love be sweeter far / Than all other pleasures are.

JOHN DRYDEN, *TYRANNIC LOVE* (1669), 4.1

51. Love, love, love. All th' wurruld is love. Soft an' sweet an' sticky it covers th' globe.

FINLEY PETER DUNNE, "ON THE POWER OF MUSIC," *MR. DOOLEY ON MAKING A WILL* (1919)

52. The richest love is that which submits to the arbitration of time.

LAWRENCE DURRELL, *CLEA* (1960), 3.2

53. Love joins and then divides. How else would we be growing?

LAWRENCE DURRELL [GEORGE], *BALTHAZAR* (1958)

54. Love compels cruelty / To those who do not understand love.

T. S. ELIOT, *THE FAMILY REUNION* (1939), 2.2

55. He that loveth maketh his own the grandeur he loves.

EMERSON, "COMPENSATION," *ESSAYS: FIRST SERIES* (1841)

56. Love is the bright foreigner, the foreign self.

EMERSON, *JOURNALS,* 1849

57. No love can be bound by oath or covenant to secure it against a higher love.

EMERSON, "CIRCLES," *ESSAYS: FIRST SERIES* (1841)

58. They love too much that die for love.

ENGLISH PROVERB

59. Love won't be tampered with, love won't go away. Push it to one side and it creeps to the other.

LOUISE ERDRICH, "RELIGIOUS WARS," *THE BINGO PALACE* (1994)

60. Love. The black hook. The spear singing through the mind.

LOUISE ERDRICH, "SAINT MARIE," *LOVE MEDICINE* (1984)

61. Love is all we have, the only way / that each can help the other.

EURIPIDES, *ORESTES* (408 B.C.), TR. WILLIAM ARROWSMITH

62. Love must not touch the marrow of the soul. / Our affections must be breakable chains that we / can cast them off or tighten them.

EURIPIDES, *HIPPOLYTUS* (428 B.C.), TR. DAVID GRENE

63. They [the Shoshone] know that it [romantic love] exists. But they also recognize it for what it is—in their case, a form of madness.

PETER FARB, *MAN'S RISE TO CIVILIZATION* (1968)

64. To love nothing is not to live; to love but feebly is to languish rather than live.

FÉNELON, *À UN HOMME DU MONDE* (1699)

65. Love is a tyrant, / Resisted.

JOHN FORD, *THE LOVER'S MELANCHOLY* (1629), 1.3

66. Love is a great force in private life; it is indeed the greatest of all things; but love in public affairs does not work.

E. M. FORSTER, "TOLERANCE," *TWO CHEERS FOR DEMOCRACY* (1951)

67. Love makes the time pass. Time makes love pass.

FRENCH PROVERB

68. Erotic love begins with separateness, and ends in oneness. Motherly love begins with oneness, and leads to separateness.

ERICH FROMM, *THE SANE SOCIETY* (1955), 3

69. Love is often nothing but a favorable exchange between two people who get the most of what they can expect, considering their value on the personality market.

ERICH FROMM, *THE SANE SOCIETY* (1955), 5

70. Love is union with somebody, or something, outside oneself, under the condition of retaining the separateness and integrity of one's own self.

ERICH FROMM, *THE SANE SOCIETY* (1955), 3

71. There is hardly any activity, any enterprise, which is started with such tremendous hopes and expectations, and yet which fails so regularly, as love.

ERICH FROMM, *THE ART OF LOVING* (1956), 1

72. It seems that it is madder never to abandon one's self than often to be infatuated; better to be wounded, a captive and a slave, than always to walk in armor.

MARGARET FULLER, *SUMMER ON THE LAKES* (1844), 5

73. There is more pleasure in loving than in being beloved.

THOMAS FULLER, M.D., *GNOMOLOGIA* (1732), 4900

74. Love, the itch, and a cough cannot be hid.

THOMAS FULLER, M.D., *GNOMOLOGIA* (1732), 3298

75. Love makes use of the worst traps. The least noble. The rarest. It exploits coincidence.

JEAN GENET, *OUR LADY OF THE FLOWERS* (1949)

76. We must resemble each other a little in order to understand each other, but we must be a little different to love each other.

PAUL GÉRALDY, *L'HOMME ET L'AMOUR* (1951)

77. Love knows hidden paths.

German Proverb

78. Even as love crowns you so shall he crucify you. Even as he is for your growth so is he for your pruning.

Kahlil Gibran, "On Love," *The Prophet* (1923)

79. Love is the irresistible desire to be desired irresistibly.

Louis Ginsberg, reading at St. Mark's in the Bowery, April 1, 1968

80. A life without love, without the presence of the beloved, is nothing but a mere magic-lantern show. We draw out slide after slide, swiftly tiring of each, and pushing it back to make haste for the next.

Goethe, *Elective Affinities* (1809), 27

81. Friendship is a disinterested commerce between equals; love, an object intercourse between tyrants and slaves.

Oliver Goldsmith, *The Good-Natured Man* (1768), 1

82. When one loves somebody, everything is clear—where to go, what to do—it all takes care of itself and one doesn't have to ask anybody about anything.

Maxim Gorky, *The Zykovs* (1914), 4

83. 'Tis much to gain universal admiration; more, universal love.

Baltasar Gracián, *The Art of Worldly Wisdom* (1647), 40, tr. Joseph Jacobs

84. Love is a universal migraine, / A bright stain on the vision, / Blotting out reason.

Robert Graves, "Symptoms of Love," *Collected Poems* (1961)

85. They are always saying God loves us. If that's love I'd rather have a bit of kindness.

Graham Greene, *The Captain and the Enemy* (1988)

86. Because love has been so perverted, it has in many cases come to involve a measure of hatred. X

Germaine Greer, *The Female Eunuch* (1970)

87. Words have no language which can utter the secrets of love; and beyond the limits of expression is the expounding of desire.

Hāfiz, ghazals from the *Divan* (14th c.), 46, tr. Justin Huntly McCarthy

88. What is first love worth, except to prepare for a second? / What does second love bring? Only regret for the first.

John Hay, "Distichs" (1871?), 5

89. Love is that condition in which the happiness of another person is essential to your own.

Robert A. Heinlein, *Stranger in a Strange Land* (1961), 34

90. When you love you wish to do things for. You wish to sacrifice for. You wish to serve.

Ernest Hemingway, *A Farewell to Arms* (1929)

91. Love is the true price of love.

George Herbert, *Jacula Prudentum* (1651)

92. The love we give away is the only love we keep.

Elbert Hubbard, *The Note Book* (1927)

93. When peoples care for you and cry for you, they can straighten out your soul.

Langston Hughes, *Simple Speaks His Mind* (1950)

94. The supreme happiness of life is the conviction that we are loved.

Victor Hugo, "Fantine," *Les Misérables* (1862), 5.4, tr. Charles E. Wilbour

95. The word "love" bridges for us those chasms of momentary indifference and boredom which gape from time to time between even the most ardent lovers.

Aldous Huxley, *The Olive Tree* (1937)

96. No matter what you've done for yourself or for humanity, if you can't look back on having given love and attention to your own family, what have you really accomplished?

Lee Iacocca, *Talking Straight* (1988), with Sonny Kleinfeld

97. Love is the wisdom of the fool and the folly of the wise.

Samuel Johnson, quoted in Birkbeck Hill's *Johnsonian Miscellanies* (1897), v. 2

98. As selfishness and complaint pervert and cloud the mind, so love with its joy clears and sharpens the vision.

Helen Keller, *My Religion* (1927)

99. Love is a great thing, a great good in every wise; it alone maketh light every heavy thing and beareth evenly every uneven thing.

Thomas à Kempis, *The Imitation of Christ* (1426), 2.6

100. Though a man excels in everything, unless he has been a lover his life is lonely, and he may be likened to a jewelled cup which can contain no wine.

Yoshida Kenkō, "The Consideration of Women," *The Harvest of Leisure (Tsure-Zure Gusa,* c. 1330–35), tr. Ryukichi Kurata

101. If a love is to be unforgettable, fortuities must immediately start fluttering down to it like birds to Francis of Assisi's shoulder.

MILAN KUNDERA, *THE UNBEARABLE LIGHTNESS OF BEING* (1984)

102. Love does not make itself felt in the desire for copulation (a desire that extends to an infinite number of women) but in the desire for shared sleep (a desire limited to one woman).

MILAN KUNDERA, *THE UNBEARABLE LIGHTNESS OF BEING* (1984)

103. Time, which strengthens friendship, weakens love.

LA BRUYÈRE, *CHARACTERS* (1688), 4.4

104. We perceive when love begins and when it declines by our embarrassment when alone together.

LA BRUYÈRE, *CHARACTERS* (1688), 4.33, TR. HENRI VAN LAUN

105. In love deceit nearly always goes further than mistrust.

LA ROCHEFOUCAULD, *MAXIMS* (1665), TR. KENNETH PRATT

106. Love, all agreeable as it is, charms more by the fashion in which it displays itself, than by its own true merit.

LA ROCHEFOUCAULD, *MAXIMS* (1665), TR. KENNETH PRATT

107. Sometimes we are less unhappy in being deceived by those we love, than in being undeceived by them.

LA ROCHEFOUCAULD, *MAXIMS* (1665), TR. KENNETH PRATT

108. The restraints we impose on ourselves to refrain from loving are often more cruel than the severities of our beloved.

LA ROCHEFOUCAULD, *MAXIMS* (1665), TR. KENNETH PRATT

109. There is no disguise which can hide love for long where it exists, or simulate it where it does not.

LA ROCHEFOUCAULD, *MAXIMS* (1665), TR. KENNETH PRATT

110. The pleasure of love is in loving, and we are made happier by the passion that we experience than by that which we inspire.

LA ROCHEFOUCAULD, *MAXIMS* (1665), TR. KENNETH PRATT

111. True love is like ghosts, which everybody talks about and few have seen.

LA ROCHEFOUCAULD, *MAXIMS* (1665), TR. KENNETH PRATT

112. What the bloom is on fruit, the charm of novelty is to love; it imparts a lustre which is easily effaced and which never returns.

LA ROCHEFOUCAULD, *MAXIMS* (1665), TR. KENNETH PRATT

113. When we are in love we often doubt that which we most believe.

LA ROCHEFOUCAULD, *MAXIMS* (1665), TR. KENNETH PRATT

114. Love should be practiced like Lent, secretly and dumbly.

PARIS LEARY, "ONAN," *A CONTROVERSY OF POETS* (1965)

115. Him that I love, I wish to be / Free— / Even from me.

ANNE MORROW LINDBERGH, "EVEN—," *THE UNICORN AND OTHER POEMS,* 1935–55 (1956)

116. There is no harvest for the heart alone; / The seed of love must be / Eternally / Resown.

ANNE MORROW LINDBERGH, "SECOND SOWING," *THE UNICORN AND OTHER POEMS 1935–55* (1956)

117. To a person in love, the value of the individual is intuitively known. Love needs no logic for its mission.

CHARLES A. LINDBERGH, "OUT OF EDEN," *AUTOBIOGRAPHY OF VALUES* (1978)

118. That love for one, from which there doth not spring / Wide love for all, is but a worthless thing.

JAMES RUSSELL LOWELL, "SONNET 3" (1840)

119. True love is but a humble, low-born thing, / And hath its food served up in earthen ware.

JAMES, RUSSELL LOWELL, "LOVE" (1840)

120. I am of this mind, that both might and malice, deceit and treachery, all perjury, any impiety may lawfully be committed in love, which is lawless.

JOHN LYLY, *EUPHUES: THE ANATOMY OF WIT* (1579)

121. Love is simple to understand if you haven't got a mind soft and full of holes. It's a crutch, that's all, and there isn't a one of us doesn't need a crutch.

NORMAN MAILER, *BARBARY SHORE* (1951), 19

122. This was love at first sight, love everlasting: a feeling unknown, unhoped for, unexpected—in so far as it could be a matter of conscious awareness; it took entire possession of him, and he understood, with joyous amazement, that this was for life.

THOMAS MANN, "DISORDER AND EARLY SORROW" (1925)

123. He who loves the more is the inferior and must suffer.

Thomas Mann, "Tonio Kröger" (1903), *Death in Venice,*, tr. H. T. Lowe-Porter

124. It is love, not reason, that is stronger than death.

Thomas Mann, *The Magic Mountain* (1924), 6.7, tr. H. T. Lowe-Porter

125. We don't love qualities, we love persons; sometimes by reason of their defects as well as of their qualities.

Jacques Maritain, *Reflections on America* (1958), 3

126. Who ever loved, that loved not at first sight?

Christopher Marlowe, "Hero and Leander" (1598), 1

127. It takes two to make a love affair and a man's meat is too often a woman's poison.

W. Somerset Maugham, *The Summing Up* (1938), 52

128. Love is not always blind and there are few things that cause greater wretchedness than to love with all your heart someone who you know is unworthy of love.

W. Somerset Maugham, *The Summing Up* (1938), 77

129. We are not the same persons this year as last; nor are those we love. It is a happy chance if we, changing, continue to love a changed person.

W. Somerset Maugham, *The Summing Up* (1938), 77

130. Human love is often but the encounter of two weaknesses.

François Mauriac, "All Soul's Day," *Cain, Where Is Your Brother?* (1962)

131. The most disgusting cad in the world is the man who, on grounds of decorum and morality, avoids the game of love. He is one who puts his own ease and security above the most laudable of philanthropies.

H. L. Mencken, *Prejudices: Second Series* (1920), 10

132. Prepare, / You lovers, to know Love a thing of moods: / Not like hard life, of laws.

George Meredith, *Modern Love* (1862), 10

133. We cannot love ourselves unless we love others, and we cannot love others unless we love ourselves. But a selfish love of ourselves makes us incapable of loving others.

Thomas Merton, *No Man Is an Island* (1955)

134. He that would eat of love must eat it where it hangs.

Edna St. Vincent Millay, "Never May the Fruit Be Plucked," *The Harp-Weaver* (1923)

135. Love is not all: it is not meat nor drink / Nor slumber nor a roof against the rain; / Nor yet a floating spar to men that sink.

Edna St. Vincent Millay, *Fatal Interview* (1931), 30

136. There is something inexpressibly charming in falling in love and, surely, the whole pleasure lies in the fact that love isn't lasting.

Molière, *Don Juan* (1665), 1, tr. John Wood

137. In love, 'tis no other than frantic desire for that which flies from us.

Montaigne, "Of friendship," *Essays* (1580–88), tr. W. C. Hazlitt

138. Romantic love is an illusion. Most of us discover this truth at the end of a love affair or else when the sweet emotions of love lead us into marriage and then turn down their flames.

Thomas Moore, *Soul Mates* (1994)

139. Alas! how light a cause may move / Dissension between hearts that love!

Thomas Moore, "The Light of the Harem," *Lalla Rookh* (1817)

140. There's nothing half so sweet in life / As love's young dream.

Thomas Moore, "Love's Young Dream," *Irish Melodies* (1807–35)

141. Intense mutual erotic love, love which involves with the flesh all the most refined sexual being of the spirit, which reveals and perhaps even ex nihilo creates spirit as sex, is comparatively rare in this inconvenient world.

Iris Murdoch, *The Sacred and Profane Love Machine* (1974)

142. To love, that's the point—what matters whom? / What does the bottle matter provided we can be drunk?

Alfred De Musset, "La Coupe et les lèvres," *Premières poésies* (1829–35)

143. The only victory in love is flight.

Napoleon I, *Maxims* (1804–15)

144. A man reserves his true and deepest love not for the species of woman in whose company he finds himself electrified and enkindled, but for that one in whose company he may feel tenderly drowsy.

George Jean Nathan, "The Ultimately Desirable Woman," *The Theatre Book of the Year, 1949–1950*

145. A broken heart is a monument to a love that will never die; fulfillment is a monument to a love that is already on its deathbed.

George Jean Nathan, "Attitude toward Love and Marriage," *The Autobiography of an Attitude* (1925)

146. Love is more afraid of change than destruction.

Nietzsche, *Miscellaneous Maxims and Opinions* (1879), 280, tr. Paul V. Cohn

147. There is always some madness in love. But there is also always some reason in madness.

Nietzsche, "On Reading and Writing," *Thus Spoke Zarathustra* (1883–92), 1, tr. Walter Kaufmann

148. When a man is in love he endures more than at other times; he submits to everything.

Nietzsche, *The Antichrist* (1888), 23, tr. Anthony M. Ludovici

149. I am the least difficult of men. All I want is boundless love.

Frank O'Hara, title poem, *Meditations in an Emergency* (1967)

150. Family love is messy, clinging, and of an annoying and repetitive pattern, like bad wallpaper.

P. J. O'Rourke, *Modern Manners* (1988)

151. If you'd be loved, be worthy to be loved.

Ovid, *The Art of Love* (c. A.D. 8), 2, tr. J. Lewis May

152. Love fed fat soon turns to boredom.

Ovid, *The Loves* (c. A.D. 8), 2.19, tr. Rolfe Humphries

153. Love is a driver, bitter and fierce if you fight and resist him, / Easy-going enough once you acknowledge his power.

Ovid, *The Loves* (c. A.D. 8), 1.2, tr. Rolfe Humphries

154. Love is a naked child: do you think he has pockets for money?

Ovid, *The Loves* (c. A.D. 8), 1.10, tr. Rolfe Humphries

155. Love's dominion, like a king's, admits of no partition.

Ovid, *The Art of Love* (c. A.D. 8), 3, tr. J. Lewis May

156. Every love's the love before / In a duller dress.

Dorothy Parker, "Summary," *Death and Taxes* (1931)

157. We conceal it from ourselves in vain—we must always love something. In those matters seemingly removed from love, the feeling is secretly to be found, and man cannot possibly live for a moment without it.

Pascal, *Discours sur les passions de l'amour* (1653)

158. We never, then, love a person, but only qualities.

Pascal, *Pensées* (1670), 323, tr. W. F. Trotter

159. 'Tis never for their wisdom that one loves the wisest, or for their wit that one loves the wittiest; 'tis for benevolence and virtue and honest fondness one loves people.

Hester Lynch Piozzi, letter to Fanny Burney, 1781

160. [Love is] the joy of the good, the wonder of the wise, the amazement of the gods; desired by those who have no part in him, and precious to those who have the better part in him.

Plato, *The Symposium* (4th c. B.C.), tr. Benjamin Jowett

161. Love, free as air at sight of human ties, / Spreads his light wings, and in a moment flies.

Alexander Pope, "Eloisa to Abelard" (1717), 74

162. Cupid is naked and does not like artifices contrived by beauty.

Propertius, *Elegies* (c. 28-c. 16 B.C.), 1.2.8

163. There can be no peace of mind in love, since the advantage one has secured is never anything but a fresh starting-point for further desires.

Marcel Proust, *Remembrance of Things Past: Within a Budding Grove* (1913–27), tr. C. K. Scott-Moncrieff

164. Those whose suffering is due to love are, as we say of certain invalids, their own physicians.

Marcel Proust, *Remembrance of Things Past: Within a Budding Grove* (1913–27), tr. C. K. Scott-Moncrieff

165. We are ordinarily so indifferent to people that when we have invested one of them with the possibility of giving us joy, or suffering, it seems as if he must belong to some other universe, he is imbued with poetry.

Marcel Proust, *Remembrance of Things Past: Swann's Way* (1913–27)

166. A god could hardly love and be wise.

Publilius Syrus, *Moral Sayings* (1st c. B.C.), 25, tr. Darius Lyman

167. Love, like a tear, rises in the eye and falls upon the breast.

PUBLILIUS SYRUS, *MORAL SAYINGS* (1ST C. B.C.), 42, TR. DARIUS LYMAN

168. When you are in love you are not wise; or, when you are wise you are not in love.

PUBLILIUS SYRUS, *MORAL SAYINGS* (1ST C. B.C.), 816, TR. DARIUS LYMAN

169. Love is not dumb. The heart speaks many ways.

RACINE, *BRITANNICUS* (1669), 3, TR. ROBERT HENDERSON

170. None love, but they who wish to love.

RACINE, *BRITANNICUS* (1669), 3, TR. ROBERT HENDERSON

171. The man who has never made a fool of himself in love will never be wise in love.

THEODOR REIK, *OF LOVE AND LUST* (1957), 1.3.14

172. There is need of variety in sex, but not in love.

THEODOR REIK, *OF LOVE AND LUST* (1957), 1.1.5

173. Beyond the wounds of the child and the scars of the man, there is something in the heart of love itself that makes love pathetic.

PHILIP RIEFF, "SEXUALITY AND DOMINATION," *FREUD: THE MIND OF THE MORALIST* (1959)

174. For one human being to love another: that is perhaps the most difficult of all our tasks, the ultimate, the last test and proof, the work for which all other work is but preparation.

RAINER MARIA RILKE, *LETTERS TO A YOUNG POET,* MAY 14, 1904, TR. M. D. HERTER NORTON

175. To be loved means to be consumed. To love is to give light with inexhaustible oil. To be loved is to pass away, to love is to endure.

RAINER MARIA RILKE, *THE NOTEBOOKS OF MALTE LAURIDS BRIGGE* (1910), TR. M. D. HERTER NORTON

176. As long as we love, we lend to the beloved object qualities of mind and heart which we deprive him of when the day of misunderstanding arrives.

JOSEPH ROUX, *MEDITATIONS OF A PARISH PRIEST* (1886), 9.25, TR. ISABEL F. HAPGOOD

177. Love is something far more than desire for sexual intercourse; it is the principal means of escape from the loneliness which afflicts most men and women throughout the greater part of their lives.

BERTRAND RUSSELL, "THE PLACE OF LOVE IN HUMAN LIFE," *MARRIAGE AND MORALS* (1929)

178. To love means to give, and to give means to build, while to hate is to destroy.

ANWAR EL-SADAT, "THE LIBERATION OF -SELF'—CELL 54," *IN SEARCH OF IDENTITY* (1977)

179. Life has taught us that love does not consist in gazing at each other but in looking outward together in the same direction.

SAINT-EXUPÉRY, *WIND, SAND, AND STARS* (1939), 9.6, TR. LEWIS GALANTIÈRE

180. Love does not cause suffering: what causes it is the sense of ownership, which is love's opposite.

SAINT-EXUPÉRY, *THE WISDOM OF THE SANDS* (1948), 49, TR. STUART GILBERT

181. There is a warning love sends and the cost of it is never written till long afterward.

CARL SANDBURG, "EXPLANATIONS OF LOVE," *COMPLETE POEMS* (1950)

182. Love, whether sexual, parental, or fraternal, is essentially sacrificial, and prompts a man to give his life for his friends.

GEORGE SANTAYANA, *THE LIFE OF REASON: REASON IN RELIGION* (1905–06), 14

183. Not to believe in love is a great sign of dulness. There are some people so indirect and lumbering that they think all real affection must rest on circumstantial evidence.

GEORGE SANTAYANA, *THE LIFE OF REASON: REASON IN SOCIETY* (1905–06), 1

184. When we love animals and children too much, we love them at the expense of men.

JEAN-PAUL SARTRE, *THE WORDS* (1964), 1

185. Love rules the court, the camp, the grove, / And men below, and saints above; / For love is heaven, and heaven is love.

SIR WALTER SCOTT, *THE LAY OF THE LAST MINSTREL* (1805), 3.2

186. True love's the gift which God has given / To man alone beneath the heaven.

SIR WALTER SCOTT, *THE LAY OF THE LAST MINSTREL* (1805), 5.8

187. You can end love more easily than you can moderate it.

SENECA THE ELDER, *CONTROVERSIAE* (1ST C.), 2

188. Base men being in love have then a nobility in their natures more than is native to them.

SHAKESPEARE, *OTHELLO* (1604–05), 2.1.218

189. I may command where I adore.

Shakespeare, *Twelfth Night* (1599–1600), 2.5.115

190. If thou remember'st not the slightest folly / That ever love did make thee run into, / Thou hast not loved.

Shakespeare, *As You Like It* (1599–1600), 2.4.33

191. Love is a spirit all compact of fire.

Shakespeare, *Venus and Adonis* (1593), 149

192. Love looks not with the eyes, but with the mind; / And therefore is winged Cupid painted blind.

Shakespeare, *A Midsummer Night's Dream* (1595–96), 1.1.234

193. Love sought is good, but given unsought, is better.

Shakespeare, *Twelfth Night* (1599–1600), 3.1.168

194. Love's best habit is a soothing tongue.

Shakespeare, *The Passionate Pilgrim* (1599), 1.11

195. The course of true love never did run smooth.

Shakespeare, *A Midsummer Night's Dream* (1595–96), 1.1.134

196. There's beggary in the love that can be reckoned.

Shakespeare, *Antony and Cleopatra* (1606–07), 1.1.15

197. They do not love that do not show their love.

Shakespeare, *The Two Gentlemen of Verona* (1594–95), 1.2.31

198. All love is sweet, / Given or returned. Common as light is love, / And its familiar voice wearies not ever.

Shelley, *Prometheus Unbound* (1818–19), 2.5

199. One word / Frees us of all the weight and pain of life: / That word is love.

Sophocles, *Oedipus at Colonus* (401 B.C.), tr. Robert Fitzgerald

200. Love is like war: you begin when you like and leave off when you can.

Spanish Proverb

201. Where there is love, there is pain.

Spanish Proverb

202. We cease loving ourselves if no one loves us.

Mme De Staël, quoted by Sainte-Beuve in *Portraits de femmes* (1832–48)

203. A woman holds dreadful power over a man who is in love with her but she should realize that the quality and force of his love is the index of his potential contempt and hatred.

John Steinbeck

204. Romance is a means to the end of self-completion, but love is an end in itself.

Gloria Steinem, *Revolution from Within* (1992)

205. A very small degree of hope is sufficient to cause the birth of love.

Stendhal, *On Love* (1822), 3, tr. H. B. V., under direction of C. K. Scott-Moncrieff

206. To be loved at first sight, a man should have at the same time something to respect and something to pity in his face.

Stendhal, *On Love* (1822), 21, tr. H. B. V., under direction of C. K. Scott-Moncrieff

207. Let the dead have the immortality of fame, but the living the immortality of love.

Rabindranath Tagore, *Stray Birds* (1916), 279

208. Love remains a secret even when spoken, / for only a lover truly knows that he is loved.

Rabindranath Tagore, *Fireflies* (1928)

209. Love is an endless mystery, / for it has nothing else to explain it.

Rabindranath Tagore, *Fireflies* (1928)

210. Love's gift cannot be given, / it waits to be accepted.

Rabindranath Tagore, *Fireflies* (1928)

211. The loving are the daring.

Bayard Taylor, *The Song of the Camp*

212. O, beauty, are you not enough? / Why am I crying after love?

Sara Teasdale, "Spring Night," *Rivers to the Sea* (1915)

213. Take love when love is given, / But never think to find it / A sure escape from sorrow / Or a complete repose.

Sara Teasdale, "Day's Ending," *Dark of the Moon* (1926)

214. He that shuts Love out, in turn shall be / Shut out from Love, and on her threshold lie / Howling in the outer darkness.

Lord Tennyson, "To—" (1832)

215. 'Tis better to have loved and lost / Than never to have loved at all.

Lord Tennyson, "In Memoriam A. H. H." (1850), 27

216. Love is the only gold.

Lord Tennyson, *Becket* (1884), 4.1

217. For you to ask advice on the rules of love is no better than to ask advice on the rules of madness.

Terence, *The Eunuch* (161 B.C.), tr. Robert Graves

218. There is no remedy for love but to love more.

Thoreau, *Journal*, July 25, 1839

219. The Love-god inflames / more fiercely / those he sees are reluctant to surrender.

Tibullus, *Elegies* (1st c. B.C.), 1.8, tr. Hubert Creekmore

220. One cannot be strong without love. For love is not an irrelevant emotion; it is the blood of life, the power of reunion of the separated.

Paul Tillich, *The Eternal Now* (1963), 3.13.2

221. If so many men, so many minds, certainly so many hearts, so many kinds of love.

Leo Tolstoy, *Anna Karenina* (1873–76), 2.7, tr. Constance Garnett

222. Love is like those shabby hotels in which all the luxury is in the lobby.

Paul Jean Toulet, *Le Carnet de M. du Paur, homme public* (1898)

223. The absolute value of love makes life worth while, and so makes Man's strange and difficult situation acceptable. Love cannot save life from death; but it can fulfill life's purpose.

Arnold J. Toynbee, "Why and How I Work," *Saturday Review*, April 5, 1969

224. Love is the child of illusion and the parent of disillusion.

Miguel De Unamuno, "Love, Suffering, Pity and Personality," *Tragic Sense of Life* (1913), tr. J. E. Crawford Flitch

225. Love is an act of endless forgiveness, a tender look which becomes a habit.

Peter Ustinov, *Christian Science Monitor*, Dec. 9, 1958

226. Love, like a sense of humor, is now claimed by everyone even though Love, like a sense of humor, is rather more rare than not, and to most of us poor muddlers unbearable at full strength.

Gore Vidal, *Rocking the Boat* (1962)

227. Love has features which pierce all hearts, he wears a bandage which conceals the faults of those beloved. He has wings, he comes quickly and flies away the same.

Voltaire, "Fable," *Philosophical Dictionary* (1764)

228. Love has various lodgings; the same word does not always signify the same thing.

Voltaire, "Abuse of Words," *Philosophical Dictionary* (1764)

229. Whatever pains disease may bring / Are but the tangy seasoning / To Love's delicious fare.

Richard Wilbur, "Pangloss's Song: A Comic-Opera Lyric," *Advice to a Prophet* (1961)

230. Each man kills the thing he loves, / By each let this be heard, / Some do it with a bitter look, / Some with a flattering word. / The coward does it with a kiss, / The brave man with a sword!

Oscar Wilde, *The Ballad of Reading Gaol* (1898), 1.7

231. When one is in love one begins by deceiving one's self. And one ends by deceiving others. That is what the world calls a romance.

Oscar Wilde, *A Woman of No Importance* (1893), 3

232. There may be two equally good, equally gifted, equally beautiful, but there may never be two that love one another equally well.

Thornton Wilder, *The Bridge of San Luis Rey* (1927)

233. Love is / unworldly / and nothing / comes of it but love.

William Carlos Williams, "Rain," *Selected Poems* (1949)

234. Love is what we were born with. Fear is what we learned here.

Marianne Williamson, "Introduction," *A Return to Love* (1992)

235. We must try to love one another.... The terrible and beautiful sentence, the last, the final wisdom that the earth can give, is remembered at the end, is spoken too late, wearily. It stands there, awful and untraduced, above the dusty racket of our lives. No forgetting, no forgiving, no denying, no explaining, no hating.

Thomas Wolfe, *Look Homeward, Angel* (1929)

236. You must love him, ere to you / He will seem worthy of your love.

William Wordsworth, "A Poet's Epitaph" (1799)

237. A pity beyond all telling / Is in the heart of love.

William Butler Yeats, "The Pity of Love" (1893)

552. LOVE, LOSS OF

See also 301. Estrangement; 472. Infidelity; 550. Loss; 553. Love, Unrequited; 793. Rejection

1. [L]ove was an appalling bore once you had ceased loving. All that time wasted.

Simone de Beauvoir, *Les Belles Images* (1966), tr. Patrick O'Brian (1968)

2. It is obviously quite difficult to be no longer loved when we are still in love, but it is incomparably more painful to be loved when we ourselves no longer love.

Georges Courteline, *La Philosophie de G. Courteline* (1917)

3. The loss of love is a terrible thing; / They lie who say that death is worse.

Countee Cullen, "Variations on a Theme (The Loss of Love)," *On These I Stand* (1947)

4. We are never so defenceless against suffering as when we love, never so helplessly unhappy as when we have lost our loved object or its love.

Sigmund Freud, *Civilization and Its Discontents* (1930), 2, tr. James Strachey

5. It is impossible to love a second time what we have really ceased to love.

La Rochefoucauld, *Maxims* (1665), tr. Kenneth Pratt

6. There are scarcely any who are not ashamed of being beloved, when they love no more themselves.

La Rochefoucauld, *Maxims* (1665), tr. Kenneth Pratt

7. A girl (and perhaps the same thing applies to a boy) would find life less broken apart after a misguided love affair if she could feel that she had been sinful rather than a fool.

Phyllis McGinley, "In Defense of Sin," *The Province of the Heart* (1959)

8. Women's hearts are like old china, none the worse for a break or two.

W. Somerset Maugham, *Lady Frederick* (1907), 1

9. After all, my erstwhile dear, / My no longer cherished, / Need we say it was no love, / Just because it perished?

Edna St. Vincent Millay, "Passer Mortuus Est," *Second April* (1921)

10. 'Tis not love's going hurts my days, / But that it went in little ways.

Edna St. Vincent Millay, "The Spring and the Fall," *The Harp-Weaver* (1923)

11. It is not because other people are dead that our affection for them grows faint, it is because we ourself are dying.

Marcel Proust, *Remembrance of Things Past: The Sweet Cheat Gone* (1913–27), tr. C. K. Scott-Moncrieff

12. The heart that can no longer / Love passionately, must with fury hate.

Racine, *Andromache* (1667), 1, tr. Robert Henderson

13. Where love fails we espy all faults.

John Ray, *English Proverbs* (1670)

14. Love is not love / Which alters when it alteration finds.

Shakespeare, *Sonnets* (1609), 116.2

15. When love begins to sicken and decay / It useth an enforced ceremony. / There are no tricks in plain and simple faith.

Shakespeare, *Julius Caesar* (1599–1600), 4.2.20

16. Warmed-over loves and soups are generally not recommended.

Elie Wiesel, *The Testament* (1981), tr. Marion Wiesel

553. LOVE, UNREQUITED

See also 793. Rejection

1. A mighty pain to love it is, / And 'tis a pain that pain to miss; / But of all pains, the greatest pain / It is to love, but love in vain.

Abraham Cowley, "Gold," *From Anacreon* (1656)

2. It is the missed opportunity that counts, and in a love that vainly yearns from behind prison bars you have perchance the love supreme.

Saint-Exupéry, *The Wisdom of the Sands* (1948), 45, tr. Stuart Gilbert

554. LOVE AND HATE

See also 412. Hatred; 551. Love

1. When Love is suppressed Hate takes its place.

Havelock Ellis, *On Life and Sex: Essays of Love and Virtue* (1937), 1

2. Hatred is blind, as well as love.

Thomas Fuller, M.D., *Gnomologia* (1732), 1805

3. Love that is ignorant and hatred have almost the same ends.

Ben Jonson, "Explorata," *Timber* (1640)

4. Hatred paralyzes life; love releases it. Hatred confuses life; love harmonizes it. Hatred darkens life; love illumines it.

Martin Luther King, Jr., *Strength to Love* (1963), 14.3

5. If we judge of love by its usual effects, it resembles hatred more than friendship.

La Rochefoucauld, *Maxims* (1665), tr. Kenneth Pratt

6. As the best wine doth make the sharpest vinegar, so the deepest love turneth to the deadliest hate.

John Lyly, *Euphues: The Anatomy of Wit* (1579)

7. Oh, I have loved him too much to feel no hate for him.

Racine, *Andromache* (1667), 2.1

8. We love without reason, and without reason we hate.

Jean-François Regnard, *Les Folies amoureuses* (1704), 2.2

9. Hatred, as well as love, renders its votaries credulous.

Rousseau, *Confessions* (1766–70), 5

10. Hatred which is entirely conquered by love passes into love, and love on that account is greater than if it had not been preceded by hatred.

Spinoza, *Ethics* (1677), 3, tr. Andrew Boyle

11. As love, if love be perfect, casts out fear, / So hate, if hate be perfect, casts out fear.

Lord Tennyson, "Merlin and Vivien," *Idylls of the King* (1859)

12. Our mother gives us our earliest lessons in love—and its partner, hate. Our father—our "second other"—elaborates on them.

Judith Viorst, *Necessary Losses* (1986)

555. LOVERS

See also 551. Love; 552. Love, Loss of; 553. Love, Unrequited; 554. Love and Hate

1. The face of a lover is an unknown, precisely because it is invested with so much of oneself. It is a mystery, containing, like all mysteries, the possibility of torment.

James Baldwin, *Another Country* (1962)

2. Everything disturbs an absent lover.

Cervantes, *Don Quixote* (1605–15), 1.2.6, tr. John Ozell

3. Lovers are commonly industrious to make themselves uneasy.

Cervantes, *Don Quixote* (1605–15), 1.3.10, tr. John Ozell

4. For lovers, touch is metamorphosis. All the parts of their bodies seem to change, and seem to become something different and better.

John Cheever, "The Bus to St. James's," *The Stories of John Cheever* (1978)

5. All mankind love a lover.

Emerson, "Love," *Essays: First Series* (1841)

6. The lover is made happier by his love than the object of his affection.

Emerson, *Journals,* 1832

7. There is desire / in those who love to hear about their loved ones' pains.

Euripides, *Helen* (412 B.C.), tr. Richmond Lattimore

8. Lovers who love truly do not write down their happiness.

Anatole France, *The Crime of Sylvestre Bonnard* (1881), 1, tr. Lafcadio Hearn

9. When a love relationship is at its height there is no room left for any interest in the environment; a pair of lovers are sufficient to themselves.

Sigmund Freud, *Civilization and Its Discontents* (1930), 5, tr. James Strachey

10. A lover without indiscretion is no lover at all.

Thomas Hardy, *The Hand of Ethelberta* (1876)

11. All lovers unconsciously establish their own rules of the game, which from the outset admit of no transgression.

Milan Kundera, *The Unbearable Lightness of Being* (1984)

12. The reason why lovers are never weary of one another is this: they are always talking of themselves.

La Rochefoucauld, *Maxims* (1665)

13. Like any lover, he desired to please; suffered agonies at the thought of failure, and brightened his dress with smart ties and handkerchiefs and other youthful touches.

Thomas Mann, *Death in Venice* (1911)

14. Of all affliction taught a lover yet, / 'Tis sure the hardest science to forget.

Alexander Pope, "Eloisa to Abelard" (1717)

15. An angry lover tells himself many lies.

PUBLILIUS SYRUS, *MORAL SAYINGS* (1ST C. B.C.), 19, TR. DARIUS LYMAN

16. Lovers know what they want, but not what they need.

PUBLILIUS SYRUS, *MORAL SAYINGS* (1ST C. B.C.), 21, TR. DARIUS LYMAN

17. The lover is a monotheist who knows that other people worship different gods but cannot himself imagine that there could be other gods.

THEODOR REIK, *OF LOVE AND LUST* (1957), 1.3.1

18. They say all lovers swear more performance than they are able and yet reserve an ability that they never perform, vowing more than the perfection of ten and discharging less than the tenth part of one.

SHAKESPEARE, *TROILUS AND CRESSIDA* (1601–02), 3.2.91

19. I once fell in love with a man only because we both belonged to that large and secret club of children who had "crazy mothers." We traded stories of the shameless houses to which we could never invite our friends.

GLORIA STEINEM, "RUTH'S SONG," *OUTRAGEOUS ACTS AND EVERYDAY REBELLIONS* (1983)

20. The anger of lovers renews their love.

TERENCE, *THE WOMAN OF ANDROS* (166 B.C.)

LOWER CLASS

See 682. THE PEOPLE

556. LOYALTY

See also 181. CONSTANCY AND INCONSTANCY; 491. INTEGRITY

1. Loyalty is still the same, / Whether it win or lose the game; / True as a dial to the sun, / Although it be not shined upon.

SAMUEL BUTLER (D. 1680), *HUDIBRAS* (1663), 3.2

2. When young we are faithful to individuals, when older we grow more loyal to situations and to types.

CYRIL CONNOLLY, *THE UNQUIET GRAVE* (1945), 2

3. To require a citizen to sign a loyalty oath is to destroy some of the loyalty he could otherwise claim, since any subsequent loyal behavior may then be attributed to the oath.

B.F. SKINNER, *BEYOND FREEDOM AND DIGNITY* (1971)

LUCK

See 360. FORTUNE

557. LUXURY

See also 312. EXCESS; 324. EXTRAVAGANCE; 750. PROSPERITY

1. Minds, like bodies, will often fall into a pimpled, ill-conditioned state from mere excess of comfort.

CHARLES DICKENS, *BARNABY RUDGE* (1841), 7

2. Our expense is almost all for conformity. It is for cake that we all run in debt.

EMERSON, *JOURNALS,* 1840

3. The lust for comfort, that stealthy thing that enters the house a guest, and then becomes a host, and then a master.

KAHLIL GIBRAN, "ON HOUSES," *THE PROPHET* (1923)

4. Luxury either comes of riches or makes them necessary; it corrupts at once rich and poor, the rich by possession and the poor by covetousness.

ROUSSEAU, *THE SOCIAL CONTRACT* (1762), 3.4, TR. G. D. H. COLE

5. They must know but little of mankind who can imagine that, after they have been once seduced by luxury, they can ever renounce it.

ROUSSEAU, *A DISCOURSE ON POLITICAL ECONOMY* (1758), TR. G. D. H. COLE

6. What nature requires is obtainable, and within easy reach. It's for the superfluous we sweat.

SENECA, *LETTERS TO LUCILIUS* (1ST C.), 4.11, TR. E. PHILLIPS BARKER

7. Men first feel necessity, then look for utility, next attend to comfort, still later amuse themselves with pleasure, thence grow dissolute in luxury, and finally go mad and waste their substance.

GIAMBATTISTA VICO, *THE NEW SCIENCE* (1725–44), 1.2

8. Give me the luxuries of life and I will willingly do without the necessities.

FRANK LLOYD WRIGHT, QUOTED IN HIS OBITUARY, APRIL 9, 1959

558. LYING

See also 224. DECEPTION; 864. SELF-DECEPTION; 999. TRUTH AND FALSEHOOD; 998. TRUTH; 1000. TRUTHFULNESS

1. A liar will not be believed, even when he speaks the truth.

AESOP, "THE SHEPHERD'S BOY," *FABLES* (6TH C. B.C.?), TR. JOSEPH JACOBS

2. One falsehood spoils a thousand truths.

ASHANTI PROVERB

3. A lie faces God and shrinks from man.

FRANCIS BACON, "OF TRUTH," *ESSAYS* (1625)

4. A lie always needs a truth for a handle to it.

HENRY WARD BEECHER, *PROVERBS FROM PLYMOUTH PULPIT* (1887)

5. Any fool can tell the truth, but it requires a man of some sense to know how to tell a lie well.

SAMUEL BUTLER (D. 1902), "TRUTH AND CONVENIENCE," *NOTE-BOOKS* (1912)

6. Lying has a kind of respect and reverence with it. We pay a person the compliment of acknowledging his superiority whenever we lie to him.

SAMUEL BUTLER (D. 1902), "TRUTH AND CONVENIENCE," *NOTE-BOOKS* (1912)

7. The best liar is he who makes the smallest amount of lying go the longest way.

SAMUEL BUTLER (D. 1902), *THE WAY OF ALL FLESH* (1903), 39

8. And, after all, what is a lie? 'Tis but / The truth in masquerade; and I defy / Historians—heroes—lawyers—priests, to put / A fact without some leaven of a lie.

BYRON, *DON JUAN* (1819–24), 11.37

9. Lying is the only art form that the public sanctions and instinctively prefers to reality.

JEAN COCTEAU, *DIARY OF AN UNKNOWN* (1952; 1988)

10. A falsehood is, in one sense, a dead thing; but too often it moves about, galvanized by self-will, and pushes the living out of their seats.

SAMUEL TAYLOR COLERIDGE, "PRELIMINARY OBSERVATIONS," *AIDS TO REFLECTION* (1825)

11. Falsehood is often rocked by truth, but she soon outgrows her cradle and discards her nurse.

CHARLES CALEB COLTON, *LACON* (1825), 1.550

12. A child of today can detect a lie quicker than the wisest adult of two decades ago. When I want to know what is true, I ask my children.

PHILIP K. DICK, *I HOPE I SHALL ARRIVE SOON* (1985)

13. Every violation of truth is not only a sort of suicide in the liar, but is a stab at the health of human society.

EMERSON, "PRUDENCE," *ESSAYS: FIRST SERIES* (1841)

14. He saw she was lying but it was a brave lie. They talked from their hearts—with the half truths and evasions peculiar to that organ, which has never been famed as an instrument of precision.

F. SCOTT FITZGERALD, *THE CRACK-UP* (1945)

15. Without lies humanity would perish of despair and boredom.

ANATOLE FRANCE, AFTERWORD TO *THE BLOOM OF LIFE* (1922)

16. Falsehood is the jockey of misfortune.

JEAN GIRAUDOUX, *SIEGFRIED* (1928), 2, TR. PETER H. JUDD

17. A single lie destroys a whole reputation for integrity.

BALTASAR GRACIÁN, *THE ART OF WORLDLY WISDOM* (1647), 181, TR. JOSEPH JACOBS

18. The most mischievous liars are those who keep sliding on the verge of truth.

AUGUSTUS WILLIAM HARE, *GUESSES AT TRUTH* (1827)

19. As hypocrisy is said to be the highest compliment to virtue, the art of lying is the strongest acknowledgment of the force of truth.

WILLIAM HAZLITT, "ON PATRONAGE AND PUFFING," *TABLE TALK* (1821–22)

20. The great masses of the people ... will more easily fall victims to a big lie than to a small one.

ADOLF HITLER, *MEIN KAMPF* (1924), 1.10

21. Sin has many tools, but a lie is the handle which fits them all.

OLIVER WENDELL HOLMES, SR., *THE AUTOCRAT OF THE BREAKFAST TABLE* (1858), 6

22. Americans detest all lies except lies spoken in public or printed lies.

EDGAR WATSON HOWE, *VENTURES IN COMMON SENSE* (1919), 2.6

23. Life is a system of half-truths and lies, / Opportunistic, convenient evasion.

LANGSTON HUGHES, "ELDERLY POLITICIANS," *THE LANGSTON HUGHES READER* (1958)

24. If there were no falsehood in the world, there would be no doubt, if there were no doubt, there would be no inquiry; if no inquiry, no wisdom, no knowledge, no genius; and Fancy herself would lie muffled up in her robe, inactive, pale, and bloated.

WALTER SAVAGE LANDOR, "EPICURUS, LEONTION, AND TERNISSA," *IMAGINARY CONVERSATIONS* (1824–53)

25. Lying is not only excusable; it is not only innocent, and instinctive; it is, above all, necessary and unavoidable. Without the ameliorations that it offers life would become a mere syllogism, and hence too metallic to be borne.

H. L. MENCKEN, *PREJUDICES: FOURTH SERIES* (1924), 15

26. People on the Continent either tell you the truth or lie; in England they hardly ever lie, but they would not dream of telling you the truth.

GEORGE MIKES, *HOW TO BE AN ALIEN* (1946)

27. I do myself a greater injury in lying than I do him of whom I tell a lie.

MONTAIGNE, "OF PRESUMPTION," *ESSAYS* (1580–88), TR. W. C. HAZLITT

28. In plain truth, lying is an accursed vice. We are not men, nor have other tie upon one another, but by our word.

MONTAIGNE, "OF LIARS," *ESSAYS* (1580–88), TR. W. C. HAZLITT

29. That lies should be necessary to life is part and parcel of the terrible and questionable character of existence.

NIETZSCHE, *THE WILL TO POWER* (1888), 853, TR. ANTHONY M. LUDOVICI

30. A liar should have a good memory.

QUINTILIAN, *INSTITUTIO ORATORIA* (C. A.D. 95), 4.2, TR. H. E. BUTLER

31. Repetition does not transform a lie into a truth.

FRANKLIN D. ROOSEVELT, RADIO ADDRESS, OCT. 26, 1939

32. To tell a falsehood is like the cut of a sabre; for though the wound may heal, the scar of it will remain.

SA'DI, *GULISTAN* (1258), 8.98, TR. JAMES ROSS

33. A liar goes in fine clothes, / A liar goes in rags. / A liar is a liar, clothes or no clothes.

CARL SANDBURG, "THE LIARS," *COMPLETE POEMS* (1950)

34. People lie because they don't remember clear what they saw. / People lie because they can't help making a story better than it was the way it happened.

CARL SANDBURG, *THE PEOPLE, YES* (1936)

35. O, what a goodly outside falsehood hath!

SHAKESPEARE, *THE MERCHANT OF VENICE* (1596–97), 1.3.103

36. It is a general rule that when the grain of truth cannot be found, men will swallow great helpings of falsehood.

ISAAC BASHEVIS SINGER, "YENTL THE YESHIVA BOY" (1962)

37. False words are not only evil in themselves, but they infect the soul with evil.

SOCRATES, IN PLATO'S *PHAEDO* (4TH–3RD C. B.C.), TR. BENJAMIN JOWETT

38. A lie is troublesome, and sets a man's invention upon the rack, and one trick needs a great many more to make it good.

RICHARD STEELE, *THE SPECTATOR* (1711–12), 352

39. A lie is an abomination unto the Lord, and a very present help in trouble.

ADLAI STEVENSON, SPEECH, SPRINGFIELD, ILL., JANUARY 1951

40. The cruellest lies are often told in silence.

ROBERT LOUIS STEVENSON, TITLE ESSAY, 4, *VIRGINIBUS PUERISQUE* (1881)

41. A lie which is half a truth is ever the blackest of lies.

LORD TENNYSON, "THE GRANDMOTHER" (1864), 8

42. One man lies in his words, and gets a bad reputation; another in his manners, and enjoys a good one.

THOREAU, *JOURNAL*, JUNE 25, 1851

43. It is often the case that a man who can't tell a lie thinks that he is the best judge of one.

MARK TWAIN, *NOTEBOOK* (1935)

44. One of the most striking differences between a cat and a lie is that a cat has only nine lives.

MARK TWAIN, "PUDD'NHEAD WILSON'S CALENDAR," *PUDD'NHEAD WILSON* (1894), 7

45. What we have to do, what at any rate it is our duty to do, is to revive the old art of Lying.

OSCAR WILDE, *THE ARTIST AS CRITIC: CRITICAL WRITINGS OF OSCAR WILDE*, ED. RICHARD ELLMANN (1969)

M

MACHINES

See 966. TECHNOLOGY

559. MADNESS

See also 627. NEUROSIS; 842. SANITY

1. We are all born mad. Some remain so.

SAMUEL BECKETT, *WAITING FOR GODOT* (1952), 2

2. The wily lunatic is lost if through the narrowest crack he allows a sane eye to peer into his locked universe and thus profane it.

COLETTE, "FREEDOM," *EARTHLY PARADISE* (1966), 2

3. There is less harm to be suffered in being mad among madmen than in being sane all by oneself.

DENIS DIDEROT, *SUPPLEMENT TO BOUGAINVILLE'S "VOYAGE"* (1796)

4. There is a pleasure sure / In being mad which none but madmen know.

JOHN DRYDEN, *THE SPANISH FRIAR* (1681), 2.1

5. Sanity is very rare: every man almost, and every woman, has a dash of madness.

EMERSON, *JOURNALS*, 1836

6. What is madness / To those who only observe, is often wisdom / To those to whom it happens.

CHRISTOPHER FRY, *A PHOENIX TOO FREQUENT* (1950)

7. The world is so full of simpletons and madmen, that one need not seek them in a madhouse.

GOETHE, QUOTED IN JOHANN PETER ECKERMANN'S *CONVERSATIONS WITH GOETHE*, MARCH 17, 1830

8. Better mad with the rest of the world than wise alone.

BALTASAR GRACIÁN, *THE ART OF WORLDLY WISDOM* (1647), 133, TR. JOSEPH JACOBS

9. Everyone is more or less mad on one point.

RUDYARD KIPLING, "ON THE STRENGTH OF A LIKENESS," *PLAIN TALES FROM THE HILLS* (1888)

10. Sometimes accidents happen in life from which we have need of a little madness to extricate ourselves successfully.

LA ROCHEFOUCAULD, *MAXIMS* (1665), TR. KENNETH PRATT

11. Here's an object more of dread / Than aught the grave contains— / A human form with reason fled, / While wretched life remains.

ABRAHAM LINCOLN, LETTER TO ANDREW JOHNSON, SEPT. 6, 1846

12. The great proof of madness is the disproportion of one's designs to one's means.

NAPOLEON I, *MAXIMS* (1804–15)

13. Men are so necessarily mad, that not to be mad would amount to another form of madness.

PASCAL, *PENSÉES* (1670), 414, TR. W. F. TROTTER

14. Whom Fortune wishes to destroy she first makes mad.

PUBLILIUS SYRUS, *MORAL SAYINGS* (1ST C. B.C.), 911, TR. DARIUS LYMAN

15. A body seriously out of equilibrium, either with itself or with its environment, perishes outright. Not so a mind. Madness and suffering can set themselves no limit.

GEORGE SANTAYANA, *THE LIFE OF REASON: REASON IN COMMON SENSE* (1905–06), 2

16. The lunatic, the lover, and the poet / Are of imagination all compact.

SHAKESPEARE, *A MIDSUMMER NIGHT'S DREAM* (1595–96), 5.1.7

17. In the twentieth century, the repellent, harrowing disease that is made the index of a superior sensitivity, the vehicle of "spiritual" feelings and "critical" discontent, is insanity.

SUSAN SONTAG, *ILLNESS AS METAPHOR* (1978)

18. When we remember that we are all mad, the mysteries disappear and life stands explained.

MARK TWAIN, *NOTEBOOK* (1935)

19. What is madness? To have erroneous perceptions and to reason correctly from them.

VOLTAIRE, "MADNESS," *PHILOSOPHICAL DICTIONARY* (1764)

560. MAILMEN

1. Neither snow, nor rain, nor heat, nor gloom of night stays these couriers from the swift completion of their appointed rounds.

INSCRIPTION ON THE GENERAL POST OFFICE, NEW YORK CITY, ADAPTED FROM HERODOTUS' *THE HISTORIES* (5TH C. B.C.)

561. MALICE

See also 295. ENVY; 905. SLANDER

1. A truth that's told with bad intent / Beats all the Lies you can invent.

WILLIAM BLAKE, "AUGURIES OF INNOCENCE" (1800–10)

2. I am convinced that we have a degree of delight, and that no small one, in the real misfortunes and pains of others.

EDMUND BURKE, *A PHILOSOPHICAL INQUIRY INTO THE ORIGIN OF OUR IDEAS OF THE SUBLIME AND BEAUTIFUL* (1756), 1.14

3. Man's life is a warfare against the malice of men.

BALTASAR GRACIÁN, *THE ART OF WORLDLY WISDOM* (1647), 13, TR. JOSEPH JACOBS

4. Malice often takes the garb of truth.

WILLIAM HAZLITT, "ON DEPTH AND SUPERFICIALITY," *THE PLAIN SPEAKER* (1826)

5. The malicious have a dark happiness.

VICTOR HUGO, "FANTINE," *LES MISÉRABLES* (1862), 5.9, TR. CHARLES E. WILBOUR

6. In the misfortune of our best friends we always discover something not unpleasing to us.

LA ROCHEFOUCAULD, *MAXIMS* (1665), TR. KENNETH PRATT

7. Man loves malice, but not against one-eyed men nor the unfortunate, but against the fortunate and proud.

MARTIAL, *EPIGRAMS* (A.D. 86)

8. Malicious tongues spread their poison abroad and nothing here below is proof against them.

MOLIÈRE, *TARTUFFE* (1664), 5, TR. JOHN WOOD

9. Do not trust a malicious man because you have long been intimate with him. A serpent will still bite, though it may have been kept and tended a long time.

PANCHATANTRA (C. 5TH C.), 1, TR. FRANKLIN EDGERTON

10. When malice has reason on its side it becomes proud, and parades reason in all its splendour.

PASCAL, *PENSÉES* (1670), 407, TR. W. F. TROTTER

11. Often on earth the gentlest heart is fain / To feed and banquet on another's woe.

PETRARCH, "LAURA DEAD," *CANZONIERE* (1360), 294

12. Malice swallows the greater part of its own venom.

PUBLILIUS SYRUS, *MORAL SAYINGS* (1ST C. B.C.), 1030, TR. DARIUS LYMAN

13. If there were in the world today any large number of people who desired their own happiness more than they desired the unhappiness of others, we could have a paradise in a few years.

BERTRAND RUSSELL, *THE NEW YORK TIMES,* MAY 18, 1961

14. One likes people much better when they're battered down by a prodigious siege of misfortunate than when they triumph.

VIRGINIA WOOLF, *A WRITER'S DIARY,* AUG. 13, 1921

MAN, AGES OF

See 540. LIFE, STAGES OF

MANAGEMENT

See 13. ADMINISTRATION; 315. EXECUTIVES

562. MANKIND

See also 431. HUMAN NATURE; 539. LIFE

1. Man *becomes* man only by the intelligence, but he *is* man only by the heart.

HENRI FRÉDÉRIC AMIEL, *JOURNAL,* APRIL 7, 1851, TR. MRS. HUMPHRY WARD

2. Not in innocence, and not in Asia, was mankind born. The home of our fathers was that African highland reaching north from the Cape to the Lakes of the Nile. Here we came about—slowly, ever so slowly—on a sky-swept savannah glowing with menace.

ROBERT ARDREY, *AFRICAN GENESIS* (1961)

3. Man, when perfected, is the best of animals, but, when separated from law and justice, he is the worst of all.

ARISTOTLE, *POLITICS* (4TH C. B.C.), 1.2, TR. BENJAMIN JOWETT

4. Know, man hath all which Nature hath, but more, / And in that *more* lie all his hopes of good.

MATTHEW ARNOLD, "TO AN INDEPENDENT PREACHER" (1849)

5. Is a man a salvage at heart, skinned o'er with fragile Manners? Or is salvagery but a faint taint in the natural man's gentility, which erupts now and again like pimples on an angel's arse?

JOHN BARTH, *THE SOT-WEED FACTOR* (1960), 3.12

6. We drink without thirst and we make love anytime, madame; only this distinguishes us from the other animals.

BEAUMARCHAIS, *THE MARRIAGE OF FIGARO* (1784), 2.21

7. Man is at the bottom an animal, midway a citizen, and at the top divine. But the climate of this world is such that few ripen at the top.

HENRY WARD BEECHER, *PROVERBS FROM PLYMOUTH PULPIT* (1887)

8. So God created man in his own image, in the image of God created he him; male and female created he them.

BIBLE, GENESIS 1:27

9. Man is unique not because he does science, and he is unique not because he does art, but because science and art equally are expressions of his marvelous plasticity of mind.

JACOB BRONOWSKI, *THE ASCENT OF MAN* (1973)

10. Man is a singular creature. He has a set of gifts which make him unique among the animals: so that, unlike them, he is not a figure in the landscape—he is a shaper of the landscape.

JACOB BRONOWSKI, *THE ASCENT OF MAN* (1973)

11. O man! thou feeble tenant of an hour, / Debased by slavery, or corrupt by power, / Who knows thee well must quit thee with disgust, / Degraded mass of animated dust! / Thy love is lust, thy friendship all a cheat, / Thy smiles hypocrisy, thy word deceit! / By nature vile, ennobled but by name, / Each kindred brute might bid thee blush for shame.

BYRON, "ON THE MONUMENT OF A NEWFOUNDLAND DOG" (1808)

12. Every people is a chosen people in its own mind. And it is rather amusing that their name for themselves usually means mankind.

JOSEPH CAMPBELL, *THE POWER OF MYTH* (1988)

13. Man is an exception, whatever else he is. If he is not the image of God, then he is a disease of the dust.

G. K. CHESTERTON, "WINE WHEN IT IS RED," *ALL THINGS CONSIDERED* (1908)

14. A wonderful fact to reflect upon, that every human creature is constituted to be that profound secret and mystery to every other.

CHARLES DICKENS, *A TALE OF TWO CITIES* (1859), 1.3

15. What is man, when you come to think upon him, but a minutely set, ingenious machine for turning, with infinite artfulness, the red wine of Shiraz into urine?

ISAK DINESEN, "THE DREAMERS," *SEVEN GOTHIC TALES* (1934)

16. Man is not only a contributary creature, but a total creature; he does not only make one, but he is all; he is not a piece of the world, but the world itself; and next to the glory of God, the reason why there is a world.

JOHN DONNE, *SERMONS,* NO. 35, 1625

17. Men are but children of a larger growth.

JOHN DRYDEN, *ALL FOR LOVE* (1678), 4.1

18. Biologically, man is still the great amateur of the animal kingdom; he is unique in his lack of anatomical and physiological specialization.

RENÉ DUBOS, "THE PURSUIT OF SIGNIFICANCE," *SO HUMAN AN ANIMAL* (1968)

19. Each human being is unique, unprecedented, unrepeatable.

RENÉ DUBOS, FOREWORD TO *SO HUMAN AN ANIMAL* (1968)

20. What if I am, in some way, only a sophisticated fire that has acquired an ability to regulate its rate of combustion and to hoard its fuel in order to see and walk?

LOREN EISELEY, "THE LAST NEANDERTHAL," *THE STAR THROWER* (1978)

21. The majority of mankind is lazyminded, incurious, absorbed in vanities, and tepid in emotion, and is therefore incapable of either much doubt or much faith.

T. S. ELIOT, INTRODUCTION TO PASCAL'S *PENSÉES* (1931)

22. Man is physically as well as metaphysically a thing of shreds and patches, borrowed unequally from good and bad ancestors, and a misfit from the start.

EMERSON, "BEAUTY," *THE CONDUCT OF LIFE* (1860)

23. It were no slight attainment could we merely fulfil what the nature of man implies.

EPICTETUS, *DISCOURSES* (2ND C.), 2.9, TR. THOMAS W. HIGGINSON

24. Man is Nature's sole mistake!

W. S. GILBERT, *PRINCESS IDA* (1884), 2

25. It is because nations tend to stupidity and baseness that mankind moves so slowly; it is because individuals have a capacity for better things that it moves at all.

GEORGE GISSING, "SPRING," *THE PRIVATE PAPERS OF HENRY RYECROFT* (1903)

26. Man is a simple being. And however rich, varied, and unfathomable he may be, the cycle of his situations is soon run through.

GOETHE, QUOTED IN JOHANN PETER ECKERMANN'S *CONVERSATIONS WITH GOETHE,* MAY 1, 1825

27. Mankind are earthen jugs with spirits in them.

NATHANIEL HAWTHORNE, *AMERICAN NOTE-BOOKS,* 1842

28. Among all creatures that breathe on earth and crawl on it / there is not anywhere a thing more dismal than man is.

HOMER, *ILIAD* (9TH C. B.C.), 17.446, TR. RICHMOND LATTIMORE

29. Man as we know him is a poor creature; but he is half-way between an ape and a god, and he is travelling in the right direction.

WILLIAM RALPH INGE, "CONFESSIO FIDEI," *OUTSPOKEN ESSAYS: SECOND SERIES* (1922)

30. The Family of Man is more than three billion strong. It lives in more than one hundred nations. Most of its members are not white. Most of them are not Christians. Most of them know nothing about free enterprise, or due process of law or the Australian ballot.

JOHN F. KENNEDY, ADDRESS, PROTESTANT COUNCIL OF NEW YORK CITY, NOV. 8, 1963

31. [Man] is the only one in whom the instinct of life falters long enough to enable it to ask the question "Why?"

JOSEPH WOOD KRUTCH, "THE GENESIS OF A MOOD," *THE MODERN TEMPER* (1929)

32. The world's five thousand extant languages are products of our shared ability, but the five thousand cultures they create are separate from each other.

RICHARD LEAKEY, *THE ORIGIN OF HUMANKIND* (1994)

33. We are bipedal apes, and it should not be surprising to see that fact reflected in the way our ancestors lived.

RICHARD LEAKEY, *THE ORIGIN OF HUMANKIND* (1994)

34. [T]he human mind, in taking us down the path of technocracy, has become the adversary of life itself and collaterally the adversary of the human soul.

KONRAD LORENZ, *THE WANING OF HUMANENESS* (1983), TR. ROBERT WARREN KICKER

35. Man would be *otherwise.* That is the essence of the specifically human.

ANTONIO MACHADO, *JUAN DE MAIRENA* (1943), 44, TR. BEN BELITT

36. Whatever profits man, that is the truth. In him all nature is comprehended, in all nature only he is created, and all nature only for him. He is the measure of all things, and his welfare is the sole and single criterion of truth.

THOMAS MANN, *THE MAGIC MOUNTAIN* (1924), 6.3, TR. H. T. LOWE-PORTER

37. i suppose the human race / is doing the best it can / but hells bells thats / only an explanation / its not an excuse.

DON MARQUIS, "ARCHY SAYS," *ARCHY DOES HIS PART* (1935)

38. Man, in the ideal, is so noble and so sparkling, such a grand and glowing creature, that over any ignominious blemish in him all his fellows should run to throw their costliest robes.

HERMAN MELVILLE, *MOBY-DICK* (1851), 26

39. Man is a beautiful machine that works very badly. He is like a watch of which the most that can be said is that its cosmetic effect is good.

H. L. MENCKEN, *MINORITY REPORT* (1956), 20

40. Every other man is a piece of myself, for I am a part and a member of mankind.

THOMAS MERTON, *NO MAN IS AN ISLAND* (1955)

41. Every man carries the entire form of human condition.

MONTAIGNE, "OF REPENTANCE," *ESSAYS* (1580–88), TR. W. C. HAZLITT

42. I have never seen greater monster or miracle in the world than myself.

MONTAIGNE, "OF CRIPPLES," *ESSAYS* (1580–88), TR. W. C. HAZLITT

43. Man, in good earnest, is a marvelous vain, fickle, and unstable subject, and on whom it is very hard to form any certain and uniform judgment.

MONTAIGNE, "THAT MEN BY VARIOUS WAYS ARRIVE AT THE SAME END," *ESSAYS* (1580–88), TR. W. C. HAZLITT

44. Man exists only insofar as he is separated from his surroundings. The cranium is a space-traveler's helmet. Stay inside or you perish.

VLADIMIR NABOKOV, *PNIN* (1953)

45. Alas for this mad melancholy beast man! What phantasies invade it, what paroxysms of perversity, hysterical senselessness, and mental bestiality break out immediately, at the very slightest check on its being the beast of action.

NIETZSCHE, *THE GENEALOGY OF MORALS* (1887), 2.22, TR. HORACE B. SAMUEL

46. For in fact what is man in nature? A Nothing in comparison with the Infinite, an All in comparison with Nothing, a mean between nothing and everything.

PASCAL, *PENSÉES* (1670), 72, TR. W. F. TROTTER

47. What a chimera then is man! What a novelty! What a monster, what a chaos, what a contradiction, what a prodigy! Judge of all things, imbecile worm of the earth; depository of truth, a sink of uncertainty and error; the pride and refuse of the universe!

PASCAL, *PENSÉES* (1670), 434, TR. W. F. TROTTER

48. There are three classes of men—lovers of wisdom, lovers of honor, lovers of gain.

PLATO, *THE REPUBLIC* (4TH C. B.C.), 9, TR. BENJAMIN JOWETT

49. It is exciting and emancipating to believe we are one of nature's latest experiments, but what if the experiment is unsuccessful?

V. S. PRITCHETT, "THE SCIENTIFIC ROMANCES," *THE LIVING NOVEL & LATER APPRECIATIONS* (1964)

50. A man has many parts, he is virtually everything, and you are free to select in him that part which pleases you.

SAINT-EXUPÉRY, *THE WISDOM OF THE SANDS* (1948), 96, TR. STUART GILBERT

51. The mass of mankind is divided into two classes, the Sancho Panzas who have a sense for reality, but no ideals, and the Don Quixotes with a sense for ideals, but mad.

GEORGE SANTAYANA, PREFACE TO *INTERPRETATIONS OF POETRY AND RELIGION* (1900)

52. Lord, what fools these mortals be!

SHAKESPEARE, *A MIDSUMMER NIGHT'S DREAM* (1595–96), 3.2.115

53. What a piece of work is man! how noble in reason! how infinite in faculties! in form and moving how express and admirable! in action how like an angel! in apprehension how like a god! the beauty of the world! the paragon of animals!

SHAKESPEARE, *HAMLET* (1600), 2.2.315

54. Twenty-five hundred years ago it might have been said that man understood himself as well as any other part of the world. Today he is the thing he understands least.

B.F. SKINNER, *BEYOND FREEDOM AND DIGNITY* (1971)

55. In the traditional view, a person is free. He is autonomous in the sense that his behavior is uncaused. He can therefore be held responsible for what he does and justly punished if he offends.

B.F. SKINNER, *BEYOND FREEDOM AND DIGNITY* (1971)

56. The fish in the water is silent, the animal on the earth is noisy, the bird in the air is singing. / But Man has in him the silence of the sea, the noise of the earth and the music of the air.

RABINDRANATH TAGORE, *STRAY BIRDS* (1916), 43

57. I am a man; I consider nothing human alien to me.

TERENCE, *THE SELF-TORMENTOR* (163 B.C.)

58. I will confess that I have no more sense of what goes on in the mind of mankind than I have for the mind of an ant.

LEWIS THOMAS, "COMPUTERS," *THE LIVES OF A CELL* (1974)

59. Man has gone long enough, or even too long, without being man enough to face the simple truth that the trouble with man is Man.

JAMES THURBER, "THE TROUBLE WITH MAN IS MAN," *LANTERNS AND LANCES* (1961)

60. The noblest work of God? Man. Who found it out? Man.

MARK TWAIN, *AUTOBIOGRAPHY* (1924), V. 2

61. We should expect the best and the worst from mankind, as from the weather.

VAUVENARGUES, *REFLECTIONS AND MAXIMS* (1746), 102, TR. F. G. STEVENS

62. What is man? Ally of God or simply his toy? His triumph or his fall?

ELIE WIESEL, *LEGENDS OF OUR TIMES* (1968)

63. We're all of us guinea pigs in the laboratory of God. Humanity is just a work in progress.

TENNESSEE WILLIAMS, *CAMINO REAL* (1953), 12

563. MANNERS

See also 114. CEREMONY; 197. COURTESY; 213. CUSTOM; 378. GENTLEMAN; 391. GOOD BREEDING; 408. HANDSHAKE; 749. PROPRIETY; 914. SOCIETY, POLITE; 961. TACT

1. Manners are the hypocrisy of a nation.

BALZAC, QUOTED IN ANDRÉ GIDE'S *JOURNALS*, 1911, TR. JUSTIN O'BRIEN

2. Manners maketh man. Yes, but they make woman still more.

SAMUEL BUTLER (D. 1902), "HIGGLEDY-PIGGLEDY," *NOTE-BOOKS* (1912)

3. Society is smoothed to that excess, / That manners hardly differ more than dress.

BYRON, *DON JUAN* (1819–24), 13.94

4. Good manners are the settled medium of social, as specie is of commercial, life; returns are equally expected for both.

LORD CHESTERFIELD, *LETTERS TO HIS SON*, DEC. 25, 1753

5. Manners must adorn knowledge and smooth its way through the world.

LORD CHESTERFIELD, *LETTERS*, JULY 1, 1748

6. We are justified in enforcing good morals, for they belong to all mankind; but we are not justified in enforcing good manners, for good manners always mean our own manners.

G. K. CHESTERTON, "LIMERICKS AND COUNSELS OF PERFECTION," *ALL THINGS CONSIDERED* (1908)

7. Nothing seems at first sight less important than the outward form of human actions, yet there is nothing upon which men set more store: they grow used to everything except to living in a society which has not their own manners.

ALEXIS DE TOCQUEVILLE, *DEMOCRACY IN AMERICA* (1835–39), 2.3.14

8. Fine manners need the support of fine manners in others.

EMERSON, "BEHAVIOR," *THE CONDUCT OF LIFE* (1860)

9. Manners are the happy ways of doing things; each once a stroke of genius or of love, now repeated and hardened into usage.

EMERSON, "BEHAVIOR," *THE CONDUCT OF LIFE* (1860)

10. Manners make the fortune of the ambitious youth.

EMERSON, "BEHAVIOR," *THE CONDUCT OF LIFE* (1860)

11. Manners require time, as nothing is more vulgar than haste.

EMERSON, "BEHAVIOR," *THE CONDUCT OF LIFE* (1860)

12. There is nothing settled in manners, but the laws of behavior yield to the energy of the individual.

EMERSON, "MANNERS," *ESSAYS: SECOND SERIES* (1844)

13. A man without ceremony had need of great merit in its place.

THOMAS FULLER, M.D., *GNOMOLOGIA* (1732), 315

14. A bad manner spoils everything, even reason and justice; a good one supplies everything, gilds a No, sweetens truth, and adds a touch of beauty to old age itself.

BALTASAR GRACIÁN, *THE ART OF WORLDLY WISDOM* (1647), 14, TR. JOSEPH JACOBS

15. Etiquette is what you are doing and saying when people are looking and listening. What you are thinking is your business.

VIRGINIA CARY HUDSON, *O YE JIGS & JULEPS!* (1962)

16. People who put slipcovers, doilies, plastic protectors, and cellophane on everything good that they own rarely live to see an occasion so good that all these covers are removed.

JUDITH MARTIN, *MISS MANNERS' GUIDE TO EXCRUCIATINGLY CORRECT BEHAVIOR* (1979)

17. Fashionably amusing table manners are a matter of breaking the right rule at the right time.

P.J. O'ROURKE, *MODERN MANNERS* (1988)

18. Good manners consist of doing precisely what everyone thinks should be done, especially when no one knows quite what that is.

P.J. O'ROURKE, *MODERN MANNERS* (1988)

19. I'd discovered, after a lot of extreme apprehension about what spoons to use, that if you do something incorrect at table with a certain arrogance, as if you knew perfectly well you were doing it improperly, you can get away with it and nobody will think you are bad-mannered or poorly brought up.

SYLVIA PLATH, *THE BELL JAR* (1963)

20. Etiquette can be at the same time a means of approaching people and of staying clear of them.

DAVID RIESMAN, "A JURY OF THEIR PEERS," *THE LONELY CROWD* (1950)

21. Manners are not idle, but the fruit / Of loyal nature and of noble mind.

LORD TENNYSON, "GUINEVERE," *IDYLLS OF THE KING* (1859)

22. To the real artist in humanity, what are called bad manners are often the most picturesque and significant of all.

WALT WHITMAN, "EMERSON'S BOOKS," *NOTES LEFT OVER* (1881)

MARCH

See 854. SEASONS

564. MARRIAGE

See also 66. BACHELORS; 123. CHILDREN; 198. COURTSHIP; 262. DIVORCE; 334. FAMILY; 472. INFIDELITY; 499. INTIMACY; 670. PARENTHOOD; 892. SEX; 1051. WEDDINGS

1. The capacity of women to make unsuitable marriages must be considered as the cornerstone of society.

HENRY ADAMS, *DEMOCRACY: AN AMERICAN NOVEL* (1880)

2. Married love between / man and woman is bigger than oaths guarded by right of nature.

AESCHYLUS, *THE EUMENIDES* (458 B.C.), TR. RICHMOND LATTIMORE

3. When a match has equal partners / then I fear not.

AESCHYLUS, *PROMETHEUS BOUND* (C. 478 B.C.), TR. DAVID GRENE

4. Wives are young men's mistresses, companions for middle age, and old men's nurses.

FRANCIS BACON, "OF MARRIAGE AND SINGLE LIFE," *ESSAYS* (1625)

5. [I]t had been from the first her great mistake—to meet him, to marry him, to love him as she so bitterly had. Looking at his face, it sometimes came to her that all women had been cursed from the cradle; all, in one fashion or another, being given the same cruel destiny, born to suffer the weight of men.

JAMES BALDWIN, *GO TELL IT ON THE MOUNTAIN* (1953)

6. A long association—prolonged human contact, when a man and woman live together—this ends up producing a sort of rot, a poison.

UGO BETTI, *THE INQUIRY* (1944–45), 1.10

7. Can two walk together, except they be agreed?

BIBLE, AMOS 3:3

8. It is better to dwell in a corner of the housetop, than with a brawling woman in a wide house.

BIBLE, PROVERBS 21:9 AND 25:24

9. Whoso findeth a wife findeth a good thing.

BIBLE, PROVERBS 18:22

10. That is partly why women marry—to keep up the fiction of being in the hub of things.

ELIZABETH BOWEN, *THE HOUSE IN PARIS* (1935), 2.2

11. The bitterest creature under heaven is the wife who discovers that her husband's bravery is only bravado, that his strength is only a uniform, that his power is but a gun in the hands of a fool.

PEARL S. BUCK, "LOVE AND MARRIAGE," *TO MY DAUGHTERS, WITH LOVE* (1967)

12. One was never married, and that's his hell; another is, and that's his plague.

ROBERT BURTON, *THE ANATOMY OF MELANCHOLY* (1621), 2.4.2.1

13. In matrimony, to hesitate is sometimes to be saved.

SAMUEL BUTLER (D. 1902), "HIGGLEDY-PIGGLEDY," *NOTE-BOOKS* (1912)

14. But I had not quite fixed whether to make him [Don Juan] end in Hell—or in an unhappy marriage,—not knowing which would be the severest.

BYRON, *SELECTED LETTERS AND JOURNALS* (1982), ED. LESLIE A. MARCHAND

15. People marry through a variety of other reasons, and with varying results; but to marry for love is to invite inevitable tragedy.

JAMES BRANCH CABELL, *THE CREAM OF THE JEST* (1917)

16. When you make the sacrifice in marriage, you're sacrificing not to each other but to unity in a relationship.

JOSEPH CAMPBELL, *THE POWER OF MYTH* (1988)

17. Marriage is not a simple love affair, it's an ordeal, and the ordeal is the sacrifice of ego to a relationship in which two have become one.

JOSEPH CAMPBELL, *THE POWER OF MYTH* (1988)

18. When people get married because they think it's a long-time love affair, they'll be divorced very soon, because all love affairs end in disappointment. But marriage is a recognition of a spiritual identity.

JOSEPH CAMPBELL, *THE POWER OF MYTH* (1988)

19. To marry a woman you love and who loves you is to lay a wager with her as to who will stop loving the other first.

ALFRED CAPUS, *NOTES ET PENSÉES* (1926)

20. That was their marriage then—not the highest paving of the stair, the clatter of Italian fountains, the

wind in the alien olive trees, but this: a jay-naked male and female discussing their bowels.

JOHN CHEEVER, *THE FALCONER* (1977)

21. Oh! how many torments lie in the small circle of a wedding-ring!

COLLEY CIBBER, *THE DOUBLE GALLANT* (1707), 1.2

22. Show me one couple unhappy merely on account of their limited circumstances, and I will show you ten who are wretched from other causes.

SAMUEL TAYLOR COLERIDGE, *TABLE TALK*, JUNE 10, 1824

23. Marriage is a feast where the grace is sometimes better than the dinner.

CHARLES CALEB COLTON, *LACON* (1825), 2.47

24. Marriage indeed may qualify the fury of his passion, but it very rarely mends a man's manners.

WILLIAM CONGREVE, *LOVE FOR LOVE* (1695), 1.1

25. Most of the beauty of women evaporates when they achieve domestic happiness at the price of their independence.

CYRIL CONNOLLY, *THE UNQUIET GRAVE* (1945), 2

26. The dread of loneliness is greater than the fear of bondage, so we get married.

CYRIL CONNOLLY, *THE UNQUIET GRAVE* (1945), 1

27. I suppose I shall marry eventually. One does that, one drifts into stability.

PETER DE VRIES, *COMFORT ME WITH APPLES* (1956)

28. Every woman should marry—and no man.

BENJAMIN DISRAELI, *LOTHAIR* (1870), 30

29. The chains of marriage are so heavy that it takes two to bear them, sometimes three.

ALEXANDRE DUMAS FILS, QUOTED IN L. TREICH'S *L'ESPRIT D'ALEXANDRE DUMAS*

30. As Thoreau nearly said: "Most wives lead lives of quiet disapprobation."

LAWRENCE DURRELL, *MONSIEUR* (1974)

31. Having once embarked on your marital voyage, it is impossible not to be aware that you make no way and that the sea is not within sight—that, in fact, you are exploring an enclosed basin.

GEORGE ELIOT, *MIDDLEMARCH* (1871–72), 20

32. A man's wife has more power over him than the state has.

EMERSON, *JOURNALS*, 1836

33. Marriage is the perfection which love aimed at, ignorant of what it sought.

EMERSON, *JOURNALS*, 1850

34. Wedlock, a padlock.

ENGLISH PROVERB

35. A rare spoil for a man / Is the winning of a good wife; very / Plentiful are the worthless women.

EURIPIDES, *IPHIGENIA IN AULIS* (C. 405 B.C.), TR. CHARLES R. WALKER

36. All other woes a woman bears are minor / But lose her husband!—might as well be dead.

EURIPIDES, *ANDROMACHE* (C. 426 B.C.), TR. JOHN F. NIMS

37. One man should love and honor one: / A bride-bed / Theirs alone till life's done.

EURIPIDES, *ANDROMACHE* (C. 426 B.C.), TR. JOHN F. NIMS

38. Man's best possession is a sympathetic wife.

EURIPIDES, *ANTIGONE* (5TH C. B.C.), 164, TR. M. H. MORGAN

39. Marry, and with luck / it may go well. But when a marriage fails, / then those who marry live at home in hell.

EURIPIDES, *ORESTES* (408 B.C.), TR. WILLIAM ARROWSMITH

40. Having whipped single women into high marital panic—or "nuptialitis," as one columnist called it—the press hastened to soothe fretted brows with conjugal tonic.

SUSAN FALUDI, *BACKLASH* (1991)

41. To be unwed and female was to succumb to an illness with only one known cure: marriage.

SUSAN FALUDI, *BACKLASH* (1991)

42. Marriage is simply an economic necessity, and so there are no elaborate courtship displays or marriage celebrations among the Eskimo.

PETER FARB, *MAN'S RISE TO CIVILIZATION* (1968)

43. Keep your eyes wide open before marriage, half shut afterwards.

BENJAMIN FRANKLIN, *POOR RICHARD'S ALMANACK* (1732–57)

44. You can bear your own faults, and why not a fault in your wife?

BENJAMIN FRANKLIN, *POOR RICHARD'S ALMANACK* (1732–57)

45. Choose a wife rather by your ear than your eye.

THOMAS FULLER, M.D., *GNOMOLOGIA* (1732), 1107

46. More belongs to marriage than four legs in a bed.
THOMAS FULLER, M.D., *GNOMOLOGIA* (1732), 3450

47. The comfortable estate of widowhood, is the only hope that keeps up a wife's spirits.
JOHN GAY, *THE BEGGAR'S OPERA* (1728), 1.8, AIR 10

48. A wife loves out of duty, and duty leads to constraint, and constraint kills desire.
JEAN GIRAUDOUX, *AMPHITRYON 38* (1929), 1, TR. PETER H. JUDD

49. Half the human race can change its name and sometimes its nation without suffering—at least half! All women!
JEAN GIRAUDOUX, *SIEGFRIED* (1928), 3, TR. PETER H. JUDD

50. If the Lord had appointed her to marriage, He would have arranged it all in His own good time.
ELLEN GLASGOW, *VEIN OF IRON* (1935)

51. The sum which two married people owe to one another defies calculation. It is an infinite debt, which can only be discharged through all eternity.
GOETHE, *ELECTIVE AFFINITIES* (1809), 9

52. When a woman gets married it's like jumping into a hole in the ice in the middle of winter: you do it once, and you remember it the rest of your days.
MAXIM GORKY, *THE LOWER DEPTHS* (1903), 1, TR. ALEXANDER BAKSHY

53. Marriage is the only evil that men pray for.
GREEK PROVERB

54. Marriage cannot be a *job* as it has become.
GERMAINE GREER, *THE FEMALE EUNUCH* (1970)

55. Maidens! why should you worry in choosing whom you shall marry? / Choose whom you may, you will find you have got somebody else.
JOHN HAY, "DISTICHS" (1871?), 10

56. He had married on the rebound from the rotten time he had in college, and Frances took him on the rebound from his discovery that he had not been everything to his first wife.
ERNEST HEMINGWAY, *THE SUN ALSO RISES* (1926)

57. Two days are the best of a man's wedded life, / The days when he marries and buries his wife.
HIPPONAX (6TH C. B.C.)

58. There is nothing nobler or more admirable than when two people who see eye to eye keep house as man and wife, confounding their enemies and delighting their friends.
HOMER, *ODYSSEY* (9TH C. B.C.), 6, TR. E. V. RIEU

59. A man should be taller, older, heavier, uglier, and hoarser than his wife.
EDGAR WATSON HOWE, *COUNTRY TOWN SAYINGS* (1911)

60. For every quarrel a man and wife have before others, they have a hundred when alone.
EDGAR WATSON HOWE, *COUNTRY TOWN SAYINGS* (1911)

61. A man who marries a woman to educate her falls a victim to the same fallacy as the woman who marries a man to reform him.
ELBERT HUBBARD, *THE NOTE BOOK* (1927)

62. No man knows what the wife of his bosom is until he has gone with her through the fiery trials of this world.
WASHINGTON IRVING, "THE WIFE," *THE SKETCH BOOK OF GEOFFREY CRAYON, GENT.* (1819–20)

63. Those men are most apt to be obsequious and conciliating abroad who are under the discipline of shrews at home.
WASHINGTON IRVING, "RIP VAN WINKLE," *THE SKETCH BOOK OF GEOFFREY CRAYON, GENT.* (1819–20)

64. The common impulse is not to sustain a marriage by finding satisfaction elsewhere, but to end the marriage and set up a new one which will provide the comfort lacking in the first.
ELIZABETH JANEWAY, *MAN'S WORLD, WOMAN'S PLACE* (1971), 16

65. A gentleman who had been very unhappy in marriage, married immediately after his wife died: Johnson said, it was the triumph of hope over experience.
SAMUEL JOHNSON, QUOTED IN BOSWELL'S *LIFE OF SAMUEL JOHNSON,* 1770

66. I would advise no man to marry who is not likely to propagate understanding.
SAMUEL JOHNSON, QUOTED IN BIRKBECK HILL'S *JOHNSONIAN MISCELLANIES* (1897), V. 1

67. It is so far from being natural for a man and woman to live in a state of marriage, that we find all the motives which they have for remaining in that connection, and the restraints which civilised society imposes to prevent separation, are hardly sufficient to keep them together.
SAMUEL JOHNSON, QUOTED IN BOSWELL'S *LIFE OF SAMUEL JOHNSON,* MARCH 31, 1772

68. It is not from reason and prudence that people marry, but from inclination.

SAMUEL JOHNSON, QUOTED IN BOSWELL'S *LIFE OF SAMUEL JOHNSON*, OCT. 26, 1769

69. Always see a fellow's weak point in his wife.

JAMES JOYCE, *ULYSSES* (1922)

70. Marrying a man is like buying something you've been admiring for a long time in a shop window. You may love it when you get it home, but it doesn't always go with everything else in the house.

JEAN KERR, "THE TEN WORST THINGS ABOUT A MAN," *THE SNAKE HAS ALL THE LINES* (1960)

71. Daughters-in-law lived with their husbands' parents, not their own; a synonym for marriage in Chinese is "taking a daughter-in-law."

MAXINE HONG KINGSTON, *THE WOMAN WARRIOR* (1976)

72. There are few wives so perfect as not to give their husbands at least once a day good reason to repent of ever having married, or at least of envying those who are unmarried.

LA BRUYÈRE, *CHARACTERS* (1688), 3.78, TR. HENRI VAN LAUN

73. Nothing is to me more distasteful than that entire complacency and satisfaction which beam in the countenances of a new-married couple,—in that of the lady particularly; it tells you that her lot is disposed of in this world; that *you* can have no hopes of her.

CHARLES LAMB, "A BACHELOR'S COMPLAINT OF THE BEHAVIOUR OF MARRIED PEOPLE," *ESSAYS OF ELIA* (1823)

74. There are some good marriages, but no delightful ones.

LA ROCHEFOUCAULD, *MAXIMS* (1665), TR. KENNETH PRATT

75. The men that women marry, / And why they marry them, will always be / A marvel and a mystery to the world.

LONGFELLOW, *MICHAEL ANGELO* (1883), 1.6

76. There is no more lovely, friendly and charming relationship, communion or company than a good marriage.

MARTIN LUTHER, *TABLE TALK* (1569)

77. The wives who are not deserted, but who have to feed and clothe and comfort and scold and advise, are the true objects of commiseration; wives whose existence is given over to a ceaseless vigil of cantankerous affection.

WILLIAM MCFEE, "KNIGHTS AND TURCOPOLIERS," *HARBOURS OF MEMORY* (1921)

78. Marriage is a lot of things—an alliance, a sacrament, a comedy, or a mistake; but it is definitely not a partnership because that implies equal gain. And every right-thinking woman knows the profit in matrimony is by all odds hers.

PHYLLIS MCGINLEY, "HOW TO GET ALONG WITH MEN," *THE PROVINCE OF THE HEART* (1959)

79. Marriage was all a woman's idea, and for man's acceptance of the pretty yoke it becomes us to be grateful.

PHYLLIS MCGINLEY, "HOW TO GET ALONG WITH MEN," *THE PROVINCE OF THE HEART* (1959)

80. The fundamental trouble with marriage is that it shakes a man's confidence in himself, and so greatly diminishes his general competence and effectiveness. His habit of mind becomes that of a commander who has lost a decisive and calamitous battle. He never quite trusts himself thereafter.

H. L. MENCKEN, *PREJUDICES: SECOND SERIES* (1920), 10

81. Hail, wedded love, mysterious law, true source / Of human offspring.

MILTON, *PARADISE LOST* (1667), 4.750

82. Nothing lovelier can be found / In woman, than to study household good, / And good works in her husband to promote.

MILTON, *PARADISE LOST* (1667), 9.232

83. Marriage is three parts love and seven parts forgiveness of sins.

LANGDON MITCHELL, *THE NEW YORK IDEA* (1907), 2

84. A good husband be the best sort of plaster for to cure a young woman's ailments.

MOLIÈRE, *A DOCTOR IN SPITE OF HIMSELF* (1666), 2, TR. JOHN WOOD

85. Wives rarely fuss about their beauty / To guarantee their mate's affection.

MOLIÈRE, *THE SCHOOL FOR WIVES* (1662), 3.2, TR. DONALD M. FRAME

86. [Marriage] can be compared to a cage: birds outside it despair to enter, and birds within, to escape.

MONTAIGNE, "UPON SOME VERSES OF VIRGIL," *ESSAYS* (1580–88)

87. Men are monopolists / of "stars, garters, buttons / and other shining baubles"— / unfit to be the guardians / of another person's happiness.

MARIANNE MOORE, "MARRIAGE," *COLLECTED POEMS* (1951)

88. Marriage is an Athenic weaving together of families, of two souls with their individual fates and destinies, of time and eternity—everyday life married to the timeless mysteries of the soul.

Thomas Moore, *Soul Mates* (1994)

89. Marriage isn't a tram. It doesn't have to get anywhere.

Iris Murdoch, *A Severed Head* (1961)

90. People who boast of happy marriages are, I submit, usually self-deceivers, if not actually liars.

Iris Murdoch, *The Black Prince* (1973)

91. A husband is a man who two minutes after his head / touches the pillow is snoring like an overloaded / omnibus.

Ogden Nash, "The Trouble with Women Is Men," *Marriage Lines* (1964)

92. Marriage is based on the theory that when a man discovers a particular brand of beer exactly to his taste he should at once throw up his job and go to work in the brewery.

George Jean Nathan, "General Conclusions about the Coarse Sex," *The Theatre, the Drama, the Girls* (1921)

93. If married couples did not live together, happy marriages would be more frequent.

Nietzsche, *Human, All Too Human* (1878), 393, tr. Helen Zimmern

94. Man is for woman a means: the end is always the child.

Nietzsche, "On Little Old and Young Women," *Thus Spoke Zarathustra* (1883–92), 1, tr. Walter Kaufmann

95. When marrying, one should ask oneself this question: Do you believe that you will be able to converse well with this woman into your old age?

Nietzsche, *Human, All Too Human* (1878), 406, in *The Portable Nietzsche*, tr. Walter Kaufmann

96. Quarrels are the dowry which married folk bring one another.

Ovid, *The Art of Love* (c. A.D. 8), 2, tr. J. Lewis May

97. What makes men indifferent to their wives is that they can see them when they please.

Ovid, *The Art of Love* (c. A.D. 8), 3, tr. J. Lewis May

98. Between a man and his wife nothing ought to rule but love. Authority is for children and servants, yet not without sweetness.

William Penn, *Some Fruits of Solitude* (1693), 1.100

99. Never marry but for love; but see that thou lovest what is lovely.

William Penn, *Some Fruits of Solitude* (1693), 1.79

100. Strange to say what delight we married people have to see these poor fools decoyed into our condition.

Samuel Pepys, *Diary*, Dec. 25, 1665

101. This seemed a dreary and wasted life for a girl with fifteen years of straight A's, but I knew that's what marriage was like, because cook and clean and wash was just what Buddy Willard's mother did from morning till night, and she was the wife of a university professor and had been a private school teacher herself.

Sylvia Plath, *The Bell Jar* (1963)

102. A good marriage is that in which each appoints the other guardian of his solitude.

Rainer Maria Rilke, *Letters* (1892–1910; 1910–26), tr. Jane Barnard Greene and M. D. Herter Norton

103. Romance calls for "the faraway love" of the troubadours; marriage for love of "one's neighbor."

Denis de Rougemont, *Love in the Western World* (1939), 7.7, tr. Montgomery Belgion

104. Marriage is for women the commonest mode of livelihood, and the total amount of undesired sex endured by women is probably greater in marriage than in prostitution.

Bertrand Russell, "Prostitution," *Marriage and Morals* (1929)

105. It takes patience to appreciate domestic bliss; volatile spirits prefer unhappiness.

George Santayana, *The Life of Reason: Reason in Society* (1905–06), 2

106. A light wife doth make a heavy husband.

Shakespeare, *The Merchant of Venice* (1596–97), 5.1.130

107. Men are April when they woo, December when they wed. Maids are May when they are maids, but the sky changes when they are wives.

Shakespeare, *As You Like It* (1599–1600), 4.1.147

108. What is wedlock forced but a hell, / An age of discord and continual strife? Whereas the contrary bringeth bliss / And is a pattern of celestial peace.

Shakespeare, *1 Henry VI* (1591–92), 5.5.62

109. It is a woman's business to get married as soon as possible, and a man's to keep unmarried as long as he can.

George Bernard Shaw, *Man and Superman* (1903), 2

110. Marriage is tolerable enough in its way if youre easygoing and dont expect too much from it. But it doesnt bear thinking about.

George Bernard Shaw, *Getting Married* (1911)

111. Marriage is popular because it combines the maximum of temptation with the maximum of opportunity.

George Bernard Shaw, "Maxims for Revolutionists," *Man and Superman* (1903)

112. 'Tis safest in matrimony to begin with a little aversion.

Richard Brinsley Sheridan, *The Rivals* (1775), 1.2

113. Esther could not conceive. In every other way she was a good wife; she knew how to knit, sew a wedding gown, bake gingerbread and tarts, tear out the pip of a chicken, apply a cupping glass or leeches, even bleed a patient.

Isaac Bashevis Singer, *The Magician of Lublin* (1960)

114. It is a matter of life and death for married people to interrupt each other's stories; for it they did not, they would burst.

Logan Pearsall Smith, *Afterthoughts* (1931), 3

115. Marriage resembles a pair of shears, so joined that they cannot be separated; often moving in opposite directions, yet always punishing anyone who comes between them.

Sydney Smith, quoted in Lady S. Holland's *Memoir* (1855), v. 1.11

116. Woe to the house where the hen crows and the rooster keeps still.

Spanish Proverb

117. The married state, with and without the affection suitable to it, is the compleatest image of heaven and hell we are capable of receiving in this life.

Richard Steele, *The Spectator* (1711–12), 479

118. American married life is the doormat to the whorehouse.

John Steinbeck, *Steinbeck: A Life in Letters,* eds. Elaine Steinbeck and Robert Wallsten (1975)

119. The American girl makes a servant of her husband and then finds him contemptible for being a servant.

John Steinbeck, *Steinbeck: A Life in Letters,* eds. Elaine Steinbeck and Robert Wallsten (1975)

120. I've yet to be on a campus where most women weren't worrying about some aspect of combining marriage, children, and a career. I've yet to find one where many men were worrying about the same thing.

Gloria Steinem, "Why Young Women Are More Conservative," *Outrageous Acts and Everyday Rebellions* (1983)

121. [T]he nineteenth-century wave of feminism was started by older women who had been through the radicalizing experience of getting married and becoming the legal chattel of their husbands (or the equally radicalizing experience of *not* getting married and being treated as spinsters).

Gloria Steinem, "Why Young Women Are More Conservative," *Outrageous Acts and Everyday Rebellions* (1983)

122. Marriage is like life in this—that it is a field of battle, and not a bed of roses.

Robert Louis Stevenson, title essay, 1, *Virginibus Puerisque* (1881)

123. Marriage is one long conversation, checkered by disputes.

Robert Louis Stevenson, "Talk and Talkers" (1882), 2

124. We study ourselves three weeks, we love each other three months, we squabble three years, we tolerate each other thirty years, and then the children start all over again.

Hippolyte Taine, *Vie et opinions de Thomas Graingorge* (1867)

125. An ideal wife is any woman who has an ideal husband.

Booth Tarkington, *Looking Forward to the Great Adventure* (1926)

126. Long-married couples balance their checkbooks as a substitute for love-making, or they refuse each other love by protesting one another's financial error or excess.

Diana Trilling, *Mrs. Harris: The Death of the Scarsdale Doctor* (1981)

127. Both marriage and death ought to be welcome: the one promises happiness, doubtless the other assures it.

Mark Twain, letter to Will Bowen, Nov. 4, 1888

128. Love seems the swiftest, but it is the slowest of all growths. No man or woman really knows what perfect love is until they have been married a quarter of a century.

Mark Twain, *Notebook* (1935)

129. There isn't a wife in the world who has not taken the exact measure of her husband, weighed him and settled him in her own mind, and knows him as well as if she had ordered him after designs and specifications of her own.

CHARLES DUDLEY WARNER, "THIRD STUDY," *BACKLOG STUDIES* (1873)

130. How marriage ruins a man. It's as demoralizing as cigarettes, and far more expensive.

OSCAR WILDE, *LADY WINDERMERE'S FAN* (1892), 3

131. In married life three is company and two is none.

OSCAR WILDE, *THE IMPORTANCE OF BEING EARNEST* (1895), 1

132. Men marry because they are tired; women because they are curious. Both are disappointed.

OSCAR WILDE, *A WOMAN OF NO IMPORTANCE* (1893), 3

133. The one charm of marriage is that it makes a life of deception absolutely necessary for both parties.

OSCAR WILDE, *THE PICTURE OF DORIAN GRAY* (1891), 1

134. Twenty years of romance makes a woman look like a ruin; but twenty years of marriage make her something like a public building.

OSCAR WILDE, *A WOMAN OF NO IMPORTANCE* (1893), 1

135. When a woman marries again it is because she detested her first husband. When a man marries again, it is because he adored his first wife. Women try their luck; men risk theirs.

OSCAR WILDE, *THE PICTURE OF DORIAN GRAY* (1891), 15

136. [Married men] are horribly tedious when they are good husbands, and abominably conceited when they are not.

OSCAR WILDE, *A WOMAN OF NO IMPORTANCE* (1893), 2

137. Marriage is a bribe to make a housekeeper think she's a householder.

THORNTON WILDER, *THE MATCHMAKER* (1955), 1

565. MARTYRS AND MARTYRDOM

See also 125. CHRISTIANITY; 797. RELIGION; 837. SACRIFICE; 840. SAINTS AND SAINTHOOD; 847. SCAPEGOAT

1. It is often pleasant to stone a martyr, no matter how much we may admire him.

JOHN BARTH, *THE FLOATING OPERA* (1956)

2. To die for a religion is easier than to live it absolutely.

JORGE LUIS BORGES, "DEUTSCHES REQUIEM," *LABYRINTHES* (1962)

3. The martyr endured tortures to affirm his belief in truth but he never asserted his disbelief in torture.

G. K. CHESTERTON, "ABOUT IMPENITENCE," *AS I WAS SAYING* (1936)

4. Opposition may become sweet to a man when he has christened it persecution.

GEORGE ELIOT, *JANET'S REPENTANCE* (1857), 8

5. The few of understanding, vision rare, / Who veiled not from the herd their hearts, but tried, / Poor generous fools, to lay their feelings bare, / Them have men always burnt and crucified.

GOETHE, "NIGHT," *FAUST: PART I* (1808), TR. PHILIP WAYNE

6. Perhaps there is no happiness in life so perfect as the martyr's.

O. HENRY, "THE COUNTRY OF ELUSION," *THE TRIMMED LAMP* (1907)

7. Everyone hates a martyr; it's no wonder martyrs were burned at the stake.

EDGAR WATSON HOWE, *COUNTRY TOWN SAYINGS* (1911)

8. Our admiration is so given to dead martyrs that we have little time for living heroes.

ELBERT HUBBARD, *THE NOTE BOOK* (1927)

9. To die in agony upon a cross / Does not create a martyr; he must first / Will his own execution.

HENRIK IBSEN, *BRAND* (1866), 3

10. If a man is in doubt whether it would be better for him to expose himself to martyrdom or not, he should not do it. He must be convinced that he has a delegation from heaven.

SAMUEL JOHNSON, QUOTED IN BOSWELL'S *LIFE OF SAMUEL JOHNSON*, APRIL–MAY 1773

11. It is not the least of a martyr's scourges to be canonized by the persons who burned him.

MURRAY KEMPTON, "THE DRY BONES," *PART OF OUR TIME* (1955)

12. It is the cause and not the death that makes the martyr.

NAPOLEON I, *MAXIMS* (1804–15)

13. Must then a Christ perish in torment in every age to save those that have no imagination?

GEORGE BERNARD SHAW, EPILOGUE TO *SAINT JOAN* (1923)

14. It is truer to say that martyrs make faith than that faith makes martyrs.

Miguel de Unamuno, "Faith, Hope, and Charity," *Tragic Sense of Life* (1913), tr. J. E. Crawford Flitch

15. A thing is not necessarily true because a man dies for it.

Oscar Wilde, *Sebastian Melmoth* (1904)

566. MASCULINITY AND FEMININITY

See also 581. Men and Women

1. As vivacity is the gift of women, gravity is that of men.

Joseph Addison, *The Spectator* (1711–12), 128

2. The finest people marry the two sexes in their own person.

Emerson, *Journals,* 1843

3. Neither sex, without some fertilization of the complementary characters of the other, is capable of the highest reaches of human endeavor.

H. L. Mencken, "The Feminine Mind," *In Defense of Women* (1922)

4. The wholly manly man lacks the wit necessary to give objective form to his soaring and secret dreams, and the wholly womanly woman is apt to be too cynical a creature to dream at all.

H. L. Mencken, "The Feminine Mind," *In Defense of Women* (1922)

5. In our civilization, men are afraid that they will not be men enough and women are afraid that they might be considered only women.

Theodor Reik, *Esquire,* November 1958

6. What is most beautiful in virile men is something feminine; what is most beautiful in feminine women is something masculine.

Susan Sontag, "Notes on Camp," *Against Interpretation* (1961)

MASKS

See 45. Appearance; 165. Concealment; 688. Personality, Dual; 732. Pretension

THE MASSES

See 682. The People

567. MASOCHISM

See also 866. Self-Destruction

1. If he has no other burden, he'll take up a load of stones.

Malay Proverb

568. MASS MOVEMENTS

See also 111. Causes; 232. Demagoguery; 353. Following; 445. Ideology; 819. Revolution

1. Mass movements can rise and spread without belief in a God, but never without belief in a devil.

Eric Hoffer, *The True Believer* (1951), 3.14.65

2. There is nothing more explosive than a skilled population condemned to inaction. Such a population is likely to become a hotbed of extremism and intolerance, and be receptive to any proselytizing ideology, however absurd and vicious, which promises vast action.

Eric Hoffer, "Automation, Leisure, and the Masses," *The Temper of Our Time* (1967), 2

3. Social movements are at once the symptoms and the instruments of progress. Ignore them and statesmanship is irrelevant; fail to use them and it is weak.

Walter Lippmann, "Revolution and Culture," *A Preface to Politics* (1914)

569. MATERIALISM

See also 646. Objects; 927. Spirituality

1. Materialism is decadent and degenerate only if the spirit of the nation has withered and if individual people are so unimaginative that they wallow in it.

Brooks Atkinson, "January 22," *Once Around the Sun* (1951)

2. We live in a world of things, and our only connection with them is that we know how to manipulate or to consume them.

Erich Fromm, *The Sane Society* (1955), 5

3. The steady pressure to consume, absorb, participate, receive, by eye, ear, mouth, and mail involves a cruelty to intestines, blood pressure, and psyche unparalleled in history.

Herbert Gold, *The Age of Happy Problems* (1962)

4. Acquisition means life to miserable mortals.

Hesiod, *Works and Days* (8th c. b.c.), 686, tr. Richmond Lattimore

5. Those who live by bread alone will submit, for the sake of it, to the vilest abuse, like a hungry dog.

Jami, "The Dog and the Loaf of Bread," *Baharistan* (15th c.)

6. The materialistic idealism that governs American life, that on the one hand makes a chariot of every grocery wagon, and on the other a mere hitching post of every star, lets every man lead a very enticing double life.

LOUIS KRONENBERGER, *COMPANY MANNERS* (1954), 3.3

570. MATHEMATICS

1. If a man's wit be wandering, let him study the mathematics.

FRANCIS BACON, "OF STUDIES," *ESSAYS* (1625)

2. Here, where we reach the sphere of mathematics, we are among processes which seem to some the most inhuman of all human activities and the most remote from poetry. Yet it is here that the artist has the fullest scope of his imagination.

HAVELOCK ELLIS, *THE DANCE OF LIFE* (1923), 2

3. There is no royal road to geometry.

EUCLID (300 B.C.), QUOTED IN PROCLUS' *COMMENTARIA IN EUCLIDEM* (5TH C. A.D.), 2.4

4. One has to be able to count if only so that at fifty one doesn't marry a girl of twenty.

MAXIM GORKY, *THE ZYKOVS* (1914), 2

5. Mathematicians who are only mathematicians have exact minds, provided all things are explained to them by means of definitions and axioms; otherwise they are inaccurate and insufferable, for they are only right when the principles are quite clear.

PASCAL, *PENSÉES* (1670), 1, TR. W. F. TROTTER

6. Uncle Scrooge preferred to let the poor die "and decrease the surplus population." Scrooge may not have had God on his side, but his arithmetic was impeccable.

ROGER ROSENBLATT, "DO YOU FEEL THE DEATHS OF STRANGERS?" *THE MAN IN THE WATER* (1994)

7. Mathematics may be defined as the subject in which we never know what we are talking about, nor whether what we are saying is true.

BERTRAND RUSSELL, "MATHEMATICS AND THE METAPHYSICIANS," *MYSTICISM AND LOGIC* (1917)

8. The true spirit of delight, the exaltation, the sense of being more than Man, which is the touchstone of the highest excellence, is to be found in mathematics as surely as in poetry.

BERTRAND RUSSELL, *MYSTICISM AND LOGIC* (1917)

9. Arithmetic is where the answer is right and everything is nice and you can look out of the window and see the blue sky—or the answer is wrong and you have to start all over and try again and see how it comes out this time.

CARL SANDBURG, "ARITHMETIC," *COMPLETE POEMS* (1950)

10. A man has one hundred dollars and you leave him with two dollars, that's subtraction.

MAE WEST, IN *MY LITTLE CHICKADEE* (1940)

571. MATURITY

See also 404. GROWTH AND DEVELOPMENT; 452. IMMATURITY; 586. MIDDLE AGE; 653. OLD AGE; 1071. YOUTH

1. Strong meat belongeth to them that are of full age.

BIBLE, HEBREWS 5:14

2. When I was a child, I spake as a child, I understood as a child, I thought as a child: but when I became a man, I put away childish things.

BIBLE, 1 CORINTHIANS 13:11

3. Grown up, and that is a terribly hard thing to do. It is much easier to skip it and go from one childhood to another.

F. SCOTT FITZGERALD, "NOTE-BOOKS," *THE CRACK-UP* (1945)

4. How do you know that the fruit is ripe? Simply because it leaves the branch.

ANDRÉ GIDE, "PORTRAITS AND APHORISMS," *PRETEXTS* (1903), TR. OTHERS

5. Those of us who have come to years of discretion and more, must often take to retrospect, and seek to appraise the outcome of our lives.

LEARNED HAND, *THE SPIRIT OF LIBERTY* (1959)

6. We have not passed that subtle line between childhood and adulthood until we move from the passive voice to the active voice—that is, until we have stopped saying "It got lost," and say, "I lost it."

SYDNEY J. HARRIS, *ON THE CONTRARY* (1962), 7

7. It is unjust to claim the privileges of age, and retain the playthings of childhood.

SAMUEL JOHNSON, *THE RAMBLER* (1750–52), 50

8. The turning point in the process of growing up is when you discover the core of strength within you that survives all hurt.

MAX LERNER, "FAUBUS AND LITTLE ROCK," *THE UNFINISHED COUNTRY* (1959), 4

9. The process of maturing is an art to be learned, an effort to be sustained. By the age of fifty you have

made yourself what you are, and if it is good, it is better than your youth.

Marya Mannes, *More in Anger* (1958), 1.3

10. Understanding and love require a wisdom that comes only with age.

Rollo May, *The Courage to Create* (1975)

11. To be grown up is to sit at the table with people who have died, who neither listen nor speak; / Who do not drink their tea, though they always said / Tea was such a comfort.

Edna St. Vincent Millay, "Childhood Is the Kingdom Where Nobody Dies," *Wine from These Grapes* (1934)

12. A man's maturity consists in having found again the seriousness one had as a child, at play.

Nietzsche, *Beyond Good and Evil* (1886), 94, tr. Walter Kaufmann

13. To be adult is to be alone.

Jean Rostand, *Pensées d'un biologiste* (1939)

14. Nature, in denying us perennial youth, has at least invited us to become unselfish and noble.

George Santayana, *The Life of Reason: Reason in Religion* (1905–06), 14

15. 'Tis but an hour ago since it was nine, / And after one hour more 'twill be eleven; / And so, from hour to hour, we ripe and ripe, / And then, from hour to hour, we rot and rot; / And thereby hangs a tale.

Shakespeare, *As You Like It* (1599–1600), 2.7.24

16. When I was very young and the urge to be someplace else was upon me, I was assured by mature people that maturity would cure this itch. When years described me as mature, the remedy prescribed was middle age. In middle age I was assured that greater age would calm my fever and now that I am fifty-eight perhaps senility will do the job.

John Steinbeck, *Travels with Charley* (1962)

17. The latter part of a wise man's life is taken up in curing the follies, prejudices, and false opinions he had contracted in the former.

Jonathan Swift, *Thoughts on Various Subjects* (1711)

18. When we rejoice in our fullness, then we can part with our fruits with joy.

Rabindranath Tagore, *Stray Birds* (1916), 159

19. When I can look Life in the eyes, / Grown calm and very coldly wise, / Life will have given me the Truth, / And taken in exchange—my youth.

Sara Teasdale, "Wisdom," *Dark of the Moon* (1926)

20. To live with fear and not be afraid is the final test of maturity.

Edward Weeks, "A Quarter Century: Its Retreats," *Look*, July 18, 1961

21. One of the signs of passing youth is the birth of a sense of fellowship with other human beings as we take our place among them.

Virginia Woolf, "Hours in a Library," *Times Literary Supplement*, Nov. 30, 1916

572. MAXIMS

See also 296. Epigrams; 773. Quotations

1. The proverbist knows nothing of the two sides of a question. He knows only the roundness of answers.

Karl Shapiro, *The Bourgeois Poet* (1964), 1.19

2. A short saying oft contains much wisdom.

Sophocles, *Aletes* (5th c. B.C.), 99, tr. M. H. Morgan

3. It is more trouble to make a maxim than it is to do right.

Mark Twain, "Pudd'nhead Wilson's New Calendar," *Following the Equator* (1897), 1.3

MAY

See 854. Seasons

573. MEANING

See also 3. The Absurd; 959. Symbols and Symbolism; 1064. Words

1. There is no meaning to life except the meaning man gives his life by the unfolding of his powers, by living productively.

Erich Fromm, *Man for Himself* (1947), 3

2. We must each find our separate meaning / In the persuasion of our days / Until we meet in the meaning of the world.

Christopher Fry, *The Firstborn* (1946), 3.2

3. A thing in itself never expresses anything. It is the relation between things that gives meaning to them and that formulates a thought. A thought functions only as a fragmentary part in the formulation of an idea.

Hans Hofmann, *Search for the Real* (1967)

4. If we have our own *why* of life, we shall get along with almost any *how*.

Nietzsche, "Maxims and Missiles," 12, *Twilight of the Idols* (1888), tr. Walter Kaufmann

5. Oh, it is not death that frightens me, but the impossibility of imparting some meaning to my past.

ELIE WIESEL, *THE TESTAMENT* (1981), TR. MARION WIESEL

MEANNESS

See 693. PETTINESS; 936. STINGINESS

574. MEANS AND ENDS

See also 319. EXPEDIENCY; 585. METHOD

1. When we deliberate it is about means and not ends.

ARISTOTLE, *NICOMACHEAN ETHICS* (4TH C. B.C.), 3.3, TR. J.A.K. THOMSON

2. The first sign of corruption in a society that is still alive is that the end justifies the means.

GEORGES BERNANOS, "WHY FREEDOM?" *THE LAST ESSAYS OF GEORGES BERNANOS* (1955), TR. BARRY ULANOV

3. Most of the great results of history are brought about by discreditable means.

EMERSON, "CONSIDERATIONS BY THE WAY," *THE CONDUCT OF LIFE* (1860)

4. The means prepare the end, and the end is what the means have made it.

JOHN MORLEY, "CARLYLE," *CRITICAL MISCELLANIES* (1871–1908)

5. When the journey from means to end is not too long, the means themselves are enjoyed if the end is ardently desired.

BERTRAND RUSSELL, "TECHNIQUE AND HUMAN NATURE," *AUTHORITY AND THE INDIVIDUAL* (1949)

6. A good man would prefer to be defeated than to defeat injustice by evil means.

SALLUST, *JUGURTHINE WAR* (1ST C. B.C.), 42

575. MEDDLING

See also 394. GOSSIP

1. "If everybody minded their own business," the Duchess said in a hoarse growl, "the world would go round a deal faster than it does."

LEWIS CARROLL, *ALICE'S ADVENTURES IN WONDERLAND* (1865), 6

2. Those who in quarrels interpose, / Must often wipe a bloody nose.

JOHN GAY, "THE MASTIFFS," *FABLES* (1727–38)

3. A man is likely to mind his own business when it is worth minding.

ERIC HOFFER, *THE TRUE BELIEVER* (1951), 1.2.10

4. For prying into any human affairs, none are equal to those whom it does not concern.

VICTOR HUGO, "FANTINE," *LES MISÉRABLES* (1862), 5.8, TR. CHARLES E. WILBOUR

5. A person should be free to do as he likes in his own concerns; but he ought not to be free to do as he likes in acting for another, under the pretext that the affairs of the other are his own affairs.

JOHN STUART MILL, *ON LIBERTY* (1859), 5

6. Have you so much time to spare from your own affairs that you can attend to another man's with which you have no concern?

TERENCE, *THE SELF-TORMENTOR* (163 B.C.)

576. MEDIA

See also 292. ENTERTAINMENT; 364. FREE SPEECH; 611. MOVIES; 630. NEWSPAPERS; 731. PRESS, FREEDOM OF THE; 764. PUBLISHING; 967. TELEVISION

1. What the mass media offer is not popular art, but entertainment which is intended to be consumed like food, forgotten, and replaced by a new dish.

W. H. AUDEN, "THE POET AND THE CITY," *THE DYER'S HAND* (1962)

2. The hand that rules the press, the radio, the screen and the far-spread magazine, rules the country.

LEARNED HAND, MEMORIAL ADDRESS FOR JUSTICE BRANDEIS, DEC. 21, 1942

3. When distant and unfamiliar and complex things are communicated to great masses of people, the truth suffers a considerable and often a radical distortion. The complex is made over into the simple, the hypothetical into the dogmatic, and the relative into an absolute.

WALTER LIPPMANN, *THE PUBLIC PHILOSOPHY* (1955), 2.3

4. It is not enough to show people how to *live* better: there is a mandate for any group with enormous powers of communication to show people how to *be* better.

MARYA MANNES, "A WORD TO THE WIZARDS," *BUT WILL IT SELL?* (1955–64)

577. MEDICINE

See also 243. DIAGNOSIS; 263. DOCTORS; 413. HEALTH; 757. PSYCHIATRY; 798. REMEDIES; 896. SICKNESS

1. Oh, the powers of nature! She knows what we need, and the doctors know nothing.

BENVENUTO CELLINI, *AUTOBIOGRAPHY* (1558–66), TR. GEORGE BULL

2. Patience is the best medicine.

JOHN FLORIO, *FIRST FRUTES* (1578)

3. Keep a watch also on the faults of the patients, which often make them lie about the taking of things prescribed.

HIPPOCRATES, *DECORUM* (C. 400 B.C.), 14, TR. W.H.S. JONES

4. The true miracle of modern medicine is diabolical. It consists in making not only individuals but whole populations survive on inhumanly low levels of personal health.

IVAN ILLICH, *MEDICAL NEMESIS* (1976)

5. All interest in disease and death is only another expression of interest in life.

THOMAS MANN, *THE MAGIC MOUNTAIN* (1924), 6.7, TR. H. T. LOWE-PORTER

6. The general order of things that takes care of fleas and moles also takes care of men, if they will have the same patience that fleas and moles have, to leave it to itself.

MONTAIGNE, "OF THE RESEMBLANCE OF CHILD REN TO THEIR FATHERS," *ESSAYS* (1580–88), TR. W. C. HAZLITT

7. Medicine being a compendium of the successive and contradictory mistakes of medical practitioners, when we summon the wisest of them to our aid, the chances are that we may be relying on a scientific truth the error of which will be recognized in a few years' time.

MARCEL PROUST, *REMEMBRANCE OF THINGS PAST: THE GUERMANTES WAY* (1913–27), TR. C. K. SCOTT-MONCRIEFF

8. It is medicine, not scenery, for which a sick man must go searching.

SENECA, *LETTERS TO LUCILIUS* (1ST C.), 104.18

9. By medicine life may be prolonged, yet death / Will seize the doctor too.

SHAKESPEARE, *CYMBELINE* (1609–10), 5.5.29

10. There is one thing pleasantly unconfusing about medicine. The direction and the end are fixed and the patient never works backward.

JOHN STEINBECK, *STEINBECK: A LIFE IN LETTERS,* EDS. ELAINE STEINBECK AND ROBERT WALLSTEN (1975)

11. I doubt not that in due time, when the arts are brought to perfection, some means will be found to give a sound head to a man who has none at all.

VOLTAIRE, "SERPENTS," *PHILOSOPHICAL DICTIONARY* (1764)

578. MEDIOCRITY

See also 311. EXCELLENCE

1. There is always a heavy demand for fresh mediocrity. In every generation the least cultivated taste has the largest appetite.

THOMAS BAILEY ALDRICH, "LEAVES FROM A NOTEBOOK," *PONKAPOG PAPERS* (1903)

2. When half-gods go, / The gods arrive.

EMERSON, "GIVE ALL TO LOVE," *POEMS* (1847)

3. Mediocrity has no greater consolation than in the thought that genius is not immortal.

GOETHE, *ELECTIVE AFFINITIES* (1809), 23

4. The way to get on in the world is to be neither more nor less wise, neither better nor worse than your neighbours.

WILLIAM HAZLITT, "ON KNOWLEDGE OF THE WORLD," *SKETCHES AND ESSAYS* (1839)

5. As a rule, the man who can do all things equally well is a very mediocre individual.

ELBERT HUBBARD, *THE PHILISTINE* (1895–1915)

6. When small men attempt great enterprises, they always end by reducing them to the level of their mediocrity.

NAPOLEON I, *MAXIMS* (1804–15)

MEDITATION

See 183. CONTEMPLATION; 818. REVERIE; 975. THOUGHT

MEEKNESS

See 435. HUMILITY; 980. TIMIDITY

579. MEETINGS

See also 147. COMMITTEES

1. Committees are to get everybody together and homogenize their thinking.

ART LINKLETTER, *A CHILD'S GARDEN OF MISINFORMATION* (1965), 12

580. MEMORY

See also 639. NOSTALGIA

1. We forget because we must / And not because we will.

MATTHEW ARNOLD, "SWITZERLAND," 6, *EMPEDOCLES ON ETNA, AND OTHER POEMS* (1852)

2. Not the power to remember, but its very opposite, the power to forget, is a necessary condition for our existence.

SHOLEM ASCH, *THE NAZARENE* (1939), 1

3. Any given program will expand to fill all available memory.

ARTHUR BLOCH, "LAWS OF COMPUTER PROGRAMMING," *MURPHY'S LAW* (1979)

4. As we grow older, the memories of early life brighten, those of maturity and senescence grow dim and confused.

ANTHONY BURGESS, *YOU'VE HAD YOUR TIME* (1990)

5. How strange are the tricks of memory, which, often hazy as a dream about the most important events of a man's life, religiously preserve the merest trifles.

SIR RICHARD BURTON, *SIND REVISITED* (1851), V. 1

6. Oblivion is the dark page, whereon Memory writes her light-beam characters, and makes them legible; were it all light, nothing could be read there, any more than if it were all darkness.

THOMAS CARLYLE, "ON HISTORY AGAIN" (1833)

7. Memory is the thing you forget with.

ALEXANDER CHASE, *PERSPECTIVES* (1966)

8. Memory is often the attribute of stupidity; it generally belongs to heavy spirits whom it makes even heavier by the baggage it loads them down with.

CHATEAUBRIAND, *MÉMOIRES D'OUTRE-TOMBE* (1848–50), 1

9. Our memories are card-indexes consulted, and then put back in disorder by authorities whom we do not control.

CYRIL CONNOLLY, *THE UNQUIET GRAVE* (1945), 3

10. Each and all, we are riding into the dark. Even living, we cannot remember half the events of our own days.

LOREN EISELEY, "THE LAST NEANDERTHAL," *THE STAR THROWER* (1978)

11. It is a funny thing what the brain will do with memories and how it will treasure them and finally bring them into odd juxtapositions with other things, as though it wanted to make a design, or get some meaning out of them, whether you want it or not, or even see it.

LOREN EISELEY, "THE BIRD AND THE MACHINE," *THE STAR THROWER* (1978)

12. Memory is a net; one finds it full of fish when he takes it from the brook; but a dozen miles of water have run through it without sticking.

OLIVER WENDELL HOLMES, SR., *THE AUTOCRAT OF THE BREAKFAST TABLE* (1858), 12

13. A retentive memory may be a good thing, but the ability to forget is the true token of greatness.

ELBERT HUBBARD, *THE NOTE BOOK* (1927)

14. It would add much to human happiness, if an art could be taught of forgetting all of which the remembrance is at once useless and afflictive ... that the mind might perform its functions without incumbrance, and the past might no longer encroach upon the present.

SAMUEL JOHNSON, *THE IDLER* (1758–60), 72

15. Memory is like all other human powers, with which no man can be satisfied who measures them by what he can conceive, or by what he can desire.

SAMUEL JOHNSON, *THE IDLER* (1758–60), 74

16. To be able to enjoy one's past life is to live twice.

MARTIAL, *EPIGRAMS* (A.D. 86), 10.23.7

17. A strong memory is commonly coupled with infirm judgment.

MONTAIGNE, "OF LIARS," *ESSAYS* (1580–88), TR. W. C. HAZLITT

18. The memory represents to us not what we choose but what it pleases.

MONTAIGNE, "APOLOGY FOR RAIMOND DE SEBONDE," *ESSAYS* (1580–88), TR. W. C. HAZLITT

19. Bliss in possession will not last; / Remembered joys are never past.

JAMES MONTGOMERY, "THE LITTLE CLOUD" (1825)

20 Disguise our bondage as we will, / 'Tis woman, woman, rules us still.

THOMAS MOORE (1779–1852), "SOVEREIGN WOMAN"

21. Memories may escape the action of the will, may sleep a long time, but when stirred by the right influence, though that influence be light as a shadow, they flash into full stature and life with everything in place.

JOHN MUIR, *A THOUSAND-MILE WALK TO THE GULF* (1916), 6

22. It is strange how a memory will grow into a wax figure, how the cherub grows suspiciously prettier as its frame darkens with age—strange, strange are the mishaps of memory.

VLADIMIR NABOKOV, *THE GIFT* (1963)

23. The sweetest memory is that which involves something which one should not have done; the bitterest, that which involves something which one should not have done, and which one did not do.

GEORGE JEAN NATHAN, "GENERAL CONCLUSIONS ABOUT THE COARSE SEX," *THE THEATRE, THE DRAMA, THE GIRLS* (1921)

24. A great memory does not make a philosopher, any more than a dictionary can be called a grammar.

JOHN HENRY NEWMAN, *THE IDEA OF A UNIVERSITY* (1853–58), 1.6.5

25. What beastly incidents our memories insist on cherishing—the ugly and disgusting—the beautiful things we have to keep diaries to remember.

EUGENE O'NEILL, *STRANGE INTERLUDE* (1928), 2

26. What we remember from childhood we remember forever—permanent ghosts, stamped, imprinted, eternally seen.

CYNTHIA OZICK, "THE SHOCK OF TEAPOTS," *METAPHOR & MEMORY* (1989)

27. I remember that night as a magical night, and the way the city looked. I always meant to go back there, but maybe it would be better not to, for things are never the same the second time.

MAXWELL PERKINS, *EDITOR TO AUTHOR: THE LETTERS OF MAXWELL PERKINS*, ED. JOHN HALL WHEELOCK (1950)

28. Forgetfulness transforms every occurrence into a non-occurrence.

PLUTARCH, "CONTENTMENT," *MORALIA* (C. A.D. 100), TR. MOSES HADAS

29. Memory is not so brilliant as hope, but it is more beautiful, and a thousand times as true.

GEORGE DENNISON PRENTICE, *PRENTICEANA* (1860)

30. We may with advantage at times forget what we know.

PUBLILIUS SYRUS, *MORAL SAYINGS* (1ST C. B.C.), 234, TR. DARIUS LYMAN

31. Better by far you should forget and smile / Than that you should remember and be sad.

CHRISTINA ROSSETTI, "REMEMBER" (1862)

32. Human memory works its own wheel, and stops where it will, entirely without reference to the last stop, and with no connection with the next.

WILLIAM SAROYAN, *CHANCE MEETINGS* (1978)

33. It is a curious fact that in bad days we can very vividly recall the good time that is now no more; but that in good days we have only a very cold and imperfect memory of the bad.

SCHOPENHAUER, "FURTHER PSYCHOLOGICAL OBSERVATIONS," *PARERGA AND PARALIPOMENA* (1851), TR. T. BAILEY SAUNDERS

34. Reminiscences make one feel so deliciously aged and sad.

GEORGE BERNARD SHAW, *THE IRRATIONAL KNOT* (1885–87), 14

35. Music, when soft voices die, / Vibrates in the memory; / Odours, when sweet violets sicken, / Live within the sense they quicken.

SHELLEY, "TO—, MUSIC, WHEN SOFT VOICES DIE" (1821)

36. Our memories are independent of our wills. It is not so easy to forget.

RICHARD BRINSLEY SHERIDAN, *THE RIVALS* (1775), 1.2

37. A man's real possession is his memory. In nothing else is he rich, in nothing else is he poor.

ALEXANDER SMITH, "OF DEATH AND THE FEAR OF DYING," *DREAMTHORP* (1863)

38. Memory, the priestess, / kills the present / and offers its heart to the shrine of the dead past.

RABINDRANATH TAGORE, *FIREFLIES* (1928)

39. Oh better than the minting / Of a gold-crowned king / Is the safe-kept memory / Of a lovely thing.

SARA TEASDALE, "THE COIN," *FLAME AND SHADOW* (1920)

40. We seem but to linger in manhood to tell the dreams of our childhood, and they vanish out of memory ere we learn the language.

THOREAU, *JOURNAL*, FEB. 19, 1841

41. In memory's telephoto lens, far objects are magnified.

JOHN UPDIKE, "FIRST WIVES AND TROLLEY CARS," *ODD JOBS* (1991)

42. Memory has the singular characteristic of recalling in a friend absent, as in a journey long past, only that which is agreeable.

CHARLES DUDLEY WARNER, "FIFTH STUDY," *BACKLOG STUDIES* (1873)

43. What would the future of man be if it were devoid of memory?

ELIE WIESEL, "PREFACE," *FROM THE KINGDOM OF MEMORY* (1990)

44. Memory is the diary that we all carry about with us.

OSCAR WILDE, *THE IMPORTANCE OF BEING EARNEST* (1895), 1

45. In memory everything seems to happen to music.

TENNESSEE WILLIAMS, *THE GLASS MENAGERIE* (1945), 1

46. What's memory but the ash / That chokes our fires that have begun to sink?

WILLIAM BUTLER YEATS, *THE COUNTESS CATHLEEN* (1892), 2

581. MEN AND WOMEN

See also 566. MASCULINITY AND FEMININITY; 582. MEN; 1062. WOMEN

1. Women like silent men. They think they're listening.

MARCEL ACHARD, *QUOTE,* NOV. 4, 1956

2. The woman who is known only through a man is known wrong.

HENRY ADAMS, *THE EDUCATION OF HENRY ADAMS* (1907), 23

3. The innumerable conflicts that set men and women against one another come from the fact that neither is prepared to assume all the consequences of this situation which the one has offered and the other accepted.

SIMONE DE BEAUVOIR, *THE SECOND SEX* (1949)

4. [A]*ll* literature up to today is sexist. The Muses never sang to the poets about liberated women. It's the same old *chanson* from the Bible and Homer through Joyce and Proust.

ALLAN BLOOM, "BOOKS," *THE CLOSING OF THE AMERICAN MIND* (1987)

5. In the forties [1940s] in Washington it was still unusual for a rich and socially well-connected married woman to work. If she did, her husband was assumed by his peers to be unable to support a household on his own and somehow to be inadequate.

DAVID BRINKLEY, *WASHINGTON GOES TO WAR* (1988)

6. The most casual examination will reveal the fact that all the jokes about the horrible results of masculine cooking and sewing are written by men. It is all part of a great scheme of sex propaganda.

HEYWOOD BROUN, "HOLDING A BABY," IN *FIFTY GREAT ESSAYS* (1964)

7. When Adam delved and Eve spun, the fiction that man is incapable of housework was first established.

HEYWOOD BROUN, "HOLDING A BABY," IN *FIFTY GREAT ESSAYS* (1964)

8. Most women have all other women as adversaries; most men have all other men as their allies.

GELETT BURGESS, "THE GENTLEMAN'S CODE," *THE ROMANCE OF THE COMMONPLACE* (1916)

9. Verily, men do foolish things thoughtlessly, knowing not why; but no woman doeth aught without a reason.

GELETT BURGESS, *THE MAXIMS OF METHUSELAH* (1907), 2

10. Man's love is of man's life a thing apart, / 'Tis a Woman's whole existence.

BYRON, *DON JUAN* (1819–24), 1.194

11. In the sex-war thoughtlessness is the weapon of the male, vindictiveness of the female.

CYRIL CONNOLLY, *THE UNQUIET GRAVE* (1945), 1

12. The last thing a woman will consent to discover in a man whom she loves, or on whom she simply depends, is want of courage.

JOSEPH CONRAD, *VICTORY* (1915), 2.5

13. I'm not denyin' the women are foolish: God Almighty made 'em to match the men.

GEORGE ELIOT, *ADAM BEDE* (1859), 53

14. Men live by forgetting—women live on memories.

T. S. ELIOT, *THE ELDER STATESMAN* (1958), 2

15. Keeping the peace with the particular man in one's life becomes more essential than battling the mass male culture.

SUSAN FALUDI, *BACKLASH* (1991)

16. The economic victims of the era are men who who know someone has made off with their future—and they suspect the thief is a woman.

SUSAN FALUDI, *BACKLASH* (1991)

17. When man and woman die, as poets sung, / His heart's the last part moves, her last, the tongue.

BENJAMIN FRANKLIN, *POOR RICHARD'S ALMANACK* (1732–57)

18. The women I have loved I have desired for themselves, but also because I feared myself.

CARLOS FUENTES, "HOW I STARTED TO WRITE," IN *THE ART OF THE PERSONAL ESSAY* (1994), ED. PHILLIP LOPATE

19. If the heart of a man is depressed with cares, / The mist is dispelled when a woman appears.

JOHN GAY, *THE BEGGAR'S OPERA* (1728), 2.3, AIR 21

20. The man who discovers a woman's weakness is like the huntsman in the heat of the day who finds a cool spring. He wallows in it.

JEAN GIRAUDOUX, *TIGER AT THE GATES* (1935), 1, TR. CHRISTOPHER FRY

21. At the same time as woman was becoming the showcase for wealth and caste, while men were slipping into relative anonymity and "handsome is as handsome does," she was emerging as the central emblem of western art.

GERMAINE GREER, *THE FEMALE EUNUCH* (1970)

22. Strange difference of sex, that time and circumstance, which enlarge the views of most men, narrow the views of women almost invariably.

THOMAS HARDY, *JUDE THE OBSCURE* (1895), 6.10

23. Man is a wretch without woman; but woman is a monster—and thank Heaven, an almost impossible and hitherto imaginary monster—without man, as her acknowledged principal!

NATHANIEL HAWTHORNE, *THE BLITHEDALE ROMANCE* (1852), 14

24. I should like to see any kind of a man, distinguishable from a gorilla, that some good and even pretty woman could not shape a husband out of.

OLIVER WENDELL HOLMES, SR., *THE PROFESSOR AT THE BREAKFAST TABLE* (1860), 7

25. The average woman sees only the weak points in a strong man, and the good points in a weak one.

ELBERT HUBBARD, *THE NOTE BOOK* (1927)

26. You don't work no harder than me and yet you expects me to do the shopping, cooking, cleaning, and wash your filthy clothes, too, when I come home.

LANGSTON HUGHES, *SIMPLE SPEAKS HIS MIND* (1950)

27. The consequence of a very free commerce between the sexes, and of their living much together, will often terminate in intrigues and gallantry.

DAVID HUME, *A DIALOGUE*

28. Women speak because they wish to speak, whereas a man speaks only when driven to speech by something outside himself—like, for instance, he can't find any clean socks.

JEAN KERR, "HOW TO TALK TO A MAN," *THE SNAKE HAS ALL THE LINES* (1960)

29. A woman's guess is much more accurate than a man's certainty.

RUDYARD KIPLING, "THREE AND—AN EXTRA," *PLAIN TALES FROM THE HILLS* (1888)

30. Men are the reason that women do not love one another.

LA BRUYÈRE, *CHARACTERS* (1688), 3.55, TR. HENRI VAN LAUN

31. Women become attached to men by the favors they grant them; men are cured by these same favors.

LA BRUYÈRE, *CHARACTERS* (1688), 3.16

32. The clarity of gender makes possible the human dialectic. Let the lines of balanced tension go slack and the structure dissolves into the ooze of androgyny and narcissism.

LEWIS LAPHAM, *IMPERIAL MASQUERADE* (1990)

33. Nowadays beautiful women are counted among the talents of their husbands.

GEORG CHRISTOPH LICHTENBERG, *APHORISMS* (1764–99), TR. H. HATFIELD

34. The worldly relations of men and women often form an equation that cancels out without warning when some insignificant factor has been added to either side.

WILLIAM MCFEE, *CASUALS OF THE SEA* (1916), 1.1.14

35. Women are not men's equals in anything except responsibility. We are not their inferiors, either, or even their superiors. We are quite simply different races.

PHYLLIS MCGINLEY, "THE HONOR OF BEING A WOMAN," *THE PROVINCE OF THE HEART* (1959)

36. A woman can forgive a man for the harm he does her, but she can never forgive him for the sacrifices he makes on her account.

W. SOMERSET MAUGHAM, *THE MOON AND SIXPENCE* (1919), 41

37. When a man's in love, he at once makes a pedestal of the Ten Commandments and stands on the top of them with his arms akimbo. When a woman's in love she doesn't care two straws for Thou Shalt and Thou Shalt Not.

W. SOMERSET MAUGHAM, *LADY FREDERICK* (1907), 2

38. Women want mediocre men, and men are working hard to be as mediocre as possible.

MARGARET MEAD, *QUOTE*, MAY 15, 1958

39. The allurement that women hold out to men is precisely the allurement that Cape Hatteras holds out to sailors: they are enormously dangerous and hence enormously fascinating.

H. L. MENCKEN, "THE INCOMPARABLE BUZZ-SAW," *THE SMART SET,* MAY 1919

40. A man's women folk, whatever their outward show of respect for his merit and authority, always regard him secretly as an ass, and with something akin to pity.

H.L. MENCKEN, "THE FEMININE MIND," IN *FIFTY FAMOUS ESSAYS* (1964)

41. In argument with men a woman ever / Goes by the worse, whatever be her cause.

MILTON, *SAMSON AGONISTES* (1671), 903

42. Women, as they grow older, rely more and more on cosmetics. Men, as they grow older, rely more and more on a sense of humor.

GEORGE JEAN NATHAN, "COSMETICS VS. HUMOR," *AMERICAN MERCURY,* JULY 1925

43. Only he who is man enough will release the woman in woman.

NIETZSCHE, "ON VIRTUE THAT MAKES SMALL," *THUS SPOKE ZARATHUSTRA* (1883–92), 3, TR. WALTER KAUFMANN

44. Woman understands children better than man does, but man is more childlike than woman.

NIETZSCHE, "ON LITTLE OLD AND YOUNG WOMEN," *THUS SPOKE ZARATHUSTRA* (1883–92), 1, TR. WALTER KAUFMANN

45. Men go to musicals. Women are the ones who buy the tickets for plays.

JOHN O'HARA, *THE INSTRUMENT* (1967)

46. Woman's life must be wrapped up in a man, and the cleverest woman on earth is the biggest fool with a man.

DOROTHY PARKER, QUOTED IN OBITUARY, *THE NEW YORK TIMES,* JUNE 8, 1967

47. Women have many faults, but the worst of them all is that they are too pleased with themselves and take too little pains to please the men.

PLAUTUS, *THE LITTLE CARTHAGINIAN* (2ND C. B.C.), 5.4.1203

48. No woman ever hates a man for being in love with her, but many a woman hates a man for being a friend to her.

ALEXANDER POPE, *THOUGHTS ON VARIOUS SUBJECTS* (1727)

49. If she is pleasing to one man, a girl is taken care of.

PROPERTIUS, *ELEGIES* (C. 28—C. 16 B.C.), 1.2.26

50. Even the wisest men make fools of themselves about women, and even the most foolish women are wise about men.

THEODOR REIK, *THE NEED TO BE LOVED* (1963)

51. There's something every woman wants, and that's a man to blame.

PHILIP ROTH, *THE COUNTERLIFE* (1987)

52. In their hearts women think that it is men's business to earn money and theirs to spend it.

SCHOPENHAUER, "ON WOMEN," *PARERGA AND PARALIPOMENA* (1851), TR. T. BAILEY SAUNDERS

53. Women upset everything. When you let them into your life, you find that the woman is driving at one thing and you're driving at another.

GEORGE BERNARD SHAW, *PYGMALION* (1913), 2

54. I have thought that men and women should never come together except in bed. There is the only place where their natural hatred of each other is not so apparent.

JOHN STEINBECK, *STEINBECK: A LIFE IN LETTERS,* EDS. ELAINE STEINBECK AND ROBERT WALLSTEN (1975)

55. [T]he warfare between the unaroused male and female is constant and ferocious. Each blames the other for his loss of soul.

JOHN STEINBECK, *STEINBECK: A LIFE IN LETTERS,* EDS. ELAINE STEINBECK AND ROBERT WALLSTEN (1975)

56. [M]en were valued by what they did, women by how they looked and then by what their husbands did, and all of life was arranged (or so we thought) from the outside in.

GLORIA STEINEM, *REVOLUTION FROM WITHIN* (1992)

57. Women can be vivacious. We are allowed more varieties of facial expression and gestures. Men must be rocklike.

GLORIA STEINEM, "MEN AND WOMEN TALKING," *OUTRAGEOUS ACTS AND EVERYDAY REBELLIONS* (1983)

58. More men feel comfortable doing "public speaking," while more women feel comfortable doing "private" speaking.

DEBORAH TANNEN, *YOU JUST DON'T UNDERSTAND* (1990)

59. The chivalrous man who holds a door open or signals a woman to go ahead of him when he's driving is negotiating both status and connection.

DEBORAH TANNEN, *YOU JUST DON'T UNDERSTAND* (1990)

60. Men at most differ as heaven and earth, / But women, worst and best, as heaven and hell.

Lord Tennyson, "Merlin and Vivien," *Idylls of the King* (1859)

61. There is trouble with a wife, but it's even worse with a woman who is not a wife.

Leo Tolstoy, *Anna Karenina* (1873–76), 5.33

62. While husbands and lovers in the stories [of the 14th century] are of all kinds, ranging from sympathetic to disgusting, women are invariably deceivers: inconstant, unscrupulous, quarrelsome, querulous, lecherous, shameless, although not necessarily all of these at once.

Barbara W. Tuchman, *A Distant Mirror* (1978)

63. God created man and, finding him not sufficiently alone, gave him a companion to make him feel his solitude more keenly.

Paul Valéry, *Tel quel* (1943)

64. Woman is man's confusion.

Vincent of Beauvais, *Speculum Majus* (13th c.), 346

65. Women are not so sentimental as men, and are not so easily touched with the unspoken poetry of nature; being less poetical, and having less imagination, they are more fitted for practical affairs, and would make less failures in business.

Charles Dudley Warner, "Ninth Study," *Backlog Studies* (1873)

66. There is nothing that disgusts a man like getting beaten at chess by a woman.

Charles Dudley Warner, "Third Study," *Backlog Studies* (1873)

67. If a woman wants to hold a man, she has merely to appeal to what is worst in him. We make gods of men, and they leave us. Others make brutes of them and they fawn and are faithful.

Oscar Wilde, *Lady Windermere's Fan* (1892), 3

68. Men always want to be a woman's first love. That is their clumsy vanity. We women have a more subtle instinct about things. What we like is to be a man's last romance.

Oscar Wilde, *A Woman of No Importance* (1893), 2

69. There's nothing like mixing with woman to bring out all the foolishness in a man of sense.

Thornton Wilder, *The Matchmaker* (1955), 1

70. Hysteria is a natural phenomenon, the common denominator of the female nature. It's the big female weapon, and the test of a man is his ability to cope with it.

Tennessee Williams, *The Night of the Iguana* (1961), 1

MENTAL HEALTH

See 559. Madness; 842. Sanity

582. MEN

See also 66. Bachelors; 378. Gentleman; 566. Masculinity and Femininity; 581. Men and Women; 1062. Women

1. Poor little men! Poor little strutting peacocks! They spread out their tails as conquerors almost as soon as they are able to walk.

Jean Anouilh, *Cécile* (1949), tr. Arthur Klein

2. Men, unlike mockingbirds, have the capacity for systematic self-delusion. We echo each other with equal precision, equal eloquence, equal assurance.

Robert Ardrey, *The Territorial Imperative* (1966)

3. Male, n. A member of the unconsidered, or negligible sex. The male of the human race is commonly known (to the female) as Mere Man. The genus has two varieties: good providers and bad providers.

Ambrose Bierce, *The Devil's Dictionary* (1881–1911)

4. Men build bridges and throw railroads across deserts, and yet they contend successfully that the job of sewing on a button is beyond them. Accordingly, they don't have to sew buttons.

Heywood Broun, "Holding a Baby," *Seeing Things at Night* (1921)

5. Men's men: gentle or simple, they're much of a muchness.

George Eliot, *Daniel Deronda* (1874–76), 4.31

6. History is bright and fiction dull with homely men who have charmed women.

O. Henry, "Next to Reading Matter," *Roads of Destiny* (1909)

7. Man, without a saving touch of woman in him, is too doltish, too naïve and romantic, too easily deluded and lulled to sleep by his imagination to be anything above a cavalryman, a theologian or a corporation director.

H.L. Mencken, "The Feminine Mind," in *Fifty Famous Essays* (1964)

8. The beauty of stature is the only beauty of men.

Montaigne, "Of presumption," *Essays* (1580–88), tr. W. C. Hazlitt

9. Men should not care too much for good looks; neglect is becoming.

OVID, *THE ART OF LOVE* (C. A.D. 8), 1, TR. ROLFE HUMPHRIES

10. There was, I think, never any reason to believe in any innate superiority of the male, except his superior muscle.

BERTRAND RUSSELL, "IDEAS THAT HAVE HARMED MANKIND," *UNPOPULAR ESSAYS* (1950)

11. A man is like a phonograph with half-a-dozen records. You soon get tired of them all; and yet you have to sit at table whilst he reels them off to every new visitor.

GEORGE BERNARD SHAW, *GETTING MARRIED* (1911)

12. A man who has no office to go to—I don't care who he is—is a trial of which you can have no conception.

GEORGE BERNARD SHAW, *THE IRRATIONAL KNOT* (1885–87), 18

13. A handsome man is not quite poor.

SPANISH PROVERB

14. For many men the denial of dependency on their mother is repeated in their subsequent relationships, sometimes by an absence of any sexual interest in women, sometimes by a pattern of loving and leaving them.

JUDITH VIORST, *NECESSARY LOSSES* (1986)

15. In fact, men are outliving their usefulness. All you need are sperm banks to keep the species going, and those are coming along now. Most men are rotten lovers, women say, so there's not much loss in replacing sex with science.

ROBERT JAMES WALLER, *THE BRIDGES OF MADISON COUNTY* (1992)

583. MERCY

See also 359. FORGIVENESS; 534. LENIENCY; 698. PITY

1. We hand folks over to God's mercy, and show none ourselves.

GEORGE ELIOT, *ADAM BEDE* (1859), 42

2. Teach me to feel another's woe, / To hide the fault I see; / That mercy I to others show, / That mercy show to me.

ALEXANDER POPE, "THE UNIVERSAL PRAYER" (1738), 10

3. One time you smash a bug with no mercy. Another time you find one helpless on his back with his legs flailing the air, and you flip him over and let him go on his way. The struggle that touches the heart.

CHARLES PORTIS, *GRINGOS* (1991)

4. Clemency is the support of justice.

RUSSIAN PROVERB

5. Nothing emboldens sin so much as mercy.

SHAKESPEARE, *TIMON OF ATHENS* (1607–08), 3.5.3

6. Sweet mercy is nobility's true badge.

SHAKESPEARE, *TITUS ANDRONICUS* (1592–93), 1.1.119

7. The quality of mercy is not strained; / It droppeth as the gentle rain from heaven / Upon the place beneath. It is twice blessed— / It blesseth him that gives, and him that takes.

SHAKESPEARE, *THE MERCHANT OF VENICE* (1596–97), 4.1.184

8. A second-century rabbi said that if 999 angels gave a bad account of a man and one angel reported favorably, God would hear the one angel; even if 999 parts of that one angel's report were unfavorable, God would hearken to the favorable part.

ISRAEL SHENKER, *COAT OF MANY COLORS* (1985)

584. MERIT

See also 311. EXCELLENCE; 332. FAME; 722. PRAISE; 804. REPUTATION; 952. SUPERIORITY

1. Merit and knowledge will not gain hearts, though they will secure them when gained.

LORD CHESTERFIELD, *LETTERS TO HIS SON,* NOV. 24, 1749

2. The assumption of merit is easier, less embarrassing, and more effectual than the actual attainment of it.

WILLIAM HAZLITT, *CHARACTERISTICS* (1823), 21

3. The world more often rewards the appearances of merit than merit itself.

LA ROCHEFOUCAULD, *MAXIMS* (1665), TR. KENNETH PRATT

4. The erection of a monument is superfluous; our memory will endure if our lives have deserved it.

PLINY THE YOUNGER, *LETTERS* (C. 97–110), 9.19.3

5. Let none presume / To wear an undeservèd dignity. / O that estates, degrees, and offices / Were not derived corruptly, and that clear honour / Were purchased by the merit of the wearer!

SHAKESPEARE, *THE MERCHANT OF VENICE* (1596–97), 2.9.39

585. METHOD

See also 280. EFFICIENCY; 574. MEANS AND ENDS; 661. ORDER; 677. PATIENCE; 702. PLANS;

721. Practice; 737. Problems; 832. Rules; 903. Single-Mindedness; 939. Strategy

1. Better one safe way than a hundred on which you cannot reckon.

Aesop, "The Fox and the Cat," *Fables* (6th c. B.C.?), tr. Joseph Jacobs

2. If there are obstacles, the shortest line between two points may be the crooked line.

Bertolt Brecht, *Galileo* (1938; 1947), 13, tr. Charles Laughton

3. There is time enough for everything in the course of the day if you do but one thing at once; but there is not time enough in the year if you will do two things at a time.

Lord Chesterfield, *Letters to His Son,* April 14, 1747

4. There is always a best way of doing everything, if it be to boil an egg.

Emerson, "Behavior," *The Conduct of Life* (1860)

5. It is not always by plugging away at a difficulty and sticking at it that one overcomes it; but, rather, often by working on the one next to it. Certain people and certain things require to be approached on an angle.

André Gide, *Journals,* Oct. 26, 1924, tr. Justin O'Brien

6. Attempt easy tasks as if they were difficult, and difficult as if they were easy: in the one case that confidence may not fall asleep, in the other that it may not be dismayed.

Baltasar Gracián, *The Art of Worldly Wisdom* (1647), 204, tr. Joseph Jacobs

7. While Honey lies in Every Flower, no doubt, / It takes a Bee to get the Honey out.

Arthur Guiterman, *A Poet's Proverbs* (1924)

8. We often get in quicker by the back door than by the front.

Napoleon I, *Maxims* (1804–15)

9. Look for a tough wedge for a tough log.

Publilius Syrus, *Moral Sayings* (1st c. B.C.), 723, tr. Darius Lyman

10. To do two things at once is to do neither.

Publilius Syrus, *Moral Sayings* (1st c. B.C.), 7, tr. Darius Lyman

11. What sets us against one another is not our aims—they all come to the same thing—but our methods, which are the fruit of our varied reasoning.

Saint-Exupéry, *Wind, Sand, and Stars* (1939), 9.6, tr. Lewis Galantière

12. One arrow does not bring down two birds.

Turkish Proverb

586. MIDDLE AGE

See also 540. Life, Stages of; 571. Maturity; 653. Old Age; 1071. Youth

1. The Indian Summer of life should be a little sunny and a little sad, like the season, and infinite in wealth and depth of tone—but never hustled.

Henry Adams, *The Education of Henry Adams* (1907), 35

2. Men of age object too much, consult too long, adventure too little, repent too soon, and seldom drive business home to the full period, but content themselves with a mediocrity of success.

Francis Bacon, "Of Fortune," *Essays* (1625)

3. In middle life politics are not a mental acquisition; they are a temperament.

Frank Moore Colby, "Notes and Comments," *The Colby Essays* (1926), v. 2

4. When a middle-aged man says in a moment of weariness that he is half dead, he is telling the literal truth.

Elmer Davis, "On Not Being Dead, As Reported," *By Elmer Davis* (1964)

5. [T]hough we are perpetually bragging of it [the middle class] as our safety, it is nothing but a poor fringe on the mantle of the upper class.

Charles Dickens, *The Selected Letters of Charles Dickens*, (1960), ed. F.W. Dupee

6. The years between fifty and seventy are the hardest. You are always being asked to do things, and yet you are not decrepit enough to turn them down.

T. S. Eliot, *Time,* Oct. 23, 1950

7. After thirty, a man wakes up sad every morning, excepting perhaps five or six, until the day of his death.

Emerson, *Journals,* 1834

8. Whoever, in middle age, attempts to realize the wishes and hopes of his early youth, invariably deceives himself. Each ten years of a man's life has its own fortunes, its own hopes, its own desires.

Goethe, *Elective Affinities* (1809), 30

9. As you got older, and felt yourself to be at the centre of your time, and not at a point in its circumference, as you felt when you were little, you were seized with a sort of shuddering.

THOMAS HARDY, *JUDE THE OBSCURE* (1895), 1.2

10. Men, like peaches and pears, grow sweet a little while before they begin to decay.

OLIVER WENDELL HOLMES, SR., *THE AUTOCRAT OF THE BREAKFAST TABLE* (1858), 4

11. Middle age is when your age starts to show around the middle.

BOB HOPE, NEWS SUMMARIES, FEB. 15, 1954

12. Whenever a man's friends begin to compliment him about looking young, he may be sure that they think he is growing old.

WASHINGTON IRVING, "BACHELORS," *BRACEBRIDGE HALL* (1822)

13. The blush that flies at seventeen / Is fixed at forty-nine.

RUDYARD KIPLING, "MY RIVAL," *DEPARTMENTAL DITTIES* (1886)

14. She was in a petticoat now, and corsets which bulged, and unaware of being seen in bulgy corsets. She had become so dully habituated to married life that in her full matronliness she was as sexless as an anemic nun.

SINCLAIR LEWIS, *BABBITT* (1922)

15. By the time a man notices that he is no longer young, his youth has long since left him.

FRANÇOIS MAURIAC, "THE AGE OF SUCCESS," *SECOND THOUGHTS* (1961), TR. ADRIENNE FOULKE

16. Middle age is when you've met so many / people that every new person you / meet reminds you of someone else.

OGDEN NASH, "LET'S NOT CLIMB THE WASHINGTON MONUMENT TONIGHT," *VERSUS* (1949)

17. There is more felicity on the far side of baldness than young men can possibly imagine.

LOGAN PEARSALL SMITH, *AFTERTHOUGHTS* (1931), 2

18. Jamie is fifty and feels thirty: Judy is thirty and feels twenty. That's only ten years difference.

FAY WELDON, *REMEMBER ME* (1976)

19. In a man's middle years there is scarcely a part of the body he would hesitate to turn over to the proper authorities.

E. B. WHITE, "A WEEKEND WITH THE ANGELS," *THE SECOND TREE FROM THE CORNER* (1954)

587. MIDDLE CLASS

See also 52. ARISTOCRACY; 135. CLASS; 682. THE PEOPLE; 780. RANK; 913. SOCIETY; 933. STATUS

1. [I]t was difficult for me to distinguish one class from another [in America], everybody looked middle-class in European eyes, including the black students in the university and the beggars in the street.

LUIGI BARZINI, *O AMERICA* (1977)

2. I call bourgeois anyone who says no to himself, who gives up struggle and renounces love in favor of his security. I call bourgeois anyone who places anything above feeling.

LÉON-PAUL FARGUE, "BANALITÉ," *SOUS LA LAMPE* (1921)

3. [T]he very development of the American city has removed poverty from the living, emotional experience of millions upon millions of middle-class Americans.

MICHAEL HARRINGTON, *THE OTHER AMERICA* (1963)

4. [The bourgeois] prefers comfort to pleasure, convenience to liberty, and a pleasant temperature to that deathly inner consuming fire.

HERMANN HESSE, "TREATISE ON THE STEPPENWOLF," *DER STEPPENWOLF* (1927), TR. BASIL CREIGHTON, REV. WALTER SORELL

5. A moderately honest man with a moderately faithful wife, moderate drinkers both, in a moderately healthy house: that is the true middle class unit.

GEORGE BERNARD SHAW, "MAXIMS FOR REVOLUTIONISTS," *MAN AND SUPERMAN* (1905)

6. I have to live for others and not for myself; that's middle class morality.

GEORGE BERNARD SHAW, *PYGMALION* (1913), 5

7. [B]ehind the contained and orderly lives we lead as members of the respectable middle class there's a terrible human capacity that may one day overwhelm any of us.

DIANA TRILLING, *MRS. HARRIS: THE DEATH OF THE SCARSDALE DOCTOR* (1981)

8. The provincial, the middle-class, the bourgeois, are to be found everywhere; they are necessary, I suppose—only, when you differ from their own narrow molds, they may try to crucify you.

THOMAS WOLFE, *THOMAS WOLFE'S LETTERS TO HIS MOTHER* (1943)

588. THE MILITARY

See also 939. STRATEGY; 1042. WAR; 1049. WEAPONS

THE MILITARY

1. Industrial-strength foolishness sets in—in males, at least—at about the age of 18. This is why the military prefers males in the 18-to-25-year-old range when there's combat to be done.

RUSSELL BAKER, *THE NEW YORK TIMES*, APRIL 1, 1994

2. Lucky are soldiers who strive in a just war; / for them it is an easy entry into heaven.

BHAGAVADGITA, 2, TR. P. LAL

3. Raw in the fields the rude militia swarms, / Mouth without hands; maintained at vast expense, / In peace a charge, in war a weak defence.

JOHN DRYDEN, *CYMON AND IPHIGENIA* (1699)

4. A sojer's life is on'y gloryous in times iv peace. Thin he can wear his good clothes with th' goold lace on thim, an' sthrut in scarlet an' blue through th' sthreets.

FINLEY PETER DUNNE, "ON PAST GLORIES," *MR. DOOLEY ON MAKING A WILL* (1919)

5. It is characteristic of the military mentality that non-human factors ... are held essential, while the human being, his desires and thoughts—in short, the psychological factors—are considered as unimportant and secondary.

EINSTEIN, *OUT OF MY LATER LIFE* (1950), 36

6. He who loves the bristle of bayonets, only sees in their glitter what beforehand he feels in his heart.

EMERSON, "WAR," *MISCELLANIES* (1884)

7. It is essential to persuade the soldier that those he is being urged to massacre are bandits who do not deserve to live; before killing other good, decent fellows like himself, his gun would fall from his hands.

ANDRÉ GIDE, *JOURNALS*, FEB. 10, 1943, TR. JUSTIN O'BRIEN

8. I am the very model of a modern Major-General, / I've information vegetable, animal, and mineral, / I know the kings of England, and I quote the fights historical, / From Marathon to Waterloo, in order categorical.

W. S. GILBERT, *THE PIRATES OF PENZANCE* (1879), 1

9. Our business in the field of fight / Is not to question, but to prove our might.

HOMER, *ILIAD* (9TH C. B.C.), 20.304, TR. ALEXANDER POPE

10. The sound of the drum drives out thought; for that very reason it is the most military of instruments.

JOSEPH JOUBERT, *PENSÉES* (1842), 12.5, TR. KATHARINE LYTTELTON

11. The soldier, above all other people, prays for peace, for he must suffer and bear the deepest wounds and scars of war.

DOUGLAS MACARTHUR, ADDRESS, U. S. MILITARY ACADEMY, WEST POINT, N.Y., MAY 12, 1962

12. He [Gen. Douglas MacArthur] was a great thundering paradox of a man, noble and ignoble, inspiring and outrageous, arrogant and shy, the best of men and the worst of men, the most protean, most ridiculous, and most sublime.

WILLIAM MANCHESTER, *AMERICAN CAESAR* (1978)

13. The military caste did not originate as a party of patriots, but as a party of bandits.

H. L. MENCKEN, *MINORITY REPORT* (1956), 317

14. A cause breaks or exalts a soldier's strength; unless that cause is just, shame will make him throw his weapons away.

PROPERTIUS, *ELEGIES* (C. 28–C. 16 B.C.), 4.6.51

15. You cannot organize civilization around the core of militarism and at the same time expect reason to control human destinies.

FRANKLIN D. ROOSEVELT, RADIO ADDRESS, OCT. 26, 1938

16. A man who is good enough to shed his blood for his country is good enough to be given a square deal afterwards.

THEODORE ROOSEVELT, SPEECH, SPRINGFIELD, ILL., JULY 4, 1903

17. Theirs not to make reply, / Theirs not to reason why, / Theirs but to do and die.

LORD TENNYSON, "THE CHARGE OF THE LIGHT BRIGADE" (1854)

18. The pitifulest thing out is a mob; that's what an army is—a mob; they don't fight with courage that's born in them, but with courage that's borrowed from their mass, and from their officers.

MARK TWAIN, *THE ADVENTURES OF HUCKLEBERRY FINN* (1884), 22

19. The army is a nation within the nation; it is a vice of our time.

ALFRED DE VIGNY, *SERVITUDE ET GRANDEUR MILITAIRES* (1835), 1.2

20. We want to get rid of the militarist not simply because he hurts and kills, but because he is an intolerable thick-voiced blockhead who stands hectoring and blustering in our way to achievement.

H. G. WELLS, *THE OUTLINE OF HISTORY* (1920, 1921), 40.4

589. MIND AND BODY

See also 90. BODY; 413. HEALTH; 590. MIND; 882. SENSES; 919. SOUL; 927. SPIRITUALITY

1. So much are our minds influenced by the accidents of our bodies, that every man is more the man of the day than a regular and consequential character.

LORD CHESTERFIELD, *LETTERS TO HIS SON*, AUG. 30, 1748

2. The flesh believes that pleasure is limitless and that it requires unlimited time; but the mind, understanding the end and limit of the flesh and ridding itself of fears of the future, secures a complete life and has no longer any need for unlimited time.

EPICURUS, "PRINCIPAL DOCTRINES" (3RD C. B.C.), 20, IN *LETTERS, PRINCIPAL DOCTRINES, AND VATICAN SAYINGS*, TR. RUSSEL M. GEER

3. The flesh endures the storms of the present alone, the mind those of the past and future as well as the present.

EPICURUS, (4TH–3RD C. B.C.), QUOTED IN DIOGENES LAERTIUS' *LIVES AND OPINIONS OF EMINENT PHILOSOPHERS* (3RD C. A.D.), TR. R. D. HICKS

4. [A]t three o'clock in the morning, a forgotten package has the same tragic importance as a death sentence, and the cure doesn't work—and in a real dark night of the soul it is always three o'clock in the morning, day after day.

F. SCOTT FITZGERALD, *THE CRACK-UP* (1945)

5. Man is a mind betrayed, not served, by his organs.

JULES DE GONCOURT, *JOURNAL*, JULY 30, 1861, TR. ROBERT BALDICK

6. What we think and feel and are is to a great extent determined by the state of our ductless glands and our viscera.

ALDOUS HUXLEY, "MEDITATION ON EL GRECO," *MUSIC AT NIGHT* (1931)

7. [J]ust make someone who has fallen in love listen to his stomach rumble, and the unity of body and soul, that lyrical illusion of the age of science, instantly falls away.

MILAN KUNDERA, *THE UNBEARABLE LIGHTNESS OF BEING* (1984)

8. If the mind, which rules the body, ever forgets itself so far as to trample upon its slave, the slave is never generous enough to forgive the injury; but will rise and smite its oppressor.

LONGFELLOW, *HYPERION* (1839), 1.7

9. Man is to himself the most wonderful object in nature; for he cannot conceive what the body is, still less what the mind is, and least of all how a body should be united to a mind.

PASCAL, *PENSÉES* (1670), 72, TR. W. F. TROTTER

10. All the soarings of my mind begin in my blood.

RAINER MARIA RILKE, LETTER TO A YOUNG GIRL, JULY 1921, IN *WARTIME LETTERS*, TR. M. D. HERTER NORTON

11. Depression is melancholy minus its charms—the animation, the fits.

SUSAN SONTAG, *ILLNESS AS METAPHOR* (1978)

590. MIND

See also 450. IMAGINATION; 492. INTELLECTUALS AND INTELLECTUALISM; 493. INTELLIGENCE; 589. MIND AND BODY; 818. REVERIE; 975. THOUGHT; 1006. UNCONSCIOUSNESS; 1007. UNDERSTANDING

1. Mind is a light which the Gods mock us with, / To lead those false who trust it.

MATTHEW ARNOLD, *EMPEDOCLES ON ETNA* (1852), 1.2

2. There are some things the arrogant mind does not see; it is blinded by its vision of what it desires.

WENDELL BERRY, "PEOPLE, LAND, AND COMMUNITY," *STANDING BY WORDS* (1983)

3. The mind covers more ground than the heart but goes less far.

CHINESE PROVERB

4. The mind wants the world to return its love, or its awareness; the mind wants to know all the world, and all eternity, and God.

ANNIE DILLARD, "TOTAL ECLIPSE," *TEACHING A STONE TO TALK* (1982)

5. Mind is a most delicate evidence. / Not a soul has seen it yet.

RICHARD EBERHART, "ON THE FRAGILITY OF MIND," *SELECTED POEMS 1930–1965* (1965)

6. We should take care not to make the intellect our god; it has, of course, powerful muscles, but no personality.

EINSTEIN, *OUT OF MY LATER LIFE* (1950), 51

7. Outside, among your fellows, among strangers, you must preserve appearances, a hundred things you cannot do; but inside, the terrible freedom!

EMERSON, *JOURNALS*, 1832

8. It is the mind which creates the world about us, and even though we stand side by side in the same meadow, my eyes will never see what is beheld by yours, my heart will never stir to the emotions with which yours is touched.

George Gissing, "Summer," *The Private Papers of Henry Ryecroft* (1903)

9. The direction of the mind is more important than its progress.

Joseph Joubert, *Pensées* (1842), 18.13, tr. Katharine Lyttelton

10. The limits of thought are not so much set from outside, by the fullness or poverty of experiences that meet the mind, as from within, by the power of conception, the wealth of formulative notions with which the mind meets experiences.

Susanne K. Langer, *Philosophy in a New Key* (1942)

11. The understanding, like the eye, whilst it makes us see and perceive all things, takes no notice of itself; and it requires art and pains to set it at a distance and make it its own subject.

John Locke, *An Essay Concerning Human Understanding* (1690), 1.1.1

12. The mind is its own place, and in itself / Can make a heaven of hell, a hell of heaven.

Milton, *Paradise Lost* (1667), 1.254

13. The mind is a dangerous weapon, even to the possessor, if he knows not discreetly how to use it.

Montaigne, "Apology for Raimond de Sebonde," *Essays* (1580–88), tr. W. C. Hazlitt

14. Order and reason, beauty and benevolence, are characteristics and conceptions which we find solely associated with the mind of man.

Karl Pearson, quoted in Henry Adams' *The Education of Henry Adams* (1907), 31

15. We are less justified in saying that the thinking life of humanity is a miraculous perfectioning of animal and physical life than that it is an imperfection in the organization of spiritual life as rudimentary as the communal existence of protozoa in colonies.

Marcel Proust, *Remembrance of Things Past: The Past Recaptured* (1913–27), tr. Stephen Hudson

16. Men are not prisoners of fate, but only prisoners of their own minds.

Franklin D. Roosevelt, Pan American Day address, April 15, 1939

17. The mind is the expression of the soul, which belongs to God and must be let alone by government.

Adlai Stevenson, speech, Salt Lake City, Utah, Oct. 14, 1952

18. The human mind is not meant to be governed, certainly not by any book of rules yet written; it is supposed to run itself, and we are obliged to follow it along, trying to keep up with it as best we can.

Lewis Thomas, "The Attic of the Brain," *Late Night Thoughts on Listening to Mahler's Ninth Symphony* (1983)

19. How few things can a man measure with the tape of his understanding! How many greater things might he be seeing in the meanwhile.

Thoreau, *Journal*, Feb. 14, 1851

20. Mind has transformed the world, and the world is repaying it with interest. It has led man where he had no idea how to go.

Paul Valéry, "Our Destiny and Literature," *Reflections on the World Today* (1931), tr. Francis Scarfe

21. The mind of man is more intuitive than logical, and comprehends more than it can coordinate.

Vauvenargues, *Reflections and Maxims* (1746), 2, tr. F. G. Stevens

22. Minds differ still more than faces.

Voltaire, "Wit, Spirit, Intellect," *Philosophical Dictionary* (1746)

23. Strongest minds / Are often those of whom the noisy world / Hears least.

William Wordsworth, *The Excursion* (1814), 1

591. MINORITIES

See also 85. Blacks; 775. Racial Prejudice

1. Because half a dozen grasshoppers under a fern make the field ring with their importunate chink...do not imagine that those who make the noise are the only inhabitants of the field.

Edmund Burke, *Reflections on the Revolution in France* (1790)

2. A resolute minority has usually prevailed over an easygoing or wobbly majority whose prime purpose was to be left alone.

James Reston, *Sketches in the Sand* (1967)

3. No democracy can long survive which does not accept as fundamental to its very existence the recognition of the rights of minorities.

Franklin D. Roosevelt, letter to the National Association for the Advancement of Colored People, June 25, 1938

592. MIRACLES

See also 953. Supernatural

1. True miracles are created by men when they use the courage and intelligence that God gave them.

Jean Anouilh, *The Lark* (1955), 2, adapted by Lillian Hellman

2. Picasso said that everything is a miracle, that it's a miracle that we don't dissolve in our baths.

Jean Cocteau, *Diary of an Unknown* (1952; 1988)

3. There is in every miracle a silent chiding of the world, and a tacit reprehension of them who require, or who need miracles.

John Donne, *Sermons,* No. 47, 1627

4. Religion seems to have grown an infant with age, and requires miracles to nurse it, as it had in its infancy.

Jonathan Swift, *Thoughts on Various Subjects* (1711)

5. Men talk about Bible miracles because there is no miracle in their lives. Cease to gnaw that crust. There is ripe fruit over your head.

Thoreau, *Journal,* June 1850

6. I have come to know that the miracle rarely happens in human affairs; Lazarus is uncured and bleeds from his sores.

Thomas Wolfe, *Thomas Wolfe's Letters to His Mother* (1943)

593. MIRRORS

See also 444. Identity

1. Every man carries with him through life a mirror, as unique and impossible to get rid of as his shadow.

W. H. Auden, "Hic et Ille," *The Dyer's Hand* (1962)

2. The best mirror is an old friend.

German Proverb

3. The image in the mirror was instantaneously transformed: suddenly it was a woman in her undergarments, a beautiful, distant, indifferent woman with a terribly out-of-place bowler hat on her head, holding the hand of a man in a gray suit and tie.

Milan Kundera, *The Unbearable Lightness of Being* (1984)

4. [Mirrors] are there when we are and yet they never give anything back to us but our own image. Never, never shall we know what they are when they are alone or what is behind them.

Erich Maria Remarque, *The Black Obelisk* (1957), 6, tr. Denver Lindley

5. There was never yet fair woman but she made mouths in a glass.

Shakespeare, *King Lear* (1605–06), 3.2.35

6. All mirrors are magical mirrors, and we never see our faces in them.

Logan Pearsall Smith, *Afterthoughts* (1931), 1

594. MISANTHROPY

See also 255. Dislike; 412. Hatred; 433. Humanitarianism

1. I do not want people to be very agreeable, as it saves me the trouble of liking them a great deal.

Jane Austen, letter to her sister Cassandra, Dec. 24, 1798

2. True misanthropes are not found in solitude, but in the world: because it is practical experience of the world and not philosophy that makes men hate.

Giacomo Leopardi, *Pensieri* (1834–37), 89, tr. William Fense Weaver

3. Any man who hates dogs and babies can't be all bad.

Leo Rosten, speaking of W. C. Fields at a banquet for the latter given by the Masquers' Club in Hollywood, Feb. 16, 1939

4. I love mankind—it's people I can't stand.

Charles M. Schulz, *Go Fly a Kite, Charlie Brown* (1963)

595. MISERS

See also 403. Greed; 936. Stinginess

1. Misers take care of property as if it belonged to them, but derive no more benefit from it than if it belonged to others.

Bion (2nd c. b.c.?), quoted in Diogenes Laertius' *Lives and Opinions of Eminent Philosophers* (3rd c. a.d.), tr. R. D. Hicks

2. The miser is the man who starves himself, and everybody else, in order to worship wealth in its dead form, as distinct from its living form.

G. K. Chesterton, "About Bad Comparisons," *As I Was Saying* (1936)

3. He [the miser] falls down and worships the god of this world, but will have neither its pomps, its vanities nor its pleasures for his trouble.

CHARLES CALEB COLTON, *LACON* (1825), 1.24

4. The miser and the pig are of no use until dead.

FRENCH PROVERB

5. The miser puts his gold pieces into a coffer; but as soon as the coffer is closed, it is as if it were empty.

ANDRÉ GIDE, "CONCERNING INFLUENCE IN LITERATURE," *PRETEXTS* (1903), TR. OTHERS

6. What greater evil could you wish a miser, than long life?

PUBLILIUS SYRUS, *MORAL SAYINGS* (1ST C. B.C.), 68, TR. DARIUS LYMAN

MISERY

See 946. SUFFERING; 1011. UNHAPPINESS

MISFORTUNE

See 17. ADVERSITY; 360. FORTUNE

596. MISSIONARIES

See also 841. SALVATION

1. Go ye into the world, and preach the gospel to every creature. He that believeth and is baptized shall be saved; but he that believeth not shall be damned.

BIBLE, MARK 16:15–16

2. If he have faith, the believer cannot be restrained. He betrays himself. He breaks out. He confesses and teaches this gospel to the people at the risk of life itself.

MARTIN LUTHER, PREFACE TO HIS TRANSLATION OF THE *NEW TESTAMENT* (1522)

MISTAKES

See 88. BLUNDER; 299. ERROR

MISTRUST

See 259. DISTRUST

597. MOB

See also 208. CROWDS; 682. THE PEOPLE

1. The best university that can be recommended to a man of ideas is the gauntlet of the mob.

EMERSON, *SOCIETY AND SOLITUDE* (1870)

2. In the hands of vicious men, / a mob will do anything. But under good leaders / it's quite a different story.

EURIPIDES, *ORESTES* (408 B.C.), TR. WILLIAM ARROWSMITH

3. Mobs in their emotions are much like children, / subject to the same tantrums and fits of fury.

EURIPIDES, *ORESTES* (408 B.C.), TR. WILLIAM ARROWSMITH

4. The mob gets out of hand, runs wild, worse / than raging fire, while the man who stands apart / is called a coward.

EURIPIDES, *HECUBA* (C. 425 B.C.), TR. WILLIAM ARROWSMITH

5. Isolation from power makes men look for a mob in which they can be strong.

HERBERT GOLD, "LET'S KILL THE FIRST RED-HAIRED MAN WE SEE...," *THE MAGIC WILL* (1971)

6. There is no grievance that is a fit object of redress by mob law.

ABRAHAM LINCOLN, SPEECH, SPRINGFIELD, ILL., JAN. 27, 1838

7. The nose of a mob is its imagination. By this, at any time, it can be quietly led.

EDGAR ALLAN POE, *MARGINALIA* (1844–49), 13

MODEL

See 310. EXAMPLE

598. MODERATION

See also 312. EXCESS; 494. INTEMPERANCE; 748. PROPORTION; 755. PRUDENCE; 947. SUFFICIENCY; 970. TEMPERANCE

1. Ask the gods nothing excessive.

AESCHYLUS, *THE SUPPLIANT MAIDENS* (463 B.C.), TR. SETH G. BERNARDETE

2. Give me more love or more disdain; / The torrid or the frozen zone / Bring equal ease unto my pain; / The temperate affords me none.

THOMAS CAREW, "MEDIOCRITY IN LOVE REJECTED," *POEMS* (1640)

3. There is a mistaken idea, ancient but still with us, that an overdose of anything from fornication to hot chocolate will teach restraint by the very results of its abuse.

M.F.K. FISHER, "ONCE A TRAMP, ALWAYS...," IN *THE ART OF THE PERSONAL ESSAY* (1994), ED. PHILLIP LOPATE

4. It is only through restraint that man can manage not to suppress himself.

André Gide, *Journals*, 1911, translated and edited by Justin O'Brien

5. Moderation is the silken string running through the pearl chain of all virtues.

Joseph Hall, introduction to *Christian Moderation* (1601)

6. I have almost reached the regrettable conclusion that the Negroes' great stumbling block in the stride toward freedom is not the White Citizens' "Councilor" or the Ku Klux Klanner, but the white moderate who is more devoted to "order" than to justice.

Martin Luther King, Jr., "Letter from Birmingham City Jail"

7. Is not moderation an old refrain / Ringing in our ears? from which we all refrain.

La Fontaine, "Moderation," *Fables* (1668–94), tr. Marianne Moore

8. The moderate are not usually the most sincere, for the same circumspection which makes them moderate makes them likewise retentive of what could give offense.

Walter Savage Landor, "Diogenes and Plato," *Imaginary Conversations* (1824–53)

9. Moderation has been created a virtue to limit the ambition of great men, and to console undistinguished people for their want of fortune and their lack of merit.

La Rochefoucauld, *Maxims* (1665), tr. Kenneth Pratt

10. Moderation is the languor and indolence of the soul, as ambition is its ardour and activity.

La Rochefoucauld, *Maxims* (1665), tr. Kenneth Pratt

11. Ah, men do not know how much strength is in poise, / That he goes the farthest who goes far enough.

James Russell Lowell, *A Fable for Critics* (1848)

12. It is circumstance and proper measure that give an action its character, and make it either good or bad.

Plutarch, "Life of Agesilaus II," *Parallel Lives* (1st–2nd c. A.D.), tr. John Dryden

13. The heart is great which shows moderation in the midst of prosperity.

Seneca The Elder, *Suasoriae* (1st c.), 1

14. Nothing in excess.

Solon (7th–6th c. B.C.), quoted in Diogenes Laertius' *Lives and Opinions of Eminent Philosophers* (3rd c. A.D.), tr. R. D. Hicks

599. MODERNITY

See also 184. Contemporaneousness

1. A seventeenth-century painting can be "modern" because the living eye finds it fresh and new. A "modern" painting can be outdated because it was a product of the moment and not of time.

Marya Mannes, *More in Anger* (1958), 3.2

2. It is only the modern that ever becomes old-fashioned.

Oscar Wilde, "The Decay of Lying," *Intentions* (1891)

600. MODESTY

See also 435. Humility

1. A just and reasonable modesty does not only recommend eloquence, but sets off every great talent which a man can be possessed of.

Joseph Addison, *The Spectator* (1711–12), 231

2. Nothing is more amiable than true modesty, and nothing more contemptible than the false. The one guards virtue, the other betrays it.

Joseph Addison, *The Spectator* (1711–12), 458

3. Modesty is the only sure bait when you angle for praise.

Lord Chesterfield, *Letters to His Son*, May 17, 1750

4. Pocket all your knowledge with your watch, and never pull it out in company unless desired.

Lord Chesterfield, *Letters to His Son*, Nov. 1, 1750

5. He who speaks without modesty will find it difficult to make his words good.

Confucius, *Analects* (6th c. B.C.), 14.21, tr. James Legge

6. Loquacity storms the ear, but modesty takes the heart.

Thomas Fuller, M.D., *Gnomologia* (1732), 3276

7. There speaks the man of truly noble ways, / Who will not listen to the words of praise. / In modesty averse, and with deaf ears, / He acts as though the others were his peers.

Goethe, "On the Lower Peneus," *Faust: Part II* (1832), tr. Philip Wayne

8. The sage never seems to know his own merits, for only by not noticing them can you call others' attention to them.

Baltasar Gracián, *The Art of Worldly Wisdom* (1647), 123, tr. Joseph Jacobs

9. True modesty does not consist in an ignorance of our merits, but in a due estimate of them.

Augustus William Hare, *Guesses at Truth* (1827)

10. None of the adults I knew ever touched in public, much less kneaded each other's flesh.

Maureen Howard, *Facts of Life* (1978)

11. A modest man is usually admired—if people ever hear of him.

Edgar Watson Howe, *Ventures in Common Sense* (1919), 4.7

12. Modesty and diffidence make a man unfit for public affairs; they also make him unfit for brothels.

Walter Savage Landor, "Diogenes and Plato," *Imaginary Conversations* (1824–53)

13. With people of only moderate ability modesty is a mere honesty; but with those who possess great talent it is hypocrisy.

Schopenhauer, "Further Psychological Observations," *Parerga and Paralipomena* (1851), tr. T. Bailey Saunders

14. Modesty—is a quality in a lover more praised by women than liked.

Richard Brinsley Sheridan, *The Rivals* (1775), 2.2

601. MONASTICISM

See also 122. Chastity; 138. Clergy; 183. Contemplation; 840. Saints and Sainthood; 865. Self-Denial; 927. Spirituality

1. Monastic incarceration is castration.

Victor Hugo, "Cosette," *Les Misérables* (1862), 7.3, tr. Charles E. Wilbour

2. The convent is supreme egotism resulting in supreme self-denial.

Victor Hugo, "Cosette," *Les Misérables* (1862), 7.7, tr. Charles E. Wilbour

3. I cannot praise a fugitive and cloistered virtue, unexercised and unbreathed, that never sallies out and sees her adversary, but slinks out of the race where that immortal garland is to be run for, not without dust and heat.

Milton, *Areopagitica* (1644)

602. MONEY

See also 8. Acquisition; 69. Banking; 104. Business and Commerce; 503. Investment; 680. Payment; 750. Prosperity; 977. Thrift; 1048. Wealth; 1058. Wills and Inheritance

1. It seems to be a law of American life that whatever enriches us anywhere except in the wallet inevitably becomes uneconomic.

Russell Baker, "Observer," *The New York Times,* March 24, 1968

2. Money, it turned out, was exactly like sex, you thought of nothing else if you didn't have it and thought of other things if you did.

James Baldwin, "The Black Boy Looks at the White Boy," *Nobody Knows My Name* (1961)

3. If you would know what the Lord God thinks of money, you have only to look at those to whom he gives it.

Maurice Baring, quoted by Dorothy Parker in *Writers at Work: First Series* (1958)

4. The love of money is the root of all evil.

Bible, 1 Timothy 6:10

5. Money, n. A blessing that is of no advantage to us excepting when we part with it.

Ambrose Bierce, *The Devil's Dictionary* (1881–1911)

6. People who can least afford to pay rent, pay rent. People who can most afford to pay rent, build up equity.

Arthur Bloch, "Perlsweig's Law," *Murphy's Law* (1979)

7. One must choose, in life, between making money and spending it. There's no time to do both.

Edouard Bourdet, *Les Temps difficiles* (1934), 4

8. Life is short and so is money.

Bertolt Brecht, *The Threepenny Opera* (1928), 3.3, tr. Eric Bentley

9. Money has a power above / The stars and fate, to manage love: / Whose arrows, learned poets hold, / That never miss, are tipped with gold.

Samuel Butler (d. 1680), *Hudibras* (1663), 3.3

10. What makes all doctrines plain and clear? / About two hundred pounds a year. / And that which was proved true before, / Prove false again? Two hundred more.

Samuel Butler (d. 1680), *Hudibras* (1663), 3.1

11. Ready money is Aladdin's lamp.

BYRON, *DON JUAN* (1819–24), 12.12

12. No honest hardworking official likes to see good money disappearing into the hands of the Treasury at the end of the financial year.

JOYCE CARY, *MISTER JOHNSON* (1939)

13. My mother taught me never to speak about money when there was a shirtful, and I've always been very reluctant to speak about it when there was any scarcity, so I cannot paint much of a picture of what ensued in the next six months.

JOHN CHEEVER, "THE HOUSEBREAKER OF SHADY HILL," *THE STORIES OF JOHN CHEEVER* (1980)

14. A moderate addiction to money may not always be hurtful; but when taken in excess it is nearly always bad for the health.

CLARENCE DAY, "IMPROVING THE LIVES OF THE RICH," *THE CROW'S NEST* (1921)

15. Money is coined liberty, and so it is ten times dearer to a man who is deprived of freedom. If money is jingling in his pocket, he is half consoled, even though he cannot spend it.

DOSTOYEVSKY, *THE HOUSE OF THE DEAD* (1862), 1.1, TR. CONSTANCE GARNETT

16. If a man is wise, he gets rich an' if he gets rich, he gets foolish, or his wife does. That's what keeps th' money movin' around.

FINLEY PETER DUNNE, "NEWPORT," *OBSERVATIONS BY MR. DOOLEY* (1902)

17. The value of a dollar is social, as it is created by society.

EMERSON, "WEALTH," *THE CONDUCT OF LIFE* (1860)

18. Money helps, though not so much as you think when you don't have it.

LOUISE ERDRICH, "INSULATION," *THE BINGO PALACE* (1994)

19. Money's the wise man's religion.

EURIPIDES, *THE CYCLOPS* (C. 425 B.C.), TR. WILLIAM ARROWSMITH

20. Never ask of money spent / Where the spender thinks it went. / Nobody was ever meant / To remember or invent / What he did with every cent.

ROBERT FROST, "THE HARDSHIP OF ACCOUNTING," *A FURTHER RANGE* (1936)

21. Be the business never so painful, you may have it done for money.

THOMAS FULLER, M.D., *GNOMOLOGIA* (1732), 857

22. Money, like dung, does no good till 'tis spread.

THOMAS FULLER, M.D., *GNOMOLOGIA* (1732), 3444

23. God makes, and apparel shapes: but it's money that finishes the man.

THOMAS FULLER, M.D., *GNOMOLOGIA* (1732), 1680

24. Help me to money and I'll help myself to friends.

THOMAS FULLER, M.D., *GNOMOLOGIA* (1732), 1030

25. To have money is to be virtuous, honest, beautiful and witty. And to be without is to be ugly and boring and stupid and useless.

JEAN GIRAUDOUX, *THE MADWOMAN OF CHAILLOT* (1945), 2, ADAPTED BY MAURICE VALENCY

26. Money is time. With money I buy for cheerful use the hours which otherwise would not in any sense be mine; nay, which would make me their miserable bondsman.

GEORGE GISSING, "WINTER," *THE PRIVATE PAPERS OF HENRY RYECROFT* (1903)

27. With his own money a person can live as he likes—a ruble that's your own is dearer than a brother.

MAXIM GORKY, *THE ZYKOVS* (1914), 4

28. Politics, war, marriage, crime, adultery. Everything that exists in the world has something to do with money.

GRAHAM GREENE, *THE CAPTAIN AND THE ENEMY* (1988)

29. If a man has money, it is usually a sign, too, that he knows how to take care of it; don't imagine his money is easy to get simply because he has plenty of it.

EDGAR WATSON HOWE, *COUNTRY TOWN SAYINGS* (1911)

30. To learn the value of money, it is not necessary to know the nice things it can get for you, you have to have experienced the trouble of getting it.

PHILIPPE HÉRIAT, *LA FAMILLE BOUSSARDEL* (1946), 17

31. Go into the street, and give one man a lecture on morality, and another a shilling, and see which will respect you most.

SAMUEL JOHNSON, QUOTED IN BOSWELL'S *LIFE OF SAMUEL JOHNSON*, JULY 20, 1763

32. Some men make money not for the sake of living, but ache / In the blindness of greed and live just for their fortune's sake.

JUVENAL, *SATIRES* (C. 100), 12.49, TR. HUBERT CREEKMORE

33. Like grain in a time of famine, the immense resources which the nation does in fact possess go

not to the child in the greatest need but to the children of the highest bidder—the child of parents who, more frequently than not, have also enjoyed the same abundance when they were schoolchildren.

Jonathan Kozol, *Savage Inequalities* (1991)

34. In our culture we make heroes of the men who sit on top of a heap of money, and we pay attention not only to what they say in their field of competence, but to their wisdom on every other question in the world.

Max Lerner, "The Epic of Model T," *Actions and Passions* (1949)

35. Moral principle is a looser bond than pecuniary interest.

Abraham Lincoln, speech, October 1856

36. It is extraordinary how many emotional storms one may weather in safety if one is ballasted with ever so little gold.

William McFee, *Casuals of the Sea* (1916), 1.1.10

37. Money is not an aphrodisiac: the desire it may kindle in the female eye is more for the cash than the carrier.

Marya Mannes, "A Plea for Flirtation," *But Will It Sell?* (1955–64)

38. Money is the alienated essence of man's work and existence; this essence dominates him and he worships it.

Karl Marx, "The capacity of the present-day Jews and Christians to become free" (1884), *Early Writings*

39. Money is like a sixth sense without which you cannot make a complete use of the other five.

W. Somerset Maugham, *Of Human Bondage* (1915), 51

40. Much work is merely a way to make money; much leisure is merely a way to spend it.

C. Wright Mills, "Diagnosis of Our Moral Uneasiness," *Power, Politics and People* (1963)

41. Cultivated people should be superior to any consideration so sordid as a mercenary interest.

Molière, *The Would-be Gentleman* (1670), 1, tr. John Wood

42. Gold is the key, whatever else we try; / And that sweet metal aids the conqueror / In every case, in love as well as war.

Molière, *The School for Wives* (1662), 1.4, tr. Donald M. Frame

43. Money writes books, money sells them. Give me not righteousness, O Lord, give me money, only money.

George Orwell, *Keep the Aspidistra Flying* (1936)

44. Gold will buy the highest honours; and gold will purchase love.

Ovid, *The Art of Love* (c. A.D. 8), 2, tr. J. Lewis May

45. He that has a penny in his purse, is worth a penny: Have and you shall be esteemed.

Petronius, *Satyricon* (1st c.), tr. William Burnaby

46. Even genius is tied to profit.

Pindar, *Odes* (5th c. B.C.), Pythia 3, tr. Richmond Lattimore

47. You, O money, are the cause of a restless life! Because of you we journey toward a premature death; you provide cruel nourishment for the evils of men; the seed of our cares sprouts from your head.

Propertius, *Elegies* (c. 28-c. 16 B.C.), 3.7.1

48. Money alone sets all the world in motion.

Publilius Syrus, *Moral Sayings* (1st c. B.C.), 656, tr. Darius Lyman

49. When Gold argues the cause, eloquence is impotant.

Publilius Syrus, *Moral Sayings* (1st c. B.C.), 65, tr. Darius Lyman

50. When reason rules, money is a blessing.

Publilius Syrus, *Moral Sayings* (1st c. B.C.), 50, tr. Darius Lyman

51. I finally know what distinguishes man from the other beasts: financial worries.

Jules Renard, *Journal* (1887–1910)

52. When money speaks, the truth keeps silent.

Russian Proverb

53. Money is power, freedom, a cushion, the root of all evil, the sum of blessings.

Carl Sandburg, *The People, Yes* (1936)

54. Nothing comes amiss, so money comes withal.

Shakespeare, *The Taming of the Shrew* (1593–94), 1.2.82

55. Money is indeed the most important thing in the world; and all sound and successful personal and national morality should have this fact for its basis.

George Bernard Shaw, preface, *The Irrational Knot* (1885–87)

56. Money is the counter that enables life to be lived socially: it is life as truly as sovereigns and banknotes are money.

George Bernard Shaw, preface, *Major Barbara* (1905)

57. There was a time when a fool and his money were soon parted, but now it happens to everybody.

Adlai Stevenson, *The Stevenson Wit* (1966)

58. The jingling of the guinea helps the hurt that Honor feels.

Lord Tennyson, "Locksley Hall" (1842)

59. Almost any man knows how to earn money, but not one in a million knows how to spend it. If he had known so much as this, he would never have earned it.

Thoreau, *Journal*, 1841

60. I began to think of F. Scott Fitzgrald, the only writer this country had ever produced who knew to the last dollar and cent the moral worth of money.

Diana Trilling, *Mrs. Harris: The Death of the Scarsdale Doctor* (1981)

61. Some men worship rank, some worship heroes, some worship power, some worship God, and over these ideals they dispute—but they all worship money.

Mark Twain, *Notebook* (1935)

62. Money is only useful when you get rid of it. It is like the odd card in "Old Maid"; the player who is finally left with it has lost.

Evelyn Waugh, "Kicking Against the Goad," *Commonweal* magazine, March 11, 1949

63. It is better to have a permanent income than to be fascinating.

Oscar Wilde, "The Model Millionaire" (1887)

64. The difference between a little money and no money at all is enormous—and can shatter the world. And the difference between a little money and an enormous amount of money is very slight—and that, also, can shatter the world.

Thornton Wilder, *The Matchmaker* (1955), 4

65. Money, big money (which is actually a relative concept) is always, under any circumstances, a seduction, a test of morals, a temptation to sin.

Boris Yeltsin, *The Struggle for Russia* (1994), tr. Catherine A. Fitzpatrick

66. With money in your pocket, you are wise and you are handsome and you sing well too.

Yiddish Proverbs (1949)

MOODS

See 284. Emotions; 969. Temperament

603. MOON

See also 415. The Heavens; 921. Space

1. So there he is at last. Man on the moon. The poor magnificent bungler! He can't even get to the office without undergoing the agonies of the damned, but give him a little metal, a few chemicals, some wire and twenty or thirty billion dollars and, vroom! there he is, up on a rock a quarter of a million miles up in the sky.

Russell Baker, in *The New York Times*, July 21, 1969

2. There is something haunting in the light of the moon; it has all the dispassionateness of a disembodied soul, and something of its inconceivable mystery.

Joseph Conrad, *Lord Jim* (1900), 24

3. Evening had fallen. A rim of the young moon cleft the pale waste of sky line, the rim of a silver hoop embedded in grey sand: and the tide was flowing in fast to the land with a low whisper of her waves, islanding a few last figures in distant pools.

James Joyce, *A Portrait of the Artist as a Young Man* (1916)

4. Treading the soil of the moon, palpitating its pebbles, tasting the panic and splendor of the event, feeling in the pit of one's stomach the separation from terra—these form the most romantic sensation an explorer has ever known.

Vladimir Nabokov, in *The New York Times*, July 21, 1969

5. The moon is a friend for the lonesome to talk to.

Carl Sandburg, "Moonlight and Maggots," *Complete Poems* (1950)

604. MORALITY

See also 77. Behavior; 174. Conscience; 393. Goodness; 491. Integrity; 1033. Virtue

1. Morality is a private and costly luxury.

Henry Adams, *The Education of Henry Adams* (1907), 22

2. Decalogue, n. A series of commandments, ten in number—just enough to permit an intelligent selection for observance, but not enough to embarrass the choice.

Ambrose Bierce, *The Devil's Dictionary* (1881–1911)

3. There is a perennial and unobtrusive view that morality consists in such things as telling the truth,

paying one's debts, respecting one's parents and doing no voluntary harm to anyone. Those are all things easy to say and hard to do; they do not attract much attention, and win little honor in the world.

ALLAN BLOOM, *THE CLOSING OF THE AMERICAN MIND* (1987)

4. Morality, thou deadly bane, / Thy tens o' thousands thou hast slain! / Vain is his hope, whose stay an' trust is / In moral mercy, truth, and justice!

ROBERT BURNS, "A DEDICATION TO GAVIN HAMILTON, ESQ." (1786)

5. Morality turns on whether the pleasure precedes or follows the pain.

SAMUEL BUTLER (D. 1902), "ELEMENTARY MORALITY," *NOTE-BOOKS* (1912)

6. Morality is the custom of one's country and the current feeling of one's peers.

SAMUEL BUTLER (D. 1902), "ELEMENTARY MORALITY," *NOTE-BOOKS* (1912)

7. The only absolute morality is absolute stagnation.

SAMUEL BUTLER (D. 1902), "CASH AND CREDIT," *NOTE-BOOKS* (1912)

8. If there is one thing worse than the modern weakening of major morals it is the modern strengthening of minor morals.

G. K. CHESTERTON, "ON LYING IN BED," *TREMENDOUS TRIFLES* (1909)

9. A man may not transgress the bounds of major morals, but may make errors in minor morals.

CONFUCIUS, *ANALECTS* (6TH C. B.C.), 19.11, TR. CH'U CHAI AND WINBERG CHAI

10. Too many moralists begin with a dislike of reality.

CLARENCE DAY, *THIS SIMIAN WORLD* (1920), 13

11. Every man takes care that his neighbor shall not cheat him. But a day comes when he begins to care that he do not cheat his neighbor. Then all goes well.

EMERSON, "WORSHIP," *THE CONDUCT OF LIFE* (1860)

12. How can we be scrupulous / In a life which, from birth onwards, is so determined / To wring us dry of any serenity at all?

CHRISTOPHER FRY, *THE FIRSTBORN* (1946), 3.1

13. The success of any great moral enterprise does not depend upon numbers.

WILLIAM LLOYD GARRISON, *LIFE* (1885–89), V. 3

14. He who defines his conduct by ethics imprisons his song-bird in a cage.

KAHLIL GIBRAN, "ON RELIGION," *THE PROPHET* (1923)

15. What is moral is what you feel good after and what is immoral is what you feel bad after.

ERNEST HEMINGWAY, *DEATH IN THE AFTERNOON* (1932), 1

16. Our system of morality is a body of imperfect social generalizations expressed in terms of emotion.

OLIVER WENDELL HOLMES, JR., "IDEALS AND DOUBTS," *ILLINOIS LAW REVIEW* (1915), V. 10

17. Morality is largely a matter of geography.

ELBERT HUBBARD, *THE PHILISTINE* (1895–1915)

18. There can be no final truth in ethics any more than in physics, until the last man has had his experience and said his say.

WILLIAM JAMES, "THE MORAL PHILOSOPHER AND THE MORAL LIFE," *THE WILL TO BELIEVE* (1896)

19. Be not too hasty to trust or to admire the teachers of morality: they discourse like angels, but they live like men.

SAMUEL JOHNSON, *RASSELAS* (1759), 18

20. Rhetoric takes no real account of the art in literature and morality takes no account of the art in life.

JOSEPH WOOD KRUTCH, "LIFE, ART, AND PEACE," *THE MODERN TEMPER* (1929)

21. Abstractions about right and wrong, whether they are as old as Thou Shalt Not Kill or as modern as Do Your Own Thing, often serve only to confuse and weaken genuine moral decision.

URSULA K. LE GUIN, "MORAL AND ETHICAL IMPLICATIONS," *DANCING AT THE EDGE OF THE WORLD* (1989)

22. Every man has his moral backside too, which he doesn't expose unnecessarily but keeps covered as long as possible by the trousers of decorum.

GEORG CHRISTOPH LICHTENBERG, *APHORISMS* (1764–99), TR. H. HATFIELD

23. The whole speculation about morality is an effort to find a way of living which men who live it will instinctively feel is good.

WALTER LIPPMANN, "SOME NECESSARY ICONOCLASM," *A PREFACE TO POLITICS* (1914)

24. There is nothing so bad but it can masquerade as moral.

WALTER LIPPMANN, "SOME NECESSARY ICONOCLASM," *A PREFACE TO POLITICS* (1914)

25. There cannot any one moral rule be proposed whereof a man may not justly demand a reason.

JOHN LOCKE, *AN ESSAY CONCERNING HUMAN UNDERSTANDING* (1690), 1.3.4

26. The difference between a moral man and a man of honor is that the latter regrets a discreditable act, even when it has worked and he has not been caught.

H. L. Mencken, *Prejudices: Fourth Series* (1924), 11

27. Sometimes I feel something akin to rage / At the corrupted morals of this age!

Molière, *The School for Husbands* (1661), 1.3, tr. Donald M. Frame

28. The essence of morality is the subjugation of nature in obedience to social needs.

John Morley, "Carlyle," *Critical Miscellanies* (1871–1908)

29. Social taboos are shy like virtue; once lost, there is no remedy.

Gunnar Myrdal, *Beyond the Welfare State* (1960)

30. Physical science will not console me for the ignorance of morality in the time of affliction. But the science of ethics will always console me for the ignorance of the physical sciences.

Pascal, *Pensées* (1670), 67, tr. W. F. Trotter

31. When reason and instinct are reconciled, there will be no higher appeal.

Jean-Philippe Rameau, *Observations sur notre instinct pour la musique et sur son principe* (1734)

32. Ethics is in origin the art of recommending to others the sacrifices required for co-operation with oneself.

Bertrand Russell, "On Scientific Method in Philosophy," *Mysticism and Logic* (1917)

33. Without civic morality communities perish; without personal morality their survival has no value.

Bertrand Russell, "Individual and Social Ethics," *Authority and the Individual* (1949)

34. Our virtues / Lie in th' interpretation of the time.

Shakespeare, *Coriolanus* (1607–08), 4.7.49

35. Morality consists of suspecting other people of not being legally married.

George Bernard Shaw, *The Doctor's Dilemma* (1913), 3

36. The great secret of morals is love.

Shelley, *A Defence of Poetry* (1821)

37. "It is written, better to be a fool all your days than for one hour to be evil. You are not a fool. They are the fools. For he who causes his neighbor to feel shame loses Paradise himself."

Isaac Bashevis Singer, "Gimpel the Fool," , tr. Saul Bellow, *Partisan Review* (1953)

38. We must never delude ourselves into thinking that physical power is a substitute for moral power, which is the true sign of national greatness.

Adlai Stevenson, speech, Hartford, Conn., Sept. 18, 1952

39. To make our morality centre on forbidden acts is to defile the imagination and to introduce into our judgments of our fellow-men a secret element of gusto.

Robert Louis Stevenson, *Across the Plains* (1892), 12

40. If your morals make you dreary, depend upon it, they are wrong.

Robert Louis Stevenson, *Across the Plains* (1892), 12

41. Our whole life is startlingly moral. There is never an instant's truce between virtue and vice.

Thoreau, "Higher Laws," *Walden* (1854)

42. It is not best that we use our morals week days; it gets them out of repair for Sundays.

Mark Twain, *Notebook* (1935)

43. Morals are an acquirement—like music, like a foreign language, like piety, poker, paralysis—no man is born with them.

Mark Twain, "Seventieth Birthday" (1910)

44. The moral sense enables one to perceive morality—and avoid it. The immoral sense enables one to perceive immorality and enjoy it.

Mark Twain, *Notebook* (1935)

45. Our errors and our controversies, in the sphere of morality, arise sometimes from looking on men as though they could be altogether bad, or altogether good.

Vauvenargues, *Reflections and Maxims* (1746), 31, tr. F. G. Stevens

46. All sects differ, because they come from men; morality is everywhere the same, because it comes from God.

Voltaire, "Theism," *Philosophical Dictionary* (1764)

47. Much of our adult morality, in books and out of them, has a stuffiness unworthy of childhood. Our grown-up conclusions often rest on perilously soft bottom.

E.B. White, *One Man's Meat* (1944)

48. As society is now constituted, a literal adherence to the moral precepts scattered throughout the Gospels would mean sudden death.

Alfred North Whitehead, *Adventures in Ideas* (1933), 2

49. A man who moralizes is usually a hypocrite, and a woman who moralizes is invariably plain.

OSCAR WILDE, *LADY WINDERMERE'S FAN* (1892), 3

50. Morality is simply the attitude we adopt towards people whom we personally dislike.

OSCAR WILDE, *AN IDEAL HUSBAND* (1895), 2

605. MORNING

See also 73. BED; 633. NIGHT; 906. SLEEP

1. It is only your habitual late riser who takes in the full flavor of Nature at those rare intervals when he gets up to go afishing. He brings virginal emotions and unsatiated eyes to the sparkling freshness of earth and stream and sky.

THOMAS BAILEY ALDRICH, "ASIDES: WRITERS AND TALKERS," *PONKAPOG PAPERS* (1903)

2. It was a splendid summer morning and it seemed as if nothing could go wrong.

JOHN CHEEVER, "THE COMMON DAY," *THE STORIES OF JOHN CHEEVER* (1980)

3. So far as I know, anything worth hearing is not usually uttered at seven o'clock in the morning; and if it is, it will generally be repeated at a more reasonable hour for a larger and more wakeful audience.

MOSS HART, *ACT ONE* (1959)

4. Oft when the white, still dawn / Lifted the skies and pushed the hills apart, / I have felt it like a glory in my heart.

EDWIN MARKHAM, "JOY OF THE MORNING" (1899)

5. For the mind disturbed, the still beauty of dawn is nature's finest balm.

EDWIN WAY TEALE, "APRIL 21," *CIRCLE OF THE SEASONS* (1953)

6. The long morning shadows lay as still and dark as lakes and patterned the rough ground with straight margins.

PAUL THEROUX, *THE OLD PATAGONIAN EXPRESS* (1979)

7. It is true, I never assisted the sun materially in his rising, but doubt not, it was of the last importance only to be present at it.

THOREAU, "ECONOMY," *WALDEN* (1854)

8. Only that day dawns to which we are awake. There is more day to dawn. The sun is but a morning star.

THOREAU, "CONCLUSION," *WALDEN* (1854)

9. Only dull people are brilliant at breakfast.

OSCAR WILDE, *AN IDEAL HUSBAND* (1895), 1

10. For what human ill does not dawn seem to be an alleviation?

THORNTON WILDER, *THE BRIDGE OF SAN LUIS REY* (1927), 3

606. MORTALITY

See also 221. DEATH; 454. IMMORTALITY; 990. TRANSIENCE

1. Most men eddy about / Here and there—eat and drink, / Chatter and love and hate, / Gather and squander, are raised / Aloft, are hurled in the dust, / Striving blindly, achieving / Nothing; and then they die— / Perish;—and no one asks / Who or what they have been.

MATTHEW ARNOLD, "RUGBY CHAPEL," *NEW POEMS* (1867)

2. To live, to have so much ambition, to suffer, to cry, to fight and, at the end, forgetfulness ... as if I had never existed.

MARIE BASHKIRTSEV, PREFACE TO *JOURNAL* (1887)

3. All flesh is grass, and all the goodliness thereof is as the flower of the field.

BIBLE, ISAIAH 40:6

4. Let us eat and drink; for tomorrow we shall die.

BIBLE, ISAIAH 22:13

5. What will die with me when I die, what pathetic or fragile form will the world lose?

JORGE LUIS BORGES, "PARABLES," IN *FIFTY GREAT ESSAYS* (1964)

6. The gay will laugh / When thou art gone, the solemn brood of care / Plod on, and each one as before will chase / His favourite phantom; yet all these shall leave / Their mirth and their employments, and shall come, / And make their bed with thee.

WILLIAM CULLEN BRYANT, "THANATOPSIS" (1811)

7. To venerate the simple days / Which lead the seasons by, / Needs but to remember / That from you or I / They may take the trifle / Termed mortality!

EMILY DICKINSON, POEM (C. 1858)

8. The fall of a leaf is a whisper to the living.

ENGLISH PROVERB

9. Such is the frailty of man that even where he makes the truest and most forcible impression—in the memory, in the heart of his beloved—, there also he must perish.

GOETHE, *THE SORROWS OF YOUNG WERTHER* (1774), 2, OCT. 26, 1772, TR. VICTOR LANGE

10. Come, for the House of Hope is built on sand: bring wine, for the fabric of life is as weak as the wind.

Hāfiz, ghazals from the *Divan* (14th c.), 12, tr. Justin Huntly McCarthy

11. Our brains are seventy-year clocks. The Angel of Life winds them up once for all, then closes the case, and gives the key into the hand of the Angel of the Resurrection.

Oliver Wendell Holmes, Sr., *The Autocrat of the Breakfast Table* (1858), 8

12. Art is long, and Time is fleeting, / And our hearts, though stout and brave, / Still, like muffled drums, are beating / Funeral marches to the grave.

Longfellow, "A Psalm of Life" (1839), 4

13. One thing is certain and the rest is Lies; / The Flower that once has blown for ever dies.

Omar Khayyám, *Rubáiyát* (11th–12th c.), tr. Edward FitzGerald, 4th

14. Mortality has its compensations: one is that all evils are transitory, another that better times may come.

George Santayana, *The Life of Reason: Reason in Common Sense* (1905–06), 12

15. Our life's a moment and less than a moment, but even this mite nature has mockingly humored with some appearance of a longer span.

Seneca, *Letters to Lucilius* (1st c.), 49.3, tr. E. Phillips Barker

16. We are such stuff / As dreams are made on, and our little life / Is rounded with a sleep.

Shakespeare, *The Tempest* (1611–12), 4.1.156

17. Old and young, we are all on our last cruise.

Robert Louis Stevenson, "Crabbed Age and Youth," *Virginibus Puerisque* (1881)

18. For all the compasses in the world, there's only one direction, and time is its only measure.

Tom Stoppard, *Rosencrantz & Guildenstern Are Dead* (1967), 2

19. Man comes and tills the field and lies beneath, / And after many a summer dies the swan.

Lord Tennyson, "Tithonus" (1860)

20. What fools men are to weep the dead and gone! / Unwept, youth drops its petals one by one.

Theognis (6th c. b.c.)

21. I've made a long voyage and been to a strange country, and I've seen the dark man very close; and I don't think I was too much afraid of him, but so much of mortality still clings to me—I wanted most desperately to live and still do.

Thomas Wolfe, *Editor to Author: The Letters of Maxwell Perkins* (1950), ed. John Hall Wheelock

607. MOTHERS

See also 670. Parenthood

1. Every beetle is a gazelle in the eyes of its mother.

Moorish Proverb

608. MOTIVES

See also 286. Ends; 771. Purpose

1. All that we do is done with an eye to something else.

Aristotle, *Nicomachean Ethics* (4th c. b.c.), 3.3, tr. J. A. K. Thomson

2. 'Tis e'er the wont of simple folk to prize the deed and o'erlook the motive, and of learned folk to discount the deed and lay open the soul of the doer.

John Barth, *The Sot-Weed Factor* (1960), 3.9

3. He advised people to have intellect, and to look beneath what he called "the epithelium of things," though he did discourage scrutiny of his own motives.

Peter De Vries, *Comfort Me With Apples* (1956)

4. A good intention clothes itself with sudden power. When a god wishes to ride, any chip or pebble will bud and shoot out winged feet, and serve him for a horse.

Emerson, "Fate," *The Conduct of Life* (1860)

5. The scientist seeking to advance the frontiers of his discipline, the missionary seeking to convert infidels to the true faith, the philanthropist seeking to bring comfort to the needy—all are pursuing their interests, as they see them, as they judge them by their own values.

Milton Friedman & Rose Friedman, *Free to Choose* (1980)

6. We should often feel ashamed of our best actions if the world could see all of the motives which produced them.

La Rochefoucauld, *Maxims* (1665), tr. Kenneth Pratt

7. Men can be stimulated by hope or driven by fear, but the hope and the fear must be vivid and immedi-

ate if they are to be effective without producing weariness.

BERTRAND RUSSELL, "TECHNIQUE AND HUMAN NATURE," *AUTHORITY AND THE INDIVIDUAL* (1949)

8. The Light of Lights / Looks always on the motive, not the deed, / The Shadow of Shadows on the deed alone.

WILLIAM BUTLER YEATS, *THE COUNTESS CATHLEEN* (1892), 5

609. MOUNTAINS

1. The influence of fine scenery, the presence of mountains, appeases our irritations and elevates our friendships.

EMERSON, "CULTURE," *THE CONDUCT OF LIFE* (1860)

2. Mountains are the beginning and the end of all natural scenery.

JOHN RUSKIN, *MODERN PAINTERS* (1843–60), V. 4, 5.20.1

3. Yonder were mountains: the sunlight revealed their tiny heads and wide shoulders, craggy and purple, with small black trees, delicate as eyelashes, on their slopes.

PAUL THEROUX, *THE OLD PATAGONIAN EXPRESS* (1979)

610. MOURNING

See also 103. BURIAL; 367. FUNERALS; 918. SORROW; 1052. WEEPING

1. Ah! surely Nothing dies but Something mourns!

BYRON, *DON JUAN* (1819–24), 3.108

2. Let mourning stop when one's grief is fully expressed.

CONFUCIUS, *ANALECTS* (6TH C. B.C.), 19.14, TR. CH'U CHAI AND WINBERG CHAI

3. The vastest earthly Day / Is shrunken small / By one Defaulting Face / Behind a Pall.

EMILY DICKINSON, POEM (C. 1874)

4. The dead sleep in their moonless night; my business is with the living.

EMERSON, *JOURNALS*, 1825

5. To weep excessively for the dead is to affront the living.

THOMAS FULLER, M.D., *GNOMOLOGIA* (1732), 5251

6. We who are left how shall we look again / Happily on the sun or feel the rain / Without remembering how they who went / Ungrudgingly and spent / Their lives for us loved, too, the sun and rain?

WILFRED WILSON GIBSON, "LAMENT" (1917?)

7. The sorrow for the dead is the only sorrow from which we refuse to be divorced.

WASHINGTON IRVING, "RURAL FUNERALS," *THE SKETCH BOOK OF GEOFFREY CRAYON, GENT.* (1819–20)

8. When we lose one we love, our bitterest tears are called forth by the memory of hours when we loved not enough.

MAURICE MAETERLINCK, *WISDOM AND DESTINY* (1898), 44, TR. ALFRED SUTRO

9. What we call mourning for our dead is perhaps not so much grief at not being able to call them back as it is grief at not being able to want to do so.

THOMAS MANN, *THE MAGIC MOUNTAIN* (1924), 7.8, TR. H. T. LOWE-PORTER

10. Not louder shrieks to pitying heaven are cast, / When husbands, or when lapdogs breathe their last.

ALEXANDER POPE, *THE RAPE OF THE LOCK* (1712), 3.157

11. Now let the weeping cease; / Let no one mourn again. / These things are in the hands of God.

SOPHOCLES, *OEDIPUS AT COLONUS* (401 B.C.), TR. ROBERT FITZGERALD

12. None mourn more ostentatiously than those who most rejoice at it [a death].

TACITUS, *ANNALS* (A.D. 115–117?), 2.78, TR. ALFRED J. CHURCH AND WILLIAM J. BRODRIBB

13. One friend dies and we remain indifferent; another dies, perhaps less intimate, and we see ourselves as dead, and weep, mourn, tear our hair or find ourselves caught up in the madness of the wake, competing with others as to who was closest, now suffers most.

FAY WELDON, *REMEMBER ME* (1976)

611. MOVIES

See also 421. HOLLYWOOD; 576. MEDIA

1. In the world of movie personalities the distance between popularity and politics is short.

SHIRLEY TEMPLE BLACK, *CHILD STAR* (1988)

2. The tragedy of film history is that it is fabricated, falsified, by the very people who make film history.

LOUISE BROOKS, "THE OTHER FACE OF W. C. FIELDS," *LULU IN HOLLYWOOD* (1982)

3. "Clutch your chest. Fall off that horse," they directed. That was it. Death was the extent of Indian acting in the movie theater.

LOUISE ERDRICH, "THE PLUNGE OF THE BRAVE," *LOVE MEDICINE* (1984)

4. A wide screen just makes a bad film twice as bad.

Samuel Goldwyn, *Quote,* Sept. 9, 1956

5. The stultifying effect of the movies is *not* that the children see them but that their parents do, as if Hollywood provided a plausible adult recreation to grow up into.

Paul Goodman, *Growing Up Absurd* (1960), 4.4

6. Since films and television have staged everything imaginable before it happens, a true event, taking place in the real world, brings to mind the landscape of films.

Elizabeth Hardwick, "The Apotheosis of Martin Luther King," *Bartleby in Manhattan* (1983)

7. A film is a boat which is always on the point of sinking—it always tends to break up as you go along and drag you under with it.

François Truffaut, interview in Peter Graham's *The New Wave* (1968)

8. Movies are, like sharp sunlight, merciless; we do not imagine, we view.

John Updike, "Being on TV—II," *Odd Jobs* (1991)

9. All Americans born between 1890 and 1945 wanted to be movie stars.

Gore Vidal, *The Second American Revolution and Other Essays* (1982)

612. THE MUNDANE

See also 333. Familiarity; 996. Trifles; 1012. Unimportance

1. There is health in table talk and nursery play. We must wear old shoes and have aunts and cousins.

Emerson, *Journals,* 1836

2. That which one cannot experience in daily life is not true for oneself.

D. H. Lawrence, *The Rainbow* (1915), 11

3. Not to know at large of things remote / From use, obscure and subtle, but to know / That which before us lies in daily life, / Is the prime wisdom.

Milton, *Paradise Lost* (1667), 8.191

4. 'Tis the taste of effeminacy that disrelishes ordinary and accustomed things.

Montaigne, "Of experience," *Essays* (1580–88), tr. W. C. Hazlitt

5. A mind too proud to unbend over the small ridiculosa of life is as painful as a library with no trash in it.

Christopher Morley, *Inward Ho!* (1923), 14

6. Commonplaces are the tramways of intellectual transportation.

José Ortega y Gasset, *The Revolt of the Masses* (1930), 14

7. Objects which are usually the motives of our travels by land and by sea are often overlooked and neglected if they lie under our eye.

Pliny the Younger, *Letters* (c. 97–110), 8.20.1, tr. William Melmoth

8. If your daily life seems poor, do not blame it; blame yourself, tell yourself that you are not poet enough to call forth its riches.

Rainer Maria Rilke, *Letters to a Young Poet,* Feb. 17, 1903, tr. M. D. Herter Norton

9. Most people become bankrupt through having invested too heavily in the prose of life.

Oscar Wilde, *The Picture of Dorian Gray* (1891), 4

10. The commonest thing is delightful if one only hides it.

Oscar Wilde, *The Picture of Dorian Gray* (1891), 1

MURDER

See 518. Killing

613. MUSEUMS

1. Each living art object, taken out of its native habitat so we can conveniently gaze at it, is like an animal in a zoo. Something about it has died in the removal.

Daniel J. Boorstin, *The Image* (1962), 3.4

2. I seldom ... go into a natural history museum without feeling as if I were attending a funeral.

John Burroughs, *Indoor Studies* (1889)

3. The Museum is not meant either for the wanderer to see by accident or for the pilgrim to see with awe. It is meant for the mere slave of a routine of self-education to stuff himself with every sort of incongruous intellectual food in one indigestible meal.

G. K. Chesterton, "On Sightseeing," *All Is Grist* (1931)

614. MUSIC

See also 615. Musical Instruments; 655. Opera; 902. Singing

1. Nothing is capable of being well set to music that is not nonsense.

Joseph Addison, *The Spectator,* March 21, 1711

2. A verbal art like poetry is reflective; it stops to think. Music is immediate, it goes on to become.

W. H. AUDEN, "NOTES ON MUSIC AND OPERA," *THE DYER'S HAND* (1962)

3. The most exciting rhythms seem unexpected and complex, the most beautiful melodies simple and inevitable.

W. H. AUDEN, "NOTES ON MUSIC AND OPERA," *THE DYER'S HAND* (1962)

4. Whether the angels play only Bach in praising God I am not quite sure; I am sure, however, that *en famille* they play Mozart.

KARL BARTH, QUOTED IN HIS OBITUARY, *THE NEW YORK TIMES,* DEC. 11, 1968

5. The piano is the social instrument par excellence. It is drawing-room furniture, a sign of bourgeois prosperity, the most massive of the devices by which the young are tortured in the name of education, and the grown-up in the name of entertainment.

JACQUES BARZUN, "MEN, WOMEN, AND PIANOS," *CRITICAL QUESTIONS* (1982)

6. Composers should write tunes that chauffeurs and errand boys can whistle.

SIR THOMAS BEECHAM, *THE NEW YORK TIMES,* MARCH 9, 1961

7. Even experimental composers, revolutionary composers, self-styled radicals are, in writing revolutionary music, recognizing the music that preceded them precisely by trying to avoid it.

LEONARD BERNSTEIN, "SOMETHING TO SAY...," *THE INFINITE VARIETY OF MUSIC* (1962)

8. Nothing is more singular about this generation than its addiction to music.

ALLAN BLOOM, "MUSIC," *THE CLOSING OF THE AMERICAN MIND* (1987)

9. Classical music is now a special taste, like the Greek language or pre-Columbian archeology, not a common culture of reciprocal communication and psychological shorthand.

ALLAN BLOOM, *THE CLOSING OF THE AMERICAN MIND* (1987)

10. Rock gives children, on a silver platter, with all the public authority of the entertainment industry, everything their parents always used to tell them they had to wait for until they grew up and would understand later.

ALLAN BLOOM, *THE CLOSING OF THE AMERICAN MIND* (1987)

11. Music is a part of us, and either ennobles or degrades our behavior.

BOETHIUS, *DE INSTITUTIONE MUSICA* (6TH C. A.D.)

12. Who hears music, feels his solitude / Peopled at once.

ROBERT BROWNING, *BALAUSTION'S ADVENTURE* (1871)

13. Many men are melancholy by hearing music, but it is a pleasing melancholy that it causeth; and therefore to such as are discontent, in woe, fear, sorrow, or dejected, it is a most present remedy.

ROBERT BURTON, *THE ANATOMY OF MELANCHOLY* (1621)

14. To know whether you are enjoying a piece of music or not you must see whether you find yourself looking at the advertisements of Pear's soap at the end of the program.

SAMUEL BUTLER (D. 1902), "UNPROFESSIONAL SERMONS," *NOTE-BOOKS* (1912)

15. Oh! there is an organ playing in the street—a waltz too! I must leave off to listen.

BYRON, *SELECTED LETTERS AND JOURNALS* (1982), ED. LESLIE A. MARCHAND

16. Music is edifying, for from time to time it sets the soul in operation.

JOHN CAGE, "FORERUNNERS OF MODERN MUSIC," *SILENCE* (1961)

17. Music is well said to be the speech of angels; in fact, nothing among the utterances allowed to man is felt to be so divine. It brings us near to the Infinite.

THOMAS CARLYLE, "THE OPERA" (1852)

18. Where there's music there can be no evil.

CERVANTES, *DON QUIXOTE* (1605–15), 2.4.34

19. Music has charms to soothe a savage breast—but not the unmusical one.

ALEXANDER CHASE, *PERSPECTIVES* (1966)

20. Music with dinner is an insult both to the cook and violinist.

G. K. CHESTERTON, QUOTED IN *THE NEW YORK TIMES,* NOV. 16, 1967

21. Music has charms to soothe a savage breast, / To soften rocks, or bend a knotted oak.

WILLIAM CONGREVE, *THE MOURNING BRIDE* (1697), 1.1

22. Civil disobeyers commit crimes fraught with drama; rappers commit drama fraught with crime.

MARK COSTELLO AND DAVID FOSTER WALLACE, *SIGNIFYING RAPPERS* (1990)

23. Rap is a fortress protected by twin moats of talk and technology.

MARK COSTELLO AND DAVID FOSTER WALLACE, *SIGNIFYING RAPPERS* (1990), P. 53

24. Rap, whether fecund or sterile, is today's pop music's lone cutting edge, the new, the unfamiliar, the brain-resisted-while-body-boogies.

MARK COSTELLO AND DAVID FOSTER WALLACE, *SIGNIFYING RAPPERS* (1990), P. 27

25. By making radically new use of old sounds, rap confounds intellectual property law as it confounds critics, sitcoms, heavy metal, Black Power, and whatever else it tosses in its blender, exposing a set of truths the music industry has kept nicely under wraps.

MARK COSTELLO, AND DAVID FOSTER WALLACE, *SIGNIFYING RAPPERS* (1990)

26. Music is my weapon. I believe in music, in its spirituality, its exaltation, its ecstatic nobility, its humor, its power to penetrate to the basic fineness of every human being.

HENRY COWELL, QUOTED IN *STEREO REVIEW*, DECEMBER 1974

27. Professional musicians sometimes like to give the impression that theirs is the best job of all in that they're being paid to do what they would be doing just for fun.

FRANCIS DAVIS, "HIS OWN JUKEBOX," *THE ATLANTIC MONTHLY*, OCTOBER 1994

28. Music is composed for people. People are not assembled merely to observe a musical ritual. But a conductor rules otherwise. So the audience behaves like the well-trained flunky that it is in the interpreter's presence.

OLIN DOWNES, *OLIN DOWNES ON MUSIC* (1957), ED. IRENE DOWNES

29. We constantly hear about the necessity of an open mind in listening to new music. Does it occur to many that an open mind is also a necessity with old music?

OLIN DOWNES, *OLIN DOWNES ON MUSIC* (1957), ED. IRENE DOWNES

30. As poetry is the harmony of words, so music is that of notes.

JOHN DRYDEN, DEDICATION TO PURCELL'S *THE PROPHETESS* (1690)

31. Music was invented to confirm human loneliness.

LAWRENCE DURRELL, *CLEA* (1960), 1.3

32. [Music] takes us out of the actual and whispers to us dim secrets that startle our wonder as to who we are, and for what, whence, and whereto.

EMERSON, *JOURNALS*, 1836

33. Music is nothing else but wild sounds civilized into time and tune.

THOMAS FULLER, D.D., *WORTHIES OF ENGLAND*, (1662), 10

34. A nation creates music—the composer only arranges it.

MIKHAIL GLINKA, QUOTED IN *THEATRE ARTS*, JUNE 1958

35. Schoenberg does not write against the piano, but neither can he be accused of writing for it.

GLENN GOULD, "THE PIANO MUSIC OF ARNOLD SCHOENBERG," *THE GLENN GOULD READER* (1984)

36. Take a music-bath once or twice a week for a few seasons, and you will find that it is to the soul what the water-bath is to the body.

OLIVER WENDELL HOLMES, SR., *OVER THE TEACUPS* (1891), 5

37. No one can get really drunk on a novel or a painting, but who can help getting drunk on Beethoven's Ninth, Bartok's Sonata for Two Pianos and Percussion, or the Beatles' White Album?

MILAN KUNDERA, *THE UNBEARABLE LIGHTNESS OF BEING* (1984)

38. And the night shall be filled with music, / And the cares that infest the day, / Shall fold their tents, like the Arabs, / And as silently steal away.

LONGFELLOW, "THE DAY IS DONE" (1844), 11

39. Music quickens time, she quickens us to the finest enjoyment of time.

THOMAS MANN, *THE MAGIC MOUNTAIN* (1924), 4.4, TR. H. T. LOWE-PORTER

40. A bad performance haunts the artist like a nightmare for days and days, and the memory of it is erased only by a good performance.

GERALD MOORE, *AM I TOO LOUD? A MUSICAL AUTOBIOGRAPHY* (1962)

41. You may read music as fluently as you read a newspaper, but it does not make an artist of you, and I count it just as clever to be a good stenographer.

GERALD MOORE, *AM I TOO LOUD? A MUSICAL AUTOBIOGRAPHY* (1962)

42. To produce music is also in a sense to produce children.

NIETZSCHE, *THE WILL TO POWER* (1888), 800, TR. ANTHONY M. LUDOVICI

43. Without music, life would be an error. The German imagines even God singing songs.

Nietzsche, "Maxims and Missiles," 33, *Twilight of the Idols* (1888), tr. Walter Kaufmann

44. Jazz may be thought of as a current that bubbled forth from a spring in the slums of New Orleans to become the main spring of the twentieth century.

Henry Pleasants, news summaries, Dec. 30, 1955

45. When I am not too sad to listen, music is my consolation.

Marcel Proust, *Letters of Marcel Proust* (1949), tr. Mina Curtiss

46. We must have recourse to the rules [of music] only when our genius and our ear seem to deny what we are seeking.

Jean-Philippe Rameau, *Le nouveau système de musique théorique* (1726)

47. What strange impulse is it which induces otherwise truthful people to say they like music when they do not, and thus expose themselves to hours of boredom?

Agnes Repplier, "The Idolatrous Dog," *Under Dispute* (1924)

48. [Of music]. Thou speakest to me of things which in all my endless life I have not found and shall not find.

Jean Paul Richter, quoted in Emerson's "Love," *Essays: First Series* (1841)

49. Why, after all, must everyone like music? That they are missing something is just the lover's opinion.

Ned Rorem, "Listening and Hearing," *Music from Inside Out* (1967)

50. Music is essentially useless, as life is.

George Santayana, *The Life of Reason: Reason in Art* (1905–06), 4

51. Music is a means of giving form to our inner feelings without attaching them to events or objects in the world.

George Santayana, *Little Essays* (1920), 54

52. The notes I handle no better than many pianists. But the pauses between the notes—ah, that is where the art resides!

Artur Schnabel, *Chicago Daily News,* June 11, 1958

53. The man that hath no music in himself, / Nor is not moved with concord of sweet sounds, / Is fit for treasons, stratagems, and spoils; / The motions of his spirit are dull as night, / And his affections dark as Erebus. / Let no such man be trusted.

Shakespeare, *The Merchant of Venice* (1596–97), 5.1.83

54. Music revives the recollections it would appease.

Mme de Staël, *Corinne* (1807), 9.2

55. When a man is not disposed to hear music, there is not a more disagreeable sound in harmony than that of the violin.

Richard Steele, *The Tatler,* April 1, 1710

56. The one true comment on a piece of music is another piece of music.

Igor Stravinsky, "Stravinsky on the Musical Scene and Other Matters," *The New York Review of Books* (May 12, 1966)

57. The performance of performance has developed to such an extent in recent years that it challenges the music itself and will soon threaten it with relegation.

Igor Stravinsky, "Stravinsky on the Musical Scene and Other Matters," *The New York Review of Books* (May 12, 1966)

58. The trouble with music appreciation in general is that people are taught to have too much respect for music; they should be taught to love it instead.

Igor Stravinsky, *The New York Times Magazine,* Sept. 27, 1964

59. Conductors must give unmistakable and suggestive signals to the orchestra—not choreography to the audience.

George Szell, *Newsweek,* Jan. 28, 1963

60. Men profess to be lovers of music, but for the most part they give no evidence in their opinions and lives that they have heard it. It would not leave them narrow-minded and bigoted.

Thoreau, *Journal,* Aug. 5, 1851

61. The harmony of a concert, to which you listen with delight, must have on certain classes of minute animals the effect of terrible thunder; perhaps it kills them.

Voltaire, "Appearance," *Philosophical Dictionary* (1764)

62. I mean jazz. I don't mean rock and roll. I mean the never-the-same-way-twice music the American black people gave the world.

Kurt Vonnegut, *Hocus Pocus* (1990)

63. There are songs that come free from the blue-eyed grass, from the dust of a thousand country roads.

Robert James Waller, *The Bridges of Madison County* (1992)

64. Muzak pervades Las Vegas from the time you walk into the airport upon landing to the last time you leave the casinos.

Tom Wolfe, *The Kandy-Kolored Tangerine-Flake Streamline Baby* (1965)

65. Believe it or not, there are places in the world where music is important. There are places in the world where all the arts are a matter of national pride.

Frank Zappa, *The Real Frank Zappa Book* (1989), with Peter Occhiogrosso

66. "Conducting" is when you draw "designs" in the nowhere—with a stick, or with your hands—which are interpreted as "instructional messages" by guys wearing bow ties who wish they were fishing.

Frank Zappa, *The Real Frank Zappa Book* (1989), with Peter Occhiogrosso

615. MUSICAL INSTRUMENTS

See also 614. Music

1. Accordion, n. An instrument in harmony with the sentiments of an assassin.

Ambrose Bierce, *The Devil's Dictionary* (1881–1911)

2. The cello is like a beautiful woman who has not grown older, but younger with time, more slender, more supple, more graceful.

Pablo Casals, *Time,* April 29, 1957

3. Violins are the lively, forward, importunate wits, that distinguish themselves by the flourishes of imagination, sharpness of repartee, glances of satire, and bear away the upper part in every consort.

Richard Steele, *The Tatler,* April 1, 1710

616. MYSTICISM

See also 278. Ecstasy; 927. Spirituality

1. Without mysticism man can achieve nothing great.

André Gide, *The Counterfeiters* (1925), 2.5, tr. Dorothy Bussy

2. Mysticism is, in essence, little more than a certain intensity and depth of feeling in regard to what is believed about the universe.

Bertrand Russell, title essay, *Mysticism and Logic* (1917)

3. Mystics always hope that science will some day overtake them.

Booth Tarkington, *Looking Forward to the Great Adventure* (1926)

617. MYTH

See also 449. Illusion

1. Myths are clues to the spiritual potentialities of the human life.

Joseph Campbell, *The Power of Myth* (1988)

2. The South is one of those kingdoms of the mind, like India or Scotland, that are neat and understandable only to people who have never been there.

Alistair Cooke, "Change in the Deep South," *America Observed: From the 1940s to the 1980s* 4(1988)

3. The American myth is of free will in its simple, primary sense. One can choose oneself and will oneself; and this absurdly optimistic assumption so dominates the republic that it has bred all its gross social injustices.

John Fowles, *Daniel Martin* (1977)

4. The tricky or boastful gods of ancient myths and primitive folk tales are characters of the same kind that turn up in Faulkner or Tennessee Williams.

Northrop Frye, *The Educated Imagination* (1964)

5. The great enemy of the truth is very often not the lie—deliberate, contrived and dishonest—but the myth—persistent, persuasive and unrealistic.

John F. Kennedy, commencement address, Yale University, New Haven, Conn., June 11, 1962

6. When myth meets myth, the collision is very real.

Stanislaw Lec, *Unkempt Thoughts* (1962), tr. Jacek Galazka

7. A false idea of Florence [Italy] grew up in the nineteenth century, thanks in great part to the Brownings and their readers—a tooled-leather idea of Florence as a dear bit of the old world.

Mary McCarthy, *The Stones of Florence* (1959)

8. Mythology is what grown-ups believe, folklore is what they tell the children, and religion is both.

Cedric Whitman, letter to Edward Tripp, Feb. 28, 1969

N

618. NAÏVETÉ

See also 202. CREDULITY; 447. IGNORANCE; 478. INNOCENCE

1. The greenhorn is the ultimate victor in everything; it is he that gets the most out of life.

G. K. CHESTERTON, "THE FAIRY PICKWICK," *A SHILLING FOR MY THOUGHTS* (1916)

2. The ignorance of the world leaves one at the mercy of its malice.

WILLIAM HAZLITT, "ON THE DISADVANTAGES OF INTELLECTUAL SUPERIORITY," *TABLE TALK* (1821–22)

3. I like peasants—they are not sophisticated enough to reason speciously.

MONTESQUIEU, *VARIÉTÉS*

4. They fall for the latest isms gullibly as pups for rubber bones.

DYLAN THOMAS, *QUITE EARLY ONE MORNING* (1954)

619. NAMES

See also 444. IDENTITY

1. For every man there is something in the vocabulary that would stick to him like a second skin. His enemies have only to find it.

AMBROSE BIERCE, "OLEAGINOUS," *THE DEVIL'S DICTIONARY* (1881–1911)

2. Names are but noise and smoke, / Obscuring heavenly light.

GOETHE, "MARTHA'S GARDEN," *FAUST: PART I* (1808), TR. PHILIP WAYNE

3. Of all eloquence a nickname is the most concise; of all arguments the most unanswerable.

WILLIAM HAZLITT, "ON NICKNAMES," *SKETCHES AND ESSAYS* (1839)

4. Great names abase, instead of elevating, those who do not know how to bear them.

LA ROCHEFOUCAULD, *MAXIMS* (1665), TR. KENNETH PRATT

5. The name of a man is a numbing blow from which he never recovers.

MARSHALL MCLUHAN, *UNDERSTANDING MEDIA* (1964), 2

6. Titles are but nicknames, and every nickname is a title.

THOMAS PAINE, *THE RIGHTS OF MAN* (1791), 1

7. "My first name is Esmé. I don't think I shall tell you my full name, for the moment. I have a title and you may just be impressed by titles. Americans are, you know."

J.D. SALINGER, "FOR ESMÉ—WITH LOVE AND SPLENDOR," IN *NINE STORIES BY J.D. SALINGER* (1953)

8. What's in a name? That which we call a rose / By any other name would smell as sweet.

SHAKESPEARE, *ROMEO AND JULIET* (1594–95), 2.2.43

9. It still may take some explaining, but many more women are keeping their *birth* names (and not calling them *maiden* names, with all the sexual double standard that implies).

GLORIA STEINEM, "WORDS AND CHANGE," *OUTRAGEOUS ACTS AND EVERYDAY REBELLIONS* (1983)

NARCISSISM

See 876. SELF-LOVE

620. NARROWNESS

See also 335. FANATICISM; 500. INTOLERANCE; 654. OPEN-MINDEDNESS; 726. PREJUDICES; 903. SINGLE-MINDEDNESS

1. Beware of the man of one book.

ST. THOMAS AQUINAS, QUOTED IN ISAAC D'ISRAELI'S *CURIOSITIES OF LITERATURE* (1791–93)

2. The most fatal illusion is the settled
point of view. Since life is growth and motion,
a fixed point of view kills anybody who has one.

BROOKS ATKINSON, "APRIL 29," *ONCE AROUND THE SUN* (1951)

3. It is as though nature must needs make men narrow in order to give them force.

W. E. B. DU BOIS, *THE SOULS OF BLACK FOLK* (1903), 3

4. There is no more certain sign of a narrow mind, of stupidity, and of arrogance, than to stand aloof from those who think differently from us.

Walter Savage Landor, "Marcus Tullius and Quinctus Cicero," *Imaginary Conversations* (1824–53)

5. He who knows only his own side of the case, knows little of that.

John Stuart Mill, *On Liberty* (1859), 2

6. The poverty of goods is easily cured; the poverty of the soul is irreparable.

Montaigne, "Of managing the will," *Essays* (1580–88), tr. W. C. Hazlitt

7. Blessed is the satirist; and blessed the ironist; blessed the witty scoffer, and blessed the sentimentalist; for each, having seen one spoke of the wheel, thinks to have seen all, and is content.

Christopher Morley, *Inward Ho!* (1923), 1

8. It is with narrow-souled people as with narrow-necked bottles: the less they have in them, the more noise they make in pouring it out.

Alexander Pope, *Thoughts on Various Subjects* (1727)

9. All living souls welcome whatsoever they are ready to cope with; all else they ignore, or pronounce to be monstrous and wrong, or deny to be possible.

George Santayana, *Dialogues in Limbo* (1925), 4

10. Narrow / The heart that loves, the brain that contemplates, / The life that wears, the spirit that creates / One object, and one form, and builds thereby / A sepulchre for its eternity.

Shelley, *Epipsychidion* (1821)

11. Minds that have nothing to confer / Find little to perceive.

William Wordsworth, "Yes! Thou Art Fair, Yet Be Not Moved" (1845)

621. NATION

See also 453. Immigration; 622. Nationalism; 678. Patriotism; 930. State

1. The ruin of a nation begins in the homes of its people.

Ashanti Proverb

2. We travel by plane, oftener than not, and yet the spirit of our country [United States of America] seems to have remained a country of railroads.

John Cheever, *Bullet Park* (1960)

3. A nation will not count the sacrifice it makes, if it supposes it is engaged in a struggle for its fame, its influence and its existence.

Benjamin Disraeli, speech, "Prosecution of War," May 24, 1855

4. The quality of the thought differences the Egyptian and the Roman, the Austrian and the American.

Emerson, "Fate," *The Conduct of Life* (1860)

5. There is a genius of a nation, which is not to be found in the numerical citizens, but which characterizes the society.

Emerson, "Nominalist and Realist," *Essays: Second Series* (1844)

6. The spirit of a nation is what counts—the look in its eyes.

Jean Giraudoux, *Electra* (1937), 2, tr. Peter H. Judd

7. Nothing is good for a nation but that which arises from its own core and its own general wants, without apish imitation of another.

Goethe, quoted in Johann Peter Eckermann's *Conversations with Goethe,* Jan. 24, 1824

8. Men may be linked in friendship. Nations are linked only by interests.

Rolf Hochhuth, *The Soldiers* (1967)

9. A nation without dregs and malcontents, is orderly, decent, peaceful and pleasant, but perhaps without the seed of things to come.

Eric Hoffer, *The True Believer* (1951), 2.4.18

10. Size is not grandeur, and territory does not make a nation.

Thomas Henry Huxley, "On University Education" (1876)

11. Every country should realize that its turn at world domination, domination because its rights coincided more or less with the character or progress of the epoch, must terminate with the change brought about by this progress.

Juan Ramón Jiménez, "Heroic Reason," *Selected Writings* (1957), tr. H. R. Hays

12. A nation reveals itself not only by the men it produces but also by the men it honors, the men it remembers.

John F. Kennedy, address, Amherst College, Mass., Oct. 26, 1963

13. A nation can be no stronger abroad than she is at home. Only an America which practices what it preaches about equal rights and social justice will be respected by those whose choice affects our future.

JOHN F. KENNEDY, UNDELIVERED ADDRESS, DALLAS, TEXAS, NOV. 22, 1963

14. We must recognize that every nation determines its policies in terms of its own interests.

JOHN F. KENNEDY, ADDRESS, MORMON TABERNACLE, SALT LAKE CITY, UTAH, SEPT. 26, 1963

15. A nation may be said to consist of its territory, its people, and its laws. The territory is the only part which is of certain durability.

ABRAHAM LINCOLN, MESSAGE TO CONGRESS, DEC. 1, 1862

16. It is in times of difficulty that great nations, like great men, display the whole energy of their character and become an object of admiration to posterity.

NAPOLEON I, *MAXIMS* (1804–15)

17. A nation usually renews its youth on a political sick-bed, and there finds again the spirit which it had gradually lost in seeking and maintaining power.

NIETZSCHE, *HUMAN, ALL TOO HUMAN* (1878), 464, TR. HELEN ZIMMERN

18. Nations, like individuals, have to limit their objectives, or take the consequences.

JAMES RESTON, *SKETCHES IN THE SAND* (1967)

19. The driving force of a nation lies in its spiritual purpose, made effective by free, tolerant but unremitting national will.

FRANKLIN D. ROOSEVELT, MESSAGE TO CONGRESS, APRIL 14, 1938

20. Every nation thinks its own madness normal and requisite; more passion and more fancy it calls folly, less it calls imbecility.

GEORGE SANTAYANA, *DIALOGUES IN LIMBO* (1925), 3

21. For total greed, rapacity, heartlessness, and irresponsibility there is nothing to match a nation.

LEWIS THOMAS, "THE IKS," *THE LIVES OF A CELL* (1974)

22. Growing nations should remember that, in nature, no tree, though placed in the best conditions of light, soil, and plot, can continue to grow and spread indefinitely.

PAUL VALÉRY, "GREATNESS AND DECADENCE OF EUROPE," *REFLECTIONS ON THE WORLD TODAY* (1931), TR. FRANCIS SCARFE

23. Energy in a nation is like sap in a tree; it rises from bottom up.

WOODROW WILSON, SPEECH, OCT. 28, 1912

24. We can afford to exercise the self-restraint of a really great nation which realizes its own strength and scorns to misuse it.

WOODROW WILSON, MESSAGE TO CONGRESS, AUG. 27, 1913

622. NATIONALISM

See also 498. INTERNATIONAL RELATIONS; 621. NATION; 678. PATRIOTISM

1. Patriotism is a lively sense of responsibility. Nationalism is a silly cock crowing on its own dunghill.

RICHARD ALDINGTON, *THE COLONEL'S DAUGHTER* (1931)

2. Nationalism is our form of incest, is our idolatry, is our insanity. "Patriotism" is its cult.

ERICH FROMM, *THE SANE SOCIETY* (1955), 3

3. Altogether, national hatred is something peculiar. You will always find it strongest and most violent where there is the lowest degree of culture.

GOETHE, QUOTED IN JOHANN PETER ECKERMANN'S *CONVERSATIONS WITH GOETHE*, MARCH 14, 1830

4. The efficiency of the truly national leader consists primarily in preventing the division of the attention of a people, and always in concentrating it on a single enemy.

ADOLF HITLER, *MEIN KAMPF* (1924), 1.3

5. The closer one gets to either the eastern or the southern fringe of the German-speaking world—the closer one gets, in other words, to the threatening and more numerous Slavs—the more insecure and dangerous nationalism becomes.

ROBERT D. KAPLAN, *BALKAN GHOSTS* (1993)

6. All nations have present, or past, or future reasons for thinking themselves incomparable.

PAUL VALÉRY, "EXTRANEOUS REMARKS," *SELECTED WRITINGS* (1964)

7. To wish the greatness of our own country is often to wish evil to our neighbors. He who could bring himself to wish that his country should always remain as it is, would be a citizen of the universe.

VOLTAIRE, "COUNTRY," *PHILOSOPHICAL DICTIONARY* (1764)

8. Nationalism has two fatal charms for its devotees: it presupposes local self-sufficiency, which is a pleasant and desirable condition, and it suggests, very sub-

tly, a certain personal superiority by reason of one's belonging to a place which is definable and familiar, as against a place which is strange, remote.

E. B. WHITE, "INTIMATIONS," *ONE MAN'S MEAT* (1944)

9. Nationalism is blamed for this century's wars, but nationalism need not mean militarism. And the nation-state has been the laboratory of liberty.

GEORGE F. WILL, "GORBACHEV, MEET JEFFERSON," *SUDDENLY: THE AMERICAN IDEA ABROAD AND AT HOME, 1986–1990* (1990)

623. NATURE

See also 177. CONSERVATION; 272. EARTH; 308. EVOLUTION; 352. FLOWERS; 415. THE HEAVENS; 431. HUMAN NATURE; 481. INSECTS; 486. INSTINCT; 603. MOON; 609. MOUNTAINS; 824. RIVERS; 853. SEA; 854. SEASONS; 911. SNOW; 950. SUN; 995. TREES; 1046. WATER; 1050. WEATHER; 1059. WIND

1. Nature, with equal mind, / Sees all her sons at play; / Sees man control the wind, / The wind sweep man away; / Allows the proudly-riding and the foundering bark.

MATTHEW ARNOLD, *EMPEDOCLES ON ETNA* (1852), 1.2

2. Nature is often hidden, sometimes overcome, seldom extinguished.

FRANCIS BACON, "OF NATURE IN MEN," *ESSAYS* (1625)

3. Nature, to be commanded, must be obeyed.

FRANCIS BACON, *NOVUM ORGANUM* (1620)

4. Into every empty corner, into all forgotten things and nooks, Nature struggles to pour life, pouring life into the dead, life into life itself.

HENRY BESTON, "LANTERN ON THE BEACH," *THE OUTERMOST HOUSE* (1928)

5. The three great elemental sounds in nature are the sound of rain, the sound of wind in a primeval wood, and the sound of outer ocean on a beach.

HENRY BESTON, "THE HEADLONG WAVE," *THE OUTERMOST HOUSE* (1928)

6. To see a World in a Grain of Sand / And a Heaven in a Wild Flower, / Hold Infinity in the palm of your hand / And Eternity in an hour.

WILLIAM BLAKE, "AUGURIES OF INNOCENCE" (1800–10)

7. Man is wise and constantly in quest of more wisdom; but the ultimate wisdom, which deals with beginnings, remains locked in a seed. There it lies, the simplest fact of the universe and at the same time the one which calls forth faith rather than reason.

HAL BORLAND, "THE CERTAINTY—APRIL 5," *SUNDIAL OF THE SEASONS* (1964)

8. You can't be suspicious of a tree, or accuse a bird or a squirrel of subversion or challenge the ideology of a violet.

HAL BORLAND, "SPRING IS FOR LAUGHTER—APRIL 13," *SUNDIAL OF THE SEASONS* (1964)

9. Man masters nature not by force but by understanding.

JACOB BRONOWSKI, "THE CREATIVE MIND," *SCIENCE AND HUMAN VALUES* (1956)

10. To him who in the love of Nature holds / Communion with her visible forms, she speaks / A various language.

WILLIAM CULLEN BRYANT, "THANATOPSIS" (1811)

11. Gie me ae spark o' Nature's fire, / That's a' the learning I desire.

ROBERT BURNS, "EPISTLE TO JOHN LAPRAIK NO. 1" (1786)

12. There is a pleasure in the pathless woods, / There is a rapture on the lonely shore / There is society, where none intrudes, / By the deep Sea, and Music in its roar: / I love not Man the less, but Nature more.

BYRON, *CHILDE HAROLD'S PILGRIMAGE* (1812–18), 4.178

13. I have never been happier, more exhilarated, at peace, rested, inspired, and aware of the grandeur of the universe and the greatness of God than when I find myself in a natural setting not much changed from the way He made it.

JIMMY CARTER, *AN OUTDOOR JOURNAL: ADVENTURES AND REFLECTIONS* (1988)

14. Like music and art, love of nature is a common language that can transcend political or social boundaries.

JIMMY CARTER, *AN OUTDOOR JOURNAL: ADVENTURES AND REFLECTIONS* (1988)

15. Modern nature-worship is all upside down. Trees and fields ought to be the ordinary things; terraces and temples ought to be extraordinary. I am on the side of the man who lives in the country and wants to go to London.

G. K. CHESTERTON, "THE SURRENDER OF A COCKNEY," *ALARMS AND DISCURSIONS* (1910)

16. The only words that ever satisfied me as describing Nature are the terms used in fairy books,

"charm," "spell," "enchantment." They express the arbitrariness of the fact and its mystery.

G. K. Chesterton, "The Logic of Elfland," *Orthodoxy* (1908)

17. I long for scenes, where man hath never trod, / A place where woman never smiled or wept- / There to abide with my Creator, God, / And Sleep as I in childhood sweetly slept, / Untroubling, and untroubled where I lie, / The grass below—above the vaulted sky.

John Clare, "I Am" (1845)

18. Nature is the art of God.

Dante, *On World Government* (c. 1313), 1.3

19. Although gravity is by far the weakest force of nature, its insidious and cumulative action serves to determine the ultimate fate not only of individual astronomical objects but of the entire cosmos. The same remorseless attraction that crushes a star operates on a much grander scale on the universe as a whole.

Paul Davies, *The Last Three Minutes* (1994)

20. The peace of nature and of the innocent creatures of God seems to be secure and deep, only so long as the presence of man and his restless and unquiet spirit are not there to trouble its sanctity.

Thomas de Quincey, "Preliminary Confessions," *Confessions of an English Opium-Eater* (1821–56)

21. Nature's silence is its one remark, and every flake of world is a chip off that old mute and immutable block.

Annie Dillard, "Teaching a Stone to Talk," *Teaching a Stone to Talk* (1982)

22. It has been said repeatedly that one can never, try as he will, get around to the front of the universe. Man is destined to see only its far side, to realize nature only in retreat.

Loren Eiseley, "The Innocent Fox," *The Star Thrower* (1978)

23. How cunningly nature hides every wrinkle of her inconceivable antiquity under roses and violets and morning dew!

Emerson, "The Progress of Culture," *Letters and Social Aims* (1876)

24. Nature is a mutable cloud which is always and never the same.

Emerson, "History," *Essays: First Series* (1841)

25. Nature is no spendthrift, but takes the shortest way to her ends.

Emerson, "Fate," *The Conduct of Life* (1860)

26. Nature is reckless of the individual. When she has points to carry, she carries them.

Emerson, "Culture," *The Conduct of Life* (1860)

27. When a man says to me, "I have the intensest love of nature," at once I know that he has none.

Emerson, *Journals*, 1857

28. Why should we fear to be crushed by savage elements, we who are made up of the same elements?

Emerson, "Fate," *The Conduct of Life* (1860)

29. Numbers, time, inches, feet. All are just ploys for cutting nature down to size.

Louise Erdrich, "The Good Tears," *Love Medicine* (1984)

30. And after reading Thoreau I felt how much I have lost by leaving nature out of my life.

F. Scott Fitzgerald, *The Crack-Up* (1945)

31. How nature loves the incomplete. She knows / If she drew a conclusion it would finish her.

Christopher Fry, *Venus Observed* (1950), 2.2

32. Forget not that the earth delights to feel your bare feet and the winds long to play with your hair.

Kahlil Gibran, "On Clothes," *The Prophet* (1923)

33. The true return to nature is the definitive return to the elements—death.

André Gide, "The Limits of Art," *Pretexts* (1903), tr. others

34. A plant is like a self-willed man, out of whom we can obtain all which we desire, if we will only treat him his own way.

Goethe, *Elective Affinities* (1809), 27

35. Nature goes her own way, and all that to us seems an exception is really according to order.

Goethe, quoted in Johann Peter Eckermann's *Conversations with Goethe*, Dec. 9, 1824

36. Bring out your social remedies! They will fail, they will fail, every one, until each man has his feet somewhere upon the soil.

David Grayson, *Adventures in Contentment* (1907), 6

37. Nature herself is not always unambiguous. Sometimes a girl child may have so well-developed a clitoris that it is assumed she is a boy. Likewise, many male children may be underdeveloped, or their genitals deformed or hidden and it is assumed that they are girls.

Germaine Greer, *The Female Eunuch* (1970)

38. People thought they could explain and conquer nature—yet the outcome is that they destroyed it and disinherited themselves from it.

Václav Havel, "Politics and Conscience," *Open Letters: Selected Writings 1965–1990* (1991) selected and edited by Paul Wilson

39. We do not see nature with our eyes, but with our understandings and our hearts.

William Hazlitt, "On Taste," *Sketches and Essays* (1839)

40. Deviation from Nature is deviation from happiness.

Samuel Johnson, *Rasselas* (1759), 22

41. Never does nature say one thing and wisdom another.

Juvenal, *Satires* (c. 100), 14.21

42. The roaring of the wind is my wife and the stars through the window pane are my children.

Keats, letter to George and Georgiana Keats, Oct. 14, 1818

43. Nature, in her blind thirst for life, has filled every possible cranny of the rotting earth with some sort of fantastic creature.

Joseph Wood Krutch, "The Genesis of a Mood," *The Modern Temper* (1929)

44. Nature takes no account of even the most reasonable of human excuses.

Joseph Wood Krutch, "The Paradox of Humanism," *The Modern Temper* (1929)

45. Only those within whose own consciousness the sun rise and set, the leaves burgeon and wither, can be said to be aware of what living is.

Joseph Wood Krutch, "March," *The Twelve Seasons* (1949)

46. Culture represents a novelty in the world of nature, and it could have added an effective, unifying edge to the forces of natural selection.

Richard Leakey, *The Origin of Humankind* (1994)

47. The visible marks of extraordinary wisdom and power appear so plainly in all the works of creation that a rational creature who will but seriously reflect on them cannot miss the discovery of a diety.

John Locke, *An Essay Concerning Human Understanding* (1690), 1.4.9

48. There is not so contemptible a plant or animal that does not confound the most enlarged understanding.

John Locke, *An Essay Concerning Human Understanding* (1690), 3.6.9

49. Thoreau gave an otherwise hidden passion and drew from woods and water the love affair with earth and sky he'd recorded in his journals.

Bernard Malamud, *Dubin's Lives* (1979)

50. The child of civilization, remote from wild nature and all her ways, is more susceptible to her grandeur than is her untutored son who has looked at her and lived close to her from childhood up, on terms of prosaic familiarity.

Thomas Mann, *The Magic Mountain* (1924), 6.7, tr. H. T. Lowe-Porter

51. What is too often forgotten is that nature obviously intends the botched to die, and that every interference with that benign process is full of dangers.

H. L. Mencken, "Chiropractic," *The Vintage Mencken* (1955)

52. God, I can push the grass apart / And lay my finger on Thy heart!

Edna St. Vincent Millay, title poem, *Renascence* (1917)

53. Accuse not Nature! she hath done her part; / Do thou but thine!

Milton, *Paradise Lost* (1667), 8.561

54. Nature is a gentle guide, but not more sweet and gentle than prudent and just.

Montaigne, "Of experience," *Essays* (1580–88), tr. W. C. Hazlitt

55. Nature, in her most dazzling aspects or stupendous parts, is but the background and theatre of the tragedy of man.

John Morley, "Byron," *Critical Miscellanies* (1871–1908)

56. Let children walk with Nature, let them see the beautiful blendings and communions of death and life, their joyous inseparable unity,... and they will learn that death is stingless indeed, and as beautiful as life, and that the grave has no victory, for it never fights.

John Muir, *A Thousand-Mile Walk to the Gulf* (1916), 4

57. Nature has some perfections to show that she is the image of God, and some defects to show that she is only His image.

PASCAL, *PENSÉES* (1670), 579, TR. W. F. TROTTER

58. Those honour Nature well, who teach that she can speak on everything, even on theology.

PASCAL, *PENSÉES* (1670), 29, TR. W. F. TROTTER

59. It were happy if we studied nature more in natural things, and acted according to nature, whose rules are few, plain, and most reasonable.

WILLIAM PENN, *SOME FRUITS OF SOLITUDE* (1693), 1.9

60. The day, water, sun, moon, night—I do not have to purchase these things with money.

PLAUTUS, *THE COMEDY OF ASSES* (3RD C. B.C.)

61. All nature is but art, unknown to thee; / All chance, direction, which thou canst not see; / All discord, harmony not understood; / All partial evil, universal good.

ALEXANDER POPE, *AN ESSAY ON MAN* (1733–34), 1.289

62. Nature's instructions are always slow, those of men are generally premature.

ROUSSEAU, *ÉMILE* (1762), 4

63. The works of nature first acquire a meaning in the commentaries they provoke.

GEORGE SANTAYANA, *LITTLE ESSAYS* (1920), 1

64. True wisdom consists in not departing from nature and in molding our conduct according to her laws and model.

SENECA, "ON A HAPPY LIFE," *MORAL ESSAYS* (1ST C.), TR. AUBREY STEWART

65. In nature two things do not occur—the wheel and good taste.

JOHN STEINBECK, *STEINBECK: A LIFE IN LETTERS*, EDS. ELAINE STEINBECK AND ROBERT WALLSTEN (1975)

66. In choosing where to live or vacation, we may be setting the stage for the play of ourselves, treating nature as prop.

DEBORAH TALL, "HERE," *FROM WHERE WE STAND* (1993)

67. Commonly we stride through the out-of-doors too swiftly to see more than the most obvious and prominent things. For observing nature, the best pace is a snail's pace.

EDWIN WAY TEALE, "JULY 14," *CIRCLE OF THE SEASONS* (1953)

68. In nature, there is less death and destruction than death and transmutation.

EDWIN WAY TEALE, "JULY 5," *CIRCLE OF THE SEASONS* (1953)

69. Nature is one with rapine, a harm no preacher can heal; / The Mayfly is torn by the swallow, the sparrow speared by the shrike, / And the whole little wood where I sit is a world of plunder and prey.

LORD TENNYSON, "MAUD; A MONODRAMA" (1856), 4.4

70. Man is embedded in nature.

LEWIS THOMAS, "THE LIVES OF A CELL," *THE LIVES OF A CELL* (1974)

71. It is the marriage of the soul with Nature that makes the intellect fruitful, and gives birth to imagination.

THOREAU, *JOURNAL*, AUG. 21, 1851

72. Nature refuses to sympathize with our sorrow. She seems not to have provided for, but by a thousand contrivances against, it.

THOREAU, *JOURNAL*, JULY 27, 1840

73. Nature will bear the closest inspection. She invites us to lay our eye level with her smallest leaf, and take an insect view of its plain.

THOREAU, *JOURNAL*, OCT. 22, 1839

74. We soon get through with Nature. She excites an expectation which she cannot satisfy. The merest child which has rambled into a copsewood dreams of a wildness so wild and strange and inexhaustible as Nature can never show him.

THOREAU, *JOURNAL*, MAY 23, 1854

75. We can never have enough of nature.

THOREAU, "SPRING," *WALDEN* (1854)

76. Nature is, in fact, a suggester of uneasiness, a promoter of pilgrimages and of excursions of the fancy which never come to any satisfactory haven.

CHARLES DUDLEY WARNER, "NINTH STUDY," *BACKLOG STUDIES* (1873)

77. Nature is entirely indifferent to any reform. She perpetuates a fault as persistently as a virtue.

CHARLES DUDLEY WARNER, "FIFTH STUDY," *BACKLOG STUDIES* (1873)

78. It is only now and then, in a jungle, or amidst the towering white menace of a burnt or burning Australian forest, that Nature strips the moral veils from vegetation and we apprehend its stark ferocity.

H. G. WELLS, *THE HAPPY TURNING* (1946), 33–34

79. I would feel more optimistic about a bright future for man if he spent less time proving that he can outwit Nature and more time tasting her sweetness and respecting her seniority.

E.B. White, "Coon Tree," *Essays of E. B. White* (1977)

80. The eye is pleased when nature stoops to art.

Richard Wilbur, "A Courtyard Thaw," *Ceremony* (1950)

81. A vacuum is a hell of a lot better than some of the stuff that nature replaces it with.

Tennessee Williams, *Cat on a Hot Tin Roof* (1955), 2

82. Come forth into the light of things, / Let Nature be your teacher.

William Wordsworth, "The Tables Turned" (1798)

83. I have learned / To look on nature, not as in the hour / Of thoughtless youth; but hearing oftentimes / The still, sad music of humanity.

William Wordsworth, "Lines Composed a Few Miles Above Tintern Abbey" (1798)

84. Nature never did betray / The heart that loved her.

William Wordsworth, "Lines Composed a Few Miles Above Tintern Abbey" (1798)

NAKEDNESS

See 642. Nudity

624. NECESSITY

See also 129. Circumstance; 240. Destiny; 340. Fate; 360. Fortune; 625. Need

1. Against necessity, / against its strength, no one can fight and win.

Aeschylus, *Prometheus Bound* (c. 478 B.C.), tr. David Grene

2. Hold it wise ... / To make a virtue of necessity.

Chaucer, "The Knight's Tale," *The Canterbury Tales* (c. 1387–1400), tr. Nevill Coghill

3. When they were on their uppers, she worked—first at the Steuben glass store, on Fifth Avenue, and then she went to Jensen's, where she got into trouble by insisting on her right to smoke.

John Cheever, "Just One More Time," *The Stories of John Cheever* (1980)

4. Necessity is an evil; but there is no necessity for continuing to live subject to necessity.

Epicurus, "Vatican Sayings" (3rd c. B.C.), 9, in *Letters, Principal Doctrines, and Vatican Sayings*, tr. Russel M. Geer

5. How base a thing it is / when a man will struggle with necessity! / We have to die.

Euripides, *Heracles* (c. 422 B.C.), tr. William Arrowsmith

6. Nothing has more strength than dire necessity.

Euripides, *Helen* (412 B.C.), tr. Richmond Lattimore

7. Necessity never made a good bargain.

Benjamin Franklin, *Poor Richard's Almanack* (1732–57)

8. Necessity is the theme and the inventress, the eternal curb and law of nature.

Leonardo Da Vinci, *Notebooks* (c. 1500), tr. Jean Paul Richter

9. There is no good in arguing with the inevitable. The only argument available with an east wind is to put on your overcoat.

James Russell Lowell, "Democracy," *Democracy and Other Addresses* (1887)

10. Necessity is not an established fact, but an interpretation.

Nietzsche, *The Will to Power* (1888), 552, tr. Anthony M. Ludovici

11. Necessity turns lion into fox.

Persian Proverb

12. Necessity is the argument of tyrants, it is the creed of slaves.

William Pitt the Younger, speech on the India Bill, November 1783

13. The true creator is necessity, who is the mother of our invention.

Plato, *The Republic* (4th c. B.C.), 2, tr. Benjamin Jowett

14. A wise man never refuses anything to necessity.

Publilius Syrus, *Moral Sayings* (1st c. B.C.), 540, tr. Darius Lyman

15. We give to necessity the praise of virtue.

Quintilian, *Institutio Oratoria* (c. A.D. 95), 1.8.14

16. What is necessary is never a risk.

Cardinal de Retz, *Mémoires* (1718)

17. Necessity relieves us from the embarrassment of choice.

Vauvenargues, *Reflections and Maxims* (1746), 592, tr. F. G. Stevens

625. NEED

See also 236. DEPRIVATION; 624. NECESSITY; 718. POVERTY

1. The finest poems of the world have been expedients to get bread.

EMERSON, *JOURNALS*, 1834

2. No living being is held by anything so strongly as by its own needs. Whatever therefore appears a hindrance to these, be it brother, or father, or child, or mistress, or friend, is hated, abhorred, execrated.

EPICTETUS, *DISCOURSES* (2ND C.), 2.22, TR. THOMAS W. HIGGINSON

3. That was the worst of being poor, you couldn't give the right things in sickness.

ELLEN GLASGOW, *VEIN OF IRON* (1935)

4. Want gave tongue, and, at her howl, / Sin awakened with a growl.

JAMES RUSSELL LOWELL, "THE GHOST SEER" (1845)

5. The constant demands of the heart and the belly can allow man only an incidental indulgence in the pleasures of the eye and the understanding.

GEORGE SANTAYANA, *LITTLE ESSAYS* (1920), 49

6. The greater part of humanity is too much harassed and fatigued by the struggle with want, to rally itself for a new and sterner struggle with error.

SCHILLER, *ON THE AESTHETIC EDUCATION OF MAN* (1795), 8, TR. REGINALD SNELL

7. Understanding human needs is half the job of meeting them.

ADLAI STEVENSON, SPEECH, COLUMBUS, OHIO, OCT. 3, 1952

NEGOTIATION

See 994. TREATIES

NEGROES

See 85. BLACKS

626. NEIGHBORS

1. Every man is the architect of his own fortunes, but the neighbors superintend the construction.

GEORGE ADE, "THE RISE AND FLIGHT OF THE WINGED INSECT," *HAND-MADE FABLES* (1920)

2. Thou shalt love thy neighbor as thyself.

BIBLE, LEVITICUS 19:18

3. Where life is fully and consciously lived in our own neighborhood, we are cushioned a little from the impact of great far-off events which should be of only marginal concern to us.

HUBERT BUTLER, "BESIDE THE NORE," IN *THE ART OF THE PERSONAL ESSAY* (1994), ED. PHILLIP LOPATE

4. Your next-door neighbour ... is not a man; he is an environment. He is the barking of a dog; he is the noise of a pianola; he is a dispute about a party wall; he is drains that are worse than yours, or roses that are better than yours.

G. K. CHESTERTON, "THE IRISHMAN," *THE USES OF DIVERSITY* (1920)

5. The correlative to loving our neighbors as ourselves is hating ourselves as we hate our neighbors.

OLIVER WENDELL HOLMES, SR., *THE PROFESSOR AT THE BREAKFAST TABLE* (1860), 11

6. People have discovered that they can fool the Devil; but they can't fool the neighbors.

EDGAR WATSON HOWE, *VENTURES IN COMMON SENSE* (1919), 3.34

7. Happiness puts on as many shapes as discontent, and there is nothing odder than the satisfaction of one's neighbor.

PHYLLIS MCGINLEY, "PIPELINE AND SINKER," *THE PROVINCE OF THE HEART* (1959)

8. Of the good things given / between man and man, I say that a neighbor, / true and loving in heart, to neighbor is a joy beyond / all things else.

PINDAR, *ODES* (5TH C. B.C.), NEMEA 7, TR. RICHMOND LATTIMORE

9. Where there are children, people become neighbors; they don't merely hold property adjacent to one another.

DIANA TRILLING, *MRS. HARRIS: THE DEATH OF THE SCARSDALE DOCTOR* (1981)

10. Each man is afraid of his neighbor's disapproval—a thing which, to the general run of the race, is more dreaded than wounds and death.

MARK TWAIN, "THE UNITED STATES OF LYNCHERDOM" (1923)

11. Mix with the neighbors, and you learn what's doing in your own house.

YIDDISH PROVERBS (1949)

NERVOUSNESS

See 43. ANXIETY; 343. FEAR; 627. NEUROSIS

627. NEUROSIS

See also 43. Anxiety; 163. Compulsiveness; 559. Madness; 651. Obsession; 757. Psychiatry; 758. Psychoanalysis; 842. Sanity; 866. Self-Destruction

1. What a curious creature is man! With what a variety of powers and faculties is he endued! Yet how easily is he disturbed and put out of order!

James Boswell, *London Journal,* March 22, 1763

2. The mistake which is commonly made about neurotics is to suppose that they are interesting. It is not interesting to be always unhappy, engrossed with oneself, ungrateful and malignant, and never quite in touch with reality.

Cyril Connolly, *The Unquiet Grave* (1945), 2

3. Oh the nerves, the nerves; the mysteries of this machine called man! Oh the little that unhinges it: poor creatures that we are!

Charles Dickens, "Third Quarter," *The Chimes* (1844)

4. There are characters which are continually creating collisions and nodes for themselves in dramas which nobody is prepared to act with them.

George Eliot, *Middlemarch* (1871–72), 19

5. The multitude of the sick shall not make us deny the existence of health.

Emerson, "Worship," *The Conduct of Life* (1860)

6. We may say that hysteria is a caricature of an artistic creation, a compulsion neurosis a caricature of a religion, and a paranoiac delusion a caricature of a philosophic system.

Sigmund Freud, *Totem and Taboo* (1918), tr. A. A. Brill

7. If you be sick, your own thoughts make you sick.

Ben Jonson, *Every Man in His Humour* (1598), 4.8

8. Has there ever been an age so rife with neurotic sensibility, with that state of near shudders, or near hysteria, or near nausea, much of it induced by trifles, which used to belong to people who were at once ill-adjusted and overcivilized?

Louis Kronenberger, "The Spirit of the Age," *Company Manners* (1954)

9. Modern neurosis began with the discoveries of Copernicus. Science made man feel small by showing him that the earth was not the center of the universe.

Mary McCarthy, "Tyranny of the Orgasm," *On the Contrary* (1961)

10. The "sensibility" claimed by neurotics is matched by their egotism; they cannot abide the flaunting by others of the sufferings to which they pay an ever increasing attention in themselves.

Marcel Proust, *Remembrance of Things Past: The Guermantes Way* (1913–27), tr. C. K. Scott-Moncrieff

11. We are all prone to the malady of the introvert, who, with the manifold spectacle of the world spread out before him, turns away and gazes only upon the emptiness within. But let us not imagine that there is anything grand about the introvert's unhappiness.

Bertrand Russell, *The Conquest of Happiness* (1930), 11

12. Living with golden fantasies of an endlessly nurtured infancy can be a neurotic refusal to grow up.

Judith Viorst, *Necessary Losses* (1986)

NEUTRALITY

See 455. Impartiality; 498. International Relations

628. NEW ENGLAND

1. The most serious charge which can be brought against New England is not Puritanism but February.

Joseph Wood Krutch, "February," *The Twelve Seasons* (1949)

2. The New England spirit does not seek solutions in a crowd; raw light and solitariness are less dreaded than welcomed as enhancers of our essential selves.

John Updike, "New England Churches," *Hugging the Shore* (1983)

NEWNESS

See 479. Innovation; 640. Novelty

629. NEWS

See also 630. Newspapers

1. What's wan man's news is another man's throubles.

Finley Peter Dunne, "The News of a Week," *Observations by Mr. Dooley* (1902)

2. News is history shot on the wing. The huntsmen from the Fourth Estate seek to bag only the peacock or the eagle of the swifting day.

Gene Fowler, *Skyline* (1961)

3. Nowadays truth is the greatest news.

Thomas Fuller, M.D., *Gnomologia* (1732), 3689

4. No news at 4:30 a.m. is good.

Lady Bird Johnson, *A White House Diary* (1970)

5. A reporter is always concerned with tomorrow. There's nothing tangible of yesterday. All I can say I've done is agitate the air ten or fifteen minutes and then boom—it's gone.

EDWARD R. MURROW, NEWS SUMMARIES, DEC. 31, 1955

6. If it's far away, it's news, but if it's close at home, it's sociology.

JAMES RESTON, *WALL STREET JOURNAL*, MAY 27, 1963

7. Give to a gracious message / An host of tongues, but let ill tidings tell / Themselves when they be felt.

SHAKESPEARE, *ANTONY AND CLEOPATRA* (1606–07), 2.5.86

8. Nobody likes the bringer of bad news.

SOPHOCLES, *ANTIGONE* (442–41 B.C.), TR. ELIZABETH WYCKOFF

9. To a philosopher all news, as it is called, is gossip, and they who edit and read it are old women over their tea.

THOREAU, "WHERE I LIVED, AND WHAT I LIVED FOR," *WALDEN* (1854)

10. By giving us the opinions of the uneducated, [journalism] keeps us in touch with the ignorance of the community.

OSCAR WILDE, *THE ARTIST AS CRITIC: CRITICAL WRITINGS OF OSCAR WILDE*, ED. RICHARD ELLMANN (1969)

11. Someday, before we all die, perhaps I shall get from home a letter in which all the news will be pleasant. I never have thus far.

THOMAS WOLFE, *THOMAS WOLFE'S LETTERS TO HIS MOTHER* (1943)

630. NEWSPAPERS

See also 364. FREE SPEECH; 576. MEDIA; 629. NEWS; 731. PRESS, FREEDOM OF THE; 764. PUBLISHING

1. Have you noticed that life, real honest-to-goodness life, with murders and catastrophes and fabulous inheritances, happens almost exclusively in the newspapers?

JEAN ANOUILH, *THE REHEARSAL* (1950), 2, TR. LUCIENNE HILL

2. A man doesn't amount to something because he has been successful at a third-rate career like journalism. It is evidence, that's all: evidence that if he buckled down and worked hard, he might some day do something really worth doing.

RUSSELL BAKER, *THE GOOD TIMES* (1989)

3. After two years studying what rewrite men did with the facts I phoned them, I knew that journalism was essentially a task of stringing together seamlessly an endless series of clichés.

RUSSELL BAKER, *GROWING UP* (1982)

4. Reporters thrive on the world's misfortune. For this reason they often take an indecent pleasure in events that dismay the rest of humanity.

RUSSELL BAKER, *THE GOOD TIMES* (1989)

5. Nowhere else can one find so miscellaneous, so various, an amount of knowledge as is contained in a good newspaper.

HENRY WARD BEECHER, *PROVERBS FROM PLYMOUTH PULPIT* (1887)

6. There was a time when the reader of an unexciting newspaper would remark, "How dull is the world today!" Nowadays he says, "What a dull newspaper!"

DANIEL J. BOORSTIN, *THE IMAGE* (1962), 1

7. At one time he was employed on one of the Yiddish dailies, but lost his job during a political campaign, when he refused to write two editorials advocating the election of two opposing candidates, both to appear in the same issue of the newspaper.

ABRAHAM CAHAN, *GRANDMA NEVER LIVED IN AMERICA* (1985), ED. MOSES RISCHIN

8. Do not, oh do not indulge such a wild idea that a newspaper might err! If so what have we to trust in this age of sham?

LEWIS CARROLL, *THE LETTERS OF LEWIS CARROLL*, ED. MORTON N. COHEN (1979)

9. Journalism is popular, but it is popular mainly as fiction. Life is one world, and life seen in the newspapers another.

G. K. CHESTERTON, "ON THE CRYPTIC AND THE ELLIPTIC," *ALL THINGS CONSIDERED* (1908)

10. That ephemeral sheet of paper, the newspaper, is the natural enemy of the book, as the whore is of the decent woman.

JULES DE GONCOURT, *JOURNAL*, JULY 1858, TR. ROBERT BALDICK

11. Newspapers are horror happening to other people.

NADINE GORDIMER, *A SPORT OF NATURE* (1987)

12. The man who never looks into a newspaper is better informed than he who reads them; inasmuch as he who knows nothing is nearer to truth than he whose mind is filled with falsehood and errors.

THOMAS JEFFERSON, LETTER TO JOHN NORVELL, JUNE 11, 1807

13. Were it left to me to decide whether we should have a government without newspapers, or newspapers without a government, I should not hesitate a moment to prefer the latter.

Thomas Jefferson, letter to Col. Edward Carrington, Jan. 16, 1787

14. It is the gossip columnist's business to write about what is none of his business.

Louis Kronenberger, "Fashions in Vulgarity," *The Cart and the Horse* (1964), 2

15. Newspapers always excite curiosity. No one ever lays one down without a feeling of disappointment.

Charles Lamb, "Detached Thoughts on Books and Reading," *Last Essays of Elia* (1833)

16. Journalism, like history, has no therapeutic value; it is better able to diagnose than to cure, and it provides society with a primitive means of psychoanalysis that allows the patient to judge the distance between fantasy and reality.

Lewis Lapham, *Imperial Masquerade* (1990)

17. The window to the world can be covered by a newspaper.

Stanislaw Lec, *Unkempt Thoughts* (1962), tr. Jacek Galazka

18. A politician wouldn't dream of being allowed to call a columnist the things a columnist is allowed to call a politician.

Max Lerner, "Love and Hate in Politics," *Actions and Passions* (1949)

19. People everywhere confuse / What they read in newspapers with news.

A. J. Liebling, "A Talkative Something or Other," *The New Yorker,* April 7, 1956

20. I take a grave view of the plight of the press. It is the weak slat under the bed of democracy.

A.J. Liebling, *The Press* (1961)

21. The function of the press in society is to inform, but its role is to make money.

A.J. Liebling, *The Press* (1961)

22. There is a healthy American newspaper tradition of not taking yourself seriously. It is the story you must take that way.... And if you do take yourself seriously, according to this sound convention, you are supposed to do your best not to let anyone else know about it. (Like bed-wetting.)

A.J. Liebling, *The Press* (1961)

23. One of the most valuable philosophical features of journalism is that it realizes that truth is not a solid but a fluid.

Christopher Morley, *Inward Ho!* (1923), 4

24. Surely the glory of journalism is its transience.

Malcolm Muggeridge, introduction to *The Most of Malcolm Muggeridge* (1966)

25. Four hostile newspapers are more to be feared than a thousand bayonets.

Napoleon I, *Maxims* (1804–15)

26. We live under a government of men and morning newspapers.

Wendell Phillips, speech, Jan. 28, 1852

27. One reads the papers as one wants to with a bandage over one's eyes without trying to understand the facts, listening to the soothing words of the editor as to the words of one's mistress.

Marcel Proust, *Remembrance of Things Past: The Past Recaptured* (1913–27), tr. Stephen Hudson

28. A newspaper column, like a fish, should be consumed when fresh; otherwise it is not only undigestible but unspeakable.

James Reston, *Sketches in the Sand* (1967)

29. The trouble with daily journalism is that you get so involved with "Who hit John?" that you never really know why John had his chin out in the first place.

Chalmers Roberts, *Newsweek,* Jan. 6, 1958

30. The hard-drinking newspaperman is, or used to be, a stock character of fiction. Now he is being phased out of literature just as he is being phased out of life.

Waverly Root, "The Pressure Mounts," *The Paris Edition* (1987)

31. In America journalism is apt to be regarded as an extension of history: in Britain, as an extension of conversation.

Anthony Sampson, *Anatomy of Britain* (1962)

32. A newspaper, not having to act on its descriptions and reports, but only to sell them to idly curious people, has nothing but honor to lose by inaccuracy and unveracity.

George Bernard Shaw, *The Doctor's Dilemma* (1913), 4

33. The journalistic vision sharpens to the point of maximum impact every event, every individual and social configuration; but the honing is uniform.

George Steiner, *Real Presences* (1989)

34. We [journalists] tell the public which way the cat is jumping. The public will take care of the cat.

Arthur Hays Sulzberger, *Time,* May 8, 1950

35. Don't forget that the only two things people read in a [news] story are the first and last sentences. Give them blood in the eye on the first one.

Herbert Bayard Swope, statement recalled in obituaries after his death on June 20, 1958

36. The First Duty of a newspaper is to be Accurate. If it be Accurate, it follows that it is Fair.

Herbert Bayard Swope, letter to *New York Herald Tribune,* March 16, 1958

37. How many beautiful trees gave their lives that today's scandal should, without delay, reach a million readers!

Edwin Way Teale, "March 13," *Circle of the Seasons* (1953)

38. [I]f you work in either journalism or politics...you will be flogged for being right and flogged for being wrong, and it hurts both ways—but it doesn't hurt as much when you're right.

Hunter S. Thompson, Introduction to *Generation of Swine* (1988)

39. In modern America, anyone who attempts to write satirically about the events of the day finds it difficult to concoct a situation so bizarre that it may not actually come to pass while his article is still on the presses.

Calvin Trillin, Introduction to *Uncivil Liberties* (1982)

40. You can never get all the facts from just one newspaper, and unless you have the facts, you cannot make proper judgments about what is going on.

Harry S Truman, *Mr. Citizen* (1960)

41. You should never form judgments from front page headlines. As with a contract, the fine print on the inside pages should be carefully studied.

Harry S Truman, *Mr. Citizen* (1960)

42. Journalism—an ability to meet the challenge of filling the space.

Rebecca West, *New York Herald Tribune,* April 22, 1956

631. THE NEW YEAR

1. Drop the last year into the silent limbo of the past. Let it go, for it was imperfect, and thank God that it can go.

Brooks Atkinson, "December 31," *Once Around the Sun* (1951)

2. Year's end is neither an end nor a beginning but a going on, with all the wisdom that experience can instill in us.

Hal Borland, "The Tomorrows—December 30," *Sundial of the Seasons* (1964)

3. Time has no divisions to mark its passage, there is never a thunder-storm or blare of trumpets to announce the beginning of a new month or year. Even when a new century begins it is only we mortals who ring bells and fire off pistols.

Thomas Mann, *The Magic Mountain* (1924), 5.4, tr. H. T. Lowe-Porter

4. Now the New Year reviving old Desires, / The thoughtful Soul to Solitude retires.

Omar Khayyám, *Rubáiyát* (11th–12th c.), tr. Edward FitzGerald, 4th ed., 4

5. Ring out the old, ring in the new, / Ring, happy bells, across the snow: / The year is going, let him go; / Ring out the false, ring in the true.

Lord Tennyson, "In Memoriam A. H. H." (1850), 106

632. NEW YORK

See also 131. Cities

1. New York was the glamorous town that you only see now in old movies and on Broadway stages. The sky was lit up with dancing neon signs. It was safe to walk out in the streets.

Art Buchwald, *Leaving Home: A Memoir* (1993)

2. All of this—the shared apartment in the Village, the illicit relationship, the Friday-night train to a country house—was what he had imagined life in New York to be, and he was intensely happy.

John Cheever, "Torch Song," *The Stories of John Cheever* (1980)

3. I was in love with New York. I do not mean "love" in any colloquial way, I mean that I was in love with the city, the way you love the first person who ever touches you and never love anyone quite that way again.

Joan Didion, "Goodbye to All That," in *The Art of the Personal Essay* (1994), ed. Phillip Lopate

4. It is often said that New York is a city for only the very rich and the very poor. It is less often said that New York is also, at least for those of us who came there from somewhere else, a city for only the very young.

Joan Didion, "Goodbye to All That," in *The Art of the Personal Essay* (1994), ed. Phillip Lopate

5. I lived in New York for a couple months. It seemed to me at first an incredibly clean place with well-dressed people and washed cars and bright-painted red-and-yellow streetcars and white buildings.

E.L. DOCTOROW, *LOON LAKE* (1980)

6. Nearly all th' most foolish people in th' country an' manny iv th' wisest goes to Noo York. Th' wise people ar-re there because th' foolish wint first. That's th' way th' wise men make a livin'.

FINLEY PETER DUNNE, "SOME POLITICAL OBSERVATIONS," *MR. DOOLEY'S OPINIONS* (1901)

7. Ernest [Hemingway] was always uneasy in New York and liked being there less than in any other city he frequented.

A.E. HOTCHNER, *PAPA HEMINGWAY* (1966)

8. He lives with his mother and sister in Brooklyn and next week he is bringing Mary Agnes Keely home—in the grand tradition. I expect a delicious kielbasa and a picture of Kosciuszko in the front room.

MAUREEN HOWARD, *BRIDGEPORT BUS* (1965)

9. [A]s long as what *is* is—and Georgia is Georgia—I will take Harlem for mine. At least, if trouble comes, I will have *my own window* to shoot from.

LANGSTON HUGHES, *SIMPLE SPEAKS HIS MIND* (1950)

10. Melting pot Harlem—Harlem of honey and chocolate and caramel and rum and vinegar and lemon and lime and gall. Dusky dream Harlem rumbling into a nightmare tunnel where the subway from the Bronx keeps right on downtown.

LANGSTON HUGHES, "IN LOVE WITH HARLEM," *FREEDOMWAYS,* SUMMER 1963

11. It is one of the sublime provincialities of New York that its inhabitants lap up trivial gossip about essential nobodies they've never set eyes on, while continuing to boast that they could live somewhere for twenty years without so much as exchanging pleasantries with their neighbors across the hall.

LOUIS KRONENBERGER, *COMPANY MANNERS* (1954), 2.2

12. The beauty of New York is unintentional; it arose independent of human design, like a stalagmite cavern.

MILAN KUNDERA, *THE UNBEARABLE LIGHTNESS OF BEING* (1984)

13. [New York] is the place where all the aspirations of the Western World meet to form one vast master aspiration, as powerful as the suction of a steam dredge. It is the icing on the pie called Christian civilization.

H. L. MENCKEN, *PREJUDICES: SIXTH SERIES* (1927), 9

14. Almost all the people I met in New York were trying to reduce.

SYLVIA PLATH, *THE BELL JAR* (1963)

15. When New Yorkers tell one about the dangers of their city, the muggings, the dinner parties to which no one turns up for fear of being attacked on the way, the traffic snarl-ups, the bland indifference of the city cops, they are unmistakably bragging.

JONATHAN RABAN, *SOFT CITY* (1974)

16. In all my years of New York cab riding I have yet to find the colorful, philosophical cabdriver that keeps popping up on the late movies.

JEAN SHEPHERD, "FUN CITY," *THE FERRARI IN THE BEDROOM* (1972)

17. Manhattan cabs are born old.

JEAN SHEPHERD, "FUN CITY," *THE FERRARI IN THE BEDROOM* (1972)

18. New York is a wonderful city.... It is going to be the capital of the world.

JOHN STEINBECK, *STEINBECK: A LIFE IN LETTERS,* EDS. ELAINE STEINBECK AND ROBERT WALLSTEN (1975)

19. The utter insanity of living in a place like this doesn't occur to the 9,000,000 people who inhabit New York. Except for visits I think I shall not be here any more as a resident.

JOHN STEINBECK, *STEINBECK: A LIFE IN LETTERS,* EDS. ELAINE STEINBECK AND ROBERT WALLSTEN (1975)

20. [New York] isn't like the rest of the country—it's like a nation itself—more tolerant than the rest in a curious way. Littleness gets swallowed up here. All the viciousness that makes other cities vicious is sucked up and absorbed in New York.

JOHN STEINBECK, *STEINBECK: A LIFE IN LETTERS,* EDS. ELAINE STEINBECK AND ROBERT WALLSTEN (1975)

21. New York is of course many cities, and an exile does not return to the one he left.

JOHN UPDIKE, "IS NEW YORK INHABITABLE?" *ODD JOBS* (1991)

22. This great city has fed my imagination—it has allowed me to dream.

THOMAS WOLFE, *THOMAS WOLFE'S LETTERS TO HIS MOTHER* (1943)

23. "Anyway, I don't want to live in New York. I want some place more like where we used to live in New Jersey. I don't like living here. There aren't any trees."

Tom Wolfe, *The Kandy-Kolored Tangerine-Flake Streamline Baby* (1965)

NICKNAMES

See 619. Names

633. NIGHT

See also 217. Darkness; 605. Morning; 906. Sleep

1. Learn to reverence night and to put away the vulgar fear of it, for, with the banishment of night from the experience of man, there vanishes as well a religious emotion, a poetic mood, which gives depth to the adventure of humanity.

Henry Beston, "Night on the Great Beach," *The Outermost House* (1928)

2. We of the age of the machines, having delivered ourselves of nocturnal enemies, now have a dislike of night itself. With lights and ever more lights, we drive the holiness and beauty of night back to the forests and the sea.

Henry Beston, "Night on the Great Beach," *The Outermost House* (1928)

3. The night / Shows stars and women in a better light.

Byron, *Don Juan* (1819–24), 2.152

4. You have to have spent the night at sea, sitting in a life raft and looking at your watch, to know that the night is immeasurably longer than the day.

Gabriel García Márquez, *The Story of a Shipwrecked Sailor* (1986)

5. To make ourselves invisible to creditors or to the envious, and even to our own worries, we can take advantage here on earth of a great democratic institution—in fact, democracy's only success—the night.

Jean Giraudoux, *Amphitryon 38* (1929), 1, tr. Peter H. Judd

6. It is awfully easy to be hard-boiled about everything in the daytime, but at night it is another thing.

Ernest Hemingway, *The Sun Also Rises* (1926)

7. The day is done, and the darkness / Falls from the wings of Night, / As a feather is wafted downward / From an eagle in his flight.

Longfellow, "The Day Is Done" (1844), 1

8. Night, when words fade and things come alive. When the destructive analysis of day is done, and all that is truly important becomes whole and sound again.

Saint-Exupéry, *Flight to Arras* (1942), 1, tr. Lewis Galantière

9. Night brings our troubles to the light, rather than banishes them.

Seneca, *Letters to Lucilius* (1st c.), 56.6

634. NIHILISM

1. To think is to say no.

Alain, *Le Citoyen contre les pouvoirs* (1925)

2. The Stars are setting and the Caravan / Starts for the Dawn of Nothing—Oh, make haste!

Omar Khayyám, *Rubáiyát* (11th–12th c.), tr. Edward FitzGerald, 1st ed., 38

635. NOBILITY

See also 491. Integrity; 952. Superiority

1. The nobler a man, the harder it is for him to suspect inferiority in others.

Cicero, *Ad Quintum Fratrem* (1st c. b.c.), 1

2. All that is noble is in itself of a quiet nature, and appears to sleep until it is aroused and summoned forth by contrast.

Goethe, quoted in Johann Peter Eckermann's *Conversations with Goethe,* April 1, 1827

3. Be noble! and the nobleness that lies / In other men, sleeping, but never dead, / Will rise in majesty to meet thine own.

James Russell Lowell, "Sonnet 4" (1840)

4. To be nobly wrong is more manly than to be meanly right.

Thomas Paine, *The American Crisis* (1776–83), 10

5. True nobility is exempt from fear.

Shakespeare, *2 Henry VI* (1590–91), 4.1.129

6. Put more trust in nobility of character than in an oath.

Solon, (7th–6th c. b.c.), quoted in Diogenes Laertius' *Lives and Opinions of Eminent Philosophers* (3rd c. a.d.), tr. R. D. Hicks

7. Let a man nobly live or nobly die.

Sophocles, *Ajax* (c. 447 b.c.), tr. John Moore

636. NOISE

1. The [Italian] air is in fact filled with so much noise that one must usually talk in a very loud voice to be understood, thereby increasing the total uproar. Lovers sometimes have to whisper "I love you" to each other in the tones of newsboys selling the afternoon paper.

LUIGI BARZINI, *THE ITALIANS* (1964)

2. Noise has one advantage. It drowns out words.

MILAN KUNDERA, *THE UNBEARABLE LIGHTNESS OF BEING* (1984)

3. All ideas advanced to deal with the Florentine noise problem, the Florentine traffic problem, are utopian, and nobody believes in them, just as nobody believed in Machiavelli's Prince, a utopian image of the ideally self-interested despot.

MARY MCCARTHY, *THE STONES OF FLORENCE* (1959)

4. Noise is the most impertinent of all forms of interruption.

SCHOPENHAUER, "ON NOISE," *PARERGA AND PARALIPOMENA* (1851), TR. T. BAILEY SAUNDERS

5. I have often lamented that we cannot close our ears with as much ease as we can our eyes.

RICHARD STEELE, *THE SPECTATOR* (1711–12), 148

6. Noise is evolving not only the endurers of noise but the needers of noise.

EDWIN WAY TEALE, *JOURNEY INTO SUMMER* (1960), 3

7. Nowadays most men lead lives of noisy desperation.

JAMES THURBER, "THE GRIZZLY AND THE GADGETS," *FURTHER FABLES FOR OUR TIME* (1956)

NONCONFORMITY

See 91. BOHEMIANS; 258. DISSENT; 468. INDIVIDUALISM; 469. INDIVIDUALITY

NONSENSE

See 881. SENSE AND NONSENSE

NONVIOLENCE

See 665. PACIFISM

637. NORMALITY

See also 171. CONFORMITY

1. The normal is what you find but rarely. The normal is an ideal. It is a picture that one fabricates of the average characteristics of men, and to find them all in a single man is hardly to be expected.

W. SOMERSET MAUGHAM, *THE SUMMING UP* (1938), 20

NOSE

See 326. FACE

638. NORTH AND SOUTH

1. I know no South, no North, no East, no West, to which I owe any allegiance. The Union, sir, is my country.

HENRY CLAY, SPEECH, U.S. SENATE, 1848

639. NOSTALGIA

See also 550. LOSS; 580. MEMORY; 676. PAST

1. I suddenly recall the arpeggios of laughter lilting across the tender, springtime grass—gay-welling, far-floating, fluent, spontaneous, a bell-like feminine fluting, then suppressed; as though snuffed swiftly and irrevocably beneath the quiet solemnity of the vespered air now vibrant with somber chapel bells.

RALPH ELLISON, *THE INVISIBLE MAN* (1952)

2. Her heart of compressed ash, which had resisted the most telling blows of daily reality without strain, fell apart with the first waves of nostalgia.

GABRIEL GARCÍA MÁRQUEZ, *ONE HUNDRED YEARS OF SOLITUDE* (1970)

3. Nostalgia is a dangerous emotion, both because it is powerless to act in the real world, and because it glides so easily into hatred and resentment against those who have taken our Eden from us.

CAROLYN G. HEILBRUN, *THE NEW YORK TIMES*, DEC. 25, 1992

4. For a long time he had wanted to express somehow that it was in his feet that he had the feeling of Russia, that he could touch and recognize all of her with his soles, as a blind man feels with his palms. And it was a pity when he reached the end of that stretch of rich brown earth and once again had to step along the resonant sidewalk.

VLADIMIR NABOKOV, *THE GIFT* (1963)

5. It is easy to recollect the good things of life, the times when one's heart rejoices and expands, when everything is enfolded in kindness and love; it is easy to recollect the fineness of life—how noble one was, how generous one felt, what courage one showed in the face of adversity.

OLIVER SACKS, *A LEG TO STAND ON* (1984)

6. We are so habitually nostalgic by now that we anticipate looking back in the midst of enjoyment, look forward to watching the videos we're taking of our children even as we make them.

DEBORAH TALL, "DWELLING," *FROM WHERE WE STAND* (1993)

7. The deeper the nostalgia and the more complete the fear, the purer, the richer the word and the secret.

ELIE WIESEL, *LEGENDS OF OUR TIMES* (1968)

NOVELS

See 344. FICTION

640. NOVELTY

See also 117. CHANGE; 338. FASHION; 479. INNOVATION; 502. INVENTION

1. There is no new thing under the sun.

BIBLE, ECCLESIASTES 1:9

2. Novelties *please* less than they *impress*.

BYRON, *DON JUAN* (1819–24), 12.69

3. The wise man, the sage, is hostile to the new. Disabused, he abdicates: that is his form of protest.

E.M. CIORAN, "SOME BLIND ALLEYS: A LETTER," IN THE ART OF THE PERSONAL ESSAY (1994), ED. PHILLIP LOPATE

4. Only God and some few rare geniuses can keep forging ahead into novelty.

DENIS DIDEROT, *RAMEAU'S NEPHEW* (1762), TR. RALPH H. BOWEN

5. A brand new mediocrity is thought more of than accustomed excellence.

BALTASAR GRACIÁN, *THE ART OF WORDLY WISDOM* (1647), 269, TR. JOSEPH JACOBS

6. We have learned so well how to absorb novelty that receptivity itself has turned into a kind of tradition—"the tradition of the new." Yesterday's avant-garde experiment is today's chic and tomorrow's cliché.

RICHARD HOFSTADTER, *ANTI-INTELLECTUALISM IN AMERICAN LIFE* (1963), 6.15

7. It is always the latest song that an audience applauds the most.

HOMER, *ODYSSEY* (9TH C. B.C.), 1, TR. E. V. RIEU

8. As soon as we are shown the existence of something old in a new thing, we are pacified.

NIETZSCHE, *THE WILL TO POWER* (1888), 551, TR. ANTHONY M. LUDOVICI

9. "What's new?" is an interesting and broadening eternal question, but one which, if pursued exclusively, results only in an endless parade of trivia and fashion, the silt of tomorrow.

ROBERT M. PIRSIG, *ZEN AND THE ART OF MOTORCYCLE MAINTENANCE* (1974)

NOVEMBER

See 854. SEASONS

641. NUCLEAR POWER

See also 956. SURVIVAL; 966. TECHNOLOGY; 1049. WEAPONS

1. [John F. Kennedy:] Above all, while defending our own vital interests, nuclear powers must avert those confrontations which bring down an adversary to the choice of either a humiliating retreat or a nuclear war.

ELIE ABEL, *THE MISSILE CRISIS* (1966)

2. Gods are born and die, but the atom endures.

ALEXANDER CHASE, *PERSPECTIVES* (1966)

3. No country without an atom bomb could properly consider itself independent.

CHARLES DE GAULLE, QUOTED IN *THE NEW YORK TIMES MAGAZINE,* MAY 12, 1968

4. The content of physics is the concern of physicists, its effect the concern of all men.

FRIEDRICH DÜRRENMATT, "21 POINTS," *THE PHYSICISTS* (1962), TR. JAMES KIRKUP

5. After the great destructions / Everyone will prove that he was innocent.

GÜNTER EICH, "THINK OF THIS" (1955), TR. VERNON WATKINS

6. At Hiroshima, on the bright clear morning of August 6, 1945, thousands were killed, more thousands were fatally injured, and the homes of a quarter million people were destroyed, within seconds of the falling of a single bomb.

MICHIHIKO HACHIYA, *HIROSHIMA DIARY,* TRANSLATOR'S FOREWORD (1955)

7. Scorching winds howled around us, whipping dust and ashes into our eyes and up our noses. Our mouths became dry, our throats raw and sore from the biting smoke pulled into our lungs. Coughing was uncontrollable.

MICHIHIKO HACHIYA, *HIROSHIMA DIARY* (1955)

8. [T]each us *all* to do right, Lord, *please*, and to get along together with that atom bomb on this earth—

because I do not want it to fall on me—nor Thee-nor anybody living. Amen!

LANGSTON HUGHES, *SIMPLE SPEAKS HIS MIND* (1950)

9. [T]he time is not far off when many nations in many parts of the world of many political shades and commitments will possess nuclear or even thermonuclear weapons.

JOHN F. KENNEDY, *THE STRATEGY OF PEACE* (1960)

10. We will not act prematurely or unnecessarily risk the costs of world-wide nuclear war in which even the fruits of victory would be ashes in our mouth. But neither will we shrink from that risk at any time it must be faced.

JOHN F. KENNEDY, TELEVISION ADDRESS OCT. 22, 1962

11. We have genuflected before the god of science only to find that it has given us the atomic bomb, producing fears and anxieties that science can never mitigate.

MARTIN LUTHER KING JR, *STRENGTH TO LOVE* (1963), 13.3

12. It is impossible, except for theologians, to conceive of a world-wide scandal or a universe-wide scandal; the proof of this is the way people have settled down to living with nuclear fission, radiation poisoning, hydrogen bombs, satellites, and space rockets.

MARY MCCARTHY, "THE FACT IS FICTION," *ON THE CONTRARY* (1961)

13. We are, to put it mildly, in a mess, and there is a strong chance that we shall have exterminated ourselves but the end of the century. Our only consolation will have to be that, as a species, we have had an exciting term of office.

DESMOND MORRIS, *THE NAKED APE* (1967), 5

14. Man has wrested from nature the power to make the world a desert or to make the deserts bloom. there is no evil in the atom; only in men's souls.

ADLAI STEVENSON, SPEECH, HARTFORD, CONN., SEPT. 18, 1952

15. The H-bomb rather favors small nations that doesn't as yet possess it; they feel slightly more free to jostle other nations, having discovered that a country can stick its tongue out quite far these days without provoking war, so horrible are war's consequences.

E. B. WHITE, "LETTER FROM THE EAST," *THE POINTS OF MY COMPASS* (1956)

16. The terror of the atom age is not the violence of the new power but the speed of man's adjustment to it-the speed of his acceptance. Already bombproofing is on approximately the same level as mothproofing.

E. B. WHITE, "NOTES ON OUR TIME," *THE SECOND TREE FROM THE CORNER* (1954)

642. NUDITY

See also 749. PROPRIETY; 756. PRUDERY; 893. SHAME

1. I saw them come out and I saw that they were naked, unshy, beautiful, and full of grace, and I watched the naked women walk out of the sea.

JOHN CHEEVER, "GOODBYE, MY BROTHER," *THE STORIES OF JOHN CHEEVER* (1980)

2. Man is the sole animal whose nudities offend his own companions, and the only one who, in his natural actions, withdraws and hides himself from his own kind.

MONTAIGNE, "APOLOGY FOR RAIMOND DE SEBONDE," *ESSAYS* (1580–88), TR. W. C. HAZLITT

O

643. OATHS

See also 743. PROMISES

1. It is not the oath that makes us believe the man, but the man the oath.

AESCHYLUS, *FRAGMENTS* (525–456 B.C.), 385, TR. M. H. MORGAN

2. Oaths are but words, and words but wind, / Too feeble implements to bind.

SAMUEL BUTLER (D. 1680), *HUDIBRAS* (1663), 2.2

644. OBEDIENCE

See also 61. AUTHORITY; 256. DISOBEDIENCE; 353. FOLLOWING; 531. LEADERSHIP

1. This free will business is a bit terrifying anyway. It's almost pleasanter to obey, and make the most of it.

UGO BETTI, *STRUGGLE TILL DAWN* (1949), 2, TR. G. H. MCWILLIAM

2. The height of ability in the least able consists in knowing how to submit to the good leadership of others.

LA ROCHEFOUCAULD, *MAXIMS* (1665), TR. KENNETH PRATT

3. It is right that what is just should be obeyed; it is necessary that what is strongest should be obeyed.

PASCAL, *PENSÉES* (1670), 298, TR. W. F. TROTTER

4. He who yields a prudent obedience, exercises a partial control.

PUBLILIUS SYRUS, *MORAL SAYINGS* (1ST C. B.C.), 752, TR. DARIUS LYMAN

5. The man who obeys is nearly always better than the man who commands.

ERNEST RENAN, "CERTITUDES," *DIALOGUES ET FRAGMENTS PHILOSOPHIQUES* (1876)

6. The man who does something under orders is not unhappy; he is unhappy who does something against his will.

SENECA, *LETTERS TO LUCILIUS* (1ST C.), 61.3

7. Obedience, / Bane of all genius, virtue, freedom, truth, / Makes slaves of men, and, of the human frame, / A mechanized automaton.

SHELLEY, *QUEEN MAB* (1813), 3

8. Learn to obey before you command.

SOLON (7TH–6TH C. B.C.), QUOTED IN DIOGENES LAERTIUS' *LIVES AND OPINIONS OF EMINENT PHILOSOPHERS* (3RD C. A.D.), TR. R. D. HICKS

645. OBESITY

1. If all the world were fat there would be no more wars.

ANONYMOUS, SIGN OVER ENTRANCE TO FAT MAN'S SHOP IN NEW YORK CITY

2. Count no matron happy until she hath passed thirty, and hath not waxed fat.

GELETT BURGESS, *THE MAXIMS OF METHUSELAH* (1907), 10

3. Imprisoned in every fat man a thin one is wildly signalling to be let out.

CYRIL CONNOLLY, *THE UNQUIET GRAVE* (1945), 2

4. The one way to get thin is to reestablish a purpose in life.

CYRIL CONNOLLY, *THE UNQUIET GRAVE* (1945), 1

5. More die in the United States of too much food than of too little.

JOHN KENNETH GALBRAITH, *THE AFFLUENT SOCIETY* (1958), 9.2

6. A fat man is never so happy as when he is describing himself as "robust."

GEORGE ORWELL, *KEEP THE ASPIDISTRA FLYING* (1936)

OBJECTIVITY

See 455. IMPARTIALITY

646. OBJECTS

See also 569. MATERIALISM

1. Inanimate objects are classified scientifically into three major categories—those that don't work, those that break down and those that get lost.

RUSSELL BAKER, "OBSERVER," *THE NEW YORK TIMES*, JUNE 18, 1968

2. The goal of all inanimate objects is to resist man and ultimately to defeat him.

RUSSELL BAKER, "OBSERVER," *THE NEW YORK TIMES*, JUNE 18, 1968

3. After inside upheavals, it is important to fix on imperturbable *things.* Their imperturbableness, their air that nothing has happened renews our guarantee.

ELIZABETH BOWEN, *THE DEATH OF THE HEART* (1938), 2.6

4. Things have their laws as well as men, and things refuse to be trifled with.

EMERSON, "POLITICS," *ESSAYS: SECOND SERIES* (1844)

5. We are the slaves of objects around us, and appear little or important according as these contract or give us room to expand.

GOETHE, QUOTED IN JOHANN PETER ECKERMANN'S *CONVERSATIONS WITH GOETHE,* SEPT. 11, 1828

6. You throw the ball, and three things can happen. Two of them are bad.

DARRELL ROYAL, *DARRELL ROYAL TALKS FOOTBALL* (1963)

7. The superior gratification derived from the use and contemplation of costly and supposedly beautiful products is, commonly, in great measure a gratification of our sense of costliness masquerading under the name of beauty.

THORSTEIN VEBLEN, *THE THEORY OF THE LEISURE CLASS* (1899), 6

8. All men feel an habitual gratitude, and something of an honourable bigotry, for the objects which have long continued to please them.

WILLIAM WORDSWORTH, PREFACE TO 2ND EDITION OF *LYRICAL BALLADS* (1800)

647. OBLIGATION

See also 222. DEBT; 271. DUTY; 384. GIFTS AND GIVING; 399. GRATITUDE; 475. INGRATITUDE; 787. RECEIVING

1. We cannot render benefits to those from whom we receive them, or only seldom. But the benefits we receive must be rendered again line for line, deed for deed to somebody.

EMERSON, *JOURNALS,* 1836

2. There are minds so impatient of inferiority that their gratitude is a species of revenge, and they return benefits, not because recompense is a pleasure, but because obligation is a pain.

SAMUEL JOHNSON, *THE RAMBLER,* JAN. 15, 1751

3. Pride does not wish to owe, and self-love does not wish to pay.

LA ROCHEFOUCAULD, *MAXIMS* (1665), TR. KENNETH PRATT

4. Too great an eagerness to discharge an obligation is a species of ingratitude.

LA ROCHEFOUCAULD, *MAXIMS* (1665), TR. KENNETH PRATT

5. We are nearer loving those who hate us than those who owe us more than we wish.

LA ROCHEFOUCAULD, *MAXIMS* (1665), TR. KENNETH PRATT

6. A refined nature is vexed by knowing that some one owes it thanks, a coarse nature by knowing that it owes thanks to some one.

NIETZSCHE, *HUMAN, ALL TOO HUMAN* (1878), 330, TR. HELEN ZIMMERN

7. Benefits received are a delight to us as long as we think we can requite them; when that possibility is far exceeded, they are repaid with hatred instead of gratitude.

TACITUS, *ANNALS* (A.D. 115–117?), 4.18, TR. WILLIAM J. BRODRIBB

8. The soil in return for her service / keeps the tree tied to her, / the sky asks nothing and leaves it free.

RABINDRANATH TAGORE, *FIREFLIES* (1928)

648. OBSCURANTISM

See also 149. COMMUNICATION

1. Untruth being unacceptable to the mind of man, there is no other defence left for absurdity but obscurity.

JOHN LOCKE, *AN ESSAY CONCERNING HUMAN UNDERSTANDING* (1690), 3.10.9

2. Sanity, soundness, and sincerity, of which gleams and strains can still be found in the human brain under powerful microscopes, flourish only in a culture of clarification, which is now becoming harder and harder to detect with the naked eye.

JAMES THURBER, "THE NEW VOCABULARIANISM," *LANTERNS AND LANCES* (1961)

3. Where misunderstanding serves others as an advantage, one is helpless to make oneself understood.

LIONEL TRILLING, "ART AND FORTUNE," *THE LIBERAL IMAGINATION* (1950)

649. OBSCURITY

See also 400. GREAT AND SMALL; 908. SMALLNESS; 1012. UNIMPORTANCE

1. Obscurity often brings safety.

AESOP, "THE TREE AND THE REED," *FABLES* (6TH C. B.C.?), TR. JOSEPH JACOBS

2. When the oak-tree is felled, the whole forest echoes with it; but a hundred acorns are planted silently by some unnoticed breeze.

THOMAS CARLYLE, "ON HISTORY" (1830)

3. That which comes into the world to disturb nothing deserves neither respect nor patience.

RENÉ CHAR, "TO THE HEALTH OF THE SERPENT," *LE POÈME PULVÉRISÉ* IN *HYPNOS WAKING* (1956), TR. OTHERS

4. Full many a flower is born to blush unseen, / And waste its sweetness on the desert air.

THOMAS GRAY, "ELEGY WRITTEN IN A COUNTRY CHURCHYARD" (1742?–50), 14

5. To be forgotten is to sleep in peace with the undisturbed myriads, no longer subject to the chills and heats, the blasts, the sleet, the dust, which assail in endless succession that shadow of a man which we call his reputation.

OLIVER WENDELL HOLMES, SR., *THE POET AT THE BREAKFAST TABLE* (1872), 6

6. He is happiest of whom the world says least, good or bad.

THOMAS JEFFERSON, LETTER TO JOHN ADAMS, 1786

7. Not a day passes over the earth, but men and women of no note do great deeds, speak great words and suffer noble sorrows.

CHARLES READE, *THE CLOISTER AND THE HEARTH* (1861), 1

8. It is better to be looked over than overlooked.

MAE WEST, *BELLE OF THE NINETIES* (1934)

650. OBSERVATION

See also 59. AUDIENCE; 219. DEADNESS, SPIRITUAL; 466. INDIFFERENCE; 683. PERCEPTION; 897. SIGHT

1. When we try to observe things that are very small, the act of observation itself will significantly disturb the state we are seeking to measure.

JOHN D. BARROW, *THE ORIGIN OF THE UNIVERSE* (1994)

2. Time, I thought, strips us rudely of the privileges of the bystander, and in the end that couple chatting loudly in bad French in the lobby of the Grande Bretagne (Athens) turns out to be us.

JOHN CHEEVER, "A VISION OF THE WORLD," *THE STORIES OF JOHN CHEEVER* (1978)

3. Cultivated men and women who do not skim the cream of life, and are attached to the duties, yet escape the harsher blows, make acute and balanced observers.

GEORGE MEREDITH, *AN ESSAY ON COMEDY* (1897)

4. A stander-by may sometimes, perhaps, see more of the game than he that plays it.

JONATHAN SWIFT, *A TRITICAL ESSAY UPON THE FACULTIES OF THE MIND* (1707)

5. Observation is an old man's memory.

JONATHAN SWIFT, *THOUGHTS ON VARIOUS SUBJECTS* (1711)

6. To become the spectator of one's own life is to escape the suffering of life.

OSCAR WILDE, *THE PICTURE OF DORIAN GRAY* (1891), 9

651. OBSESSION

See also 163. COMPULSIVENESS; 627. NEUROSIS

1. [W]hat necessity impels a writer who has produced fifty books to write still one more? Why this proliferation, this fear of being forgotten, this debased coquetry?

E.M. CIORAN, "SOME BLIND ALLEYS: A LETTER," IN *THE ART OF THE PERSONAL ESSAY* (1994), ED. PHILLIP LOPATE

652. OBSTINACY

See also 264. DOGMATISM; 350. FLEXIBILITY

1. Obstinacy / standing alone is the weakest of all things / in one whose mind is not possessed by wisdom.

AESCHYLUS, *PROMETHEUS BOUND* (C. 478 B.C.), TR. DAVID GRENE

2. No man is good for anything who has not some particle of obstinacy to use upon occasion.

HENRY WARD BEECHER, *PROVERBS FROM PLYMOUTH PULPIT* (1887)

3. An obstinacy's ne'er so stiff, / As when 'tis in a wrong belief.

SAMUEL BUTLER (D. 1680), *HUDIBRAS* (1663), 3.2

4. Obstinacy alone is not a virtue.

ALBERT CAMUS, "HOMAGE TO AN EXILE," *RESISTANCE, REBELLION, AND DEATH* (C. 1950)

5. The obstinacy of human beings is exceeded only by the obstinacy of inanimate objects.

ALEXANDER CHASE, *PERSPECTIVES* (1966)

6. A man will do more for his stubbornness than for his religion or his country.

EDGAR WATSON HOWE, *COUNTRY TOWN SAYINGS* (1911)

7. There are some men who turn a deaf ear to reason and good advice, and wilfully go wrong for fear of being controlled.

La Bruyère, *Characters* (1688), 4.71, tr. Henri Van Laun

8. Smallness of mind is the cause of stubbornness, and we do not credit readily what is beyond our view.

La Rochefoucauld, *Maxims* (1665), tr. Kenneth Pratt

9. Obstinacy and dogmatism are the surest signs of stupidity. Is there anything more confident, resolute, disdainful, grave and serious than an ass?

Montaigne, "Of the Art of Conference," *Essays* (1580–88)

10. Obstinacy is the sister of constancy, at least in vigor and stability.

Montaigne, "Defense of Seneca and Plutarch," *Essays* (1580–88), tr. W. C. Hazlitt

11. Stubbornness and stupidity are twins.

Sophocles, *Antigone* (442–41 B.C.), tr. Elizabeth Wyckoff

OCEAN

See 853. Sea

OCTOBER

See 854. Seasons

OFFENSE

See 476. Injury

653. OLD AGE

See also 226. Decline; 374. Generations; 540. Life, Stages of; 548. Longevity; 571. Maturity; 586. Middle Age; 813. Retirement; 1072. Youth and Age

1. Beyond age, leaf / withered, man goes three footed / no stronger than a child is, / a dream that falters in daylight.

Aeschylus, *Agamemnon* (458 B.C.), tr. Richmond Lattimore

2. Old men are always young enough to learn, with profit.

Aeschylus, *Agamemnon* (458 B.C.), tr. Richmond Lattimore

3. To keep the heart unwrinkled, to be hopeful, kindly, cheerful, reverent—that is to triumph over old age.

Thomas Bailey Aldrich, "Leaves from a Notebook," *Ponkapog Papers* (1903)

4. When you're forty, half of you belongs to the past—and when you are seventy, nearly all of you.

Jean Anouilh, *Time Remembered* (1939), 2.2, tr. Patricia Moyes

5. Age has a good mind and sorry shanks.

Pietro Aretino, letter to Bernardo Tasso, 1537, tr. Samuel Putnam

6. To me, old age is always fifteen years older than I am.

Bernard Baruch, news reports, Aug. 20, 1955

7. With the ancient is wisdom; and in length of days understanding.

Bible, Job 12:12

8. We ought not to heap reproaches on old age, seeing that we all hope to reach it.

Bion (2nd c. B.C.?), quoted in Diogenes Laertius' *Lives and Opinions of Eminent Philosophers* (3rd c. A.D.), tr. R. D. Hicks

9. Age doth not rectify, but incurvate our natures, turning bad dispositions into worser habits.

Sir Thomas Browne, *Religio Medici* (1642), 1

10. Grow old along with me! / The best is yet to be, / The last of life, for which the first was made: / Our times are in His hand / Who saith "A whole I planned, / Youth shows but half; trust God: see all nor be afraid!"

Robert Browning, "Rabbi Ben Ezra," *Dramatis Personae* (1864), 1

11. What is the worst of woes that wait on Age? / What stamps the wrinkle deeper on the brow? / To view each loved one blotted from Life's page, / And be alone on earth, as I am now.

Byron, *Childe Harold's Pilgrimage* (1812–18), 2.98

12. Years steal / Fire from the mind as vigour from the limb; / And Life's enchanted cup but sparkles near the brim.

Byron, *Childe Harold's Pilgrimage* (1812–18), 3.8

13. In looking back, I see nothing to regret and little to correct.

John C. Calhoun, quoted in Richard Hofstadter, *The American Political Tradition* (1948)

14. Old men when they begin to hear the last trumpet, on the morning breeze, often have a kind of absent-minded smile; like people listening. And their smiles are just politeness.

Joyce Cary, *The Horse's Mouth* (1944)

15. [A]n old man's memories, like his bones, grow sharp with age and show their true shapes.

JOYCE CARY, *TO BE A PILGRIM* (1942)

16. The heart never grows better by age; I fear rather worse, always harder.

LORD CHESTERFIELD, *LETTERS TO HIS SON,* MAY 17, 1750

17. No one is so old that he does not think he could live another year.

CICERO, *DE SENECTUTE* (44 B.C.)

18. Regrets are the natural property of grey hairs.

CHARLES DICKENS, *MARTIN CHUZZLEWIT* (1844), 10

19. When a man fell into his anecdotage it was a sign for him to retire from the world.

BENJAMIN DISRAELI, *LOTHAIR* (1870), 28

20. No spring, nor summer beauty hath such grace, / As I have seen in one autumnal face.

JOHN DONNE, ELEGY 9, "THE AUTUMNAL" (1635)

21. I grow old ... I grow old ... / I shall wear the bottoms of my trousers rolled.

T. S. ELIOT, "THE LOVE SONG OF J. ALFRED PRUFROCK" (1915)

22. As we grow old,... the beauty steals inward.

EMERSON, *JOURNALS,* 1845

23. We do not count a man's years until he has nothing else to count.

EMERSON, *JOURNALS,* 1840

24. Within, I do not find wrinkles and used heart, but unspent youth.

EMERSON, *JOURNALS,* 1864

25. Age is a bad traveling companion.

ENGLISH PROVERB

26. Alas, how right the ancient saying is: / We, who are old, are nothing else but noise / And shape. Like mimicries of dreams we go, / And have no wits, although we think us wise.

EURIPIDES, *AEOLUS* (BEFORE 423 B.C.)

27. Oftener than not the old are uncontrollable; / Their tempers make them difficult to deal with.

EURIPIDES, *ANDROMACHE* (C. 426 B.C.), TR. JOHN F. NIMS

28. Old age is not / a total misery. Experience helps.

EURIPIDES, *THE PHOENICIAN WOMEN* (C. 411–409 B.C.), TR. ELIZABETH WYCKOFF

29. Old men's prayers for death are lying prayers, in which they abuse old age and long extent of life. But when death draws near, not one is willing to die, and age no longer is a burden to them.

EURIPIDES, *ALCESTIS* (438 B.C.), 669, TR. M. H. MORGAN

30. The power of love itself weakens and gradually becomes lost with age, like all the other energies of man.

ANATOLE FRANCE, *THE CRIME OF SYLVESTRE BONNARD* (1881), 2, TR. LAFCADIO HEARN

31. An old goat is never the more reverend for his beard.

THOMAS FULLER, M.D., *GNOMOLOGIA* (1732), 646

32. Let others hail the rising sun: / I bow to that whose course is run.

DAVID GARRICK, "AN ODE ON THE DEATH OF MR. PELHAM" (1754)

33. An old man loved is winter with flowers.

GERMAN PROVERB

34. It is not becoming to lay to virtue the weariness of old age.

ANDRÉ GIDE, *JOURNALS,* JULY 25, 1934, TR. JUSTIN O'BRIEN

35. It's not that age brings childhood back again, / Age merely shows what children we remain.

GOETHE, "PRELUDE IN THE THEATRE," *FAUST: PART I* (1808), TR. PHILIP WAYNE

36. People always fancy that we must become old to become wise; but, in truth, as years advance, it is hard to keep ourselves as wise as we were.

GOETHE, QUOTED IN JOHANN PETER ECKERMANN'S *CONVERSATIONS WITH GOETHE,* FEB. 17, 1831

37. We must not take the faults of our youth into our old age, for old age brings with it its own defects.

GOETHE, QUOTED IN JOHANN PETER ECKERMANN'S *CONVERSATIONS WITH GOETHE,* AUGUST 16, 1824

38. Old age is wasted on the elderly: the young know what to do with it—insist on something different.

HERBERT GOLD, "ISRAEL," *BOHEMIA* (1993)

39. I love everything that's old: old friends, old times, old manners, old books, old wines.

OLIVER GOLDSMITH, *SHE STOOPS TO CONQUER* (1773), 1

40. Time goes by: reputation increases, ability declines.

DAG HAMMARSKJÖLD, "1945–1949: TOWARDS NEW SHORES—?" *MARKINGS* (1964), TR. W. H. AUDEN

41. I can't think of anything better to do with a life than to wear it out in efforts to be useful to the world.

ARMAND HAMMER, *HAMMER* (1987), WITH NEIL LYNDON

42. The private decision of real-estate developers to ring a city with carefully zoned, relatively expensive suburbs exacerbates racial tensions, segregates education on the basis of color and class, modifies the urban tax base and consequently the political order, and embitters the experience of old age for those who are left behind.

MICHAEL HARRINGTON, *THE ACCIDENTAL CENTURY* (1966)

43. Unto each man comes a day when his favorite sins all forsake him, / And he complacently thinks he has forsaken his sins.

JOHN HAY, "DISTICHS" (1871?), 11

44. As we grow old, our sense of the value of time becomes vivid. Nothing else, indeed, seems of any consequence.

WILLIAM HAZLITT, "ON THE FEELING OF IMMORTALITY IN YOUTH," *LITERARY REMAINS* (1836)

45. It may be made a question whether men grow wiser as they grow older, any more than they grow stronger or healthier or honester.

WILLIAM HAZLITT, "ON KNOWLEDGE OF THE WORLD," *SKETCHES AND ESSAYS* (1839)

46. We do not die wholly at our deaths: we have mouldered away gradually long before. Faculty after faculty, interest after interest, attachment after attachment disappear: we are torn from ourselves while living.

WILLIAM HAZLITT, "ON THE FEELING OF IMMORTALITY IN YOUTH," *LITERARY REMAINS* (1836)

47. Envy not the old man the tranquillity of his existence, nor yet blame him if it sometimes looks like apathy. Time, the inexorable, does not threaten him with the scythe so often as with the sand-bag. He does not cut, but he stuns and stupefies.

OLIVER WENDELL HOLMES, SR., *OVER THE TEACUPS* (1891), 2

48. Our years / Glide silently away. No tears, / No loving orisons repair / The wrinkled cheek, the whitening hair / That drop forgotten to the tomb.

HORACE, *ODES* (23–C. 15 B.C.), 2.14

49. How good we all are, in theory, to the old; and how in fact we wish them to wander off like old dogs, die without bothering us, and bury themselves.

EDGAR WATSON HOWE, *VENTURES IN COMMON SENSE* (1919), 18.2

50. The misery of a child is interesting to a mother, the misery of a young man is interesting to a young woman, the misery of an old man is interesting to nobody.

VICTOR HUGO, "SAINT DENIS," *LES MISÉRABLES* (1862), 9.3, TR. CHARLES E. WILBOUR

51. When grace is joined with wrinkles, it is adorable. There is an unspeakable dawn in happy old age.

VICTOR HUGO, "JEAN VALJEAN," *LES MISÉRABLES* (1862), 5.2, TR. CHARLES E. WILBOUR

52. Age is rarely despised but when it is contemptible.

SAMUEL JOHNSON, *THE RAMBLER* (1750–52), 50

53. Life is a country that the old have seen, and lived in. Those who have to travel through it can only learn the way from them.

JOSEPH JOUBERT, *PENSÉES* (1842), 6.32, TR. KATHARINE LYTTELTON

54. Old age deprives the intelligent man only of qualities useless to wisdom.

JOSEPH JOUBERT, *PENSÉES* (1842), 7.35

55. The brief span of our poor unhappy life to its final hour / Is hastening on; and while we drink and call for gay wreaths, / Perfumes, and young girls, old age creeps upon us, unperceived.

JUVENAL, *SATIRES* (C. 100), 9.126, TR. HUBERT CREEKMORE

56. I warmed both hands before the fire of life; / It sinks, and I am ready to depart.

WALTER SAVAGE LANDOR, "DYING SPEECH OF AN OLD PHILOSOPHER" (1849)

57. Few people know how to be old.

LA ROCHEFOUCAULD, *MAXIMS* (1665), TR. KENNETH PRATT

58. Old age is a tyrant who forbids, upon pain of death, all the pleasures of youth.

LA ROCHEFOUCAULD, *MAXIMS* (1665), TR. KENNETH PRATT

59. Old men like to give good advice in order to console themselves for not being any longer able to set bad examples.

LA ROCHEFOUCAULD, *MAXIMS* (1665), TR. KENNETH PRATT

60. Nature, with her customary beneficence, has ordained that man shall not learn how to live until the reasons for living are stolen from him, that he shall find no enjoyment until he has become incapable of vivid pleasure.

GIACOMO LEOPARDI, *PENSIERI* (1834–37), 79, TR. WILLIAM FENSE WEAVER

61. Age is opportunity no less / Than youth itself, though in another dress, / And as the evening twilight

fades away / The sky is filled with stars, invisible by day.

LONGFELLOW, *MORITURI SALUTAMUS* (1874)

62. Old age has its pleasures, which, though different, are not less than the pleasures of youth.

W. SOMERSET MAUGHAM, *THE SUMMING UP* (1938), 73

63. Growing old is no more than a bad habit which a busy man has no time to form.

ANDRÉ MAUROIS, QUOTED IN *THE AGING AMERICAN* (1961)

64. Old age is always wakeful; as if, the longer linked with life, the less man has to do with aught that looks like death.

HERMAN MELVILLE, *MOBY-DICK* (1851), 29

65. Wiser in relish, if sedate, / Come graybeards to their roses late.

HERMAN MELVILLE, "L'ENVOI," *WEEDS AND WILDINGS CHIEFLY: WITH A ROSE OR TWO* (1924)

66. Here's a song was never sung: / Growing old is dying young.

EDNA ST. VINCENT MILLAY, "TO A POET THAT DIED YOUNG," *SECOND APRIL* (1921)

67. 'Tis well for old age that it is always accompanied with want of perception, ignorance, and a facility of being deceived. For should we see how we are used and would not acquiesce, what would become of us?

MONTAIGNE, "OF THE AFFECTIONS OF FATHERS TO THEIR CHILDREN," *ESSAYS* (1580–88), TR. W. C. HAZLITT

68. Age imprints more wrinkles in the mind than it does on the face.

MONTAIGNE, "OF REPENTANCE," *ESSAYS* (1580–88), TR. W. C. HAZLITT

69. Senescence begins / And middle age ends / The day your descendents / Out-number your friends.

OGDEN NASH, "CROSSING THE BOARDER," *MARRIAGE LINES* (1964)

70. The old men know when an old man dies.

OGDEN NASH, "OLD MEN," *VERSES FROM 1929 ON* (1959)

71. Age's terms of peace, after the long interlude of war with life, have still to be concluded—Youth must keep decently away—so many old wounds may have to be unbound, and old scars pointed to with pride, to prove to ourselves we have been brave and noble.

EUGENE O'NEILL, *STRANGE INTERLUDE* (1928), 9

72. The old—like children—talk to themselves, for they have reached that hopeless wisdom of experience which knows that though one were to cry it in the streets to multitudes, or whisper it in the kiss to one's beloved, the only ears that can ever hear one's secret are one's own!

EUGENE O'NEILL, *LAZARUS LAUGHED* (1927), 4.1

73. When the roses are gone, nothing is left but the thorn.

OVID, *THE ART OF LOVE* (C. A.D. 8), 2, TR. ROLFE HUMPHRIES

74. Old age has a great sense of calm and freedom; when the passions relax their hold, then ... we are freed from the grasp not of one mad master only, but of many.

PLATO, *THE REPUBLIC* (4TH C. B.C.), 1, TR. BENJAMIN JOWETT

75. Old men, for the most part, are like old chronicles that give you dull but true accounts of times past, and are worth knowing only on that score.

ALEXANDER POPE, *THOUGHTS ON VARIOUS SUBJECTS* (1727)

76. Death laughs when old women frolic.

PUBLILIUS SYRUS, *MORAL SAYINGS* (1ST C. B.C.), 56, TR. DARIUS LYMAN

77. He has existed only, not lived, who lacks wisdom in old age.

PUBLILIUS SYRUS, *MORAL SAYINGS* (1ST C. B.C.), 55, TR. DARIUS LYMAN

78. Old men grasp more at life than babies, and leave it with a much worse grace than young people. It is because all their labours having been for this life, they perceive at last their trouble lost.

ROUSSEAU, *REVERIES OF A SOLITARY WALKER* (1782), 3

79. Old places and old persons in their turn, when spirit dwells in them, have an intrinsic vitality of which youth is incapable; precisely the balance and wisdom that comes from long perspectives and broad foundations.

GEORGE SANTAYANA, *PERSONS AND PLACES: MY HOST THE WORLD* (1953), 7

80. For inside all the weakness of old age, the spirit, God knows, is as mercurial as it ever was.

MAY SARTON, *KINDS OF LOVE* (1974)

81. Growing old is, of all things we experience, that which takes the most courage, and at a time when we have the least resources, especially with which to meet frustration.

MAY SARTON, "SUNDAY, AUGUST 3RD (ON GREENINGS ISLAND)," *THE HOUSE BY THE SEA: A JOURNAL* (1977)

82. It is, I assume, quite easy to wither into old age, and hard to grow into it.

MAY SARTON, "WEDNESDAY, NOVEMBER 20TH," *THE HOUSE BY THE SEA: A JOURNAL* (1977)

83. What does long life avail? The best seats at the funerals of friends.

DELMORE SCHWARTZ, QUOTED IN *THE NEW YORK TIMES*, OCT. 25, 1993

84. No one's so old that he mayn't with decency hope for one more day.

SENECA, *LETTERS TO LUCILIUS* (1ST C.), 12.6, TR. E. PHILLIPS BARKER

85. I wasted time, and now doth time waste me.

SHAKESPEARE, *RICHARD II* (1595–96), 5.5.49

86. Last scene of all, / That ends this strange eventful history, / Is second childishness and mere oblivion, / Sans teeth, sans eyes, sans taste, sans everything.

SHAKESPEARE, *AS YOU LIKE IT* (1599–1600), 2.7.163

87. What [Time] hath scanted men in hair, he hath given them in wit.

SHAKESPEARE, *THE COMEDY OF ERRORS* (1592–93), 2.2.81

88. When the age is in, the wit is out.

SHAKESPEARE, *MUCH ADO ABOUT NOTHING* (1598–99), 3.5.38

89. Growing old is not a gradual decline, but a series of drops, full of sorrow, from one ledge to another below it.

LOGAN PEARSALL SMITH, *AFTERTHOUGHTS* (1931), 2

90. The denunciation of the young is a necessary part of the hygiene of older people, and greatly assists the circulation of the blood.

LOGAN PEARSALL SMITH, *AFTERTHOUGHTS* (1931), 2

91. The mere process of growing old together will make our slightest acquaintances seem like bosom-friends.

LOGAN PEARSALL SMITH, *AFTERTHOUGHTS* (1931), 2

92. There are people who are beautiful in dilapidation, like old houses that were hideous when new.

LOGAN PEARSALL SMITH, *AFTERTHOUGHTS* (1931), 2

93. Nobody loves life like an old man.

SOPHOCLES, *ACRISIUS* (5TH C. B.C.), 63, TR. M. H. MORGAN

94. Being over seventy is like being engaged in a war. All our friends are going or gone and we survive amongst the dead and dying as on a battlefield.

MURIEL SPARK, *MEMENTO MORI* (1959)

95. Age in a virtuous person, of either sex, carries in it an authority which makes it preferable to all the pleasures of youth.

RICHARD STEELE, *THE SPECTATOR* (1711–12), 153

96. A kind of second childhood falls on so many men. They trade their violence for the promise of a small increase of life span. In effect, the head of the house becomes the youngest child.

JOHN STEINBECK, *TRAVELS WITH CHARLEY* (1962)

97. If a man lives to any considerable age, it can not be denied that he laments his imprudences, but I notice he often laments his youth a deal more bitterly and with a more genuine intonation.

ROBERT LOUIS STEVENSON, "CRABBED AGE AND YOUTH," *VIRGINIBUS PUERISQUE* (1881)

98. Old men and comets have been reverenced for the same reason: their long beards, and pretences to foretell events.

JONATHAN SWIFT, *THOUGHTS ON VARIOUS SUBJECTS* (1711)

99. It is the common vice of all, in old age, to be too intent upon our interests.

TERENCE, *THE BROTHERS* (160 B.C.), 5.8.30, TR. HENRY THOMAS RILEY

100. Medical science has oppressed us with a new huge burden of longevity. It is in that last undesired decade, when passion is cold, appetites feeble, curiosity dulled and experience has begotten cynicism, that accidia lies in wait as the final temptation to destruction.

EVELYN WAUGH, *SUNDAY TIMES* (LONDON), JANUARY 7, 1962

101. Drawn to childhood, the old man will seek it in a thousand different ways.

ELIE WIESEL, "MAKING THE GHOSTS SPEAK," *FROM THE KINGDOM OF MEMORY* (1990)

102. An aged man is but a paltry thing, / A tattered coat upon a stick, unless / Soul clap its hands and sing, and louder sing / For every tatter in its mortal dress.

WILLIAM BUTLER YEATS, "SAILING TO BYZANTIUM" (1928), 2

654. OPEN-MINDEDNESS

See also 117. CHANGE; 350. FLEXIBILITY; 404. GROWTH AND DEVELOPMENT; 620. NARROWNESS; 901. SINCERITY

1. Openness, as currently conceived, is a way of making surrender to whatever is most powerful, or worship of vulgar success, look principled.

ALLAN BLOOM, "INTRODUCTION: OUR VIRTUE," *THE CLOSING OF THE AMERICAN MIND* (1987)

2. Oh, would that my mind could let fall its dead ideas, as the tree does its withered leaves! And without too many regrets, if possible! Those from which the sap has withdrawn. But, good Lord, what beautiful colors!

ANDRÉ GIDE, *JOURNALS,* 1947, TR. JUSTIN O'BRIEN

3. The only means of strengthening one's intellect is to make up one's mind about nothing—to let the mind be a thoroughfare for all thoughts.

KEATS, LETTER TO GEORGE AND GEORGIANA KEATS, SEPT. 17–27, 1819

4. Where there is an open mind, there will always be a frontier.

CHARLES F. KETTERING, QUOTED IN *PROFILE OF AMERICA* (1954)

5. Ah, snug lie those that slumber / Beneath Conviction's roof. / Their floors are sturdy lumber, / Their windows weatherproof. / But I sleep cold forever / And cold sleep all my kind, / For I was born to shiver / In the draft from an open mind.

PHYLLIS MCGINLEY, "LAMENT FOR A WAVERING VIEWPOINT," *A POCKETFUL OF WRY* (1940)

6. The beautiful souls are they that are universal, open, and ready for all things.

MONTAIGNE, "OF PRESUMPTION," *ESSAYS* (1580–88), TR. W. C. HAZLITT

655. OPERA

See also 902. SINGING

1. An opera may be allowed to be extravagantly lavish in its decorations, as its only design is to gratify the senses and keep up an indolent attention in the audience.

JOSEPH ADDISON, *THE SPECTATOR,* MARCH 6, 1711

2. Whenever I go to an opera, I leave my sense and reason at the door with my half-guinea, and deliver myself up to my eyes and my ears.

LORD CHESTERFIELD, *LETTERS TO HIS SON,* JAN. 23, 1752

656. OPINION

See also 51. ARGUMENT; 252. DISCORD; 350. FLEXIBILITY; 443. IDEAS; 591. MINORITIES; 762. PUBLIC OPINION

1. Some men are just as sure of the truth of their opinions as are others of what they know.

ARISTOTLE, *NICOMACHEAN ETHICS* (4TH C. B.C.), 7.3, TR. J. A. K. THOMSON

2. We tolerate differences of opinion in people who are familiar to us. But differences of opinion in people we do not know sound like heresy or plots.

BROOKS ATKINSON, "FEBRUARY 4," *ONCE AROUND THE SUN* (1951)

3. Men get opinions as boys learn to spell, / By reiteration chiefly.

ELIZABETH BARRETT BROWNING, *AURORA LEIGH* (1856), 6.6

4. The more unpopular an opinion is, the more necessary is it that the holder should be somewhat punctilious in his observance of conventionalities generally.

SAMUEL BUTLER (D. 1902), "THE POSITION OF A HOMO UNIUS LIBRI," *NOTE-BOOKS* (1912)

5. A man should take to himself no discomfort from an opinion expressed or implied by his adversary, but it is difficult, and oftentimes humiliating to attempt to justify the kindness of one's friends.

EUGENE V. DEBS, *WALLS AND BARS* (1927)

6. We are of different opinions at different hours, but we always may be said to be at heart on the side of truth.

EMERSON, "WORSHIP," *THE CONDUCT OF LIFE* (1860)

7. If all men saw the fair and wise the same / men would not have debaters' double strife.

EURIPIDES, *THE PHOENICIAN WOMEN* (C. 411–409 B.C.), TR. ELIZABETH WYCKOFF

8. An opinion, though it is original, does not necessarily differ from the accepted opinion; the important thing is that it does not try to conform to it.

ANDRÉ GIDE, *JOURNALS,* FEB. 6, 1929, TR. JUSTIN O'BRIEN

9. So many young men get their likes and dislikes from Mencken.

ERNEST HEMINGWAY, *THE SUN ALSO RISES* (1926)

10. With effervescing opinions, as with the not yet forgotten champagne, the quickest way to let them go flat is to let them get exposed to the air.

OLIVER WENDELL HOLMES, JR., OPINION, U.S. SUPREME COURT (1920)

11. A man's opinions are generally of much more value than his arguments.

OLIVER WENDELL HOLMES, SR., *THE PROFESSOR AT THE BREAKFAST TABLE* (1860), 5

12. It is often easier as well as more advantageous to conform to other men's opinions than to bring them over to ours.

La Bruyère, *Characters* (1688), 5.48, tr. Henri Van Laun

13. We credit scarcely any persons with good sense except those who are of our opinion.

La Rochefoucauld, *Maxims* (1665), tr. Kenneth Pratt

14. One must judge men not by their opinions, but by what their opinions have made of them.

Georg Christoph Lichtenberg, *Aphorisms* (1764–99), tr. H. Hatfield

15. New opinions are always suspected, and usually opposed, without any other reason but because they are not already common.

John Locke, "The Epistle Dedicatory," *An Essay Concerning Human Understanding* (1690)

16. In the human mind, one-sidedness has always been the rule, and many-sidedness the exception. Hence, even in revolutions of opinion, one part of the truth usually sets while another rises.

John Stuart Mill, *On Liberty* (1859), 2

17. Where there is much desire to learn, there of necessity will be much arguing, much writing, many opinions; for opinion in good men is but knowledge in the making.

Milton, *Areopagitica* (1644)

18. Opinion is a powerful party, bold, and without measure.

Montaigne, "That the relish of good and evil depends in a great measure upon the opinion we have of them," *Essays* (1580–88), tr. W. C. Hazlitt

19. Our opinions are less important than the spirit and temper with which they possess us, and even good opinions are worth very little unless we hold them in a broad, intelligent, and spacious way.

John Morley, "Robespierre," *Critical Miscellanies* (1871–1908)

20. One often contradicts an opinion when it is really only the tone in which it has been presented that is unsympathetic.

Nietzsche, *Human, All Too Human* (1878), 303, in *The Portable Nietzsche*, tr. Walter Kaufmann

21. It is safer to learn than teach; and who conceals his opinion has nothing to answer for.

William Penn, *Some Fruits of Solitude* (1693), 2.118

22. Truth is one forever absolute, but opinion is truth filtered through the moods, the blood, the disposition of the spectator.

Wendell Phillips, lecture, "Idols," Boston, Oct. 4, 1859

23. Refusing to have an opinion is a way of having one, isn't it?

Luigi Pirandello, *Each in His Own Way* (1924), 1, tr. Arthur Livingston

24. To observations which ourselves we make, / We grow more partial for th' observer's sake.

Alexander Pope, *Moral Essays* (1731–35), 1.11

25. To reign by opinion, begin by trampling it under your feet.

Rousseau, *Émile* (1762), 3

26. The sentiments of an adult are compounded of a kernal of instinct surrounded by a vast husk of education.

Bertrand Russell, *Sceptical Essays* (1928)

27. If a man would register all his opinions upon love, politics, religion, learning, etc., beginning from his youth, and so go to old age, what a bundle of inconsistencies and contradictions would appear at last!

Jonathan Swift, *Thoughts on Various Subjects* (1711)

28. Men seldom take the opinion of their equal, or of a man like themselves, upon trust.

Alexis de Tocqueville, *Democracy in America* (1835–39), 2.3.21

29. It were not best that we should all think alike; it is difference of opinion that makes horse-races.

Mark Twain, "Pudd'nhead Wilson's Calendar," *Pudd'nhead Wilson* (1894), 19

30. Opinion is called the queen of the world; it is so, for when reason opposes it, it is condemned to death. It must rise twenty times from its ashes to gradually drive away the usurper.

Voltaire, "Opinion," *Philosophical Dictionary* (1764)

31. The chief effect of talk on any subject is to strengthen one's own opinions, and, in fact, one never knows exactly what he does believe until he is warmed into conviction by the heat of attack and defence.

Charles Dudley Warner, "Sixth Study," *Backlog Studies* (1873)

32. It is only about things that do not interest one that one can give a really unbiased opinion, which is

no doubt the reason why an unbiased opinion is always absolutely valueless.

Oscar Wilde, "The Critic as Artist," *Intentions* (1891)

657. OPPORTUNITY

See also 717. Potential

1. The impossible often has a kind of integrity which the merely improbable lacks.

Douglas Adams, *The Long Dark Tea-Time of the Soul* (1988)

2. A wise man will make more opportunities than he finds.

Francis Bacon, "Of Ceremonies and Respects," *Essays* (1625)

3. A door that seems to stand open must be of a man's size, or it is not the door that Providence means for him.

Henry Ward Beecher, *Proverbs from Plymouth Pulpit* (1887)

4. Intentions often melt in the face of unexpected opportunity.

Shirley Temple Black, *Child Star* (1988)

5. Opporchunity knocks at ivry man's dure wanst. On some men's dures it hammers till it breaks down th' dure an' thin it goes in an' wakes him up if he's asleep, an' iver aftherward it wurruks f'r him as a night-watchman.

Finley Peter Dunne, "Mr. Carnegie's Gift," *Mr. Dooley's Opinions* (1901)

6. Remember that you ought to behave in life as you would at a banquet. As something is being passed around, it comes to you; stretch out your hand, take a portion of it politely. It passes on; do not detain it. Or it has not come to you yet; do not project your desire to meet it, but wait until it comes in front of you.

Epictetus, *Enchiridion* (2nd c.), 15, tr. Thomas W. Higginson

7. That's what this democracy was for us, a huge supermarket of mass man where we could take a piece here and a piece there to make our personalities for ourselves instead of putting up with what was given at the beginning.

Seymour Krim, "For My Brothers and Sisters in the Failure Business," in *The Art of the Personal Essay* (1994), ed. Phillip Lopate

8. In great affairs we ought to apply ourselves less to creating chances than to profiting from those that offer.

La Rochefoucauld, *Maxims* (1665), tr. Kenneth Pratt

9. Know thine opportunity.

Pittacus (7th–6th c. b.c.), quoted in Diogenes Laertius' *Lives and Opinions of Eminent Philosophers* (3rd c. a.d.), tr. R. D. Hicks

10. Look what can happen in this country, they'd say. A girl lives in some out-of-the-way town for nineteen years, so poor she can't afford a magazine, and then she gets a scholarship to college and wins a prize here and a prize there and ends up steering New York like her own private car.

Sylvia Plath, *The Bell Jar* (1963)

11. While we stop to think, we often miss our opportunity.

Publilius Syrus, *Moral Sayings* (1st c. b.c.), 185, tr. Darius Lyman

12. There is a tide in the affairs of men / Which, taken at the flood, leads on to fortune; / Omitted, all the voyage of their life / Is bound in shallows and in miseries.

Shakespeare, *Julius Caesar* (1599–1600), 4.3.218

OPPOSITES

See 187. Contrast

658. OPPOSITION

See also 252. Discord; 258. Dissent; 753. Protest; 786. Rebellion; 819. Revolution; 1032. Violence

1. Many a man's strength is in opposition, and when that faileth, he groweth out of use.

Francis Bacon, "Of Faction," *Essays* (1625)

2. Opposition, n. In politics the party that prevents the Government from running amuck by hamstringing it.

Ambrose Bierce, *The Devil's Dictionary* (1881–1911)

3. He that wrestles with us strengthens our nerves and sharpens our skill. Our antagonist is our helper.

Edmund Burke, *Reflections on the Revolution in France* (1790)

4. I respect only those who resist me, but I cannot tolerate them.

Charles de Gaulle, quoted in *The New York Times Magazine,* May 12, 1968

5. No government can be long secure without formidable opposition.

Benjamin Disraeli, *Coningsby* (1844), 2.1

6. Opposition brings concord. Out of discord comes the fairest harmony.

Heraclitus, *Fragments* (c. 500 B.C.), 98, tr. Philip Wheelwright

7. What country can preserve its liberties, if its rulers are not warned from time to time, that this people preserve the spirit of resistance?

Thomas Jefferson, letter to Col. William S. Smith, Nov. 13, 1787

8. Men naturally despise those who court them, but respect those who do not give way to them.

Thucydides, *The Peloponnesian War* (c. 400 B.C.), 3.39, tr. Benjamin Jowett

9. The man who is swimming against the stream knows the strength of it.

Woodrow Wilson, speech, "The New Freedom" (1913)

OPPRESSION

See 889. Servitude; 1002. Tyranny

659. OPTIMISM

See also 660. Optimism and Pessimism; 692. Pessimism

1. Optimism approves of everything, submits to everything, believes everything; it is the virtue above all of the taxpayer.

Georges Bernanos, "France Before the World of Tomorrow," *The Last Essays of Georges Bernanos* (1955), tr. Joan and Barry Ulanov

2. Optimism, n. The doctrine or belief that everything is beautiful, including what is ugly, everything good, especially the bad, and everything right that is wrong.

Ambrose Bierce, *The Devil's Dictionary* (1881–1911)

3. The essence of optimism is that it takes no account of the present, but it is a source of inspiration, of vitality and hope where others have resigned; it enables a man to hold his head high, to claim the future for himself and not to abandon it to his enemy.

Dietrich Bonhoeffer, "After Ten Years," *Letters and Papers from Prison* (1953), tr. Eberhard Bethge

4. The year's at the spring / And day's at the morn; / Morning's at seven; / The hillside's dew-pearled; / The lark's on the wing; / The snail's on the thorn: / God's in his heaven—/ All's right with the world!

Robert Browning, "Morning," *Pippa Passes* (1841)

5. Children drown, beautiful women are mangled in automobile accidents, cruise ships founder, and men die lingering deaths in mines and submarines, but you will find none of this in my accounts.

John Cheever, "The Jewels of the Cabots," *The Stories of John Cheever* (1978)

6. Optimism is the content of small men in high places.

F. Scott Fitzgerald, "Note-Books," *The Crack-Up* (1945)

7. Optimism is a kind of heart stimulant—the digitalis of failure.

Elbert Hubbard, *A Thousand and One Epigrams* (1911)

8. Now, as never before, hundreds of millions of men and women—who had formerly believed that stoic resignation in the face of hunger and disease and darkness was the best one could could do—have come alive with a new sense that the means are at hand with which to make for themselves a better life.

John F. Kennedy, *The Strategy of Peace* (1960)

9. a optimist is a guy / that has never had / much experience.

Don Marquis, "certain maxims of archy," *Archy and Mehitabel* (1927)

10. There is an optimism which nobly anticipates the eventual triumph of great moral laws, and there is an optimism which cheerfully tolerates unworthiness.

Agnes Repplier, "Are Americans Timid?" *Under Dispute* (1924)

11. One day everything will be well, that is our hope: / Everything's fine today, that is our illusion.

Voltaire, *Poème sur le désastre de Lisbonne* (1756)

12. [Optimism] is the mania of maintaining that everything is well when we are wretched.

Voltaire, *Candide* (1759), 19

13. If you pretend to be good, the world takes you very seriously. If you pretend to be bad, it doesn't. Such is the astounding stupidity of optimism.

Oscar Wilde, *Lady Windermere's Fan* (1892), 1

660. OPTIMISM AND PESSIMISM

See also 659. Optimism; 692. Pessimism

1. Our notion of an optimist is a man who, knowing that each year was worse than the preceding, thinks next year will be better. And a pessimist is a man who knows the next year can't be any worse than the last one.

Franklin P. Adams, *Nods and Becks* (1944)

2. The optimist proclaims that we live in the best of all possible worlds; and the pessimist fears this is true.

JAMES BRANCH CABELL, *THE SILVER STALLION* (1926)

3. O, merry is the Optimist, / With the troops of courage leaguing. / But a dour trend / In any friend / Is somehow less fatiguing.

PHYLLIS MCGINLEY, "SONG AGAINST SWEETNESS AND LIGHT," *A POCKETFUL OF WRY* (1940)

4. The man who is a pessimist before forty-eight knows too much; if he is an optimist after it, he knows too little.

MARK TWAIN, *NOTEBOOK* (1935)

ORATORY

See 763. PUBLIC SPEAKING

661. ORDER

See also 257. DISORDER; 410. HARMONY; 529. LAW AND ORDER; 585. METHOD; 702. PLANS; 828. ROUTINE

1. Some people like to make a little garden out of life and walk down a path.

JEAN ANOUILH, *THE LARK* (1955), 2, ADAPTED BY LILLIAN HELLMAN

2. Let all things be done decently and in order.

BIBLE, 1 CORINTHIANS 14:40

3. Good order is the foundation of all things.

EDMUND BURKE, *REFLECTIONS ON THE REVOLUTION IN FRANCE* (1790)

4. It is meritorious to insist on forms; religion and all else naturally clothes itself in forms. Everywhere the formed world is the only habitable one.

THOMAS CARLYLE, *ON HEROES, HERO-WORSHIP AND THE HEROIC IN HISTORY* (1841), 6

5. "Begin at the beginning," the King said, gravely, "and go till you come to the end; then stop."

LEWIS CARROLL, *ALICE'S ADVENTURES IN WONDERLAND* (1865), 12

6. Watch out for the fellow who talks about putting things in order! Putting things in order always means getting other people under your control.

DENIS DIDEROT, *SUPPLEMENT TO BOUGAINVILLE'S "VOYAGE"* (1796)

7. It is best to do things systematically, / since we are only human, and disorder is our worst enemy.

HESIOD, *WORKS AND DAYS* (8TH C. B.C.), 471, TR. RICHMOND LATTIMORE

8. Symmetry is ennui, and ennui is the very essence of grief and melancholy. Despair yawns.

VICTOR HUGO, "COSETTE," *LES MISÉRABLES* (1862), 4.1, TR. CHARLES E. WILBOUR

9. The virtue of the soul does not consist in flying high, but in walking orderly.

MONTAIGNE, "OF REPENTANCE," *ESSAYS* (1580–88), TR. W. C. HAZLITT

10. We have lost faith in the formal powers of the mind, not, as some suppose, because our universe is too difficult to grasp, but because we lack the inner principle of order.

LEWIS MUMFORD, *FINDINGS AND KEEPINGS. ANALECTS FOR AN AUTOBIOGRAPHY* (1975)

11. Order marches with weighty and measured strides; disorder is always in a hurry.

NAPOLEON I, *MAXIMS* (1804–15)

12. Peace is present when man can see the face that is composed of things that have meaning and are in their place. Peace is present when things form part of a whole greater than their sum, as the diverse minerals in the ground collect to become the tree.

SAINT-EXUPÉRY, *FLIGHT TO ARRAS* (1942), 13, TR. LEWIS GALANTIÈRE

13. Order always weighs on the individual. Disorder makes him wish for the police or for death. These are two extreme circumstances in which human nature is not at ease.

PAUL VALÉRY, PREFACE TO MONTESQUIEU'S *PERSIAN LETTERS* (1926)

14. It seemed to me that I should have a desk, even though I had no real need for a desk. I was afraid that if I had no desk in my room my life would seem too haphazard.

E.B. WHITE, *ONE MAN'S MEAT* (1944)

662. ORIGINALITY

See also 276. ECCENTRICITY; 468. INDIVIDUALISM; 469. INDIVIDUALITY; 1014. UNIQUENESS

1. He is great who is what he is from nature and who never reminds us of others.

EMERSON, "USES OF GREAT MEN," *REPRESENTATIVE MEN* (1850)

2. Where do we now meet an original nature? and where is the man who has the strength to be true, and to show himself as he is?

GOETHE, QUOTED IN JOHANN PETER ECKERMANN'S *CONVERSATIONS WITH GOETHE,* JAN. 2, 1824

3. When people are free to do as they please, they usually imitate each other. Originality is deliberate and forced, and partakes of the nature of a protest.

ERIC HOFFER, *THE PASSIONATE STATE OF MIND* (1954), 33

4. It is perfectly easy to be original by violating the laws of decency and the canons of good taste.

OLIVER WENDELL HOLMES, SR., *OVER THE TEACUPS* (1891), 5

5. All good things which exist are the fruits of originality.

JOHN STUART MILL, *ON LIBERTY* (1859), 3

6. Originality is the one thing which unoriginal minds cannot feel the use of.

JOHN STUART MILL, *ON LIBERTY* (1859), 3

663. OTHERS

See also 515. JUDGING OTHERS; 794. RELATIONSHIPS, HUMAN; 1008. UNDERSTANDING OTHERS

1. We are better able to study our neighbors than ourselves, and their actions than our own.

ARISTOTLE, *NICOMACHEAN ETHICS* (4TH C. B.C.), 9.9, TR. J. A. K. THOMSON

2. I often marvel how it is that though each man loves himself beyond all else, he should yet value his own opinion of himself less than that of others.

MARCUS AURELIUS, *MEDITATIONS* (2ND C.), 12.4, TR. MAXWELL STANIFORTH

3. It is when we try to grapple with another man's intimate need that we perceive how incomprehensible, wavering, and misty are the beings that share with us the sight of the stars and the warmth of the sun.

JOSEPH CONRAD, *LORD JIM* (1900), 16

4. We cannot forgive another for not being ourselves.

EMERSON, *JOURNALS* 1841

5. None knows the weight of another's burden.

THOMAS FULLER, M.D., *GNOMOLOGIA* (1732), 3655

6. Most often it happens that one attributes to others only the feelings of which one is capable oneself.

ANDRÉ GIDE, *JOURNALS,* JAN. 11, 1932, TR. JUSTIN O'BRIEN

7. At last you are no longer searching for yourself, but for another—you are saved.

JEAN GIRAUDOUX, *SIEGFRIED* (1928), 4, TR. PETER H. JUDD

8. Just as much as we see in others we have in ourselves.

WILLIAM HAZLITT, "COMMONPLACES," *THE ROUND TABLE* (1817), 14

9. The longer we live, the more we find we are like other persons.

OLIVER WENDELL HOLMES, SR., *OVER THE TEACUPS* (1891), 1

10. Others are to us like the "characters" in fiction, eternal and incorrigible; the surprises they give us turn out in the end to have been predictable—unexpected variations on the theme of being themselves.

MARY MCCARTHY, "CHARACTERS IN FICTION," *ON THE CONTRARY* (1961)

11. We are never the same with others as when we are alone; we are different, even, when we are in the dark with them.

MAURICE MAETERLINCK, "THE PRE-DESTINED, " *THE TREASURE OF THE HUMBLE* (1896), TR. ALFRED SUTRO

12. It is the tragedy of other people that they are to us merely showcases for the very perishable collections of our own mind.

MARCEL PROUST, *REMEMBRANCE OF THINGS PAST: THE SWEET CHEAT GONE* (1913–27), TR. C. K. SCOTT-MONCRIEFF

13. Do not base your life on the judgments of others; first, because they are as likely to be mistaken as you are, and further, because you cannot know that they are telling you their true thoughts.

JEAN-JACQUES ROUSSEAU, QUOTED IN *BOSWELL ON THE GRAND TOUR: GERMANY AND SWITZERLAND* (1928; 1953)

14. Other people are quite dreadful. The only possible society is one's self.

OSCAR WILDE, *AN IDEAL HUSBAND* (1895), 3

664. OVERCONFIDENCE

See also 860. SELF-CONFIDENCE

1. Let him that thinketh he standeth take heed lest he fall.

BIBLE, 1 CORINTHIANS 10:12

2. Danger breeds best on too much confidence.

CORNEILLE, *LE CID* (1636), 2.6, TR. PAUL LANDIS

3. How fortune brings to earth the oversure!

PETRARCH, "LAURA DEAD," *CANZONIERE* (1360), 270

OVERPOPULATION

See 84. BIRTH CONTROL; 713. POPULATION

OWNERSHIP

See 716. POSSESSION; 746. PROPERTY

P

665. PACIFISM

See also 357. FORCE; 476. INJURY; 681. PEACE

1. Whosoever shall smite thee on thy right cheek, turn to him the other also.

BIBLE, MATTHEW 5:39

2. If you have a nation of men who have risen to that height of moral cultivation that they will not declare war or carry arms, for they have not so much madness left in their brains, you have a nation of lovers, of benefactors, of true, great, and able men.

EMERSON, "WAR," *MISCELLANIES* (1884)

3. The peace of the man who has forsworn the use of the bullet seems to me not quite peace, but a canting impotence.

EMERSON, *JOURNALS,* 1839

4. It is open to a war resister to judge between the combatants and wish success to the one who has justice on his side. By so judging he is more likely to bring peace between the two than by remaining a mere spectator.

MOHANDAS K. GANDHI, *NON-VIOLENCE IN PEACE AND WAR* (1948), 1.241

5. Mental violence has no potency and injures only the person whose thoughts are violent. It is otherwise with mental nonviolence. It has potency which the world does not yet know.

MOHANDAS K. GANDHI, *NON-VIOLENCE IN PEACE AND WAR* (1948), 1.256

6. Non-violence is not a garment to be put on and off at will. Its seat is in the heart, and it must be an inseparable part of our very being.

MOHANDAS K. GANDHI, *NON-VIOLENCE IN PEACE AND WAR* (1948), 1.61

7. The noble art of losing face / may one day save the human race / and turn into eternal merit / what weaker minds would call disgrace.

PIET HEIN, "LOSING FACE," *GROOKS* (1966)

8. The distant Trojans never injured me.

HOMER, *ILIAD* (9TH C. B.C.), 1.200, TR. ALEXANDER POPE

9. Rendering oneself unarmed when one had been the best-armed, out of a height of feeling—that is the means to real peace, which must always rest on a peace of mind.

NIETZSCHE, *THE WANDERER AND HIS SHADOW* (1880), 284, IN *THE PORTABLE NIETZSCHE*, TR. WALTER KAUFMANN

10. Sometime they'll give a war and nobody will come.

CARL SANDBURG, *THE PEOPLE, YES* (1936)

11. Beware of the man who does not return your blow: he neither forgives you nor allows you to forgive yourself.

GEORGE BERNARD SHAW, "MAXIMS FOR REVOLUTIONISTS," *MAN AND SUPERMAN* (1903)

12. One ought not to return injustice, nor do evil to anybody in the world, no matter what one may have suffered from them.

SOCRATES, IN PLATO'S *CRITO* (4TH C. B.C.), TR. LANE COOPER

13. There is such a thing as man being too proud to fight. There is such a thing as a nation being so right that it does not need to convince others by force that it is right.

WOODROW WILSON, ADDRESS, PHILADELPHIA, MAY 10, 1915

PAIN

See 946. SUFFERING

666. PAINTING

See also 53. ART AND ARTISTS; 143. COLOR

1. In painting, the most brilliant colors, spread at random and without design, will give far less pleasure than the simplest outline of a figure.

ARISTOTLE, *POETICS* (4TH C. B.C.), 2.3, TR. THOMAS TWINING

2. Painting, n. The art of protecting flat surfaces from the weather and exposing them to the critic.

AMBROSE BIERCE, *THE DEVIL'S DICTIONARY* (1881–1911)

3. All art is bad, but modern art is the worst.

JOYCE CARY, *THE HORSE'S MOUTH* (1944)

4. There are only two styles of portrait painting: the serious and the smirk.

Charles Dickens, *Nicholas Nickleby* (1838–39), 10

5. The picture waits for my verdict; it is not to command me, but I am to settle its claim to praise.

Emerson, "Self-Reliance," *Essays: First Series* (1841)

6. That which probably hears more stupidities than anything else in the world is a painting in a museum.

Edmond and Jules de Goncourt, *Idées et sensations* (1866)

7. One picture in ten thousand, perhaps, ought to live in the applause of mankind, from generation to generation until the colors fade and blacken out of sight or the canvas rot entirely away.

Nathaniel Hawthorne, *The Marble Faun* (1860)

8. I would rather see the portrait of a dog that I know, than all the allegorical paintings they can shew me in the world.

Samuel Johnson, quoted in Birkbeck Hill's *Johnsonian Miscellanies* (1897), v. 2

9. The painter who draws by practise and judgment of the eye without the use of reason is like the mirror which reproduces within itself all the objects which are set opposite to it without knowledge of the same.

Leonardo da Vinci, *Notebooks* (c. 1500)

10. How vain painting is—we admire the realistic depiction of objects which in their original state we don't admire at all.

Pascal, *Pensées* (1670), 134

11. You want to know how to paint a perfect painting? It's easy. Make yourself perfect and then just paint naturally.

Robert M. Pirsig, *Zen and the Art of Motorcycle Maintenance* (1974)

12. A little amateur painting in water-colour shows the innocent and quiet mind.

Robert Louis Stevenson, title essay, *Virginibus Puerisque* (1881)

13. Every portrait that is painted with feeling is a portrait of the artist, not of the sitter.

Oscar Wilde, *The Picture of Dorian Gray* (1891), 1

667. PARADES

1. Parades should be classed as a Nuisance and participants should be subject to a term in prison. They stop more work, inconvenience more people, stop more traffic, cause more accidents, entail more expense, and commit and cause I don't remember the other hundred misdemeanors.

Will Rogers, "Let's Treat Our Presidents Like Human Beings," *The Illiterate Digest* (1924)

668. PARADOXES

1. Paradoxes are useful to attract attention to ideas.

Mandell Creighton, *Life and Letters* (1904)

2. He who confronts the paradoxical exposes himself to reality.

Friedrich Dürrenmatt, "21 Points," *The Physicists* (1962), tr. James Kirkup

3. Life is a paradox. Every truth has its counterpart which contradicts it; and every philosopher supplies the logic for his own undoing.

Elbert Hubbard, *The Note Book* (1927)

4. Why can't a state that launches cosmonauts into space provide enough eggs and milk for its city children during the winter months?

Harrison E. Salisbury, *Russia* (1965)

669. PARASITES

1. All the wise world is little else, in nature, / But parasites or subparasites.

Ben Jonson, *Volpone* (1605), 3.1

2. Great fleas have little fleas upon their backs to bite 'em, / And little fleas have lesser fleas, and so on *ad infinitum*.

Augustus de Morgan, *A Budget of Paradoxes* (c. 1850)

3. The parasites live where the great have little secret sores.

Nietzsche, "On Old and New Tablets," *Thus Spoke Zarathustra* (1883–92), 3, tr. Walter Kaufmann

PARDON

See 359. Forgiveness

670. PARENTHOOD

See also 65. Babies; 97. Boys; 123. Children; 218. Daughters; 334. Family; 385. Girls; 417. Heredity; 916. Sons; 988. Training

1. We are the buffoons of our children.

Pietro Aretino, letter to Sebastiano the Painter, June 15, 1537, tr. Samuel Putnam

2. This is the reason why mothers are more devoted to their children than fathers: it is that they suffer more in giving them birth and are more certain that they are their own.

Aristotle, *Nicomachean Ethics* (4th c. B.C.), 9.7, tr. J. E. C. Welldon

3. Children sweeten labours, but they make misfortunes more bitter; they increase the cares of life, but they mitigate the remembrance of death.

Francis Bacon, "Of Parents and Children," *Essays* (1625)

4. The joys of parents are secret, and so are their griefs and fears: they cannot utter the one, nor they will not utter the other.

Francis Bacon, "Of Parents and Children," *Essays* (1625)

5. I could never become accustomed to American mothers' reckless disregard for their daughters' moral welfare.

Luigi Barzini, *O America* (1977)

6. We never know the love of our parents for us till we have become parents.

Henry Ward Beecher, *Proverbs from Plymouth Pulpit* (1887)

7. A man should love his sons in equal measure, for him that he loves best and in whom he reposes his hope, the wheel will suddenly ravish away; but him that he hated and kept afar will restore his soul and sustain his old age.

Berechiah ben Natronai ha-Nakdan, *Fables of a Jewish Aesop* (1967)

8. When a woman is twenty, a child deforms her; when she is thirty, he preserves her; and when forty, he makes her young again.

Léon Blum, *Du Mariage* (1907), 6

9. Some are kissing mothers and some are scolding mothers, but it is love just the same, and most mothers kiss and scold together.

Pearl S. Buck, "To You on Your First Birthday," *To My Daughters, With Love* (1967)

10. In the mind of a woman, to give birth to a child is the short cut to omniscience.

Gelett Burgess, *The Maxims of Methuselah* (1907), 10

11. How often do we not see children ruined through the virtues, real or supposed, of their parents?

Samuel Butler (d. 1902), "Elementary Morality," *Note-Books* (1912)

12. One of the most visible effects of a child's presence in the household is to turn the worthy parents into complete idiots when, without him, they would perhaps have remained mere imbeciles.

Georges Courteline, *La Philosophie de G. Courteline* (1917)

13. To have a son in wartime is the worst curse that can befall a mother, no matter what anyone says.

Slavenka Drakulic, *The Balkan Express* (1993)

14. All men know their children / Mean more than life. If childless people sneer— / Well, they've less sorrow. But what lonesome luck!

Euripides, *Andromache* (c. 426 B.C.), tr. John F. Nims

15. Here all mankind is equal: / rich and poor alike, they love their children.

Euripides, *Heracles* (c. 422 B.C.), tr. William Arrowsmith

16. Lucky that man / whose children make his happiness in life / and not his grief, the anguished disappointment of his hopes.

Euripides, *Orestes* (408 B.C.), tr. William Arrowsmith

17. Oh, what a power is motherhood, possessing / A potent spell. All women alike / Fight fiercely for a child.

Euripides, *Iphigenia in Aulis* (c. 405 B.C.), tr. Charles R. Walker

18. The new-come stepmother hates the children born / to a first wife.

Euripides, *Alcestis* (438 B.C.), tr. Richmond Lattimore

19. A father is a banker provided by nature.

French Proverb

20. The mother-child relationship is paradoxical and, in a sense, tragic. It requires the most intense love on the mother's side, yet this very love must help the child grow away from the mother, and to become fully independent.

Erich Fromm, *The Sane Society* (1955), 3

21. You don't have to deserve your mother's love. You have to deserve your father's. He's more particular.

Robert Frost, interview, *Writers at Work: Second Series* (1963)

22. The character and history of each child may be a new and poetic experience to the parent, if he will let it.

Margaret Fuller, *Summer on the Lakes* (1844), 7

23. There is not so much comfort in the having of children as there is sorrow in parting with them.

Thomas Fuller, M.D., *Gnomologia* (1732), 4932

24. Parenthood is an endless series of small events, periodic conflicts, and sudden crises which call for a response. The response is not without consequence: it affects personality for better or for worse.

Haim G. Ginott, *Between Parent & Teenager* (1969)

25. [Lincoln, speaking of his mother:] "God bless my mother; all that I am or ever hope to be I owe to her."

William H. Herndon, *Herndon's Life of Lincoln* (1888)

26. The most ferocious animals are disarmed by caresses to their young.

Victor Hugo, "Fantine," *Les Misérables* (1862), 4.1, tr. Charles E. Wilbour

27. I perceive affection makes a fool / Of any man too much the father.

Ben Jonson, *Every Man in His Humour* (1598), 1.2

28. The greatest reverence is due to a child! If you are contemplating a disgraceful act, despise not your child's tender years.

Juvenal, *Satires* (c. 100), 14.47

29. Mothers may still want their favorite sons to grow up to be President, but, according to a famous Gallup poll of some years ago, they do not want them to become politicians in the process.

John F. Kennedy, *Profiles in Courage* (1956)

30. The real menace in dealing with a five-year-old is that in no time at all you begin to sound like a five-year-old.

Jean Kerr, "How to Get the Best of Your Children," *Please Don't Eat the Daisies* (1957)

31. It is ... sometimes easier to head an institute for the study of child guidance than it is to turn one brat into a decent human being.

Joseph Wood Krutch, "Whom Do We Picket Tonight?" *If You Don't Mind My Saying So* (1964)

32. There are some extraordinary fathers, who seem, during the whole course of their lives, to be giving their children reasons for being consoled at their death.

La Bruyère, *Characters* (1688), 11.17, tr. Henri Van Laun

33. If you and your child were going to be killed tomorrow, would you not give him to eat today?

Primo Levi, *Survival in Auschwitz* (1959)

34. Our [women's] bodies are shaped to bear children, and our lives are a working-out of the processes of creation. All our ambitions and intelligence are beside that great elemental point.

Phyllis McGinley, "The Honor of Being a Woman," *The Province of the Heart* (1959)

35. A father is very miserable who has no other hold on his children's affection than the need they have of his assistance, if that can be called affection.

Montaigne, "Of the affections of fathers to their children," *Essays* (1580–88), tr. W. C. Hazlitt

36. "Planned parenthood" in the social history of the Western countries is, indeed, a phenomenon instrinsically related to those very changes in people's attitudes which, on the political plane, have been causing the trend towards economic planning.

Gunnar Myrdal, *Beyond the Welfare State* (1960)

37. Through the survival of their children, happy parents are able to think calmly, and with a very practical affection, of a world in which they are to have no direct share.

Walter Pater, *Marius the Epicurean* (1885), 25

38. Men are generally more careful of the breed of their horses and dogs than of their children.

William Penn, *Some Fruits of Solitude* (1693), 1.85

39. An angry father is most cruel toward himself.

Publilius Syrus, *Moral Sayings* (1st c. b.c.), 638, tr. Darius Lyman

40. Romance fails us and so do friendships, but the relationship of parent and child, less noisy than all others, remains indelible and indestructible, the strongest relationship on earth.

Theodor Reik, *Of Love and Lust* (1957), 1.3.10

41. I opine ... "Judicious mothers will always keep in mind, that they are the first book read, and the last put aside, in every child's library."

C. Lenox Remond, *The Mind of the Negro As Reflected in Letters Written During the Crisis, 1800–1860* (1926)

42. The fundamental defect of fathers is that they want their children to be a credit to them.

Bertrand Russell, *The New York Times,* June 9, 1963

43. Parents lend children their experience and a vicarious memory; children endow their parents with a vicarious immortality.

George Santayana, *The Life of Reason: Reason in Society* (1905–06), 2

44. It is impossible for any woman to love her children twenty-four hours a day.

MILTON R. SAPIRSTEIN, *PARADOXES OF EVERYDAY LIFE* (1955), 3

45. The ideal mother, like the ideal marriage, is a fiction.

MILTON R. SAPIRSTEIN, *PARADOXES OF EVERYDAY LIFE* (1955), 3

46. We never make sport of religion, politics, race, or mothers. A mother never gets hit with a custard pie. Mothers-in-law—yes. But mothers—never.

MACK SENNETT, *THE NEW YORK TIMES,* NOV. 6, 1960

47. It is a wise father that knows his own child.

SHAKESPEARE, *THE MERCHANT OF VENICE* (1596–97), 2.2.80

48. To make the child in your own image is a capital crime, for your image is not worth repeating. The child knows this and you know it. Consequently you hate each other.

KARL SHAPIRO, *THE BOURGEOIS POET* (1964), 3.72

49. Parentage is a very important profession; but no test of fitness for it is ever imposed in the interest of the children.

GEORGE BERNARD SHAW, *EVERYBODY'S POLITICAL WHAT'S WHAT* (1944), 9

50. The father who raises a son to have a profession he once dreamed of, and the mother who uses her daughter as the adult companion her husband is not; the parents who urge their children into accomplishments as status symbols—all these and many more are ways of subordinating a child's authentic self to a parent's needs.

GLORIA STEINEM, *REVOLUTION FROM WITHIN* (1992)

51. Now, we've made the revolutionary discovery that children have two parents. A decade ago even the kindly Dr. Spock held mothers solely responsible for children.

GLORIA STEINEM, "WORDS AND CHANGE," *OUTRAGEOUS ACTS AND EVERYDAY REBELLIONS* (1983)

52. In the bad sixties, when drugs came into widespread use among adolescents and when Scarsdale mothers developed the habit of not asking about each other's children for fear of what they'd hear, one knew that they were speaking—or not speaking, keeping their unhappy silence—on behalf of stricken motherhood everywhere in the country.

DIANA TRILLING, *MRS. HARRIS: THE DEATH OF THE SCARSDALE DOCTOR* (1981)

53. I have found the best way to give advise to your children is to find out what they want and then advise them to do it.

HARRY S TRUMAN, TELEVISION INTERVIEW, MAY 27, 1955

54. All the critics in the world may say it's good but a man's own mother will know.

THOMAS WOLFE, *THOMAS WOLFE'S LETTERS TO HIS MOTHER* (1943)

55. Schoolmasters and parents exist to be grown out of.

JOHN WOLFENDEN, *SUNDAY TIMES,* LONDON, JULY 13, 1958

56. The mealy look of men today is the result of momism and so is the pinched and baffled fury in the eyes of womankind.

PHILIP WYLIE, *GENERATION OF VIPERS* (1942), 11

57. We could improve worldwide mental health if we acknowledged that parents can make you crazy.

FRANK ZAPPA, *THE REAL FRANK ZAPPA BOOK* (1989), WITH PETER OCCHIOGROSSO

671. PARIS

See also 361. FRANCE AND FRENCHMEN

1. If you are lucky enough to have lived in Paris as a young man, then wherever you go for the rest of your life, it stays with you, for Paris is a moveable feast.

ERNEST HEMINGWAY, EPIGRAPH TO *A MOVEABLE FEAST* (1964)

2. To err is human. To loaf is Parisian.

VICTOR HUGO, "MARIUS," *LES MISÉRABLES* (1862), 4.1, TR. CHARLES E. WILBOUR

3. Paris: city of encounters, of furtive and painful discoveries. All isms converge there, including the anti-isms, all the revolutionaries too, including the counterrevolutionaries.

ELIE WIESEL, *THE TESTAMENT* (1981), TR. MARION WIESEL

672. PARTIES

1. Parties organized primarily for the purpose of meeting eligible men and women are, by their own nature, ideal opportunities for self-torture and misery.

DAN GREENBURG WITH MARCIA JACOBS, *HOW TO MAKE YOURSELF MISERABLE* (1966)

2. [T]hink of a dinner party as a club of revolutionaries, a technocratic elite whose social interactions that night are a dry run for some future takeover of the state.

PHILLIP LOPATE, "THE DINNER PARTY," IN *THE ART OF THE PERSONAL ESSAY* (1994), ED. PHILLIP LOPATE

3. A cocktail party is what you call it when you invite everyone you know to come over to your house at six p.m., put cigarettes out on your rug, and leave at eight to go somewhere more interesting for dinner without inviting you.

P.J. O'Rourke, *Modern Manners* (1988)

4. A debutante party is basically a bar mitzvah with sex in the parking lot. The same rules of egregious display, inedible food, and ridiculous expense are enforced.

P.J. O'Rourke, *Modern Manners* (1988)

673. PARTING

See also 2. Absence

1. Going away: I can generally bear the separation, but I don't like the leave-taking.

Samuel Butler (d. 1902), "Higgledy-Piggledy," *Note-Books* (1912)

2. There's a kind of release / And a kind of torment in every goodbye for every man.

C. Day-Lewis, "Departure in the Dark," *Short Is the Time* (1943)

3. Ever has it been that love knows not its own depth until the hour of separation.

Kahlil Gibran, "The Coming of the Ship," *The Prophet* (1923)

4. To leave is to die a little; / It is to die to what one loves. / One leaves behind a little of oneself / At any hour, any place.

Edmond Haraucourt, "Rondel de l'adieu," *Choix de poésies* (1891)

5. The return makes one love the farewell.

Alfred de Musset, "À mon frère revenant d'Italie," *Poésies nouvelles* (1836–52)

6. Every parting gives a foretaste of death; every coming together again a foretaste of the resurrection.

Schopenhauer, "Further Psychological Observations," *Parerga and Paralipomena* (1851), tr. T. Bailey Saunders

7. There is a time to separate from our mother. But unless we are ready to separate—unless we are ready to leave her and be left—anything is better than separation.

Judith Viorst, *Necessary Losses* (1986)

8. We shall not come again. We never shall come back again.

Thomas Wolfe, *Look Homeward, Angel* (1929)

674. PARTISANSHIP

See also 111. Causes; 335. Fanaticism; 455. Impartiality; 710. Political Parties

1. A sect or party is an elegant incognito devised to save a man from the vexation of thinking.

Emerson, *Journals,* 1831

2. He who is as faithful to his principles as he is to himself is the true partisan.

William Hazlitt, "On the Spirit of Partisanship," *Sketches and Essays* (1839)

3. The great issues facing us today are not Republican issues or Democratic issues. The political parties can debate the means, but both parties must embrace the end objective, which is to make America great again.

Lee Iacocca, *Iacocca: An Autobiography* (1984) with William Novak

4. Party loyalty lowers the greatest men to the petty level of the masses.

La Bruyère, *Characters* (1688), 11.63

5. No new sect ever had humor; no disciples either, even the disciples of Christ.

Anne Morrow Lindbergh, "Theodore," *Dearly Beloved* (1962)

6. The less reasonable a cult is, the more men seek to establish it by force.

Rousseau, *Correspondance á Monseigneur l'Archevêque de Paris*

7. A man doesn't save a century, or a civilization, but a militant party wedded to a principle can.

Adlai Stevenson, address, Democratic National Convention, July 21, 1952

8. Party is the madness of many for the gain of a few.

Jonathan Swift, *Thoughts on Various Subjects* (1711)

9. There is no greater hindrance to the progress of thought than an attitude of irritated party-spirit.

Alfred North Whitehead, *Adventures in Ideas* (1933), 8

PARTY, POLITICAL

See 710. Political Parties

675. PASSION

See also 238. Desires; 284. Emotions; 551. Love

1. The way to avoid evil is not by maiming our passions, but by compelling them to yield their vigor to our moral nature.

HENRY WARD BEECHER, *PROVERBS FROM PLYMOUTH PULPIT* (1887)

2. Vanity plays lurid tricks with our memory, and the truth of every passion wants some pretence to make it live.

JOSEPH CONRAD, *LORD JIM* (1900), 41

3. One declaims endlessly against the passions; one imputes all of man's suffering to them. One forgets that they are also the source of all his pleasures.

DENIS DIDEROT, *PENSÉES PHILOSOPHIQUES* (1746), 1

4. Only passions, great passions, can elevate the soul to great things.

DENIS DIDEROT, *PENSÉES PHILOSOPHIQUES* (1746), 1

5. Passions destroy more prejudices than philosophy does.

DENIS DIDEROT, *DISCOURS SUR LA POÉSIE DRAMATIQUE* (1773–78)

6. Passion, though a bad regulator, is a powerful spring.

EMERSON, "CONSIDERATIONS BY THE WAY," *THE CONDUCT OF LIFE* (1860)

7. Serving one's own passions is the greatest slavery.

THOMAS FULLER, M.D., *GNOMOLOGIA* (1732), 4103

8. Nothing great in the world has been accomplished without passion.

HEGEL, INTRODUCTION TO *PHILOSOPHY OF HISTORY* (1832), TR. JOHN SIBREE

9. Passions are spiritual rebels and raise sedition against the understanding.

BEN JONSON, "EXPLORATA," *TIMBER* (1640)

10. If we resist our passions, it is more on account of their weakness than of our own strength.

LA ROCHEFOUCAULD, *MAXIMS* (1665), TR. KENNETH PRATT

11. In the human heart there is a ceaseless birth of passions, so that the destruction of one is almost always the establishment of another.

LA ROCHEFOUCAULD, *MAXIMS* (1665), TR. KENNETH PRATT

12. Those who have had great passions find themselves all their lives both happy and unhappy at being cured of them.

LA ROCHEFOUCAULD, *MAXIMS* (1665), TR. KENNETH PRATT

13. The duration of our passions is no more dependent on ourselves than the duration of our lives.

LA ROCHEFOUCAULD, *MAXIMS* (1665), TR. KENNETH PRATT

14. The passions are the only orators which always persuade.

LA ROCHEFOUCAULD, *MAXIMS* (1665), TR. KENNETH PRATT

15. Take heed lest passion sway / Thy judgement to do aught, which else free will / Would not admit.

MILTON, *PARADISE LOST* (1667), 8.635

16. All passions that suffer themselves to be relished and digested are but moderate.

MONTAIGNE, "OF SORROW," *ESSAYS* (1580–88), TR. W. C. HAZLITT

17. When the passions become masters, they are vices.

PASCAL, *PENSÉES* (1670), 502, TR. W. F. TROTTER

18. The ruling passion, be it what it will, / The ruling passion conquers reason still.

ALEXANDER POPE, *MORAL ESSAYS* (1731–35), 3.153

19. Passion is like genius: a miracle.

ROMAIN ROLLAND, "LE BUISSON ARDENT," *JEAN CHRISTOPHE* (1904–12), 2

20. Give me that man / That is not passion's slave, and I will wear him / In my heart's core.

SHAKESPEARE, *HAMLET* (1600), 3.2.76

21. What to ourselves in passion we propose, / The passion ending, doth the purpose lose.

SHAKESPEARE, *HAMLET* (1600), 3.2.204

22. The mind is the soul's eye, not its source of power. That lies in the heart, in other words, in the passions.

VAUVENARGUES, *REFLECTIONS AND MAXIMS* (1746), 149, TR. F. G. STEVENS

PASSIVITY

See 219. DEADNESS, SPIRITUAL; 235. DEPENDENCE; 459. IMPOTENCE; 466. INDIFFERENCE; 650. OBSERVATION

676. PAST

See also 42. ANTIQUITY; 298. ERA; 368. FUTURE; 419. HISTORY AND HISTORIANS; 507. IRREVOCABLENESS; 639. NOSTALGIA; 729. PRESENT; 986. TRADITION

PAST

1. This only is denied even to God: the power to undo the past.

AGATHON, QUOTED IN ARISTOTLE'S *NICOMACHEAN ETHICS* (4TH C. B.C.), 6.2

2. Have you ever heard one civilized person whose opinion you respect, at any time, anywhere, in any civilized country anywhere, say the good new days?

CLEVELAND AMORY, "WHY YOURS TRULY WAS THE ONLY ONE TO CARRY THE SPEAR," *THE TROUBLE WITH NOWADAYS* (1979

3. Obligations, hatreds, injuries—What did I expect memories to be? And I was forgetting remorse. I have a complete past now.

JEAN ANOUILH, *TRAVELER WITHOUT LUGGAGE* (1936), 2.1, TR. LUCIENNE HILL

4. Man is a history-making creature who can neither repeat his past nor leave it behind.

W. H. AUDEN, "D. H. LAWRENCE," *THE DYER'S HAND* (1962)

5. The passing minute is every man's equal possession, but what has once gone by is not ours.

MARCUS AURELIUS, *MEDITATIONS* (2ND C.), 2.14, TR. MAXWELL STANIFORTH

6. The past is our definition. We may strive, with good reason, to escape it, or to escape what is bad in it, but we will escape it only by adding something better to it.

WENDELL BERRY, "THE SPECIALIZATION OF POETRY," *STANDING BY WORDS* (1983)

7. One may return to the place of his birth, / He cannot go back to his youth.

JOHN BURROUGHS, "THE RETURN," *BIRD AND BOUGH* (1906)

8. The Past is such a curious Creature / To look her in the Face / A Transport may receipt us / Or a Disgrace—.

EMILY DICKINSON, POEM (C. 1871)

9. The Things that never can come back, are several— / Childhood—some forms of Hope—the Dead— / Though Joys—like Men—may sometimes make a Journey— / And still abide—.

EMILY DICKINSON, POEM (C. 1881)

10. We make a mistake to condescend to the past as if it were preparatory to our own time.

E.L. DOCTOROW, "THE NINETEENTH NEW YORK," *JACK LONDON, HEMINGWAY, AND THE CONSTITUTION* (1993)

11. We have to do with the past only as we can make it useful to the present and the future.

FREDERICK DOUGLASS, *THE LIFE AND WRITINGS OF FREDERICK DOUGLASS* (1950), V. 2

12. We are not free to use today, or to promise tomorrow, because we are already mortgaged to yesterday.

EMERSON, *JOURNALS*, 1858

13. It was like the good gone times when we still believed in summer hotels and the philosophies of popular songs.

F. SCOTT FITZGERALD, *THE CRACK-UP* (1945)

14. It is sadder to find the past again and find it inadequate to the present than it is to have it elude you and remain forever a harmonious conception of memory.

F. SCOTT FITZGERALD, "SHOW MR. AND MRS. F. TO NUMBER—," *THE CRACK-UP* (1945)

15. If only the sense of actuality can be lulled—and it sleeps for ever in most historians—there is no passion that cannot be gratified in the past.

E.M. FORSTER, "THE CONSOLATION OF HISTORY," *ABINGER HARVEST* (1936)

16. To what a degree the same past can leave different marks—and especially admit of different interpretations.

ANDRÉ GIDE, *JOURNALS*, SEPTEMBER 1931, TR. JUSTIN O'BRIEN

17. The past, with its pleasures, its rewards, its foolishness, its punishments, is there for each of us forever, and it should be.

LILLIAN HELLMAN, *SCOUNDREL TIME* (1976)

18. There is nothing like the dead cold hand of the Past to take down our tumid egotism and lead us into the solemn flow of the life of our race.

OLIVER WENDELL HOLMES, SR., "IRIS, HER BOOK," *THE PROFESSOR AT THE BREAKFAST TABLE* (1860)

19. Respect the past in the full measure of its deserts, but do not make the mistake of confusing it with the present nor seek in it the ideals of the future.

JOSÉ INGENIEROS, *PROPOSICIONES RELATIVAS AL PORVENIR DE LA FILOSOFIA* (1918)

20. Nothing impresses the mind with a deeper feeling of loneliness than to tread the silent and deserted scene of former throng and pageant.

WASHINGTON IRVING, "WESTMINSTER ABBEY," *THE SKETCH BOOK OF GEOFFREY CRAYON, GENT.* (1819–20)

21. Why doesn't the past decently bury itself, instead of sitting waiting to be admired by the present?

D. H. LAWRENCE, *ST. MAWR* (1925)

22. Look not mournfully into the Past. It comes not back again. Wisely improve the Present. It is thine. Go forth to meet the shadowy Future, without fear, and with a manly heart.

LONGFELLOW, *HYPERION* (1839), 4.7

23. It is unlikely that there has ever been a nation more reckless with its past than ours, so quick to tear down its monuments for the sake of a better real-estate deal, so careless with the genius of its architects and artists if they happened to stand in the way of what we call progress when what we mean is profit.

RUSSELL LYNES, "A MAGNET FOR AMERICANS," *ARCHITECTURAL DIGEST* (1975)

24. The past is immortalized; that is to say, it is dead; and death is the root of all godliness and all abiding significance.

THOMAS MANN, "DISORDER AND EARLY SORROW" (1925)

25. To excel the past we must not allow ourselves to lose contact with it; on the contrary, we must feel it under our feet because we raised ourselves upon it.

JOSÉ ORTEGA Y GASSET, "IN SEARCH OF GOETHE FROM WITHIN, LETTER TO A GERMAN," *PARTISAN REVIEW*, DECEMBER 1949, TR. WILLARD R. TRASK

26. The past not merely is not fugitive, it remains present.

MARCEL PROUST, *REMEMBRANCE OF THINGS PAST: THE GUERMANTES WAY* (1913–27), TR. C. K. SCOTT-MONCRIEFF

27. Mad is the man who is forever gritting his teeth against that granite block, complete and changeless, of the past.

SAINT-EXUPÉRY, *THE WISDOM OF THE SANDS* (1948), 50, TR. STUART GILBERT

28. I tell you the past is a bucket of ashes.

CARL SANDBURG, "PRAIRIE," *COMPLETE POEMS* (1950)

29. Those who do not remember the past are condemned to relive it.

GEORGE SANTAYANA, *THE LIFE OF REASON* (1905–06)

30. All things are taken from us, and become / Portions and parcels of the dreadful past.

LORD TENNYSON, "THE LOTOS-EATERS" (1842), 4

31. All the past is here, present to be tried; let it approve itself if it can.

THOREAU, *JOURNAL*, NOV. 5, 1839

32. We live in reference to past experience and not to future events, however inevitable.

H. G. WELLS, *MIND AT THE END OF ITS TETHER* (1946), 2

677. PATIENCE

See also 456. IMPATIENCE; 585. METHOD; 1040. WAITING

1. Sad patience, too near neighbor to despair.

MATTHEW ARNOLD, "THE SCHOLAR-GIPSY," *POEMS* (1853)

2. Patience, n. A minor form of despair, disguised as a virtue.

AMBROSE BIERCE, *THE DEVIL'S DICTIONARY* (1881–1911)

3. Our patience will achieve more than our force.

EDMUND BURKE, *REFLECTIONS ON THE REVOLUTION IN FRANCE* (1790)

4. They also serve who only stand wait for the two-fifteen [train].

G.K. CHESTERTON, "A PIECE OF CHALK," IN *THE ART OF THE PERSONAL ESSAY* (1994), ED. PHILLIP LOPATE

5. Patience, and the mulberry leaf becomes a silk gown.

CHINESE PROVERB

6. Beware the fury of a patient man.

JOHN DRYDEN, *ABSALOM AND ACHITOPHEL* (1681), 1.1005

7. Abused patience turns to fury.

THOMAS FULLER, M.D., *GNOMOLOGIA* (1732), 757

8. All commend patience, but none can endure to suffer.

THOMAS FULLER, M.D., *GNOMOLOGIA* (1732), 508

9. Let him that hath no power of patience retire within himself, though even there he will have to put up with himself.

BALTASAR GRACIÁN, *THE ART OF WORLDLY WISDOM* (1647), 159, TR. JOSEPH JACOBS

10. Patience, that blending of moral courage with physical timidity.

THOMAS HARDY, *TESS OF THE D'URBERVILLES* (1891), 43

11. Patience makes lighter / What sorrow may not heal.

HORACE, *ODES* (23–C. 15 B.C.), 1.24

12. You can't set a hen in one morning and have chicken salad for lunch.

GEORGE HUMPHREY, *TIME*, JAN. 26, 1953

13. We shall sooner have the fowl by hatching the egg than by smashing it.

ABRAHAM LINCOLN, SPEECH, APRIL 11, 1865

14. Only with winter-patience can we bring / The deep-desired, long-awaited spring.

ANNE MORROW LINDBERGH, "AUTUMN 1939," *THE UNICORN AND OTHER POEMS, 1935–1955* (1956)

15. Patience and diligence, like faith, remove mountains.

WILLIAM PENN, *SOME FRUITS OF SOLITUDE* (1693), 1.234

16. Though patience be a tired mare, yet she will plod.

SHAKESPEARE, *HENRY V* (1598–99), 2.1.26

17. A wise man does not try to hurry history. Many wars have been avoided by patience and many have been precipitated by reckless haste.

ADLAI STEVENSON, SPEECH, SAN FRANCISCO, SEPT. 5, 1952

18. The Colombians are good-tempered people. They are used to waiting for buses that are late, used to riding buses and trains that do not arrive.

PAUL THEROUX, *THE OLD PATAGONIAN EXPRESS* (1979)

19. Patience is the art of hoping.

VAUVENARGUES, *REFLECTIONS AND MAXIMS* (1746), 251

PATIENTS

See 263. DOCTORS

678. PATRIOTISM

See also 423. HOMELAND; 622. NATIONALISM

1. Patriotism is in political life what faith is in religion.

LORD ACTON, "NATIONALITY," *THE HOME AND FOREIGN REVIEW,* JULY 1862

2. What a pity is it / That we can die but once to save our country!

JOSEPH ADDISON, *CATO* (1713), 1.4

3. When a whole nation is roaring Patriotism at the top of its voice, I am fain to explore the cleanness of its hands and purity of its heart.

EMERSON, *JOURNALS,* 1824

4. A person does not belong to a place until there is someone dead under the ground.

GABRIEL GARCÍA MÁRQUEZ, *ONE HUNDRED YEARS OF SOLITUDE* (1970)

5. He who loves not his home and country which he has seen, how shall he love humanity in general which he has not seen?

WILLIAM RALPH INGE, "PATRIOTISM," *OUTSPOKEN ESSAYS: FIRST SERIES* (1919)

6. Patriotism is the last refuge of a scoundrel.

SAMUEL JOHNSON, QUOTED IN BOSWELL'S *LIFE OF SAMUEL JOHNSON,* APRIL 7, 1775

7. There are things a man must not do even to save a nation.

MURRAY KEMPTON, "TO SAVE A NATION," *AMERICA COMES OF MIDDLE AGE* (1963)

8. Ask not what your country can do for you: Ask what you can do for your country.

JOHN F. KENNEDY, INAUGURAL ADDRESS, JAN. 20, 1961

9. With a good conscience our only sure reward, with history the final judge of our deeds, let us go forth to lead the land we love, asking His blessing and His help, but knowing that here on earth God's work must truly be our own.

JOHN F. KENNEDY, INAUGURAL ADDRESS, JAN. 20, 1961

10. I am, we are, patriots so outrageously old-fashioned that we incorporated the spirit of the country in our very heads, took literally its every invitation to the greatest kind of self-fulfillment ever known.

SEYMOUR KRIM, "FOR MY BROTHERS AND SISTERS IN THE FAILURE BUSINESS," IN *THE ART OF THE PERSONAL ESSAY* (1994), ED. PHILLIP LOPATE

11. When a nation is filled with strife, then do patriots flourish.

LAO TZU, *THE SIMPLE WAY* (6TH C. B.C.)

12. You're not supposed to be so blind with patriotism that you can't face reality. Wrong is wrong, no matter who does it or who says it.

MALCOLM X, *MALCOLM X SPEAKS* (1965), 12

13. The love of Americans for their country is not an indulgent, it is an exacting and chastising love; they cannot tolerate its defects.

JACQUES MARITAIN, *REFLECTIONS ON AMERICA* (1958), 5

14. Patriotism is a kind of religion; it is the egg from which wars are hatched.

GUY DE MAUPASSANT, *MY UNCLE SOSTHENES*

15. Not for the flag / Of any land because myself was born there / Will I give up my life. / But I will

love that land where man is free, / And that will I defend.

Edna St. Vincent Millay, "Not for a Nation," *Mine the Harvest* (1954)

16. Who saves his country violates no law.

Napoleon I, *Maxims* (1804–15)

17. There can be no fifty-fifty Americanism in this country. There is room here for only hundred per cent Americanism.

Theodore Roosevelt, speech, Saratoga, N.Y., July 19, 1918

18. Do we wish men to be virtuous? Then let us begin by making them love their country.

Rousseau, *A Discourse on Political Economy* (1758), tr. G. D. H. Cole

19. No one loves his country for its size or eminence, but because it's his own.

Seneca, *Letters to Lucilius* (1st c.), tr. E. Phillips Barker

20. Patriotism is not a short and frenzied outburst of emotion but the tranquil and steady dedication of a lifetime.

Adlai Stevenson, Speech to American Legion Convention, Aug. 30, 1952

21. To strike freedom of the mind with the fist of patriotism is an old and ugly subtlety.

Adlai Stevenson, speech, New York City, Aug. 27, 1952

22. My kind of loyalty was loyalty to one's country, not to its institutions or its office-holders.

Mark Twain, *A Connecticut Yankee at King Arthur's Court* (1889)

23. Talking of patriotism, what humbug it is; it is a word which always commemorates a robbery.

Mark Twain, *Notebook* (1935)

24. The things that the flag stands for were created by the experiences of a great people. Everything that it stands for was written by their lives. The flag is the embodiment, not of sentiment, but of history.

Woodrow Wilson, speech, June 14, 1915

679. PATRONAGE

1. Is not a patron one who looks with unconcern on a man struggling for life in the water, and, when he has reached ground, encumbers him with help?

Samuel Johnson, letter to Lord Chesterfield, Feb. 7, 1755, quoted in Boswell's *Life of Samuel Johnson*

680. PAYMENT

See also 647. Obligation; 789. Recompense

1. They [an entire family] got a dollar and a quarter a day five days a week and seventy-five cents on Saturday, seven dollars a week, ten hours' work a day.

James Agee, *Let Us Now Praise Famous Men* (1941)

2. The House took a large twenty-five percent raise. We [Senators] took a three percent raise, but we kept our right to earn an outside income. In this way the taxpayers don't have to pay.

Senator Alfonse D'Amato, quoted in *Senator Pothole* (1994), by Leonard Lurie

3. Always pay; for first or last you must pay your entire debt.

Emerson, "Compensation," *Essays: First Series* (1841)

4. In nature nothing can be given, all things are sold.

Emerson, "Compensation," *Essays: First Series* (1841)

5. In every work / a reward added makes the pleasure twice as great.

Euripides, *Rhesus* (c. 455–441 B.C.), tr. Richmond Lattimore

6. He that payeth beforehand shall have his work ill done.

Thomas Fuller, M.D., *Gnomologia* (1732), 2245

7. People will always work harder if they're getting well paid and if they're afraid of losing a job which they know will be hard to equal. As is well known, if you pay peanuts, you get monkeys.

Armand Hammer, *Hammer* (1987), with Neil Lyndon

8. "There are bullfighters who do it just for the money—they are worthless [said Hemingway]. The only one who matters is the bullfighter who feels it, so that if he did it for nothing, he would do it just as well. Same holds true for damn near everyone."

A.E. Hotchner, *Papa Hemingway* (1966)

9. One pays for everything, the trick is not to pay too much of anything for anything.

John Steinbeck, *Steinbeck: A Life in Letters*, eds. Elaine Steinbeck and Robert Wallsten (1975)

681. PEACE

See also 167. Conciliation; 173. Conquest; 228. Defeat; 665. Pacifism; 989. Tranquility; 1042. War

PEACE

1. Better beans and bacon in peace than cakes and ale in fear.

AESOP, "THE TOWN MOUSE AND THE COUNTRY MOUSE," *FABLES* (6TH C. B.C.?), TR. JOSEPH JACOBS

2. He knows peace who has forgotten desire.

BHAGAVADGITA, 2, TR. CHRISTOPHER ISHERWOOD

3. Peace is liberty in tranquillity.

CICERO, *PHILIPPICS* (44–43 B.C.), 2.44

4. The name of peace is sweet and the thing itself good, but between peace and slavery there is the greatest difference.

CICERO, *PHILIPPICS* (44–43 B.C.), 2

5. I take it that what all men are really after is some form or perhaps only some formula of peace.

JOSEPH CONRAD, PROLOGUE TO PART I, *UNDER WESTERN EYES* (1911)

6. No one can have peace longer than his neighbor pleases.

DUTCH PROVERB

7. On all the peaks lies peace.

GOETHE, "WANDERERS NACHTLIED."

8. Peace. The upland serenity of high altitude, the openness of grassland without indigenous bush or trees; the greening, yellowing or silver-browning that prevailed, according to season.

NADINE GORDIMER, *THE CONSERVATIONIST* (1975)

9. War makes rattling good history; but Peace is poor reading.

THOMAS HARDY, *THE DYNASTS* (1904–08), 2.5

10. Mankind has grown strong in eternal struggles and it will only perish through eternal peace.

ADOLF HITLER, *MEIN KAMPF* (1924), 1.4

11. The passions that incline men to peace are fear of death, desire of such things as are necessary to commodious living, and a hope by their industry to obtain them.

THOMAS HOBBES, *LEVIATHAN* (1651), 1.13

12. The only condition of peace in this world is to have no ideas, or, at least, not to express them.

OLIVER WENDELL HOLMES, SR., *THE PROFESSOR AT THE BREAKFAST TABLE* (1860), 4

13. Mutual cowardice keeps us in peace.

SAMUEL JOHNSON, QUOTED IN BOSWELL'S *LIFE OF SAMUEL JOHNSON*, APRIL 28, 1778

14. Now we suffer the woes of long peace. Luxury, more savage / Than war, has smothered us, avenging the world we ravage.

JUVENAL, *SATIRES* (C. 100), 6.292, TR. HUBERT CREEKMORE

15. Peace is a daily, a weekly, a monthly process, gradually changing opinions, slowly eroding old barriers, quietly building new structures.

JOHN F. KENNEDY, ADDRESS TO UNITED NATIONS GENERAL ASSEMBLY, SEPT. 20, 1963

16. The mere absence of war is not peace.

JOHN F. KENNEDY, STATE OF THE UNION MESSAGE, JAN. 14, 1963

17. My aunt once said the world would never find peace until men fell at their women's feet and asked for forgiveness.

JACK KEROUAC, *ON THE ROAD* (1957)

18. You may call for peace as loudly as you wish, but where there is no brotherhood there can in the end be no peace.

MAX LERNER, "THE GIFTS OF THE MAGI," *ACTIONS AND PASSIONS* (1949)

19. Certain peace is better and safer than anticipated victory.

LIVY, *AB URBE CONDITA* (C. 29 B.C.), 30.30

20. If there is to be any peace it will come through being, not having.

HENRY MILLER, "THE WISDOM OF THE HEART," *THE WISDOM OF THE HEART* (1941)

21. Peace hath her victories no less renowned than war.

MILTON, SONNET 16 (1652)

22. There is no way to peace. Peace is the way.

A. J. MUSTE, QUOTED IN AN EDITORIAL IN *THE NEW YORK TIMES*, NOV. 16, 1967

23. Because of the realities of human nature, perfect peace is achieved in two places only: in the grave and at the typewriter.

RICHARD M. NIXON, *REAL PEACE* (1984)

24. Peace demands more, not less, from a people. Peace lacks the clarity of purpose and the cadence of war. War is scripted: peace is improvisation.

RICHARD M. NIXON, *BEYOND PEACE* (1994)

25. Fair peace is becoming to men; fierce anger belongs to beasts.

OVID, *THE ART OF LOVE* (C. A.D. 8), 3.502

26. It is better to have a war for justice than peace in injustice.

Charles Péguy, "The Rights of Man," *Basic Verities* (1943), tr. Julian Green

27. Peace is not made with friends. Peace is made with enemies.

Yitzhak Rabin, quoted in *The New York Times,* Sept. 5, 1993

28. Peace, like war, can succeed only where there is a will to enforce it, and where there is available power to enforce it.

Franklin D. Roosevelt, speech at the Foreign Policy Association, New York City, Oct. 21, 1944

29. I believe that for peace a man may, even should, do everything in his power. Nothing in this world could rank higher than peace.

Anwar el-Sadat, "The Road to Peace," *In Search of Identity* (1977)

30. Peace is when time doesn't matter as it passes by.

Maria Schell, *Time,* March 3, 1958

31. It is expedient for the victor to wish for peace restored; for the vanquished it is necessary.

Seneca, *Hercules Furens* (1st c.), 369

32. A peace is of the nature of a conquest; / For then both parties nobly are subdued, / And neither party loser.

Shakespeare, *2 Henry IV* (1597–98), 4.2.89

33. Since wars begin in the minds of men, it is in the minds of men that the defenses of peace must be constructed.

Unesco, constitution (1945)

34. Peace is a virtual, mute, sustained victory of potential powers against probable greeds.

Paul Valéry, "Greatness and Decadence of Europe," *Reflections on the World Today* (1931), tr. Francis Scarfe

35. What we dignify with the name of peace is really only a short truce, in accordance with which the weaker party renounces his claims, whether just or unjust, until such time as he can find an opportunity of asserting them with the sword.

Vauvenargues, *Reflections and Maxims* (1746), 413, tr. F. G. Stevens

36. Where men had once howled and hacked at one another, and fought nip-and-tuck with nature as well, the machines hummed and whirred and clicked, and made parts for baby carriages and bottle caps, motorcycles and refrigerators, television sets and tricycles—the fruits of peace.

Kurt Vonnegut, *Player Piano* (1952)

37. Most people think of peace as a state of Nothing Bad Happening, or Nothing Much Happening. Yet if peace is to overtake us and make us the gift of serenity and well-being, it will have to be the state of Something Good Happening.

E.B. White, "Unity," *Essays of E. B. White* (1977)

38. The deliberate aim at Peace very easily passes into its bastard substitute, Anaesthesia.

Alfred North Whitehead, *Adventures of Ideas* (1935)

39. Peace hath higher tests of manhood / Than battle ever knew.

John Greenleaf Whittier, "The Hero" (1853), 19

40. Only a peace between equals can last.

Woodrow Wilson, address to U.S. Senate, 1917

41. There is a price which is too great to pay for peace, and that price can be put in one word. One cannot pay the price of self-respect.

Woodrow Wilson, speech, Des Moines, Iowa, Feb. 1, 1916

42. An insincere peace is better than a sincere war.

Yiddish proverb, *A Treasury of Jewish Folklore* (1948), ed. Nathan Ausubel

PEDANTRY

See 522. Knowledge; 848. Scholars and Scholarship

682. THE PEOPLE

See also 52. Aristocracy; 135. Class; 208. Crowds; 233. Democracy; 587. Middle Class; 597. Mob; 913. Society

1. The few have not strength to achieve great changes unaided; the many have not wisdom to be moved by truth unmixed.

Lord Acton, "Nationality" (1862), reprinted in *Essays on Freedom and Power* (1948)

2. Civilization exists precisely so that there may be no masses but rather men alert enough never to constitute masses.

Georges Bernanos, "Why Freedom?" *The Last Essays of Georges Bernanos* (1955), tr. Barry Ulanov

3. People on the whole are very simple-minded, in whatever country one finds them. They are so simple as to take literally, more often than no, the things their leaders tell them.

Pearl S. Buck, *What America Means to Me* (1943), 5

4. The general public knows practically nothing about the prison and appears to be little concerned about how it is managed and how prisoners are treated.

Eugene V. Debs, *Walls and Bars* (1927)

5. The instinct of the people is right.

Emerson, "Power," *The Conduct of Life* (1860)

6. The populace drag down the gods to their own level.

Emerson, *Journals,* 1858

7. The public always prefers to be reassured. There are those whose job this is. There are only too many.

André Gide, *Journal of "The Counterfeiters,"* Second Notebook, Mar. 29, 1925, tr. Justin O'Brien

8. The people like neither the true nor the simple; they like novels and charlatans.

Edmond and Jules De Goncourt, *Journal,* March 31, 1861

9. The efforts of governments alone will never be enough. In the end, the people must choose and the people must help themselves.

John F. Kennedy, at reception for Latin-American diplomats, Washington, D.C., March 13, 1961

10. We hold the view that the people make the best judgment in the long run.

John F. Kennedy, campaign remarks, rally, Greensboro, N. C., Sept. 17, 1960

11. While the people retain their virtue and vigilance, no administration, by any extreme of wickedness or folly, can very seriously injure the government in the short space of four years.

Abraham Lincoln, first Inaugural Address, March 4, 1861

12. Why should there not be a patient confidence in the ultimate justice of the people? Is there any better or equal hope in the world?

Abraham Lincoln, first Inaugural Address, March 4, 1861

13. The people, and the people alone, are the motive force in the making of world history.

Mao Tse-Tung, *Quotations from Chairman Mao Tse-Tung* (1966), 11

14. In our popular mythology, the lower classes are decent, hardworking, and possessed of simple piety and common sense—as long as they stay downwind.

P.J. O'Rourke, *Modern Manners* (1988)

15. Of the whole public not a handful can understand the artist's point of view or the writer's conscience.

Maxwell Perkins, *Editor to Author: The Letters of Maxwell Perkins* (1950), ed. John Hall Wheelock

16. An habitation giddy and unsure / Hath he that buildeth on the vulgar heart.

Shakespeare, *2 Henry IV* (1597–98), 1.3.89

17. For the truth is that men do not desire to be the Common Man any more than they are the Common Man. They need greatness in others and the occasion to discover the greatness in themselves.

C.V. Wedgwood, *History and Hope* (1987)

18. Every country is renewed out of the unknown ranks and not out of the ranks of those already famous and powerful and in control.

Woodrow Wilson, speech, Chester, Pa., Oct. 28, 1912

683. PERCEPTION

See also 87. Blindness, Spiritual; 325. Eyes; 501. Intuition; 689. Perspective; 882. Senses; 883. Sensibility; 897. Sight; 1007. Understanding; 1035. Vision

1. A fool sees not the same tree that a wise man sees.

William Blake, "Proverbs of Hell," *The Marriage of Heaven and Hell* (1790)

2. The Eye altering alters all.

William Blake, "The Mental Traveller" (1800–10)

3. No object is mysterious. The mystery is your eye.

Elizabeth Bowen, *The House in Paris* (1935), 2.6

4. People only see what they are prepared to see.

Emerson, *Journals,* 1863

5. Women see better than men. Men see lazily, if they do not expect to act. Women see quite without any wish to act.

Emerson, *Journals* 1839

6. The vision of an entire world becoming just like us is at least as discomfiting as the thought that most of it won't.

Eva Hoffman, *Exit Into History* (1933)

7. The searcher's eye / Not seldom finds more than he wished to find.

GOTTHOLD EPHRAIM LESSING, *NATHAN THE WISE* (1779), 2.7, TR. BAYARD QUINCY MORGAN

8. Some eyes want spectacles to see things clearly and distinctly: but let not those that use them therefore say nobody can see clearly without them.

JOHN LOCKE, *AN ESSAY CONCERNING HUMAN UNDERSTANDING* (1690), 4.17.4

9. Resemblances are the shadows of differences. Different people see different similarities and similar differences.

VLADIMIR NABOKOV, "COMMENTARY," *PALE FIRE* (1962), 894

10. The man who sees little always sees less than there is to see; the man who hears badly always hears something more than there is to hear.

NIETZSCHE, *HUMAN, ALL TOO HUMAN* (1878), 544, TR. HELEN ZIMMERN

11. Not only is there but one way of doing things rightly, but there is only one way of seeing them, and that is, seeing the whole of them.

JOHN RUSKIN, *THE TWO PATHS* (1859), 2

684. PERFECTION

See also 299. ERROR; 342. FAULTS; 457. IMPERFECTION

1. When a man says that he is perfect already, there is only one of two places for him, and that is heaven or the lunatic asylum.

HENRY WARD BEECHER, *PROVERBS FROM PLYMOUTH PULPIT* (1887)

2. All mankind / Is born for perfection / And each shall attain it / Will he but follow / His nature's duty.

BHAGAVADGITA, 18, TR. CHRISTOPHER ISHERWOOD

3. If thou wilt be perfect, go and sell that thou hast, and give to the poor, and thou shalt have treasure in heaven.

BIBLE, MATTHEW 19:21

4. Total freedom from error is what none of us will allow to our neighbors; however we may be inclined to flirt a little with such spotless perfection ourselves.

CHARLES CALEB COLTON, *LACON* (1825), 1.17

5. The wise man, the true friend, the finished character, we seek everywhere, and only find in fragments.

EMERSON, *JOURNALS,* 1833

6. People who have no weaknesses are terrible; there is no way of taking advantage of them.

ANATOLE FRANCE, *THE CRIME OF SYLVESTRE BONNARD* (1881), 2.4, TR. LAFCADIO HEARN

7. We shall never have friends, if we expect to find them without fault.

THOMAS FULLER, M.D.,, *GNOMOLOGIA* (1732), 5456

8. Could everything be done twice everything would be done better.

GERMAN PROVERB

9. Trifles make perfection, but perfection is no trifle.

ITALIAN PROVERB

10. In small proportions we just beauties see, / And in short measures life may perfect be.

BEN JONSON, "TO THE IMMORTAL MEMORY OF SIR LUCIUS CARY AND SIR HENRY MORISON," *UNDERWOODS* (1640), 3

11. He whose preoccupation is with excellence longs fervently to find rest in perfection; and is not nothingness a form of perfection?

THOMAS MANN, *DEATH IN VENICE* (1911)

12. Perfection has one grave defect: it is apt to be dull.

W. SOMERSET MAUGHAM, *THE SUMMING UP* (1938), 10

13. The most vigilant self-criticism of course is necessary, but the time comes when the artist must tell himself he is good or he will go under.

GERALD MOORE, *AM I TOO LOUD? A MUSICAL AUTOBIOGRAPHY* (1962)

14. Whoever thinks a faultless piece to see, / Thinks what ne'er was, nor is, nor shall be.

ALEXANDER POPE, *AN ESSAY ON CRITICISM* (1711), 2.53

15. Perfection is no more a requisite to art than to heroes. Frigidaires are perfect. Beauty limps. My frigidaire has had to be replaced.

NED ROREM, "RANDOM NOTES FROM A DIARY," *MUSIC FROM INSIDE OUT* (1967)

16. In anything at all, perfection is finally attained not when there is no longer anything to add, but when there is no longer anything to take away.

SAINT-EXUPÉRY, *WIND, SAND, AND STARS* (1939), 3, TR. LEWIS GALANTIÈRE

17. Striving to better, oft we mar what's well.

SHAKESPEARE, *KING LEAR* (1605–06), 1.4.369

18. The indefatigable pursuit of an unattainable Perfection, even though it consist in nothing more

than the pounding of an old piano, alone gives a meaning to our life on this unavailing star.

LOGAN PEARSALL SMITH, *AFTERTHOUGHTS* (1931), 5

19. The abuse of grace is affectation, as the abuse of the sublime is absurdity; all perfection is nearly a fault.

VOLTAIRE, "GRACE," *PHILOSOPHICAL DICTIONARY* (1764)

20. It is through Art, and through Art only, that we can realise our perfection.

OSCAR WILDE, "THE CRITIC AS ARTIST," *INTENTIONS* (1891)

685. PERFUME

See also 192. COSMETICS

1. To smell, though well, is to stink.

MONTAIGNE, "OF SMELLS," *ESSAYS* (1580–88), TR. W. C. HAZLITT

2. A basic ingredient in the manufacture of perfume, the attar—a heavy, pale-yellow oil stored in small metal drums—had been put up as collateral by Bulgaria, in lieu of gold, at the Moscow Narodny Bank, a Communist finance house for East-West trade.

S.J. PERELMAN, *THE RISING GORGE* (1961)

3. A woman smells well when she smells of nothing.

PLAUTUS, *MOSTELLARIA* (3RD C. B.C.)

PERMANENCE

See 118. CHANGELESSNESS

686. PERSEVERANCE

See also 281. EFFORT; 287. ENDURANCE; 585. METHOD

1. The person who makes a success of living is the one who sees his goal steadily and aims for it unswervingly. That is dedication.

CECIL B. DE MILLE, *SUNSHINE AND SHADOW* (1955)

2. To persevere, trusting in what hopes he has, / is courage in a man. The coward despairs.

EURIPIDES, *HERACLES* (C. 422 B.C.), TR. WILLIAM ARROWSMITH

3. Somehow life doesn't always pay off to those who are most insistent.

MAX LERNER, "THE POSTPONED GENERATION," *ACTIONS AND PASSIONS* (1949)

4. Perseverance can lend the appearance of dignity and grandeur to many actions, just as silence in company affords wisdom and apparent intelligence to a stupid person.

GEORG CHRISTOPH LICHTENBERG; *APHORISMS* (1764–99), TR. H. HATFIELD

5. Many strokes overthrow the tallest oaks.

JOHN LYLY, *EUPHUES: THE ANATOMY OF WIT* (1579)

6. Perseverance is more prevailing than violence; and many things which cannot be overcome when they are together, yield themselves up when taken little by little.

PLUTARCH, "LIFE OF SERTORIUS," *PARALLEL LIVES* (1ST–2ND C. A.D.), TR. JOHN DRYDEN

7. The wind-footed steed is broken down in his speed, whilst the camel-driver jogs on with his beast to the end of his journey.

SA'DI, *GULISTAN* (1258), 8.37, TR. JAMES ROSS

8. Even after a bad harvest there must be sowing.

SENECA, *LETTERS TO LUCILIUS* (1ST C.), 81.1, TR. E. PHILLIPS BARKER

687. PERSONALITY

See also 119. CHARACTER; 688. PERSONALITY, DUAL; 969. TEMPERAMENT

1. Few men are of one plain, decided color; most are mixed, shaded, and blended; and vary as much, from different situations, as changeable silks do from different lights.

LORD CHESTERFIELD, *LETTERS TO HIS SON*, APRIL 30, 1752

2. He was a lot like those Currier and Ives prints which, having outgrown them, one then laps the field of Sensibility to approach again from behind and see as "wonderful."

PETER DE VRIES, *COMFORT ME WITH APPLES* (1956)

3. A man is like a bit of Labrador spar, which has no lustre as you turn it in your hand, until you come to a particular angle; then it shows deep and beautiful colors.

EMERSON, "EXPERIENCE," *ESSAYS: SECOND SERIES* (1844)

4. Many of the twisted minds and crippled characters in the world were made by careless parents who kept their children away from knives and fires, but put permanent scars on their souls.

GILBERT HIGHET, *THE ART OF TEACHING* (1950)

5. The juvenile delinquent does not feel his *disturbed personality*. The intelligent man does not feel his *intelligence* or the introvert his *introversion*.

B.F. SKINNER, *BEYOND FREEDOM AND DIGNITY* (1971)

688. PERSONALITY, DUAL

See also 440. HYPOCRISY; 444. IDENTITY; 687. PERSONALITY

1. The image of myself which I try to create in my own mind in order that I may love myself is very different from the image which I try to create in the minds of others in order that they may love me.

W. H. AUDEN, "HIC ET ILLE," *THE DYER'S HAND* (1962)

2. God be thanked, the meanest of his creatures / Boasts two soul-sides, one to face the world with, / One to show a woman when he loves her!

ROBERT BROWNING, "ONE WORD MORE," *MEN AND WOMEN* (1855), 17

3. A man must ride alternately on the horses of his private and his public nature.

EMERSON, "FATE," *THE CONDUCT OF LIFE* (1860)

4. There is no one so bound to his own face that he does not cherish the hope of presenting another to the world.

ANTONIO MACHADO, *JUAN DE MAIRENA* (1943), 17, TR. BEN BELITT

689. PERSPECTIVE

See also 58. ATTITUDE; 333. FAMILIARITY; 683. PERCEPTION; 795. RELATIVENESS

1. It is very much easier to divide your outlook on the world into two halves, to say that you know this belongs to the daily half and this belongs to the Sunday half.

JACOB BRONOWSKI, *MAGIC, SCIENCE, AND CIVILIZATION* (1978)

2. 'Tis distance lends enchantment to the view, / And robes the mountain in its azure hue.

THOMAS CAMPBELL, *PLEASURES OF HOPE* (1799), 1.7

3. What you see, yet can not see over, is as good as infinite.

THOMAS CARLYLE, *SARTOR RESARTUS* (1833–34), 2.1

4. It is the eye which makes the horizon.

EMERSON, "EXPERIENCE," *ESSAYS: SECOND SERIES* (1844)

5. The field cannot well be seen from within the field.

EMERSON, "CIRCLES," *ESSAYS: FIRST SERIES* (1841)

6. Distance has the same effect on the mind as on the eye.

SAMUEL JOHNSON, *RASSELAS* (1759), 35

7. Every man takes the limits of his own field of vision for the limits of the world.

SCHOPENHAUER, "FURTHER PSYCHOLOGICAL OBSERVATIONS," *PARERGA AND PARALIPOMENA* (1851), TR. T. BAILEY SAUNDERS

690. PERSUASION

See also 51. ARGUMENT; 158. COMPLIANCE; 283. ELOQUENCE; 745. PROPAGANDA

1. Most people have ears, but few have judgment; tickle those ears, and, depend upon it, you will catch their judgments, such as they are.

LORD CHESTERFIELD, *LETTERS TO HIS SON,* DEC. 9, 1749

2. To please people is a great step towards persuading them.

LORD CHESTERFIELD, *LETTERS TO HIS SON,* NOV. 1, 1739

3. He who wants to persuade should put his trust not in the right argument, but in the right word. The power of sound has always been greater than the power of sense.

JOSEPH CONRAD, "A FAMILIAR PREFACE," *A PERSONAL RECORD* (1912)

4. I am guilty of believing that the human race can be humanized and enriched in every spiritual inference through the saner and more beneficent processes of peaceful persuasion applied to material problems rather than through wars, riots and bloodshed.

EUGENE V. DEBS, *WALLS AND BARS* (1927)

5. Too much zeal offends / where indirection works.

EURIPIDES, *ORESTES* (408 B.C.), TR. WILLIAM ARROWSMITH

6. Charming women can true converts make, / We love the precepts for the teacher's sake.

GEORGE FARQUHAR, *THE CONSTANT COUPLE* (1699), 5.3

7. Would you persuade, speak of interest, not of reason.

BENJAMIN FRANKLIN, *POOR RICHARD'S ALMANACK* (1732–57)

8. The persuasion of a friend is a strong thing.

HOMER, *ILIAD* (9TH C. B.C.), 15.404, TR. RICHMOND LATTIMORE

9. People are generally better persuaded by the reasons which they have themselves discovered than by those which have come into the mind of others.

PASCAL, *PENSÉES* (1670), 10, TR. W. F. TROTTER

10. I see / that everywhere among the race of men / it is the tongue that wins and not the deed.

SOPHOCLES, *PHILOCTETES* (409 B.C.), TR. DAVID GRENE

691. PERVERSENESS

See also 170. CONFLICT, INNER; 866. SELF-DESTRUCTION

1. Man never knows what he wants; he aspires to penetrate mysteries and as soon as he has, wants to re-establish them. Ignorance irritates him and knowledge cloys.

HENRI FRÉDÉRIC AMIEL, *JOURNAL* (1882–84)

2. There is in the human race some dark spirit of recalcitrance, always pulling us in the direction contrary to that in which we are reasonably expected to go.

MAX BEERBOHM, "SOME DAMNABLE ERRORS ABOUT CHRISTMAS," *A CHRISTMAS GARLAND* (1895)

3. The good that I would do not; but the evil which I would not, that I do.

BIBLE, ROMANS 7:19

4. What rapture, oh, it is to know / A good thing when you see it / And having seen a good thing, oh, / What rapture 'tis to flee it.

BERTOLT BRECHT, *THE GOOD WOMAN OF SETZUAN* (1938–40), 10, TR. MAJA APELMAN

5. We trifle with, make sport of, and despise those who are attached to us, and follow those that fly from us.

WILLIAM HAZLITT, "ON THE CONDUCT OF LIFE," *LITERARY REMAINS* (1836)

6. Look round the habitable world: how few / Know their own good, or knowing it, pursue.

JUVENAL, *SATIRES* (C. 100), 10, TR. JOHN DRYDEN

7. Few people want the pleasures they are free to take.

OVID, *THE LOVES* (C. A.D. 8), 3.4, TR. J. LEWIS MAY

8. Man is neither angel nor beast, and the misfortune is that he who would act the angel acts the beast.

PASCAL, *PENSÉES* (1670), 358

9. The heart *prefers* to move against the grain of circumstance; perversity is the soul's very life.

JOHN UPDIKE, "MORE LOVE IN THE WESTERN WORLD," *ASSORTED PROSE* (1965)

10. The instinct of a man is to pursue everything that flies from him, and to fly from all that pursue him.

VOLTAIRE, "ENCHANTMENT," *PHILOSOPHICAL DICTIONARY* (1764)

692. PESSIMISM

See also 659. OPTIMISM; 660. OPTIMISM AND PESSIMISM

1. To a profound pessimist about life, being in danger is not depressing.

F. SCOTT FITZGERALD, QUOTED IN ANDREW TURNBULL'S *SCOTT FITZGERALD* (1962), 6

2. He that hopes no good fears no ill.

THOMAS FULLER, M.D., *GNOMOLOGIA* (1732), 2166

3. A pessimist is a man who has been compelled to live with an optimist.

ELBERT HUBBARD, *THE NOTE BOOK* (1927)

4. Logic and sermons never convince, / The damp of the night drives deeper into my soul.

WALT WHITMAN, "SONG OF MYSELF," 30, *LEAVES OF GRASS* (1855–92)

693. PETTINESS

See also 525. LARGENESS; 578. MEDIOCRITY; 996. TRIFLES; 1012. UNIMPORTANCE

1. No sadder proof can be given by a man of his own littleness than disbelief in great men.

THOMAS CARLYLE, *ON HEROES, HERO-WORSHIP AND THE HEROIC IN HISTORY* (1841), 1

2. To the mean eye all things are trivial, as certainly as to the jaundiced they are yellow.

THOMAS CARLYLE, *ON HEROES, HERO-WORSHIP AND THE HEROIC IN HISTORY* (1841), 3

3. That is the consolation of a little mind; you have the fun of changing it without impeding the progress of mankind.

FRANK MOORE COLBY, "SIMPLE SIMON," *THE COLBY ESSAYS* (1926), V.1

4. When we play the part of a great man too much, we seem very small.

PHILIPPE DESTOUCHES, *LE GLORIEUX* (1732), 3.5

5. The pettiness of a mind can be measured by the pettiness of its adoration or its blasphemy.

ANDRÉ GIDE, *JOURNALS,* JANUARY 1902, TR. JUSTIN O'BRIEN

6. Poor fool! in whose petty estimation all things are little.

GOETHE, *THE SORROWS OF YOUNG WERTHER* (1774), 1, AUG. 18, 1771, TR. VICTOR LANGE

7. Small minds are much distressed by little things. Great minds see them all but are not upset by them.

LA ROCHEFOUCAULD, *MAXIMS* (1665), TR. KENNETH PRATT

8. To the mean all becomes mean.

NIETZSCHE, "ON OLD AND NEW TABLETS," *THUS SPOKE ZARATHUSTRA* (1883–92), 3, TR. WALTER KAUFMANN

9. Small things make base men proud.

SHAKESPEARE, *2 HENRY VI* (1590–91), 4.1.106

10. We cannot be kind to each other here for an hour; / We whisper, and hint, and chuckle, and grin at a brother's shame; / However we brave it out, we men are a little breed.

LORD TENNYSON, "MAUD; A MONODRAMA" (1856), 4.5

PHILANTHROPY

See 433. HUMANITARIANISM

694. PHILOSOPHERS AND PHILOSOPHY

See also 317. EXISTENTIALISM; 432. HUMANISM; 573. MEANING; 634. NIHILISM; 785. REASON; 904. SKEPTICISM; 937. STOICISM; 974. THEORY; 975. THOUGHT; 1019. THE UNKNOWN

1. A little philosophy inclineth man's mind to atheism, but depth in philosophy bringeth men's minds about to religion.

FRANCIS BACON, "OF ATHEISM," *ESSAYS* (1625)

2. Professors of Greek forget or are unaware that Thomas Aquinas, who did not know Greek, was a better interpreter of Aristotle than any of them have proved to be, not only because he was smarter but because he took Aristotle more seriously.

ALLAN BLOOM, *THE CLOSING OF THE AMERICAN MIND* (1987)

3. The facile economic and psychological debunking of the theoretical life cannot do away with its irreducible beauties.

ALLAN BLOOM, *THE CLOSING OF THE AMERICAN MIND* (1987)

4. All philosophies, if you ride them home, are nonsense; but some are greater nonsense than others.

SAMUEL BUTLER (D. 1902), "FIRST PRINCIPLES," *NOTE-BOOKS* (1912)

5. There is nothing so strange and so unbelievable that it has not been said by one philosopher or another.

DESCARTES, *DISCOURSE ON METHOD* (1639), 2

6. Posterity for the philosopher is what the other world is for the religious man.

DENIS DIDEROT, *LETTRE À FALCONET,* 1765

7. What is it to be a philosopher? Is it not to be prepared against events?

EPICTETUS, *DISCOURSES* (2ND C.), 3.10, TR. THOMAS W. HIGGINSON

8. Let no young man delay the study of philosophy, and let no old man become weary of it; for it is never too early nor too late to care for the well-being of the soul.

EPICURUS, LETTER TO MENOECEUS (3RD C. B.C.), IN *LETTERS, PRINCIPAL DOCTRINES, AND VATICAN SAYINGS,,* TR. RUSSEL M. GEER

9. You can't do without philosophy, since everything has its hidden meaning which we must know.

MAXIM GORKY, *THE ZYKOVS* (1914), 2

10. The difference between gossip and philosophy lies only in one's way of taking a fact.

OLIVER WENDELL HOLMES, JR., "THE BAR AS A PROFESSION," *YOUTH'S COMPANION,* 1896

11. The object of studying philosophy is to know one's own mind, not other people's.

WILLIAM RALPH INGE, "CONFESSIO FIDEI," *OUTSPOKEN ESSAYS: SECOND SERIES* (1922)

12. Pretend what we may, the whole man within us is at work when we form our philosophical opinions.

WILLIAM JAMES, "THE SENTIMENT OF RATIONALITY," *THE WILL TO BELIEVE* (1896)

13. Do not all charms fly / At the mere touch of cold philosophy?

KEATS, "LAMIA" (1819), 2

14. Philosophy will clip an Angel's wings, / Conquer all mysteries by rule and line, / Empty the haunted air, and gnomed mine— / Unweave a rainbow.

KEATS, "LAMIA" (1819), 2

15. All schools of philosophy, and almost all authors, are rather to be frequented for exercise than for weight.

WALTER SAVAGE LANDOR, "EPICURUS, LEONTION, AND TERNISSA," *IMAGINARY CONVERSATIONS* (1824–53)

16. The continual pursuit of meanings—wider, clearer, more negotiable, more articulate meanings—is philosophy.

SUSANNE K. LANGER, *PHILOSOPHY IN A NEW KEY* (1942)

17. A philosophy is characterized more by the formulation of its problem than by its solution of them.

SUSANNE K. LANGER, *PHILOSOPHY IN A NEW KEY* (1942)

18. The constancy of philosophers is nothing but the art of concealing their disquietude in their hearts.

La Rochefoucauld, *Maxims* (1665), tr. Kenneth Pratt

19. Oh! speculators on things, boast not of knowing the things that nature ordinarily brings about; but rejoice if you know the end of those things which you yourself devise.

Leonardo Da Vinci, *Notebooks* (c. 1500), tr. Jean Paul Richter

20. When philosophers try to be politicians they generally cease to be philosophers.

Walter Lippmann, "The Changing Focus," *A Preface to Politics* (1914)

21. The great philosophers are poets who believe in the reality of their poems.

Antonio Machado, *Juan de Mairena* (1943), 22, tr. Ben Belitt

22. It has been said that metaphysics is the finding of bad reasons for what we believe upon instinct.

W. Somerset Maugham, *The Summing Up* (1938), 15

23. Metaphysics is almost always an attempt to prove the incredible by an appeal to the unintelligible.

H. L. Mencken, *Minority Report* (1956), 357

24. Wonder is the foundation of all philosophy, inquiry the progress, ignorance the end.

Montaigne, "Of cripples," *Essays* (1580–88)

25. Philosophy is such an impertinently litigious lady that a man had as good be engaged in lawsuits as have to do with her.

Isaac Newton, letter to Edmund Halley, June 20, 1687

26. A married philosopher belongs to comedy.

Nietzsche, *The Genealogy of Morals* (1887), 3.7, tr. Horace B. Samuel

27. Philosophers.—We are full of things which take us out of ourselves.

Pascal, *Pensées* (1670), 464, tr. W. F. Trotter

28. To make light of philosophy is to be a true philosopher.

Pascal, *Pensées* (1670), 4, tr. W. F. Trotter

29. It is a proof of philosophical mediocrity, today, to look for a philosophy.

Pierre-Joseph Proudhon, *La Révolution sociale* (1852)

30. The philosopher spends in becoming a man the time which the ambitious man spends in becoming a personage.

Joseph Roux, *Meditations of a Parish Priest* (1886), 4.94, tr. Isabel F. Hapgood

31. Ethical metaphysics is fundamentally an attempt, however disguised, to give legislative force to our own wishes.

Bertrand Russell, "On Scientific Method in Philosophy," *Mysticism and Logic* (1917)

32. For the learning of every virtue there is an appropriate discipline, and for the learning of suspended judgment the best discipline is philosophy.

Bertrand Russell, "Philosophy for Laymen," *Unpopular Essays* (1950)

33. Philosophers, for the most part, are constitutionally timid, and dislike the unexpected. Few of them would be genuinely happy as pirates or burglars. Accordingly they invent systems which make the future calculable, at least in its main outlines.

Bertrand Russell, "Philosophy's Ulterior Motives," *Unpopular Essays* (1950)

34. At best, the true philosopher can fulfil his mission very imperfectly, which is to pilot himself, or at most a few voluntary companions who may find themselves in the same boat.

George Santayana, *Character and Opinion in the United States* (1921), 2

35. Philosophers are as jealous as women; each wants a monopoly of praise.

George Santayana, *Dialogues in Limbo* (1925), 2

36. Philosophy has a fine saying for everything.—For Death it has an entire set.

Laurence Sterne, *Tristram Shandy* (1759–67), 5.3

37. That's why I love philosophy: no one wins.

Daisetz Teitaro Suzuki, quoted in John Cage's "Composition as Process," *Silence* (1961), 2

38. The various opinions of philosophers have scattered through the world as many plagues of the mind as Pandora's box did those of the body; only with this difference, that they have not left hope at the bottom.

Jonathan Swift, *A Tritical Essay Upon the Faculties of the Mind* (1707)

39. To be a philosopher is not merely to have subtle thoughts, nor even to found a school, but so to love

wisdom as to live according to its dictates, a life of simplicity, independence, magnanimity, and trust.

THOREAU, *WALDEN* (1854)

40. All the persecutors declare against each other mortal war, while the philosopher, oppressed by them all, contents himself with pitying them.

VOLTAIRE, "PHILOSOPHER," *PHILOSOPHICAL DICTIONARY* (1764)

41. When one man speaks to another man who doesn't understand him, and when the man who's speaking no longer understands, it's metaphysics.

VOLTAIRE, *CANDIDE* (1759)

42. Every philosophy is tinged with the colouring of some secret imaginative background, which never emerges explicitly into its trains of reasoning.

ALFRED NORTH WHITEHEAD, *SCIENCE AND THE MODERN WORLD* (1925), 1

43. Philosophy begins in wonder. And, at the end, when philosophic thought has done its best, the wonder remains.

ALFRED NORTH WHITEHEAD, *MODES OF THOUGHT* (1938)

695. PHOTOGRAPHY

1. On others of these [grave]stones, as many as a dozen of them, there is something I have never seen before: by some kind of porcelain reproduction, a photograph of the person who is buried there; the last or the best likeness that had been made, in a small-town studio, or at home with a snapshot camera.

JAMES AGEE, *LET US NOW PRAISE FAMOUS MEN* (1941)

2. The virtue of the camera is not the power it has to transform the photographer into an artist, but the impulse it gives him to keep on looking.

BROOKS ATKINSON, "AUGUST 28," *ONCE AROUND THE SUN* (1951)

3. There was a group of Americans taking photographs. "What barbarians!" said Papa. "They take photographs so that they do not have to look."

SIMONE DE BEAUVOIR, *LES BELLES IMAGES* (1966), TR. PATRICK O'BRIAN (1968)

4. Nobody ever discovered ugliness through photographs. But many, through photographs, have discovered beauty.

SUSAN SONTAG, *ON PHOTOGRAPHY* (1977)

5. The possession of a camera can inspire something akin to lust. And like all credible forms of lust, it cannot be satisfied.

SUSAN SONTAG, *ON PHOTOGRAPHY* (1977)

6. To collect photographs is to collect the world.

SUSAN SONTAG, *ON PHOTOGRAPHY* (1977)

7. Photography records the gamut of feelings written on the human face, the beauty of the earth and skies that man has inherited, and the wealth and confusion man has created. It is a major force in explaining man to man.

EDWARD STEICHEN, *TIME,* APRIL 7, 1961

8. I hate cameras. They are so much more sure than I am about everything.

JOHN STEINBECK, *STEINBECK: A LIFE IN LETTERS,* EDS. ELAINE STEINBECK AND ROBERT WALLSTEN (1975)

9. For half a century photography has been the "art form" of the untalented. Obviously some pictures are more satisfactory than others, but where is credit due? To the designer of the camera? to the finger on the button? to the law of averages?

GORE VIDAL, *THE SECOND AMERICAN REVOLUTION AND OTHER ESSAYS* (1982)

696. PHYSICAL FITNESS

See also 929. SPORTS; 1041. WALKING

1. Bodily exercise profiteth little; but godliness is profitable unto all things.

BIBLE, 1 TIMOTHY 4:8

2. Oh, the wild joys of living! the leaping from rock up to rock, / The strong rending of boughs from the fir-tree, the cool silver shock / Of the plunge in a pool's living water.

ROBERT BROWNING, "SAUL," *MEN AND WOMEN* (1855), 9

3. Bodily exercises are to be done discreetly; not to be taken evenly and alike by all men.

THOMAS À KEMPIS, *THE IMITATION OF CHRIST* (1426), 1.19

4. There is nothing, I think, more unfortunate than to have soft, chubby, fat-looking children who go to watch their school play basketball every Saturday and regard that as their week's exercise.

JOHN F. KENNEDY, ADDRESS AT U.S. CHILDREN'S BUREAU, WASHINGTON, D.C., APRIL 9, 1962

5. In all important respects, the man who has nothing but his physical power to sell has nothing to sell which it is worth anyone's money to buy.

NORBERT WIENER, *THE HUMAN USE OF HUMAN BEINGS* (1954), 9

PHYSICIANS

See 263. DOCTORS

PHYSICS

See 849. SCIENCE

697. PIETY

See also 393. GOODNESS; 506. IRREVERENCE; 723. PRAYER

1. The strength of a man consists in finding out the way in which God is going, and going in that way too.

HENRY WARD BEECHER, *PROVERBS FROM PLYMOUTH PULPIT* (1887)

2. At the first sound of the priest's voice in the vestarium she was on her feet and she fired out her amens and her mercies in a stern and resonant voice, timed well ahead of the rest of the congregation as if she were involved in a sort of ecclesiastical footrace.

JOHN CHEEVER, *BULLET PARK* (1960)

3. Fear God, and where you go men shall think they walk in hallowed cathedrals.

EMERSON, "WORSHIP," *THE CONDUCT OF LIFE* (1860)

4. The best way to see divine light is to put out thy own candle.

THOMAS FULLER, M.D., *GNOMOLOGIA* (1732), 4421

5. Piety, like nobility, has its aristocracy.

GOETHE, QUOTED IN JOHANN PETER ECKERMANN'S *CONVERSATIONS WITH GOETHE*, FEB. 25, 1824

6. Love of God is not always the same as love of good.

HERMANN HESSE, *NARCISSUS AND GOLDMUND* (1930), 3, TR. URSULE MOLINARO

7. A devout man is he who would be an atheist if the king were.

LA BRUYÈRE, *CHARACTERS* (1688), 13.21

8. Piety with some people, but especially with women, is either a passion, or an infirmity of age, or a fashion which must be followed.

LA BRUYÈRE, *CHARACTERS* (1688), 3.16, TR. HENRI VAN LAUN

9. Experience makes us see an enormous difference between piety and goodness.

PASCAL, *PENSÉES* (1670), 496, TR. W. F. TROTTER

10. It is rash to intrude upon the piety of others: both the depth and the grace of it elude the stranger.

GEORGE SANTAYANA, *DIALOGUES IN LIMBO* (1925), 4

11. Religion in its humility restores man to his only dignity, the courage to live by grace.

GEORGE SANTAYANA, *DIALOGUES IN LIMBO* (1925), 4

12. Live with men as if God saw you: speak to God as if men heard you.

SENECA, *LETTERS TO LUCILIUS* (1ST C.), 10.5, TR. E. PHILLIPS BARKER

698. PITY

See also 583. MERCY; 877. SELF-PITY; 960. SYMPATHY; 1008. UNDERSTANDING OTHERS

1. One cannot weep for the entire world. It is beyond human strength. One must choose.

JEAN ANOUILH, *CÉCILE* (1949), TR. ARTHUR KLEIN

2. The response man has the greatest difficulty in tolerating is pity, especially when he warrants it. Hatred is a tonic, it makes one live, it inspires vengeance, but pity kills, it makes our weakness weaker.

BALZAC, *LA PEAU DE CHAGRIN* (1831), 3

3. Pity would be no more / If we did not make somebody Poor; / And Mercy no more could be / If all were as happy as we.

WILLIAM BLAKE, "THE HUMAN ABSTRACT," *SONGS OF EXPERIENCE* (1794)

4. There are a few things that'll move people to pity, a few, but the trouble is, when they've been used several times, they no longer work.

BERTOLT BRECHT, *THE THREEPENNY OPERA* (1928), 1.1, TR. ERIC BENTLEY

5. By compassion we make others' misery our own, and so, by relieving them, we relieve ourselves also.

SIR THOMAS BROWNE, *RELIGIO MEDICI* (1642), 2

6. A tear dries quickly, especially when it is shed for the troubles of others.

CICERO, *PARTITIONES ORATORIAE* (C. 55 B.C.)

7. Most of our misfortunes are more supportable than the comments of our friends upon them.

CHARLES CALEB COLTON, *LACON* (1825), 1.517

8. Endow the Living—with the Tears— / You squander on the Dead.

EMILY DICKINSON, POEM (C. 1862)

9. Pity melts the mind to love.

JOHN DRYDEN, "ALEXANDER'S FEAST" (1687), 96

10. You may regret calamities if you can thereby help the sufferer, but if you cannot, mind your own business.

EMERSON, *JOURNALS*, 1836

11. Pity wraps the student of the past in an ambrosial cloud, and washes his limbs with eternal youth.

E.M. FORSTER, "THE CONSOLATION OF HISTORY," *ABINGER HARVEST* (1936)

12. Sacrifice not thy heart upon every altar.

THOMAS FULLER, M.D., *GNOMOLOGIA* (1732), 4062

13. We may have uneasy feelings for seeing a creature in distress without pity; for we have not pity unless we wish to relieve them.

SAMUEL JOHNSON, QUOTED IN BOSWELL'S *LIFE OF SAMUEL JOHNSON*, JULY 20, 1763

14. We all have enough strength to bear the misfortunes of others.

LA ROCHEFOUCAULD, *MAXIMS* (1665), TR. KENNETH PRATT

15. Compassion for the friend should conceal itself under a hard shell.

NIETZSCHE, "ON THE FRIEND," *THUS SPOKE ZARATHUSTRA* (1883–92), 1, TR. WALTER KAUFMANN

16. Verily, I do not like them, the merciful who feel blessed in their pity: they are lacking too much in shame. If I must pity, at least I do not want it known; and if I do pity, it is preferably from a distance.

NIETZSCHE, "ON THE PITYING," *THUS SPOKE ZARATHUSTRA* (1883–92), 2, TR. WALTER KAUFMANN

17. What value has compassion that does not take its object in its arms?

SAINT-EXUPÉRY, *THE WISDOM OF THE SANDS* (1948), 26, TR. STUART GILBERT

18. The entire world would perish, if pity were not to limit anger.

SENECA THE ELDER, *CONTROVERSIAE* (1ST C. A.D.), 1

19. Worse than idle is compassion / If it end in tears and sighs.

WILLIAM WORDSWORTH, "THE ARMENIAN LADY'S LOVE" (1830), 4

699. PLACE

See also 992. TRAVEL

1. All places are distant from heaven alike.

ROBERT BURTON, *THE ANATOMY OF MELANCHOLY* (1621), 2.2.4

2. One always begins to forgive a place as soon as it's left behind.

CHARLES DICKENS, *LITTLE DORRIT* (1857–58), 1.2

3. The difference between landscape and landscape is small, but there is a great difference in the beholders.

EMERSON, "NATURE," *ESSAYS: SECOND SERIES* (1844)

4. The axis of the earth sticks out visibly through the centre of each and every town or city.

OLIVER WENDELL HOLMES, SR., *THE AUTOCRAT OF THE BREAKFAST TABLE* (1858), 6

5. A blade of grass is always a blade of grass, whether in one country or another.

SAMUEL JOHNSON, QUOTED IN HESTER LYNCH PIOZZI'S *ANECDOTES OF SAMUEL JOHNSON* (1786)

6. God gives all men all earth to love, / But, since man's heart is small, / Ordains for each one spot shall prove / Beloved over all.

RUDYARD KIPLING, "SUSSEX" (1902)

7. A place is nothing, not even space, / Unless at its heart a figure stands.

AMY LOWELL, "THORN PIECE," *A SHARD OF SILENCE* (1957)

8. All places are alike, / And every earth is fit for burial.

CHRISTOPHER MARLOWE, *EDWARD II* (C. 1593), 5.2

9. Free people have a serious problem with place, being in a place, using up a place, deciding which new place to rotate to. Americans ricochet around the United States like billiard balls.

WALKER PERCY, "WHY I LIVE WHERE I LIVE," *SIGNPOSTS IN A STRANGE LAND* (1991)

10. No place is a place until things that have happened in it are remembered in history, ballads, yarns, legends, or monuments. Fictions serve as well as facts.

WALLACE STEGNER, "THE SENSE OF PLACE," *WHEN THE BLUEBIRD SINGS IN THE LEMONADE SPRINGS* (1992)

700. PLAGIARISM

See also 451. IMITATION

1. If we steal thoughts from the moderns, it will be cried down as plagiarism; if from the ancients, it will be cried up as erudition.

CHARLES CALEB COLTON, *LACON* (1825), 1.546

2. Begin with another's to end with your own.

BALTASAR GRACIÁN, *THE ART OF WORLDLY WISDOM* (1647), 144, TR. JOSEPH JACOBS

3. We are all of us richer than we think we are; but we are taught to borrow and to beg, and brought up

more to make use of what is another's than of our own.

MONTAIGNE, "OF PHYSIOGNOMY," *ESSAYS* (1580–88), TR. W. C. HAZLITT

4. Immature artists imitate. Mature artists steal.

LIONEL TRILLING, *ESQUIRE*, SEPTEMBER 1962

PLAIN DEALING

See 362. FRANKNESS; 425. HONESTY; 901. SINCERITY

701. PLAIN LIVING

See also 186. CONTENTMENT; 977. THRIFT

1. Give me neither poverty nor riches; feed me with food convenient for me.

BIBLE, PROVERBS 30:8

2. Were a man to order his life by the rules of true reason, a frugal substance joined to a contented mind is for him great riches; for never is there any lack of a little.

LUCRETIUS, *ON THE NATURE OF THINGS* (1ST C. B.C.), 5, TR. H. A. J. MUNRO

3. Plain living is nothing but voluntary poverty.

SENECA, *LETTERS TO LUCILIUS* (1ST C.), 17.5, TR. E. PHILLIPS BARKER

4. Reduce the complexity of life by eliminating the needless wants of life, and the labors of life reduce themselves.

EDWIN WAY TEALE, "FEBRUARY 4," *CIRCLE OF THE SEASONS* (1953)

5. An elegant sufficiency, content, / Retirement, rural quiet, friendship, books.

JAMES THOMSON, "SPRING," *THE SEASONS* (1726–30), 1156

6. Plain living and high thinking are no more: / The homely beauty of the good old cause / Is gone; our peace, our fearful innocence, / And pure religion breathing household laws.

WILLIAM WORDSWORTH, "O FRIEND! I KNOW NOT WHICH WAY I MUST LOOK" (1802)

702. PLANS

See also 585. METHOD; 661. ORDER; 939. STRATEGY

1. Make no little plans: they have no magic to stir men's blood.

DANIEL H. BURNHAM, MOTTO OF CITY PLANNERS, QUOTED IN CHARLES MOORE'S *DANIEL H. BURNHAM* (1921), 2.25

2. The best-laid schemes o' mice an' men / Gang aft agley, / An' lea'e us nought but grief an' pain, / For promis'd joy!

ROBERT BURNS, "TO A MOUSE" (1785), 7

3. There are so many plans, so many schemes, and so many reasons why there should be neither plans nor schemes.

BENJAMIN DISRAELI, *DISRAELI*, SARAH BRADFORD (1982)

4. The very madness of the scheme protects it.

IRIS MURDOCH, *A WORD CHILD* (1975)

5. Amid a multitude of projects, no plan is devised.

PUBLILIUS SYRUS, *MORAL SAYINGS* (1ST C. B.C.), 319, TR. DARIUS LYMAN

6. It is a bad plan that admits of no modification.

PUBLILIUS SYRUS, *MORAL SAYINGS* (1ST C. B.C.), 469, TR. DARIUS LYMAN

7. Plans get you into things but you got to work your way out.

WILL ROGERS, *THE AUTOBIOGRAPHY OF WILL ROGERS* (1949), 16

8. Our lives are not totally random. We make commitments, we cause things to happen.

WENDY WASSERSTEIN, "THE MESSIAH," *BACHELOR GIRLS* (1990)

PLANTS

See 337. FARMS AND FARMING; 352. FLOWERS; 371. GARDENING; 623. NATURE; 995. TREES

703. PLAY

See also 533. LEISURE; 929. SPORTS

1. Play so that you may be serious.

ANACHARSIS (C. 600 B.C.), QUOTED IN ARISTOTLE'S *NICOMACHEAN ETHICS* (4TH C. B.C.), 10.6, TR. J. A. K. THOMSON

2. The true object of all human life is play. Earth is a task garden; heaven is a playground.

G. K. CHESTERTON, "OXFORD FROM WITHOUT," *ALL THINGS CONSIDERED* (1908)

3. It is a happy talent to know how to play.

EMERSON, *JOURNALS*, 1834

4. There are toys for all ages.

ENGLISH PROVERB

5. Our minds need relaxation, and give way / Unless we mix with work a little play.

MOLIÈRE, *THE SCHOOL FOR HUSBANDS* (1661), 1.3, TR. DONALD M. FRAME

6. In our play we reveal what kind of people we are.

OVID, *THE ART OF LOVE* (C. A.D. 8), 3, TR. ROLFE HUMPHRIES

7. To condemn spontaneous and delightful occupations because they are useless for self-preservation shows an uncritical prizing of life irrespective of its content.

GEORGE SANTAYANA, *THE SENSE OF BEAUTY* (1896), 4

8. To the art of working well a civilized race would add the art of playing well.

GEORGE SANTAYANA, *LITTLE ESSAYS* (1920), 61

PLAYS

See 972. THEATER

704. PLEASURE

See also 409. HAPPINESS; 513. JOIE DE VIVRE; 705. PLEASURE AND PAIN; 706. PLEASURE-SEEKING; 739. PROFLIGACY

1. It is not abstinence from pleasures that is best, but mastery over them without being worsted.

ARISTIPPUS (5TH–4TH C. B.C.), ED IN DIOGENES LAERTIUS' *LIVES AND OPINIONS OF EMINENT PHILOSOPHERS* (3RD C. A.D.), TR. R. D. HICKS

2. When Pleasure is at the bar the jury is not impartial.

ARISTOTLE, *NICOMACHEAN ETHICS* (4TH C. B.C.), 2.9, TR. J. A. K. THOMSON

3. One half of the world cannot understand the pleasures of the other.

JANE AUSTEN, *EMMA* (1816), 9

4. People seem to enjoy things more when they know a lot of other people have been left out on the pleasure.

RUSSELL BAKER, "OBSERVER," *THE NEW YORK TIMES,* NOV. 2, 1967

5. 'Twere too absurd to slight / For the hereafter the today's delight!

ROBERT BROWNING, *SORDELLO* (1840), 6

6. Pleasures are like poppies spread: You seize the flow'r, its bloom is shed.

ROBERT BURNS, "TAM O' SHANTER" (1793)

7. Though sages may pour out their wisdom's treasure, / There is no sterner moralist than Pleasure.

BYRON, *DON JUAN* (1819–24), 3.65

8. Enjoying things which are pleasant; that is not the evil: it is the reducing of our moral self to slavery by them that is.

THOMAS CARLYLE, *ON HEROES, HERO-WORSHIP AND THE HEROIC IN HISTORY* (1841), 2

9. Enjoy pleasures, but let them be your own, and then you will taste them.

LORD CHESTERFIELD, *LETTERS TO HIS SON,* MAY 8, 1750

10. It is often a mistake to combine two pleasures, because pleasures, like pains, can act as counter-irritants to each other.

G. K. CHESTERTON, "ON MISUNDERSTANDING," *GENERALLY SPEAKING* (1928)

11. Pleasure is none, if not diversified.

JOHN DONNE, ELEGY 19, "VARIETY" (1635)

12. The pleasure of life is according to the man who lives it, and not according to the work or the place.

EMERSON, "FATE," *THE CONDUCT OF LIFE* (1860)

13. Life is to be enjoyed, not simply endured. Pleasure and goodness and joy support the pursuit of survival.

WILLARD GAYLIN, *FEELINGS: OUR VITAL SIGNS* (1979)

14. Enjoyment is *not* a goal, it is a feeling that accompanies important ongoing activity.

PAUL GOODMAN, *GROWING UP ABSURD* (1960), 11.12

15. Mankind is safer when men seek pleasure than when they seek the power and the glory.

GEOFFREY GORER, *THE NEW YORK TIMES MAGAZINE,* NOV. 27, 1966

16. We have more days to live through than pleasures. Be slow in enjoyment, quick at work, for men see work ended with pleasure, pleasure ended with regret.

BALTASAR GRACIÁN, *THE ART OF WORLDLY WISDOM* (1647), 174, TR. JOSEPH JACOBS

17. Enjoying living was learning to get your money's worth and knowing when you had it.

ERNEST HEMINGWAY, *THE SUN ALSO RISES* (1926)

18. Each day was a challenge of enjoyment, and he [Hemingway] would plan it out as a field general plans a campign.

A.E. HOTCHNER, *PAPA HEMINGWAY* (1966)

19. In all pleasure hope is a considerable part.

SAMUEL JOHNSON, QUOTED IN BOSWELL'S *LIFE OF SAMUEL JOHNSON*, APRIL 7, 1779

20. No man is a hypocrite in his pleasures.

SAMUEL JOHNSON, QUOTED IN BOSWELL'S *LIFE OF SAMUEL JOHNSON*, JUNE 1784

21. A bookworm in bed with a new novel and a good reading lamp is as much prepared for pleasure as a pretty girl at a college dance.

PHYLLIS MCGINLEY, "YOU TAKE THE HIGH ROAD," *THE PROVINCE OF THE HEART* (1959)

22. The spirit is often most free when the body is satiated with pleasure; indeed, sometimes the stars shine more brightly seen from the gutter than from the hilltop.

W. SOMERSET MAUGHAM, *THE SUMMING UP* (1938), 15

23. Enjoyment and innocence are the most bashful things: both do not want to be sought.

NIETZSCHE, "ON OLD AND NEW TABLETS," *THUS SPOKE ZARATHUSTRA* (1883–92), 3, TR. WALTER KAUFMANN

24. Better be jocund with the fruitful Grape / Than sadden after none, or bitter, Fruit.

OMAR KHAYYÁM, *RUBÁIYÁT* (11TH–12TH C.), TR. EDWARD FITZGERALD, 4TH

25. A safe pleasure is a tame pleasure.

OVID, *THE ART OF LOVE* (C. A.D. 8), 3, TR. J. LEWIS MAY

26. The pleasure that is granted to me from a sense of duty ceases to be a pleasure at all.

OVID, *THE ART OF LOVE* (C. A.D. 8), 2, TR. J. LEWIS MAY

27. Too much pleasure disagrees with us. Too many concords are annoying in music; too many benefits irritate us; we wish to have the wherewithal to overpay our debts.

PASCAL, *PENSÉES* (1670), 72, TR. W. F. TROTTER

28. Music and women I cannot but give way to, whatever my business is.

SAMUEL PEPYS, *DIARY*, MARCH 9, 1666

29. Man's pleasure is a short time growing / And it falls to the ground / As quickly.

PINDAR, *ODES* (5TH C. B.C.), PYTHIA 8.88

30. No pleasure endures unseasoned by variety.

PUBLILIUS SYRUS, *MORAL SAYINGS* (1ST C. B.C.), 406, TR. DARIUS LYMAN

31. There is more of fear than delight in a secret pleasure.

PUBLILIUS SYRUS, *MORAL SAYINGS* (1ST C. B.C.), 990, TR. DARIUS LYMAN

32. Pleasure once tasted satisfies less than the desire experienced for its torments.

JOSEPH ROUX, *MEDITATIONS OF A PARISH PRIEST* (1886), 5.21, TR. ISABEL F. HAPGOOD

33. Vain is the hope of finding pleasure in that which one has hitherto disdained; as when the warrior hopes to find pleasure in the joys of the sedentaries.

SAINT-EXUPÉRY, *THE WISDOM OF THE SANDS* (1948), 29, TR. STUART GILBERT

34. Pleasure dies at the very moment when it charms us most.

SENECA, "ON A HAPPY LIFE," *MORAL ESSAYS* (1ST C.), TR. AUBREY STEWART

35. No profit grows where is no pleasure ta'en.

SHAKESPEARE, *THE TAMING OF THE SHREW* (1593–94), 1.1.39

36. The daintiest last, to make the end most sweet.

SHAKESPEARE, *RICHARD II* (1595–96), 1.3.68

37. There are two things to aim at in life: first, to get what you want; and, after that, to enjoy it. Only the wisest of mankind achieve the second.

LOGAN PEARSALL SMITH, *AFTERTHOUGHTS* (1931), 1

38. Pleasure is the object, the duty, and the goal of all rational creatures.

VOLTAIRE, *ÉPÎTRE À MADAME DE G.* (1716)

705. PLEASURE AND PAIN

See also 704. PLEASURE; 946. SUFFERING

1. Sweet is pleasure after pain.

JOHN DRYDEN, "ALEXANDER'S FEAST" (1687), 58

2. No pleasure is evil in itself; but the means by which certain pleasures are gained bring pains many times greater than the pleasures.

EPICURUS, "PRINCIPAL DOCTRINES" (3RD C. B.C.), 8, IN *LETTERS, PRINCIPAL DOCTRINES, AND VATICAN SAYINGS*, TR. RUSSEL M. GEER

3. There is no gathering the rose without being pricked by the thorns.

FABLES OF BIDPAI (C. 750)

4. Ay, in the very temple of Delight / Veiled Melancholy has her sovran shrine.

KEATS, "ODE ON MELANCHOLY" (1819)

5. The heart can ne'er a transport know / That never feels a pain.

George Lyttleton, "Song."

6. I conceive that pleasures are to be avoided if greater pains be the consequence, and pains to be coveted that will terminate in greater pleasures.

Montaigne, "The story of Spurina," *Essays* (1580–88), tr. W. C. Hazlitt

7. The most intolerable pain is produced by prolonging the keenest pleasure.

George Bernard Shaw, "Maxims for Revolutionists," *Man and Superman* (1903)

8. Marred pleasure's best, shadow makes the sun strong.

Stevie Smith, "The Queen and the Young Princess," *Selected Poems* (1964)

9. All fits of pleasure are balanced by an equal degree of pain or langour; 'tis like spending this year part of the next year's revenue.

Jonathan Swift, *Thoughts on Various Subjects* (1711)

10. There is a pleasure in not being pleased.

Voltaire, *Candide* (1759), 25

706. PLEASURE-SEEKING

See also 704. Pleasure; 739. Profligacy

1. Let us have Wine and Woman, Mirth and Laughter, / Sermons and soda-water the day after.

Byron, *Don Juan* (1819–24), 2.178

2. The man of pleasure, by a vain attempt to be more happy than any man can be, is often more miserable than most men are.

Charles Caleb Colton, *Lacon* (1825), 1.177

3. Many seek good nights and lose good days.

Dutch Proverb

4. Gather ye rosebuds while ye may, / Old Time is still a-flying, / And this same flower that smiles to-day / To-morrow will be dying.

Robert Herrick, "To the Virgins to make much of Time," *Hesperides* (1648)

5. By comparison with a night-club, churches are positively gay.

Aldous Huxley, *Do What You Will* (1929)

6. We torment ourselves rather to make it appear that we are happy than to become so.

La Rochefoucauld, *Maxims* (1665), tr. Kenneth Pratt

7. The fly that prefers sweetness to a long life may drown in honey.

George Santayana, *Dialogues in Limbo* (1925), 3

8. Pleasure seizes the whole man who addicts himself to it, and will not give him leisure for any good office in life which contradicts the gayety of the present hour.

Richard Steele, *The Spectator* (1711–12), 151

707. PLUMBERS

See also 891. Sewers

1. Anybody who has any doubt about the ingenuity and resourcefulness of a plumber never got a bill from one.

George Meany, CBS-TV, Jan. 8, 1954

708. POETRY AND POETS

See also 201. Creation and Creativity; 524. Language; 1069. Writing and Writers

1. One thing I feel is this: that a great deal of poetry is the product of adolescence—or of an emotionally adolescent frame of mind: and that as this state of mind changes, poetry is likely to dry up.

James Agee, *Letters of James Agee to Father Flye* (1962)

2. Poetry is a whim of Nature in her lighter moods; it requires nothing but its own madness and, lacking that, it becomes a soundless cymbal, a belfry without a bell.

Pietro Aretino, letter to Nicolò Franco, June 25, 1537, tr. Samuel Putnam

3. A poet is, before anything else, a person who is passionately in love with language.

W. H. Auden, *The New York Times,* Oct. 9, 1960

4. Poetry makes nothing happen: it survives / In the valley of its saying.

W. H. Auden, "In Memory of W. B. Yeats," *Another Time* (1940)

5. Not philosophy, after all, not humanity, just sheer joyous power of song, is the primal thing in poetry.

Max Beerbohm, "No. 2, The Pines," *And Even Now* (1920)

6. The form of a poem is invisible. A poem is not an "object." This is hard to accept in a mechanical age.

Wendell Berry, "Notes: Unspecializing Poetry," *Standing by Words* (1983)

7. Poetry is the impish attempt to paint the color of the wind.

MAXWELL BODENHEIM, QUOTED IN BEN HECHT'S PLAY *WINKELBERG* (1958)

8. No one is a poet from eight to twelve and from two to six. Whoever is a poet is one always, and continually assaulted by poetry.

JORGE LUIS BORGES, "BLINDNESS," IN *THE ART OF THE PERSONAL ESSAY* (1994), ED. PHILLIP LOPATE

9. All poetry is difficult to read, /—The sense of it is, anyhow.

ROBERT BROWNING, *THE RING AND THE BOOK* (1868–69), 7

10. Nothing so difficult as a beginning / In poesy, unless perhaps the end.

BYRON, *DON JUAN* (1819–24), 4.1

11. Who forgives the Senior's ceaseless verse, / Whose hairs grow hoary as his rhymes grow worse?

BYRON, *ENGLISH BARDS AND SCOTCH REVIEWERS* (1809)

12. I can never get people to understand that poetry is the expression of excited passion, and that there is no such thing as a life of passion any more than a continuous earthquake, or an eternal fever. Besides who would ever shave themselves in such a state?

BYRON, *SELECTED LETTERS AND JOURNALS* (1982), ED. LESLIE A. MARCHAND

13. Wise poets that wrapt Truth in tales, / Knew her themselves through all her veils.

THOMAS CAREW, "INGRATEFUL BEAUTY THREATENED," *POEMS* (1640)

14. How does the poet speak to men with power, but by being still more a man than they?

THOMAS CARLYLE, "BURNS," *EDINBURGH REVIEW*, 1828

15. When you are describing / A shape, or sound, or tint; / Don't state the matter plainly, / But put it in a hint; / And learn to look at all things / With a sort of mental squint.

LEWIS CARROLL, "POETA FIT, NON NASCITUR" (1869)

16. Would you be a poet / Before you've been to school? / Ah, well! I hardly thought you / So absolute a fool.

LEWIS CARROLL, "POETA FIT, NON NASCITUR" (1869)

17. Prose,—words in their best order; poetry,—the best words in their best order.

SAMUEL TAYLOR COLERIDGE, *TABLE TALK* (1835)

18. Poetry does not necessarily have to be beautiful to stick in the depths of our memory, there to occupy most mischievously the place doomed to invasion by certain melodies which, however blameworthy, can never be expunged.

COLETTE, "UNDER THE BLUE LANTERN," *EARTHLY PARADISE* (1966), 6

19. To a poet, silence is an acceptable response, even a flattering one.

COLETTE, "THE OCCUPATION," *EARTHLY PARADISE* (1966), 6

20. All poets pretend to write for immortality, but the whole tribe have no objection to present pay and present praise.

CHARLES CALEB COLTON, *LACON* (1825), 1.23

21. Poets arguing about modern poetry: jackals snarling over a dried-up well.

CYRIL CONNOLLY, *THE UNQUIET GRAVE* (1945), 1

22. There is a pleasure in poetic pains / Which only poets know.

WILLIAM COWPER, "THE TIMEPIECE," *THE TASK* (1785), 285

23. The poets of each generation seldom sing a new song. They turn to themes men always have loved, and sing them in the mode of their times.

CLARENCE DAY, "HUMPTY-DUMPTY AND ADAM," *THE CROW'S NEST* (1921)

24. Poetry's unnat'ral; no man ever talked poetry 'cept a beadle on boxin' day.

CHARLES DICKENS, *PICKWICK PAPERS* (1836–37), 33

25. Poetry is a counterfeit creation, and makes things that are not, as though they were.

JOHN DONNE, *SERMONS*, NO. 13, 1622

26. All good poetry is forged slowly and patiently, link by link, with sweat and blood and tears.

LORD ALFRED DOUGLAS, INTRODUCTION TO *COLLECTED POEMS* (1919)

27. Only the poet who writes speaks his message across the millennia to other hearts. Only in writing can the cry from the great cross on Golgotha still be heard in the minds of men.

LOREN EISELEY, "THE LONG LONELINESS," *THE STAR THROWER* (1978)

28. Maturing as a poet means maturing as the whole man, experiencing new emotions appropriate to one's

age, and with the same intensity as the emotions of youth.

T. S. ELIOT, "YEATS" (1940)

29. The business of the poet is not to find new emotions, but to use the ordinary ones and, in working them up into poetry, to express feelings which are not in actual emotions at all.

T. S. ELIOT, "TRADITION AND THE INDIVIDUAL TALENT" (1919)

30. The majority of poems one outgrows and outlives, as one outgrows and outlives the majority of human passions.

T. S. ELIOT, "DANTE" (1929)

31. The poet's mind is in fact a receptacle for seizing and storing up numberless feelings, phrases, images, which remain there until all the particles which can unite to form a new compound are present together.

T. S. ELIOT, "TRADITION AND THE INDIVIDUAL TALENT" (1919)

32. I can understand your wanting to write poems, but I don't quite know what you mean by "being a poet."

T.S. ELIOT, LETTER TO STEPHEN SPENDER, *WORLD WITHIN WORLD* (1951)

33. A poem is made up of thoughts, each of which filled the whole sky of the poet in its turn.

EMERSON, *JOURNALS,* 1834

34. Poetry makes its own pertinence, and a single stanza outweighs a book of prose.

EMERSON, *JOURNALS,* 1839

35. The people fancy they hate poetry, and they are all poets and mystics.

EMERSON, "THE POET," *ESSAYS: SECOND SERIES* (1844)

36. When a man does not write his poetry, it escapes by other vents through him.

EMERSON, "BEHAVIOR," *THE CONDUCT OF LIFE* (1860)

37. A poem is true if it hangs together. Information points to something else. A poem points to nothing but itself.

E. M. FORSTER, "ANONYMITY: AN ENQUIRY," *TWO CHEERS FOR DEMOCRACY* (1951)

38. A true sonnet goes eight lines and then takes a turn for better or worse and goes six or eight lines more.

ROBERT FROST, NEWS SUMMARIES, MARCH 29, 1954

39. I have never started a poem yet whose end I knew. Writing a poem is discovering.

ROBERT FROST, *THE NEW YORK TIMES,* NOV. 7, 1955

40. Horace, in a particularly boastful mood, once said his verse would last as long as the vestal virgins kept going up the Capitoline Hill to worship at the temple of Jupiter. But Horace's poetry has lasted longer than Jupiter's religion, and Jupiter himself has only survived because he disappeared into literature.

NORTHROP FRYE, *THE EDUCATED IMAGINATION* (1964)

41. The poet is a bird of strange moods. He descends from his lofty domain to tarry among us, singing; if we do not honor him he will unfold his wings and fly back to his dwelling place.

KAHLIL GIBRAN, "THE POET FROM BAALBEK," *THOUGHTS AND MEDITATIONS* (1960), TR. ANTHONY R. FERRIS

42. At bottom, no real object is unpoetical, if the poet knows how to use it properly.

GOETHE, QUOTED IN JOHANN PETER ECKERMANN'S *CONVERSATIONS WITH GOETHE,* JULY 5, 1827

43. If a poet would work politically, he must give himself up to a party; and so soon as he does that, he is lost as a poet.

GOETHE, QUOTED IN JOHANN PETER ECKERMANN'S *CONVERSATIONS WITH GOETHE,* MARCH 1832

44. Poetry is the universal possession of mankind, revealing itself everywhere, and at all times, in hundreds and hundreds of men.

GOETHE, QUOTED IN JOHANN PETER ECKERMANN'S *CONVERSATIONS WITH GOETHE,* JAN. 31, 1827

45. The poet should seize the Particular, and he should, if there be anything sound in it, thus represent the Universal.

GOETHE, QUOTED IN JOHANN PETER ECKERMANN'S *CONVERSATIONS WITH GOETHE,* JUNE 11, 1825

46. The world is so great and rich, and life so full of variety, that you can never lack occasions for poems.

GOETHE, QUOTED IN JOHANN PETER ECKERMANN'S *CONVERSATIONS WITH GOETHE,* SEPT. 18, 1823

47. A verse may find him who a sermon flies, / And turn delight into sacrifice.

GEORGE HERBERT, "THE CHURCH PORCH," 1, *THE TEMPLE* (1633)

48. Most Americans do not like poetry. We may respect it, but we do not enjoy it.

GILBERT HIGHET, *THE POWERS OF POETRY* (1960)

49. Poetry is halfway between prose and music: it is sometimes like an intimate conversation, in words and phrases which need not be fully uttered, and sometimes like dancing and wordless music.

GILBERT HIGHET, *THE POWERS OF POETRY* (1960)

50. An artist who works in marble or colors has them all to himself and his tribe, but the man who moulds his thought in verse has to employ the materials vulgarized by everybody's use, and glorify them by his handling.

OLIVER WENDELL HOLMES, SR., *THE POET AT THE BREAKFAST TABLE* (1872), 4

51. When you write in prose you say what you mean. When you write in rhyme you say what you must.

OLIVER WENDELL HOLMES, SR., *OVER THE TEACUPS* (1891), 2

52. True poetry, the best of it, is but the ashes of a burnt-out passion.

OLIVER WENDELL HOLMES, SR., *OVER THE TEACUPS* (1891), 4

53. It is not enough for poems to be fine; they must charm, and draw the mind of the listener at will.

HORACE, *ARS POETICA* (13–8 B.C.)

54. Poetry is like painting: one piece takes your fancy if you stand close to it, another if you keep at some distance.

HORACE, *ARS POETICA* (13–8 B.C.)

55. Literature is a state of culture, poetry a state of grace, before and after culture.

JUAN RAMÓN JIMÉNEZ, "POETRY AND LITERATURE," *SELECTED WRITINGS* (1957), TR. H. R. HAYS

56. A good poet's made as well as born.

BEN JONSON, "TO THE MEMORY OF SHAKESPEARE" (1616)

57. All good verses are like impromptus made at leisure.

JOSEPH JOUBERT, *PENSÉES* (1842)

58. A drainless shower / Of light is poesy; 'tis the supreme of power; / 'Tis might half slumb'ring on its own right arm.

KEATS, "SLEEP AND POETRY" (1816)

59. If Poetry comes not as naturally as the leaves to a tree it had better not come at all.

KEATS, LETTER TO JOHN TAYLOR, FEB. 27, 1818

60. Poetry should be great and unobtrusive, a thing which enters into one's soul, and does not startle it or amaze it with itself but with its subject.

KEATS, LETTER TO JOHN HAMILTON REYNOLDS, FEB. 3, 1818

61. When power leads man toward arrogance, poetry reminds him of his limitations. When power narrows the areas of man's concern, poetry reminds him of the richness and diversity of his existence. When power corrupts, poetry cleanses.

JOHN F. KENNEDY, ADDRESS, AMHERST COLLEGE, MASS., OCT. 26, 1963

62. The vain poet is of the opinion that nothing of his can be too much: he sends to you basketful after basketful of juiceless fruit, covered with scentless flowers.

WALTER SAVAGE LANDOR, "ARCHDEACON HARE AND WALTER LANDOR," *IMAGINARY CONVERSATIONS* (1824–53)

63. Prose on certain occasions can bear a great deal of poetry; on the other hand, poetry sinks and swoons under a moderate weight of prose.

WALTER SAVAGE LANDOR, "ARCHDEACON HARE AND WALTER LANDOR," *IMAGINARY CONVERSATIONS* (1824–53)

64. As to the pure mind all things are pure, so to the poetic mind all things are poetical.

LONGFELLOW, "TWICE-TOLD TALES," *DRIFTWOOD* (1857)

65. The true poet is a friendly man. He takes to his arms even cold and inanimate things, and rejoices in his heart.

LONGFELLOW, "TWICE-TOLD TALES," *DRIFTWOOD* (1857)

66. He who would be the tongue of this wide land / Must string his harp with chords of sturdy iron / And strike it with a toil-imbrowned hand.

JAMES RUSSELL LOWELL, "ODE" (1841), 3

67. A poem should not mean / But be.

ARCHIBALD MACLEISH, "ARS POETICA," *STREETS IN THE MOON* (1926)

68. Poetry is the plough that turns up time in such a way that the abyssal strata of time, its black earth, appear on the surface.

OSIP MANDELSHTAM, *THE COMPLETE CRITICAL PROSE AND LETTERS*, ED. JANE GARY HARRIS

69. The crown of literature is poetry. It is its end and aim. It is the sublimest activity of the human mind. It is the achievement of beauty and delicacy. The writer of prose can only step aside when the poet passes.

W. SOMERSET MAUGHAM, *SATURDAY REVIEW*, JULY 20, 1957

70. The arrogance of poets is only a defense; doubt gnaws the greatest among them; they need our testimony to escape despair.

FRANÇOIS MAURIAC, "L'ORGUEIL DES POÈTES," *JOURNAL* (1936–53), V. 2

71. The poem is the dream made flesh, in a two-fold sense: as work of art, and as life, which is a work of art.

HENRY MILLER, "CREATIVE DEATH," *THE WISDOM OF THE HEART* (1941)

72. The courage of the poet is to keep ajar the door that leads into madness.

CHRISTOPHER MORLEY, *INWARD HO!* (1923), 2

73. The world, in its sheer exuberance of kindness, will try to bury the poet with warm and lovely human trivialities. It will even ask him to autograph books.

CHRISTOPHER MORLEY, *INWARD HO!* (1923), 8

74. A poet, any real poet, is simply an alchemist who transmutes his cynicism regarding human beings into an optimism regarding the moon, the stars, the heavens, and the flowers, to say nothing of Spring, love, and dogs.

GEORGE JEAN NATHAN, "POET," *MONKS ARE MONKS* (1929)

75. The great poet draws his creations only from out of his own reality.

NIETZSCHE, *ECCE HOMO* (1888), TR. ANTHONY M. LUDOVICI

76. The poet presents his thoughts festively, on the carriage of rhythm: usually because they could not walk.

NIETZSCHE, *HUMAN, ALL TOO HUMAN* (1878), 189, IN *THE PORTABLE NIETZSCHE*, TR. WALTER KAUFMANN

77. Prose—it might be speculated—is discourse; poetry ellipsis. Prose is spoken aloud; poetry overheard.

JOYCE CAROL OATES, "THE ROMANCE OF EMILY DICKINSON'S POETRY," *(WOMAN) WRITER: OCCASIONS AND OPPORTUNITIES* (1988)

78. Poetry is adolescence fermented and thus preserved.

JOSÉ ORTEGA Y GASSET, "IN SEARCH OF GOETHE FROM WITHIN, LETTER TO A GERMAN," *PARTISAN REVIEW*, DECEMBER 1949, TR. WILLARD R. TRASK

79. The poet begins where the man ends. The man's lot is to live his human life, the poet's to invent what is nonexistent.

JOSÉ ORTEGA Y GASSET, *THE DEHUMANIZATION OF ART* (1925)

80. To read a poem is to hear it with our eyes; to hear it is to see it with our ears.

OCTAVIO PAZ, "RECAPITULATIONS," *ALTERNATING CURRENT* (1973)

81. Poetry is the revelation of a feeling that the poet believes to be interior and personal [but] which the reader recognizes as his own.

SALVATORE QUASIMODO, *THE NEW YORK TIMES*, MAY 14, 1960

82. The void yields up nothing. You have to be a great poet to make it ring.

JULES RENARD, *JOURNAL*, DECEMBER 1906, TR. ELIZABETH ROGET

83. Poetry is the opening and closing of a door, leaving those who look through to guess about what is seen during a moment.

CARL SANDBURG, "TENTATIVE (FIRST MODEL) DEFINITIONS OF POETRY," *COMPLETE POEMS* (1950)

84. If artists and poets are unhappy, it is after all because happiness does not interest them.

GEORGE SANTAYANA, *THE SENSE OF BEAUTY* (1896)

85. Popular poets are the parish priests of the Muse, retailing her ancient divinations to a long since converted public.

GEORGE SANTAYANA, *THE LIFE OF REASON: REASON IN ART* (1905–06), 6

86. Ne'er / Was flattery lost on poet's ear; / A simple race! they waste their toil / For the vain tribute of a smile.

SIR WALTER SCOTT, *THE LAY OF THE LAST MINSTREL* (1805), 4, CONCLUSION

87. The forms of things unknown, the poet's pen / Turns them to shapes, and gives to airy nothing / A local habitation and a name.

SHAKESPEARE, *A MIDSUMMER NIGHT'S DREAM* (1595–96), 5.1.15

88. Poets of course are even more unpredictable than other writers, overwhelmed as they are by the moment they inhabit and finding it difficult to connect yesterday with tomorrow.

KARL SHAPIRO, *REPORTS OF MY DEATH* (1990)

89. A poet is a nightingale, who sits in darkness and sings to cheer its own solitude with sweet sounds.

SHELLEY, *A DEFENCE OF POETRY* (1821)

90. Most wretched men / Are cradled into poetry by wrong. / They learn in suffering what they teach in song.

SHELLEY, "JULIAN AND MADDALO" (1818–19)

91. Poetry lifts the veil from the hidden beauty of the world, and makes familiar objects be as if they were not familiar.

SHELLEY, *A DEFENCE OF POETRY* (1821)

92. Poets are the unacknowledged legislators of the world.

SHELLEY, *A DEFENCE OF POETRY* (1821)

93. Poets are the hierophants of an unapprehended inspiration; the mirrors of the gigantic shadows which futurity casts upon the present.

SHELLEY, *A DEFENCE OF POETRY* (1821)

94. Not by wisdom do they [poets] make what they compose, but by a gift of nature and an inspiration similar to that of the diviners and the oracles.

SOCRATES, IN PLATO'S *APOLOGY* (4TH C. B.C.), TR. LANE COOPER

95. The poet is the priest of the invisible.

WALLACE STEVENS, "ADAGIA," *OPUS POSTHUMOUS* (1957)

96. Ah God! the petty fools of rhyme / That shriek and sweat in pigmy wars.

LORD TENNYSON, "LITERARY SQUABBLES" (1846)

97. I do but sing because I must, / And pipe but as the linnets sing.

LORD TENNYSON, "IN MEMORIAM A. H. H." (1850), 21

98. In America they make too much fuss of poets; in London they make too little.

CAITLIN THOMAS, *CAITLIN* (1986), WITH GEORGE TREMLETT

99. Families, like countries, take their prophets unkindly, but a verse-speaker in the house is dishonor to be hooted.

DYLAN THOMAS, *QUITE EARLY ONE MORNING* (1954)

100. Poetry is the rhythmic, inevitably narrative, movement from an overclothed blindness to a naked vision that depends in its intensity on the strength of the labour put into the creation of the poetry.

DYLAN THOMAS, *QUITE EARLY ONE MORNING* (1954)

101. Reading one's own poems aloud is letting the cat out of the bag. You may have always suspected bits of a poem to be overweighted, overviolent, or daft, and then, suddenly, with the poet's tongue around them, your suspicion is made certain.

DYLAN THOMAS, *QUITE EARLY ONE MORNING* (1954)

102. A good poem is a contribution to reality. The world is never the same once a good poem has been added to it.

DYLAN THOMAS, "ON POETRY," *QUITE EARLY ONE MORNING* (1960)

103. Poetry is what in a poem makes you laugh, cry, prickle, be silent, makes your toenails twinkle, makes you want to do this or that or nothing, makes you know that you are alone in the unknown world, that your bliss and suffering is forever shared and forever all your own.

DYLAN THOMAS, INTRODUCTORY REMARKS TO A READING GIVEN AT MASSACHUSETTS INSTITUTE OF TECHNOLOGY, JULY 3, 1952

104. Color, which is the poet's wealth, is so expensive that most take to mere outline sketches and become men of science.

THOREAU, *JOURNAL*, FEB. 13, 1851

105. The best poets, after all, exhibit only a tame and civil side of nature. They have not seen the west side of any mountain.

THOREAU, *JOURNAL*, AUG. 18, 1841

106. The poet is he that hath fat enough, like bears and marmots, to suck his claws all winter.

THOREAU, "SUNDAY," *A WEEK ON THE CONCORD AND MERRIMACK RIVERS* (1849)

107. A farmer, a hunter, a soldier, a reporter, even a philosopher, may be daunted; but nothing can deter a poet, for he is actuated by pure love.

THOREAU, "FORMER INHABITANTS; AND WINTER VISITORS," *WALDEN* (1854)

108. Who can predict his comings and goings? His business calls him out at all hours, even when doctors sleep.

THOREAU, "FORMER INHABITANTS; AND WINTER VISITORS," *WALDEN* (1854)

109. Feeble verses are those which sin not against rules, but against genius.

VOLTAIRE, "STYLE," *PHILOSOPHICAL DICTIONARY* (1764)

110. Song is not Truth, not Wisdom, but the rose / Upon Truth's lips, the light in Wisdom's eyes.

SIR WILLIAM WATSON, "ODE TO J. C. COLLINS," *COLLECTED POEMS* (1905)

111. A poet's pleasure is to withhold a little of his meaning, to intensify by mystification. He unzips the veil from beauty, but does not remove it.

E. B. WHITE, "POETRY," *ONE MAN'S MEAT* (1944)

112. All poets who, when reading from their own works, experience a choked feeling, are major.

E. B. WHITE, "HOW TO TELL A MAJOR POET," *QUO VADIMUS?* (1939)

113. Of all mankind the great poet is the equable man. Not in him but off from him things are grotesque or eccentric or fail of their sanity.

Walt Whitman, preface to *Leaves of Grass* (1855)

114. A great poet, a really great poet, is the most unpoetical of all creatures. But inferior poets are absolutely fascinating.

Oscar Wilde, *The Picture of Dorian Gray* (1891), 4

115. It is difficult / to get the news from poems / yet men die miserably every day / for lack / of what is found there.

William Carlos Williams, "Asphodel, That Greeny Flower," *Pictures from Brueghel* (1962), 1

116. Poets are not supposed to write epics any longer, despite the fact that the only poets who have endured and will endure are poets who have written epics.

Tom Wolfe, *The Bonfire of the Vanities* (1987)

117. Poetry is the spontaneous overflow of powerful feelings: it takes its origin from emotion recollected in tranquility.

William Wordsworth, preface to 2nd edition of *Lyrical Ballads* (1800)

118. The Poet, gentle creature as he is, / Hath, like the Lover, his unruly times; / His fits when he is neither sick nor well, / Though no distress be near him but his own / Unmanageable thoughts.

William Wordsworth, *The Prelude* (1799–1805), 1

119. We Poets in our youth begin in gladness; / But thereof come in the end despondency and madness.

William Wordsworth, "Resolution and Independence" (1802), 7

709. POLICE

See also 529. Law and Order

1. A vague uneasiness: the police. It's like when you suddenly understand you have to undress in front of the doctor.

Ugo Betti, *The Inquiry* (1944–45), 1.10

2. A polisman goes afther vice as an officer iv th' law an' comes away as a philosopher.

Finley Peter Dunne, "The Crusade Against Vice," *Mr. Dooley's Opinions* (1901)

3. There's more joy over wan sinner ray-turned to th' station thin f'r ninety an' nine that've rayformed.

Finley Peter Dunne, "The Crusade Against Vice," *Mr. Dooley's Opinions* (1901)

4. When constabulary duty's to be done, / The policeman's lot is not a happy one!

W. S. Gilbert, *The Pirates of Penzance* (1879), 2

5. There is a sleeping cop in all of us. He must be killed.

Graffito written during French student revolt, May 1968

6. For the middle class, the police protect property, give directions, and help old ladies. For the urban poor, the police are those who arrest you.

Michael Harrington, *The Other America* (1962), 1.2

POLITENESS

See 197. Courtesy; 563. Manners

710. POLITICAL PARTIES

See also 178. Conservatism; 536. Liberalism; 674. Partisanship; 711. Politics and Politicians; 776. Radicalism

1. All political parties die at last of swallowing their own lies.

John Arbuthnot, quoted in Richard Garnett's *Life of Emerson* (1887)

2. Those who think that all virtue is to be found in their own party principles push matters to extremes; they do not consider that disproportion destroys a state.

Aristotle, *Politics* (4th c. b.c.), 5.9, tr. Benjamin Jowett

3. The Republicans believe the wagon train will not make it to the frontier unless some of our old, some of our young, and some of our weak are left behind by the side of the trail. We Democrats believe that we can make it all the way with the whole family intact.

Mario Cuomo, Speech to the Democratic National Convention, 1984

4. Whin a man gets to be my age, he ducks pol-itical meetin's, an' r-reads th' papers an' weighs th' ividence an' th' argymints,—pro-argymints an' con-argymints,—an' makes up his mind ca'mly, an' votes th' Dimmycratic ticket.

Finley Peter Dunne, "On the Hero in Politics," *Mr. Dooley in Peace and in War* (1898)

5. I am invariably and have been since adolescence inimical to the Republican mind which shows at the most inflated size the bad qualities of the bourgeoisie

rather than the good qualities of the middle class which the Democrats call forth.

JANET FLANNER, *DARLINGHISSIMA: LETTERS TO A FRIEND* (1960), ED. NATALIA DANESI MURRAY

6. He serves his party best who serves the country best.

RUTHERFORD B. HAYES, INAUGURAL ADDRESS, MARCH 5, 1877

7. Let us not seek the Republican answer or the Democratic answer, but the right answer. Let us not seek to fix the blame for the past. Let us accept our own responsibility for the future.

JOHN F. KENNEDY, ADDRESS, LOYOLA COLLEGE ALUMNI BANQUET, BALTIMORE, MD., FEB. 18, 1958

8. Under democracy one party always devotes its chief energies to trying to prove that the other party is unfit to rule—and both commonly succeed, and are right.

H. L. MENCKEN, *MINORITY REPORT* (1956), 330

9. The amount of effort put into a campaign by a worker expands in proportion to the personal benefits that he will derive from his party's victory.

MILTON RAKOVE, *THE VIRGINIA QUARTERLY REVIEW*, SUMMER 1965

10. There is a hundred things to single you out for promotion in party politics besides ability.

WILL ROGERS, *THE AUTOBIOGRAPHY OF WILL ROGERS* (1949), 13

11. Even more important than winning the election is governing the nation. That is the test of a political party—the acid, final test.

ADLAI STEVENSON, ACCEPTANCE SPEECH, DEMOCRATIC NATIONAL CONVENTION, JULY 26, 1952

12. The elephant has a thick skin, a head full of ivory, and as everyone who has seen a circus parade knows, proceeds best by grasping the tail of his predecessor.

ADLAI STEVENSON, "THE ART OF POLITICS," *THE STEVENSON WIT* (1966)

13. Our political parties exist for no other reason than to win power; they are not ideological debating societies designed to present a particular political philosophy and to persuade voters to accept it.

TOM WICKER, *JFK AND LBJ* (1968)

711. POLITICS AND POLITICIANS

See also 132. CITIZENS; 172. CONGRESS; 232. DEMAGOGUERY; 395. GOVERNMENT; 498. INTERNATIONAL RELATIONS; 621. NATION; 710. POLITICAL PARTIES; 730. PRESIDENCY; 761. PUBLIC OFFICE; 930. STATE; 931. STATESMEN AND STATESMANSHIP; 1038. VOTING

1. The trouble with this country is that there are too many politicians who believe, with a conviction based on experience, that you can fool all of the people all of the time.

FRANKLIN P. ADAMS, *NODS AND BECKS* (1944)

2. When the political columnists say "Every thinking man" they mean themselves, and when the candidates appeal to "Every intelligent voter" they mean everybody who is going to vote for them.

FRANKLIN P. ADAMS, *NODS AND BECKS* (1944)

3. Politics cannot stop to study psychology. Its methods are rough; its judgments rougher still.

HENRY ADAMS, *THE EDUCATION OF HENRY ADAMS* (1907)

4. Whenever a man reaches the top of the political ladder, his enemies unite to pull him down. His friends become critical and exacting.

HENRY ADAMS, *DEMOCRACY: AN AMERICAN NOVEL* (1880)

5. Knowledge of human nature is the beginning and end of political education.

HENRY ADAMS, *THE EDUCATION OF HENRY ADAMS* (1907), 12

6. Modern politics is, at bottom, a struggle not of men but of forces. The men become every year more and more creatures of force, massed about central powerhouses.

HENRY ADAMS, *THE EDUCATION OF HENRY ADAMS* (1907), 28

7. Politics, as a practice, whatever its professions, has always been the systematic organization of hatreds.

HENRY ADAMS, *THE EDUCATION OF HENRY ADAMS* (1907), 1

8. As far as I'm concerned, the only difference between the Republicans and the Democrats is the Republicans are Socialists and the Democrats are Bolsheviks.

CLEVELAND AMORY, "WHY YOURS TRULY WAS THE ONLY ONE TO CARRY THE SPEAR," *THE TROUBLE WITH NOWADAYS* (1979)

9. It is evident that the state is a creation of nature, and that man is by nature a political animal.

ARISTOTLE, *POLITICS* (4TH C. B.C.), 1.2, TR. BENJAMIN JOWETT

10. The politician is an acrobat. He keeps his balance by saying the opposite of what he does.

MAURICE BARRÈS, *MES CAHIERS* (1896–1923), 12

11. A political leader must keep looking over his shoulder all the time to see if the boys are still there. If they aren't still there, he's no longer a political leader.

BERNARD M. BARUCH, QUOTED IN OBITUARY, *THE NEW YORK TIMES,* JUNE 21, 1965

12. Public sentiment is to public officers what water is to the wheel of the mill.

HENRY WARD BEECHER, *PROVERBS FROM PLYMOUTH PULPIT* (1887)

13. Politics, n. A strife of interests masquerading as a contest of principles.

AMBROSE BIERCE, *THE DEVIL'S DICTIONARY* (1881–1911)

14. Late into the [1944 election] night, [Gov. Thomas E.] Dewey still had not sent the usual polite message of congratulation to the winner. And so Roosevelt finally went upstairs to bed, riding up in the small elevator originally installed in the [Hyde Park] house to carry the family's trunks up and down. He said of Dewey, "He's still a son of a bitch."

DAVID BRINKLEY, *WASHINGTON GOES TO WAR* (1992)

15. Nowhere are prejudices more mistaken for truth, passion for reason, and invective for documentation than in politics. That is a realm, peopled only by villains or heroes, in which everything is black or white and gray is a forbidden color.

JOHN MASON BROWN, *THROUGH THESE MEN* (1956)

16. Magnanimity in politics is not seldom the truest wisdom; and a great empire and little minds go ill together.

EDMUND BURKE, SPEECH, "ON CONCILIATION WITH THE AMERICAN COLONIES," MARCH 22, 1775

17. Politics, and the fate of mankind, are shaped by men without ideals and without greatness.

ALBERT CAMUS, *NOTEBOOKS 1935–1942* (1962), 2, TR. PHILIP THODY

18. Politics interests people who don't know how to make money or love.

CBS NEWS MEMORANDUM, QUOTED IN LEWIS LAPHAM, *IMPERIAL MASQUERADE* (1990)

19. [Political skill] is the ability to foretell what is going to happen tomorrow, next week, next month, and next year. And to have the ability afterwards to explain why it didn't happen.

SIR WINSTON CHURCHILL, "POLITICS," *THE CHURCHILL WIT* (1965)

20. Persistence in one opinion has never been considered a merit in political leaders.

CICERO, *AD FAMILIARES* (1ST C. B.C.), 1

21. Politics is a place of humble hopes and strangely modest requirements, where all are good who are not criminal and all are wise who are not ridiculously otherwise.

FRANK MOORE COLBY, "ON SEEING TEN BAD PLAYS," *THE COLBY ESSAYS* (1926), V. 1

22. In politics as in religion, it so happens that we have less charity for those who believe the half of our creed, than for those that deny the whole of it.

CHARLES CALEB COLTON, *LACON* (1825), 1.27

23. The political is replacing the metaphysical as the characteristic mode of grasping reality.

HARVEY COX, *THE SECULAR CITY* (1966), 11

24. A politician is an arse upon which everyone has sat except a man.

E.E. CUMMINGS, *100 SELECTED POEMS* (1926)

25. Since a politician never believes what he says, he is surprised when others believe him.

CHARLES DE GAULLE, *NEWSWEEK,* OCT. 1, 1962

26. A man ought to be honest to start with an' afther that he ought to be crafty. A pollytician who's on'y honest is jus' th' same as bein' out in a winther storm without anny clothes on.

FINLEY PETER DUNNE, "REFORM ADMINISTRATION," *OBSERVATIONS BY MR. DOOLEY* (1902)

27. Spare me the sight / of this thankless breed, these politicians / who cringe for favors from a screaming mob / and do not care what harm they do their friends, / providing they can please a crowd!

EURIPIDES, *HECUBA* (C. 425 B.C.), TR. WILLIAM ARROWSMITH

28. Politics is not the art of the possible. It consists in choosing between the disastrous and the unpalatable.

JOHN KENNETH GALBRAITH, *AMBASSADOR'S JOURNAL* (1969)

29. I could not be leading a religious life unless I identified myself with the whole of mankind, and that I could not do unless I took part in politics.

MOHANDAS K. GANDHI, *NON-VIOLENCE IN PEACE AND WAR* (1948), 1.170

30. A newly elected representative quickly discovers that his job in government—aside from making new laws—is to act as a broker, middleman, special pleader and finagler.

William Greider, *Who Will Tell the People* (1992)

31. Because the slums are no longer centers of powerful political organizations, the politicians need not really care about their inhabitants.

Michael Harrington, *The Other America* (1962)

32. Probably the most distinctive characteristic of the successful politician is selective cowardice.

Richard Harris, "Annals of Legislation," *The New Yorker,* Dec. 14, 1968

33. A "penchant for telling the truth" can cripple a candidate's chances faster than being caught *in flagrante delicto* with the governor's wife.

Sydney J. Harris, "Honesty Not the Best Policy for Winning Votes," *Clearing the Ground* (1986)

34. Genuine politics—politics worthy of the name, and the only politics I am willing to devote myself to—is simply a matter of serving those around us: serving the community, and serving those who will come after us.

Václav Havel, "Politics, Morality, and Civility," *Summer Meditations* (1992), tr. Paul Wilson

35. When we get sick, we want an uncommon doctor. If we have a construction job, we want an uncommon engineer. When we get into a war, we dreadfully want an uncommon admiral and an uncommon general. Only when we get into politics are we content with the common man.

Herbert Hoover, quoted in his obituary notice in *The New York Times,* Oct. 21, 1964

36. The greatest superstition now entertained by public men is that hypocrisy is the royal road to success.

Robert G. Ingersoll, speech, Dec. 13, 1886

37. Good thing we've still got politics in Texas—finest form of free entertainment ever invented.

Molly Ivins, *Molly Ivins Can't Say That, Can She?* (1991)

38. The tragedy of all political action is that some problems have no solution; none of the alternatives are intellectually consistent or morally uncompromising; and whatever decision is taken will harm somebody.

James Joll, *Three Intellectuals in Politics* (1960)

39. Popular men, / They must create strange monsters, and then quell them, / To make their arts seem something.

Ben Jonson, *Catiline His Conspiracy* (1611), 3.1

40. A political convention is just not a place from which you can come away with any trace of faith in human nature.

Murray Kempton, "All in Favor Say Aye," *America Comes of Middle Age* (1963)

41. All of us in the Senate live in an iron lung—the iron lung of politics, and it is no easy task to emerge from that rarified atmosphere in order to breathe the same fresh air our constituents breathe.

John F. Kennedy, *Profiles in Courage* (1956)

42. Political action is the highest responsibility of a citizen.

John F. Kennedy, campaign remarks, Pat Clancy Dinner, Astor Hotel, New York City, Oct. 20, 1960

43. In Massachusetts they [Democratic politicians] steal, in California they feud, and in New York they lie.

Robert Kennedy, quoted by Jack Newfield in *Robert Kennedy* (1969)

44. Politicians are the same all over. They promise to build a bridge even where there is no river.

Nikita Khrushchev, comment to reporters, Glen Cove, N.Y., October 1960

45. The public life of every political figure is a continual struggle to rescue an element of choice from the pressure of circumstance.

Henry Kissinger, *White House Years* (1979)

46. Politics is the art of making civilization work.

Louis L'Amour, *Education of a Wandering Man* (1989)

47. We demand of our political life greater certainty and greater perfection than we demand of our personal life.

Max Lerner, "Politics and the Connective Tissue," *Actions and Passions* (1949)

48. The man who raises new issues has always been distasteful to politicians. He musses up what had been so tidily arranged.

Walter Lippmann, "The Red Herring," *A Preface to Politics* (1914)

49. Politicians tend to live "in character," and many a public figure has come to imitate the journalism which describes him.

Walter Lippmann, "The Changing Focus," *A Preface to Politics* (1914)

50. Successful democratic politicians are insecure and intimidated men. They advance politically only as they placate, appease, bribe, seduce, bamboozle, or otherwise manage to manipulate the demanding and threatening elements in their constituencies.

Walter Lippmann, *The Public Philosophy* (1955), 2.4

51. There comes a time when even the reformer is compelled to face the fairly widespread suspicion of the average man that politics is an exhibition in which there is much ado about nothing.

Walter Lippmann, introduction, *A Preface to Politics* (1914)

52. [Senator] Al[fonse] D'Amato resides in a town that resembles a medieval fortress whose political leaders peer out at the countryside in search of opportunities to plunder.

Leonard Lurie, *Senator Pothole* (1994)

53. Politics, in a sense, has always been a con game.

Joe McGinniss, *The Selling of the President 1968* (1969)

54. The friend of humanity cannot recognize a distinction between what is political and what is not. There is nothing that is not political.

Thomas Mann, *The Magic Mountain* (1924), 6.8, tr. H. T. Lowe-Porter

55. A candidate for office can have no greater advantage than muddled syntax; no greater liability than a command of language.

Marya Mannes, *More in Anger* (1958), 1.1

56. Political power grows out of the barrel of a gun.

Mao Tse-Tung, *Quotations from Chairman Mao Tse-tung* (1966), 5

57. Politics is war without bloodshed while war is politics with bloodshed.

Mao Tse-Tung, *Quotations from Chairman Mao Tse-tung* (1966), 5

58. did you ever / notice that when / a politician / does get an idea / he usually / gets it all wrong.

Don Marquis, "archy-grams," *Archy's Life of Mehitabel* (1933)

59. If experience teaches us anything at all, it teaches us this: that a good politician, under democracy, is quite as unthinkable as an honest burglar.

H. L. Mencken, *Prejudices: Fourth Series* (1924), 6

60. Politics, as hopeful men practise it in the world, consists mainly of the delusion that a change in form is a change in substance.

H. L. Mencken, *Prejudices: Fourth Series* (1924), 13

61. The public weal requires that men should betray, and lie, and massacre.

Montaigne, "Of profit and honesty," *Essays* (1580–88), tr. W. C. Hazlitt

62. In politics, as in womanizing, failure is decisive. It sheds its retrospective gloom on earlier endeavor which at the time seemed full of promise.

Malcolm Muggeridge, "Boring for England," *The Most of Malcolm Muggeridge* (1966)

63. Politics is the diversion of trivial men who, when they succeed at it, become important in the eyes of more trivial men.

George Jean Nathan, news summaries, July 9, 1954

64. But they were as different as fire and ice. [Robert] Kennedy thought [Eugene] McCarthy was pompous, petty, and venal. McCarthy thought Kennedy was a spoiled, unintelligent demagogue.

Jack Newfield, *Robert Kennedy* (1969)

65. There are men who desire power simply for the sake of the happiness it will bring; these belong chiefly to political parties.

Nietzsche, *The Will to Power* (1888), 721, tr. Anthony M. Ludovici

66. All politics is local.

Tip O'Neill, *Man of the House* (1987)

67. In our time, political speech and writing are largely the defense of the indefensible.

George Orwell, "Politics and the English Language," *Shooting an Elephant* (1950)

68. Political language—and with variations this is true of all political parties, from Conservatives to Anarchists—is designed to make lies sound truthful and murder respectable, and to give an appearance of solidity to pure wind.

George Orwell, "Politics and the English Language," *Shooting an Elephant* (1950)

69. In business, people are held accountable. In Washington, nobody is held accountable. In business,

people are judged on results. In Washington, people are measured by their ability to get reelected.

Ross Perot, *United We Stand: How We Can Take Back Our Country* (1992)

70. Modern politics has become little more than shirking responsibility and blaming somebody else.

Ross Perot, *United We Stand: How We Can Take Back Our Country* (1992)

71. [T]he state Republican chairman, Gaylord Parkinson, postulated what he called the Eleventh Commandment: *Thou shalt not speak ill of any fellow Republican*.

Ronald Reagan, *An American Life* (1990)

72. All politics are based on the indifference of the majority.

James Reston, "New York," *The New York Times,* June 12, 1968

73. The future lies with those wise political leaders who realize that the great public is interested more in government than in politics.

Franklin D. Roosevelt, speech, Washington, D.C., Jan. 8, 1940

74. Our great democracies still tend to think that a stupid man is more likely to be honest than a clever man, and our politicians take advantage of this prejudice by pretending to be even more stupid than nature made them.

Bertrand Russell, *New Hopes for a Changing World* (1951)

75. Politics in a democracy is, at the end, an educational process.

Arthur Schlesinger, Jr., quoted in the *New York Times,* April 15, 1993

76. Experience suggests that the first rule of politics is never to say never. The ingenious human capacity for maneuver and compromise may make acceptable tomorrow what seems outrageous or impossible today.

William V. Shannon, "Vietnam: America's Dreyfus Case," *The New York Times,* March 3, 1968

77. He knows nothing and he thinks he knows everything. That points clearly to a political career.

George Bernard Shaw, *Major Barbara* (1905), 3

78. The politician who once had to learn to flatter Kings has now to learn how to fascinate, amuse, coax, humbug, frighten, or otherwise strike the fancy of the electorate.

George Bernard Shaw, "The Revolutionist's Handbook," *Man and Superman* (1903)

79. If you let Barnum & Bailey interpret a plot by Stendahl, it might come out to be something like the 1972 Democratic convention.

Gloria Steinem, "Campaigning," *Outrageous Acts and Everyday Rebellions* (1983)

80. [W]omen are never again going to be mindless coffee-makers or mindless policy-makers in politics.

Gloria Steinem, "Campaigning," *Outrageous Acts and Everyday Rebellions* (1983)

81. Why is it that when political ammunition runs low, inevitably the rusty artillery of abuse is always wheeled into action?

Adlai Stevenson, speech, New York City, Sept. 22, 1952

82. Unless we insist that politics is imagination and mind, we will learn that imagination and mind are politics, and of a kind we will not like.

Lionel Trilling, "The Function of the Little Magazine," *The Liberal Imagination* (1950)

83. A politician is a man who understands government, and it takes a politician to run a government. A statesman is a politician who's been dead 10 or 15 years.

Harry S Truman, *New York World Telegram & Sun,* April 12, 1958

84. As the master politician navigates the ship of state, he both creates and responds to public opinion. Adept at tacking with the wind, he also succeeds, at times, in generating breezes of his own.

Stewart L. Udall, *The Quiet Crisis* (1963), 11

85. Politics is the art of preventing people from taking part in affairs which properly concern them.

Paul Valéry, *Tel quel* (1943)

86. In a society like ours, politics is improvisation. To the artful dodger rather than the true believer goes the prize.

Gore Vidal, *Rocking the Boat* (1962)

87. One of the most fascinating aspects of politician-watching is trying to determine to what extent any politician believes what he says.

Gore Vidal, *Reflections Upon a Sinking Ship* (1969)

88. Yet in a society of conflicting interests the only democratic way in which matters can be improved is

through politics, and politics means the compromising of extremes in order to achieve that notorious half loaf which the passionate and the outraged never find sufficient.

Gore Vidal, *Reflections Upon a Sinking Ship* (1969)

89. Consensus politics is a cyclical thing—in order to accumulate power, one must dispose of it, and as one disposes of it, one must accumulate more power to replace it. In financial terms, a dollar must be spent to make a dollar—or two, if things go well.

Tom Wicker, *JFK and LBJ* (1968)

90. There seldom is enmity between seasoned old politicians, who know as much as men can of human weakness and human strength.

Tom Wicker, *JFK and LBJ* (1968)

91. Politics is a war of causes; a joust of principles. Government is too serious a matter to admit of meaningless courtesies.

Woodrow Wilson, quoted in Richard Hofstadter, *The American Political Tradition* (1948)

92. Tolerance is an admirable intellectual gift; but it is of little worth in politics.

Woodrow Wilson, quoted in Richard Hofstadter, *The American Political Tradition* (1948)

93. Prosperity is necessarily the first theme of a political campaign.

Woodrow Wilson, address, Sept. 4, 1912

94. A politician must have some scruples, a certain decency; he cannot smear himself in the mud for the sake of a high ideal.

Boris Yeltsin, *The Struggle for Russia* (1994), tr. Catherine A. Fitzpatrick

95. There are numerous bugbears in the profession of politician. First, ordinary everyday life suffers. Second, there are many temptations to ruin you and those around you. And I suppose, third, and this is rarely discussed, people at the top generally have no friends.

Boris Yeltsin, *The Struggle for Russia* (1994), tr. Catherine A. Fitzpatrick

POOR

See 718. Poverty

712. POPULARITY

See also 49. Approval; 474. Ingratiation

1. He that has many friends, has no friends.

Aesop, "The Hare with Many Friends," *Fables* (6th c. b.c.?), tr. Joseph Jacobs

2. The man with a host of friends who slaps on the back everybody he meets is regarded as the friend of nobody.

Aristotle, *Nicomachean Ethics* (4th c. b.c.), 9.10, tr. J. A. K. Thomson

3. Woe unto you, when all men shall speak well of you!

Bible, Luke 6:26

4. When a man is familiar with many people he must expect many disagreeable familiarities.

James Boswell, *London Journal*, Feb. 17, 1763

5. There must be something good in a thing that pleases so many; even if it cannot be explained, it is certainly enjoyed.

Baltasar Gracián, *The Art of Worldly Wisdom* (1647), 270, tr. Joseph Jacobs

6. A dish around which I see too many people doesn't tempt me.

Julien Green, *Journal* (1938)

7. What is popular is not necessarily vulgar; and that which we try to rescue from fatal obscurity had in general much better remain where it is.

William Hazlitt, "On Taste," *Sketches and Essays* (1839)

8. The more one pleases everybody, the less one pleases profoundly.

Stendhal, "Miscellaneous Fragments," *On Love* (1822)

9. It is an unhappy lot which finds no enemies.

Publilius Syrus, *Moral Sayings* (1st c. b.c.), 499, tr. Darius Lyman

10. The most popular persons in society are those who take the world as it is, find the least fault, and have [ride] no hobbies.

Charles Dudley Warner, "Fifth Study," *Backlog Studies* (1873)

713. POPULATION

See also 84. Birth Control; 208. Crowds; 802. Reproduction

1. All that tread / The globe are but a handful to the tribes / That slumber in its bosom.

William Cullen Bryant, "Thanatopsis" (1811)

2. Over-population is a phenomenon connected with the survival of the unfit, and it is a mechanism which has created conditions favourable to the survival of the unfit and the elimination of the fit.

William Ralph Inge, "The Dilemma of Civilisation," *Outspoken Essays: Second Series* (1922)

3. Creation destroys as it goes, throws down one tree for the rise of another. But ideal mankind would abolish death, multiply itself million upon million, rear up city upon city, save every parasite alive, until the accumulation of mere existence is swollen to a horror.

D. H. Lawrence, *St. Mawr* (1925)

4. If people waited to know one another before they married, the world wouldn't be so grossly over-populated as it is now.

W. Somerset Maugham, *Mrs. Dot* (1912), 2

5. We have been God-like in our planned breeding of our domesticated plants and animals, but we have been rabbit-like in our unplanned breeding of ourselves.

Arnold Toynbee, *National Observer,* June 10, 1963

6. It is obvious that the best qualities in man must atrophy in a standing-room-only environment.

Stewart L. Udall, *The Quiet Crisis* (1963), 13

714. PORNOGRAPHY

1. A taste for dirty stories may be said to be inherent in the human animal.

George Moore, *Confessions of a Young Man* (1888), 9

2. Nine-tenths of the appeal of pornography is due to the indecent feelings concerning sex which moralists inculcate in the young; the other tenth is physiological, and will occur in one way or another whatever the state of the law may be.

Bertrand Russell, "The Taboo on Sex Knowledge," *Marriage and Morals* (1929)

3. Though both erotica and pornography refer to verbal or pictorial representations of sexual behavior, they are as different as a room with doors open and one with doors locked. The first might be a home, but the second could only be a prison.

Gloria Steinem, "Erotica vs. Pornography," *Outrageous Acts and Everyday Rebellions* (1983)

715. PORTENT

See also 306. Evidence; 755. Prudence

1. One swallow does not make a summer; neither does one fine day.

Aristotle, *Nicomachean Ethics* (4th c. b.c.), 1.7, tr. J. A. K. Thomson

2. Every cloud engenders not a storm.

Shakespeare, 3 *Henry VI* (1590–91), 5.3.13

POSITION

See 780. Rank

716. POSSESSION

See also 8. Acquisition; 108. Capitalism; 746. Property

1. What a man has honestly acquired is absolutely his own, which he may freely give, but cannot be taken from him without his consent.

Samuel Adams, Massachusetts circular letter, Feb. 11, 1768

2. Fie on possession, / But if a man be vertuous withal.

Chaucer, "The Squire's Tale," *The Canterbury Tales* (1387–1400), 686

3. To keep demands as much skill as to win.

Chaucer, *Troilus and Cressida* (c. 1385), 3.234, tr. George Phillip Krapp

4. To possess, is past the instant / We achieve the Joy—/ Immortality contented / Were Anomaly.

Emily Dickinson, poem (c. 1865)

5. Our life on earth is, and ought to be, material and carnal. But we have not yet learned to manage our materialism and carnality properly; they are still entangled with the desire for ownership.

E. M. Forster, "My Wood," *Abinger Harvest* (1936)

6. How sweet an emotion is possession! What charm is inherent in ownership! What a foundation for vanity, even for the greater quality of self-respect, lies in a little property!

David Grayson, *Adventures in Contentment* (1907), 3

7. Nothing can be so perfect while we possess it as it will seem when remembered.

Oliver Wendell Holmes, Sr., *The Poet at the Breakfast Table* (1872), 12

8. It is disastrous to own more of anything than you can possess, and it is one of the most fundamental laws of human nature that our power actually to possess is limited.

Joseph Wood Krutch, "The Miracle of Grass," *If You Don't Mind My Saying So* (1964)

9. He who possesses most must be most afraid of loss.

Leonardo Da Vinci, *Notebooks* (c. 1500), tr. Jean Paul Richter

10. Clutter is what happens to things when they become useless but friendly.

Russell Lynes, "Things," *Horizon* (1968)

11. An object in possession seldom retains the same charm that it had in pursuit.

Pliny The Younger, *Letters* (c. 97–110), 2.15.1, tr. William Melmoth

12. Most people seek after what they do not possess and are thus enslaved by the very things they want to acquire.

Anwar el-Sadat, *In Search of Identity* (1977)

13. It is as unjust to possess a woman exclusively as to possess slaves.

Marquis De Sade, *La Philosophie dans le boudoir* (1795), tr. Paul Dinnage

14. An ill-favoured thing, sir, but mine own.

Shakespeare, *As You Like It* (1599–1600), 5.4.60

15. When we desire or solicit any thing, our minds run wholly on the good side or circumstances of it; when it is obtained, our minds run wholly on the bad ones.

Jonathan Swift, *Thoughts on Various Subjects* (1711)

16. No one worth possessing / Can be quite possessed.

Sara Teasdale, "Advice to a Girl," *Strange Victory* (1933)

17. The want of a thing is perplexing enough, but the possession of it is intolerable.

Sir John Vanbrugh, *The Confederacy* (1705), 1.2

POSSIBILITIES

See 657. Opportunity; 717. Potential

POSTPONEMENT

See 231. Delay

717. POTENTIAL

See also 657. Opportunity; 1010. Unfulfillment

1. The important thing is this: to be able at any moment to sacrifice what we are for what we could become.

Charles du Bos, *Approximations* (1922–37), 3

2. Nothing is unthinkable, nothing impossible to the balanced person, provided it arises out of the needs of life and is dedicated to life's further developments.

Lewis Mumford, "The Way and the Life," *The Conduct of Life* (1951)

3. Man is as full of potentiality as he is of impotence.

George Santayana, *The Life of Reason: Reason in Common Sense* (1905–06), 9

4. Man is not the sum of what he has already, but rather the sum of what he does not yet have, of what he could have.

Jean-Paul Sartre, "Temporalité," *Situations* (1947–49), v. 1

5. So many worlds, so much to do, / So little done, such things to be.

Lord Tennyson, "In Memoriam A. H. H." (1850), 73

6. The world which credits what is done / Is cold to all that might have been.

Lord Tennyson, "In Memoriam A. H. H." (1850), 75

718. POVERTY

See also 17. Adversity; 74. Beggars; 236. Deprivation; 437. Hunger; 602. Money; 625. Need; 746. Property; 1009. Unemployment; 1048. Wealth

1. The possession of gold has ruined fewer men than the lack of it. What noble enterprises have been checked and what fine souls have been blighted in the gloom of poverty the world will never know.

Thomas Bailey Aldrich, "Leaves from a Notebook," *Ponkapog Papers* (1903)

2. Is it possible that the environmental severity of the 1930's induced—particularly in the most aware, alert, and compassionate of [British] men—a morality which makes no sense today?

Robert Ardrey, *The Territorial Imperative* (1966)

3. Poverty is the parent of revolution and crime.

Aristotle, *Politics* (4th c. b.c.), 2.6, tr. Benjamin Jowett

4. What they [impecunious expatriates] like, of course, is not only low prices and sunshine but a place where indigence looks like modest affluence by contrasting with the surrounding poverty, where poverty can be worn with dignity, as it is not noticeable or embarrassing.

Luigi Barzini, *The Italians* (1964)

5. Poverty is very good in poems, but it is very bad in a house. It is very good in maxims and in sermons, but it is very bad in practical life.

Henry Ward Beecher, *Proverbs from Plymouth Pulpit* (1887)

6. The poor man's wisdom is despised, and his words are not heard.

Bible, Ecclesiastes 9:16

7. Poverty is taking your children to the hospital and spending the whole day waiting with no one even taking your name—and then coming back the next day, and the next, until they finally get around to you.

Mrs. Janice Bradshaw, quoted by Sargent Shriver in April 12, 1965 hearing of the House Committee on Education and Labor

8. To be a poor man is hard, but to be a poor race in a land of dollars is the very bottom of hardships.

W. E. B. Du Bois, *The Souls of Black Folk* (1903), 1

9. I didn't feel poor, I just felt that I didn't have any money.

Joseph Campbell, *The Power of Myth* (1988)

10. For the poor of this world, two major ways of expiring are available: either by the absolute indifference of your fellow-men in peace-time, or by the homicidal passion of these same when war breaks out.

Louis-Ferdinand Céline, *Voyage au bout de la nuit* (1932)

11. The rich man may never get into heaven, but the pauper is already serving his term in hell.

Alexander Chase, *Perspectives* (1966)

12. The honest poor can sometimes forget poverty. The honest rich can never forget it.

G. K. Chesterton, "Cockneys and Their Jokes," *All Things Considered* (1908)

13. Those who produce should have, but we know that those who produce the most—that is, those who work hardest, and at the most difficult and most menial tasks, have the least.

Eugene V. Debs, *Walls and Bars* (1927)

14. Is there not yet oppression in the country? A starving of men and pampering of dogs?

John Donne, *Sermons,* No. 68, 1630

15. Those who have not, and live in want, are a menace, / Ridden with envy and fooled by demagogues.

Euripides, *The Suppliant Women* (c. 421 B.C.), tr. Frank W. Jones

16. There is no scandal like rags, nor any crime so shameful as poverty.

George Farquhar, *The Beaux' Strategem* (1707), 1.1

17. Poor men's reasons are not heard.

Thomas Fuller, M.D., *Gnomologia* (1732), 3897

18. For every talent that poverty has stimulated it has blighted a hundred.

John W. Gardner, *Excellence* (1961)

19. Even when the money finally trickles down, even when a school is built in a poor neighborhood, for instance, the poor are still deprived.

Michael Harrington, *The Other America* (1962)

20. The American poor are pessimistic and defeated, and they are victimized by mental suffering to a degree unknown in Suburbia.

Michael Harrington, *The Other America* (1962)

21. The millions who are poor in the United States tend to become increasingly invisible.

Michael Harrington, *The Other America* (1962)

22. America has the best-dressed poverty the world has ever known.

Michael Harrington, *The Other America* (1962)

23. Beauty and myths are perennial masks of poverty.

Michael Harrington, *The Other America* (1962)

24. People who are much too sensitive to demand of cripples that they run races ask of the poor that they get up and act just like everyone else in the society.

Michael Harrington, *The Other America* (1962)

25. The teacher's chief difficulty is poverty. He (or she) belongs to a badly paid profession. He cannot dress and live like a workman, but he is sometimes paid as little as an unskilled laborer.

Gilbert Highet, *The Art of Teaching* (1950)

26. [M]any of the snarly bad-tempered teachers whom we remember with hatred were really nice people soured by years of anxiety and penny-pinching.

Gilbert Highet, *The Art of Teaching* (1950)

27. The poor on the borderline of starvation live purposeful lives. To be engaged in a desperate struggle for food and shelter is to be wholly free from a sense of futility.

Eric Hoffer, *The True Believer* (1951), 2.5.21

28. Poverty comes pleading, not for charity, for the most part, but imploring us to find a purchaser for its unmarketable wares.

OLIVER WENDELL HOLMES, SR., *OVER THE TEACUPS* (1891), 6

29. There is always more misery among the lower classes than there is humanity in the higher.

VICTOR HUGO, "FANTINE," *LES MISÉRABLES* (1862), 1.2, TR. CHARLES E. WILBOUR

30. This growing poverty in the midst of growing population constitutes a permanent menace to peace. And not only to peace, but also to democratic institutions and personal liberty. For overpopulation is not compatible with freedom.

ALDOUS HUXLEY, "THE DOUBLE CRISIS," *THEMES AND VARIATIONS* (1950)

31. It is not poverty so much as pretense that harasses a ruined man—the struggle between a proud mind and an empty purse—the keeping up of a hollow show that must soon come to an end.

WASHINGTON IRVING, "THE WIFE," *THE SKETCH BOOK OF GEOFFREY CRAYON, GENT* (1819–20)

32. It is easy enough to say that poverty is no crime. No; if it were men wouldn't be ashamed of it. It's a blunder, though, and is punished as such.

JEROME K. JEROME, "ON BEING HARD UP," *THE IDLE THOUGHTS OF AN IDLE FELLOW* (1889)

33. When I was young, poverty was so common that we didn't know it had a name.

LYNDON B. JOHNSON, WHITE HOUSE NEWS CONFERENCE, JULY 29, 1965

34. Poverty has many roots, but the tap root is ignorance.

LYNDON B. JOHNSON, MESSAGE TO CONGRESS, JAN. 12, 1965

35. All the arguments which are brought to represent poverty as no evil, show it to be evidently a great evil. You never find people laboring to convince you that you may live very happily upon a plentiful fortune.

SAMUEL JOHNSON, QUOTED IN BOSWELL'S *LIFE OF SAMUEL JOHNSON* JULY 20, 1763

36. Poverty is a great enemy to human happiness; it certainly destroys liberty, and it makes some virtues impracticable and others extremely difficult.

SAMUEL JOHNSON, QUOTED IN BOSWELL'S *LIFE OF SAMUEL JOHNSON* DEC. 7, 1782

37. Poverty has, in large cities, very different appearances; it is often concealed in splendour, and often in extravagance.

SAMUEL JOHNSON, *RASSELAS* (1759), 25

38. Slow rises worth by poverty depressed.

SAMUEL JOHNSON, *LONDON* (1738)

39. Of the woes / Of unhappy poverty, none is more difficult to bear / Than that it heaps men with ridicule.

JUVENAL, *SATIRES* (C. 100), 3.152, TR. HUBERT CREEKMORE

40. Seldom do people discern / Eloquence under a threadbare cloak.

JUVENAL, *SATIRES* (C. 100), 7.145, TR. HUBERT CREEKMORE

41. Love in a hut, with water and a crust, / Is—Love, forgive us!—cinders, ashes, dust.

KEATS, "LAMIA" (1819), 2

42. If a free society cannot help the many who are poor, it cannot save the few who are rich.

JOHN F. KENNEDY, INAUGURAL ADDRESS, JAN. 20, 1961

43. Political sovereignty is but a mockery without the means of meeting poverty and illiteracy and disease. Self-determination is but a slogan if the future holds no hope.

JOHN F. KENNEDY, ADDRESS TO UNITED NATIONS GENERAL ASSEMBLY, SEPT. 25, 1961

44. If thy wealth waste, they wit will give but small warmth.

JOHN LYLY, *EUPHUES: THE ANATOMY OF WIT* (1579)

45. We have two American flags always; one for the rich and one for the poor. When the rich fly it it means that things are under control; when the poor fly it it means danger, revolution, anarchy.

HENRY MILLER, "GOOD NEWS! GOD IS LOVE!" *THE AIR-CONDITIONED NIGHTMARE* (1945)

46. Lack of money means discomfort, means squalid worries, means shortage of tobacco, means ever-present consciousness of failure—above all, it means loneliness.

GEORGE ORWELL, *KEEP THE ASPIDISTRA FLYING* (1936)

47. Short of genius, a rich man cannot imagine poverty.

CHARLES PÉGUY, "SOCIALISM AND THE MODERN WORLD," *BASIC VERITIES* (1943), TR. JULIAN GREEN

48. In a change of government, the poor change nothing beyond the change of their master.

PHAEDRUS, "THE ASS AND THE OLD SHEPHERD," *FABLES* (1ST C.), TR. THOMAS JAMES

49. I should like to live like a poor man, with a great deal of money.

PABLO PICASSO, QUOTED IN JANET FLANNER, *JANET FLANNER'S WORLD, UNCOLLECTED WRITINGS 1932–1975* (1979)

50. The more humanity owes him [the poor man], the more society denies him. Every door is shut against him, even when he has a right to its being opened: and if he ever obtains justice, it is with much greater difficulty than others obtain favours.

ROUSSEAU, *A DISCOURSE ON POLITICAL ECONOMY* (1758), TR. G. D. H. COLE

51. The poor don't know that their function in life is to exercise our generosity.

JEAN-PAUL SARTRE, *THE WORDS* (1964), 1

52. Poverty with joy isn't poverty at all. The poor man is not one who has little, but one who hankers after more.

SENECA, *LETTERS TO LUCILIUS* (1ST C.), 2, TR. E. PHILLIPS BARKER

53. Security, the chief pretence of civilization, cannot exist where the worst of dangers, the danger of poverty, hangs over everyone's head.

GEORGE BERNARD SHAW, PREFACE *MAJOR BARBARA* (1905)

54. Poverty is no disgrace to a man, but it is confoundedly inconvenient.

SYDNEY SMITH, *WIT AND WISDOM* (1900)

55. We who are liberal and progressive know that the poor are our equals in every sense except that of being equal to us.

LIONEL TRILLING, "THE PRINCESS CASAMASSIMA," *THE LIBERAL IMAGINATION* (1950)

56. Forgive us for pretending to care for the poor, when we do not like poor people and do not want them in our homes.

UNITED PRESBYTERIAN CHURCH, *LITANY FOR HOLY COMMUNION* (1968)

57. Bankruptcy is a sacred state, a condition beyond conditions, as theologians might say, and attempts to investigate it are necessarily obscene, like spiritualism.

JOHN UPDIKE, "THE BANKRUPT MAN," *HUGGING THE SHORE* (1983)

58. The poor must be wisely visited and liberally cared for, so that mendicity shall not be tempted into mendacity, nor want exasperated into crime.

ROBERT C. WINTHROP, YORKTOWN ORATION, 1881

719. POWER

See also 61. AUTHORITY; 459. IMPOTENCE; 940. STRENGTH; 1002. TYRANNY

1. There is no evidence to support the belief that [Soviet Premier Nikita] Khrushchev ever questioned America's power. He questioned only the President's [John F. Kennedy's] readiness to use it.

ELIE ABEL, *THE MISSILE CRISIS* (1966)

2. Power tends to corrupt and absolute power corrupts absolutely.

LORD ACTON, LETTER TO MANDELL CREIGHTON, APRIL 5, 1887

3. A friend in power is a friend lost.

HENRY ADAMS, *THE EDUCATION OF HENRY ADAMS* (1907), 7

4. Power when wielded by abnormal energy is the most serious of facts.

HENRY ADAMS, *THE EDUCATION OF HENRY ADAMS* (1907), 28

5. For the mighty even to give way is grace.

AESCHYLUS, *AGAMEMNON* (458 B.C.), TR. RICHMOND LATTIMORE

6. The possession of unlimited power will make a despot of almost any man. There is a possible Nero in the gentlest human creature that walks.

THOMAS BAILEY ALDRICH, "LEAVES FROM A NOTEBOOK," *PONKAPOG PAPERS* (1903)

7. Power can corrupt, but absolute power is absolutely delightful.

ANONYMOUS

8. We thought, because we had power, we had wisdom.

STEPHEN VINCENT BENÉT, *LITANY FOR DICTATORSHIPS* (1935)

9. The central opposition between magic and science is the opposition between power and knowledge.

JACOB BRONOWSKI, *MAGIC, SCIENCE, AND CIVILIZATION* (1978)

10. The greater the power, the more dangerous the abuse.

EDMUND BURKE, SPEECH, "ON THE MIDDLESEX ELECTION," 1771

11. We can't do without dominating others or being served. ... Even the man on the bottom rung still has his wife, or his child. If he's a bachelor, his dog. The essential thing, in sum, is being able to get angry without the other person being able to answer back.

ALBERT CAMUS, *THE FALL* (1956)

12. To know the pains of power, we must go to those who have it; to know its pleasures, we must go to those who are seeking it.

CHARLES CALEB COLTON, *LACON* (1825), 1.427

13. No man is wise enough nor good enough to be trusted with unlimited power.

CHARLES CALEB COLTON, *LACON* (1825), 1.522

14. To be a great autocrat you must be a great barbarian.

JOSEPH CONRAD, *THE MIRROR OF THE SEA* (1906), 29

15. Omnipotence is bought with ceaseless fear.

CORNEILLE, *CINNA* (1639), 4.1, TR. PAUL LANDIS

16. God is usually on the side of big squadrons against little ones.

ROGER DE BUSSY-RABUTIN, LETTER TO THE COMTE DE LIMOGES, OCT. 18, 1667

17. When the reality of power has been surrendered, it's playing a dangerous game to seek to retain the appearance of it; the external aspect of vigor can sometimes support a debilitated body, but most often it manages to deal it the final blow.

ALEXIS DE TOCQUEVILLE, *ÉTAT SOCIAL ET POLITIQUE DE LA FRANCE* (1834), 1

18. Power doesn't have to show off. Power is confident, self-assuring, self-starting and self-stopping, self-warming and self-justifying. When you have it, you know it.

RALPH ELLISON, *THE INVISIBLE MAN* (1952)

19. All power is of one kind, a sharing of the nature of the world. The mind that is parallel with the laws of nature will be in the current of events, and strong with their strength.

EMERSON, "POWER," *THE CONDUCT OF LIFE* (1860)

20. Life is a search after power; and this is an element with which the world is so saturated,—there is no chink or crevice in which it is not lodged,—that no honest seeking goes unrewarded.

EMERSON, "POWER," *THE CONDUCT OF LIFE* (1860)

21. You shall have joy, or you shall have power, said God; you shall not have both.

EMERSON, *JOURNALS* 1842

22. Oh, it is vile for a man, if he be noble, / And when he has won to the heights of power, / To put on new manners for old and change / His countenance.

EURIPIDES, *IPHIGENIA IN AULIS* (C. 405 B.C.), TR. CHARLES R. WALKER

23. Power gives no purchase / to the hand, it will not hold, soon perishes, / and greatness goes.

EURIPIDES, *HECUBA* (C. 425 B.C.), TR. WILLIAM ARROWSMITH

24. Power is not something that can be assumed or discarded at will like underwear.

JOHN KENNETH GALBRAITH, *THE NEW INDUSTRIAL STATE* (1967)

25. Lost in the solitude of his immense power, he began to lose direction.

GABRIEL GARCÍA MÁRQUEZ, *ONE HUNDRED YEARS OF SOLITUDE* (1970)

26. The sole advantage of power is that you can do more good.

BALTASAR GRACIÁN, *THE ART OF WORLDLY WISDOM* (1647), 286, TR. JOSEPH JACOBS

27. Money is power in American politics. It always has been.

WILLIAM GREIDER, *WHO WILL TELL THE PEOPLE* (1992)

28. Power is pleasure; and pleasure sweetens pain.

WILLIAM HAZLITT, "ON APPLICATION TO STUDY," *THE PLAIN SPEAKER* (1826)

29. It is when power is wedded to chronic fear that it becomes formidable.

ERIC HOFFER, *THE PASSIONATE STATE OF MIND* (1954), 43

30. Our sense of power is more vivid when we break a man's spirit than when we win his heart.

ERIC HOFFER, *THE PASSIONATE STATE OF MIND* (1954), 90

31. The only prize much cared for by the powerful is power. The prize of the general is not a bigger tent, but command.

OLIVER WENDELL HOLMES JR., SPEECH, HARVARD LAW SCHOOL ASSOCIATION OF NEW YORK, FEB. 15, 1913

32. An honest man can feel no pleasure in the exercise of power over his fellow citizens.

THOMAS JEFFERSON, LETTER TO JOHN MELISH, JAN. 13, 1813

33. The problem of power is how to achieve its responsible use rather than its irresponsible and indulgent use—of how to get men of power to live *for* the public rather than *off* the public.

ROBERT F. KENNEDY, "I REMEMBER, I BELIEVE," *THE PURSUIT OF JUSTICE* (1964)

34. Tutelage is a comfortable relationship for the senior partner, but it is demoralizing in the long run. It breeds illusions of omniscience on one side and attitudes of impotent irresponsibility on the other.

HENRY A. KISSINGER, *AMERICAN FOREIGN POLICY* (1969)

35. Great power constitutes its own argument, and it never has much trouble drumming up friends, applause, sympathetic exegesis, and a band.

LEWIS LAPHAM, *IMPERIAL MASQUERADE* (1990)

36. What makes human power erupt like a volcano? What destroys it? The civilizations of Rome, Greece, Egypt, China were all eruptions from a human core.

CHARLES A. LINDBERGH, "PLASTIC DISCS AND MARBLE BONES," *AUTOBIOGRAPHY OF VALUES* (1978)

37. The first principle of a civilized state is that power is legitimate only when it is under contract.

WALTER LIPPMANN, *THE PUBLIC PHILOSOPHY* (1955), 11.3

38. One of the most dangerously vicious circles menacing the continued existence of all mankind arises through that grim striving for the highest possible position within the ranked order, in other words, the reckless pursuit of power which combines with an insatiable greed of neurotic proportions that the results of acquired power confer.

KONRAD LORENZ, *THE WANING OF HUMANENESS* (1983), TR. ROBERT WARREN KICKER

39. Deny a strong man his due, and he will take all he can get.

LUCAN, *ON THE CIVIL WAR* (1ST C.), TR. ROBERT GRAVES

40. To ask for power is forcing uphill a stone which after all rolls back again from the summit and seeks in headlong haste the levels of the plain.

LUCRETIUS, *ON THE NATURE OF THINGS* (1ST C. B.C.), 3, TR. H. A. J. MUNRO

41. [W]hoever is the cause of another becoming powerful, is ruined himself; for that power is produced by him either through craft or force; and both of these are suspected by the one who has been raised to power.

NICCOLO MACHIAVELLI, *THE PRINCE* (1517)

42. Power never takes a back step—only in the face of more power.

MALCOLM X, *MALCOLM X SPEAKS* (1965), 12

43. Every high degree of power always involves a corresponding degree of freedom from good and evil.

NIETZSCHE, *THE WILL TO POWER* (1888), TR. ANTHONY M. LUDOVICI

44. There is a universal need to exercise some kind of power, or to create for one's self the appearance of some power, if only temporarily, in the form of intoxication.

NIETZSCHE, *THE WILL TO POWER* (1888), 721, TR. ANTHONY M. LUDOVICI

45. Economic power is not the same as strength of national character. Our country may be rich in goods, but we are poor in spirit.

RICHARD M. NIXON, *BEYOND PEACE* (1994)

46. Rich white Protestant men have held on to some measure of power in America almost solely by getting women, blacks, and other disadvantaged groups to wear crippling foot fashions. This keeps them too busy with corns and bunions to compete in the job market.

P.J. O'ROURKE, *MODERN MANNERS* (1988)

47. Power-worship blurs political judgment because it leads, almost unavoidably, to the belief that present trends will continue. Whoever is winning at the moment will always seem to be invincible.

GEORGE ORWELL, "SECOND THOUGHTS ON JAMES BURNHAM," *SHOOTING AN ELEPHANT* (1950)

48. The property of power is to protect.

PASCAL, *PENSÉES* (1670), 310, TR. W. F. TROTTER

49. Hares can gambol over the body of a dead lion.

PUBLILIUS SYRUS, *MORAL SAYINGS* (1ST C. B.C.), 420, TR. DARIUS LYMAN

50. There is a homely adage which runs: "Speak softly and carry a big stick; you will go far."

THEODORE ROOSEVELT, SPEECH, MINNESOTA STATE FAIR, SEPT. 2, 1901

51. The strongest is never strong enough to be always the master, unless he transforms strength into right, and obedience into duty.

ROUSSEAU, *THE SOCIAL CONTRACT* (1762), 1.3, TR. G. D. H. COLE

52. O, it is excellent / To have a giant's strength; but it is tyrannous / To use it like a giant.

SHAKESPEARE, *MEASURE FOR MEASURE* (1604–05), 2.2.107

53. The eagle suffers little birds to sing.

SHAKESPEARE, *TITUS ANDRONICUS* (1592–93), 4.4.83

54. Power, like a desolating pestilence, / Pollutes whate'er it touches.

SHELLEY, *QUEEN MAB* (1813), 3

55. Legions and fleets are not such sure bulwarks of imperial power as a numerous family.

TACITUS, *HISTORIES* (A.D. 104–109), 4.52, TR. WILLIAM J. BRODRIBB

56. Power takes as ingratitude the writhing of its victims.

RABINDRANATH TAGORE, *STRAY BIRDS* (1916), 158

57. It is natural for men to want power. But to seek power actively takes a temperament baffling to both the simple and the wise. The simple cannot fathom how any man would dare presume to prevail, while the wise are amazed that any reasonable man would want the world, assuming he could get it.

GORE VIDAL, *ROCKING THE BOAT* (1962)

58. True power and true politeness are above vanity.

VOLTAIRE, "CEREMONIES," *PHILOSOPHICAL DICTIONARY* (1764)

59. Offices are not powerful because they exist; men make them so. Rights are not honored because they exist; men compel their recognition.

TOM WICKER, *JFK AND LBJ* (1968)

60. There is no need to fear the strong. All one needs is to know the method of overcoming them. There is a special jujitsu for every strong man.

YEVGENY YEVTUSHENKO, *A PRECOCIOUS AUTOBIOGRAPHY* (1963), TR. ANDREW R. MACANDREW

POWERLESSNESS

See 459. IMPOTENCE

720. PRACTICALITY

See also 148. COMMON SENSE; 319. EXPEDIENCY; 755. PRUDENCE; 785. REASON; 1023. USEFULNESS

1. I like a man who likes to see a fine barn as well as a good tragedy.

EMERSON, *JOURNALS,* 1828

2. The Arab who built himself a hut with marbles from the temple of Palmyra is more philosophical than all the curators of the museums of London, Paris and Munich.

ANATOLE FRANCE, *THE CRIME OF SYLVESTRE BONNARD* (1881), 2

3. A mariner must have his eye upon rocks and sands, as well as upon the North Star.

THOMAS FULLER, M.D., *GNOMOLOGIA* (1732), 319

4. I had rather ride on an ass that carries me than a horse that throws me.

GEORGE HERBERT, *JACULA PRUDENTUM* (1651)

721. PRACTICE

See also 532. LEARNING; 585. METHOD

1. Practice is nine-tenths.

EMERSON, "POWER," *THE CONDUCT OF LIFE* (1860)

2. However much thou art read in theory, if thou hast no practice thou art ignorant.

SA'DI, *GULISTAN* (1258), 8.3, TR. JAMES ROSS

722. PRAISE

See also 47. APPRECIATION; 49. APPROVAL; 584. MERIT

1. A man who does not love praise is not a full man.

HENRY WARD BEECHER, *PROVERBS FROM PLYMOUTH PULPIT* (1887)

2. The advantage of doing one's praising to oneself is that one can lay it on so thick and exactly in the right places.

SAMUEL BUTLER (D. 1902), *THE WAY OF ALL FLESH* (1903), 34

3. No doubt any connoisseur, any collector, some bored old millionaire when he shows off his treasures, is seeking in your praise the resurrection and the life.

JOYCE CARY, *TO BE A PILGRIM* (1942)

4. Expect not praise without envy until you are dead.

CHARLES CALEB COLTON, *LACON* (1825), 1.245

5. Praise to the undeserving is severe satire.

BENJAMIN FRANKLIN, *POOR RICHARD'S ALMANACK* (1732–57)

6. Praise makes good men better and bad men worse.

THOMAS FULLER, M.D., *GNOMOLOGIA* (1732), 3918

7. Praises from an enemy imply real merit.

THOMAS FULLER, M.D., *GNOMOLOGIA* (1732), 3924

8. Praises from wicked men are reproaches.

THOMAS FULLER, M.D., *GNOMOLOGIA* (1732), 3925

9. Just about the only interruption we don't object to is applause.

SYDNEY J. HARRIS, "WHY I DON'T WRITE ABOUT POLITICS," *CLEARING THE GROUND* (1986)

10. The safest kind of praise is to foretell that another will become great in some particular way. It has the greatest show of magnanimity, and the least of it in reality.

WILLIAM HAZLITT, *CHARACTERISTICS* (1823), 415

11. Unmerited abuse wounds, while unmerited praise has not the power to heal.

THOMAS JEFFERSON, LETTER TO EDWARD RUTLEDGE, DEC. 27, 1796

12. Praise, like gold and diamonds, owes its value only to its scarcity.

SAMUEL JOHNSON, *THE RAMBLER*, JUNE 6, 1751

13. The applause of a single human being is of great consequence.

SAMUEL JOHNSON, QUOTED IN BOSWELL'S *LIFE OF SAMUEL JOHNSON*, 1781

14. We cannot at once catch the applauses of the vulgar and expect the approbation of the wise.

WALTER SAVAGE LANDOR, "LUCULLUS AND CAESAR," *IMAGINARY CONVERSATIONS* (1824–53)

15. The deafest man can hear praise, and is slow to think any an excess.

WALTER SAVAGE LANDOR, "MILTON AND MARVEL," *IMAGINARY CONVERSATIONS* (1824–53)

16. An ingenuous mind feels in unmerited praise the bitterest reproof.

WALTER SAVAGE LANDOR, "BOSSUET AND THE DUCHESS DE FONTANGES," *IMAGINARY CONVERSATIONS* (1824–53)

17. Generally we praise only to be praised.

LA ROCHEFOUCAULD, *MAXIMS* (1665), TR. KENNETH PRATT

18. Refusal of praise is a desire to be praised twice.

LA ROCHEFOUCAULD, *MAXIMS* (1665), TR. KENNETH PRATT

19. There are reproaches which praise, and praises which defame.

LA ROCHEFOUCAULD, *MAXIMS* (1665), TR. KENNETH PRATT

20. There's no praise to beat the sort you can put in your pocket.

MOLIÈRE, *THE WOULD-BE GENTLEMAN* (1670), 1, TR. JOHN WOOD

21. Praise is always pleasing, let it come from whom, or upon what account it will.

MONTAIGNE, "OF VANITY," *ESSAYS* (1580–88), TR. W. C. HAZLITT

22. Praise is more obtrusive than a reproach.

NIETZSCHE, *BEYOND GOOD AND EVIL* (1886), 170, TR. WALTER KAUFMANN

23. Better to be despised, then, than to be ignored; or damned with condescending praise.

JOYCE CAROL OATES, "(WOMAN) WRITER: THEORY AND PRACTICE," *(WOMAN) WRITER: OCCASIONS AND OPPORTUNITIES* (1988)

24. Envy bestrides praise.

PINDAR, *ODES* (5TH C. B.C.), OLYMPIA 2, TR. RICHMOND LATTIMORE

25. Every artist loves applause. The praise of his contemporaries is the most valuable part of his recompense.

ROUSSEAU, *A DISCOURSE ON THE MORAL EFFECTS OF THE ARTS AND SCIENCES* (1750), 2, TR. G. D. H. COLE

26. Persons of delicate taste endure stupid criticism better than they do stupid praise.

JOSEPH ROUX, *MEDITATIONS OF A PARISH PRIEST* (1886), 1.26, TR. ISABEL F. HAPGOOD

27. True praise comes often even to the lowly; false praise only to the strong.

SENECA, *THYESTES* (1ST C.), 211

28. Praise is the best diet for us, after all.

SYDNEY SMITH, QUOTED IN LADY S. HOLLAND'S *MEMOIR* (1855), V. 1.9

29. The praise of an ignorant man is only good-will, and you should receive his kindness as he is a good neighbour in society, and not as a good judge of your actions in point of fame and reputation.

RICHARD STEELE, *THE SPECTATOR* (1711–12), 188

30. All panegyrics are mingled with an infusion of poppy.

JONATHAN SWIFT, *THOUGHTS ON VARIOUS SUBJECTS* (1711)

31. Praise shames me, for I secretly beg for it.

RABINDRANATH TAGORE, *STRAY BIRDS* (1916), 207

32. We begin to praise when we begin to see a thing needs our assistance.

THOREAU, *JOURNAL*, JUNE 20, 1840

33. Mankind are tolerant of the praises of others so long as each hearer thinks he can do as well or nearly well himself.

THUCYDIDES, *THE PELOPONNESIAN WAR* (C. 400 B.C.), 2.35, TR. BENJAMIN JOWETT

34. It is a great sign of mediocrity to praise always moderately.

VAUVENARGUES, *REFLECTIONS AND MAXIMS* (1746), 12

35. Men sometimes feel injured by praise because it assigns a limit to their merit.

VAUVENARGUES, *REFLECTIONS AND MAXIMS* (1746), 66, TR. F. G. STEVENS

36. I'm sick of praise; I want money.

THOMAS WOLFE, *THOMAS WOLFE'S LETTERS TO HIS MOTHER* (1943)

723. PRAYER

See also 183. CONTEMPLATION; 1068. WORSHIP

1. It is in vain to expect our prayers to be heard, if we do not strive as well as pray.

AESOP, "HERCULES AND THE WAGGONER," *FABLES* (6TH C. B.C.?), TR. THOMAS JAMES

2. It is not well for a man to pray cream and live skim milk.

HENRY WARD BEECHER, *PROVERBS FROM PLYMOUTH PULPIT* (1887)

3. The wish to pray is a prayer in itself.

GEORGES BERNANOS, *THE DIARY OF A COUNTRY PRIEST* (1936), 4, TR. PAMELA MORRIS

4. Pray, v. To ask that the laws of the universe be annulled in behalf of a single petitioner confessedly unworthy.

AMBROSE BIERCE, *THE DEVIL'S DICTIONARY* (1881–1911)

5. Prayers are to men as dolls are to children. They are not without use and comfort, but it is not easy to take them very seriously.

SAMUEL BUTLER (D. 1902), "UNPROFESSIONAL SERMONS," *NOTE-BOOKS* (1912)

6. To say this sacred prayer [the Kaddish, prayer for the dead] for a Gentile is a most uncommon proceeding, but so unanimous and ardent is the feeling of the people of the [New York] ghetto in the present instance that [Pres. William] McKinley is spoken of in that quarter as "the loving brother of all of us," as one who "died a martyr to the freedom of Jew and Gentile."

ABRAHAM CAHAN, *GRANDMA NEVER LIVED IN AMERICA* (1985), ED. MOSES RISCHIN

7. I have had prayers answered—most strangely so sometimes—but I think our heavenly Father's loving-kindness has been even more evident in what He has refused me.

LEWIS CARROLL, *THE LETTERS OF LEWIS CARROLL*, ED. MORTON N. COHEN (1979)

8. He prayeth best, who loveth best / All things both great and small; / For the dear God who loveth us, / He made and loveth all.

SAMUEL TAYLOR COLERIDGE, *THE RIME OF THE ANCIENT MARINER* (1798), 7.23

9. A prayer may chance to rise / From one whose heart lives in the grace of God. / A prayer from any other is unheeded.

DANTE, "PURGATORIO," *THE DIVINE COMEDY* (C. 1300–21), TR. LAWRENCE GRANT WHITE

10. Prayer is the little implement / Through which Men reach / Where Presence—is denied them.

EMILY DICKINSON, POEM (C. 1862)

11. Prayer as a means to effect a private end is theft and meanness.

EMERSON, "SELF-RELIANCE," *ESSAYS: FIRST SERIES* (1841)

12. Prayer is the contemplation of the facts of life from the highest point of view.

EMERSON, "SELF-RELIANCE," *ESSAYS: FIRST SERIES* (1841)

13. None can pray well but he that lives well.

THOMAS FULLER, M.D., *GNOMOLOGIA* (1732), 3647

14. Prayer should be the key of the day and the lock of the night.

THOMAS FULLER, M.D., *GNOMOLOGIA* (1732), 3927

15. Prayer is not an old woman's idle amusement. Properly understood and applied, it is the most potent instrument of action.

MOHANDAS K. GANDHI, *NON-VIOLENCE IN PEACE AND WAR* (1948), 2.77

16. Men have prayed in prison, men have prayed in slums and concentration camps. It's only the middle class who demand to pray in suitable surroundings.

GRAHAM GREENE, *A BURNT-OUT CASE* (1960)

17. Your cravings as a human animal do not become a prayer just because it is God whom you must ask to attend to them.

DAG HAMMARSKJÖLD, "1941–1942: THE MIDDLE YEARS," *MARKINGS* (1964), TR. W. H. AUDEN

18. We all have our prayer-wheels which we set up on the steppes. The indifferent winds come and carry most of them away to gasp out their little lives in the desert, for few reach heaven.

LEARNED HAND, ADDRESS, BRYN MAWR COLLEGE, JUNE 2, 1927

19. Certain thoughts are prayers. There are moments when, whatever be the attitude of the body, the soul is on its knees.

VICTOR HUGO, "SAINT DENIS," *LES MISÉRABLES* (1862), 5.4, TR. CHARLES E. WILBOUR

20. Affliction teacheth a wicked person sometime to pray; prosperity never.

BEN JONSON, "RANDOM NOTES," *TIMBER* (1640)

21. How ready is heaven to those that pray!

BEN JONSON, *VOLPONE* (1605), 5.12

22. Do not pray for easy lives. Pray to be stronger men.

JOHN F. KENNEDY, ADDRESS, PRAYER BREAKFAST, WASHINGTON, D.C., FEB. 7, 1963

23. Prayer is a strong wall and fortress of the church; it is a goodly Christian's weapon.

MARTIN LUTHER, *TABLE TALK* (1569)

24. Who rises from prayer a better man, his prayer is answered.

GEORGE MEREDITH, *THE ORDEAL OF RICHARD FEVEREL* (1859), 12

25. There are few men who durst publish to the world the prayers they make to Almighty God.

MONTAIGNE, "OF PRAYERS," *ESSAYS* (1580–88), TR. W. C. HAZLITT

26. So let us all who pray ask for what most of them need badly, a sense of humor to lighten their way through life, making it merrier for themselves and easier for others.

SEAN O'CASEY, "THE POWER OF LAUGHTER: WEAPON AGAINST EVIL," *FIFTY FAMOUS ESSAYS* (1964)

27. Night after night I prayed, with a fervour never previously attained in my prayers, "Please God, do not let me wet my bed! Oh, please God, do not let me wet my bed!"

GEORGE ORWELL, "SUCH, SUCH WERE THE JOYS," *A COLLECTION OF ESSAYS* (1954)

28. In his prayers he says, thy will be done: but means his own, at least acts so.

WILLIAM PENN, *SOME FRUITS OF SOLITUDE* (1693), 1.26

29. Who cared if there was really any Being to pray to? What mattered was the sense of giving thanks and praise, the feeling of a humble and grateful heart.

OLIVER SACKS, *A LEG TO STAND ON* (1984)

30. Prayer, among sane people, has never superseded practical efforts to secure the desired end.

GEORGE SANTAYANA, *THE LIFE OF REASON: REASON IN RELIGION* (1905–06), 4

31. My words fly up, my thoughts remain below. / Words without thoughts never to heaven go.

SHAKESPEARE, *HAMLET* (1600), 3.3.97

32. The unlettered man who prayed to his maker would be heard; the pedant reciting a faultless invocation would be ignored.

ISRAEL SHENKER, *COAT OF MANY COLORS* (1985)

33. Complaint is the largest tribute Heaven receives, and the sincerest part of our devotion.

JONATHAN SWIFT, *THOUGHTS ON VARIOUS SUBJECTS* (1711)

34. More things are wrought by prayer / Than this world dreams of.

LORD TENNYSON, "THE PASSING OF ARTHUR," *IDYLLS OF THE KING* (1869)

35. What are men better than sheep or goats / That nourish a blind life within the brain, / If knowing God, they lift not hands of prayer / Both for themselves and those who call them friend?

LORD TENNYSON, "THE PASSING OF ARTHUR," *IDYLLS OF THE KING* (1869)

36. We offer up prayers to God only because we have made Him after our own image. We treat Him like a pasha, or a sultan, who is capable of being exasperated and appeased.

VOLTAIRE, "PRAYER," *PHILOSOPHICAL DICTIONARY* (1764)

724. PREACHING AND PREACHERS

See also 128. CHURCHGOING; 138. CLERGY

1. He that does not know how wisely to meddle with public affairs in preaching the gospel, does not know how to preach the gospel.

HENRY WARD BEECHER, *PROVERBS FROM PLYMOUTH PULPIT* (1887)

2. He preaches well that lives well.

CERVANTES, *DON QUIXOTE* (1605–15), 2.3.20, TR. JOHN OZELL

3. Among provocatives, the next best thing to good preaching is bad preaching.

EMERSON, *JOURNALS*, 1836

4. Go into one of our cool churches, and begin to count the words that might be spared, and in most places the entire sermon will go.

EMERSON, *JOURNALS*, 1834

5. The sermon which I write inquisitive of truth is good a year after, but that which is written because a sermon must be writ is musty the next day.

EMERSON, *JOURNALS*, 1832

6. What do our clergy lose by reading their sermons? They lose preaching, the preaching of the voice in many cases, the preaching of the eye almost always.

AUGUSTUS WILLIAM HARE, *GUESSES AT TRUTH* (1827)

7. The preacher's garment is cut according to the pattern of that of the hearers, for the most part.

Oliver Wendell Holmes, Sr., *Over the Teacups* (1891), 10

8. He that has but one word of God before him, and out of that word cannot make a sermon, can never be a preacher.

Martin Luther, *Table Talk* (1569), 10

9. Preaching has become a by-word for a long and dull conversation of any kind; and whoever wishes to imply, in any piece of writing, the absence of everything agreeable and inviting, calls it a sermon.

Sydney Smith, quoted in Lady S. Holland's *Memoir* (1855), v. 1.3

10. The preaching of divines helps to preserve well-inclined men in the course of virtue, but seldom or never reclaims the vicious.

Jonathan Swift, *Thoughts on Various Subjects* (1711)

PREDICTION

See 368. Future; 715. Portent; 747. Prophecies; 1035. Vision

725. PREFERENCE

See also 124. Choice; 963. Taste

1. There is no banquet but some dislike something in it.

Thomas Fuller, M.D., *Gnomologia* (1732), 4904

2. There are as many preferences as there are men.

Horace, *Satires* (35–30 B.C.), 2.1

3. I don't care anything about reasons, but I know what I like.

Henry James, *The Portrait of a Lady* (1881), 24

4. Esteem must be founded on some sort of preference. Bestow it on everybody and it ceases to have any meaning at all.

Molière, *The Misanthrope* (1666), 1, tr. John Wood

5. Let us prefer, let us not exclude.

Joseph Roux, *Meditations of a Parish Priest* (1886), 5.5, tr. Isabel F. Hapgood

6. I know of no redeeming qualities in myself but a sincere love for some things, and when I am reproved I fall back on to this ground.

Thoreau, "Sunday," *A Week on the Concord and Merrimack Rivers* (1849)

PREJUDICE, RACIAL

See 775. Racial Prejudice

726. PREJUDICES

See also 264. Dogmatism; 500. Intolerance; 620. Narrowness

1. Above all, the ability to feel the force of an argument apart from the substance it deals with is the strongest weapon against prejudice.

Jacques Barzun, *Teacher in America* (1944)

2. In a day of footloose movements of people and of mixed marriages in the ancestry of the most desirable elements of the community, we preach unabashed the gospel of the pure race.

Ruth Benedict, *Patterns of Culture* (1934)

3. Prejudice, n. A vagrant opinion without visible means of support.

Ambrose Bierce, *The Devil's Dictionary* (1881–1911)

4. Our prejudices are our mistresses; reason is at best our wife, very often heard indeed, but seldom minded.

Lord Chesterfield, *Letters to His Son*, April 13, 1752

5. As in political so in literary action a man wins friends for himself mostly by the passion of his prejudices and by the consistent narrowness of his outlook.

Joseph Conrad, "A Familiar Preface," *A Personal Record* (1912)

6. Prejudice is never easy unless it can pass itself off for reason.

William Hazlitt, "On Prejudice," *Sketches and Essays* (1839)

7. Prejudice is the child of ignorance.

William Hazlitt, "On Prejudice," *Sketches and Essays* (1839)

8. There is no prejudice so strong as that which arises from a fancied exemption from all prejudice.

William Hazlitt, "On the Tendency of Sects," *The Round Table* (1817)

9. The tendency of the casual mind is to pick out or stumble upon a sample which supports or defies its prejudices, and then to make it the representative of a whole class.

Walter Lippmann, *Public Opinion* (1929), 3.10

10. Order a purge for your brain, it will there be much better employed than upon your stomach.

MONTAIGNE, "OF THE RESEMBLANCE OF CHILDREN TO THEIR FATHERS," *ESSAYS* (1580–88), TR. W. C. HAZLITT

11. Knowledge humanizes mankind, and reason inclines to mildness; but prejudices eradicate every tender disposition.

MONTESQUIEU, *L'ESPRIT DES LOIS* (1748), 15.3

12. Everyone is a prisoner of his own experiences. No one can eliminate prejudices—just recognize them.

EDWARD R. MURROW, DEC. 31, 1955

13. No man is prejudiced in favor of a thing knowing it to be wrong. He is attached to it on the belief of its being right.

THOMAS PAINE, *THE RIGHTS OF MAN* (1791), 2

14. Some men, under the notion of weeding out prejudices, eradicate virtue, honesty, and religion.

JONATHAN SWIFT, *THOUGHTS ON VARIOUS SUBJECTS* (1711)

727. PREMATURENESS

See also 231. DELAY; 979. TIMELINESS

1. Boast not thyself of tomorrow; for thou knowest not what a day may bring forth.

BIBLE, PROVERBS 27:1

2. Count no mortal happy till / he has passed the final limit of his life secure from pain.

SOPHOCLES, *OEDIPUS THE KING* (C. 430 B.C.), TR. DAVID GRENE

728. PREPAREDNESS

See also 1035. VISION

1. We are all, it seems, saving ourselves for the Senior Prom. But many of us forget that somewhere along the way we must learn to dance.

ALAN HARRINGTON, *LIFE IN THE CRYSTAL PALACE* (1959)

2. For all your days prepare, / And meet them all alike: / When you are the anvil, bear— / When you are the hammer, strike.

EDWIN MARKHAM, "PREPAREDNESS" (1918)

3. Shape your heart to front the hour, but dream not that the hour will last.

LORD TENNYSON, "LOCKSLEY HALL SIXTY YEARS AFTER" (1886), 106

729. PRESENT

See also 368. FUTURE; 676. PAST

1. It is not the weight of the future or the past that is pressing upon you, but ever that of the present alone. Even this burden, too, can be lessened if you confine it strictly to its own limits.

MARCUS AURELIUS, *MEDITATIONS* (2ND C.), 8.36, TR. MAXWELL STANIFORTH

2. Remember that the sole life which a man can lose is that which he is living at the moment.

MARCUS AURELIUS, *MEDITATIONS* (2ND C.), 2.14, TR. MAXWELL STANIFORTH

3. All our yesterdays are summarized in our now, and all the tomorrows are ours to shape.

HAL BORLAND, "THE TOMORROWS—DECEMBER 30," *SUNDIAL OF THE SEASONS* (1964)

4. The Will-be and the Has-been touch us more nearly than the Is. So we are more tender towards children and old people than to those who are in the prime of life.

SAMUEL BUTLER (D. 1902), "HIGGLEDY-PIGGLEDY," *NOTE-BOOKS* (1912)

5. Real generosity toward the future lies in giving all to the present.

ALBERT CAMUS, "BEYOND NIHILISM," *THE REBEL* (1951), TR. ANTHONY BOWER

6. The present time has one advantage over every other—it is our own.

CHARLES CALEB COLTON, *LACON* (1825), 1.81

7. I would not fear nor wish my fate, / But boldly say each night, / To-morrow let my sun his beams display, / Or in clouds hide them; I have lived today.

ABRAHAM COWLEY, "OF MYSELF" (17TH C.)

8. It is the fashion to style the present moment an extraordinary crisis.

BENJAMIN DISRAELI, SPEECH, HIGH WYCOMBE, DEC. 16, 1834

9. Happy the man, and happy he alone, / He who can call to-day his own; / He who, secure within, can say, / To-morrow, do thy worst, for I have lived to-day.

JOHN DRYDEN, *IMITATION OF HORACE* (1697), 3.29.65

10. The vanishing, volatile froth of the Present which any shadow will alter, any thought blow away, any event annihilate, is every moment converted into the Adamantine Record of the Past.

EMERSON, *JOURNALS*, 1832

11. We can see well into the past; we can guess shrewdly into the future; but that which is rolled up and muffled in impenetrable folds is today.

EMERSON, *JOURNALS*, 1854

12. With the Past, as past, I have nothing to do; nor with the Future as future. I live now, and will verify all past history in my own moments.

EMERSON, *JOURNALS*, 1839

13. If we could wake each morning with no memory / Of living before we went to sleep, we might / Arrive at a faultless day, once in a great many.

CHRISTOPHER FRY, *THE DARK IS LIGHT ENOUGH* (1954), 2

14. Today is yesterday's pupil.

THOMAS FULLER, M.D., *GNOMOLOGIA* (1732), 5153

15. Today is always partly tomorrow and can only be understood in movement, futuristically, speculatively.

MICHAEL HARRINGTON, *THE ACCIDENTAL CENTURY* (1966)

16. No mind is much employed upon the present; recollection and anticipation fill up almost all our moments.

SAMUEL JOHNSON, *RASSELAS* (1759), 30

17. The present, like a note in music, is nothing but as it appertains to what is past and what is to come.

WALTER SAVAGE LANDOR, "AESOP AND RHODOPE," *IMAGINARY CONVERSATIONS* (1824–53)

18. Each day the world is born anew / For him who takes it rightly.

JAMES RUSSELL LOWELL, "GOLD EGG: A DREAM-FANTASY," *UNDER THE WILLOWS AND OTHER POEMS* (1868)

19. Each day provides its own gifts.

MARTIAL, *EPIGRAMS* (A.D. 86), 8.78, TR. WALTER C. A. KERR

20. The passing moment is all we can be sure of; it is only common sense to extract its utmost value from it; the future will one day be the present and will seem as unimportant as the present does now.

W. SOMERSET MAUGHAM, *THE SUMMING UP* (1938), 15

21. Ah, take the Cash, and let the Credit go, / Nor heed the rumble of a distant Drum!

OMAR KHAYYÁM, *RUBÁIYÁT* (11TH–12TH C.), TR. EDWARD FITZGERALD, 4TH ED., 13

22. The present age is demented. It is possessed by a sense of dislocation, a loss of personal identity, an alternating sentimentality and rage which, in an individual patient, could be characterized as dementia.

WALKER PERCY, "WHY ARE YOU A CATHOLIC?" *SIGNPOSTS IN A STRANGE LAND* (1991)

23. The present offers itself to our touch for only an instant of time and then eludes the senses.

PLUTARCH, "CONTENTMENT," *MORALIA* (C. A.D. 100), TR. MOSES HADAS

24. Past, and to come, seems best; things present, worst.

SHAKESPEARE, *2 HENRY IV* (1597–98), 1.3.108

25. Do not say, "It is morning," and dismiss it with a name of yesterday. See it for the first time as a newborn child that has no name.

RABINDRANATH TAGORE, *STRAY BIRDS* (1916), 233

730. PRESIDENCY

See also 395. GOVERNMENT; 761. PUBLIC OFFICE

1. Every damn President since I can remember has been so in love with foreign policy that they're just like a schoolboy with a new girl.

CLEVELAND AMORY, "FOREIGN AFFAIRS," *THE TROUBLE WITH NOWADAYS* (1979)

2. Presidency, n. The greased pig in the field game of American politics.

AMBROSE BIERCE, *THE DEVIL'S DICTIONARY* (1881–1911)

3. Abraham Lincoln was not all brooding and melancholy and patient understanding. There was a hard core in him, and plenty of toughness. He could recognize a revolutionary situation when he saw one, and he could act fast and ruthlessly to meet it.

BRUCE CATTON, *THIS HALLOWED GROUND* (1956)

4. The president we get is the country we get. With each new president the nation is conformed spiritually.

E.L. DOCTOROW, "THE CHARACTER OF PRESIDENTS," *JACK LONDON, HEMINGWAY, AND THE CONSTITUTION* (1993)

5. Th' prisidincy is th' highest office in th' gift iv th' people. Th' vice-prisidincy is th' next highest an' the lowest. It isn't a crime exactly. Ye can't be sint to jail f'r it, but it's a kind iv a disgrace.

FINLEY PETER DUNNE, "THE VICE-PRESIDENT," *DISSERTATIONS BY MR. DOOLEY* (1906)

6. No *easy* problems ever come to the President of the United States. If they are easy to solve, somebody else has solved them.

DWIGHT D. EISENHOWER, QUOTED BY JOHN F. KENNEDY, *PARADE*, APRIL 8, 1962

7. The second office of this government is honorable and easy, the first is but a splendid misery.

Thomas Jefferson, letter to Elbridge Gerry, May 13, 1797

8. A President's hardest task is not to do what is right, but to know what is right.

Lyndon B. Johnson, State of the Union Message, Jan. 4, 1965

9. Whatever the political affiliation of our next President, whatever his views may be on all the issues and problems that rush in upon us, he must above all be the chief executive in every sense of the word.

John F. Kennedy, quoted in Tom Wicker, *JFK and LBJ* (1968)

10. The function and responsibility of the President is to set before the American people the unfinished business, the things we must do if we are going to succeed as a nation.

John F. Kennedy, campaign remarks, Crestwood, Mo., Oct. 22, 1960

11. In Washington, as we learned from the White House transcripts, a president may speak of kicking butts, call a problem a can of worms, decide not to be in the position of basically hunkering down, anticipate something hitting the fan, propose to tough it through, sight minefields down the road, see somebody playing hard ball, claim political savvy, and wonder what stroke some of his associates have with others.

Edwin Newman, *Strictly Speaking* (1974)

12. I don't know what I expected, but my first morning in the Oval Office had a surprising ring of familiarity to it. It reminded me a lot of my job as governor.

Ronald Reagan, *An American Life* (1990)

13. There is far less to the Presidency, in terms of essential activity, than meets the eye.

Arthur M. Schlesinger, Jr., quoting George Reedy, press secretary to Lyndon Johnson, in *The Imperial Presidency* (1973)

14. Every President reconstructs the Presidency to meet his own psychological needs.

Arthur M. Schlesinger, Jr., *The Imperial Presidency* (1973)

15. While the Nixon Presidency induced a momentary sense of congressional unity, a more skillful President could readily restore the customary situation where members of Congress felt more solidarity with a President of their own party than with colleagues of the opposite party.

Arthur M. Schlesinger, Jr., *The Imperial Presidency* (1973)

16. What higher obligation does a President have than to explain his intentions to the people and persuade them that the direction he wishes to go is right?

Arthur Schlesinger, Jr., *The New York Times*, April 15, 1993

17. In the White House, the future rapidly becomes the past; and delay is itself a decision.

Theodore Sorensen, *Nation's Business*, June 1963

18. The President is the representative of the whole nation and he's the only lobbyist that all the 160 million people in this country have.

Harry S Truman, lecture, Columbia University, April 27, 1959

19. [President George] Bush talked to us like we were a bunch of morons and we ate it up. Can you imagine, the Pledge of Allegiance, read my lips—can you imagine such crap in this day and age?

John Updike, *Rabbit at Rest* (1990)

20. When the Presidential virus attacks the system there is a tendency for the patient in his fever to move from the Right or the Left to the Center where the curative votes are.

Gore Vidal, *Rocking the Boat* (1962)

21. The President's decisions make the weather, and if he is great enough, change the climate, too.

Theodore H. White, *In Search of History* (1978)

22. He [John F. Kennedy] might have envisioned himself being "alone, at the top" but, like [Woodrow] Wilson, he would find out that not even a President moves free of human entanglement, human needs, human illusions; not even a President can be independent of those around him.

Tom Wicker, *JFK and LBJ* (1968)

23. Most presidents come to Washington bright as freshly minted dimes and leave much diminished.

George F. Will, "Ronald Reagan: The Captain Who Calmed the Sea," *Suddenly: The American Idea Abroad and At Home, 1986–1990* (1990)

24. I want the people to love me, but I suppose they never will.

Woodrow Wilson, quoted in Richard Hofstadter, *The American Political Tradition* (1948)

25. The main problem with being president is the constant sense that you are inside a glass bowl for everyone to see, or in a kind of barometric chamber with an artificial atmosphere where you must stay all the time.

BORIS YELTSIN, *THE STRUGGLE FOR RUSSIA* (1994), TR. CATHERINE A. FITZPATRICK

731. PRESS, FREEDOM OF THE

See also 113. CENSORSHIP; 258. DISSENT; 364. FREE SPEECH; 630. NEWSPAPERS; 764. PUBLISHING; 823. RIGHTS

1. In America, the majority raises formidable barriers around the liberty of opinion: within these barriers, an author may write what he pleases; but woe to him if he goes beyond them.

ALEXIS DE TOCQUEVILLE, *DEMOCRACY IN AMERICA* (1835–39), 1.15

2. Freedom of the press is not an end in itself but a means to the end of a free society.

FELIX FRANKFURTER, *THE NEW YORK TIMES,* NOV. 28, 1954

3. The liberty of the press is most generally approved when it takes liberties with the other fellow, and leaves us alone.

EDGAR WATSON HOWE, *COUNTRY TOWN SAYINGS* (1911)

4. The press exerts the pressure of dissent on officials otherwise inclined to rest content with the congratulations of their retainers.

LEWIS LAPHAM, *IMPERIAL MASQUERADE* (1990)

5. The freedom of the press is one of the great bulwarks of liberty, and can never be restrained but by despotic government.

GEORGE MASON, VIRGINIA BILL OF RIGHTS, JUNE 12, 1776

6. A free press stands as one of the great interpreters between the government and the people. To allow it to be fettered is to be fettered ourselves.

JUSTICE GEORGE SUTHERLAND, *GROSJEAN V. AMERICAN PRESS CO.* (1935)

PRETENSE

See 165. CONCEALMENT; 224. DECEPTION; 440. HYPOCRISY; 450. IMAGINATION; 732. PRETENSION

732. PRETENSION

See also 45. APPEARANCE; 54. ARTIFICIALITY; 451. IMITATION; 484. INSINCERITY; 733. PRIDE; 825. ROLE-PLAYING; 1027. VANITY

1. Excusations, cessions, modesty itself well governed, are but arts of ostentation.

FRANCIS BACON, "OF VAIN-GLORY," *ESSAYS* (1625)

2. All human beings have gray little souls—and they all want to rouge them up.

MAXIM GORKY, *THE LOWER DEPTHS* (1903), 3, TR. ALEXANDER BAKSHY

3. Some degree of affection is as necessary to the mind as dress is to the body; we must overact our part in some measure, in order to produce any effect at all.

WILLIAM HAZLITT, "ON CANT AND HYPOCRISY," *SKETCHES AND ESSAYS* (1839)

4. We all wear some disguise, make some professions, use some artifice, to set ourselves off as being better than we are; and yet it is not denied that we have some good intentions and praiseworthy qualities at bottom.

WILLIAM HAZLITT, "ON CANT AND HYPOCRISY," *SKETCHES AND ESSAYS* (1839)

5. Almost every man wastes part of his life in attempts to display qualities which he does not possess, and to gain applause which he cannot keep.

SAMUEL JOHNSON, *THE RAMBLER* (1750–52), 189

6. Hypocrisy is the necessary burden of villainy, affectation part of the chosen trappings of folly; the one completes a villain, the other only finishes a fop.

SAMUEL JOHNSON, *THE RAMBLER* (1750–52), 20

7. Nothing prevents our being natural so much as the desire to appear so.

LA ROCHEFOUCAULD, *MAXIMS* (1665)

8. The qualities we have do not make us so ridiculous as those which we affect.

LA ROCHEFOUCAULD, *MAXIMS* (1665), TR. KENNETH PRATT

9. Affectation is an awkward and forced imitation of what should be genuine and easy, wanting the beauty that accompanies what is natural.

JOHN LOCKE, *SOME THOUGHTS CONCERNING EDUCATION* (1693), 66

10. Foreign diplomats could have modeled their conduct on the way the Negro postmen, Pullman porters, and dining car waiters of Roxbury [Massachusetts] acted, striding around as if they were wearing top hats and cutaways.

MALCOLM X, *THE AUTOBIOGRAPHY OF MALCOLM X* (1964)

11. It is in vain that we get upon stilts, for, once on them, it is still with our legs that we must walk. And on the highest throne in the world we are still sitting on our own ass.

MONTAIGNE, "OF EXPERIENCE," *ESSAYS* (1580–88)

12. Pretending is a virtue. If you can't pretend, you can't be king.

LUIGI PIRANDELLO, *LIOLÀ* (1916), 1, TR. GERARDO GUERRIERI

13. Those who wish to seem learned to fools, seem fools to the learned.

QUINTILIAN, *INSTITUTIO ORATORIA* (C. A.D. 95), 10.7, TR. CLYDE MURLEY

14. Very probably, it was not part of the sofa vaudeville of a showoff but, rather, the private, exposed achievement of a young man who, at one time or another, might have tried shaving himself left-handed.

J.D. SALINGER, "JUST BEFORE THE WAR WITH THE ESKIMOS," IN *NINE STORIES BY J.D. SALINGER* (1953)

15. I used to think that once a writer became a man of letters, if only for a half hour, he was done for. And here I am now, at the very *moment* of such an odious, though respectable, danger.

DYLAN THOMAS, *QUITE EARLY ONE MORNING* (1954)

733. PRIDE

See also 89. BOASTING; 156. COMPLACENCY; 166. CONCEIT; 435. HUMILITY; 871. SELF-ESTEEM; 873. SELF-IMPORTANCE; 876. SELF-LOVE; 910. SNOBBERY; 1027. VANITY

1. It's a fine thing to rise above pride, but you must have pride in order to do so.

GEORGES BERNANOS, *THE DIARY OF A COUNTRY PRIEST* (1936), 7, TR. PAMELA MORRIS

2. Pride goeth before destruction, and an haughty spirit before a fall.

BIBLE, PROVERBS 16:18

3. There is a paradox in pride—it makes some men ridiculous, but prevents others from becoming so.

CHARLES CALEB COLTON, *LACON* (1825), 1.207

4. Pride, like the magnet, constantly points to one object, self; but, unlike the magnet, it has no attractive pole, but at all points repels.

CHARLES CALEB COLTON, *LACON* (1825), 1.111

5. Pride, avarice, and envy are the tongues men know and heed, a Babel of despair.

DANTE, "INFERNO," 6, *THE DIVINE COMEDY* (C. 1300–21), TR. JOHN CIARDI

6. Pride that dines on vanity sups on contempt.

BENJAMIN FRANKLIN, "THE WAY TO WEALTH" (JULY 7, 1757)

7. Pride is said to be the last vice the good man gets clear of.

BENJAMIN FRANKLIN, *POOR RICHARD'S ALMANACK* (1732–57)

8. Pride, perceiving humility honourable, often borrows her cloak.

THOMAS FULLER, M.D., *GNOMOLOGIA* (1732), 3948

9. A proud man is satisfied with his own good opinion, and does not seek to make converts to it.

WILLIAM HAZLITT, *CHARACTERISTICS* (1823), 98

10. The truly proud man knows neither superiors nor inferiors. The first he does not admit of—the last he does not concern himself about.

WILLIAM HAZLITT, *CHARACTERISTICS* (1823), 112

11. Pride is the mask of one's own faults.

HEBREW PROVERB

12. Pride is seldom delicate; it will please itself with very mean advantages.

SAMUEL JOHNSON, *RASSELAS* (1759), 9

13. It is as proper to have pride in oneself as it is ridiculous to show it to others.

LA ROCHEFOUCAULD, *MAXIMS* (1665), TR. KENNETH PRATT

14. Pride dwells in the thought; the tongue can have but a very little share in it.

MONTAIGNE, "USE MAKES PERFECT," *ESSAYS* (1580–88), TR. W. C. HAZLITT

15. The hurricane does not uproot grasses, which are pliant and bow low before it on every side. It is only the lofty trees that it attacks.

PANCHATANTRA (C. 5TH C.), 1, TR. FRANKLIN EDGERTON

16. There is but a step between a proud man's glory and his disgrace.

PUBLILIUS SYRUS, *MORAL SAYINGS* (1ST C. B.C.), 138, TR. DARIUS LYMAN

17. I do not believe that any peacock envies another peacock his tail, because every peacock is persuaded that his own tail is the finest in the world. The consequence of this is that peacocks are peaceable birds.

BERTRAND RUSSELL, *THE CONQUEST OF HAPPINESS* (1930), 6

18. All men who would surpass the other animals should do their best not to pass through life silently like the beasts whom nature made prone, obedient to their bellies.

SALLUST, *CONSPIRACY OF CATILINE* (1ST C. B.C.), 1

19. He that is proud eats up himself. Pride is his own glass, his own trumpet, his own chronicle; and whatever praises itself but in the deed, devours the deed in the praise.

SHAKESPEARE, *TROILUS AND CRESSIDA* (1601–02), 2.3.164

20. None are more taken in by flattery than the proud, who wish to be the first and are not.

SPINOZA, *ETHICS* (1677), 4, TR. ANDREW BOYLE

21. Pride is over-estimation of oneself by reason of self-love.

SPINOZA, *ETHICS* (1677), 3, TR. ANDREW BOYLE

22. Pride destroys all symmetry and grace, and affectation is a more terrible enemy to fine faces than the small-pox.

RICHARD STEELE, *THE SPECTATOR* (1711–12), 33

23. Dust are our frames; and, gilded dust, our pride / Looks only for a moment whole and sound.

LORD TENNYSON, "AYLMER'S FIELD" (1864)

PRIESTS

See 138. CLERGY

734. PRINCIPLE

See also 491. INTEGRITY; 822. RIGHT

1. [F]alse principles, which correspond with the bad as well as with the just aspirations of mankind, are a normal and necessary element in the social life of nations.

LORD ACTON, "NATIONALITY" (1862), REPRINTED IN *ESSAYS ON FREEDOM AND POWER* (1948)

2. Expedients are for the hour, but principles are for the ages.

HENRY WARD BEECHER, *PROVERBS FROM PLYMOUTH PULPIT* (1887)

3. We speak of being anchored to our principles. But if the weather turns nasty you up with an anchor and let it down where there's less wind, and the fishing's better.

ROBERT BOLT, *A MAN FOR ALL SEASONS* (1962), 1

4. Men of principle are sure to be bold, but those who are bold may not always be men of principle.

CONFUCIUS, *ANALECTS* (6TH C. B.C.), 14.5, TR. JAMES LEGGE

5. One of the most ordinary weaknesses of the human intellect is to seek to reconcile contrary principles, and to purchase peace at the expense of logic.

ALEXIS DE TOCQUEVILLE, *DEMOCRACY IN AMERICA* (1835–39), 2.1.6

6. General principles are not the less true or important because from their nature they elude immediate observation; they are like the air, which is not the less necessary because we neither see nor feel it.

WILLIAM HAZLITT, "EDMUND BURKE," *THE ELOQUENCE OF THE BRITISH SENATE* (1807)

7. Amid the pressure of great events, a general principle gives no help.

HEGEL, INTRODUCTION TO *PHILOSOPHY OF HISTORY* (1832), TR. JOHN SIBREE

8. Everywhere the basis of principle is tradition.

OLIVER WENDELL HOLMES, JR., SPEECH, BOSTON, JAN. 8, 1897

9. A man is usually more careful of his money than he is of his principles.

EDGAR WATSON HOWE, *VENTURES IN COMMON SENSE* (1919), 30.4

10. A man may be very sincere in good principles, without having good practice.

SAMUEL JOHNSON, QUOTED IN BOSWELL'S *JOURNAL OF A TOUR TO THE HEBRIDES WITH SAMUEL JOHNSON*, OCT. 25, 1773

11. Principles—and I have in mind such principles as states' rights or national sovereignty or the free market or pacifism—have a way of drying up while the sap of life goes flowing in another direction.

MAX LERNER, "POLITICS AND THE CONNECTIVE TISSUE," *ACTIONS AND PASSIONS* (1949)

12. Manners with fortunes, humours turn with climes, / Tenets with books, and principles with times.

ALEXANDER POPE, *MORAL ESSAYS* (1731–35), 1.172

13. The fate of America cannot depend on any one man. The greatness of America is grounded in principles and not on any single personality.

FRANKLIN D. ROOSEVELT, SPEECH, NEW YORK CITY, NOV. 5, 1932

14. Ideas and principles that do harm are, as a rule, though not always, cloaks for evil passions.

BERTRAND RUSSELL, "IDEAS THAT HAVE HARMED MANKIND," *UNPOPULAR ESSAYS* (1950)

15. It is often easier to fight for principles than to live up to them.

Adlai Stevenson, speech, New York City, Aug. 27, 1952

16. Prosperity is the best protector of principle.

Mark Twain, "Pudd'nhead Wilson's New Calendar," *Following the Equator* (1897), 2.2

PRINTING

See 764. Publishing

735. PRISON

See also 109. Captivity

1. All prisons are brimming over with innocence. It is those who cram their fellows into them, in the name of empty ideas, who are the only guilty ones.

Jean Anouilh, *Catch as Catch Can* (1960), tr. Lucienne Hill

2. A prison is a cross section of society in which every human strain is clearly revealed.

Eugene V. Debs, *Walls and Bars* (1927)

3. In the very progress of society, the prison has in the very nature of things undergone some improvement, but there are vast stretches yet to be covered before the prison becomes, if it ever does, an institution for the reclamation and rehabilitation of erring and unfortunate men and women.

Eugene V. Debs, *Walls and Bars* (1927)

4. The prison, above all others, should be the most human of institutions.

Eugene V. Debs, *Walls and Bars* (1927)

5. Wherever any one is against his will, that is to him a prison.

Epictetus, *Discourses* (2nd c.), 1.7, tr. Thomas W. Higginson

6. A prison is a house of care, a place where none can thrive; / A touchstone true to try a friend, a grave for one alive. / Sometimes a place of right, sometimes a place of wrong, / Sometimes a place of rogues and thieves and honest men among.

Inscription on Edinburgh's old Tolbooth prison (demolished in 1817)

7. It is this refrain that we hear repeated by everyone: you are not at home, this is not a sanatorium, the only exit is by way of the Chimney. (What did it mean? Soon we were all to learn what it meant.)

Primo Levi, *Survival in Auschwitz* (1959)

8. Stone walls do not a prison make, / Nor iron bars a cage; / Minds innocent and quiet take / That for an hermitage.

Richard Lovelace, "To Althea from Prison" (1649), 4

9. Prison is not a mere physical horror. It is using a pickaxe to no purpose that makes a prison.

Saint-Exupéry, *Wind, Sand, and Stars* (1939), 9.6, tr. Lewis Galantière

10. Every prison that men build / Is built with bricks of shame, / And bound with bars lest Christ should see / How men their brothers maim.

Oscar Wilde, *The Ballad of Reading Gaol* (1898), 5.3

11. I know not whether Laws be right, / Or whether Laws be wrong; / All that we know who lie in gaol / Is that the wall is strong; / And that each day is like a year, / A year whose days are long.

Oscar Wilde, *The Ballad of Reading Gaol* (1898), 5.1

12. The vilest deeds like poison weeds / Bloom well in prison-air: / It is only what is good in Man / That wastes and withers there: / Pale Anguish keeps the heavy gate, / And the warder is Despair.

Oscar Wilde, *The Ballad of Reading Gaol* (1898), 5.5

736. PRIVACY

See also 760. Publicity; 915. Solitude

1. The personal life of every individual is based on secrecy, and perhaps it is partly for that reason that civilized man is so nervously anxious that personal privacy should be respected.

Anton Chekhov, "The Lady with the Pet Dog" (1899)

2. To construct a proper privacy, making it a privilege rather than a burden, we first need to construct a community—love, family, politics, art.

Herbert Gold, "Programming the Peculiar Things," *The Magic Will* (1971)

3. The human animal needs a freedom seldom mentioned, freedom from intrusion. He needs a little privacy quite as much as he wants understanding or vitamins or exercise or praise.

Phyllis McGinley, "A Lost Privilege," *The Province of the Heart* (1959)

4. In a crowd, on a journey, at a banquet even, a line of thought can itself provide its own seclusion.

Quintilian, *Institutio Oratoria* (c. A.D. 95), 10.3, tr. Clyde Murley

5. [P]rivacy, after all, was the most relative of privileges. It was granted us by society under ungenerous

conditions, the most fundamental of them that whether for pain or profit, by design or accident, we not call public attention to ourselves.

Diana Trilling, *Mrs. Harris: The Death of the Scarsdale Doctor* (1981)

6. The essence of government is concern for the widest possible public interest; the essence of the humanities, it seems to me, is private study, thought, and passion. Publicity is a essential to the one as privacy is to the other.

John Updike, "On One's Own Oeuvre," *Hugging the Shore* (1983)

7. In large Victorian houses with many rooms and heavy doors, the occupants could be mysterious and exciting to one another in a way that those who live in rackety developments can never hope to be. Not even the lust of a Lord Byron could survive the fact of Levittown.

Gore Vidal, "On Pornography," *New York Review of Books,* March 31, 1966

8. Commercial society regards people as bundles of appetites, a conception that turns human beings inside out, leaving nothing to be regarded as inherently private.

George F. Will, "Privacy in the Republic of Appetites," *The Pursuit of Happiness and Other Sobering Thoughts* (1978)

PRIVILEGE

See 15. Advantage

737. PROBLEMS

See also 585. Method

1. The unsolved problems pile up and inevitably produce catastrophes at regular intervals. The Italians always see the next one approaching with a clear eye, but, like sleepers in a nightmare, cannot do anything to ward it off.

Luigi Barzini, *The Italians* (1964)

2. Every major industrial society believes it has a serious youth problem.

Edgar Z. Friedenberg, *Coming of Age in America* (1963)

3. Problems are only opportunities in work clothes.

Henry J. Kaiser (1882–1967), maxim

4. Our problems are man-made, therefore they may be solved by man. And man can be as big as he wants. No problem of human destiny is beyond human beings.

John F. Kennedy, address, The American University, Washington, D.C., June 10, 1963

PROCRASTINATION

See 231. Delay

PROFANITY

See 957. Swearing

PROFESSIONS

See 1037. Vocations

738. PROFITEERING

See also 104. Business and Commerce; 105. Buying and Selling

1. When a man sells eleven ounces for twelve, he makes a compact with the devil, and sells himself for the value of an ounce.

Henry Ward Beecher, *Proverbs from Plymouth Pulpit* (1887)

2. He that maketh haste to be rich shall not be innocent.

Bible, Proverbs 28:20

3. Prefer a loss to a dishonest gain: the one brings pain at the moment, the other for all time.

Chilon (6th c. b.c.), quoted in Diogenes Laertius' *Lives and Opinions of Eminent Philosophers* (3rd c. a.d.), tr. R. D. Hicks

4. What is a man if he is not a thief who openly charges as much as he can for the goods he sells?

Mohandas K. Gandhi, *Non-Violence in Peace and War* (1948), 2.124

5. Gain not base gains; base gains are the same as losses.

Hesiod, *Works and Days* (8th c. b.c.), 353, tr. J. Banks

6. Greenmail, in case you're wondering, is when a company pays a raider a premium for his holdings—if he'll go away. What I think it really is is blackmail in a pin-striped suit.

Lee Iacocca, *Talking Straight* (1988), with Sonny Kleinfeld

7. The smell of profit is clean / And sweet, whatever the source.

Juvenal, *Satires* (c. 100), 14.204, tr. Hubert Creekmore

8. He who wishes to be rich in a day will be hanged in a year.

LEONARD DA VINCI, *NOTEBOOKS* (C. 1500), TR. JEAN PAUL RICHTER

9. More men come to doom / through dirty profits than are kept by them.

SOPHOCLES, *ANTIGONE* (442–41 B.C.), TR. ELIZABETH WYCKOFF

739. PROFLIGACY

See also 494. INTEMPERANCE; 706. PLEASURE-SEEKING

1. It is the hour to be drunken! To escape being the martyred slaves of time, be ceaselessly drunken. On wine, on poetry, or on virtue, as you wish.

CHARLES BAUDELAIRE, "ENIVREZ-VOUS," *PARIS SPLEEN* (1869)

2. An unrestricted satisfaction of every need presents itself as the most enticing method of conducting one's life, but it means putting enjoyment before caution, and soon brings its own punishment.

SIGMUND FREUD, *CIVILIZATION AND ITS DISCONTENTS* (1930), 2, TR. JAMES STRACHEY

3. Debauchery is perhaps an act of despair in the face of infinity.

JULES DE GONCOURT, *JOURNAL*, JULY 30, 1861, TR. ROBERT BALDICK

4. An orgy looks particularly alluring seen through the mists of righteous indignation.

MALCOLM MUGGERIDGE, "DOLCE VITA IN A COLD CLIMATE," *THE MOST OF MALCOLM MUGGERIDGE* (1966)

5. Not joy but joylessness is the mother of debauchery.

NIETZSCHE, *MISCELLANEOUS MAXIMS AND OPINIONS* (1879), 71, TR. PAUL V. COHN

6. Violent pleasures which reach the soul through the body are generally of this sort—they are reliefs of pain.

PLATO, *THE REPUBLIC* (4TH C. B.C.), 9, TR. BENJAMIN JOWETT

740. PROFUNDITY

See also 886. SERIOUSNESS; 951. SUPERFICIALITY; 1060. WISDOM

1. The profound thinker always suspects that he is superficial.

BENJAMIN DISRAELI, *CONTARINI FLEMING* (1832), 4.5

2. Errors, like straws, upon the surface flow; / He who would search for pearls must dive below.

JOHN DRYDEN, PROLOGUE TO *ALL FOR LOVE* (1678)

3. There's no one so transparent as the person who thinks he's devilish deep.

W. SOMERSET MAUGHAM, *LADY FREDERICK* (1907), 1

4. Smooth runs the water where the brook is deep.

SHAKESPEARE, *2 HENRY VI* (1590–91), 3.1.53

741. PROGRESS

See also 308. EVOLUTION

1. A thousand things advance; nine hundred and ninety-nine retreat: that is progress.

HENRI FRÉDÉRIC AMIEL, *JOURNAL* (1882–84)

2. The most powerful drive in the ascent of man is his pleasure in his own skill. He loves to do what he does well and, having done it well, he loves to do it better.

JACOB BRONOWSKI, *THE ASCENT OF MAN* (1973)

3. All progress is based upon a universal innate desire on the part of every organism to live beyond its income.

SAMUEL BUTLER (D. 1902), "LORD, WHAT IS MAN?" *NOTE-BOOKS* (1912)

4. The distance from nothing to a little, is ten thousand times more, than from it to the highest degree in this life.

JOHN DONNE, *SERMONS*, NO. 5, 1619

5. All that is human must retrograde if it do not advance.

EDWARD GIBBON, *DECLINE AND FALL OF THE ROMAN EMPIRE* (1776), 71

6. The world owes all its onward impulses to men ill at ease. The happy man inevitably confines himself within ancient limits.

NATHANIEL HAWTHORNE, *THE HOUSE OF THE SEVEN GABLES* (1851), 20

7. In human affairs, the best stimulus for running ahead is to have something we must run from.

ERIC HOFFER, *THE ORDEAL OF CHANGE* (1964), 9

8. The natural progress of the works of men is from rudeness to convenience, from convenience to elegance, and from elegance to nicety.

SAMUEL JOHNSON, *THE IDLER* (1758–60), 63

9. The best road to progress is freedom's road.

JOHN F. KENNEDY, MESSAGE TO CONGRESS, MARCH 14, 1961

10. There can be no progress if people have no faith in tomorrow.

John F. Kennedy, address, Inter-American Press Association, Miami Beach, Fla., Nov. 18, 1963

11. If freedom makes social progress possible, so social progress strengthens and enlarges freedom. The two are inseparable partners in the great adventure of humanity.

Robert F. Kennedy, "Berlin East and West," *The Pursuit of Justice* (1964)

12. Obviously, computers have made differences. They have fostered the development of spaceships—as well as a great increase in junk mail.

Tracy Kidder, *The Soul of a New Machine* (1981)

13. All progress is precarious, and the solution of one problem brings us face to face with another problem.

Martin Luther King, Jr., *Strength to Love* (1963), 8.3

14. Is it progress if a cannibal uses knife and fork?

Stanislaw Lec, *Unkempt Thoughts* (1962), tr. Jacek Galazka

15. Human progress is furthered, not by conformity, but by aberration.

H. L. Mencken, *Prejudices: Third Series* (1922), 18

16. Progress—progress is the dirtiest word in the language—who ever told us— / And made us believe it—that to take a step forward was necessarily, was always / A good idea?

Edna St. Vincent Millay, untitled poem, *Make Bright the Arrows* (1940)

17. Whatever there be of progress in life comes not through adaptation but through daring, through obeying the blind urge.

Henry Miller, "Reflections on Writing," *The Wisdom of the Heart* (1941)

18. The magnitude of a "progress" is gauged by the greatness of the sacrifice that it requires.

Nietzsche, *The Genealogy of Morals* (1887), 2.12, tr. Horace B. Samuel

19. All history teaches us that these questions that we think the pressing ones will be transmuted before they are answered, that they will be replaced by others, and that the very process of discovery will shatter the concepts that we today use to describe our puzzlement.

J. Robert Oppenheimer, "Prospects in the Arts and Sciences," *Fifty Great Essays* (1964)

20. Every step of progress the world has made has been from scaffold to scaffold, and from stake to stake.

Wendell Phillips, speech, Oct. 15, 1851

21. It was old President Díaz who said that nothing ever happens in Mexico until it happens. Things rock along from day to day, and then all at once you are caught up in a rush of unforeseen events.

Charles Portis, *Gringos* (1991)

22. The desire to understand the world and the desire to reform it are the two great engines of progress, without which human society would stand still or retrogress.

Bertrand Russell, "The Place of Sex Among Human Values," *Marriage and Morals* (1929)

23. All progress means war with Society.

George Bernard Shaw, *Getting Married* (1911)

24. Nothing is ever done in this world until men are prepared to kill one another if it is not done.

George Bernard Shaw, *Major Barbara* (1905), 4

25. The reasonable man adapts himself to the world: the unreasonable one persists in trying to adapt the world to himself. Therefore all progress depends on the unreasonable man.

George Bernard Shaw, "Maxims for Revolutionists," *Man and Superman* (1903)

26. Let's talk sense to the American people. Let's tell them the truth, that there are no gains without pains.

Adlai Stevenson, acceptance speech, Democratic National Convention, July 26, 1952

27. I doubt not through the ages one increasing purpose runs, / And the thoughts of men are widened with the process of the suns.

Lord Tennyson, "Locksley Hall" (1842)

28. The policy of man consists, at first, in endeavoring to arrive at a state equal to that of animals, whom nature has furnished with food, clothing, and shelter.

Voltaire, "Policy," *Philosophical Dictionary* (1764)

29. We have our arts, the ancients had theirs.... We cannot raise obelisks a hundred feet high in a single piece, but our meridians are more exact.

Voltaire, "Antiquity," *Philosophical Dictionary* (1764)

742. PROMISCUITY

See also 472. Infidelity; 857. Seduction; 892. Sex

PROMISES

1. Many [Italian men] are disposed to make love at the drop of a hat, anywhere, in a car, on a beach, behind a bush, on mountain summits, under water, or even in a bed, during the day or at night.

LUIGI BARZINI, *THE ITALIANS* (1964)

2. Like the bee its sting, the promiscuous leave behind them in each encounter something of themselves by which they are made to suffer.

CYRIL CONNOLLY, *THE UNQUIET GRAVE* (1945), 2

3. Give but a grain of the heart's rich seed, / Confine some under cover, / And when love goes, bid him God-speed. / And find another lover.

COUNTEE CULLEN, "SONG IN SPITE OF MYSELF," *ON THESE I STAND* (1947)

4. Loving everybody is polygamy. I care for no friend who loves his enemy equally well.

EDGAR WATSON HOWE, *VENTURES IN COMMON SENSE* (1919), 15.5

5. My aunt could not have been the lone romantic who gave up everything for sex. Women in the old China did not choose. Some man had commanded her to lie with him and be his secret evil.

MAXINE HONG KINGSTON, *THE WOMAN WARRIOR* (1976)

6. Accursed from birth they be / Who seek to find monogamy, / Pursuing it from bed to bed— / I think they would be better dead.

DOROTHY PARKER, "REUBEN'S CHILDREN," *SUNSET GUN* (1928)

743. PROMISES

See also 643. OATHS

1. I've broken all the good promises. When I was a little girl, I used to make promises on the new moon and the first snow. I've broken everything good.

JOHN CHEEVER, "THE HARTLEYS," *THE STORIES OF JOHN CHEEVER* (1980)

2. Promises are not to be kept, if the keeping of them would prove harmful to those to whom you have made them.

CICERO, *DE OFFICIIS* (44 B.C.), 1.10.32

3. A promise is binding in the inverse ratio of the numbers to whom it is made.

THOMAS DE QUINCEY, APPENDIX, *CONFESSIONS OF AN ENGLISH OPIUM-EATER* (1821–56)

4. Better break your word than do worse in keeping it.

THOMAS FULLER, M.D., *GNOMOLOGIA* (1732), 883

5. He that promises too much means nothing.

THOMAS FULLER, M.D., *GNOMOLOGIA* (1732), 2253

6. We promise according to our hopes, and perform according to our fears.

LA ROCHEFOUCAULD, *MAXIMS* (1665), TR. KENNETH PRATT

7. Ease would recant / Vows made in pain, as violent and void.

MILTON, *PARADISE LOST* (1667), 4.96

8. The best way to keep one's word is not to give it.

NAPOLEON I, *MAXIMS* (1804–15)

9. Everyone's a millionaire where promises are concerned.

OVID, *THE ART OF LOVE* (C. A.D. 8), 1, TR. J. LEWIS MAY

10. A promise made is a debt unpaid.

ROBERT W. SERVICE, "THE CREMATION OF SAM MCGEE," *THE SPELL OF THE YUKON* (1907)

11. Promises and pie-crust are made to be broken.

JONATHAN SWIFT, *POLITE CONVERSATION* (1738), 1

12. The vow that binds too strictly snaps itself.

LORD TENNYSON, "THE LAST TOURNAMENT," *IDYLLS OF THE KING* (1871)

13. To promise not to do a thing is the surest way in the world to make a body want to go and do that very thing.

MARK TWAIN, *THE ADVENTURES OF TOM SAWYER* (1876), 22

14. We promise much to avoid giving little.

VAUVENARGUES, *REFLECTIONS AND MAXIMS* (1746), 436

15. To make a vow for life is to make oneself a slave.

VOLTAIRE, "VOWS," *PHILOSOPHICAL DICTIONARY* (1764)

PROMPTNESS

See 979. TIMELINESS

744. PROOF

See also 306. EVIDENCE; 785. REASON

1. He that, in the ordinary affairs of life, would admit of nothing but direct plain demonstration would be sure of nothing in this world but of perishing quickly.

JOHN LOCKE, *AN ESSAY CONCERNING HUMAN UNDERSTANDING* (1690), 4.11.10

2. That which needs to be proved cannot be worth much.

NIETZSCHE, "THE PROBLEM OF SOCRATES," 5, *TWILIGHT OF THE IDOLS* (1888), TR. ANTHONY M. LUDOVICI

745. PROPAGANDA

See also 18. ADVERTISING; 760. PUBLICITY

1. In the first World War British propaganda had to invent the stories of German soldiers bayoneting Belgian babies, because there were too few real atrocities to feed the hatred against the enemy.

ERICH FROMM, *THE ANATOMY OF HUMAN DESTRUCTIVENESS* (1973)

2. Public-relations specialists make flower arrangements of the facts, placing them so that the wilted and less attractive petals are hidden by sturdy blooms.

ALAN HARRINGTON, "PUBLIC RELATIONS," *LIFE IN THE CRYSTAL PALACE* (1959)

3. The greatest triumphs of propaganda have been accomplished, not by doing something, but by refraining from doing. Great is truth, but still greater, from a practical point of view, is silence about truth.

ALDOUS HUXLEY, FOREWORD, *BRAVE NEW WORLD* (1932)

4. The propagandist's purpose is to make one set of people forget that certain other sets of people are human.

ALDOUS HUXLEY, *THE OLIVE TREE* (1937)

5. I give you bitter pills in sugar coating. The pills are harmless; the poison is in the sugar.

STANISLAW LEC, *UNKEMPT THOUGHTS* (1962), TR. JACEK GALAZKA

6. There is no nonsense so arrant that it cannot be made the creed of the vast majority by adequate governmental action.

BERTRAND RUSSELL, "AN OUTLINE OF INTELLECTUAL RUBBISH," *UNPOPULAR ESSAYS* (1950)

7. Why is propaganda so much more successful when it stirs up hatred than when it tries to stir up friendly feeling?

BERTRAND RUSSELL, *THE CONQUEST OF HAPPINESS* (1930), 6

8. Man is a creature who lives not upon bread alone, but principally by catchwords; and the little rift betwen the sexes is astonishingly widened by simply teaching one set of catchwords to the girls and another to the boys.

ROBERT LOUIS STEVENSON, "ON MARRIAGE," IN *THE ART OF THE PERSONAL ESSAY* (1994), ED. PHILLIP LOPATE

746. PROPERTY

See also 8. ACQUISITION; 108. CAPITALISM; 430. HOUSES; 602. MONEY; 716. POSSESSION; 718. POVERTY; 1048. WEALTH

1. It is not the possessions but the desires of mankind which require to be equalized.

ARISTOTLE, *POLITICS* (4TH C. B.C.), 2.7, TR. BENJAMIN JOWETT

2. Where all of the man is what property he owns, it does not take long to annihilate him.

HENRY WARD BEECHER, *PROVERBS FROM PLYMOUTH PULPIT* (1887)

3. Where your treasure is, there will your heart be also.

BIBLE, MATTHEW 6:21

4. Property is in its nature timid and seeks protection, and nothing is more gratifying to government than to become a protector.

JOHN C. CALHOUN, SPEECH, MARCH 21, 1834

5. If a man own land, the land owns him. Now let him leave home, if he dare.

EMERSON, "WEALTH," *THE CONDUCT OF LIFE* (1860)

6. A pig that has two owners is sure to die of hunger.

ENGLISH PROVERB

7. Men honor property above all else; / it has the greatest power in human life.

EURIPIDES, *THE PHOENICIAN WOMEN* (C. 411–409 B.C.), TR. ELIZABETH WYCKOFF

8. Of all obstacles to that complete democracy of which we dream, is there a greater than property?

DAVID GRAYSON, *ADVENTURES IN CONTENTMENT* (1907), 3

9. The legal relations between the individual and the community which arise out of the production and distribution of property, comprise by far the greater, and more important, part of the law; subtract these and very little content would be left.

LEARNED HAND, *THE SPIRIT OF LIBERTY* (1959)

10. What we call real estate—the solid ground to build a house on—is the broad foundation on which nearly all the guilt of this world rests.

NATHANIEL HAWTHORNE, *THE HOUSE OF THE SEVEN GABLES* (1851), 17

11. There is a desire of property in the sanest and best men, which Nature seems to have implanted as conservative of her works, and which is necessary to encourage and keep alive the arts.

WALTER SAVAGE LANDOR, "ARISTOTELES AND CALLISTHENES," *IMAGINARY CONVERSATIONS* (1824–53)

12. In our rich consumers' civilization we spin cocoons around ourselves and get possessed by our possessions.

MAX LERNER, "WHAT SHALL I SAVE?" *THE UNFINISHED COUNTRY* (1959), 1

13. Where there is no property there is no injustice.

JOHN LOCKE, *AN ESSAY CONCERNING HUMAN UNDERSTANDING* (1690), 4.3.18

14. An acre in Middlesex is better than a principality in Utopia.

THOMAS BABINGTON MACAULAY, "LORD BACON" (1837)

15. Like Michelangelo and Cellini, Florentines of every station are absorbed in acquiring real estate: a little apartment that can be rented to foreigners; a farm that will supply the owner with oil, wine, fruit, and flowers for the house.

MARY MCCARTHY, *THE STONES OF FLORENCE* (1959)

16. No man divulges his revenue, or at least which way it comes in: but every one publishes his acquisitions.

MONTAIGNE, "OF THE EDUCATION OF CHILDREN," *ESSAYS* (1580–88), TR. W. C. HAZLITT

17. Property is theft.

PIERRE-JOSEPH PROUDHON, *QU'EST-CE QUE LA PROPRIÉTÉ?* (1840)

18. It should be remembered that the foundation of the social contract is property; and its first condition, that every one should be maintained in the peaceful possession of what belongs to him.

ROUSSEAU, *A DISCOURSE ON POLITICAL ECONOMY* (1758), TR. G. D. H. COLE

19. The first man to fence in a piece of land, saying "This is mine," and who found people simple enough to believe him, was the real founder of civil society.

ROUSSEAU, *DISCOURSE ON THE ORIGIN AND BASES OF INEQUALITY AMONG MEN* (1754)

20. So soon as the possession of property becomes the basis of popular esteem, therefore, it becomes also a requisite to that complacency which we call self-respect.

THORSTEIN VEBLEN, *THE THEORY OF THE LEISURE CLASS* (1899), 2

21. The spirit of property doubles a man's strength.

VOLTAIRE, "PROPERTY," *PHILOSOPHICAL DICTIONARY* (1764)

22. What good is a planet called Earth, after all, if you own no land?

KURT VONNEGUT, "TRIAGE," *PALM SUNDAY* (1981)

23. Broad acres are a patent of nobility; and no man but feels more of a man in the world if he have a bit of ground that he can call his own. However small it is on the surface, it is four thousand miles deep; and that is a very handsome property.

CHARLES DUDLEY WARNER, "PRELIMINARY," *MY SUMMER IN A GARDEN* (1871)

747. PROPHECIES

1. [W]e can predict the present without having to know everything about the past.

JOHN D. BARROW, *THE ORIGIN OF THE UNIVERSE* (1994)

2. I always avoid prophesying beforehand, because it is a much better policy to prophesy after the event has already taken place.

SIR WINSTON CHURCHILL, PRESS CONFERENCE, CAIRO, FEB. 1, 1943

3. Prophecy is the most gratuitous form of error.

GEORGE ELIOT, *MIDDLEMARCH* (1871–72), 10

4. It was her [Cassandra's] fate always to know the disaster that was coming and be unable to avert it.

EDITH HAMILTON, *MYTHOLOGY* (1940)

5. As a forecaster, Marx shared the common destiny of all prophets: to be belied by events.

GUNNAR MYRDAL, *BEYOND THE WELFARE STATE* (1960)

6. Prognostics do not always prove prophecies,—at least the wisest prophets make sure of the event first.

HORACE WALPOLE, LETTER TO THOMAS WALPOLE, FEB. 19, 1785

748. PROPORTION

See also 324. EXTRAVAGANCE; 410. HARMONY; 598. MODERATION

1. Proportion is almost impossible to human beings. There is no one who does not exaggerate.

EMERSON, "NOMINALIST AND REALIST," *ESSAYS: SECOND SERIES* (1844)

2. Without a sense of proportion there can be neither good taste nor genuine intelligence, nor perhaps moral integrity.

ERIC HOFFER, *THE PASSIONATE STATE OF MIND* (1954), 233

3. How sour sweet music is / When time is broke and no proportion kept! / So is it in the music of men's lives.

SHAKESPEARE, *RICHARD II* (1595–96), 5.5.42

749. PROPRIETY

See also 114. CEREMONY; 197. COURTESY; 391. GOOD BREEDING; 563. MANNERS; 642. NUDITY; 756. PRUDERY; 809. RESPECTABILITY

1. A prig always finds a last refuge in responsibility.

JEAN COCTEAU, PREFACE TO *THE WEDDING ON THE EIFFEL TOWER* (1921), TR. MICHAEL BENEDIKT

2. Blue laws once frowned on Sunday labor, also loud recreation, unseemly dress, and any "deportment inconsistent with proper reverence," and those laws still frown but do it in private, in the book of old ordinances, in a section unread for many years.

GARRISON KEILLOR, *LAKE WOBEGON DAYS* (1985)

3. Propriety is the least of all laws, and the most observed.

LA ROCHEFOUCAULD, *MAXIMS* (1665), TR. KENNETH PRATT

4. Ceremony forbids us to express by words things that are lawful and natural, and we obey it; reason forbids us to do things unlawful and ill, and nobody obeys it.

MONTAIGNE, "OF PRESUMPTION," *ESSAYS* (1580–88), TR. W. C. HAZLITT

5. Politeness requires this thing; decorum that; ceremony has its forms, and fashion its laws, and these we must always follow, never the promptings of our own nature.

ROUSSEAU, *A DISCOURSE ON THE MORAL EFFECTS OF THE ARTS AND SCIENCES* (1750), 1, TR. G. D. H. COLE

750. PROSPERITY

See also 17. ADVERSITY; 557. LUXURY; 751. PROSPERITY AND ADVERSITY; 945. SUCCESS; 1048. WEALTH

1. They who prosper take on airs of vanity.

AESCHYLUS, *AGAMEMNON* (458 B.C.), TR. RICHMOND LATTIMORE

2. Happiness seems to require a modicum of external prosperity.

ARISTOTLE, *NICOMACHEAN ETHICS* (4TH C. B.C.), 1.8, TR. J. A. K. THOMSON

3. If prosperity is regarded as the reward of virtue it will be regarded as the symptom of virtue.

G. K. CHESTERTON, "THE BOOK OF JOB," *G. K. C. AS M. C.* (1929)

4. Prosperity is only an instrument to be used, not a deity to be worshiped.

CALVIN COOLIDGE, SPEECH, JUNE 11, 1928

5. The taste for well-being is the prominent and indelible feature of democratic times.

ALEXIS DE TOCQUEVILLE, *DEMOCRACY IN AMERICA* (1835–39), 2.1.5

6. Some men never find prosperity, / For all their voyaging, / While others find it with no voyaging.

EURIPIDES, *IPHIGENIA IN TAURIS* (C. 414–12 B.C.), TR. WITTER BYNNER

7. Hardship is vanishing, but so is style, and the two are more closely connected than the present generation supposes.

E. M. FORSTER, "CAMBRIDGE," *TWO CHEERS FOR DEMOCRACY* (1951)

8. The human race has had long experience and a fine tradition in surviving adversity. But we now face a task for which we have little experience, the task of surviving prosperity.

ALAN GREGG, *THE NEW YORK TIMES*, NOV. 4, 1956

9. It is the curse of prosperity that it takes work away from us, and shuts that door to hope and health of spirit.

WILLIAM DEAN HOWELLS, *THE RISE OF SILAS LAPHAM* (1885), 17

10. Social prosperity means man happy, the citizen free, the nation great.

VICTOR HUGO, "SAINT DENIS," *LES MISÉRABLES* (1862), 1.4, TR. CHARLES E. WILBOUR

11. I should like to bring a case to trial: / Prosperity versus Beauty, / Cash registers teetering in a balance against the comfort of the soul.

AMY LOWELL, "CHARLESTON, SOUTH CAROLINA," *WHAT'S O'CLOCK* (1925)

12. When all is well who cannot be wise?

PANCHATANTRA (C. 5TH C.), 1, TR. FRANKLIN EDGERTON

13. We have produced a world of contented bodies and discontented minds.

ADAM CLAYTON POWELL, "THE TEMPTATIONS OF MODERNITY," *KEEP THE FAITH, BABY!* (1967)

14. Prosperity's the very bond of love, / Whose fresh complexion and whose heart together / Affliction alters.

SHAKESPEARE, *THE WINTER'S TALE* (1610–11), 4.4.584

15. Few of us can stand prosperity. Another man's, I mean.

MARK TWAIN, "PUDD'NHEAD WILSON'S NEW CALENDAR," *FOLLOWING THE EQUATOR* (1897), 2.4

16. When you ascend the hill of prosperity, may you not meet a friend.

MARK TWAIN, "PUDD'NHEAD WILSON'S NEW CALENDAR," *FOLLOWING THE EQUATOR* (1897), 2.5

17. Prosperity doth bewitch men, seeming clear; / But seas do laugh, show white, when rocks are near.

JOHN WEBSTER, *THE WHITE DEVIL* (1612), 5.6

751. PROSPERITY AND ADVERSITY

See also 17. ADVERSITY; 360. FORTUNE; 750. PROSPERITY

1. In the day of prosperity, adversity is forgotten and in the day of adversity, prosperity is not remembered.

APOCRYPHA, ECCLESIASTICUS 11:25

2. They merit more praise who know how to suffer misery than those who temper themselves in contentment.

PIETRO ARETINO, LETTER TO THE KING OF FRANCE, APRIL 24, 1525, TR. SAMUEL PUTNAM

3. The virtue of prosperity is temperance; the virtue of adversity is fortitude.

FRANCIS BACON, "OF ADVERSITY," *ESSAYS* (1625)

4. In the day of prosperity be joyful, but in the day of adversity consider.

BIBLE, ECCLESIASTES 7:14

5. Adversity is sometimes hard upon a man; but for one man who can stand prosperity, there are a hundred that will stand adversity.

THOMAS CARLYLE, *ON HEROES, HERO-WORSHIP AND THE HEROIC IN HISTORY* (1841), 5

6. In prosperity friends do not leave you unless desired, whereas in adversity they stay away of their own accord.

DEMETRIUS (4TH–3RD C. B.C.), QUOTED IN DIOGENES LAERTIUS' *LIVES AND OPINIONS OF EMINENT PHILOSOPHERS* (3RD C. A.D.), TR. R. D. HICKS

7. Misfortunes tell us what fortune is.

THOMAS FULLER, M.D., *GNOMOLOGIA* (1732), 3420

8. One who was abhorred by all in prosperity is adored by all in adversity.

BALTASAR GRACIÁN, *THE ART OF WORLDLY WISDOM* (1647), 163, TR. JOSEPH JACOBS

9. Prosperity is a great teacher; adversity is a greater.

WILLIAM HAZLITT, "ON THE CONVERSATION OF LORDS," *SKETCHES AND ESSAYS* (1839)

10. Sometimes it looks as if, the better off they [nations] become, the bigger do they conceive the gap between what is actually their lot and what would be desirable, while in the poor countries large masses of people seem to be satisfied by merely surviving.

GUNNAR MYRDAL, *BEYOND THE WELFARE STATE* (1960)

11. Prosperity makes friends, adversity tries them.

PUBLILIUS SYRUS, *MORAL SAYINGS* (1ST C. B.C.), 872, TR. DARIUS LYMAN

12. Prosperity has no power over adversity.

PUBLILIUS SYRUS, *MORAL SAYINGS* (1ST C. B.C.), 692, TR. DARIUS LYMAN

13. A man is insensible to the relish of prosperity till he has tasted adversity.

SA'DI, *GULISTAN* (1258), 5.10, TR. JAMES ROSS

14. In victory even the cowardly like to boast, while in adverse times even the brave are discredited.

SALLUST, *JUGURTHINE WAR* (1ST C. B.C.), 53

15. Mankind apparently find it easier to drive away adversity than to retain prosperity.

THUCYDIDES, *THE PELOPONNESIAN WAR* (C. 400 B.C.), 3.39, TR. BENJAMIN JOWETT

752. PROSTITUTION

1. Experienced travelers, and the Italians themselves, naturally enough, believe that no professional courtesan in Europe beats the Italian.

LUIGI BARZINI, *THE ITALIANS* (1964)

2. Prostitution, black marketeering, and informing on one's neighbors and friends all had such a deep-rooted tradition in Romania that there was a charming naturalness and innocence about it.

ROBERT D. KAPLAN, *BALKAN GHOSTS* (1993)

753. PROTEST

See also 258. DISSENT; 658. OPPOSITION; 786. REBELLION

1. Sometimes a scream is better than a thesis.

EMERSON, *JOURNALS,* 1836

PROTESTANTISM

See 125. CHRISTIANITY

PROVERBS

See 572. MAXIMS

754. PROVIDENCE

See also 240. DESTINY; 340. FATE; 387. GOD; 880. SELF-SUFFICIENCY

1. There is a Power whose care / Teaches thy way along that pathless coast,— / The desert and illimitable air,— / Lone wandering, but not lost.

WILLIAM CULLEN BRYANT, "TO A WATERFOWL" (1818)

2. To put one's trust in God is only a longer way of saying that one will chance it.

SAMUEL BUTLER (D. 1902), "HIGGLEDY-PIGGLEDY," *NOTE-BOOKS* (1912)

3. The Infinite Goodness has such wide arms that it takes whatever turns to it.

DANTE, "PURGATORIO," 3, *THE DIVINE COMEDY* (C. 1300–21), TR. CHARLES ELIOT NORTON

4. God tempers the wind to the shorn lamb.

ENGLISH PROVERB

5. How dark are all the ways of god to man!

EURIPIDES, *HERACLES* (C. 422 B.C.), TR. WILLIAM ARROWSMITH

6. The man whom heaven helps / has friends enough.

EURIPIDES, *ORESTES* (408 B.C.), TR. WILLIAM ARROWSMITH

7. God never sends the mouth but he sendeth meat.

JOHN HEYWOOD, *PROVERBS* (1546), 1.4

8. Know from the bounteous heaven all riches flow; / And what man gives, the gods by man bestow.

HOMER, *ODYSSEY* (9TH C. B.C.), 18.26, TR. ALEXANDER POPE

9. The gods give to mortals not everything at the same time.

HOMER, *ILIAD* (9TH C. B.C.), 4.320, TR. RICHMOND LATTIMORE

10. The wisdom of providence is as much revealed in the rarity of genius, as in the circumstance that not everyone is deaf or blind.

GEORG CHRISTOPH LICHTENBERG, *APHORISMS* (1764–99), TR. H. HATFIELD

11. Men almost universally have acknowledged a Providence, but that fact has had no force to destroy natural aversions and fears in the presence of events.

GEORGE SANTAYANA, *THE LIFE OF REASON: REASON IN RELIGION* (1905–06), 4

12. I know not where His islands lift / Their fronded palms in air; / I only know I cannot drift / Beyond His love and care.

JOHN GREENLEAF WHITTIER, "THE ETERNAL GOODNESS" (1867), 20

755. PRUDENCE

See also 112. CAUTIOUSNESS; 148. COMMON SENSE; 354. FOLLY; 598. MODERATION; 720. PRACTICALITY; 748. PROPORTION; 781. RASHNESS; 1060. WISDOM

1. No one tests the depth of a river with both feet.

ASHANTI PROVERB

2. I would rather worry without need than live without heed.

BEAUMARCHAIS, *THE BARBER OF SEVILLE* (1775), 2, TR. ALBERT BERMEL

3. Prudence is a rich, ugly old maid courted by Incapacity.

WILLIAM BLAKE, "PROVERBS OF HELL," *THE MARRIAGE OF HEAVEN AND HELL* (1790)

4. 'Tis the part of a wise man to keep himself today for tomorrow, and not venture all his eggs in one basket.

CERVANTES, *DON QUIXOTE* (1605–15), 1.3.9, TR. JOHN OZELL

5. Judgment is not upon all occasions required, but discretion always is.

LORD CHESTERFIELD, *LETTERS TO HIS GODSON,* 1766

6. In order to try whether a vessel be leaky, we first prove it with water before we trust it with wine.

CHARLES CALEB COLTON, *LACON* (1825), 1.46

7. Act so in the valley that you need not fear those who stand on the hill.

DANISH PROVERB

8. The eye of prudence may never shut.

EMERSON, "PRUDENCE," *ESSAYS: FIRST SERIES* (1841)

9. If thy heart fails thee, climb not at all.

THOMAS FULLER, D.D., *WORTHIES OF ENGLAND* (1662), V. 1

10. When you have nothing to say, or to hide, there is no need to be prudent.

ANDRÉ GIDE, *JOURNALS,* 1922, TR. JUSTIN O'BRIEN

11. Prudence is but experience, which equal time equally bestows on all men, in those things they equally apply themselves unto.

THOMAS HOBBES, *LEVIATHAN* (1651), 1.13

12. Prudence is sometimes stretched too far, until it blocks the road of progress.

TEHYI HSIEH, *CHINESE EPIGRAMS INSIDE OUT AND PROVERBS* (1948), 261

13. A prudent man does not make the goat his gardener.

HUNGARIAN PROVERB

14. Tell not all you know, believe not all you hear, do not all you are able.

ITALIAN PROVERB

15. Although it rain, cast not away the watering pot.

MALAY PROVERB

16. Sincerity is glass, discretion is diamond.

ANDRÉ MAUROIS, *CONSEILS À UNE JEUNE FILLE QUI DIT TOUT CE QU'ELLE PENSE* (1947)

17. He who is not a bird should not build his nest over abysses.

NIETZSCHE, "ON THE FAMOUS WISE MEN," *THUS SPOKE ZARATHUSTRA* (1883–92), 2, TR. WALTER KAUFMANN

18. If thou thinkest twice before thou speakest once, thou wilt speak twice the better for it.

WILLIAM PENN, *SOME FRUITS OF SOLITUDE* (1693), 1.131

19. Be moderate in prosperity, prudent in adversity.

PERIANDER (D. 585 B.C.), QUOTED IN DIOGENES LAERTIUS' *LIVES AND OPINIONS OF EMINENT PHILOSOPHERS* (3RD C. A.D.), TR. R. D. HICKS

20. He who wants a rose must respect the thorn.

PERSIAN PROVERB

21. Consider the little mouse, how sagacious an animal it is which never entrusts its life to one hole only.

PLAUTUS, *TRUCULENTUS* (C. 191–186 B.C.), 4.4.15, TR. HENRY THOMAS RILEY

22. It is well to moor your bark with two anchors.

PUBLILIUS SYRUS, *MORAL SAYINGS* (1ST C. B.C.), 119, TR. DARIUS LYMAN

23. Never exceed your rights, and they will soon become unlimited.

ROUSSEAU, *A DISCOURSE ON POLITICAL ECONOMY* (1758), TR. G. D. H. COLE

24. Reveal not every secret you have to a friend, for how can you tell but that friend may hereafter become an enemy. And bring not all the mischief you are able to do upon an enemy, for he may one day become your friend.

SA'DI, *GULISTAN* (1258), 8.10, TR. JAMES ROSS

25. We are prudent people. We are afraid to let go of our petty reality in order to grasp at a great shadow.

SAINT-EXUPÉRY, *WIND, SAND, AND STARS* (1939), 9.5, TR. LEWIS GALANTIÈRE

26. Around the year 2023 the American people would be well advised to go on the alert and start nailing down everything in sight.

ARTHUR M. SCHLESINGER, JR., *THE IMPERIAL PRESIDENCY* (1973)

27. The better part of valour is discretion.

SHAKESPEARE, *I HENRY IV* (1597–98), 5.4.121

28. If you are out of trouble, watch for danger. / And when you live well, then consider the most / your life, lest ruin take it unawares.

SOPHOCLES, *PHILOCTETES* (409 B.C.), TR. DAVID GRENE

29. So soon as prudence has begun to grow up in the brain, like a dismal fungus, it finds its first expression in a paralysis of generous acts.

ROBERT LOUIS STEVENSON, "AES TRIPLEX," *VIRGINIBUS PUERISQUE* (1881)

30. No wise man stands behind an ass when he kicks.

TERENCE, *THE EUNUCH* (161 B.C.), TR. ROBERT GRAVES

31. The prudent man does himself good; the virtuous one does it to other men.

VOLTAIRE, "VIRTUE," *PHILOSOPHICAL DICTIONARY* (1764)

756. PRUDERY

See also 642. NUDITY; 749. PROPRIETY; 769. PURITANS AND PURITANISM

1. A private sin is not so prejudicial in this world as a public indecency.

CERVANTES, *DON QUIXOTE* (1605–15), 2.3.22, TR. JOHN OZELL

2. Decency, not to dare to do that in public which it is decent enough to do in private.

MONTAIGNE, "APOLOGY FOR RAIMOND DE SEBONDE," *ESSAYS* (1580–88), TR. W. C. HAZLITT

3. Prudery is a kind of avarice, the worst of all.

STENDHAL, "MISCELLANEOUS FRAGMENTS," *ON LOVE* (1822), TR. H. B. V., UNDER DIRECTION OF C. K. SCOTT-MONCRIEFF

4. Nature knows no indecencies; man invents them.

MARK TWAIN, *NOTEBOOK* (1935)

PRYING

See 575. MEDDLING

757. PSYCHIATRY

See also 627. NEUROSIS; 758. PSYCHOANALYSIS; 759. PSYCHOLOGY

1. Canst thou not minister to a mind diseased, / Pluck from the memory a rooted sorrow, / Raze out the written troubles of the brain, / And with some sweet oblivious antidote / Cleanse the stuffed bosom of that perilous stuff / Which weighs upon the heart?

SHAKESPEARE, *MACBETH* (1605–06), 5.3.40

2. I suspect that our own faith in psychiatry will seem as touchingly quaint to the future as our grandparents' belief in phrenology seems now to us.

GORE VIDAL, *REFLECTIONS UPON A SINKING SHIP* (1969)

3. A neurotic is the man who builds a castle in the air. A psychotic is the man who lives in it. And a psychiatrist is the man who collects the rent.

UNIDENTIFIED AUTHOR

758. PSYCHOANALYSIS

See also 43. ANXIETY; 627. NEUROSIS; 757. PSYCHIATRY; 759. PSYCHOLOGY; 875. SELF-KNOWLEDGE

1. Do you not know, Prometheus, that words are healers of the sick temper?

AESCHYLUS, *PROMETHEUS BOUND* (C. 478 B.C.), TR. DAVID GRENE

2. Once read thy own breast right, / And thou hast done with fears.

MATTHEW ARNOLD, *EMPEDOCLES ON ETNA* (1852), 1.2

3. The greatest happiness is to know the source of unhappiness.

DOSTOYEVSKY, *A DIARY OF A WRITER* (1876), 4, JULY-AUGUST

4. All cases are unique, and very similar to others.

T. S. ELIOT, *THE COCKTAIL PARTY* (1949), 2

5. It might be said of psychoanalysis that if you give it your little finger it will soon have your whole hand.

SIGMUND FREUD, *INTRODUCTORY LECTURES ON PSYCHOANALYSIS* (1917), TR. JOAN RIVIERE

6. Look into the depths of your own soul and learn first to know yourself, then you will understand why this illness was bound to come upon you and perhaps you will thenceforth avoid falling ill.

SIGMUND FREUD, "ONE OF THE DIFFICULTIES OF PSYCHOANALYSIS," *COLLECTED PAPERS* (1924–50), TR. JOAN RIVIERE

7. The examined life has always been pretty well confined to a privileged class.

EDGAR Z. FRIEDENBERG, "THE IMPACT OF THE SCHOOL," *THE VANISHING ADOLESCENT* (1959)

8. The man who once cursed his fate, now curses himself—and pays his psychoanalyst.

JOHN W. GARDNER, *NO EASY VICTORIES* (1968), 1

9. There were 117 psychoanalysts on the Pan Am flight to Vienna and I'd been treated by at least six of them. And married a seventh.

ERICA JONG, *FEAR OF FLYING* (1973)

10. Why do analysts always answer a question with a question?

ERICA JONG, *FEAR OF FLYING* (1973)

11. To have known how to change the past into a few saddened smiles—is this not to master the future?

MAURICE MAETERLINCK, "THE STAR," *THE TREASURE OF THE HUMBLE* (1896), TR. ALFRED SUTRO

12. Every life is, more or less, a ruin among whose debris we have to discover what the person ought to have been.

JOSÉ ORTEGA Y GASSET, "IN SEARCH OF GOETHE FROM WITHIN, LETTER TO A GERMAN," *PARTISAN REVIEW*, DECEMBER 1949, TR. WILLARD R. TRASK

13. Man is tied to the weight of his own past, and even by a great therapeutic labor little more can be accomplished than a shifting of the burden.

PHILIP RIEFF, PREFACE TO *FREUD: THE MIND OF THE MORALIST* (1959)

14. To understand oneself is the classic form of consolation; to elude oneself is the romantic.

GEORGE SANTAYANA, *WINDS OF DOCTRINE* (1913)

15. Let us not seek our disease out of ourselves; 'tis in us, and planted in our bowels; and the mere fact that we do not perceive ourselves to be sick, renders us more hard to be cured.

SENECA, *LETTERS TO LUCILIUS* (1ST C.)

16. The unexamined life is not worth living.

SOCRATES, IN PLATO'S *APOLOGY* (4TH C. B.C.), TR. LANE COOPER

17. Paradoxically, only journeying backward in time and reentering the home we once knew allows us to go forward to the home we've always wanted.

GLORIA STEINEM, *REVOLUTION FROM WITHIN* (1992)

18. Until a man can quit talking loudly to himself in order to shout down the memories of blunderings and gropings, he is in no shape for the painstaking examination of distress.

JAMES THURBER, "A NOTE AT THE END," *THE THURBER CARNIVAL* (1945)

759. PSYCHOLOGY

See also 590. MIND; 627. NEUROSIS; 757. PSYCHIATRY; 758. PSYCHOANALYSIS

1. There are almost no limits to the discoveries of how the human brain operates—in illness and health, in sleep and waking and dreaming, in calm and under tension. The question is how far man can put these discoveries to use without using them not for cure but for power.

MAX LERNER, "MANIPULATING LIFE," IN THE *NEW YORK POST,* JAN. 24, 1968

2. Idleness is the parent of all psychology.

NIETZSCHE, "MAXIMS AND MISSILES," 1, *TWILIGHT OF THE IDOLS* (1888), TR. ANTHONY M. LUDOVICI

3. The object of psychology is to give us a totally different idea of the things we know best.

PAUL VALÉRY, *TEL QUEL* (1943)

THE PUBLIC

See 682. THE PEOPLE

760. PUBLIC OFFICE

See also 172. CONGRESS; 395. GOVERNMENT; 711. POLITICS AND POLITICIANS; 730. PRESIDENCY; 762. PUBLIC OPINION

1. It is not easy for a person to do any great harm when his tenure of office is short, whereas long possession begets tyranny.

ARISTOTLE, *POLITICS* (4TH C. B.C.), 5.8, TR. BENJAMIN JOWETT

2. Nowadays, for the sake of the advantage which is to be gained from the public revenues and from office, men want to be always in office.

ARISTOTLE, *POLITICS* (4TH C. B.C.), 3.6, TR. BENJAMIN JOWETT

3. The very essence of a free government consists in considering offices as public trusts, bestowed for the good of the country, and not for the benefit of an individual or a party.

JOHN C. CALHOUN, SPEECH, FEB. 13, 1835

4. A man ain't got no right to be a public man, unless he meets the public views.

CHARLES DICKENS, *MARTIN CHUZZLEWIT* (1844), 34

5. He that puts on a public gown must put off a private person.

THOMAS FULLER, M.D., *GNOMOLOGIA* (1732), 2257

6. The public official must pick his way nicely, must learn to placate though not to yield too much, to have the art of honeyed words but not to seem neutral, and above all to keep constantly audible, visible, likable, even kissable.

LEARNED HAND, SPEECH, WASHINGTON, D.C., MARCH 8, 1932

7. A situation in a public office is secure, but laborious and mechanical, and without the two great springs of life, Hope and Fear.

WILLIAM HAZLITT, "ON THE CONDUCT OF LIFE," *LITERARY REMAINS* (1836)

8. Offices are as acceptable here as elsewhere, and whenever a man has cast a longing eye on them, a rottenness begins in his conduct.

THOMAS JEFFERSON, LETTER TO TENCH COXE, MAY 21, 1799

9. When a man assumes a public trust, he should consider himself as public property.

THOMAS JEFFERSON, REMARK TO BARON VON HUMBOLDT, 1807

10. In government offices which are sensitive to the vehemence and passion of mass sentiment public men have no sure tenure. They are in effect perpetual office seekers, always on trial for their political lives, always required to court their restless constituents.

WALTER LIPPMANN, *THE PUBLIC PHILOSOPHY* (1955), 2.4

11. The best servants of the people, like the best valets, must whisper unpleasant truths in the master's ear. It is the court fool, not the foolish courtier, whom the king can least afford to lose.

WALTER LIPPMANN, "SOME NECESSARY ICONOCLASM," *A PREFACE TO POLITICS* (1914)

12. In our democracy officers of the government are the servants, and never the masters of the people.

FRANKLIN D. ROOSEVELT, SPEECH, HOLLYWOOD, CALIF., FEB. 27, 1941

13. As soon as public service ceases to be the chief business of the citizens, and they would rather serve with their money than with their persons, the State is not far from its fall.

ROUSSEAU, *THE SOCIAL CONTRACT* (1762), 3.15, TR. G. D. H. COLE

14. Your public servants serve you right; indeed often they serve you better than your apathy and indifference deserve.

ADLAI STEVENSON, SPEECH, LOS ANGELES, SEPT. 11, 1952

761. PUBLIC OPINION

See also 656. OPINION

1. There is nothing that makes more cowards and feeble men than public opinion.

HENRY WARD BEECHER, *PROVERBS FROM PLYMOUTH PULPIT* (1887)

2. Your representative owes you, not his industry only, but his judgment; and he betrays instead of serving you if he sacrifices it to your opinion.

EDMUND BURKE, SPEECH TO THE ELECTORS OF BRISTOL, NOV. 3, 1774

3. The public buys its opinions as it buys its meat, or takes in its milk, on the principle that it is cheaper to do this than to keep a cow. So it is, but the milk is more likely to be watered.

SAMUEL BUTLER (D. 1902), "MATERIAL FOR A PROJECTED SEQUEL TO *ALPS AND SANCTUARIES*," *NOTE-BOOKS* (1912)

4. Nothing is more dangerous in wartime than to live in the temperamental atmosphere of a Gallup Poll, always feeling one's pulse and taking one's temperature.

SIR WINSTON CHURCHILL, SPEECH, HOUSE OF COMMONS, SEPT. 30, 1941

5. When the multitude detests a man, inquiry is necessary; when the multitude likes a man, inquiry is equally necessary.

CONFUCIUS, *ANALECTS* (6TH C. B.C.), 15.27, TR. WINBERG CHAI

6. What we call public opinion is generally public sentiment.

BENJAMIN DISRAELI, SPEECH, AUG. 3, 1880

7. According to the experience of all but the most accomplished jugglers, it is easier to keep one ball in the air than many.

JOHN KENNETH GALBRAITH, *THE NEW INDUSTRIAL STATE* (1967)

8. The idea of what the public will think prevents the public from ever thinking at all, and acts as a spell on the exercise of private judgment.

WILLIAM HAZLITT, "ON LIVING TO ONE'S-SELF," *TABLE TALK* (1821–22)

9. A straw vote only shows which way the hot air blows.

O. HENRY, "A RULER OF MEN," *ROLLING STONES* (1912)

10. Public opinion, a vulgar, impertinent, anonymous tyrant who deliberately makes life unpleasant for anyone who is not content to be the average man.

WILLIAM RALPH INGE, "OUR PRESENT DISCONTENTS," *OUTSPOKEN ESSAYS: FIRST SERIES* (1919)

11. [A]ny court which undertakes by its legal processes to enforce civil liberties needs the support of an enlightened and vigorous public opinion which will be intelligent and discriminating as to what cases really are civil liberties cases and what questions really are involved in those cases.

ROBERT H. JACKSON, "THE SUPREME COURT AS A POLITICAL INSTITUTION," GODKIN LECTURE PREPARED FOR HARVARD UNIVERSITY

12. About things on which the public thinks long it commonly attains to think right.

SAMUEL JOHNSON, *LIVES OF THE POETS: ADDISON* (1779–81)

13. A universal feeling, whether well or ill founded, cannot be safely disregarded.

ABRAHAM LINCOLN, SPEECH, PEORIA, ILL., OCT. 16, 1854

14. With public sentiment, nothing can fail; without it, nothing can succeed. Consequently he who molds public sentiment goes deeper than he who enacts statutes or pronounces decisions.

ABRAHAM LINCOLN, SPEECH, OTTAWA, ILL., JULY 31, 1858

15. All becomes easy when we follow the current of opinion; it is the ruler of the world.

NAPOLEON I, *MAXIMS* (1804–15)

16. Public opinion is the thermometer a monarch should constantly consult.

NAPOLEON I, *MAXIMS* (1804–15)

17. A government can be no better than the public opinion which sustains it.

FRANKLIN D. ROOSEVELT, SPEECH, WASHINGTON, D.C., JAN. 8, 1936

18. There is no group in America that can withstand the force of an aroused public opinion.

FRANKLIN D. ROOSEVELT, STATEMENT ON SIGNING THE NATIONAL INDUSTRIAL RECOVERY ACT, JUNE 16, 1933

19. One should respect public opinion in so far as is necessary to avoid starvation and to keep out of prison, but anything that goes beyond this is voluntary submission to an unnecessary tyranny.

BERTRAND RUSSELL, *THE CONQUEST OF HAPPINESS* (1930), 9

20. A man must know how to brave public opinion, a woman how to submit to it.

MME DE STAËL, *DELPHINE* (1802)

PUBLIC RELATIONS

See 18. ADVERTISING; 745. PROPAGANDA; 760. PUBLICITY

762. PUBLIC SPEAKING

See also 232. DEMAGOGUERY; 283. ELOQUENCE; 923. SPEAKING

1. Great orators who are not also great writers become very indistinct shadows to the generations following them. The spell vanishes with the voice.

THOMAS BAILEY ALDRICH, "LEAVES FROM A NOTEBOOK," *PONKAPOG PAPERS* (1903)

2. It fell to me in these coming days and months to express their sentiments on suitable occasions. This I was able to do, because they were mine also. There was a white glow, overpowering, sublime, which ran through our island from end to end.

SIR WINSTON CHURCHILL, *THEIR FINEST HOUR* (1949)

3. Nothing is so unbelievable that oratory cannot make it acceptable.

CICERO, *PARADOXA STOICORUM* (46 B.C.)

4. Eloquence is the language of nature, and cannot be learned in the schools; but rhetoric is the creature of art, which he who feels least will most excel in.

CHARLES CALEB COLTON, *LACON* (1825), 1.435

5. Ivry gr-reat orator ought to be accompanied by an orchesthry or, at worst, a pianist who wud play trills while th' artist was refreshin' himself with a glass iv ice wather.

FINLEY PETER DUNNE, "ON THE GIFT OF ORATORY," *MR. DOOLEY ON MAKING A WILL* (1919)

6. All the great speakers were bad speakers at first.

EMERSON, "POWER," *THE CONDUCT OF LIFE* (1860)

7. An orator can hardly get beyond commonplaces: if he does, he gets beyond his hearers.

WILLIAM HAZLITT, "ON THE DIFFERENCE BETWEEN WRITING AND SPEAKING," *THE PLAIN SPEAKER* (1826)

8. Speeches measured by the hour die with the hour.

THOMAS JEFFERSON, LETTER TO DAVID HARDING, APRIL 20, 1824

9. Ike [Pres. Dwight Eisenhower] usually fought a speech to a draw.

NORMAN MAILER, *CANNIBALS AND CHRISTIANS* (1967)

10. It is true that despite occasional gleams of Churchillian eloquence he [Gen. Douglas MacArthur] usually spoke poorly. He was far more effective in conversations *à deux*. But those who dismiss him as shallow because his rhetoric was fustian err.

WILLIAM MANCHESTER, *AMERICAN CAESAR* (1978)

11. What orators lack in depth they make up to you in length.

MONTESQUIEU, *LETTERS* (1767)

12. All that is necessary to raise imbecility into what the mob regards as profundity is to lift it off the floor and put it on a platform.

GEORGE JEAN NATHAN, "PROFUNDITY," *AMERICAN MERCURY* SEPTEMBER 1929

13. Oratory is just like prostitution: you must have little tricks.

VITTORIO EMANUELE ORLANDO, *TIME*, DEC. 8, 1952

14. When orators and auditors have the same prejudices, those prejudices run a great risk of being made to stand for incontestable truths.

JOSEPH ROUX, *MEDITATIONS OF A PARISH PRIEST* (1886), 2.35, TR. ISABEL F. HAPGOOD

15. It is terrible to speak well and be wrong.

SOPHOCLES, *ELECTRA* (C. 418–14 B.C.), TR. DAVID GRENE

16. In oratory the greatest art is to hide art.

JONATHAN SWIFT, *A TRITICAL ESSAY UPON THE FACULTIES OF THE MIND* (1707)

763. PUBLICITY

See also 18. ADVERTISING; 736. PRIVACY; 745. PROPAGANDA

1. Formerly, a public man needed a *private* secretary for a barrier between himself and the public. Nowadays he has a *press* secretary, to keep him properly in the public eye.

DANIEL J. BOORSTIN, *THE IMAGE* (1962), 2.4

2. There is a photographer in every bush, going about like a roaring lion seeking whom he may devour.

SAMUEL BUTLER (D. 1902), "UNPROFESSIONAL SERMONS," *NOTE-BOOKS* (1912)

3. I am happy to exhibit, but not to put myself on exhibition.

JEAN COCTEAU, *DIARY OF AN UNKNOWN* (1952; 1988)

4. We march through life an' behind us marches th' phottygrafer an' th' rayporther. There are no such things as private citizens.

FINLEY PETER DUNNE, "NEWSPAPER PUBLICITY," *OBSERVATIONS BY MR. DOOLEY* (1902)

PUBLIC LIFE

See 332. FAME; 761. PUBLIC OFFICE

764. PUBLISHING

See also 364. FREE SPEECH; 630. NEWSPAPERS; 731. PRESS, FREEDOM OF THE

1. The printing-press is either the greatest blessing or the greatest curse of modern times, one sometimes forgets which.

J. M. BARRIE, *SENTIMENTAL TOMMY* (1896)

2. Things evidently false are not only printed, but many things of truth most falsely set forth.

SIR THOMAS BROWNE, "TO THE READER," *RELIGIO MEDICI* (1642)

3. 'Tis pleasant, sure, to see one's name in print; / A Book's a Book, altho' there's nothing in't.

BYRON, *ENGLISH BARDS AND SCOTCH REVIEWERS* (1809)

4. Th' printin'-press isn't wondherful. What's wondherful is that annybody shud want it to go on doin' what it does.

FINLEY PETER DUNNE, "ON THE MIDWAY," *MR. DOOLEY'S OPINIONS* (1901)

5. Great editors do not discover nor produce great authors; great authors create and produce great publishers.

JOHN FARRAR, *WHAT HAPPENS IN BOOK PUBLISHING* (1957)

6. What are the publications that succeed? Those that pretend to teach the public that the persons they have been accustomed unwittingly to look up to as the lights of the earth are no better than themselves.

WILLIAM HAZLITT, "ON READING NEW BOOKS," *SKETCHES AND ESSAYS* (1839)

7. A presentation copy, reader,—if haply you are yet innocent of such favours—is a copy of a book which does not sell, sent you by the author.

CHARLES LAMB, "POPULAR FALLACIES, II," *LAST ESSAYS OF ELIA* (1833)

8. Since the discovery of printing, knowledge has been called to power, and power has been used to make knowledge a slave.

NAPOLEON I, *MAXIMS* (1804–15)

9. The job of editor in a publishing house is the dullest, hardest, most exciting, exasperating and rewarding of perhaps any job in the world.

MAXWELL PERKINS, *EDITOR TO AUTHOR: THE LETTERS OF MAXWELL PERKINS* (1950), ED. JOHN HALL WHEELOCK

10. What we publishers think is that our function is to bring everything out into the open, on the theory that we have an adult population that knows values, or can learn them, and let them decide.

MAXWELL PERKINS, *EDITOR TO AUTHOR: THE LETTERS OF MAXWELL PERKINS* (1950), ED. JOHN HALL WHEELOCK

11. Printing links the present with forever. It carries personal identity into realms unknown.

NEIL POSTMAN, "THE PRINTING PRESS AND THE NEW ADULT," *THE DISAPPEARANCE OF CHILDHOOD* (1982)

12. Editing is the same as quarreling with writers—same thing exactly.

HAROLD ROSS, *TIME,* MARCH 6, 1950

13. Zuckerman, sucker though he was for seriousness, was still not going to be drawn into a discussion about agents and editors. If ever there was a reason for an American writer to seek asylum in Red China, it would be to put ten thousand miles between himself and those discussions.

PHILIP ROTH, *ZUCKERMAN UNBOUND* (1981)

14. An editor is one who separates the wheat from the chaff and prints the chaff.

ADLAI STEVENSON, *THE STEVENSON WIT* (1966)

15. Television wrecked the short-story branch of the industry, and now accountants and business school graduates dominate book publishing. They feel that money spent on someone's first novel is good money down a rat hole.

KURT VONNEGUT, "THE FIRST AMENDMENT," *PALM SUNDAY* (1981)

16. Editing is the most companionable form of education.

EDWARD WEEKS, *IN FRIENDLY CANDOR* (1959)

765. PUNCTUALITY

See also 231. DELAY

1. We are not saints, but we have kept our appointment. How many people can boast as much?

SAMUEL BECKETT, *WAITING FOR GODOT* (1952), 2

2. Men count up the faults of those who keep them waiting.

FRENCH PROVERB

3. Few things tend more to alienate friendship than a want of punctuality in our engagements.

WILLIAM HAZLITT, "ON THE SPIRIT OF OBLIGATIONS," *THE PLAIN SPEAKER* (1826)

4. Better three hours too soon than a minute too late.

SHAKESPEARE, *THE MERRY WIVES OF WINDSOR* (1597), 2.2.327

PUNCTUATION

See 942. STYLE

766. PUNISHMENT

See also 250. DISCIPLINE; 735. PRISON; 767. PUNISHMENT, CAPITAL; 815. RETRIBUTION; 890. SEVERITY

1. [W]hatever the punishment, once a specific crime has appeared for the first time, its reappearance is more likely than its initial emergence could ever have been.

HANNAH ARENDT, *EICHMANN IN JERUSALEM* (1963)

2. All punishment is mischief. All punishment in itself is evil.

JEREMY BENTHAM, *INTRODUCTION TO PRINCIPLES OF MORALS AND LEGISLATION* (1789), 15

3. He that spareth his rod hateth his son.

BIBLE, PROVERBS 13:24

4. Speak roughly to your little boy, / And beat him when he sneezes: / He only does it to annoy, / Because he knows it teases.

LEWIS CARROLL, *ALICE'S ADVENTURES IN WONDERLAND* (1865), 6

5. Beat your child once a day. If you don't know why, he does.

CHINESE PROVERB

6. Rather than waste precious time arguing, I went up and started serving my "sentence" without delay. It was usually about an hour for epigrams; somewhat longer for a paradox.

PETER DE VRIES, *COMFORT ME WITH APPLES* (1956)

7. Crime and punishment grow out of one stem.

EMERSON, "COMPENSATION," *ESSAYS: FIRST SERIES* (1841)

8. Fellow senators balked at punishing Senator Alfonse D'Amato of New York though he was caught in a series of transactions that earned him the label "Senator Sleaze." D'Amato explained their reluctance as he defended his own behavior. "There but for the grace of God go most of my colleagues," he said.

WILLIAM GREIDER, *WHO WILL TELL THE PEOPLE?* (1992)

9. Texas is not a civilized place. Texans shoot one another a lot. They also knife, razor, and stomp one another to death with some frequency. And they fight in bars all the time.

MOLLY IVINS, *MOLLY IVINS CAN'T SAY THAT, CAN SHE?* (1991)

10. Many punishments sometimes, and in some cases, as much discredit a prince as many funerals a physician.

BEN JONSON, "OF STATECRAFT," *TIMBER* (1640)

11. Many a man spanks his / children for / things his own / father should have / spanked out of him.

DON MARQUIS, "CERTAIN MAXIMS OF ARCHY," *ARCHY AND MEHITABEL* (1927)

12. I have never observed other effects of whipping than to render boys more cowardly, or more willfully obstinate.

MONTAIGNE, "OF THE AFFECTIONS OF FATHERS TO THEIR CHILDREN," *ESSAYS* (1580–88), TR. W. C. HAZLITT

13. Speaking generally, punishment hardens and numbs, it produces concentration, it sharpens the consciousness of alienation, it strengthens the power of resistance.

NIETZSCHE, *THE GENEALOGY OF MORALS* (1887), 2.14, TR. HORACE B. SAMUEL

14. After all, it's not where a man lands that marks his punishment. It's how far he falls.

TIP O'NEILL, *MAN OF THE HOUSE* (1987)

15. The fact that the beating had not hurt was a sort of victory and partially wiped out the shame of the bed-wetting. I was even incautious enough to wear a grin on my face.

GEORGE ORWELL, "SUCH, SUCH WERE THE JOYS," *A COLLECTION OF ESSAYS* (1954)

16. The first of all laws is to respect the laws: the severity of penalties is only a vain resource, invented by little minds in order to substitute terror for that respect which they have no means of obtaining.

ROUSSEAU, *A DISCOURSE ON POLITICAL ECONOMY* (1758), TR. G. D. H. COLE

17. Except when physically restrained, a person is least free or dignified when he is under threat of

punishment, and unfortunately most people often are.

B.F. Skinner, *Beyond Freedom and Dignity* (1971)

18. He only may chastise who loves.

Rabindranath Tagore, "The Judge," *The Crescent Moon* (1913)

19. Punishment is a vital need of the human soul.

Simone Weil, *The Need for Roots* (1952), tr. Arthur Wills

20. While punishing a recalcitrant pupil he suffered; he did not allow it to show because he did not want us to think him weak. He revealed himself only to God.

Elie Wiesel, *Legends of Our Times* (1968)

767. PUNISHMENT, CAPITAL

See also 766. Punishment

1. It is fairly obvious that those who are in favor of the death penalty have more affinity with assassins than those who are not.

Rémy de Gourmont, *Pensees inedites* (1924?)

2. When a man knows he is to be hanged in a fortnight, it concentrates his mind wonderfully.

Samuel Johnson, quoted in Boswell's *Life of Samuel Johnson,* Sept. 19, 1777

3. The compensation for a death sentence is knowledge of the exact hour when one is to die. A great luxury, but one that is well earned.

Vladimir Nabokov, *Invitation to a Beheading* (1934), 1

4. It is far more ignominious to die by justice than by an unjust sedition.

Pascal, *Pensées* (1670), 789, tr. W. F. Trotter

5. There is no great difficulty to separate the soul from the body, but it is not so easy to restore life to the dead.

Sa'di, *Gulistan* (1258), 8.56, tr. James Ross

768. PUNS

See also 1061. Wit

1. There is no kind of false wit which has been so recommended by the practice of all ages, as that which consists in a jingle of words, and is comprehended under the general name of *Punning*.

Joseph Addison, *The Spectator* (1711–12), 61

2. The goodness of the true pun is in the direct ratio of its intolerability.

Edgar Allan Poe, *Marginalia* (1844–49), 1

769. PURITANS AND PURITANISM

See also 756. Prudery

1. Puritanism—The haunting fear that someone, somewhere, may be happy.

H. L. Mencken, "Sententiae," *A Book of Burlesques* (1920)

2. Puritanism had fallen into such disrepair that not even the oldest spinster thought of putting Susanna in a ducking stool; not even the oldest farmer suspected that Susanna's diabolical beauty had made his cow run dry.

Kurt Vonnegut, *Welcome to the Monkey House* (1970)

770. PURITY

See also 57. Association; 478. Innocence

1. The sun, though it passes through dirty places, yet remains as pure as before.

Francis Bacon, *The Advancement of Learning* (1605), 2

2. When he has no lust, no hatred, / A man walks safely among the things of lust and hatred

Bhagavadgita, 2, tr. Christopher Isherwood

3. Unto the pure all things are pure.

Bible, Titus 1:15

4. Whoso doth no evil is apt to suspect none.

Thomas Fuller, M.D., *Gnomologia* (1732), 5727

5. Purity / Is obscurity.

Ogden Nash, "Reflection on a Wicked World," *Verses from 1929 On* (1959)

6. My strength is as the strength of ten, / Because my heart is pure.

Lord Tennyson, "Sir Galahad" (1842), 3

771. PURPOSE

See also 225. Decision; 286. Ends; 465. Indecision; 608. Motives; 807. Resolution; 867. Self-Determination; 1056. Will; 1057. Willingness

1. A man should have any number of little aims about which he should be conscious and for which he should have names, but he should have neither name for, nor consciousness concerning, the main aim of his life.

Samuel Butler (d. 1902), "Unprofessional Sermons," *Note-Books* (1912)

2. A windmill is eternally at work to accomplish one end, although it shifts with every variation of the weathercock, and assumes ten different positions in a day.

CHARLES CALEB COLTON, *LACON* (1825), 2.63

3. The secret of success is constancy to purpose.

BENJAMIN DISRAELI, SPEECH, JUNE 24, 1870

4. The idea of life having a purpose stands and falls with the religious system.

SIGMUND FREUD, *CIVILIZATION AND ITS DISCONTENTS* (1930), 2, TR. JAMES STRACHEY

5. Obstacles cannot crush me / Every obstacle yields to stern resolve / He who is fixed to a star does not change his mind.

LEONARDO DA VINCI, *NOTEBOOKS* (C. 1500), TR. JEAN PAUL RICHTER

6. He who would make serious use of his life must always act as though he had a long time to live and must schedule his time as though he were about to die.

ÉMILE LITTRÉ, *DICTIONNAIRE DE LA LANGUE FRANÇAISE* (1877), 3

7. The great and glorious masterpiece of man is to know how to live to purpose.

MONTAIGNE, "OF EXPERIENCE," *ESSAYS* (1580–88), TR. W. C. HAZLITT

8. The soul that has no established aim loses itself.

MONTAIGNE, "OF IDLENESS," *ESSAYS* (1580–88), TR. W. C. HAZLITT

9. There is one quality more important than "know-how" and we cannot accuse the United States of any undue amount of it. This is "know-what" by which we determine not only how to accomplish our purposes, but what our purposes are to be.

NORBERT WIENER, *THE HUMAN USE OF HUMAN BEINGS* (1954), 10

Q

772. QUARRELING

See also 51. Argument; 252. Discord; 345. Fighting

1. The quarrels of friends are the opportunities of foes.

Aesop, "The Lions and the Bulls," *Fables* (6th c. b.c.?), tr. Thomas James

2. Little quarrels often prove / To be but new recruits of love.

Samuel Butler (d. 1680), *Hudibras* (1663), 3.1

3. Looking at God instantly reduces our disposition to dissent from our brother.

Emerson, *Journals,* 1831

4. When we quarrel, how we wish we had been blameless.

Emerson, *Journals,* 1863

5. Most quarrels amplify a misunderstanding.

André Gide, *Journals,* 1920, tr. Justin O'Brien

6. [E]ven when I was a grown woman, he [Father] would leave me on the edge of hysteria in all our arguments: though I married and lived as far as I could spiritually from Bridgeport, he reduced me in a matter of hours to a wriggling child, pleading to go free.

Maureen Howard, *Facts of Life* (1978)

7. You can make up a quarrel, but it will always show where it was patched.

Edgar Watson Howe, *Country Town Sayings* (1911)

8. An association of men who will not quarrel with one another is a thing which never yet existed, from the greatest confederacy of nations down to a town-meeting or a vestry.

Thomas Jefferson, letter to John Taylor, 1798

9. Quarrels would not last long if the fault was only on one side.

La Rochefoucauld, *Maxims* (1665), tr. Kenneth Pratt

10. Friendships ought to be immortal, hostilities mortal.

Livy, *Ab Urbe Condita* (c. 29 b.c.), 40.46

11. The same reason that makes us wrangle with a neighbor, causes a war between princes.

Montaigne, "Apology for Raimond de Sebonde," *Essays* (1580–88), tr. W. C. Hazlitt

12. I say, when there are spats, kiss and make up before the day is done and live to fight another day.

Randolph Ray, *New York World-Telegram & Sun,* June 30, 1956

13. Beware / Of entrance to a quarrel; but being in, / Bear't that th' opposed may be beware of thee.

Shakespeare, *Hamlet* (1600), 1.3.65

14. For souls in growth, great quarrels are great emancipations.

Logan Pearsall Smith, *Afterthoughts* (1931), 1

15. It is in disputes as in armies, where the weaker side sets up false lights, and makes a great noise, to make the enemy believe them more numerous and strong than they really are.

Jonathan Swift, *Thoughts on Various Subjects* (1711)

QUESTIONS

See 480. Inquiry

QUICKNESS

See 411. Haste; 926. Speed

773. QUOTATIONS

See also 296. Epigrams; 572. Maxims

1. The majority of those who put together collections of verses or epigrams resemble those who eat cherries or oysters: they begin by choosing the best and end by eating everything.

Chamfort, *Maxims et pensées* (1805), 1

2. I hate quotations. Tell me what you know.

Emerson, *Journals,* 1849

3. Though old the thought and oft exprest, / 'Tis his at last who says it best.

James Russell Lowell, "For an Autograph," *Under the Willows and Other Poems* (1868)

4. Most men are rich in borrowed sufficiency: a man may very well say a good thing, give a good answer, cite a good sentence, without at all seeing the force of either the one or the other.

MONTAIGNE, "OF THE ART OF CONFERENCE," *ESSAYS* (1580–88), TR. W. C. HAZLITT

5. A good aphorism is too hard for the tooth of time, and is not worn away by all the centuries, although it serves as food for every epoch.

NIETZSCHE, *MISCELLANEOUS MAXIMS AND OPINIONS* (1879), 168, TR. PAUL V. COHN

6. A fine quotation is a diamond on the finger of a man of wit, and a pebble in the hand of a fool.

JOSEPH ROUX, *MEDITATIONS OF A PARISH PRIEST* (1886), I.74, TR. ISABEL F. HAPGOOD

R

774. RACE

See also 40. Anglo-Saxons; 85. Blacks; 775. Racial Prejudice; 1054. Whites

1. It is not races but individuals that are noble and courageous or ignoble and craven or considerate or persistent or philosophical or reasonable. The race gets credit when the percentage of noble individuals is high.

Edwin Way Teale, "January 9," *Circle of the Seasons* (1953)

775. RACIAL PREJUDICE

See also 85. Blacks; 774. Race; 1054. Whites

1. Sometimes, it's [racial prejudice] like a hair across your cheek. You can't see it, you can't find it with your fingers, but you keep brushing at it because the feel of it is irritating.

Marian Anderson, *Ladies' Home Journal*, September 1960

2. The plague of racism is insidious, entering into our minds as smoothly and quietly and invisibly as floating airborne microbes enter into our bodies to find lifelong purchase in our bloodstreams.

Maya Angelou, "Our Boys," *Wouldn't Take Nothing for My Journey Now* (1993)

3. Race prejudice is not only a shadow over the colored—it is a shadow over all of us, and the shadow is darkest over those who feel it least and allow its evil effects to go on.

Pearl S. Buck, *What America Means to Me* (1943), 1

4. Cannot the nation that has absorbed ten million foreigners into its political life without catastrophe absorb ten million Negro Americans into that same political life at less cost than their unjust and illegal exclusion will involve?

W. E. B. Du Bois, "No Cowards or Trucklers," *In Their Own Words: 1865–1916*, v. 2

5. Race prejudice decreases values both real estate and human; crime, ignorance and filth decrease values.

W. E. B. Du Bois, "What Would You Do?" *In Their Own Words: 1916–1966*, v. 3

6. The problem of the Twentieth Century is the problem of the color-line.

W. E. B. Du Bois, *The Souls of Black Folk* (1903), 2

7. Who makes and keeps the Jew or the Negro base, who but you, who exclude them from the rights which others enjoy?

Emerson, *Journals* 1867

8. Racial prejudice boils down to the deeply anti-American message that some people are born to fail.

James Fallows, *More Like Us* (1989), 6

9. To live anywhere in the world today and be against equality because of race or color, is like living in Alaska and being against snow.

William Faulkner, "On Fear: Deep South in Labor: Mississippi," *Essays, Speeches & Public Letters* (1965)

10. There is a tendency to judge a race, a nation or any distinct group by its least worthy members.

Eric Hoffer, *The True Believer* (1951), 1.3.18

11. Everybody should take each other as they are, white, black, Indians, Creole. Then there would be no prejudice, nations would get along.

Langston Hughes, *Simple Speaks His Mind* (1950)

12. I have a dream that my four little children will one day live in a nation where they will not be judged by the color of their skin but by the content of their character.

Martin Luther King, Jr., speech, Washington, D.C., June 15, 1963

13. Segregation is on its deathbed—the question now is, how costly will the segregationists make the funeral?

Martin Luther King, Jr., address, Villanova University, Jan. 20, 1965

14. In the end, as any successful teacher will tell you, you can only teach the things that you are. If we practice racism then it is racism that we teach.

Max Lerner, "We Teach What We Are," *Actions and Passions* (1949)

15. Why should anyone think a white skin superior in evaluating the qualities of human life? I did not really admire a white skin so much myself. Did I not prefer the brown that came with exposure to the sun?

Charles A. Lindbergh, "Atlantis," *Autobiography of Values* (1978)

16. A segregated school system produces children who, when they graduate, graduate with crippled minds.

Malcolm X, *Malcolm X Speaks* (1965), 3

17. While some [Quakers] preached the golden rule, others practiced segregation within their own churches; some even carried it to the church pew and the graveyard.

Gilbert Osofsky, *The Burden of Race* (1967)

18. Shame on the cant and hypocrisy of those who can teach virtue, preach righteousness, and pray blessings for those only with skins colored like their own.

C. Lenox Remond, *The Mind of the Negro As Reflected in Letters Written During the Crisis 1800–1860* (1926)

776. RADICALISM

See also 178. Conservatism; 536. Liberalism; 710. Political Parties

1. I've always felt, as a writer, that radicals are fascinating because they're relations, they have a place in the American family. They're the relatives everyone wishes would go away. They're the embarrassments to decorum and good taste.

E.L. Doctorow, Interview, 1993

2. The spirit of our American radicalism is destructive and aimless: it is not loving, it has no ulterior and divine ends; but is destructive only out of hatred and selfishness.

Emerson, "Politics," *Essays: Second Series* (1844)

3. I never dared to be radical when young / For fear it would make me conservative when old.

Robert Frost, "Ten Mills," *A Further Range* (1936)

4. Radicalism itself ceases to be radical when absorbed mainly in preserving its control over a society or an economy.

Eric Hoffer, *The Passionate State of Mind* (1954), 21a

5. We need our radicals.

Eleanor Roosevelt, Lecture at Duke University, 1957

6. You sometimes find something good in the lunatic fringe. In fact, we have got as part of our social and economic government today a whole lot of things which in my boyhood were considered lunatic fringe, and yet they are now part of everyday life.

Franklin D. Roosevelt, press conference, May 30, 1944

7. The radical of one century is the conservative of the next.

Mark Twain, *Notebook* (1935)

777. RADIO

1. The radio is now something people listen to while they are doing something else.

Tom Wolfe, *The Kandy-Kolored Tangerine-Flake Streamline Baby* (1965)

778. RAIN

See also 778. Rainbows; 854. Seasons; 1050. Weather

1. Rain! whose soft architectural hands have power to cut stones, and chisel to shapes of grandeur the very mountains.

Henry Ward Beecher, *Proverbs from Plymouth Pulpit* (1887)

2. The good rain, like a bad preacher, does not know when to leave off.

Emerson, *Journals*, 1834

3. It rained for four years, eleven months, and two days. There were periods of drizzle during which everyone put on his full dress and a convalescent look to celebrate the clearing, but people soon grew accustomed to interpret the pauses as a sign of redoubled rain.

Gabriel García Márquez, *One Hundred Years of Solitude* (1970)

4. Rain is good for vegetables, and for the animals who eat those vegetables, and for the animals who eat those animals.

Samuel Johnson, quoted in Boswell's *Life of Samuel Johnson*, July 6, 1763

5. One can find so many pains when the rain is falling.

John Steinbeck, Steinbeck: A Life in Letters, eds. Elaine Steinbeck and Robert Wallsten (1975)

779. RAINBOWS

See also 778. Rain

1. After a debauch of thunder-shower, the weather takes the pledge and signs it with a rainbow.

THOMAS BAILEY ALDRICH, "LEAVES FROM A NOTEBOOK," *PONKAPOG PAPERS* (1903)

2. My heart leaps up when I behold / A rainbow in the sky: / So was it when my life began; / So is it now I am a man; / So be it when I shall grow old, / Or let me die!

WILLIAM WORDSWORTH, "MY HEART LEAPS UP WHEN I BEHOLD" (1802)

780. RANK

See also 52. ARISTOCRACY; 135. CLASS; 649. OBSCURITY; 669. PARASITES; 910. SNOBBERY; 933. STATUS; 1012. UNIMPORTANCE

1. The defeats and victories of the fellows at the top aren't always defeats and victories for the fellows at the bottom.

BERTOLT BRECHT, *MOTHER COURAGE* (1939), 3, TR. ERIC BENTLEY

2. Detestation of the high is the involuntary homage of the low.

CHARLES DICKENS, *A TALE OF TWO CITIES* (1859), 2.9

3. Even workhouses have their aristocracy.

ENGLISH PROVERB

4. The greatest monarch on the proudest throne / is obliged to sit upon his own arse.

BENJAMIN FRANKLIN, *POOR RICHARD'S ALMANACK* (1732–57)

5. When everyone is somebodee, / Then no one's anybody.

W. S. GILBERT, *THE GONDOLIERS* (1889), 2

6. The man who occupies the first place seldom plays the principal part.

GOETHE, *THE SORROWS OF YOUNG WERTHER* (1774), 2, JAN. 8, 1772, TR. VICTOR LANGE

7. A cat may look on a king.

JOHN HEYWOOD, *PROVERBS* (1546), 2.5

8. It is a very curious fact that, with all our boasted "free and equal" superiority over the communities of the Old World, our people [Americans] have the most enormous appetite for Old World titles of distinction.

OLIVER WENDELL HOLMES, SR., *OVER THE TEACUPS* (1891), 9

9. A fly, Sir, may sting a stately horse and make him wince; but one is but an insect, and the other is a horse still.

SAMUEL JOHNSON, QUOTED IN BOSWELL'S *LIFE OF SAMUEL JOHNSON,* FOOTNOTE ON WARBURTON, 1754

10. Subordination tends greatly to human happiness. Were we all upon an equality, we should have no other enjoyment than mere animal pleasure.

SAMUEL JOHNSON, QUOTED IN BOSWELL'S *LIFE OF SAMUEL JOHNSON,* JULY 20, 1763

11. No man is safe above but he that will gladly be beneath.

THOMAS À KEMPIS, *THE IMITATION OF CHRIST* (1426), 1.20

12. There is merit without rank, but there is no rank without some merit.

LA ROCHEFOUCAULD, *MAXIMS* (1665), TR. KENNETH PRATT

13. When fortune surprises us by giving us an important position, without having led us to it by degrees, or without our being elevated to it by our hopes, it is almost impossible for us to maintain ourselves suitably in it, and appear worthy of possessing it.

LA ROCHEFOUCAULD, *MAXIMS* (1665), TR. KENNETH PRATT

14. Bottom is bottom, even if it is turned upside down.

STANISLAW LEC, *UNKEMPT THOUGHTS* (1962), TR. JACEK GALAZKA

15. The good Lord sees your heart, not the braid on your jacket, before Him we are all in our birthday suits, generals and common men alike.

THOMAS MANN, *THE MAGIC MOUNTAIN* (1924), 6.8, TR. H. T. LOWE-PORTER

16. A throne is only a bench covered with velvet.

NAPOLEON I, *MAXIMS* (1804–15)

17. There may be as much nobility in being last as in being first, because the two positions are equally necessary in the world, the one to complement the other.

JOSÉ ORTEGA Y GASSET, "PRELIMINARY MEDITATION," *MEDITATIONS ON QUIXOTE* (1914)

18. To call a king "Prince" is pleasing, because it diminishes his rank.

PASCAL, *PENSÉES* (1670), 42, TR. W. F. TROTTER

19. That in the captain's but a choleric word / Which in the soldier is flat blasphemy.

SHAKESPEARE, *MEASURE FOR MEASURE* (1604–05), 2.2.130

20. Titles distinguish the mediocre, embarrass the superior, and are disgraced by the inferior.

George Bernard Shaw, "Maxims for Revolutionists," *Man and Superman* (1903)

21. It is a maxim, that those to whom everybody allows the second place, have an undoubted title to the first.

Jonathan Swift, dedication, *The Tale of a Tub* (1704)

22. The sparrow is sorry for the peacock at the burden of its tail.

Rabindranath Tagore, *Stray Birds* (1916), 58

23. It is an interesting question how far men would retain their relative rank if they were divested of their clothes.

Thoreau, "Economy," *Walden* (1854)

781. RASHNESS

See also 112. Cautiousness; 354. Folly; 755. Prudence

1. If you leap into a well, Providence is not bound to fetch you out.

Thomas Fuller, M.D., *Gnomologia* (1732), 2795

2. Rashness succeeds often, still more often fails.

Napoleon I, *Maxims* (1804–15)

782. RATIONALIZATION

See also 314. Excuses; 322. Explanation

1. The fox condemns the trap, not himself.

William Blake, "Proverbs of Hell," *The Marriage of Heaven and Hell* (1790)

2. We do what we can, and then make a theory to prove our performance the best.

Emerson, *Journals,* 1834

3. In the conduct of life we make use of deliberation to justify ourselves in doing what we want to do.

W. Somerset Maugham, *The Summing Up* (1938), 15

4. There's nothing people can't contrive to praise or condemn and find justification for doing so, according to their age and their inclinations.

Molière, *The Misanthrope* (1666), 3, tr. John Wood

READING

See 93. Books and Reading

783. REALISM

See also 304. Evasion; 720. Practicality; 784. Reality

1. Realists do not fear the results of their study.

Dostoyevsky, "The Latest Literary Phenomenon," *Polnoye Sobraniye Sochinyeni* (*Complete Collected Works,* 1895), v. 9

2. Let us replace sentimentalism by realism, and dare to uncover those simple and terrible laws which, be they seen or unseen, pervade and govern.

Emerson, "Worship," *The Conduct of Life* (1860)

3. It is only by knowing how little life has in store for us that we are able to look on the bright side and avoid disappointment.

Ellen Glasgow, *The Sheltered Life* (1932)

4. Is it strange, then, that in a literature so concerned with realism and with personal liberation this refusal and impoverishment of the life of the spirit have always nourished the screamers, the eccentrics, the pseudo-Whitmans, the calculating terrorists?

Alfred Kazin, *On Native Grounds* (1942)

5. Intuition? Bosh! Women, in fact, are the supreme realists of the race.

H.L. Mencken, "The Feminine Mind," in *Fifty Famous Essays* (1964)

6. Our safety is not in blindness, but in facing our dangers.

Schiller, "The Sublime" (1793?)

784. REALITY

See also 328. Facts; 449. Illusion; 783. Realism

1. We take our shape, it is true, within and against that cage of reality bequeathed us at our birth; and yet it is precisely through our dependence on this reality that we are most endlessly betrayed.

James Baldwin, "Everybody's Protest Novel" (1949), *Notes of a Native Son* (1955)

2. If it were possible to talk to the unborn, one could never explain to them how it feels to be alive, for life is washed in the speechless real.

Jacques Barzun, *The House of Intellect* (1959), 6

3. You ride astride the imaginary in order to hunt down the real.

Breyten Breytenbach, *Return to Paradise* (1993)

4. Facts as facts do not always create a spirit of reality, because reality is a spirit.

G. K. Chesterton, "On the Classics," *Come to Think of It* (1930)

5. Everything is a dangerous drug except reality, which is unendurable.

CYRIL CONNOLLY, *THE UNQUIET GRAVE* (1945), 1

6. The sky is not less blue because the blind man does not see it.

DANISH PROVERB

7. The real world is not easy to live in. It is rough; it is slippery. Without the most clear-eyed adjustments we fall and get crushed. A man must stay sober: not always, but most of the time.

CLARENCE DAY, "IN HIS BABY BLUE SHIP," *THE CROW'S NEST* (1921)

8. Reality is that which, when you stop believing in it, doesn't go away.

PHILIP K. DICK, *I HOPE I SHALL ARRIVE SOON* (1985)

9. What is actual is actual only for one time / And only for one place.

T. S. ELIOT, "ASH WEDNESDAY" (1930), 1

10. There is no reality except the one contained within us. That is why so many people live such an unreal life. They take the images outside them for reality and never allow the world within to assert itself.

HERMANN HESSE, *DEMIAN* (1919), 6, TR. MICHAEL LEBECK

11. To mention a loved object, a person, or a place to someone else is to invest that object with reality.

ANNE MORROW LINDBERGH, "BAKER LAKE," *NORTH TO THE ORIENT* (1935)

12. What was once called the objective world is a sort of Rorschach ink blot, into which each culture, each system of science and religion, each type of personality, reads a meaning only remotely derived from the shape and color of the blot itself.

LEWIS MUMFORD, "ORIENTATION TO LIFE," *THE CONDUCT OF LIFE* (1951)

13. You too must not count overmuch on your reality as you feel it today, since, like that of yesterday, it may prove an illusion for you tomorrow.

LUIGI PIRANDELLO, *SIX CHARACTERS IN SEARCH OF AN AUTHOR* (1921), 3, TR. EDWARD STORER

14. The past exists only in our memories, the future only in our plans. The present is our only reality.

ROBERT M. PIRSIG, *ZEN AND THE ART OF MOTORCYCLE MAINTENANCE* (1974)

15. More wisdom is latent in things-as-they-are than in all the words men use.

SAINT-EXUPÉRY, *THE WISDOM OF THE SANDS* (1948), 22, TR. STUART GILBERT

16. Monotheism owes its existence not to philosophic speculation about the nature of reality or knowledge or virtue, but to acceptance of reality identified with a supreme being.

ISRAEL SHENKER, *COAT OF MANY COLORS* (1985)

17. Images are more real than anyone could have supposed.

SUSAN SONTAG, *ON PHOTOGRAPHY* (1977)

18. In the American metaphysic, reality is always material reality, hard, resistant, unformed, impenetrable, and unpleasant.

LIONEL TRILLING, "REALITY IN AMERICA," *THE LIBERAL IMAGINATION* (1950)

19. The very greatest mystery is in unsheathed reality itself.

EUDORA WELTY, "REALITY IN CHEKHOV'S STORIES," *THE EYE OF THE STORY* (1978)

785. REASON

See also 51. ARGUMENT; 493. INTELLIGENCE; 744. PROOF; 974. THEORY; 975. THOUGHT; 1020. UNREASON

1. The mind resorts to reason for want of training.

HENRY ADAMS, *THE EDUCATION OF HENRY ADAMS* (1907), 24

2. Analysis kills spontaneity. The grain once ground into flour springs and germinates no more.

HENRI FRÉDÉRIC AMIEL, *JOURNAL*, NOV. 7, 1878, TR. MRS. HUMPHRY WARD

3. Logic, n. The art of thinking and reasoning in strict accordance with the limitations and incapacities of the human misunderstanding.

AMBROSE BIERCE, *THE DEVIL'S DICTIONARY* (1881–1911)

4. Logic is like the sword—those who appeal to it shall perish by it.

SAMUEL BUTLER (D. 1902), "FIRST PRINCIPLES," *NOTE-BOOKS* (1912)

5. Peace rules the day, where reason rules the mind.

WILLIAM COLLINS, *PERSIAN ECLOGUES* (1742), 2

6. Reason flies / When following the senses, on clipped wings.

DANTE, "PARADISO," 2, *THE DIVINE COMEDY* (C. 1300–21), TR. LAWRENCE GRANT WHITE

7. The difference between the reason of man and the instinct of the beast is this, that the beast does but know, but the man knows that he knows.

JOHN DONNE, *SERMONS*, NO. 57, 1628

8. Man has such a predilection for systems and abstract deductions that he is ready to distort the truth intentionally, he is ready to deny the evidence of his senses only to justify his logic.

Dostoyevsky, *Notes from Underground* (1864), 1.7, tr. Constance Garnett

9. To a reasonable creature, that alone is insupportable which is unreasonable; but everything reasonable may be supported.

Epictetus, *Discourses* (2nd c.), 1.2, tr. Thomas W. Higginson

10. Reason can wrestle / And overthrow terror.

Euripides, *Iphigenia in Aulis* (c. 405 B.C.), tr. Charles R. Walker

11. 'Tis in vain to speak reason where 'twill not be heard.

Thomas Fuller, M.D., *Gnomologia* (1732), 5088

12. Reason, ruling alone, is a force confining; and passion, unattended, is a flame that burns to its own destruction.

Kahlil Gibran, "On Reason and Passion," *The Prophet* (1923)

13. The want of logic annoys. Too much logic bores. Life eludes logic, and everything that logic alone constructs remains artificial and forced.

André Gide, *Journals,* May 12, 1927, tr. Justin O'Brien

14. What eludes logic is the most precious element in us, and one can draw nothing from a syllogism that the mind has not put there in advance.

André Gide, *Journals,* June 1927, tr. Justin O'Brien

15. [T]he growing chasm between private and social cost, the corporate control of a technology which is essentially public, called into question a most basic assumption of Western thought: that man frees himself through reason.

Michael Harrington, *The Accidental Century* (1966)

16. Logic is not satisfied with assertion. It cares nothing for the opinions of the great—nothing for the prejudices of the many, and least of all for the superstitions of the dead.

Robert G. Ingersoll, *Prose-Poems and Selections* (1884)

17. We may take Fancy for a companion, but must follow Reason as our guide.

Samuel Johnson, letter to James Boswell, c. March 15, 1774, quoted in Boswell's *Life of Samuel Johnson*

18. Logic is the art of making truth prevail.

La Bruyère, *Characters* (1688), 1.55, tr. Henry Van Laun

19. At the very smallest wheel of our reasoning it is possible for a handful of questions to break the bank of our answers.

Antonio Machado, *Juan de Mairena* (1943), 43, tr. Ben Belitt

20. Reason also is choice.

Milton, *Paradise Lost* (1667), 3.108

21. Rational thought is interpretation according to a scheme which we cannot escape.

Nietzsche, "Notes" (1887), 522, in *The Portable Nietzsche,* tr. Walter Kaufmann

22. Reason commands us far more imperiously than a master; in disobeying the latter we are made unhappy, in disobeying the former, fools.

Pascal, *Pensées* (1670), 345

23. The last function of reason is to recognize that there are an infinity of things which surpass it.

Pascal, *Pensées* (1670), 267

24. Logic is one thing, the human animal another. You can quite easily propose a logical solution to something and at the same time hope in your heart of hearts it won't work out.

Luigi Pirandello, *The Pleasure of Honesty* (1917), 2, tr. William Murray

25. Say first, of God above or man below, / What can we reason but from what we know?

Alexander Pope, *An Essay on Man* (1733–34), 1.17

26. Reason cannot save us, nothing can; but reason can mitigate the cruelty of living.

Philip Rieff, preface to *Freud: The Mind of the Moralist* (1959)

27. Reason? That dreary shed, that hutch for grubby schoolboys.

Theodore Roethke, "I Cry, Love! Love!" *The Collected Verse of Theodore Roethke* (1961)

28. We distrust our heart too much, and our head not enough.

Joseph Roux, *Meditations of a Parish Priest* (1886), 9.4, tr. Isabel F. Hapgood

29. Reason may be a small force, but it is constant, and works always in one direction, while the forces of unreason destroy one another in futile strife.

Bertrand Russell, "The Harm That Good Men Do," *Fifty Famous Essays* (1964)

30. Pure logic is the ruin of the spirit.

SAINT-EXUPÉRY, *FLIGHT TO ARRAS* (1942), 2, TR. LEWIS GALANTIÈRE

31. The seed haunted by the sun never fails to find its way between the stones in the ground. And the pure logician, if no sun draws him forth, remains entangled in his logic.

SAINT-EXUPÉRY, *FLIGHT TO ARRAS* (1942), 22, TR. LEWIS GALANTIÈRE

32. Reason and happiness are like other flowers—they wither when plucked.

GEORGE SANTAYANA, *THE LIFE OF REASON: REASON AND RELIGION* (1905–06), 10

33. Reason in my philosophy is only a harmony among irrational impulses.

GEORGE SANTAYANA, *PERSONS AND PLACES: THE MIDDLE SPAN* (1945), 4

34. Reason deserves to be called a prophet; for in showing us the consequence and effect of our actions in the present, does it not tell us what the future will be?

SCHOPENHAUER, "FURTHER PSYCHOLOGICAL OBSERVATIONS," *PARERGA AND PARALIPOMENA* (1851), TR. T. BAILEY SAUNDERS

35. In these anxious times many of us are less astonished that reason is ever suspended than that it should ever prevail, even during the briefest of intervals.

MORTON IRVING SEIDEN, *THE PARADOX OF HATE: A STUDY IN RITUAL MURDER* (1967), 1

36. The man who listens to Reason is lost: Reason enslaves all whose minds are not strong enough to master her.

GEORGE BERNARD SHAW, "MAXIMS FOR REVOLUTIONISTS," *MAN AND SUPERMAN* (1903)

37. A mind all logic is like a knife all blade. It makes the hand bleed that uses it.

RABINDRANATH TAGORE, *STRAY BIRDS* (1916), 193

38. Reason deceives us more often than does nature.

VAUVENARGUES, *REFLECTIONS AND MAXIMS* (1746), 123

786. REBELLION

See also 256. DISOBEDIENCE; 258. DISSENT; 658. OPPOSITION; 819. REVOLUTION; 1032. VIOLENCE

1. Rebel, n. A proponent of a new misrule who has failed to establish it.

AMBROSE BIERCE, *THE DEVIL'S DICTIONARY* (1881–1911)

2. When I refuse to obey an unjust law, I do not contest the right of the majority to command, but I simply appeal from the sovereignty of the people to the sovereignty of mankind.

ALEXIS DE TOCQUEVILLE, *DEMOCRACY IN AMERICA* (1835–39), 1.15

3. In a nutshell—I fear authority but at the same time I resent it—the authority *and* my own fear. So I rebel.

PHILIP K. DICK, *THE GOLDEN MAN* (1980)

4. No one can go on being a rebel too long without turning into an autocrat.

LAWRENCE DURRELL, *BALTHAZAR* (1958), 2.6

5. Who draws his sword against the prince must throw away the scabbard.

ENGLISH PROVERB

6. At certain times and in certain schools it is orthodox to be a rebel; and in general it is a very poor class that does not contain at least three pupils who can be counted on to oppose the teacher's authority and loudly and persistently to question everything he says.

GILBERT HIGHET, *THE ART OF TEACHING* (1950)

7. A little rebellion, now and then, is a good thing, and as necessary in the political world as storms in the physical.

THOMAS JEFFERSON, LETTER TO JAMES MADISON, JAN. 30, 1787

8. For self-realization, a rebel demands a strong authority, a worthy opponent, God to his Lucifer.

MARY MCCARTHY, *HOW I GREW* (1987)

787. RECEIVING

See also 384. GIFTS AND GIVING; 399. GRATITUDE; 475. INGRATITUDE; 647. OBLIGATION; 789. RECOMPENSE

1. Nothing costs so much as what is given us.

THOMAS FULLER, M.D., *GNOMOLOGIA* (1732), 3660

2. The art of acceptance is the art of making someone who has just done you a small favor wish that he might have done you a greater one.

RUSSELL LYNES, *READER'S DIGEST,* DECEMBER 1961

788. RECIPROCITY

1. Men seldom give pleasure when they are not pleased themselves.

SAMUEL JOHNSON, *THE RAMBLER* (1750–52), 74

2. He who loves others is constantly loved by them. He who respects others is constantly respected by them.

MENCIUS, *WORKS* (4TH–3RD C. B.C.), 4, TR. CHARLES A. WONG

3. Evidence of trust begets trust, and love is reciprocated by love.

PLUTARCH, "MARRIAGE COUNSEL," *MORALIA* (C. A.D. 100), TR. MOSES HADAS

RECKLESSNESS

See 92. BOLDNESS; 216. DANGER; 781. RASHNESS

RECOGNITION

See 47. APPRECIATION

789. RECOMPENSE

See also 476. INJURY; 680. PAYMENT; 817. REVENGE

1. Recompense injury with justice, and recompense kindness with kindness.

CONFUCIUS, *ANALECTS* (6TH C. B.C.), 14.36, TR. JAMES LEGGE

2. Men are more prone to revenge injuries than to requite kindnesses.

THOMAS FULLER, M.D., *GNOMOLOGIA* (1732), 3389

790. REFORM

See also 433. HUMANITARIANISM; 442. IDEALISM; 460. IMPROVEMENT; 477. INJUSTICE; 1025. UTOPIA

1. Nobody expects to find comfort and companionability in reformers.

HEYWOOD BROUN, "WHIMS," *NEW YORK WORLD,* FEB. 6, 1928

2. Many—have too rashly charged the troops of error, and remain as trophies unto the enemies of truth.

SIR THOMAS BROWNE, *RELIGIO MEDICI* (1642), 1

3. Men reform a thing by removing the reality from it, and then do not know what to do with the unreality that is left.

G. K. CHESTERTON, "ON DOMESTIC SERVANTS," *GENERALLY SPEAKING* (1928)

4. Attempts at reform, when they fail, strengthen despotism, as he that struggles tightens those cords he does not succeed in breaking.

CHARLES CALEB COLTON, *LACON* (1825), 1.440

5. Experience has two things to teach: the first is that we must correct a great deal; the second, that we must not correct too much.

DELACROIX, *LETTRE À PHILARÈTE CHASLES,* MARCH 8, 1860

6. A man that'd expict to thrain lobsters to fly in a year is called a loonytic; but a man that thinks men can be tur-rned into angels be an iliction is called a rayformer an' remains at large.

FINLEY PETER DUNNE, "CASUAL OBSERVATIONS," *MR. DOOLEY'S PHILOSOPHY* (1900)

7. [Th' rayformer] don't understand that people wud rather be wrong an' comfortable thin right in jail.

FINLEY PETER DUNNE, "REFORM ADMINISTRATION," *OBSERVATIONS BY MR. DOOLEY* (1902)

8. Every reform was once a private opinion, and when it shall be a private opinion again, it will solve the problem of the age.

EMERSON, "HISTORY," *ESSAYS: FIRST SERIES* (1841)

9. The religions are obsolete when the reforms do not proceed from them.

EMERSON, *JOURNALS,* 1872

10. It is one of the ironies of history that reformers so often misjudge the consequences of their reforms.

JOHN W. GARDNER, "THE DECLINE OF HEREDITARY PRIVILEGE," *EXCELLENCE* (1961)

11. All the evil in the world is the fault of the self-styled pure in heart, a result of their eagerness to unearth secrets and expose them to the light of the sun.

JEAN GIRAUDOUX, *ELECTRA* (1937), 2, TR. PETER H. JUDD

12. Those who are fond of setting things to rights, have no great objection to seeing them wrong.

WILLIAM HAZLITT, *CHARACTERISTICS* (1823)

13. As soon as the people fix one Shame of the World, another turns up.

EDGAR WATSON HOWE, *VENTURES IN COMMON SENSE* (1919), 2.24

14. Every man is a reformer until reform tramps on his toes.

EDGAR WATSON HOWE, *COUNTRY TOWN SAYINGS* (1911)

15. One great flaw in the reforming passion is that in its eagerness to remedy social wrongs it tends to neglect, certainly to undervalue, the experience of those whose lives it wishes to improve.

IRVING HOWE, "KIPLING'S *KIM*: ECSTASIES," *A CRITIC'S NOTEBOOK* (1994)

16. Long customs are not easily broken: he that attempts to change the course of his own life very often labours in vain: and how shall we do that for others, which we are seldom able to do for ourselves?

Samuel Johnson, *Rasselas* (1759), 29

17. You've tried to reform what will not learn. / Shut doors on traits that you wish were dead; / They will open a window and return.

La Fontaine, "The Cat Changed to a Woman," *Fables* (1668–94), tr. Marianne Moore

18. Unless the reformer can invent something which substitutes attractive virtues for attractive vices, he will fail.

Walter Lippmann, "The Taboo," *A Preface to Politics* (1914)

19. The urge to save humanity is almost always only a false-face for the urge to rule it.

H. L. Mencken, *Minority Report* (1956), 369

20. The spirit of improvement is not always a spirit of liberty, for it may aim at forcing improvements on an unwilling people.

John Stuart Mill, *On Liberty* (1859), 3

21. The man who is forever disturbed about the condition of humanity either has no problems of his own or has refused to face them.

Henry Miller, *Sunday after the War* (1944)

22. It is a folly second to none, / To try to improve the world.

Molière, *The Misanthrope* (1666), 1.1

23. All reformers are bachelors.

George Moore, *The Bending of the Bough* (1900), 1

24. The men who have changed the universe have never accomplished it by changing officials but always by inspiring the people.

Napoleon I, *Maxims* (1804–15)

25. Whoever fights monsters should see to it that in the process he does not become a monster.

Nietzsche, *Beyond Good and Evil* (1886), 146, tr. Walter Kaufmann

26. A long habit of not thinking a thing wrong, gives it a superficial appearance of being right, and raises at first a formidable outcry in defense of custom.

Thomas Paine, introduction to *Common Sense* (1776)

27. To give up the task of reforming society is to give up one's responsibility as a free man.

Alan Paton, "The Challenge of Fear," *Saturday Review*, Sept. 9, 1967

28. The reformer is careless of numbers, disregards popularity, and deals only with ideas, conscience, and common sense. He feels, with Copernicus, that as God waited long for an interpreter, so he can wait for his followers.

Wendell Phillips, quoted in Richard Hofstadter, *The American Political Tradition* (1948)

29. The men with the muck-rake are often indispensable to the well-being of society, but only if they know when to stop raking the muck.

Theodore Roosevelt, address, Washington, D.C., April 14, 1906

30. The superannuated bawd feels no hesitation in forswearing fornication, nor the displaced police magistrate in foregoing oppression.

Sa'di, *Gulistan* (1258), 8.120, tr. James Ross

31. It is one of the consolations of middle-aged reformers that the good they inculcate must live after them if it is to live at all.

Saki, "The Byzantine Omelette," *Beasts and Super-Beasts* (1914)

32. Think of [your contemporaries] as they ought to be when you have to influence them, but think of them as they are when you are tempted to act on their behalf.

Schiller, *On the Aesthetic Education of Man* (1795), 9, tr. Reginald Snell

33. If anything ail a man, so that he does not perform his functions, if he have a pain in his bowels even,—for that is the seat of sympathy,—he forthwith sets about reforming the world.

Thoreau, "Economy," *Walden* (1854)

34. There are a thousand hacking at the branches of evil to one who is striking at the root.

Thoreau, "Economy," *Walden* (1854)

35. Nothing so needs reforming as other people's habits.

Mark Twain, "Pudd'nhead Wilson's Calendar," *Pudd'nhead Wilson* (1894), 15

36. I am a correctionist. If something is wrong in society, it must be fixed. At least one should try to fix it.

Gore Vidal, *Rocking the Boat* (1962)

37. Every abuse ought to be reformed, unless the reform is more dangerous than the abuse itself.

VOLTAIRE, *PHILOSOPHICAL DICTIONARY* (1764)

791. REFUSAL

See also 805. REQUEST

1. A soft refusal is not always taken, but a rude one is immediately believed.

ALEXANDER CHASE, *PERSPECTIVES* (1966)

2. He who awaits the call, but sees the need, / Already sets his spirit to refuse it.

DANTE, "PURGATORIO," 17, *THE DIVINE COMEDY* (C. 1300–21), TR. LAWRENCE GRANT WHITE

3. Better a friendly denial than unwilling compliance.

GERMAN PROVERB

4. The prompter the refusal, the less the disappointment.

PUBLILIUS SYRUS, *MORAL SAYINGS* (1ST C. B.C.), 492, TR. DARIUS LYMAN

5. He who never says "no" is no true man.

SAINT-EXUPÉRY, *THE WISDOM OF THE SANDS* (1948), 29, TR. STUART GILBERT

6. No is no negative in a woman's mouth.

SIR PHILIP SIDNEY, *ARCADIA* (1590), 3

7. In refusing benefits caution must be used lest we seem to despise or to refuse them for fear of having to repay them in kind.

SPINOZA, *ETHICS* (1677), 4, TR. ANDREW BOYLE

792. REGRET

See also 44. APOLOGY

1. Regrets and recriminations only hurt your soul.

ARMAND HAMMER, *HAMMER* (1987), WITH NEIL LYNDON

2. We as often repent the good we have done as the ill.

WILLIAM HAZLITT, *CHARACTERISTICS* (1823)

3. Ah, in this world, where every guiding thread / Ends suddenly in the one sure centre, death, / The visionary hand of Might-have-been / Alone can fill Desire's cup to the brim!

JAMES RUSSELL LOWELL, "ON THE DEATH OF A FRIEND'S CHILD" (1844)

4. I have loved badly, loved the great / Too soon, withdrawn my words too late; / And eaten in an echoing hall / Alone and from a chipped plate / The words that I withdrew too late.

EDNA ST. VINCENT MILLAY, "THEME AND VARIATIONS," *HUNTSMAN, WHAT QUARRY?* (1939)

5. Let us not burden our remembrance with / A heaviness that's gone.

SHAKESPEARE, *THE TEMPEST* (1611–12), 5.1.199

6. To regret deeply is to live afresh.

THOREAU, *JOURNAL*, NOV. 13, 1839

793. REJECTION

See also 552. LOVE, LOSS OF; 553. LOVE, UNREQUITED

1. Heaven has no rage like love to hatred turned, / Nor hell a fury like a woman scorned.

WILLIAM CONGREVE, *THE MOURNING BRIDE* (1697), 3.8

2. Spurn not the nobly-born / With love affected, / Nor treat with virtuous scorn / The well-connected.

W. S. GILBERT, *IOLANTHE* (1882), 1

3. To find oneself jilted is a blow to one's pride. One must do one's best to forget it and if one doesn't succeed, at least one must pretend to.

MOLIÈRE, *TARTUFFE* (1664), 2, TR. JOHN WOOD

4. Oh, seek, my love, your newer way; / I'll not be left in sorrow. / So long as I have yesterday, / Go take your damned to-morrow!

DOROTHY PARKER, "GODSPEED," *ENOUGH ROPE* (1926), 2

794. RELATIONSHIPS, HUMAN

See also 499. INTIMACY; 663. OTHERS; 1008. UNDERSTANDING OTHERS

1. Almost all of our relationships begin and most of them continue as forms of mutual exploitation, a mental or physical barter, to be terminated when one or both parties run out of goods.

W. H. AUDEN, "HIC ET ILLE," *THE DYER'S HAND* (1962)

2. Persons are fine things, but they cost so much! for thee I must pay me.

EMERSON, *JOURNALS*, 1843

3. The famous carry about with them a great weight of patriarchal baggage—the footnotes of their lives.

ELIZABETH HARDWICK, "WIVES AND MISTRESSES," *BARTLEBY IN MANHATTAN* (1983)

4. Without wearing any mask we are conscious of, we have a special face for each friend.

Oliver Wendell Holmes, Sr., *The Professor at the Breakfast Table* (1860), 8

5. The first thing to learn in intercourse with others is non-interference with their own peculiar ways of being happy, provided those ways do not assume to interfere by violence with ours.

William James, "What Makes a Life Significant?" *Talks to Teachers and to Students* (1899)

6. To really know someone is to have loved and hated him in turn.

Marcel Jouhandeau, "Erotologie," *Défense de l'enfer* (1935)

7. We can't all be friends and relatives as the world is; most of us have to be strangers.

Bernard Malamud, *Dubin's Lives* (1979)

8. The only thing as challenging as getting tangled in the underbrush of relationship is trying to write about it.

Thomas Moore, *Soul Mates* (1994)

9. The bonds that unite another person to ourself exist only in our mind.

Marcel Proust, *Remembrance of Things Past: The Sweet Cheat Gone* (1913–27), tr. C. K. Scott-Moncrieff

10. The opinions which we hold of one another, our relations with friends and kinsfolk are in no sense permanent, save in appearance, but are as eternally fluid as the sea itself.

Marcel Proust, *Remembrance of Things Past: The Guermantes Way* (1913–27), tr. C. K. Scott-Moncrieff

11. Man is a knot, a web, a mesh into which relationships are tied. Only those relationships matter.

Saint-Exupéry, *Flight to Arras* (1942), 19, tr. Lewis Galantière

12. There is no hope of joy except in human relations.

Saint-Exupéry, *Wind, Sand, and Stars* (1939), 2.1, tr. Lewis Galantière

13. Those whom we can love, we can hate; to others we are indifferent.

Thoreau, *Journal*, Feb. 24, 1857

795. RELATIVENESS

See also 153. Comparison

1. In the country of the blind, the one-eyed man is king.

Michael Apostolius, *Proverbs* (15th c.)

2. When the moon is not full, the stars shine more brightly.

Buganda Proverb

3. Bad is never good until worse happens.

Danish Proverb

4. When a man sits with a pretty girl for an hour, it seems like a minute. But let him sit on a hot stove for a minute—and it's longer than any hour. That's relativity.

Einstein, quoted in his obituary, *The New York Times,* April 19, 1955

796. RELATIVES

See also 334. Family; 794. Relationships, Human

1. It is a melancholy truth that even great men have their poor relations.

Charles Dickens, *Bleak House* (1852), 28

2. Blood's thicker than water, and when one's in trouble / Best to seek out a relative's open arms.

Euripides, *Andromache* (c. 426 b.c.), tr. John F. Nims

3. A poor relation—is the most irrelevant thing in nature,—a piece of impertinent correspondency,—an odious approximation,—a haunting conscience,—a preposterous shadow, lengthening in the noontide of our prosperity.

Charles Lamb, "Poor Relations," *Last Essays of Elia* (1833)

4. When our relatives are at home, we have to think of all their good points or it would be impossible to endure them.

George Bernard Shaw, *Heartbreak House* (1929), 1

797. RELIGION

See also 78. Belief; 80. Bible; 125. Christianity; 126. Church; 127. Church and State; 128. Churchgoing; 138. Clergy; 264. Dogmatism; 265. Doubt, Religious; 330. Faith; 565. Martyrs and Martyrdom; 596. Missionaries; 601. Monasticism; 616. Mysticism; 697. Piety; 723. Prayer; 724. Preaching and Preachers; 769. Puritans and Puritanism; 816. Revelation, Divine;

835. SABBATH; 840. SAINTS AND SAINTHOOD; 841. SALVATION; 850. SCIENCE AND RELIGION; 973. THEOLOGY; 1068. WORSHIP

1. One's religion is whatever he is most interested in.

J. M. BARRIE, *THE TWELVE-POUND LOOK* (1910)

2. Pure religion and undefiled before God and the Father is this, To visit the fatherless and widows in their affliction, and to keep himself unspotted from the world.

BIBLE, JAMES 1:27

3. Religion, n. A daughter of Hope and Fear, explaining to Ignorance the nature of the Unknowable.

AMBROSE BIERCE, *THE DEVIL'S DICTIONARY* (1881–1911)

4. These sociologists who talk so facilely about the sacred are like a man who keeps a toothless old circus lion around the house in order to experience the thrills of the jungle.

ALLAN BLOOM, *THE CLOSING OF THE AMERICAN MIND* (1987)

5. It may be that religion is dead, and if it is, we had better know it and set ourselves to try to discover other sources of moral strength before it is too late.

PEARL S. BUCK, *WHAT AMERICA MEANS TO ME* (1947), 11

6. Nothing is so fatal to religion as indifference.

EDMUND BURKE, LETTER TO WILLIAM SMITH, JAN. 29, 1795

7. The true laws of God are the laws of our own well-being.

SAMUEL BUTLER (D. 1902), "ELEMENTARY MORALITY," *NOTE-BOOKS* (1912)

8. I am always most religious upon a sunshiny day.

BYRON, *SELECTED LETTERS AND JOURNALS* (1982), ED. LESLIE A. MARCHAND

9. I am no Platonist, I am nothing at all; but I would sooner be a Paulician, Manichean, Spinozist, Gentile, Pyrrhonian, Zoroastrian, than one of the seventy-two villainous sects who are tearing each other to pieces for the love of the Lord and hatred of each other.

BYRON, *SELECTED LETTERS AND JOURNALS* (1982), ED. LESLIE A. MARCHAND

10. Every religion is true one way or another. It is true when understood metaphorically. But when it gets stuck in its own metaphors, interpreting them as facts, then you are in trouble.

JOSEPH CAMPBELL, *THE POWER OF MYTH* (1988)

11. More and more people care about religious tolerance as fewer and fewer care about religion.

ALEXANDER CHASE, *PERSPECTIVES* (1966)

12. A cosmic philosophy is not constructed to fit a man; a cosmic philosophy is constructed to fit a cosmos. A man can no more possess a private religion than he can possess a private sun and moon.

G. K. CHESTERTON, "THE BOOK OF JOB," *G. K. C. AS M. C.* (1929)

13. Men will wrangle for religion, write for it, fight for it, die for it; anything but live for it.

CHARLES CALEB COLTON, *LACON* (1825), 1.25

14. Where true religion has prevented one crime, false religions have afforded a pretext for a thousand.

CHARLES CALEB COLTON, *LACON* (1825), 1.189

15. In my religion there would be no exclusive doctrine; all would be love, poetry and doubt.

CYRIL CONNOLLY, *THE UNQUIET GRAVE* (1945), 1

16. Persecution, religious pride, the love of contradiction, are the food of what the world commonly calls religion.

MICHEL GUILLAUME JEAN DE CRÈVECOEUR, *LETTERS FROM AN AMERICAN FARMER* (1782), 3

17. Intellectually, religious emotions are not creative but conservative. They attach themselves readily to the current view of the world and consecrate it.

JOHN DEWEY, "THE INFLUENCE OF DARWINSIM ON PHILOSOPHY" (1909)

18. All religions are ancient monuments to superstition, ignorance, ferocity; and modern religions are only ancient follies rejuvenated.

BARON D'HOLBACH, *LE BON SENS, OU IDÉES NATURELLES OPPOSÉES AUX IDÉES SURNATURELLES* (1772), 120

19. The cosmic religious experience is the strongest and the noblest driving force behind scientific research.

EINSTEIN, QUOTED IN HIS OBITUARY, APRIL 19, 1955

20. For a great nature, it is a happiness to escape a religious training,—religion of character is so apt to be invaded.

EMERSON, "WORSHIP," *THE CONDUCT OF LIFE* (1860)

21. God enters by a private door into every individual.

EMERSON, "INTELLECT," *ESSAYS: FIRST SERIES* (1841)

22. The religions of the world are the ejaculations of a few imaginative men.

EMERSON, "THE POET," *ESSAYS: SECOND SERIES* (1844)

23. The test of a religion or philosophy is the number of things it can explain.

EMERSON, *JOURNALS*, 1836

24. No man's religion ever survived his morals.

ENGLISH PROVERB

25. Men make their choice: one man honors one God, / and one another.

EURIPIDES, *HIPPOLYTUS* (428 B.C.), TR. DAVID GRENE

26. What is god, what is not god, what is between man / and god, who shall say?

EURIPIDES, *HELEN* (412 B.C.), TR. RICHMOND LATTIMORE

27. Nature teaches us to love our friends, but religion our enemies.

THOMAS FULLER, M.D., *GNOMOLOGIA* (1732), 3508

28. Religion is the best armour in the world, but the worst cloak.

THOMAS FULLER, M.D., *GNOMOLOGIA* (1732), 4011

29. Many of the men who had come to the wilderness to practice religion appeared to have forgotten its true nature.

ELLEN GLASGOW, *VEIN OF IRON* (1935)

30. The founders of the great world religions, Gautama Buddha, Jesus, Lao-Tzu, Mohammed, all seem to have striven for a worldwide brotherhood of man; but none of them could develop institutions which would include the enemy, the unbeliever.

GEOFFREY GORER, *THE NEW YORK TIMES MAGAZINE*, NOV. 27, 1966

31. Religion either makes men wise and virtuous, or it makes them set up false pretences to both.

WILLIAM HAZLITT, "ON RELIGIOUS HYPOCRISY," *THE ROUND TABLE* (1817)

32. The garb of religion is the best cloak for power.

WILLIAM HAZLITT, "ON THE CLERICAL CHARACTER," *POLITICAL ESSAYS* (1819)

33. Civil religion gives American culture its direction and defines its fundamental values, but it does not determine the diversified contents of American national culture.

E.D. HIRSCH, JR., *CULTURAL LITERACY* (1987)

34. The great end of being is to harmonize man with the order of things, and the church has been a good pitch-pipe, and may be so still.

OLIVER WENDELL HOLMES, SR., *THE PROFESSOR AT THE BREAKFAST TABLE* (1860), 1

35. It is well that the stately synagogue should lift its walls by the side of the aspiring cathedral, a perpetual reminder that there are many mansions in Father's earthly house as well as in the heavenly ones.

OLIVER WENDELL HOLMES, SR., *OVER THE TEACUPS* (1891), 8

36. Nobody can have the consolations of religion or philosophy unless he has first experienced their desolations.

ALDOUS HUXLEY, "VARIATIONS ON A BAROQUE TOMB," *THEMES AND VARIATIONS* (1950)

37. Religion is always a patron of the arts, but its taste is by no means impeccable.

ALDOUS HUXLEY, "FAITH, TASTE, AND HISTORY," *TOMORROW AND TOMORROW AND TOMORROW* (1956)

38. No man with any sense of humor ever founded a religion.

ROBERT G. INGERSOLL, *PROSE-POEMS AND SELECTIONS* (1884)

39. To hate man and worship God seems to be the sum of all creeds.

ROBERT G. INGERSOLL, *SOME MISTAKES OF MOSES* (1879)

40. There can be but little liberty on earth while men worship a tyrant in heaven.

ROBERT G. INGERSOLL, *PROSE-POEMS AND SELECTIONS* (1884)

41. In prosperity no altars smoke.

ITALIAN PROVERB

42. He who steadily observes those moral precepts in which all religions concur, will never be questioned at the gates of heaven as to the dogmas in which they all differ.

THOMAS JEFFERSON, LETTER TO WILLIAM CANBY, SEPT. 18, 1813

43. Men have torn up the roads which led to Heaven, and which all the world followed; now we have to make our own ladders.

JOSEPH JOUBERT, *PENSÉES* (1842), 17.5, TR. KATHARINE LYTTELTON

44. One man finds in religion his literature and his science, another finds in it his joy and his duty.

JOSEPH JOUBERT, *PENSÉES* (1842), 1.30, TR. KATHARINE LYTTELTON

45. A religion which has lost its basic conviction about the interconnection of men with men in their

common struggles for the human, will never command belief in the realm of the superhuman.

MAX LERNER, "LAISSEZ-FAIRE IN SOCIAL JUSTICE," *ACTIONS AND PASSIONS* (1949)

46. I count religion but a childish toy, / And hold there is no sin but ignorance.

CHRISTOPHER MARLOWE, *THE JEW OF MALTA* (C. 1589), 1

47. Religion is the sign of the oppressed creature, the sentiment of a heartless world, and the soul of soulless conditions. It is the opium of the people.

KARL MARX, INTRODUCTION TO "CONTRIBUTION TO THE CRITIQUE OF HEGEL'S PHILOSOPHY OF RIGHT" (1884), *EARLY WRITINGS*

48. In religion above all things the only thing of use is an objective truth. The only God that is of use is a being who is personal, supreme and good, and whose existence is as certain as that two and two make four.

W. SOMERSET MAUGHAM, *THE SUMMING UP* (1938), 69

49. We must respect the other fellow's religion, but only in the sense and to the extent that we respect his theory that his wife is beautiful and his children smart.

H. L. MENCKEN, *MINORITY REPORT* (1956), 1

50. Religion has the same relation to man's heavenly condition that mathematics has to his earthly one: both the one and the other are merely the rules of the game. Belief in God and belief in numbers: local truth and truth of location.

VLADIMIR NABOKOV, *THE GIFT* (1963)

51. Knowledge and history are the enemies of religion.

NAPOLEON I, *MAXIMS* (1804–15)

52. Religion indeed enlightens, terrifies, subdues; it gives faith, it inflicts remorse, it inspires resolutions, it draws tears, it inflames devotion, but only for the occasion.

JOHN HENRY NEWMAN, *THE IDEA OF A UNIVERSITY* (1853–58), 1.8.3

53. True religion is slow in growth, and, when once planted, is difficult of dislodgement; but its intellectual counterfeit has no root in itself: it springs up suddenly, it suddenly withers.

JOHN HENRY NEWMAN, *THE IDEA OF A UNIVERSITY* (1853–58), 1.8.8

54. Wherever on earth the religious neurosis has appeared we find it tied to three dangerous dietary demands: solitude, fasting, and sexual abstinence.

NIETZSCHE, *BEYOND GOOD AND EVIL* (1886), 47, TR. WALTER KAUFMANN

55. In the long term we can hope that religion will change the nature of man and reduce conflict. But history is not encouraging in this respect. The bloodiest wars in history have been religious wars.

RICHARD M. NIXON, *REAL PEACE* (1984)

56. Men despise religion; they hate it, and fear it is true.

PASCAL, *PENSÉES* (1670), 187, TR. W. F. TROTTER

57. Religion is so great a thing that it is right that those who will not take the trouble to seek it, if it be obscure, should be deprived of it.

PASCAL, *PENSÉES* (1670), 573, TR. W. F. TROTTER

58. That a religion may be true, it must have knowledge of our nature.

PASCAL, *PENSÉES* (1670), 433, TR. W. F. TROTTER

59. You corrupt religion either in favour of your friends, or against your enemies.

PASCAL, *PENSÉES* (1670), 854, TR. W. F. TROTTER

60. To be furious in religion is to be irreligiously religious.

WILLIAM PENN, *SOME FRUITS OF SOLITUDE* (1693), 1.533

61. Religion blushing, veils her sacred fires, / And unawares Morality expires.

ALEXANDER POPE, *THE DUNCIAD* (1743), 4.642

62. Religion may have been the original cure; Freud reminds us that it was also the original disease.

PHILIP RIEFF, "THE RELIGION OF THE FATHERS," *FREUD: THE MIND OF THE MORALIST* (1959)

63. Religion is something infinitely simple, ingenuous. It is not knowledge, not content of feeling,... it is not duty and not renunciation, it is not restriction: but in the infinite extent of the universe it is a direction of the heart.

RAINER MARIA RILKE, LETTER TO ILSE BLUMENTHAL-WEISS, DEC. 28, 1921, IN *WARTIME LETTERS*,, TR. M. D. HERTER NORTON

64. Religions which have any very strong hold over men's actions have generally some instinctive basis.

BERTRAND RUSSELL, "WHERE FATHERHOOD IS UNKNOWN," *MARRIAGE AND MORALS* (1929)

65. Each religion, by the help of more or less myth which it takes more or less seriously, proposes some method of fortifying the human soul and enabling it to make its peace with its destiny.

GEORGE SANTAYANA, *PERSONS AND PLACES: MY HOST THE WORLD* (1953), 1

66. Matters of religion should never be matters of controversy. We neither argue with a lover about his taste, nor condemn him, if we are just, for knowing so human a passion.

George Santayana, *The Life of Reason: Reason in Religion* (1905–06), 6

67. Religion is the love of life in the consciousness of impotence.

George Santayana, *Winds of Doctrine* (1913)

68. Religion should be disentangled as much as possible from history and authority and metaphysics, and made to rest honestly on one's fine feelings, on one's indomitable optimism and trust in life.

George Santayana, *Character and Opinion in the United States* (1921), 1

69. Religion is indeed a convention which a man must be bred in to endure with any patience; and yet religion, for all its poetic motley, comes closer than work-a-day opinion to the heart of things.

George Santayana, *Dialogues in Limbo* (1925), 4

70. There is only one religion, though there are a hundred versions of it.

George Bernard Shaw, preface, *Arms and the Man* (1894)

71. Without their fictions the truths of religion would for the multitude be neither intelligible nor even apprehensible; and the prophets would prophesy and the teachers teach in vain.

George Bernard Shaw, preface, *Back to Methuselah* (1921)

72. Religion pervades intensely the whole frame of society, and is according to the temper of the mind which it inhabits, a passion, a persuasion, an excuse, a refuge; never a check.

Shelley, preface, *The Cenci* (1819)

73. If things are going well, religion and legislation are beneficial; if not, they are of no avail.

Solon (7th–6th c. B.C.), quoted in Diogenes Laertius' *Lives and Opinions of Eminent Philosophers* (3rd c. A.D.), tr. R. D. Hicks

74. Religion has nothing more to fear than not being sufficiently understood.

Stanislaus I of Poland, *Maxims* (c. 18th c.), 36

75. We have just religion enough to make us hate, but not enough to make us love one another.

Jonathan Swift, *Thoughts on Various Subjects* (1711)

76. We are self-uncertain creatures, and we may / Yea, even when we know not, mix our spites / And private hates with our defence of Heaven.

Lord Tennyson, *Becket* (1884), 5.2

77. Let us meet four times a year in a grand temple with music, and thank God for all his gifts. There is one sun. There is one God. Let us have one religion. Then all mankind will be brethren.

Voltaire, quoted in *Boswell on the Grand Tour: Germany and Switzerland* (1928; 1953)

78. Just because I don't harass it like some peoples us know don't mean I ain't got religion.

Alice Walker, *The Color Purple* (1982)

79. Religions are such stuff as dreams are made of.

H. G. Wells, *The Happy Turning* (1946)

80. Once or twice a year we go to church, as we might visit the Museum of Natural History, on a sudden impulse to see a strange sight, such as a whale suspended in air.

E.B. White, *One Man's Meat* (1944)

81. The fact of the religious vision, and its history of persistent expansion, is our one ground for optimism. Apart from it, human life is a flash of occasional enjoyments lighting up a mass of pain and misery, a bagatelle of transient experience.

Alfred North Whitehead, *Science and the Modern World* (1925), 12

82. Religion is the reaction of human nature to its search for God.

Alfred North Whitehead, *Science and the Modern World* (1925), 12

83. No religion can be considered in abstraction from its followers, or even from its various types of followers.

Alfred North Whitehead, *Adventures in Ideas* (1933), 2

798. REMEDIES

See also 180. Consolations; 243. Diagnosis; 577. Medicine

1. What destroys one man preserves another.

Corneille, *Cinna* (1639), 2.1, tr. Paul Landis

2. The remedy for all blunders, the cure of blindness, the cure of crime, is love.

Emerson, "Worship," *The Conduct of Life* (1860)

3. Life as we find it is too hard for us; it entails too much pain, too many disappointments, impossible tasks. We cannot do without palliative remedies.

SIGMUND FREUD, *CIVILIZATION AND ITS DISCONTENTS* (1930), TR. JOAN RIVIERE

4. Extreme remedies are very appropriate for extreme diseases.

HIPPOCRATES, *APHORISMS* (C. 400 B.C.), 1.6

5. Most men die of their remedies, not of their diseases.

MOLIÈRE, *THE IMAGINARY INVALID* (1673), 3, TR. JOHN WOOD

6. Peace is a great goal, but it is not a panacea. Neither is material wealth.

RICHARD M. NIXON, *BEYOND PEACE* (1994)

7. A thousand ills require a thousand cures.

OVID, *LOVE'S CURE* (C. A.D. 8), TR. J. LEWIS MAY

8. A pharmacist in the Rue de Vaugirard, absorbed in bottling leeches and obviously a figment of René Clair's imagination, paused long enough to patch me up grudgingly, and I went into a *brasserie* hard by for a restorative.

S.J. PERELMAN, *THE RISING GORGE* (1961)

9. Gout is not relieved by a fine shoe nor a hangnail by a costly ring nor migraine by a tiara.

PLUTARCH, "CONTENTMENT," *MORALIA* (C. A.D. 100), TR. MOSES HADAS

10. There are some remedies worse than the disease.

PUBLILIUS SYRUS, *MORAL SAYINGS* (1ST C. B.C.), 301, TR. DARIUS LYMAN

11. Diseases desperate grown / By desperate appliances are relieved, / Or not at all.

SHAKESPEARE, *HAMLET* (1600), 4.3.9

12. Our remedies oft in ourselves do lie, / Which we ascribe to heaven.

SHAKESPEARE, *ALL'S WELL THAT ENDS WELL* (1602–03), 1.1.231

REMINISCENCES

See 580. MEMORY

799. RENUNCIATION

See also 806. RESIGNATION

1. Renunciation—is a piercing Virtue—/ The letting go / A Presence—for an Expectation—.

EMILY DICKINSON, POEM (C. 1863)

2. How seek the way which leadeth to our wishes? By renouncing our wishes. The crown of excellence is renunciation.

HĀFIZ, GHAZALS FROM THE *DIVAN* (14TH C.), 15, TR. JUSTIN HUNTLY MCCARTHY

REPAYMENT

See 789. RECOMPENSE

800. REPETITION

1. There is repetition everywhere, and nothing is found only once in the world.

GOETHE, QUOTED IN JOHANN PETER ECKERMANN'S *CONVERSATIONS WITH GOETHE,* OCT. 29, 1823

2. What if one does say the same things,—of course in a little different form each time,—over and over? If he has anything to say worth saying, that is just what he ought to do.

OLIVER WENDELL HOLMES, SR., *OVER THE TEACUPS* (1891), 1

3. What so tedious as a twice-told tale?

HOMER, *ODYSSEY* (9TH C. B.C.), 12.538, TR. ALEXANDER POPE

4. After people have repeated a phrase a great number of times, they begin to realize it has meaning and may even be true.

H. G. WELLS, *THE HAPPY TURNING* (1946), 3–4

REPRESENTATIVE ASSEMBLY

See 172. CONGRESS

801. REPRESSION

See also 109. CAPTIVITY; 357. FORCE; 1002. TYRANNY

1. The barricade closes the street but opens the way.

GRAFFITO WRITTEN DURING FRENCH STUDENT REVOLT, MAY 1968

2. Prison, blood, death, create enthusiasts and martyrs, and bring forth courage and desperate resolution.

NAPOLEON I, *MAXIMS* (1804–15)

3. A little fire is quickly trodden out, / Which, being suffered, rivers cannot quench.

SHAKESPEARE, *3 HENRY VI* (1590–91), 4.8.7

REPROACH

See 803. REPROOF

802. REPRODUCTION

See also 84. BIRTH CONTROL; 417. HEREDITY; 713. POPULATION

1. The love of posterity is the consequence of the necessity of death. If a man were sure of living forever here, he would not care about his offspring.

NATHANIEL HAWTHORNE, *AMERICAN NOTE-BOOKS* (1868)

2. Monks, nuns, long-term spinsters and bachelors and permanent homosexuals are all, in a reproductive sense, aberrant. Society has bred them, but they have failed to return the compliment.

DESMOND MORRIS, *THE NAKED APE* (1967), 2

3. The turtle lives 'twixt plated decks / Which practically conceal its sex. / I think it clever of the turtle / In such a fix to be so fertile.

OGDEN NASH, "THE TURTLE," *MANY LONG YEARS AGO* (1945)

803. REPROOF

See also 206. CRITICISM; 342. FAULTS; 515. JUDGING OTHERS

1. There is no defence against reproach, but obscurity; it is a kind of concomitant to greatness.

JOSEPH ADDISON, *THE SPECTATOR* (1711–12), 101

2. The best preservative to keep the mind in health is the faithful admonition of a friend.

FRANCIS BACON, "OF FRIENDSHIP," *ESSAYS* (1625)

3. Reprove not a scorner, lest he hate thee: rebuke a wise man, and he will love thee.

BIBLE, PROVERBS 9:8

4. The man who acts the least, upbraids the most.

HOMER, *ILIAD* (9TH C. B.C.), 2.311, TR. ALEXANDER POPE

5. Rash and incessant scolding runs into custom and renders itself despised.

MONTAIGNE, "OF ANGER," *ESSAYS* (1580–88), TR. W. C. HAZLITT

6. I wonder how anyone can have the face to condemn others when he reflects upon his own thoughts.

W. SOMERSET MAUGHAM, *THE SUMMING UP* (1938), 16

7. Fear not the anger of the wise to raise; / Those best can bear reproof who merit praise.

ALEXANDER POPE, *AN ESSAY ON CRITICISM* (1711), 3.23

8. Blame is especially useful in situations in which there is no apparent villain—those moments that prove, despite our advancement of learning, how susceptible we are to high winds and wet roads.

ROGER ROSENBLATT, "AN INESCAPABLE NEED TO BLAME," *THE MAN IN THE WATER* (1994)

9. Better a little chiding than a great deal of heartbreak.

SHAKESPEARE, *THE MERRY WIVES OF WINDSOR* (1597), 5.3.10

10. The correction of silence is what kills; when you know you have transgressed, and your friend says nothing and avoids your eye.

ROBERT LOUIS STEVENSON, "TALK AND TALKERS" (1882), 2

11. Be thou, in rebuking evil, / Conscious of thine own.

JOHN GREENLEAF WHITTIER, "WHAT THE VOICE SAID" (1847), 15

REPUBLICANS

See 710. POLITICAL PARTIES

804. REPUTATION

See also 57. ASSOCIATION; 584. MERIT; 905. SLANDER

1. A good name is rather to be chosen than great riches.

BIBLE, PROVERBS 22:1

2. Shall I be remembered after death? I sometimes think and hope so. But I trust I may not be found out before my death.

SAMUEL BUTLER (D. 1902), "THE LIFE OF THE WORLD TO COME," *NOTE-BOOKS* (1912)

3. Men are much more unwilling to have their weaknesses and their imperfections known than their crimes.

LORD CHESTERFIELD, *LETTERS TO HIS SON,* SEPT. 5, 1748

4. There are two modes of establishing our reputation; to be praised by honest men, and to be abused by rogues.

CHARLES CALEB COLTON, *LACON* (1825), 1.218

5. There are many who dare not kill themselves for fear of what the neighbors will say.

CYRIL CONNOLLY, *THE UNQUIET GRAVE* (1945), 2

6. A man's real life is that accorded to him in the thoughts of other men by reason of respect or natural love.

JOSEPH CONRAD, *UNDER WESTERN EYES* (1911), 1.1

7. What shall I do to be for ever known, / And make the age to come my own?

ABRAHAM COWLEY, "THE MOTTO" (17TH C.)

8. If you would not be known to do anything, never do it.

EMERSON, "SPIRITUAL LAWS," *ESSAYS: FIRST SERIES* (1841)

9. When the man is at home, his standing in society is well known and quietly taken; but when he is abroad, it is problematical, and is dependent on the success of his manners.

EMERSON, *JOURNALS,* 1827

10. Reputation is often got without merit and lost without fault.

ENGLISH PROVERB

11. Reputation is commonly measured by the acre.

THOMAS FULLER, M.D., *GNOMOLOGIA* (1732), 4023

12. What people say behind your back is your standing in the community in which you live.

EDGAR WATSON HOWE, *COUNTRY TOWN SAYINGS* (1911)

13. Be it true or false, what is said about men often has as much influence upon their lives, and especially upon their destinies, as what they do.

VICTOR HUGO, "FANTINE," *LES MISÉRABLES* (1862), 1.1, TR. CHARLES E. WILBOUR

14. Those who are well assured of their own standing are least apt to trepass on that of others.

WASHINGTON IRVING, "THE COUNTRY CHURCH," *THE SKETCH BOOK OF GEOFFREY CRAYON, GENT.* (1819–20)

15. One who has the reputation of an early riser may safely lie abed till noon.

JEWISH PROVERB, *A TREASURY OF JEWISH FOLKLORE* (1948)

16. The Englishman wants to be recognized as a gentleman, or as some other suitable species of human being; the American wants to be considered a good guy.

LOUIS KRONENBERGER, *COMPANY MANNERS* (1954), 3.3

17. When we are dead we are praised by those who survive us, though we frequently have no other merit than that of being no longer alive.

LA BRUYÈRE, *CHARACTERS* (1688), 12.78, TR. HENRI VAN LAUN

18. A Negro just can't be whipped by somebody white and return with his head up in the neighborhood, especially in those days, when sports and, to a lesser extent show business, were the only fields open to Negroes, and when the ring was the only place a Negro could whip a white man and not be lynched.

MALCOLM X, *THE AUTOBIOGRAPHY OF MALCOLM X* (1964)

19. Some men seem remarkable to the world in whom neither their wives nor their valets saw anything extraordinary. Few men have been admired by their servants.

MONTAIGNE, "OF REPENTANCE," *ESSAYS* (1580–88)

20. But what do I care whether or not I receive attention during my lifetime, if I am not certain that the world will remember me until its last darkest winter, marveling like Ronsard's old woman?

VLADIMIR NABOKOV, *THE GIFT* (1963)

21. A great reputation is a great noise, the more there is of it, the further does it swell. Land, monuments, nations, all fall, but the noise remains, and will reach to other generations.

NAPOLEON I, *MAXIMS* (1804–15)

22. Who has not, for the sake of his good reputation—sacrificed himself once?

NIETZSCHE, *BEYOND GOOD AND EVIL* (1886), 92, TR. WALTER KAUFMANN

23. We do not content ourselves with the life we have in ourselves and in our own being; we desire to live an imaginary life in the mind of others, and for this purpose we endeavour to shine.

PASCAL, *PENSÉES* (1670), 147, TR. W. F. TROTTER

24. It is generally much more shameful to lose a good reputation than never to have acquired it.

PLINY THE YOUNGER, *LETTERS* (C. 97–110), 8.24, TR. ALFRED P. DORJAHN

25. It is easier to add to a great reputation than to get it.

PUBLILIUS SYRUS, *MORAL SAYINGS* (1ST C. B.C.), 250, TR. DARIUS LYMAN

26. Posterity is always just.

JEAN-JACQUES ROUSSEAU, QUOTED IN *BOSWELL ON THE GRAND TOUR: GERMANY AND SWITZERLAND* (1928; 1953)

27. Reputation is an idle and most false imposition; oft got without merit and lost without deserving.

SHAKESPEARE, *OTHELLO* (1604–05), 2.3.268

28. The Purest treasure mortal times afford / Is spotless reputation.

SHAKESPEARE, *RICHARD II* (1595–96), 1.1.177

29. One can survive everything nowadays, except death, and live down anything except a good reputation.

OSCAR WILDE, *A WOMAN OF NO IMPORTANCE* (1893), I

30. He who is known for an early riser may lie abed till noon.

YIDDISH PROVERBS (1949)

805. REQUEST

See also 791. REFUSAL

1. To be happy with human beings, we should not ask them for what they cannot give.

TRISTAN BERNARD, *L'ENFANT PRODIGUE DU VÉSINET* (1921)

2. Not to ask is not to be denied.

JOHN DRYDEN, *THE HIND AND THE PANTHER* (1687), I.1536

3. The highest price we can pay for anything, is to ask it.

WALTER SAVAGE LANDOR, "ESCHINES AND PHOCION," *IMAGINARY CONVERSATIONS* (1824–53)

4. Even the gods are moved by the voice of entreaty.

OVID, *THE ART OF LOVE* (C. A.D. 8), I, TR. J. LEWIS MAY

5. Never ask of him who has, but of him who wishes you well.

SPANISH PROVERB

RESERVE

See 31. ALOOFNESS; 142. COLDNESS

806. RESIGNATION

See also 287. ENDURANCE; 507. IRREVOCABLENESS; 624. NECESSITY; 799. RENUNCIATION; 937. STOICISM

1. Resignation, not mystic, not detached, but resignation open-eyed, conscious, and informed by love, is the only one of our feelings for which it is impossible to become a sham.

JOSEPH CONRAD, "A FAMILIAR PREFACE," *A PERSONAL RECORD* (1912)

2. We must like what we have when we don't have what we like.

ROGER DE BUSSY-RABUTIN, LETTER TO MME. DE SÉVIGNÉ, MAY 23, 1667

3. Teach us to care and not to care / Teach us to sit still.

T. S. ELIOT, "ASH WEDNESDAY" (1930), I

4. The doctrine of Necessity or Destiny is the doctrine of Toleration.

EMERSON, *JOURNALS,* 1841

5. What cannot be altered must be borne, not blamed.

THOMAS FULLER, M.D., *GNOMOLOGIA* (1732), 5481

6. The mind which renounces, once and for ever, a futile hope, has its compensation in ever-growing calm.

GEORGE GISSING, "SPRING," *THE PRIVATE PAPERS OF HENRY RYECROFT* (1903)

7. Mankind are more disposed to suffer, while evils are sufferable, than to right themselves by abolishing the forms to which they are accustomed.

THOMAS JEFFERSON, *DECLARATION OF INDEPENDENCE,* JULY 4, 1776

8. Happy he who learns to bear what he cannot change!

SCHILLER, "THE SUBLIME" (1793?)

9. It's the great soul that surrenders itself to fate, but a puny degenerate thing that struggles.

SENECA, *LETTERS TO LUCILIUS* (1ST C.), 107.12, TR. E. PHILLIPS BARKER

10. A calm despair, without angry convulsions or reproaches directed at heaven, is the essence of wisdom.

ALFRED DE VIGNY, *JOURNAL D'UN POÈTE* (1832)

RESISTANCE

See 658. OPPOSITION; 786. REBELLION

807. RESOLUTION

See also 225. DECISION; 771. PURPOSE; 867. SELF-DETERMINATION; 1056. WILL

1. We shall go on to the end, we shall fight in France, we shall fight in the seas and oceans, we shall fight with growing confidence and growing strength in the air, we shall defend our island, whatever the cost may be, we shall fight on the beaches, we shall fight on the landing-grounds, we shall fight in the fields and in the streets, we shall fight in the hills; we shall never surrender, and even if, which I do not for a moment believe, this island or a large part of it were subjugated and starving, then our Empire beyond the seas, armed and guarded by the British Fleet, would carry on the struggle, until, in God's good time, the New World, with all its power and might, steps forth to the rescue and the liberation of the Old.

SIR WINSTON CHURCHILL, SPEECH TO BRITISH PARLIAMENT, JUNE 4, 1940

2. Resolve to perform what you ought. Perform without fail what you resolve.

BENJAMIN FRANKLIN, *AUTOBIOGRAPHY* (1791), 2

3. A resolution to avoid an evil is seldom framed till the evil is so far advanced as to make avoidance impossible.

THOMAS HARDY, *FAR FROM THE MADDING CROWD* (1874), 18

4. You can't have a country or a city or a state that's worth a damn unluss you govern within yourself in your day-to-day life.

LEE IACOCCA, *TALKING STRAIGHT* (1988), WITH SONNY KLEINFELD

5. We have more ability than will power, and it is often an excuse to ourselves that we imagine that things are impossible.

LA ROCHEFOUCAULD, *MAXIMS* (1665), TR. KENNETH PRATT

6. Good resolutions are useless attempts to interfere with scientific laws.

OSCAR WILDE, *THE PICTURE OF DORIAN GRAY* (1891), 8

808. RESPECT

See also 14. ADMIRATION; 426. HONORS; 1068. WORSHIP

1. Reverence is a good thing, and part of its value is that the more we revere a man, the more sharply are we struck by anything in him (and there is always much) that is incongruous with his greatness.

MAX BEERBOHM, "LAUGHTER," *AND EVEN NOW* (1920)

2. Reverence makes it possible to be whole, though ignorant. It is the wholeness of understanding.

WENDELL BERRY, "NOTES: UNSPECIALIZING POETRY," *STANDING BY WORDS* (1983)

3. Without feelings of respect, what is there to distinguish men from beasts?

CONFUCIUS, *ANALECTS* (6TH C. B.C.), 2.7, TR. WINBERG CHAI

4. The Porcupine, whom one must Handle, gloved, / May be respected, but is never Loved.

ARTHUR GUITERMAN, *A POET'S PROVERBS* (1924)

5. Man is still a savage to the extent that he has little respect for anything that cannot hurt him.

EDGAR WATSON HOWE, *VENTURES IN COMMON SENSE* (1919), 4.16

6. It is difficult to like those whom we do not esteem; but it is no less so to like those whom we esteem more than ourselves.

LA ROCHEFOUCAULD, *MAXIMS* (1665), TR. KENNETH PRATT

7. We can always make ourselves liked provided we act likable, but we cannot always make ourselves esteemed, no matter what our merits are.

NICOLAS MALEBRANCHE, *TRAITÉ DE LA MORALE* (1867), 11

8. If you have any shame, forbear to pluck the beard of a dead lion.

MARTIAL, *EPIGRAMS* (A.D. 86), 10.90, TR. WALTER C. A. KERR

9. The honor we receive from those that fear us, is not honor; those respects are paid to royalty and not to me.

MONTAIGNE, "OF THE INEQUALITY AMONG US," *ESSAYS* (1580–88), TR. W. C. HAZLITT

10. Concerning great things one should either be silent or speak loftily.

NIETZSCHE, *THE WILL TO POWER* (1888), TR. ANTHONY M. LUDOVICI

809. RESPECTABILITY

See also 749. PROPRIETY

1. Respectability, n. The offspring of a liaison between a bald head and a bank account.

AMBROSE BIERCE, *THE DEVIL'S DICTIONARY* (1881–1911)

2. The world of shabby gentility is like no other; its sacrifices have less logic, its standards are harsher, its relation to reality is dimmer than comfortable property or plain poverty can understand.

MURRAY KEMPTON, "THE SHELTERED LIFE," *PART OF OUR TIME* (1955)

3. The genteel is a mighty catafalque of service-with-a-smile and flattering solicitude smothering every spontaneous movement of thought or feeling.

MARSHALL MCLUHAN, "L'IL ABNER," *THE MECHANICAL BRIDE* (1951)

4. The more things a man is ashamed of, the more respectable he is.

GEORGE BERNARD SHAW, *MAN AND SUPERMAN* (1903), 1

5. No man is inherently respectable, but all women are by nature.

LIN YUTANG, "I LIKE TO TALK WITH WOMEN," *WITH LOVE AND IRONY* (1934–40)

810. RESPONSIBILITY

See also 271. DUTY

1. That which is common to the greatest number has the least care bestowed upon it.

ARISTOTLE, *POLITICS* (4TH C. B.C.), 2.3, TR. BENJAMIN JOWETT

2. Unto whomsoever much is given, of him shall much be required.

Bible, Luke 12:48

3. Responsibility, n. A detachable burden easily shifted to the shoulders of God, Fate, Fortune, Luck or one's neighbor. In the days of astrology it was customary to unload it upon a star.

Ambrose Bierce, *The Devil's Dictionary* (1881–1911)

4. One can pass on responsibility, but not the discretion that goes with it.

Benvenuto Cellini, *Autobiography* (1558–66), tr. George Bull

5. Man must now assume the responsibility for his world. He can no longer shove it off on religious power.

Harvey Cox, *The Secular City* (1966), 10

6. Everybody's business is nobody's business.

English Proverb

7. Man's responsibility increases as that of the gods decreases.

André Gide, *Journals*, Sept. 27, 1940, tr. Justin O'Brien

8. I am inclined to believe that a man may be free to do anything he pleases if only he will accept responsibility for whatever he does.

Ellen Glasgow, *Vein of Iron* (1935)

9. Though the wisdom or virtue of one can very rarely make many happy, the folly or vice of one man often make many miserable.

Samuel Johnson, *Rasselas* (1759), 26

10. To be a man is, precisely, to be responsible.

Saint-Exupéry, *Wind, Sand, and Stars* (1939), 2.2, tr. Lewis Galantière

11. The fault, dear Brutus, is not in our stars, / But in ourselves, that we are underlings.

Shakespeare, *Julius Caesar* (1599–1600), 1.2.140

12. A burden in the bush is worth two on your hands.

James Thurber, "The Hunter and the Elephant," *Fables for Our Time* (1943)

811. REST

See also 446. Idleness; 533. Leisure; 813. Retirement

1. We combat obstacles in order to get repose, and, when got, the repose is insupportable.

Henry Adams, *The Education of Henry Adams* (1907), 29

2. One cannot rest except after steady practice.

George Ade, "The Man Who Was Going to Retire," *Forty Modern Fables* (1901)

3. Too much rest itself becomes a pain.

Homer, *Odyssey* (9th c. b.c.), 15.429, tr. William Broome

4. Nothing gives rest but the sincere search for truth.

Pascal, *Pensées* (1670), 907, tr. W. F. Trotter

5. In all things rest is sweet; there is sur feit / even in honey, even in Aphrodite's lovely flowers.

Pindar, *Odes* (5th c. b.c.), Nemea 7, tr. Richmond Lattimore

6. Rest is the sauce of labor.

Plutarch, "The Education of Children," *Moralia* (c. a.d. 100), tr. Moses Hadas

812. RESTLESSNESS

See also 10. Activity; 456. Impatience; 1040. Waiting

1. A wanderer is man from his birth. / He was born in a ship / On the breast of the river of Time.

Matthew Arnold, "The Future" (1852)

2. Never have I been able to settle in life. Always seated askew, as if on the arm of a chair; ready to get up, to leave.

André Gide, *Journals*, July 14, 1930, tr. Justin O'Brien

3. I would like to sit still for a while but I'm restless you know and sitting still is only an ideal like celibacy and complete cleanliness.

John Steinbeck, *Travels with Charley* (1962)

RESTRAINT

See 598. Moderation; 947. Sufficiency

813. RETIREMENT

See also 446. Idleness; 533. Leisure; 811. Rest

1. Cessation of work is not accompanied by cessation of expenses.

Cato the Elder, *De Agri Cultura* (2nd c. b.c.)

2. Dismiss the old horse in good time, lest he fail in the lists and the spectators laugh.

Horace, *Epistles* (20-c. 8 b.c.), 1.1.8

3. [I]t is one of the enjoyments of retirement that you are able to drift through the day at your own pace,

easy in the knowledge that you have put hard work and achievement behind you.

Kazuo Ishiguro, *An Artist of the Floating World* (1986)

4. I am Retired Leisure. I am to be met with in trim gardens. I am already come to be known by my vacant face and careless gesture, perambulating at no fixed pace nor with any settled purpose. I walk about; not to and from.

Charles Lamb, "The Superannuated Man," *Last Essays of Elia* (1833)

5. Few men of action have been able to make a graceful exit at the appropriate time.

Malcolm Muggeridge, "Twilight of Greatness," *The Most of Malcolm Muggeridge* (1966)

814. RETREAT

See also 300. Escape

1. To withdraw is not to run away, and to stay is no wise action, when there's more reason to fear than to hope.

Cervantes, *Don Quixote* (1605–15), 1.3.9, tr. John Ozell

815. RETRIBUTION

See also 110. Cause and Effect; 176. Consequences; 766. Punishment; 789. Recompense; 817. Revenge

1. He who makes his law a curse, / By his own law shall surely die.

William Blake, "To the Jews," *Jerusalem* (1804–20)

2. There's no need to hang about waiting for the Last Judgement—it takes place every day.

Albert Camus, *The Fall* (1956)

3. And if any mischief follow, then thou shalt give life for life, / Eye for eye, tooth for tooth, hand for hand, foot for foot, / Burning for burning, wound for wound, stripe for stripe.

Bible, Exodus 21:23–25

4. Whatsoever a man soweth, that shall he also reap.

Bible, Galatians 6:7

5. God gives each his due at the time allotted.

Euripides, *Electra* (413 b.c.), tr. John McLean

6. The gods visit the sins of the fathers upon the children.

Euripides, *Phrixus* (c. 412 b.c.), 970, tr. M. H. Morgan

7. He that plants thorns must never expect to gather roses.

Fables of Bidpai (c. 750)

8. Though the mills of God grind slowly, yet they grind exceeding small; / Though with patience He stands waiting, with exactness grinds He all.

Friedrich Von Logau, *Retribution* (1654)

9. Justice divine / Mends not her slowest pace for prayers or cries.

Milton, *Paradise Lost* (1667), 10.858

10. The laws of changeless justice bind / Oppressor and oppressed; / And, close as sin and suffering joined, / We march to Fate abreast.

John Greenleaf Whittier, "At Port Royal" (1862)

11. Jupiter is slow looking into his notebook, but he always looks.

Zenobius, *Sententiae* (2nd c.), 4.11

REVELATION

See 816. Revelation, Divine; 878. Self-Revelation

816. REVELATION, DIVINE

See also 387. God

1. My own mind is the direct revelation which I have from God and far least liable to mistake in telling his will of any revelation.

Emerson, *Journals,* 1831

2. There is a sort of transcendental ventriloquy through which men can be made to believe that something which was said on earth came from heaven.

Georg Christoph Lichtenberg, *Aphorisms* (1764–99), tr. F. H. Hatfield

3. Instead of complaining that God had hidden Himself, you will give Him thanks for having revealed so much of Himself.

Pascal, *Pensées* (1670), 288, tr. W. F. Trotter

4. You go up the mountaintop and all you're gonna get is a great big heavy stone tablet handed to you with a bunch of rules on it.

Robert M. Pirsig, *Zen and the Art of Motorcycle Maintenance* (1974)

817. REVENGE

See also 476. Injury; 789. Recompense; 815. Retribution

1. Men regard it as their right to return evil for evil—and, if they cannot, feel they have lost their liberty.

ARISTOTLE, *NICOMACHEAN ETHICS* (4TH C. B. C.), 5.5, TR. J. A. K. THOMSON

2. A man that studieth revenge keeps his own wounds green, which otherwise would heal and do well.

FRANCIS BACON, "OF REVENGE," *ESSAYS* (1625)

3. In taking revenge, a man is but even with his enemy; but in passing it over, he is superior.

FRANCIS BACON, "OF REVENGE," *ESSAYS* (1625)

4. Since women do most delight in revenge, it may seem but feminine manhood to be vindictive.

SIR THOMAS BROWNE, *CHRISTIAN MORALS* (1716), 3

5. Sweet is revenge—especially to women.

BYRON, *DON JUAN* (1819–24), 1.124

6. "Put your face in the dirt. *Put your face in the dirt!* Do what I say. Put your face in the dirt." He fell forward in the filth.

JOHN CHEEVER, "THE FIVE-FORTY-EIGHT," *THE STORIES OF JOHN CHEEVER* (1980)

7. Just vengeance does not call for punishment.

CORNEILLE, *LE CID* (1636), 2.8, TR. PAUL LANDIS

8. Revenge is a dish that should be eaten cold.

ENGLISH PROVERB

9. This is sweet: to see your foe / perish and pay to justice all he owes.

EURIPIDES, *HERACLES* (C. 422 B.C.), TR. WILLIAM ARROWSMITH

10. Revenge proves its own executioner.

JOHN FORD, *THE BROKEN HEART* (1633), 5.3

11. Revenge is a luscious fruit which you must leave to ripen.

ÉMILE GABORIAU, *FILE 113* (1867), 10

12. It is difficult to fight against anger; for a man will buy revenge with his soul.

HERACLITUS (C. 500 B.C.), QUOTED IN ARISTOTLE'S *POLITICS* (4TH C. B.C.), 5.11, TR. BENJAMIN JOWETT

13. Revenge is always the joy of narrow, / Sick, and petty minds.

JUVENAL, *SATIRES* (C. 100), 13.189, TR. HUBERT CREEKMORE

14. Revenge, at first though sweet, / Bitter ere long back on itself recoils.

MILTON, *PARADISE LOST* (1667), 9.171

15. It is folly to punish your neighbor by fire when you live next door.

PUBLILIUS SYRUS, *MORAL SAYINGS* (1ST C. B.C.), 910, TR. DARIUS LYMAN

16. Heat not a furnace for your foe so hot / That it do singe yourself.

SHAKESPEARE, *HENRY VIII* (1612–13), 1.1.140

17. God will not punish the man / Who makes return for an injury.

SOPHOCLES, *OEDIPUS AT COLONUS* (401 B.C.), TR. ROBERT FITZGERALD

18. [O]ur children are the only people on whom we can safely take revenge for what was done to us.

GLORIA STEINEM, *REVOLUTION FROM WITHIN* (1992)

REVERENCE

See 808. RESPECT; 1068. WORSHIP

818. REVERIE

See also 450. IMAGINATION; 336. FANTASY; 975. THOUGHT

1. To make a prairie it takes a clover and one bee, / One clover, and a bee, / And revery, / The revery alone will do, / If bees are few.

EMILY DICKINSON, *POEMS* (C. 1862–86)

2. Thought is the labour of the intellect, reverie is its pleasure.

VICTOR HUGO, "SAINT DENIS," *LES MISÉRABLES* (1862), 2.1, TR. CHARLES E. WILBOUR

3. Reverie is the groundwork of creative imagination; it is the privilege of the artist that with him it is not as with other men an escape from reality, but the means by which he accedes to it.

W. SOMERSET MAUGHAM, *THE SUMMING UP* (1938), 23

4. What a wee little part of a person's life are his acts and his words! His real life is led in his head, and is known to none but himself.

MARK TWAIN, *AUTOBIOGRAPHY* (1924), V. 1

5. Let us leave every man at liberty to seek into himself and to lose himself in his ideas.

VOLTAIRE, "SOUL," *PHILOSOPHICAL DICTIONARY* (1764)

REVIEWS

See 207. CRITICISM, PROFESSIONAL

819. REVOLUTION

See also 258. DISSENT; 441. ICONOCLASM; 568. MASS MOVEMENTS; 658. OPPOSITION; 786. REBELLION; 801. REPRESSION; 1002. TYRANNY; 1032. VIOLENCE

1. Inferiors revolt in order that they may be equal, and equals that they may be superior.

ARISTOTLE, *POLITICS* (4TH C. B.C.), 5.2, TR. BENJAMIN JOWETT

2. If there be fuel prepared, it is hard to tell whence the spark shall come that shall set it on fire.

FRANCIS BACON, "OF SEDITIONS AND TROUBLES," *ESSAYS* (1625)

3. Revolutions are not made by fate but by men.

JACOB BRONOWSKI, *THE ASCENT OF MAN* (1973)

4. All oppressed people are authorized, whenever they can, to rise and break their fetters.

HENRY CLAY, SPEECH, U.S. HOUSE OF REPRESENTATIVES, MARCH 24, 1818

5. The revolutionary spirit is mighty convenient in this, that it frees one from all scruples as regards ideas.

JOSEPH CONRAD, "A FAMILIAR PREFACE," *A PERSONAL RECORD* (1912)

6. Plots, true or false, are necessary things, / To raise up commonwealths, and ruin kings.

JOHN DRYDEN, *ABSALOM AND ACHITOPHEL* (1681), 1.83

7. The overwhelming pressure of mediocrity, sluggish and indomitable as a glacier, will mitigate the most violent, and depress the most exalted revolution.

T. S. ELIOT, "THE IDEA OF A CHRISTIAN SOCIETY" (1939)

8. Every revolution was first a thought in one man's mind; and when the same thought occurs to another man, it is the key to that era.

EMERSON, "HISTORY," *ESSAYS: FIRST SERIES* (1841)

9. The world is always childish, and with each new gewgaw of a revolution or new constitution that it finds, thinks it shall never cry any more.

EMERSON, *JOURNALS*, 1847

10. The successful revolutionary is a statesman, the unsuccessful one a criminal.

ERICH FROMM, *ESCAPE FROM FREEDOM* (1941), 7

11. The Keynesian Revolution occurred at the moment in history when other change had made it indispensable.

JOHN KENNETH GALBRAITH, *THE NEW INDUSTRIAL STATE* (1967)

12. A non-violent revolution is not a program of seizure of power. It is a program of transformation of relationships, ending in a peaceful transfer of power.

MOHANDAS K. GANDHI, *NON-VIOLENCE IN PEACE AND WAR* (1948), 2.8

13. In troublesome times, nothing is more common than the alliance of audacious vice and turbulent virtue.

PIERRE GAXOTTE, "THÈME ET VARIATIONS," *PROPOS SUR LA LIBERTÉ*

14. Though a revolution may call itself "national," it always marks the victory of a single party.

ANDRÉ GIDE, *JOURNALS*, OCT. 17, 1941, TR. JUSTIN O'BRIEN

15. A great revolution is never the fault of the people, but of the government.

GOETHE, QUOTED IN JOHANN PETER ECKERMANN'S *CONVERSATIONS WITH GOETHE*, JAN. 4, 1824

16. Everywhere revolutions are painful yet fruitful gestations of a people: they shed blood but create light, they eliminate men but elaborate ideas.

MANUEL GONZÁLEZ PRADA, *HORAS DE LUCHA* (1908)

17. A successful revolution establishes a new community. A missed revolution makes irrelevant the community that persists. And a compromised revolution tends to shatter the community that was, without an adequate substitute.

PAUL GOODMAN, *GROWING UP ABSURD* (1960), 11.1

18. Revolution is the festival of the oppressed.

GERMAINE GREER, *THE FEMALE EUNUCH* (1970)

19. The profound revolution manifest in Megalopolis came into existence without the intervention of the masses in the streets.

MICHAEL HARRINGTON, *THE ACCIDENTAL CENTURY* (1966)

20. Not actual suffering but the hope of better things incites people to revolt.

ERIC HOFFER, *THE ORDEAL OF CHANGE* (1964), 10

21. We used to think that revolutions are the cause of change. Actually it is the other way around: change prepares the ground for revolution.

ERIC HOFFER, "A TIME OF JUVENILES," *THE TEMPER OF OUR TIME* (1967), 1

22. When hopes and dreams are loose in the streets, it is well for the timid to lock doors, shutter windows and lie low until the wrath has passed.

ERIC HOFFER, *THE TRUE BELIEVER* (1951), 1.1.5

23. The wind of revolutions is not tractable.

VICTOR HUGO, "SAINT DENIS," *LES MISÉRABLES* (1862), 10.4, TR. CHARLES E. WILBOUR

24. One should never put on one's best trousers to go out to battle for freedom and truth.

HENRIK IBSEN, *AN ENEMY OF THE PEOPLE* (1882), 5

25. The tree of liberty must be refreshed from time to time, with the blood of patriots and tyrants. It is its natural manure.

THOMAS JEFFERSON, LETTER TO COL. WILLIAM S. SMITH, NOV. 13, 1787

26. If the abuse be enormous, nature will rise up, and claiming her original rights, overturn a corrupt political system.

SAMUEL JOHNSON, QUOTED IN BOSWELL'S *LIFE OF SAMUEL JOHNSON,* JULY 6, 1763

27. A revolution requires of its leaders a record of unbroken infallibility; if they do not possess it, they are expected to invent it.

MURRAY KEMPTON, "IT'S TIME TO GO, I HEARD THEM SAY," *PART OF OUR TIME* (1955)

28. Every social war is a battle between the very few on both sides who care and who fire their shots across a crowd of spectators.

MURRAY KEMPTON, "FATHER AND SONS," *PART OF OUR TIME* (1955)

29. We live in a hemisphere whose own revolution has given birth to the most powerful force of the modern age—the search for the freedom and self-fulfillment of man.

JOHN F. KENNEDY, MESSAGE TO THE INTER-AMERICAN ECONOMIC AND SOCIAL CONFERENCE, PUNTA DEL ESTE, URUGUAY, AUG. 5, 1961

30. Revolutionaries are rarely motivated primarily by material considerations—though the illusion that they are persists in the West.

HENRY A. KISSINGER, *AMERICAN FOREIGN POLICY* (1969)

31. To revolutionaries the significant reality is the world which they are fighting to bring about, not the world they are fighting to overcome.

HENRY A. KISSINGER, *AMERICAN FOREIGN POLICY* (1969)

32. It is a quality of revolutions not to go by old lines or old laws; but to break up both, and make new ones.

ABRAHAM LINCOLN, SPEECH, HOUSE OF REPRESENTATIVES, JAN. 12, 1848

33. Women hate revolutions and revolutionists. They like men who are docile, and well-regarded at the bank, and never late at meals.

H. L. MENCKEN, *PREJUDICES: FOURTH SERIES* (1924), 5

34. If obedience is the result of the instinct of the masses, revolt is the result of their thought.

NAPOLEON I, *MAXIMS* (1804–15)

35. Revolt is the violence of an entire people; rebellion the unruliness of an individual or an uprising by a minority; both are spontaneous and blind. Revolution is both planned and spontaneous, a science and an art.

OCTAVIO PAZ, "REVOLT, REVOLUTION, REBELLION," *ALTERNATING CURRENT* (1973)

36. Revolutions are not made: they come. A revolution is as natural a growth as an oak. It comes out of the past. Its foundations are laid far back.

WENDELL PHILLIPS, SPEECH, BOSTON, JAN. 28, 1852

37. We made a revolution in 1917 to make things better, not worse. Since then we have sacrificed one generation after another. We have known nothing but hardship. Now we want to live.

HARRISON E. SALISBURY, *RUSSIA* (1965)

38. Revolution is a transfer of property from class to class.

LEON SAMSON, *THE NEW HUMANISM* (1930), 16

39. Revolutions have never lightened the burden of tyranny: they have only shifted it to another shoulder.

GEORGE BERNARD SHAW, PREFACE, "THE REVOLUTIONIST'S HANDBOOK," *MAN AND SUPERMAN* (1903)

40. In most cases, when the lion, weary of obeying its master, has torn and devoured him, its nerves are pacified and it looks round for another master before whom to grovel.

PAUL VALÉRY, "FLUCTUATIONS ON LIBERTY," *REFLECTIONS ON THE WORLD TODAY* (1931), TR. FRANCIS SCARFE

RICHES

See 1048. WEALTH

820. RIDICULE

See also 4. ABSURDITY; 434. HUMILIATION; 436. HUMOR; 526. LAUGHTER; 893. SHAME

1. The talent of turning men into ridicule, and exposing to laughter those one converses with, is the qualification of little ungenerous tempers.

JOSEPH ADDISON, *THE SPECTATOR* (1711–12), 249

2. To make fun of a person to his face is a brutal way of amusing one's self; be delicate and cunning, and keep your laugh in your sleeve, lest you frighten away your game.

GELETT BURGESS, "THE USE OF FOOLS," *THE ROMANCE OF THE COMMONPLACE* (1916)

3. Mockery is often the result of a poverty of wit.

LA BRUYÈRE, *CHARACTERS* (1688), 5.57

4. Ridicule dishonours more than dishonour.

LA ROCHEFOUCAULD, *MAXIMS* (1665), TR. KENNETH PRATT

5. The most effective way of attacking vice is to expose it to public ridicule. People can put up with rebukes but they cannot bear being laughed at: they are prepared to be wicked but they dislike appearing ridiculous.

MOLIÈRE, PREFACE TO *TARTUFFE* (1664), TR. JOHN WOOD

6. There is no character, howsoever good and fine, but it can be destroyed by ridicule, howsoever poor and witless.

MARK TWAIN, "PUDD'NHEAD WILSON'S CALENDAR: A WHISPER TO THE READER," *PUDD'NHEAD WILSON* (1894)

821. RIDING

1. There is no secret so close as that between a rider and his horse.

ROBERT SMITH SURTEES, *MR. SPONGE'S SPORTING TOUR* (1853), 31

822. RIGHT

See also 174. CONSCIENCE; 227. DEEDS; 299. ERROR; 319. EXPEDIENCY; 393. GOODNESS; 734. PRINCIPLE; 1033. VIRTUE; 1070. WRONGDOING

1. How forcible are right words.

BIBLE, JOB 6:25

2. The humblest citizen of all the land, when clad in the armor of a righteous cause, is stronger than all the hosts of error.

WILLIAM JENNINGS BRYAN, SPEECH, DEMOCRATIC NATIONAL CONVENTION, CHICAGO, JULY 8, 1896

3. You cannot make yourself feel something you do not feel, but you can make yourself do right in spite of your feelings.

PEARL S. BUCK, "MY NEIGHBOR'S SON," *TO MY DAUGHTERS, WITH LOVE* (1967)

4. From a worldly point of view there is no mistake so great as that of being always right.

SAMUEL BUTLER (D. 1902), "HIGGLEDY-PIGGLEDY," *NOTE-BOOKS* (1912)

5. Might and right do differ frightfully from hour to hour; but give them centuries to try it in, they are found to be identical.

THOMAS CARLYLE, *CHARTISM* (1839), 8

6. Be always sure you are right—then go ahead.

DAVID CROCKETT, *AUTOBIOGRAPHY* (1834)

7. Good and bad are but names very readily transferable to that or this; the only right is what is after my constitution; the only wrong what is against it.

EMERSON, "SELF-RELIANCE," *ESSAYS: FIRST SERIES* (1841)

8. What is the freedom of the most free? To do what is right!

GOETHE, *EGMONT* (1788), TR. MICHAEL HAMBURGER

9. We uniformly applaud what is right and condemn what is wrong, when it costs us nothing but the sentiment.

WILLIAM HAZLITT, *CHARACTERISTICS* (1823)

10. Right is right only when entire.

VICTOR HUGO, "MARIUS," *LES MISÉRABLES* (1862), 4.4, TR. CHARLES E. WILBOUR

11. Those who believe that they are exclusively in the right are generally those who achieve something.

ALDOUS HUXLEY, *PROPER STUDIES* (1927)

12. The assailant is often in the right; the assailed is always.

WALTER SAVAGE LANDOR, "JOHN OF GAUNT AND JOANNA OF KENT," *IMAGINARY CONVERSATIONS* (1824–53)

13. I'm armed with more than complete steel—/ The justice of my quarrel.

CHRISTOPHER MARLOWE, *LUST'S DOMINION* (1657), 4.3, ATTRIBUTED TO

14. May God prevent us from becoming "right-thinking men"—that is to say men who agree perfectly with their own police.

THOMAS MERTON, QUOTED IN HIS OBITUARY, *THE NEW YORK TIMES*, DEC. 11, 1968

15. Few sometimes may know, when thousands err.

MILTON, *PARADISE LOST* (1667), 6.148

16. I will follow the right side even to the fire, but excluding the fire if I can.

MONTAIGNE, "OF PROFIT AND HONESTY," *ESSAYS* (1580–88), TR. W. C. HAZLITT

17. He who practices right, but in the hope of acquiring great renown, is very near to vice.

NAPOLEON I, *MAXIMS* (1804–15)

18. To do a great right, do a little wrong.

SHAKESPEARE, *THE MERCHANT OF VENICE* (1596–97), 4.1.216

19. One's belief that one is sincere is not so dangerous as one's conviction that one is right. We all feel we are right; but we felt the same way twenty years ago and today we know we weren't always right.

IGOR STRAVINSKY, *CONVERSATIONS WITH IGOR STRAVINSKY* (1959)

20. Because right is right, to follow right / Were wisdom in the scorn of consequence.

LORD TENNYSON, "OENONE" (1842)

21. It is not desirable to cultivate a respect for the law, so much as for the right.

THOREAU, *CIVIL DISOBEDIENCE* (1849)

22. The Moral Sense teaches us what is right, and how to avoid it—when unpopular.

MARK TWAIN, "THE UNITED STATES OF LYNCHERDOM" (1923)

23. The right is more precious than peace.

WOODROW WILSON, ADDRESS TO CONGRESS, APRIL 2, 1917

823. RIGHTS

See also 297. EQUALITY; 364. FREE SPEECH; 537. LIBERTY; 731. PRESS, FREEDOM OF THE

1. Considered together, the ten amendments in the Bill of Rights outline the most comprehensive protection of individual freedom ever written.

ELLEN ALDERMAN AND CAROLINE KENNEDY, *IN OUR DEFENSE* (1991)

2. In guaranteeing the fundamental right of assembly, the Supreme Court has recognized that protecting individual rights in times of stability and social harmony is easy. It becomes more difficult in times of crisis, but that is precisely when the right to assemble, to speak out, and to disagree with the prevailing orthodoxy must be vigilantly protected.

ELLEN ALDERMAN AND CAROLINE KENNEDY, *IN OUR DEFENSE* (1991)

3. Although it is one of the best known of the rights in the first ten amendments, the right against self-incrimination is also one of the least popular. It is often perceived as a shield for the guilty rather than a shelter for the innocent, the argument being that those who are innocent have nothing to hide and no reason to remain silent.

ELLEN ALDERMAN AND CAROLINE KENNEDY, *IN OUR DEFENSE* (1991)

4. It is fair to judge peoples by the rights they will sacrifice most for.

CLARENCE DAY, *THIS SIMIAN WORLD* (1920), 6

5. An accurate charting of American women's progress through history might look more like a corkscrew tilted slightly to one side, its loops inching closer to the line of freedom with the passage of time—but, like a mathematical curve approaching infinity, never touching its goal.

SUSAN FALUDI, *BACKLASH* (1991)

6. Rights that do not flow from duty well performed are not worth having.

MOHANDAS K. GANDHI, *NON-VIOLENCE IN PEACE AND WAR* (1948), 2.269

7. Wherever there is a human being, I see God-given rights inherent in that being, whatever may be the sex or complexion.

WILLIAM LLOYD GARRISON, *LIFE* (1885–89), V. 3

8. Civil rights took us all by surprise. Every night we'd wait until the news to see what "Dr. King and dem" were doing. It was like watching the Olympics or the World Series when somebody colored was on.

HENRY LOUIS GATES, JR., "PRIME TIME," *COLORED PEOPLE* (1994)

9. He was pursuing the dream of a free country, the dream of a country so vast that each man would have room to bury his dead on his own land.

ELLEN GLASGOW, *VEIN OF IRON* (1935)

10. If the government can set aside some spot for a elk *to be a elk* without being bothered, or a buffalo *to be a buffalo* without being shot down, there ought to be some place where a Negro can be a Negro without being Jim Crowed.

LANGSTON HUGHES, *SIMPLE SPEAKS HIS MIND* (1950)

11. All, too, will bear in mind this sacred principle, that though the will of the majority is in all cases to prevail, that will to be rightful must be reasonable; that the minority possess their equal rights, which

equal law must protect, and to violate would be oppression.

THOMAS JEFFERSON, FIRST INAUGURAL ADDRESS, MARCH 4, 1801

12. I am not so much concerned with the right of everyone to say anything he pleases as I am about our need as a self-governing people to hear everything relevant.

JOHN F. KENNEDY, ADDRESS, NATIONAL CIVIL LIBERTIES CONFERENCE, WASHINGTON, D.C., APRIL 16, 1959

13. In giving rights to others which belong to them, we give rights to ourselves and to our country.

JOHN F. KENNEDY, MESSAGE ON 100TH ANNIVERSARY OF EMANCIPATION PROCLAMATION, WASHINGTON, D.C., SEPT. 22, 1962

14. This nation was founded by men of many nations and backgrounds. It was founded on the principle that all men are created equal, and that the rights of every man are diminished when the rights of one man are threatened.

JOHN F. KENNEDY, TELEVISION ADDRESS, JUNE 11, 1963

15. Let us have faith that right makes might, and in that faith let us to the end do our duty as we understand it.

ABRAHAM LINCOLN, SPEECH, NEW YORK CITY, FEB. 27, 1860

16. They have rights who dare maintain them.

JAMES RUSSELL LOWELL, "THE PRESENT CRISIS" (1844)

17. What men value in this world is not rights but privileges.

H. L. MENCKEN, *MINORITY REPORT* (1956), 36

18. The rights which a man arrogates to himself are relative to the duties which he sets himself, and to the tasks which he feels capable of performing.

NIETZSCHE, *THE WILL TO POWER* (1888), 872, TR. ANTHONY M. LUDOVICI

19. Unless we see a job as part of every citizen's right to autonomy and personal fulfillment, we will continue to be vulnerable to someone else's idea of what "need" is, and whose "need" counts the most.

GLORIA STEINEM, "THE IMPORTANCE OF WORK," *OUTRAGEOUS ACTS AND EVERYDAY REBELLIONS* (1983)

20. The greatest achievement of the civil-rights movement is that it has restored the dignity of indignation.

FREDERIC WERTHAM, *A SIGN FOR CAIN: AN EXPLORATION IN HUMAN VIOLENCE* (1966)

21. A right is worth fighting for only when it can be put into operation.

WOODROW WILSON, ADDRESS, CHATTANOOGA, TENN., AUG. 31, 1910

RISING

See 73. BED; 605. MORNING

RITUAL

See 114. CEREMONY

RIVALRY

See 155. COMPETITION

824. RIVERS

See also 853. SEA; 1046. WATER

1. If the voice of the brook was not the first song of celebration, it must have been at least an obbligato for that event.

HAL BORLAND, "THE SONG OF THE BROOK—MARCH 25," *SUNDIAL OF THE SEASONS* (1964)

2. The Mississippi River carries the mud of thirty states and two provinces 2,000 miles south to the delta and deposits 500 million tons of it there every year. The business of the Mississippi, which it will accomplish in time, is methodically to transport all of Illinois to the Gulf of Mexico.

CHARLES KURALT, *A LIFE ON THE ROAD* (1990)

3. The Nile seems to be impervious to change. It flows on now, as it always flowed, perpetually renewing itself from year to year and from century to century, a never-ending flood of warm, life-giving water that spans half Africa from the Equator to the Mediterranean, and it is still the mightiest river on earth.

ALAN MOOREHEAD, *THE WHITE NILE* (1971)

4. Rivers are roads which move, and which carry us whither we desire to go.

PASCAL, *PENSÉES* (1670), 17, TR. W. F. TROTTER

5. The only real river I knew was hardly more than a brook. It spilled through a tumbledown mill at the bottom of our road, opened into a little trouty pool, then ran on through water meadows over graveled shallows into Fakenham [England], where it slowed and deepened, gathering strength for the long drifts across muddy flatlands to Norwich and the North Sea.

JONATHAN RABAN, *OLD GLORY* (1981)

6. All this piling up of one technology on top of another—railroad on steamboat, interstate highway on railroad, hydroelectric dam on watermill—had reduced the Mississippi from a wonder of nature to this sluggish canal on the wrong side of the tracks.

JONATHAN RABAN, *OLD GLORY* (1981)

7. It [the Mississippi] belonged to the same category as vandalized public housing projects, junked automobiles and dead cats. I was appalled. No one would have dared do such a thing to the river in my head.

JONATHAN RABAN, *OLD GLORY* (1981)

8. I chatter, chatter, as I flow, / To join the brimming river, / For men may come and men may go, / But I go on forever.

LORD TENNYSON, "THE BROOK" (1887)

9. The Hudson River is like old October and tawny Indians in their camping places long ago; it is like long pipes and old tobacco; it is like cool depths and opulence; it is like the shimmer of liquid green on summer days.

THOMAS WOLFE, *OF TIME AND THE RIVER* (1935), 58

ROBBERY

See 934. STEALING

825. ROLE-PLAYING

See also 45. APPEARANCE; 732. PRETENSION

1. Play out the game, act well your part, and if the gods have blundered, we will not.

EMERSON, *JOURNALS,* 1856

2. We accept every person in the world as that for which he gives himself out, only he must give himself out for something. We can put up with the unpleasant more easily than we can endure the insignificant.

GOETHE, *ELECTIVE AFFINITIES* (1809), 23

3. Perhaps one never seems so much at one's ease as when one has to play a part.

OSCAR WILDE, *THE PICTURE OF DORIAN GRAY* (1891), 15

826. ROMANCE

See also 198. COURTSHIP; 827. ROMANTICISM

1. Why one man rather than another? It was odd. You find yourself involved with a fellow for life just because he was the one you met when you were nineteen.

SIMONE DE BEAUVOIR, *LES BELLES IMAGES* (1966), TR. PATRICK O'BRIAN (1968)

2. Romance dies hard, because its very nature is to want to live.

ANDRÉ DUBUS, "OF ROBIN HOOD AND WOMANHOOD," *BROKEN VESSELS* (1991)

3. Romance only dies with life. No pair of pincers will ever pull it out of us. But there is a spurious sentiment which cannot resist the unexpected and the incongruous and the grotesque.

E.M. FORSTER, *WHERE ANGELS FEAR TO TREAD* (1920)

4. Romance, like alcohol, should be enjoyed but must not be allowed to become necessary.

EDGAR Z. FRIEDENBERG, "EMOTIONAL DEVELOPMENT IN ADOLESCENCE," *THE VANISHING ADOLESCENT* (1959)

5. [Romance] was a game, like bridge, in which you said things instead of playing cards. Like bridge you had to pretend you were playing for money or playing for some stakes.

ERNEST HEMINGWAY, *A FAREWELL TO ARMS* (1929)

6. Following each divorce, he discovered anew that unmarried a man had to take women places: out to restaurants, for walks in the park, to museums and the opera and the movies—not only had to go to the movies but afterwards had to discuss them.

PHILIP ROTH, *THE ANATOMY LESSON* (1983)

7. Nothing spoils a romance so much as a sense of humour in the woman.

OSCAR WILDE, *A WOMAN OF NO IMPORTANCE* (1893), I

827. ROMANTICISM

1. It is not irregular hours or irregular diet that make the romantic life.

EMERSON, *JOURNALS,* 1840

2. It may be that, while we plodding realists go on, for ever preoccupied with our daily chores, abstracting a microscopic pleasure from each microscopic duty, your true romantic has the truer vision, and beholds, afar off, in all its lurid splendour and terrible proportions, the piquant adventure we call life.

WILLIAM MCFEE, "THE CRUSADERS," *HARBOURS OF MEMORY* (1921)

3. Is not this the true romantic feeling—not to desire to escape life, but to prevent life from escaping you?

THOMAS WOLFE, QUOTED IN ANDREW TURNBULL'S *THOMAS WOLFE* (1968)

828. ROUTINE

See also 406. HABIT; 661. ORDER

1. Men fall into a routine when they are tired and slack: it has all the appearance of activity with few of its burdens.

Walter Lippmann, "Revolution and Culture," *A Preface to Politics* (1914)

2. It is the leisured, I have noticed, who rebel the most at an interruption of routine.

Phyllis McGinley, "A Garland of Kindness," *The Province of the Heart* (1959)

3. After you've done a thing the same way for two years, look it over carefully. After five years, look at it with suspicion. And after ten years, throw it away and start all over.

Alfred Edward Perlman, *The New York Times,* July 3, 1958

4. Routine is the god of every social system; it is the seventh heaven of business, the essential component in the success of every factory, the ideal of every statesman. The social machine should run like clockwork.

Alfred North Whitehead, *Adventures in Ideas* (1933), 6

5. If the human being is condemned and restricted to perform the same functions over and over again, he will not even be a good ant, not to mention a good human being.

Norbert Wiener, *The Human Use of Human Beings* (1954), 3

829. ROYALTY

See also 196. Court, Royal; 520. Kings

1. Royalty does good and is badly spoken of.

Antisthenes (5th–4th c. b.c.), quoted in Diogenes Laertius' *Lives and Opinions of Eminent Philosophers* (3rd c. a.d.), tr. R. D. Hicks

2. A prince is a gr-reat man in th' ol' counthry, but he niver is as gr-reat over there as he is here [in America].

Finley Peter Dunne, "Prince Henry's Reception," *Observations by Mr. Dooley* (1902)

830. RUDENESS

See also 197. Courtesy; 488. Insult; 961. Tact

1. Except in streetcars one should never be unnecessarily rude to a lady.

O. Henry, "The Gold That Glittered," *Strictly Business* (1910)

2. Rudeness is the weak man's imitation of strength.

Eric Hoffer, *The Passionate State of Mind* (1954), 241

3. Folly often goes beyond her bounds, but impudence knows none.

Ben Jonson, "Explorata," *Timber* (1640)

4. A man must have very eminent qualities to hold his own without being polite.

La Bruyère, *Characters* (1688), 5.32, tr. Henri Van Laun

5. If somebody tells you an obviously untrue story, on the Continent you would remark, "You are a liar, Sir, and a rather dirty one at that." In England you just say, "Oh, is that so?" Or "That's rather an unusual story, isn't it?"

George Mikes, *How to Be an Alien* (1946)

6. Spiritual strength and passion, when accompanied by bad manners, only provoke loathing.

Nietzsche, *The Will to Power* (1888), tr. Anthony M. Ludovici

RUINS

See 42. Antiquity

831. RULERS

See also 61. Authority; 395. Government; 520. Kings; 531. Leadership; 730. Presidency

1. Every ruler is harsh whose rule is new.

Aeschylus, *Prometheus Bound* (c. 478 b.c.), tr. David Grene

2. If men think that a ruler is religious and has a reverence for the Gods, they are less afraid of suffering injustice at his hands.

Aristotle, *Politics* (4th c. b.c.), 5.11, tr. Benjamin Jowett

3. Princes are like heavenly bodies, which cause good or evil times, and which have much veneration, but no rest.

Francis Bacon, "Of Empire," *Essays* (1625)

4. Those who see and observe kings, heroes, and statesmen, discover that they have headaches, indigestion, humors and passions, just like other people; every one of which in their turns determine their wills in defiance of their reason.

Lord Chesterfield, *Letters to His Son,* Dec. 5, 1749

5. Power educates the potentate.

Emerson, "Power," *The Conduct of Life* (1860)

6. The subject's love is the king's best guard.

THOMAS FULLER, M.D., *GNOMOLOGIA* (1732), 4773

7. He who would rule must hear and be deaf, see and be blind.

GERMAN PROVERB

8. The art of governing is a great *métier,* requiring the whole man, and it is therefore not well for a ruler to have too strong tendencies for other affairs.

GOETHE, QUOTED IN JOHANN PETER ECKERMANN'S *CONVERSATIONS WITH GOETHE,* FEB. 18, 1831

9. To appear at church every Sunday; to look down upon, and let himself be looked at for an hour by the congregation, is the best means of becoming popular which can be recommended to a young sovereign.

GOETHE, QUOTED IN JOHANN PETER ECKERMANN'S *CONVERSATIONS WITH GOETHE,* APRIL 2, 1829

10. Whom hatred frights, / Let him not dream on sovereignty.

BEN JONSON, *SEJANUS HIS FALL* (1603), 2.2

11. He that would govern others, first should be / The master of himself.

PHILIP MASSINGER, *THE BONDMAN* (C. 1624), 1.3

12. We owe subjection and obedience to all our kings, whether good or bad, alike, for that has respect unto their office; but as to esteem and affection, these are only due to their virtue.

MONTAIGNE, "THAT OUR AFFECTIONS CARRY THEMSELVES BEYOND US," *ESSAYS* (1580–88), TR. W. C. HAZLITT

13. Rigorous authority and justice are the kindness of kings.

NAPOLEON I, *MAXIMS* (1804–15)

14. To rule is not so much a question of the heavy hand as the firm seat.

JOSÉ ORTEGA Y GASSET, *THE REVOLT OF THE MASSES* (1930), 14

15. Better have as king a vulture advised by swans than a swan advised by vultures.

PANCHATANTRA (C. 5TH C.), 1, TR. ARTHUR W. RYDER

16. The power of kings is founded on the reason and on the folly of the people, and specially on their folly.

PASCAL, *PENSÉES* (1670), 330, TR. W. F. TROTTER

17. Where princes are concerned, a man who is able to do good is as dangerous and almost as criminal as a man who intends to do evil.

CARDINAL DE RETZ, *MÉMOIRES* (1718)

18. Not the least of the qualities that go into the making of a great ruler is the ability of letting others serve him.

CARDINAL RICHELIEU, *POLITICAL TESTAMENT* (1687), 1.4

19. If you have but a single ruler, you lie at the discretion of a master who has no reason to love you: and if you have several, you must bear at once their tyranny and their divisions.

ROUSSEAU, *A DISCOURSE ON POLITICAL ECONOMY* (1758), TR. G. D. H. COLE

20. One can't reign and be innocent.

LOUIS ANTOINE LÉON DE SAINT-JUST, *DISCOURS À LA CONVENTION,* NOV. 13, 1792

21. Uneasy lies the head that wears a crown.

SHAKESPEARE, *2 HENRY IV* (1597–98), 3.1.31

22. Within the hollow crown / That rounds the mortal temples of a king / Keeps Death his court.

SHAKESPEARE, *RICHARD II* (1595–96), 3.2.160

23. To know nor faith, nor love, nor law; to be / Omnipotent but friendless is to reign.

SHELLEY, *PROMETHEUS UNBOUND* (1818–19), 2.4

24. Ill can he rule the great that cannot reach the small.

EDMUND SPENSER, *THE FAERIE QUEENE* (1596), 5.2.43

25. A doubtful throne is ice on summer seas.

LORD TENNYSON, "THE COMING OF ARTHUR," *IDYLLS OF THE KING* (1869)

832. RULES

See also 585. METHOD

1. In reading and writing, you cannot lay down rules until you have learnt to obey them. Much more so in life.

MARCUS AURELIUS, *MEDITATIONS* (2ND C.), 11.29, TR. MAXWELL STANIFORTH

2. A technical objection is the first refuge of a scoundrel.

HEYWOOD BROUN, "'JAM-TOMORROW' PROGRESSIVES," *NEW REPUBLIC,* DEC. 15, 1937

3. No rule is so general, which admits not some exception.

ROBERT BURTON, *THE ANATOMY OF MELANCHOLY* (1621), 1.2.2.3

4. There is no useful rule without an exception.

THOMAS FULLER, M.D., *GNOMOLOGIA* (1732), 4925

5. The important thing is to abide by the rule of threes. Either you see a woman three times in quick succession and then never again, or you maintain relations over the years but make sure that the rendezvous are at least three weeks apart.

MILAN KUNDERA, *THE UNBEARABLE LIGHTNESS OF BEING* (1984)

6. Any fool can make a rule / And every fool will mind it.

THOREAU, *JOURNAL,* FEB. 3, 1860

833. RUMORS

See also 394. GOSSIP; 846. SCANDAL

1. Rumor is a pipe / Blown by surmises, jealousies, conjectures.

SHAKESPEARE, INDUCTION TO *2 HENRY IV* (1597–98), 15

2. Rumour doth double, like the voice and echo, / The numbers of the feared.

SHAKESPEARE, *2 HENRY IV* (1597–98), 3.1.97

3. Rumor goes forth at once, Rumor than whom / No other speedier evil thing exists; / She thrives by rapid movement, and acquires / Strength as she goes; small at the first from fear, / She presently uplifts herself aloft, / And stalks upon the ground and hides her head / Among the clouds.

VERGIL, *AENEID* (30–19 B.C.), 4.173, TR. T. H. DELABERE-MAY

834. RUSSIA AND RUSSIANS

1. I cannot forecast to you the action of Russia. It is a riddle wrapped in a mystery inside an enigma.

SIR WINSTON CHURCHILL, RADIO BROADCAST, OCT. 1, 1939

2. Don't you forget what's divine in the Russian soul—and that's resignation.

JOSEPH CONRAD, *UNDER WESTERN EYES* (1911), 1.1

3. The Russians train; they do not dare educate.

MAX LERNER, "FOUR FALLACIES OF OUR SCHOOLS," *THE UNFINISHED COUNTRY* (1959), 2

4. Ideas in modern Russia are machine-cut blocks coming in solid colors; the nuance is outlawed, the interval walled up, the curve grossly stepped.

VLADIMIR NABOKOV, "COMMENTARY," *PALE FIRE* (1962), 681

5. Not a single reform effort in Russia has ever been completed.

BORIS YELTSIN, *THE STRUGGLE FOR RUSSIA* (1994), TR. CATHERINE A. FITZPATRICK

6. We [Russians] are already living, not getting ready to live.

BORIS YELTSIN, *THE STRUGGLE FOR RUSSIA* (1994), TR. CATHERINE A. FITZPATRICK

S

835. SABBATH

1. Remember the sabbath day, to keep it holy. Six days shalt thou labour, and do all thy work: But the seventh day is the sabbath of the Lord thy God: in it thou shalt not do any work.

Bible, Exodus 20:8–10

2. Sabbath, n. A weekly festival having its origin in the fact that God made the world in six days and was arrested on the seventh.

Ambrose Bierce, *The Devil's Dictionary* (1881–1911)

3. The [Jewish] Sabbath was not intended to be simply a desert of prohibitions, but rather an oasis for moral restoration and seemly pleasure—one was to eat, drink, even be merry.

Israel Shenker, *Coat of Many Colors* (1985)

836. SACRAMENT

See also 959. Symbols and Symbolism

1. I mean by this word Sacrament an outward and visible sign of an inward and spiritual grace.

Offices of Instruction, *The Book of Common Prayer* (1549, 1789, 1928)

837. SACRIFICE

See also 565. Martyrs and Martyrdom; 888. Services

1. Greater love hath no man than this, that a man lay down his life for his friends.

Bible, John 15:13

2. Sacrificers are not the ones to pity. The ones to pity are those they sacrifice.

Elizabeth Bowen, *The Death of the Heart* (1938), 1.6

3. Drown not thyself to save a drowning man.

Thomas Fuller, M.D., *Gnomologia* (1732), 1340

4. The very act of sacrifice magnifies the one who sacrifices himself to the point where his sacrifice is much more costly to humanity than would have been the loss of those for whom he is sacrificing himself. But in his abnegation lies the secret of his grandeur.

André Gide, *Journals*, June 23, 1931, tr. Justin O'Brien

5. One unfortunate maiden after another beloved of the gods had had to kill her child secretly or be killed herself. The best such a one could expect was exile, and many women thought that worse than death.

Edith Hamilton, *Mythology* (1940)

6. Where else, in a non-totalitarian country, but in the political profession is the individual expected to sacrifice all—including his own career—for the national good?

John F. Kennedy, *Profiles in Courage* (1956)

7. Sacrifice may be a flower that virtue will pluck on its road, but it was not to gather this flower that virtue set forth on its travels.

Maurice Maeterlinck, *Wisdom and Destiny* (1898), 65, tr. Alfred Sutro

8. Only he can understand what a farm is, what a country is, who shall have sacrificed part of himself to his farm or country.

Saint-Exupéry, *Flight to Arras* (1942), 23, tr. Lewis Galantière

9. Nothing so much enhances a good as to make sacrifices for it.

George Santayana, *The Sense of Beauty* (1896), 26

10. Self-sacrifice enables us to sacrifice other people without blushing.

George Bernard Shaw, "Maxims for Revolutionists," *Man and Superman* (1903)

11. Too long a sacrifice / Can make a stone of the heart.

William Butler Yeats, "Easter 1916" (1916)

838. SADISM

See also 567. Masochism; 209. Cruelty

1. We know well enough when we're being unjust and despicable. But we don't restrain ourselves

because we experience a certain pleasure, a primitive sort of satisfaction in moments like that.

Ugo Betti, *Landslide* (1936), 2, tr. G. H. McWilliam

2. Pleasure is sweetest when 'tis paid for by another's pain.

Ovid, *The Art of Love* (c. A.D. 8), 1, tr. J. Lewis May

3. Tears gratify a savage nature, they do not melt it.

Publilius Syrus, *Moral Sayings* (1st c. B.C.), 163, tr. Darius Lyman

SADNESS

See 1011. Unhappiness

SAFETY

See 856. Security

839. SAILING

See also 895. Ships and Boats

1. Land was created to provide a place for steamers to visit.

Brooks Atkinson, "January 20," *Once Around the Sun* (1951)

2. Ports are necessities, like postage stamps or soap, / but they seldom seem to care what impressions they make.

Elizabeth Bishop, "Arrival at Santos," *Questions of Travel* (1965)

3. Nowhere else than upon the sea do the days, weeks, and months fall away quicker into the past. They seem to be left astern as easily as the light air-bubbles in the swirls of the ship's wake.

Joseph Conrad, *The Mirror of the Sea* (1906), 2

4. There is nothing more enticing, disenchanting, and enslaving than the life at sea.

Joseph Conrad, *Lord Jim* (1900), 2

5. The happiest hour a sailor sees / Is when he's down / At an inland town, / With his Nancy on his knees, yo ho! / And his arm around her waist!

W. S. Gilbert, *The Mikado* (1885), 1

6. Being in a ship is being in a jail, with the chance of being drowned.

Samuel Johnson, quoted in Boswell's *Life of Samuel Johnson*, March 16, 1759

840. SAINTS AND SAINTHOOD

See also 565. Martyrs and Martyrdom; 927. Spirituality

1. I'm an alcoholic. I'm a drug addict. I'm homosexual. I'm a genius. Of course, I could be all four of these dubious things and still be a saint. But I shonuf ain't no saint yet, nawsuh.

Truman Capote, *Music for Chameleons* (1980)

2. Many of the insights of the saint stem from his experience as a sinner.

Eric Hoffer, *The Passionate State of Mind* (1954), 9

3. Those we call saints rebelled against an outmoded and inadequate form of God on the basis of their new insights into divinity.

Rollo May, *The Courage to Create* (1975)

4. We are content to place a statue of Francis of Assisi in the middle of a bird bath and let the whole business of the Saints go at that.

C. Kilmer Myers, *The New York Times*, March 19, 1962

5. He [Gandhi] was not one of those saints who are marked out by their phenomenal piety from childhood onwards, nor one of the other kind who forsake the world after sensational debaucheries.

George Orwell, "Reflections on Gandhi," *A Collection of Essays* (1954)

6. Many people genuinely do not wish to be saints, and it is probable that some who achieve or aspire to sainthood have never felt much temptation to be human beings.

George Orwell, "Reflections on Gandhi," *Shooting an Elephant* (1950)

7. No doubt alcohol, tobacco, and so forth, are things that a saint must avoid, but sainthood is also a thing that human beings must avoid.

George Orwell, "Reflections on Gandhi," *Shooting an Elephant* (1950)

8. Saints should always be judged guilty until they are proved innocent.

George Orwell, "Reflections on Gandhi," *Shooting an Elephant* (1950)

9. Grace is indeed needed to turn a man into a saint; and he who doubts it does not know what a saint or a man is.

Pascal, *Pensées* (1670), 508, tr. W. F. Trotter

10. It is easier to make a saint out of a libertine than out of a prig.

George Santayana, *The Life of Reason: Reason in Religion* (1905–06), 11

11. Sanctity and genius are as rebellious as vice.

GEORGE SANTAYANA, *LITTLE ESSAYS* (1920), 49

12. It's the bad that's in the best of us / Leaves the saint so like the rest of us.

ARTHUR STRINGER, "HUMANITY" (1912)

13. The only difference between the saint and the sinner is that every saint has a past, and every sinner has a future.

OSCAR WILDE, *A WOMAN OF NO IMPORTANCE* (1893), 3

841. SALVATION

See also 596. MISSIONARIES; 900. SIN

1. Strait is the gate, and narrow is the way, which leadeth unto life, and few there be that find it.

BIBLE, MATTHEW 7:14

2. As life draws nearer to its end, I feel more and more clearly that it will not matter in the least, at the last day, what form of religion a man has professed—nay, that many who have never even heard of Christ, will in that day find themselves saved by His blood.

LEWIS CARROLL, *THE LETTERS OF LEWIS CARROLL*, ED. MORTON N. COHEN (1979)

3. Salvation, the prophets tell us, is preconditioned by repentance. The redeeming act of God waits upon man's initiative.

ABBA EBAN, *MY PEOPLE* (1968)

4. Souls are not saved in bundles.

EMERSON, "WORSHIP," *THE CONDUCT OF LIFE* (1860)

5. What is most contrary to salvation is not sin but habit.

CHARLES PÉGUY, "SINNERS AND SAINTS," *BASIC VERITIES* (1943), TR. ANN AND JULIAN GREEN

842. SANITY

See also 413. HEALTH; 559. MADNESS; 627. NEUROSIS

1. Our health is our sound relation to external objects; our sympathy with external being.

EMERSON, *JOURNALS*, 1836

2. The criterion of mental health is not one of individual adjustment to a given social order, but a universal one, valid for all men, of giving a satisfactory answer to the problem of human existence.

ERICH FROMM, *THE SANE SOCIETY* (1955), 2

3. Sanity is a madness put to good uses; waking life is a dream controlled.

GEORGE SANTAYANA, *INTERPRETATIONS OF POETRY AND RELIGION* (1900)

4. I detest "love lyrics." I think one of the causes of bad mental health in the United States is that people have been raised on "love lyrics."

FRANK ZAPPA, *THE REAL FRANK ZAPPA BOOK* (1989), WITH PETER OCCHIOGROSSO

843. SARCASM

See also 1061. WIT

1. Sarcasm: the last refuge of modest and chaste-souled people when the privacy of their soul is coarsely and intrusively invaded.

DOSTOYEVSKY, *NOTES FROM UNDERGROUND* (1864), 2.4, TR. CONSTANCE GARNETT

844. SATIRE

See also 1061. WIT

1. One man's pointlessness is another's barbed satire.

FRANKLIN P. ADAMS, *NODS AND BECKS* (1944)

2. Satire is not a social dynamite. But it is a social indicator: it shows that new men are knocking at the door.

JACOB BRONOWSKI, *THE ASCENT OF MAN* (1973)

3. By rights, satire is a lonely and introspective occupation, for nobody can describe a fool to the life without much patient self-inspection.

FRANK MOORE COLBY, "SIMPLE SIMON," *THE COLBY ESSAYS* (1926), V. 1

4. Satirists gain the applause of others through fear, not through love.

WILLIAM HAZLITT, *CHARACTERISTICS* (1823), 72

5. Satire should, like a polished razor keen, / Wound with a touch that's scarcely felt or seen.

LADY MARY WORTLEY MONTAGU, "TO THE IMITATOR OF THE FIRST SATIRE OF HORACE, BOOK II" (1733)

6. Satire's my weapon, but I'm too discreet / To run amuck, and tilt at all I meet.

ALEXANDER POPE, *IMITATIONS OF HORACE* (1733–38), 2.1.69

7. Satire is a sort of glass, wherein beholders do generally discover everybody's face but their own.

JONATHAN SWIFT, PREFACE TO *THE BATTLE OF THE BOOKS* (1704)

8. If satire is to be effective, the audience must be aware of the thing satirized.

Gore Vidal, *Rocking the Boat* (1962)

845. SATISFACTION

See also 186. Contentment; 238. Desires; 947. Sufficiency

1. Satisfaction in a job may compensate for low wages. On the other hand, higher wages may compensate for a disagreeable job.

Milton Friedman & Rose Friedman, *Free to Choose* (1980)

2. From the satisfaction of desire there may arise, accompanying joy and as it were sheltering behind it, something not unlike despair.

André Gide, *The Counterfeiters* (1925), 1.7, tr. Dorothy Bussy

3. So whatever else has happened, I am figgerin this: I can always look back an say, at least I ain't led no hum-drum life.

Winston Groom, *Forrest Gump* (1986)

4. The sovereign source of melancholy is repletion. Need and struggle are what excite and inspire us; our hour of triumph is what brings the void.

William James, "Is Life Worth Living?" *The Will to Believe* (1896)

5. When we reside in an attic we enjoy a supper of fried fish and stout. When we occupy the first floor it takes an elaborate dinner at the Continental to give us the same amount of satisfaction.

Jerome K. Jerome, "On Furnished Apartments," *The Idle Thoughts of an Idle Fellow* (1889)

6. He is well paid that is well satisfied.

Shakespeare, *The Merchant of Venice* (1596–97), 4.1.415

7. The journey, not the arrival, matters; the voyage, not the landing.

Paul Theroux, *The Old Patagonian Express* (1979)

8. In the world there are only two tragedies. One is not getting what one wants, and the other is getting it.

Oscar Wilde, *Lady Windermere's Fan* (1892), 3

SAVAGERY

See 70. Barbarism

846. SCANDAL

See also 394. Gossip; 833. Rumors

1. Love and scandal are the best sweeteners of tea.

Henry Fielding, *Love in Several Masques* (1728), 2.11

2. A lie has no leg, but a scandal has wings.

Thomas Fuller, M.D., *Gnomologia* (1732), 263

3. Every age has a keyhole to which its eye is pasted. Spicy court-memoirs, the lives of gallant ladies, recollections of an ex-nun, a monk's confession, an atheist's repentance, true-to-life accounts of prostitution and bastardy gave our ancestors a penny peep into the forbidden room.

Mary McCarthy, "My Confession," in *The Art of the Personal Essay* (1994), ed. Phillip Lopate

4. Greatest scandal waits on greatest state.

Shakespeare, *The Rape of Lucrece* (1594), 1006

5. There never was a scandalous tale without some foundation.

Richard Brinsley Sheridan, *The School for Scandal* (1777), 2.2

847. SCAPEGOAT

See also 405. Guilt; 565. Martyrs and Martyrdom

1. For some high-profile men in trouble, women, especially feminist women, became the all-purpose scapegoats—charged with crimes that often descended into the absurd.

Susan Faludi, *Backlash* (1991)

2. The scapegoat has always had the mysterious power of unleashing man's ferocious pleasure in torturing, corrupting, and befouling.

François Mauriac, "Child Martyrs," *Second Thoughts* (1961), tr. Adrienne Foulke

848. SCHOLARS AND SCHOLARSHIP

See also 279. Education; 522. Knowledge; 532. Learning; 924. Specialists; 965. Teaching

1. Learning is the property of those who fear to do disagreeable things.

Pietro Aretino, letter to the Cardinal of Ravenna, Aug. 29, 1537, tr. Samuel Putnam

2. To spend too much time in studies is sloth; to use them too much for ornament is affectation; to make judgment wholly by their rules is the humor of a scholar.

Francis Bacon, "Of Studies," *Essays* (1625)

3. Erudition, n. Dust shaken out of a book into an empty skull.

AMBROSE BIERCE, *THE DEVIL'S DICTIONARY* (1881–1911)

4. Never did I think that the university was properly ministerial to the society around it. Rather I thought and think that society is ministerial to the university, and I bless a society that tolerates and supports an eternal childhood for some, a childhood whose playfulness can in turn be a blessing to society.

ALLAN BLOOM, *THE CLOSING OF THE AMERICAN MIND* (1987)

5. University convention submerges nature. It issues licenses, and hunting without one is forbidden.

ALLAN BLOOM, *THE CLOSING OF THE AMERICAN MIND* (1987)

6. Things take indeed a wondrous turn / When learned men do stoop to learn.

BERTOLT BRECHT, *GALILEO* (1938; 1947), 5, TR. CHARLES LAUGHTON

7. We want a Society for the Suppression of Erudite Research and the Decent Burial of the Past. The ghosts of the dead past want quite as much laying as raising.

SAMUEL BUTLER (D. 1902), "CASH AND CREDIT," *NOTE-BOOKS* (1912)

8. When nature exceeds culture, we have the rustic. When culture exceeds nature, we have the pedant.

CONFUCIUS, *ANALECTS* (6TH C. B.C.), 6.16, TR. WINBERG CHAI

9. A great man will find a great subject, or which is the same thing, make any subject great.

EMERSON, *JOURNALS,* 1833

10. A scholar is a man with this inconvenience, that, when you ask him his opinion of any matter, he must go home and look up his manuscripts to know.

EMERSON, *JOURNALS,* 1855

11. How we hate this solemn Ego that accompanies the learned, like a double, wherever he goes.

EMERSON, *JOURNALS* 1839

12. The office of the scholar is to cheer, to raise, and to guide men by showing them facts amidst appearances.

EMERSON, *THE AMERICAN SCHOLAR* (1837)

13. In truth man is made rather to eat ices than to pore over old texts.

ANATOLE FRANCE, *THE CRIME OF SYLVESTRE BONNARD* (1881), 1, TR. LAFCADIO HEARN

14. Tim was so learned that he could name a horse in nine languages: so ignorant that he bought a cow to ride on.

BENJAMIN FRANKLIN, *POOR RICHARD'S ALMANACK* (1732–57)

15. The esteem or approval of fellow scholars serves very much the same function that monetary reward does in the economic market.

MILTON FRIEDMAN & ROSE FRIEDMAN, *FREE TO CHOOSE* (1980)

16. Economists, on the whole, think well of what they do themselves and much less well of what their professional colleagues do.

JOHN KENNETH GALBRAITH, *THE NEW INDUSTRIAL STATE* (1967)

17. It is the vice of scholars to suppose that there is no knowledge in the world but that of books.

WILLIAM HAZLITT, "ON THE CONDUCT OF LIFE," *LITERARY REMAINS* (1836)

18. Learning is the knowledge of that which none but the learned know.

WILLIAM HAZLITT, "ON THE IGNORANCE OF THE LEARNED," *TABLE TALK* (1821–22)

19. The humblest painter is a true scholar; and the best of scholars—the scholar of nature.

WILLIAM HAZLITT, "ON THE PLEASURE OF PAINTING," *TABLE TALK* (1821–22)

20. The world's great men have not commonly been great scholars, nor its great scholars great men.

OLIVER WENDELL HOLMES, SR., *THE AUTOCRAT OF THE BREAKFAST TABLE* (1858), 6

21. Pedantry is the dotage of knowledge.

HOLBROOK JACKSON, *THE ANATOMY OF BIBLIOMANIA* (1930–31)

22. Life is surely given us for higher purposes than to gather what our ancestors have wisely thrown away, and to learn what is of no value but because it has been forgotten.

SAMUEL JOHNSON, *THE RAMBLER* (1750–52), 121

23. Two evils, of almost equal weight, may befall the man of erudition: never to be listened to, and to be listened to always.

WALTER SAVAGE LANDOR, "EPICURUS, LEONTION, AND TERNISSA," *IMAGINARY CONVERSATIONS* (1824–53)

24. The ordinary man is ruined by the flesh lusting against the spirit; the scholar by the spirit lusting too much against the flesh.

GEORG CHRISTOPH LICHTENBERG, *APHORISMS* (1764–99), TR. H. HATFIELD

25. The mind of the scholar, if you would have it large and liberal, should come in contact with other minds. It is better that his armor should be somewhat bruised by rude encounters even, than hang for ever rusting on the wall.

LONGFELLOW, *HYPERION* (1839), 1.8

26. Don't appear so scholarly, pray. Humanize your talk, and speak to be understood. Do you think a Greek name gives more weight to your reasons?

MOLIÈRE, *THE CRITIQUE OF THE SCHOOL FOR WIVES* (1663), 6, TR. DONALD M. FRAME

27. Everything that's prose isn't verse and everything that isn't verse is prose. Now you see what it is to be a scholar!

MOLIÈRE, *THE WOULD-BE GENTLEMAN* (1670), 3, TR. JOHN WOOD

28. Difficulty is a coin the learned make use of like jugglers, to conceal the inanity of their art.

MONTAIGNE, "APOLOGY FOR RAIMOND DE SEBONDE," *ESSAYS* (1580–88), TR. W. C. HAZLITT

29. This is ever the test of the scholar: whether he allows intellectual fastidiousness to stand between him and the great issues of his time.

JOHN MORLEY, "EMERSON," *CRITICAL MISCELLANIES* (1871–1908)

30. Abraham Lincoln was on the side of the social scientists when he said, "God must have loved the people of lower and middle socioeconomic status, because he made such a multiplicity of them."

EDWIN NEWMAN, *STRICTLY SPEAKING* (1974)

31. The range of human knowledge today is so great that we're all specialists and the distance between specializations has become so great that anyone who seeks to wander freely among them almost has to forego closeness with the people around him.

ROBERT M. PIRSIG, *ZEN AND THE ART OF MOTORCYCLE MAINTENANCE* (1974)

32. The idea that the majority of students attend a university for an education independent of the degree and grades is a little hypocrisy everyone is happier not to expose.

ROBERT M. PIRSIG, *ZEN AND THE ART OF MOTORCYCLE MAINTENANCE* (1974)

33. Scholarship is polite argument.

PHILIP RIEFF, *NEW YORK HERALD TRIBUNE,* JAN. 1, 1961

34. The scholar is early acquainted with every department of the impossible.

JOHN RUSKIN, REVIEW OF LORD LINDSAY'S *SKETCHES OF THE HISTORY OF CHRISTIAN ART*

35. A learned man is an idler who kills time with study.

GEORGE BERNARD SHAW, "MAXIMS FOR REVOLUTIONISTS," *MAN AND SUPERMAN* (1903)

36. In Jewish tradition, death-defying devotion to scholarship was the stuff of saintliness.

ISRAEL SHENKER, *COAT OF MANY COLORS* (1985)

37. This is the great vice of academicism, that it is concerned with ideas rather than with thinking.

LIONEL TRILLING, "THE SENSE OF THE PAST," *THE LIBERAL IMAGINATION* (1950)

849. SCIENCE

See also 641. NUCLEAR POWER; 850. SCIENCE AND RELIGION; 921. SPACE; 966. TECHNOLOGY; 974. THEORY

1. The quick harvest of applied science is the usable process, the medicine, the machine. The shy fruit of pure science is Understanding.

LINCOLN BARNETT, *LIFE,* JAN. 9, 1950

2. Every judgment in science stands on the edge of error, and is personal.

JACOB BRONOWSKI, *THE ASCENT OF MAN* (1973)

3. One aim of the physical sciences has been to give an exact picture of the material world. One achievement of physics in the twentieth century has been to prove that that aim is unattainable.

JACOB BRONOWSKI, *THE ASCENT OF MAN* (1973)

4. There's always wan encouragin' thing about th' sad scientific facts that come out ivry week in th' papers. They're usually not thrue.

FINLEY PETER DUNNE, "ON THE DESCENT OF MAN," *MR. DOOLEY ON MAKING A WILL* (1919)

5. Science is the attempt to make the chaotic diversity of our sense-experience correspond to a logically uniform system of thought.

EINSTEIN, *OUT OF MY LATER YEARS* (1950), 14

6. The whole of science is nothing more than a refinement of everyday thinking.

EINSTEIN, *OUT OF MY LATER YEARS* (1950), 13.1

7. 'Tis a short sight to limit our faith in laws to those of gravity, of chemistry, of botany, and so forth.

EMERSON, "WORSHIP," THE CONDUCT OF LIFE (1860)

8. In place of science, the Eskimo has only magic to bridge the gap between what he can understand and what is not known. Without magic, his life would be one long panic.

PETER FARB, *MAN'S RISE TO CIVILIZATION* (1968)

9. Scientist alone is true poet he gives us the moon / he promises the stars he'll make us a new universe if it comes to that.

ALLEN GINSBERG, "POEM ROCKET," *KADDISH AND OTHER POEMS* (1961)

10. As soon as any one belongs to a narrow creed in science, every unprejudiced and true perception is gone.

GOETHE, QUOTED IN JOHANN PETER ECKERMANN'S *CONVERSATIONS WITH GOETHE,* MAY 18, 1824

11. The whole history of science has been the gradual realization that events do not happen in an arbitrary manner, but that they reflect a certain underlying order, which may or may not be divinely inspired.

STEPHEN W. HAWKING, *A BRIEF HISTORY OF TIME* (1988)

12. Science is the knowledge of consequences, and dependence of one fact upon another.

THOMAS HOBBES, *LEVIATHAN* (1651), 1.5

13. Astronomers work always with the past; because light takes time to move from one place to another, they see things as they were, not as they are.

NEALE E. HOWARD, *THE TELESCOPE HANDBOOK AND STAR ATLAS* (1967), 3

14. Science is nothing but trained and organized common sense.

THOMAS HENRY HUXLEY, "THE METHOD OF ZADIG" (1878)

15. The great tragedy of Science—the slaying of a beautiful hypothesis by an ugly fact.

THOMAS HENRY HUXLEY, "BIOGENESIS AND ABIOGENESIS" (1870)

16. Science herself consults her heart when she lays it down that the infinite ascertainment of fact and correction of false belief are the supreme goods for man.

WILLIAM JAMES, TITLE ESSAY, *THE WILL TO BELIEVE* (1896)

17. Let both sides seek to invoke the wonders of science instead of its terrors. Together let us explore the stars, conquer the deserts, eradicate disease, tap the ocean depths, and encourage the arts and commerce.

JOHN F. KENNEDY, INAUGURAL ADDRESS, JAN. 20, 1961

18. The means by which we live have outdistanced the ends for which we live. Our scientific power has outrun our spiritual power. We have guided missiles and misguided men.

MARTIN LUTHER KING, JR., *STRENGTH TO LOVE* (1963), 7.3

19. Nominally a great age of scientific inquiry, ours has actually become an age of superstition about the infallibility of science; of almost mystical faith in its nonmystical methods; above all ... of external verities; of traffic-cop morality and rabbit-test truth.

LOUIS KRONENBERGER, *COMPANY MANNERS* (1954), 1.4

20. Science has always promised two things not necessarily related—an increase first in our powers, second in our happiness or wisdom, and we have come to realize that is the first and less important of the two promises which it has kept most abundantly.

JOSEPH WOOD KRUTCH, "THE DISILLUSION WITH THE LABORATORY," *THE MODERN TEMPER* (1929)

21. Though many have tried, no one has ever yet explained away the decisive fact that science, which can do so much, cannot decide what it ought to do.

JOSEPH WOOD KRUTCH, "THE LOSS OF CONFIDENCE," *THE MEASURE OF MAN* (1954)

22. Science itself is a humanist in the sense that it doesn't discriminate between human beings, but it is also morally neutral. It is no better or worse than the ethos with and for which it is used.

MAX LERNER, "MANIPULATING LIFE," IN THE *NEW YORK POST,* JAN. 24, 1968

23. In science, all facts, no matter how trivial or banal, enjoy democratic equality.

MARY MCCARTHY, "THE FACT IN FICTION," *ON THE CONTRARY* (1961)

24. It is proper to the role of the scientist that he not merely find new truth and communicate it to his fellows, but that he teach, that he try to bring the most honest and intelligible account of new knowledge to all who will try to learn.

J. ROBERT OPPENHEIMER, "PROSPECTS IN THE ARTS AND SCIENCES," *FIFTY GREAT ESSAYS* (1964)

25. It is not merely the truth of science that makes it beautiful, but its simplicity.

WALKER PERCY, "FROM FACT TO FICTION," *SIGNPOSTS IN A STRANGE LAND* (1991)

26. Give me an underground laboratory, half a dozen atom-smashers, and a beautiful girl in a diaphanous veil waiting to be turned into a chimpanzee, and I care not who writes the nation's laws.

S.J. PERELMAN, *THE MOST OF S.J. PERELMAN* (1958)

27. The major producer of the social chaos, the indeterminacy of thought and values that rational knowledge is supposed to eliminate, is none other than science itself.

ROBERT M. PIRSIG, *ZEN AND THE ART OF MOTORCYCLE MAINTENANCE* (1974)

28. Science is built of facts the way a house is built of bricks; but an accumulation of facts is no more science than a pile of bricks is a house.

HENRI POINCARÉ, *LA SCIENCE ET L'HYPOTHÈSE* (1902)

29. The simplest schoolboy is now familiar with truths for which Archimedes would have sacrificed his life.

ERNEST RENAN, *SOUVENIRS D'ENFANCE ET DE JEUNESSE* (1883)

30. In art nothing worth doing can be done without genius; in science even a very moderate capacity can contribute to a supreme achievement.

BERTRAND RUSSELL, "SCIENCE AND CULTURE," *MYSTICISM AND LOGIC* (1917)

31. Science, by itself, cannot supply us with an ethic. It can show us how to achieve a given end, and it may show us that some ends cannot be achieved.

BERTRAND RUSSELL, "THE SCIENCE TO SAVE US FROM SCIENCE," *THE NEW YORK TIMES MAGAZINE,* MARCH 19, 1950

32. Science is a way of thinking much more than it is a body of knowledge. Its goal is to find out how the world works, to seek what regularities there may be, to penetrate to the connections of things—from subatomic particles, which may be the constituents of all matter, to living organisms, the human social community, and thence to the cosmos as a whole.

CARL SAGAN, *BROCA'S BRAIN: REFLECTIONS ON THE ROMANCE OF SCIENCE* (1979)

33. People must understand that science is inherently neither a potential for good nor for evil. It is a potential to be harnessed by man to do his bidding.

GLENN T. SEABORG, ASSOCIATED PRESS INTERVIEW WITH ALTON BLAKESLEE, SEPT. 29, 1964

34. The true scientist never loses the faculty of amazement. It is the essence of his being.

HANS SELYE, *NEWSWEEK,* MARCH 31, 1958

35. Science is always simple and always profound. It is only the half-truths that are dangerous.

GEORGE BERNARD SHAW, *THE DOCTOR'S DILEMMA* (1913), 1

36. Science is the great antidote to the poison of enthusiasm and superstition.

ADAM SMITH, *THE WEALTH OF NATIONS* (1776), 5.3

37. The truth is, that those who have never entered upon scientific pursuits know not a tithe of the poetry by which they are surrounded.

HERBERT SPENCER, *EDUCATION: INTELLECTUAL, MORAL AND PHYSICAL* (1861)

38. Science when well digested is nothing but good sense and reason.

STANISLAUS I OF POLAND, *MAXIMS* (C. 18TH C.), 43

39. Science has zipped the atom open in a dozen places, it can read the scrawlings on the Rosetta stone as glibly as a literary critic explains Hart Crane, but it doesn't know anything about playwrights.

JAMES THURBER, "ROAMING IN THE GLOAMING," *COLLECTING HIMSELF* (1989)

40. Science is the most intimate school of resignation and humility, for it teaches us to bow before the seemingly most insignificant of facts.

MIGUEL DE UNAMUNO, "FAITH, HOPE, AND CHARITY," *TRAGIC SENSE OF LIFE* (1913), TR. J. E. CRAWFORD FLITCH

41. Scientific discovery consists in the interpretation for our own convenience of a system of existence which has been made with no eye to our convenience at all.

NORBERT WIENER, *THE HUMAN USE OF HUMAN BEINGS* (1954), 7

42. Sweet is the lore which Nature brings; / Our meddling intellect / Mis-shapes the beauteous forms of things:— / We murder to dissect.

WILLIAM WORDSWORTH, "THE TABLES TURNED" (1798)

850. SCIENCE AND RELIGION

See also 797. RELIGION; 849. SCIENCE

1. We know that Jesus could not have ascended to heaven because there is no physical heaven anywhere in the universe. Even ascending at the speed of light, Jesus would still be in the galaxy.

JOSEPH CAMPBELL, *THE POWER OF MYTH* (1988)

2. "Faith" is a fine invention / When Gentlemen can *see*— / But *Microscopes* are prudent / In an Emergency.

EMILY DICKINSON, POEM (C. 1860)

3. Science without religion is lame, religion without science is blind.

EINSTEIN, "SCIENCE AND RELIGION," *OUT OF MY LATER YEARS* (1950)

4. Don't set out to teach theism from your natural history.... You spoil both.

EMERSON, *JOURNALS*, 1857

5. The religion that is afraid of science dishonors God and commits suicide.

EMERSON, *JOURNALS*, 1831

6. Science investigates; religion interprets. Science gives man knowledge which is power; religion gives man wisdom which is control.

MARTIN LUTHER KING, JR., *STRENGTH TO LOVE* (1963), 1.1

7. The effort to reconcile science and religion is almost always made, not by theologians, but by scientists unable to shake off altogether the piety absorbed with their mother's milk.

H. L. MENCKEN, *MINORITY REPORT* (1956), 232

8. Religion will not regain its old power until it can face change in the same spirit as does science. Its principles may be eternal, but the expression of those principles requires continual development.

ALFRED NORTH WHITEHEAD, *SCIENCE AND THE MODERN WORLD* (1925), 12

9. Religions die when they are proved to be true. Science is the record of dead religions.

OSCAR WILDE, "PHRASES AND PHILOSOPHIES FOR THE USE OF THE YOUNG" (1891)

10. An undevout astronomer is mad.

EDWARD YOUNG, *NIGHT THOUGHTS* (1742–46), 9.771

SCORN

See 185. CONTEMPT

851. SCOTSMEN

1. A Scotchman must be a very sturdy moralist who does not love Scotland better than truth.

SAMUEL JOHNSON, *JOURNEY TO THE HEBRIDES* (1775)

852. SCRATCHING

1. Scratching is one of nature's sweetest gratifications, and nearest at hand.

MONTAIGNE, "OF EXPERIENCE," *ESSAYS* (1580–88), TR. W. C. HAZLITT

2. One bliss for which / There is no match / Is when you itch / To up and scratch.

OGDEN NASH, "TABOO TO BOOT," *VERSES FROM 1929 ON* (1959)

3. If you are with the quality, or at a funeral, or trying to go to sleep when you ain't sleepy—if you are anywheres where it won't do for you to scratch, why you will itch all over in upwards of a thousand places.

MARK TWAIN, *THE ADVENTURES OF HUCKLEBERRY FINN* (1884), 2

853. SEA

See also 347. FISH; 824. RIVERS; 839. SAILING; 895. SHIPS AND BOATS; 1046. WATER

1. The seas are the heart's blood of the earth. Plucked up and kneaded by the sun and the moon, the tides are systole and diastole of earth's veins.

HENRY BESTON, "THE HEADLONG WAVE," *THE OUTERMOST HOUSE* (1928)

2. All the rivers run into the sea; yet the sea is not full; unto the place from whence the rivers come, thither they return again.

BIBLE, ECCLESIASTES 1:7

3. Little islands are all large prisons: one cannot look at the sea without wishing for the wings of a swallow.

SIR RICHARD BURTON, *WANDERINGS IN WEST AFRICA* (1863)

4. Roll on, thou deep and dark blue Ocean—roll! / Ten thousand fleets sweep over thee in vain; / Man marks the earth with ruin—his control / Stops with the shore.

BYRON, *CHILDE HAROLD'S PILGRIMAGE* (1812–18), 4.179

5. It is a curious situation that the sea, from which life first arose, should now be threatened by the activities of one form of that life. But the sea, though changed in a sinister way, will continue to exist; the threat is rather to life itself.

RACHEL CARSON, PREFACE TO REVISED EDITION OF *THE SEA AROUND US* (1950)

6. For all that has been said of the love that certain natures (on shore) have professed to feel for it, for all the celebrations it has been the object of in prose and song, the sea has never been friendly to man. At most it has been the accomplice of human restlessness.

JOSEPH CONRAD, *THE MIRROR OF THE SEA* (1906), 35

7. Some of us, regarding the ocean with understanding and affection, have seen it looking old, as if the

immemorial ages had been stirred up from the undisturbed bottom of ooze. For it is a gale of wind that makes the sea look old.

JOSEPH CONRAD, *THE MIRROR OF THE SEA* (1906), 22

8. The sea—this truth must be confessed—has no generosity. No display of manly qualities—courage, hardihood, endurance, faithfulness—has ever been known to touch its irresponsible consciousness of power.

JOSEPH CONRAD, *THE MIRROR OF THE SEA* (1906), 36

9. The sea pronounces something, over and over, in a hoarse whisper; I cannot quite make it out.

ANNIE DILLARD, "TEACHING A STONE TO TALK," *TEACHING A STONE TO TALK* (1982)

10. Every time we walk along a beach some ancient urge disturbs us so that we find ourselves shedding shoes and garments or scavenging among seaweed and whitened timbers like the homesick refugees of a long war.

LOREN EISELEY, "THE HIDDEN TEACHER," *THE STAR THROWER* (1978)

11. To Gold, the smell of the sea at Sheepshead Bay was a powerful call to clams on the half shell, shrimp, lobster or broiled flounder or bass.

JOSEPH HELLER, *GOOD AS GOLD* (1979)

12. The ocean doesn't care about you. It makes your boat feel tiny. The oceans are great promoters of religion, or at least of humility—but not in everyone.

TRACY KIDDER, *THE SOUL OF A NEW MACHINE* (1981)

13. Implacable I, the implacable Sea; / Implacable most when most I smile serene— / Pleased, not appeased, by myriad wrecks in me.

HERMAN MELVILLE, "PEBBLES," *JOHN MARR AND OTHER SAILORS* (1888)

14. Consider the sea's listless chime: / Time's self it is, made audible.

DANTE GABRIEL ROSSETTI, "THE SEA LIMITS" (1850)

15. 'Tis said, fantastic ocean doth enfold / The likeness of whate'er on land is seen.

WILLIAM WORDSWORTH, "FISH-WOMEN.—ON LANDING AT CALAIS" (1821)

854. SEASONS

See also 778. RAIN; 911. SNOW; 1050. WEATHER

1. It is the middle and pure height and whole of summer and a summer night, the held breath, of a planet's year; high shored sleeps the crested tide: what day of the month I do not know, which day of the week I am not sure, far less what hour of the night.

JAMES AGEE, *LET US NOW PRAISE FAMOUS MEN* (1941)

2. Let us love winter, for it is the spring of genius.

PIETRO ARETINO, LETTER TO AGOSTINO RICCHI, JULY 10, 1537, TR. SAMUEL PUTNAM

3. The quality of life, which in the ardour of spring was personal and sexual, becomes social in midsummer.

HENRY BESTON, "THE YEAR AT HIGH TIDE," *THE OUTERMOST HOUSE* (1928)

4. Here comes February, a little girl with her first valentine, a red bow in her windblown hair, a kiss waiting on her lips, a tantrum just back of her laughter.

HAL BORLAND, "FEBRUARY–FEBRUARY 1," *SUNDIAL OF THE SEASONS* (1964)

5. March is a tomboy with tousled hair, a mischievous smile, mud on her shoes and a laugh in her voice.

HAL BORLAND, "MARCH–MARCH 1," *SUNDIAL OF THE SEASONS* (1964)

6. No Winter lasts forever, no Spring skips its turn. April is a promise that May is bound to keep, and we know it.

HAL BORLAND, "A PROMISE—APRIL 29," *SUNDIAL OF THE SEASONS* (1964)

7. October is the fallen leaf, but it is also a wider horizon more clearly seen. It is the distant hills once more in sight, and the enduring constellations above them once again.

HAL BORLAND, "AUTUMN IS FOR UNDERSTANDING—OCTOBER 25," *SUNDIAL OF THE SEASONS* (1964)

8. Summer ends, and Autumn comes, and he who would have it otherwise would have high tide always and a full moon every night.

HAL BORLAND, "AUTUMN ON THE DOORSTEP—SEPTEMBER 13," *SUNDIAL OF THE SEASONS* (1964)

9. Autumn arrives in the early morning, but spring at the close of a winter day.

ELIZABETH BOWEN, *THE DEATH OF THE HEART* (1938), 2.1

10. It is in this unearthly first hour of spring twilight that earth's almost agonized livingness is most felt. This hour is so dreadful to some people that they hurry indoors and turn on the lights.

ELIZABETH BOWEN, *THE DEATH OF THE HEART* (1938), 2.1

11. The lonely season in lonely lands, when fled / Are half the birds, and mists lie low, and the sun / Is rarely seen, nor strayeth far from his bed; / The short days pass unwelcomed one by one.

ROBERT BRIDGES, "NOVEMBER," *NEW POEMS* (1899)

12. Autumn wins you best by this, its mute / Appeal to sympathy for its decay.

ROBERT BROWNING, *PARACELSUS* (1835), I

13. The melancholy days are come, the saddest of the year, / Of wailing winds, and naked woods, and meadows brown and sere.

WILLIAM CULLEN BRYANT, "THE DEATH OF THE FLOWERS" (1825)

14. Long stormy spring-time, wet contentious April, winter chilling the lap of very May; but at length the season of summer does come.

THOMAS CARLYLE, *CHARTISM* (1839), 8

15. Hard is the heart that loveth nought / In May.

CHAUCER, *THE ROMAUNT OF THE ROSE* (C. 1370)

16. Spring never is Spring unless it comes too soon.

G. K. CHESTERTON, "THE GARDENER AND THE GUINEA," *A MISCELLANY OF MEN* (1912)

17. It was one of those March days when the sun shines hot and the wind blows cold: when it is summer in the light, and winter in the shade.

CHARLES DICKENS, *GREAT EXPECTATIONS* (1860–1861)

18. April is the cruellest month, breeding / Lilacs out of the dead land, mixing / Memory and desire, stirring / Dull roots with spring rain.

T. S. ELIOT, "THE WASTE LAND" (1922), I

19. I should like to enjoy this summer flower by flower, as if it were to be the last one for me.

ANDRÉ GIDE, *JOURNALS,* MAY 18, 1930, TR. JUSTIN O'BRIEN

20. Honest winter, snow-clad and with the frosted beard, I can welcome not uncordially; but that long deferment of the calendar's promise, that weeping gloom of March and April, that bitter blast outraging the honour of May—how often has it robbed me of heart and hope.

GEORGE GISSING, "SPRING," *THE PRIVATE PAPERS OF HENRY RYECROFT* (1903)

21. There is no season when such pleasant and sunny spots may be lighted on, and produce so pleasant an effect on the feelings, as now in October.

NATHANIEL HAWTHORNE, *AMERICAN NOTE-BOOKS,* OCT. 7, 1841

22. Every mile is two in winter.

GEORGE HERBERT, *JACULA PRUDENTUM* (1651)

23. Sweet spring, full of sweet days and roses, / A box where sweets compacted lie.

GEORGE HERBERT, "VIRTUE," 3, *THE TEMPLE* (1633)

24. Summer is when we believe, all of a sudden, that if we just walked out the back door and kept on going long enough and far enough we would reach the Rocky Mountains.

EDWARD HOAGLAND, "A YEAR AS IT TURNS," *THE TUGMAN'S PASSAGE* (1982)

25. The changing year's successive plan / Proclaims mortality to man.

HORACE, *ODES* (23-C. 15 B.C.), 4.7

26. Nobody can keep spring out of Harlem. I stuck my head out the window this morning and spring kissed me bang in the face.

LANGSTON HUGHES, *SIMPLE SPEAKS HIS MIND* (1950)

27. Summer was made to give you a taste of what hell is like. Winter was made for landladies to charge high rents and keep cold radiators and make a fortune off of poor tenants.

LANGSTON HUGHES, *SIMPLE SPEAKS HIS MIND* (1950)

28. Season of mists and mellow fruitfulness, / Close bosom-friend of the maturing sun.

KEATS, "TO AUTUMN" (1819)

29. August creates as she slumbers, replete and satisfied.

JOSEPH WOOD KRUTCH, "AUGUST," *THE TWELVE SEASONS* (1949)

30. In our hearts those of us who know anything worth knowing know that in March a new year begins, and if we plan any new leaves, it will be when the rest of Nature is planning them too.

JOSEPH WOOD KRUTCH, "MARCH," *THE TWELVE SEASONS* (1949)

31. No price is set on the lavish summer; / June may be had by the poorest comer.

JAMES RUSSELL LOWELL, PRELUDE TO PART I, "THE VISION OF SIR LAUNFAL" (1848)

32. What is so rare as a day in June? / Then, if ever, come perfect days; / Then Heaven tries the earth if it be in tune, / And over it softly her warm ear lays.

JAMES RUSSELL LOWELL, PRELUDE TO PART I, "THE VISION OF SIR LAUNFAL" (1848)

33. Wag the world how it will, / Leaves must be green in Spring.

HERMAN MELVILLE, "MALVERN HILL," *BATTLEPIECES AND ASPECTS OF THE WAR* (1866)

34. April / Comes like an idiot, babbling and strewing flowers.

EDNA ST. VINCENT MILLAY, "SPRING," *SECOND APRIL* (1921)

35. Winter is cold-hearted, / Spring is yea and nay, / Autumn is a weather-cock / Blown every way. / Summer days for me / When every leaf is on its tree.

CHRISTINA ROSSETTI, "SUMMER" (1862)

36. November's sky is chill and drear, / November's leaf is red and sear.

SIR WALTER SCOTT, *MARMION* (1808), I, INTRODUCTION

37. Rough winds do shake the darling buds of May, / And summer's lease hath all too short a date.

SHAKESPEARE, *SONNETS* (1609), 18.3

38. Sing a song of seasons! / Something bright in all! / Flowers in the Summer, / Fires in the Fall.

ROBERT LOUIS STEVENSON, "AUTUMN FIRES" (1885)

39. For man, autumn is a time of harvest, of gathering together. For nature, it is a time of sowing, of scattering abroad.

EDWIN WAY TEALE, *AUTUMN ACROSS AMERICA* (1956), 14

40. How sad would be November if we had no knowledge of the spring!

EDWIN WAY TEALE, "NOVEMBER 21," *CIRCLE OF THE SEASONS* (1953)

41. The world's favorite season is the spring. All things seem possible in May.

EDWIN WAY TEALE, *NORTH WITH THE SPRING* (1951), 3

42. A hush is over everything— / Silent as women wait for love, / The world is waiting for the spring.

SARA TEASDALE, "CENTRAL PARK AT DUSK," *HELEN OF TROY* (1911)

43. In the spring a young man's fancy lightly turns to thoughts of love.

LORD TENNYSON, "LOCKSLEY HALL" (1842)

44. Spring is come home with her world-wandering feet, / And all things are made young with young desires.

FRANCIS THOMPSON, "FROM THE NIGHT OF FOREBEING" (1897)

45. Summer set lip to earth's bosom bare, / And left the flushed print in a poppy there.

FRANCIS THOMPSON, "THE POPPY" (1891)

46. In a pleasant spring morning all men's sins are forgiven.

THOREAU, "SPRING," *WALDEN* (1854)

47. Children hold spring so tightly in their brown fists—just as grownups, who are less sure of it, hold it in their hearts.

E.B. WHITE, "A REPORT IN SPRING," *ESSAYS OF E. B. WHITE* (1977)

48. Caught Summer is always an imagined time. / Time gave it, yes, but time out of any mind. / There must be prime / In the heart to beget that season, to reach past rain and find / Riding the palest days / Its perfect blaze.

RICHARD WILBUR, "MY FATHER PAINTS THE SUMMER," *THE BEAUTIFUL CHANGES* (1947)

49. Hot summer has exhausted her intent / To the last rose and roundelay and seed. / No leaf has changed, and yet these leaves now read / Like a love-letter that's no longer meant.

RICHARD WILBUR, "TWO QUATRAINS FOR FIRST FROST," *ADVICE TO A PROPHET* (1961)

50. [H]e had heard an inarticulate promise: he had been pierced by Spring, that sharp knife.

THOMAS WOLFE, *LOOK HOMEWARD, ANGEL* (1929)

51. All things on earth point home in old October: sailors to sea, travellers to walls and fences, hunters to field and hollow and the long voice of the hounds, the lover to the love he has forsaken.

THOMAS WOLFE, *OF TIME AND THE RIVER* (1935), 39

52. Spring, the cruelest and fairest of the seasons, will come again. And the strange and buried men will come again, in flower and leaf the strange and buried men will come again, and death and the dust will never come again, for death and the dust will die.

THOMAS WOLFE, *LOOK HOMEWARD, ANGEL* (1929), 37

855. SECRETS

See also 169. CONFIDENCES

1. [W]e can never know the origins of *the* universe. The deepest secrets are the ones that keep themselves.

JOHN D. BARROW, *THE ORIGIN OF THE UNIVERSE* (1994)

2. To know that one has a secret is to know half the secret itself.

HENRY WARD BEECHER, *PROVERBS FROM PLYMOUTH PULPIT* (1887)

3. Little secrets are commonly told again, but great ones generally kept.

LORD CHESTERFIELD, *LETTERS TO HIS SON*, SEPT. 13, 1748

4. A woman only obliges a man to secrecy, that she may have the pleasure of telling herself.

WILLIAM CONGREVE, *LOVE FOR LOVE* (1695), 1.1

5. In the mind and nature of a man a secret is an ugly thing, like a hidden physical defect.

ISAK DINESEN, "OF HIDDEN THOUGHTS AND OF HEAVEN," *LAST TALES* (1957)

6. Nothing is so burdensome as a secret.

FRENCH PROVERB

7. Would you know secrets? Look for them in grief or pleasure.

THOMAS FULLER, M.D., *GNOMOLOGIA* (1732), 5828

8. He that communicates his secret to another makes himself that other's slave.

BALTASAR GRACIÁN, *THE ART OF WORLDLY WISDOM* (1647), 237, TR. JOSEPH JACOBS

9. Many a deep secret that cannot be pried out by curiosity can be drawn out by indifference.

SYDNEY J. HARRIS, *ON THE CONTRARY* (1962), 7

10. At no time are people so sedulously careful to keep their trifling appointments, attend to their ordinary occupations, and thus put a commonplace aspect on life, as when conscious of some secret that if suspected would make them look monstrous in the general eye.

NATHANIEL HAWTHORNE, *THE MARBLE FAUN* (1860), 20

11. We don't know each other's secrets quite so well as we flatter ourselves we do. We don't always know our own secrets as well as we might.

OLIVER WENDELL HOLMES, SR., *THE POET AT THE BREAKFAST TABLE* (1872), 6

12. How can we expect another to keep our secret if we have been unable to keep it ourselves?

LA ROCHEFOUCAULD, *MAXIMS* (1665), TR. KENNETH PRATT

13. A good many men and women want to get possession of secrets just as spendthrifts want to get money—for circulation.

GEORGE DENNISON PRENTICE, *PRENTICEANA* (1860)

14. None can be so true to your secret as yourself.

SA'DI, *GULISTAN* (1258), 8.10, TR. JAMES ROSS

15. Few secret undertakings ever did any nation any good.

ARTHUR M. SCHLESINGER, JR., *THE IMPERIAL PRESIDENCY* (1973)

16. There are no secrets except the secrets that keep themselves.

GEORGE BERNARD SHAW, *BACK TO METHUSELAH* (1921), 3

17. It always hurts when you lose a secret.

ELIE WIESEL, *THE TESTAMENT* (1981), TR. MARION WIESEL

SECT

See 674. PARTISANSHIP

856. SECURITY

See also 115. CERTAINTY; 229. DEFENSE; 482. INSECURITY

1. The eternal God is thy refuge, and underneath are the everlasting arms.

BIBLE, DEUTERONOMY 33:27

2. Uncertainty and expectation are the joys of life. Security is an insipid thing, and the overtaking and possessing of a wish, discovers the folly of the chase.

WILLIAM CONGREVE, *LOVE FOR LOVE* (1695), 4.3

3. Nothing's as good as holding on to safety.

EURIPIDES, *THE PHOENICIAN WOMEN* (C. 411–409 B.C.), TR. ELIZABETH WYCKOFF

4. Our military plans should be based on the assumption of unpredictability, rather than on carefully drawn, static models of the world.

JAMES FALLOWS, *NATIONAL DEFENSE* (1981)

5. They that can give up essential liberty to obtain a little temporary safety deserve neither liberty nor safety.

BENJAMIN FRANKLIN, (ATTRIB.), *AN HISTORICAL REVIEW OF PENNSYLVANIA* (1759)

6. Monopoly or the full control of supply, and hence of price, by a single firm was the ultimate security. But there were many very habitable half-way houses.

JOHN KENNETH GALBRAITH, *THE AFFLUENT SOCIETY* (1958)

7. The most beaten paths are certainly the surest; but do not hope to scare up much game on them.

ANDRÉ GIDE, *JOURNALS*, MAY 1930, TR. JUSTIN O'BRIEN

8. The protected man doesn't need luck; therefore it seldom visits him.

ALAN HARRINGTON, "IT'S COLD OUT THERE," *LIFE IN THE CRYSTAL PALACE* (1959)

9. God Himself is not secure, having given man dominion over His works.

HELEN KELLER, *LET US HAVE FAITH* (1940)

10. Security depends not so much upon how much you have, as upon how much you can do without.

JOSEPH WOOD KRUTCH, "IF YOU DON'T MIND MY SAYING SO," *THE AMERICAN SCHOLAR* (SUMMER 1967)

11. Only in growth, reform, and change, paradoxically enough, is true security to be found.

ANNE MORROW LINDBERGH, *THE WAVE OF THE FUTURE* (1940)

12. Most people want security in this world, not liberty.

H. L. MENCKEN, *MINORITY REPORT* (1956), 170

13. Not a gift of a cow, nor a gift of land, nor yet a gift of food, is so important as the gift of safety, which is declared to be the great gift among all gifts in this world.

PANCHATANTRA (C. 5TH C.), 1, TR. FRANKLIN EDGERTON

14. People wish to learn to swim and at the same time to keep one foot on the ground.

MARCEL PROUST, *REMEMBRANCE OF THINGS PAST: THE SWEET CHEAT GONE* (1913–27), TR. C. K. SCOTT-MONCRIEFF

15. Happy he whoe'er, content with the common lot, with safe breeze hugs the shore, and, fearing to trust his skiff to the wider sea, with unambitious oar keeps close to the land.

SENECA, *AGAMEMNON* (1ST C.), 102, TR. FRANK JUSTUS MILLER

16. To keep oneself safe does not mean to bury oneself.

SENECA, "ON PEACE OF MIND," *MORAL ESSAYS* (1ST C.), TR. AUBREY STEWART

17. [N]ational security rests on the credible threat of a form of warfare universally condemned since the Dark Ages, the wholesale slaughter of noncombatants.

GEORGE F. WILL, "IN COLD BLOOD," *THE PURSUIT OF HAPPINESS AND OTHER SOBERING THOUGHTS* (1978)

857. SEDUCTION

See also 198. COURTSHIP; 351. FLIRTATION; 551. LOVE; 742. PROMISCUITY; 892. SEX

1. Brisk Confidence still best with woman copes: / Pique her and soothe in turn—soon Passion crowns thy hopes.

BYRON, *CHILDE HAROLD'S PILGRIMAGE* (1812–18), 2.34

2. Once a woman parts with her virtue, she loses the esteem even of the man whose vows and tears won her to abandon it.

CERVANTES, *DON QUIXOTE* (1605–15), 1.4.7, TR. JOHN OZELL

3. Every man is to be had one way or another, and every woman almost any way.

LORD CHESTERFIELD, *LETTERS TO HIS SON*, JUNE 5, 1750

4. A woman that loves to be at the window is a bunch of grapes on the highway.

ENGLISH PROVERB

5. To win a woman in the first place one must please her, then undress her, and then somehow get her clothes back on her. Finally, so that she will allow you to leave her, you've got to annoy her.

JEAN GIRAUDOUX, *AMPHITRYON 38* (1929), 1, TR. PETER H. JUDD

6. She kept the man's name to herself throughout her labor and dying; she did not accuse him that he be punished with her. To save her inseminator's name she gave silent birth.

MAXINE HONG KINGSTON, *THE WOMAN WARRIOR* (1976)

7. A man can deceive a woman by his sham attachment to her provided he does not have a real attachment elsewhere.

LA BRUYÈRE, *CHARACTERS* (1688), 3.69

8. All really great lovers are articulate, and verbal seduction is the surest road to actual seduction.

MARYA MANNES, *MORE IN ANGER* (1958), 4.3

9. Had we but world enough, and time, / This coyness, lady, were no crime.

ANDREW MARVELL, "TO HIS COY MISTRESS" (1650)

10. Women can always be caught; that's the first rule of the game.

OVID, *THE ART OF LOVE* (C. A.D. 8), 1, TR. ROLFE HUMPHRIES

11. Venus yields to caresses, not to compulsion.

PUBLILIUS SYRUS, *MORAL SAYINGS* (1ST C. B.C.), 101, TR. DARIUS LYMAN

12. Don't fear to pledge. By winds the perjuries of love / Are blown, null and void, across the land and farthest seas.

TIBULLUS, *ELEGIES* (1ST C. B.C.), 1.4, TR. HUBERT CREEKMORE

13. It is not enough to conquer; one must know how to seduce.

VOLTAIRE, *MÉROPE* (1743), 1.4

SEEING

See 897. SIGHT

SEGREGATION

See 775. RACIAL PREJUDICE

858. SELF

See also 45. APPEARANCE; 444. IDENTITY; 469. INDIVIDUALITY; 593. MIRRORS

1. Our entire life, with our fine moral code and our precious freedom, consists ultimately in accepting ourselves as we are.

JEAN ANOUILH, *TRAVELER WITHOUT LUGGAGE* (1936), 2.1, TR. LUCIENNE HILL

2. The self cannot be escaped, but it can be, with ingenuity and hard work, distracted.

DONALD BARTHELME, "DAUMIER," *SADNESS* (1972)

3. When the self is one's exclusive subject and limit, reference and measure, one has no choice but to make a world of words.

WENDELL BERRY, "THE SPECIALIZATION OF POETRY," *STANDING BY WORDS* (1983)

4. When I say "I," I mean a thing absolutely unique, not to be confused with any other.

UGO BETTI, *THE INQUIRY* (1944–45), 2.2

5. We carry with us the wonders we seek without us.

SIR THOMAS BROWNE, *RELIGIO MEDICI* (1642), 1

6. My care is for myself; / Myself am whole and sole reality.

ROBERT BROWNING, "MR. SLUDGE, THE MEDIUM," *DRAMATIS PERSONAE* (1864)

7. Inside myself is a place where I live all alone and that's where you renew your springs that never dry up.

PEARL S. BUCK, *NEW YORK POST*, APRIL 26, 1959

8. The ideal is in thyself, the impediment too is in thyself.

THOMAS CARLYLE, *SARTOR RESARTUS* (1833–34), 2.9

9. One may understand the cosmos, but never the ego; the self is more distant than any star.

G. K. CHESTERTON, "THE LOGIC OF ELFLAND," *ORTHODOXY* (1908)

10. The spirit is the true self, not that physical figure which can be pointed out by your finger.

CICERO, *DE RE PUBLICA* (C. 51 B.C.), 6

11. We are all serving a life-sentence in the dungeon of self.

CYRIL CONNOLLY, *THE UNQUIET GRAVE* (1945), 2

12. So much of our time is preparation, so much is routine, and so much retrospect, that the pith of each man's genius contracts itself to a very few hours.

EMERSON, "EXPERIENCE," *ESSAYS: SECOND SERIES* (1844)

13. It was strange to have no self—to be like a little boy left alone in a big house, who knew that now he could do anything he wanted to do, but found that there was nothing that he wanted to do.

F. SCOTT FITZGERALD, *THE CRACK-UP* (1945)

14. Man can be defined as the animal that can say "I," that can be aware of himself as a separate entity.

ERICH FROMM, *THE SANE SOCIETY* (1955), 3

15. What other dungeon is so dark as one's own heart! What jailer so inexorable as one's self!

NATHANIEL HAWTHORNE, *THE HOUSE OF THE SEVEN GABLES* (1851), 11

16. No man would, I think, exchange his existence with any other man, however fortunate. We had as lief not be, as not be ourselves.

WILLIAM HAZLITT, "ON THE FEAR OF DEATH," *TABLE TALK* (1821–22)

17. The remarkable thing is that we really love our neighbor as ourselves: we do unto others as we do unto ourselves. We hate others when we hate ourselves. We are tolerant toward others when we tolerate ourselves.

ERIC HOFFER, *THE PASSIONATE STATE OF MIND* (1954), 100

18. No one has ever seen the self. It has no visible shape, nor does it occupy measurable space. It is an abstraction, like other abstractions equally elusive: the individual, the mind, the society.

IRVING HOWE, "THE SELF IN LITERATURE," *A CRITIC'S NOTEBOOK* (1994)

19. Anytime you make a person into something other than himself, you make a monster.

ROGER ROSENBLATT, SY JACKSON, QUOTED BY ROGER ROSENBLATT IN "PORTRAIT OF A PRISONER," *THE MAN IN THE WATER* (1994)

20. Be rich for yourself and poor to your friends.

JUVENAL, *SATIRES* (C. 100), 5.113, TR. HUBERT CREEKMORE

21. The self-evident truth which makes men invincible is that inalienably they are inviolable persons.

WALTER LIPPMANN, *THE GOOD SOCIETY* (1943), 4.17

22. Not in the clamour of the crowded street, / Not in the shouts and plaudits of the throng, / But in ourselves, are triumph and defeat.

LONGFELLOW, "THE POETS" (1876)

23. Each one is all in all to himself; for being dead, all is dead to him.

PASCAL, *PENSÉES* (1670), 457, TR. W. F. TROTTER

24. Man is the creature that cannot emerge from himself, that knows his fellows only in himself; when he asserts the contrary, he is lying.

MARCEL PROUST, *REMEMBRANCE OF THINGS PAST: THE SWEET CHEAT GONE* (1913–27), TR. C. K. SCOTT-MONCRIEFF

25. You live and die according to what goes on in yourself, which no one else can even begin to know, not even father, mother, wife, son, or daughter.

WILLIAM SAROYAN, "THE LIGHT FANTASTIC OF GEORGE JEAN NATHAN," *SONS COME & GO, MOTHERS HANG IN FOREVER* (1979)

26. Every man is correct in asking God why he is stuck with himself, and his rotten luck.

WILLIAM SAROYAN, *CHANCE MEETINGS* (1978)

27. One does not "find oneself" by pursuing one's self, but on the contrary by pursuing something else and learning through some discipline or routine (even the routine of making beds) who one is and wants to be.

MAY SARTON, "THURSDAY, JANUARY 8TH," *THE HOUSE BY THE SEA: A JOURNAL* (1977)

28. Self-reverence, self-knowledge, self-control, / These three alone lead life to sovereign power.

LORD TENNYSON, "OENONE" (1842)

29. The whole dear notion of one's own Self—marvelous old free-willed, free- enterprising, autonomous, independent, isolated island of a Self—is a myth.

LEWIS THOMAS, "ON PROBABILITY AND POSSIBILITY," *THE LIVES OF A CELL* (1974)

30. But ceremony never did conceal, / Save to the silly eye, which all allows, / How much we are the woods we wander in.

RICHARD WILBUR, TITLE POEM, *CEREMONY* (1950)

859. SELF-ASSERTION

See also 92. BOLDNESS

1. The perfection preached in the Gospels never yet built an empire. Every man of action has a strong dose of egotism, pride, hardness, and cunning.

CHARLES DE GAULLE, QUOTED IN *THE NEW YORK TIMES MAGAZINE,* MAY 12, 1968

2. [H]aving tried to give pattern to the chaos which lives within the pattern of your certainties, I must come out, I must emerge.

RALPH ELLISON, *THE INVISIBLE MAN* (1952)

3. Take the place and attitude to which you see your unquestionable right, and all men acquiesce.

EMERSON, *JOURNALS,* 1836

4. You must either conquer and rule or serve and lose, suffer or triumph, be the anvil or the hammer.

GOETHE, *DER GROSS-COPHTA* (1792), 2

5. Nobody can give you freedom. Nobody can give you equality or justice or anything. If you're a man, you take it.

MALCOLM X, *MALCOLM X SPEAKS* (1965), 9

6. The price of being oneself is so high and involves so much ruthlessness toward others (or what looks like ruthlessness in our duty-bound culture) that very few people can afford it.

MAY SARTON, "WEDNESDAY, JANUARY 20TH," *THE HOUSE BY THE SEA: A JOURNAL* (1977)

860. SELF-CONFIDENCE

See also 664. OVERCONFIDENCE; 868. SELF-DOUBT

1. Self-trust is the essence of heroism.

EMERSON, "HEROISM," *ESSAYS: FIRST SERIES* (1841)

2. In a world where survival is always seen as a struggle, and in which some pitfalls always exist, if something brings into question our confidence in our own coping ability, it will threaten our safety.

WILLARD GAYLIN, *FEELINGS: OUR VITAL SIGNS* (1979)

3. It generally happens that assurance keeps an even pace with ability.

SAMUEL JOHNSON, *THE RAMBLER* (1750–52), 159

4. All those happy confusions of himself with God, those identifications with divinity and genius, and that supreme self-confidence—all of them were as lost as the smoke of Gettysburg, the tears of Gethsemane.

JOHN O'HARA, *THE INSTRUMENT* (1967)

5. Assurance is contemptible and fatal unless it is self-knowledge.

GEORGE SANTAYANA, *CHARACTER AND OPINION IN THE UNITED STATES* (1921), 3

6. There's one blessing only, the source and cornerstone of beatitude—confidence in self.

SENECA, *LETTERS TO LUCILIUS* (1ST C.), 31.3, TR. E. PHILLIPS BARKER

7. Perhaps well-to-do women and unemployed ghetto teenagers have something in common. Neither group has been allowed to develop the self-confidence that comes from knowing you can support yourselves.

GLORIA STEINEM, "COLLEGE REUNION," *OUTRAGEOUS ACTS AND EVERYDAY REBELLIONS* (1983)

8. They can do all because they think they can.

VERGIL, *AENEID* (30–19 B.C.), 5.231, TR. T. H. DELABERE-MAY

861. SELF-CONSCIOUSNESS

See also 893. SHAME

1. Self-consciousness is the curse of the city and all that sophistication implies.

ANNIE DILLARD, "THE PRESENT," *PILGRIM AT TINKER CREEK* (1974)

2. If you happen to have a wart on your nose or forehead, you cannot help imagining that no one in the world has anything else to do but stare at your wart, laugh at it, and condemn you for it, even though you have discovered America.

DOSTOYEVSKY, *THE IDIOT* (1868), 3.1, TR. DAVID MAGARSHACK

3. Those people who are uncomfortable in themselves are disagreeable to others.

WILLIAM HAZLITT, "ON DISAGREEABLE PEOPLE," *SKETCHES AND ESSAYS* (1839)

4. When we are *self*-conscious, we cannot be wholly aware; we must throw ourselves out first. This throwing ourselves away is the act of creativity.

MADELEINE L'ENGLE, *A CIRCLE OF QUIET* (1972)

862. SELF-CONTROL

See also 250. DISCIPLINE

1. If one shed tears, they must be shed on one's pillow.

HENRY ADAMS, *THE EDUCATION OF HENRY ADAMS* (1907)

2. I am, / indeed, / a king, because I know how to rule myself.

PIETRO ARETINO, LETTER TO AGOSTINO RICCHI, MAY 10, 1537, TR. SAMUEL PUTNAM

3. What it lies in our power to do, it lies in our power not to do.

ARISTOTLE, *NICOMACHEAN ETHICS* (4TH C. B.C.), 3.4, TR. J. A. K. THOMSON

4. Freedom is not procured by a full enjoyment of what is desired, but by controlling the desire.

EPICTETUS, *DISCOURSES* (2ND C.), 4.1, TR. THOMAS W. HIGGINSON

5. We learn to curb our will and keep our overt actions within the bounds of humanity, long before we can subdue our sentiments and imaginations to the same mild tone.

WILLIAM HAZLITT, "ON THE PLEASURE OF HATING," *THE PLAIN SPEAKER* (1826)

6. He that would be superior to external influences must first become superior to his own passions.

SAMUEL JOHNSON, *THE IDLER* (1758–60), 52

7. There is a raging tiger inside every man whom God put on this earth. Every man worthy of the respect of his children spends his life building inside himself a cage to pen that tiger in.

MURRAY KEMPTON, "SNAPPING THE LEASH," *AMERICA COMES OF MIDDLE AGE* (1963)

8. The Russian leaders are keen judges of human psychology, and as such they are highly conscious that loss of temper and of self-control is never a source of strength in political affairs.

GEORGE F. KENNAN, *AMERICAN DIPLOMACY 1900–1950* (1951)

9. He who conquers others is strong; / He who conquers himself is mighty.

LAO TZU, *THE CHARACTER OF TAO* (6TH C. B.C.), 33, TR. LIN YUTANG

10. Not being able to govern events, I govern myself, and apply myself to them, if they will not apply themselves to me.

MONTAIGNE, "OF PRESUMPTION," *ESSAYS* (1580–88), TR. W. C. HAZLITT

11. The strong man is the one who is able to intercept at will the communication between the senses and the mind.

NAPOLEON I, *MAXIMS* (1804–15)

12. How shall I be able to rule over others, that have not full power and command of myself?

RABELAIS, *GARGANTUA AND PANTAGRUEL* (1532–64), 1.52

13. It is a new road to happiness, if you have strength enough to castigate a little the various impulses that sway you in turn.

George Santayana, *Winds of Doctrine* (1913)

14. Man who man would be, / Must rule the empire of himself.

Shelley, "Political Greatness" (1821)

15. A man who is master of himself can end a sorrow as easily as he can invent a pleasure.

Oscar Wilde, *The Picture of Dorian Gray* (1891), 9

863. SELF-CRITICISM

See also 868. Self-Doubt; 872. Self-Hatred

1. How shall we expect charity towards others, when we are uncharitable to ourselves?

Sir Thomas Browne, *Religio Medici* (1642), 2

2. What is this self inside us, this silent observer, / Severe and speechless critic, who can terrorize us / And urge us on to futile activity, / And in the end, judge us still more severely / For the errors into which his own reproaches drove us?

T. S. Eliot, *The Elder Statesman* (1958), 2

3. He who makes great demands upon himself is naturally inclined to make great demands on others.

André Gide, *Journals,* Feb. 1, 1938, tr. Justin O'Brien

4. He is a man whom it is impossible to please, because he is never pleased with himself.

Goethe, *The Sorrows of Young Werther* (1774), 2, Dec. 24, 1771, tr. Victor Lange

5. Any one is to be pitied who has just sense enough to perceive his deficiencies.

William Hazlitt, *Characteristics* (1823), 213

6. All censure of a man's self is oblique praise. It is in order to show how much he can spare.

Samuel Johnson, quoted in Boswell's *Life of Samuel Johnson,* April 25, 1778

7. Self-criticism is an art not many are qualified to practice.

Joyce Carol Oates, "The Art of Self-Criticism," *(Woman) Writer: Occasions and Opportunities* (1988)

864. SELF-DECEPTION

See also 876. Self-Love; 1027. Vanity

1. Never can true courage dwell with them, / Who, playing tricks with conscience, dare not look / At their own vices.

Samuel Taylor Coleridge, *Fears in Solitude* (1798)

2. Self-deception is sometimes as necessary a tool as a crowbar.

Moss Hart, *Act One* (1959)

3. No estimate is more in danger of erroneous calculations than those by which a man computes the force of his own genius.

Samuel Johnson, *The Rambler* (1750–52), 154

4. The greatest deception men suffer is from their own opinions.

Leonardo da Vinci, *Notebooks* (c. 1500), tr. Jean Paul Richter

5. Nixon has not only developed the use of the platitude, he's raised it to an art form. It's mashed potatoes. It appeals to the lowest common denominator of American taste. It's a farce, a delicious farce; self-deception carried to the nth degree.

Joe McGinniss, *The Selling of the President 1968* (1969)

6. A woman wishes to mother a man simply because she sees into his helplessness, his need of an amiable environment, his touching self-delusion.

H.L. Mencken, "The Feminine Mind," in *Fifty Famous Essays* (1964)

7. The most common sort of lie is the one uttered to one's self.

Nietzsche, *The Antichrist* (1888), 55, tr. Anthony M. Ludovici

8. We are only falsehood, duplicity, contradiction; we both conceal and disguise ourselves from ourselves.

Pascal, *Pensées* (1670), 377, tr. W. F. Trotter

9. Nature never deceives us; it is we who deceive ourselves.

Rousseau, *Émile* (1762), 3

865. SELF-DENIAL

See also 122. Chastity; 601. Monasticism

1. The abstinent run away from what they desire / But carry their desires with them.

Bhagavadgita, 2, tr. Swami Prabhavananda and Christopher Isherwood

2. Abstainer, n. A weak person who yields to the temptation of denying himself a pleasure.

Ambrose Bierce, *The Devil's Dictionary* (1881–1911)

3. To refuse the sweets of life because they once must leave us, is as preposterous as to wish to have been born old, because we one day must be old.

WILLIAM CONGREVE, *THE WAY OF THE WORLD* (1700), 2.1

4. Refrain to-night, / And that shall lend a kind of easiness / To the next abstinence; the next more easy; / For use almost can change the stamp of nature.

SHAKESPEARE, *HAMLET* (1600), 3.4.165

5. Self-denial is not a virtue: it is only the effect of prudence on rascality.

GEORGE BERNARD SHAW, "MAXIMS FOR REVOLUTIONISTS," *MAN AND SUPERMAN* (1903)

6. Self-denial is simply a method by which man arrests his progress, and self-sacrifice a survival of the mutilation of the savage.

OSCAR WILDE, "THE CRITIC AS ARTIST," *INTENTIONS* (1891)

7. I really can't stand any more to pay for a burst of animation when someone comes in for drinks with a depressed and low-keyed next day, in which I have to go around on my hands and knees.

EDMUND WILSON, *THE SIXTIES* (1993)

866. SELF-DESTRUCTION

See also 691. PERVERSENESS; 872. SELF-HATRED; 948. SUICIDE

1. We often give our enemies the means for our own destruction.

AESOP, "THE EAGLE AND THE ARROW," *FABLES* (6TH C. B.C.?), TR. JOSEPH JACOBS

2. I, who have never willfully pained another, have no business to pain myself.

MARCUS AURELIUS, *MEDITATIONS* (2ND C.), 8.42, TR. MAXWELL STANIFORTH

3. Our greatest foes, and whom we must chiefly combat, are within.

CERVANTES, *DON QUIXOTE* (1605–15), 2.3.8, TR. JOHN OZELL

4. He invites future injuries who rewards past ones.

THOMAS FULLER, M.D., *GNOMOLOGIA* (1732), 1905

5. If he has no other burden, he'll take up a load of stones.

MALAY PROVERB

6. A hair shirt does not always render those chaste who wear it.

MONTAIGNE, "THE STORY OF SPURINA," *ESSAYS* (1580–88), TR. W. C. HAZLITT

7. Troubles hurt the most / when they prove self-inflicted.

SOPHOCLES, *OEDIPUS THE KING* (C. 430 B.C.), TR. DAVID GRENE

8. Why, since we are always complaining of our ills, are we constantly employed in redoubling them?

VOLTAIRE, "WHYS," *PHILOSOPHICAL DICTIONARY* (1764)

9. A man's worst enemy can't wish him what he thinks up for himself.

YIDDISH PROVERBS (1949)

867. SELF-DETERMINATION

See also 444. IDENTITY; 771. PURPOSE; 807. RESOLUTION; 880. SELF-SUFFICIENCY; 1056. WILL

1. I have discovered that we may be in some degree whatever character we choose. Besides, practice forms a man to anything.

JAMES BOSWELL, *LONDON JOURNAL,* NOV. 21, 1762

2. Every man is the son of his own works.

CERVANTES, *DON QUIXOTE* (1605–15), 1.1.4, TR. JOHN OZELL

3. Every spirit makes its house; but afterwards the house confines the spirit.

EMERSON, "FATE," *THE CONDUCT OF LIFE* (1860)

4. If we must accept Fate, we are not less compelled to affirm liberty, the significance of the individual, the grandeur of duty, the power of character.

EMERSON, "FATE," *THE CONDUCT OF LIFE* (1860)

5. In the history of the individual is always an account of his condition, and he knows himself to be a party to his present estate.

EMERSON, "FATE," *THE CONDUCT OF LIFE* (1860)

6. You will fetter my leg, but not Zeus himself can get the better of my free will.

EPICTETUS, *DISCOURSES* (2ND C.), 1.1, TR. THOMAS W. HIGGINSON

7. The wisest men follow their own direction.

EURIPIDES, *IPHIGENIA IN TAURIS* (C. 414–12 B.C.), TR. WITTER BYNNER

8. Some minds seem almost to create themselves, springing up under every disadvantage and working their solitary but irresistible way through a thousand obstacles.

WASHINGTON IRVING, "ROSCOE," *THE SKETCH BOOK OF GEOFFREY CRAYON, GENT.* (1819–20)

9. Life is what our character makes it. We fashion it, as a snail does its shell. A man can say: "I never made a fortune because it is not in my character to be rich."

JULES RENARD, *JOURNAL,* FEBRUARY 1908, TR. ELIZABETH ROGET

10. Every man is the architect of his own fortune.

SALLUST, SPEECH TO CAESAR ON THE STATE (1ST C. B.C.), 1

11. We can't reach old age by another man's road.

MARK TWAIN, "SEVENTIETH BIRTHDAY" (1910)

868. SELF-DOUBT

See also 43. ANXIETY; 482. INSECURITY; 860. SELF-CONFIDENCE; 863. SELF-CRITICISM; 871. SELF-ESTEEM

1. The fearful Unbelief is unbelief in yourself.

THOMAS CARLYLE, *SARTOR RESARTUS* (1833–34), 2.7

2. You must not on any account give me credit for being penetrating. I have impressed people that way before, and the result is always disaster.

T.S. ELIOT, *LETTERS*, ED. VALERIE ELIOT

3. Any work looks wonderful to me except the one which I can do.

EMERSON, *JOURNALS,* 1836

4. He that listens after what people say of him shall never have peace.

THOMAS FULLER, M.D., *GNOMOLOGIA* (1732), 2218

5. He who undervalues himself is justly undervalued by others.

WILLIAM HAZLITT, "ON THE KNOWLEDGE OF CHARACTER," *TABLE TALK* (1821–22)

6. No one can make you feel inferior without your consent.

ELEANOR ROOSEVELT, *CATHOLIC DIGEST,* AUGUST 1960

7. It is easy—terribly easy—to shake a man's faith in himself. To take advantage of that to break a man's spirit is devil's work.

GEORGE BERNARD SHAW, *CANDIDA* (1903), 1

869. SELF-ESTEEM

See also 733. PRIDE; 868. SELF-DOUBT; 872. SELF-HATRED; 876. SELF-LOVE

1. It is easy to live for others; everybody does. I call on you to live for yourselves.

EMERSON, *JOURNALS,* 1845

2. So there was not an "I" anymore—not a basis on which I could organize my self-respect—save my limitless capacity for toil that it seemed I possessed no more.

F. SCOTT FITZGERALD, *THE CRACK-UP* (1945)

3. Be a friend to thyself, and others will be so too.

THOMAS FULLER, M.D., *GNOMOLOGIA* (1732), 847

4. Respect yourself if you would have others respect you.

BALTASAR GRACIÁN, *THE ART OF WORLDLY WISDOM* (1647), 284, TR. JOSEPH JACOBS

5. Let a man's talents or virtues be what they may, we only feel satisfaction in his society as he is satisfied in himself.

WILLIAM HAZLITT, *CHARACTERISTICS* (1823), 40

6. It is difficult to make a man miserable while he feels worthy of himself and claims kindred to the great God who made him.

ABRAHAM LINCOLN, SPEECH, WASHINGTON, D.C., SEPT. 14, 1862

7. Oft times nothing profits more / Than self-esteem, grounded on just and right / Well-managed.

MILTON, *PARADISE LOST* (1667), 8.571

8. If we must live with a perpetual sense that the world and the men in it are greater than we and too much for us, let it be the measure of our virtue that we know this and seek no comfort.

J. ROBERT OPPENHEIMER, "PROSPECTS IN THE ARTS AND SCIENCES," *FIFTY GREAT ESSAYS* (1964)

9. All through my boyhood I had a profound conviction that I was no good, that I was wasting my time, wrecking my talents, behaving with monstrous folly and wickedness and ingratitude—and all this, it seemed, was inescapable, because I lived among laws which were absolute, like the law of gravity, but which it was not possible for me to keep.

GEORGE ORWELL, "SUCH, SUCH WERE THE JOYS," *A COLLECTION OF ESSAYS* (1954)

10. So much is a man worth as he esteems himself.

RABELAIS, *GARGANTUA AND PANTAGRUEL* (1532–64), 2.29

11. Self-respect will keep a man from being abject when he is in the power of enemies, and will enable him to feel that he may be in the right when the world is against him.

BERTRAND RUSSELL, "TECHNIQUE AND HUMAN NATURE," *AUTHORITY AND THE INDIVIDUAL* (1949)

12. I began to understand that self-esteem isn't everything; it's just that there's nothing without it.

GLORIA STEINEM, *REVOLUTION FROM WITHIN* (1992)

13. I'm still the same person who grew up mostly in a Midwestern, factory-working neighborhood where talk about "self-esteem" would have seemed like a luxury.

GLORIA STEINEM, *REVOLUTION FROM WITHIN* (1992)

14. A man cannot be comfortable without his own approval.

MARK TWAIN, "WHAT IS MAN?" (1906)

15. Only individuals with an aberrant temperament can in the long run retain their self-esteem in the face of the disesteem of their fellows.

THORSTEIN VEBLEN, *THE THEORY OF THE LEISURE CLASS* (1899), 2

870. SELF-EXPRESSION

See also 201. CREATION AND CREATIVITY

1. The man is only half himself, the other half is his expression.

EMERSON, "THE POET," *ESSAYS: SECOND SERIES* (1844)

2. Self-expression is a hard and selfish thing. It eats everything, even the self. At the end you find you haven't even got a self to express.

GRAHAM GREENE, *A BURNT-OUT CASE* (1960)

871. SELF-GOVERNMENT

See also 862. SELF-CONTROL

1. For better or worse, man is the tool-using animal, and as such he has become the lord of creation. When he is lord also of himself, he will deserve his self-chosen title *homo sapiens*.

WILLIAM RALPH INGE, "THE DELEMMA OF CIVILISATION," *OUTSPOKEN ESSAYS: SECOND SERIES* (1922)

872. SELF-HATRED

See also 863. SELF-CRITICISM; 866. SELF-DESTRUCTION; 868. SELF-DOUBT; 871. SELF-ESTEEM

1. The self-despisers are less intent on their own increase than on the diminution of others. Where self-esteem is unobtainable, envy takes the place of greed.

ERIC HOFFER, *THE PASSIONATE STATE OF MIND* (1954), 114

2. A man must first despise himself, and then others will despise him.

MENCIUS, *WORKS* (4TH–3RD C. B.C.), 4, TR. CHARLES A. WONG

873. SELF-IMPORTANCE

See also 166. CONCEIT; 876. SELF-LOVE; 1027. VANITY

1. Man errs not that he deems / His welfare his true aim, / He errs because he dreams / The world does but exist that welfare to bestow.

MATTHEW ARNOLD, *EMPEDOCLES ON ETNA* (1852), I.2

2. Man desires to be free and he desires to feel important. This places him in a dilemma, for the more he emancipates himself from necessity the less important he feels.

W. H. AUDEN, "POSTSCRIPT: THE FRIVOLOUS AND THE EARNEST," *THE DYER'S HAND* (1962)

3. Half of the harm that is done in this world / Is due to people who want to feel important.

T. S. ELIOT, *THE COCKTAIL PARTY* (1949), 2

4. We all wish to be of importance in one way or another. The child coughs with might and main, since it has no other claim on the company.

EMERSON, *JOURNALS*, 1836

5. When they came to shoe the horses, the beetle stretched out his leg.

ENGLISH PROVERB

6. What, will the world be quite overturned when you die?

EPICTETUS, *DISCOURSES* (2ND C.), 3.10, TR. THOMAS W. HIGGINSON

7. Every cock is proud on his own dunghill.

THOMAS FULLER, M.D., *GNOMOLOGIA* (1732), 1412

8. Everyone thinks that all the bells echo his own thoughts.

GERMAN PROVERB

9. A sick man that gets talking about himself, a woman that gets talking about her baby, and an author that begins reading out of his own book, never know when to stop.

OLIVER WENDELL HOLMES, SR., *THE POET AT THE BREAKFAST TABLE* (1872), 11

10. There's a world of difference between a strong ego, which is essential, and a large ego—which can be destructive.

Lee Iacocca, *Iacocca: An Autobiography* (1984) with William Novak

11. But enough of me. Let's talk about you. What do you think of me?

Ed Koch, Interview

12. The extreme pleasure we take in speaking of ourselves should make us apprehensive that it gives hardly any to those who listen to us.

La Rochefoucauld, *Maxims* (1665), tr. Kenneth Pratt

13. We would rather speak badly of ourselves than not talk about ourselves at all.

La Rochefoucauld, *Maxims* (1665)

14. Egotism is the anesthetic that dulls the pain of stupidity.

Frank Leahy, *Look,* Jan. 10, 1955

15. The turtle lays thousands of eggs without anyone knowing, but when the hen lays an egg, the whole country is informed.

Malay Proverb

16. It was his [Gen. Douglas MacArthur's] relationship with the administration In Washington which became poisoned by his egomania. Link upon link the bond between events on the battlefield and his own ruin was forged, and, as is essential in genuine tragedy, the gods used the victim himself to forge the links.

William Manchester, *American Caesar* (1978)

17. Glory consists of two parts: the one in setting too great a value upon ourselves, and the other in setting too little a value upon others.

Montaigne, "Of presumption," *Essays* (1580–88), tr. W. C. Hazlitt

18. The big drum only sounds well from afar.

Persian Proverb

19. It astounds us to come upon other egoists, as though we alone had the right to be selfish, and be filled with eagerness to live.

Jules Renard, *Journal,* Nov. 18, 1887, tr. Elizabeth Roget

20. [Norman] Mailer records in his recent essays and public appearances his perfecting of himself as a virile instrument of letters; he is perpetually in training, getting ready to launch himself from his own missile pad into a high, beautiful orbit; even his failures may yet be turned to successes.

Susan Sontag, "Michel Leiris' *Manhood,*" *Against Interpretation* (1966)

SELF-IMPROVEMENT

See 460. Improvement

SELF-INDULGENCE

See 470. Indulgence

SELF-INTEREST

See 495. Interest; 874. Selfishness; 876. Self-Love

874. SELFISHNESS

See also 495. Interest; 876. Self-Love; 936. Stinginess

1. The men who made the Industrial Revolution are usually pictured as hardfaced businessmen with no other motive than self-interest. That is certainly wrong. For one thing, many of them were inventors who had come into business that way.

Jacob Bronowski, *The Ascent of Man* (1973)

2. Human history is the sad result of each one looking out for himself.

Julio Cortázar, *The Winners* (1960), 17, tr. Elaine Kerrigan

3. i have noticed / that when / chickens quit / quarreling over their / food they often / find that there is / enough for all of them / i wonder if / it might not / be the same way / with the / human race.

Don Marquis, "random thoughts by archy," *Archy's Life of Mehitabel* (1933)

4. He who lives only for himself is truly dead to others.

Publilius Syrus, *Moral Sayings* (1st c. b.c.), 771, tr. Darius Lyman

5. Selfishness is not living as one wishes to live, it is asking others to live as one wishes to live.

Oscar Wilde, *The Soul of Man Under Socialism* (1891)

875. SELF-KNOWLEDGE

See also 183. Contemplation; 444. Identity; 758. Psychoanalysis; 858. Self

1. The questions which one asks oneself begin, at last, to illuminate the world, and become one's key to the experience of others.

JAMES BALDWIN, INTRODUCTION, *NOBODY KNOWS MY NAME* (1961)

2. There is no purifier like knowledge in this world: / time makes man find himself in his heart.

BHAGAVADGITA, 4, TR. P. LAL

3. O wad some Power the giftie gie us / To see oursels as ithers see us! / It wad frae monie a blunder free us, / An' foolish notion.

ROBERT BURNS, "TO A LOUSE" (1786)

4. To know oneself, one should assert oneself.

ALBERT CAMUS, *NOTEBOOKS 1935–1942* (1962), I, TR. PHILIP THODY

5. Full wise is he that can himselven knowe.

CHAUCER, "THE MONK'S TALE," *THE CANTERBURY TALES* (1387–1400), 3329

6. The test of a civilized person is first self-awareness, and then depth after depth of sincerity in self-confrontation.

CLARENCE DAY, "A WILD POLISH HERO," *THE CROW'S NEST* (1921)

7. It is not enough to understand what we ought to be, unless we know what we are; and we do not understand what we are, unless we know what we ought to be.

T. S. ELIOT, "RELIGION AND LITERATURE" (1935)

8. It is doubtless a vice to turn one's eyes inward too much, but I am my own comedy and tragedy.

EMERSON, *JOURNALS*, 1833

9. Wherever we go, whatever we do, self is the sole subject we study and learn.

EMERSON, *JOURNALS*, 1833

10. Know thyself! A maxim as pernicious as it is ugly. Whoever observes himself arrests his own development. A caterpillar who wanted to know itself well would never become a butterfly.

ANDRÉ GIDE, *LES NOUVELLES NOURRITURES* (1935)

11. Let a man once see himself as others see him, and all enthusiasm vanishes from his heart.

ELBERT HUBBARD, *THE NOTE BOOK* (1927)

12. Hardly anybody recognizes the most significant moments of their life at the time they happen.

W.P. KINSELLA, *SHOELESS JOE* (1982)

13. He who knows others is learned; / He who knows himself is wise.

LAO TZU, *THE CHARACTER OF TAO* (6TH C. B.C.), 33, TR. LIN YUTANG

14. When one is a stranger to oneself then one is estranged from others too.

ANNE MORROW LINDBERGH, "MOON SHELL," *GIFT FROM THE SEA* (1955)

15. In moments of despair, we look on ourselves leadenly as objects; we see ourselves, our lives, as someone else might see them and may even be driven to kill ourselves if the separation, the "knowledge," seems sufficiently final.

MARY MCCARTHY, "CHARACTERS IN FICTION," *ON THE CONTRARY* (1961)

16. It is far more important that one's life should be perceived than that it should be transformed; for no sooner has it been perceived, than it transforms itself of its own accord.

MAURICE MAETERLINCK, "THE DEEPER LIFE," *THE TREASURE OF THE HUMBLE* (1896), TR. ALFRED SUTRO

17. Knowledge of the soul would unfailingly make us melancholy if the pleasures of expression did not keep us alert and of good cheer.

THOMAS MANN, "TONIO KRÖGER" (1903), *DEATH IN VENICE*, TR. H. T. LOWE-PORTER

18. We are nearer neighbors to ourselves than the whiteness of snow or the weight of stones are to us: if man does not know himself, how should he know his functions and powers?

MONTAIGNE, "APOLOGY FOR RAIMOND DE SEBONDE," *ESSAYS* (1580–88), TR. W. C. HAZLITT

19. It [his brother's assassination] made Robert Kennedy, a man unprepared for introspection, think for the first time in his life, what *he* wanted to do, and what *he* stood for.

JACK NEWFIELD, *ROBERT KENNEDY* (1969)

20. If men knew themselves, God would heal and pardon them.

PASCAL, *PENSÉES* (1670), 778, TR. W. F. TROTTER

21. Learn what you are and be such.

PINDAR, *ODES* (5TH C. B.C.), PYTHIA 2, TR. RICHMOND LATTIMORE

22. Know then thyself, presume not God to scan; / The proper study of mankind is man.

ALEXANDER POPE, *AN ESSAY ON MAN* (1733–34), 2.1

23. We may fail of our happiness, strive we ever so bravely; but we are less likely to fail if we measure with judgment our chances and our capabilities.

AGNES REPPLIER, "THE SPINSTER," *COMPROMISES* (1904)

24. Who's not sat tense before his own heart's curtain?

RAINER MARIA RILKE, "THE FOURTH ELEGY," *DUINO ELEGIES* (1923), TR. STEPHEN SPENDER

25. Two places in this world make it impossible for a man to escape from himself: a battlefield and a prison cell.

ANWAR EL-SADAT, *IN SEARCH OF IDENTITY* (1977)

26. If a man really knew himself he would utterly despise the ignorant notions others might form on a subject in which he had such matchless opportunities for observation.

GEORGE SANTAYANA, *THE LIFE OF REASON: REASON IN SOCIETY* (1905–06), 6

27. A man may call to mind the face of his friend, but not his own. Here, then, is an initial difficulty in the way of applying the maxim, *Know Thyself*.

SCHOPENHAUER, "FURTHER PSYCHOLOGICAL OBSERVATIONS," *PARERGA AND PARALIPOMENA* (1851), TR. T. BAILEY SAUNDERS

28. Go to your bosom; / Knock there, and ask your heart what it doth know.

SHAKESPEARE, *MEASURE FOR MEASURE* (1604–05), 2.2.136

29. Self-knowledge is a dangerous thing, tending to make man shallow or insane.

KARL SHAPIRO, *THE BOURGEOIS POET* (1964), 3.74

30. Explore thyself. Herein are demanded the eye and the nerve.

THOREAU, "CONCLUSIONS," *WALDEN* (1854)

31. All men should strive to learn before they die what they are running from, and to, and why.

JAMES THURBER, "THE SHORE AND THE SEA," *FURTHER FABLES FOR OUR TIME* (1956)

SELFLESSNESS

See 435. HUMILITY; 887. SERVICE; 1021. UNSELFISHNESS

876. SELF-LOVE

See also 166. CONCEIT; 733. PRIDE; 864. SELF-DECEPTION; 871. SELF-ESTEEM; 874. SELFISHNESS; 1027. VANITY

1. Our own self-love draws a thick veil between us and our faults.

LORD CHESTERFIELD, *LETTERS TO HIS SON,* JUNE 21, 1748

2. Narcissus never wrote well nor was a friend.

EDWARD DAHLBERG, "ON WRITERS AND WRITING," *REASONS OF THE HEART* (1965)

3. What is an obstacle in our loving men is the love they have for themselves, which is touchy, exclusive, inordinate, tragic. We could never love them as much as that.

PAUL GÉRALDY, *L'HOMME ET L'AMOUR* (1951)

4. Self-love is an idolatry. Self-hatred is a tragedy.

ELIZABETH HARDWICK, "MILITANT NUDES," *BARTLEBY IN MANHATTAN* (1983)

5. We prefer ourselves to others, only because we have a more intimate consciousness and confirmed opinion of our own claims and merits than of any other person's.

WILLIAM HAZLITT, *CHARACTERISTICS* (1823), 25

6. Self-love is the greatest of all flatterers.

LA ROCHEFOUCAULD, *MAXIMS* (1665), TR. KENNETH PRATT

7. We feel good and ill only in proportion to our self-love.

LA ROCHEFOUCAULD, *MAXIMS* (1665), TR. KENNETH PRATT

8. He who is in love with himself has at least this advantage—he won't encounter many rivals.

GEORG CHRISTOPH LICHTENBERG, *APHORISMS* (1764–99), TR. H. HATFIELD

9. Simple narcissism gives the power of beasts to politicians, professional wrestlers and female movie stars.

NORMAN MAILER, *MIAMI AND THE SIEGE OF CHICAGO* (1968), 2.24

10. The Europeans wanted gold and slaves, like everybody else; but at the same time they wanted statues put up to themselves as people who had done good things for the slaves.

V.S. NAIPAUL, *A BEND IN THE RIVER* (1979)

11. One must learn to love oneself ... with a wholesome and healthy love, so that one can bear to be with oneself and need not roam.

NIETZSCHE, "ON THE SPIRIT OF GRAVITY," *THUS SPOKE ZARATHUSTRA* (1883–92), 3, TR. WALTER KAUFMANN

12. No person loving or admiring himself is alone.

THEODOR REIK, *OF LOVE AND LUST* (1957), 1.1.6

13. We believe, first and foremost, what makes us feel that we are fine fellows.

Bertrand Russell, "An Outline of Intellectual Rubbish," *Unpopular Essays* (1950)

14. Self-love, my liege, is not so vile a sin / As self-neglecting.

Shakespeare, *Henry V* (1598–99), 2.4.75

15. We cannot love others as others unless we possess suficient self-love, a love we learn from being loved in infancy.

Judith Viorst, *Necessary Losses* (1986)

16. It is not love we should have painted as blind, but self-love.

Voltaire, *Correspondance, à M. Damilaville,* May 11, 1764

17. Self-love is the instrument of our preservation; it resembles the provision for the perpetuity of mankind; it is necessary, it is dear to us, it gives us pleasure, and we must conceal it.

Voltaire, "Self-Love," *Philosophical Dictionary* (1764)

18. I dote on myself, there is that lot of me and all so luscious.

Walt Whitman, "Song of Myself," *Leaves of Grass* (1855–92)

19. I find no sweeter fat than sticks to my own bones.

Walt Whitman, "Song of Myself," *Leaves of Grass* (1855–92)

20. To love oneself is the beginning of a life-long romance.

Oscar Wilde, *An Ideal Husband* (1895), 3

877. SELF-PITY

See also 698. Pity

1. Every man supposes himself not to be fully understood or appreciated.

Emerson, *Journals,* 1840

2. Life, I fancy, would very often be insupportable, but for the luxury of self-compassion.

George Gissing, "Spring," *The Private Papers of Henry Ryecroft* (1903)

3. Self-pity comes so naturally to all of us, that the most solid happiness can be shaken by the compassion of a fool.

André Maurois, *Ariel* (1924), 16, tr. Ella D'Arcy

4. Shall a man go and hang himself because he belongs to the race of pygmies, and not be the biggest pygmy that he can?

Thoreau, "Conclusion," *Walden* (1854)

SELF-PRESERVATION

See 229. Defense; 956. Survival

SELF-RELIANCE

See 867. Self-Determination; 880. Self-Sufficiency

SELF-RESPECT

See 871. Self-Esteem; 876. Self-Love

878. SELF-REVELATION

See also 169. Confidences

1. His Cheek is his Biographer— / As long as he can blush.

Emily Dickinson, poem (c. 1879)

2. When I speak to you about myself, I am speaking to you about yourself. How is it you don't see that?

Victor Hugo, quoted in John Hall Wheelock's "The Poem in the Nuclear Age," *What Is Poetry?* (1963)

3. The most difficult secret for a man to keep is his own opinion of himself.

Marcel Pagnol, news summaries, March 15, 1954

4. Self-exposure is commendable in art only when it is of a quality and complexity that allows other people to learn about themselves from it.

Susan Sontag, "Going to Theater, Etc.," *Against Interpretation* (1966)

879. SELF-RIGHTEOUSNESS

See also 264. Dogmatism; 335. Fanaticism

1. Self-righteousness is a loud din raised to drown the voice of guilt within us.

Eric Hoffer, *The True Believer* (1951), 3.14.69

2. Men never do evil so completely and cheerfully as when they do it from a religious conviction.

Pascal, *Pensées* (1670), 894, tr. W. F. Trotter

3. Forgive us for cheering legislators who promise low taxes, but deny homes and schools and help to those in need; for self-righteousness that blames the poor for their poverty or the oppressed for their oppression.

United Presbyterian Church, *Litany for Holy Communion* (1968)

SELF-SACRIFICE

See 837. SACRIFICE

SELF-SEEKING

See 495. INTEREST; 874. SELFISHNESS; 876. SELF-LOVE

880. SELF-SUFFICIENCY

See also 235. DEPENDENCE; 291. ENTERPRISE; 867. SELF-DETERMINATION

1. How much time he gains who does not look to see what his neighbor says or does or thinks, but only at what he does himself, to make it just and holy.

MARCUS AURELIUS, *MEDITATIONS* (2ND C.), 4.18, TR. MORRIS HICKEY MORGAN

2. The foundations which we would dig about and find are within us, like the Kingdom of Heaven, rather than without.

SAMUEL BUTLER (D. 1902), "ELEMENTARY MORALITY," *NOTE-BOOKS* (1912)

3. Who to himself is law no law doth need, / Offends no law, and is a king indeed.

GEORGE CHAPMAN, *BUSSY D'AMBOIS* (C. 1604), 2.1

4. Her passion for independence had reached into her manipulation of their joint checking account.

JOHN CHEEVER, *THE FALCONER* (1977)

5. Be thine own palace, or the world's thy jail.

JOHN DONNE, "TO SIR HENRY WOTTON" (1633)

6. The great man is he who in the midst of the crowd keeps with perfect sweetness the independence of solitude.

EMERSON, "SELF-RELIANCE," *ESSAYS: FIRST SERIES* (1841)

7. We must be our own before we can be another's.

EMERSON, "FRIENDSHIP," *ESSAYS: FIRST SERIES* (1841)

8. It is folly for a man to pray to the gods for that which he has the power to obtain for himself.

EPICURUS, "VATICAN SAYINGS" (3RD C. B.C.), 65, IN *LETTERS, PRINCIPAL DOCTRINES, AND VATICAN SAYINGS*, TR. RUSSEL M. GEER

9. Teenagers crave independence. The more self-sufficient we make them feel, the less hostile they are toward us.

HAIM G. GINOTT, *BETWEEN PARENT & TEENAGER* (1969)

10. Be yourself and think for yourself; and while your conclusions may not be infallible they will be nearer right than the conclusions forced upon you by those who have a personal interest in keeping you in ignorance.

ELBERT HUBBARD, *THE NOTE BOOK* (1927)

11. Formal learning can teach you a great deal, but many of the essential skills in life are the ones you have to develop on your own.

LEE IACOCCA, *IACOCCA: AN AUTOBIOGRAPHY* (1984) WITH WILLIAM NOVAK

12. A great maxim of personal responsibility and mature achievement—Do It Yourself—is now the enthroned cliché for being occupied with nonessentials.

LOUIS KRONENBERGER, "UNBRAVE NEW WORLD," *THE CART AND THE HORSE* (1964), 2

13. Who / cannot resolve upon a moment's notice / To live his own life, he forever lives / A slave to others.

GOTTHOLD EPHRAIM LESSING, *NATHAN THE WISE* (1779), 2.9, TR. BAYARD QUINCY MORGAN

14. A learned man is not learned in all things; but a sufficient man is sufficient throughout, even to ignorance itself.

MONTAIGNE, "OF REPENTANCE," *ESSAYS* (1580–88), TR. W. C. HAZLITT

15. A wise man never loses anything if he have himself.

MONTAIGNE, "OF SOLITUDE," *ESSAYS* (1580–88), TR. W. C. HAZLITT

16. I care not so much what I am in the opinion of others, as what I am in my own; I would be rich of myself, and not by borrowing.

MONTAIGNE, "OF GLORY," *ESSAYS* (1580–88), TR. W. C. HAZLITT

17. If you want a thing done well, do it yourself.

NAPOLEON I, *MAXIMS* (1804–1815)

18. Independence is for the very few; it is a privilege of the strong.

NIETZSCHE, *BEYOND GOOD AND EVIL* (1886), 29, TR. WALTER KAUFMANN

19. Now I know the things I know, / And do the things I do; / And if you do not like me so, / To hell, my love, with you!

DOROTHY PARKER, "INDIAN SUMMER," *ENOUGH ROPE* (1926), 2

20. I do my intellectual work inside myself, and once I am with my fellow creatures it is more or less a mat-

ter of indifference to me whether or not they are intelligent as long as they are kind, sincere, etc.

MARCEL PROUST, *LETTERS OF MARCEL PROUST* (1949), TR. MINA CURTISS

21. Any man who is really a man must learn to be alone in the midst of others, to think alone for others, and, if necessary, against others.

ROMAIN ROLLAND, INTRODUCTION, *CLÉRAMBAULT* (1919)

22. Whatever the time or circumstances, the feeling that I am a peasant gives me a rare self-sufficiency. Indeed, the land is always there. I can go back to it at any time.

ANWAR EL-SADAT, *IN SEARCH OF IDENTITY* (1977)

23. We never reflect how pleasant it is to ask for nothing.

SENECA, *LETTERS TO LUCILIUS* (1ST C.), 15.9, TR. E. PHILLIPS BARKER

24. If you want good service, serve yourself.

SPANISH PROVERB

25. The most affluent man is he that confronts all the shows he sees by equivalents out of the stronger wealth of himself.

WALT WHITMAN, PREFACE TO *LEAVES OF GRASS* (1855)

SELLING

See 105. BUYING AND SELLING

881. SENSE AND NONSENSE

1. To appreciate nonsense requires a serious interest in life.

GELETT BURGESS, "THE SENSE OF HUMOR," *THE ROMANCE OF THE COMMONPLACE* (1916)

2. Even God has been defended with nonsense.

WALTER LIPPMANN, "THE GOLDEN RULE AND AFTER," *A PREFACE TO POLITICS* (1914)

3. Nonsense is good only because common sense is so limited.

GEORGE SANTAYANA, "THE COMIC," *THE SENSE OF BEAUTY* (1896)

4. Given any new technology for transmitting information, we seem bound to use it for great quantities of small talk. We are only saved by music from being overwhelmed by nonsense.

LEWIS THOMAS, "THE MUSIC OF *THIS* SPHERE," *THE LIVES OF A CELL* (1974)

882. SENSES

See also 220. DEAFNESS; 325. EYES; 326. FACE; 589. MIND AND BODY; 683. PERCEPTION; 884. SENSUALITY; 897. SIGHT

1. The ear tends to be lazy, craves the familiar, and is shocked by the unexpected: the eye, on the other hand, tends to be impatient, craves the novel and is bored by repetition.

W. H. AUDEN, "HIC ET ILLE," *THE DYER'S HAND* (1962)

2. It was a rich compound of whiskey, after-shave lotion, shoe polish, woolens, and the rankness of a mature male.

JOHN CHEEVER, "REUNION," *THE STORIES OF JOHN CHEEVER* (1978)

3. The soul may be a mere pretense, / the mind makes very little sense. / So let us value the appeal / of that which we can taste and feel.

PIET HEIN, "A TOAST," *GROOKS* (1966)

4. Men trust their ears less than their eyes.

HERODOTUS, *THE HISTORIES* (5TH C. B.C.), 1.8, TR. A. D. GODLEY

5. Nothing awakens a reminiscence like an odour.

VICTOR HUGO, "JEAN VALJEAN," *LES MISÉRABLES* (1862), 9.4, TR. CHARLES E. WILBOUR

6. The air was so sweet in New Orleans it seemed to come in soft bandannas; and you could smell the river and really smell the people, and mud, and molasses, and every kind of tropical exhalation, with your nose suddenly removed from the dry ices of a Northern winter.

JACK KEROUAC, *ON THE ROAD* (1957)

7. What can give us surer knowledge than our senses? With what else can we better distinguish the true from the false?

LUCRETIUS, *ON THE NATURE OF THINGS* (1ST C. B.C.), 1

8. All credibility, all good conscience, all evidence of truth come only from the senses.

NIETZSCHE, *BEYOND GOOD AND EVIL* (1886), 134, TR. WALTER KAUFMANN

9. The loss of a sense adds as much beauty to the world as its acquisition.

MARCEL PROUST, *REMEMBRANCE OF THINGS PAST: THE GUERMANTES WAY* (1913–27), TR. C. K. SCOTT-MONCRIEFF

10. The air I was breathing wasn't air: it was a compound of smells, of meat, sweat, popcorn, cooking fat and passed gas.

JONATHAN RABAN, *OLD GLORY* (1981)

11. We are astonished at thought, but sensation is equally wonderful.

VOLTAIRE, "SENSATION," *PHILOSOPHICAL DICTIONARY* (1764)

12. Seeing, hearing, feeling, are miracles, and each part and tag of me is a miracle.

WALT WHITMAN, "SONG OF MYSELF," 24, *LEAVES OF GRASS* (1855–92)

13. Devils can be driven out of the heart by the touch of a hand on a hand, or a mouth on a mouth.

TENNESSEE WILLIAMS, *THE MILK TRAIN DOESN'T STOP HERE ANYMORE* (1963), 5

883. SENSIBILITY

See also 175. CONSCIOUSNESS; 284. EMOTIONS; 483. INSENSITIVITY; 501. INTUITION; 683. PERCEPTION

1. Chords that vibrate sweetest pleasure / Thrill the deepest notes of woe.

ROBERT BURNS, "ON SENSIBILITY" (1791)

2. If we had keen vision and feeling of all ordinary human life, it would be like hearing the grass grow and the squirrel's heart beat, and we should die of that roar which lies on the other side of silence.

GEORGE ELIOT, *MIDDLEMARCH* (1871–72), 20

3. The great man, that is, the man most imbued with the spirit of the time, is the impressionable man.

EMERSON, "FATE," *THE CONDUCT OF LIFE* (1860)

4. Great eaters and great sleepers are incapable of anything else that is great.

HENRY IV OF FRANCE (1553–1610), EPIGRAM

5. Nothing is little to him that feels it with great sensibility.

SAMUEL JOHNSON, LETTER TO JOSEPH BARETTI, JULY 20, 1762, QUOTED IN BOSWELL'S *LIFE OF SAMUEL JOHNSON*

6. The heart that is soonest awake to the flowers / Is always the first to be touched by the thorns.

THOMAS MOORE, "OH, THINK NOT MY SPIRITS ARE ALWAYS AS LIGHT," *IRISH MELODIES* (1807–35)

7. The sensibility of man to trifles, and his insensibility to great things, indicates a strange inversion.

PASCAL, *PENSÉES* (1670), 198, TR. W. F. TROTTER

8. The two pioneering forces of modern sensibility are Jewish moral seriousness and homosexual aestheticism and irony.

SUSAN SONTAG, "NOTES ON CAMP," *AGAINST INTERPRETATION* (1961)

SENSITIVITY

See 883. SENSIBILITY

884. SENSUALITY

See also 882. SENSES

1. Moral qualities rule the world, but at short distances the senses are despotic.

EMERSON, "MANNERS," *ESSAYS: SECOND SERIES* (1844)

2. How much more sensuality invites to art than does sentimentality.

ANDRÉ GIDE, *JOURNALS*, 1912, TRANSLATED AND EDITED BY JUSTIN O'BRIEN

3. "I could walk with Jack [John F. Kennedy] into a room full of a hundred women," fellow Congressman and friend Frank Thompson said, "and at least eighty-five of them would be willing to sacrifice their honor and everything else if they could get into a pad with him."

DORIS KEARNS GOODWIN, *THE FITZGERALDS AND THE KENNEDYS* (1987)

4. He could distinguish the approach of Milly like that of a police car from a long way off. Whistles instead of sirens warned him of her coming.

GRAHAM GREENE, *OUR MAN IN HAVANA* (1958)

5. Attraction eludes control so stubbornly that whole societies designed to organize relationships among people cannot keep order, not even when they bind people to one another from childhood and raise them together.

MAXINE HONG KINGSTON, *THE WOMAN WARRIOR* (1976)

6. Sensuality, too, which used to show itself coarse, smiling, unmasked, and unmistakable, is now serious, analytic, and so burdened with a sense of its responsibilities that it passes muster half the time as a new type of asceticism.

AGNES REPPLIER, "FICTION IN THE PULPIT," *POINTS OF VIEW* (1891)

885. SENTIMENTALITY

1. Sentimentality, the ostentatious parading of excessive and spurious emotion, is the mark of dishonesty, the inability to feel.

JAMES BALDWIN, "EVERYBODY'S PROTEST NOVEL" (1949), *NOTES OF A NATIVE SON* (1955)

2. If there is anybody I detest, it is weak-minded sentimentalists—all those melancholy people who, out of an excess of sympathy for others, miss the thrill of

their own essence and drift through life without identity, like a human fog, feeling sorry for everyone.

JOHN CHEEVER, "THE HOUSEBREAKER OF SHADY HILL," *THE STORIES OF JOHN CHEEVER* (1980)

3. To the modern spirit, disillusioned, or at least unillusioned, the great evil to be avoided is sentimentality.

IRWIN EDMAN, "HOW TO BE SWEET THOUGH SOPHISTICATED," *ADAM, THE BABY, AND THE MAN FROM MARS* (1929)

4. Sentimentality is only sentiment that rubs you up the wrong way.

W. SOMERSET MAUGHAM, *A WRITER'S NOTEBOOK*, 1941

5. I hope my tongue in prune juice smothers / If I belittle dogs and mothers.

OGDEN NASH, "COMPLIMENTS OF A FRIEND," *VERSUS* (1949)

6. Sentimentality is a failure of feeling.

WALLACE STEVENS, "ADAGIA," *OPUS POSTHUMOUS* (1957)

7. I don't trust sentimentality in men; it goes with tyranny; you can't have one without the other.

CAITLIN THOMAS, *CAITLIN* (1986), WITH GEORGE TREMLETT

8. A sentimentalist is a man who sees an absurd value in everything and doesn't know the market price of any single thing.

OSCAR WILDE, *LADY WINDERMERE'S FAN* (1892), 3

9. There is no more subtle dissolvent of morals than sentimentality.

WOODROW WILSON, ADDRESS, PRINCETON UNIVERSITY, JUNE 7, 1908

SEPARATION

See 673. PARTING

SERENITY

See 989. TRANQUILITY

886. SERIOUSNESS

See also 740. PROFUNDITY

1. A serious life means being fully aware of the alternatives, thinking about them with all the intensity one brings to bear on life-and-death questions, in full recognition that every choice is a great risk with necessary consequences that are hard to bear.

ALLAN BLOOM, *THE CLOSING OF THE AMERICAN MIND* (1987)

2. Oh, that ludicrous virile earnestness!

HEINRICH BÖLL, *WHAT'S TO BECOME OF THE BOY?* (1981)

3. Earnest people are often people who habitually look on the serious side of things that have no serious side.

VAN WYCK BROOKS, *FROM A WRITER'S NOTEBOOK* (1958)

4. Every man is grave alone.

EMERSON, *JOURNALS*, 1824

5. There is ever a slight suspicion of the burlesque about earnest, good men.

EMERSON, *JOURNALS*, 1840

6. A human action becomes genuinely important when it springs from the soil of a clearsighted awareness of the temporality and the ephemerality of everything human.

VÁCLAV HAVEL, *DISTURBING THE PEACE* (1990)

7. Taking fun / as simply fun / and earnestness / in earnest / shows how thoroughly / thou none / of the two / discernest.

PIET HEIN, "THE ETERNAL TWINS," *GROOKS* (1966)

8. There are people who think that everything one does with a serious face is sensible.

GEORG CHRISTOPH LICHTENBERG, *APHORISMS* (1764–99), TR. H. HATFIELD

9. Solemnity is the shield of idiots.

MONTESQUIEU, *PENSÉES ET JUGEMENTS* (1899)

10. Taking sides is the beginning of sincerity, and earnestness follows shortly afterwards, and the human being becomes a bore.

OSCAR WILDE, *A WOMAN OF NO IMPORTANCE* (1893), 1

SERMONS

See 724. PREACHING AND PREACHERS

887. SERVICE

See also 56. ASSISTANCE; 227. DEEDS; 433. HUMANITARIANISM; 1023. USEFULNESS

1. All service ranks the same with God— / With God, whose puppets, best and worst, / Are we: there is no last nor first.

ROBERT BROWNING, "NIGHT," *PIPPA PASSES* (1841)

2. To serve is beautiful, but only if it is done with joy and a whole heart and a free mind.

PEARL S. BUCK, "MEN AND WOMEN," *TO MY DAUGHTERS, WITH LOVE* (1967)

3. Pressed into service means pressed out of shape.

ROBERT FROST, "THE SELF-SEEKER," *NORTH OF BOSTON* (1914)

4. "Let me light my lamp," / says the star, / "And never debate / if it will help to remove the darkness."

RABINDRANATH TAGORE, *FIREFLIES* (1928)

5. There is something better, if possible, that a man can give than his life. That is his living spirit to a service that is not easy, to resist counsels that are hard to resist, to stand against purposes that are difficult to stand against.

WOODROW WILSON, SPEECH, MAY 30, 1919

888. SERVICES

See also 227. DEEDS; 384. GIFTS AND GIVING; 433. HUMANITARIANISM; 837. SACRIFICE

1. The man who confers a favour would rather not be repaid in the same coin.

ARISTOTLE, *NICOMACHEAN ETHICS* (4TH C. B.C.), 4.1, TR. J. A. K. THOMSON

2. We should render a service to a friend to bind him closer to us, and to an enemy in order to make a friend of him.

CLEOBULUS (6TH C. B.C.), QUOTED IN DIOGENES LAERTIUS' *LIVES AND OPINIONS OF EMINENT PHILOSOPHERS* (3RD C. A.D.), TR. R. D. HICKS

3. Verily the kindness that gazes upon itself in a mirror turns to stone, / And a good deed that calls itself by tender names becomes the parent to a curse.

KAHLIL GIBRAN, "THE FAREWELL," *THE PROPHET* (1923)

4. To oblige persons often costs little and helps much.

BALTASAR GRACIÁN, *THE ART OF WORLDLY WISDOM* (1647), 226, TR. JOSEPH JACOBS

5. The pleasure we derive from doing favors is partly in the feeling it gives us that we are not altogether worthless.

ERIC HOFFER, *THE PASSIONATE STATE OF MIND* (1954), 113

6. The charity that is a trifle to us can be precious to others.

HOMER, *ODYSSEY* (9TH C. B.C.), 6, TR. E. V. RIEU

7. Men become attached to us not by reason of the services we render them, but by reason of the services they render us.

EUGÈNE LABICHE, *LE VOYAGE DE M. PERRICHON* (1860), 4.8

8. He who boasts of a favor bestowed, would like it back again.

PUBLILIUS SYRUS, *MORAL SAYINGS* (1ST C. B.C.), 91, TR. DARIUS LYMAN

9. A favour well bestowed is almost as great an honour to him who confers it as to him who receives it.

RICHARD STEELE, *THE SPECTATOR* (1711–12), 497

889. SERVITUDE

See also 109. CAPTIVITY; 537. LIBERTY; 1002. TYRANNY

1. He who is by nature not his own but another's man, is by nature a slave.

ARISTOTLE, *POLITICS* (4TH C. B.C.), 1.4, TR. BENJAMIN JOWETT

2. Virtue cannot dwell with slaves, nor reign / O'er those who cower to take a tyrant's yoke.

WILLIAM CULLEN BRYANT, "THE AGES" (1821)

3. Slavery they can have anywhere. It is a weed that grows in every soil.

EDMUND BURKE, SPEECH, "ON CONCILIATION WITH THE AMERICAN COLONIES," MARCH 22, 1775

4. As contraband, fugitive slaves could be collected and used by a Union army just as any other property could be collected and used, and nobody was in any way committed on any side of the slavery issue itself.

BRUCE CATTON, *THIS HALLOWED GROUND* (1956)

5. The feeling of the nation must be quickened; the conscience of the nation must be roused; the propriety of the nation must be startled; the hypocrisy of the nation must be exposed; and its crimes against God and man must be proclaimed and denounced.

FREDERICK DOUGLASS, IN A SPEECH ON SLAVERY, JULY 4, 1852

6. I didn't know I was a slave until I found out I couldn't do the things I wanted.

FREDERICK DOUGLASS, *NARRATIVE OF THE LIFE OF FREDERICK DOUGLASS* (1845)

7. This is what it means / to be a slave: to be abused and bear it, / compelled by violence to suffer wrong.

EURIPIDES, *HECUBA* (C. 425 B.C.), TR. WILLIAM ARROWSMITH

8. Whatever day / Makes man a slave, takes half his worth away.

HOMER, *ODYSSEY* (9TH C. B.C.), 17.392, TR. ALEXANDER POPE

9. Freedom is indivisible, and when one man is enslaved, all are not free.

JOHN F. KENNEDY, ADDRESS, WEST BERLIN, JUNE 26, 1963

10. This is a world of compensation; and he who would be no slave must consent to have no slave. Those who deny freedom to others deserve it not for themselves, and, under a just God, cannot long retain it.

ABRAHAM LINCOLN, LETTER TO H. L. PIERCE AND OTHERS, APRIL 6, 1859

11. This is servitude, / To serve the unwise.

MILTON, *PARADISE LOST* (1667), 6.178

12. Every aspect of the slave regime attempted to obliterate the slave's being. The simplest and most sacred forms by which humans acquire identity and dignity were denied slaves—the right to a name, knowledge of a birthday, occasional privacy, the ability to maintain the most basic family relationships, protection from physical and sexual savagery, and so on.

GILBERT OSOFSKY, *THE BURDEN OF RACE* (1967)

13. Art thou less a slave by being loved and favoured by thy master? Thou art indeed well off, slave. Thy master favours thee; he will soon beat thee.

PASCAL, *PENSÉES* (1670), 209, TR. W. F. TROTTER

14. Coercion created slavery, the cowardice of the slaves perpetuated it.

ROUSSEAU, *THE SOCIAL CONTRACT* (1762), 1.2

15. Slaves lose everything in their chains, even the desire of escaping from them.

ROUSSEAU, *THE SOCIAL CONTRACT* (1762), 1.2, TR. G. D. H. COLE

16. Slavery holds few men fast; the greater number hold fast their slavery.

SENECA, *LETTERS TO LUCILIUS* (1ST C.), 22.11, TR. E. PHILLIPS BARKER

17. No man is good enough to be another man's master.

GEORGE BERNARD SHAW, *MAJOR BARBARA* (1905), 3

18. All spirits are enslaved which serve things evil.

SHELLEY, *PROMETHEUS UNBOUND* (1818–19), 2.4

19. Servitude debases men to the point where they end up liking it.

VAUVENARGUES, *REFLECTIONS AND MAXIMS* (1746), 22

890. SEVERITY

See also 534. LENIENCY; 766. PUNISHMENT

1. If you hit a pony over the nose at the outset of your acquaintance, he may not love you, but he will take a deep interest in your movements ever afterwards.

RUDYARD KIPLING, "FALSE DAWN," *PLAIN TALES FROM THE HILLS* (1888)

2. Excessive severity misses its own aim.

PUBLILIUS SYRUS, *MORAL SAYINGS* (1ST C. B.C.), 62, TR. DARIUS LYMAN

3. Be not so severe as to cause shyness, nor so clement as to encourage boldness.

SA'DI, *GULISTAN* (1258), 8.19, TR. JAMES ROSS

4. Nothing comes of severity if there be no leanings towards a change of heart. And if there be natural leanings towards a change of heart, what need for severity?

SAINT-EXUPÉRY, *THE WISDOM OF THE SANDS* (1948), 43, TR. STUART GILBERT

5. I must be cruel, only to be kind.

SHAKESPEARE, *HAMLET* (1600), 3.4.178

891. SEWERS

See also 707. PLUMBERS

1. A sewer is a cynic. It tells All.

VICTOR HUGO, JEAN VALJEAN, *LES MISERABLES* (1862), 2.2, TR. CHARLES E. WILBOUR

892. SEX

See also 122. CHASTITY; 351. FLIRTATION; 424. HOMOSEXUALITY; 521. KISSING; 551. LOVE; 566. MASCULINITY AND FEMININITY; 714. PORNOGRAPHY; 742. PROMISCUITY; 752. PROSTITUTION; 857. SEDUCTION; 884. SENSUALITY

1. Desire is poison at lunch and wormwood at dinner; your bed is a stone, friendship is hateful and your fancy is always fixed on one thing.

PIETRO ARETINO, LETTER TO COUNT DI SAN SECONDO, JUNE 24, 1537, TR. SAMUEL PUTNAM

2. There was scarcely a woman alive, it seemed, who could resist the urge to haul men down onto beds, car seats, kitchen floors, dining-room tables, park grass, parlor sofas, or packing crates, entwine warm thighs around them, and pant in ecstasy.

RUSSELL BAKER, *GROWING UP* (1982)

3. [H]is mother and father, who went to church on Sundays, they did it too, and sometimes John heard them in the bedroom behind him, over the sound of

rats' feet, and rat screams, and the music and cursing from the harlot's house downstairs.

JAMES BALDWIN, *GO TELL IT ON THE MOUNTAIN* (1953)

4. Sexuality is the lyricism of the masses.

CHARLES BAUDELAIRE, *INTIMATE JOURNALS* (1887), 93, TR. CHRISTOPHER ISHERWOOD

5. She transformed his miseries into sexual excitements and, to give credit where it was due, turned his grief in a useful direction.

SAUL BELLOW, *HERZOG* (1964)

6. What I seem to do, thought Herzog, is to inflame myself with my drama, with ridicule, failure, denunciation, distortion, to inflame myself voluptuously, esthetically, until I reach sexual climax. And that climax looks like a resolution and an answer to many "higher" problems.

SAUL BELLOW, *HERZOG* (1964)

7. If venereal delight and the power of propagating the species were permitted only to the virtuous, it would make the world very good.

JAMES BOSWELL, *LONDON JOURNAL,* MARCH 26, 1763

8. Sex was invented as a biological instrument by (say) the green algae. But as an instrument in the ascent of man which is basic to his cultural evolution, it was invented by man himself.

JACON BRONOWSKI, *THE ASCENT OF MAN* (1973)

9. I don't know whether it's normal or not, but sex has always been something that I take seriously. I would put it higher than tennis on my list of constructive things to do.

ART BUCHWALD, *LEAVING HOME: A MEMOIR* (1993)

10. He then joins her on her side of the bed and they engage in a back-breaking labor of love that occupies them for twenty minutes and leaves them both with a grueling headache.

JOHN CHEEVER, *BULLET PARK* (1960)

11. [H]ow can we describe the most exalted experience of our physical lives [sex], as if—jack, wrench, hubcap, and nuts—we were describing the changing of a flat tire?

JOHN CHEEVER, "A MISCELLANY OF CHARACTERS THAT WILL NOT APPEAR," *THE STORIES OF JOHN CHEEVER* (1978)

12. His imagery for a big orgasm was winning the sailboat race, the Renaissance, high mountains.

JOHN CHEEVER, *THE FALCONER* (1977)

13. If our elaborate and dominating bodies are given us to be denied at every turn, if our nature is always wrong and wicked, how ineffectual we are—like fishes not meant to swim.

CYRIL CONNOLLY, *THE UNQUIET GRAVE* (1945), I

14. Sex is the great amateur art. The professional, male or female, is frowned on; he or she misses the whole point and spoils the show.

DAVID CORT, *SOCIAL ASTONISHMENTS* (1963)

15. Well, one thing you can say for masturbation...you certainly don't have to look your best.

MART CROWLEY, *THE BOYS IN THE BAND* (1968)

16. What most men desire is a virgin who is a whore.

EDWARD DAHLBERG, "ON LUST," *REASONS OF THE HEART* (1965)

17. Love's mysteries in souls do grow, / But yet the body is his book.

JOHN DONNE, "THE ECSTASY," *SONGS AND SONNETS* (1633)

18. Whoever loves, if he do not propose / The right true end of love, he's one that goes / To sea for nothing but to make him sick.

JOHN DONNE, ELEGY 18, "LOVE'S PROGRESS" (1661)

19. The sexual embrace can only be compared with music and with prayer.

HAVELOCK ELLIS, *ON LIFE AND SEX: ESSAYS OF LOVE AND VIRTUE* (1937), I

20. If your life at night is good, you think you have / Everything; but, if in that quarter things go wrong, / You will consider your best and truest interests / Most hateful.

EURIPIDES, *MEDEA* (431 B.C.), TR. REX WARNER

21. Sex begins before adolescence, and survives sterility; it is indeed coeval with our lives, although at the mating age its effects are more obvious to Society.

E.M. FORSTER, "PEOPLE," *ASPECTS OF THE NOVEL* (1927)

22. Retrospectively, I would agree with Luis Buñuel that sex without sin is like an egg without salt.

CARLOS FUENTES, "HOW I STARTED TO WRITE," IN *THE ART OF THE PERSONAL ESSAY* (1994), ED. PHILLIP LOPATE

23. Women are silver dishes into which we put golden apples.

GOETHE, QUOTED IN JOHANN PETER ECKERMANN'S *CONVERSATIONS WITH GOETHE,* OCT. 22, 1828

24. My own view, for what it's worth, is that sexuality is lovely, there cannot be too much of it, it is self-lim-

iting if it is satisfactory, and satisfaction diminishes tension and clears the mind for attention and learning.

Paul Goodman, *Compulsory Miseducation* (1964)

25. Sex for many has become a sorry business, a mechanical release involving neither discovery nor triumph, stressing human isolation more dishearteningly than ever before.

Germaine Greer, *The Female Eunuch* (1970)

26. The castration of women has been carried out in terms of a masculine-feminine polarity, in which men have commandeered all the energy and streamlined it into an aggressive conquistadorial power, reducing all heterosexual contact to a sadomasochistic pattern.

Germaine Greer, *The Female Eunuch* (1970)

27. If a woman hasn't got a tiny streak of a harlot in her, she's a dry stick as a rule.

D. H. Lawrence, *Pornography and Obscenity* (1930)

28. Virginity is now a mere preamble or waiting room to be got out of as soon as possible; it is without significance.

Ursula K. Le Guin, "The Space Crone," *Dancing at the Edge of the World* (1989)

29. The old man, especially if he is in society, in the privacy of his thoughts, though he may protest the opposite, never stops believing that, through some singular exception of the universal rule, he can in some unknown and inexplicable way still make an impression on women.

Giacomo Leopardi, *Pensieri* (1834–37), 54, tr. William Fense Weaver

30. The body searches for that which has injured the mind with love.

Lucretius, *On the Nature of Things* (1st c. b.c.), 4

31. The truly erotic sensibility, in evoking the image of woman, never omits to clothe it. The robing and disrobing: that is the true traffic of love.

Antonio Machado, *Juan de Mairena* (1943), 46, tr. Ben Belitt

32. Most creatures have a vague belief that a very precarious hazard, a kind of transparent membrane, divides death from love; and that the profound idea of nature demands that the giver of life should die at the moment of giving.

Maurice Maeterlinck, *The Life of the Bee* (1901), tr. Alfred Sutro

33. Looking back now on the whole sexual scene we can see that our species has remained much more loyal to its basic biological urges than we might at first imagine. Its primate sexual system with carnivore modifications has survived all the fantastic technological advances remarkably well.

Desmond Morris, *The Naked Ape* (1967)

34. The orgasm has replaced the Cross as the focus of longing and the image of fulfillment.

Malcolm Muggeridge, "Down with Sex," *The Most of Malcolm Muggeridge* (1966)

35. There is nothing like early promiscuous sex for dispelling life's bright mysterious expectations.

Iris Murdoch, *A Word Child* (1975)

36. When a lady's erotic life is vexed / God knows what God is coming next.

Ogden Nash, "The Seven Spiritual Ages of Mrs. Marmaduke Moore," *Verses from 1929 On* (1959)

37. Christianity gave Eros poison to drink: he did not die of it but degenerated—into vice.

Nietzsche, *Beyond Good and Evil* (1886), 168, tr. Walter Kaufmann

38. The degree and kind of a man's sexuality reach up into the ultimate pinnacle of his spirit.

Nietzsche, *Beyond Good and Evil* (1886), 75, tr. Walter Kaufmann

39. I hate a woman who offers herself because she ought to do so, and, cold and dry, thinks of her sewing when she's making love.

Ovid, *The Art of Love* (c. a.d. 8), 2, tr. J. Lewis May

40. Modern feminism's most naive formulation is its assertion that rape is a crime of violence but not of sex, that it is merely power masquerading as sex. But sex is power, and all power is inherently aggressive.

Camille Paglia, *Sexual Personae: Art and Decadence from Nefertiti to Emily Dickinson* (1990)

41. Sex is the point of contact between man and nature, where morality and good intentions fall to primitive urges.

Camille Paglia, *Sexual Personae: Art and Decadence from Nefertiti to Emily Dickinson* (1990)

42. I sometimes think novelists write about sex in order to avoid boring themselves to death.

Walker Percy, "How To Be a Novelist In Spite of Being Southern and Catholic," *Signposts in a Strange Land* (1991)

43. It often puzzles me when people think that matters connected with sex ought to be suppressed. Sex

itself cannot be suppressed, and the efforts to do it, it seems to me, result in greater damage than it can do itself. After all, it was not an invention of man, but of God.

Maxwell Perkins, *Editor to Author: The Letters of Maxwell Perkins* (1950), ed. John Hall Wheelock

44. I'd call it love if love / didn't take so many years / but lust too is a jewel.

Adrienne Rich, "Two Songs," *Necessities of Life* (1966)

45. Some have held the Eye to be / The instrument of lechery, / More furtive than the Hand in low / And vicious venery—Not so! / Its rape is gentle, never more / Violent than a metaphor.

Theodore Roethke, "Prayer," *The Collected Verse of Theodore Roethke* (1961)

46. Civilized people cannot fully satisfy their sexual instinct without love.

Bertrand Russell, "The Place of Love in Human Life," *Marriage and Morals* (1929)

47. Much contention and strife will arise in that house where the wife shall get up dissatisfied with her husband.

Sa'di, *Gulistan* (1258), 6.2, tr. James Ross

48. Is it not strange that desire should so many years outlive performance?

Shakespeare, *2 Henry IV* (1597–98), 2.4.283

49. Certainly nothing is unnatural that is not physically impossible.

Richard Brinsley Sheridan, *The Critic* (1779), 2.1

50. The eyes of men love to pluck / the blossoms; from the faded flowers they turn away.

Sophocles, *The Women of Trachis* (c. 413 B.C.), tr. Michael Jameson

51. Obviously, untangling sex from aggression and violence or the threat of it is going to take a very long time. And the process is going to be greatly resisted as a challenge to the very heart of male dominance and male centrality.

Gloria Steinem, "Erotica vs. Pornography," *Outrageous Acts and Everyday Rebellions* (1983)

52. [I]t is no mere accident (as Orwell knew) that the standardization of sexual life, either through controlled license or compelled puritanism, should accompany totalitarian politics.

George Steiner, *Language and Silence* (1967)

53. Sex builds no roads, writes no novels, and sex certainly gives no meaning to anything in life but itself.

Gore Vidal, *Rocking the Boat* (1962)

893. SHAME

See also 405. Guilt; 434. Humiliation; 820. Ridicule; 861. Self-Consciousness

1. We never forgive those who make us blush.

Jean-François De La Harpe, *Mélanie* (1770), 3.1

2. Blushing is the color of virtue.

Diogenes The Cynic (4th c. B.C.), quoted in Diogenes Laertius' *Lives and Opinions of Eminent Philosophers* (3rd c. A.D.), tr. R. D. Hicks

3. One of the misfortunes of our time is that in getting rid of false shame we have killed off so much real shame as well.

Louis Kronenberger, *Company Manners* (1954), 2.1

4. I remember one thing that marred this time for me; the movie "Gone with the Wind." When it played in Mason [Michigan], I was the only Negro in the theater, and when Butterfly McQueen went into her act, I felt like crawling under the rug.

Malcolm X, *The Autobiography of Malcolm X* (1964)

5. The only shame is to have none.

Pascal, *Pensées* (1670), 194, tr. W. F. Trotter

6. Give your friend cause to blush, and you will be likely to lose him.

Publilius Syrus, *Moral Sayings* (1st c. B.C.), 848, tr. Darius Lyman

7. I never wonder to see men wicked, but I often wonder to see them not ashamed.

Jonathan Swift, *Thoughts on Various Subjects* (1711)

8. Man is the only animal that blushes. Or needs to.

Mark Twain, "Pudd'nhead Wilson's New Calendar," *Following the Equator* (1897), 1.27

9. The man that blushes is not quite a brute.

Edward Young, *Night Thoughts* (1742–46), 7.496

894. SHARING

See also 384. Gifts and Giving

1. The ass that is common property is always the worst saddled.

English Proverb

2. Infinite sharing is the law of God's inner life.

Thomas Merton, *No Man Is an Island* (1955)

3. If wisdom were offered me with the proviso that I should keep it shut up and refrain from declaring it, I should refuse. There's no delight in owning anything unshared.

SENECA, *LETTERS TO LUCILIUS* (1ST C.), 6.4, TR. E. PHILLIPS BARKER

4. I never share credit or desserts.

BEVERLY SILLS, INTERVIEW IN *THE NEW YORK TIMES*

5. He who divides gets the worst share.

SPANISH PROVERB

6. Grief can take care of itself, but to get the full value of joy you must have somebody to divide it with.

MARK TWAIN, *NOTEBOOK* (1935)

895. SHIPS AND BOATS

See also 839. SAILING

1. A ship in dock, surrounded by quays and the walls of warehouses, has the appearance of a prisoner meditating upon freedom in the sadness of a free spirit put under restraint.

JOSEPH CONRAD, *THE MIRROR OF THE SEA* (1906), 33

2. Believe me, my young friend, there is *nothing*—absolutely nothing—half so much worth doing as simply messing about in boats.

KENNETH GRAHAME, *THE WIND IN THE WILLOWS* (1908), 1

3. Somewhere far at the back of the fleet of barges, now lost behind the island, now printing blots of smoke on the sky, was a boat that wasn't a boat, but a blunt white four-story house, all balconies and verandas, mounted over the top of an enormous engine.

JONATHAN RABAN, *OLD GLORY* (1981)

4. A boat to your average woman is just one more damn house to take care of, only it's more uncomfortable, and the man orders her around like Captain Bligh, and she doesn't trust the machinery or the plumbing, and she has to walk six blocks to buy groceries or to get the laundry done.

KURT VONNEGUT, *WAMPETERS FOMA & GRANFALLOONS (OPINIONS)*

SHYNESS

See 980. TIMIDITY

896. SICKNESS

See also 382. GERMS; 413. HEALTH; 577. MEDICINE

1. Diseases crucify the soul of man, attenuate our bodies, dry them, wither them, shrivel them up like old apples, make them so many anatomies.

ROBERT BURTON, *THE ANATOMY OF MELANCHOLY* (1621), 1

2. I reckon being ill as one of the great pleasures of life, provided one is not too ill and is not obliged to work till one is better.

SAMUEL BUTLER (D. 1902), *THE WAY OF ALL FLESH* (1903), 80

3. Can there be worse sickness, than to know / that we are never well, nor can be so?

JOHN DONNE, *AN ANATOMY OF THE WORLD; THE FIRST ANNIVERSARY* (1612)

4. Ivry sick man is a hero, if not to th' wurruld or aven to th' fam'ly, at laste to himself.

FINLEY PETER DUNNE, "GOING TO SEE THE DOCTOR," *MR. DOOLEY ON MAKING A WILL* (1919)

5. All diseases run into one, old age.

EMERSON, *JOURNALS,* 1840

6. There is one topic peremptorily forbidden to all well-bred, to all rational mortals, namely, their distempers. If you have not slept, or if you have slept, or if you have headache, or sciatica, or leprosy, or thunderstroke, I beseech you, by all angels, to hold your peace, and not pollute the morning.

EMERSON, "BEHAVIOR," *THE CONDUCT OF LIFE* (1860)

7. We forget ourselves and our destinies in health, and the chief use of temporary sickness is to remind us of these concerns.

EMERSON, *JOURNALS,* 1821

8. Sleep to the sick is half health.

GERMAN PROVERB

9. Those who have never been ill are incapable of real sympathy for a great many misfortunes.

ANDRÉ GIDE, *JOURNALS,* JULY 25, 1930, TR. JUSTIN O'BRIEN

10. A human being sheds its leaves like a tree. Sickness prunes it down; and it no longer offers the same silhouette to the eyes which loved it, to the people to whom it afforded shade and comfort.

JULES DE GONCOURT, *JOURNAL,* JULY 22, 1862, TR. ROBERT BALDICK

11. A bodily disease, which we look upon as whole and entire within itself, may, after all, be but a symptom of some ailment in the spiritual part.

NATHANIEL HAWTHORNE, *THE SCARLET LETTER* (1850), 10

12. To be sick and helpless is a humiliating experience. Prolonged illness also carries the hazard of narcissistic self-absorption.

RICHARD HOFSTADTER, *THE AMERICAN POLITICAL TRADITION* (1948)

13. One of the most difficult things to contend with in a hospital is the assumption on the part of the staff that because you have lost your gall bladder you have also lost your mind.

JEAN KERR, "OPERATION OPERATION," *PLEASE DON'T EAT THE DAISIES* (1957)

14. How convalescence shrinks a man back to his pristine stature! where is now the space, which he occupied so lately, in his own, in the family's eye?

CHARLES LAMB, "THE CONVALESCENT," *LAST ESSAYS OF ELIA* (1833)

15. How sickness enlarges the dimensions of a man's self to himself! he is his own exclusive object. Supreme selfishness is inculcated upon him as his only duty.

CHARLES LAMB, "THE CONVALESCENT," *LAST ESSAYS OF ELIA* (1833)

16. Disease makes men more physical, it leaves them nothing but body.

THOMAS MANN, *THE MAGIC MOUNTAIN* (1924), 4.10, TR. H. T. LOWE-PORTER

17. A man can be riddled with malaria for years on end, with its chills and its fevers and its nightmares, but if one day he sees that the water from his kidneys is black, he knows he will not leave that place again, wherever he is, or wherever he hoped to be.

BERYL MARKHAM, *WEST WITH THE NIGHT* (1942)

18. A cough is something that you yourself can't help, but everybody else does on purpose just to torment you.

OGDEN NASH, "CAN I GET YOU A GLASS OF WATER? OR PLEASE CLOSE THE GLOTTIS AFTER YOU," *YOU CAN'T GET THERE FROM HERE* (1957)

19. The sick woman especially: no one surpasses her in refinements for ruling, oppressing, tyrannising.

NIETZSCHE, *THE GENEALOGY OF MORALS* (1887), 3.14, TR. HORACE B. SAMUEL

20. I've got Bright's disease and he has mine.

S.J. PERELMAN, *THE MOST OF S.J. PERELMAN* (1958)

21. Show him death, and he'll be content with fever.

PERSIAN PROVERB

22. When he is sick, every man wants his mother; if she's not around, other women must do. Zuckerman was making do with four other women.

PHILIP ROTH, *THE ANATOMY LESSON* (1983)

23. First thing about being a patient—you have to learn patience.

OLIVER SACKS, *A LEG TO STAND ON* (1984)

24. I was set apart, we were set apart, we patients in white nightgowns, and avoided clearly, though unconsciously, like lepers.

OLIVER SACKS, *A LEG TO STAND ON* (1984)

25. Recovery was not to be seen as a smooth slope, but as a series of radical steps, each inconceivable, impossible, from the step below.

OLIVER SACKS, *A LEG TO STAND ON* (1984)

26. The diseases which destroy a man are no less natural than the instincts which preserve him.

GEORGE SANTAYANA, *DIALOGUES IN LIMBO* (1925), 3

27. There was never yet philosopher / That could endure the toothache patiently.

SHAKESPEARE, *MUCH ADO ABOUT NOTHING* (1598–99), 5.1.35

28. I enjoy convalescence. It is the part that makes the illness worth while.

GEORGE BERNARD SHAW, *BACK TO METHUSELAH* (1921), 2

29. Illness is the night-side of life, a more onerous ciizenship. Everyone who is born holds dual citizenship, in the kingdom of the well and in the kingdom of the sick.

SUSAN SONTAG, *ILLNESS AS METAPHOR* (1978)

30. The sleep of a sick man has keen eyes. / It is a sleep unsleeping.

SOPHOCLES, *PHILOCTETES* (409 B.C.), TR. DAVID GRENE

31. I dislike helplessness in other people and in myself, and this is by far my greatest fear of illness.

JOHN STEINBECK, *TRAVELS WITH CHARLEY* (1962)

32. I do not find illness an eminence, and I do not understand how people can use it to draw attention to themselves since the attention they draw is nearly always reluctantly given and unpleasantly carried out.

JOHN STEINBECK, *TRAVELS WITH CHARLEY* (1962)

33. We are so fond of one another, because our ailments are the same.

JONATHAN SWIFT, *JOURNAL TO STELLA*, FEB. 1, 1711

897. SIGHT

See also 86. BLINDNESS, PHYSICAL; 325. EYES; 683. PERCEPTION; 882. SENSES; 1035. VISION

1. Our sight is the most perfect and most delightful of all our senses. It fills the mind with the largest variety of ideas, converses with its objects at the greatest distance, and continues the longest in action without being tired or satiated with its proper enjoyments.

JOSEPH ADDISON, *THE SPECTATOR* (1711–12), 411

2. The hunger of the eye is not to be despised; and they are to be pitied who have starvation of the eye.

HENRY WARD BEECHER, *PROVERBS FROM PLYMOUTH PULPIT* (1887)

3. When I walk with a camera, I walk from shot to shot, reading the light on a calibrated meter. When I walk without a camera, my own shutter opens, and the moment's light prints on my own silver gut. When I see this second way I am above all an unscrupulous observer.

ANNIE DILLARD, "SEEING," IN *THE ART OF THE PERSONAL ESSAY* (1994), ED. PHILLIP LOPATE

4. The eye obeys exactly the action of the mind.

EMERSON, "BEHAVIOR," *THE CONDUCT OF LIFE* (1860)

5. Eyes are more accurate witnesses than ears.

HERACLITUS, *FRAGMENTS* (C. 500 B.C.), 12, TR. PHILIP WHEELWRIGHT

6. New ways of seeing can disclose new things: the radio telescope revealed quasars and pulsars, and the scanning electron microscope showed the whiskers of the dust mite. But turn the question around: Do new *things* make for new ways of seeing?

WILLIAM LEAST HEAT MOON, *BLUE HIGHWAYS* (1982)

7. Things seen are mightier than things heard.

LORD TENNYSON, "ENOCH ARDEN" (1864)

SIGNS

See 306. EVIDENCE; 715. PORTENT

898. SILENCE

See also 923. SPEAKING

1. Speech is of time, silence is of eternity.

THOMAS CARLYLE, *SARTOR RESARTUS* (1833–34), 3.3

2. Silence is all we dread. / There's Ransom in a Voice— / But Silence is Infinity.

EMILY DICKINSON, POEM (1873)

3. The words the happy say / Are paltry melody / But those the silent feel / Are beautiful—.

EMILY DICKINSON, *POEMS* (C. 1862–86)

4. Nothing is often a good thing to say, and always a clever thing to say.

WILL DURANT, *NEW YORK WORLD-TELEGRAM & SUN,* JUNE 6, 1958

5. Better say nothing than nothing to the purpose.

ENGLISH PROVERB

6. The stillest tongue can be the truest friend.

EURIPIDES, *IPHIGENIA IN TAURIS* (C. 414–12 B.C.), TR. WITTER BYNNER

7. Silence is exhilarating at first—as noise is—but there is a sweetness to silence outlasting exhilaration, akin to the sweetness of listening and the velvet of sleep.

EDWARD HOAGLAND, "THE RIDGE-SLOPE FOX AND THE KNIFE THROWER," *THE TUGMAN'S PASSAGE* (1982)

8. Elected Silence, sing to me / And beat upon my whorlèd ear, / Pipe me to pastures still and be / The music that I care to hear.

GERARD MANLEY HOPKINS, "THE HABIT OF PERFECTION" (C. 1866)

9. Silence is as full of potential wisdom and wit as the unhewn marble of great sculpture.

ALDOUS HUXLEY, *POINT COUNTER POINT* (1928), 1

10. Your highest female grace is silence.

BEN JONSON, *VOLPONE* (1605), 3.4

11. Three Silences there are: the first of speech, / The second of desire, the third of thought.

LONGFELLOW, "THE THREE SILENCES OF MOLINOS" (1877)

12. Silence is sorrow's best food.

JAMES RUSSELL LOWELL, *A FABLE FOR CRITICS* (1848)

13. Sticks and stones are hard on bones. / Aimed with angry art, / Words can sting like anything. / But silence breaks the heart.

PHYLLIS MCGINLEY, "BALLADE OF LOST OBJECTS," *THE LOVE LETTERS OF PHYLLIS MCGINLEY* (1954)

14. Silence is the element in which great things fashion themselves together, that at length they may emerge, full-formed and majestic, into the daylight of Life, which they are henceforth to rule.

MAURICE MAETERLINCK, "SILENCE," *THE TREASURE OF THE HUMBLE* (1896), TR. ALFRED SUTRO

15. Do not the most moving moments of our lives find us all without words?

MARCEL MARCEAU, *READER'S DIGEST,* JUNE 1958

16. We need a reason to speak, but none to keep silent.

PIERRE NICOLE, *DE LA PAIX AVEC LES HOMMES,* 2.1

17. Do you wish people to believe good of you? Don't speak.

PASCAL, *PENSÉES* (1670), 44, TR. W. F. TROTTER

18. By diminishing the value of silence, publicity has also diminished that of language. The two are inseparable: knowing how to speak has always meant knowing how to keep silent, knowing that there are times when one should say nothing.

OCTAVIO PAZ, "THE SYMPOSIUM AND THE HERMIT," *ALTERNATING CURRENT* (1973)

19. Many a time the thing left silent makes for happiness.

PINDAR, *ODES* (5TH C. B.C.), ISTHMIA 1, TR. RICHMOND LATTIMORE

20. A sage thing is timely silence, and better than any speech.

PLUTARCH, "THE EDUCATION OF CHILDREN," *MORALIA* (C. A.D. 100), TR. MOSES HADAS

21. I have often regretted my speech, never my silence.

PUBLILIUS SYRUS, *MORAL SAYINGS* (1ST C. B.C.), 1070, TR. DARIUS LYMAN

22. Let a fool hold his tongue and he will pass for a sage.

PUBLILIUS SYRUS, *MORAL SAYINGS* (1ST C. B.C.), 914, TR. DARIUS LYMAN

23. An absolute silence leads to sadness: it is the image of death.

ROUSSEAU, *REVERIES OF A SOLITARY WALKER* (1782), 5

24. What, O wise man, is the tongue in the mouth? It is a key to the casket of the intellectual treasurer; so long as the lid remains shut how can any person say whether he be a dealer in gems or in pedlery?

SA'DI, INTRODUCTION, *GULISTAN* (1258), TR. JAMES ROSS

25. I do know of these / That therefore only are reputed wise / For saying nothing.

SHAKESPEARE, *THE MERCHANT OF VENICE* (1596–97), 1.1.95

26. The silence often of pure innocence / Persuades when speaking fails.

SHAKESPEARE, *THE WINTER'S TALE* (1610–11), 2.2.41

27. The uncomfortable truth seems to be that the amount of talk by women has been measured less against the amount of men's talk than against the expectation of female silence.

GLORIA STEINEM, "MEN AND WOMEN TALKING," *OUTRAGEOUS ACTS AND EVERYDAY REBELLIONS* (1983)

28. Silence will save me from being wrong (and foolish), but it will also deprive me of the possibility of being right.

IGOR STRAVINSKY, "CONTINGENCIES," *THEMES AND EPISODES* (1966)

29. In human intercourse the tragedy begins, not when there is misunderstanding about words, but when silence is not understood.

THOREAU, "THE ATLANTIDES," *A WEEK ON THE CONCORD AND MERRIMACK RIVERS* (1849)

30. The right word may be effective, but no word was ever as effective as a rightly timed pause.

MARK TWAIN, INTRODUCTION, *SPEECHES* (1923)

31. The philosophers are wrong: it is not words that kill, it is silence.

ELIE WIESEL, *THE TESTAMENT* (1981), TR. MARION WIESEL

899. SIMPLICITY

See also 478. INNOCENCE; 701. PLAIN LIVING

1. Less is more.

ROBERT BROWNING, "ANDREA DEL SARTO," *MEN AND WOMEN* (1855), 78. MAXIM OF LUDWIG MIES VAN DER ROHE

2. To be simple is the best thing in the world; to be modest is the next best thing. I am not so sure about being quiet.

G. K. CHESTERTON, "THE WORSHIP OF THE WEALTHY," *ALL THINGS CONSIDERED* (1908)

3. It is proof of high culture to say the greatest matters in the simplest way.

EMERSON, "BEAUTY," *THE CONDUCT OF LIFE* (1860)

4. There is / one art, / no more, / no less: / to do / all things / with art— / lessness.

PIET HEIN, "ARS BREVIS," *GROOKS* (1966)

5. The ability to simplify means to eliminate the unnecessary so that the necessary may speak.

HANS HOFMANN, *SEARCH FOR THE REAL* (1967)

6. Give me a look, give me a face, / That makes simplicity a grace; / Robes loosely flowing, hair as free, / Such sweet neglect more taketh me / Than all the

adulteries of art: / They strike mine eyes, but not my heart.

BEN JONSON, *EPICENE, OR THE SILENT WOMAN* (1609), 1.1

7. Teach us Delight in simple things, / And Mirth that has no bitter springs.

RUDYARD KIPLING, "THE CHILDREN'S SONG," *PUCK OF POOK'S HILL* (1906)

8. Affected simplicity is an elegant imposture.

LA ROCHEFOUCAULD, *MAXIMS* (1665), TR. KENNETH PRATT

9. Perfect simplicity is unconsciously audacious.

GEORGE MEREDITH, *THE ORDEAL OF RICHARD FEVEREL* (1859), 1

10. And all the loveliest things there be / Come simply, so, it seems to me.

EDNA ST. VINCENT MILLAY, "THE GOOSE-GIRL," *THE HARP-WEAVER* (1923)

11. Simplicity of character is no hindrance to subtlety of intellect.

JOHN MORLEY, *LIFE OF GLADSTONE* (1903)

12. Beauty of style and harmony and grace and good rhythm depend on simplicity.

PLATO, *THE REPUBLIC* (4TH C. B.C.), 3, TR. BENJAMIN JOWETT

13. Simplicity is the mean between ostentation and rusticity.

ALEXANDER POPE, PREFACE TO THE *ILIAD* (1715–20)

14. Simplicity, simplicity, simplicity! I say, let your affairs be as two or three, and not a hundred or a thousand; instead of a million count half a dozen, and keep your accounts on your thumb-nail.

THOREAU, "WHERE I LIVED, AND WHAT I LIVED FOR," *WALDEN* (1854)

15. The art of art, the glory of expression and the sunshine of the light of letters, is simplicity.

WALT WHITMAN, PREFACE TO *LEAVES OF GRASS* (1855–92)

900. SIN

See also 307. EVIL; 448. ILLEGALITY; 841. SALVATION; 971. TEMPTATION; 1055. WICKEDNESS; 1070. WRONGDOING

1. A man does not sin by commission only, but often by omission.

MARCUS AURELIUS, *MEDITATIONS* (2ND C.), 9.5, TR. MAXWELL STANIFORTH

2. [H]e saw, in this wandering, how far his people had wandered from God. They had all turned aside, and gone out into the wilderness, to fall down before idols of gold and silver, and wood and stone, false gods that could not heal them.

JAMES BALDWIN, *GO TELL IT ON THE MOUNTAIN* (1953)

3. Be sure your sin will find you out.

BIBLE, NUMBERS 32:23

4. Earth reserves no blessing / For the unblessed of Heaven!

EMILY BRONTË, "A.E." (1845)

5. Pleasure's a sin, and sometimes Sin's a pleasure.

BYRON, *DON JUAN* (1819–24), 1.133

6. Without the spice of guilt, sin cannot be fully savored.

ALEXANDER CHASE, *PERSPECTIVES* (1966)

7. I have committed many sins in my life. This precise sin—the sin against poets—is without absolution.

E.L. DOCTOROW, *LOON LAKE* (1980)

8. Between these two, the denying of sins, which we have done, and the bragging of sins, which we have not done, what a space, what a compass is there, for millions of millions of sins!

JOHN DONNE, *SERMONS,* NO. 2, 1618

9. In best understandings, sin began, / Angels sinned first, then Devils, and then Man.

JOHN DONNE, "TO SIR HENRY WOTTON," *LETTERS TO SEVERAL PERSONAGES* (1651)

10. It's harder to confess the sin that no one believes in / Than the crime that everyone can appreciate. / For the crime is in relation to the law / And the sin is in relation to the sinner.

T. S. ELIOT, *THE ELDER STATESMAN* (1958), 3

11. Oh, Lord, it is not the sins I have committed that I regret, but those which I have had no opportunity to commit.

GHALIB, *PRAYER* (C. 1800)

12. A curse seemed to hang over the family, making men sin in spite of themselves and bringing suffering and death down upon the innocent as well as the guilty.

EDITH HAMILTON, *MYTHOLOGY* (1940)

13. We do ourselves wrong, and too meanly estimate the holiness above us, when we deem that any act or enjoyment good in itself, is not good to do religiously.

NATHANIEL HAWTHORNE, *THE MARBLE FAUN* (1860)

14. Really to sin you have to be serious about it.

HENRIK IBSEN, *PEER GYNT* (1867), 5

15. The mind sins, not the body; if there is no intention, there is no blame.

LIVY, *AB URBE CONDITA* (C. 29 B.C.), 1.58

16. People are no longer sinful, they are only immature or underprivileged or frightened or, more particularly, sick.

PHYLLIS MCGINLEY, "IN DEFENSE OF SIN," *THE PROVINCE OF THE HEART* (1959)

17. Sin is a dangerous toy in the hands of the virtuous. It should be left to the congenitally sinful, who know when to play with it and when to let it alone.

H. L. MENCKEN, "A GOOD MAN GONE WRONG," *THE AMERICAN MERCURY*, FEBRUARY 1929

18. The public scandal is what constitutes the offence: sins sinned in secret are no sins at all.

MOLIÈRE, *TARTUFFE* (1664), 4, TR. JOHN WOOD

19. There were sins that were too subtle to be explained, and there were others that were too terrible to be clearly mentioned. For example, there was sex, which was always smouldering just under the surface and which suddenly blew up into a tremendous row when I was about twelve.

GEORGE ORWELL, "SUCH, SUCH WERE THE JOYS," *A COLLECTION OF ESSAYS* (1954)

20. The twin conceptions of sin and vindictive punishment seem to be at the root of much that is most vigorous, both in religion and politics.

BERTRAND RUSSELL, "IDEAS THAT HAVE HARMED MANKIND," *UNPOPULAR ESSAYS* (1950)

21. At first sin was as fragile as a spider's thread, and finally as stout as a ship's hawser; sin arrived as a passerby, next lingered for a moment, then came as a visitor, and finally became master of the house.

ISRAEL SHENKER, *COAT OF MANY COLORS* (1985)

22. Sins cannot be undone, only forgiven.

IGOR STRAVINSKY, *CONVERSATIONS WITH IGOR STRAVINSKY* (1959)

23. We cannot well do without our sins; they are the highway of our virtue.

THOREAU, *JOURNAL*, MARCH 22, 1842

24. There is a charm about the forbidden that makes it unspeakably desirable.

MARK TWAIN, *NOTEBOOK* (1935)

901. SINCERITY

See also 362. FRANKNESS; 425. HONESTY; 440. HYPOCRISY; 484. INSINCERITY; 491. INTEGRITY; 1000. TRUTHFULNESS

1. No one means all he says, and yet very few say all they mean.

HENRY ADAMS, *THE EDUCATION OF HENRY ADAMS* (1907), 31

2. Men are always sincere. They change sincerities, that's all.

TRISTAN BERNARD, *CE QUE L'ON DIT AUX FEMMES* (1923)

3. The spontaneity of slaps is sincerity, whereas the ceremonial of caresses is largely convention.

UGO BETTI, *THE GAMBLER* (1950), 2.3

4. I should say sincerity, a deep, great, genuine sincerity, is the first characteristic of all men in any way heroic.

THOMAS CARLYLE, *ON HEROES, HERO-WORSHIP AND THE HEROIC IN HISTORY* (1841), 2

5. A friend is a person with whom I may be sincere. Before him I may think aloud.

EMERSON, "FRIENDSHIP," *ESSAYS: FIRST SERIES* (1841)

6. Nature forever puts a premium on reality. What is done for effect is seen to be done for effect; what is done for love is felt to be done for love. A man inspires affection and honor because he was not lying in wait for these.

EMERSON, "BEHAVIOR," *THE CONDUCT OF LIFE* (1860)

7. Sincerity is the highest compliment you can pay.

EMERSON, *JOURNALS*, 1836

8. Be as you would seem to be.

THOMAS FULLER, M.D., *GNOMOLOGIA* (1732), 849

9. What is uttered from the heart alone / Will win the hearts of others to your own.

GOETHE, "NIGHT," *FAUST: PART I* (1808), TR. PHILIP WAYNE

10. Sincerity that thinks it is the sole possessor of the truth is a deadlier sin than hypocrisy, which knows better.

SYDNEY J. HARRIS, "SINCERITY CAN BE DANGEROUS," *CLEARING THE GROUND* (1986)

11. [T]he young do not demand omniscience. They know it is unattainable. They do demand sincerity.

GILBERT HIGHET, *THE ART OF TEACHING* (1950)

12. Civility is not a sign of weakness, and sincerity is always subject to proof.

JOHN F. KENNEDY, INAUGURAL ADDRESS, JAN. 20, 1961

13. Sincerity is an opening of the heart; we find it in very few persons; and that which we see ordinarily is only a cunning deceit to attract the confidence of others.

LA ROCHEFOUCAULD, *MAXIMS* (1665), TR. KENNETH PRATT

14. Weak people cannot be sincere.

LA ROCHEFOUCAULD, *MAXIMS* (1665), TR. KENNETH PRATT

15. It's never what you say, but how / You make it sound sincere.

MARYA MANNES, "CONTROVERSE," *BUT WILL IT SELL?* (1955–64)

16. A man must not always tell all, for that were folly: but what a man says should be what he thinks.

MONTAIGNE, "OF PRESUMPTION," *ESSAYS* (1580–88), TR. W. C. HAZLITT

17. The primary condition for being sincere is the same as for being humble: not to boast of it, and probably not even to be aware of it.

HENRI PEYRE, *LITERATURE AND SINCERITY* (1963)

18. Suit the action to the word, the word to the action.

SHAKESPEARE, *HAMLET* (1600), 3.2.19

19. I only desire sincere relations with the worthiest of my acquaintance, that they may give me an opportunity once in a year to speak the truth.

THOREAU, *JOURNAL*, AUG. 24, 1851

20. A little sincerity is a dangerous thing, and a great deal of it is absolutely fatal.

OSCAR WILDE, *THE ARTIST AS CRITIC: CRITICAL WRITINGS OF OSCAR WILDE*, ED. RICHARD ELLMAN (1969)

21. A little sincerity is a dangerous thing, and a great deal of it is absolutely fatal.

OSCAR WILDE, *THE CRITIC AS ARTIST* (1891), 2

902. SINGING

See also 614. MUSIC; 655. OPERA

1. [H]ard as I try, daddy-o, I really do not like concert singers. They are always singing in some foreign language.

LANGSTON HUGHES, *SIMPLE SPEAKS HIS MIND* (1950)

2. Her voice was distinctly separate from the other children's voices, and not just because she was seated nearest me. It had the best upper register, the sweetest-sounding, the surest, and it automatically led the way.

J.D. SALINGER, "FOR ESMÉ—WITH LOVE AND SPLENDOR," IN *NINE STORIES BY J.D. SALINGER* (1953)

903. SINGLE-MINDEDNESS

See also 620. NARROWNESS

1. One should always think of what one is about; when one is learning, one should not think of play; and when one is at play, one should not think of one's learning.

LORD CHESTERFIELD, *LETTERS TO HIS SON*, JULY 24, 1739

2. A straight path never leads anywhere except to the objective.

ANDRÉ GIDE, *JOURNALS*, 1922, TR. JUSTIN O'BRIEN

3. It is in self-limitation that a master first shows himself.

GOETHE, *NATUR UND KUNST*

4. As any action or posture, long continued, will distort and disfigure the limbs, so the mind likewise is crippled and contracted by perpetual application to the same set of ideas.

SAMUEL JOHNSON, *THE RAMBLER* (1750–52), 173

5. When you are at sea, keep clear of the land.

PUBLILIUS SYRUS, *MORAL SAYINGS* (1ST C. B.C.), 480, TR. DARIUS LYMAN

6. There's some end at last for the man who follows a path: mere rambling is interminable.

SENECA, *LETTERS TO LUCILIUS* (1ST C.), 16.9, TR. E. PHILLIPS BARKER

904. SKEPTICISM

See also 265. DOUBT, RELIGIOUS; 1004. UNBELIEF

1. Doubt is not below knowledge, but above it.

ALAIN, *LIBRES-PROPOS* (1908–14)

2. There is one thing a professor can be absolutely certain of: almost every student entering the university believes, or says he believes, that truth is relative.

ALLAN BLOOM, "INTRODUCTION: OUR VIRTUE," *THE CLOSING OF THE AMERICAN MIND* (1987)

3. Doubt is the vestibule which all must pass, before they can enter into the temple of truth.

CHARLES CALEB COLTON, *LACON* (1825), 1.251

4. What has not been examined impartially has not been well examined. Skepticism is therefore the first step toward truth.

DENIS DIDEROT, *PENSÉES PHILOSOPHIQUES* (1746), 31

5. Doubt is an element of criticism, and the tendency of criticism is necessarily skeptical.

BENJAMIN DISRAELI, "CHURCH POLICY," Nov. 25, 1864

6. Man's most valuable trait / is a judicious sense of what not to believe.

EURIPIDES, *HELEN* (412 B.C.), TR. RICHMOND LATTIMORE

7. A wise skepticism is the first attribute of a good critic.

JAMES RUSSELL LOWELL, "SHAKESPEARE ONCE MORE," *AMONG MY BOOKS* (1870)

8. Let the greatest part of the news thou hearest be the least part of what thou believest, lest the greater part of what thou believest be the least part of what is true.

FRANCIS QUARLES, *ENCHIRIDION* (1640), 2.50

9. When all beliefs are challenged together, the just and necessary ones have a chance to step forward and to re-establish themselves alone.

GEORGE SANTAYANA, *THE LIFE OF REASON: REASON IN SCIENCE* (1905–06), 11

10. Modest doubt is called / The beacon of the wise, the tent that searches / To th' bottom of the worst.

SHAKESPEARE, *TROILUS AND CRESSIDA* (1601–02), 2.2.15

11. The skeptic does not mean him who doubts, but him who investigates or researches, as opposed to him who asserts and thinks that he has found.

MIGUEL DE UNAMUNO, "MY RELIGION," *ESSAYS AND SOLILOQUIES* (1924), TR. J. E. CRAWFORD FLITCH

SKILL

See 1. ABILITY

905. SLANDER

See also 5. ACCUSATION; 394. GOSSIP; 804. REPUTATION; 846. SCANDAL

1. There is nothing that more betrays a base ungenerous spirit than the giving of secret stabs to a man's reputation. Lampoons and satires, that are written with wit and spirit, are like poisoned darts, which not only inflict a wound, but make it incurable.

JOSEPH ADDISON, *THE SPECTATOR* (1711–12), 23

2. Every one in a crowd has the power to throw dirt: nine out of ten have the inclination.

WILLIAM HAZLITT, "ON READING NEW BOOKS," *SKETCHES AND ESSAYS* (1839)

3. Into the space of one little hour sins enough may be conjured up by evil tongues to blast the fame of a whole life of virtue.

WASHINGTON IRVING, "THE WIDOW'S ORDEAL," *WOLFERT'S ROOST* (1855)

4. If a man could say nothing against a character but what he can prove, history could not be written.

SAMUEL JOHNSON, QUOTED IN BOSWELL'S *LIFE OF SAMUEL JOHNSON*, APRIL 3, 1776

5. People are more slanderous from vanity than from malice.

LA ROCHEFOUCAULD, *MAXIMS* (1665), TR. KENNETH PRATT

6. Folk whose own behavior is most ridiculous are always to the fore in slandering others.

MOLIÈRE, *TARTUFFE* (1664), 1, TR. JOHN WOOD

7. Calumny ever pursues the great, even as the winds hurl themselves on high places.

OVID, *LOVE'S CURE* (C. A.D. 8), TR. J. LEWIS MAY

8. Whole surfaces are carried away even from a mountain when undermined by a gentle flow of water; how much more the soft hearts of men by clever persons who attack them with slander!

PANCHATANTRA (C. 5TH C.), 1, TR. FRANKLIN EDGERTON

9. What is slander? A verdict of "guilty" pronounced in the absence of the accused, with closed doors, without defence or appeal, by an interested and prejudiced judge.

JOSEPH ROUX, *MEDITATIONS OF A PARISH PRIEST* (1886), 4.67, TR. ISABEL F. HAPGOOD

10. Be thou as chaste as ice, as pure as snow, thou shalt not escape calumny.

SHAKESPEARE, *HAMLET* (1600), 3.1.140

11. Slander lives upon succession, / For ever housed where it gets possession.

SHAKESPEARE, *THE COMEDY OF ERRORS* (1592–93), 3.1.105

12. Slander, / Whose edge is sharper than the sword, whose tongue / Outvenoms all the worms of Nile, whose breath / Rides on the posting winds and doth belie / All corners of the world.

SHAKESPEARE, *CYMBELINE* (1609–10), 3.4.35

13. Strike at a great man, and you will not miss.

SOPHOCLES, *AJAX* (C. 447 B.C.), TR. JOHN MOORE

14. It takes your enemy and your friend, working together, to hurt you to the heart; the one to slander you and the other to get the news to you.

MARK TWAIN, "PUDD'NHEAD WILSON'S NEW CALENDAR," *FOLLOWING THE EQUATOR* (1897), 2.9

SLANG

See 524. LANGUAGE

SLAVERY

See 889. SERVITUDE

906. SLEEP

See also 73. BED; 266. DREAMS; 605. MORNING; 633. NIGHT

1. You would probably not say that he was sleeping the sleep of the just, unless you meant the just asleep, but it was certainly the sleep of someone who was not fooling about when he climbed into bed of a night and turned off the light.

DOUGLAS ADAMS, *THE LONG DARK TEA-TIME OF THE SOUL* (1988)

2. Sleep hath its own world, / And a wide realm of wild reality, / And dreams in their development have breath, / And tears, and tortures, and the touch of Joy.

BYRON, "THE DREAM" (1816), 1

3. Now blessings light on him that first invented this same sleep. It covers a man all over, thoughts and all, like a cloak.

CERVANTES, *DON QUIXOTE* (1605–15), 2.4.68, TR. JOHN OZELL

4. Oh sleep! It is a gentle thing, / Beloved from pole to pole!

SAMUEL TAYLOR COLERIDGE, *THE RIME OF THE ANCIENT MARINER* (1798), 5.1

5. Sleep is pain's easiest salve, and doth fulfill / All offices of death, except to kill.

JOHN DONNE, "THE STORM: TO MR. CHRISTOPHER BROOKE," *LETTERS TO SEVERAL PERSONAGES* (1651)

6. Care-charming Sleep, thou easer of all woes, / Brother to Death.

FLETCHER, *VALENTINIAN* (1647), 5.2

7. The pillow is a silent Sibyl, and it is better to sleep on things beforehand than lie awake about them afterwards.

BALTASAR GRACIÁN, *THE ART OF WORLDLY WISDOM* (1647), 151, TR. JOSEPH JACOBS

8. Even sleepers are workers and collaborators in what goes on in the universe.

HERACLITUS, *FRAGMENTS* (C. 500 B.C.), 124, TR. PHILIP WHEELWRIGHT

9. Even where sleep is concerned, too much is a bad thing.

HOMER, *ODYSSEY* (9TH C. B.C.), 15, TR. E. V. RIEU

10. That we are not much sicker and much madder than we are is due exclusively to that most blessed and blessing of all natural graces, sleep.

ALDOUS HUXLEY, "VARIATIONS ON A PHILOSOPHER," *THEMES AND VARIATIONS* (1950)

11. You can't sleep until noon with the proper élan unless you have some legitimate reason for staying up until three (parties don't count).

JEAN KERR, INTRODUCTION, *PLEASE DON'T EAT THE DAISIES* (1957)

12. For sleep, one needs endless depths of blackness to sink into; daylight is too shallow, it will not cover one.

ANNE MORROW LINDBERGH, "DARK," *NORTH TO THE ORIENT* (1935)

13. Cut if you will, with Sleep's dull knife, / Each day to half its length, my friend,—/ The years that Time takes off *my* life, / He'll take off the other end!

EDNA ST. VINCENT MILLAY, "MIDNIGHT OIL," *A FEW FIGS FROM THISTLES* (1920)

14. It is interesting that amongst children of preschool age, the more intelligent ones tend to sleep less than the dull ones. After the age of seven this relationship is reversed, the more intelligent schoolchildren sleeping more than the dull ones.

DESMOND MORRIS, *THE NAKED APE* (1967)

15. Not to have been born is undoubtedly best, but sound sleep is second best.

IRIS MURDOCH, *A WORD CHILD* (1975)

16. Then blessings on thee, my afternoon torpor/Thou makest a prince of a mental porpor.

OGDEN NASH, "CAT NAPS ARE TOO GOOD FOR CATS," *A SUBTREASURY OF AMERICAN HUMOR* (1941)

17. Sleeping is no mean art: for its sake one must stay awake all day.

NIETZSCHE, "ON THE TEACHERS OF VIRTUE," *THUS SPOKE ZARATHUSTRA* (1883–92), 1, TR. WALTER KAUFMANN

18. He sleeps well who knows not that he sleeps ill.

PUBLILIUS SYRUS, *MORAL SAYINGS* (1ST C. B.C.), 77, TR. DARIUS LYMAN

19. Sleep does make us all equal, it seems to me, like his big brother—Death.

ARTHUR SCHNITZLER, *LA RONDE* (1900), 10

20. Sleep that knits up the ravelled sleave of care, / The death of each day's life, sore labour's bath, / Balm of hurt minds, great nature's second course, / Chief nourisher in life's feast.

SHAKESPEARE, *MACBETH* (1605–06), 2.2.37

21. Weariness / Can snore upon the flint when resty sloth / Finds the down pillow hard.

SHAKESPEARE, *CYMBELINE* (1609–10), 3.6.33

22. We still think of human disease as the work of an organized, modernized kind of demonology, in which the bacteria are the most visible and centrally placed of our adversaries. We assume that they must somehow relish what they do.

LEWIS THOMAS, "GERMS," *THE LIVES OF A CELL* (1974)

23. In Sleep we lie all naked and alone, in Sleep we are united at the heart of night and darkness, and we are strange and beautiful asleep; for we are dying in the darkness, and we know no death.

THOMAS WOLFE, "DEATH THE PROUD BROTHER," *FROM DEATH TO MORNING* (1935)

907. SLOWNESS

See also 231. DELAY; 411. HASTE; 926. SPEED

1. There is a slowness in affairs which ripens them, and a slowness which rots them.

JOSEPH ROUX, *MEDITATIONS OF A PARISH PRIEST* (1886), 4.93, TR. ISABEL F. HAPGOOD

SLYNESS

See 200. CRAFTINESS

908. SMALLNESS

See also 400. GREAT AND SMALL; 525. LARGENESS; 649. OBSCURITY; 693. PETTINESS; 996. TRIFLES; 1012. UNIMPORTANCE

1. A big man knows he don't have to fight, but whin a man is little an' knows he's little an' is thinkin' all th' time he's little an' feels that ivrybody else is thinkin' he's little, look out f'r him.

FINLEY PETER DUNNE, "THE JAPANESE SCARE," *MR. DOOLEY SAYS* (1910)

2. In the ant's house the dew is a flood.

PERSIAN PROVERB

SMELLING

See 882. SENSES

SMILING

See 526. LAUGHTER

SMOKING

See 982. TOBACCO

909. SMUGNESS

See also 156. COMPLACENCY

1. Of all the horrid, hideous notes of woe, / Sadder than owl-songs or the midnight blast, / Is that portentous phrase, "I told you so," / Uttered by friends, those prophets of the *past*.

BYRON, *DON JUAN* (1819–24), 14.50

2. Next to "I win," "I told you so" are the sweetest words.

GORE VIDAL, "UNITED STATES," *ESSAYS 1952–1992* (1993)

910. SNOBBERY

See also 135. CLASS; 725. PREFERENCE; 733. PRIDE; 780. RANK; 914. SOCIETY, POLITE

1. Men hate the haughty of heart who will not be / the friend of every man.

EURIPIDES, *HIPPOLYTUS* (428 B.C.), TR. DAVID GRENE

2. We must exclude someone from our gathering, or we shall be left with nothing.

E. M. FORSTER, *A PASSAGE TO INDIA* (1924), 1.4

3. There was a certain inner comfort in knowing he could knock down anybody who was snooty toward him, although, being very shy and a throughly nice boy, he never fought except in the gym.

ERNEST HEMINGWAY, *THE SUN ALSO RISES* (1926)

4. Levellers wish to level *down* as far as themselves; but they cannot bear levelling *up* to themselves.

SAMUEL JOHNSON, QUOTED IN BOSWELL'S *LIFE OF SAMUEL JOHNSON*, JULY 21, 1763

5. All the people like us are We, / And every one else is They.

RUDYARD KIPLING, "WE AND THEY" (1926)

6. [S]nobbery is not merely a silly human weakness but something basic in the mentality of modern man—a symptom which reflects the general sickness, the dislocation of social and cultural values in contemporary civilization.

Arthur Koestler, "The Anatomy of Snobbery," *The Anchor Review* (1955)

7. The true snob never rests; there is always a higher goal to attain, and there are, by the same token, always more and more people to look down upon.

Russell Lynes, "The New Snobbism," *Harper's Magazine,* November 1950

8. In men this blunder still you find,— / All think their little set mankind.

Hannah More, *Florio* (1786), 1

9. [They were] quiet intelligent surreptitious beavering-away snobs, as most cultured middle-class people are, unless there is some positive quality of character or education to stop them.

Iris Murdoch, *A Word Child* (1975)

10. Snobbishness, like hypocrisy, is a check upon behaviour whose value from a social point of view has been underrated.

George Orwell, "Raffles and Miss Blandish," *A Collection of Essays* (1954)

911. SNOW

See also 854. Seasons

1. His soul swooned slowly as he heard the snow falling faintly through the universe and faintly falling, like the descent of their last end, upon all the living and the dead.

James Joyce, "The Dead," *Dubliners* (1914)

2. The snow itself is lonely or, if you prefer, self-sufficient. There is no other time when the whole world seems composed of one thing and one thing only.

Joseph Wood Krutch, "December," *The Twelve Seasons* (1949)

912. SOCIALISM

See also 150. Communism; 395. Government

1. In England the more horses a nobleman has, the more popular he is. So long as the English are devoted to racing, Socialism has no chance with you.

Bismarck, quoted in Sarah Bradford, *Disraeli* (1982)

2. In effect, according to Lenin, socialism and democracy are indivisible. By gaining democratic freedoms the working masses come to power.

Mikhail Gorbachev, *Perestroika* (1987)

3. There is the fundamental paradox of the welfare state: that it is not built for the desperate, but for those who are already capable of helping themselves.

Michael Harrington, *The Other America* (1962), 9.1

4. The fact is that life has become a sweepstake. Millions of people who have lost the sense of being able to make anything of the collective effort of shaping their economic society, now expect fortune to descend like pie from the sky.

Max Lerner, "I'm Dreaming of a Bright Sweepstake," *Actions and Passions* (1949)

5. It [Socialism] was a kind of political hockey played by big, gaunt, dyspeptic girls in pants.

Mary McCarthy, "My Confession," in *The Art of the Personal Essay* (1994), ed. Phillip Lopate

6. What the collectivist age wants, allows, and approves is the perpetual holiday from the self.

Thomas Mann, "Europe, Beware," *The Thomas Mann Reader* (1950), tr. H. T. Lowe-Porter

SOCIAL WORK

See 433. Humanitarianism

913. SOCIETY

See also 36. Anarchy; 52. Aristocracy; 133. Civilization; 135. Class; 395. Government; 487. Institutions; 587. Middle Class; 682. The People; 930. State

1. Society is immoral and immortal; it can afford to commit any kind of folly, and indulge in any sort of vice; it cannot be killed, and the fragments that survive can always laugh at the dead.

Henry Adams, *The Education of Henry Adams* (1907), 18

2. No scheme for a change of society can be made to appear immediately palatable, except by falsehood, until society has become so desperate that it will accept any change.

T. S. Eliot, "The Idea of a Christian Society" (1939)

3. Society acquires new arts and loses old instincts.

Emerson, "Self-Reliance," *Essays: First Series* (1841)

4. The power that keeps cities of men together / Is noble preservation of law.

EURIPIDES, *THE SUPPLIANT WOMEN* (C. 421 B.C.), TR. FRANK W. JONES

5. Societies are healthiest when their radius of trust is broad and when people feel they can influence their own fate.

JAMES FALLOWS, *MORE LIKE US* (1989)

6. Successful societies—those which progress economically and politically and can control the terms on which they deal with the outside world—succeed because they have found ways to match individual self-interest to the collective good.

JAMES FALLOWS, *MORE LIKE US* (1989), 1

7. A complex society is not necessarily more advanced than a simple one; it has just adapted to conditions in a more complicated way.

PETER FARB, *MAN'S RISE TO CIVILIZATION* (1968)

8. Human life in common is only made possible when a majority comes together which is stronger than any separate individual and which remains united against all separate individuals.

SIGMUND FREUD, *CIVILIZATION AND ITS DISCONTENTS* (1930), 3, TR. JAMES STRACHEY

9. Society must be organized in such a way that man's social, loving nature is not separated from his social existence, but becomes one with it.

ERICH FROMM, *THE ART OF LOVING* (1956)

10. In the mouth of Society are many diseased teeth, decayed to the bones of the jaws. But Society makes no effort to have them extracted and be rid of the affliction. It contents itself with gold fillings.

KAHLIL GIBRAN, "DECAYED TEETH," *THOUGHTS AND MEDITATIONS* (1960), TR. ANTHONY R. FERRIS

11. Life in a great society, or for that matter in a small, is a web of tangled relations of all sorts, whose adjustment so that it may be endurable is an extraordinarily troublesome matter.

LEARNED HAND, *THE SPIRIT OF LIBERTY* (1959)

12. There is only one institution in the society capable of acting to abolish poverty. That is the Federal Government.

MICHAEL HARRINGTON, *THE OTHER AMERICA* (1963)

13. One cannot raise the bottom of a society without benefiting everyone above.

MICHAEL HARRINGTON, *THE OTHER AMERICA* (1962), 9.1

14. Time and time again I have been persuaded that a huge potential of goodwill is slumbering within our society. It's just that it's incoherent, suppressed, confused, crippled and perplexed.

VÁCLAV HAVEL, "POLITICS, MORALITY, AND CIVILITY," *SUMMER MEDITATIONS* (1992), TR. PAUL WILSON

15. The best school in the world will scarcely save a boy who hates the school and the purpose it serves and the society that created it.

GILBERT HIGHET, *THE ART OF TEACHING* (1950)

16. We will be able to achieve a just and prosperous society only when our schools ensure that everyone commands enough shared background knowledge to be able to communicate effectively with everyone else.

E.D. HIRSCH, JR., *CULTURAL LITERACY* (1987)

17. Society is always trying in some way or other to grind us down to a single flat surface.

OLIVER WENDELL HOLMES, SR., *THE PROFESSOR AT THE BREAKFAST TABLE* (1860), 2

18. The great society is a place where men are more concerned with the quality of their goals than the quantity of their goods.

LYNDON B. JOHNSON, SPEECH, UNIVERSITY OF MICHIGAN, MAY 22, 1964

19. In civilized society we all depend upon each other, and our happiness is very much owing to the good opinion of mankind.

SAMUEL JOHNSON, QUOTED IN BOSWELL'S *LIFE OF SAMUEL JOHNSON*, JULY 20, 1763

20. The conviction of tragedy that rises out of his [John Dos Passos's] work is the steady protest of a sensitive democratic conscience against the tyranny and the ugliness of society, against the failure of a complete human development under industrial capitalism.

ALFRED KAZIN, *ON NATIVE GROUNDS* (1942)

21. The principles of the good society call for a concern with an order of being—which cannot be proved existentially to the sense organs—where it matters supremely that the human person is inviolable, that reason shall regulate the will, that truth shall prevail over error.

WALTER LIPPMANN, *THE PUBLIC PHILOSOPHY* (1955), 11.4

22. In civilized communities men's idiosyncrasies are mitigated by the necessity of conforming to certain rules of behaviour. Culture is a mask that hides their faces.

W. SOMERSET MAUGHAM, *THE SUMMING UP* (1938), 53

23. Necessity reconciles and brings men together; and this accidental connection afterward forms itself into laws.

Montaigne, "Of vanity," *Essays* (1580–88), tr. W. C. Hazlitt

24. A decrepit society shuns humor as a decrepit individual shuns drafts.

Malcolm Muggeridge, "Tread Softly for You Tread on My Jokes," *The Most of Malcolm Muggeridge* (1966)

25. [P]eople become less inhibited from wanting to change social and economic conditions in a radical fashion according to their own interests, and from being prepared to think of state intervention in ever wider spheres as possible and useful for this purpose.

Gunnar Myrdal, *Beyond the Welfare State* (1960)

26. Man did not enter into society to become worse than he was before, nor to have fewer rights than he had before, but to have those rights better secured.

Thomas Paine, *The Rights of Man* (1791), 1

27. Sociology and anthropology are not disciplines which take easily to situations where people are able to live out their fantasies, not just in the symbolic action of ritual, but in the concrete theater of society at large.

Jonathan Raban, *Soft City* (1974)

28. What man loses by the social contract is his natural liberty and an unlimited right to everything he tries to get and succeeds in getting; what he gains is civil liberty and the proprietorship of all he possesses.

Rousseau, *The Social Contract* (1762), 1.8, tr. G. D. H. Cole

29. Society itself is an accident to the spirit, and if society in any of its forms is to be justified morally it must be justified at the bar of the individual conscience.

George Santayana, *Dialogues in Limbo* (1925), 6

30. Society is a kind of parent to its members. If it, and they, are to thrive, its values must be clear, coherent and generally acceptable.

Milton R. Sapirstein, *Paradoxes of Everyday Life* (1955), 8

31. Nature holds no brief for the human experiment: it must stand or fall by its results.

George Bernard Shaw, preface to *Back to Methuselah* (1921)

32. Many social practices essential to the welfare of the species involve the control of one person by another, and no one can suppress them who has any concern for human achievements.

B.F. Skinner, *Beyond Freedom and Dignity*, 2

33. Cursed be the social lies that warp us from the living truth.

Lord Tennyson, "Locksley Hall" (1842)

34. Every social system is more or less against nature, and at every moment nature is at work to reclaim her rights.

Paul Valéry, "The Idea of Dictatorship," *Reflections on the World Today* (1931), tr. Francis Scarfe

35. Society soon grows used to any state of things which is imposed upon it without explanation.

Edith Wharton, "The Spark," *Old New York* (1924)

36. A great society is a society in which its men of business think greatly of their functions.

Alfred North Whitehead, *Adventures in Ideas* (1933), 6

914. SOCIETY, POLITE

See also 152. Company; 563. Manners; 672. Parties; 910. Snobbery

1. Society is a masked ball, where every one hides his real character, and reveals it in hiding.

Emerson, "Worship," *The Conduct of Life* (1860)

2. The secret of success in society is a certain heartiness and sympathy.

Emerson, "Manners," *Essays: Second Series* (1844)

3. If all your clothes are worn to the same state, it means you go out too much.

F. Scott Fitzgerald, "Note-Books," *The Crack-Up* (1945)

4. Society is a more level surface than we imagine. Wise men or absolute fools are hard to be met with, as there are few giants or dwarfs.

William Hazlitt, *Characteristics* (1823), 52

5. There are people whom one should like very well to drop, but would not wish to be dropped by.

Samuel Johnson, quoted in Boswell's *Life of Samuel Johnson*, March 26, 1781

6. Men would not live in society long if they were not each other's dupes.

La Rochefoucauld, *Maxims* (1665)

7. Human society is founded on mutual deceit; few friendships would endure if each knew what his friend said of him in his absence.

Pascal, *Pensées* (1670), 100, tr. W. F. Trotter

SOLITUDE

8. Teas, / Where small talk dies in agonies.

SHELLEY, "PETER BELL THE THIRD" (1819), 3.12

9. The path of social advancement is, and must be, strewn with broken friendships.

H. G. WELLS, *KIPPS* (1905), 2.5

10. To be in it [society] is merely a bore. But to be out of it simply a tragedy.

OSCAR WILDE, *A WOMAN OF NO IMPORTANCE* (1893), 3

11. To get into the best society nowadays, one has either to feed people, amuse people, or shock people.

OSCAR WILDE, *A WOMAN OF NO IMPORTANCE* (1893), 3

SOLACE

See 180. CONSOLATIONS; 960. SYMPATHY

SOLDIERS

See 588. THE MILITARY

SOLEMNITY

See 886. SERIOUSNESS

915. SOLITUDE

See also 30. ALIENATION; 31. ALOOFNESS; 547. LONELINESS; 736. PRIVACY

1. He who is unable to live in society, or who has no need because he is sufficient for himself, must be either a beast or a god.

ARISTOTLE, *POLITICS* (4TH C. B.C.), 1.2, TR. BENJAMIN JOWETT

2. Yes! in the sea of life enisled, / With echoing straits between us thrown, / Dotting the shoreless watery wild, / We mortal millions live *alone*.

MATTHEW ARNOLD, "SWITZERLAND," 5, *EMPEDOCLES ON ETNA, AND OTHER POEMS* (1852)

3. Little do men perceive what solitude is, and how far it extendeth. For a crowd is not company, and faces are but a gallery of pictures, and talk but a tinkling cymbal, where there is no love.

FRANCIS BACON, "OF FRIENDSHIP," *ESSAYS* (1625)

4. Those that want friends to open themselves unto are cannibals of their own hearts.

FRANCIS BACON, "OF FRIENDSHIP," *ESSAYS* (1625)

5. The person who tries to live alone will not succeed as a human being. His heart withers if it does not answer another heart. His mind shrinks away if he hears only the echoes of his own thoughts and finds no other inspiration.

PEARL S. BUCK, "TO YOU ON YOUR FIRST BIRTHDAY," *TO MY DAUGHTERS, WITH LOVE* (1967)

6. If from society we learn to live, / 'Tis Solitude should teach us how to die; / It hath no flatterers.

BYRON, *CHILDE HAROLD'S PILGRIMAGE* (1812–18), 4.33

7. To fly from, need not be to hate, mankind: / All are not fit with them to stir and toil, / Nor is it discontent to keep the mind / Deep in its fountain.

BYRON, *CHILDE HAROLD'S PILGRIMAGE* (1812–18), 3.69

8. Only solitary men know the full joys of friendship. Others have their family; but to a solitary and an exile his friends are everything.

WILLA CATHER, *SHADOWS ON THE ROCK* (1931)

9. Solitary trees, if they grow at all, grow strong.

SIR WINSTON CHURCHILL, QUOTED IN RANDOLPH S. CHURCHILL'S *WINSTON S. CHURCHILL* (1966), V. 1

10. There are days when solitude is a heady wine that intoxicates you with freedom, others when it is a bitter tonic, and still others when it is a poison that makes you beat your head against the wall.

COLETTE, "FREEDOM," *EARTHLY PARADISE* (1966), 2

11. To dare to live alone is the rarest courage; since there are many who had rather meet their bitterest enemy in the field, than their own hearts in their closet.

CHARLES CALEB COLTON, *LACON* (1825), 1.445

12. Maybe each human being lives in a unique world, a private world, a world different from those inhabited and experienced by all other humans.

PHILIP K. DICK, *I HOPE I SHALL ARRIVE SOON* (1985)

13. It is sometimes advantageous to be unseen, although it is most often rather wearing on the nerves.

RALPH ELLISON, *THE INVISIBLE MAN* (1952)

14. Isolation must precede true society.

EMERSON, "SELF-RELIANCE," *ESSAYS: FIRST SERIES* (1841)

15. We never touch but at points.

EMERSON, *JOURNALS,* 1836

16. When you have shut your doors and darkened your room, remember, never to say that you are alone; for you are not alone, but God is within, and your genius is within.

EPICTETUS, *DISCOURSES* (2ND C.), 1.14, TR. THOMAS W. HIGGINSON

17. He never is alone that is accompanied with noble thoughts.

FLETCHER, *LOVE'S CURE* (1647), 3.3

18. Better be alone than in bad company.

THOMAS FULLER, M.D., *GNOMOLOGIA* (1732), 872

19. Solitude is bearable only with God.

ANDRÉ GIDE, *JOURNALS*, SEPT. 1, 1942, TR. JUSTIN O'BRIEN

20. To every man it is decreed: Thou shalt live alone. Happy they who imagine that they have escaped the common lot; happy, whilst they imagine it.

GEORGE GISSING, "SPRING," *THE PRIVATE PAPERS OF HENRY RYECROFT* (1903)

21. He that can live alone resembles the brute beast in nothing, the sage in much, and God in everything.

BALTASAR GRACIÁN, *THE ART OF WORLDLY WISDOM* (1647), 137, TR. JOSEPH JACOBS

22. A solitude is the audience-chamber of God.

WALTER SAVAGE LANDOR, "LORD BROOKE AND SIR PHILIP SIDNEY," *IMAGINARY CONVERSATIONS* (1824–53)

23. What a commentary on our civilization, when being alone is considered suspect; when one has to apologize for it, make excuses, hide the fact that one practices it—like a secret vice!

ANNE MORROW LINDBERGH, "MOON SHELL," *GIFT FROM THE SEA* (1955)

24. It is in solitude that the works of hand, heart and mind are always conceived, and in solitude that individuality must be affirmed.

ROBERT LINDNER, "THE MUTINY OF THE YOUNG," *MUST YOU CONFORM?* (1956)

25. Ships that pass in the night, and speak each other in passing, / Only a signal shown and a distant voice in the darkness; / So on the ocean of life, we pass and speak one another, / Only a look and a voice, then darkness again and a silence.

LONGFELLOW, "ELIZABETH," 4, *TALES OF A WAYSIDE INN* (1863)

26. Solitude is as needful to the imagination as society is wholesome for the character.

JAMES RUSSELL LOWELL, "DRYDEN," *AMONG MY BOOKS* (1870)

27. The nurse of full-grown souls is solitude.

JAMES RUSSELL LOWELL, "COLUMBUS" (1844)

28. A solitary, unused to speaking of what he sees and feels, has mental experiences which are at once more intense and less articulate than those of a gregarious man.

THOMAS MANN, *DEATH IN VENICE* (1911)

29. Solitude gives birth to the original in us, to beauty unfamiliar and perilous—to poetry. But also, it gives birth to the opposite: to the perverse, the illicit, the absurd.

THOMAS MANN, TITLE STORY (1913), *DEATH IN VENICE*, TR. H. T. LOWE-PORTER

30. Solitude sometimes is best society, / And short retirement urges sweet return.

MILTON, *PARADISE LOST* (1667), 9.249

31. Nature has presented us with a large faculty of entertaining ourselves alone; and often calls us to it, to teach us that we owe ourselves in part to society, but chiefly and mostly to ourselves.

MONTAIGNE, "ON GIVING THE LIE," *ESSAYS* (1580–88), TR. W. C. HAZLITT

32. Solitude is the playfield of Satan.

VLADIMIR NABOKOV, "COMMENTARY," *PALE FIRE* (1962), 62

33. Life is for each man a solitary cell whose walls are mirrors.

EUGENE O'NEILL, *LAZARUS LAUGHED* (1927), 2.1

34. We are fools to depend upon the society of our fellow-men. Wretched as we are, powerless as we are, they will not aid us; we shall die alone.

PASCAL, *PENSÉES* (1670), 211, TR. W. F. TROTTER

35. Solitude is the profoundest fact of the human condition. Man is the only being who knows he is alone.

OCTAVIO PAZ, *THE LABYRINTH OF SOLITUDE* (1950)

36. There are some solitary wretches who seem to have left the rest of mankind, only, as Eve left Adam, to meet the devil in private.

ALEXANDER POPE, *THOUGHTS ON VARIOUS SUBJECTS* (1727)

37. He who lives in solitude may make his own laws.

PUBLILIUS SYRUS, *MORAL SAYINGS* (1ST C. B.C.), 432, TR. DARIUS LYMAN

38. Solitude is the mother of anxieties.

PUBLILIUS SYRUS, *MORAL SAYINGS* (1ST C. B.C.), 222, TR. DARIUS LYMAN

39. I picked at an omelette which had been cooked to the texture of chamois leather and drank, rather more enthusiastically, a bottle of California chablis, feeling my soiltude as a conspicuous caste mark.

JONATHAN RABAN, *OLD GLORY* (1982)

40. There are places and moments in which one is so completely alone that one sees the world entire.

Jules Renard, *Journal,* December 1900, tr. Elizabeth Roget

41. Children love to be alone because alone is where they know themselves, and where they dream.

Roger Rosenblatt, "Children of War," *The Man in the Water* (1994)

42. Solitude vivifies; isolation kills.

Joseph Roux, *Meditations of a Parish Priest* (1886), 5.60, tr. Isabel F. Hapgood

43. You and I possess manifold ideal bonds in the interests we share; but each of us has his poor body and his irremediable, incommunicable dreams.

George Santayana, *The Life of Reason: Reason in Science* (1905–06), 9

44. And if I go alone, I don't even have to talk.

John Steinbeck, *Travels with Charley* (1962)

45. One can acquire everything in solitude except character.

Stendhal, "Miscellaneous Fragments," *On Love* (1822)

46. The man who goes alone can start today; but he who travels with another must wait till that other is ready, and it may be a long time before they get off.

Thoreau, "Economy," *Walden* (1854)

47. I love to be alone. I never found the companion that was so companionable as solitude.

Thoreau, "Solitude," *Walden* (1854)

48. I find it wholesome to be alone the better part of the time. To be in company, even with the best, is soon wearisome and dissipating.

Thoreau, "Solitude," *Walden* (1854)

49. You may live a long while with some people, and be on friendly terms with them, and never once speak openly with them from your soul.

Ivan Turgenev, "The District Doctor," *A Sportsman's Sketches* (1852), v. 1, tr. Constance Garnett

50. Only in solitude do we find ourselves; and in finding ourselves, we find in ourselves all our brothers in solitude.

Miguel de Unamuno, "Solitude," *Essays and Soliloquies* (1924), tr. J. E. Crawford Flitch

51. We are rarely proud when we are alone.

Voltaire, "Laughter," *Philosophical Dictionary* (1764)

52. Isolation breeds conceit.

Charles Dudley Warner, "Sixth Study," *Backlog Studies* (1873)

53. We're all of us sentenced to solitary confinement inside our own skins, for life.

Tennessee Williams, *Orpheus Descending* (1957), 2.1

54. Which of us has known his brother? Which of us has looked into his father's heart? Which of us has not remained forever prison-pent? Which of us is not forever a stranger and alone?

Thomas Wolfe, flyleaf, *Look Homeward, Angel* (1929)

916. SONS

See also 97. Boys; 670. Parenthood

1. Most sons of famous men lead mediocre lives, particularly those who have their fathers' Christian names and follow in their footsteps.

Luigi Barzini, *O America* (1977)

2. Everyone calls his son his son, whether he has talents or has not talents.

Confucius, *Analects* (6th c. b.c.), 11.7, tr. James Legge

3. In order to get as much fame as one's father one has to be much more able than he.

Denis Diderot, *Rameau's Nephew* (1762), tr. Ralph H. Bowen

4. Few sons, indeed, are like their fathers. Generally they are worse; but just a few are better.

Homer, *Odyssey* (9th c. b.c.), 2, tr. E. V. Rieu

5. Sons have always a rebellious wish to be disillusioned by that which charmed their fathers.

Aldous Huxley, "Vulgarity in Literature," *Music at Night* (1931)

6. There must always be a struggle between a father and son, while one aims at power and the other at independence.

Samuel Johnson, quoted in Boswell's *Life of Samuel Johnson,* July 14, 1763

7. Greatness of name in the father oftentimes overwhelms the son; they stand too near one another. The shadow kills the growth.

Ben Jonson, *Timber* (1640)

8. Sons do not need you. They are always out of your reach, / Walking strange waters.

Phyllis McGinley, "The Old Woman with Four Sons," *A Pocketful of Wry* (1940)

9. Like Franklin Roosevelt and Adlai Stevenson, he was a wellborn victim of *Uberängstlichkeit*, a mama's boy who reached his fullest dimensions in following maternal orders to be mercilessly ambitious.

William Manchester, *American Caesar* (1978)

10. How easily a father's tenderness is recalled, and how quickly a son's offenses vanish at the slightest word of repentance!

Molière, *Don Juan* (1665), 5.1, tr. Donald M. Frame

11. Any father whose son raises his hand against him is guilty: of having produced a son who raised his hand against him.

Charles Péguy, *Les Cahiers de la quinzaine,* Dec. 2, 1906

12. You don't raise heroes, you raise sons. And if you treat them like sons, they'll turn out to be heroes, even if it's just in your own eyes.

Walter Schirra, Sr., *This Week,* Feb. 3, 1963

13. 'Tis a happy thing / To be the father unto many sons.

Shakespeare, *3 Henry VI* (1590–91), 3.2.104

14. This is what a father ought to be about: helping his son to form the habit of doing right on his own initiative, rather than because he's afraid of some serious consequence.

Terence, *The Brothers* (160 b.c.), tr. William A. Oldfather

15. Our genes keep unfolding as long as we live. Harry tastes in his teeth a sourness that offended him on his father's breath. Poor Pop. His face yellowed like a dried apricot at the end.

John Updike, *Rabbit at Rest* (1990)

16. My father provided; he gathered things to himself and let them fall upon the world; my clothes, my food, my luxurious hopes had fallen to me from him, and for the first time his death seemed, even at its immense stellar remove of impossibility, a grave and dreadful threat.

John Updike, *The Centaur* (1963)

17. The time not to become a father is eighteen years before a world war.

E. B. White, "Answers to Hard Questions," *The Second Tree from the Corner* (1954)

917. SOPHISTICATION

See also 193. Cosmopolitanism; 321. Experience

1. Sophistication demands honesty; it does not require ill temper.

Irwin Edman, "How to Be Sweet Though Sophisticated," in *Fifty Great Essays* (1964)

2. The finished man of the world must eat of every apple once.

Emerson, "Culture," *The Conduct of Life* (1860)

3. The mark of the man of the world is absence of pretension.

Emerson, "Culture," *The Conduct of Life* (1860)

4. "Sophistication" is another word for that inventive mix of tolerance, resilience, and resourcefulness city people develop.

Edward Hoagland, "A Year As It Turns," *The Tugman's Passage* (1982)

5. I find those sophisticated girls were wrong—it was much easier to be brittle at the age of twenty when wisdom is easily come by.

Maureen Howard, *Facts of Life* (1978)

6. Be wisely worldly, be not worldly wise.

Francis Quarles, *Emblems* (1635), 2.2

918. SORROW

See also 610. Mourning; 946. Suffering; 1011. Unhappiness; 1052. Weeping

1. Grief drives men into habits of serious reflection, sharpens the understanding and softens the heart.

John Adams, letter to Thomas Jefferson, May 6, 1816

2. Grief is no more necessary when we understand death than fear is necessary when we understand flying.

Richard Bach, *Running from Safety* (1994)

3. Sorrow is better than laughter: for by the sadness of the countenance the heart is made better.

Bible, Ecclesiastes 7:3

4. Joys impregnate. Sorrows bring forth.

William Blake, "Proverbs of Hell," *The Marriage of Heaven and Hell* (1790)

5. The finer the nature, and the higher the level at which it seeks to live, the lower in grief it not only sinks but dives: it goes to weep with beggars and mountebanks, for these make the shame of being unhappy less.

Elizabeth Bowen, *The Death of the Heart* (1938), 3.3

6. There is no doubt that sorrow brings one down in the world. The aristocratic privilege of silence

belongs, you soon find out, to only the happy state—or, at least, to the state when pain keeps within bounds.

Elizabeth Bowen, *The Death of the Heart* (1938), 3.3

7. When we grieve, tears and guilt get mixed together.

Art Buchwald, *Leaving Home: A Memoir* (1993)

8. Grief should be the instructor of the wise; / Sorrow is Knowledge.

Byron, *Manfred* (1817) 1.1

9. She cried for herself, she cried because she was afraid that she herself might die in the night, because she was alone in the world, because her desperate and empty life was not an overture but an ending, and through it all she could see the rough, brutal shape of a coffin.

John Cheever, "The Hartleys," *The Stories of John Cheever* (1980)

10. Grief is not in the nature of things, but in opinion.

Cicero, *Tusculan Disputations* (44 B.C.), 3

11. There is something pleasurable in calm remembrance of a past sorrow.

Cicero, *Ad Familiares* (1st c. B.C.), 5

12. Melancholy and remorse form the deep leaden keel which enables us to sail into the wind of reality.

Cyril Connolly, *The Unquiet Grave* (1945), 3

13. Grief even in a child hates the light and shrinks from human eyes.

Thomas de Quincey, "The Affliction of Childhood," *Suspiria de Profundis* (1845)

14. I measure every Grief I meet / With narrow, probing Eyes— / I wonder if It weighs like Mine— / Or has an Easier size.

Emily Dickinson, poem (c. 1862)

15. Man sheds grief as his skin sheds rain.

Emerson, *Journals*, 1843

16. Sorrow makes us all children again.

Emerson, *Journals*, 1842

17. There are some men above grief and some men below it.

Emerson, *Journals*, 1836

18. Sadness flies on the wings of the morning and out of the heart of darkness comes the light.

Jean Giraudoux, *The Madwoman of Chaillot* (1945), 2, adapted by Maurice Valency

19. It is better to drink of deep griefs than to taste shallow pleasures.

William Hazlitt, *Characteristics* (1823), 306

20. Learn weeping, and thou shalt gain laughing.

George Herbert, *Jacula Prudentum* (1651)

21. There is not / any advantage to be won from grim lamentation.

Homer, *Iliad* (9th c. B.C.), 24.523, tr. Richmond Lattimore

22. Great grief is a divine and terrible radiance which transfigures the wretched.

Victor Hugo, "Fantine," *Les Misérables* (1862), 5.13, tr. Charles E. Wilbour

23. When a man or woman loves to brood over a sorrow and takes care to keep it green in their memory, you may be sure it is no longer a pain to them.

Jerome K. Jerome, "On Being in the Blues," *The Idle Thoughts of an Idle Fellow* (1889)

24. Grief is a species of idleness.

Samuel Johnson, letter to Mrs. Henry Thrale, March 17, 1773

25. While grief is fresh, every attempt to divert only irritates.

Samuel Johnson, quoted in Boswell's *Life of Samuel Johnson,* April 10, 1776

26. Real sorrow is incompatible with hope. No matter how great that sorrow may be, hope raises it one hundred cubits higher.

Comte de Lautréamont, *Poésies* (1870), 1

27. We collected in a group in front of their door, and we experienced within ourselves a grief that was new for us, the ancient grief of the people that has no land, the grief without hope of the exodus which is renewed in every century.

Primo Levi, *Survival in Auschwitz* (1959)

28. Grief can't be shared. Everyone carries it alone, his own burden, his own way.

Anne Morrow Lindbergh, "Theodore," *Dearly Beloved* (1962)

29. Take this sorrow to thy heart, and make it a part of thee, and it shall nourish thee till thou art strong again.

Longfellow, *Hyperion* (1839), 4.2

30. The first pressure of sorrow crushes out from our hearts the best wine; afterwards the constant weight

of it brings forth bitterness, the taste and stain from the lees of the vat.

LONGFELLOW, "TABLE-TALK," *DRIFTWOOD* (1857)

31. Rapture's self is three parts sorrow.

AMY LOWELL, "HAPPINESS," *SWORD BLADES AND POPPY SEEDS* (1914)

32. There is a sort of pleasure in indulging of grief.

THOMAS FULLER, M.D., *GNOMOLOGIA* (1732), 4883

33. There is far too much talk of love and grief benumbing the faculties, turning the hair gray, and destroying a man's interest in his work. Grief has made many a man look younger.

WILLIAM MCFEE, "ON A BALCONY," *HARBOURS OF MEMORY* (1921)

34. He truly sorrows who sorrows unseen.

MARTIAL, *EPIGRAMS* (A.D. 86), 1.33, TR. WALTER C. A. KERR

35. Why not leave their private sorrows to people? Is sorrow not, one asks, the only thing in the world people really possess?

VLADIMIR NABOKOV, *PNIN* (1957), 2.5

36. We were born to die; we were born to endure, on the way to death, sorrow—sorrow in manifold shapes.

CYNTHIA OZICK, "THE BIOLOGICAL PREMISES OF OUR SAD EARTH-SPECK," *ART & ARDOR* (1983)

37. Hope is incredible to the slave of grief.

PETRARCH, "LAURA LIVING," *CANZONIERE* (1360), 117

38. It is our human lot, it is heaven's will, that sorrow follow joy.

PLAUTUS, *AMPHITRYON* (3RD C. B.C.)

39. Sorrows remembered sweeten present joy.

ROBERT POLLOK, *THE COURSE OF TIME* (1827), 1.464

40. Happiness is beneficial for the body, but it is grief that develops the powers of the mind.

MARCEL PROUST, *REMEMBRANCE OF THINGS PAST: THE PAST RECAPTURED* (1913–27)

41. There is in this world in which everything wears out, everything perishes, one thing that crumbles into dust, that destroys itself still more completely, leaving behind still fewer traces of itself than Beauty: namely Grief.

MARCEL PROUST, *REMEMBRANCE OF THINGS PAST: THE SWEET CHEAT GONE* (1913–27), TR. C. K. SCOTT-MONCRIEFF

42. We wasters of sorrows! / How we stare away into sad endurance beyond them, / trying to foresee their end! Whereas they are nothing else / than our winter foliage, our sombre evergreen, *one* / of the seasons of our interior year.

RAINER MARIA RILKE, "THE TENTH ELEGY," *DUINO ELEGIES* (1923), TR. STEPHEN SPENDER

43. That sorrow which is the harbinger of joy is preferable to the joy which is followed by sorrow.

SA'DI, *GULISTAN* (1258), 8.107, TR. JAMES ROSS

44. It is sweet to mingle tears with tears; / Griefs, where they wound in solitude, / Wound more deeply.

SENECA, *AGAMEMNON* (1ST C.), 664

45. No emotion falls into dislike so readily as sorrow.

SENECA, *LETTERS TO LUCILIUS* (1ST C.), 63.3, TR. E. PHILLIPS BARKER

46. Every one can master a grief but he that has it.

SHAKESPEARE, *MUCH ADO ABOUT NOTHING* (1598–99), 3.2.28

47. Give sorrow words. The grief that does not speak / Whispers the o'erfraught heart and bids it break.

SHAKESPEARE, *MACBETH* (1605–06), 4.3.209

48. Gnarling sorrow hath less power to bite / The man that mocks at it and sets it light.

SHAKESPEARE, *RICHARD II* (1595–96), 1.3.292

49. I will instruct my sorrows to be proud; / For grief is proud, and makes his owner stoop.

SHAKESPEARE, *KING JOHN* (1596–97), 3.1.68

50. Sorrow breaks seasons and reposing hours, / Makes the night morning and the noontide night.

SHAKESPEARE, *RICHARD III* (1592–93), 1.4.76

51. When sorrows come, they come not single spies, / But in battalions!

SHAKESPEARE, *HAMLET* (1600), 4.5.78

52. Winter is come and gone, / But grief returns with the revolving year.

SHELLEY, *ADONAIS* (1821), 18

53. When people fall in deep distress, their native sense departs.

SOPHOCLES, *ANTIGONE* (442–41 B.C.), TR. ELIZABETH WYCKOFF

54. A sorrow's crown of sorrow is remembering happier things.

LORD TENNYSON, "LOCKSLEY HALL" (1842)

55. Where there is sorrow there is holy ground.

OSCAR WILDE, *DE PROFUNDIS* (1905)

56. A deep distress hath humanised my Soul.

William Wordsworth, "Elegiac Stanzas" (1805)

57. In heaven above, / And earth below, they best can serve true gladness / Who meet most feelingly the calls of sadness.

William Wordsworth, "'Tis He Whose Yester-Evening's High Disdain" (1838)

919. SOUL

See also 927. Spirituality

1. The soul is that which denies the body. For example, that which refuses to run when the body trembles, to strike when the body is angry, to drink when the body is thirsty.

Alain, *Definitions* (1953)

2. Foreigners have souls; the English haven't.

George Mikes, *How to Be an Alien* (1946)

3. Our soul is cast into a body, where it finds number, time, dimension. Thereupon it reasons, and calls this nature necessity, and can believe nothing else.

Pascal, *Pensées* (1670), 233, tr. W. F. Trotter

4. Nothing can so pierce the soul as the uttermost sigh of the body.

George Santayana, *The Life of Reason: Reason in Art* (1905–06), 6

5. The soul is the voice of the body's interests.

George Santayana, *The Life of Reason: Reason in Common Sense* (1905–06), 9

6. The lusts and greeds of the Body scandalize the Soul; but it has to come to heel.

Logan Pearsall Smith, *Afterthoughts* (1931), 1

7. Body and spirit are twins: God only knows which is which: / The soul squats down in the flesh, like a tinker drunk in a ditch.

Algernon Charles Swinburne, "The Higher Pantheism in a Nutshell," *The Heptalogia* (1880)

8. I have said that the soul is not more than the body, / And I have said that the body is not more than the soul, / And nothing, not God, is greater to one than one's self is.

Walt Whitman, "Song of Myself," 48, *Leaves of Grass* (1855–92)

9. Nothing can cure the soul but the senses, just as nothing can cure the senses but the soul.

Oscar Wilde, *The Picture of Dorian Gray* (1891), 2

10. The human body is the best picture of the human soul.

Ludwig Wittgenstein, *Philosophical Investigations* (1953), 2.4, tr. G. E. M. Anscombe

SOUND

See 614. Music; 636. Noise; 882. Senses

920. SOUR GRAPES

See also 185. Contempt; 249. Disappointment

1. It is easy to despise what you cannot get.

Aesop, "The Fox and the Grapes," *Fables* (6th c. b.c.?), tr. Joseph Jacobs

2. Believe not much them that seem to despise riches, for they despise them that despair of them.

Francis Bacon, "Of Riches," *Essays* (1625)

3. He whose mouth is out of taste says the wine is flat.

Montaigne, "Apology for Raimond de Sebonde," *Essays* (1580–88), tr. W. C. Hazlitt

SOUTH

See 638. North and South

921. SPACE

See also 415. The Heavens; 603. Moon; 1017. Universe

1. If all the stars and galaxies in the universe today were smoothed out into a uniform sea of atoms, there would only be about one atom in every cubic meter of space.

John D. Barrow, *The Origin of the Universe* (1994)

2. Everything in space obeys the laws of physics. If you know these laws, and obey them, space will treat you kindly. And don't tell me man doesn't belong out there. Man belongs wherever he wants to go—and he'll do plenty well when he gets there.

Wernher von Braun, *Time*, Feb. 17, 1958

3. The secret of our success on planet Earth is space. Lots of it. Our solar system is a tiny island of activity in an ocean of emptiness.

Paul Davies, *The Last Three Minutes* (1994)

4. Space flights are merely an escape, a fleeing away from oneself, because it is easier to go to Mars or to the moon than it is to penetrate one's own being.

Carl Gustav Jung, quoted in Miguel Serrano's "The Farewell," *C. G. Jung and Hermann Hesse* (1966), tr. Frank MacShane

5. The eternal silence of these infinite spaces frightens me.

PASCAL, *PENSÉES* (1670), 206, TR. W. F. TROTTER

922. SPAIN AND SPANIARDS

1. In Spain, the dead are more alive than the dead of any other country in the world.

FEDERICO GARCÍA LORCA, "THE DUENDE: THEORY AND DIVERTISSEMENT," *POET IN NEW YORK* (1940), APPENDIX 6, TR. BEN BELITT

2. The first meal in Spain was always a shock with the hors d'oeuvres, an egg course, two meat courses, vegetables, salad, and dessert and fruit.

ERNEST HEMINGWAY, *THE SUN ALSO RISES* (1926)

923. SPEAKING

See also 98. BREVITY; 134. CLARITY; 149. COMMUNICATION; 188. CONVERSATION; 283. ELOQUENCE; 524. LANGUAGE; 543. LISTENING; 763. PUBLIC SPEAKING; 898. SILENCE; 961. TACT; 1064. WORDS

1. If human beings don't keep exercising their lips, he thought, their mouths probably seize up. After a few months' consideration and observation he abandoned this theory in favor of a new one. If they don't keep on exercising their lips, he thought, their brains start working.

DOUGLAS ADAMS, *THE HITCHHIKER'S GUIDE TO THE GALAXY* (1979)

2. The most difficult thing in the world is to say thinkingly what everybody says without thinking.

ALAIN, *HISTOIRE DE MES PENSÉES* (1936)

3. To speak agreeably to him with whom we deal is more than to speak in good words or in good order.

FRANCIS BACON, "OF DISCOURSE," *ESSAYS* (1625)

4. Many [foreign tourists] try to speak Italian. A few creditably manage this in a short time. Others think they do.

LUIGI BARZINI, *THE ITALIANS* (1964)

5. Words [spoken by Americans] were usually ejected in lumps, at enormous speed, groups of them strung together like rushing railroad cars without perceptible separations.

LUIGI BARZINI, *O AMERICA* (1977)

6. The voice is a second face.

GÉRARD BAUËR, *CARNETS INÉDITS*

7. None love to speak so much, when the mood of speaking comes, as they who are naturally taciturn.

HENRY WARD BEECHER, *PROVERBS FROM PLYMOUTH PULPIT* (1887)

8. A fool uttereth all his mind.

BIBLE, PROVERBS 29:11

9. Let your speech be alway with grace, seasoned with salt.

BIBLE, COLOSSIANS 4:6

10. Loquacity, n. A disorder which renders the sufferer unable to curb his tongue when you wish to talk.

AMBROSE BIERCE, *THE DEVIL'S DICTIONARY* (1881–1911)

11. Speech is too often not the art of concealing thought, but of quite stifling and suspending thought, so that there is none to conceal.

THOMAS CARLYLE, *SARTOR RESARTUS* (1833–34), 3.3

12. Little said is soon amended.

CERVANTES, *DON QUIXOTE* (1605–15), 1.3.11, TR. JOHN OZELL

13. Her voice was sweet, and reminded him of elms, of lawns, of those glass arrangements that used to be hung from porch ceilings to tinkle in the summer wind.

JOHN CHEEVER, "TORCH SONG," *THE STORIES OF JOHN CHEEVER* (1980)

14. One never repents of having spoken too little, but often of having spoken too much.

PHILIPPE DE COMMYNES, *MÉMOIRES* (1524), 1.14

15. Let thy speech be better than silence, or be silent.

DIONYSIUS THE ELDER, EXTANT FRAGMENT (4TH C. B.C.)

16. Do not say things. What you are stands over you the while and thunders so that I cannot hear what you say to the contrary.

EMERSON, *JOURNALS*, 1840

17. Must we always talk for victory, and never once for truth, for comfort, and joy?

EMERSON, *JOURNALS*, 1856

18. First learn the meaning of what you say, and then speak.

EPICTETUS, *DISCOURSES* (2ND C.), 3.23, TR. THOMAS W. HIGGINSON

19. When you speak to a man, look on his eyes; when he speaks to you, look on his mouth.

BENJAMIN FRANKLIN, *POOR RICHARD'S ALMANACK* (1732–57)

20. Is there any place where there is no traffic in empty talk? Is there on this earth one who does not worship himself talking?

KAHLIL GIBRAN, "MISTER GABBER," *THOUGHTS AND MEDITATIONS* (1960), TR. ANTHONY R. FERRIS

21. In much of your talking, thinking is half murdered. / For thought is a bird of space, that in a cage of words may indeed unfold its wings but cannot fly.

KAHLIL GIBRAN, "ON TALKING," *THE PROPHET* (1923)

22. The true use of speech is not so much to express our wants as to conceal them.

OLIVER GOLDSMITH, *THE BEE*, OCT. 20, 1759

23. There is always time to add a word, never to withdraw one.

BALTASAR GRACIÁN, *THE ART OF WORLDLY WISDOM* (1647), 160, TR. JOSEPH JACOBS

24. People do not seem to talk for the sake of expressing their opinions, but to maintain an opinion for the sake of talking.

WILLIAM HAZLITT, "ON COFFEE-HOUSE POLITICIANS," *TABLE TALK* (1821–22)

25. If no thought / your mind does visit, / make your speech / not too explicit.

PIET HEIN, "THE CASE FOR OBSCURITY," *GROOKS* (1966)

26. The English talked with inflected phrases. One phrase to mean everything.

ERNEST HEMINGWAY, *THE SUN ALSO RISES* (1926)

27. Talking is like playing on the harp; there is as much in laying the hand on the strings to stop their vibrations as in twanging them to bring out their music.

OLIVER WENDELL HOLMES, SR., *THE AUTOCRAT OF THE BREAKFAST TABLE* (1858), 1

28. Nobody talks much that doesn't say unwise things—things he did not mean to say; as no person plays much without striking a false note sometimes.

OLIVER WENDELL HOLMES, SR., *THE PROFESSOR AT THE BREAKFAST TABLE* (1860), 1

29. Many people would be more truthful were it not for their uncontrollable desire to talk.

EDGAR WATSON HOWE, *COUNTRY TOWN SAYINGS* (1911)

30. A man is hid under his tongue.

ALI IBN-ABI-TALIB, *SENTENCES* (7TH C.), 83, TR. SIMON OCKLEY

31. No glass renders a man's form or likeness so true as his speech.

BEN JONSON, "OF LANGUAGE IN ORATORY," *TIMBER* (1640)

32. Whom the disease of talking still once possesseth, he can never hold his peace.

BEN JONSON, "OF TALKING OVERMUCH," *TIMBER* (1640)

33. Sometimes when we have to speak suddenly we come closer to the truth than when we have time to think.

MADELEINE L'ENGLE, *A CIRCLE OF QUIET* (1972)

34. Babies and language are the essential ingredients of civilization, and speakers of language no more know where it came from than babies know where they come from.

CHARLTON LAIRD, *THE MIRACLE OF LANGUAGE* (1953)

35. [T]he great arbiters of language are the women who speak it in the presence of children.... What the women pass on to the next generation is "right" and what they do not bother to pass on to their children sooner or later becomes "wrong."

CHARLTON LAIRD, *THE MIRACLE OF LANGUAGE* (1953)

36. The trumpet does not more stun you by its loudness, than a whisper teases you by its provoking inaudibility.

CHARLES LAMB, "THE OLD AND THE NEW SCHOOLMASTER," *ESSAYS OF ELIA* (1823)

37. We oftener say things because we can say them well, than because they are sound and reasonable.

WALTER SAVAGE LANDOR, "MARCUS TULLIUS AND QUINCTUS CICERO," *IMAGINARY CONVERSATIONS* (1824–53)

38. He who talks more is sooner exhausted.

LAO TZU, *THE CHARACTER OF TAO* (6TH C. B.C.), 5, TR. CH'U TA-KAO

39. It is never more difficult to speak well than when we are ashamed of keeping silent.

LA ROCHEFOUCAULD, *MAXIMS* (1665), TR. KENNETH PRATT

40. We talk little when vanity does not make us.

LA ROCHEFOUCAULD, *MAXIMS* (1665), TR. KENNETH PRATT

41. "I'm with an old family" was the euphemism used to dignify the professions of white folks' cooks and maids who talked so affectedly among their own kind

in Roxbury [Massachusetts] that you couldn't even understand them.

MALCOLM X, *THE AUTOBIOGRAPHY OF MALCOLM X* (1964)

42. Speech is civilization itself. The word, even the most contradictious word, preserves contact—it is silence which isolates.

THOMAS MANN, *THE MAGIC MOUNTAIN* (1924), 6.8, TR. H. T. LOWE-PORTER

43. Every man may speak truly, but to speak methodically, prudently, and fully is a talent that few men have.

MONTAIGNE, "OF THE ART OF CONFERENCE," *ESSAYS* (1580–88), TR. W. C. HAZLITT

44. The unluckiest insolvent in the world is the man whose expenditure of speech is too great for his income of ideas.

CHRISTOPHER MORLEY, *INWARD HO!* (1923), 9

45. Pleasant words are the food of love.

OVID, *THE ART OF LOVE* (C. A.D. 8), 2, TR. J. LEWIS MAY

46. One who speaks aright never says his say at an unsuitable place or time, nor before one of immature faculties or without excellence. This is why his words are not spoken in vain.

PANCHATANTRA (C. 5TH C.), 1, TR. FRANKLIN EDGERTON

47. There are some who speak well and write badly. For the place and the audience warm them, and draw from their minds more than they think of without that warmth.

PASCAL, *PENSÉES* (1670), 47, TR. W. F. TROTTER

48. It is easy to utter what has been kept silent, but impossible to recall what has been uttered.

PLUTARCH, "THE EDUCATION OF CHILDREN," *MORALIA* (C. A.D. 100), TR. MOSES HADAS

49. Speech is a mirror of the soul: as a man speaks, so is he.

PUBLILIUS SYRUS, *MORAL SAYINGS* (1ST C. B.C.), 1073, TR. DARIUS LYMAN

50. In the faculty of speech man excels the brute; but if thou utterest what is improper, the brute is they superior.

SA'DI, INTRODUCTION, *GULISTAN* (1258), TR. JAMES ROSS

51. His voice was oddly and beautifully rough cut, as some small boys' voices are. Each of his phrasings was rather like a little ancient island, inundated by a miniature sea of whiskey.

J.D. SALINGER, "TEDDY," IN *NINE STORIES BY J.D. SALINGER* (1953)

52. When I think over what I have said, I envy dumb people.

SENECA, "ON A HAPPY LIFE," *MORAL ESSAYS* (1ST C.), TR. AUBREY STEWART

53. Her voice was ever soft, / Gentle, and low—an excellent thing in woman.

SHAKESPEARE, *KING LEAR* (1605–06), 5.3.272

54. Talkers are no good doers.

SHAKESPEARE, *RICHARD III* (1592–93), 1.3.351

55. Speech is the mirror of action.

SOLON (7TH–6TH C. B.C.), QUOTED IN DIOGENES LAERTIUS' *LIVES AND OPINIONS OF EMINENT PHILOSOPHERS* (3RD C. A.D.), TR. R. D. HICKS

56. Surely human affairs would be far happier if the power in men to be silent were the same as that to speak. But experience more than sufficiently teaches that men govern nothing with more difficulty than their tongues, and can moderate their desires more easily than their words.

SPINOZA, *ETHICS* (1677), 3, TR. ANDREW BOYLE

57. Just as our bread, mixed and baked, packaged and sold without benefit of accident or human frailty, is uniformly good and uniformly tasteless, so will our speech become one speech.

JOHN STEINBECK, *TRAVELS WITH CHARLEY* (1962)

58. [A] rejection of the way a woman speaks is often a way of blaming or dismissing her without dealing with the content of what she is saying.

GLORIA STEINEM, "MEN AND WOMEN TALKING," *OUTRAGEOUS ACTS AND EVERYDAY REBELLIONS* (1983)

59. There can be no fairer ambition than to excel in talk; to be affable, gay, ready, clear, and welcome.

ROBERT LOUIS STEVENSON, "TALK AND TALKERS" (1882), 1

60. Nature, which gave us two eyes to see, and two ears to hear, has given us but one tongue to speak.

JONATHAN SWIFT, *A TRITICAL ESSAY UPON THE FACULTIES OF THE MIND* (1707)

61. I know in London a Welsh hairdresser who has striven so vehemently to abolish his accent that he sounds like a man speaking with the Elgin marbles in his mouth.

DYLAN THOMAS, *QUITE EARLY ONE MORNING* (1954)

62. It is the man determines what is said, not the words.

THOREAU, *JOURNAL*, JULY 11, 1840

SPECIALISTS

63. A dog is not considered good because of his barking, and a man is not considered clever because of his ability to talk.

CHUANG TZU, *WORKS* (4TH–3RD C. B.C.), 32.1, TR. LIN YUTANG

924. SPECIALISTS

See also 848. SCHOLARS AND SCHOLARSHIP; 1037. VOCATIONS

1. An expert is a person who avoids the small errors while sweeping on to the grand fallacy.

ARTHUR BLOCH, "WEINBERG'S COROLLARY," *MURPHY'S LAW* (1979)

2. A poet on Pegasus, reciting his own verses, is hardly more to be dreaded than a mounted specialist.

OLIVER WENDELL HOLMES, SR., *OVER THE TEACUPS* (1891), 7

3. Specialized meaninglessness has come to be regarded, in certain circles, as a kind of hall mark of true science.

ALDOUS HUXLEY, "BELIEFS," *ENDS AND MEANS* (1937)

4. The essence of the expert is that his field shall be very special and narrow: one of the ways in which he inspires confidence is to rigidly limit himself to the little toe; he would scarcely venture an off-the-record opinion on an infected little finger.

LOUIS KRONENBERGER, *COMPANY MANNERS* (1954), 1.4

5. Wherever learning breeds specialists, the sum of human culture is enhanced thereby. That is the illusion and consolation of specialists.

ANTONIO MACHADO, *JUAN DE MAIRENA* (1943), 1, TR. BEN BELITT

925. SPECTACLES

1. Wearing spectacles makes men conceited, because spectacles raise them to a degree of sensual perfection which is far above the power of their own nature.

JOHANN PETER ECKERMANN, *CONVERSATIONS WITH GOETHE,* APRIL 5, 1830

SPECTATORS

See 59. AUDIENCE; 650. OBSERVATION

SPEECH

See 188. CONVERSATION; 364. FREE SPEECH; 763. PUBLIC SPEAKING; 923. SPEAKING

926. SPEED

See also 411. HASTE; 907. SLOWNESS

1. There is no secrecy comparable to celerity.

FRANCIS BACON, "OF DELAY," *ESSAYS* (1625)

2. In skating over thin ice our safety is in our speed.

EMERSON, "PRUDENCE," *ESSAYS: FIRST SERIES* (1841)

3. The day started off, as all mine do, at a snail's pace.

S.J. PERELMAN, *THE RISING GORGE* (1961)

4. Celerity is never more admired / Than by the negligent.

SHAKESPEARE, *ANTONY AND CLEOPATRA* (1606–07), 3.7.25

SPIRIT

See 590. MIND; 927. SPIRITUALITY

927. SPIRITUALITY

See also 183. CONTEMPLATION; 490. THE INTANGIBLE; 569. MATERIALISM; 589. MIND AND BODY; 601. MONASTICISM; 616. MYSTICISM; 840. SAINTS AND SAINTHOOD

1. Spirit is an invisible force made visible in all life.

MAYA ANGELOU, "IN THE SPIRIT," *WOULDN'T TAKE NOTHING FOR MY JOURNEY NOW* (1993)

2. I am certainly convinced that it is one of the greatest impulses of mankind to arrive at something higher than a natural state.

JAMES BALDWIN, "THE MALE PRISON," *NOBODY KNOWS MY NAME* (1961)

3. One of our problems today is that we are not well acquainted with the literature of the spirit. We're interested in the news of the day and the problems of the hour.

JOSEPH CAMPBELL, *THE POWER OF MYTH* (1988)

4. Give unto us this day the daily manna / Without which, in this desert where we dwell, / He must go backward who would most advance.

DANTE, "PURGATORIO," 11, *THE DIVINE COMEDY* (C. 1300–21), TR. LAWRENCE GRANT WHITE

5. The soul may ask God for anything, and never fail.

ANNIE DILLARD, "TEACHING A STONE TO TALK," *TEACHING A STONE TO TALK* (1982)

6. To the poet, to the philosopher, to the saint, all things are friendly and sacred, all events profitable, all days holy, all men divine.

EMERSON, "HISTORY," *ESSAYS: FIRST SERIES* (1841)

7. Our spirituality is our opening to one another as whole human beings, each different and precious, and our exploring how we can truly learn to love.

JEAN GRASSO FITZPATRICK, *SOMETHING MORE* (1991)

8. There is one spectacle grander than the sea, that is the sky; there is one spectacle grander than the sky, that is the interior of the soul.

VICTOR HUGO, "FANTINE," *LES MISÉRABLES* (1862), 7.3, TR. CHARLES E. WILBOUR

9. The human soul is very much older than the human mind.

KONRAD LORENZ, *THE WANING OF HUMANENESS* (1983), TR. ROBERT WARREN KICKER

10. Physical strength can never permanently withstand the impact of spiritual force.

FRANKLIN D. ROOSEVELT, SPEECH, STAUNTON, VA., MAY 4, 1941

11. I mean it's very hard to meditate and live a spiritual life in America. People think you're a freak if you try to.

J.D. SALINGER, *RAISE HIGH THE ROOF BEAM, CARPENTERS* (1963)

12. All spiritual interests are supported by animal life.

GEORGE SANTAYANA, *THE LIFE OF REASON: REASON IN SOCIETY* (1905–06), I

13. Pressed, I would define spirituality as the shadow of light humanity casts as it moves through the darkness of everything that can be explained.

JOHN UPDIKE, "SPIRITUALITY," *ODD JOBS* (1991)

14. To be rooted is perhaps the most important and least recognized need of the human soul.

SIMON WEIL, *THE NEED FOR ROOTS* (1952), TR. ARTHUR WILLS

15. Nuns fret not at their convent's narrow room; / And hermits are contented with their cells.

WILLIAM WORDSWORTH, "NUNS FRET NOT AT THEIR CONVENT'S NARROW ROOM" (1807)

928. SPONTANEITY

See also 293. ENTHUSIASM; 461. IMPULSIVENESS; 1036. VITALITY; 1053. WHIM

1. Great art must be guided by an invisible technique; it must seem the spontaneous blossom of the moment's mood and impulse.

LUIGI BARZINI, *THE ITALIANS* (1964)

2. Improvisation is the essence of good talk. Heaven defend us from the talker who doles out things prepared for us! But let heaven not less defend us from the beautifully spontaneous writer who puts his trust in the inspiration of the moment!

MAX BEERBOHM, "LYTTON STRACHEY," *MAINLY ON THE AIR* (1946)

3. The individual never asserts himself more than when he forgets himself.

ANDRÉ GIDE, "PORTRAITS AND APHORISMS," *PRETEXTS* (1903), TR. OTHERS

4. We never do anything well till we cease to think about the manner of doing it. This is the reason why it is so difficult for any but natives to speak a language correctly or idiomatically.

WILLIAM HAZLITT, "ON PREJUDICE," *SKETCHES AND ESSAYS* (1839)

5. Too much improvisation leaves the mind stupidly void.

VICTOR HUGO, "FANTINE," *LES MISÉRABLES* (1862), 3.7, TR. CHARLES E. WILBOUR

929. SPORTS

See also 348. FISHING; 438. HUNTING; 696. PHYSICAL FITNESS; 703. PLAY; 821. RIDING; 1041. WALKING

1. Baseball is slovenly and excessive in midsummer, with its onrolling daily cascade of line scores and box scores, shifting statistics, highlights and lowlights, dingers and shutouts, streaks and slumps.

ROGER ANGELL, "HARDBALL," *THE NEW YORKER*, OCT. 17, 1994

2. Losing is the bane and bugbear of every professional athlete's existence, but in baseball the monster seems to hang closer than in other sports, its chilly claws and foul breath palpable around the neck hairs of the infielder bending for his crosshand scoop or the reliever slipping his first two fingers off-center on the ball seams before delivering his two-and-two cut fastball.

ROGER ANGELL, "HARD LINES," *BASEBALL* (1994), BY GEOFFREY C. WARD AND KEN BURNS

3. [I]nfield practice is more mystic ritual than preparation, encouraging the big-leaguer, no less than the duffer in the stands, to believe in spite of all evidence to the contrary, that playing ball is a snap.

ROGER ANGELL, "HARD LINES," *BASEBALL* (1994), BY GEOFFREY C. WARD AND KEN BURNS

4. [W]hat really makes baseball so hard is its retributive capacity for disaster if the smallest thing is done wrong, and the invisible presence of defeat that attends every game.

ROGER ANGELL, "HARD LINES," *BASEBALL* (1994), BY GEOFFREY C. WARD AND KEN BURNS

5. In America, it is sport that is the opiate of the masses.

RUSSELL BAKER, "OBSERVER," *THE NEW YORK TIMES,* OCT. 3, 1967

6. No myth dies harder, and none is more regularly debunked by the facts, than the one about international sports contributing to international friendship.

ALISTAIR COOKE, "AN EPIC OF COURAGE," *AMERICA OBSERVED: FROM THE 1940S TO THE 1980S* (1988)

7. Pro football is like nuclear warfare. There are no winners, only survivors.

FRANK GIFFORD, *SPORTS ILLUSTRATED,* JULY 4, 1960

8. A golf course is the epitome of all that is purely transitory in the universe, a space not to dwell in, but to get over as quickly as possible.

JEAN GIRAUDOUX, *THE ENCHANTED* (1933), 1, ADAPTED BY MAURICE VALENCY

9. The human spirit sublimates / the impulses it thwarts; / a healthy sex life mitigates / the lust for other sports.

PIET HEIN, "HINT AND SUGGESTION," *GROOKS* (1966)

10. When I were a young man, I used to play baseball and steal bases just like Jackie [Robinson]. If the empire would rule me out, I would get mad and hit the empire.

LANGSTON HUGHES, *SIMPLE SPEAKS HIS MIND* (1950)

11. We are inclined to think that if we watch a football game or a baseball game, we have taken part in it.

JOHN F. KENNEDY, INTERVIEW WITH DAVE GARROWAY, JAN. 31, 1961

12. America has been erased like a blackboard, only to be rebuilt and then erased again. But baseball has marked time while America has rolled by like a procession of steamrollers.

W.P. KINSELLA, *SHOELESS JOE* (1982)

13. Rodeoing is about the only sport you can't fix. You'd have to talk to the bulls and horses, and they wouldn't understand you.

BILL LINDERMAN, NEWS SUMMARIES, MARCH 8, 1954

14. Little boys are still playing the game [baseball], more little girls are playing, and it is still the world's most interesting game, a duel, a chess match, a foot race, a gymnastics exhibition, that rare opportunity for individuals to be recognized within a group effort.

ROBERT LIPSYTE, "ON BASEBALL," *THE NEW YORK TIMES,* SEPT. 15, 1994

15. A college boy cannot successfully go through life by graduating in football, baseball, or highballs, for the responsibilities of life are not ball-bearing.

WILLIAM H. MURRAY, SPEECH QUOTED IN *A TREASURY OF SOUTHERN FOLKLORE* (1949)

16. Serious sport has nothing to do with fair play. It is bound up with hatred, jealousy, boastfulness, disregard of all rules and sadistic pleasure in witnessing violence: in other words it is war minus the shooting.

GEORGE ORWELL, "THE SPORTING SPIRIT," *SHOOTING AN ELEPHANT* (1950)

17. Going to college offered me the chance to play football for four more years.

RONALD REAGAN, *AN AMERICAN LIFE* (1990)

18. Ideally, the umpire should combine the integrity of a Supreme Court justice, the physical agility of an acrobat, the endurance of Job and the imperturbability of Buddha.

"THE VILLAINS IN BLUE," *TIME,* AUG. 25, 1961

19. Baseball is meant to be fun, and not all the solemn money-men in fur-collared greatcoats, not all the scruffy media cameramen and sour-faced reporters that crowd around the dugouts can quite smother the exhilarating spaciousness and grace of this impudently relaxed sport, a game of innumerable potential redemptions and curious disappointments.

JOHN UPDIKE, *ODD JOBS* (1991)

20. Baseball, it is said, is only a game. True. And the Grand Canyon is only a hole in Arizona. Not all holes, or games, are created equal.

GEORGE F. WILL, *MEN AT WORK: THE CRAFT OF BASEBALL* (1990)

21. Greek philosophers considered sport a religious and civic—in a word, moral—undertaking. Sport, they said, is morally serious because mankind's noblest aim is the loving contemplation of worthy things, such as beauty and courage.

GEORGE F. WILL, *MEN AT WORK: THE CRAFT OF BASEBALL* (1990)

22. It is an old baseball joke that big-inning baseball is affirmed in the Bible, in Genesis. "In the big inning, God created...."

GEORGE F. WILL, *MEN AT WORK: THE CRAFT OF BASEBALL* (1990)

23. Football brings out the sociologist that lurks in some otherwise respectable citizens. They say football is a metaphor for America's sinfulness.

GEORGE F. WILL, "WOODY HAYES," *THE PURSUIT OF HAPPINESS AND OTHER SOBERING THOUGHTS* (1978)

SPRING

See 854. SEASONS

STARS

See 415. THE HEAVENS

STARTING

See 75. BEGINNING

930. STATE

See also 127. CHURCH AND STATE; 132. CITIZENS; 395. GOVERNMENT; 621. NATION; 913. SOCIETY

1. We weed out the darnel from the corn and the unfit in war, but do not excuse evil men from the service of the state.

ANTISTHENES (5TH–4TH C. B.C.), QUOTED IN DIOGENES LAERTIUS' *LIVES AND OPINIONS OF EMINENT PHILOSOPHERS* (3RD C. A.D.), TR. R. D. HICKS

2. The state exists for the sake of a good life, and not for the sake of life only.

ARISTOTLE, *POLITICS* (4TH C. B.C.), 3.9, TR. BENJAMIN JOWETT

3. Nothing doth more hurt in a state than that cunning men pass for wise.

FRANCIS BACON, "OF CUNNING," *ESSAYS* (1625)

4. The modern state no longer has anything but rights; it does not recognize duties any more.

GEORGES BERNANOS, "WHY FREEDOM?" *THE LAST ESSAYS OF GEORGES BERNANOS* (1955), TR. BARRY ULANOV

5. A state without some means of change is without the means of its conservation.

EDMUND BURKE, *REFLECTIONS ON THE REVOLUTION IN FRANCE* (1790)

6. A thousand years scarce serve to form a state; / An hour may lay it in the dust.

BYRON, *CHILDE HAROLD'S PILGRIMAGE* (1812–18), 2.84

7. A state worthy of the name has no friends—only interests.

CHARLES DE GAULLE, QUOTED IN *THE NEW YORK TIMES MAGAZINE*, MAY 12, 1968

8. The State is made for man, not man for the State.

EINSTEIN, "THE DISARMAMENT CONFERENCE OF 1932," *THE WORLD AS I SEE IT* (1934), TR. ALAN HARRIS

9. The State is a poor, good beast who means the best: it means friendly.

EMERSON, *JOURNALS*, 1846

10. The State is our neighbors; our neighbors are the State.

EMERSON, *JOURNALS*, 1845

11. When fear enters the heart of a man at hearing the names of candidates and the reading of laws that are proposed, then is the State safe, but when these things are heard without regard, as above or below us, then is the Commonwealth sick or dead.

EMERSON, *JOURNALS*, 1836

12. The state is the servant of the citizen, and not his master.

JOHN F. KENNEDY, STATE OF THE UNION MESSAGE, JAN. 11, 1962

13. The State not seldom tolerates a comparatively great evil to keep out millions of lesser ills and inconveniences which otherwise would be inevitable and without remedy.

LA BRUYÈRE, *CHARACTERS* (1688), 10.7, TR. HENRI VAN LAUN

14. While the state exists there is no freedom; when there is freedom there will be no state.

LENIN, *THE STATE AND REVOLUTION* (1917)

15. As great edifices collapse of their own weight, so Heaven sets a similar limit to the growth of prosperous states.

LUCAN, *ON THE CIVIL WAR* (1ST C.), TR. ROBERT GRAVES

16. Each State can have for enemies only other States, and not men; for between things disparate in nature there can be no real relation.

ROUSSEAU, *THE SOCIAL CONTRACT* (1762), 1.4, TR. G. D. H. COLE

17. The responsibility of great states is to serve and not to dominate the world.

HARRY S TRUMAN, MESSAGE TO CONGRESS, APRIL 16, 1945

931. STATESMEN AND STATESMANSHIP

See also 247. DIPLOMATS AND DIPLOMACY; 711. POLITICS AND POLITICIANS

1. It is seldom that statesmen have the option of choosing between a good and an evil.

CHARLES CALEB COLTON, *LACON* (1825), 1.73

2. The difference between being an elder statesman / And posing successfully as an elder statesman / Is practically negligible.

T. S. ELIOT, *THE ELDER STATESMAN* (1958), 2

3. The minds of some of our statesmen, like the pupil of the human eye, contract themselves the more, the stronger light there is shed upon them.

THOMAS MOORE, PREFACE TO *CORRUPTION AND INTOLERANCE* (1808)

4. In statesmanship there are predicaments from which it is impossible to escape without some wrongdoing.

NAPOLEON I, *MAXIMS* (1804–15)

5. The heart of a statesman should be in his head.

NAPOLEON I, *MAXIMS* (1804–15)

6. You can always get the truth from an American statesman after he has turned seventy, or given up all hope of the Presidency.

WENDELL PHILLIPS, SPEECH, NOV. 7, 1860

7. There are some whom the applause of the multitude has deluded into the belief that they are really statesmen.

PLATO, *THE REPUBLIC* (4TH C. B.C.), 4, TR. BENJAMIN JOWETT

8. Statesmen are not only liable to give an account of what they say or do in public, but there is a busy inquiry made into their very meals, beds, marriages, and every other sportive or serious action.

PLUTARCH, "POLITICAL PRECEPTS," *MORALIA* (C. A.D. 100)

9. In statesmanship get formalities right, never mind about the moralities.

MARK TWAIN, "PUDD'NHEAD WILSON'S NEW CALENDAR," *FOLLOWING THE EQUATOR* (1897), 2.29

932. STATISTICS

1. You and I are forever at the mercy of the census-taker and the census-maker. That impertinent fellow who goes from house to house is one of the real masters of the statistical situation. The other is the man who organizes the results.

WALTER LIPPMANN, "THE GOLDEN RULE AND AFTER," *A PREFACE TO POLITICS* (1914)

2. There are three kinds of lies—lies, damned lies and statistics.

MARK TWAIN, *AUTOBIOGRAPHY* (1924), V. 1

933. STATUS

See also 171. CONFORMITY; 780. RANK

1. Grass is the least rewarding of all status symbols.... The grass does nothing but drink money, exhaust energies, crush spirits, destroy sleep, create tensions and interfere with the watching of baseball games, and sprout insolent signs ordering humans to keep off it.

RUSSELL BAKER, "GREEN ELEPHANT," *ALL THINGS CONSIDERED* (1962)

2. I mean the shoestring aristocrats of the upper East Side—the elegant, charming, and shabby men who work for brokerage houses, and their high-flown wives, with their thrift-shop minks and their ash-can fur pieces, their alligator shoes and their snotty ways with doormen and with the cashiers in supermarkets, their gold jewelry and their dregs of Je Reviens and Chanel.

JOHN CHEEVER, "JUST ONE MORE TIME," *THE STORIES OF JOHN CHEEVER* (1980)

3. The prestige you acquire by being able to tell your friends that you know famous men proves only that you are yourself of small account.

W. SOMERSET MAUGHAM, *THE SUMMING UP* (1938), 2

4. The poor man is ruined as soon as he begins to ape the rich.

PUBLILIUS SYRUS, *MORAL SAYINGS* (1ST C. B.C.), 941, TR. DARIUS LYMAN

5. Girls are not accustomed to jockeying for status in an obvious way; they are more concerned that they be liked.

DEBORAH TANNEN, *YOU JUST DON'T UNDERSTAND* (1990)

934. STEALING

See also 191. CORRUPTION; 204. CRIME

1. Some go to prison for stealing, and others for believing that a better system can be provided and maintained than one that makes it necessary for a man to steal in order to live.

EUGENE V. DEBS, *WALLS AND BARS* (1927)

2. All stealing is comparative. If you come to absolutes, pray who does not steal?

EMERSON, "EXPERIENCE," *ESSAYS: SECOND SERIES* (1844)

3. A thief passes for a gentleman when stealing has made him rich.

THOMAS FULLER, M.D., *GNOMOLOGIA* (1732), 431

4. Old burglars never die, they just steal away.

GLEN GILBREATH, ON FACING HIS THIRTEENTH ROBBERY CHARGE, *CHICAGO SUN-TIMES*, APRIL 26, 1958

5. A thief believes everybody steals.

EDGAR WATSON HOWE, *COUNTRY TOWN SAYINGS* (1911)

6. The fact of the matter is that poor men do not often steal, and when they do, it is petty theft, something to eat or perhaps an item of clothing to keep them from the cold. Thieves are usually those who have something and want more.

LOUIS L'AMOUR, *EDUCATION OF A WANDERING MAN* (1989)

7. The faults of the burglar are the qualities of the financier.

GEORGE BERNARD SHAW, PREFACE, *MAJOR BARBARA* (1905)

935. STEREOTYPES

See also 171. CONFORMITY

1. There's nothing the world loves more than a ready-made description which they can hang on to a man, and so save themselves all trouble in future.

W. SOMERSET MAUGHAM, *MRS. DOT* (1912), 2

2. Every society has a tendency to reduce its opponents to caricatures.

NIETZSCHE, *THE WILL TO POWER* (1888), TR. ANTHONY M. LUDOVICI

936. STINGINESS

See also 384. GIFTS AND GIVING; 595. MISERS

1. Who will not feed the cats, must feed the mice and rats.

GERMAN PROVERB

2. Meanness is more in half-doing than in omitting acts of generosity.

ELBERT HUBBARD, *THE NOTE BOOK* (1927)

3. We often excuse our own want of philanthropy by giving the name of fanaticism to the more ardent zeal of others.

LONGFELLOW, "TABLE-TALK," *DRIFTWOOD* (1857)

STOCK MARKET

See 503. INVESTMENT

937. STOICISM

See also 287. ENDURANCE; 806. RESIGNATION

1. Here is a rule to remember in future, when anything tempts you to feel bitter: not, "This is a misfortune," but "To bear this worthily is good fortune."

MARCUS AURELIUS, *MEDITATIONS* (2ND C.), 4.49, TR. MAXWELL STANIFORTH

2. He who has calmly reconciled his life to fate, and set proud death beneath his feet, can look fortune in the face, unbending both to good and bad: his countenance unconquered he can shew.

BOETHIUS, *THE CONSOLATION OF PHILOSOPHY* (A.D. 524), 1, TR. W. V. COOPER

3. He who despises life is his life's master.

CORNEILLE, *CINNA* (1639), 1.2, TR. PAUL LANDIS

4. Let a man accept his destiny, / No pity and no tears.

EURIPIDES, *IPHIGENIA IN TAURIS* (C. 414–12 B.C.), TR. WITTER BYNNER

5. Be content with what you are, and wish not change; nor dread your last day, nor long for it.

MARTIAL, *EPIGRAMS* (A.D. 86), 10.47, TR. WALTER C. A. KERR

6. Whoever has nothing to hope, let him despair of nothing.

SENECA, *MEDEA* (1ST C.), 163, TR. FRANK JUSTUS MILLER

7. Why, courage then! What cannot be avoided / 'Twere childish weakness to lament or fear.

SHAKESPEARE, 3 *HENRY VI* (1590–91), 5.4.37

8. The chief difference between mankind and the cockroach is that the one continually bitches over his fate while the other stoically plods on, uncomplaining, with never a glance backward nor a sigh for what might have been.

JEAN SHEPHERD, "FUN CITY," *THE FERRARI IN THE BEDROOM* (1972)

9. The stoical scheme of supplying our wants by lopping off our desires, is like cutting off our feet, when we want shoes.

JONATHAN SWIFT, *THOUGHTS ON VARIOUS SUBJECTS* (1711)

938. STORYTELLING

See also 344. FICTION; 1069. WRITING AND WRITERS

1. A story has been thought to its conclusion when it has taken its worst possible turn.

FRIEDRICH DÜRRENMATT, "21 POINTS," *THE PHYSICISTS* (1962), TR. JAMES KIRKUP

2. Neanderthal man listened to stories, if one may judge by the shape of his skull.

E.M. FORSTER, "THE STORY," *ASPECTS OF THE NOVEL* (1927)

3. There is much good sleep in an old story.

GERMAN PROVERB

4. A story with a moral appended is like the bill of a mosquito. It bores you, and then injects a stinging drop to irritate your conscience.

O. HENRY, "THE GOLD THAT GLITTERED," *STRICTLY BUSINESS* (1910)

5. A touch of science, even bogus science, gives an edge to the superstitious tale.

V.S. PRITCHETT, "AN IRISH GHOST," *THE LIVING NOVEL & LATER APPRECIATIONS* (1964)

6. An honest tale speeds best being plainly told.

SHAKESPEARE, *RICHARD III* (1592–93), 4.4.358

STRANGERS

See 358. FOREIGNERS AND FOREIGNNESS

939. STRATEGY

See also 585. METHOD

1. Unhappy the general who comes on the field of battle with a system.

NAPOLEON I, *MAXIMS* (1804–15)

2. Those oft are stratagems which errors seem, / Nor is it Homer nods, but we that dream.

ALEXANDER POPE, *AN ESSAY ON CRITICISM* (1711), 1.177

3. Divide the fire, and you will the sooner put it out.

PUBLILIUS SYRUS, *MORAL SAYINGS* (1ST C. B.C.), 201, TR. DARIUS LYMAN

4. In baiting a mouse-trap with cheese, always leave room for the mouse.

SAKI, "THE INFERNAL PARLIAMENT," *THE SQUARE EGG* (1924)

940. STRENGTH

See also 195. COURAGE; 1047. WEAKNESS

1. The high strength of men / knows no content with limitation.

AESCHYLUS, *AGAMEMNON* (458 B.C.), TR. RICHMOND LATTIMORE

2. The strength of even the strongest individual can always be overpowered by the many, who often will combine for no other purpose than to ruin strength precisely because of its peculiar independence.

HANNAH ARENDT, *ON VIOLENCE* (1969)

3. Nobody can honestly think of himself as a strong character because, however successful he may be in overcoming them, he is necessarily aware of the doubts and temptations that accompany every important choice.

W. H. AUDEN, FOREWORD TO DAG HAMMARSKJÖLD'S *MARKINGS* (1964)

4. When is man strong until he feels alone?

ROBERT BROWNING, *COLOMBE'S BIRTHDAY* (1844), 3

5. The awareness of our own strength makes us modest.

PAUL CÉZANNE, *LETTERS* (1937), ED. JOHN REWALD

6. When strong, be merciful, if you would have the respect, not the fear of your neighbors.

CHILON (6TH C. B.C.), QUOTED IN DIOGENES LAERTIUS' *LIVES AND OPINIONS OF EMINENT PHILOSOPHERS* (3RD C. A.D.), TR. R. D. HICKS

7. It is as easy for the strong man to be strong, as it is for the weak to be weak.

EMERSON, "SELF-RELIANCE," *ESSAYS: FIRST SERIES* (1841)

8. If you're strong enough, there *are* no precedents.

F. SCOTT FITZGERALD, "NOTE-BOOKS," *THE CRACK-UP* (1945)

9. A weak man is just by accident. A strong but non-violent man is unjust by accident.

MOHANDAS K. GANDHI, *NON-VIOLENCE IN PEACE AND WAR* (1948), 1.354

10. Like strength is felt from hope, and from despair.

HOMER, *ILIAD* (9TH C. B.C.), 15.852, TR. ALEXANDER POPE

11. Strength and strength's will are the supreme ethic. All else are dreams from hospital beds, the sly, crawling goodness of sneaking souls.

ELBERT HUBBARD, *THE PHILISTINE* (1895–1915)

12. Strong men can always afford to be gentle. Only the weak are intent on "giving as good as they get."

ELBERT HUBBARD, *THE NOTE BOOK* (1927)

13. So long as some are strong and some are weak, the weak will be driven to the wall.

W. SOMERSET MAUGHAM, *THE SUMMING UP* (1938), 73

14. What is strength without a double share / Of wisdom?

Milton, *Samson Agonistes* (1671), 53

15. The strongest iron, hardened in the fire, / most often ends in scraps and shatterings.

Sophocles, *Antigone* (442–41 B.C.), tr. Elizabeth Wyckoff

STRIFE

See 252. Discord

STRIKES

See 1013. Unions

STUBBORNNESS

See 652. Obstinacy

STUDY

See 532. Learning

941. STUPIDITY

See also 270. Dullness; 354. Folly; 356. Fools; 447. Ignorance; 493. Intelligence

1. Idiot, n. A member of a large and powerful tribe whose influence in human affairs has always been dominant and controlling.

Ambrose Bierce, *The Devil's Dictionary* (1881–1911)

2. With stupidity and sound digestion man may front much.

Thomas Carlyle, *Sartor Resartus* (1833–34), 2.7

3. When a finger points at the moon, the imbecile looks at the finger.

Chinese Proverb

4. An ass may bray a good while before he shakes the stars down.

George Eliot, *Romola* (1863), 3.50

5. He that hath a head of wax must not walk in the sun.

English Proverb

6. A learned blockhead is a greater blockhead than an ignorant one.

Benjamin Franklin, *Poor Richard's Almanack* (1732–57)

7. He that makes himself an ass must not take it ill if men ride him.

Thomas Fuller, M.D., *Gnomologia* (1732), 2232

8. Persons of slender intellectual stamina dread competition, as dwarfs are afraid of being run over in the street.

William Hazlitt, *Characteristics* (1823), 30

9. The hardest thing to cope with is not selfishness or vanity or deceitfulness, but sheer stupidity.

Eric Hoffer, *The Passionate State of Mind* (1954), 210

10. Stupidity often saves a man from going mad.

Oliver Wendell Holmes, Sr., *The Autocrat of the Breakfast Table* (1858), 2

11. Every two years, one of the most hotly contested elections in Texas is the poll taken among members of the capitol press corps to determine who are actually *the* ten stupidest members of the Legislature. Two years ago, there were thirty-seven official nominees and several write-ins.

Molly Ivins, *Molly Ivins Can't Say That, Can She?* (1991)

12. It is so pleasant to come across people more stupid than ourselves. We love them at once for being so.

Jerome K. Jerome, "On Cats and Dogs," *The Idle Thoughts of an Idle Fellow* (1889)

13. He that reads and grows no wiser seldom suspects his own deficiency, but complains of hard words and obscure sentences, and asks why books are written which cannot be understood.

Samuel Johnson, *The Idler* (1758–60), 70

14. If poverty is the mother of all crimes, lack of intelligence is their father.

La Bruyère, *Characters* (1688), 11.13, tr. Henri Van Laun

15. To serve an unintelligent man is like crying in the wilderness, massaging the body of a dead man, planting water-lilies on dry land, whispering in the ear of the deaf.

Panchatantra (c. 5th c.), 1, tr. Franklin Edgerton

16. Nothing sways the stupid more than arguments they can't understand.

Cardinal de Retz, *Mémoires* (1718)

17. Against stupidity the very gods / Themselves contend in vain.

Schiller, *The Maid of Orleans* (1801), 3.6

18. One great mistake made by intelligent people is to refuse to believe that the world is as stupid as it is.

Mme de Tencin, quoted in Chamfort's *Caractères et anecdotes* (1771)

19. Whenever a man does a thoroughly stupid thing it is always from the noblest motive.

Oscar Wilde, *The Picture of Dorian Gray* (1891)

20. Some scientists claim that hydrogen, because it is so plentiful, is the basic building block of the universe. I dispute that. I say there is more stupidity than hydrogen, and that is the basic building block of the universe.

Frank Zappa, *The Real Frank Zappa Book* (1989), with Peter Occhiogrosso

942. STYLE

See also 282. Elegance; 398. Grammar; 1069. Writing and Writers

1. The style is the man himself.

Georges Buffon, discourse on his reception into the French Academy, 1750

2. Epithets, like pepper, / Give zest to what you write; / And if you strew them sparely, / They whet the appetite: / But if you lay them on too thick, / You spoil the matter quite!

Lewis Carroll, "Poeta Fit, Non Nascitur" (1869)

3. Style is the dress of thoughts; and let them be ever so just, if your style is homely, coarse, and vulgar, they will appear to as much disadvantage.

Lord Chesterfield, *Letters to His Son,* Nov. 24, 1749

4. Manner is all in all, whate'er is writ, / The substitute for genius, sense, and wit.

William Cowper, *Table Talk* (1782), 542

5. Style is the perfection of a point of view.

Richard Eberhart, "Meditation Two," *Selected Poems 1930–1965* (1965)

6. All progress in literary style lies in the heroic resolve to cast aside accretions and exuberances, all the conventions of a past age that were once beautiful because alive and are now false because dead.

Havelock Ellis, *The Dance of Life* (1923), 4

7. The great writer finds style as the mystic finds God, in his own soul.

Havelock Ellis, *The Dance of Life* (1923), 4

8. I just couldn't make the grade as a hack—that, like everything else, requires a certain practiced excellence.

F. Scott Fitzgerald, *The Letters of F. Scott Fitzgerald* (1963), ed. Andrew Turnbull

9. If any man wish to write a clear style, let him be first clear in his thoughts; and if any would write in a noble style, let him first possess a noble soul.

Goethe, quoted in Johann Peter Eckermann's *Conversations with Goethe,* April 14, 1824

10. I might say that what amateurs call a style is usually only the unavoidable awkwardness in first trying to make something that has not heretofore been made.

Ernest Hemingway, interview, *Writers at Work: Second Series* (1963)

11. One has to dismount from an idea, and get into the saddle again, at every parenthesis.

Oliver Wendell Holmes, Sr., *The Autocrat of the Breakfast Table* (1858), 8

12. In all pointed sentences, some degree of accuracy must be sacrificed to conciseness.

Samuel Johnson, "On the Bravery of the English Common Soldier," *Works* (1787), v. 10

13. Read over your compositions, and wherever you meet with a passage which you think is particularly fine, strike it out.

Samuel Johnson, quoting a college tutor, in Boswell's *Life of Samuel Johnson,* April 30, 1773

14. The most important things must be said simply, for they are spoiled by bombast; whereas trivial things must be described grandly, for they are supported only by aptness of expression, tone and manner.

La Bruyère, *Characters* (1688), 5.77

15. A good style should show no sign of effort. What is written should seem a happy accident.

W. Somerset Maugham, *The Summing Up* (1938), 13

16. Style is the hallmark of a temperament stamped upon the material at hand.

André Maurois, *The Art of Writing* (1960)

17. When we see a natural style, we are astonished and delighted; for we expected to see an author, and we find a man.

Pascal, *Pensées* (1670), 29, tr. W. F. Trotter

18. Mere elegance of language can produce at best but an empty renown.

Petrarch, *Letter to Posterity* (1367–72)

19. Style is a magic wand, and turns everything to gold that it touches.

Logan Pearsall Smith, *Afterthoughts* (1931), 5

20. Proper words in proper places, make the true definition of a style.

JONATHAN SWIFT, LETTER TO A YOUNG CLERGYMAN, JAN. 9, 1720

21. Style, like the human body, is specially beautiful when the veins are not prominent and the bones cannot be counted.

TACITUS, *A DIALOGUE ON ORATORY* (C. A.D. 81), 21, TR. WILLIAM J. BRODRIBB

22. As to the adjective: when in doubt, strike it out.

MARK TWAIN, "PUDD'NHEAD WILSON'S CALENDAR," *PUDD'NHEAD WILSON* (1894), 11

23. He most honors my style who learns under it to destroy the teacher.

WALT WHITMAN, "SONG OF MYSELF," *47, LEAVES OF GRASS* (1855–92)

24. In matters of grave importance, style, not sincerity, is the vital thing.

OSCAR WILDE, *THE IMPORTANCE OF BEING EARNEST* (1895), 3

943. SUBTLETY

See also 139. CLEVERNESS; 200. CRAFTINESS

1. I like to have a thing suggested rather than told in full. When every detail is given, the mind rests satisfied, and the imagination loses the desire to use its own wings.

THOMAS BAILEY ALDRICH, "LEAVES FROM A NOTEBOOK," *PONKAPOG PAPERS* (1903)

2. There be many wise men that have secret hearts and transparent countenances.

FRANCIS BACON, "OF CUNNING," *ESSAYS* (1625)

3. Be ye therefore wise as serpents, and harmless as doves.

BIBLE, MATTHEW 10:16

4. In the early days, computers inspired widespread awe and the popular press dubbed them giant brains. In fact, the computer's power resembled that of a bulldozer; it did not harness subtlety, though subtlety went into its design.

TRACY KIDDER, *THE SOUL OF A NEW MACHINE* (1981)

5. Some people take more care to hide their wisdom than their folly.

JONATHAN SWIFT, *THOUGHTS ON VARIOUS SUBJECTS* (1711)

944. SUBURBS

See also 131. CITIES; 194. THE COUNTRY

1. Slums may well be breeding-grounds of crime, but middle-class suburbs are incubators of apathy and delirium.

CYRIL CONNOLLY, *THE UNQUIET GRAVE* (1945), 1

2. Conformity may not always reign in the prosperous bourgeois suburb, but it ultimately always governs.

LOUIS KRONENBERGER, *COMPANY MANNERS* (1954), 3.3

3. The dinner party is a suburban form of entertainment. Its spread in our big cities represents an insidious Fifth Column suburbanization of the metropolis.

PHILLIP LOPATE, "THE DINNER PARTY," IN *THE ART OF THE PERSONAL ESSAY* (1994), ED. PHILLIP LOPATE

4. The children themselves, before they get access to a car, are captives of their suburb, save for those families where the housewives surrender continuity in their own lives to chauffeur their children to lessons, doctors, and other services that could be reached via public transport in the city.

DAVID RIESMAN, *ABUNDANCE FOR WHAT?* (1964)

5. The modern suburb is the product of the car, the five-day week, and the "bankers' hours" of the masses.

DAVID RIESMAN, *ABUNDANCE FOR WHAT?* (1964)

945. SUCCESS

See also 6. ACHIEVEMENT; 33. AMBITION; 173. CONQUEST; 329. FAILURE; 750. PROSPERITY

1. Yes, success is everything. Failure is more common. Most achieve a sort of middling thing, but fortunately one's situation is always blurred, you never know absolutely quite where you are.

DONALD BARTHELME, "THE CRISIS," *GREAT DAYS* (1979)

2. The ability to convert ideas to things is the secret of outward success.

HENRY WARD BEECHER, *PROVERBS FROM PLYMOUTH PULPIT* (1887)

3. The toughest thing about success is that you've got to keep on being a success.

IRVING BERLIN, *THEATRE ARTS,* FEBRUARY 1958

4. Too much success can ruin you as surely as too much failure.

MARLON BRANDO, QUOTED IN *THE NEW YORKER,* NOV. 9, 1957

5. A minute's success pays the failure of years.

Robert Browning, "Apollo and the Fates" (1886)

6. Constant success shows us but one side of the world. For as it surrounds us with friends who will tell us only our merits, so it silences those enemies from whom alone we can learn our defects.

Charles Caleb Colton, *Lacon* (1825), 1.513

7. Success seems to be that which forms the distinction between confidence and conceit.

Charles Caleb Colton, *Lacon* (1825), 1.75

8. To win without risk is to triumph without glory.

Corneille, *Le Cid* (1636), 2.2

9. A man who raises himself by degrees to wealth and power, contracts, in the course of this protracted labor, habits of prudence and restraint which he cannot afterwards shake off. A man cannot gradually enlarge his mind as he does his house.

Alexis De Tocqueville, *Democracy in America* (1835–39), 2.3.19

10. Success is counted sweetest / By those who ne'er succeed.

Emily Dickinson, poem (c. 1859)

11. Success is relative: It is what we can make of the mess we have made of things.

T. S. Eliot, *The Family Reunion* (1939), 2.3

12. According to success do we gain a reputation for judgment.

Euripides, *Hippolytus* (428 b.c.), tr. Moses Hadas and John McLean

13. Premature success gives one an almost mystical conception of destiny as opposed to will power—at its worst the Napoleonic delusion.

F. Scott Fitzgerald, *The Crack-Up* (1945)

14. The compensation of a very early success is a conviction that life is a romantic matter. In the best sense one stays young.

F. Scott Fitzgerald, "Early Success," *The Crack-Up* (1945)

15. Nothing is more humiliating than to see idiots succeed in enterprises we have failed in.

Flaubert, *Sentimental Education* (1869), 5

16. There are some things we do simply because the doing is a success.

Nikki Giovanni, "Memories Are Selective," *Racism 101* (1994)

17. The way to secure success is to be more anxious about obtaining than about deserving it.

William Hazlitt, "On the Qualifications Necessary to Success in Life," *The Plain Speaker* (1826)

18. A successful man cannot realize how hard an unsuccessful man finds life.

Edgar Watson Howe, *Country Town Sayings* (1911)

19. The key to success isn't much good until one discovers the right lock to insert it in.

Tehyi Hsieh, *Chinese Epigrams Inside Out and Proverbs* (1948), 7

20. Pray that success will not come any faster than you are able to endure it.

Elbert Hubbard, *The Note Book* (1927)

21. Some men succeed by what they know; some by what they do; and a few by what they are.

Elbert Hubbard, *The Note Book* (1927)

22. The ability to concentrate and to use your time well is everything if you want to succeed in business—or almost anywhere else, for that matter.

Lee Iacocca, *Iacocca: An Autobiography* (1984) with William Novak

23. The way to rise is to obey and please.

Ben Jonson, *Sejanus His Fall* (1603), 3.3

24. The technique of winning is so shoddy, the terms of winning are so ignoble, the tenure of winning is so brief; and the specter of the has-been—a shameful rather than a pitiable sight today—brings a sudden chill even to our sunlit moments.

Louis Kronenberger, "The Spirit of the Age," *Company Manners* (1954)

25. There are two ways of rising in the world, either by your own industry or by the folly of others.

La Bruyère, *Characters* (1688), 6.52, tr. Henri Van Laun

26. It is almost as easy to be enervated by triumph as by defeat.

Max Lerner, "The Consequences of the Atom," *Actions and Passions* (1949)

27. Success makes men rigid and they tend to exalt stability over all the other virtues; tired of the effort of willing they become fanatics about conservatism.

Walter Lippmann, "Routineer and Inventor," *A Preface to Politics* (1914)

28. Failure makes people bitter and cruel. Success improves the character of the man.

W. Somerset Maugham, *The Summing Up* (1938), 48

29. The success of most things depends upon knowing how long it will take to succeed.

MONTESQUIEU, *PENSÉES DIVERSES* (1750)

30. There is only one success—to be able to spend your life in your own way.

CHRISTOPHER MORLEY, *WHERE THE BLUE BEGINS* (1922)

31. If a man be self-controlled, truthful, wise, and resolute, is there aught that can stay out of the reach of such a man?

PANCHATANTRA (C. 5TH C.), 3, TR. FRANKLIN EDGERTON

32. Most men that do thrive in the world do forget to take pleasure during the time that they are getting their estate, but reserve that till they have got one, and then it is too late for them to enjoy it.

SAMUEL PEPYS, *DIARY*, MARCH 10, 1666

33. Success / for the striver washes away the effort of striving.

PINDAR, *ODES* (5TH C. B.C.), OLYMPIA 2, TR. RICHMOND LATTIMORE

34. Success abides longer among men / when it is planted by the hand of God.

PINDAR, *ODES* (5TH C. B.C.), NEMEA 8, TR. RICHMOND LATTIMORE

35. When men succeed, even their neighbors think them wise.

PINDAR, *ODES* (5TH C. B.C.), OLYMPIA 5, TR. RICHMOND LATTIMORE

36. Success causes us to be more praised than known.

JOSEPH ROUX, *MEDITATIONS OF A PARISH PRIEST* (1886), 4.46, TR. ISABEL F. HAPGOOD

37. Unless a man has been taught what to do with success after getting it, the achievement of it must inevitably leave him a prey to boredom.

BERTRAND RUSSELL, *THE CONQUEST OF HAPPINESS* (1930), 3

38. I do not care for socially recognizable success. I only value that success which I can feel within me, which satisfies me, and which basically stems from self-knowledge.

ANWAR EL-SADAT, *IN SEARCH OF IDENTITY* (1977)

39. Success is not greedy, as people think, but insignificant. That's why it satisfies nobody.

SENECA, *LETTERS TO LUCILIUS* (1ST C.), 118.6, TR. E. PHILLIPS BARKER

40. Lowliness is young ambition's ladder, / Whereto the climber-upward turns his face; / But when he once attains the upmost round, / He then unto the ladder turns his back, / Looks in the clouds, scorning the base degrees / By which he did ascend.

SHAKESPEARE, *JULIUS CAESAR* (1599–1600), 2.1.22

41. [Norman] Mailer in his writings is ultimately more concerned with success than with danger; danger is only a means to success.

SUSAN SONTAG, "MICHEL LEIRIS' *MANHOOD*," *AGAINST INTERPRETATION* (1966)

42. There is no success without hardship.

SOPHOCLES, *ELECTRA* (C. 418–14 B.C.), TR. DAVID GRENE

43. Is there anything in life so disenchanting as attainment?

ROBERT LOUIS STEVENSON, "THE ADVENTURE OF THE HANSOM CAB," *NEW ARABIAN NIGHTS* (1882)

44. I know that unremitting attention to business is the price of success, but I don't know what success is.

CHARLES DUDLEY WARNER, "FIRST STUDY," *BACKLOG STUDIES* (1873)

45. I'm perpetually curious as to what happened to all those supposed prodigies who were singled out while I and my coterie of far more interesting malcontents passed on.

WENDY WASSERSTEIN, "WINNER TAKE ALL," *BACHELOR GIRLS* (1990)

46. Success means we go to sleep at night knowing that our talents and abilities were used in a way that served others.

MARIANNE WILLIAMSON, "WORK," *A RETURN TO LOVE* (1992)

946. SUFFERING

See also 17. ADVERSITY; 476. INJURY; 704. PLEASURE; 705. PLEASURE AND PAIN; 877. SELF-PITY; 918. SORROW; 1011. UNHAPPINESS; 1052. WEEPING

1. For sufferers it is sweet to know before-hand clearly the pain that still remains for them.

AESCHYLUS, *PROMETHEUS BOUND* (C. 478 B.C.), TR. DAVID GRENE

2. Who, except the gods, / can live time through forever without any pain?

AESCHYLUS, *AGAMEMNON* (458 B.C.), TR. RICHMOND LATTIMORE

3. If you are distressed by anything external, the pain is not due to the thing itself but to your own estimate of it; and this you have the power to revoke at any moment.

Marcus Aurelius, *Meditations* (2nd c.), 8.47, tr. Maxwell Staniforth

4. His mother, her eyes raised to heaven, hands arched before her, moving, made real for John that patience, that endurance, that long suffering, which he had read of in the Bible and found so hard to imagine.

James Baldwin, *Go Tell It on the Mountain* (1953)

5. It is infinitely easier to suffer in obedience to a human command than to accept suffering as free, responsible men.

Dietrich Bonhoeffer, "After Ten Years," *Letters and Papers from Prison* (1953), tr. Eberhard Bethge

6. There is no point in being overwhelmed by the appalling total of human suffering; such a total does not exist. Neither poverty nor pain is accumulable.

Jorge Luis Borges, "A New Refutation of Time," *Other Inquisitions* (1952), 1, tr. R. L. Simms

7. We cannot live, sorrow or die for somebody else, for suffering is too precious to be shared.

Edward Dahlberg, *Because I Was Flesh* (1963)

8. Either the human being must suffer and struggle as the price of a more searching vision, or his gaze must be shallow and without intellectual revelation.

Thomas De Quincey, "Vision of Life," *Suspiria de Profundis* (1845)

9. A *Wounded* Deer—leaps highest.

Emily Dickinson, poem (c. 1860)

10. Pain—has an Element of Blank— / It cannot recollect / When it begun—or if there were / A time when it was not—.

Emily Dickinson, poem (c. 1862)

11. Suffering is the sole origin of consciousness.

Dostoyevsky, *Notes from Underground* (1864), 1.9, tr. Constance Garnett

12. Pain and death are a part of life. To reject them is to reject life itself.

Havelock Ellis, "On Life and Sex: Essays of Love and Virtue" (1937), 2.5

13. Pain, indolence, sterility, endless ennui have also their lesson for you, if you are great.

Emerson, *Journals,* 1845

14. An hour of pain is as long as a day of pleasure.

English Proverb

15. At some point, you no longer feel pain. Sensation disappears and reason is dulled, until you lose all grasp of time and place.

Gabriel García Márquez, *The Story of a Shipwrecked Sailor* (1986)

16. Much of your pain is self-chosen. / It is the bitter potion by which the physician within you heals your sick self.

Kahlil Gibran, "On Pain," *The Prophet* (1923)

17. Each one of us must suffer long to himself before he can learn that he is but one in a great community of wretchedness which has been pitilessly repeating itself from the foundation of the world.

William Dean Howells, *The Rise of Silas Lapham* (1885), 17

18. God will not look you over for medals, degrees or diplomas, but for scars!

Elbert Hubbard, *The Note Book* (1927)

19. Culture makes pain tolerable by interpreting its necessity; only pain perceived as curable is intolerable.

Ivan Illich, *Medical Nemesis* (1976)

20. The new experience that has replaced dignified suffering is artificially prolonged, opaque, depersonalized maintenance.

Ivan Illich, *Medical Nemesis* (1976), 3

21. Pleasure is oft a visitant; but pain / Clings cruelly to us.

Keats, *Endymion* (1817), 1

22. Although the world is full of suffering, it is full also of the overcoming of it.

Helen Keller, *Optimism* (1903), 1

23. We feel and weigh soon enough what we suffer from others: but how much others suffer from us, of this we take no heed.

Thomas à Kempis, *The Imitation of Christ* (1426), 2.5

24. He had learned that every *known* physical pain was bearable; if one knew beforehand exactly what was going to happen to one, one stood it as a surgical operation—for instance, the extraction of a tooth.

Arthur Koestler, *Darkness at Noon* (1940)

25. Beauty cannot disguise nor music melt / A pain undiagnosable but felt.

ANNE MORROW LINDBERGH, "THE STONE," *THE UNICORN AND OTHER POEMS, 1935–1955* (1956)

26. Know how sublime a thing it is / To suffer and be strong.

LONGFELLOW, "THE LIGHT OF THE STARS," *VOICES OF THE NIGHT* (1839)

27. Even pain / Pricks to livelier living.

AMY LOWELL, "HAPPINESS," *SWORD BLADES AND POPPY SEEDS* (1914)

28. To be good we must needs have suffered; but perhaps it is necessary to have caused suffering before we can become better.

MAURICE MAETERLINCK, "THE INVISIBLE GOODNESS," *THE TREASURE OF THE HUMBLE* (1896), TR. ALFRED SUTRO

29. It is not true that suffering ennobles the character; happiness does that sometimes, but suffering, for the most part, makes men petty and vindictive.

W. SOMERSET MAUGHAM, *THE MOON AND SIXPENCE* (1919), 17

30. Suffering for truth's sake / Is fortitude to highest victory, / And to the faithful death the gate of life.

MILTON, *PARADISE LOST* (1667), 12.569

31. He who fears he shall suffer, already suffers what he fears.

MONTAIGNE, "OF EXPERIENCE," *ESSAYS* (1580–88), TR. W. C. HAZLITT

32. We are more sensible of one little touch of a surgeon's lancet than of twenty wounds with a sword in the heat of fight.

MONTAIGNE, "THAT THE RELISH OF GOOD AND EVIL DEPENDS IN A GREAT MEASURE UPON THE OPINION WE HAVE OF THEM," *ESSAYS* (1580–88), TR. W. C. HAZLITT

33. What really raises one's indignation against suffering is not suffering intrinsically, but the senselessness of suffering.

NIETZSCHE, *THE GENEALOGY OF MORALS* (1887), 2.7, TR. HORACE B. SAMUEL

34. Most people get a fair amount of fun out of their lives, but on balance life is suffering, and only the very young or the very foolish imagine otherwise.

GEORGE ORWELL, "LEAR, TOLSTOY AND THE FOOL," *SHOOTING AN ELEPHANT* (1950)

35. Pain makes man think. Thought makes man wise. Wisdom makes life endurable.

JOHN PATRICK, *THE TEAHOUSE OF THE AUGUST MOON* (1953)

36. Man never reasons so much and becomes so introspective as when he suffers; since he is anxious to get at the cause of his sufferings, to learn who has produced them, and whether it is just or unjust that he should have to bear them.

LUIGI PIRANDELLO, *SIX CHARACTERS IN SEARCH OF AN AUTHOR* (1921), 3, TR. EDWARD STORER

37. Who breathes must suffer, and who thinks must mourn; / And he alone is blessed who ne'er was born.

MATTHEW PRIOR, *SOLOMON ON THE VANITY OF THE WORLD* (1718), 3

38. To a great extent, suffering is a sort of need felt by the organism to make itself familiar with a new state, which makes it uneasy, to adapt its sensibility to that state.

MARCEL PROUST, *REMEMBRANCE OF THINGS PAST: THE GUERMANTES WAY* (1913–27), TR. C. K. SCOTT-MONCRIEFF

39. We are healed of a suffering only by experiencing it to the full.

MARCEL PROUST, *REMEMBRANCE OF THINGS PAST: THE SWEET CHEAT GONE* (1913–27), TR. C. K. SCOTT-MONCRIEFF

40. Pain will force even the truthful to speak falsely.

PUBLILIUS SYRUS, *MORAL SAYINGS* (1ST C. B.C.), 232, TR. DARIUS LYMAN

41. Pain is unjust, and all the arguments / That cannot soothe it only rouse suspicion.

RACINE, *BRITANNICUS* (1669), 1, TR. ROBERT HENDERSON

42. If pain could have cured us we should long ago have been saved.

GEORGE SANTAYANA, *THE LIFE OF REASON: REASON IN COMMON SENSE* (1905–06), 9

43. A man who suffers before it is necessary, suffers more than is necessary.

SENECA, *LETTERS TO LUCILIUS* (1ST C.), 98, TR. E. PHILLIPS BARKER

44. One fire burns out another's burning; / One pain is lessened by another's anguish.

SHAKESPEARE, *ROMEO AND JULIET* (1594–95), 1.2.46

45. Oh, lift me as a wave, a leaf, a cloud! / I fall upon the thorns of life! I bleed!

SHELLEY, "ODE TO THE WEST WIND" (1819), 4

46. Perhaps the worst thing about suffering is that it finally hardens the hearts of those around it.

Gloria Steinem, "Ruth's Song," *Outrageous Acts and Everyday Rebellions* (1983)

47. The history of a soldier's wound beguiles the pain of it.

Laurence Sterne, *Tristram Shandy* (1759–67), 1.25

48. How vivid is the suffering of the few when the people are few and how the suffering of nameless millions in two world wars is blurred over by numbers.

Edwin Way Teale, *Autumn Across America* (1956), 19

49. Nothing begins and nothing ends / That is not paid with moan; / For we are born in other's pain, / And perish in our own.

Francis Thompson, "Daisy" (1890)

50. The pain seemed to be displacing with its own hairy segments his heart and lungs; as its grip swelled in his throat he felt he was holding his brain like a morsel on a platter high out of hungry reach.

John Updike, *The Centaur* (1963)

51. Clergymen and people who use phrases without wisdom sometimes talk of suffering as a mystery. It is really a revelation.

Oscar Wilde, *De Profundis* (1905)

52. Hearts live by being wounded.

Oscar Wilde, *A Woman of No Importance* (1893), 3

53. Suffering is one very long moment. We can not divide it by seasons. We can only record its moods and chronicle their return.

Oscar Wilde, *De Profundis* (1905)

54. Suffering is permanent, obscure and dark, / And shares the nature of infinity.

William Wordsworth, *The Borderers* (1795–96)

947. SUFFICIENCY

See also 312. Excess; 598. Moderation; 845. Satisfaction

1. You never know what is enough unless you know what is more than enough.

William Blake, "Proverbs of Hell," *The Marriage of Heaven and Hell* (1790)

2. Sufficiency's enough for men of sense.

Euripides, *The Phoenician Women* (c. 411–409 B.C.), tr. Elizabeth Wyckoff

3. Enough is as good as a feast.

John Heywood, *Proverbs* (1546), 1.11

4. There is satiety in all things, in sleep, and love-making, / in the loveliness of singing and the innocent dance.

Homer, *Iliad* (9th c. B.C.), 13.636, tr. Richmond Lattimore

948. SUICIDE

See also 866. Self-Destruction

1. To run away from trouble is a form of cowardice and, while it is true that the suicide braves death, he does it not for some noble object but to escape some ill.

Aristotle, *Nicomachean Ethics* (4th c. B.C.), 3.7, tr. J. A. K. Thomson

2. That is what chills your spine when you read an account of a suicide: not the frail corpse hanging from the window bars but what happened inside that heart immediately before.

Simone de Beauvoir, *Les Belles Images* (1966), tr. Patrick O'Brian (1968)

3. Judging whether life is or is not worth living amounts to answering the fundamental question of philosophy. All the rest—whether or not the world has three dimensions, whether the mind has nine or twelve categories—comes afterward.

Albert Camus, *The Myth of Sisyphus* (1955), tr. Justin O'Brien

4. There is but one truly serious philosophical problem, and that is suicide. Judging whether life is or is not worth living amounts to answering the fundamental question of philosophy.

Albert Camus, "An Absurd Reasoning," *The Myth of Sisyphus* (1942), tr. Justin O'Brien

5. To attempt suicide is a criminal offense. Any man who, of his own will, tries to escape the treadmill to which the rest of us feel chained incites our envy, and therefore our fury. We do not suffer him to go unpunished.

Alexander Chase, *Perspectives* (1966)

6. He emptied the ashtray containing his nail parings and cigarette butts into the toilet, and swept the floor with a shirt, so that there would be no trace of his life, of his body, when that lewd and searching shape of death came there to find him in the morning.

John Cheever, "Torch Song," *The Stories of John Cheever* (1980)

7. When even despair ceases to serve any creative purpose, then surely we are justified in suicide.

CYRIL CONNOLLY, *THE UNQUIET GRAVE* (1945), 1

8. Comedians are the nearest to suicide.

LAWRENCE DURRELL, *MONSIEUR* (1974)

9. The question is whether [suicide] is the way *out*, or the way *in*.

EMERSON, *JOURNALS*, 1839

10. If life's a joke, then suicide's a bad punch line.

LOUISE ERDRICH, "RELIGIOUS WARS," *THE BINGO PALACE* (1994)

11. He who saves a man against his will as good as murders him.

HORACE, *ARS POETICA* (13–8 B.C.)

12. On July 2, 1961, a writer whom many critics call the greatest writer of this century, a man who had a zest for life and adventure as big as his genius, a winner of the Nobel Prize and the Pulitzer Prize, a soldier of fortune with a home in Idaho's Sawtooth Mountains, where he hunted in the winter, an apartment in New York, a specially rigged yacht to fish the Gulf Stream, an available apartment at the Ritz in Paris and the Gritti in Venice, a solid marriage, no serious physical ills, good friends everywhere—on that July day, that man [Hemingway], the envy of other men, put a shotgun to his head and killed himself.

A.E. HOTCHNER, *PAPA HEMINGWAY* (1966)

13. No sane society chooses to commit national suicide.

JOHN F. KENNEDY, *THE STRATEGY OF PEACE* (1960)

14. In China your father had a sister who killed herself. She jumped into the family well. We say that your father has all brothers because it is as if she had never been born.

MAXINE HONG KINGSTON, *THE WOMAN WARRIOR* (1976)

15. When all the blandishments of life are gone, / The coward sneaks to death, the brave live on.

MARTIAL, *EPIGRAMS* (A.D. 86), 11.56, TR. SEWELL

16. Why dost thou complain of this world? It detains thee not; thy own cowardice is the cause, if thou livest in pain.

MONTAIGNE, "A CUSTOM OF THE ISLE OF CEA," *ESSAYS* (1580–88), TR. W. C. HAZLITT

17. Guns are always the best method for a private suicide.... Drugs are too chancy. You might miscalculate the dosage and just have a good time.

P.J. O'ROURKE, *MODERN MANNERS* (1988)

18. Razors pain you; / Rivers are damp; / Acids stain you; / And drugs cause cramp. / Guns aren't lawful; / Nooses give; / Gas smells awful; / You might as well live.

DOROTHY PARKER, "RÉSUMÉ," *ENOUGH ROPE* (1926), 2

19. The journey over the bridge had unnerved me. The river water passed me by like an untouched drink. I suspected that even if my mother and brother had not been there I would have made no move to jump.

SYLVIA PLATH, *THE BELL JAR* (1963)

20. Amid the sufferings of life on earth, suicide is God's best gift to man.

PLINY THE ELDER, *NATURAL HISTORY* (1ST C.), 2

21. He cocked the piece. Then he went over and sat down on the unoccupied twin bed, looked at the girl, aimed the pistol, and fired a bullet through his right temple.

J.D. SALINGER, "A PERFECT DAY FOR BANANAFISH," IN *NINE STORIES BY J.D. SALINGER* (1953)

22. We cannot tear out a single page from our life, but we can throw the whole book into the fire.

GEORGE SAND, *MAUPRAT* (1837)

23. Is it sin / To rush into the secret house of death / Ere death dare come to us?

SHAKESPEARE, *ANTONY AND CLEOPATRA* (1606–07), 4.15.80

24. It is great / To do that thing that ends all other deeds, / Which shackles accidents and bolts up change.

SHAKESPEARE, *ANTONY AND CLEOPATRA* (1606–07), 5.2.4

25. Whatever crazy sorrow saith, / No life that breathes with human breath / Has ever truly longed for death.

LORD TENNYSON, "THE TWO VOICES" (1842)

26. The man who, in a fit of melancholy, kills himself today, would have wished to live had he waited a week.

VOLTAIRE, "CATO," *PHILOSOPHICAL DICTIONARY* (1764)

27. The paintings by dead men who were poor most of their lives are the most valuable pieces in my collection. And if an artist wants to really jack up the prices of his creations, may I suggest this: suicide.

KURT VONNEGUT, *BLUEBEARD* (1987)

949. SUITABILITY

See also 979. TIMELINESS

1. Send not for a hatchet to break open an egg with.

THOMAS FULLER, M.D., *GNOMOLOGIA* (1732), 4097

2. With our mortal minds we should seek from the gods that which becomes us.

PINDAR, *ODES* (5TH C. B.C.), PYTHIA 3, TR. RICHMOND LATTIMORE

3. Every beauty, when out of its place, is a beauty no longer.

VOLTAIRE, "WIT, SPIRIT, INTELLECT," *PHILOSOPHICAL DICTIONARY* (1764)

SUMMER

See 854. SEASONS

950. SUN

See also 140. CLIMATE; 415. THE HEAVENS

1. The adventure of the sun is the great natural drama by which we live, and not to have joy in it and awe of it, not to share in it, is to close a dull door on nature's sustaining and poetic spirit.

HENRY BESTON, "MIDWINTER," *THE OUTERMOST HOUSE* (1928)

2. There is a muscular energy in sunlight corresponding to the spiritual energy of wind.

ANNIE DILLARD, "SPRING," *PILGRIM AT TINKER CREEK* (1974)

3. The sun beats down with a merciless white fire until the cloudless sky is scarcely blue but rather like the blade of a knife that for days has been ground to the stone.

CONRAD RICHTER, *THE SEA OF GRASS* (1937)

4. The Florida sun seems not much a single thing overhead but a set of klieg lights that pursue you everywhere with an even white illumination.

JOHN UPDIKE, *RABBIT AT REST* (1990)

5. Goodness comes out of people who bask in the sun, as it does out of a sweet apple roasted before the fire.

CHARLES DUDLEY WARNER, "SEVENTEENTH WEEK," *MY SUMMER IN A GARDEN* (1871)

951. SUPERFICIALITY

See also 54. ARTIFICIALITY; 740. PROFUNDITY

1. We are the hollow men / We are the stuffed men / Leaning together.

T. S. ELIOT, "THE HOLLOW MEN" (1925), 1

2. God will have life to be real; we will be damned, but it shall be theatrical.

EMERSON, *JOURNALS*, 1843

3. Anyone who has looked deeply into the world may guess how much wisdom lies in the superficiality of men. The instinct that preserves them teaches them to be flighty, light, and false.

NIETZSCHE, *BEYOND GOOD AND EVIL* (1886), 59, TR. WALTER KAUFMANN

4. Light boats sail swift, though greater hulks draw deep.

SHAKESPEARE, *TROILUS AND CRESSIDA* (1601–02), 2.3.277

5. Only the shallow know themselves.

OSCAR WILDE, "PHRASES AND PHILOSOPHIES FOR THE USE OF THE YOUNG" (1891)

952. SUPERIORITY

See also 311. EXCELLENCE; 584. MERIT; 635. NOBILITY

1. He who ascends to mountain tops, shall find / The loftiest peaks most wrapt in clouds and snow; / He who surpasses or subdues mankind, / Must look down on the hate of those below.

BYRON, *CHILDE HAROLD'S PILGRIMAGE* (1812–18), 3.45

2. What the superior man seeks is in himself. What the mean man seeks is in others.

CONFUCIUS, *ANALECTS* (6TH C. B.C.), 15.20, TR. JAMES LEGGE

3. Be more than man, or thou'rt less than an ant.

JOHN DONNE, *AN ANATOMY OF THE WORLD; THE FIRST ANNIVERSARY* (1612)

4. To me one man is worth ten thousand if he is first-rate.

HERACLITUS, *FRAGMENTS* (C. 500 B.C.), 84, TR. PHILIP WHEELWRIGHT

5. Whoever rises above those who once pleased themselves with equality, will have many malevolent gazers at his eminence.

SAMUEL JOHNSON, *THE RAMBLER* (1750–52), 172

6. The highest summits and those elevated above the level of other things are mostly blasted by envy as by a thunderbolt.

LUCRETIUS, *ON THE NATURE OF THINGS* (1ST C. B.C.), 5, TR. H. A. J. MUNRO

7. we parted each feeling / superior to the other / and is not that / feeling after all one of the great / desiderata of social intercourse.

DON MARQUIS, "THE MERRY FLEA," *ARCHY AND MEHITABEL* (1927)

8. The suggestion that Jews were selected from among all nations of the earth to be God's chosen people suggested a kind of group arrogance, especially when the good news was first reported by Jews. However, the choice was interpreted not as tribute to superior virtue but as divine challenge.

ISRAEL SHENKER, *COAT OF MANY COLORS* (1985)

9. We are wrong to fear superiority of mind and soul; this superiority is very moral, for understanding everything makes a person tolerant and the capacity to feel deeply inspires great goodness.

MME DE STAËL, *CORINNE* (1807), 18.5

10. Superiority and inferiority are individual, not racial or national.

PHILIP WYLIE, *GENERATION OF VIPERS* (1942), 1

953. SUPERNATURAL

See also 383. GHOSTS; 592. MIRACLES

1. The supernatural is the natural not yet understood.

ELBERT HUBBARD, *THE NOTE BOOK* (1927)

2. Faith in the supernatural is a desperate wager made by man at the lowest ebb of his fortunes.

GEORGE SANTAYANA, *THE LIFE OF REASON: REASON IN SCIENCE* (1905–06), 10

3. There are more things in heaven and earth, Horatio, / Than are dreamt of in your philosophy.

SHAKESPEARE, *HAMLET* (1600), 1.5.166

954. SUPERSTITION

See also 78. BELIEF

1. In all superstition wise men follow fools.

FRANCIS BACON, "OF SUPERSTITION," *ESSAYS* (1625)

2. We may be living in the twentieth century, in resplendent sophistication. But deep down, most of us find ourselves still in the Stone Age of superstition.

HELEN HAYES, "PSYCHO-LOGIC," *LOVING LIFE* (1987), WITH MARION GLASSEROW GLADNEY

3. All people have their blind side—their superstitions.

CHARLES LAMB, "MRS. BATTLE'S OPINIONS ON WHIST," *ESSAYS OF ELIA* (1823)

4. The superstition in which we grew up, / Though we may recognize it, does not lose / Its power over us.—Not all are free / Who make mock of their chains.

GOTTHOLD EPHRAIM LESSING, *NATHAN THE WISE* (1779), 4.4, TR. BAYARD QUINCY MORGAN

5. Men become superstitious, not because they have too much imagination, but because they are not aware that they have any.

GEORGE SANTAYANA, *LITTLE ESSAYS* (1920), 25

SURFEIT

See 312. EXCESS

955. SURPRISE

See also 202. CREDULITY; 1063. WONDER

1. A man surprised is half beaten.

THOMAS FULLER, M.D., *GNOMOLOGIA* (1732), 310

2. Stupefaction, when it persists, becomes stupidity.

JOSÉ ORTEGA Y GASSET, "IN SEARCH OF GOETHE FROM WITHIN, LETTER TO A GERMAN," *PARTISAN REVIEW*, DECEMBER 1949, TR. WILLARD R. TRASK

3. Surprise is the greatest gift which life can grant us.

BORIS PASTERNAK, "ON MODESTY AND BOLDNESS," SPEECH AT THE WRITERS' PLENUM, MINSK, FEBRUARY 1936

4. Unfamiliarity lends weight to misfortune, and there was never a man whose grief was not heightened by surprise.

SENECA, *LETTERS TO LUCILIUS* (1ST C.), 91.3, TR. E. PHILLIPS BARKER

956. SURVIVAL

See also 229. DEFENSE; 287. ENDURANCE; 641. NUCLEAR POWER; 1049. WEAPONS

1. It isn't important to come out on top, what matters is to be the one who comes out alive.

BERTOLT BRECHT, *JUNGLE OF CITIES* (1924), 10, TR. ANSELM HOLLO

2. We must live in groups; other people are like nutrients for us, and are absolutely essential for our survival.

WILLARD GAYLIN, *FEELINGS: OUR VITAL SIGNS* (1979)

3. Self-preservation is the first principle of our nature.

ALEXANDER HAMILTON, *A FULL VINDICATION ...*, DEC. 15, 1774

4. At that time I had not yet been taught the doctrine I was later to learn so hurriedly in the Lager: that man is bound to pursue his own ends by all possible means, while he who errs but once pays dearly.

PRIMO LEVI, *SURVIVAL IN AUSCHWITZ* (1959)

5. Whether science—and indeed civilization in general—can long survive depends upon psychology, that is to say, it depends upon what human beings desire.

BERTRAND RUSSELL, "THE SCIENCE TO SAVE US FROM SCIENCE," *THE NEW YORK TIMES MAGAZINE,* MARCH 19, 1950

6. Accommodation to change, the thoughtful pursuit of alternative futures are keys to the survival of civilization and perhaps of the human species.

CARL SAGAN, *BROCA'S BRAIN: REFLECTIONS ON THE ROMANCE OF SCIENCE* (1979)

7. Nature is indifferent to the survival of the human species, including Americans.

ADLAI STEVENSON, SPEECH, RADIO AND TELEVISION, SEPT. 29, 1952

SUSPICION

See 259. DISTRUST

957. SWEARING

See also 212. CURSING; 643. OATHS

1. Th' best thing about a little judicyous swearin' is that it keeps th' temper. 'Twas intinded as a compromise between runnin' away an' fightin'.

FINLEY PETER DUNNE, "SWEARING," *OBSERVATIONS BY MR. DOOLEY* (1902)

2. When you're lying awake with a dismal headache, and repose is tabooed by anxiety, / I conceive you may use any language you choose to indulge in without impropriety.

W. S. GILBERT, *IOLANTHE* (1882), 2

958. SWITZERLAND AND THE SWISS

1. Geneva has the sleepy tidiness of a man who combs his hair while yet in his pyjamas.

LEWIS MUMFORD, *FINDINGS AND KEEPINGS. ANALECTS FOR AN AUTOBIOGRAPHY* (1975)

2. I look upon Switzerland as an inferior sort of Scotland.

SYDNEY SMITH, LETTER TO LORD HOLLAND, 1815

959. SYMBOLS AND SYMBOLISM

See also 573. MEANING; 836. SACRAMENT

1. A person gets from a symbol the meaning he puts into it, and what is one man's comfort and inspiration is another's jest and scorn.

JUSTICE ROBERT JACKSON, *WEST VIRGINIA STATE BOARD V. BARNETTE* (1943)

960. SYMPATHY

See also 169. CONFIDENCES; 698. PITY; 1008. UNDERSTANDING OTHERS

1. Unto a broken heart / No other one may go / Without the high prerogative / Itself hath suffered too.

EMILY DICKINSON, *POEMS* (C. 1862–86)

2. A sympathetic person is placed in the dilemma of a swimmer among drowning men, who all catch at him, and if he gives so much as a leg or a finger, they will drown him.

EMERSON, "EXPERIENCE," *ESSAYS: SECOND SERIES* (1844)

3. Sympathy is a supporting atmosphere, and in it we unfold easily and well.

EMERSON, *JOURNALS,* 1836

4. Search not a wound too deep lest thou make a new one.

THOMAS FULLER, M.D., *GNOMOLOGIA* (1732), 4084

5. Our sympathy is cold to the relation of distant misery.

EDWARD GIBBON, *DECLINE AND FALL OF THE ROMAN EMPIRE* (1776), 49

6. When you are in trouble, people who call to sympathize are really looking for the particulars.

EDGAR WATSON HOWE, *COUNTRY TOWN SAYINGS* (1911)

7. Wisdom must go with Sympathy, else the emotions will become maudlin and pity may be wasted on a poodle instead of a child—on a field-mouse instead of a human soul.

ELBERT HUBBARD, *THE NOTE BOOK* (1927)

8. Pity may represent little more than the impersonal concern which prompts the mailing of a check, but true sympathy is the personal concern which demands the giving of one's soul.

MARTIN LUTHER KING, JR., *STRENGTH TO LOVE* (1963), 3.3

9. Of all cruelties those are the most intolerable that come under the name of condolence and consolation.

Walter Savage Landor, letter to Robert Southey, 1816

10. No one is so accursed by fate, / No one so utterly desolate, / But some heart, though unknown, / Responds unto his own.

Longfellow, "Endymion" (1842), 8

11. There is nothing sweeter than to be sympathized with.

George Santayana, *The Life of Reason: Reason in Common Sense* (1905–06), 6

12. Before an affliction is digested, consolation ever comes too soon; and after it is digested, it comes too late.

Laurence Sterne, *Tristram Shandy* (1759–67), 3.29

T

961. TACT

See also 830. RUDENESS

1. You never know till you try to reach them how accessible men are; but you must approach each man by the right door.

HENRY WARD BEECHER, *PROVERBS FROM PLYMOUTH PULPIT* (1887)

2. Silence is not always tact and it is tact that is golden, not silence.

SAMUEL BUTLER (D. 1902), "HIGGLEDY-PIGGLEDY," *NOTE-BOOKS* (1912)

3. Some people mistake weakness for tact. If they are silent when they ought to speak and so feign an agreement they do not feel, they call it being tactful. Cowardice would be a much better name.

SIR FRANK MEDLICOTT, *READER'S DIGEST,* JULY 1958

4. Talk to every woman as if you loved her, and to every man as if he bored you, and at the end of your first season you will have the reputation of possessing the most perfect social tact.

OSCAR WILDE, *A WOMAN OF NO IMPORTANCE* (1893), 3

5. He spoke with a certain what-is-it in his voice, and I could see that, if not actually disgruntled, he was far from being gruntled.

P.G. WODEHOUSE, *THE CODE OF THE WOOSTERS* (1938)

962. TALENT

See also 1. ABILITY; 311. EXCELLENCE; 377. GENIUS VS. TALENT

1. Talent is like a faucet; while it is open, one must write. Inspiration is a farce that poets have invented to give themselves importance.

JEAN ANOUILH, *THE NEW YORK TIMES,* OCT. 2, 1960

2. The handsome gifts that fate and nature lend us / Most often are the very ones that end us.

CHAUCER, "WORDS OF THE HOST TO THE PHYSICIAN AND TO THE PARDONER," *THE CANTERBURY TALES* (C. 1387–1400), TR. NEVILL COGHILL

3. There is hardly anybody good for everything, and there is scarcely anybody who is absolutely good for nothing.

LORD CHESTERFIELD, *LETTERS TO HIS SON,* JAN. 2, 1748

4. Every form of talent involves a certain shamelessness.

E.M. CIORAN, "SOME BLIND ALLEYS: A LETTER," IN *THE ART OF THE PERSONAL ESSAY* (1994), ED. PHILLIP LOPATE

5. Mediocrity knows nothing higher than itself, but talent instantly recognizes genius.

SIR ARTHUR CONAN DOYLE, *THE VALLEY OF FEAR* (1915)

6. A forte always makes a foible.

EMERSON, *JOURNALS,* 1859

7. Nothing is so frequent as to mistake an ordinary human gift for a special and extraordinary endowment.

OLIVER WENDELL HOLMES, SR., *THE POET AT THE BREAKFAST TABLE* (1872), 6

8. Never to be cast away are the gifts of the gods, magnificent, / which they give of their own will, no man could have them for wanting them.

HOMER, *ILIAD* (9TH C. B.C.), 3.65, TR. RICHMOND LATTIMORE

9. There is no so wretched and coarse a soul wherein some particular faculty is not seen to shine.

MONTAIGNE, "OF PRESUMPTION," *ESSAYS* (1580–88), TR. W. C. HAZLITT

10. Behind a remarkable scholar one finds, not infrequently, a mediocre man, and behind a mediocre artist quite often—a very remarkable man.

NIETZSCHE, *BEYOND GOOD AND EVIL* (1886), 137, TR. WALTER KAUFMANN

11. What a man *is* begins to betray itself when his talent decreases—when he stops showing what he *can do.*

NIETZSCHE, *BEYOND GOOD AND EVIL* (1886), 130, TR. WALTER KAUFMANN

12. Most of your clean-cut types don't have any talent. When they get done washing their face in the morning that's about the end of their contribution.

JOHN O'HARA, *THE INSTRUMENT* (1967)

13. Talent is a question of quantity. Talent does not write one page: it writes three hundred.

JULES RENARD, *JOURNAL*, 1887, TR. ELIZABETH ROGET

14. It is a very rare thing for a man of talent to succeed by his talent.

JOSEPH ROUX, *MEDITATIONS OF A PARISH PRIEST* (1886), 4.88, TR. ISABEL F. HAPGOOD

15. I concluded that my mind was so ordinary, which is to say empty, that I could never be anything but a reasonably good camera. So I would content myself with a more common and general sort of achievement than serious art, which was money.

KURT VONNEGUT, *BLUEBEARD* (1987)

16. Be equal to your talent, not your age. / At times let the gap between them be embarrassing.

YEVGENY YEVTUSHENKO, "OTHERS MAY JUDGE YOU," *THE POETRY OF YEVGENY YEVTUSHENKO: 1953–1965* (1965), TR. GEORGE REAVEY

TALKING

See 923. SPEAKING

963. TASTE

See also 282. ELEGANCE; 725. PREFERENCE

1. Every one carries his own inch-rule of taste, and amuses himself by applying it, triumphantly, wherever he travels.

HENRY ADAMS, *THE EDUCATION OF HENRY ADAMS* (1907), 12

2. Between friends differences in taste or opinion are irritating in direct proportion to their triviality.

W. H. AUDEN, "HIC ET ILLE," *THE DYER'S HAND* (1962)

3. People care more about being thought to have taste than about being thought either good, clever, or amiable.

SAMUEL BUTLER (D. 1902), *NOTE-BOOKS* (1912)

4. The art of taxation consists in so plucking the goose as to obtain the largest possible amount of feathers with the smallest possible amount of hissing.

ATTRIBUTED TO JEAN BAPTISTE COLBERT (C. 1665)

5. Taste is the fundamental quality which sums up all other qualities. It is the ne plus ultra of the intelligence.

COMTE DE LAUTRÉAMONT, *POÉSIES* (1870), 1

6. The diffusion of taste is not the same thing as the improvement of taste.

WILLIAM HAZLITT, "WHY THE ARTS ARE NOT PROGRESSIVE," *ROUND TABLE* (1817)

7. Those who are pleased with the fewest things know the least, as those who are pleased with everything know nothing.

WILLIAM HAZLITT, "ON TASTE," *SKETCHES AND ESSAYS* (1839)

8. Taste speaks through a turn of phrase, a curl of the lip, a shrug of the shoulder: it makes an atmosphere.

IRVING HOWE, "NATURALISM AND TASTE," *A CRITIC'S NOTEBOOK* (1994)

9. One of the surest signs of the Philistine is his reverence for the superior tastes of those who put him down.

PAULINE KAEL, "ZEITGEIST AND POLTERGEIST," *I LOST IT AT THE MOVIES* (1965)

10. Tastes in young people are changed by natural impetuosity, and in the aged are preserved by habit.

LA ROCHEFOUCAULD, *MAXIMS* (1665), TR. KENNETH PRATT

11. The shaping of taste is essentially the science of merchandising, whether of detergents or cars or books or objects of fine and decorative art.

RUSSELL LYNES, *THE PHENOMENON OF CHANGE* (1984)

12. In literature as in love, we are astonished at what is chosen by others.

ANDRÉ MAUROIS, *THE NEW YORK TIMES*, APRIL 14, 1963

13. A person's taste is as much his own peculiar concern as his opinion or his purse.

JOHN STUART MILL, *ON LIBERTY* (1859), 4

14. All of life is a dispute over taste and tasting.

NIETZSCHE, "ON THOSE WHO ARE SUBLIME," *THUS SPOKE ZARATHUSTRA* (1883–92), 2, TR. WALTER KAUFMANN

15. Taste is the enemy of creativeness.

PABLO PICASSO, *QUOTE*, MARCH 24, 1957

16. "Good taste" is a virtue of the keepers of museums. If you scorn bad taste, you will have neither painting nor dancing, neither palaces nor gardens.

SAINT-EXUPÉRY, *THE WISDOM OF THE SANDS* (1948), 9, TR. STUART GILBERT

17. Beautiful things, when taste is formed, are obviously and unaccountably beautiful.

GEORGE SANTAYANA, *THE LIFE OF REASON: REASON IN SOCIETY* (1905–06), 1

18. Taste has no system and no proofs.

SUSAN SONTAG, "NOTES ON CAMP," *AGAINST INTERPRETATION* (1961)

19. "Loud" dress becomes offensive to people of taste, as evincing an undue desire to reach and impress the untrained sensibilities of the vulgar.

THORSTEIN VEBLEN, *THE THEORY OF THE LEISURE CLASS* (1899), 7

964. TAXES

See also 101. BUDGET; 277. ECONOMICS

1. The state is never so efficient as when it wants money.

ANTHONY BURGESS, *YOU'VE HAD YOUR TIME* (1990)

2. To tax and to please, no more than to love and be wise, is not given to men.

EDMUND BURKE, SPEECH, "ON AMERICAN TAXATION," APRIL 19, 1774

3. There is one difference between a tax collector and a taxidermist—the taxidermist leaves the hide.

MORTIMER CAPLAN, *TIME*, FEB. 1, 1963

4. The point to remember is that what the government gives it must first take away.

JOHN S. COLEMAN, ADDRESS TO THE DETROIT CHAMBER OF COMMERCE

5. It is inseparably essential to the freedom of a people that no taxes be imposed on them but with their own consent, given personally or by their representatives.

ATTRIBUTED TO JOHN DICKINSON, RESOLUTIONS OF THE STAMP ACT CONGRESS, OCT. 19, 1765

6. Aside from sending someone to war or to prison, government's ability to make people involuntarily give over their money is its strongest exercise of authority over private citizens and their institutions.

WILLIAM GREIDER, *WHO WILL TELL THE PEOPLE?* (1992)

7. The wisdom of man never yet contrived a system of taxation that would operate with perfect equality.

ANDREW JACKSON, PROCLAMATION TO THE PEOPLE OF SOUTH CAROLINA, DEC. 10, 1832

8. [T]here is apparently nowhere a workable majority in the representative assemblies for making the specific cuts in expenditure which could bring down the taxes, and in election after election the people vote into power representatives who are as unable as they are unwilling to do anything about it.

GUNNAR MYRDAL, *BEYOND THE WELFARE STATE* (1960)

9. Taxes, after all, are the dues that we pay for the privileges of membership in an organized society.

FRANKLIN D. ROOSEVELT, SPEECH, WORCESTER, MASS., OCT. 21, 1936

10. It is the part of a good shepherd to shear his flock, not to flay it.

TIBERIUS, QUOTED IN SUETONIUS' *LIVES OF THE CAESARS: TIBERIUS* (2ND C. A.D.), 32.2

11. The ceiling on taxation of capital gains reflects the national belief that speculation is a more worthwhile way to make a living than work.

CALVIN TRILLIN, "TAXING PROBLEMS," *UNCIVIL LIBERTIES* (1982)

965. TEACHING

See also 279. EDUCATION; 532. LEARNING

1. A teacher affects eternity; he can never tell where his influence stops.

HENRY ADAMS, *THE EDUCATION OF HENRY ADAMS* (1907), 20

2. Nothing is more tiresome than a superannuated pedagogue.

HENRY ADAMS, *THE EDUCATION OF HENRY ADAMS* (1907), 23

3. Never try to teach a pig to sing...it wastes your time and annoys the pig.

ANONYMOUS, TEXAS SAYING

4. Teachers, who educate children, deserve more honor than parents, who merely gave them birth; for the latter provided mere life, while the former ensure a good life.

ARISTOTLE (4TH C. B.C.), QUOTED IN DIOGENES LAERTIUS' *LIVES AND OPINIONS OF EMINENT PHILOSOPHERS* (3RD C. A.D.), TR. R. D. HICKS

5. Every real teacher is myself in disguise.

RICHARD BACH, *RUNNING FROM SAFETY* (1994)

6. Teaching is not a lost art, but the regard for it is a lost tradition.

JACQUES BARZUN, *TEACHER IN AMERICA* (1944)

7. The dons are too busy educating the young men to be able to teach them anything.

SAMUEL BUTLER (D. 1902), "HIGGLEDY-PIGGLEDY," *NOTE-BOOKS* (1912)

8. First he wrought, and afterwards he taught.

CHAUCER, "PROLOGUE," *THE CANTERBURY TALES* (1387–1400), 496

9. If a man keeps cherishing his old knowledge, so as continually to be acquiring new, he may be a teacher of others.

Confucius, *Analects* (6th c. B.C.), 2.11, tr. James Legge

10. The theory of the teacher with all these immigrant kids was that if you spoke English loudly enough they would eventually understand.

E.L. Doctorow, *Loon Lake* (1980)

11. The whole secret of the teacher's force lies in the conviction that men are convertible.

Emerson, *Journals,* 1834

12. I pay the schoolmaster, but 'tis the schoolboys that educate my son.

Emerson, *Journals,* 1849

13. The whole art of teaching is only the art of awakening the natural curiosity of young minds for the purpose of satisfying it afterwards.

Anatole France, *The Crime of Sylvestre Bonnard* (1881), 2, tr. Lafcadio Hearn

14. No man can reveal to you aught but that which already lies half asleep in the dawning of your knowledge.

Kahlil Gibran, "On Teaching," *The Prophet* (1923)

15. A teacher who can arouse a feeling for one single good action, for one single good poem, accomplishes more than he who fills our memory with rows and rows of natural objects, classified with name and form.

Goethe, *Elective Affinities* (1809), 25

16. Bad teaching wastes a great deal of effort, and spoils many lives which might have been full of energy and happiness.

Gilbert Highet, *The Art of Teaching* (1950)

17. If you do not actually like boys and girls, or young men and young women, give up teaching.

Gilbert Highet, *The Art of Teaching* (1950)

18. You [the teacher] do not merely insert a lot of facts, if you teach them [the students] properly. It is not like injecting 500 cc. of serum, or administering a year's dose of vitamins.

Gilbert Highet, *The Art of Teaching* (1950)

19. He that teaches us anything which we knew not before is undoubtedly to be reverenced as a master.

Samuel Johnson, *The Idler* (1758–60), 85

20. To teach is to learn twice over.

Joseph Joubert, *Pensées* (1842), 18.18, tr. Katharine Lyttelton

21. In public schooling, social policy has been turned back almost one hundred years.

Jonathan Kozol, *Savage Inequalities* (1991)

22. On Mondays and Fridays in early May, nearly 18,000 children—the equivalent of all the elementary students in suburban Glencoe, Wilmette, Glenview, Kenilworth, Winnetka, Deerfield, Highland Park and Evanston—are assigned to classes with no teacher.

Jonathan Kozol, *Savage Inequalities* (1991)

23. He [the schoolmaster] is awkward, and out of place, in the society of his equals. He comes like Gulliver from among his little people, and he cannot fit the stature of his understanding to yours.

Charles Lamb, "The Old and the New Schoolmaster," *Essays of Elia* (1823)

24. The greater part of the people we assign to educate our sons we know for certain are not educated. Yet we do not doubt that they can give what they have not received, a thing which cannot be otherwise acquired.

Giacomo Leopardi, *Pensieri* (1834–37), 10, tr. William Fense Weaver

25. It is easier for a tutor to command than to teach.

John Locke, *Some Thoughts Concerning Education* (1693), 50

26. A man who knows a subject thoroughly, a man so soaked in it that he eats it, sleeps it and dreams it—this man can always teach it with success, no matter how little he knows of technical pedagogy.

H. L. Mencken, *Prejudices: Third Series* (1922), 13

27. I maintain, in truth, / That with a smile we should instruct our youth, / Be very gentle when we have to blame, / And not put them in fear of virtue's name.

Molière, *The School for Husbands* (1661), 1.2, tr. Donald M. Frame

28. An educator never says what he himself thinks, but only that which he thinks it is good for those whom he is educating to hear.

Nietzsche, *The Will to Power* (1888), 980, tr. Anthony M. Ludovici

29. Men must be taught as if you taught them not, / And things unknown proposed as things forgot.

Alexander Pope, *An Essay on Criticism* (1711), 3.15

30. The severity of the master is more useful than the indulgence of the father.

SA'DI, *GULISTAN* (1258), 7.4, TR. JAMES ROSS

31. My joy in learning is partly that it enables me to teach.

SENECA, *LETTERS TO LUCILIUS* (1ST C.), 6.4, TR. E. PHILLIPS BARKER

32. He who can, does. He who cannot, teaches.

GEORGE BERNARD SHAW, "MAXIMS FOR REVOLUTIONISTS," *MAN AND SUPERMAN* (1903)

33. One good teacher in a lifetime may sometimes change a delinquent into a solid citizen.

PHILIP WYLIE, *GENERATION OF VIPERS* (1942), 7

966. TECHNOLOGY

See also 502. INVENTION; 641. NUCLEAR POWER; 849. SCIENCE; 1001. TWENTIETH CENTURY

1. Whatever the country, capitalist or socialist, man was everywhere crushed by technology, made a stranger to his own work, imprisoned, forced into stupidity.

SIMONE DE BEAUVOIR, *LES BELLES IMAGES* (1966), TR. PATRICK O'BRIAN (1968)

2. As industrial technology advances and enlarges, and in the process assumes greater social, economic, and political force, it carries people away from where they belong by history, culture, deeds, association, and affection.

WENDELL BERRY, "STANDING BY WORDS," *STANDING BY WORDS* (1983)

3. Have you ever looked inside one of those t hings [computers]? It's a whole hierarchy of angels—all on slats. And those little tubes—those are miracles.

JOSEPH CAMPBELL, *THE POWER OF MYTH* (1988)

4. When a machine begins to run without human aid, it is time to scrap it—whether it be a factory or a government.

ALEXANDER CHASE, *PERSPECTIVES* (1966)

5. Only science can hope to keep technology in some sort of moral order.

EDGAR Z. FRIEDENBERG, "THE IMPACT OF THE SCHOOL," *THE VANISHING ADOLESCENT* (1959)

6. It is a commonplace of modern technology that there is a high measure of certainty that problems have solutions before there is knowledge of how they are to be solved.

JOHN KENNETH GALBRAITH, *THE NEW INDUSTRIAL STATE* (1967)

7. The miraculousness of technology is a popular article of Western faith.

MICHAEL HARRINGTON, *THE ACCIDENTAL CENTURY* (1966)

8. If there is technological advance without social advance, there is, almost automatically, an increase in human misery.

MICHAEL HARRINGTON, APPENDIX TO *THE OTHER AMERICA* (1962)

9. Is it a fact—or have I dreamt it—that, by means of electricity, the world of matter has become a great nerve, vibrating thousands of miles in a breathless point of time?

NATHANIEL HAWTHORNE, *THE HOUSE OF THE SEVEN GABLES* (1851), 17

10. Watt with his steam engine, Faraday with his electric motor, and Edison with his incandescent light bulb did not have it as their goal to contribute to a fuel shortage someday that would place their countries at the mercy of Arab oil.

JOSEPH HELLER, *GOOD AS GOLD* (1979)

11. Where there is the necessary technical skill to move mountains, there is no need for the faith that moves mountains.

ERIC HOFFER, *THE PASSIONATE STATE OF MIND* (1954), 12

12. It is said that one machine can do the work of fifty ordinary men. No machine, however, can do the work of one extraordinary man.

TEHYI HSIEH, *CHINESE EPIGRAMS INSIDE OUT AND PROVERBS* (1948), 470

13. Applied Science is a conjuror, whose bottomless hat yields impartially the softest of Angora rabbits and the most petrifying of Medusas.

ALDOUS HUXLEY, *TOMORROW AND TOMORROW AND TOMORROW* (1956)

14. Man is still the most extraordinary computer of all.

JOHN F. KENNEDY, MAY 21, 1963

15. Electronic calculators can solve problems which the man who made them cannot solve; but no government-subsidized commission of engineers and physicists could create a worm.

JOSEPH WOOD KRUTCH, "MARCH," *THE TWELVE SEASONS* (1949)

16. Technology made large populations possible; large populations now make technology indispensable.

Joseph Wood Krutch, "The Nemesis of Power," *Human Nature and the Human Condition* (1959)

17. We have forgotten the beast and the flower not in order to remember either ourselves or God, but in order to forget everything except the machine.

Joseph Wood Krutch, "March," *The Twelve Seasons* (1949)

18. You cannot endow even the best machine with initiative; the jolliest steam-roller will not plant flowers.

Walter Lippmann, "Routineer and Inventor," *A Preface to Politics* (1914)

19. It is critical vision alone which can mitigate the unimpeded operation of the automatic.

Marshall McLuhan, "Magic That Changes Mood," *The Mechanical Bride* (1951)

20. Everywhere in the world the industrial regime tends to make the unorganized or unorganizable individual, the pauper, into the victim of a kind of human sacrifice offered to the gods of civilization.

Jacques Maritain, *Reflections on America* (1958), 19.2

21. [T]he danger always exists that our technology will serve as a buffer between us and nature, a block between us and the deeper dimensions of our own experience.

Rollo May, *The Courage to Create* (1975)

22. By his very success in inventing labor-saving devices, modern man has manufactured an abyss of boredom that only the privileged classes in earlier civilizations have ever fathomed.

Lewis Mumford, "The Challenge to Renewal," *The Conduct of Life* (1951)

23. One has to look out for engineers—they begin with sewing machines and end up with the atomic bomb.

Marcel Pagnol, *Critique des critiques* (1949), 3

24. The nihilism of technology lies not only in the fact that it is the most perfect expression of the will to power, as Heidegger believes, but also in the fact that it lacks meaning. *Why?* and *To what purpose?* are questions that technology does not ask itself.

Octavio Paz, "The Channel and the Signs," *Alternating Current* (1973)

25. Technology presumes there's just one right way to do things and there never is.

Robert M. Pirsig, *Zen and the Art of Motorcycle Maintenance* (1974)

26. The shock of twentieth-century technology numbed our brains and we are just beginning to notice the spiritual and social debris that our technology has strewn about us.

Neil Postman, "Six Questions," *The Disappearance of Childhood* (1982)

27. Sometimes you might think the machines we worship make all the chief appointments, promoting the human beings who seem closest to them.

J. B. Priestley, "Candles Burning Low," *Thoughts in the Wilderness* (1957)

28. We cannot get grace from gadgets. In the bakelite house of the future, the dishes may not break, but the heart can.

J. B. Priestley, news summaries, April 1, 1956

29. The machine does not isolate man from the great problems of nature but plunges him more deeply into them.

Saint-Exupéry, *Wind, Sand, and Stars* (1939), 3, tr. Lewis Galantière

30. The machine yes the machine / never wastes anybody's time / never watches the foreman / never talks back.

Carl Sandburg, *The People, Yes* (1936)

31. I have never received a telephone call that justified the excitement and fuss of the electronics involved. If I can't see somebody I love, for instance, such as a daughter, or a son, I would rather receive a letter.

William Saroyan, "Let's Just Nobody Ever Forget Joan Castle," *Sons Come & Go, Mothers Hang In Forever* (1979)

32. No medicine man these days can afford to be without a portable tape recorder. Without the aid of this modern device, which may be easily concealed in the undergrowth of the jungle, the old tribal authority will rapidly become undermined by the mounting influenece of modern skepticism.

Muriel Spark, *The Ballad of Peckham Rye* (1960)

33. Those who live by electronics die by electronics. *Sic semper tyrannis.*

Kurt Vonnegut, *Player Piano* (1952)

34. The thing I longed for as a teenager is now an object of neglect and scorn. I've grown to hate my telephone.

Wendy Wasserstein, "A Phone of Her Own," *Bachelor Girls* (1990)

TEEN-AGERS

See 1071. YOUTH

967. TELEVISION

1. Situation comedy on television has thrived for years on "canned" laughter grafted to gaglines by technicians using records of guffawing audiences that have been dead for years.

RUSSELL BAKER, "THE INVISIBLE ARTISTS," *ALL THINGS CONSIDERED* (1962)

2. The charm of television entertainment is its ability to bridge the chasm between dinner and bedtime without mental distraction.

RUSSELL BAKER, "ON WITH MINDLESSNESS," *ALL THINGS CONSIDERED* (1962)

3. [T]elevision *doomed* us to the Family, whose household instrument it has become—what the hearth used to be, flanked by the communal kettle.

ROLAND BARTHES, "LEAVING THE MOVIE THEATER," IN *THE ART OF THE PERSONAL ESSAY* (1994), ED. PHILLIP LOPATE

4. Authors are now marketed like promising movie starlets and must rattle around the nation's television stations to try to assert a salable identity different from that of the other starlets.

ALISTAIR COOKE, "THE BEST OF HIS KIND," *AMERICA OBSERVED: FROM THE 1940S TO THE 1980S* (1988)

5. It [television] is a medium of entertainment which permits millions of people to listen to the same joke at the same time, and yet remain lonesome.

T. S. ELIOT, *NEW YORK POST,* SEPT. 22, 1963

6. In 1957, when I was in second grade, black children integrated Central High School in Little Rock, Arkansas. We watched it on TV. All of us watched it. I don't mean Mama and Daddy and Rocky. I mean *all* the colored people in America watched it, together, with one set of eyes.

HENRY LOUIS GATES, JR., "PRIME TIME," *COLORED PEOPLE* (1994)

7. Television watching does reduce reading and often encroaches on homework. Much of it is admittedly the intellectual equivalent of junk food. But in some respects, such as its use of standard written English, television watching is acculturative.

E.D. HIRSCH, JR., *CULTURAL LITERACY* (1987)

8. There are days when any electrical appliance in the house, including the vacuum cleaner, seems to offer more entertainment possibilities than the TV set.

HARRIET VAN HORNE, *NEW YORK WORLD-TELEGRAM AND SUN,* JUNE 7, 1957

9. Movies are a combination of art and mass medium, but television is so single in its purpose—selling—that it operates without that painful, poignant mixture of aspiration and effort and compromise.

PAULINE KAEL, "MOVIES ON TELEVISION," *KISS KISS BANG BANG* (1965)

10. Murrow regarded television as a sound-equipped mirror held behind American society, reflecting its good and its bad, both only too real. He affixed to the electronic mirror a magnifying lens and a powerful focusing searchlight.

ALEXANDER KENDRICK, *PRIME TIME* (1969)

11. [Ed] Murrow was always conscious that television's power for good was no greater than its power for evil.

ALEXANDER KENDRICK, *PRIME TIME* (1969)

12. In an automobile civilization, which was one of constant motion and activity, there was almost no time to think; in a television one, there is small desire.

LOUIS KRONENBERGER, *COMPANY MANNERS* (1954), I.3

13. For all its flexibility, television is more a mirror of taste than a shaper of it.

RUSSELL LYNES, *THE PHENOMENON OF CHANGE* (1984)

14. Americans have never quite digested television. The mystique which should fade grows stronger. We make celebrities not only of the men who cause events but of the men who read reports of them aloud.

JOE MCGINNISS, *THE SELLING OF THE PRESIDENT 1968* (1969)

15. Over and over again, on every television set in Houston, George Bush was seen with his coat slung over a shoulder; his sleeves rolled up; walking the streets of his district; grinning, gripping, sweating, letting the voter know he cared. About what, was never made clear.

JOE MCGINNISS, *THE SELLING OF THE PRESIDENT 1968* (1969)

16. With the coming of television, and the knowledge of how it could be used to seduce voters, the old political values disappeared. Something new, murky, undefined started to rise from the mists.

JOE MCGINNISS, *THE SELLING OF THE PRESIDENT 1968* (1969)

17. [T]he time is soon coming, thinks Rusty, when fornication will be professional athletics, and everybody will watch the national eliminations on TV.

NORMAN MAILER, *WHY ARE WE IN VIETNAM?* (1967)

18. It is television's primary damage that it provides ten million children with the same fantasy, ready-made and on a platter.

MARYA MANNES, *MORE IN ANGER* (1958), 3.1

19. Television was not intended to make human beings vacuous, but it is an emanation of their vacuity.

MALCOLM MUGGERIDGE, "I LIKE DWIGHT," *THE MOST OF MALCOLM MUGGERIDGE* (1966)

20. Many Americans feel themselves inferior in the presence of anyone with an English accent, which is why an English accent has become fashionable in television commercials; it is thought to sound authoritative.

EDWIN NEWMAN, *STRICTLY SPEAKING* (1974)

21. Millions who endure poverty and bad government can now know what they are missing. To see how the other half lives all they have to do is switch on their television sets.

RICHARD M. NIXON, *REAL PEACE* (1984)

22. Above all, a book is the riverbank for the river of language. Language without the riverbank is only television talk—a free fall, a loose splash, a spill.

CYNTHIA OZICK, "THE QUESTION OF OUR SPEECH: THE RETURN TO AURAL CULTURE," *METAPHOR & MEMORY* (1989)

23. I used to pride myself on being impervious to the sentimentalities of soap opera, but when that loveliest of actresses, Rachel Gurney, of *Upstairs, Downstairs*, perished on the *Titanic*, I wept so convulsively and developed such anorexia that I had to be force-fed.

S.J. PERELMAN, *THE LAST LAUGH* (1981)

24. If we may say that the Age of Andrew Jackson took political life out of the hands of aristocrats and turned it over to the masses, then we may say, with equal justification, that the Age of Television has taken politics away from the adult mind altogether.

NEIL POSTMAN, "THE ADULT CHILD," *THE DISAPPEARANCE OF CHILDHOOD* (1982)

25. Already we Viewers, when not viewing, have begun to whisper to one another that the more we elaborate our means of communication, the less we communicate.

J. B. PRIESTLEY, "TELEVIEWING," *THOUGHTS IN THE WILDERNESS* (1957)

26. Words, isolated in the velvet of radio, took on a jeweled particularity. Television has quite the opposite effect: words are drowned in the visual soup in which they are obliged to be served.

FREDERIC RAPHAEL, "THE LANGUAGE OF TELEVISION," IN *THE STATE OF THE LANGUAGE* (1980) ED. BY LEONARD MICHAELS AND CHRISTOPHER RICKS

27. [O]ne can watch hours and hours of TV without actually losing interest, but, as with Chinese food, one is rarely left with much residue of nourishment.

FREDERIC RAPHAEL, "THE LANGUAGE OF TELEVISION," IN *THE STATE OF THE LANGUAGE* (1980) ED. BY LEONARD MICHAELS AND CHRISTOPHER RICKS

28. Being on TV is like being alive, only more so.

JOHN UPDIKE, "BEING ON TV—I," *ODD JOBS* (1991)

29. One [television] program was an interminable exploration of the question: can a woman with a low I.Q. be happily married to a man with a high one? The answer seemed to be yes and no.

KURT VONNEGUT, *PLAYER PIANO* (1952)

30. I hate television. I hate it as much as peanuts. But I can't stop eating peanuts.

ORSON WELLES, *NEW YORK HERALD TRIBUNE*, OCT. 12, 1956

31. We shall stand or fall by television—of that I am quite sure.

E.B. WHITE, *ONE MAN'S MEAT* (1944)

32. Disparagement of television is second only to watching television as an American pastime.

GEORGE F. WILL, "PRISONERS OF TV," *THE PURSUIT OF HAPPINESS AND OTHER SOBERING THOUGHTS* (1978)

968. TEMPER, BAD

See also 39. ANGER; 392. GOOD NATURE; 969. TEMPERAMENT

1. All music jars when the soul's out of tune.

CERVANTES, *DON QUIXOTE* (1605–15), 2.4.44, TR. JOHN OZELL

2. A tart temper never mellows with age, and a sharp tongue is the only edged tool that grows keener with constant use.

WASHINGTON IRVING, "RIP VAN WINKLE," *THE SKETCH BOOK OF GEOFFREY CRAYON, GENT.* (1819–20)

3. I'm half Scotch-Irish on both sides, and when I lose my temper—brother, I go.

S.J. PERELMAN, *THE RISING GORGE* (1961)

4. He who is of a calm and happy nature will hardly feel the pressure of age, but to him who is of an opposite disposition youth and age are equally a burden.

PLATO, *THE REPUBLIC* (4TH C. B.C.), 1, TR. BENJAMIN JOWETT

969. TEMPERAMENT

See also 284. EMOTIONS; 392. GOOD NATURE; 687. PERSONALITY; 968. TEMPER, BAD

1. There is no harbor of peace / From the changing waves of joy and despair.

EURIPIDES, *ION* (C. 421–08 B.C.), TR. RONALD F. WILLETTS

2. Temperament, like liberty, is important despite how many crimes are committed in its name.

LOUIS KRONENBERGER, *COMPANY MANNERS* (1954), 1.2

3. The tranquility or agitation of our temper does not depend so much on the big things which happen to us in life, as on the pleasant or unpleasant arrangements of the little things which happen daily.

LA ROCHEFOUCAULD, *MAXIMS* (1665), TR. KENNETH PRATT

4. The happiness and unhappiness of men depend as much on their turn of mind as on fortune.

LA ROCHEFOUCAULD, *MAXIMS* (1665), TR. KENNETH PRATT

5. A human being tends to believe that the mood of the moment, be it troubled or blithe, peaceful or stormy, is the true, native, and permanent tenor of his existence ... whereas the truth is that he is condemned to improvisation and morally lives from hand to mouth all the time.

THOMAS MANN, "A MAN AND HIS DOG" (1918), *DEATH IN VENICE*, TR. H. T. LOWE-PORTER

6. If health and a fair day smile upon me, I am a very good fellow; if a corn trouble my toe, I am sullen, out of humor, and inaccessible.

MONTAIGNE, "APOLOGY FOR RAIMOND DE SEBONDE," *ESSAYS* (1580–88), TR. W. C. HAZLITT

7. Certainly there are good and bad times, but our mood changes more often than our fortune.

JULES RENARD, *JOURNAL*, JANUARY 1905, ED. AND, TR. ELIZABETH ROGET

970. TEMPERANCE

See also 268. DRINKING; 494. INTEMPERANCE; 598. MODERATION

1. Subdue your appetites, my dears, and you've conquered human natur.

CHARLES DICKENS, *NICHOLAS NICKLEBY* (1838–39), 5

2. Sobriety is love of health, or inability to eat much.

LA ROCHEFOUCAULD, *MAXIMS* (1665), TR. KENNETH PRATT

3. Intemperate temperance injures the cause of temperance, while temperate temperance helps it in its fight against intemperate intemperance.

MARK TWAIN, *NOTEBOOK* (1935)

971. TEMPTATION

See also 99. BRIBERY; 191. CORRUPTION; 900. SIN

1. All men are tempted. There is no man that lives that can't be broken down, provided it is the right temptation, put in the right spot.

HENRY WARD BEECHER, *PROVERBS FROM PLYMOUTH PULPIT* (1887)

2. No temptation can ever be measured by the value of its object.

COLETTE, "HUMAN NATURE," *EARTHLY PARADISE* (1966), 4

3. Though the bird may fly over your head, let it not make its nest in your hair.

DANISH PROVERB

4. There is a certain degree of temptation which will overcome any virtue. Now, in so far as you approach temptation to a man, you do him an injury; and, if he is overcome, you share his guilt.

SAMUEL JOHNSON, QUOTED IN BOSWELL'S *LIFE OF SAMUEL JOHNSON*, APRIL 3, 1778

5. Who will not judge him worthy to be robbed / That sets his doors wide open to a thief, / And shows the felon where his treasure lies?

BEN JONSON, *EVERY MAN IN HIS HUMOUR* (1598), 3.3

6. I have a simple principle for the conduct of life—never to resist an adequate temptation.

MAX LERNER, "THE LAW OF AUSTERE HEDONISM," *THE UNFINISHED COUNTRY* (1959), 1

7. Blessed is he who has never been tempted; for he knows not the frailty of his rectitude.

CHRISTOPHER MORLEY, *INWARD HO!* (1923), 1

8. There are several good protections against temptations, but the surest is cowardice.

MARK TWAIN, "PUDD'NHEAD WILSON'S NEW CALENDAR," *FOLLOWING THE EQUATOR* (1897), 1.36

9. I generally avoid temptation unless I can't resist it.

MAE WEST, IN *MY LITTLE CHICKADEE* (1940)

10. I can resist everything except temptation.

OSCAR WILDE, *LADY WINDERMERE'S FAN* (1892), 1

11. The only way to get rid of a temptation is to yield to it. Resist it, and your soul grows sick with longing for the things it has forbidden to itself.

Oscar Wilde, *The Picture of Dorian Gray* (1891), 2

THANKS

See 399. Gratitude

THANKSGIVING DAY

See 420. Holidays

972. THEATER

See also 11. Actors; 144. Comedians; 145. Comedy; 215. Dancing; 611. Movies; 655. Opera; 987. Tragedy

1. There is as much difference between the stage and the films as between a piano and a violin. Normally you can't become a virtuoso in both.

Ethel Barrymore, *New York Post,* June 7, 1956

2. Plays, gentlemen, are to their authors what children are to women: they cost more pain than they give pleasure.

Beaumarchais, preface to *The Barber of Seville* (1775), tr. Joyce Bermel

3. Throughout the play everything possible was done to show the virtue, innocence and helplessness of the poor, and the abandoned cruelty, the heartless self-indulgence of the rich.

Joyce Cary, *Except the Lord* (1953)

4. Don't put your daughter on the stage, Mrs. Worthington,/Don't put your daughter on the stage,/The profession is overcrowded/ And the struggle's pretty tough/ And admitting t he fact/She's burning to act,/That isn't quite enough.

Noël Coward, Song, "Mrs. Worthington"

5. In London, theatregoers expect to laugh; in Paris, they wait grimly for proof that they should.

Robert Dhéry, *Look,* March 4, 1958

6. A play should give you something to think about. When I see a play and understand it the first time, then I know it can't be much good.

T. S. Eliot, *New York Post,* Sept. 22, 1963

7. Like hungry guests, a sitting audience looks: / Plays are like suppers; poets are the cooks. / The founder's you: the table is this place: / The carvers we: the prologue is the grace. / Each act a course, each scene, a different dish.

George Farquhar, prologue to *The Inconstant* (1702)

8. In my plays I want to look at life—at the commonplace of existence—as if we had just turned a corner and run into it for the first time.

Christopher Fry, *Time,* Nov. 20, 1950

9. The stage-play is a trial, not a deed of violence. The soul is opened, like the combination of a safe, by means of a word. You don't require an acetylene torch.

Jean Giraudoux, quoted in introduction to *Jean Giraudoux: Four Plays* (1958), adapted by Maurice Valency

10. One's roused by this, another finds that fit: / Each loves the play for what he brings to it.

Goethe, "Prelude in the Theatre," *Faust: Part I* (1808), tr. Philip Wayne

11. You need three things in the theatre—the play, the actors and the audience, and each must give something.

Kenneth Haigh, *Theatre Arts,* July 1958

12. Playwriting, like begging in India, is an honorable but humbling profession.

Moss Hart, *Act One* (1959)

13. The frivolity with which all theatrical activity is conducted has one consoling feature—there are no rules of behavior that apply regularly to any part of the theatre.

Moss Hart, *Act One* (1959)

14. There is nothing that one can say about acting, writing, producing or directing that cannot be revoked in the next breath. Nothing is immutable. The logic of one year is a folly of the next.

Moss Hart, *Act One* (1959)

15. I think theatre should always be somewhat suspect.

Václav Havel, *Disturbing the Peace* (1990)

16. The stage but echoes back the public voice. / The drama's laws the drama's patrons give, / For we that live to please, must please to live.

Samuel Johnson, *Prologue at the Opening of the Drury Lane Theatre* (1747)

17. In New York people don't go to the theatre—they go to see hits.

Attributed to Louis Jourdan

18. We do not go [to the theatre], like our ancestors, to escape from the pressure of reality, so much as to confirm our experience of it.

CHARLES LAMB, "ON THE ARTIFICIAL COMEDY OF THE LAST CENTURY," *ESSAYS OF ELIA* (1823)

19. Words can be deceitful, but pantomime necessarily is simple, clear and direct.

MARCEL MARCEAU, *THEATRE ARTS,* MARCH 1958

20. If the audience never understands the plot, it can be counted on to be attentive to the very end.

BENEDETTO MARCELLO, *IL TEATRO ALLA MODA* (1720)

21. The inclination to digress is human. But the dramatist must avoid it even more strenuously than the saint must avoid sin, for while sin may be venial, digression is mortal.

W. SOMERSET MAUGHAM, *THE SUMMING UP* (1938), 35

22. The drama is make-believe. It does not deal with truth but with effect.

W. SOMERSET MAUGHAM, *THE SUMMING UP* (1938), 39

23. The theater, when all is said and done, is not life in miniature, but life enormously magnified, life hideously exaggerated.

H. L. MENCKEN, *PREJUDICES: FIRST SERIES* (1919), 17

24. Great drama is the souvenir of the adventure of a master among the pieces of his own soul.

GEORGE JEAN NATHAN, "GREAT DRAMA," *THE WORLD IN FALSEFACE* (1923)

25. Men go to the theatre to forget; women, to remember.

GEORGE JEAN NATHAN, "THE THEATRE," *AMERICAN MERCURY,* JULY 1926

26. He was done with tinsel and sawdust, he declaimed; he wanted no more of the theater and its cutthroat machinations.

S.J. PERELMAN, *THE RISING GORGE* (1961)

27. A novelist may lose his readers for a few pages; a playwright never dares lose his audience for a minute.

TERENCE RATTIGAN, IN *NEW YORK JOURNAL-AMERICAN,* OCT. 29, 1956

28. Not to go to the theatre is like making one's toilet without a mirror.

SCHOPENHAUER, "FURTHER PSYCHOLOGICAL OBSERVATIONS," *PARERGA AND PARALIPOMENA* (1851), TR. T. BAILEY SAUNDERS

29. The public voice in the theater today is crude and raucous, and, all too often, weak-minded.

SUSAN SONTAG, "GOING TO THEATER, ETC.," *AGAINST INTERPRETATION* (1966)

30. I see the playwright as a lay preacher peddling the ideas of his time in popular form.

AUGUST STRINDBERG, PREFACE TO *MISS JULIE* (1888), TR. ELIZABETH SPRIGGE

31. It is the destiny of the theater nearly everywhere and in every period to struggle even when it is flourishing.

HOWARD TAUBMAN, *THE NEW YORK TIMES,* AUG. 4, 1964

32. Surely no other American institution is so bound around and tightened up by rules, strictures, adages, and superstitions as the Broadway theatre.

JAMES THURBER, "THE QUALITY OF MIRTH," *COLLECTING HIMSELF* (1989)

33. A good many inconveniences attend playgoing in any large city, but the greatest of them is usually the play itself.

KENNETH TYNAN, *NEW YORK HERALD TRIBUNE,* FEB. 17, 1957

34. The theater needs continual reminders that there is nothing more debasing than the work of those who do well what is not worth doing at all.

GORE VIDAL, *ROCKING THE BOAT* (1962)

35. A talent for drama is not a talent for writing, but is an ability to articulate human relationships.

GORE VIDAL, *THE NEW YORK TIMES,* JUNE 17, 1956

36. A dramatist is one who from his earliest years has found that sheer gazing at the shocks and countershocks among people is quite sufficiently engrossing without having to encase it in comment.

THORNTON WILDER, INTERVIEW, *WRITERS AT WORK: FIRST SERIES* (1958)

37. On the stage it is always *now;* the personages are standing on that razor-edge, between the past and the future, which is the essential character of conscious being.

THORNTON WILDER, INTERVIEW, *WRITERS AT WORK: FIRST SERIES* (1958)

38. The unencumbered stage encourages the truth operative in everyone. The less seen, the more heard. The eye is the enemy of the ear in real drama.

THORNTON WILDER, *THE NEW YORK TIMES,* NOV. 6, 1961

39. We live in what is, but we find a thousand ways not to face it. Great theater strengthens our faculty to face it.

THORNTON WILDER, INTERVIEW, *WRITERS AT WORK: FIRST SERIES* (1958)

40. Some mystery should be left in the revelation of character in a play, just as a great deal of mystery is always left in the revelation of character in life, even in one's own character to himself.

TENNESSEE WILLIAMS, STAGE DIRECTIONS, *CAT ON A HOT TIN ROOF* (1955)

41. Every now and then, when you're on stage, you hear the best sound a player can hear. It's a sound you can't get in movies or in television. It is the sound of a wonderful, deep silence that means you've hit them where they live.

SHELLEY WINTERS, *THEATRE ARTS,* JUNE 1956

THEFT

See 934. STEALING

973. THEOLOGY

See also 387. GOD; 797. RELIGION

1. The theologian who has no joy in his work is not a theologian at all. Sulky faces, morose thoughts and boring ways of speaking are intolerable in this science.

KARL BARTH, QUOTED IN HIS OBITUARY, *THE NEW YORK TIMES,* DEC. 11, 1968

2. Doctrine is nothing but the skin of truth set up and stuffed.

HENRY WARD BEECHER, *PROVERBS FROM PLYMOUTH PULPIT* (1887)

3. First, I hate all theological controversy: it is wearing to the temper, and is I believe (at all events when viva voce) worse than useless.

LEWIS CARROLL, *THE LETTERS OF LEWIS CARROLL,* ED. MORTON N. COHEN (1979)

4. The cure for false theology is motherwit. Forget your books and traditions, and obey your moral perceptions at this hour.

EMERSON, "WORSHIP," *THE CONDUCT OF LIFE* (1860)

5. The most tedious of all discourses are on the subject of the Supreme Being.

EMERSON, *JOURNALS,* 1836

6. Hypotheses are only the pieces of scaffolding which are erected round a building during the course of construction, and which are taken away as soon as the edifice is completed.

GOETHE (1749–1832), QUOTED IN ANTHONY M. LUDOVICI'S INTRODUCTION TO NIETZSCHE'S *THE WILL TO POWER*

7. Theology is an attempt to explain a subject by men who do not understand it. The intent is not to tell the truth but to satisfy the questioner.

ELBERT HUBBARD, *THE PHILISTINE* (1895–1915)

8. Theology in religion is what poisons are in food.

NAPOLEON I, *MAXIMS* (1804–15)

9. Theology emerged not as a course of knowledge but as a feast of homily and imagination and exaggeration in which every man could find his image and his portion. And yet there were limits.

ISRAEL SHENKER, *COAT OF MANY COLORS* (1985)

10. Theological religion is the source of all imaginable follies and disturbances; it is the parent of fanaticism and civil discord; it is the enemy of mankind.

VOLTAIRE, "RELIGION," *PHILOSOPHICAL DICTIONARY* (1764)

974. THEORY

See also 9. ACTION; 328. FACTS; 694. PHILOSOPHERS AND PHILOSOPHY; 849. SCIENCE

1. Professors in every branch of the sciences prefer their own theories to truth; the reason is that their theories are private property, but truth is common stock.

CHARLES CALEB COLTON, *LACON* (1825), 1.378

2. It is a capital mistake to theorize before one has data.

SIR ARTHUR CONAN DOYLE, "SCANDAL IN BOHEMIA," *THE ADVENTURES OF SHERLOCK HOLMES* (1891)

3. The astonishment of life is the absence of any appearances of reconciliation between the theory and the practice of life.

EMERSON, *JOURNALS,* 1844

4. In theory, there is nothing to hinder our following what we are taught, but in life there are many things to draw us aside.

EPICTETUS, *DISCOURSES* (2ND C.), 1.26, TR. THOMAS W. HIGGINSON

5. No theory is good except on condition that one use it to go beyond.

ANDRÉ GIDE, *JOURNALS,* 1918, TR. JUSTIN O'BRIEN

6. To be sure, theory is useful. But without warmth of heart and without love it bruises the very ones it claims to save.

ANDRÉ GIDE, *JOURNALS,* 1937, TR. JUSTIN O'BRIEN

7. All theory, my friend, is grey, / But green is life's glad golden tree.

GOETHE, "NIGHT," *FAUST: PART I* (1808), TR. PHILIP WAYNE

8. It is so much easier to talk of poverty than to think of the poor, to argue the rights of capital than to see its results. Pretty soon we come to think of the theories and abstract ideas as things in themselves.

WALTER LIPPMANN, "SOME NECESSARY ICONOCLASM," *A PREFACE TO POLITICS* (1914)

9. For every fact there is an *infinity* of hypotheses. The more you *look* the more you *see*.

ROBERT M. PIRSIG, *ZEN AND THE ART OF MOTORCYCLE MAINTENANCE* (1974)

10. It is only theory that makes men completely incautious.

BERTRAND RUSSELL, "IDEAS THAT HAVE HARMED MANKIND," *UNPOPULAR ESSAYS* (1950)

11. Theory helps us to bear our ignorance of facts.

GEORGE SANTAYANA, "THE AVERAGE MODIFIED IN THE DIRECTION OF PLEASURE," *THE SENSE OF BEAUTY* (1896)

12. It is better to emit a scream in the shape of a theory than to be entirely insensible to the jars and incongruities of life and take everything as it comes in a forlorn stupidity.

ROBERT LOUIS STEVENSON, "CRABBED AGE AND YOUTH," *VIRGINIBUS PUERISQUE* (1881)

13. Let us work without theorizing ... 'tis the only way to make life endurable.

VOLTAIRE, *CANDIDE* (1759), 30

14. The utmost abstractions are the true weapons with which to control our thought of concrete fact.

ALFRED NORTH WHITEHEAD, *SCIENCE AND THE MODERN WORLD* (1925), 2

THIEF

See 934. STEALING

THINGS

See 646. OBJECTS

THINKING

See 975. THOUGHT

975. THOUGHT

See also 24. AFTERTHOUGHT; 443. IDEAS; 492. INTELLECTUALS AND INTELLECTUALISM; 493. INTELLIGENCE; 590. MIND; 694. PHILOSOPHERS AND PHILOSOPHY; 785. REASON; 818. REVERIE

1. Our life is what our thoughts make it.

MARCUS AURELIUS, *MEDITATIONS* (2ND C.), 4.3, TR. MORRIS HICKEY MORGAN

2. Since it is seldom clear whether intellectual activity denotes a superior mode of being or a vital deficiency, opinion swings between considering intellect a privilege and seeing it as a handicap.

JACQUES BARZUN, *THE HOUSE OF INTELLECT* (1959), 2

3. One thought fills immensity.

WILLIAM BLAKE, "PROVERBS OF HELL," *THE MARRIAGE OF HEAVEN AND HELL* (1790)

4. In itself, a thought, / A slumbering thought, is capable of years, / And curdles a long life into one hour.

BYRON, "THE DREAM" (1816), 1

5. We get into the habit of living before acquiring the habit of thinking. In that race which daily hastens us toward death, the body maintains its irreparable lead.

ALBERT CAMUS, *THE MYTH OF SISYPHUS* (1955), TR. JUSTIN O'BRIEN

6. The highest possible stage in moral culture is when we recognize that we ought to control our thoughts.

CHARLES DARWIN, *THE DESCENT OF MAN* (1871), 4

7. I think, therefore I am.

DESCARTES, *DISCOURSE ON METHOD* (1639), 4

8. What was once thought can never be unthought.

FRIEDRICH DÜRRENMATT, *THE PHYSICISTS* (1962), 2, TR. JAMES KIRKUP

9. If a man sits down to think, he is immediately asked if he has the headache.

EMERSON, *JOURNALS,* 1833

10. Intellect annuls fate. So far as a man thinks, he is free.

EMERSON, "FATE," *THE CONDUCT OF LIFE* (1860)

11. Thought makes every thing fit for use.

EMERSON, "THE POET," *ESSAYS: SECOND SERIES* (1844)

12. To think is to act.

EMERSON, "SPIRITUAL LAWS," *ESSAYS: FIRST SERIES* (1841)

13. What is the hardest task in the world? To think.

EMERSON, *JOURNALS,* 1836

14. All thought is a feat of association: having what's in front of you bring up something in your mind that you almost didn't know you knew.

ROBERT FROST, INTERVIEW, *WRITERS AT WORK: SECOND SERIES* (1963)

15. Those that think must govern those that toil.

OLIVER GOLDSMITH, *THE TRAVELLER* (1765), 372

16. Thinking is hard work. One can't bear burdens and ideas at the same time.

RÉMY DE GOURMONT, *PROMENADES PHILOSOPHIQUES* (1905–09)

17. The secret thoughts of a man run over all things, holy, profane, clean, obscene, grave, and light, without shame or blame.

THOMAS HOBBES, *LEVIATHAN* (1651), 1.7

18. There is one disadvantage which the man of philosophical habits of mind suffers, as compared with the man of action. While he is taking an enlarged and rational view of the matter before him, he lets his chance slip through his fingers.

OLIVER WENDELL HOLMES, SR., *THE PROFESSOR AT THE BREAKFAST TABLE* (1860), 11

19. We find it hard to get and to keep any private property in thought. Other people are all the time saying the same things we are hoarding to say when we get ready.

OLIVER WENDELL HOLMES, SR., *THE POET AT THE BREAKFAST TABLE* (1872), 11

20. Every real thought on every real subject knocks the wind out of somebody or other.

OLIVER WENDELL HOLMES, SR., *THE AUTOCRAT OF THE BREAKFAST TABLE* (1858), 5

21. To think great thoughts you must be heroes as well as idealists.

OLIVER WENDELL HOLMES, JR., LECTURE, HARVARD UNIVERSITY, FEB. 17, 1886

22. To meditate is to labour; to think is to act.

VICTOR HUGO, "COSETTE," *LES MISÉRABLES* (1862), 7.8, TR. CHARLES E. WILBOUR

23. You may derive thoughts from others; your way of thinking, the mould in which your thoughts are cast, must be your own.

CHARLES LAMB, "THE OLD AND THE NEW SCHOOLMASTER," *ESSAYS OF ELIA* (1823)

24. We do not at present educate people to think but, rather, to have opinions, and that is something altogether different.

LOUIS L'AMOUR, *EDUCATION OF A WANDERING MAN* (1989)

25. My thoughts are my company; I can bring them together, select them, detain them, dismiss them.

WALTER SAVAGE LANDOR, "DIOGENES AND PLATO," *IMAGINARY CONVERSATIONS* (1824–53)

26. The thoughts that come often unsought, and, as it were, drop into the mind, are commonly the most valuable of any we have.

JOHN LOCKE, LETTER TO SAMUEL BOLD, MAY 16, 1699

27. Horror films do not prepare us for the hours lost in searching after one clear thought.

NORMAN MAILER, *TOUGH GUYS DON'T DANCE* (1984)

28. All deep, earnest thinking is but the intrepid effort of the soul to keep the open independence of her sea, while the wildest winds of heaven and earth conspire to cast her on the treacherous, slavish shore.

HERMAN MELVILLE, *MOBY-DICK* (1851), 23

29. Thinking is, or ought to be, a coolness and a calmness; and our poor hearts throb, and our poor brains beat too much for that.

HERMAN MELVILLE, *MOBY-DICK* (1851), 135

30. Most thinkers write badly, because they communicate not only their thoughts, but also the thinking of them.

NIETZSCHE, *HUMAN, ALL TOO HUMAN* (1878), 188, TR. HELEN ZIMMERN

31. Profundity of thought belongs to youth, clarity of thought to old age.

NIETZSCHE, *MISCELLANEOUS MAXIMS AND OPINIONS* (1879), 289, TR. PAUL V. COHN

32. Thought is not a gift to man but a laborious, precarious and volatile acquisition.

JOSÉ ORTEGA Y GASSET, "IN SEARCH OF GOETHE FROM WITHIN, LETTER TO A GERMAN," *PARTISAN REVIEW,* DECEMBER 1949, TR. WILLARD R. TRASK

33. Thinking is the endeavor to capture reality by means of ideas.

JOSÉ ORTEGA Y GASSET, *THE DEHUMANIZATION OF ART* (1925)

34. By space the universe encompasses and swallows me up like an atom; by thought I comprehend the world.

PASCAL, *PENSÉES* (1670), 348, TR. W. F. TROTTER

35. Man is but a reed, the feeblest thing in nature; but he is a thinking reed.

PASCAL, *PENSÉES* (1670), 347, TR. W. F. TROTTER

36. Man is obviously made to think. It is his whole dignity and his whole merit.

PASCAL, *PENSÉES* (1670), 146, TR. W. F. TROTTER

37. Mental reflection is so much more interesting than TV it's a shame more people don't switch over to it.

ROBERT M. PIRSIG, *ZEN AND THE ART OF MOTORCYCLE MAINTENANCE* (1974)

38. All the mind's activity is easy if it is not subjected to reality.

MARCEL PROUST, *REMEMBRANCE OF THINGS PAST: CITIES OF THE PLAIN* (1913–27)

39. Thought is essentially practical in the sense that but for thought no motion would be an action, no change a progress.

GEORGE SANTAYANA, *THE LIFE OF REASON: REASON IN COMMON SENSE* (1905–06), 9

40. Nimble thought can jump both sea and land.

SHAKESPEARE, *SONNETS* (1609), 44.7

41. The body always ends by being a bore. Nothing remains beautiful and interesting except thought, because the thought is the life.

GEORGE BERNARD SHAW, *BACK TO METHUSELAH* (1921), 5

42. We pass thoughts around, from mind to mind, so compulsively and with such speed that the brains of mankind often appear, functionally, to be undergoing fusion.

LEWIS THOMAS, "ON PROBABILITY AND POSSIBILITY," *THE LIVES OF A CELL* (1974)

43. Great thoughts come from the heart.

VAUVENARGUES, *REFLECTIONS AND MAXIMS* (1746), 127, TR. F. G. STEVENS

44. When a thought is too weak to be expressed simply, it should be rejected.

VAUVENARGUES, *REFLECTIONS AND MAXIMS* (1746), 3

45. I have thought too much to deign to act.

VILLIERS DE L'ISLE-ADAM, *AXEL* (1890), 4.2

46. Those who think are excessively few; and those few do not set themselves to disturb the world.

VOLTAIRE, "SOUL," *PHILOSOPHICAL DICTIONARY* (1764)

47. Thought depends absolutely on the stomach, but in spite of that, those who have the best stomachs are not the best thinkers.

VOLTAIRE, LETTER TO D'ALEMBERT, AUG. 20, 1770

48. I know what I'm thinking bout, I think. Nothing. And as much of it as I can.

ALICE WALKER, *THE COLOR PURPLE* (1982)

49. Mind is the great lever of all things; human thought is the process by which human ends are ultimately answered.

DANIEL WEBSTER, ADDRESS ON LAYING THE CORNERSTONE OF THE BUNKER HILL MONUMENT, BOSTON, MASS., JUNE 17, 1825

50. There's nothing of so infinite vexation / As man's own thoughts.

JOHN WEBSTER, *THE WHITE DEVIL* (1612), 5.6

51. It belongs to the self-respect of intellect to pursue every tangle of thought to its final unravelment.

ALFRED NORTH WHITEHEAD, *SCIENCE AND THE MODERN WORLD* (1925), 12

52. The importance of an individual thinker owes something to chance. For it depends upon the fate of his ideas in the minds of his successors.

ALFRED NORTH WHITEHEAD, *SCIENCE AND THE MODERN WORLD* (1925), 2

53. It is so easy for people to have sympathy with suffering. It is so difficult for them to have sympathy with thought.

OSCAR WILDE, *THE ARTIST AS CRITIC: CRITICAL WRITINGS OF OSCAR WILDE,* ED. RICHARD ELLMAN (1969)

54. The essence of thought, as the essence of life, is growth.

OSCAR WILDE, *THE ARTIST AS CRITIC: CRITICAL WRITINGS OF OSCAR WILDE,* RICHARD ELLMAN, ED. (1969)

55. Thinking is the most unhealthy thing in the world, and people die of it just as they die of any other disease.

OSCAR WILDE, "THE DECAY OF LYING," *INTENTIONS* (1891)

56. Uncompromising thought is the luxury of the closeted recluse. Untrammeled reasoning is the indulgence of the philosopher, of the dreamer of sweet dreams.

WOODROW WILSON, ADDRESS, UNIVERSITY OF TENNESSEE, JUNE 17, 1890

57. A man's thinking goes on within his consciousness in a seclusion in comparison with which any physical seclusion is an exhibition to public view.

LUDWIG WITTGENSTEIN, *PHILOSOPHICAL INVESTIGATIONS* (1953), 2.2, TR. G. E. M. ANSCOMBE

58. Things thought too long can be no longer thought, / For beauty dies of beauty, worth of worth, / And ancient lineaments are blotted out.

WILLIAM BUTLER YEATS, "THE GYRES," *NEW POEMS* (1938)

976. THREAT

See also 216. DANGER

1. A bluff taken seriously is more useful than a serious threat interpreted as a bluff.

HENRY A. KISSINGER, *AMERICAN FOREIGN POLICY* (1969)

2. The rattling thunderbolt hath but his clap, the lightning but his flash, and as they both come in a moment, so do they both end in a minute.

JOHN LYLY, *EUPHUES: THE ANATOMY OF WIT* (1579)

977. THRIFT

See also 324. EXTRAVAGANCE

1. Men are divided between those who are as thrifty as if they would live forever, and those who are as extravagant as if they were going to die the next day.

ARISTOTLE (4TH C. B.C.), QUOTED IN DIOGENES LAERTIUS' *LIVES AND OPINIONS OF EMINENT PHILOSOPHERS* (3RD C. A.D.), TR. R. D. HICKS

2. I am money's medium. It passes through me—taxes, insurance, mortgage, child support, rent, legal fees. All this dignified blundering costs plenty.

SAUL BELLOW, *HERZOG* (1964)

3. A penny saved is a penny to squander.

AMBROSE BIERCE, "SAW," *THE DEVIL'S DICTIONARY* (1881–1911)

4. Economy is a distributive virtue, and consists not in saving but in selection.

EDMUND BURKE, *LETTER TO A NOBLE LORD* (1796)

5. Expense, and great expense, may be an essential part of true economy.

EDMUND BURKE, *LETTER TO A NOBLE LORD* (1796)

6. Men do not realize how great an income thrift is.

CICERO, *PARADOXA STOICORUM* (46 B.C.)

7. Annual income twenty pounds, annual expenditure nineteen nineteen six, result happiness. Annual income twenty pounds, annual expenditure twenty pounds ought and six, result misery.

CHARLES DICKENS, *DAVID COPPERFIELD* (1849–50), 12

8. A man often pays dear for a small frugality.

EMERSON, "COMPENSATION," *ESSAYS: FIRST SERIES* (1841)

9. Economy, in the estimation of common minds, often means the absence of all taste and comfort.

SYDNEY SMITH, QUOTED IN LADY S. HOLLAND'S *MEMOIR* (1855), V. 1.8

10. Anyone who lives within his means suffers from a lack of imagination.

LIONEL STANDER, QUOTED IN HELEN LAWRENSON'S "LIONEL STANDER," *PLAYBOY*, DECEMBER 1967

11. Let us all be happy, and live within our means, even if we have to borrer money to do it with.

ARTEMUS WARD, "SCIENCE AND NATURAL HISTORY," *ARTEMUS WARD IN LONDON* (1872)

12. I have noticed that it is the easy-going ones among us who have the best time; in this climate, at the rate a stove eats wood, if a man were to grow too thrifty or forehanded he'd never be able to crawl out from under his woodpile.

E.B. WHITE, *ONE MAN'S MEAT* (1944)

978. TIME

See also 302. ETERNITY; 540. LIFE, STAGES OF; 990. TRANSIENCE

1. Time brings all things to pass.

AESCHYLUS, *THE LIBATION BEARERS* (458 B.C.), TR. RICHMOND LATTIMORE

2. Time in his aging overtakes all things alike.

AESCHYLUS, *THE EUMENIDES* (458 B.C.), TR. RICHMOND LATTIMORE

3. Time in its aging course teaches all things.

AESCHYLUS, *PROMETHEUS BOUND* (C. 478 B.C.), TR. DAVID GRENE

4. Time and space are fragments of the infinite for the use of finite creatures.

HENRI FRÉDÉRIC AMIEL, *JOURNAL*, NOV. 16, 1864, TR. MRS. HUMPHRY WARD

5. Since time is the one immaterial object which we cannot influence—neither speed up nor slow down, add to nor diminish—it is an imponderably valuable gift.

MAYA ANGELOU, "THE SWEETNESS OF CHARITY," *WOULDN'T TAKE NOTHING FOR MY JOURNEY NOW* (1993)

6. There was no "before" the beginning of the universe, because once upon a time there was no time.

John D. Barrow, *The Origin of the Universe* (1994)

7. Killing time is the chief end of our society.

Ugo Betti, *The Fugitive* (1953), 1, tr. G. H. McWilliam

8. The ruins of Time build mansions in Eternity.

William Blake, letter to William Hayley, May 6, 1800

9. Time lost is time when we have not lived a full human life, time unenriched by experience, creative endeavor, enjoyment and suffering.

Dietrich Bonhoeffer, "After Ten Years," *Letters and Papers from Prison* (1953), tr. Eberhard Bethge

10. Time is the only true purgatory.

Samuel Butler (d. 1902), "Higgledy-Piggledy," *Note-Books* (1912)

11. Time! the Corrector where our judgments err, / The test of Truth, Love—sole philosopher, / For all beside are sophists.

Byron, *Childe Harold's Pilgrimage* (1812–18), 4.130

12. Time ripens all things. No man's born wise.

Cervantes, *Don Quixote* (1605–15), 2.4.33, tr. John Ozell

13. Time heals nothing—which should make us better able to minister.

Peter De Vries, *The Blood of the Lamb* (1962)

14. Time is a Test of Trouble— / But not a Remedy— / If such it prove, it prove too / There was no Malady—.

Emily Dickinson, poem (c. 1863)

15. Time is the continuous loop, the snakeskin with scales endlessly overlapping without beginning or end, or time is an ascending spiral if you will, like a child's toy Slinky.

Annie Dillard, "Untying the Knot," *Pilgrim at Tinker Creek* (1974)

16. The days come and go like muffled and veiled figures sent from a distant friendly party, but they say nothing, and if we do not use the gifts they bring, they carry them as silently away.

Emerson, *Journals,* 1847

17. Time is a file that wears and makes no noise.

English Proverb

18. Time was rushing around me like water around a big wet rock. The only difference is, I was not so durable as stones. Very quickly I would be smoothed away.

Louise Erdrich, "The Plunge of the Brave," *Love Medicine* (1984)

19. [I]t is never possible for a novelist to deny time inside the fabric of his novel: he must cling, however lightly, to the thread of his story, he must touch the interminable tapeworm, otherwise he becomes unintelligible, which, in his case, is a blunder.

E.M. Forster, "The Story," *Aspects of the Novel* (1927)

20. Time deals gently only with those who take it gently.

Anatole France, *The Crime of Sylvestre Bonnard* (1881), 2, tr. Lafcadio Hearn

21. Dost thou love life, then do not squander time, for that's the stuff life is made of.

Benjamin Franklin, "The Way to Wealth" (July 7, 1757)

22. Modern man thinks he loses something—time—when he does not do things quickly; yet he does not know what to do with the time he gains—except kill it.

Erich Fromm, *The Art of Loving* (1956), 4

23. Time cures one of everything—even of living.

Jules de Goncourt, *Journal,* Oct. 14, 1856, tr. Robert Baldick

24. God Himself chasteneth not with a rod but with time.

Baltasar Gracián, *The Art of Worldly Wisdom* (1647), 55, tr. Joseph Jacobs

25. The weeks go by so slow I almost think time passin backwards.

Winston Groom, *Forrest Gump* (1986)

26. Time is love, above all else. It is the most precious commodity in the world and should be lavished on those we care most about.

Sydney J. Harris, "Money Is Time," *Clearing the Ground* (1986)

27. I have had the irreplaceable opportunity of learning my profession with the proper tools, the most important of which is not a pencil or a typewriter, but the necessary time to think before using them.

Moss Hart, *Act One* (1959)

28. The laws of science do not distinguish between the past and the future.

Stephen W. Hawking, *A Brief History of Time* (1988)

29. Time flies over us, but leaves its shadow behind.

Nathaniel Hawthorne, *The Marble Faun* (1860), 24

30. Most of the methods for measuring the lapse of time have, I believe, been the contrivance of monks and religious recluses, who, finding time hang heavy on their hands, were at some pains to see how they got rid of it.

William Hazlitt, "On a Sundial," *Sketches and Essays* (1839)

31. Time is the rider that breaks youth.

George Herbert, *Jacula Prudentum* (1651)

32. City people try to buy time as a rule, when they can, whereas country people are prepared to kill time, although both try to cherish in their mind's eye the notion of a better life ahead.

Edward Hoagland, "The Ridge-Slope Fox and the Knife Thrower," *The Tugman's Passage* (1982)

33. The most intractable of our experiences is the experience of Time—the intuition of duration, combined with the thought of perpetual perishing.

Aldous Huxley, *Tomorrow and Tomorrow and Tomorrow* (1956)

34. Time is but the shadow of the world upon the background of Eternity.

Jerome K. Jerome, "Clocks," *The Idle Thoughts of an Idle Fellow* (1889)

35. We know all along that time is squeezing us into a corner while we mentally rocket to each new star that flares across our sky, and yet we can't help ourselves.

Seymour Krim, "For My Brothers and Sisters in the Failure Business," in *The Art of the Personal Essay* (1994), ed. Phillip Lopate

36. Those who make the worst use of their time are the first to complain of its brevity.

La Bruyère, *Characters* (1688), 12.101, tr. Henri Van Laun

37. The only way men or women can be judged is against the canvas of their own time.

Louis L'Amour, *Education of a Wandering Man* (1989)

38. Time is an abstraction which, on earth, exists only for the human brain it has evolved.

Charles A. Lindbergh, "The Reefs of Biak," *Autobiography of Values* (1978)

39. For tribal man space was the uncontrollable mystery. For technological man it is time that occupies the same role.

Marshall McLuhan, "Magic That Changes Mood," *The Mechanical Bride* (1951)

40. When one day is like all the others, then they are all like one; complete uniformity would make the longest life seem short, and as though it had stolen away from us unawares.

Thomas Mann, *The Magic Mountain* (1924), 4.2, tr. H. T. Lowe-Porter

41. But at my back I always hear / Time's wingèd chariot hurrying near.

Andrew Marvell, "To His Coy Mistress" (1650)

42. Time is a great legalizer, even in the field of morals.

H. L. Mencken, *A Book of Prefaces* (1917), 4.6

43. [T]he convenience of timekeeping is greatly overrated; and the people who practice it so faithfully that they lose the capacity for appreciating the fixed and the static and the spatially related experiences cut themselves off from a good part of reality.

Lewis Mumford, *Findings and Keepings. Analects for an Autobiography* (1975)

44. There is one kind of robber whom the law does not strike at, and who steals what is most precious to men: time.

Napoleon I, *Maxims* (1804–15)

45. Time flies apace—we would fain believe that everything flies forward with it.

Nietzsche, *The Will to Power* (1888), tr. Anthony M. Ludovici

46. Time at length becomes justice.

Cynthia Ozick, "Truman Capote Reconsidered," *Art & Ardor* (1983)

47. Time makes more converts than reason.

Thomas Paine, introduction to *Common Sense* (1776)

48. Time heals griefs and quarrels, for we change and are no longer the same persons.

Pascal, *Pensées* (1670), 122, tr. W. F. Trotter

49. You are all right on time, except for the fact that time is the enemy of us all, and especially of the writer.

Maxwell Perkins, *Editor to Author: The Letters of Maxwell Perkins* (1950), ed. John Hall Wheelock

TIME

50. Life hurries on, a frantic refugee, / And Death, with great forced marches, follows fast; / And all the present leagues with all the past / And all the future to make war on me.

PETRARCH, "LAURA DEAD," *CANZONIERE* (1360), 231

51. Years following years steal something every day; / At last they steal us from ourselves away.

ALEXANDER POPE, *IMITATIONS OF HORACE* (1733–38), 2.2.72

52. It seems no more than right that men should seize time by the forelock, for the rude old fellow, sooner or later, pulls all their hair out.

GEORGE DENNISON PRENTICE, *PRENTICEANA* (1860)

53. In theory one is aware that the earth revolves, but in practice one does not perceive it, the ground upon which one treads seems not to move, and one can live undisturbed. So it is with Time in one's life.

MARCEL PROUST, *REMEMBRANCE OF THINGS PAST: WITHIN A BUDDING GROVE* (1913–27), TR. C. K. SCOTT-MONCRIEFF

54. Time, which changes people, does not alter the image we have retained of them.

MARCEL PROUST, *REMEMBRANCE OF THINGS PAST: THE PAST RECAPTURED* (1913–27)

55. Don't keep saying, "I don't know where the time goes." It goes the same place it's always gone and no one has ever known where that is.

ANDREW A. ROONEY, "A PENNY SAVED IS A WASTE OF TIME," *PIECES OF MY MIND* (1984)

56. Time can be such a menace to a man. By this age do that; by that age do better.

ROGER ROSENBLATT, "REAL MEN DON'T DIE," *THE MAN IN THE WATER* (1994)

57. Both in thought and in feeling, even though time be real, to realise the unimportance of time is the gate of wisdom.

BERTRAND RUSSELL, TITLE ESSAY, *MYSTICISM AND LOGIC* (1917)

58. Time is like an enterprising manager always bent on staging some new and surprising production, without knowing very well what it will be.

GEORGE SANTAYANA, "TIPPERARY," *SOLILOQUIES IN ENGLAND* (1922)

59. Time is that in which all things pass away.

SCHOPENHAUER, "THE VANITY OF EXISTENCE," *PARERGA AND PARALIPOMENA* (1851), TR. T. BAILEY SAUNDERS

60. Time heals what reason cannot.

SENECA, *AGAMEMNON* (1ST C.)

61. Come what come may, / Time and the hour runs through the roughest day.

SHAKESPEARE, *MACBETH* (1605–06), 1.3.146

62. The whirligig of time brings in his revenges.

SHAKESPEARE, *TWELFTH NIGHT* (1599–1600), 5.1.384

63. Time's glory is to calm contending kings, / To unmask falsehood and bring truth to light.

SHAKESPEARE, *THE RAPE OF LUCRECE* (1594), 939

64. Great Time makes all things dim.

SOPHOCLES, *AJAX* (C. 447 B.C.), TR. JOHN MOORE

65. Time is a kindly God.

SOPHOCLES, *ELECTRA* (C. 418–14 B.C.), TR. DAVID GRENE

66. No preacher is listened to but Time, which gives us the same train and turn of thought that elder people have in vain tried to put into our heads before.

JONATHAN SWIFT, *THOUGHTS ON VARIOUS SUBJECTS* (1711)

67. Time turns the old days to derision, / Our loves into corpses or wives.

ALGERNON CHARLES SWINBURNE, "DOLORES" (1866)

68. The butterfly counts not months but moments, / and has time enough.

RABINDRANATH TAGORE, *FIREFLIES* (1928)

69. Time is a wealth of change, but the clock in its parody makes it mere change and no wealth.

RABINDRANATH TAGORE, *STRAY BIRDS* (1916), 139

70. We lack not rhymes and reasons, / As on this whirligig of Time / We circle with the seasons.

LORD TENNYSON, "WILL WATERPROOF'S LYRICAL MONOLOGUE" (1842)

71. Our costliest expenditure is time.

THEOPHRASTUS (C. 370–287 B.C.), QUOTED IN DIOGENES LAERTIUS' *LIVES AND OPINIONS OF EMINENT PHILOSOPHERS* (3RD C. A.D.), TR. R. D. HICKS

72. We must expect everything and fear everything from time and from men.

VAUVENARGUES, *REFLECTIONS AND MAXIMS* (1746), 102

73. Time bears away all things, even the mind.

VERGIL, *ECLOGUES* (37 B.C.), 9.51, TR. T. F. ROYDS

74. Time moves slowly, but passes quickly.

ALICE WALKER, *THE COLOR PURPLE* (1982)

75. Time is anonymous; when we give it a face, it's the same face the world over.

EUDORA WELTY, "SOME NOTES ON TIME IN FICTION," *THE EYE OF THE STORY* (1978)

76. I think time is a merciless thing. I think life is a process of burning oneself out and time is the fire that burns you. But I think the spirit of man is a good adversary.

TENNESSEE WILLIAMS, *NEW YORK POST,* APRIL 30, 1958

77. Time is the longest distance between two places.

TENNESSEE WILLIAMS, *THE GLASS MENAGERIE* (1945), 1

78. The years like great black oxen tread the world, / And God the herdsman goads them on behind, / And I am broken by their passing feet.

WILLIAM BUTLER YEATS, *THE COUNTESS CATHLEEN* (1892), 5

79. We take no note of time / But from its loss.

EDWARD YOUNG, *NIGHT THOUGHTS* (1742–46), 1.55

80. A composer's job involves the decoration of fragments of time. Without music to decorate it, time is just a bunch of boring production deadlines or dates by which bills must be paid.

FRANK ZAPPA, *THE REAL FRANK ZAPPA BOOK* (1989), WITH PETER OCCHIOGROSSO

979. TIMELINESS

See also 231. DELAY; 727. PREMATURENESS; 765. PUNCTUALITY; 949. SUITABILITY

1. A word spoken in due season, how good is it!

BIBLE, PROVERBS 15:23

2. To every thing there is a season, and a time to every purpose under the heaven.

BIBLE, ECCLESIASTES 3:1

3. If you trap the moment before it's ripe, / The tears of repentence you'll certainly wipe; / But if once you let the ripe moment go / You can never wipe off the tears of woe.

WILLIAM BLAKE, "THE MARRIAGE RING" (1793–99)

4. There are times when sense may be unseasonable, as well as truth.

WILLIAM CONGREVE, *THE DOUBLE-DEALER* (1694), 1.1

5. I hate it in friends when they come too late to help.

EURIPIDES, *RHESUS* (C. 455–41 B.C.), TR. RICHMOND LATTIMORE

6. Timeliness is best in all matters.

HESIOD, *WORKS AND DAYS* (8TH C. B.C.), 694, TR. RICHMOND LATTIMORE

7. To each thing belongs / its measure. Occasion is best to know.

PINDAR, *ODES* (5TH C. B.C.), OLYMPIA 13, TR. RICHMOND LATTIMORE

8. How many things by season seasoned are / To their right praise and true perfection!

SHAKESPEARE, *THE MERCHANT OF VENICE* (1596–97), 5.1.107

9. In season, all is good.

SOPHOCLES, *OEDIPUS THE KING* (C. 430 B.C.), TR. DAVID GRENE

THE TIMES

See 298. ERA

980. TIMIDITY

See also 92. BOLDNESS; 112. CAUTIOUSNESS; 304. EVASION; 343. FEAR; 435. HUMILITY

1. There is that destroyeth his own soul through bashfulness.

APOCRYPHA, ECCLESIASTICUS 20:22

2. Shyness has a strange element of narcissism, a belief that how we look, how we perform, is truly important to other people.

ANDRÉ DUBUS, "UNDER THE LIGHTS," *BROKEN VESSELS* (1991)

3. Do not be too timid and squeamish about your actions. All life is an experiment.

EMERSON, *JOURNALS,* 1842

4. There are men whose language is strong and defying enough, yet their eyes and their actions ask leave of other men to live.

EMERSON, *JOURNALS,* 1832

5. He suddenly became shy and developed a conceited grin—the grin of the village yokel whose cricket score is mentioned before a stranger.

E.M. FORSTER, *WHERE ANGELS FEAR TO TREAD* (1920)

6. He will never have true friends who is afraid of making enemies.

WILLIAM HAZLITT, *CHARACTERISTICS* (1823), 401

7. Happiness hates the timid! So does Science!

EUGENE O'NEILL, *STRANGE INTERLUDE* (1928), 4

8. What is more mortifying than to feel that you have missed the plum for want of courage to shake the tree?

LOGAN PEARSALL SMITH, *AFTERTHOUGHTS* (1931), 1

981. TIPPING

1. Perhaps the five-pound note I slipped into his hand was excessive, but, lacking a diamond the size of the Cullinan, I had no adequate means of expressing my gratitude.

S.J. PERELMAN, *THE RISING GORGE* (1961)

TIREDNESS

See 341. FATIGUE

TITLES

See 619. NAMES

982. TOBACCO

1. He who doth not smoke hath either known no great griefs, or refuseth himself the softest consolation, next to that which comes from heaven.

BULWER-LYTTON, *WHAT WILL HE DO WITH IT?* (1859), 1.6

2. To the average cigarette smoker the world is his ashtray.

ALEXANDER CHASE, *PERSPECTIVES* (1966)

3. Smokers, male and female, inject and excuse idleness in their lives every time they light a cigarette.

COLETTE, "FREEDOM," *EARTHLY PARADISE* (1966), 2

4. A man of no conversation should smoke.

EMERSON, *JOURNALS,* 1866

5. The believing we do something when we do nothing is the first illusion of tobacco.

EMERSON, *JOURNALS,* 1859

6. A custom [smoking] loathsome to the eye, harmful to the brain, dangerous to the lungs, and in the black stinking fume thereof, nearest resembling the horrible Stygian smoke of the pit that is bottomless.

JAMES I OF ENGLAND, *COUNTERBLASTE TO TOBACCO* (1604)

7. A woman is only a woman, but a good cigar is a smoke.

RUDYARD KIPLING, "THE BETROTHED", *DEPARTMENTAL DITTIES* (1886)

8. It is now proved beyond doubt that smoking is one of the leading causes of statistics.

FLETCHER KNEBEL, *READER'S DIGEST,* DECEMBER 1961

9. For thy sake, tobacco, I / Would do anything but die.

CHARLES LAMB, *A FAREWELL TO TOBACCO* (1805)

10. This very night I am going to leave off tobacco! Surely there must be some other world in which this unconquerable purpose shall be realized.

CHARLES LAMB, LETTER TO THOMAS MANNING, DEC. 26, 1815

11. He stopped smoking at least once a month. He went through with it like the solid citizen he was: admitted the evils of tobacco, courageously made resolves, laid out plans to check the vice, tapered off his allowance of cigars, and expounded the pleasures of virtuousness to every one he met. He did everything, in fact, except stop smoking.

SINCLAIR LEWIS, *BABBITT* (1922)

12. Some things are better eschewed than chewed, tobacco is one of them.

GEORGE DENNISON PRENTICE, *PRENTICEANA* (1860)

13. Idly, but not idle—for in leisure there is neither idleness nor haste—I watched the slow wreathing of smoke, into the still air, from my pipe.

OLIVER SACKS, *A LEG TO STAND ON* (1984)

14. Tilting his head back, he slowly released an enormous quantity of smoke from his mouth and drew it up through his nostrils. He continued to smoke in this "French-inhale" style.

J.D. SALINGER, "JUST BEFORE THE WAR WITH THE ESKIMOS," IN *NINE STORIES BY J.D. SALINGER* (1953)

15. Fuller's cigar in the night was a beacon warning carefree, frivolous people away. It was plainly a cigar smoked in anger.

KURT VONNEGUT, *WELCOME TO THE MONKEY HOUSE* (1968)

TODAY

See 729. PRESENT

983. TOGETHERNESS

See also 31. ALOOFNESS; 151. COMMUNITY; 152. COMPANY; 499. INTIMACY

1. Something there is that doesn't love a wall, / That wants it down.

ROBERT FROST, "MENDING WALL," *NORTH OF BOSTON* (1914)

2. We go right enough, darling, if we go wrong together!

GEORGE SANTAYANA, *PERSONS AND PLACES: MY HOST THE WORLD* (1953), 2

3. Togetherness is a substitute sense of community, a counterfeit communion.

GABRIEL VAHANIAN, *THE DEATH OF GOD* (1962), 1

984. TOLERANCE

See also 120. CHARITY; 500. INTOLERANCE; 519. KINDNESS

1. The peak of tolerance is most readily achieved by those who are not burdened with convictions.

ALEXANDER CHASE, *PERSPECTIVES* (1966)

2. If you will please people, you must please them in their own way; and as you cannot make them what they should be, you must take them as they are.

LORD CHESTERFIELD, *LETTERS TO HIS SON*, DEC. 5, 1749

3. Persecution was at least a sign of personal interest. Tolerance is composed of nine parts of apathy to one of brotherly love.

FRANK MOORE COLBY, "TRIALS OF AN ENCYCLOPEDIST," *THE COLBY ESSAYS* (1926), V. 1

4. True goodness is not without that germ of greatness that can bear with patience the mistakes of the ignorant.

CHARLES CALEB COLTON, *LACON* (1825), 2.39

5. Racist, sexist, and homophobic thoughts cannot, alas, be abolished by fiat but only by the time-honored methods of persuasion, education and exposure to the other guy's—or excuse me, woman's—point of view.

BARBARA EHRENREICH, "TEACH DIVERSITY WITH A SMILE," *TIME* MAGAZINE, APRIL 8, 1991

6. Laws alone cannot secure freedom of expression; in order that every man present his views without penalty there must be a spirit of tolerance in the entire population.

EINSTEIN, *OUT OF MY LATER YEARS* (1950), 6

7. [Tolerance] is just a makeshift, suitable for an overcrowded and overheated planet. It carries on when love gives out, and love generally gives out as soon as we move away from our home and our friends.

E. M. FORSTER, "TOLERANCE," *TWO CHEERS FOR DEMOCRACY* (1951)

8. We are all tolerant enough of those who do not agree with us, provided only they are sufficiently miserable.

DAVID GRAYSON, *ADVENTURES IN CONTENTMENT* (1907), 10

9. People tolerate those they fear further than those they love.

EDGAR WATSON HOWE, *COUNTRY TOWN SAYINGS* (1911)

10. It does me no injury for my neighbor to say there are twenty gods, or no God.

THOMAS JEFFERSON, *NOTES ON THE STATE OF VIRGINIA* (1784–85)

11. The highest result of education is tolerance.

HELEN KELLER, *OPTIMISM* (1903), 2

12. Mankind are greater gainers by suffering each other to live as seems good to themselves, than by compelling each to live as seems good to the rest.

JOHN STUART MILL, *ON LIBERTY* (1859), 1

13. It is a good thing to demand liberty for ourselves and for those who agree with us, but it is a better thing and a rarer thing to give liberty to others who do not agree with us.

FRANKLIN D. ROOSEVELT, RADIO ADDRESS, NOV. 22, 1933

14. So long as a man rides his hobbyhorse peaceably and quietly along the King's highway, and neither compels you or me to get up behind him,—pray, Sir, what have either you or I to do with it?

LAURENCE STERNE, *TRISTRAM SHANDY* (1759–67), 1.7

985. TOTALITARIANISM

See also 395. GOVERNMENT; 1002. TYRANNY

1. It belongs among the refinements of totalitarian government in our century that they don't permit their opponents to die a great, dramatic martyr's death for their convictions.

HANNAH ARENDT, *EICHMANN IN JERUSALEM* (1963)

2. I suspect that in our loathing of totalitarianism, there is infused a good deal of admiration for its efficiency.

T. S. ELIOT, "THE IDEA OF A CHRISTIAN SOCIETY" (1939)

3. I have read somewhere that in a totalitarian system martyrdom does better than thought.

VÁCLAV HAVEL, "SIX ASIDES ABOUT CULTURE," *OPEN LETTERS: SELECTED WRITINGS 1965–1990* (1991) SELECTED AND EDITED BY PAUL WILSON

4. Totalitarianism spells simplification: an enormous reduction in the variety of aims, motives, interests, human types, and, above all, in the categories and units of power.

ERIC HOFFER, *THE ORDEAL OF CHANGE* (1964), 12

5. You have not converted a man because you have silenced him.

JOHN MORLEY, *ON COMPROMISE* (1874)

TOUCH

See 882. SENSES

TOURISM

See 992. TRAVEL

TRADE

See 104. BUSINESS AND COMMERCE; 1037. VOCATIONS

986. TRADITION

See also 42. ANTIQUITY; 136. CLASSICS; 213. CUSTOM; 441. ICONOCLASM; 676. PAST

1. They that reverence too much old times are but a scorn to the new.

FRANCIS BACON, "OF INNOVATIONS," *ESSAYS* (1625)

2. It is pure illusion to think that an opinion which passes down from century to century, from generation to generation, may not be entirely false.

PIERRE BAYLE, *THOUGHTS ON THE COMET* (1682)

3. We must accept all the implications of our human inheritance, one of the most important of which is the small scope of biologically transmitted behavior, and the enormous role of the cultural process of the transmission of tradition.

RUTH BENEDICT, *PATTERNS OF CULTURE* (1934)

4. Hardened round us, encasing wholly every notion we form, is a wrappage of traditions, hearsays, mere words.

THOMAS CARLYLE, *ON HEROES, HERO-WORSHIP AND THE HEROIC IN HISTORY* (1841), I

5. A love for tradition has never weakened a nation, indeed it has strengthened nations in their hour of peril; but the new view must come, the world must roll forward.

SIR WINSTON CHURCHILL, SPEECH, HOUSE OF COMMONS, NOV. 29, 1944

6. The dead govern the living.

AUGUSTE COMTE, *CATÉCHISME POSITIVISTE* (1852)

7. Tradition, thou art for suckling children, / Thou art the enlivening milk for babes, / But no meat for men is in thee.

STEPHEN CRANE, *THE BLACK RIDERS AND OTHER LINES* (1896), 45

8. A precedent embalms a principle.

BENJAMIN DISRAELI, SPEECH, FEB. 22, 1848

9. A tradition without intelligence is not worth having.

T. S. ELIOT, "AFTER STRANGE GODS" (1934)

10. There is no creation without tradition. No one creates from nothing.

CARLOS FUENTES, "HOW I STARTED TO WRITE," IN *THE ART OF THE PERSONAL ESSAY* (1994), ED. PHILLIP LOPATE

11. Much of this world's wisdom is still acquired by necromancy,—by consulting the oracular dead.

JULIUS CHARLES HARE AND AUGUSTUS WILLIAM HARE, *GUESSES AT TRUTH* (1827)

12. To rest upon a formula is a slumber that, prolonged, means death.

OLIVER WENDELL HOLMES, JR., "IDEALS AND DOUBTS," *ILLINOIS LAW REVIEW* (1915), V. 10

13. Old ways will always remain unless some one invents a new way and then lives and dies for it.

ELBERT HUBBARD, *THE NOTE BOOK* (1927)

14. Few people have ever seriously wished to be exclusively rational. The good life which most desire is a life warmed by passions and touched with that ceremonial grace which is impossible without some affectionate loyalty to traditional forms and ceremonies.

JOSEPH WOOD KRUTCH, "IGNOBLE UTOPIAS," *THE MEASURE OF MAN* (1954)

15. Worshippers of light ancestral make the present light a crime.

JAMES RUSSELL LOWELL, "THE PRESENT CRISIS" (1844)

16. Tradition is a guide and not a jailer.

W. SOMERSET MAUGHAM, *THE SUMMING UP* (1938), 60

17. Every tradition grows continually more venerable, and the more remote its origin, the more this is lost sight of. The veneration paid the tradition accumulates from generation to generation, until it at last becomes holy and excites awe.

NIETZSCHE, *HUMAN, ALL TOO HUMAN* (1878), 96, TR. HELEN ZIMMERN

18. The less men are fettered by tradition, the greater becomes the inward activity of their motives; the greater, again, in proportion thereto, the outward restlessness, the confused flux of mankind, the polyphony of strivings.

NIETZSCHE, *HUMAN, ALL TOO HUMAN* (1878), 23, TR. HELEN ZIMMERN

19. Tradition is no longer a continuity but a series of sharp breaks. The modern tradition is the tradition of revolt.

OCTAVIO PAZ, "INVENTION, UNDERDEVELOPMENT, MODERNITY," *ALTERNATING CURRENT* (1973)

20. No way of thinking or doing, however ancient, can be trusted without proof.

THOREAU, "ECONOMY," *WALDEN* (1854)

21. Loyalty to petrified opinion never yet broke a chain or freed a human soul.

MARK TWAIN, INSCRIBED BENEATH HIS BUST IN THE HALL OF FAME FOR GREAT AMERICANS, NEW YORK UNIVERSITY

987. TRAGEDY

See also 145. COMEDY; 972. THEATER

1. Tragedy, no matter how sad, becomes boring to those not caught in its addictive caress.

MAYA ANGELOU, *ALL GOD'S CHILDREN NEED TRAVELING SHOES* (1986)

2. Why is it that man desires to be made sad, beholding doleful and tragical things, which yet himself would by no means suffer?

ST. AUGUSTINE, *CONFESSIONS* (5TH C.), 3, TR. E. B. PUSEY

3. Only a great mind overthrown yields tragedy.

JACQUES BARZUN, *THE HOUSE OF INTELLECT* (1959), 2

4. One cannot balance tragedy in the scales / Unless one weighs it with the tragic heart.

STEPHEN VINCENT BENÉT, *JOHN BROWN'S BODY* (1928), 4

5. A tragedy means always a man's struggle with that which is stronger than man.

G. K. CHESTERTON, "THE BLUFF OF THE BIG SHOPS," *OUTLINE OF SANITY* (1926)

6. I suspect tragedy in the American countryside because all the people capable of it move to the big towns at twenty.

F. SCOTT FITZGERALD, *THE LETTERS OF F. SCOTT FITZGERALD* (1963), ED. ANDREW TURNBULL

7. Tragedy and comedy are simply questions of value; a little misfit in life makes us laugh; a great one is tragedy and cause for expression of grief.

ELBERT HUBBARD, *THE NOTE BOOK* (1927)

8. A tragic writer does not have to believe in God, but he must believe in man.

JOSEPH WOOD KRUTCH, "THE TRAGIC FALLACY," *THE MODERN TEMPER* (1929)

9. Ours is essentially a tragic age, so we refuse to take it tragically.

D. H. LAWRENCE, *LADY CHATTERLEY'S LOVER* (1928), 1

10. In tragedy great men are more truly great than in history. We see them only in the crises which unfold them.

NAPOLEON I, *MAXIMS* (1804–15)

11. Men play at tragedy because they do not believe in the reality of the tragedy which is actually being staged in the civilised world.

JOSÉ ORTEGA Y GASSET, *THE REVOLT OF THE MASSES* (1930), 11

12. A tragic situation exists precisely when virtue does *not* triumph but when it is still felt that man is nobler than the forces which destroy him.

GEORGE ORWELL, "LEAR, TOLSTOY AND THE FOOL," *SHOOTING AN ELEPHANT* (1950)

13. Modern discussions of the possibility of tragedy are not exercises in literary analysis; they are exercises in cultural diagnostics, more or less disguised.

SUSAN SONTAG, "THE DEATH OF TRAGEDY," *AGAINST INTERPRETATION* (1966)

14. Tragedy is a vision of nihilism, a heroic or ennobling vision of nihilism.

SUSAN SONTAG, "THE DEATH OF TRAGEDY," *AGAINST INTERPRETATION* (1966)

15. Writers of comedy have outlook, whereas writers of tragedy have, according to them, insight.

JAMES THURBER, "THE CASE FOR COMEDY," *LANTERNS AND LANCES* (1961)

16. The essence of dramatic tragedy is not unhappiness. It resides in the solemnity of the remorseless working of things.

ALFRED NORTH WHITEHEAD, *SCIENCE AND THE MODERN WORLD* (1925), 1

988. TRAINING

See also 250. DISCIPLINE; 279. EDUCATION; 404. GROWTH AND DEVELOPMENT

1. Train up a child in the way he should go: and when he is old he will not depart from it.

BIBLE, PROVERBS 22:6

2. The fear of hell, the punishment of sin, how the modern parent revolts from such teaching. Yet I will assert that far from doing us children harm, it was a

sure foundation to the world of our confidence, a master girder in our palace of delight.

JOYCE CARY, *EXCEPT THE LORD* (1953)

3. Art is long, life short; judgment difficult, opportunity transient.

GOETHE, *WILHELM MEISTER'S APPRENTICESHIP* (1795–96), 7.9

4. Life is short and the art long.

HIPPOCRATES, *APHORISMS* (C. 400 B.C.), 1.1

5. It is no hard matter to get children; but after they are born, then begins the trouble, solicitude, and care rightly to train, principle, and bring them up.

MONTAIGNE, "OF THE EDUCATION OF CHILDREN," *ESSAYS* (1580–88), TR. W. C. HAZLITT

6. Man is the only one that knows nothing, that can learn nothing without being taught. He can neither speak nor walk nor eat, and in short he can do nothing at the prompting of nature only, but weep.

PLINY THE ELDER, *NATURAL HISTORY* (1ST C.), 7.4, TR. H. T. RILEY

7. 'Tis education forms the common mind, / Just as the twig is bent the tree's inclined.

ALEXANDER POPE, *MORAL ESSAYS* (1731–35), 1.149

8. There's so much horseshit about babies; schools change every ten years. [My sister] raised a couple of nice ones by forcing them to be considerate or leave the room.... I think people act the way they're expected to act.

JOHN STEINBECK, *STEINBECK: A LIFE IN LETTERS,* (1975), EDS. ELAINE STEINBECK AND ROBERT WALLSTEN

9. Children should be led into the right paths, not by severity, but by persuasion.

TERENCE, *THE BROTHERS* (160 B.C.)

10. A man can seldom—very, very, seldom—fight a winning fight against his training: the odds are too heavy.

MARK TWAIN, "AS REGARDS PATRIOTISM" (1923)

TRAITORS

See 993. TREASON

989. TRANQUILITY

See also 160. COMPOSURE; 186. CONTENTMENT; 681. PEACE

1. Calm's not life's crown, though calm is well.

MATTHEW ARNOLD, "YOUTH AND CALM," *EMPEDOCLES ON ETNA, AND OTHER POEMS* (1852)

2. There's nought, no doubt, so much the spirit calms / As rum and true religion.

BYRON, *DON JUAN* (1819–24), 2.34

3. Tranquillity! thou better name / Than all the family of Fame.

SAMUEL TAYLOR COLERIDGE, "ODE TO TRANQUILLITY" (1801)

4. No one can achieve Serenity until the glare of passion is past the meridian.

CYRIL CONNOLLY, *THE UNQUIET GRAVE* (1945), 1

5. When we are unable to find tranquility within ourselves, it is useless to seek it elsewhere.

LA ROCHEFOUCAULD, *MAXIMS* (1665), TR. KENNETH PRATT

6. The world is fleeting; all things pass away; / Or is it we that pass and they that stay?

LUCIAN (C. 120–200)

7. We are used to the actions of human beings, not to their stillness.

V. S. PRITCHETT, "THE HYPOCRITE," *THE LIVING NOVEL & LATER APPRECIATIONS* (1964)

8. There is no joy but calm.

LORD TENNYSON, "THE LOTOS-EATERS" (1842), 2

9. If you want inner peace find it in solitude, not speed, and if you would find yourself, look to the land from which you came and to which you go.

STEWART L. UDALL, *THE QUIET CRISIS* (1963), 14

10. Nothing but stillness can remain when hearts are full / Of their own sweetness, bodies of their loveliness.

WILLIAM BUTLER YEATS, "MEDITATIONS IN TIME OF CIVIL WAR" (1923), 7

990. TRANSIENCE

See also 117. CHANGE; 302. ETERNITY; 606. MORTALITY; 978. TIME

1. The entire most beautiful order of things that are very good, when their measures have been accomplished, is to pass away.

ST. AUGUSTINE, *CONFESSIONS* (5TH C.), 13, TR. JOHN K. RYAN

2. All is ephemeral,—fame and the famous as well.

MARCUS AURELIUS, *MEDITATIONS* (2ND C.), 4.35, TR. MORRIS HICKEY MORGAN

3. As for man, his days are as grass: as a flower of the field, so he flourisheth.

BIBLE, PSALMS 103:15

4. We are but of yesterday, and know nothing, because our days upon earth are a shadow.

BIBLE, JOB 8:9

5. Loveliest of lovely things are they, / On earth, that soonest pass away.

WILLIAM CULLEN BRYANT, "A SCENE ON THE BANK OF THE HUDSON" (1827)

6. Ambition is a meteor-gleam; / Fame a restless airy dream; / Pleasures, insects on the wing / Round Peace, th' tend'rest flow'r of spring.

ROBERT BURNS, "WRITTEN IN FRIARS CARSE HERMITAGE" (1793)

7. Our lives ... are but a little while, / so let them run as sweetly as you can, / and give no thought to grief from day to day. / For time is not concerned to keep our hopes, / but hurries on its business, and is gone.

EURIPIDES, *HERACLES* (C. 422 B.C.), TR. WILLIAM ARROWSMITH

8. Would that life were like the shadow cast by a wall or a tree, but it is like the shadow of a bird in flight.

HAGGADAH, *PALESTINIAN TALMUD* (4TH C.)

9. Life is but a day; / A fragile dew-drop on its perilous way / From a tree's summit.

KEATS, "SLEEP AND POETRY" (1816)

10. The Worldly Hope men set their Hearts upon / Turns Ashes—or it prospers; and anon, / Like Snow upon the Desert's dusty Face, / Lighting a little hour or two—is gone.

OMAR KHAYYÁM, *RUBÁIYÁT* (11TH–12TH C.), TR. EDWARD FITZGERALD, 4TH ED., 16

11. Nothing mortal is enduring, and there is nothing sweet which does not presently end in bitterness.

PETRARCH, *LETTER TO POSTERITY* (1367–72)

12. We are things of a day. What are we? What are we not? The shadow of a dream / is man, no more.

PINDAR, *ODES* (5TH C. B.C.), PYTHIA 8, TR. RICHMOND LATTIMORE

13. Joy and sorrow, beauty and deformity, equally pass away.

SA'DI, *GULISTAN* (1258), 1.30, TR. JAMES ROSS

14. No reliance can be placed on the friendship of kings, nor vain hope put in the melodious voice of boys; for that passes away like a vision, and this vanishes like a dream.

SA'DI, *GULISTAN* (1258), 8.9, TR. JAMES ROSS

15. Worlds on worlds are rolling ever / From creation to decay, / Like the bubbles on a river / Sparkling, bursting, borne away.

SHELLEY, *HELLAS* (1821)

16. We are not sure of sorrow, / And joy was never sure; / Today will die tomorrow; / Time stoops to no man's lure.

ALGERNON CHARLES SWINBURNE, "THE GARDEN OF PROSERPINE," *POEMS AND BALLADS: FIRST SERIES* (1866)

17. The fairest things have fleetest end, / Their scent survives their close: / But the rose's scent is bitterness / To him that loved the rose.

FRANCIS THOMPSON, "DAISY" (1890)

18. Fame is a vapor, popularity an accident; the only earthly certainty is oblivion.

MARK TWAIN, *NOTEBOOK* (1935)

19. As generations come and go, / Their arts, their customs, ebb and flow; / Fate, fortune, sweep strong powers away, / And feeble, of themselves, decay.

WILLIAM WORDSWORTH, "THE HIGHLAND BROACH" (1831)

TRANSLATION

See 524. LANGUAGE

991. TRANSPORTATION

See also 28. AIRPLANES; 64. AUTOMOBILES

1. Bypasses are devices that allow some people to dash from point A to point B very fast while other people dash from point B to point A very fast.

DOUGLAS ADAMS, *THE HITCHHIKER'S GUIDE TO THE GALAXY* (1979)

2. It can hardly be a coincidence that no language on earth has ever produced the expression "as pretty as an airport."

DOUGLAS ADAMS, *THE LONG DARK TEA-TIME OF THE SOUL* (1988)

3. God Almighty Himself must have been hilarious when human beings so mingled iron and water and fire as to make a railroad train!

KURT VONNEGUT, *BLUEBEARD* (1987)

992. TRAVEL

See also 28. AIRPLANES; 64. AUTOMOBILES; 429. HOTELS; 699. PLACE; 839. SAILING; 991. TRANSPORTATION

TRAVEL

1. The less a tourist knows, the fewer mistakes he need make, for he will not expect himself to explain ignorance.

HENRY ADAMS, *THE EDUCATION OF HENRY ADAMS* (1907), 27

2. Perhaps travel cannot prevent bigotry, but by demonstrating that all peoples cry, laugh, eat, worry, and die, it can introduce the idea that if we try to understand each other, we may even become friends.

MAYA ANGELOU, "PASSPORTS TO UNDERSTANDING," *WOULDN'T TAKE NOTHING FOR MY JOURNEY NOW* (1993)

3. The worst thing about being a tourist is having other tourists recognize you as a tourist.

RUSSELL BAKER, "SUMMER IN FLORIDA," *ALL THINGS CONSIDERED* (1962)

4. There are sultry days in July and August when the [Italian] cities, emptied by the natives, are almost completely taken over by the swarms of dusty and perspiring foreigners.

LUIGI BARZINI, *THE ITALIANS* (1964)

5. In Europe, where human relations like clothes are supposed to last, one's got to be wearable. In France one has to be interesting, in Italy pleasant, in England one has to fit.

SYBILLE BEDFORD, *THE SUDDEN VIEW* (1953), 1

6. Many shall run to and fro, and knowledge shall be increased.

BIBLE, DANIEL 12:4

7. Road, n. A strip of land along which one may pass from where it is too tiresome to be to where it is futile to go.

AMBROSE BIERCE, *THE DEVIL'S DICTIONARY* (1881–1911)

8. The traveler used to go about the world to encounter the natives. A function of travel agencies now is to prevent this encounter.

DANIEL J. BOORSTIN, *THE IMAGE: A GUIDE TO PSEUDO-EVENTS IN AMERICA* (1961)

9. The traveler was active; he went strenuously in search of people, of adventure, of experience. The tourist is passive; he expects interesting things to happen to him. He goes "sight-seeing."

DANIEL J. BOORSTIN, *THE IMAGE* (1962), 3.2

10. Travellers, like poets, are mostly an angry race.

SIR RICHARD BURTON, "NARRATIVE OF A TRIP TO HARAR," *ROYAL GEOGRAPHICAL SOCIETY JOURNAL* (1855), 25

11. One can see them playing hearts in the lounge car and eating cheese sandwiches in the railroad stations as they traveled through Kansas and Nebraska—over the mountains and on to the Coast.

JOHN CHEEVER, "O CITY OF BROKEN DREAMS," *THE STORIES OF JOHN CHEEVER* (1980)

12. There was this to be said about the journey: It made one fully conscious of the terrestrial distance that separated the hot city from the leafy and ingenuous streets of the junction village.

JOHN CHEEVER, "THE SUMMER FARMER," *THE STORIES OF JOHN CHEEVER* (1980)

13. What affects men sharply about a foreign nation is not so much finding or not finding familiar things; it is rather not finding them in the familiar place.

G. K. CHESTERTON, "ON FLAGS," *GENERALLY SPEAKING* (1928)

14. Why do the wrong people travel, travel, travel,/When the right people stay back home?

NOËL COWARD, SONG, "WHY DO THE WRONG PEOPLE TRAVEL?"

15. How much a dunce that has been sent to roam / Excels a dunce that has been kept at home!

WILLIAM COWPER, *THE PROGRESS OF ERROR* (1782), 415

16. To roam / Giddily, and be everywhere but at home, / Such freedom doth a banishment become.

JOHN DONNE, "TO MR. ROWLAND WOODWARD," *LETTERS TO SEVERAL PERSONAGES* (1651)

17. Men run away to other countries because they are not good in their own, and run back to their own because they pass for nothing in the new places.

EMERSON, "CULTURE," *THE CONDUCT OF LIFE* (1860)

18. No man should travel until he has learned the language of the country he visits. Otherwise he voluntarily makes himself a great baby,—so helpless and so ridiculous.

EMERSON, *JOURNALS*, 1833

19. The world is his who has money to go over it.

EMERSON, "WEALTH," *THE CONDUCT OF LIFE* (1860)

20. Travelling is a fool's paradise. We owe to our first journeys the discovery that place is nothing.

EMERSON, "SELF-RELIANCE," *ESSAYS: FIRST SERIES* (1841)

21. The heaviest baggage for a traveler is an empty purse.

ENGLISH PROVERB

22. As a member of an escorted tour, you don't even have to know the Matterhorn isn't a tuba.

TEMPLE FIELDING, *FIELDING'S GUIDE TO EUROPE*, 1963

23. I don't much care where I am anymore, nor expect very much from places.

F. SCOTT FITZGERALD, *THE LETTERS OF F. SCOTT FITZGERALD* (1963), ED. ANDREW TURNBULL

24. Your first most typical figure in any new place turns out to be a bluff or a local nuisance.

F. SCOTT FITZGERALD, *THE CRACK-UP* (1945)

25. Each traveler should know what he has to see, and what properly belongs to him, on a journey.

GOETHE, QUOTED IN JOHANN PETER ECKERMANN'S *CONVERSATIONS WITH GOETHE,* NOV. 3, 1823

26. When traveling with someone, take large doses of patience and tolerance with your morning coffee.

HELEN HAYES, "GLOBE-TROTTING," *LOVING LIFE* (1987), WITH MARION GLASSEROW GLADNEY

27. To live is to see, and traveling sometimes speeds up the process.

EDWARD HOAGLAND, "HEADING OUT FROM HOME," *THE TUGMAN'S PASSAGE* (1982)

28. They change their climate, not their soul, who rush across the sea.

HORACE, *EPISTLES* (20-C. 8 B.C.), 1.10

29. One travels more usefully when alone, because he reflects more.

THOMAS JEFFERSON, LETTER TO J. BANNISTER, JR., JUNE 19, 1787

30. Travelling. This makes men wiser, but less happy.

THOMAS JEFFERSON, LETTER TO PETER CARR, AUG. 10, 1787

31. In traveling: a man must carry knowledge with him, if he would bring home knowledge.

SAMUEL JOHNSON, QUOTED IN BOSWELL'S *LIFE OF SAMUEL JOHNSON,* APRIL 17, 1778

32. The use of travelling is to regulate imagination by reality, and instead of thinking how things may be, to see them as they are.

SAMUEL JOHNSON, QUOTED IN HESTER LYNCH PIOZZI'S *ANECDOTES OF SAMUEL JOHNSON* (1786)

33. [E]very native of every place is a potential tourist, and every tourist is a native of somewhere. Every native everywhere lives a life of overwhelming and crushing banality and boredom and desperation and depression, and every deed, good and bad, is an attempt to forget this.

JAMAICA KINCAID, *A SMALL PLACE* (1988)

34. A tourist is an ugly human being.

JAMAICA KINCAID, *A SMALL PLACE* (1988)

35. The Uffizi [in Florence, Italy] is invaded by barbarian hordes from the North, squadrons of tourists in shorts, wearing sandals or hiking shoes, carrying metal canteens and cameras, smelling of sweat and suntan oil, who have been hustled in here by their guides to contemplate "Venus on the Half-Shell."

MARY MCCARTHY, *THE STONES OF FLORENCE* (1959)

36. My heart is warm with the friends I make, / And better friends I'll not be knowing; / Yet there isn't a train I wouldn't take, / No matter where it's going.

EDNA ST. VINCENT MILLAY, "TRAVEL," *SECOND APRIL* (1921)

37. Nothing is so awesomely unfamiliar as the familiar that discloses itself at the end of a journey. Nothing shakes the heart so much as meeting—far, far away—what you last met at home.

CYNTHIA OZICK, "THE SHOCK OF TEAPOTS," *METAPHOR & MEMORY* (1989)

38. If travel has taught me nothing more, and it certainly has, it's this: you never know when some trifling incident, utterly without significance, may pitchfork you into adventure or, by the same token, may not.

S.J. PERELMAN, *THE RISING GORGE* (1961)

39. We cannot learn to love other tourists,—the laws of nature forbid it,—but, meditating soberly on the impossibility of their loving us, we may reach some common platform of tolerance, some common exchange of recognition and amenity.

AGNES REPPLIER, "THE TOURIST," *COMPROMISES* (1904)

40. Against my will, in the course of my travels, the belief that everything worth knowing was known at Cambridge gradually wore off. In this respect my travels were very useful to me.

BERTRAND RUSSELL, *THE AUTOBIOGRAPHY OF BERTRAND RUSSELL: 1872–1914* (1967)

41. A traveller without knowledge is a bird without wings.

SA'DI, *GULISTAN* (1258), 8.82, TR. JAMES ROSS

42. Roam abroad in the world, and take thy fill of its enjoyments before the day shall come when thou must quit it for good.

SA'DI, *GULISTAN* (1258), 3.28, TR. JAMES ROSS

43. He who would travel happily must travel light.

SAINT-EXUPÉRY, *WIND, SAND, AND STARS* (1939), 8, TR. LEWIS GALANTIÈRE

44. The traveller must be somebody and come from somewhere, so that his definite character and moral

traditions may supply an organ and a point of comparison for his observations.

GEORGE SANTAYANA, *PERSONS AND PLACES: MY HOST THE WORLD* (1953), 3

45. Those who pass their lives in foreign travel find they contract many ties of hospitality, but form no friendships.

SENECA, *LETTERS TO LUCILIUS* (1ST C.), 2, TR. E. PHILLIPS BARKER

46. When I was at home, I was in a better place; but travellers must be content.

SHAKESPEARE, *AS YOU LIKE IT* (1599–1600), 2.4.17

47. I know people who are so immersed in road maps that they never see the countryside they pass through, and others who, having traced a route, are held to it as though held by flanged wheels to rails.

JOHN STEINBECK, *TRAVELS WITH CHARLEY* (1962)

48. Niagara Falls is very nice. I'm very glad I saw it, because from now on if I am asked whether I have seen Niagara Falls I can say yes, and be telling the truth for once.

JOHN STEINBECK, *TRAVELS WITH CHARLEY* (1962)

49. Wealth I ask not, hope nor love, / Nor a friend to know me; / All I seek, the heaven above / And the road below me.

ROBERT LOUIS STEVENSON, "THE VAGABOND," *SONGS OF TRAVEL* (1886)

50. For my part, I travel not to go anywhere, but to go. I travel for travel's sake. The great affair is to move.

ROBERT LOUIS STEVENSON, "CHEYLARD AND LUC," *TRAVELS WITH A DONKEY* (1879)

51. Travel is a vanishing act, a solitary trip down a pinched line of geography to oblivion.

PAUL THEROUX, *THE OLD PATAGONIAN EXPRESS* (1979)

52. [T]ruly, the worst trains take one across the best landscapes.

PAUL THEROUX, *THE OLD PATAGONIAN EXPRESS* (1979)

53. [R]ailways are irresistible bazaars, snaking along perfectly level no matter what the landscape, improving your mood with speed, and never upsetting your drink.

PAUL THEROUX, *THE GREAT RAILWAY BAZAAR* (1975)

54. To forget pain is to be painless; to forget care is to be rid of it; to go abroad is to accomplish both.

MARK TWAIN, *AUTOBIOGRAPHY* (1924), V. 2

55. To go abroad has something of the same sense that death brings. I am no longer of ye—what ye say of me is now of no consequence.

MARK TWAIN, *NOTEBOOK* (1935)

56. If one's object is ascetic, it is far better to stay in London or Paris or New York; there is practically no extreme of heat or cold, physical risk, loneliness, hunger or thirst that cannot, with a little ingenuity, be conveniently achieved in the centres of civilization.

EVELYN WAUGH, "THE TOURIST'S MANUAL," VOGUE MAGAZINE, JULY 1, 1935

57. Most of / the beauties of travel are due to / the strange hours we keep to see them.

WILLIAM CARLOS WILLIAMS, "JANUARY MORNING," *SELECTED POEMS* (1949), 1

58. No one realizes how beautiful it is to travel until he comes home and rests his head on his old, familiar pillow.

LIN YUTANG, "A TRIP TO ANHWEI," *WITH LOVE AND IRONY* (1934–40)

993. TREASON

See also 79. BETRAYAL

1. The treason pleases, but the traitors are odious.

CERVANTES, *DON QUIXOTE* (1605–15), 1.4.12, TR. JOHN OZELL

2. Treason doth never prosper: what's the reason? / For if it prosper, none dare call it treason.

SIR JOHN HARINGTON, "OF TREASON," *EPIGRAMS* (1615)

994. TREATIES

See also 46. APPEASEMENT; 162. COMPROMISE; 167. CONCILIATION; 498. INTERNATIONAL RELATIONS

1. Treaties are like roses and young girls. They last while they last.

CHARLES DE GAULLE, *TIME,* JULY 12, 1963

2. Let us never negotiate out of fear. But let us never fear to negotiate.

JOHN F. KENNEDY, INAUGURAL ADDRESS, JAN. 20, 1961

3. Peace does not rest in charters and covenants alone. It lies in the hearts and minds of the people.

JOHN F. KENNEDY, ADDRESS, UNITED NATIONS GENERAL ASSEMBLY, SEPT. 20, 1963

4. Treaties are observed as long as they are in harmony with interests.

NAPOLEON I, *MAXIMS* (1804–15)

5. History is a pathetic junkyard of broken treaties.

RICHARD M. NIXON, *REAL PEACE* (1984)

6. The only treaties that ought to count are those which would effect a settlement between ulterior motives.

PAUL VALÉRY, "GREATNESS AND DECADENCE OF EUROPE," *REFLECTIONS ON THE WORLD TODAY* (1931), TR. FRANCIS SCARFE

7. There is nothing more likely to start disagreement among people or countries than an agreement.

E. B. WHITE, "MY DAY," *ONE MAN'S MEAT* (1944)

995. TREES

1. No town can fail of beauty, though its walks were gutters and its houses hovels, if venerable trees make magnificent colonnades along its streets.

HENRY WARD BEECHER, *PROVERBS FROM PLYMOUTH PULPIT* (1887)

2. A woodland in full color is awesome as a forest fire, in magnitude at least; but a single tree is like a dancing tongue of flame to warm the heart.

HAL BORLAND, "AUTUMN IN YOUR HAND" *SUNDIAL OF THE SEASONS* (1964)

3. We recently had a referendum in New York about extending the forest preserve. The city voted for it by a large majority; yet as I walk the streets I do not see afforestation written with conviction on the harried faces of my fellow citizens.

LEARNED HAND, *THE SPIRIT OF LIBERTY* (1959)

4. The forest is the poor man's overcoat.

NEW ENGLAND PROVERB

5. Trees are the earth's endless effort to speak to the listening heaven.

RABINDRANATH TAGORE, *FIREFLIES* (1928)

6. Any fine morning a power saw can fell a tree that took a thousand years to grow.

EDWIN WAY TEALE, *AUTUMN ACROSS AMERICA* (1956), 29

7. Us sing and dance, make faces and give flower bouquets, trying to be loved. You ever notice that trees do everything to git attention we do, except walk?

ALICE WALKER, *THE COLOR PURPLE* (1982)

TRICKERY

See 200. CRAFTINESS; 224. DECEPTION; 939. STRATEGY

996. TRIFLES

See also 400. GREAT AND SMALL; 612. THE MUNDANE; 693. PETTINESS; 908. SMALLNESS; 1012. UNIMPORTANCE

1. Little things seem nothing, but they give peace, like those meadow flowers which individually seem odorless but all together perfume the air.

GEORGES BERNANOS, *THE DIARY OF A COUNTRY PRIEST* (1936), 6

2. The displacement of a little sand can change occasionally the course of deep rivers.

MANUEL GONZÁLEZ PRADA, *HORAS DE LUCHA* (1908)

3. Men trip not on mountains, they stumble on stones.

HINDUSTANI PROVERB

4. Those who apply themselves too much to little things usually become incapable of great ones.

LA ROCHEFOUCAULD, *MAXIMS* (1665), TR. KENNETH PRATT

5. It's the people who're comfortable who have time to worry over little trivial things.

WILLIAM MCFEE, *CASUALS OF THE SEA* (1916), 2.1.6

6. Trifles make the sum of human things, / And half our misery from our foibles springs.

HANNAH MORE, *SENSIBILITY* (1783)

7. A toothache will cost a battle, a drizzle cancel an insurrection.

VLADIMIR NABOKOV, *THE EYE* (1930)

8. For the person for whom small things do not exist, the great is not great.

JOSÉ ORTEGA Y GASSET, "TO THE READER," *MEDITATIONS ON QUIXOTE* (1914)

9. A mere trifle consoles us, for a mere trifle distresses us.

PASCAL, *PENSÉES* (1670), 136, TR. W. F. TROTTER

10. What dire offence from amorous causes springs! / What mighty contests rise from trivial things!

ALEXANDER POPE, *THE RAPE OF THE LOCK* (1712), 1.1

11. Trifles make up the happiness or the misery of human life.

ALEXANDER SMITH, "MEN OF LETTERS," *DREAMTHORP* (1863)

12. Small causes are sufficient to make a man uneasy, when great ones are not in the way: for want of a block he will stumble at a straw.

JONATHAN SWIFT, *THOUGHTS ON VARIOUS SUBJECTS* (1711)

13. Think naught a trifle, though it small appear; / Small sands the mountain, moments make the year, / And trifles life.

Edward Young, *Love of Fame* (1728), 6.208

TRIVIALITY

See 68. Banality; 996. Trifles

TROUBLE

See 17. Adversity

997. TRUST

See also 79. Betrayal; 259. Distrust

1. Thrust ivrybody—but cut th' ca-ards.

Finley Peter Dunne, "Casual Observations," *Mr. Dooley's Philosophy* (1900)

2. The essence of friendship is entireness, a total magnanimity and trust.

Emerson, "Friendship," *Essays: First Series* (1841)

3. Trust men and they will be true to you; treat them greatly and they will show themselves great.

Emerson, "Prudence," *Essays: First Series* (1841)

4. He got a corporation mind. He don't believe in nature; he puts his trust and distrust in man.

Norman Mailer, *Why Are We in Vietnam?* (1967)

5. No man ever quite believes in any other man. One may believe in an idea absolutely, but not in a man.

H. L. Mencken, "The Skeptic," *The Smart Set*, May 1919

6. Various are the uses of friends, beyond all else / in difficulty, but joy also looks for trust that is clear / in the eyes.

Pindar, *Odes* (5th c. b.c.), Nemea 8, tr. Richmond Lattimore

7. Confidence is the only bond of friendship.

Publilius Syrus, *Moral Sayings* (1st c. b.c.), 34, tr. Darius Lyman

8. A man who doesn't trust himself can never really trust anyone else.

Cardinal de Retz, *Mémoires* (1718)

9. It's a vice to trust all, and equally a vice to trust none.

Seneca, *Letters to Lucilius* (1st c.), 3.4, tr. E. Phillips Barker

10. Love all, trust a few.

Shakespeare, *All's Well That Ends Well* (1602–03), 1.1.74

998. TRUTH

See also 299. Error; 331. Falsehood; 668. Paradoxes; 999. Truth and Falsehood; 1000. Truthfulness

1. Once in a while there are things the brain simply refuses to accept as being true because they appear too improbable, too unlikely, too preposterous.

Walter Abish, *How German Is It* (1979)

2. Too much *Truth* / Is uncouth.

Franklin P. Adams, *Nods and Becks* (1944)

3. Every truth has two sides; it is well to look at both, before we commit ourselves to either.

Aesop, "The Mule," *Fables* (6th c. b.c.?), tr. Thomas James

4. Great is truth and strongest of all.

Apocrypha, 1 Esdras 4:22

5. It would be wrong to put friendship before the truth.

Aristotle, *Nicomachean Ethics* (4th c. b.c.), 1.6, tr. J. A. K. Thomson

6. Truth sits upon the lips of dying men.

Matthew Arnold, "Sohrab and Rustum," *Poems* (1853)

7. I search after truth, by which man never yet was harmed.

Marcus Aurelius, *Meditations* (2nd c.), 6.21, tr. Morris Hickey Morgan

8. Every step in every proud life is a run from safety to the dark, and the only thing to trust is what we think is true.

Richard Bach, *Running from Safety* (1994)

9. How often have I said to you that when you have eliminated the impossible, whatever remains, *however improbable*, must be the truth?

John D. Barrow, "The Sign of the Four," by A. Conan Doyle, quoted in *The Origin of the Universe* (1994)

10. Pushing any truth out very far, you are met by a counter-truth.

Henry Ward Beecher, *Proverbs from Plymouth Pulpit* (1887)

11. The truth shall make you free.

Bible, John 8:32

12. So absolutely good is truth, truth never hurts / The teller.

Robert Browning, *Fifine at the Fair* (1872), 32

13. Look on this beautiful world, and read the truth / In her fair page.

William Cullen Bryant, "The Ages" (1821)

14. There is no permanent absolute unchangeable truth; what we should pursue is the most convenient arrangement of our ideas.

Samuel Butler (d. 1902), "Truth and Convenience," *Note-Books* (1912)

15. Truth's fountains may be clear—her streams are muddy, / And cut through such canals of contradiction, / That she must often navigate o'er fiction.

Byron, *Don Juan* (1819–24), 15.88

16. There exists an obvious fact that seems utterly moral: namely, that a man is always a prey to his truths. Once he has admitted them, he cannot free himself from them. One has to pay something.

Albert Camus, *The Myth of Sisyphus* (1955), tr. Justin O'Brien

17. How could sincerity be a condition of friendship? A taste for truth at any cost is a passion which spares nothing.

Albert Camus, *The Fall* (1956)

18. We call first truths those we discover after all the others.

Albert Camus, *The Fall* (1956)

19. To know, to get into the truth of anything, is ever a mystic act, of which the best logics can but babble on the surface.

Thomas Carlyle, *On Heroes, Hero-Worship and the Heroic in History* (1841), 2

20. The stupid believe that to be truthful is easy; only the artist, the great artist, knows how difficult it is.

Willa Cather, *The Song of the Lark* (1915)

21. The form of truth will bear exposure, as well as that of beauty herself.

Samuel Taylor Coleridge, "Preliminary Observations," *Aids to Reflection* (1825)

22. Pure truth, like pure gold, has been found unfit for circulation, because men have discovered that it is far more convenient to adulterate the truth than to refine themselves.

Charles Caleb Colton, *Lacon* (1825), 2.108

23. The superior man is anxious lest he should not get truth; he is not anxious lest poverty should come upon him.

Confucius, *Analects* (6th c. b.c.), 15.31, tr. James Legge

24. They who know the truth are not equal to those who love it, and they who love it are not equal to those who delight in it.

Confucius, *Analects* (6th c. b.c.), 6.18, tr. James Legge

25. Truth is a river that is always splitting up into arms that reunite. Islanded between the arms the inhabitants argue for a lifetime as to which is the main river.

Cyril Connolly, *The Uniquiet Grave* (1945), 3

26. Opinion is a flitting thing, / But Truth, outlasts the Sun— / If then we cannot own them both— / Possess the oldest one—.

Emily Dickinson, poem (c. 1879)

27. The Truth must dazzle gradually / Or every man be blind—.

Emily Dickinson, poem (c. 1868)

28. On a huge hill, / Cragged and steep, Truth stands, and he that will / Reach her, about must, and about must go.

John Donne, Satire 3 (1635)

29. How often have I said to you that when you have eliminated the impossible, whatever remains, however improbable, must be the truth?

Sir Arthur Conan Doyle, *The Sign of Four* (1889)

30. The Truth has such a face and such a mien, / As to be loved needs only to be seen.

John Dryden, *The Hind and the Panther* (1687), 11.33

31. Truth is a matter of direct apprehension—you can't climb a ladder of mental concepts to it.

Lawrence Durrell, *Balthazar* (1958), 2.6

32. Truth disappears with the telling of it.

Lawrence Durrell, *Clea* (1960), 2.2

33. Truth is what most contradicts itself.

Lawrence Durrell, *Balthazar* (1958), 1.5

34. Truth is a woman. That is why it is enigmatic.

Lawrence Durrell [George], *Balthazar* (1958)

35. Ethical axioms are found and tested not very differently from the axioms of science. Truth is what stands the test of experience.

Einstein, *Out of My Later Years* (1950), 16

36. All necessary truth is its own evidence.

Emerson, *Journals,* 1833

37. God offers to every mind its choice between truth and repose.

EMERSON, "INTELLECT," *ESSAYS: FIRST SERIES* (1841)

38. No man has a right perception of any truth, who has not been reacted on by it, so as to be ready to be its martyr.

EMERSON, "FATE," *THE CONDUCT OF LIFE* (1860)

39. Truth has already ceased to be itself if polemically said.

EMERSON, *JOURNALS*, 1836

40. The soul is unwillingly deprived of truth.

EPICTETUS, *DISCOURSES* (2ND C.), 1.28, TR. THOMAS W. HIGGINSON

41. The world can absorb only doses of truth... too much would kill it.

WILLIAM MAXWELL EVARTS, QUOTED IN *THE EDUCATION OF HENRY ADAMS* (1907)

42. Truth—that long clean clear simple undeviable unchallengeable straight and shining line, on one side of which black is black and on the other white is white, has now become an angle, a point of view.

WILLIAM FAULKNER, "ON PRIVACY," *ESSAYS, SPEECHES & PUBLIC LETTERS* (1965)

43. Truth is child of Time.

JOHN FORD, *THE BROKEN HEART* (1633), 4.3

44. Truth is a flower in whose neighbourhood others must wither.

E. M. FORSTER, "JOSEPH CONRAD: A NOTE," *ABINGER HARVEST* (1936)

45. Truth fears no trial.

THOMAS FULLER, M.D., *GNOMOLOGIA* (1732), 5297

46. Truth may sometimes come out of the Devil's mouth.

THOMAS FULLER, M.D., *GNOMOLOGIA* (1732), 5308

47. Truth has a handsome countenance but torn garments.

GERMAN PROVERB

48. Say not, "I have found the truth," but rather, "I have found a truth."

KAHLIL GIBRAN, "ON SELF-KNOWLEDGE," *THE PROPHET* (1923)

49. To love the truth is to refuse to let oneself be saddened by it.

ANDRÉ GIDE, *JOURNALS*, OCT. 14, 1940, TR. JUSTIN O'BRIEN

50. The truths of life are not discovered by us. At moments unforeseen, some gracious influence descends upon the soul, touching it to an emotion which, we know not how, the mind transmutes into thought.

GEORGE GISSING, "AUTUMN," *THE PRIVATE PAPERS OF HENRY RYECROFT* (1903)

51. The brilliant passes, like the dew at morn; / The true endures, for ages yet unborn.

GOETHE, "PRELUDE IN THE THEATRE," *FAUST: PART I* (1808), TR. PHILIP WAYNE

52. Truth always lags last, limping along on the arm of Time.

BALTASAR GRACIÁN, *THE ART OF WORLDLY WISDOM* (1647), 146, TR. JOSEPH JACOBS

53. One truth discovered, one pang of regret at not being able to express it, is better than all the fluency and flippancy in the world.

WILLIAM HAZLITT, "MY FIRST ACQUAINTANCE WITH POETS," *THE PLAIN SPEAKER* (1826)

54. Political truth is a libel—religious truth blasphemy.

WILLIAM HAZLITT, "COMMONPLACES," *THE ROUND TABLE* (1817), 42

55. Truth is a torch which gleams in the fog but does not dispel it.

CLAUDE-ADRIEN HELVÉTIUS, PREFACE TO *DE L'ESPRIT* (1758)

56. Unless you expect the unexpected you will never find [truth], for it is hard to discover and hard to attain.

HERACLITUS, *FRAGMENTS* (C. 500 B.C.), 19, TR. PHILIP WHEELWRIGHT

57. Such truth as opposeth no man's profit nor pleasure is to all men welcome.

THOMAS HOBBES, "A REVIEW AND CONCLUSION," *LEVIATHAN* (1651)

58. Add a few drops of venom to a half truth and you have an absolute truth.

ERIC HOFFER, *THE PASSIONATE STATE OF MIND* (1954), 216

59. As with the pursuit of happiness, the pursuit of truth is itself gratifying whereas the consummation often turns out to be elusive.

RICHARD HOFSTADTER, *ANTI-INTELLECTUALISM IN AMERICAN LIFE* (1963), 1.2

60. Truth is tough. It will not break, like a bubble, at a touch; nay, you may kick it about all day like a football, and it will be round and full at evening.

OLIVER WENDELL HOLMES, SR., *THE PROFESSOR AT THE BREAKFAST TABLE* (1860), 5

61. It is the customary fate of new truths to begin as heresies and to end as superstitions.

THOMAS HENRY HUXLEY, "THE COMING OF AGE OF *THE ORIGIN OF SPECIES*" (1880)

62. One point is certain, that truth is one and immutable; until the jurors all agree, they cannot all be right.

WASHINGTON IRVING, "THE WIDOW'S ORDEAL," *WOLFERT'S ROOST* (1855)

63. In order that all men may be taught to speak truth, it is necessary that all likewise should learn to hear it.

SAMUEL JOHNSON, *THE RAMBLER* (1750–52), 96

64. It is dangerous for mortal beauty, or terrestrial virtue, to be examined by too strong a light. The torch of Truth shows much that we cannot, and all that we would not, see.

SAMUEL JOHNSON, *THE RAMBLER* (1750–52), 10

65. It profits not me to have any man fence or fight for me, to flourish or take a side. Stand for truth and 'tis enough.

BEN JONSON, "OF LIBERAL STUDIES," *TIMBER* (1640)

66. The dignity of truth is lost / With much protesting.

BEN JONSON, *CATILINE HIS CONSPIRACY* (1611), 3.2

67. Truth is man's proper good, and the only immortal thing was given to our mortality to use.

BEN JONSON, "EXPLORATA," *TIMBER* (1640)

68. What the imagination seizes as beauty must be truth.

KEATS, LETTER TO BENJAMIN BAILEY, NOV. 22, 1817

69. [Quoting Ed Murrow:] "It takes two to speak the truth—one to speak and another to hear."

ALEXANDER KENDRICK, *PRIME TIME* (1969)

70. Truth, like the juice of the poppy, in small quantities, calms men; in larger, heats and irritates them, and is attended by fatal consequences in its excess.

WALTER SAVAGE LANDOR, "MIDDLETON AND MAGLIABECCHI," *IMAGINARY CONVERSATIONS* (1824–53)

71. Truth is a point, the subtlest and finest; harder than adamant; never to be broken, worn away, or blunted. Its only bad quality is, that it is sure to hurt those who touch it; and likely to draw blood, perhaps the life blood, of those who press earnestly upon it.

WALTER SAVAGE LANDOR, "DIOGENES AND PLATO," *IMAGINARY CONVERSATIONS* (1824–53)

72. Truth does not lie beyond humanity, but is one of the products of the human mind and feeling.

D. H. LAWRENCE, *THE RAINBOW* (1915), 12

73. Duration is not a test of true or false.

ANNE MORROW LINDBERGH, "DOUBLE-SUNRISE," *GIFT FROM THE SEA* (1955)

74. We say that the truth will make us free. Yes, but that truth is a thousand truths which grow and change.

WALTER LIPPMANN, "THE GOLDEN RULE AND AFTER," *A PREFACE TO POLITICS* (1914)

75. To love truth for truth's sake is the principal part of human perfection in this world, and the seed-plot of all other virtues.

JOHN LOCKE, LETTER TO ANTHONY COLLINS, OCT. 29, 1703

76. Truth, like gold, is not less so for being newly brought out of the mine.

JOHN LOCKE, "THE EPISTLE DEDICATORY," *AN ESSAY CONCERNING HUMAN UNDERSTANDING* (1690)

77. Truth forever on the scaffold, Wrong forever on the throne,—/ Yet that scaffold sways the future.

JAMES RUSSELL LOWELL, "THE PRESENT CRISIS" (1844)

78. Man's passion for truth is such that he will welcome the bitterest of all postulates so long as it strikes him as true.

ANTONIO MACHADO, *JUAN DE MAIRENA* (1943), 1, TR. BEN BELITT

79. If truth is a value it is because it is true and not because it is brave to speak it.

W. SOMERSET MAUGHAM, *THE SUMMING UP* (1938), 75

80. To believe fully and at the same moment to have doubts is not at all a contradiction: it presupposes a greater respect for truth, an awareness that truth always goes beyond anything that can be said or done at any given moment.

ROLLO MAY, *THE COURAGE TO CREATE* (1975)

81. To be mistaken is a misfortune to be pitied; but to know the truth and not to conform one's actions to it is a crime which Heaven and Earth condemn.

GIUSEPPE MAZZINI, *THE DUTIES OF MAN AND OTHER ESSAYS* (1910)

82. The smallest atom of truth represents some man's bitter toil and agony; for every ponderable chuck of it there is a brave truth-seeker's grave upon some lonely ash-dump and a soul roasting in hell.

H. L. Mencken, *Prejudices: Third Series* (1922), 14

83. Indeed, the dictum that truth always triumphs over persecution, is one of those pleasant falsehoods which men repeat after one another till they pass into commonplaces, but which all experience refutes.

John Stuart Mill, *On Liberty* (1859), 2

84. The real advantage which truth has, consists in this, that when an opinion is true, it may be extinguished once, twice, or many times, but in the course of ages there will generally be found persons to rediscover it.

John Stuart Mill, *On Liberty* (1859), 2

85. The truth of these days is not that which really is, but what every man persuades another man to believe.

Montaigne, "On giving the lie," *Essays* (1580–88), tr. W. C. Hazlitt

86. There is an innate decorum in man, and it is not fair to thrust Truth upon people when they don't expect it. Only the very generous are ready for Truth impromptu.

Christopher Morley, *Inward Ho!* (1923), 1

87. Here is the end of the Eternal Verities, when one lets them bulk so big in his eyes as to shut out that perishable speck, the human race.

John Morley, "Carlyle," *Critical Miscellanies* (1871–1908)

88. The love of truth has its reward in heaven and even on earth.

Nietzsche, *Beyond Good and Evil* (1886), 45, tr. Walter Kaufmann

89. The will to truth is merely the longing for a stable world.

Nietzsche, *The Will to Power* (1888), 585, tr. Anthony M. Ludovici

90. There are many kind of eyes. Even the Sphinx has eyes—therefore there must be many kinds of "truths," and consequently there can be no truth.

Nietzsche, *The Will to Power* (1888), 540, tr. Anthony M. Ludovici

91. Such is the irresistible nature of truth that all it asks, and all it wants, is the liberty of appearing.

Thomas Paine, *The Rights of Man* (1791), 2

92. There would be too great darkness, if truth had not visible signs.

Pascal, *Pensées* (1670), 856, tr. W. F. Trotter

93. We have an idea of truth, invincible to all scepticism.

Pascal, *Pensées* (1670), 395, tr. W. F. Trotter

94. We know the truth, not only by the reason, but also by the heart.

Pascal, *Pensées* (1670), 10.1, tr. O. W. Wight

95. He who does not bellow the truth when he knows the truth makes himself the accomplice of liars and forgers.

Charles Péguy, "The Honest People," *Basic Verities* (1943), tr. Julian Green

96. Truth often suffers more by the heat of its defenders than from the arguments of its opposers.

William Penn, *Some Fruits of Solitude* (1693), 1.142

97. The truth knocks on your door and you say, "Go away. I'm looking for the truth." And so it goes away.

Robert M. Pirsig, *Zen and the Art of Motorcycle Maintenance* (1974)

98. The greater amount of truth is impulsively uttered; thus the greater amount is spoken, not written.

Edgar Allan Poe, *Marginalia* (1844–49), 1

99. Why do we not hear the truth? Because we do not speak it.

Publilius Syrus, *Moral Sayings* (1st c B.C.), 963, tr. Darius Lyman

100. Truth is no road to fortune.

Rousseau, *The Social Contract* (1762), 2.2, tr. G. D. H. Cole

101. The words "question" and "quest" are cognates. Only through inquiry can we discover truth.

Carl Sagan, *Broca's Brain: Reflections on the Romance of Science* (1979)

102. No truth is proved, no truth achieved, by argument, and the ready-made truths men offer you are mere conveniences or drugs to make you sleep.

Saint-Exupéry, *The Wisdom of the Sands* (1948), 44, tr. Stuart Gilbert

103. Truth is not that which is demonstrable but that which is ineluctable.

Saint-Exupéry, *Wind, Sand, and Stars* (1939), 9.6, tr. Lewis Galantière

104. Truths may clash without contradicting each other.

SAINT-EXUPÉRY, *THE WISDOM OF THE SANDS* (1948), 22, TR. STUART GILBERT

105. Even under the most favourable circumstances no mortal can be asked to seize the truth in its wholeness or at its centre.

GEORGE SANTAYANA, *CHARACTER AND OPINION IN THE UNITED STATES* (1921), 1

106. The truth, my friends, is not eloquent, except unspoken; its vast shadow lends eloquence to our sparks of thought as they die into it.

GEORGE SANTAYANA, *DIALOGUES IN LIMBO* (1925), 3

107. The truth is cruel, but it can be loved, and it makes free those who have loved it.

GEORGE SANTAYANA, *LITTLE ESSAYS* (1920), 44

108. Truth lives on in the midst of deception.

SCHILLER, *ON THE AESTHETIC EDUCATION OF MAN* (1795), 9, TR. REGINALD SNELL

109. Truth's open to everyone, and the claims aren't all staked yet.

SENECA, *LETTERS TO LUCILIUS* (1ST C.), 33.11, TR. E. PHILLIPS BARKER

110. Truth hath a quiet breast.

SHAKESPEARE, *RICHARD II* (1595–96), 1.3.96

111. Truth is truth / To th' end of reck'ning.

SHAKESPEARE, *MEASURE FOR MEASURE* (1604–05), 5.1.45

112. Deep truth is imageless.

SHELLEY, *PROMETHEUS UNBOUND* (1818–19), 2.4

113. The truth will always have a market.

JEAN SHEPHERD, INTRODUCTION, *THE FERRARI IN THE BEDROOM* (1972)

114. The truth is always the strongest argument.

SOPHOCLES, *PHAEDRA* (C. 435–29 B.C.), TR. M. H. MORGAN

115. You will find that the truth is often unpopular and the contest between agreeable fancy and disagreeable fact is unequal. For, in the vernacular, we Americans are suckers for good news.

ADLAI STEVENSON, *THE NEW YORK TIMES,* JUNE 9, 1958

116. Everything has to be taken on trust; truth is only that which is taken to be true. It's the currency of living. There may be nothing behind it, but it doesn't make any difference so long as it is honored.

TOM STOPPARD, *ROSENCRANTZ & GUILDENSTERN ARE DEAD* (1967), 2

117. Truth looks tawdry when she is overdressed.

RABINDRANATH TAGORE, INTRODUCTION TO *THE CYCLE OF SPRING* (1915)

118. It is morally as bad not to care whether a thing is true or not, so long as it makes you feel good, as it is not to care how you got your money so long as you have got it.

EDWIN WAY TEALE, "FEBRUARY 18," *CIRCLE OF THE SEASONS* (1953)

119. You can prove almost anything with the evidence of a small enough segment of time. How often, in any search for truth, the answer of the minute is positive, the answer of the hour qualified, the answers of the year contradictory!

EDWIN WAY TEALE, "JANUARY 6," *CIRCLE OF THE SEASONS* (1953)

120. Nowadays flattery wins friends, truth hatred.

TERENCE, *THE WOMAN OF ANDROS* (166 B.C.)

121. Between whom there is hearty truth there is love.

THOREAU, "THE ATLANTIDES," *A WEEK ON THE CONCORD AND MERRIMACK RIVERS* (1849)

122. Rather than love, than money, than fame, give me truth.

THOREAU, "CONCLUSION," *WALDEN* (1854)

123. So little trouble do men take in the search after truth; so readily do they accept whatever comes first to hand.

THUCYDIDES, *THE PELOPONNESIAN WAR* (C. 400 B.C.), 1.20, TR. BENJAMIN JOWETT

124. Truth is more of a stranger than fiction.

MARK TWAIN, *NOTEBOOK* (1935)

125. Truth is mighty and will prevail. There is nothing the matter with this, except that it ain't so.

MARK TWAIN, *NOTEBOOK* (1935)

126. Knowledge for the sake of knowledge! Truth for truth's sake! This is inhuman.

MIGUEL DE UNAMUNO, "THE STARTING-POINT," *TRAGIC SENSE OF LIFE* (1913), TR. J. E. CRAWFORD FLITCH

127. There are certain truths so true that they are practically unbelievable.

GORE VIDAL, *THE SECOND AMERICAN REVOLUTION AND OTHER ESSAYS* (1982)

128. The only truths we can point to / are the ever-changing truths of our own experience.

PETER WEISS, *MARAT / SADE* (1964), 1.15, TR. ADRIAN MITCHELL

129. Heaven knows what seeming nonsense may not tomorrow be demonstrated truth.

Alfred North Whitehead, *Science and the Modern World* (1925), 7

130. Whatever satisfies the soul is truth.

Walt Whitman, preface to *Leaves of Grass* (1855–92)

131. For what is Truth? In matters of religion, it is simply the opinion that has survived. In matters of science, it is the ultimate sensation. In matters of art, it is one's last mood.

Oscar Wilde, *The Artist as Critic: Critical Writings of Oscar Wilde,* ed. Richard Ellman (1969)

132. Every thing to be true must become a religion.

Oscar Wilde, *De Profundis* (1905)

133. The truth is rarely pure and never simple.

Oscar Wilde, *The Importance of Being Earnest* (1895), 1

134. Truth is on the march; nothing can stop it now.

Émile Zola, "J'accuse," *Aurore* (1898)

999. TRUTH AND FALSEHOOD

See also 1000. Truthfulness; 299. Error; 331. Falsehood; 998. Truth

1. Truth exists. Only lies are invented.

Georges Braque, Pensées sur l'art (20th Century)

2. It is only a good, sound, truthful person who can lie to any good purpose; if a man is not habitually truthful his very lies will be false to him and betray him.

Samuel Butler (d. 1902), "Truth and Convenience," *Note-Books* (1912)

3. Would that I could discover truth as easily as I can uncover falsehood.

Cicero, *De Natura Deorum* (44 B.C.), 1

4. Though truth and falsehood be / Near twins, yet truth a little elder is.

John Donne, Satire 3 (1635)

5. If a man fasten his attention on a single aspect of truth and apply himself to that alone for a long time, the truth becomes distorted and not itself but falsehood.

Emerson, "Intellect," *Essays: First Series* (1841)

6. Lies are the religion of slaves and bosses. Truth is the god of the free man.

Maxim Gorky, *The Lower Depths* (1903), 4, tr. Alexander Bakshy

7. Irrationally held truths may be more harmful than reasoned errors.

Thomas Henry Huxley, "The Coming of Age of *The Origin of Species*" (1880)

8. It is error alone which needs the support of government. Truth can stand by itself.

Thomas Jefferson, *Notes on the State of Virginia* (1784–85), 17

9. Truth does not do as much good in the world as its imitations do harm.

La Rochefoucauld, *Maxims* (1665), tr. Kenneth Pratt

10. Truth gains more even by the errors of one who, with due study and preparation, thinks for himself, than by the true opinions of those who only hold them because they do not suffer themselves to think.

John Stuart Mill, *On Liberty* (1859), 2

11. What kind of truth is it which has these mountains as its boundary and is a lie beyond them?

Montaigne, "Apology for Raimond de Sebonde," *Essays* (1580–88)

12. A Hair perhaps divides the False and True.

Omar Khayyám, *Rubáiyát* (11th–12th c.), tr. Edward FitzGerald, 4th ed., 49

13. We perceive an image of truth, and possess only a lie.

Pascal, *Pensées* (1670), 434, tr. W. F. Trotter

14. A peace-mingling falsehood is preferable to a mischief-stirring truth.

Sa'di, *Gulistan* (1258), 1.1, tr. James Ross

15. The truth is balance, but the opposite of truth, which is unbalance, may not be a lie.

Susan Sontag, "Simon Weil," *Against Interpretation* (1961)

16. The history of our race, and each individual's experience, are sown thick with evidence that a truth is not hard to kill and that a lie told well is immortal.

Mark Twain, "Advice to Youth" (1923)

1000. TRUTHFULNESS

See also 331. Falsehood; 362. Frankness; 425. Honesty; 901. Sincerity; 998. Truth; 999. Truth and Falsehood

1. I love you and, because I love you, I would sooner have you hate me for telling you the truth than adore me for telling you lies.

Pietro Aretino, letter to Giovanni Pollastra, Aug. 28, 1537, tr. Samuel Putnam

2. The highest compact we can make with our fellow is, "Let there be truth between us two for evermore."

EMERSON, "BEHAVIOR," *THE CONDUCT OF LIFE* (1860)

3. Whatever games are played with us, we must play no games with ourselves, but deal in our privacy with the last honesty and truth.

EMERSON, "ILLUSIONS," *THE CONDUCT OF LIFE* (1860)

4. All truth is not to be told at all times.

THOMAS FULLER, M.D., *GNOMOLOGIA* (1732), 567

5. He that does not speak truth to me does not believe me when I speak truth.

THOMAS FULLER, M.D., *GNOMOLOGIA* (1732), 2084

6. To be wiser than other men is to be honester than they; and strength of mind is only courage to see and speak the truth.

WILLIAM HAZLITT, "ON KNOWLEDGE OF THE WORLD," *SKETCHES AND ESSAYS* (1839)

7. Dare to be true: nothing can need a lie; / A fault which needs it most, grows two thereby.

GEORGE HERBERT, "THE CHURCH PORCH," 13, *THE TEMPLE* (1633)

8. Veracity is the heart of morality.

THOMAS HENRY HUXLEY, "UNIVERSITIES, ACTUAL AND IDEAL" (1874)

9. It is always the best policy to speak the truth, unless of course you are an exceptionally good liar.

JEROME K. JEROME, *THE IDLER,* FEBRUARY 1892

10. A man's word / Is believed just to the extent of the wealth in his coffers stored.

JUVENAL, *SATIRES* (C. 100), 3.143, TR. HUBERT CREEKMORE

11. Who speaks the truth stabs Falsehood to the heart.

JAMES RUSSELL LOWELL, "L'ENVOI" (1843)

12. On the one hand, we may tell the truth, regardless of consequences, and on the other hand we may mellow it and sophisticate it to make it humane and tolerable.

H. L. MENCKEN, "THE ART ETERNAL," *THE NEW YORK EVENING MAIL,* 1918

13. I speak truth, not so much as I would, but as much as I dare; and I dare a little the more, as I grow older.

MONTAIGNE, "OF REPENTANCE," *ESSAYS* (1580–88), TR. W. C. HAZLITT

14. To be believed, make the truth unbelievable.

NAPOLEON I, *MAXIMS* (1804–15)

15. All truths that are kept silent become poisonous.

NIETZSCHE, "ON SELF-OVERCOMING," *THUS SPOKE ZARATHUSTRA* (1883–92), 2, TR. WALTER KAUFMANN

16. The inability to lie is far from the love of truth.

NIETZSCHE, "ON THE HIGHER MAN," *THUS SPOKE ZARATHUSTRA* (1883–92), 4, TR. WALTER KAUFMANN

17. They deem him their worst enemy who tells them the truth.

PLATO, *THE REPUBLIC* (4TH C. B.C.), 4, TR. BENJAMIN JOWETT

18. There are few nudities so objectionable as the naked truth.

AGNES REPPLIER, "THE GAYETY OF LIFE," *COMPROMISES* (1904)

19. O, while you live, tell truth and shame the devil!

SHAKESPEARE, *1 HENRY IV* (1597–98), 3.1.62

20. If you tell the truth you don't have to remember anything.

MARK TWAIN, *NOTEBOOK* (1935)

21. Often, the surest way to convey misinformation is to tell the strict truth.

MARK TWAIN, "PUDD'NHEAD WILSON'S NEW CALENDAR," *FOLLOWING THE EQUATOR* (1897), 2.23

22. Truth is the most valuable thing we have. Let us economize it.

MARK TWAIN, "PUDD'NHEAD WILSON'S NEW CALENDAR," *FOLLOWING THE EQUATOR* (1897), 1.7

TRYING

See 281. EFFORT

TURN

See 32. ALTERNATION

1001. TWENTIETH CENTURY

See also 3. THE ABSURD; 298. ERA; 641. NUCLEAR POWER; 966. TECHNOLOGY; 1067. WORLD

1. The fin is coming early this siècle.

ANGELA CARTER, QUOTED IN LEWIS LAPHAM, *IMPERIAL MASQUERADE* (1990)

2. It is easy enough to praise men for the courage of their convictions. I wish I could teach the sad young of this mealy generation the courage of their confusions.

JOHN CIARDI, *SATURDAY REVIEW,* JUNE 2, 1962

3. [The Jazz Age] was borrowed time anyhow—the whole upper tenth of a nation living with the insouciance of grand ducs and the casualness of chorus girls.

F. SCOTT FITZGERALD, *THE CRACK-UP* (1945)

4. It takes a kind of shabby arrogance to survive in our time, and a fairly romantic nature to want to.

EDGAR Z. FRIEDENBERG, *THE VANISHING ADOLESCENT* (1959)

5. In a contrary and perhaps cruel way the twentieth century has relieved us of labor without at the same time relieving us of the conviction that only labor is meaningful.

WALTER C. A. KERR, *THE DECLINE OF PLEASURE* (1962)

6. The trouble with our age is that it is all signpost and no destination.

LOUIS KRONENBERGER, "THE SPIRIT OF THE AGE," *COMPANY MANNERS* (1954)

7. Modern man—whether in the womb of the masses, or with his workmates, or with his family, or alone—can never for one moment forget that he is living in a world in which he is a means and whose end is not his business.

ALBERTO MORAVIA, TITLE ESSAY, *MAN AS AN END* (1964), TR. BERNARD WALL

8. We have created an industrial order geared to automatism, where feeble-mindedness, native or acquired, is necessary for docile productivity in the factory; and where a pervasive neurosis is the final gift of the meaningless life that issues forth at the other end.

LEWIS MUMFORD, "THE FULFILLMENT OF MAN," *THE CONDUCT OF LIFE* (1951)

9. Whoever has not felt the danger of our times palpitating under his hand, has not really penetrated to the vitals of destiny, he has merely pricked its surface.

JOSÉ ORTEGA Y GASSET, *THE REVOLT OF THE MASSES* (1930), 2

10. The atom bombs are piling up in the factories, the police are prowling through the cities, the lies are streaming from the loudspeakers, but the earth is still going round the sun.

GEORGE ORWELL, "THOUGHTS ON THE COMMON TOAD," *SHOOTING AN ELEPHANT* (1950)

11. In these times you have to be an optimist to open your eyes when you awake in the morning.

CARL SANDBURG, *NEW YORK POST*, SEPT. 9, 1960

12. Artists have no less talents than ever; their taste, their vision, their sentiment are often interesting; they are mighty in their independence and feeble only in their works.

GEORGE SANTAYANA, *WINDS OF DOCTRINE* (1913)

13. Time and space—time to be alone, space to move about—these may well become the great scarcities of tomorrow.

EDWIN WAY TEALE, *AUTUMN ACROSS AMERICA* (1956), 33

1002. TYRANNY

See also 357. FORCE; 458. IMPERIALISM; 719. POWER; 801. REPRESSION; 819. REVOLUTION; 889. SERVITUDE; 985. TOTALITARIANISM

1. [T]hough oppression may give rise to violent and repeated outbreaks, like the convulsions of a man in pain, it cannot mature a settled purpose and plan of regeneration, unless a new notion of happiness is joined to the sense of present evil.

LORD ACTON, "NATIONALITY" (1862), REPRINTED IN *ESSAYS ON FREEDOM AND POWER* (1948)

2. Death is a softer thing by far than tyranny.

AESCHYLUS, *AGAMEMNON* (458 B.C.), TR. RICHMOND LATTIMORE

3. This is a sickness rooted and inherent / in the nature of a tyranny: / that he that holds it does not trust his friends.

AESCHYLUS, *PROMETHEUS BOUND* (C. 478 B.C.), TR. DAVID GRENE

4. Any excuse will serve a tyrant.

AESOP, "THE WOLF AND THE LAMB," *FABLES* (6TH C. B.C.?), TR. JOSEPH JACOBS

5. [I]t is in fact far easier to act under conditions of tyranny than it is to think.

HANNAH ARENDT, "THE VITA ACTIVA AND THE MODERN AGE," *THE HUMAN CONDITION* (1958)

6. Make men large and strong, and tyranny will bankrupt itself in making shackles for them.

HENRY WARD BEECHER, *PROVERBS FROM PLYMOUTH PULPIT* (1887)

7. The slave begins by demanding justice and ends by wanting to wear a crown. He must dominate in his turn.

ALBERT CAMUS, "METAPHYSICAL REBELLION," *THE REBEL* (1951), TR. ANTHONY BOWER

8. The laws can't be enforced against the man who is the laws' master.

BENVENUTO CELLINI, *AUTOBIOGRAPHY* (1558–66), TR. GEORGE BULL

9. When a nation has allowed itself to fall under a tyrannical regime, it cannot be absolved from the faults due to the guilt of that regime.

SIR WINSTON CHURCHILL, MESSAGE AFTER VISIT TO ITALY, JULY 28, 1944

10. The dictator, in all his pride, is held in the grip of his party machine. He can go forward; he cannot go back. He must blood his hounds and show them sport, or else, like Actaeon of old, be devoured by them. All-strong without, he is all-weak within.

SIR WINSTON CHURCHILL, RADIO ADDRESS TO THE UNITED STATES, OCT. 16, 1938

11. Of all the tyrannies on humankind, / The worst is that which persecutes the mind.

JOHN DRYDEN, *THE HIND AND THE PANTHER* (1687), 11.239

12. Tyranny is tyranny, no matter what its form; the free man will resist it if his courage serves.

LEARNED HAND, *THE SPIRIT OF LIBERTY* (1959)

13. Dictators ride to and fro upon tigers from which they dare not dismount.

HINDUSTANI PROVERB, QUOTED IN SIR WINSTON CHURCHILL'S *WHILE ENGLAND SLEPT* (1936)

14. The benevolent despot who sees himself as a shepherd of the people still demands from others the submissiveness of sheep.

ERIC HOFFER, *THE ORDEAL OF CHANGE* (1964), 15.2

15. So long as men worship the Caesars and Napoleons, Caesars and Napoleons will duly rise and make them miserable.

ALDOUS HUXLEY, *ENDS AND MEANS* (1937)

16. Resistance to tyrants is obedience to God.

THOMAS JEFFERSON, MOTTO FOUND AMONG HIS PAPERS

17. If a sovereign oppresses his people to a great degree, they will rise and cut off his head. There is a remedy in human nature against tyranny that will keep us safe under every form of government.

SAMUEL JOHNSON, QUOTED IN BOSWELL'S *LIFE OF SAMUEL JOHNSON,* MARCH 31, 1772

18. Tyrants never perish from tyranny, but always from folly,—when their fantasies have built up a palace for which the earth has no foundation.

WALTER SAVAGE LANDOR, "ANACREON AND POLYCRATES," *IMAGINARY CONVERSATIONS* (1824–53)

19. When the white man governs himself, that is self-government; but when he governs himself and also governs another man, that is more than self-government—that is despotism.

ABRAHAM LINCOLN, SPEECH, PEORIA, ILL., OCT. 16, 1854

20. Tyrants are but the spawn of Ignorance, / Begotten by the slaves they trample on.

JAMES RUSSELL LOWELL, "PROMETHEUS" (1843)

21. I believe there are more instances of the abridgment of the freedom of the people by gradual and silent encroachments of those in power than by violent and sudden usurpations.

JAMES MADISON, SPEECH, VIRGINIA CONVENTION, JUNE 16, 1788

22. Time is on the side of the oppressed today, it's against the oppressor. Truth is on the side of the oppressed today, it's against the oppressor. You don't need anything else.

MALCOLM X, *MALCOLM X SPEAKS* (1965), 6

23. Beware the People weeping / When they bare the iron hand.

HERMAN MELVILLE, "THE MARTYR," *BATTLEPIECES AND ASPECTS OF THE WAR* (1866)

24. He whom many fear, has himself many to fear.

PUBLILIUS SYRUS, *MORAL SAYINGS* (1ST C. B.C.), 522, TR. DARIUS LYMAN

25. The face of tyranny / Is always mild at first.

RACINE, *BRITANNICUS* (1669), 1, TR. ROBERT HENDERSON

26. There is a cowardly propensity in the human heart that delights in oppressing somebody else, and in the gratification of this base desire we always select a victim that can be outraged with safety.

JAMES T. RAPIER, *CONGRESSIONAL GLOBE,* 1873

27. I never could believe that Providence had sent a few men into the world, ready booted and spurred to ride, and millions ready saddled and bridled to be ridden.

RICHARD RUMBOLD, ON THE SCAFFOLD, QUOTED IN MACAULAY'S *HISTORY OF ENGLAND* (1685), 5

28. To pardon the oppressor is to deal harshly with the oppressed.

SA'DI, *GULISTAN* (1258), 8.8, TR. JAMES ROSS

29. The tyrant claims freedom to kill freedom / and yet to keep it for himself.

RABINDRANATH TAGORE, *FIREFLIES* (1928)

30. To succeed in chaining the multitude you must seem to wear the same fetters.

VOLTAIRE, "CHRISTIANITY," *PHILOSOPHICAL DICTIONARY* (1764)

U

1003. UGLINESS

See also 72. BEAUTY

1. When the eye fails to find beauty—alias solace—it commands the body to create it, or, failing that, adjusts itself to perceive virtue in ugliness.

JOSEPH BRODSKY, *WATERMARK* (1992)

2. The secret of ugliness consists not in irregularity, but in being uninteresting.

EMERSON, "BEAUTY," *THE CONDUCT OF LIFE* (1860)

3. Since our persons are not of our own making, when they are such as appear defective or uncomely, it is, methinks, an honest and laudable fortitude to dare to be ugly.

RICHARD STEELE, *THE SPECTATOR* (1711–12), 17

4. I don't mind plain women being Puritans. It is the only excuse they have for being plain.

OSCAR WILDE, *A WOMAN OF NO IMPORTANCE* (1893), I

1004. UNBELIEF

See also 78. BELIEF; 265. DOUBT, RELIGIOUS; 330. FAITH; 797. RELIGION; 904. SKEPTICISM

1. Atheism is rather in the lip than in the heart of man.

FRANCIS BACON, "OF ATHEISM," *ESSAYS* (1625)

2. The fool hath said in his heart, There is no God.

BIBLE, PSALMS 14:1 AND 53:1

3. There is no proselyter half so energetic as the hard-shelled atheist.

HEYWOOD BROUN, "A NEW PREFACE TO AN OLD STORY," *BROWN'S NUTMEG*, AUG. 19, 1939

4. All we have gained then by our unbelief / Is a life of doubt diversified by faith, / For one of faith diversified by doubt: / We called the chess-board white,— we call it black.

ROBERT BROWNING, "BISHOP BLOUGRAM'S APOLOGY," *MEN AND WOMEN* (1855)

5. The writers against religion, whilst they oppose every system, are wisely careful never to set up any of their own.

EDMUND BURKE, PREFACE TO *A VINDICATION OF NATURAL SOCIETY* (1756)

6. To lose one's faith—surpass / The loss of an Estate— / Because Estates can be / Replenished— faith cannot—.

EMILY DICKINSON, POEM (C. 1862)

7. The unbelief of the age is attested by the loud condemnation of trifles.

EMERSON, *JOURNALS*, 1836

8. If there are none [gods], / All our toil is without meaning.

EURIPIDES, *IPHIGENIA IN AULIS* (C. 405 B.C.), TR. CHARLES R. WALKER

9. Atheism. There is not a single exalting and emancipating influence that does not in turn become inhibitory.

ANDRÉ GIDE, *JOURNALS*, JAN. 13, 1929, TR. JUSTIN O'BRIEN

10. If there is a God, atheism must strike Him as less of an insult than religion.

JULES DE GONCOURT, *JOURNAL*, JAN. 24, 1868, TR. ROBERT BALDICK

11. When incredulity becomes a faith, it is less rational than a religion.

JULES DE GONCOURT, *JOURNAL*, MARCH 1, 1862

12. Anti-clericalism and non-belief, have their bigots just as orthodoxy does.

JULIEN GREEN, *JOURNAL*, JULY 23, 1945

13. There seems to be a terrible misunderstanding on the part of a great many people to the effect that when you cease to believe you may cease to behave.

LOUIS KRONENBERGER, "THE SPIRIT OF THE AGE," *COMPANY MANNERS* (1954)

14. Atheists put on a false courage and alacrity in the midst of their darkness and apprehensions, like chil-

dren who, when they fear to go in the dark, will sing for fear.

Alexander Pope, *Thoughts on Various Subjects* (1727)

15. When faith burns itself out, 'tis God who dies and thenceforth proves unavailing.

Saint-Exupéry, *The Wisdom of the Sands* (1948), 11, tr. Stuart Gilbert

16. By night an atheist half believes a God.

Edward Young, *Night Thoughts* (1742–46), 5.177

1005. UNCERTAINTY

See also 115. Certainty; 465. Indecision; 482. Insecurity; 904. Skepticism

1. Doubt of the reality of love ends by making us doubt everything.

Henri Frédéric Amiel, *Journal*, Dec. 26, 1868, tr. Mrs. Humphry Ward

2. We are not certain, we are never certain. If we were, we could reach some conclusions, and we could, at last, make others take us seriously.

Albert Camus, *The Fall* (1956)

3. Diffidence is the better part of knowledge.

Charles Caleb Colton, preface, *Lacon* (1825)

4. Oft from new truths, and new phrase, new doubts grow, / As strange attire aliens the men we know.

John Donne, "To the Countess of Bedford," *Letters to Several Personages* (1651)

5. The quest for certainty blocks the search for meaning. Uncertainty is the very condition to impel man to unfold his powers.

Erich Fromm, *Man for Himself* (1947), 3

6. Doubt and mistrust are the mere panic of timid imagination, which the steadfast heart will conquer, and the large mind transcend.

Helen Keller, *Optimism* (1903), 1

7. All uncertainty is fruitful ... so long as it is accompanied by the wish to understand.

Antonio Machado, *Juan de Mairena* (1943), 43, tr. Ben Belitt

8. It is infinitely safer to know that the man at the top has his doubts, as you and I have ours, yet has the courage to move ahead in spite of these doubts.

Rollo May, *The Courage to Create* (1975)

9. We sail within a vast sphere, ever drifting in uncertainty, driven from end to end.

Pascal, *Pensées* (1670), 72, tr. W. F. Trotter

10. Our doubts are traitors / And make us lose the good we oft might win / By fearing to attempt.

Shakespeare, *Measure for Measure* (1604–05), 1.4.77

1006. UNCONSCIOUSNESS

See also 175. Consciousness; 590. Mind; 1020. Unreason

1. It is our less conscious thoughts and our less conscious actions which mainly mould our lives and the lives of those who spring from us.

Samuel Butler (d. 1902), *The Way of All Flesh* (1903), 5

2. How should men know what is coming to pass within them, when there are no words to grasp it? How could the drops of water know themselves to be a river? Yet the river flows on.

Saint-Exupéry, *The Wisdom of the Sands* (1948), 43, tr. Stuart Gilbert

3. Our unconscious is like a vast subterranean factory with intricate machinery that is never idle, where work goes on day and night from the time we are born until the moment of our death.

Milton R. Sapirstein, *Paradoxes of Everyday Life* (1955), 8

1007. UNDERSTANDING

See also 493. Intelligence; 501. Intuition; 522. Knowledge; 590. Mind; 683. Perception; 883. Sensibility; 960. Sympathy; 1008. Understanding Others; 1019. The Unknown; 1060. Wisdom

1. Light; or, failing that, lightning: the world can take its choice.

Thomas Carlyle, *On Heroes, Hero-Worship and the Heroic in History* (1841), 5

2. A man goes to knowledge as he goes to war, wide-awake, with fear, with respect, and with absolute assurance. Going to knowledge or going to war in any other manner is a mistake, and whoever makes it will live to regret his steps.

Carlos Castaneda, *The Teachings of Don Juan: A Yaqui Way of Knowledge* (1968)

3. One who understands much displays a greater simplicity of character than one who understands little.

Alexander Chase, *Perspectives* (1966)

4. Things and men have always a certain sense, a certain side by which they must be got hold of if one wants to obtain a solid grasp and a perfect command.

JOSEPH CONRAD, *UNDER WESTERN EYES* (1911), 4.1

5. You never know where you're going to find the same thoughts in another brain, but when it happens you know it right off, just like you were connected by a small electrical wire that suddenly glows red hot and sparks.

LOUISE ERDRICH, "THE BINGO VAN," *THE BINGO PALACE* (1994)

6. Understanding is the beginning of approving.

ANDRÉ GIDE, *JOURNALS,* 1902, TR. JUSTIN O'BRIEN

7. In what we really understand, we reason but little.

WILLIAM HAZLITT, "ON THE CONDUCT OF LIFE," *LITERARY REMAINS* (1836)

8. A moment's insight is sometimes worth a life's experience.

OLIVER WENDELL HOLMES, SR., "IRIS, HER BOOK," *THE PROFESSOR AT THE BREAKFAST TABLE* (1860)

9. Perfect understanding will sometimes almost extinguish pleasure.

A. E. HOUSMAN, *THE NAME AND NATURE OF POETRY* (1933)

10. Calling George Bush shallow is like calling a dwarf short.

MOLLY IVINS, *MOLLY IVINS CAN'T SAY THAT, CAN SHE?* (1991)

11. It is less dishonour to hear imperfectly than to speak imperfectly. The ears are excused: the understanding is not.

BEN JONSON, "OF FLATTERERS," *TIMBER* (1640)

12. Nothing can be loved or hated unless it is first known.

LEONARDO DA VINCI, *NOTEBOOKS* (C. 1500), TR. JEAN PAUL RICHTER

13. You can be totally rational with a machine. But if you work with people, sometimes logic often has to take a backseat to understanding.

AKIO MORITA, "AMERICAN AND JAPANESE STYLES," *MADE IN JAPAN* (1986), TR. EDWIN M. REINGOLD AND MITSUKO SHIMOMURA

14. All the glory of greatness has no lustre for people who are in search of understanding.

PASCAL, *PENSÉES* (1670), 792, TR. W. F. TROTTER

15. Quality...you know what it is, yet you don't know what it is.

ROBERT M. PIRSIG, *ZEN AND THE ART OF MOTORCYCLE MAINTENANCE* (1974)

16. Time which diminishes all things increases understanding for the aging.

PLUTARCH, "THE EDUCATION OF CHILDREN," *MORALIA* (C. A.D. 100), TR. MOSES HADAS

17. Insight doesn't happen often on the click of the moment, like a lucky snapshot, but comes in its own time and more slowly and from nowhere but within.

EUDORA WELTY, "PREFACE," *ONE TIME, ONE PLACE* (1971)

18. The first act of insight is throw away the labels.

EUDORA WELTY, "MUST THE NOVELIST CRUSADE?" *THE EYE OF THE STORY* (1978)

1008. UNDERSTANDING OTHERS

See also 67. BACKGROUND; 663. OTHERS; 683. PERCEPTION; 698. PITY; 960. SYMPATHY; 1007. UNDERSTANDING

1. It takes longer for man to find out man than any other creature that is made.

HENRY WARD BEECHER, *PROVERBS FROM PLYMOUTH PULPIT* (1887)

2. To understand is to forgive, even oneself.

ALEXANDER CHASE, *PERSPECTIVES* (1966)

3. If you do not understand a man you cannot crush him. And if you do understand him, very probably you will not.

G. K. CHESTERTON, "HUMANITARIANISM AND STRENGTH," *ALL THINGS CONSIDERED* (1908)

4. Insight—the titillating knack for hurting!

COLETTE, "THE PURE AND THE IMPURE," *EARTHLY PARADISE* (1966), 5

5. Grieve not that men do not know you; grieve that you do not know men.

CONFUCIUS, *ANALECTS* (6TH C. B.C.), 1.16, TR. WINBERG CHAI

6. Herein lies the tragedy of the age: not that men are poor,—all men know something of poverty; not that men are wicked,—who is good? not that men are ignorant,—what is truth? Nay, but that men know so little of men.

W. E. B. DU BOIS, *THE SOULS OF BLACK FOLK* (1903), 12

7. All persons are puzzles until at last we find in some word or act the key to the man, to the woman;

straightway all their past words and actions lie in light before us.

EMERSON, *JOURNALS*, 1842

8. In daily life we never understand each other, neither complete clairvoyance nor complete confessional exists.

E.M. FORSTER, "PEOPLE," *ASPECTS OF THE NOVEL* (1927)

9. [I]n the novel we can know people perfectly, and, apart from the general pleasure of reading, we can find here a compensation for their dimness in life.

E.M. FORSTER, "PEOPLE," *ASPECTS OF THE NOVEL* (1927)

10. God grant me to contend with those that understand me.

THOMAS FULLER, M.D., *GNOMOLOGIA* (1732), 1673

11. Each of us really understands in others only those feelings he is capable of producing himself.

ANDRÉ GIDE, *JOURNAL OF "THE COUNTERFEITERS,"* SECOND NOTEBOOK, AUGUST 1921, TR. JUSTIN O'BRIEN

12. To sense when a teenager needs understanding and when misunderstanding is a difficult and delicate task. The sad truth is that no matter how wise we are, we cannot be right for any length of time in our teenagers' eyes.

HAIM G. GINOTT, *BETWEEN PARENT & TEENAGER* (1969)

13. It is profound philosophy to sound the depths of feeling and distinguish traits of character. Men must be studied as deeply as books.

BALTASAR GRACIÁN, *THE ART OF WORLDLY WISDOM* (1647), 157, TR. JOSEPH JACOBS

14. It is easier to know (and understand) men in general than one man in particular.

LA ROCHEFOUCAULD, *MAXIMS* (1665), TR. KENNETH PRATT

15. We like to read others but we do not like to be read.

LA ROCHEFOUCAULD, *MAXIMS* (1665), TR. KENNETH PRATT

16. Until we know what motivates the hearts and minds of men we can understand nothing outside ourselves, nor will we ever reach fulfillment as that greatest miracle of all, the human being.

MARYA MANNES, *MORE IN ANGER* (1958), 2.2

17. The best that can be said for anybody is probably that you misunderstood him favorably.

WILLIAM SAROYAN, *CHANCE MEETINGS* (1978)

18. A man, to be greatly good, must imagine intensely and comprehensively; he must put himself in the place of another and of many others; the pains and pleasures of his species must become his own.

SHELLEY, *A DEFENCE OF POETRY* (1821)

19. Many men honestly do not know what women want, and women honestly do not know why men find what they want so hard to comprehend and deliver.

DEBORAH TANNEN, *YOU JUST DON'T UNDERSTAND* (1990)

20. One learns peoples through the heart, not the eyes or the intellect.

MARK TWAIN, "WHAT PAUL BOURGET THINKS OF US," *NORTH AMERICAN REVIEW*, JANUARY 1895

1009. UNEMPLOYMENT

1. A man willing to work, and unable to find work, is perhaps the saddest sight that fortune's inequality exhibits under this sun.

THOMAS CARLYLE, *CHARTISM* (1839), 4

2. It were depression, too. They cut my wages down once at the foundry. They cut my wages down again. Then they cut my wages *out*, also the job.

LANGSTON HUGHES, *SIMPLE SPEAKS HIS MIND* (1950)

3. Anyone who has ever experienced dehumanized life on welfare or any other confidence-shaking dependency knows that a paid job may be preferable to the dole, even when the handout is coming from a family member.

GLORIA STEINEM, "THE IMPORTANCE OF WORK," *OUTRAGEOUS ACTS AND EVERYDAY REBELLIONS* (1983)

UNFAIRNESS

See 477. INJUSTICE

1010. UNFULFILLMENT

See also 366. FRUSTRATION; 717. POTENTIAL

1. What we have never had, remains; / It is the things we have that go.

SARA TEASDALE, "WISDOM," *DARK OF THE MOON* (1926)

1011. UNHAPPINESS

See also 251. DISCONTENT; 409. HAPPINESS; 918. SORROW; 920. SOUR GRAPES; 946. SUFFERING; 1052. WEEPING

1. A man should always consider how much he has more than he wants, and how much more unhappy he might be than he really is.

JOSEPH ADDISON, *THE SPECTATOR* (1711–12; 1714), 574

2. Nothing is miserable unless you think it so.

BOETHIUS, *THE CONSOLATION OF PHILOSOPHY* (A.D. 524), 2

3. Melancholy cannot be clearly proved to others, so it is better to be silent about it.

JAMES BOSWELL, *LONDON JOURNAL,* MAY 17, 1763

4. Naught so sweet as melancholy.

ROBERT BURTON, "AUTHOR'S ABSTRACT," *THE ANATOMY OF MELANCHOLY* (1621)

5. There are no grounds for supposing that one can live a life without pain and sadness, but is it wrong to believe that somehow, somewhere, this is possible?

HUBERT BUTLER, "AUNT HARRIET," IN *THE ART OF THE PERSONAL ESSAY* (1994), ED. PHILLIP LOPATE

6. For the unhappy man death is the commutation of a sentence of life imprisonment.

ALEXANDER CHASE, *PERSPECTIVES* (1966)

7. The Morning after Woe— / 'Tis frequently the Way— / Surpasses all that rose before— / For utter Jubilee—.

EMILY DICKINSON, POEM (C. 1862)

8. All artists today are expected to cultivate a little fashionable unhappiness.

LAWRENCE DURRELL, *JUSTINE* (1957), 2

9. Fate finds for every man / His share of misery.

EURIPIDES, *IPHIGENIA IN AULIS* (C. 405 B.C.), TR. CHARLES R. WALKER

10. Where there are two, one cannot be wretched, and one not.

EURIPIDES, *HELEN* (412 B.C.), TR. RICHMOND LATTIMORE

11. This is what I think now: that the natural state of the sentient adult is a qualified unhappiness.

F. SCOTT FITZGERALD, *THE CRACK-UP* (1945)

12. Unhappiness does make people look stupid.

ANATOLE FRANCE, *THE CRIME OF SYLVESTRE BONNARD* (1881), 2, TR. LAFCADIO HEARN

13. Is there anything men take more pains about than to render themselves unhappy?

BENJAMIN FRANKLIN, *POOR RICHARD'S ALMANACK* (1732–57)

14. Sadness is almost never anything but a form of fatigue.

ANDRÉ GIDE, *JOURNALS,* 1922, TR. JUSTIN O'BRIEN

15. Man can only endure a certain degree of unhappiness; what is beyond that either annihilates him or passes by him and leaves him apathetic.

GOETHE, *ELECTIVE AFFINITIES* (1809), 22

16. For fate has wove the thread of life with pain, / And twins ev'n from the birth are misery and man!

HOMER, *ODYSSEY* (9TH C. B.C.), 7.263, TR. ALEXANDER POPE

17. The world will never be long without some good reason to hate the unhappy; their real faults are immediately detected; and if those are not sufficient to sink them into infamy, an additional weight of calumny will be superadded.

SAMUEL JOHNSON, *THE ADVENTURER* (1753), 99

18. True melancholy breeds your perfect, fine wit, sir.

BEN JONSON, *EVERY MAN IN HIS HUMOUR* (1598), 3.1

19. When the melancholy fit shall fall / Sudden from heaven like a weeping cloud, / That fosters the droop-headed flowers all, / And hides the green hill in an April shroud; / Then glut thy sorrow on a morning rose.

KEATS, "ODE ON MELANCHOLY" (1819)

20. A person who longs to leave the place where he lives is an unhappy person.

MILAN KUNDERA, *THE UNBEARABLE LIGHTNESS OF BEING* (1984)

21. Sooner or later in life everyone discovers that perfect happiness is unrealizable, but there are few who pause to consider the antithesis: that perfect unhappiness is equally unattainable.

PRIMO LEVI, *SURVIVAL IN AUSCHWITZ* (1959)

22. Into each life some rain must fall, / Some days must be dark and dreary.

LONGFELLOW, "THE RAINY DAY" (1842)

23. What makes man most unhappy is to be deprived not of that which he had, but of that which he did not have, and did not really know.

JACQUES MARITAIN, *REFLECTIONS ON AMERICA* (1958), 16

24. Oh the piercing sadness of life in the midst of its ordinariness!

IRIS MURDOCH, *A WORD CHILD* (1975)

25. Life is a well of joy; but for those out of whom an upset stomach speaks, which is the father of melancholy, all wells are poisoned.

NIETZSCHE, "ON OLD AND NEW TABLETS," *THUS SPOKE ZARATHUSTRA* (1883–92), 3, TR. WALTER KAUFMANN

26. I have discovered that all man's unhappiness derives from only one source—not being able to sit quietly in a room.

PASCAL, *PENSÉES* (1670), 139

27. How quick the old woe follows a little bliss!

PETRARCH, "LAURA LIVING," *CANZONIERE* (1360), 166

28. The wretched reflect either too much or too little.

PUBLILIUS SYRUS, *MORAL SAYINGS* (1ST C. B.C.), 225, TR. DARIUS LYMAN

29. Life is so full of miseries, minor and major; they press so close upon us at every step of the way, that it is hardly worthwhile to call one another's attention to their presence.

AGNES REPPLIER, "THE GAYETY OF LIFE," *COMPROMISES* (1904)

30. Only those sadnesses are dangerous and bad which one carries about among people in order to drown them out.

RAINER MARIA RILKE, *LETTERS TO A YOUNG POET,* AUG. 12, 1904, TR. M. D. HERTER NORTON

31. Since unhappiness excites interest, many, in order to render themselves interesting, feign unhappiness.

JOSEPH ROUX, *MEDITATIONS OF A PARISH PRIEST* (1886), 5.24, TR. ISABEL F. HAPGOOD

32. It would hardly be possible to exaggerate man's wretchedness if it were not so easy to overestimate his sensibility.

GEORGE SANTAYANA, *THE LIFE OF REASON: REASON IN RELIGION* (1905–06), 10

33. Our aches and pains conform to opinion. A man's as miserable as he thinks he is.

SENECA, *LETTERS TO LUCILIUS* (1ST C.), 78.13, TR. E. PHILLIPS BARKER

34. Is anyone in all the world / Safe from unhappiness?

SOPHOCLES, *OEDIPUS AT COLONUS* (401 B.C.), TR. ROBERT FITZGERALD

35. If misery loves company, misery has company enough.

THOREAU, *JOURNAL,* SEPT. 1, 1851

36. Like all the cultivated he believed that only the widely read could be said to *know* that they were unhappy.

THORNTON WILDER, *THE BRIDGE OF SAN LUIS REY* (1927)

1012. UNIMPORTANCE

See also 320. EXPENDABILITY; 400. GREAT AND SMALL; 469. INDIVIDUALITY; 612. THE MUNDANE; 649. OBSCURITY; 693. PETTINESS; 908. SMALLNESS; 996. TRIFLES

1. Our insignificance is often the cause of our safety.

AESOP, "THE GREAT AND THE LITTLE FISHES," *FABLES* (6TH C. B.C.?), TR. THOMAS JAMES

2. Rightly viewed no meanest object is insignificant; all objects are as windows, through which the philosophic eye looks into infinitude itself.

THOMAS CARLYLE, *SARTOR RESARTUS* (1833–34), 1.11

3. A man can look upon his life and accept it as good or evil; it is far, far harder for him to confess that it has been unimportant in the sum of things.

MURRAY KEMPTON, "O'ER MOOR AND FEN," *PART OF OUR TIME* (1955)

4. Strange how few, / After all's said and done, the things that are / Of moment.

EDNA ST. VINCENT MILLAY, "INTERIM," *RENASCENCE* (1917)

1013. UNIONS

See also 1066. WORKERS

1. There is no right to strike against the public safety by anybody, anywhere, any time.

CALVIN COOLIDGE, TELEGRAM TO SAMUEL GOMPERS, SEPT. 14, 1919

2. With all their faults, trade-unions have done more for humanity than any other organization of men that ever existed. They have done more for decency, for honesty, for education, for the betterment of the race, for the developing of character in man, than any other association of men.

CLARENCE S. DARROW, IN *THE RAILROAD TRAINMAN,* NOVEMBER 1909

3. Sthrikes are a great evil f'r th' wurrukin' man, but so are picnics an' he acts th' same at both.

FINLEY PETER DUNNE, "WORK," *MR. DOOLEY SAYS* (1910)

4. Unionism seldom, if ever, uses such power as it has to insure better work; almost always it devotes a large part of that power to safeguarding bad work.

H. L. MENCKEN, *PREJUDICES: THIRD SERIES* (1922), 4

1014. UNIQUENESS

See also 260. DIVERSITY; 469. INDIVIDUALITY; 662. ORIGINALITY

1. There never were, since the creation of the world, two cases exactly parallel.

LORD CHESTERFIELD, *LETTERS TO HIS SON*, FEB. 22, 1748

2. The poetry of art is in beholding the single tower; the poetry of nature in seeing the single tree; the poetry of love in following the single woman; the poetry of religion in worshipping the single star.

G. K. CHESTERTON, "THE ADVANTAGES OF HAVING ONE LEG," *TREMENDOUS TRIFLES* (1909)

3. Every man is more than just himself; he also represents the unique, the very special and always significant and remarkable point at which the world's phenomena intersect, only once in this way and never again.

HERMANN HESSE, PROLOGUE TO *DEMIAN* (1919), TR. MICHAEL LEBECK

1015. UNITED NATIONS

See also 498. INTERNATIONAL RELATIONS

1. Our instrument and our hope is the United Nations, and I see little merit in the impatience of those who would abandon this imperfect world instrument because they dislike our imperfect world.

JOHN F. KENNEDY, STATE OF THE UNION MESSAGE, JAN. 11, 1962

2. This 122-nation body, United Nations, is far from being a Parliament of Man, but it is a kind of mirror of our world, warts and all.

EDITORIAL, "U.N. ASSEMBLY AT 22," *THE NEW YORK TIMES*, SEPT. 19, 1967

1016. UNITY

See also 100. BROTHERHOOD; 151. COMMUNITY; 190. COOPERATION; 260. DIVERSITY

1. A common danger unites even the bitterest enemies.

ARISTOTLE, *POLITICS* (4TH C. B.C.), 5.5, TR. BENJAMIN JOWETT

2. Behold, how good and how pleasant it is for brethren to dwell together in unity!

BIBLE, PSALMS 133:1

3. We must all hang together, or assuredly we shall all hang separately.

BENJAMIN FRANKLIN, AT SIGNING OF THE DECLARATION OF INDEPENDENCE, JULY 4, 1776

4. It is always possible to bind together a considerable number of people in love, so long as there are other people left over to receive the manifestations of their aggressiveness.

SIGMUND FREUD, *CIVILIZATION AND ITS DISCONTENTS* (1930), 5, TR. JAMES STRACHEY

5. Not vain the weakest, if their force unite.

HOMER, *ILIAD* (9TH C. B.C.), 13.311, TR. ALEXANDER POPE

6. With malice toward none, with charity for all, with firmness in the right as God gives us to see the right, let us strive on to finish the work we are in, to bind up the nation's wounds.

ABRAHAM LINCOLN, SECOND INAUGURAL ADDRESS, MARCH 4, 1865

7. There are only two forces that unite men—fear and interest.

NAPOLEON I, *MAXIMS* (1804–15)

8. Plurality which is not reduced to unity is confusion; unity which does not depend on plurality is tyranny.

PASCAL, *PENSÉES* (1670), 870, TR. W. F. TROTTER

9. Horror causes men to clench their fists, and in horror men join together.

SAINT-EXUPÉRY, *WIND, SAND, AND STARS* (1939), 9.3, TR. LEWIS GALANTIÈRE

1017. UNIVERSE

See also 415. THE HEAVENS; 921. SPACE; 1067. WORLD

1. There is no reason that the universe should be designed for our convenience.

JOHN D. BARROW, *THE ORIGIN OF THE UNIVERSE* (1994)

2. The idea that the universe is running down comes from a simple observation about machines. Every machine consumes more energy than it renders.

JACOB BRONOWSKI, *THE ASCENT OF MAN* (1973)

3. A universe that came from nothing in the big bang will disappear into nothing at the big crunch. Its glorious few zillion years of existence not even a memory.

PAUL DAVIES, *THE LAST THREE MINUTES* (1994)

4. I do not wonder at a snowflake, a shell, a summer landscape, or the glory of the stars; but at the necessity of beauty under which the universe lies.

EMERSON, "FATE," *THE CONDUCT OF LIFE* (1860)

5. Law rules throughout existence, a Law which is not intelligent but Intelligence.

EMERSON, "FATE," *THE CONDUCT OF LIFE* (1860)

6. The universe does not jest with us, but is in earnest.

EMERSON, *JOURNALS,* 1841

7. The usual approach of science of constructing a mathematical model cannot answer the questions of why there should be a universe for the model to describe. Why does the universe go to all the bother of existing?

STEPHEN W. HAWKING, *A BRIEF HISTORY OF TIME* (1988)

8. The progress of the human race in understanding the universe has established a small corner of order in an increasingly disordered universe.

STEPHEN W. HAWKING, *A BRIEF HISTORY OF TIME* (1988)

9. The universe is not hostile, nor yet is it friendly. It is simply indifferent.

JOHN HAYNES HOLMES, *THE SENSIBLE MAN'S VIEW OF RELIGION* (1933)

10. Nothing puzzles me more than time and space; and yet nothing troubles me less.

CHARLES LAMB, LETTER TO THOMAS MANNING, JAN. 2, 1810

11. The cosmos is a gigantic fly-wheel making 10,000 revolutions a minute. Man is a sick fly taking a dizzy ride on it. Religion is the theory that the wheel was designed and set spinning to give him the ride.

H. L. MENCKEN, *PREJUDICES: THIRD SERIES* (1922), 5

12. The whole visible world is only an imperceptible atom in the ample bosom of nature. No idea approaches it.

PASCAL, *PENSÉES* (1670), 72, TR. W. F. TROTTER

13. All are but parts of one stupendous whole, / Whose body Nature is, and God the soul.

ALEXANDER POPE, *AN ESSAY ON MAN* (1733–34), 1.267

14. To be happy in this world, especially when youth is past, it is necessary to feel oneself not merely an isolated individual whose day will soon be over, but part of the stream of life flowing on from the first germ to the remote and unknown future.

BERTRAND RUSSELL, *THE CONQUEST OF HAPPINESS* (1930), 13

15. The universe forces those who live in it to understand it.

CARL SAGAN, *BROCA'S BRAIN: REFLECTIONS ON THE ROMANCE OF SCIENCE* (1979)

16. I do not value any view of the universe into which man and the institutions of man enter very largely and absorb much of the attention. Man is but the place where I stand, and the prospect hence is infinite.

THOREAU, *JOURNAL,* APRIL 2, 1852

1018. UNKINDNESS

See also 209. CRUELTY; 519. KINDNESS

1. Now that another is suffering pain at thy hand, trust not that thy heart shall be exempt from affliction.

SA'DI, *GULISTAN* (1258), 3.28, TR. JAMES ROSS

2. O! many a shaft, at random sent / Finds mark the archer little meant!

SIR WALTER SCOTT, *THE LORD OF THE ISLES* (1815), 5.18

1019. THE UNKNOWN

See also 522. KNOWLEDGE; 1007. UNDERSTANDING

1. 'Tis very puzzling on the brink / Of what is called Eternity to stare, / And know no more of what is *here,* than *there*.

BYRON, *DON JUAN* (1819–24), 10.20

2. The fairest thing we can experience is the mysterious. It is the fundamental emotion which stands at the cradle of true art and true science.

EINSTEIN, TITLE ESSAY, *THE WORLD AS I SEE IT* (1934), TR. ALAN HARRIS

3. Between the idea / And the reality / Between the motion / And the act / Falls the Shadow.

T. S. ELIOT, "THE HOLLOW MEN" (1925), 5

4. All is riddle, and the key to a riddle is another riddle.

EMERSON, "ILLUSIONS," *THE CONDUCT OF LIFE* (1860)

5. Grieve not, because thou understandest not life's mystery; behind the veil is concealed many a delight.

HĀFIZ, GHAZALS FROM THE *DIVAN* (14TH C.), 18, TR. JUSTIN HUNTLY MCCARTHY

6. Penetrating so many secrets, we cease to believe in the unknowable. But there it sits nevertheless, calmly licking its chops.

H. L. MENCKEN, *MINORITY REPORT* (1956), 364

7. Would there be this eternal seeking if the found existed?

ANTONIO PORCHIA, *VOCES* (1968), TR. W. S. MERWIN

8. Our dream dashes itself against the great mystery like a wasp against a window pane. Less merciful than man, God never opens the window.

JULES RENARD, *JOURNAL,* AUGUST 1906, TR. ELIZABETH ROGET

9. We are ignorant of the Beyond because this ignorance is the condition *sine qua non* of our own life. Just as ice cannot know fire except by melting, by vanishing.

JULES RENARD, *JOURNAL,* SEPTEMBER 1890, TR. ELIZABETH ROGET

10. Once men are caught up in an event they cease to be afraid. Only the unknown frightens men.

SAINT-EXUPÉRY, *WIND, SAND, AND STARS* (1939), 2.2, TR. LEWIS GALANTIÈRE

11. The unknown always passes for the marvellous.

TACITUS, *AGRICOLA* (C. A.D. 98), 30, TR. WILLIAM J. BRODRIBB

12. Perhaps some day someone will explain how, on the level of man, Auschwitz was possible; but on the level of God, it will forever remain the most disturbing of mysteries.

ELIE WIESEL, *LEGENDS OF OUR TIMES* (1968)

1020. UNREASON

See also 785. REASON; 1006. UNCONSCIOUSNESS

1. A life based on reason will always require to be balanced by an occasional bout of violent and irrational emotion, for the instinctual drives must be satisfied.

CYRIL CONNOLLY, *THE UNQUIET GRAVE* (1945), 1

1021. UNSELFISHNESS

See also 375. GENEROSITY; 433. HUMANITARIANISM; 874. SELFISHNESS; 887. SERVICE

1. To reach perfection, we must all pass, one by one, through the death of self-effacement.

DAG HAMMARSKJÖLD, "1945–1949: TOWARDS NEW SHORES—?" *MARKINGS* (1964), TR. W. H. AUDEN

2. The small share of happiness attainable by man exists only insofar as he is able to cease to think of himself.

THEODOR REIK, AUTHOR'S NOTE, *OF LOVE AND LUST* (1957)

3. In every part and corner of our life, to lose oneself is to be gainer; to forget oneself is to be happy.

ROBERT LOUIS STEVENSON, "OLD MORTALITY" (1884), 2

4. The only thing that saves the world is the little handful of disinterested men that are in it.

WOODROW WILSON, ADDRESS, WASHINGTON, D.C., MAY 15, 1916

1022. UNWILLINGNESS

See also 1057. WILLINGNESS

1. There is nothing so easy but that it becomes difficult when you do it with reluctance.

TERENCE, *THE SELF-TORMENTOR* (163 B.C.), 4.6.1, TR. HENRY THOMAS RILEY

1023. USEFULNESS

See also 720. PRACTICALITY; 887. SERVICE; 1024. USELESSNESS

1. We often despise what is most useful to us.

AESOP, "THE HART AND THE HUNTER," *FABLES* (6TH C. B.C.?), TR. JOSEPH JACOBS

2. It is a great misfortune to be of use to nobody; scarcely less to be of use to everybody.

BALTASAR GRACIÁN, *THE ART OF WORLDLY WISDOM* (1647), 85, TR. JOSEPH JACOBS

3. A man cannot sleep in his cradle: whatever is useful must in the nature of life become useless.

WALTER LIPPMANN, "THE TABOO," *A PREFACE TO POLITICS* (1914)

4. Success can corrupt; usefulness can only exalt.

DMITRI MITROPOULOS, *HI-FI MUSIC AT HOME,* MAY–JUNE 1956

5. Utility is the great idol of the age, to which all powers must do service and all talents swear allegiance.

SCHILLER, *ON THE AESTHETIC EDUCATION OF MAN* (1795), 2, TR. REGINALD SNELL

6. I have known some men possessed of good qualities which were very serviceable to others, but useless to themselves; like a sun-dial on the front of a house, to inform the neighbours and passengers, but not the owner within.

JONATHAN SWIFT, *THOUGHTS ON VARIOUS SUBJECTS* (1711)

7. The difference between utility and utility plus beauty is the difference between telephone wires and the spider's web.

EDWIN WAY TEALE, "SEPTEMBER 18," *CIRCLE OF THE SEASONS* (1953)

8. The sure way of knowing nothing about life is to try to make oneself useful.

OSCAR WILDE, "THE CRITIC AS ARTIST," *INTENTIONS* (1891)

1024. USELESSNESS

See also 1023. USEFULNESS

1. A scarecrow in a garden of cucumbers keepeth nothing.

APOCRYPHA, BARUCH 6:70

2. A useless life is early death.

GOETHE, *IPHIGENIA IN TAURIS* (1787), 1, TR. CHARLES E. PASSAGE

3. Uselessness is a fatal accusation to bring against any act which is done for its presumed utility, but those which are done for their own sake are their own justification.

GEORGE SANTAYANA, *THE SENSE OF BEAUTY* (1896), 4

UTILITY

See 1023. USEFULNESS

1025. UTOPIA

See also 442. IDEALISM; 790. REFORM

1. Utopias rest on the fallacy that perfection is a legitimate goal of human existence.

LEWIS MUMFORD, *FINDINGS AND KEEPINGS. ANALECTS FOR AN AUTOBIOGRAPHY* (1975)

2. Every one who has ever built anywhere a "new heaven" first found the power thereto in his own hell.

NIETZSCHE, *THE GENEALOGY OF MORALS* (1887), 3.10, TR. HORACE B. SAMUEL

3. Ah, Love! could thou and I with Fate conspire / To grasp this sorry Scheme of Things entire, / Would not we shatter it to bits—and then / Re-mould it nearer to the Heart's Desire!

OMAR KHAYYÁM, *RUBÁIYÁT* (11TH–12TH C.), TR. EDWARD FITZGERALD, 1ST ED., 73

4. Ideal society is a drama enacted exclusively in the imagination.

GEORGE SANTAYANA, *THE LIFE OF REASON: REASON IN SOCIETY* (1905–06), 6

V

VALOR

See 195. COURAGE

1026. VALUE

See also 47. APPRECIATION

1. *Nothing* is intrinsically valuable; the value of everything is attributed to it, assigned to it from outside the thing itself, by people.

JOHN BARTH, *THE FLOATING OPERA* (1956)

2. [T]he hierarchy of power is not the same as the hierarchy of value. A good human is higher than the animals on both scales; an evil human is high on the scale of power, but at the very bottom of the scale of values.

WENDELL BERRY, "POETRY AND PLACE," *STANDING BY WORDS* (1983)

3. Authentic values are those by which a life can be lived, which can form a people that produces great deeds and thoughts.

ALLAN BLOOM, "VALUES," *THE CLOSING OF THE AMERICAN MIND* (1987)

4. The world is an old woman, and mistakes any gilt farthing for a gold coin; whereby being often cheated, she will thenceforth trust nothing but the common copper.

THOMAS CARLYLE, *SARTOR RESARTUS* (1833–34) 2.4

5. That which cost little is less valued.

CERVANTES, *DON QUIXOTE* (1605–15) 1.4.7, TR. JOHN OZELL

6. Let him go where he will, he can only find so much beauty or worth as he carries.

EMERSON, "CULTURE," *THE CONDUCT OF LIFE* (1860)

7. The world is always curious, and people become valuable merely for their inaccessibility.

F. SCOTT FITZGERALD, "NOTE-BOOKS," *THE CRACK-UP* (1945)

8. What we must decide is perhaps how we are valuable rather than how valuable we are.

EDGAR Z. FRIEDENBERG, "THE IMPACT OF THE SCHOOL," *THE VANISHING ADOLESCENT* (1959)

9. Having lost religious faith and the humanistic values bound up with it, he [man] concentrated on technical and material values and lost the capacity for deep emotional experiences, for the joy and sadness that accompany them.

ERICH FROMM, *THE REVOLUTION OF HOPE* (1968)

10. We cannot be sure that we have something worth living for unless we are ready to die for it.

ERIC HOFFER, *THE TRUE BELIEVER* (1951) 1.2.13

11. Every time a value is born, existence takes on a new meaning; every time one dies, some part of that meaning passes away.

JOSEPH WOOD KRUTCH, "LOVE—OR THE LIFE AND DEATH OF A VALUE," *THE MODERN TEMPER* (1929)

12. Life's values originate in circumstances over which the individual has no control.

CHARLES A. LINDBERGH, "LIFE STREAM," *AUTOBIOGRAPHY OF VALUES* (1978)

13. Armed with all the powers, enjoying all the riches they owe to science, our societies are still trying to live by and to teach systems of values already blasted at the root by science itself.

JACQUES MONOD, *CHANCE AND NECESSITY* (1970)

14. Those things are dearest to us that have cost us most.

MONTAIGNE, "OF THE AFFECTIONS OF FATHERS TO THEIR CHILDREN," *ESSAYS* (1580–88), TR. W. C. HAZLITT

15. The value of a man can only be measured with regard to other men.

NIETZSCHE, *THE WILL TO POWER* (1888) 878, TR. ANTHONY M. LUDOVICI

16. What we obtain too cheap, we esteem too lightly; it is dearness only that gives everything its value.

THOMAS PAINE, *THE AMERICAN CRISIS* (1776–83) 1

17. Men understand the worth of blessings only when they have lost them.

PLAUTUS, *THE CAPTIVES* (3RD C. B.C.)

18. Everything is worth what its purchaser will pay for it.

PUBLILIUS SYRUS, *MORAL SAYINGS* (1ST C. B.C.), 847, TR. DARIUS LYMAN

19. If a piece of worthless stone can bruise a cup of gold, its worth is not increased, nor that of the gold diminished.

SA'DI, *GULISTAN* (1258) 8.57, TR. JAMES ROSS

20. What is false in the science of facts may be true in the science of values.

GEORGE SANTAYANA, *INTERPRETATIONS OF POETRY AND RELIGION* (1900)

21. Together they [President Nixon and Secretary Kissinger] pursued ends that frequently had a tenuous link with reality, using means that were not merely disproportionate but counterproductive and untrue to those values they were meant to defend. In fact neither man demonstrated much faith in those values.

WILLIAM SHAWCROSS, *SIDESHOW* (1979)

22. The real price of everything, what everything really costs to the man who wants to acquire it, is the toil and trouble of acquiring it.

ADAM SMITH, *THE WEALTH OF NATIONS* (1776) 1.5

23. Values, both those that we approve and those that we don't, have roots as deep as creosote rings, and live as long and grow as slowly.

WALLACE STEGNER, "A CAPSULE HISTORY OF CONSERVATION," *WHEN THE BLUEBIRD SINGS IN THE LEMONADE SPRINGS* (1992)

24. The timid man yearns for full value and demands a tenth. The bold man strikes for double value and compromises on par.

MARK TWAIN, "PUDD'NHEAD WILSON'S NEW CALENDAR," *FOLLOWING THE EQUATOR* (1897) 1.13

25. There is no such thing as absolute value in this world. You can only estimate what a thing is worth to *you*.

CHARLES DUDLEY WARNER, "SIXTEENTH WEEK," *MY SUMMER IN A GARDEN* (1871)

1027. VANITY

See also 166. CONCEIT; 732. PRETENSION; 733. PRIDE; 864. SELF-DECEPTION; 871. SELF-ESTEEM; 873. SELF-IMPORTANCE; 876. SELF-LOVE

1. A desire to be observed, considered, esteemed, praised, beloved, and admired by his fellows is one of the earliest as well as the keenest dispositions discovered in the heart of man.

JOHN ADAMS, *DISCOURSES ON DAVILA* (1789), 1

2. Fools take to themselves the respect that is given to their office.

AESOP, "THE JACKASS IN OFFICE," *FABLES* (6TH C. B.C.?), TR. THOMAS JAMES

3. There is no such flatterer as is a man's self.

FRANCIS BACON, "OF FRIENDSHIP," *ESSAYS* (1625)

4. The vain should be wise, for a giant is sometimes strangled by a fly, and there are times when towering giants stumble into pitfalls, and lions fear sheep.

BERECHIAH BEN NATRONAI HA-NAKDAN, *FABLES OF A JEWISH AESOP* (1967)

5. None of us are so much praised or censured as we think.

CHARLES CALEB COLTON, *LACON* (1825) 1.506

6. The anxiety we have for the figure we cut, for our personage, is constantly cropping out. We are showing off and are often more concerned with making a display than with living. Whoever feels observed observes himself.

ANDRÉ GIDE, *JOURNALS* MARCH 12, 1938, TR. JUSTIN O'BRIEN

7. Until the Donkey tried to clear / The Fence, he thought himself a Deer.

ARTHUR GUITERMAN, *A POET'S PROVERBS* (1924)

8. Without vanity a writer's work is tepid, and he must accept his vanity as part of his stock in trade and live with it as one of the hazards of his profession.

MOSS HART, *ACT ONE* (1959)

9. Vanity is truly the motive-power that moves humanity, and it is flattery that greases the wheels.

JEROME K. JEROME, "ON VANITY AND VANITIES," *THE IDLE THOUGHTS OF AN IDLE FELLOW* (1889)

10. The most violent passions sometimes leave us at rest, but vanity agitates us constantly.

LA ROCHEFOUCAULD, *MAXIMS* (1665), TR. KENNETH PRATT

11. What renders other people's vanity insufferable is that it wounds our own.

LA ROCHEFOUCAULD, *MAXIMS* (1665), TR. KENNETH PRATT

12. He wanted to be the bride at every wedding and the corpse at every funeral.

ALICE ROOSEVELT LONGWORTH, QUOTED IN *NEW YORK TIMES BOOK REVIEW,* NOVEMBER 9, 1993

13. He who denies his own vanity usually possesses it in so brutal a form that he instinctively shuts his eyes to avoid the necessity of despising himself.

NIETZSCHE, *MISCELLANEOUS MAXIMS AND OPINIONS* (1879) 38, TR. PAUL V. COHN

14. The most vulnerable and yet most unconquerable of things is human vanity; nay, through being wounded its strength increases and can grow to giant proportions.

NIETZSCHE, *MISCELLANEOUS MAXIMS AND OPINIONS* (1879) 46, TR. PAUL V. COHN

15. We crave support in vanity, as we do in religion, and never forgive contradictions in that sphere.

GEORGE SANTAYANA, *THE LIFE OF REASON: REASON IN SOCIETY* (1905–06) 6

16. It is not vain-glory for a man and his glass to confer in his own chamber.

SHAKESPEARE, *CYMBELINE* (1609–10), 4.1.8

17. A vain man may become proud and imagine himself pleasing to all when he is in reality a universal nuisance.

SPINOZA, *ETHICS* (1677) 3, TR. ANDREW BOYLE

18. Such is the weakness of our nature, that when men are a little exalted in their condition they immediately conceive they have additional senses, and their capacities enlarged not only above other men, but above human comprehension itself.

RICHARD STEELE, *THE SPECTATOR* (1711–12) 193

19. There are no grades of vanity, there are only grades of ability in concealing it.

MARK TWAIN, *NOTEBOOK* (1935)

20. Man habitually sacrifices his life to his purse, but he sacrifices his purse to his vanity.

MIGUEL DE UNAMUNO, "THE HUNGER OF IMMORTALITY," *TRAGIC SENSE OF LIFE* (1913), TR. J. E. CRAWFORD FLITCH

1028. VEGETARIANISM

See also 355. FOOD

1. Most vigitaryans I iver see looked enough like their food to be classed as cannybals.

FINLEY PETER DUNNE, "CASUAL OBSERVATIONS," *MR. DOOLEY'S PHILOSOPHY* (1900)

2. I have no doubt that it is a part of the destiny of the human race, in its gradual improvement, to leave off eating animals, as surely as the savage tribes have left off eating each other when they came in contact with the more civilized.

THOREAU, "HIGHER LAWS," *WALDEN* (1854)

VENGEANCE

See 815. RETRIBUTION; 817. REVENGE

1029. VENICE

See also 509. ITALY AND ITALIANS

1. The sweet life has always attracted travelers, to Venice in the months of the famous Carnival and elsewhere at different times of the year, down the centuries.

LUIGI BARZINI, *THE ITALIANS* (1964)

2. Venice is like eating an entire box of chocolate liqueurs in one go.

TRUMAN CAPOTE, NEWS SUMMARIES, NOV. 26, 1961

3. The perennial wonder of Venice is to peer at herself in her canals and find that she exists—incredible as it seems. It is the same reassurance that a looking-glass offers us: the guarantee that we are real.

MARY MCCARTHY, *VENICE OBSERVED* (1956)

4. The rationalist mind has always had its doubts about Venice. The watery city receives a dry inspection, as though it were a myth for the credulous—poets and honeymooners.

MARY MCCARTHY, *VENICE OBSERVED* (1956)

5. This grossly advertised wonder [Venice], this gold idol with clay feet, this *trompe-l'oeil*, this painted deception, this cliché—what intelligent iconoclast could fail to experience a destructive impulse in her presence?

MARY MCCARTHY, *VENICE OBSERVED* (1956)

6. Venice is the world's unconscious: a miser's glittering hoard, guarded by a Beast whose eyes are made of white agate, and by a saint who is really a prince who has just slain a dragon.

MARY MCCARTHY, *VENICE OBSERVED* (1956)

7. Is there anyone but must repress a secret thrill, on arriving in Venice for the first time—or returning thither after long absence—and stepping into a Venetian gondola?

THOMAS MANN, *DEATH IN VENICE* (1911)

8. Looking, he thought that to come to Venice by the station is like entering a palace by the back door.

THOMAS MANN, *DEATH IN VENICE* (1911)

1030. VICE

See also 204. CRIME; 900. SIN; 1033. VIRTUE; 1034. VIRTUE AND VICE; 1055. WICKEDNESS; 1070. WRONGDOING

1. Vices are their own punishment.

AESOP, "AVARICIOUS AND ENVIOUS," *FABLES* (6TH C. B.C.?), TR. JOSEPH JACOBS

2. We make a ladder of our vices, if we trample those same vices underfoot.

ST. AUGUSTINE, "DE ASCENSIONE," *SERMONS* (5TH C.)

3. Half the vices which the world condemns most loudly have seeds of good in them and require moderate use rather than total abstinence.

SAMUEL BUTLER (D. 1902), *THE WAY OF ALL FLESH* (1903) 52

4. It is the function of vice to keep virtue within reasonable bounds.

SAMUEL BUTLER (D. 1902), *NOTE-BOOKS* (1912)

5. Let them show me a cottage where there are not the same vices of which they accuse courts.

LORD CHESTERFIELD, *LETTERS TO HIS SON,* JUNE 6, 1751

6. We are more apt to catch the vices of others than their virtues, as disease is far more contagious than health.

CHARLES CALEB COLTON, *LACON* (1825) 1.247

7. When all run by common consent into vice, none appear to do so.

CHARLES CALEB COLTON, *LACON* (1825) 2.61

8. Vice is a creature of such heejous mien, as Hogan says, that th' more ye see it th' betther ye like it.

FINLEY PETER DUNNE, "THE CRUSADE AGAINST VICE," *MR. DOOLEY'S OPINIONS* (1901)

9. Every vice is only an exaggeration of a necessary and virtuous function.

EMERSON, *JOURNALS* 1836

10. Vice often rides triumphant in virtue's chariot.

THOMAS FULLER, M.D., *GNOMOLOGIA* (1732) 5538

11. Many a man's vices have at first been nothing worse than good qualities run wild.

AUGUSTUS WILLIAM HARE, *GUESSES AT TRUTH* (1827)

12. This is the danger, when vice becomes a precedent.

BEN JONSON, "OF THE DIVERSITY OF WITS," *TIMBER* (1640)

13. He who hates vices hates men.

JOHN MORLEY, "ROBESPIERRE," *CRITICAL MISCELLANIES* (1871–1908)

14. Men are more easily governed through their vices than through their virtues.

NAPOLEON I, *MAXIMS* (1804–15)

15. Jupiter has loaded us with a couple of wallets: the one, filled with our own vices, he has placed at our backs; the other, heavy with those of others, he has hung before.

PHAEDRUS, *FABLES* (1ST C.) 4.10.1, TR. H. T. RILEY

16. For lawless joys a bitter ending waits.

PINDAR, *ODES* (5TH C. B.C.) ISTHMIA 7.23

17. Vice is a monster of so frightful mien, / As to be hated needs but to be seen; / Yet seen too oft, familiar with her face, / We first endure, then pity, then embrace.

ALEXANDER POPE, *AN ESSAY ON MAN* (1733–34) 2.217

18. Every vice has its excuse ready.

PUBLILIUS SYRUS, *MORAL SAYINGS* (1ST C. B.C.), 986, TR. DARIUS LYMAN

19. The little vices of the great must needs be accounted very great.

PUBLILIUS SYRUS, *MORAL SAYINGS* (1ST C. B.C.) 1004, TR. DARIUS LYMAN

20. We tolerate without rebuke the vices with which we have grown familiar.

PUBLILIUS SYRUS, *MORAL SAYINGS* (1ST C. B.C.), 150, TR. DARIUS LYMAN

21. Vice, like virtue, / Grows in small steps, and no true innocence / Can ever fall at once to deepest guilt.

RACINE, *PHAEDRA* (1677) 4, TR. ROBERT HENDERSON

22. Astronomy was born of superstition; eloquence of ambition, hatred, falsehood, and flattery; geometry of avarice; physics of an idle curiosity; and even moral philosophy of human pride. Thus the arts and sciences owe their birth to our vices.

ROUSSEAU, *A DISCOURSE ON THE MORAL EFFECTS OF THE ARTS AND SCIENCES* (1750) 2, TR. G. D. H. COLE

23. The gods are just, and of our pleasant vices / Make instruments to scourge us.

SHAKESPEARE, *KING LEAR* (1605–06) 5.3. 170

24. There is no vice so simple but assumes / Some mark of virtue on his outward parts.

SHAKESPEARE, *THE MERCHANT OF VENICE* (1596–97) 3.2.81

25. Through tattered clothes small vices do appear; / Robes and furred gowns hide all. Plate sin with gold, / And the strong lance of justice hurtless breaks; / Arm it in rags, a pygmy's straw does pierce it.

SHAKESPEARE, *KING LEAR* (1605–06) 4.6. 168

26. Nurse one vice in your bosom. Give it the attention it deserves and let your virtues spring up modestly around it. Then you'll have the miser who's no liar; and the drunkard who's the benefactor of a whole city.

THORNTON WILDER, *THE MATCHMAKER* (1955) 3

VICTORY

See 173. CONQUEST

VIEWPOINT

See 58. ATTITUDE; 689. PERSPECTIVE

1031. VICE-PRESIDENCY

See also 730. PRESIDENCY

1. Th' prisidincy is th' highest office in th' gift iv th' people. Th' vice-prisidincy is th' next highest an' the lowest. It isn't a crime exactly. Ye can't be sint to jail f'r it, but it's a kind iv a disgrace.

FINLEY PETER DUNNE, "THE VICE-PRESIDENT," *DISSERTATIONS BY MR. DOOLEY* (1906)

2. The second office of this government is honorable and easy, the first is but a splendid misery.

THOMAS JEFFERSON, LETTER TO ELBRIDGE GERRY, MAY 13, 1797

1032. VIOLENCE

See also 26. AGGRESSION; 357. FORCE; 518. KILLING; 786. REBELLION; 1042. WAR

1. Now at last the slowly gathered, long-pent-up fury of the storm broke upon us. Four or five millions of men met each other in the first shock of the most merciless of all the wars of which record has been kept.

SIR WINSTON CHURCHILL, *THEIR FINEST HOUR* (1949)

2. Violence is just where kindness is vain.

CORNEILLE, *HÉRACLIUS* (1647) I

3. God hates violence. He has ordained that all men / fairly possess their property, not seize it.

EURIPIDES, *HELEN* (412 B.C.), TR. RICHMOND LATTIMORE

4. Not only do most people accept violence
if it is perpetuated by legitimate authority,
they also regard violence against certain kinds of people as inherently legitimate, no matter who commits it.

EDGAR Z. FRIEDENBERG, *NEW YORK REVIEW OF BOOKS,* OCT. 20, 1966

5. Most Americans would say that they disapproved of violence. But what they really mean is that they believe it should be the monopoly of the state.

EDGAR Z. FRIEDENBERG, *NEW YORK REVIEW OF BOOKS,* OCT. 20, 1966

6. It is better to be violent, if there is violence in our hearts, than to put on the cloak of non-violence to cover impotence.

MOHANDAS K. GANDHI, *NON-VIOLENCE IN PEACE AND WAR* (1948) 1.240

7. Liberty and democracy become unholy when their hands are dyed red with innocent blood.

MOHANDAS K. GANDHI, *NON-VIOLENCE IN PEACE AND WAR* (1948) 1.357

8. The most heterogeneous ideas are yoked by violence together.

SAMUEL JOHNSON, *LIVES OF THE POETS: COWLEY* (1779–81)

9. The pornography of violence of course far exceeds, in volume and general acceptance, sexual pornography, in this Puritan land of ours.

URSULA K. LE GUIN, "FACING IT," *DANCING AT THE EDGE OF THE WORLD* (1989)

10. Violence is essentially wordless, and it can begin only where thought and rational communication have broken down.

THOMAS MERTON, INTRODUCTION TO SELECTED TEXTS FROM MOHANDAS K. GANDHI'S *NON-VIOLENCE IN PEACE AND WAR* (1948)

11. To-day violence is the rhetoric of the period.

JOSÉ ORTEGA Y GASSET, *THE REVOLT OF THE MASSES* (1930) II

12. It is possible, I suppose, that we are returning to a Dark Age. What is frightening is that violence is not only represented by nations, but everywhere walks among us freely.

MAY SARTON, "THURSDAY, DECEMBER 5TH," *THE HOUSE BY THE SEA: A JOURNAL* (1977)

13. A child who has been severely punished for sex play is not necessarily less inclined to continue; and a

man who has been imprisoned for violent assault is not necessarily less inclined toward violence.

B.F. SKINNER, *BEYOND FREEDOM AND DIGNITY* (1971)

14. Wherever a people has grown savage in arms so that human laws have no longer any place among it, the only powerful means of reducing it is religion.

GIAMBATTISTA VICO, *THE NEW SCIENCE* (1725–44) 1.2

1033. VIRTUE

See also 393. GOODNESS; 491. INTEGRITY; 604. MORALITY; 822. RIGHT; 1030. VICE; 1034. VIRTUE AND VICE

1. All sober inquirers after truth, ancient and modern, pagan and Christian, have declared that the happiness of man, as well as his dignity, consists in virtue.

JOHN ADAMS, *THOUGHTS ON GOVERNMENT* (1776)

2. Public virtue cannot exist in a nation without private, and public virtue is the only foundation of republics.

JOHN ADAMS, LETTER TO MERCY WARREN, APRIL 16, 1776

3. A state of temperance, sobriety and justice without devotion is a cold, lifeless, insipid condition of virtue, and is rather to be styled philosophy than religion.

JOSEPH ADDISON, *THE SPECTATOR* (1711–12) 201

4. Virtue is more clearly shown in the performance of fine actions than in the nonperformance of base ones.

ARISTOTLE, *NICOMACHEAN ETHICS* (4TH C. B.C.) 4.1, TR. J. A. K. THOMSON

5. Virtue is like precious odours,—most fragrant when they are incensed or crushed.

FRANCIS BACON, "OF ADVERSITY," *ESSAYS* (1625)

6. A virtue to be serviceable must, like gold, be alloyed with some commoner but more durable metal.

SAMUEL BUTLER (D. 1902), *THE WAY OF ALL FLESH* (1903) 19

7. Abstract qualities begin / With capitals alway: / The True, the Good, the Beautiful— / Those are the things that pay!

LEWIS CARROLL, "POETA FIT, NON NASCITUR" (1869)

8. Virtue is not the absence of vices or the avoidance of moral dangers; virtue is a vivid and separate thing, like pain or a particular smell.

G. K. CHESTERTON, "A PIECE OF CHALK," *TREMENDOUS TRIFLES* (1909)

9. The existence of virtue depends entirely upon its use.

CICERO, *DE RE PUBLICA* (C. 51 B.C.) 1

10. The good opinion of our fellow men is the strongest, though not the purest motive to virtue.

CHARLES CALEB COLTON, *LACON* (1825) 2.104

11. If a superior man abandon virtue, how can he fulfil the requirements of that name?

CONFUCIUS, *ANALECTS* (6TH C. B.C.) 4.5, TR. JAMES LEGGE

12. Seldom indeed does human virtue rise / From trunk to branch.

DANTE, "PURGATORIO," 7, *THE DIVINE COMEDY* (C. 1300–21), TR. LAWRENCE GRANT WHITE

13. Virtue is praised, but hated. People run away from it, for it is ice-cold and in this world you must keep your feet warm.

DENIS DIDEROT, *RAMEAU'S NEPHEW* (1762), TR. RALPH H. BOWEN

14. Who knows his virtue's name or place, hath none.

JOHN DONNE, "A LETTER TO THE LADY CAREY, AND MRS. ESSEX RICHE, FROM AMYENS," *LETTERS TO SEVERAL PERSONAGES* (1651)

15. Virtue, though in rags, will keep me warm.

JOHN DRYDEN, *IMITATION OF HORACE* (1697) 3.29.87

16. The essence of greatness is the perception that virtue is enough.

EMERSON, "HEROISM," *ESSAYS: FIRST SERIES* (1841)

17. The highest virtue is always against the law.

EMERSON, "WORSHIP," *THE CONDUCT OF LIFE* (1860)

18. The order of things consents to virtue.

EMERSON, *JOURNALS* 1834

19. Silver and gold are not the only coin; virtue too passes current all over the world.

EURIPIDES, *OEDIPUS* (5TH C. B.C.) 546, TR. M. H. MORGAN

20. He hath no mean portion of virtue that loveth it in another.

THOMAS FULLER, M.D., *GNOMOLOGIA* (1732) 1894

21. Virtue is despised if it be seen in a threadbare cloak.

THOMAS FULLER, M.D., *GNOMOLOGIA* (1732) 5374

22. That virtue which requires to be ever guarded is scarce worth the sentinel.

OLIVER GOLDSMITH, *THE VICAR OF WAKEFIELD* (1766) 5

23. The measure of any man's virtue is what he would do, if he had neither the laws nor public opinion, nor even his own prejudices, to control him.

WILLIAM HAZLITT, *CHARACTERISTICS* (1823) 128

24. I don't believe the Devil would give half as much for the services of a sinner as he would for those of one of these folks that are always doing virtuous acts in a way to make them unpleasing.

OLIVER WENDELL HOLMES, SR., *THE PROFESSOR AT THE BREAKFAST TABLE* (1860) 4

25. Even virtue followed beyond reason's rule / May stamp the just man knave, the sage a fool.

HORACE, *EPISTLES* (20-C. 8 B.C.) 1.6

26. Every man prefers virtue, when there is not some strong incitement to transgress its precepts.

SAMUEL JOHNSON, QUOTED IN BOSWELL'S *LIFE OF SAMUEL JOHNSON* JULY 21, 1763

27. There are people who are virtuous only in a piece-meal way; virtue is a fabric from which they never make themselves a whole garment.

JOSEPH JOUBERT, *PENSÉES* (1842) 9.37

28. If it be usual to be strongly impressed by things that are scarce, why are we so little impressed by virtue?

LA BRUYÈRE, *CHARACTERS* (1688) 2.20, TR. HENRI VAN LAUN

29. He is a truly virtuous man who wishes always to be open to the observation of honest men.

LA ROCHEFOUCAULD, *MAXIMS* (1665), TR. KENNETH PRATT

30. Virtue would not go to such lengths if vanity did not keep her company.

LA ROCHEFOUCAULD, *MAXIMS* (1665), TR. KENNETH PRATT

31. Happiness cannot be the reward of virtue; it must be the intelligible consequence of it.

WALTER LIPPMANN, *A PREFACE TO MORALS* (1929) 1.7.7

32. Love Virtue, she alone is free, / She can teach ye how to climb / Higher than the sphery chime; / Or, if Virtue feeble were, / Heav'n itself would stoop to her.

MILTON, *COMUS* (1634) 1019

33. Most men admire / Virtue who follow not her lore.

MILTON, *PARADISE REGAINED* (1671) 1.482

34. Virtue cannot be followed but for herself, and if one sometimes borrows her mask to some other purpose, she presently pulls it away again.

MONTAIGNE, "OF THE INCONSTANCY OF OUR ACTIONS," *ESSAYS* (1580–88), TR. W. C. HAZLITT

35. It is a distinction to have many virtues, but a hard lot.

NIETZSCHE, "ON ENJOYING AND SUFFERING THE PASSIONS," *THUS SPOKE ZARATHUSTRA* (1883–92) 1, TR. WALTER KAUFMANN

36. When we are planning for posterity, we ought to remember that virtue is not hereditary.

THOMAS PAINE, "OF THE PRESENT ABILITY OF AMERICA," *COMMON SENSE* (1776)

37. Virtues are virtues only to those who can appreciate them.

PANCHATANTRA (C. 5TH C.) 1, TR. FRANKLIN EDGERTON

38. The strength of a man's virtue must not be measured by his efforts, but by his ordinary life.

PASCAL, *PENSÉES* (1670) 352, TR. W. F. TROTTER

39. There may be guilt when there is too much virtue.

RACINE, *ANDROMACHE* (1667) 3, TR. ROBERT HENDERSON

40. The chief cause of our misery is less the violence of our passions than the feebleness of our virtues.

JOSEPH ROUX, *MEDITATIONS OF A PARISH PRIEST* (1886) 5.25, TR. ISABEL F. HAPGOOD

41. We know that the exercise of virtue should be its own reward, and it seems to follow that the enduring of it on the part of the patient should be its own punishment.

BERTRAND RUSSELL, "THE HARM THAT GOOD MEN DO," *FIFTY FAMOUS ESSAYS* (1964)

42. The glory that goes with wealth and beauty is fleeting and fragile; virtue is a possession glorious and eternal.

SALLUST, *CONSPIRACY OF CATILINE* (1ST C. B.C.) 4

43. Virtue is bold, and goodness never fearful.

SHAKESPEARE, *MEASURE FOR MEASURE* (1604–05) 3.1.215

44. Virtue herself is her own fairest reward.

SILIUS ITALICUS, *PUNICA* (1ST C.) 13.663

45. Nothing can be more puritanical in application than the virtues.

MURIEL SPARK, *CURRICULUM VITAE* (1992)

46. When men grow virtuous in their old age, they only make a sacrifice to God of the devil's leavings.

JONATHAN SWIFT, *THOUGHTS ON VARIOUS SUBJECTS* (1711)

47. Virtue must shape itself in deed.

LORD TENNYSON, "TIRESIAS" (1885)

48. Virtue in a man doesn't make you want to grab him.

CAITLIN THOMAS, *CAITLIN* (1986), WITH GEORGE TREMLETT

49. I have seen men incapable of the sciences, but never any incapable of virtue.

VOLTAIRE, "PHILOSOPHER," *PHILOSOPHICAL DICTIONARY* (1764)

50. Virtue between men is a commerce of good actions: he who has no part in this commerce must not be reckoned.

VOLTAIRE, "VIRTUE," *PHILOSOPHICAL DICTIONARY* (1764)

51. Virtue is the roughest way, / But proves at night a bed of down.

SIR HENRY WOTTON, "UPON THE SUDDEN RESTRAINT OF THE EARL OF SOMERSET," *POEMS* (1842)

1034. VIRTUE AND VICE

See also 1030. VICE; 1033. VIRTUE

1. Show me a community or a country where all the minor vices are discouraged and I will show you one bereft of major virtues.

HEYWOOD BROUN, "SARATOGA FADES," *NEW YORK WORLD TELEGRAM,* AUG. 19, 1939

2. They that endeavour to abolish vice, destroy also virtue; for contraries, though they destroy one another, are yet the life of one another.

SIR THOMAS BROWNE, *RELIGIO MEDICI* (1642) 2

3. Vice has more martyrs than virtue; and it often happens that men suffer more to be lost than to be saved.

CHARLES CALEB COLTON, *LACON* (1825) 1.170

4. This is the tax a man must pay to his virtues—they hold up a torch to his vices, and render those frailties notorious in him which would have passed without observation in another.

CHARLES CALEB COLTON, *LACON* (1825) 1.237

5. Men imagine that they communicate their virtue or vice only by overt actions, and do not see that virtue or vice emit a breath every moment.

EMERSON, "SELF-RELIANCE," *ESSAYS: FIRST SERIES* (1841)

6. There is a capacity of virtue in us, and there is a capacity of vice to make your blood creep.

EMERSON, *JOURNALS,* 1831

7. Search others for their virtues, thy self for thy vices.

BENJAMIN FRANKLIN, *POOR RICHARD'S ALMANACK* (1732–57)

8. Our virtues are most frequently but vices disguised.

LA ROCHEFOUCAULD, *MAXIMS* (1665)

9. Vices are ingredients of virtues just as poisons are ingredients of remedies. Prudence mixes and tempers them and uses them effectively against life's ills.

LA ROCHEFOUCAULD, *MAXIMS* (1665)

10. It is convention and arbitrary rewards which make all the merit and demerit of what we call vice and virtue.

JULIEN OFFROY DE LA METTRIE, *ANTI-SÉNÈQUE OU DISCOURS SUR LE BONHEUR*

11. The absence of vices adds so little to the sum of one's virtues.

ANTONIO MACHADO, *JUAN DE MAIRENA* (1943) 28, TR. BEN BELITT

12. If virtue cannot shine bright, but by the conflict of contrary appetites, shall we then say that she cannot subsist without the assistance of vice, and that it is from her that she derives her reputation and honor?

MONTAIGNE, "OF CRUELTY," *ESSAYS* (1580–88), TR. W. C. HAZLITT

13. When I religiously confess myself to myself, I find that the best virtue I have has in it some tincture of vice.

MONTAIGNE, "THAT WE TASTE NOTHING PURE," *ESSAYS* (1580–88), TR. W. C. HAZLITT

14. When virtue has slept, she will get up more refreshed.

NIETZSCHE, *HUMAN, ALL TOO HUMAN* (1878) 83, IN *THE PORTABLE NIETZSCHE*, TR. WALTER KAUFMANN

15. Virtue and vice, evil and good, are siblings, or next-door neighbors, / Easy to make mistakes, hard to tell them apart.

OVID, *THE REMEDIES FOR LOVE* (C. A.D. 8), TR. ROLFE HUMPHRIES

16. Who does not sufficiently hate vice, / Does not sufficiently love virtue.

JEAN-BAPTISTE ROUSSEAU, *FABLES, OEUVRES* (1743)

17. Some rise by sin, and some by virtue fall.

SHAKESPEARE, *MEASURE FOR MEASURE* (1604–05) 2.1.38

18. Virtue itself turns vice, being misapplied, / And vice sometime's by action dignified.

SHAKESPEARE, *ROMEO AND JULIET* (1594–95) 2.3.21

19. More people are flattered into virtue than bullied out of vice.

ROBERT SMITH SURTEES, *THE ANALYSIS OF THE HUNTING FIELD* (1846) 1

20. I never was so rapid in my virtue but my vice kept up with me.

THOREAU, *JOURNAL* FEB. 8, 1841

21. If a man has no vices, he's in great danger of making vices about his virtues, and there's a spectacle.

THORNTON WILDER, *THE MATCHMAKER* (1955) 3

1035. VISION

See also 683. PERCEPTION; 897. SIGHT

1. No man sees far; the most see no farther than their noses.

THOMAS CARLYLE, "COUNT CAGLIOSTRO" (1833)

2. A great mind is one that can forget or look beyond itself.

WILLIAM HAZLITT, "COMMONPLACES," *THE ROUND TABLE* (1817), 67

3. Visionary people are visionary partly because of the very great many things they don't see.

BERKELEY RICE, *THE NEW YORK TIMES MAGAZINE,* MARCH 17, 1968

4. Hundreds of people can talk for one who can think, but thousands can think for one who can see. To see clearly is poetry, prophecy, and religion—all in one.

JOHN RUSKIN, *MODERN PAINTERS* (1843–60), V. 3, 4.16.28

5. A rock pile ceases to be a rock pile the moment a single man contemplates it, bearing within him the image of a cathedral.

SAINT-EXUPÉRY, *FLIGHT TO ARRAS* (1942), 22, TR. LEWIS GALANTIÈRE

6. Vision is the art of seeing things invisible.

JONATHAN SWIFT, *THOUGHTS ON VARIOUS SUBJECTS* (1711)

VISITING

See 428. HOSPITALITY

1036. VITALITY

See also 293. ENTHUSIASM; 513. JOIE DE VIVRE; 928. SPONTANEITY

1. Vitality shows in not only the ability to persist but the ability to start over.

F. SCOTT FITZGERALD, "NOTE-BOOKS," *THE CRACK-UP* (1945)

2. The difference between the university graduate and the autodidact lies not so much in the extent of knowledge as in the extent of vitality and self-confidence.

MILAN KUNDERA, *THE UNBEARABLE LIGHTNESS OF BEING* (1984)

3. When vitality runs high, death takes men by surprise. But if they close their eyes to this possibility, what they gain in peace they lose in sensibility and significance.

LEWIS MUMFORD, "COSMOS AND PERSON," *THE CONDUCT OF LIFE* (1951)

4. Human vitality is so exuberant that in the sorriest desert it still finds a pretext for glowing and trembling.

JOSÉ ORTEGA Y GASSET, *NOTES ON THE NOVEL* (1925)

5. Nature drives with a loose rein and vitality of any sort can blunder through many a predicament in which reason would despair.

GEORGE SANTAYANA, *THE SENSE OF BEAUTY* (1896)

1037. VOCATIONS

See also 1. ABILITY; 311. EXCELLENCE; 988. TRAINING; 1065. WORK

1. The price one pays for pursuing any profession, or calling, is an intimate knowledge of its ugly side.

JAMES BALDWIN, "THE BLACK BOY LOOKS AT THE WHITE BOY," *NOBODY KNOWS MY NAME* (1961)

2. Vocations which we wanted to pursue, but didn't, bleed, like colors, on the whole of our existence.

BALZAC, "SCÈNES DE LA VIE PARISIENNE," *LA MAISON NUCINGEN* (1838), V. 3

3. The professionals resemble and recognize each other by virtue of the stigmata that their trade has left upon them. They are like the dog in the fable, whose collar has made an indelible mark around his neck. The amateur is the shaggy wolf whom no dog had better trust too far.

JACQUES BARZUN, "THE INDISPENSABLE AMATEUR," *CRITICAL QUESTIONS* (1982)

4. Blessed is he who has found his work; let him ask no other blessedness.

THOMAS CARLYLE, *PAST AND PRESENT* (1843), 3.11

5. Every man has his own vocation. The talent is the call.

EMERSON, "SPIRITUAL LAWS," *ESSAYS: FIRST SERIES* (1841)

6. The player envies only the player, the poet envies only the poet.

WILLIAM HAZLITT, "ENVY," *SKETCHES AND ESSAYS* (1839)

7. Every calling is great when greatly pursued.

OLIVER WENDELL HOLMES, JR., SPEECH, SUFFOLK BAR ASSOCIATION, FEB. 5, 1885

8. The artisan or scientist or the follower of whatever discipline who has the habit of comparing himself not with other followers but with the discipline itself will have a lower opinion of himself, the more excellent he is.

GIACOMO LEOPARDI, *PENSIERI* (1834–37), 64, TR. WILLIAM FENSE WEAVER

9. Every science has for its basis a system of principles as fixed and unalterable as those by which the universe is regulated and governed. Man cannot make principles; he can only discover them.

THOMAS PAINE, *THE AGE OF REASON* (1794, 1796), I

10. When men are rightly occupied, their amusement grows out of their work, as the colour-petals out of a fruitful flower.

JOHN RUSKIN, *SESAME AND LILIES* (1865), 1.39

11. All professions are conspiracies against the laity.

GEORGE BERNARD SHAW, *THE DOCTOR'S DILEMMA* (1913), I

12. The sure way of knowing nothing about life is to try to make oneself useful.

OSCAR WILDE, *THE ARTIST AS CRITIC: CRITICAL WRITINGS OF OSCAR WILDE*, ED. RICHARD ELLMAN (1969)

1038. VOTING

See also 132. CITIZENS; 233. DEMOCRACY; 395. GOVERNMENT; 711. POLITICS AND POLITICIANS

1. Elections are won by men and women chiefly because most people vote against somebody, rather than for somebody.

FRANKLIN P. ADAMS, *NODS AND BECKS* (1944)

2. Vote for the man who promises least; he'll be the least disappointing.

BERNARD BARUCH, QUOTED IN MEYER BERGER'S *NEW YORK* (1960)

3. A man without a vote is in this land like a man without a hand.

HENRY WARD BEECHER, *PROVERBS FROM PLYMOUTH PULPIT* (1887)

4. At the bottom of all the tributes paid to democracy is the little man, walking into the little booth, with a little pencil, making a little cross on a little bit of paper—no amount of rhetoric or voluminous discussion can possibly diminish the overwhelming importance of the point.

SIR WINSTON CHURCHILL, SPEECH, HOUSE OF COMMONS, OCT. 31, 1944

5. Disfranchisement is the deliberate theft and robbery of the only protection of poor against rich and black against white.

W. E. B. DU BOIS, "WE RETURN—FIGHTING," *IN THEIR OWN WORDS: 1916–1966*, V. 3

6. Those who stay away from the election think that one vote will do no good: 'Tis but one step more to think one vote will do no harm.

EMERSON, *JOURNALS*, 1854

7. The apathy of the modern voter is the confusion of the modern reformer.

LEARNED HAND, SPEECH, WASHINGTON, D.C., MARCH 8, 1932

8. The vote is the most powerful instrument ever devised by man for breaking down injustice and destroying the terrible walls which imprison men because they are different from other men.

LYNDON B. JOHNSON, ADDRESS ON SIGNING THE VOTING-RIGHTS BILL, WASHINGTON, D.C., AUG. 6, 1965

9. There are more Negroes in jail with me than there are on the voting rolls.

MARTIN LUTHER KING, JR., LETTER FROM SELMA, ALA., FEBRUARY 1, 1965

10. To make democracy work, we must be a nation of participants, not simply observers. One who does not vote has no right to complain.

LOUIS L'AMOUR, *EDUCATION OF A WANDERING MAN* (1989)

11. An American presidential campaign resembles a forced march through enemy country.

LEWIS LAPHAM, *IMPERIAL MASQUERADE* (1990)

12. Ballots are the rightful and peaceful successors to bullets.

ABRAHAM LINCOLN, MESSAGE TO CONGRESS, JULY 7, 1861

13. Football strategy does not originate in a scrimmage: it is useless to expect solutions in a political campaign.

WALTER LIPPMANN, "THE CHANGING FOCUS," *A PREFACE TO POLITICS* (1914)

14. No candidate too pallid, / No issue too remote, / But it can snare / A questionnaire / To analyze our vote.

PHYLLIS MCGINLEY, "BALLAD OF THE PREELECTION VOTE," *A POCKETFUL OF WRY* (1940)

15. Voting is simply a way of determining which side is the stronger without putting it to the test of fighting.

H. L. MENCKEN, *MINORITY REPORT* (1956), 312

16. More men have been elected between Sundown and Sunup than ever were elected between Sunup and Sundown.

WILL ROGERS, "MR. FORD AND OTHER POLITICAL SELF-STARTERS," *THE ILLITERATE DIGEST* (1924)

17. Let us never forget that government is *ourselves* and not an alien power over us. The ultimate rulers of our democracy are not a President and senators and congressmen and government officials, but the voters of this country.

FRANKLIN D. ROOSEVELT, SPEECH, MARIETTA, OHIO, JULY 8, 1938

18. An election is a moral horror, as bad as a battle except for the blood: a mud bath for every soul concerned in it.

GEORGE BERNARD SHAW, *BACK TO METHUSELAH* (1921), 2

19. The idea that you can merchandise candidates for high office like breakfast cereal—that you can gather votes like box tops—is, I think, the ultimate indignity to the democratic process.

ADLAI STEVENSON, ACCEPTANCE SPEECH, DEMOCRATIC NATIONAL CONVENTION, AUG. 18, 1956

20. In years divisible by two we expect the truth to be trashed and decency to be mugged.

GEORGE F. WILL, "THE POLLUTION OF POLITICS," *SUDDENLY: THE AMERICAN IDEA ABROAD AND AT HOME, 1986–1990* (1990)

VOWS

See 743. PROMISES

1039. VULGARITY

1. The vulgar man is always the most distinguished, for the very desire to be distinguished is vulgar.

G. K. CHESTERTON, "THE BOY," *ALL THINGS CONSIDERED* (1908)

2. [T]hose who are addicted to the phrase "to use a vulgarism" expect to achieve the feat of being at once vulgar and superior to vulgarity.

H.W. FOWLER, *A DICTIONARY OF MODERN ENGLISH USAGE*, 2ND ED. (1926)

3. It is disgusting to pick your teeth; what is vulgar is to use a gold toothpick.

LOUIS KRONENBERGER, "FASHIONS IN VULGARITY," *THE CART AND THE HORSE* (1964), 2

W

1040. WAITING

See also 318. EXPECTATION; 427. HOPE; 456. IMPATIENCE; 677. PATIENCE

1. Serene, I fold my hands and wait, / Nor care for wind, nor tide, nor sea; / I rave no more 'gainst time or fate, / For lo! my own shall come to me.

JOHN BURROUGHS, "WAITING" (1862)

2. How much of human life is lost in waiting!

EMERSON, "PRUDENCE," *ESSAYS: FIRST SERIES* (1841)

3. The philosophy of waiting is sustained by all the oracles of the universe.

EMERSON, *JOURNALS,* 1847

4. They also serve who only stand and wait.

MILTON, SONNET 19 (1655)

5. Half the agony of living is waiting.

ALEXANDER ROSE, *MEMOIRS OF A HETEROSEXUAL* (1968)

6. Long ailments wear out pain, and long hopes, joy.

STANISLAUS I OF POLAND, *MAXIMS* (C. 18TH C.)

1041. WALKING

See also 696. PHYSICAL FITNESS; 929. SPORTS

1. People seem to think there is something inherently noble and virtuous in the desire to go for a walk.

MAX BEERBOHM, "GOING OUT FOR A WALK," *AND EVEN NOW* (1920)

2. These feet have walked ten thousand miles working for white folks and another ten thousand keeping up with colored.

LANGSTON HUGHES, *SIMPLE SPEAKS HIS MIND* (1950)

3. A sedentary life is the real sin against the Holy Spirit. Only those thoughts that come by walking have any value.

NIETZSCHE, "MAXIMS AND MISSILES," 34, *TWILIGHT OF THE IDOLS* (1888), TR. ANTHONY M. LUDOVICI

WANDERING

See 812. RESTLESSNESS; 992. TRAVEL

WANTS

See 238. DESIRES; 625. NEED

1042. WAR

See also 173. CONQUEST; 228. DEFEAT; 229. DEFENSE; 252. DISCORD; 345. FIGHTING; 518. KILLING; 588. THE MILITARY; 641. NUCLEAR POWER; 665. PACIFISM; 681. PEACE; 939. STRATEGY; 1032. VIOLENCE; 1043. WAR, CIVIL; 1049. WEAPONS

1. The art of war is like the art of the courtesan—indeed, they might be called sisters, since both are the slaves of desperation.

PIETRO ARETINO, LETTER TO AMBROGIO EUSEBIO, NOV. 28, 1537, TR. SAMUEL PUTNAM

2. A just fear of an imminent danger, though there be no blow given, is a lawful cause of war.

FRANCIS BACON, "OF EMPIRE," *ESSAYS* (1625)

3. Youth is the first victim of war; the first fruit of peace. It takes twenty years or more of peace to make a man; it takes only twenty seconds of war to destroy him.

BAUDOUIN I OF BELGIUM, ADDRESS TO JOINT SESSION OF U.S. CONGRESS, MAY 12, 1959

4. It is not merely cruelty that leads men to love war, it is excitement.

HENRY WARD BEECHER, *PROVERBS FROM PLYMOUTH PULPIT* (1887)

5. A general and a bit of shooting makes you forget your troubles ... it takes your mind off the cost of living.

BRENDAN BEHAN, *THE HOSTAGE* (1958), 3

6. If we justify war, it is because all peoples always justify the traits of which they find themselves possessed, not because war will bear an objective examination of its merits.

RUTH BENEDICT, *PATTERNS OF CULTURE* (1934)

7. We do not fight for the real but for shadows we make. / A flag is a piece of cloth and a word is a

sound, / But we make them something neither cloth nor a sound, / Totems of love and hate, black sorcery-stones.

STEPHEN VINCENT BENÉT, *JOHN BROWN'S BODY* (1928), 4

8. War is like love, it always finds a way.

BERTOLT BRECHT, *MOTHER COURAGE* (1939), 6, TR. ERIC BENTLEY

9. No one ever mentioned it, but thousands of men welcomed World War II as a way to escape their humdrum lives rather than a chance to fight for God and country.

ART BUCHWALD, *LEAVING HOME: A MEMOIR* (1993)

10. War for most men is not fighting or marching in parades. It is sitting around somewhere wondering what the hell you are supposed to be doing.

ART BUCHWALD, *LEAVING HOME: A MEMOIR* (1993)

11. Clear undeniable right, clear undeniable might: either of these once ascertained puts an end to battle. All battle is a confused experiment to ascertain one and both of these.

THOMAS CARLYLE, *CHARTISM* (1839), 1

12. There is nothing so subject to the inconstancy of fortune as war.

CERVANTES, *DON QUIXOTE* (1605–15), 1.1.8, TR. JOHN OZELL

13. There is no working middle course in wartime.

SIR WINSTON CHURCHILL, SPEECH, HOUSE OF COMMONS, JULY 2, 1942

14. Boys are the cash of war. Whoever said / we're not free-spenders doesn't know our likes.

JOHN CIARDI, "NEW YEAR'S EVE," *THIS STRANGEST EVERYTHING* (1966)

15. Laws are silent in time of war.

CICERO, *PRO MILONE* (52 B.C.)

16. War is nothing but a duel on a larger scale.

KARL VON CLAUSEWITZ, *WAR, POLITICS & POWER* (1962), 1, TR. EDWARD M. COLLINS

17. War is the province of chance. In no other sphere of human activity must such a margin be left for this intruder. It increases the uncertainty of every circumstance and deranges the course of events.

KARL VON CLAUSEWITZ, *WAR, POLITICS & POWER* (1962), 3, TR. EDWARD M. COLLINS

18. War is a continuation of policy by other means. It is not merely a political act but a real political instrument.

KARL VON CLAUSEWITZ, *WAR, POLITICS & POWER* (1962), 1, TR. EDWARD M. COLLINS

19. All the gods are dead except the god of war.

ELDRIDGE CLEAVER, "FOUR VIGNETTES," *SOUL ON ICE* (1968)

20. As wounded men may limp through life, so our war minds may not regain the balance of their thoughts for decades.

FRANK MOORE COLBY, "WAR MINDS," *THE COLBY ESSAYS* (1926), V. 2

21. Boys and girls, / And women, that would groan to see a child / Pull off an insect's leg, all read of war, / The best amusement for our morning meal.

SAMUEL TAYLOR COLERIDGE, *FEARS IN SOLITUDE* (1798)

22. For what are the triumphs of war, planned by ambition, executed by violence, and consummated by devastation? The means are the sacrifice of many, the end, the bloated aggrandizement of the few.

CHARLES CALEB COLTON, *LACON* (1825), 2.283

23. War is a game in which princes seldom win, the people never.

CHARLES CALEB COLTON, *LACON* (1825), 1.534

24. The disasters of the world are due to its inhabitants not being able to grow old simultaneously. There is always a raw and intolerant nation eager to destroy the tolerant and mellow.

CYRIL CONNOLLY, *THE UNQUIET GRAVE* (1945), 2

25. War's a game which were their subjects wise / Kings would not play at.

WILLIAM COWPER, "THE WINTER MORNING WALK," *THE TASK* (1785), 187

26. As peace is of all goodness, so war is an emblem, a hieroglyphic, of all misery.

JOHN DONNE, *SERMONS*, NO. 12, 1622

27. All delays are dangerous in war.

JOHN DRYDEN, *TYRANNIC LOVE* (1669), 1.1

28. A war expert is a man ye niver heerd iv befure. If ye can think iv annywan whose face is onfamilyar to ye an' ye don't raymimber his name, an' he's got a job on a pa-aper ye didn't know was published, he's a war expert.

FINLEY PETER DUNNE, "THE WAR EXPERT," *MR. DOOLEY'S PHILOSOPHY* (1900)

29. War is a generality, so are the inevitabilities of war, including death.

MARGUERITE DURAS, *THE WAR: A MEMOIR* (1986), TR. BARBARA BRAY

30. War educates the senses, calls into action the will, perfects the physical constitution, brings men into such swift and close collision in critical moments that man measures man.

EMERSON, "WAR," *MISCELLANIES* (1884)

31. The most disadvantageous peace is better than the most just war.

ERASMUS, *ADAGIA* (1500)

32. Men love war because it allows them to look serious. Because it is the one thing that stops women laughing at them.

JOHN FOWLES, *THE MAGUS* (1965), 52

33. There never was a good war or a bad peace.

BENJAMIN FRANKLIN, LETTER TO JOSIAH QUINCY, SEPT. 11, 1773

34. Morality is contraband in war.

MOHANDAS K. GANDHI, *NON-VIOLENCE IN PEACE AND WAR* (1948), 1.268

35. War is an unmitigated evil. But it certainly does one good thing. It drives away fear and brings bravery to the surface.

MOHANDAS K. GANDHI, *NON-VIOLENCE IN PEACE AND WAR* (1948), 1.270

36. What difference does it make to the dead, the orphans and the homeless, whether the mad destruction is wrought under the name of totalitarianism or the holy name of liberty or democracy?

MOHANDAS K. GANDHI, *NON-VIOLENCE IN PEACE AND WAR* (1948), 1.357

37. It is easier to lead men to combat and to stir up their passions than to temper them and urge them to the patient labors of peace.

ANDRÉ GIDE, *JOURNALS*, SEPT. 13, 1938, TR. JUSTIN O'BRIEN

38. During war we imprison the rights of man.

JEAN GIRAUDOUX, *TIGER AT THE GATES* (1935), 2, TR. CHRISTOPHER FRY

39. Everyone, when there's war in the air, learns to live in a new element: falsehood.

JEAN GIRAUDOUX, *TIGER AT THE GATES* (1935), 2, TR. CHRISTOPHER FRY

40. There's a kind of permission for war which can be given only by the world's mood and atmosphere, the feel of its pulse. It would be madness to undertake a war without that permission.

JEAN GIRAUDOUX, *TIGER AT THE GATES* (1935), 2, TR. CHRISTOPHER FRY

41. Who would prefer peace to the glory of hunger and thirst, of wading through mud, and dying in the service of one's country?

JEAN GIRAUDOUX, *AMPHITRYON 38* (1929), 1, TR. PETER H. JUDD

42. "Terrorism" is what we call the violence of the weak, and we condemn it; "war" is what we call the violence of the strong, and we glorify it.

SYDNEY J. HARRIS, "NATIONS SHOULD SUBMIT TO THE RULE OF LAW," *CLEARING THE GROUND* (1986)

43. She, Ruin, is strong and sound on her feet, and therefore / far outruns all Prayers, and wins into every country / to force men astray; and the Prayers follow as healers after her.

HOMER, *ILIAD* (9TH C. B.C.), 9.505, TR. RICHMOND LATTIMORE

44. Older men declare war. But it is youth that must fight and die.

HERBERT HOOVER, SPEECH, REPUBLICAN NATIONAL CONVENTION, CHICAGO, JUNE 27, 1944

45. The most shocking fact about war is that its victims and its instruments are individual human beings, and that these individual beings are condemned by the monstrous conventions of politics to murder or be murdered in quarrels not their own.

ALDOUS HUXLEY, *THE OLIVE TREE* (1937)

46. It is but seldom that any one overt act produces hostilities between two nations; there exists, more commonly, a previous jealousy and ill will, a predisposition to take offense.

WASHINGTON IRVING, "ENGLISH WRITERS ON AMERICA," *THE SKETCH BOOK OF GEOFFREY CRAYON, GENT.* (1819–20)

47. I am tired—my heart is sick and sad. From where the sun now stands I will fight no more forever.

CHIEF JOSEPH, STATEMENT OF SURRENDER OF THE NEZ PERCÉ TRIBE

48. No man who witnessed the tragedies of the last war, no man who can imagine the unimaginable possibilities of the next war can advocate war out of irritability or frustration or impatience.

JOHN F. KENNEDY, VETERANS DAY ADDRESS, ARLINGTON NATIONAL CEMETERY, NOV. 11, 1961

49. [Man] is, perhaps, no more prone to war than he used to be and no more inclined to commit other evil deeds. But a given amount of ill will or folly will go further than it used to.

JOSEPH WOOD KRUTCH, "THE LOSS OF CONFIDENCE," *THE MEASURE OF MAN* (1954)

50. The slaying of multitudes should be mourned with sorrow. / A victory should be celebrated with the funeral rite.

LAO TZU, *THE CHARACTER OF TAO* (6TH C. B.C.), 31, TR. LIN YUTANG

51. Small wars are always teetering on the brink of becoming big ones.

MAX LERNER, "HIC SUNT DRACONES," *THE AGE OF OVERKILL* (1962)

52. The way to prevent war is to bend every energy toward preventing it, not to proceed by the dubious indirection of preparing for it.

MAX LERNER, "ON PEACETIME MILITARY TRAINING," *ACTIONS AND PASSIONS* (1949)

53. This is war: / Boys flung into a breach / Like shoveled earth; / And old men, / Broken, / Driving rapidly before crowds of people / In a glitter of silly decorations. / Behind the boys / And the old men, / Life weeps, / And shreds her garments / To the blowing winds.

AMY LOWELL, "IN THE STADIUM," *A SHARD OF SILENCE* (1957)

54. It is fatal to enter any war without the will to win it.

DOUGLAS MACARTHUR, SPEECH, REPUBLICAN NATIONAL CONVENTION, JULY 7, 1952

55. One believes in the coming of war if one does not sufficiently abhor it.

THOMAS MANN, *THE MAGIC MOUNTAIN* (1924), 6.2, TR. H. T. LOWE-PORTER

56. War can only be abolished through war, and in order to get rid of the gun it is necessary to take up the gun.

MAO TSE-TUNG, *QUOTATIONS FROM CHAIRMAN MAO TSE-TUNG* (1966), 5

57. Blood is the god of war's rich livery.

CHRISTOPHER MARLOWE, *TAMBURLAINE THE GREAT* (C. 1587), 2.3.2

58. All wars are boyish, and are fought by boys.

HERMAN MELVILLE, "THE MARCH INTO VIRGINIA," *BATTLEPIECES AND ASPECTS OF THE WAR* (1866)

59. War may make a fool of man, but it by no means degrades him; on the contrary, it tends to exalt him, and its net effects are much like those of motherhood on women.

H. L. MENCKEN, *MINORITY REPORT* (1956), 17

60. We think—although of course, now, we very seldom / Clearly think— / That the other side of War is Peace.

EDNA ST. VINCENT MILLAY, UNTITLED POEM, *MAKE BRIGHT THE ARROWS* (1940)

61. How different the new order would be if we could consult the veteran instead of the politician.

HENRY MILLER, "THE ALCOHOLIC VETERAN WITH THE WASHBOARD CRANIUM," *THE WISDOM OF THE HEART* (1941)

62. We kill because we're afraid of our own shadow, afraid that if we used a little common sense we'd have to admit that our glorious principles were wrong.

HENRY MILLER, "THE ALCOHOLIC VETERAN WITH THE WASHBOARD CRANIUM," *THE WISDOM OF THE HEART* (1941)

63. War has become an affair of machines...and soldiers are little more than clever mechanics.

ALBERTO MORAVIA, *TWO WOMEN* (1959)

64. War is both the product of an earlier corruption and a producer of new corruptions.

LEWIS MUMFORD, "THE CHALLENGE TO RENEWAL," *THE CONDUCT OF LIFE* (1951)

65. Against war it may be said that it makes the victor stupid and the vanquished revengeful.

NIETZSCHE, *HUMAN, ALL TOO HUMAN* (1878), 444, TR. HELEN ZIMMERN

66. How good bad music and bad reasons sound when one marches against an enemy!

NIETZSCHE, *THE DAWN* (1881), 557, IN *THE PORTABLE NIETZSCHE*, TR. WALTER KAUFMANN

67. The quickest way of ending a war is to lose it.

GEORGE ORWELL, "SECOND THOUGHTS ON JAMES BURNHAM," *SHOOTING AN ELEPHANT* (1950)

68. Wars, invented and organized by the highest available consciousnesses (do the worms go to war? do the fish? do the paramecia?), are the planet's chief source and cause of torment.

CYNTHIA OZICK, "THE BIOLOGICAL PREMISES OF OUR SAD EARTH-SPECK," *ART & ARDOR* (1983)

69. He who is the author of a war lets loose the whole contagion of hell and opens a vein that bleeds a nation to death.

THOMAS PAINE, *THE AMERICAN CRISIS* (1776–83), 5

70. War involves in its progress such a train of unforeseen and unsupposed circumstances that no human wisdom can calculate the end. It has but one thing certain, and that is to increase taxes.

THOMAS PAINE, *PROSPECTS ON THE RUBICON* (1787)

71. Life and fame and wealth—all these must, I say, be defended by fighting. Death in battle is the most glorious for men. Who lives under the sway of his foe—it is he that is dead.

PANCHATANTRA (C. 5TH C.), 1, TR. FRANKLIN EDGERTON

72. Can anything be more ridiculous than that a man should have the right to kill me because he lives on the other side of the water, and because his ruler has a quarrel with mine, though I have none with him?

PASCAL, *PENSÉES* (1670), 294, TR. W. F. TROTTER

73. The cause of some going to war, and of others avoiding it, is the same desire in both, attended with different views.

PASCAL, *PENSÉES* (1670), 425, TR. W. F. TROTTER

74. The grim fact is that we prepare for war like precocious giants and for peace like retarded pygmies.

LESTER PEARSON, NEWS SUMMARIES, MARCH 15, 1955

75. [W]e must love men more than things, and I admire and weep more for the soldiers than for the churches which were only the recording of an heroic gesture which today is reenacted at every moment.

MARCEL PROUST, *LETTERS OF MARCEL PROUST* (1949). MINA CURTISS, TRANSLATOR-EDITOR

76. Diplomats are just as essential to starting a war as Soldiers are for finishing it. You take Diplomacy out of war and the thing would fall flat in a week.

WILL ROGERS, *THE AUTOBIOGRAPHY OF WILL ROGERS* (1949), 12

77. I find war detestable but those who praise it without participating in it even more so.

ROMAIN ROLLAND, *INTER ARMA CARITAS, JOURNAL DE GENÈVE,* OCT. 30, 1914

78. I have seen children starving. I have seen the agony of mothers and wives. I hate war.

FRANKLIN D. ROOSEVELT, SPEECH, CHAUTAUQUA, N.Y., AUG. 14, 1936

79. For those at home, as well as for those in battle, war is curiously disabling. The mere realization that one's country is at war poisons the bloodstream, creates an incessant mood of worry that infiltrates even the most casual moments.

ROGER ROSENBLATT, "GONE TO SOLDIERS EVERYONE," *THE MAN IN THE WATER* (1994)

80. World War III will be triggered off not by suppressed nationalists seeking political independence, as happened the first time around when the Serbs at Sarajevo shot the heir to the Austrian throne, but by some semiliterate, whacked-out "loner" who lobs a rocket into a nuclear arsenal in order to impress Brooke Shields.

PHILIP ROTH, *THE COUNTERLIFE* (1987)

81. When the whole world turns clown, and paints itself red with its own heart's blood instead of vermilion, it is something else than comic.

JOHN RUSKIN, *THE CROWN OF WILD OLIVE* (1866), 2.59

82. People who are vigorous and brutal often find war enjoyable, provided that it is a victorious war and that there is not too much interference with rape and plunder. This is a great help in persuading people that wars are righteous.

BERTRAND RUSSELL, "IDEAS THAT HAVE HARMED MANKIND," *UNPOPULAR ESSAYS* (1950)

83. It is the savor of bread broken with comrades that makes us accept the values of war.

SAINT-EXUPÉRY, *WIND, SAND, AND STARS* (1939), 9.6, TR. LEWIS GALANTIÈRE

84. War is not an adventure. It is a disease.

SAINT-EXUPÉRY, *FLIGHT TO ARRAS* (1942), 8, TR. LEWIS GALANTIÈRE

85. To call war the soil of courage and virtue is like calling debauchery the soil of love.

GEORGE SANTAYANA, *THE LIFE OF REASON: REASON IN SOCIETY* (1905–06), 3

86. To delight in war is a merit in the soldier, a dangerous quality in the captain, and a positive crime in the statesman.

GEORGE SANTAYANA, *THE LIFE OF REASON: REASON IN SOCIETY* (1905–06), 3

87. Of war men ask the outcome, not the cause.

SENECA, *HERCULES FURENS* (1ST C.), 407, TR. FRANK JUSTUS MILLER

88. Every war is its own excuse. That's why they're all surrounded with ideals. That's why they're all crusades.

KARL SHAPIRO, *THE BOURGEOIS POET* (1964), 1.6

89. Cambodia was not a mistake; it was a crime. The world is diminished by the experience.

WILLIAM SHAWCROSS, *SIDESHOW* (1979)

90. War is cruelty, and you cannot refine it.

WILLIAM T. SHERMAN, *MEMOIRS* (1875), V. 1

91. They make a desert and call it peace.

TACITUS, *AGRICOLA* (C. A.D. 98), 30

92. What madness is this, inviting sable Death by warfare? / It always hovers close and comes unforeseen on silent steps.

TIBULLUS, *ELEGIES* (1ST C. B.C.), I.10, TR. HUBERT CREEKMORE

93. The butter to be sacrificed because of the war always turns out to be the margarine of the poor.

JAMES TOBIN, SPEECH, SOCIAL SCIENCES ASSOCIATION, WASHINGTON, D.C., DEC. 27, 1967

94. Vice foments war; it is virtue which actually fights. If there were no virtue, we would live in peace forever.

VAUVENARGUES, *REFLECTIONS AND MAXIMS* (1746), 225

95. It is said that God is always on the side of the heaviest battalions.

VOLTAIRE, LETTER TO M. LE RICHE, FEB. 6, 1770

96. Men appear to prefer ruining one another's fortunes, and cutting each other's throats about a few paltry villages, to extending the grand means of human happiness.

VOLTAIRE, "ROADS," *PHILOSOPHICAL DICTIONARY* (1764)

97. Nowadays, of course, just about our only solvent industry is the merchandising of death, bankrolled by our grandchildren.

KURT VONNEGUT, *BLUEBEARD* (1987)

98. [A] nice thing about war—not that anything about war is nice, I guess—is that while it's going on and you're in it, you never worry about doing the right thing.

KURT VONNEGUT, *PLAYER PIANO* (1952)

99. How many wars have been caused by fits of indigestion, and how many more dynasties have been upset by the love of woman than by the hate of man.

CHARLES DUDLEY WARNER, "EIGHTEENTH WEEK," *MY SUMMER IN A GARDEN* (1871)

100. Once we thought a few hundred corpses would be enough / then we saw thousands were still too few / and today we can't even count all the dead / Everywhere you look.

PETER WEISS, *MARAT / SADE* (1964), I.8, TR. ADRIAN MITCHELL

101. Nothing except a battle lost can be half so melancholy as a battle won.

DUKE OF WELLINGTON, DISPATCH, 1815

102. Granted that every war is madness—civil war, fratricide, is the worst of all; it reaches deeper into ugliness, cruelty and absurdity.

ELIE WIESEL, *THE TESTAMENT* (1981), TR. MARION WIESEL

103. Though we talk peace, we wage war. Sometimes we even wage war in the name of peace. Does that seem paradoxical? Well, war is not afraid of paradoxes.

ELIE WIESEL, "ARE WE AFRAID OF PEACE?" *FROM THE KINGDOM OF MEMORY* (1990)

104. As long as war is regarded as wicked, it will always have its fascination. When it is looked upon as vulgar, it will cease to be popular.

OSCAR WILDE, "THE CRITIC AS ARTIST," *INTENTIONS* (1891)

1043. WAR, CIVIL

See also 1042. WAR

1. If a house be divided against itself, that house cannot stand.

BIBLE MARK 3:25

2. Soldiers who had been in the army long enough to know what a bloody swindle war really is would begin to feel that army life was really kind of fun, as long as [General Philip] Sheridan was up front.

BRUCE CATTON, *BANNERS AT SHENANDOAH* (1955)

3. It is notorious that no war between countries elicits as much hate and cruelty as civil war, in which there is no lack of acquaintance between the two warring sides.

ERICH FROMM, *THE ANATOMY OF HUMAN DESTRUCTIVENESS* (1973)

1044. WASHINGTON, D.C.

1. In any election year, Washington vibrates early.

SHIRLEY TEMPLE BLACK, *CHILD STAR* (1988)

2. Washington is a city of Southern efficiency and Northern charm.

JOHN F. KENNEDY, QUOTED IN WILLIAM MANCHESTER'S *PORTRAIT OF A PRESIDENT* (1962)

3. Washington—appropriately, since it is the capital of the United States—is the place where language is most thoroughly debased—more than Hollywood, which is not what it used to be.

EDWIN NEWMAN, *STRICTLY SPEAKING* (1974)

4. People only leave [Washington] by way of the box—ballot or coffin.

CLAIBORNE PELL, *VOGUE*, AUG. 1, 1963

5. Once upon a time Washington's charm was that people here thought mostly about power, its sources and uses, rather than money. It wasn't pretty, but at least it wasn't New York, where money is on most minds.

GEORGE F. WILL, "GEORGE THE GOOD, IF HE DOES SAY SO HIMSELF," *SUDDENLY: THE AMERICAN IDEA ABROAD AND AT HOME, 1986–1990* (1990)

6. There are no .400 hitters in Washington.

GEORGE F. WILL, *MEN AT WORK: THE CRAFT OF BASEBALL* (1990)

1045. WASTEFULNESS

See also 324. EXTRAVAGANCE

1. See a pin and let it lie, you'll want a pin before you die.

FRENCH PROVERB

1046. WATER

See also 778. RAIN; 824. RIVERS; 853. SEA

1. Water, thou hast no taste, no color, no odor; canst not be defined, art relished while ever mysterious. Not necessary to life, but rather life itself, thou fillest us with a gratification that exceeds the delight of the senses.

SAINT-EXUPÉRY, *WIND, SAND, AND STARS* (1939), 8, TR. LEWIS GALANTIÈRE

2. My life is like water that has passed the mill; it turns no wheel.

THOMAS WOLFE, *THOMAS WOLFE'S LETTERS TO HIS MOTHER* (1943)

1047. WEAKNESS

See also 342. FAULTS; 459. IMPOTENCE; 542. LIMITATIONS; 940. STRENGTH; 980. TIMIDITY

1. The spirit indeed is willing, but the flesh is weak.

BIBLE MATTHEW 26:41

2. The weakest and most timorous are the most revengeful and implacable.

THOMAS FULLER, M.D., *GNOMOLOGIA* (1732), 4822

3. It was not the violence of our enemies [in World War I] that would undo us, I thought, but our own spiritual weakness, the shallowness of our convictions.

LEARNED HAND, *THE SPIRIT OF LIBERTY* (1959)

4. He is a fool who tries to match his strength with the stronger. / He will lose his battle, and with the shame will be hurt also.

HESIOD, *WORKS AND DAYS* (8TH C. B.C.), 210, TR. RICHMOND LATTIMORE

5. It is to escape the responsibility for failure that the weak so eagerly throw themselves into grandiose undertakings.

ERIC HOFFER, *THE ORDEAL OF CHANGE* (1964), 15.5

6. We cannot win the weak by sharing our wealth with them. They feel our generosity as oppression.

ERIC HOFFER, *THE ORDEAL OF CHANGE* (1964), 2

7. We have allowed a soft sentimentalism to form the atmosphere we breathe. And in that kind of atmosphere, a diffuse desire to do good has become a substitute for tough-minded plans and operations—a substitute for strategy.

JOHN F. KENNEDY, *THE STRATEGY OF PEACE* (1960)

8. Often we are firm from weakness, and audacious from timidity.

LA ROCHEFOUCAULD, *MAXIMS* (1665), TR. KENNETH PRATT

9. There is nothing so imperious as feebleness which feels itself supported by force.

NAPOLEON I, *MAXIMS* (1804–15)

10. I have often laughed at the weaklings who thought themselves good because they had no claws.

NIETZSCHE, "ON THOSE WHO ARE SUBLIME," *THUS SPOKE ZARATHUSTRA* (1883–92), 2, TR. WALTER KAUFMANN

11. The sick are the greatest danger for the healthy; it is not from the strongest that harm comes to the strong, but from the weakest.

NIETZSCHE, *THE GENEALOGY OF MORALS* (1887), 3.14, TR. HORACE B. SAMUEL

12. The weak can be terrible / because they try furiously to appear strong.

RABINDRANATH TAGORE, *FIREFLIES* (1928)

13. Oh, you weak, beautiful people who give up with such grace. What you need is someone to take hold of you—gently, with love, and hand your life back to you.

TENNESSEE WILLIAMS, *CAT ON A HOT TIN ROOF* (1955), 3

1048. WEALTH

See also 8. ACQUISITION; 403. GREED; 557. LUXURY; 602. MONEY; 718. POVERTY; 746. PROPERTY; 750. PROSPERITY

1. Riches attract the attention, consideration, and congratulations of mankind.

JOHN ADAMS, *DISCOURSES ON DAVILA* (1789), 2

2. Let there be / wealth without tears; enough for / the wise man who will ask no further.

AESCHYLUS, *AGAMEMNON* (458 B.C.), TR. RICHMOND LATTIMORE

3. Wealth unused might as well not exist.

AESOP, "THE MISER AND HIS GOLD," *FABLES* (6TH C. B.C.?), TR. JOSEPH JACOBS

4. Be not penny-wise: riches have wings, and sometimes they fly away of themselves; sometimes they must be set flying to bring in more.

FRANCIS BACON, "OF RICHES," *ESSAYS* (1625)

5. All wealth is relative; and so is its absence.

SYBILLE BEDFORD, *THE SUDDEN VIEW* (1953), 10

6. It is easier for a camel to go through the eye of a needle, than for a rich man to enter the kingdom of God.

BIBLE MATTHEW 1924

7. Riches certainly make themselves wings; they fly away as an eagle toward heaven.

BIBLE PROVERBS 23:5

8. Wealth maketh many friends.

BIBLE PROVERBS 19:4

9. If a man who is born to a fortune cannot make himself easier and freer than those who are not, he gains nothing.

JAMES BOSWELL, *LONDON JOURNAL*, FEB. 25, 1763

10. In big houses in which things are done properly, there is always the religious element. The diurnal cycle is observed with more feeling when there are servants to do the work.

ELIZABETH BOWEN, *THE DEATH OF THE HEART* (1938), 1.6

11. He is rich who hath enough to be charitable.

SIR THOMAS BROWNE, *RELIGIO MEDICI* (1642), 2

12. To be poor without murmuring is difficult. To be rich without being proud is easy.

CONFUCIUS, *ANALECTS* (6TH C. B.C.), 14.11, TR. JAMES LEGGE

13. All heiresses are beautiful.

JOHN DRYDEN, *KING ARTHUR* (1691), 1.1

14. It requires a great deal of boldness and a great deal of caution to make a great fortune, and when you have got it, it requires ten times as much wit to keep it.

EMERSON, "POWER," *THE CONDUCT OF LIFE* (1860)

15. There is a time when a man distinguishes the idea of felicity from the idea of wealth; it is the beginning of wisdom.

EMERSON, *JOURNALS*, 1830

16. Without the rich heart, wealth is an ugly beggar.

EMERSON, "MANNERS," *ESSAYS: SECOND SERIES* (1844)

17. Natural wealth is limited and easily obtained; the wealth defined by vain fancies is always beyond reach.

EPICURUS, "PRINCIPAL DOCTRINES" (3RD C. B.C.), 15, IN *LETTERS, PRINCIPAL DOCTRINES, AND VATICAN SAYINGS*, TR. RUSSEL M. GEER

18. If some appalling disaster befalls, there's / Always a way for the rich.

EURIPIDES, *ANDROMACHE* (C. 426 B.C.), TR. JOHN F. NIMS

19. That glittering hope is immemorial / And beckons many men / To their undoing.

EURIPIDES, *IPHIGENIA IN TAURIS* (C. 414–12 B.C.), TR. WITTER BYNNER

20. Wealth stays with us a little moment if at all; / only our characters are steadfast, not our gold.

EURIPIDES, *ELECTRA* (413 B.C.), TR. EMILY TOWNSEND VERMEULE

21. Riches have never fascinated me, unless combined with the greatest charm or distinction.

F. SCOTT FITZGERALD, *THE LETTERS OF F. SCOTT FITZGERALD* (1963), ED. ANDREW TURNBULL

22. He is not fit for riches who is afraid to use them.

THOMAS FULLER, M.D., *GNOMOLOGIA* (1732), 1934

23. Not possession, but use, is the only riches.

THOMAS FULLER, M.D., *GNOMOLOGIA* (1732), 3681

24. Rich men feel misfortunes that fly over poor men's heads.

THOMAS FULLER, M.D., *GNOMOLOGIA* (1732), 4035

25. Riches rather enlarge than satisfy appetites.

THOMAS FULLER, M.D., *GNOMOLOGIA* (1732), 4048

26. Wealth is not without its advantages and the case to the contrary, although it has often been made, has never proved widely persuasive.

KENNETH GALBRAITH, *THE AFFLUENT SOCIETY* (1958)

27. In the Protestant version of the capitalist morality, riches were the reward of the righteously ascetic.

MICHAEL HARRINGTON, *THE ACCIDENTAL CENTURY* (1966)

28. All else—valor, a good name, glory, everything in heaven and earth—is secondary to the charm of riches.

HORACE, *SATIRES* (35–30 B.C.), 2.3

29. It is better to live rich than to die rich.

SAMUEL JOHNSON, QUOTED IN BOSWELL'S *LIFE OF SAMUEL JOHNSON*, APRIL 17, 1778

30. Let me smile with the wise, and feed with the rich.

SAMUEL JOHNSON, QUOTED IN BOSWELL'S *LIFE OF SAMUEL JOHNSON*, OCT. 6, 1769

31. Majestic mighty Wealth is the holiest of our gods.

JUVENAL, *SATIRES* (C. 100), 1.112, TR. HUBERT CREEKMORE

32. Wealth is the means, and people are the ends. All our material riches will avail us little if we do not use them to expand the opportunities of our people.

JOHN F. KENNEDY, STATE OF THE UNION MESSAGE, JAN. 11, 1962

33. It is in vain to ridicule a rich fool, for the laughers will be on his side.

LA BRUYÈRE, *CHARACTERS* (1688), 6.10, TR. HENRI VAN LAUN

34. Wherever there is excessive wealth, there is also in the train of it excessive poverty; as, where the sun is brightest, the shade is deepest.

WALTER SAVAGE LANDOR, "ARISTOTELES AND CALLISTHENES," *IMAGINARY CONVERSATIONS* (1824–53)

35. Old money is fully as moronic as new money but it has inherited an appearance of cultivation.

MARY MCCARTHY, *HOW I GREW* (1987)

36. The most valuable of all human possessions, next to a superior and disdainful air, is the reputation of being well to do. Nothing else so neatly eases one's way through life, especially in democratic countries.

H. L. MENCKEN, *PREJUDICES: THIRD SERIES* (1922), 18

37. Let none admire that riches grow in hell; that soil may best / Deserve the precious bane.

MILTON, *PARADISE LOST* (1667), 1.690

38. Every man who is worth thirty millions and is not wedded to them, is dangerous to the government.

NAPOLEON I, *MAXIMS* (1804–15)

39. In his heart everyone knows that the only people who get rich from the "get rich quick" books are those who write them.

RICHARD M. NIXON, *REAL PEACE* (1984)

40. Get wealth when you have it not; guard what you have got; increase what you have guarded; and bestow on worthy persons what you have increased.

PANCHATANTRA (C. 5TH C.), 1, TR. FRANKLIN EDGERTON

41. The makers of fortunes have a second love of money as a creation of their own, resembling the affection of authors for their own poems, or of parents for their children, besides that natural love of it for the sake of use and profit.

PLATO, *THE REPUBLIC* (4TH C. B.C.), 1, TR. BENJAMIN JOWETT

42. Wealth is well known to be a great comforter.

PLATO, *THE REPUBLIC* (4TH C. B.C.), 1, TR. BENJAMIN JOWETT

43. Get place and wealth, if possible, with grace; / If not, by any means get wealth and place.

ALEXANDER POPE, *EPILOGUE TO THE SATIRES* (1738), 1.1.103

44. We may see the small value God has for riches by the people he gives them to.

ALEXANDER POPE, *THOUGHTS ON VARIOUS SUBJECTS* (1727)

45. There are men who gain from their wealth only the fear of losing it.

ANTOINE RIVAROLI, *L'ESPRIT DE RIVAROL* (1808)

46. Most of us aren't that interested in getting rich—we just don't want to get poor.

ANDREW A. ROONEY, "MONEY IN STRESS," *PIECES OF MY MIND* (1984)

47. True wealth is not a static thing. It is a living thing made out of the disposition of men to create and to distribute the good things of life with rising standards of living.

FRANKLIN D. ROOSEVELT, SPEECH, WASHINGTON, D.C., OCT. 24, 1934

48. It is an unfortunate human failing that a full pocketbook often groans more loudly than an empty stomach.

FRANKLIN D. ROOSEVELT, SPEECH, BROOKLYN, N.Y., NOV. 1, 1940

49. As long as there are rich people in the world, they will be desirous of distinguishing themselves from the poor.

ROUSSEAU, *A DISCOURSE ON POLITICAL ECONOMY* (1758), TR. G. D. H. COLE

50. Riches are intended for the comfort of life, and not life for the purpose of hoarding riches.

SA'DI, *GULISTAN* (1258), 8.1, TR. JAMES ROSS

51. The rich man is everywhere expected and at home.

SA'DI (12TH–13TH C.), QUOTED IN EMERSON'S "WEALTH," *THE CONDUCT OF LIFE* (1860)

52. A great fortune is a great slavery.

SENECA, *AD POLYBIUM DE CONSOLATIONE* (1ST C.)

53. Many a man has found the acquisition of wealth only a change, not an end of miseries.

SENECA, *LETTERS TO LUCILIUS* (1ST C.), 17.11, TR. E. PHILLIPS BARKER

54. O, what a world of vile ill-favoured faults / Looks handsome in three hundred pounds a year!

SHAKESPEARE, *THE MERRY WIVES OF WINDSOR* (1597), 3.4.32

55. In an ugly and unhappy world the richest man can purchase nothing but ugliness and unhappiness.

GEORGE BERNARD SHAW, "MAXIMS FOR REVOLUTIONISTS," *MAN AND SUPERMAN* (1903)

56. Every man is rich or poor according to the degree in which he can afford to enjoy the necessaries, conveniences, and amusements of human life.

ADAM SMITH, *THE WEALTH OF NATIONS* (1776), 1.5

57. Wealth breeds satiety, satiety outrage.

SOLON (7TH–6TH C. B.C.), QUOTED IN DIOGENES LAERTIUS' *LIVES AND OPINIONS OF EMINENT PHILOSOPHERS* (3RD C. A.D.), TR. R. D. HICKS

58. Just as war is waged with the blood of others, fortunes are made with other people's money.

ANDRÉ SUARÈS, *VOICI L'HOMME* (1906)

59. Superfluous wealth can buy superfluities only.

THOREAU, "CONCLUSION," *WALDEN* (1854)

60. Men living in democratic times have many passions, but most of their passions either end in the love of riches, or proceed from it.

ALEXIS DE TOCQUEVILLE, *DEMOCRACY IN AMERICA* (1835–39), 2.3.17

61. In order to stand well in the eyes of the community, it is necessary to come up to a certain, somewhat indefinite, conventional standard of wealth.

THORSTEIN VEBLEN, *THE THEORY OF THE LEISURE CLASS* (1899), 2

1049. WEAPONS

See also 229. DEFENSE; 641. NUCLEAR POWER; 956. SURVIVAL; 1042. WAR

1. Far from the truth lay the antique assumption that man had fathered the weapon. The weapon, instead, had fathered man.

ROBERT ARDREY, *AFRICAN GENESIS* (1961)

2. [In war] the latest refinements of science are linked with the cruelties of the Stone Age.

SIR WINSTON CHURCHILL, SPEECH, LONDON, MARCH 26, 1942

3. We can do without butter, but, despite all our love of peace, not without arms. One cannot shoot with butter but with guns.

PAUL JOSEPH GOEBBELS, SPEECH, BERLIN, JAN. 17, 1936

4. You may be obliged to wage war, but not to use poisoned arrows.

BALTASAR GRACIÁN, *THE ART OF WORLDLY WISDOM* (1647), 164, TR. JOSEPH JACOBS

5. At exactly fifteen minutes past eight in the morning, on August 6, 1945, Japanese time, at the moment when the atomic bomb flashed above Hiroshima, Miss Toshiko Sasaki, a clerk in the personnel department of the East Asia Tin Works, had just sat down at her place in the plant office and was turning her head to speak to the girl at the next desk.

JOHN HERSEY, *HIROSHIMA* (1946)

6. Only technology has permitted us to put a city to the sword without quite realizing what we are doing.

JOSEPH WOOD KRUTCH, "IF YOU DON'T MIND MY SAYING SO," *THE AMERICAN SCHOLAR* (SUMMER 1967)

7. Remote control. Ingenious contradiction of terms. Fits like a handshake. Aims like a gun.

ROGER ROSENBLATT, "GONE TO SOLDIERS EVERYONE," *THE MAN IN THE WATER* (1994)

1050. WEATHER

See also 140. CLIMATE; 778. RAIN; 854. SEASONS; 911. SNOW; 950. SUN; 1059. WIND

1. A cloudy day, or a little sunshine, have as great an influence on many constitutions as the most real blessings or misfortunes.

JOSEPH ADDISON, *THE SPECTATOR* (1711–12), 162

2. There it is, fog, atmospheric moisture still uncertain in destination, not quite weather and not altogether mood, yet partaking of both.

HAL BORLAND, "FOG—SEPTEMBER 27," *SUNDIAL OF THE SEASONS* (1964)

3. The air was so damp that fish could have come in through the doors and swum out the windows, floating through the atmosphere in the rooms.

Gabriel García Márquez, *One Hundred Years of Solitude* (1970)

4. For the man sound in body and serene of mind there is no such thing as bad weather; every sky has its beauty, and storms which whip the blood do but make it pulse more vigorously.

George Gissing, "Winter," *The Private Papers of Henry Ryecroft* (1903)

5. We shall never be content until each man makes his own weather and keeps it to himself.

Jerome K. Jerome, "On the Weather," *The Idle Thoughts of an Idle Fellow* (1889)

6. Weather in towns is like a skylark in a counting-house—out of place and in the way.

Jerome K. Jerome, "On the Weather," *The Idle Thoughts of an Idle Fellow* (1889)

7. Who knows whither the clouds have fled? / In the unscarred heaven they leave no wake; / And the eyes forget the tears they have shed, / The heart forgets its sorrow and ache.

James Russell Lowell, prelude to part 1, "The Vision of Sir Launfal" (1848)

8. On the Continent there is one topic which should be avoided—the weather; in England, if you do not repeat the phrase "Lovely day, isn't it?" at least two hundred times a day, you are considered a bit dull.

George Mikes, *How to Be an Alien* (1946)

9. There is nothing more universally commended than a fine day; the reason is, that people can commend it without envy.

William Shenstone, *Essays on Men and Manners* (1764)

10. One thing about cold weather: it brings out the statistician in everyone.

Paul Theroux, *The Old Patagonian Express* (1979)

11. Extreme cold when it first arrives seems to generate cheerfulness and sociability. For a few hours all life's dubious problems are dropped in favor of the clear and congenial task of keeping alive.

E. B. White, "Cold Weather," *One Man's Meat* (1944)

1051. WEDDINGS

See also 564. Marriage

1. If it were not for the presents, an elopement would be preferable.

George Ade, "The General Manager of the Love Affair," *Forty Modern Fables* (1901)

2. Bride, n. A woman with a fine prospect of happiness behind her.

Ambrose Bierce, *The Devil's Dictionary* (1881–1911)

3. Girls usually have a papier mâché face on their wedding day.

Colette, "Wedding Day," *Earthly Paradise* (1966), 2

4. Weddings seem to be magnets for mishap and for whatever craziness lurks in family closets. In more ways than one, weddings bring out the ding-dong on everybody involved.

Robert Fulghum, *It Was on Fire When I Lay Down on It* (1989)

5. Let there be no more weddings. Get thee to a nunnery.

William Shakespeare, *Hamlet* (1600)

6. [A]t American weddings, the quality of the food is in inverse proportion to the social position of the bride and groom.

Calvin Trillin, "Understanding Preppies," *Uncivil Liberties* (1982)

1052. WEEPING

See also 526. Laughter; 527. Laughter and Tears; 610. Mourning; 918. Sorrow; 946. Suffering; 1011. Unhappiness

1. Weeping may endure for a night, but joy cometh in the morning.

Bible Psalms 30:5

2. Heaven knows we need never be ashamed of our tears, for they are rain upon the blinding dust of earth, overlying our hard hearts.

Charles Dickens, *Great Expectations* (1860–1861)

3. They who are sad find somehow sweetness in tears.

Euripides, *The Trojan Women* (415 B.C.), tr. Richmond Lattimore

4. Waste not fresh tears over old griefs.

Euripides, *Alexander* (c. 415 B.C.), 44, tr. M. H. Morgan

5. Who would recognize the unhappy if grief had no language?

Publilius Syrus, *Moral Sayings* (1st c. B.C.), 791, tr. Darius Lyman

6. Cries of despair, misery, sobbing grief are a kind of wealth.

SAINT-EXUPÉRY, *WIND, SAND, AND STARS* (1939), 8, TR. LEWIS GALANTIÈRE

7. Let tears flow of their own accord: their flowing is not inconsistent with inward peace and harmony.

SENECA, *LETTERS TO LUCILIUS* (1ST C.), 99.20, TR. E. PHILLIPS BARKER

8. How much better is it to weep at joy than to joy at weeping!

SHAKESPEARE, *MUCH ADO ABOUT NOTHING* (1598–99), 1.1.28

9. To weep is to make less the depth of grief.

SHAKESPEARE, *3 HENRY VI* (1590–91), 2.1.85

WEST

See 273. EAST AND WEST

1053. WHIM

See also 461. IMPULSIVENESS; 928. SPONTANEITY

1. The pleasure of gratifying whim is very great. It is known only by those who are whimsical.

JAMES BOSWELL, *LONDON JOURNAL,* DEC. 12, 1762

2. The only difference between a caprice and a lifelong passion is that the caprice lasts a little longer.

OSCAR WILDE, *THE PICTURE OF DORIAN GRAY* (1891), 2

1054. WHITES

See also 85. BLACKS; 775. RACIAL PREJUDICE

1. This world is white no longer, and it will never be white again.

JAMES BALDWIN, "STRANGER IN THE VILLAGE" (1953), *NOTES OF A NATIVE SON* (1955)

2. There can be no whiter whiteness than this one: / An insurance man's shirt on its morning run.

GWENDOLYN E. BROOKS, "MRS. SMALL," *THE BEAN EATERS* (1960)

3. He [liberal white person] may stand with you through thin, but not thick; when the chips are down, you'll find that as fixed in him as his bone structure is his sometimes subconscious conviction that he's better than anybody black.

MALCOLM X, *THE AUTOBIOGRAPHY OF MALCOLM X* (1964)

4. There are many humorous things in the world, among them the white man's notion that he is less savage than the other savages.

MARK TWAIN, "THE WHITE MAN'S NOTION," *FOLLOWING THE EQUATOR* (1897)

1055. WICKEDNESS

See also 191. CORRUPTION; 307. EVIL; 900. SIN; 971. TEMPTATION; 1030. VICE; 1070. WRONGDOING

1. There is no peace, saith the Lord, unto the wicked.

BIBLE ISAIAH 48:22

2. As for an authentic villain, the real thing, the absolute, the artist, one rarely meets him even once in a lifetime. The ordinary bad hat is always in part a decent fellow.

COLETTE, "THE SOUTH OF FRANCE," *EARTHLY PARADISE* (1966), 4

3. A belief in a supernatural source of evil is not necessary; men alone are quite capable of every wickedness.

JOSEPH CONRAD, *UNDER WESTERN EYES* (1911), 2.4

4. Wicked is not much worse than indiscreet.

JOHN DONNE, *AN ANATOMY OF THE WORLD; THE FIRST ANNIVERSARY* (1612)

5. It is an esoteric doctrine of society, that a little wickedness is good to make muscle; as if conscience were not good for hands and legs.

EMERSON, "POWER," *THE CONDUCT OF LIFE* (1860)

6. The unrighteous are never really fortunate.

EURIPIDES, *HELEN* (412 B.C.), TR. RICHMOND LATTIMORE

7. Wickedness is always easier than virtue, for it takes the short cut to everything.

SAMUEL JOHNSON, QUOTED IN BOSWELL'S *JOURNAL OF A TOUR TO THE HEBRIDES WITH SAMUEL JOHNSON,* SEPT. 17, 1773

8. No man ever became extremely wicked all at once.

JUVENAL, *SATIRES* (C. 100), 2.83

9. [O]ne's worst enormities remain within, and it is only one's vulgar commonplaces of error and folly that turn into murders and suicides, treasons, infidelities, and betrayals.

LEWIS MUMFORD, *FINDINGS AND KEEPINGS. ANALECTS FOR AN AUTOBIOGRAPHY* (1975)

10. One man's wickedness may easily become all men's curse.

PUBLILIUS SYRUS, *MORAL SAYINGS* (1ST C. B.C.), 463, TR. DARIUS LYMAN

11. Man is not born wicked; he becomes so, as he becomes sick.

VOLTAIRE, "WICKED," *PHILOSOPHICAL DICTIONARY* (1764)

12. Wickedness is a myth invented by good people to account for the curious attractiveness of others.

Oscar Wilde, "Phrases and Philosophies for the Use of the Young" (1891)

1056. WILL

See also 124. Choice; 771. Purpose; 807. Resolution; 867. Self-Determination; 1057. Willingness

1. The will is never free—it is always attached to an object, a purpose. It is simply the engine in the car—it can't steer.

Joyce Cary, interview, *Writers at Work: First Series* (1958)

2. Will cannot be quenched against its will.

Dante, "Paradiso," 4, *The Divine Comedy* (c. 1300–21), tr. Lawrence Grant White

3. Will and Wisdom are both mighty leaders. Our times worship Will.

Clarence Day, "Humpty-Dumpty and Adam," *The Crow's Nest* (1921)

4. The good or ill of man lies within his own will.

Epictetus, *Discourses* (2nd c.), 1.25, tr. Thomas W. Higginson

5. A fat kitchen, a lean will.

Benjamin Franklin, *Poor Richard's Almanack* (1732–57)

6. The magic will which makes us see the other side of our natures—dream and disaster, catastrophe and fulfillment—is the great permanent challenge of humanity.

Herbert Gold, "The Magic Will," *The Magic Will* (1971)

7. I wish it, I command it. Let my will take the place of a reason.

Juvenal, *Satires* (c. 100), 6.223

8. Man's will creates the things that paralyze his brain and brutalize his heart.

Max Lerner, "The Human Heart and the Human Will," *Actions and Passions* (1949)

9. Will springs from the two elements of moral sense and self-interest.

Abraham Lincoln, speech, Springfield, Ill., June 26, 1857

10. Our wills and fates do so contrary run / That our devices still are overthrown; / Our thoughts are ours, their ends none of our own.

Shakespeare, *Hamlet* (1600), 3.2.221

1057. WILLINGNESS

See also 771. Purpose; 1022. Unwillingness; 1056. Will

1. When a man's / Willing and eager, god joins in.

Aeschylus, *The Persians* (472 b.c.), tr. Seth G. Bernardete

2. A willing mind makes a light foot.

Thomas Fuller, M.D., *Gnomologia* (1732), 467

3. Nothing is impossible to a willing heart.

John Heywood, *Proverbs* (1546), 1.4

4. Nothing is troublesome that we do willingly.

Thomas Jefferson, letter to Thomas Jefferson Smith, Feb. 21, 1825

1058. WILLS AND INHERITANCE

See also 1048. Wealth

1. Posthumous charities are the very essence of selfishness when bequeathed by those who, when alive, would part with nothing.

Charles Caleb Colton, *Lacon* (1825), 1.341

2. When it comes to divide an estate, the politest men quarrel.

Emerson, *Journals* 1863

3. They that marry ancient people, merely in expectation to bury them, hang themselves in hope that one will come and cut the halter.

Thomas Fuller, D.D, "Of Marriage," *The Holy State and the Profane State* (1642)

4. One of my father's most precious legacies to me was spiritual. I learned from him the value of courage and the strength of will.

Armand Hammer, *Hammer* (1987), with Neil Lyndon

5. The art of will-making chiefly consists in baffling the importunity of expectation.

William Hazlitt, "On Will-Making," *Table Talk* (1821–22)

6. There is nothing earthly that lasts so well, on the whole, as money. A man's learning dies with him; even his virtues fade out of remembrance; but the

dividends on the stocks he bequeaths to his children live and keep his memory green.

OLIVER WENDELL HOLMES SR., *THE PROFESSOR AT THE BREAKFAST TABLE* (1860), 6

7. A son can bear with composure the death of his father, but the loss of his inheritance might drive him to despair.

MACHIAVELLI, *THE PRINCE* (1517), 17

1059. WIND

See also 854. SEASONS

1. The wind goeth toward the south, and turneth about unto the north; it whirleth about continually, and the wind returneth again according to his circuits.

BIBLE ECCLESIASTES 1:6

2. The East Wind, an interloper in the dominions of Westerly Weather, is an impassive-faced tyrant with a sharp poniard held behind his back for a treacherous stab.

JOSEPH CONRAD, *THE MIRROR OF THE SEA* (1906), 28

3. The Westerly Wind asserting his sway from the south-west quarter is often like a monarch gone mad, driving forth with wild imprecations the most faithful of his courtiers to shipwreck, disaster, and death.

JOSEPH CONRAD, *THE MIRROR OF THE SEA* (1906), 26

4. The substance of the winds is too thin for human eyes, their written language is too difficult for human minds, and their spoken language mostly too faint for the ears.

JOHN MUIR, *A THOUSAND-MILE WALK TO THE GULF* (1916), 8

5. Who has seen the wind? / Neither you nor I: / But when the trees bow down their heads / The wind is passing by.

CHRISTINA ROSSETTI, "SING-SONG" (1872)

6. O wild West Wind, thou breath of Autumn's being, / Thou, from whose unseen presence the leaves dead / Are driven, like ghosts from an enchanter fleeing, / Yellow, and black, and pale, and hectic red, / Pestilence-stricken multitudes.

SHELLEY, "ODE TO THE WEST WIND" (1819), 1

7. O wind, a-blowing all day long, / O wind, that sings so loud a song!

ROBERT LOUIS STEVENSON, "THE WIND" (1885)

WINE

See 268. DRINKING

WINNERS

See 15. ADVANTAGE; 945. SUCCESS

WINTER

See 854. SEASONS

1060. WISDOM

See also 493. INTELLIGENCE; 522. KNOWLEDGE; 740. PROFUNDITY; 755. PRUDENCE; 1007. UNDERSTANDING

1. Wisdom / comes alone through suffering.

AESCHYLUS, *AGAMEMNON* (458 B.C.), TR. RICHMOND LATTIMORE

2. Knowing what is right does not make sagacious man.

ARISTOTLE, *NICOMACHEAN ETHICS* (4TH C. B.C.), 7.10, TR. J. A. K. THOMSON

3. To wisdom belongs the intellectual apprehension of eternal things; to knowledge, the rational knowledge of temporal things.

ST. AUGUSTINE, *ON THE TRINITY* (5TH C.), 12

4. The fear of the Lord is the beginning of wisdom.

BIBLE PSALMS 111:10 AND PROVERBS 9:10

5. The price of wisdom is above rubies.

BIBLE JOB 28:18

6. Wisdom is the principal thing; therefore get wisdom; and with all thy getting get understanding.

BIBLE PROVERBS 4:7

7. It may be a mistake to mix different wines, but old and new wisdom mix admirably.

BERTOLT BRECHT, PROLOGUE, *THE CAUCASIAN CHALK CIRCLE* (1944–45),, TR. MAJA APELMAN

8. Such are the sages! What must they be, when such as I can stumble on their mistakes or misstatements?

BYRON, *SELECTED LETTERS AND JOURNALS* (1982). LESLIE A. MARCHAND, ED.

9. What we're learning in our schools is not the wisdom of life. We're learning technologies, we're getting information.

JOSEPH CAMPBELL, *THE POWER OF MYTH* (1988)

10. The function of wisdom is to discriminate between good and evil.

CICERO, *DE OFFICIIS* (44 B.C.), 3.17.71

11. There is this difference between happiness and wisdom: he that thinks himself the happiest man, really is so; but he that thinks himself the wisest, is generally the greatest fool.

CHARLES CALEB COLTON, *LACON* (1825), 1.326

12. If one is too lazy to think, too vain to do a thing badly, too cowardly to admit it, one will never attain wisdom.

CYRIL CONNOLLY, *THE UNQUIET GRAVE* (1945), 1

13. Knowledge is proud that he has learned so much; / Wisdom is humble that he knows no more.

WILLIAM COWPER, "WINTER WALK AT NOON," *THE TASK* (1785), 95

14. The wisest people are the clowns, like Harpo Marx, who would not speak. If I could have anything I want I would like God to listen to what Harpo was not saying, and understand why Harpo would not talk.

PHILIP K. DICK, *THE GOLDEN MAN* (1980)

15. Life is a festival only to the wise.

EMERSON, "HEROISM," *ESSAYS: FIRST SERIES* (1841)

16. Wisdom has its root in goodness, and not goodness its root in wisdom.

EMERSON, *JOURNALS*, 1857

17. Wise men are not wise at all times.

EMERSON, "WEALTH," *THE CONDUCT OF LIFE* (1860)

18. Fortune seldom troubles the wise man. Reason has controlled his greatest and most important affairs, controls them throughout his life, and will continue to control them.

EPICURUS, "PRINCIPAL DOCTRINES" (3RD C. B.C.), 16, IN *LETTERS, PRINCIPAL DOCTRINES, AND VATICAN SAYINGS*, TR. RUSSEL M. GEER

19. Those who are held / Wise among men and who search the reasons of things / Are those who bring the most sorrow on themselves.

EURIPIDES, *MEDEA* (431 B.C.), TR. REX WARNER

20. The heart of a fool is in his mouth, but the mouth of a wise man is in his heart.

BENJAMIN FRANKLIN, *POOR RICHARD'S ALMANACK* (1732–57)

21. He is no wise man that cannot play the fool upon occasion.

THOMAS FULLER, M.D., *GNOMOLOGIA* (1732), 1929

22. Wisdom rises upon the ruins of folly.

THOMAS FULLER, M.D., *GNOMOLOGIA* (1732), 5770

23. The wise are always impatient, for he that increases knowledge increases impatience of folly.

BALTASAR GRACIÁN, *THE ART OF WORLDLY WISDOM* (1647), 159, TR. JOSEPH JACOBS

24. The sage has one advantage: he is immortal. If this is not his century, many others will be.

BALTASAR GRACIÁN, *THE ART OF WORLDLY WISDOM* (1647), 20, TR. JOSEPH JACOBS

25. The seat of knowledge is in the head; of wisdom, in the heart. We are sure to judge wrong if we do not feel right.

WILLIAM HAZLITT, *CHARACTERISTICS* (1823), 380

26. The road to wisdom?—Well, it's plain / and simple to express: / Err / and err / and err again / but less / and less / and less.

PIET HEIN, "THE ROAD TO WISDOM," *GROOKS* (1966)

27. Men who love wisdom should acquaint themselves with a great many particulars.

HERACLITUS, *FRAGMENTS* (C. 500 B.C.), 3, TR. PHILIP WHEELWRIGHT

28. Knowledge can be communicated, but not wisdom. One can find it, live it, be fortified by it, do wonders through it, but one cannot communicate and teach it.

HERMANN HESSE, "GOVINDA," *SIDDHARTHA* (1923), TR. HILDA ROSNER

29. Such is the nature of men, that howsoever they may acknowledge many others to be more witty, or more eloquent, or more learned, yet they will hardly believe there be many so wise as themselves.

THOMAS HOBBES, *LEVIATHAN* (1651), 1.13

30. How prone to doubt, how cautious are the wise!

HOMER, *ODYSSEY* (9TH C. B.C.), 13.375, TR. ALEXANDER POPE

31. Wisdom is an affair of values, and of value judgments. It is intelligent conduct of human affairs.

SIDNEY HOOK, "DOES PHILOSOPHY HAVE A FUTURE?" *SATURDAY REVIEW*, NOV. 11, 1967

32. Wisdom consists not so much in knowing what to do in the ultimate as in knowing what to do next.

HERBERT HOOVER, *READER'S DIGEST*, JULY 1958

33. "Age has nothing to do with wisdom," said Simple. "I know a man fifty-two years old who never does go home except to take a bath and change his underwear."

LANGSTON HUGHES, *SIMPLE SPEAKS HIS MIND* (1950)

34. The tongue of a wise man lieth behind his heart.

ALI IBN-ABI-TALIB, *SENTENCES* (7TH C.), 95, TR. SIMON OCKLEY

35. Wisdom, I know, is social. She seeks her fellows, but Beauty is jealous, and illy bears the presence of a rival.

THOMAS JEFFERSON, LETTER TO ABIGAIL ADAMS, SEPT. 25, 1785

36. Common sense suits itself to the ways of the world. Wisdom tries to conform to the ways of Heaven.

JOSEPH JOUBERT, *PENSÉES* (1842), 8.6, TR. KATHARINE LYTTELTON

37. If it be true that a man is rich who wants nothing, a wise man is a very rich man.

LA BRUYÈRE, *CHARACTERS* (1688), 6.49, TR. HENRI VAN LAUN

38. It is easier to be wise on behalf of others than to be so for ourselves.

LA ROCHEFOUCAULD, *MAXIMS* (1665),, TR. KENNETH PRATT

39. It is very foolish to wish to be exclusively wise.

LA ROCHEFOUCAULD, *MAXIMS* (1665), TR. KENNETH PRATT

40. It requires wisdom to understand wisdom; the music is nothing if the audience is deaf.

WALTER LIPPMANN, *A PREFACE TO MORALS* (1929), 3.15.2

41. Wisdom requires no form; her beauty must vary, as varies the beauty of flame. She is no motionless goddess, for ever couched on her throne.

MAURICE MAETERLINCK, *WISDOM AND DESTINY* (1898), 24, TR. ALFRED SUTRO

42. The contradictory remarks of politicians are forgotten; the more asinine predictions of pundits are buried with mercy.

NORMAN MAILER, *CANNIBALS AND CHRISTIANS* (1967)

43. Wisdom enough to leech us of our ill / Is daily spun; but there exists no loom / To weave it into fabric.

EDNA ST. VINCENT MILLAY, *SONNETS* (1941), 137

44. Wisdom is a solid and entire building, of which every piece keeps its place and bears its mark.

MONTAIGNE, "OF EXPERIENCE," *ESSAYS* (1580–88), TR. W. C. HAZLITT

45. The growth of wisdom may be gauged exactly by the diminution of ill-temper.

NIETZSCHE, *THE WANDERER AND HIS SHADOW* (1880), 348, TR. PAUL V. COHN

46. Wisdom is always an overmatch for strength.

PHAEDRUS, *FABLES* (1ST C.), 1.13.13, TR. HENRY THOMAS RILEY

47. Not by years but by disposition is wisdom acquired.

PLAUTUS, *THE THREE-PENNY DAY* (C. 194 B.C.), 2.2.48, TR. HENRY THOMAS RILEY

48. He bids fair to grow wise who has discovered that he is not so.

PUBLILIUS SYRUS, *MORAL SAYINGS* (1ST C. B.C.), 598, TR. DARIUS LYMAN

49. Wisdom had rather be buffeted than not listened to.

PUBLILIUS SYRUS, *MORAL SAYINGS* (1ST C. B.C.), 152, TR. DARIUS LYMAN

50. Nine-tenths of wisdom is being wise in time.

THEODORE ROOSEVELT, SPEECH, LINCOLN, NEB., JUNE 14, 1917

51. Youth is the time to study wisdom; old age is the time to practice it.

ROUSSEAU, *REVERIES OF A SOLITARY WALKER* (1782), 3

52. The first step in wisdom, as well as in morality, is to open the windows of the ego as wide as possible.

BERTRAND RUSSELL, "FORTITUDE," *NEW HOPES FOR A CHANGING WORLD* (1951)

53. The fool doth think he is wise, but the wise man knows himself to be a fool.

SHAKESPEARE, *AS YOU LIKE IT* (1599–1600), 5.1.34

54. To be wise and love / Exceeds man's might: that dwells with gods above.

SHAKESPEARE, *TROILUS AND CRESSIDA* (1601–02), 3.2.163

55. One rabbi compared wise men studying the law to children tossing a ball to one another: a first sage said the meaning was this, another said the meaning was that, one gave his opinion, another begged to differ.

ISRAEL SHENKER, *COAT OF MANY COLORS* (1985)

56. How terrible is wisdom when / it brings no profit to the man that's wise!

SOPHOCLES, *OEDIPUS THE KING* (C. 430 B.C.), TR. DAVID GRENE

57. Sciences may be learned by rote, but wisdom not.

LAURENCE STERNE, *TRISTRAM SHANDY* (1759–67), 5.32

58. Knowledge comes, but wisdom lingers, and he bears a laden breast, / Full of sad experience, moving toward the stillness of his rest.

LORD TENNYSON, "LOCKSLEY HALL" (1842)

59. It is a characteristic of wisdom not to do desperate things.

THOREAU, "ECONOMY," *WALDEN* (1854)

60. Not by constraint or severity shall you have access to true wisdom, but by abandonment, and childlike mirthfulness. If you would know aught, be gay before it.

THOREAU, *JOURNAL*, JUNE 23, 1840

61. Of the demonstrably wise there are but two; those who commit suicide, and those who keep their reasoning faculties atrophied with drink.

MARK TWAIN, *NOTEBOOK* (1935)

62. The well-bred contradict other people. The wise contradict themselves.

OSCAR WILDE, "PHRASES AND PHILOSOPHIES FOR THE USE OF THE YOUNG" (1891)

63. To be free is not necessarily to be wise. Wisdom comes with counsel, with the frank and free conference of untrammeled men united in the common interest.

WOODROW WILSON, ACCEPTANCE SPEECH, DEMOCRATIC NATIONAL CONVENTION, JULY 7, 1912

64. Wisdom is ofttimes nearer when we stoop / Than when we soar.

WILLIAM WORDSWORTH, *THE EXCURSION* (1814), 3

65. It takes a wise man to recognize a wise man.

XENOPHANES (6TH–5TH C. B.C.), QUOTED IN DIOGENES LAERTIUS' *LIVES AND OPINIONS OF EMINENT PHILOSOPHERS* (3RD C. A.D.), TR. R. D. HICKS

WISHES

See 238. DESIRES

1061. WIT

See also 139. CLEVERNESS; 145. COMEDY; 436. HUMOR; 526. LAUGHTER; 768. PUNS; 843. SARCASM; 844. SATIRE

1. The mere wit is only a human bauble. He is to life what bells are to horses—not expected to draw the load, but only to jingle while the horses draw.

HENRY WARD BEECHER, *PROVERBS FROM PLYMOUTH PULPIT* (1887)

2. Humorous persons have pleasant mouths turned up at the corners.... But the mouth of a merely witty man is hard and sour until the moment of its discharge.

CHARLES S. BROOKS, "ON THE DIFFERENCE BETWEEN WIT AND HUMOR," IN *I WAS JUST THINKING* (1959)

3. A man must have a good share of wit himself to endure a great share in another.

LORD CHESTERFIELD, *LETTERS TO HIS GODSON*, DEC. 18, 1765

4. Wit is so shining a quality that everybody admires it; most people aim at it, all people fear it, and few love it unless in themselves.

LORD CHESTERFIELD, *LETTERS TO HIS GODSON*, DEC. 18, 1765

5. The more wit we have, the less satisfied we are with it.

JEAN LE ROND D'ALEMBERT, "ESSAI SUR LES GENS DE LETTRES," *OEUVRES PHILOSOPHIQUE* (1805), V. 3

6. Wit makes its own welcome and levels all distinctions.

EMERSON, "THE COMIC," *LETTERS AND SOCIAL AIMS* (1876)

7. Men never think their fortune too great, nor their wit too little.

THOMAS FULLER, M.D., *GNOMOLOGIA* (1732), 3400

8. A delicate wit is a corruption which a nation takes a long time to acquire. It is only worn-out nations that possess it.

EDMOND AND JULES DE GONCOURT, *JOURNAL*, MAY 2, 1858, TR. ROBERT BALDICK

9. Many get the repute of being witty, but thereby lose the credit of being sensible. Jest has its little hour, seriousness should have all the rest.

BALTASAR GRACIÁN, *THE ART OF WORLDLY WISDOM* (1647), 75, TR. JOSEPH JACOBS

10. The wit we wish we had spoils the wit we have.

JEAN BAPTISTE LOUIS GRESSET, *LE MÉCHANT* (1745), 4.7

11. Wit is the salt of conversation, not the food.

WILLIAM HAZLITT, "ON WIT AND HUMOUR," *LECTURES ON THE ENGLISH COMIC WRITERS* (1819)

12. Impertinent wits are a kind of insect which are in everybody's way and plentiful in all countries.

LA BRUYÈRE, *CHARACTERS* (1688), 5.3, TR. HENRI VAN LAUN

13. True wit, to every man, is that which falls on another.

WALTER SAVAGE LANDOR, "ALEXANDER AND THE PRIEST OF HAMMON," *IMAGINARY CONVERSATIONS* (1824–53)

14. A wit would often be embarrassed without the company of fools.

LA ROCHEFOUCAULD, *MAXIMS* (1665), TR. KENNETH PRATT

15. The greatest fault of a penetrating wit is to go beyond the mark.

La Rochefoucauld, *Maxims* (1665)

16. In the midst of the fountain of wit there arises something bitter, which stings in the very flowers.

Lucretius, *On the Nature of Things* (1st c. B.C.), 4.1133

17. I have ever thought so superstitiously of wit, that I fear I have committed idolatry against wisdom.

John Lyly, *Euphues: The Anatomy of Wit* (1579)

18. Wit has a deadly aim and it is possible to prick a large pretense with a small pin.

Marya Mannes, "Controverse," *But Will It Sell?* (1955–64)

19. Impropriety is the soul of wit.

W. Somerset Maugham, *The Moon and Sixpence* (1919), 4

20. Wit is the epitaph of an emotion.

Nietzsche, *Miscellaneous Maxims and Opinions* (1879), 202, tr. Paul V. Cohn

21. Wit has truth in it; wisecracking is simply calisthenics with words.

Dorothy Parker, interview, *Writers at Work: First Series* (1958)

22. The greatest advantage I know of being thought a wit by the world is, that it gives one the greater freedom of playing the fool.

Alexander Pope, *Thoughts on Various Subjects* (1727)

23. True wit is Nature to advantage dressed, / What oft was thought, but ne'er so well expressed.

Alexander Pope, *An Essay on Criticism* (1711), 2.97

24. To be over much facetious is the accomplishment of courtiers and blemish of the wise.

Sa'di, *Gulistan* (1258), 1.15, tr. James Ross

25. The quality of wit inspires more admiration than confidence.

George Santayana, "Wit," *The Sense of Beauty* (1896)

26. Brevity is the soul of wit.

Shakespeare, *Hamlet* (1600), 2.2.90

27. There is hardly that person to be found who is not more concerned for the reputation of wit and sense, than honesty and virtue.

Richard Steele, *The Spectator* (1711–12), 6

28. Wit isn't a useful instrument of defense; it may make a short-run appeal, but it creates a backlash—one saw this in the Hiss case and the Oppenheimer hearings; certainly one saw it in the trial of Oscar Wilde.

Diana Trilling, *Mrs. Harris: The Death of the Scarsdale Doctor* (1981)

29. Wit is the sudden marriage of ideas which before their union were not perceived to have any relation.

Mark Twain, *Notebook* (1935)

30. He who cannot shine by thought, seeks to bring himself into notice by a witticism.

Voltaire, "Wit, Spirit, Intellect," *Philosophical Dictionary* (1764)

1062. WOMEN

See also 121. Charm; 192. Cosmetics; 267. Dress; 338. Fashion; 566. Masculinity and Femininity; 581. Men and Women; 593. Mirrors; 685. Perfume

1. Women have, commonly, a very positive moral sense; that which they will is right; that which they reject is wrong; and their will, in most cases, ends by settling the moral.

Henry Adams, *The Education of Henry Adams* (1907), 6

2. Forgetting is woman's first and greatest art.

Richard Aldington, *The Colonel's Daughter* (1931)

3. Women wish to be loved without a why or a wherefore; not because they are pretty, or good, or well-bred, or graceful, or intelligent, but because they are themselves.

Henri Frédéric Amiel, *Journal,* March 17, 1868

4. These impossible women! How they do get around us! / The poet was right: can't live with them, or without them.

Aristophanes, *Lysistrata* (411 B.C.), tr. Dudley Fitts

5. With women, the heart argues, not the mind.

Matthew Arnold, *Merope* (1858)

6. A lady's imagination is very rapid; it jumps from admiration to love, from love to matrimony in a moment.

Jane Austen, *Pride and Prejudice* (1813), 6

7. A woman can be anything that the man who loves her would have her be.

J. M. Barrie, *Tommy and Grizel* (1900)

8. There is no other purgatory but a woman.

Beaumont and Fletcher, *The Scornful Lady* (c. 1614), 3.1

9. The women of today are in a fair way to dethrone the myth of femininity; they are beginning to affirm their independence in concrete ways; but they do not easily succeed in living completely the life of a human being.

Simone de Beauvoir, *The Second Sex* (1953)

10. Woman is determined not by her hormones or by mysterious instincts, but by the manner in which her body and her relation to the world are modified through the action of others than herself.

Simone de Beauvoir, *The Second Sex* (1949)

11. As a jewel of gold in a swine's snout, so is a fair woman which is without discretion.

Bible Proverbs 11:22

12. Here's to woman! Would that we could fall into her arms without falling into her hands.

Ambrose Bierce, quoted in C. H. Grattan's *Bitter Bierce* (1929)

13. Intimacies between women often go backwards, beginning in revelations and ending up in small talk without loss of esteem.

Elizabeth Bowen, *The Death of the Heart* (1938), 2.1

14. In the nineteenth century, government agencies in Washington had, almost without exception, flatly refused to hire even one female.

David Brinkley, *Washington Goes to War* (1988)

15. As the cat lapses into savagery by night, and barbarously explores the dark, so primal and titanic is a woman with the love-madness.

Gelett Burgess, "The Gentleman's Code," *The Romance of the Commonplace* (1916)

16. Alas! the love of Women! it is known / To be a lovely and a fearful thing.

Byron, *Don Juan* (1819–24), 2.199

17. Now what I love in women is, they won't / Or can't do otherwise than lie, but do it / So well, the very truth seems falsehood to it.

Byron, *Don Juan* (1819–24), 11.36

18. A woman is a vehicle of life. Life has overtaken her. Woman is what it is all about—the giving of birth and the giving of nourishment.

Joseph Campbell, *The Power of Myth* (1988)

19. For women in those days, the break-up of a home was often a break-up of their lives. Many a girl in the bad times passed in a year from bridehood and motherhood to the workhouse or the streets.

Joyce Cary, *Except the Lord* (1953)

20. What a woman says to an eager lover, / write it on running water, write it on air.

Catullus, *Poems* (1st c. b.c.), 70, tr. Gilbert Highet

21. Old, that's an affront no woman can well bear.

Cervantes, *Don Quixote* (1605–15), 2.3.31, tr. John Ozell

22. That's the nature of women, not to love when we love them, and to love when we love them not.

Cervantes, *Don Quixote* (1605–15), 1.3.6, tr. John Ozell

23. She was a well-mannered woman of perhaps thirty-five, Mr. Bruce decided, with a well-ordered house and a perfect emotional digestion—one of those women who, through their goodness, can absorb anything.

John Cheever, "The Bus to St. James's," *The Stories of John Cheever* (1980)

24. Women who are either indisputably beautiful, or indisputably ugly, are best flattered upon the score of their understandings.

Lord Chesterfield, *Letters to His Son,* Sept. 5, 1748

25. Variability is one of the virtues of a woman. It avoids the crude requirement of polygamy. So long as you have one good wife you are sure to have a spiritual harem.

G. K. Chesterton, "The Glory of Grey," *Alarms and Discursions* (1910)

26. Women singly do a good deal of harm. Women in bulk are chastening.

Frank Moore Colby, "Some of the Difficulties of Frollicking," *The Colby Essays* (1926), v. 1

27. Women generally consider consequences in love, seldom in resentment.

Charles Caleb Colton, *Lacon* (1825), 1.517

28. Most females will forgive a liberty rather than a slight.

Charles Caleb Colton, *Lacon* (1825), 1.557

29. Women are like tricks by sleight of hand, / Which, to admire, we should not understand.

William Congreve, *Love for Love* (1695), 4.3

30. Women, like flames, have a destroying power, / Ne'er to be quenched till they themselves devour.

WILLIAM CONGREVE, *THE DOUBLE-DEALER* (1694), 4.5

31. A woman's desire for revenge outlasts all her other emotions.

CYRIL CONNOLLY, *THE UNQUIET GRAVE* (1945), I

32. There is no fury like a woman searching for a new lover.

CYRIL CONNOLLY, *THE UNQUIET GRAVE* (1945), I

33. A woman never sees what we do for her, she only sees what we don't do.

GEORGES COURTELINE, *LA PAIX CHEZ SOI* (1903), 4

34. Women are better than they are reputed to be: they don't mock the tears men shed unless they themselves are responsible for them.

GEORGES COURTELINE, *LA PHILOSOPHIE DE G. COURTELINE* (1917)

35. What is woman?—only one of Nature's agreeable blunders.

HANNAH COWLEY, *WHO'S THE DUPE?* (1779), 2

36. Women are never stronger than when they arm themselves with their weaknesses.

MARQUISE DU DEFFAND, *LETTERS TO VOLTAIRE* (1759–75)

37. Women never use their intelligence—except when they need to prop up their intuition.

JACQUES DEVAL, NEWS SUMMARIES, MAY 10, 1954

38. Women are most fascinating between the age of thirty-five and forty after they have won a few races and know how to pace themselves. Since few women ever pass forty, maximum fascination can continue indefinitely.

CHRISTIAN DIOR, *COLLIER'S,* JUNE 10, 1955

39. Women are like the arts, forced unto none, / Open to all searchers, unprized, if unknown.

JOHN DONNE, ELEGY 3, "CHANGE" (1635)

40. There are only three things to be done with a woman. You can love her, suffer for her, or turn her into literature.

LAWRENCE DURRELL, *JUSTINE* (1957), I

41. Of women, the most we can say, not being Frenchmen, is that they are burrowing animals.

LAWRENCE DURRELL [GEORGE], *BALTHAZAR* (1958)

42. A woman's hopes are woven of sunbeams; a shadow annihilates them.

GEORGE ELIOT, *FELIX HOLT* (1866), I

43. Half the sorrows of women would be averted if they could repress the speech they know to be useless—nay, the speech they have resolved not to utter.

GEORGE ELIOT, *FELIX HOLT* (1866), 2

44. The happiest women, like the happiest nations, have no history.

GEORGE ELIOT, *THE MILL ON THE FLOSS* (1860), 6.3

45. A beautiful woman is a practical poet.

EMERSON, "BEAUTY," *THE CONDUCT OF LIFE* (1860)

46. A woman should always challenge our respect, and never move our compassion.

EMERSON, *JOURNALS,* 1836

47. A woman's strength is the unresistible might of weakness.

EMERSON, *JOURNALS,* 1836

48. All are good maids, but whence come the bad wives?

ENGLISH PROVERB

49. When women age into their power, no wind can upset them, no hand turn aside their knowledge, no fact can deflect their point of view.

LOUISE ERDRICH, "LIPSHA MORRISEY," *THE BINGO PALACE* (1994)

50. Love's all in all to women.

EURIPIDES, *ANDROMACHE* (C. 426 B.C.), TR. JOHN F. NIMS

51. Neither earth nor ocean / produces a creature as savage and monstrous / as woman.

EURIPIDES, *HECUBA* (C. 425 B.C.), TR. WILLIAM ARROWSMITH

52. There seems to be some pleasure / for women in sick talk of one another.

EURIPIDES, *THE PHOENICIAN WOMEN* (C. 411–409 B.C.), TR. ELIZABETH WYCKOFF

53. What else goes wrong for a woman—except her marriage?

EURIPIDES, *ANDROMACHE* (C. 426 B.C.), TR. JOHN F. NIMS

54. Woman is woman's natural ally.

EURIPIDES, *ALOPE* (5TH C. B.C.), 109, TR. M. H. MORGAN

55. The American woman has not yet slipped into a cocoon, but she has tumbled down a rabbit hole into sudden isolation.

SUSAN FALUDI, *BACKLASH* (1991)

56. How a little love and good company improves a woman!

GEORGE FARQUHAR, *THE BEAUX' STRATEGEM* (1707), 4.1

57. To most women art is a form of scandal.

F. SCOTT FITZGERALD, "THE NOTE-BOOKS," *THE CRACK-UP* (1945)

58. Ugly women may be naturally quite as capricious as pretty ones; but as they are never petted and spoiled, and as no allowances are made for them, they soon find themselves obliged either to suppress their whims or to hide them.

ANATOLE FRANCE, *THE CRIME OF SYLVESTRE BONNARD* (1881), 1, TR. LAFCADIO HEARN

59. Women are equal because they are not different any more.

ERICH FROMM, *THE ART OF LOVING* (1956), 2

60. A woman scoffs at evidence. Show her the sun, tell her it is daylight, at once she will close her eyes and say to you, "No, it is night."

ÉMILE GABORIAU, *MONSIEUR LECOQ* (1869), 10

61. Women never confess; even when they seemingly resign themselves to such a course, they are never sincere.

ÉMILE GABORIAU, *MONSIEUR LECOQ* (1869), 10

62. Women have no sense of the abstract—a woman admiring the sky is a woman caressing the sky. In a woman's mind beauty is something she needs to touch.

JEAN GIRAUDOUX, *THE APOLLO OF BELLAC* (1942), ADAPTED BY MAURICE VALENCY

63. Only the woman of the world is a woman; the rest are females.

JULES DE GONCOURT, *JOURNAL*, OCT. 13, 1855, TR. ROBERT BALDICK

64. A woman prefers a man without money to money without a man.

GREEK PROVERB

65. A woman's vanity is interested in making the object of her choice the God of her idolatry.

WILLIAM HAZLITT, "ON THE SPIRIT OF OBLIGATIONS," *THE PLAIN SPEAKER* (1826)

66. Women never reason, and therefore they are (comparatively) seldom wrong.

WILLIAM HAZLITT, *CHARACTERISTICS* (1823)

67. If men knew how women pass the time when they are alone, they'd never marry.

O. HENRY, "MEMOIRS OF A YELLOW DOG," *THE FOUR MILLION* (1906)

68. A woman never forgets her sex. She would rather talk with a man than an angel, any day.

OLIVER WENDELL HOLMES, SR., *THE POET AT THE BREAKFAST TABLE* (1872), 4

69. Oh woman, woman! when to ill thy mind / Is bent, all hell contains no fouler fiend.

HOMER, *ODYSSEY* (9TH C. B.C.), 11.531, TR. ALEXANDER POPE

70. The part we play is not as we want it, but as we are made—with the genitals God gave us.

MAUREEN HOWARD, *BRIDGEPORT BUS* (1965)

71. A woman is as old as she looks before breakfast.

EDGAR WATSON HOWE, *COUNTRY TOWN SAYINGS* (1911)

72. A woman does not spend all her time in buying things; she spends part of it in taking them back.

EDGAR WATSON HOWE, *COUNTRY TOWN SAYINGS* (1911)

73. At first a woman doesn't want anything but a husband, but just as soon as she gets one, she wants everything else in the world.

EDGAR WATSON HOWE, *COUNTRY TOWN SAYINGS* (1911)

74. A woman will doubt everything you say except it be compliments to herself.

ELBERT HUBBARD, *THE NOTE BOOK* (1927)

75. I know how to handle women who act like ladies, but my landlady ain't no lady. Sometimes I even wish I was living with my wife again so I could have my own place and not have no landladies.

LANGSTON HUGHES, *SIMPLE SPEAKS HIS MIND* (1950)

76. One of the magnanimities of woman is to yield.

VICTOR HUGO, "SAINT DENIS," *LES MISÉRABLES* (1862), 8.1, TR. CHARLES E. WILBOUR

77. A woman's whole life is a history of the affections.

WASHINGTON IRVING, "THE BROKEN HEART," *THE SKETCH BOOK OF GEOFFREY CRAYON, GENT.* (1819–20)

78. There is in every true woman's heart a spark of heavenly fire, which lies dormant in the broad daylight of prosperity, but which kindles up and beams and blazes in the dark hour of adversity.

WASHINGTON IRVING, "THE WIFE," *THE SKETCH BOOK OF GEOFFREY CRAYON, GENT.* (1819–20)

79. When female minds are embittered by age or solitude, their malignity is generally exerted in a rigorous and spiteful superintendence of domestic trifles.

SAMUEL JOHNSON, *THE RAMBLER* (1750–52), 113

80. A woman, the more curious she is about her face, is commonly the more careless about her house.

Ben Jonson, "Random Thoughts," *Timber* (1640)

81. There's no effrontery like that of a woman caught in the act; her very guilt inspires her with wrath and insolence.

Juvenal, *Satires* (c. 100), 6.284

82. Never praise a sister to a sister, in the hope of your compliments reaching the proper ears.

Rudyard Kipling, "The False Dawn," *Plain Tales from the Hills* (1888)

83. If a handsome woman allows that another woman is beautiful, we may safely conclude she excels her.

La Bruyère, *Characters* (1688), 12.8, tr. Henri Van Laun

84. In their first passion women love their lovers, in all the others they love love.

La Rochefoucauld, *Maxims* (1665)

85. One must choose between loving women and knowing them.

Attributed to Ninon De Lenclos (1620–1705)

86. The pleasure of talking is the inextinguishable passion of a woman, coeval with the act of breathing.

Alain-René Lesage, *Histoire de Gil Blas de Santillane* (1715–35), 7.7

87. Woman's normal occupations in general run counter to creative life, or contemplative life, or saintly life.

Anne Morrow Lindbergh, "Channelled Whelk," *Gift from the Sea* (1955)

88. Women, like princes, find few real friends.

George Lyttleton, "Advice to a Lady" (1733)

89. Women like other women fine. The more feminine she is, the more comfortable a woman feels with her own sex. It is only the occasional and therefore noticeable adventuress who refuses to make friends with us.

Phyllis McGinley, "Some of My Best Friends...," *The Province of the Heart* (1959)

90. To be married to a good woman is to live with tender surprise.

Norman Mailer, *Harlot's Ghost* (1991)

91. the females of all species are most / dangerous when they appear to retreat.

Don Marquis, "a farewell," *Archy Does His Part* (1935)

92. A woman will always sacrifice herself if you give her the opportunity. It is her favorite form of self-indulgence.

W. Somerset Maugham, *The Circle* (1921), 3

93. We don't love a woman for what she says, we like what she says because we love her.

André Maurois, *De la conversation* (1921)

94. There are many wild beasts on land and in the sea, but the beastliest of all is woman.

Menander, *The Changeling* (4th–3rd c. b.c.), 488

95. When women kiss it always reminds one of prize-fighters shaking hands.

H. L. Mencken, "Sententiae," *A Book of Burlesques* (1920)

96. Women have simple tastes. They can get pleasure out of the conversation of children in arms and men in love.

H. L. Mencken, "Sententiae," *A Book of Burlesques* (1920)

97. Woman's reason is in the milk of her breasts.

George Meredith, *The Ordeal of Richard Feveral* (1859), 43

98. To inspire love is a woman's greatest ambition, believe me. It's the one thing women care about and there's no woman so proud that she doesn't rejoice at heart in her conquests.

Molière, *The Sicilian* (1666), 1, tr. John Wood

99. It costs an unreasonable woman no more to pass over one reason than another; they cherish themselves most where they are most wrong.

Montaigne, "Of the affections of fathers to their children," *Essays* (1580–88), tr. W. C. Hazlitt

100. American Women: How they mortify the flesh in order to make it appetizing! Their beauty is a vast industry, their enduring allure a discipline which nuns or athletes might find excessive.

Malcolm Muggeridge, "Women of America," *The Most of Malcolm Muggeridge* (1966)

101. Women would rather be right than reasonable.

Ogden Nash, "Frailty, Thy Name Is a Misnomer," *Marriage Lines* (1964)

102. Let man fear woman when she loves: then she makes any sacrifice, and everything else seems without value to her.

Nietzsche, "On Little Old and Young Women," *Thus Spoke Zarathustra* (1883–92), 1, tr. Walter Kaufmann

103. Where neither love nor hatred is in the game, a woman's game is mediocre.

NIETZSCHE, *BEYOND GOOD AND EVIL* (1886), 115, TR. WALTER KAUFMANN

104. Woman was God's second mistake.

NIETZSCHE, *THE ANTICHRIST* (1888), 48, TR. ANTHONY M. LUDOVICI

105. Women themselves always still have in the background of all personal vanity an impersonal contempt for "woman."

NIETZSCHE, *BEYOND GOOD AND EVIL* (1886), 86, TR. WALTER KAUFMANN

106. Every woman thinks herself attractive; even the plainest is satisfied with the charms she deems that she possesses.

OVID, *THE ART OF LOVE* (C. A.D. 8), I, TR. J. LEWIS MAY

107. Many women long for what eludes them, and like not what is offered them.

OVID, *THE ART OF LOVE* (C. A.D. 8), I, TR. J. LEWIS MAY

108. What one beholds of a woman is the least part of her.

OVID, *LOVE'S CURE* (C. A.D. 8), TR. J. LEWIS MAY

109. Women's words are as light as the doomed leaves whirling in autumn, / Easily swept by the wind, easily drowned by the wave.

OVID, *THE LOVES* (C. A.D. 8), 2.16, TR. ROLFE HUMPHRIES

110. Women who write with an overriding consciousness that they write *as women* are engaged not in aspiration toward writing, but chiefly in a politics of sex.

CYNTHIA OZICK, "LITERATURE AND THE POLITICS OF SEX: A DISSENT," *ART & ARDOR* (1983)

111. Women are in league with each other, a secret conspiracy of hearts and pheromones.

CAMILLE PAGLIA, *SEX, ART, AND AMERICAN CULTURE* (1992)

112. Kings, women, and creeping vines as a rule embrace whatever is beside them.

PANCHATANTRA (C. 5TH C.), I, TR. FRANKLIN EDGERTON

113. All right, so call me Miss Cliché of 1960, but the thing about the married ones that always spooks me is how sweet and attentive they are at first, when they're on the prowl.

S.J. PERELMAN, *THE RISING GORGE* (1961)

114. Women are one and all a set of vultures.

PETRONIUS, *SATYRICON* (1ST C.), 42

115. Women are like dreams—they are never the way you would like to have them.

LUIGI PIRANDELLO, *EACH IN HIS OWN WAY* (1924), I, TR. ARTHUR LIVINGSTON

116. There's no such thing, you know, as picking out the best woman: it's only a question of comparative badness, brother.

PLAUTUS, *THE POT OF GOLD* (C. 200 B.C.), 2.1.139, TR. PAUL NIXON

117. Woman is certainly the daughter of Delay personified!

PLAUTUS, *THE BRAGGART WARRIOR* (C. 205 B.C.), 4.7.1292, TR. PAUL NIXON

118. It is a high distinction for a homely woman to be loved for her character rather than for beauty.

PLUTARCH, "MARRIAGE COUNSEL," *MORALIA* (C. A.D. 100), TR. MOSES HADAS

119. Women, as they are like riddles in being unintelligible, so generally resemble them in this, that they please us no longer once we know them.

ALEXANDER POPE, *THOUGHTS ON VARIOUS SUBJECTS* (1727)

120. Woman loves or hates: she knows no middle course.

PUBLILIUS SYRUS, *MORAL SAYINGS* (1ST C. B.C.), 66, TR. DARIUS LYMAN

121. She wavers, she hesitates: in a word, she is a woman.

RACINE, *ATHALIAH* (1691), 3.3

122. Women see through each other, but they rarely look into themselves.

THEODOR REIK, *OF LOVE AND LUST* (1957), 4.48

123. [Woman] is quick to revere genius, but in her secret soul she seldom loves it.

AGNES REPPLIER, "ENGLISH LOVE-SONGS," *POINTS OF VIEW* (1891)

124. Women and elephants never forget an injury.

SAKI, "REGINALD ON BESETTING SINS," *REGINALD* (1904)

125. My gosh, if I'd just read about one-tenth of what that woman's read and forgotten, I'd be happy. I mean she's *taught*, she's worked on a *news*paper, she designs her own *clothes*, she does every single bit of her own *house*work.

J.D. SALINGER, *RAISE HIGH THE ROOF BEAM, CARPENTERS* (1963)

WOMEN

126. A woman is a dish for the gods, if the devil dress her not.

SHAKESPEARE, *ANTONY AND CLEOPATRA* (1606–07), 5.2.275

127. A woman moved is like a fountain troubled, / Muddy, ill-seeming, thick, bereft of beauty.

SHAKESPEARE, *THE TAMING OF THE SHREW* (1593–94), 5.2.142

128. Do you not know I am a woman? When I think, I must speak.

SHAKESPEARE, *AS YOU LIKE IT* (1599–1600), 3.2.263

129. Kindness in women, not their beauteous looks, / Shall win my love.

SHAKESPEARE, *THE TAMING OF THE SHREW* (1593–94), 4.2.41

130. Women are as roses, whose fair flower, / Being once displayed, doth fall that very hour.

SHAKESPEARE, *TWELFTH NIGHT* (1599–1600), 2.4.39

131. What will not woman, gentle woman dare, / When strong affection stirs her spirit up?

ROBERT SOUTHEY, *MADOC IN WALES* (1805), 2.2

132. No woman can be handsome by the force of features alone, any more than she can be witty only by the help of speech.

RICHARD STEELE, *THE SPECTATOR* (1711–12), 33

133. The difficulty of course is that I like women. It is only wives I am in trouble with.

JOHN STEINBECK, *STEINBECK: A LIFE IN LETTERS,* (1975), EDS. ELAINE STEINBECK AND ROBERT WALLSTEN,

134. There's more to Bunnyhood than stuffing bosoms.

GLORIA STEINEM, "I WAS A PLAYBOY BUNNY," *OUTRAGEOUS ACTS AND EVERYDAY REBELLIONS* (1983)

135. Even when educators survey grade school texts and create new bibliographies to help teachers include Asians, Eskimos, and other Americans, females in and out of those groups may be downplayed or forgotten.

GLORIA STEINEM, *REVOLUTION FROM WITHIN* (1992)

136. Women are always eagerly on the lookout for any emotion.

STENDHAL, *ON LOVE* (1822), 7H. B. V., UNDER DIRECTION OF C. K. SCOTT-MONCRIEFF

137. I know the disposition of women: when you will, they won't; when you won't, they set their hearts upon you of their own inclination.

TERENCE, *THE EUNUCH* (161 B.C.), 4.7.42, TR. HENRY THOMAS RILEY

138. Most women have small waists the world throughout, / But their desires are thousand miles about.

CYRIL TOURNEUR, *THE REVENGER'S TRAGEDY* (1607), 5

139. The nastiness of women [in the 14th century] was generally perceived at the close of life when a man began to worry about hell, and his sexual desire in any case fading.

BARBARA W. TUCHMAN, *A DISTANT MIRROR* (1978)

140. Woman [in the 14th century] was the Church's rival, the temptress, the distraction, the obstacle to holiness, the Devil's decoy.

BARBARA W. TUCHMAN, *A DISTANT MIRROR* (1978)

141. A woman springs a sudden reproach upon you which provokes a hot retort—and then she will presently ask you to apologize.

MARK TWAIN, *NOTEBOOK* (1935)

142. She hasn't been attending a weekly women's discussion group down here for nothing. She feels indignant enough, independent enough, to get up and march into the kitchen and open the cabinet doors and pull down the Campari bottle and an orange-juice glass.

JOHN UPDIKE, *RABBIT AT REST* (1990)

143. The worst thing in the world is a bitter woman. That's one thing about your mother, she's never been bitter.

JOHN UPDIKE, *THE CENTAUR* (1963)

144. It's a man's world, they say; but in its daily textures it is a world created by and for women.

JOHN UPDIKE, "WOMEN," *ODD JOBS* (1991)

145. Womankind / Is ever a fickle and a changeful thing.

VERGIL, *AENEID* (30–19 B.C.), 4.569, TR. T. H. DELABERE-MAY

146. Woman is perpetual revolution, and is that element in the world which continually destroys and recreates.

CHARLES DUDLEY WARNER, "NINTH STUDY," *BACKLOG STUDIES* (1873)

147. No woman should ever be quite accurate about her age. It looks so calculating.

OSCAR WILDE, *THE IMPORTANCE OF BEING EARNEST* (1895), 3

148. The only way to behave to a woman is to make love to her, if she is pretty, and to someone else if she is plain.

OSCAR WILDE, *THE IMPORTANCE OF BEING EARNEST* (1895), 1

149. Women are a decorative sex. They never have anything to say, but they say it charmingly.

OSCAR WILDE, *THE PICTURE OF DORIAN GRAY* (1891), 4

150. If woman had no existence save in the fiction written by men, one would imagine her a person of the utmost importance; very various; heroic and mean; splendid and sordid; infinitely beautiful and hideous in the extreme; as great as a man, some think even greater.

VIRGINIA WOOLF, *A ROOM OF ONE'S OWN* (1929), 3

1063. WONDER

See also 955. SURPRISE

1. Wonder is the basis of worship.

THOMAS CARLYLE, *SARTOR RESARTUS* (1833–34), 1.10

2. Wherever life takes us, there are always moments of wonder.

JIMMY CARTER, *AN OUTDOOR JOURNAL: ADVENTURES AND REFLECTIONS* (1988)

3. Men love to wonder, and that is the seed of our science.

EMERSON, "WORKS AND DAYS," *SOCIETY AND SOLITUDE* (1870)

4. What happens to the hopes and dreams and wonder with which every child is born? Can it be that in working so hard to prepare them for their future roles in society, we are neglecting to offer a vision of their place in the universe?

JEAN GRASSO FITZPATRICK, *SOMETHING MORE* (1991)

1064. WORDS

See also 93. BOOKS AND READING; 134. CLARITY; 230. DEFINITION; 244. DICTIONARIES; 398. GRAMMAR; 524. LANGUAGE; 544. LITERALNESS; 573. MEANING; 923. SPEAKING; 1069. WRITING AND WRITERS

1. Words may be deeds.

AESOP, "THE TRUMPETER TAKEN PRISONER," *FABLES* (6TH C. B.C.?), TR. JOSEPH JACOBS

2. I'm very anxious not to fall into archaism or "literary" diction. I want my vocabulary to have a very large range, but the words *must* be alive.

JAMES AGEE, *LETTERS OF JAMES AGEE TO FATHER FLYE* (1962)

3. Man is a talking animal and he will always let himself be swayed by the power of the word. Machines won't change human nature.

SIMONE DE BEAUVOIR, *LES BELLES IMAGES* (1966), TR. PATRICK O'BRIAN (1968)

4. All words are pegs to hang ideas on.

HENRY WARD BEECHER, *PROVERBS FROM PLYMOUTH PULPIT* (1887)

5. Thought itself needs words. It runs on them like a long wire. And if it loses the habit of words, little by little it becomes shapeless, somber.

UGO BETTI, *GOAT ISLAND* (1946), 1.4

6. It is extremely natural for us to desire to see such our thoughts put into the dress of words, without which indeed we can scarce have a clear and distinct idea of them our selves.

EUSTACE BUDGELL, IN *THE SPECTATOR* (1711–12), 379

7. At all periods of the [English] language it is difficult to assign a beginning date to most new words and meanings. They tend to slip into the language silently, and are placed in date order only when scholars subsequently get to work.

ROBERT BURCHFIELD, *UNLOCKING THE ENGLISH LANGUAGE* (1989)

8. Vulgarity finds its antidote; old crudities become softened with time. Distinctions, both those that are useful and those that are burdensome, flourish and die, reflourish and die again.

ROBERT BURCHFIELD, *UNLOCKING THE ENGLISH LANGUAGE* (1989)

9. A word carries far—very far—deals destruction through time as the bullets go flying through space.

JOSEPH CONRAD, *LORD JIM* (1900), 15

10. Words, as is well known, are the great foes of reality.

JOSEPH CONRAD, PROLOGUE TO PART 1, *UNDER WESTERN EYES* (1911)

11. A word is dead / When it is said, / Some say. / I say it just / Begins to live / That day.

EMILY DICKINSON, POEM (1872?)

12. It's strange that words are so inadequate. / Yet, like the asthmatic struggling for breath, / So the lover must struggle for words.

T. S. ELIOT, *THE ELDER STATESMAN* (1958), 3

13. Letters to the editors of English and American newspapers often contain expressions of horror about

the new terms that creep into the language, and these expressions are usually accompanied by dire predictions about ruination of the mother tongue.

PETER FARB, *WORD PLAY* (1973)

14. You can stroke people with words.

F. SCOTT FITZGERALD, "THE NOTE-BOOKS," *THE CRACK-UP* (1945)

15. It need hardly be said that shortness is a merit in words.

H.W. FOWLER, *A DICTIONARY OF MODERN ENGLISH USAGE*, 2ND ED. (1926)

16. Those who run to long words are mainly the unskillful and tasteless; they confuse pomposity with dignity, flaccidity with ease, and bulk with force.

H.W. FOWLER, *A DICTIONARY OF MODERN ENGLISH USAGE*, 2ND ED. (1926)

17. The word is the most imprecise of signs. Only a science-obsessed age could fail to comprehend that this is its great virtue, not its defect.

JOHN FOWLES, *DANIEL MARTIN* (1977)

18. If a people have no word for something, either it does not matter to them or it matters too much to talk about.

EDGAR Z. FRIEDENBERG, "ADOLESCENCE," *THE VANISHING ADOLESCENT* (1959)

19. English is such a deliciously complex and undisciplined language, we can bend, fuse, distort words to all our purposes. We give old words new meanings, and we borrow new words from any language that intrudes into our intellectual environment.

WILLARD GAYLIN, *FEELINGS: OUR VITAL SIGNS* (1979)

20. Words are wise men's counters, they do but reckon by them; but they are the money of fools.

THOMAS HOBBES, *LEVIATHAN* (1651), 1.4

21. Action can give us the feeling of being useful, but only words can give us a sense of weight and purpose.

ERIC HOFFER, *THE PASSIONATE STATE OF MIND* (1954), 98

22. We must think things not words, or at least we must constantly translate our words into the facts for which they stand, if we are to keep the real and the true.

OLIVER WENDELL HOLMES, JR., ADDRESS, NEW YORK STATE BAR ASSOCIATION, JAN. 17, 1889

23. Words form the thread on which we string our experiences.

ALDOUS HUXLEY, *THE OLIVE TREE* (1937)

24. Words have users, but as well, users have words. And it is the users that establish the world's realities.

LE ROI JONES, "EXPRESSIVE LANGUAGE," *HOME* (1966)

25. Words, like glass, obscure when they do not aid vision.

JOSEPH JOUBERT, *PENSÉES* (1842), 21.15, TR. KATHARINE LYTTELTON

26. Any euphemism ceases to be euphemistic after a time and the true meaning begins to show through. It's a losing game, but we keep on trying.

JOSEPH WOOD KRUTCH, TITLE ESSAY, 1, *IF YOU DON'T MIND MY SAYING SO* (1964)

27. Who steals my purse steals trash, but he who filches from me a good word steals that which now enriches him, and leaves me none the poorer.

CHARLTON LAIRD, *THE MIRACLE OF LANGUAGE* (1953)

28. *Jazz* was formerly a crude term for indulging in an action which in polite society is referred to, if at all, only with such vague Latin terms as *intercourse* and *cohabitation*.

CHARLTON LAIRD, *THE MIRACLE OF LANGUAGE* (1953)

29. I hate false words, and seek with care, difficulty, and moroseness, those that fit the thing.

WALTER SAVAGE LANDOR, "BISHOP BURNET AND HUMPHREY HARDCASTLE," *IMAGINARY CONVERSATIONS* (1824–53)

30. We should have a great many fewer disputes in the world if words were taken for what they are, the signs of our ideas only, and not for things themselves.

JOHN LOCKE, *AN ESSAY CONCERNING HUMAN UNDERSTANDING* (1690), 3.10

31. Words, in their primary or immediate signification, stand for nothing but the ideas in the mind of him who uses them.

JOHN LOCKE, *AN ESSAY CONCERNING HUMAN UNDERSTANDING* (1690), 3.2.2

32. How strangely do we diminish a thing as soon as we try to express it in words.

MAURICE MAETERLINCK, "MYSTIC MORALITY," *THE TREASURE OF THE HUMBLE* (1896), TR. ALFRED SUTRO

33. Usually when he forgot words he would wait for them to seep back into consciousness like fish drawn up to the hungry surface of a stream. He would remember the initial letter of the forgotten word or sense sounds in it; soon the word reappeared in an illumination.

BERNARD MALAMUD, *DUBIN'S LIVES* (1979)

34. Words have weight, sound and appearance; it is only by considering these that you can write a sentence that is good to look at and good to listen to.

W. Somerset Maugham, *The Summing Up* (1938), 13

35. [In England] a fishmonger is the man who mongs fish; the ironmonger and the warmonger do the same with iron and war. They just mong them.

George Mikes, *How to Be an Alien* (1946)

36. It's when the thing itself is missing that you have to supply the word.

Henry de Montherlant, *Queen After Death* (1942), 2.1

37. Those things for which we find words, are things we have already overcome.

Nietzsche, "Skirmishes in a War with the Age," 26, *Twilight of the Idols* (1888), tr. Anthony M. Ludovici

38. It [modern writing at its worst] consists in gumming together long strips of words which have already been set in order by someone else, and making the results presentable by sheer humbug.

George Orwell, "Politics and the English Language," *A Collection of Essays* (1954)

39. Meanings receive their dignity from words instead of giving it to them.

Pascal, *Pensées* (1670), 50, tr. W. F. Trotter

40. A word is not the same with one writer as with another. One tears it from his guts. The other pulls it out of his overcoat pocket.

Charles Péguy, "The Honest People," *Basic Verities* (1943), tr. Ann and Julian Green

41. Clichés and stereotypes such as "beatnik" or "hippie" have been invented for the antitechnologists, the antisystem people, and will continue to be. But one does not convert individuals into mass people with the simple coining of a mass term.

Robert M. Pirsig, *Zen and the Art of Motorcycle Maintenance* (1974)

42. Words are like leaves; and where they most abound, / Much fruit of sense beneath is rarely found.

Alexander Pope, *An Essay on Criticism* (1711), 2.109

43. How describe the delicate thing that happens when a brilliant insect alights on a flower? Words, with their weight, fall upon the picture like birds of prey.

Jules Renard, *Journal*, September 1893, tr. Elizabeth Roget

44. Words are the small change of thought.

Jules Renard, *Journal*, November 1888, tr. Elizabeth Roget

45. Words not only affect us temporarily; they change us, they socialize or unsocialize us.

David Riesman, "Storytellers as Tutors," *The Lonely Crowd* (1950)

46. [H]alf the population (I guess) thinks that any plural ending in *s* requires an apostrophe, and the other half stands idly by without squirming, if, in fact, it even notices.

John Simon, "The Corruption of English," in *The State of the Language* (1980), eds. Leonard Michaels and Christopher Ricks

47. Many ideas have been transformed by adding one crucial adjective—*women's* bank, *women's* music, *women's* studies, *women's* caucus. That adjective did more than change a phrase. It implied a lot of new content: child care, flexible work hours, new standards of creditworthiness, new symbolism, new lyrics.

Gloria Steinem, "Words and Change," *Outrageous Acts and Everyday Rebellions* (1983)

48. Man does not live by words alone, despite the fact that sometimes he has to eat them.

Adlai Stevenson, speech, Denver, Colo., Sept. 5, 1952

49. Man is a creature who lives not upon bread alone, but principally by catchwords.

Robert Louis Stevenson, title essay, 2, *Virginibus Puerisque* (1881)

50. Words, like Nature, half reveal / And half conceal the Soul within.

Lord Tennyson, "In Memoriam A. H. H." (1850), 5

51. Words should be an intense pleasure just as leather should be to a shoemaker.

Evelyn Waugh, *The New York Times*, Nov. 19, 1950

1065. WORK

See also 281. Effort; 463. Incompetence; 680. Payment; 811. Rest; 813. Retirement; 924. Specialists; 1009. Unemployment; 1013. Unions; 1037. Vocations; 1066. Workers

1. Of all human activities, only labor, and neither action nor work, is unending, progressing automatically in accordance with life itself and outside the range of willful decisions or humanly meaningful purposes.

Hannah Arendt, *The Human Condition* (1958), 14

2. Most men in a brazen prison live, / Where, in the sun's hot eye, / With heads bent o'er their toil, they languidly / Their lives to some unmeaning taskwork give, / Dreaming of nought beyond their prison-wall.

MATTHEW ARNOLD, "A SUMMER NIGHT," *EMPEDOCLES ON ETNA, AND OTHER POEMS* (1852)

3. Don't condescend to unskilled labor. Try it for half a day first.

BROOKS ATKINSON, "MARCH 27," *ONCE AROUND THE SUN* (1951)

4. Capitalism arose and took off its pajamas. Another day, another dollar. Each man is valued at what he will bring in the marketplace. Meaning has been drained from work and assigned instead to remuneration.

DONALD BARTHELME, "THE RISE OF CAPITALISM," *SADNESS* (1972)

5. Often in other countries, one is waited on by people who obviously believe they were destined for better things but were forced by cruel fate to accept a degrading occupation, so degrading in fact as to bring them in contact with people like you. This never happens in Italy.

LUIGI BARZINI, *THE ITALIANS* (1964)

6. It is necessary to work, if not from inclination, at least from despair. Everything considered, work is less boring than amusing oneself.

CHARLES BAUDELAIRE, *MON COEUR MIS À NU* (1887), 18

7. Work would be terribly boring if one did not play the game all out, passionately.

SIMONE DE BEAUVOIR, *LES BELLES IMAGES* (1966), TR. PATRICK O'BRIAN (1968)

8. Work is not the curse, but drudgery is.

HENRY WARD BEECHER, *PROVERBS FROM PLYMOUTH PULPIT* (1887)

9. A man's work is rather the needful supplement to himself than the outcome of it.

MAX BEERBOHM, "HETHWAY SPEAKING," *MAINLY ON THE AIR* (1946)

10. No fine work can be done without concentration and self-sacrifice and toil and doubt.

MAX BEERBOHM, "BOOKS WITHIN BOOKS," *AND EVEN NOW* (1920)

11. What is work? and what is not work? are questions that perplex the wisest of men.

BHAGAVADGITA, 4, TR. P. LAL

12. In the sweat of thy face shalt thou eat bread, till thou return unto the ground; for out of it wast thou taken.

BIBLE, GENESIS 3:16

13. Investment in reliability will increase until it exceeds the probable cause of errors, or until someone insists on getting some useful work done.

ARTHUR BLOCH, "GILBS LAW OF UNRELIABILITY," *MURPHY'S LAW* (1979)

14. Whether our work is art or science or the daily work of society, it is only the form in which we explore our experience which is different.

JACOB BRONOWSKI, "THE SENSE OF HUMAN DIGNITY," *SCIENCE AND HUMAN VALUES* (1956)

15. Most people spend most of their days doing what they do not want to do in order to earn the right, at times, to do what they may desire.

JOHN MASON BROWN, *ESQUIRE*, APRIL 1960

16. He that can work is a born king of something.

THOMAS CARLYLE, *CHARTISM* (1839), 3

17. He that will not work according to his faculty, let him perish according to his necessity: there is no law juster than that.

THOMAS CARLYLE, *CHARTISM* (1839), 3

18. He who considers his work beneath him will be above doing it well.

ALEXANDER CHASE, *PERSPECTIVES* (1966)

19. The ant is knowing and wise; but he doesn't know enough to take a vacation.

CLARENCE DAY, *THIS SIMIAN WORLD* (1920), 5

20. Originality and the feeling of one's own dignity are achieved only through work and struggle.

DOSTOYEVSKY, *A DIARY OF A WRITER* (1873), 3

21. To crush, to annihilate a man utterly, to inflict on him the most terrible of punishments so that the most ferocious murderer would shudder at it and dread it beforehand, one need only give him work of an absolutely, completely useless and irrational character.

DOSTOYEVSKY, *THE HOUSE OF THE DEAD* (1862), 1.2, TR. CONSTANCE GARNETT

22. Where there is most labour there is not always most life.

HAVELOCK ELLIS, PREFACE, *THE DANCE OF LIFE* (1923)

23. Every man's task is his life-preserver.

Emerson, "Worship," *The Conduct of Life* (1860)

24. It is the privilege of any human work which is well done to invest the doer with a certain haughtiness.

Emerson, "Wealth," *The Conduct of Life* (1860)

25. The life of labor does not make men, but drudges.

Emerson, *Journals,* 1843

26. We put our love where we have put our labor.

Emerson, *Journals,* 1836

27. Toil, says the proverb, is the sire of fame.

Euripides, *Licymnius* (c. 450 B.C.), 477, tr. M. H. Morgan

28. If the building of a bridge does not enrich the awareness of those who work on it, then that bridge ought not to be built.

Frantz Fanon, "The Pitfalls of National Consciousness," *The Wretched of the Earth* (1961), tr. Constance Farrington

29. One of the saddest things is that the only thing a man can do for eight hours a day, day after day, is work. You can't eat eight hours a day nor drink for eight hours a day nor make love for eight hours.

William Faulkner, interview, *Writers at Work: First Series* (1958)

30. Day's work is still to do, / Whatever the day's doom.

Christopher Fry, *Thor, with Angels* (1948)

31. I and you—we are infinite, rich, large, contradictory, living, breathing miracles—free human beings, children of God and the everlasting universe. That's what we do.

Robert Fulghum, *It Was on Fire When I Lay Down on It* (1989)

32. Men for the sake of getting a living forget to live.

Margaret Fuller, *Summer on the Lakes* (1844), 7

33. All work is empty save when there is love.

Kahlil Gibran, "On Work," *The Prophet* (1923)

34. Most people work the greater part of their time for a mere living; and the little freedom which remains to them so troubles them that they use every means of getting rid of it.

Goethe, *The Sorrows of Young Werther* (1774), 1, May 17, 1771, tr. Victor Lange

35. When work is a pleasure, life is a joy! When work is a duty, life is slavery.

Maxim Gorky, *The Lower Depths* (1903), 1, tr. Alexander Bakshy

36. Human happiness is the true odour of growth, the sweet exhalation of work.

David Grayson, *Adventures in Contentment* (1907), 6

37. Unless the concepts of work and play and reward for work change absolutely, women must continue to provide cheap labor, and even more, free labor exacted of right by an employer possessed of a contract for life, made out in his favor.

Germaine Greer, *The Female Eunuch* (1970)

38. Raking over the past and sifting its dust is an occupation for the idle or the elderly retired.

Armand Hammer, *Hammer* (1987), with Neil Lyndon

39. Serious occupation is labor that has reference to some want.

Hegel, *Philosophy of History* (1832), 1.2.1, tr. John Sibree

40. It is weariness to keep toiling at the same things so that one becomes ruled by them.

Heraclitus, *Fragments* (c. 500 B.C.), 89, tr. Philip Wheelwright

41. To labour is the lot of man below; / And when Jove gave us life, he gave us woe.

Homer, *Iliad* (9th c. B.C.), 10.78, tr. Alexander Pope

42. There is only one thing for a man to do who is married to a woman who enjoys spending money, and that is to enjoy earning it.

Edgar Watson Howe, *Country Town Sayings* (1911)

43. A man is not idle because he is absorbed in thought. There is a visible labour and there is an invisible labour.

Victor Hugo, "Cosette," *Les Misérables* (1862), 7.8, tr. Charles E. Wilbour

44. Work is prayer. Work is also stink. Therefore stink is prayer.

Aldous Huxley, *Jesting Pilate* (1926), 1

45. I like work: it fascinates me. I can sit and look at it for hours. I love to keep it by me: the idea of getting rid of it nearly breaks my heart.

Jerome K. Jerome, *Three Men in a Boat* (1889), 15

46. The world is sown with good; but unless I turn my glad thoughts into practical living and till my own field, I cannot reap a kernel of the good.

HELEN KELLER, *OPTIMISM* (1903), 1

47. If thou be not busy for thyself now, who shall be busy for thee in time to come?

THOMAS À KEMPIS, *THE IMITATION OF CHRIST* (1426), 1.23

48. Who first invented work and bound the free / And holiday-rejoicing spirit down?

CHARLES LAMB, "WORK" (1819)

49. Thou, O God, dost sell us all good things at the price of labor.

LEONARDO DA VINCI, *NOTEBOOKS* (C. 1500), TR. JEAN PAUL RICHTER

50. Where there is no desire, there will be no industry.

JOHN LOCKE, *SOME THOUGHTS CONCERNING EDUCATION* (1693), 126

51. a great many people / who spend their time mourning / over the brevity of life / could make it seem longer / if they did a little more work.

DON MARQUIS, "ARCHY ON THIS AND THAT," *ARCHY DOES HIS PART* (1935)

52. Constant labor of one uniform kind destroys the intensity and flow of a man's animal spirits, which find recreation and delight in mere change of activity.

KARL MARX, *CAPITAL* (1867–94), 2.9, TR. STEPHEN L. TRASK

53. There is no pleasure subtler than the sensation of being a good workman; and in work there is the sense of consanguinity—unconscious as a rule but sometimes conscious.

MARIANNE MOORE, "IF A MAN DIE," *THE COMPLETE PROSE OF MARIANNE MOORE* (1986)

54. Japanese people tend to be much better adjusted to the notion of work, any kind of work, as honorable.

AKIO MORITA, "AMERICAN AND JAPANESE STYLES," *MADE IN JAPAN* (1986), TR. EDWIN M. REINGOLD AND MITSUKO SHIMOMURA

55. How Sunday into Monday melts!

OGDEN NASH, "TIME MARCHES ON," *I'M A STRANGER HERE MYSELF* (1938)

56. Work expands to fill the time available for its completion.

C. NORTHCOTE PARKINSON, *PARKINSON'S LAW* (1962)

57. Love labor: for if thou dost not want it for food, thou mayest for physic. It is wholesome for thy body and good for thy mind.

WILLIAM PENN, *SOME FRUITS OF SOLITUDE* (1693), 1.57

58. If you direct your whole thought to work itself, none of the things which invade eyes or ears will reach the mind.

QUINTILIAN, *INSTITUTIO ORATORIA* (C. A.D. 95), 10.3, TR. CLYDE MURLEY

59. Though top executives may work as hard as ever—in part perhaps because, being trained in an earlier day, they can hardly help doing so—their subordinates are somewhat less work-minded.

DAVID RIESMAN, *ABUNDANCE FOR WHAT?* (1964)

60. [T]he closest thing we have to the traditional ideology of the leisure class is a group of artists and intellectuals who regard their work as play and their play as work.

DAVID RIESMAN, *ABUNDANCE FOR WHAT?* (1964)

61. Far and away the best prize that life offers is the chance to work hard at work worth doing.

THEODORE ROOSEVELT, LABOR DAY ADDRESS, SYRACUSE, N. Y., 1903

62. It is only by labour that thought can be made healthy, and only by thought that labour can be made happy, and the two cannot be separated with impunity.

JOHN RUSKIN, "THE NATURE OF GOTHIC," *THE STONES OF VENICE* (1851–53), V. 2.6

63. My nature is subdued / To what it works in, like the dyer's hand.

SHAKESPEARE, *SONNETS* (1609), 111.6

64. One can't be happy as I have been for very long. There's a law against it. I have worked hard and enjoyed my work and it is the punishment of man to hate his work. Sooner or later I will have work that I hate.

JOHN STEINBECK, *NEWSWEEK*, DEC. 24, 1962

65. Before feminism, work was largely defined as what men did or would do. Thus, a *working woman* was someone who labored outside the home for money, masculine-style.

GLORIA STEINEM, "WORDS AND CHANGE," *OUTRAGEOUS ACTS AND EVERYDAY REBELLIONS* (1983)

66. All things have rest: why should we toil alone, / We only toil, who are the first of things, / And make perpetual moan.

LORD TENNYSON, "THE LOTOS-EATERS" (1842), 2

67. Death is the end of life; ah, why / Should life all labor be?

LORD TENNYSON, "THE LOTOS-EATERS" (1842), 4

68. Those who work much do not work hard.

THOREAU, *JOURNAL,* MARCH 31, 1841

69. Let us be grateful to Adam our benefactor. He cut us out of the "blessing" of idleness and won for us the "curse" of labor.

MARK TWAIN, "PUDD'NHEAD WILSON'S NEW CALENDAR," *FOLLOWING THE EQUATOR* (1897), 1.33

70. Work spares us from three great evils: boredom, vice, and need.

VOLTAIRE, *CANDIDE* (1759), 30

71. No race can prosper till it learns there is as much dignity in tilling a field as in writing a poem.

BOOKER T. WASHINGTON, ADDRESS, ATLANTA EXPOSITION, SEPT. 18, 1895

72. Work is a way of shutting out ambiguous sentiment.

WENDY WASSERSTEIN, "JEAN HARLOW'S WEDDING NIGHT," *BACHELOR GIRLS* (1990)

73. No task, rightly done, is truly private. It is part of the world's work.

WOODROW WILSON, ADDRESS, PRINCETON UNIVERSITY, NOV. 1, 1902

1066. WORKERS

See also 315. EXECUTIVES; 1009. UNEMPLOYMENT; 1013. UNIONS; 1065. WORK

1. A good horse should be seldom spurred.

THOMAS FULLER, M.D, *GNOMOLOGIA* (1732), 156

2. His brow is wet with honest sweat, / He earns whate'er he can, / And looks the whole world in the face, / For he owes not any man.

LONGFELLOW, "THE VILLAGE BLACKSMITH" (1839), 2

3. Slave of the wheel of labor, what to him / Are Plato and the swing of Pleiades?

EDWIN MARKHAM, "THE MAN WITH THE HOE" (1899)

4. When white-collar people get jobs, they sell not only their time and energy, but their personalities as well. They sell by the week, or month, their smiles and their kindly gestures, and they must practice that prompt repression of resentment and aggression.

C. WRIGHT MILLS, *WHITE COLLAR* (1956)

5. The really efficient laborer will be found not to crowd his day with work, but will saunter to his task surrounded by a wide halo of ease and leisure.

THOREAU, *JOURNAL,* MARCH 31, 1841

6. If you do things by the job, you are perpetually driven: the hours are scourges. If you work by the hour, you gently sail on the stream of Time, which is always bearing you on to the haven of Pay, whether you make any effort, or not.

CHARLES DUDLEY WARNER, "ELEVENTH WEEK," *MY SUMMER IN A GARDEN* (1871)

1067. WORLD

See also 272. EARTH; 539. LIFE; 1001. TWENTIETH CENTURY; 1017. UNIVERSE

1. Ah, love, let us be true / To one another! for the world, which seems / To lie before us like a land of dreams, / So various, so beautiful, so new, / Hath really neither joy, nor love, nor light, / Nor certitude, nor peace, nor help for pain.

MATTHEW ARNOLD, "DOVER BEACH," *NEW POEMS* (1867)

2. The pleasure of Italy comes from living in a world made by man, for man, on man's measurements.

LUIGI BARZINI, *THE ITALIANS* (1964)

3. The world is a gambling-table so arranged that all who enter the casino must play and all must lose more or less heavily in the long run, though they win occasionally by the way.

SAMUEL BUTLER (D. 1902), "LORD, WHAT IS MAN?" *NOTE-BOOKS* (1912)

4. I have not loved the World, nor the World me; / I have not flattered its rank breath, nor bowed / To its idolatries a patient knee, / Nor coined my cheek to smiles,—nor cried aloud / In worship of an echo.

BYRON, *CHILDE HAROLD'S PILGRIMAGE* (1812–18), 3.113

5. The world is a bundle of hay, / Mankind are the asses who pull; / Each tugs it a different way,— / And the greatest of all is John Bull!

BYRON, "EPIGRAM" (1821)

6. This world, after all our science and sciences, is still a miracle; wonderful, inscrutable, magical and more, to whosoever will think of it.

THOMAS CARLYLE, *ON HEROES, HERO-WORSHIP AND THE HEROIC IN HISTORY* (1841), 1

7. The world is a great volume, and man the index of that book; even in the body of man, you may turn to the whole world.

JOHN DONNE, *SERMONS*, NO. 42, 1626

8. The world is hard to love, though we must love it because we have no other, and to fail to love it is not to exist at all.

MARK VAN DOREN, *AUTOBIOGRAPHY OF MARK VAN DOREN* (1958)

9. The most incomprehensible thing about the world is that it is comprehensible.

EINSTEIN, QUOTED IN HIS OBITUARY, APRIL 19, 1955

10. This is the way the world ends / Not with a bang but a whimper.

T. S. ELIOT, "THE HOLLOW MEN" (1925), 5

11. What's wrong with this world is, it's not finished yet. It is not completed to that point where man can put his final signature to the job and say, "It is finished. We made it, and it works."

WILLIAM FAULKNER, ADDRESS, WELLESLEY, MASS., JUNE 8, 1953

12. The world, as a rule, does not live on beaches and in country clubs.

F. SCOTT FITZGERALD, *THE LETTERS OF F. SCOTT FITZGERALD* (1963), ED. ANDREW TURNBULL

13. The world only exists in your eyes—your conception of it. You can make it as big or as small as you want to.

F. SCOTT FITZGERALD, "THE CRACK-UP" *THE CRACK-UP* (1945)

14. The world is a bride of surpassing beauty—but remember that this maiden is never bound to anyone.

HĀFIZ, GHAZALS FROM THE *DIVAN* (14TH C.), 34, TR. JUSTIN HUNTLY MCCARTHY

15. That cold accretion called the world, so terrible in the mass, is so unformidable, even pitiable, in its units.

THOMAS HARDY, *TESS OF THE D'URBERVILLES* (1891), 13

16. Books are a world in themselves, it is true; but they are not the only world. The world itself is a volume larger than all the libraries in it.

WILLIAM HAZLITT, "ON THE CONVERSATION OF AUTHORS," *THE PLAIN SPEAKER* (1826)

17. To him who looks upon the world rationally, the world in its turn presents a rational aspect.

HEGEL, INTRODUCTION TO *PHILOSOPHY OF HISTORY* (1832), TR. JOHN SIBREE

18. The world is a fine place and worth the fighting for and I hate very much to leave it.

ERNEST HEMINGWAY, *FOR WHOM THE BELL TOLLS* (1940), 43

19. The unrest which keeps the never stopping clock of metaphysics going is the thought that the nonexistence of this world is just as possible as its existence.

WILLIAM JAMES, "THE PROBLEM OF BEING," *SOME PROBLEMS OF PHILOSOPHY* (1911)

20. The world has narrowed to a neighborhood before it has broadened to brotherhood.

LYNDON B. JOHNSON, ADDRESS, NEW YORK CITY, DEC. 17, 1963

21. The world in all doth but two nations bear, / The good, the bad; and these mixed everywhere.

ANDREW MARVELL, "THE LOYAL SCOT" (1650)

22. The world goes on because a few men in every generation believe in it utterly, accept it unquestioningly; they underwrite it with their lives.

HENRY MILLER, "WITH EDGAR VARÈSE IN THE GOBI DESERT," *THE AIR-CONDITIONED NIGHTMARE* (1945)

23. For in and out, above, about, below, / 'Tis nothing but a Magic Shadow-show, / Played in a Box whose Candle is the Sun, / Round which we Phantom Figures come and go.

OMAR KHAYYÁM, *RUBÁIYÁT* (11TH–12TH C.), TR. EDWARD FITZGERALD, 1ST ED., 46

24. The world is a thing we must of necessity either laugh at or be angry at; if we laugh at it, they say we are proud; if we are angry at it, they say we are ill-natured.

ALEXANDER POPE, *THOUGHTS ON VARIOUS SUBJECTS* (1727)

25. All the world's a stage, / And all the men and women merely players. / They have their exists and their entrances, / And one man in his time plays many parts.

SHAKESPEARE, *AS YOU LIKE IT* (1599–1600), 2.7.139

26. The world is so full of a number of things, / I'm sure we should all be as happy as kings.

ROBERT LOUIS STEVENSON, "HAPPY THOUGHT," *A CHILD'S GARDEN OF VERSES* (1885)

27. How do we accurately evoke land we love? What should we even call the world we walk and drive through—scenery, landscape?

DEBORAH TALL, "HERE," *FROM WHERE WE STAND* (1993)

28. "To what end was this world formed?" said Candide. "To infuriate us," replied Martin.

VOLTAIRE, *CANDIDE* (1759), 21

29. The world is a comedy to those that think; a tragedy to those that feel.

HORACE WALPOLE, LETTER TO HORACE MANN, DEC. 31, 1769

30. We milk the cow of the world, and as we do / We whisper in her ear, "You are not true."

RICHARD WILBUR, "EPISTEMOLOGY," *CEREMONY* (1950)

31. The beauty of the world which is so soon to perish, has two edges, one of laughter, one of anguish, cutting the heart asunder.

VIRGINIA WOOLF, *A ROOM OF ONE'S OWN* (1929), 1

WORLDLINESS

See 917. SOPHISTICATION

WORRY

See 43. ANXIETY

1068. WORSHIP

See also 14. ADMIRATION; 353. FOLLOWING; 441. ICONOCLASM; 506. IRREVERENCE; 723. PRAYER; 797. RELIGION

1. Heathen, n. A benighted creature who has the folly to worship something that he can see and feel.

AMBROSE BIERCE, *THE DEVIL'S DICTIONARY* (1881–1911)

2. Many infidels have maintained that Ignorance is the mother of Devotion.

JAMES BOSWELL, *BOSWELL ON THE GRAND TOUR: GERMANY AND SWITZERLAND* (1928; 1953)

3. Does not every true man feel that he is himself made higher by doing reverence to what is really above him?

THOMAS CARLYLE, *ON HEROES, HERO-WORSHIP AND THE HEROIC IN HISTORY* (1841), 1

4. It [idolatry] nourishes man's ambition to domineer over his fellow man. Idolatry, therefore, is the source of all social and moral evil in the world.

ABBA EBAN, *MY PEOPLE* (1968)

5. Men are idolaters, and want something to look at and kiss and hug, or throw themselves down before; they always did, they always will; and if you don't make it of wood, you must make it of words.

OLIVER WENDELL HOLMES, SR., *THE POET AT THE BREAKFAST TABLE* (1872), 5

6. Every idol, however exalted, turns out, in the long run, to be a Moloch, hungry for human sacrifice.

ALDOUS HUXLEY, *THE DEVILS OF LOUDON* (1952)

7. Where it is a duty to worship the sun, it is pretty sure to be a crime to examine the laws of heat.

JOHN MORLEY, *VOLTAIRE* (1872)

8. He worships God who knows him.

SENECA, *LETTERS TO LUCILIUS* (1ST C.), 95.47, TR. E. PHILLIPS BARKER

9. God waits to win back his own flowers as gifts from man's hands.

RABINDRANATH TAGORE, *STRAY BIRDS* (1916), 215

10. God prefers bad verses recited with a pure heart, to the finest verses possible chanted by the wicked.

VOLTAIRE, "PRAYER," *PHILOSOPHICAL DICTIONARY* (1764)

11. We adore, we invoke, we seek to appease, only that which we fear.

VOLTAIRE, "RELIGION," *PHILOSOPHICAL DICTIONARY* (1764)

12. It is Sunday, mid-morning—Sunday in the living room, Sunday in the kitchen, Sunday in the woodshed, Sunday down the road in the village: I hear the bells, calling me to share God's grace.

E.B. WHITE, *ONE MAN'S MEAT* (1944)

13. The worship of God is not a rule of safety—it is an adventure of the spirit, a flight after the unattainable.

ALFRED NORTH WHITEHEAD, *SCIENCE AND THE MODERN WORLD* (1925), 12

WORTH

See 1026. VALUE

1069. WRITING AND WRITERS

See also 62. AUTOBIOGRAPHY; 81. BIOGRAPHY; 93. BOOKS AND READING; 134. CLARITY; 201. CREATION AND CREATIVITY; 344. FICTION; 398. GRAMMAR; 524. LANGUAGE; 545. LITERATURE; 708. POETRY AND POETS; 938. STORYTELLING; 942. STYLE; 1064. WORDS

1. Having imagination, it takes you an hour to write a paragraph that, if you were unimaginative, would take you only a minute. Or you might not write the paragraph at all.

FRANKLIN P. ADAMS, *HALF A LOAF* (1927)

2. The universal object and idol of men of letters is reputation.

JOHN ADAMS, *DISCOURSES ON DAVILA* (1789), 2

3. Among all kinds of writing, there is none in which authors are more apt to miscarry than in works of humour, as there is none in which they are more ambitious to excel.

JOSEPH ADDISON, *THE SPECTATOR* (1711–12), 35

4. Dreiser's English is bum, yet it has a peculiar beauty and excellence. You feel you're reading a rather inadequate translation of a very great foreign novel—Russian, probably.

JAMES AGEE, *LETTERS OF JAMES AGEE TO FATHER FLYE* (1962)

5. Between the reputation of the author living and the reputation of the same author dead there is ever a wide discrepancy.

THOMAS BAILEY ALDRICH, "LEAVES FROM A NOTEBOOK," *PONKAPOG PAPERS* (1903)

6. I detest professional anythings but particularly professional writers. Most of them today are just garbage collectors.

CLEVELAND AMORY, "WHY YOURS TRULY WAS THE ONLY ONE TO CARRY THE SPEAR," *THE TROUBLE WITH NOWADAYS* (1979

7. For the creation of a master-work of literature two powers must concur, the power of the man and the power of the moment.

MATTHEW ARNOLD, "THE FUNCTION OF CRITICISM" (1864)

8. Writing comes more easily if you have something to say.

SHOLEM ASCH, *NEW YORK HERALD TRIBUNE,* NOV. 6, 1955

9. Nothing a man writes can please him as profoundly as something he does with his back, shoulders and hands. For writing is an artificial activity. It is a lonely and private substitute for conversation.

BROOKS ATKINSON, "JUNE 13," *ONCE AROUND THE SUN* (1951)

10. In relation to a writer, most readers believe in the Double Standard: they may be unfaithful to him as often as they like, but he must never, never be unfaithful to them.

W. H. AUDEN, "READING," *THE DYER'S HAND* (1962)

11. No poet or novelist wishes he were the only one who ever lived, but most of them wish they were the only one alive, and quite a number fondly believe their wish has been granted.

W. H. AUDEN, "WRITING," *THE DYER'S HAND* (1962)

12. Does anybody learn writing, or do they just touch someone who lets them see the power of the deleted word?

RICHARD BACH, *RUNNING FROM SAFETY* (1994)

13. Reading maketh a full man, conference a ready man, and writing an exact man.

FRANCIS BACON, "OF STUDIES," *ESSAYS* (1625)

14. The writer's greed is appalling. He wants, or seems to want, everything and practically everybody; in another sense, and at the same time, he needs no one at all.

JAMES BALDWIN, "ALAS, POOR RICHARD," *NOBODY KNOWS MY NAME* (1961)

15. Writers are really people who write books not because they are poor, but because they are dissatisfied with the books which they could buy but do not like.

WALTER BENJAMIN, "UNPACKING MY LIBRARY," IN *THE ART OF THE PERSONAL ESSAY* (1994), ED. PHILLIP LOPATE

16. Poets are sultans, if they had their will; / For every author would his brother kill.

ROGER BOYLE, *PROLOGUES* (C. 17TH C.)

17. The pen is mightier than the sword.

BULWER-LYTTON, *RICHELIEU* (1838), 2.2

18. The writer's life seethes within but not without.

ANTHONY BURGESS, *YOU'VE HAD YOUR TIME* (1990)

19. One hates an author that's *all author*—fellows / In foolscap uniforms turned up with ink, / So very anxious, clever, fine, and jealous, / One don't know what to say to them, or think, / Unless to puff them with a pair of bellows.

BYRON, *BEPPO* (1818), 75

20. I think you must remember that a writer is a simple-minded person to begin with and go on that basis. He's not a great mind, he's not a great thinker, he's not a great philosopher, he's a story-teller.

ERSKINE CALDWELL, *THE ATLANTIC MONTHLY,* JULY 1958

21. Writing has laws of perspective, of light and shade, just as painting does, or music. If you are born knowing them, fine. If not, learn them. Then rearrange the rules to suit yourself.

TRUMAN CAPOTE, INTERVIEW, *WRITERS AT WORK: FIRST SERIES* (1958)

22. Considering the multitude of mortals that handle the pen in these days, and can mostly spell, and write without glaring violations of grammar, the question

naturally arises: How is it, then, that no work proceeds from them, bearing any stamp of authenticity and permanence; of worth for more than one day?

THOMAS CARLYLE, "BIOGRAPHY" (1832)

23. If a book come from the heart, it will contrive to reach other hearts; all art and authorcraft are of small amount to that.

THOMAS CARLYLE, *ON HEROES, HERO-WORSHIP AND THE HEROIC IN HISTORY* (1841), 2

24. The literary man? An indiscreet man, who devaluates his miseries, divulges them, tells them like so many beads: immodesty—the sideshow of second thoughts—is his rule; he *offers himself*.

E.M. CIORAN, "SOME BLIND ALLEYS: A LETTER," IN *THE ART OF THE PERSONAL ESSAY* (1994), ED. PHILLIP LOPATE

25. To write books is to have a certain relation with original sin. For what is a book if not a loss of innocence, an act of aggression, a repetition of our Fall?

E.M. CIORAN, "SOME BLIND ALLEYS: A LETTER," IN *THE ART OF THE PERSONAL ESSAY* (1994), ED. PHILLIP LOPATE

26. There ought to be some sign in a book about Man, that the writer knows thoroughly one man at least.

FRANK MOORE COLBY, "SIMPLE SIMON," *THE COLBY ESSAYS* (1926), V. 1

27. The writer who loses his self-doubt, who gives way as he grows old to a sudden euphoria, to prolixity, should stop writing immediately: the time has come for him to lay aside his pen.

COLETTE, "LADY OF LETTERS," *EARTHLY PARADISE* (1966), 4

28. Our admiration of fine writing will always be in proportion to its real difficulty and its apparent ease.

CHARLES CALEB COLTON, *LACON* (1825), 2.143

29. In plucking the fruit of memory one runs the risk of spoiling its bloom, especially if it has got to be carried into the marketplace.

JOSEPH CONRAD, "AUTHOR'S NOTE," *THE ARROW OF GOLD* (1919)

30. In America only the successful writer is important, in France all writers are important, in England no writer is important, and in Australia you have to explain what a writer is.

GEOFFREY COTTERELL, *NEW YORK JOURNAL-AMERICAN*, SEPT. 22, 1961

31. Authors are sometimes like tomcats: they distrust all the other toms, but they are kind to kittens.

MALCOLM COWLEY, INTRODUCTION TO *WRITERS AT WORK: FIRST SERIES* (1958)

32. I tried to write worse but it was no good; my generalizations came out as before, each more exquisite than the last. I grew discouraged.

PETER DE VRIES, *COMFORT ME WITH APPLES* (1956)

33. I myself, I am not a character in this novel; I am the novel.

PHILIP K. DICK, *A SCANNER DARKLY* (1977)

34. An author who speaks about his own books is almost as bad as a mother who talks about her own children.

BENJAMIN DISRAELI, SPEECH, GLASGOW, NOV. 19, 1873

35. Writers are not just people who sit down and write. They hazard themselves. Every time you compose a book your composition of yourself is at stake.

E.L. DOCTOROW, INTERVIEW, 1933

36. A poem, a sentence, causes us to see ourselves. I be, and I see my being, at the same time.

EMERSON, *JOURNALS*, 1836

37. He that writes to himself writes to an eternal public.

EMERSON, "SPIRITUAL LAWS," *ESSAYS: FIRST SERIES* (1841)

38. In good writing, words become one with things.

EMERSON, *JOURNALS*, 1831

39. The maker of a sentence launches out into the infinite and builds a road into Chaos and old Night, and is followed by those who hear him with something of wild, creative delight.

EMERSON, *JOURNALS*, 1834

40. If you would be a reader, read; if a writer, write.

EPICTETUS, *DISCOURSES* (2ND C.), 2.18, TR. THOMAS W. HIGGINSON

41. He [the writer] must teach himself that the basest of all things is to be afraid; and, teaching himself that, forget it forever, leaving no room in his workshop for anything but the old verities and truths of the heart, the old universal truths lacking which any story is ephemeral and doomed—love and honor and pity and pride and compassion and sacrifice.

WILLIAM FAULKNER, IN A SPEECH ACCEPTING THE NOBEL PRIZE, DEC. 10, 1950

42. A writer needs three things, experience, observation, and imagination, any two of which, at times any one of which, can supply the lack of the others.

WILLIAM FAULKNER, INTERVIEW, *WRITERS AT WORK: FIRST SERIES* (1958)

43. No man can write who is not first a humanitarian.

WILLIAM FAULKNER, *TIME,* FEB. 25, 1957

44. An author ought to write for the youth of his own generation, the critics of the next, and the schoolmasters of ever afterward.

F. SCOTT FITZGERALD, *THE LETTERS OF F. SCOTT FITZGERALD* (1963), ANDREW TURNBULL, ED.

45. You don't write because you want to say something; you write because you've got something to say.

F. SCOTT FITZGERALD, "THE NOTE-BOOKS," *THE CRACK-UP* (1945)

46. A writer's desire to write can only have come from previous experience of literature, and he'll start by imitating whatever he's read, which usually means what the people around him are writing.

NORTHROP FRYE, *THE EDUCATED IMAGINATION* (1964)

47. For the serious mediocre writer convention makes him sound like a lot of other people; for the popular writer it gives him a formula he can exploit; for the serious good writer it releases his experiences or emotions from himself and incorporates them into literature, where they belong.

NORTHROP FRYE, *THE EDUCATED IMAGINATION* (1964)

48. You start by writing to live. You end by writing so as not to die.

CARLOS FUENTES, "HOW I STARTED TO WRITE," IN *THE ART OF THE PERSONAL ESSAY* (1994), ED. PHILLIP LOPATE

49. To one who has enjoyed the full life of any scene, of any hour, what thoughts can be recorded about it seem like the commas and semicolons in the paragraph—mere stops.

MARGARET FULLER, *SUMMER ON THE LAKES* (1844), 1

50. Authorship of any sort is a fantastic indulgence of the ego.

JOHN KENNETH GALBRAITH, *THE AFFLUENT SOCIETY* (1958)

51. A writer's life stands in relation to his work as a house does to a garden, related but distinct.

MAVIS GALLANT, "ELIZABETH BOWEN," *PARIS NOTEBOOKS* (1986)

52. Enduring fame is promised only to those writers who can offer to successive generations a substance constantly renewed; for every generation arrives upon the scene with its own particular hunger.

ANDRÉ GIDE, "BAUDELAIRE AND M. FAGUET," *PRETEXTS* (1903), TR. OTHERS

53. Great authors are admirable in this respect: in every generation they make for disagreement. Through them we become aware of our differences.

ANDRÉ GIDE, "THIRD IMAGINARY INTERVIEW," *PRETEXTS* (1903), TR. OTHERS

54. The most beautiful things are those that madness prompts and reason writes.

ANDRÉ GIDE, *JOURNALS,* 1894, TR. JUSTIN O'BRIEN

55. He who does not expect a million readers should not write a line.

GOETHE, QUOTED IN JOHANN PETER ECKERMANN'S *CONVERSATIONS WITH GOETHE,* MAY 12, 1825

56. Even monarchs have need of authors, and fear their pens more than ugly women the painter's pencil.

BALTASAR GRACIÁN, *THE ART OF WORLDLY WISDOM* (1647), 281, TR. JOSEPH JACOBS

57. Thought flies and words go on foot. Therein lies all the drama of a writer.

JULIEN GREEN, *JOURNAL,* MAY 4, 1943

58. A writer doesn't write for his readers, does he? Yet he has to take elementary precautions all the same, to make them comfortable.

GRAHAM GREENE, *A BURNT-OUT CASE* (1960)

59. They're fancy talkers about themselves, writers. If I had to give young writers advice. I would say don't listen to writers talking about writing or themselves.

LILLIAN HELLMAN, *THE NEW YORK TIMES,* FEB. 21, 1960

60. Nobody that ever left their own country ever wrote anything worth printing. Not even in the newspapers.

ERNEST HEMINGWAY, *THE SUN ALSO RISES* (1926)

61. Writing, at its best, is a lonely life. Organizations for writers palliate the writer's loneliness, but I doubt if they improve his writing.

ERNEST HEMINGWAY, ACCEPTANCE SPEECH FOR THE NOBEL PRIZE, DEC. 10, 1954

62. An old author is constantly rediscovering himself in the more or less fossilized productions of his earlier years.

OLIVER WENDELL HOLMES, SR., *OVER THE TEACUPS* (1891), 12

63. The secret of all good writing is sound judgment.

HORACE, *ARS POETICA* (13–8 B.C.)

64. He [Hemingway] used a stand-up work place he had fashioned out of the top of of a bookcase near his bed. His portable typewriter was snugged in there and papers were spread along the top of the bookcase on either side of it. He used a reading board for long-hand writing.

A.E. HOTCHNER, *PAPA HEMINGWAY* (1966)

65. A writer and nothing else: a man alone in a room with the English language, trying to get human feelings right.

JOHN K. HUTCHENS, *NEW YORK HERALD TRIBUNE,* SEPT. 10, 1961

66. The fact that many people should be shocked by what he writes practically imposes it as a duty upon the writer to go on shocking them.

ALDOUS HUXLEY, "VULGARITY IN LITERATURE," *MUSIC AT NIGHT* (1931)

67. A man may write at any time, if he will set himself doggedly to it.

SAMUEL JOHNSON, QUOTED IN BOSWELL'S *JOURNAL OF A TOUR TO THE HEBRIDES WITH SAMUEL JOHNSON,* AUG. 16, 1773

68. No man but a blockhead ever wrote except for money.

SAMUEL JOHNSON, QUOTED IN BOSWELL'S *LIFE OF SAMUEL JOHNSON,* APRIL 5, 1776

69. What is written without effort is in general read without pleasure.

SAMUEL JOHNSON, QUOTED IN BIRKBECK HILL'S *JOHNSONIAN MISCELLANIES* (1897), V. 2

70. An inveterate and incurable itch for writing besets many and grows old with their sick hearts.

JUVENAL, *SATIRES* (C. 100), 7.51

71. Lost and forever writing the history of their loss, they [writers of the lost generation] became specialists in anguish; and as they sentimentalized themselves, so they were easily sentimentalized.

ALFRED KAZIN, *ON NATIVE GROUNDS* (1942)

72. We never know how much has been missing from our lives until a true writer comes along.

ALFRED KAZIN, "THEODORE DREISER AND HIS CRITICS," *THE STATURE OF THEODORE DREISER* (1955)

73. What happens whenever we convert a writer into a symbol is that we lose the writer himself in all his indefeasible singularity, his particular inimitable genius.

ALFRED KAZIN, "THEODORE DREISER AND HIS CRITICS," *THE STATURE OF THEODORE DREISER* (1955)

74. A mediocre mind thinks it writes divinely; a good mind thinks it writes reasonably.

LA BRUYÈRE, *CHARACTERS* (1688), 1.18, TR. HENRI VAN LAUN

75. It is the glory and the merit of some men to write well, and of others not to write at all.

LA BRUYÈRE, *CHARACTERS* (1688), 1.59, TR. HENRI VAN LAUN

76. The same common sense which makes an author write good things, makes him dread they are not good enough to deserve reading.

LA BRUYÈRE, *CHARACTERS* (1688), 1.18, TR. HENRI VAN LAUN

77. To make a book is as much a trade as to make a clock; something more than intelligence is required to become an author.

LA BRUYÈRE, *CHARACTERS* (1688), 1.3, TR. HENRI VAN LAUN

78. Clear writers, like fountains, do not seem so deep as they are; the turbid look the most profound.

WALTER SAVAGE LANDOR, "SOUTHEY AND PORSON," *IMAGINARY CONVERSATIONS* (1824–53)

79. Every great writer is a writer of history, let him treat on almost what subject he may. He carries with him for thousands of years a portion of his times.

WALTER SAVAGE LANDOR, "DIOGENES AND PLATO," *IMAGINARY CONVERSATIONS* (1824–53)

80. Authors are like cattle going to a fair: those of the same field can never move on without butting one another.

WALTER SAVAGE LANDOR, "ARCHDEACON HARE AND WALTER LANDOR," *IMAGINARY CONVERSATIONS* (1824–53)

81. The great authors share their souls with us—"literally."

URSULA K. LE GUIN, "WHERE DO YOU GET YOUR IDEAS FROM?" *DANCING AT THE EDGE OF THE WORLD* (1989)

82. If you once understand an author's character, the comprehension of his writings becomes easy.

LONGFELLOW, *HYPERION* (1839), 1.5

83. The unpublished manuscript is like an unconfessed sin that festers in the soul, corrupting and contaminating it.

ANTONIO MACHADO, *JUAN DE MAIRENA* (1943), 48, TR. BEN BELITT

84. It is one test of a fully developed writer that he reminds us of no one but himself.

MELVIN MADDOCKS, *CHRISTIAN SCIENCE MONITOR,* MAY 2, 1963

85. Writing is a mode of being. If I write I live.

BERNARD MALAMUD, *DUBIN'S LIVES* (1979)

86. If you have one strong idea, you can't help repeating it and embroidering it. Sometimes I think that authors should write one novel and then be put in a gas chamber.

JOHN P. MARQUAND, *NEW YORK HERALD TRIBUNE*, OCT. 5, 1958

87. i never think at all when i write / nobody can do two things at the same time / and do them both well.

DON MARQUIS, "ARCHY ON THE RADIO," *ARCHY'S LIFE OF MEHITABEL* (1933)

88. 'Tis easy to write epigrams nicely, but to write a book is hard.

MARTIAL, *EPIGRAMS* (A.D. 86), 7.85, TR. WALTER C. A. KERR

89. It has been said that good prose should resemble the conversation of a well-bred man.

W. SOMERSET MAUGHAM, *THE SUMMING UP* (1938), 12

90. The writer is more concerned to know than to judge.

W. SOMERSET MAUGHAM, *THE MOON AND SIXPENCE* (1919), 41

91. A writer is essentially a man who does not resign himself to loneliness.

FRANÇOIS MAURIAC, *DIEU ET MAMMON* (1929), 5

92. Sin is the writer's element.

FRANÇOIS MAURIAC, "LITERATURE AND SIN," *SECOND THOUGHTS* (1961), TR. ADRIENNE FOULKE

93. No man would set a word down on paper if he had the courage to live out what he believed in.

HENRY MILLER, *SUNDAY AFTER THE WAR* (1944)

94. I always do the first line well, but I have trouble doing the others.

MOLIÈRE, *THE RIDICULOUS PRÉCIEUSES* (1659), 11, TR. DONALD M. FRAME

95. The only people who can be excused for letting a bad book loose on the world are the poor devils who have to write for a living!

MOLIÈRE, *THE MISANTHROPE* (1666), 1, TR. JOHN WOOD

96. All the world knows me in my book, and my book in me.

MONTAIGNE, "UPON SOME VERSES OF VIRGIL," *ESSAYS* (1580–88), TR. W. C. HAZLITT

97. Writing is an undertaking for the modest.

MARIANNE MOORE, "*THE DIAL*: A RETROSPECT," *THE COMPLETE PROSE OF MARIANNE MOORE* (1986)

98. When writing is good, everything is symbolic, but symbolic writing is seldom good.

WRIGHT MORRIS, *A BILL OF RITES, A BILL OF WRONGS, A BILL OF GOODS* (1967), 6

99. Writing became such a process of discovery that I couldn't wait to get to work in the morning: I wanted to find out what I was going to say.

SHARON O'BRIEN, *THE NEW YORK TIMES BOOK REVIEW*, FEB. 20, 1994

100. When I sit down to write a book, I do not say to myself, "I am going to produce a work of art." I write it because there is some lie that I want to expose, some fact to which I want to draw attention, and my initial concern is to get a hearing.

GEORGE ORWELL, "WHY I WRITE," *A COLLECTION OF ESSAYS* (1954)

101. Money, money, all is money! Could you write even a penny novelette without money to put heart in you?

GEORGE ORWELL, *KEEP THE ASPIDISTRA FLYING* (1936)

102. I measure my life in sentences pressed out, line by line, like the lustrous ooze on the underside of the snail, the snail's secret open seam, its wound, leaking attar.

CYNTHIA OZICK, "THE SEAM OF THE SNAIL," *METAPHOR & MEMORY* (1989)

103. The last thing one settles in writing a book is what one should put in first.

PASCAL, *PENSÉES* (1670), 19, TR. W. F. TROTTER

104. The writer is the Faust of modern society,
the only surviving individualist in a mass age.
To his orthodox contemporaries he seems a semi-madman.

BORIS PASTERNAK, *THE OBSERVER*, DEC. 20, 1959

105. I do not think you should read about writing while you are writing.

MAXWELL PERKINS, *EDITOR TO AUTHOR: THE LETTERS OF MAXWELL PERKINS* (1950), ED. JOHN HALL WHEELOCK

106. Writing, like drawing is an art, and whatever conveys the meaning is justified.

MAXWELL PERKINS, *EDITOR TO AUTHOR: THE LETTERS OF MAXWELL PERKINS* (1950), ED. JOHN HALL WHEELOCK

107. There is no lighter burden, nor more agreeable, than a pen.

PETRARCH, *LETTER TO POSTERITY* (1367–72)

108. An essayist is a lucky person who has found a way to discourse without being interrupted.

CHARLES POORE, *THE NEW YORK TIMES*, MAY 31, 1962

109. True ease in writing comes from art, not chance, / As those move easiest who have learned to dance.

ALEXANDER POPE, *AN ESSAY ON CRITICISM* (1711), 2.162

110. Most people won't realize that writing is a craft. You have to take your apprenticeship in it like anything else.

KATHERINE ANNE PORTER, *SATURDAY REVIEW*, MARCH 31, 1962

111. The pen is a formidable weapon, but a man can kill himself with it a great deal more easily than he can other people.

GEORGE DENNISON PRENTICE, *PRENTICEANA* (1860)

112. The businessman who is a novelist is able to drop in on literature and feel no suicidal loss of esteem if the lady is not at home, and he can spend his life preparing without fuss for the awful interview.

V. S. PRITCHETT, "AN AMATEUR," *THE LIVING NOVEL & LATER APPRECIATIONS* (1964)

113. Our passions shape our books, repose writes them in the intervals.

MARCEL PROUST, *REMEMBRANCE OF THINGS PAST: THE PAST RECAPTURED* (1913–27), TR. STEPHEN HUDSON

114. From writing rapidly it does not result that one writes well, but from writing well it results that one writes rapidly.

QUINTILIAN, *INSTITUTIO ORATORIA* (C. A.D. 95), 10.3, TR. CLYDE MURLEY

115. In literature, there are only oxen. The biggest ones are the geniuses—the ones who toil eighteen hours a day without tiring.

JULES RENARD, *JOURNAL*, 1887, TR. ELIZABETH ROGET

116. Writing the last page of a book was as close as he'd ever come to sublimity, and that hadn't happened in four years.

PHILIP ROTH, *THE ANATOMY LESSON* (1983)

117. [A] life of writing books is a trying adventure in which you cannot find out where you *are* unless you lose your way.

PHILIP ROTH, *THE COUNTERLIFE* (1987)

118. Even after you've won fame and fortune, every time you write you've got to write, there's no shortcut, you have to start your career all over again.

WILLIAM SAROYAN, "FAME AND FORTUNE AND FUN AT THE HAMPSHIRE HOUSE," *SONS COME & GO, MOTHERS HANG IN FOREVER* (1979)

119. Writers are a fascinating breed, because there are so many kinds of them, they are made by so many circumstances, conditions, and mysteries, and there are so many ways for writing to be done.

WILLIAM SAROYAN, "POET LARSEN OF *O CITY CITIES*," *SONS COME & GO, MOTHERS HANG IN FOREVER* (1979)

120. No one can ever write about anything that happened to him after he was twelve years old.

IGNAZIO SILONE, QUOTED IN MURRAY KEMPTON'S *AMERICA COMES OF MIDDLE AGE* (1963)

121. Writing is not a profession but a vocation of unhappiness.

GEORGES SIMENON, INTERVIEW, *WRITERS AT WORK: FIRST SERIES* (1958)

122. Every author, however modest, keeps a most outrageous vanity chained like a madman in the padded cell of his breast.

LOGAN PEARSALL SMITH, *AFTERTHOUGHTS* (1931), 5

123. I learned that all of my manuscripts have been rejected three or four times since I last heard. It is a nice thing to know that so many people are reading my books. That is one way of getting an audience.

JOHN STEINBECK, *NEWSWEEK*, DEC. 24, 1962

124. The profession of book writing makes horse racing seem like a solid, stable business.

JOHN STEINBECK, *NEWSWEEK*, DEC. 24, 1962

125. The difficulty of literature is not to write, but to write what you mean.

ROBERT LOUIS STEVENSON, TITLE ESSAY, 4, *VIRGINIBUS PUERISQUE* (1881)

126. The good writing of any age has always been the product of *someone's* neurosis, and we'd have a mighty dull literature if all the writers that came along were a bunch of happy chuckleheads.

WILLIAM STYRON, INTERVIEW, *WRITERS AT WORK: FIRST SERIES* (1958)

127. Every country has the writers she requires and deserves, which is why Nicaragua, in two hundred years of literacy, has produced one writer—a mediocre poet.

PAUL THEROUX, *THE OLD PATAGONIAN EXPRESS* (1979)

128. The condition of the world *today* is such that most writers feel they cannot truthfully be "comic" about it.

DYLAN THOMAS, *QUITE EARLY ONE MORNING* (1954)

129. Nothing goes by luck in composition. It allows of no tricks. The best you can write will be the best you are.

THOREAU, *JOURNAL*, FEB. 28, 1841

130. There are two classes of authors: the one write the history of their times, the other their biography.

THOREAU, *JOURNAL*, APRIL 22, 1841

131. [T]he act of writing is either something the writer dreads or actually likes, and I actually like it. Even re-writing's fun. You're getting somewhere, whether it seems to move or not.

JAMES THURBER, "SPEAKING OF HIS OWN WRITING...," *COLLECTING HIMSELF* (1989)

132. Writers who teach tend to prefer literary theory to literature and tenure to all else. Writers who do not teach prefer the contemplation of Careers to art of any kind.

GORE VIDAL, *ESSAYS*, 1952–1992 (1993)

133. Ideally, the writer needs no audience other than the few who understand. It is immodest and greedy to want more.

GORE VIDAL, "FRENCH LETTERS: THEORIES OF THE NEW NOVEL," *ENCOUNTER*, DECEMBER 1967

134. I wonder now what Ernest Hemingway's dictionary looked like, since he got along so well with dinky words that anybody can spell and truly understand.

KURT VONNEGUT, *WELCOME TO THE MONKEY HOUSE* (1968)

135. The only way to get anything out of a writer's brains is to leave him or her alone until he or she is damn well ready to write it down.

KURT VONNEGUT, "SELF-INTERVIEW," *PALM SUNDAY* (1981)

136. You can't teach people to write well. Writing well is something God lets you do or declines to let you do.

KURT VONNEGUT, *WAMPETERS, FOMA, & GRANFALOONS* (1974)

137. Your business as a writer is not to illustrate virtue but to show how a fellow may move toward it or away from it.

ROBERT PENN WARREN, *PARIS REVIEW*, SPRING-SUMMER 1957

138. Those huge novels from North America are not the product of diligence; hard labour would refine and clarify them.

EVELYN WAUGH, "SLOTH," *SUNDAY TIMES* (LONDON), JANUARY 7, 1962

139. The writing of a novel is taking life as it already exists, not to report it but to make an object, toward the end that the finished work might contain this life inside it, and offer it to the reader.

EUDORA WELTY, "MUST THE NOVELIST CRUSADE?" *THE EYE OF THE STORY* (1978)

140. There is no royal path to good writing; and such paths as exist do not lead through neat critical gardens, various as they are, but through the jungles of self, the world, and of craft.

JESSAMYN WEST, *SATURDAY REVIEW*, SEPT. 21, 1957

141. I have just been refining the room in which I sit, yet I sometimes doubt that a writer should refine or improve his workroom by so much as a dictionary: one thing leads to another and the first thing you know he has a stuffed chair and is fast asleep in it.

E.B. WHITE, *ONE MAN'S MEAT* (1944)

142. In the nature of things, a person engaged in the flimsy business of expressing himself on paper is dependent on the large general privilege of being heard. Any intimation that this privilege may be revoked throws a writer into panic.

E.B. WHITE, *ONE MAN'S MEAT* (1944)

143. The essayist is a self-liberated man, sustained by the childish belief that everything he thinks about, everything that happens to him, is of general interest.

E.B. WHITE, "FOREWORD," *ESSAYS OF E. B. WHITE* (1977)

144. To speak in literature with the perfect rectitude and insouciance of the movements of animals and the unimpeachableness of the sentiment of trees in the woods and grass by the roadside is the flawless triumph of art.

WALT WHITMAN, PREFACE TO *LEAVES OF GRASS* (1855)

145. [T]he act of writing is for me often nothing more than the secret or conscious desire to carve words on a tombstone: to the memory of a town forever vanished, to the memory of a childhood in exile, to the memory of all those I loved and who, before I could tell them I loved them, went away.

ELIE WIESEL, *LEGENDS OF OUR TIMES* (1968)

146. If there is a single theme that dominates all my writings, all my obsessions, it is that of memory—

because I fear forgetfulness as much as hatred and death.

Elie Wiesel, "Preface," *From the Kingdom of Memory* (1990)

147. The great play is yet unwritten; the great novel beats with futile hands against the portals of my brain.

Thomas Wolfe, *Thomas Wolfe's Letters to His Mother* (1943)

148. Literature is strewn with the wreckage of men who have minded beyond reason the opinion of others.

Virginia Woolf, *A Room of One's Own* (1929), 3

149. Every great and original writer, in proportion as he is great and original, must himself create the taste by which he is to be relished.

William Wordsworth, preface to 2nd edition of *Lyrical Ballads* (1800)

WRONG

See 299. Error; 476. Injury; 477. Injustice; 1070. Wrongdoing

1070. WRONGDOING

See also 174. Conscience; 191. Corruption; 204. Crime; 227. Deeds; 307. Evil; 815. Retribution; 900. Sin; 1030. Vice; 1055. Wickedness

1. The act of evil / breeds others to follow, / young sins in its own likeness.

Aeschylus, *Agamemnon* (458 B.C.), tr. Richmond Lattimore

2. The sinner sins against himself; the wrongdoer wrongs himself, becoming the worse by his own action.

Marcus Aurelius, *Meditations* (2nd c.), 9.4, tr. Maxwell Staniforth

3. Whoso diggeth a pit shall fall therein.

Bible Proverbs 26:27

4. If once a man indulges himself in murder, very soon he comes to think little of robbing; and from robbing he comes next to drinking and Sabbath-breaking, and from that to incivility and procrastination.

Thomas De Quincey, "On Murder Considered as One of the Fine Arts" (1827–54)

5. Throughout our life, our worst weaknesses and meannesses are usually committed for the sake of the people whom we most despise.

Charles Dickens, *Great Expectations* (1860–61), 27

6. You cannot do wrong without suffering wrong.

Emerson, "Compensation," *Essays: First Series* (1841)

7. For a wrongdoer to be undetected is difficult; and for him to have confidence that his concealment will continue is impossible.

Epicurus, "Vatican Sayings" (3rd c. B.C.), 7, in *Letters, Principal Doctrines, and Vatican Sayings,*, tr. Russel M. Geer

8. If one must do a wrong, it's best to do it / pursuing power—otherwise, let's have virtue.

Euripides, *The Phoenician Women* (c. 411–409 B.C.), tr. Elizabeth Wyckoff

9. A small demerit extinguishes a long service.

Thomas Fuller, M.D., *Gnomologia* (1732), 404

10. As a single leaf turns not yellow but with the silent knowledge of the whole tree, so the wrong-doer cannot do wrong without the hidden will of you all.

Kahlil Gibran, "On Crime and Punishment," *The Prophet* (1923)

11. A good man can be stupid and still be good. But a bad man must have brains—absolutely.

Maxim Gorky, *The Lower Depths* (1903), 4, tr. Alexander Bakshy

12. Most vices may be committed very genteelly: a man may debauch his friend's wife genteelly: he may cheat at cards genteelly.

Samuel Johnson, quoted in Boswell's *Life of Samuel Johnson,* April 6, 1775

13. Many might go to heaven with half the labour they go to hell, if they would venture their industry the right way.

Ben Jonson, "Random Thoughts," *Timber* (1640)

14. There is scarcely any man sufficiently clever to appreciate all the evil he does.

La Rochefoucauld, *Maxims* (1665), tr. Kenneth Pratt

15. Violence and wrong enclose all who commit them in their meshes and do mostly recoil on him from whom they begin.

Lucretius, *On the Nature of Things* (1st c. B.C.), 5, tr. H. A. J. Munro

16. Men of most renowned virtue have sometimes by transgressing most truly kept the law.

MILTON, *TETRACHORDON* (1645)

17. There is no shame in the accidents of chance, but only in the consequence of our own misdeeds.

PHAEDRUS, "THE CRIPPLE AND THE BULLY," *FABLES* (1ST C.), TR. THOMAS JAMES

18. He who is bent on doing evil can never want occasion.

PUBLILIUS SYRUS, *MORAL SAYINGS* (1ST C. B.C.), 459,, TR. DARIUS LYMAN

19. It is so often on the *name* of a misdeed that a life goes to pieces, not the nameless and personal action itself, which was perhaps a perfectly definite necessity of that life and would have been absorbed by it without effort.

RAINER MARIA RILKE, *LETTERS TO A YOUNG POET,* AUG. 12, 1904, TR. M. D. HERTER NORTON

20. How oft the sight of means to do ill deeds / Make deeds ill done!

SHAKESPEARE, *KING JOHN* (1596–97), 4.2.219

21. Men whose wit has been mother of villainy once / have learned from it to be evil in all things.

SOPHOCLES, *PHILOCTETES* (409 B.C.), TR. DAVID GRENE

22. No female iniquity was more severely condemned [in the 14th century] than the habit of plucking eyebrows and the hairline to heighten the forehead.

BARBARA W. TUCHMAN, *A DISTANT MIRROR* (1978)

Y

YANKEES

See 34. AMERICA AND AMERICANS

1071. YOUTH

See also 97. BOYS; 123. CHILDREN; 385. GIRLS; 540. LIFE, STAGES OF; 1072. YOUTH AND AGE

1. Young men have a passion for regarding their elders as senile.

HENRY ADAMS, *THE EDUCATION OF HENRY ADAMS* (1907), 11

2. The young are permanently in a state resembling intoxication; for youth is sweet and they are growing.

ARISTOTLE, *NICOMACHEAN ETHICS* (4TH C. B.C.), 7.14, TR. J. A. K. THOMSON

3. Young men are fitter to invent than to judge, fitter for execution than for counsel, fitter for new projects than for settled business.

FRANCIS BACON, "OF YOUTH AND AGE," *ESSAYS* (1625)

4. Americans began by loving youth, and now, out of adult self-pity, they worship it.

JACQUES BARZUN, *THE HOUSE OF INTELLECT* (1959), 4

5. Money is sullen / And wisdom is sly, / But youth is the pollen / That blows through the sky / And does not ask why.

STEPHEN VINCENT BENÉT, *JOHN BROWN'S BODY* (1928), 1

6. Our youth we can have but to-day, / We may always find time to grow old.

GEORGE BERKELEY, *CAN LOVE BE CONTROLLED BY ADVICE?* (1713)

7. I can now say without hesitation the Marine Corps was the best foster home I ever had.

ART BUCHWALD, *LEAVING HOME: A MEMOIR* (1993)

8. I was eleven, then I was sixteen. Though no honors came my way, those were the lovely years.

TRUMAN CAPOTE, *THE GRASS HARP* (1951)

9. The excesses of our youths are drafts upon our old age, payable with interest, about thirty years after date.

CHARLES CALEB COLTON, *LACON* (1825), 1.76

10. A youth is to be regarded with respect. How do you know that his future will not be equal to our present?

CONFUCIUS, *ANALECTS* (6TH C. B.C.), 9.22, TR. JAMES LEGGE

11. It is better to waste one's youth than to do nothing with it at all.

GEORGES COURTELINE, *LA PHILOSOPHIE DE G. COURTELINE* (1917)

12. All young people want to kick up their heels and defy convention; most of them would prefer to do it at a not too heavy cost.

ELMER DAVIS, "ON THE EVE: REMINISCENCES OF 1913," *BY ELMER DAVIS* (1964)

13. While we are young the idea of death or failure is intolerable to us; even the possibility of ridicule we cannot bear.

ISAK DINESEN, "THE DELUGE AT NORDERNEY," *SEVEN GOTHIC TALES* (1934)

14. The youth of a nation are the trustees of posterity.

BENJAMIN DISRAELI, *SYBIL* (1845), 6.13

15. If youth is the season of hope, it is often so only in the sense that our elders are hopeful about us; for no age is so apt as youth to think its emotions, partings and resolves are the last of their kind.

GEORGE ELIOT, *MIDDLEMARCH* (1871–72), 55

16. In youth, we clothe ourselves with rainbows, and go as brave as the zodiac.

EMERSON, "FATE," *THE CONDUCT OF LIFE* (1860)

17. The mind of a little child is fascinating, for it looks on old things with new eyes—but at about twelve this changes. The adolescent offers nothing, can do nothing, say nothing that the adult cannot do better.

F. SCOTT FITZGERALD, *THE LETTERS OF F. SCOTT FITZGERALD* (1963), ED. ANDREW TURNBULL

18. Human life is a continuous thread which each of us spins to his own pattern, rich and complex in meaning. There are no natural knots in it. Yet knots form, nearly always in adolescence.

EDGAR Z. FRIEDENBERG, *COMING OF AGE IN AMERICA* (1963)

19. Those who love the young best stay young longest.

EDGAR Z. FRIEDENBERG, "ADULT IMAGERY AND FEELING," *THE VANISHING ADOLESCENT* (1959)

20. Adolescents tend to be passionate people, and passion is no less real because it is directed toward a hot-rod, a commercialized popular singer, or the leader of a black-jacketed gang.

EDGAR Z. FRIEDENBERG, "EMOTIONAL DEVELOPMENT IN ADOLESCENCE," *THE VANISHING ADOLESCENT* (1959)

21. I go to school to youth to learn the future.

ROBERT FROST, "WHAT FIFTY SAID," *WEST RUNNING BROOK* (1928)

22. Youth's the season made for joys, / Love is then our duty.

JOHN GAY, *THE BEGGAR'S OPERA* (1728), 2.4, AIR 22

23. Adolescence can be a time of turmoil and turbulence, of stress and storm. Rebellion against authority and against convention is to be expected and tolerated for the sake of learning and growth.

HAIM G. GINOTT, *BETWEEN PARENT & TEENAGER* (1969)

24. Wise parents know that fighting a teenager, like fighting a riptide, is inviting doom.

HAIM G. GINOTT, *BETWEEN PARENT & TEENAGER* (1969)

25. [Adolescence] is the age of cosmic yearnings and private passions, of social concern and personal agony. It is the age of inconsistency and ambivalence.

HAIM G. GINOTT, *BETWEEN PARENT & TEENAGER* (1969)

26. Every one believes in his youth that the world really began with him, and that all merely exists for his sake.

GOETHE, QUOTED IN JOHANN PETER ECKERMANN'S *CONVERSATIONS WITH GOETHE,* DEC. 6, 1829

27. Give me those days with heart in riot, / The depths of bliss that touched on pain, / The force of hate, and love's disquiet— / Ah, give me back my youth again!

GOETHE, "PRELUDE IN THE THEATRE," *FAUST: PART I* (1808), TR. PHILIP WAYNE

28. Here in the city the worst thing that can happen to a nation has happened: we are a people afraid of its youth.

ELIZABETH HARDWICK, "DOMESTIC MANNERS," *BARTLEBY IN MANHATTAN* (1983)

29. The teenager, an afterthought of social history, became a more genuine example of the "new man" than any of the calculated personalities which the Communists held up for emulation.

MICHAEL HARRINGTON, *THE ACCIDENTAL CENTURY* (1966)

30. No young man believes he shall ever die.

WILLIAM HAZLITT, "ON THE FEELING OF IMMORTALITY IN YOUTH," *LITERARY REMAINS* (1836)

31. Young people are thoughtless as a rule.

HOMER, *ODYSSEY* (9TH C. B.C.), 7, TR. E. V. RIEU

32. His story is the usual one of adolescence: endless tortures and temptations, insatiable desires, a satisfying rebellion and at rare moments an exhilarating freedom.

MAUREEN HOWARD, *BEFORE MY TIME* (1974)

33. Youth, even in its sorrows, always has a brilliancy of its own.

VICTOR HUGO, "SAINT DENIS," *LES MISÉRABLES* (1862), 3.8, TR. CHARLES E. WILBOUR

34. A majority of young people seem to develop mental arteriosclerosis forty years before they get the physical kind.

ALDOUS HUXLEY, INTERVIEW, *WRITERS AT WORK: SECOND SERIES* (1963)

35. Eyes fading. Embarrassed at any seriousness in me. Left outside I lose it all. My youth wasted on the bare period of my desires.

LEROI JONES, *THE SYSTEM OF DANTE'S HELL* (1963)

36. A riotous youth; / There's little hope of him. / That fault his age / Will, as it grows, correct.

BEN JONSON, *SEJANUS HIS FALL* (1603), 1.1

37. The imagination of a boy is healthy, and the mature imagination of a man is healthy; but there is a space of life between, in which the soul is in a ferment, the character undecided, the way of life uncertain, the ambition thicksighted.

KEATS, PREFACE, *ENDYMION* (1818)

38. It is not possible for civilization to flow backward while there is youth in the world. Youth may be headstrong, but it will advance its allotted length.

HELEN KELLER, *MIDSTREAM* (1930)

39. Fond youth flatters itself that all must heed its prayer.

LA FONTAINE, "THE OLD CAT AND THE YOUNG MOUSE," *FABLES* (1668–94), TR. MARIANNE MOORE

40. Youth is perpetual intoxication; it is a fever of the mind.

LA ROCHEFOUCAULD, *MAXIMS* (1665), TR. KENNETH PRATT

41. Not childhood alone, but the young man till thirty, never feels practically that he is mortal.

CHARLES LAMB, "NEW YEAR'S EVE," *ESSAYS OF ELIA* (1823)

42. We were happier when we were poorer, but we were also younger.

CHARLES LAMB, "OLD CHINA," *LAST ESSAYS OF ELIA* (1833)

43. How beautiful is youth! how bright it gleams / With its illusions, aspirations, dreams!

LONGFELLOW, *MORITURI SALUTAMUS* (1874)

44. It is an illusion that youth is happy, an illusion of those who have lost it.

W. SOMERSET MAUGHAM, *OF HUMAN BONDAGE* (1915), 29

45. It is, indeed, one of the capital tragedies of youth—and youth is the time of real tragedy—that the young are thrown mainly with adults they do not quite respect.

H. L. MENCKEN, "TRAVAIL," *THE BALTIMORE EVENING SUN*, OCT. 8, 1928

46. You never see the old austerity / That was the essence of civility; / Young people hereabouts, unbridled, now / Just want.

MOLIÈRE, *THE SCHOOL FOR HUSBANDS* (1661), 1.3, TR. DONALD M. FRAME

47. The response of teenagers to their idols is relevant. As an audience, they enjoy themselves, not by screaming with laughter, but screaming with screams.

DESMOND MORRIS, *THE NAKED APE* (1967)

48. Immature is the love of the youth, and immature his hatred of man and earth. His mind and the wings of his spirit are still tied down and heavy.

NIETZSCHE, "ON FREE DEATH," *THUS SPOKE ZARATHUSTRA* (1883–92), 1, TR. WALTER KAUFMANN

49. When one is young, one venerates and despises without that art of nuances which constitutes the best gain of life.

NIETZSCHE, *BEYOND GOOD AND EVIL* (1886), 31, TR. WALTER KAUFMANN

50. Alas, that Spring should vanish with the Rose! / That Youth's sweet-scented Manuscript should close!

OMAR KHAYYÁM, *RUBÁIYÁT* (11TH–12TH C.), TR. EDWARD FITZGERALD, 1ST ED., 72

51. It [England] is a family in which the young are generally thwarted and most of the power is in the hands of irresponsible uncles and bedridden aunts.

GEORGE ORWELL, "ENGLAND YOUR ENGLAND," *A COLLECTION OF ESSAYS* (1954)

52. The old Happiness is unreturning. / Boy's griefs are not so grievous as youth's yearning, / Boys have no sadness sadder than our hope.

WILFRED OWEN, "HAPPINESS," *COLLECTED POEMS* (1920)

53. The ripeness of adolescence is prodigal in pleasures, skittish, and in need of a bridle.

PLUTARCH, "THE EDUCATION OF CHILDREN," *MORALIA* (C. A.D. 100), TR. MOSES HADAS

54. So much of adolescence is an ill-defined dying, / An intolerable waiting, / A longing for another place and time, / Another condition.

THEODORE ROETHKE, "I'M HERE," *THE COLLECTED VERSE OF THEODORE ROETHKE* (1961)

55. As a result of all his education, from everything he hears and sees around him, the child absorbs such a lot of lies and foolish nonsense, mixed in with essential truths, that the first duty of the adolescent who wants to be a healthy man is to disgorge it all.

ROMAIN ROLLAND, *JEAN CHRISTOPHE* (1904–12)

56. In early youth, as we contemplate our coming life, we are like children in a theatre before the curtain is raised, sitting there in high spirits and eagerly waiting for the play to begin.

SCHOPENHAUER, "ON THE SUFFERINGS OF THE WORLD," *PARERGA AND PARALIPOMENA* (1851), TR. T. BAILEY SAUNDERS

57. Don't laugh at a youth for his affectations; he is only trying on one face after another to find a face of his own.

LOGAN PEARSALL SMITH, *AFTERTHOUGHTS* (1931), 2

58. The right way to begin is to pay attention to the young, and make them just as good as possible.

SOCRATES, IN PLATO'S *EUTHYPHRO* (4TH–3RD C. B.C.), TR. LANE COOPER

59. Youth is the time to go flashing from one end of the world to the other, both in mind and body.

ROBERT LOUIS STEVENSON, "CRABBED AGE AND YOUTH," *VIRGINIBUS PUERISQUE* (1881)

60. Youth smiles without any reason. It is one of its chiefest charms.

OSCAR WILDE, *THE PICTURE OF DORIAN GRAY* (1891), 14

61. The world lay before him for his picking—full of opulent cities, golden vintages, glorious triumphs, lovely women, full of a thousand unmet and magnificent possibilities. Nothing was dull or tarnished. The strange enchanted coasts were unvisited. He was young and he could never die.

THOMAS WOLFE, *LOOK HOMEWARD, ANGEL* (1929)

62. A young man is so strong, so mad, so certain, and so lost. He has everything and he is able to use nothing.

Thomas Wolfe, *Of Time and the River* (1935), 51

63. For youthful faults ripe virtues shall atone.

William Wordsworth, "Artegal and Elidure" (1815)

64. Heaven lies about us in our infancy! / Shades of the prison-house begin to close / Upon the growing boy.

William Wordsworth, "Intimations of Immortality" (1803), 5

1072. YOUTH AND AGE

See also 540. Life, Stages of; 653. Old Age; 1071. Youth

1. Believe me, all evil comes from the old. They grow fat on ideas and young men die of them.

Jean Anouilh, *Catch as Catch Can* (1960), tr. Lucienne Hill

2. If age, which is certainly / Just as wicked as youth, look any wiser, / It is only that youth is still able to believe / It will get away with anything, while age / Knows only too well that it has got away with nothing.

W. H. Auden, "The Sea and the Mirror," *Collected Poetry* (1945), 1

3. The old repeat themselves and the young have nothing to say. The boredom is mutual.

Jacques Bainville, "Charme de la conversation," *Lectures* (1937)

4. Young men think old men are fools; but old men know young men are fools.

George Chapman, *All Fools* (c. 1599), 5.1

5. The young fancy that their follies are mistaken by the old for happiness. The old fancy that their gravity is mistaken by the young for wisdom.

Charles Caleb Colton, *Lacon* (1825), 2.92

6. A youth without fire is followed by an old age without experience.

Charles Caleb Colton, *Lacon* (1825), 1.89

7. In youth the life of reason is not in itself sufficient; afterwards the life of emotion, except for short periods, becomes unbearable.

Cyril Connolly, *The Unquiet Grave* (1945), 1

8. Old hands soil, it seems, what they caress; but they too have their beauty when they are joined in prayer. Young hands are made for caresses and the sheathing of love; it is a pity to make them join too soon.

André Gide, *Journals,* Jan. 21, 1929, tr. Justin O'Brien

9. Old people are a kind of monsters to little folks; mild manifestations of the terrible, it may be, but still, with their white locks and ridged and grooved features, which those horrid little eyes exhaust of their details like so many microscopes, not exactly what human beings ought to be.

Oliver Wendell Holmes, Sr., *The Poet at the Breakfast Table* (1872), 1

10. Age looks with anger on the temerity of youth, and youth with contempt on the scrupulosity of age.

Samuel Johnson, *Rasselas* (1759), 26

11. He that would pass the latter part of life with honour and decency must, when he is young, consider that he shall one day be old; and remember, when he is old, that he has once been young.

Samuel Johnson, *The Rambler* (1750–52), 50

12. In youth, it is common to measure right and wrong by the opinion of the world, and in age, to act without any measure but interest, and to lose shame without substituting virtue.

Samuel Johnson, *The Rambler* (1750–52), 197

13. Now we are all fallen, youth from their fear, / And age from that which bred it, good example.

Ben Jonson, *Every Man in His Humour* (1598), 2.5

14. The passions of the young are vices in the old.

Joseph Joubert, *Pensées* (1842), 7.13

15. Most men spend the first half of their lives making the second half miserable.

La Bruyère, *Characters* (1688), 11.102

16. If you will be cherished when you are old, be courteous while you be young.

John Lyly, *Euphues: The Anatomy of Wit* (1579)

17. Youth is immortal; / 'Tis the elderly only grow old!

Herman Melville, "The Wise Virgins to Madam Mirror," *At the Hostelry* (1925)

18. What though youth gave love and roses, / Age still leaves us friends and wine.

Thomas Moore, "Spring and Autumn," *National Airs* (1815)

19. The aged love what is practical, while impetuous youth longs only for what is dazzling.

Petrarch, *Letter to Posterity* (1367–72)

20. The young man who has not wept is a savage, and the older man who will not laugh is a fool.

GEORGE SANTAYANA, *DIALOGUES IN LIMBO* (1925)

21. Crabbed age and youth cannot live together: / Youth is full of pleasance, age is full of care.

SHAKESPEARE, *THE PASSIONATE PILGRIM* (1599), 12.1

22. It's all that the young can do for the old, to shock them and keep them up to date.

GEORGE BERNARD SHAW, "INDUCTION," *FANNY'S FIRST PLAY* (1912)

23. Youth, which is forgiven everything, forgives itself nothing: age, which forgives itself everything, is forgiven nothing.

GEORGE BERNARD SHAW, "MAXIMS FOR REVOLUTIONISTS," *MAN AND SUPERMAN* (1903)

24. To the old our mouths are always partly closed; we must swallow our obvious retorts and listen. They sit above our heads, on life's raised dais, and appeal at once to our respect and pity.

ROBERT LOUIS STEVENSON, "TALK AND TALKERS" (1882), 2

25. All sorts of allowances are made for the illusions of youth; and none, or almost none, for the disenchantments of age.

ROBERT LOUIS STEVENSON, "CRABBED AGE AND YOUTH," *VIRGINIBUS PUERISQUE* (1881)

26. Dignity, high station, or great riches, are in some sort necessary to old men, in order to keep the younger at a distance, who are otherwise too apt to insult them upon the score of their age.

JONATHAN SWIFT, *THOUGHTS ON VARIOUS SUBJECTS* (1711)

27. Age is no better, hardly so well, qualified for an instructor as youth, for it has not profited so much as it has lost.

THOREAU, "ECONOMY," *WALDEN* (1854)

28. Life should begin with age and its privileges and accumulations, and end with youth and its capacity to splendidly enjoy such advantages.

MARK TWAIN, LETTER TO EDWARD L. DIMMIT, JULY 19, 1901

29. The young suffer less from their own errors than from the cautiousness of the old.

VAUVENARGUES, *REFLECTIONS AND MAXIMS* (1746), 158

30. The old believe everything, the middle-aged suspect everything, the young know everything.

OSCAR WILDE, "PHRASES AND PHILOSOPHIES FOR THE USE OF THE YOUNG" (1891)

Z

1073. ZEAL

See also 293. ENTHUSIASM; 335. FANATICISM

1. Zeal without knowledge is fire without light.

THOMAS FULLER, M.D., *GNOMOLOGIA* (1732), 6069

2. Zeal will do more than knowledge.

WILLIAM HAZLITT, "ON THE DIFFERENCE BETWEEN WRITING AND SPEAKING," *THE PLAIN SPEAKER* (1826)

3. Let a man in a garret but burn with enough intensity and he will set fire to the world.

SAINT-EXUPÉRY, *WIND, SAND, AND STARS* (1939), 9.1, TR. LEWIS GALANTIÈRE

ZEN

See 798. RELIGION

Index of Authors and Sources

This index contains brief identifications of all persons quoted and of works that cannot be ascribed to an author. The numbers in the entries refer not to page numbers but to individual quotations. That part of the number before the period indicates the category; the second part indicates the quotation within the category. Titles of categories appear at the tops of the text pages.

A

Abel, Elie (1920–) American journalist and educator. 205.1; 236.1; 241.1; 641.1; 719.1

Abish, Walter (1931–) American novelist and poet. 355.1; 361.1; 381.1; 998.1

Achard, Marcel (1899–1974) French playwright. 581.1

Acton, Lord (Sir John Emerich Edward Dalberg-Acton, 1st Baron Acton) (1834–1902) English historian. 119.1; 332.1; 419.1; 487.1; 537.1; 537.2; 678.1; 682.1; 719.2; 734.1; 1002.1

Adams, Douglas (1952–) English radio and television writer, producer, author. 43.1; 343.1; 454.1; 535.1; 657.1; 906.1; 923.1; 991.1; 991.2

Adams, Franklin P. (1881–1960) American journalist and humorist. 113.1; 324.1; 464.1; 660.1; 711.1; 711.2; 844.1; 998.2; 1038.1; 1069.1

Adams, Henry [Brooks] (1838–1918) American historian, scholar, man of letters. 97.1; 116.1; 119.2; 254.1; 254.2; 257.1; 279.1; 293.1; 301.1; 319.1; 365.1; 365.2; 365.3; 419.2; 419.3; 435.1; 551.1; 551.2; 564.1; 581.2; 586.1; 604.1; 711.3; 711.4; 711.5; 711.6; 711.7; 719.3; 719.4; 785.1; 811.1; 862.1; 901.1; 913.1; 963.1; 965.1; 965.2; 992.1; 1062.1; 1071.1

Adams, John (1735–1826) Second President of the United States (1797–1801). 279.2; 376.1; 395.1; 395.2; 395.3; 446.1; 918.1; 1027.1; 1033.1; 1033.2; 1048.1; 1069.2

Adams, Samuel (1722–1803) American pamphleteer, member of Continental Congress. 716.1

Addison, Joseph (1672–1719) English essayist, critic, poet. 14.1; 19.1; 41.1; 143.1; 188.1; 198.1; 209.1; 226.1; 332.2; 351.1; 391.1; 392.1; 407.1; 409.1; 510.1; 566.1; 600.1; 600.2; 614.1; 655.1; 678.2; 768.1; 803.1; 820.1; 897.1; 905.1; 1011.1; 1033.3; 1050.1; 1069.3

Ade, George (1866–1944) American humorist and playwright. 188.2; 333.1; 422.1; 626.1; 811.2; 1051.1

Adler, Renata (1866–1944) Contemporary American film critic. 374.1

Aeschylus (525–456 B.C.) Greek tragic playwright. 17.1; 19.2; 139.1; 157.1; 221.1; 268.1; 295.1; 343.2; 343.3; 356.1; 368.1; 387.1; 428.1; 440.1; 519.1; 528.1; 564.2; 564.3; 598.1; 624.1; 643.1; 652.1; 653.1; 653.2; 719.5; 750.1; 758.1; 831.1; 940.1; 946.1; 946.2; 978.1; 978.2; 978.3; 1002.2; 1002.3; 1048.2; 1057.1; 1060.1; 1070.1

Aesop (c. 620–c. 560 B.C.) Greek fabulist. 17.2; 19.3; 19.4; 22.1; 45.1; 46.1; 57.1; 60.1; 166.1; 186.1; 195.1; 238.1; 238.2; 251.1; 252.1; 288.1; 288.2; 307.1; 310.1; 356.2; 363.1; 365.4; 400.1; 436.1; 444.1; 449.1; 474.1; 476.1; 508.1; 558.1; 585.1; 649.1; 681.1; 712.1; 723.1; 772.1; 866.1; 920.1; 998.3; 1002.4; 1012.1; 1023.1; 1027.2; 1030.1; 1048.3; 1064.1

African Proverbs. 23.1

Agathon (second half of 5th c. B.C.) Athenian tragic poet. 53.1; 676.1

Agee, James (1909–1955) American poet, film writer, novelist. 45.2; 77.1; 103.1; 131.1; 334.1; 364.1; 404.1; 428.2; 493.1; 680.1; 695.1; 708.1; 854.1; 1064.2; 1069.4

Alain. Pen name of Emile [Auguste] Chartier (1868–1951) French philosopher, essayist, teacher. Alain 443.1; 634.1; 904.1; 919.1; 923.2

Alcmaeon of Crotona (fl. c. 500 B.C.) Greek physician and Pythagorean philosopher. 76.1

Alderman, Ellen (1958–) American attorneys. 823.1; 823.2; 823.3

Aldington, Richard (1892–1962) English poet, novelist, biographer, translator. 622.1; 1062.2

Aldrich, Thomas Bailey (1836–1907) American poet, editor, novelist, playwright. 53.2; 73.1; 93.1; 95.1; 133.1; 500.1; 524.1; 578.1; 605.1; 653.3; 718.1; 719.6; 762.1; 779.1; 943.1; 1069.5

Ali ibn-abi-Talib (c. 600–661) Cousin and son-in-law of Mohammed; fourth caliph of the Moslems. 77.14; 184.5; 240.13; 288.13; 365.60; 393.23; 403.11; 923.30; 1060.34

Allen, Fred. Real name, John F. Sullivan (1894–1956) American comedian. 144.1; 332.3

Altrincham, Lord *See* Grigg, John

Amiel, Henri Frédéric (1821–1881) Swiss philosopher and poet. 121.1; 123.1; 225.1; 233.1; 240.1; 259.1; 377.1; 406.1; 440.2; 487.2; 491.1; 562.1; 691.1; 741.1; 785.2; 978.4; 1005.1; 1062.3

Amory, Cleveland (1917–) American writer and social critic. 62.1; 104.1; 279.3; 328.1; 367.1; 676.2; 711.8; 730.1; 1069.6

Amphis (4th c. B.C.) Greek playwright. 53.3

Anacharsis (fl. c. 600 B.C.) Scythian philosopher. 268.2; 703.1

Anaxagoras (c. 500–c. 428 B.C.) Greek philosopher and scientist. 221.2

Anderson, Marian (1902–) American contralto. 775.1

Angell, Roger (1920–) American editor and author. 929.1; 929.2; 929.3; 929.4

Angelou, Maya (1928–) American writer, musician, teacher. 221.3; 422.2; 775.2; 927.1; 978.5; 987.1; 992.2

Anonymous. 129.1; 221.4; 416.1; 419.4; 528.2; 645.1; 719.7; 965.3

Anouilh, Jean (1910–) French playwright and screen writer. 43.2; 53.4; 72.1; 72.2; 72.3; 195.2; 221.5; 239.1; 343.4; 361.2; 387.2; 504.1; 528.3; 539.1; 540.1; 542.1; 551.3; 582.1; 592.1; 630.1; 653.4; 661.1; 676.3; 698.1; 735.1; 858.1; 962.1; 1072.1

Antisthenes (c. 445–365 B.C.) Greek philosopher, founder of the Cynic school. 288.3; 295.2; 334.2; 829.1; 930.1

Apocrypha (c. 445–365 B.C.) A part of the sacred literature of the Alexandrian Jews. 43.3; 57.2; 98.1; 165.1; 206.1; 216.1; 221.6; 241.2; 284.1; 286.1; 356.3; 365.5; 365.6; 387.3; 409.2; 510.2; 751.1; 980.1; 998.4; 1024.1

Apostolius, Michael (1422–1480) Greek scholar in Italy during Renaissance. 795.1

Aquinas, St. Thomas (c. 1225–1274) Italian theologian and philosopher. 620.1

Arabic Proverbs. 56.1; 57.3; 96.1; 104.2; 157.2; 191.1; 212.1; 357.1; 386.1; 516.1

Arbuthnot, John (1667–1735) Scottish writer and physician. 710.1

Ardrey, Robert (1908–1980) American writer. 41.2; 77.2; 110.1; 308.1; 308.2; 343.5; 524.2; 562.2; 582.2; 718.2; 1049.1
Arendt, Hannah (1906–1975) German-born American author, political theorist. 201.1; 204.1; 393.1; 405.1; 526.1; 766.1; 940.2; 985.1; 1002.5; 1065.1
Aretino, Pietro (1492–1556) Italian Renaissance satirist. 17.3; 39.1; 83.1; 349.1; 365.7; 491.2; 516.2; 530.1; 539.2; 653.5; 670.1; 708.2; 751.2; 848.1; 854.2; 862.2; 892.1; 1000.1; 1042.1
Ariosto, Lodovico (1474–1533) Italian poet. 209.2
Aristippus (fl. c. 435–c. 356 B.C.) Greek philosopher, founder of Cyrenaic School. 704.1
Aristophanes (c. 445–380 B.C.) Greek comic playwright. 1062.4
Aristotle (384–322 B.C.) Greek philosopher. 9.1; 10.1; 17.4; 21.1; 39.2; 53.5; 72.4; 72.5; 116.2; 123.2; 131.2; 131.3; 132.1; 166.2; 176.1; 207.1; 227.1; 232.1; 233.2; 233.3; 279.4; 279.5; 297.1; 297.2; 307.2; 334.3; 334.4; 365.8; 365.9; 365.10; 365.11; 366.1; 376.2; 393.2; 395.4; 409.3; 409.4; 409.5; 427.1; 494.1; 514.1; 517.1; 519.2; 528.4; 528.5; 531.1; 532.1; 539.3; 547.1; 562.3; 574.1; 608.1; 656.1; 663.1; 666.1; 670.2; 704.2; 710.2; 711.9; 712.2; 714.1; 718.3; 746.1; 750.2; 760.1; 760.2; 810.1; 817.1; 819.1; 831.2; 862.3; 888.1; 889.1; 915.1; 930.2; 948.1; 965.4; 977.1; 998.5; 1016.1; 1033.4; 1060.2; 1071.2
Arnold, Matthew (1822–1888) English critic, essayist, poet. 77.3; 116.3; 117.1; 210.1; 238.3; 367.2; 387.4; 444.2; 444.3; 504.2; 562.4; 580.1; 590.1; 606.1; 623.1; 677.1; 758.2; 812.1; 873.1; 915.2; 989.1; 998.6; 1062.5; 1065.2; 1067.1; 1069.7
Aron, Raymond [Claude Ferdinand] (1905–) French educator and writer. 361.3
Asch, Sholem (1880–1957) Polish-born American novelist. 580.2; 1069.8
Ashanti Proverbs. 268.3; 558.2; 621.1; 755.1
Athenodorus [Cananites] (c. 74 B.C.–A.D. 8) Greek Stoic philosopher. 548.1
Atkinson, [Justin] Brooks (1894–) American dramatic critic and essayist. 53.6; 82.1; 108.1; 126.1; 202.1; 207.2; 279.6; 298.1; 443.2; 504.3; 539.4; 542.2; 569.1; 620.2; 631.1; 656.2; 695.2; 839.1; 1065.3; 1069.9
Attlee, Clement [Richard], 1st Earl (1883–1967) British political leader. Prime Minister of Great Britain (1945–1951). 233.4
Auden, W[ystan] H[ugh] (1907–1973) English-born American poet and playwright. 20.1; 34.1; 93.2; 207.3; 208.1; 330.1; 376.3; 393.3; 469.1; 549.1; 551.4; 576.1; 593.1; 614.2; 614.3; 676.4; 688.1; 708.3; 708.4; 794.1; 873.2; 882.1; 940.3; 963.2; 1069.10; 1069.11; 1072.2
Augustine, St. Latin name, Aurelius Augustinus (A.D. 354–430) Early Christian church father and philosopher. 55.1; 122.1; 330.2; 409.6; 987.2; 990.1; 1030.2; 1060.3
Aurelius, Marcus. Full name, Marcus Aurelius Antoninus (121–180) Roman emperor and Stoic philosopher. 33.1; 72.6; 151.1; 183.1; 209.3; 219.1; 227.2; 240.2; 368.2; 393.4; 393.5; 409.7; 451.1; 476.2; 539.5; 539.6; 548.2; 550.1; 663.2; 676.5; 729.1; 729.2; 832.1; 866.2; 880.1; 900.1; 937.1; 946.3; 975.1; 990.2; 998.7; 1070.2
Austen, Jane (1775–1817) English novelist. 66.1; 194.1; 292.1; 365.12; 523.1; 594.1; 704.3; 1062.6

B

Babylonian Proverbs. 348.2
Bacchylides (c. 505–c. 450 B.C.) Greek lyric poet. 221.7
Bach, Richard (1936–) American writer and aviator. 124.1; 269.1; 343.6; 454.2; 480.1; 918.2; 965.5; 998.8; 1069.12
Bacon, Francis (1561–1626) English philosopher, statesman, essayist. 1.1; 8.1; 19.5; 39.3; 87.1; 93.3; 93.4; 104.3; 169.1; 195.3; 201.2; 207.4; 213.1; 216.2; 221.8; 221.9; 295.3; 299.1; 332.4; 334.5; 354.1; 360.1; 365.13; 365.14; 401.1; 428.3; 476.3; 479.1; 480.2; 514.2; 522.1; 551.5; 558.3; 564.4; 570.1; 586.2; 623.2; 623.3; 657.2; 658.1; 670.3; 670.4; 694.1; 732.1; 751.3; 770.1; 803.2; 817.2; 817.3; 819.2; 831.3; 848.2; 915.3; 915.4; 920.2; 923.3; 926.1; 930.3; 943.2; 954.1; 986.1; 1004.1; 1027.3; 1033.5; 1042.2; 1048.4; 1069.13; 1071.3
Bainville, Jacques (1879–1936) French historian, journalist, essayist. 1072.3
Baker, Russell [Wayne] (1925–) American journalist and author. 123.3; 267.1; 588.1; 602.1; 603.1; 630.2; 630.3; 630.4; 646.1; 646.2; 704.4; 892.2; 929.5; 933.1; 967.1; 967.2; 992.3
Baldwin, James (1924–1987) American novelist and essayist. 34.2; 53.7; 65.1; 85.1; 85.2; 85.3; 87.2; 123.4; 131.4; 146.1; 199.1; 204.2; 221.10; 235.1; 303.1; 329.1; 329.2; 363.2; 368.3; 412.1; 538.1; 555.1; 564.5; 602.2; 784.1; 875.1; 885.1; 892.3; 900.2; 927.2; 946.4; 1037.1; 1054.1; 1069.14
Balzac [Honoré de] (1799–1850) French novelist. 537.3; 563.1; 698.2; 1037.2
Barbey d'Aurevilly, Jules (1808–1889) French novelist and critic. 409.8
Baring, Maurice (1874–1945) English novelist, essayist, poet, playwright. 602.3
Barnes, Djuna (1892–) American novelist, short-story writer, playwright. 284.2; 444.4
Barnett, Lincoln [Kinnear] (1909–) American writer. 849.1
Barr, A[lfred] H[amilton], Jr (1902–) American art historian and museum director. 64.1
Barrès, [Augustin-] Maurice (1862–1923) French novelist, journalist, politician. 711.10
Barrie, Sir J[ames] M[atthew] (1860–1937) Scottish dramatist and novelist. 121.2; 195.4; 332.5; 539.7; 764.1; 797.1; 1062.7
Barron, Frank (1860–1937) Contemporary American educator and writer. 201.3
Barrow, John D. (1952–) English cosmologist. 415.1; 444.5; 650.1; 747.1; 855.1; 921.1; 978.6; 998.9; 1017.1
Barrymore, Ethel (1879–1959) American actress. 11.1; 972.1
Bartók, Béla (1881–1945) Hungarian composer, pianist, collector of folk songs. 155.1
Barth, John [Simmons] (1930–) American novelist. 419.5; 478.1; 562.5; 565.1; 608.2; 1026.1
Barth, Karl (1886–1968) Swiss Protestant Reformed theologian and educator. 331.1; 614.4; 973.1
Barthélémy, Auguste [Marseille] (1796–1867) French poet and satirist. 117.2
Barthelme, Donald (1931–1989) American short-story writer and novelist. 217.1; 279.7; 858.2; 945.1; 1065.4
Barthes, Roland (1915–1980) French literary critic. 967.3
Baruch, Bernard M[annes] (1870–1965) American businessman and statesman. 395.5; 653.6; 711.11; 1038.2
Barzini, Luigi (Jr.) (1908–1984) Italian journalist and author. 34.3; 34.4; 34.5; 34.6; 72.7; 77.4; 190.1; 351.2; 355.2; 355.3; 385.1; 479.2; 493.2; 509.1; 509.2; 524.3; 538.2; 587.1; 636.1; 670.5; 718.4; 737.1; 742.1; 752.1; 916.1; 923.4; 923.5; 928.1; 992.4; 1029.1; 1065.5; 1067.2
Barzun, Jacques [Martin] (1907–) French-born American critic and educator. 1.2; 53.8; 117.3; 201.4; 297.3; 321.1; 442.1; 449.2; 614.5; 726.1; 784.2; 965.6; 975.2; 987.3; 1037.3; 1071.4
Bashkirtsev, Marie (1860–1884) Russian painter and diarist. 606.2
Bauër, Gérard (1888–) French writer. 923.6
Baudelaire, Charles [Pierre] (1821–1867) French poet. 27.1; 104.4; 739.1; 892.4; 1065.6
Baudouin I (1951–) King of Belgium. 1042.3

Baxter, Richard (1615–1691) English divine. 119.3
Bayle, Pierre (1647–1706) French philosopher. 986.2
Bazin, Hervé (1917–) French novelist. 412.2
Beaumarchais, Pierre Augustin Caron de (1732–1799) French playwright, courtier, watchmaker to Louis XV. 562.6; 755.2; 972.2
Beaumont, Francis (c. 1584–1616) English playwright. 17.5; 338.1; 1062.8
Beauvoir, Simone de (1908–1986) French existentialist novelist and essayist. 252.2; 297.4; 316.1; 363.3; 552.1; 581.3; 695.3; 826.1; 948.2; 966.1; 1062.9; 1062.10; 1064.3; 1065.7
Beckett, Samuel (1906–1989) Irish author and playwright. 406.2; 559.1; 765.1
Bedford, Sybille (1911–) English novelist and travel writer. 992.5; 1048.5
Beecham, Sir Thomas (1879–1961) English conductor. 289.1; 614.6
Beecher, Henry Ward (1813–1887) American clergyman, editor, writer. 6.1; 18.1; 39.4; 41.40; 51.1; 85.4; 93.5; 97.2; 99.1; 104.5; 104.6; 105.1; 119.4; 123.5; 139.2; 165.2; 174.1; 178.1; 206.2; 213.2; 222.1; 228.1; 233.5; 238.4; 267.2; 271.1; 284.3; 293.2; 349.2; 368.4; 392.2; 393.6; 395.6; 395.7; 409.9; 422.3; 433.1; 436.2; 447.1; 514.3; 522.3; 528.6; 528.7; 533.1; 537.4; 540.2; 558.4; 562.7; 630.5; 652.2; 657.3; 670.6; 675.1; 684.1; 697.1; 711.12; 718.5; 722.1; 723.2; 724.1; 734.2; 738.1; 746.2; 761.1; 778.1; 855.2; 897.2; 923.7; 945.2; 961.1; 971.1; 973.2; 995.1; 998.10; 1002.6; 1008.1; 1038.3; 1042.4; 1061.1; 1064.4; 1065.8
Beerbohm, Sir Max (1872–1956) English essayist and caricaturist. 14.2; 131.5; 166.3; 192.1; 207.5; 227.3; 289.2; 332.6; 342.1; 384.1; 401.2; 418.1; 428.4; 428.5; 517.2; 526.2; 691.2; 708.5; 808.1; 928.2; 1041.1; 1065.9; 1065.10
Behan, Brendan (1923–1964) Irish playwright and wit. 1042.5
Belloc, [Joseph] Hilaire [Pierre] (1870–1953) English writer. 41.3; 115.1; 365.15
Bellow, Saul (1915–) American novelist, playwright, short-story writer. 124.2; 221.11; 343.7; 416.2; 892.5; 892.6; 977.2
Benét, Stephen Vincent (1898–1943) American poet and short-story writer. 34.7; 307.3; 443.3; 719.8; 987.4; 1042.7; 1071.5
Benedict, Ruth F[ulton] (1887–1948) American anthropologist and poet. 53.9; 77.5; 133.3; 151.2; 210.2; 210.3; 500.2; 726.2; 986.3; 1042.6
Benjamin, Walter (1892–1940) German essayist. 93.6; 1069.15
Bentham, Jeremy (1748–1832) English philosopher. 409.10; 766.2
Bentley, Eric (1916–) English-born American drama critic, teacher, editor. 54.1; 145.1; 338.2
Berechiah ben Natronai ha-Nakdan (13th century) Jewish philosopher. 17.6; 670.7; 1027.4
Berenson, Bernard (1865–1959) Lithuanian-born American art connoisseur. 53.10
Bergson, Henri (1859–1941) French philosopher. 493.3
Berkeley, George (1685–1753) Irish-born English bishop and philosopher. 1071.6
Berle, Milton. Real name, Milton Berlinger (1908–) American actor and comedian. 147.1
Berlin, Irving. Real name, Israel Baline (1888–) Russian-born American composer. 945.3
Bernanos, Georges (1888–1948) French novelist and political writer. 9.2; 62.2; 416.3; 427.2; 574.2; 659.1; 682.2; 723.3; 733.1; 930.4; 996.1
Bernard, Tristan. Pen name of Paul Bernard (1866–1947) French playwright and novelist. 409.11; 805.1; 901.2
Bernstein, Leonard (1918–1990) American composer, conductor, lecturer. 614.7
Berry, John (1915–) American poet and fiction writer. 409.12
Berry, Wendell (1934–) American poet, novelist, essayist. 9.3; 522.2; 590.2; 676.6; 708.6; 808.2; 858.3; 966.2; 1026.2
Beston, Henry [Sheahan] (1888–1968) American writer. 54.2; 90.1; 177.1; 177.2; 272.1; 294.1; 623.4; 623.5; 633.1; 633.2; 853.1; 854.3; 950.1
Betti, Ugo (1892–1953) Italian playwright. 78.1; 103.2; 271.2; 334.6; 343.8; 444.6; 482.1; 517.3; 564.6; 644.1; 709.1; 838.1; 858.4; 901.3; 978.7; 1064.5
Bhagavadgita (1892–1953) (Sanskrit, The Song of God). (2) 588.2; 681.2; 770.2; 865.1; (4) 9.4; 522.4; 875.2; 1065.11; (5) 10.2; 447.2; (16) 416.4; (17) 9.5; 17 330.3; (18) 684.2
Bias (fl. middle of 6th c. B.C.) Greek philosopher, one of the Seven Sages of Greece. 365.16
Bible (fl. middle of 6th c. B.C.) The Authorized King James Version (1611). 6.2; 19.6; 33.2; 39.5; 39.6; 45.3; 48.1; 57.4; 73.2; 76.2; 80.1; 83.2; 93.7; 96.2; 100.1; 105.2; 112.1; 119.5; 126.2; 127.1; 167.1; 167.3; 167.4; 176.2; 186.2; 206.3; 206.4; 221.12; 221.13; 227.4; 247.1; 252.3; 274.1; 281.1; 288.4; 300.1; 307.4; 329.3; 330.4; 330.5; 356.4; 356.5; 359.1; 359.2; 365.17; 375.1; 384.2; 384.3; 387.5; 387.6; 387.7; 388.1; 393.7; 394.1; 405.2; 409.13; 415.2; 426.1; 427.3; 428.6; 433.2; 433.3; 433.4; 444.7; 446.2; 447.3; 448.1; 473.1; 491.3; 497.1; 510.3; 522.5; 526.3; 528.8; 530.2; 539.8; 544.1; 551.6; 551.7; 562.8; 564.7; 564.8; 564.9; 571.1; 571.2; 596.1; 602.4; 606.3; 606.4; 626.2; 640.1; 653.7; 661.2; 664.1; 665.1; 684.3; 691.3; 696.1; 701.1; 712.3; 718.6; 727.1; 733.2; 738.2; 746.3; 751.4; 766.3; 770.3; 797.2; 803.3; 804.1; 810.2; 815.3; 815.4; 822.1; 835.1; 837.1; 841.1; 853.2; 856.1; 900.3; 918.3; 923.8; 923.9; 943.3; 979.1; 979.2; 988.1; 990.3; 990.4; 992.6; 998.11; 1004.2; 1016.2; 1043.1; 1047.1; 1048.6; 1048.7; 1048.8; 1052.1; 1055.1; 1059.1; 1060.4; 1060.5; 1060.6; 1062.11; 1065.12; 1070.3
Bierce, Ambrose [Gwinett] (1842–?1914) American journalist, short-story writer, poet. 6.3; 7.1; 8.2; 14.3; 19.7; 51.2; 57.5; 72.8; 77.6; 95.2; 98.2; 103.3; 104.7; 105.3; 114.1; 130.1; 156.1; 162.1; 171.1; 178.2; 188.3; 197.1; 225.2; 234.1; 240.3; 247.2; 264.1; 269.2; 279.8; 293.3; 315.1; 338.3; 348.1; 367.3; 368.5; 383.1; 395.8; 398.1; 406.3; 409.14; 419.6; 435.2; 437.1; 440.3; 450.1; 463.1; 494.2; 498.1; 506.1; 519.3; 528.9; 537.5; 582.3; 602.5; 604.2; 615.1; 619.1; 658.2; 659.2; 666.2; 677.2; 711.13; 723.4; 726.3; 730.2; 785.3; 786.1; 797.3; 809.1; 810.3; 835.2; 848.3; 865.2; 923.10; 941.1; 977.3; 992.7; 1051.2; 1062.12; 1068.1
Bion (probably 2nd c. B.C.) Greek poet. 17.7; 595.1; 653.8
Bird, [Cyril] Kenneth. Pseudonym, Fougasse (1887–) English illustrator, cartoonist, editor. 436.3
Bishop, Elizabeth (1911–) American poet. 839.2
Bishop, Jim [James Alonzo] (1907–) American writer, editor, newspaperman. 207.6; 419.7
Bishop, Morris (1893–1973) American author, editor, translator. 363.4
Bismarck-Schönhausen, Otto Eduard Leopold von (1815–1898) Prussian statesman and first chancellor of the German Empire, "the Iron Chancellor". 381.2; 912.1
Black, Hugo L[aFayette] (1886–1971) American jurist. 364.2
Black, Shirley Temple (1928–) American actress and diplomat. 360.2; 611.1; 657.4; 1044.1
Blake, William (1757–1827) English poet, engraver, painter, mystic. 33.3; 39.7; 78.2; 125.1; 264.2; 299.2; 312.1; 330.6; 354.2; 356.6; 359.3; 409.15; 435.3; 446.3; 460.1; 478.2; 513.1; 527.1; 561.1; 623.6; 683.1; 683.2; 698.3; 755.3; 782.1; 815.1; 918.4; 947.1; 975.3; 978.8; 979.3

Bloch, Arthur McBride (1938–) American author and teacher. 17.10; 17.11; 580.3; 602.6; 924.1; 1065.13.
Bloom, Allan 34.8; 53.11; 123.6; 171.2; 210.4; 279.9; 279.10; 279.11; 419.8; 419.9; 431.1; 537.6; 581.4; 604.3; 614.8; 614.9; 614.10; 654.1; 694.2; 694.3; 797.4; 848.4; 848.5; 886.1; 904.2; 1026.3
Blum, Léon (1872–1950) French statesman and critic. 670.8
Bodenheim, Maxwell (1893–1954) American poet and novelist. 708.7
Boethius, Anicius Manlius Severinus (c. 480–525) Roman philosopher. 17.12; 409.16; 551.8; 614.11; 937.2; 1011.2
Bohlen, Charles E[ustis] (1904–1974). American diplomat. 150.1
Boileau [-Despréaux], Nicolas (1636–1711) French poet and critic. 134.1; 298.2; 447.4; 491.4
Böll, Heinrich (1971–1985) German novelist and short-story writer. 886.2
Bolt, Robert (1924–) English playwright. 221.14; 734.3
Bonhoeffer, Dietrich (1906–1945) German theologian, imprisoned and executed by Nazis. 122.2; 221.15; 225.3; 387.8; 659.3; 946.5; 978.9
Bonnot, Étienne *See* Condillac, Étienne Bonnot, Abbé de
Boorstin, Daniel J. (1914–) American educator and writer. 18.2; 34.9; 34.10; 53.12; 93.8; 309.1; 332.7; 387.9; 418.2; 449.3; 613.1; 630.6; 763.1; 992.8; 992.9
Booth, Shirley (1909–) American actress. 59.1
Borges, Jorge Luis (1899–1986) Argentine short-story writer, essayist, poet. 86.1; 266.1; 541.1; 551.9; 565.2; 606.5; 708.8; 946.6
Borland, Hal [Harold Glen] (1900–) American newspaperman and nature writer. 82.2; 623.7; 623.8; 631.2; 729.3; 824.1; 854.4; 854.5; 854.6; 854.7; 854.8; 995.2; 1050.2
Boswell, James (1740–1795) Scottish lawyer, man of letters, biographer of Samuel Johnson. 96.3; 307.5; 333.2; 365.18; 375.2; 538.3; 627.1; 712.4; 867.1; 892.7; 1011.3; 1048.9; 1053.1; 1068.2
Bourdaloue, Louis (1632–1704) French Jesuit preacher. 206.5
Bourdet, Edouard (1887–) French playwright. Bourdet, Edouard 602.7
Bourget, Paul [Charles Joseph] (1852–1935) French novelist, critic, poet. 551.10
Bowen, Catherine [Shober] Drinker (1897–1973) American biographer. 81.1
Bowen, Elizabeth [Dorothea Cole] (1899–1973). Anglo-Irish novelist and short-story writer. 2.1; 58.1; 123.7; 123.8; 131.6; 239.2; 249.1; 321.2; 404.2; 449.4; 469.2; 542.3; 551.11; 564.10; 646.3; 683.3; 837.2; 854.9; 854.10; 918.5; 918.6; 1048.10; 1062.13
Bowles, Jane [Sydney Auer] (1917–1973) American novelist and playwright. 15.1; 539.9; 539.10
Boyle, Roger, 1st Earl of Orrery (1621–1679) Irish playwright and soldier. 1069.16
Boyle, T. Coraghesson (1948–) American novelist and short-story writer. 18.3; 34.11; 268.4
Bradbury, Robert (1621–1679) Contemporary Liverpool city official. 64.2
Bradshaw, Mrs. Janice Contemporary American mother, housewife. 718.7
Brancusi, Constantin (1876–1957) Rumanian sculptor. 50.1
Brando, Marlon (1924–) American film actor. 945.4
Braque, Georges (1882–1963) French painter. 53.13; 999.1
Brecht, Bertolt (1898–1956) German playwright. 9.6; 251.2; 267.3; 291.1; 360.3; 393.8; 400.2; 409.17; 412.3; 489.1; 504.4; 532.2; 585.2; 602.8; 691.4; 698.4; 780.1; 848.6; 956.1; 1042.8; 1060.7
Breytenbach, Breyten (1939–) South African-born French painter and writer. 257.2; 784.3
Bridges, Robert (1844–1930) English poet, appointed poet laureate in 1913. 854.11
Brillat-Savarin, Anthelme (1755–1826) French politician and gourmet. 189.1; 274.2
Brinkley, David (1920–) American broadcast journalist. 50.2; 524.4; 581.5; 711.14; 1062.14
Brodsky, Joseph [Iosif Alexandrovich] (1940–) Russian-born American poet, essayist. 53.14; 201.5; 214.1; 221.16; 387.10; 551.12; 1003.1
Bronowski, Jacob (1908–1974) English scientist, mathematician, lecturer, philosopher. 65.2; 242.1; 308.3; 337.1; 404.3; 450.2; 493.4; 522.6; 532.3; 562.9; 562.10; 623.9; 689.1; 719.9; 741.2; 819.3; 844.2; 849.2; 849.3; 874.1; 892.8; 1017.2; 1065.14
Brontë, Emily [Jane] (1818–1848) English novelist and poet. 900.4
Brooks, Charles S. (1878–1934) American playwright and essayist. 1061.2
Brooks, Gwendolyn E[lizabeth] (1917–) American poet and novelist. 1054.2
Brooks, Louise (1907–1985) American film actress and writer. 81.2; 311.2; 611.2
Brooks, Van Wyck (1886–1963) American poet, novelist, critic, biographer. 307.6; 886.3
Brougham, Lord (Henry Peter Brougham, Baron Brougham and Vaux) (1778–1868) Scottish jurist and political leader. 279.12
Broun, [Matthew] Heywood [Campbell] (1888–1939) American journalist and novelist. 53.15; 65.3; 65.4; 207.7; 329.4; 355.4; 364.3; 419.10; 581.6; 581.7; 582.4; 790.1; 832.2; 1004.3; 1034.1
Brown, John Mason (1900–1969) American literary critic, essayist, lecturer. 121.3; 711.15; 1065.15
Browne, Sir Thomas (1605–1682) English writer and scholar. 87.3; 111.1; 152.1; 186.3; 195.5; 221.17; 221.18; 261.1; 284.4; 295.4; 298.3; 321.3; 326.1; 330.7; 349.3; 357.2; 375.3; 504.5; 653.9; 698.5; 764.2; 790.2; 817.4; 858.5; 863.1; 1034.2; 1048.11
Browning, Elizabeth Barrett (1806–1861) English poet, wife of Robert Browning. 93.9; 261.2; 284.5; 289.3; 298.4; 393.9; 551.13; 656.3
Browning, Robert (1812–1889) English poet. 17.13; 53.16; 55.2; 82.3; 272.2; 279.13; 284.6; 329.5; 387.11; 387.12; 390.1; 390.2; 393.10; 400.3; 447.5; 533.2; 539.11; 539.12; 539.13; 551.14; 614.12; 653.10; 659.4; 688.2; 696.2; 704.5; 708.9; 854.12; 858.6; 887.1; 899.1; 940.4; 945.5; 998.12; 1004.4
Bruyère, Jean de la (1812–1889) English poet. 674.4
Bryan, William Jennings (1860–1925) American political leader and orator. 337.2; 822.2
Bryant, William Cullen (1794–1878) American poet, critic, editor. 117.4; 221.19; 299.3; 340.1; 551.15; 606.6; 623.10; 713.1; 754.1; 854.13; 889.2; 990.5; 998.13
Buchwald, Art (1925–) American columnist, humorist and author. 279.14; 434.1; 436.4; 632.1; 892.9; 918.7; 1042.9; 1042.10; 1071.7
Buck, Pearl S[ydenstricker] (1892–1973) American novelist and humanitarian. 9.7; 85.5; 299.4; 404.4; 442.2; 458.1; 537.7; 551.16; 564.11; 670.9; 682.3; 775.3; 797.5; 822.3; 858.7; 887.2; 915.5
Budgell, Eustace (1686–1737) English essayist and man of letters. 51.3; 173.1; 365.19; 1064.6
Buffon, Comte Georges Louis Leclerc de (1707–1788). 376.4; 942.1
Buganda Proverbs. 795.2
Bulwer-Lytton, Edward George Earle Lytton, 1st Baron Lytton (1803–1873) English novelist and playwright. 982.1; 1069.17
Buonarroti, Michelangelo *See* Michelangelo Buonarroti
Burchfield, Robert [William] (1923–) New Zealand-born English scholar and lexicographer.

164.1; 244.1; 299.5; 398.2; 524.5; 524.6; 524.7; 1064.7; 1064.8

Burgess, Anthony (1917–93) English novelist. 53.17; 93.10; 262.1; 263.1; 338.4; 344.1; 454.3; 545.1; 580.4; 964.1; 1069.18

Burgess, [Frank] Gelett (1866–1951) American humorist and illustrator. 155.2; 309.2; 365.20; 450.3; 581.8; 581.9; 645.2; 670.10; 820.2; 881.1; 1062.15

Burke, Edmund (1729–1797) English statesman, orator, writer. 17.14; 162.2; 213.3; 216.3; 329.6; 343.9; 357.3; 368.6; 395.9; 529.1; 561.2; 591.1; 658.3; 661.3; 677.3; 711.16; 719.10; 761.2; 797.6; 889.3; 930.5; 964.2; 977.4; 977.5; 1004.5

Burmese Proverbs. 33.4; 48.2; 238.5; 274.3; 428.7; 551.17

Burnham, Daniel H[udson] (1846–1912) American architect. 702.1

Burns, Robert (1756–1796) Scottish poet. 152.2; 209.4; 604.4; 623.11; 702.2; 704.6; 875.3; 883.1; 990.6

Burroughs, John (1837–1921) American naturalist, essayist, poet. 93.11; 411.1; 613.2; 676.7; 1040.1

Burton, Robert (1577–1640) English clergyman and writer. 19.8; 189.2; 191.2; 338.5; 435.4; 564.12; 614.13; 699.1; 832.3; 896.1; 1011.4

Burton, Sir Richard Francis (1821–1890) English explorer and writer of travel books. 580.5; 853.3; 992.10

Butler, Hubert. 393.11; 626.3; 1011.5

Butler, Samuel (1612–1680) English poet and satirist. 158.1; 199.2; 227.5; 300.2; 340.2; 556.1; 602.9; 602.10; 643.2; 652.3; 772.2

Butler, Samuel (1835–1902) English novelist, scholar, translator. 3.1; 17.15; 35.1; 41.4; 51.4; 53.18; 53.19; 98.3; 115.2; 115.3; 138.1; 174.2; 201.6; 221.20; 221.21; 230.1; 242.2; 264.3; 271.3; 274.4; 299.6; 299.7; 313.1; 330.8; 330.9; 334.7; 335.21; 341.1; 387.13; 387.14; 387.15; 401.3; 404.5; 419.11; 452.1; 477.1; 539.14; 539.15; 541.2; 558.5; 558.6; 558.7; 563.2; 564.13; 604.5; 604.6; 604.7; 614.14; 656.4; 670.11; 673.1; 694.4; 722.2; 723.5; 729.4; 741.3; 754.2; 761.3; 763.2; 771.1; 785.4; 797.7; 804.2; 822.4; 848.7; 880.2; 896.2; 961.2; 963.3; 965.7; 978.10; 998.14; 999.2; 1006.1; 1030.3; 1030.4; 1033.6; 1067.3

Byrd, William (1540?–1623) English composer. 333.3

Byron, George Gordon [Noel], 6th Baron Byron of Rochdale. Called Lord Byron (1788–1824) English poet. 9.8; 17.16; 31.1; 94.2; 122.3; 125.2; 140.1; 142.1; 145.2; 207.8; 207.9; 207.10; 221.22; 221.23; 268.5; 274.5; 289.4; 298.5; 354.3; 365.22; 387.16; 409.18; 412.4; 449.5; 454.4; 489.2; 519.4; 527.2; 528.10; 537.8; 548.3; 551.18; 558.8; 562.11; 563.3; 564.14; 581.10; 602.11; 610.1; 614.15; 623.12; 633.3; 640.2; 653.11; 653.12; 704.7; 706.1; 708.10; 708.11; 708.12; 764.3; 797.8; 797.9; 817.5; 853.4; 857.1; 900.5; 906.2; 909.1; 915.6; 915.7; 918.8; 930.6; 952.1; 975.4; 978.11; 989.2; 998.15; 1019.1; 1060.8; 1062.16; 1062.17; 1067.4; 1067.5; 1069.19

C

Cabell, James Branch (1879–1958) American novelist and essayist. 564.15; 660.2

Caesar, [Caius] Julius (100–44 B.C.) Roman general and statesman. 43.4; 252.4; 528.11

Cage, John (1912–) American composer. 53.20; 539.16; 614.16

Cahan, Abraham (1860–1951) American novelist and journalist. 355.5; 630.7; 723.6

Caldwell, Erskine [Preston] (1903–) American novelist and short-story writer. 1069.20

Calhoun, John C[aldwell] (1782–1850) American statesman, Vice President of the United States under John Q. Adams and Andrew Jackson (1825–1832). 34.12; 117.5; 653.13; 746.4; 760.3

Cameroonian Proverbs. 151.3; 480.3

Campbell, Joseph (1904–1987) American educator and author. 115.4; 126.3; 233.6; 233.7; 387.17; 387.18; 418.3; 418.4; 457.1; 468.1; 562.12; 564.16; 564.17; 564.18; 617.1; 718.9; 797.10; 850.1; 927.3; 966.3; 1060.9; 1062.18

Campbell, Thomas (1777–1844) Scottish poet. 287.1; 409.19; 454.5; 689.2

Camus, Albert (1913–1960) French philosopher, novelist, playwright, journalist. 3.2; 4.1; 51.5; 53.21; 53.22; 72.9; 169.2; 175.1; 185.1; 221.24; 284.7; 321.4; 344.2; 363.5; 365.23; 405.3; 405.4; 409.20; 409.21; 433.5; 493.5; 541.3; 652.4; 711.17; 719.11; 729.5; 815.2; 875.4; 948.3; 948.4; 975.5; 998.16; 998.17; 998.18; 1002.7; 1005.2

Canning, George (1740–1827) English statesman. 362.1

Caplan, Mortimer M[axwell] (1916–) American lawyer and public official. 964.3

Capote, Truman (1924–1984) American novelist and short-story writer. 188.4; 266.2; 387.19; 840.1; 1029.2; 1069.21; 1071.8

Capus, Alfred (1858–1922) French journalist and playwright. 510.4; 564.19

Cardarelli, Vincenzo (1887–) Italian poet and critic. 452.2

Carew, Thomas (c. 1598–c. 1639) English poet. 551.19; 598.2; 708.13

Carlyle, Thomas (1795–1881) Scottish-born English prose writer. 9.9; 9.10; 9.11; 26.1; 39.8; 81.3; 81.4; 93.12; 172.1; 197.2; 213.4; 221.25; 222.2; 224.1; 241.3; 261.3; 279.15; 284.8; 321.5; 328.2; 342.2; 387.20; 395.10; 401.4; 419.12; 477.2; 477.3; 501.1; 516.3; 526.4; 526.5; 538.4; 580.6; 614.17; 649.2; 661.4; 689.3; 693.1; 693.2; 704.8; 708.14; 751.5; 822.5; 854.14; 858.8; 868.1; 898.1; 901.4; 923.11; 941.2; 986.4; 998.19; 1007.1; 1009.1; 1012.2; 1026.4; 1035.1; 1037.4; 1042.11; 1063.1; 1065.16; 1065.17; 1067.6; 1068.3; 1069.22; 1069.23

Carroll, Lewis. Pen name of Charles Lutwidge Dodgson (1832–1898) English writer and mathematician. 93.13; 188.5; 221.26; 385.2; 521.1; 526.6; 575.1; 630.8; 661.5; 708.15; 708.16; 723.7; 766.4; 841.2; 942.2; 973.3; 1033.7

Carson, Rachel [Louise] (1907–1964) American writer and scientist. 853.5

Carter, Angela (1940–) English journalist and novelist. 1001.1

Carter, Jimmy (1924–) Thirty-ninth President of the United States. 177.3; 395.11; 395.12; 438.1; 491.5; 623.13; 623.14; 1063.2

Cary, Joyce (1888–1957) Anglo-Irish novelist. 11.2; 61.1; 61.2; 77.7; 201.7; 236.2; 268.6; 367.4; 374.2; 511.1; 517.4; 551.20; 602.12; 653.14; 653.15; 666.3; 722.3; 972.3; 988.2; 1056.1; 1062.19

Casals, Pablo (1876–1973) Spanish cellist and conductor. 615.2

Castaneda, Carlos (1931–) Brazilian anthropologist and author. 1007.2

Cather, Willa [Sibert] (1873–1947) American novelist and short-story writer. 201.8; 221.27; 409.22; 545.2; 915.8; 998.20

Cato the Elder. Full name, Marcus Porcius, Cato. Also known as Cato the Censor (234–149 B.C.) Roman statesman. 337.3; 813.1

Catton, Bruce (1899–1978) American journalist, Civil War historian. 34.13; 240.4; 340.3; 730.3; 889.4; 1043.2

Catullus. Full Latin name, Gaius Valerius Catullus (c. 84–c. 54 B.C.) Roman poet. 170.1; 1062.20

CBS News memorandum. 711.18

Céline, Louis-Ferdinand. Pen name of the doctor Louis-Ferdinand Destouches (1894–1961) French novelist. 718.10

Cellini, Benvenuto (1500–1571) Florentine goldsmith, sculptor, writer of an autobiography. 37.1; 360.4; 577.1; 810.4; 1002.8

Cervantes [Saavedra], Miguel de (1547–1616) Spanish novelist, dramatist, poet. 57.6; 110.2; 116.4; 151.4; 163.1; 195.6; 201.9; 227.6; 231.1; 268.7; 268.8; 306.1; 343.10; 360.5; 365.24; 379.1; 387.21; 387.22; 409.23; 422.4; 425.1; 437.2; 528.12; 555.2; 555.3; 614.18; 724.2; 755.4; 756.1; 814.1; 857.2; 866.3; 867.2; 906.3; 923.12; 968.1; 978.12; 993.1; 1026.5; 1042.12; 1062.21; 1062.22

Cézanne, Paul (1839–1906) French painter. 940.5

Chamfort, Sébastien Roch Nicolas (1741–1794) French writer and wit. 77.8; 93.14; 93.15; 332.8; 440.4; 526.7; 539.17; 540.3; 773.1

Chanel, Coco [Gabrielle Bonheur] (1883–1971) French fashion designer and perfumer. 338.6

Chapman, George (1559?–1634) English poet, translator, playwright. 393.12; 551.21; 880.3; 1072.4

Char, René (1907–) French poet. 9.12; 649.3

Chase, Alexander (1926–) American journalist, editor of the Tipton, Nebraska, *Courier*. 11.3; 28.1; 68.1; 117.6; 202.2; 233.8; 373.1; 433.6; 539.18; 580.7; 614.19; 641.2; 652.5; 718.11; 791.1; 797.11; 900.6; 948.5; 966.4; 982.2; 984.1; 1007.3; 1008.2; 1011.6; 1065.18

Chateaubriand, Vicomte François René de (1768–1848) French writer. 386.2; 580.8

Chaucer, Geoffrey (c. 1343–1400) English poet. 211.1; 338.7; 354.4; 405.5; 411.2; 450.4; 507.1; 624.2; 716.2; 716.3; 854.15; 875.5; 962.2; 965.8

Cheever, John (1912–1982) American short-story writer and novelist. 45.4; 120.1; 221.28; 269.3; 365.25; 365.26; 367.5; 420.1; 429.1; 555.4; 564.20; 602.13; 605.2; 621.2; 624.3; 632.2; 642.1; 650.2; 659.5; 697.2; 743.1; 817.6; 880.4; 882.2; 885.2; 892.10; 892.11; 892.12; 918.9; 923.13; 933.2; 948.6; 992.11; 992.12; 1062.23

Chekhov, Anton Pavlovich (1860–1904) Russian author and physician. 53.23; 485.1; 736.1

Chesterfield, (Lord Philip Dormer Stanhope, 4th Earl of Chesterfield) (1694–1773) English statesman and man of letters. 51.6; 104.8; 136.1; 208.2; 224.2; 226.2; 262.2; 284.9; 284.10; 321.6; 338.8; 369.1; 391.2; 391.3; 411.3; 431.2; 447.6; 451.2; 476.4; 499.1; 522.7; 522.8; 563.4; 563.5; 584.1; 585.3; 589.1; 600.3; 600.4; 653.16; 655.2; 687.1; 690.1; 690.2; 704.9; 726.4; 755.5; 804.3; 831.4; 855.3; 857.3; 876.1; 903.1; 942.3; 962.3; 984.2; 1014.1; 1030.5; 1061.3; 1061.4; 1062.24

Chesterton, G[ilbert] K[eith] (1874–1936) English journalist, essayist, novelist, poet. 3.3; 16.1; 34.14; 53.24; 102.1; 123.9; 133.4; 133.5; 136.2; 137.1; 143.2; 195.7; 198.2; 208.3; 209.5; 264.4; 264.5; 284.11; 321.7; 334.8; 340.4; 345.1; 403.1; 411.4; 413.1; 419.13; 436.5; 446.4; 450.5; 455.1; 497.2; 562.13; 563.6; 565.3; 595.2; 604.8; 613.3; 614.20; 618.1; 623.15; 623.16; 626.4; 630.9; 677.4; 703.2; 704.10; 718.12; 750.3; 784.4; 790.3; 797.12; 854.16; 858.9; 899.2; 987.5; 992.13; 1008.3; 1014.2; 1033.8; 1039.1; 1062.25

Chevalier, Maurice (1888–1972) French singer and actor. 53.25

Chilon (fl. 1st half of 6th c. B.C.) Greek sage, one of the Seven Sages of Greece. 245.1; 738.3; 940.6

Chinese Proverbs. 33.5; 37.2; 75.1; 105.4; 279.16; 321.8; 332.9; 336.1; 401.5; 409.24; 433.7; 503.1; 590.3; 677.5; 766.5; 941.3

Christie, Agatha, [Miller] (1891–1976) English detective-story writer and playwright. 42.1

Chuang Tzu (369?–?286 B.C.) Chinese philosopher and teacher. 149.1; 354.17; 522.61; 923.63

Churchill, Sir Winston [Leonard Spencer] (1874–1965) British statesman and writer. Prime Minister of Great Britain (1940–1945; 1951–1955). 46.2; 50.3; 53.26; 111.2; 150.2; 173.2; 206.6; 229.1; 233.9; 240.5; 284.12; 289.5; 300.3; 335.1; 426.2; 507.2; 711.19; 747.2; 761.4; 762.2; 807.1; 834.1; 915.9; 986.5; 1002.9; 1002.10; 1032.1; 1038.4; 1042.13; 1049.2

Ciardi, John (1916–) American poet, teacher, critic. 1001.2; 1042.14

Cibber, Colley (1671–1757) English playwright, poet, actor. 2.2; 338.9; 460.2; 564.21

Cicero, Marcus Tullius (106–43 B.C.) Roman orator, statesman, man of letters. 55.3; 119.6; 166.4; 181.1; 246.1; 299.9; 363.6; 365.27; 386.3; 389.1; 419.14; 431.3; 454.6; 517.5; 531.2; 540.4; 635.1; 653.17; 681.3; 681.4; 698.6; 711.20; 743.2; 762.3; 858.10; 918.10; 918.11; 977.6; 999.3; 1033.9; 1042.15; 1060.10

Cioran, E. M. (1911–) Rumanian essayist. 94.3; 184.1; 376.5; 640.3; 651.1; 962.4; 1069.24; 1069.25

Clare, John (1793–1864) English poet. 623.17

Clausewitz, Karl von (1780–1831) Prussian army officer and writer. 1042.16; 1042.17; 1042.18

Clay, Henry (1777–1852) American statesman. 127.2; 395.13; 638.1; 819.4

Cleaver, Eldridge (1935–) American writer and a leader of the Black Panther movement. 34.15; 188.6; 424.1; 1042.19

Clemens, Samuel Langhorne *See* Twain, Mark

Cleobulus (fl. 6th c. B.C.) Greek poet, one of Seven Sages of Greece. 888.2

Cocteau, Jean (1889–1963) French poet, novelist, playwright, essayist, film writer, director. 41.5; 53.27; 92.1; 273.1; 282.1; 332.10; 338.10; 365.28; 365.29; 558.9; 592.2; 749.1; 763.3

Colbert, Jean Baptiste (1619–1683) French statesman and Minister of Finance to Louis XIV of France. 963.4

Colby, Frank Moore (1865–1925) American teacher, editor, essayist, humorist. Colby, Frank Moore 27.2; 39.9; 39.10; 131.7; 147.2; 152.3; 188.7; 208.4; 436.6; 586.3; 693.3; 711.21; 844.3; 984.3; 1042.20; 1062.26; 1069.26

Coleman, John S[trider] (1897–1958) American businessman and corporate official. 964.4

Coleridge, Samuel Taylor (1772–1834) English poet, essayist, critic. 39.11; 272.3; 296.1; 299.10; 305.1; 321.9; 401.6; 551.22; 551.23; 551.24; 558.10; 564.22; 708.17; 723.8; 864.1; 906.4; 989.3; 998.21; 1042.21

Colette. Pen name of Sidonie Gabrielle Colette (1873–1954) French novelist. 2.3; 93.16; 165.3; 197.3; 365.30; 385.3; 435.5; 510.5; 550.2; 559.2; 708.18; 708.19; 915.10; 971.2; 982.3; 1008.4; 1051.3; 1055.2; 1069.27

Collins, John Churton (1848–1908) English critic. 88.1

Collins, William (1721–1759) English poet. 785.5

Colton, Charles Caleb (1780–1832) English writer and clergyman. 6.4; 17.17; 17.18; 19.9; 27.3; 31.2; 42.2; 73.3; 93.17; 93.18; 98.4; 111.3; 120.2; 131.8; 131.9; 140.2; 156.2; 166.5; 170.2; 173.3; 191.3; 198.3; 199.3; 201.10; 202.3; 206.7; 213.5; 216.4; 224.3; 235.3; 252.5; 258.1; 290.1; 295.5; 298.6; 299.11; 307.7; 338.11; 338.12; 349.4; 349.5; 356.7; 365.31; 384.4; 396.1; 401.7; 403.2; 406.4; 409.25; 412.5; 414.1; 419.15; 427.4; 428.8; 440.5; 447.7; 451.3; 468.2; 476.5; 479.3; 480.4; 491.6; 517.6; 518.1; 522.9; 528.13; 551.25; 558.11; 564.23; 595.3; 684.4; 698.7; 700.1; 706.2; 708.20; 711.22; 719.12; 719.13; 722.4; 729.6; 733.3; 733.4; 755.6; 762.4; 771.2; 790.4; 797.13; 797.14; 804.4; 904.3; 915.11; 931.1; 945.6; 945.7; 974.1; 984.4; 998.22; 1005.3; 1027.5;

1030.6; 1030.7; 1033.10; 1034.3; 1034.4; 1042.22; 1042.23; 1058.1; 1060.11; 1062.27; 1062.28; 1069.28; 1071.9; 1072.5; 1072.6

Comden, Betty (1919–) American playwright and lyricist. 253.1; 548.4

Commynes, Philippe de (c. 1445–1511) French statesman and historian. 923.14

Comte, [Isidore] Auguste [Marie Francois] (1798–1857) French philosopher and mathematician; founder of positivism. 986.6

Confucius (551?–?479 B.C.) Chinese philosopher. 45.5; 92.2; 112.2; 250.1; 312.2; 334.9; 342.3; 362.2; 388.2; 395.14; 411.5; 433.8; 433.9; 452.3; 493.6; 522.10; 522.11; 524.8; 531.3; 532.4; 551.26; 600.5; 604.9; 610.2; 734.4; 761.5; 789.1; 808.3; 848.8; 916.2; 952.2; 965.9; 998.23; 998.24; 1008.5; 1033.11; 1048.12; 1071.10

Congolese Proverbs. 118.1; 392.3

Congreve, William (1670–1729) English playwright. 72.10; 156.3; 198.4; 224.4; 231.2; 241.4; 405.6; 476.6; 551.27; 551.28; 564.24; 614.21; 793.1; 855.4; 856.2; 865.3; 979.4; 1062.29; 1062.30

Conklin, Edwin Grant (1863–1952) American zoologist. 363.7

Connolly, Cyril [Vernon] (1903–1974) English essayist, critic, novelist. 53.28; 93.19; 125.3; 131.10; 133.6; 133.7; 194.2; 321.10; 329.7; 409.26; 412.6; 416.5; 449.6; 450.6; 472.1; 504.6; 539.19; 556.2; 564.25; 564.26; 580.9; 581.11; 627.2; 645.3; 645.4; 708.21; 742.2; 784.5; 797.15; 804.5; 858.11; 892.13; 918.12; 944.1; 948.7; 989.4; 998.25; 1020.1; 1042.24; 1060.12; 1062.31; 1062.32; 1072.7

Conrad, Joseph. Original name, Teodor Jósef Konrad Korzeniowski (1857–1924) Polish-born English novelist. 9.13; 33.6; 53.29; 79.1; 115.5; 116.5; 145.3; 219.2; 288.5; 315.2; 343.11; 344.3; 387.23; 395.15; 423.1; 441.1; 443.4; 449.7; 449.8; 450.7; 524.9; 539.20; 547.2; 581.12; 603.2; 663.3; 675.2; 681.5; 690.3; 719.14; 726.5; 804.6; 806.1; 819.5; 834.2; 839.3; 839.4; 853.6; 853.7; 853.8; 895.1; 1007.4; 1055.3; 1059.2; 1059.3; 1064.9; 1064.10; 1069.29

Constant, Benjamin. Full name, Henri Benjamin Constant de Rebecque (1767–1830) Swiss-born French politician, journalist, novelist. 395.16

Cooke, [Alfred] Alistair (1908–) English-born American essayist and journalist. 34.16; 297.5; 617.2; 929.6; 967.4

Coolidge, [John] Calvin (1872–1933) Thirtieth President of the United States (1923–1929). 104.9; 229.2; 750.4; 1013.1

Cooper, Leonard American historian. 173.4

Corneille, Pierre (1606–1684) French playwright. 226.3; 227.7; 271.4; 307.8; 360.6; 412.7; 519.5; 537.9; 551.29; 551.30; 664.2; 719.15; 798.1; 817.7; 937.3; 945.8; 1032.2

Cort, David (1904–) American editor and writer. 259.2; 892.14

Cortázar, Julio (1914–) Argentine novelist, short-story writer, poet. 406.5; 545.3; 874.2; 614.22

Costello, Mark American writer. 614.23; 614.24; 614.25

Cotterell, Geoffrey (1919–) English writer. 1069.30

Courteline, Georges. Pseudonym of Georges Moineaux (1860–1929) French humorist, sometimes called "the Mark Twain of France." 470.1; 552.2; 670.12; 1062.33; 1062.34; 1071.11

Cousin, Victor (1792–1867) French philosopher and teacher. 445.1

Coward, Noël [Pierce] (1899–1973) English playwright, composer, actor. 194.3; 358.1; 972.4; 992.14

Cowell, Henry Dixon (1897–1965) American composer. 614.26

Cowley, Abraham (1618–1667) English poet and essayist. 131.11; 539.21; 553.1; 729.7; 804.7

Cowley, Hannah (1743–1809) English playwright. 1062.35

Cowley, Malcolm (1898–) American critic and poet. 1069.31

Cowper, William (1731–1800) English poet. 194.4; 194.5; 363.8; 401.8; 409.27; 446.5; 708.22; 942.4; 992.15; 1042.25; 1060.13

Cox, Harvey [Gallagher] (1929–) American educator and writer. 85.6; 126.4; 131.12; 492.1; 711.23; 810.5

Crébillon, Prosper Jolyot. Pen name of Prosper Jolyot, sieur de Crais-Billon (1674–1762) French playwright. 520.1

Crèvecoeur, Michel Guillaume Jean de. Pen name, J. Hector St. John (1735–1813) French writer, agronomist, traveler, settler in America. 797.16

Crane, Stephen [Townley] (1871–1900) American novelist, short-story writer, poet, war correspondent. 986.7

Crashaw, Richard (1612–1649) English metaphysical poet. 66.2

Cratinus (c. 520–c. 423 B.C.) Greek playwright. 268.9

Cravens, Kathryn (c. 520–c. 423 B.C.) Contemporary American journalist, writer, radio news commentator. 349.6

Creeley, Robert [White] (1926–) American poet, editor, novelist. 399.1

Creighton, Mandell (1843–1901) English prelate and historian. 668.1

Crockett, David (1786–1836) American frontiersman, soldier, public official. 822.6

Crowley, Mart (1925–) American playwright. 41.6; 72.11; 424.2; 892.15

Cruse, Heloise (1599–1658) Contemporary American writer. 137.2

Cullen, Countee (1903–1946) American poet. 541.4; 552.3; 742.3

Cumberland, Richard (1632–1718) English bishop. 10.3

Cummings, E[dward] E[stlin]. *Also* e. e. cummings (1894–1962) American poet. 271.5; 444.8; 447.8; 521.2; 711.24

Cuomo, Mario (1932–) Former Governor of New York. 710.3

Curran, John Philpot (1750–1817) Irish orator and magistrate. 537.10

D

Dahlberg, Edward (1900–) American novelist and critic. 21.2; 30.1; 56.2; 116.6; 119.7; 161.1; 235.4; 299.12; 342.4; 496.1; 517.7; 539.22; 876.2; 892.16; 946.7

Daily Mail. 326.2

d'Alembert, Jean Le Rond (1717–1783) French mathematician and skeptical philosopher. 1061.5

D'Amato, Senator Alfonse (19??–) American politician. 680.2

Daniels, Jonathan [Worth] (1902–) American newspaperman, writer, public official. 93.20

Daninos, Pierre (1913–) French writer. 289.6; 289.7; 289.8; 378.1

Danish Proverbs. 97.3; 123.10; 221.29; 222.3; 268.10; 295.6; 356.8; 400.4; 428.9; 480.5; 528.14; 755.7; 784.6; 795.3; 971.3

Dankevich, Konstantin (1902–) Contemporary Russian composer. 207.11

Dante. Full name, Dante Alighieri (1265–1321) Italian poet. 167.2; 176.3; 238.6; 240.6; 329.8; 332.11; 415.3; 450.8; 516.4; 517.8; 551.31; 551.32; 623.18; 723.9; 733.5; 754.3; 785.6; 791.2; 927.4; 1033.12; 1056.2

Darrow, Clarence S. (1857–1938) American lawyer, lecturer, reformer, writer. 1013.2

Darwin, Charles [Robert] (1809–1882) English naturalist. 308.4; 975.6

d'Aurevilly, Jules Barbey (1808–1889) French novelist and critic. 53.30; 94.1; 133.2

Davies, Paul (1946–) American scientist and writer. 285.1; 415.4; 623.19; 921.3; 1017.3

Davies, W[illiam] H[enry] (1871–1940) Welsh-born English poet. 533.3

Davis, Elmer [Holmes] (1890–1958) American journalist and radio commentator. 586.4; 1071.12

Davis, Francis (1946–) American author and jazz critic. 614.27
Davis, David (1815–1886) American jurist. Associate justice of the U.S. Supreme Court. 182.1
Day, Clarence [Shepard], Jr. (1874–1935) American writer. 10.4; 41.7; 41.8; 42.3; 53.31; 65.5; 83.3; 211.2; 293.4; 299.13; 308.5; 365.32; 438.2; 522.12; 602.14; 604.10; 708.23; 784.7; 823.4; 875.6; 1056.3; 1065.19
Day-Lewis, C[ecil] (1904–1972) Irish-born English poet laureate and writer of detective stories. 673.2
de Bussy-Rabutin, Roger (1618–1693) French soldier and writer. 719.16; 806.2
de Florian, Jean Pierre Claris (1755–1794) French novelist, playwright, fabulist. 551.33
de Goncourt, Edmond (1830–1870) French writers and collaborators, known as the Brothers Goncourt. 70.2; 188.15; 666.6; 682.8; 1061.8
de Goncourt, Jules [Alfred Huot] (1830–1870) French writers and collaborators, known as the Brothers Goncourt. 42.4; 70.2; 188.15; 207.24; 307.17; 344.16; 419.26; 589.5; 630.10; 666.6; 682.8; 739.3; 896.10; 978.23; 1004.10; 1004.11; 1061.8; 1062.63
de Kooning, Willem (1904–) Dutch painter. 53.32
de La Harpe, Jean-François (1739–1803) French poet and playwright. 893.1
de Laclos, Pierre [Ambrose François] Choderlos (1741–1803) French artillery officer and writer. 198.5
deLacretelle, Jacques (1888–) French novelist. 194.6
de Lautréamont, Comte. Pen name of Isidore Lucien Ducasse (1846–1870) French poet. 963.5
De Mille, Agnes [George] (1905–) American dancer, choreographer, writer. 215.1
De Mille, Cecil B[lount] (1881–1959) American motion-picture producer and director. 686.1
de Montherlant, Henry [Millon] (1896–1972) French playwright, novelist, poet, essayist. 21.3; 221.30
De Quincey, Thomas (1785–1859) English essayist and critic. 165.4; 174.3; 623.20; 743.3; 918.13; 946.8; 1070.4
de Staël, Mme. Born Anne Louise Germaine Necker (1766–1817) Swiss-born French writer. 94.4
de Tocqueville, Count Alexis [Charles Henri Maurice Clérel] (1805–1859) French political leader, historian, writer. 34.17; 233.11; 233.12; 233.13; 374.3; 395.17; 471.1; 563.7; 719.17; 731.1; 734.5; 750.5; 786.2; 945.9
de Vigny Alfred [Victor] (1797–1863) French poet, playwright, novelist. 70.5
De Vries, Peter (1910–1993) American novelist and humorist. 16.2; 205.2; 237.1; 239.3; 499.2; 521.3; 564.27; 608.3; 687.2; 766.6; 978.13; 1069.32
Debs, Eugene V[ictor] (1855–1926) American socialist leader. 100.2; 109.1; 204.3; 656.5; 682.4; 690.4; 718.13; 735.2; 735.3; 735.4; 934.1
Deffand [Marie de Vichy-Chamrond], Marquise du. Also called Mme. du Deffand (1697–1780) French noblewoman, leader in social, literary, philosophical circles. 1062.36
Defoe, Daniel (1660–1731) Born Daniel Foe. English novelist, pamphleteer, journalist, political agent. 517.9
de Gaulle, Charles [André Joseph Marie] (1890–1970) French general and statesman. President of the Fifth Republic of France (1958–1969). 247.3; 361.4; 531.4; 641.3; 658.4; 711.25; 859.1; 930.7; 994.1
Delacroix [Ferdinand Victor Eugène] (1799–1863) French painter; leader of the romantic school of painting. 790.5
Dement, William (1928–) American psychiatrist. 266.3
Demetrius of Phalerum (c. 345–c. 280 B.C.) Greek orator and statesman. 283.1; 751.6
Democritus (c. 460–c. 370 B.C.) Thracian philosopher. 186.4
De Morgan, Augustus (1806–1871) English mathematician and logician. 669.2
Descartes, René (1596–1650) French philosopher and mathematician. 93.21; 148.1; 401.9; 409.28; 493.7; 694.5; 975.7
Destouches, Louis-Ferdinand *See* Céline, Louis-Ferdinand
Destouches, Philippe. Pen name of Philippe Néricault (1680–1754) French playwright. 207.12; 693.4
Deval, Jacques (1894–1972) French playwright. 1062.37
Dewey, John (1859–1952) American teacher, philosopher, educational reformer. 117.7; 279.17; 443.5; 797.17
Dhéry, Robert (1921–) French actor, director, writer. 972.5
d'Holbach, [Paul Henri Dietrich] Baron (1723–1789) French materialist philosopher. 797.18
Dick, Philip K. (1928–1982) American novelist and short-story writer. 225.4; 344.4; 418.5; 517.10; 558.12; 784.8; 786.3; 915.12; 1060.14; 1069.33
Dickens, Charles (1812–1870) English novelist. 34.18; 34.19; 65.6; 97.4; 123.11; 123.12; 152.4; 260.1; 267.4; 267.5; 267.6; 334.10; 363.9; 376.6; 422.5; 422.6; 438.3; 443.6; 489.3; 509.3; 528.15; 546.1; 557.1; 562.14; 586.5; 627.3; 653.18; 666.4; 699.2; 708.24; 760.4; 780.2; 796.1; 854.17; 970.1; 977.7; 1052.2; 1070.5
Dickinson, Emily [Elizabeth] (1830–1886) American poet. 17.20; 39.13; 72.12; 82.4; 93.22; 175.2; 187.1; 221.31; 221.32; 221.33; 221.34; 239.4; 258.2; 278.1; 330.10; 332.12; 332.13; 336.2; 340.5; 360.7; 387.24; 409.29; 422.7; 427.5; 450.9; 481.1; 482.2; 503.2; 519.6; 526.8; 551.34; 551.35; 551.36; 606.7; 610.3; 676.8; 676.9; 698.8; 716.4; 723.10; 799.1; 818.1; 850.2; 878.1; 898.2; 898.3; 918.14; 945.10; 946.9; 946.10; 960.1; 978.14; 998.26; 998.27; 1004.6; 1011.7; 1064.11
Dickinson, John. Pen name, Fabius (1732–1808), American lawyer and pamphleteer. 964.5
Diderot, Denis (1713–1784) French encyclopedist, materialistic philosopher, novelist, satirist, playwright, art critic. 57.7; 433.10; 528.16; 559.3; 640.4; 661.6; 675.3; 675.4; 675.5; 694.6; 904.4; 916.3; 1033.13
Didion, Joan (1934–) American novelist and essayist. 76.3; 632.3; 632.4
Dillard, Annie (1945–) American writer. 72.13; 90.2; 126.5; 308.6; 478.3; 539.23; 539.24; 539.25; 541.5; 590.4; 623.21; 853.9; 861.1; 897.3; 927.5; 950.2; 978.15
Dimnet, Ernest (1866–1954) French abbé and writer. 93.23; 321.11; 376.7
Dinesen, Isak. Pen name of Baroness Karen Blixen, née Dinesen (1885–1962) Danish short-story writer. 551.37; 562.15; 855.5; 1071.13
Diogenes the Cynic (c. 400–c. 325 B.C.) Greek philosopher. 57.8; 193.1; 204.4; 893.2
Dionysius the Elder (c. 430–367 B.C.) Tyrant of Syracuse, politician, militarist. 923.15
Dior, Christian (1905–1957) French fashion designer. 513.2; 1062.38
Dirksen, Everett M[cKinley] (1896–1969) American political leader. 117.8
Disraeli, Benjamin, 1st Earl of Beaconsfield (1804–1881) English statesman and novelist. 44.1; 51.7; 81.5; 129.2; 133.8; 135.1; 178.3; 206.8; 207.13; 322.1; 376.8; 447.9; 487.3; 487.4; 518.2; 522.13; 540.5; 564.28; 621.3; 653.19; 658.5; 702.3; 729.8; 740.1; 761.6; 771.3; 904.5; 986.8; 1069.34; 1071.14
Doctorow, E. L. (1931–) American novelist, drama-

tist, short-story writer. 53.33; 178.4; 182.2; 238.7; 328.3; 344.5; 344.6; 419.16; 632.5; 676.10; 730.4; 776.1; 900.7; 965.10; 1069.35
Doddridge, Philip (1702–1751) English non-conformist clergyman. 513.3
Donne, John (1572?–1631) English metaphysical poet and divine. 2.4; 122.4; 125.4; 144.2; 151.5; 152.5; 174.4; 183.2; 195.8; 221.35; 221.36; 334.11; 342.5; 387.25; 393.13; 409.30; 433.11; 466.1; 514.4; 535.2; 541.6; 551.38; 551.39; 551.40; 551.41; 551.42; 551.43; 551.44; 562.16; 592.3; 653.20; 704.11; 708.25; 718.14; 741.4; 785.7; 880.5; 892.17; 892.18; 896.3; 900.8; 900.9; 906.5; 952.3; 992.16; 998.28; 999.4; 1005.4; 1033.14; 1042.26; 1055.4; 1062.39; 1067.7
Dooley, Mr. *See* Dunne, Finley Peter
Dorris, Michael (1945–) American writer and teacher. 34.20; 274.6; 450.10; 551.45
Dos Passos, John [Roderigo] (1896–1970) American novelist, poet, playwright, essayist. 355.6; 545.4
Dostoyevsky, Fyodor Mikhailovich (1821–1881) Russian novelist. 4.2; 58.2; 111.4; 124.3; 149.2; 175.3; 239.5; 251.3; 409.31; 431.4; 433.12; 479.4; 522.14; 526.9; 551.46; 551.47; 602.15; 758.3; 783.1; 785.8; 843.1; 861.2; 946.11; 1065.20; 1065.21
Douglas, Lord Alfred [Bruce] (1870–1945) English poet. 708.26
Douglass, Frederick (1817?–1895) American abolitionist, orator, journalist. 85.7; 676.11; 889.5; 889.6
Downes, [Edwin] Olin (1886–1955) American music critic. 207.14; 614.28; 614.29
Doyle, Sir Arthur Conan (1859–1930) English physician and detective-story writer. 194.7; 204.6; 522.15; 546.2; 962.5; 974.2; 998.29
Drakulic, Slavenka Yugoslavian journalist (1933–). 670.13
Dryden, John (1631–1700) English poet, dramatist, critic. 195.9; 221.37; 221.38; 233.14; 240.7; 262.3; 359.4; 359.5; 401.10; 409.32; 510.6; 539.26; 551.48; 551.49; 551.50; 559.4; 562.17; 588.3; 614.30; 677.6; 698.9; 705.1; 729.9; 740.2; 805.2; 819.6; 998.30; 1002.11; 1033.15; 1042.27; 1048.13
du Bartas, Seigneur, Guillaume de Salluste (1544–1590) French poet and soldier. 311.1
du Bartas, Seigneur, Guillaume de Salluste (1544–1590) French poet and soldier. 481.2
Du Bois, W[illiam] E[dward] B[urghardt] (1868–1963) American writer, editor, teacher, lecturer. 34.21; 204.5; 279.18; 620.3; 718.8; 775.4; 775.5; 775.6; 1008.6; 1038.5
Du Bos, Charles (1882–1939) French critic. 471.2; 717.1
Dubos, René Jules (1901–1982) French-born American bacteriologist. 562.18; 562.19
Dubus, André (1936–) American short-story writer and essayist. 28.2; 344.7; 454.7; 545.5; 826.2; 980.2
Duhamel, Georges. Pen name Denis Thévenin (1884–1966) French playwright, novelist, critic, poet. 299.14
Dumas, Alexandre. Known as Dumas fils (1824–1895) French playwright, illegitimate son of Alexandre Dumas, the novelist. 279.19; 564.29
Dunbar, Paul Laurence (1872–1906) American poet. 539.27
Dunne, Finley Peter (1867–1936) American journalist and humorist, creator of "Mr. Dooley." 34.22; 40.1; 70.1; 133.9; 263.2; 308.7; 382.1; 403.3; 420.2; 475.1; 490.1; 517.11; 517.12; 551.51; 588.4; 602.16; 629.1; 632.6; 657.5; 709.2; 709.3; 710.4; 711.26; 730.5; 762.5; 763.4; 764.4; 790.6; 790.7; 829.2; 849.4; 896.4; 908.1; 957.1; 997.1; 1013.3; 1028.1; 1030.8; 1031.1; 1042.28
Durant, Will[iam James] (1885–) American teacher, philosopher, historian. 898.4
Duras, Marguerite (1914–) French writer. 343.12; 1042.29
Dürrenmatt, Friedrich (1921–) Swiss novelist, playwright, short-story writer, writing in German. 17.21; 17.22; 53.34; 53.35; 53.36; 169.3; 201.11; 207.15; 405.7; 450.11; 510.7; 521.4; 551.52; 551.53; 564.30; 614.31; 786.4; 948.8; 998.31; 998.32; 998.33; 998.34; 1011.8; 1062.40; 1062.41
Dürrenmatt, Friedrich (1921–) Swiss novelist, playwright, short-story writer, writing in German. 432.1; 641.4; 668.2; 938.1; 975.8
Dutch Proverbs. 87.4; 111.5; 238.8; 281.2; 320.1; 463.2; 681.6; 706.3

E

Eban, Abba (1915–) South African-born Israeli diplomat and politician. 419.17; 841.3; 1068.4
Eberhart, Richard (1904–) American poet and teacher. 590.5; 942.5
Echeverría, Esteban (1809–1851) Argentine poet and political leader. 491.7
Eckermann, Johann Peter (1792–1854) German writer, friend, literary assistant to Goethe. 925.1
Edman, Irwin (1896–1954) American philosopher and educator. 197.4; 307.9; 418.6; 885.3; 917.1
Egyptian Proverbs. 75.2; 299.15; 366.2
Ehrenburg, Ilya [Grigoryevich] (1891–1967) Russian novelist, poet, journalist. 53.37; 53.38; 279.20; 299.16
Ehrenreich, Barbara (1941–) American author. 984.5
Eich, Günter (1907–) German poet. 641.5
Einstein, Albert (1879–1955) German-Swiss-American physicist. 30.2; 150.3; 194.8; 328.4; 363.10; 395.18; 406.6; 588.5; 590.6; 795.4; 797.19; 849.5; 849.6; 850.3; 930.8; 984.6; 998.35; 1019.2; 1067.9.
Eiseley, Loren 53.39; 73.4; 242.3; 346.1; 352.1; 368.7; 532.5; 539.28; 540.6; 562.20; 580.10; 580.11; 623.22; 708.27; 853.10
Eisenhower, Dwight D[avid] (1890–1969) American general and thirty-fourth President of the United States (1953–1961). 34.23; 291.2; 337.4; 345.2; 386.4; 419.18; 730.6; 101.1
Eliot, George. Pen name of Mary Ann or Marian Evans (1819–1880) English novelist. 15.2; 41.9; 166.6; 227.8; 259.3; 318.1; 365.33; 404.6; 436.7; 492.2; 524.10; 564.31; 565.4; 581.13; 582.5; 583.1; 627.4; 747.3; 883.2; 941.4; 1062.42; 1062.43; 1062.44; 1071.15
Eliot, T[homas] S[tearns] (1888–1965) American-born English poet, critic, editor, playwright. 9.14; 12.1; 41.10; 53.40; 53.41; 80.2; 93.24; 117.9; 207.16; 210.5; 219.3; 221.39; 254.3; 295.7; 305.2; 334.12; 376.9; 413.2; 416.6; 419.19; 473.2; 524.11; 539.29; 545.6; 551.54; 562.21; 581.14; 586.6; 653.21; 708.28; 708.29; 708.30; 708.31; 708.32; 758.4; 784.9; 806.3; 819.7; 854.18; 863.2; 868.2; 873.3; 875.7; 900.10; 913.2; 931.2; 945.11; 951.1; 967.5; 972.6; 985.2; 986.9; 1019.3; 1064.12; 1067.10
Elkin, Stanley (1930–) American author. 53.42
Elliott, Ebenezer (1781–1849) English poet, called the Corn-Law Rhymer. 150.4
Ellis, [Henry] Havelock (1859–1939) English psychologist, essayist, art critic. 53.43; 117.10; 215.2; 216.5; 510.8; 539.30; 554.1; 570.2; 892.19; 942.6; 942.7; 946.12; 1065.22
Ellison, Ralph [Waldo] (1914–1994) American writer and educator. 30.3; 53.44; 344.8; 639.1; 719.18; 859.2; 915.13

Emerson, Ralph Waldo (1803–1882) American poet, essayist, philosopher. 1.3; 6.5; 6.6; 7.2; 9.15; 9.16; 9.17; 10.5; 15.3; 17.23; 19.10; 20.2; 21.4; 30.4; 34.24; 45.6; 53.45; 53.46; 53.47; 55.4; 56.3; 65.7; 72.14; 72.15; 72.16; 72.17; 72.18; 72.19; 75.3; 77.9; 93.25; 93.26; 93.27; 93.28; 95.3; 110.3; 110.4; 119.8; 119.9; 119.10; 123.13; 123.14; 123.15; 124.4; 125.5; 125.6; 125.7; 125.8; 126.6; 126.7; 128.1; 128.2; 131.13; 131.14; 132.2; 133.10; 137.3; 148.2; 148.3; 148.4; 149.3; 149.4; 152.6; 154.1; 171.3; 171.4; 173.5; 174.5; 176.4; 178.5; 178.6; 179.1; 184.2; 188.8; 188.9; 188.10; 195.10; 197.5; 199.4; 201.12; 204.7; 205.3; 206.9; 207.17; 207.18; 208.5; 210.6; 210.7; 210.8; 211.3; 216.6; 221.40; 227.9; 229.3; 231.3; 233.15; 241.5; 244.2; 246.2; 261.4; 264.6; 266.4; 268.11; 268.12; 269.4; 271.6; 279.21; 279.22; 279.23; 279.24; 283.2; 286.2; 289.9; 293.5; 295.8; 298.7; 300.4; 303.2; 305.3; 307.10; 307.11; 316.2; 319.2; 319.3; 321.12; 321.13; 325.1; 326.3; 328.5; 328.6; 328.7; 330.11; 333.4; 333.5; 335.2; 335.3; 340.6; 341.2; 342.6; 343.13; 344.9; 344.10; 344.11; 349.7; 360.8; 363.11; 363.12; 363.13; 363.14; 365.34; 365.35; 365.36; 365.37; 367.6; 368.8; 372.1; 376.10; 376.11; 376.12; 377.2; 377.3; 378.2; 384.5; 384.6; 384.7; 387.26; 387.27; 387.28; 387.29; 390.3; 391.4; 392.4; 392.5; 393.14; 393.15; 393.16; 400.5; 401.11; 401.12; 401.13; 401.14; 403.4; 404.7; 408.1; 409.33; 410.1; 413.3; 414.2; 415.5; 418.7; 418.8; 419.20; 419.21; 422.8; 422.9; 422.10; 427.6; 428.10; 428.11; 430.1; 435.6; 440.6; 442.3; 449.9; 450.12; 450.13; 453.1; 460.3; 464.2; 464.3; 467.1; 469.3; 469.4; 473.3; 473.4; 480.6; 480.7; 485.2; 486.1; 487.5; 487.6; 492.3; 493.8; 496.2; 501.2; 504.7; 504.8; 507.3; 515.1; 519.7; 522.16; 522.17; 524.12; 526.10; 528.17; 528.18; 531.5; 533.4; 538.5; 539.31; 539.32; 542.4; 551.55; 551.56; 551.57; 555.5; 555.6; 557.2; 558.13; 559.5; 562.22; 563.8; 563.9; 563.10; 563.11; 563.12; 564.32; 564.33; 566.2; 574.3; 578.2; 585.4; 586.7; 588.6; 590.7; 597.1; 602.17; 604.11; 608.4; 609.1; 610.4; 612.1; 614.32; 621.4; 621.5; 623.23; 623.24; 623.25; 623.26; 623.27; 623.28; 625.1; 627.5; 646.4; 647.1; 653.22; 653.23; 653.24; 656.6; 662.1; 663.4; 665.2; 665.3; 666.5; 674.1; 675.6; 676.12; 678.3; 680.3; 680.4; 682.5; 682.6; 683.4; 683.5; 684.5; 687.3; 688.3; 689.4; 689.5; 697.3; 698.10; 699.3; 703.3; 704.12; 708.33; 708.34; 708.35; 708.36; 719.19; 719.20; 719.21; 720.1; 721.1; 723.11; 723.12; 724.3; 724.4; 724.5; 729.10; 729.11; 729.12; 746.5; 748.1; 753.1; 755.8; 762.6; 766.7; 775.7; 776.2; 778.2; 782.2; 783.2; 790.8; 790.9; 794.2; 797.20; 797.21; 797.22; 797.23; 798.2; 804.8; 804.9; 806.4; 816.1; 819.8; 819.9; 822.7; 825.1; 827.1; 831.5; 841.4; 842.1; 848.9; 848.10; 848.11; 848.12; 849.7; 850.4; 850.5; 858.12; 859.3; 860.1; 867.3; 867.4; 867.5; 868.3; 869.1; 870.1; 873.4; 875.8; 875.9; 877.1; 880.6; 880.7; 883.3; 884.1; 886.4; 886.5; 896.5; 896.6; 896.7; 897.4; 899.3; 901.5; 901.6; 901.7; 913.3; 914.1; 914.2; 915.14; 915.15; 917.2; 917.3; 918.15; 918.16; 918.17; 923.16; 923.17; 926.2; 927.6; 930.9; 930.10; 930.11; 934.2; 940.7; 946.13; 948.9; 951.2; 960.2; 960.3; 962.6; 965.11; 965.12; 973.4; 973.5; 974.3; 975.9; 975.10; 975.11; 975.12; 975.13; 977.8; 978.16; 980.3; 980.4; 982.4; 982.5; 992.17; 992.18; 992.19; 992.20; 997.2; 997.3; 998.36; 998.37; 998.38; 998.39; 999.5; 1000.2; 1000.3; 1003.2; 1004.7; 1008.7; 1017.4; 1017.5; 1017.6; 1019.4; 1026.6; 1030.9; 1033.16; 1033.17; 1033.18; 1034.5; 1034.6; 1037.5; 1038.6; 1040.2; 1040.3; 1042.30; 1048.14; 1048.15; 1048.16; 1055.5; 1058.2; 1060.15; 1060.16; 1060.17; 1061.6; 1062.45; 1062.46; 1062.47; 1063.3; 1065.23; 1065.24; 1065.25; 1065.26; 1069.36; 1069.37; 1069.38; 1069.39; 1070.6; 1071.16

"Endless Volumes" editorial. 93.56

English Proverbs. 1.4; 2.5; 17.24; 45.7; 48.3; 56.4; 75.4; 76.4; 84.1; 87.5; 88.2; 89.1; 93.29; 104.10; 109.2; 118.2; 120.3; 123.16; 139.3; 155.3; 174.6; 189.3; 213.6; 216.7; 221.41; 222.4; 224.5; 231.4; 245.2; 245.3; 263.3; 274.7; 274.8; 281.3; 281.4; 321.14; 342.7; 342.8; 354.5; 356.9; 369.2; 379.2; 399.2; 417.1; 476.7; 551.58; 564.34; 606.8; 653.25; 703.4; 746.6; 754.4; 780.3; 786.5; 797.24; 804.10; 810.6; 817.8; 857.4; 873.5; 894.1; 898.5; 941.5; 946.14; 978.17; 992.21; 1062.48

Epictetus (fl. A.D. 100) Greek philosopher. 9.18; 55.5; 61.3; 124.5; 166.7; 221.42; 245.4; 267.7; 279.25; 343.14; 363.15; 373.2; 393.17; 401.15; 542.5; 562.23; 625.2; 657.6; 694.7; 735.5; 785.9; 862.4; 867.6; 873.6; 915.16; 923.18; 974.4; 998.40; 1056.4; 1069.40

Epicurus (341–270 B.C.) Greek philosopher. 9.19; 17.25; 51.8; 119.11; 186.5; 221.43; 221.44; 238.9; 343.15; 363.16; 365.38; 368.9; 368.10; 409.34; 426.3; 494.3; 517.13; 541.7; 589.2; 589.3; 624.4; 694.8; 705.2; 880.8; 1048.17; 1060.18; 1070.7

Erasmus, Desiderius (1466–1536) Dutch scholar and philosopher. 1042.31

Erdrich, Louise (1954–) American novelist and poet. 221.45; 330.12; 390.4; 415.6; 447.10; 539.33; 551.59; 551.60; 602.18; 611.3; 623.29; 948.10; 978.18; 1007.5; 1062.49

Erikson, Erik H[omburger] (1902–) German-born American psychoanalyst and educator. 34.25; 174.7; 363.17; 541.8

Ethiopian Proverbs. 165.5; 307.12

Euclid (fl. 300 B.C.) Greek mathematician. 570.3

Euripides (480–405 B.C.) Greek tragic playwright. 1.5; 17.26; 17.27; 17.28; 17.29; 24.1; 39.14; 55.6; 57.9; 61.4; 61.5; 72.20; 99.2; 100.3; 103.4; 111.6; 116.7; 117.11; 117.12; 132.3; 139.4; 148.5; 155.4; 171.5; 173.6; 174.8; 176.5; 181.2; 186.6; 195.11; 195.12; 216.8; 218.1; 221.46; 221.47; 221.48; 250.2; 265.1; 268.13; 274.9; 279.26; 281.5; 281.6; 284.13; 287.2; 288.6; 288.7; 304.1; 307.13; 311.3; 321.15; 330.13; 336.3; 340.7; 342.9; 356.10; 360.9; 360.10; 360.11; 360.12; 360.13; 365.39; 365.40; 365.41; 365.42; 365.43; 368.11; 384.8; 387.30; 387.31; 389.2; 389.3; 390.5; 394.2; 395.19; 401.16; 409.35; 409.36; 423.2; 425.2; 426.4; 427.7; 440.7; 472.2; 475.2; 477.4; 482.3; 493.9; 498.2; 516.5; 517.14; 522.18; 528.19; 528.20; 539.34; 539.35; 541.9; 541.10; 551.61; 551.62; 555.7; 564.35; 564.36; 564.37; 564.38; 564.39; 597.2; 597.3; 597.4; 602.19; 624.5; 624.6; 653.26; 653.27; 653.28; 653.29; 656.7; 670.14; 670.15; 670.16; 670.17; 670.18; 680.5; 686.2; 690.5; 711.27; 718.15; 719.22; 719.23; 746.7; 750.6; 754.5; 754.6; 785.10; 796.2; 797.25; 797.26; 815.5; 815.6; 817.9; 856.3; 867.7; 889.7; 892.20; 898.6; 904.6; 910.1; 913.4; 937.4; 945.12; 947.2; 969.1; 979.5; 990.7; 1004.8; 1011.9; 1011.10; 1032.3; 1033.19; 1048.18; 1048.19; 1048.20; 1052.3; 1052.4; 1055.6; 1060.19; 1062.50; 1062.51; 1062.52; 1062.53; 1062.54; 1065.27; 1070.8

Evans, Bergen (1904–) American educator and writer. 531.6

Evarts, William Maxwell (1818–1901) American lawyer and statesman. 998.41

Evenus [of Paros] (5th c. B.C.)

Greek elegist and sophist. 406.7

F
Faber, Harold Contemporary American newspaperman and editor. 528.21
Fabius *See* Dickinson, John
Fables of Bidpai. 705.3; 815.7
Fadiman, Clifton (1904–) American critic, lecturer, radio entertainer, editor. 355.7; 398.3
Fallows, James M[ackenzie] (1949–) American writer and editor. 13.1; 34.26; 102.2; 229.4; 241.6; 775.8; 856.4; 913.5; 913.6
Faludi, Susan (1959–) American journalist. 267.8; 297.6; 297.7; 338.13; 564.40; 564.41; 581.15; 581.16; 823.5; 847.1; 1062.55
Fanon, Frantz (1925–1961) French psychiatrist and writer. 132.4; 210.9; 1065.28
Farb, Peter (1929–1980) American linguist, anthropologist, author. 77.10; 117.13; 123.17; 149.5; 149.6; 188.11; 213.7; 213.8; 244.3; 294.2; 398.4; 412.8; 502.1; 551.63; 564.42; 849.8; 913.7; 1064.13
Fargue, Léon-Paul (1876–1947) French poet. 587.2
Farouk or Faruk I (1920–1965) King of Egypt, 1936–1952. 520.2
Farquhar, George (1678–1707) English playwright. 690.6; 718.16; 972.7; 1062.56
Farrar, John [Chipman] (1896–1974) American editor, publisher, poet. 764.5
Farrell, James T[homas] (1904–) American novelist. 34.27
Faulkner, William (1897–1962) American novelist and short-story writer. 53.48; 53.49; 125.9; 775.9; 998.42; 1065.29; 1067.11; 1069.41; 1069.42; 1069.43
Fénelon [François de Salignac de la Mothe-] (1651–1715) French prelate and writer. 469.5; 551.64
Fielding, Henry (1707–1754) English novelist. 138.2; 207.19; 221.49; 263.4; 329.9; 409.37; 846.1
Fielding, Temple [Hornaday] (1913–) American writer, foreign correspondent, travel writer. 992.22
Fisher, M[ary] F[rances] K[ennedy] (1908–1992) American writer. 598.3
Fitch, James Marston (1909–) American educator. 64.3
Fitzgerald, F[rancis] Scott [Key] (1896–1940) American novelist and short-story writer. 34.28; 34.29; 53.50; 72.21; 94.5; 123.18; 123.19; 188.12; 225.5; 239.6; 253.2; 254.4; 289.10; 307.14; 334.13; 359.6; 360.14; 365.44; 376.13; 376.14; 385.4; 387.32; 418.9; 421.1; 421.2; 424.3; 425.3; 446.6; 493.10; 521.5; 545.7; 549.2; 558.14; 571.3; 589.4; 623.30; 676.13; 676.14; 692.1; 858.13; 869.2; 914.3; 940.8; 942.8; 945.13; 945.14; 987.6; 992.23; 992.24; 1001.3; 1011.11; 1026.7; 1036.1; 1048.21; 1062.57; 1064.14; 1067.12; 1067.13; 1069.44; 1069.45; 1071.17
Fitzpatrick, Jean Grasso (1954–) American author and psychotherapist. 387.33; 404.8; 927.7; 1063.4
Flanner, Janet (1892–1978) American journalist and novelist. 710.5
Flaubert, Gustave (1821–1880) French novelist. 207.20; 513.4; 945.15
Flers, Robert [Pellevé de La Motte-Ango, marquis de] (1872–1927) French playwright. 233.10
Fletcher and Massinger *See* Fletcher, John or Massinger, Philip
Fletcher, John (1579–1625) English playwright. *See also* Massinger, Philip. 338.1; 906.6; 915.17; 1062.8
Florio, John (1553–1625) English lexicographer and translator. 577.2
Fontenelle, Bernard le Bovier de (1657–1757) French man of letters. 409.38
Ford, John (1586–c. 1640) English playwright. 287.3; 363.18; 491.8; 507.4; 551.65; 817.10; 998.43
Forster, E[dward] M[organ] (1879–1970) English novelist, short-story writer, essayist. 53.51; 79.2; 92.3; 93.30; 93.31; 113.2; 203.1; 207.21; 207.22; 211.4; 233.16; 284.14; 289.11; 297.8; 330.14; 340.8; 344.12; 344.13; 344.14; 401.17; 418.10; 419.22; 419.23; 435.7; 443.7; 501.3; 509.4; 524.13; 537.11; 541.11; 545.8; 551.66; 676.15; 698.11; 708.37; 716.5; 750.7; 826.3; 892.21; 910.2; 938.2; 978.19; 980.5; 984.7; 998.44; 1008.8; 1008.9
Fortas, Abe (1910–1982) American lawyer and jurist. 258.3; 528.22
Fouché, Joseph, Duc d'Otrante (1763–1820) French statesman and Minister of Police. 88.3
Fougasse *See* Bird, [Cyril] Kenneth
Fowler, Gene [Eugene Devlan] (1890–1960) American editor and writer. 495.1; 629.2
Fowler, H[enry] W[atson] (1858–1933) English lexicographer. 436.8; 1039.2; 1064.15; 1064.16
Fowles, John (1926–) English-born American novelist. 188.13; 271.7; 318.2; 542.6; 617.3; 1042.32; 1064.17
France, Anatole. Pen name of Jacques Anatole François Thibault (1844–1924) French novelist, poet, critic. 53.52; 100.4; 117.14; 123.20; 207.23; 213.9; 279.27; 284.15; 539.36; 555.8; 558.15; 684.6; 720.2; 848.13; 965.13; 978.20; 1011.12; 1062.58
Frankfurter, Felix (1882–1965) American jurist and teacher. 119.12; 469.6; 528.23; 731.2
Franklin, Benjamin (1706–1790) American statesman, writer, inventor, printer, scientist. 58.3; 73.5; 105.5; 155.5; 188.14; 195.13; 222.5; 238.10; 263.5; 342.10; 356.11; 395.20; 409.39; 419.24; 420.3; 427.8; 446.7; 472.3; 484.1; 522.19; 528.24; 528.25; 530.3; 564.43; 564.44; 581.17; 624.7; 690.7; 722.5; 733.6; 733.7; 780.4; 807.2; 848.14; 856.5; 923.19; 941.6; 978.21; 1011.13; 1016.3; 1034.7; 1042.33; 1056.5; 1060.20
French Proverbs. 65.8; 126.8; 268.14; 268.15; 274.10; 288.8; 295.9; 314.1; 386.5; 396.2; 397.1; 403.5; 427.9; 447.11; 539.37; 539.38; 551.67; 595.4; 670.19; 765.2; 855.6; 1045.1
French Saying. 267.9
Freud, Anna (1895–) Austrian psychoanalyst, daughter of Sigmund Freud. 201.13
Freud, Sigmund (1856–1939) Austrian psychologist and originator of psychoanalysis. 21.5; 35.2; 55.7; 123.21; 187.2; 409.40; 541.12; 552.4; 555.9; 627.6; 739.2; 758.5; 758.6; 771.4; 798.3; 913.8; 1016.4
Friedenberg, Edgar Z[odiag] (1921–) American sociologist. 1.6; 34.30; 204.8; 279.28; 367.7; 737.2; 758.7; 826.4; 966.5; 1001.4; 1026.8; 1032.4; 1032.5; 1064.18; 1071.18; 1071.19; 1071.20
Friedman, Milton and Rose (1912–) American economist. 102.3; 363.19; 395.21; 468.3; 524.14; 608.5; 845.1; 848.15
Friedman, Thomas L[oren] (1953–) American journalist. 39.15
Fromm, Erich (1900–1980) German-born American psychoanalyst and philosopher. 26.2; 31.3; 63.1; 77.11; 94.6; 104.11; 105.6; 119.13; 175.4; 181.3; 201.14; 201.15; 221.50; 221.51; 238.11; 240.8; 297.9; 308.8; 316.3; 330.15; 404.9; 404.10; 409.41; 414.3; 418.11; 427.10; 431.5; 467.2; 468.4; 469.7; 486.2; 504.9; 529.2; 539.39; 541.13; 541.14; 551.68; 551.69; 551.70; 551.71; 569.2; 573.1; 622.2; 670.20; 745.1; 819.10; 842.2; 858.14; 913.9; 978.22; 1005.5; 1026.9; 1043.3; 1062.59
Frost, Robert (1874–1963) American poet. 152.7; 221.52; 279.29; 334.14; 409.42; 415.7; 422.11; 602.20; 670.21; 708.38; 708.39; 776.3; 887.3; 975.14; 983.1; 1071.21
Fry, Christopher (1907–) English playwright. 12.2; 145.4; 228.2; 387.34; 470.2; 482.4; 559.6; 573.2; 604.12; 623.31; 729.13; 972.8; 1065.30

Frye, Northrop (1912–1991) Canadian literary critc and educator. 136.3; 450.14; 524.15; 545.9; 545.10; 617.4; 708.40; 1069.46; 1069.47

Fuentes, Carlos (1928–) Mexican novelist. 133.11; 209.6; 493.11; 524.16; 581.18; 892.22; 986.10; 1069.48

Fulbright, J[ames] William (1905–) American political leader. 27.4

Fulghum, Robert (1937–) American writer. 517.15; 527.3; 539.40; 1051.4; 1065.31

Fuller, [Sara] Margaret. Marchesa Ossoli (1810–1850) American editor, essayist, poet, teacher. 128.3; 133.12; 184.3; 238.12; 336.4; 401.18; 401.19; 480.8; 491.9; 551.72; 670.22; 1065.32; 1069.49

Fuller, D.D., Thomas (1608–1661) English clergyman and writer. 39.12; 50.4; 93.32; 614.33; 755.9; 1058.3; 1066.1

Fuller, M.D., Thomas 1654–1734 English physician, writer, compiler. 1.7; 2.6; 5.1; 5.2; 6.7; 7.3; 9.20; 10.6; 15.4; 32.1; 33.7; 45.8; 45.9; 51.9; 51.10; 53.53; 57.10; 76.5; 78.3; 88.4; 99.3; 99.4; 105.7; 111.7; 112.3; 128.4; 131.15; 138.3; 153.1; 158.2; 174.9; 186.7; 197.6; 199.5; 200.1; 211.5; 213.10; 216.9; 220.1; 221.53; 221.54; 222.6; 227.10; 243.1; 245.5; 245.6; 249.2; 259.4; 262.4; 268.16; 279.30; 281.7; 283.3; 288.9; 295.10; 301.2; 307.15; 321.16; 332.14; 332.15; 338.14; 342.11; 343.16; 349.8; 349.9; 356.12; 356.13; 362.3; 368.12; 384.9; 384.10; 393.18; 394.3; 401.20; 403.6; 403.7; 403.8; 405.8; 407.2; 409.43; 409.44; 411.6; 413.4; 425.4; 427.11; 428.12; 436.9; 437.3; 447.12; 447.13; 455.2; 463.3; 466.2; 471.3; 475.4; 476.8; 476.9; 480.9; 493.12; 499.3; 503.3; 507.5; 517.16; 517.17; 519.8; 522.20; 526.11; 528.26; 528.27; 531.7; 537.12; 539.41; 541.15; 541.16; 542.7; 549.3; 551.73; 551.74; 554.2; 563.13; 564.45; 564.46; 600.6; 602.21; 602.22; 602.23; 602.24; 610.5; 629.3; 670.23; 675.7; 677.7; 677.8; 680.6; 684.7; 692.2; 697.4; 698.12; 718.17; 720.3; 722.6; 722.7; 722.8; 723.13; 723.14; 725.1; 729.14; 733.8; 743.4; 743.5; 751.7; 760.5; 770.4; 781.1; 785.11; 787.1; 789.2; 797.27; 797.28; 804.11; 806.5; 831.6; 832.4; 837.3; 846.2; 855.7; 866.4; 868.4; 869.3; 873.7; 901.8; 915.18; 918.32; 934.3; 941.7; 949.1; 955.1; 960.4; 998.45; 998.46; 1000.4; 1000.5; 1008.10; 1030.10; 1033.20; 1033.21; 1047.2; 1048.22; 1048.23; 1048.24; 1048.25; 1057.2; 1060.21; 1060.22; 1061.7; 1070.9; 1073.1

G

Géraldy, Paul. Pen name of Paul Le Fèvre (1885–) French poet and playwright. 551.76; 876.3

Gaboriau, Émile (1835–1873) French writer of detective stories. 817.11; 1062.60; 1062.61

Galbraith, John Kenneth (1908–) Canadian-born American economist, diplomat, writer. 104.12; 104.13; 105.8; 108.2; 178.7; 277.1; 305.4; 437.4; 437.5; 480.10; 645.5; 711.28; 719.24; 761.7; 819.11; 848.16; 856.6; 966.6; 1048.26; 1069.50

Gallant, Mavis (1922–) Canadian short-story writer and essayist. 344.15; 539.42; 545.11; 1069.51

Gallico, Paul [William] (1897–1976) American journalist, novelist, short-story writer. 488.1

Galsworthy, John (1867–1933) English novelist and playwright. 55.8; 528.28

Gandhi, Mohandas K[aramchand], called Mahatma (1869–1948) Hindu nationalist leader. 100.5; 104.14; 111.8; 233.17; 274.11; 307.16; 363.20; 511.2; 528.29; 537.13; 665.4; 665.5; 665.6; 711.29; 723.15; 738.4; 819.12; 823.6; 940.9; 1032.6; 1032.7; 1042.34; 1042.35; 1042.36

García Lorca, Federico (1898–1936) Spanish poet and playwright. 922.1

García Márquez, Gabriel (1928–) Colombian novelist and short-story writer. 82.5; 332.16; 343.17; 633.4; 639.2; 678.4; 719.25; 778.3; 946.15; 1050.3

Gardner, John W. (1912–) American foundation executive and public official. 335.4; 419.25; 491.10; 718.18; 758.8; 790.10

Garrick, David (1717–1779) English actor and theater manager. 653.32

Garrison, William Lloyd (1805–1879) American abolitionist. 100.6; 233.18; 494.4; 604.13; 823.7

Gary, Romain (1914–) Russian-born French novelist and diplomat. 436.10; 545.12

Gasset, José Ortega y *See* Ortega y Gasset, José

Gates, Henry Louis, Jr. (1950–) American scholar and writer. 135.2; 823.8; 967.6

Gaxotte, Pierre (1895–) French historian. 819.13

Gay, John (1685–1732) English poet and playwright. 3.4; 31.4; 224.6; 268.17; 295.11; 351.3; 564.47; 575.2; 581.19; 1071.22

Gaylin, Willard (1925–) American physician and educator. 43.5; 124.6; 284.16; 404.11; 510.9; 704.13; 860.2; 956.2; 1064.19

Genet, Jean (1910–1986) French playwright, novelist, poet, essayist. 62.3; 238.13; 269.5; 278.2; 450.15; 518.3; 551.75

German Proverbs. 108.3; 126.9; 159.1; 186.8; 204.9; 224.7; 268.18; 321.17; 357.4; 384.11; 447.14; 457.2; 462.1; 480.11; 510.10; 528.30; 551.77; 593.2; 653.33; 684.8; 791.3; 831.7; 873.8; 896.8; 936.1; 938.3; 998.47

Ghalib (Asad Allah Khan) (1796–1869) Turkish poet. 900.11

Gibbon, Edward (1737–1794) English historian. 399.3; 741.5; 960.5

Gibran, Kahlil (1883–1931) Syrian-American mystic, poet, painter. 2.7; 123.22; 174.10; 336.5; 384.12; 390.6; 409.45; 551.78; 557.3; 604.14; 623.32; 673.3; 708.41; 785.12; 888.3; 913.10; 923.20; 923.21; 946.16; 965.14; 998.48; 1065.33; 1070.10

Gibson, Wilfred Wilson (1878–1962) English poet. 610.6

Gide, André (1869–1951) French novelist, critic, essayist, editor, translator. 16.3; 20.3; 53.54; 53.55; 53.56; 76.6; 78.4; 78.5; 93.33; 117.15; 122.5; 122.6; 125.10; 125.11; 142.2; 162.3; 184.4; 227.11; 238.14; 242.4; 279.31; 281.8; 284.17; 347.1; 363.21; 387.35; 389.4; 409.46; 440.8; 469.8; 469.9; 479.5; 493.13; 493.14; 516.6; 519.9; 542.8; 545.13; 571.4; 585.5; 588.7; 595.5; 598.4; 616.1; 623.33; 653.34; 654.2; 656.8; 663.6; 676.16; 682.7; 693.5; 755.10; 772.5; 785.13; 785.14; 810.7; 812.2; 819.14; 837.4; 845.2; 854.19; 856.7; 863.3; 875.10; 884.2; 896.9; 903.2; 915.19; 928.3; 974.5; 974.6; 998.49; 1004.9; 1007.6; 1008.11; 1011.14; 1027.6; 1042.37; 1069.52; 1069.53; 1069.54; 1072.8

Gifford, Frank (1930–) Sports announcer and professional football player. 929.7

Gilbert, Sir W[illiam] S[chwenck] (1836–1911) English dramatist, librettist, writer of humorous verse. 45.10; 89.2; 186.9; 204.10; 210.10; 221.55; 308.9; 340.9; 400.6; 539.43; 539.44; 562.24; 588.8; 709.4; 780.5; 793.2; 839.5; 957.2

Gilbreath, Glen (1886–) Contemporary American thief. 934.4

Ginott, Haim G. (1922–1973) Israeli-born American psychologist and writer. 250.3; 444.9; 482.5; 670.24; 880.9; 1008.12; 1071.23; 1071.24; 1071.25

Ginsberg, Allen (1926–) American poet. 849.9

Ginsberg, Louis (1896–1976) American poet, father of Allen Ginsberg. 551.79
Giovanni, Nikki (1943–) American poet and writer. 50.6; 117.16; 149.7; 182.3; 279.32; 539.45; 543.1; 945.16
Giraldi, Giglio Gregorio *See* Gyraldus, Lilius Gregorius
Giraudoux, [Hippolyte] Jean (1882–1944) French dramatist, novelist, essayist, diplomat. 102.4; 138.4; 191.4; 221.56; 221.57; 240.9; 260.2; 279.33; 351.4; 352.2; 387.36; 401.21; 418.12; 527.4; 528.31; 541.17; 558.16; 564.48; 564.49; 581.20; 602.25; 621.6; 633.5; 663.7; 790.11; 857.5; 918.18; 929.8; 972.9; 1042.38; 1042.39; 1042.40; 1042.41; 1062.62
Gissing, George [Robert] (1857–1903) English novelist, critic, essayist. 93.34; 131.16; 409.47; 562.25; 590.8; 602.26; 806.6; 854.20; 877.2; 915.20; 998.50; 1050.4
Glasgow, Ellen [Anderson Gholson] (1874–1945) American novelist. 564.50; 625.3; 783.3; 797.29; 810.8; 823.9
Glinka, Mikhail [Ivanovich] (1804–1857) Russian composer. 614.34
Goebbels, Paul Joseph (1897–1945) German Nazi propagandist. 1049.3
Goethe [Johann Wolfgang von] (1749–1832) German poet, playwright, novelist. 15.5; 19.11; 50.7; 53.57; 72.22; 77.12; 78.6; 88.5; 104.15; 105.9; 119.14; 171.6; 176.6; 197.7; 216.10; 238.15; 240.10; 254.5; 271.8; 279.34; 284.18; 298.8; 299.17; 342.12; 342.13; 363.22; 401.22; 406.8; 422.12; 427.12; 431.6; 444.10; 454.8; 469.10; 507.6; 517.18; 526.12; 532.6; 535.3; 551.80; 559.7; 562.26; 564.51; 565.5; 578.3; 586.8; 600.7; 606.9; 619.2; 621.7; 622.3; 623.34; 623.35; 635.2; 646.5; 653.35; 653.36; 653.37; 662.2; 681.7; 693.6; 697.5; 708.42; 708.43; 708.44; 708.45; 708.46; 780.6; 800.1; 819.15; 822.8; 825.2; 831.8; 831.9; 849.10; 859.4; 863.4; 892.23; 901.9; 903.3; 942.9; 965.15; 972.10; 973.6; 974.7; 988.3; 992.25; 998.51; 1011.15; 1024.2; 1065.34; 1069.55; 1071.26; 1071.27
Gogol, Nikolai Vasilyevich (1809–1852) Russian novelist, playwright, short-story writer. 369.3
Gold, Herbert (1924–) American novelist, short-story writer, essayist. 53.58; 171.7; 201.16; 238.16; 431.7; 569.3; 597.5; 653.38; 736.2; 1056.6
Golden, Harry [Lewis] (1902–1981) American writer and publisher. 17.30; 178.8
Goldsmith, Oliver (1730?–1774) Irish-born English poet, playwright, novelist. 104.16; 174.11; 318.3; 528.32; 551.81; 653.39; 923.22; 975.15; 1033.22
Goldwater, Barry [Morris] (1909–) American political leader. 335.5; 395.22
Goldwyn, Samuel (1882–1974) Polish-born American motion-picture producer. 611.4
Goncourt, Brothers *See* de Goncourt, Edmond or *see* de Goncourt, Jules
González Prada, Manuel (1848–1918) Peruvian politician and writer. 996.2; 819.16
Goodman, Paul (1911–1972) American writer, educator, psychoanalyst. 34.31; 34.32; 91.1; 104.17; 113.3; 201.17; 279.35; 279.36; 401.23; 504.10; 533.5; 611.5; 704.14; 819.17; 892.24
Goodwin, Doris Kearns (1943–) American biographer and journalist. 69.1; 135.3; 334.15; 505.1; 884.3
Gorbachev, Mikhail (1931–) Former president of USSR. 294.3; 419.27; 912.2
Gordimer, Nadine (1923–) South African novelist and short-story writer. 343.18; 630.11; 681.8
Gorer, Geoffrey (1905–) English psychologist and historian. 41.11; 704.15; 797.30
Gorky, Maxim. Pen name of Aleksei Maximovich Peshkov (1868–1936) Russian writer. 289.13; 368.13; 393.19; 409.48; 437.6; 518.4; 528.33; 551.82; 564.52; 570.4; 602.27; 694.9; 732.2; 999.6; 1065.35; 1070.11
Gould, Glenn (1932–1982) Canadian pianist. 614.35
Gourmont, Rémy de (1858–1915) French literary critic and novelist. 767.1; 975.16
Gracián, Baltasar (1601–1658) Spanish prose writer and Jesuit priest. 1.8; 33.8; 33.9; 45.11; 53.59; 173.7; 188.16; 197.8; 210.11; 235.5; 288.10; 295.12; 309.3; 311.4; 338.15; 345.3; 358.2; 360.15; 360.16; 365.45; 365.46; 365.47; 365.48; 389.5; 390.7; 427.13; 532.7; 533.6; 551.83; 558.17; 559.8; 561.3; 563.14; 585.6; 600.8; 640.5; 677.9; 700.2; 704.16; 712.5; 719.26; 751.8; 855.8; 869.4; 888.4; 906.7; 915.21; 923.23; 978.24; 998.52; 1008.13; 1023.2; 1049.4; 1060.23; 1060.24; 1061.9; 1069.56
Graffito, French student revolt, May 1968. 709.5; 801.1
Grahame, Kenneth (1859–1932) English essayist and writer of children's books. 895.2
Grant, Ulysses S[impson] (1822–1885) American soldier and eighteenth President of the United States (1869–1877). 528.34
Grass, Günter [Wilhelm] (1927–) German novelist, poet and essayist. 6.8; 9.21; 234.2
Graves, Robert [Ranke] (1895–) English poet, novelist, critic. 221.58; 551.84
Gray, Thomas (1716–1771) English poet. 386.6; 447.15; 649.4
Grayson, David. Pen name of Ray Stannard Baker (1870–1946) American journalist, biographer, essayist. 93.35; 105.10; 131.17; 355.8; 365.49; 393.20; 623.36; 716.6; 746.8; 984.8; 1065.36
Greek Anthology (7th c. B.C.–A.D. 10th c.) A collection of several thousand poems, songs, epigrams and epitaphs by numerous Greek writers, known and unknown. 263.6; 268.19; 362.4
Greek Proverbs. 9.22; 186.10; 266.5; 311.5; 564.53; 1062.64
Green, Adolph (1915–) American lyricist and playwright. 253.1
Green, Julien (1900–) French novelist of American parentage. 180.1; 712.6; 1004.12; 1069.57
Greenburg, Dan (1936–) American author. 672.1
Greene, Graham (1904–1991) English novelist, short-story writer, playwright. 50.8; 68.2; 80.3; 118.3; 123.23; 150.5; 201.18; 239.7; 330.16; 332.17; 344.17; 551.85; 602.28; 723.16; 870.2; 884.4; 1069.58
Greer, Germaine (1939–) Australian-born English journalist and author. 551.86; 564.54; 581.21; 623.37; 819.18; 892.25; 892.26; 1065.37
Gregg, Alan (1890–1957) American physician and foundation official. 750.8
Gregory, Dick (1932–) American comedian and civil rights activist. 85.8
Greider, William (1936–) American journalist and author. 191.5; 711.30; 719.27; 766.8; 964.6
Gresset, Jean Baptiste Louis (1709–1777) French poet and playwright. 1061.10
Grigg, John [Edward Poynder] (1924–) English political journalist; renounced the title of Lord Altrincham in 1963. 62.4
Griswold, [Alfred] Whitney (1909–1963) American educator. 443.8
Groom, Winston (1943–) American novelist. 77.13; 186.11; 266.6; 845.3; 978.25
Grumbach, Doris (1918–) American novelist, editor, critic. 211.6; 218.2
Guiterman, Arthur (1871–1943) American poet. 207.25; 585.7; 808.4; 1027.7
Gutman, Walter Knowleton (1903–) American economist and writer. 503.4

H

Hāfiz. Pen name of Shams-ud-din Muhammad (c. 1300–1388) Persian poet. 606.10; 799.2; 1019.5; 116.8; 186.12; 291.3; 427.14; 541.18; 551.87; 1067.14

Haberman, Phillip W., Jr. (1479–1552) Contemporary American writer. 274.12

Hachiya, Michihiko (1903–) Japanese physician. 641.6; 641.7

Haggadah Palestinian Talmud (4th c.). 262.5; 491.11; 990.8

Haigh, Kenneth (c. 1300–1388) Contemporary English actor. 972.11

Hailsham, 2nd Viscount (Quintin McGarel Hogg) (1907–) British government official. 51.11

Hall, Joseph (1574–1656) English clergyman and satirist. 221.59; 598.5

Hamilton, Alexander (1757–1804) American statesman. 223.1; 297.10; 395.23; 956.3

Hamilton, Edith (1867–1963) American essayist, classical scholar, translator. 309.4; 747.4; 837.5; 900.12

Hammarskjöld, Dag (1905–1961) Swedish statesman. United Nations Secretary-General (1953–1961). 9.23; 195.14; 221.60; 240.11; 246.3; 359.7; 435.8; 442.4; 653.40; 723.17; 1021.1

Hammer, Armand (1898–1990) American industrialist and businessman. 53.60; 150.6; 524.17; 653.41; 680.7; 792.1; 1058.4; 1065.38

Hammurabi (2067–2025 B.C.) King of Babylon. 517.19

Hand, Learned (1872–1961) American jurist. 9.24; 117.17; 120.4; 134.2; 177.4; 182.4; 190.2; 233.19; 233.20; 258.4; 259.5; 363.23; 514.5; 514.6; 517.20; 528.35; 528.36; 532.8; 537.14; 537.15; 539.46; 571.5; 576.2; 723.18; 746.9; 760.6; 913.11; 995.3; 1002.12; 1038.7; 1047.3

Haraucourt, Edmond (1856–1941) French novelist, poet, playwright. 673.4

Hardwick, Elizabeth (1916–) American novelist and critic. 349.10; 368.14; 611.6; 794.3; 876.4

Hardy, Thomas (1840–1928) English novelist and poet. 133.14; 209.7; 272.4; 360.17; 387.37; 539.47; 548.5; 555.10; 581.22; 586.9; 677.10; 681.9; 807.3; 1067.15

Hare, Augustus William *See* Hare, Julius Charles

Hare, Julius Charles (1795–1855) and his brother Augustus William (1792–1834) English clergymen, joint authors of *Guesses at Truth.* 76.7; 207.26; 238.17; 307.18; 330.17; 365.50; 444.11; 465.1; 470.3; 541.19; 558.18; 600.9; 724.6; 986.11; 1030.11

Harington or Harrington, Sir John (1561–1612) English satirist and miscellaneous writer. 93.36; 165.6; 360.18; 993.2

Harkness, Richard [Long] (1907–) American radio and television commentator and journalist. 147.3

Harpe, Jean-François de la (1739–1803) French poet and playwright. 309.5

Harriman, W[illiam] Averell (1891–) American businessman, politician, diplomat. 498.3

Harrington, Alan (1919–) American social critic and writer. 728.1; 745.2; 856.8

Harrington, Michael (1928–) American writer and social critic. 17.31; 34.33; 34.34; 85.9; 108.4; 108.5; 108.6; 132.5; 151.6; 217.2; 226.4; 261.5; 317.1; 374.4; 468.5; 517.21; 587.3; 653.42; 709.6; 711.31; 718.19; 718.20; 718.21; 718.22; 718.23; 718.24; 729.15; 785.15; 819.19; 912.3; 913.12; 913.13; 966.7; 966.8; 1048.27

Harris, Richard (1928–) Contemporary American journalist. 711.32

Harris, Sydney J[ustin] (1917–1986) English-born American newspaper columnist, writer, teacher. 78.7; 214.2; 419.28; 454.9; 571.6; 711.33; 722.9; 855.9; 901.10; 978.26; 1042.42

Hart, Moss (1904–1961) American playwright and librettist. 11.4; 120.5; 209.8; 334.16; 436.11; 605.3; 864.2; 972.12; 972.13; 972.14; 978.27; 1027.8

Hável, Václav (1936–) Czech playwright and essayist, president of Czechoslovakia and of the Czech Republic. 150.7; 433.13; 445.2; 526.13; 545.14; 623.38; 711.34; 886.6; 913.14; 972.15; 985.3

Hawking, Stephen W. (1942–) English theoretical physicist. 849.11; 978.28; 1017.7; 1017.8

Hawthorne, Nathaniel (1804–1864) American novelist and short-story writer. 48.4; 53.61; 103.5; 122.7; 142.3; 165.7; 194.9; 198.6; 274.13; 362.5; 375.4; 376.15; 390.8; 401.24; 418.13; 431.8; 454.10; 524.18; 539.48; 562.27; 581.23; 666.7; 741.6; 746.10; 802.1; 854.21; 855.10; 858.15; 896.11; 900.13; 966.9; 978.29

Hay, John [Milton] (1838–1905) American statesman and man of letters. 171.8; 247.4; 268.20; 365.51; 369.4; 394.4; 551.88; 564.55; 653.43

Hayes, Helen (1900–1993) American actress. 123.24; 221.61; 954.2; 992.26

Hayes, Rutherford B[irchard] (1822–1893) Nineteenth President of the United States, (1877–1881). 710.6

Hays, Brooks (1898–) American lawyer, educator, presidential aide, congressman. 6.9

Hazlitt, William (1778–1830) English essayist and critic. 9.25; 53.62; 93.37; 113.4; 120.6; 125.12; 145.5; 166.8; 178.9; 181.4; 188.17; 188.18; 221.62; 221.63; 221.64; 238.18; 238.19; 266.7; 266.8; 271.9; 279.37; 279.38; 289.14; 311.6; 311.7; 318.4; 321.19; 329.10; 332.18; 333.6; 334.17; 338.16; 342.14; 363.24; 365.52; 365.53; 375.5; 376.16; 376.17; 394.5; 396.3; 400.7; 401.25; 401.26; 401.27; 412.9; 412.10; 414.4; 427.15; 431.9; 449.10; 508.2; 516.7; 524.19; 530.4; 532.9; 539.49; 539.50; 541.20; 558.19; 561.4; 578.4; 584.2; 618.2; 619.3; 623.39; 653.44; 653.45; 653.46; 663.8; 674.2; 691.5; 712.7; 719.28; 722.10; 726.6; 726.7; 726.8; 732.3; 732.4; 733.9; 733.10; 734.6; 751.9; 760.7; 761.8; 762.7; 764.6; 765.3; 790.12; 792.2; 797.31; 797.32; 822.9; 844.4; 848.17; 848.18; 848.19; 858.16; 861.3; 862.5; 863.5; 868.5; 869.5; 876.5; 905.2; 914.4; 918.19; 923.24; 928.4; 941.8; 945.17; 963.6; 963.7; 978.30; 980.6; 998.53; 998.54; 1000.6; 1007.7; 1033.23; 1035.2; 1037.6; 1058.5; 1060.25; 1061.11; 1062.65; 1062.66; 1067.16; 1073.2

Hebrew Proverbs. 733.11

Hegel, Georg Friedrich Wilhelm (1770–1831) German philosopher. 206.10; 363.25; 419.29; 539.51; 675.8; 734.7; 1065.39; 1067.17

Heilbrun, Carolyn G[old] (1926–) American author and scholar. 639.3

Hein, Piet (1905–) Dutch inventor and poet. 6.10; 539.52; 665.7; 882.3; 886.7; 899.4; 923.25; 929.9; 1060.26

Heine, Heinrich (1797–1856) German poet, satirist, journalist. 298.9

Heinlein, Robert A. Pen name, Anson MacDonald (1907–) American novelist and science fiction writer. 551.89

Heller, Joseph (1923–) American novelist. 19.12; 329.11; 512.1; 853.11; 966.10

Hellman, Lillian (1905–1984) American playwright. 676.17; 1069.59

Helvétius, Claude-Adrien (1715–1771) French encyclopedist and materialist philosopher. 998.55

Hemingway, Ernest [Miller] (1899–1961) American novelist and short-story writer. 53.63; 72.23; 221.65; 303.3; 344.18; 365.54; 366.3; 424.4; 521.6; 551.90; 564.56; 604.15; 633.6; 656.9; 671.1; 704.17; 826.5; 910.3; 922.2; 923.26; 942.10; 1067.18; 1069.60; 1069.61

Henry IV of France. Also Henry of Navarre (1553–1610) King of France (1589–1610). 883.4

Henry, O. Pen name of William Sydney Porter (1862–1910) American short-story writer. 91.2; 131.18; 425.5; 437.7; 539.53; 539.54; 565.6; 582.6; 761.9; 830.1; 938.4; 1062.67

Henry, Patrick (1736–1799) American statesman and orator. 321.20; 427.16; 537.16

Heraclitus (fl. c. 500 B.C.) Greek philosopher. 17.32; 87.6; 117.18; 117.19; 119.15; 187.3; 238.20; 238.21; 261.6; 263.7; 266.9; 268.21; 279.39; 387.38; 410.2; 528.37; 658.6; 817.12; 897.5; 906.8; 952.4; 998.56; 1060.27; 1065.40

Herbert, Edward, 1st Baron Herbert of Cherbury (1583–1648) English philosopher, diplomat, historian, poet. Brother of George Herbert. 472.4

Herbert, George (1593–1633) English clergyman and metaphysical poet. 1.9; 105.11; 162.4; 224.8; 268.22; 325.2; 359.8; 507.7; 550.3; 551.91; 708.47; 720.4; 854.22; 854.23; 918.20; 978.31; 1000.7

Hériat, Philippe. Pen name of Raymond-Gérard Payelle (1898–1971) French actor and writer. 602.30

Hermant, Abel (1862–1950) French novelist and essayist. 362.6; 418.14; 425.6

Herndon, James (1929–) American educator and writer. 93.38; 123.25; 228.3; 532.10

Herndon, William H. (1818–1891) American lawyer, biographer of Abraham Lincoln. 518.5; 670.25

Herodotus (c. 480–c. 425 B.C.) Greek historian. 295.13; 459.1; 882.4

Herrick, Robert (1591–1674) English poet. 706.4

Hersey, John [Richard] (1914–1993) American novelist and journalist. 228.4; 344.19; 1049.5

Hershey, General Lewis B[laine] (1893–) American general. Former director of Selective Service. 97.5

Herzog, Emile *See* Maurois, André

Hesiod (8th century B.C.) Greek poet, known as the father of Greek didactic poetry. 155.6; 198.7; 288.11; 307.19; 321.21; 334.18; 365.55; 393.21; 394.6; 569.4; 661.7; 738.5; 979.6; 1047.4

Hesse, Hermann (1877–1962) German novelist. 195.15; 210.12; 221.66; 442.5; 528.38; 587.4; 697.6; 784.10; 1014.3; 1060.28

Heywood, John (1497?–1580) English poet. 297.11; 754.7; 780.7; 947.3; 1057.3

Higginson, Thomas Wentworth (1823–1911) American clergyman, editor, writer. 193.2

Highet, [Karl] Gilbert (1906–1987) Scottish-born American classical scholar and writer. 62.5; 276.1; 447.16; 511.3; 532.11; 533.7; 687.4; 708.48; 708.49; 718.25; 718.26; 786.6; 901.11; 913.15; 965.16; 965.17; 965.18

Hill, Sir Rowland (1795–1879) English postal authority, originator of "penny postage." 242.5

Hindustani Proverbs. 50.9; 149.8; 310.2; 455.3; 996.3; 1002.13

Hippocrates (460?–377 B.C.) Greek physician, the father of medicine. 577.3; 798.4; 988.4

Hipponax (fl. c. 540 B.C.) Greek poet. 564.57

Hirsch, E[ric] D[onald], Jr. (1928–) American educator and author. 279.40; 279.41; 522.21; 797.33; 913.16; 967.7

Hitler, Adolf (1889–1945) German Nazi and Führer of the Third Reich (1933–1945). 357.5; 558.20; 622.4; 681.10

Hoagland, Edward (1932–) American essayist and novelist. 344.20; 431.10; 547.3; 854.24; 898.7; 917.4; 978.32; 992.27

Hobbes, Thomas (1588–1679) English philosopher. 4.3; 125.13; 136.4; 258.5; 526.14; 681.11; 755.11; 849.12; 975.17; 998.57; 1060.29; 1064.20

Hoch, Edward Wallis (1849–1925) American politician. 206.11

Hochhuth, Rolf (1931–) German playwright and editor. 621.8

Hocking, William Ernest (1873–1966) American philosopher. 221.67

Hoffer, Eric (1902–) American longshoreman and philosopher. 9.26; 10.7; 12.3; 53.64; 100.7; 111.9; 111.10; 117.20; 165.8; 201.19; 202.4; 221.68; 221.69; 231.5; 238.22; 238.23; 251.4; 258.6; 264.7; 271.10; 291.4; 297.12; 307.20; 316.4; 329.12; 335.6; 336.6; 338.17; 363.26; 363.27; 368.15; 368.16; 384.13; 386.7; 395.24; 401.28; 406.9; 409.49; 411.7; 412.11; 419.30; 427.17; 435.9; 444.12; 447.17; 451.4; 451.5; 477.5; 479.6; 519.10; 568.1; 568.2; 575.3; 621.9; 662.3; 718.27; 719.29; 719.30; 741.7; 748.2; 775.10; 776.4; 819.20; 819.21; 819.22; 830.2; 840.2; 858.17; 872.1; 879.1; 941.9; 966.11; 985.4; 998.58; 1002.14; 1026.10; 1047.5; 1047.6; 1064.21; 888.6

Hoffman, Eva (1945–) Polish-born American teacher and writer. 42.5; 60.2; 174.12; 436.12; 515.2; 536.1; 683.6

Hofmann, Hans (1880–1966) German-born American abstract painter. 53.65; 573.3; 899.5

Hofstadter, Richard (1916–1970) American historian. 178.10; 335.7; 492.4; 492.5; 640.6; 896.12; 998.59

Holmes, John Haynes (1879–1964) American clergyman. 138.5; 1017.9

Holmes, Oliver Wendell, Jr. (1841–1935) American jurist. 115.6; 213.11; 233.23; 279.42; 401.29; 504.11; 514.7; 522.22; 528.39; 539.55; 604.16; 656.10; 694.10; 719.31; 734.8; 975.21; 986.12; 1037.7; 1064.22

Holmes, Oliver Wendell, Sr. (1809–1894) American physician, professor, man of letters. 12.4; 19.13; 33.10; 34.35; 44.2; 69.2; 93.39; 95.4; 156.4; 178.11; 207.27; 219.4; 244.4; 265.2; 284.19; 307.21; 328.8; 328.9; 332.19; 338.18; 364.4; 365.56; 367.8; 374.5; 376.18; 377.4; 377.5; 377.6; 391.5; 413.5; 430.2; 435.10; 441.2; 441.3; 443.9; 443.10; 464.4; 493.15; 499.4; 522.23; 539.56; 542.9; 558.21; 580.12; 581.24; 586.10; 606.11; 614.36; 626.5; 649.5; 653.47; 656.11; 662.4; 663.9; 676.18; 681.12; 699.4; 708.50; 708.51; 708.52; 716.7; 718.28; 724.7; 780.8; 794.4; 797.34; 797.35; 800.2; 848.20; 855.11; 873.9; 913.17; 923.27; 923.28; 924.2; 941.10; 942.11; 962.7; 975.18; 975.19; 975.20; 998.60; 1007.8; 1033.24; 1058.6; 1062.68; 1068.5; 1069.62

Homer (9th c. B.C.) Greek poet. 3.5; 6.11; 92.4; 92.5; 139.5; 173.8; 268.23; 300.5; 312.3; 332.20; 350.1; 365.57; 374.6; 387.39; 390.9; 403.9; 423.3; 428.13; 433.14; 440.9; 477.6; 520.3; 531.8; 542.10; 562.28; 564.58; 588.9; 640.7; 665.8; 690.8; 754.8; 754.9; 800.3; 803.4; 811.3; 889.8; 906.9; 916.4; 918.21; 940.10; 947.4; 962.8; 1011.16; 1016.5; 1042.43; 1060.30; 1062.69; 1065.41

Hook, Sidney (1902–) American philosopher, educator, writer. 1060.31

Hoover, Helen (1910–) American naturalist and writer. 41.12

Hoover, Herbert [Clark] (1874–1964) Thirty-first President of the United States (1929–1933). 711.35; 1042.44; 1060.32

Hope, Bob (1904–) English-born American radio, film, television comedian. 69.3; 586.11

Hopkins, Gerard Manley (1844–1889) English poet and Jesuit priest. 898.8

Horace. Full name, Quintus Horatius Flaccus (65–8 B.C.) Roman poet and

Horace (*cont.*) satirist. 42.6; 53.66; 75.5; 98.5; 151.7; 185.2; 221.70; 226.5; 251.5; 268.24; 268.25; 318.5; 340.10; 342.15; 354.6; 357.6; 360.19; 384.14; 403.10; 417.2; 427.18; 431.11; 436.13; 517.22; 530.5; 653.48; 677.11; 708.53; 708.54; 725.2; 813.2; 854.25; 948.11; 992.28; 1033.25; 1048.28; 1069.63

Hostos [y Bonilla], Eugenio María de (1839–1903) Puerto Rican educator, social reformer, journalist. 393.22; 443.11; 517.23

Hotchner, A[aron] E[dward] (1920–) American writer and dramatist. 18.4; 274.14; 418.15; 541.21; 632.7; 680.8; 704.18; 948.12; 1069.64

Housman, A[lfred] E[dward] (1859–1936) English poet and classical scholar. 268.26; 1007.9

Howard, Maureen (1930–) American novelist and memoirist. 45.12; 50.10; 79.3; 125.14; 215.3; 218.3; 218.4; 276.2; 334.19; 444.13; 526.15; 600.10; 632.8; 917.5; 1062.70

Howard, Neale E. (1911–) American astronomer, teacher, writer. 849.13

Howe, Edgar Watson (1853–1937) American journalist, novelist, essayist. 17.33; 55.9; 105.12; 115.7; 198.8; 259.6; 274.15; 288.12; 297.13; 330.18; 341.3; 343.19; 356.14; 425.7; 427.19; 428.14; 440.10; 467.3; 476.10; 477.7; 539.57; 558.22; 564.59; 564.60; 565.7; 600.11; 602.29; 626.6; 652.6; 653.49; 731.3; 734.9; 742.4; 790.13; 790.14; 804.12; 808.5; 923.29; 934.5; 945.18; 960.6; 984.9; 1062.71; 1062.72; 1062.73; 1065.42

Howe, Irving (1920–1993) American author, editor, teacher. 93.40; 145.6; 450.16; 545.15; 790.15; 858.18; 963.8

Howells, William Dean (1837–1920) American novelist, poet, editor, critic. 750.9; 946.17

Hoyle, Sir Fred (1915–) British astronomer, mathematician, educator. 340.11

Hubbard, Elbert [Green] (1856–1915) American businessman, writer, printer. 8.3; 10.8; 56.5; 93.41; 125.15; 174.13; 178.12; 201.20; 221.71; 259.7; 264.8; 299.18; 316.5; 318.6; 322.2; 326.4; 329.13; 329.14; 343.20; 356.15; 359.9; 363.28; 365.58; 401.30; 409.50; 418.16; 428.15; 504.12; 526.16; 539.59; 539.58; 551.92; 564.61; 565.8; 578.5; 580.13; 581.25; 604.17; 659.7; 668.3; 692.3; 875.11; 880.10; 936.2; 940.11; 940.12; 945.20; 945.21; 946.18; 953.1; 960.7; 973.7; 986.13; 987.7; 1062.74

Hudson, Virginia Cary (1894–1954) American who, at the age of ten, wrote *O Ye Jigs & Juleps!*, a collection of essays. 45.13; 563.15

Hughes, [James] Langston (1902–1967) American poet. 41.13; 72.24; 93.42; 123.26; 222.7; 268.27; 274.16; 426.5; 500.3; 511.4; 551.93; 558.23; 581.26; 632.9; 632.10; 641.8; 775.11; 823.10; 854.26; 854.27; 902.1; 929.10; 1009.2; 1041.2; 1060.33; 1062.75

Hugo, Victor [Marie] (1802–1885) French poet, novelist, playwright. 39.16; 78.8; 87.7; 88.6; 123.27; 131.19; 159.2; 216.11; 219.5; 222.8; 268.28; 283.4; 300.6; 324.2; 360.20; 368.17; 387.40; 418.17; 446.8; 482.6; 518.6; 537.18; 551.94; 561.5; 575.4; 601.1; 601.2; 653.50; 653.51; 661.8; 670.26; 671.2; 718.29; 723.19; 750.10; 804.13; 818.2; 819.23; 822.10; 878.2; 882.5; 891.1; 918.22; 927.8; 928.5; 975.22; 1062.76; 1065.43

Hulme, Thomas Ernest (1883–1917) English poet, critic, philosopher. 524.20

Humboldt, Baron Wilhelm von (1767–1835) German philologist and diplomat. 515.3

Hume, David (1711–1776) Scottish philosopher and historian. 125.16; 581.27

Humphrey, George [Magoffin] (1890–) American industrialist. U.S. Secretary of the Treasury (1953–1957). 277.2; 677.12

Humphrey, Hubert H[oratio] (1911–) American political leader. Vice-President of the United States (1965–1969). 364.5; 528.40

Hungarian Proverbs. 755.13

Hutchens, John K[ennedy] (1905–) American journalist and editor. 1069.65

Hutcheson, Francis (1694–1746) Scottish philosopher and professor. 433.15

Huxley, Aldous [Leonard] (1894–1963) English novelist, essayist, satirist. 12.5; 93.43; 100.8; 114.2; 123.28; 156.5; 179.2; 210.13; 221.72; 241.7; 274.17; 321.22; 321.23; 335.8; 395.25; 404.13; 409.51; 414.5; 419.31; 442.6; 479.7; 551.95; 589.6; 706.5; 718.30; 745.3; 745.4; 797.36; 797.37; 822.11; 898.9; 906.10; 916.5; 924.3; 966.13; 978.33; 1002.15; 1042.45; 1064.23; 1065.44; 1068.6; 1069.66

Huxley, Thomas Henry (1825–1895) English biologist, teacher, writer. 9.28; 176.7; 279.44; 308.10; 329.15; 395.26; 431.12; 469.11; 522.24; 621.10; 849.14; 849.15; 998.61; 999.7; 1000.8

I

Iacocca, Lee (1924–) American business executive. 17.34; 39.17; 88.7; 104.18; 108.7; 123.29; 155.7; 157.3; 178.13; 240.12; 277.3; 281.9; 299.19; 315.3; 334.20; 340.12; 365.59; 444.14; 528.41; 551.96; 674.3; 738.6; 807.4; 873.10; 880.11; 945.22

Ibarruri, Dolores. Called La Pasionaria (1895–) Spanish Communist leader. 363.29

Ibsen, Henrik [Johan] (1828–1906) Norwegian playwright and poet. 365.61; 383.2; 442.7; 449.11; 469.12; 565.9; 819.24; 900.14

Illich, Ivan (1926–) Austrian-born American author. 577.4; 946.19; 946.20

Inge, Dean William Ralph (1860–1954) English prelate and writer. 41.14; 274.18; 279.45; 358.3; 374.7; 395.27; 458.2; 487.7; 520.4; 522.25; 545.16; 562.29; 678.5; 694.11; 713.2; 761.10; 871.1; 676.19

Ingersoll, Robert G[reen] (1833–1899) American lawyer, public official, agnostic. 16.4; 127.3; 279.46; 357.7; 387.41; 435.11; 455.4; 517.24; 711.36; 785.16; 797.38; 797.39; 797.40

Irving, Washington (1783–1859) American essayist, biographer, historian. 53.67; 66.3; 117.21; 198.9; 207.28; 289.15; 351.5; 446.9; 454.11; 503.5; 545.17; 545.18; 564.62; 564.63; 586.12; 610.7; 676.20; 718.31; 804.14; 867.8; 905.3; 968.2; 998.62; 1042.46; 1062.77; 1062.78

Ishiguro, Kazuo (1954–) Japanese novelist and short-story writer. 252.6; 813.3

Italian Proverbs. 37.3; 56.6; 72.25; 98.6; 105.13; 109.3; 162.5; 191.6; 199.6; 221.73; 280.1; 476.11; 517.25; 684.9; 755.14; 797.41

Ivins, Molly (1944–) American political commentator and writer. 432.2; 436.14; 493.16; 711.37; 766.9; 941.11; 1007.10

J

Jackson, Andrew (1767–1845) Seventh President of the United States (1829–1837). 395.28; 964.7

Jackson, Holbrook (1874–1948) English literary scholar and editor. 848.21

Jackson, Robert H[oughwout] (1892–1954) American jurist, Justice of the Supreme Court (1941–1954). 258.7; 761.11; 959.1

Jacob, Max (1876–1944) French poet, prose writer, painter. 53.68

Jacobs, Jane (1916–) American social critic and writer. 131.20

Jacobs, Jane (1916–) American social critic and writer. 43.6; 672.1

James I of England (1566–1625) King of Great

Britain (1603–1625); also ruled as James VI of Scotland (1567–1625). 982.6

James, Henry [Jr.] (1843–1916) American novelist, short-story writer, man of letters. 289.16; 504.13; 725.3

James, William (1842–1910) American philosopher, physiologist, psychologist, teacher. 78.9; 203.2; 451.6; 465.2; 604.18; 694.12; 794.5; 845.4; 849.16; 1067.19

Jami. Pen name of Nur ud-din 'Abd-ur-rahman ibn Ahmad (1414–1492) Persian poet, mystic, short-story writer. 569.5

Janeway, Elizabeth (Hall) (1913–) American critic, novelist, lecturer. 564.64

Japanese Proverbs. 92.6; 186.13; 287.4; 451.7; 491.12

Jefferson, Thomas (1743–1826) American statesman, Third President of the United States (1801–1809). 10.9; 34.36; 43.7; 50.11; 52.1; 104.19; 105.14; 113.5; 178.14; 182.5; 182.6; 197.9; 231.6; 233.21; 233.22; 265.3; 271.11; 272.5; 279.47; 297.14; 299.20; 395.29; 409.52; 447.18; 493.17; 528.42; 533.8; 539.60; 630.12; 630.13; 649.6; 658.7; 719.32; 722.11; 730.7; 760.8; 760.9; 762.8; 772.8; 786.7; 797.42; 806.7; 819.25; 823.11; 984.10; 992.29; 992.30; 999.8; 1002.16; 1031.2; 1057.4; 1060.35

Jerome, Jerome K[lapka] (11859–1927) English novelist and playwright. 33.11; 186.14; 268.29; 446.10; 718.32; 845.5; 918.23; 941.12; 978.34; 1000.9; 1027.9; 1050.5; 1050.6; 1065.45

Jerrold, Douglas (1803–1857) English playwright and humorist. 549.4

Jewish Proverbs. 221.74; 343.21; 804.15

Jiménez, Juan Ramón (1881–1958) Spanish poet. 67.1; 131.21; 336.7; 411.8; 539.61; 621.11; 708.55

Johnson, Lady Bird (19??–) Wife of Lyndon B. Johnson. 629.4

Johnson, Lyndon B[aines] (1908–1973) Thirty-sixth President of the United States (1963–1969). 100.9; 229.5; 368.18; 395.30; 718.33; 718.34; 730.8; 913.18; 1038.8; 1067.20

Johnson, Samuel. Also known as Dr. Johnson (1709–1784) English lexicographer, essayist, poet. 7.4; 10.10; 11.5; 18.5; 18.6; 19.14; 26.3; 52.2; 61.6; 66.4; 81.6; 93.44; 93.45; 134.3; 138.6; 152.8; 152.9; 165.9; 181.5; 185.3; 188.19; 200.2; 206.12; 207.29; 209.9; 211.7; 238.24; 238.25; 244.5; 245.7; 267.10; 267.11; 268.30; 268.31; 274.19; 274.20; 281.10; 291.5; 295.14; 297.15; 311.8; 318.7; 332.21; 336.8; 343.22; 349.11; 349.12; 355.9; 360.21; 365.62; 365.63; 369.5; 374.8; 376.19; 384.15; 384.16; 390.10; 393.24; 395.31; 401.31; 404.14; 409.53; 409.54; 409.55; 423.4; 427.20; 433.16; 436.15; 438.4; 440.11; 446.11; 450.17; 451.8; 493.18; 495.2; 504.14; 505.2; 509.5; 519.11; 522.26; 522.27; 522.28; 522.29; 524.21; 528.43; 530.6; 533.9; 538.6; 539.62; 541.22; 546.3; 548.6; 551.97; 564.65; 564.66; 564.67; 564.68; 565.10; 571.7; 580.14; 580.15; 602.31; 604.19; 623.40; 647.2; 653.52; 666.8; 678.6; 679.1; 681.13; 689.6; 698.13; 699.5; 704.19; 704.20; 718.35; 718.36; 718.37; 718.38; 722.12; 722.13; 729.16; 732.5; 732.6; 733.12; 734.10; 741.8; 761.12; 767.2; 778.4; 780.9; 780.10; 785.17; 788.1; 790.16; 810.9; 819.26; 839.6; 848.22; 851.1; 860.3; 862.6; 863.6; 864.3; 883.5; 903.4; 905.4; 910.4; 913.19; 914.5; 916.6; 918.24; 918.25; 941.13; 942.12; 942.13; 952.5; 965.19; 971.4; 972.16; 992.31; 992.32; 998.63; 998.64; 1002.17; 1011.17; 1032.8; 1033.26; 1048.29; 1048.30; 1055.7; 1062.79; 1069.67; 1069.68; 1069.69; 1070.12; 1072.10; 1072.11; 1072.12

Johnston, Eric [Allen] (1896–1963) American business association official and motion picture industry executive. 312.4

Joll, James (1918–) American political analyst. 711.38

Jones, James (1921–1977) American novelist. 361.5

Jones, LeRoi (1934–) American writer and militant civil rights advocate. 30.5; 85.10; 363.30; 1064.24; 1071.35

Jong, Erica [Mann] (1942–) American novelist and poet. 28.3; 73.6; 285.2; 289.17; 394.7; 424.5; 502.2; 758.9; 758.10

Jonson, Ben (1573–1637) English playwright and poet. 8.4; 17.35; 33.12; 138.7; 203.3; 343.23; 349.13; 357.8; 360.22; 360.23; 393.25; 405.9; 426.6; 433.17; 440.12; 476.12; 550.4; 554.3; 627.7; 669.1; 670.27; 675.9; 684.10; 708.56; 711.39; 723.20; 723.21; 766.10; 830.3; 831.10; 898.10; 899.6; 916.7; 923.31; 923.32; 945.23; 971.5; 998.65; 998.66; 998.67; 1007.11; 1011.18; 1030.12; 1062.80; 1070.13; 1071.36; 1072.13

Joseph, Chief (19??–) Native American leader. 1042.47

Joubert, Joseph (1754–1824) French essayist and moralist. 93.46; 123.30; 271.12; 365.64; 480.12; 517.26; 588.10; 590.9; 653.53; 653.54; 708.57; 797.43; 797.44; 965.20; 1033.27; 1060.36; 1064.25; 1072.14

Jouhandeau, Marcel. Pen name, Marcel Provence (1888–) French fiction writer, essayist, playwright. 794.6

Jourdan, Louis (1922–) French actor. 972.17

Joyce, James (1882–1941) Irish novelist, short-story writer, poet. 65.9; 174.14; 470.4; 564.69; 603.3; 911.1

Jung, Carl Gustav (1875–1961) Swiss psychiatrist. 921.4

Juvenal. Full name, Decimus Junius Juvenalis (A.D. 60?–?140) Roman satirist. 90.3; 209.10; 337.5; 405.10; 413.6; 425.8; 426.7; 457.3; 491.13; 519.12; 602.32; 623.41; 653.55; 670.28; 681.14; 691.6; 718.39; 718.40; 738.7; 817.13; 858.20; 1000.10; 1048.31; 1055.8; 1056.7; 1062.81; 1069.70

K

Kael, Pauline (1919–) American film critic. 53.69; 516.8; 963.9; 967.9

Kaiser, Henry J (1882–1967) American industrialist. 737.3

Kant, Immanuel (1724–1804) German philosopher. 9.29

Kaplan, Robert D. (1952–) Journalist and author. 498.4; 518.7; 622.5; 752.2

Karr, [Jean-Baptiste] Alphonse (1808–1890) French journalist and novelist. 117.22; 409.56

Kaufman, Bel (1808–1890) Contemporary German-born American educator and writer. 123.31

Kazin, Alfred (1915–) American literary critic, teacher, editor, memoirist. 53.70; 104.20; 221.75; 545.19; 783.4; 913.20; 1069.71; 1069.72; 1069.73

Keats, John (1795–1821) English poet. 72.26; 72.27; 86.2; 160.1; 188.20; 251.6; 268.32; 321.24; 329.16; 333.7; 335.9; 336.9; 401.32; 401.33; 431.13; 450.18; 450.19; 522.30; 539.63; 623.42; 654.3; 694.13; 694.14; 705.4; 708.58; 708.59; 708.60; 718.41; 854.28; 946.21; 990.9; 998.68; 1011.19; 1071.37

Keillor, Garrison (1942–) American humorist, writer, radio host. 45.14; 355.10; 359.10; 387.42; 539.64; 749.2

Keller, Helen [Adams] (1880–1968) American memoirist and essayist. 16.5; 112.4; 119.16; 153.2; 271.13; 321.25; 409.57; 409.58; 551.98; 856.9; 946.22; 984.11; 1005.6; 1065.46; 1071.38

Kempis, Thomas à (1880–1968) American memoirist and essayist. 6.12; 17.37; 183.3; 213.12; 221.76; 342.16; 444.15; 460.4; 516.9; 522.31; 548.7; 551.99; 696.3; 780.11; 946.23; 1065.47

Kempton, Murray (1917–) American journalist. 85.11; 131.22; 146.2; 150.8; 150.9; 378.3; 443.12; 565.11; 678.7; 711.40; 809.2; 819.27; 819.28; 862.7; 1012.3

Kendrick, Alexander American journalist and broadcaster. 149.9; 967.10; 967.11; 998.69
Kenkō, Yoshida (1283–1350) Japanese court official and Buddhist monk. 284.20; 454.12; 551.100
Kennan, George F[rost] (1904–) American diplomat and historian. 108.8; 250.4; 395.32; 498.5; 862.8
Kennedy, Caroline & Alderman, Ellen (1957–) (1958–) American attorneys. 823.1; 823.2; 823.3
Kennedy, John F[itzgerald] (1917–1963) Thirty-fifth President of the United States. 34.37; 53.71; 53.72; 85.12; 100.10; 100.11; 100.12; 101.2; 107.1; 109.4; 115.8; 117.23; 131.23; 131.24; 132.6; 150.10; 162.6; 195.16; 205.4; 205.5; 216.12; 225.6; 229.6; 229.7; 233.24; 233.25; 245.8; 247.5; 252.8; 277.4; 279.48; 363.31; 365.65; 395.33; 395.34; 443.13; 450.20; 498.6; 498.7; 522.32; 528.44; 537.19; 537.20; 562.30; 617.5; 621.12; 621.13; 621.14; 641.9; 641.10; 659.8; 670.29; 678.8; 678.9; 681.15; 681.16; 682.9; 682.10; 696.4; 708.61; 710.7; 711.41; 711.42; 718.42; 718.43; 723.22; 730.9; 730.10; 737.4; 741.9; 741.10; 819.29; 823.12; 823.13; 823.14; 837.6; 849.17; 889.9; 901.12; 929.11; 930.12; 948.13; 966.14; 994.2; 994.3; 1015.1; 1042.48; 1044.2; 1047.7; 1048.32
Kennedy, Robert F[rancis] (1925–1968) American political leader. 117.24; 335.10; 517.27; 711.43; 719.33; 741.11
Kerouac, Jack (1922–1969) American novelist and poet. 102.5; 131.25; 449.12; 681.17; 882.6
Kerr, Clark (1911–) American educator. 279.49
Kerr, Jean (1923–) American essayist and playwright. 11.6; 73.7; 564.70; 581.28; 670.30; 896.13; 906.11
Kerr, Walter C. A. (1913–) American drama critic. 1001.5
Kettering, Charles F[ranklin] (1876–1958) American engineer and inventor. 654.4
Khrushchev, Nikita [Sergeyevich] (1894–1971) Russian political leader and Premier of the Soviet Union (1953–1964). 162.7; 711.44
Kidder, John Tracy (1945–) American writer. 741.12; 853.12; 943.4
Kincaid, Jamaica (1949–) West Indian author. 992.33; 992.34
King, Martin Luther, Jr. (1929–1968) American clergyman and civil rights leader. 85.13; 127.4; 171.9; 201.21; 252.7; 307.22; 433.18; 447.19; 528.45; 554.4; 598.6; 641.11; 741.13; 775.12; 775.13; 849.18; 850.6; 960.8; 1038.9
Kingsley, Rev. Charles (1819–1875) English clergyman, novelist, poet. 393.26; 539.65
Kingston, Maxine Hong (1940–) American memoirist and novelist. 37.4; 45.15; 149.10; 437.8; 564.71; 742.5; 857.6; 884.5; 948.14
Kinsella, William P. (1935–) Canadian novelist and short-story writer. 78.10; 414.6; 418.18; 875.12; 929.12
Kipling, Rudyard (1865–1936) English novelist, poet, short-story writer. 19.15; 46.3; 100.13; 312.5; 356.16; 422.13; 480.13; 518.8; 559.9; 581.29; 586.13; 699.6; 890.1; 899.7; 910.5; 982.7; 1062.82
Kirk, Marshall (19??–). 424.6
Kissinger, Henry A[lfred] (1923–) American foreign policy expert and diplomat. 14.4; 52.3; 498.8; 498.9; 498.10; 711.45; 719.34; 819.30; 819.31; 976.1
Klee, Paul (1879–1940) Swiss painter. 53.73
Knebel, Fletcher (1911–) American journalist and writer. 982.8
Knight, G. Wilson (1897–1985) English critic and teacher. 149.11
Koch, Edward (1924–) American political figure and columnist. 873.11
Koestler, Arthur (1905–1983) Hungarian-born English journalist, novelist, critic. 150.11; 174.15; 174.16; 299.21; 419.32; 910.6; 946.24
Kogon, Eugen (1903–) German scholar and educator. 232.2; 288.14
Koran (6th and 7th c.) Sacred book of the Muslims. 271.14
Kozol, Jonathan (1936–) American author. 123.32; 131.26; 279.50; 602.33; 965.21; 965.22
Kramer, Hilton (6th and 7th c.) Contemporary American art critic and writer. 53.74
Krishna Menon, V. K. (1897–1974) Indian statesman and lawyer. 498.13
Krim, Seymour (1922–1989) American critic and essayist. 657.7; 678.10; 978.35
Kronenberger, Louis (1904–) American critic, essayist, novelist, editor. 12.6; 34.38; 43.8; 53.75; 72.28; 104.21; 105.15; 117.25; 152.10; 171.10; 210.14; 210.15; 235.6; 276.3; 298.10; 304.2; 329.17; 332.22; 353.1; 394.8; 411.9; 432.3; 436.16; 468.6; 468.7; 496.3; 496.4; 569.6; 627.8; 630.14; 632.11; 804.16; 849.19; 880.12; 893.3; 924.4; 944.2; 945.24; 967.12; 969.2; 1001.6; 1004.13; 1039.3
Krutch, Joseph Wood (1893–1970) American critic, essayist, teacher. 18.7; 34.39; 41.15; 77.15; 105.16; 105.17; 133.15; 170.3; 194.10; 213.13; 233.26; 241.8; 298.11; 328.10; 368.19; 431.14; 449.13; 481.3; 482.7; 491.14; 562.31; 604.20; 623.43; 623.44; 623.45; 628.1; 670.31; 716.8; 849.20; 849.21; 854.29; 854.30; 856.10; 911.2; 966.15; 966.16; 966.17; 986.14; 987.8; 1026.11; 1042.49; 1049.6; 1064.26; 41.16
Kundera, Milan (1929–) Czech novelist and short-story writer. 35.3; 77.16; 116.9; 210.16; 218.5; 266.10; 332.23; 423.5; 459.2; 551.101; 551.102; 555.11; 589.7; 593.3; 614.37; 632.12; 636.2; 832.5; 1011.20; 1036.2
Kuralt, Charles (1934–) American broadcast journalist. 824.2

L
Labiche, Eugène [Marin] (1815–1888) French playwright. 888.7
La Chaussé, Pierre-Claude Nivelle de (1692–1754) French playwright. 299.8
L'Amour, Louis [Dearborn] (1908–1988) American novelist and short-story writer. 16.6; 93.49; 279.51; 332.25; 447.20; 522.33; 711.46; 934.6; 975.24; 978.37; 1038.10
L'Engle, Madeleine (1918–) American novelist. 18.8; 201.22; 387.43; 491.15; 861.4; 923.33
La Bruyère, Jean de (1645–1696) French writer and moralist. 33.13; 93.47; 188.21; 200.3; 226.6; 238.26; 263.8; 264.9; 329.18; 332.24; 342.17; 372.2; 412.12; 425.9; 540.7; 551.103; 551.104; 564.72; 581.30; 581.31; 652.7; 656.12; 670.32; 697.7; 697.8; 785.18; 804.17; 820.3; 830.4; 857.7; 930.13; 941.14; 942.14; 945.25; 978.36; 1033.28; 1048.33; 1060.37; 1061.12; 1062.83; 1069.74; 1069.75; 1069.76; 1069.77; 1072.15
La Fontaine [Jean de] (1621–1695) French fabulist. 1.10; 45.16; 202.5; 221.79; 349.14; 437.9; 598.7; 790.17; 1071.39
La Mettrie, Julien Offroy de (1709–1751) French physician and materialist philosopher. 477.8; 1034.10
La Rochefoucauld, François, Duc de (1613–1680) French writer. 1.11; 2.9; 7.5; 14.5; 15.6; 17.38; 19.16; 21.6; 33.15; 45.17; 89.3; 116.10; 139.6; 165.10; 165.11; 168.1; 181.6; 181.7; 181.8; 188.22; 188.23; 195.17; 195.18; 195.19; 199.8; 200.4; 211.8; 221.80; 224.9; 224.10; 227.13; 238.27; 258.8; 259.8; 259.9; 271.15; 283.5; 283.6; 284.21; 288.15; 295.15; 295.16; 295.17; 305.5; 321.26; 332.27; 338.19; 342.18; 342.19; 342.20; 349.15; 351.6;

354.7; 354.8; 360.24; 360.25; 365.66; 365.67; 365.68; 365.69; 367.9; 384.19; 390.11; 393.28; 399.4; 399.5; 401.34; 403.12; 409.59; 409.60; 413.7; 418.19; 427.21; 435.12; 435.13; 440.13; 478.4; 493.19; 495.4; 510.11; 510.12; 510.13; 510.14; 516.10; 522.34; 551.105; 551.106; 551.107; 551.108; 551.109; 551.110; 551.111; 551.112; 551.113; 552.5; 552.6; 554.5; 555.12; 559.10; 561.6; 564.74; 584.3; 598.9; 598.10; 608.6; 619.4; 644.2; 647.3; 647.4; 647.5; 652.8; 653.57; 653.58; 653.59; 656.13; 657.8; 675.10; 675.11; 675.12; 675.13; 675.14; 693.7; 694.18; 698.14; 706.6; 722.17; 722.18; 722.19; 732.7; 732.8; 733.13; 743.6; 749.3; 772.9; 780.12; 780.13; 807.5; 808.6; 820.4; 855.12; 873.12; 873.13; 876.6; 876.7; 899.8; 901.13; 901.14; 905.5; 914.6; 923.39; 923.40; 963.10; 969.3; 969.4; 970.2; 989.5; 996.4; 999.9; 1008.14; 1008.15; 1027.10; 1027.11; 1033.29; 1033.30; 1034.8; 1034.9; 1047.8; 1060.38; 1060.39; 1061.14; 1061.15; 1062.84; 1070.14; 1071.40

Laird, Charlton (1901–) American linguist and writer. 41.17; 133.16; 262.6; 398.5; 398.6; 398.7; 524.22; 524.23; 524.24; 923.34; 923.35; 1064.27; 1064.28

Lamartine, Alphonse Marie Louis de (1790–1869) French poet, writer, statesman. 2.8; 261.7

Lamb, Charles. Pen name, Elia (1775–1834) English essayist. 93.48; 93.50; 96.4; 97.6; 123.33; 155.8; 199.7; 202.6; 227.12; 268.33; 274.21; 369.6; 384.17; 384.18; 389.6; 428.16; 436.17; 474.2; 526.17; 538.7; 564.73; 630.15; 764.7; 796.3; 813.4; 896.14; 896.15; 923.36; 954.3; 965.23; 972.18; 975.23; 982.9; 982.10; 1017.10; 1065.48; 1071.41; 1071.42

Lamb, Mary [Ann] (1764–1847) English writer, sister of Charles Lamb. 123.34

Landor, Walter Savage (1775–1864) English poet and prose writer. 33.14; 47.1; 51.12; 93.51; 131.27; 189.5; 207.30; 295.18; 333.8; 393.27; 400.8; 402.1; 426.8; 495.3; 524.25; 528.46; 539.66; 540.8; 541.23; 558.24; 598.8; 600.12; 620.4; 653.56; 694.15; 708.62; 708.63; 722.14; 722.15; 722.16; 729.17; 746.11; 805.3; 822.12; 848.23; 915.22; 923.37; 960.9; 975.25; 998.70; 998.71; 1002.18; 1048.34; 1061.13; 1064.29; 1069.78; 1069.79; 1069.80

Lane, Kenneth Jay (1932–) American designer. 332.26

Lang, Paul Henry (1901–) Hungarian-born American musicologist and author. 207.31

Langer, Susanne K. (1895–1985) American philosopher and teacher. 480.14; 590.10; 694.16; 694.17

Lao Tzu [Laotse or La-tsze] (c. 604–531 B.C.) Chinese philosopher and founder of Taoism. 55.10; 186.15; 229.8; 327.1; 678.11; 862.9; 875.13; 923.38; 1042.50

Lapham, Lewis (1935–) American editor and writer. 233.27; 233.28; 359.11; 581.32; 630.16; 719.35; 731.4; 1038.11

Latin American Proverbs. 109.5

Latin Proverbs. 5.3; 48.5; 57.11; 195.20; 338.20

Lautréamont, Comte de. Pen name of Isidore Lucien Ducasse (1846–1870) French poet. 918.26

Lavater, Johann Kaspar (1741–1801) Swiss divine and poet. 474.3

Lawrence, D[avid] H[erbert] (1885–1930) English novelist, short-story writer, poet, essayist. 26.4; 133.17; 363.32; 374.9; 486.3; 612.2; 676.21; 713.3; 892.27; 987.9; 998.72

Leach, Edmund (1910–) English anthropologist, educator and writer. 419.33

Leahy, Frank [William] (1908–) American football coach. 873.14

Leakey, Richard [Erskine] (1944–) Kenyan-born American paleoanthropologist. 53.76; 103.6; 210.17; 308.11; 404.15; 524.26; 524.27; 562.32; 562.33; 623.46

Leary, Paris (1931–) American poet and educator. 551.114

Least Heat Moon, William (1939–) American writer. 16.7; 34.53; 117.27; 189.6; 443.22; 897.6

Lec, Stanislaw [Jerzy] (1909–) Polish poet and aphorist. 19.17; 409.61; 414.7; 441.4; 476.13; 617.6; 630.17; 741.14; 745.5; 780.14

Lee, Robert E[dward] (1807–1870) American general, commander in chief of Confederate armies. 271.17

Legge, Walter and Schwarzkopf, Elisabeth (19??–). 53.77; 53.128

Le Guin, Ursula K. (1929–) American novelist and short-story writer. 93.52; 133.13; 321.18; 368.20; 604.21; 892.28; 1032.9; 1069.81

Lenclos, Ninon. Pen name of Anne Lenclos (1620–1705) French wit and lady of fashion. 1062.85

Lenin, Nikolai, Pseudonym of Vladimir Ilyich Ulyanov (1870–1924) Russian Communist leader. 233.29; 930.14

Leonardo da Vinci (1452–1519) Italian artist, inventor, scientist. 51.13; 82.6; 152.11; 321.27; 343.24; 360.26; 430.3; 522.35; 532.12; 541.24; 624.8; 666.9; 694.19; 716.9; 738.8; 771.5; 864.4; 1007.12; 1065.49

Leopardi, Count Giacomo (1798–1837) Italian poet and essayist. 95.5; 165.12; 206.13; 594.2; 653.60; 892.29; 965.24; 1037.8

Lerner, Max (1902–) Russian-born American teacher, editor, journalist. 34.40; 108.9; 133.18; 202.7; 229.9; 233.30; 241.9; 281.11; 307.23; 307.24; 358.4; 387.44; 495.5; 498.11; 522.36; 571.8; 602.34; 630.18; 681.18; 686.3; 711.47; 734.11; 746.12; 759.1; 775.14; 797.45; 834.3; 849.22; 912.4; 945.26; 971.6; 1042.51; 1042.52; 1056.8

Lesage, Alain-René (1668–1747) French playwright and novelist. 409.62; 1062.86

Lessing, Gotthold Ephraim (1729–1781) German playwright, aesthetician, critic. 57.12; 393.29; 418.20; 683.7; 880.13; 954.4

Levi, Primo (1919–1987) Italian memoirist and novelist. 195.21; 381.3; 434.2; 670.33; 735.7; 918.27; 956.4; 1011.21

Lévi-Strauss, Claude (1908–) French social anthropologist and author. 419.34

Lewis, Cecil Day. *See* Day-Lewis, C.

Lewis, [Harry] Sinclair (1885–1951) American novelist. 64.4; 77.17; 105.18; 233.31; 406.10; 422.14; 430.4; 472.5; 586.14; 982.11

Lichtenberg, Georg Christoph (1742–1799) German physicist and writer. 78.11; 93.53; 93.54; 152.12; 363.33; 376.20; 401.35; 404.16; 466.3; 581.33; 604.22; 656.14; 686.4; 754.10; 816.2; 848.24; 876.8; 886.8

Liebling, A[bbott] J[oseph] (1904–1963) American journalist and satirist. 131.28; 522.37; 630.19; 630.20; 630.21; 630.22

Lily, John (19??–). 51.14

Lincoln, Abraham (1861–1865) Sixteenth President of the United States. 8.5; 34.41; 109.6; 179.3; 233.32; 241.10; 374.10; 376.21; 395.35; 395.36; 537.21; 559.11; 597.6; 602.35; 621.15; 677.13; 682.11; 682.12; 761.13; 761.14; 819.32; 823.15; 869.6; 889.10; 1002.19; 1016.6; 1038.12; 1056.9

Lindbergh, Anne Morrow (1906–) American writer. 8.6; 34.42; 59.2; 149.12; 484.2; 492.6; 551.115; 551.116; 674.5; 677.14; 784.11; 856.11; 875.14; 906.12; 915.23; 918.28; 946.25; 998.73; 1062.87

Lindbergh, Charles A[ugustus] (1902–1974) American aviator and writer. 133.19; 155.9; 209.11; 221.81; 238.28; 308.12; 363.34; 486.4; 539.67; 551.117; 719.36; 775.15; 978.38; 1026.12

Linderman, Bill (1922?–1961) American rodeo performer. 929.13
Lindner, Robert [Mitchell] (1914–1956) American psychoanalyst and writer. 12.7; 61.7; 111.11; 150.12; 171.11; 171.12; 208.6; 468.8; 915.24
Linkletter, Art (1912–) Canadian-born American radio and television personality. 540.9; 579.1
Lin Yutang *See* Yutang, Lin
Lippmann, Walter (1889–1974) American teacher, editor, journalist. 53.78; 61.8; 70.3; 119.17; 174.17; 201.23; 233.33; 233.34; 233.35; 238.29; 242.6; 335.11; 368.21; 395.37; 395.38; 395.39; 432.4; 435.14; 442.8; 443.14; 491.16; 528.47; 531.9; 568.3; 576.3; 604.23; 604.24; 694.20; 711.48; 711.49; 711.50; 711.51; 719.37; 726.9; 760.10; 760.11; 790.18; 828.1; 858.21; 881.2; 913.21; 932.1; 945.27; 966.18; 974.8; 998.74; 1023.3; 1033.31; 1038.13; 1060.40
Lipsyte, Robert (1938–) American journalist and writer. 929.14
Lithgow, William (1582–c. 1645) Scottish traveler and writer. 274.22
Littré, [Maximilien Paul] Émile (1801–1881) French scholar and lexicographer. 771.6
Livy. Full name, Titus Livius (59 B.C.–A.D.17) Roman historian. 92.7; 208.7; 246.4; 475.3; 528.48; 681.19; 772.10; 900.15
Locke, John (1632–1704) English philosopher. 9.30; 93.55; 213.14; 224.11; 299.22; 299.23; 321.29; 333.9; 336.10; 413.8; 442.9; 480.15; 516.11; 528.49; 542.11; 590.11; 604.25; 623.47; 623.48; 648.1; 656.15; 683.8; 732.9; 744.1; 746.13; 965.25; 975.26; 998.75; 998.76; 1064.30; 1064.31; 1065.50
Lodge, Henry Cabot, Jr. (1902–) American politician and diplomat. 437.10
Logau, Baron Friedrich von (1604–1655) German poet and epigrammatist. 815.8
Longfellow, Henry Wadsworth (1807–1882) American poet and translator. 6.13; 21.7; 55.11; 76.8; 93.57; 123.35; 131.29; 131.30; 142.4; 166.9; 194.11; 279.52; 287.5; 288.16; 299.24; 325.3; 336.11; 401.36; 422.15; 427.22; 440.14; 532.13; 564.75; 589.8; 606.12; 614.38; 633.7; 653.61; 676.22; 708.64; 708.65; 848.25; 858.22; 898.11; 915.25; 918.29; 918.30; 936.3; 946.26; 960.10; 1011.22; 1066.2; 1069.82; 1071.43
Longworth, Alice Roosevelt (19?? –) Daughter of American President Theodore Roosevelt. 1027.12
Lopate, Phillip (1943–) American essayist. 672.2; 944.3
Lord, James (1922–) American biographer and memoirist. 454.13
Lord, Louise Bennett (1895–1989) Mother of biographer James Lord. 19.18
Lorenz, Konrad Z. (1903–) Viennese-born zoologist and writer. 201.24; 201.25; 308.13; 308.14; 562.34; 719.38; 927.9; 41.18
Lovelace, Richard (1618–1658) English poet. 491.17; 735.8
Lowell, Amy [Lawrence] (1874–1925) American poet, critic, biographer. 34.43; 93.58; 131.31; 203.4; 316.6; 386.8; 525.1; 699.7; 750.11; 918.31; 946.27; 1042.53
Lowell, James Russell (1819–1891) American poet, critic, editor, diplomat. 72.29; 113.6; 123.36; 136.5; 201.26; 207.32; 221.82; 227.14; 238.30; 287.6; 321.30; 359.12; 360.27; 363.35; 371.1; 377.7; 384.20; 387.45; 412.13; 431.15; 522.38; 547.4; 551.118; 598.11; 624.9; 625.4; 635.3; 708.66; 729.18; 773.3; 792.3; 823.16; 854.31; 854.32; 898.12; 904.7; 915.26; 915.27; 986.15; 998.77; 1000.11; 1002.20; 1050.7; 551.119
Lowenstein, Allard (1929–1980) American public official. 286.3
Lucan (full name, Marcus Annaeus Lucanus) (A.D. 39–65) Roman poet and prose writer. 92.8; 401.37; 403.13; 549.5; 719.39; 930.15
Lucas, E[dward] V[errall] (1868–1938) English novelist, poet, essayist, man of letters. 197.10; 279.53; 344.21
Lucian (c. 120–200) Greek satirist. 989.6
Lucretius. Full name, Titus Lucretius Carus (98?–55 B.C.) Roman poet and natural philosopher. 110.5; 117.26; 216.13; 221.83; 374.11; 701.2; 719.40; 882.7; 892.30; 952.6; 1061.16; 1070.15
Lurie, Leonard (19?? –) American historian. 491.18; 491.19; 711.52
Luther, Martin (1483–1546) German theologian and founder of the Protestant Reformation. 38.1; 284.22; 330.19; 564.76; 596.2; 723.23; 724.8
Lyly, John (1554?–1606) English prose writer, poet, playwright. 58.4; 268.34; 321.31; 469.13; 551.120; 554.6; 686.5; 718.44; 976.2; 1061.17; 1072.16
Lynd, Robert (1879–1949) Anglo-Irish essayist and journalist. 480.16
Lynes, [Joseph] Russell (Jr.) (1910–) American editor, critic, writer. 267.12; 676.23; 716.10; 787.2; 910.7; 963.11; 967.13
Lyttleton, George. 1st Baron Lyttleton of Frankley (1709–1773) English statesman, patron, writer. 705.5; 1062.88

M

MacArthur, Douglas (1880–1964) American general. 588.11; 1042.54
Macaulay, Thomas Babington, 1st Baron Macaulay of Rothley (1800–1859) English statesman, poet, historian, essayist, biographer. 80.4; 201.27; 746.14
MacDonald, Anson *See* Heinlein, Robert A.
Machado [y Ruiz], Antonio (1875–1939) Spanish poet. 78.12; 321.32; 416.7; 506.2; 524.28; 562.35; 688.4; 694.21; 785.19; 892.31; 924.5; 998.78; 1005.7; 1034.11; 1069.83
Machiavelli, Niccolo (1469–1527) Florentine statesman and political philosopher. 349.16; 719.41; 1058.7
MacLeish, Archibald (1892–1982) American poet, dramatist. 221.84; 399.6; 708.67
Macmillan, [Maurice] Harold (1894–) Prime Minister of Great Britain (1957–1963). 206.14; 216.14
Madagascan Proverbs. 465.3
Maddocks, Melvin (1883–1970) Contemporary American writer. 1069.84
Madison, James (1751–1836) Fourth President of the United States (1809–1817). 1002.21
Madsen, Hunter (19??–). 424.6
Maeterlinck, Count Maurice (1862–1949) Belgian poet, dramatist, essayist. 221.85; 305.6; 307.25; 368.22; 393.30; 517.28; 610.8; 663.11; 758.11; 837.7; 875.16; 892.32; 898.14; 946.28; 1060.41; 1064.32
Mailer, Norman (1923–) American novelist and essayist. 18.10; 53.80; 119.18; 133.20; 178.15; 195.22; 221.86; 403.14; 409.63; 424.7; 551.121; 762.9; 876.9; 967.17; 975.27; 997.4; 1060.42; 1062.90
Malamud, Bernard (1914–1986) American novelist and short-story writer. 62.6; 77.19; 81.7; 103.7; 123.37; 175.5; 217.3; 266.11; 316.7; 321.33; 321.34; 351.7; 418.21; 444.16; 504.15; 539.69; 540.10; 623.49; 794.7; 1064.33; 1069.85
Malay Proverbs. 33.16; 109.7; 171.13; 221.87; 235.7; 247.6; 271.16; 314.2; 400.9; 401.38; 540.11; 567.1; 755.15; 866.5; 873.15
Malcolm X. Original name, Malcolm Little (1925–1965) American civil-rights activist and orator. 39.18; 363.36; 678.12; 719.42; 732.10; 775.16; 804.18; 859.5; 893.4; 923.41; 1002.22; 1054.3
Malebranche, Nicolas

(1638–1715) French philosopher and theologian. 443.15; 450.21; 808.7

Mallarmé, Stéphane (1842–1898) French poet. 290.2

Malraux, André (1901–1976) French novelist and critic. 50.12; 53.81; 345.4

Manchester, William (1922–) American novelist and historian. 195.23; 330.20; 418.22; 588.12; 762.10; 873.16; 916.9

Mandelshtam, Osip (1891–1938) Russian poet. 708.68

Mann, Horace (1796–1859) American educator. 279.54

Mann, Thomas (1875–1955) German novelist and essayist. 41.19; 53.82; 53.83; 65.10; 72.30; 93.59; 124.7; 174.18; 184.6; 201.28; 221.88; 238.31; 284.23; 367.10; 406.11; 432.5; 443.16; 551.122; 551.123; 551.124; 555.13; 562.36; 577.5; 610.9; 614.39; 623.50; 631.3; 676.24; 684.11; 711.54; 780.15; 875.17; 896.16; 912.6; 915.28; 915.29; 923.42; 969.5; 978.40; 1029.7; 1029.8; 1042.55

Mannes, Marya (1904–) American essayist and journalist. 8.7; 34.48; 64.8; 125.17; 177.5; 178.16; 351.8; 392.6; 491.20; 493.20; 516.12; 533.11; 571.9; 576.4; 599.1; 602.37; 711.55; 857.8; 901.15; 967.18; 1008.16; 1061.18

Mao Tse-tung (1893–) Chairman of the Central Committee of the Chinese Communist Party. 135.4; 150.13; 156.7; 178.17; 682.13; 711.56; 711.57; 1042.56

Marceau, Marcel (1923–) French actor and pantomimist. 898.15; 972.19

Marcello, Benedetto (1686–1739) Italian composer. 972.20

Maritain, Jacques (1882–1973) French philosopher and man of letters. 34.49; 205.6; 233.36; 298.13; 399.7; 443.17; 551.125; 678.13; 966.20; 1011.23

Markham, Beryl (1902–1986) English aviator. 28.4; 217.4; 896.17

Markham, Edwin (1852–1940) American poet. 133.21; 271.18; 605.4; 728.2; 1066.3

Marlowe, Christopher (1564–1593) English dramatist and poet. 520.5; 551.126; 699.8; 797.46; 822.13; 1042.57

Marquand, John P[hillips] (1893–1960) American novelist. 1069.86

Marquis, Don[ald Robert Perry] (1878–1937) American newspaperman and humorist. Marquis, Don 72.31; 204.11; 231.7; 268.35; 277.5; 319.4; 395.40; 409.64; 427.23; 481.4; 508.4; 562.37; 659.9; 711.58; 766.11; 874.3; 952.7; 1062.91; 1065.51; 1069.87

Marshall, John (1755–1835) American jurist. Chief Justice of the U.S. Supreme Court (1801–1835). 104.22

Martí, José [Julian] (1853–1895) Cuban patriot, poet, essayist. 363.37; 401.39; 406.12

Martial. Full name, Marcus Valarius Martialis (A.D. 42?–?102) Latin epigrammatist born in Spain. 45.18; 384.21; 386.9; 413.9; 418.23; 444.17; 513.5; 539.70; 561.7; 580.16; 729.19; 808.8; 918.34; 937.5; 948.15; 1069.88

Martin, Judith, (1938–) American author. 77.20; 224.13; 563.16

Martin-Chauffier, Louis (1894–) French writer. 221.89

Marvell, Andrew (1621–1678) English poet. 221.90; 857.9; 978.41; 1067.21

Marx, Karl (1818–1883) German philosopher and socialist. 108.10; 512.2; 602.38; 797.47; 1065.52

Mason, George (1725–1792) American statesman, author of the Virginia Constitution and Bill of Rights, on which were modeled the Federal Constitution and Bill of Rights. 731.5

Massinger, Philip (1583–1640) English playwright. *See also* Fletcher, John. 33.17; 221.91; 268.36; 268.37; 831.11

Maugham, W[illiam] Somerset (1874–1965) English novelist and playwright. 11.7; 17.40; 21.8; 31.5; 53.84; 53.85; 59.3; 59.4; 72.32; 91.3; 93.60; 93.61; 115.9; 145.7; 149.13; 174.19; 188.24; 201.29; 206.15; 210.18; 270.1; 289.18; 307.26; 312.6; 344.22; 365.71; 365.72; 390.12; 393.31; 395.41; 398.8; 400.10; 401.40; 405.11; 436.18; 449.14; 450.22; 499.5; 515.4; 515.5; 522.39; 526.18; 539.71; 540.12; 551.127; 551.128; 551.129; 552.8; 581.36; 581.37; 602.39; 637.1; 653.62; 684.12; 694.22; 704.22; 708.69; 713.4; 729.20; 740.3; 782.3; 797.48; 803.6; 818.3; 885.4; 913.22; 933.3; 935.1; 940.13; 942.15; 945.28; 946.29; 972.21; 972.22; 986.16; 998.79; 1061.19; 1062.92; 1064.34; 1069.89; 1069.90; 1071.44

Maupassant, [Henri René Albert] Guy de (1850–1893) French short-story writer and novelist. 678.14

Mauriac, François (1885–1970) French novelist, essayist, playwright. 53.86; 81.8; 103.8; 199.9; 207.33; 551.130; 586.15; 708.70; 847.2; 1069.91; 1069.92

Maurois, André. Pen name of Emile Herzog (1885–1967) French biographer, novelist, essayist. 21.9; 210.19; 653.63; 755.16; 877.3; 942.16; 963.12; 1062.93

May, Rollo (1909–1994) American psychoanalyst and writer. 174.20; 195.24; 201.30; 201.31; 258.9; 278.3; 431.16; 499.6; 531.10; 571.10; 840.3; 966.21; 998.80; 1005.8

Mazzini, Giuseppe (1805–1872) Italian patriot and writer. 998.81

Mc Carthy, Mary [Therese] (1912–1989) American novelist, short-story writer, critic. 34.44; 34.45; 34.46; 64.5; 66.5; 74.1; 77.18; 119.19; 131.32; 131.33; 168.2; 172.2; 185.4; 224.12; 227.15; 279.55; 282.2; 285.3; 298.12; 355.11; 365.70; 419.35; 443.18; 474.4; 477.9; 477.10; 533.10; 539.68; 617.7; 627.9; 636.3; 641.12; 663.10; 746.15; 786.8; 846.3; 849.23; 875.15; 912.5; 992.35; 1029.3; 1029.4; 1029.5; 1029.6; 1048.35

McDonagh, Edward C[harles] (1915–) Canadian-born American sociologist. 64.6

McFee, William [Morley Punshon] (1881–1966) English-born American novelist and essayist. 17.39; 43.9; 53.79; 83.4; 169.4; 289.19; 340.13; 443.19; 472.6; 564.77; 581.34; 602.36; 827.2; 918.33; 996.5

Mc Ginley, Phyllis (1905–) American essayist and writer of light verse and books for children. 19.19; 95.6; 152.13; 508.3; 552.7; 564.78; 564.79; 581.35; 626.7; 654.5; 660.3; 670.34; 704.21; 736.3; 828.2; 898.13; 900.16; 916.8; 1038.14; 1062.89

McGinniss, Joe (1942–) American journalist and author. 711.53; 864.5; 967.14; 967.15; 967.16

McLuhan, [Herbert] Marshall (1911–) Canadian educator, author, media expert. McLuhan, Marshall 18.9; 34.47; 64.7; 229.10; 279.56; 283.7; 289.20; 362.7; 619.5; 809.3; 966.19; 978.39

Mead, Margaret (1901–) American anthropologist and psychologist. 91.4; 581.38

Meany, George (1894–) American labor leader. 707.1

Medlicott, Sir Frank (1903–) English solicitor. 961.3

Melville, Herman (1819–1891) American novelist, short-story writer, poet. 160.2; 219.6; 227.16; 330.21; 330.22; 476.14; 498.12; 526.19; 562.38; 653.64; 653.65; 853.13; 854.33; 975.28; 975.29; 1002.23; 1042.58; 1072.17

Menander (342–?292 B.C.) Greek comic playwright. 321.41; 321.42; 1062.94

Mencius (372–289 B.C.) Chinese philosopher. 119.20; 357.9; 395.42; 478.5; 788.2; 872.2

Mencken, H[enry] L[ouis] (1880–1956) American newspaperman, editor, writer. 34.50; 50.13; 104.23; 115.10; 125.18; 137.4; 150.14; 173.9; 174.21; 191.7; 207.34; 210.20; 233.37; 233.38; 262.7; 271.19; 279.57; 330.23; 330.24; 332.28; 334.21; 355.12; 365.73; 387.46; 387.47; 418.24; 422.16; 433.19; 433.20; 442.10; 442.11; 472.7; 493.21; 517.29; 526.20; 539.72; 551.131; 558.25; 562.39; 564.80; 566.3; 566.4; 581.39; 581.40; 582.7; 588.13; 604.26; 623.51; 632.13; 694.23; 710.8; 711.59; 711.60; 741.15; 769.1; 783.5; 790.19; 797.49; 819.33; 823.17; 850.7; 856.12; 864.6; 900.17; 965.26; 972.23; 978.42; 997.5; 998.82; 1000.12; 1013.4; 1017.11; 1019.6; 1038.15; 1042.59; 1048.36; 1062.95; 1062.96; 1071.45

Menon, V. K. Krishna *See* Krishna Menon, V. K.

Meredith, George (1828–1909) English novelist, poet, critic. 521.7; 551.132; 650.3; 723.24; 899.9; 1062.97

Merton, Thomas (1915–1968) French-born poet, writer, Trappist monk. Merton, Thomas 43.10; 409.65; 469.14; 539.73; 551.133; 562.40; 822.14; 894.2; 1032.10

Michaux, Henri (1899–) Belgian poet and artist. 39.19

Michelangelo Buonarroti (1475–1564) Italian painter, sculptor, poet. 53.87; 53.88; 221.92

Mikes, George (1912–1993) Hungarian-born English critic, broadcaster, writer. 41.20; 198.10; 213.15; 558.26; 830.5; 919.2; 1050.8; 1064.35

Mill, John Stuart (1806–1873) English philosopher and economist. 15.7; 213.16; 213.17; 276.4; 279.58; 363.38; 364.6; 376.22; 409.66; 409.67; 431.17; 575.5; 620.5; 656.16; 662.5; 662.6; 790.20; 963.13; 984.12; 998.83; 998.84; 999.10

Millay, Edna St. Vincent (1892–1950) American poet. 72.33; 73.8; 103.9; 123.38; 181.9; 221.93; 279.59; 284.24; 307.27; 330.25; 336.12; 363.39; 417.3; 466.4; 483.1; 537.22; 539.74; 547.5; 551.134; 551.135; 552.9; 552.10; 571.11; 623.52; 653.66; 678.15; 741.16; 792.4; 854.34; 899.10; 906.13; 992.36; 1012.4; 1042.60; 1060.43

Miller, Henry (1891–) American writer. 3.6; 34.51; 34.52; 53.89; 53.90; 188.25; 231.8; 233.39; 289.21; 297.16; 361.6; 404.17; 419.36; 443.20; 479.8; 504.16; 517.30; 522.40; 522.41; 531.11; 539.75; 541.25; 681.20; 708.71; 718.45; 741.17; 790.21; 1042.61; 1042.62; 1067.22; 1069.93

Mills, C[harles] Wright (1916–1962) American sociologist. 279.60; 292.2; 340.14; 602.40; 1066.4

Milton, John (1608–1674) English poet and prose writer. 72.34; 72.35; 93.62; 93.63; 219.7; 330.26; 330.27; 357.10; 387.48; 387.49; 393.32; 393.33; 399.8; 409.68; 416.8; 522.42; 539.76; 564.81; 564.82; 581.41; 590.12; 601.3; 612.3; 623.53; 656.17; 675.15; 681.21; 743.7; 785.20; 815.9; 817.14; 822.15; 869.7; 889.11; 915.30; 940.14; 946.30; 1033.32; 1033.33; 1040.4; 1048.37; 1070.16

Mimnermus (7th c. B.C.) Greek elegiac poet. 332.29

Mishler, Judge Jacob. 418.25

Mistinguett. Stage name of Jeanne Bourgeois (1874?–1956) French dancer and singer. 521.8

Mitchell, Langdon [Elwyn] (1862–1935) American playwright and poet. 396.4; 564.83

Mitford, Jessica (1917–) English writer. 41.21; 140.3; 404.18; 519.13

Mitropoulos, Dmitri (1896–1960) Greek-born American conductor. 1023.4

Moineaux, Georges *See* Courteline, Georges

Molière. Pen name of Jean Baptiste Poquelin (1622–1673) French comic playwright. 37.5; 171.14; 202.8; 206.16; 207.35; 207.36; 221.94; 227.17; 263.9; 264.10; 267.13; 279.61; 342.21; 356.17; 389.7; 409.69; 431.18; 440.15; 488.2; 522.43; 539.77; 551.136; 561.8; 564.84; 564.85; 602.41; 602.42; 604.27; 703.5; 722.20; 725.4; 782.4; 790.22; 793.3; 798.5; 820.5; 848.26; 848.27; 900.18; 905.6; 916.10; 965.27; 1062.98; 1069.94; 1069.95; 1071.46

Monod, Jacques (1910–1976) French chemist, Nobel Prize winner. 1026.13

Montagu, Lady Mary Wortley (1689–1762) English letter writer and poet. 844.5

Montaigne, Michel [Eyquem] de (1533–1592) French moralist and essayist. 17.41; 27.5; 39.20; 75.6; 77.21; 78.13; 93.64; 93.65; 93.66; 123.39; 125.19; 152.14; 174.22; 188.26; 191.8; 197.11; 206.17; 207.37; 207.38; 209.12; 211.9; 213.18; 213.19; 221.95; 221.96; 226.7; 227.18; 228.5; 245.9; 260.3; 263.10; 266.12; 274.23; 279.62; 279.63; 332.30; 332.31; 334.22; 362.8; 365.74; 368.23; 386.10; 386.11; 390.13; 393.34; 395.43; 403.15; 409.70; 413.10; 413.11; 419.37; 427.24; 435.15; 444.18; 447.21; 447.22; 465.4; 481.5; 493.22; 494.5; 504.17; 516.13; 516.14; 517.31; 541.26; 548.8; 551.137; 558.27; 558.28; 562.41; 562.42; 562.43; 564.86; 577.6; 580.17; 580.18; 582.8; 590.13; 612.4; 620.6; 623.54; 642.2; 652.9; 652.10; 653.67; 653.68; 654.6; 656.18; 661.9; 670.35; 675.16; 685.1; 694.24; 700.3; 705.6; 711.61; 722.21; 723.25; 726.10; 732.11; 733.14; 746.16; 749.4; 756.2; 766.12; 771.7; 771.8; 772.11; 773.4; 803.5; 804.19; 808.9; 822.16; 831.12; 848.28; 852.1; 862.10; 866.6; 873.17; 875.18; 880.14; 880.15; 880.16; 901.16; 913.23; 915.31; 920.3; 923.43; 946.31; 946.32; 948.16; 962.9; 969.6; 988.5; 998.85; 999.11; 1000.13; 1026.14; 1033.34; 1034.12; 1034.13; 1060.44; 1062.99; 1069.96

Montale, Eugenio (1896–) Italian poet. 420.4

Montesquieu [Charles de Secondat, Baron de la Brède et de] (1689–1755) French philosopher, man of letters, lawyer. 83.5; 93.67; 125.20; 191.9; 213.20; 227.19; 365.75; 387.50; 528.50; 537.23; 618.3; 726.11; 762.11; 886.9; 945.29

Montgomery, James (1771–1854) English poet and editor. 541.27; 580.19

Montherlant, Henry [Millon] de (1896–1972) French playwright, novelist, poet, essayist. 443.21; 1064.36

Moore, George (1852–1933) Irish novelist, playwright, poet, critic. 714.1; 790.23

Moore, Gerald (1899–1987) English musician and writer. 332.32; 614.40; 614.41; 684.13; 524.29

Moore, Marianne (1887–1972) American poet. 41.22; 53.91; 72.36; 214.3; 450.23; 465.5; 564.87; 1065.53; 1069.97

Moore, Thomas (1779–1852) Irish poet. 188.27; 198.11; 330.28; 334.23; 361.7; 387.51; 472.8; 499.7; 551.138; 551.139; 551.140; 564.88; 580.20; 794.8; 883.6; 931.3; 1072.18

Moorehead, Alan (1910–1983) Australian journalist and historical writer. 824.3

Moorish Proverbs. 607.1

Mora, José María Luis (1794–1850) Mexican historian. 537.24

Moravia, Alberto. Pen name of Alberto Pincherle (1907–) Italian novelist, short-story writer, essayist. 1001.7; 1042.63

More, Hannah (1745–1833) English writer and philanthropist. 910.8; 996.6

Morita, Akio (1921–) Japanese business executive. 1007.13; 1065.54

Morley, Christopher. 26.5; 34.54; 72.37; 213.21; 612.5; 620.7; 630.23;

708.72; 708.73; 923.44; 945.30; 971.7; 998.86
Morley, John, Viscount Morley of Blackburn (1838–1923) English statesman and man of letters. Morley, John 119.21; 207.39; 298.14; 335.12; 401.41; 433.21; 443.23; 539.78; 574.4; 604.28; 623.55; 656.19; 848.29; 899.11; 985.5; 998.87; 1030.13; 1068.7
Morris, Desmond (1928–) English zoologist. 198.12; 208.8; 424.8; 499.8; 641.13; 802.2; 892.33; 906.14; 1071.47
Morris, Wright (1910–) American novelist. 468.9; 1069.98
Mosely, Philip E[dward] (1905–1972) American foreign policy expert, teacher. 34.55
Moyers, Bill (1934–) American journalist. 34.56
Muggeridge, Malcolm (1903–) English editor and writer. 34.57; 34.58; 279.64; 289.22; 436.19; 630.24; 711.62; 739.4; 813.5; 892.34; 913.24; 967.19; 1062.100
Muir, John (1838–1914) Scottish-born American naturalist and writer. 137.5; 352.3; 580.21; 623.56; 1059.4
Mumford, Lewis (1895–1990) American writer, philosopher, historian, teacher. 50.14; 53.92; 64.9; 104.24; 111.12; 175.6; 257.3; 266.13; 321.35; 374.12; 409.71; 443.24; 493.23; 533.12; 539.79; 661.10; 717.2; 784.12; 958.1; 966.22; 978.43; 1001.8; 1025.1; 1036.3; 1042.64; 1055.9
Munro, H. H. *See* Saki
Murdoch, Iris (1919–) Irish-born novelist and philosopher. 53.93; 123.40; 221.97; 257.4; 266.14; 499.9; 545.20; 551.141; 564.89; 564.90; 702.4; 892.35; 906.15; 910.9; 1011.24
Murray, William H. Former Governor of Oklahoma. 929.15
Murrow, Edward R[oscoe] (1908–1965) American news commentator. 65.11; 629.5; 726.12
Musset, Alfred de (1810–1857) French poet, novelist, playwright. 551.142; 673.5
Muste, A[braham] J[ohannes] (1885–1967) American clergyman and pacifist. 681.22
Myers, C. Kilmer (1916–) Episcopalian bishop of California. 840.4
Myrdal, [Karl] Gunnar (1898–1987) Swedish economist. 15.8; 69.4; 118.4; 179.4; 277.6; 277.7; 524.30; 536.2; 604.29; 670.36; 747.5; 751.10; 913.25; 964.8

N
Nabokov, Vladimir (1899–1977) Russian-born American novelist, poet, critic. 541.28; 562.44; 580.22; 603.4; 639.4; 683.9; 767.3; 797.50; 804.20; 834.4; 915.32; 918.35; 996.7
Naipaul, V[idiadhar] S[urajprasad] (1932) West Indian novelist and essayist. 108.11; 303.4; 455.5; 876.10
Napoleon I (Napoleon Bonaparte) (1769–1821) Emperor of France (1804–1815). 4.4; 36.1; 74.2; 112.5; 133.22; 157.4; 172.3; 195.25; 204.12; 225.7; 247.7; 267.14; 329.19; 332.33; 335.13; 338.21; 356.18; 357.11; 360.28; 361.9; 393.35; 395.44; 400.11; 401.42; 414.8; 416.9; 425.10; 447.23; 452.4; 458.3; 495.6; 498.14; 504.18; 517.32; 531.12; 531.13; 537.25; 539.80; 551.143; 559.12; 565.12; 578.6; 585.8; 621.16; 630.25; 661.11; 678.16; 743.8; 761.15; 761.16; 764.8; 780.16; 781.2; 790.24; 797.51; 801.2; 804.21; 819.34; 822.17; 831.13; 862.11; 880.17; 931.4; 931.5; 939.1; 973.8; 978.44; 987.10; 994.4; 1000.14; 1016.7; 1030.14; 1047.9; 1048.38
Nash, Ogden (1902–1971) American writer of light verse. 17.42; 18.11; 27.6; 41.23; 41.24; 64.10; 137.6; 139.7; 174.23; 206.18; 267.15; 268.38; 321.36; 334.24; 394.9; 420.5; 463.4; 481.6; 539.81; 564.91; 586.16; 653.69; 653.70; 770.5; 802.3; 852.2; 885.5; 892.36; 896.18; 906.16; 1062.101; 1065.55
Nathan, George Jean (1882–1958) American drama and social critic, editor, memoirist. 53.94; 66.6; 144.3; 207.40; 214.4; 267.16; 365.76; 551.144; 551.145; 564.92; 580.23; 581.42; 708.74; 711.63; 762.12; 972.24; 972.25
National Geographic Society. 415.8
New England Proverbs. 995.4
Newfield, Jack (1938–) American journalist. 6.14; 17.43; 549.6; 711.64; 875.19
Newman, Barnett (1905–1970) American painter. 20.4
Newman, Edwin (1919–) American news commentator and writer. 134.4; 149.14; 283.8; 309.6; 443.25; 524.31; 730.11; 848.30; 967.20; 1044.3
Newman, John Henry, Cardinal (1801–1890) English churchman and writer. 265.4; 378.4; 404.19; 522.44; 580.24; 797.52; 797.53
Newton, Isaac (1642–1727) English physicist and mathematician. 694.25
Nicole, Pierre (1625–1695) French essayist and teacher. 898.16
Niebuhr, Reinhold (1892–1971) American theologian. 100.14; 477.11
Nietzsche, Friedrich [Wilhelm] (1844–1900) German philosopher. 1.12; 17.44; 39.21; 53.95; 53.96; 56.7; 74.3; 78.14; 80.5; 90.4; 90.5; 93.68; 93.69; 118.5; 125.21; 134.5; 137.7; 165.13; 174.24; 174.25; 176.8; 185.5; 185.6; 189.7; 195.26; 207.41; 209.13; 221.98; 221.99; 227.20; 227.21; 233.40; 240.14; 267.17; 284.25; 288.19; 297.17; 299.25; 301.3; 307.28; 321.37; 321.38; 321.39; 341.4; 342.22; 351.9; 353.2; 353.3; 359.13; 363.40; 365.77; 365.78; 368.24; 376.23; 376.24; 384.22; 384.23; 387.52; 393.36; 401.43; 409.72; 419.38; 427.25; 427.26; 431.19; 433.22; 435.16; 435.17; 440.16; 442.12; 442.13; 455.6; 461.1; 476.15; 491.21; 492.7; 516.15; 522.45; 526.21; 526.22; 526.23; 531.14; 532.14; 537.26; 539.82; 547.6; 547.7; 551.146; 551.147; 551.148; 558.29; 562.45; 564.93; 564.94; 564.95; 571.12; 573.4; 581.43; 581.44; 614.42; 614.43; 621.17; 624.10; 640.8; 647.6; 656.20; 665.9; 669.3; 683.10; 693.8; 694.26; 698.15; 698.16; 704.23; 708.75; 708.76; 711.65; 719.43; 719.44; 722.22; 739.5; 741.18; 744.2; 755.17; 759.2; 766.13; 773.5; 785.21; 790.25; 797.54; 804.22; 808.10; 823.18; 830.6; 864.7; 876.11; 880.18; 882.8; 892.37; 892.38; 896.19; 906.17; 935.2; 946.33; 951.3; 962.10; 962.11; 963.14; 965.28; 975.30; 975.31; 978.45; 986.17; 986.18; 998.88; 998.89; 998.90; 1000.15; 1000.16; 1011.25; 1025.2; 1026.15; 1027.13; 1027.14; 1033.35; 1034.14; 1041.3; 1042.65; 1042.66; 1047.10; 1047.11; 1060.45; 1061.20; 1062.102; 1062.103; 1062.104; 1062.105; 1064.37; 1071.48; 1071.49
Nigerian Proverbs. 92.9; 235.8; 365.79
Nin, Anaïs (1914–1977) French-born American novelist, short-story writer, dancer. 404.20
Nixon, Richard M. (1913–1994) Thirty-seventh President of the United States. 34.59; 119.22; 150.15.; 681.23; 681.24; 719.45; 797.55; 798.6; 967.21; 994.5; 1048.39

O
O'Brien, Sharon (19??–). 1069.99
O'Casey, Sean (1884–1964) Irish playwright. 145.8; 436.20; 436.21; 443.26; 526.24; 526.25; 526.26; 723.26
O'Hara, Frank (1926–1966) American poet and art critic. 45.19; 551.149
O'Hara, John (1905–1970) American novelist and short-story writer. 113.7; 135.5; 581.45; 860.4; 962.12

O'Neill, Eugene [Gladstone] (1888–1953) American playwright. 129.3; 186.16; 336.13; 539.83; 547.8; 580.25; 653.71; 653.72; 915.33; 980.7
O'Neill, Thomas P. "Tip," Jr. (1912–1993) American political leader. 711.66; 766.14
O'Reilly, John Boyle (1844–1890) Irish-born American journalist, poet, novelist. 336.14
O'Rourke, P.J. (1947–) American author, editor. 332.35; 334.25; 408.2; 551.150; 563.17; 563.18; 672.3; 672.4; 682.14; 719.46; 948.17
Oates, Joyce Carol (1938–) American novelist, short-story writer, essayist, poet. 53.97; 321.28; 332.34; 345.5; 708.77; 722.23; 863.7
Ochs, Adolph S[imon] (1858–1935) American publisher and editor. 18.12
Offices of Instruction, The Book of Common Prayer. 836.1
Omar Khayyám (d. 1123) Persian astronomer and poet. 221.77; 221.78; 226.8; 240.15; 268.39; 268.40; 340.15; 414.9; 606.13; 631.4; 634.2; 704.24; 729.21; 990.10; 999.12; 1025.3; 1067.23; 1071.50
Oppenheimer, J[ulius] Robert (1904–1967) American physicist. 117.28; 479.9; 741.19; 849.24; 869.8
Orlando, Vittorio Emanuele (1860–1952) Italian statesman. 762.13
Ormsby Gore, [William] David, 5th Baron Harlech (1918–) British diplomat. 289.12
Ortega y Gasset, José (1883–1955) Spanish philosopher and statesman. 30.6; 35.4; 53.98; 53.99; 53.100; 55.12; 156.6; 173.10; 201.32; 281.12; 311.9; 376.25; 389.8; 412.14; 419.39; 493.24; 495.7; 539.84; 539.85; 612.6; 676.25; 708.78; 708.79; 758.12; 780.17; 831.14; 955.2; 975.32; 975.33; 987.11; 996.8; 1001.9; 1032.11; 1036.4
Orwell, George. Pen name of Eric Blair (1903–1950) English novelist, essayist, critic. 31.6; 123.41; 134.6; 271.20; 284.26; 289.23; 289.24; 390.14; 418.26; 431.20; 436.22; 458.4; 492.8; 524.32; 524.33; 524.34; 541.30; 545.21; 602.43; 645.6; 711.67; 711.68; 718.46; 719.47; 723.27; 766.15; 840.5; 840.6; 840.7; 840.8; 869.9; 900.19; 910.10; 929.16; 946.34; 987.12; 1001.10; 1042.67; 1064.38; 1069.100; 1069.101; 1071.51
Osofsky, Gilbert (1935–1974) American scholar. 775.17; 889.12
Ostrovsky, Alexander Nikolayevich (1823–1886) Russian playwright. 102.6
Ovid. Full name, Publius Ovidius Naso (43 B.C.—? A.D. 17) Roman poet. 72.38; 72.39; 119.23; 155.10; 198.13; 229.11; 240.16; 268.41; 338.22; 351.10; 351.11; 384.24; 385.5; 392.7; 403.16; 406.13; 446.12; 510.15; 551.151; 551.152; 551.153; 551.154; 551.155; 564.96; 564.97; 582.9; 602.44; 653.73; 681.25; 691.7; 703.6; 704.25; 704.26; 743.9; 798.7; 805.4; 838.2; 857.10; 892.39; 905.7; 923.45; 1034.15; 1062.106; 1062.107; 1062.108; 1062.109
Owen, Wilfred (1893–1918) English poet. 1071.52
Ozick, Cynthia (1928–) American novelist, short-story writer and essayist. 91.5; 145.9; 238.32; 363.41; 539.86; 543.2; 580.26; 918.36; 967.22; 978.46; 992.37; 1042.68; 1062.110; 1069.102

P

Paglia, Camille (1947–) American writer and teacher. 34.60; 368.25; 517.33; 892.40; 892.41; 1062.111
Pagnol, Marcel (1895–1974) French playwright, screenwriter, film critic. 878.3; 966.23
Paine, Thomas (1737–1809) English pamphleteer, political radical; influential in French and American revolutions. 119.24; 126.10; 191.10; 223.2; 297.18; 298.15; 374.13; 395.45; 395.46; 395.47; 395.48; 403.17; 537.27; 537.28; 619.6; 635.4; 726.13; 790.26; 913.26; 978.47; 998.91; 1026.16; 1033.36; 1037.9; 1042.69; 1042.70
Palladas (fl. 400) Greek epigrammatist. 115.11; 297.19
Paley, William (1743–1805) English theologian and philosopher. 185.7
Parker, Dorothy [Rothschild] (1893–1967) American writer of short stories, verse, criticism. 10.11; 16.8; 33.18; 88.8; 221.100; 267.18; 436.23; 504.19; 551.156; 581.46; 742.6; 793.4; 880.19; 948.18; 1061.21
Parkinson, C. Northcote (1909–) American historian and writer. 1065.56
Parmenter, Ross (1912–) Canadian-born American music critic and writer. 146.3; 294.4
Pascal, Blaise (1623–1662) French philosopher, scientist, mathematician, writer. 9.31; 10.12; 44.3; 51.15; 61.9; 78.15; 87.8; 93.70; 114.3; 116.11; 117.29; 176.9; 213.22; 213.23; 221.101; 221.102; 227.22; 233.41; 238.33; 268.42; 279.65; 281.13; 283.9; 284.27; 299.26; 330.29; 330.30; 332.37; 342.23; 357.12; 387.53; 387.54; 387.55; 389.9; 412.16; 435.18; 446.13; 452.5; 479.10; 493.25; 517.34; 518.9; 522.48; 528.51; 539.87; 539.88; 551.157; 551.158; 559.13; 561.10; 562.46; 562.47; 570.5; 589.9; 604.30; 623.57; 623.58; 644.3; 666.10; 675.17; 690.9; 691.8; 694.27; 694.28; 697.9; 704.27; 719.48; 767.4; 780.18; 785.22; 785.23; 797.56; 797.57; 797.58; 797.59; 804.23; 811.4; 816.3; 824.4; 831.16; 840.9; 858.23; 864.8; 875.20; 879.2; 883.7; 889.13; 893.5; 898.17; 914.7; 915.34; 919.3; 921.5; 923.47; 942.17; 975.34; 975.35; 975.36; 978.48; 996.9; 998.92; 998.93; 998.94; 999.13; 1005.9; 1007.14; 1011.26; 1016.8; 1017.12; 1033.38; 1042.72; 1042.73; 1064.39; 1069.103
Pasionara, La *See* Ibarruri, Dolores
Pasternak, Boris [Leonidovich] (1890–1960) Russian lyric poet and novelist. 201.33; 955.3; 1069.104
Pasteur, Louis (1822–1895) French chemist. 116.12
Pater, Walter [Horatio] (1839–1894) English essayist and critic. 53.101; 53.102; 670.37
Paterson, Isabel (1839–1894) Contemporary American writer. 433.23
Paton, Alan [Stewart] (1903–) South African writer. 790.27
Patrick, John (1905–) American playwright. 946.35
Pavese, Cesare (1908–1950) Italian novelist, poet, translator. 33.19; 539.89
Payelle, Raymond-Gérard *See* Hériat, Philippe
Paz, Octavio (1914–) Mexican writer and poet. 34.61; 53.103; 269.6; 524.35; 541.31; 708.80; 819.35; 898.18; 915.35; 966.24; 986.19
Peacock, Thomas Love (1785–1866) English novelist and poet. 268.43
Pearson, Hesketh (1887–1964) English writer. 52.4
Pearson, Karl (1857–1936) English scientist and writer. 590.14
Pearson, Lester B[owles] (1963–1968) Canadian prime minister. 1042.74
Péguy, Charles [Pierre] (1873–1914) French poet and essayist. 53.104; 365.80; 419.40; 425.11; 478.6; 537.29; 681.26; 718.47; 841.5; 916.11; 998.95; 1064.40
Pell, Clairborne (1918–) American diplomat and United States senator. 1044.4
Pemberton, Gayle (1948–) American teacher and essayist. 421.3
Penn, William (1644–1718) English Quaker, founder of Pennsylvania. 33.20; 104.25; 206.19; 222.9; 233.42; 339.1; 403.18; 427.27; 447.24; 510.16; 541.32; 564.98; 564.99; 623.59; 656.21; 670.38;

677.15; 723.28; 755.18; 797.60; 998.96; 1065.57
Pepys, Samuel (1633–1703) English statesman and diarist. 274.24; 289.25; 564.100; 704.28; 945.32
Percy, Walker (1919–1990) American novelist and essayist. 123.42; 344.23; 412.17; 447.25; 699.9; 729.22; 849.25; 892.42
Perelman, S[idney] J[oseph] (1904–1979) American humorist. 108.12; 131.34; 188.28; 234.3; 267.19; 267.20; 274.25; 289.26; 318.8; 329.20; 340.16; 355.13; 355.14; 366.4; 371.2; 391.6; 407.3; 407.4; 429.2; 472.9; 532.15; 685.2; 798.8; 849.26; 896.20; 926.3; 967.23; 968.3; 972.26; 981.1; 992.38; 1062.113
Periander (d. 585 B.C.) Greek tyrant, one of the Seven Sages of Greece. 755.19
Perkins, Maxwell [Evarts] (1884–1947) American editor and publisher. 19.20; 93.71; 93.72; 264.11; 580.27; 682.15; 764.9; 764.10; 892.43; 978.49; 1069.105; 1069.106
Perlman, Alfred Edward (1902–) American railroad executive. 828.3
Perot, H. Ross (1930–) American businessman. 55.13; 223.3; 233.43; 711.69; 711.70
Persian Proverbs. 17.45; 87.9; 153.3; 166.10; 221.103; 226.9; 239.8; 259.11; 291.6; 321.43; 404.21; 422.17; 477.12; 624.11; 755.20; 873.18; 896.21; 908.2
Persius. Full name, Aulus Persius Flaccus (A.D. 34–62) Roman satiric poet. 437.11
Petrarch. Italian name, Francesco Petrarca (1304–1374) Italian poet and scholar. 550.5; 561.11; 664.3; 918.37; 942.18; 978.50; 990.11; 1011.27; 1069.107; 1072.19
Petronius, Gaius. Also known as Petronius Arbiter (d. c. A.D. 65) Roman writer, probable author of the Satyricon. 104.26; 387.56; 414.10; 427.28; 602.45; 1062.114
Peyre, Henri [Maurice] (1901–) French-born American educator and critic. 901.17
Phaedrus (1st c.) Roman fabulist. 224.14; 307.29; 357.13; 718.48; 1030.15; 1060.46; 1070.17
Phillips, Wendell (1811–1884) American abolitionist, orator, reformer. 233.44; 387.57; 395.49; 528.52; 537.30; 630.26; 656.22; 741.20; 790.28; 819.36; 931.6
Picasso, Pablo [Ruiz y] (1881–1973) Spanish painter and sculptor. 53.105; 718.49; 963.15
Pike, James A[lbert] (1913–1969) American Episcopalian bishop. 128.5
Pilpay *See* Bidpai
Pindar (522 or 518–432 or 438 B.C.) Greek poet. 1.13; 9.32; 33.21; 55.14; 117.30; 201.34; 221.104; 224.15; 283.10; 287.7; 295.19; 362.9; 387.58; 400.12; 409.73; 542.12; 602.46; 626.8; 704.29; 722.24; 811.5; 875.21; 898.19; 945.33; 945.34; 945.35; 949.2; 979.7; 990.12; 997.6; 1030.16
Pinero, Sir Arthur Wing (1855–1934) English playwright, actor, essayist. 368.26
Piozzi, Hester Lynch. Born Salusbury; also known as Mrs. Thrale (1741–1821) English writer, intimate of Samuel Johnson. 263.11; 551.159
Pirandello, Luigi (1867–1936) Italian playwright and novelist. 4.5; 165.14; 266.15; 328.11; 328.12; 344.24; 350.2; 378.5; 405.12; 409.74; 443.27; 444.19; 539.90; 539.91; 656.23; 732.12; 784.13; 785.24; 946.36; 1062.115
Pirsig, Robert M. (1928–) American writer and philosopher. 264.12; 335.14; 370.1; 411.10; 433.24; 456.1; 502.3; 640.9; 666.11; 784.14; 816.4; 848.31; 848.32; 849.27; 966.25; 974.9; 975.37; 998.97; 1007.15; 1064.41
Pitt, William (1759–1806) English statesman, called "the Younger Pitt." 624.12
Pittacus (c. 650–c. 569 B.C.) Greek statesman and poet, one of the Seven Sages of Greece. 657.9
Plath, Sylvia (1932–1963) American poet, essayist and novelist. 103.10; 563.19; 564.101; 632.14; 657.10; 948.19.
Plato 53.106; 188.29; 195.27; 233.45; 251.7; 279.66; 279.67; 425.12; 454.14; 454.15; 477.13; 514.8; 517.35; 522.49; 522.50; 532.16; 551.160; 562.48; 624.13; 653.74; 739.6; 899.12; 931.7; 968.4; 1000.17; 1048.41; 1048.42
Plautus. Full name, Titus Maccius Plautus (254?–184 B.C.) Roman comic playwright. 271.21; 358.5; 495.8; 550.6; 581.47; 623.60; 685.3; 755.21; 918.38; 1026.17; 1060.47; 1062.116; 1062.117
Pleasants, Henry (1910?–) American music critic. 614.44
Pliny the Elder. Full name, Caius Plinius Secundus (A.D. 23–79) Latin writer and scientist. 17.46; 268.44; 948.20; 988.6
Pliny the Younger. Full name, Gaius Plinius Caecilius Secundus (c. A.D. 61–c. 114) Roman statesman and letter writer. 6.15; 43.11; 386.12; 584.4; 612.7; 716.11; 804.24
Plutarch (c. a.d. 46–c. 120) Greek biographer and essayist. 37.6; 57.14; 119.25; 213.24; 279.68; 295.20; 390.16; 580.28; 598.12; 686.6; 729.23; 788.3; 798.9; 811.6; 898.20; 923.48; 931.8; 1007.16; 1062.118
Poe, Edgar Allan (1809–1849) American poet, critic, short-story writer. 93.73; 195.28; 376.26; 376.27; 409.75; 597.7; 768.2; 998.98
Poincaré, [Jules] Henri (1854–1912) French mathematician and physicist. 849.28
Polish Proverbs. 428.17
Pollok, Robert (1798–1827) Scottish poet. 918.39
Poore, Charles [Graydon] (1902–1971) American editor, book critic, writer. 1069.108
Pope, Alexander (1688–1744) English poet and satirist. 14.6; 17.47; 19.21; 51.16; 51.17; 58.5; 72.40; 80.6; 120.7; 120.8; 148.6; 188.30; 207.42; 207.43; 227.23; 318.9; 332.38; 334.26; 338.23; 342.24; 356.19; 359.14; 374.14; 392.8; 393.37; 404.22; 407.5; 422.18; 425.13; 427.29; 435.19; 436.24; 440.17; 476.16; 478.7; 491.22; 516.16; 522.51; 551.161; 555.14; 581.48; 583.2; 610.10; 620.8; 623.61; 653.75; 656.24; 675.18; 684.14; 734.12; 785.25; 797.61; 803.7; 844.6; 875.22; 899.13; 915.36; 939.2; 965.29; 978.51; 988.7; 996.10; 1004.14; 1017.13; 1030.17; 1048.43; 1048.44; 1061.22; 1061.23; 1062.119; 1064.42; 1067.24; 1069.109
Popper, Sir Karl R[aimund] (1902–) Austrian-born English educator and philosopher of science. 419.41
Porchia, Antonio (1886–) Italian-born Argentine typographer and writer. 115.12; 168.3; 201.35; 284.28; 473.5; 539.92; 1019.7
Porter, Katherine Anne (1890–) American novelist and short-story writer. 1069.110
Porter, William Sydney *See* Henry, O.
Portis, Charles (1933–) American newspaperman and novelist. 210.21; 231.9; 430.5; 583.3; 741.21
Portuguese Proverbs. 229.12; 357.14; 497.3
Postman, Neil (1931–) American teacher and writer. 93.74; 123.43; 764.11; 966.26; 967.24
Pound, Ezra [Loomis] (1885–1972) American poet and critic. 93.75; 93.76; 376.28; 524.36
Pound, Roscoe (1870–1964) American jurist, educator, writer. 528.53
Powell, Adam Clayton (1908–1972) American politician, clergyman, writer. 85.15; 297.20; 750.13
Prentice, George Dennison (1802–1870) American newspaperman and editor. 160.3; 404.23; 413.12; 474.5; 494.6; 580.29; 855.13; 978.52; 982.12; 1069.111
Presbyterian Church,

United. 718.56
Price, Reynolds. 53.107
Priestley, J[ohn] B[oynton] (1894–) English novelist, playwright, essayist. 105.19; 106.1; 376.29; 966.27; 966.28; 967.25
Prior, Matthew (1664–1721) English poet and diplomat. 53.108; 447.26; 946.37
Pritchett, V[ictor] S[awdon] (1900–) English novelist, short-story writer, literary critic. 436.25; 562.49; 938.5; 989.7; 1069.112
Propertius. Full name, Sextus Propertius (50–48 B.C.—before A.D. 2) Roman poet. 485.3; 551.162; 581.49; 588.14; 602.47
Proudhon, Pierre-Joseph (1809–1865) French libertarian and socialist. 694.29; 746.17
Proust, Marcel (1871–1922) French novelist. 53.109; 53.110; 53.111; 78.16; 93.77; 152.15; 225.8; 227.24; 238.34; 326.5; 426.9; 433.25; 551.163; 551.164; 551.165; 552.11; 577.7; 590.15; 614.45; 627.10; 630.27; 663.12; 676.26; 794.9; 794.10; 856.14; 858.24; 880.20; 882.9; 918.40; 918.41; 946.38; 946.39; 975.38; 978.53; 978.54; 1042.75; 1069.113
Provence, Marcel *See* Jouhandeau, Marcel
Proverbs *See* individual countries or groups—i.e., Spanish Proverbs
Publilius Syrus (fl. 1st century B.C.) Latin writer of mimes. 6.16; 8.8; 15.9; 17.48; 27.7; 33.22; 39.22; 39.23; 39.24; 48.6; 57.15; 92.10; 119.26; 152.16; 152.17; 152.18; 168.4; 173.11; 174.26; 174.27; 200.7; 206.20; 221.105; 222.10; 224.16; 227.25; 240.17; 252.9; 268.45; 279.69; 281.14; 288.17; 288.18; 300.7; 332.39; 343.25; 360.29; 360.30; 360.31; 365.83; 365.84; 365.85; 367.11; 368.27; 384.25; 393.38; 394.10; 401.45; 403.19; 404.24; 405.13; 409.76; 409.77; 411.11; 412.18; 425.14; 434.3; 435.20; 444.20; 447.27; 450.24; 451.9; 454.16; 469.15; 477.14; 478.8; 516.17; 517.36; 517.37; 531.15; 534.1; 539.93; 548.14; 550.7; 550.8; 551.166; 551.167; 551.168; 555.15; 555.16; 559.14; 561.12; 580.30; 585.9; 585.10; 595.6; 602.48; 602.49; 602.50; 624.14; 644.4; 653.76; 653.77; 657.11; 670.39; 702.5; 702.6; 704.30; 704.31; 712.9; 719.49; 733.16; 751.11; 751.12; 755.22; 791.4; 798.10; 804.25; 817.15; 838.3; 857.11; 874.4; 888.8; 890.2; 893.6; 898.21; 898.22; 903.5; 906.18; 915.37; 915.38; 923.49; 933.4; 939.3; 946.40; 997.7; 998.99; 1002.24; 1011.28; 1026.18; 1030.18; 1030.19; 1030.20; 1052.5; 1055.10; 1060.48; 1060.49; 1062.120; 1070.18

Q
Quarles, Francis (1592–1644) English metaphysical poet. Quarles, Francis 904.8; 917.6
Quasimodo, Salvatore (1901–) Italian poet and critic. 708.81
Quintilian. Full name, Marcus Fabius Quintilianus (c. 35–c. 99) Roman rhetorician. 558.30; 624.15; 732.13; 736.4; 1065.58; 1069.114

R
Raban, Jonathan (1942–) English author and journalist. 34.62; 64.11; 131.35; 131.36; 131.37; 151.8; 204.13; 208.9; 267.21; 348.3; 453.2; 481.7; 632.15; 824.5; 824.6; 824.7; 882.10; 895.3; 913.27; 915.39
Rabelais, François (1494?–1553) French scholar, humanist, physician, writer. 522.52; 526.27; 862.12; 869.10
Rabin, Yitzhak (1922–1995) Israeli soldier and public official. 681.27
Racine, Jean [Baptiste] (1639–1699) French playwright. 204.14; 300.8; 491.23; 517.38; 551.169; 551.170; 552.12; 554.7; 946.41; 1002.25; 1030.21; 1033.39; 1062.121
Radford, Arthur William (1896–1973) American admiral and business consultant. 315.4
Radiguet, Raymond (1903–1923) French novelist and poet. 406.14
Rakove, Milton (1903–1923) Contemporary American educator and political adviser. 710.9
Rameau, Jean-Philippe (1683–1764) French composer and musical theorist. 604.31; 614.46
Randall, Clarence B[elden] (1891–) American industrialist. 531.16
Raphael, Frederic (1931–) American-born English author. 149.15; 967.26; 967.27
Rapier, James T[homas] (1837–1883) American lawyer, journalist, congressman. 1002.26
Rattigan, Terence [Mervyn] (1911–) English playwright. 972.27
Ray, John (1627–1705) English naturalist. 123.44; 275.1; 552.13
Ray, Randolph (1886–1963) American clergyman and writer. 772.12
Reade, Charles (1814–1884) English novelist. 649.7
Reagan, Ronald (1911–) Fortieth President of the United States. 108.13; 116.13; 132.7; 395.50; 421.4; 711.71; 730.12; 929.17
Redfield, William (1927–) American actor and writer. 466.5
Reeves, Richard (1936–) American journalist and critic. 34.63
Regnard, Jean-François (1655–1709) French playwright. 554.8
Reich, Robert B. (1946–) American economist and public official. 443.28
Reid, Alastair (1926–) American poet and writer. 123.45
Reik, Theodor (1888–1969) Austrian-born American psychologist and writer. 551.171; 551.172; 555.17; 566.5; 581.50; 670.40; 876.12; 1021.2; 1062.122
Remarque, Erich Maria (1898–1970) German journalist and novelist. 593.4
Remond, C. Lenox (1810–1873) American anti-slavery lecturer and orator. 670.41; 775.18
Renan, [Joseph] Ernest (1823–1892) French writer, critic, scholar. 78.17; 265.5; 392.9; 418.27; 419.42; 644.5; 849.29
Renard, Jules (1864–1910) French novelist and playwright. 4.6; 19.22; 134.7; 265.6; 316.8; 387.59; 409.78; 517.39; 519.14; 526.28; 530.7; 602.51; 708.82; 867.9; 873.19; 915.40; 962.13; 969.7; 1019.8; 1019.9; 1064.43; 1064.44; 1069.115
Repplier, Agnes (1855–1950) American essayist, biographer, historian, poet. 17.49; 41.25; 41.26; 53.112; 206.21; 213.25; 495.9; 498.15; 513.6; 526.29; 543.3; 614.47; 659.10; 875.23; 884.6; 992.39; 1000.18; 1011.29; 1062.123
Reston, James [Barrett] (1909–) Scottish-born American journalist and editor. 247.8; 498.16; 498.17; 591.2; 621.18; 629.6; 630.28; 711.72
Retz [Jean François-Paul de Gondi], Cardinal de (1614–1679) French prelate and writer. 204.15; 259.12; 299.27; 343.26; 624.16; 831.17; 941.16; 997.8
Rice, Berkeley (1937–) Contemporary American writer. 1035.3
Rice, Robert (1916–) American criminologist. 204.16
Rich, Adrienne (1929–) American poet. 892.44
Richelieu, Armand-Jean du Plessis, duc de. Known as Cardinal Richelieu (1585–1642) French statesman and prelate. 395.51; 831.18
Richter, Conrad (1890–1968) American novelist and short-story writer. 266.16; 950.3
Richter, Jean Paul [Friedrich] (1763–1825) German novelist and aesthetician. 187.4; 614.48
Rieff, Philip (1922–) American sociologist and writer. 551.173; 758.13; 785.26; 797.62; 848.33
Riesman, David (1909–) American sociologist, writer, lecturer. 8.9; 64.12; 105.20;

131.38; 171.15; 178.18; 210.22; 279.70; 292.3; 293.6; 374.15; 418.28; 528.54; 533.13; 563.20; 944.4; 944.5; 1064.45; 1065.59; 1065.60

Rilke, Rainer Maria (1875–1926) German poet. 53.113; 56.8; 195.29; 207.44; 245.10; 284.29; 326.6; 332.40; 368.28; 404.25; 539.94; 551.174; 551.175; 564.102; 589.10; 612.8; 797.63; 875.24; 918.42; 1011.30; 1070.19

Rivarol, Comte de *See* Rivaroli, Antoine

Rivaroli, Antoine. Known as Comte de Rivarol (1753–1801) French journalist of Italian parentage. 1048.45

Robb, Charles S. (1939–) Virginia government official. 477.15

Roberts, Chalmers [McGeagh] (1910–) American writer. 630.29

Robsjohn-Gibbings, T[erence] H[arold] (1905–) English interior decorator and writer. 430.6

Rochefoucauld, François, Duc de la *See* La Rochefoucauld, François, Duc de

Rodman, Frances (1905–) Contemporary American writer. 195.30

Roethke, Theodore (1908–1963) American poet. 785.27; 892.45; 1071.54

Rogers, Will[iam Penn Adair] (1879–1935) American actor and humorist. 34.64; 62.7; 101.3; 104.27; 133.23; 150.16; 233.46; 247.9; 297.21; 414.11; 418.29; 436.26; 503.6; 520.6; 537.31; 537.32; 667.1; 702.7; 710.10; 1038.16; 1042.76

Roland, Jeanne Manon Phlipon. Known as Madame Roland (1754–1793) During the French Revolution her salon was the meeting place for the Girondists. 537.33

Rolland, Romain (1866–1944) French novelist, playwright, essayist, musicologist. 418.30; 675.19; 880.21; 1042.77; 1071.55

Ronan, Thomas P. (1885–) Contemporary journalist; London correspondent of *The New York Times*. 171.16

Rooney, Andrew A. (1919–) American newspaper columnist, author and television journalist. 53.114; 188.31; 201.36; 231.10; 443.29; 978.55; 1048.46

Roosevelt, [Anna] Eleanor (1884–1962) American humanitarian, columnist, lecturer, wife of President Franklin D. Roosevelt. 776.5; 868.6

Roosevelt, Franklin D[elano] (1933–1945) Thirty-second President of the United States. 34.65; 34.66; 46.4; 172.4; 177.6; 178.19; 178.20; 205.7; 223.4; 229.13; 233.47; 233.48; 297.22; 343.27; 357.15; 363.42; 395.52; 420.6; 487.8; 498.18; 519.15; 522.53; 532.17; 536.3; 537.34; 537.35; 558.31; 588.15; 590.16; 591.3; 621.19; 681.28; 711.73; 734.13; 760.12; 761.17; 761.18; 776.6; 927.10; 964.9; 984.13; 1038.17; 1042.78; 1048.47; 1048.48

Roosevelt, Theodore (1901–1909) Twenty-sixth President of the United States. 34.67; 46.5; 132.8; 528.55; 588.16; 678.17; 719.50; 790.29; 1060.50; 1065.61

Root, Waverly [Lewis] (1903–1982) American essayist, journalist, food historian. 630.30

Rorem, Ned (1923–) American composer and writer. 53.115; 53.116; 62.8; 365.81; 401.46; 614.49; 684.15

Rose, Alexander (1901–) American writer. 1040.5

Rosenblatt, Roger (1940–) American writer and newspaper columnist. 41.27; 62.9; 72.41; 93.78; 123.46; 182.7; 221.106; 570.6; 803.8; 858.19; 915.41; 978.56; 1042.79; 1049.7

Ross, Harold [Wallace] (1892–1951) American editor, founder of *The New Yorker*. 764.12

Ross, Leonard Q *See* Rosten, Leo Calvin

Rossetti, Christina [Georgina] (1830–1894) English poet. 194.12; 539.95; 580.31; 854.35; 1059.5

Rossetti, Dante Gabriel. Full name, Gabriel Charles Dante Rossetti (1828–1882) English poet and painter. 853.14

Rostand, Edmond (1868–1918) French poet and playwright. 521.9

Rostand, Jean (1894–) French biologist and writer. 518.10; 571.13

Rosten, Leo [Calvin]. Pen name, Leonard Q. Ross (1908–) Polish-born American writer and political scientist. 594.3

Roth, Philip (1933–) American novelist and short-story writer. 367.12; 367.13; 421.5; 512.3; 522.54; 581.51; 764.13; 826.6; 896.22; 1042.80; 1069.116; 1069.117

Rougemont, Denis de (1906–) Swiss writer, writing in French. 409.79; 564.103

Rousseau, Jean-Baptiste (1671–1741) French poet. 109.8; 113.8; 125.22; 133.24; 168.5; 173.12; 177.7; 233.49; 279.71; 389.10; 389.11; 395.53; 409.80; 443.30; 478.9; 515.6; 528.56; 537.36; 539.96; 548.9; 554.9; 557.4; 557.5; 623.62; 653.78; 656.25; 674.6; 678.18; 718.50; 719.51; 722.25; 746.18; 746.19; 749.5; 755.23; 760.13; 766.16; 831.19; 864.9; 889.14; 889.15; 898.23; 913.28; 930.16; 998.100; 1030.22; 1034.16; 1048.49; 1060.51

Rousseau, Jean-Jacques (1712–1778) Swiss-born French philosopher, novelist, political theorist. 307.30; 361.8; 663.13; 804.26

Roux, Joseph (1834–1905) French priest and writer. 227.26; 238.35; 271.22; 279.72; 284.30; 284.31; 299.28; 321.44; 354.9; 365.86; 409.81; 427.30; 449.15; 450.25; 476.17; 517.40; 517.41; 551.176; 694.30; 704.32; 722.26; 725.5; 762.14; 773.6; 785.28; 905.9; 907.1; 915.42; 945.36; 962.14; 1011.31; 1033.40

Rowan, Carl [Thomas] (1925–) American journalist and diplomat. 247.10; 480.17

Royal, Darrell (1924–) American football head coach, formerly of the University of Texas Longhorns. 646.6

Rumbold, Richard (1622?–1685) English conspirator and soldier. 1002.27

Ruskin, John (1819–1900) English writer and critic. 50.15; 50.16; 50.17; 50.18; 53.117; 53.118; 53.119; 53.120; 72.42; 72.43; 93.79; 123.47; 133.25; 143.3; 279.73; 285.4; 395.54; 425.15; 435.21; 457.4; 473.6; 539.97; 609.2; 683.11; 848.34; 1035.4; 1037.10; 1042.81; 1065.62

Russell, Bertrand [Arthur William], 3rd Earl Russell (1872–1970) English philosopher, mathematician, social reformer. 16.9; 21.10; 51.18; 77.22; 78.18; 78.19; 93.80; 117.31; 123.48; 129.4; 133.26; 133.27; 151.9; 206.22; 209.14; 219.8; 276.5; 279.74; 295.21; 297.23; 335.15; 343.28; 343.29; 354.10; 358.6; 389.12; 393.39; 393.40; 395.55; 401.47; 409.82; 409.83; 412.19; 427.31; 431.21; 442.14; 442.15; 445.3; 446.14; 454.17; 504.20; 513.7; 528.57; 536.4; 537.37; 539.98; 551.177; 561.13; 564.104; 570.7; 570.8; 574.5; 582.10; 604.32; 604.33; 608.7; 616.2; 627.11; 656.26; 670.42; 694.31; 694.32; 694.33; 711.74; 714.2; 733.17; 734.14; 741.22; 745.6; 745.7; 761.19; 785.29; 797.64; 849.30; 849.31; 869.11; 876.13; 892.46; 900.20; 945.37; 956.5; 974.10; 978.57; 992.40; 1017.14; 1033.41; 1042.82; 1060.52

Russell, Rosalind (1911–1976) American actress. 329.21

Russian Proverb. 104.28; 263.12; 345.6; 358.7; 394.11; 437.12; 442.16; 583.4; 602.52

S

Sa'di. Pen name of Musharrif-uddin (born Muslih-uddin; c. 1184–1291) Persian poet.

Sa'di. *(cont.)*

19.23; 37.7; 41.28; 57.16; 72.44; 127.5; 166.11; 169.5; 186.19; 188.32; 206.23; 216.15; 284.32; 288.20; 326.7; 342.25; 343.31; 358.8; 358.9; 375.6; 393.41; 411.12; 412.20; 417.4; 433.26; 435.22; 437.13; 447.28; 457.5; 493.26; 519.16; 520.7; 522.55; 534.2; 558.32; 686.7; 721.2; 751.13; 755.24; 767.5; 790.30; 855.14; 890.3; 892.47; 898.24; 918.43; 923.50; 965.30; 990.13; 990.14; 992.41; 992.42; 999.14; 1002.28; 1018.1; 1026.19; 1048.50; 1048.51; 1061.24

Saarinen, [Gottlieb] Eliel (1873–1950) Finnish-American architect. 237.2

Sacks, Oliver (1933–) English neurologist and writer. 186.18; 263.13; 533.14; 546.4; 639.5; 723.29; 896.23; 896.24; 896.25; 982.13

Sackville-West, Vita [Victoria Mary] (1892–1962) English novelist, poet and critic. 352.4; 371.3; 371.4; 371.5

Sadat, Anwar el- (1918–1981) Egyptian political leader and President of Egypt (1970–1981). 330.31; 343.30; 469.16; 528.58; 551.178; 681.29; 716.12; 875.25; 880.22; 945.38

Sade, Comte Donatien Alphonse François de. Known as Marquis de Sade (1740–1814) French soldier, writer. 716.13

Sagan, Carl (1934–) American scientist and author. 78.20; 211.10; 261.8; 308.15; 344.25; 479.11; 480.18; 493.27; 849.32; 956.6; 998.101; 1017.15

Sagan, Françoise. Pen name of Françoise Quoirez (1935–) French novelist. 510.17

Saint-Éxupéry, Antoine de (1900–1944) French novelist, essayist, aviator. 3.7; 8.10; 13.2; 30.7; 53.121; 55.15; 78.21; 123.49; 221.107; 252.10; 271.23; 284.33; 328.13; 404.26; 433.27; 469.17; 504.21; 524.37; 531.17; 539.99; 547.9; 551.179; 551.180; 553.2; 562.50; 585.11; 633.8; 661.12; 676.27; 684.16; 698.17; 704.33; 735.9; 755.25; 784.15; 785.30; 785.31; 791.5; 794.11; 794.12; 810.10; 837.8; 890.4; 963.16; 966.29; 992.43; 998.102; 998.103; 998.104; 1004.15; 1006.2; 1016.9; 1019.10; 1035.5; 1042.83; 1042.84; 1046.1; 1052.6; 1073.3

Saint-Just, Louis Antoine Léon de (1767–1794) French revolutionary leader, intimate of Robespierre. 831.20

Saint-Évremond, seigneur de (Charles de Marguetel de Saint-Denis) (1613–1703) French wit and man of letters. 475.5

Saki. Pen name of Hector Hugh Munto (1870–1916) Scottish novelist and short-story writer. 790.31; 939.4; 1062.124

Salinger, J[erome] D[avid] (1919–) American novelist and short-story writer. 45.20; 123.50; 221.108; 267.22; 385.6; 407.6; 407.7; 409.84; 619.7; 732.14; 902.2; 923.51; 927.11; 948.21; 982.14; 1062.125

Salisbury, Harrison E. (1909–1993) American journalist and editor. 55.16; 124.8; 368.29; 668.4; 819.37

Sallust. Full name, Gaius Valerius Sallustius Crispus (86–35 B.C.) Roman historian. 365.87; 574.6; 733.18; 751.14; 867.10; 1033.42

Sampson, Anthony (1926–) English journalist and biographer. 630.31

Samson, Leon (1926–) Contemporary writer. 819.38

Sand, George. Pen name of Amandine Lucie Aurore Dupin, Baronne Dudevant (1804–1876) French writer. 948.22

Sandburg, Carl (1878–1967) American poet. 195.31; 286.4; 354.11; 356.20; 363.43; 416.10; 427.32; 524.38; 551.181; 558.33; 558.34; 570.9; 602.53; 603.5; 665.10; 676.28; 708.83; 966.30; 1001.11

Sanger, Margaret [Higgins] (1883–1966) American birth-control leader. 84.2

Sanskrit Proverb. 532.18

Santayana, George (1863–1952) Spanish-born American philosopher, poet, novelist, author. 34.68; 50.19; 53.122; 53.123; 53.124; 53.125; 20.5; 22.2; 22.3; 26.6; 27.8; 70.4; 72.45; 72.46; 90.7; 98.7; 123.51; 125.23; 174.28; 193.3; 207.45; 207.46; 213.26; 238.36; 239.9; 255.1; 266.17; 274.26; 279.75; 284.34; 289.27; 294.5; 308.16; 316.9; 321.45; 330.32; 335.16; 336.15; 336.16; 345.7; 354.12; 365.88; 365.89; 387.60; 390.17; 401.48; 401.49; 404.27; 406.15; 409.85; 410.4; 414.12; 415.9; 418.31; 422.19; 423.6; 436.27; 443.31; 450.26; 454.18; 457.6; 457.7; 473.7; 477.16; 486.5; 487.9; 487.10; 493.28; 516.18; 539.100; 539.101; 542.13; 548.10; 551.182; 551.183; 559.15; 562.51; 564.105; 571.14; 606.14; 614.50; 614.51; 620.9; 621.20; 623.63; 625.5; 653.79; 670.43; 676.29; 694.34; 694.35; 697.10; 697.11; 703.7; 703.8; 706.7; 708.84; 708.85; 717.3; 723.30; 754.11; 758.14; 785.32; 785.33; 797.65; 797.66; 797.67; 797.68; 797.69; 837.9; 840.10; 840.11; 842.3; 860.5; 862.13; 875.26; 881.3; 896.26; 904.9; 913.29; 915.43; 919.4; 919.5; 927.12; 946.42; 953.2; 954.5; 960.11; 963.17; 974.11; 975.39; 978.58; 983.2; 992.44; 998.105; 998.106; 998.107; 1001.12; 1011.32; 1024.3; 1025.4; 1026.20; 1027.15; 1036.5; 1042.85; 1042.86; 1061.25; 1072.20.

Sapirstein, Milton R. 72.47; 279.76; 279.77; 334.27; 335.17; 670.44; 670.45; 913.30; 1006.3

Saroyan, William (1908–1981) American short-story writer, novelist, playwright. 7.6; 53.126; 144.4; 145.10; 224.17; 365.90; 387.61; 393.42; 393.43; 409.86; 527.5; 580.32; 858.25; 858.26; 966.31; 1008.17; 1069.118; 1069.119

Sarton, May (1912–) Belgian-born American poet, playwright, novelist. 43.12; 425.16; 653.80; 653.81; 653.82; 858.27; 859.6; 1032.12

Sartre, Jean-Paul (1905–) French existentialist philosopher, playwright, novelist, teacher. 3.8; 9.33; 125.24; 149.16; 317.2; 387.62; 412.21; 444.21; 551.184; 717.4; 718.51

Saurin, Bernard Joseph (1706–1781) French poet. 541.33

Schell, Maria (1926–) Austrian actress. 681.30

Schiller, [Johann Christoph] Friedrich von (1759–1805) German playwright, poet, historian. 53.127; 53.128; 116.14; 271.24; 469.18; 625.6; 783.6; 790.32; 806.8; 941.17; 998.108; 1023.5

Schirra, Walter, Sr. Father of the American astronaut (1759–1805) German playwright, poet, historian. 916.12

Schlesinger, Arthur M., Jr. (1917–) American historian. 277.8; 548.11; 711.75; 730.13; 730.16; 730.14; 730.15; 755.26; 855.15

Schnabel, Artur (1882–1951) Austrian-born American pianist, teacher, composer. 614.52

Schnitzler, Arthur (1862–1931) Austrian novelist and playwright. 906.19

Schopenhauer, Arthur (1788–1860) German philosopher. 10.13; 41.29; 116.15; 142.5; 197.12; 342.26; 409.87; 418.32; 481.8; 539.102; 539.103; 539.104; 580.33; 581.52; 600.13; 636.4; 673.6; 689.7; 785.34; 875.27; 972.28; 978.59; 1071.56

Schulz, Charles M[onroe] (1922–) American cartoonist, creator of Peanuts. 594.4

Schwartz, Delmore (1913–1966) American poet and short-story writer. 653.83

Schwarzkopf, Elizabeth & Legge, Walter (19??–). 53.77

Schwarzkopf, H. Norman

(1934–) American general. 418.33
Scott, Geoffrey (1885–1929) English writer. 50.20; 50.21
Scott, Sir Walter (1771–1832) Scottish novelist and poet. 386.13; 423.7; 427.33; 551.185; 551.186; 708.86; 854.36; 1018.2
Seaborg, Glenn T[heodore] (1912–) American chemist and government official. 849.33
Seiden, Morton Irving (1921–) American teacher and essayist. 405.14; 785.35
Selden, John (1584–1654) English jurist, scholar, orientalist. 80.7; 138.8; 311.10; 435.23
Selye, Hans (1907–) Austrian-born American physician. 849.34
Seneca the Elder. Full name, Lucius (or Marcus) Annaeus Seneca. Also known as Seneca the Rhetorician (55 B.C.–c. A.D. 39) Roman rhetorician. 4.7; 10.14; 17.50; 17.51; 43.13; 59.5; 77.23; 83.6; 90.8; 116.16; 149.17; 155.11; 180.2; 180.3; 184.7; 195.32; 195.33; 201.37; 204.17; 219.9; 221.109; 221.110; 221.111; 226.10; 227.27; 268.46; 304.3; 307.31; 307.32; 310.3; 311.11; 318.10; 340.17; 343.32; 343.33; 360.32; 360.33; 363.44; 376.30; 376.31; 384.26; 387.63; 403.20; 403.21; 409.88; 413.13; 431.22; 476.18; 493.29; 516.19; 518.11; 520.8; 520.9; 528.59; 539.105; 539.106; 539.107; 541.34; 541.35; 541.36; 548.12; 551.187; 557.6; 577.8; 598.13; 606.15; 623.64; 633.9; 644.6; 653.84; 678.19; 681.31; 686.8; 697.12; 698.18; 701.3; 704.34; 718.52; 722.27; 758.15; 806.9; 856.15; 856.16; 860.6; 880.23; 889.16; 894.3; 903.6; 918.44; 918.45; 923.52; 937.6; 945.39; 946.43; 955.4; 965.31; 978.60; 992.45; 997.9; 998.109; 1011.33; 1042.87; 1048.52; 1048.53; 1052.7; 1068.8
Senegalese Proverb. 169.6
Sennett, Mack. Original name, Michael Sinnott (1884–1960) American actor and pioneer motion-picture producer and director. 670.46
Service, Robert W[illiam] (1874–1958) English-born Canadian writer. 743.10
Shahn, Ben (1898–1969) Lithuanian-born American artist. 53.129
Shakespeare, William (1564–1616) English playwright, poet, most widely known writer in English literature. 6.17; 10.15; 11.8; 17.52; 17.53; 17.54; 19.24; 29.1; 39.25; 55.17; 56.9; 57.17; 61.10; 72.48; 72.49; 79.4; 92.11; 96.5; 98.8; 110.6; 120.9; 122.8; 131.39; 132.9; 139.8; 152.19; 155.12; 156.8; 167.5; 174.29; 174.30; 174.31; 181.10; 181.11; 186.20; 186.21; 191.11; 191.12; 192.2; 195.34; 198.14; 199.10; 204.18; 206.24; 218.6; 221.112; 221.113; 221.114; 221.115; 221.116; 222.11; 224.18; 224.19; 226.11; 230.2; 231.11; 240.18; 252.11; 259.13; 259.14; 264.13; 266.18; 267.23; 267.24; 268.47; 268.48; 268.49; 271.25; 281.15; 287.8; 307.33; 307.34; 318.11; 319.5; 320.2; 332.41; 333.10; 338.24; 338.25; 340.18; 342.27; 343.34; 356.21; 356.22; 360.34; 365.91; 365.92; 368.30; 368.31; 384.27; 384.28; 386.14; 387.64; 389.13; 390.18; 390.19; 393.44; 399.9; 401.50; 401.51; 405.15; 405.16; 409.89; 409.90; 409.91; 411.13; 411.14; 420.7; 422.20; 425.17; 427.34; 427.35; 428.18; 431.23; 431.24; 433.28; 436.28; 440.18; 440.19; 450.27; 460.5; 475.6; 475.7; 483.2; 491.24; 491.25; 491.26; 507.8; 510.18; 512.4; 514.9; 517.42; 517.43; 518.12; 518.13; 520.10; 522.56; 528.60; 528.61; 531.18; 537.38; 539.108; 539.109; 539.110; 539.111; 541.37; 543.4; 550.9; 551.188; 551.189; 551.190; 551.191; 551.192; 551.193; 551.194; 551.195; 551.196; 551.197; 552.14; 552.15; 555.18; 558.35; 559.16; 562.52; 562.53; 564.106; 564.107; 564.108; 571.15; 577.9; 583.5; 583.6; 583.7; 584.5; 593.5; 602.54; 604.34; 606.16; 614.53; 619.8; 629.7; 635.5; 653.85; 653.86; 653.87; 653.88; 657.12; 670.47; 675.20; 675.21; 677.16; 681.32; 682.16; 684.17; 693.9; 704.35; 704.36; 708.87; 715.2; 716.14; 719.52; 719.53; 723.31; 729.24; 733.19; 740.4; 748.3; 750.14; 755.27; 757.1; 765.4; 772.13; 780.19; 792.5; 798.11; 798.12; 801.3; 803.9; 804.27; 804.28; 810.11; 817.16; 822.18; 831.21; 831.22; 833.1; 833.2; 845.6; 846.4; 854.37; 865.4; 875.28; 876.14; 890.5; 892.48; 896.27; 898.25; 898.26; 901.18; 904.10; 905.10; 905.11; 905.12; 906.20; 906.21; 916.13; 918.46; 918.47; 918.48; 918.49; 918.50; 918.51; 923.53; 923.54; 926.4; 937.7; 938.6; 945.40; 946.44; 948.23; 948.24; 951.4; 953.3; 975.40; 978.61; 978.62; 978.63; 979.8; 992.46; 997.10; 998.110; 998.111; 1000.19; 1005.10; 1027.16; 1030.23; 1030.24; 1030.25; 1033.43; 1034.17; 1034.18; 1048.54; 1051.5; 1052.8; 1052.9; 1056.10; 1060.53; 1060.54; 1061.26; 1062.126; 1062.127; 1062.128; 1062.129; 1062.130; 1065.63; 1067.25; 1070.20; 1072.21
Shannon, William V[incent] (1927–) American newspaperman and editor. 711.76
Shapiro, Karl [Jay] (1913–) American poet, critic, editor. 305.7; 430.7; 528.62; 572.1; 670.48; 708.88; 875.29; 1042.88
Shaw, George Bernard (1856–1950) Irish playwright, critic, social reformer. 53.130; 53.131; 53.132; 94.7; 113.9; 123.52; 129.5; 129.6; 148.7; 153.4; 185.8; 195.35; 201.38; 209.15; 221.117; 233.50; 233.51; 235.9; 256.1; 263.14; 271.26; 279.78; 289.28; 289.29; 289.30; 299.30; 312.7; 321.46; 321.47; 328.14; 338.26; 354.13; 354.14; 363.45; 388.3; 391.7; 409.92; 412.22; 413.14; 418.34; 466.6; 472.10; 491.27; 506.3; 512.5; 517.44; 518.14; 518.15; 522.57; 532.19; 537.39; 539.112; 540.13; 541.38; 564.109; 564.110; 564.111; 565.13; 580.34; 581.53; 582.11; 582.12; 587.5; 587.6; 602.55; 602.56; 604.35; 630.32; 665.11; 670.49; 705.7; 711.77; 711.78; 718.53; 741.23; 741.24; 741.25; 780.20; 785.36; 796.4; 797.70; 797.71; 809.4; 819.39; 837.10; 848.35; 849.35; 855.16; 865.5; 868.7; 889.17; 896.28; 913.31; 934.7; 965.32; 975.41; 1037.11; 1038.18; 1048.55; 1072.22; 1072.23
Shawcross, William (1946–) English journalist and writer. 162.8; 355.15; 1026.21; 1042.89
Shawn, Ted (1891–1972) American dancer and choreographer. 215.4
Shelley, Percy Bysshe (1792–1822) English poet. 53.133; 100.15; 180.4; 207.47; 221.118; 221.119; 242.7; 298.16; 333.11; 416.11; 427.36; 454.19; 520.11; 524.39; 526.30; 551.198; 580.35; 604.36; 620.10; 644.7; 708.89; 708.90; 708.91; 708.92; 708.93; 719.54; 797.72; 831.23; 862.14; 889.18; 914.8; 918.52; 946.45; 990.15; 998.112; 1008.18; 1059.6
Shenker, Israel (1925–) American author and journalist. 34.69; 80.8; 84.3; 123.53; 262.8; 387.65; 435.24; 512.6; 512.7; 524.40; 583.8; 723.32; 784.16; 835.3; 848.36; 900.21; 952.8; 973.9; 1060.55
Shenstone, William (1714–1763) English poet, known for his pastoral verse. 1050.9
Shepherd, Jean (1929–) American writer and humorist. 64.13; 64.14; 632.16; 632.17; 937.8; 998.113
Sheppard, Eugenia (1714–1763) Contemporary American fashion writer. 267.25
Sheridan, Richard Brinsley

(1751–1816) Irish-born English playwright, orator, statesman. 120.10; 218.7; 268.50; 295.22; 517.45; 564.112; 580.36; 600.14; 846.5; 892.49
Sherman, William T[ecumseh] (1820–1891) American general. 1042.90
Sherwood, Robert E[mmet] (1896–1955) American playwright and editor. 43.14
Shirley, James (1596–1666) English playwright. 221.120; 227.28; 340.19
Shostakovich, Dmitri [Dmitrievich] (1906–1975) Russian composer. 201.39
Sidney, Sir Philip (1554–1586) English poet, scholar, soldier, courtier. 791.6
Silius Italicus, Tiberius Catius Asconius (A.D. c. 25–101) Roman statesman and poet. 1033.44
Sills, Beverley (1929–) American soprano and opera company director. 894.4
Silone, Ignazio. Original name, Secondo Tranquilli (1900–) Italian novelist. 17.19; 1069.120
Simenon, Georges (1903–) Belgian-born French novelist. 1069.121
Simon, John (1925–) Contemporary Yugoslav-born American drama critic. 524.41; 545.22; 1064.46
Simpson, Louis (1923–) American poet. 34.70
Singer, Isaac Bashevis (1904–1991) Polish-born Yiddish novelist and short-story writer. 77.24; 265.7; 266.19; 387.66; 472.11; 499.10; 558.36; 564.113; 604.37
Skinner, B[urrhus] F[rederick] (1904–1990) American behavioral psychologist and writer. 14.7; 26.7; 49.1; 77.25; 210.23; 279.79; 294.6; 308.17; 395.56; 398.9; 524.42; 556.3; 562.54; 562.55; 687.5; 766.17; 913.32; 1032.13
Smith, Adam (1723–1790) Scottish philosopher and economist. 104.29; 369.7; 849.36; 1026.22; 1048.56
Smith, Alexander (1830–1867) Scottish poet and essayist. 119.27; 216.16; 221.121; 332.42; 404.28; 442.17; 580.37; 996.11
Smith, Logan Pearsall (1865–1946) American-born English man of letters. 22.4; 62.10; 93.81; 93.82; 94.8; 121.4; 184.8; 321.48; 332.43; 365.93; 447.29; 479.12; 497.4; 564.114; 586.17; 593.6; 653.89; 653.90; 653.91; 653.92; 684.18; 704.37; 772.14; 919.6; 942.19; 980.8; 1069.122; 1071.57
Smith, Stevie. Real name Florence Margaret Smith (1902–1971) English poet and novelist. 19.25; 41.30; 125.25; 239.10; 276.6; 365.94; 705.8
Smith, Sydney (1771–1845) English clergyman, wit, essayist. 93.83; 104.30; 189.8; 194.13; 274.27; 386.15; 401.52; 564.115; 718.54; 722.28; 724.9; 958.2; 977.9
Snow, Carmel (1890–1961) Irish-born American fashion editor. 282.3
Sockman, Ralph W[ashington] (1889–1970) American Methodist clergyman. 387.67
Socrates (469–399 B.C.) Greek philosopher. 51.19; 221.122; 319.6; 386.16; 393.45; 539.113; 539.114; 558.37; 665.12; 708.94; 758.16; 1071.58
Solon (c. 640–c. 558 B.C.) Greek statesman, poet, one of the Seven Sages of Greece. 19.26; 528.63; 598.14; 635.6; 644.8; 797.73; 923.55; 1048.57
Solzhenitsyn, Aleksandr Isayevich (1918–) Russian novelist. 545.23
Sontag, Susan (1933–) American essayist and novelist. 20.6; 72.50; 108.14; 145.11; 207.48; 207.49; 413.15; 443.32; 545.24; 545.25; 559.17; 566.6; 589.11; 695.4; 695.5; 695.6; 784.17; 873.20; 878.4; 883.8; 896.29; 945.41; 963.18; 972.29; 987.13; 987.14; 999.15
Sophocles (496–406 B.C.) Greek tragic playwright. 17.55; 17.56; 19.27; 19.28; 24.2; 39.26; 86.3; 111.13; 116.17; 123.54; 173.13; 181.12; 217.5; 221.123; 221.124; 227.29; 240.19; 250.5; 300.9; 329.22; 340.20; 354.15; 360.35; 360.36; 365.95; 365.96; 368.32; 384.29; 409.93; 409.94; 431.25; 493.30; 517.46; 517.47; 517.48; 519.17; 519.18; 531.20; 532.20; 539.115; 551.199; 572.2; 610.11; 629.8; 635.7; 652.11; 653.93; 690.10; 727.2; 738.9; 755.28; 762.15; 817.17; 866.7; 892.50; 896.30; 905.13; 918.53; 940.15; 945.42; 978.64; 978.65; 979.9; 998.114; 1011.34; 1060.56; 1070.21
Sorensen, Theodore [Chalkin] (1928–) American lawyer and writer. 730.17
Southey, Robert (1774–1843) English poet and man of letters. 1062.131
Spanish Proverb. 12.8; 17.57; 37.8; 57.18; 58.6; 66.7; 105.21; 122.9; 122.10; 150.17; 169.7; 218.8; 226.12; 263.15; 268.51; 321.49; 334.28; 334.29; 393.46; 394.12; 405.17; 434.4; 455.7; 473.8; 476.19; 551.200; 551.201; 564.116; 582.13; 805.5; 880.24; 894.5
Spark, Muriel (1918–) Scottish novelist, short-story writer and critic. 221.125; 224.20; 365.97; 412.23; 653.94; 966.32; 1033.45
Spencer, Herbert (1820–1903) English philosopher and social scientist. 849.37
Spenser, Edmund (1552?–1599) English poet. 327.2; 378.6; 831.24
Spinoza, Baruch [or Benedict] (1632–1677) Dutch philosopher. 173.14; 207.50; 332.44; 387.68; 390.20; 426.10; 431.26; 435.25; 454.20; 554.10; 733.20; 733.21; 791.7; 923.56; 1027.17
Spock, Benjamin [McLane] (1903–) American pediatrician, educator, civil rights leader. 123.55
St. John, Henry, 1st Viscount Bolingbroke (1678–1751) English statesman, orator, man of letters. 299.29
Staël, Mme de. Born Anne Louise Germaine Necker (1766–1817) Swiss-born French writer. 537.40; 551.202; 614.54; 761.20; 952.9
Stander, Lionel (1908–) Contemporary American actor. 977.10
Stanislaus I (Stanislaus or Stanislas Leszczynski) (1677–1766) King of Poland 1704–1709 and 1733–1735. 797.74; 849.38; 1040.6
St. Augustine *See* Augustine, St.
Steele, Richard (1672–1729) Irish-born English playwright, essayist, editor. 96.6; 535.4; 188.33; 188.34; 188.35; 349.17; 392.10; 413.16; 472.12; 491.28; 558.38; 564.117; 614.55; 615.3; 636.5; 653.95; 706.8; 722.29; 733.22; 888.9; 1003.3; 1027.18; 1061.27; 1062.132
Stegner, Wallace (1909–1993) American writer. 221.126; 401.53; 419.43; 443.33; 468.10; 539.116; 699.10; 1026.23
Steichen, Edward (1879–1973) American photographer. 695.7
Stein, Gertrude (1874–1946) American poet, novelist, critic. 376.32; 444.22
Steinbeck, John [Ernst] (1902–1968) American novelist and short-story writer. 39.27; 41.31; 41.32; 93.84; 93.85; 102.7; 201.40; 207.51; 263.16; 340.21; 365.98; 367.14; 380.1; 405.18; 437.14; 437.15; 545.26; 551.203; 564.118; 564.119; 571.16; 577.10; 581.54; 581.55; 623.65; 632.18; 632.19; 632.20; 653.96; 680.9; 695.8; 778.5; 812.3; 896.31; 896.32; 915.44; 923.57; 988.8; 992.47; 992.48; 1062.133; 1065.64; 1069.123; 1069.124
Steinem, Gloria (1934–) American publisher, editor, writer. 49.2; 6.18; 135.6; 279.80; 334.30; 512.8; 512.9; 524.43; 531.21; 539.117; 551.204; 555.19; 564.120; 564.121; 581.56; 581.57; 619.9; 670.50; 670.51; 711.79; 711.80; 714.3; 758.17; 817.18; 823.19; 860.7; 869.12; 869.13; 892.51; 898.27; 923.58; 946.46; 1009.3; 1062.134; 1062.135; 1064.47; 1065.65
Steiner, George (1929–)

French-born American author. 363.46; 450.28; 492.9; 630.33; 892.52

Stendhal. Pen name of Marie Henri Beyle (1783–1842) French novelist and critic. Stendhal 72.51; 227.30; 551.205; 551.206; 712.8; 756.3; 915.45; 1062.136

Sterne, Laurence (1713–1768) English novelist. 174.32; 207.52; 263.17; 267.26; 436.29; 522.58; 539.118; 694.36; 946.47; 960.12; 984.14; 1060.57

Stevens, Wallace (1879–1955) American poet. 708.95; 885.6

Stevenson, Adlai E[wing] (1900–1965) American statesman. 34.71; 34.72; 41.33; 13.3; 121.5; 150.18; 233.52; 233.53; 328.15; 349.18; 363.47; 364.7; 368.33; 374.16; 406.16; 419.44; 474.6; 522.59; 558.39; 590.17; 602.57; 604.38; 625.7; 641.14; 674.7; 677.17; 678.20; 678.21; 710.11; 710.12; 711.81; 734.15; 741.26; 760.14; 764.14; 956.7; 998.115; 1038.19; 1064.48

Stevenson, Robert Louis [Balfour] (1850–1894) Scottish novelist, poet, essayist. 2.10; 37.9; 41.34; 55.18; 93.86; 104.31; 123.56; 179.5; 271.27; 281.16; 321.50; 330.33; 344.26; 354.16; 409.95; 446.15; 459.3; 539.119; 545.27; 547.10; 558.40; 564.122; 564.123; 604.39; 604.40; 606.17; 653.97; 666.12; 745.8; 755.29; 803.10; 854.38; 923.59; 945.43; 974.12; 992.49; 992.50; 1021.3; 1059.7; 1064.49; 1067.26; 1069.125; 1071.59; 1072.24; 1072.25

St. John, J. Hector *See* Crèvecoeur, Michel Guillaume Jean de

Stone, I[sidor] F[einstein] (1907–) American journalist and social commentator; editor and publisher of *I. F. Stone's Weekly*. 229.14

Stoppard, Tom (1937–) English playwright. 76.9; 221.127; 289.31; 302.1; 606.18; 998.116

Stravinsky, Igor Feodorovitch (1882–1971) Russian-born American composer. 53.134; 59.6; 201.41; 207.53; 332.45; 374.17; 401.54; 532.21; 614.56; 614.57; 614.58; 822.19; 898.28; 900.22

Strindberg, [Johan] August (1849–1912) Swedish playwright, novelist, poet. 334.31; 334.32; 409.96; 972.30

Stringer, Arthur [John Arbuthnott] (1874–1950) American novelist and poet. 72.52; 254.6; 840.12

St. Thomas Aquinas *See* Aquinas, St. Thomas

Styron, William [Clark, Jr.] (1925–) American novelist. 93.87; 1069.126

Suarès, André (1868–1948) French poet, critic, essayist. 258.10; 1048.58

Suckling, Sir John (1609–1642) English poet. 181.13; 318.12

Sulzberger, Arthur Hays (1891–1968) American newspaper publisher. 630.34

Sulzberger, C[yrus] L[eo] (1912–) American newspaperman and political writer. 361.10

Surtees, Robert Smith (1803–1864) English novelist and sports writer. 194.14; 267.27; 821.1; 1034.19

Sutherland, George (1862–1942) American jurist. Associate Justice of the U.S. Supreme Court (1922–1938). 731.6

Suzuki, Daisetz Teitaro (1870–1966) Japanese Zen Buddhist scholar and writer. 694.37

Swift, Jonathan (1667–1745) English satirist. 31.7; 33.23; 66.8; 73.9; 181.14; 196.1; 206.25; 207.54; 263.18; 264.14; 299.31; 299.32; 339.2; 349.19; 360.37; 376.33; 392.11; 405.19; 414.13; 539.120; 548.13; 550.7; 571.17; 592.4; 650.4; 650.5; 653.98; 656.27; 674.8; 694.38; 705.9; 716.15; 722.30; 723.33; 724.10; 726.14; 743.11; 762.16; 772.15; 780.21; 797.75; 844.7; 893.7; 896.33; 923.60; 937.9; 942.20; 943.5; 978.66; 996.12; 1023.6; 1033.46; 1035.6; 1072.26

Swinburne, Algernon Charles (1837–1909) English poet and man of letters. 221.128; 330.34; 511.5; 919.7; 978.67; 990.16

Swope, Herbert Bayard (1882–1958) American newspaperman, editor, public official. 630.35; 630.36

Syrus, Publilius *See* Publilius Syrus

Szell, George (1897–1970) Hungarian-born American conductor, composer, pianist. 614.59

T

Tacitus, Cornelius (55?–117) Roman historian. 2.11; 33.24; 173.15; 319.7; 342.28; 376.34; 386.17; 390.21; 476.20; 491.29; 610.12; 647.7; 719.55; 942.21; 1019.11; 1042.91

Taft, William Howard (1857–1930) Twenty-seventh President of the United States (1909–1913). 182.8

Tagore, [Sir] Rabindranath (1861–1941) Bengali poet, novelist, essayist, composer. 53.135; 56.10; 72.53; 72.54; 117.32; 123.57; 126.11; 209.16; 242.8; 264.15; 266.20; 316.10; 332.46; 357.16; 363.48; 384.30; 384.31; 387.69; 399.10; 433.29; 433.30; 435.26; 459.4; 504.22; 519.19; 539.121; 539.122; 541.39; 551.207; 551.208; 551.209; 551.210; 562.56; 571.18; 580.38; 647.8; 719.56; 722.31; 729.25; 766.18; 780.22; 785.37; 887.4; 978.68; 978.69; 995.5; 998.117; 1002.29; 1047.12; 1068.9

Taine, Hippolyte [Adolphe] (1828–1893) French philosopher, critic, historian. 564.124

Tall, Deborah (1951–) American teacher and writer. 444.23; 444.24; 468.11; 623.66; 639.6; 1067.27

Tannen, Deborah (1945–) American teacher and writer. 149.18; 225.9; 235.10; 366.5; 499.11; 581.58; 581.59; 933.5; 1008.19

Tarkington, [Newton] Booth (1869–1946) American novelist and playwright. 51.20; 409.97; 564.125; 616.3

Taubman, [Hyman] Howard (1907–) American journalist and essayist. 972.31

Taylor, Bayard (1825–1878) American poet, journalist, novelist. 551.211

Taylor, Jeremy (1613–1667) English clergyman and writer. 263.19; 334.33

Teale, Edwin Way (1899–) American teacher, editor, writer, naturalist. 41.35; 131.40; 177.8; 415.10; 533.15; 539.123; 605.5; 623.67; 623.68; 630.37; 636.6; 701.4; 774.1; 854.39; 854.40; 854.41; 946.48; 995.6; 998.118; 998.119; 1001.13; 1023.7

Teasdale, Sara (1884–1933) American poet. 72.55; 72.56; 72.57; 129.7; 321.51; 521.10; 539.124; 539.125; 551.212; 551.213; 571.19; 580.39; 716.16; 854.42; 1010.1

Tehyi Hsieh (1884–) Chinese educator, writer, diplomat. 9.27; 273.2; 279.43; 404.12; 410.3; 537.17; 755.12; 945.19; 966.12

Temple, Sir William (1628–1699) English diplomat, statesman, essayist. 93.88

Tencin [Claudine-Alexandrine Guérin] Mme de (1682–1749) French letter writer, novelist and leader in Parisian intellectual circles. 941.18

Tennyson, Alfred, 1st Baron Tennyson. Commonly called Alfred, Lord Tennyson (1809–1892) English poet. 72.58; 117.33; 151.10; 193.4; 197.13; 218.9; 221.129; 265.8; 266.21; 288.21; 321.52; 330.35; 387.70; 390.22; 447.30; 454.21; 457.8; 459.5; 476.21; 478.10; 519.20; 551.214; 551.215; 551.216; 554.11; 558.41; 563.21; 581.60; 588.17; 602.58; 606.19; 623.69; 631.5; 676.30; 693.10; 708.96; 708.97; 717.5; 717.6; 723.34; 723.35; 728.3; 733.23; 741.27; 743.12; 770.6; 797.76; 822.20; 824.8; 831.25; 854.43; 858.28; 897.7; 913.33; 918.54; 948.25; 978.70; 989.8; 1033.47; 1060.58; 1064.50; 1065.66; 1065.67

Terence. Full name, Publius

Terentius After (195?–159 B.C.) Roman playwright. 167.6; 213.27; 321.53; 360.38; 413.17; 469.19; 528.64; 551.217; 555.20; 562.57; 575.6; 653.99; 755.30; 916.14; 988.9; 998.120; 1022.1; 1062.137
Tertullian. Full name, Quintus Septimius Florens Tertullianus (160?–?230) Latin ecclesiastical writer; a father of the church. 300.10; 387.71
Thackeray, William Makepeace (1811–1863) English novelist. 344.27
Theobald, Lewis (1688–1744) English essayist, playwright, Shakespearian critic. 469.20
Theocritus (fl. c. 270 B.C.) Greek pastoral poet. 384.32
Theognis (6th c. B.C.) Greek elegiac and gnomic poet. 221.130; 606.20
Theophrastus (c. 370–287 B.C.) Greek philosopher and man of letters. 978.71
Theroux, Paul Edward (1941–) American writer. 28.5; 93.89; 332.47; 361.11; 605.6; 609.3; 677.18; 845.7; 992.51; 992.52; 992.53; 1050.10; 1069.127
Thévenin, Denis *See* Duhamel, Georges
Thomas Aquinas, St *See* Aquinas, St. Thomas
Thomas, Caitlin [Macnamara] (1913–1994) Irish writer, widow of Dylan Thomas. 201.42; 708.98; 885.7; 1033.48
Thomas, Dylan [Marlais] (1914–1953) Welsh poet and prose writer. 66.9; 78.22; 90.9; 221.131; 228.6; 241.11; 268.52; 436.30; 436.31; 485.4; 618.4; 708.99; 708.100; 708.101; 708.102; 708.103; 732.15; 923.61; 1069.128
Thomas Lewis (1913–) American physician, scientist and writer. 41.36; 77.26; 77.27; 368.34; 413.18; 433.31; 443.34; 524.44; 562.58; 590.18; 621.21; 623.70; 858.29; 881.4; 906.22; 975.42
Thompson, Francis (1859–1907) English poet. 387.72; 854.44; 854.45; 946.49; 990.17
Thompson, Hunter S[tockton] (1939–) American writer. 630.38
Thomson, James (1700–1748) Scottish-born English poet. 72.59; 413.19; 701.5
Thoreau, Henry David (1817–1862) American essayist, naturalist, poet. 19.29; 31.8; 35.5; 72.60; 93.90; 93.91; 93.92; 93.93; 93.94; 110.7; 128.6; 148.8; 152.20; 152.21; 152.22; 152.23; 165.15; 184.9; 191.13; 206.26; 208.10; 227.31; 239.11; 254.7; 258.11; 267.28; 271.28; 279.81; 284.35; 306.2; 316.11; 321.54; 336.17; 336.18; 337.6; 338.27; 342.29; 346.2; 363.49; 365.99; 393.47; 395.57; 409.98; 414.14; 419.45; 430.8; 430.9; 433.32; 435.27; 468.12; 478.11; 493.31; 504.23; 515.7; 518.16; 524.45; 528.65; 528.66; 539.126; 551.218; 558.42; 580.40; 590.19; 592.5; 602.59; 604.41; 605.7; 605.8; 614.60; 623.71; 623.72; 623.73; 623.74; 623.75; 629.9; 676.31; 694.39; 708.104; 708.105; 708.106; 708.107; 708.108; 722.32; 725.6; 780.23; 790.33; 790.34; 792.6; 794.13; 822.21; 832.6; 854.46; 875.30; 877.4; 898.29; 899.14; 900.23; 901.19; 915.46; 915.47; 915.48; 923.62; 986.20; 998.121; 998.122; 1011.35; 1017.16; 1028.2; 1034.20; 1048.59; 1060.59; 1060.60; 1065.68; 1066.5; 1069.129; 1069.130; 1072.27
Thrale, Mrs. *See* Piozzi, Hester Lynch
Thucydides (c. 460–c. 400 B.C.) Greek historian. 195.36; 216.17; 233.54; 402.2; 658.8; 722.33; 751.15; 998.123
Thurber, James [Grover] (1894–1961) American essayist, short-story writer, humorist. 34.73; 53.136; 10.16; 33.25; 73.10; 145.12; 145.13; 149.19; 224.21; 258.12; 271.29; 274.28; 395.58; 403.22; 431.27; 436.32; 436.33; 446.16; 465.6; 522.60; 524.46; 527.6; 562.59; 636.7; 648.2; 758.18; 810.12; 849.39; 875.31; 972.32; 987.15; 1069.131
Tiberius. Full Latin name Tiberius Claudius Nero (42 B.C.–A.D. 37) Roman emperor, called a cruel tyrant and a sound administrator. 964.10; 409.99; 551.219; 857.12; 1042.92
Tillich, Paul (1886–1965) German-born American philosopher and theologian. 6.19; 221.132; 330.36; 359.15; 390.23; 551.220
Tillotson, John (1630–1694) English writer and prelate. 387.73
Tobin, James (1918–) American educator. 1042.93
Tobin, John (1770–1804) English playwright. 267.29
Tocqueville, Count Alexis [Charles Henri Maurice Clérel] de (1805–1859) French political leader, historian, writer. 104.32; 297.24; 297.25; 656.28; 1048.60
Tolbooth prison inscription. 735.6
Tolkien, J[ohn] R[onald] R[enel] (1892–1973) English scholar and writer. 211.11
Tolstoy, Count Leo [or Lev] Nikolayevich. Also Tolstoi (1828–1910) Russian novelist and moral philosopher. 12.9; 94.9; 334.34; 440.20; 551.221; 581.61
Toulet, Paul Jean (1867–1920) French poet and novelist. Jean 551.222
Tourneur, Cyril (c. 1575–1626) English playwright. 1062.138
Toynbee, Arnold J[oseph] (1889–1975) English historian. 133.28; 713.5; 34.74; 43.15; 551.223
Trillin, Calvin (1935–) American author. 520.12; 630.39; 964.11; 1051.6
Trilling, Diana Ruben (1905–) American writer. 355.16; 365.100; 422.21; 445.4; 510.19; 512.10; 517.49; 564.126; 587.7; 602.60; 626.9; 670.52; 736.5; 1061.28
Trilling, Lionel (1905–1975) American critic, short-story writer, educator, novelist. 53.137; 135.7; 445.5; 545.28; 648.3; 700.4; 711.82; 718.55; 784.18; 848.37
Truffaut, François (1932–) French film director and critic. 611.7
Truman, Harry S (1884–1972) Thirty-third President of the United States (1945–1953). 41.37; 233.55; 630.40; 630.41; 670.53; 711.83; 730.18; 930.17
Tsang Sin (5th c. B.C.) Disciple of Confucius. 531.19
Tuchman, Barbara W[ertheim] (1912–1989) American historian and journalist. 104.33; 108.15; 122.11; 126.12; 138.9; 195.37; 512.11; 581.62; 1062.139; 1062.140; 1070.22
Turgenev, Ivan Sergeyevich (1818–1883) Russian novelist. 221.133; 409.100; 915.49
Turkish Proverb. 57.19; 112.6; 141.1; 157.5; 288.22; 446.17; 585.12
Twain, Mark. Pen name of Samuel Langhorne Clemens (1835–1910) American writer and humorist. 17.58; 21.11; 34.75; 34.76; 34.77; 39.28; 41.38; 65.12; 80.9; 81.9; 100.16; 133.29; 159.3; 165.16; 172.5; 178.21; 179.6; 186.22; 195.38; 199.11; 209.17; 213.28; 221.134; 239.12; 242.9; 242.10; 268.53; 268.54; 279.82; 279.83; 295.23; 298.17; 308.18; 310.4; 330.37; 333.12; 349.20; 356.23; 361.12; 365.101; 381.4; 391.8; 393.48; 398.10; 399.11; 406.17; 409.101; 419.46; 420.8; 429.3; 436.34; 443.35; 450.29; 458.5; 475.8; 498.19; 502.4; 504.24; 506.4; 520.13; 527.7; 537.41; 537.42; 539.127; 541.40; 541.41; 541.42; 558.43; 558.44; 559.18; 562.60; 564.127; 564.128; 572.3; 588.18; 602.61; 604.42; 604.43; 604.44; 626.10; 656.29; 660.4; 678.22; 678.23; 734.16; 743.13; 750.15; 750.16; 756.4; 776.7; 790.35; 818.4; 820.6; 822.22; 852.3; 867.11; 869.14; 893.8; 894.6; 898.30; 900.24; 905.14; 931.9; 932.2; 942.22; 970.3; 971.8; 986.21; 988.10; 990.18; 992.54; 992.55; 998.124; 998.125; 999.16;

1000.20; 1000.21; 1000.22; 1008.20; 1026.24; 1027.19; 1054.4; 1060.61; 1061.29; 1062.141; 1065.69; 1072.28

Tynan, Kenneth [Peacock] (1927–) English drama critic. 207.55; 972.33

Tze-sze (5th c. B.C.) Grandson of Confucius. 519.21; 532.22

U

Udall, Stewart L[ee] (1961–1969) American political leader. Former U.S. Secretary of the Interior. 711.84; 713.6; 989.9

Unamuno [y Jugo], Miguel de (1864–1936) Spanish philosopher, poet, novelist. 126.13; 178.22; 188.36; 265.9; 330.38; 387.74; 443.36; 541.43; 551.224; 565.14; 849.40; 904.11; 915.50; 998.126; 1027.20

Unesco. 681.33

Unidentified Author. 757.3

United Presbyterian Church. 105.22; 879.3

Updike, John [Hoyer] (1932–) American novelist, short-story writer, poet. 17.59; 50.22; 53.138; 53.139; 53.140; 54.3; 95.7; 123.58; 123.59; 225.10; 267.30; 279.84; 329.23; 344.28; 374.18; 451.10; 540.14; 580.41; 611.8; 628.2; 632.21; 691.9; 718.57; 730.19; 736.6; 916.15; 916.16; 927.13; 929.19; 946.50; 950.4; 967.28; 1062.142; 1062.143; 1062.144

Ustinov, Peter [Alexander] (1921–) English actor, producer, playwright. 551.225

V

Vahanian, Gabriel [Antoine] (1927–) American educator and writer. 265.10; 317.3; 983.3

Valency, Maurice (1903–) American educator, playwright, translator. 443.37

Valéry, [Ambroise] Paul [Toussaint Jules] (1871–1945) French poet and critic. 3.9; 78.23; 381.5; 419.47; 537.43; 581.63; 590.20; 621.22; 622.6; 661.13; 681.34; 711.85; 759.3; 819.40; 913.34; 994.6

de Valois, Dame Ninette (1898–) Irish-born English ballet director. 376.35

Van Doren, Mark (1894–1972) American poet, critic, educator, novelist, short-story writer, editor. 1067.8

Van Horne, Harriet (1920–) American newspaper columnist and critic. 189.4; 967.8

Van Loon, Hendrik Willem (1882–1944) Dutch-born American journalist and historian. 133.30

Van Vechten, Carl (1880–1964) American author. 41.39

Vanbrugh, Sir John (1664–1726) English playwright. 472.13; 716.17

Vauvenargues, marquis de Luc de Clapiers (1715–1747) French moralist. 6.20; 19.30; 33.26; 224.22; 254.8; 284.36; 299.33; 332.48; 342.30; 375.7; 375.8; 427.37; 539.128; 562.61; 590.21; 604.45; 624.17; 675.22; 677.19; 681.35; 722.34; 722.35; 743.14; 785.38; 889.19; 975.43; 975.44; 978.72; 1042.94; 1072.29

Veblen, Thorstein [Bunde] (1857–1929) American economist and social philosopher. 105.23; 457.9; 524.47; 533.16; 646.7; 746.20; 869.15; 963.19; 1048.61

Vergil. Full name, Publius Vergilius Maro (70–19 B.C.) Roman poet. 8.11; 56.11; 259.15; 287.9; 343.35; 360.39; 833.3; 860.8; 978.73; 1062.145

Vico, Giambattista or Giovanni Battista (1668–1744) Italian philosopher and jurist. 450.30; 557.7; 1032.14

Vidal, Gore (1929–) American novelist and playwright. 34.78; 34.79; 53.141; 53.142; 102.8; 207.56; 288.23; 328.16; 334.35; 344.29; 419.48; 424.9; 424.10; 451.11; 528.67; 545.29; 551.226; 611.9; 695.9; 711.86; 711.87; 711.88; 719.57; 730.20; 736.7; 757.2; 790.36; 844.8; 892.53; 909.2; 972.34; 972.35; 998.127; 1069.132; 1069.133

Vigny, Alfred [Victor] de (1797–1863) French poet, playwright, novelist. 539.129; 588.19; 806.10

Villiers de l'Isle-Adam [Comte Jean Marie Mathias Philippe Auguste de] French writer of fiction and drama (1838–1889). 975.45

Vincent of Beauvais (fl. 13th c.) Dominican monk and scholar. 581.64

Vinci, Leonardo da *See* Leonardo da Vinci

Vinokurov, Yevgeniy [Mikhaylovich] (1925–) Russian poet. 444.25

Viorst, Judith (1931–) American poet, author. 2.12; 336.19; 404.29; 499.12; 550.10; 554.12; 582.14; 627.12; 673.7; 876.15

Virgil *See* Vergil

Voltaire. Pen name of François Marie Arouet (1694–1778) French satirist, essayist, dramatist, philosopher, historian. 38.2; 42.7; 72.61; 72.62; 93.95; 95.8; 98.98.9; 101.4; 119.28; 132.10; 174.33; 184.10; 185.9; 188.37; 189.9; 204.19; 262.9; 263.20; 289.32; 299.34; 299.35; 299.36; 309.7; 330.39; 332.49; 335.18; 338.28; 343.36; 344.30; 361.13; 365.102; 387.75; 387.76; 389.14; 390.24; 395.59; 401.55; 403.23; 427.38; 431.28; 436.35; 440.21; 472.14; 479.13; 502.5; 514.10; 516.20; 517.50; 518.17; 528.68; 528.69; 535.5; 537.44; 551.227; 551.228; 559.19; 577.11; 590.22; 604.46; 614.61; 622.7; 656.30; 659.11; 659.12; 684.19; 691.10; 694.40; 694.41; 704.38; 705.10; 708.109; 719.58; 723.36; 741.28; 741.29; 743.15; 746.21; 755.31; 790.37; 797.77; 818.5; 857.13; 866.8; 876.16; 876.17; 882.11; 915.51; 948.26; 949.3; 973.10; 974.13; 975.46; 975.47; 1002.30; 1033.49; 1033.50; 1042.95; 1042.96; 1055.11; 1061.30; 1065.70; 1067.28; 1068.10; 1068.11

von Braun, Wernher 1912– German-born American rocket engineer. 921.2

Vonnegut, Kurt (1922–) American novelist, short-story writer, playwright, essayist. 34.80; 84.4; 105.24; 133.31; 238.37; 244.6; 246.5; 293.7; 431.29; 464.5; 547.11; 547.12; 614.62; 681.36; 746.22; 764.15; 769.2; 895.4; 948.27; 962.15; 966.33; 967.29; 982.15; 991.3; 1042.97; 1042.98; 1069.134; 1069.135; 1069.136

Voznesensky, Andrey (1934–) Russian poet. 201.43

Vreeland, Diana (1934–) Contemporary French-born American fashion editor. 282.4

W

Walker, Alice (1944–) American novelist, poet and short-story writer. 143.4; 387.77; 414.15; 522.62; 797.78; 975.48; 978.74; 995.7

Walker, David (1785–1830) American abolitionist. 85.16; 614.22; 614.23; 614.24; 614.25

Waller, Edmund (1606–1687) English poet. 414.16; 460.6

Waller, Robert James (1939–) American writer and photographer. 26.8; 115.13; 171.17; 201.44; 266.22; 492.10; 582.15; 614.63

Walpole, Horace, 4th Earl of Orford (1717–1797) English writer and historian. 289.33; 747.6; 1067.29

Walsh, William (1663–1708) English critic and poet. 295.24

Walton, Izaak (1593–1683) English writer and lover of fishing. 152.24; 348.4; 413.20; 550.11

Ward, Artemus. Pen name of Charles Farrar Browne (1834–1867) American humorist, newspaperman, editor, lecturer. 17.60; 376.36; 398.11; 977.11

Ward, Barbara [Lady (Robert) Jackson] (1914–) English economist and writer. 332.50

Warner, Charles Dudley (1829–1900) American essayist, editor, novelist. 51.21; 54.4; 55.19; 93.96; 128.7; 131.41; 171.18; 188.38; 204.20; 221.135; 224.23; 248.1; 298.18; 337.7; 337.8; 344.31;

Warner, Charles Dudley (*cont.*)

355.17; 371.6; 412.24; 419.49; 542.14; 564.129; 580.42; 581.65; 581.66; 623.76; 623.77; 656.31; 712.10; 746.23; 915.52; 945.44; 950.5; 1026.25; 1042.99; 1062.146; 1066.6

Warren, Earl (1953–1968) American jurist. Chief Justice of U. S. Supreme Court. 132.11

Warren, Robert Penn (1905–) American poet, novelist, educator. 419.50; 1069.137

Washington, Booker T[aliaferro] (1856–1915) American educator and writer. 25.1; 1065.71

Washington, George (1789–1797) First President of the United States. 229.15; 425.18

Wasserstein, Wendy (1950–) American playwright and writer. 274.29; 334.36; 436.36; 702.8; 945.45; 966.34; 1065.72

Watson, Sir William (1858–1935) English poet. 708.110

Watts, Isaac (1674–1748) English theologian and hymn writer. 41.41; 267.31; 416.12

Waugh, Evelyn [Arthur St. John] (1903–1966) English novelist. 131.42; 524.48; 524.49; 602.62; 653.100; 992.56; 1064.51; 1069.138

Webster, Daniel (1782–1852) American statesman and orator. 132.12; 337.9; 517.51; 522.63; 522.64; 537.45; 975.49

Webster, John (1580?–1625) English playwright. 263.21; 360.40; 360.41; 386.18; 414.17; 750.17; 975.50

Wedgwood, C[icely] V[eronica] (1910–) English historian. 418.35; 418.36; 419.51; 419.52; 522.65; 682.17

Weeks, Edward [Augustus], Jr. (1898–) American editor, lecturer, essayist. 571.20; 764.16

Weil, Simone (1909–1943) French philosophical writer. 210.24; 279.85; 401.56; 766.19; 927.14

Weiler, A. H. (1909–1943) Contemporary American editor and newspaperman. 315.5

Weiss, Peter (1916–) German-born painter, film director, novelist, playwright. 221.136; 450.31; 998.128; 1042.100

Weldon, Fay (1933–) English novelist. 92.12; 499.13; 586.18; 610.13

Welles, [George] Orson (1915–1985) American actor, producer, film director. 11.9; 17:61; 967.30

Wellington, 1st Duke of (Arthur Wellesley) (1769–1852) English general and statesman. 1042.101

Wells, H[erbert] G[eorge] (1866–1946) English novelist and journalist. 12.10; 100.17; 419.53; 588.20; 623.78; 676.32; 797.79; 800.4; 914.9

Welsh Proverb. 96.7; 356.24

Welty, Eudora [Alice] (1909–) American novelist and short-story writer. 53.143; 66.10; 336.20; 491.30; 521.11; 784.19; 978.75; 1007.17; 1007.18; 1069.139

Wertham, Frederic (1895–) German-born American psychiatrist, writer, teacher. 823.20

Wescott, Glenway (1901–1989) American poet and novelist. 545.30

West, Jessamyn (1907–) American novelist and short-story writer. 1069.140

West, Mae (1892–) American actress. 62.11; 307.35; 528.70; 570.10; 649.8; 971.9

West, Nathanael [Nathan Wallenstein Weinstein] (1906–1940) American novelist. 257.5

West, Rebecca. Pen name of Mrs. Cicily Maxwell Andrews, born Fairfield (1892–) English novelist, critic, essayist. 630.42

Westcott, Edward Noyes (1846–1898) American banker and novelist. 41.42; 388.4

Wharton, Edith [Newbold Jones] (1862–1937) American novelist and short-story writer. 539.130; 539.131; 913.35

Wheelock, John Hall (1886–) American poet. 524.50

White, E[lwyn] B[rooks] (1899–1985) American humorist and essayist. 34.81; 34.82; 34.83; 64.15; 100.18; 104.34; 108.16; 110.8; 130.2; 131.43; 189.10; 234.4; 247.11; 288.24; 289.34; 333.13; 337.10; 360.42; 376.37; 398.12; 409.102; 436.37; 460.7; 537.46; 537.47; 586.19; 604.47; 622.8; 623.79; 641.15; 641.16; 661.14; 681.37; 708.111; 708.112; 797.80; 854.47; 916.17; 967.31; 977.12; 994.7; 1050.11; 1068.12; 1069.141; 1069.142; 1069.143

White, Theodore (1915–1986) American writer and journalist. 233.56; 730.21

Whitehead, Alfred North (1861–1947) English philosopher and mathematician. 9.35; 53.144; 117.34; 298.19; 321.55; 387.78; 395.60; 443.38; 528.71; 604.48; 674.9; 681.38; 694.42; 694.43; 797.81; 797.82; 797.83; 828.4; 850.8; 913.36; 974.14; 975.51; 975.52; 987.16; 998.129; 1068.13

Whitman, Cedric (1916–) American educator and classical scholar. 617.8

Whitman, Walt[er] (1819–1892) American poet, journalist, essayist. Whitman, Walt 41.43; 59.7; 90.10; 120.11; 131.44; 171.19; 221.137; 362.10; 384.33; 395.61; 419.54; 447.31; 464.6; 537.48; 539.132; 563.22; 692.4; 708.113; 876.18; 876.19; 880.25; 882.12; 899.15; 919.8; 942.23; 998.130; 1069.144

Whittier, John Greenleaf (1807–1892) American poet and editor. 271.30; 491.31; 507.9; 681.39; 754.12; 803.11; 815.10

Wicker, Tom (1926–) American newspaperman and author. 119.29; 395.62; 710.13; 711.89; 711.90; 719.59; 730.22

Wiener, Norbert (1894–1964) American mathematician and educator. 34.84; 177.9; 522.66; 696.5; 771.9; 828.5; 849.41

Wiesel, Elie (1928–) Rumanian-born American novelist and essayist. 204.21; 221.138; 334.37; 358.10; 363.50; 363.51; 365.103; 423.8; 466.7; 512.12; 527.8; 532.23; 552.16; 562.62; 573.5; 580.43; 639.7; 653.101; 671.3; 766.20; 855.17; 898.31; 1019.12; 1042.102; 1042.103; 1069.145; 1069.146

Wilbur, Richard (1921–) American poet. 134.8; 551.229; 623.80; 854.48; 854.49; 858.30; 1067.30

Wilcox, Ella Wheeler (1850–1919) American poet and novelist. 527.9

Wilde, Oscar [Fingal O'Flahertie Wills] (1854–1900) Irish-born English poet, playwright, novelist. 10.17; 19.31; 20.7; 34.85; 34.86; 45.21; 51.22; 53.145; 53.146; 53.147; 53.148; 53.149; 53.150; 53.151; 54.5; 55.20; 68.3; 72.63; 78.24; 81.10; 93.97; 121.6; 121.7; 123.60; 136.6; 148.9; 159.4; 160.4; 165.17; 174.34; 181.15; 201.45; 201.46; 207.57; 207.58; 214.5; 227.32; 251.8; 256.2; 266.23; 267.32; 270.2; 271.31; 279.86; 279.87; 279.88; 279.89; 284.37; 298.20; 305.8; 321.56; 321.57; 329.24; 342.31; 342.32; 343.37; 373.3; 376.38; 393.49; 394.13; 438.5; 440.22; 443.39; 444.26; 446.18; 450.32; 468.13; 472.15; 472.16; 484.3; 484.4; 522.67; 526.31; 531.22; 539.133; 539.134; 551.230; 551.231; 558.45; 564.130; 564.131; 564.132; 564.133; 564.134; 564.135; 564.136; 565.15; 580.44; 581.67; 581.68; 599.2; 602.63; 604.49; 604.50; 605.9; 612.9; 612.10; 629.10; 650.6; 656.32; 659.13; 663.14; 666.13; 684.20; 708.114; 735.10; 735.11; 735.12; 804.29; 807.6; 825.3; 826.7; 840.13; 845.8; 850.9; 862.15; 865.6; 874.5; 876.20; 885.8; 886.10; 901.20; 901.21; 914.10; 914.11; 918.55; 919.9; 941.19; 942.24; 946.51; 946.52; 946.53; 951.5; 961.4; 971.10; 971.11; 975.53; 975.54; 975.55; 998.131; 998.132; 998.133; 1003.4; 1023.8; 1037.12; 1042.104; 1053.2; 1055.12; 1060.62; 1062.147; 1062.148; 1062.149; 1071.60; 1072.30

Wilder, Thornton [Niven] (1897–1975) American novelist and playwright. 41.44; 116.18; 265.11; 422.22; 470.5; 551.232; 564.137; 581.69; 602.64; 605.10; 972.36; 972.37; 972.38; 972.39; 1011.36; 1030.26; 1034.21
Will, George F[rederick] (1941–) American writer, editor, commentator. 18.13; 71.1; 118.6; 123.61; 294.7; 361.14; 419.55; 622.9; 730.23; 736.8; 856.17; 929.20; 929.21; 929.22; 929.23; 967.32; 1038.20; 1044.5; 1044.6
Williams, Tennessee. Pen name of Thomas Lanier Williams (1914–) American playwright and writer of fiction. 117.35; 259.16; 362.11; 367.15; 541.44; 562.63; 580.45; 581.70; 623.81; 882.13; 915.53; 972.40; 978.76; 978.77; 1047.13
Williams, William Carlos (1883–1963) American poet and physician. 359.16; 450.33; 551.233; 708.115; 992.57
Williamson, Marianne (1952–) American lecturer and writer. 359.17; 551.234; 945.46
Wilson, Angus (1913–) English novelist and short-story writer. 344.32
Wilson, Charles Erwin (1886–1972) American industrialist. 104.35
Wilson, Edmund (1895–1972) American literary and social critic, novelist, playwright, short-story writer and poet. 289.35; 303.5; 470.6; 865.7
Wilson, [Thomas] Woodrow (1856–1924) Twenty-eighth President of the United States (1913–1921). 34.87; 34.88; 34.89; 46.6; 104.36; 173.16; 233.57; 233.58; 312.8; 365.104; 395.63; 395.64; 401.57; 459.6; 498.20; 498.21; 517.52; 528.72; 537.49; 537.50; 537.51; 537.52; 621.23; 621.24; 658.9; 665.13; 678.24; 681.40; 681.41; 682.18; 711.91; 711.92; 711.93; 730.24; 822.23; 823.21; 885.9; 887.5; 975.56; 1021.4; 1060.63; 1065.73
Windsor, Duke of (1894–1972) Former king of Great Britain, as Edward VIII. 34.90
Winters, Shelly (1922–) American actress. 972.41
Winthrop, Robert C (1809–1894) American politician. 718.58
Wittgenstein, Ludwig (1889–1951) Austrian philosopher. 919.10; 975.57
Wodehouse, P[elham] G[renville] (1881–1975) English writer and humorist. 207.59; 961.5
Wolfe, Thomas [Clayton] (1900–1938) American novelist and short-story writer. 38.3; 53.152; 64.16; 72.64; 78.25; 97.7; 112.7; 119.30; 131.45; 133.32; 217.6; 221.139; 221.140; 221.141; 221.142; 221.143; 224.24; 269.7; 332.51; 334.38; 368.35; 387.79; 399.12; 420.9; 446.19; 492.11; 492.12; 503.7; 540.15; 551.235; 587.8; 592.6; 606.21; 614.64; 629.11; 632.22; 632.23; 670.54; 673.8; 708.116; 722.36; 777.1; 824.9; 827.3; 854.50; 854.51; 854.52; 906.23; 915.54; 1046.2; 1069.147; 1071.61; 1071.62
Wolfenden, John (1906–) English educator. 670.55
Woolf, [Adeline] Virginia (1882–1941) English novelist, critic, essayist. 16.10; 93.98; 274.30; 336.21; 344.33; 401.58; 436.38; 561.14; 571.21; 1062.150; 1067.31; 1069.148
Wordsworth, William (1770–1850) English poet. 43.16; 104.37; 118.7; 123.62; 131.46; 289.36; 352.5; 384.34; 404.30; 519.22; 551.236; 590.23; 620.11; 623.82; 623.83; 623.84; 646.8; 698.19; 701.6; 708.117; 708.118; 708.119; 779.2; 849.42; 853.15; 918.56; 918.57; 927.15; 946.54; 990.19; 1060.64; 1069.149; 1071.63; 1071.64
Wotton, Sir Henry (1568–1639) English diplomat and poet. 126.14; 247.12; 491.32; 1033.51
Wright, Frank Lloyd (1869–1959) American architect. 50.23; 106.2; 557.8
Wright, Richard [Nathaniel] (1908–1960) American novelist and short-story writer. 444.27
Wylie, Philip [Gordon] (1902–1971) American writer. 133.33; 191.14; 419.56; 670.56; 952.10; 965.33

X

Xenophanes (c. 570–c. 480 B.C.) Greek philosopher. 1060.65

Y

Yeats, William Butler (1865–1939) Irish poet and playwright. 88.9; 336.22; 457.10; 522.68; 551.237; 580.46; 608.8; 653.102; 837.11; 975.58; 978.78; 989.10
Yeltsin, Boris (1931–) Russian political leader. 357.17; 602.65; 711.94; 711.95; 730.25; 834.5; 834.6
Yevtushenko, Yevgeny (1933–) Russian poet. 119.31; 719.60; 962.16
Yiddish proverb. 681.42
Young, Edward (1683–1765) English poet and playwright. 55.21; 83.7; 226.13; 231.12; 387.80; 401.59; 454.22; 850.10; 893.9; 978.79; 996.13; 1004.16
Yutang, Lin (1895–1976) Chinese-born American author. 210.25; 355.18; 537.53; 809.5; 992.58

Z

Zappa, Frank Vincent (1940–1993) American composer and musician. 123.63; 299.37; 413.21; 419.57; 425.19; 522.69; 614.65; 614.66; 670.57; 842.4; 941.20; 978.80
Zeno of Citium (fl. 300 B.C.) Greek philosopher, founder of Stoicism. 88.10; 186.23; 543.5
Zenobius (fl. early 2nd c. A.D.) Greek Sophist who lived in Rome. 200.6; 815.11
Zola, Émile (1840–1902) French writer and critic. 53.153; 998.134

Index of Key Words

This index is intended primarily to help the user in finding a quotation that he only half recalls. One or more key words—that is, important words most likely to be remembered—are given here, surrounded by related words. These word-clusters form brief synopses of the quotations by which they can be readily identified.

The numbers that follow the precis refer not to the pages but to individual quotations. That part of the number before the period indicates the category; the second part locates the quotation within the category.

Because key words may often be the subjects of their quotations, this index can supplement category headings. However, a user who is looking for quotations on a subject, rather than a specific saying, should also turn to the Index of Categories for an overview of the subject headings and cross references.

A

abandon: it is madder never to a. one's self than often to be infatuated 551.72

abdomen: a. is why man does not take self for god 90.5

abecedarian: what a contemptible thing is an old a. 279.62

abilities: natural a. need pruning by study 1.1

ability: a. to imbue foreigner with inferiority 289.8
- assurance keeps even pace with a. 860.3
- God obligeth no man to more than he hath given him a. to perform 271.14
- great a. in knowing how to conceal a. 200.4
- height of a. in the least able is knowing how to submit to good leadership 644.2
- pills didn't interfere with a. to reproduce 84.4
- reputation increases, a. declines 653.40

abject: those believed a., usually ambitious 435.25

abnormal: to be independent is to be a. 171.1

above: all we know of a. is that they happy are 414.16
- no man is safe a. but he that will gladly be beneath 780.11

abridgment: every a. of a good book is a stupid a. 93.64

abroad: man's standing a. is problematical 804.9
- to go a. has same sense death brings 992.55
- to go a. is to forget pain, care 992.54

absence: a. lessens small passions, augments great 2.9
- a. makes the heart grow frozen 2.12
- a. sharpens love 2.6
- a. tries how long this love will be 2.4
- hours in a. have crutches 2.2
- love reckons every a. an age 551.49
- senses know that a. blots people out 2.1
- what you love most in friend may be clearer in his a. 2.7

absences: a. are a good influence in love 2.10

absent: after death, the a. take on a firmer outline 2.3
- greater things are believed of those a. 2.11
- those who are a. are always wrong 2.5

absent-minded: I believe they are completely absent-minded 387.36

absents: presents, I often say, endear a. 384.17

absolute: no such thing as a. value in this world 1026.25

abstainer: a.: weak person who yields to temptation of denying himself a pleasure 865.2

abstinence: mastery of pleasures better than a. 704.1
- vices require moderate use, not total a. 1030.3

abstinent: the a. carry their desires with them 865.1

abstract: a. qualities all have capitals: Good, True 1033.7
- women have no sense of the a. 1062.62

abstractions: a. are weapons to control fact 974.14

absurd: a. man is he who never changes 117.2
- But Lord! To see the a. nature of Englishmen 289.25
- if life is a., death is insupportable 3.8
- the a. is essentially a divorce 3.2

absurdities: life is full of infinite a. 4.5

absurdity: feeling a. can strike any man in the face 4.1
- no defence for a. but obscurity 648.1
- privilege of a. accorded to none but man 4.3

abundance: desolation of an empty a. 34.34

abuse: a. man unjustly: make friends for him 477.7
- a. to be reformed, unless reform worse 790.37
- men let you a., if you make them laugh 436.2
- unmerited a. wounds 722.11
- who live by bread alone submit to a. 569.5

abysses: only a bird should build nest over a. 755.17

academicism: a. is concerned with ideas, not thinking 848.37

academies: great men formed independent of a. 401.55
- they teach in a. much that is useless 279.34

accent: inferior in the presence of anyone with an English a. 967.20

acceptance: art of a. of favors 787.2

accepted: not right to shun a. ways from spite 171.14

accepting: a. what we are inhibits what we ought to be 542.6
- life consists in a. ourselves as we are 858.1

accessible: each man is a. by the right door 961.1

accident: a. counts for much in companionship 116.1
- a. is greatest of all inventors 502.4
- what reason of the ant drags into a heap, wind of a. collects in a breath 116.14

accidents: a. will happen in best-regulated families 334.10
- ambush is everywhere from the army of a. 116.8
- no shame in the a. of chance 1070.17

acclaimed: greatest reward is to have one's work a. 207.36

accomplishes: nobody a. all he feels he can do 542.14

accordion: a.: instrument in harmony with sentiments of an assassin 615.1
- wheezing like an a. by the time I unpacked 429.2

accounts: keep your a. on your thumb-nail 899.14

accusation: guilty man justifies himself before a. 405.8

accusations: even doubtful a. leave a stain 5.2

accused: it is honorable to be a. by those who deserve to be a. 5.3

accusing: a. is proving, with Malice as judge 5.1

accustomed: no conditions to which man can't grow a. 12.9
- 'Tis the taste of effeminacy that disrelishes ordinary and a. things 612.4
- unpleasant to miss things we are a. to 406.8

ache: no deadlier a. than striving to be oneself 444.25

achieve: to a. great things, live as if never to die 6.20

achievement: a. death of endeavor, birth of disgust 6.3
behind each a. is surprised mother-in-law 6.9
happiness lies in the a. of it 409.31
achievements: awareness of the ambiguity of one's a. 6.19
life overgrows a. as well as ruins 539.131
aching: better a tooth out than always a. 262.4
acquaintance: a.: person we know well enough to borrow from but not well enough to lend to 7.1
acquaintances: chance a. sometimes the most memorable 7.6
how casually we make our most valued a. 7.2
we like new a. in hope of more admiration 7.5
acquiescence: no peace from a. in wrong 46.6
acquired: what man has honestly a. is his own 716.1
acquiring: price of everything is trouble of a. it 1026.22
acquisition: a. means life to miserable mortals 569.4
acquisitions: every man publishes his a. 746.16
act: a. done for its own sake is its own justification 1024.3
a. only on maxim you can will to be universal law 9.29
a. quickly, think slowly 9.22
a. so in valley that you need not fear those who stand on the hill 755.7
a. well your part, there all honour lies 491.22
last a. tragic however happy the rest 221.102
our passivity would be an a. 9.33
people who can a. are never preachers 9.17
play out the game, a. well your part 825.1
thought too much to deign to a. 975.45
to a. is to be committed 146.1
to think is to a. 975.12
when Butterfly McQueen went into her a. 893.4
worst pain: know much, be impotent to a. 459.1
acting: between a. dreadful thing and first motion, all the interim is a hideous dream 204.18
extent of Indian a. in movie theater 611.3
action: a. can give us feeling of being useful 1064.21
a. is the proper fruit of knowledge 9.20
a. not from thought is nothing at all 9.2
a. should culminate in wisdom 9.4
a. started because one must do something 9.14
a. that is moved by love for good 9.3
a. the great business of mankind 9.30
a. will remove doubt theory cannot solve 9.27
all sentiments weigh less than lovely a. 227.14
artist is a man of a. 53.29
but for thought no motion would be an a. 975.39
can a. be active resignation? 9.21
circumstance gives an a. its character 598.12
do good a. stealthily, have it found out 227.12
every a. is an idea before it is an a. 443.33
every great a. is extreme when undertaken 227.30
few men of a. make graceful exit 813.5
great end of life is a., not knowledge 9.28
in a. be primitive 9.12
in arena of life, honours fall to those who show their good qualities in a. 9.1
in each a. we must look beyond the a. 176.9
life made up of constant calls to a. 9.24
man of a. has strong dose of egotism 859.1
materials of a. variable, their use constant 9.18
men of a. are generally fools 493.13
"Men of a.," whose minds are too busy 9.7
no human a. which custom has not at one time justified and at another condemned 213.13
one knows bad a. in flash of regret 227.15
our a. only fitfully guided by thought 9.35
profit on good a. is to have done it 227.27
speech is the mirror of a. 923.55
suit a. to word, the word to a. 901.18
test of any man lies in a. 9.32
the road to holiness passes through world of a. 9.23
to dispose a soul to a. we must upset its equilibrium 9.26
unreal is a. without discipline 9.5
actions: a. are our epochs 9.8
do not be too timid about your a. 980.3
easier to dream than do good a. 393.29
great a. not sons of great resolutions 227.5
human a. are second causes 227.16
life's decisive a. are often unconsidered 227.11
lust and force source of all a. 9.31
man's most open a. have secret side 9.13
not always a. show the man 227.23
only a. of the just smell sweet 227.28
our less conscious thoughts, a., mold lives 1006.1
stellar universe not so difficult to comprehend as the a. of other people 227.24
we are used to a., not stillness, of humans 989.7
we learn to curb a. long before sentiments 862.5
activity: men, inactive within, need external a. 10.13
self urges us on to futile a. 863.2
actor: a. believes bad things printed about him 11.9
a. remembers briefest notice into old age 11.6
by the time an a. knows how to act any part he is too old to act any but a few 11.7
movie a. is a god in captivity 11.3
actors: a. should be overheard, not listened to 59.1
actress: for an a. to be a success 11.1
acts: a. and words are wee part of a life 818.4
familiar a. are beautiful through love 333.11
make morality center on forbidden a. 604.39
nameless, unremembered a. of kindness 519.22
actual: music takes us out of the a. 614.32
what is a. is a. only for one time 784.9
ad: today models of eloquence are a. agencies 283.7
Adam: we owe deep debt of gratitude to A. 541.42
Adam's: all A. children, but silk distinguishes 471.3
adapt: a. or perish is nature's imperative 12.10
adaptation: a. is an essentially cognitive process 308.13
adequate: no a. means of expressing my gratitude 981.1
who ever is a. 542.3
adjective: a. is banana peel of parts of speech 398.3
a. *women's* did more than change a phrase 1064.47
when in doubt, strike out a. 942.22
adjustment: a. is the theme of our swan song 12.7
every new a. is crisis in self-esteem 12.3
for young people things move so fast there's no problem of a. 117.25
our goal is not fulfillment but a. 12.6
administration: a. does not create; it carries on 13.2
a. receives kicks due the president 395.8
bad a. can destroy good policy 13.3
no government matters as much as the a. 395.40
while people retain vigilance, no a. can injure government in four years 682.11
administrative: geniuses ordered by a. types 376.29
administrators: a. of justice like cat protecting cheese 514.10
admiration: a. involves obliquity of vision 14.2
a. is a short-lived passion 14.1
a.: our recognition of another's resemblance to ourselves 14.3
familiarity takes off the edge of a. 333.6
modern world not given to uncritical a. 332.50
admirations: some molded by a., others hostilities 404.2
admire: a. others, not my most fully developed trait 14.4
fools a., men of sense approve 14.6
we a. people when we cannot explain what they do 14.7
we do not always like those whom we a. 14.5

admired: desire to be a. early disposition of man 1027.1
admirer: it's the a. and watcher who provoke us to all the insanities we commit 59.5
admirers: woman with staff of a. 351.4
adolescence: a. can be a time of turmoil and turbulence 1071.23
a great deal of poetry is the product of a. 708.1
chaste a. makes for a dissolute old age 122.6
ripeness of a. is in need of a bridle 1071.53
since a., inimical to the Republican party 710.5
so much of a. is an ill-defined dying 1071.54
adolescents: a. tend to be passionate people 1071.20
adore: I may command where I a. 551.189
adorn: know who you are; a. self accordingly 267.7
adorned: she's a. that in husband's eye is lovely 267.29
when unadorned, loveliness is most a. 72.59
ads: he watched the a., not the road 64.10
adult: boy is a. before parents think so 97.5
to be a. is to be alone 571.13
adultery: a. is an evil inasmuch as it is a theft 472.14
a. is more common where climate's sultry 140.1
a. is the application of democracy to love 472.7
adulthood: most mammalians progress directly from infancy to a. 404.15
we pass into a. when we stop saying, It got lost, and say I lost it 571.6
adults: most a. I knew never touched in public 600.10
advance: not to go back is to a. 404.22
advantage: every a. has its tax 15.3
no way to take a. of those with no weaknesses 684.6
them as take a. get a. i' this world 15.2
advantages: little a. produce felicity 409.39
adventure: a.: an inconvenience rightly considered 16.1
a. becomes romantic when safe at home 16.6
adventurers who hope to find a. 16.7
every a. wears the shape of our thoughts 305.6
it is only in a. that some people succeed in knowing themselves 16.3
life is either daring a. or nothing 16.5
[A] life of writing books is a trying a. 1069.117
life without a. is unsatisfying 16.9
some trifling incident may pitchfork you into a. 992.38
we pay for a. with bother 16.2
adventuring: not once had he hazarded respectability by a. 472.5
adversaries: law a. strive mightily, eat as friends 155.12
adversary: right to hear advice of a., not follow it 19.23
adverse: in a. times even brave are discredited 751.14
adversity: a. in immunological doses has its uses 17.59
a. is greater teacher than prosperity 751.9
a. is more supportable than prosperity 17.15
a. is the first path to truth 17.16
be prudent in a. 755.19
education is a refuge in a. 279.4
fire is test of gold, a. of strong men 17.50
firmest friendships are formed in a. 365.31
in a., bitter to remember happiness 17.12
in prosperity be joyful, in a. consider 751.4
in the day of prosperity, a. is forgotten 751.1
knows not own strength who hasn't met a. 17.36
man insensible to prosperity till has a. 751.13
many who are struggling with a. are happy 390.21
no comfort in a. more sweet than art 53.3
none can smile in face of a. and mean it 17.33
one abhorred in prosperity is adored in a. 751.8
prosperity has no power over a. 751.12
prosperity makes friends, a. tries them 751.11
sweet are the uses of a. 17.53
virtue of a. is fortitude 751.3
we can learn to endure another man's a. 17.58
who has not suffered extreme a. knows not extent of his depravation 17.18
advertisement: promise, large promise, is soul of a. 18.6
advertisements: a. get attention by magnificent promises 18.5
a. have more knowledge concerning the community 18.1
advertiser: a. is court jester at democratic court 18.7
advertising: a. and salesmanship create needs 105.19
a. in final analysis should be news 18.12
first syllable of valuable or even earnest a. 19.29
forgive us for a. the unnecessary 105.22
we want to be deceived in a. 18.2
advice: a. of elders to young apt to be unreal 19.13
a. should help, not please 19.26
a.: the smallest current coin 19.7
a grave danger, the a. of friends 11.4
best way to give a. to your children 670.53
distrust interested a. 19.3
easy for one outside calamity to give a. 19.2
give a. and buy a foe 19.19
good scare is worth more than good a. 343.19
men ignore good a., fear being controlled 652.7
never trust a. of man in difficulties 19.4
no enemy is worse than bad a. 19.28
to give good a. is absolutely fatal 19.31
we ask a., but mean approbation 19.9
we receive nothing so reluctantly as a. 19.1
when well, all have a. for the ill 413.17
wrong to follow a. of adversary 19.23
advise: we are so happy to a. others 19.22
aeon: altar cloth of one a. is doormat of next 298.17
aesthetics: a. is for artists as ornithology for birds 20.4
a. make life lovely and wonderful 20.7
affairs: every man's a. important to himself 495.2
have you time to spare from your own a. that you can attend to another man's 575.6
in great a. profit from chances offered 657.8
let your a. be as two or three 899.14
slowness in a. ripens them or rots them 907.1
there is a tide in the a. of men 657.12
affect: qualities we have do not make us so ridiculous as those which we a. 732.8
affectation: a. as necessary to mind as dress to body 732.3
a.: imitation of what should be natural 732.9
a. is more enemy to faces than small-pox 733.22
a. only finishes a fop 732.6
affectations: by a. youth is seeking a face of his own 1071.57
affection: a. is created by habit 21.8
a. makes fool of man too much the father 670.27
a. most precious reward man can win 21.11
a. never was wasted 21.7
human nature gives a. most readily to those who seem least to demand it 21.10
measure a. by constancy, not ardor 181.1
mix admiration, pity as sure recipe for a. 21.9
most would rather get than give a. 21.1
natural a. is a prejudice 334.17
some think a. rests on circumstantial evidence 551.183
what woman dares, when a. stirs her 1062.131
affectionate: we are uneasy with an a. man 21.2
affections: a. left untouched diminish imperceptibly 21.5
a. must be breakable chains 551.62
it's often interest, vanity that cause a. 21.6
most a. are habits we lack courage to end 21.3
the a. cannot keep their youth 21.4
affinities: profoundest a. are most readily felt 22.3
affirmations: our a. are mere matters of chronology 184.8
affliction: a. sometime teacheth wicked to pray

723.20
before a. digested, consolation comes too soon 960.12
afflictions: one can't shed light on a. he's never had 321.32
affluence: many amid great a. are utterly miserable 390.21
affluent: a. man confronts all he sees by equivalents out of stronger wealth of self 880.25
afforestation: a. written on the faces of citizens 995.3
afraid: I am a. I shall not find Him 265.6.
who possesses most is most a. of loss 716.9
afterthought: a. makes first resolve a liar 24.2
against: men not a. you; merely for themselves 495.1
age: a. has a good mind and sorry shanks 653.5
a. in the virtuous carries an authority 653.95
a. is a bad traveling companion 653.25
a. is despised but when it is contemptible 653.52
a. is opportunity no less than youth 653.61
a. knows it has got away with nothing 1072.2
a. looks with anger on temerity of youth 1072.10
a. not as qualified to instruct as youth 1072.27
a. of anxiety: along with what weighs on our minds is what grates on our nerves 43.8
a. prints more wrinkles on mind than face 653.68
a. shows what children we remain 653.35
a. still leaves us friends and wine 1072.18
almost no allowances are made for the disenchantments of a. 1072.25
be equal to your talent, not your a. 962.16
beyond a., man no stronger than child is 653.1
crabbed a. and youth cannot live together 1072.21
each a. has choice of death it will die 298.18
each a. selects philosophy apt for it 298.14
every a. beheld too close is ill-discerned 298.4
every a. has a keyhole to which its eye is pasted 298.12
every a. has its pleasures, wit, and ways 298.2
every a. is fed on illusions 449.8
every a. thinks its battle most important 298.9
fear of a. is prime cause of infidelity 472.1
happy man will not feel pressure of a. 968.4
heart grows not better but worse with a. 653.16
in every a., "good old days" were a myth 298.1
it is unjust to claim the privileges of a. and retain playthings of childhood 571.7
knowledge is shelter in advanced a. 522.7
let a., not envy, wrinkle thy cheeks 295.4
let me stand in my a. 184.3
life should begin with a., end with youth 1072.28
love weakens with a. like all human energies 653.30
men of a. object, consult too much 586.2
middle a. is when a. shows around middle 586.11
middle a., when you've met so many people 586.16
now a. is fallen from good example 1072.13
no woman should ever be accurate about her a. 1062.147
our a. is all signpost, no destination 1001.6
our bad taste is the bad taste of our a. 184.8
ours is essentially a tragic a. 987.9
ours is the a. of substitutes 54.1
riotous youth, growing a. will correct 1071.36
the a.: a few profound and active men 298.7
the a. of the overworked and undereducated 298.20
'Tis hard to find a whole a. to imitate 298.3
we must place ourselves on the level of our a. before we can rise above it 184.10
what is the worst of woes that wait on a. 653.11
when the a. is in, the wit is out 653.88
woe to those with no appetite for dish of their a. 184.4
aged: a. man is but a paltry thing 653.102
the a. love what is practical 1072.19
age's: a. peace terms with life are yet to be made 653.71
aggression: extent to which a. exemplifies innate tendencies 26.7
aggressiveness: possible to bind people in love if others are left to receive their a. 1016.4
aging: time increases understanding for the a. 1007.16
agnostic: most satisfying faith is purely a. 330.24
agony: I have seen the a. of mothers and wives 1042.78
agree: by universal misunderstanding, all a. 27.1
if brothers a., no fortress so strong 334.2
we tolerate those who do not a. with us 984.8
agreeable: conversation passing for a. is made up of civility and falsehood 440.17
custom determines what is a. 213.23
few men shine, but most can be a. 392.11
gentle-breeding lies in wish to be a. 391.5
people not a. save me trouble of liking them 594.1
agreed: can two walk together except they be a. 564.7
men are not a. about any one thing 27.5
agreement: a. made more precious by disagreement 27.7
nothing starts disagreement like an a. 994.7
too much a. kills a chat 188.6
agrees: nobody a. with anybody; infants show it 27.6
agriculture: blessed be a. if one doesn't have too much 337.7
ahead: passion to get a. is sometimes born of fear lest we be left behind 291.4
aid: only a. we can give is incidental 56.3
ail: if anything a. a man, he sets about reforming the world 790.33
ailments: fond of each other because a. the same 896.33
long a. wear out pain, and long hopes, joy 1040.6
aim: despair: price for setting impossible a. 239.7
if you would hit the mark, a. above it 55.11
name little aims, but neither name nor be conscious of main a. of your life 771.1
aims: our methods, not our a., set us at odds 585.11
air: lovers of a. travel hang poised between illusion of immortality, fact of death 28.1
opening my lips and receiving bad a. 29.1
airplane: not much to say about most a. journeys 28.5
airport: as pretty as an a. 991.2
air travel: vowed to give up sex, bacon, and a. t. 28.3
Alaska: nine of ten in A. had drinking problem 268.4
alert: go on the a. and start nailing down everything 755.26
alien: America shudders at anything a. 358.4
consider nothing human a. to me 562.57
nothing that is real is a. to me 450.26
alike: before the Lord we're all a. 780.15
alimony: a.: the ransom the happy pay to the devil 262.7
alive: being on TV is like being a., only more so 967.28
one only stays a. for fear of death 541.30
to be a. at all involves some risk 216.14
to preserve a man a. is a miracle 263.19
what matters is to come out a., not on top 956.1
you die because you're a. 541.36
all: each one is a. in a. to himself 858.23
we a. breathe same air, are mortal 100.10
allegory: a man's life is a continual a. 539.63
alliance: a.: union of two thieves who cannot separately plunder a third 498.1
lofty words cannot construct an a. 247.5
ally: a. need not own the land he helps 498.2
alms: not a soul who does not have to beg a. 235.4
on a. given from pity beggar would starve 433.22
when thou doest a., let not

thy left hand know what thy right doeth 433.4
alone: a., you are your own master 152.11
basest pattern of relatedness better than being a. 504.9
better be a. than in bad company 915.18
children love to be a. 915.41
decreed to every man: thou shalt live a. 915.20
every man is grave a. 886.4
if I go a. I don't have to talk 915.44
I love to be a. 915.47
in our civilization, being a. is suspect 915.23
inside myself is place where I live a. 858.7
in the most important things, we are a. 56.8
in the sea of life we millions live a. 915.2
in travel books, word a. implied on every page 93.89
live a.: you won't succeed as human being 915.5
man is the only being who knows he's a. 915.35
man who goes a. can start today 915.46
man who walks a. soon trailed by F.B.I. 468.9
never same with others as when a. 663.11
no person loving himself is a. 876.12
not a. if accompanied by noble thoughts 915.17
there are places, moments, in which one is so a. one sees the world entire 915.40
to be adult is to be a. 571.13
to dare to live a. is the rarest courage 915.11
true man must learn to be a. 880.21
we shall die a. 915.34
when is man strong until he feels a. 940.4
which of us is not forever a stranger, a. 915.54
who can live a. resembles sage and God 915.21
woe to him that is a. when he falleth 329.3
you are not a.; God and your genius within 915.16
alphabet: a. enabled men to store and learn 524.42
altar: acolyte knows what boys do behind a. 321.49
altars: in prosperity no a. smoke 797.41
altered: what cannot be a. must be borne 806.5
alternatives: a. grow only on imaginary trees 124.2
altruism: a. grounded on fact that it is uncomfortable to have unhappy people about one 433.19
a., one of biology's deep mysteries 433.31
a. which is not egoism is sterile 433.25
amateur: a. is a man of enthusiasm 207.2
amazement: true scientist never loses faculty of a. 849.34
ambassador: a. is an honest man sent abroad to lie 247.12
ambassadors: a. of peace shall weep bitterly 247.1
ambiguity: character of human life is a. 390.23
ambition: a. does not see earth she treads on 33.14
a. is a meteor-gleam 990.6
a. is only vanity ennobled 33.11
a. makes more trusty slaves than need 33.12
a. puts men doing meanest offices 33.23
greatest evil: small talents, great a. 33.26
no fairer a. than to excel in talk 923.59
nothing so arouses a. as another's fame 33.9
sense of inferiority, called a. 33.19
to succeed, vein a. with humanity 33.5
we hardly ever return from a. to love 33.15
ambition's: lowliness is young a. ladder 945.40
ambitions: all a. lawful but those based on misery 33.6
man's worth no greater than worth of a. 33.1
ambitious: a. man has as many masters as there are people useful in bettering his position 33.13
a. man spends time becoming a personage 694.30
a. men most liable to fortune's blasts 33.20
mama's boy following orders to be a. 916.9
those believed abject, usually a. 435.25
amended: little said is soon a. 923.12
America: A. is now liberty-conscious 34.82
a rigid A. is weak and vulnerable 34.26
discussion in A. means dissent 258.12
fate of A. in its principles, not in one man 734.13
future A. to match its military strength with moral restraint, power with purpose 34.37
he would rather have been in A. 303.3
I don't see A. as a mainland, but as a sea, a big ocean 205.6
in A. everybody is of opinion he has no social superiors 297.23
in A., ivry man's as good as ivry other man 34.22
in A. journalism governs for ever and ever 34.85
in A., majority bars liberty of opinion 731.1
in A. man presoomed guilty ontil proved so 517.12
in A. nature is autocratic 34.25
in A. only successful writer is important 1069.30
in A. parents obey their children 34.90
in A., sport is the opiate of the masses 929.5
little of beauty has A. given the world 34.21
not healthy when nation lives within a nation, as colored are living within A. 85.5
what A. hopes to bring to pass in world must come to pass first in A.'s heart 34.23
youth of A. is their oldest tradition 34.86
America's: supermarket is A. temple 34.72
American: A. citizen tries to perpetuate youth 34.57
A. vice reduces everything unique 297.16
a rowdy strain in A. life 34.13
clothes, money and new fear constitute differences between A. and Attila's men 133.33
each A. sure he has a sense of humor 34.81
if A. men are obsessed with money, A. women are obsessed with weight 34.48
inside polling booth every A. equal 297.22
in the A. metaphysic, reality is always material reality 784.18
it isn't oceans which cut us off from the world—it's the A. way of looking at things 34.52
it's complicated, being an A. 34.70
law of A. life: what enriches other than wallet is uneconomic 602.1
learning to be an A. is learning not to let individuality become a nuisance 34.30
life for the A. is a hazard 539.68
mass production of distraction a part of the A. way of life 292.2
materialistic idealism of A. life 569.6
more A. than Miss America 72.7
no characteristic can be labeled A. 34.75
no crime in cynical A. calendar more humiliating than to be a sucker 202.7
part of A. dream: live long, die young 367.7
spirit of A. radicalism is destructive 776.2
the A.: a titan enamored of progress 34.61
the A. girl makes a servant of her husband 564.119
the making of an A. begins when he rejects all other ties, any other history 34.2
two A. flags; one for the rich and one for the poor 718.45
typical A. believes no necessity of soul is free and few cannot be bought 34.39
Americanism: room only for hundred per cent A. 678.17
Americanized: we go to Europe to be A. 303.2
Americans: A. are possessed of two great qualities 34.66
A. (as seen from a distance) were known to get things done 34.4
A. began by loving youth 1071.4
A. don't understand studied insult 488.1
A. ricochet around the United States like billiard balls 699.9
art for most A. is a very queer fish 53.75
for A., progress is fact and principle 34.84
in modern world, A. are old inhabitants 34.31
kindness and hospitality in so many A. 519.13

love of A. for their country is exacting 678.13
nature is indifferent to survival of A. 956.7
nothing wrong with A. except ideals 34.14
serious leisure not genius of A. 533.5
we A. suffer primarily from illusions 449.3
amity: a. maintained only by reciprocal respect 498.12
Amor: nothing heals while A. remembers wrong 476.14
amorous: what dire offence from a. causes springs 996.10
amusement: men rightly occupied derive a. from work 1037.10
analogy: a. is the least misleading thing we have 35.1
perception of truth is detection of a. 35.5
analysis: a. destroys wholes 492.10
a. kills spontaneity 785.2
analyze: when a man is happy he doesn't a. it 409.74
anarchy: a. and competition are the laws of death 395.54
a. is the stepping stone to absolute power 36.1
a., the amateur's natural element 1.2
ancestor: reverse a. worship 37.4
ancestors: atop tree of a. sits Probably Arboreal 37.9
to forget a. is to be a tree without a root 37.2
ancestors': good birth fine, but merit is a. 37.6
ancestral: worshippers of light a. make the present light a crime 986.15
ancestry: man who prides himself on a. 37.8
anchors: it is well to moor your bark with two a. 755.22
ancient: praise of a. authors proceeds from mutual envy of the living 136.4
with the a. is wisdom 653.7
ancients: speak of a. without idolatry 136.1
we have our arts, the a. had theirs 741.29
anecdotage: a. was sign for man to retire from world 653.19
anecdote: a. will pitch talk off track 188.38
anecdotes: a., tastier spiced with expensive names 81.2
angel: a guardian a. gives you dispensation 15.1
a. is a spiritual creature 38.1
each sees a. in his future self 460.3
he who would act the a. acts the beast 691.8
angels: better to be improvement on monkey thin such a fallin' off fr'm th' a. 308.7
fools rush in where a. fear to tread 356.19
he did not believe in a. with soft faces 38.3
it is not known precisely where a. dwell 38.2
it's a whole hierarchy of a. 966.3
Whether the a. play only Bach 614.4
anger: a.: a power when great mind moved by it 39.1
a. as soon as fed is dead 39.13
a. due to a cause will be appeased 412.15
a. is one of the sinews of the soul 39.12
a. may be foolish and absurd 39.16
a. of lovers renews their love 555.20
a. wishes its judgment to seem just 516.19
a. would inflict punishment on another; meanwhile, it tortures itself 39.23
bare recollection of a. kindles a. 39.24
fear not the a. of the wise to raise 803.7
fierce a. belongs to beasts 681.25
hell has three gates: lust, a., greed 416.4
it is difficult to fight against a. 817.12
jealousy, a., and anxiety shorten life 43.2
more violent the love, more violent the a. 551.17
no old age for a man's a., only death 39.26
plow your a. into something positive 39.17
to tear out foe's brain washes away a. 288.20
who doesn't know a. doesn't know anything 39.19
who is slow to a. is better than mighty 39.5
world would perish did pity not limit a. 698.18
angle: certain people and certain things require to be approached on an a. 585.5
from right a., man shows depth, beauty 687.3
angling: a. like mathematics: never fully learnt 348.4
angry: always shun whatever may make you a. 39.22
essential thing is being able to get a. 719.11
feeling a. without anybody to be a. at 39.9
no man is a. that feels not himself hurt 39.3
not easy to be a. with right person, to right extent, at right time 39.2
people when a. bring about a change 39.18
shun a. man a moment—enemy forever 288.17
when a., count four; when very a., swear 39.28
who cannot be a. cannot be good 39.4
anguish: beauty of world is of laughter and a. 1067.31
mirth is the mail of a. 526.8
no man without some manner of a. 17.37
specialists in a. were easily sentimentalized 1069.71
animal: a. confounds the understanding 623.48
a. horizons from which we made our march 41.2
a. would depict Devil in human form 41.14
be a good a., true to your a. instincts 486.3
bringing out the a. in an a. 41.27
love of a. parent violent while it lasts 41.1
man is worse than an a. when he's an a. 209.16
spiritual interests supported by a. life 927.12
who forgets man is a. is made less humane 431.14
animal's: stunned by the beauty of an a. skin 41.22
animals: a. are disarmed by caresses to their young 670.26
a. are such agreeable friends 41.9
best about a. is they don't talk much 41.44
destiny of human race to stop eating a. 1028.2
excessive love of a. at expense of men 551.184
higher a. follow from war of nature 308.4
if a. had a Pope 289.7
man tries to equal a. 741.28
rain is good for the a. who eat a. 778.4
those who respect natures of wild a. 41.35
annihilate: to a. a man, give him useless work 1065.21
annuities: persons living on a. are longer lived 489.2
annuity: a. makes your life interesting to yourself 489.3
anonymous: killer and mugger come out of the a. dark 204.13
anorexia: developed such a. I had to be force-fed 967.23
another: true wit is that which falls on a. 1061.13
we cannot forgive a. for not being ourselves 663.4
another's: begin with a. to end with your own 700.2
we must be our own before a. 880.7
answer: a. of the minute is positive 998.119
not every question deserves a. 480.9
the a. seemed to be yes and no 967.29
answers: many people today don't want honest a. 304.2
who asks questions cannot avoid the a. 480.3
ant: go to the a., thou sluggard 530.2
antagonist: our a. is our helper 658.3
anticipation: pleasures and trouble greatest in a. 318.6
recollection and a. fill our moments 729.16
anti-Communism: simplistic a., used to perpetuate power 232.2
antique: precious pleasure to meet an a. book 93.22
antiquity: a. full of praises of a more remote a. 42.7
a. provides professors with bread 42.4
if we look backwards to a., it should be as those that are winning a race 42.3
ants: a. and savages put strangers to death 358.6
ant's: in a. house dew is a flood 908.2
anvil: either suffer or triumph, be a. or hammer 859.4
every man is either an a. or a hammer 361.13
if you're the a., bear; if hammer, strike 728.2
anxieties: solitude is the mother of a. 915.38
anxiety: age of a.: along with what weighs on our minds is what grates on our nerves 43.8
a. and conscience are pow-

erful dynamos 43.15
a. is the mark of spiritual insecurity 43.10
character forms at first pinch of a. 119.31
jealousy, anger, and a. shorten life 43.2
our reasoning powers facilitate a. 43.5
people want soft answer that turneth away a. 304.2
without a. life would have little savor 43.12
anxious: tenterhooks are upholstery of a. seat 43.14
anything: a man free to do a. he pleases 810.8
apartment: cast from the womb without an a. 550.10
apes: we are bipedal a. 562.33
aphorism: good a. too hard for tooth of time 773.5
Apollo: words of Mercury harsh after songs of A. 271.25
apologies: a. only account for what they don't alter 44.1
apology: a. is egotism wrong side out 44.2
Apostles: That all the A. would have done as they did 125.2
apostrophe: thinks any plural ending in *s* requires an a. 1064.46
apparel: a. shapes, but money finishes, the man 602.23
the a. oft proclaims the man 267.24
appearance: a.: looking the best you can for the money 45.13
insinuating a. seldom linked with virtue 45.5
man looketh on the outward a. 45.3
appearances: always scorn a. and you always may 45.6
publicly you must preserve a. 590.7
shallow people do not judge by a. 45.21
appeasement: no a. with ruthlessness 46.4
appeaser: a. feeds crocodile so he's eaten last 46.2
appetite: a.: solution to labor question 437.1
it took me till noon to get my a. back 274.16
nothing so incontinent as man's a. 403.9
appetites: others' a. appear excessive if unshared 238.14
riches more enlarge than satisfy a. 1048.25
subdue your a., you conquer human nature 970.1
applauded: When I hear a man a. by the mob 332.28
applauds: audience always a. latest song most 640.7
applause: a. of single human is of great consequence 722.13
every artist loves a. 722.25
interruption we don't object to is a. 722.9
apple: finished man of world eats of every a. 917.2
appointment: we aren't saints, but we have kept our a. 765.1
appreciated: each supposes himself not fully a. 877.1
apprehension: grief has limits, a. none 43.11
apprehensions: my a. come in crowds 43.16
approval: man isn't comfortable without his own a. 869.14
simulated a. and affection 49.1
approve: fools admire, men of sense a. 14.6
approving: understanding is the beginning of a. 1007.6
April: first day of A. reminds us of what we always are 420.8
weeping gloom of March and A. 854.20
aptitude: most do violence to their natural a. 1.8
Arab: place their countries at the mercy of A. oil 966.10
arbiters: the great a. of langauge are women 923.35
arch: a. never sleeps 50.9
archeologist: an a. is the best husband 42.1
Archimedes: simplest schoolboy knows truths for which A. would have given his life 849.29
architect: if not a sculptor or painter, can't be a. 50.17
job of a. more difficult in this secular age 50.6
life's brevity makes a.'s trade sad 50.4
architects: a., like clients, want to show off 430.6
architecture: a. is inhabited sculpture 50.1
a., the art of organizing craftsmen 50.20
genius of a. has shed maledictions over land 50.11
I call a. "petrified music" 50.7
no a. is so haughty as the simple 50.16
no such thing as good and bad a. 50.22
promise and ruin seen in Gothic a. 50.19
the a. of empty space 50.12
are: what you a. drowns out what you say 923.16
what you a. must displease, if you would attain to what you a. not 55.1
you a., when all is done, just what you a. 444.10
arguing: a. of shadow, we forgo the substance 51.14
there is no good a. with the inevitable 624.9
argument: America is the longest a. in the world 34.56
a nickname: the most unanswerable a. 619.3
a. seldom convinces against inclinations 51.9
if in a. make man angry, we overcome him 51.12
in a. with men a woman goes by worse 581.41
no truth is proved or achieved by a. 998.102
scholarship is polite a. 848.33
somebody has last word in every a. 51.5
to win a.: start by being right 51.11
truth is always the strongest a. 998.114
unjust a., sick, needs clever medicine 528.19
when a. is over, how many reasons does man recollect which heat made him forget 51.3
arguments: a. are always vulgar 51.22
a. only confirm people in own opinions 51.20
opinions are of much more value than a. 656.11
aristocracy: even workhouses have their a. 780.3
piety, like nobility, has its a. 697.5
there is a natural a. among men 52.1
aristocrats: the shoestring a. of the upper East Side 933.2
arithmetic: a. is where the answer is right 570.9
Scrooge may not have had God on his side, but his a. was impeccable 570.6
Ark: there will be no second Noah's A. 294.3
arms: a. race is based on optimistic view of technology, pessimistic view of man 229.14
fear is stronger than a. 343.2
prudent person tries everything before a. 167.6
wherever a people has grown savage in a. 1032.14
army: a. fights with borrowed courage 588.18
a. is a nation within a nation 588.19
a. life was really kind of fun 1043.2
no a. large enough to guarantee against attack or insure victory 229.2
arrogance: do something incorrect with a certain a. 563.19
it takes shabby a. to survive in our time 1001.4
arrogant: some things the a. mind does not see 590.2
arrow: one a. does not bring down two birds 585.12
arsenals: were half power, wealth given to redeem mind from error, no need of a. 299.24
art: all a. aspires towards condition of music 53.101
all a. is at once surface and symbol 53.148
all a. is bad, but modern a. is the worst 666.3
apply to a. as much discrimination as to work 53.6
a. admits us to inner life of others 53.78
a. affirms, blesses, deifies existence 53.95
a. and the human striving for comprehension 201.25
a., by-product of attempt to do something well 53.114
a. changes, but it never improves 53.70
a. distills sensation, enhances meaning 53.8
a. does not reproduce the visible 53.73
a.: domain where the divine is visible 53.81
a. for Americans is a very queer fish 53.75
a. helps nature, and experience a. 53.53
a. imitates nature: not to dare is to dwindle 53.138
a. is a jealous mistress 53.45
a. is a kind of confession 53.7
a. is for fertilisation of the soul 53.144
a. is in love with luck, luck with a. 53.1
a. is lie that makes us realize

truth 53.105
a. is like baby shoes 53.139
a. is long and time is fleeting 606.12
a. is long, life short 988.3
a. is meant to disturb; science reassures 53.13
a. is most intense mode of individualism 468.13
a. is nature seen through a temperament 53.55
a. is not propaganda, but a form of truth 53.72
a. is not the same as cerebration 545.21
a. is only great if it is one all may enjoy 53.84
a. is ship in which man conquers life's formlessness 53.44
a. is the right hand of nature 53.127
a. is the sex of the imagination 53.94
a. is to bring something into existence 53.5
a. leads to more profound concept of life 53.65
a., like life, should be free 53.123
a. never didactic, doesn't take to facts 53.112
a. nourishes culture that sets artist free 53.71
a. object taken out of its habitat 613.1
a. of a. is simplicity 899.15
a. postulates communion 53.134
a. produces ugly things that often become beautiful with time 338.10
a. proposes to give the highest quality to your moments 53.102
a. raises its head where creeds relax 53.96
a.: response to demand for entertainment 53.122
a. should be appreciated with passion 53.85
a. teaches the significance of life 53.89
a., the dance before the yawning abyss 53.103
a. usually has ingredient of impudence 53.129
a. without practice is nothing 530.1
a. work measured by its reproduction 53.12
beginnings of a. acquire a greater celebrity than a. in perfection 479.13
connoisseurs in a. reveal its beauty 207.24
criticism is easy, a. is difficult 207.12
criticism is the windows of a. 207.40
delight in a. is growth of taste, knowledge 53.62
difficult for man to realize his life an a. 539.30
does a. have higher function than to make one enjoy natural objects 53.10
every work of a. is an abstraction from time 53.92
eye is pleased when nature stoops to a. 623.80
fashion: to realize a. in living forms 338.18
for the best we must have recourse to a. 53.59
giving oneself up completely to a. 470.6
great a., contempt of a great man for small a. 53.50
great a. is expression of great men 53.119
great a. is the night thought of man 53.39
great a., remarkably separate from religion 53.9
greatness of a. lies in perpetual tension 53.21
great works of a. do not begin by giving us all their best 53.110
if a. were to redeem man, it could do so only by restoring him to boyishness 53.99
illusions are a. and by a. we live 449.4
in a., as in love, instinct is enough 53.52
in a. nothing can be done without genius 849.30
in fine a., hand, head, heart go together 53.118
interpretation is revenge of intellect on a. 207.49
it makes a. into an article for use 207.48
it's the aim of a. to give life form 53.4
life imitates a. more than a., life 539.133
life is short and the a. long 988.4
man who would emancipate a. from discipline 53.124
man works to recover, through a., images that first gained access to his heart 53.22
maybe there should be a law against a. 53.42
minimal a., maximum explanation 53.74
mirror reflects your face, a. your soul 53.132
mood means more than object in a. 53.46
morality takes no account of the a. in life 604.20
more inexpressible than all else is a. 53.113
no better deliverance from world than a. 53.57
no comfort in adversity sweeter than a. 53.3
no generation interested in a. in same way 53.40
not strength, but a., obtains prize 139.5
one may do whate'er one likes in a. 53.16
perfection not requisite to a. 684.15
power of great a. to transcend boundaries 53.60
prig, philistine, Ph.D., C.P.A. hate a. 210.15
thanks to a., many words are at our disposal 53.111
there is no progress in a. 53.38
there is one a.: to do all artlessly 899.4
to follow a. for sake of being great is surest way of ending in total extinction 53.120
to make us feel small is a function of a. 53.51
to most women a. is a form of scandal 1062.57
to reveal a., conceal artist, is a.'s aim 53.151
trend toward pure a. shows modesty 53.98
true a. selects and paraphrases 53.2
under-tow of time can't drag true a. back 53.28
we cannot appreciate the a. of any age 321.1
we don't like a. that is artificial 53.91
without a. reality is unbearable 53.131
without innovation, a. is a corpse 53.26
work of a. is the exaggeration of an idea 53.56
works of a. are of an infinite loneliness 207.44
youth of an a. is its most interesting period 53.19
arteriosclerosis: young people develop mental a. 1071.34
article: Should let itself be snuffed out by an a. 207.8
articulate: a. voice distracts more than mere noise 149.17
artifacts: a. tell more about ourselves than confessions 201.5
artifice: customary use of a. is sign of small mind 165.10
artificial: first duty in life is to be a. 54.5
to know only a. night is absurd 54.2
artist: aim of a. is to arrest motion 53.49
America is essentially against the a. 53.90
art in which a. is in danger of death 53.63
a. cannot get along without a public 53.54
a. cannot speak about his art 53.27
a. finds greater pleasure in painting 201.37
a. has conversation with public 53.25
a. has need to share joy with others 53.134
a. has never been a dictator 53.15
a. in teens who is happy is a charlatan 53.79
a. is a man of action 53.29
a. is as dissatisfied as revolutionary 53.64
a. like everyone else, only more so 53.115
a.: lover of nature, her slave and master 53.135
a. moves in a direction and hopes he arrives before death overtakes him 53.20
a. must blow trumpet of defiance 53.80
a.: one who creates something not here before with tools of human spirit 53.48
a. produces for the liberation of his soul 201.29
a. should be fit for best society 53.117
a. to keep awake sense of wonder 53.24
a. works on next composition because he was not satisfied with his previous one 201.39
behind mediocre a. find remarkable man 962.10
being an a. means ceasing to take seriously person we are when we are not an a. 53.100
cheat for sake of beauty, you're an a. 53.68
every a. is an unhappy lover 53.93
every a. is in everything he creates 53.126
every a. loves applause 722.25
every a. writes his own autobiography 53.43

every master knows material teaches the a. 53.37
first prerogative of a. in any medium is to make a fool of himself 53.69
life lived *in potentia* until a. deploys it 53.35
no a. has his complete meaning alone 53.41
no a. sees things as they really are 53.150
nobody ought to look at pictures who cannot find more in them than a. expressed 53.61
no fate more distressing for an a. than to have to show his work to fools 207.35
no longing sweeter to a. than longing after bliss of the commonplace 53.82
society must let a. follow vision anywhere 53.71
that a. puts order into nature is absurd 53.32
the a. has power to shape the material of pain we all have 53.137
the good a. addresses himself to life 53.142
this is the a., then—life's hungry man 53.152
true a. will let his wife starve 53.130
when critics disagree, the a. is in accord with himself 207.58
who fears nothing cannot be an a. 53.23
with an a. no sane man quarrels 207.46
woe to a. if he is disciple of his time 53.128
artistic: a. impulse seems not to wish to produce finished work 53.31
artist's: a. joy: thought and feeling merged 53.83
a. morality: truth, force of description 53.30
a. work constitutes the only relationship he can have with fellow men 53.36
artists: all men are creative but few are a. 201.17
a. don't steal, but borrow 53.116
a. have no less talents than ever 1001.12
a., poets uninterested in happiness 708.84
a. reproduce themselves or each other 207.57
a. today expected to cultivate unhappiness 1011.8
a. whom love inspires have light of fame 53.106
competitions are for horses, not a. 155.1
for a. waits the compromise through art 53.34
good a. exist in what they make 53.149
immature a. imitate; mature a. steal 700.4
refusal to rest content distinguishes a. from entertainers 53.140
arts: a. and sciences owe birth to our vices 1030.22
a. must study their occasions 53.125
a. will one day give headless man head 577.11
religion always a patron of the a. 797.37
society acquires new a. and loses old instincts 913.3
ascent: agriculture, largest step in a. of man 337.1
most powerful drive in a. of man 741.2
ascetic: if a., far better to stay in London or Paris 992.56
riches, the reward of the righteously a. 1048.27
ashamed: more a man a. of, more respectable he is 809.4
often wonder to see them not a. 893.7
Asia: not in A. was mankind born 562.2
asides: character comes out best in a. 119.27
ask: a. of him who wishes you well 805.5
better a. twice than lose your way once 480.5
how pleasant it is to a. for nothing 880.23
not to a. is not to be denied 805.2
we should not a. people for what they cannot give 805.1
aspiration: a. is a joy for ever 55.18
I drink the wine of a. and the drug of illusion 55.8
path made clear, a. of everyone 115.5
whole of satisfaction not from single a. 55.7
aspirations: life's a. come in the guise of children 123.57
the hopes and a. of all the peoples on earth 55.13
aspire: if you a. to the highest place 55.3
ass: a. may bray long before he shakes stars 941.4
a. that is common property is always the worst saddled 894.1
hay is more acceptable to an a. than gold 48.5
hood a. with purple, he shall pass for cathedral doctor 138.7
rather ride on a. that carries me 720.4
regard him secretly as an a. 334.21
who makes himself an a., men will ride 941.7
wise do not stand behind kicking a. 755.30
assailant: a. often in the right; assailed, always 822.12
assassination: a. has never changed history of the world 518.2
a. is always possible 518.5
a. the extreme form of censorship 113.9
assent: a., and you are sane 258.2
assert: to know oneself, a. oneself 875.4
asserts: individual never a. himself more than when he forgets himself 928.3
associating: a. with men, one acquires their virtues, vices 57.13
wise man a. with vicious becomes idiot 57.3
association: all thought is a feat of a. 975.14
long a. ends up producing a sort of rot 564.6
unquarreling a. of men never existed 772.8
assurance: a. contemptible unless self-knowledge 860.5
a. keeps even pace with ability 860.3
nothing gives more a. than a mask 165.3
astray: some go a. because no right path for them 124.7
astronomer: undevout a. is mad 850.10
astronomers: a. work always with the past 849.13
asylum: a reason to seek a. in Red China 764.13
atheism: a. must insult God less than religion 1004.10
a. rampant in community without blasphemy 506.2
a. rather in lip than heart of man 1004.1
a.: there's not a single emancipating influence that doesn't become inhibitory 1004.9
little philosophy inclineth to a. 694.1
to put faith in lies and hate is true a. 412.13
atheist: by night an a. half believes a God 1004.16
fight between theist, a. is whether God shall be called God or some other name 387.15
no proselyter so energetic as a. 1004.3
atheists: a. put on a false courage and alacrity 1004.14
atom: an a. tossed in a chaos made of yeasting worlds; whence have I come 316.6
a. bombs pile up, but earth still goes round the sun 1001.10
gods are born and die; the a. endures 641.2
no country without a. bomb independent 641.3
no evil in a., only in men's souls 641.14
terror of a. age: man's adjustment to it 641.16
atom bomb: get along together with that a. 641.8
atomic: god of science gave us a. bomb 641.11
atrocities: a. to feed the hatred against the enemy 745.1
attached: men are a. to us for services they render 888.7
attack: a. is the reaction 26.3
isn't the best defense always a good a. 229.11
attainable: let me strive for a. things 55.14
attainment: is anything in life disenchanting as a. 945.43
attempted: nothing ever a., if all objections must first be overcome 291.5
attention: we despise no source paying us pleasing a. 349.20
attic: in an a. we enjoy supper of fried fish 845.5
attraction: a. stubbornly eludes control 884.5
attractions: men by sympathetic a. lead human race 531.5
auctioneer: a.: proclaims with hammer that he has picked a pocket with his tongue 105.3
audacious: often we are a. from timidity 1047.8
perfect simplicity is unconsciously a. 899.9
audacity: a. augments courage; hesitation, fear 92.10
fly should be used as symbol of a. 481.8
tact in a. is knowing how far

to go 92.1
audience: a. an abstraction, it has no taste 59.6
a. is a very curious animal 59.3
a. is fifty percent of performance 59.1
a. is not least important actor in the play 59.4
a. must be aware of the thing satirized 844.8
his a., wife and children, in the palm of his hand 334.19
if a. never understands plot, it will be very attentive 972.20
one can't exchange thoughts with an a. 59.2
solitude is a.-chamber of God 915.22
the a. behaves like a well-trained flunky 614.28
writer needs no a. other than the few 1069.133
audiences: to have great poets, must have great a. 59.7
August: A. creates as she slumbers 854.29
austerity: a. of line, simplicity, economy of effect 282.2
authentic: the a. is almost never found by being pursued 60.2
author: a. needs more than intelligence 1069.77
a. reading his own book can't stop 873.9
a. who speaks about his books as bad as mother about children 1069.34
every a. keeps an outrageous vanity 1069.122
every a. would his brother kill 1069.16
every production must resemble its a. 201.9
old a. rediscovers himself in fossilized production of earlier years 1069.62
one hates an a. that's all a. 1069.19
same common sense makes a. write good things, dread they are not good enough 1069.76
we expected to see a., we find a man 942.17
when characters are alive before their a. 344.24
who first praises book, next in merit to a. 207.30
wide discrepancy between reputation of a. living and dead 1069.5
author's: a. work furnishes critics with food 207.27
understand a. character, comprehension of his writings becomes easy 1069.82
authority: age has an a. making it preferable to youth 653.95
anyone who in discussion relies on a. 51.13
a. has every reason to fear the skeptic 61.7
a. is dangerous, selfish, inexplicable 61.2
a. is for children and servants 564.98
a. is never without hate 61.4
a. seldom resisted when well employed 61.6
I fear a. but at the same time I resent it 786.3
most men after freedom prefer a. 61.8
new faces have more a. than old 61.5
power of a. among the poor and uneducated 61.1
proud man, dressed in a little brief a. 61.10
rigorous a., justice: kindness of kings 831.13
way to undermine a. is laughter 526.1
we have to hate our immediate predecessors to get free of their a. 374.9
authors: a., a natural and irresistible aristocracy 93.93
a. are like cattle going to a fair 1069.80
a. are sometimes like tomcats 1069.31
a. marketed like promising movie starlets 967.4
a. should write one novel, then be gassed 1069.86
even monarchs have need of a. 1069.56
great a. make for disagreement 1069.53
great a. produce great publishers 764.5
of a. there is great scarcity 207.37
one class of a. write history of their times; the other, biography 1069.130
the great a. share their souls with us 1069.81
authors': some judge of a. names, not works 207.43
autobiography: a. is now as common as adultery 62.4
every artist writes his own a. 53.43
the sonnets have the fascination of an a. 62.5
wrote a., never mentioned his wife 62.1
autocrat: to be great a., must be great barbarian 719.14
autograph: few not flattered by a request for an a. 332.32
automatic: critical vision can mitigate a. operation 966.19
automatism: we have created an industrial order geared to a. 1001.8
automobile: a. has dissolved living tissue of city 64.3
except the American woman, nothing interests eye of American man more than a. 64.1
to the a. to satisfy love of aggression 64.16
autonomy: a job as citizen's right to a. 823.19
men lose individual a. seeking to be alike 171.15
autumn: a. arrives in the early morning 854.9
a.: season of mists, friend of sun 854.28
a. time for gathering, scattering 854.39
a. wins you by mute appeal to sympathy 854.12
summer ends, and a. comes 854.8
autumnal: grace I have seen in one a. face 653.20
autumn's: wild west wind, breath of a. being 1059.6
avarice: a. hoards itself poor 384.11
a. is a cursed vice 403.13
a. is a fine, absorbin' passion 403.3
a. is as destitute as poverty 403.19
a. makes man too timorous to be wealthy 403.17
extreme a. misapprehends itself always 403.12
miser's a. is sepulchre of other passions 403.2
pride, a., envy are tongues men heed 733.5
prudery is the worst kind of a. 756.3
to hazard much for much is a., not wisdom 403.18
when other sins are old, a. is young 403.5
avaricious: men hate the a.; nothing gained from him 403.23
avoided: weakness to lament what cannot be a. 937.7
awake: only that day dawns to which we are a. 605.8
aware: to live means to be divinely a. 539.75
awareness: if building a bridge does not enrich a. of builders, don't build 1065.28
awful: anything a. makes me laugh 526.17
awkwardness: a. has no forgiveness in heaven or earth 372.1
B
Babbitt: but one thing wrong with the B. house 422.14
babies: all b. look like Winston Churchill 65.11
man who hates dogs and b. can't be all bad 594.3
baby: b. is angel whose wings decrease 65.8
cradle is rocked but b. is pinched 271.16
each b. is a finer one than the last 65.6
human b., a mosaic of animal and angel 65.2
one hundred and fifty-two distinctly different ways of holding a b. 65.4
Babylon: perfumed to exude suggestions of nights in B. 267.1
bachelor: he's such an old b. 66.10
no character harder to play well than old b. 66.3
bachelor's: b. admired freedom is often a yoke 66.6
b. fare is bread, cheese, kisses 66.8
bachelors: all reformers are b. 790.23
background: a product of his b. 119.29
b. reveals the true being of man or thing 67.1
every philosophy tinged with secret imaginative b. 694.42
bad: b. in best of us leaves saint like rest of us 840.12
b. is never good until worse happens 795.3
b. man must have brains 1070.11
better fare hard with good men than feast with b. 57.10
good and b. is helping or hurting 390.3
good and b. may not be dissevered 390.5
good is good doctor, b. sometimes better 307.11
good so good that b. when b. can't be b. 389.7
man not good or b. for one action 227.10
no benefit in gifts of a b. man 384.8
nothing good for him for

whom nothing b. 390.7
nothing good, b. but thinking makes it so 389.13
nothing so b. but can masquerade as moral 604.24
one knows b. action in flash of regret 227.15
the b. often let you see how b. they are 165.15
the good suffers while the b. prevails 390.9
when the b. imitate the good, there is no knowing what mischief is intended 451.9
world bears two nations: good and b. 1067.21
badness: good people make b. very important 393.49
balance: false b. is an abomination 105.2
fortune holds even, scrupulous b. 116.5
truth is b., but unbalance not a lie 999.15
balanced: nothing is unthinkable to the b. person 717.2
baldness: more felicity on the far side of b. 586.17
ball: easier to keep one b. in the air than many 762.7
ballots: b. rightful successors to bullets 1038.12
bandannas: the air seemed to come in soft b. 882.6
bang: world ends not with a b. but a whimper 1067.10
bank: b. lends money if you don't need it 69.3
banker: father is a b. provided by nature 670.19
bankers: American b. believe in the personal touch 68.2
b., legendary figures in public imagination 69.1
bankrupt: people become b. having invested too heavily in the prose of life 612.9
bankruptcy: b. is a sacred state 718.57
banquet: don't come giving me a big b. that you eat 426.5
some dislike something in every b. 725.1
barbarian: man born b., raises self by culture 210.11
to be great autocrat, must be great b. 719.14
barbarians: men have been b. much longer than civilized 70.3
barbarism: b. is the condition of past customs 213.9
b. naturally has its apologists 70.4
civilization is b. in lamb's skin 133.1
soldier is grievous vestige of b. 70.5
barber: one b. shaves not so close but another finds work 155.3
bard: wine to gifted b. is mount that races 268.9
bargain: unpleasant to get more than you b. for 312.7
bargains: someone always cheated in b. 105.10
bark: let no dog b.! 264.13
barricade: b. closes the street but opens the way 801.1
base: b. men in love gain a nobility 551.188
small things make b. men proud 693.9
what b. things fear makes men do 343.23
baseball: b., a game; Grand Canyon, a hole in Arizona 929.20
b., a game of innumerable redemptions 929.19
b. is slovenly and excessive in midsummer 929.1
big-inning b., affirmed in the Bible 929.22
baseness: two infinities: God above, human b. below 307.17
basest: the b. of all things is to be afraid 1069.41
bashfulness: there is that destroyeth his soul by b. 980.1
bath: I test my b. before I sit 137.6
bathing suit: a canary-yellow two-piece b. 267.22
bathroom: a royal b. of porcelain and glazed tile 430.4
bathrooms: nation of b. with humanist in each tub 34.46
battle: all b. is a confused experiment to ascertain clear undeniable might or right 1042.11
life, a b. between Bad and Worse 214.1
nothing except a b. lost can be half so melancholy as a b. won 1042.101
peace hath higher tests than b. 681.39
toothache will cost a b. 996.7
unhappy the general who comes on field of b. with a system 939.1
bayonets: lover of b. sees in glitter what he feels 588.6
be: b. as you would seem to b. 901.8
b. what you are 444.11
b. what you wish to be thought to b. 386.16
b. yourself and think for yourself 880.10
every moment, one is what one will b. 444.26
tell yourself what you would b. 55.5
beach: along a b., some ancient urge disturbs us 853.10
beaches: we shall fight on the b. 807.1
bear: who learns to b. what he cannot change 806.8
beard: b. does not make philosopher 407.2
old goat not more reverend for b. 653.31
beards: safety razors make it hard to grow b. in America 34.58
bearing: we may be masters of our lot by b. it 287.9
beast: guarded by a B. whose eyes are made of white agate 1029.6
he who would act the angel acts the b. 691.8
when human being says b. in him aroused 431.27
beasts: men not to live silently like b. 733.18
who will pity any who go near wild b. 216.1
world is full of nothing but b. of prey 26.1
beat: b. your child once a day 766.5
they used to b. your head right in public 500.3
beaten: man surprised is half b. 955.1
beating: that the b. had not hurt was a sort of victory 766.15
beauties: all b. to be honored, only one embraced 72.45
a procession of sinuous long-stemmed b. 267.19
statesmen, b., rarely sense own decay 226.2
beautifier: no b. like wish to scatter joy 519.7
beautiful: b. derives its beauty from itself 72.6
b. rests on foundations of the necessary 72.17
b. souls are they that are open and ready 654.6
b. things, when taste is formed 963.17
it's easy to be b., hard to appear so 45.19
man makes b. what he loves 78.17
most b. things are those that madness prompts and reason writes 1069.54
most b. things in world are most useless 72.43
no woman can be b. who can be false 472.12
some people are b. in dilapidation 653.92
things are b. if you love them 72.3
things not b. until they speak to the imagination 72.18
beauty: a b. you notice; a charmer notices you 121.5
a little b. is preferable to much wealth 72.44
ask a toad what is b.—a female toad 72.61
as we grow old, b. steals inward 653.22
b., after offense returning, regains love 72.35
b., a grace wholly gratuitous 72.13
b. a greater recommendation than any letter of introduction 72.5
b. and deformity equally pass away 990.13
b. corrodes, corrupts all it touches 72.20
b. deprived of adjuncts ceases to be b. 72.42
b. dies of b., worth dies of worth 975.58
b. draws us with a single hair 407.5
b. fades, leaves record upon face as to what became of it 326.4
b., find self in love, not thy mirror 72.54
b. gets the best of it in this world 72.31
b. hath no true glass, but loving eyes 72.29
b., invisible, has visible reflection 72.22
b. is an ecstasy; it's as simple as hunger 72.32
b. is everlasting; dust is for a time 72.36
b. is its own excuse for being 72.16
b. is joint force and full result of all 72.40
b. is not immortal 72.52
b. is one of the rare things that do not lead to doubt of God 72.1
b. is the promise of happiness 72.51
b. is truth, truth b. 72.27
b. is unbearable, drives us to despair 72.9
b. is wherever there is a soul to admire 72.60
b. more than bitterness

breaks the heart 72.55
b. must not be hoarded 72.34
b. of American women is vast industry 1062.100
b. of world is of laughter and anguish 1067.31
b. persuades eyes of men without orator 72.48
b.: power by which woman charms lover and terrifies husband 72.8
b. provoketh thieves sooner than gold 72.49
b.: truth's smile beholding her own face 72.53
b. without expression tires 72.15
better to be happy and burned up with b. 409.64
cannot hope for b. in all things 72.33
chase b. and it ceases 72.12
cheat for sake of b., you're an artist 53.68
culture opens the sense of b. 210.8
every b., out of place, is a b. no longer 949.3
extraordinary b. involves a moral charm 72.14
exuberance is b. 513.1
frigidaires perfect, b. limps 684.15
from b. we draw conception of divine life 410.4
genius lasts longer than b. 279.89
glory of b. is fleeting; virtue, eternal 1033.42
how long does b. last? 72.11
is b. not enough, why do I cry for love? 551.212
judgment of b. can err with wine, dark 72.38
little of b. has America given the world 34.21
looking for b. makes us see shortcomings 457.6
love built on b., soon as b., dies 551.41
mightiest of Puritans who first insisted b. is only skin deep 72.28
narrow souls dare not to admire true b. 72.10
not enough to see and know b. of a work 72.62
nothing lasts except b. 72.64
offered himself up in spirit to create b. 72.30
one finds only so much b. as one carries 1026.6
outstanding b. tends to hamper happiness 72.47
personal b. requires that one be tall 72.4
poet unzips veil of b., doesn't remove it 708.111
prosperity versus b.; cash against soul 750.11
real b. is something very grave 72.2
scale of 1 to 10 for grading woman's b. 13.1
she who is born a b. is born betrothed 72.25
the moment of b. was there 72.21
thing of b. is a joy forever 72.26
to keep b. in place makes all beautiful 72.46
to the elect, beautiful things mean b. 72.63
truth will bear exposure as well as b. 998.21
universe lies under necessity of b. 1017.4
vast, confused b. 34.43
we fly to b. from terrors of the finite 72.19
what imagination seizes as b. is truth 998.68
wisdom is social, b. is jealous 1060.35
without grace b. is an unbaited hook 396.2
zest is the secret of all b. 513.2

become: man needs only to b. 8.10
sacrifice what we are for what we could b. 717.1
we b. what we are by radical refusal 444.21

bed: bride b.: theirs alone till life's done 564.37
in b., I prefer beauty before goodness 188.26
man's b. his cradle; woman's her rack 73.10
marriage more than four legs in b. 564.46
very warm weather when one's in b. 73.9
we go to b. with reluctance 73.3

bedfellows: misery acquaints a man with strange b. 17.52

bee: honey in every flower, takes b. to get it 585.7
not good for swarm, not good for b. 151.1

beer: running b. gathers no foam 928.5

bees: b. sip honey and hum their thanks 399.10
is any polity better ordered than that of b. 481.5
what state excels b. for government 481.2

beetle: when they came to shoe the horses, the b. stretched out his leg 873.5

beg: not a soul who does not have to b. alms 235.4

beggar: a b., offered alms a second time, refuses 74.1
poor command respect; b. excites anger 74.2

beggars: b. should be abolished entirely 74.3

begin: b. at beginning, go on to end; then stop 661.5
better to b. in evening than not at all 75.4
in creating, only hard thing's to b. 201.26
you b. well only in what you end well 76.5

beginner: merit goes to b. if successor does better 75.2

beginning: art of ending greater than that of b. 76.8
bad b. makes a bad ending 176.5
good b. makes a good ending 76.4
men perish because they cannot join b. with end 76.1

beginnings: easy to see the b. of things 76.3
most men are bundles of b. 75.3
we should have our eyes intent on b. 75.6

begun: once task b., half work is done 75.5

behave: b. in life as if at a banquet 657.6
cease to believe, you may cease to b. 1004.13
in great matters men b. as expected 77.8
men who b. well may be creatures of habit 77.15

behavior: beautiful b. better than beautiful form 77.9
b.: conduct determined by breeding 77.6
b. is the index of the man 77.14
b.: mirror where one displays his image 77.12
b. toward each other is unpredictable 77.27
call bad b. righteous indignation 241.7
in our collective b. we are mysterious 77.26
laws of b. yield to energy of individual 563.12
loyal b. may be attributed to the oath 556.3
man, not committed to particular variety of b. 77.5
no rules of b. that apply to the theatre 972.13
we attribute b. to a person we cannot see 77.25
what leads the evolutionary procession is b. 77.2

beholders: less difference in landscapes than in b. 699.3

Being: who cared if there was any B. to pray to? 723.29

being: a problem-recognizing and -accepting b. 431.1
b. is the great explainer 316.11
each must form himself as a particular b. 469.10
every life is its own excuse for b. 316.5
man needs to die in fullness of b. 8.10
peace will come through b. 681.20
sanctity hangs about sources of our b. 316.9

belief: b. which allows me best use of my strength 78.4
eloquent man is drunk with a certain b. 283.2
it is desire that engenders b. 78.16
widespread b. is likely to be foolish 78.19

beliefs: there is a multitude of individual b. 78.5
when all b. are challenged together 904.9

believe: b. in something for another world 414.11
b. not all you hear 755.14
b. that life is worth living 78.9
cease to b., you may cease to behave 1004.13
childish to expect men to b. like fathers 374.5
faith is to b. what you do not yet see 330.2
first we b. everything, then nothing, then everything again 78.11
he does not b. who does not so live 78.3
he's a fool who tries to make blockhead b. 330.6
hundreds b., but each has to b. by himself 330.1
man as big as number who b. in him 401.57
man is credulous and must b. something 78.18
no man ready to b. all he is told does well 104.26
reason should make you b. 330.30
to b. in something you have to b. in everything necessary for belief 78.1
under all that we think, lives all we b. 78.12
valuable trait is sense of

what not to b. 904.6
we b. the most incredible things 78.6
we b. what makes us feel fine fellows 876.13
we b. what we want to b. 78.7
what will make us b. in what we must do 442.2
believed: everything b. is an image of truth 78.2
nothing so b., as what we least know 78.13
that b. by all has every chance of being false 78.23
to be b., make truth unbelievable 1000.14
believer: b. cannot be restrained 596.2
b. undisturbed that others do not yet see 330.11
believest: let greatest part of what thou hearest be the least part of what thou b. 904.8
believing: b. that a better system can be provided 934.1
loving is half of b. 78.8
people enjoy b. things they know untrue 202.1
bell: never send to know for whom the b. tolls 221.35
bellies: b. big enough to have names 45.14
bells: everyone thinks b. echo his thoughts 873.8
belly: afraid every time her b. began to swell 65.1
b. is ungrateful 437.12
constant demands of heart and b. 625.5
belongs: man b. wherever he wants to go 921.2
beloved: ashamed of being b. when we no longer love 552.6
beneath: nothing is b. you if it is in direction of your life 435.6
benefactor: every evil not yielded to is a b. 307.10
beneficent: be b., but defend your rights 229.3
benefits: b. we receive must be rendered again 647.1
in refusing b. caution should be used 791.7
more pleased seeing those on whom we confer b. than those from whom we receive b. 384.19
unrequitable b. repaid with hatred 647.7
who talk of b. do them to talk of them 433.17
benevolence: great exercise of b.: loving relatives 519.21
best: each entitled to be valued by b. moment 515.1
there is always b. way to do everything 585.4
'Tis his at last who says it b. 773.3
bestiality: any check on human action brings mental b. 562.45
best seller: b. is celebrity among books 93.8
b. is gilded tomb of mediocre talent 93.82
betray: all a man can b. is his conscience 79.1
I hope I should have the guts to b. my country 79.2
to take refuge with inferior is to b. self 57.15
betrayal: distrust is our only defense against b. 259.16
betrayed: those that are b. feel treason sharply 79.4
better: b. to be despised than ignored 722.23
be what you are: first step to being b. 444.11
have zeal first to b. thyself 460.4
striving to b., oft we mar what's well 684.17
who rises from prayer a b. man 723.24
beves: more a man dreams, less he b. 115.10
bewilderment: b. cause of much unhappiness 149.2
Bible: the Iliad and and the B. are sad books 93.72
big: a man as b. as number who believe in him 401.57
b. drum only sounds well from afar 873.18
you take b. paces, you leave b. spaces 33.4
bigness: overabundance of b. not good 312.4
bigot: b.: one with opinion you don't entertain 264.1
one who has thought thoroughly called a b. 264.5
bigotry: b. holds truth with a grip that kills it 264.15
religion is destroyed by b. 264.6
bigots: anti-clericalism, nonbelief, have their b. 1004.12
billboard: A b. lovely as a tree 18.11
binding: better the book, less it demands from b. 93.49
biographies: b. are but clothes and buttons of a man 81.9
history is the essence of innumerable b. 419.12
biography: in b., fact, fiction shouldn't be mixed 81.1
read no history: read only b. 81.5
the last act in b. is that of death 418.4
there is no history, only b. 419.21
bird: b. of paradise alights on ungrasping hand 409.12
b. thinks it kindness to give fish a lift 56.10
don't let b. make its nest in your hair 971.3
if you can't catch a b. of paradise 162.7
no b. soars too high, with his own wings 33.3
no ladder needs the b. but skies 82.4
one beats bush, another catches the b. 108.3
only a b. should build nest over abysses 755.17
birds: only admirable event is migration of b. 82.1
birth: at b., death stands but a little aside 221.14
b., copulation, death: all the facts 539.29
b. is nothing without virtue 37.5
death borders upon our b. 221.59
good b. fine, but merit is ancestors' 37.6
high b. is a poor dish at table 37.3
man's task is to give b. to himself 201.15
mourn not death of men, but b. 83.5
only cure for b., death, is to enjoy interval 539.101
our b. is nothing but our death begun 83.7
to give b. is short-cut to omniscience 670.10
birthright: where position is felt to be a b. 52.3
bitten: b. by snake, fears piece of string 321.43
bitter: no fruit not b. before it is ripe 404.24
nothing so b. a patient mind can't find solace for it 180.3
worst thing in the world is a b. woman 1062.143
bitterness: nothing sweet which does not end in b. 990.11
black: b. boy's badness is badness 85.14
b. children integrated Central High School 967.6
b. man is striding freedom road 85.15
if you are b. only roads into American life are through subservience 85.10
blackmail: b. in a pin-striped suit 738.6
blade: each b. of grass has spot on earth 423.1
blame: every woman wants a man to b. 581.51
if there is no intention, there is no b. 900.15
keep alive justice, much b. will pass you by 517.14
blamed: what cannot be altered must not be b. 806.5
blameless: when we quarrel, we wish we had been b. 772.4
blasphemies: all great truths begin as b. 506.3
blasphemy: where b. does not exist, atheism rampant 506.2
blessing: earth has no b. for unblessed of Heaven 900.4
one b. only: confidence in self 860.6
blessings: b. on thee, afternoon torpor 906.16
good government greatest of human b. 395.27
men slower to recognize b. than evils 475.3
men value b. only when they lose them 1026.17
blind: all have their b. side—superstitions 954.3
b. lead b., it's democratic way 233.39
b. man who sees is better than seeing man who is b. 87.9
B. she is, an' deef an' dumb an' has a wooden leg! 517.11
he has the greatest b. side who thinks he has none 87.4
if b. lead b. both shall fall into ditch 447.3
in land of the b., one-eyed man is king 795.1
it is we that are b., not Fortune 87.3
none so b. as they that won't see 87.5
sky is not less blue because the b. man does not see it 784.6
sounds are things b. see 86.3
the b. esteem it be enough estate to see 187.1
we b. ourselves in order not to be disturbed 240.8
blindness: b., one of the

styles of living 86.1
there is a triple sight in b. keen 86.2
bliss: how quick old woe follows a little b. 1011.27
one moment may with b. repay hours of pain 409.19
blockhead: learned b. worse than ignorant b. 941.6
blood: b. is the god of war's rich livery 1042.57
ounce of b. worth more than pound of friendship 334.28
prison, b., death create enthusiasts 801.2
there is no sure foundation set on b. 518.13
blood's: b. thicker than water 796.2
bloom: It's [charm] a sort of b. on a woman 121.2
blossoms: b. of the heart no wind can touch 284.20
eyes of men love to pluck the b. 892.50
blow: a b. with a walking-stick as delightful tickling 289.24
a fate-determined b. which must be endured 330.31
bluff: a b. may be more useful than a threat 976.1
blunder: worse than a crime, it is a b. 88.3
blundering: All this dignified b. costs plenty 977.2
blunders: great b. made of multitude of fibres 88.6
pain of our b. never passes away 88.9
blush: b. that flies at seventeen is fixed at forty-nine 586.13
give friend cause to b.: likely lose him 893.6
his cheek is his biographer, as long as he can b. 878.1
we never forgive those who make us b. 893.1
blushes: man is only animal that b.—or needs to 893.8
man that b. is not quite a brute 893.9
whoever b. is already guilty 478.9
blushing: b. is the color of virtue 893.2
boast: b. not thyself of tomorrow 727.1
boasting: tonsillitis to prevent a Frenchman from b. 361.11
boat: a b., just one more damn house to take care of 895.4
boats: light b. sail swift 951.4
nothing so worth doing as messing in b. 895.2
bodies: we have a world of contented b. 750.13
what is more important than our b. 90.7
body: b. always ends by being a bore 975.41
b. am I entirely, and nothing else 90.4
b. is a house of windows 547.10
b. is as easily satisfied as a spaniel 90.2
b. is love's book 892.17
b. never forgives injury by mind 589.8
b. seeks what injured the mind with love 892.30
death reveals what a nothing the b. is 90.3
happiness is spirit fulfilled through b. 409.26
if any thing sacred the b. is sacred 90.10
in middle years scarcely a part of b. man would hesitate to turn over to authorities 586.19
mind sins, not the b. 900.15
nature the b., God the soul 1017.13
poor b., time taught you use of clothes 90.1
pray for a sane mind in a sound b. 413.6
sound mind in sound b. is a happy state 413.8
though disfigured, to whom is b. not dear 90.6
trouble with preserving health of b. is to do it without destroying mind 413.1
we are ashamed of our own b. 431.4
body's: he is slave of many masters who is his b. slave 90.8
bold: be b., but not too b. 92.12
b. are helpless without cleverness 139.4
b. are not always men of principle 734.4
b. man does best, at home or abroad 92.5
b. man strikes for double value and compromises on par 1026.24
boldest: when hope is feeble, b. plans are safest 92.7
boldness: be not so clement as to encourage b. 890.3
b. without propriety is insubordination 92.2
decent b. ever meets with friends 92.4
Bolshevik: philosophy of the Russian B. 150.2
Bolsheviks: Republicans are Socialists and the Democrats are B. 711.8
bomb: god of science has given us the atomic b. 641.11
no country without atom b. independent 641.3
no reasoning with an incendiary b. 46.4
the falling of a single b. 641.6
bombs: guns and b. are witness to human folly 229.5
people have settled down to living with b. 641.12
bond: a great b. to dislike the same things 22.2
bondage: familiarize yourself with chains of b. 109.6
bonds: b. that unite us exist only in our mind 794.9
bones: reduced my b. to rubber, my brain to gruel 521.3
bonus: b. is salve applied to conscience of rich 104.34
book: all know me in my b., and my b. in me 1069.96
as much trickery required to grow rich by a stupid b. as is folly in buying it 93.47
bad b. as hard to write as good b. 93.43
better the b., less it demands from binding 93.49
beware of the man of one b. 620.1
b. is a b., altho' there's nothing in't 764.3
b. is a mirror 93.53
b. is good company 93.5
b. is made better by good readers 93.68
b. is not harmless because no one is offended by it 93.24
b. on cheap paper does not convince 93.41
b. writing makes horse racing look solid 1069.124
easy to write epigrams, hard to write b. 1069.88
favorable hours for reading a b. 93.57
have you ever bought a b. by a Negro writer? 93.42
he who destroys a b. kills reason itself 93.63
if a b. come from the heart 1069.23
I know every b. of mine by its scent 93.34
important thing in a b.: its meaning for you 93.61
last thing one settles in writing b. 1069.103
making a b.: a trade like clockmaking 1069.77
many date new era in life from reading b. 93.91
newspaper is natural enemy of the b. 630.10
no man understands a deep b. 93.75
no such thing as a moral or immoral b. 93.97
only people who have to write for a living can be excused for letting bad b. loose 1069.95
pleasing picture of a child peering into a b. 93.78
possession of b. substitutes for reading 93.10
precious pleasure to meet an antique b. 93.22
presentation copy is b. which does not sell 764.7
"Reader, I am myself the subject of my b.;" 62.6
reading all my b. in originals 93.26
we should gloat over a b. 93.86
what use is a b. without pictures or talk 93.13
when a man sees nothing in a b., he often means he does not see himself in it 207.26
who first praises b. next in merit to author 207.30
wicked b. is wickeder; it can't repent 93.29
you live many lives when reading great b. 93.87
books: all b. are either dreams or swords 93.58
all great b. contain boring portions 401.47
best seller is a celebrity among b. 93.8
borrowers of b. 538.7
b. are own world, but not the only world 1067.16
b. for all the world are foul-smelling 93.69
b. give not wisdom where was none before 93.36
b. have much one does not want to know 93.11
b. preserve the intellect that bred them 93.62
b. receive chief value from stamp of ages 93.88
b. speak plain when counselors blanch 93.3
b. succeed, and lives fail 93.9
b. take their place by specific gravity 93.25
b. that influence us are

those a little farther down our path than we 93.30
B. think for me 93.48
b. to be read as deliberately as written 93.90
b., treasured wealth of the world 93.92
children have a natural antipathy to b. 279.86
conversation with wise man better than b. 279.52
hard-covered b. break up friendships 93.85
in b. lies the soul of the whole past 93.12
in b. resurrecting the lives of others 539.69
in great b. mind finds room to put much 93.46
many b. require no thought from reader 93.17
many good b. suffer from inefficient beginnings 93.73
more b. upon b. than any other subject 207.38
no b. are undeservedly remembered 93.2
no furniture so charming as b. 93.83
no reason man should like same b. at eighteen and forty-eight 93.76
of all the ways of acquiring b. 93.6
of making many b. there is no end 93.7
passions shape b., repose writes them 1069.113
second-hand b. are wild b., homeless b. 93.98
security in an old b. criticized by Time 136.5
seek in reading b. only to please myself 93.66
small number of b. play great part 93.95
some b. are to be tasted 93.4
the flesh is sad, and I've read all b. 290.2
there are b. of the hour, b. of all time 93.79
they like my b. better in England 93.77
today's b. seem to be written in one day 93.14
true university is a collection of b. 538.4
we are too civil to b. 93.27
world of b. is delightful if you enter it as an adventurer 93.35
bookworm: b. with new novel is prepared for pleasure 704.21
b. wraps himself in web of generalities 93.37
bore: best you can hope for is to be a b. 524.48
b. consumes each year one and a half times his own weight in others' patience 95.7
b. is the last to find himself out 95.4
b.: person who talks when you wish him to listen 95.2
God is a b. 125.18
if you are a thinker you must be a frowning b. 34.49
secret of being b. is to tell everything 95.8
bored: better to be happy for moment than long b. 409.64
man only animal that can be b. 94.6
boredom: b. can become the sublimest of emotions 94.8
b. dismantles the mind, renders it superficial 94.3
b. is an early stage in life and art 94.5
b.: the desire for desires 94.9
modern man has manufactured an abyss of b. 966.22
one must choose between b. and torment 94.4
passions are less mischievous than b. 94.1
bores: b. we have with us even to the end 95.6
society is formed of b. and the bored 94.2
so many intensified b. in the United States 34.18
boring: work, terribly b. if one did not play 1065.7
born: being b. is undeniably a start 83.4
he alone is blessed who ne'er was b. 946.37
it is as if she had never been b. 948.14
man always dies before he is fully b. 404.10
man should be b., and b., die at once 83.1
we are b. crying, live complaining 539.41
borne: what cannot be altered must be b. 806.5
borrow: have own horse and you may b. another's 96.7
human species made of men who b., lend 96.4
borrowed: b. cloak does not keep one warm 96.1
most men are rich in b. sufficiency 773.4
borrower: b. is servant to the lender 96.2
neither a b. nor a lender be 96.5
borrowers: b. of books, mutilators of collections 538.7
bosoms: more to Bunnyhood than stuffing b. 1062.134
botany: laws of gravity, chemistry, b. 849.7
bottle: it's only the first b. that's expensive 268.14
over the b. many a friend is found 268.55
bottom: b. is b., even if turned upside down 780.14
victories of fellows at the top aren't always victories for fellows at the b. 780.1
bounty: b. receives value from manner of bestowal 384.15
bourgeois: b.: one who places anything above feeling 587.2
b. prefers convenience to liberty 587.4
bow: stretch a b. very full, you will wish you had stopped in time 229.8
bowels: jay-naked male and female discussing their b. 564.20
boy: a b. with an almost full-grown head 407.6
b. is adult before parents think so 97.5
b. is a piece of existence quite separate 97.2
imagination of a b. is healthy 1071.37
prison-house shades close on growing b. 1071.64
speak roughly to your little b. 766.4
boyhood: our b. is what any boy in our environment would have had 123.59
boy's: white b. badness is animal spirits; black b. badness is badness 85.14
boys: acolyte knows what b. do behind altar 321.49
b. are the cash of war 1042.14
b. are unwholesome companions for grown people 97.6
b. have no sadness sadder than our hope 1071.52
b. look on all force as an enemy 97.1
b. spirited but not tender as daughter 218.1
no hope be put in melodious voice of b. 990.14
bragging: they are unmistakably b. 632.15
brain: a girl's b. is mysterious, in a superficial way 493.1
almost no limits to the discoveries of how the human b. operates 759.1
a man should keep his b. attic stocked with usable furniture 522.15
half a b. is enough if one says little 98.6
his b. like a morsel on a platter 946.50
things the b. refuses to accept as true 998.1
where the heart lies, let the b. lie also 284.6
brains: b. of mankind, undergoing fusion 975.42
each is satisfied with his own b. 156.2
many complain of looks, none of their b. 493.32
our b. are seventy-year clocks 606.11
we can't all combine good looks, b. 542.10
brandy: b. is lead in the morning, gold at night 268.18
who aspires to be a hero must drink b. 268.30
brassiere: redefine their shape with a b. 499.8
brave: all are b. on observing one who despairs 195.26
b. creature is part coward 195.38
b. man thinks no one his superior who does him an injury 476.16
b. men can make any danger spot tenable 216.12
coward shuns but b. chooses danger 195.11
coward sneaks to death, the b. live on 948.15
easy to be b. from a safe distance 195.1
fortune favors the b. 360.38
in misfortune even b. are discredited 751.14
man not b. who is afraid to be a coward 195.28
none but the b. deserves the fair 195.9
we become b. by performing b. actions 227.1
bravery: all b. stands upon comparisons 195.3
bravest: b. spirits do not shrink from danger 195.36
bread: better loaf wet with tears than unsalted b. 504.19
cast thy b. upon the waters 375.1
eaten b. is forgotten 475.4
finest poems are expedients

to get b. 625.1
in sweat of thy face shalt thou eat b. 1065.12
it's hard to pay for b. that's eaten 222.3
who live by b. alone submit to abuse 569.5
breakfast: only dull people are brilliant at b. 605.9
pleasantest prospect indoors: b. table 274.13
breaks: he that b. a thing to find out what it is 211.11
breasts: trying to find those lusty prairie b. 266.16
breath: one possession outvalues others: last b. 539.127
the held b. of a planet's year 854.1
breed: men are more careful of the b. of their dogs, horses, than of their children 670.38
breeding: good b.: concealing how much we think of ourselves, how little of others 391.8
good b. finds favor at first sight 391.2
good b. is man's substitute for good nature 391.1
good b.: union of kindness, independence 391.4
lay aside good b., intimacy degenerates into coarse familiarity 499.1
scholar without good b. is a pedant 391.3
test of b. how one acts in quarrel 391.7
we are rabbit-like in our unplanned b. 713.5
breeze: there, wasn't it a b.? he asked gaily 234.3
brethren: as ye have done it unto one of the least of my b., ye have done it unto me 433.2
brevity: b. good when we are or aren't understood 98.3
b. is the soul of wit 1061.26
life's b. makes architect's trade sad 50.4
brewer: best b. sometimes makes bad beer 457.2
bride: b.: woman with fine prospect of happiness behind her 1051.2
bridge: the finest b. in all Peru broke 116.18
brief: honest b. has its own eloquence 528.20
to be b. is almost to be inspired 98.7
brilliant: only dull people are b. at breakfast 605.9
the b. passes; the true endures 998.51
Britain: in B. journalism is apt to be regarded as an extension of conversation 630.31
British: maxim of B. people: "business as usual" 289.5
no one can be as calculatedly rude as B. 488.1
brittle: much easier to be b. at the age of twenty 917.5
broken: unto a b. heart no other one may go 960.1
bronze: b. is the mirror of form; wine, of heart 268.1
brook: a river that was hardly more than a b. 824.5
voice of b. an obbligato of creation 824.1
brothels: modesty, diffidence make man unfit for public affairs, b. 600.12
brother: sympathetic friend can be dear as b. 365.57
when you deal with your b., be pleasant, but get a witness 334.18
which of us has known his b. 915.54
brotherhood: America is a human b. or it is a chaos 34.40
b. of man precious—what there is of it 100.16
low capacity for getting along with those near goes with receptivity to idea of b. 100.7
where no b. there can be no peace 681.18
world is a neighborhood before becoming b. 1067.20
brother's: primal eldest curse on a b. murder 518.12
brothers: because men are unequal they need to be b. 471.2
between b., two witnesses and a notary 334.29
cruel is the strife of b. 334.3
freedom is to share chains our b. wear 363.35
if b. agree, no fortress so strong 334.2
live like b., do business like strangers 104.2
browsing: b., time for formation of impressions 446.14
brute: man that blushes is not quite a b. 893.9
brutes: b. show wisdom in enjoying the present 41.29
Buchenwald: my father gave back his soul at B. 221.138
budget: b. is a mythical bean bag 101.3
federal b. reflects need of the people 101.2
buffoons: we are the b. of our children 670.1
build: if you b. it, he will come 78.10
too low they b., who b. beneath the stars 55.21
when we b., let us think we b. for ever 50.18
why b. cities, if man unbuilded goes 133.21
building: b. filled with books and unimaginably vast 538.1
if design of b. bad, antiquity is its only virtue 50.15
light is a principal beauty in a b. 50.5
no b. was safe from the furniture 50.8
buildings: we shape b.; thereafter they shape us 50.3
builds: when one b. and another tears down, what do they gain but toil 241.2
bullet: aimed and fired a b. through his right temple 948.21
man who has forsworn b. is impotent 665.3
bullets: ballots rightful successors to b. 1038.12
bullfighter: the one who matters is the b. 680.8
burden: b. in bush worth two on your hands 810.12
lacking b. he'll take up load of stones 866.5
none knows weight of another's b. 663.5
same b. weighs more heavily on some 199.9
to bear b. of others' faults worst 342.9
burdensome: nothing is so b. as a secret 855.6
bureaucrat: a b. does not like a poem 102.8
burglar: faults of b. are qualities of financier 934.7
burglars: old b. never die; just steal away 934.4
burial: after sixty, b. service becomes personal 367.8
all places alike, every earth fit for b. 699.8
buried: small difference to dead if b. in luxury 103.4
burlesque: something of b. in earnest, good men 886.5
burn: let a man b. with intensity, he will set fire to the world 1073.3
little fire to warm, a great one to b. 186.7
burnt: b. child can't wait to get back at fire 321.36
who has b. his mouth blows his soup 321.17
bury: room to b. his dead on his own land 823.9
burying: We're b. the statue today 263.6
bush: one beats b., another catches the bird 108.3
business: attention to b. is price of success 945.44
big b. dangerous because of privileges 104.36
bonus is one great give-away in b. 104.34
build b. up big enough, it's respectable 104.27
b. of America is b. 104.9
b., reduced to people, product, and profits 104.18
crime is extension of behavior in b. 204.16
dispatch is the soul of b. 104.8
end of this day's b. ere it come! 368.30
everybody's b. is nobody's b. 810.6
if everybody minded their own b., the world would go round faster 575.1
it's better to be at ease than at b. 533.6
live like brothers, do b. like strangers 104.2
man in b. puts up affronts if he loves quiet 104.25
man minds his b., if it's worth minding 575.3
perpetual devotion to b. is sustained by neglect of many other things 104.31
time is the measure of b. 104.3
we must keep b. separate from life 104.15
without dissimulation no b. possible 224.2
businessman: b. buys at ten, is happy to get out at twelve 108.11
b. who is novelist drops in on literature 1069.112
no b. who believes all he is told does well 104.26
what need had b. to scribble or philosophize? 104.20
busy: aging is a habit b. man hasn't time for 653.63
being b. is proof of happiness 10.14
b. life is nearest to a purposeful life 10.7
if thou be not b. for thyself now, who shall be b. for thee in time to come 1065.47
if you want work well done, select b. man 10.8
butter: one cannot shoot with

b. but with guns 1049.3
butterfly: b. counts moments and has time enough 978.68
b. is sure flowers owe thanks to him 399.10
consider ways of b. and get wise 324.1
buy: friend you b. will be bought from you 99.3
he that speaks ill of the mare will b. her 105.5
he who findeth fault meaneth to b. 105.7
if you don't want prosperity to falter, b. 105.16
buying: forgive us for frantic b. and selling 105.22
man's happiness consists in b. all he can 409.41
by-and-by: b. is easily said 231.11
C
cabdriver: philosophical c. on late movies 632.16
cabs: Manhattan c. are born old 632.17
Caesar: render to C. the things that are C.'s 127.1
Cain: he who bears brand of C. shall rule 518.14
Cajun: somewhere lives a bad C. cook 189.6
calamities: c. of two kinds: misfortune to ourselves and good fortune to others 17.8
high heart ought to bear c. and not flee 17.3
regret c. only if it helps the sufferer 698.10
calamity: c. is man's true touchstone 17.5
easy for one outside c. to give advice 19.2
every c. is a spur and valuable hint 17.23
get bored enough with c. and learn to laugh 17.21
he that fashions c. for his neighbor 17.6
in another's c., see what ills to avoid 17.48
public c. is a mighty leveller 17.14
call: he who awaits the c., but sees the need, already sets his spirit to refuse it 791.2
calling: c. George Bush shallow, like c. a dwarf short 1007.10
every c. great when greatly pursued 1037.7
calls: c. and the theater propagate platitudes 188.36
calm: any can hold helm when sea is c. 531.15
calm's not life's crown, though c. is well 989.1
mind which renounces hope grows c. 806.6
there is no joy but c. 989.8
to bear truths with c. is sovereignty 160.1
calmness: nothing is so aggravating as c. 160.4
calumny: be chaste as ice, thou shan't escape c. 905.10
c. ever pursues the great 905.7
mysterious power of flattery and c. 202.4
Cambridge: belief that everything worth knowing at C. wore off 992.40
camel: c.-driver jogs on to end of journey 686.7
easier for c. to go through eye of needle than rich man to enter kingdom of God 1048.6
if c. once get his nose in the tent 191.1
camera: c. can inspire something akin to lust 695.5
c. encourages photographer to keep on looking 695.2
camera's: bleak buildings look beautiful through c. eye 72.50
cameras: c. are much more sure than I am 695.8
camouflage: c. is a game we all like to play 267.12
campaign: effort put into c. by worker 710.9
presidential c. resembles a forced march 1038.11
prosperity first theme of political c. 711.93
solutions not expected in political c. 1038.13
campus: three administrative problems on c. 279.49
Canada: geography made America and C. neighbors 107.1
canal: sluggish c. on the wrong side of the tracks 824.6
candid: save me from the c. friend 362.1
candidate: c. for office can have no greater advantage than muddled syntax 711.55
candidates: merchandise c. like breakfast cereal 1038.19
to c., "every intelligent voter" means those who will vote for them 711.2
candle: better to light a c. than curse darkness 433.7
how far that little c. throws his beams 433.28
Played in a Box whose C. is the Sun 1067.23
unnecessary to light a c. to the sun 56.4
candles: all c. out, all cats gray 297.11
candor: faults forgiven of man of perfect c. 362.10
world of vested interests doesn't want c. 495.9
cannibal: my mother and I play a c. game 218.3
cant: c. of criticism is the most tormenting 207.52
cap: once you have the c. and gown whatever nonsense you talk becomes wisdom 279.61
capacity: c. to accept common sacrifices 190.1
capital: It is going to be the c. of the world 632.18
much cant of common interests of c., labor 108.1
capitalism: c., first step away from fatalism 108.5
c., given us a weapon against Communism 108.13
c. is moving toward its end imperceptibly 108.4
capitalist: c. man was accomplishing moral virtue 108.6
caprice: c. lasts longer than lifelong passion 1053.2
captain's: c. choleric word is blasphemy in soldier 780.19
car: c. has become secular sanctuary 64.6
c. is dress without which we are unclad 64.7
everything in life is somewhere else, and you get there in a c. 64.15
caravan: dogs bark, but the c. moves on 157.2
cards: all men are equal—at c. 369.3
c. are war, in disguise of sport 369.6
sorry I have not learnt to play at c. 369.5
true luck consists not in holding best c. 369.4
care: c. and diligence bring luck 281.7
not to c. is never to be born 466.5
teach us to c. and not to c. 806.3
cares: c. fold tents like Arabs, steal away 614.38
if desires are endless, c. will be so 403.7
those with no c. fear next life 414.4
caresses: ceremonial of c. is convention 901.3
Venus yields to c. 857.11
caricatures: each society reduces its opponents to c. 935.2
carnal: our life ought to be material and c. 716.5
carpenter: the house praises the c. 6.5
the worse the c., the more the chips 463.2
you may scold c. who has made bad table 206.12
carried: who is c. does not realize how far the town is 235.8
cars: people in c. look worse 64.8
case: who can't mend own c. will impair other's 295.3
cases: all c. are unique, and similar to others 758.4
cash: ah, take the c. and let the credit go 729.21
if a little doesn't go, much c. will not come 503.1
caste: ideas are fatal to c. 443.7
castles: if you have built c. in the air 336.18
castration: monastic incarceration is c. 601.1
cat: c. may look on a king 780.7
c. pent up becomes a lion 109.3
escort a c. abroad on a leash 41.33
the c. is never vulgar 41.39
to cross man with c. would improve man, deteriorate c. 41.38
trouble with a kitten is it becomes a c. 41.24
what comes of a c. will catch mice 417.1
catastrophes: c. at regular intervals 737.1
c. come when dominant institution crumbles at the touch of what seems an idea 487.9
catching: with c. end pleasures of chase 8.5
catchwords: one set of c. to girls, another to boys 1064.49
catfish: for the c. he'd bought a pound of steak 348.3
cathedral: synagogue lifts its walls by side of c. 797.35
who bears in his heart a c. 55.15
Catholic: The C. must adopt the decision handed down to him 125.22

Catholic Church: the C., inviolate to my mother and father 125.14
cats: all candles out, all c. gray 297.11
c., a rebuke to behavioral scientists 41.36
c. are delicate but never suffer insomnia 41.15
c. seem to think it never harms to ask 41.16
c. worshipped as in ancient Egypt 41.20
scalded c. fear even cold water 321.16
who won't feed c. must feed mice, rats 936.1
cause: best c. requires a good pleader 111.5
c. breaks or exalts soldier's strength 588.14
faith in c. substitute for faith in self 111.9
faith in holy c. must be extravagant 111.10
First C. worked automatically like a somnambulist 387.37
good c., yet money must carry it 111.7
if a c. be good, attack will not injure it so much as injudicious defense 111.3
in a just c. the weak beat the strong 111.13
just c. needs no interpreting 528.19
just c. never lacks good arguments 111.6
just c. not ruined by a few mistakes 111.4
nothing can be lower than c. of all things 387.60
our least deed wends its way to sea of c. and effect 110.7
strong men believe in c. and effect 110.3
take away c. and effect ceases 110.2
truth never damages a c. that is just 111.8
causes: no more lectures on behalf of good c. 111.12
small c. can make a man uneasy 996.12
cautious: if you cannot be chaste, be c. 122.9
look beyond each action, be very c. 176.9
when a man feels the difficulty of doing, can he be other than c. 112.2
celebrated: we imagine works of c. men are commonly admired because their names are 332.18
celebrity: c. in politics or trade gains esteem for intellectual taste or skill 492.3
c.: I picture myself as a bust with legs 332.10
c.: known by those who don't know you 332.8
c.'s name is worth more than services 332.7
c. works to be known, then shields face 332.3
the c. is created by the media 418.2
we have made God the biggest c. 387.9
celebrities: We make c. not only of the men who cause events 967.14
celerity: c. never more admired than by negligent 926.4
no secrecy comparable to c. 926.1
celestial: one c. father gives to all 387.49
celibacy: marriage has pains, c. no pleasures 66.4
purpose of fasting and c. 122.11
cello: c. is like woman grown younger 615.2
cemetery: c.: only place we do not meet dead again 103.8
censoriousness: hating leaves to virtue nothing but c. 412.10
censors: no government ought to be without c. 113.5
censorship: assassination is extreme form of c. 113.9
c. a stupid giant traffic policeman 113.1
c. may preserve, but not restore, morality 113.8
we get nervous about freedom and admit c. 113.2
where official c., speech is serious 113.3
censure: c. is tax paid for being eminent 206.25
c. of man's self is oblique praise 863.6
folly to c. him whom all the world adores 206.20
he has right to c. who has heart to help 206.19
let such c. freely who have written well 207.42
take each man's c., but reserve judgment 206.24
censured: none are so much praised, c., as we think 1027.5
census: we are at mercy of c.-taker and c.-maker 932.1
century: problem of twentieth c. is color-line 775.6
ceremony: c. forbids, we obey; reason forbids, nobody obeys 749.4
man without c. needs great merit 563.13
certain: it is c. that nothing is c. 115.3
there is little about which one can be c. 115.9
we are not c., we are never c. 1005.2
certainties: c. are arrived at only on foot 115.12
certainty: belief in divine mission a form of c. 335.15
c. generally is illusion 115.6
one unchangeable c. is nothing is certain 115.8
only earthly c. is oblivion 990.18
quest for c. blocks the search for meaning 1005.5
reasonable probability is only c. 115.7
this kind of c. comes only once 115.13
woman's guess is more accurate than man's c. 581.29
chaining: in c. multitude, seem to wear same fetters 1002.30
chains: if any in c., all freedom endangered 109.4
intelligence in c. loses in lucidity 493.5
chair: a c. in which a man could move and sit still 479.2
challenge: measure of a man: his stand in time of c. 252.7
chamber pots: ivory knickknacks, fly whisks, and musical c. 318.8
chance: be a football to time and c. 504.7
call life today your own, rest belongs to c. 116.7
c. favors the prepared mind 116.12
c. gives and removes thoughts 116.11
c. makes a football of man's life 116.16
c. to fight for God and country 1042.9
does random c., change, control the world 265.1
great actions often are result only of c. 227.13
no shame in the accidents of c. 1070.17
we are ruled by c. 116.6
who await no gifts from c., conquer fate 116.3
why need man fear since c. is all in all 116.17
chances: life is full of c. and changes 116.2
change: accept past till need for c. cries out 117.17
all is c.; all yields place and goes 117.11
as nature abhors a vacuum, humans resist c. 117.16
be content with what you are; wish not c. 937.5
c. as c. is flux, and insults intelligence 117.7
c. is death of that which was 117.26
c. is scientific, progress is ethical 117.31
c. is the law of life 117.23
c. prepares the ground for revolution 819.21
displacement of a little sand can c. the course of deep rivers 996.2
for happiness, man needs hope and c. 409.83
from c. to c. men's being rolls 117.1
habit will reconcile us to all but c. 406.4
happy who learns to bear what he cannot c. 806.8
in c. unhappiness remembers happiness 117.12
in worst of fortune is best chance for c. 360.13
loss is c. and c. is nature's delight 550.1
love fears c. more than destruction 551.146
man delights in mere c. of activity 1065.52
more things c., more they remain same 117.22
nothing is permanent but c. 117.19
only in c. is true security to be found 856.11
progress is a nice word but c. is its motivator 117.24
state without c. is without means of conservation 930.5
there's relief in c.—even bad to worse 117.21
time works c. for better or worse 117.30
to remain young one must c. 117.6
we only c. our fancies 452.5
when the man you like switches, he has courage to c. his mind 464.1
who tries to c. his life tries in vain 790.16
changed: universe c. by inspiring people 790.24
changelessness: happiness is never so welcome as c. 118.3
changes: absurd man is he

who never c. 117.2
c. are melancholy; part of us is left behind 117.14
cultural c. begin in affectation 117.3
life is full of chances and c. 116.2
many social c. are irreversible 118.4
weep not that the world c. 117.4
changing: it's a happy chance if we, c., continue to love a changed person 551.129
chaos: c., more fruitful than a regularity 257.3
c. often breeds life; order, habit 257.1
Out of c. God made a world 387.16
tried to give pattern to the c. 859.2
chap: give it up, old c.! sleep it off! 470.4
character: all c. can be destroyed by ridicule 820.6
American c. looks always as if it had just had a rather bad haircut 34.44
between selves and real natures we put our c. 119.17
can't smell c. unless it stinks 119.7
c. forms at first pinch of anxiety 119.31
c. is inured habit 119.25
c. much easier kept than recovered 119.24
c. not developed in ease and quiet 119.16
c. tested by sentiments more than conduct 119.1
conscience is the frame of c. 174.1
genius formed in quiet; c., in life stream 119.14
happiness is not the end of life: c. is 119.4
his own c. is arbiter of one's fortune 119.26
judge your c. by your dreams 266.4
knowledge has outstripped c. development 279.20
life is what our c. makes it 867.9
look at eye: how can man conceal c. 119.20
man's c. is his guardian divinity 119.15
man's real c. comes out in asides 119.27
more peculiarly his own a man's c. is, the better it fits him 119.6
mystery should be left in c. 972.40
nobody can think himself a strong c. 940.3
no man can climb out beyond the limitations of his own c. 119.21
no public c. ever stood revelation of private utterance, correspondence 332.1
one can acquire all in solitude but c. 915.45
opinion of world is confession of c. 119.10
people betray c. in what they laugh at 526.12
people with courage, c., seem sinister 195.15
religion of c. apt to be invaded by religious training 797.20
society: masked ball where all hide c. 914.1
space of life in which c. is undecided 1071.37
terrible and questionable c. of existence 558.29
trust c. more than an oath 635.6
ultimate test of nation's c. 119.22
value of culture is its effect on c. 210.18
we find the finished c. only in fragments 684.5
we may be whatever c. we choose 867.1
we need someone on whom to mould our c. 310.3
what a man is depends on his c. 129.6
who plays deep must lose money or c. 369.1
character's: when c. right, looks are greater delight 119.23
characters: as if our own handiwork, we value our c. 119.11
others are to us like c. in fiction 663.10
wealth with us a moment; only our c. steadfast 1048.20
when c. are alive before their author 344.24
chariot: Time's wingéd c. hurrying near 978.41
charitable: he is rich who hath enough to be c. 1048.11
charities: posthumous c. are selfish made by those who, when alive, would part with nothing 1058.1
charity: all mankind's concern is c. 120.8
c. gives itself rich 384.11
c., personal force are the only worthwhile investments 120.11
c. that is trifle to us can be precious to others 888.6
did universal c. prevail, earth would be a heaven, hell a fable 120.2
generosity relinquished to practice c. 433.5
he that has no c. deserves no mercy 120.3
how shall we expect c. towards others, when we are uncharitable to ourselves 863.1
in all things, c. 119.3
little fear that God will damn a man that has c. 120.7
silver ore of c. an expensive article 120.10
unreal is c. without sympathy 9.5
with malice toward none, c. for all 1016.6
would we hold liberty, we must have c. 120.4
charm: c. is glow that casts light on others 121.3
c. of women and the courage of men 545.7
c.: that quality in others of making us more satisfied with ourselves 121.1
charmer: a beauty you notice; a c. notices you 121.5
charming: all c. people, I fancy, are spoiled 121.6
c. people live up to edge of charm 121.4
city of Southern efficiency and Northern c. 1044.2
people are either c. or tedious 121.7
charms: do not all c. fly at touch of philosophy 694.13
chase: with catching end pleasures of c. 8.5
chaste: be warm, but pure; be amorous, but be c. 122.3
I flee who c. me, and c. who flees me 198.13
if you cannot be c., be cautious 122.9
only c. woman is one not asked 122.10
twenty lascivious turtles found ere c. man 122.8
chastise: he only may c. who loves 766.18
chastity: c. in old man: disability to be unchaste 122.4
c. is orientation of life towards goal 122.2
c. often the effect of lack of appetite 122.5
give me c., but not just now 122.1
woman's c., like onion, is series of coats 122.7
chatter: I c., c., as I flow 824.8
Chautauqua: When you've got a C. in your head 335.14
cheap: never buy what you do not want because it is c.; it will be costly to you 105.14
what we obtain too c., we esteem lightly 1026.16
cheat: c. me in price, not in goods 105.21
man must be careful not to c. neighbor 604.11
cheated: when c., wife or husband feels same 472.2
cheating: better fail with honor than win by c. 329.22
checking: her manipulation of their joint c. account 880.4
cheek: where's the c. that doth not fade 333.7
whoever shall smite thee, turn other c. 665.1
cheer: the more skillful the performance of false c. 224.13
cheerfulness: c. is a habit of mind; mirth, an act 392.1
c. is proper to the cock 82.6
the more c. is spent, the more remains 392.4
cheese: can't govern country with 246 kinds of c. 361.4
c.—milk's leap toward immortality 355.7
chemistry: laws of gravity, c., botany 849.7
chess: man hates to be beaten at c. by woman 581.66
Chicago: just as long as I'd be in C. tomorrow 131.25
chiding: c. is better than heartbreak 803.9
chief: c. assumes responsibility 531.17
chiefs: multiple c. disappear for lack of unity 531.13
child: a c. is a person 123.63
a c. looks on old things with new eyes 1071.17
all women fight fiercely for a c. 670.17
beat your c. once a day; he knows why 766.5
burnt c. can't wait to get back at fire 321.36
c. does not fear thought of aging 123.49
c. fussed over gets feeling of destiny 123.55

c. is father of the man 404.30
c., not a prisoner of its inheritance 404.3
c. not smiled on by mother is not worthy of the gods 123.20
c. should always say what's true 123.56
c. understands fear, hurt, and hate 343.18
depend on c.: blindness in one eye 235.7
each c. may be new, poetic experience 670.22
easier to head institute for c. guidance than make brat into decent human 670.31
energy which makes c. hard to manage is energy which later makes him manage life 123.5
everyone thinks own c. handsome 166.11
give little love to c., get great deal 123.47
greatest reverence is due to a c. 670.28
hard words bruise the heart of a c. 123.35
more to be learned from questions of c. 480.15
mother glad to get loveliest c. asleep 123.14
presence of c. turns parents into idiots 670.12
sharper than serpent's tooth: thankless c. 475.7
the c. is small, and its world is small 123.12
the most important influence on a c. 404.9
to make c. in your own image a capital crime; your image not worth repeating 670.48
train up a c. in the way he should go 988.1
what should a simple c. know of death 123.62
when a woman is twenty, a c. deforms her; at forty, he makes her her young again 670.8
when c. has left room, toys are affecting 123.13
when I was a c., I spake as a c. 571.2
who takes c. by hand takes mother by heart 123.10
wise father knows his own c. 670.47
wretched c. does not return parents' care 475.2
childhood: as I get older, c. self is more accessible 540.14
c. brings heaven to our rough earthliness 123.1
c. is a short season 123.24
c. is the kingdom where nobody dies 123.38
c., old man will seek it in a thousand ways 653.101
moment in c. when world changes forever 123.23
our c. is what we alone have had 123.59
people who talk about the joys of c. 123.3
second c. falls on so many men 653.96
supports an eternal c. for some 848.4
the great golden goal of every c. 404.18
what we remember from c. we remember forever 580.26
childishness: last scene of all is second c., oblivion 653.86
childless: noblest works come from c. men 201.2
childlike: c. man not one whose development has been arrested 404.13
children: after c. born begins the trouble, care 988.5
age shows what c. we remain 653.35
all c. find chaos congenial 123.61
all men know their c. mean more than life 670.14
best way to advise your c. 670.53
can't a state provide eggs and milk for c.? 668.4
capable men are c. more than once a day 452.4
c. are always cruel 209.9
c. are anchors that hold a mother to life 123.54
c. are completely egoistic 123.21
c. are God's apostles of love and hope 123.36
c. are natural mythologists 123.51
c. are poor men's riches 123.16
c. are ruined through virtues of parents 670.11
c. are the true connoisseurs 123.31
c., better observers of adults' character 123.6
c. discern true law of life 539.126
c. don't understand they are being cheated 123.32
c. endow parents with immortality 670.43
c. entitled to otherness, as anyone is 123.45
c. have intelligence, ardor, clarity 123.28
c. have never failed to imitate elders 123.4
c. have reverted to being little devils 123.48
c., living messages we send to time 123.43
c. need models rather than critics 123.30
c. notice things first, people later 123.42
c., on whom we can safely take revenge 817.18
c. perceive injustice 123.11
c. pick up words as pigeons peas 123.44
c. rarely forgive their parents 123.60
c. should be led by persuasion 988.9
c. sweeten labours but make misfortunes more bitter 670.3
c. were strangers you loved 123.37
c. will not fear life if their elders do not fear death 541.8
excessive love of c. at expense of men 551.184
gods visit sins of fathers on the c. 815.6
hypocrisy deceives men; c. recognize it 440.20
impossible to love one's c. all day long 670.44
in America parents obey their c. 34.90
in survival of c., parents can think of world in which they will have no share 670.37
less comfort having c. than sorrow in parting with them 670.23
let c. walk with nature, and they will learn that death is stingless 623.56
life of c. is wholly governed by desires 123.2
life's aspirations come in the guise of c. 123.57
love, c., work are sources of contact 504.20
man lucky if c. make his happiness 670.16
men are but c. of a larger growth 562.17
men more careful of breed of dogs than c. 670.38
men not on speaking terms with c. cease to be men, become machines 123.58
mothers more devoted to c. than fathers 670.2
no end to violations by c. on c. 123.8
no greater pain for mortals than seeing their c. dead 221.48
no test for parentage in interest of c. 670.49
resources go to c. of highest bidder 602.33
rich and poor alike love their c. 670.15
some seem as if they were never c. 404.23
sorrow makes us all c. again 918.16
stars through window pane are my c. 623.42
the c. have left for school 123.18
to know what is true, I ask my c. 558.12
to produce music is also to produce c. 614.42
unfortunate for chubby c. to watch basketball, regard it as their exercise 696.4
we are more taken with the games of our c. than with their complete actions 123.39
we are the buffoons of our c. 670.1
we delight in beauty, happiness of c. 123.15
who loves not c. broods nest of sorrows 334.33
wife and c. hostages to fortune 334.5
your c. are sons and daughters of life's longing for itself 123.22
child's: c. liberty concealed from him 363.3
c. nature too serious to be regarded as a mere appendage to another being 123.33
entering into the c. point of view 123.41
great man is he who does not lose c. heart 478.5
chill: November's sky is c. and drear 854.36
chimera: what a c. then is man 562.47
chimney: exit is by way of the c. 735.7
China: a natural Great Wall of C. 380.1
chivalries: by c. the seeds of smiles are planted 519.6
choice: c. compels c. 124.5
door of c. is not open to thee or me 186.12
doubts and temptations accompany every important c. 940.3
every c. is a risk, with consequences 886.1

life's terrible c. is between good, bad 390.2
necessity relieves us from c. 624.17
principle of growth lies in human c. 404.6
reason also is c. 785.20
very few live by c. 360.21
what man wants is independent c. 124.3
who does anything by custom makes no c. 213.17
chlorophyll: I have no truck with lettuce, cabbage and similar c. 274.25
chocolate: eating an entire box of c. liqueurs 1029.2
choices: men have thousand desires to bushel of c. 238.4
choose: you c., you live the consequences 124.1
chooseth: as a man c. so is he 124.4
Christ: C. wrote nothing 545.20
must then a C. perish in every age 565.13
Christendom: with the Pope, one of two great defenders of C. 330.20
Christian: in Christendom where is the C. 125.6
no man a C. who cheats his fellows 125.17
the C. idea of a perfect heaven 414.5
true C. a pilgrim and a stranger 125.23
Christianity: glory of C. is to conquer by forgiveness 125.1
idealistic C. is attacked by idealists 125.8
most sects of C. pervert its essence 125.12
no one is without C. 125.9
truth is only a horse for C. 125.7
Christians: great clots of white C. 520.12
in visible church true C. are invisible 126.9
own dealing teaches C. to suspect others 259.14
what makes good C. makes good citizens 132.12
Christian's: prayer is a goodly C. weapon 723.23
Christmas: irony of C. is upon the poor in heart 420.1
Christ's: no kingdom suffered as many wars as C. 125.20
Church: the C. gave ceremony and dignity to lives 126.12
church: beautiful to have c. always open 128.1
c. must be the conscience of the state 127.4
disputation will prove scab of c. 126.14
end of being is to harmonize man with order; c. has been a good pitch-pipe 797.34
go to funeral, not c., to be uplifted 367.10
holy man without learning: enemy of c. 127.5
how often we go to c. only to see company 152.5
if you talked in c., you were bad 119.19
in c. false sentiment is frequent 126.7
in c., true Christians are invisible 126.9
many bring clothes to c., not selves 128.4
my own mind is my own c. 126.10
once or twice a year we go to c. 797.80
who builds c. to God, not to fame 435.19
who is near the c. is often far from God 126.8
churches: no objection to c. so long as they do not interfere with God's work 126.1
people in c. seem like cheerful tourists 126.5
cigar: a c. smoked in anger 982.15
good c. is a smoke 982.7
cigarette: smokers inject idleness with every c. 982.3
circulation: feel the c. of the communal blood 514.6
circumstance: c. gives an action its character 598.12
circumstances: c. are the creatures of man, not man of c. 129.2
c. over which individual has no control 1026.12
it is futile to rail at c. 129.1
some look for c., or make them 129.5
what a man does depends on his c. 129.6
circus: a toothless old c. lion kept around the house 797.4
c.: where horses see men acting the fool 130.1
citadel: man, like spider, may spin his own c. 450.18
cities: c. are, by definition, full of strangers 131.20
c. degrade us by magnifying trifles 131.13
c. produce corrupt, ferocious men 131.19
in c. poverty has different appearances 718.37
in great c. men are more callous 131.8
neglecting our c., we neglect the nation 131.24
sweetest souls soon canker in c. 131.27
citizen: c. wiser than fathers of country 132.3
humblest c., with righteous cause, stronger than all the hosts of error 822.2
not same to be good man and good c. 132.1
political action highest responsibility of c. 711.42
requisite of good c. is to pull weight 132.8
state is servant, not master, of the c. 930.12
citizens: before man made us c. nature made us men 431.15
c. are free to invent for themselves 359.11
c. equally free, not equally powerful 132.10
in America there must be only c. 132.6
no such things as private c. 760.4
what makes good Christians makes good c. 132.12
citizenship: c.: the right to have rights 132.11
city: a c. for only the very young 632.4
a large c. is a chaos of details 131.37
an inner c. without an outer c. 131.26
c.: aggregate of incongruous materials 131.14
c. has a face; country, a soul 194.6
c. man knows nothing of midnight 131.40
commuters give c. its restlessness; natives give it solidity; settlers give it passion 131.43
confusion, epitome of what c. is herself 131.46
God the first garden made, and the first c. Cain 131.11
great c. has greatest men and women 131.44
great c. is not the same as populous one 131.2
illness of American c. is voicelessness 131.12
I mean that I was in love with the c. 632.3
in the big c. a man will disappear suddenly 131.18
it takes a real c. to keep renewing itself 131.28
men, not houses, make the c. 131.15
no c. should be too large for a man to walk out of in a morning 131.10
quiet c. is a contradiction in terms 131.5
the c. is squalid and sinister 131.31
thing generally raised on c. land: taxes 131.41
this great c. has allowed me to dream 632.22
to know and be not known, live in a c. 131.9
very populous c. is rarely well governed 131.3
we don't get life in the c. 131.17
what is the c. but the people 131.39
civic: without c. morality communities perish 604.33
civil war: as much hate and cruelty as c. 1043.3
civil: c. dissension is a viperous worm 252.11
c.-rights movement has restored dignity of indignation 823.20
c. service a fortress of forms, red tape 102.6
civility: c. not sign of weakness 901.12
civilization: a long last night over c. 133.20
an increasingly manipulated mass c. 468.4
babies and language, essential ingredients of c. 923.34
can't make c. around core of militarism 588.15
child of c. susceptible to nature 623.50
c. advances; each war they kill a new way 133.23
c. could not exist until there was written language 133.16
c. exists so there may be no masses 682.2
c. favors mind at expense of body 133.22
c. has forgotten the chief business of life 104.24
c. is a movement, not a condition 133.28
c. is barbarism in lamb's skin 133.1
c. is condition of present customs 213.9
c. is the making of civil persons 133.25

c. of one epoch becomes manure of next 133.7
combustion of present with past forms c. 133.6
crimes of c. worse than those of barbarism 133.2
every advance in c. has been denounced as unnatural while recent 133.26
farmers are founders of human c. 337.9
good c., a tree; bad c., an umbrella 133.4
In an automobile c. 967.12
model of modern Western c. is the virus 133.13
provision for poor is true test of c. 433.16
savagery is necessary antidote to c. 70.2
shall we confer our c. on peoples that sit in darkness 458.5
social moulds c. fits us into 133.14
speech is c. itself 923.42
survival of c. depends on what man desires 956.5
test of c. is kind of man it turns out 133.10
there is no high c. without ample leisure 533.1
too many imagine they belong to higher c. 133.31
triumph of c.: taming of human male 133.18
Western c., because of fortuitous historical circumstances 133.3

civilizations: activities introducing c. to each other 133.11
ancient c., eruptions from a human core 719.36
c. die from philosophical calm 133.15

civilized: anybody can gain a reputation for being c. 267.32
c. get more out of life than uncivilized 504.6
c. man: free, talking of what he may do 133.5
c. man is a larger mind but more imperfect nature than the savage 133.12
c. man's pastime: croolty to other c. man 133.9
c. race would add art of playing well 703.8
men have been barbarians longer than c. 70.3
nature is rarely allowed into c. society 133.30
test of a c. person is self-awareness 875.6

clams: a powerful call to c. on the half shell 853.11

clarification: sanity, soundness, flourish in culture of c. 648.2

clarity: c. is politeness of man of letters 134.7

class: diminution of reality of c. lessens our ability to see difference, specialness 135.7
in c. society, thinking branded by its c. 135.4
independence: that's middle class c. blasphemy 235.9
live for others: middle c. morality 587.6
middle c. unit: couple living moderately 587.5
planning ahead is a measure of c. 135.6

classic: all true art is c. 53.109
c.: man one can praise without reading 136.2
the literary model we call the c. 136.3

classical: c. artist recognized by his sincerity 53.104

classics: public swallow their c. whole 136.6

claws: thought themselves good because they had no c. 1047.10

clay: one can't make pure c. of time's mud 321.34

clean: c. glove often hides dirty hand 224.5
God looks at the c. hands 425.14

cleanliness: c. is not next to godliness nowadays 137.1
what separates people most is sense of c. 137.7

clear: error would die if given c. expression 299.33
matter becomes c., ceases to concern us 134.5
there is a poignancy in all things c. 134.8

clearly: what is conceived well is expressed c. 134.1

clearness: c. produces despair, despair produces c. 239.9

clemency: c. is the support of justice 583.4

clement: be not so c. as to encourage boldness 890.3

clergy: c. are men as well as other folks 138.2
c., no more lecherous than other men 138.9
c. would have us believe them against our own reason 138.8

clergyman: c. the father of too large a family 138.6
we expect c. to be a kind of human Sunday 138.1

clever: all c. men are birds of prey 139.3
be good, and let who will be c. 393.26
desire to appear c. prevents us being so 139.6
good rule of thumb: too c. is dumb 139.7
if just they are better than c. 517.47
progress in cunning: not to seem too c. 200.3

cleverness: bold are helpless without c. 139.4

climate: lands favoured in c. not always happiest 12.1
who rush across sea change c., not soul 992.28

climax: that c. looks like a resolution 892.6

climb: if thy heart fails thee, c. not at all 755.9
when you feel how slowly you c. 6.10

climbed: who never c. high never fell low 33.7

climber: c. scorns degrees by which he did ascend 945.40

climbing: c. performed in creeping posture 33.23

clock: c. makes time mere change and no wealth 978.69

closer: c. is He than breathing 387.70

clothes: beware enterprises that require new c. 267.28
c., manners, greatly improve appearance 267.2
fine c. are good only as they supply the want of other means of procuring respect 267.11
fine c. may disguise a fool 356.2
if your c. are worn to the same state, it means you go out too much 914.3
in c. as well as speech, the man of sense shuns extremes 267.13
many bring c. to church, not themselves 128.4
poor body, time taught you use of c. 90.1
wash your filthy c. when I come home 581.26
would men retain rank without their c. 780.23

cloud: every c. engenders not a storm 715.2

clouds: he that regardeth the c. shall not reap 112.1
who knows whither the c. have fled 1050.7

cloudy: c. day has influence on constitutions 1050.1

clown: art of the c.: comic mirror of tragedy, tragic mirror of comedy 144.3

clowns: wisest people are the c., like Harpo Marx 1060.14

cloy: best of things, beyond their measure, c. 312.3

clubs: c. produce words, not thought 188.8

clutter: c., things useless but friendly 716.10

coat: man with good c. meets better reception 267.10

cocaine: c. sets their bodies adrift 269.5

cock: cheerfulness is proper to the c. 82.6
every c. is proud on his own dunghill 873.7
when the c. is drunk, he forgets the hawk 268.3

cockroach: chief difference between mankind and c. 937.8

cocks: crow in the company of c. 171.13

cocktail party: c., what you call it when you invite everyone 672.3

cocoon: American woman has not yet slipped into a c. 1062.55

coffee: c. should be black as hell 141.1

coffee-makers: women, never again going to be mindless c. 711.80

coffin: he who is not in c. has enough 539.132

coiffures: with c. squeezed from an icing gun 407.4

coin: every word from the mouth is a c. lost 149.10

Cokes: there ain't no C. in hell 416.1

cold: c. in clime are c. in blood 142.1
c. is agreeable that we may get warm 117.29
first extreme c. generates sociability 1050.11
we call a man c., when he's only sad 142.4

collar: Englishman never takes his c. off when he is writing 289.19

colleagues: there but for the grace of God go my c. 766.8

collections: who assemble c. are like cherry eaters 773.1

collectivist: c. age wants perpetual holiday from self 912.6

collector: c. sees nothing but the prize 8.6
first-rate c. can collect his wits 160.3
college: aim of c. is to eliminate need for c. 279.60
c. offered chance to play football 929.17
takes five years to recover from c. education 279.6
the c. years are civilization's only chance 279.11
colleges: c.: where pebbles polished, diamonds dimmed 279.46
concourses of youth are flocking to our c. 532.8
meek young men grow up slaves in c. 279.21
color: c. is the poet's wealth 708.104
not be judged by the c. of their skin but by the content of their character 775.12
problem of twentieth century is c.-line 775.6
purest and thoughtful minds love c. most 143.3
regardless of c. all need same nourishment 297.21
colored: not healthy when nation lives within a nation, as the c. live inside America 85.5
colors: c. speak all languages 143.1
columnist's: gossip c. business not his business 630.14
columnists: to political c., "every thinking man" means themselves 711.2
combat: easier to lead men to c. than peace 1042.37
come: we never shall c. back again 673.8
comedian: all c. has to show is echo of laughter 144.1
comedians: c. consider human experience unbearable ordeal 144.4
c., nearest to suicide 948.8
comedy: c.: an experience of underinvolvement 145.13
c. is escape from despair into faith 145.4
c. naturally wears itself out 145.5
people you like invariably have a sense of c. 145.10
rules of c. those of taste; limitations, of libel 145.12
tragedy, c., are simply questions of value 987.7
we couldn't live without c. 145.8
world is a c. to those that think 1067.29
writers of c. have outlook 987.15
comets: c. are the nearest thing to nothing 415.8
old men and c. reverenced for same reason 653.98
comfort: bourgeois prefers c. to pleasure 587.4
c. in knowing he could knock down anybody 910.3
c.: state of mind produced by contemplation of neighbor's uneasiness 156.1
lust for c. enters the house a guest 557.3
no c. in adversity more sweet than art 53.3
society in shipwreck is a c. to all 152.17
comfortable: c. people worry over trivial things 996.5
man cannot be c. without own approval 869.14
more men feel c. doing public speaking 581.58
you canna expect to be baith grand and c. 332.5
comic: the c., when human, takes face of pain 145.3
command: c. wisely, be obeyed cheerfully 531.7
do not c. what you cannot enforce 531.20
harder to c. great things than to do them 531.14
how shall I rule others without c. of myself 862.12
learn to obey before you c. 644.8
only one in c. in home or state 395.19
commander: who has not learned to obey cannot be c. 531.1
commandment: the eleventh c. 711.71
commandments: accepting God's c. because they come from God 435.24
decalogue: enough c. to permit selection 604.2
easier to keep holidays than c. 420.3
commands: c. to be obeyed when issued by a woman 521.4
man who c. must have obeyed in the past 531.2
men not important; what counts is who c. 531.4
who obeys is usually better than who c. 644.5
commentaries: every place swarms with c. 207.37
works of nature acquire meaning by c. 623.63
commentator: science brought forth radio c. 576.2
commerce: c. is led by the strong, works against weak 104.6
honour sinks where c. long prevails 104.16
in democracies, nothing is greater than c. 104.32
commercial: c. society: people as bundles of appetites 736.8
singing c.: America's litany 34.72
the c., invention of a Christian nation 18.10
commercials: modern Little Red Riding Hood, reared on singing c. 18.9
commitment: beauty of strong c. often best understood by a man incapable of it 146.2
committee: c. is group of unwilling, picked from unfit, to do unnecessary 147.3
c. keeps the minutes and loses hours 147.1
we carry out by c. anything in which one of us would be too reasonable to persist 147.2
commodity: man feels himself to be a c. 105.6
common: c. man may have no soul, but he consumes 105.17
life in c. only possible when majority stronger than any separate individual 913.8
only in politics are we content with c. man 711.35
sweets grown c. lose their dear delight 333.10
that held most in c. gets least care 810.1
commonest: c. thing is delightful if one hides it 612.10
common law: c., combination of custom and adaptations 517.20
commonplace: no longing sweeter to artist than longing after bliss of the c. 53.82
nothing so c. as wish to be remarkable 33.10
commonplaces: c.: tramways of intellectual transportation 612.6
communicate: being "Homo sapiens" was to c. 149.7
gestures and facial expressions do c. 149.5
it is easier to c. with spirits 149.11
communicating: c. of self to friend doubles joys 365.14
communication: a medium for c. and reflection 524.27
c. is a continual balancing act 149.1
c., not to be confused with communications 149.9
good c. is stimulating as black coffee 149.12
mass c. communicates massively 149.15
more we elaborate our means of c., the less we communicate 967.25
precision of c. more important than ever 149.18
communism: color of c. was not red but gray 150.15
c. is corruption of dream of justice 150.18
c. is like Prohibition 150.16
c. overthrown by life, thought, dignity 150.7
c., not red but gray 150.154
c. succeeded as scavenger, never as leader 150.10
Lenin told me, in effect, that C. was not working 150.6
success of c. is much that of religion 150.12
Communist: a C. finance house for East-West trade 685.2
communist: c. one who hath yearnings for equal division of unequal earnings 150.4
c. system has some character of religion 150.3
objection to c.: he is not a gentleman 150.14
communists: c. are seeds and the people, soil 150.13
c. committed crimes but didn't stand aside 150.5
c. have done less to damage our society than those who defend us 150.8
c. take away sense of sin 150.9
with c., what is secret is serious and what is public is propaganda 150.1
communities: without civic morality c. perish 604.33
community: a cynical c. is a corrupt c. 491.10
if a c. decides that some conduct is prejudicial 258.4
life is lived in common, but not in c. 151.6
standing in c. requires wealth 1048.61

commuters: c. give city its tidal restlessness 131.43
compact: highest c. with fellow is for truth 1000.2
companion: agreeable c. on journey is as good as a carriage 152.16
c. loves man's qualities; friend, the man 365.18
gave him a c. to make him feel his solitude more keenly 581.63
man knows his c. in a long journey 499.3
no man pleased with c. who does not increase fondness of himself 152.9
with one c., you are half your own 152.11
companionship: accident counts for much in c. 116.1
profounder need for devotion than for c. 146.3
company: A man is known by the c. he organizes 57.5
bad c. is as instructive as debauchery 57.7
better be alone than in bad c. 915.18
did you expect justice from a c. 104.30
every man is like the c. he keeps 57.9
good c., discourse, are sinews of virtue 152.24
how often we go to church only to see c. 152.5
if misery loves c., misery has c. enough 1011.35
learning makes man fit c. for himself 279.30
man known by the c. he organizes 93.1
man loves c. even if only a small candle 152.12
tell me thy c. and I'll tell thee what thou art 57.6
that c. we leave feeling most satisfied with ourselves, we leave most bored 95.5
the c. of the great is good c. 418.35
to be in c. is wearisome 915.48
we do not mind not arriving so much as not having c. on the way 152.3
who must have c. must have at times bad c. 152.1
comparative: all human excellence is c. 311.8
comparison: c. makes men happy or wretched 153.1
comparisons: all bravery stands upon c. 195.3
compassion: by c. we make others' misery our own 698.5
c. for friend should conceal itself 698.15
what value has c. that does not embrace its object 698.17
woman should never move our c. 1062.46
worse than idle is c. if ends in tears 698.19
compensation: this is a world of c. 889.10
compete: too busy with corns and bunions to c. 719.46
competing: c. with others as to who was closest 610.13
competition: men of small intellectual stamina dread c. 941.8
competitions: c. are for horses, not artists 155.1
competitiveness: country's c. starts in the classroom 155.7
complacency: c. is enemy of study 156.7
complain: French c. of everything, and always 361.9
people who cease to c., cease to think 157.4
complaint: c. is the largest tribute to heaven 723.33
compliance: better friendly denial than unwilling c. 791.3
much c., much craft 158.2
complicated: no limit to how c. things can get 110.8
complies: he that c. against his will, is of his own opinion still 158.1
compliment: c. is like a kiss through a veil 159.2
if you cannot get a c., pay yourself one 159.3
sincerity is highest c. you can pay 901.7
compliments: c. are the only things we can pay 159.4
c. cost nothing, yet many pay for them 159.1
woman will doubt everything except c. 1062.74
compose: if two c. one song, the muse fans wrath 155.4
composer: nation creates music; c. arranges it 614.34
composers: c. should write tunes chauffeurs can whistle 614.6
composition: nothing goes by luck in c. 1069.129
things are much finer in c. than alone 410.1
compositions: read over c., strike out passage which you think particularly fine 942.13
compound: a c. of whiskey and after-shave lotion 882.2
compromise: c. may make the outrageous acceptable 711.76
c.: when each feels deprived of just due 162.1
every human benefit is founded on c. 162.2
lean c. better than fat lawsuit 162.4
life is a long second-best, perpetual c. 539.98
compromising: c., the fine art of conciliating 162.6
compulsion: c. neurosis is a caricature of a religion 627.6
computer: man is still the most extraordinary c. 966.14
computers: c. have fostered increase in junk mail 741.12
powers of c., based on avoidance of error 299.5
comrades: bread broken with c. makes us accept values of war 1042.83
comradeship: in c. is danger countered best 216.10
conceal: ability in knowing how to c. ability 200.4
we c. ourselves from ourselves 864.8
concealed: man trying to escape never sufficiently c. 300.6
concealment: commit a crime and there is no c. 204.7
conceals: who c. his disease cannot be cured 165.5
conceit: chief c. concerns ancestry 37.1
c. is vanity forced to appeal to itself 166.8
hole in mind plastered over with c. 166.9
isolation breeds c. 915.52
riskiness of corporate life, a harmless c. 104.12
smaller the mind, the greater the c. 166.1
conceited: c. people carry their comfort with them 166.6
effect on himself satisfies c. man 166.3
concentrate: ability to c. and use time well 945.22
concentrates: knowing one is to be hanged c. the mind 767.2
concert: c. must have on minute animals the effect of terrible thunder 614.61
concessions: rational institution suffers not by c. 487.10
conciseness: pointed sentences sacrifice accuracy to c. 942.12
conclusions: empiricism has sworn never to draw c. 321.45
grown-up c. rest on soft bottom 604.47
concrete: c. cloverleaf our national flower 64.9
condemn: have the face to c. others 803.6
justice will not c. even Devil wrongfully 517.16
there is something to c. in everything 359.13
condemns: fox c. the trap, not himself 782.1
condescend: Don't c. to unskilled labor 1065.3
condition: every man carries entire human c. 562.41
conditioned: c. to behave in almost every desired way 77.11
conditioning: c. aims to make us like our destiny 12.5
condolence: worst cruelties come under the name of c. 960.9
conduct: c. is largest concern of life 77.3
fine c. is always spontaneous 77.23
our c. is true mirror of our doctrine 77.21
right c. is never promoted by ignorance 77.22
we may give advice, but can't inspire c. 19.16
conducting: c., when you draw designs in the nowhere 614.66
conductor: audience depends on c. for its taste 59.6
conductors: c. not to give choreography to audience 614.59
conference: c. maketh a ready man 1069.13
conferences: c. at top level are always courteous 498.3
confess: ridiculous things hardest to c. 168.5
to deny all is to c. all 405.17
confession: c. of faults is next to innocence 168.4
c. of one man humbles all 168.3
confide: we rarely c. in those better than we 169.2
confidence: brisk c. still best with woman copes 857.1
c. is the only bond of friend-

ship 997.7
danger breeds best on too much c. 664.2
no c. in man whose faults you can't see 342.4
one blessing only: c. in self 860.6
public c. is basis of effective government 395.34
skill, c., are an unconquered army 1.9
too dangerous to live through with c. 151.8
we need the c. of friends' help in need 365.38
conflict: any spot on the globe where dispute and c. may erupt 34.15
c., a necessary part of child's education 279.76
conform: public opinion or fear makes all c. 171.5
conformist: c. keeps worried eye on what is in wind 468.7
intelligence lends itself to c. error 171.12
conformists: quality of non-conformists same as c. 91.4
conformity: adjustment is modern synonym for c. 12.7
c., inevitable when folks huddle in rebellion 171.7
c. is the ape of harmony 171.3
c. is to pay our fares to paradise 171.11
c. ultimately governs the suburb 944.2
our expense is almost all for c. 557.2
saddest thing about c. is the ghastly sort of non-conformity it breeds 171.10
we are half ruined by c. 171.18
confrontations: c. causing retreat or war 641.1
confused: I came, I saw, I was c. 257.2
confusion: c., epitome of what the city is herself 131.46
guilt ever at a loss, and c. waits upon it 405.6
Jews are a singular c. 512.7
confusions: happy c. of himself with God 860.4
teach the young the courage of their c. 1001.2
confuted: one may be c. and yet not convinced 51.10
Congress: no American criminal class except C. 172.5
privilege of C. to dispose 172.4
connoisseurs: children are the true c. 123.31
real c. in art reveal its beauty 207.24
conquer: to c. with arms is temporary conquest 173.16
you must c. and rule or serve and lose 859.4
conqueror: a c. is like a cannonball 173.4
only one way of fighting: to be the c. 345.4
conquerors: men, poor strutting peacocks, spread their tails as c. as soon as they can walk 582.1
conquers: who c. others is strong; c. self, mighty 862.9
conquest: right of c. is right of strongest 173.12
conscience: a c. from which memory is not easily erased 174.12
all a man can betray is his c. 79.1
anxiety and c. are powerful dynamos 43.15
bite of c. teaches men to bite 174.25
c. and cowardice are the same things 174.34
c. does make cowards of us all 174.30
c.: guardian of rules of the community 174.19
c. is a coward 174.11
c. is a just but a weak judge 174.10
c. is a warning that someone may be looking 174.21
c. is good for hands and legs 1055.5
c. is not vessel of eternal verities 174.17
c. is the frame of character 174.1
c. is well-bred: stops talking if one wishes 174.2
c. often more expensive than wife, carriage 174.3
creating the c. of the race 174.20
even when there is no law, there is c. 174.27
evil c. is often quiet, but never secure 174.26
few can understand the writer's c. 682.15
friends, books, sleepy c. is ideal life 186.22
good c. is the best divinity 174.9
guilty c. needs no accuser 174.6
human c. remains partially infantile for life 174.7
laws of c. proceed from custom 174.22
my c. hath a thousand tongues 174.31
one thing stands brunt of life: quiet c. 174.8
only happiness: a clear c. or none 174.23
peace above earthly dignities, a still c. 174.29
policy sits above c. 319.5
sell oneself to c., abandon mankind 174.16
state of c. is higher than of innocence 174.18
strongest feelings assigned to the c. express physical antipathies 174.28
value health next to a good c. 413.20
we invent c. and prey on ourselves 174.13
wild liberty breeds iron c. 363.14
conscientious: c. men are less encouraged than tolerated 271.22
nothing as dangerous as c. stupidity 447.19
conscious: gift of c. life is a sense of mystery 175.6
our less c. thoughts, actions, mold lives 1006.1
to be too c. is an illness 175.3
consciousness: c. makes clerk and conqueror equal 175.1
c. of a fact is not knowing it 328.14
suffering is the sole origin of c. 946.11
That awful stranger C. 175.2
the Depression has never disappeared from my c. 178.13
consensus: c. as reconciliation is a fine thing 27.4
c. politics is a cyclical thing 711.89
consent: c. of people is foundation of government 395.1
essence of republican government is c. 233.53
none good enough to govern without c. 395.36
consequences: c. indifferent to our improvement 176.8
conservatism: c. drives the children into radicalism 178.6
success makes men rigid, fanatics about c. 945.27
conservative: c. government is organised hypocrisy 178.3
c. has two good legs, can't walk forward 178.19
c.: statesman enamored of existing evils 178.2
c., willing to pay price of people's suffering 178.4
radical invents views, c. adopts 178.21
radical of one century is c. of next 776.7
Santa Barbara people are c.—not like in L.A. 131.34
the c. is a tame man 528.66
when nation's young men are c., its funeral bell is already rung 178.1
conservatives: all c. are such from personal defects 178.5
c. know institutions conserved by adjusting 487.8
c. nearly always tolerate the demagogue 178.8
in history of mankind, baseness makes c. 419.26
considerateness: c.: not to wound feelings of fellows 517.5
consistency: c. is simply a confession of failures 181.15
foolish c. is hobgoblin of little minds 179.1
lawyer's truth is not truth but c. 528.65
to stick in a rut is called c. 179.6
consistent: can't remain c. with world save by growing inconsistent with our past selves 117.10
c. thinker may be a monomaniac 179.2
who mean to be true contradict selves less than those who try to be c. 464.4
consolation: before affliction digested, c. comes too soon 960.12
classic form of c. is to understand oneself; to elude oneself is the romantic 758.14
worst cruelties come under the name of c. 960.9
consolations: great treasure-chamber of ingenious c. 125.21
consoles: Christianity, above all, c. 125.10
conspiracy: a nation obsessed with the idea of c. 34.78
constancy: c. in love is a perpetual inconstancy 181.6
fickleness of women I love equaled by c. of women who love me 472.10
foolish to experiment on c.

of friend 181.5
measure affection by c. 181.1
obstinacy in bad cause is but c. in a good 111.1
two sorts of c. in love 181.7
constant: there is nothing c. but inconstancy 181.14
were man c., he were perfect 181.11
constituents: breathe the fresh air our c. breathe 711.41
Constitution: C. is more than literature 182.7
one stands in awe of the C. 182.3
constitutions: c. are checks on hasty action of majority 182.8
society's blessings depend on c. 395.2
some deem c. too sacred to be touched 182.5
written c. furnish text to rally people 182.6
construct: those who cannot c. take to pieces 207.18
consul: c.: given office on condition that he leave the country 247.2
consume: it is the duty of the citizen to c. 132.5
urge to c. is fathered by value system 105.8
consumers: future of moppets is to be skilled c. 105.20
consumes: thank God, the common man c. 105.17
consumption: conspicuous c. is a means of reputability 105.23
contemplates: rock pile ceases to be rock pile when man c. it 1035.5
contemporaries: man lives the life of his c. 184.6
think of c. as they ought to be when you have to influence them 790.32
contempt: everything can be borne except c. 185.9
moral c. is greater insult than any crime 185.5
pride that dines on vanity sups on c. 733.6
to be low, but above c., may be high enough to be happy 186.3
contend: never c. with man who has nothing to lose 345.3
content: be c. to seem what you really are 45.18
be c. with what you are, wish not change 937.5
be c. with your lot 186.1
c. may dwell in all stations 186.3
happy and c. because I think I am 409.62
happy who, c. with common lot, hugs shore 856.15
he is poor who does not feel c. 186.13
in whatsoever state I am, to be c. 186.2
my crown is called c. 186.20
nothing will c. him who is not c. with a little 186.10
poor and c. is rich, and rich enough 186.21
subtract these and very little c. would be left 746.9
contented: all fortune belongs to him with c. mind 186.17
he who is c. is rich 186.15
if foolish enough be c., don't show it 186.14
world of c. bodies, discontented minds 750.13
contention: spread the table and c. will cease 274.7
contentment: butterfly preaches c. to toad under harrow 19.15
c. is a warm sty for eaters, sleepers 186.16
c. preserves one even from catching cold 267.17
familiarity breeds c. 333.1
if thou covetest riches, ask but for c. 186.19
seat of c. is in the head 156.2
to know c., let your deeds be few 186.4
continence: give me c., but not just now 122.1
continuation: her life was merely a c. of her mother's 218.5
continuity: c. in everything is unpleasant 117.29
contradict: men c. themselves every day of lives 299.32
speak what you think tomorrow, though it c. what you said today 464.3
tomorrow perhaps I shall c. it all 464.2
contradiction: what a c. is man 562.47
contrast: we derive intense enjoyment only from c. 187.2
contrasts: we live a life of c. and patchwork 539.32
contribution: only c. is to warm a seat at the table 446.6
control: he who yields a prudent obedience exercises a partial c. 644.4
social practices, c. of one person by another 913.32
controlled: some wilfully go wrong for fear of being c. 652.7
controversial: all who reflect on c. matters should be free from hatred, friendship, anger, pity 252.4
controversies: most savage c. are those to which there is no good evidence either way 51.18
controversy: theological c. is worse than useless 973.3
who shows better temper scores most in c. 51.4
convalescence: c. makes illness worth while 896.28
c. shrinks man back to pristine stature 896.14
convenience: bourgeois prefers c. to liberty 587.4
convent: c. is supreme egotism 601.2
convention: supposed to be a delegate to a visiting c. 267.21
there is nothing sacred about c. 213.26
conversation: art of c. is a certain self-control 188.9
art of c. is hearing as well as being heard 188.18
confidence gives more to c. than wit 188.22
c. a dialogue, not a monologue 188.4
c., an interpenetration of worlds 188.27
c.: display of minor mental commodities 188.3
c. is an endeavour at effect 188.20
c.: one of the greatest pleasures in life 188.24
c. on very gentle subjects 188.12
c. which passes for agreeable is made up of civility and falsehood 440.17
c. with wise man better than books 279.52
happiest c. is calm quiet interchange 188.19
in c. consider whether man has inclination to hear you or that you hear him 188.33
it is a fault in c. for one man to take up all the discourse 188.34
listen closely, reply well is art of c. 188.23
man of no c. should smoke 982.4
marriage is one long c. 564.123
mingle c. with instruction 532.7
more the pleasures of the body fade, greater is the pleasure of c. 188.29
private, accidental c. breeds thought 188.8
repose as necessary in c. as in picture 188.17
success in c.: bringing out wit in others 188.21
the best of life is c. 188.10
wit in c. is a quick conception and an easy delivery 188.30
wit is salt of c., not the food 1061.11
writing is lonely substitute for c. 1069.9
conversations: rules about taking turns in c. 188.11
converse: many c. by giving history of their pains 188.35
converted: man not c. because he is silenced 985.5
convertible: teacher's conviction that men are c. 965.11
converts: charming women can true c. make 690.6
time makes more c. than reason 978.47
conviction: a profound c. that I was no good 869.9
it is your own c. that compels you 124.5
my c. that the public always shows itself more honest 123.53
conviction's: snug lie those slumbering beneath c. roof 654.5
convictions: c. are worse enemies of truth than lies 78.14
easy to praise men for courage of c. 1001.2
painless c. are worthless 78.21
tolerance best achieved by those without c. 984.1
convince: to c., seem open to conviction 51.6
convinced: men c. of your sincerity only by your death 221.24
one may be confuted and yet not c. 51.10
conviviality: what is the odds when the fire of soul is kindled at the taper of c. 152.4
cook: good c. is a certain slow poisoner 189.9
good c. is the peculiar gift of the gods 189.5

cookery: c. is now noble science; cook, a gentleman 189.2
kissing don't last: c. do 521.7
cooking: c. should be entered into with abandon 189.4
the odor of c. goes on forever 189.10
cooks: bad c. have delayed human development 189.7
c. and maids who talked so affectedly 923.41
God sends meat and the Devil sends c. 189.3
our lives are in the lap of our c. 355.18
coolly: to do anything c. is to do it genteelly 160.2
cooperation: c. whose maintenance is the stuff of law 190.2
cop: sleeping c. in all of us must be killed 709.5
cope: all living welcome what they can c. with 620.9
copulation: birth, c., death: that's all the facts 539.29
coquetry: love's greatest miracle is curing of c. 351.6
why this proliferation, this debased c.? 651.1
coquette: he who keeps undisputed sway over heart of a c. is indeed a hero 351.5
life is too short for all tricks of a c. 351.1
coronets: kind hearts are more than c. 519.20
corporation: a rough picture of life in a c. 315.3
c.: device for individual profit without individual responsibility 104.7
c. is an artificial being 104.22
correct: it is easier to be critical than to be c. 206.8
we must c. a great deal, but not too much 790.5
when we wish to c. with advantage 51.15
correction: c. of silence is what kills 803.10
corrupt: nature will overturn c. political system 819.26
power tends to c. 719.2
corruption: c. is like a ball of snow 191.3
c. made up of contribution of individuals 191.8
c. of government begins with principles 191.9
c. sees everything stained, impure 191.10
c. wins not more than honesty 191.11
sign of c. when end justifies means 574.2
corruptions: war is a producer of new c. 1042.64
cosmic: no object can't be looked at from c. view 58.2
our impotence in the face of c. forces 133.27
cosmopolitan: truly c. man is at home even in own country 193.2
cosmopolite: best c. loves his native country best 193.4
cost: c. of living not bad if you don't pay it 277.5
persons c. much; for thee I must pay me 794.2
that which c. little is less valued 1026.5
costliness: c. masquerades as beauty 646.7
costs: nothing c. so much as what is given 787.1
we condemn wrong when it c. us nothing 822.9
cottage: c. has same vices as courts 1030.5
cough: c. is something you can't help 896.18
love, itch, and c. cannot be hid 551.74
counsel: another's c. gives purer light than own 19.5
friendly c. cuts off many foes 19.24
where's the man who c. can bestow 19.21
who cannot give good c.; 'tis cheap 19.8
counselors: books will speak plain when c. blanch 93.3
in the multitude of c. there is safety 19.6
counsels: c. of old age give light without heat 19.30
count: one must be able to c. 570.4
countenance: man's heart changes his c. 284.1
countenances: many wise men have transparent c. 943.2
countries: c. are like fruit, worms are inside 191.4
c. assume burdens because necessary 498.8
little c. apologize when they do wrong 498.19
not good in own c., men run to others 992.17
country: a c. can stick its tongue out quite far these days without provoking war 641.15
a pity we can die but once to save our c. 678.2
ask not what your c. can do for you 678.8
best cosmopolite loves his native c. 193.4
city has a face: c., a soul 194.6
c. belongs to people who inhabit it 233.32
c. has its charms—cheapness for one 194.14
c. renewed by unknown, not powerful 682.18
God made the c., and man made the town 194.4
good thing about the c. is no bad weather 194.10
he serves party best who serves c. best 710.6
he who could wish his c. to remain as it is, would be a citizen of the universe 622.7
in c. quiet life stimulates creative mind 194.8
in love of home, love of c. has rise 422.6
it is right to prefer own c. to others 423.6
I tremble for my c. when I reflect that God is just 34.36
man good enough to shed blood for c. should be given a square deal afterwards 588.16
man must be quiet, happy to endure c. 194.11
man's feet should be planted in own c. 193.3
my c. is world; countrymen, mankind 100.6
my loyalty was to c., not office-holders 678.22
nobody that left their own c. wrote anything 1069.60
no sweeter sight than one's own c. 423.3
one day in c. is worth month in town 194.12
one loves his c. because it's his own 678.19
only in c. we get to know person or book 194.2
our c., a c. of railroads 621.2
sacrifice to c. teaches what c. is 837.8
schools taught love of c. and penmanship 279.3
self-important fathers of their c. think they're above the people 132.3
to make men virtuous, make them love their c. 678.18
we have become a conservative c. 178.18
what is good for c. is good for General Motors, and vice versa 104.35
when in Rome you long for the c. 251.5
who loves not his c., how shall he love humanity 678.5
who saves his c. violates no law 678.16
countryside: as much sin in smiling c. as in vile London alleys 194.7
people who never see the c. 992.47
couple: c. is unhappy not merely from limited means 564.22
courage: a nation which has forgotten c. 195.16
beware ready-made ideas about cowardice, c. 199.9
charm of women and the c. of men 545.7
c. does not always march to a bugle 195.30
c. for the strange, the inexplicable 195.29
c. gives reality to all other virtues and values 195.24
c. imperils life, fear protects it 343.24
c. is a kind of salvation 195.27
c. is the thing; all goes if c. goes 195.4
c. is to bear fate unflinchingly 195.12
c. mounteth with occasion 195.34
c. must have hope for nourishment 195.25
c. not in those who won't look at own vices 864.1
c. of all one really knows comes late 491.21
c. of convictions, confusions 1001.2
c. raises the blood to crimson splendor 195.35
c. resistance to fear—not its absence 195.38
c. to move ahead in spite of doubts 1005.8
even to live sometimes act of c. 195.33
every man has his own c. 195.10
great crises produce great deeds of c. 205.4
last thing woman will consent to discover in man she loves is want of c. 581.12
life without c. for death is slavery 195.32
many would be cowards if they had the c. 199.5
men often bear little grievances with less c. than they do large misfortunes

508.1
miss plum for want of c. to shake tree 980.8
narrow souls dare not to admire true c. 72.10
no man would set a word down on paper if he had c. to live what he believed in 1069.93
no one can answer for his c. when he has never been in danger 195.18
paradox of c.: man must be a little careless of life even in order to keep it 195.7
people with c., character, seem sinister 195.15
perfect c., utter cowardice rarely occur 199.8
to persevere is c. in a man 686.2
until day of death, no man sure of c. 195.2
value of c., strength of will 1058.4
where guilt is, rage and c. abound 405.9
will of God to be borne with c. 240.19
will to jump after drowning man doubles in presence of people lacking c. 56.7
without justice, c. is weak 195.13
couriers: neither snow nor rain stays these c. 560.1
course: I bow to that whose c. is run 653.32
courteous: if c. when young, then cherished when old 1072.16
courtesan: no professional c. in Europe beats the Italian 752.1
war and c. are slaves of desperation 1042.1
courtesies: no man gains credit for cowardly c. 199.4
courtesy: all doors open to c. 197.6
c. is politic witchery of the great 197.8
c. is the due of man to man 197.2
gratitude is most exquisite form of c. 399.7
greater man, the greater c. 197.13
knowledge of c. is a necessary study 197.11
no defense like elaborate c. 197.10
there is a c. of the heart 197.7
courts: cottages have same vices as c. 1030.5
courtship: best marriages are preceded by long c. 198.1
c. is a witty prologue to a dull play 198.4
covetous: c. man fares worse than poor man 403.15
c. man's penny is a stone 403.11
covetousness: c. has made few rich men 403.8
cow: c. crunching surpasses any statue 41.43
c. of many: well milked, badly fed 150.17
just one c. with a wistful moo 194.3
coward: brave creature is part c. 195.38
c. sneaks to death, the brave live on 948.15
man not brave who is afraid to be a c. 195.28
man who stands apart from mob called c. 597.4
cowardice: between c. and despair valour is born 195.8
beware ready-made ideas about c., courage 199.9
conscience and c. are the same things 174.34
c. is incorrigible which love of power cannot overcome 199.3
c.: surest protection against temptation 971.8
hidden valor is as bad as c. 195.20
if thou livest in pain, c. is the cause 948.16
mortifying infirmity in human nature is c. 199.7
mutual c. keeps us in peace 681.13
perfect courage, utter c. rarely occur 199.8
to run away from trouble is a form of c. 948.1
cowardly: in victory even c. like to boast 751.14
no man gains credit for c. courtesies 199.4
coward's: hatred is the c. revenge 412.22
cowards: between two c., he has the advantage who first detects the other 199.6
c. die many times before their deaths 199.10
c. never use might, but against such as will not fight 199.2
human race is race of c. 199.11
many would be c. if they had the courage 199.5
coyness: had we time, c. would be no crime 857.9
crab: c. instructs young: walk straight ahead 310.2
crabgrass: lie down and listen to the c. grow 533.11
cradle: c. is rocked but the baby is pinched 271.16
craft: much compliance, much c. 158.2
cranium: the c. is a space-traveler's helmet 562.44
crank: c. insists on laying down law to others 276.3
cranks: c. take up unfashionable errors 276.5
crap: all that David Copperfield kind of c. 123.
craves: he is poor that c. much 403.6
what the eye sees not, the heart c. not 238.8
create: impulse to destroy as ancient as to c. 241.8
long and hard and painful to c. life 518.15
to c. there must be a dynamic force 201.41
who knows not how to c. should not know 201.35
created: no great thing is c. suddenly 401.15
creates: man, like Deity, c. in his own image 201.20
creating: in c., the only hard thing's to begin 201.26
creation: artist's c. must become multitude's desire 53.121
art of c. is older than art of killing 201.43
c. destroys as it goes 713.3
c. is but a succession of battles 201.4
c. of a work of art is our one small "yes" 53.141
destruction is new c. on a wider scale 241.3
human c. is never perfect 201.22
if I bind my will I strangle c. 201.38
in our time, man believes he's capable of c. 201.32
man unites with world in process of c. 201.14
rational being will discover deity in c. 623.47
women's lives work out processes of c. 670.34
creative: all men are c. but few are artists 201.17
c. minds known to survive bad training 201.13
c. person is more primitive and cultivated than average person 201.3
gifted members of the human species are at c. best when they cannot have their way 201.19
man is a free c. spirit 201.7
the c. accomplishments of humans 201.24
creativeness: taste is the enemy of c. 963.15
creative person: c. does not have rest of life in proportion 201.42
creativity: c. is a by-product of hard work 201.36
c., the definition of man 53.11
in c., every person must start at the beginning 201.31
throwing ourselves away is act of c. 861.4
creator: one must die to life to be a c. 201.28
spirit of c. not evoked by opium or wine 269.4
creature: c. that creates space vehicles can cope 294.7
nature has filled each cranny with fantastic c. 623.43
creatures: we love c. with two, four legs, but not six 481.3
credit: never share c. or desserts 894.4
who has enough c. to pay for mistakes 299.12
creditor: c. worse than master; c. has your dignity 222.8
creditors: c. are great observers of set days 222.5
credulity: c. greatest about things we know least 202.4
c. is man's weakness, child's strength 202.6
credulous: imaginative people are the most c. 202.2
man is c. and must believe something 78.18
most positive men are the most c. 264.14
creed: at back of every c. lies something hard 203.1
no nonsense that cannot be made c. 745.6
our c. tested only in emergencies of life 203.2
we have less charity for those who believe half our c. 711.22
when one belongs to narrow c. in science 849.10
creeds: art raises its head where c. relax 53.96
hate man, worship God seems sum of all c. 797.39
cries: c. of despair are a kind of wealth 1052.6
he that falls by himself

never c. 157.5
crime: Cambodia was not a mistake; it was a c. 1042.89
cause of idleness, c. is deferring hopes 427.6
commit a c. and there is no concealment 204.7
commonplace c. difficult to solve 204.6
c. and punishment grow out of one stem 766.7
c. is extension of behavior in business 204.16
for one c. expiated in prison ten thousand committed by those who condemn 517.30
harder to confess sin no one believes in than c. everyone can appreciate 900.10
once a c. has appeared for the first time 766.1
poverty is parent of revolution and c. 718.3
problem of community cursed with c. is preventing the young from training in c. 204.5
punishment of c. is fear 204.19
successful, fortunate c. called virtue 204.17
there is no absolute c. 477.8
want should not be exasperated into c. 718.58
worse than a c., it is a blunder 88.3
crimes: account for the c. that are visited upon them 204.3
baseness of c. requires wise not only to be angry but to go insane 307.31
collective c. incriminate no one 204.12
c. of civilization worse than those of barbarism 133.2
fantastic c. imputed to the degraded 204.2
great c. linked to sins that went before 204.14
lack of intelligence is father of all c. 941.14
men incapable of c. don't suspect others 478.4
men more willing to have c. known than weaknesses 804.3
most men only commit great c. because of their scruples about petty ones 204.15
criminal: c. acts are not more unnatural than virtues 431.17
judge condemned when c. is acquitted 517.37
no American c. class except Congress 172.5
society forgives c., never the dreamer 450.32
cripple: if live with c., you will learn to limp 57.14
crises: c. frighten weak, inspire strong 498.16
great c. produce great men, great deeds 205.4
nationwide planning will prevent c. 205.7
crisis: c. means danger and opportunity 205.5
no blare of trumpets announces modern c. 205.1
present moment an extraordinary c. 729.8
critic: a c., lug-worm in the liver of literature 207.15
c. knows the way but can't drive the car 207.55
c. must get into the mind of artist 207.34
c.: sorcerer who makes hidden spring gush 207.33
c. who justly admires many things simultaneously cannot love any of them 207.5
dramatic c. comes out after dark, up to no good 207.59
good c. is the man who describes his adventures among masterpieces 207.23
good writer is not per se good book c. 207.6
man is a c. when he cannot be an artist 207.20
the c. must keep some seats reserved 53.145
wise skepticism is attribute of good c. 904.7
critical: author furnishes c. larvae with food 207.27
c. vision can mitigate automatic operation 966.19
every nation has own c. turn of mind 207.16
it is easier to be c. than to be correct 206.8
pleasure is least fallible c. guide 20.1
the c. spirit creates 201.46
criticism: art can hardly be reached with c. 207.44
cant of c. is the most tormenting 207.52
confusion of reporting with art c. 207.31
c., a study by which men grow important 207.29
c. is easy, art is difficult 207.12
c. is never inhibited by ignorance 206.14
c. is the windows and chandeliers of art 207.40
c. of the elite, like opening shot of an uprising 178.10
c. should not be querulous but guiding 206.9
c. that overlays text with windy sermon 207.39
I do not resent c. 206.6
judgments of fact, not of value, a sign of pedantic c. 207.45
no effective c. until a man provoked 206.26
people ask for c., but only want praise 206.15
rain of c. makes garden of music flourish 207.11
should be a dash of the amateur in c. 207.2
stupid c. versus stupid praise 722.26
tomes of c. hang on moments of delight 20.5
criticized: one can be c. only by a greater man 207.17
critics: c. all are ready made 207.9
c. are like brushers of nobles' clothes 207.4
c., like insects, desire blood, not pain 207.41
c.: men who have failed in literature, art 207.13
if c. were as clear-sighted as malignant 207.47
seek roses in December before you trust c. 207.10
stones c. hurl man may use for monument 207.25
we have paid too great a compliment to c. 207.19
what c. often ask for is the impossible 53.17
when c. disagree, the artist is in accord with himself 207.58
Cross: orgasm has replaced the C. 892.34
cross-section: not a representative c. of the English working class 289.23
crow: c. that mimics cormorant gets drowned 451.7
crowd: c. has a generalized stink 208.1
c. is not company without love 915.3
everyone in c. has power to throw dirt 905.2
I live in the c. of jollity 152.8
in the c. a mass-mind operates 208.6
no human happier for being lost in a c. 208.3
nothing so unpredictable as feelings of c. 208.7
we may better join the foolish c. 171.14
crowds: as c. increase we build forts of inattention 208.4
crown: c. of roses makes the prettier appearance 61.3
uneasy lies the head that wears a c. 831.21
within c. of king keeps Death his court 831.22
crucified: men of rare vision are always c. 565.5
cruel: c. describe themselves as frank 362.11
man adds to grief by being c. to man 209.1
cruelest: man is the c. animal 209.13
cruelties: worst c. come under name of condolence 960.9
cruelty: c., excitement, lead men to love war 1042.4
c. is law pervading nature, society 209.7
c. stems from vile mind, cowardly heart 209.2
c. to intestines, blood pressure, psyche 569.3
c. to other civilized man 133.9
fear is one of the main sources of c. 343.28
intellectual c. is the worst kind of c. 209.5
is c. a moral judgment? 209.11
love compels c. 551.54
opinions which justify c. are inspired by cruel impulses 209.14
there is in man a specific lust for c. 209.15
the theatre breeds its own kind of c. 209.8
cruise: old and young, all on last c. 606.17
crusades: psychopathic element rises to top of c. 111.11
crutch: love is a c. 551.121
nothing more frightening than to be divested of a c. 235.1
cubs: must enter tiger's den to take c. 92.6
cucumber: c. should be seasoned, then thrown out 355.9
cult: less reasonable a c. is, more men seek to establish it by force 674.6
cultivated: c. man is end to which nature works 210.7
c. man make acute, balanced observers 650.3

c. people need not speak at all 210.14
c. people should be superior to mercenary interest 602.41
cultivation: c. of weeds at the expense of occasional flowers 207.56
cultural: c. changes begin in affectation 117.3
culture: a c. must be reasonably stable 210.23
birth within a particular c. decides 77.10
business men are not likely to contribute to c. 210.25
cheerful, intelligent face is end of c. 210.6
c.: acquainting ourselves with best known, thus with history of human spirit 210.1
c., a novelty in the world of nature 623.46
c. as art, expression of man's creativity 210.4
c., a subject upon which we need enlightenment 210.2
c. can't be deliberately aimed at 210.5
c. is a mask that hides men's faces 913.22
c. is an atmosphere and a heritage 210.20
c. is an instrument wielded by professors to manufacture professors 210.24
c. opens the sense of beauty 210.8
c., to say great things in simplest way 899.3
custom is the deterioration of c. 210.9
if you're anxious to be a man of c., you must get transcendental terms 210.10
man born barbarian, raises self by c. 210.11
permitted to despise only your own c. 210.21
realization that the old formal c.—the "New England idea"—could no longer serve 545.19
value of c. is its effect on character 210.18
what really binds men together is their c. 210.3
what we call education and c. is nothing but substitution of literature for life 279.78
cunning: knowledge without justice is c. 522.50
More in the c. purchase of my wealth 8.4
progress in c.: not to seem too clever 200.3
state hurt when c. pass for wise 930.3
they who cannot be wise are c. 200.2
cup: many a slip 'twixt c. and lip 115.11
Cupid: C. is naked and does not like artifices contrived by beauty 551.162
cure: we labour against our own c., for death is the c. of all diseases 221.18
cured: disease known is half c. 243.1
cures: thousand ills require thousand c. 798.7
curiosity: creatures whose mainspring is c. enjoy accumulating facts 211.2
c. is permanent trait of vigorous intellect 211.7
glory and c. are two scourges of the soul 211.9
newspapers always excite c. 630.15
there are various sorts of c.; one is from interest, and the other from pride 211.8
we have no c. about sun which warms us 480.7
curriculum: only one c.: basics of human experience 279.36
world's c. doesn't include Latin and Greek 279.53
curse: "blessing" of idleness and won for us the "c." of labor 1065.69
cursed: none so c. but Eternal Love may return 551.32
curves: with c. like the hull of a racing yacht 72.23
custom: c. adapts itself to expediency 319.7
c. can't conquer nature, she's unconquered 431.3
c. creates the whole of equity 213.22
c. determines what is agreeable 213.23
c., fashion are blind to what is to come 213.5
c. is principal magistrate of life 213.1
c. is second nature and no less powerful 213.18
c. is the deterioration of culture 210.9
c. is the guide of the ignorant 213.6
c. makes all things easy 213.10
c. reconciles us to everything 213.3
habit raises outcry in defense of c. 790.26
innumerable are the illusions of c. 213.4
laws of conscience proceed from c. 174.22
lest one good c. should corrupt the world 117.33
morality is the c. of one's country 604.6
no human action which c. has not at one time justified and at another condemned 213.13
old c. is hard to break 213.12
things both just, unjust sanctioned by c. 213.27
universality of a c.: pledge of its worth 213.25
we are more sensible of what is done against c. than against nature 213.24
what humanity abhors, c. recommends 213.14
who does anything by c. makes no choice 213.17
customer: c. is an object to be manipulated 104.11
if you're a c. today you're an intruder 104.1
customs: c. are made for customary circumstances 213.16
c. represent the experience of mankind 213.2
don't change laws to change c. 213.20
long c. are not easily broken 790.16
new c., though ridiculous, are followed 338.24
sense of guilt on approaching c. barrier 405.18
cut: measure a thousand times and c. once 112.6
cynic: c. is prematurely disappointed in future 214.2
c. knows the price of everything 214.5
c. might suggest motto of modern life—"Just as good as the real." 54.4
cynicism: only alternative to perfection is c. 449.2
only the c. born of success is valid 214.4
cynics: c. do things for people who don't want them 214.3

D

daintiest: d. last, to make the end most sweet 704.36
damage: television's primary d. 967.18
dance: d. is only art wherein we are stuff of which it is made 215.4
either d. well or quit the ballroom 311.5
men must walk before they d. 404.22
danced: consider day lost on which we have not d. 409.72
dancer: good education usually harmful to a d. 215.1
dancing: d. is attempt to get into life's rhythm 215.4
d. loftiest, most beautiful of the arts 215.2
Dane: once you have paid the D.-geld you never get rid of the D. 46.3
danger: any d. spot is tenable—by brave men 216.12
avoiding d. no safer than exposure to it 112.4
common d. unites even enemies 1016.1
d. and delight grown on one stalk 216.7
d. breeds best on too much confidence 664.2
d. is only a means to success 945.41
d. past, God is forgotten 216.9
delay breeds d. 231.1
if not in trouble, watch for d. 755.28
in comradeship is d. countered best 216.10
life of d. moderates dread of death 9.25
mystery magnifies d. as fog the sun 216.4
out of d., man forgets his fears 216.8
the path is smooth that leadeth on to d. 156.8
to pessimist d. is not depressing 692.1
whoever has not felt the d. of our times 1001.9
wise man prays not for safety from d. 216.6
dangerous: all fame is d. 332.15
dangers: d., by being despised, grow great 216.3
who won't sail till d. are over sails not 112.3
dare: d. a little the more, as I grow older 1000.13
not to d. is to dwindle 53.138
dares: fortune sides with him who d. 360.39
daring: best mask for demoralization is d. 92.8
progress in life comes through d. 741.17
the loving are the d. 551.211

dark: each and all, we are riding into the d. 580.10
much easier to tell intimate things in d. 169.4
darkness: better to light candle than to curse d. 433.7
in d., shameful deed brings no disgrace 217.5
none who passed door of d. return to tell 221.78
there is in d. a unity 217.3
darknesses: we move between two d. 541.11
data: mistake to theorize without d. 974.2
dates: d. by which bills must be paid 978.80
daughter: d. am I in my mother's house 422.13
don't put your d. on the stage 972.4
to old father, nothing sweeter than d. 218.1
daughters: he who has d. is always a shepherd 218.8
little d. of doctors and dentists 218.4
daughters': trust not d. minds by what they act 218.6
dawn: still beauty of d. is nature's balm 605.5
what human ill not alleviated by d. 605.10
day: cloudy d. has influence on constitutions 1050.1
d. is done, and the darkness falls 633.7
each d. provides its own gifts 729.19
if one d. like all, all are like one 978.40
life loses in a d. what many years amassed 550.5
nothing more commended than fine d. 1050.9
prayer should be the key of the d. 723.14
sufficient unto the d. is the evil thereof 307.4
thou knowest not what a d. may bring forth 727.1
time and hour runs through roughest d. 978.61
what d. fails to reveal some theft 457.3
days: a dollar and a quarter five d. a week 680.1
aren't d. long when nothing goes wrong 186.9
d. come and go like veiled figures 978.16
one of these d. is none of these d. 231.4
upon the sea d. fall away quicker 839.3
we've more d. to live than pleasures 704.16
dead: a funeral isn't for the d. 367.14
d. are all holy, even they that were base 221.25
d. govern the living 986.6
d. men have no victory 173.6
d. to them as they are d. to me 224.24
distance the d. have gone does not at first appear 221.32
drive your plow over the bones of the d. 221.11
earth belongs to living, not to d. 539.60
few wholly d.: blow embers, flame starts 221.58
for the d. there are no more toils 221.124
in Spain d. more alive than d. elsewhere 922.1
it takes many years to learn that one is d. 219.3
let the d. have fame, but the living love 551.207
living dog is better than a d. lion 539.8
not easy to restore life to the d. 767.5
one being d., all is d. to him 858.23
one cannot live with the d. 221.89
only two topics of interest: sex, the d. 522.68
our affection for the d. grows faint because we ourself are dying 552.11
pity is for the living, envy for the d. 541.41
praised when d., we often have no other merit than that of being no longer alive 804.17
ritual disposal of the d., awareness of self 103.6
small difference to d. if buried in luxury 103.4
sorrow for the d. is only one from which we refuse to be divorced 610.7
the d. sleep in their moonless night 610.4
those most like d. are most loath to die 221.79
those who fear life are three parts d. 219.8
to ashes of d. glory comes too late 386.9
today we can't even count all the d. 1042.100
to mourn d. unduly affronts the living 610.5
to the d. rugs are no richer than thorns 221.130
we aren't honest, we embalm our d. 103.2
we rob selves when we make presents to d. 367.11
you never find the d. making any complaint against the doctor who killed them 263.9
deaf: it is folly to sing twice to a d. man 48.3
music is nothing if the audience is d. 1060.40
none so d. as he who will not hear 220.1
deal: to d. only with honest men, stop dealing 425.4
dealing: nothing astonishes men like plain d. 148.3
plain d. is a jewel out of fashion 362.3
plain d. is kicked out of doors 349.8
dearest: those things d. that have cost us most 1026.14
Death: I answer the heroic question "D., where is thy sting?" 221.3
if D. stepped miraculously through the glass 221.108
waiting in the last room, the Red D. 221.143
death: action, danger moderate dread of d. 9.25
a d. is the most terrible of facts 221.97
all our life is but a going out to d. 541.6
ants and savages put strangers to d. 358.6
any man's d. diminishes me 221.35
as men, we are all equal in presence of d. 221.105
as to d., we live in city without walls 221.44
at birth, d. stands but a little aside 221.14
belief in hell never prevented people from behaving as though d. were a rumor 221.72
better a quiet d. than public misfortune 434.4
children will not fear life if their elders do not fear d. 541.8
compensation for a d. sentence 767.3
d. always comes too early or too late 221.41
d., a spur to ride life across the barriers 221.142
d. a stake put up to play game of life 541.17
d. borders upon our birth 221.59
d. but an instant, life a long torment 541.33
d. by justice is ignominious 767.4
d. came there to find him in the morning 948.6
d. cancels everything but truth 221.4
d., certification to the end of pain 221.126
d. cuts in marble what would sink to dust 221.93
d. does not blow a trumpet 221.29
d. drowns in the indifference of nature 221.136
d. either destroys or unhusks us 221.109
d. explodes like a car bomb 123.46
d. guide of life, no goal but d. 221.85
d. has no sting, but life has 541.40
d. has one terror: it has no tomorrow 221.68
d. hath a thousand doors to let out life 221.91
d. in battle is the most glorious for men 1042.71
d. is always sad 221.26
d. is a thing which makes men weep 221.22
d. is camel that lies down at every door 221.103
d. is greatest evil, for it cuts off hope 427.15
d. is like a fisherman 221.133
d. is never sweet 221.50
d. is not the greatest misfortune 539.80
d. is nothing; we fear what we know not 221.38
d. is of no concern to us 221.43
d. is one moment, life so many of them 541.44
d. is perpetual retirement without pay 221.57
d. is stingless, grave never fights 623.56
d. is supreme festival on the road to freedom 221.15
d. is the absence of presence 221.127
d. is the cure of all diseases 221.18
d. is the supple suitor that wins at last 221.31
d. is the veil those who live call life 454.19
d. is ultimate horror of life 221.56
d. laughs when old women frolic 653.76
d. lays his icy hands on kings 340.19
d. must be waiting at end of ride before you see earth, feel heart, love world 221.5
d. must be, like the rest, a

mockery 221.118
d. must not be taken too seriously 3.1
d. ought not to take one by surprise 221.125
d. reveals what a nothing the body is 90.3
d. softer thing by far than tyranny 1002.2
d. surprises us amidst our hopes 221.53
d. takes away commonplace of life 221.121
d. takes us piecemeal, not at a gulp 221.110
d. wanted when anguish of living too great 541.9
do not fear d., but the inadequate life 504.4
do not seek d.; d. will find you 221.60
each age has choice of d. it will die 298.18
end of all is d. 221.76
even Rome can't grant dispensation from d. 221.94
even the bold fly when d. draws close 221.123
fear of d. or pain is to be dreaded 343.14
for the unhappy man d. is end of life imprisonment 1011.6
give me liberty or give me d. 537.16
good life fears not life nor d. 541.15
hardest of deaths is d. one sees ahead 221.7
haunted itself with rumors of own d. 17.31
He seemed to seek d. on battlefields 195.23
he who has set d. beneath his feet 937.2
honorable d. man's immortality 454.16
however long you live, d. awaits you 221.83
how little room do we take up in d. 221.120
how shall man know d., which he hath not seen 541.2
ideal mankind would abolish d. 713.3
if life is absurd, d. is insupportable 3.8
in every d. is a celebration 221.86
in great measure d. is past already 541.35
instinct serves end of bringing about d. 541.12
interest in d. is interest in life 577.5
in the midst of life we are in d. 541.29
inviting sable d. by warfare 1042.92
is it sin to rush into d. ere d. come 948.23
is life a boon? If so, d. is too soon 221.55
life a great surprise; d. even greater one 541.28
life, d., appear ours, yet are hardly so 541.23
life feels different once you greet d. 221.45
life hurries on, and d. follows fast 978.50
life levels all men; d. reveals eminent 221.117
life without courage for d. is slavery 195.32
long life, and short, are by d. made one 541.26
love of posterity caused by d. 802.1
man is only animal that doubts d. 221.67
man sorry for himself doubles d. 221.47
marriage promises happiness, d. assures it 564.127
men convinced of your sincerity only by your d. 221.24
men fear d. as children fear dark 221.9
men's natural sentiment in face of d. 454.18
nearest friends can go with anyone to d. 221.52
nobody knows what d. is, yet we fear it 221.122
no certain life achieved by others' d. 518.13
no life that breathes has longed for d. 948.25
no preaching has made d. other than d. 221.82
nothing after d., and d. itself nothing 221.111
obloquy is more painful than d. 206.22
old men's prayers for d. are lying prayers 653.29
one can survive everything except d. 804.29
one only stays alive for fear of d. 541.30
only cure for birth, d., is to enjoy interval 539.101
only solvent industry is merchandising of d. 1042.97
only way to be prepared for d.: be sated 221.30
opium eater understands the pain of d. 269.3
origin of evils not d., but the fear of d. 221.42
our birth is nothing but our d. begun 83.7
our life is made by the d. of others 541.24
philosophy has a set of sayings for d. 694.36
prison, blood, d. create enthusiasts 801.2
prolonged rest on a formula means d. 986.12
rejoice not over anyone's d. 221.6
repugnance to d. is proportionate to our consciousness of having lived in vain 221.62
rich and poor alike move toward d. 221.104
Shall I be remembered after d.? 804.2
shown d., he'll be content with fever 896.21
some think d. the only reality in life 541.19
spare me the ceremonious air of gloom—which makes d. a hideous show 367.2
spring will come, d. and dust will die 854.52
sun and d. cannot be looked at steadily 221.80
suspense is hostiler than d. 482.2
the artist's eyes destroy d. 53.58
there is no God stronger than d. 221.128
the sense of d. is most in apprehension 221.114
the strong good medicine of d. 221.140
the weariest and most loathed worldly life is a paradise to what we fear of d. 541.37
this sergeant, d., is strict in arrest 221.116
this very d. which I cannot escape 221.101
those who favor d. penalty have more affinity with assassins than those who don't 767.1
time and d. will ultimately claim us all 431.16
to cure fear of d. set just value on life 541.20
to defeat d. man obliged to defeat life 541.25
to have the universe bear one company would be a great consolation in d. 152.18
to live a life half dead, a living d. 219.7
to reject pain, d., is to reject life 946.12
to the faithful d. is the gate of life 946.30
true return to nature is d. 623.33
useless life is early d. 1024.2
weakest arm can take away life, but the strongest cannot deprive us of d. 221.17
we dread d. as the close of hope 221.64
we face facts of sex but not of d. 328.10
we fear d. as we fear a short summer 221.40
we find in d. not meaning, but an end 541.31
what is this d.—a quiet of the heart 221.23
what lives is granted breath by d. 541.4
what should a simple child know of d. 123.62
when vitality runs high, d. takes men by surprise 1036.3
while young, idea of d., failure, intolerable 1071.13
without d., no awareness of life 221.81
work of life is to lay foundation of d. 221.96

death's: d. dark way must be trodden once 221.70
d. stamp gives value to the coin of life 541.39

deaths: few go to their d. with dignity 195.21
he must die more d. than one 440.22

debaters': if all saw fair, wise, the same, no d. strife 656.7

debauchee: d.: has pursued pleasure and overtaken it 494.2

debauchery: d. is despair in face of infinity 739.3
joylessness, not joy, is mother of d. 739.5

debt: d., a crazy aunt we keep in the basement 223.3
first or last you must pay entire d. 680.3
national d. if not excessive is a blessing 223.1
national d. is a national bond 223.2
national d. owed by and to nation 223.4
no nation ought to be without a d. 223.2
poor man's d. makes a great noise 222.6
promise made is d. unpaid 743.10
two ways of paying d. 222.2

debtor: if a d. prove insolvent, don't ruin him 222.9

debts: forgive us our d. 359.2
he that dies pays all d.

221.112
say nothing of my d. or pay them 222.4
we shall have to pay d. to world when it may be inconvenient for survival 177.9
words pay no d. 222.11
debunking: facile d. of theoretical life cannot 694.3
decade: that last undesired d. 653.100
decadence: d., not a function of the economy 226.4
decay: all human things are subject to d. 221.37
men, like fruit, grow sweet before d. 586.10
deceit: fooled with hope, men favor life's d. 539.26
human society founded on mutual d. 914.7
in love d. goes further than mistrust 551.105
deceive: d. not thy physician, confessor, lawyer 224.8
man can d. a woman by sham attachment 857.7
nature never deceives us; we d. ourselves 864.9
deceived: happier d. than undeceived in love 551.107
life is art of being well d. 449.10
more tolerable to be refused than d. 224.16
we're most easily d. deceiving others 224.9
who will not be d. must have many eyes 224.7
deceives: hope d. more men than cunning does 427.37
reason d. us more often than does nature 785.38
that which d. and does harm also undeceives and does good 476.17
deceiving: vain to find fault with arts of d. 224.11
December: thoughts suitable to 25th of D. 420.5
decency: as simians we have done well as to d. 308.5
d.: not to dare do in public what is decent enough in private 756.2
decent: if we cannot be d., let us be graceful 396.4
decently: man lives d. as discipline saves his life 250.5
deception: men suffer d. from their own opinions 864.4
people always overdo it in attempting d. 224.23
truth lives on in the midst of d. 998.108
deceptive: Russian is a very d. language 524.17
decide: d.: to succumb to preponderance of one set of influences over another set 225.2
nothing more difficult than ability to d. 225.7
decision: d. is action taken when incomplete information does not suggest answer 315.4
delay is itself a d. 730.17
never a d. not one hundred per cent selfish 225.10
strong man advances issues, makes a d. 225.3
decisions: impelled by a state of mind destined not to last, we make our irrevocable d. 225.8
decisive: life's d. actions are often unconsidered 227.11
decorum: follow d., never promptings of nature 749.5
man keeps moral backside covered by d. 604.22
decree: hot temper leaps o'er a cold d. 39.25
dedicated: people d. to dogmas in doubt 264.12
deed: among men, the tongue wins, not the d. 690.10
good d. shines in a naughty world 433.28
man makes no noise over a good d. 227.2
our least d. wends its way to sea of cause and effect 110.7
virtue must shape itself in d. 1033.47
deeds: d. determine us as we determine our d. 227.8
gentle mind by gentle d. is known 378.6
great to do that which ends all other d. 948.24
means to do ill d. makes d. ill done 1070.20
men alike in promises, differ in d. 227.17
noble d. most estimable when hidden 227.22
only concrete d. can maintain an alliance 247.5
to know contentment, let your d. be few 186.4
ugly d. are taught by ugly d. 227.29
words may be d. 1064.1
deep: smooth runs water where the brook is d. 740.4
deer: d. with chain of gold will eat grass 109.7
defaulting: vastest day is shrunken by one d. face 610.3
defeat: as easy to be enervated by triumph as d. 945.26
d. attends every game 929.4
d. is school in which truth grows strong 228.1
d. preferable to defeating injustice by evil 574.6
if the idea is good it will survive d. 443.3
in ourselves are triumph and d. 858.22
defeats: there are d. more triumphant than victories 228.5
who can see any difference between our victories and d. 228.2
defect: easier to confess d. than claim a quality 342.1
one shining quality hides glaring d. 311.7
defects: a man must thank his d. 342.6
d. can be pointed out and corrected 233.55
defense: d. is faith in institutions defended 229.13
diplomacy, d. not substitutes for each other 229.6
isn't the best d. always a good attack 229.11
no d. like elaborate courtesy 197.10
spent the same amount on d. every year 229.4
defer: d. not till to-morrow to be wise 231.2
defiance: artist must blow trumpet of d. 53.80
deficiencies: pity one whose only sense is to see his d. 863.5
deficiency: easier to see a d. than import or value 206.10
defiled: sun visits cesspools and is not d. 57.8
whoever touches pitch will be d. 57.2
define: d., d., well-educated infant 230.2
definition: d.: wilderness of idea within wall of words 230.1
deformity: beauty and d. equally pass away 990.13
no d. but saves us from a dream 457.10
degenerates: everything d. in the hands of man 177.7
degradation: readers felt pleasure reading about d. 211.6
the work of bestial d. 381.3
dehumanization: d. of Negro indivisible from d. of ourselves 85.3
deity: rational being discovers d. in creation 623.47
delay: d. breeds danger 231.1
d. is itself a decision 730.17
d. is preferable to error 231.6
woman is the daughter of d. 1062.117
delays: all d. are dangerous in war 1042.27
deliberation: we use d. to justify doing what we want 782.3
delight: absurd to slight today's d. for the hereafter 704.5
danger and d. grow on one stalk 216.7
in temple of d. melancholy has shrine 705.4
some d. smiles on us even in melancholy 409.70
teach us d. in simple things 899.7
tomes of criticism hang on moments of d. 20.5
delinquency: juvenile d. provides adults with fantasies 204.8
delinquent: teacher may change d. into solid citizen 965.33
deliverance: liberation is not d. 537.18
delusion: America died from a d. that she had moral leadership. 34.64
ignorance prevents wisdom; d. is result 447.2
demagogues: where laws are not supreme, d. arise 232.1
demands: who makes great d. upon himself is inclined to make great d. on others 863.3
demerit: small d. extinguishes long service 1070.9
democracies: great d. tend to think stupid man is more likely to be honest than clever man 711.74
in d., nothing is greater than commerce 104.32
democracy: armed forces cannot protect our d. 229.9
at bottom of d. is little man making a little cross on a little bit of paper 1038.4
bipartisan d. presupposes the individual 233.19
d. admits variety and permits criticism 233.16
d., a euphemism for deterioration 53.77
d. best, for it respects man

as reasonable 233.24
d.: covenant among men to respect rights 233.47
d. effective only if people can stop talking 233.4
d.: election by incompetent many 233.50
d. furthered when minorities cancel each other out 233.8
d. is a charming form of government 233.45
d. is the theory that the common people know what they want and deserve to get it 233.37
d. is worst form of government except all other forms 233.9
d.: name for the people when we need them 233.10
d. needs a party that will separate the good in it from evils that beset it 233.38
d. not static but an everlasting march 233.48
d. offers great hope for mankind 233.28
d. represents disbelief in all great men 233.40
d.: subjection of minority to majority 233.29
evil of d., to put up with man you elect 233.46
fight to save wild beauty is d. at its best 177.8
in a d., administration is by many, not few 233.54
in a d. the free are rulers 233.2
in d. officers of government are servants 761.12
justice delayed is d. denied 517.27
liberty in d. when all share government 233.3
masses are the material of d. 233.1
modern democracies do not yet effect d. 233.36
no difference in destruction wrought under name of totalitarianism or d. 1042.36
nothing will make d. of illiterate people 233.33
obstacle to d. is property 746.8
our d. must contend for the cause of human freedom 537.19
rulers of d. are the voters 1038.17
self-criticism is secret weapon of d. 233.52
socialism and d. are indivisible 912.2
taste of d. bitter when full d. denied 233.30
under d. the weakest should have the same opportunity as the strongest 233.17
what chance has d. if it requires a whole population of capable voters 233.51
world must be made safe for d. 233.58
democracy's: d. only success—the night 633.5
democratic: amongst d. nations, each new generation is a new people 374.3
blind lead blind, it's the d. way 233.39
d. American idea is not one level for all but liberty for each to be what he is 233.5
d. disease reduces everything unique 297.16
d. government too perfect for mere men 233.49
d. institutions do not renew themselves effortlessly 233.27
d. institutions give men lofty notion of their country, themselves 233.11
d. movement loves crowd, fears individuals 233.34
d. nations are haunted by what will be 233.13
freemen have d. feeling which will not submit to arrogance, servility 233.23
man of d. principles must overcome physical repugnances 100.8
passions of men in d. times end in love of riches, or proceed from it 1048.60
taste for well-being is feature of d. times 750.5
that a peasant may become king does not render the kingdom d. 233.57
demonstration: he who admits only d. can be sure only of perishing quickly 744.1
demoralization: best mask for d. is daring 92.8
denial: better d. than unwilling compliance 791.3
denied: not to ask is not to be d. 805.2
dentist: d.: puts metal in your mouth, pulls coins out of your pocket 234.1
deny: to d. all is to confess all 405.17
depart: fire of life sinks and I am ready to d. 653.56
departure: time for d. even when no place to go 117.35
depend: in civilized society we d. on each other 913.19
to d. on child is blindness in one eye 235.7
we put up with most from those on whom we most d. 235.5
depressed: if didn't live venturously, never be d. 16.10
depression: d. is melancholy minus its charms 589.11
deprived: unhappy man d. of what he did not have 1011.23
when money finally trickles down, poor still d. 718.19
depth: no one tests d. of river with both feet 755.1
deride: men learn more quickly what they d. 185.2
describe: how d. delicate thing that happens when brilliant insect alights on flower 1064.43
describing: when d. don't state the matter plainly 708.15
description: world loves a ready-made d. to hang on a man 935.1
desert: d. speaks of man's insignificance 415.10
I scare myself with my own d. places 415.7
they make a d. and call it peace 1042.91
use every man after his d. 517.43
deserted: wives invariably flourish when d. 472.6
wives not d.: objects of commiseration 564.77
deserting: d. male often ends in disaster 472.6
design: color without d. less pleasing than simple outline 666.1
d. a thing by considering it in next larger context 237.2
things difficult to d. easy to perform 245.7
designers: interior d., like clients, want to show off 430.6
desire: all envy is proportionate to d. 295.14
boredom: the d. for desires 94.9
catastrophe and d. are linked in our lives 238.16
d. for imaginary benefits often involves loss of present blessings 238.1
d. is poison at lunch, wormwood at dinner 892.1
d. outlives performance many years 892.48
d. projected itself visually 238.31
first d. easier to extinguish than successors 238.27
freedom won by controlling d. 862.4
from satisfaction of d. may arise despair 845.2
great d. obtains little 238.5
he knows peace who has forgotten d. 681.2
if you d. many things, they will seem few 238.10
it is d. that engenders belief 78.16
it is hard to fight against impulsive d. 238.20
make us, not fly to dreams, but moderate d. 238.3
most men d. a virgin who is a whore 892.16
pleasure tasted satisfies less than d. 704.32
some d. necessary to keep life in motion 238.25
some, from dread of losing what they ardently d., leave nothing undone to lose it 238.26
'Tis very certain the d. of life / Prolongs it 548.3
to d. is in some sense to enjoy 238.19
we do not succeed in changing things to our d.; gradually our d. changes 238.34
when we d. or solicit any thing, our minds run wholly on the good side of it 716.15
where no d., no industry 1065.50
desire's: only might-have-been can fill d. cup 792.3
desires: a mixture of d. beyond man's knowledge 238.28
can't abolish by law or axe d. of men 238.29
d., realized, haunt us less readily 238.12
each believes what he fears or d. 202.5
if d. are endless, cares will be so 403.7
ignore a man's d.: ignore source of power 528.47
men have thousand d. to bushel of choices 238.4
not possessions, but d., need equalizing 746.1
supplying wants by lopping off d. is like cutting off feet 937.9
the abstinent carry their d.

with them 865.1
those d. that do not bring pain if they are not satisfied are not necessary 238.9
desiring: don't spoil what you have by d. more 186.5
desk: if I had no d. in my room 661.14
despair: after d., one is almost happy 239.1
between cowardice and d. valour is born 195.8
calm d. is the essence of wisdom 806.10
clearness produces d. 239.9
cries of d. are a kind of wealth 1052.6
debauchery is d. in face of infinity 739.3
d.: price for setting an impossible aim 239.7
ennui makes more suicides than d. 290.1
from satisfaction of desire may arise d. 845.2
in d. are intense enjoyments 239.5
in d. we look on ourselves as objects 875.15
lest I wither by d. 9.34
like strength is felt from hope, d. 940.10
no adult misery can be compared with a child's d. 123.40
no peace in changing waves of joy, d. 969.1
sad patience, neighbor to d. 677.1
safe d. raves—agony is frugal 239.4
suicide justified if no purpose to d. 948.7
who has nothing to hope should d. of nothing 937.6
desperate: wisdom does not do d. things 1060.59
desperation: d. a grandiose form of funk 239.2
men lead lives of quiet d. 239.11
nowadays most lead lives of noisy d. 636.7
despise: it is easy to d. what you cannot get 920.1
man must d. himself, then others will 872.2
men d. those who court them 658.8
those whom men have injured they d. 476.18
despisers: great d. are the great reverers 185.6
despot: benevolent d. demands from others the submissiveness of sheep 1002.14
despotism: d. does great things illegally 537.3
failure of reform strengthens d. 790.4
man about the same with d. or freedom 395.61
when white man governs another man, that is d. 1002.19
destination: our age is all signpost and no d. 1001.6
destinies: greater dooms win greater d. 17.32
our d. are decided by nothings, accident 240.1
destiny: an almost mustical conception of d. 945.13
conditioning aims to make us like our d. 12.5
d. grants our wishes, but in its own way 240.10
d. is relentless logic of each day 240.9
d.: tyrant's authority for crime and fool's excuse for failure 240.3
efforts to escape d. lead us into it 300.4
how easy it is, when d. is kind 240.7
let a man accept his d. 937.4
love only that which is woven in your d. 240.2
no problem of human d. is beyond human beings 737.4
one link of chain of d. at a time 240.5
our d. rules over us 240.14
sometimes better to abandon one's self to d. 112.5
we are not permitted to choose our d. 240.11
where d. blunders, prudence will not avail 240.17
Where D. with Men for Pieces plays: 240.15
who glories in luck may be overthrown by d. 360.12
whoever has not felt the danger of our times has not penetrated to vitals of d. 1001.9
destroy: d. 73 percent of oil-refining capacity 241.6
fortune, to d., first makes mad 559.14
if a man d. another's eye, d. his eye 517.19
impulse to d. as ancient as to create 241.8
minute can d. what an age must rebuild 241.4
short, easy to d. life others have made 518.15
to be able to d. with good conscience 241.7
to give means to build; to hate is to d. 551.178
destroys: what d. one man preserves another 798.1
destruction: d. is new creation on a wider scale 241.3
destructions: after the great d. everyone will prove he was innocent 641.5
detachment: d. excludes ability to experience happiness 31.3
detail: if every d. given, imagination loses desire 943.1
detest: men love in haste, but they d. at leisure 412.4
detractions: happy they that put their d. to mending 460.5
detractor: next to joy of egotist is joy of d. 206.21
developed: do not seek so anxiously to be d. 435.27
devil: animal would depict d. in human form 41.14
apology for the d.: we hear only one side of case; God has written all the books 242.2
d. always insists on having the last word 242.4
d. does not punish you for behaving well 242.1
d. gets to belfry by vicar's skirts 307.15
d. is merely a fallen angel 242.6
d. seeks slaves and claims obedience 242.8
God without the d. is dead, being alone 387.13
idle men tempt the d. 446.17
mass movements need belief in a d. 568.1
sometimes the d. is a gentleman 242.7
they must needs go whom the d. drives 163.1
where God hath a temple, d. hath a chapel 191.2
why should d. have all the good tunes 242.5
with pious action we sugar o'er the d. 440.19
devil's: truth may come from the d. mouth 998.46
devils: d. driven from heart by touch of hand 882.13
devotion: ignorance is the mother of d. 1068.2
need for d. to something outside ourselves 146.3
temperance, justice without d. is cold virtue 1033.3
devotion's: with d. visage we sugar o'er the devil 440.19
devour: men would d. men but for power of hiding 165.2
devout: d. man would be an atheist if king were 697.7
if man is d., we accuse him of hypocrisy 206.5
most d., harshest in their antipathy 512.11
dialect: d. with slang admirable medium for those with nothing to say 524.1
diary: keep a d. and someday it'll keep you 62.11
dice: best throw of d.: throw them away 369.2
dictator: artist has never been a d. 53.15
d. held in grip of party machine 1002.10
dictators: d. ride on tigers they dare not dismount 1002.13
dictionary: neither is a d. a bad book to read 244.2
one d. is as good as another 244.6
the d. is a closed system 244.3
to read poetry I take down my d. 244.4
what Ernest Hemingway's d. looked like 1069.134
die: afraid that she herself might d. in the night 918.9
anxiety of having to d. is anxiety of being eternally forgotten 221.132
a pity we can d. but once to save country 678.2
as natural to d. as to be born 221.8
base to fight necessity; we have to d. 624.5
cannot love to live if cannot bear to d. 541.32
d. proudly when one cannot live proudly 221.98
d. to life to be a creator 201.28
greatest good luck: to d. at right time 401.28
he was young and could never d. 1071.61
he who hath lived ill cannot d. well 221.54
"I'm going to d.," she said; then waited and said, "I hate it." 221.65
I shall d. of having lived 221.27.
it is better to d. on your feet than to live on your knees 363.29
knowledge of hour when one is to d. 767.3

longest-lived, shortest-lived lose same thing when they d. 548.2
man should be born, and born, d. at once 83.1
man thinks he was not made to d. 454.21
men eddy about, achieving nothing; then d. 606.1
must spend all one's life learning to d. 541.34
nothing to d.; frightful not to live 219.5
no young man believes he shall ever d. 1071.30
old men must d., or the world would only breed the past again 221.129
only benefit of old age: to d. by degrees 221.95
people can d. of mere imagination 450.4
theirs but to do and d. 588.17
there are two respectable ways to d. 221.71
those most like dead are most loath to d. 221.79
to d. completely, one must be forgotten 221.21
to d. is different from what anyone supposed 221.137
to d. is to go into the Collective Unconscious 221.66
to d. is to stop dying and finally do it 221.20
to d. with glory is still pain for dier 221.46
to d. without having lived is unbearable 221.51
to live in hearts we leave is not to d. 454.5
to work, live, d. hard and go to hell 416.10
we cannot d., we cannot be destroyed 454.2
we can't be sure of something worth living for unless we are ready to d. for it 1026.10
we d. disappointed 539.41
we have mouldered away long before we d. 653.46
we must d. to one life to enter another 117.14
we must needs d., and are as water spilt 221.13
we shall d. alone 915.34
what will d. with me when I d.? 606.5
when man and woman d., his heart's the last part to move 581.17
will world be overturned when you d. 873.6
you d. because you're alive 541.36
you'll find it when you try to d. the easier to let go 221.34
died: can't know a man's life until he has d. 539.115
most persons have d. before they expire 219.4
dies: after many a summer d. the swan 606.19
flower that once has blown for ever d. 606.13
he that d. pays all debts 221.112
it matters not how a man d. 541.22
man always d. before he is fully born 404.10
man d. whether he's done nothing or much 6.11
surely nothing d. but something mourns 610.1
diet: anxiety about d. no better than disease 413.12
differ: freedom to d. is not limited 258.7
we hate for points on which we d. 27.3
differed: we owe our knowledge to those who have d. 258.1
difference: d. between university graduate and autodidact 1036.2
Jamie is fifty and feels thirty: Judy is thirty and feels twenty. That's only ten years d. 586.18
little d. whether committed to a farm or jail 337.6
wit, not much d. between half and whole 493.31
differences: resemblances are shadows of d. 683.9
different: anybody who is any good is d. from others 469.6
d. men seek happiness in d. ways 409.3
men are born equal and d. 469.7
men are created d. 171.15
them of other naturs think d. 260.1
they were as d. as fire and ice 711.64
we must be d. in order to love each other 551.76
difficult: all things are d. before they are easy 245.5
attempt d. tasks as if they were easy 585.6
easy is d. when done with reluctance 1022.1
history has made life d. for us all 245.8
in the d. are the friendly forces 245.10
things d. to design easy to perform 245.7
to do nothing at all is most d. 10.17
difficulties: d. are things that show what men are 245.4
he who accounts all things easy will have many d. 327.1
never trust advice of man in d. 19.4
ten thousand d. do not make one doubt 265.4
difficulty: d.: coin used by learned to conceal inanity 848.28
plugging away at a d. 585.5
diffidence: d. is the better part of knowledge 1005.3
digestion: with sound d. man may front much 941.2
dignity: d. achieved only through struggle 1065.20
d.: a matter which concerns only mankind 246.4
d. is genuine which is not diminished by the indifference of others 246.3
essential that a citizen see d. in others 246.5
let none wear an undeserved d. 584.5
let not a man guard his d. 246.2
man's d. reduced by largesse 433.27
what is d. without honesty 246.1
digression: sin may be venial, d. is mortal 972.21
dilapidation: some people are beautiful in d. 653.92
diligence: care and d. bring luck 281.7
few things impossible to d. and skill 281.10
patience, d., like faith, remove mountains 677.15
what is the use of such terrible d. 271.13
dined: many are d. out of their religion, politics 99.1
one cannot think well, love well, sleep well if one has not d. well 274.30
dining: the art of d. well is no slight art 274.23
dinner: d. is to a day what dessert is to d. 274.6
good d., feasting reconciles everybody 274.24
in France everything is a pretext for d. 361.2
man thinks more earnestly of d. than anything 274.19
music with d. is an insult both to the cook and violinist 614.20
people must have d. table laid as usual 213.21
the tocsin of the soul—the d.-bell 274.5
dinner party: the d. is a suburban form of entertainment 944.3
dinosaur's: d. lesson: overabundance of bigness 312.4
diplomacy: d., defense not substitutes for each other 229.6
d. is the lowest form of politeness 247.11
d. is the police in grand costume 247.7
real d. when diplomat deceives his own people 247.9
diplomat: d. should be yielding, supple as liana 247.6
my advice to d. is to have kids and dog 247.10
diplomatic triumph: the d. of this century or any other 309.6
diplomats: d. are essential to starting a war 1042.76
d. are useful only in fair weather 247.3
d., women, crabs seem coming when going 247.4
direction: change in d. clothes itself in rightness 225.5
nothing below you if in d. of your life 435.6
only one d. in world, time its measure 606.18
we have no sense of d., only impetus 483.1
with rifles aimed in the right d. 120.5
directness: the weak and confused worship brutal d. 362.7
dirt: everyone in crowd has power to throw d. 905.2
dirty: clean glove often hides d. hand 224.5
only man, civilized animals become d. 137.5
so long as we are d., we are pure 248.1
taste for d. stories inherent in humans 714.1
disagreeable: those uncomfortable in themselves are d. to others 861.3
disagreement: agreement made more precious by d. 27.7
disappointed: he who expects nothing shall never be d. 318.9
we look for reward and are d. 459.3
disappointment: prompter

the refusal, the less d. 791.4
look on bright side and avoid d. 783.3
disappoints: man appoints and God d. 387.21
disapproval: each man is afraid of neighbor's d. 626.10
disaster: d. crushes one now, afterward another 17.26
know d. was coming, be unable to avert it 747.4
man does better to run from d. than be caught 300.5
disastrous: no events so d. adroit men don't advance 305.5
disavowed: least said is soonest d. 98.2
disciple: every master has but one d. 353.2
disciples: having d. is like having children 353.1
discipline: d. requires recognition of infallibility 250.4
man lives decently, as d. saves his life 250.5
who compares self with the d., not followers of the d., has lower opinion of self 1037.8
discontent: d. first step in progress of man, nation 251.8
nor is it d. to keep the mind deep in its fountain 915.7
discontented: d. one place, seldom happy in another 251.1
discord: d. gives a relish for concord 252.9
harmony needs background of d. 410.3
out of d. comes the fairest harmony 658.6
discouragement: trouble has no connection with d. 253.2
discourse: d. is index of a man's understanding 77.14
d. makes a clear man 188.14
good company, d., are sinews of virtue 152.24
discourses: most tedious d. those on Supreme Being 973.5
discoverers: ill d. think there's no land when they see only sea 87.1
discoveries: bring forth d. in art 53.143
discovery: d. follows d. 479.9
scientific d.: interpretation for our own convenience 849.41
the d. that children have two parents 670.51
Writing became such a process of d. 1069.99
discretion: d., deadly to genius, ruinous to talent 376.5
d. is on all occasions required 755.5
one can pass on responsibility, not d. 810.4
sincerity is glass, d. is diamond 755.16
the better part of valor is d. 755.27
discriminations: social d. with effects so profound 252.2
discussion: anyone who in d. relies on authority 51.13
d. in America means dissent 258.12
no d. between two persons can be of use 188.5
disease: bodily d. may be symptom of spiritual d. 896.11
d. known is half cured 243.1
d. makes men more physical 896.16
every physician has his favourite d. 263.4
got Bright's d. and he has mine 896.20
human d. as the work of demonology 906.22
interest in d. is interest in life 577.5
it is by d. that health is pleasant 187.3
life is an incurable d. 539.21
some remedies worse than the d. 798.10
who conceals his d. cannot be cured 165.5
diseased: canst thou not minister to a mind d. 757.1
diseases: all d. run into one, old age 896.5
d. crucify the soul of man 896.1
d. desperate grown by desperate appliances are relieved, or not at all 798.11
d. which destroy a man are natural 896.26
extreme remedies appropriate to extreme d. 798.4
disenchanting: is anything so d. as attainment 945.43
disfranchisement: d. robs poor of only protection against rich 1038.5
disgrace: in darkness shameful deed brings no d. 217.5
Ye can't be sint to jail f'r it, but it's a kind iv a d. 730.5
disguise: accustomed to d. ourselves to others, we become disguised to ourselves 165.11
man is practised in d. 224.6
to go naked is the best d. 224.4
we all wear some d. 732.4
we d. ourselves from ourselves 864.8
dish: d. around which I see too many people doesn't tempt me 712.6
high birth is a poor d. at table 37.3
dishonesty: d. is the raw material of dupes 224.1
d., the rule; honesty, the exception 425.19
hatred of d. is from fear of being deceived 224.22
honesty is less profitable than d. 425.12
no clear boundary separates honesty, d. 425.5
dishonor: do no d. to the earth 177.1
verse-speaker in the house, d. to be hooted 708.99
disillusion: d. can become illusion if we rest in it 254.3
hope is only good thing d. respects 254.8
disinterested: world saved by handful of d. men 1021.4
dislike: some d. something in every banquet 725.1
sorrow falls readily into d. 918.45
dismal: nothing on earth more d. than man 562.28
disobedience: d. is man's original virtue 256.2
d. is seldom distinguished from neglect 256.1
disorder: d. immediately defeats itself 312.8
d. is always in a hurry 661.11
d. is our worst enemy 661.7
d. makes one wish for police or death 661.13
disovery: d. will shatter concepts we use today 741.19
dispatch: d. is the soul of business 104.8
display: young animals need to d. 267.30
disposition: best part of health is fine d. 392.5
good d. is virtue in itself and is lasting 392.7
disputant: d. no more cares for truth than sportsman for the hare 51.16
disputants: d. like sportsmen; delight in pursuit 51.17
disputation: itch of d. will prove scab of Church 126.14
dispute: in philosophical d., defeated gains most 51.8
dissatisfied: we are less d. when we lack many things 238.23
dissect: we murder to d. 849.42
dissension: civil d. is a viperous worm 252.11
dissent: discussion in America means d. 258.12
looking at God reduces our disposition to human d. 772.3
dissenters: d. have no monopoly on freedom 258.3
dissimulation: without d. no business possible 224.2
world is so full of d. that words are empty 349.17
dissolute: if their pleasures drove away the fears of the d., we'd find no fault in them 494.3
distance: d. has same effect on mind as on eye 689.6
d. lends enchantment to the view 689.2
greatest d. is from nothing to little 741.4
if a man makes me keep my d., the comfort is, he keeps his as well 31.7
distant: d. Trojans never injured me 665.8
eyes upon the d. soaring ranges 368.35
superiority of the d. over the present 238.36
distempers: one topic, their d., forbidden to all well-bred mortals 896.6
distinction: d. that Jews have themselves always made 512.10
envy is tax d. must pay 295.8
distortion: a d. to picture the human as teetering 413.18
distress: deep d. hath humanised my soul 918.56
in deep d. native sense departs 918.53
until man stops shouting down his blunderings, he's not in shape to examine d. 758.18
what end served by running to meet d. 318.10
distressed: knowing sorrow I learn to succor the d. 56.11
distrust: better traitors escape than have spirit of d. 259.5

d. is our only defense against betrayal 259.16
he puts his trust and d. in man 997.4
our d. justifies the deceit of others 259.9
what loneliness is more lonely than d. 259.3
disturb: what comes into the world to d. nothing deserves neither respect nor patience 649.3
diverse: d. elements joined in heart of man 260.2
diversity: the most universal quality is d. 260.3
divide: d. the fire, and you will put it out 939.3
divided: house d. against itself cannot stand 1043.1
divides: he who d. gets the worst share 894.5
divination: come to realize their powers of d. 182.4
divine: belief in d. mission a form of certainty 335.15
from beauty we draw conception of d. life 410.4
God is what man finds that is d. in himself 387.44
held by his fellows as almost d. 123.50
only domain where d. visible: art 53.81
pretenders to d. knowledge are possessed with the sin of pride 335.11
to see d. light put out thy candle 697.4
what is d. escapes men's notice 261.6
divinity: d. is in crisis 261.5
good conscience is the best d. 174.9
I will work out the d. that is busy within my mind 201.34
there is surely a piece of d. in us 261.1
there's a d. that shapes our ends 240.18
divorce: amoebas practice d. but no remarriage 262.6
children have a right to the d. experience 262.1
d. the first before marrying the second 19.12
marriage some weeks more ancient than d. 262.9
divorced: four minds in bed of d. man who marries d. woman 262.5
do: all seek to d. what they please 363.15
can d. all because they think they can 860.8
d. and have done; the former is easiest 76.7
d. it yourself—now enthroned cliché for being occupied with nonessentials 880.12
d. not all you are able 755.14
don't d. to others as you would they d. to you 388.3
d. unto the other feller the way he'd like to d. unto you 388.4
d. what you have to d. 55.5
hideous to assume we can d. something for others 56.2
if to d. were as easy as to know what were good to d. 393.44
if you would not be known to d. anything, never d. it 804.8
man may d. or know but little 9.15
people always neglect something they can d. trying to d. something they can't 55.9
people who d. things exceed endurance 33.18
somebody must make us d. what we can 473.3
theirs but to d. and die 588.17
to d. nothing is most difficult thing 446.18
to promise not to d. a thing 743.13
want thing done well, d. it yourself 880.17
we d. all with an eye to something else 608.1
we d. nothing well till we cease to think about the manner of doing it 928.4
we d. what we can, then make a theory 782.2
we d. what we must 319.3
what I must d. is all that concerns me 227.9
what it lies in our power to d., it lies in our power not to d. 862.3
what men daily d. not knowing what they d. 483.2
whatsoever thy hand findeth to d. 227.4
what ye would men d. to you, d. to them 388.1
what you d. not want done to yourself, d. not to others 388.2
doctor: a d., a friend with special knowledge 263.16
death will seize the d. too 577.9
d. and patient are employer and employee 263.14
God heals, and the d. takes the fees 263.5
hood ass with purple, he shall pass for cathedral d. 138.7
only a fool will make a d. his heir 263.12
doctors: best d. are Diet, Quiet, Merryman 263.18
d. torture the sick and demand a fee 263.7
nature knows needs; d. know nothing 577.1
there are more old drunkards than old d. 268.15
doctrine: d. is the skin of truth set up and stuffed 973.2
no d. does good where nature is wanting 203.3
doctrines: what makes all d. clear? two hundred pounds a year 602.10
doers: talkers are no good d. 923.54
dog: a deep-lying patriarchal instinct in the d. 41.19
a d. gets lonesome just like a human 41.13
Charley is a mind-reading d. 41.31
d. is a lion in his own house 422.17
d., pampered by mistress, is lamentable 41.25
d. was created specially for children 41.40
d. will never forget crumb thou gavest 41.28
large, friendly d. in a very small room 34.74
make d. prosperous, he will not bite you 475.8
no faith never broken save that of a d. 41.18
pleasure of a d. is that you may make a fool of yourself with him 41.4
reasonable amount of fleas is good for d. 41.42
dogma: danger lies in the uncompromisingness with whieh d. is held, not in the d. 264.3
d.: the pleasure of answering questions 480.16
dogmas: he who observes moral precepts of religions won't be questioned in heaven as to d. 797.42
dogmatic: profound ignorance makes a man d. 264.9
unconscious dogmatists most d. 264.4
dogmatism: obstinacy, d., surest signs of stupidity 652.9
dogmatize: no man should d. except on theology 264.8
dog's: d. best friend is his illiteracy 41.23
dogs: d. bark, but the caravan moves on 157.2
d. have more love than integrity 41.7
d. live with man as courtiers 41.34
England, where they feed the d. steak and let people in the slums die 41.21
I dreamed of d. last night 41.32
if I belittle d. or mothers 885.5
let d. delight to bark and bite 41.41
O happy d. of England 41.30
our d. will love the meanest of us 41.26
who hates d. and babies can't be all bad 594.3
who lies with d. shall rise with fleas 57.11
doing: anything worth d. has been done 227.3
d. is overrated 329.7
no d. till thing to be done is recognized 9.11
saying is one thing and d. is another 227.18
step from knowing to d. rarely taken 9.16
we spend days d. what we don't want 1065.15
what is worth d. is worth trouble of asking somebody to do it 315.1
dollar: use his last d. for anything but food 437.5
value of a d. is social 602.17
domestic: d. as a plate, I retire half-past eight 73.8
female malignity exerted in d. trifles 1062.79
gaining d. happiness, women lose beauty 564.25
it takes patience to appreciate d. bliss 564.105
dominate: slave must d. in his turn 1002.7
dominating: we can't do without d. others 719.11
domination: country's turn at world d. ends with change 621.11
done: he that has d. nothing has known nothing 9.9
what is well d. is d. soon enough 311.1
what's d. is d.; spend not time in tears 507.4
Don Quixotes: mankind either Sancho Panzas or D.Q. 562.51

donkey: until the d. tried to clear fence, he thought himself a deer 1027.7
doom: he deposes d. who hath suffered him 17.20
dooms: greater d. win greater destinies 17.32
door: each man is accessible by right d. 961.1
he's on the wrong side of every d. 41.10
open d. must be of a man's size 657.3
room with d. open, one with d. locked 714.3
we often get in quicker by back d. 585.8
doors: all d. open to courtesy 197.6
dote: I d. on myself 876.18
double-tongued: words of the d. reach to the bowels 224.20
doubt: authority rarely survives in face of d. 61.7
cleave to the sunnier side d. 330.35
d. is an element of criticism 904.5
d. is not below knowledge, but above it 904.1
d. is the vestibule of temple of truth 904.3
d., mistrust: panic of timid imagination 1005.6
d. of reality of love makes us d. all 1005.1
d. springs eternal in the human breast 265.11
faith embraces itself and d. 330.36
faith had dissociated itself from d. 265.10
let us never d. what nobody is sure about 115.1
majority of mankind incapable of d., faith 562.21
man with humility will acquire in his beliefs the saving d. of his certainty 435.14
modest d. called the beacon of the wise 904.10
ten thousand difficulties do not make one d. 265.4
there lives more faith in honest d. 265.8
wilt Thou not take d. of Thy children 265.2
doubtful: d. friend is worse than certain enemy 365.4
doubts: d. make us lose good we oft might win 1005.10
from new truths, new phrase, new d. grow 1005.4
the skeptic does not mean him who d. 904.11
doughnut: keep eye upon the d., not upon the whole 274.29
dour: d. friend is less fatiguing than optimist 660.3
dove: oh that I had wings like a d. 300.1
doves: be ye therefore harmless as d. 943.3
downwind: lower classes, decent as long as they stay d. 682.14
drama: d. deals not with truth, but with effect 972.22
eye is the enemy of ear in real d. 972.38
great d. is the souvenir of the adventure of a master among pieces of his own soul 972.24
rappers commit d. fraught with crime 614.22
talent for d. is not talent for writing 972.35
drama's: d. laws the d. patrons give 972.16
dramas: some always create parts for selves in d. which nobody is prepared to act with them 627.4
dramatist: d. finds watching shocks among men engrossing enough without comment 972.36
d. must avoid digression more than a saint does sin 972.21
dread: d. gives you your freedom 343.7
dreaded: he is to be d. who dreads poverty 33.22
dream: a d. pursued and found wanting 131.36
d. is always below the surface of speech 336.15
lie of pipe d. is what gives us life 336.13
luckily I have learned to d. 201.40
man that is born falls into d. 449.7
man who doesn't d. stores up a lot of poison 266.2
no deformity but saves us from a d. 457.10
our d. dashes against the great mystery 1019.8
shadow of a d. is man, no more 990.12
sleep that allows me to d. 266.15
the memory of a d. to end all dreams 381.1
there's nothing like d. to create future 368.17
we need men who can d., not skeptics 450.20
we wake from one d. into another d. 449.9
where all is d., reasoning is useless 336.10
dreamed: oh, to have d. harder! 266.13
whatever doesn't really happen is d. 266.19
dreamer: d. can know no truth but by awaking 336.16
d. lives forever; toiler dies in a day 336.14
only d. shall understand realities 336.4
society forgives criminal, never the d. 450.32
dreaming: d. is a game of the imagination 266.10
d. permits us to be insane every night 266.3
dreams: believe in d., spend life asleep 336.1
d. are dower that make us rich an hour 336.2
d. are interpreters of our inclinations 266.12
d. are the children of an idle brain 266.18
d. are true while they last 266.21
d. have breath, tears, and the touch of joy 906.2
d. live deaf amid cries of real world 266.17
each of us has his irremediable d. 915.43
easier to swoon in d. than do good 393.29
he who passes not his days in d. is slave of the days 336.5
in manhood we tell d. of childhood 580.40
in our d. submerged truth comes to top 336.21
in the mind, d. build nest with fragments 266.20
I still got d. like anybody else 266.6
joy of d. which none can take away 336.3
judge your character by your d. 266.4
let d. visit, like birds 266.14
make us, not fly to d., but moderate desire 238.3
old age brings red flare of d. again 336.22
old d. were good d. 266.22
religions such stuff as d. are made of 797.79
she entered his d. sane and left mad 266.11
the d. with which every child is born 1063.4
truest life is when we are in d. awake 336.17
we are not really grateful to those who make our d. come true 336.6
we are such stuff as d. are made on 606.16
we forget our d. so speedily 266.8
when hopes and d. are loose in streets 819.22
who walks in loneliness and d. 266.23
dress: loud d. offends people of taste 963.19
man can't d. without clothing his ideas 267.27
dressed: any may be in good spirits when well d. 267.5
d. fine as I will, flies exceed me still 267.31
lady wants to be d. like everybody else 267.15
drink: d., for you know not whence you came, nor why 268.39
d. not the third glass 268.22
d. today, and drown all sorrow 268.36
drove millions of the weaker nerve to d. 268.6
every man should eat and d. 274.1
lechery d. provokes, and unprovokes 268.48
let us eat and d., for tomorrow we die 606.4
passed me by like an untouched d. 948.19
we d. each other's healths, spoil our own 268.29
drinker: under a bad cloak there's often a good d. 268.8
drinkers: old stomach reforms more d. than new resolve 268.35
drinketh: he that d. well sleepeth well 274.22
drinking: d. man never less himself than when sober 268.33
there are two reasons for d. 268.43
driven: we sail, ever d. in uncertainty 1005.9
drivers: d. in a traffic jam are not amiable 64.12
drop: there are people one should like to d. 914.5
drown: d. not thyself to save a drowning man 837.3
it is folly to d. on dry land 354.5
drowned: Bacchus hath d. more men than Neptune 268.16
drowning: d. man is not troubled by rain 17.45

not waving but d. 239.10
drudgery: work is not the curse, but d. is 1065.8
drudges: life of labor makes d., not men 1065.25
drug: a d. for everything is madness 269.1
d. misuse is not a disease, it is a decision 225.4
everything is a dangerous d. but reality 784.5
drugs: beautifully narrowed into the crux of d. 221.28
d. are nihilistic 269.6
drum: big d. only sounds well from afar 873.18
d. drives out thought, is military instrument 588.10
take cash, nor heed rumble of distant d. 729.21
drummer: because he hears a different d. 468.12
drunk: good d. is not always a good bartender 207.6
man, being reasonable, must get d. 268.5
when the cock is d., he forgets the hawk 268.3
who can help getting d. on Beethoven's Ninth? 614.37
wise man stays home when d. 268.13
drunkard: to dispute d. is to debate empty house 268.45
drunkards: there are more old d. than old doctors 268.15
drunken: be d., on wine, poetry, virtue, as you wish 739.1
what the sober man has in his heart, the d. man has on his lips 268.10
drunkenness: d. doesn't create vices 268.46
d. insulates us in thought 268.12
d. neither keeps a secret nor observes a promise 268.7
what does d. not accomplish 268.24
due: each his d. at the time allotted 815.5
dull: d. man is always sure, sure man always d. 115.10
to the d. mind all nature is leaden 493.8
dullness: d. is the coming of age of seriousness 270.2
d. makes life supportable, welcome 219.2
gentle d. ever loves a joke 436.24
dumbness: d. in the speech of men more agonizing than d. in the eyes of animals 149.8
dung: money and d. are no good till spread 602.22
duped: who fears being d. cannot be magnanimous 259.1
dupes: dishonesty is the raw material of d. 224.1
most mistrustful are often greatest d. 259.12
duration: d. is not a test of true or false 998.73
that formed for long d. matures slowly 404.14
dusk: d., when streetlights make little difference 217.6
dust: beauty is everlasting; d. is for a time 72.36
d. are our frames 733.23
d. into d., and under d. to lie 221.77
d. thou art, and unto d. shalt return 221.12
duties: modern state has only rights, no d. 930.4
to be righteous is the first of all d. 491.14
when habit has strengthened sense of d., they leave us no time for other things 271.11
duty: always some who think they know your d. 271.6
do your d. and leave the rest to the gods 271.4
d. is the sublimest word in our language 271.17
d. is what one expects from others 271.31
d. leads to constraint, kills desire 564.48
d.: pretending that trivial is critical 271.7
d. toward others is a way of attaching our drowning selves to a passing raft 271.10
he gives worthless gold who gives from d. 384.20
it is not hard to do one's d. if one knows it 271.3
last pleasure in life is discharging our d. 271.9
no d. so underrated as being happy 271.27
paths of d. may not get you anywhere 271.29
rights that do not flow from d. are not worth having 823.6
sense of d. enables man to do prodigies 271.19
there's life in d., rest in striving 271.30
to the honest, an honor to do d. 271.21
what is your d.; what the day demands 271.8
when d. comes a-knocking, welcome him in 271.18
when d. grows thy law, enjoyment fades 271.24
when stupid man does thing he is ashamed of, he declares that it is his d. 271.26
without d., life is soft and boneless 271.12
dwarf: the d. remnants of our sun will cool and dim 285.1
dwelling: style in d., emblem of identity 444.24
dying: arts of living well and d. well are one 541.7
d. is as natural as living 541.16
d. is more the survivors' affair 221.88
d. was nobody's business but his own 221.75
for d., you always have time 221.74
growing old is d. young 653.66
it is not death but d. which is terrible 221.49
reason for living also reason for d. 541.3
the d. pray at the last, "thank you" 541.5
the tongues of d. men enforce attention 221.115
to our real, naked selves there is nothing on earth or heaven worth d. for 221.69
truth sits upon the lips of d. men 998.6

E

eager: when a man's willing and e., god joins in 1057.1
eagle: e. clasps the crag with crooked hands 82.7
e. never lost so much time as when he submitted to learn of the crow 435.3
the e. suffers little birds to sing 719.53
ear: eye is the painter and e. the singer 20.2
give every man thine e., few thy voice 543.4
early: fate of worm shows danger of e. rising 73.1
genius always finds itself a century e. 376.10
who is known as e. riser may sleep late 804.30
earnest: e. men have no time to patch naked truth 113.6
e. people habitually look on serious side of things that have no serious side 886.3
something of burlesque in e., good men 886.5
earnestness: taking fun as fun and e. in earnest 886.7
ears: eyes are more accurate witnesses than e. 897.5
hungry stomach has no e. 437.9
men trust their e. less than their eyes 882.4
most have e., few have judgment 690.1
two e., one mouth: listen more, talk less 543.5
we cannot close our e. easily as eyes 636.5
earth: ambition does not see e. she treads on 33.14
axis of e. through center of every town 699.4
do no dishonour to the e. 177.1
e. being so good, would Heaven seem best 272.2
e. delights to feel your bare feet 623.32
e. is given as a common stock 272.5
e. we abuse will take revenge 177.5
e., with her thousand voices, praises God 272.3
let me enjoy the e. no less 272.4
more things in heaven, e., than dreamt of 953.3
our days upon e. are a shadow 990.4
the e. has killed itself 241.11
touch, love, and honour the e. 272.1
earthquake: e. achieves equality of all men 17.19
earth's: e. crammed with heaven 261.2
ease: e. would recant vows made in pain 743.7
East: there is neither E. nor West, when two strong men stand face to face 100.13
easy: all things are difficult before e. 245.5
attempt e. tasks as if difficult 585.6
do not pray for e. lives 723.22
for e. things men set little store 327.2
he who accounts all things e. will have many difficulties 327.1
nothing is e. to the unwilling 245.6
eat: every man should e. and drink 274.1
[Americans] expect to e. and stay thin 34.10
let us e. and drink, for

tomorrow we die 606.4
nature a conjugation of the verb to e. 274.18
tell what you e., I will tell who you are 274.2
eaten: e. bread is forgotten 475.4
eaters: great e. are incapable of all else great 883.4
eateth: he that e. well drinketh well 274.22
eating: destiny of human race to stop e. animals 1028.2
e. is believing 274.28
when e. can't be a habit, neither can seeing 437.8
eccentric: at liberty to be as e. as they please 276.6
e. is a man who is a law unto himself 276.3
eccentricity: e. abounds when character abounds 276.4
paradise of individuality, e., heresy, anomalies, hobbies, and humours 289.27
eccentrics: e. are explosive mixtures 276.1
ecclesiastical: a sort of e. footrace 697.2
economics: questions that are beyond the reach of e. 480.10
economists: e. are as useful as astrologers 277.8
e. think well of what they do themselves 848.16
economy: e. consists not in saving but in selection 977.4
e. in common minds means no taste, comfort 977.9
expense may be essential part of true e. 977.5
the fully planned e. is warmly regarded 277.1
ecstasy: e., intensity in the creative act 278.3
entwine thighs around them, pant in e. 892.2
lit up with a quiet e. 278.2
take all away from me, but leave me e. 278.1
ecumenical: e. crisis is between traditional and experimental forms of church life 126.4
Eden: E. is that old-fashioned House 409.29
edge: finest e. is made with blunt whetstone 321.31
editing: e. is most companionable form of education 764.16
e. is same as quarreling with writers 764.12
editor: e. separates wheat from chaff, prints chaff 764.14
the job of e., dullest of any in the world 764.9
editorial: advertisements have more knowledge concerning the community than e. columns 18.1
editorials: e. advocating election of opposing candidates 630.7
educate: people that e. aren't always educated 965.24
educated: e. people speak the same languages 210.14
higher than God's tribunal—the e. man's 279.13
only the e. are free 279.25
educates: power e. the potentate 831.5
educating: dons are too busy e. to be able to teach 965.7
education: by nature men alike; by e., very different 279.16
e. accumulates ignorance in inert facts 279.1
educational progress is national concern, e. private 279.32
e.: balance wheel of the social machinery 279.54
e. can even seem to be an impediment 279.9
e. consists in creating motives 279.85
e. consists in what we have unlearned 279.82
e. determines a man's future life 279.67
e.: discloses to wise and disguises from foolish their lack of understanding 279.8
e. in a technological world is neuter 279.56
e. instills nonsense, unifies people 279.74
e. is an admirable thing 522.67
e. is an emancipation 279.31
e. is an ornament in prosperity 279.4
e. is leading souls to what is best 279.73
e. is listening without losing temper 279.29
e. is that which teaches discernment 279.72
e.: learning how to make facts live 279.42
e., like neurosis, begins at home 279.77
e. makes a people easy to govern, but impossible to enslave 279.12
e. makes greater difference between man and man 279.2
e. makes straight ditch of free brook 279.81
e. makes us more stupid than brutes 279.33
e. produces and erases intuitions 279.65
e. that fails to cultivate will depraves mind 279.27
e. that would leave out history and the past 34.29
e., the movement from darkness to light 279.10
experience, travel an e. in themselves 321.15
first duty of adolescent is to disgorge all his e. 1071.55
goal of e. is advancement of knowledge and dissemination of truth 279.48
good deal of e. consists of unlearning 279.55
great difficulty in e. 279.75
higher e. is booming in the U.S. 279.64
highest result of e. is tolerance 984.11
history a race between e., catastrophe 419.53
how is it children are intelligent, men stupid; it must be e. that does it 279.19
it is only the ignorant who despise e. 279.69
making children honest is beginning of e. 425.15
nature has always had more power than e. 431.28
no one can "get" an e. 279.51
philosophic aim of e. to get one out of isolated class into humanity 279.35
putting man on the moon, easier than improving e. 279.79
roots of e. are bitter, fruit is sweet 279.5
soap and e. are deadly in the long run 133.29
students attend university for an e. 848.32
takes five years to recover from college e. 279.6
things taught in schools are not an e. 279.22
we need to unlearn some respect for e. 279.80
what we call e. and culture is nothing but substitution of literature for life 279.78
what we do not call e. is more precious than what we call e. 279.24
educator: e. says what he thinks pupils should hear 965.28
effect: best e. of fine persons felt afterward 473.4
take away cause and e. ceases 110.2
what is done for e. is seen to be done for e. 901.6
efficiency: city of Southern e. and Northern charm 1044.2
efficient: e. laborer will not crowd day with work 1066.5
superlatively e. government is anti-human 395.25
effort: do for themselves through local and private e. 277.4
e. is only e. when it begins to hurt 281.12
law of human life is e. 457.4
men moved not by goal, but by the e. 281.11
much e., much prosperity 281.5
efforts: man's virtue not measured by his e. 1033.38
effrontery: no e. like that of woman caught in act 1062.81
egg: e. source of all, everyone's ancestral hall 83.3
send not for a hatchet to break open an e. 949.1
sex without sin, like an e. without salt 892.22
sooner have fowl by hatching the e. 677.13
eggs: wise do not venture all e. in one basket 755.4
ego: contribute vastly to a comforting glow in the ego of the grown-up 65.3
difference between strong e. and large e. 873.10
fantastic indulgence of the e. 1069.50
solemn e. accompanies the learned 848.11
egoism: altruism which is not e. is sterile 433.25
our e. leads us to judge people by their relations to ourselves 515.4
egoistic: children are completely e. 123.21
egoists: it astounds us to come upon other e. 873.19
egotism: apology is e. wrong side out 44.2
e.: anesthetic dulling pain of stupidity 873.14
egotist: next to joy of e. is joy of detractor 206.21
elbow: e. grease is the best polish 281.3
elders: advice of e. apt to be unreal 19.13

elected: more men e. between sundown and sunup 1038.16
election: democracy is e. by incompetent many 233.50
e. is a moral horror 1038.18
more important than winning e. is governing nation 710.11
elections: in e. people vote against, not for 1038.1
electricity: by e. matter became great vibrating nerve 966.9
electronics: justified the excitement and fuss of the e. involved 966.31
those who live by e. die by e. 966.33
elegance: e. ceases to exist when it is noticed 282.1
e. is good taste plus dash of daring 282.3
mere e. of language produces empty renown 942.18
only real e. is in the mind 282.4
elemental: world to-day: sick for lack of e. things 177.2
elements: invention successful if necessary e. are present 502.1
why fear savage e. that we are made of 623.28
elephant: e. has thick skin, head full of ivory 710.12
elephants: e. suffer from too much patience 41.8
trumpet in a herd of e. 171.13
elopement: if not for presents, e. preferable 1051.1
eloquence: continuous e. wearies 283.9
e. has departed; simple speech as well 134.4
e. is the language of nature 763.4
e. lies in voice and eyes as much as words 283.5
honest brief has its own e. 528.20
occasional gleams of Churchillian e. 763.10
seldom discern e. under threadbare cloak 718.40
today models of e. are ad agencies 283.7
true e. says all to be said and that only 283.6
we can't all combine good looks and e. 542.10
when gold argues cause, e. impotent 602.49
eloquent: e. man is drunk with a certain belief 283.2
emancipation: e. from the soil is no freedom for a tree 363.48
embalm: nature is honest, we aren't; we e. dead 103.2
embarrassing: no e. questions; just e. answers 480.17
embrace: kings, women, vines e. what is nearest 1062.112
emergencies: in e. we fall back on our gods 203.2
eminence: a plague on e. 332.44
false praise says e. comes from nobility 332.36
men of e. get as much flattery as censure 332.2
whoever rises will have many malevolent gazers at his e. 952.5
eminent: censure is tax paid for being e. 206.25
emotion: after youth life of e. becomes unbearable 1072.7
e. has taught mankind to reason 284.36
e. is primarily about nothing 284.34
life of reason balanced by irrational e. 1020.1
never have an e. that is unbecoming 284.37
no e. or wave can long retain its form 284.3
poetry: e. recollected in tranquillity 708.117
women are eagerly on lookout for any e. 1062.136
emotional: well-ordered house and perfect e. digestion 1062.23
emotions: e. are pure which gather and lift you up 284.29
intelligent able to control e. 493.20
nothing vivifies and kills like the e. 284.30
oversensitiveness makes e. seem disgusting 284.26
the e. may be endless 284.14
to experience only one's own e. would be a sorry limitation 284.17
emphatic: difficult to be e. when other side is not 51.21
empire: great e., little minds, go ill together 711.16
if the e. would rule me out, I would hit the e. 929.10
perfection of Gospels never built e. 859.1
to e. builders, men are instruments 458.3
who man would be, must rule e. of himself 862.14
who seek e. have no alternative between success and downfall 33.24
empiricism: e. has sworn never to draw conclusions 321.45
emptiness: greatest pretenses built up to hide e. 165.8
empty: better an e. purse than an e. head 447.11
cannot scare me with their e. spaces 415.7
enchanter: spell of true e. operates upon imagination and heart 53.67
encounter: people do not heed the things they e. 87.6
end: better the e. of a thing than beginning 76.2
e. is what the means have made it 574.4
it was not clear how it would e. 285.2
little earth, that is the e. 221.102
means are enjoyed if e. is desired 574.5
men perish because they cannot join beginning with e. 76.1
no man can see what e. waits for him 368.32
remember the e., thou shalt never do amiss 286.1
the educational process has no e. beyond itself 279.17
you begin well only in what you e. well 76.5
ended: nothing is ever e., all is only begun 539.125
ending: art of e. greater than that of beginning 76.8
bad beginning makes a bad e. 176.5
good beginning makes a good e. 76.4
ends: great to do that which e. all other deeds 948.24
more e. in world than anything else 286.4
there's a divinity that shapes our e. 240.18
endurance: e. is crowning quality of great hearts 287.6
patient e. is godlike 287.5
endure: art of life: how to enjoy and e. 539.50
to e. unendurable is true endurance 287.4
enemies: common danger unites even e. 1016.1
e. are first to discover your mistakes 288.3
for ten jokes thou hast an hundred e. 436.29
friends provoked become bitterest e. 365.47
from e. alone we can learn our defects 945.6
if we read secret history of e., we should find sorrow enough to disarm 288.16
it is unhappy lot which finds no e. 712.9
we often give e. means for our own ruin 866.1
who fears making e. will have no friends 980.6
wise man gets more from his e. than a fool from his friends 288.10
you only injure yourself if you take notice of despicable e. 288.2
enemies': e. promises were made to be broken 288.1
enemy: be thine e. an ant, see him as elephant 288.22
bound to forgive e., not trust him 288.9
bring not all mischief on an e. 755.24
concentrating attention of people on e. 622.4
e. becomes friend when underground 288.7
e. can't wish what man thinks up for self 866.9
have nothing to do with your e. 288.11
how good bad music and bad reasons sound when one marches against an e. 1042.66
if thine e. hunger, feed him 288.4
kisses of an e. are deceitful 365.17
know e. as he is, not as one wishes him to be 288.14
men put e. in mouths to steal away brains 268.49
no e. so annoying as one who was a friend 365.90
no safety in regaining favor of e. 288.18
nothing like sight of e. down on his luck 288.6
one active e. is worth two friends 288.12
praises from an e. imply real merit 722.7
prove to e. that he did you some good 288.19
their worst e.: who tells them the truth 1000.17
there is no little e. 288.8
time-consuming to have an e. 288.24
to befriend e. is essence of true religion 100.5

whoever has foe at his mercy and does not kill is his own e. 534.2
who has one e. shall meet him everywhere 288.13
enemy's: e. gift is ruinous and no gift 384.29
energy: e. in nation like sap in a tree 621.23
e. which makes child hard to manage is e. which later makes him manager of life 123.5
repeated shocks exhaust the e. of strongest souls 117.1
too much work and e. kill a man 312.5
worshipper of e. is too energetic 10.4
enforce: do not command what you cannot e. 531.20
engine: four-story house, mounted over an enormous e. 895.3
engineers: e. cannot create a worm 966.15
one has to look out for e. 966.23
England: in E. stables centre of household 289.29
in E. the rich own the poor 289.31
to ensure summer in E., have it framed 289.33
English: correct E.: slang of prigs writing essays 524.10
curious race, the E. 289.26
foreigners have souls; the E. haven't 919.2
if you spoke E. loudly enough they would understand 965.10
look to standard man for standard E. 524.45
modern E. is full of bad habits 134.6
the E. are the slaves of law 289.32
the E. language is in a bad way 524.33
the E. talked with inflected phrases 923.26
the two main forms of E. are continuing to move apart 524.5
varieties of spoken E. could not be counted 524.3
will America be the death of E.? 524.31
Englishman: guard against E. who speaks French perfectly 289.18
impossible for any E. to be happy here 34.19
Englishmen: mad dogs and E. go out in the midday sun 358.1
enjoy: art of life: how to e. and endure 539.50
people e. things more knowing others have been left out 704.4
two aims: to get what you want and e. it 704.37
enjoying: e. things is not evil 704.8
enjoyment: each day was a challenge of e. 704.18
e. before caution soon brings punishment 739.2
e.: feeling accompanying ongoing activity 704.14
e. good in itself is good religiously 900.13
e. is bashful, does not want to be sought 704.23
life is not a progress from e. to e. 238.24
no e. for man until incapable of pleasure 653.60
we derive intense e. only from contrast 187.2
enjoyments: in despair there are intense e. 239.5
enmity: e. is catching 412.23
seldom e. between seasoned politicians 711.90
to eye of e. virtue seems ugliest blemish 412.20
ennui: e. has made more gamblers than avarice 290.1
symmetry is e., the essence of grief 661.8
enormities: one's worst e. remain within 1055.9
enough: e. is as good as a feast 947.3
you never know what is e. unless you know what is more than e. 947.1
enriches: what e. other than wallet is uneconomic 602.1
enslaved: all spirits e. which serve evil 889.18
enterprise: for happiness, man needs e. and change 409.83
on young man no gem so gracious as e. 291.3
entertaining: man who can be e. for a full day 496.1
entertainment: art is response to demand for e. 53.122
mass e., dominated by documentary realism 292.3
mass media offer e. to be consumed 576.1
enthusiasm: e.: a distemper of youth 293.3
nothing great was ever done without e. 293.5
science is antidote to poison of e. 849.36
entreaty: even the gods are moved by voice of e. 805.4
entry: every exit is an e. somewhere else 76.9
envied: man will do all things to get himself e. 295.23
much better to be e. than to be pitied 295.13
envies: no peacock e. another peacock his tail 733.17
player e. only player, poet only poet 1037.6
envious: e. consumed by their own passion 295.2
e. die as oft as envied win applause 295.12
not even success softens heart of e. 295.19
those believed humble, usually e. 435.25
environment: adaptation between man and e. 12.1
e. does not determine man's culture 294.2
grateful e. is substitute for happiness 294.5
Never have people been more the masters of their e. 34.9
qualities atrophy in standing-room-only e. 713.6
envy: all e. is proportionate to desire 295.14
e. a sharper spur than pay 295.11
e. bestrides praise 722.24
e. blasts things elevated above rest 952.6
e. is destroyed by true friendship 295.16
e. is everywhere 295.7
e. is more irreconcilable than hatred 295.15
e. is the tax distinction must pay 295.8
e. lasts longer than happiness of envied 295.17
e.: see things only in their relations 295.21
expect not praise without e. until death 722.4
great are spoken against from e. 295.18
great power incites e., destruction 426.7
if e. were fever, all world would be ill 295.6
let age, not e., wrinkle thy cheeks 295.4
men e. those who fare well 431.26
no passion so strong in the heart as e. 295.22
nothing sharpens sight like e. 295.10
our nature holds much e. and malice 295.20
people commend fine day without e. 1050.9
pity is for the living, e. for the dead 541.41
pride, avarice, e. are tongues men heed 733.5
ephemeral: all is e.—even fame and the famous 990.2
epic: e. vanished with age of personal heroism 418.27
epicure: e. says, fate cannot harm me, I've dined 274.27
epigram: what is an e.? a dwarfish whole 296.1
epigrams: an hour for e., longer for a paradox 766.6
easy to write e., but hard to write book 1069.88
epiphany: he went faint with gastric e. 18.3
epitaph: e.: inscription showing that virtues acquired by death have retroactive effect 103.3
epithelium: look beneath the e. of things 608.3
epithets: e., like pepper, give zest to your writing 942.2
epoch: at each e., world was lost, saved 298.13
every e. has character determined by way population react to material events 298.19
every e. has deified its peculiar errors 298.16
man lives the life of his e. 184.6
to make an e. in the world, good head and great inheritance are essential 401.22
equal: all have e. right to government protection 297.10
all men are created e. 297.14
all men are e.—at cards 369.3
as men, we are all e. in presence of death 221.105
in company of e., fortune must decline 57.16
in polling booth every American e. 297.22
men are born e. but also born different 469.7
men seldom trust the opinion of their e. 656.28
quarrels arise when those who are e. have not got e. shares, or vice versa 297.2
equality: can be friends only on terms of e. 365.104
e. in democracy when all share rule 233.3
e. is treating similar men

alike 297.1
e. lowers flight of imagination 297.25
earthquake achieves e. of all men 17.19
intellect respects e. as a convention 297.3
nobody can give you e. 859.5
on e. we would have only animal pleasure 780.10
perfect e. affords no temptation 297.18
some unhappy is better than none happy, which would be the case in a state of e. 297.15
standardization of man is called e. 297.9
to be against e. today like living in Alaska and being against snow 775.9
unless man believes all mankind his brothers, he labors vainly in vineyards of e. 297.20
we clamor for e. in matters in which we cannot hope to obtain excellence 297.12
When a match has e. partners / then I fear not 564.3
equals: e. revolt to be superior 819.1
friendship seldom lasting but between e. 365.62
little friendship in world; least between e. 365.13
equity: custom creates the whole of e. 213.22
there is no real e. 477.8
erotic: truly e. sensibility in evoking the image of woman never omits to clothe it 892.31
when a lady's e. life is vexed 892.36
err: experience does not e. 321.27
few sometimes know, when thousands e. 822.15
road to wisdom: e. and e., less and less 1060.26
striving, man must e. 299.17
the most may e. as grossly as the few 233.14
to e. is human, to forgive divine 359.14
errands: pleasure we treasure is to run e. for the Ministers of State 400.6
erroneous: e. ideas would perish if clearly expressed 299.33
error: all liable to e.; most tempted to it 299.22
beware barking close to heels of an e. 299.10
cause of e. is war of senses, reason 299.26
delay is preferable to e. 231.6
e. alone needs support of government 999.8
e. flies from mouth to mouth, pen to pen 299.34
e. is the rule; truth, accident of e. 299.14
e.: scribbled sheet we must first erase 299.11
e. venges itself unto the seventh generation 299.21
e., wounded, writhes in pain and dies 299.3
humanity too harassed by want to struggle with e. 625.6
ignorance preferable to e. 447.18
in practice e. and truth do not consort 9.10
intelligence lends itself to conformist e. 171.12
love truth, but pardon e. 299.35
man who can own up to his e. is greater than he who merely avoids making it 299.27
many have rashly charged troops of e. 790.2
no e. is such as pursuit of absolute truth 299.7
progress of rivers to ocean is not so rapid as that of man to e. 299.36
prophecy is most gratuitous form of e. 747.3
to show e. is not to give truth 299.23
truth lies within compass, e. is immense 299.29
we don't allow freedom from e. to our neighbors 684.4
were half power, wealth given to redeem mind from e., no need of arsenals 299.24
errors: cranks take up unfashionable e. 276.5
e. of young men are ruin of business 299.1
e. on surface flow, for pearls dive below 740.2
every epoch has deified its peculiar e. 298.16
general, abstract ideas: source of e. 443.30
make your rule the e. of a wise man 299.2
men positive in e. out of zeal to truth 299.32
those oft are stratagems which e. seem 939.2
errs: to show another that he e. 51.15
erudition: e.: dust shaken from book into empty skull 848.3
if we steal thoughts from ancients, it's e. 700.1
two evils for man of e.: never be listened to, and be listened to always 848.23
escape: man trying to e. never concealed enough 300.6
space flights are an e. from oneself 921.4
two places impossible for a man to e. from 875.25
Eskimos: always find some E. ready to instruct Congolese on heat waves 19.17
essayist: e. can discourse without interruption 1069.108
e. is a self-liberated man 1069.143
essence: e. of thought is growth 975.54
establish: to e. himself, a man appears established 45.17
estate: politest men quarrel at division of e. 1058.2
real e. is foundation of world's guilt 746.10
esteem: difficult to like those whom we don't e. 808.6
e. must be founded on preference 725.4
esteemed: have, and you shall be e. 602.45
we cannot always make ourselves e. 808.7
estrangement: e. of opinions: for two to speak ironically and neither to feel the irony 301.3
eternal: I have seen the e. Footman hold my coat, and snicker 221.39
past is e., the sea will wash it up again 118.5
we feel and know that we are e. 454.20
eternity: e. is terrible thought 302.1
hold e. in an hour 623.6
I am not e., but a man 542.5
eternity's: he who kisses joy as it flies lives in e. sun rise 409.15
ethic: science, by itself, cannot supply an e. 849.31
strength and strength's will are supreme e. 940.11
ethical: e. axioms are like axioms of science 998.35
ethics: do not confuse vested interests with e. 495.5
e. is recommending to others sacrifices required for co-operation with oneself 604.32
e. make existence possible 20.7
no final truth in e. 604.18
science of e. consoles me for ignorance of physical sciences 604.30
who defines his conduct by e. imprisons his song-bird in cage 604.14
Ethiopian: can E. change skin, or leopard, spots 444.7
etiquette: e. is what you do, say, when others looking 563.15
e.: means of approaching, avoiding people 563.20
euphemism: e. ceases to be euphemistic after a time 1064.26
Europe: E., I feel, that also introduced us to the lie 303.4
mistake about E. is taking countries seriously 303.5
we go to E. to be Americanized 303.2
European: life for the E. is a career 539.68
evening: in e. man walks only with his legs 341.2
evasion: American social life constitutes an e. of talking to people 152.10
event: an e. is only actualization of thoughts 305.3
do we not all spend lives under shadow of e. not yet come 368.22
no man before the e. can see 368.32
person makes e. and e. person 110.4
events: cushioned a little from the impact of great e. 626.3
enemy of wisdom is the march of e. 305.4
in pressure of e., principle is no help 734.7
most e. are inexpressible 53.113
people to whom nothing has happened cannot understand unimportance of e. 305.2
spirits of great e. stride on before the e. 305.1
to be philosopher is to be prepared against e. 694.7
eventually: e.: has the soothing effect of a promise 231.5
everybody: e. should take each other as they are

775.11
everything happens to e. in time 321.46
everybody's: e. business is nobody's business 810.6
everyday: e. life is order and haphazardry 539.119
everyone: like a human fog, feeling sorry for e. 885.2
everything: e. happens to everybody in time 321.46
e. with six legs and wings and stings 481.7
the only solution is to plow e. under 371.2
everywhere: he that is e. is nowhere 10.6
evidence: all necessary truth is its own e. 998.36
circumstantial e. is very strong 306.2
more than sufficient e. that all is not right with the world 307.9
evil: act of e. breeds others to follow 1070.1
all are spirits enslaved which serve e. 889.18
all e. comes from the old 1072.1
all e. is universal good 623.61
always fair sailing if you escape e. 300.9
a thousand hack at branches of e. 790.34
be good and let people speak e. of thee 393.41
belief in supernatural e. unnecessary 1055.3
defeat preferable to victory by e. means 574.6
destroy seed of e. lest it grow 307.1
every e. hath its good 154.1
e. alone has oil for every wheel 307.27
e. attracts the weak by promise of power 307.20
e. communications corrupt good manners 473.1
e. condoned if compensated by good 390.12
e. done to another is e. done to oneself 307.19
e. enters like needle, spreads like oak 307.12
e., fault of self-styled pure in heart 790.11
e. in us is intolerant of e. in others 307.25
e. is a necessary part of the universe 307.26
e. is uncertain in same degree as good 343.22
e. men by their nature cannot ever prosper 307.13
e. men not excused from service of state 930.1
e. not yielded to is a benefactor 307.10
e. tongues may blast a whole life of virtue 905.3
e. which I would not, that I do 691.3
good preventing greater good is e. 390.20
great epochs come when we rechristen e. as what is best in us 307.28
harmful ideas are cloaks for e. passions 734.14
he who accepts e. is involved in it 307.22
he who does e. that good may come 307.18
if men were basically e. 307.6
in rebuking e. be conscious of own 803.11
instruments of e. believe what they do is not e. but honorable 307.23
it by e. that good is pleasant 187.3
judge should have learned to know e. 514.8
life's a field for good and e. 539.106
love of money is root of all e. 602.4
marriage is the only e. men pray for 564.53
men do e. from religious conviction 879.2
men's e. manners live in brass 307.33
men think it a right to return e. for e. 817.1
must I do all the e. I can before I shun it? 307.16
no e. in atom, only in men's souls 641.14
no man appreciates all the e. he does 1070.14
no notice is taken of a little e. 307.2
no resolve for good or e. until execution 390.8
not all those to whom we do e. hate us 227.26
oldest e. more supportable than the new 17.41
omission of good is no less reprehensible than commission of e. 390.16
one ought not to return e. to anybody 665.12
overcome e. with good 393.7
real e. is to cringe to the evils 307.32
resolution is too late to avoid e. 807.3
six well-spent years will pay off all e. 307.30
some men wish e. and accomplish it 307.3
state tolerates e. to keep out lesser ills 930.13
submit to present e. lest greater befall 307.29
sufficient unto the day is the e. thereof 307.4
Than one more clever who is e. too 365.41
the e. that men do lives after them 390.19
there is some goodness in things e. 307.34
those who would extirpate e. from world 307.5
to a good man there can come no e. 393.45
to avoid e. utilize passions, not maim them 675.1
where there's music there's no e. 614.18
who doth no e. is apt to suspect none 770.4
who is bent on e. never wants occasion 1070.18
worst e.: give up living before one dies 219.9
evils: all e. are equal when they are extreme 307.8
between two e., pick the one never tried 307.35
cause of e. inability to apply principles 373.2
how much pain have cost us the e. which have never happened 43.7
lesser of two e. is still an evil 307.24
mankind are disposed to suffer e. 806.7
men slower to recognize blessings than e. 475.3
mitigating e. of a pyramidal social system 135.3
real e. deliver us from petty despotism of imaginary e. 307.7
to great e. we submit; we resent little provocations 508.2
evolution: e. does not signify increased perfection 308.10
e. loves death more than you or me 308.6
first to take e. into own hands 308.15
genetic endowment, product of e. of species 308.17
tide of e. carries everything before it 308.16
when e. destroyed the picture of God 308.8
exaggerate: proportion almost impossible: all e. 748.1
to e. is to weaken 309.5
exaggeration: a tendency to e. was a Roman trait 309.4
e., inseparable companion of greatness 309.7
e. is prodigality of judgment 309.3
exalted: men a little e. conceive their capacities enlarged above human comprehension 1027.18
examinations: e. are formidable even to best prepared 480.4
examined: e. life confined to privileged class 758.7
example: e. is the best precept 310.1
few things harder to endure than good e. 310.4
now age is fallen from good e. 1072.13
exasperation: men live lives of quiet e. 508.3
excel: men of genius labour because they e. 311.6
excellence: all human e. is comparative 311.8
e., a result of ceaseless concentration 311.2
e. nothing without consent of God 311.3
less excellent the man, more he claims e. for nation, religion, race 335.6
excellency: we measure e. in others by e. in self 311.10
excellent: man's heart doesn't tolerate absence of the e. 311.9
none so e. but he is excelled 311.4
exception: man is an e., whatever else he is 562.13
no rule is so general which admits no e. 832.3
no useful rule without an e. 832.4
exceptional: we are all e. cases 405.4
excess: e. on occasion is exhilarating 312.6
nothing in e. 598.14
quality carried to e. defeats itself 41.8
road of e. leads to the palace of wisdom 312.1
excesses: e. accomplish nothing 312.8
excitement: cruelty, e., lead men to love war 1042.4
exclude: every individual strives to grow and e. 469.3
let us prefer, let us not e. 725.5
we must e. someone from our gathering 910.2
exclusive: Christianity (Christian orthodoxy) is e.

125.11
excuse: any e. will serve a tyrant 1002.4
every vice has its e. ready 1030.18
excuses: nature takes no account of human e. 623.44
executive: chief e. in every sense of the word 730.9
e. officers not made out of saints 319.2
must be granted the possession of e. abilities of the loftiest order 242.9
executives: top e. may work as hard as ever 1065.59
exercise: bodily e. profiteth little 696.1
e. is the vital principle of health 413.19
philosophy for e. rather than freight 694.15
unfortunate for chubby children to watch basketball, regard it as their e. 696.4
exercises: bodily e. are to be done discreetly 696.3
exile: an e. does not return to the one he left 632.21
e., many women thought that worse than death 837.5
existence: best proof of Almighty's e. 221.16
e. requires closeness and distance 499.12
human e. is not a tragedy, but a bore 539.72
its glorious few zillion years of e. 1017.3
man is only animal for whom e. is a problem 316.3
problem of e.: we should love, do not 100.14
robbed of one half of his e. 34.17
true tenor of e. is improvisation 969.5
existentialism: a conservative e. which protested against the rationalization of life 317.1
e. is possible only in world where God and Christianity are dead 317.3
first principle of e.: man is nothing but what he makes of himself 317.2
exit: every e. is an entry somewhere else 76.9
expect: we e. more of ourselves than we should 542.9
we must e., fear, everything from time, men 978.72
expectation: oft e. fails where most it promises 318.11
'tis e. makes a blessing dear 318.12
uncertainty and e. are the joys of life 856.2
expects: who e. nothing shall not be disappointed 318.9
expediency: alloy of e. improves the gold of morality 319.4
custom adapts itself to e. 319.7
expedients: e. are for an hour; principles, for ages 734.2
expenditure: our costliest e. is time 978.71
expense: e. may be essential part of true economy 977.5
our e. is almost all for conformity 557.2
expenses: cessation of work not accompanied by cessation of e. 813.1
experience: art helps nature, and e. art 53.53
drink e. or die in desert of ignorance 321.40
ever-changing truths of our own e. 998.128
e. and travel are an education 321.15
e.: comb nature gives us when we're bald 321.8
e. differentiates piety, goodness 697.9
e. does not err 321.27
e. has two things to teach 790.5
e.: illusions lost, not wisdom acquired 449.15
e. in fingers, head, not heart 321.54
e. is hardly e. until it repeats itself 321.2
e. is hut made from ruins of illusions 321.44
e. is like the stern lights of a ship 321.9
e. is the banker of hope 427.4
e. is the name everyone gives to mistakes 321.56
e. is the only teacher 321.12
e. of any human soul is real knowledge 321.5
e. seems to lead to conclusions 321.45
e.: what you do with what happens to you 321.22
innocence is full, e. is empty 478.6
man deaf to that to which e. has given him no access 532.14
measure life by e., not length 548.5
men wise in proportion to capacity for e. 321.47
moderns ask what can we e. 321.55
most of worth is what own e. preaches 321.52
my feet are guided by lamp of e. 321.20
no man's knowledge can go beyond his e. 321.29
not data but purposes constitute human e. 321.35
nothing so unfair as man without e. 321.53
old age not total misery; e. helps 653.28
people know little beyond their own e. 321.25
prudence is but e. 755.11
questions asked self are key to others' e. 875.1
removed poverty from the e. of millions 587.3
secondhand e. breaks down a block from the car lot 321.18
studies should be bounded in by e. 1.1
that which one cannot e. in daily life is not true for oneself 612.2
the most exalted e. of our physical lives 892.11
thorn of e. worth a wilderness of warning 321.30
to get e. out of ideas 279.75
we live in reference to past e. 676.32
when you have really exhausted an e., you always reverence and love it 321.7
whether our work is art, science, only the form in which we explore e. is different 1065.14
why the need to verify e. by way of language? 321.28
you cannot create e.; you must undergo it 321.4
experiences: everyone is prisoner of own e. 726.12
e. more intense and less articulate 915.28
lost the capacity for deep emotional e. 1026.9
only the simplest e. open to all 210.13
single right idea saves labor of e. 443.17
strong man digests his e. 321.37
to regret e. is to arrest development 321.57
experiment: all life is an e. 980.3
exciting to think we are nature's latest e. 562.49
experiments: we are all e. in enthusiasms 293.7
expert: e. limits himself to the little toe 924.4
e., one who avoids the small errors 924.1
experts: e. in keeping boys in frenzied uncertainty 351.2
explain: never e. 322.2
explanation: the American vice is e. 34.79
explanations: no waste of time in life like making e. 322.1
exploitation: relationships are forms of e. 794.1
exploration: age of e. unparalleled since Renaissance 479.11
explore: e. thyself 875.30
explorer: most romantic sensation an e. has known 603.4
exposed: inner as well as outer life can be e. 93.31
expressed: what is conceived well is e. clearly 134.1
expressing: a person engaged in the business of e. himself 1069.142
expression: American feels so rich in his opportunities for free e. 363.17
beauty without e. tires 72.15
e. is only altered by a man of genius 376.9
glory of e. is simplicity 899.15
great e. furnishes its own standards 401.18
he whose genius seems truest excels in e. 376.15
man is half himself, other half is his e. 870.1
pleasures of e. keep us alert 875.17
exquisite: each more e. than the last 1069.32
extramarital: with e. courtship, deception was prolonged 224.12
extravagance: poverty often concealed in e. 718.37
extravagant: some e. as if they would die tomorrow 977.1
extreme: every great action is e. when undertaken 227.30
nothing so e. that's not allowed by some 213.19
extremism: e. in the defense of liberty is no vice 335.5
political e. involves two ingredients 335.4
extremists: evil of e. is that they are intolerant 335.10
extremities: manlike to bear e., godlike to forgive 287.3

exuberance: decline of e. barely noticeable 293.6
e. is beauty 513.1
e. is better than taste 513.4
eye: beautiful e. luminous, not sparkling 325.3
e. altering alters all 683.2
e. is the painter and ear the singer 20.2
e. obeys exactly action of the mind 897.4
e. of the master fattens the steed 58.6
he who has one e. is prince among those with none 15.4
hunger of the e. is not to be despised 897.2
if a man destroy another's e., destroy his 517.19
if e. too near, opal's hues not seen 333.5
it is the e. which makes the horizon 689.4
listen to man's words and look at his e. 119.20
no object mysterious; mystery is your e. 683.3
some held e. to be instrument of lechery 892.45
the e. commands the body to perceive virtue 1003.1
thou shalt give e. for e. 815.3
to know e. will mark our coming is sweet 551.18
what e. ne'er sees, heart ne'er rues 110.2
what e. sees not, heart craves not 238.8
what makes impression on heart seems lovely in the e. 284.32
eyes: e. are more accurate witnesses than ears 897.5
e. have one language everywhere 325.2
e. indicate the antiquity of the soul 325.1
e. not responsible when mind does seeing 450.24
men are born with two e., one tongue 98.4
men of cold passions have quick e. 142.3
men trust their ears less than their e. 882.4
practised man trusts e. more than tongue 149.4
when you speak to man, look on his e. 923.19

F

fable: f.: recital of facts presented as fiction 344.30
find my biography in every f. that I read 344.10
face: beauty leaves record on f. as to what became of it 326.4
cheerful, intelligent f. is end of culture 210.6
f. shows family traits, history, wants 326.3
five-year-old can judge a f. as a f. 72.41
happy the man who never puts on a f. 428.10
losing f. may one day save human race 665.7
lovely f. is the solace of wounded hearts 326.7
man remembers friend's f., not his own 875.27
mask tells us more than a f. 165.17
none so bound to his own f. that he doesn't hope of presenting another to world 688.4
no one can wear one f. to self, one to multitude and not forget which is true 165.7
often noble f. hides filthy ways 440.7
put your f. in the dirt 817.6
the voice is a second f. 923.6
we have a special f. for each friend 794.4
woman careful about her f. is careless about her house 1062.80
faces: looking at f., take advice of the day 72.39
minds differ still more than f. 590.22
more f. than humans; each has several 326.6
our f. carry in them motto of our souls 326.1
we never see our f. in mirrors 593.6
facetious: to be f. is accomplishment of courtiers 1061.24
fact: abstractions are weapons to control f. 974.14
a f. is like a sack which won't stand when it is empty 328.11
consciousness of a f. is not knowing it 328.14
for every f., an infinity of hypotheses. 974.9
new f. enhances constant f. of life 328.6
rejected f. will always return 328.5
science makes ascertainment of f., correction of false belief the supreme goods 849.16
spirit of the age to believe any f. superior to any imaginative exercise 328.16
wise man bows to authority of f. 328.8
facts: accumulation of f. is not science 849.28
conclusive f. are separated from inclusive only by head that already understands 328.2
education: learning to make f. live 279.42
f. are like an unlit oil-lamp 328.13
f. as f. do not create reality 784.4
f.: brute beasts of intellectual domain 328.9
f. of life are very stubborn things 328.1
historian who seeks truth falsifies f. 419.3
images are the f. of fiction. 328.3
in science, all f. enjoy democratic equality 849.23
theory helps us to bear ignorance of f. 974.11
time dissipates the angularity of f. 328.7
we are all imprisoned by f. 328.12
we must translate words into f. 1064.22
what is false in science of f. may be true in science of values 1026.20
fade: where's the cheek that doth not f. 333.7
faded: eyes of men turn from f. flowers 892.50
fail: books succeed, lives f. 93.9
f. I alone—all men strive, who succeeds 329.5
no freedom without freedom to f. 363.26
some people are born to f. 775.8
sooner f. than not be among the greatest 401.33
to f. is something too awful to think of 329.17
when we f., pride supports us 6.4
failing: aware of own f., won't find fault with others' 342.25
scarcely a man lacks some f. that diminishes his family's regret at his loss 342.17
failings: expose not the secret f. of mankind 206.23
f. bind us together as closely as virtue 342.30
failure: f. is allotted to men by their stars 340.8
f. is the Siberian end of the line 329.2
f. makes people bitter and cruel 945.28
f. not only punishment for laziness 530.7
f., the only thing that worked predictably 329.11
fine line between f. and success 329.13
kicking against the goads is way to f. 287.7
no f. except in no longer trying 329.14
no fiercer hell than f. in great object 329.16
optimism is the digitalis of f. 659.7
success is undesirable, f. more so 329.7
the f. is a stranger in his own house 329.12
the good have come to wisdom through f. 393.43
while young, idea of death, f., intolerable 1071.13
failures: awareness of the ambiguity of one's f. 6.19
benefit in making a few f. early in life 329.15
f. arise from pulling in horse as he leaps 465.1
women adore f. 329.24
faint-hearted: fortune is not on side of the f. 360.35
fair: he injures f. lady who beholds her not 466.2
I like not f. terms and a villain's mind 224.18
none but the brave deserves the f. 195.9
fair weather: And am like to love three more, / If it prove f. w. 181.13
fairies: f.: nature's attempt to get rid of soft boys by sterilizing them 424.3
fairness: f. with one's own enables one to do justice in the state 517.46
fairyland: f. the sunny country of common sense 450.5
faith: all men created equal, irksome f. to live by 297.5
cling to f. beyond the forms of f. 330.35
doubt has become immune to f. 265.10
easy to shake a man's f. in himself 868.7
f., belief even when gods don't deliver 330.12
f., conviction about the not yet proven 330.15
f. counts on failure 330.33
f. embraces contradictory truths 330.29
f. embraces itself and doubt 330.36

f.: illogical belief in the improbable 330.23
f. in a cause is a substitute for f. in selves 111.9
f. in a holy cause has to be extravagant 111.10
f. in supernatural is desperate wager 953.2
f. is a fine invention when gentlemen can see 850.2
f. is a stiffening process 330.14
f. is believing what seems false 330.39
f. is believing what you know ain't so 330.37
f. is but a kind of betting, speculation 330.8
f. is the evidence of things not seen 330.4
f. is the pierless bridge 330.10
f. is to believe what you do not yet see 330.2
f. is wishing that God may exist 330.38
f., like a jackal, feeds among the tombs 330.21
f., not truth, keeps the world alive 330.25
f. opposed to experience, learning, investigation is not worth expression 330.18
f. speaks when hope dissembles 330.34
f. that sets bounds to itself is none 330.17
f., wed to falsehood, hugs it to the last 330.28
f. which does not doubt is a dead f. 265.9
f. without works is dead 330.5
give me stormy thought, not dead calm of f. 16.4
he wears his f. as fashion of his hat 181.10
if one f. abandoned, don't abandon all f. 330.16
it is truer that martyrs make f. than f. makes martyrs 565.14
let none seek cause to approve their f. 330.27
majority of mankind incapable of doubt, f. 562.21
man consists of the f. that is in him 330.3
man would die a thousand deaths for f. 330.19
most satisfying f. is purely agnostic 330.24
never believe on f., see for yourself 532.2
no f. never broken save that of a dog 41.18
only f. comprehends mysteries of religion 125.19
relation of f. between subject and object is unique in every case 330.1
terrors of truth, death are vain to f. 330.22
there lives more f. in honest doubt 265.8
to believe only possibilities is not f. 330.7
to lose one's f. surpass loss of estate 1004.6
what is f., love, virtue alone 330.26
when f. burns out, 'tis God who dies 1004.15
when f. lost, honor dies, man is dead 491.31
where technical skill, no need for f. 966.11
you can do little with f., nothing without it 330.9
faithful: f. know the trivial side of love 472.15
he who is f. in little is f. in much 491.3
person who has faith in himself can be f. to others 181.3
violence we do ourselves to remain f. is hardly better than an infidelity 181.8
young men want to be f., and are not 472.16
faithfulness: f. is simply a confession of failures 181.15
faithless: f. know love's tragedies 472.15
fall: flowers and buds f., and old and ripe f. 221.87
haughty spirit goeth before a f. 733.2
he that lies on the ground cannot f. 329.25
if a man f., all will tread on him 549.3
soar not too high to f.; stoop to rise 33.17
stumble may prevent a f. 88.4
who thinks he stands beware lest he f. 664.1
why do ye f. at such a little wind 329.8
falls: he that f. by himself never cries 157.5
false: f. balance is an abomination 105.2
f. friend, shadow, attend while sun shines 484.1
f. words infect the soul with evil 558.37
hair perhaps divides the f. and true 999.12
how often are we angry against truth, being moved under a f. cause 39.20
I hate f. words 1064.29
in church f. sentiment is frequent 126.7
no woman can be beautiful who can be f. 472.12
falsehood: f. is a dead thing but often moves about 558.10
f. is like a sabre cut: the scar remains 558.32
f. is the jockey of misfortune 558.16
f., rocked by truth, outgrows her cradle 558.11
long attention to single aspect of truth leads to f. 999.5
one f. spoils a thousand truths 558.2
O, what a goodly outside f. hath! 558.35
peace-mingling f. preferable to mischievous truth 999.14
truth and f. be near twins 999.4
we are only f., duplicity 864.8
when war in air everyone learns f. 1042.39
who speaks truth stabs f. to the heart 1000.11
without f., there would be no knowledge 558.24
fame: all f. is dangerous 332.15
all is ephemeral—even f. and the famous 990.2
blessed is he whose f. does not outshine his truth 332.46
book against f. bears author's name 440.6
charm of f. is so great 332.37
do good by stealth and blush to find it f. 393.37
drawback of f. pleasing other men 332.43
drying up a single tear has more of honest f. than shedding seas of gore 519.4
f. but an inscription on a grave 332.41
f. drowns things weighty and solid 332.4
f. has often created something of nothing 332.14
f. is a bee 332.12
f. is a vapor, popularity an accident 990.18
f.: public destruction of one in process of becoming 332.39
f. usually comes to those who are thinking about something else 332.19
folly loves the martyrdom of f. 354.3
for a good man, f. is always a problem 332.17
he lives in f. who died in virtue's cause 332.40
he who seeks f. by the practice of virtue 332.48
men have a solicitude about f. 332.21
nothing so arouses ambition as another's f. 33.9
nothing so troublesome as pursuit of f. 332.24
to get as much f. as one's father 916.3
toil is the sire of f. 1065.27
who builds church to God, not to f. 435.19
who hankers after f. has no idea what f. is 332.23
fame's: f. carapace does not allow for easy breathing 332.34
familiar: f. acts are beautiful through love 333.11
f. use of things cures not ignorance 333.9
man f. with many must expect familiarities 712.4
poetry makes f. be as if not f. 708.91
unfamiliar as the f. at end of a journey 992.37
familiarity: coarse f. productive of contempt 499.1
f. breeds contempt—and children 333.12
f. breeds contentment 333.1
f. confounds all traits of distinction 516.7
f. grants exemption from all evil 333.13
f. takes off the edge of admiration 333.6
families: f. are all mysterious 334.30
f. break up when people take hints you don't intend 334.14
f. should have parliament within doors 334.11
family: bringing up a f. should be an adventure 334.27
chief conceit is about f. 37.1
f. is chief source of unhappiness 334.7
f. is the home of all social evils 334.32
f. is where most ridiculous things go on 334.6
f. is where self-respect is smothered 334.31
f. of man more than three billion strong 562.30
f. often a commonwealth of malignants 334.26
happy the f. that can eat

onions together 355.17
less trouble governing f. than kingdom 334.22
nature set up f. to supply man's wants 334.4
no vocabulary for love within a f. 334.12
numerous f. is bulwark of power 719.55
only institution that works is the f. 334.20
small f. is soon provided for 84.1
the f. in the West is finished 334.35
the f. is the test of freedom 334.8
unhappy f. is unhappy in its own way 334.34
we need absence of pain, presence of f. 221.61
without love to f., what have you accomplished 551.96
family quarrels: f., like splits in the skin that won't heal 334.13
famine: all's good in a f. 437.3
famous: prestige you acquire by knowing f. men 933.3
rich parents are f. for miserliness 334.25
the f. carry the footnotes of their lives 794.3
to be f., have a f. relative 332.35
we are clever at envying a f. man while alive, at praising him when he's dead 332.29
whole segments of population wake up f. 332.22
fanatic: f. can't change mind, won't change subject 335.1
there is nobody as enslaved as the f. 335.17
fanaticism: f. consists in redoubling effort when you have forgotten aim 335.16
strong performance needs f. in performer 335.3
we give name of f. to zeal of others 936.3
fanatic's: no place in f. head for reason 335.13
fanatics: f. have dreams, weave paradise for sect 335.9
to make f., persuade before you instruct 335.18
fancy: a young man's f. turns to a f. young man 424.2
ever let the f. roam 336.9
f. is a balloon that soars at wind's will 450.3
we may take f. for a companion 785.17
fantasy: childish f. like sheath over bud 123.7
f. can be equivalent to a paradise 336.7
f. no good unless it springs from truth 336.20
farce: f. appeals to the collective belly 145.7
f. bears animus against civilization 145.6
farces: like dreams, f. show fulfillment of wishes 145.1
farewell: the return makes one love the f. 673.5
farm: remote though your f. may be 337.5
sacrifice to f. teaches what a f. is 837.8
farmer: good f. is handy man with sense of humus 337.10
farmers: complain about f. with your mouth full 157.3
f. are founders of human civilization 337.9
farming: f. looks easy when your plow is a pencil 337.4
in f., do one thing late, you will be late in everything 337.3
farms: destroy f. and grass will grow in cities 337.2
farthest: he goes f. who goes far enough 598.11
fascinating: evening with f. person leaves vivid memories; with interesting person, bouquet 496.3
fascination: f. that goes beyond public achievements 334.15
fashion: as good be out of world as out of f. 338.9
custom, f. are blind to what is to come 213.5
even knowledge has to be in f. 338.15
f. condemns us to many follies 338.21
f.: despot whom wise ridicule and obey 338.3
f. elevates bad to level of good 338.2
f. has brought all into vogue but virtue 338.11
f. is issue of ostentation, egotism 338.16
f. is made to become unfashionable 338.6
f. is more powerful than any tyrant 338.20
f. produces beautiful things that become ugly with time 338.10
f.: to realize art in living forms 338.18
f. wears out more apparel than the man 338.25
he is fantastical who is not in f. 338.5
if not in f., you are nobody 338.8
ladies of f. starve love to feed pride 338.12
no new f. worth salt is ever wearable 267.25
parade of f., the silt of tomorrow 640.9
present f. is always handsome 338.14
there's never a new f. but it's old 338.7
fashionable: destroying a man by making him f. 332.47
f. idea is an adulterated one 443.12
fashioned: used a stand-up work place he had f. 1069.64
fashions: every generation laughs at the old f. 338.27
fancy, not taste, produces many new f. 338.28
f. are only induced epidemics 338.26
fast: they stumble that run f. 411.14
fat: f. hens lay few eggs 186.8
imprisoned in every f. man a thin one is wildly signalling to be let out 645.3
let me have men about me that are f. 57.17
sweetest f. sticks to my own bones 876.19
when served, it is fairly dripping with f. 355.5
fatal: God was satisfied with his own work, and that is f. 201.6
fate: an evil f. drives men on 340.3
a part of f. is freedom of man 363.11
book of nature is book of f. 507.3
difficulty of f. lies in complexity 539.94
f. as the handmaiden of morality 80.8
f. can be surmounted by scorn 185.1
f. falls on men unless they act 340.4
f. finds for every man his share of misery 1011.9
f., fortune, sweep strong powers away 990.19
f. has terrible power none can avoid 340.20
f. has to do with the unintended results of innumerable men 340.14
f. hath but one law for small and great 340.10
f. is at your elbow 393.4
f. leads the willing 340.17
f. shaped by men without greatness 711.17
f. was dealing from the bottom of the deck 340.16
great soul surrenders itself to f. 806.9
if f. means you to lose, give a fight 340.13
if we accept f., we must affirm liberty 867.4
intellect annuls f. 975.10
man once cursed his f., now curses himself 758.8
men are not prisoners of f. 590.16
necessity is harsh; f. has no reprieve 340.7
superiority to f. is difficult to gain 340.5
there is no armor against f. 340.19
to bear is to conquer our f. 287.1
to be wise in misfortune is to conquer f. 17.49
we have not the smallest clue to our own f. 340.11
we march to f. abreast 815.10
whatever limits us we call f. 340.6
whatever we perpetrate we're steered by f. 340.2
when f. summons, monarchs must obey 221.37
who await no gifts from chance, conquer f. 116.3
who fights against his f. is a fool 287.2
who has calmly reconciled his life to f. 937.2
fate's: granting our wish: f. saddest joke 238.30
fates: our wills and f. do contrary run 1056.10
see how the f. their gifts allot 340.9
what f. impose men must needs abide 340.18
father: affection makes fool of man too much the f. 670.27
angry f. is most cruel toward himself 670.39
child is f. of the man 404.30
f. is a banker provided by nature 670.19
f. miserable who holds children's affection because they need his assistance 670.35
f. should help son form habit of doing right on his own initiative 916.14

f. unto many sons 916.13
f. whose son raises his hand to him is guilty 916.11
greatness in f. often overwhelms son 916.7
have we not all one f. 100.1
it is a wise f. that knows his own child 670.47
must be struggle between f. and son 916.6
My f. provided 916.16
one celestial f. gives to all 387.49
son can bear death of his f. 1058.7
time not to become a f. is eighteen years before a war 916.17
to be famous as one's f.: be more able 916.3
to old f. nothing sweeter than daughter 218.1
father's: f. nature lives anew in infant 417.2
how easily a f. tenderness is recalled 916.10
you have to deserve your f. love 670.21
fathers: childish to expect men to believe like f. 374.5
fundamental defect of f. 670.42
men more like own time than like f. 184.5
some f. never stop giving their children reasons for being consoled at their death 670.32
sons are generally worse than their f. 916.4
we do things because our f. have done them 213.11
fatigue: sadness is almost always a form of f. 1011.14
fault: f. is not in our stars, but in ourselves 810.11
he who findeth f. meaneth to buy 105.7
one without f. would not have a friend 342.14
real f.: to have faults, not amend them 342.3
we desire to make other men perfect but we will not amend our own f. 342.16
we won't have friends if we expect no f. 684.7
why not bear a f. in your wife 564.44
faultless: he is lifeless that is f. 342.7
whoever thinks a f. piece to see 684.14
faults: benevolent man should allow f. in himself 342.10
best men are moulded out of f. 342.27
confession of f. next to innocence 168.4
faultfinder will find f. in paradise 342.29
f. forgiven man of perfect candor 362.10
f. look handsome in three hundred pounds 1048.54
f. of those who keep men waiting 765.2
for youthful f. ripe virtues shall atone 1071.63
greatest of f. is to be conscious of none 342.2
man whose f. you cannot see 342.4
more f. committed while obliging 342.28
must not take f. of youth into old age 653.37
no one is born without f. 342.15
our f. are not seen, but past us 342.5
our f. more pardonable than the shifts we make to hide them 342.20
people impatient if have to lay f. aside 342.13
pride is the mask of one's own f. 733.11
rich men's f. are covered with money 342.8
self-love veils our f. from us 876.1
telling man his f. helps, if with love 206.2
they see only f. who seek nothing else 342.11
to bear burden of others' f. worst 342.9
to suffer from one's own f. is the sting of life 342.31
truly an evil to be full of f. 342.23
we acknowledge our f. to repair the damage they've done us in others' eyes 168.1
we can't stand other people having our f. 342.32
we only admit to minor f. 342.19
when a man laughs he shows all his f. 526.10
when f. seen in others, we behold our own 342.26
where love fails we espy all f. 552.13
whoe'er tells my f., I hate him mortally 342.24
without our own f. we wouldn't enjoy seeing them in others 342.18
favor: easier to get than keep f. from fortune 360.30
f. well bestowed is almost as great an honour to the giver as to the receiver 888.9
man who confers f. would rather not be repaid in same coin 888.1
who boasts of f. bestowed, wants it back 888.8
favors: art of acceptance of f. 787.2
pleasure we derive doing f. is in the feeling that we are not worthless 888.5
pretty woman likes to be asked for her f. 351.11
to confer f. with grace 384.4
façade: city hidden inside its own f. 131.35
fear: as love casts out f., hate casts out f. 554.11
behind all we feel, there is sense of f. 343.8
better beans and bacon in peace than cakes and ale in f. 681.1
courage imperils life, f. protects it 343.24
death is nothing; we f. what we know not 221.38
expect, f., everything from time and men 978.72
f. betrays unworthy souls 343.35
f., born of stern matron Responsibility 43.9
f. could never make virtue 343.36
f. created gods; audacity, kings 520.1
f., effective in destroying the soul 343.30
f. first brought gods into the world 387.56
f. is an instructor of great sagacity 343.13
f. is herald of all revolutions 343.13
f. is sharp-sighted 343.10
f. is stronger than arms 343.2
f. is the main source of superstition 343.28
f. of death or pain is to be dreaded 343.14
f. succeeds crime, is its punishment 204.19
hate is the consequence of f. 412.6
he whom many f., has himself many to f. 1002.24
hope, f., must be vivid to be effective 608.7
hope should no more be a virtue than f. 427.38
how does one kill f., I wonder 343.11
how vain and vile a passion is this f. 343.23
I f. the Greeks even when they bring gifts 259.15
I f. the man who drinks water 268.19
maturity: to live with f., not be afraid 571.20
never negotiate out of f. 994.2
none act humanely under influence of f. 343.29
nothing robs the mind of its powers as f. 343.9
of all passions, f. weakens judgment most 343.26
one has f. on every side of a fool 343.21
one may attribute petty actions to f. 227.20
only f. and interest unite men 1016.7
only thing we have to f. is f. itself 343.27
ought not to f. with too much dejection 343.22
overcome f., behold wonder 343.6
people tolerate those they f. 984.9
perfect love casteth out f. 551.7
scalded cats f. even cold water 321.16
there are situations in which hope and f. run together and destroy one another 427.12
there are times when f. is good 343.3
there is no devil but f. 343.20
to stay is no wise action when there's more reason to f. than to hope 814.1
true nobility is exempt from f. 635.5
we adore, invoke, seek to appease what we f. 1068.11
weakness to f. what cannot be avoided 937.7
we are in deadly f. of life 363.23
we are in deadly f. of life 539.46
we poison our lives with f. of burglary 43.3
what frees one from f. of others is good 343.15
what we f. comes to pass more speedily than what we hope 343.25
where f. is, happiness is not 343.33
who shrinks from knowledge of calamities aggravates his f. 304.3
wise man prays for deliver-

ance from f. 216.6
feareth: he who killeth a lion when absent f. a mouse when present 89.1
fearful: f. are caught as often as the bold 112.4
fears: belief in providence has not allayed f. 754.11
each believes what he f. or desires 202.5
if desires are endless, f. will be so 403.7
out of danger, man forgets his f. 216.8
present f. are less than imaginings 343.34
read thy own breast right, and thou hast done with f. 758.2
we perform according to our f. 743.6
who f. from near at hand f. less 343.32
who f. he shall suffer, suffers what he f. 946.31
who f. you present will hate you absent 343.16
feast: a f. of homily and imagination 973.9
enough is as good as a f. 947.3
he of a merry heart hath a continual f. 409.13
feasts: true f. are solemn and rare 114.2
features: the f. of our face are gestures which have become permanent 326.5
February: here comes F., a kiss waiting on her lips 854.4
most serious charge against New England is F. 628.1
feeble: 'Tis not enough to help the feeble up 56.9
feebleness: supported by force, f. is imperious 1047.9
feed: who won't f. cats must f. mice, rats 936.1
feel: behind all we f., there is sense of fear 343.8
can't make yourself f. what you don't f. 822.3
It is not that the Englishman can't f. 289.11
let us value that which we can taste, f. 882.3
thinking when we ought to f. 88.1
what we think, f., determined by glands 589.6
feeling: bourgeois: one who places anything above f. 587.2
f. merged with thought, artist's joy 53.83
universal f. cannot be disregarded 762.13
feelings: English are loth to express their f. 284.12
everyone's f. have a front and side door 284.19
f. shape decision-making 284.16
great f. take with them their own universe 284.7
often one attributes to others only f. of which one is capable oneself 663.6
understand in others f. we're capable of 1008.11
feet: these f. have walked ten thousand miles 1041.2
until I met a man who had no f. 153.3
felicity: human f. is produced by little advantages 409.39
one cannot but mistrust a prospect of f. 409.69
seldom that f. not tempered by sorrow 409.23
fell: who never climbed high never f. low 33.7
fellow: how comfortable to know our f. creature 81.4
who love not f.-beings live unfruitfully 100.15
fellows: you're a bad set of f. 97.4
fellowship: good f. is commonly but the virtue of pigs in a litter 152.21
more f. among snakes than among mankind 209.10
sign of passing youth: birth of f. 571.21
felon's: f. capacity for innocent enjoyment is just as great as any honest man's 204.10
female: f. malignity exerted in domestic trifles 1062.79
highest f. grace is silence 898.10
hysteria is phenomenon of f. nature 581.70
to be unwed and f. was to succumb to an illness 564.41
females: f. may be downplayed or forgotten 1062.135
f. most dangerous when appear to retreat 1062.91
f. will forgive a liberty, not a slight 1062.28
feminine: f. ardor for clothes shopping 267.8
f. woman feels comfortable with women 1062.89
festival: life is a f. only to the wise 1060.15
fetters: f. of gold are still f. 109.2
fever: shown death, he'll be content with f. 896.21
few: f. sometimes know, when thousands err 822.15
fickle: womankind ever f. and changeful thing 1062.145
fickleness: f. of women I love equaled by constancy of women who love me 472.10
fiction: f. gives opportunity to live history 344.19
f. is a kind of magic and trickery 344.32
f. is like a spider's web 344.33
f. puts ideas into the head 344.1
f., subtlest instrument for self-examination 344.28
f. takes the measure of a life 344.15
f. to man what play is to child 344.26
good f. made of that which is real 344.8
little mansions in f. acclaimed to their detriment 207.22
readers of new f. are film producers 344.6
truth is more of a stranger than f. 998.124
writing f. had little effect on the world 344.7
field: f. not well seen from within 689.5
fifty: years between f. and seventy are hardest 586.6
fight: fine thing to f. for another's freedom 537.41
From where the sun now stands I will f. no more forever 1042.47
he who flees will f. again 300.10
in f. our business is to prove our might 588.9
in f. rich man saves face; poor man, coat 345.6
kiss and make up: live to f. another day 772.12
people seem to f. about things very unsuitable for fighting 345.1
there is such a thing as a nation being too right to f. 665.13
they f. in bars all the time 766.9
those that fly may f. again 300.2
to f. is a radical instinct 345.7
we do not f. for the real 1042.7
what counts is size of f. in dog 345.2
fighting: defend life, fame, wealth by f. 1042.71
man is a f. animal 443.31
only one way of f.: to be the conqueror 345.4
to love life for some men is to love f. 345.5
fights: learn not to have f. with the other boys 19.18
figure: your first f. turns out to be a bluff 992.24
film: f.: boat always on the point of sinking 611.7
tragedy of f. history is that it is fabricated 611.2
wide screen makes bad f. twice as bad 611.4
films: a true event brings to mind the landscape of f. 611.6
you can't be virtuoso in stage and f. 972.1
financial: f. worries distinguishes man from beast 602.51
financier: faults of burglar are qualities of f. 934.7
fine: best effect of f. persons felt afterward 473.4
finest: f. edge is made with blunt whetstone 321.31
finger: moving f. writes and having writ moves on 340.15
finished: f. product has already seen better days 285.4
one must be thrust out of f. cycle in life 404.20
fire: a little f. is quickly trodden out 801.3
by labor f. is got out of a stone 281.2
can a man take f. in his bosom 57.4
divide the f., and you will put it out 939.3
f. has an insatiable hunger to be fed 346.1
f. is the most tolerable third party 346.2
go to the land of infernal f. 271.28
heap coals of f. on enemy's head 288.4
how great a matter a little f. kindleth 176.2
it may be a f.—tomorrow, ashes 386.1
let a man burn with intensity, he will set f. to the world 1073.3
little f. warms, a great one burns 186.7
one f. burns out another's burning 946.44
people's sympathies are with the f. 313.1

what if I am only a sophisticated f.? 562.20
fireside: you are a king by your own f. 422.4
firm: often we are f. from weakness 1047.8
firmness: f. without intellect is perverseness 493.26
first: I always do the f. line well 1069.94
one cannot be f. in everything 186.1
who has f. place seldom has principal part 780.6
first-rate: one man is worth ten thousand if f. 952.4
fish: air so damp f. could come through doors 1050.3
f. die belly-upward and fall to the surface 347.1
net of the sleeper catches f. 266.5
fishes: he f. on who catches one 427.9
fishing: gods do not deduct hours spent in f. 348.2
fishmonger: a f. is the man who mongs fish 1064.35
five: menace in dealing with a f.-year-old 670.30
flag: f. is embodiment of history, not sentiment 678.24
gaudiest f. the world has ever seen 34.77
not for f. of birthplace will I give life 678.15
flame: mighty f. followeth a tiny spark 176.3
flattered: beautiful women f. for understandings 1062.24
flatterer: every f. lives at flattered listener's cost 349.14
f., unlike physician, must administer strongest dose to the weakest patient 349.5
no such f. as is a man's self 1027.3
of all tame beasts, preserve me from f. 349.13
flattery: f. is a challenge 349.10
f. is a juggler, no kin unto sincerity 349.3
f. is all right—if you don't inhale 349.18
f. may turn one's stomach 349.9
f. pleases very generally 349.11
f. sits in the parlour 349.8
greater the love, the less room for f. 206.16
imitation is the sincerest f. 451.3
love of f. stems from mean opinion men have of selves 349.19
mysterious power of f. and calumny 202.4
necessary that f. be accommodated to circumstances or characters 349.12
ne'er was f. lost on poet's ear 708.86
none more taken in by f. than proud 733.20
no other way of guarding against f. 349.16
nowadays f. wins friends 998.120
some profess to despise all f. 349.4
some whom gold would not seduce, f. would 349.2
too much f. never lost a gentleman 349.6
vanity moves humanity; f. greases wheels 1027.9
we don't hate f., but manner of flattering 349.15
we love f. even when not deceived 349.7
fleas: great f. have little f. upon their backs 669.2
haste in nothing but catching f. 411.6
reasonable amount of f. is good for dog 41.42
who lies with dogs shall rise with f. 57.11
flees: he who f. will fight again 300.10
fleeting: world is f., all things pass—or do we 989.6
flesh: all f. is grass 606.3
f. endures the storms of the present alone 589.3
f. must bear only storms of present 589.1
spirit is willing but the f. is weak 1047.1
the f. is sad, and I've read all books 290.2
flight: f. is lawful, when one flies from tyrants 300.8
flirtation: f.: expression of considered desire 351.8
flood: in the ant's house the dew is a f. 908.2
flops: f. are a part of life's menu 329.21
Florence: those who know F. compare it to Boston 131.33
tooled-leather idea of F. as a dear bit of the old world 617.7
flower: f. is the poetry of reproduction 352.2
f. may at time control braggart lords 352.3
f. that once has blown for ever dies 606.13
f. you single out is rejection of all others 469.17
full many a f. is born to blush unseen 649.4
meanest f. can give thoughts that often lie too deep for tears 352.5
our national f. is concrete cloverleaf 64.9
weed is no more than a f. in disguise 371.1
flowerless: a f. room is a soulless room 352.4
flowers: f. as gifts from man's hands 1068.9
take honey from f. of creation 201.16
without f., man and bird would be unrecognizable 352.1
fluency: one truth discovered is better than all f. 998.53
fly: f. may sting horse and make him wince 780.9
f. ought to be used as symbol of audacity 481.8
God in His wisdom made the f. 481.6
then would I f. away and be at rest 300.1
those that f. may fight again 300.2
foe: heat not a furnace so hot for your f. 817.16
he makes no friend who never made a f. 288.21
sweet to see your f. perish 817.9
foe's: tear out thy f. brain 288.20
foes: our greatest f. are within 866.3
you shall judge a man by friends, f. 288.5
fog: f.: not weather and not mood, yet both 1050.2
foible: forte always makes a f. 962.6
most powerful f.: love of living 539.77
folklore: f. is what they tell the children 617.8
folkways: careful to observe complicated f. 213.7
follies: others' f. teach us not 321.52
what is life but a series of inspired f. 354.14
follow: we f. those that fly from us 691.5
followers: every man with idea has two or three f. 443.2
great man's f. put out eyes that they may better sing his praise 353.3
following: most lives spent in seeming and f. 171.4
folly: be fool without shame, learn from f. 354.11
f. is perennial, yet human race survives 354.10
f. loves the martyrdom of fame 354.3
f. of one can make many miserable 810.9
f. of one man is fortune of another 354.1
f. often goes beyond her bounds 830.3
f. pursues us at all periods of our lives 354.7
f. to censure him whom world adores 206.20
if thou rememberest not the f. of love 551.190
it is f. to drown on dry land 354.5
it is f. to sing twice to a deaf man 48.3
kings' power founded on f. of people 831.16
living without f. not so wise as believed 354.8
riches forsake a man, we discover his f. 226.6
what use is wisdom when f. reigns 354.18
who realize their f. are not true fools 354.17
wisdom at times is found in f. 354.6
wisdom rises upon the ruins of f. 1060.22
fond: f. of each other because ailments same 896.33
food: f. in America has become eatable 355.3
nothing to which men with f. and drink cannot reconcile themselves 274.26
to him stinted of f. a boiled turnip will be relished like a roast fowl 437.13
fool: answer a f. according to his folly 356.4
any f. can make a rule, every f. minds it 832.6
better to be a f. than to be evil 604.37
dullness of f. is whetstone of wits 356.21
every man hath a f. in his sleeve 356.13
fine clothes may disguise, but foolish words will disclose a f. 356.2
f. can ask more than wisest can answer 480.4
f. cannot enter Heaven, be he ever so holy 356.6
f. doesn't know to cash in on foolishness 356.15
f. hath said there is no G. 1004.2
f. is always satisfied with

himself 356.18
f. knows after he's suffered 321.21
f. matches strength with stronger 1047.4
f. publishes the triumph of the deceiver 356.7
f. sees not the same tree a wise man sees 683.1
f. uttereth all his mind 923.8
f. who holdeth his peace counted wise 356.5
give me the young man who has brains enough to make a f. of himself 354.16
heart of a f. is in his mouth 1060.20
how ill white hairs become a f., jester 356.22
if every f. wore a crown, we should all be kings 356.24
learned f. sillier than an ignorant one 356.17
let f. hold tongue, he will pass for sage 898.22
life of the f. is worse than death 356.3
misfortune of wise better than prosperity of f. 17.25
need very clever woman to manage a f. 356.16
nobody can describe a f. without much self-inspection 844.3
people can f. Devil, but not neighbors 626.6
prosperous f. is a grievous burden 356.1
sometimes wisdom to seem a f. 356.12
talk sense to f., he calls you foolish 356.10
tell him to be a f. every so often 354.11
the f. doth think he is wise 1060.53
there's no need to fasten a bell to a f. 356.8
to never see f. smash looking-glass 356.20
too many politicians believe you can f. all the people all the time 711.1
who fights against his fate is a f. 287.2
who has not made a f. of himself in love 551.171
wise man can play the f. on occasion 1060.21
you can f. too many too much of the time 224.21
fooled: superior man may be imposed upon, not f. 493.6
foolish: if others had not been f., we should be 354.2
if we're not f. young, we're f. old 354.4
profitable if one is wise to seem f. 139.1
foolishness: f. revenges self by excommunicating world 354.12
f. sets in at about the age of 18 588.1
my seeming f. may be in fool's eye 354.15
fool's: f. head never whitens 356.9
fools: absolute f. are hard to be met with 914.4
better to weep with wise men than laugh with f. 57.18
f. admire, men of sense approve 14.6
f. rush in where angels fear to tread 356.19
I am two f., I know, for loving, and for saying so 551.39
if f. do not control world, it isn't because they are not in majority 356.14
learning begets arrogance in f. 522.47
let us be thankful for the f. 356.23
Lord, what f. these mortals be! 562.52
only f. strain at high C all their lives 55.19
there are two f. in every market 104.28
things people make f. of themselves for 354.13
we think fathers f., sons think us so 374.14
who are a little wise, the best f. be 144.2
who realize their folly are not true f. 354.17
who seem learned to f. seem f. to learned 732.13
young think the old f. 1072.4
foot: willing mind makes a light f. 1057.2
football: be a f. to time and chance 504.7
f., a metaphor for America's sinfulness 929.23
in pro f. as in nuclear warfare, no winners 929.7
forbearance: who shows f. scores most in controversy 51.4
forbidden: there is a charm about the f. 900.24
to make idea of morality center on f. acts 604.39
force: accusing is proving, with f. as judge 5.1
against naked f. only defense is naked f. 357.15
as if nature makes men narrow to give f. 620.3
boys look on all f. as an enemy 97.1
easiest victor over reason: terror, f. 357.5
f. may subdue for a moment 357.3
f. overcomes but half the foe 357.10
f. without justice is tyranny 357.12
f. without reason falls of own weight 357.6
f. works on servile natures, not free 357.8
knowledge is more than f. 522.29
lust and f. source of all actions 9.31
not take another's house by f. 100.3
there is no real f. without justice 357.11
when fact can be demonstrated, f. is unnecessary; when it cannot, f. is infamous 357.7
forcible: f. ways do not end evil, but leave hatred 357.2
how f. are right words 822.1
foreign: everything f. is respected 358.2
for a f. place, it was remarkably clean 355.1
f. affairs will not conform to whim 498.17
f. relations endless, like human relations 247.8
international incidents should not govern f. policy 498.14
nation needs f. stock to thrive well 453.1
what affects men about f. nation is not finding things in the familiar place 992.13
foreigners: admiration for ourselves too often measured by our contempt for f. 358.3
swarms of dusty and perspiring f. 992.4
foresight: in action be primitive; in f. a strategist 9.12
forest: f. is the poor man's overcoat 995.4
forget: ability to f. is true token of greatness 580.13
advantage at times to f. what we know 580.30
better f. and smile than remember, be sad 580.31
eyes f. the tears they have shed 1050.7
it is not easy to f. 580.36
memory is the thing you f. with 580.7
to f. is a necessary condition of life 580.2
to f. oneself is to be happy 1021.3
we f. because we must, not because we will 580.1
forgetfulness: f. transforms occurrence to nonoccurrence 580.28
I fear f. as much as hatred and death 1069.146
forgetting: f. a wrong is a mild revenge 476.9
f. is woman's first and greatest art 1062.2
it would add to happiness if art of f. could be taught 580.14
men live by f.—women live on memories 581.14
forgive: bound to f. enemy, not to trust him 288.9
did man e'er live saw priest, woman f. 359.12
f. us our debts 359.2
how unhappy is he who cannot f. himself 405.13
it is easier to f. an enemy than a friend 359.3
manlike to bear extremities, godlike to f. 287.3
men offend where they find goodness to f. 476.6
to err is human, to f. divine 359.14
to understand is to f., even oneself 1008.2
we f. a place as soon as it's left behind 699.2
we never f. those who make us blush 893.1
who does you ill will not f. you 476.7
forgiven: forgotten is f. 359.6
injuries may be f., but not forgotten 476.1
forgiveness: f., important to healing of world 359.17
f. is the answer to the child's dream 359.7
f. to the injured does belong 359.4
glory of Christianity is to conquer by f. 125.1
love is an act of endless f. 551.225
until men fell at women's feet and asked for f. 681.17
what power has love but f. 359.16
forgives: man who does not return your blow neither f. you nor allows you to forgive self 665.11

forgiving: be tenderhearted, f. one another 359.1
f. presupposes remembering 359.15
joy of f. might well arouse envy of gods 359.9
to be social is to be f. 152.7
forgotten: celebrities wake to find themselves f. 332.22
f. is forgiven 359.6
he who is not f. is not dead 221.21
to be f. is to sleep in peace 649.5
what I fear is not being enough f. 81.8
form: government defines may by printed f. 102.4
pay attention to f.; emotion will come 20.3
picture, sculpture are festivities of f. 53.47
formalities: superstition to put hope in f. 114.3
forms: it is meritorious to insist on f. 661.4
formula: new f. is virtually old at appearance 443.9
to rest on a f. is a slumber 986.12
formulative: f. notions with which mind meets experiences 590.10
fornication: old bawd hesitates not to forswear f. 790.30
when f. will be professional athletics 967.17
forte: f. always makes a foible 962.6
fortitude: heaven has space for all modes of f. 414.2
fortuities: f. must immediately start fluttering 551.101
fortunate: be f., and you will be thought great 360.20
f. persons hardly ever amend their ways 360.24
no events so f. that the imprudent cannot turn to their own prejudice 305.5
'Tis better to be f. than wise 360.40
unrighteous are never really f. 1055.6
fortune: ambitious men most liable to blasts of f. 33.20
behind, f. is bald 360.26
boldness, caution, make f.; wit keeps it 1048.14
folly of one man is f. of another 354.1
f. and humour govern the world 116.10
f. belongs to him with contented mind 186.17
f. blind to those she does no good 360.25
f. brings in boats that are not steered 360.34
f. confers aura of worth, unworthily 360.10
f. favors the bold and the young 360.16
f. favors the brave 360.38
f. gives advantage to those she favours. 15.6
f. gives much to many, never enough to any 360.18
f. had no deity if men had wisdom 360.22
f. holds even, scrupulous balance 116.5
f. is not on side of fainthearted 360.35
f. like market where price may fall 360.1
f. makes a fool of him whom she favors too much 360.29
f. never takes her favorite unawares 360.28
f. seldom troubles the wise man 1060.18
f. sides with him who dares 360.39
f. soon tires of carrying any one long 360.15
f., to destroy, first makes mad 559.14
f., what god is more cruel than thou 360.19
good f. leads one to the highest glory, but to renounce it calls for equal courage 360.6
great f. is a great slavery 1048.52
how f. brings to earth the oversure 664.3
how many cards f. has up her sleeve 360.4
ill f. never crushed that man whom good f. deceived not 360.23
in worst of f. is best chance for change 360.13
it is f. with nature that makes heroes 418.19
it is we that are blind, not f. 87.3
men balance between good and bad f. 360.36
men never think their f. too great 1061.7
misfortunes tell us what f. is 751.7
near-missing of happiness looks like insult of f. 409.37
none can hold f. still and make it last 360.11
our mood changes more than our f. 969.7
own character the arbiter of one's f. 119.26
power of f. confessed only by the miserable 360.37
truth is no road to f. 998.100
war is subject to inconstancy of f. 1042.12
when f. flatters, she does it to betray 360.31
when f. on our side, popular favor also 15.9
when f. surprises us with a position, it is almost impossible to maintain it 780.13
who is born to a f. must be freer than those who are not, or he gains nothing 1048.9
fortune's: f. a right whore 360.41
f. expensive smile is earned 360.7
f. not content with knocking a man down 360.32
f. slave has one foot in gravy, one in grave 33.25
some live just for their f. sake 602.32
yield not thy neck to f. yoke 92.11
fortunes: every man architect of own f., but neighbors superintend construction 867.10
f. are made with other people's money 1048.58
man's f. are fruit of his character 119.9
forty: to hold same views at f. as at twenty 179.5
when f., half of you belongs to the past 653.4
foster: Marine Corps best f. home I ever had 1071.7
foundations: loftiest edifices need deepest f. 401.49
our f. are within us, not without 880.2
fountain: what f. sends forth returns to f. 21.7
fox: f. condemns the trap, not himself 782.1
f. knows many tricks 200.6
lion is ashamed when he hunts with f. 57.12
with foxes we must play the f. 200.1
France: in F. everything is a pretext for dinner 361.2
political thought in F. is nostalgic or utopian 361.3
who cannot love F., which taught us 685 ways to dress eggs 361.7
frankness: cruel describe selves as paragons of f. 362.11
lies kill love: what about f.. 362.6
fraternity: a f. is the antithesis of f. 100.18
great perils bring out the f. of strangers 216.11
fraud: the f. delights my soul 224.17
whoever has become notorious by f. 224.14
frauds: some f. are so well conducted 224.3
free: better starve f. than be a fat slave 363.1
butterflies are f. 363.9
essence of f. government 761.3
for a people to be f., the governed must be sages 537.25
force works on servile natures, not f. 357.8
f. government consists in control of rivalries 395.3
f. human beings, children of God 1065.31
him I love, I wish to be f. even from me 551.115
history of f. men written by choice 419.18
if you cannot be f., be as f. as you can 363.12
I will love, defend land where man is f. 678.15
live f. and uncommitted 363.49
lord of one green lizard—and f. 337.5
man believes he acts as a f. being 363.33
man desires to be f. and feel important 873.2
man f. to do as likes only in own concerns 575.5
man is born f., is everywhere in chains 109.8
man's belief that he is f. causes remorse 174.24
modesty is a virtue of f. men 233.23
most powerful force in world today is man's desire to be f. and independent 363.31
nation has character only when it is f. 537.40
no man can be just who is not f. 517.52
no man f.; slaves of money or necessity 171.5
not all are f. who mock their chains 954.4
only the educated are f. 279.25
renew pledge to man, his right to be f. 363.39
so far as a man thinks, he is f. 975.10

strive to live f., caught in own toils 363.18
this f. will business is a bit terrifying 644.1
to be f. is not necessarily to be wise 1060.63
truth shall make you f. 998.11
we have confused f. with f. and easy 363.47
while a soul is in prison, I am not f. 100.2
who would be f. themselves must act 537.8
who would keep land f. must be martyred 537.22
freedom: abridgment of f. by gradual encroachments 1002.21
all this presupposes a belief in f. 363.5
a part of fate is f. of man 363.11
at rare moments an exhilarating f. 1071.32
bachelor's admired f. is often a yoke 66.6
black man is striding f. road 85.15
civilized men impose own restraint against abuse of f. 537.34
comprehensive protection of individual f. 823.1
dagger plunged in name of f. is plunged into the breast of f. 363.37
death is supreme festival on road to f. 221.15
don't wear best trousers to battle for f. 819.24
economic and political f. produced golden age 363.19
everything great is created by the individual who can labor in f. 363.10
fine thing to fight for another man's f. 537.41
f. and slavery are mental states 363.20
f., a principal goal of human endeavor 363.7
f. baffling: known only when gone 363.43
f. can't be bestowed, it must be achieved 537.35
f. can't be bought for nothing 363.44
f. from self-imposed limitation 363.28
f. has thousand charms slaves never know 363.8
f. is greatest fruit of self-sufficiency 363.16
f. is indivisible 889.9
f. is not something anybody can be given 363.2
f. is to share chains our brothers wear 363.35
f. means, above all, f. from lies 363.32
f., more than absence of legal restraints 537.6
f. never relied on uniformity of opinion 252.8
f. of press a bulwark of liberty 731.5
f. of press a means, not end 731.2
f. of speech means you shall not do something to people for their views 364.2
f. of the most free: to do what is right 822.8
f. praised when she is tucked away in past 113.2
f. suppressed, regained bites with keener fangs than f. never endangered 363.6
f. to differ is not limited 258.7
f. to learn the first part of being free 532.17
f.: will to be responsible to ourselves 363.40
f. won by controlling desire 862.4
genius can only breathe in atmosphere of f. 376.22
he earns f. who daily conquers it anew 363.22
history: progress of consciousness of f. 363.25
if any in chains anywhere, f. endangered everywhere 109.4
if God exists, how can we lay claim to f. 363.50
if world knew how to use f. 537.17
in f. people take care of government 395.63
inside, the terrible f. 590.7
it is by his f. that a man knows himself 363.51
laws alone cannot secure f. of expression 984.6
leaving man the f. to accept or scoff, to obey or disregard 387.65
man about the same with despotism or f. 395.61
men lose social f. seeking to become alike 171.15
me this unchartered f. tires 118.7
more joy hollering for f. than getting it 537.31
most men after f. prefer authority 61.8
nobody can give you f. 859.5
no one can be at peace unless he has f. 363.36
no real f. without economic security 363.42
nurturing earth is made for f. 363.41
overpopulation is not compatible with f. 718.30
peace and f. walk together 131.23
people demand f. when they have no power 537.26
people use every means to get rid of f. 1065.34
real evil is to surrender f. 307.32
real f. lies in wildness 363.34
search for f. greatest force of modern age 819.29
social progress strengthens f. 741.11
there can be no f. without f. to fail 363.26
there can't be any apprenticeship for f. 363.30
thing is to know what to do with f. 363.21
those always free can't understand power of hope of f. to those who are not free 537.7
those who deny f. deserve it not 889.10
to march to f., men must deal with political as with scientific questions 395.26
to obey God is f. 387.63
to reap blessings of f., men must undergo fatigue of supporting it 537.28
to strike f. of the mind with fist of patriotism is old, ugly subtlety 678.21
tyranny is always better organized than f. 537.29
tyrant claims f. to kill f. and yet to keep it for himself 1002.29
unless a man has talents to make something of himself, f. is an irksome burden 363.27
we have f. of speech and conscience, and prudence never to practice them 537.42
we love goodness, but also f. 363.13
we prate of f.; we are in fear of life 539.46
we stand for f.: that is our only commitment to others 537.20
when there is f. there will be no state 930.14
freedom's: best road to progress is f. road 741.9
freedoms: four sandwiches vs. four f. 437.10
free economy: public debate dominated by adherents of a f. 277.7
free speech: prefer a little f. to no f. at all 364.1
freight: philosophy for exercise rather than f. 694.15
French: the F. are a contemptible nation 361.8
the F. are individualistic, ungovernable 361.10
Frenchman: F. is first and foremost a *man* 361.6
friend: admonition of f. best preservative of mind's health 803.2
a true f. is the greatest of all blessings 365.66
be a f. to thyself, others will be too 869.3
best f. can show and accept kindness 519.18
best mirror is an old f. 593.2
better lose a jest than a f. 436.9
communicating self to f. doubles joys 365.14
compassion for f. should conceal itself 698.15
doubtful f. is worse than certain enemy 365.4
faithful are the wounds of a f. 365.17
false f., shadow, attend while sun shines 484.1
foolish to experiment on constancy of f. 181.5
forsake not an old f. 365.6
f. in power is a f. lost 719.3
f. is person with whom I may be sincere 901.5
f. knows all about you, still likes you 365.58
f. loves whole man; companion, his qualities 365.18
f. may be reckoned masterpiece of nature 365.34
f. often chosen to flatter our self-love 365.53
f. should bear his friend's infirmities 365.91
f. should guess and keep still 365.77
f. that you buy will be bought from you 99.3
f. to everybody and nobody is same thing 455.7
give f. cause to blush: likely lose him 893.6
he makes no f. who never made a foe 288.21
he's a f. that speaks well behind back 394.3
he that wrongs f. wrongs self more 476.21
hold a true f. with both your hands 365.79
I care for no f. who loves his enemy equally well 742.4

if each knew what his f. said of him 914.7
if f. is equal to brother, don't wrong him 365.55
in misfortune what f. remains a f. 17.29
invite your f. to dinner 288.11
longest journey is search for a sincere f. 365.60
must eat peck of salt with f. to know him 365.24
my best f. wishes me well for my sake 365.9
new f. is like new wine 365.5
no love for f. whose love is words 365.95
no man can be happy without a f. 409.44
not f. if cannot open honest mind 425.2
nothing openeth the heart but a f. 169.1
office of a f. is to side with you when you are wrong 365.101
one afraid of laughing at f. lacks love 365.50
one f. in a lifetime is much; two are many 365.3
one f. worth ten thousand relatives 365.42
only way to have f. is to be one 365.37
over the bottle many a f. is found 268.55
persuasion of a f. is a strong thing 690.8
reveal not every secret to a f. 755.24
save me from the candid f. 362.1
stillest tongue can be truest f. 898.6
stranger has no f., unless a stranger 358.9
successful man can satisfy one f. 365.99
sympathetic f. can be dear as brother 365.57
to throw away honest f. is to throw your life away 365.96
we die as often as we lose a f. 365.85
we find the true f. only in fragments 684.5
we have a special face for each f. 794.4
what you love most in f. may be clearer in his absence 2.7
what you share with f. you save from heir 384.14

friendless: no one would choose f. life on condition of having all other things 547.1

friendly: social, f. man fulfills nature's plan 152.2

friends: a good man will never suspect f. of shady actions 393.39
all our f. are going or gone 653.94
all's dear that comes from f. 384.32
best loved man would perish if he heard all his f. say in a day 394.4
between f., differences in taste 963.2
between f. there is no need of justice 365.8
can be f. only on terms of equality 365.104
count not him among f. who will retail your privacies to the world 394.10
delight to make f. with someone despised 365.30
don't be honest with f. who ask it 365.23
easily made f. and yet was friendless 365.100
f. are born, not made 365.1
f. are generally of the same sex 27.8
f. are the sunshine of life 365.51
f. are to be feared for what they keep us from doing 365.61
f. become critical and exacting 711.4
f. provoked become bitterest enemies 365.47
f. show love in times of trouble 365.39
God save me from my f. 365.82
God send me over all such f. victorious 365.94
hateful in f. to help too late 979.5
have f., 'tis a second existence 365.48
help me to money and I'll have f. 602.24
he that is neither one thing nor the other has no f. 444.1
hoarder of documents and trusted f. 365.97
if f. are one-eyed, look at them in profile 365.64
if you have five real f. 365.59
I keep my f. as misers do their treasure 365.7
in adversity f. stay away of own accord 751.6
in the thirties we want f. 365.44
love f. as if they might become your enemies 365.16
make your f. your teachers 532.7
man's growth seen in succession of f. 404.7
man with host of f. who slaps everyone on back is regarded as friend of nobody 712.2
more shameful to mistrust one's f. than to be deceived by them 259.8
most f. are those of circumstances 365.45
old f. are best, we say, when disillusionment shakes faith in new comrade 365.20
one active enemy is worth two f. 288.12
one can be stupid with old f. 365.36
one uses early f. to mark progress 365.56
ornament of house is f. who frequent it 422.10
people at the top generally have no f. 711.95
procure yourself critical f. 447.4
scarcity of friendship but not of f. 7.3
those that lack f. to open themselves unto are cannibals of own hearts 915.4
true f. are punctilious equals 498.12
various are the uses of f. 997.6
wealth maketh many f. 1048.8
we can't all be f. and relatives 794.7
we have really no absent f. 2.1
we know our f. by their defects 365.72
we need new f. 365.93
we regret loss of f. because of our needs 365.69
we won't have f. if we expect no fault 684.7
who fears making enemies will have no f. 980.6
who has many f. has no f. 712.1
who has thousand f. hasn't one to spare 288.13
whom heaven helps has f. enough 754.6
who treats f., foes the same lacks love, justice 455.4
win f. by prejudices, narrowness 726.5
women, like princes, find few real f. 1062.88
yield to f. and you win victory 173.13
you shall judge a man by f., foes 288.5
you've heard all f. have to say 365.81

friendship: broken f. soldered is never sound 301.2
business may bring money, f. does rarely 365.12
can sincerity be condition of f. 998.17
characteristic of f. to take without enquiry the unseen doings of our friends 365.88
confidence is the only bond of f. 997.7
date evolving mind by rings of f. 365.70
for women to preserve f. with men, slight physical antipathy helpful 365.78
f. admits of difference of character 365.86
f. either finds or makes equals 365.83
f. ends in love; but love in f.—never 551.25
f. has no paraphernalia at all 365.25
f.: inclination to promote other's good 365.19
f. is a single soul in two bodies 365.11
f. is a slow-ripening fruit 365.10
f. is constant in all things save love 365.92
f. is disinterested commerce of equals 551.81
f. is like money, easier made than kept 365.21
f. is love without his wings 365.22
f. is marriage of the soul 365.102
f. is reciprocal conciliation of interests 365.67
f. is sole remedy against misfortune 365.46
f. is too time-consuming for busy men 533.4
f. makes prosperity more brilliant 365.27
f. marks a life more deeply than love 365.103
f. needs a parallelism of life 365.2
f. seldom lasting but between equals 365.62
f. that can come to an end, never began 365.84
in f. is sympathy; in love, antipathy 551.23
in f. we render small services for big 365.75
it is wise to apply politeness to f. 197.3
it would be wrong to put f.

before truth 998.5
lack of punctuality alienates f. 765.3
laughter is not a bad beginning for a f. 526.31
little f. in world; least between equals 365.13
love demands infinitely less than f. 365.76
love rarer than genius, f. rarer than love 365.80
man passes life in seeking f. 365.35
man should keep f. in constant repair 7.4
minds tend to change in hate and f. 181.12
nobody chooses already unfortunate for f. 549.5
no f. made without initial clashing 365.49
ounce of blood worth more than pound of f. 334.28
real f. shown in times of trouble 365.43
same likes, dislikes make solid f. 365.87
scarcity of f. but not of friends 7.3
steady f. best proves strength of mind 181.4
that f. be lasting, virtue must be equal 365.63
the essence of f. is entireness 997.2
to cement a new f. a spark must fly 365.89
true f. is self-love at secondhand 365.52
true love is less rare than true f. 365.68
friendships: firmest f. are formed in adversity 365.31
f. begin with liking or gratitude 365.33
f. of nations built on interests 498.15
f. ought to be immortal 772.10
it's no good trying to keep up old f. 365.71
man of active mind outwears f. 365.73
real f. among men are rare 365.32
frightened: is there anything uglier than a f. man 343.4
we are more often f. than hurt 43.13
frog: f. would leap from throne of gold to puddle 48.6
frolic: dog was made for children, is god of f. 41.40
frontier: the wagon train will not make it to the f. 710.3
where there is open mind, there will be f. 654.4
frugality: man often pays dear for a small f. 977.8
fruit: f. which rotted before it had a chance to ripen 34.51
how do you know that the f. is ripe 571.4
no f. not bitter before it is ripe 404.24
people throw stones at tree loaded with f. 295.9
there are cases where the plant flowers, but no f. is produced 452.3
vine made to bear f. in spring dies soon 279.71
fruitfully: joy at eventide if day spent f. 6.12
fruits: by their f. ye shall know them 6.2
fuel: if f. prepared, hard to tell whence spark shall come 819.2
fulfillment: f. as human being is greatest miracle 1008.16
indulgences, not f., is what world permits 470.2
only peace, only security is in f. 504.16
seek the road which makes death a f. 221.60
full: f. gut supports moral precepts .1
fullness: when we rejoice in our f., then we can part with our fruits with joy 571.18
fun: f. good when it spoils nothing better 436.27
taking f. as f., earnestness in earnest 886.7
to make f. of person to his face 820.2
fundamental: as f. a problem as getting enough to eat 524.15
funeral: chief mourner not always at f. 367.6
f.: pageant whereby we attest respect for dead by enriching undertaker 367.3
go into a natural history museum without feeling as if I were attending a f. 613.2
go to f., not church, to be uplifted 367.10
I misbehaved once at a f. 526.17
no American attends his f. without services of cosmeticians 367.7
people ask me what makes a good f. 367.1
funerals: f. are pretty compared to death 367.15
f. have more regard to vanity of the living 367.9
many f. discredit a physician 766.10
the best seats at the f. of friends 653.83
funny: anyone considered f., deep inside they are serious 436.36
everything's f. if it happens to others 436.26
life remains f. when people die 541.38
furnace: heat not a f. so hot for your foe 817.16
furniture: no f. so charming as books 93.83
fury: abused patience turns to f. 677.7
a f. that would take form instantly 240.4
beware the f. of a patient man 677.6
futility: a mortal breed most full of f. 33.21
f.: playing a harp before a buffalo 48.2
future: cynic is prematurely disappointed in f. 214.2
do not seek ideals of f. in the past 676.19
each sees angel in his f. self 460.3
fear, desire, hope, push us on toward f. 368.23
f. cannot be repetition of past 368.21
f. enters us to transform itself 368.28
f. is like heaven 368.3
f. is neither ours nor wholly not ours 368.9
f. is past entered through another gate 368.26
f. makes laws for our to-day 240.14
f.: period when affairs prosper, friends are true and happiness is assured 368.5
f. struggles not to become the past 368.27
generosity to f. is giving to present 729.5
he who fears not f. may enjoy present 368.12
how much man lives in the f. 368.8
I go to school to youth to learn the f. 1071.21
if I bind the f. I bind my will 201.38
if we do not grasp f., others will 368.33
if we open a quarrel between the past and present, we shall lose the f. 507.2
in contempt of what is, some strain into f. 33.21
meet f. without fear, with manly heart 676.22
men know someone has made off with their f. 581.16
never let the f. disturb you 368.2
no way of judging f. but by past 321.20
only mothers can think of the f. 368.13
only way to predict f. is to have power to shape f. 368.16
preoccupation with the f. prevents seeing the present, prompts rearranging of past 368.15
schools are the f. in miniature 279.43
the f. is interesting and dangerous 368.34
the f. may be an enemy 368.14
the great past is the best door to the f. 368.25
there's nothing like dream to create the f. 368.17
to be part of the f. 1017.14
to change past into sad smiles is to master the f. 758.11
we are diminishing our f. 177.5
we can chart f. clearly only when we know path which has led to present 419.44
you can never plan the f. by the past 368.6
you shall know f. when it has come 368.1
futurity: fate of man to seek consolations in f. 318.7
G
gadgeteer: the insight and imagination of a g. 34.80
gadgets: we cannot get grace from g. 966.28
gaiety: g. of life, like beauty, is saving grace 513.6
gain: prefer loss to dishonest g. 738.3
sometimes better incur loss than make g. 550.6
gainer: to lose oneself is to be g. 1021.3
gains: base g. are the same as losses 738.5
there are no g. without pains 741.26
Galilean: thou hast conquered, O pale G. 511.5
gallantry: g. is more common where climate's sultry 140.1

gambling: g. is the great leveller 369.3
world is a g.-table 1067.3
game: one vexed at losing g. by a single hole 329.10
play out the g., act well your part 825.1
stander-by may see more of g. than player 650.4
the world's most interesting g. 929.14
we think if we watch g. we have taken part 929.11
game's: genius loves play for own sake; the g. the thing 155.2
games: we must play no g. with ourselves 1000.3
gaming: man is g. animal, trying to get the better 155.8
garden: some make a g. of life, walk down a path 661.1
you could dig the g. with him 90.9
gardener: g. should have nine times as many lives as a cat 371.3
gardening: grow anything anywhere, surely the art of g. 371.5
successful g. is a question of love 371.4
garlic: peasant dishes, mostly composed of g. and tomatoes 355.2
garment: new g. ever fails wearer's expectation 267.4
our last g. is made without pockets 221.73
gate: strait is the g., narrow the way 841.1
gather: g. thyself together, at least once a day 183.3
g. ye rosebuds while ye may 706.4
gay person: the recognizable g. is treated like a freak 424.6
gender: clarity of g. makes possible dialectic 581.32
general: g. makes you forget your troubles 1042.5
prize of g. not tent, but command 719.31
unhappy the g. who comes on field of battle with a system 939.1
generalities: bookworm wraps himself in web of g. 93.37
g. in morals mean absolutely nothing 373.3
generality: for parlor use vague g. is a life-saver 188.2
generalization: g. necessary to advancement of knowledge 201.27
God is our name for the last g. to which we can arrive 387.27
generalizations: all g. are false, including this one 373.1
generation: each g. can be a world of its own 34.63
each g. removes parents' household gods 374.7
each new g. is a new people 374.3
each new g. looked back to its youth 374.4
every g. laughs at the old fashions 338.27
every g. must be free to act for itself 374.13
every g. revolts against its fathers 374.12
every old man complains of the rising g. 374.8
immortality is attained only by g. 454.15
no g. interested in art in same way 53.40
older g. bewails indolence of young 374.15
self-defeating to pretend to style of younger g. than your own 374.1
strife hushed by passing of one g. 374.10
the injustice of one g. to another 374.2
to decry younger g. dates a man 374.16
who thinks only of own g. born for few 184.7
world is a whole g. older and wiser 374.5
generations: as g. come and go, their arts ebb, flow 990.19
g. passing like grass 42.5
g. quickly change, pass on torches of life 374.11
we feel closer to distant g. 374.17
generosity: function of poor to exercise our g. 718.51
g. gives assistance, rather than advice 375.7
g. is the flower of justice 375.4
g. relinquished to practice charity 433.5
sea has no g. 853.8
the weak feel our g. as oppression 1047.6
generous: be just before you're g. 517.45
far fewer g. men than we think 475.5
if a man is g., we call his courage pride 206.5
impossible to be just if one is not g. 517.40
prodigal man cannot be truly g. 375.2
prudence engenders paralysis of g. acts 755.29
genitals: with the g. God gave us 1062.70
genius: a zest for life as big as his g. 948.12
beware of notions like g., inspiration 376.25
coffee good for talent; g. needs prayer 377.2
concept of g. as akin to madness fostered by public's inferiority complex 376.28
crooked roads without improvement are roads of g. 460.1
danger of erroneous calculations when man computes force of his own g. 864.3
even g. is tied to profit 602.46
everyone is a g. at least once a year 376.20
g. acts unconsciously 376.17
g. always finds itself a century early 376.10
g. and morality are often bitter enemies 376.36
g. belongs to individuals 377.4
g. can only breathe in atmosphere of freedom 376.22
g. depends upon the data within reach 376.7
g. is but greater aptitude for patience 376.4
g. is formed in quiet; character, in life stream 119.14
g. is sorrow's child 376.1
g. is that in whose power a man is 377.7
g. lasts longer than beauty 279.89
g. loves play for its own sake 155.2
g. more often in cracked pot than whole 376.37
g. native to soil where it grows 376.16
g. never accepted without a measure of condonement 376.30
g. says things he has never heard 377.3
g. seems to consist in trueness of sight 376.11
g. should marry person of character 376.18
g.: to effect what's in your mind 376.13
g. will fight against oblivion 376.31
if men of g. never complained of critics 207.54
it takes a g. to whine appealingly 549.2
it takes a lot of time to be a g. 376.32
lucky person passes for a g. 360.10
man's g. contracts itself to a few hours 858.12
men of g. are far more abundant 376.26
men of g. labour because they excel 311.6
men of g. regarded as fools 479.4
never imitate the eccentricities of g. 376.6
no great g. without some madness 376.2
one type of g. begets, other gives birth 376.24
patience is a necessary ingredient of g. 376.8
persecution of g. fosters its influence 376.34
profound g. baffled by trivial questions 480.6
public forgives everything except g. 376.38
sanctity, g., are as rebellious as vice 840.11
sign of g.: dunces are against him 376.33
talent is to be envied, g. pitied 377.6
the g. is necessarily a squanderer 376.23
to do what is impossible for talent is g. 377.1
towering g. disdains beaten path 376.21
true g. is mind of large general powers 376.19
true g. prefers silence to incompleteness 376.27
wisdom of providence seen in rarity of g. 754.10
with g., throes are in conception 201.10
woman seldom loves g. 1062.123
world does not know what to do with g. 377.5
you cannot create g.; only nurture it 376.35
young g. apologizes for his large feet 376.14
young man reveres men of g. 376.12
geniuses: biggest oxen are the g. 1069.115

g. ordered by administrative types 376.29
what g. must do is what they most want to 376.3
genocide: expulsion and g. must remain distinct 204.1
genteel: g.: catafalque smothering spontaneity 809.3
genteelly: to do anything coolly is to do it g. 160.2
gentility: world of shabby g. is like no other 809.2
gentle: g. mind by g. deeds is known 378.6
strong men can always afford to be g. 940.12
gentleman: Englishman wants to be recognized as a g. 804.16
g. dies without pronouncing the word g. 378.1
g. is one who never inflicts pain 378.4
repose and cheerfulness are badge of g. 378.2
rich thief passes for a g. 934.3
sometimes the devil is a g. 242.7
to be a g. is to be oneself 378.3
you have to be a g. all the time 378.5
gentlest: possible Nero in g. human 719.6
the g. feeds on another's woe 561.11
geography: history is all explained by g. 419.50
morality is largely matter of g. 604.17
geometry: there is no royal road to g. 570.3
German: virtues of G. people have created evils 381.5
when literary G. dives into a sentence 381.4
Germans: we G. fear God, but nothing else 381.2
Germany: most important result, invention of G. 361.14
get: easy to g. everything you want 8.3
it is easy to despise what you cannot g. 920.1
not to g. heart's desire bad as getting nothing 366.1
gettings: end to our g. is only end to our losses 8.8
ghetto: g. improved one way: out of existence 131.4
ghost: g.: outward sign of an inward fear 383.1
ghosts: I think we are all g., every one of us 383.1
modern mansion has no place for g. 430.2
you can't live with g. or without them 383.2
giant: tyrannous to use giant's strength like g. 719.52
giants: when towering g. stumble 1027.4
gift: a g. deprives us of our liberty 384.10
enemy's g. is ruinous and no g. 384.29
every good g. is from above 384.2
g. in season is a double favor to needy 384.25
g., with kind countenance, is double 384.9
hasten to give while g. can be enjoyed 384.16
intention, not value, of g. is weighed 384.26
loving-kindness may go with a little g. 384.32
nothing so frequent as to mistake an ordinary human g. for a special endowment 962.7
only g. is a portion of thyself 384.6
painful to give g. to man of sensibility 384.5
surprise is greatest g. life can grant 955.3
gifts: each day provides its own g. 729.19
g. are like hooks 384.21
g. fate and nature lend us often end us 962.2
gods themselves moved by g. 99.2
I fear the Greeks even when they bring g. 259.15
if we do not use g. the days bring, they carry them silently away 978.16
never to be cast away are g. of the gods 962.8
no benefit in g. of a bad man 384.8
rich g. wax poor when givers prove unkind 384.27
girl: dear to heart of a g. is her beauty, charm 385.5
if pleasing to one man, g. is taken care of 581.49
little g. without doll as unfortunate as woman without children 123.27
girls: a lot of g. together is a romantic thing 385.4
cannot even pretend to feel as much interest in boys as in g. 385.2
g., not accustomed to jockeying for status 933.5
there is no need to waste pity on young g. 385.3
give: do not g. like hen that lays egg, cackles 433.1
g. all thou canst 384.34
it is more blessed to g. than to receive 384.3
well to g. when asked, better unasked 384.12
when I g. I g. myself 384.33
given: nothing costs so much as what is g. 787.1
to whom much is g., much is required 810.2
you pay too dear for what's g. freely 384.28
giver: we do not quite forgive a g. 384.7
givers: rich gifts wax poor when g. prove unkind 384.27
gives: he g. worthless gold who g. from duty 384.20
what man g., the gods by man bestow 754.8
giving: to give, but not feel it: best way of g. 384.1
we promise much to avoid g. little 743.14
glad: one can bear grief, takes two to be g. 409.50
gladness: g. of heart is the life of man 409.2
they serve g. who meet calls of sadness 918.57
glamorous: thought that Lake Forest was the most g. place in the world 254.4
glass: it is not vain-glory for man and his g. to confer 1027.16
glories: g., like glow-worms, afar off shine 386.18
glorious: hour of g. life worth age without name 386.13
glory: better live miserably than die in g. 541.10
desire of g. last infirmity, even of wise 386.17
g. and curiosity are two scourges of soul 211.9
g. and repose can't inhabit same place 386.10
g. consists of two parts 873.17
g. is largely a theatrical concept 386.7
g. is like a circle in the water 386.14
g. melancholy blazon on coffin lid 332.41
g. should be a consequence, not a motive 386.12
good fortune leads one to the highest g. 360.6
I have felt it like a g. in my heart 605.4
paths of g. at least lead to grave 271.29
paths of g. lead but to the grave 386.6
shortest way to g. is to be what you would be thought to be 386.16
shortest way to g. is to do that for conscience which we do for g. 386.11
sudden g. makes grimaces called laughter 526.14
take away writing, you take away g. 386.2
those most desirous of honour or g. cry out loudest of its abuse 426.10
to ashes of dead g. comes too late 386.9
to die with g. is still pain for dier 221.46
when g. comes, memory departs 386.5
glove: clean g. often hides dirty hand 224.5
glow: a white g., overpowering, sublime 763.2
glutton: g. digs his grave with his teeth 274.8
gluttony: g. makes drowsy without tranquility 530.6
goal: successful person sees g. and aims for it 686.1
goats: bleat in a flock of g. 171.13
God: all service ranks the same with G. 887.1
an honest G. is the noblest work of man 387.41
any G. I felt in church I brought with me 387.77
any G. who can invent hell 387.18
before Kepler, heavens told glory of G. 415.9
by night atheist half believes a G. 1004.16
canst thou by searching find out G. 387.5
closer is G. than breathing 387.70
damned by men, we are absolved by G. 387.71
danger past, G. is forgotten 216.9
do not ask G. the way to heaven 414.7
do not speak of G. much 387.26
do we seek G. or G.'s gifts 387.67
even G. has been defended with nonsense 881.2
every common bush afire with G. 261.2
every man thinks G. is on his side 387.2
excellence nothing without consent of G. 311.3
fear G., and where you are

will be like a cathedral 697.3
fool hath said there is no G. 1004.2
give G. thanks for revealing Himself 816.3
G. finds a way for what none foresaw 368.11
G. gives almonds to those who have no teeth 17.57
G. has delegated himself to a million deputies 174.5
G. is day and night, winter and summer, war and peace, satiety and want 387.38
G. is the indwelling 387.68
G. is usually on the side of big squadrons against little ones 719.16
G. knows what G. is coming next 892.36
G. seeks comrades and claims love 242.8
G. was well aware of Lake Wobegon 387.42
G. who loveth us made and loveth all 723.8
G. works wonders now and then 528.24
good thing G. doesn't let you look into future 240.12
great man stands on G. 400.5
heart experiences G., not reason 387.54
heavens declare the glory of G. 415.2
he revealed himself only to G. 766.20
he worships G. who knows him 1068.8
how do you expect to search out G. 387.3
hymnbooks resound with cursing of G. 128.6
idea of G. ends in a meeting-house 128.2
if G. created us in his own image, we have more than reciprocated 387.75
if G. did not exist, would be invented 387.76
if I ascend to heaven, thou, G., art there 387.7
if men knew selves, G. would pardon 875.20
if one religion, G. would be manifest 387.53
is there no G., then, but an absentee G. 387.20
it does me no injury for my neighbor to say there are twenty gods or no G. 984.10
it is through us that G. is achieved 387.35
just are the ways of G. 387.48
let none mourn; these things are in the hands of G. 610.11
looking at G. reduces our disposition to human dissent 772.3
love of G. is not always love of good 697.6
malt justifies G. to man 268.27
man appoints and G. disappoints 387.21
man is G. by his faculty for 261.7
man's strength is to find, follow way of G. 697.1
man wrong who thinks to swindle G. 224.15
mills of G. grind slowly 815.8
nature is the art of G. 623.18
one man has one G., and one another G. 797.25
perfections of nature show image of G. 623.57
perhaps the sun was G. 387.66
poorest worm tells me there is a G. 387.25
question even the existence of a G. 265.3
render to G. the things that are G.'s 127.1
respectable society believed in G. to avoid having to speak about him 387.62
solitude is audience-chamber of G. 915.22
solitude is bearable only with G. 915.19
speak to G. as if men heard you 697.12
terror of G. is the secret of religion 343.37
the eternal G. is thy refuge 856.1
the only money of G. is G. 387.29
the only useful G. is one whose existence is certain 797.48
there is no G. stronger than death 221.128
they are always saying G. loves us 551.85
to obey G. is freedom 387.63
to put trust in G. means one will chance it 754.2
true laws of G. are laws of our well-being 797.7
trust in G., but tie your camel 259.11
try first thyself, and after call in G. 281.6
we have made G. the biggest celebrity 387.9
we make G. accomplice to legalize our sins 440.2
we need G. to give a meaning to the Universe 387.74
we should find G. in what we know 387.8
we treat G. like a pasha, or a sultan 723.36
weigh gain, loss in wagering that G. is 387.55
when faith burns out, G. dies 1004.15
when G. hands you a gift, he hands you a whip 387.19
where G. hath a temple, Devil hath chapel 191.2
while G. waits for His temple to be built of love, men bring stones 126.11
who can speak to G., or rather who can't? 387.61
whom heart of man shuts out, G. takes in 547.4
whom man kills, G. restoreth to life 518.6
who serve G. and Mammon lose faith in G. 497.4
who's near the Church is often far from G. 126.8
will of G. to be borne with courage 240.19
worship of G. is flight after unattainable 1068.13

god: as if some lesser g. had made the world 457.8
curiosity and intelligence provided by a g. 261.8
g. of cannibal will be a cannibal 387.28
how dark the ways of g. to man 754.5
if triangles had g., he'd have three sides 387.50
though a g., I've learned to obey the times 297.19
to do all one would like: to be a g. 504.18
true g. is perfect, lacking nothing 387.30
when a man's willing and eager, g. joins in 1057.1
who shall say what is or is not g. 797.26

God's: it is G. giving if we laugh or weep 409.93
on earth G. work must truly be our own 678.9
one on G. side is a majority 387.57
people who use G. name most frequently 387.43

godliness: g. is profitable unto all things 696.1

gods: all g. dead except god of war 1042.19
ask the g. nothing excessive 598.1
do we deceive ourselves that g. exist 265.1
false g. that could not heal them 900.2
fear created g.; audacity, kings 520.1
fear first brought g. into the world 387.56
g. give mortals not everything at once 754.9
g. used the victim himself to forge links 873.16
if man obeys g., they listen to him also 387.39
if no g. all toil is without meaning 1004.8
in emergencies we fall back on our g. 203.2
injustice makes us doubt g. 477.4
many roads to happiness if g. assent 409.73
never to be cast away are gifts of the g. 962.8
only g. can live forever without pain 946.2
populace drag down g. to their own level 682.6
should seek from g. that which becomes us 949.2
skirts of the g. drag in our mud 387.34
the g. kill us for their sport 387.64
we make g. to whom to impute the ills we ought to bear 387.4
we meet no g. if we harbor none 261.4
when half-gods go, the g. arrive 578.2

going: keep on g. right on until you die 316.1
men must endure their g. and coming 221.113
we never know we go when we are g. 221.33

gold: Europeans wanted g. and slaves 876.10
deer with chain of g. will eat grass 109.7
fetters of g. are still fetters 109.2
g. aids the conqueror in love and war 602.42
g. buys honours; g. will purchase love 602.44
g. has ruined fewer men than lack of it 718.1
greed for g., to what does thou drive man 8.11
hay is more acceptable to an ass than g. 48.5
if stone bruises g., worth undiminished 1026.19
love is the only g. 551.216
weather emotional storms with g. ballast 602.36

when g. argues cause, eloquence impotent 602.49
golden: the g. years are slipping by 540.15
golf: g. course is epitome of the transitory 929.8
gone: the gay will laugh when thou art g. 606.6
good: advantage of power: you can do more g. 719.26
all evil is universal g. 623.61
all g. things will pass away 990.1
anybody who is any g. is different 469.6
apprehension of the g. gives but the greater feeling to the worse 390.18
be g. and let people speak evil of thee 393.41
be g., and let who will be clever 393.26
better to fare hard with g. men 57.10
better ungrateful men than miss chance to do g. 433.10
do g. action stealthily, have it found it out 227.12
do g. by stealth 393.37
do g. even to the wicked 433.26
do not argue what g. man should be 393.5
do not call painful what is g. for you 250.2
do not require evil with g. 288.19
easier to swoon in dreams than do g. 393.29
easy to do g. action, but not as habit 393.2
enjoyment g. in itself is g. religiously 900.13
everyone has as much of g. as he can 389.14
finer wits say knowledge is the g. 522.49
forget the g., the bad has more punch 390.4
g. and bad is simply helping or hurting 390.3
g. and bad may not be dissevered 390.5
g., communicated, more abundant grows 393.32
g. deed shines in a naughty world 433.28
g. humor is a philosophic state of mind 392.9
g. is g. doctor, bad is sometimes better 307.11
g. is not g. unless a thousand it possess 393.13
g. man can be stupid and still be g. 1070.11
g. man must rather sit with loss than rise unjust 550.4
g. man prefers defeat to using evil to win 574.6
g. man's pedigree is little hunted up 393.46
g. men are stars, illustrate the times 393.25
g. men join one g. act to another 393.6
g. men must not obey laws too well 393.14
g. nature is better in conversation than wit 188.1
g. nature is worth more than knowledge 392.2
g. not achieved when sought directly 389.12
g. people make badness very important 393.49
g. shall not compensate bad in man 390.2
g. so g. that bad when bad can't be bad 389.7
g. that I would I do not 691.3
g. things are fruits of originality 662.5
g. things of life come with a mixture 389.6
g. things when short are twice as g. 389.5
g. to be tired by search for true g. 389.9
g. which prevents greater g. is evil 390.20
g. will be the final goal of ill 390.22
great and g. are seldom the same man 401.20
hardly anybody g. for everything 962.3
he is not g. who speaks well of all 455.2
he that hopes no g. fears no ill 692.2
he too busy doing g. has no time to be g. 433.29
how few know their own g., or pursue it 691.6
idiot the g. man, he doesn't know any better 393.42
if you are happy you will be g. 393.40
if you pretend to be g., the world takes you seriously 659.13
in g. days we've cold memory of bad times 580.33
it is by evil that g. is pleasant 187.3
it is hard to be simple enough to be g. 393.16
it's wiser being g. than bad 390.1
jail doesn't teach anyone to do g. 393.19
life's a field for g. and evil 539.106
love of God is not always love of g. 697.6
man makes no noise over a g. deed 227.2
man not g. or bad for one action 227.10
man's g. or ill lies in his own will 1056.4
man who insists he is as g. as anybody believes he is better 297.13
may the g. God pardon all g. men 393.9
men are g. when free from passion, error 393.22
men become g. creatures, but so slow 393.10
men love g., but can't judge what is g. 389.10
men more capable of great actions than g. 227.19
moral g. is effect of physical evil 390.10
more hope in death of g. than in life of wicked 393.18
most harmful harm is done by the g. 393.36
nature, not standing, makes g. man 393.38
no man g. enough to be another's master 889.17
no man so g. he wouldn't deserve hanging 393.34
no resolve for g. or evil until execution 390.8
no society can be kept up without g. nature 391.1
not all those to whom we do g. love us 227.26
not enough to do g. 433.21
nothing g., bad but thinking makes it so 389.13
nothing g. for all 389.4
nothing g. for him for whom nothing bad 390.7
nothing is so g. as it seems beforehand 318.1
nothing so enhances a g. as sacrifices 837.9
often g. things have hurtful consequences 176.1
omission of g. is no less reprehensible than commission of evil 390.16
profit on g. action is to have done it 227.27
prudence does not always lead to g. 176.6
pure g. soon grows insipid 412.9
question of g. and evil remains in chaos 390.24
seek not g. from without, but from within 393.17
some men have g. qualities useless to themselves 1023.6
the g. have come to wisdom through failure 393.43
the g. is landscape man advances through 389.8
the g. is oft interred with men's bones 390.19
the g. suffers while the bad prevails 390.9
there is so much g. in the worst of us 206.11
there must be g. in what pleases many 712.5
they're only truly great who are truly g. 393.12
to a g. man there can come no evil 393.45
to become a g. man, one must have faithful friends or outright enemies 393.35
to be g. we must needs have suffered 946.28
to be greatly g., a man must imagine intensely 1008.18
to show others how to be g. is noble and no trouble 393.48
we as often repent g. we have done as ill 792.2
we do g. to accomplish evil with impunity 390.11
we do not always see our own g. 389.11
we know the g., can't achieve it 389.2
we look for g. but do not recognize it 389.3
we slight man whose g. will can't help 495.8
what falls in accordance with nature is g. 389.1
what rapture to know g. thing when you see it 691.4
when the bad imitate the g., there is no knowing what mischief is intended 451.9
who cannot be angry cannot be g. 39.4
who wants to do g. knocks at gate; who loves finds it open 433.30
world bears two nations: g. and bad 1067.21
world is sown with g. 1065.46
youngster who does not know what he is g. at 1.6
good-bye: there's release and torment in every g. 673.2
good-humored: man who thinks himself unequalled sure to be g. 156.4
good-natured: g. man has world to be happy in 392.8
goodness: capacity to feel deeply inspires g. 952.9
experience differentiates piety, g. 697.9

g. can bear mistakes of the ignorant 984.4
g. comes out of people who bask in sun 950.5
g. is born of wisdom 393.30
g. is easier to recognize than to define 393.3
g. is only investment that never fails 393.47
g. is uneventful 393.20
g. makes men happy, happiness good 393.27
g. that assumes a public role is no longer good 393.1
g. that preaches undoes itself 393.15
g. thinks no ill where no ill seems 393.33
greatness and g. are not means, but ends 401.6
Infinite G. has such wide arms 754.3
loving-kindness is the better part of g. 393.31
nobody deserves to be praised for his g. if he has not power to be wicked 393.28
no odor so bad as that from g. tainted 191.13
no one can be good if g. is not in demand 393.8
one good action after another: perfection of g. 393.23
there is some soul of g. in things evil 307.34
virtue is bold, g. never fearful 1033.43
we love g., but also freedom 363.13
wisdom has its root in g. 1060.16

goodwill: g. is slumbering within society 913.14

gospel: believer teaches g. at risk of life 596.2
go ye into the world and preach the g. 596.1

gossip: difference between g. and philosophy 694.10
g. columnist's business not his business 630.14
g. is light to lift up, hard to put down 394.6
g. needs no carriage 394.11
g. within everybody's reach 394.9
lap up trivial g. about essential nobodies 632.11
men have always detested women's g. 394.7
whoever gossips to you will g. about you 394.12

gossips: who g. well has a reputation for being good company, a wit, but never a gossip 394.8

Gothic: G. is at once the most logical and the most beautiful 50.13
promise, ruin seen in G. architecture 50.19

Goths: an army of rampaging G. 208.9

gourmet: g. is glutton with brains 274.12
nine chefs, because I am a g. 355.15

gout: g. is not relieved by a fine shoe 798.9

govern: can't g. country having 246 cheeses 361.4
dead g. the living 986.6
g. by counting, not breaking, heads 233.20
let the people think they g. 233.42
men have choice to g., or be governed 395.6
none good enough to g. without consent 395.36
not being able to g. events, I g. myself 862.10
nothing as dangerous for state as those who would g. with maxims found in books 395.51
to g. a nation you need specific talent 395.41
unless you g. within yourself 807.4
who would g. others should master self 831.11

governed: consent of g. safeguard against both ignorant tyrants and benevolent despots 233.35
nation perpetually conquered is not g. 357.3
very populous city is rarely well g. 131.3

governing: art of g.: not let men grow old in jobs 395.44
art of g. requires the whole man 831.8
pleasure of g. must certainly be exquisite 395.59

government: a dose of smaller and less intrusive g. 102.3
all are interested in struggle for better living conditions, not in form of g. 395.5
all g. is founded on compromise and barter 162.2
America is still a g. of the naïve, for the naïve, and by the naïve 34.54
basis of g. is justice, not pity 395.64
compassionate g. is servant of people 395.30
consent of people is foundation of g. 395.1
conservative g. is organised hypocrisy 178.3
corruption of g. begins with principles 191.9
each man has equal right to protection of g. 297.10
easy to accuse g. of imperfection 395.43
effective g. based on public confidence 395.34
essence of free g. is considering offices as public trusts 761.3
essence of g., concern for public interest 736.6
essence of republican g. is consent 233.53
even for neutrality you must have strong g. 395.23
every central g. worships uniformity 395.17
every g. is exact symbol of its people 395.10
every man who is not wedded to his millions is dangerous to the g. 1048.38
forms of g. arise from differences in men 409.3
forms of g. forged in the fire of practice 395.32
free g. consists in control of rivalries 395.3
freedom when people take care of g. 395.63
good g. greatest human blessing 395.27
good laws, disobeyed, are not good g. 528.4
g. and co-operation are the laws of life 395.54
g. a trust, officers of g. trustees 395.13
g. can easily exist without law 528.57
g. consists in taking money from one part of citizens to give to the other 101.4
g. defines man by the printed form 102.4
g. expands to absorb revenue, then some 395.62
g. gratified to become a protector 746.4
g. is a contrivance of human wisdom 395.11
g. is ourselves, not alien power 1038.17
g. is produced by our wickedness 395.46
g. is science of social happiness 395.2
g. makes it easy for people to do good 395.12
g. no better than public opinion sustaining it 762.17
g., organism with appetite for money 395.50
g. refused to hire even one female 1062.14
g. requires sufficient food, military equipment, confidence of people in ruler 395.14
g. that functions in pinches survives 395.33
g., too serious to admit of courtesies 711.91
great revolution is the fault of the g. 819.15
guilt of g. is crime of whole country 395.48
if a g. blurs decency it is an evil g. 395.24
in change of g., poor only change masters 718.48
in g., justice means force, virtue 517.32
in g. offices sensitive to mass sentiment, no sure tenure 761.10
invisible g. is malign 395.39
job in g., act as broker 711.30
liberty is limitation of g. power 537.51
mind, soul, must be let alone by g. 590.17
next to anarchy, g. is the worst thing 395.7
no broader basis for g. than that which includes all people 233.18
no g. has provision for own termination 395.35
no g. matters as much as the administration 395.40
no g. ought to be without censors 113.5
no g. secure without opposition 658.5
object of g.: secure happiness to mass 395.29
officers of g. are servants 761.12
people are the safe depositories of g. 233.21
permissive g. leaves control to other sources 395.56
popular g. awakens spirit and energy 233.15
popular g. not proved to guarantee good g. 395.38
public interested more in g. than politics 711.73
purpose of g. to conserve rights of many 395.52
society a blessing, g. necessary evil 395.47
superlatively efficient g. is anti-human 395.25
test of a g. 491.5
that g. best which provides most 395.37
the deadening effects of g. control 468.3

there are no necessary evils in g. 395.28
there can be g. without initiative 395.55
virtue alone not sufficient for g. 395.42
we live under g. of men, newspapers 630.26
what g. gives it must first take away 964.4
when g. tries to handle our affairs, it costs more and the results are worse 395.16
where's the state that excels bees for g. 481.2
governments: efforts of g. not enough without the people 682.9
g. arise out of people or over people 395.45
g. classified by considering who are the somebodies they endeavor to satisfy 395.60
g. exist to protect rights of minorities 395.49
most g. are usually inexpedient 395.57
nations may have fashioned their g. 395.15
grace: abuse of g. is affectation 684.19
calling me to share God's g. 1068.12
deformed men ponder g. 187.1
g. is the absence of all that indicates pain, difficulty, hesitation, incongruity 396.3
g. needed to turn man into saint 840.9
highest female g. is silence 898.10
no spring, nor summer beauty hath such g. 653.20
religion restores courage to live by g. 697.11
to confer favors with g. 384.4
we cannot get g. from gadgets 966.28
when g. is joined with wrinkles 653.51
without g. beauty is an unbaited hook 396.2
graceful: if we cannot be decent, let us be g. 396.4
graces: g. which encourage imitation are inimitable 396.1
grades: kids who got bad g., who were a pain in the ass 123.25
gradually: everything comes g. at its appointed hour 240.16
graft: first gold star child gets in school is its first lesson in g. 191.14
grammar: g. can be discovered but not invented 398.6
g. is common speech formulated 398.8
g., rich and diverse linguistic system 398.2
g.: system of pitfalls for feet of the self-made man 398.1
scholars assumed that Latin g. was g. itself 398.5
grammatical: speakers know intuitively whether a sentence is g. 398.4
grandeur: if g. in you, you find it in all 261.4
granted: men have infinite capacity for taking things for g. 156.5
grape: better be jocund with the fruitful g. 704.24
grapes: the g. of wrath are growing heavy 39.27
grasp: man's reach should exceed his g. 55.2
people do not g. the things they learn 87.6
grass: all flesh is g. 606.3
as for man, his days are as g. 990.3
blade of g. is always a blade of g. 699.5
they chewed gum instead of g. 385.1
grateful: g. mind by owing owes not 399.8
people ar-re not g. because they niver feel they get half that they deserve 475.1
gratefulness: g. is the poor man's payment 399.2
gratify: I'll climb the highest mountain, swim the deepest ocean to g. it 391.6
gratitude: all men feel g. for pleasing objects 646.8
child shows g. the way woman shows a dress 399.6
for some, g. is a species of revenge 647.2
g. is a debt like blackmail 399.11
g. is most exquisite form of courtesy 399.7
g. is veiled desire for more benefaction 399.4
I loathe a friend whose g. grows old 365.40
revenge is profitable, g. is expensive 399.3
some have knack of putting upon you gifts of no value to engage substantial g. 384.18
you can't extract g. as you would a tooth 498.11
grave: every man is g. alone 886.4
good man's g. is his Sabbath 221.36
hearts beating funeral marches to g. 606.12
it is a kind of healthy g. 194.13
no pulpit sends voice far as g. 473.6
paths of glory lead but to the g. 386.6
sustained and soothed, approach thy g. 221.19
who is not in g. has enough 539.132
grave's: g. a fine place, but none there embrace 221.90
gravity: g., by far the weakest force of nature 623.19
laws of g., chemistry, botany 849.7
vivacity is gift of women, g. that of men 566.1
gray: g. a colour always on eve of change 143.2
graybeards: wiser, if sedate, come g. to roses late 653.65
great: a g. man profits by his good fortune 401.34
a g. man will find a g. subject 848.9
banalities of g. man pass for wit 68.1
calumny ever pursues the g. 905.7
come nearest the g. when g. in humility 435.26
errors of g. men are more fruitful than truths of little men 299.25
every g. action is extreme when undertaken 227.30
everything g. is created by individual who can labor in freedom 363.10
few g. men could pass Personnel 401.23
first test of g. man is humility 435.21
for the person for whom small things don't exist, the g. is not g. 996.8
g. actions not always sons of g. resolutions 227.5
g. and good are seldom the same man 401.20
g. crises produce g. men, g. deeds 205.4
g. eaters incapable of all else g. 883.4
g. fleas have little fleas to bite 'em 669.2
g. ideas are not charitable 443.21
g. life is young idea lived by mature man 539.129
g. man doesn't lose his self-possession 401.44
g. man is ganglion in nerves of society 401.29
g. man is he who does not lose child's-heart 478.5
g. man is the impressionable man 883.3
g. man need not be virtuous 401.48
g. man resents partner in greatness 401.37
g. man stands on God 400.5
g. men are but life-sized 401.2
g. men, comets, are eccentric in courses 401.7
g. men hallow a whole people 401.52
g. men lose greatness by being near us 333.8
g. men must be lifted on world's shoulders 401.24
g. men toiling upward in the night 6.13
g. men too make many mistakes 401.35
g. men too often have greater faults than little men can find room for 400.8
g. mind can look beyond itself 1035.2
g. offices will have g. talents 401.8
g. society concerned with goals not goods 913.18
g. soul surrenders itself to fate 806.9
g. things are made of little things 400.3
g. welcome the herd out of vanity 400.11
hearts of the g. can be changed 350.1
he is g. who is what he is from nature 662.1
height from which the g. look down makes all the rest of mankind seem equal 400.7
if we play g. man too much, we seem small 693.4
in narrow sphere g. men are blunderers 401.42
in tragedy g. men are more truly great than in history 987.10
let him be g. and love shall follow him 401.11
little vices of g. must be accounted g. 1030.19

lives of g. men all remind us 401.36
men in g. places are thrice servants 401.1
men more capable of g. actions than good 227.19
men of no note do g. deeds 649.7
men worship the shows of g. men 401.4
no g. thing is created suddenly 401.15
no man was ever g. by imitation 401.31
no really g. man ever thought himself so 401.27
none think the g. unhappy but the g. 401.59
nothing g. accomplished without passion 675.8
nothing g. ever done without enthusiasm 293.5
of g. things, be silent or speak loftily 808.10
only passions can raise soul to g. things 675.4
our g. men not commonly g. scholars 848.20
privilege of the g. is to see catastrophes from a terrace 401.21
strike at g. man, you will not miss 905.13
the g. man is often all of a piece 400.10
they're only truly g. who are truly good 393.12
to be g. is to be misunderstood 401.13
to know g. men dead is compensation for having to live with mediocre 401.30
treat men greatly and they will be g. 997.3
when a g. man dies no successor comes 401.14
when g. men don't know how g. they are 401.41
when house of a g. one collapses, many little ones are slain 400.2
without mysticism man can do nothing g. 616.1

greater: g. dooms win g. destinies 17.32
g. man, the g. courtesy 197.13

greatest: g. man is man most in men's good thoughts 401.3
g. monarch sits on his own arse 780.4
g. spirits capable of g. vices and virtues 401.9

greatness: all g. affects minds differently 401.19
conquest is an ersatz g. 401.56
desire of g. is a godlike sin 401.10
do not despise the bottom-rungs in the ascent to g. 401.45
exaggeration inseparable companion of g. 309.7
g. and goodness are not means, but ends 401.6
g. brings no profit to people 401.16
g. confers intense happiness with insignificant gifts 401.43
g. has no lustre for those in search of understanding 1007.14
g. is perception that virtue is enough 1033.16
g. not effect of inspiration 401.46
g. of father often overwhelms son 916.7
men need g. in others 682.17
men win g. unawares working to other aim 286.2
must be humility to go on to g. 435.18
some have g. thrust upon them 401.50
some owe their g. to detecting needed strength in those they destine for tools 315.2
test of g. is the page of history 401.26
who meets own idea of g. has low standard 401.25

Greece: spirit of G. animated universal nature 402.1

greed: for g. all nature is too little 403.20
g. for gold, to what does thou drive man 8.11
hell has three gates: lust, anger, g. 416.4
some ache in the blindness of g. 602.32

greed's: g. worst point is its ingratitude 403.21

greedy: g. have extraordinary capacity for waste 403.14
there is something g. about trying to enjoy dinner, concert at same time 403.1

Greek: subtle of God to learn G. 80.5

greenhorn: g. is the ultimate victor in everything 618.1

gregariousness: one who may be known by the development of his organ of g. 152.20

grief: every one can master g. but he that has it 918.46
great g. transfigures the wretched 918.22
g. can take care of itself 894.6
g. can't be shared; one carries it alone 918.28
g. drives men into serious reflection 918.1
g. has limits, apprehension none 43.11
g. has made many a man look younger 918.33
g. hates the light and shrinks from eyes 918.13
g. is always heightened by surprise 955.4
g. is a species of idleness 918.24
g. is in opinion, not in nature of things 918.10
g. is proud, and makes his owner stoop 918.49
g. returns with the revolving year 918.52
g. should be the instructor of the wise 918.8
g. that does not speak bids heart break 918.47
happiness benefits body, g. develops mind 918.40
hope is incredible to the slave of g. 918.37
I measure every G. I meet 918.14
lighten g. with hopes of brighter morrow 318.5
look for secrets in g. or pleasure 855.7
man sheds g. as his skin does rain 918.15
one can bear g., takes two to be glad 409.50
one thing in this world that destroys itself more completely than beauty: g. 918.41
some are above and some below g. 918.17
stop mourning when g. is fully expressed 610.2
the g. without hope of the exodus 918.27
there is pleasure in indulging g. 918.32
to spare oneself from g. achieved only at price of total detachment 31.3
to weep is to make less the depth of g. 1052.9
what's past help should be past g. 507.8
while g. fresh, attempt to divert only irritates 918.25

griefs: better deep g. than shallow pleasures 918.19
g. that wound in solitude wound deeply 918.44
no temple can still g. and strifes 128.3
of all g. most bitter is scornful jest 436.15
waste not fresh tears over old g. 1052.4

grievance: g. is most poignant when almost redressed 477.5
no g. fit for redress by mob law 597.6
to have a g. is to have a purpose in life 251.4

grin: a conceited g., the g. of a village yokel 980.5

grind: mills of God g. slowly 815.8

ground: he that lies on the g. cannot fall 329.25
loftiest towers rise from the g. 401.5
man feels more a man if he has a bit of g. 746.23
never test g. before taking your next step 442.4
out of the g. wast thou taken 1065.12
there is life in the g. 337.8

grow: every individual strives to g. and exclude 469.3

growing: g. up: discovering inner core of strength 571.8

grown: g. up is to sit with people who have died 571.11
g. up, that is a hard thing to do 571.3
wisest man is boy grieving that he's g. 452.2

growth: all g. is a leap in the dark 404.17
g. is the only evidence of life 404.19
g. itself contains the germ of happiness 404.4
human happiness is true odour of g. 1065.36
life is cut to allow for g. 404.25
love dies only when g. stops 551.16
man's g. seen in succession of friends 404.7
only g. is in fulfilling obligations 271.23
only in g. is true security to be found 856.11
principle of g. lies in human choice 404.6

gruntled: he was far from being g. 961.5

guardians: men unfit as g. of another's happiness 564.87

guess: I try not to g. 115.4

guest: equally offensive to speed a g. who'd like to stay as detain one who'd leave 428.13
g. sees more in hour than

host in year 428.17
I'll not be a g. for less than a hundred 428.15
man should behave in own house as g. 422.9
to be an ideal g., stay at home 428.14
what is there more kindly than the feeling between host and g. 428.1
guest's: seven days is the length of a g. life 428.7
guests: fish and g. smell at three days old 428.9
unbidden g. are welcomest when gone 428.18
where g. are well-acquainted, they eat more 274.15
guidance: message of g. that neither politics nor philosophy nor religion 545.15
guilt: g. ever at a loss, confusion waits on it 405.6
g. hurries towards punishment 405.7
g. spills itself in fearing to be spilt 405.15
real estate: foundation of world's g. 746.10
self-righteousness drowns our g. 879.1
sin, g., fruit of tree of knowledge 522.41
tears and g. get mixed together 918.7
there may be g. if too much virtue 1033.39
where g. is, rage and courage abound 405.9
without spice of g., sin can't be savored 900.6
guilty: better to save g. than condemn innocent 517.50
easy to compel sensitive being to feel g. 405.14
g. conscience needs no accuser 174.6
g. man justifies self before accusation 405.8
g. think all talk is of themselves 405.5
in America man presoomed g. ontil proved g. 517.12
in his own heart no g. man is acquitted 405.10
no g. persons, only responsible ones 405.3
where all are g., no one is 405.1
whoever blushes is already g. 478.9
guinea: jingling of the g. helps honor's hurt 602.58
gullibly: g. as pups for rubber bones 618.4
gun: fits like a handshake, aims like a g. 1049.7
political power grows out of g. barrel 711.56
to get rid of g. necessary to take up g. 1042.56
guns: g. and bombs are witness to human folly 229.5
one cannot shoot with butter but with g. 1049.3
gutter: we are all in g., but some look at stars 55.20
guys: tough g. don't dance, better believe it 195.22

H

habit: chaos often breeds life; order breeds h. 257.1
character is inured h. 119.25
costly thy h. as thy purse can buy 267.23
evolution from happiness to h. is one of death's best weapons 406.5
h.: a shackle for the free 406.3
h. does not make the monk 45.8
h. is a great deadener 406.2
h. is coaxed downstairs, not flung out 406.17
h. is practice that becomes man himself 406.7
h. is stronger than reason 406.15
h. will reconcile us to all but change 406.4
in h. we find the greatest pleasure 406.14
one may attribute average actions to h. 227.20
progress has no greater enemy than h. 406.12
what is most contrary to salvation is h. 841.5
who behave well may be creatures of h. 77.15
habits: ill h. gather by unseen degrees 406.13
laws are never as effective as h. 406.16
life is but a tissue of h. 406.1
nothing so needs reforming as others' h. 790.35
wise living consists in acquiring as few h. as possible 406.9
habituation: h. a falling asleep of sense of time 406.11
hack: a h. requires a practiced excellence 942.8
Hades: descent to H. same from all starting places 221.2
hair: don't let bird make its nest in your h. 971.3
every h. makes its shadow on ground 473.8
h. shirt doesn't render the wearer chaste 866.6
time hath scanted men in h. 653.87
time pulls men's h. out 978.52
hamburger: eat straight h. in a Renaissance palazzo 274.14
ham sandwich: a grand jury will indict a h. if asked 477.15
hammer: either suffer or triumph, be anvil or h. 859.4
hand: h.: commonly thrust into somebody's pocket 8.2
hard to close open h. because one loves 384.23
let not left h. know what right doeth 433.4
hands: go around on my h. and knees 865.7
if we shake h. with icy fingers 321.48
old h. soil what they caress 1072.8
one head better than a hundred h. 493.12
handshake: a firm h. gives a good first impression 408.2
handshakes: more history made by secret h. 419.5
handsome: h. man is not quite poor 582.13
no woman is h. by features alone 1062.132
hand-wrought: imperfections of h. goods accounted marks of superiority 457.9
hang: we must all h. together 1016.3
hanged: who knows he is to be h. concentrates well 767.2
hangnail: h. is not relieved by a costly ring 798.9
happen: best way to live, by not knowing what will h. 217.1
no man can say, This shall not h. to me 321.42
happened: nothing has h. to you unless you make much of it 321.41
happens: how something h., business of historians 305.7
nothing h. in Mexico until it h. 741.21
we want to know what h. next 211.4
happier: h. when we were poorer, but also younger 1071.42
happiest: h. is he who suffers the least pain 409.80
h. lives from day to day, asks no more 186.6
he is h. of whom world says least 649.6
he that thinks self h. really is so 1060.11
happily: live in ascending scale when we live h. 409.95
happiness: artists, poets uninterested in h. 708.84
bitter to see h. through another's eyes 409.90
different men seek h. in different ways 409.3
discovery of a new dish does more for man's h. than discovery of a star 189.1
dry h. is like dry bread 324.2
every h. lent by chance for uncertain time 116.15
flaw in h., to see beyond our bourn 251.6
for h. we need hope, enterprise, change 409.83
goodness makes men happy, h. good 393.27
grateful environment a substitute for h. 294.5
greatest h. of greatest number is foundation of morals and legislation 409.10
growth itself contains the germ of h. 404.4
h. always looks small in your hands 409.48
h. a sunbeam the least shadow intercepts 409.24
h. attained when man ceases to think of self 1021.2
h. bound up in circumstances demands of life more than it has to give 129.4
h. cannot be the reward of virtue 1033.31
h. depends less on exteriors than supposed 409.27
h. depends on turn of mind 969.4
h. depends upon ourselves 409.4
h. enjoyed only in proportion as known 409.54
h. forgiven if you share it 409.21
h. hates the timid; so does science 980.7
h. is a Eurydice, vanishing when gazed on 409.79
h. is a solid and joy a liquid 409.84
h. is beneficial for the body 918.40
h. is brief and will not stay 409.35
h. is composed of misfortunes avoided 409.56

h. is fulfillment of spirit through body 409.26
h. is in the taste, and not the things 409.59
h. is knowing you don't require it 409.86
h. is never so welcome as changelessness 118.3
h. is never to be found 409.55
h. is not the end of life: character is 119.4
h. is owing to good opinion of mankind 913.19
h. is to know source of unhappiness 758.3
h. lacking makes h. one has unbearable 409.81
h. leads none of us by the same route 409.25
h. lies on the surface 409.71
h., like a flower, withers when plucked 785.32
h. makes up in height what it lacks in length 409.42
h. not achieved when sought directly 389.12
h. not in h. but achievement of it 409.31
h. of life is to be measured by the extent it has been free from suffering 409.87
h. of man consists in virtue 1033.1
h. of people is end of government 395.1
h. of the passing moment 409.47
h. puts on as many shapes as discontent 626.7
h. requires a modicum of prosperity 750.2
h. resides in imaginative reflection 409.85
h.: satisfaction of dammed-up needs 409.40
h.: sensation arising from contemplating misery of another 409.14
h. sought for ourselves alone 409.65
h.: soul expressed in considered actions 409.5
h., to be dissolved into something great 409.22
h.: to look back on a life usefully and virtuously employed 504.14
h. was born a twin 409.18
happy men are grave; carry h. cautiously 409.8
human h. is true odour of growth 1065.36
if h. in self-content is placed, the wise are wretched, fools only blessed 156.3
if one door of h. closes, another opens 409.58
if we can't buy h., we mustn't gaze on it 409.11
income 20 pounds, expenditure 19.19.6: h. 977.7
It is of no moment to the h. of an individual 395.31
keep from telling h. to the unhappy 409.101
knowledge of possible is beginning of h. 542.13
life bursts in too cruelly for h. 53.79
love: h. of another essential to own h. 551.89
malicious have a dark h. 561.5
man feels h. is his indisputable right 409.57
man's h. built on other's unhappiness 409.100
man's h.: to do things proper to man 409.7
many roads to h. if gods assent 409.73
men unfit as guardians of another's h. 564.87
modern man's h. consists in buying all he can 409.41
near-missing of h. looks like insult of fortune 409.37
new road to h.: castigate impulses 862.13
nineteen-twentieths of mankind do without h. 409.67
no h. in life so perfect as martyr's 565.6
no right to consume h. without producing it 409.92
nothing so fatal to h. as remembrance of h. 409.46
obstacle to h.: to anticipate great h. 409.38
old h. is unreturning 1071.52
only h.: a clear conscience or none 174.23
our h. depends on wisdom always 409.94
outstanding beauty tends to hamper h. 72.47
pursuit of h. makes Americans try to perpetuate youth 34.57
right to h. is fundamental 409.17
rob man of illusion, rob him of his h. 449.11
search for h. is source of unhappiness 409.49
so long as we can lose h., we possess some 409.97
subordination tends greatly to h. 780.10
supreme h. is conviction we are loved 551.94
that action is best which procures greatest h. for greatest numbers 433.15
thing left silent often makes for h. 898.19
to beg daily h. from others 235.3
to fill the hour,—that is h. 409.33
tranquility and occupation give h. 409.52
true h. is of a retired nature 409.1
universal h. keeps the wheels turning 409.51
we are less likely to fail of h. if we measure our chances and capabilities 875.23
where fear is, h. is not 343.33
whose h. is so established that he has no quarrel with his estate of life 409.16
with love one can live without h. 551.47
happy: after despair, one is almost h. 239.1
ask if you are h. and you cease to be so 409.66
better to be h. for a moment 409.64
bitter to remember that one once was h. 17.12
count no mortal h. before he has died secure from pain 727.2
h. ending is America's national belief 34.45
h. families are all alike 334.34
h. is he that serveth not another's will 491.32
h. man seems thus to himself 409.77
h. man will not feel pressure of age 968.4
h. the man content in his own ground 422.18
h. the man who calls to-day his own 729.9
he is h. that knoweth not otherwise 409.43
if you are h. you will be good 393.40
it is not enough to be h. 409.78
I were little h. if I could say how much 409.91
man's life h. expecting it soon to be so 409.75
man wishes to be h. even when his life is such as to make happiness impossible 409.6
never so h. as when describing himself as robust 645.6
no duty we so underrate as being h. 271.27
no man h. who does not think himself so 409.76
noninterference with others' ways of being h. 794.5
of mortals there is none who is h. 409.36
others look at what I have and think me h. 238.35
peasant and philosopher not equally h. 409.53
poor man thinks rich man h. 153.4
that thou art h., owe to God 409.68
to be h. by means of the heart—have none 551.10
to be h., must not be too concerned with others 409.20
to be h., resign self to seeing others h. 151.9
to forget oneself is to be h. 1021.3
we appear h. rather than become so 706.6
we are always preparing to be h. 539.88
we must be doing something to be h. 530.4
we're never so h. or unhappy as we imagine 409.60
when man is h. he doesn't analyze it 409.74
wine is only sweet to h. men 268.32
hard-boiled: easy to be h. in the daytime 633.6
harder: h. and h. to tell government from show business 395.58
hardhearted: what makes people h. is this, each has as much as he can bear in his own troubles 142.5
hardship: h. is vanishing, but so is style 750.7
there is no success without h. 945.42
we have known nothing but h. 819.37
hares: h. can gambol over body of dead lion 719.49
Harlem: I will take H. for mine 632.9
melting pot H.—H. of honey, chocolate 632.10
harlot's: cursing from the h. house downstairs 892.3
harm: h. done by people who want to feel important 873.3
most harmful h. is done by the good 393.36
harmless: be ye wise as serpents and h. as doves 943.3

harmony: conformity is the ape of h. 171.3
h. needs background of discord 410.3
hidden h. is better than the obvious 410.2
harms: wise men learn by other's h. 356.11
Harper & Brothers: leave it to H. to select our reading 93.94
harrow: butterfly preaches contentment to toad under h. 19.15
harvest: must be sowing even after bad h. 686.8
has-been: fear of becoming a h. keeps some people from becoming anything 338.17
haste: greatest assassin of life is h. 411.8
nothing is more vulgar than h. 563.11
stars setting and caravan starts, make h. 634.2
that produced in h. goes hastily to waste 411.12
hastily: do nothing h. but flea-catching 411.6
no werkman may both werken wel and h. 411.2
nothing done at once h., prudently 411.11
hat: broad h. not always on venerable head 138.3
none look so ungentlemanly as in a bad h. 267.26
hatchet: send not for a h. to break open an egg 949.1
hate: all men naturally h. one another 412.16
all victories breed h. 173.7
authority is never without h. 61.4
deepest love turneth to deadliest h. 554.6
h., compressed in heart, burns fiercer 412.7
h. fears to be delivered of itself 412.2
h., if h. be perfect, casts out fear 554.11
h. is the consequence of fear 412.6
h. man, worship God seems sum of creeds 797.39
it is human to h. those you've injured 476.20
loved him too much to feel no h. for him 554.7
minds tend to change in h., friendship 181.12
only one man need h. for h. to gain mankind 412.21
practical experience makes men h. 594.2
those whom we can love, we can h. 794.13
to put faith in h. is the true atheism 412.13
we h. for points on which we differ 27.3
we love and h. without reason 554.8
when love suppressed, h. takes its place 554.1
who fears you present will h. you absent 343.16
who harbours h., how shall another appease 412.15
you need to h. somebody 412.24
hated: nothing can be h. unless it is known 1007.12
hates: he who h. vices h. men. 1030.13
heart that no longer loves, h. 552.12
who h. dogs and babies can't be all bad 594.3
hath: he is not poor that h. not much 403.6
hating: h. eats into the heart of religion 412.10
hatred: even h. of vileness distorts features 412.3
foremost art of kings is enduring h. 520.9
for love of the Lord and h. of each other 797.9
h. alone is immortal 412.9
h. can be concealed in countenance, kiss 412.18
h. conquered by love passes into love 554.10
h., ignorant love have same ends 554.3
h. is a tonic, it makes one live 698.2
h. is blind, as well as love 554.2
h. is by far the longest pleasure 412.4
h. is often felt, seldom avowed 412.5
h. is so lasting, stubborn that reconciliation on sickbed certainly forebodes death 412.12
h. is the coward's revenge 412.22
h. leads to the extinction of values 412.14
h., like love, renders votaries credulous 554.9
h. never failed to destroy the man who hated 412.1
h. paralyzes life; love releases it 554.4
heart is more prone to h. 412.19
honest h. serves better than love corrupted 412.17
let us forget words like h., bitterness 363.39
national h. is the most violent where there is the lowest degree of culture 622.3
propaganda successful when it stirs h. 745.7
to wrong those we hate is to add fuel to h. 412.11
who has no h. is safe among things of h. 770.2
whom h. frights, let him dream not on sovereignty 831.10
hatreds: politics is the organization of h. 711.7
haughtiness: work well done invests doer with h. 1065.24
haughty: men hate h. who will not be friend 910.1
have: h., and you shall be esteemed 602.45
having: peace comes through being, not h. 681.20
hawk: when the cock is drunk, he forgets the h. 268.3
hazard: the h. of narcissistic self-absorption 896.12
head: arts will one day give headless man h. 577.11
better empty purse than empty h. 447.11
bigger a man's h., the worse his headache 166.10
h. doesn't know how to play heart's part 284.21
he with h. of wax must not walk in sun 941.5
knowing h. is second blessing 493.17
no one dares to speak well of his h. 493.19
one h. better than a hundred hands 493.12
we distrust heart too much, h. not enough 785.28
when h. aches, all members share pain 151.4
headache: bigger a man's head, the worse his h. 166.10
when you're lying awake with a dismal h. 957.2
headaches: kings have h. like other people 831.4
headdress: nothing is so variable as a lady's h. 407.1
headlines: never form judgments from front page h. 630.41
healing: wish for h. half of health 413.13
health: best part of h. is fine disposition 392.5
fear of women is basis of good h. 66.7
h. in table talk and nursery play 612.1
h. is a blessing that money cannot buy 413.20
h. is sound relation to external objects 842.1
h. is the vital principle of bliss 413.19
h. is worth more than learning 533.8
h. merits that a man lay out his life to obtain it 413.10
h., to be enjoyed, must be interrupted 187.4
if h. smile upon me, I'm a good fellow 969.6
in h. we forget ourselves and destinies 896.7
in the decay of h., let us endeavour at such temper as may be our best support 413.16
it is by disease that h. is pleasant 187.3
life is not living, but living in h. 413.9
many sick do not make us deny h. exists 627.5
preserving h. by severe rule is a malady 413.7
sickness is felt, but h. not at all 413.4
the first wealth is h. 413.3
to keep well, think little about h. 413.5
use your h., to the point of wearing it out 413.14
what some call h. no better than disease 413.12
wish for healing half of h. 413.13
healthy: h. ear can stand hearing sick words 169.6
we'll always be young, rich, and h. 413.21
hear: be swift to h., slow to speak 167.3
less dishonor to h. than speak imperfectly 1007.11
one to speak and another to h. 998.69.
heard: h. melodies are sweet 450.19
things seen are mightier than things h. 897.7
hearest: let greatest part of what thou h. be the least part of what thou believest 904.8
hearing: anything worth h. is not uttered at 7 a.m. 605.3
conversation is h. as well as being heard 188.18
my initial concern is to get a h. 1069.100
hears: who h. badly h. more than there is 683.10
heart: a h. that could not know despair 551.20

adhering to life with last muscle: h. 284.2
all can acquire my knowledge, but not my h. 284.18
blossoms of the h. no wind can touch 284.20
broken h.: monument to never-dying love 551.145
constant demands of h. and belly 625.5
diverse elements joined in h. of man 260.2
give me those days with h. in riot 1071.27
go to your bosom, ask h. what it knows 875.28
h. errs like the head, no less fatally 284.15
h. experiences God, not reason 387.54
h. grows not better but worse with age 653.16
h. has its reasons 284.27
h. influences the understanding 284.10
h. is forever inexperienced 284.35
h. is more prone to hatred 412.19
h. must break or become as bronze 539.17
h. prefers to move against circumstance 691.9
h. sees before the head can see 501.1
h. soon wearies of what it loved awhile 181.9
h. speaks many ways 551.169
h. that is soonest awake to flowers is always first to be touched by thorns 883.6
honest h. first blessing 493.17
human h. is like a ship on a stormy sea 284.22
idea of getting rid of it nearly breaks my h. 1065.45
if maiden's h. stolen, she steals after it 198.11
if they h. fails thee, climb not at all 755.9
I know I am but summer to your h. 466.4
in a full h. there is room for everything 284.28
it is one thing to lack a h. 516.18
lay my finger on Thy h.! 623.52
let go of h., one loses control of head 284.25
let h. be wise; it is gods' best gift 284.13
man is man only by the h. 562.1
man's h. changes his countenance 284.1
mind goes less far than h. 590.3
my h. leaps up when I behold a rainbow 779.2
narrow h. that loves one object 620.10
no harvest for h.; love must be resown 551.116
no room in God's army for the coward h. 199.1
not to get what you have set your h. on 366.1
one learns peoples through the h. 1008.20
only with the h. can one see rightly 284.33
pity me that the h. is slow to learn 284.24
place to improve world is first one's h. 433.24
put self on bosom of one whose h. you'd eat 440.12
sacrifice not thy h. upon every altar 698.12
shape your h. to front the hour 728.3
soul's power lies in the h. 675.22
strange how often h. must be broken before the years can make it wise 321.51
teeth are smiling, but is the h. 392.3
tender h. our noblest quality 519.12
the h. is inexperienced 321.54
the h. is not a puzzle that can't be solved 387.51
to be happy by means of the h.—have none 551.10
unto a broken h. no other one may go 960.1
we distrust h. too much, head not enough 785.28
we know truth by reason and by the h. 998.94
what dungeon is so dark as one's own h. 858.15
what eye ne'er sees, h. ne'er rues 110.2
what happened inside that h. 948.2
what is uttered from h. alone wins hearts 901.9
what makes impression on h. seems lovely 284.32
where the h. lies, let the brain lie also 284.6
where your treasure is your h. will be 746.3
whom the h. of man shuts out, God takes in 547.4
without hopes the h. would break 427.11
without rich h. wealth is an ugly beggar 1048.16
you cannot plumb depths of human h. 387.3

heart's: give but a grain of the h. rich seed 742.3
who's not sat tense before own h. curtain 875.24

hearts: all are oftener led by h. than by understandings 284.9
h. live by being wounded 946.52
h. of the great can be changed 350.1
home-keeping h. are happiest 422.15
many wise men have secret h. 943.2
merit and knowledge do not gain h. 584.1
so many h., so many kinds of love 551.221
we do not see nature with eyes, but h. 623.39
we have h. within: warm, live, indecent 284.5

heartstrings: cut your h. if they extend across the barricade 365.29

heathen: h.: has folly to worship something he can see and feel 1068.1

heaven: a H. for your friends 125.15
all I seek is h. above, the road below 992.49
all places are distant from h. alike 699.1
complaint is largest tribute to h. 723.33
earth being so good, would h. seem best 272.2
for modern man h. is big department store 414.3
from the bounteous h. all riches flow 754.8
God will show you the hardest way to h. 414.7
h. always bears proportion to earth 387.28
h. equally distant everywhere 414.10
h.-gates not so highly arched as palaces 414.17
h. has space for all modes of love 414.2
h. is under our feet 414.14
h. lies about us in our infancy 1071.64
h. rejects the lore of less or more 384.34
h. were not h. if we knew what it were 318.12
how ready is h. to those that pray 723.21
in h., what they do not do is marry 414.13
many might go to h. with half labour they go to hell 1070.12
men conceived h. only to find it insipid 414.12
men tore up roads to h.; now make ladders 797.43
more things in h., earth, than dreamt of 953.3
see h. in a wild flower 623.6
short arm man needs to reach to h. 387.72
there is no humor in h. 436.34
this must be h.; no, it's Iowa 414.6
'Tis h. alone that is given away 387.45
we mix our spites and hates with our defence of h. 797.76
when were you in h.? 77.24
who bears sword of h. should be holy 514.9
who built new h. took power from own hell 1025.2
whom h. helps has friends enough 754.6

heaven's: h. help better than early rising 360.5
h. joys do not satisfy cravings of nature 431.9

heavens: before Kepler, h. told glory of Lord 415.9
h. call; your eye gazes only to earth 415.3
h. declare the glory of God 415.2

hedgehog's: h. one trick is best of all 200.6

heights: warmer on h. than those in valley suppose 492.7

heir: only a fool will make a doctor his h. 263.12
what you share with friend you save from h. 384.14

heiresses: all h. are beautiful 1048.13

hell: belief in h. distorts judgement on life 416.5
h. has three gates: lust, anger, greed 416.4
h. is the bloodcurdling mansion of time 416.7
h., madame, is to love no longer 416.3
h. populous, smoky city much like London 416.11
many might go to heaven with half labour they go to h. 1070.12
men conceived h. only to find it ridiculous 414.12
no fiercer h. than failure 329.16
pauper is already serving his term in h. 718.11
there is a dreadful h. 416.12

to work, live, die hard and go to h. 416.10
what is h.? h. is oneself 416.6
when we have known h. through and through 416.2
which way I fly is h.; myself am h. 416.8
who built heaven took power from own h. 1025.2
hellbent: the h. get where they are going 10.16
help: hate friends who come too late to h. 979.5
he has right to censure who has heart to h. 206.19
h. like that he didn't need 34.11
love is only way each can h. other 551.61
often we can h. most by leaving alone 56.5
we need the confidence of friends' h. 365.38
what's past h. should be past grief 507.8
helping: good and bad is simply h. or hurting 390.3
helplessness: h., my greatest fear of illness 896.31
Hemingway: an affliction common to my generation: H. Awe 418.15
she knew everything Mr. H. had written 532.15
hemorrhage: an intercontinental bronchial h. 64.11
hen: when h. lays egg, whole country informed 873.15
woe to house where h. crows 564.116
you can't set a h. in one morning and have chicken salad for lunch 677.12
hens: fat h. lay few eggs 186.8
herd: h. seek out the great for their influence 400.11
hereafter: absurd to slight for the h. today's delight 704.5
heresies: in a dead religion there are no more h. 258.10
heresy: h. springs only from system in full vigor 258.6
those misliking private opinion call it h. 258.5
hermits: h. are contented with their cells 927.15
hero: better not be a h. than work oneself into heroism by shouting lies 418.31
doesn't take a h. to order men into battle 418.33
every h. becomes a bore at last 418.7
every h. is a Samson 418.32
h. cannot be h. unless in heroic world 418.13
h. has given life to something bigger 418.3
h. he who, without death, can win praise 418.23
h. is a man who does what he can 418.30
h. is suffered to be himself 418.8
in war-time a man is called a h. 418.12
show me a h. and I'll write you a tragedy 418.9
the h. created himself 418.2
to be h., main thing is know when to die 418.29
we expect smallest h. to act as demigod 418.20
we have no h.; we suspect hero worship 418.6
heroes: admiration given to dead martyrs rather than living h. 565.8
change in h. within the working class 418.28
chief business of nation: setting up h. 418.24
efficiency regime can't be run without h. 418.10
h. don't talk about what they did 418.18
it is fortune with nature that makes h. 418.19
misfortunes, poverty have their h. 418.17
most h. are easily touched by praise 418.1
we make h. of men sitting on money heap 602.34
without h. we're all plain people 418.21
you don't raise h., you raise sons 916.12
heroic: anyone can be h. from time to time 378.5
h. man does not pose 418.16
sincerity is first quality of h. men 901.4
when a man bears with composure one mischance after another, he is of h. temper 17.4
heroism: epic vanished with age of personal h. 418.27
h. does not require spiritual maturity 418.14
self-trust is the essence of h. 860.1
you cannot throw away a word like h. 491.20
hesitate: it's all right to h. if you then go ahead 9.6
hesitates: he who h. is sometimes saved 465.6
hesitation: audacity augments courage; h., fear 92.10
heterogeneous: h. ideas yoked by violence together 1032.8
heterosexual: reducing h. contact to a sadomasochistic pattern 892.26
hid: man is h. under his tongue 923.30
hide: h. nothing from confessor, lawyer, doctor 165.6
hardest thing to h. is what's not there 165.8
hides: h. one thing in the depths of his heart, and speaks forth another 440.9
hiding: men would devour men but for power of h. 165.2
hierarchy: h. of power, not same as h. of value 1026.2
high: detestation of h. is homage of the low 780.2
h. people, sir, are the best 52.2
they that stand h. have blasts shake them 401.51
highest: h. are blasted by envy 952.6
if you aspire to the h. place 55.3
highway: on old h. maps main routes were red 117.27
himself: man asking God why he is stuck with h. 858.26
must decide for h. the course to follow 225.6
who lives only for h. truly dead to others 874.4
Hiroshima: the moment when the atomic bomb flashed above H. 1049.5
historian: Britain will be honored by the h. 289.12
h. must not try to know truth 419.3
historian's: the h. business is to illuminate 419.51
historians: h. creates true ensemble from half-true 419.42
h. relate what they would have believed 419.24
the middle sort of h. spoil all 419.37
historic: h. picks up individual and deposits him in trend 419.35
historical: h. sense is perception of past 419.19
our h. beginnings are mysterious 53.97
histories: if h. properly told romances unneeded 419.54
history: all that is observable falls into the domain of h. 419.23
at each epoch of h. world was lost, saved 298.13
educate the masses: make h. personal 132.4
every great writer writes h. 1069.79
fiction gives opportunity to live h. 344.19
functionaries are clubbing h. dumb 419.16
game of h. is played by the best and worst over the heads of the majority 419.30
good writer of h. is suspicious 419.7
good writing is the concomitant of good h. 419.52
h.: account mostly false of events mostly unimportant 419.6
h.: action, reaction of nature, thought 419.20
h. always enunciates new truths 419.38
h., baggage we threw overboard 419.43
h. concerned with arranging good entrances for people 419.10
h., gradual liberation from provincialism 78.20
h. has made life difficult for us all 245.8
h. is a hill, high point of vantage 419.13
h. is all explained by geography 419.50
h. is amoral, has no conscience 174.15
h. is a novel which did take place 344.16
h. is a tangled skein 419.2
h. is attractive to the timid 419.22
h. is essence of innumerable biographies 419.12
h. is one long regret 419.49
h., junkyard of broken treaties 994.5
h. justifies whatever we want it to 419.47
h. knows no scruples and no hesitation 419.32
h. never looks like h. when being lived 419.25
h. of free men is written by choice 419.18
h. of institutions, a h. of deceptions 487.1
h. of the world is the record of the weakness 419.11
h. of world is the h. of privileged few 419.36
h.: progress of consciousness of freedom 363.25
h. provides neither compensation for suffering nor penalties for wrong 419.1

h.: race between education, catastrophe 419.53
h.: recital of facts represented as true 344.30
h. repeats itself, but in disguise 419.28
h. sacrifices totality for continuity 419.33
h.: sad result of each looking out for self 874.2
h. spread as evenly as honey on toast 419.55
h., written for amusement of ruling classes 419.57
human life worthless unless woven into that of ancestors by h. 419.14
if a man said only what was proven, h. could not be written 905.4
in an individual's h. is an account of his condition 867.5
ink in which h. written: fluid prejudice 419.46
it is impossible to write modern h. 419.40
language is the archives of h. 524.12
man hasn't learned from h. 419.4
moment in h. when other change made it indispensable 819.11
more h. made by secret handshakes 419.5
need h. to see if we can escape from it 419.39
no wise or brave man lies on tracks of h. 291.2
our h. is every human h. 419.56
people are makers of h. 419.27
peoples, governments never learn from h. 419.29
read no h.: read only biography 81.5
shape of h. seldom clear to men who live it 298.11
test of greatness is the page of h. 401.26
that men do not learn from h. is the most important lesson of h. 419.31
the more we know h., the less we esteem subjects of it 419.15
there is no h. of mankind 419.41
there is no h., only biography 419.21
we need h. to make a future possible 419.9
wise man does not try to hurry h. 677.17
world h. made by the people alone 682.13
hit: if you h. pony on nose at outset 890.1
hits: don't go to the theatre—they go to see h. 972.17
hoax: victims of a mighty h. 398.7
hobbies: popular persons ride no h. 712.10
hobby: he that rides h. gently must cede to him that rides his h. hard 335.2
hobbyhorse: as long as a man rides his h. peaceably 984.14
hockey: political h. played by dyspeptic girls in pants 912.5
holidays: easier to keep h. than commandments 420.3
h. have no pity 420.4
if year all h., sport as tedious as work 420.7
holiness: the road to h. passes through the world of action 9.23
hollow: we are the h. men leaning together 951.1
Hollywood: in H.: do everything to conceal individuality 421.1
holocaust: the impact of the h. on believers 512.12
holy: faith in a h. cause has to be extravagant 111.10
h. cannot rise beyond highest in you 390.6
h. man without learning: enemy of church 127.5
man makes h. what he believes 78.17
my h. of holies is the human body 485.1
remember the sabbath, to keep it h. 835.1
they are not all saints who use h. water 45.7
home: ache for h. lives in all of us 422.2
a most miserable thing to feel ashamed of h. 422.5
dunce sent to roam excels dunce kept h. 992.15
essence of a h. lies in its permanence 422.16
for man of sluggish mind, no place like h. 422.19
Giddily, and be everywhere but at h. 992.16
go forward to the h. we've always wanted 758.17
h. is where they must take you in 422.11
h.-keeping hearts are happiest 422.15
h., the place where the books are kept 93.84
in love of h., love of country has rise 422.6
make wherever we're lost in look like h. 12.2
men are merriest when they are from h. 422.20
no place like h. for wearing what you like 422.1
only one in command in h. or state 395.19
we shall be judged more by what we do at h. than what we preach abroad 498.6
when at h., I was in a better place 992.46
where thou art, that is h. 422.7
who makes young happy at h. benefits public 422.3
whose welfare is assured at h. is fortunate 422.12
homes: Mexican h. as a rule are closed off to the world 430.5
ruin of a nation begins in its h. 621.1
homosexual person: no such thing as a h. 424.9
homosexual: h. aestheticism and irony 883.8
homosexuality: h. a sickness as is baby-rape 424.1
probably no sensitive heterosexual alive not preoccupied with his latent h. 424.7
homosexuals: that defensive contempt for h. 424.5
honest: don't be h. with friends who ask it 365.23
friendly, h. man fulfills nature's plan 152.2
happy he whose armour is h. thought 491.32
h. brief has its own eloquence 528.20
h. man's the noblest work of God 425.13
h. man's word is as good as his bond 425.1
I keep six h. serving-men 480.13
life of h. man is perpetual infidelity 425.11
mind of an h. man is terrifying 425.6
most enviable of all titles: an h. man 425.18
no such thing as man willing to be h. 425.3
O grant an h. fame, or grant me none! 332.38
praised by h. men, abused by rogues 804.4
rogue in limelight acts like h. man 332.33
surest way to remain poor, be h. 425.10
to deal only with h. men, stop dealing 425.4
too afraid of being disliked to be h. 425.16
honesty: for merchant, h. is financial speculation 104.4
h., delightful pastime at other's expense 362.5
h. is beginning of education 425.15
h. is incompatible with amassing fortune 104.14
h. is knowing dishonesty is a mistake 425.7
h. is less profitable than dishonesty 425.12
no clear boundary separates h., dishonesty 425.5
no legacy is so rich as h. 425.17
show of h. is the surest way to riches 425.9
we must deal in privacy with h. and truth 1000.3
what is dignity without h. 246.1
workmanship instinct will take care of h. 201.23
honesty's: h. praised, then left to freeze 425.8
honey: h. in every flower, takes a bee to get it 585.7
honor: act well your part, there all the h. lies 491.22
better fail with h. than win by cheating 329.22
difference between moral man, man of h. 604.26
few have ethical energy enough for more than one inflexible point of h. 491.27
great people face war rather than purchase prosperity at price of national h. 46.5
h. confirms men's opinion of themselves 166.2
h. is a steep island without a shore 491.4
h. makes enemies as it condemns opposite 491.29
h. received from those who fear us is not h. 808.9
h. regulates man's acts as public man 491.7
h. sinks where commerce long prevails 104.16
h. travels in a narrow strait 491.24
he has h. if he holds himself to an ideal of conduct 491.16
hold it great wrong to prefer life to h. 491.13
how we fight weakness to preserve h. 491.8
if you want to h. me, give

that child some help 123.26
jingling of the guinea helps h.'s hurt 602.58
man who permits his h. to be taken, permits his life to be taken 491.2
many men set high the show of h. 440.1
O that h. were purchased by merit 584.5
prophet is without h. in his own country 426.1
those most desirous of h. or glory cry out loudest of its abuse 426.10
when faith lost, h. dies, man is dead 491.31
without money, h. is a malady 491.23
would that public and private h. might become identical 491.9
you cannot throw away a word like h. 491.20

honorable: notion of work, any kind of work, as h. 1065.54

honor's: quarrel at a straw when h. is at stake 491.25

honors: great h. are great burdens 426.6
great power drowns some men in h. 426.7
high h. sweet but they stand close to grief 426.4
nation reveals itself by men it h. 621.12
Though no h. came my way, those were the lovely years 1071.8

honour: Loved I not h. more 491.17

hope: all that I am or ever h. to be I owe to her 670.25
around-the-corner h. prompts action 427.17
come, for house of h. is built on sand 606.10
courage must have h. for nourishment 195.25
death is end, not of enjoyment, but of h. 221.64
death is greatest evil, for it cuts off h. 427.15
faith speaks when h. dissembles 330.34
first we h. too much, later, not enough 427.30
fooled with h., men favor life's deceit 539.26
glittering h. beckons many to undoing 1048.19
good h. that there is something after death 454.14
he that lives upon h. will die fasting 427.8
h. an echo, ties itself yonder 427.32
h. beyond reason shows desire, not judgment 427.27
h. deceives more men than cunning does 427.37
h. deferred maketh the heart sick 427.3
h., fear, must be vivid to be effective 608.7
h. has as many lives as cat, king 427.22
h. is a great falsifier of truth 427.13
h. is a risk that must be run 427.2
h. is a strange invention 427.5
h. is a waking dream 427.1
h. is brightest when it dawns from fears 427.33
h. is incredible to the slave of grief 918.37
h. is necessary in every condition 427.20
h. is only good thing disillusion respects 254.8
h. is worst evil, it prolongs torments 427.25
h. leads us agreeably to end of our lives 427.21
h. looks for unqualified success 330.33
h. makes meaner creatures kings 427.35
h. more brilliant than memory, less true 580.29
h. prodigal heir, experience his banker 427.4
h. should no more be a virtue than fear 427.38
h. springs eternal in the human breast 427.29
h. stimulates life more than realised joy 427.26
humans not caught without nibble of h. 427.28
if h. is feeble, boldest plans are safest 92.7
in all pleasure h. is considerable part 704.19
leader is a dealer in h. 531.12
like strength is felt from h., despair 940.10
love lives on h., dies when h. is dead 551.30
mind which renounces h. grows calm 806.6
natural to indulge in illusions of h. 427.16
not suffering but h. incites revolt 819.20
real sorrow is incompatible with h. 918.26
small h. sufficient for birth of love 551.205
the miserable have no medicine but h. 427.34
there are situations in which h. and fear run together and destroy one another 427.12
to keep h. in world, change population 427.23
we expect something for nothing and call it h. 427.19
what a valiant faculty is h. 427.24
what we fear comes to pass more speedily than what we h. 343.25
whoever has nothing to h., let him despair of nothing 937.6
worldly h. turns ashes or prospers, is gone 990.10

hopeful: consciously h. and unconsciously hopeless 175.4

hopes: all have h., most of which go awry 427.7
cause of idleness, crime is deferring h. 427.6
death surprises us amidst our h. 221.53
extreme h. are born of extreme misery 427.31
he that h. no good fears no ill 692.2
long ailments wear out pain; long h., joy 1040.6
short life forbids far-reaching h. 427.18
when h. and dreams are loose in streets 819.22
without h. the heart would break 427.11
woman's h. are woven of sunbeams 1062.42

horizon: it is the eye which makes the h. 689.4
no h. is especially interesting by itself 495.7
who keeps his eye fixed on the h. will find the right road 442.4

hormones: curse of modern times, preponderance of h. 26.8

horror: death is ultimate h. of life 221.56
h. causes men to clench fists, unite 1016.9

horse: difference of opinion makes h.-races 656.29
dismiss old h. in good time 813.2
good h. should be seldom spurred 1066.1
h. fastest when has others to outpace 155.10
never join friend in abuse of h. or wife 206.7
no secret so close as between rider, h. 821.1

horses: more h. a nobleman has, more popular he is 912.1
not best to swap h. crossing river 179.3
people on h. look better 64.8

horseshit: there's so much h. about babies 988.8

hospitable: h. instinct is not wholly altruistic 428.4

hospital: h. staff assumes if you lose gall bladder you also lose your mind 896.13

hospitality: when h. becomes an art, it loses its soul 428.5

host: what is there more kindly than the feeling between h. and guest 428.1

hostile: the wise man is h. to the new 640.3

hostilities: h. should be mortal; friendships, immortal 772.10
one act seldom produces h. in nations 1042.46
some molded by admirations, others h. 404.2

hostility: h. lurks at the heart of our relations 152.15

hotel: saints can do miracles, few can keep a h. 429.3

hotels: love is like shabby h. 551.222
when we still believed in summer h. 676.13

hour: all of us are but creatures of the h. 332.25
from h. to h., we ripe and ripe 571.15
shape your heart to front the h. 728.3

hours: h. in love have wings 2.2

house: dog is lion in his own h. 422.17
every spirit makes its h. 867.3
every spot, the possible site of a h. 430.9
except Lord build h., labour is in vain 126.2
h. divided against itself cannot stand 1043.1
h. draws visitors, possessor detains them 428.8
let not houseless pull down other's h. 241.10
man builds h.; now he has master for life 430.1
man should behave in own h. as guest 422.9
man's h. is his stage 430.7
on finishing h., we realize

we have learned what we needed to know before start 321.39
ornament of h. is friends who frequent it 422.10
the h. praises the carpenter 6.5
when the h. of a great one collapses, many little ones are slain 400.2
woman careful with face, careless with h. 1062.80
householders: surroundings h. crave are glorified, ghost-written autobiographies 430.6
houses: graveyards full of women whose h. were spotless 137.2
in big h. always religious element 1048.10
in Victorian h. occupants could be mysterious and exciting to one another 736.7
men, not h., make the city 131.15
more want to break out of h. than in 422.22
old h. mended cost little less than new 460.2
our h. are such unwieldy property 430.8
human: a h. capacity that may overwhelm any of us 587.7
astonishing what h. beings have achieved 133.27
character of h. life is ambiguity 390.23
could we perfect h. nature 431.6
each h. is profound secret to every other 562.14
every man carries the entire h. condition 562.41
fulfillment as h. being is greatest miracle 1008.16
h. actions are second causes 227.16
h. action springs from clear-sighted awareness 886.6
h. being doing same thing over and over 828.5
h. being sheds its leaves like a tree 896.10
h. nature is not a machine but a tree 279.58
h. nature is the same everywhere 431.2
h. nature loves more readily than hates 431.8
h. nature so constituted that we are reassured as foolishly as we are alarmed 482.6
h. nature to stand in middle of a thing 465.5
h. race is a race of cowards 199.11
h. race is doing the best it can 562.37
h. species made of men who borrow, lend 96.4
humans become h. through learning of culture 210.17
in prison every h. strain is revealed 735.2
it's a burden to us even to be h. beings 431.4
logic is one thing, h. animal another 785.24
man would be otherwise, essence of the h. 562.35
nature holds no brief for the h. experiment 913.31
no h. characteristic can be labeled American 34.75
no problem of h. destiny is beyond h. beings 737.4
only hope of joy is in h. relations 794.12
our history is every h. history 419.56
political education: knowledge of h. nature 711.5
scenery is fine—but h. nature is finer 431.13
spirit of recalcitrance in h. race 691.2
the h. mind, adversary of life 562.34
the most sadistic and destructive man is h. 431.5
to be h. is not to seek perfection 431.20
to flea, h. being is something good to eat 481.4
we must accept the implications of h. inheritance 986.3
what is h. must retrograde if not advance 741.5
when h. being says beast in him aroused 431.27
who would extirpate all evil know little of h. nature 307.5
human being: each h. is unique, unprecedented, unrepeatable 562.19
living completely the life of a h. 1062.9
the perfect h. is uninteresting 457.1
human beings: h. mingled iron, water, fire to make railroad 991.3
if h. don't keep exercising lips 923.1
when it comes to the pinch, h. are heroic 418.26
human nature: h. cannot be changed, a tiresome platitude 431.21
when we study language we study h. 524.22
human relations: h. like clothes are supposed to last 992.5
human rights: h. are universal and indivisible 433.13
humane: who forgets man is animal is made less h. 431.14
humanely: none act h. under influence of fear 343.29
humanism: h. is not alive and well in Texas 432.2
in all h. there is an element of weakness 432.5
humanist: nation of bathrooms with h. in each tub 34.46
unless the h. tradition survives, there can be no civilization 432.3
humanists: men no longer theists must become h. 432.4
humanitarian: h. wishes to be prime mover 433.23
no man can write who is not first a h. 1069.43
humanitarians: h. constantly overestimate suffering 433.20
humanity: his h. tells him that life has a meaning 539.73
h. is just a work in progress 562.63
in abstract love of h. one loves oneself 433.12
man forever disturbed about condition of h. has no problems of his own 790.21
man of h. is one who, in seeking to establish self, finds a foothold for others 433.8
more misery among lower classes than h. in the higher 718.29
religion of h. has no faith in humans 233.34
who loves not his home, how shall he love h. 678.5
humble: condition for being h.: not to boast of it 901.17
if a man is h., we call this weakness 206.5
if not h. as dust, men are less than men 435.22
many wish to be devout, no one to be h. 435.13
one may be h. out of pride 435.15
those believed h., usually envious 435.25
humbleth: he that h. himself wishes to be exalted 435.16
humiliate: nothing ought more to h. great men than their care to boast of little things 89.3
humiliating: h. to see idiots succeed 945.15
humility: come nearest the great when great in h. 435.26
first test of a great man is his h. 435.21
h., a quality for which I have limited admiration 435.7
h. begins in awareness of unworthiness 435.5
h. has the toughest hide 435.17
h. is first of virtues—for other people 435.10
h. is often only feigned submission which people use to render others submissive 435.12
h. is the opposite of self-abasement 435.8
h. is the virtue all preach, none practice 435.23
h. must be portion of any man whose acclaim is earned in the blood of his followers 386.4
h. neither falls far, nor heavily 435.20
h. reveals the heavenly lights 435.27
h.: substitution of one pride for another 435.9
man with h. will acquire in his beliefs the saving doubt of his certainty 435.14
must be h. to go to greatness 435.18
pride often borrows cloak of h. 733.8
they are proud in h. 435.4
humor: closest thing to h. is tragedy 436.32
decrepit society shuns h. 913.24
each American sure he has sense of h. 34.81
fortune and h. govern the world 116.10
good h. is a philosophic state of mind 392.9
good h. is dress to appear in when we meet 392.10
good taste, h.: contradiction in terms 436.19
happy consciousness of possessing a deep sense of h. 289.20
h. first to perish in foreign tongue 436.38
h. is an affirmation of dignity 436.10

h. is chaos remembered in tranquility 436.33
h. is encapsulated in criticism 436.23
h. is falling downstairs while warning your wife not to 436.3
H. is only thing about which English are utterly serious 289.22
h. simultaneously wounds and heals 436.16
h. teaches tolerance 526.18
man with h. never founded a religion 797.38
men confess to murder, but not lack of h. 436.6
no new sect or its disciples ever had h. 674.5
no writing is more apt to miscarry than h. 1069.3
secret source of h. not joy but sorrow 436.34
what most need badly, a sense of h. 723.26
with h., I'm trying to get even 436.4
world treats h. patronizingly 436.37
humorist: h. has a good eye for humbug, not saint 436.18
the h. is above honor, above faith 436.21
humorous: h. man realizes perfection is beyond man 542.2
h. persons have pleasant turned-up mouths 1061.2
h. writers are responsive to the hopeless concatenations of life 436.25
hunger: all vile acts are done to satisfy h. 437.6
good meal ought to begin with h. 274.10
h. is the teacher of arts 437.11
no sauce in world like h. 437.2
what h. is to food, zest is to life 513.7
world needs redemption from h., oppression 432.1
hungry: h. do not care about liberty 537.11
h. man is more interested in four sandwiches than in four freedoms 437.10
h. people: stuff of which dictatorships made 363.42
h. stomach has no ears 437.9
hunting: it is strange that we call h. a pleasure 438.4
passion for h. implanted in human breast 438.3
hurricane: h. attacks only the lofty trees 733.15
hurry: great disadvantage of h.: takes time 411.4
in such a h. we never get a chance to talk 456.1
one is in a h., leaving things behind 411.9
people in a h. cannot think, grow, decay 411.7
we cannot outrun the demon of h. 411.1
when you want to h. something 411.10
whoever is in a h. is doing a thing too big for him 411.3
hurt: it doesn't h. as much when you're right 630.38
it takes enemy and friend working together to h. you to the heart 905.14
no man is angry that feels not himself h. 39.3
hurting: good and bad is simply helping or h. 390.3
hurtling: h. from one point to another 64.13
husband: an archeologist is the best h. 42.1
h. is best plaster for woman's ailments 564.84
h.: man who snores like overloaded bus 564.91
if woman loses h.—might as well be dead 564.36
light wife doth make a heavy h. 564.106
seen the paper before her h. sixty-seven times 406.10
some good and even pretty woman could not shape a h. out of 581.24
strife where wife is dissatisfied with h. 892.47
when cheated, wife and h. feel same 472.2
wife takes exact measure of her h. 564.129
husband's: she's adorned that in h. eye is lovely 267.29
husbands: becoming the legal chattel of h. 564.121
married men are tedious when good h. 564.136
no shrieks cast louder to heaven than when h. or lap-dogs die 610.10
hygiene: h. is corruption of medicine by morality 137.4
hymnbooks: h. resound with cursing of God 128.6
hypocrisy: h. completes a villain 732.6
h. deceives men; children recognize it 440.20
h. is a fashionable vice 440.15
h. is royal road to success 711.36
h. is the homage vice pays to virtue 440.13
manners are the h. of a nation 563.1
there is very little h. in the world 440.11
who pretends to be what he's not and hides what he is knows h. 440.5
hypocrite: h. always playing same part stops being h. 440.16
man who moralizes is usually a h. 604.49
no man is a h. in his pleasures 704.20
true h. lies with sincerity 440.8
hypocrites: cant of h. may be the worst 123.52
Christians, a powerful subtribe of the H. 440.3
liars, and fools, and h. 221.139
we are not h. in our sleep 266.7
hypotheses: h. are pieces of scaffolding 973.6
hysteria: he would leave me on the edge of h. 772.6
h. common denominator of female nature 581.70
h. is a caricature of an artistic creation 627.6

I

ice cream: first i. is soul-stirring surprise 355.4
iconoclasm: i.—the only way to get at truth 441.2
idea: between i. and reality falls the shadow 1019.3
dangerous commitment to constricting i. 335.7
dismount from an i., and get into the saddle again, at every parenthesis 942.11
every man with an i. has followers 443.2
fashionable i. is an adulterated one 443.12
give up the i. of Spain 19.20
historical peoples export i. by war 445.1
i. does not pass from one language to another without change 443.36
i., if right, saves labor of experiences 443.17
if an i. cannot move on its own 443.34
if the i. is good, it will survive defeat 443.3
if you have one strong i., you repeat it 1069.86
is there a dead i. that does not live on 443.11
nations rise and fall, but an i. lives on 443.13
no man can establish title to an i. 443.37
nothing is more dangerous than an i., when it is the only i. 443.1
one may believe in an i., but not a man 997.5
originator of i. always called a crank 443.10
possessed by i., you even smell it 443.16
the creative phase of an i. 443.32
there is no i. that cannot be vulgarized 4.2
you can't put rope around neck of i. 443.26
ideal: i. is in thyself, the impediment, too 858.8
i. man is noble and sparkling 562.38
i. society is an imaginary drama 1025.4
power of devotion to an i. 34.67
sitting still is only an i. 812.3
idealism: chief curse of the world is i. 442.11
i. and a politician's will to power 442.6
i. springs from deep feelings 442.1
idealist: i. can make ideal out of heaven or hell 442.12
i. notices a rose smells better than a cabbage, concludes it will make better soup 442.10
idealists: idealistic Christianity attacked by i. 125.8
i. obtain what they have struggled for in a form which destroys their ideals 442.15
ideals: bitterest wine drained from crushed i. 254.6
i. are understanding of that which is desirable in that which is possible 442.8
in marriage with world our i. bear fruit 442.14
men do the incredible if i. threatened 442.5
ideas: all great i. are dangerous 443.39
general, abstract i. source of errors 443.30
great i. are not charitable 443.21
hang i.; they are tramps, vagabonds 443.4

harmful i. are cloaks for evil passions 734.14
heterogeneous i. yoked by violence 1032.8
i. are fatal to caste 443.7
i. in Russia are machine-cut blocks 834.4
man's i. get clothed when he dresses 267.27
men are mortal; but i. are immortal 443.14
mind crippled by same set of i. 903.4
minds need i. to conceive 443.15
new i. one of most overrated concepts 443.29
old i. are habits, ingrained attitudes 443.5
one part of world is slow to adopt valuable i. of another part 443.35
one thing to study i. historically 443.23
only condition of peace is to have no i. 681.12
only weapon against bad i. is better i. 443.8
paradoxes useful to attract attention to i. 668.1
revolutionary spirit frees one from scruples as regards i. 819.5
secret of success: to convert i. to things 945.2
that my mind could let fall its dead i. 654.2
to get experience out of i. 279.75
we should pursue best arrangement of our i. 998.14
words stand for i. in mind of user 1064.31
young man must let his i. grow 443.19
identity: faculty for idleness implies sense of i. 446.15
opiate: unlocked door in prison of i. 269.2
strong sense of i. gives man idea he can do no wrong; too little does same 444.4
the search for a personal i. 444.9
ideology: i. is the habit of showing respect for certain formulas 445.5
i. is the sterner face of myth 445.4
religion is now called an i. 445.3
idiosyncrasies: i. are mitigated by necessity of conforming 913.22
idiot: bein a i. is no box of chocolates 186.11
i., babbling and strewing flowers 854.34
i.: member of tribe whose influence has always been dominant and controlling 941.1
only i. persists in his error 299.9
idiots: In the first place God made i. 279.83
solemnity is the shield of i. 886.9
idle: determine never to be i. 10.9
i. men tempt the devil 446.17
if you are i., be not solitary 446.11
man not i. because absorbed in thought 1065.43
idleness: faculty for i. implies catholic appetite 446.15
i. and pride tax with heavy hand 446.7
i. has a son, robbery 446.8
i. is the parent of all psychology 759.2
i., like kisses, to be sweet must be stolen 446.10
i. was a sin against Mammon 446.19
love is born of i. and fostered by it 446.12
reason of i., crime is deferring hopes 427.6
idler: no man so methodical as complete i. 446.9
idol: every i. turns out to be a Moloch 1068.6
i. shattered to prove God's dust greater 387.69
no one is unhappier than superannuated i. 226.1
this gold i. with clay feet 1029.5
idolaters: men are i.; want something to kiss, hug 1068.5
idolatry: i., source of all social and moral evil 1068.4
idolence: i. is delightful but distressing state 530.4
idols: civilized man bows to flesh-and-blood i. 418.34
not merely the i. fell 254.1
we must not smash other people's i. 441.3
if: your i. is the only peacemaker 167.5
ignominies: no pursuit more elegant than collecting and showing the i. of our nature 62.10
ignoramus: an i., but many people don't mind that 545.9
ignorance: all i. toboggans into know 447.8
a man is ignorant with i. of his time 184.9
criticism is never inhibited by i. 206.14
drink experience or die in desert of i. 321.40
expanding knowledge we but increase i. 522.40
familiar use of things cures not i. 333.9
from i. our comfort flows 447.26
genuine victories are those over i. 447.23
great pleasure of i. is asking questions 480.16
i.: a blank sheet on which we may write 299.11
i. delivers judgments on all things 447.30
i., incuriosity two very soft pillows 447.13
i. irritates man, knowledge cloys 691.1
i. is always ready to admire itself 447.4
i. is not innocence but sin 447.5
i. is the womb of monsters 447.1
i., more fruitful than appearance of knowledge 447.25
i. of Beyond *sine qua non* of our life 1019.9
i. of world puts one at mercy of its malice 618.2
i. preferable to error 447.18
nothing is more dangerous than sincere i. 447.19
one who has learned much can appreciate i. 447.20
poverty has many roots; tap root is i. 718.34
prejudice is the child of i. 726.7
pride and i. mutually beget each other 447.7
profound i. makes a man dogmatic 264.9
sky just about size of my i. 447.10
there is no sin but i. 797.46
things that reveal our i. or insufficiency 209.6
to hide our i. is hard to do over wine 268.21
tyrants are but the spawn of i. 1002.20
where i. is bliss, 'tis folly to be wise 447.15
who displays his knowledge shows his i. 188.32
who would be cured of i. must confess it 447.22
ignorant: better be i. than half know matter 447.27
conscious you're i. is first step to knowledge 447.9
custom is the guide of the i. 213.6
goodness can bear mistakes of the i. 984.4
if thou hast no practice thou art i. 721.2
i. man insignificant and contemptible 447.6
it is only the i. who despise education 279.69
millions live, die, i. of selves, of world 447.24
nothing so good for i. man as silence 447.28
praise from i. man is only good-will 722.29
ill: being i. is a great pleasure, provided one is not too i. and does not have to work 896.2
given amount of i. will goes further now 1042.49
good will be the final goal of i. 390.22
he that hopes no good fears no i. 692.2
means to do i. deeds makes deeds i. done 1070.20
to be unable to bear i. is great i. 17.9
what human i. not alleviated by dawn 605.10
when well, all have advice for the i. 413.17
who does you i. will not forgive you 476.7
who have never been i. are incapable of real sympathy for many misfortunes 896.9
ill-favoured: an i. thing, but my own 716.14
ill-luck: some are so fond of i. they run to it 549.4
illiteracy: dog's best friend is his i. 41.23
illiterate: indescribable freshness about an i. person 447.31
nothing will make democracy of i. people 233.33
illness: convalescence makes i. worth while 896.28
I do not find i. an eminence 896.32
i. is the night-side of life 896.29
know self and you'll understand this i. 758.6
ills: see in other's calamity i. to avoid 17.48
thousand i. require thousand cures 798.7
why are we constantly redoubling our i. 866.8
illusion: disillusion can become i. if we rest in it 254.3

everything's fine today, that is our i. 659.11
love is the child of i. 551.224
rob man of life i., rob his happiness 449.11
romantic love is an i. 551.138
to be happy, we select i. and embrace it 449.6
today's reality may prove an i. tomorrow 784.13
young girls will recover their i. 385.3
illusions: Americans suffer primarily from i. 449.3
best part of our lives takes place in i. 449.13
every age is fed on i. 449.8
flowers of life are but i. 254.5
i. are art and by art we live 449.4
time strips our i. of their hue 449.5
image: i. of myself in my own mind 688.1
So God created man in his own i. 562.8
the i. in the mirror was instantaneously transformed 593.3
imageless: deep truth is i. 998.112
imagery: i. for big orgasm was winning the sailboat race 892.12
images: i. more real than could have supposed 784.17
imagination: a picture always present to our i. 511.1
cannot gratify i. and senses together 450.12
having i., it takes longer to write 1069.1
I have i.; nothing real is alien to me 450.26
i. and mind are politics 711.82
i., a way of engaging reality 450.16
i. begins by analyzing nature 450.2
i. grows by exercise 450.22
i. is the mad boarder 450.21
i. is the liquid solution in which art develops the snapshots of reality 450.6
i. like lofty building reared to meet sky 450.3
i. robust in proportion as reasoning weak 450.30
i. so abstracts us that we are not aware 450.8
i. supreme master of art, life 450.7
i. that towers can reproduce evanescence 450.23
i.: warehouse of facts with poet and liar in joint ownership 450.1
instant all we have unless i. startle us 450.33
in the world of the i., anything goes 450.14
marriage of soul with nature gives birth to i. 623.71
memorable days vibrate to i. 450.13
men are not aware they have any i. 954.5
people can die of mere i. 450.4
principle of equality lowers flight of i. 297.25
solitude is needful to the i. 915.26
so powerful a spell on the young i. 11.2
such tricks hath strong i. 450.27
the i. imitates 201.46
the possible's slow fuse is lit by i. 450.9
things not beautiful until they speak to the i. 72.18
truths judged first through i. 450.10
were it not for i., a man would be happy in arms of chambermaid 450.17
who lives within means suffers lack of i. 977.10
woe to him who tries to stretch the i. 450.31
you can't depend on judgment when i. is out of focus 450.29
imaginative: capacity for i. reflex is not limitless 450.28
i. people are the most credulous 202.2
imagine: I i., therefore I belong and am free 450.11
imaginery: ride astride the i. to hunt down the real 784.3
imaginings: present fears are less than horrible i. 343.34
imbecile: i. looks at finger pointing to moon 941.3
imbecility: to raise i. to profundity, put it on a platform 763.12
imitate: free to do as we please, we i. 662.3
they usually i. each other 451.5
imitated: no one so low as not to be i. by somebody 451.6
imitation: absurdity of conduct arises from the i. of those whom we cannot resemble 451.8
act of i. breeds resentment 451.4
i. chemical vanilla 34.6
i. is the sincerest flattery 451.3
men often applaud i. and his real thing 60.1
no man was ever great by i. 401.31
to refrain from i. is the best revenge 451.1
we are what we are mainly by i. 451.2
immature: i. is love and hatred of the youth 1071.48
immigrant: the first positive move that the i. makes 453.2
imminent: the death of every art form seems i. 53.107
immoral: what is i. is what you feel bad after 604.15
immorality: immoral sense enables one to perceive i. and enjoy it 604.44
immortal: aspire not to i. life; exhaust the possible 542.12
mortal nature is seeking to be i. 454.15
people I respect behave as if they were i. 92.3
truth only i. thing given us to use 998.67
would not have lovely days, hearts to enjoy them, unless we were meant to be i. 454.10
immortality: all the doctrines about i. 454.18
efforts to attain i., vain in long run 454.9
if belief in soul's i. is mere delusion, it is a pleasing one 454.6
i. of the soul is a "grand peut-être" 454.4
intimations of i. seem to arise out of Art 53.136
let him who believes in i. enjoy his happiness in silence 454.8
life is short; honorable death man's i. 454.16
longing for i., considered beneath dignity 454.13
love is i. 551.36
ne'er crowned with i. who fears to follow where airy voices lead 401.32
thing well said walks in i. 283.10
to occupy inch of dusty shelf is i. 454.11
immortals: i. are what you wanted 454.1
impartiality: i. may simply mean indifference 455.1
justice is i. 517.44
impatient: wise are always i. 1060.23
impediment: ideal is in thyself, the i., too 858.8
imperfections: i. make handmade goods superior 457.9
things better for divinely appointed i. 457.4
imperialism: i., a sort of forcible evangelizing 458.4
in i. nothing fails like success 458.2
impertinent: i. wits are a kind of universal insect 1061.12
impiety: i.: your irreverence toward my deity 506.1
importance: but doubt not, it was of the last i. only to be present at it 605.7
we all wish to be of i. in some way 873.4
important: harm done by people who want to feel i. 873.3
man desires to be free and feel i. 873.2
say i. things simply; bombast spoils them 942.14
impossible: dwelling-place of i.: dreams of impotent 459.4
few things i. to diligence and skill 281.10
nothing is i. for the man who doesn't have to do it himself 315.5
nothing is i. to a willing heart 1057.3
impostors: made wary by i., men look for wrong 259.10
impotence: man is as full of potentiality as of i. 717.3
man who has forsworn bullet has i. 665.3
religion: love of life, conscious of i. 797.67
impotent: dwelling-place of impossible: dreams of i. 459.4
impoverishment: i. of life of the spirit 783.4
impressed: not very much i. any more by anything 540.6
impressionable: the great man is the i. man 883.3
improbable: however i., must be the truth? 998.29
man can never believe the i. 78.24
impropriety: i. is the soul of wit 1061.19

improve: none will i. your lot if you do not 291.1
improvement: he who reads for i. is beyond hope of i. 93.20
i. makes straight roads 460.1
spirit of i. not always spirit of liberty 790.20
improvements: half a life is devoted to i. 460.7
improvisation: human being is condemned to i. 969.5
i. is the essence of good talk 928.2
too much i. leaves mind void 928.5
imprudences: man laments i., but his youth more 653.97
impudence: i. knows no bounds 830.3
impulse: to its own i. every creature stirs 444.3
impulses: i. expressed in sadism or masochism 486.2
new road to happiness: castigate i. 862.13
impulsive: it is hard to fight against i. desire 238.20
inaccessibility: people become valuable merely for their i. 1026.7
inaccuracy: I do not mind lying, but I hate i. 299.6
inaction: population condemned to i. is explosive 568.2
inanimate: goal of i. objects is to resist, defeat man 646.2
obstinacy of i. objects 652.5
three scientific classes of i. objects: those that don't work, break down, get lost 646.1
incautious: theory makes men i. 974.10
inclinations: argument seldom convinces against i. 51.9
income: better to have a permanent i. 602.63
we kept our right to earn an outside i. 680.2
incommunicable: distrust the i.; it is source of violence 149.16
we have bonds, but each has i. dreams 915.43
incomplete: nature loves the i. 623.31
incomprehensible: how i. are beings who share with us sight of stars, warmth of sun 663.3
inconsistency: the age of i. and ambivalence 1071.25
to climb out of a rut is called i. 179.6
inconstancy: i. no sin will prove 472.4
there is nothing constant but i. 181.14
incontinent: impulses of i. man carry him in opposite direction from that aimed at 494.1
nothing so i. as man's appetite 403.9
inconvenience: i.: an adventure wrongly considered 16.1
incredulity: i. as faith is less rational than religion 1004.11
incuriosity: ignorance, i. are two very soft pillows 447.13
indecencies: nature knows no i.; man invents them 756.4
indecency: private sin not so prejudicial as public i. 756.1
indecision: he is most miserable whose only habit is i. 465.2
i. is like the stepchild 465.3
independence: in crowd, great man keeps i. of solitude 880.6
i. is a privilege of the strong 880.18
i.: that's middle class blasphemy 235.9
the desire for freedom and i. 235.10
thinking is effort of soul to keep i. 975.28
independent: to be i. is to be abnormal 171.1
what man wants is i. choice 124.3
indifference: i. a mode of bearing ills of life 17.17
opposite of love not hate but i. 466.7
price of eternal vigilance is i. 229.10
secret can be drawn out by i. 855.9
indifferent: communists have not been i. 150.5
we are so i. to people 551.165
worst sin to be i. to others 466.6
indigence: where i. looks like modest affluence 718.4
indigestion: how many wars have been caused by i. 1042.99
indignation: a good i. brings out one's powers 467.1
call bad behavior righteous i. 241.7
civil-rights movement has restored dignity of i. 823.20
i. is no good unless backed with a club 467.3
moral i. permits envy and hate 467.2
no more sovereign eloquence than truth in i. 283.4
indirection: too much zeal offends where i. works 690.5
indiscreet: wicked is not much worse than i. 1055.4
indiscretion: lover without i. is no lover at all 555.10
individual: every i. strives to grow and exclude 469.3
function of society, to cultivate i. 468.1
God enters by a private door into every i. 797.21
go from i. to i. to gain totality of race 469.18
i. at the apex of his species' past 308.12
i. expected to sacrifice all 837.6
i. man tries to escape the race 469.9
liberty of i. must be limited 363.38
men speaking in i. manner are interesting 496.2
nature is reckless of the i. 623.26
to damage the sovereignty of the i. 469.16
individualism: i. and mobility, core of American identity 468.11
i.: developed without its corrective, belonging 468.10
i. is like innocence 468.6
the sober virtues of Protestant i. 468.5
individualists: i. tend to be unobservant 468.7
individuality: defects are necessary for existence of i. 342.12
i. must be affirmed in solitude 915.24
learning to be an American is learning not to let your i. become a nuisance 34.30
without i. society doesn't advance 469.11
individualizes: man whom God wills to slay he first i. 469.12
individuals: convert i. into mass people 1064.41
not races but i. that are noble 774.1
we think men i.; so are pumpkins 469.4
world events are the work of i. 419.48
indivisibility: supreme reality is our i. as God's children 100.11
indolent: man is by nature i. 406.6
indulgence: excessive i. is only self-i. 470.3
i. is what the world permits us 470.2
severity is more useful than i. 965.30
Industrial Revolution: men who made I. pictured as businessmen 874.1
industrial: pauper a human sacrifice in i. regime 966.20
industrialized society: everyone in i. must give up the past 108.14
industry: rising in life by own i., others' folly 945.25
where no desire, no i. 1065.50
ineffectual: if bodies are to be denied, nature wicked, we are i.—fishes not meant to swim 892.13
inequality: individuals seek an i. to their advantage 471.1
inevitable: there is no good in arguing with the i. 624.9
inexperienced: heart is forever i. 284.35
infancy: a love we learn in i. 876.15
heaven lies about us in our i. 1071.64
i. conforms to none, but all to it 65.7
infant: happy to be the trustful i. 478.10
what am I: an i. crying in the night 459.5
infant's: father's nature lives anew in i. breast 417.2
infants: nobody agrees with anybody; i. show it 27.6
infected: all seems i. that the i. spy 58.5
inferior: no one can make you feel i. without your consent 868.6
to take refuge with i. is to betray self 57.15
inferiority: sense of i., called ambition 33.19
superiority and i. are individual 952.10
inferiors: i. revolt to be equal 819.1
what man dislikes in superiors, let him not display in treatment of his i. 531.19

infidelity: i., that infallible rejuvenator 472.1
life of honest man is perpetual i. 425.11
only i.; for man to vote himself dead 219.6
infield: i. practice is mystic ritual 929.3
infinite: eternal silence of these i. spaces 921.5
what you see, yet can not see over, is as good as i. 689.3
infinities: two i.: God above, human baseness below 307.17
infinity: hold i. in the palm of your hand 623.6
like a mathematical curve approaching i. 823.5
suffering shares the nature of i. 946.54
influenced: unconscious selection exercised in being i. 473.2
information: diminishment of commonly shared i. 279.40
live effectively: live with adequate i. 522.66
trade ideas or i. or gossip 524.14
informer: man is i. when he cannot be a soldier 207.20
ingenuous: i. mind feels reproof in unmerited praise 722.16
ingratitude: greed's worst point is its i. 403.21
too great an eagerness to discharge an obligation is a species of i. 647.4
wind, thou art not so unkind as man's i. 475.6
inheritance: loss of i. might drive son to despair 1058.7
inhuman: take care not to feel i. towards i. men 209.3
inhumanity: man's i. to man makes thousands mourn 209.4
nature has imprinted in man instinct of i. 209.12
iniquity: female i., habit of plucking eyebrows 1070.22
initiative: no fruitful i. without government 395.55
you cannot endow machine with i. 966.18
injure: to i., then beg forgiveness, shows power 476.15
injured: he threatens many that hath i. one 476.12
it is human to hate those you have i. 476.20
those whom men have i. they despise 476.18
injures: he i. fair lady who beholds her not 466.2
injuries: he invites i. who rewards past ones 866.4
i. may be forgiven, but not forgotten 476.1
men more prone to revenge i. 789.2
injury: brave man thinks no one his superior who does him an i. 476.16
hard to keep secret, employ leisure, bear i. 245.1
I do myself a greater i. in lying 558.27
i. sooner forgotten than insult 476.4
reject your sense of i. and i. disappears 476.2
women, elephants never forget an i. 1062.124
injustice: defeat preferable to defeating i. by evil 574.6
feeling of i. is insupportable to men 477.2
if i. prevails we must doubt gods 477.4
i. all around is justice 477.12
i. feared less if ruler is religious 831.2
i. has a terrible way of lingering 477.9
i. is not something comparative 477.16
i. sweeps the earth and tramples mankind 477.6
i.: whatever prevents my doing what I like 477.1
justice can't subsist without mixture of i. 517.31
justice discreet; i. makes big noise 517.39
mankind censure i., fearing they may be victims of it 477.13
no man at bottom means i. 477.3
one ought not to return i. to anybody 665.12
rectify an i. or set a record straight 477.10
rigid justice is the greatest i. 517.17
rigorous law is often rigorous i. 528.64
source of justice was fear of i. 517.22
war for justice better than peaceful i. 681.26
where no property, no i. 746.13
innocence: all prisons are brimming over with i. 735.1
childish fantasy protects world from power of i. 123.7
confession of faults next to i. 168.4
courage of children is a function of i. 478.3
i. and truth are always ready for expression 405.6
i. dwells with wisdom, never with ignorance 478.2
i. is bashful, does not want to be sought 704.23
i. is full, experience is empty 478.6
loss of i. brings loss of prejudice 57.7
silence of i. often persuades 898.26
through our recovered i. we discern i. of neighbors 478.11
true i. never falls at once to deep guilt 1030.21
when i. trembles, it condemns the judge 477.14
who blushes is guilty; true i. not ashamed 478.9
innocent: after the great destructions everyone will prove he was i. 641.5
better to save guilty man than condemn i. 517.50
each man insists on being i. 405.4
every man is i. in his own eyes 517.9
he's armed without that's i. within 478.7
lot of i. in world to fly to the wolf for succor from the lion 478.1
man who was completely i. 511.2
one can't reign and be i. 831.20
somebody's responsible and somebody's i. 517.3
who hastes to be rich shall not be i. 738.2
innocently: if you would live i., seek solitude 478.8
innovation: be not over-anxious to encourage i. 479.3
without i., art is a corpse 53.26
innovator: time is the greatest i. 479.1
inquire: i. not what boils in another's pot 211.5
inquiry: no i. is forbidden to man to pursue 480.8
inquisitive: one shouldn't be too i. in life about God or one's wife 211.1
inquisitor: true i. is a creature of policy 335.12
insanity: i., the disease made the index of sensitivity 559.17
insatiable: i. appetite for the future 34.42
insensible: better to emit scream than to be i. 974.12
insensitivity: suggests an i. to conflict-of-interest rules 491.19
insight: first act of i. is throw away labels 1007.18
i. doesn't happen often on click of the moment 1007.17
i. of any human soul is real knowledge 321.5
i.—the titillating knack for hurting 1008.4
moment's i. is sometimes worth a life's experience 1007.8
insignificance: our i. is often the cause of our safety 1012.1
insignificant: easier to bear the unpleasant than the i. 825.2
no meanest object is i. 1012.2
insincere: most exhausting thing in life is being i. 484.2
insincerity: by i. we can multiply our personalities 484.4
great enemy of clear language is i. 524.34
i., by which we can multiply our personalities 484.3
insistent: life doesn't pay off to those most i. 686.3
insolvency: all roads to i. open to my profession 329.20
inspiration: beware of notions like genius and i. 376.25
defend us from the i. of the moment 928.2
greatness not effect of i. 401.46
i. is a farce that poets have invented 962.1
inspired: to be brief is almost to be i. 98.7
instant: i., trivial as it is, is all we have 450.33
instinct: i. is enough in art, as in love 53.52
i. serves end of bringing about death 541.12
justice substituted for i. in civil state 133.24
the i. of the people is right 682.5
trust i. though you cannot explain why 486.1
well-bred i. meets reason half-way 486.5
when reason and i. are rec-

onciled 604.31
instincts: be true to your animal i. 486.3
society acquires new arts, loses old i. 913.3
institution: every i. prepares way for its rival 487.7
i. capable of acting to abolish poverty 913.12
i. is lengthened shadow of one man 487.5
rational i. suffers not by concessions 487.10
institutions: i. alone can create a nation 487.3
i. hand in hand with progress of mind 528.42
we fall into i. already made 487.6
instruct: with a smile we should i. our youth 965.27
instruction: man seldom has so much knowledge of another as necessary to make i. useful 19.14
tigers of wrath are wiser than horses of i. 39.7
instructions: nature's i. slow, those of men premature 623.62
insult: Americans don't understand studied i. 488.1
injury sooner forgotten than i. 476.4
insults: best reply to i.: patience, moderation 488.2
insurance: when praying does no good, i. does help 489.1
integrity: impossible has a kind of i. 657.1
i. can neither be lost nor concealed 491.30
i. vanishes the moment we are conscious of it 491.15
simple i. baffles one full of duplicity 491.6
intellect: do everything with i. except understand another 493.23
everyone thinks own i. perfect 166.11
greater i. one has, more originality one finds in men 493.25
human i. functions to solve problems which the man's inner destiny sets it 493.24
i. mis-shapes the beauteous things 849.42
i. respects equality as a convention 297.3
i. should pursue thought to unravelment 975.51
i. without firmness is craft, chicanery 493.26
marriage of soul with nature makes i. fruitful 623.71
means of strengthening i. is to make up one's mind about nothing 654.3
not clear if i. is privilege or handicap 975.2
take care not to make the i. our god 590.6
thought is the labor of the i. 818.2
weakness of the human i.: seeks to reconcile contrary principles 734.5
intellectual: commonplaces: tramways of i. transportation 612.6
incapacity for mastering small i. tricks 493.21
i., a reader with pencil in hand 492.9
i. betrayed by own vanity, assuming he can express everything in words 492.6
i. treatment of any datum, any experience 480.14
it is the task of the i. to "think otherwise" 492.1
men of slender i. stamina dread competition 941.8
our credulity as to i. powers of others 202.3
the i. is pledged, committed, enlisted 492.5
those who know supremacy of i. life 492.2
to do nothing is the most i. thing 446.18
tongue is a key to the i. treasure 898.24
intellectualism: i. is often the sole piety of the skeptic 492.4
intellectuals: i. no longer take jazz seriously 492.11
i. suppose previous ages less sick 298.10
rock and roll, much in vogue now among i. 492.12
intelligence: greatest i. suffers most from own limits 493.14
i. has an incomprehension of life 493.3
i. in chains loses in lucidity 493.5
i. is inseparable from maliciousness 493.11
i. is quickness in seeing things as they are 493.28
i. is the ability to hold two opposed ideas in the mind 493.10
i. tinged with limeadish sarcasm 77.1
lack of i. is father of all crimes 941.14
man becomes man only by the i. 562.1
intelligent: a man i. and Fascist is not honest 493.2
cheerful, i. face is end of culture 210.6
high price for being i.; wisdom hurts 493.9
i. people able to control emotions 493.20
i. people are generally paralytics 493.13
kings need the company of the i. 520.7
intemperance: i. is the only vulgarity 268.11
i. is the plague of sensuality 494.5
no tyrant like i. 494.4
intemperate: blush of an i. man painted by liquor 494.6
life of i. is wholly governed by desires 123.2
intention: good i. clothes itself with sudden power 608.4
if there is no i., there is no blame 900.15
interactions: friendly i. become reduced 208.8
interest: in danger, none blamed looking to own i. 216.17
i. does not tie nations together 498.20
i. even plays part of disinterestedness 495.4
i. gnaws at a man's substance 222.1
only fear and i. unite men 1016.7
we talk on principle, act on i. 495.3
would you persuade, speak of i., not reason 690.7
interesting: evening with fascinating person leaves vivid memories; with i. person, bouquet 496.3
life's perplexity: too many i. things 497.2
men speaking in individual manner are i. 496.2
test of i. people is that subject matter doesn't matter 496.4
the obligation of great art to be continually i. 20.6
to render themselves i., many feign unhappiness 1011.31
interests: all pursuing their i. as they see them 608.5
do not confuse vested i. with ethics 495.5
man fights harder for i. than rights 495.6
nations linked by i., not friendship 621.8
nation's policies determined by its i. 621.14
world of vested i. doesn't want candour 495.9
interludes: our lives are merely strange dark i. 539.83
international: i. crises frighten weak, inspire strong 498.16
i. incidents should not govern foreign policy 498.14
the greatest need of the contemporary i. system 498.10
interpretation: i. is the revenge of intellect upon art 207.49
our virtues lie in the i. of the time 604.34
interpretations: more ado to interpret i. than things 207.38
interpreter: Thomas Aquinas, who did not know Greek, was a better i. of Aristotle 694.2
interruption: noise is most impertinent form of i. 636.4
intimacies: i. between women often go backwards 1062.13
intimacy: i. begins with oneself 499.7
i. requires courage because risk is inescapable 499.6
intimate: having been, up to then, merely i. 499.2
much easier to tell i. things in the dark 169.4
intolerance: i., a local and temporal culture trait 500.2
i.: to oppose death penalty but electrocute those who disagree 500.1
intoxication: man must get drunk: best of life is i. 268.5
one creates power for self by way of i. 719.44
introspection: a man unprepared for i. 875.19
introspective: man becomes i. when he suffers 946.36
introvert: i. gazes only upon the emptiness within 627.11
the i. does not feel his introversion 687.5
intuition: i. attracts those who wish to be spiritual without any bother 501.3
women use intelligence to prop up i. 1062.37

intuitions: i. produced and erased by education 279.65
intuitive: mind of man is more i. than logical 590.21
invalids: when elderly i. with same ailment converse, life is delicious 22.4
invention: diabolically new i. 34.5
hunger is the bestower of i. 437.11
necessity, the mother of our i. 624.13
inventions: our i. mirror our secret wishes 201.11
inventor: was the i. of the bathtub plug a man? 502.2
inventors: greatest of i.: accident 502.4
i. almost always regarded as fools 479.4
i. of the mechanical arts have been much more useful than i. of syllogisms 502.5
investment: goodness is the only i. that never fails 393.47
i. and lending at interest of money 108.15
investments: charity, personal force only worthwhile i. 120.11
invincible: men are i. because inviolable 858.21
invisible: I am an i. man 30.3
i. government is malign 395.39
poet is the priest of the i. 708.95
to make ourselves i. to creditors 633.5
Irishman: not a single I. on board of a major bank 505.1
iron: strong i. often ends in shatterings 940.15
irony: i. and pity are two good counselors 539.36
i. can penetrate rage and puncture self-pity 436.11
irregular: romantic life not made by i. hours, diet 827.1
irreverence: i. is the champion of liberty 506.4
irritations: fine scenery appeases our i. 609.1
island: Englishmen must have an i. 289.10
little i. inundated by a miniature sea of whiskey 923.51
no man is an i., entire of itself 151.5
islanding: i. a few last figures in distant pools 603.3
islands: little i. are all large prisons 853.3
isolation: i. breeds conceit 915.52
i. must precede true society 915.42
Israel: we will never turn our back on friends in I. 365.65
issues: i. today not Republican or Democratic i. 674.3
Italian: many try to speak I. 923.4
Italy: in I. I feel that everybody's dead 34.28
I., and the spring and first love all together 409.82
jealously guarded beauties in I. 509.2
man who has not been in I. is inferior 509.5
itch: bliss: when you i., to up and scratch 852.2
if you are anywheres where it won't do to scratch, you will i. all over 852.3
love, i., and cough cannot be hid 551.74

J

jail: be thine own palace, or world's thy j. 880.5
in j. each day is like a year 735.11
j. doesn't teach anyone to do good 393.19
need ways to keep people out of j. 204.20
jailer: he was his own bitter j. 470.5
janitor: he was looking about for a job as j. 25.1
jargon: instead of language, we have j. 54.1
jaundiced: all looks yellow to the j. eye 58.5
Jazz Age: the J. was borrowed time 1001.3
jazz: j. is main spring of twentieth century 614.44
jealous: art is a j. mistress 53.45
God is indeed a j. God 387.24
j. ear hears all things 510.2
j. man fares worse than cuckold 403.15
j. troubles others, but torment selves 510.16
philosophers are as j. as women 694.35
she'll make you so j., you'll bust 72.24
tramp is j. of tramp 155.6
trifles are to the j. strong proofs 510.18
jealousy: in j. there is more self-love than love 510.11
it is not love that is blind, but j. 510.7
j., anger, and anxiety shorten life 43.2
J. feeds upon suspicion 510.12
j. is beautiful only on a young face 510.4
j. is born with love, doesn't die with it 510.13
j. is cruel as the grave 510.3
j. is not low, but it catches us humbled 510.5
j. is pain from fear of not being equally loved 510.1
j. is the greatest of all evils 510.14
j. serves the struggle for survival 510.9
j. slays love under pretense of keeping it alive 510.8
love that is fed by j. dies hard 510.15
nothing is more frightful to j. than laughter 510.17
sexual j., that most destructive of emotions 510.19
where there is no j. there is no love 510.10
jealousy's: j. a proof of love, but can't cure it 510.6
jest: better lose a j. than a friend 436.9
j. often decides matters of importance 436.13
of all griefs most bitter is scornful j. 436.15
jest's: j. prosperity lies in the ear of hearer 436.28
jesting: clumsy j. is no joke 436.1
Jew: hath not a J. eyes, hands, organs 512.4
he makes J. base who denies him rights 775.7
the J. has an anchorage in time 512.9
Jewish: my mother taught me pride in J. tradition 512.8
the J. cemetery, only place where I felt at home 423.8
jilted: one must forget being j. or pretend to 793.3
job: gotten the j. I wanted at Montgomery Ward 116.13
jobs: when white-collar people get j. 1066.4
joke: clumsy jesting is no j. 436.1
gentle dullness ever loves a j. 436.24
vulgar j.: a subtle and spiritual idea 436.5
jokes: differing taste in j. strains affections 436.7
for ten j. thou has an hundred enemies 436.29
journalism: glory of j. is its transience 630.24
in America j. governs for ever and ever 34.85
in Britain j. extension of conversation 630.31
j. allows readers to witness history 344.19
j., giving us the opinions of the uneducated 629.10
j. has no therapeutic value 630.16
j. is meeting challenge of filling space 630.42
j. is popular mainly as fiction 630.9
j. realizes truth is fluid, not solid 630.23
j., stringing endless series of clichés 630.3
trouble with daily j. 630.29
journalistic: j. vision sharpens every event 630.33
journalists: j. tell public which way cat is jumping 630.34
journey: agreeable companion on a j. is as good as a carriage 152.16
count every step, you make j. long 6.7
j. of thousand miles begins with step 75.1
man knows his companion in a long j. 499.3
the j., not the arrival, matters 845.7
Will the day's j. take the whole long day? 539.95
joy: all who j. would win must share it 409.18
better to weep at j. than j. at weeping 1052.8
excess of j. weeps; of sorrow, laughs 527.1
heaven wills that sorrow follow j. 918.38
illusory j. worth more than real sorrow 409.28
inch of j. surmounts a span of grief 526.27
j. and sorrow equally pass away 990.13
j. at eventide if day spent fruitfully 6.12
j. cometh in the morning 1052.1
j. consists in forgetting life 504.12
j. of life is to put out one's power 504.11
my j. of living is in the battles of life 409.96
no beautifier like wish to scatter j. 519.7
no peace in changing waves of j., despair 969.1
only hope of j. is in human

relations 794.12
silence is the perfectest herald of j. 409.91
sorrow before j. better than after it 918.43
sorrows remembered sweeten present j. 918.39
temper j. in fear of changed fortune 318.5
there is no j. but calm 989.8
the world, so various, hath neither j. nor love 1067.1
thing of beauty is a j. forever 72.26
to get full value of j. you must divide it 894.6
tomorrow's j. is possible only if today's makes way for it 117.15
to possess is past the instant we achieve the j. 716.4
to win j. through struggle is better than to yield to melancholy 281.8
true j. is the earnest we have of heaven 409.30
well of j. is poisoned for those out of whom an upset stomach speaks 1011.25
when you jump for j., beware that no one moves the ground from beneath your feet 409.61
who binds j. to self destroys winged life 409.15
wise man sings his j. in his heart 409.99
your j. is your sorrow unmasked 409.45
joylessness: j., not joy, is the mother of debauchery 739.5
joys: bitter ending awaits lawless j. 1030.16
j. are often tender shadows of sorrows 409.9
j. impregnate; sorrows bring forth 918.4
j. may make a journey and still abide 676.9
live life as it were spoil, pluck the j. 513.5
man fond of counting troubles, not j. 251.3
oh, the wild j. of living 696.2
present j. are more to flesh and blood 409.32
remembered j. are never past 580.19
undeserved j. are they that sing 409.98
Judas: it is usually J. who writes the biography 81.10
judge: as long as the j. is happy 516.1
do not j., and you will never be mistaken 515.6
j. is condemned when criminal acquitted 517.37
j. men by what their opinions made of them 656.14
j. not, that ye be not judged 206.3
j. should not be young 514.8
men j. men by their fashion and fortune 338.19
no one should be j. in his own cause 517.36
our tendency to j. others 498.5
there is a tendency to j. a race, nation, group, by its least worthy members 775.10
to an incompetent j. I may be silent 514.4
to j. a man, ask about concept of humanity if he were its sole representative 515.3
to j., get away from what one is judging 516.6
we j. others by an image we have formed of ourselves 515.5
we j. wrong if we do not feel right 1060.25
when innocence trembles, it condemns the j. 477.14
you shall j. a man by friends, foes 288.5
judged: only way men or women can be j. 978.37
judges: j. are elderly men likely to hate analysis 514.7
j. must also be performers 207.1
j. must beware of hard constructions 514.2
robes of all good j. that ever lived could not cover iniquity of one corrupt judge 514.3
judgest: thou j. another, condemnest thyself 206.4
judgeth: as a man is inwardly so he j. outwardly 516.9
judging: interest, prejudice take away power of j. 516.7
without informing himself to utmost, one can't acquit himself of j. amiss 516.11
judgment: an advantage in j. we yield to none 516.14
don't wait for last j.; it's every day 815.2
everyone complains of memory, none of j. 516.10
for learning suspended j., best discipline is philosophy 694.32
for right j., it's essential to see good qualities before pronouncing on bad 516.3
hasty j. first step to recantation 516.17
in j. be ye not too confident 516.4
in success we gain reputation for j. 945.12
j. is not always required 755.5
most have ears, but few have j. 690.1
nothing of greater value than power of j. 516.2
of all passions, fear weakens j. most 343.26
rightness of j. is bitterness to the heart 516.5
the j. is proper for all, has oar in all 516.13
the people make best j. in long run 682.10
too much anxiety about j. is fatal 516.8
ultimate cynicism is to suspend j. so you are not judged 516.12
we praise or blame, whichever exhibits j. 516.15
you can't depend on j. when imagination is out of focus 450.29
judgments: do not base your life on j. of others 663.13
ignorance delivers j. on all things 447.30
j. as watches, each believes his own 516.16
jujitsu: special j. to overcome every strong man 719.60
June: what is so rare as a day in J. 854.32
jurisdiction: j. given not for judge but litigant 61.9
jury: j. may in the sworn twelve have a thief 517.42
just: be j. before you're generous 517.45
if j. they are better than clever 517.47
impossible to be j. if one not generous 517.40
in a j. cause the weak beat the strong 111.13
I tremble for my country when I reflect that God is j. 34.36
j. and unjust things sanctioned by custom 213.27
j. are the ways of God 387.48
j. cause is not ruined by a few mistakes 111.4
j. cause needs no interpreting 528.19
j. cause never lacks good arguments 111.6
men are too unstable to be j. 517.7
no man can be j. who is not free 517.52
only actions of the j. smell sweet 227.28
right that j. should be obeyed 644.3
to possess eyes and a j. imagination 516.18
we become j. by performing j. actions 227.1
when you cannot be j. through virtue, be so through pride 517.23
justice: administrators of j. are like a cat set to take care of a cheese 514.10
armed with more than steel: j. of quarrel 822.13
at times even j. brings harm with it 517.48
basis of government is j., not pity 395.64
between friends there is no need of j. 365.8
clemency is the support of j. 583.4
death by j. is ignominious 767.4
do not expect j. where might is right 357.13
each loves j. in the affairs of another 517.25
extreme j. is often unjust 517.38
fairness with one's own enables one to do j. in the state 517.46
generosity is the flower of j. 375.4
how can j. fall victim to right? 517.10
in government, j. means force, virtue 517.32
injustice all around is j. 477.12
injustice easy to bear; what stings is j. 517.29
it is from reason that j. springs 393.30
it is not j. that holds a balance 116.5
j. comes not without council to the bow 517.8
j. condemns not even Devil wrongfully 517.16
j. delayed is democracy denied 517.27
j. discreet; injustice makes noise 517.39
j. divine mends not slow pace for cries 815.9
j. injustice change with climate 517.34
j. is impartiality 517.44
j. is last concern of universe 517.28

j. is the great interest of man on earth 517.51
j. is the right of the weakest 517.26
j. is violent to the party offending 517.9
j.: my being allowed to do whatever I like 477.1
j.: not to do wrong to fellow men 517.5
j. should remove her bandage to distinguish between vicious and unfortunate 517.24
j. substituted for instinct in civil state 133.24
j. without force is impotent 357.12
keep alive j., much blame will pass you by 517.14
knowledge without j. is cunning 522.50
laws of j. bind oppressor and oppressed 815.10
liberty plucks j. by the nose 537.38
many set high show of honor yet break j. 440.1
most may be done by impartial j. 517.18
nobody can give you j. 859.5
no such thing as j. in the abstract 517.13
not interpersonal warmth but institutional j. 85.6
our sense of j. sleeps till others have been aroused by sense of injustice 517.2
ranks of those who seek after j. and mercy 517.15
rigid j. is the greatest injustice 517.17
rigorous authority, j.: kindness of kings 831.13
social force impelled toward practice of j. 517.21
source of j. was fear of injustice 517.22
the more laws, the less j. 528.30
there is no real force without j. 357.11
there is one principle of j.: the interest of the stronger 517.35
we love j. greatly, and just men little 517.41
we will not be satisfied until j. rolls down like waters 85.13
where might is master, j. is servant 357.4
why not confidence in j. of the people 682.12
without j., courage is weak 195.13
justifiable: all bad precendents began as j. measures 528.11
justification: people can praise anything and find j. 782.4
justifies: guilty man j. himself before accusation 405.8
justify: he who must j. his existence by own efforts is in eternal bondage to himself 316.4
juvenile: j. delinquency provides adults with fantasies 204.8
K
kaleidoscope: k. of fragments, positions held and abandoned 512.6
keep: to k. demands as much skill as to win 716.3
keyhole: every age has k. to which eye is pasted 846.3
kids: life comes into focus: there stand my k. 123.29
kielbasa: a delicious k. and picture of Kosciuszko 632.8
kill: must we k. to prevent any wicked 518.9
not by wrath does one k. but by laughter 526.23
nothing is done until men are prepared to k. one another if it is not done 741.24
ridiculous to k. for rulers' quarrel 1042.72
we k. because we're afraid of our shadow 1042.62
killed: if your child were to be k. tomorrow 670.33
killer's: sword is but a tool in k. hand 518.11
killing: a quiet k. on the stock market 105.24
art of creation is older than art of k. 201.43
driving a car, you are in danger of k. 64.5
what can you do by k. 518.4
kills: each man k. the thing he loves 551.230
man who k. himself today, would have wished to live had he waited a week 948.26
one k. a man, one is an assassin; one k. everybody, one is a god 518.10
whom man k., God restoreth to life 518.6
kin: less danger from wiles of stranger if one's own k., kith were more fun to be with 334.24
one touch of nature makes whole world k. 431.24
kind: be ye k. one to another 359.1
do not ask me to be k. 519.14
gift, with k. countenance, is double 384.9
k. hearts are more than coronets 519.20
men are cruel, but man is k. 519.19
not necessarily natural that fondness for own k. lead to subjection of others 458.1
we can't be k. to each other for an hour 693.10
who does a kindness is not always k. 227.23
kind-hearted: majority of men are secretly k. 209.17
kindness: best friend knows how to show, accept k. 519.18
bird thinks it a k. to take fish in air 56.10
hated hand makes k. odious 519.5
k.: brief preface to volumes of exaction 519.3
k. brings forth k. always 519.17
k. can become its own motive 519.10
k. imagines others' joys, suffering as own 519.9
k. that gazes in a mirror turns to stone 888.3
nameless, unremembered acts of k. 519.22
set a high value on spontaneous k. 519.11
to justify the k. of one's friends 656.5
unreasonable k. gets no thanks 519.8
violence is just where k. is vain 1032.2
kindnesses: men not prone to requite k. 789.2
king: better have as k. vulture advised by swans 831.15
cat may look on a k. 780.7
if you can't pretend, you can't be k. 732.12
it is no bad thing to be a k. 520.3
k. can't last if people start thinking 520.6
k. is he who has laid fear aside 520.8
k. without clemency is enemy of state 127.5
not all the water can wash balm off k. 520.10
sail, quoth the k.; hold, saith the wind 626.11
to call k. "Prince" is pleasing 780.18
within crown of k. keeps Death his court 831.22
you are a k. by your own fire-side 422.4
kingdom: good mind possesses a k. 493.29
k. of the well, k. of the sick 413.15
king's: k. power founded on people's folly 831.16
subject's love is k. best guard 831.6
kings: a crown it is that seldom k. enjoy 186.20
all k. is mostly rapscallions 520.13
fear created gods; audacity created k. 520.1
foremost art of k. is to endure hatred 520.9
if men are shrewd, they may serve k. 200.5
k. have headaches like other people 831.4
k. have worship of world, but no repose 520.11
k. need company of the intelligent 520.7
k., women, vines embrace what is nearest 1062.112
no reliance placed on friendship of k. 990.14
priests put crowns on thieves, called k. 127.3
soon only five k. in world—king of England and four k. in pack of cards 520.2
we owe obedience to our k.; but esteem, affection are due only to their virtue 831.12
what are k., when regiment is gone 520.5
kiss: hatred can be concealed in countenance, k. 412.18
k. can be a comma, a question mark 521.8
k., make up: live to fight another day 772.12
k. originated when first male reptile licked first female 521.5
k. was not so wonderful as dreams I had 521.10
k., when all is said, what is it 521.9
must learn to k. the cold worm's mouth 221.84
she returned him k. for k. 521.11
when women k. it always reminds one of prizefighters shaking hands 1062.95
kissed: I k. her hard and held her tight 521.6
kisses: k. are a better fate than wisdom 521.2
k. of an enemy are deceitful 365.17
kissing: k. don't last: cookery

do 521.7
kitchen: fat k., lean will 1056.5
kitten: trouble with k. is that it becomes a cat 41.24
knew: if a man k. himself he would despise the ignorant notions others might form 875.26
if men k. themselves, God would pardon 875.20
knife: like the blade of a k. ground for days 950.3
knock: few sounds exceed interest of k. at door 428.16
to k. a thing down is a delight 26.6
know: advantage at times to forget what we k. 580.30
all ignorance toboggans into k. 447.8
beast does but k., man knows he knows 785.7
better be ignorant than half k. matter 447.27
don't k. nothing, and glad of it. 522.62
each thinks he must k. best about himself 19.11
full wise is he that can himselven k. 875.5
grieve not that men do not k. you 1008.5
if man does not k. himself, how should he know his functions and powers 875.18
if you would k. aught, be gay before it 1060.60
k. self and perhaps you'll avoid illness 758.6
k. thine opportunity 657.9
k. thyself: maxim as pernicious as ugly 875.10
k.-what more important than k.-how 771.9
k. who you are; adorn self accordingly 267.7
live by what one does k. 77.19
man may do or k. but little 9.15
more crucial than what we k. is what we do not want to k. 447.17
nothing I would not rather k. than not 522.27
right to k. is like right to live 522.57
thirst to k., understand, is excellent 532.22
those who k. the least of others think the highest of themselves 166.5
to each belongs its measure, best to k. 979.7
to k. a little often brings ridicule 522.8
to k. a man is to have loved, hated him 794.6
to k. is to grasp end realized through changes 117.7
to k. oneself, assert oneself 875.4
to k. others is learned; k. self, wise 875.13
to k. what none k., read things year later 522.17
we k. little, but have presentiment of much 450.25
we k. ourselves chiefly by hearsay 444.12
we k. what we are, not what we may be 368.31
we ought to k. a little about everything 522.48
what can we reason but from what we k. 785.25
wisest professed to k. he knew nothing 522.42
you never k. absolutely where you are 945.1
know-how: know-what more important than k. 771.9
knowing: If I cannot brag of k. something, then I brag of not k. it 522.16
k. beats unknowing 522.54
k. what is useful makes a wise man 522.20
nothing worth k. can be taught 522.67
speculators, boast not of k. things 694.19
step from k. to doing rarely taken 9.16
knowledge: acquisition of k., revelation of ignorance 522.2
action is the proper fruit of k. 9.20
all can acquire my k., but not my heart 284.18
all k. is of itself of some value 522.27
a man goes to k. as he goes to war 1007.2
any kind of k. is its own reward 522.44
conscious you're ignorant is first step to k. 447.9
conversation is not a search after k. 188.20
desire for k. increases with acquisition 522.58
desire of k. natural feeling of mankind 522.26
diffidence is the better part of k. 1005.3
doubt is not below k., but above it 904.1
enough k. to be able to communicate 913.16
even k. has to be in fashion 338.15
expanding k. we but increase ignorance 522.40
experience of anybody is real k. 321.5
extensive k. needful to thinking people 522.30
finer wits say k. is the good 522.49
fruit of tree of k. always drives man from paradise 522.25
general k. may have to be slight 522.65
human k. so great, we're all specialists 848.31
if little k. dangerous, who's out of danger 522.24
if we value k., we must be free 522.59
ignorance irritates man, k. cloys 691.1
information is not k., k. not wisdom 522.69
k. acquired under compulsion 279.66
k. can be communicated, but not wisdom 1060.28
k. comes, but wisdom lingers 1060.58
k. equalizes social condition of man 522.13
k. for the sake of k.! this is inhuman 998.126
k. has outstripped character development 279.20
k. humanizes mankind 726.11
k. is in the head; wisdom, in the heart 1060.25
k. is of two kinds 522.28
k. is power; dupes of this saying will read until their initiative is stunned 522.12
k. is proud that he has learned so much 1060.13
k. is shelter in advanced age 522.7
k. is the fountain of human liberty 522.63
k. is the great sun in the firmament 522.64
k. is true organ of sight, not the eyes 522.46
k. is two-fold 522.9
k., like money, must circulate 522.33
k., not confined to atomic scale 522.6
k. of the world acquired in world 321.6
k. the best protection against prejudice 522.53
k., timber not to be used till seasoned 522.23
k.: to hold to what you know, admit when you do not know 522.11
k. which stops at what it does not know is highest k. 522.61
k. without justice is cunning 522.50
leisure and curiosity might make advances in k. 533.9
man can reveal to you only what already lies in dawning of your k. 965.14
man is not weak, k. is more than force 522.29
man seldom has so much k. of another as necessary to make instruction useful 19.14
many men are stored full of unused k. 522.3
many will run to and fro, k. will grow 992.6
merit and k. will not gain hearts 584.1
no man's k. can go beyond his experience 321.29
no purifier like k. in this world 875.2
nowhere is k. as varied as in a newspaper 630.5
our k. is always superficial and imperfect 522.34
pedantry is the dotage of k. 848.21
pocket all your k. with your watch 600.4
power is used to make k. a slave 764.8
raft of k. ferries worst sinner to safety 522.4
sin, guilt, neurosis: fruit of tree of k. 522.41
special k. required to describe picture, fix car 522.39
step by which men add to their k. is step also by which they can control other men 522.36
to be fond of learning is to be near k. 532.21
to be proud of k. is to be blind with light 522.19
to conceal limits of k. don't overstep them 165.12
to k. belongs rational k. of temporal things 1060.3
to master any branch of k. you must master those next to it 522.22
traveler without k. is bird without wings 992.41
we are least open to precise k. concerning things we are most vehement about 264.7
we owe our k. to those who have differed 258.1
what harm in getting k. from

a sot, pot 522.52
who acquires k. and doesn't practise it 522.55
who displays his k. shows his ignorance 188.32
who increaseth k. increaseth sorrow 522.5
why do we make so much of k. 522.18
wisdom sets bounds even to k. 522.45
without k., life but the shadow of death 522.43
zeal will do more than k. 1073.1
zeal without k. is fire without light 1073.1
known: he that has done nothing had k. nothing 9.9
I come to be k. by my vacant face and careless gesture 813.4
if k. by everybody you know nobody 332.45
nothing can be loved, hated, unless k. 1007.12
not to be k. to do anything, never do it 804.8
what shall I do to be forever k. 804.7
knows: courage of all one really k. comes late 491.21
he that k. least presumes most 447.12
he that k. little often repeats it 447.13
what man k. is at war with what he wants 170.3
who k. only his side of the case, k. little of that 620.5

L

labor: by l. fire is got out of a stone 281.2
l. of one kind destroys man's spirits 1065.52
l.-saving devices have brought boredom 966.22
l. that has reference to a want 1065.39
life of l. makes drudges, not men 1065.25
love l.: if not for food, then for physic 1065.57
much cant of common interests of capital, l. 108.1
of all human activities, only l. is unending 1065.1
rest is the sauce of l. 811.6
slave of l. wheel, what to him is Plato 1066.3
the conviction that only l. is meaningful 1001.5
there is visible l. and invisible l. 1065.43
to l. is the lot of man 1065.41
true success is to l. 281.16
we put love where we have put l. 1065.67
where there's l. there's not always life 1065.22
why should life all l. be 1065.67
laboratory: an underground l., half a dozen atom-smashers 849.26
Labor Day: L. D. symbolizes our determination to achieve an economic freedom 420.6
laborer: if l. complain, set him to do nothing 446.13
labors: eliminate needless wants, and l. will reduce themselves 701.4
may share l. of great but not spoil 400.1
labour: Many might go to heaven with half the l. they go to hell 1070.13
lack: we are less dissatisfied when we l. many things 238.23
ladies: always very bountiful, especially the l. 120.1
in America there are no l. except salesladies 34.47
l. of fashion starve love to feed pride 338.12
take a hundred l. of quality 52.2
lady: he injures fair l. who beholds her not 466.2
l. wants to be dressed like everybody else 267.15
my landlady ain't no l. 1062.75
said a fervent young l. of Hammels 363.4
Lady Godiva: think what happened to L. 332.26
lady's: l. imagination is very rapid 1062.6
nothing so variable as l. headdress 407.1
when a l. erotic life is vexed 892.36
laity: professions are conspiracies against l. 1037.11
lamb: no absolute will make lion lie down with l. 26.4
lament: l., to win rear from audience, is worthwhile 157.1
lamentation: advantage to be won from grim l. 918.21
Lamentations: the L. of Jeremiah always pick me up 239.3
lamp: when l. shattered, light lies dead 221.119
land: American history is about l. 34.53
first man to fence in l. 746.5
he who would be the tongue of this wide l. 708.66
how do we accurately evoke l. we love 1067.27
if a man own l., the l. owns him 746.5
if you would find yourself, look to the l. 989.9
l. created as place for steamer to visit 839.1
man is rooted to the l. 423.1
this is my own, my native l. 423.7
various as your l. 34.7
landlord: as long as it means trouble for the l. 17.30
landlords: l. love to reap where they never sowed 108.10
landmarks: these are brave, free days of destroyed l. 441.1
landscape: difference between l. and l. is small 699.3
l. without theatricals 681.8
read the l. to help me through 444.23
something about the l. that might incriminate 518.7
landscapes: worst trains take one across best l. 992.52
lane: it is a long l. that has no turning 118.2
language: a book is the riverbank for the river of l. 967.22
a dog we know if better company than a man whose l. we do not understand 152.14
animal l., contagious expression of mood 524.2
do not travel before learning l. 992.18
enemy of clear l. is insincerity 524.34
English is such a deliciously complex and undisciplined l. 1064.19
eyes have one l. everywhere 325.2
idea does not pass from one l. to another without change 443.36
if l. be not in accordance with the truth, affairs cannot be carried to success 524.8
if thought corrupts l., l. can also corrupt thought 524.32
infants reared together cannot develop a l. 123.17
it is advisable to know numerals in any l. 524.49
l., culminating event in emergence of humanity 524.26
l. does not stand still 117.13
l. is by nature communal 524.20
l. is full of illogicalities 524.30
l. is little better than croak of fowls 524.18
l. is the archives of history 524.12
l. lies outside of society 524.35
l. must survive in men's minds and on their tongues 524.23
l., not desires, sets men at variance 252.10
l. of Johnson, stately l. of the time 524.7
l. of law foreign to the ears 134.2
l., setting us apart from rest of life 524.44
l. veils ideas, but softens, refines them 524.25
love of nature is a common l. 623.14
mere elegance of l. produces empty renown 942.18
new words slip into the l. silently 1064.7
next to him who violates the laws of his country is he who violates the l. 524.25
no l. expresses all human comprehension 524.36
only living l.: one in which we think 524.28
ours is a precarious l. 524.46
people who speak the same l. can hate one another 412.8
poet is in love with l. 708.3
pressure on l. to deteriorate 524.41
publicity has diminished value of l. 898.18
the l. of the working neighborhood 524.4
transfuse from one l. into another the creations of a poet 524.39
use any l., you say only what you are 149.3
wars fought between people who speak the same l. 149.6
we use l. of past to grasp present 524.37
where l. is most thoroughly debased 1044.3
who would recognize the unhappy if grief had no l. 1052.5
you and I have little effect on l. 524.24
languages: colors speak all l. 143.1

five thousand l., products of shared ability 562.32
l. are the pedigree of nations 524.21
to teacher of l. world but place of words 524.9
largesse: man reduced to vassalage by l. 433.27
lascivious: twenty l. turtles found ere chaste man 122.8
last: old and young, all on l. cruise 606.17
somebody has to have the l. word 51.5
there may be nobility in being l. 780.17
late: better hours too soon than minute too l. 765.4
hate friends who come too l. to help 979.5
he that riseth l. must trot all day 73.5
only habitual l. riser, up early, takes in full flavor of nature 605.1
latest: audience always applauds l. song most 640.7
laugh: absurdities have crumbled before a l. 526.29
a l. is the loud echo of a sigh 526.24
all of those I love make me l. 551.4
always gone in for the loud l., the wow 34.73
anything awful makes me l. 526.17
better to l. at life than lament over it 539.105
call truth false if not accompanied by l. 409.72
if I l., 'tis that I may not weep 527.2
it is God's giving if we l. or weep 409.93
l., and the world laughs with you 527.9
man who cannot l. is fit for treasons 526.5
men let you abuse, if you make them l. 436.2
One can know a man from his l. 526.7
people betray character in what they l. at 526.12
the only creatures that both l. and weep 527.3
to l. is proper to the man 526.27
we are in the world to l. 526.28
we l., cry—then feebler l., then die 527.7
wouldn't a l. serve us better? 526.15
laughed: he is not l. at who laughs first at self 526.11
who has once l. cannot be altogether bad 526.4
laughing: learn weeping and gain l. 918.20
one afraid of l. at friend lacks love 365.50
laugh's: l. wisest answer to all that's queer 526.19
laughs: he who l. best to-day also l. last 526.21
no one laughable who l. at himself 4.7
when a man l. he shows all his faults 526.10
laughter: all comedian has to show is echo of l. 144.1
arpeggios of l. lilting across the grass 639.1
beauty of world is l. and anguish 1067.31
even in l. the heart is sorrowful 526.3
in l. evil is absolved of its own bliss 526.22
l. is God's mistake 527.8
l. is higher than all pain 526.16
l. is not a bad beginning for friendship 526.31
l. is wine for the soul 526.25
l. of amusement should be kept apart 526.6
l. of man more terrible than his tears 527.6
l. tends to mock the pompous and pretentious 526.26
make faces and produce l., like dancing dogs 11.5
not by wrath does one kill but by l. 526.23
not one has died of l. 526.2
only l., love are worth wear of winning 365.15
our sincerest l. with pain is fraught 526.30
sudden glory maketh grimaces called l. 526.14
unextinguished l. shakes the skies 3.5
laurels: do we want l. or that no one else shall have any 386.8
law: absolute loyalty to authoritative l. 514.5
by transgressing men have kept the l. 1070.16
can't abolish by l. or axe desires of men 238.29
commercial l. prohibited innovation 104.33
cultivate respect not for l. but right 822.21
defiance of l. is surest road to tyranny 528.44
Englishman walks before the l. like a trained horse in the circus 289.13
even when no l., there is conscience 174.27
every new time will give its l. 528.33
highest virtue is always against the l. 1033.17
if there isn't a l., there will be 528.21
in l., what plea so tainted and corrupt 528.60
it takes a hundred to make a l., then a hundred years to get rid of it 528.6
language of l. must not be foreign 528.36
l. and reason only things between us and tyranny 528.23
l. cannot exist without government 528.57
l. cannot persuade where it cannot punish 528.26
l., introduced without reason, has become reasonable 528.51
l. is an edifice sheltering all of us 528.28
l. is experience developed by reason 528.53
l. is good, if a man uses it lawfully 528.8
l. is passionless 528.5
l. is the last result of human wisdom 528.43
l. is the witness of our moral life 528.39
l. rules throughout existence 1017.5
l. was not preferable to man 528.67
man for whom l. exists is a tame man 528.66
men in l. firms do not glory in night work 528.54
nobody has a more sacred obligation to obey the l. that those who make the l. 528.3
no grievance fit for redress by mob l. 597.6
no l. quite appropriate for all 528.48
no man above l. or below it 528.55
none can enforce l. not supported by people 528.40
opinion of all lawyers, unanimous cry of nation, good of state are l. 528.69
our bodies can be mobilized by l. 442.2
people say l. but they mean wealth 528.18
people should fight for their l. 528.37
power that keeps cities together is l. 913.4
rigorous l. is often rigorous injustice 528.64
unjust l. is itself a species of violence 528.29
victim to too severe a l. is considered martyr 517.6
we must not make a scarecrow of the l. 528.61
when I refuse to obey an unjust l. 786.2
wherever l. ends, tyranny begins 528.49
who make his l. a curse dies by his l. 815.1
who saves his country violates no l. 678.16
who takes it upon himself to break bad l. 528.16
who to himself is l. no l. doth need 880.3
lawless: bitter ending awaits l. joys 1030.16
laws: all l. would become meaningless 528.58
best use of good l. 528.52
blue l. still frown but do it in private 749.2
brain may devise l. for the blood 39.25
don't change l. to change customs 213.20
first of all l. is to respect the l. 766.16
good l., disobeyed, not good government 528.4
good l. lead to better; bad to worse 528.56
good men must not obey l. too well 393.14
if soul cannot breathe, l. are too tight 537.4
it ain't no sin if you crack a few l. 528.70
l. alone cannot secure freedom of expression 984.6
l. are like spider's webs 528.63
l. are never as effective as habits 406.16
l. are silent in time of war 1042.15
l. cannot carry themselves into practice 395.42
l. can't be enforced against master 1002.8
l. grind the poor, rich men rule law 528.32
l. hand in hand with progress of mind 528.42
l. of gravity, chemistry, botany 849.7
l. of nature are human inventions 502.3
l. that only threaten are soon scorned 528.12
l. too gentle are seldom obeyed 528.25
many l. make bad men, bad

men make many l. 528.46
no worse torture than torture of l. 514.2
run against the grain of a nation's genius and see where you get with your l. 528.47
some sense their own l. within them 528.38
strict execution best way to repeal bad l. 528.34
the more l., the less justice 528.30
the more l., the more offenders 528.27
things have l. as well as men 646.4
to interpret l. is to corrupt them 528.68
unwritten l. more fixed than the written 528.59
useless l. weaken necessary ones 528.50
where l. are not supreme, demagogues arise 232.1
who lives in solitude may make own l. 915.37
lawsuit: lean compromise better than fat l. 162.4
lawyer: behold a l., an honest man 528.24
deceive not thy physician, confessor, l. 224.8
hide nothing from confessor, l., doctor 165.6
poet never interpreted nature as freely as l. interprets truth 528.31
thought a l. was an honest man 528.2
lawyer's: l. truth is not truth but consistency 528.65
lawyers: if no bad people there would be no good l. 528.15
l. eat, sleep and dream paper 528.62
laziness: don't yield to that alluring witch, l. 530.5
doom of l. to be inactive without ease 530.6
failure not our only punishment for l. 530.7
flee l., it ends in sorrow of repentance 530.1
l. travels slowly, poverty overtakes him 530.3
lazy: l. boy, warm bed are difficult to part 97.3
lead: men by sympathetic attractions l. nations 531.5
leader: efficiency of the national l. 622.4
l. is a dealer of hope 531.12
l. is in common mass of matter lost 531.8
l. leaves in others the will to carry on 531.9
l. must know, must know he knows 531.16
[O]ne longs for the presence of a l. like Lincoln 531.10
real l. is content to point the way 531.11
leaders: most l. merely follow in front 531.6
leadership: what l. has gone undiscovered 531.21
leaf: fall of a l. is a whisper to the living 606.8
leaky: to try whether a vessel be l., we prove it with water before wine 755.6
lean: yond Cassius has a l. and hungry look 57.17
leaps: the sequence of l. spun from her endlessly 215.3
learn: freedom to l. first part of being free 532.17
it is safer to l. than teach 656.21
l. as if you'd never be able to master it 532.4
l. what you are and be such 875.21
men l. only what their passions allow 321.23
no dishonor to l. from others 19.27
old men still young enough to l. 653.2
to l. is a pleasure common to all men 532.6
we l. geology morning after earthquake 205.3
we l. not for life but for the debating-room 155.11
we l. only from those we love 532.6
we l. to-day what our better advanced judgments will unteach us to-morrow 321.3
what we l. depends upon powers of insight 532.5
what you yourself don't l., you don't know 532.2
where there is desire to l., there is arguing 656.17
learned: l. blockhead is worse than ignorant one 941.6
l. discount deed, open soul of doer 608.2
l. fool is sillier than ignorant one 356.17
l. man: idler who kills time with study 848.35
l. man so ignorant he bought cow to ride 848.14
no profit to have l. well, if you neglect to do well 227.25
solemn ego accompanies the l. 848.11
to master torrent of life, l. man meditates 539.85
when l. men do stoop to learn 848.6
who seem l. to fools seem fools to l. 732.13
learning: joy in l.: it enables me to teach 965.31
l. acquired in youth helps in old age 522.35
l. apart from nature is fractional 279.68
l. begets arrogance in fools 522.47
l. gained most on books by which printer lost 93.32
l. is but an adjunct to ourself 522.56
l. is for those fearing disagreeable action 848.1
l. is its own exceeding great reward 532.9
l.: knowledge of what none but learned know 848.18
l. makes man fit company for himself 279.30
l. nothing without cultivated manners 210.19
l. to get your money's worth 704.17
l. without liberty is always in vain 522.32
l. without thought is labour lost 522.10
little l. is a dangerous thing 522.51
make l. of books your own wisdom 532.18
much l. does not teach understanding 279.39
my pleasure comes from l. something 409.96
nature's fire is all the l. I desire 623.11
to be fond of l. is to be near knowledge 532.21
what one has been long l. unwillingly, he unlearns with eagerness, haste 279.38
when l. one should not think of play 903.1
whoso neglects l. in his youth, loses the past and is dead for the future 279.26
wise man not ashamed to l. more 532.20
learnt: to have l. feels like losing something 532.19
least: those who work hardest have the l. 718.13
leave: to l. is to die a little 673.4
lechery: l. drink provokes, and unprovokes 268.48
legacies: eras die, l. are left to strange police 42.2
legal: l. broom's a moral chimney-sweeper 528.10
legislation: if all is well, l. is beneficial 797.73
in l. as in medicine, it's easier to show what does harm than what does good 528.13
legislative: large l. bodies resolve into coteries 172.3
legislators: poets are unacknowledged l. of the world 708.92
leisure: hard to keep secret, employ l., bear injury 245.1
increased means, l., two civilisers of man 133.8
l., sine qua non of the full Renaissance 533.10
l., the privilege teachers most often misuse 533.7
life of l. is beautiful and ennobling 533.16
much l. merely a way to spend money 602.40
no high civilization exists without ample l. 533.1
serious l. not genius of Americans 533.5
when a man's busy, l. strikes him as pleasure 533.2
without l. there can be neither art nor science 533.12
leisured: l. rebel most at interruption of routine 828.2
lend: human species made of men who borrow, l. 96.4
lender: borrower is servant to the l. 96.2
neither a borrower nor a l. be 96.5
leopard: can Ethiopian change skin, or l., spots 444.7
lesbians: l. under their skin 424.4
less: l. is more 899.1
lesson: pain, sterility, ennui teach l. 946.13
lessons: Life is a succession of l. which must be lived to be understood 321.13
letter: a l. in which all the news will be pleasant 629.11
l. killeth, but spirit giveth life 544.1
letters: more than kisses, l. mingle souls 535.2
we destroy l., a beautiful breath of life 535.3
levelers: l. wish to level down 910.4
lexicographer: l.: writer of dictionaries, harmless drudge 244.5
lexicography: l. is a chastening art 244.1
liar: best l. makes the least

lying go farthest 558.7
each lie is a sort of suicide in the l. 558.13
l. denies truth to others, not self 442.13
l. goes in fine clothes 558.33
l. not believed even when he speaks truth 558.1
l. should have a good memory 558.30
you are a l., sir, a rather dirty one at that 830.5
liars: mischevious l.: those on the verge of truth 558.18
liberal: essence of the l. outlook lies in how opinions are held 536.4
l. uses legs, hands at command of his head 536.3
l. wishes to replace existing evils with others 178.2
mellowing rigorist is pleasanter than tightening l. 178.11
that man has had a l. education whose body is the servant of his will 279.44
liberalism: the cultural bloom of economic l. 536.2
the idea of l. recurs in politics 536.1
liberality: hand of l. stronger than arm of power 375.6
liberals: we l. know the poor are our equals in every sense except being equal to us 718.55
liberation: l. is not deliverance 537.18
liberties: country preserves l. if rulers warned that people preserve spirit of resistance 658.7
libertine: easier to make a saint out of a l. 840.10
liberty: a gift deprives us of our l. 384.10
as child, man's l. is concealed from him 363.3
by social contract man gains civil l. 913.28
eternal vigilance is the price of l. 537.10
freedom of press a bulwark of l. 731.5
give l. to those not agreeing with us 984.13
give me l. or give me death 537.16
he that would make own l. secure must guard even enemy from oppression 537.32
hungry do not care about l. 537.11
if we must accept fate we must also affirm l. 867.4
in chains, laurels, l. knows only victory 537.30
in doubtful things, l. 119.3
irreverence is the champion of l. 506.4
knowledge is the fountain of human l. 522.63
lean l. is better than fat slavery 740.4
l. a mockery if price is the destruction of those who are to enjoy l. 537.13
l. and democracy become unholy when dyed with innocent blood 1032.7
l. doesn't even do small things legally 537.3
l. exists in proportion to restraint 537.45
l. in democracy when all share rule 233.3
l. is hardest test inflicted on a people 537.43
l. is independence maintained by force 537.44
l. is itself the highest political end 537.1
l. is its own reward 537.49
l. is latitude the powerful accord to weak 537.14
l. is limitation of government power 537.51
l. is the only true riches 363.24
l. is the right to do what laws permit 537.23
l. is the soul's right to breathe 537.4
l. may do no more than stir up civil wars 537.9
l. motive for good, pretext for crime 537.2
l. never out of bounds or off limits 537.46
l. not as good in practice as in speech 537.32
l. of the individual must be limited 363.38
l. plucks justice by the nose 537.38
l.: precious possession of imagination 537.5
l. translation of declarations into action 537.50
l. without learning is always in peril 522.32
little l. on earth while tyrant is in heaven 797.40
money is coined l. 602.15
most people want security, not l. 756.4
observance of law is safeguard of l. 528.44
Oh l., what crimes are committed in your name! 537.33
religions united with government inimical to l. 127.2
spirit of improvement not always of l. 790.20
spirit of l. not too sure it is right 537.15
they that give up l. to obtain safety 856.5
to discover and maintain l. among men 34.87
too little l. brings stagnation and too much brings chaos 537.37
to renounce l. is to renounce being a man 537.36
to whom you tell your secrets you resign your l. 169.7
tree of l. refreshed by patriots' blood 819.25
when we demand l. of a person 537.53
wild l. breeds iron conscience 363.14
wise see in l. the potent Law of Laws 537.48
wolf says shepherd is destroyer of l. 537.21
word l. has served for destruction of l. 537.24
you cannot tear up ancient rootages and safely plant tree of l. 537.52
library: a man's l. is sort of his harem 538.5
hours spent in l., intimidated and embarrassed 538.2
public l. shows vanity of human hopes 538.6
what can a man see of a l.? 538.3
lie: Europe, I feel, that also introduced us to the l. 303.4
fool can tell truth: sense is needed to l. 558.5
inability to l. is far from love of truth 1000.16
in England they hardly ever l. 558.26
l. always needs truth for a handle 558.4
l. faces God and shrinks from man 558.3
l. has no leg, but scandal has wings 846.2
l. is a very present help in trouble 558.39
l. is but the truth in masquerade 558.8
l. is handle that fits all sin's tools 558.21
l. needs great many more to make it good 558.38
l. of pipe dream is what gives us life 336.13
l. told well is immortal 999.16
l. which is half a truth is blackest l. 558.41
man who can't tell a l. thinks he is the best judge of one 558.43
masses will fall victims to a big l. 558.20
most common l.: one uttered to one's self 864.7
most striking difference between cat l. is cat has only nine lives 558.44
not one of us can l. or pretend 444.19
only a truthful man can l. to any purpose 999.2
people l. because they don't remember 558.34
repetition doesn't transform l. into truth 558.31
single l. destroys whole reputation 558.17
we admit superiority of man we l. to 558.6
we perceive image of truth, possess a l. 999.13
when I l. down 73.2
who serves two has to l. to one 497.3
women l. so well that truth seems false 1062.17
lies: Americans detest all l. except l. spoken in public or printed l. 558.22
art of living: knowing how to believe l. 539.89
cruellest l. told in silence 558.40
cursed be the social l. 913.33
freedom means freedom from l. 363.32
l. are the religion of slaves 999.6
life is a system of half-truths and l. 558.23
man had rather a hundred l. told of him 165.9
no mask like truth to cover l. 224.4
of l., false modesty is the most decent 440.4
one l. in words, gets bad reputation 558.42
sooner hate for truth than adore for l. 1000.1
there are l., damned l., and statistics 932.2
to put faith in l. is the true atheism 412.13
truth exists; only l. are invented 999.1
without l., man dies of despair, boredom 558.15
life: aim of l. is to live 539.75
a l. without pain and sadness 1011.5
all l. is an experiment 980.3

all of l. was arranged from outside in 581.56
all our l. is but a going out to death 541.6
all we do passes into great machine of l. 227.32
a man's l. is a continual allegory 539.63
a man wants to get to where he left his l. 539.9
art, a mold in which to imprison l. itself 201.8
art is long, l. short 988.3
art, like l., should be free 53.123
art of l.: how to enjoy and endure 539.50
art teaches the significance of l. 53.89
at least I ain't led no humdrum l. 845.3
behave in l. as if at a banquet 657.6
believe l. is worth living 78.9
believe more in l., fling less to moment 461.1
best way to prepare for l. is to live 539.58
better a moment of l. than epoch-long unconsciousness of a stone 539.123
better to laugh at l. than to lament over it 539.105
brief span of l. is hastening on 653.55
call l. you live today your own 116.7
cannot evaluate man's l. till he is dead 539.115
character of human l. is ambiguity 390.23
complete l. includes old age 540.12
death has no sting, but l. has 541.40
death is an instant, l. a long torment 541.33
death is ultimate horror of l. 221.56
death's stamp gives value to coin of l. 541.39
death takes away commonplace of l. 221.121
deem not l. a thing of consequence 539.5
determine quality of l. by its activities 10.1
difficult for man to realize his l. an art 539.30
do not fear death, but the inadequate l. 504.4
dost thou love l., do not squander time 978.21
dullness makes l. supportable 219.2
each ten year's of man's l. has own hopes 586.8
easy to recollect good things of l. 639.5
everyday l. is order and haphazardry 539.119
every l. is its own excuse for being 316.5
every l. is, more or less, a ruin 758.12
every man lives to give meaning to l. 539.90
flowers of l. are but illusions 254.5
full l. cannot be recorded 1069.49
giver of l. should die at moment of giving 892.32
good l. fears not l. nor death 541.15
growth is the only evidence of l. 404.19
hard for man to confess his l. was unimportant 1012.3
having tasted l. in this world, one has no wish to begin as a new boy in another 454.17
he who despises l. is his l.'s master 937.3
hold it wrong to prefer l. to honor 491.13
hour which hives us l. begins to take it 83.6
however mean your l. is, live it 504.23
how much of human l. lost in waiting 1040.2
human l., a continuous thread 1071.18
I do not cut my l. up into days 539.61
if daily l. seems poor, you are not poet 612.8
if l. is absurd, death is insupportable 3.8
if money can answer, wrong to endanger l. 216.15
if we had keen vision, feeling of l. 883.2
in morn of l. we are alert, we are heated in its noon, in its decline we repose 540.8
in short measures l. may perfect be 684.10
instinct of l. falters only in man 562.31
in the midst of l. we are in death 541.29
interest in death is interest in l. 577.5
is l. a boon? If so, death is interest in l. 577.5
I warmed both hands before the fire of l. 653.56
joy of l. is to put out one's power 504.11
judging whether l. is worth living 948.3
just conception of l. too large to grasp in short lifetime 539.47
knowing how little l. has in store for us 783.3
last of l. is best: youth shows but half 653.10
later l. flings itself along faster 406.11
leave l. blessing it rather than in love with it 221.99
leaves of l. keep falling one by one 226.8
l., accommodation to patterns and standards 151.2
l., a faint tracing on the surface of mystery 539.24
l. an end in itself 539.55
l. a petty thing unless moved by the indomitable urge to extend its boundaries 55.12
l. as we find it is too hard for us 798.3
l. consists in accepting ourselves 858.1
l., death, appear ours, yet are hardly so 541.23
l. difficult because of its simplicity 539.94
l. driven forward by apprehension of notions too general for language 443.38
l. finds its wealth by claims of world 504.22
l. force is vigorous 539.71
l. for girl with years of straight A's 564.101
l. for the American is a hazard 539.68
l. full of stairs to go up and come down 235.6
l. given to us, we earn it by giving it 539.122
l. given us for higher purposes than to gather what ancestors have thrown away 848.22
l. has become a sweepstake 912.4
l. has meaning if bartered for something else 539.99
l. has to be given a meaning 3.6
l. has value when it has valuable object 539.51
l. hurries on, and death follows fast 978.50
l. imitates art more than art imitates l. 539.133
l. in itself is neither good nor evil 390.13
l. insupportable but for self-pity 877.2
l. is a child playing around your feet 540.1
l. is a country the old have seen, lived in 653.53
l. is a diary in which man means to write one story, and writes another 539.7
l. is a disease 540.13
l. is a fatal, contagious complaint 539.56
l. is a festival only to the wise 1060.15
l. is a Gordian knot, cut sooner or later 539.14
l. is a great surprise 541.28
l. is a jest 3.4
l. is a maze in which we take the wrong turning before we have learnt to walk 539.19
l. is an incurable disease 539.21
l. is an irreversible process 368.21
l. is a process where people mix and match 539.45
l. is a progress from want to want 238.24
l. is a search after power 719.20
l. is a stuff to try soul's strength 539.12
l. is a succession of lessons 321.11
l. is a system of half-truths and lies 558.23
l. is a task to be done 539.103
l. is a toy made of glass 539.2
l. is a well of joy 1011.25
l. is art of being well deceived 449.10
l. is art of drawing sufficient conclusions from insufficient premises 115.2
l. is as tedious as a twice-told tale 539.108
l. is but a day; a fragile dew-drop 990.9
l. is but a series of inspired follies 354.14
l. is compromise between ideal, possible 539.98
l. is cut to allow for growth 404.25
l. is either daring adventure or nothing 16.5
l. is external text from which God speaks 539.84
l. is fleeting—and therefore endurable 539.18
l. is for most one long postponement 231.8
l. is frail moth caught in web of years 539.124
l. is half spent before one knows l. 539.37
l. is like an onion one peels crying 539.38
l. is like shadow of bird in flight 990.8

LIFE

l. is little more than a loan shark 539.91
l. is made up of marble and mud 539.48
l. is made up of sobs, sniffles, smiles 539.53
l. is not a static thing 117.8
l. is not governed by will or intention 539.134
l. is not living, but living in health 413.9
l. is one damn thing over and over 539.74
l. is one damned thing after another 539.59
l. is one long process of getting tired 341.1
l. is paradox: each truth has counterpart 668.3
l. is pill none can swallow without gilding 539.62
l. is short and the art long 988.4
l. is short, but its ills make it seem long 539.93
l. is solitary cell 915.33
l. is struggle to be, do, what we cannot 539.49
l. is suffering 946.34
l. is the only reality in death 541.19
l. is that which interrupts 539.86
l. is thorny; youth is vain 39.11
l. is to be enjoyed, not simply endured 704.13
l. is too short to take seriously 539.112
l. is tragedy: we're spectators, actors 539.120
l. is washed in the speechless real 784.2
l. is what our character makes it 867.9
l. laughs shaking its rattle of death 539.121
l. levels all men 221.117
l. like after-dinner hour with cigar 539.20
l. looked at one way is cause for alarm 58.1
l. loses in a day what many years amassed 550.5
l. made up of constant calls to action 9.24
l. must always be full of risks 216.5
l. not bound to the physical world of science 539.67
l.: not having been told floor just waxed 539.81
l. of man to shift from sorrow to sorrow 539.118
l. only art we practice without preparation 539.79
l. only avails, not the having lived 539.31
l. only demands the strength you possess 195.14
l. ought to be material and carnal 716.5
l. passeth away suddenly as a shadow 221.76
l. perceived transforms itself 875.16
l. protracted is protracted woe 548.6
l. reduced to hell when cultures overlap 210.12
l. remains funny when people die 541.38
l., saddest thing there is, next to death 539.130
l. seems cursed to be a wiggle merely 539.23
l. seldom as unendurable as it logically ought to be 539.4
l. short; should try to make it smooth 539.35
l. should begin with age, end with youth 1072.28
l. the frailest thing in the world 539.87
l. we learn with, l. we live with 316.7
l. without absorbing occupation is hell 504.12
l. without adventure is unsatisfying 16.9
l. without courage for death: slavery 195.32
l. wonderful to talk about, not to live 539.1
living well, one must have pleasant l. 409.34
long and hard and painful to create l. 518.15
long quaffing maketh a short l. 268.34
love cannot save l. from death 551.223
love earth too much to contemplate l. apart 454.7
man arrives as novice at each age of l. 540.3
man lives the l. of his epoch 184.6
man wastes part of l. to display qualities he does not possess 732.5
man's l. accorded him in thoughts of others 804.6
man's l. happy expecting it soon to be so 409.75
man's l. is warfare against men's malice 561.3
man's virtue measured by his l. 1033.38
measure l. by experience, not length 548.5
men cling to l. even in misfortune 539.3
minute to smile, hour to weep: that is l. 539.27
moments make the year, and trifles l. 996.13
motto of modern l.: just as good as real 54.3
music is essentially useless, as l. is 614.50
must be thrust out of finished cycle in l. 404.20
my l. is a flight and I lose everything 541.1
new fact enhances constant fact of l. 328.6
nobody can write l. of a man but friends 81.6
no easy path out of l., few easy within 539.66
no man has tasted full flavor of l. until he has known poverty, love, and war 539.54
no man quick enough to enjoy l. 539.70
none can help things l. has done to us 129.3
no one would accept l. as gift, if he had knowledge of it 539.107
nor love l., nor hate; but live well 539.76
not easy to restore l. to the dead 767.5
nothing is unthinkable provided it arises out of the needs of l. 717.2
one's real l. is led in his head 818.4
only in the microscope that l. looks big 539.102
our l. is made by the death of others 541.24
our l. is what our thoughts make it 975.1
our whole l. is startlingly moral 604.41
responsibilities of l. are not ball-bearing 929.15
scenes of l. beautiful only from distance 539.104
shame on soul, to falter on road of l. 219.1
sharing is the law of God's inner l. 894.2
short l. forbids far-reaching hopes 427.18
shortness of l. cannot dissuade us from its pleasures, console us for its pains 539.128
significant moments of l. 875.12
skills in l. develop on your own 880.11
sole l. man loses is l. he is now living 729.2
so long as we do not blow brains out, l. is worth living 539.57
some make a garden of l., walk down path 661.1
something better man can give than his l. 887.5
strait is the gate which leadeth to l. 841.1
sure way of knowing nothing about l. 1037.12
thank you God for this good l. 539.64
that I exist is a surprise which is l. 316.10
the art of l., using what happens to us 539.117
the l. he left starving like an old dog 539.10
the l. we all live begins in accident 539.116
the notion of a better l. ahead 978.32
the story of my l. is always guarded 444.13
the time of l. is short 539.110
theory and practice of l. not reconciled 974.3
there is l. in the ground 337.8
there is no wealth but l. 539.97
there is one meaning of l.: living itself 539.39
this l. soon be over 414.15
thou shalt give l. for l. 815.3
three modes of bearing ills of l. 17.17
time in l. when we need to strut our stuff 404.29
to cure fear of death, set just value on l. 541.20
to defeat death man obliged to defeat l. 541.25
to fear love is to fear l. 219.8
to feel part of the stream of l. 1017.14
tragedy of l. is that man almost wins 329.4
trifles make up happiness, misery of l. 996.11
truest l. is when we are in dreams awake 336.17
unexamined l. is not worth living 758.16
uniformity makes the longest l. short 978.40
useless l. is early death 1024.2
vanity to want long l., heed not good l. 548.7
we are in a l. that passes understanding 539.16
we are in deadly fear of l. 539.46
we cannot tear page from our l. but can throw whole book into fire 948.22
we cross the ocean of this world, each in his average

cabin of a l. 539.13
we desire to live an imaginary l. 804.23
we face facts of sex but not of l. 328.10
we live l. of contrasts and patchwork 539.32
we love l. because we are used to loving 539.82
we spend lives talking of mystery: l. 316.8
wear l. out in efforts to be useful 653.41
web of l. is a mingled yarn 539.111
well-written l. is rare as well-spent one 81.3
what a miserable thing l. is 251.2
what am I if not a participant in l. 504.21
what is l. without time to stand, stare 533.3
when l. goes stale, junk it! 34.62
when one realizes his l. is worthless 30.1
when work is a duty, l. is slavery 1065.35
where l. is more terrible than death, it is truest valour to dare to live 195.5
who regards l. as meaningless is almost disqualified for l. 30.2
who would tread again the scene he trod through l. before 541.27
why should l. all labor be 1065.67
work of l. is to lay foundation of death 221.96
writing of a novel, taking l. as it exists 1069.139
life's: all theory is grey, but green is l. tree 974.7
flops are a part of l. menu 329.21
l. a moment and less than a moment 606.15
l. a pudding full of plums 539.43
l. brevity makes architect's trade sad 50.4
l. business: be, do, do without, go 539.78
l. but a walking shadow 539.109
l. enchanted cup but sparkles near the brim 653.12
l. like a play 311.11
l. neither a good nor an evil 539.106
l. the only riddle we don't give up 539.44
lifeblood: their l. ran in different directions 499.11
lifeless: he is l. that is faultless 342.7
light: lamp was no longer giving any l. beyond its own daylighted chimney 428.2
l. boats sail swift 951.4
l. is a principal beauty in a building 50.5
l. or, failing that, lightning 1007.1
man, like a picture, deserves advantage of good l. 197.5
no one is a l. unto himself 473.5
out of heart of darkness comes l. 918.18
there is l. in the darkness 217.2
to see divine l. put out thy candle 697.4
lightning: l. hath but his flash 976.2
light, or, failing that, l. 1007.1
lights: l. that pursue you everywhere 950.4
with l. we drive night to forest and sea 633.2
like: all the people l. us are We 910.5
don't care about reasons, know what I l. 725.3
to l., dislike, same things makes a solid friendship 365.87
we must l. what we have when we don't have what we l. 806.2
liked: how I like to be l.; what I do to be l. 474.2
since I wronged you, I have never l. you 476.19
we can always make ourselves l. 808.7
likeness: little liking where there is no l. 22.1
no glass renders man's l. as his speech 923.31
likings: man's road marked by graves of l. 404.28
lilacs: L. out of the dead land 854.18
lilies: consider l. of the field: they toil not 446.2
l. that fester smell worse than weeds 191.12
limitation: freedom from self-imposed l. 363.28
limitations: art, organism's reaction against retentive l. 53.14
men cease to interest us when we find l. 542.4
limits: thing I am most aware of is my l. 542.8
we take l. of vision for l. of the world 689.7
whatever l. us we call fate 340.6
line: queuemania is a compulsive urge to l. up 171.16
shortest l. may be crooked l. 585.2
lion: cat pent up becomes a l. 109.3
dog is a l. in his own house 422.17
forbear to pluck beard of a dead l. 808.8
hares can gambol over body of dead l. 719.49
l. is ashamed when he hunts with the fox 57.12
no absolute will make l. lie down with lamb 26.4
who has cut claws of l. will not be secure till he has drawn teeth 173.3
lip: many a slip 'twixt cup and l. 115.11
liquor: blush of an intemperate man painted by l. 494.6
candy is dandy but l. is quicker 268.38
l. will end a contest quicker 268.50
men are disguised by sobriety, not by l. 165.4
listen: l. to crabgrass grow, faucet leak 533.11
to l. acutely is to be powerless 543.2
two ears, one mouth: l. more, talk less 543.5
listened: two evils: never be l. to, always be l. to 848.23
listening: language is a gift, l. is a responsibility 543.1
only l. that counts is l. of the talker 543.3
the sweetness of l., the velvet of sleep 898.7
listens: who l. for what people say has no peace 868.4
literacy: l., key to improvement of education 279.41
literary: in l. action a man wins friends by prejudices 726.5
l. sensibility geared to the timeless 545.22
l. world made of little confederacies 545.17
llama is like an unsuccessful l. man 41.3
progress in l. style lies in the resolve to cast aside conventions of past 942.6
literature: always some pretentiousness about l. 545.30
by thought, l. becomes escape into living 93.19
convention incorporates emotions into l. 1069.47
desire to write comes from experience of l. 1069.46
difficulty of l.: to write what you mean 1069.125
for creation of l. two powers must concur 1069.7
great l. brings to birth in us the creative impulse 545.8
greatness of l. not determined by literary standards 545.6
in l. as in love, we are astonished at what is chosen by others 963.12
in l., there are only oxen 1069.115
I refuse to see l. as amusement, as a game 545.23
l. belongs to the world man constructs 545.10
l. flourishes when half trade, half art 545.16
l. is a matter of life and death 545.11
l. is a state of culture 708.55
l. is an inspiration for reality 545.12
l. is as useless as astronomy 545.5
l. is fairy land at a distance 545.18
l. is human activity that takes the fullest account of possibility, difficulty 545.28
l. strewn with wreckage of men minding others' opinion 1069.148
l. usually begets l. 545.24
l. will end up as cottage industry 545.1
perversity is the muse of modern l. 545.25
rhetoric takes no account of the art in l. 604.20
to devote oneself to l. alone is deceptive 545.14
to speak in l. with perfect rectitude of movements of animals is triumph of art 1069.144
unusual is exactly what makes l. 545.3
we hear too much of scenery in l. 545.27
with noble sentiments bad l. gets written 545.13
writers who teach tend to prefer literary theory to l. 1069.132
litigant: jurisdiction for l., not judge 61.9
l.: person about to give up skin for hope of retaining his bones 528.9
little: great fleas have l. fleas to bite 'em 669.2

in fool's petty estimate all things are l. 693.6
l. man is a bundle of contradictory elements 400.10
l. people may have charm, not beauty 72.4
l. things go lessening till God comes behind them 400.3
l. things seem nothing, but give peace 996.1
never is there any lack of a l. 701.2
whin man knows he's l., look out f'r him 908.1
who apply themselves too much to l. things become incapable of great ones 996.4
littleness: no sadder proof by man of his own l. than disbelief in great men 693.1
live: act as if you had long time to l. 771.6
ask who wants to l. to be a hundred 548.4
better l. wretched than die famous 541.10
better to die on your feet than l. on your knees 363.29
better to l. rich than to die rich 1048.29
cannot love to l. if cannot bear to die 541.32
even to l. sometimes act of courage 195.33
for the sake of a living men forget to l. 1065.32
he does not believe who does not so l. 78.3
it's nothing to die; frightful not to l. 219.5
let us l. while we l. 513.3
let us l. within our means 977.11
let us so l. that when we die even the undertaker will be sorry 221.134
l. all you can; it's a mistake not to 504.13
l. by thy light, and earth will l. by hers 444.3
l. life as it were spoil, pluck the joys 513.5
l. not as though you had a thousand years 393.4
l. with men as if God saw you 697.12
longer we l., more we find we are like others 663.9
man can't l. until reasons for living are stolen 653.60
mankind gain by suffering each other to l. 984.12
man pines to l., can't endure days of life 539.22
man should l. if only to satisfy curiosity .1
men are unconscious of their birth, suffer when they die, and neglect to l. 540.7
men should learn to deserve to l. 539.96
must spend all one's life learning to l. 541.34
my trade and art is to l. 504.17
none takes thought to l. well, only to l. long 548.12
nooses give, you might as well l. 948.18
nor love life, nor hate; but l. well 539.76
nothing meaner than anxiety to l. on 548.10
right to know is like right to l. 522.57
they l. ill who expect to l. always 548.14
to l. a life half dead, a living death 219.7
to l. is like to love—reason is against it 539.15
to l. is to be slowly born 404.26
to l. is to feel oneself lost 30.6
to l., to suffer, to fight, and to forget 606.2
to love a thing means wanting it to l. 551.26
to work, l., die hard and go to hell 416.10
we are always getting ready to l. 231.3
we l. complaining 539.41
we l. everything as it comes, without warning 77.16
we never l., but we hope to l. 539.88
what counts is not to l., but l. aright 539.114
who can l. alone resembles sage and God 915.21
who can't l. his own life lives a slave 880.13
lived: boldly say each night, I have l. today 729.7
he who hath l. ill cannot die well 221.54
man of great sensibility has l. long 548.9
lives: all great l. have contained uninteresting stretches 401.47
all l. are interesting 539.42
he preaches well that l. well 724.2
he who l. more than one life 440.22
live half our waking l. in insensible waters 539.25
matters not how man dies but how he l. 541.22
men lead l. of quiet desperation 239.11
men live l. of quiet exasperation 508.3
men spend first half of their l. making second half miserable 1072.15
most l. were alike in stages of living 540.10
one l. in the hope of becoming a memory 539.92
only he can pray well who l. well 723.13
our l. are merely strange dark interludes 539.83
our l. are not totally random 702.8
sons of famous men lead mediocre l. 916.1
we all got holes in our l. 539.33
we pass best part of l. counting on future 318.4
what l. is granted breath by death 541.4
who l. within means lacks imagination 977.10
living: all l. welcome what they can cope with 620.9
art of l. is knowing how to believe lies 539.89
art of l. is like wrestling 539.6
arts of l. well and dying well are one 541.7
cost of l. not bad if you don't have to pay for it 277.5
dying is as as natural as l. 541.16
earth belongs to l., not to the dead 539.60
half the agony of l. is waiting 1040.5
how good is mere l. 539.11
if we could wake with no memory of l. we might arrive at a faultless day 729.13
let the dead have fame, but the l. love 551.207
l. dog is better than a dead lion 539.8
l. the good life and l. a good life 539.40
l. well, beautifully, justly, are one 539.113
love of l. is the most powerful foible 539.77
my business is with the l. 610.4
my joy of l. is in battles of life 409.96
oh, the wild joys of l. 696.2
only those within whose consciousness the suns rise and set can be aware of what l. is 623.45
plain l. and high thinking are no more 701.6
reason for l. also reason for dying 541.3
reason mitigates the cruelty of l. 785.26
secret of l. is to find a pivot 443.27
snow falling faintly upon all the l. and dead 911.1
to mourn dead unduly affronts the l. 610.5
we are l., not getting ready to live 834.6
we are sentenced to death for crime of l. 12.4
we cannot be sure we have something worth l. for unless we are ready to die for it 1026.10
worst evil to give up l. before one dies 219.9
llama: l. is like an unsuccessful literary man 41.3
loaf: to err human; to l., Parisian 671.2
loafed: better to have l. and lost than never to have l. 446.16
loan: good man whom you favor with l. will feel indebted after he has paid you 96.6
l. oft loses both itself and friend 96.5
small l. makes debtor, great l. enemy 222.10
lobbyist: president only l. of whole nation 730.18
loftiest: l. edifices need deepest foundations 401.49
l. towers rise from the ground 401.5
lofty: hurricane attacks only the l. trees 733.15
logic: l. and sermons never convince 692.4
l.: art of reasoning in accordance with limitations of human misunderstanding 785.3
l. is like sword: appeal to it, perish by it 785.4
l. is not satisfied with assertion 785.16
l. is one thing, human animal another 785.24
l. is the art of making truth prevail 785.18
men purchase peace at expense of l. 734.5
mind all l. is like knife all blade 785.37
pure l. is the ruin of the spirit 785.30
the l. of one year is a folly of the next 972.14
want of l. annoys; too much l. bores 785.13

what eludes l. is our most precious element 785.14
logical: l. consequences are the scarecrows of fools 176.7
mind of man is more intuitive than l. 590.21
logician: l. needs sun to draw him forth from his logic 785.31
London: hell a populous, smoky city much like L. 416.11
the nightglow of L., city of cities 546.4
there is in L. all life can afford 546.3
loneliness: a l. they are not liable to notice 334.1
create communities in which l. can be cured 547.12
fearing l. more than bondage, we marry 564.26
lack of money, above all, means l. 718.46
l. is bred of a mind grown earthbound 547.9
love is principal means of escape from l. 551.177
man's l. is but his fear of life 547.8
most pervasive American disease was l. 547.11
music was invented to confirm human l. 614.31
no deeper l. than to tread silent, deserted scene of former throng 676.20
no l. is greater than l. of a failure 329.12
our l. makes us avid column readers 547.3
the l. that only the sleepless know 73.4
what l. is more lonely than distrust 259.3
who knows what true l. is 547.2
lonely: l. man is eaten up by himself 547.6
l. one offers his hand too quickly 547.7
we go l., side by side but not together 149.13
lonesome: millions listen to the same joke, yet remain l. 967.5
long: man wants to live l. but not be old 548.13
longing: l., unwavering passion of commerce 238.7
look: l. at all things with a mental squint 708.15
only those at levers of control have chance to l. out for themselves 459.6
looks: if character's right, l. are a delight 119.23
many complain of l., none of brains 493.32
we can't all combine good l. and brains 542.10
we love good l., though they may destroy 45.16
loquacity: l.: renders sufferer unable to curb tongue when you wish to talk 923.10
l. storms the ear, modesty the heart 600.6
Lord: except L. build house, labour is in vain 126.2
if the L. had appointed her to marriage 564.50
lose: better to l. the saddle than the horse 162.5
if fate means you to l., give a fight 340.13
it is more necessary to l. than gain 201.33
never contend with man who has nothing to l. 345.3
no man can l. what he never had 550.11
to l. oneself is to be gainer 1021.3
whatever you can l., reckon of no account 550.8
when we l. one we love, bitterest tears are for hours we loved not enough 610.8
you must l. a fly to catch a trout 550.3
loser's: in life the l. score is always zero 549.1
losers: all men are mortal and therefore l. 329.23
loses: who l. all often l. himself 434.2
wise man never l. anything if he has self 880.15
losing: by l. himself man becomes something 504.10
l., bane of every athlete's existence 929.2
one vexed at l. game by single hole 329.10
loss: good man must rather sit with l. than rise unjust 550.4
l. is nothing else but change 550.1
l. shapes image of lost treasures 550.2
l. which is unknown is no l. at all 550.7
prefer l. to dishonest gain 738.3
sometimes better incur l. than make gain 550.6
who possesses most is most afraid of l. 716.9
world so quickly readjusts after l. 221.135
losses: base gains are the same as l. 738.5
end to gettings is only end to l. 8.8
lost: lived and loved and died, always l. 228.6
make wherever we're l. in look like home 12.2
lottery: adventure all tickets in l., you lose 369.7
love: absence sharpens l. 2.6
absences a good influence in l. 2.10
advice on rules of l. like advice on rules of madness 551.217
against great advantages in another, no means of defending ourselves except l. 15.5
alas! how light a cause may move dissension between hearts that l. 551.139
all is lawful in l., which is lawless 551.120
all I want is boundless l. 551.149
all l. is sweet, given or returned 551.198
all of those I l. make me laugh 551.4
all thoughts, passions are ministers of l. 551.24
all wurruld is l., soft, sweet an' sticky 551.51
always some madness in l. 551.147
as l. crowns so shall he crucify you 551.78
back-breaking labor of l. for twenty minutes 892.10
base men in l. gain a nobility 551.188
beggary in the l. that can be reckoned 551.196
begin l. when you like, stop when you can 551.200
best of a man's life, his acts of l. 519.22
between whom there is truth there is l. 998.121
body seeks what injured the mind with l. 892.30
broken heart: monument to never-dying l. 551.145
cannot satisfy sexual instinct without l. 892.46
charm of falling in l.: l. isn't lasting 551.136
course of true l. never did run smooth 551.195
deepest l. turneth to deadliest hate 554.6
defenceless against suffering when we l. 552.4
desire in those who l. to hear of lovers' pains 555.7
disposed to make l. at the drop of a hat 742.1
doubting l., we end by doubting everything 1005.1
embarrassed alone together when l. begins, dies 551.104
erotic l. begins with separateness, ends in oneness 551.68
eternal l. doth keep earth, air, deep 551.15
every l.'s the l. before in duller dress 551.156
exploring how we can truly learn to l. 927.7
familiar acts are beautiful through l. 333.11
family l. is messy 551.150
far from lips we l., we make l. to lips near 472.8
fill a woman with l. of herself 198.3
for one human to l. another is the most difficult of all tasks 551.174
give little l. to child, get great deal 123.47
give me more l. or more disdain 598.2
god could hardly l. and be wise 551.166
greater l. hath no man than this, that he lay down his life for his friends 837.1
greatest pain is to l. in vain 553.1
great secret of morals is l. 604.36
hail, wedded l. 564.81
hardly any activity is started with such hopes, and fails so regularly, as l. 551.71
hatred conquered by l. passes into l. 554.10
hatred, ignorant l. have same ends 554.3
hatred is blind, as well as l. 554.2
hatred paralyzes life; l. releases it 554.4
heaven has no rage like l. turned to hate 793.1
he that shuts l. out, shall be shut out from l. 551.214
he whom l. touches not walks in darkness 53.106
hell, madame, is to l. no longer 416.3
hours in l. have wings 2.2
how great l. is, presence best trial 2.4
if delight in l., 'tis when I see heart which others bleed for, bleed for me 551.27

if he do not propose right true end of l. 892.18
if thou rememberest not the folly of l. 551.190
impossible to l. again what we ceased to l. 552.5
in abstract l. of humanity one loves oneself 433.12
in friendship is sympathy; in l., antipathy 551.23
in l. not wise; when wise not in l. 551.168
in l. one begins by deceiving one's self 551.231
intense mutual erotic l. is rare 551.141
is beauty not enough, why do I cry for l. 551.212
it is impossible to l. and be wise 551.5
it is not l. that is blind, but jealousy 510.7
it is possible to bind people in l. 1016.4
it takes two to make a l. affair 551.127
lasting l. best proves strength of mind 181.4
let him be great and l. shall follow him 401.11
let the dead have fame, but the living l. 551.207
lies kill l.: what about frankness 362.6
life finds its worth by the claims of l. 504.22
life less broken after l. affair if one can feel sinful rather than a fool 552.7
life without l.: mere magic-lantern show 551.80
loss of l. is a terrible thing 552.3
l., a disease to be born with patience 551.1
l. affair with earth and sky 623.49
l., all alike, no season knows, nor clime 551.43
l. all l. of other sights controls 551.40
l. and scandal are best sweeteners of tea 846.1
l., appalling bore once you cease loving 552.1
l. at first sight, l.[ove] everlasting 551.122
l. based on good disposition endures 392.7
l. built on beauty soon as beauty dies 551.41
l. cannot save life from death 551.223
l. charms by display, not by merit 551.106
l., children, work: sources of contact 504.20
l. compels cruelty to those who do not understand l. 551.54
l.: cure for blunders, blindness, crime 798.2
l. demands infinitely less than friendship 365.76
l.: desire for that which flies from us 551.137
l. dies only when growth stops 551.16
l., exhausting by its steady drain on strength 551.2
l. fears change more than destruction 551.146
l. fed fat soon turns to boredom 551.152
l., felt in the desire for shared sleep 551.102
l. flies at sight of human ties 551.161
l. for one, from which springs not l. for all, is but worthless 551.118
l. frees us of weight and pain of life 551.199
l.-god inflames more fiercely the reluctant 551.219
l. goes out gate which suspicion enters 259.4
l.: happiness of another essential to own 551.89
l. has come to involve a measure of hatred 551.86
l. has features which pierce all hearts 551.227
l. has no language to be heard 551.28
l. has various lodgings 551.228
l., if l. be perfect, casts our fear 554.11
l. in a hut is cinders, ashes, dust 718.41
l. in public affairs does not work 551.66
l. is admiring, cherishing the beloved, on condition you are object of their action 551.22
l. is a driver, bitter if you fight him 551.153
l. is a great good in every wise 551.99
l. is a migraine, blotting out reason 551.84
l. is a naked child 551.154
l. is an end in itself 551.204
l. is a spirit all compact of fire 551.191
l. is a tender look that becomes a habit 551.225
l. is a thing of moods, not of law 551.132
l. is a tyrant sparing none 551.29
l. is a tyrant, resisted 551.65
l. is all we have, only way to help 551.61
l. is born of and fostered by idleness 446.12
l. is done when l.'s begun 551.35
l. is essentially sacrificial 551.182
l. is growing or full constant light 551.42
l. is heaven, and heaven is l. 551.185
l. is immortality 551.36
l. is intercourse between tyrants, slaves 551.81
l. is like shabby hotels 551.222
l. is nature's second sun 551.21
l. is not all: it is not meat nor drink 551.135
l. is not always blind 551.128
l. is not dumb; heart speaks many ways 551.169
l. is not l. which alters 552.14
l. is reciprocated by l. 788.3
l. is strong as death 510.3
l. is the bright foreigner 551.56
l. is the child of illusion and the parent of disillusion 551.224
l. is the irresistible desire to be desired irresistibly 551.79
l. is the joy of the good 551.160
l. is the only gold 551.216
l. is the slowest of all growths 564.128
l. is the true price of l. 551.91
l. is to gaze outward together 551.179
l. is true seed of every merit in you 551.31
l. is unbearable at full strength 551.226
l. is union retaining separateness 551.70
l. is unto itself a higher law 551.8
l. is what we were born with 551.234
l. is wisdom of the fool, folly of the wise 551.97
l. is woman's whole existence, not man's 581.10
l. is, above all, the gift of oneself 551.3
l., itch, and cough cannot be hid 551.74
l. joins and then divides 551.53
l. knows hidden paths 551.77
l. knows not own depth until separation 673.3
l., let us be true to one another 1067.1
l., like a tear, rises in the eye 551.167
l. limits our possibilities 551.45
l. lives on hope, dies when hope is dead 551.30
l. looks not with eyes, but with mind 551.192
l. makes time pass; time makes l. pass 551.67
l. makes use of the worst traps 551.75
l.: means of escape from loneliness 551.177
l. must not touch marrow of soul 551.62
l.: mystery nothing else can explain 551.209
l. needs no logic for its mission 551.117
l. never ends in friendship 551.25
l., not reason, stronger than death 551.124
l. of life can defeat l. for the dead 541.14
l. often but encounter of two weaknesses 551.130
l.: often nothing but a favorable exchange 551.69
l. of women is lovely and fearful 1062.16
l. only what is woven in your destiny 240.2
l. or perish not same as mingle or fail 152.13
l. rarer than genius, friendship more rare 365.80
l. reckons every absence an age 551.49
l. remains a secret even when spoken 551.208
l. resembles hatred more than friendship 554.5
lover made happier by l. than loved one 555.6
l. should be practiced like Lent 551.114
l. simple to understand: it's a crutch 551.121
l. sought is good; given unsought, better 551.193
l. that is fed by jealousy dies hard 510.15
l., the spear singing through the mind 551.60
l. to meet the guy I'm supposed to be 444.14
l. unworldly; nothing comes of it but l. 551.233
l. we give away is only l. we keep 551.92
l. weakens with age like all human energies 653.30
l., which, sexual or non-sexual, is hard work 31.6

l. with its joy clears the vision 551.98
l., with very young, is heartless 551.37
l. won't be tampered with 551.59
l. yourself with wholesome, healthy l. 876.11
man saves l. for woman with whom he may feel drowsy 551.144
man who, on grounds of decorum and morality, avoids game of l. is a cad 551.131
many waters cannot quench l. 551.6
marriage is the perfection l. aimed at 564.33
marriage without l., l. without marriage 472.3
minds conquered by l., magnanimity 173.14
money has a power to manage l. 602.9
more easy to end l. than moderate it 551.187
more violent the l., more violent the anger 551.17
much may be done by l. 517.18
need outward show to conclude inward l. 551.44
need we say it was no l. because it perished 552.9
no disguise can hide l. or simulate it 551.109
no harvest for heart; l. must be resown 551.116
no l. for friend whose l. is words 365.95
no man dies for l., but on the stage 551.48
none l., but they who wish to l. 551.170
no oath secures l. against a higher l. 551.57
no redeeming qualities in me but sincere l. for some things 725.6
no remedy for l. but to l. more 551.218
no vocabulary for l. within a family 334.12
not to believe in l. is sign of dullness 551.183
O Lyric L., half angel and half bird 551.14
one cannot be strong without l. 551.220
one must eat of l. where it hangs 551.134
only l. of friends is worth wear of winning 365.15
only l. should rule between man and wife 564.98
only they conquer l. that run away 551.19
only victory in l. is flight 551.143
ownership, not l., causes suffering 551.180
pains of l. sweeter than all pleasures 551.50
perfect l. casteth out fear 551.7
perjuries of l. blown away by winds 857.12
pity beyond telling is in heart of l. 551.237
pity melts the mind to l. 698.9
pleasant words are the food of l. 923.45
pleasure of l. is in loving 551.110
pleasure of l. lasts but a moment, pain of l. lasts a lifetime 551.33
problem of existence is we do not l. 100.14
proof of l.: to be unsparing in criticism 206.16
prosperity's the very bond of l. 750.14
richest l. submits to arbitration of time 551.52
robing, disrobing, is true traffic of l. 892.31
small hope sufficient for birth of l. 551.205
so many hearts, so many kinds of l. 551.221
something in heart of l. is pathetic 551.173
so primal is a woman with the l.-madness 1062.15
take l. when l. is given 551.213
there are always some whom one can l. 100.4
there can be no peace of mind in l. 551.163
there is a warning l. sends 551.181
they do not l. that do not show their l. 551.197
they l. too much that die for l. 551.58
things are beautiful if you l. them 72.3
thinks of her sewing when she's making l. 892.39
this bane, the boon of all alive, is l. 551.34
those who l. not fellow-beings live unfruitful lives 100.15
those whom we can l., we can hate 794.13
those whose suffering is due to l. are their own physicians 551.164
though got by chance, l. is kept by art 551.38
time strengthens friendship, weakens l. 551.103
'Tis much to gain universal admiration; more, universal l. 551.83
'Tis not l.'s going hurts my days 552.10
to be wise and l. exceeds man's might 1060.54
to fall in l.: to create a religion that has a fallible god 551.9
to fear l. is to fear life 219.8
to hell, my l., with you 880.19
to inspire l. is woman's ambition 1062.98
to live is like to l.—reason is against it 539.15
to l. a thing means wanting it to live 551.26
to l. feebly is to languish 551.64
to l. is to endure 551.175
to l. nothing is not to live 551.64
to l. oneself is to begin a long romance 876.20
to l. simply, know how to show l. 551.46
to l., that's the point 551.142
true l. is but a humble, low-born thing 551.119
true l. like ghosts, talked of but unseen 551.111
two that l. one another equally well 551.232
variety needed in sex, but not in l. 551.172
we cry on passers-by to l. us 547.10
we don't l. qualities, we l. persons 551.125
we l. and hate without reason 554.8
we l. animals, children at expense of men 551.184
we l. each other three months 564.124
we learn only from those we l. 532.6
we must always l. something 551.157
we must be different to l. each other 551.76
we never know the l. of our parents for us till we have become parents 670.6
we never l. a person, but qualities 551.158
we often pass from l. to ambition 33.15
we put l. where we have put labor 1065.26
we really l. our neighbor as ourselves 858.17
what bloom is to fruit, novelty is to l. 551.112
what force is more potent than l. 201.41
what is done for l. is felt to be done for l. 901.6
what is faith, l., virtue alone 330.26
what is first l. worth 551.88
what power has l. but forgiveness 359.16
whatever is done for l. always occurs beyond good and evil 227.21
when in l. a man submits to everything 551.148
when l. sickens, it useth ceremony 552.15
when l. suppressed, hate takes its place 554.1
when we lose one we l., bitterest tears are for hours we loved not enough 610.8
when we l. we lend qualities to beloved 551.176
when we l., we doubt what we most believe 551.113
when you l. you wish to do things for 551.90
when you l., saved-up wishes come out 551.11
where l. fails we espy all faults 552.13
where there is l., there is pain 551.201
where there's no jealousy there's no l. 510.10
while God waits for His temple to be built of l., men bring stones 126.11
who cares not whom I l., loves not me 466.1
who has not made a fool of himself in l. 551.171
who is in l. with himself has few rivals 876.8
with l. one can live without happiness 551.47
you don't have to deserve your mother's l. 670.21
you must l. him, ere to you he seem worthy of your l. 551.236

love's: at l. height no interest in environment 555.9
l. all in all to women 1062.50
l. best habit is a soothing tongue 551.194
l. gift waits to be accepted 551.210
l. mysteries in souls do grow 892.17
l. of king's dominion admits of no partition 551.155
nothing half so sweet as l. young dream 551.140
pains are seasoning to l. delicious fare 551.229

the faithless know l. tragedies 472.15
true l. the gift God gave to man alone 551.186
loved: better to have l. and lost 551.215
if you'd be l., be worthy to be l. 551.151
is it so small a thing to have l. 504.2
l., because it was he, because it was I 365.74
nothing can be l. unless it is known 1007.12
painful to be l. when we no longer love 552.2
supreme happiness is conviction we are l. 551.94
to be l. at first sight 551.206
to be l. long 351.9
to be l. means to be consumed 551.175
to mention thing l.: to invest it with reality 784.11
who ever l., that l. not at first sight 551.126
women I have l. I have desired for themselves 581.18
loveless: better be left by dears than lie in l. bed 504.19
loveliest: l. are things that soonest pass away 990.5
l. things come simply 899.10
loveliness: l. is when unadorned adorned the most 72.59
spend all you have for l. 72.57
lovely: look for l. thing and you will find it 72.56
l. face is the solace of wounded hearts 326.7
lover: all mankind love a l. 555.5
an angry l. tells himself many lies 555.15
everything disturbs an absent l. 555.2
like any l., he desired to please 555.13
l. is a monotheist 555.17
l. made happier by love than loved one 555.6
l., poet, are of imagination all compact 559.16
l. without indiscretion no l. at all 555.10
no fury like woman searching for new l. 1062.32
of all affliction taught a l. yet 555.14
only a l. truly knows that he is loved 551.208
the face of a l. is an unknown 555.1
who has not been l. is like unused cup 551.100
write what woman says to l. on water 1062.20
lovers: all really great l. are articulate 857.8
anger of l. renews their love 555.20
for l., touch is metamorphosis 555.4
l. are always talking of themselves 555.12
l. establish their own rules of the game 555.11
l. industrious to make selves uneasy 555.3
l. know what they want, not what they need 555.16
l. swear more performance than they are able 555.18
pair of l. are sufficient to themselves 555.9
there are no ugly l. nor handsome prisons 58.3
true l. do not write of their happiness 555.8
loves: each man kills the thing he l. 551.230
fear woman who l.; all else has no value 1062.102
half our standards come from first l. 473.7
hardest to close open hand because one l. 384.23
heart that no longer l., hates 552.12
he only may chastise who l. 766.18
he who l. others is loved by them 788.2
he who l. the more is the inferior 551.123
human nature l. more readily than hates 431.8
no good comes of having two l. 181.2
one l. people for benevolence and virtue 551.159
time turns l. into corpses or wives 978.67
warmed-over l. and soups not recommended 552.16
when one l. somebody, everything is clear 551.82
who wants to do good knocks at gate; who l. finds it open 433.30
whoso l. believes the impossible 551.13
loveth: he prayeth best who l. best 723.8
he that l. maketh his own the grandeur he loves 551.55
loving: beauty hath no true glass, but l. eyes 72.29
l. becomes one with social existence 913.9
l. everybody is polygamy 742.4
l. is half of believing 78.8
l. more pleasant than being loved 551.73
nearer l. those who hate us than owe us 647.5
no person l. himself is alone 876.12
obstacle in our l. men is their self-love 876.3
restraints to refrain from l. often more cruel than severities of our beloved 551.108
the l. are the daring 551.211
we cease l. ourselves if no one loves us 551.202
loving-kindness: l. is the better part of goodness 393.31
low: destestation of the high is homage of l. 780.2
lowliness: l. is young ambition's ladder 945.40
loyal: young l. to individuals, old to types 556.2
loyalty: l. the same if it win or lose the game 556.1
my l. to country, not officeholders 678.22
luck: art is in love with l., and l. with art 53.1
care and diligence bring l. 281.7
don't envy men because they have run of l. 360.9
go and wake up your l. 291.6
good l. needs no explanation 360.2
greatest good l.: to die at right time 401.28
have but l., you will have the rest 360.20
l. is not chance—it's toil 360.7
l. isn't mentioned before self-made men 360.42
l. is the prerogative of valiant souls 360.27
l. never made a man wise 360.33
pleasant to see enemy have ill l. 288.6
protected man doesn't need l. 856.8
shallow men believe in l. 110.3
some folk want their l. buttered 360.17
to believe in l. is skepticism 360.8
true l. consists not in holding best cards 369.4
who glories in l. may be overthrown 360.12
who has good l. is good 360.3
women try their l.; men risk theirs 564.135
lucky: l. person passes for a genius 360.10
ludicrous: any idea may be shown in l. light 4.2
lunatic: l. is lost if he allows a sane eye to peer into his locked universe 559.2
l., lover, are of imagination all compact 559.16
sometimes find something good in l. fringe 776.6
lunch: man may be a pessimistic determinist before l. 274.17
lust: hell has three gates: l., anger, greed 416.4
l. and force source of all actions 9.31
l. too is a jewel 892.44
who has no l. is safe among things of l. 770.2
luxuries: give me l.; will do without necessities 557.8
luxury: a l.: talk about self-esteem 869.13
l. corrupts rich and poor 557.4
l., more savage than war 681.14
mankind seduced by l. cannot renounce it 557.5
men grow dissolute in l., then go mad 557.7
lying: in plain truth, l. is an accursed vice 558.28
l. is acknowledgment of force of truth 558.19
l. is necessary and unavoidable 558.25
l. is the proper aim of art 53.147
l., the art form the public sanctions 558.9
she was l. but it was a brave lie 558.14
we have to revive the old art of l. 558.45

M

macaroni: boil up m. and then grate cheese on it 355.10
machine gun: amid m. fire you notice your skin 343.12
machine: m. consumes more energy than it renders 1017.2
m. never wastes anybody's time 966.30
m. plunges man more deeply into problems of nature 966.29

no m. can do work of extraordinary man 966.12
nothing inhuman about an intelligent m. 493.27
we have forgotten beast and flower in order to forget everything except the m. 966.17
when m. runs without human aid, scrap it 966.4
you cannot endow m. with initiative 966.18
machines: seems m. make all the chief appointments 966.27
mad: better m. with the rest than wise alone 559.8
everyone is more or less m. on one point 559.9
fortune, to destroy, first makes m. 559.14
I hope He comes back *mad* His own self 511.4
imagination is the m. boarder 450.21
less harm in being m. among madmen 559.3
most men are m. when they act 9.19
pleasure in being m. none but madmen know 559.4
stupidity often saves a man from going m. 941.10
the m. also laugh 527.5
we are all born m.; some remain so 559.1
when we remember we are all m. 559.18
made: stick to the thing for which one was m. 1.10
madmen: world is full of simpletons and m. 559.7
madness: almost every man, woman has dash of m. 559.5
always m. in love but also reason in m. 551.147
be sure your m. corresponds to your era 332.49
carry common sense itself almost to the point of m. 34.38
in some accidents need m. to extricate us 559.10
m. is to reason correctly from erroneous perceptions 559.19
m. is wisdom to those to whom it happens 559.6
m., suffering can set themselves no limit 559.15
no great genius without some m. 376.2
not to be mad would be form of m. 559.13
proof of m. is disproportion of designs to means 559.12
recognize romantic love as a form of m. 551.63
sanity is a m. put to good uses 842.3
society's m. seems normal to itself 171.2
magic: opposition between m. and science 719.9
where we have buried the silent races we've buried much of m. of life 133.17
without m., life would be one long panic 849.8
magnanimity: m. in politics is the truest wisdom 711.16
m. is the rarest virtue 375.5
m. will not consider prudence of its motives 375.8
minds conquered by love, m. 173.14
magnanimous: who fears being duped cannot be m. 259.1
Mahomet: The merit of M. is that he founded a religion without an inferno 416.9
maiden: if heart of m. stolen, m. steals after it 198.11
maids: all are good m.—whence come bad wives 1062.48
m. are May when they are m. 564.107
mail: m. is the consolation of life 535.5
m. on the doormat, the usual things 535.1
majority: all politics based on indifference of m. 711.72
in thinking, the m. is always wrong 233.7
m. best, yet opinion of least able 233.41
m. is always the best repartee 51.7
one on God's side is a m. 387.57
security of identification with the m. 171.9
will of m. in all cases to prevail 823.11
wobbly m. falls to resolute minority 591.2
make-believe: man lives not by truth but by m. 449.14
maladjusted: salvation lies in hands of creatively m. 201.21
maladjustment: much m. is caused by ignorance 447.16
malaria: riddled with m. for years on end 896.17
malcontents: nation without m. is without seed of future 621.9
male: challenge to m. dominance and m. centrality 892.51
innate superiority of m. is in muscle 582.10
m.: member of the negligible sex 582.3
triumph of civilization: taming human m. 133.18
malice: accusing is proving, with m. as judge 5.1
m. often takes the garb of truth 561.4
m. swallows greater part of its own venom 561.12
man loves m. against the fortunate, proud 561.7
man's life is warfare against m. of men 561.3
meekness is the mask of m. 435.11
miseries spring from stupidity, m. 335.8
our nature holds much envy and m. 295.20
when m. has reason on its side 561.10
with m. toward none, charity for all 1016.6
world's ignorance exposes one to its m. 618.2
malicious: don't trust a m. man 561.9
m. have a dark happiness 561.5
nothing is proof against m. tongues 561.8
malt: m., more than Milton, justifies God to man 268.27
mammal: man can be defined as a languagized m. 41.17
Mammon: who serve God and M. find there is no God 497.4
man: a bad odor about a m. who's been betrayed 79.3
absence of pretension marks m. of world 917.3
alas for this mad melancholy beast m. 562.45
a m. has his personal scent 208.1
a m. is always a prey to his truths 998.16
a m. is virtually everything 562.50
a m. should love his sons in equal measure 670.7
a m. who combs his hair while still in pyjamas 958.1
as an infant, m. is wrapped in mother's womb; grown up, in custom; dead, in earth 540.11
as for m., his days are as grass 990.3
be more than m. or thou'rt less than ant 952.3
by losing himself m. becomes something 504.10
ceases to be simply a black m. 85.1
child is father of the m. 404.30
disappointed in monkey, God invented m. 308.18
diverse elements joined in heart of m. 260.2
each has day when he must accept he is a m. 542.1
every m. is a m. of the day 589.1
every m. is to be had some way 857.3
every other m. is a piece of myself 562.40
family of m. more than three billion strong 562.30
finished m. of world eats of each apple 917.2
from right angle, m. shows depth, beauty 687.3
God makes, but money finishes, the m. 602.23
how dark the ways of god to m. 754.5
how easily m. is disturbed, put out of order 627.1
if a m. is vain, flatter him 349.6
it is m. who has destroyed m. 241.9
it takes longer for m. to find out m. than any other creature 1008.1
keeping the peace with the m. in one's life 581.15
like leaves on trees the race of m. is found 374.6
machine cannot do work of extraordinary m. 966.12
m., an island in only sense that matters 504.15
m. appoints and God disappoints 387.21
m.: beautiful machine that works badly 562.39
m. can be as big as he wants 737.4
m. can be best or worst of animals 562.3
m. can be justly punished if he offends 562.55
m. can deceive a woman by sham attachment 857.7
m. cannot emerge from himself 858.24
m. consists of the faith that is in him 330.3
m. determines what is said,

not words 923.62
m. drinks without thirst, makes love anytime 562.6
m. exists for his own sake 132.2
m. feels himself to be a commodity 105.6
m. half-way between ape and god 562.29
m. has in him water's silence, earth's noise, and bird's song 562.56
m. has risen so far above other species 155.9
m. hath all which nature hath, but more 562.4
m., in the ideal, is noble and sparkling 562.38
m. is a fighting animal 443.31
m. is a free creative spirit 201.7
m. is a masterpiece of creation 363.33
m. is a mind betrayed by his organs 589.5
m. is a misfit from the start 562.22
m. is an exception, whatever else he is 562.13
m. is a shaper of the landscape 562.10
m. is a simple being 562.26
m. is at bottom an animal, midway a citizen, at top divine 562.7
m. is a wolf to those he does not know 358.5
m. is a wretch without woman 581.23
m. is bound to pursue his own ends 956.4
m. is but a reed, a thinking reed 975.35
m. is but the place where I stand 1017.16
m. is by nature a political animal 711.9
m. is by nature indolent 406.6
m. is depressed until woman appears 581.19
m. is for woman a means to a child 564.94
m. is God by his faculty for thought 261.7
m. is like phonograph with few records 582.11
m. is machine for turning wine into urine 562.15
m. is m. only by the heart 562.1
m. is more childlike than woman 581.44
m. is more interesting than men 469.8
m. is nature's sole mistake 562.24
m. is neither angel nor beast 691.8
m. is not contributary but total creature 562.16
m. is obviously made to think 975.36
m. is only animal for whom existence is a problem 316.3
m. is only animal that blushes 893.8
m. is only animal that doubts death 221.67
m. is rooted to the land 423.1
m. is the animal that can say "I" 858.14
m. is the cruelest animal 209.13
m. is the measure of all things 562.36
m. is the most extraordinary computer 966.14
m. is the sum of what he could have 717.4
m. is the thing that m. understands least 562.54
m. knows nothing without being taught 988.6
m., like Deity, creates in own image 201.20
m., like spider, may spin his citadel 450.18
m. loves woman with whom he may feel drowsy 551.144
m. made to eat ices, not pore over texts 848.13
m. only animal that can be bored 94.6
m. readier to feel than to think 284.8
m.'s inhumanity to m. makes thousands mourn 209.4
m.'s misfortunes occasioned by m. 17.46
m. speaks when he can't find clean socks 581.28
m., subject hard to form any judgment on 562.43
m., the great amateur of the animal kingdom 562.18
m., the most complicated of the animals 404.11
m. the only being who knows he's alone 915.35
m., thou feeble tenant of an hour 562.11
m., unconscious of primitive elements of life 133.19
m. wants what he is supposed to want 238.11
m. who is really a m. must learn to be alone 880.21
m. who m. would be must rule himself 862.14
m. without a saving touch of woman in him 582.7
m.: worse than animal when he's an animal 209.16
manly m. lacks wit to realize dreams 566.4
measure of a m.: his stand at time of challenge 252.7
measure value of m. only by other men 1026.15
men are cruel, but m. is kind 519.19
modern m. a means; end not his business 1001.7
noblest work of God: m.; who found it out: m. 562.60
no m. worth having is true to his wife 472.13
no slight attainment to fulfill what nature of m. implies 562.23
nothing on earth more dismal than m. 562.28
oh the little that unhinges m. 627.3
only m. works on self with inborne stings 174.4
pity is not natural to m. 209.9
principal difference between dog and m. 475.8
proper study of mankind is m. 875.22
raging tiger inside every m. 862.7
shadow of a dream is m., no more 990.12
shall m. hang self because he is pygmy 877.4
silliest woman can manage a clever m. 356.16
so many times is he a m. as he has languages, friends, arts, trades 1.3
stages of m.: infancy, childhood, adolescence, obsolescence 540.9
state made for m., not m. for state 930.8
talk to every m. as if he bored you 961.4
test of m.: coping with female hysteria 581.70
that m. is wolf to m. is a libel on the wolf 41.11
the fiction that m. is incapable of housework 581.7
there must be something unique about m. 493.4
to be a m. is to be responsible 810.10
to do all one able to do: to be a m. 504.18
to himself m. is most wonderful object 589.9
tragic writer must believe in m. 987.8
trouble with m. is m. 562.59
what a chimera then is m. 562.47
what a piece of work is m. 562.53
what is m., ally of God or simply his toy? 562.62
what is m. in nature? nothing, all 562.46
when a m., I put away childish things 571.2
where's m. could ease heart like satin gown 267.18
where there are no men, strive to be a m. 491.11
while a m. exists there is need of him 316.2
who is m. enough releases woman in woman 581.43
why does m. wish to be made sad by seeing tragical things 987.2
world is a great volume, m. the index 1067.7
manhood: in m. we tell dreams of childhood 580.40
m. and sagacity ripen of themselves 404.27
mankind: all think their little set m. 910.8
expect best, worst from m. and weather 562.61
expose not the secret failings of m. 206.23
know more of m., expect less of them 393.24
m. are disposed to suffer evils 806.7
m. are earthen jugs with spirits in them 562.27
m. either Sancho Panzas or Quixotes 562.51
m. has become so much one family 151.9
m. moves so slowly 562.25
m. will perish through eternal peace 681.10
more fellowship among snakes than m. 209.10
my country is world; countrymen, m. 100.6
no sense of what goes on in mind of m. 562.58
our true nationality is m. 100.17
to be religious, identify with m. 711.29
to fly from, need not be to hate, m. 915.7
to think ill of m., and not wish m. ill, is perhaps highest wisdom, virtue 120.6
mankind's: all m. concern is charity 120.8
manly: Florence is a m. town 131.32
man of letters: once a writer became a m., he was done

for 732.15
man's: every m. life ends the same way 541.21
m. main task is to give birth to himself 201.15
m. marvelous plasticity of mind 562.9
m. meat is often a woman's poison 551.127
m. women folk regard him as an ass 581.40
woman is m. confusion 581.64
manna: without daily m., he must go backward who would most advance 927.4
manner: bad m. spoils everything; good one supplies everything 563.14
m. is substitute for genius, sense, wit 942.4
manners: evil communications corrupt good m. 473.1
fine m. need support of others' fine m. 563.8
good m., what everyone thinks should be done 563.18
is man a savage with fragile m. 562.5
learning nothing without cultivated m. 210.19
man in power puts on new m. 719.22
marriage very rarely mends a man's m. 564.24
men grow used to everything but living in society which has not their own m. 563.7
there is nothing settled in m. 563.12
we are not justified in enforcing good m. 563.6
manuscript: unpublished m. is like unconfessed sin 1069.83
manuscripts: I learned that all of my m. have been rejected three or four times 1069.123
many: cow of m.: well milked, badly fed 150.17
March: in M. a new year begins 854.30
weeping gloom of M. and April 854.20
mariner: m. must have his eye upon rocks 720.3
smooth sea never made a skillful m. 245.2
marital: on m. voyage, you explore enclosed basin 564.31
mark: if you would hit the m., aim above it 55.11
market: a m. system that has proved so obdurate 279.50
fortune like m. where price may fall 360.1
there are two fools in every m. 104.28
marksman: good m. may miss 542.7
marriage: accident counts for much in m. 116.1
birds outside m. despair to enter cage 564.86
chains of m. are so heavy 564.29
combining m., children, and career 564.120
common impulse is not to sustain a m. 564.64
courtship to m. is a witty prologue to a dull play 198.4
far from natural to live in state of m. 564.67
ideal mother, like ideal m., is a fiction 670.45
if m. fails, those married live in hell 564.39
in good m. each appoints the other guardian of his solitude 564.102
keep your eyes wide open before m. 564.43
m., a recognition of spiritual identity 564.18
m., a weaving together of families 564.88
m. based on theory that man who likes a certain beer should work in the brewery 564.92
m. calls for love of one's neighbor 564.103
m. cannot be a *job* 564.54
m. combines temptation and opportunity 564.111
m. doesn't have to get anywhere 564.89
m.: feast where grace better than dinner 564.23
m. field of battle, not bed of roses 564.122
m. has pains, celibacy no pleasures 66.4
m. is a bribe to make a housekeeper think she's a householder 564.137
m. is an economic necessity 564.42
m. is an ordeal 564.17
m. is as demoralizing as cigarettes 564.130
m. is one long conversation 564.123
m. is the only evil men pray for 564.53
m. is the perfection love aimed at 564.33
m. is three parts love and seven parts forgiveness of sins 564.83
m. is tolerable if you're easy-going 564.110
m. is to morality as licensed liquor traffic is to sobriety 268.54
m. makes a woman like a public building 564.134
m. makes life of deception necessary 564.133
m. may qualify the fury of man's passion 564.24
m. not a partnership, for gain is unequal 564.78
m. promises happiness, death assures it 564.127
m. resembles a pair of shears 564.115
m., sacrifice to unity in a relationship 564.16
m. shakes a man's confidence in himself 564.80
m. was all a woman's idea 564.79
m. without love, love without m. 472.3
more to m. than four legs in bed 564.46
mother weeps at her daughter's m. 218.9
our m. is dead when pleasure is fled 262.3
second m.: triumph of hope over experience 564.65
there's no lovelier relationship than good m. 564.76
tragedies end by death; comedies, by m. 145.2
what else goes wrong for woman but her m. 1062.53
whether to make him end in Hell or in an unhappy m. 564.14
marriages: best m. are preceded by long courtship 198.1
capacity of women to make unsuitable m. 564.1
if couples lived apart m. would be happier 564.93
there are some good m., none delightful 564.74
married: dread of loneliness is greater than the fear of bondage, so we get m. 564.26
he had m. on the rebound 564.56
in m. life three is company and two is none 564.131
m. life, the doormat to the whorehouse 564.118
m. love is bigger than oaths 564.2
m. people interrupt each other's stories 564.114
m. state is compleatest image of heaven and hell we can have in this life 564.117
one was never m., and that's his hell 564.12
strange delight we m. people have to see these fools decoyed to our condition 564.100
sum m. couple owe to each other infinite 564.51
when a woman gets m. it's like jumping into a hole in the ice 564.52
when m. people don't get on they separate; if they're not m., it's impossible 499.5
woman's business to get m. soon as possible 564.109
marries: who m. woman to educate her falls victim to fallacy of woman who m. to reform 564.61
woman m. again because she detested her first husband 564.135
marry: at fifty one doesn't m. a girl of twenty 570.4
every woman should m.—and no man 564.28
maidens, why worry whom to m. 564.55
m. but for love, but love the lovely 564.99
m. for love, invite tragedy 564.15
men m. because they are tired 564.132
men women m. will always be a marvel 564.75
people m. from inclination, not reason 564.68
they that m. old people hang themselves 1058.3
to m. a woman you love is to lay a wager as to who will stop loving first 564.19
women m. to be in hub of things 564.10
marrying: m. a man is like buying what you admired a long time in a shop window 564.70
m., ask if you can converse into old age 564.95
men always wooing goddesses, m. mortals 198.9
martyr: a m. to the freedom of Jew and Gentile 723.6
cause, not death, makes m. 565.12
everyone hates a m. 565.7
m. never asserted his disbelief in torture 565.3
often pleasant to stone a m. 565.1

to die a m., one must will own execution 565.9
martyrdom: for m., man must be convinced he has delegation from heaven 565.10
martyred: m. many times must be who would keep his country free 537.22
martyr's: no happiness in life is so perfect as m. 565.6
not the least of m. scourges to be canonized by persons who burned him 565.11
martyrs: truer that m. make faith than faith makes m. 565.14
vice has more m. than virtue 1034.3
marvelous: unknown always passes for m. 1019.11
masculine: the m. blunder of mixing smartness with character 119.2
mask: m. tells us more than a face 165.17
nothing gives more assurance than a m. 165.3
woe to him who doesn't know how to wear his m. 165.14
you cannot unmask a m. 3.3
masquerade: English life is nothing but a huge m. ball 289.6
mass: m.-mind of crowd, gang is uncivilized 208.6
m. movements cannot rise without belief in a devil 568.1
Massachusetts: in M. Democratic politicians steal 711.43
massacre: each successful m. consecrated by Te Deum 440.2
masses: away with this hurrah of m. 208.5
civilization exists so men may not be m. 682.2
m. will fall victims to a big lie 558.20
obedience is result of instinct of the m. 819.34
sexuality is the lyricism of the m. 892.4
mass media: misled by m. m. notoriously phony 34.32
master: creditor is worse than a m. 222.8
every m. has but one disciple 353.2
eye of the m. fattens the steed 58.6
man who is m. of himself can end sorrow 862.15
m. eventually wins all to his opinion 401.12
m. shows himself in self-limitation 903.3
no man good enough to be another's m. 889.17
slave has but one m.; ambitious man, many 33.13
when lion weary of obeying m. has devoured him, it looks for another m. 819.40
masterpieces: m. are not single and solitary births 401.58
nothing likely about m. 401.54
masters: half our standards come from our first m. 473.7
no man can serve two m. 497.1
we cannot all be m. 531.18
we may be m. of lot by bearing it 287.9
mastery: no one has m. of his art 53.88
masturbation: for m. you don't have to look your best 892.15
material: a great deal of dark, unseen m. exists 415.1
our life ought to be m. and carnal 716.5
materialism: m. decadent only if nation's spirit withered 569.1
materialistic: m. idealism of American life 569.6
mathematicians: m. who are only m. have exact minds 570.5
mathematics: exaltation found in m. as in poetry 570.8
if a man's wit wanders, let him study m. 570.1
m. gives artist fullest scope of imagination 570.2
m. the subject in which we never know what we are talking about 570.7
matrimony: in m., to hesitate may be to be saved 564.13
lady's imagination jumps to m. in a moment 1062.6
safest in m. to begin with some aversion 564.112
matron: no m. happy till past thirty and not fat 645.2
maturing: process of m. is an art to be learned 571.9
maturity: assured that m. would cure this itch 571.16
awareness of ambiguity of one's achievements and failures is a symptom of m. 6.19
m., to find seriousness of child at play 571.12
to live with fear is final test of m. 571.20
whatever is formed for long duration arrives slowly to its m. 404.14
maxim: more trouble to make m. than do right 572.3
maxims: govern kingdoms with m. 395.51
May: all things seem possible in M. 854.41
hard is heart that loveth nought in M. 854.15
must's a schoolroom in the month of M. 271.5
rough winds shake the darling buds of M. 854.37
mayor: m. who won't steal is a triumph 131.7
meal: good m. ought to begin with hunger 274.10
the m., of course, was ghastly 355.13
mean: none m. all they say, few say all they m. 901.1
some men have a necessity to be m. 307.14
to the m. all becomes m. 693.8
to the m. eye all things are trivial 693.2
what m. man seeks is in others, not self 952.2
meaning: each culture reads m. into objective world 784.12
every man lives to give a m. to life 539.90
impossibility of imparting m. to my past 573.5
learn m. of what you say, then speak 923.18
life has to be given m. since it has no m. 3.6
m. eludes the murderer's mind 518.3
pursuit of perfection gives m. to life 684.18
quest for certainty blocks search for m. 1005.5
repeated phrase gains m. 800.4
there is no m. to life except the m. man gives by living productively 573.1
we find in death not m., but an end 541.31
we must find our separate m. 573.2
meaninglessness: specialized m. a hallmark of science 924.3
meanings: m. receive dignity from words 1064.39
meanness: m. is in half-doing 936.2
means: increased m., leisure, two civilisers 133.8
let us live within our m. 977.11
m. are enjoyed if the end is desired 574.5
m. prepare the end 574.4
the m. with which to make a better life 659.8
we deliberate about m. and not ends 574.1
measure: m. a thousand times and cut once 112.6
to each thing belongs its m. 979.7
meat: God never sends the mouth but he sendeth m. 754.7
strong m. belongeth to them of full age 571.1
medal: m. glitters, also casts a shadow 426.2
media: mass m. offer entertainment to be consumed, forgotten and replaced 576.1
medicine: by m. life may be prolonged 577.9
hygiene is corruption of m. by morality 137.4
m. a compendium of successive and contradictory mistakes of its practitioners 577.7
miracle of modern m. is diabolical 577.4
one thing pleasantly unconfusing about m. 577.10
patience is the best m. 577.2
sick man must search for m., not scenery 577.8
medicine man: no m. can be without a tape recorder 966.32
mediocre: m. mind thinks it writes divinely 1069.74
who can do all things equally well is m. 578.5
women want m. men; men work to be m. 581.38
mediocrity: always heavy demand for fresh m. 578.1
consolation of m.: genius isn't immortal 578.3
m. knows nothing higher than itself 962.5
m. mitigates the most violent revolution 819.7
men of age content with m. of success 586.2
new m. thought more of than accustomed excellence 640.5
rapport between m. of author's and public's ideas 93.15
sign of m. to praise always moderately 722.34

meditate: to m. is to labor; to think is to act 975.22
meditation: m. makes a profound man 188.14
meek: it's safer being m. than fierce 390.1
meekness: m. is the mask of malice 435.11
m.: patience in planning revenge 435.2
meeting: m. people unlike oneself confirms one's idea that one is unique 469.2
meetings: observe any m. of people 208.2
Megalopolis: the profound revolution in M. 819.19
melancholy: in temple of delight m. has her shrine 705.4
m. and remorse are our keel 918.12
m. cannot be proved to others, so be silent 1011.3
m. days are come, saddest of year 854.13
music causeth m., but it is pleasing m. 614.13
naught so sweet as m. 1011.4
sovereign source of m. is repletion 845.4
to win joy through struggle is better than to yield to m. 281.8
true m. breeds perfect, fine wit 1011.18
when the m. fit shall fall 1011.19
mellowing: m. rigorist is much pleasanter than a tightening liberal 178.11
melodies: heard m. are sweet, those unheard sweeter 450.19
most beautiful m. seem simple and inevitable 614.3
memoirs: m. is to put down good, leave out bad 62.7
memorable: m. days vibrate to imagination 450.13
memories: an old man's m. grow sharp with age 653.15
as we age, m. of early life brighten 580.4
funny what the brain will do with m. 580.11
m. may sleep a long time 580.21
men live by forgetting—women live on m. 581.14
our m. are disorderly card-indexes 580.9
our m. independent of our wills 580.36
our m. insist on cherishing the ugly 580.25
memory: better than minting of king is lovely m. 580.39
bitterest m. involves what one should not have done, and which one did not do 580.23
everyone complains of m., none of judgment 516.10
great m. does not make a philosopher 580.24
human m. works its own wheel 580.32
in good days we've cold m. of bad times 580.33
in m., dead more present than living 221.107
in m. everything seems to happen to music 580.45
liar should have a good m. 558.30
man dies even in the m. of his beloved 606.9
man's real possession is his m. 580.37
m. but ash choking sinking fires 580.46
m. is a net, full of fish but not water 580.12
m. is diary we all carry about with us 580.44
m. is often the attribute of stupidity 580.8
m. is the thing you forget with 580.7
m. kills present, offers its heart to past 580.38
m. may be good, to forget is greatness 580.13
m. not brilliant as hope; more beautiful 580.29
m. of man is as old as misfortune 17.22
m. preserves the merest trifles 580.5
m. recalls agreeable traits of friend 580.42
no man can be satisfied with m. 580.15
oblivion is the page whereon m. writes 580.6
one lives in the hope of becoming a m. 539.92
our m. will endure if we deserve it 584.4
plucking fruit of m., one runs risk 1069.29
strange are the mishaps of m. 580.22
strong m. is coupled with infirm judgment 580.17
study without liking spoils the m. 532.12
the m. represents what it pleases 580.18
vanity plays lurid tricks with m. 675.2
we labor to stuff m. and leave rest void 279.63
what would future of man be devoid of m.? 580.43
when glory comes, m. departs 386.5
memory's: in m. telephoto lens, objects are magnified 580.41
men and women: how many great m. a small house will contain 152.23
m. should never come together except in bed 581.54
men: all m. accessible by the right door 961.1
all m. be not cast in one mold 469.13
all m. naturally hate one another 412.16
as m. grow older, rely on sense of humor 581.42
as many m., so many minds 469.19
beautiful in m. is something feminine 566.6
by keeping m. off, you keep them on 31.4
conflicts that set m. and w[omen] against each other 581.3
easier to know m. in general than one man 1008.14
expect, fear, everything from time and m. 978.72
few m. are of one plain color 687.1
gravity is the gift of m. 566.1
he who hates vices hates m. 1030.13
history is bright and fiction dull with homely m. who have charmed women 582.6
if m. are shrewd, they may dally with women 200.5
if not humble, m. are less than m. 435.22
it disturbs me no more to find m. base than to see apes mischievous 431.18
m. all seek their satisfaction 238.33
m. always want to be woman's first love 581.68
m. and women agree only in conclusions 27.8
m. are April when they woo 564.107
m. are afraid they won't be m. enough 566.5
m. are born equal and different 469.7
m. are but children of a larger growth 562.17
m. are children more than once a day 452.4
m. are created different 171.15
m. are cured by women's favors 581.31
m. are inviolable persons 858.21
m. are like stars: some make own light, others reflect brilliance they receive 401.39
m. are my teachers 532.16
m. are necessarily mad 559.13
m. are of no importance 531.4
m. are what their mothers made them 119.8
m. contend sewing is beyond them 582.4
m. die—no one asks who, what they've been 606.1
m. differ as heaven and earth 581.60
m., like fruit, grow sweet before decay 586.10
m. love flattery from low opinion of themselves 349.19
m. make new experience a ploughshare 321.38
m. may come and m. may go 824.8
m. must be studied as deeply as books 1008.13
m. must work and women must weep 539.65
m., not houses, make the city 131.15
m. not to live silently like beasts 733.18
m. of few words are the best m. 98.8
m. see lazily when not expecting to act 683.5
m. shouldn't care too much for good looks 582.9
m.'s m.: they're much of a muchness 582.5
m. under discipline of shrews at home 564.63
m. woo goddesses, marry mortals 198.9
many m. honestly do not know what women want 1008.19
most m. have all other m. as allies 581.8
real friendships among m. are rare 365.32
relations of m. and women like equation 581.34
things and m. have always a certain sense 1007.4
three classes of m.—lovers of wisdom, lovers of honor, lovers of gain 562.48
to empire builders, m. are instruments 458.3
tragedy of age: m. know so

little of m. 1008.6
we make gods of m. and they leave us 581.67
we m. are a little breed 693.10
what m. daily do not knowing what they do 483.2
where m. once howled and hacked at one another 681.36
women and m. are simply different races 581.35
mend: who cannot m. own case will impair other's 295.3
mended: old houses m. cost little less than new 460.2
mental: m. health not individual adjustment to society 842.2
merchandising: information, subject to rules of m. 522.37
merchant: for m., honesty is financial speculation 104.4
whoever reigns, the m. reigns 104.5
merchants: m. have no country 104.19
Mercury: words of M. harsh after songs of Apollo 271.25
mercy: he that has no charity deserves no m. 120.3
his mercy is more attractive and pleasing in our eyes than his justice 387.22
law of human judgment is m. 457.4
m. blesses him that gives, him that takes 583.7
m. I to others show, that m. show to me 583.2
m. no more could be if all were as happy as we 698.3
nothing emboldens sin so much as m. 583.5
reason is law, but m. prerogative 359.5
sweet m. is nobility's true badge 583.6
we give folks to God's m. and show none 583.1
merit: assumption of m. easier than its attainment 584.2
how vain, without the m., is the name 332.20
m. and knowledge do not gain hearts 584.1
man without ceremony needs great m. 563.13
more reward the appearance of m. than m. 584.3
O that honour were purchased by m. 584.5
praises from an enemy imply real m. 722.7
merits: modesty consists in a due estimate of m. 600.9
sage never seems to know own m. 600.8
merriest: men are m. when they are from home 422.20
merry: he of a m. heart hath a continual feast 409.13
m. heart goes all day, sad tires in mile 409.89
mess: we are, to put it mildly, in a m. 641.13
message: give to a gracious m. an host of tongues 629.7
messes: not tragedies that kill us, it's m. 88.8
metaphor: a single m. can give birth to love 35.3
m.: its efficacy verges on magic 35.4
metaphysics: ethical m. is an attempt to give legislative force to our wishes 694.31
m.: attempt to prove the incredible by appeal to the unintelligible 694.23
m. is the finding of bad reasons for what we believe upon instinct 694.22
when speaker no longer understands, it's m. 694.41
method: m. most important in dispatch 104.8
methods: our m., not our aims, set us at odds 585.11
meting: heart, hand become callous from m. out 384.22
Mexicans: language of M. springs from abysmal extremes 524.16
Michelangelo: like M., absorbed in acquiring real estate 746.15
microscopes: m. are prudent in an emergency 850.2
middle class: m., nothing but a poor fringe 586.5
the m. demand to pray in suitable surroundings 723.16
middle: human nature to stand in m. of a thing 465.5
independence: that's m. class blasphemy 235.9
in m. life, politics are a temperament 586.3
live for others: m. class morality 587.6
m. age is when age shows around m. 586.11
m. age, when you've met so many people 586.16
m. class unit: couple living moderately 587.5
true way is the m. one 33.8
middle-aged: consolation of m. reformers 790.31
if m. man says he's half dead, it's true 586.4
m. suspect everything 1072.30
youth plans bridge to moon, m. man concludes to build a woodshed 254.7
middle-class: everybody looked m. in European eyes 587.1
Middlesex: acre in M. better than realm in Utopia 746.14
midnight: there is a budding morrow in m. 86.2
midsummer: quality of life is social in m. 854.3
might: do not expect justice where m. is right 357.13
m., right, over centuries found identical 822.5
right makes m. 823.15
saddest words: it m. have been 507.9
where m. is master, justice is servant 357.4
where there is no m. right loses itself 357.14
might-have-been: m. can fill desire's cup 792.3
mighty: for m. even to give way is grace 719.5
migraine: m. not relieved by a tiara 798.9
militarism: can't make civilization around core of m. 588.15
militarist: we want to get rid of the m. 588.20
military: drum drives out thought, is m. instrument 588.10
in m. mentality, non-human factors essential, human being considered secondary 588.5
m. caste originated as party of bandits 588.13
militia: raw in the fields the rude m. swarms 588.3
milk's: cheese: m. leap toward immortality 355.7
mill: m. can't grind with water that's past 507.7
mills: m. of God grind slowly 815.8
mimics: crow that m. cormorant gets drowned 451.7
mind: All the soarings of my m. begin in my blood 589.10
base m. mounts no higher than bird soars 55.17
best preservative to keep m. in health 803.2
body never forgives injury by m. 589.8
canst thou not minister to a m. diseased 757.1
consolation of a little m.: changing it without impeding mankind 693.3
direction of m. more important than progress 590.9
eye obeys exactly the action of the m. 897.4
eyes not responsible when m. does seeing 450.24
for m. disturbed, dawn is balm 605.5
free m. not to be tethered on chain 522.59
good m. possesses a kingdom 493.29
great m. can look beyond itself 1035.2
happiness depends on turn of m. 969.4
he who is fixed does not change his m. 771.5
human m. is not meant to be governed 590.18
imagination and m. are politics 711.82
I shiver in the draft from an open m. 654.5
it is natural for m. to believe 78.15
lasting love best proves strength of m. 181.4
let m. be thoroughfare for all thoughts 654.3
man cannot gradually enlarge his m. 945.9
man is a m. betrayed by his organs 589.5
man of active m. outwears friendships 365.73
m. all logic is like knife all blade 785.37
m. cleansed of temporal concerns 387.17
m. creates the world about us 590.8
m. crippled by same set of ideas 903.4
m. goes less far than heart 590.3
m. grows old as well as body 514.1
m. has transformed the world 590.20
m. is a light the gods mock us with 590.1
m. is a most delicate evidence 590.5
m. is dangerous if discreet use not known 590.13
m. is the great lever of all things 975.49

m. is the soul's eye 675.22
m. its own place, makes heaven of hell 590.12
m. leaps through immensities of space 482.7
m. must bear storms of past and future as well as of present 589.1
m. must be let alone by government 590.17
m. of an honest man is terrifying 425.6
m. of man is more intuitive than logical 590.21
m. quite vacant is a m. distressed 446.5
m. sins, not the body 900.15
m. too proud to unbend over ridiculosa 612.5
m., unlike flesh, secures complete life 589.2
m. wants to know world, eternity, God 590.4
my m. is my direct revelation from God 816.1
my own m. is my own church 126.10
nothing robs the m. of its powers as fear 343.9
not enough to have good m. 493.7
of all tyrannies, worst persecutes m. 1002.11
order, reason, beauty are characteristics associated with the m. of man 590.14
pray for a sane m. in a sound body 413.6
sharp m. gives edge to pains, pleasures 493.22
small rooms discipline the m. 430.3
smaller the m., greater the conceit 166.1
sound m. in sound body is a happy state 413.8
strength of m.: courage to see, speak truth 1000.6
strong m. can embrace great and small 493.18
study philosophy to know one's own m. 694.11
tendency of casual m. is to pick a sample which supports its prejudices 726.9
that m. draws me which I cannot read 211.3
time bears away all, even the m. 978.73
to illumined m. world burns with light 493.8
whatever diverts m. from itself 175.5
who can't open honest m. won't be friend 425.2
mindful: for all you have done, I am ever m. 399.12
mind's: m. activity easy, if never meets reality 975.38
questions show the m. range 480.12
minds: as many men, so many m. 469.19
great m. are not upset by little things 693.7
m. conquered by love, magnanimity 173.14
m. differ still more than faces 590.22
m. do not act together in public 27.2
m. give way unless we mix work with play 703.5
m., like bodies, fall into ill-conditioned state from excess of comfort 557.1
m. need ideas in order to conceive 443.15
m. that have nothing to confer find little to perceive 620.11
our m. are influenced much by our bodies 589.1
some m. seem almost to create themselves 867.8
strongest m. are often those of whom noisy world hears least 590.23
uncultivated m. not full of wild flowers 447.29
wars begin in m. of men 681.33
we have a world of discontented m. 750.13
we must satisfy our own m. in what we do 491.28
mine: an ill-favored thing, but m. own 716.14
mingle: love or perish is not same as m. or fail 152.13
minorities: governments exist to protect rights of m. 395.49
no democracy can survive without recognition of the rights of m. 591.3
minority: democracy: subjection of m. to majority 233.29
to violate m. rights would be oppression 823.11
wobbly majority falls to resolute m. 591.2
minute: passing m. is every man's possession 676.5
miracle: in each m. is silent chiding of the world 592.3
Picasso said that everything is a m. 592.2
the m. rarely happens in human affairs 592.6
there lay the little m. among the pillows 65.10
this world is still a m. 1067.6
miracles: Christian religion not only was at first attended with m. 125.16
men talk of Bible m. because there is no miracle in their lives 592.5
seeing, hearing, feeling, are m. 882.12
true m. are created by men when they use the courage God gave them 592.1
miraculous: m. by repetition ceases to be m. 213.4
mirror: best m. is an old friend 593.2
every man carries through life a m. 593.1
mirrors: all m. are magical 593.6
m. never give anything back but our image 593.4
mirth: cheerfulness is habit; m., a transient act 392.1
end of m. is heaviness 526.3
m. is the mail of anguish 526.8
teach us m. that has no bitter springs 899.7
mirthful: in m. tale we're content with less truth 436.17
misanthropes: true m. found not in solitude but in world 594.2
mischance: ride in triumph over all m. 92.11
misdeed: on name of a m. a life goes to pieces 1070.19
miser: m. and pig are no use until dead 595.4
m. worships god of this world 595.3
m. worships wealth in its dead form 595.2
what greater evil for m. than long life 595.6
when coffer of m. closed, it's as if empty 595.5
miserable: difficult to make man m. while he feels worthy and claims kindred to God 869.6
man's as m. as he thinks he is 1011.33
men spend first half of their lives making second half m. 1072.15
most m. is he who enjoys least pleasure 409.80
nothing m. unless you think so 1011.2
the m. have no other medicine but hope 427.34
what a m. thing life is 251.2
miseries: an indiscreet man who devaluates his m. 1069.24
life is so full of m. 1011.29
m. spring from idealism, dogmatism, zeal 335.8
misers: m. tend property but don't benefit from it 595.1
misery: cause of m. is feebleness of our virtues 1033.40
child's m. interesting to mother, young man's to young woman, old man's to nobody 653.50
extreme hopes are born of extreme m. 427.31
fate finds for every man his share of m. 1011.9
half our m. from our foibles springs 996.6
he who finds himself, loses his m. 444.2
if m. loves company, m. has enough 1011.35
income 20 pounds, expenditure 20.0.6: m. 977.7
merit praise who know how to suffer m. 751.2
m. acquaints man with strange bedfellows 17.52
m. must somewhere have a stop 17.27
more m. among lower classes than humanity in the higher 718.29
must be green isles in sea of m. 180.4
relieving others' m., we relieve ourselves 698.5
second office of this government is honorable and easy, the first is but a splendid m. 730.7
solace from company in m. is spiteful 180.2
sympathy is cold to relation of distant m. 960.5
technological advance without social advance usually increases human m. 966.8
there is no recourse to mention of pure m. 17.35
To see so much m. everywhere, I suspect that God is not rich 387.40
twins even from birth are m. and man 1011.16
misfit: man is a m. from the start 562.22
misfortune: better a quiet death than public m. 434.4
doing what's right's no guarantee against m. 17.39
falsehood is the jockey of m. 558.16
friendship is sole remedy against m. 365.46
in friends' m. we find something pleasing 561.6
in m. what friend remains a friend 17.29
men cling to life even in

great m. 539.3
m. lights now upon one, now upon another 17.1
one likes people better when battered down with m. than when they triumph 561.14
the memory of man is as old as m. 17.22
to bear m. worthily is good fortune 937.1
world quickly bored by recital of m. 17.40
misfortunes: better be wise by m. of others 17.2
happiness is composed of m. avoided 409.56
if man talks of his m. there is something in them that is not disagreeable to him 17.35
ignorance of one's m. is clear gain 17.28
man bears another's m. like a Christian 17.47
m. are battlefields which have heroes 418.17
m. more supportable than friends' comments 698.7
m. one can endure—they come from outside 342.31
m. tell us what fortune is 751.7
m. when asleep are not to be awakened 17.24
rich men feel m. that miss the poor 1048.24
to be wise in m. is to conquer fate 17.49
we all have strength to bear others' m. 698.14
we delight in real m. and pains of others 561.2
with man, most m. are occasioned by man 17.46
misinformation: to convey m. tell the strict truth 1000.21
miss: good marksman may m. 542.7
missile: a m. is a m. 241.1
missiles: we have guided m. and misguided men 849.18
missing: one person m. can make world depopulated 2.8
missionaries: the East should have sent us m. 273.1
mistake: every m. has a halfway moment 299.4
every m. must be paid for in full 299.13
greatest m. is fearing you will make one 299.18
no m. is so great as being always right 822.4
mistaken: do not judge, and you will never be m. 515.6
mistakes: any man can make m. 299.9
enemies are first to discover your m. 288.3
experience is name everyone gives to m. 321.56
great men too make m., many do it often 401.35
just cause is not ruined by a few m. 111.4
making m. is more honorable than doing nothing 299.30
m. are part of life; you can't avoid them 88.7
m. arise from feeling when we ought to think, thinking when we ought to feel 88.1
only things one never regrets are m. 148.9
own up to m. so you don't suffer 299.19
people seldom learn from m. of others 299.16
we don't forget m. in Lake Woebegon 359.10
when such as I can stumble on their m. 1060.8
who has enough credit to pay for his m. 299.12
mistress: daughter in my mother's house, m. in own 422.13
mistrust: doubt, m., are panic of timid imagination 1005.6
more shameful to m. one's friends 259.8
mistrustful: most m. are often greatest dupes 259.12
To rest m. where a noble heart 259.13
misunderstanding: most quarrels amplify a m. 772.5
where m. serves others as advantage, one cannot make self understood 648.3
misunderstood: best you can say is you m. him favorably 1008.17
do not complain of being m. 184.1
to be great is to be m. 401.13
mixture: good things of life come to us with a m. 389.6
mob: best university for man of ideas: gauntlet of the m. 597.1
in hands of vicious, m. will do anything 597.2
isolation from power makes men look for a m. 597.5
man who stands apart from m. called coward 597.4
most timorous, sniveling, poltroonish, ignominious m. of serfs and goose-steppers 34.50
no grievance fit for redress by m. law 597.6
nose of m. is its imagination 597.7
pitifulest thing is a m. 588.18
mobs: m. in emotions are like children 597.3
mockery: m. is often the result of poverty of wit 820.3
model: I am the very m. of a modern Major-General 588.8
moderate: be m. in prosperity 755.19
m. are not usually the most sincere 598.8
moderately: m. honest man with m. faithful wife 587.5
moderation: excess prevents m. from acquiring the deadening effect of a habit 312.6
heart great which shows m. in prosperity 598.13
m. in the pursuit of justice is no virtue 335.5
m. is a refrain from which we all refrain 598.7
m. is the languor and indolence of soul 598.10
m. runs through all virtues 598.5
m. was created to limit and console men 598.9
modern: a m. painting can be outdated 599.1
in m. world, Americans are old inhabitants 34.31
m. man a means; end not his business 1001.7
m. man wants what he is supposed to want 238.11
m. mansion has no place for ghosts 430.2
motto of m. life: just as good as real 54.3
only the m. ever becomes old-fashioned 599.2
moderns: m. ask what can we experience 321.55
speak of m. without contempt 136.1
modest: awareness of our strength makes us m. 940.5
m. man is usually admired—if people ever hear of him 600.11
to be simple is best, m. next best 899.2
modesty: as simians we have done well as to m. 308.5
for those of great talent m. is hypocrisy 600.13
he who speaks without m. will find it difficult to make his words good 600.5
loquacity storms ear, m. the heart 600.6
m. and reverence are virtues of freemen 233.23
m., diffidence make man unfit for public affairs, brothels 600.12
m. guards virtue; false m. betrays it 600.2
m. is not a spontaneous flower 901.4
m. more praised in lover than liked 600.14
m. sets off every great talent 600.1
m. the only sure bait for praise 600.3
of lies, false m. is the most decent 440.4
true m. consists in due estimate of merits 600.9
modification: bad plan admits of no m. 702.6
mold: all men be not cast in one m. 469.13
moment: believe more in life, fling less to m. 461.1
if you let the ripe m. go, you can never wipe off tears of woe 979.3
life's a m. and less than a m. 606.15
passing m. is all we can be sure of 729.20
strange how few things of m. 1012.4
that m. which stamped past and future 204.21
the m. had come for her to tell her husband 168.2
moments: m. of reckoning, m. of truth 340.12
m. make the year 996.13
momism: mealy look of men is the result of m. 670.56
monarch: greatest m. sits on his own arse 780.4
m. represents his subjects better than elected assembly 520.4
monarchy: we have been born under a m. 387.63
monastic: m. incarceration is castration 601.1
Monday: how Sunday into M. melts 1065.55
money: a more serious art, m. 962.15
a poor man with a great deal of m. 718.49

all men worship m. 602.61
all morality should have m. as basis 602.55
any man knows how to earn m., but few how to spend it 602.59
big m., always a temptation to sin 602.65
difference between little and no m. is enormous 602.64
do you think love has pockets for m. 551.154
everything has something to do with m. 602.28
excessive addiction to m. is hurtful 602.14
federal m. in large amounts looks like free m. 101.1
fortunes made with other people's m. 1048.58
Give me not righteousness, O Lord, give me m., only m. 602.43
good cause, yet m. must carry it 111.7
having m. and bad conscience 34.70
help me to m. and I'll have friends 602.24
heroes: men who sit on top of heap of m. 602.34
if a man has m., he knows how to take care of it 602.29
if m. can answer, wrong to endanger life 216.15
in race for m. man comes last 8.7
it's m. that finishes the man 602.23
knew the moral worth of m. 602.60
life is short and so is m. 602.8
love of m. is root of all evil 602.4
makers of fortunes love m. as their own creation 1048.41
man is more careful of m. than principles 734.9
man married to woman who enjoys spending m. must enjoy earning it 1065.42
men make m. not for the sake of living 602.32
m.: alienated essence of man's existence 602.38
m. alone sets all the world in motion 602.48
m. and dung are no good till spread 602.22
m.: blessing of no advantage excepting when we part with it 602.5
m. enables life to be lived socially 602.56
m. helps, though not so much as you think 602.18
m. in pocket, you are wise, handsome 602.66
m. is coined liberty 602.15
m. is like a sixth sense 602.39
m. is not an aphrodisiac 602.37
m. is root of evil, sum of blessings 602.53
m. is time 602.26
m. is useful only when you get rid of it 602.62
m., m., all is m.! 1069.101
m. not needed to buy day, water, sun 623.60
m., power to manage love 602.9
m. the cause of a restless life 602.47
m. was exactly like sex 602.2
morally bad not to care how you got m. 998.118
much work merely a way to make m. 602.40
never ask of m. spent where it went 602.20
never so efficient as when it wants m. 964.1
nothing comes amiss, so m. comes withal 602.54
old m. is as moronic as new m. 1048.35
once fool, m. parted, now happens to all 602.57
only a blockhead ever wrote except for m. 1069.68
outrage about political m. and what it buys 191.5
public m. like holy water—taken by all 191.6
put no trust in m., but m. in trust 69.2
ready m. is Aladdin's lamp 602.11
soul buried under dungheap or pile of m. 194.9
there is nothing that lasts so well as m. 1058.6
there's no time to both make and spend m. 602.7
'Tis m. that begets m. 503.3
to have m. is to be virtuous, honest, beautiful and witty 602.25
to know what God thinks of m., look at those to whom he gives it 602.3
to learn the value of m. 602.30
when m. speaks, truth keeps silent 602.52
when reason rules, m. is a blessing 602.50
who plays deep must lose m. or character 369.1
with his own m. a person can live as he likes 602.27
without m., honor is a malady 491.23
woman prefers man without m. to m. alone 1062.64
women think it their business to spend m. 581.52
world is his who has m. to go over it 992.19
you may have painful thing done for m. 602.21
money's: m. the wise man's religion 602.19
monk: habit does not make the m. 45.8
monkey: better to be improvement on m. thin such a fallin' off fr'm th' angels 308.7
disappointed in the m., God invented man 308.18
monks: m., soldier-saints, the city's heroes 66.5
monogamy: accursed from birth those who seek m. 742.6
monopolists: men are m. of stars, garters, buttons 564.87
monopoly: it should be the m. of the state 1032.5
m., the ultimate security 856.6
monotheist: lover is a m. 555.17
monsters: who fights m. must beware of becoming one 790.25
month: the first of the m. falls every m. 222.7
monument: erection of a m. is superfluous 584.4
no man who needs m. ever should have one 103.5
monuments: when smashing m., save the pedestals 441.4
moocow: there was a m. coming down along the road 65.9
mood: m. means more than object in art 53.46
m. of moment believed permanent 969.5
no m. is unaltered through hours 284.23
our m. changes more often than fortune 969.7
moon: everyone is a m. and has a dark side 165.16
m. a friend for lonesome to talk to 603.5
something haunting in light of m. 603.2
there he is at last, man on the m. 603.1
treading the soil of the m. 603.4
when m. not full, stars shine brightly 795.2
moral: difference between m. man, man of honor 604.26
disregard for their daughters' m. welfare 670.5
Englishman thinks he is m. when he is only uncomfortable 289.28
every man has his m. backside too 604.22
full gut supports m. precepts .1
highest stage in m. culture: control of our thoughts 975.6
if we can't be m., we can avoid being vulgar 396.4
is there any m. shut in bosom of rose 72.58
law is the witness of our m. life 528.39
man may demand reason for every m. rule 604.25
m. contempt is greater insult than crime 185.5
m. good is effect of physical evil 390.10
m. indignation permits envy and hate 467.2
m. principle is a looser bond than pecuniary interest 602.35
m. qualities rule the world 884.1
m. sense teaches how to avoid the right 822.22
national greatness is m. power 604.38
no such thing as a m. or immoral book 93.97
nothing so bad but can masquerade as m. 604.24
our whole life is startlingly m. 604.41
state a m. case to a ploughman 279.47
story with m. is like bill of a mosquito 938.4
success of any great m. enterprise does not depend upon numbers 604.13
what is m. is what you feel good after 604.15
women have a very positive m. sense 1062.1
moralists: many m. begin with a dislike of reality 604.10
m. suppose previous ages less sinful 298.10
morality: absolute m. is absolute stagnation 604.7
a dirty joke, not a serious attack on m. 436.22
a m. which makes no sense today 718.2
all m. should have money

for basis 602.55
alloy of expediency improves gold of m. 319.4
artist's m.: truth, force of description 53.30
censorship may preserve, but not restore, m. 113.8
genius and m. are often bitter enemies 376.36
in name of m., saintly old people hinder removal of legal brutalities 528.71
live for others: middle class m. 587.6
marriage is to m. as licensed liquor traffic is to sobriety 268.54
m. cannot be legislated, but behavior can be regulated 528.45
m. consists of suspecting people of not being legally married 604.35
m. is a private and costly luxury 604.1
m. is body of imperfect generalizations 604.16
m. is contraband in war 1042.34
m. is everywhere the same 604.46
m. is the attitude we adopt towards people we personally dislike 604.50
m. is the custom of one's country 604.6
m. largely matter of geography 604.17
m. regulates man's acts as private individual 491.7
m.: subjugation of nature to social needs 604.28
m. takes no account of the art in life 604.20
m., telling the truth, paying one's debts 604.3
m., thy tens o'thousands thou hast slain 604.4
m. turns on whether pleasure precedes or follows pain 604.5
moral sense enables one to perceive m. and avoid it 604.44
our errors, controversies in sphere of m. arise from seeing men as all bad, all good 604.45
religion veils sacred fires, m. expires 797.61
speculation about m.: effort to find way of living which men feel is good 604.23
teachers of m. discourse like angels 604.19
to make idea of m. center on forbidden acts 604.39
traffic-cop m. and rabbit-test truth 849.19
veracity is the heart of m. 1000.8
without civic m. communities perish 604.33
moralizes: man who m. is usually a hypocrite 604.49
morals: corrupted m. of this age! 604.27
France has neither winter nor summer nor m. 361.12
generalities in m. mean absolutely nothing 373.3
great secret of m. is love 604.36
if your m. make you dreary, they're wrong 604.40
make errors in minor m., not major ones 604.9
m. are an acquirement, like music 604.43
m. in art like legislature in sex 53.94
not best that we use our m. weekdays 604.42
religion has never survived m. 797.24
sentimentality is dissolvent of m. 885.9
terror of society is the basis of m. 343.37
time is a great legalizer, even of m. 978.42
worse than weakening of major m. is strengthening of minor m. 604.8
more: less is m. 899.1
less is m. where m.[ore] is no good 50.23
morning: healthy adult awakes in m. feeling terrible 73.7
in m. man walks with his whole body 341.2
it is always three o'clock in the m. 589.4
m. comes whether you set the alarm or not 368.20
see m. as new-born child with no name 729.25
morons: talked to us like we were a bunch of m. 730.19
morrow: man least dependent on m. meets m. happily 368.10
mortal: all men think all men m. but themselves 454.22
m. nature is seeking to be immortal 454.15
we all breathe same air, are m. 100.10
young man never feels that he is m. 1071.41
mortality: changing year's plan proclaims m. to man 854.25
m. has its compensations 606.14
much of m. still clings to me 606.21
why alas; it's m. we experience 539.34
mortals: gods give to m. not everything at once 754.9
Lord, what fools these m. be! 562.52
Moses: was M. a hero? 418.25
mother: a man's own m. will know 670.54
children are anchors that hold m. to life 123.54
ideal m., like ideal marriage, is fiction 670.45
m.-child relation is paradoxical, tragic 670.20
m. gives us earliest lessons in love 554.12
m. glad to get loveliest child asleep 123.14
m. taught me never to speak about money 602.13
m. weeps at her daughter's marriage 218.9
no woman free unless she can choose whether to be a m. 84.2
the poor child who has lost its m. 236.2
when sick, every man wants his m. 896.22
who takes child by hand takes m. by heart 123.10
motherhood: from bridehood and m. to the workhouse 1062.19
oh, what a power is m. 670.17
speaking on behalf of stricken m. everywhere 670.52
mother-in-law: back of every achievement is surprised m. 6.9
motherly: m. love begins with oneness, leads to separateness 551.68
mother's: tender are a m. dreams 65.5
you don't have to deserve your m. love 670.21
mothers: if I belittle dogs or m. 885.5
in love with man because we had crazy m. 555.19
men are what their m. made them 119.8
most m. kiss and scold together 670.9
m. are the first book read, last put aside 670.41
m. more devoted to children than fathers 670.2
only m. can think of the future 368.13
we never make sport of m. 670.46
motion: aim of artist is to arrest m. 53.49
our nature consists in m. 10.12
scoured to nothing with perpetual m. 10.15
motive: stupid thing done from noblest m. 941.19
motives: feel ashamed of best actions if m. seen 608.6
motor car: his m. was poetry and tragedy, love and heroism 64.4
mountain: there are many paths to the m. top 332.9
mountains: men trip not on m., but on stones 996.3
m.: beginning and end of natural scenery 609.2
m. with tiny heads and wide shoulders 609.3
mourn: let none m.; these things are in the hands of God 610.11
none m. more ostentatiously than those who rejoice at a death 610.12
one must m. birth, not death 83.5
mourner: chief m. does not always attend funeral 367.6
mourning: all m. fears its end 412.2
m. is grief at not wanting back the dead 610.9
stop m. when grief is fully expressed 610.2
mourns: surely nothing dies but something m. 610.1
mouse: if m. laughs at cat, there is hole nearby 92.9
m. miracle enough to stagger infidels 41.43
m. never trusts its life to one hole 755.21
mousetrap: in baiting m., leave room for mouse 939.4
moustache: my m., however sparse, was all mine 407.7
mouth: man overboard, a m. the less 320.1
two ears, one m.: listen more, talk less 543.5
when man speaks to you, look on his m. 923.19
mouths: men put enemy in m. to steal away brains 268.49
never fair woman but made m. in a glass 593.5
move: the great affair is to m. 992.50
movement: vitality of new m.

gauged by fury aroused 479.12
movements: psychopathic element rises to top of m. 111.11
movie: all Americans wanted to be m. stars 611.9
m. actor is a god in captivity 11.3
movies: m. are, like sharp sunlight, merciless 611.8
not only go to the m. but discuss them 826.6
stultifying effect of m.: parents see them 611.5
much: the trick is not to pay too m. 680.9
muckrake: men with m. often indispensable 790.29
muddlers: we're all m. 257.4
mule: a m. has more horse sense than a horse 41.37
multiplicity: he made such a m. of them 848.30
multitude: if m. detests a man, inquiry is necessary 762.5
without fictions the truths of religion would not be intelligible to the m. 797.71
murder: if man indulges in m., soon he thinks little of robbing 1070.4
no humane being will m. any creature 518.16
primal eldest curse on a brother's m. 518.12
we m. to dissect 849.42
murderers: m. punished who kill not in large companies and to the sound of trumpets 518.17
muses: no wide road leads to the m. 485.3
museum: m. meant for slave of self-education 613.3
painting in m. hears most stupidities 666.6
music: all art aspires towards condition of m. 53.101
all m. jars when soul's out of tune 968.1
and the night shall be filled with m. 614.38
an open mind is a necessity with old m. 614.29
classical m. is now a special taste 614.9
criticism makes m. flourish 207.11
lived long in m. and short in life 81.7
man without m. in him fit for treasons 614.53
men profess to be lovers of m. 614.60
m. and women I cannot but give way to 704.28
m. ennobles or degrades our behavior 614.11
M. has charms to soothe a savage breast 614.21
m. is a most present remedy 614.13
m. is essentially useless, as life is 614.50
m. is immediate, it goes on to become 614.2
m. is my consolation 614.45
m. is my weapon 614.26
m. is well said to be speech of angels 614.17
m. is wild sounds civilized 614.33
m. quickens us to enjoyment of time 614.39
m. revives memories it would appease 614.54
m. sets the soul in operation 614.16
m. speaks to me of things I have not found and shall not 614.48
m. takes us out of the actual 614.32
m. the American black people gave the world 614.62
m. was invented to confirm human loneliness 614.31
m.: way of giving form to inner feelings 614.51
m., when soft voices die, vibrates in the memory 580.35
m. with dinner is an insult both to the cook and violinist 614.20
nation creates m.; composer arranges it 614.34
nothing can be well set to m. but nonsense 614.1
only in m. has Negro been able to tell his story 85.2
only true comment on m. is other m. 614.56
people say they like m. when they do not 614.47
people taught too much respect for m. 614.58
performance challenges m. itself 614.57
poetry is harmony of words; m., notes 614.30
read m. as fluently as you read a newspaper 614.41
recognizing the m. that preceded 614.7
saved by m. from being overwhelmed 881.4
sweet m. is sour when no proportion kept 748.3
take a m. bath once or twice a week 614.36
there are places where m. is important 614.65
The still, sad m. of humanity 623.83
this generation's addiction to m. 614.8
to know if you are enjoying m. see if you are looking at advertisements in program 614.14
to produce m. is also to produce children 614.42
we must have recourse to rules of m. 614.46
where there's m. there's no evil 614.18
who hears m., feels his solitude peopled 614.12
why, after all, must everyone like m. 614.49
without m., life would be an error 614.43
musicals: men go to m.; women to plays 581.45
must: m.'s a schoolroom in month of May 271.5
we do what we m. 319.3
Muzak: M. pervades Las Vegas 614.64
myself: image of m. in my own mind 688.1
inside m. is place where I live alone 858.7
my care is for m.; m. am whole reality 858.6
never seen greater monster, miracle than m. 562.42
when I speak to you about m., I am speaking to you about yourself 878.2
mysterious: fairest we can experience is the m. 1019.2
no object m.; mystery is your eye 683.3
mystery: gift of conscious life is sense of m. 175.6
grieve not for not understanding life's m. 1019.5
m. magnifies danger as fog the sun 216.4
m. of a person is divine to him that has a sense for the godlike 261.3
m. should be left in character 972.40
our dream dashes against the great m. 1019.8
we spend lives talking of m.: life 316.8
mystic: to get into the truth is a m. act 998.19
mysticism: m. is intensity of feeling about beliefs held of universe 616.2
without m. man can achieve nothing great 616.1
mystics: m. hope that science will overtake them 616.3
myth: American m. is of free will 617.3
enemy of truth is often not lie but m. 617.5
m. about international sports 929.6
when m. meets m., collision is very real 617.6
mythologists: children are natural m. 123.51
mythology: m. is what grown-ups believe 617.8
myths: m., clues to spiritual potentialities 617.1
tricky gods of ancient m. and folk tales 617.4

N

naked: N. I came into the world, n. I shall go out of it! 297.8
they were n., beautiful, full of grace 642.1
to go n. is the best disguise 224.4
name: God, he whom everyone knows, by n. 387.59
good n. rather to be chosen than riches 804.1
how vain, without the merit, is the n. 332.20
leave out my n., but keep my song 384.30
man's n.: blow he never recovers from 619.5
on n. of misdeed a life collapses 1070.19
she kept the man's n. to herself 857.6
women can change n. and nation 564.49
names: great n. abase those unable to bear them 619.4
n. are but noise and smoke 619.2
scattering of our n. into many mouths, we call making them more great 332.30
some judge of authors' n., not works 207.43
nap: n. overtakes the old when they try to entertain unwelcome visitors 94.7
narcissism: n. gives the power of beasts 876.9
Narcissus: N. never wrote well nor was a friend 876.2
narrow: as if nature makes men n. to give force 620.3
n. heart that loves one object 620.10
n.-souled people like narrow-necked bottles 620.8
narrowness: n., prerogative of the creative artist 207.21
nation: chief business of n.: setting up heroes 418.24

driving force of n. is spiritual purpose 621.19
educate the n.: make history personal 132.4
energy in n. like sap in a tree 621.23
every n. determines policies in terms of its own interests 621.14
every n. thinks its own madness normal 621.20
for total greed, nothing to match a n. 621.21
genius of a n. characterizes the society 621.5
healthy n.: balance of people, government 395.18
institutions alone can create a n. 487.3
n. can be no stronger abroad than at home 621.13
n. consists of territory, people, laws 621.15
n. doesn't have to be cruel to be tough 519.15
n. has character only when it is free 537.40
n., if has anything to say, should say it 247.11
n. needs foreign stock to thrive 453.1
n. renews youth on political sick-bed 621.17
n. revealed by men it honors, remembers 621.12
n. will not count sacrifices in struggle 621.3
n. without dregs, malcontents, is without the seed of things to come 621.9
n. writes its history in image of its ideal 419.17
nothing good for a n. but that which arises from its own core and general wants 621.7
ruin of a n. begins in its homes 621.1
spirit of n. is what counts 621.6
territory does not make a n. 621.10
the conscience of the n. must be roused 889.5
there are things a man must not do even to save a n. 678.7
there is always a raw and intolerant n. eager to destroy the tolerant and mellow 1042.24
we are not a n., but a union 34.12
when n. is in strife, patriots flourish 678.11
women can change name and n. 564.49
nation-state: n., the laboratory of liberty 622.9
national: n. debt a blessing if not excessive 223.1
n. debt is a n. bond 223.2
n. debt owed by and to nation 223.4
n. greatness moral, not physical, power 604.38
n. hatred is something peculiar 622.3
nationalism: n.: a silly cock crowing on own dunghill 622.1
n. is our form of incest, insanity 622.2
n. supposes self-sufficiency, superiority 622.8
the more dangerous n. becomes 622.5
nationality: only great country whose intellectuals are ashamed of their own n. 492.8
our true n. is mankind 100.17
nations: all n. think they are incomparable 622.6
because n. tend to stupidity, baseness, mankind moves slowly 562.25
friendship links men; only interests link n. 621.8
friendships of n. built on interests 498.15
growing n. should remember that no tree can continue to grow indefinitely 621.22
in difficulty great n., like great men, display energy of character 621.16
interest does not tie n. together 498.20
languages are the pedigree of n. 524.21
n. have to limit their objectives 621.18
n. may have fashioned governments 395.15
one act seldom produces hostilities in n. 1042.46
world bears two n.: good and bad 1067.21
nationwide: n. thinking, planning, prevent n. crises 205.7
native: best cosmopolite loves his n. country 193.4
every man has a lurking wish to appear considerable in his n. place 423.4
no sorrow above loss of n. land 423.2
natural: Englishman is never so n. as when he's holding his tongue 289.16
never happier than in a n. setting 623.13
nothing prevents being n. as wish to be so 732.7
one of greatest impulses of mankind is to arrive at something higher than n. state 927.2
supernatural is n. not yet understood 953.1
to be n. is to be as immoral as nature 431.19
natural selection: n. operates according to immediate circumstances 308.11
n. rewards procreative success 308.14
nature: accuse not n., she hath done her part 623.53
all n. is but art, unknown to thee 623.61
art helps n., and experience art 53.53
art imitates n. in this: not to dare is to dwindle 53.138
art is the right hand of n. 53.127
artist: lover of n., her slave and master 53.135
before man made us citizens, n. made us men 431.15
book of n. is book of fate 507.3
child of civilization susceptible to n. 623.50
cultivated man is goal of n. 210.7
custom can't conquer n., she's unconquered 431.3
custom is second n. and no less powerful 213.18
deviation from n. is deviation from happiness 623.40
drive n. away and she will return again 431.11
eye is pleased when n. stoops to art 623.80
felt how much I have lost by leaving n. out of my life 623.30
for observing n., snail's pace best 623.67
gifts fate and n. lend us often end us 962.2
heaven's joys do not satisfy cravings of n. 431.9
he who claims deep love of n. has none 623.27
in America n. is autocratic 34.25
in man all n. is comprehended 562.36
in n. nothing is given, all is sold 680.4
in n. two things do not occur 623.65
in n., there is death and transmutation 623.68
in remaking world we violate kinship of n. 294.4
let n. be your teacher 623.82
little we see in n. that is ours 104.37
man, destined to realize n. only in retreat 623.22
Man is embedded in n. 623.70
man learned pugnaciousness from n. 26.5
man masters n. not by force but by understanding 623.9
marriage of soul with n. 623.71
mind parallel with laws of n. will be strong with their strength 719.19
modern n.-worship is all upside down 623.15
my n. is subdued to what it works in 1065.63
n. a conjugation of the verb to eat 274.18
n. always has more power than education 431.28
n. can speak on everything 623.58
n. drives with a loose rein 1036.5
n. goes her own way 623.35
n. has filled every cranny of the earth 623.43
n. has given us two eyes, two ears, and one tongue 923.60
n. her custom holds 431.23
n. herself is not always unambiguous 623.37
n. hides wrinkles of antiquity under rose 623.23
n. holds no brief for the human experiment 913.31
n. is a guide, not more gentle than just 623.54
n. is a mutable cloud 623.24
n. is a rag merchant 201.12
n. is a suggester of uneasiness 623.76
n. is but theater of the tragedy of man 623.55
n. is entirely indifferent to any reform 623.77
n. is honest, we aren't; we embalm dead 103.2
n. is indifferent to survival of Americans 956.7
n. is one with rapine 623.69
n. is rarely allowed into civilization 133.30
n. is reckless of the individual 623.26
n. is the art of God 623.18
n. knows no indecencies; man invents them 756.4
n. knows what we need

577.1
n. loves the incomplete 623.31
n. never betrayed heart that loved her 623.84
n. never deceives us 864.9
n. never says one thing, wisdom another 623.41
n., not standing, makes the good man 393.38
n. obviously intends the botched to die 623.51
n. often hidden, sometimes overcome 623.2
n. pours life into dead, into life 623.4
n. refuses to sympathize with sorrow 623.72
n. scarcely ever gives us very best 53.59
n. speaks a various language 623.10
n. suits the man to his fortunes 119.9
n. takes no account of human excuses 623.44
n. takes shortest way to her ends 623.25
n. teaches us to love our friends 797.27
n., to be commanded, must be obeyed 623.3
n. will bear the closest inspection 623.73
n., with equal mind, sees her sons at play 623.1
n. without learning is blind 279.68
n. would watch unmoved if we destroyed entire human race 221.136
necessity is curb and law of n. 624.8
no doctrine does good where n. is wanting 203.3
one touch of n. makes whole world kin 431.24
only habitual late riser, up early, takes in full flavor of n. 605.1
our n. consists in motion 10.12
peace of n. secure so long as man not there 623.20
people thought they could conquer n. 623.38
perfections of n. show image of God 623.57
ploys for cutting n. down to size 623.29
reason deceives us more often than n. 785.38
reason demands man live in accord with his own n. 431.22
sounds in n.: rain, wind, ocean 623.5
sweet is the lore which n. brings 849.42
thief and murderer follow n. just as much as the philanthropist 431.12
time spent proving he can outwit n. 623.79
to do what misfits one's n. is disgust 431.25
transpose faith in n. to faith in man 431.10
treating n. as prop 623.66
true religion must know our n. 797.58
true return to n. is death 623.33
true wisdom is not departing from n. 623.64
we can never have enough of n. 623.75
we do not see n. with eyes, but hearts 623.39
we should study n. more in natural things 623.59
we soon get through with n. 623.74
what falls in accordance with n. is good 389.1
what is man in n.? nothing, all 562.46
when n. strips veils from vegetation, we apprehend its ferocity 623.78
where n. does most, man does the least 140.2
words describing n. found in fairy books 623.16
works of n. acquire meaning by commentary 623.63
world an atom in ample bosom of n. 1017.12
nature's: adapt or perish is n. imperative 12.10
exciting that we are n. latest experiment 562.49
honest man fulfills n. plan 152.2
man is n. sole mistake 562.24
n. fire is all the learning I desire 623.11
n. instructions are always slow 623.62
n. silence is its one remark 623.21
natures: them of other n. thinks different 260.1
nausea: close to n. with empty promises 178.15
navigation: how can a man learn n. where there's no rudder 482.4
near: if eye too n., hues of opal not seen 333.5
slight not what's n. aiming at what's far 55.6
necessary: beautiful rests on foundations of the n. 72.17
grief, no more n. when we understand death 918.2
If God were not a n. Being of Himself 387.73
what is n. is never a risk 624.16
necessities: give me the luxuries; will do without n. 557.8
necessity: against n. no one can fight and win 624.1
doctrine of n. is that of toleration 806.4
everything that occurs because of n. is mute 116.9
how base to struggle with n. 624.5
men first feel n., then look for utility 557.7
n.: argument of tyrants, creed of slaves 624.12
n. is an interpretation, not fixed fact 624.10
n. is harsh; fate has no reprieve 340.7
n. is the theme and the inventress 624.8
n. never made a good bargain 624.7
n. prompts to do things at thought of which one would start at other times 227.6
n. reconciles men, forms itself into laws 913.23
n. relieves us of embarrassment of choice 624.17
n. turns lion into fox 624.11
nothing has more strength than dire n. 624.6
there is no n. to live subject to n. 624.4
true creator is n. 624.13
we give to n. the praise of virtue 624.15
wise man never refuses anything to n. 624.14
wise to make a virtue of n. 624.2
necrophilia: powerful attraction of n. in the world 529.2
need: ambition makes more trusty slaves than n. 33.12
he who awaits the call but sees the n. 791.2
when we grapple with another man's n. 663.3
while a man exists there is n. of him 316.2
needs: happiness: satisfaction of dammed-up n. 409.40
living being held most by own n. 625.2
subordinating child's self to parent's n. 670.50
understanding human n. is half the job of meeting them 625.7
needy: gift in season is a double favor to n. 384.25
neglect: Englishman is too apt to n. the present good 289.15
I n. God and his angles for the noise of a fly 183.2
such sweet n. more taketh me 899.6
negligent: celerity never more admired than by n. 926.4
negotiate: never n. out of fear, but never fear to n. 994.2
Negro: being N. doesn't make you expert on race 85.8
can't the nation that absorbed foreigners absorb N. Americans 775.4
dehumanization of N. is indivisible from dehumanization of ourselves 85.3
for N. in America, winning smallest things takes so long they become miracles 85.11
he makes N. base who denies him rights 775.7
N. is superior to the white race 85.4
only in case of N. has melting pot failed 85.12
only in music has N. been able to tell his story 85.2
to be N.: to participate in culture of poverty and fear 85.9
where a N. can be a N. without being Jim Crowed 823.10
Negroes: having despised us N. it's not strange that Americans render us despicable 85.7
more N. in jail with me than on the voting rolls 1038.9
treat us N. like men; we'll live in peace 85.16
neighbor: a n. who never lets you feel at home 39.15
as man draws nearer to the stars, why shouldn't he also draw nearer to his n. 100.9
folly to punish n. by fire 817.15
he gains time who does not watch his n. 880.1
n. true and loving is joy beyond all else 626.8
nothing odder than satisfactions of n. 626.7
pity for all means hardness to n. 455.6
we really love our n. as ourselves 858.17

your next-door n. is an environment 626.4
neighbor's: each man is afraid of n. disapproval 626.10
if a n. apples fell into your yard 528.41
withdraw thy foot from thy n. house 428.6
your safety at stake if n. wall burns 151.7
neighborhood: n.: where, when you go out, you get beat up 131.22
neighbors: be no better nor worse than your n. 578.4
correlative to loving n. as ourselves is hating ourselves as we hate n. 626.5
mix with n.; learn what's doing at home 626.11
people can fool Devil, but not n. 626.6
the state is our n.; n. are the state 930.10
there are many who dare not kill themselves for fear of what the n. will say 804.5
thou shalt love thy n. as thyself 626.2
we can better study our n. than ourselves 663.1
we do things because our n. do them 213.11
we make sport for our n., laugh at them 292.1
when men succeed, even n. think them wise 945.35
where there are children, people become n. 626.9
nerves: life is a question of n. 539.134
n., the n., mysteries of this machine, man 627.3
neurosis: education, like n., begins at home 279.77
good writing is product of someone's n. 1069.126
n. began with discoveries of Copernicus 627.9
n. is final gift of industrial order 1001.8
religious n. is tied to dietary demands 797.54
sin, n., fruit of tree of knowledge 522.41
neurotic: a n. refusal to grow up 627.12
has there ever been an age so rife with n. sensibility 627.8
n. is man who builds castle in air 757.3
neurotics: mistake to suppose n. are interesting 627.2
neutral: before the arrival of the white men, I had considered myself n. 455.5
neutrality: even for n. a government must be strong 395.23
there can be no positive n. 498.13
New England: most serious charge against N. E. is February 628.1
New York: all foolish an' manny wise men go to N.Y. 632.6
always uneasy in N. 632.7
cleaning the teeth is called "prophylaxis" in N. 234.4
cut out dirty stuff, put it back in N. 113.7
in N.Y. aspirations of Western world meet 632.13
the beauty of N. is unintentional 632.12
what he had imagined life in N. to be 632.2
new: be not the first by whom the n. are tried 338.23
experience of the n. is rarely without foreboding 117.20
from n. truths, n. phrase, n. doubts grow 1005.4
heard one person say the good n. days 676.2
if we see old in n. thing we are pacified 640.8
let no one say I've said nothing n. 479.10
n. carries sense of sacrilege, violation 479.8
n. faces have more authority than old 61.5
no n. garment lives up to expectation 267.4
no subject too old for n. comment 522.14
nothing thought rare which is not n. 338.1
old remains unless one lives, dies for n. 986.13
old tracks lost, n. country is revealed 117.32
there is no n. thing under the sun 640.1
to discover n. lands, lose sight of shore 479.5
news: if far, it's n.; if close, it's sociology 629.6
n. is history shot on the wing 629.2
nobody likes the bringer of bad n. 629.8
no n. at 4:30 a.m. is good 629.4
nowadays truth is the greatest n. 629.3
to a philosopher, all n. is gossip 629.9
wan man's n. is another man's throubles 629.1
newspaper: first duty of a n. is to be accurate 630.36
man who never looks into a n. is better informed than he who reads them 630.12
n. column, like fish, to be consumed fresh 630.28
n. has nothing but honor to lose 630.32
n. is the natural enemy of the book 630.10
nowhere is knowledge as varied as in a n. 630.5
reader of an unexciting n. 630.6
window to world can be covered by a n. 630.17
you never get all the facts from one n. 630.40
newspaperman: the hard-drinking n., a stock character 630.30
newspapers: books and n. assume a common reader 522.21
government without n., or n. without a government 630.13
hostile n. more fearful than bayonets 630.25
life one world, life seen in n. another 630.9
n. always excite curiosity 630.15
n., horror happening to other people. 630.11
people confuse that read in n. with news 630.19
real life happens exclusively in the n. 630.1
we live under government of men, n. 630.26
nicknames: of all eloquence a n. is most concise 619.3
titles but n.; every n. a title 619.6
night: and the n. shall be filled with music 614.38
at n. words fade and things come alive 633.8
by n. an atheist half believes a God 1004.16
damp of the n. drives deeper into my soul 692.4
darkness falls from the wings of n. 633.7
democracy's only success—the n. 633.5
do not go gentle into that good n. 221.131
for a bad n., a mattress of wine 268.51
if life at n. good you think you have all 892.20
lamps defend man from age-old n. 131.40
learn to reverence n. 633.1
n. brings our troubles to the light 633.9
n. is immeasurably longer than day 633.4
n. shows stars and women in better light 633.3
prayer should be the lock of the n. 723.14
the tender desolations of profoundest n. 131.1
to know only artificial n. is absurd 54.2
we now have a dislike of n. itself 633.2
when shall the n. be gone 73.2
nightclub: in comparison to n. churches are gay 706.5
nights: many seek good n. and lose good days 706.3
Nile: the N. seems impervious to change 824.3
nineteen: the one you met when you were n. 826.1
nipples: her dark sweated n. show through 45.2
no: he who never says n. is n. true man 791.5
n. is n. negative in a woman's mouth 791.6
to think is to say n. 634.1
nobility: there may be n. in being last 780.17
true n. is exempt from fear 635.5
you cannot throw away a word like n. 491.20
noble: man of truly n. ways listens not to praise 600.7
men of no note suffer n. sorrows 649.7
nature has invited us to become n. 571.14
n. deed most estimable hidden 227.22
often n. face hides filthy ways 440.7
to write n. style, possess a n. soul 942.9
what is n. is in itself of a quiet nature 635.2
nobleness: n. in others will rise to meet thine own 635.3
nobler: n. a man, harder it is for him to suspect inferiority in others 635.1
noblest: honest man's the n. work of God 425.13
stupid thing done from n. motive 941.19
nobly: let a man n. live or n. die 635.7
spurn not the n.-born 793.2
nobody's: everybody's business is n. business 810.6
noise: ideas to deal with Florentine n. are utopian 636.3
n. has one advanatge: it drowns out words 636.2

n. is evolving endurers, needers of n. 636.6
n.: most impertinent form of interruption 636.4
so much n. that one must talk in a loud voice 636.1
who make the n. are not only inhabitants of field 591.1
noisy: most men lead lives of n. desperation 636.7
nonconformism: n. is the major sin of our time 468.8
nonconformists: quality of n. same as of conformists 91.4
noninterference: n. with others' ways of being happy 794.5
nonsense: even God has been defended with n. 881.2
n. good because common sense limited 881.3
n. may tomorrow be demonstrated truth 998.129
there is no n. that cannot be made creed 745.6
to appreciate n. requires serious interest in life 881.1
nonviolence: n. is not a garment to be put on at will 665.6
nonviolent: n. revolution not a seizure of power 819.12
strong, n. man is unjust by accident 940.9
normal: n. is an ideal 637.1
North America: language of N., not dissimilar from that of mother country 524.6
nosebleeds: where D'Amato is subject to n. 491.18
noses: when you're down and out, something always turns up; usually friends' n. 17.61
nostalgia: deeper the n., more complete the fear 639.7
heart fell apart with first waves of n. 639.2
n. is a dangerous emotion 639.3
note: men of n. do great deeds 649.7
nothing: caravan starts for the dawn of n. 634.2
how pleasant it is to ask for n. 880.23
it seemed as if n. could go wrong 605.2
many find n. within themselves 321.25
no one creates from n. 986.10
n. can come of n. 281.15
n. comes from n. 110.5
n. is always a clever thing to say 898.4
n. like a gleam of humor 436.12
n. would be easier than to fall again 329.1
people do not practise doing n. 446.4
we brought n. into world, carry n. out 83.2
we were able to agree that we didn't know n. 228.3
while you can't resolve what you are, at last you will be n. 444.17
nothingness: is not n. a form of perfection? 684.11
notion: An' foolish n. 875.3
notions: airy n. tyrannize in all men's minds 336.8
life driven forward by apprehension of n. too general for language 443.38
nourishment: one is rarely left with much residue of n. 967.27
regardless of color all require same n. 297.21
novel: a n. is based on evidence 344.13
don't write n. to establish a principle 344.9
final test for n. is affection for it 344.12
I am the n. 1069.33
not really a bad n. as the critics called it 344.18
n. is conviction of fellowmen's existence 344.3
n. is history that could take place 344.16
n., through which flows reader's life 344.5
n., what won't sell if called poems or short stories 344.23
the great n. beats with futile hands 1069.147
the subject of a n. is not the plot 344.17
what, in fact, is a n. but a universe 344.2
novelist: never possible for a n. to deny time 978.19
n. businessman drops in on literature 1069.112
n. floats original design upon invented ocean 344.20
painter thinks with brush, n. with story 344.22
novelists: n. write about sex to avoid boring themselves 892.42
novels: have you any right to read n. 93.96
huge n., hard labor would clarify them 1069.138
n. are sweets 344.27
n. play no part in contemporary life 344.29
readers of n. are a strange folk 344.21
to love n. is to prefer sentiment 344.11
novelties: n. please less than they impress 640.2
try n. for salesman's bait 105.9
novelty: had Greeks disdained n., what ancient work would now exist 42.6
only God and some few rare geniuses can keep forging ahead into n. 640.4
we have learned so well how to absorb n. 640.6
what bloom is to fruit, n. is to love 551.112
November: how sad N. if no knowledge of spring 854.40
novice: man arrives a n. at each age of his life 540.3
novices: we arrive at various stages of life as n. 321.26
nowhere: he that is everywhere is n. 10.6
nuclear: we will not unnecessarily risk n. war 641.10
nudities: man sole animal whose n. offend own kind 642.2
nuisance: vain man in reality a universal n. 1027.17
number: greatest happiness of greatest n. is foundation of morals and legislation 409.10
numbers: suffering of millions blurred by n. 946.48
numerous: if the sailors too n., the ship sinks 56.1
nun: she was as sexless as an anemic n. 586.14
nunnery: get thee to a n. 1051.5
nuns: n. fret not at their narrow room 927.15
O
oak: when o. is felled, the forest echoes 649.2
oaks: many strokes overthrow the tallest o. 686.5
oath: no o. secures love against higher love 551.57
o. doesn't make us believe man, man the o. 643.1
trust character more than an o. 635.6
oaths: o. are but words, and words but wind 643.2
obedience: he who yields a prudent o., exercises a partial control 644.4
it is a bitter dose to be taught o. after you have learned to rule 434.3
o., bane of all genius, virtue, freedom 644.7
o. is result of instinct of the masses 819.34
obedient: men not to live like beasts, prone, o. 733.18
obey: it's almost pleasanter to o. 644.1
learn to o. before you command 644.8
way to rise is to o. and please 945.23
who has not learned to o. cannot command 531.1
obeyed: command wisely, be o. cheerfully 531.7
man who commands must have o. in the past 531.2
obeys: who o. usually better than who commands 644.5
object: at bottom, no real o. is unpoetical 708.42
no meanest o. is insignificant 1012.2
objection: technical o. is refuge of scoundrel 832.2
objective: o. world is a sort of Rorschach ink blot 784.12
objects: goal of inanimate o. is to defeat man 646.2
men feel gratitude for pleasing o. 646.8
obstinacy of inanimate o. 652.5
we are the slaves of o. around us 646.5
obligation: none bound by o. unless freely accepted 271.2
What higher o. does a President have 730.16
obligations: only growth is in fulfillment of o. 271.23
oblige: to o. costs little and helps much 888.4
oblivion: o. is the page whereon memory writes 580.6
only earthly certainty is o. 990.18
obloquy: o. is, to most, more painful than death 206:22
obnoxious: nothing as o. as other people's luck 360.14
obscurity: no defense for absurdity but o. 648.1
o. often brings safety 649.1
only defence against reproach is o. 803.1
things in o. had better remain there 712.7

observation: o. is an old man's memory 650.5
o. will disturb what we try to measure 650.1
observations: make o. of others we might make of self 206.17
to o. which ourselves we make, we grow more partial for observer's sake 656.24
observed: whoever feels o. observes himself 1027.6
observers: cultivated men make acute, balanced o. 650.3
observeth: he that o. the wind shall not sow 112.1
obstacles: if there are o., shortest line between two points may be crooked line 585.2
o. cannot crush me 771.5
we combat o. to get repose 811.1
obstinacy: firmness without intellect is o. 493.26
no man is any good without some o. 652.2
o. alone is not a virtue 652.4
o., dogmatism, surest signs of stupidity 652.9
o. in bad cause is but constancy in a good 111.1
o. is the sister of constancy 652.10
o. of human beings is exceeded only by the o. of inanimate objects 652.5
o. weakest of things in one without wisdom 652.1
obstinacy's: o. ne'er so stiff as in a wrong belief 652.3
occupation: an o. for idle or elderly retired 1065.38
future o. is to be skilled consumers 105.20
life without absorbing o. is hell 504.12
serious o. has reference to some want 1065.39
tranquility and o. give happiness 409.52
occupations: woman's o. run counter to creative life 1062.87
worse o. than feeling a woman's pulse 263.17
ocean: fantastic o. doth enfold the likeness of whate'er on land is seen 853.15
roll on, thou deep and dark blue o. 853.4
you cannot speak of o. to a well-frog 149.1
oceans: o. are great promoters of religion 853.12
October: all things on earth point home in old O. 854.51
never such pleasant, sunny spots as in O. 854.21
O. is the fallen leaf 854.7
odor: no o. so bad as from goodness tainted 191.13
nothing awakens a memory like an o. 882.5
odors: o., when sweet violets sicken, live within the sense they quicken 580.35
offend: men o. where they find goodness to forgive 476.6
offended: who is o. writes on marble 476.11
offender: o. never pardons 359.8
offenders: the more laws, the more o. 528.27
offends: O, it o. me to the soul 11.8
who o. writes on sand 476.11
offense: pardon one o. and encourage many 534.1
office: fools take to selves respect given to o. 1027.2
man who has no o. to go to, a trial 582.12
men want public o. for its advantage 761.2
public o. is secure, but lacks hope, fear 761.7
offices: great o. will have great talents 401.8
man casts eye on o., rottenness begins 761.8
official: o. must be audible, visible, kissable 761.6
Ohio: why did you ever leave O.? 253.1
old: all diseases run into one, o. age 896.5
all evil comes from the o. 1072.1
as we grow o., beauty steals inward 653.22
as we grow o., it is hard to keep wise 653.36
as we grow o., value of time becomes vivid 653.44
be not the last to lay the o. aside 338.23
chaste adolescence makes dissolute o. age 122.6
chastity is not chastity in an o. man 122.4
complete life includes o. age 540.12
counsels of o. age give light without heat 19.30
denunciation of young necessary to o. 653.90
dignity, riches necessary to o. men 1072.26
dismiss o. horse in time 813.2
envy not the o. man his tranquillity 653.47
every o. man complains of rising generation 374.8
few people know how to be o. 653.57
good o. times.: all times when o. are good. 298.5
growing o. is dying young 653.66
growing o. is no more than a bad habit 653.63
growing o. is not a gradual decline 653.89
growing o. takes most courage when we have least 653.81
grow o. with me; the best is yet to be 653.10
if we see o. in new thing we are pacified 640.8
if we're not foolish young, we're foolish o. 354.4
I love everything that's o. 653.39
in o. age common to act from interest 1072.12
learning acquired in youth helps o. age 522.35
like children, the o. talk to themselves 653.72
man wants to live long but not be o. 548.13
mind grows o. as well as body 514.1
misery of o. man interesting to nobody 653.50
nobody loves life like an o. man 653.93
no subject too o. for new comment 522.14
none so o. he does not think he could live another year 653.17
none so o. that he may not hope for one more day 653.84
oftener than not the o. are uncontrollable 653.27
o. age brings out essential characteristics 119.12
o. age brings red flare of dreams again 336.22
o. age brings with it its own defects 653.37
o. age creeps upon us, unperceived 653.55
o. age deprives the intelligent man only of qualities useless to wisdom 653.54
o. age has great sense of calm, freedom 653.74
o. age has its pleasures 653.62
o. age has no precise boundary 540.4
o. age is always wakeful 653.64
o. age is fifteen years older than I 653.6
o. age is forgiven nothing 1072.23
o. age is tyrant who forbids pleasures 653.58
o. age not total misery; experience helps 653.28
o. age should burn and rave at close 221.131
o. age: too intent on our interests 653.99
o. age turns bad dispositions into worse habits 653.9
o. and the ripe fall 221.87
o. believe everything 1072.30
o. deeds for o. people, new deeds for new 227.31
o. goat not more reverend for beard 653.31
o. hands soil what they caress 1072.8
o. man loved is winter with flowers 653.33
o. man never stops believing that he can still make an impression on women 892.29
o. men and comets reverenced for same reason 653.98
o. men are like old chronicles 653.75
o. men give good advice to console selves 653.59
o. men grasp more at life than babies 653.78
o. men know when an o. man dies 653.70
o. men still young enough to learn 653.2
o. men want to be faithless, and cannot 472.16
o. men's prayers for death are lying ones 653.29
o. order changeth 117.33
o. people are monsters to little folk 1072.9
o. persons, places, have intrinsic vitality 653.79
o. remains unless one lives, dies for new 986.13
o., that's affront no woman can bear 1062.21
o. words die, new melodies break forth 117.32
one must, when o., remember one's youth 1072.11
only benefit of o. age: to die by degrees 221.95
passions of the young are vices in the o. 1072.14
people don't conform to instructions of us o. ones 19.11

some o. in years have only age to prove they have lived long 548.1
the o. appeal to our respect and pity 1072.24
the o. fancy their gravity is mistaken by the young for wisdom 1072.5
the o. repeat themselves 1072.3
the o. sit on life's raised dais 1072.24
there is unspeakable dawn in happy o. age 653.51
they that reverence too much o. times are but a scorn to the new 986.1
those we grow o. with seem bosom-friends 653.91
to be hopeful is to triumph over o. age 653.3
to lay to virtue the weariness of o. age 653.34
way through life must be learned from o. 653.53
we can't reach o. age by another's road 867.11
we may always find time to grow o. 1071.6
we should not reproach o. age. 653.8
we who are o. are but noise and shape 653.26
we wish the o. to wander off, die, and bury themselves 653.49
well that o. age accompanied by ignorance 653.67
when friends compliment a man about looking young, they think he is growing o. 586.12
when snake is o., frog will tease him 226.9
who lacks wisdom in o. age has existed only 653.77
woman is as o. as she looks before breakfast 1062.71
young can shock and keep o. up to date 1072.22
young think o. fools, o. know young are 1072.4
youth is a blunder; o. age a regret 540.5
youth must study wisdom, o. practice it 1060.51
old age: experience of o. for those left behind 653.42
it is easy to wither into o. 653.82
o. is wasted on the elderly 653.38
old-fashioned: only the modern ever becomes o. 599.2
patriots so outrageously o. 678.10
older: as men grow o., rely on a sense of humor 581.42
do men grow wiser as they grow o. 653.45
o. and at centre of your time 586.9
o. man who will not laugh is a fool 1072.20
young loyal to individuals, o. to types 556.2
old men: o. when they begin to hear the last trumpet 653.14
Olympics: it was like watching the O. 823.8
omnipotence: o. is bought with ceaseless fear 719.15
omnipotent: to be o. but friendless is to reign 831.23
one: o. arrow does not bring down two birds 585.12
o. man should love and honor o. 564.37
only o. in command in home or state 395.19
one-eyed: in land of the blind, the o. man is king 795.1
oneself: no ache more deadly than striving to be o. 444.25
one does not find o. by pursuing one's self 858.27
price of being o. so high few can afford it 859.6
writing of o. one should show no mercy 62.2
onion: life is like an o. one peels crying 539.38
onions: happy is family that can eat o. together 355.17
o. within the bowl animate the whole 189.8
onward: world owes o. impulses to men ill at ease 741.6
ooze: like the lustrous o. on the underside of the snail 1069.102
open: nothing won to admit men with o. door, and to receive them with shut countenance 428.3
openly: you may live with people and not speak o. 915.49
opera: music-lover may accept o. for music in it 655.2
o. may be allowed lavish decorations 655.1
opiate: o.: unlocked door in prison of identity 269.2
opinion: all mankind not justified in silencing one person of contrary o. 364.6
American majority bar liberty of o. 731.1
care not so much what I am in the o. of others 880.16
current of o. is ruler of the world 762.15
difference of o. makes horse-races 656.29
error of o. may be tolerated where reason is left free to combat it 299.20
every reform was once a private o. 790.8
freedom never relied on uniformity of o. 252.8
government no better than public o. sustaining it 762.17
having no o. conducive to peace of mind 466.3
illusion to think ancient o. may not be false 986.2
loyalty to petrified o. never freed a soul 986.21
majority best, yet o. of least able 233.41
man must brave public o., woman submit 762.20
man values own o. of self less 663.2
men seldom trust the o. of their equal 656.28
more unpopular an o., more its holder should observe conventionalities 656.4
my o. is a view I hold until I find out something that changes it 350.2
no group can withstand public o. 762.18
nothing makes more cowards than public o. 762.1
one often contradicts o. because of unsympathetic tone 656.20
o. in good men is knowledge in the making 656.17
o. is a flitting thing 998.26
o. is a powerful party, without measure 656.18
o. is called the queen of the world 656.30
o. is truth filtered through moods 656.22
o. of world is confession of character 119.10
original o. does not necessarily differ from the accepted o. 656.8
people maintain o. for sake of talking 923.24
proud man satisfied with his own good o. 733.9
public o. is generally public sentiment 762.6
public o. is the thermometer a monarch should constantly consult 762.16
public o. makes life unpleasant for one not content to be the average man 762.10
refusing to have an o. is having one 656.23
respect public o. as far as necessary 762.19
scholar needs manuscripts to know his o. 848.10
they that approve private o. call it o. 258.5
to reign by o., begin by trampling it 656.25
unbiased o. is absolutely valueless 656.32
we tolerate differences of o. only in people familiar to us 656.2
who hides his o. has nothing to answer for 656.21
who never alters his o. is like standing water 264.2
youth measures right by world o. 1072.12
opinions: arguments confirm people in own o. 51.20
chief effect of talk: strengthens own o. 656.31
different hours, we are of different o. 656.6
easier to conform to o. than to sway o. 656.12
effervescing o., like champagne, get flat when exposed to the air 656.10
judge men by what their o. made of them 656.14
men get o. by reiteration chiefly 656.3
men suffer deception from their own o. 864.4
new o. are suspected because they are not already common 656.15
o. are of much more value than arguments 656.11
o. from youth to age are inconsistent and contradictory 656.27
o. printed in a newspaper are for the wastebasket 207.14
our o. are less important than the spirit with which they possess us 656.19
our o. of others are not permanent 794.10
people oppose established o. from pride 258.8
public buys its o. as it buys meat, milk 762.3
some men are as sure of truth of their o. as others are of what they know 656.1
sound of tireless voices is price we pay to hear music of our own o. 364.7
there never were two o. alike 260.3

opium: religion is o. of the people 797.47
spirit of world not evoked by o. or wine 269.4
opportunities: greatest of o. and the worst of influences 34.68
problems are only o. in work clothes 737.3
wise man makes more o. than he finds 657.2
opportunity: intentions melt in face of o. 657.4
it is the missed o. that counts 553.2
know thine o. 657.9
o. knocks wanst; on some dures it hammers 657.5
those which I have had no o. to commit 900.11
while we stop to think, we often miss o. 657.11
opposition: many a man's strength is in o. 658.1
no government secure without o. 658.5
o. becomes sweet when called persecution 565.4
o. brings concord 658.6
o.: party that prevents government from running amuck by hamstringing it 658.2
oppressed: greatest consolation of the o. is to consider themselves superior to their tyrants 180.1
o. people authorized to break fetters 819.4
pardon oppressor is to deal harshly with o. 1002.28
truth, time, on the side of the o. today 1002.22
oppressing: we delight in o. somebody else 1002.26
oppression: displaced police magistrate feels no hesitation in foregoing o. 790.30
must guard even his enemy from o. 537.27
o. cannot mature a settled purpose 1002.1
world needs redemption from hunger and o. 432.1
oppressor: pardon o. is to deal harshly with oppressed 1002.28
optimism: o. approves, submits, believes all 659.1
o.: belief that everything is beautiful, including the ugly 659.2
o.: content of small men in high places 659.6
o. is kind of heart stimulant 659.7
o. maintains all is well when wretched 659.12
o. takes no account of the present 659.3
there is o. which tolerates unworthiness 659.10
optimist: dour friend is less fatiguing than o. 660.3
must be o. to open your eyes in morning 1001.11
o. after forty-eight knows too little 660.4
o. is guy that never had much experience 659.9
o. knows each year worse, thinks next year will be better 660.1
pessimist is a man who's lived with an o. 692.3
orator: no o. ever thought another better 166.4
o. can hardly get beyond commonplaces 763.7
o. should be accompanied by an orchesthry 763.5
orators: o. not also great writers are shadows to following generations 763.1
passions are only o. that always persuade 675.14
what o. lack in depth they make up to you in length 763.11
oratory: in o. greatest art is to hide art 763.16
nothing so unbelievable that o. cannot make it acceptable 763.3
o. is like prostitution; must have tricks 763.13
order: chaos often breeds life; o., habit 257.1
events reflect a certain underlying o. 849.11
good o. is the foundation of all things 661.3
He moves the pieces and they come / somehow into a kind of o. 387.31
let all things be done decently and in o. 661.2
old o. changeth 117.33
o. always weighs on the individual 661.13
o. marches with measured strides 661.11
putting things in o. 661.6
the o. of things consents to virtue 1033.18
the o. of things that takes care of fleas and moles also takes care of men 577.6
to put some o. into ourselves 53.32
orders: who does thing under o. is not unhappy 644.6
ordinary: o. men gain greatness by being near us 333.8
o. persons find no differences in men 493.25
organization: large o. is loose o. 102.1
orgasm: o. has replaced the Cross 892.34
orgy: o. made alluring by righteous indignation 739.4
original: it is easy to be o. by violating taste 662.4
where do we now meet an o. nature 662.2
originality: all good things are fruits of o. 662.5
o., dignity achieved only through struggle 1065.20
o.: one thing unoriginal cannot feel use of 662.6
original sin: to write books is to have a relation with o. 1069.25
orthodoxy: o. can't eliminate old idea or absorb new 178.12
ostentation: arts of o.: excusations, cessions, modesty 732.1
other: o. people are quite dreadful 663.14
o. people are showcases for our ideas 663.12
others: it is easy to live for o. 869.1
just as much as we see in o. is in us 663.8
o. are to us like characters in fiction 663.10
o. can never tell you who you really are 469.14
our life is made by the death of o. 541.24
see in o. who you are 444.16
those who know the least of o. 166.5
unhappiness of o. 561.13
ourselves: everything intercepts us from o. 30.4
nothing befalls us not of nature of o. 305.6
we cannot forgive another for not being o. 663.4
we cannot love o. unless we love others 551.133
we had as lief not be, as not be o. 858.16
we know o. chiefly by hearsay 444.12
we owe o. to society, but chiefly to o. 915.31
we prefer o. to others 876.5
we see, read, acquire only o. 93.28
out: it is easier to stay o. than get o. 504.24
outcome: seek to appraise the o. of our lives 571.5
outdoors: beauties of o., here forever 177.3
outgrow: as we o. trousers, we o. acquaintances 404.16
outlive: most I ever did for you was to o. you 547.5
outraged: man never o. unless at bottom right 39.16
Oval Office: first morning in O. had a ring of familiarity 730.12
overact: we must o. to produce any effect at all 732.3
overboard: man o., a mouth the less 320.1
overcomes: who o. by force o. but half the foe 357.10
overcrowding: o., corrected by inducing people not to crowd 294.6
overdose: an o. of anything will [not] teach restraint 598.3
overlooked: better to be looked over than o. 649.8
object often o. if it lies under our eye 612.7
overpopulated: if people waited to know one another before they married, world wouldn't be so o. 713.4
overpopulation: o. connected with survival of unfit 713.2
oversure: how fortune brings to earth the o. 664.3
overwork: o.: disorder affecting functionaries who want to go fishing 348.1
owes: he looks world in face, o. not any 1066.2
owing: grateful mind by o. owes not 399.8
owl: o. is a question wrapped in insulation 82.2
own: ally need not o. the land he helps 498.2
an ill-favoured thing, but mine o. 716.14
begin with another's to end with your o. 700.2
if a man o. land, the land owns him 746.5
o. a horse, and you may borrow another's 96.7
sweetest fat sticks to my o. bones 876.19
we must be our o. before another's 880.7
owners: pig with two o. dies of hunger 746.6
ownership: o., not love, causes suffering 551.180
owning: no delight in o. anything unshared 894.3
ox: o. remains an o., even if driven to Vienna 941.10

P

pace: if a man does not keep p. 468.12
the day started off at a snail's p. 926.3
paces: if you take big p. you leave big spaces 33.4
pad: if they could get into a p. with him 884.3
paid: he is well p. that is well satisfied 845.6
p. to do what they would do for fun 614.27
pain: advantage in wisdom won from p. 343.3
another suffering p. at thy hand, thy heart not exempt from affliction 1018.1
at some point, you no longer feel p. 946.15
culture makes p. tolerable 946.19
ease would recant vows made in p. 743.7
even p. pricks to livelier living 946.27
every known physical p. was bearable 946.24
fate has wove the thread of life with p. 1011.16
gentleman never inflicts p. 378.4
give no heart p. so long as can avoid it 519.16
greatest p. is to love in vain 553.1
have no business to p. myself 866.2
heart can ne'er a transport know that never feels a p. 705.5
history of soldier's wound beguiles its p. 946.47
hour of p. as long as a day of pleasure 946.14
if p. cured, we should have been saved 946.42
much of your p. is self-chosen 946.16
neither poverty nor p. is accumulable 946.6
no p. in wound received in victory 173.11
nothing helps a p. undiagnosable but felt 946.25
nothing is got without p. but dirt and long nails 281.4
one moment may with bliss repay hours of p. 409.19
one p. is lessened by another's anguish 946.44
only gods can live forever without p. 946.2
p. cannot recollect when it began 946.10
p. forces even truthful to speak falsely 946.40
p. from anything external is due to your estimate of it 946.3
p. is deeper than all thought 526.16
p. is produced by prolonging pleasure 705.7
p. is unjust 946.41
p. lays not its touch upon a corpse 221.1
p. makes man think 946.35
p. others give passes away 88.9
pleasure is a visitant; p. clings to us 946.21
pleasure sweetest if paid for by other's p. 838.2
sincerest laughter with p. is fraught 526.30
sweet is pleasure after p. 705.1
the comic, when human, takes face of p. 145.3
to reject p., death, is to reject life 946.12
we are born in other's p., perish in own 946.49
when head aches, all members share p. 151.4
where there is love, there is p. 551.201
you can learn from p., sterility, ennui 946.13
painful: do not consider p. what is good for you 250.2
you may have p. business done for money 602.21
pains: many converse by giving history of their p. 188.35
p. are seasoning to love's fare 551.229
p. of love sweeter than all pleasures 551.50
p. to be coveted that end in pleasures 705.6
there are no gains without p. 741.26
we delight in others' misfortunes and p. 561.2
painter: humblest p. is true scholar—of nature 848.19
p. who draws without use of reason 666.9
painters: lawyers, p., can change white to black 528.14
painting: amateur p. in watercolour shows innocent and quiet mind 666.12
a modern p. can be outdated 599.1
how to paint a perfect p. 666.11
p. in museum hears most stupidities 666.6
p. is measured by its reproduction 53.12
p.: protecting flat surfaces from weather 666.2
we admire realistic depiction in p. 666.10
paintings: p. by dead men who were poor most of their lives 948.27
palace: be thine own p. or the world's they jail 880.5
come and see my shining p. built upon the sand 336.12
like entering a p. by the back door 1029.8
panegyrics: all p. mingled with an infusion of poppy 722.30
panic: don't p. 343.1
pantomime: p. is simple, clear and direct 972.19
papacy: p. is the ghost of the Roman empire 125.13
paper: white wall is the fool's p. 397.1
papers: one reads the p. as one wants to with a bandage over one's eyes 630.27
parades: p. should be classed as a nuisance 667.1
paradise: fantasy can be equivalent to a p. 336.7
if you can't catch a bird of p. 162.7
p.: center whither all souls proceeding 414.8
paradox: a p. of a man, noble and ignoble 588.12
life is a p.; every truth has counterpart 668.3
paradoxes: p. useful to attract attention to ideas 668.1
paradoxical: who confronts p. exposes self to reality 668.2
parallel: never two cases exactly p. 1014.1
none but himself can be his p. 469.20
paranoiac: p. delusion: caricature of a philosophic system 627.6
paranoids: the p. are after us 431.7
parasites: all the wise world is little else but p. 669.1
p. live where great have secret sores 669.3
pardon: if men knew selves, God would p. them 875.20
may the good God p. all good men 393.9
p. one offence and encourage many 534.1
they ne'er p. who have done the wrong 359.4
we are least ready to p. folly we ourselves might have committed 354.9
pardons: offender never p. 359.8
parent: government's role is to serve as a p. 395.21
p. and child: strongest relationship of all 670.40
the modern p. revolts from such teaching 988.2
parentage: no test of fitness for p. imposed 670.49
pride thyself on virtue, not on p. 37.7
parenthood: p., an endless series of small events 670.24
planned p. in social history of West 670.36
parents: boy is adult before p. think so 97.5
children are ruined through virtues of p. 670.11
children rarely forgive their p. 123.60
how p. love us is not known till we are p. 670.6
in America p. obey their children 34.90
in survival of children, p. can think of world in which they will have no share 670.37
joys of p. secret, as are griefs, fears 670.4
p. can make you crazy 670.57
p. lend children experience and memory 670.43
p. who put permanent scars on children's souls 687.4
presence of child turns p. into idiots 670.12
schoolmasters, p., to be grown out of 670.55
teachers deserve more honor than p. 965.4
parents': must remember p. age for joy, anxiety 334.9
wretched child does not return p. care 475.2
Paris: in London theatregoers laugh; in P. they wait grimly for proof they should 972.5
Parisian: to err human; to loaf, P. 671.2
park: silence of shut p. tense, confined 131.6
parks: p. are but pavement disguised with grass 131.16
partiality: p. may simply mean mental activity 455.1

participant: what am I if not a p. in life 504.21
particular: each must form himself as a p. being 469.10
poet should seize the p. 708.45
particularity: p. necessary to creations of imagination 201.27
parties: p., ideal opportunities for misery 672.1
parting: every p. gives a foretaste of death 673.6
partisan: p. is anxious only to convince his hearers 51.19
true p. as true to principles as to self 674.2
partner: great man resents p. in greatness 401.37
partners: it is natural to consult with p. 225.9
Party: the P., comrade, is more than you and I 150.11
party: a debutante p., a bar mitzvah with sex 672.4
acid test of political p. is governing 710.11
he serves p. best who serves country best 710.6
in democracy each p. proves other unfit 710.8
p.: incognito to save man from thinking 674.1
p. is madness of many for gain of few 674.8
p. loyalty lowers great men to mass level 674.4
p.-spirit a hindrance to thought 674.9
p. wedded to principle can save century 674.7
pass: all good things will p. away 990.1
all things p. away—or is it we who p. 989.6
passion: a p. to live beyond one's death 201.30
a sanitizing distance from crimes of p. 517.49
caprice lasts longer than lifelong p. 1053.2
deep p. for the rights of man 34.89
Hamlet came out of his soul, and Romeo out of his p. 201.45
If he is quite mad with p. 198.10
market kills artistic p. 201.44
no p. that cannot be gratified 676.15
nothing great accomplished without p. 675.8
p., a bad regulator, is powerful spring 675.6
p. is like genius: a miracle 675.19
p. must ever sway the heart of man 528.5
p. sways to what free will wouldn't admit 675.15
p., unattended, is flame that burns to its own destruction 785.12
ruling p. conquers reason still 675.18
strong p. for any object ensures success 238.18
tear a p. to tatters 11.8
truth of p. wants pretence to make it live 675.2
what to ourselves in p. we propose 675.21
passion's: give me that man that is not p. slave 675.20
passions: all p. relished and digested are moderate 675.16
duration of our p. is not dependent on us 675.13
human heart has a ceaseless birth of p. 675.11
if we resist our p., the p. are weak 675.10
men of cold p. have quick eyes 142.3
one imputes all suffering to the p. forgetting p. are source of all pleasures 675.3
only p. can elevate soul to great things 675.4
p. are less mischievous than boredom 94.1
p. are only orators that always persuade 675.14
p. kill more prejudices than philosophy 675.5
p. of the young are vices in the old 1072.14
p. raise sedition against understanding 675.9
p. transform man from thing into hero 418.11
p., when masters, become vices 675.17
serving one's own p. is greatest slavery 675.7
soul's power lies in the p. 675.22
those who have great p. are happy and unhappy at being cured of them 675.12
to avoid evil utilize p., not maim them 675.1
who would be superior to external influences must become superior to his p. 862.6
passive: the female, of course, would be p. 235.2
passivity: were we mute as stones, our very p. would be an act 9.33
Passover: this was our last P. meal as a family 334.37
past: accept p. till need for change cries out 117.17
all the p. is here, to be tried 676.31
all things are taken from us, and become portions of the dreadful p. 676.30
a nation reckless with its p. 676.23
condescend to p., preparatory to own time 676.10
denied even to God: power to undo the p. 676.1
ghosts of the p. want both laying and raising 848.7
in books lies the soul of the whole p. 93.12
it is sadder to find the p. inadequate to the present than to have it elude you 676.14
look not mournfully into the p. 676.22
mad is he who opposes the p. 676.27
man can't repeat p. or leave it behind 676.4
man is tied to the weight of his own p. 758.13
mill cannot grind with water that's p. 507.7
no way of judging future but by p. 321.20
obligations, hatreds, injuries, remorse: memories; I have a complete p. now 676.3
old men must die, or the world would only breed the p. again 221.129
p., and to come, seems best 729.24
p. is a bucket of ashes 676.28
p. is not fugitive, but remains present 676.26
p. is such a curious creature 676.8
p. takes down our egotism and leads us into life of race 676.18
respect p.; do not confuse with present 676.19
same p. can leave different marks 676.16
the p. is immortalized; it is dead 676.24
the p. is our definition 676.6
the p. is there for each of us forever 676.17
time flies, and what is p. is done 507.6
to change p. into sad smiles is to master the future 758.11
to enjoy p. life is to live twice 580.16
to excel p., mustn't lose contact with it 676.25
volatile present changes to adamantine p. 729.10
we have to do with the p. only as it is useful to the present and future 676.11
who do not remember p. must relive it 676.29
who look only to p. are sure to miss future 117.23
why doesn't p. decently bury itself 676.21
with the p. as p. I have nothing to do 729.12
you can never plan the future by the p. 368.6
path: end at last for man who follows p. 903.6
every p. has its puddle 245.3
no easy p. out of life, few easy within 539.66
p. made clear, aspiration of everyone 115.5
paths: most beaten p. are the surest 856.7
patience: abused p. turns to fury 677.7
all commend p., none can endure to suffer 677.8
genius is but greater aptitude for p. 376.4
let him with no p. retire within himself 677.9
our p. will achieve more than our force 677.3
p., and mulberry leaf becomes silk gown 677.5
p., diligence, like faith, remove mountains 677.15
p.: form of despair disguised as virtue 677.2
p. is a necessary ingredient of genius 376.8
p. is all the passion of great hearts 287.6
p. is the art of hoping 677.19
p. is the best medicine 577.2
p. lightens what sorrow can't heal 677.11
p.: moral courage, physical timidity 677.10
p., neighbor to despair 677.1
though p. be a tired mare, she will plod 677.16
patient: a p. must learn patience 896.23
beware the fury of a p. man 677.6
doctor and p. are employer and employee 263.14
nothing so bitter a p. mind

can't find solace for it 180.3
p. like hero in hands of a story writer 263.2
patients: a presumption of stupidity in p. 263.13
p., avoided unsconsciously like lepers 896.24
p. lie about taking of things prescribed 577.3
patriotism: don't be so blind with p. you can't face reality 678.12
hating makes p. an excuse for war 412.10
p. is a word which commemorates a robbery 678.23
p. is lively sense of responsibility 622.1
p. is steady dedication of a lifetime 678.20
p. is the egg from which wars are hatched 678.14
p. is the last refuge of a scoundrel 678.6
p. is to politics as faith to religion 678.1
to strike freedom of the mind with fist of p. is an old, ugly subtlety 678.21
when a nation roars p., I question the cleanness of its hands 678.3
patriots: p. those who love America enough to see her as a model for mankind 34.71
when nation is in strife, p. flourish 678.11
patron: p. looks with unconcern on man struggling for life in the water 679.1
patronage: spotted also with the gravy of political p. 172.2
pauper: p. is already serving his term in hell 718.11
p. is human sacrifice in industrial regime 966.20
pause: no word was ever as effective as a p. 898.30
pauses: pianist's art resides in p. 614.52
pay: first or last you must p. entire debt 680.3
if you p. peanuts, you get monkeys 680.7
it's hard to p. for bread that's eaten 222.3
you p. too dear for what's given freely 384.28
payeth: who p. beforehand has work ill done 680.6
peace: all men after form or formula of p. 681.5
ambassadors of p. shall weep bitterly 247.1
better beans and bacon in p. than cakes and ale in fear 681.1
better just war than unjust p. 681.26
certain p. better than anticipated victory 681.19
chief enemy of p., spirit of unreason 443.24
deliberate aim at p. passes into its bastard substitute, anaesthesia 681.38
disadvantageous p. better than just war 1042.31
easier to lead men to combat than p. 1042.37
fair p. is becoming to men 681.25
find inner p. in solitude, not speed 989.9
greatest difference between p., slavery 681.4
having no opinion conducive to p. of mind 466.3
he knows p. who has forgotten desire 681.2
insincere p. better than sincere war 681.42
little things seem nothing but give p. 996.1
mankind will perish through eternal p. 681.10
mere absence of war is not p. 681.16
mutual cowardice keeps us in p. 681.13
never was a good war or a bad p. 1042.33
no one can have p. longer than his neighbor pleases 681.6
nothing could rank higher than p. 681.29
now we suffer the woes of long p. 681.14
on all the peaks lies p. 681.7
only a p. between equals can last 681.40
only condition of p. is to have no ideas 681.12
only p., only security is in fulfillment 504.16
passions toward p.: fear of death, desire for commodious living 681.11
p. and freedom walk together 131.23
p. does not rest in charters, covenants 994.3
p. expedient for victor, necessary for vanquished 681.31
p. found only in grave and at typewriter 681.23
p. gives victory to both sides 173.5
p. hath her victories no less than war 681.21
p. hath higher tests than battle 681.39
p. is an emblem of all goodness 1042.26
p. is daily, weekly, monthly process 681.15
p. is liberty in tranquility 681.3
p. is made with enemies 681.27
p. is of the nature of a conquest 681.32
p. is poor reading 681.9
p. is victory against probable greeds 681.34
p., not a panacea 798.6
p. of man who has forsworn bullet 665.3
p. requires a personal framework 30.7
p. rules day where reason rules mind 785.5
p. succeeds only with power to enforce it 681.28
p., the tenderest flower of spring 990.6
p.: when time doesn't matter passing by 681.30
p., when whole is greater than parts 661.12
p. will come through being, not having 681.20
p. with a cudgel in hand is war 229.12
people think of p. as state of Nothing Bad Happening 681.37
preparedness for war best means of p. 229.15
real p. must always rest on p. of mind 665.9
resister of war can bring p. 665.4
right is more precious than p. 822.23
self-respect too great a price for p. 681.41
separation only p. for man and wife 262.2
since wars begin in minds of men, it is there defenses of p. must be constructed 681.33
soldier, above all others, prays for p. 588.11
there can be no p. of mind in love 551.163
there is no p. unto the wicked 1055.1
there is no way to p.; p. is the way 681.22
there is p. in being what one is 444.6
there must be an organized p. 498.21
they make a desert and call it p. 1042.91
war is scripted, p. is improvisation 681.24
we can secure p. only by preparing for war 229.7
we prepare for p. like retarded pygmies 1042.74
we think the other side of war is p. 1042.60
what we dignify as p. is only a short truce 681.35
When at p. they [Americans] are reluctant to think of the possibility of war 34.55
where no brotherhood there can be no p. 681.18
who listens for what people say has no p. 868.4
who would prefer p. to glory of hunger, thirst and dying 1042.41
world p. requires mutual tolerance, not love 498.7
you can't separate p. from freedom 363.36
peacemaker: your If is the only p. 167.5
peacemakers: blessed are p.; they are freed from wrath 167.2
blessed are the p. 167.4
peacock: no p. envies another p. his tail 733.17
p. blushing at sight of his ugly feet 457.5
sparrow sorry for p. at burden of tail 780.22
peaks: on all the p. lies peace 681.7
peanuts: But I can't stop eating p. 967.30
pearl: diver thinking of shark would not get p. 343.31
somewhere along the line the p. would be handed to me 449.12
pearls: errors on surface flow, for p. dive below 740.2
neither cast ye p. before swine 48.1
peasant: p. and philosopher equally satisfied 409.53
sour look of a starved p. 45.12
peasants: p. not sophisticated enough to reason speciously 618.3
pecuniary: moral principle is a looser bond than p. interest 602.35
pedagogue: nothing tiresome as superannuated p. 965.2
pedant: when culture exceeds nature, we have the p. 848.8
pedantic: judgments of fact, not of value, a sign of p. criticism 207.45
pedantry: p. is the dotage of knowledge 848.21

pedestrian: p.: man with two cars driven by family 64.2
pedigree: good man's p. is little hunted up 393.46
peers: morality is the feeling of one's p. 604.6
pegs: words are p. to hang ideas on 1064.4
pen: man can kill himself with p. more easily than others 1069.111
no lighter burden, nor more agreeable than p. 1069.107
p. is mightier than sword 1069.17
slanders of the p. pierce to the heart 207.28
penalties: severity of p. is a vain resource 766.16
penetrating: must not give me credit for being p. 868.2
penitentiary: guns on the walls index the character of the p. 109.1
penny: p. saved is a p. to squander 977.3
who has a p. in his purse is worth a p. 602.45
Pentagon: the day the P. was finished, it was too small 50.2
people: ability to make p. give over their money 964.6
ambitious fantasies make p. blush 336.19
best servants of p. must whisper unpleasant truths in the master's ear 761.11
beware the p. weeping 1002.23
every p. a chosen p. in its own mind 562.12
in the novel we can know p. perfectly 1008.9
I want the p. to love me, but I suppose they never will 730.24
let the p. think they govern 233.42
masses of p. satisfied by merely surviving 751.10
most p., enslaved by things they want to acquire 716.12
my own kind of p., bums and drinkers 365.98
not because of what government did for p. but because of what p. did for themselves 34.59
observe any meetings of p. 208.2
ordinary p. say no to the tyrant 418.5
other p. are quite dreadful 663.14
other p. are showcases for our ideas 663.12
p. and p. alone make world history 682.13
p. are government's safe depositories 233.21
p. asked why he was looking so worried 43.1
p. dash from point to point very fast 991.1
p. hungry, ill-clad, unsheltered or diseased 437.4
p. like us are We, everyone else is They 910.5
p. of two kinds, from the Valley, from Elsewhere 135.2
p. pick and choose what they learn from the Bible 80.3
p. want to hear you talk about yourself 332.16
p. who believe they were destined for better things 1065.5
p. who boast of happy marriages 564.90
p. who know they are right do great damage 264.11
p. who put slipcovers on everything good 563.16
p. who were born to stay home 422.21
p. will fall victims to a big lie 558.20
reject p. less educated than themselves 131.38
the awful thing about p. is their caution 112.7
the fun of catching p. behaving disgustingly 77.20
the instinct of the p. is right 682.5
the p. like novels and charlatans 682.8
the p. make best judgment in long run 682.10
the p. must help themselves 682.9
universe changed by inspiring the p. 790.24
we are so indifferent to p. 551.165
wealth is the means, p. are the ends 1048.32
what is the city but the p. 131.39
what p. see and hear makes them unutterably sad 409.102
when p. care for you and cry for you 551.93
when p. rule, they must be made happy 233.12
why not confidence in justice of the p. 682.12
you must take p. as they are 984.2
people's: p. voice can be a great roar 233.43
peoples: one learns p. through the heart 1008.20
perceived: life p. transforms itself 875.16
perception: why level downward to our dullest p. 148.8
perceptions: the authenticity of complex, sophisticated p. 515.2
perfect: could we p. human nature 431.6
everything is p. coming from Creator 177.7
if thou wilt be p., give to the poor 684.3
in short measures life may p. be 684.10
nothing so p. possessed as remembered 716.7
there was no place p. on it, so he created France 361.5
we desire to make other men p. 342.16
when a man says he is p. already, he belongs in heaven or in a lunatic asylum 684.1
perfection: all p. is nearly a fault 684.19
a straining toward p. 62.9
dance of the water sings pebbles into p. 357.16
humorous man realizes p. is beyond man 542.2
marriage is the p. love aimed at 564.33
one good action after another: p. of goodness 393.23
our sense misses the p. it demands 457.6
p. is apt to be dull 684.12
p. not a requisite to art 684.15
p. of Gospels never built an empire 859.1
p., when there is nothing to remove 684.16
pursuit of p. gives meaning to our life 684.18
the fallacy that p. is a legitimate goal 1025.1
things by season are seasoned to p. 979.8
through Art only, that we can realize our p. 53.146
through art we can realize p. 684.20
to be human is not to seek p. 431.20
to reach p. we must pass through death of self-effacement 1021.1
trifles make p., but p. is no trifle 684.9
who follows his nature's duty attains p. 684.2
perfections: p. of nature show image of God 623.57
perform: resolve to p. what you ought 807.2
performance: a bad p. haunts the artist 614.40
p. of p. threatens music 614.57
strong p. needs fanaticism in performer 335.3
performers: judges must also be p. 207.1
perils: great p. bring to light fraternity of strangers 216.11
p. ask to be paid in pleasures 216.2
period: all men of one p. are related 184.2
perjuries: p. of love blown away by winds 857.12
permanent: nothing is p. but change 117.19
the spiny coiffure was in actuality a home p. 407.3
perpetrate: whatsoe'er we p., we are steered by fate 340.2
perpetual: with agonizing finality, p. night will fall 415.4
persecution: opposition becomes sweet when called p. 565.4
p. was a sign of personal interest 984.3
truth does not always triumph over p. 998.83
perseverance: p. can lend actions appearance of dignity 686.4
p. is more prevailing than violence 686.6
persevere: to p. is courage in a man 686.2
person: invite everyone who knew the p. 367.13
make a p. into something other than himself 858.19
one p. missing can depopulate world 2.8
p. makes event and event p. 110.4
Personnel: few great men could pass P. 401.23
persons: all p. are puzzles 1008.7
p. cost much; for thee I must pay me 794.2
persuade: law cannot p. where cannot punish 528.26
persuaded: people better p. by own reasons 690.9
persuading: to please is great

step toward p. 690.2
persuasion: children should be led by p. 988.9
p. of a friend is a strong thing 690.8
the beneficent processes of peaceful p. 690.4
when gentle p. falls on deaf ears 250.3
perversion: connotations of intellectual and moral p. 277.6
perversity: p. is the muse of modern literature 545.25
p. is the soul's very life 691.9
pessimist: optimist proclaims we live in best of worlds; p. fears this is true 660.2
p. before forty-eight knows too much 660.4
p. is a man who's lived with an optimist 692.3
p. knows next year can't be any worse than the last 660.1
to a profound p. danger is not depressing 692.1
pet: everyone's p. is the most outstanding 41.5
petrify: quickly p. and become own statue 526.13
pettiness: p. of a mind can be measured by the p. of its adoration or its blasphemy 693.5
petty: in fool's p. estimate all things are little 693.6
Philadelphia: just been in a play that closed in P. 45.20
philanthropy: economic injustice which makes p. necessary 433.18
p. is almost only virtue appreciated 433.32
we excuse our lack of p. 936.3
Philistine: One of the surest signs of the P. 963.9
philosopher: a p. does not know what he is talking about 254.2
beard does not make p. 407.2
great memory does not make a p. 580.24
married p. belongs to comedy 694.26
never yet p. that could endure toothache 896.27
nothing so strange that it has not been said by one p. or another 694.5
peasant and p. may be equally satisfied 409.53
p. contents self with pitying persecutors 694.40
p. fulfills his mission imperfectly 694.34
p. spends time becoming a man 694.30
p. without good breeding is a cynic 391.3
posterity for the p. is what the other world is for the religious man 694.6
to be p. is not to have subtle thoughts 694.39
to be p. is to be prepared against events 694.7
to the p. all things are friendly and sacred 927.6
true p. makes light of philosophy 694.28
philosophers: constancy of p. conceals their disquietude 694.18
great p.: poets believing poems' reality 694.21
p. are as jealous as women 694.35
p. are timid and dislike the unexpected 694.33
p. cannot arise where is no prying beast 390.17
p. have scattered as many plagues as Pandora's box, but without hope at bottom 694.38
p. who try to be politicians no longer p. 694.20
say, Not so, and you will outcircle p. 258.11
we p. are full of things which take us out of ourselves 694.27
philosophical: in p. dispute, the defeated gains most 51.8
p. man lets his chance escape 975.18
whole man within us forms our p. opinions 694.12
philosophies: some p. are greater nonsense than others 694.4
philosophy: a p. centered on the priorities of life 541.13
business of p.: to part with self-conceit 166.7
difference between gossip and p. 694.10
do not all charms fly at mere touch of p. 694.13
every p. tinged with secret imaginative background 694.42
for learning of suspended judgment the best discipline is p. 694.32
let no young man delay the study of p. 694.8
little p. inclineth to atheism 694.1
nation struggling to find new p. of existence 368.29
no consolations of religion or p. unless one experiences their desolations 797.36
passions kill more prejudices than p. 675.5
p. a mode of bearing ills of life 17.17
p. begins in wonder and the wonder remains 694.43
p. doesn't triumph over the present evils 17.38
p. forms us for ourselves, not others 444.18
p. has a fine saying for everything 694.36
p. is characterized more by formulation of problems than by solution of them 694.17
p. is such a litigious lady 694.25
p., the continual pursuit of meanings 694.16
p. will clip an angel's wings 694.14
proof today of philosophical mediocrity is to look for a p. 694.29
schools of p. frequented for exercise 694.15
study p. to know own mind, not others' 694.11
suicide only serious question of p. 948.4
test of p. is how much it explains 797.23
that's why I love p.: no one wins 694.37
wonder is foundation of all p. 694.24
you can't do without p. 694.9
photograph: a p. of the person who is buried there 695.1
photographer: p. is in every bush like lion seeking prey 760.2
photographs: collect p., collect the world 695.6
take p. so they don't have to look 695.3
photography: p.: major force in explaining man to man 695.7
p., the art form of the untalented 695.9
physical: man with nothing but p. power to sell 696.5
physician: as long as men die and desire to live, a p. will be made fun of but well paid 263.8
deceive not thy p., confessor, lawyer 224.8
every p. has his favourite disease 263.4
hide nothing from confessor, lawyer, p. 165.6
p. has no power over sand in hourglass 263.11
physicians: p. leave cure to nature, but take credit 263.1
p., like kings, brook no contradiction 263.21
physicians': p. faults are covered with earth 342.8
physics: the effect of p. is concern of all men 641.4
pianists: art of p. resides in pauses 614.52
piano: p., the social instrument par excellence 614.5
Schoenberg does not write against the p., but neither can he be accused of writing for it 614.35
picture: one p. in 10,000 ought to live in applause 666.7
p. and sculpture are festivities of form 53.47
the p. awaits my verdict 666.5
piety: experience differentiates p., goodness 697.9
p., like nobility, has its aristocracy 697.5
p. of some is passion, infirmity, fashion 697.8
rash to intrude upon the p. of others 697.10
pig: p. with two owners dies of hunger 746.6
pillow: p. is a silent Sibyl 906.7
pilots: for p. there exists a kind of guild 28.4
pinches: only wearer knows where the shoe p. 321.14
pioneers: p. are invariably mess-makers 370.1
pious: with p. action we sugar o'er the devil 440.19
pit: whoso diggeth a p. shall fall therein 1070.3
pitch: whoever touches p. will be defiled 57.2
pitied: much better to be envied than to be p. 295.13
pity: a few things move people to p. 698.4
irony and p. are two good counselors 539.36
men p. those who fare badly 431.26
p. beyond telling is in heart of love 551.237
p. for all means hardness to neighbor 455.6
p. is for the living, envy for the dead 541.41

p. is not natural to man 209.9
p. is often avowed, seldom felt 412.5
p. kills, it makes our weakness weaker 698.2
p. may represent impersonal concern 960.8
p. melts the mind to love 698.9
p. would be no more if we did not make somebody poor 698.3
p. wraps student of the past in a cloud 698.11
Verily, I do not like them, the merciful who feel blessed in their p. 698.16
we have not p. unless we wish to relieve distress 698.13
world would die did p. not limit anger 698.18
pivot: secret of living is to find a p. 443.27
place: first journeys teach that p. is nothing 992.20
get p. and wealth with grace 1048.43
in the world I fill up a p. 320.2
not belong to p. until there is someone dead 678.4
one forgives a p. soon as it's left behind 699.2
p. is nothing unless at its heart a figure stands 699.7
p. not a p. until things in it are remembered 699.10
those allowed second p. have undoubted title to first 780.21
who longs to leave the p. where he lives 1011.20
places: all p. alike, every earth fit for burial 699.8
all p. are distant from heaven alike 699.1
nor expect very much from p. 992.23
plagiarism: if we steal thoughts from moderns, it's p. 700.1
plain: p. dealing is a jewel out of fashion 362.3
p. living nothing but voluntary poverty 701.3
p. speech breeds hate 362.4
plan: amid multitude of projects, no p. devised 702.5
bad p. admits of no modification 702.6
planet: what good is p. called Earth if you own no land? 746.22
plans: make no little p.; won't stir men's blood 702.1
p. get you into things, work gets you out 702.7
there should be neither p. nor schemes 702.3
plant: a p. is like a self-willed man 623.34
p. confounds the understanding 623.48
to p. seeds is commonest delight 371.6
plasticity: p. loves new moulds because it can fill them 422.19
plate: it was just as if he had dropped a p. 185.4
platform: to raise imbecility to profundity, put it on a p. 763.12
platitude: good p. makes the whole world kin 68.3
platitudes: calls and the theater propagate p. 188.36
play: at p. one should not think of learning 903.1
each loves the p. for what he brings to it 972.10
fiction to man what p. is to child 344.26
genius loves p. for its own sake 155.2
greatest inconvenience to playgoer is p. 972.33
in p. we reveal kind of people we are 703.6
it is a happy talent to know how to p. 703.3
life's like a p. 311.11
minds give way unless we mix work with p. 703.5
one is at ease if one must p. a part 825.3
p. should give something to think about 972.6
p. so that you may be serious 703.1
the true object of all human life is p. 703.2
player: best sound a p. can hear: deep silence 972.41
players: all the men and women merely p. 1067.25
playing: civilized race would add art of p. well 703.8
plays: in my p. I look at the commonplace 972.8
p. are like suppers; poets are the cooks 972.7
p. give authors more pain than pleasure 972.2
who p. deep loses money or character 369.1
playwright: p. dares not lose his audience for a minute 972.27
p. is lay preacher peddling current ideas 972.30
playwrights: science doesn't know anything about p. 849.39
playwriting: p., honorable but humbling 972.12
pleasant: must live well to live p. life 409.34
seek for the deceitful in the p. 390.15
pleasantry: p. is never good on serious points 436.35
please: it is vain to hope to p. all alike 474.5
not pleased with self, impossible to p. 863.4
p. all and you will p. none 474.1
p. God, do not let me wet my bed! 723.27
to p. is step toward persuading 690.2
to try to p. and p. not 366.2
way to rise is to obey and p. 945.23
we that live to p., must p. to live 972.16
you must p. people in their own way 984.2
pleased: men seldom give pleasure when not p. 788.1
there is a pleasure in not being p. 705.10
those p. with fewest things know least 963.7
pleases: if one p. all, one p. less profoundly 712.8
there must be good in what p. many 712.5
pleasing: art of p. lies in never speaking of yourself 188.15
if p. to one man, a girl is taken care of 581.49
p. ware is half sold 105.11
secret of displeasing none, if not of p. all, is to court mediocrity 474.3
pleasure: all p. balanced by equal pain 705.9
chords that vibrate sweet p. thrill woe 883.1
feel a little man's p. when they come a cropper 401.17
hour of pain is as long as a day of p. 946.14
in all p. hope is a considerable part 704.19
it is in habit we find the greatest p. 406.14
last p. in life is discharging our duty 271.9
let fancy roam, p. never is at home 336.9
look for secrets in grief or p. 855.7
man of p. is often most miserable 706.2
mankind is safer when men seek p., not power 704.15
men forget p. while getting their estate 945.32
men seldom give p. when not pleased 788.1
more fear than delight in secret p. 704.31
my p. comes from learning something 409.96
no p. endures unseasoned by variety 704.30
no p. is evil in itself 705.2
no profit grows where is no p. ta'en 704.35
our marriage is dead when p. is fled 262.3
pain is produced by prolonging p. 705.7
p. a short time growing, falls as fast 704.29
p. depends on the man, not on work, place 704.12
p. dies at moment when it charms us most 704.34
p. from sense of duty ceases to be p. 704.26
p. is a visitant; but pain clings to us 946.21
p. is least fallible critical guide 20.1
p. is none if not diversified 704.11
p.: object, duty, goal of rational beings 704.38
p.'s a sin, and sometimes sin's a p. 900.5
p. seizes whole man who is addicted to it 706.8
p. sweetest if paid for by other's pain 838.2
p. tasted satisfies less than desire 704.32
power is p., and p. sweetens pain 719.28
safe p. is tame p. 704.25
spirit is free when body is satiated with p. 704.22
sweet is p. after pain 705.1
there is a p. in indulging grief 918.32
there is no sterner moralist than p. 704.7
there is p. in the pathless woods 623.12
too much p. disagrees with us 704.27
understanding almost extinguishes p. 1007.9
vain is hope for p. in thing disdained 704.33
when p. is at bar, jury is not impartial 704.2
pleasure's: married p. best, shadow makes the sun strong 705.8
pleasures: better deep griefs than shallow p. 918.19
enjoy p., but let them be your own 704.9

few people want p. they are free to take 691.7
life exacts high interest rate for p. 539.91
mastery of p. better than abstinence 704.1
no man is a hypocrite in his p. 704.20
old age has its p. 653.62
one half of the world cannot understand the p. of the other 704.3
perils ask to be paid in p. 216.2
p. are like poppies spread 704.6
p. can act as counter-irritants 704.10
p., insects on the wing 990.6
p. to be avoided if greater pains result 705.6
p., trouble, greatest in anticipation 318.6
violent p. which reach soul through body 739.6
we've more days to live through than p. 704.16
pledge: don't fear to p. 857.12
Pleiades: when P. no longer part of human spirit, man lacks completeness and true humanity 294.1
plot: let Barnum & Bailey interpret p. by Stendahl 711.79
plots: p.: no more exhausted than men are 344.31
p. raise up commonwealths, ruin kings 819.6
plum: miss p. for want of courage to shake tree 980.8
plumber: anybody who has doubt about resourcefulness of p. never got bill from one 1.1
plunder: in search of opportunities to p. 711.52
plurality: p. is part of our nature 424.10
pocketbook: full p. often groans more loudly than empty stomach 1048.48
pockets: our last garment is made without p. 221.73
poem: a p. makes us see ourselves 1069.36
each thought of a p. filled poet's sky 708.33
form of a p. is invisible 708.6
good p. is a contribution to reality 708.102
great p., deep theorem, are reader's own experiences 532.3
p. is the dream made flesh 708.71
p. is true if it hangs together 708.37
p. should not mean but be 708.67
to read a p. is to hear it with our eyes 708.80
Writing a p. is discovering 708.39
poems: difficult to get the news from p. 708.115
finest p. are expedients to get bread 625.1
it is not enough for p. to be fine 708.53
majority of p. one outgrows, outlives 708.30
world so rich: never lack occasions for p. 708.46
poesy: drainless shower of light is p. 708.58
nothing so difficult as a beginning in p. 708.10
poet: beautiful woman is a practical p. 1062.45
courage of the p. is to keep ajar the door that leads into madness 708.72
for vain p., nothing of his is too much 708.62
God is the perfect p. 387.11
good p. made as well as born 708.56
great p. draws creations from own reality 708.75
great p. is the most unpoetical creature 708.114
great p. makes the void ring 708.82
how does p. speak to men with power 708.14
I don't quite know what you mean by "being a p." 708.32
lot of p.: to invent what's nonexistent 708.79
lover, p., are of imagination all compact 559.16
maturing as p. means maturing as whole man 708.28
no p. ever thought another better 166.4
nothing can deter a p. 708.107
of all mankind great p. is equable man 708.113
p. can earn more money writing about his art than he can practicing it 34.1
p. expresses feelings which are not in actual emotions 708.29
p. gives thoughts on carriage of rhythm 708.76
p. hath, like lover, his unruly times 708.118
p. is a bird of strange moods 708.41
p. is a nightingale 708.89
p. is he who hath fat enough, like bear, to suck his claws all winter 708.106
p. is in love with language 708.3
p. is the priest of the invisible 708.95
p. knows little, has presentiment of much 450.25
p. lost as p. if gives himself to a party 708.43
p. on Pegasus, reciting his own verses 924.2
p. should seize the particular 708.45
p. speaks his message across the millennia 708.27
p. transmutes cynicism into optimism 708.74
p. wishes he were the only one alive 1069.11
scientist alone is true p. 849.9
to master the torrent of life, p. quivers 539.85
to p. all things are friendly and sacred 927.6
to p., silence is an acceptable response 708.19
transfuse from one language to another the creations of a p. 524.39
true p. is a friendly man 708.65
whoever is a p. is one always 708.8
world will try to bury p. with trivialities 708.73
would you be a p. before going to school 708.16
poetic: the p. faculty of denying our universe 450.15
to p. mind all things are poetical 708.64
poetry: good p. forged with sweat, blood, tears 708.26
if p. comes not naturally 708.59
most Americans do not like p. 708.48
most wretched cradled into p. by wrong 708.90
p.,-best words in their best order 708.17
p. doesn't necessarily have to be beautiful 708.18
p.: emotion recollected in tranquillity 708.117
p. is a counterfeit creation 708.25
p. is adolescence fermented and preserved 708.78
p. is a state of grace 708.55
p. is attempt to paint color of wind 708.7
p. is but the ashes of burnt-out passion 708.52
p. is crown, end, aim of literature 708.69
p. is halfway between prose and music 708.49
p. is hard to read—its sense is, anyhow 708.9
p. is harmony of words; music, notes 614.30
p. is like painting 708.54
p. is opening and closing of a door 708.83
p. is reflective; it stops to think 614.2
p. is revelation of personal feeling the reader recognizes as his own 708.81
p. is the expression of excited passion 708.12
p. is the plough that turns up time 708.68
p. is whim of nature in her lighter moods 708.2
p. lifts veil from hidden beauty of world 708.91
p. makes its own pertinence 708.34
p. makes nothing happen 708.4
p. makes your toenails twinkle 708.103
p. of art: beholding single tower 1014.2
p. should be great and unobtrusive 708.60
p. should prevent language from changing too rapidly 524.11
p. sinks under moderate weight of prose 708.63
p.'s unnat'ral; no man ever talked p. 'cept a beadle on boxin' day 708.24
p. the universal possession of mankind 708.44
people fancy they hate p., and are poets 708.35
poets arguing about modern p.: jackals snarling over a dried-up well 708.21
prose is discourse, p. ellipsis 708.77
song is the primal thing in p. 708.5
the labor put into the creation of the p. 708.100
those who have never entered scientific pursuits know not p. surrounding them 849.37
to read p. I take down my dictionary 244.4
unwritten p. escapes by other vents 708.36
when power corrupts, p. cleanses 708.61

poet's: color is the p. wealth 708.104
ne'er was flattery lost on p. ear 708.86
p. mind receptacle for storing feelings 708.31
p. pen gives to airy nothing a habitation 708.87
p. pleasure is to withhold some meaning 708.111
the p. business calls him out at all hours 708.108
poets: all p. who, when reading from own works, experience choked feeling, are major 708.112
arrogance of p. is only a defense 708.70
artists, p. uninterested in happiness 708.84
in America, too much fuss of p. 708.98
not by wisdom do p. make what they compose 708.94
pleasure in poetic pains only p. know 708.22
p. are hierophants of unapprehended inspiration 708.93
p. are sultans, would kill their brothers 1069.16
p. creators and creations of their age 53.133
p. exhibit only civil side of nature 708.105
p. in youth begin in gladness 708.119
p. lose praise by what they discreetly blot 460.6
p., more unpredictable than other writers 708.88
p., not supposed to write epics 708.116
p. pretend to write for immortality 708.20
p. seldom sing a new song 708.23
p. unacknowledged legislators of world 708.92
p. wrap truth in tales, yet they know her 708.13
popular p. are parish priests of the Muse 708.85
to have great p., there must be great audiences too 59.7
poets and novelists: p. conducting demure and careful lives 451.11
pointlessness: one man's p. is another's satire 844.1
poise: men don't know how much strength in p. 598.11
poison: Christianity gave Eros p. 892.37
expect p. from standing water 446.3
pills are harmless; the p. is in the sugar 745.5
police: for middle class, p. help old ladies; for urban poor, p. arrest you 709.6
men who agree perfectly with their p. 822.14
vague uneasiness, the p. 709.1
policeman: p. goes afther vice as law officer an' comes away as philosopher 709.2
principle is not as powerful as a p. 425.7
policeman's: p. lot is not a happy one 709.4
policies: nation's p. determined by its interests 621.14
policy: bad administration can destroy good p. 13.3
p. sits above conscience 319.5
p. turned back almost one hundred years 965.21
polish: elbow-grease is the best p. 281.3
polite: only great man holds own without being p. 830.4
politeness: a special word, "civil," for mere p. 289.35
it is wise to apply p. to friendship 197.3
p. is artificial good humor 197.9
p. is to human nature as warmth is to wax 197.12
p. requires this thing; decorum that 749.5
p.: the most acceptable hypocrisy 197.1
true power and p. are above vanity 719.58
politic: body p. carries in itself causes of its destruction 395.53
political: French p. thought: nostalgic or utopian 361.3
ignorance, conceit, point to p. career 711.77
knowledge of human nature the beginning and end of p. education 711.5
liberty is the highest p. end 537.1
man is by nature a p. animal 711.9
nature will overturn corrupt p. system 819.26
old p. values disappeared 967.16
persistence in one opinion never considered a merit in p. leaders 711.20
p. action is citizen's highest responsibility 711.42
p. convention not place you can come away from with any faith in human nature 711.40
p. extremism involves two ingredients 335.4
p. history is elevated to world history 419.41
p. is replacing metaphysical as mode of grasping reality 711.23
p. language makes lies sound true 711.68
p. leader must keep looking over his shoulder to see if the boys are still there 711.11
p. parties die of swallowing own lies 710.1
p. party members seek power for happiness 711.65
p. power grows out of barrel of gun 711.56
p. skill is ability to foretell what will happen and to explain later why it didn't 711.19
p. sovereignty a mockery without means to meet poverty, illiteracy, disease 718.43
p. truth is libel 998.54
power-worship blurs p. judgment 719.47
solutions not expected in p. campaign 1038.13
some p. problems have no solution 711.38
test of p. institutions: condition of country whose future they regulate 487.4
there is nothing that is not p. 711.54
to master life, p. hero erects fortress 539.85
we demand more of p. life than personal 711.47
when p. ammunition low, artillery of abuse is wheeled into action 711.81
politically: educate masses p.: make history personal 132.4
political parties: p. are not debating societies 710.13
political speech: p. and writing, defense of the indefensible 711.67
politician: a p. is an arse 711.24
consult the veteran instead of the p. 1042.61
good p., under democracy, is unthinkable 711.59
idealism and a p.'s will to power 442.6
it takes a p. to run a government 711.83
most distinctive characteristic of successful p. is selective cowardice 711.32
one has to be a murderer to be a p. 443.20
p. cannot smear himself in the mud 711.94
p. can't call columnist the things columnist is allowed to call p. 630.18
p. is an acrobat 711.10
p. must learn to coax the electorate 711.78
p. never believes what he says 711.25
p. ought to be honest; afther that, crafty 711.26
p. tacks with wind, but also makes breezes 711.84
when p. gets an idea he gets it all wrong 711.58
whether any p. believes what he says 711.87
politicians: do not want their sons to become p. 670.29
p. know less now that they campaign by air 28.2
p. need not care about the slums 711.31
p. promise bridge even where no river 711.44
p. tend to live "in character" 711.49
p. want power for happiness' sake 711.65
spare me sight of thankless breed of p. 711.27
successful democratic p. insecure men 711.50
too many p. believe you can fool all the people all the time 711.1
who raises new issues is distasteful to p. 711.48
politics: all p. based on indifference of majority 711.72
all p. is local 711.66
eloquence in p. can win what is won in war 283.1
first rule of p. is never to say never 711.76
identify with mankind, take part in p. 711.29
in middle life, p. are a temperament 586.3
in p. failure is decisive 711.62
in p. gray is a forbidden color 711.15
magnanimity in p. is the truest wisdom 711.16
modern p. a struggle of forces, not men 711.6
money is power in American p. 719.27
my only p. have been friendship 365.28

only in p. are we content with common man 711.35
p., a matter of serving those around us 711.34
p., art of making civilization work 711.46
p. cannot stop to study psychology 711.3
p.: choice between the disastrous and the unpalatable 711.28
p. consists of the delusion that a change in form is a change in substance 711.60
p. has always been a con game 711.53
p. interests people who don't know how to make love 711.18
p. in Texas, finest form of free entertainment 711.37
p. is an educational process 711.75
p. is a place of modest requirements 711.21
p. is imagination and mind 711.82
p. is improvisation 711.86
p. is the diversion of trivial men 711.63
p. is the systematic organization of hatreds 711.7
p. is war without bloodshed 711.57
p. keeps us out of affairs concerning us 711.85
p. mean compromising of extremes 711.88
p. shaped by men without ideals 711.17
p.: strife of interests masquerading as contest of principles 711.13
p. suspected to be much ado about nothing 711.51
public interested more in government than p. 711.73
sin a basic concept in religion and p. 900.20
the profession I chose was p. 528.72
tolerance, of little worth in p. 711.92

poll: p. taken among members of the capitol press corps 941.11

polling: inside p. booth every American equal 297.22

poodle: p., the insignia of one's deviation 41.6

poor: a p. race in a land of dollars 718.8
be rich for yourself, p. to friends 858.20
children are p. men's riches 123.16
easier to talk of poverty than think of p. 974.8
evermore thanks, the exchequer of the p. 399.9
forest is the p. man's overcoat 995.4
forgive us blaming p. for their poverty 879.3
forgive us for pretending to care for p. 718.56
function of p. to exercise our generosity 718.51
funeral expenses are the curse of the p. 367.4
gratefulness is the p. man's payment 399.2
handsome man is not quite p. 582.13
he is p. that craves much 403.6
he is p. who does not feel content 186.13
I didn't feel p., I just felt that I didn't have any money 718.9
if free society cannot help the many who are p., it cannot save the few who are rich 718.42
in change of government, p. change masters 718.48
in fight rich man saves face; p. man, coat 345.6
man rich or p. according to whether he can afford necessaries, conveniences 1048.56
no being so p. who does not think there is somebody still poorer 185.3
one flag for the rich, one for the p. 718.45
people don't demand cripples run races, yet ask p. to act like everyone else 718.24
p. and content is rich, and rich enough 186.21
p. command respect; beggar excites anger 74.2
p. die of indifference in peace-time, or by homicidal passion if war breaks out 718.10
p. man ruined as soon as he apes the rich 933.4
p. man's debt makes a great noise 222.6
p. man's wisdom is despised 718.6
p. men's reasons are not heard 718.17
p. must be wisely visited and cared for 718.58
p. on borderline of starvation live purposeful lives 718.27
p. tend to become increasingly invisible 718.21
provision for p. is test of civilization 433.16
sell what thou hast, and give to the p. 684.3
surest way to remain p., be honest 425.10
the more humanity owes the p. man, more society denies him 718.50
to be p. without murmuring is hard 1048.12
to the p. I was p. pretending to be rich 135.5
we liberals know the p. are our equals in every sense except being equal to us 718.55
what to the p. we give, to Jove is lent 433.14
with full stomach rich and p. are alike 274.9

poorer: happier when p., but were also younger 1071.42

populace: p. drag down gods to their own level 682.6

popular: p. government awakens spirit and energy 233.15
p. government no guarantee of good government 395.38
p. men create monsters then quell them 711.39
p. persons: those who take world as it is 712.10
what is p. is not necessarily vulgar 712.7
when fortune is with us, p. favor is too 15.9

popularity: distance between p. and politics is short 611.1
fame is a vapor, p. an accident 990.18

population: natural selection deals ruthlessly with any p. 308.2
p. condemned to inaction is explosive 568.2
the p. then was two per square world 84.3
to keep hope in world, keep changing p. 427.23

populations: large p. make technology indispensable 966.16

populous: great city not same as p. one 131.2
very p. city is rarely well governed 131.3

porcupine: p. may be respected, but never loved 808.4

pornography: appeal of p. due to indecent feelings about sex which moralists inculcate in young 714.2
p. of violence far exceeds sexual p. 1032.9

portrait: I would rather see the p. of a dog that I know 666.8
p. painted with feeling is p. of artist 666.13
two styles of p. painting: serious, smirk 666.4

ports: p. don't care what impressions they make 839.2

position: holding a p. rather than doing a job 102.2
only one p. for an artist anywhere 78.22

positions: easy to appear worthy of p. we don't have 1.11

positive: most p. men the most credulous 264.14
p.: mistaken at top of one's voice 51.2

possess: as unjust to p. woman as slaves 716.13
human nature limits our power to p. 716.8
to p. is past the instant we achieve the joy 716.4

possesses: who p. most is most afraid of loss 716.9

possessing: no one worth p. can be quite possessed 716.16

possession: bliss in p. will not last 580.19
every p. lent by chance for uncertain time 116.15
fie on p. but if a man be vertuous withal 716.2
how sweet an emotion is p. 716.6
man's real p. is his memory 580.37
not p. but use is the only riches 1048.23
object in p. seldom has charm it had in pursuit 716.11
one p. outvalues all others: last breath 539.127
want of thing perplexing, p. intolerable 716.17

possessions: not p., but desires, need equalizing 746.1
we get possessed by our p. 746.12
zest for p. retains some energy 8.9

possibilities: offer more entertainment p. than the TV set 967.8
round about what is, lies world of p. 336.11

possibility: each believes he has a greater p. 55.4

possible: aspire not to immor-

tality; exhaust the p. 542.12
knowing the p. is beginning of happiness 542.13
possible's: p. slow fuse is lit by imagination 450.9
posterity: let us transmit to p. a memorial 6.15
love of p. caused by death 802.1
p. is likely to be wrong 207.7
postponement: life is for most one long p. 231.8
postscript: woman seldom writes her mind but in p. 535.4
pot: enquire not what boils in another's p. 211.5
potentiality: man is as full of p. as of impotence 717.3
potter: p. is potter's enemy 155.6
poverty: all arguments that p. is no evil, show it to be great evil 718.35
America has the best-dressed p. the world has ever known 718.22
avarice is as destitute as p. 403.19
beauty and myths: perennial masks of p. 718.23
easier to talk of p. than think of poor 974.8
for every talent that p. has stimulated it has blighted a hundred 718.18
give me neither p. nor riches 701.1
gold has ruined fewer men than p. 718.1
he is to be dreaded who dreads p. 33.22
honest rich can never forget p. 718.12
in train of excessive wealth, excessive p. 1048.34
laziness travels slowly, p. overtakes him 530.3
neither p. nor pain is accumulable 946.6
plain living is voluntary p. 701.3
p. comes imploring us to find a purchaser for its unmarketable wares 718.28
p. has many roots; tap root is ignorance 718.34
p. has very different appearances 718.37
p. heaps men with ridicule 718.39
p. is enemy to happiness, liberty, virtues 718.36
p. is good in poems, but bad in a house 718.5
p. is no crime, it's a blunder 718.32
p. is no disgrace, but it is inconvenient 718.54
p. is parent of revolution and crime 718.3
p. is the indifference of hospitals 718.7
p. of the soul is irreparable 620.6
p.-stricken man thinks rich man happy 153.4
p. the worst of dangers 718.53
p. was a specific black face for him 17.43
p. with joy isn't p. at all 718.52
pretense, more than p., harasses ruined man 718.31
rich man cannot imagine p. 718.47
slow rises worth by p. depressed 718.38
there is no crime so shameful as p. 718.16
the teacher's chief difficulty is p. 718.25
wealth, p.: parents of discontent 251.7
we didn't know p. had a name 718.33
power: absolute p. is absolutely delightful 719.7
advantage of p.: you can do more good 719.26
anarchy is stepping stone to absolute p. 36.1
by promise of p., evil attracts the weak 307.20
computer's p. resembled that of a bulldozer 943.4
cowardice is incorrigible which love of p. cannot overcome 199.3
friend in p. is a friend lost 719.3
garb of religion best cloak for p. 797.32
greater the p., more dangerous the abuse 719.10
great p. drowns some men in honors 426.7
hand of liberality stronger than arm of p. 375.6
how to get men of p. to live for rather than off the public 719.33
idealism and a politician's will to p. 442.6
if one does wrong, best to do it pursuing p. 1070.8
it is natural for men to want p. 719.57
joy of life to put out p. in useful way 504.11
kings' p. founded on people's folly 831.16
life is a search after p. 719.20
man in p. puts on new manners 719.22
mankind is safer when men seek pleasure, not p. 704.15
national greatness is moral, not physical, p. 604.38
no man is wise nor good enough to be trusted with unlimited p. 719.13
no pleasure in p. over fellow citizens 719.32
no safe depository of p. but people 233.22
not balance of p., but community of p. 498.21
numerous family is bulwark of p. 719.55
people demand freedom when they lack p. 537.26
political p. grows out of barrel of gun 711.56
politicians want p. for happiness' sake 711.65
p.: a sharing of the nature of the world 719.19
p. corrupts and absolute p., absolutely 719.2
p. doesn't have to show off 719.18
p. educates the potentate 831.5
p. for good no greater than p. for evil 967.11
p. gives no purchase to hand, will not hold 719.23
p. involves freedom from good and evil 719.43
p. is more vivid when we break a man's spirit than when we win his heart 719.30
p. is pleasure, and pleasure sweetens pain 719.28
p. is used to make knowledge a slave 764.8
p. legitimate only under contract 719.37
p. never has trouble drumming up friends 719.35
p. of the unprivileged to extort 15.7
p. pollutes whate'er it touches 719.54
p. steps back only in face of more p. 719.42
p. takes as ingratitude the writhing of its victims 719.56
p. wedded to chronic fear is formidable 719.29
p. wielded by abnormal energy is serious fact 719.4
p.-worship blurs political judgment 719.47
prize cared for by powerful is p. 719.31
property has greatest p. in life 746.7
property of p. is to protect 719.48
reckless pursuit of p. 719.38
self-reverence, self-knowledge, self-control lead life to sovereign p. 858.28
to ask for p. is forcing uphill a stone which rolls back again 719.40
to know pains of p. go to him who has it 719.12
true p. and politeness are above vanity 719.58
universal need to exercise some kind of p. 719.44
unlimited p. makes any man a despot 719.6
Washington's charm was that people here thought mostly about p. 1044.5
we thought since we had p. we had wisdom 719.8
when p. corrupts, poetry cleanses 708.61
when reality of p. has been surrendered 719.17
You shall have joy, or you shall have p., said God 719.21
powerful: liberty is latitude the p. accord weak 537.14
the p. can take your life 518.1
powers: getting and spending we lay waste our p. 104.37
practical: ignoring contradictions in principle makes the p. man 319.1
unless I turn thoughts into p. living, I cannot reap good 1065.46
practice: grand schoolmaster is p. 279.15
habit is p. that becomes man himself 406.7
if thou hast no p. thou art ignorant 721.2
in p. error and truth do not consort 9.10
man may be sincere in principles, not p. 734.10
p. aimless in absence of nature, learning 279.68
p. forms a man to anything 867.1
p. is nine-tenths 721.1
theory and p. of life not reconciled 974.3
prairie: to make a p. it takes a clover and one bee 818.1
praise: all motivated by desire for p. 386.3
censure of man's self is

oblique p. 863.6
deafest man can hear p. 722.15
envy bestrides p. 722.24
expect not p. without envy until death 722.4
generally we p. only to be praised 722.17
ingenuous mind feels reproof in unmerited p. 722.16
man of truly noble ways listens not to p. 600.7
men feel injured by p.; limits merits 722.35
modesty the only sure bait for p. 600.3
never p. a sister to a sister 1062.82
no p. beats one you can put in your pocket 722.20
nothing is made worse or better by p. 72.6
people ask for criticism, but want p. 206.15
people swallow anything seasoned with p. 202.8
p. from ignorant man is only good-will 722.29
p. is always pleasing 722.21
p. is more obtrusive than a reproach 722.22
p. is the best diet for us, after all 722.28
p., like gold, owes value to its scarcity 722.12
p. makes good men better, bad men worse 722.6
p. shames me, for I secretly beg for it 722.31
p. to the undeserving is severe satire 722.5
purr at every stranger's p.! 34.35
refusal of p. is desire for p. twice 722.18
safest p.: to foretell greatness for another 722.10
sign of mediocrity to p. moderately 722.34
stupid criticism versus stupid p. 722.26
true p. comes even to the lowly 722.27
unmerited p. has not the power to heal 722.11
we p. when a thing needs our assistance 722.32
who does not love p. is not a full man 722.1
praised: none are so much p., censured, as we think 1027.5
p. by honest men, abused by rogues 804.4
praises: p. from an enemy imply real merit 722.7
p. from wicked men are reproaches 722.8
there are p. which defame 722.19
we are tolerant of p. of others if we think we do as well 722.33
who first p. book next in merit to author 207.30
praising: good of p. self is one can lay it on thick 722.2
pray: affliction sometime teacheth wicked to p. 723.20
do not p. for easy lives 723.22
folly for a man to p. to gods for that which he has power to obtain for himself 880.8
how ready is heaven to those that p. 723.21
it is not well to p. cream, live skim milk 723.2
only he can p. well who lives well 723.13
p.: to ask laws of universe be annulled for petitioner confessedly unworthy 723.4
what we p. to ourselves for is granted 305.3
prayer: cravings do not become a p. 723.17
more things are wrought by p. than this world dreams of 723.34
p. for private end is theft and meanness 723.11
p. from other than one whose heart lives in grace of God is unheeded 723.9
p. has never superseded practical efforts 723.30
p. is a goodly Christian's weapon 723.23
p. is contemplation of facts of life 723.12
p. is not an old woman's idle amusement 723.15
p. is the implement through which men reach where presence is denied them 723.10
p. should be the key of the day 723.14
we all have p.-wheels we set up on steppes 723.18
what are men better than sheep, if knowing God, they lift not hands of p. 723.35
who rises from p. a better man 723.24
wish to pray is a p. 723.3
work is p., stink is p. 1065.44
prayers: certain thoughts are p. 723.19
few men durst publish their p. to God 723.25
for p. to be heard we must also strive 723.1
I have had p. answered—most strangely so sometimes 723.7
in p. he says, thy will be done 723.28
p. are to men as dolls to children: comforting but hard to take seriously 723.5
ruin outruns all p., forces men astray 1042.43
we offer p. to God, treat Him like a pasha 723.36
prayeth: he p. best who loveth best 723.8
praying: when p. does no good, insurance does help 489.1
preach: go ye into the world and p. the gospel 596.1
judged more by what we do at home than what we p. abroad 498.6
who cannot wisely meddle with public affairs in preaching gospel, cannot p. 724.1
preacher: no p. listened to but time 978.66
rain and bad p. do not know when to stop 778.2
who has but one word of God before him, and cannot make a sermon, cannot be a p. 724.8
preacher's: p. garment is cut to pattern of hearers 724.7
preachers: people who can act are never p. 9.17
preaches: goodness that p. undoes itself 393.15
he p. well that lives well 724.2
preaching: by reading sermons, clergy lose art of p. 724.6
next best thing to good p. is bad p. 724.3
no p. has made death other than death 221.82
p. helps preserve well-inclined men 724.10
p. is by-word for long, dull conversation 724.9
precautions: torment of p. often exceeds dangers 112.5
precedent: danger, when vice becomes a p. 1030.12
p. embalms a principle 986.8
precedents: bad p. began as justifiable measures 528.11
if you're strong enough, there are no p. 940.8
precept: example is the best p. 310.1
precipice: we run carelessly to the p. 87.8
predict: p. the present without knowing the past 747.1
prefer: let us p., let us not exclude 725.5
preference: esteem must be founded on p. 725.4
preferences: there are as many p. as there are men 725.2
prefers: how often one p. one's enemies to his friends 288.23
preindustrial: in p. cultures leisure not a burden 533.13
prejudice: ink in which history is written: fluid p. 419.46
knowledge the best protection against p. 522.53
loss of innocence brings loss of p. 57.7
natural affection is a p. 334.17
p. is the child of ignorance 726.7
p. uneasy unless it can pass for reason 726.6
p.: vagrant opinion without visible means of support 726.3
race p. decreases values 775.5
race p. is a shadow over all of us 775.3
racial p. is like hair across cheek 775.1
strongest p.: fancied exemption from all p. 726.8
the strongest weapon against p. 726.1
prejudiced: no man p. for thing he knows is wrong 726.13
prejudices: man wins friends by p., narrowness 726.5
one cannot eliminate p.—just recognize them 726.12
our p. are our mistresses 726.4
passions kill more p. than philosophy 675.5
p. eradicate every tender disposition 726.11
weeding out p., some eradicate virtue 726.14
when orators and auditors have same p., the p. run risk of standing for truths 763.14

preoccupation: p. with the choice of a mate 308.3
preparation: life is only art we practice without p. 539.79
prepare: for all your days p. 728.2
prepared: to be philosopher is to be p. against events 694.7
prescribed: patients lie about taking of things p. 577.3
prescription: who saw a physician approve another's p. 263.10
presence: good p. is letters of recommendation 45.9
how great love is, p. best trial makes 2.4
p. strengthens love 2.6
present: brutes show wisdom in enjoying the p. 41.29
building fragile p. out of pieces of past 498.4
future lies in giving all to p. 729.5
he who bringeth p. findeth door open 99.4
he who fears not future may enjoy p. 368.12
memory kills p., offers its heart to past 580.38
no mind much employed upon the p. 729.16
one is led to misjudge the p. 419.34
p. alone presses, not future or past 729.1
p. has one advantage—it is our own 729.6
p. is nothing but as it appertains to past and future 729.17
p. is our only reality 784.14
p. joys are more to flesh and blood 409.32
p. moment an extraordinary crisis 729.8
p. offers itself for only instant of time 729.23
superiority of the distant over the p. 238.36
the p. age is demented 729.22
things p. seem worst 729.24
volatile p. converts to adamantine past 729.10
we constantly abuse p. age, which our children will praise 298.6
wisely improve the p.; it is thine 676.22
presents: p., believe me, seduce both men and gods 384.24
p., I often say, endear absents 384.17
preserve: to p. a man alive is a miracle 263.19
to p., renew almost as noble as to create 263.20
presidency: far less to p. than meets the eye 730.13
p.: greased pig in game of American politics 730.2
p. is but splendid misery 1031.2
p. is highest office in gift of people 1031.1
President: not even a P. is independent 730.22
when P. and Congress agree 233.56
president: a p. may speak of kicking butts 730.11
being p., sense you're inside glass bowl 730.25
every p. reconstructs the presidency 730.14
function of p. is to set unfinished business before the American people 730.10
no easy problems ever come to the p. 730.6
p. can restore Congressional party solidarity 730.15
p. only lobbyist of whole nation 730.18
the only p. who died of overwork 548.11
the p. we get is the country we get 730.4
President's: the P. decisions make the weather 730.21
Presidential: when the P. virus attacks the system 730.20
president's: p. hardest task is to know what is right 730.8
presidents: p. arrive bright as freshly minted dimes 730.23
press: freedom of p. a bulwark of liberty 731.5
freedom of p. is means, not an end 731.2
hand that rules p. rules country 576.3
if p. free, no government lacks censors 113.5
liberty of p. is approved if it takes liberties with others 731.3
p. can't be restrained by government 731.5
p. secretary to keep man in public eye 760.1
p., weak slat under the bed of democracy 630.20
the p. and idols with feet of clay 332.50
the p. exerts the pressure of dissent 731.4
the role of the p. is to make money 630.21
to fetter p. is to fetter ourselves 731.6
pressed: p. into service means p. out of shape 887.3
presumes: he that knows least p. most 447.12
pretend: not one of us can lie or p. 444.19
pretending: p. is a virtue 732.12
pretense: possible to prick large p. with pin 1061.18
p., more than poverty, harasses ruined man 718.31
pretenses: greatest p. are built to hide emptiness 165.8
pretension: mark of man of world is absence of p. 917.3
prey: if can't p. on others, we p. on ourselves 174.13
price: highest p. can pay for anything: to ask it 805.3
p. of everything is trouble acquiring it 1026.22
p. offered is counted upon to produce result sought 108.2
sell us all good things at the p. of labor 1065.49
pride: gilded dust, our p. looks whole, sound 733.23
idleness and p. tax with heavy hand 446.7
it's a fine thing to rise above p. 733.1
one may be humble out of p. 435.15
people oppose established opinions from p. 258.8
p., avarice, envy are tongues men heed 733.5
p. destroys all symmetry and grace 733.22
p. doesn't wish to owe, self-love to pay 647.3
p. goeth before destruction 733.2
p., ignorance mutually beget each other 447.7
p. is in thought; tongue has small share 733.14
p. is last vice good man sheds 733.7
p. is seldom delicate 733.12
p. is the mask of one's own faults 733.11
p. makes some men ridiculous 733.3
p. often borrows humility's cloak 733.8
p. over-estimation by self-love 733.21
p. that dines on vanity sups on contempt 733.6
p. thyself on virtue, not on parentage 37.7
proper to have p., ridiculous to show it 733.13
unlike a magnet, p. at all points repels 733.4
unwillingness to submit to formalities is p. 114.3
when we fail, p. supports us 6.4
priests: in death and famine, reason is on the side of the p. 138.4
p. are no more necessary to religion than politicians to patriotism 138.5
p. put crowns on thieves, called kings 127.3
prig: p. finds last refuge in responsibility 749.1
primitive: more p. a society, more leisured its life 213.8
prince: p. not as gr-reat in ol' counthry as here 829.2
who draws his sword against the p. 786.5
princes: p. are like heavenly bodies 831.3
where p. are concerned, man able to do good is as dangerous as one who intends evil 831.17
principal: who has first place seldom plays p. part 780.6
principle: amid pressure of events, p. is no help 734.7
contradictions in p. easily set aside 319.1
don't make a novel to establish a p. 344.9
everywhere the basis of p. is tradition 734.8
men of p. are sure to be bold 734.4
party wedded to p. can save century 674.7
precedent embalms a p. 986.8
p. is not as powerful as a policeman 425.7
prosperity is the best protector of p. 734.16
we lack the inner p. of order 661.10
we talk on p., but we act on interest 495.3
principles: cause of evils inability to apply p. 373.2
corruption of government begins with p. 191.9
easier to fight for p. than live them 734.15
expedients are for an hour; p., for ages 734.2
false p., normal and necessary 734.1
fate of America is in its p. 734.13
general p., like air, are no

less important because they elude observation 734.6
man cannot make p.; only discover 1037.9
man is more careful of money than of p. 734.9
man may be sincere in p., not practice 734.10
p. have a way of drying up 734.11
true partisan as true to p. as to self 674.2
we speak of being anchored to our p. 734.3
print: p. never changes its mind 93.52
'tis pleasant to see one's name in p. 764.3
printed: things false not only are p., but things of truth most falsely set forth 764.2
printer: The Fates, like an absent-minded p. 457.7
printing: p. links the present with forever 764.11
printing-press: p. greatest blessing or curse 764.1
printin'-press: Th' p. isn't wondherful 764.4
prison: atmosphere not quite that of a p. 279.28
every p. is built with bricks of shame 735.10
most men in a brazen p. live 1065.2
pickaxe used to no purpose makes a p. 735.9
p., blood, death create enthusiasts 801.2
p. is a house of care, where none thrive 735.6
p. should be the most human of institutions 735.4
public knows practically nothing about p. 682.4
stone walls do not a p. make 735.8
vilest deeds bloom well in p. air 735.12
wherever one is against will is a p. 735.5
while there is soul in p., I am not free 100.2
prisoner: p. dashes for the open door 363.45
prisoners: men not p. of fate, but p. of own minds 590.16
prisons: all p. are brimming over with innocence 735.1
no ugly lovers nor handsome p. 58.3
privacies: count not him among friends who will retail your p. to the world 394.10
privacy: human needs p. as much as understanding 736.3
personal p. should be respected 736.1
to construct p. we first need community 736.2
private enterprise: nothing in Russia resembling p. 108.8
private: man uses now p., now public, nature 688.3
there are no such things as p. citizens 760.4
who dons public gown doffs p. person 761.5
privileged: comparing our lot, we are among the p. 153.2
concessions of the p. to the unprivileged 15.7
history of world is history of p. few 419.36
p. and the people formed two nations 135.1
privileges: privacy, the most relative of p. 736.5
what men value is not rights but p. 823.17
prize: let a p. lower my position 426.9
p. cared for by powerful is power 719.31
probability: reasonable p. is the only certainty 115.7
problem: no p. of human destiny beyond human beings 737.4
solution to one p. brings us to another 741.13
problems: certainty that p. have solutions 966.6
people are faced with new p. 299.16
p. are opportunities in work clothes 737.3
some political p. have no solution 711.38
procrastination: p. is art of keeping up with yesterday 231.7
p. is the thief of time 231.12
prodigal: if man is p., he cannot be truly generous 375.2
it is fun to be p. 324.1
prodigies: what happened to all those supposed p. 945.45
product: finished p. has seen better days 285.4
production: every p. must resemble its author 201.9
p. goes up and up 105.19
p. only fills void it has itself created 104.13
profession: price for pursuing any p. is intimate knowledge of its ugly side 1037.1
time gave the opportunity of learning my p. 978.27
professionals: I detest p. anythings 1069.6
p. resemble and recognize each other 1037.3
professions: all p. are conspiracies against the laity 1037.11
professor: p. led astray by artificial rules 279.47
professors: antiquity provides p. with bread, butter 42.4
culture wielded by p. to manufacture p. 210.24
p. guard the glory that was Greece 42.2
p. prefer own theories to truth 974.1
profit: even genius is tied to p. 602.46
no p. grows where is no pleasure ta'en 704.35
practice and theory of production for p. 104.17
p. system always unprofitable to most 108.16
smell of p. sweet, whatever the source 738.7
what p. to gain world and lose soul 33.2
profits: dirty p. ruin more than they keep 738.9
profound: p. thinker suspects that he is superficial 740.1
program: p. will expand to fill available memory 580.3
progress: all p. is precarious 741.13
all p. means war with society 741.23
basis of p.: desire to live beyond income 741.3
best road to p. is freedom's road 741.9
change is scientific, p. is ethical 117.31
desire to understand, to reform the world, are the two great engines of p. 741.22
discontent is the first step in p. 251.8
human p. is furthered by aberration 741.15
Is it p. if a cannibal uses knife and fork? 741.14
natural p. is from rudeness to convenience, to elegance, to nicety 741.8
no p. without faith in tomorrow 741.10
p. as fact, ethical principle 34.84
p. depends on the unreasonable man 741.25
p. has been made through disobedience 256.2
p. has no greater enemy than habit 406.12
p. in life comes through daring 741.17
p. is a nice word but change is its motivator 117.24
p. is gauged by sacrifice it requires 741.18
p. is the dirtiest word in the language 741.16
p. of the human race in understanding 1017.8
p.: to learn questions lack meaning 3.7
prudence sometimes blocks road of p. 755.12
routine of most active lives precludes p. 10.5
ruled by "p." 34.20
social movements are symptoms of p. 568.3
social p. strengthens freedom 741.11
the greatest threat to economic p. 178.7
there is no p. in art 53.38
thousand things advance; nine hundred and ninety-nine retreat: that is p. 741.1
world's p. made from scaffold to scaffold 741.20
prom: all saving ourselves for senior p. 728.1
prominent: most p. men are hard to converse with 332.6
promiscuous: as bee its sting, p. leave behind something of selves by which they must suffer 742.2
promise: April is a p. 854.6
p. binding in inverse ratio of the numbers to whom it is made 743.3
p., large p., is soul of advertisement 18.6
p. made is a debt unpaid 743.10
to p. not to do a thing 743.13
we p. much to avoid giving little 743.14
promises: enemies' p. were made to be broken 288.1
everyone's a millionaire concerning p. 743.9
men are alike in their p. 227.17
out of danger, man may forget p. 216.8
p. and pie-crust made to be broken 743.11
p. not to be kept if harmful to those to whom you have made them 743.2

p. on the new moon and the first snow 743.1
who p. too much means nothing 743.5
proof: blockhead wants p. of what he can't see 330.6
no way of thinking or doing, however ancient, can be trusted without p. 986.20
proofs: p. looked for last by religious mind 330.32
propaganda: all part of a great scheme of sex p. 581.6
p. more successful when it stirs hatred 745.7
triumphs of p. accomplished not by doing, but by refraining from doing 745.3
propagandist: p. makes one set of people forget that other sets are human 745.4
propagating: if p. the species were permitted only to the virtuous, world would be very good 892.7
property: all must fairly possess p., not seize it 1032.3
desire of p. implanted by nature 746.11
foundation of the social contract is p. 746.18
hater of p. has deed recorded 440.6
he whose all is his p. is easily destroyed 746.2
men honor p. above all; has greatest power 746.7
obstacle to democracy is p. 746.8
p. is requisite to self-respect 746.20
p. is theft 746.17
p. is timid and seeks protection 746.4
revolution is a transfer of p. 819.38
spirit of p. doubles a man's strength 746.21
what foundation for vanity lies in p. 716.6
where no p., no injustice 746.13
prophecy: p. is the most gratuitous form of error 747.3
prophesy: better to p. after event has taken place 747.2
prophet: best p. common sense, our native wit 148.5
p. is without honour in his own country 426.1
reason deserves to be called a p. 785.34
when God makes p., he doesn't unmake the man 442.9
prophets: the common destiny of all p. 747.5
wisest p. make sure of the event first 747.6
proportion: p. almost impossible; all exaggerate 748.1
without sense of p. there cannot be taste, intelligence, integrity 748.2
propose: woman might as well p. 198.8
propriety: p. is least of all laws and most observed 749.3
prose: good p. should resemble the conversation of a well-bred man 1069.89
one stanza outweighs book of p. 708.34
people become bankrupt having invested too heavily in the p. of life 612.9
p. can bear a great deal of poetry 708.63
p.,—words in their best order 708.17
when writing in p. you say what you mean 708.51
proselyter: no p. so energetic as atheist 1004.3
prospects: hours with happy p. in view more pleasing 318.3
prosper: those who p. take on airs of vanity 750.1
prosperity: adversity is greater teacher than p. 751.9
be moderate in p., prudent in adversity 755.19
curse of p.: it takes work away from us 750.9
easier to drive off adversity than keep p. 751.15
few of us can stand another man's p. 750.15
few respect p. without begrudging 295.1
for one man who can stand p., there are a hundred who can stand adversity 751.5
happiness requires a modicum of p. 750.2
heart great which shows moderation in p. 598.13
in p. be joyful, in adversity consider 751.4
in p. no altars smoke 797.41
in the day of p., adversity is forgotten 751.1
man insensible to p. till has adversity 751.13
much effort, much p. 281.5
one abhorred in p. is adored in adversity 751.8
p. doth bewitch men, seeming clear 750.17
p. first theme of political campaign 711.93
p. has no power over adversity 751.12
p. is full of friends 365.43
p. is the best protector of principle 734.16
p. makes friends, adversity tries them 751.11
p. only an instrument, not a deity 750.4
p. regarded as symptom of virtue 750.3
p. versus beauty; cash against soul 750.11
p. won't falter if you buy, buy, buy 105.16
social p. means man happy, citizen free, nation great 750.10
some never find p. for all their voyaging 750.6
to insure own p., must insure p. of all 151.9
virtue of p. is temperance 751.3
we now face task of surviving p. 750.8
when you ascend hill of p., may you not meet a friend 750.16
prosperity's: p. the very bond of love 750.14
prosperous: p. need people to be kind to 519.2
protect: property of power is to p. 719.48
protected: p. man doesn't need luck 856.8
protest: p. of a sensitive democratic conscience 913.20
Protestant: the P. must learn to decide for himself 125.22
protracted: life p. is p. woe 548.6
proud: but a step between p. man's glory, disgrace 733.16
every cock is p. on his own dunghill 873.7
he that is p. eats up himself 733.19
mind too p. to unbend over ridiculosa 612.5
p. man knows no superiors, inferiors 733.10
p. man satisfied with his own good opinion 733.9
struggle between p. mind, empty purse 718.31
the p. taken in by flattery 733.20
they are p. in humility 435.4
we are rarely p. when we are alone 915.51
proudly: die p. when one can no longer live p. 221.98
prove: p. anything with small segment of time 998.119
proved: what needs to be p. cannot be worth much 744.2
proverbist: p. knows only roundness of answers 572.1
providence: belief in p. has not allayed fears 754.11
wisdom of p. revealed in rarity of genius 754.10
provincial: the p. may try to crucify you 587.8
proving: accusing is p., with Malice as judge 5.1
proximity: human soul not framed for continued p. 499.9
prudence: misfortune attended with guilt and shame unqualifies man to act with p. 405.19
p. engenders paralysis of generous acts 755.29
p. is but experience 755.11
p. is ugly old maid courted by incapacity 755.3
p. sometimes blocks road of progress 755.12
self-made man acquires habit of p. 945.9
the eye of p. may never shut 755.8
where destiny blunders, p. will not avail 240.17
prudent: be p. in adversity 755.19
p. man does himself good 755.31
p. man doesn't make the goat gardener 755.13
p. person tries everything before arms 167.6
what is p. does not always lead to good 176.6
when you have nothing to say or hide, there is no need to be p. 755.10
prudently: nothing can be done at once hastily, p. 411.11
prudery: p. is the worst kind of avarice 756.3
pry: who p. into sewer cannot have nice noses 113.4
prying: for p. into human affairs, none equal those whom it does not concern 575.4
pseudocopulation: nothing unusual about an act of p. 424.8
psychiatrist: p. collects rent

on castle in air 757.3
psychiatry: our faith in p., touchingly quaint 757.2
psychoanalysis: 117 p. on the Pan Am flight to Vienna 758.9
p.: give it little finger, takes whole hand 758.5
psychoanalyst: man who once cursed his fate, now curses himself and pays his p. 758.8
psychology: idleness is the parent of all p. 759.2
p. gives a different idea of what we know 759.3
psychopathic: p. element rises to top of all crusades 111.11
psychotic: p. is man who lives in castle in air 757.3
puberty: phone ringing ever since she reached p. 385.6
public: artist cannot get along without a p. 53.54
best p. measures are forced by the occasion 395.20
better a quiet death than p. misfortune 434.4
can't be p. man unless man meets p. views 761.4
government no better than p. opinion sustaining it 762.17
he that writes to himself writes to an eternal p. 1069.37
how dreary to be p. like a frog 332.13
love in p. affairs does not work 551.66
man assumes p. trust, he's p. property 761.9
man must brave p. opinion, woman submit 762.20
man uses now private, now p., nature 688.3
men want p. office for its advantage 761.2
minds do not act together in p. 27.2
modesty, diffidence make man unfit for p. affairs 600.12
no group can withstand p. opinion 762.18
nothing makes more cowards than p. opinion 762.1
people before the p. live imagined life 332.42
press secretary to keep man in p. eye 760.1
p. always prefers to be reassured 682.7
p. buys opinions as it buys meat, milk 762.3
p. calamity is a mighty leveller 17.14
p. confidence is basis of effective government 395.34
p. forgives everything except genius 376.38
p. is odorless 208.1
p. men deem hypocrisy road to success 711.36
p. money like holy water—taken by all 191.6
p., more honest than judges of art 207.53
p. office is secure, but lacks hope, fear 761.7
p. official must be visible, kissable 761.6
p. opinion is generally p. sentiment 762.6
p. opinion is the thermometer a monarch should constantly consult 762.16
p. opinion makes life unpleasant for one not content to be the average man 762.10
p. sentiment is to p. officers what water is to the wheel of the mill 711.12
p. virtue is foundation of republics 1033.2
p. weal requires men betray, massacre 711.61
respect p. opinion as far as necessary 762.19
the p. swallow their classics whole 136.6
what p. will think prevents p. from thinking 762.8
when p. thinks long, it thinks right 762.12
who cannot wisely meddle with p. affairs in preaching gospel, cannot preach 724.1
who dons p. gown doffs private person 761.5
with p. sentiment nothing can fail 762.14
your p. servants serve you right 761.14
publications: p. that succeed pretend that persons admired by public are no better than public 764.6
public life: the p. of every political figure is a struggle 711.45
public opinion: court needs support of enlightened p. 762.11
public-relations: p. men make flower arrangements of facts 745.2
publishers: great authors produce great p. 764.5
p. function, bring everything out in the open 764.10
publishing: p. a first novel, money down a rat hole 764.15
puddle: every path has its p. 245.3
pugnacious: man learned habit of being p. from nature 26.5
pulse: feeling a woman's p. 263.17
pumpkin: every p. goes through all p. history 469.4
pun: goodness of p. in ratio of intolerability 768.2
punctuality: lack of p. alienates friendship 765.3
pundits: asinine predictions of p. 1060.42
punish: folly to p. neighbor by fire 817.15
God will not p. the man 817.17
law cannot persuade where cannot p. 528.26
punishment: all p. is mischief 766.2
capital p. is vestige of barbarism 70.5
crime and p. grow out of one stem 766.7
least free when under the threat of p. 766.17
not where a man lands that marks his p. 766.14
p. basic concept in religion and politics 900.20
p. hardens, numbs, produces concentration 766.13
p., vital need of the human soul 766.19
we are all sentenced to capital p. 12.4
punishments: many p. discredit a prince 766.10
punning: no false wit is so well practiced as p. 768.1
purchase: no need to p. day, water, sun, moon 623.60
purchaser: everything is worth what p. will pay 1026.18
pure: evil, fault of self-styled p. in heart 790.11
my strength is as the strength of ten, because my heart is p. 770.6
so long as we are dirty, we are p. 248.1
unto the p. all things are p. 770.3
purgatory: there is no other p. but a woman 1062.8
time is the only true p. 978.10
purge: order a p. for your brain, not stomach 726.10
Puritans: mightiest of P. who first insisted that beauty is only skin deep 72.28
we are presarvẹd fr'm th' P. 420.2
purity: p. is obscurity 770.5
purple: pisses God off if you walk by the color p. 143.4
purpose: life having p. based on religious system 771.4
masterpiece of man is knowing how to live to p. 771.7
secret of success is constancy to p. 771.3
the passion ending, doth the p. lose 675.21
through the ages one p. runs 741.27
to have a grievance is to have a p. 251.4
we all must have some p. in life 146.3
purposeful: busy life is nearest to a p. life 10.7
purposes: not data but p. constitute human experience 321.35
purse: better an empty p. than an empty head 447.11
heaviest bag for traveler is empty p. 992.21
man sacrifices his life to his p. 1027.20
should be silver in p. or on tongue 283.3
pursue: instinct of man to p. all that flies from him 691.10
thing we p. is often substitute for thing we really want 238.22
pursuit: hop on a horse in p. of youth 351.7
p. of alternative futures, keys to survival 956.6
puzzle: the four letter words of the easy p. 276.2
puzzles: all persons are p. 1008.7
pygmy: shall man hang self because he is a p. 877.4

Q

quacks: dishonesty is the raw material of q. 224.1
quaffing: long q. maketh a short life 268.34
qualities: some men have useless good q. 1023.6
we don't love q., we love persons 551.125
we love q., not a person 551.158
quality: easier to confess defect than claim a q. 342.1
one shining q. lends lustre to another 311.7
q. . . . you know what it is, yet you don't 1007.15

take a hundred ladies of q. 52.2
Yiddish has a down-to-earth q. 524.40
quarrel: association of men will always q. 772.8
beware of entrance to a q. 772.13
for every q. man and wife have before others, they have a hundred alone 564.60
justice of my q. 822.13
politest men q. at division of estate 1058.2
q. will always show where it was patched 772.7
test of breeding: how one acts in q. 391.7
we are losers when we q. with ourselves 170.2
when we q. we wish we had been blameless 772.4
quarreling: when chickens quit q., enough food for all 874.3
quarrels: great q. are great emancipations 772.14
most q. amplify a misunderstanding 772.5
q.: dowry married folk bring each other 564.96
q. of friends are opportunities of foes 772.1
q. often prove to be new recruits of love 772.2
q. wouldn't last if fault only on one side 772.9
those who interpose in q. often wipe a bloody nose 575.2
Queen Victoria: the writer's Q. is his public 436.8
to tell more about Q. than could be known 344.14
question: analysts always answer a q. with a q. 758.10
not every q. deserves an answer 480.9
q. even the existence of a God 265.3
sudden q. may surprise man, lay him open 480.2
to q. a wise man is beginning of wisdom 480.11
questioned: no evidence Khrushchev q. America's power 719.1
questions: great pleasure of ignorance is asking q. 480.16
it is possible for a handful of q. to break the bank of our answers 785.19
more to be learned from q. of child 480.15
no embarrassing q., just embarrassing answers 480.17
q. asked self are key to others' experience 875.1
q. shows the mind's range 480.12
who asks q. cannot avoid the answers 480.3
you want a few forever q. 480.1
quick: no man q. enough to enjoy life 539.70
quickly: things done q. are not done thoroughly 411.5
quiet: I am not so sure about being q. 899.2
no retreat as q. as one's own soul 183.1
quotation: fine q. is diamond on finger of a wit 773.6
quotations: I hate q. Tell me what you know 773.2

R

race: a poor r. in a land of dollars 718.8
he may well win the r. that runs by himself 155.5
individual man tries to escape the r. 469.9
no r. can prosper till it learns dignity of tilling field 1065.71
r. prejudice decreases values 775.5
r. prejudice is a shadow over all of us 775.3
we preach unabashed the gospel of the pure r. 726.2
you have to go the rounds from individual to individual to gather totality of r. 469.18
races: not r. but individuals are noble 774.1
racial: r. prejudice is like hair across cheek 775.1
racism: if we practice r. then it is r. we teach 775.14
plague of r. is insidious 775.2
racist: r. thoughts cannot be abolished by fiat 984.5
radical: I never dared to be r. when young 776.3
r. invents views, conservative adopts 178.21
r. of one century is conservative of next 776.7
radicalism: conservatism drives the children into r. 178.6
r. ceases to be radical when absorbed in preserving control over a society 776.4
spirit of American r. is destructive 776.2
radicals: r., relatives everyone wishes would go away 776.1
we need our r. 776.5
radio: hand that rules r. rules country 576.3
r., more effective than a squadron of B-52s 498.9
r., people listen while doing something else 777.1
science brought forth r. commentator 576.2
rage: where guilt is, r. and courage abound 405.9
railways: r. are irresistible bazaars 992.53
rain: drowning man is not troubled by r. 17.45
into each life some r. must fall 1011.22
r., bad preacher, do not know when to stop 778.2
r. does not fall on one roof alone 151.3
r. has soft architectural hands 778.1
r. is good for vegetables 778.4
so many pains when the r. is falling 778.5
though it r., cast not away watering pot 755.15
rainbow: after debauch of shower, r. a pledge 779.1
my heart leaps up when I behold a r. 779.2
rained: r. four years, eleven months, two days 778.3
rainy: preparing for r. day is sure to bring it on 105.16
rambling: mere r. is interminable 903.6
rank: there is no r. without some merit 780.12
would men retain r. without clothes 780.23
rap: r. confounds intellectual property law 614.25
r., fortress protected by talk and technology 614.23
r., the brain-resisted-while-body-boogies 614.24
rapine: nature is one with r. 623.69
rapture: first fine careless r. 82.3
rapture's: r. self is three parts sorrow 918.31
rare: what is so r. as a day in June 854.32
rashness: r. succeeds often, more often fails 781.2
rational: few ever wished to be exclusively r. 986.14
r. being discovers deity in creation 623.47
using r. choice to decide our futures 124.6
rationalist: r. mind has always had doubts about Venice 1029.4
rationalization: the r. of life in a machine society 317.
rationally: to him who looks upon the world r. 1067.17
reach: man's r. should exceed his grasp 55.2
reactionaries: all r. are paper tigers 178.17
r. are those at home in the present 178.22
reactionary: r. is a somnambulist walking backwards 178.20
read: better to be able neither to r., write than to be able to do nothing else 279.37
have you any right to r. novels 93.96
I do not think anyone can read *War and Peace* too much 71.
man ought to r. as inclination leads 93.44
some r. to think; majority r. to talk 93.18
thousand new books to r., with time to r. a hundred 93.39
to r. a writer is to travel with him 93.33
to r. means to borrow 93.54
we like to r. others, don't like to be r. 1008.15
what is r. now will not be r., ever 545.29
what that woman's r. and forgotten 1062.125
when we r. too fast or too slowly 93.70
you have to be able to r. to be equal 93.38
reader: if you would be a r., read 1069.40
make r. laugh, he thinks you trivial 93.60
readers: good r. make much out of little 93.40
r. may be unfaithful to a writer 1069.10
r. of novels are a strange folk 344.21
reading: a r. machine, he mastered the worthless 522.38
he that I'm r. seems to have most force 93.65
many date new era in life from r. book 93.91
no distress that r. can't relieve 93.67
people say that life is the thing, but I prefer r. 93.81
possession of book substitutes for r. 93.10
r. aloud is letting the cat out of the bag 708.101

r. furnishes mind with materials of knowledge; thinking makes what we read ours 93.55
r. good books like talking with fine men 93.21
r. is but silent conversation 93.51
r. is the scourge of childhood 93.74
r.: killing time under dignified name 93.23
r. makes a full man 188.14
r. maketh a full man 1069.13
r. should be absorbing, voluptuous 93.86
there are favorable hours for r. 93.57
where some wisdom is, r. makes it more 93.36
reads: for one who r., no limit to lives 93.50
who r. and grows no wiser seldom suspects his own deficiency 941.13
who r. for improvement is beyond hope of it 93.20
ready: be r. for that which is not yet born 427.10
to be always r. man must be able to cut knot 225.1
real: life is washed in the speechless r. 784.2
men often applaud imitation and hiss r. 60.1
nothing that is r. is alien to me 450.26
r. estate is foundation of world's guilt 746.10
the guarantee that we are r. 1029.3
realism: let us replace sentimentalism by r. 783.2
realists: r. do not fear results of study 783.1
realities: only dreamer shall understand r. 336.4
reality: acceptance of r. identified with a supreme being 784.16
between idea and r. falls the shadow 1019.3
comparison, not r., makes men happy or wretched 153.1
everything is a dangerous drug but r. 784.5
greatest mystery is in unsheathed r. 784.19
in the American metaphysic, r. is always material r. 784.18
melancholy and remorse form keel enabling us to sail into the wind of r. 918.12
mind's activity easy if r. is not met 975.38
moralists begin with a dislike of r. 604.10
no r. except the one within us 784.10
political is mode of grasping r. 711.23
r. is a spirit 784.4
r. is not an inspiration for literature 545.12
r. is that which doesn't go away 784.8
r., the world they are fighting to bring about 819.31
supreme r. of our time is common vulnerability of this planet 100.11
the ludicrous is stuck in the muck of r. 145.9
today's r. may be an illusion tomorrow 784.13
we are afraid to let go of petty r. to grasp great shadow 755.25
we take shape within and against that r. bequeathed us at birth 784.1
who confronts the paradoxical finds r. 668.2
who shut eyes to r. invite destruction 87.2
words are the great foes of r. 1064.10
realization: the r. that he was utterly powerless 459.2
reap: they that sow in tears shall r. in joy 281.1
we shall r., if we faint not 433.3
whatever a man soweth, that shall he r. 815.4
reason: all men are capable of r. 233.6
cause of error is war of senses, r. 299.26
easiest victor over r.: terror, force 357.5
emotion has taught mankind to r. 284.36
force without r. falls of own weight 357.6
frugal substance is riches for a man of r. 701.2
God must approve of the homage of r. 265.3
habit is stronger than r. 406.15
heart experiences God, not r. 387.54
in death and famine, r. is on the side of the priests 138.4
in what we understand, we r. but little 1007.7
in youth life of r. is not sufficient 1072.7
it is from r. that justice springs 393.30
law and r. only things between us and tyranny 528.23
life of r. balanced by irrational emotion 1020.1
love is a migraine, blotting out r. 551.84
love, not r., stronger than death 551.124
man frees himself through r. 785.15
man who listens to r. is lost 785.36
men live but by intervals of r. 284.4
mind resorts to r. for want of training 785.1
no place in fanatic's head for r. 335.13
object of dread is human form with r. fled, while wretched life remains 559.11
peace rules the day, where r. rules mind 785.5
peasants not sophisticated enough to r. speciously 618.3
r.: a harmony among irrational impulses 785.33
r., alone, is a force confining 785.12
r. also is choice 785.20
r. can wrestle and overthrow terror 785.10
r. can't save us but can mitigate living 785.26
r. deceives us more often than nature 785.38
r. demands man live in accord with his own nature 431.22
r. deserves to be called a prophet 785.34
r. flies, following senses, on clipped wings 785.6
r. for living is also r. for dying 541.3
r. guides but a small part of man 284.31
r. inclines to mildness 726.11
r., like a flower, withers when plucked 785.32
r., like wife, is heard but not minded 726.4
r. must keep rising to depose opinion 656.30
r. recognizes infinity of things which surpass it 785.23
r. rules more imperiously than a master 785.22
r., that hutch for grubby schoolboys 785.27
r. wishes judgment it gives be just 516.19
some men ignore r., fear being controlled 652.7
takes r. to rule, mercy to forgive 359.5
theirs not to r. why 588.17
time makes more converts than r. 978.47
'Tis in vain to speak r. 785.11
untrammeled r. is indulgence of philosopher 975.56
we are less astonished that r. is suspended than it should ever prevail 785.35
well-bred instinct meets r. half-way 486.5
we love without r., without r. we hate 554.8
we must follow r. as our guide 785.17
what can we r. but from what we know 785.25
when malice has r. on its side 561.10
when r. and instinct are reconciled 604.31
woman's r. is in milk of her breasts 1062.97
women never r. and thus are seldom wrong 1062.66
would you persuade, speak of interest, not r. 690.7
your own r. should make you believe 330.30
reasonable: to r. man everything r. may be supported 785.9
reasoning: imagination robust in proportion as r. weak 450.30
where all is dream, r. is useless 336.10
reasons: I don't care about r., know what I like 725.3
those seeking r. bring sorrow on themselves 1060.19
rebel: a r. demands a worthy opponent 786.8
in certain schools it is orthodox to be a r. 786.6
no one can be r. too long and not turn into autocrat 786.4
r.: proponent of a new misrule who has failed to establish it 786.1
rebellion: little r., now and then, is good thing 786.7
progress has been made through r. 256.2
rebuff: welcome each r. 17.13
recalcitrance: in the human race is spirit of r. 691.2
recollection: r. and anticipation fill our moments 729.16

recommendation: good presence is letters of r. 45.9
recompense: r. injury by justice; kindness by kindness 789.1
reconciles: good dinner, feasting r. everybody 274.24
recovery: r., not a smooth slope 896.25
Redeemer: tired by search after true good we stretch out arms to R. 389.9
redemption: Christian sense of sin without the saving belief in redemption 125.3
reduce: people I met were all trying to r. 632.14
reeducation: society offers little in the way of r. 279.70
refine: doubt that a writer should r. or improve his workroom 1069.141
reflection: happiness resides in imaginative r. 409.85
mental r., more interesting than TV 975.37
reform: abuse to be reformed, unless r. worse 790.37
every r. was once a private opinion 790.8
men r. a thing by removing reality 790.3
nature is entirely indifferent to any r. 623.77
no r. effort in Russia ever completed 834.5
only in r. is true security to be found 856.11
r., if it fails, strengthens despotism 790.4
you've tried to r. what will not learn 790.17
reformer: apathy of voter is confusion of r. 1038.7
man a r. until reform tramps on his toes 790.14
r. don't see that people wud rather be wrong an' comfortable thin right in jail 790.7
r. must substitute attractive virtues for attractive vices or he will fail 790.18
r. thinks election turns men into angels 790.6
the r. is careless of numbers 790.28
reformers: all r. are bachelors 790.23
consolation of middle-aged r. 790.31
nobody expects comfort from r. 790.1
r. misjudge consequences of reforms 790.10
reforming: give up r. society, give up responsibility 790.27
if anything ail a man, he sets about r. the world 790.33
nothing so needs r. as others' habits 790.35
r. passion tends to neglect experience 790.15
reforms: religions obsolete if they bring no r. 790.9
refreshment: to sit in shade on fine day is perfect r. 194.1
refuge: God is the immemorial r. of the incompetent, the helpless, the miserable 387.46
God is our r. and strength 387.6
the eternal God is thy r. 856.1
refusal: prompter the r., the less disappointment 791.4
soft r. not always taken 791.1
we become what we are by radical r. 444.21
refused: more tolerable to be r. than deceived 224.16
refute: who can r. a sneer 185.7
regression: Our closeness to nature is one reason why our problem is not repression but regression 34.60
regret: history is one long r. 419.49
looking back, I see nothing to r. 653.13
one knows bad action in flash of r. 227.15
r. calamities only if it helps sufferer 698.10
to r. deeply is to live afresh 792.6
regrets: r. and recriminations hurt the soul 792.1
r. are natural property of grey hairs 653.18
rehabilitation: r. of unfortunate men and women 735.3
reign: one can't r. and be innocent 831.20
to be omnipotent but friendless is to r. 831.23
reigns: whoever r., the merchant r. 104.5
rejection: r. is a form of self-assertion 255.1
rejoicing: r. of a man is length of days 409.2
relation: poor r. is most irrelevant thing in nature 796.3
r. between things gives meaning to them 573.3
relations: a web of tangled r. of all sorts 913.11
even great men have their poor r. 796.1
hostility lurks at the heart of our r. 152.15
renewal of broken r. is a nervous matter 301.1
relationship: caught in the underbrush of r. 794.8
strongest r. on earth: parent and child 670.40
the family the soul wants, a network of r. 334.23
relationships: man is a knot into which r. are tied 794.11
r. are forms of exploitation 794.1
relative: in trouble best to seek out r. 796.2
relatives: great exercise of benevolence: loving r. 519.21
one loyal friend worth ten thousand r. 365.42
when our r. are at home 796.4
relativity: that's r. 795.4
reliance: no man is worthy of unlimited r. 191.7
religion: atheism must insult God less than r. 1004.10
civil r. gives culture its direction 797.33
cosmos is a fly-wheel; r. is theory that the wheel was designed to give man ride 1017.11
depth in philosophy inclineth to r. 694.1
effort to reconcile science and r. 850.7
every r. is true one way or another 797.10
every thing to be true must become a r. 998.132
false r. a pretext for thousand crimes 797.14
garb of r. is best cloak for power 797.32
God is for men and r. for women 387.23
hating turns r. to spleen, bigotry 412.10
if all is well, r. is beneficial 797.73
if one r., God would be manifest 387.53
in a dead r. there are no more heresies 258.10
in my r. all would be love, poetry, doubt 797.15
in r. the only thing of use is an objective truth 797.48
it don't mean I ain't got r. 797.78
knowledge, history are enemies of r. 797.51
let us have one r. 797.77
man can no more possess a private r. than he can possess private sun, moon 797.12
man with sense of humor never founded a r. 797.38
matters of r. should never be matters of controversy 797.66
men despise r. and fear it is true 797.56
men will die for r., but not live for it 797.13
money's the wise man's r. 602.19
need new source of moral strength if r. dead 797.5
no consolations of r. or philosophy unless one experiences their desolations 797.36
no r. can be considered in abstraction from its followers 797.83
not matter what r. a man has professed 841.2
nothing so fatal to r. as indifference 797.6
nought calms the spirit as rum and true r. 989.2
one man finds in r. his literature, science; another finds in it his joy, duty 797.44
only one r., though a hundred versions 797.70
persecution, religious pride, love of contradiction are the food of r. 797.16
pure r. and undefiled before God 797.2
pure r. breathing household laws 701.6
r. a childish toy; no sin but ignorance 797.46
r. a mode of bearing ills of life 17.17
r. and mathematics are rules of the game 797.50
r. comes closer to the heart of things 797.69
r.: daughter of Hope and Fear 797.3
r. easier to die for than live absolutely 565.2
r. enlightens, terrifies, subdues 797.52
r. has never survived morals 797.24
r. has no place in public policy 395.22
r. has only to fear not being understood 797.74
r. is a direction of the heart 797.63
r. is always a patron of the arts 797.37
r. is both mythology and folklore 617.8

r. is destroyed by bigotry 264.6
r. is never a check 797.72
r. is now called an ideology 445.3
r. is opium of the people 797.47
r. is reaction of human nature to search for God 797.82
r. is the best armour, the worst cloak 797.28
r. is whatever one is most interested in 797.1
r.: loving life, conscious of impotence 797.67
r. makes men wise and virtuous, or makes them set up false pretences to both 797.31
r. of character apt to be invaded by religious training 797.20
r. only means of reducing people grown savage in arms 1032.14
r.: original cure and original disease 797.62
r. proposes method of fortifying soul 797.65
r. restores the courage to live by grace 697.11
r. seems grown an infant with age 592.4
r. should rest on one's fine feelings 797.68
r. teaches us to love our enemies 797.27
r. that fears science dishonors God 850.5
r. veils sacred fires, morality expires 797.61
r. which has lost conviction about men's struggles for the human 797.45
r. will not regain power until it can face change 850.8
r. without science is blind 850.3
science investigates; r. interprets 850.6
sin a basic concept in r. and politics 900.20
terror of God is the secret of r. 343.37
test of r. is how much it explains 797.23
theological r. is the enemy of mankind 973.10
theology in r. like poisons in food 973.8
to befriend enemy is essence of true r. 100.5
true r. must know our nature 797.58
true r. slow in growth, hard to dislodge 797.53
we crave support in vanity and r. 1027.15
we have r. enough to hate, not love 797.75
we must respect the other fellow's r. 797.49
who seek not r. should be deprived of it 797.57
without fictions the truths of r. would not be intelligible to the multitude 797.71
writers against r. never set up their own 1004.5
you corrupt r. in favour of friends 797.59
religions: all r. are monuments to superstition 797.18
founders of r. didn't include unbeliever 797.30
he who observes moral precepts of r. won't be questioned in heaven as to dogmas 797.42
r. are obsolete if they bring no reforms 790.9
r. die when they are proved to be true 850.9
r.: ejaculations of a few imaginative men 797.22
r. generally have some instinctive basis 797.64
r. such stuff as dreams are made of 797.79
r. united with government inimical to liberty 127.2
religious: all r. thinkers were doubters 265.7
in big houses always r. element 1048.10
injustice feared less if ruler is r. 831.2
life having purpose based on r. system 771.4
man can no longer shove responsibility off on r. power 810.5
men do evil from r. conviction 879.2
more and more care about r. tolerance 797.11
most r. upon a sunshiny day 797.8
proofs looked for last by r. mind 330.32
r. emotions are conservative, not creative 797.17
r. experience is force behind scientific research 797.19
r. neurosis is tied to dietary demands 797.54
r. truth is blasphemy 998.54
r. vision is our one ground for optimism 797.81
social evil sanctified by r. sentiment 477.11
to be furiously r. is irreligiously r. 797.60
to lead r. life, identify with mankind 711.29
religiously: any act good in itself is good to do r. 900.13
reluctance: easy is difficult when done with r. 1022.1
remains: what we never had r., things we have go 1010.1
remark: assified r. is often sanctified by use 213.28
remarkable: nothing so commonplace as wish to be r. 33.10
remedies: extreme r. appropriate to extreme diseases 798.4
most men die of r., not of diseases 798.5
our r. oft in ourselves do lie 798.12
social r. will fail 623.36
some r. worse than the disease 798.10
we cannot do without palliative r. 798.3
remedy: everyone suffers wrongs which have no r. 476.10
r. for all blunders is love 798.2
remember: better forget and smile than r., be sad 580.31
remembered: nothing is so perfect possessed as r. 716.7
remembering: forgiving presupposes r. 359.15
how shall we look on sun and feel rain, r. those who loved sun and rain 610.6
remembrance: burden not r. with heaviness that's gone 792.5
reminiscence: nothing awakens a r. like an odour 882.5
reminiscences: r. makes one feel aged, sad 580.34
remorse: melancholy and r. are our keel 918.12
Renaissance: bathed in the full current of the R. 545.4
rend: all we value we shall sometime r. 241.5
renounce: to work is better than to r. 10.2
renown: measure r. according to how it's acquired 332.27
r. is like hue of grass that comes, goes 332.11
to practice right in hope of r. is near to vice 822.17
rent: people who can least afford to pay r., pay r. 602.6
renunciation: crown of excellence is r. 799.2
r. is a piercing virtue 799.1
repartee: majority is always best r. 51.7
repay: in refusing benefits caution to be used, lest we seem to fear having to r. them 791.7
repeated: r. phrase gains meaning 800.4
repeateth: he that r. a matter separateth friends 394.1
repeats: he that knows little often r. it 447.13
repent: we as often r. good we have done as ill 792.2
repetition: r. everywhere: nothing found only once 800.1
repletion: sovereign source of melancholy is r. 845.4
reporter: r. is concerned with tomorrow 629.5
reporters: r. thrive on the world's misfortune 630.4
repose: choice between truth and r. 998.37
I long for r. that ever is the same 118.7
glory and r. can't inhabit same place 386.10
r. as necessary in conversation as in art 188.17
r. in energy is badge of gentleman 378.2
r. is not the destiny of man 115.6
we combat obstacles to get r. 811.1
representative: r. assembly lets parties fight by petition 172.1
your r. betrays you if he sacrifices his judgment to your opinion 762.2
representatives: r. unwilling to bring down taxes 964.8
reproach: only defence against r. is obscurity 803.1
reproaches: there are r. which praise 722.19
reproduction: flower is the poetry of r. 352.2
reproductive: monks, nuns, spinsters are not r. 802.2
reproof: ingenuous mind feels r. in unmerited praise 722.16
those best can bear r. who merit praise 803.7
reprove: r. not a scorner, lest he hate thee 803.3
republic: the r. which sinks to sleep 233.44
Republican: if Chrysler crisis had come in R. adminis-

tration 17.34
republics: public virtue is only foundation of r. 1033.2
reputability: conspicuous consumption is a means of r. 105.23
reputation: easier to add to great r. than to get it 804.25
for sake of good r., all sacrifice selves 804.22
great r. is a great noise 804.21
how many worthy men have survived own r. 226.7
more shameful to lose good r. than never to have acquired it 804.24
one can live down anything except a good r. 804.29
people care more for r. of wit than virtue 1061.27
purest treasure is spotless r. 804.28
r. got without merit, lost without fault 804.10
r. increases, ability declines 653.40
r. is an idle and most false imposition 804.27
r. is commonly measured by the acre 804.11
single lie destroys whole r. 558.17
to secretly stab a r. betrays a base spirit 905.1
two modes of establishing r. 804.4
universal idol of men of letters is r. 1069.2
valuable possession: r. of being well to do 1048.36
required: to whom much is given, much is r. 810.2
requires: who r. much from himself 250.1
resemblances: r. are the shadows of differences 683.9
resentment: nothing consumes man more quickly than r. 39.21
who requires much of self, little of others, will not be the object of r. 250.1
reserve: r. is an artificial quality 31.5
suspect emptiness if man carries on r. to a third interview 31.2
resignation: r., only feeling for which impossible to become sham 806.1
resist: I can r. everything except temptation 971.10
resistance: country preserves liberties if rulers warned that people preserve spirit of r. 658.7
resolution: r. to avoid evil is made too late 807.3
resolutions: Affirming in fervid and firm r. 178.16
good r. interfere with scientific laws 807.6
great actions not sons of great r. 227.5
resolve: afterthought makes first r. a liar 24.2
every obstacle yields to stern r. 771.5
perform without fail what you r. 807.2
respect: fools take to selves r. given to office 1027.2
give one man lecture, another shilling, and see which will r. you most 602.31
I r. only those who resist me, but I cannot tolerate them 658.4
men r. those who do not give way to them 658.8
people I r. behave as if they were immortal 92.3
r. for private enterprise and law and order 517.33
r. self if you wish others to r. you 869.4
when we know all a man's views, we lose r. for him 333.2
without r. what distinguishes man, beast 808.3
woman should always challenge our r. 1062.46
respectability: r.: offspring of liaison between bald head and bank account 809.1
respectable: build business up big enough, it's r. 104.27
more man ashamed of, more r. he is 809.4
no man is inherently r. 809.5
respects: he who r. others is respected by them 788.2
responds: no one so accursed, desolate, but some heart r. unto his own 960.10
responsibility: being grownup, assuming r. for parents 334.36
chief is a man who assumes r. 531.17
fear, born of the stern matron R. 43.9
liberty means r. 537.39
man must assume the r. for his world 810.5
man's r. increases as the gods' decreases 810.7
one can pass on r., not discretion 810.4
politics, little more than shirking r. 711.70
prig always finds a last refuge in r. 749.1
r.: detachable burden easily shifted to God, fate, fortune, luck or one's neighbor 810.3
responsible: freedom is will to be r. to ourselves 363.40
somebody's r. and somebody's innocent 517.3
there are r. persons, no guilty ones 405.3
to be a man is, precisely, to be r. 810.10
rest: absence of occupation is not r. 446.5
complete r. is death 10.12
in all things r. is sweet 811.5
most men in a coma when at r. 9.19
nothing gives r. but search for truth 811.4
one can r. only after steady practice 811.2
r. is the sauce of labor 811.6
too much r. itself becomes a pain 811.3
restorative: I went into a *brasserie* hard by for a r. 798.8
restraint: all seek to do what they please without r. 363.15
liberty exists in proportion to r. 537.45
through r., man can manage not to suppress 598.4
restraints: story of man, history of necessary r. 528.22
result: everything we do has a r. 176.6
results: most great r. of history are brought about by discreditable means 574.3
resurrection: seeking in your praise r. and life 722.3
reticence: the habit of r. is never effaced 435.1
retirement: death is perpetual r. without pay 221.57
elegant sufficiency, content, r. 701.5
r. accords with the tone of my mind 31.1
r.: you have put achievement behind you 813.3
retreat: females most dangerous when appear to r. 1062.91
no r. as quiet as one's own soul 183.1
return: the r. makes one love the farewell 673.5
reveal: do not r. your thoughts to everyone 165.1
revelation: my mind is direct r. from God 816.1
revenge: a man will buy r. with his soul 817.12
forgetting a wrong is a mild r. 476.9
in r. man but even with enemy 817.3
man that studieth r. keeps wounds green which otherwise heal 817.2
men more prone to r. injuries 789.2
r. back on itself recoils 817.14
r. is a dish to be eaten cold 817.8
r. is fruit which you must leave to ripen 817.11
r. is joy of narrow, sick, petty minds 817.13
r. is profitable, gratitude is expensive 399.3
r. proves its own executioner 817.10
since women delight in r., it may seem but feminine manhood to be vindictive 817.4
sweet is r.—especially to women 817.5
to refrain from imitation is the best r. 451.1
woman's desire for r. outlasts emotions 1062.31
revenged: I will not be r., and this I owe to my enemy 476.5
revengeful: weakest are the most r. 1047.2
revenges: whirligig of time brings in his r. 978.62
revenue: government expands to absorb r. 395.62
no man divulges which way his r. comes in 746.16
revere: more we r. a man, more we are struck by his flaws 808.1
reverence: does not man feel he is made higher by doing r. to what is above him 1068.3
r. makes it possible to be whole 808.2
reverend: old goat not more r. for beard 653.31
reverie: r. is the groundwork of creative imagination 818.3
to make a prairie, r. alone will do 818.1
review: one can't r. bad book without showing off 207.3
who would write and can't, can surely r. 207.32
reviewers: r., what lice they are 207.51

reviews: do not read the r. 207.17
revolt: inferiors r. to be equal 819.1
not suffering but hope incites men to r. 819.20
r. is result of thought of the masses 819.34
revolution: change prepares the ground for r. 819.21
childish world pleased with each new r. 819.9
compromised r. shatters community that was 819.17
every r. was first one man's thought 819.8
great r. is the fault of the government 819.15
mediocrity mitigates the most violent r. 819.7
modern search for freedom, self-fulfillment born of r. in our hemisphere 819.29
poverty is parent of r. and crime 718.3
r. always marks victory of single party 819.14
r., festival of the oppressed 819.18
r. is a science and an art 819.35
r. is a transfer of property 819.38
r. requires leaders' infallibility 819.27
woman is perpetual r. 1062.146
revolutionaries: in history of mankind, envy makes r. 419.26
r., rarely motivated by material considerations 819.30
revolutionary: artist is as dissatisfied as r. 53.64
r. spirit frees one from scruples as regards ideas 819.5
successful r. is a statesman, unsuccessful one a criminal 819.10
revolutions: quality of r. to make new lines, laws 819.32
r. are not made; they come 819.36
r. eliminate men but elaborate ideas 819.16
r. never lightened the burden of tyranny 819.39
r. not made by fate but by men 819.3
wind of r. is not tractable 819.23
women hate r. and revolutionists 819.33
reward: r. doubles pleasure of every work 680.5
r. of thing well done is to have done it 6.6
virtue herself is her own fairest r. 1033.44
we look for r., are disappointed 459.3
rewards: who r. past injuries invites more 866.4
rhetoric: r. is the creature of art 763.4
r. takes no account of the art in literature 604.20
to-day violence is the r. of the period 1032.11
rhyme: fools of r. sweat in pigmy wars 708.96
when writing in r. you say what you must 708.51
rhymes: his hairs grow hoary as his r. grow worse 708.11
we lack not r. and reasons 978.70
rhythms: most exciting r. seem unexpected and complex 614.3
r. like those of a young policeman exploding 485.4
rich: be r. for yourself, poor to friends 858.20
be r. in a day, be hanged in a year 738.8
better to live r. than to die r. 1048.29
craving of the r. for titles 52.4
easier for camel to go through eye of needle than r. man to enter kingdom of God 1048.6
he is r. who hath enough to be charitable 1048.11
he who is contented is r. 186.15
honest r. can never forget poverty 718.12
I don't think you can spend yourself r. 277.2
in fight r. man saves face; poor man, coat 345.6
it is in vain to ridicule a r. fool 1048.33
laws grind the poor, r. men rule law 528.32
man r. or poor according to whether he can afford necessaries, conveniences 1048.56
most of us aren't interested in getting r. 1048.46
poor and content is r. 186.21
poor man ruined as soon as he apes the r. 933.4
r. from writing "get rich quick" books 1048.39
r. man cannot imagine poverty 718.47
r. man is everywhere expected and at home 1048.51
r. men are to bear infirmities of poor 271.1
r. men feel misfortunes that miss poor 1048.24
r. men's faults are covered with money 342.8
r., powerful know God is on their side 387.2
r. purchase heaven by their alms 433.11
r. will ever distinguish selves from poor 1048.49
show of honesty is surest way to grow r. 425.9
smile with the wise, feed with the r. 1048.30
take no satisfaction in dying but living r. 504.5
the heartless self-indulgence of the r. 972.3
there's always a way for the r. 1048.18
to be r. without being proud is easy 1048.12
troubles of r. are troubles money can't cure 17.42
who hastes to be r. will not be innocent 738.2
wise man gets r.; if r. he gets foolish 602.16
wise man is very r., wanting nothing 1060.37
with full stomach r. and poor are alike 274.9
richer: we are all of us r. than we think we are 700.3
riches: all else is secondary to charm of r. 1048.28
all r. but liberty make us masters, slaves 363.24
as r. forsake a man we discover his folly 226.6
believe not them that seem to despise r. 920.2
children are poor men's r. 123.16
give me neither poverty nor r. 701.1
he is not fit for r. who fears to use r. 1048.22
if r. increase, think it not enough to be liberal, but munificent 375.3
if thou covetest r., ask for contentment 186.19
let none admire that r. grow in hell 1048.37
not possession but use is the only r. 1048.23
r. are for comfort, not hoarding 1048.50
r. attract the attention of mankind 1048.1
r. certainly make themselves wings 1048.7
r. have made more covetous men 403.8
r. have never fascinated me 1048.21
r. have wings; sometimes they fly away 1048.4
r. more enlarge than satisfy appetites 1048.25
r., to be enjoyed, must be interrupted 187.4
r. without law are more dangerous than poverty without law 528.7
seek not proud r. 8.1
we may see the small value God has for r. by the people he gives them to 1048.44
richest: in ugly world r. can buy only ugliness 1048.55
riddle: all is r., and the key is another r. 1019.4
life's the only r. we don't give up 539.44
riddles: women are like r.; they please us no longer once we know them 1062.119
ride: few men to r., millions to be ridden 1002.27
who makes himself an ass, men will r. 941.7
rider: no secret so close as between r., horse 821.1
ridicule: all character can be destroyed by r. 820.6
public r. is best way to attack vice 820.5
r. dishonours more than dishonour 820.4
to r. is the talent of ungenerous tempers 820.1
ridiculous: but one step from sublime to r. 4.4
in r. world nothing can be ridiculed 3.3
look for r. in all, you'll find it 4.6
r. as a man running after a wife 198.2
r. things are hardest to confess 168.5
three things render even a great man r. 188.37
right: All's r. with the world! 659.4
be always sure you are r.—then go ahead 822.6
because r. is r., to follow r. is wisdom 822.20
cultivate respect not for law but for r. 822.21
doing what's r. no guarantee against misfortune 17.39
do not expect justice where might is r. 357.13
even r. does not receive consideration if it does not seem r. 45.11

freedom of the most free: to do what is r. 822.8
God prevent us from becoming r.-thinking 822.14
if everyone is wrong, everyone is r. 299.8
I will follow the r. side even to the fire 822.16
man contends for obscure, distorted r. 477.3
man never outraged unless at bottom r. 39.16
might, r., over centuries found identical 822.5
moral sense teaches how to avoid the r. 822.22
more trouble to make maxim than do r. 572.3
nobly wrong more manly than meanly r. 635.4
no mistake is so great as being always r. 822.4
only a practicable r. is worth fighting for 823.21
r. conduct never promoted by ignorance 77.22
r. is more precious than peace 822.23
r. is r. only when entire 822.10
r. is what is after my constitution 822.7
r. makes might 823.15
r. to be heard is not r. to be heeded 364.5
r. to squawk when things go wrong 132.7
spirit of liberty not too sure it is r. 537.15
take the place which is your r. 859.3
the r. to disagree must be protected 823.2
those who believe they alone are r. succeed 822.11
to do a great r., do a little wrong 822.18
to practice r. in hope of renown is near to vice 822.17
to win argument, start by being r. 51.11
until jurors agree, they cannot all be r. 998.62
we applaud r. when it costs us nothing 822.9
we felt we were r. twenty years ago; today we know we weren't always r. 822.19
we go r. enough if we go wrong together 983.2
where there is no might r. loses itself 357.14
you can do r. in spite of your feelings 822.3
you can't let r. thing stand in yo way 77.13
right and wrong: abstractions about r. serve to confuse 604.21
righteous: call bad behavior r. indignation 241.7
hard to be r. if unrighteous have greater right 393.21
r. are bold as a lion 405.2
to be r. is the first of all duties 491.14
rights: be beneficent but defend your r. 229.3
citizenship: the right to have r. 132.11
during war we imprison r. of man 1042.38
giving others their r., we give ourselves r. 823.13
it is fair to judge peoples by r. they will sacrifice most for 823.4
man entered society to secure his r. 913.26
modern state has only r., no duties 930.4
never exceed r.: r. will become unlimited 755.23
no broader basis for government than all people with r. in their hands 233.18
r. inherent, whatever sex, complexion 823.7
r., not honored because they exist 719.59
r. of all diminish if r. of one threatened 823.14
r. that do not flow from duty are not worth having 823.6
self-given r. are relative to self-imposed duties 823.18
they have r. who dare maintain them 823.16
we magnify man's r., minimize his capacities 233.26
what men value is not r. but privileges 823.17
right stuff: to prove that you had the r. 119.30
ring: r. out the old, r. in the new 631.5
the r., where a Negro could whip a white man 804.18
ripe: from hour to hour, we r. and r. 571.15
if you trap the moment before it's r., tears of repentence you'll certainly wipe 979.3
old and the r. fall 221.87
riposte: a r. that would have seared him 188.28
rise: way to r. is to obey and please 945.23
riser: an early r. may lie abed until noon 804.15
rising: r. in life by own industry, others' folly 945.25
risk: everything is sweetened by r. 216.16
inquiries carry element of r. 480.18
to be alive at all involves some r. 216.14
what is necessary is never a r. 624.16
win without r., triumph without glory 945.8
risks: life must always be full of r. 216.5
ritual: unreal is r. without devotion 9.5
ritualism: r.: Dutch Garden of God, where He may walk in rectilinear freedom 114.1
rival: if you have a r., you must please 198.5
river: dared do such a thing to the r. in my head 824.7
to join the brimming r. 824.8
who never saw r. thought his first a sea 447.21
you cannot step twice into the same r. 117.18
rivers: all the r. run into the sea 853.2
mighty r. easily leaped at their source 6.16
r. are roads which move 824.4
road: all I seek: heaven above and r. below me 992.49
he watched the ads, not the r. 64.10
man determined never to move out of beaten r. cannot lose his way 178.9
man's r. marked by graves of likings 404.28
no r. which does not lead to an end 541.18
r. not leading to other roads must be retraced 404.12
r.: where one passes from where it's tiresome to be to where it's futile to go 992.7
we can't reach old age by another's r. 867.11
you know more of r. by having travelled it 321.19
roam: dunce sent to r. excels dunce kept home 992.15
r. abroad in the world 992.42
to r. giddily and be everywhere but home 992.15
robbed: he that is r., not wanting what's stol'n 550.9
the r. that smiles steals from the thief 120.9
worthy to be r., who shows felon where his treasure lies 971.5
robbery: idleness has a son, r. 446.8
rock: r. gives children everything they had to wait for 614.10
rocket: loner who lobs a r. into a nuclear arsenal 1042.80
rocks: mariner must have his eye upon r. 720.3
Rocky Mountains: if we just kept going we would reach R. 854.24
rod: chasteneth not with a r. but with time 978.24
he that spareth his r. hateth his son 766.3
rodeoing: r. is about only sport you can't fix 929.13
rogue: in limelight, r. acts like honest man 332.33
romance: r. calls for faraway love of troubadours 564.103
r. dies hard 826.2
r. is to deceive oneself, then others 551.231
r. only dies with life 826.3
shouldn't allow r. to become necessary 826.4
woman's sense of humour spoils r. 826.7
years of r. makes a woman look like a ruin 564.134
romances: if histories properly told r. unneeded 419.54
Romania: a deep-rooted tradition in R. 752.2
Romans: R. must have aggravated one another very much, with their noses 509.3
romantic: boys like r. tales 123.9
every ship is r. object save our own 333.4
it may be that r. has the truer vision 827.2
it takes a r. nature to want to survive 1001.4
r. artist recognized by his insincerity 53.104
r. desires to prevent life from escaping 827.3
r. life not due to irregular hours, diet 827.1
Rome: in R. one had simply to sit still and feel 509.4
roof: every r., when lifted, reveals tragedy 422.8
room: how little r. do we take up in death 221.120
love makes one little r. an everywhere 551.40
rooms: small r. discipline the

mind 430.3
rooster: woe to house where hen crows, r. still 564.116
roosters: with so many r. crowing, sun never rises 56.6
rooted: to be r. is the most important need 927.14
rose: forbear to read rood to learn r. 279.59
is there any moral shut in bosom of r. 72.58
no gathering the r. without thorn pricks 705.3
r. by any other name would smell as sweet 619.8
r. is a r. is a r. is a r. 444.22
r.'s scent is bitterness to one who loved r. 990.17
who wants a r. must respect the thorn 755.20
rosebuds: gather ye r. while ye may 706.4
roses: heap not on mound r. she cannot smell 103.9
like r. on very rickety trelliswork 393.11
when r. are gone, nothing left but thorn 653.73
who plants thorns must not expect r. 815.7
rot: from hour to hour, we r. and r. 571.15
rote: wisdom cannot be learned by r. 1060.57
roughness: r. may turn one's humour 349.9
routine: leisured rebel most at interruption of r. 828.2
men fall into r. when slack and tired 828.1
r. is god of every social system 828.4
r. of active lives precludes progress 10.5
rove: where'er we r. we find something dear 472.8
row: everyone must r. with the oars he has 1.4
royalty: r. does good and is badly spoken of 829.1
rude: except in streetcars, never be r. 830.1
no one as r. as the British 488.1
r. refusal is immediately believed 791.1
rudeness: be damned for r. than snickered at for courtesy 197.4
r. is weak man's imitation of strength 830.2
ruin: each life a r. containing what person ought to have been 758.12
if prosperous, beware of sudden r. 755.28
r. outruns all prayers, forces men astray 1042.43
ruination: predictions about r. of the mother tongue 1064.13
ruined: men are r. on the side of their natural propensities 329.6
ruining: men prefer r. one another's fortunes 1042.96
rule: he who bears brand of Cain shall r. 518.14
he who would r. must hear and be deaf 831.7
how shall I r. others without command of myself 862.12
I know how to r. myself 862.2
ill can he r. that can't reach the small 831.24
no r. so general which admits no exception 832.3
no useful r. without an exception 832.4
that r. is better which is exercised over better subjects 395.4
the important thing, abide by the r. of threes 832.5
to r. is not so much a question of the heavy hand as the firm seat 831.14
when people r., they must be made happy 233.12
ruler: every r. harsh whose rule is new 831.1
great r. able to let others serve him 831.18
if you have a single r., you lie at his discretion 831.19
injustice feared less if r. is religious 831.2
one r. after another puts guns before butter 124.8
r. shouldn't have tendency for other affairs 831.8
rulers: government degenerates when trusted to r. of people alone 233.21
insistence of r. on building powerful state 55.16
rules: cannot make r. till you can obey them 832.1
no institution so bound around by r. 972.32
professor led astray by artificial r. 279.47
you're gonna get a tablet with r. on it 816.4
rum: nought calms the spirit as r. and religion 989.2
rumor: no speedier evil thing than r. 833.3
r. doth double the numbers of the feared 833.2
r. is pipe blown by surmises, jealousies 833.1
run: many shall r. to and fro 992.6
nothing in own country, men r. to others 992.17
rungs: do not despise the bottom r. in the ascent to greatness 401.45
running: best stimulus for r. ahead is to have something we must run from 741.7
men should learn what they are r. to, from 875.31
runs: man does better who r. from disaster 300.5
rural: r. sights with r. sounds restore spirit 194.5
Russia: ideas in R. are machine-cut blocks 834.4
in his feet he had the feeling of R. 639.4
Russian: divine in R. soul—resignation 834.2
for a R. to be chivalrous 464.5
Russians: R. train; they do not dare educate 834.3
rust: better to be eaten to death with r. 10.15
it is better to wear out than r. out 10.3
rustic: when nature exceeds culture, we have the r. 848.8
rut: to stick in a r. is called consistency 179.6

S

Sabbath: good man's grave is his S. 221.36
sacrament: s.: an outward sign of an inward grace 836.1
sacrifice: s. is favorite self-indulgence of woman 1062.92
s. magnifies the one who sacrifices 837.4
s. may be flower virtue will pluck 837.7
too long a s. can make stone of heart 837.11
you cannot throw away a word like s. 491.20
sacrificers: s. are not the ones to pity 837.2
sacrifices: nothing so enhances a good as s. 837.9
sacrificial: love is essentially s. 551.182
sad: merry heart goes all day, s. tires in mile 409.89
s. find sweetness in tears 1052.3
the flesh is s., and I've read all books 290.2
when people s., they don't do anything 39.18
saddest: s. words are these: it might have been 507.9
sadness: boys have no s. sadder than our hope 1071.52
by s. of countenance, heart made better 918.3
eulogist spoke without a trace of s. 367.12
s. flies on wings of morning 918.18
s. is almost always a form of fatigue 1011.14
the piercing s. of life 1011.24
they serve gladness who meet calls of s. 918.57
sadnesses: s. are dangerous which one carries among people to drown them out 1011.30
safe: better one s. way than hundred unreckonable 585.1
easy to be brave from s. distance 195.1
to keep self s. is not to bury self 856.16
safety: gift of s. is great gift among gifts 856.13
insignificance is often the cause of s. 1012.1
nothing's as good as holding on to s. 856.3
obscurity often brings s. 649.1
s. not in blindness but in facing danger 783.6
s. will be the sturdy child of terror 229.1
they that can give up liberty to obtain s. 856.5
your s. at stake if neighbor's wall burns 151.7
sagacious: knowing what is right doesn't make s. man 1060.2
sagacity: manhood and s. ripen of themselves 404.27
no more s. is needed for business, medicine, law, than for operating taxicab 104.23
sage: let fool hold tongue, he will pass for s. 898.22
s. has one advantage: he is immortal 1060.24
s. never seems to know his own merits 600.8
sahib: a s. has got to act like a s. 271.20
said: least s. is soonest disavowed 98.2
little s. is soon amended 923.12
thing well s. walks in immortality 283.10

what is s. about men has as much influence on their lives as what they do 804.13
what's s. is s. and goes upon its way 507.1
when I think over what I have s., I envy dumb people 923.52
sail: who won't s. till danger over sails not 112.3
sailor: happiest hour a s. sees is when his Nancy is on his knees 839.5
s. should know the length of his line 542.11
sailors: if s. too numerous, the ship sinks 56.1
saint: bad in best of us leaves s. like rest of us 840.12
easier to make a s. out of a libertine 840.10
every s. has a past 840.13
grace needed to turn man into s. 840.9
many insights of the s. stem from his experience as a sinner 840.2
to s. all things are friendly and sacred 927.6
sainthood: a great collective mush of s. 454.3
s. a thing human beings must avoid 840.7
saintliness: humility is a dazzled awareness of s. 435.5
saints: executive officers not made from s. 319.2
s. can do miracles, few can keep a hotel 429.3
s. cannot arise where are no warriors 390.17
s. guilty until proved innocent 840.8
s. marked out by their phenomenal piety 840.5
s. rebelled against outmoded form of God 840.3
some s. never wanted be human 840.6
statue in bird bath: let s. go at that 840.4
they are not all s. who use holy water 45.7
salad: a s. made of shredded five-pound notes 355.14
salesman's: try novelties for s. bait 105.9
salesmanship: advertising and s. create needs 105.19
salvation: courage is a kind of s. 195.27
s. is preconditioned by repentance 841.3
s. lies in hands of creatively maladjusted 201.21
what is most contrary to s. is habit 841.5
same: if all saw fair as s., no debaters' strife 656.7
more things change, more they remain s. 117.22
when two do s. thing it is not the s. 469.15
when you've done a thing the s. way for ten years, throw it away, start over 828.3
sample: by small s. may judge of whole piece 306.1
Sancho Panzas: mankind either S.P. or Don Quixotes 562.51
sanctity: s., genius, are as rebellious as vice 840.11
sandwich: impossible to get a recognizable s. 355.16
sandwiches: compensate with a Gargantuan tea of watercress s. 366.4
eating cheese s. in the railroad stations 992.11
sane: assent, and you are s. 258.2
harm in being s. all by oneself 559.3
it's fitter being s. than mad 390.1
no man is s. who cannot be insane at times 293.2
pray for a s. mind in a sound body 413.6
sanity: s. is a madness put to good uses 842.3
s. is very rare 559.5
sans: s. teeth, s. eyes, s. taste, s. everything 653.86
sarcasm: s. the last refuge of modest people 843.1
Satan: solitude is the playful of S. 915.32
we can respect talents of S. 242.10
when God lost S. he lost one of his best lieutenants 242.6
satiety: there is s. in all things 947.4
wealth breeds s., s. outrage 1048.57
satin: where's man could ease heart like s. gown 267.18
satire: one's pointlessness is another's s. 844.1
praise to the undeserving is severe s. 722.5
s. a glass wherein everybody's face but beholder's is discovered 844.7
s. is lonely, introspective occupation 844.3
s., like a polished razor keen 844.5
s. shows that new men are at the door 844.2
satire's: s. my weapon 844.6
satires: s. not only wound, but make wound incurable 905.1
satirist: blessed is the s. 620.7
satirists: s. gain applause through fear, not love 844.4
satisfaction: job s. may compensate for low wages 845.1
men all seek their s. 238.33
whole of s. not from single aspiration 55.7
satisfied: God was s. with his own work, and that is fatal 201.6
he is well paid that is well s. 845.6
we only feel satisfaction in man's society as he is s. in himself 869.5
sauce: no s. in world like hunger 437.2
savage: civilized man is a larger mind but more imperfect nature than the s. 133.12
is a man a s. at heart 562.5
man is still a s.: he has little respect for anything that cannot hurt him 808.5
music has charms to soothe a s. breast 614.19
s. doesn't wear oncomf'rtable clothes 70.1
s.: slave talking about what he must do 133.5
white man's notion is that he is less s. 1054.4
savagery: s. necessary to bring world back to life 70.2
savages: ants and s. put strangers to death 358.6
save: drown not self to s. a drowning man 837.3
urge to s. humanity is almost always a false-face for urge to rule it 790.19
saved: if pain cured, we should have been s. 946.42
penny s. is a penny to squander 977.3
searching for another, you are s. 663.7
saves: who s. a man against his will as good as murders him 948.11
saving: we deny it is fun to be s. 324.1
say: better s. nothing than nothing apropos 898.5
nothing is always a clever thing to s. 898.4
one does s. the same things if he has anything to s. worth saying 800.2
right to s. anything is of less concern than need of people to hear everything 823.12
we oftener s. things because we s. them well 923.37
what people s. behind your back 804.12
what you are drowns out what you s. 923.16
you cannot s. anything but what you are 149.3
you're more interested in what you s. 188.31
saying: dealing with what a woman is s. 923.58
s. is one thing and doing is another 227.18
short s. oft contains much wisdom 572.2
says: half a brain is enough if one s. little 98.6
what a man s. should be what he thinks 901.16
scalded: s. cats fear even cold water 321.16
scandal: greatest s. waits on greatest state 846.4
impossible to conceive of world-wide s. 641.12
lie has no leg, but s. has wings 846.2
love and s. are best sweeteners of tea 846.1
scandalous: never a s. tale without some foundation 846.5
scapegoat: s. unleashes man's ferocious pleasure 847.2
scapegoats: women became the all-purpose s. 847.1
scarcities: time, space, may be s. of tomorrow 1001.13
scarcity: the problem of rationing permanent s. 236.1
scare: cannot s. me with their empty spaces 415.7
good s. is worth more than good advice 343.19
scarecrow: s. in a cucumber garden keepeth nothing 1024.1
we must not make a s. of the law 528.61
scars: God will not look you over for medals, degrees or diplomas, but for s.! 946.18
wounds heal and become s.; but s. grow 476.13
scenery: fine s. appeases our irritations 609.1
s. is fine—but human nature is finer 431.13
we hear too much of s. in literature 545.27
scheme: the madness of the s. protects it 702.4

to grasp this sorry s. of things entire 1025.3
schemes: best-laid s. of mice and men 702.2
schizophrenia: he was slipping into of toxic s. 269.7
scholar: all that's prose isn't verse, all that isn't verse is prose: see what it is to be a s. 848.27
behind remarkable s. find mediocre man 962.10
duty of s.: show facts amidst appearances 848.12
painter is best s.—s. of nature 848.19
s. is early acquainted with impossible 848.34
s. needs manuscripts to know his opinion 848.10
s. ruined by spirit lusting against flesh 848.24
s. should come in contact with other minds 848.25
s. without good breeding is a pedant 391.3
test of s.: if lets intellectual fastidiousness stand between him and his times 848.29
scholarly: don't appear so s., pray 848.26
scholars: esteem or approval of fellow s. 848.15
our great s. not commonly our great men 848.20
vice of s. is to suppose there is no knowledge in world but that of books 848.17
scholarship: devotion to s.: stuff of saintliness 848.36
s. is polite argument 848.33
school: best s. will scarcely save a boy who hates it 913.15
s. days are the unhappiest in all existence 279.57
segregated s. produces crippled minds 775.16
the s. never has any reasons 532.10
schoolboys: just like s. with a new girl 730.1
'tis the s. that educate my son 965.12
schoolchildren: intelligent s. sleep more than dull ones 906.14
schoolmaster: grand s. is practice 279.15
s. is awkward in society of his equals 965.23
schoolmasters: s., parents, exist to be grown out of 670.55
schools: s. are the future in miniature 279.43
s., tortures called an education 279.84
we leave s. full of words, not knowledge 279.23
science: accumulation of facts is not s. 849.28
aim of s.: to cover great number of facts by small number of hypotheses 328.4
applied s. is a conjuror 966.13
art is meant to disturb; s. reassures 53.13
art, s. create balance to material life 53.65
enthusiasm for s. among youngsters 211.10
every s. has fixed system of principles 1037.9
happiness hates the timid; so does s. 980.7
in s., all facts enjoy democratic equality 849.23
in s. a moderate capacity can contribute to a supreme achievement 849.30
in war, s. linked with Stone Age cruelties 1049.2
judgment in s. stands on edge of error 849.2
let both sides invoke wonders of s. instead of its terrors 849.17
not merely truth of s. makes it beautiful 849.25
only s. can keep technology in moral order 966.5
physical s. will not console me for ignorance of morality 604.30
producer of social chaos, s. itself 849.27
religion that fears s. dishonors God 850.5
s.: antidote to poison of enthusiasm 849.36
s., by itself, cannot supply an ethic 849.31
s. can destroy but not enrich illusions 449.13
s. cannot decide what it ought to do 849.21
s. consults her heart when she lays down supreme goods for man 849.16
s. does not distinguish past and future 978.28
s. has brought great acuity of change 117.28
s. has not destroyed the world 241.9
s. increases powers more than happiness 849.20
s. investigates; religion interprets 850.6
s. is a humanist, but morally neutral 849.22
s. is always simple and profound 849.35
s. is a refinement of everyday thinking 849.6
s. is a way of thinking 849.32
s. is inherently neither good nor evil 849.33
s. is nothing but good sense and reason 849.38
s. is the attempt to make our sense-experience correspond to a uniform system 849.5
s. is the knowledge of consequences 849.12
s. is the record of dead religions 850.9
s. is trained and organized common sense 849.14
s. made man feel small 627.9
s. says we must live, seeks means of life 541.43
s. teaches us to bow before the most insignificant of facts 849.40
s. without religion is lame 850.3
shy fruit of pure s. is understanding 849.1
specialized meaninglessness a hallmark of s. 924.3
superstition about infallibility of s. 849.19
tragedy of s.: slaying hypothesis by fact 849.15
we have genuflected before the god of s. 641.11
when one belongs to narrow creed in s. 849.10
wonder is the seed of our s. 1063.3
science fiction: s. writers really do not know anything 344.4
science-fiction: grow up with s. ideas 344.25
sciences: aim of s., give exact picture of world 849.3
arts and s. owe birth to our vices 1030.22
scientific: it's encouragin' that s. facts in pa-apers are not usually thrue 849.4
religious experience is force behind s. research 797.19
s. power has outrun spiritual power 849.18
those who have never entered s. pursuits know not poetry surrounding them 849.37
scientist: proper to the role of the s.: that he teach 849.24
s. alone is true poet, he gives us the moon 849.9
true s. never loses faculty of amazement 849.34
scientists: s. unable to shake off piety 850.7
scolding: s. runs into custom and is despised 803.5
scorn: fate can be surmounted by s. 185.1
silence is best expression of s. 185.8
scorned: hell has no fury like a woman s. 793.1
scorner: reprove not a s., lest he hate thee 803.3
scornful: of all griefs most bitter is s. jest 436.15
scratching: s.: one of nature's sweetest gratifications 852.1
scream: better to emit s. than be insensible 974.12
sometimes s. is better than a thesis 753.1
screams: they enjoy screaming with s. 1071.47
scripture: s. in time of disputes is like an open town in wartime, serving both parties 80.6
Scriptwriter: the Great S. in the Sky 436.14
scrupulous: how can we be s. in a life determined to wring us of serenity 604.12
sculpture: picture and s. are festivities of form 53.47
sea: at s. you wish for wings of swallow 853.3
gale of wind makes the s. look old 853.7
life at s.: enticing, disenchanting 839.4
s. has never been friendly to man 853.6
s. has no generosity 853.8
s. is threatened by activities of man 853.5
s. most implacable when smiles serene 853.13
s. pronounces something over and over 853.9
upon the s. days fall away quicker 839.3
when at s., keep clear of the land 903.5
yet the s. is not full 853.2
search: nothing gives rest but s. for truth 811.4
searcher's: s. eye often finds more than he wished 683.7
searching: s. for another, you are saved 663.7
searchlight: affixed to TV a powerful focusing s. 967.10

sea's: consider the s. listless chime 853.14
seas: s. are the heart's blood of the earth 853.1
season: how many things by s. seasoned are 979.8
in s., all is good 979.9
to every thing there is a s. 979.2
seasons: simple days which lead the s. by 606.7
sing a song of s. 854.38
we circle with the s. 978.70
seclusion: in a crowd thought itself can provide s. 736.4
second: nothing was worse than to finish s. 549.6
s. thoughts are ever wiser 24.1
secrecy: no s. comparable to celerity 926.1
woman obliges man to s. to have pleasure of telling 855.4
secret: can another keep our s. when even we can't 855.12
each human is profound s. to every other 562.14
few s. undertakings ever did nations good 855.15
hard to keep s., employ leisure, bear injury 245.1
he that communicates s. to another makes himself that other's slave 855.8
in a man, s. is ugly thing, like hidden defect 855.5
it always hurts when you lose a s. 855.17
man's most open actions have s. side 9.13
more fear than delight in s. pleasure 704.31
most difficult s. to keep: self-opinion 878.3
none can be so true to your s. as yourself 855.14
nothing is so burdensome as a s. 855.6
people most careful to put commonplace aspect on life when concealing s. 855.10
s. that cannot be pried out by curiosity 855.9
to know one has s. is to know half the s. 855.2
secretary: press s. to keep man in public eye 760.1
secrets: deepest s. are those that keep themselves 855.1
little s. retold, great ones kept 855.3
look for s. in grief or pleasure 855.7
many want possession of s. for circulation 855.13
there are no s. except those that keep themselves 855.16
to whom you tell your s. you resign your liberty 169.7
we don't know each other's s. so well 855.11
sect: every s. of Christianity is perversion 125.12
sects: all s. differ, as they come from men 604.46
secure: God Himself is not s. 856.9
I walk firmer and more s. up hill than down 245.9
nothing is s., nothing keeps 482.3
security: bourgeois: one who renounces love for s. 587.2
enjoy the sweet s. of streets 131.29
most people want s., not liberty 856.12
only in change is true s. to be found 856.11
s. cannot exist with danger of poverty 718.53
s. depends on how much you can do without 856.10
s. is an insipid thing 856.2
sedentary: s. life is real sin against Holy Spirit 1041.3
s., threat of slaughter of noncombatants 856.17
seduce: not enough to conquer, know how to s. 857.13
seduction: verbal s. surest road to actual s. 857.8
see: he does not weep who does not s. 87.7
if a man s. himself as others s. him 875.11
just as much as we s. in others is in us 663.8
most s. no farther than their noses 1035.1
none so blind as they that won't s. 87.5
not all eyes need spectacles to s. 683.8
people s. things in their own fashion 264.10
people s. what they are prepared to s. 683.4
to s. is poetry, prophecy, religion 1035.4
what is out of sight more disturbing than what men s. 43.4
women s. better than men 683.5
seed: destroy s. of evil lest it grow 307.1
ultimate wisdom remains locked in a s. 623.7
seeds: to plant s. is commonest delight 371.6
seeing: do new things make for new ways of s.? 897.6
s. is deceiving; eating is believing 274.28
there is only one way of s.: s. the whole 683.11
seek: let each man s. into himself 818.5
seeking: be at rest from s. after thy lot of life 240.13
would eternal s. go on if the found existed 1019.7
seem: be as you would s. to be 901.8
be content to s. what you really are 45.18
things are seldom what they s. 45.10
seeming: most lives spent in s. and following 171.4
seen: field not well s. from within 689.5
things s. are mightier than things heard 897.7
what is not s. is as if it was not 45.11
sees: who s. little s. less than there is 683.10
segregated: s. school system produces crippled minds 775.16
segregation: practiced s. within their churches 775.17
s. is on its deathbed 775.13
selection: s. by competition for space 308.1
self: censure of s. is oblique praise 863.6
it was strange to have no s. 858.13
notion of one's own s. is a myth 858.29
only possible society is one's s. 663.14
s. is an abstraction, elusive 858.18
s. is sole subject we study and learn 875.9
speaking of s. gives us pleasure 873.12
talking about s. is means to conceal s. 165.13
the s. can be distracted 858.2
the s. more distant than any star 858.9
to know s. is wise 875.13
to thine own s. be true 491.26
we serve life-sentence in dungeon of s. 858.11
what is this s. inside us 863.2
what jailer so inexorable as one's s. 858.15
when s. is one's exclusive subject 858.3
self-abasement: humility is the opposite of s. 435.8
self-assertion: rejection is a form of s. 255.1
self-awareness: test of a civilized person is s. 875.6
self-confidence: s. recovered by snubbing the dead 419.22
self-consciousness: s. is the curse of the city 861.1
self-control: art of conversation is a certain s. 188.9
self-reverence, self-knowledge, s. 858.28
self-controlled: can aught stay out of reach of s. man 945.31
self-criticism: s., an art not many qualified to practice 863.7
s. is the secret weapon of democracy 233.52
self-deception: s., as necessary a tool as a crowbar 864.2
s. carried to the nth degree 864.5
self-delusion: men have the capacity for systematic s. 582.2
self-denial: s. is man's method to arrest progress 865.6
s.: the effect of prudence on rascality 865.5
self-determination: s. but slogan if future holds no hope 718.43
self-esteem: every new adjustment is a crisis in s. 12.3
few can retain s. in face of disesteem of fellows 869.15
oft times nothing profits more than s. 869.7
understand that s. isn't everything 869.12
where s. is unobtainable, envy takes the place of greed 872.1
self-exposure: s., commendable when it allows people to learn 878.4
self-expression: s., a hard and selfish thing 870.2
self-fulfillment: search for s. greatest force of modern age 819.29
self-governing: s. people need to hear everything 823.12
self-government: s. requires self-denial and restraint 233.25
self-image: what is a s.? 18.8
self-incrimination: right against s. is one of the

least popular 823.3
self-knowledge: assurance contemptible unless it is s. 860.5
s. is a dangerous thing 875.29
self-reverence, s., self-control 858.28
self-limitation: it is in s. a master first shows himself 903.3
self-love: feel good and ill in proportion to our s. 876.7
friend often chosen to flatter our s. 365.53
pride doesn't wish to owe, s. to pay 647.3
s., an idolatry; self-hatred, a tragedy 876.4
s. is preservation; and we must conceal it 876.17
s. is the greatest of all flatterers 876.6
s. not so vile a sin as self-neglecting 876.14
s. should be painted as blind 876.16
s. veils our faults from us 876.1
self-made: in presence of s. men don't mention luck 360.42
self-opinion: most difficult secret to keep: s. 878.3
self-pity: life insupportable but for s. 877.2
s. comes so naturally to us all 877.3
self-possession: great man doesn't lose s. when afflicted 401.44
self-praise: good of s.: one can lay it on thick 722.2
self-preservation: s. is the first principle of our nature 956.3
self-realization: men can starve from lack of s. 444.27
self-respect: property is basis of s. 746.20
s. too great a price to pay for peace 681.41
s. will keep man from being abject when in the power of enemies 869.11
self-restraint: nation can afford to use s. 621.24
self-reverence: s., self-knowledge, self-control 858.28
self-righteousness: s. is a din raised to drown our guilt 879.1
self-sacrifice: s. enables us to sacrifice other people 837.10
s. is a survival of mutilation of savage 865.6
self-satisfied: form most contradictory to life: s. man 156.6
self-sufficiency: freedom is the greatest fruit of s. 363.16
feeling I am a peasant gives me s. 880.22
self-trust: s. is the essence of heroism 860.1
selfishness: s. and complaint cloud the mind 551.98
s. is asking others to live as one wishes 874.5
sell: don't imagine man trying to s. something is always so polite 105.12
he would s. even his share of the sun 105.13
time to s., any time that sells the product 18.13
to s. product, work like hell to s. self 105.15
selling: forgive us for frantic buying and s. 105.22
s. houses for more than people could afford 105.18
sells: he is a thief who charges too much for goods he s. 738.4
man s. himself, feels self to be commodity 105.6
when man s. eleven ounces for twelve, he s. himself for the value of an ounce 738.1
senescence: s.: when descendents outnumber friends 653.69
senile: young men regard elders as s. 1071.1
sensation: thought, s., equally wonderful 882.11
sense: best prophet is common s., our native wit 148.5
commonest s. is s. of men asleep 148.8
common s. and good taste—without originality or moral courage 148.7
common s. conforms to world 1060.36
common s. is as rare as genius 148.2
common s. is most fairly distributed 148.1
common s. is the wick of the candle 485.2
fairyland the sunny country of common s. 450.5
fine s. not so useful as common s. 148.6
frost, famine, rain hold us to common s. 148.4
in deep distress native s. departs 918.53
loss of a s. adds as much beauty to world as acquisition of one 882.9
most people die of creeping common s. 148.9
nonsense good because common s. limited 881.3
nothing astonishes men like common s. 148.3
power of sound greater than of s. 690.3
science is trained common s. 849.14
s., not stature, gives a man advantage 493.30
talk s. to fool, he calls you foolish 356.10
there are times when s. is unseasonable 979.4
things and men have always a certain s. 1007.4
we credit only those of our opinion with s. 656.13
senses: a quixotic inflammation of the s. 131.45
at short distances s. are despotic 884.1
cannot gratify imagination, s. together 450.12
cause of error is war of s., reason 299.26
credibility comes only from the s. 882.8
what gives us surer knowledge than our s. 882.7
sensibility: easy to overestimate man's s. 1011.32
nothing little to him with great s. 883.5
one then laps the field of s. 687.2
s. alters from generation to generation 376.9
s. claimed by neurotics matched by their egotism 627.10
s. of man to trifles 883.7
two forces of modern s.: Jewish moral seriousness and homosexual aestheticism 883.8
who has had greatest s. has lived longest 548.9
sensitive: easy to compel a s. being to feel guilty 405.14
sensuality: intemperance is the plague of s. 494.5
s. invites more to art than sentimentality 884.2
s. passes as a new type of asceticism 884.6
sentence: s. begins simply, then undulates 524.13
the maker of a s. launches out into the infinite 1069.39
when literary German dives into a s. 381.4
sentences: for a few golden s. we read whole books 93.27
sentiment: as healthy to enjoy s. as jam 284.11
in church false s. is frequent 126.7
with public s. nothing can fail 762.14
work, a way of shutting out ambiguous s. 1065.72
sentimentalism: allowed s. to form the atmosphere we breathe 1047.7
let us replace s. by realism 783.2
sentimentalist: blessed is the s. 620.7
s. sees an absurd value in everything 885.8
sentimentality: I don't trust s. in men 885.7
s. is a failure of feeling 885.6
s. is subtle dissolvent of morals 885.9
s., parading of emotion, mark of dishonesty 885.1
s.: sentiment that rubs you the wrong way 885.4
to modern spirit, evil to be avoided is s. 885.3
sentiments: all s. weigh less than a lovely action 227.14
character is tested by true s. 119.1
s. of an adult: instinct and education 656.26
separation: anything is better than s. 673.7
love knows not its own depth until s. 673.3
s. only solid peace between man and wife 262.2
serenity: achieve s. when glare of passion fades 989.4
how can we be scrupulous in a life determined to wring us of s. 604.12
serious: play so that you may be s. 703.1
some think everything done with s. face is sensible 886.8
seriousness: dullness is the coming of age of s. 270.2
s. begins to leak back in 145.11
sermon: a mandatory s. is musty the next day 724.5
count superfluous words, whole s. goes 724.4
s. implies absence of the inviting 724.9
who has one word of God before him, and cannot make a s., cannot be a

preacher 724.8
sermons: have wine, woman, then s. and soda-water 706.1
logic and s. never convince 692.4
serpents: be ye therefore wise as s. 943.3
servants: few men have been admired by their s. 804.19
men in great places are thrice s. 401.1
serve: no man can s. two masters 497.1
They also s. who only stand wait for the two-fifteen [train] 677.4
to s. is beautiful if done with whole heart 887.2
serves: he too s. who only stands, cheers 293.1
he who s. two masters has to lie to one 497.3
service: all s. ranks the same with God 887.1
civil s. a fortress of papers, red tape 102.6
if you want good s., serve yourself 880.24
pressed into s.: pressed out of shape 887.3
should render s. to friend to bind him closer and to enemy to make him friend 888.2
small demerit extinguishes long s. 1070.9
when public s. ceases to be chief business of citizens, state not far from fall 761.13
services: men are attached to us for s. they render 888.7
servile: force works on s. natures, not free 357.8
servitude: s. debases men to point where they like it 889.19
this is s., to serve the unwise 889.11
setting: men shut their doors against a s. sun 226.11
settle: never have I been able to s. in life 812.2
seventy: when s., most of you belongs to the past 653.4
severe: be not so s. as to cause shyness 890.3
severity: children should not be led by s. 988.9
excessive s. misses its own aim 890.2
much may be done by s. 517.18
s. is more useful than indulgence 965.30
s. is useless to force change of heart 890.4
sewer: who pry into s. cannot have nice noses 113.4
sewing: men contend s. on button is beyond them 582.4
sex: amount of undesired s. endured by women 564.104
good s. mitigates lust for other sports 929.9
in s.-war thoughtlessness is weapon of male, vindictiveness of the female 581.11
money was exactly like s. 602.2
neither s., without complementary characters of other, is capable of great endeavor 566.3
nothing like early promiscuous s. 892.35
not much loss in replacing s. with science 582.15
only two topics of interest: s., the dead 522.68
s. for many has become a sorry business 892.25
s. gives no meaning to anything in life but itself 892.53
s. is indeed coeval with our lives 892.21
s. is power, and all power is aggressive 892.40
s. is the great amateur art 892.14
s. itself cannot be suppressed 892.43
s., on list of constructive things to do 892.9
s. was invented by the green algae 892.8
s., where good intentions fall to primitive urges 892.41
variety needed in s., but not in love 551.172
we face facts of s. but not of death 328.10
sexes: finest people marry two s. in own person 566.2
free commerce between the s. 581.27
sexual: cannot satisfy s. instinct without love 892.46
s. embrace can be compared with music 892.19
the standardization of s. life 892.52
transformed miseries into s. excitements 892.5
sexual behavior: s. in our species goes through three phases 198.12
sexuality: degree of man's s. reaches into spirit 892.38
s. is lovely 892.24
s. is the lyricism of the masses 892.4
shade: to sit in the s. on a fine day 194.1
shadow: arguing of s., we forgo the substance 51.14
between idea and reality falls the s. 1019.3
every hair makes its s. on ground 473.8
life is like s. of bird in flight 990.8
our days upon earth are a s. 990.4
that s. would marry this s. 103.10
we are afraid to let go of petty reality to grasp great s. 755.25
you may lose substance by grasping at s. 449.1
shadows: morning s. lay still and dark as lakes 605.6
shaft: many a s. at random sent finds mark the archer little meant 1018.2
shake: if we s. hands with icy fingers 321.48
shallow: only the s. know themselves 951.5
sham: what have we to trust in this age of s.? 630.8
shame: as soon as the people fix one s. of the world, another turns up 790.13
avoid s., but do not seek glory 386.15
if you have any s., forbear to pluck the beard of a dead lion 808.8
in getting rid of false s. we have killed off much real s. as well 893.3
only s. is to have none 893.5
shameful: s. things are hardest to confess 168.5
share: happiness forgiven if you s. it 409.21
he who divides gets the worst s. 894.5
shared: mankind, why do ye set your hearts on things that, of necessity, may not be s. 238.6
shark: diver thinking of s. would not get pearl 343.31
sharp: s. men, like s. needles, break easy 139.2
s. temper easier to handle than silence 39.14
sharper: s. than serpent's tooth is thankless child 475.7
shepherd: good s. should not flay his flock 964.10
he who has daughters is always a s. 218.8
shepherds: we are like ignorant s. 419.8
shield: for impenetrable s., stand inside self 31.8
shine: few s., but most can be agreeable 392.11
no soul wherein some faculty doesn't s. 962.9
ship: being in a s. is being in a jail 839.6
every s. is romantic object save our own 333.4
s. in dock has appearance of prisoner 895.1
ships: s. that pass in the night 915.25
shipwreck: society in s. is a comfort to all 152.17
shipwrecked: who is s. twice cannot blame Neptune 88.2
shocked: most have seen worse in private than they pretend to be s. at in public 440.10
shoe: only wearer knows where the s. pinches 321.14
shoes: I murmured because I had no s. 153.3
shooting: s. takes your mind off cost of living 1042.5
shop: keep thy s., and thy s. will keep thee 104.10
man without smile must not open s. 105.4
shopping: men go s. just as men go out fishing 105.1
short: good things when s. are twice as good 389.5
let thy speech be s. 98.1
pleasantry should be s.; the serious also 98.9
shortcomings: men fall from same s. that led to rise 329.18
our s. are eyes with which we see ideal 342.22
show: outside s. poor substitute for inner worth 45.1
what this whole s. / is all about 539.52
show business: puts all the rest of s. in the shade 130.2
showoff: not part of the sofa vaudeville of a s. 732.14
shrewd: if men are s. enough they may serve kings 200.5
shun: always s. whatever may make you angry 39.22
shyness: be not so severe as to cause s. 890.3
s. has a strange element of narcissism 980.2
s. has laws 169.3

sick: healthy ear can stand hearing s. words 169.6
if s., your own thoughts make you s. 627.7
ivry s. man is a hero at laste to himsilf 896.4
man becomes wicked as he becomes s. 1055.11
many s. do not make us deny health exists 627.5
none surpass s. woman in ruling 896.19
not perceiving ourselves to be s. makes us harder to cure 758.15
people no longer sinful, only s. 900.16
s. man must go searching for medicine 577.8
s. man talking about himself can't stop 873.9
sleep of s. man has keen eyes 896.30
sleep to the s. is half health 896.8
the s. are greatest danger for the healthy 1047.11
sickness: aren't sensible to health as to least s. 413.11
s. brings out essential characteristics 119.12
s. enlarges dimensions of a man's self 896.15
s. is felt, but health not at all 413.4
temporary s. reminds us of our destinies 896.7
worst s. is to know we can never be well 896.3
side: God is always on the s. of the heaviest battalions 1042.95
who knows only his s. knows little of that 620.5
sideshow: sex, s. in the world of the animal 343.5
siècle: the fin is coming early this s. 1001.1
sigh: one s. may set whole world into a flame 519.16
sight: genius consists in trueness of s. 376.11
knowledge is true organ of s., not eyes 522.46
nothing sharpens s. like envy 295.10
s. is the most perfect of all our senses 897.1
silence: best sound a player can hear is deep s. 972.41
correction of s. is what kills 803.10
cruellest lies told in s. 558.40
elected s., sing to me 898.8
eternal s. of these infinite spaces 921.5
highest female grace is s. 898.10
I have often regretted speech, never s. 898.21
in s. great things fashion themselves together 898.14
it is not words that kill, it is s. 898.31
nothing so good for ignorant man as s. 447.28
s. is best expression of scorn 185.8
s. is full of potential wisdom and wit 898.9
s. is not tact and tact is golden, not s. 961.2
s. is sorrow's best food 898.12
s. is the perfectest herald of joy 409.91
s. leads to sadness: is the image of death 898.23
s. of a shut park tense, confined 131.6
s. often is wisest 362.9
s. saves me from being wrong or right 898.28
sorrow and s. are strong 287.5
speech is of time, s. of eternity 898.1
the expectation of female s. 898.27
there's ransom in a voice but s. is infinity 898.2
timely s. is sage, and better than speech 898.20
tragedy begins when s. is not understood 898.29
word preserves contact, s. isolates 923.42
words can sting, but s. breaks the heart 898.13
silences: three s.: of speech, desire, thought 898.11
silent: easy to utter what's been kept s. 923.48
human affairs far happier if power to be s. were the same as that to speak 923.56
misfortune to lack judgment to keep s. 372.2
thing left s. often makes for happiness 898.19
we need reason to speak, none to keep s. 898.16
women like s. men; think they listen 581.1
words the s. feel are beautiful 898.3
silently: a hundred acorns are planted s. 649.2
silver: should be s. in purse or on tongue 283.3
the moment's light prints on my own s. gut 897.3
simple: it is hard to be s. enough to be good 393.16
man is a s. being 562.26
s. folk prize deed, overlook motive 608.2
teach us delight in s. things 899.7
the people do not like the s. 682.8
to be s. is best thing in the world 899.2
simple-minded: people on the whole are very s. 682.3
simplicity: affected s. is an elegant imposture 899.8
art of art is s. 899.15
beauty of style and grace depend on s. 899.12
give me a face that makes s. a grace 899.6
perfect s. is unconsciously audacious 899.9
s. of character is no hindrance to subtlety of intellect 899.11
s.: mean between ostentation and rusticity 899.13
s., s., s. 899.14
who understands much displays greater s. 1007.3
simplify: to s.: eliminate unnecessary for necessary 899.5
simply: loveliest things come s. 899.10
sin: as much s. in smiling countryside as in vile London alleys 194.7
be sure your s. will find you out 900.3
harder to confess s. no one believes in 900.10
in best understandings, s. began 900.9
lie is handle that fits all s.'s tools 558.21
making men s. in spite of themselves 900.12
men s. by omission as well as commission 900.1
nonconformism is major s. of our time 468.8
nothing emboldens s. so much as mercy 583.5
plate s. with gold, the lance of justice breaks 1030.25
pleasure's s. and sometimes s.'s a pleasure 900.5
private s. not so prejudicial as public indecency 756.1
really to s. you must be serious about it 900.14
s. against poets is without absolution 900.7
s. basic concept in religion and politics 900.20
s. finally became master of the house 900.21
s. is dangerous in hands of the virtuous 900.17
s. is the writer's element 1069.92
some rise by s., some by virtue fall 1034.17
want gave tongue and s. awakened 625.4
without guilt's spice, s. can't be savored 900.6
worst s. to be indifferent to others 466.6
sincere: condition for being s.: not to boast of it 901.17
friend is person with whom I may be s. 901.5
I only desire s. relations 901.19
it's never what you say, but how you make it sound s. 901.15
men are always s., but change sincerities 901.2
one's belief that one is s. not so dangerous as conviction that one is right 822.19
sincerity: a little s. is a dangerous thing 901.20
can s. be condition of friendship 998.17
s. always subject to proof 901.12
s.: first characteristic of heroic men 901.4
s. is a deadlier sin than hypocrisy 901.10
s. is an opening of heart we find in few 901.13
s. is glass, discretion is diamond 755.16
s. is highest compliment you can pay 901.7
s. is not a spontaneous flower 901.4
taking sides is the beginning of s. 886.10
sinful: people no longer s., only sick 900.16
sing: I do but s. because I must, / And pipe but as the linnets s. 708.97
it is folly to s. twice to a deaf man 48.3
singing: always s. in some foreign language 902.1
in congregational s. you can join in 128.7
single: not the hurrah of masses, but the considerate vote of s. men 208.5
poetry of art: beholding s. tower 1014.2
s. man with fortune must need a wife 66.1
singularity: s. is dangerous in everything 469.5
to affect s., be very virtuous 468.2

sinner: every s. has a future 840.13
more joy over wan s. rayturned to station thin f'r ninety an' nine rayformed 709.3
s. sins against himself 1070.2
sinneth: he that sleepeth well s. not 274.22
sins: between denying s. done and bragging of s. not done is space for millions of s. 900.8
comes a day when a man's s. forsake him 653.43
gods visit s. of fathers on the children 815.6
s. are the highway of our virtue 900.23
s. cannot be undone, only forgiven 900.22
s. have origin in sense of inferiority 33.19
s. sinned in secret are no s. at all 900.18
s. too subtle to be explained 900.19
sire: with him as s., her as dam, what should I be but just what I am 417.3
sister: never praise a s. to a s. 1062.82
situation: effect a settlement of the present s. 228.4
situations: s. where there is no apparent villain 803.8
size: s. is not grandeur 621.10
skating: in s. over thin ice safety is in speed 926.2
skeptic: authority has every reason to fear s. 61.7
intellectualism is sole piety of s. 492.4
s. means him who investigates 904.11
skepticism: good critic's first attribute is wise s. 904.7
idea of truth invincible of s. 998.93
s. is the first step toward truth 904.4
to believe in luck is s. 360.8
skill: s., confidence, are unconquered army 1.9
s., not strength, governs a ship 1.7
we work for a s. not worth the effort 522.18
skilled: one man cannot be s. in everything 1.5
skillful: smooth sea never made a s. mariner 245.2
skills: s. vary with the man 1.13
skin: can the Ethiopian change his s. 444.7
skins: shame on those who preach, pray for those only with s. colored like their own 775.18
sky: as if s. were one gigantic memory 415.6
lift not your hands to s. for help 414.9
s. is all men's together 100.3
soil keeps tree tied, s. leaves it free 647.8
The grass below—above the vaulted s. 623.17
the s. is falling, and a piece of it fell on my tail 545.26
sky's: power that holds s. majesty wins worship 387.1
slander: hearts of men are undermined by s. 905.8
s. is a verdict of guilty in the absence of the accused 905.9
s. lives upon succession 905.11
s., whose edge is sharper than the sword 905.12
slandering: ridiculous folk to the fore in s. others 905.6
slanders: s. of the pen pierce to the heart 207.28
slang: dialect with s. admirable medium for those with nothing to say 524.1
s. is poor man's poetry 524.29
s. spits on hands, goes to work 524.38
strongest s. of all is s. of poets 524.10
slaps: spontaneity of s. is sincerity 901.3
slave: art thou less a s., loved by master 889.13
better starve free than be a fat s. 363.1
day making man s. takes worth away 889.8
he is s. of many masters who is his body's s. 90.8
he who is not his own man is a s. 889.1
I didn't know I was a s. 889.6
s. first wants justice, then crown 1002.7
s. regime attempted to obliterate s.'s being 889.12
to be s. means to be abused, bear it 889.7
who can't live his own life lives a s. 880.13
who would be no s. must have none 889.10
slavery: cowardice of slaves perpetuated s. 889.14
freedom and s. are mental states 363.20
great fortune is a great s. 1048.52
greatest difference between peace, s. 681.4
lean liberty is better than fat s. 537.12
serving one's own passions is greatest s. 675.7
s. holds few fast; many hold their s. 889.16
s. is a weed that grows in every soil 889.3
slaves: all are s. of money or necessity 171.5
ambition makes more trusty s. than need 33.12
Europeans wanted gold and s. 876.10
freedom has thousand charms s. never know 363.8
fugitive s. could be collected and used 889.4
necessity is the creed of s. 624.12
s. lose everything in their chains 889.15
virtue cannot dwell with s. 889.2
we are the s. of objects around us 646.5
sleep: a third of life is spent in s. 221.22
better s. on things than lie awake after 906.7
care-charming s., thou brother to death 906.6
even where s. concerned, too much is bad 906.9
for s., one needs depths of blackness 906.12
in bed my real love has always been s. 266.15
in s. we lie all naked and alone 906.23
liberty is bestowed by s. 297.17
men s. and death's veil is lifted 454.19
most blessed of all natural graces, s. 906.10
our little life is rounded with a s. 606.16
s. covers man, thoughts and all 906.3
s. cuts each day to half its length 906.13
s. hath its own world of wild reality 906.2
s. is pain's easiest slave 906.5
s., it is a gentle thing 906.4
s. makes us all equal—like death 906.19
s. of a sick man has keen eyes 896.30
s. of someone who was not fooling about 906.1
s. that knits up ravelled sleave of care 906.20
s., to be enjoyed, must be interrupted 187.4
s. to the sick is half health 896.8
sound s. is second best 906.15
there is much good s. in an old story 938.3
to be in bed and s. not 366.2
to s. until noon you need legitimate reason to stay up until three 906.11
we are not hypocrites in our s. 266.7
who is known as early riser may s. late 804.30
sleeper: net of the s. catches fish 266.5
sleepers: even s. are collaborators in what goes on in the universe 906.8
great s. are incapable of all else great 883.4
s. have each a private world of his own 266.9
sleepeth: he that s. well sinneth not 274.22
sleepiness: feeling of s. when not in bed is the meanest feeling in the world 341.3
sleeping: for sake of s. one stays awake all day 906.17
sleeplessness: the way to beat s. was to outwit it 73.6
sleeps: arch never s. 50.9
he s. well who knows not that he s. ill 906.18
slight: we s. man whose good will cannot help us 495.8
slip: many a s. 'twixt the cup and the lip 115.11
sloth: s. finds the down pillow hard 906.21
slow: so s. I almost think time passin backwards 978.25
wisely, and s.; they stumble that run fast 411.14
slowness: s. in affairs ripens them or rots them 907.1
sluggard: go to the ant, thou s. 530.2
slumber: all that tread globe are but a handful to the tribes that s. in its bosom 713.1
small: if we play great man too much, we seem s. 693.4
no man is so s. that he need never stoop 400.4
s. causes sufficient to make a man uneasy 996.12
s. man stands on a great man 400.5
s. men reduce great enterprises to level of their

mediocrity 578.6
s. rooms discipline the mind 430.3
smell: knew I was in England by the s. 289.17
not the s. of corn bread that calls us back 365.26
to s., though well, is to stink 685.1
smells: the air was a compound of s. 882.10
woman s. well when she s. of nothing 685.3
smile: minute to s., hour to weep in 539.27
one may s., and s., and be a villain 224.19
s. of a boy at his own birthday party 97.7
smiles: by chivalries the seeds of s. are planted 519.6
Nor coined my cheek to s.,—nor cried aloud 1067.4
smiling: man without s. face must not open shop 105.4
teeth are s., but is the heart 392.3
smite: whoever shall s. thee, turn other cheek 665.1
smoke: good cigar is a s. 982.7
man of no conversation should s. 982.4
slow wreathing of s. into the still air 982.13
to s. in this "French-inhale" style 982.14
who doth not s. hath known no griefs 982.1
smoker: to average s. the world is his ashtray 982.2
smokers: s. inject idleness with every cigarette 982.3
smoking: he stopped s. at least once a month 982.11
s.: a custom loathsome to the eye 982.6
s. is one of leading causes of statistics 982.8
snake: bitten by s., fears piece of string 321.43
when s. is old, frog will tease him 226.9
who will pity s. charmer bitten by a s. 216.1
snare: he avoids a s. who knows how to set one 200.7
sneer: who can refute a s. 185.7
sneezes: speak roughly to your little boy, and beat him when he s. 766.4
sniffles: life is sobs, s., smiles—s. predominate 539.53
snob: true s. never rests 910.7
snobbery: s., basic in the mentality of modern man 910.6
snobbishness: s. has been underrated 910.10
snobs: most cultured people are s. 910.9
snores: husband: man who s. like overloaded bus 564.91
snow: neither s. nor rain stays these couriers 560.1
s. is lonely, self-sufficient 911.2
soap: s., education, are deadly in the long run 133.29
soar: s. not too high to fall; stoop to rise 33.17
sob: are you unable to recognize a s. unless it has the same sound as yours 142.2
sober: he that will to bed go s. falls with leaf 268.37
man must stay s. 784.7
sobriety: most men are disguised by s., not by liquor 165.4
s. is the inability to eat much 970.2
sociable: society is no comfort to one not s. 152.19
social: American does not admit he has no s. inferiors 297.23
by s. contract man gains civil liberty 913.28
cursed be the s. lies 913.33
every s. system is against nature 913.34
inhibited from wanting to change s. conditions 913.25
path of s. advancement strewn with broken friendships 914.9
s. evil sanctified by religious sentiment 477.11
s., friendly man fulfills nature's plan 152.2
s. moulds unrelated to actual shapes 133.14
s. movements are symptoms of progress 568.3
s. process requires standardization 297.9
s. progress strengthens freedom 741.11
s. remedies will fail 623.36
s. war always between the very few 819.28
s. work is a band-aid on society's wounds 433.6
to be s. is to be forgiving 152.7
Socialists: Republicans are S. and the Democrats are Bolsheviks 711.8
societies: s. healthiest when trust is broad 913.5
s. that match self-interest to collective good 913.6
society: all progress means war with s. 741.23
complex s. not more advanced than simple s. 913.7
decrepit s. shuns humor 913.24
each lie is a stab at health of human s. 558.13
each s. reduces opponents to caricatures 935.2
first to fence in land: founder of s. 746.19
fools to depend on s. of fellow-men 915.34
great s. concerned with goals not goods 913.18
great s. is one in which men of business think greatly of their functions 913.36
human s. founded on mutual deceit 914.7
ideal s. is drama enacted in imagination 1025.4
in civilized s. we depend on each other 913.19
in class s., thinking branded by class 135.4
isolation must precede true s. 915.14
lives arranged by what s. rules right 171.19
man entered s. to secure his rights 913.26
men would not live in s. long if they were not each other's dupes 914.6
mouth of s. has many diseased teeth 913.10
national genius characterizes a s. 621.5
no change of s. palatable until s. so desperate it will accept any change 913.2
one cannot have s. on one's own terms 152.6
one for solitude, two for friendship, three for s. 152.22
only possible s. is one's self 663.14
principles of the good s. call for concern with an order of being 913.21
raising bottom of s. benefits all above 913.13
secret of success in s. is certain heartiness and sympathy 914.2
s. acquires new arts, loses old instincts 913.3
s. cannot exist without a controlling power 529.1
s. corrupt if end justifies means 574.2
s. forgives the criminal, never dreamer 450.32
s. grows used to things imposed upon it 913.35
s. in every state is a blessing 395.47
s. is always trying to grind us down to a single flat surface 913.17
s. is a more level surface than we imagine 914.4
s. is an accident to the spirit 913.29
s. is immoral and immortal 913.1
s. is no comfort to one not sociable 152.19
s. is now formed of the Bores and Bored 94.2
s. is produced by our wants 395.46
s.: masked ball where all hide character 914.1
terror of s. is the basis of morals 343.37
the concrete theater of s. at large 913.27
the prophecy of an unformed s. 50.14
to be in s. is merely a bore 914.10
to get into the best s. one has to feed, amuse, or shock people 914.11
value of a dollar is created by s. 602.17
values of s. must be clear and acceptable 913.30
who lives out of s. must be either beast or god 915.1
sociology: if far, it's news; if close, it's s. 629.6
Socrates: S. wrote nothing 545.20
sodawater: let us have wine, woman, then sermons, s. 706.1
softly: speak s. and carry a big stick 719.50
soil: nation that destroys s. destroys self 177.6
s. keeps tree tied, sky leaves it free 647.8
solace: s. from company in misery is spiteful 180.2
solar system: s., island of activity in ocean of emptiness 921.3
sold: pleasing ware is half s. 105.11
soldier: captain's choleric word is blasphemy in s. 780.19
essential to persuade s. that those he is to massacre don't deserve to live 588.7
s., above all others, prays for peace 588.11
s. is grievous vestige of bar-

barism 70.5
soldier's: s. life is on'y glorious in times iv peace 588.4
s. strength broken or exalted by a cause 588.14
soldiers: lucky are s. who strive in a just war 588.2
s., little more than clever mechanics 1042.63
weep more for s. than for churches 1042.75
solemnity: s. is the shield of idiots 886.9
solitary: if you are idle, be not s. 446.11
life is a s. cell 915.33
only s. men know the full joys of friendship 915.8
s. trees, if grow at all, grow strong 915.9
some s. wretches seem to have left mankind to meet the devil in private 915.36
we're all sentenced to s. confinement 915.53
solitude: feeling my s. as a conspicuous caste mark 915.39
find inner peace in s., not speed 989.9
he who lives in s. may make own laws 915.37
if you would live innocently, seek s. 478.8
individuality must be affirmed in s. 915.24
in the crowd, great man keeps independence of s. 880.6
little do men perceive what s. is 915.3
lost in the s. of power 719.25
Now the New Year reviving old Desires, / The thoughtful Soul to S. retires 631.4
nurse of full-grown souls is s. 915.27
one can acquire all in s. but character 915.45
only in s. do we find ourselves 915.50
s. gives birth to the original in us 915.29
s. is audience-chamber of God 915.22
s. is bearable only with God 915.19
s. is needful to the imagination 915.26
s. is the mother of anxieties 915.38
s. is the playfield of Satan 915.32
s. sometimes is best society 915.30
s. vivifies; isolation kills 915.42
some days s. a wine; other days, a poison 915.10
'Tis S. should teach us how to die 915.6
who hears music, feels his s. peopled 614.12
solutions: more dangerous than good s. to wrong problems 443.28
somebody: how dreary to be s. 332.13
when everyone is s., no one's anybody 780.5
something: if s. is wrong in society, it must be fixed 790.36
son: always struggle between father and s. 916.6
every man is the s. of his own works 867.2
everyone calls his s. his s., whether he has talents or not 916.2
greatness in father often overwhelms s. 916.7
he that spareth his rod hateth his s. 766.3
s. can bear death of his father 1058.7
son of a bitch: he's still a s. 711.14
son's: s. offenses vanish at word of repentance 916.10
song: grandeur of man lies in s., not thought 53.86
leave out my name, but keep my s. 384.30
must one swear to the truth of a s. 53.108
s. is the primal thing in poetry 708.5
s. is the rose upon truth's lips 708.110
that s. is most esteemed with which our ears are most acquainted 333.3
what is s., when world lacks taste 48.4
songs: s. that come free from the blue-eyed grass 614.63
sonnet: true s. goes eight lines; takes turn for better or worse 708.38
sons: s. are generally worse than fathers 916.4
s. do not need you 916.8
s. have rebellious wish to be disillusioned by what charmed their fathers 916.5
you don't raise heroes, you raise s. 916.12
soothing: love's best habit is a s. tongue 551.194
sophistication: s. does not require ill temper 917.1
s., resourcefulness of city people 917.4
soprano: s. with whom he had dallied in good faith 472.9
sorrow: belief in God ends burden of s. 330.13
crown of s.: remembering happier things 918.54
drink today, and drown all s. 268.36
excess of s. laughs, excess of joy weeps 527.1
first pressure of s. crushes out best wine from hearts 918.30
give s. words 918.47
glut thy s. on a morning rose 1011.19
heart forgets its s. and ache 1050.7
heaven wills that s. follow joy 918.38
illusory joy worth more than real s. 409.28
joy and s. equally pass away 990.13
knowing s. I learn to help distressed 56.11
life of man is to shift from s. to s. 539.118
loss of native land is greatest s. 423.2
nature refuses to sympathize with s. 623.72
on the way to death, s. in manifold shapes 918.36
patience lightens what s. can't heal 677.11
rapture's self is three parts s. 918.31
real s. is incompatible with hope 918.26
seldom felicity is not tempered by s. 409.23
something pleasurable in memory of past s. 918.11
s. and silence are strong 287.5
s. before joy better than s. after joy 918.43
s. brings one down in the world 918.6
s. falls readily into dislike 918.45
s. for dead is only s. from which we refuse to be divorced 610.7
s. hath less power to bite man that mocks it 918.48
s. is better than laughter 918.3
s. is knowledge 918.8
s. is only thing people really possess 918.35
s. makes night morning, noontide night 918.50
s. makes us all children again 918.16
s. one broods over is no longer a pain 918.23
s. shall nourish thee till strong 918.29
to show unfelt s. false man does easy 440.18
we are not sure of s., joy never sure 990.16
when wine is plentiful, s. takes wing 268.41
where there is s. there is holy ground 918.55
who increaseth knowledge increaseth s. 522.5
who is master of himself can end s. 862.15
your joy is your s. unmasked 409.45
sorrowful: even in laughter the heart is s. 526.3
sorrow's: genius is s. child 376.1
silence is s. best food 898.12
sorrows: heart has secret s. world knows not 142.4
he truly s. who s. unseen 918.34
joys are often tender shadows of s. 409.9
joys impregnate; s. bring forth 918.4
our cruelty to each other adds to our s. 209.1
s. are our winter foliage 918.42
s. come, not singly, but in battalions 918.51
s. remembered sweeten present joy 918.39
tell thy s. to him in whose countenance thou mayst be assured of consolation 169.5
soul: always three A.M. in dark night of s. 239.6
a man should have fine point of his s. taken off to become fit for this world 321.24
art is for fertilisation of the s. 53.144
a temple, the landscape of the s. 126.3
deep distress hath humanised my s. 918.56
every subject's s. is his own 132.9
eyes indicate antiquity of the s. 325.1
forge in smithy of my s. conscience of my race 174.14
Hamlet came out of his s., and Romeo out of his passion 201.45
knowledge of s. would make us melancholy 875.17
nature the body, God the s.

1017.13
no retreat as quiet as one's own s. 183.1
save my s., if I have a s. 265.5
shame on s. to falter when body perseveres 219.1
s. beauty seen when man bears mischances 17.4
s. buried under furrow or pile of money 194.9
s. is much older than the mind 927.9
s. is only a word for body 90.4
s. is unwillingly deprived of truth 998.40
s. may ask God for anything 927.5
s. must be let alone by government 590.17
s. with no established aim loses itself 771.8
spectacle grander than sky is interior of the s. 927.8
typical American believes no necessity of s. is free and few cannot be bought 34.39
virtue of s. consists in walking orderly 661.9
what profit to gain world and lose s. 33.2
soul's: all music jars when s. out of tune 968.1
life is a stuff to try s. strength 539.12
s. power lies in the heart, not in the mind 675.22
souls: all human beings have gray little s. 732.2
nurse of full-grown s. is solitude 915.27
s. are not saved in bundles 841.4
these are the times that try men's s. 298.15
soul-sides: God be thanked, the meanest of his creatures / Boasts two s. 688.2
sound: power of s. greater than of sense 690.3
sounds: elemental s.: rain, wind in woods, ocean 623.5
few s. exceed interest of knock at door 428.16
s. are things blind see 86.3
time that's just time will let s. be s. 919.1
soup: worries go down better with s. 43.17
South: S. is one of those kingdoms of the mind 617.2
the S., land of the sustained sibilant 34.83
Southern California: everything not fastened down slides into S. 106.2
sovereign: to appear at church is the best means of becoming popular for a young s. 831.9
sovereignty: s. of self-governing people 34.88
to bear naked truths with calm is s. 160.1
when I refuse to obey unjust law I appeal from s. of people to s. of mankind 786.2
whom hatred frights, let him not dream on s. 831.10
sow: he that observeth the wind shall not s. 112.1
they that s. in tears shall reap in joy 281.1
sower: s. sows crooked; peas show crooked line 176.4
soweth: whatsoever a man s., that shall he reap 815.4
sowing: must be s. even after bad harvest 686.8
space: about one atom in every cubic meter of s. 921.1
by s. the universe encompasses me 975.34
don't say man doesn't belong out in s. 921.2
nothing puzzles more, troubles less, than s. 1017.10
s. flights are an escape from oneself 921.4
s. fragment of the infinite for finite use 978.4
time, s.: scarcities of tomorrow 1001.13
spaces: cannot scare me with their empty s. 415.7
if you take big paces, you leave big s. 33.4
Spain: in S. dead more alive than dead elsewhere 922.1
the first meal in S. was always a shock 922.2
spanks: many a man s. children for things his father should have spanked out of him 766.11
spark: if fuel prepared, hard to tell whence s. shall come 819.2
sparrow: s. sorry for peacock's burden of tail 780.22
speak: be swift to hear, slow to s. 167.3
difficult to s. when ashamed to be silent 923.39
does not s. so much as exhale 283.8
don't s., people will believe good of you 898.17
every man may s. truly, but few s. fully 923.43
humanize your talk, s. to be understood 848.26
learn meaning of what you say, then s. 923.18
less dishonor to hear than s. imperfectly 1007.11
misfortune to lack wit to s. well 372.2
never s. of yourself to others 188.15
some s. well and write badly 923.47
s. softly and carry a big stick 719.50
s. speech of world, think thoughts of few 171.8
s. what you think today 464.3
terrible to s. well and be wrong 763.15
to s. agreeably is more than to s. in good words or in good order 923.3
we care more that men s. of us than how 332.31
we need reason to s., none to be silent 898.16
we s. badly of ourselves than not at all 873.13
when a child begins to s., it learns what it knows 524.50
When I think, I must s. 1062.128
when you s. and when you listen to yourself s. 188.13
when you s. to man, look on his eyes 923.19
woe unto you, when all s. well of you 712.3
women wish to s.; men are driven to 581.28
you may live with people and not s. openly 915.49
speaker: you may end up an after-dinner s. 421.4
speakers: all great s. were bad s. at first 763.6
speakest: think twice before thou s. once 755.18
speaking: none love s. so much as the taciturn 923.7
open way of s. draws out discoveries 362.8
s. of self gives us pleasure, others none 873.12
s. with the Elgin marbles in his mouth 923.61
speaks: he is not good who s. well of all alike 455.2
who s. aright never s. at unsuitable time 923.46
specialist: poet on Pegasus, reciting own verses, no more dreaded than mounted s. 924.2
specialists: illusion of s.: think they enhance culture 924.5
species: our s., loyal to basic biological urges 892.33
specious: ideology, s. way of relating to world 445.2
spectacle: the s. of a great man at a great moment 418.36
spectacles: not all eyes need s. to see clearly 683.8
wearing s. makes men conceited 925.1
spectator: become s. of one's life, escape suffering 650.6
spectre: how do you shoot s. through heart 343.11
speculation: s. is the romance of trade 503.5
speculators: s., boast not of knowing things 694.19
speech: dream is always below surface of s. 336.15
freedom of s. means don't do something to people for their views 364.2
free s. shoved aside for things more vital 364.3
have often regretted s., never silence 898.21
in the faculty of s. man excels the brute 923.50
let s. be better than silence or be quiet 923.15
let thy s. be short 98.1
let your s. be alway with grace 923.9
make your s. not too explicit 923.25
man whose expenditure of s. is greater than his income of ideas 923.44
men employ s. to conceal their thoughts 440.21
no glass renders man's likeness as his s. 923.31
our s. will become one s. 923.57
plain s. breeds hate 362.4
s.: art of stifling, suspending thought 923.11
s. is civilization itself 923.42
s. is of time, silence of eternity 898.1
s. is the mirror of action 923.55
s. mirror of soul: as man speaks, so is he 923.49
true use of s. is to conceal our wants 923.22
we have freedom of s. and prudence not to practice it 537.42
where there is censorship. s. is serious 113.3
speeches: s. measured by hour, die with hour 763.8

speed: in skating over thin ice safety is in s. 926.2
love comes with the s. of light 551.12
wind-footed steed is broken in his s. 686.7
sphinx: we dream of a s. to explain our horror 266.1
spider: s. as an artist has never been employed 481.1
spirit: every s. makes its house 867.3
happiness is s. fulfilled through body 409.26
home of s. is the realm of meaning 547.9
letter killeth, but s. giveth life 544.1
not acquainted with literature of the s. 927.3
our country rich in goods, poor in s. 719.45
pure logic is the ruin of the s. 785.30
s., invisible force made visible 927.1
s. is most free when body is satiated with pleasure 704.22
s. is willing but the flesh is weak 1047.1
s. longs for inverted bowl over its head 482.7
s. of man is a good adversary 978.76
s. of nation is what counts 621.6
the s. is as mercurial as ever 653.80
the s. is the true self 858.10
spirits: we learn we are s., not animals 111.2
spiritual growth: s. resembles a game of leapfrog 404.8
spiritual: hard to live a s. life in America 927.11
physical strength can't withstand s. force 927.10
scientific power has outrun s. power 849.18
s. interests supported by animal life 927.12
spirituality: s., shadow of light humanity casts 927.13
splendor: God grant me love for things of s. 55.14
splurge: she knew that his s. was over 285.3
spoil: may share labours of great but not s. 400.1
spoiled: all charming people, I fancy, are s. 121.6
spoken: one never repents of having s. too little 923.14
spontaneity: analysis kills s. 785.2
spontaneous: fine conduct is always s. 77.23
to condemn s. acts because useless 703.7
spoon: kids born with gold s. in their mouth 281.9
sport: aura of changelessness to s. 118.6
if year all holidays, s. would be dull 420.7
in America, s. is opiate of the masses 929.5
no evidence s. is motivated by aggression 26.2
only s. you can't fix is rodeoing 929.13
serious s. contains no fair play 929.16
s., a religious and civic undertaking 929.21
sports: good sex mitigates lust for other s. 929.9
spot: Ordains for each one s. shall prove / Beloved over all 699.6
spring: after stormy s. summer comes 854.14
alas, that s. should vanish with the rose 1071.50
children hold s. tightly in their fists 854.47
hush over everything—world awaits s. 854.42
if winter comes, can s. be far behind 427.36
in s. all sins are forgiven 854.46
in s. a young man's fancy lightly turns to thoughts of love 854.43
only winter-patience can bring the s. 677.14
quality of life is sexual in s. 854.3
s., a box where sweets compacted lie 854.23
s. arrives at close of winter day 854.9
s., cruel fair season, will come again 854.52
s. is come home with world-wandering feet 854.44
s. kissed me bang in the face 854.26
s. never s. unless it comes too soon 854.16
s., that sharp knife 854.50
vine made to bear fruit in s. dies soon 279.71
wag world how it will, leaves green in s. 854.33
world's favorite season is the s. 854.41
spurn: s. not the nobly-born 793.2
spurred: good horse should be seldom s. 1066.1
spurs: no need of s. if the horse is running away 300.7
squeezed: as if he had reached over and s. you 474.4
stability: One does that, one drifts into s. 564.27
stables: in England s. centre of household 289.29
stage: all the world's a s. 1067.25
no man dies for love, but on the s. 551.48
on the s. it is always now 972.37
s. but echoes back the public voice 972.16
you can't be virtuoso in s. and films 972.1
stairs: life full of s. to go up and down 235.6
stake: death a s. put up to play game of life 541.17
stand: may s. with you through thin, but not thick 1054.3
what is life without time to s. and stare 533.3
standard: look to s. man for s. English 524.45
standardization: social process requires s. of man 297.9
standard of living: highest s. the world has known 34.33
standards: great expression furnishes its own s. 401.18
half our s. come from our first masters 473.7
stander-by: s. may see more of game than player 650.4
standing: man's s. abroad depends on manners 804.9
nature, not s., makes the good man 393.38
those well assured of own s. least apt to trespass on that of others 804.14
what people say behind your back is your s. 804.12
stands: he who s. on tiptoe s. not firm 55.10
star: follow thy s., canst not fail of heaven 240.6
God is seen God / In the s. 387.12
let me light my lamp, says the s. 887.4
mariner's eye must be on rocks, North S. 720.3
toe of the s. gazer is often stubbed 442.16
we mentally rocket to each new s. that flares 978.35
stare: what is life without time to stand and s. 533.3
stars: as man draws nearer to s. he should draw nearer to his neighbors 100.9
fault is not in our s., but in ourselves 810.11
gazing on s., man at mercy of puddles 442.17
s. show men to be slight and evanescent 415.5
s. speak of man's insignificance 415.10
too low they build who build beneath the s. 55.21
we are all in gutter, but some look at s. 55.20
when moon is not full, s. shine brightly 795.2
start: there is nothing like a s. 83.4
starting: anything may be s. point, termination 76.6
starve: can s. from lack of self-realization 444.27
starving: love, art are shadows of words to s. man 437.7
s. of men, pampering of dogs 718.14
state: bungling in s. affairs produces mischief 88.5
church must be the conscience of the s. 127.4
disproportion destroys a s. 710.2
evil men not excused from service of s. 930.1
king without clemency is enemy of s. 127.5
man not just laborer for the s. 132.2
modern s. has only rights, no duties 930.4
only one in command in home or s. 395.19
s. exists for good life, not life only 930.2
s. has for enemy only other states, not men 930.16
s. has no friends—only interests 930.7
s. hurt when cunning pass for wise 930.3
s. intervention in practically all fields 15.8
s. is a creation of nature 711.9
s. is servant, not master, of the citizen 930.12
s. made for man, not man for s. 930.8
s. safe when men fear candidates, laws 930.11
s. tolerates evil to keep out lesser ills 930.13
s. without change is without means of conservation

930.5
the s. is a poor, good beast 930.9
the s. is neighbors; neighbors are s. 930.10
thousand years scarce serve to form a s. 930.6
while the s. exists there is no freedom 930.14
states: limit is set to growth of prosperous s. 930.15
responsibility of great s.: serve world 930.17
statesman: can get the truth from a s. after he's seventy 931.6
difference between being an elder s. and posing as one is negligible 931.2
heart of s. should be in his head 931.5
s. is politician dead 10 or 15 years 711.83
to delight in war is crime in the s. 1042.86
statesmanship: in s. get formalities right 931.9
s. cannot always escape wrong-doing 931.4
statesmen: inquiry made into meals and beds of s. 931.8
minds of s. contract with the light 931.3
some deluded into belief they are s. 931.7
s. and beauties rarely sense their decay 226.2
s. seldom have choice between good, evil 931.1
static: life is not a s. thing 117.8
station: train on wrong track, every s. wrong s. 321.33
statistics: there are lies, damned lies, and s. 932.2
stature: beauty of s. is the only beauty of men 582.8
being good enough to deserve s. 401.53
status: demand for equal s. began to grow exponentially 297.7
grass, least rewarding of s. symbols 933.1
negotiating both s. and connection 581.59
status quo: not those who cling to the s. 258.9
s. as a natural order of things 179.4
statute: s.: currency we stamp with our portrait 528.17
steal: artists don't s., but borrow 53.116
old burglars never die; just s. away 934.4
poor men do not often s. 934.6
stealing: all s. comparative; who does not steal 934.2
steamers: land created as place for s. to visit 839.1
steering: s. New York like her private car 657.10
step: count every s., you make journey long 6.7
thousand-mile journey begins with s. 75.1
stepchild: indecision is like the s. 465.3
stepmother: new-come s. hates children of first wife 670.18
stereotypes: the s. were broader and more offensive 421.3
sterility: pain, indolence, s., ennui teach lesson 946.13
stew: there may be things better than beef s. 355.8
stick: speak softly and carry a big s. 719.50
stillness: nothing but s. can remain when hearts are full of their own sweetness 989.10
we are use to actions, not s., of humans 989.7
stock: earth is given as a common s. 272.5
stocks: 'Tis sweet to know that s. will stand 503.2
stomach: old s. reforms more drinkers than new resolve 268.35
with full s. rich and poor are alike 274.9
stomachs: those with best s. are not best thinkers 975.47
stone: if s. bruises gold, worth undiminished 1026.19
word and s. cannot be called back 507.5
Stonehenge: simple as S. if we could but see it 50.10
stones: people throw s. at tree loaded with fruit 295.9
stoop: soar not too high to fall; s. to rise 33.17
store: for modern man heaven is a big department s. 414.3
stories: taste for dirty s. inherent in humans 714.1
there are only two or three human s. 545.2
storm: every cloud engenders not a s. 715.2
slowly gathered fury of the s. broke upon us 1032.1
they sicken of the calm, who know the s. 16.8
stories: Neanderthal man listened to s. 938.2
story: only thing read in s. are the first and last sentences 630.35
s. has been thought to its conclusion when it has taken its worst possible turn 938.1
s. with moral is like bill of mosquito 938.4
the s. you must take seriously, not yourself 630.22
there is much good sleep in an old s. 938.3
where men have lived there is a s. 419.45
straight: s. path leads only to the objective 903.2
straightforwardness: s. without propriety is rudeness 362.2
stranger: he deals harshly with s. who's not been a s. 358.8
man by definition is born a s. 358.10
s. cannot torture a human soul 499.4
s. has no friend, unless it be a s. 358.9
to depend on s. is blindness 235.7
when s. to self, estranged from others too 875.14
which of us is not forever a s. 915.54
strangers: ants and savages put s. to death 358.6
cities are, by definition, full of s. 131.20
tears of s. are only water 358.7
stratagem: let sword decide after s. has failed 357.1
stratagems: those oft are s. which errors seem 939.2
strayed: when I s. through trap-ridden compartments 62.3
street: city s., a river leading nowhere 131.31
streetcars: except in s. never be rude to a lady 830.1
washed cars and bright-painted red-and-yellow s. and white buildings 632.5
strength: awareness of our own s. makes us modest 940.5
envy man who lays down life when s. spent 226.3
fool matches s. with stronger 1047.4
growing up: discovering inner core of s. 571.8
knows not own s. who hasn't met adversity 17.36
life only demands the s. you possess 195.14
like s. is felt from hope and despair 940.10
man's s. is to find God's way, follow it 697.1
men's s. discontent with limitation 940.1
my s. is as the s. of ten 770.6
nation realizes s., scorns to misuse it 621.24
physical s. can't withstand spiritual force 927.10
skill, not s., governs a ship 1.7
s. and s.'s will are supreme ethic 940.11
s. of strongest can be overpowered 940.2
to bear lightly the neck's yoke brings s. 287.7
tyrannous to use giant's s. like a giant 719.52
what's s. without double share of wisdom 940.14
who bends under his s. the man with thoughts too high 387.58
wisdom is always an overmatch for s. 1060.46
woman's s. is might of weakness 1062.47
stretch: s. your foot to length of your blanket 404.21
striding: s. around as if wearing top hats 732.10
strife: cruel is the s. of brothers 334.3
s. hushed by passing of one generation 374.10
where there is no talebearer, the s. ceases 252.3
worse to incite to s. than to take part 252.1
strifes: no temple can still griefs and s. 128.3
strike: no right to s. against public safety 1013.1
s. at a great man, you will not miss 905.13
strikes: s. an' picnics are evils f'r wurrukin man 1013.3
strive: man must s., and striving he must err 299.17
we must s. by what is born in us 1.13
striving: success erases the effort of s. 945.33
there's life alone in duty, rest in s. 271.30
strong: adversity is the test of s. men 17.50
deny s. man his due and he'll take all 719.39
harm comes to s. from the weakest 1047.11
how shall one so weak become s. 452.5
if you're s., there are no precedents 940.8

it is easy the for s. to be s. 940.7
know how sublime to suffer and be s. 946.26
language of some men s., but their eyes and actions ask leave to live 980.4
no need to fear the s. 719.60
one cannot be s. without love 551.220
s. and weak cannot keep company 57.1
s. man advances issues, makes a decision 225.3
s. man can intercept the communication between the senses and the mind 862.11
s. man digests his experiences 321.37
s. man succumbs to the weak 418.32
s. men can always afford to be gentle 940.12
weak can be terrible trying to appear s. 1047.12
when is man s. until he feels alone 940.4
when s., be merciful to have respect 940.6
stronger: pray to be s. men 723.22
that which does not kill me makes me s. 17.44
strongest: necessary that s. should be obeyed 644.3
right of conquest is right of s. 173.12
s. have their moments of fatigue 341.4
s. iron most often ends in scraps 940.15
s. not strong enough to be always master 719.51
structure: effect of s. on the human spirit 50.21
struggle: s. alone pleases us, not victory 281.13
the s. that touches the heart 583.3
to win joy through s. is better than to yield to melancholy 281.8
stubbornness: man will do more for s. than for religion 652.6
smallness of mind is the cause of s. 652.8
s. and stupidity are twins 652.11
student: almost every s. believes truth is relative 904.2
students: s. are sure to get somewhere 6.8
studied: men must be s. as deeply as books 1008.13
studies: change of s. will fire a dull brain 532.13
to spend too much time in s. is sloth 848.2
study: complacency is enemy of s. 156.7
much s. is a weariness of the flesh 93.7
must always s., not always go to school 279.62
natural abilities need pruning by s. 1.1
people that s. more to have knowledge than to live well bring forth little fruit 522.31
proper s. of mankind is man 875.22
realists do not fear results of s. 783.1
self is sole subject we s. and learn 875.9
s. without liking spoils the memory 532.12
stumble: men s. on stones, not mountains 996.3
s. may prevent a fall 88.4
stupefaction: s., when it persists, becomes stupidity 955.2
stupid: good man can be s. and still be good 1070.11
mistake of intelligent: to refuse to believe the world as s. as it is 941.18
nothing sways the s. more than arguments they can't understand 941.16
one can be s. with old friends 365.36
pleasant to meet people more s. than we 941.12
s. thing done from noblest motive 941.19
those of delicate taste endure s. criticism better than s. praise 722.26
when s. man does thing he is ashamed of, he declares that it is his duty 271.26
stupidity: against s., even gods contend in vain 941.17
anesthetic for pain of s.: egotism 873.14
certain sign of s. to stand aloof from those who think differently from us 620.4
hardest thing to cope with is s. 941.9
memory is often the attribute of s. 580.8
miseries spring from human s., malice 335.8
nothing is more dangerous than conscientious s. 447.19
obstinacy, dogmatism, surest signs of s. 652.9
stubbornness and s. are twins 652.11
s., basic building block of universe 941.20
s. often saves a man from going mad 941.10
when stupefaction persists it becomes s. 955.2
with s. man may front much 941.2
style: Every day, so it seems, brings in a different s. 338.22
good s. should show no sign of effort 942.15
great writer finds s. in his soul 942.7
hardship is vanishing, but so is s. 750.7
progress in literary s. 942.6
proper words in proper places make s. 942.20
s. beautiful when veins not prominent 942.21
s. is temperament stamped upon material at hand 942.16
s. is the dress of thoughts 942.3
s. is the perfection of a point of view 942.5
s., not sincerity, is the vital thing 942.24
s. turns all it touches to gold 942.19
the s. is the man himself 942.1
we are delighted to see natural s. 942.17
what amateurs call s. is only awkwardness 942.10
subject: a great man will make any s. great 848.9
subject's: s. duty is king's, s. soul is his own 132.9
subjunctive: damn the s.: brings all writers to shame 398.10
sublime: abuse of the s. is absurdity 684.19
but one step from s. to ridiculous 4.4
submarines: men die lingering deaths in s. 659.5
submit: men subdued by force do not s. in heart 357.9
we s. to great evils, resent small offenses 508.2
subordination: s. tends greatly to human happiness 780.10
substance: you may lose s. by grasping at shadow 449.1
substitute: balancing checkbooks as a s. for love-making 564.126
substitutes: ours is the age of s. 54.1
subtraction: a man has one hundred dollars; you leave him with two; that's s. 570.10
suburb: children, captives of their s. 944.4
conformity ultimately governs the s. 944.2
modern s. is product of the car 944.5
suburbs: s. are incubators of apathy and delirium 944.1
subversion: communists have done less to damage us than those defending us against s. 150.8
succeed: humiliating to see idiots s. 945.15
man cannot be said to s. in this life who does not satisfy one friend 365.99
some s. by what they know, some by what they do, and a few by what they are 945.21
very rare for man of talent to s. by it 962.14
when men s., neighbors think them wise 945.35
when we s., pride betrays us 6.4
succeeding: you could stay there your whole life without s. 82.5
succeeds: fail I alone—all men strive and who s. 329.5
one s. because to fail is too awful 329.17
success: attention to business is price of s. 945.44
coming into port determines s. of voyage 6.1
compensation of early s. is a conviction that life is romantic 945.14
constant s. shows but one side of world 945.6
fine line between failure and s. 329.13
for s., aim unswervingly for goal 686.1
good-fellowship requisite for s. 392.6
hypocrisy is royal road to s. 711.36
I do not care for socially recognizable s. 945.38
in s. we gain reputation for judgment 945.12
Italian way of life cannot be considered a s. except by temporary visitors 77.4
key to s. no good until right lock found 945.19
minute's s. pays the failure

of years 945.5
near approach to good aggravates ill s. 329.9
not even s. softens heart of envious 295.19
only the cynicism born of s. is valid 214.4
pray s. won't come faster than you can endure 945.20
secret of s. is constancy to purpose 771.3
secret of s.: to convert ideas to things 945.2
some things we do because the doing is a s. 945.16
strong passion for any object ensures s. 238.18
s. abides longer when planted by God 945.34
s. can corrupt; usefulness only exalt 1023.4
s. distinguishes confidence from conceit 945.7
s. erases effort of striving 945.33
s. improves the character of the man 945.28
s. is allotted to men by their stars 340.8
s. is counted sweetest by those who ne'er succeed 945.10
s. is undesirable 329.7
s. makes men rigid; they exalt stability 945.27
s. makes us more praised than known 945.36
s. means talents used to serve others 945.46
s. not greedy, but insignificant 945.39
s. of most things depends upon knowing how long it will take to succeed 945.29
s. of others punishment for laziness 530.7
s.: to spend your life in your own way 945.30
s.: what we can make of mess we have made 945.11
there are a thousand who hate our s. 295.5
there is no s. without hardship 945.42
'Tis man's to fight, but Heaven's to give s. 173.8
too much s. can ruin you 945.4
to secure s., be more anxious about obtaining than about deserving it 945.17
toughest thing about s. is one must keep on being a s. 945.3
true s. is to labor 281.16
unless a man has been taught what to do with s. it leaves him a prey to boredom 945.37
what is responsible for s. of many works 93.15
worship of vulgar s. 654.1
successes: s. forgiven if you share them 409.21
successful: s. at a third-rate career like journalism 630.2
s. man cannot realize how hard an unsuccessful man finds life 945.18
successor: merit goes to beginner if s. does better 75.2
sucker: no crime more humiliating than to be a s. 202.7
suckers: Americans are s. for good news 328.15
suddenly: no great thing is created s. 401.15
suffer: each must s. long before he knows he is but one in a community of wretchedness 946.17
how others s. from us we take no heed 946.23
human must s. as price of vision 946.8
know how sublime to s. and be strong 946.26
mankind are disposed to s. evils 806.7
none can endure to s. 677.8
to s. in obedience to a command is easier than to accept suffering as a free man 946.5
who breathes must s. 946.37
who fears he shall s., suffers what he fears 946.31
suffered: fool knows after he's s. 321.21
sufferers: for s. sweet to know pain that remains 946.1
suffering: although world is full of s., it is full also of the overcoming of it 946.22
become spectator of one's life, escape s. 650.6
defenceless against s. when we love 552.4
it's not true that s. ennobles character 946.29
life is s. 946.34
life reduced to s. when two ages overlap 210.12
madness, s. can set themselves no limit 559.15
mental s. to degree unknown in Suburbia 718.20
only through s. can soul be strengthened 119.16
ownership, not love, causes s. 551.180
senselessness of s. raises indignation 946.33
s. for truth is fortitude to victory 946.30
s. is need felt to familiarize and adapt sensibility to a new state 946.38
s. is not a mystery but a revelation 946.51
s. is one very long moment 946.53
s. is permanent, obscure and dark 946.54
s. is the sole origin of consciousness 946.11
s. is too precious to be shared 946.7
s. of millions blurred by numbers 946.48
s., replaced by maintenance 946.20
the s. he found so hard to imagine 946.4
the worst thing about s. 946.46
they learn in s. what they teach in song 708.90
we are healed of a s. by experiencing it to the full 946.39
we cause s. before we become better 946.28
wisdom comes alone through s. 1060.1
suffers: man never reasons so much as when he s. 946.36
who s. before necessary, s. more than is necessary 946.43
suffice: would alone s. to show the whole extent of its beauty and power 80.4
sufficiency: elegant s., retirement, rural quiet 701.5
sufficiency's: s. enough for men of sense 947.2
sufficient: s. man is s., even to ignorance itself 880.14
suggested: I like things s., not told in full 943.1
suicide: guns, the best method for private s. 948.17
if despair serves no purpose s. justified 948.7
is s. the way out or the way in 948.9
no sane society chooses to commit national s. 948.13
s. does not brave death for noble object 948.1
s. is a criminal offense 948.5
s. is God's best gift to man 948.20
s. the only philosophical problem 948.4
suicide's: if life's a joke, s. a bad punch line 948.10
suicides: ennui has made as many s. as despair 290.1
summer: after many a s. dies the swan 606.19
after stormy spring-time, s. does come 854.14
caught s. is always an imagined time 854.48
enjoy this s. flower by flower 854.19
flowers in the s., fires in the fall 854.38
hot s. has exhausted her intent 854.49
no price is set on the lavish s. 854.31
one swallow does not make a s. 715.1
s. days for me when every leaf is on its tree 854.35
s. ends, and autumn comes 854.8
s. in the light, winter in the shade 854.17
s. set lip to earth's bosom bare 854.45
to ensure s. in England, have it framed 289.33
we fear death as we fear a short s. 221.40
summer's: s. lease hath all too short a date 854.37
sun: adventure of s.: drama by which we live 950.1
goodness comes from people who bask in s. 950.5
he with head of wax must not walk in s. 941.5
is it so small a thing to enjoy the s. 504.2
no need to purchase s., water, moon 623.60
s. is pure, though shines in dirty places 770.1
s. visits cesspools undefiled 57.8
unnecessary to light a candle to the s. 56.4
we have no curiosity about the s. 480.7
with many cocks crowing, s. never rises 56.6
Sunday: how S. into Monday melts 1065.55
sunlight: there is a muscular energy in s. 950.2
sunshine: s. has influence on constitutions 1050.1
superannuated: no one is unhappier than s. idol 226.1
superficiality: wisdom lies in the s. of men 951.3

superfluous: it's for the s. that we sweat 557.6
I wish for the s., the useless 324.2
superior: court the society of a s. 57.16
if s. man abandons virtue, how can he be s. 1033.11
not as tribute to s. virtue but as divine challenge 952.8
persons remain s. to what they have done 201.1
s. man anxious about truth, not poverty 998.23
s. man is easy to serve, hard to please 531.3
we parted each feeling s. to the other 952.7
what the s. man seeks is in himself 952.2
superiority: s. and inferiority are individual 952.10
s. of mind and soul is very moral 952.9
with all our boasted "free and equal" s. over the communities of the Old World 780.8
superiors: American thinks he has no social s. 297.23
what man dislikes in his s. 531.19
supermarket: a huge s. of mass man 657.7
s.: America's temple 34.72
supernatural: belief in s. evil not necessary 1055.3
faith in the s. is a desperate wager 953.2
s. is the natural not yet understood 953.1
superstition: fear is the main source of s. 343.28
in all s. wise men follow fools 954.1
most of us find ourselves in Stone Age of s. 954.2
science is antidote to poison of s. 849.36
s. though recognized doesn't lose power 954.4
superstitions: minds yield to s. of their age 184.9
superstitious: men become s. 954.5
touch of science gives edge to s. tale 938.5
support: we have greater love for those we s. than those who s. us 384.13
supreme: man's heart doesn't tolerate absence of the s. 311.9
sure: dull man always s., s. man always dull 115.10
s. things: death, taxes, and the bore 95.6
surfeit: there is s. even in honey 811.5
surgeon: best s. hath been hacked himself 263.3
no better s. than one with many scars 263.15
surgeon's: more sensitive to s. cut than sword wounds 946.32
surpasses: who s., subdues mankind must look down on the hate of those below 952.1
surprise: grief is heightened by s. 955.4
something of a s. without her clothes on 443.18
s. is the greatest gift life can grant 955.3
that I exist: perpetual s. which is life 316.10
surprised: man s. is half beaten 955.1
survival: a world where s. is seen as a struggle 860.2
groups are essential for our s. 956.2
s. will be twin brother of annihilation 229.1
survive: how to s. the educational experience 279.7
suspect: I s. his taste in higher matters 274.21
who doth no evil is apt to s. none 770.4
suspense: s. is hostiler than death 482.2
suspicion: few people can entertain s. without letting hypothesis turn into fact 259.2
love goes out the gate which s. enters 259.4
s. always haunts the guilty mind 405.16
suspicions: many low, mean s. are well founded 259.6
only wanted to have my tartar removed, though I had my s.: 234.2
suspicious: when you grow s. of a person, you will find suspicions true 259.7
swallow: one s. does not make a summer 715.1
swallowing: slow s. down to the lapping belly 268.52
swan: after many a summer dies the s. 606.19
swap: not best to s. horses crossing river 179.3
swear: if angry, count four; if very angry, s. 39.28
swearing: little judicyous s. keeps th' temper 957.1
sweat: in s. of thy face shalt thou eat bread 1065.12
sweep: you can't s. others off their feet, if you can't be swept off your own 293.4
sweepstake: fact is that life has become a s. 912.4
sweet: daintiest last, to make the end s. 704.36
every s. hath its sour 154.1
how s. and attentive they are at first 1062.113
men, like fruit, grow s. before decay 586.10
nothing s. which does not end in bitterness 990.11
the s. life has always attracted travelers 1029.1
sweetest: apples taste s. when they're going 226.10
the s. words, "I told you so" 909.2
sweetness: fly that prefers s. to a long life 706.7
sweets: s. grown common lose their dear delight 333.10
to refuse the s. of life because they must leave us is preposterous 865.3
swift: to be s. is less than to be wise 139.5
too s. arrives as tardy as too slow 411.13
swim: people wish to learn to s. but keep one foot on ground 856.14
swimming: man who is s. against the stream knows the strength of it 658.9
swindle: man wrong who to thinks to s. God 224.15
swine: neither cast ye pearls before s. 48.1
sword: artists and writers, first to take up the s. 537.47
let s. decide after stratagem has failed 357.1
overfaithful s. returns the user his heart's desire at price of blood 518.8
pen is mightier than s. 1069.17
s. is but a tool in killer's hand 518.11
who bears s. of heaven should be holy 514.9
who draws his s. against the prince 786.5
syllable: to draw nourishment out of every s. 93.59
symbol: person gets from s. what he puts into it 959.1
symbolic: good writing is s.; s. writing is seldom good 1069.98
symbolism: the human mind, spinning s. and abstraction 53.76
symmetry: s. is ennui, the essence of grief 661.8
sympathetic: s. man is like swimmer among drowning 960.2
sympathize: people who s. are really looking for the particulars 960.6
sympathized: nothing sweeter than to be s. with 960.11
sympathy: difficult to have s. with thought 975.53
s. demands the giving of one's soul 960.8
s. is a supporting atmosphere 960.3
s. is cold to relation of distant misery 960.5
s. is sound relation with external being 842.1
who have never been ill incapable of s. 896.9
wisdom must go with s. 960.7
synagogue: s. lifts its walls by side of cathedral 797.35
synonym: s. for marriage, taking a daughter-in-law 564.71
system: old s. has two advantages over new 479.3
test of every s. is the man it forms 487.2
systematically: it is best to do things s. 661.7
systems: man has predilection for s. 785.8

T

table: spread the t. and contention will cease 274.7
table manners: t., breaking the right rule at the right time 563.17
table-talk: for t., I prefer the witty to the grave 188.26
taboos: social t. are shy like virtue 604.29
taciturn: none love to speak so much as the t. 923.7
tact: some people mistake weakness for t. 961.3
t. in audacity is knowing how far to go 92.1
t., not silence, is golden 961.2
takeover: a dry run for some future t. of the state 672.2
tale: honest t. speeds best plainly told 938.6
in mirthful t. we're content with less truth 436.17
science gives an edge to superstitious t. 938.5
temptation to vivify the t. hard to deny 309.2
what so tedious as twice-told t. 800.3
talebearer: where there is no t., the strife ceaseth 252.3
talent: be equal to your t., not your age 962.16
best-seller: gilded tomb of

mediocre t. 93.82
clean-cut types don't have any t. 962.12
coffee good for t.; genius needs prayer 377.2
for every t. poverty has stimulated, it has blighted a hundred 718.18
for those of great t. modesty is hypocrisy 600.13
it is a happy t. to know how to play 703.3
t. involves a certain shamelessness 962.4
t. is a common family trait 377.4
t. is a question of quantity 962.13
t. is faucet; while open, one must write 962.1
t. is that which is in a man's power 377.7
t. is the call of vocation 1037.5
t. is to be envied, genius pitied 377.6
t. recognizes genius 962.5
t. says things he has heard only once 377.3
to do the difficult easily is mark of t. 377.1
very rare for man of t. to succeed by t. 962.14
what a man is betrays itself when his t. decreases 962.11
world receives t. with open arms 377.5

talents: greatest evil: small t., great ambition 33.26
great offices will have great t. 401.8
man must stand in terror of his t. 342.6

talk: anecdote will pitch t. off track 188.38
effect of t.: strengthens own opinions 656.31
eliminates an enormous amount of useless t. 149.14
fair ambition: to excel in t. 923.59
health in table t. and nursery play 612.1
hundreds can t. for one who can think 1035.4
if to t. to oneself is folly, it is unwise to listen to oneself in company 188.16
improvisation is the essence of good t. 928.2
let's t. about you; what do you think of me? 873.11
man not clever for his ability to t. 923.63
many would be more truthful if not for uncontrollable desire to t. 923.29
more we t., easier it is to mean little 208.4
must we always t. for victory 923.17
t. ought always to run obliquely 188.7
t. to every woman as if you loved her 961.4
two ears, one mouth: listen more, t. less 543.5
we do not t.—we bludgeon one another 188.25
we t. little when vanity doesn't make us 923.40
who t. of benefits do them to t. of them 433.17
women enjoy sick t. of one another 1062.52

talked: worse than to be t. about is not to be 394.13

talkers: t. are no good doers 923.54

talking: in t., thinking is half murdered 923.21
people maintain opinion for sake of t. 923.24
t. about self is means to conceal self 165.13
t. is like playing on the harp 923.27
t. is the passion of a woman 1062.86
who does not worship himself t. 923.20
whom t. possesseth, cannot hold his peace 923.32

talks: he who t. more is sooner exhausted 923.38
nobody t. that doesn't say unwise things 923.28

tall: beauty requires that one should be t. 72.4
no man so t. that he need never stretch 400.4

tallest: many strokes overthrow the t. oaks 686.5

task: Every man's t. is his lifepreserver 1065.23
no t., rightly done, is truly private 1065.73
to think is hardest t. in world 975.13

taste: all life is dispute over t. and tasting 963.14
beautiful things, when t. is formed 963.17
between friends, differences in t. 963.2
common sense and good t.—without originality or moral courage 148.7
diffusion of t. not same as improvement 963.6
every one carries his own inch-rule of t. 963.1
exuberance is better than t. 513.4
good t., humor: contradiction in terms 436.19
good t. is virtue of museum keepers 963.16
"It is in bad t.," most formidable word Englishman can pronounce 289.9
least cultivated t. has largest appetite 578.1
let us value that which we can t., feel 882.3
loud dress offends people of t. 963.19
our bad t. is the bad t. of our age 184.8
people want to be known for t., not virtues 963.3
person's t. is his own peculiar concern 963.13
purity of t. is almost as rare as talent 516.20
shaping of t., science of merchandising 963.11
t. has no system and no proofs 963.18
t. is enemy of creativeness 963.15
t. is the fundamental quality 963.5
t. makes an atmosphere 963.8
what is song, when world lacks t. 48.4
whose mouth out of t. says wine is flat 920.3

tastes: t. in young people are changed by impetuosity; in the aged, preserved by habit 963.10
t. may not be the same 388.3

taught: first he wrought, and afterwards he t. 965.8
man knows, learns nothing without being t. 988.6
many things draw us from what we are t. 974.4
men must be t. as if you t. them not 965.29
nothing worth knowing can be t. 522.67

tax: difference between t. collector and taxidermist: taxidermist leaves the hide 964.3
every advantage has its t. 15.3
to t. and to please is not given to men 964.2

taxation: no system of t. operates with equality 964.7
t.: plucking the goose for largest amount of feathers, with least hissing 963.4
the ceiling on t. of capital gains 964.11

taxes: forgive us for cheering legislators who promise low t. 879.3
no t. imposed without consent by people 964.5
one thing certain in war: increased t. 1042.70
t.: dues paid for membership in society 964.9
thing generally raised on city land: t. 131.41

taxpayer: optimism is above all virtue of t. 659.1

tea: you must not refuse additional caups of t. 213.15

teach: dons are too busy educating to t. 965.7
easier for tutor to command than t. 965.25
it is safer to learn than t. 656.21
joy in learning: it enables me to t. 965.31
let such t. others who themselves excel 207.42
man who knows a subject well can t. it 965.26
never try to t. a pig to sing 965.3
none who cannot t. somebody something 311.4
others' follies t. us not 321.52
our societies t. values already blasted 1026.13
t. us to care and not to care 806.3
they t. in academies much that is useless 279.34
to t. is to learn twice over 965.20

teacher: every real t. is myself in disguise 965.5
experience is the only t. 321.12
he honors my style who learns under it to destroy t. 942.23
if a man cherishes old knowledge and acquires new, he may be a t. 965.9
let nature be your t. 623.82
nearly 18,000 assigned to classes with no t. 965.22
one good t. may change a delinquent into a solid citizen 965.33
t. affects eternity 965.1
t. arousing feeling for one good action better than he filling memory with objects 965.15
to t. of languages world but place of words 524.9

teacher's: t. conviction that men are convertible 965.11

teachers: make your friends your t. 532.7
men are my t. 532.16

t. deserve more honor than parents 965.4
t. soured by anxiety and penny-pinching 718.26
we are all pupils and we are all t. 532.11
teaches: he who can, does; he who cannot, t. 965.32
who t. us anything we knew not is to be reverenced as a master 965.19
teaching: art of t. is art of awakening curiosity 965.13
bad t. spoils many lives 965.16
everybody incapable of learning has taken to t. 279.88
if you do not like boys and girls, give up t. 965.17
t. is not a lost art 965.6
t. is not like injecting vitamins 965.18
tear: t. dries quickly if for others' troubles 698.6
tears: endow the living with the t. you squander on the dead 698.8
it is sweet to mingle t. with t. 918.44
sad find somehow sweetness in t. 1052.3
shed t. on one's own pillow 862.1
t. gratify savage nature, do not melt it 838.3
t. not inconsistent with inward peace 1052.7
t. of strangers are only water 358.7
t. show a tender heart 519.12
they that sow in t. shall reap in joy 281.1
thoughts that lie too deep for t. 352.5
waste not fresh t. over old griefs 1052.4
we need never be ashamed of our t. 1052.2
teas: t., where small talk dies in agonies 914.8
technical: where t. skill, no need for faith 966.11
technicalities: wrong must not win by t. 528.1
technique: great art must be guided by an invisible t. 928.1
technological: education in a t. world is neuter 279.56
for t. man, time is uncontrollable mystery 978.39
t. advance without social advance almost automatically increases human misery 966.8
technology: man was everywhere crushed by t. 966.1
only science can keep t. in moral order 966.5
t., a buffer betwen us and nature 966.21
t., a popular article of Western faith 966.7
t. carries people from where they belong 966.2
t. has permitted us to put a city to the sword, not realizing what we are doing 1049.6
t. made large populations possible 966.16
t. presumes one right way to do things 966.25
to what purpose? a question t. does not ask 966.24
twentieth-century t. numbed our brains 966.26
tedious: each reserves to himself right to be t. 95.3
people are either charming or t. 121.7
what so t. as twice-told tale 800.3
tediousness: man who suspects his own t. not yet born 95.1
teenager: a t. needs understanding and misunderstanding 1008.12
fighting a t. is inviting doom 1071.24
the t., afterthought of social history 1071.29
teenagers: t. crave independence 880.9
t. tormented by terrors they deem personal 482.5
well-to-do women and unemployed t. 860.7
teeth: it is disgusting to pick your t. 1039.3
sans t., sans eyes, sans taste 653.86
t. are smiling, but is the heart 392.3
telephone: impossible to read in America because of t. 93.80
television: all we have to do is switch on t. 967.21
disparagement of t. second only to watching t. 967.32
t., a mirror of taste 967.13
t. bridges chasm between dinner and bedtime 967.2
t. doomed us to the Family 967.3
t. has thrived on canned laughter 967.1
t., single in its purpose—selling 967.9
t., taken politics away from adult mind 967.24
T. was not intended to make human beings vacuous 967.19
t. watching is acculturative 967.7
we shall stand or fall by t. 967.31
tell: t. not all you know 755.14
temper: hot t. leaps o'er a cold decree 39.25
loss of t. is never a source of strength 862.8
our t. depends on the daily, little things 969.3
tart t. never mellows with age 968.2
when I lose my t.—brother, I go 968.3
words are healers of the sick t. 758.1
temperament: t., like liberty, is important 969.2
temperance: intemperate t. injures the cause of t. 970.3
t. without devotion is a cold virtue 1033.3
temperate: we become t. by performing t. actions 227.1
tempers: many lose their t. seeing you keep yours 39.10
t. of old make them difficult 653.27
temple: chiefest sanctity of a t. is that men go there to weep in common 126.13
God builds his t. in the heart 126.6
no t. can still griefs and strifes 128.3
temptation: avoid t. unless I can't resist it 971.9
cowardice: surest protection against t. 971.8
degree of t. will overcome any virtue 971.4
never resist an adequate t. 971.6
no t. measurable by value of its object 971.2
way to get rid of a t. is to yield to it 971.11
tempted: all men are t. by the right temptation 971.1
blessed is he who has never been t. 971.7
tenable: any danger spot t. if brave men make it so 216.12
tender: t. heart our noblest quality 519.12
we are more t. towards children and old people than to those in prime of life 729.4
tenderness: a flush of t. that makes men horny 238.13
tenement: reminded by her lean face of a t. doorway 45.4
tenterhooks: t. are upholstery of anxious seat 43.14
tenure: long t. of office begets tyranny 761.1
terrifying: something t. about big families 334.38
territory: t. does not make a nation 621.10
t. only durable part of nation 621.15
terror: easiest victor over reason: t., force 357.5
reason can wrestle and overthrow t. 785.10
terrors: we fly to beauty from t. of the finite 72.19
terse: when I try to be t., I end being obscure 98.5
test: t. of any man lies in action 9.32
text: we pick a t. to make it serve our turn 80.7
texts: man made to eat ices, not pore over t. 848.13
thank: I have often wished there was a God to t. 387.32
thanks: evermore t., the exchequer of the poor 399.9
refined nature vexed when owed t. 647.6
Thanksgiving: we keep T. to give thanks we are preserved fr'm th' Puritans 420.2
theater: calls and t. propagate platitudes 188.36
great t. strengthens our faculty to face what is 972.39
men go to t. to forget; women to remember 972.25
not going to t.: dressing without mirror 972.28
public voice in the t. today is raucous 972.29
t. is life hideously exaggerated 972.23
t. struggles even when it flourishes 972.31
the t. and its cutthroat machinations 972.26
we go to t. to confirm experience of reality 972.18
you need three things in t.—play, actors, audience, each must give something 972.11
theatergoers: in London t. laugh; in Paris, they wait 972.5
theatre: t. should always be

somewhat suspect 972.15
theatrical: we will be damned, but it shall be t. 951.2
theism: t. taught by natural history spoils both 850.4
theist: fight between t., atheist is whether God shall be called God or some other name 387.15
theists: men no longer t. must become humanists 432.4
theologian: t. with no joy in his work is not a t. 973.1
theology: nature can speak on everything, even t. 623.58
no man should dogmatize except on t. 264.8
the cure for false t. is mother-wit 973.4
t. in religion like poisons in food 973.8
t. is attempt to explain subject by men who do not understand it 973.7
theorem: great poem, deep t., are reader's own experiences 532.3
theories: men seeking to verify erroneous t. 479.7
t., abstract ideas, things in themselves 974.8
t. are private property; truth is common 974.1
theorize: it is mistake to t. without data 974.2
theorizing: work without t. makes life endurable 974.13
theory: action will remove doubt t. cannot solve 9.27
all t. is grey, but green is life's tree 974.7
better to emit t. than be insensible 974.12
no t. is good unless used to go beyond 974.5
t. and practice of life not reconciled 974.3
t. helps us to bear ignorance of facts 974.11
t. makes men incautious 974.10
we do what we can, then make a t. 782.2
without love t. bruises the very ones it claims to save 974.6
thesis: sometimes a scream is better than a t. 753.1
thief: he is a t. who charges too much for goods he sells 738.4
he who holds ladder is as bad as t. 204.9
rich t. passes for a gentleman 934.3
t. believes everybody steals 934.5
t. doth fear each bush an officer 405.16
thieves: beauty provoketh t. sooner than gold 72.49
great t. lead away the little thief 204.4
thin: to get t., re-establish purpose in life 645.4
things: after inside upheavals, fix on imperturbable t. 646.3
be strict even in little t. 96.3
the t. of no moment remain with us 305.8
t. and men have always a certain sense 1007.4
t. are as they are regardless of what they were 444.5
t. are never the same the second time 580.27
t. have their laws as well as men 646.4
three t. can happen; two of them are bad 646.6
we live in a world of t. 569.2
we must think t., not words 1064.22
think: act quickly, t. slowly 9.22
aim of our institutions is that we may t. what we like and say what we t. 364.4
be yourself and t. for yourself 880.10
can do all because they t. they can 860.8
feeling when we ought to t. 88.1
if a man sits down to t., he is asked if he has a headache 975.9
I t., therefore I am 975.7
man is obviously made to t. 975.36
nothing miserable unless you t. so 1011.2
people who cease to complain, cease to t. 157.4
speak speech of world, t. thoughts of few 171.8
telling a man exactly what you t. of him 362.4
those that t. must govern those that toil 975.15
thousands can t. for one who can see 1035.4
to meditate is to labor; to t., to act 975.22
to t. is hardest task in world 975.13
to t. is to act 975.12
to t. is to say no. 634.1
under all we t. lives all we believe 78.12
we do not educate people to t. 975.24
what concerns me is what I must do, not what people t. 227.9
what we t., feel, is determined by glands 589.6
while we stop to t., we miss opportunity 657.11
who t. do not set selves to disturb world 975.46
thinker: importance of t. depends upon fate of his ideas in minds of his successors 975.52
t. dies, his thoughts are beyond reach 443.14
thinkers: most t. write badly 975.30
thinkest: if thou t. twice before speaking once 755.18
thinketh: as he t. in his heart, so is he 119.5
thinking: before acquiring the habit of t. 975.5
extensive knowledge needful to t. people 522.30
I know what I'm t. bout, I think 975.48
in talking, t. is half murdered 923.21
man is but a reed; but he is a t. reed 975.35
most difficult thing is to say thinkingly what others say without t. 923.2
nothing good or bad but t. makes it so 389.13
plain living and high t. are no more 701.6
sect, party, saves man from vexation of t. 674.1
t.: effort of soul to keep independence 975.28
t.: endeavor to capture reality with ideas 975.33
t. goes on in seclusion within 975.57
t. is hard work 975.16
t. is the most unhealthy thing in the world 975.55
t. life less a perfectioning of animal and physical life 590.15
t. ought to be a calmness 975.29
your way of t. must be your own 975.23
thinks: he t. too much; such men are dangerous 57.17
thirst: after days at sea, t. is a feeling unto itself 343.17
thirty: after t. a man wakes up sad every morning 586.7
no matron happy till past t. and not fat 645.2
thirty-five: no one over t. is worth meeting who has not more to teach us than does a book 321.10
thistle-down: we are like t. blown by the wind 452.1
thorn: I find the laurel also bears a t. 426.8
who wants a rose must respect the t. 755.20
thorns: I fall upon the t. of life! 946.45
no gathering roses without pricks of t. 705.3
who plants t. must not expect roses 815.7
thought: all t. is a feat of association 975.14
but for t. no motion would be an action 975.39
by t. I comprehend the world 975.34
every real t. knocks wind out of someone 975.20
every revolution was first one man's t. 819.8
give me stormy t., not calm of faith 16.4
God is a t. that makes crooked all that is straight 387.52
hours lost in searching after one clear t. 975.27
if no t. your mind does visit 923.25
if t. too weak to express simply, reject it 975.44
in a crowd t. can provide seclusion 736.4
intellect should pursue t. to end 975.51
it matters not what you are t. to be 444.20
it's hard to keep private property in t. 975.19
man is God by his faculty for t. 261.7
man not idle because absorbed in t. 1065.43
men use t. as authority for injustice 440.21
nimble t. can jump both sea and land 975.40
nothing remains beautiful except t. 975.41
one t. fills immensity 975.3
only by t. can labour be made happy 1065.62
our action only fitfully guided by t. 9.35
party-spirit a hindrance to t. 674.9
profundity of t. belongs to youth, clarity of t. to old age 975.31
quality of the t. makes nations differ 621.4
rational t. is to interpret by inescapable scheme 785.21
things t. too long can be no

longer t. 975.58
t. altereth the nature of the thing 58.4
t. depends absolutely on the stomach 975.47
t. functions as fragmentary part of idea 573.3
t. is not a gift, but an acquisition 975.32
t. is process by which ends are answered 975.49
t. is the labor of the intellect 818.2
t. itself needs words 1064.5
t. makes every thing fit for use 975.11
t. merged with feeling, artist's joy 53.83
t. spans years, curdles a life into an hour 975.4
t. without action is nothing much 9.2
t. without learning is perilous 522.10
uncompromising t. is luxury of recluse 975.56
what was once t. can never be unthought 975.8
while t. exists, words are alive 93.19
words are the small change of t. 1064.44
thoughtless: young people t. as a rule 1071.31
thoughts: all t. are always ready 298.14
all t. are ministers of love 551.24
beware t. that come in the night 443.22
certain t. are prayers 723.19
chance gives rise to and removes t. 116.11
do not reveal your t. to everyone 165.1
everyone thinks bells echo his own t. 873.8
find same t. in another brain 1007.5
great t. come from the heart 975.43
if sick, your own t. make you sick 627.7
little-minded people's t. move in small circles 493.15
man's life accorded him in t. of others 804.6
man's secret t. run over all things 975.17
man's t. are his banners 443.31
my t. are my company 975.25
not alone if accompanied by noble t. 915.17
nothing's of such vexation as own t. 975.50
our less conscious t., actions, mold lives 1006.1
our life is what our t. make it 975.1
our t. are unclear until put into words 1064.6
second t. are ever wiser 24.1
style is the dress of t. 942.3
t. of men widened by process of suns 741.27
t. that lie too deep for tears 352.5
to think great t. you must be heroes as well as idealists 975.21
unsought t.: commonly the most valuable 975.26
we ought to control our t. 975.6
you may derive t. from others 975.23
threadbare: seldom discern eloquence under t. cloak 718.40
threatens: he t. many that hath injured one 476.12
thrift: men don't realize how great an income t. is 977.6
thrifty: some t. as if they would live forever 977.1
throne: doubtful t. is ice on summer seas 831.25
frog would leap from t. of gold to puddle 48.6
on highest t. we still sit on our own ass 732.11
t. is only a bench covered with velvet 780.16
thrush: wise t. sings each song twice over 82.3
thunderbolt: t. comes in a moment, ends in a minute 976.2
thyself: be a friend to t., others will be too 869.3
explore t. 875.30
ticker: nothing like t. tape except a woman 503.4
ticket: Japanese attack could be my t. out of high school 279.14
tide: there is a t. in the affairs of men 657.12
tides: struggling t. of life are eddies of mighty stream rolling to its appointed end 340.1
t.: systole and diastole of earth's veins 853.1
tidings: let ill t. tell themselves 629.7
tiger: no man can tame a t. into a kitten 46.4
there is a raging t. inside every man 862.7
tiger's: must enter t. den to take cubs 92.6
tigers: all reactionaries are paper t. 178.17
tightrope: being in a foreign country means walking a t. 423.5
time: art is long and t. is fleeting 606.12
as we grow old, value of t. becomes vivid 653.44
baseball has marked t. 929.12
be a football to t. and chance 504.7
butterfly counts moments and has t. enough 978.68
dost thou love life, do not squander t. 978.21
earth revolves, but one lives undisturbed; so it is with t. in one's life 978.53
endless volumes prove intellectual climb, but come of having lots of t. 93.56
every new t. will give its law 528.33
everyone has t. if he likes 10.14
existence doth depend on t. 9.8
expect, fear, everything from t. and men 978.72
for technological man, t. is the mystery 978.39
God is t., or at least that His spirit is 387.10.
great t. makes all things dim 978.64
habituation is a falling asleep of sense of t. 406.11
had we but world enough, and t. 857.9
he gains t. who does not watch his neighbor 880.1
hell is t., where Satan winds a watch 416.7
in life of one man never same t. returns 117.9
I wasted t., and now doth t. waste me 653.85
keep saying "I don't know where t. goes" 978.55
killing t. is chief end of our society 978.7
late visitors should find t. in my face 428.11
love makes t. pass; t. makes love pass 551.67
men more like own t. than like fathers 184.5
men should seize t. by the forelock 978.52
methods to measure t. contrived by monks 978.30
modern man doesn't know what to do with t. 978.22
most intractable of experiences is t. 978.33
music quickens us to enjoyment of t. 614.39
nine-tenths of wisdom: being wise in t. 1060.50
none so scrupulous in measuring t. as he whose t. is worth nothing 446.9
no preacher listened to but t. 978.66
nothing puzzles more, troubles less, than t. 1017.10
nothing really belongs to us but t. 533.6
once upon a t. there was no t. 978.6
on the whirligig of t. we circle 978.70
one direction in world, t. its measure 606.18
our costliest expenditure is t. 978.71
peace: when t. doesn't matter passing by 681.30
procrastination is the thief of t. 231.12
remember that things take t. 6.10
ruins of t. build mansions in eternity 978.8
the easy-going have the best t. 977.12
the t. of life is short 539.110
t., abstraction which exists for human brain 978.38
t. and circumstance enlarge views of men, narrow views of women 581.22
t. and hour runs through roughest day 978.61
t., an imponderably valuable gift 978.5
t. at length becomes justice 978.46
t. bears away all, even the mind 978.73
t. brings all things to pass 978.1
t. can be such a menace to a man 978.56
t. cools, t. clarifies 284.23
t. cures one of everything—even living 978.23
t. deals gently only with gentle takers of t. 978.20
t. dissipates the angularity of facts 328.7
t. doesn't alter image we have of people 978.54
t. enough to do all, if one thing at a t. 585.3
t. flies, and what is past is done 507.6
t. flies apace; we would believe all flies forward with it 978.45
t. flies over us; leaves shadow behind 978.29
t.: fragment of the infinite for finite use 978.4

t. goes by: reputation increases, ability declines 653.40
t. has no divisions to mark its passage 631.3
t. heals griefs and quarrels 978.48
t. heals nothing 978.13
t. heals what reason cannot 978.60
t. increases understanding for the aging 1007.16
t. in every century has a different face 298.8
t. in its aging course teaches all things 978.3
t. is a file that wears, makes no noise 978.17
t. is a great legalizer, even of morals 978.42
t. is a kindly God 978.65
t. is a merciless thing 978.76
t. is anonymous 978.75
t. is a robber 978.44
t. is a wealth of change 978.69
t. is at fault; men become good, but so slow 393.10
t. is but shadow of world upon eternity 978.34
t. is love above all else 978.26
t. is on the side of the oppressed today 1002.22
t. is sole philosopher; all others, sophists 978.11
t. is test of trouble, but not remedy 978.14
t. is that in which all things pass away 978.59
t. is the enemy of us all 978.49
t. is the greatest innovator 479.1
t. is the measure of business 104.3
t. is the only true purgatory 978.10
t. is the rider that breaks youth 978.31
t. like manager staging new production 978.58
t.: longest distance between two places 978.77
t. lost is t. unenriched by experience 978.9
t. makes man find himself in his heart 875.2
t. makes more converts than reason 978.47
t. moves slowly, passes quickly 978.74
t. not concerned but hurries on 990.7
t. often justifies what seems unjustifiable 227.7
t. overtake all things alike 978.2
t. ripens all things; no man's born wise 978.12
t., snakeskin with scales overlapping 978.15
t., space: scarcities of tomorrow 1001.13
t. stoops to no man's lure 990.16
t. strengthens friendship, weakens l. 551.103
t. strips our illusions of their hue 449.5
t. strips us of the privileges of the bystander 650.2
t. that's just t. will let sounds be sounds 919.1
t. threatens with sand-bag, not scythe 653.47
t. to every purpose under the heaven 979.2
t. turns the old days to derision 978.67
t. was rushing around me like water 978.18
t. works change for better or worse 117.30
to realize the unimportance of t. is the gate of wisdom 978.57
travel, trouble, kiss pass my t. 10.11
truth is child of t. 998.43
truth lags last, limping on arm of t. 998.52
use t. as though you were about to die 771.6
wasted t., indispensable as sleep 446.1
we can leave footprints on sands of t. 401.36
we take no note of t. but from it loss 978.79
whirligig of t. brings in his revenges 978.62
who waste t. complain of its brevity 978.36
why trouble about t. when we cease to be 221.63
time's: t. glory is to bring truth to light 978.63
timekeeping: t. is greatly overrated 978.43
timeliness: t. is best in all matters 979.6
times: bad t. stay with you forever 277.3
good men are stars, illustrate their t. 393.25
good old t.: all t. when old are good 298.5
these are the t. that try men's souls 298.15
the t.: a few profound and active men 298.7
they that reverence too much old t. are but a scorn to the new 986.1
though a god, I've learned to obey the t. 297.19
timid: do not be too t. about your actions 980.3
happiness hates the t.; so does science 980.7
t. yearn for full value, demand a tenth 1026.24
tired: life is one long process of getting t. 341.1
titled: craving of the t. for riches 52.4
I have a t. and you may just be impressed by t. 619.7
titles: most enviable of all t.: an honest man 425.18
t. but nicknames; every nickname a title 619.6
t. distinguish the mediocre 780.20
tobacco: first illusion of t.: believing we do something when we do nothing 982.5
for thy sake, t., I'd do anything but die 982.9
other world must exist where I can quit t. 982.10
t. is better eschewed than chewed 982.12
today: boldly say each night, I have lived t. 729.7
call the life you live t. your own 116.7
in t. already walks tomorrow 305.1
mortgaged to yesterday, we cannot use t. 676.12
they who lose t. may win tomorrow 116.4
t. is always partly tomorrow 729.15
t. is muffled in impenetrable folds 729.11
t. is yesterday's pupil 729.14
t. will die tomorrow 990.16
to-morrow do thy worst, I have lived t. 729.9
together: coming t. again: foretaste of resurrection 673.6
we must all hang t. 1016.3
togetherness: t. is a counterfeit communion 983.3
toil: if no gods, all t. meaningless 1004.8
luck is not chance—it's t. 360.7
most men in a brazen prison live, with heads bent o'er their t. 1065.2
those that think must govern those who t. 975.15
t. is the sire of fame 1065.27
we only t. who are first of things 1065.66
toiler: dreamer lives forever; t. dies in a day 336.14
toiling: great men t. upward in the night 6.13
it is weariness to keep t. at same things 1065.40
told: sad is the phrase: I t. you so 909.1
tolerance: after you've heard all friends have to say, then comes t. of love 365.81
highest result of education is t. 984.11
more and more care about religious t. 797.11
t. best achieved by those without convictions 984.1
t. is makeshift for an overcrowded planet 984.7
t. is nine parts apathy to one of love 984.3
world peace requires mutual t. 498.7
tolerant: evil in us is least t. of evil in others 307.25
we are t. of those who do not agree with us 984.8
we are t. when we tolerate ourselves 858.17
tolerate: if we had to t. in others what we permit in ourselves, life would be unbearable 470.1
I respect only those who resist me, but I cannot t. them 658.4
people t. those they fear 984.9
we t. each other thirty years 564.124
toleration: doctrine of necessity is that of t. 806.4
tomboy: March is a t. with tousled hair 854.5
tombstone: together in the vault under the t. 103.7
tomorrow: boast not thyself of t. 727.1
go take your damned t. 793.4
in today already walks t. 305.1
no progress without faith in t. 741.10
the day after t. is doubtful 368.24
they who lose today may win t. 116.4
t. do thy worst, for I have lived to-day 729.9
t. is ours to win or lose 368.18
t. lurks in us 368.7
t. will be wonderful—unless it is terrible 368.19
we steal if we touch t.: it is God's 368.4
tomorrows: all the t. are ours to shape 729.3

tongue: among men, the t. wins and not the deed 690.10
blow of the t. crushes bones 206.1
fluent t. only thing mother don't like her daughter to resemble her in 218.7
he who would be the t. of this wide land 708.66
let fool hold t., he will pass for sage 898.22
man is hid under his t. 923.30
men are born with two eyes, one t. 98.4
nature has given us two eyes, two ears, and one t. 923.60
practised man trusts eyes more than t. 149.4
rather trip with feet than with t. 88.10
sharp t. grows keener with use 968.2
should be silver in purse or on t. 283.3
stillest t. can be truest friend 898.6
t. is a key to the intellectual treasure 898.24
t. of wise man lieth behind his heart 1060.34
too free a t. makes for wrangle 394.2
tongues: men govern nothing with more difficulty than their t. 923.56
tool: bad workman never gets a good t. 463.3
put away a t., need it instantly 17.11
tooth: better a t. out than always aching 262.4
toothache: man with t. thinks all without t. happy 153.4
never philosopher that could endure t. 896.27
t. will cost a battle 996.7
top: defeats of fellows at the t. aren't defeats for fellows at the bottom 780.1
many paths to the mountain t. 332.9
topic: one t. to be avoided, the weather 1050.8
torch: a gustatory t. for the entire world 108.12
torment: more estimable the offender, greater the t. 174.33
one must choose between boredom and t. 94.4
torture: stranger cannot t. a human soul 499.4
Tory: timid man fears people, is T. by nature 178.14
totalitarian: in t. system martyrdom better than thought 985.3
totalitarianism: in our loathing of t. there is admiration for its efficiency 985.2
t. doesn't permit opponents martyr's death 985.1
t. spells simplification 985.4
touch: we never t. but at points 915.15
tough: look for a t. wedge for a t. log 585.9
toughness: There was a hard core in him, and plenty of t. 730.3
tour: on escorted t. you don't even have to know the Matterhorn isn't a tuba 992.22
tourist: a t. is an ugly human being 992.34
every t. is a native of somewhere 992.33
less a t. knows, the fewer mistakes he need make 992.1
the worst thing about being a t. 992.3
t. expects things to happen to him 992.9
tourists: we cannot learn to love other t. 992.39
towel: he wiped his face on the guest t.! 77.17
town: day in country is worth month in t. 194.12
earth's axis through center of every t. 699.4
no t. can fail of beauty with trees 995.1
t. life makes one tolerant, liberal 131.30
when in country you praise distant t. 251.5
toys: there are t. for all ages 703.4
when child has left, t. become affecting 123.13
trade: it is not your t. to make tables 206.12
people of same t. seldom meet but conversation ends in conspiracy 104.29
speculation is the romance of t. 503.5
t.-unions have done more for humanity 1013.2
tradition: a way of inventing t. each morning 34.69
each t. grows continually more venerable 986.17
everywhere the basis of principle is t. 734.8
less fettered by t., greater becomes inward activity of men's motives 986.18
love for t. has never weakened a nation 986.5
modern t. is t. of revolt 986.19
Self-help and self-control are the essence of the American t. 34.65
t. is a guide and not a jailer 986.16
t. is milk for babes but no meat for men 986.7
t. seems more of a shackle to it than an inspiration 34.8
t. without intelligence not worth having 986.9
without t., art is sheep without shepherd 53.26
traditional: good life impossible without t. forms 986.14
traditions: Christian t. have lost their hold 125.5
hardened round us is a wrappage of t. 986.4
traffic: it is the white slave t. 19.25
tragedies: not t. that kill us, it's the messes 88.8
there are two t., not getting what one wants, and getting it 845.8
tragedy: discussions of t., exercises in cultural diagnostics 987.13
essence of dramatic t. not unhappiness 987.16
every roof, when lifted, reveals t. 422.8
in t. great men are more truly great than in history 987.10
life is t.: we are spectators, actors 539.120
luck or t., some people get runs 340.21
men play at t. because don't believe in reality of t. actually staged in world 987.11
nature is but theater of t. of man 623.55
only a great mind overthrown yields t. 987.3
show me a hero and I will write a t. 418.9
to balance t., weigh it with tragic heart 987.4
t., a heroic vision of nihilism 987.14
t.: an experience of hyperinvolvement 145.13
t., boring to those not in its caress 987.1
t., comedy, are simply questions of value 987.7
t. in the American countryside 987.6
t.: man's struggle with stronger 987.5
t. of life is that man almost wins 329.4
t. of the age: men know so little of men 1008.6
world is a t. to those that feel 1067.29
writers of t. say they have insight 987.15
tragic: last act t. however happy the rest 221.102
t. situation exists when virtue does not triumph 987.12
t. writer must believe in man 987.8
we refuse to take our t. age tragically 987.90
tragical: why does man wish to be made sad by seeing t. things 987.2
train: there isn't a t. I wouldn't take 992.36
t. up a child in the way he should go 988.1
training: creative minds known to survive bad t. 201.13
man can seldom win fight against his t. 988.10
t. necessary for most experiences 210.13
t. which makes men happiest 279.73
traitor: t. stands in worse case of woe 79.4
traitors: better t. escape than have spirit of distrust 259.5
treason pleases but t. are odious 993.1
traits: shut doors on t., they open windows, return 790.17
tranquility: not finding t. within, don't go elsewhere 989.5
t. and occupation give happiness 409.52
t.! better name than all family of fame 989.3
transcendent: God's merits are so t. 387.14
transgression: every major work of art is a t. 53.33
transition: in age of t. habitual dumb practice is passing, new complex of habit oncoming 117.34
period of t. always one of uncertainty 117.5
transitory: golf course is the epitome of the t. 929.8
translation: inadequate t. of a great foreign novel 1069.4
transparent: none so t. as he who thinks he's deep 740.3
transport: methodically to t.

all of Illinois to the Gulf of Mexico 824.2
trap: don't want cheese, want to get out of t. 109.5
travel: beauties of t. due to strange hours kept 992.57
do not t. before learning language 992.18
experience, t. an education in themselves 321.15
I t. not to go anywhere, but to go 992.50
no one realizes how beautiful it is to t. 992.58
perhaps t. cannot prevent bigotry 992.2
to t. happily, one must t. light 992.43
to t. hopefully better than to arrive 281.16
t. agencies prevent encounter with natives 992.8
t. is a vanishing act 992.51
who pass their lives in foreign t. 992.45
why do the wrong people t.? 992.14
traveled: I t. among unknown men 992.57
traveler: each t. should know what he has to see 992.25
heaviest baggage for a t. is empty purse 992.21
t. must come from somewhere 992.44
t. went in search of people, adventure 992.9
t. without knowledge is bird without wings 992.41
travelers: home better place, but t. must be content 992.46
t., like poets, are mostly an angry race 992.10
traveling: age is a bad t. companion 653.25
in t., carry knowledge to bring it home 992.31
to live is to see; t. speeds up the process 992.27
t. is a fool's paradise 992.20
t. is to regulate imagination by reality 992.32
t. makes men wiser but less happy 992.30
when t., take large doses of patience and tolerance 992.26
travels: man who t. alone can start today 915.46
one either commits suicide or t. 30.1
one t. more usefully alone 992.29
treading: you are t. water, playing with fire 374.18
treason: if t. prosper, none dare call it t. 993.2
t. only waits for sufficient temptation 191.7
t. pleases but traitors are odious 993.1
treasure: thou shalt have t. in heaven 684.3
where your t. is, your heart will be 746.3
Treasury: money disappearing into the T. 602.12
treaties: only t. that ought to count are those which would settle ulterior motives 994.6
t. last while they last 994.1
t. observed if in harmony with interests 994.4
tree: as the twig is bent the t.'s inclined 988.7
emancipation from soil: no freedom for t. 363.48
saw can fell t. of a thousand years 995.6
single t. like a dancing tongue of flame 995.2
though t. grow high, falling leaves return to the root 401.38
t. casts shade even upon woodcutter 455.3
you can't be suspicious of a t. 623.8
trees: how many t. gave lives that today's scandal should reach a million readers 630.37
no town can fail of beauty with t. 995.1
t. do everything to git attention 995.7
t.: earth's effort to speak to heaven 995.5
trembling: what is this t. sensation 482.1
trial: truth fears no t. 998.45
trials: pleasurable to watch great t. of another 216.13
tribulation: no man without some manner of t. 17.37
trick: we are bitter against those who t. us 224.10
tricks: fox knows many t. 200.6
tries: no one knows what he can do till he t. 281.14
trifle: mere t. consoles us, distresses us 996.9
trifles: cities degrade us by magnifying t. 131.13
moments make the year, and t. life 996.13
sensibility of man to t. 883.7
she who t. with all is less likely to fall 351.3
t. make perfection, which is no trifle 684.9
t. make the sum of human things 996.6
t. make up happiness, misery of life 996.11
unbelief shown by condemnation of t. 1004.7
trip: rather t. with feet than with tongue 88.10
t. up Alaskan Highway will do 64.14
triumph: as easy to be enervated by t. as defeat 945.26
hour of t. is what brings the void 845.4
in ourselves are t. and defeat 858.22
to win without risk is to t. without glory 945.8
t. cannot help being cruel 173.10
trivial: comfortable people worry over t. things 996.5
to the mean eye all things are t. 693.2
t. things must be described grandly 942.14
what mighty contests rise from t. things 996.10
Trojans: distant T. never injured me 665.8
trophy: killing for the sake of a t. 438.1
trouble: bringing friends to t. is hard grief 17.56
friends show love in times of t. 365.39
in t. best to seek out relative 796.2
in time of t. avert not face from hope 427.14
man born unto t., as sparks fly upward 17.7
painful to know you caused own t. 17.55
pleasures, t., greatest in anticipation 318.6
time is test of t., but not remedy 978.14
t. amiably greeted soon goes away 17.60
t. has no connection with discouragement 253.2
troubles: each has as much as he can bear in his t. 142.5
light t. speak; weighty are struck dumb 17.51
man fond of counting t., not joys 251.3
night brings our t. to the light 633.9
one man's news is another man's t. 629.1
our t. arise often from fancy 43.13
t. half seen do torture all the more 304.3
t. hurt most when self-inflicted 866.7
t. of rich are t. money can't cure 17.42
troublesome: nothing t. that we do willingly 1057.4
trousers: I shall wear the bottoms of my t. rolled 653.21
truck: today I will change the oil in my t. 231.9
true: be t.: this is highest maxim of art, life 491.1
dare to be t.; nothing can need a lie 1000.7
every thing to be t. must become a religion 998.132
hair perhaps divides the false and t. 999.12
morally bad not to care if thing t. 998.118
no man worth having is t. to his wife 472.13
the brilliant passes; the t. endures 998.51
the people do not like the t. 682.8
thing isn't t. because a man dies for it 565.15
thing to trust is what we think is t. 998.8
to thine own self be t. 491.26
t., and the opposite is probably equally t. 34.27
where is man who has strength to be t. 662.2
trumpet: t. does not more stun than whisper teases 923.36
you must blow your own t. 89.2
trust: bound to forgive enemy, not t. him 288.9
everything has to be taken on t. 998.116
evidence of t. begets t. 788.3
joy looks for t. clear in friends' eyes 997.6
love all, t. a few 997.10
put no t. in money, but money in t. 69.2
t. character more than an oath 635.6
t. in God, but tie your camel 259.11
t. ivrybody—but cut th' cards 997.1
t. men and they will be true to you 997.3
t. not man without a conscience in everything 174.32
vice to t. all, or to t. none 997.9
what can we t. in this uncertain life 482.3
who doesn't t. himself can't t. anyone 997.8

trustees: we are t. for those who come after us 177.4
trustful: takes a long while for a naturally t. person to reconcile 387.47
trusts: essence of a free government consists in considering offices as public t. 760.3
truth: add venom to a half t. and you have an absolute t. 998.58
adversity is the first path to t. 17.16
all men should learn to hear t. 998.63
all necessary t. is its own evidence 998.36
all t. is not to be told at all times 1000.4
all t. wants is liberty of appearing 998.91
apt to shut eyes against painful t. 427.16
art not propaganda but a form of t. 53.72
at heart, we are always on side of t. 656.6
atom of t. represents some man's agony 998.82
beauty is t., t. beauty 72.27
be telling the t. for once 992.48
between whom there is t. there is love 998.121
bigotry holds t. with grip that kills it 264.15
blessed is he whose fame does not outshine his t. 332.46
call t. false if not accompanied by laugh 409.72
convictions worse enemies of t. than lies 78.14
death cancels everything but t. 221.4
deep t. is imageless 998.112
defeat is school in which t. grows strong 228.1
dignity of t. is lost with much protesting 998.66
disputant no more cares for t. than sportsman for the hare 51.16
don't wear best trousers to battle for t. 819.24
doubt is the vestibule of temple of t. 904.3
dreamer can know no t. but by awaking 336.16
earnest men have no time to patch t. 113.6
eliminate the impossible, the t. remains 998.9
enemies nearer t. in judging us than we 288.15
enemy of t. is often not lie but myth 617.5
error is the rule; t., accident of error 299.14
everything believed is an image of t. 78.2
every t. has two sides; look at both 998.3
expect the unexpected, or never find t. 998.56
few nudities so objectionable as naked t. 1000.18
greater amount of t. spoken, not written 998.98
great is t. and strongest of all 998.4
great is t., greater is silence about t. 745.3
he who lies does not believe the t. 1000.5
highest compact with our fellow is for t. 1000.2
historian must not try to know t. 419.3
hope is a great falsifier of t. 427.13
iconoclasm—the only way to get at t. 441.2
idea of t. invincible to scepticism 998.93
if you tell the t. you don't have to remember anything 1000.20
inability to lie is far from love of t. 1000.16
in idleness and dreams, t. comes to top 336.21
in imagination t. finds existence 450.7
in practice error and t. do not consort 9.10
in wine there is t. 268.44
it ain't so that t. is mighty, will prevail 998.125
it is wrong to put friendship before t. 998.5
journalism realizes that t. is a fluid 630.23
lawyer's t. is not t. but consistency 528.65
let us economize on t. 1000.22
life is paradox: each t. has counterpart 668.3
long attention to single aspect of t. leads to distortion of t. 999.5
love of t. has reward in heaven, on earth 998.88
lying is acknowledgment of force of t. 558.19
malice often takes the garb of t. 561.4
man has right perception of a t. only if willing to be its martyr 998.38
man is ready to distort t. intentionally 785.8
man lives not by t. but by make-believe 449.14
man never yet harmed by t. 998.7
man's passion for t. is such he welcomes the bitterest of all postulates 998.78
men maintain errors from zeal for t. 299.32
men take little trouble in search for t. 998.123
meridian decides the t. 517.34
no error is such as pursuit of absolute t. 299.7
no final t. in ethics 604.18
no more sovereign eloquence than t. in indignation 283.4
no mortal can seize t. in its wholeness 998.105
nonsense may tomorrow be demonstrated t. 998.129
not every t. is better for showing face 362.9
nothing gives rest but search for t. 811.4
no t. is proved by argument 998.102
nowadays t. is the greatest news 629.3
nowadays t. wins hatred 998.120
on a huge hill, cragged and steep, t. stands 998.28
one part of t. sets while another rises 656.16
one t. a man does not wish told 165.9
one t. discovered is better than all fluency 998.53
only the generous ready for t. impromptu 998.86
peace-mingling falsehood preferable to mischievous t. 999.14
perception of t. is detection of analogy 35.5
political t. is libel; religious t., blasphemy 998.54
pure t., gold, are unfit for circulation 998.22
pursuit of t. is gratifying 998.59
pushing a t. far, you meet a counter-t. 998.10
rather than love, money, fame, give me t. 998.122
read the t. in world's fair page 998.13
say not I have found the t., only a t. 998.48
simple t. his utmost skill 491.32
skepticism is the first step toward t. 904.4
so good is t., t. never hurts the teller 998.12
sooner hate me for t. than adore for lies 1000.1
soul is unwillingly deprived of t. 998.40
speak suddenly, come closer to t. 923.33
speak the t. unless you're a good liar 1000.9
stand for t. and 'tis enough 998.65
telling t. can cripple candidate's chances 711.33
the many have not wisdom to be moved by t. 682.1
their worst enemy: who tells them the t. 1000.17
there are times when t. is unseasonable 979.4
there is no absolute unchangeable t. 998.14
they who know the t. are not equal to those who love it 998.24
through inquiry we discover t. 998.101
time's glory is to bring t. to light 978.63
to be believed, make t. unbelievable 1000.14
to convey misinformation tell the t. 1000.21
to get into the t. is a mystic act 998.19
to know t. and not conform to it is crime 998.81
to love the t. is to refuse to let oneself be saddened by it 998.49
to love t. for t.'s sake is part of perfection 998.75
too much t. is uncouth 998.2
too much t. would kill 998.41
torch of t. shows much we cannot see 998.64
to show error is not to give t. 299.23
traffic-cop morality, rabbit-test t. 849.19
t. and falsehood be near twins 999.4
t. a passion which spares nothing 998.17
t., a totality sacrificed by history 419.33
t. can stand by itself 999.8
t.: compost in which beauty may germinate 72.37
t., crushed to earth, shall rise again 299.3
t. disappears with the telling of it 998.32
t. does less good than imitations do harm 999.9
t. does not always triumph over persecution 998.83
t. does not lie beyond humanity 998.72
t. exists; only lies are

invented 999.1
t. fears no trial 998.45
t. for t.'s sake! this is inhuman 998.126
t. forever on scaffold, wrong on throne 998.77
t. gains more by errors of one who thinks than by true opinions of those who do not 999.10
t. goes beyond anything said at any moment 998.80
t. has advantage of being rediscovered 998.84
t. has a handsome countenance 998.47
t. has become an angle, point of view 998.42
t. has visible signs 998.92
t. hath a quiet breast 998.110
t. hurts those who touch it 998.71
t. in art is one's last mood 998.131
t. in small quantities calms men 998.70
t. is a flower that makes others wither 998.44
t. is always the strongest argument 998.114
t. is a matter of direct apprehension 998.31
t. is a torch which gleams in the fog 998.55
t. is a value because it is true 998.79
t. is balance, but unbalance not a lie 999.15
t. is child of time 998.43
t. is common stock 974.1
t. is cruel, but frees those who love it 998.107
t. is good dog, but do not bark at error 299.10
t. is man's proper good 998.67
t. is more of a stranger than fiction 998.124
t. is no road to fortune 998.100
t. is not eloquent except unspoken 998.106
t. is not hard to kill 999.16
t. is not less so for being new 998.76
t. is often unpopular 998.115
t. is on the march; nothing can stop it 998.134
t. is one and immutable 998.62
t. is one forever absolute 656.22
t. is only a horse for Christianity 125.7
t. is only that which is taken to be true 998.116
t. is on the side of the oppressed today 1002.22
t. is rarely pure and never simple 998.133
t. is river split into arms that reunite 998.25
t. is that which is ineluctable 998.103
t. is the god of the free man 999.6
t, is thousand truths which grow and change 998.74
t. is tough, won't break like a bubble 998.60
t. is t. to the end of reck'ning 998.111
t. is what man persuades man to believe 998.85
t. is what most contradicts itself 998.33
t. is what stands the test of experience 998.35
t. knocks on door; you say, "Go away" 998.97
t. lags last, limping on arm of time 998.52
t. lies within little, certain compass 299.29
t. lives on in the midst of deception 998.108
t. looks tawdry when overdressed 998.117
t. may come from the devil's mouth 998.46
t. must dazzle gradually or every man be blind 998.27
t. never damages a cause that is just 111.8
t. no longer t. if polemically said 998.39
t. opposing neither profit nor pleasure is welcome 998.57
t. outlasts the sun 998.26
t. shall make you free 998.11
t. sits upon the lips of dying men 998.6
t. suffers more from defenders than foes 998.96
t., to be loved, needs only be seen 998.30
t. told with bad intent beats all lies 561.1
t. trashed, decency mugged every two years 1038.20
t. will always have a market 998.113
t. will bear exposure as well as beauty 998.21
we know t. by reason and by the heart 998.94
we may mellow t. to make it humane 1000.12
we perceive image of t., possess a lie 999.13
whatever profits man is t. 562.36
whatever satisfies the soul is t. 998.130
what imagination seizes as beauty is t. 998.68
what kind of t. has mountains for boundary 999.11
when complex things are communicated to masses of people, t. suffers distortion 576.4
when I can look life in the eyes, it will have given me t. in exchange for youth 571.19
when money speaks, t. keeps silent 602.52
when the grain of t. cannot be found 558.36
where all is dream, t. is nothing 336.10
while you live, tell t. and shame devil 1000.19
who doesn't tell t. is liar's accomplice 998.95
who speaks t. stabs falsehood to heart 1000.11
why do we not hear the t. 998.99
will to t. is longing for a stable world 998.89
would that I could discover t. as easily as I can uncover falsehood 999.3
truth's: beauty: t. smile beholding her own face 72.53
t. fountains are clear—t. streams, muddy 998.15
t. open to all, claims not all staked 998.109
truthful: many would be more t. 923.29
only a t. man can lie to any purpose 999.2
the stupid believe that to be t. is easy 998.20
truths: all great t. begin as blasphemies 506.3
ever-changing t. of our own experience 998.128
faith embraces contradictory t. 330.29
first t. those we discover last 998.18
irrationally held t. may be more harmful than reasoned errors 999.7
many eyes means many t. and thus no truth 998.90
one falsehood spoils a thousand t. 558.2
ready-made t. are drugs 998.102
simplest schoolboy knows t. for which Archimedes would have given his life 849.29
to bear t. with calm is sovereignty 160.1
t. begin as heresies, end as superstitions 998.61
t. may clash without contradicting 998.104
t. of life are not discovered by us 998.50
t. so true they are practically unbelievable 998.127
t. that are kept silent become poisonous 1000.15
try: to t. may be to die 466.5
t. first thyself, then call in God 281.6
we are more ready to t. the untried when what we do is inconsequential 479.6
trying: is it worth t., not can it be done? 286.3
no failure except in no longer t. 329.14
tune: I dance to the t. that is played 12.8
turning: it is a long lane that has no t. 118.2
turtle: t. lives 'twixt plated decks 802.3
tutelage: t. is demoralizing in the long run 719.34
tutor: easier for t. to command than teach 965.25
twentieth: t.-century problem: color-line 775.6
twice: everything done t. would be done better 684.8
twig: as the t. is bent the tree's inclined 988.7
twilight: first hour of spring t. dreadful to some 854.10
two: if t. make one song, muse fans wrath 155.4
to do t. things at once is to do neither 585.10
when t. do same thing, it is not the same 469.15
where t., one cannot be wretched, other not 1011.10
tyrannical: nation under t. regime can't be absolved of faults due to regime's guilt 1002.9
tyrannies: of all t., worst persecutes the mind 1002.11
tyranny: death softer thing by far than t. 1002.2
defiance of law is road to t. 528.44
easier to act under t. than to think 1002.5
face of t. is always mild at first 1002.25
he that holds t. does not trust friends 1002.3
if men are strong, t. will bankrupt itself making

shackles for them 1002.6
long tenure of office begets t. 761.1
remedy in human nature against t. 1002.17
revolutions never lighten burden of t. 819.39
t. is always better organized than freedom 537.29
t. is t., no matter what its form 1002.12
t. would not exist if freedom not abused 537.17
unity without plurality is t. 1016.8
wherever law ends, t. begins 528.49
tyrant: any excuse will serve a t. 1002.4
no t. like intemperance 494.4
of all wild beasts, preserve me from t. 349.13
t. claims freedom to kill freedom and yet to keep it for himself 1002.29
tyrants: flight is lawful when one flies from t. 300.8
necessity is the argument of t. 624.12
resistance to t. is obedience to God 1002.16
t. are but the spawn of ignorance 1002.20
t. perish from folly, not tyranny 1002.18

U

ugliness: nobody discovered u. through photographs 695.4
secret of u. is in being uninteresting 1003.2
ugly: in u. world, rich can buy only ugliness 1048.55
it is laudable fortitude to dare to be u. 1003.3
u. deeds are taught by u. deeds 227.29
wise man leaves in dark everything u. 304.1
umbilical: the u. cord is made of piano wire 334.16
umpire: u. must be justice, acrobat, Job, Buddha 929.18
unbelief: all we gain by our u. is doubt diversified by faith 1004.4
u. shown by condemnation of trifles 1004.7
unbeliever: founders of religions didn't include u. 797.30
unbiased: u. opinion is absolutely valueless 656.32
uncertainty: it is u. that lends life fascination 454.12
u. and expectation are the joys of life 856.2
u. fruitful if with a wish to understand 1005.7
we sail within a vast sphere, ever drifting in u. 1005.9
unchangeable: one u. certainty is nothing is certain or u. 115.8
uncomfortable: those u. in themselves are disagreeable to others 861.3
uncommitted: as long as possible live free and u. 363.49
unconfessable: every man knows what u. things pass within the secrecy of his own heart 405.12
unconscious: our u. is a vast factory going night, day 1006.3
unconventionality: u. not difficult if convention of your set 91.3
uncultivated: u. minds are not full of wild flowers 447.29
underground: enemy becomes friend once he's u. 288.7
understand: contend with those that u. me 1008.10
if you don't u. a man you can't crush him; if you do u. him, you probably won't 1008.3
in daily life we never u. each other 1008.8
in what we really u., we reason little 1007.7
it is the acme of life to u. life 539.100
thirst to know and u. is excellent 532.22
to u. is to forgive, even oneself 1008.2
to u. oneself: classic form of consolation 758.14
we do not u. what we are, unless we know what we ought to be 875.7
you give yourself to those who least u. 169.3
understanding: advise no man to marry who is not likely to propagate u. 564.66
discourse is index of a man's u. 77.14
few things measured with tape of u. 590.19
greatest success of life is u. between sincere people 188.10
greatness has no lustre for those in search of u. 1007.14
heart has such influence over u. 284.10
in length of days is u. 653.7
logic often has to take backseat to u. 1007.13
much learning does not teach u. 279.39
passions raise sedition against the u. 675.9
perfect u. almost extinguishes pleasure 1007.9
plant and animal confound the u. 623.48
shy fruit of pure science is u. 849.1
time increases u. for the aging 1007.16
u. everything makes a person tolerant 952.9
u. is the beginning of approving 1007.6
u. needs is half job of meeting them 625.7
u. takes no notice of itself 590.11
with all thy getting, get u. 1060.6
understandings: all are led more by hearts than by u. 284.9
flatter beautiful women for u. 1062.24
understands: who u. much displays greater simplicity 1007.3
understood: each supposes himself not fully u. 877.1
every man speaks and writes to be u. 134.3
undertaker: may even the u. be sorry when we die 221.134
undervalued: who is u. by himself is justly u. by others 868.5
underwear: from cradle to coffin, u. comes first 267.3
power, not discarded at will like u. 719.24
underworld: it takes all sorts of people to make an u. 204.11
undoing: glittering hope calls many to u. 1048.19
uneasy: u. lies the head that wears a crown 831.21
we are u. with an affectionate man 21.2
unequal: because men are u. they need to be brothers 471.2
unexamined: u. life is not worth living 758.16
unexpected: expect the u., or never find truth 998.56
unfair: nothing so u. as man without experience 321.53
unfavorable: to create an u. impression, things need not be true, only said 394.5
unfortunate: nobody chooses already u. for friendship 549.5
u. need people who will be kind to them 519.2
ungrateful: belly is u. 437.12
better u. men than miss chance to do good 433.10
far fewer u. men than we believe 475.5
people are seldom u. if we are beneficial 399.5
unhappiness: artists are expected to cultivate u. 1011.8
bewilderment the cause of much u. 149.2
happiness is to know source of u. 758.3
is anyone in world safe from u. 1011.34
man can only endure certain degree of u. 1011.15
man's happiness is built on another's u. 409.100
own happiness vs. the u. of others 561.13
perfect u. is unattainable 1011.21
since u. excites interest, many feign u. 1011.31
u. makes people look stupid 1011.12
u.: not being able to sit quietly 1011.26
u. remembering happiness intolerable 117.12
u., the natural state of the sentient adult 1011.11
volatile spirits prefer u. 564.105
unhappy: couple u. not merely from limited means 564.22
Englishman is u. until he has explained America 289.34
how much more u. a man might be than he is 1011.1
how u. is he who cannot forgive himself 405.13
I look at what I have not and think myself u. 238.35
in u. world, rich buy only unhappiness 1048.55
men take pains to render themselves u. 1011.13
no one more u. than superannuated idol 226.1
only the widely read know they are u. 1011.36
that some are u. is better than none happy 297.15

u. is the man who doesn't consider himself supremely blest 409.88
u. man deprived of what he did not have 1011.23
who would recognize the u. if grief had no language 1052.5
world never without reason to hate the u. 1011.17
uniform: good u. must work its way with the women 267.6
man becomes the creature of his u. 267.14
uniformity: complete u. makes longest life short 978.40
every central government worships u. 395.17
freedom never relied on u. of pinion 252.8
lashed to the wheel of u. 171.17
unimportant: hard for man to confess sum of life u. 1012.3
unintelligent: to serve u. man like crying in wilderness 941.15
uninteresting: secret of ugliness is in being u. 1003.2
union: we are not a nation, but a u. 34.12
unionism: u. uses its power to safeguard bad work 1013.4
unions: if capitalism the right of a few to make all decisions, u. threaten capitalism 108.9
unique: democratic disease reduces everything u. 297.16
every man represents the u. 1014.3
thing absolutely u. 858.4
uniqueness: my sense of my own u. 469.1
unite: not vain the weakest if they u. 1016.5
only fear and interest u. men 1016.7
United Nations: our instrument, our hope, is the U.N. 1015.1
United States: cannot accuse U.S. of undue amount of know-what 771.9
come to the U. not knowing what to expect 318.2
unity: how pleasant for brethren to dwell in u. 1016.2
in necessary things, u. 119.3
plurality without u. is confusion 1016.8
the u. of body and soul instantly falls away 589.7
u. without plurality is tyranny 1016.8
universal: act only on maxim you can will to be u. law 9.29
I seek the u., that must be the best 184.3
u. feeling cannot be disregarded 762.13
universe: justice is the last concern of u. 517.28
no reason for u. designed for our convenience 1017.1
the u. does not jest with us 1017.6
u. changed by inspiring people 790.24
u. forces us to understand it 1017.15
u. is not hostile but simply indifferent 1017.9
why does u. go to bother of existing? 1017.7
university: best u. for man of ideas: gauntlet of mob 597.1
function of u.: to be organ of adjustment between real life, knowledge of life 279.18
true u. is a collection of books 538.4
u. convention submerges nature 848.5
unjust: he who is u. in little is u. in much 491.3
just and u. things sanctioned by custom 213.27
nothing is absolutely u. 477.8
we know when we're being u., despicable 838.1
unkind: all the world appears u. 43.16
don't care how u. things people say about me 206.18
unknowable: we cease belief in u., but there it sits 1019.6
unknown: only the u. frightens men 1019.10
u. always passes for marvellous 1019.11
unlettered man: u. who prayed to his maker would be heard 723.32
unlike: meeting people u. oneself confirms one's idea that one is unique 469.2
unnatural: nothing u. that is not physically impossible 892.49
that a thing is u. does not make it blamable 431.17
unpleasant: seek for the salutary in the u. 390.15
unpredictability: military plans should be based on u. 856.4
unprivileged: concessions of the privileged to the u. 15.7
unpublished: u. manuscript is like an unconfessed sin 1069.83
unreason: the forces of u. destroy one another 785.29
unreasonable: all progress depends on the u. man 741.25
unrighteous: u. are never really fortunate 1055.6
unsaid: u. things cause of much unhappiness 149.2
unseen: full many a flower is born to blush u. 649.4
sometimes advantageous to be u. 915.13
the torture of being the u. object 30.5
unsettled: is not man the most u. of all creatures 482.1
unstable: men are too u. to be just 517.7
untruth: u. unacceptable to mind of man 648.1
unusual: u. is rare, except in literature 545.3
unwelcomed: short days pass u. one by one 854.11
unwilling: nothing is easy to the u. 245.6
up: we may stop ourselves when going u., never when coming down 329.19
upbraids: the man who acts least, u. the most 803.4
uplifted: go to funeral, not church, to be u. 367.10
uproar: Another in my place would have made an u. 472.11
upstart: u. is sparrow eager to be betrothed to a hornbill 33.16
urban: u. man is an uprooted tree 131.21
use: it's a misfortune to be of u. to nobody 1023.2
not possession but u. is riches 1048.23
thought makes every thing fit for u. 975.11
u. almost can change the stamp of nature 865.4
useful: occasions when we have been u. 221.106
u. knowledge makes a wise man 522.20
we often despise what is most u. 1023.1
whatever is u. must become useless 1023.3
usefulness: success can corrupt; u. can only exalt 1023.4
useless: to condemn spontaneous acts because u. 703.7
whatever is useful must become u. 1023.3
u. articles called "kisses" 521.1
usher: in the hands of a gloved and obsequious u. 367.5
utility: u. is the great idol of the age 1023.5
u. plus beauty is the spider's web 1023.7
Utopia: acre in Middlesex better than realm in U. 746.14
"yes" is the password to u. 504.3
uttered: impossible to recall what has been u. 923.48

V

vacation: ant doesn't know enough to take a v. 1065.19
first v. they [convalescents] had ever had 533.14
vacuum: v. better than some of what replaces it 623.81
vague: referred to, if at all, only with such v. Latin terms 1064.28
vain: v. man may imagine himself pleasing, in reality is a nuisance 1027.17
v. man pleased with effect on others 166.3
vainglory: it is not v. for man and his glass to confer 1027.16
valiant: luck is the prerogative of v. souls 360.27
the v. never taste of death but once 199.10
valor: between cowardice and despair v. is born 195.8
hidden v. is as bad as cowardice 195.20
love of fame, fear of disgrace are often at the root of the v. men esteem 195.17
perfect v. consists in doing without witnesses what we would do before everyone 195.19
the better part of v. is discretion 755.27
v. half way between rashness and cowheartedness 195.6
v. is a gift 195.31
valuable: decide how we're v. not how v. we are 1026.8
nothing is intrinsically v. 1026.1
people become v. for their

inaccessibility 1026.7
value: all we v. we shall sometime rend 241.5
dearness gives everything its v. 1026.16
life has v. when it has valuable object 539.51
measure v. of man only by other men 1026.15
no such thing as absolute v. 1026.25
The Jews generally give v. 512.5
too many creatures estimate own v. by amount of irritation caused others 508.4
with each v. born, life takes on new meaning 1026.11
valued: each entitled to be v. by best moment 515.1
that which cost little is less v. 1026.5
values: education, knowledge not of facts but of v. 279.45
hatred leads to extinction of v. 412.14
neither man demonstrated faith in those v. 1026.21
v. by which a life can be lived 1026.3
v. have roots as deep as creosote rings 1026.23
what is false in science of facts may be true in science of v. 1026.20
vanity: difference between the v. of a Frenchman and an Englishman 289.14
every author keeps an outrageous v. 1069.122
human v. is vulnerable yet unconquerable 1027.14
man sacrifices his purse to his v. 1027.20
one may attribute extreme actions to v. 227.20
others' v. is insufferable; wounds our own 1027.11
passions leave us at rest, v. agitates us 1027.10
people slander more from v. than malice 905.5
pride that dines on v. sups on contempt 733.6
there are no grades of v. 1027.19
those who prosper take on airs of v. 750.1
true power, politeness, are above v. 719.58
v. carries more weight than self-interest 384.13
v. is motive-power that moves humanity 1027.9
v. plays lurid tricks with memory 675.2
v. wants what we do best considered hard 1.12
we crave support in v. and religion 1027.15
who denies own v. is avoiding self-hate 1027.13
woman's v. makes object of choice her idol 1062.65
writer must accept v. as part of his stock in trade 1027.8
variance: language sets men at v. 252.10
variety: no pleasure endures unseasoned by v. 704.30
vassalage: man reduced to v. by largesse 433.27
Vatican: as much gilt and gesso as the V. chapels 429.1
vegetarians: many meat eaters to be far more non-violent than v. 274.11
v. look enough like their food to be classed as cannybals 1028.1
veil: Language, if it throws a v. over our ideas 524.19
venerable: broad hat is not always on v. head 138.3
vengeance: just v. does not call for punishment 817.7
Venice: a secret thrill on first arriving in V. 1029.7
venom: malice swallows great part of own v. 561.12
ventriloquy: through transcendental v. men believe that which was said on earth came from heaven 816.2
venturously: if didn't live v., never be depressed 16.10
Venus: contemplate V. on the Half-Shell 992.35
V. favors the bold 351.10
veracity: v. is the heart of morality 1000.8
verities: eternal v. end if they bulk too big 998.87
verse: his v. would last as long as the vestal virgins kept going up the Capitoline Hill 708.40
v. may find him who a sermon flies 708.47
who forgives the senior's ceaseless v. 708.11
who moulds his thought in v. employs materials vulgarized by everybody's use 708.50
verses: feeble v. sin against genius 708.109
God prefers bad v. recited with a pure heart 1068.10
good v. are like impromptus made at leisure 708.57
veteran: consult the v. instead of the politician 1042.61
vicar's: devil gets to belfry by v. skirts 307.15
vice: alliance of audacious v., turbulent virtue 819.13
army is a v. of our time 588.19
best virtue I have has some v. 1034.13
best way to attack v. is public ridicule 820.5
convention, rewards make v., virtue 1034.10
doubtless a v. to turn one's eyes inward 875.8
every v. has its excuse ready 1030.18
let your virtues spring up around one v. 1030.26
rapid in my virtue but my v. kept up with me 1034.20
sanctity, genius, are as rebellious as v. 840.11
the danger, when v. becomes precedent 1030.12
there is a capacity of v. in us to make your blood creep 1034.6
th' more ye see v. th' betther ye like it 1030.8
v. assumes virtue's mark on outward parts 1030.24
v. function: to keep virtue within bounds 1030.4
v. has more martyrs than virtue 1034.3
v. is exaggeration of virtuous function 1030.9
v., like virtue, grows in small steps 1030.21
v. often rides in virtue's chariot 1030.10
v. seen too oft, we endure, pity, embrace 1030.17
v. to trust all, or to trust none 997.9
virtue and v. are siblings or neighbors 1034.15
virtue and v. emit a breath every moment 1034.5
virtue itself turns v., being misapplied 1034.18
we will tolerate v. 123.19
when all run into v., none seem to do so 1030.7
who doesn't hate v., doesn't love virtue 1034.16
who tries to abolish v., destroys virtue 1034.2
vice-presidency: v. isn't a crime; it's kind of disgrace 1031.1
vices: absence of v. adds little to one's virtues 1034.11
all fashionable v. pass for virtues 440.15
cottages have same v. as courts 1030.5
courage not in those who won't look at own v. 864.1
gods scourge us with our pleasant v. 1030.23
great are capable of great v., virtues 401.9
he who hates v. hates men 1030.13
little v. of great must be accounted great 1030.19
man's virtues hold a torch to his v. 1034.4
many v. are only good qualities run wild 1030.11
men more easily governed through their v. than their virtues 1030.14
most v. may be committed very genteelly 1070.11
one can't shed light on v. he doesn't have 321.32
passions, when masters, become v. 675.17
search thy self for thy v. 1034.7
through tattered clothes small v. do appear 1030.25
v. are ingredients of virtues 1034.9
v. are their own punishment 1030.1
v. require moderate use, not abstinence 1030.3
we are loaded with wallets of v. 1030.15
we are more apt to catch v. than virtues 1030.6
we make a ladder of v., if trample them 1030.2
we tolerate v. with which we're familiar 1030.20
where minor v. are discouraged, major virtues are lacking 1034.1
who has no v. makes v. about his virtues 1034.21
vicious: preaching seldom reclaims the v. 724.10
viciousness: v. is sucked up in New York 632.20
victims: friendly terms with the v. he intends to eat 274.4
victories: all v. breed hate 173.7
brave v. are never really won 539.125
genuine v. are those over ignorance 447.23
who can see any difference between our v. and defeats 228.2
victorious: who bears in his heart a cathedral to be built is v. 55.15
victory: certain peace better than anticipated v. 681.19
dead men have no v. 173.6

do not push a v. too far 173.1
god of v. is one-handed 173.5
in v. even the cowardly like to boast 751.14
moral v. degrades both victor, vanquished 173.9
no pain in wound received in moment of v. 173.11
problems of v. are more agreeable than those of defeat, but no less difficult 173.2
struggle alone pleases us, not v. 281.13
v. should be celebrated with funeral rite 1042.50
we seek not worldwide v. of one nation but worldwide v. of men 100.12
yield to friends and you win v. 173.13
videos: watching the v. we're taking 639.6
view: fatal illusion is settled point of v. 620.2
views: to hold same v. at forty as at twenty 179.5
vigilance: eternal v. is the price of liberty 537.10
price of eternal v. is indifference 229.10
vigilant: v. self-criticism is necessary 684.13
vileness: even hatred of v. distorts man's features 412.3
village: the ingenuous streets of the junction v. 992.12
to be known and not know, vegetate in v. 131.9
villain: one may smile and be a v. 224.19
one rarely meets authentic v. in lifetime 1055.2
villainy: one v. teaches men to be evil in all 1070.21
vine: v. bears grapes of pleasure, intoxication, and disgust 268.2
vintners: what do v. buy half so precious as stuff they sell 268.40
violated: no sense that is not v. 131.42
violence: Englishman, be it noted, seldom resorts to v. 289.21
heterogeneous ideas yoked by v. 1032.8
let house be safe from v. 241.10
mental v. injures only the person whose thoughts are violent 665.5
most regard v. against certain kinds of people as inherently legitimate 1032.4
not necessarily less inclined toward v. 1032.13
perseverance is more prevailing than v. 686.6
the incommunicable is source of all v. 149.16
to-day v. is the rhetoric of the period 1032.11
unjust law is a species of v. 528.29
v. enmeshes him from whom it begins 1070.15
v. everywhere walks among us freely 1032.12
v. is essentially wordless 1032.10
v. is just where kindness is vain 1032.2
violent: it is better to be v. than put on the cloak of non-violence to cover impotence 1032.6
violin: when man is not disposed to music, no sound is more disagreeable than that of v. 614.55
violins: v. are lively, forward, importunate wits 615.3
virgin: an Irish-American v. at the age of thirty 218.2
most men desire a v. who is a whore 892.16
virginal: woman who has not been pregnant remains v. 499.10
virginity: v. is now a waiting room to be got out of 892.28
virile: perfecting himself as v. instrument of letters 873.20
that ludicrous v. earnestness 886.2
virtue: all v. is summed up in dealing justly 517.1
alliance of audacious vice and turbulent v. 819.13
alloy v., like gold, with more durable metal 1033.6
best v. I have has some vice 1034.13
blushing is the color of v. 893.2
care more for reputation of wit than v. 1061.27
convention, rewards make vice, v. 1034.10
every man prefers v. 1033.26
evil tongues may blast a whole life of v. 905.3
existence of v. depends on its use 1033.9
fine words seldom associated with true v. 45.5
glory of wealth is fleeting; v., eternal 1033.42
good company, discourse, are sinews of v. 152.24
good opinion of fellow men is strongest motive to v. 1033.10
greatness: to perceive that v. is enough 1033.16
happiness must be intelligible consequence of v. 1033.31
happiness of man consists in v. 1033.1
he who seeks fame by practice of v. 332.48
highest v. is always against the law 1033.17
if no v., we would live in peace 1042.94
if v. can't shine bright but by conflict, can she subsist without vice 1034.12
impressed by rare things—why not by v. 1033.28
love v., she alone is free 1033.32
man's v. measured by his life 1033.38
measure man's v. by what he would do without laws, public opinion to control him 1033.23
men are flattered into v. 1034.19
most men admire v. who follow her not 1033.33
once a woman parts with v. 857.2
philanthropy is almost the only v. appreciated 433.32
pride thyself on v., not parentage 37.7
public v. is foundation of republics 1033.2
seldom does v. rise from trunk to branch 1033.12
sins are the highway of our v. 900.23
some incapable of sciences, but not v. 1033.49
some never make whole coat of fabric of v. 1033.27
some rise by sin, some by v. fall 1034.17
successful and fortunate crime called v. 204.17
the exercise of v. should be its own reward 1033.41
the order of things consents to v. 1033.18
there is a capacity of v. in us 1034.6
there may be guilt if too much v. 1033.39
the virtuous love v. in another 1033.20
to eye of enmity v. seems ugliest blemish 412.20
to have v. is distinction but a hard lot 1033.35
to lay to v. the weariness of old age 653.34
v. and vice emit a breath every moment 1034.5
v. and vice, evil and good, are siblings 1034.15
v. between men: commerce of good actions 1033.50
v. beyond reason makes the sage a fool 1033.25
v. cannot be followed but for herself 1033.34
v. cannot dwell with slaves 889.2
v., having slept, gets up more refreshed 1034.14
v. herself is her own fairest reward 1033.44
v. in man doesn't make you want to grab him 1033.48
v. in threadbare cloak is despised 1033.21
v. is bold, goodness never fearful 1033.43
v. is ice-cold 1033.13
v. is most fragrant when incensed, crushed 1033.5
v. is not hereditary 1033.36
v. is roughest way—proves a bed of down 1033.51
v. itself turns vice, being misapplied 1034.18
v. makes enemies as it condemns opposite 491.29
v. more clearly shown in fine actions than in nonperformance of base ones 1033.4
v. must shape itself in deed 1033.47
v. passes as currency all over the world 1033.19
v. requiring guarding not worth sentinel 1033.22
v., though in rags, will keep me warm 1033.15
v. vivid, separate; like pain, smell 1033.8
v. wouldn't go to such lengths if vanity did not keep her company 1033.30
weakness keeps us to duty, v. gets credit 271.15
what is faith, love, v. alone 330.26
who does not hate vice, does not love v. 1034.16
wickedness is always easier than v. 1055.7
wisdom and v. like two wheels of cart 491.12
wise to make a v. of necessity 624.2
writer is not to illustrate v. 1069.137
virtue's: he lives in fame who died in v. cause 332.40
vice often rides in v. chariot

1030.10
who knows his v. name, place, hath none 1033.14
virtues: absence of vices adds little to one's v. 1034.11
for youthful faults ripe v. shall atone 1071.63
great are capable of great vices, v. 401.9
if men were true, what use would v. be 342.21
let your v. spring up around one vice 1030.26
man's v. hold up a torch to his vices 1034.4
men's v. we write in water 307.33
moderation runs through all v. 598.5
nothing more puritanical than the v. 1033.45
our v. are most often but vices disguised 1034.8
search others for their v. 1034.7
social v. are commonly but the virtue of pigs in a litter 152.21
v. are v. to those who appreciate them 1033.37
v. lie in interpretation of the time 604.34
we are more apt to catch vices than v. 1030.6
where minor vices are discouraged, major v. are lacking 1034.1
virtuous: folks who do v. acts in unpleasing way 1033.24
great man need not be v. 401.48
if I am v., about whom should I not care 433.9
if you wish to be singular, be v. 468.2
men grown v. in old age make sacrifice to God of devil's leavings 1033.46
prudent do selves good; v. do to others 755.31
to make men v., make them love their country 678.18
v. man is open to honest men's observation 1033.29
visible: true mystery of the world is the v. 45.21
vision: human being must suffer as price of v. 946.8
if we had keen v., feeling of life 883.2
men of rare v. are always crucified 565.5
v. is art of seeing the invisible 1035.6
we take limits of v. for limits of world 689.7
visionary: v. denies truth to self, a liar to others 442.13
v. people are v. partly because of the great many things they don't see 1035.3
visitors: late v. should find time in my face 428.11
vitality: in sorriest desert, human v. still glows 1036.4
symptom of America's v. 34.16
v. blunders through predicaments 1036.5
v. shows in the ability to start over 1036.1
when v. runs high, death takes men by surprise 1036.3
vivacity: v. is gift of women, gravity that of men 566.1
vocabulary: for every man something in v. sticks to him like second skin 619.1
want my v. to have a very large range 1064.2
vocation: talent is the call of v. 1037.5
vocations: v. we wanted to pursue, but didn't, bleed 1037.2
voice: a sort of shucks and aw shit in the v. 119.18
give every man thine ear, but few thy v. 543.4
her v. distinctly separate from the others 902.2
her v. was sweet and reminded him of elms 923.13
there's ransom in a v. 898.2
the v. is a second face 923.6
the v. of one crying in the wilderness 531.22
v. soft, low: excellent thing in woman 923.53
voices: v. of God and Devil, scarcely distinguishable 242.3
void: hour of triumph is what brings the v. 845.4
v. yields up nothing 708.82
voluntaries: Christ is served with v. 125.4
vote: man without v. is like man without hand 1038.3
no candidate too pallid, issue too remote for questionnaire to analyze our v. 1038.14
one who does not v. has no right to complain 1038.10
straw v. shows which way the hot air blows 762.9
v. for man who promises least 1038.2
v. is most powerful instrument ever devised for breaking down injustice 1038.8
who think one v. does no good will soon think one v. will do no harm 1038.6
voter: apathy of v. is confusion of reformer 1038.7
letting the v. know he cared 967.15
voters: rulers of democracy are the v. 1038.17
voting: v.: determines stronger side without fight 1038.15
vow: to make v. for life makes self slave 743.15
v. that binds too strictly snaps itself 743.12
vows: ease would recant v. made in pain 743.7
voyage: coming into port determines success of v. 6.1
the last v., the longest, the best 221.141
voyaging: v. no help in finding prosperity 750.6
vulgar: being at once v. and superior to vulgarity 1039.2
if we can't be moral, we can avoid being v. 396.4
it is v. to use a gold toothpick 1039.3
loud dress worn to impress the v. 963.19
not at once applauses of v. and approbation of wise 722.14
unsure habitation built on v. heart 682.16
v. man always the most distinguished 1039.1
vulgarity: intemperance is the only v. 268.11
v. finds its antidote, crudities become softened 1064.8
vulgarization: ours is an age not of vulgarity but of v. 104.21
vulgarized: there is no idea that cannot be v. 4.2
vulnerable: too v. to be a confident operator 6.14

W

wages: they cut my w. out, also the job 1009.2
wags: world decorates w. with Brussels sprouts 436.37
wailing: w. over some new kitchen crisis 205.2
wait: serene, I w., for my own shall come to me 1040.1
waiter: like a w. with a tray of pastry in hand 77.18
waiters: the w. treat the clients like interlopers 355.11
waiting: faults of those who keep men w. 765.2
half the agony of living is w. 1040.5
how much of human life is lost in w. 1040.2
philosophy of w. upheld by all oracles 1040.3
used to w. for buses that are late 677.18
waking: the w. have one world in common 266.9
walk: can two w. together except they be agreed 564.7
men must w. before they dance 404.22
people think desire to w. is noble 1041.1
wall: no w. to hammer with frustrated fists 102.7
something there is that doesn't love a w. 983.1
white w. is the fool's paper 397.1
walls: stone w. do not a prison make 735.8
waltz: a w., I must leave off to listen 614.15
wanderer: a w. is man from his birth 812.1
want: easy to get everything you w. 8.3
humanity too harassed by struggle with w. to struggle with error 625.6
life is a progress from w. to w. 238.24
those in w. are menace, ridden with envy 718.15
to w. for one who comes not 366.2
w. gave tongue and sin awakened 625.4
w. of a thing is perplexing enough 716.17
we spend days doing what we don't w. 1065.15
young people, unbridled, just w. 1071.46
wanted: she only w. what she couldn't have 366.3
wants: eliminate the needless w. of life 701.4
few our real w.; how easy to satisfy them 238.17
he whose real w. are supplied must admit those of fancy 238.25
man should consider he has more than he w. 1011.1
man w. what he is supposed to want 238.11
supplying w. by lopping off desires is like cutting off feet 937.9
what man knows is at war with what he w. 170.3

war: all delays are dangerous in w. 1042.27
all gods dead except god of w. 1042.19
author of w. opens vein, bleeds nation 1042.69
begin w. when you like, stop when you can 551.200
better w. for justice than unjust peace 681.26
boys are the cash of w. 1042.14
bread broken with comrades makes us accept values of w. 1042.83
butter sacrificed because of w. 1042.93
cause of going to w. and avoiding it is same desire 1042.73
cruelty, excitement, lead men to love w. 1042.4
diplomats essential to starting a w. 1042.76
disadvantageous peace better than just w. 1042.31
during w. we imprison rights of man 1042.38
eloquence in politics wins what is won in w. 283.1
every w. is its own excuse 1042.88
every w. is madness—civil w. worst of all 1042.102
fatal to enter w. without will to win 1042.54
great nation has not madness to make w. 665.2
great people face w. rather than purchase base prosperity at price of honor 46.5
historical peoples export idea by w. 445.1
in civil w., triumphs are defeats 170.2
in every w. they kill you a new way 133.23
in w., science linked with Stone Age cruelties 1049.2
in w.-time a man is called a hero 418.12
just fear of imminent danger is lawful cause of w. 1042.2
laws are silent in time of w. 1042.15
man no more prone to w. than he once was 1042.49
men ask outcome of w., not cause 1042.87
men love w. because it allows them to look serious 1042.32
mere absence of w. is not peace 681.16
morality is contraband in w. 1042.34
never was good w. or a bad peace 1042.33
no man who witnessed tragedies of last w. can advocate w. 1042.48
not because w. will bear objective examination 1042.6
old men declare w., but youth must fight 1042.44
one believes in w. if one does not abhor it 1042.55
peace with a cudgel in hand is w. 229.12
permission for w. given by world's mood 1042.40
preparedness for w. best means of peace 229.15
quickest way to end a w. is to lose 1042.67
regarded as wicked, w. has fascination 1042.104
resister of w. can bring peace 665.4
same reason that makes us wrangle with neighbor, causes w. between princes 772.11
sometime no one will come to w. 665.10
the means of w. are sacrifice of many 1042.22
those who praise w. are detestable 1042.77
to call w. the soil of courage 1042.85
to delight in w. is a merit in soldier 1042.86
vice foments w.; virtue actually fights 1042.94
vigorous, brutal people find w. enjoyable 1042.82
w. affects men as motherhood does women 1042.59
w. and courtesan: slaves of desperation 1042.1
w.: best amusement for our morning meal 1042.21
w. drives away fear, brings bravery to surface 1042.35
w. educates senses, activates will 1042.30
w. expert is man ye niver heerd iv befure 1042.28
w.: game princes seldom win, people never 1042.23
w. increases taxes 1042.70
w. is abolished only through w. 1042.56
w. is a generality 1042.29
w. is an emblem of all misery 1042.26
w. is boys flung into a breach 1042.53
w. is but duel on a larger scale 1042.16
w. is cruelty; you cannot refine it 1042.90
w. is curiously disabling 1042.79
w. is like love, it always finds a way 1042.8
w. is not afraid of paradoxes 1042.103
w. is not an adventure but a disease 1042.84
w. is politics with bloodshed 711.57
w. is subject to inconstancy of fortune 1042.12
w. is the product of an earlier corruption 1042.64
w. is the province of chance 1042.17
w. is what we call violence of the strong 1042.42
w. lays open wounds of victorious party 173.15
w. makes rattling good history 681.9
w. makes victor stupid, loser revengeful 1042.65
w. minds may not regain their balance 1042.20
w., not fighting or marching in parades 1042.10
w.: political act, political instrument 1042.18
w.'s a game which, were their subjects wise, kings would not play at 1042.25
w.'s victims and instruments are human beings 1042.45
way to prevent w. is not by preparing for it 1042.52
we can secure peace only by preparing for w. 229.7
we prepare for w. like precocious giants 1042.74
we think the other side of w. is peace 1042.60
we will not unnecessarily risk nuclear w. 641.10
when w. in air all learn falsehood 1042.39
you may be obliged to wage w., but not to use poisoned arrows 1049.4
warfare: w. between the unaroused male and female 581.55
what madness this, inviting death by w. 1042.92
warm: better a little fire to w. us 186.7
cold is agreeable that we may get w. 117.29
warning: thorn of experience worth wilderness of w. 321.30
wars: bloodiest w. have been religious wars 797.55
liberty may do no more than stir up civil w. 537.9
many w. avoided by patience 677.17
no kingdom suffered as many w. as Christ's 125.20
small w. teetering on the brink of big ones 1042.51
w. are boyish, and are fought by boys 1042.58
w. are not won by evacuations 300.3
w. are the planet's chief source of torment 1042.68
w. of opinion are most disgraceful 252.5
we are in an epoch of w. of religion 445.3
we want end of beginning to all w. 498.18
wart: if you have a w. on your nose 861.2
wartime: dangerous in w. to live as by Gallup Poll 762.4
no working middle course in w. 1042.13
son in w., worst curse that can befall mother 670.13
wash: those who w. much talk down to those who w. little 137.3
Washington: his chief hate was W. bureaucracy 102.5
in any election year W. vibrates early 1044.1
in W., people measured by ability to get reelected 711.69
no .400 hitters in W. 1044.6
people only leave W. by way of the box 1044.4
waste: greedy have extraordinary capacity for w. 403.14
that produced in haste goes hastily to w. 411.12
under the law of conspicuous w. 524.47
wasted: The most w. day is that in which we have not laughed 526.7
waste-paper: every one should keep a mental w. basket 404.5
watch: we think if we w. game we have taken part 929.11
water: expect poison from standing w. 446.3
like w. that turns no wheel 1046.2
smooth runs w. where the brook is deep 740.4
w., not life's need but life itself 1046.1
w. taken in moderation can't hurt anyone 268.53
we'll have to w. him twice a day 493.16

when w. covers the head, a hundred fathoms are as one 239.8
water-closet: character, turn of mind connected with w. 119.28
water-colour: amateur painting in w. shows innocent and quiet mind 666.12
watt: unhappy home whose master doesn't know difference between w. and ohm 463.4
way: strait is the gate, narrow the w. 841.1
there is always best w. to do everything 585.4
weak: always see man's w. point in his wife 564.69
evil attracts w. by promise of power 307.20
how shall one so w. become strong 452.5
in a just cause w. beat the strong 111.13
only w. intent on giving as good as get 940.12
rudeness is w. man's imitation of strength 830.2
spirit is willing but the flesh is w. 1047.1
strong and w. cannot keep company 57.1
the w. feel our generosity as oppression 1047.6
the w. will be driven to the wall 940.13
the w. worship brutal directness 362.7
to escape responsibility for failure, the w. engage in grandiose undertakings 1047.5
w. can be terrible trying to appear strong 1047.12
w. man is just by accident 940.9
w. people cannot be sincere 901.14
you w. need someone to hand your life back 1047.13
weaker: w. side makes a great noise 772.15
weakest: harm comes to the strong from the w. 1047.11
not vain the w. if their force unite 1016.5
w. are the most revengeful 1047.2
weakness: man wallows in a woman's w. 581.20
some people mistake w. for tact 961.3
spiritual w., shallowness of convictions 1047.3
who can carp at human w. is held divine 207.50
woman's strength is might of w. 1062.47
weaknesses: commit worst w. for those we most despise 1070.5
men more willing to have their crimes known than their w. 804.3
people with no w. are terrible 684.6
women strongest when armed with their w. 1062.36
wealth: a little beauty is preferable to much w. 72.44
get place and w. with grace 1048.43
get w. when you have it not 1048.40
glory of w. is fleeting; virtue, eternal 1033.42
if w. waste, wit gives but small warmth 718.44
let there be w. without tears 1048.2
man discovers w. when God asks for gifts 384.31
man's word believed to extent of his w. 1000.10
many find w. change, not end, of miseries 1048.53
mighty w. is holiest of our gods 1048.31
people say law but they mean w. 528.18
some gain from w. only fear of losing it 1048.45
standing in community requires w. 1048.61
superfluous w. buys superfluities only 1048.59
the first w. is health 413.3
there is no w. but life 539.97
thirst for w. grows as our fortunes grow 403.10
true w. is not a static thing 1048.47
w. breeds satiety, satiety outrage 1048.57
w. defined by fancies is beyond reach 1048.17
w. is known to be a great comforter 1048.42
w. is not without its advantages 1048.26
w. is relative, so is its absence 1048.5
w. is the means, people are the ends 1048.32
w. maketh many friends 1048.8
w., poverty: parents of discontent 251.7
w. unused might as well not exist 1048.3
w. with us a moment; only our characters steadfast 1048.20
wherever excessive w., excessive poverty 1048.34
wise man distinguishes felicity from w. 1048.15
with w. one may be lucky but not happy 409.36
without rich heart w. is ugly beggar 1048.16
wealthy: when none but the w. had watches they were all good ones 297.24
weapon: satire's my w. 844.6
the w. fathered man 1049.1
weapons: possess nuclear or even thermonuclear w. 641.9
wear: it is better to w. out than to rust out 10.3
the problem of what to w. gave me pause 267.20
weariness: it is w. to keep toiling at same things 1065.40
w. can snore upon the flint 906.21
w. shortest way to equality, fraternity 297.17
wearing: no place like home for w. what you like 422.1
weary: let us not be w. in well doing 433.3
weather: many can brook w. that love not the wind 287.8
never content until each makes his own w. 1050.5
no bad w. at all in the country 194.10
there is no such thing as bad w. 1050.4
'tis very warm w. when one's in bed 73.9
w. brings out statistician in everyone 1050.10
w. in towns like skylark in counting-house 1050.6
w. takes pledge, signs it with rainbow 779.1
wedded: two best days of man's w. life: days when he marries and buries his wife 564.57
w. love, true source of human offspring 564.81
wedding: girls have a papier mâché face on w. day 1051.3
he wanted to be the bride at every w. 1027.12
many torments lie in circle of w. ring 564.21
weddings: at American w., the quality of the food 1051.6
w. seem to be magnets for mishap 1051.4
wedlock: w., a padlock 564.34
what is w. forced but a hell 564.108
weed: w. is no more than a flower in disguise 371.1
weeds: it is all red clay and very few w. 103.1
weep: better to w. at joy than joy at weeping 1052.8
finer nature goes to w. with beggars 918.5
he does not w. who does not see 87.7
it is God's giving if we laugh or w. 409.93
man can do nothing untaught, but w. 988.6
men w. the dead but not passing of youth 606.20
minute to smile, hour to w. in 539.27
one cannot w. for the entire world 698.1
those who w. recover more quickly 527.4
to have me w., you must feel grief 53.66
to w. is to make less the depth of grief 1052.9
w., and you w. alone 527.9
weeping: learn w. and gain laughing 918.20
w. may endure for a night 1052.1
weight: American women are obsessed with w. 34.48
born to suffer the w. of men 564.5
just w. is the Lord's delight 105.2
none knows w. of another's burden 663.5
welcome: w. is the best cheer 428.12
welfare: dehumanized life on w. 1009.3
man errs not that he deems his w. his true aim 873.1
w. state not built for the desperate, but those capable of helping themselves 912.3
well: let us not be weary in w. doing 433.3
want thing done w., do it yourself 880.17
we do nothing w. till we cease to think about manner of doing it 928.4
what is w. done is done soon enough 311.1
when w., all have advice for the ill 413.17
well-being: sense of w. with us when young 413.2
taste for w. is feature of democratic times 750.5
w. attained little by little 186.23

well-bred: w. contradict other people 1060.62
whale: however big the w., tiny harpoon can rob him of life 400.9
whim: pleasure of gratifying w. is very great 1053.1
whipping: w. renders boys more cowardly or obstinate 766.12
who should scape w. 517.43
whiskey: w. just naturally likes me 268.26
whisper: Most of the time, God speaks in a w. 387.33
trumpet does not more stun than w. teases 923.36
whistles: w. warned him of her coming 884.4
White House: in W. H. delay is a decision 730.17
white: how ill w. hairs become a fool and jester 356.22
the great stumbling block is the w. moderate 598.6
when w. man governs another man, that is despotism 1002.19
w. man's notion: that he is less savage 1054.4
why should anyone think a w. skin superior? 775.15
world is w. no longer, won't be w. again 1054.1
white-collar: when w. people get jobs 1066.4
whiteness: w.: insurance man's shirt on morning run 1054.2
whole: only one way of seeing: seeing the w. 683.11
whore: most men desire a virgin who is a w. 892.16
why: every w. hath a wherefore 110.6
if we have own w. of life, we shall get along with almost any how 573.4
instinct of life falters in man to ask w. 562.31
wicked: affliction sometime teacheth w. to pray 723.20
do good even to the w. 433.26
killing to prevent w. makes w. 518.9
man not born w.; gets so, as gets sick 1055.11
more hope in death of good than in life of w. 393.18
no man became extremely w. all at once 1055.8
praises from w. men are reproaches 722.8
there is no peace unto the w. 1055.1
w. cannot fall lower than lowest in you 390.6
w. flee when no man pursueth 405.2
w. is not much worse than indiscreet 1055.4
wickedness: a little w. makes muscle 1055.5
men capable of every w. 1055.3
one's w. may become all men's curse 1055.10
w. is always easier than virtue 1055.7
w. is a myth invented by good people 1055.12
widowhood: w.: hope that keeps up wife's spirits 564.47
widows: far more w. than widowers 221.92
wife: always see man's weak point in his w. 564.69
beaten w. with blackened eyes and torn clothes 77.7
best days of a man's wedded life: days he marries and buries his w. 564.57
bitterest creature: w. who discovers husband's bravery is only bravado 564.11
choose w. rather by ear than by eye 564.45
ideal w. any woman with an ideal husband 564.125
inducing a w. to turn against her father 252.6
in every other way, she was a good w. 564.113
I would be married, but I'd have no w. 66.2
light w. doth make a heavy husband 564.106
man is better pleased with good dinner than when his w. talks Greek 274.20
man's best possession is a sympathetic w. 564.38
man should be taller, older, heavier, uglier, and hoarser than his w. 564.59
never join friend in abuse of horse or w. 206.7
no man knows w. until he has gone with her through fiery trials 564.62
no man worth having is true to his w. 472.13
nothing nobler than when two who see eye to eye keep house as man and w. 564.58
one good w. is a spiritual harem 1062.25
one shouldn't be too inquisitive about one's w. 211.1
only love should rule between man and w. 564.98
rare spoil for man is winning of good w. 564.35
roaring of wind is my w. 623.42
single man with fortune must need a w. 66.1
strife if w. is dissatisfied with husband 892.47
when cheated, w. and husband feel same 472.2
who loves not his w., feeds a lioness 334.33
whoso findeth a w. findeth a good thing 564.9
why not bear a fault in your w. 564.44
w. and children hostages to fortune 334.5
w. dragged him reluctantly toward culture 210.22
w. has more power than state over man 564.32
w. loves out of duty 564.48
w. takes exact measure of her husband 564.129
worse trouble with a woman who is not a w. 581.61
wild: creatures that want to live a life of their own, we call wild 438.2
fight to save w. beauty is democracy at its best 177.8
those who respect natures of w. animals 41.35
who will pity any who go near w. beasts 216.1
w. things are not people 41.12
wilderness: men who came to the w. to practice religion 797.29
will: a kind of desperate w. resides even in a root 539.28
art of making a w. is baffling expectation 1058.5
fat kitchen, lean w. 1056.5
good or ill of man lies within his own w. 1056.4
he is unhappy who does thing against w. 644.6
he prays, thy w. be done: but means own w. 723.28
if I bind the future I bind my w. 201.38
ill w. goes further now 1042.49
it is natural for the w. to love 78.15
let my w. take the place of a reason 1056.7
man's w. creates the things that paralyze his brain, brutalize his heart 1056.8
not to cultivate the w. depraves the mind 279.27
not Zeus himself can get better of my free w. 867.6
our times worship w. 1056.3
our w. is always for own good 389.11
this free w. business is a bit terrifying 644.1
we have more ability than w. power 807.5
we learn to curb w. long before sentiments 862.5
wherever one is against w. is prison 735.5
w. cannot be quenched against its w. 1056.2
w. is from moral sense, self-interest 1056.9
w. is never free, is attached to a purpose 1056.1
w. makes us see other side of our natures 1056.6
willing: when a man's w. and eager, god joins in 1057.1
w. mind makes a light foot 1057.2
willingly: nothing troublesome that we do w. 1057.4
wills: our w. and fates do contrary run 1056.10
win: fatal to enter war without will to w. 1042.54
to keep demands as much skill as to w. 716.3
to w. a woman one must please her 857.5
wind: blow, blow, thou winter w. 475.6
east w. an impassive-faced tyrant 1059.2
God tempers the w. to the shorn lamb 754.4
nature sees man control the w., the w. sweep man away 623.1
no w. serves him who voyages to no port 465.4
westerly w. like monarch gone mad 1059.3
who has seen the w. 1059.5
wild west w., breath of autumn's being 1059.6
w. whirleth about continually 1059.1
windmill: w. eternally works to accomplish one end 771.2
winds: scorching w. howled around us 641.7
substance of w. too thin for human eyes 1059.4
w. long to play with your hair 623.32
Windsor: can't make Duchess of W. into Rebecca of Sunnybrook Farm 328.1
wine: after w. who talks of war or poverty 268.25
bitterest w. drained from crushed ideals 254.6
bronze is the mirror of form;

w., of heart 268.1
for a bad night, a mattress of w. 268.51
from w. what sudden friendship springs 268.17
God made only water, but man made w. 268.28
good w. is a good creature well used 268.47
in w. there is truth 268.44
it's hard to hide ignorance over w. 268.21
let us have w., woman, mirth and laughter 706.1
spirit of world not evoked by opium, w. 269.4
too much and too little w. 268.42
w. can make sage frolic, the serious smile 268.23
w. gives man neither knowledge nor wit 268.31
w. is like rain 268.20
w. is only sweet to happy men 268.32
w. to gifted bard is mount that races 268.9
with plenty of w., sorrow takes wing 268.41
wings: a bird has w. because it flies 110.1
oh that I had w. like a dove 300.1
winning: too light w. make the prize light 198.14
whoever is w. seems invincible 719.47
w. is shoddy, ignoble, brief 945.24
wins: tragedy of life is that man almost w. 329.4
winter: every mile is two in w. 854.22
freezing w. gave way to frosty spring 140.3
if w. comes, can spring be far behind 427.36
love w., for it is the spring of genius 854.2
only w.-patience can bring the long-awaited spring 677.14
w. is come and gone, but grief returns 918.52
w., made for landladies to keep cold radiators 854.27
wisdom: action should culminate in w. 9.4
age has nothing to do with w. 1060.33
a man is wise with w. of his time only 184.9
a w. that comes only with age 571.10
calm despair is the essence of w. 806.10
contrivance of human w. to provide for human wants 395.9
courage, substitute for w. in government 195.37
enemy of w. is the march of events 305.4
fear of the Lord is the beginning of w. 1060.4
first step in w., open windows of the ego 1060.52
fortune had no deity if men had w. 360.22
function of w.: discriminate good, evil 1060.10
gauge growth of w. by loss of ill-temper 1060.45
goodness is born of w. 393.30
I fear I have committed idolatry against w. 1061.17
instinct's w. impresses and disturbs me 486.4
it requires w. to understand w. 1060.40
kisses are a better fate than w. 521.2
knowledge comes, but w. lingers 1060.58
knowledge is in the head; w., in the heart 1060.25
make learning of books your own w. 532.18
men who love w. should acquaint themselves with many particulars 1060.27
much of w. still acquired by necromancy 986.11
nature never says one thing, w. another 623.41
nine-tenths of w. is being wise in time 1060.50
not by constraint shall you find w. 1060.60
one never loves wisest for their w. 551.159
our happiness depends on w. always 409.94
road to w.: err and err, less and less 1060.26
sciences may be learned by rote, w. not 1060.57
sense conforms to world, w. to Heaven 1060.36
short saying oft contains much w. 572.2
some take more care to hide w. than folly 943.5
sum of w. not contained in one language 524.36
terrible is w. that does not profit wise 1060.56
the final w. that the earth can give 551.235
the good have come to w. through failure 393.43
the price of w. is above rubies 1060.5
there is advantage in w. won from pain 343.3
'tis w. sometimes to seem a fool 356.12
to be a philosopher is to love w. 694.39
to question wise man is beginning of w. 480.11
to realize the unimportance of time is the gate of w. 978.57
to w. belongs intellectual apprehension of eternal things 1060.3
true w. is not departing from nature 623.64
ultimate w. remains locked in a seed 623.7
unlike wines, old and new w. mix admirably 1060.7
we thought since we had power we had w. 719.8
what use is w. when folly reigns 354.18
what we're learning in schools is not w. 1060.9
who is too lazy to think never attains w. 1060.12
who lacks w. in old age has existed only 653.77
will and w. are both mighty leaders 1056.3
w. and virtue like two wheels of cart 491.12
w. appears in all works of creation 623.47
w. at times is found in folly 354.6
w. cannot be communicated 1060.28
w. comes alone through suffering 1060.1
w. consists in knowing what to do next 1060.32
w., delightful pastime at other's expense 362.5
w. does not do desperate things 1060.59
w. got not by years but by disposition 1060.47
w. has its root in goodness 1060.16
w. hurts 493.9
w. is always an overmatch for strength 1060.46
w. is an affair of values, value judgments 1060.31
w. is a solid and entire building 1060.44
w. is humble that he knows no more 1060.13
w. is latent in things-as-they-are 784.15
w. is principal thing; therefore get w. 1060.6
w. is social, beauty jealous 1060.35
w.: knowing what's before us in daily life 612.3
w. makes life endurable 946.35
w. must go with sympathy 960.7
w. of one can rarely make many happy 810.9
w. ofttimes nearer when we stoop than when we soar 1060.64
w. rather buffeted than not listened to 1060.49
w. requires no form 1060.41
w. rises upon the ruins of folly 1060.22
w. seeks how to make us die well 541.43
w. sets bounds even to knowledge 522.45
w. to leech us of ill is daily spun 1060.43
w.: to live greatest number of good hours 504.8
with the ancient is w. 653.7
youth must study w., old age practice it 1060.51
wise men: w. studying the law, like children tossing a ball 1060.55
wise: all are w. for others, none for himself 19.10
as we grow old, it is hard to keep w. 653.36
better mad with the rest than w. alone 559.8
better to weep with w. men than laugh with fools 57.18
be w. as serpents and harmless as doves 943.3
be wisely worldly, be not worldly w. 917.6
conversation with w. man better than books 279.52
defer not till to-morrow to be w. 231.2
desire of glory last infirmity even of w. 386.17
fear not the anger of the w. to raise 803.7
fool sees not the same tree a w. man sees 683.1
fortune seldom troubles the w. man 1060.18
god could hardly love and be w. 551.166
he bids fair to grow w. who has discovered that he is not so 1060.48
honor paid w. man good for those honoring 426.3
how prone to doubt, cautious, are the w. 1060.30
in love not w.; when w. not in love 551.168
it is foolish to wish to be exclusively w. 1060.39
it is impossible to love and be w. 551.5
it takes w. man to recognize

w. man 1060.65
it's easier to be w. on behalf of others 1060.38
latter part of w. man's life is taken up in curing follies of the first 571.17
life is a festival only to the w. 1060.15
luck never made a man w. 360.33
men believe none so w. as themselves 1060.29
misfortune of w. better than prosperity of fool 17.25
mouth of w. man is in his heart 1060.20
not at once applauses of vulgar and approbation of w. 722.14
profitable if one is w. to seem foolish 139.1
rebuke a w. man, and he will love thee 803.3
smile with the w., feed with the rich 1048.30
state hurt when cunning pass for w. 930.3
the only wretched are the w. 447.26
these are reputed w. for saying nothing 898.25
the w. commit suicide or drink 1060.61
they who cannot be w. are cunning 200.2
time ripens all things; no man's born w. 978.12
to be free is not necessarily to be w. 1060.63
to be swift is less than to be w. 139.5
to be w. and love exceeds man's might 1060.54
to know others is learned; know self, w. 875.13
tongue of w. man lieth behind his heart 1060.34
useful knowledge makes a w. man 522.20
we find the w. man only in fragments 684.5
we old have no wits but we think us w. 653.26
when all is well, who cannot be w. 750.12
when ignorance is bliss, 'tis folly to be w. 447.15
w. among men bring most sorrow on selves 1060.19
w. are always impatient 1060.23
w. contradict themselves 1060.62
w. do not stand behind kicking ass 755.30
w. do not venture all eggs in one basket 755.4
w. heart is gods' best gift 284.13
w. man can play the fool on occasion 1060.21
w. man doth know himself to be a fool 1060.53
w. man is very rich, wanting nothing 1060.37
w. man lives as long as he ought, not can 548.8
w. man may be duped as well as a fool 356.7
w. man sings his joy in his heart 409.99
w. men are not w. at all times 1060.17
w. men are to bear mistakes of ignorant 271.1
w. men learn by others' harms 356.11
w. never refuse anything to necessity 624.14

wisecracking: w. is simply calisthenics with words 1061.21

wiser: do men grow w. as they grow older 653.45
to be w. is to be honester 1000.6

wisest: he that thinks self w. is greatest fool 1060.11
only w. can enjoy what they've got 704.37
w. man is boy grieving that he's grown 452.2
w. men follow own direction 867.7
w. men make fools of selves about women 581.50
w. professed to know he knew nothing 522.42

wish: granting our w.: fate's saddest joke 238.30
it would not be better if things happened to men just as they w. 238.21
overtaking a w. discovers folly 856.2
universal w. is a w. for heaven 238.37

wishes: like shadows, w. lengthen as sun declines 226.13
never further from our w. than when we imagine we posses what we desired 238.15
our inventions mirror our secret w. 201.11
we would be sorry if w. were gratified 238.2
when you love, saved-up w. come out 551.11

wishing: w. divorced from willing is sterile 238.32

wit: advantage of being a w.: gives one greater freedom of playing the fool 1061.22
banalities of a great man pass for w. 68.1
brevity is the soul of w. 1061.26
great fault of a w. is to go beyond mark 1061.15
if wealth waste, w. gives small warmth 718.44
impropriety is the soul of w. 1061.19
in midst of w. something bitter arises 1061.16
man must have w. to endure it in others 1061.3
men never think their w. too little 1061.7
mockery is often result of poverty of w. 820.3
more w. we have, less satisfied with it 1061.5
one never loves wittiest for their w. 551.159
people care more for reputation of w. 1061.27
quality of w. inspires more admiration than confidence 1061.25
true melancholy breeds perfect, fine w. 1011.18
true w. is that which falls on another 1061.13
who is a mere w. is only a human bauble 1061.1
wine gives man not knowledge or w. 268.31
w. has a deadly aim 1061.18
w. has truth in it 1061.21
w. in conversation is a quick conception and an easy delivery 188.30
w. is a shining quality that few love 1061.4
w. isn't a useful instrument of defense 1061.28
w. is salt of conversation, not the food 1061.11
w. is the epitaph of an emotion 1061.20
w. is the sudden marriage of ideas 1061.29
w. makes its own welcome 1061.6
w.: oft thought, ne'er so well expressed 1061.23
w. takes a nation a long time to acquire 1061.8
w. we wish we had spoils w. we have 1061.10
w. would be embarrassed without fools 1061.14

withdrawal: w. is practically a condition of safety 421.2

withdrew: The words that I w. too late 792.4

within: can men know what is w. them 1006.2
our greatest foes are w. 866.3

witnesses: eyes are more accurate w. than ears 897.5

wits: dullness of fool is whetstone of w. 356.21
first-rate collector can collect his w. 160.3
impertinent w. are a kind of universal insect 1061.12

witticism: he who cannot shine by thought, seeks to bring himself into notice by a w. 1061.30

witty: for repute of being w. many lose the credit of being sensible 1061.9
mouth of a w. man is hard until discharge 1061.2
no woman is w. only by the help of speech 1062.132

wives: all are good maids—whence come bad w. 1062.48
envy friends their w. and comforts 66.9
few w. so perfect that husbands do not daily repent marriage 564.72
most w. lead lives of quiet disapprobation 564.30
the sky changes when maids become w. 564.107
time turns our loves into corpses or w. 978.67
what makes men indifferent to their w.: they can see them when they please 564.97
w. are young men's mistresses 564.4
w. invariably flourish when deserted 472.6
w. not deserted: objects of commiseration 564.77
w. rarely fuss about their beauty 564.85

woe: how quick old w. follows a little bliss 1011.27
morning after w. surpasses all that rose before 1011.7
teach me to feel another's w. 583.2
the gentlest feeds on another's w. 561.11
when Jove gave us life, he gave us w. 1065.41

wolf: man is a w. to those he does not know 358.5
that man is a w. to man is a libel on the w. 41.11
whelp of w. must prove a w. at last 417.4
w. loses teeth, not his inclinations 226.12

woman: an unreasonable w. cherishes herself most when she is most wrong 1062.99

as a jewel of gold in a swine's snout, so is a fair w. without discretion 1062.11
as soon as w. gets husband, she wants everything else in the world 1062.73
as unjust to possess w. as slaves 716.13
a w. holds dreadful power over a man 551.203
a w. moved is like a fountain troubled 1062.127
a w. wishes to mother a man 864.6
beastliest beast of all is w. 1062.94
beautiful w. is a practical poet 1062.45
better to dwell in corner of housetop than with brawling w. in wide house 564.8
cleverest w. is biggest fool with a man 581.46
confidence still best with w. copes 857.1
did man e'er live saw priest, w. forgive 359.12
distinction for a homely w. to be loved for her character 1062.118
every w. is to be had almost any way 857.3
every w. thinks herself attractive 1062.106
fear w. who loves; all else has no value 1062.102
fill a w. with love of herself 198.3
hell has no fury like a w. scorned 793.1
how a little love, company improves a w. 1062.56
how many dynasties upset by love of w. 1042.99
if a handsome w. allows that another w. is beautiful, conclude she excels her 1062.83
if a w. wants a man, she has to appeal to what is worst in him 581.67
if w. had no existence save in the fiction written by men 1062.150
in argument with men a w. goes by worse 581.41
in new frock, faithful w. imagines a liaison 267.16
last thing w. will consent to discover in man she loves is want of courage 581.12
let no w. beguile your good sense 198.7
little girl without doll as unfortunate as w. without children 123.27
loveliest in w.: study of household good 564.82
make love to a w. if she is pretty 1062.148
man can deceive a w. by sham attachment 857.7
man is depressed until w. appears 581.19
man is for w. a means to a child 564.94
man married to w. who enjoys spending money must enjoy earning it 1065.42
man must brave public opinion, w. submit 762.20
man wants great deal here below, w. more 403.22
many a w. hates a man for being a friend to her 581.48
married to a good w., live with tender surprise 1062.90
most dangerous place for w. is her home 524.43
never fair w. but made mouths in a glass 593.5
no best w., only comparatively bad 1062.116
no creature so savage as w. 1062.51
no effrontery like that of w. 1062.81
no fouler fiend than w. with ill-bent mind 1062.69
no fury like w. searching for new lover 1062.32
none surpass sick w. in ruling 896.19
no w. doeth aught without a reason 581.9
no w. hates a man for being in love with her 581.48
no w. is beautiful who can be false 472.12
no w. is handsome by features alone 1062.132
old, that's affront no w. can bear 1062.21
one of magnanimities of w. is to yield 1062.76
only chaste w. is one not asked 122.10
only the w. of the world is a w. 1062.63
pretty w. likes to be asked for her favors 351.11
she wavers, hesitates: in short she is a w. 1062.121
silliest w. can manage a clever man 356.16
so primal is a w. with the love-madness 1062.15
talking is the passion of a w. 1062.86
talk to every w. as if you loved her 961.4
the land of emancipated and enthroned w. 355.12
there is no other purgatory but a w. 1062.8
the w. known only through a man is known wrong 581.2
to leave a w. one must annoy her 857.5
to lose husband worst woe for w. 564.36
tremble to win hand of w. unless win heart 198.6
truth is a w. 998.34
unusual for a married w. to work 581.5
variability is a virtue of a w. 1062.25
voice soft, low: excellent thing in w. 923.53
what but marriage goes wrong for w. 1062.53
what one beholds of w., least part of her 1062.108
what w. dares, when affection stirs her 1062.131
when a w. gets the idea of justice 517.4
when a w. is twenty, a child deforms her; at forty, he makes her young again 670.8
who is man enough releases w. in w. 581.43
with w.: you can love her, suffer for her, or turn her into literature 1062.40
w. brings out foolishness in man of sense 581.69
w. can be anything lover would have her be 1062.7
w. cannot forgive man for sacrifices made on her account 581.36
w. careful with face, careless with house 1062.80
w., central emblem of western art 581.21
w. dish for gods if devil dress her not 1062.126
w. doesn't spend all her time buying things 1062.72
w. don't love w. for what she says 1062.93
w. doubts everything except compliments 1062.74
w. is a monster without man as principal 581.23
w. is as old as she looks before breakfast 1062.71
w. is a vehicle of life 1062.18
w. is a w., but a good cigar is a smoke 982.7
w. is determined not by her hormones 1062.10
w. is man's confusion 581.64
w. is revolution; she destroys and creates 1062.146
w. is the daughter of Delay 1062.117
w. is woman's natural ally 1062.54
w. knows profit in matrimony is hers 564.78
w. loves or hates: no middle course 1062.120
w., man's dependent if not his slave 297.4
w. might as well propose 198.8
w. obliges man to secrecy, that she may have the pleasure of telling 855.4
w.: one of nature's agreeable blunders 1062.35
w. only sees what we don't do for her 1062.33
w. prefers man without money to money alone 1062.64
w. scoffs at evidence 1062.60
w. sees only weak points in strong man 581.25
w. seldom loves genius 1062.123
w. seldom writes her mind but in postscript 535.4
w. should always challenge our respect 1062.46
w. smells well when smells of nothing 685.3
w. springs a sudden reproach upon you 1062.141
w. talking about her baby can't stop 873.9
w. that loves to be at the window 857.4
w. understands children better than man 581.44
w. was God's second mistake 1062.104
w. was the temptress, the distraction 1062.140
w. who moralizes is invariably plain 604.49
w. will sacrifice self, given opportunity 1062.92
w. with staff of admirers 351.4
w. without bit of harlot in her is dry stick 892.27
w. would rather talk to man than angel 1062.68
womanly w. is too cynical to dream 566.4
would that we could fall into arms of w. without falling into her hands 1062.12
write what w. says to lover on water 1062.20
woman's: forgetting is w. first and greatest art 1062.2
man wallows in a w. weak-

ness 581.20
no is no negative in a w. mouth 791.6
there is in every w. heart a spark of heavenly fire 1062.78
to inspire love is w. greatest ambition 1062.98
when a w. in love she doesn't care two straws for Thou Shalt and Thou Shalt Not 581.37
w. desire for revenge outlasts emotions 1062.31
w. game is mediocre where no love, hate 1062.103
w. guess is more accurate than a man's certainty 581.29
w. hopes are woven of sunbeams 1062.42
w. life is history of the affections 1062.77
w. occupations run counter to creative life 1062.87
w. reason is in milk of her breasts 1062.97
w. strength is might of weakness 1062.47
w. vanity makes object of choice her idol 1062.65
womankind: w. ever a fickle and changeful thing 1062.145
women: American w. mortify the flesh 1062.100
amount of undesired sex endured by w. 564.104
an absence of any sexual interest in w. 582.14
as w. grow older they rely on cosmetics 581.42
at first w. love lovers, then love love 1062.84
beautiful in w. is something masculine 566.6
beautiful or ugly w. best flattered for their understandings 1062.24
beautiful w. counted among talents of husbands 581.33
beauty of w. evaporates when they trade independence for domestic happiness 564.25
charming w. can true converts make 690.6
could not possibly count the gold-digging ruses of w. 403.16
death laughs when old w. frolic 653.76
disposition of w.: when you will, they won't 1062.137
do you serve w. at this bar? 436.31
even most foolish w. are wise about men 581.50
fear of w. is basis of good health 66.7
first rule of game: w. can be caught 857.10
happiest w., like nations, have no history 1062.44
if men knew how w. pass the time when they are alone, they'd never marry 1062.67
• intimacies between w. go backwards 1062.13
kindness in w., not looks, shall win love 1062.129
kings, w., vines embrace what is nearest 1062.112
love of w. is lovely and fearful 1062.16
love's all in all to w. 1062.50
man's w. folk secretly regard him as an ass 581.40
many w. long for what eludes them 1062.107
men and w. agree only in conclusions 27.8
men are reason w. do not love one another 581.30
men must work and w. must weep 539.65
more w. are keeping their *birth* names 619.9
most w. have all other w. as adversaries 581.8
most w. have small waists, big desires 1062.138
muses never sang about liberated w. 581.4
music and w. I cannot but give way to 704.28
nastiness of w. perceived at close of life 1062.139
nature of w. not to love when we love 1062.22
offered w. the Miss America beauty pageant 297.6
one must choose loving or knowing w. 1062.85
piety in w. is passion, infirmity, fashion 697.8
relations of men and w. like an equation 581.34
sorrows of w. would be averted could they repress speech they know is useless 1062.43
sweet is revenge—especially to w. 817.5
the difficulty is that I like w. 1062.133
time, circumstance, narrow views of w. 581.22
to most w. art is a form of scandal 1062.57
ugly w. learn to suppress their whims 1062.58
vivacity is the gift of w. 566.1
whipped single w. into marital panic 564.40
with w., the heart argues, not the mind 1062.5
w. adore failures 329.24
w. alone order sole, it means something 355.6
w. and men are simply different races 581.35
w. are a decorative sex 1062.149
w. are afraid to be considered only w. 566.5
w. are as roses 1062.130
w. are best index of the coming hour 501.2
w. are burrowing animals 1062.41
w. are eagerly on lookout for any emotion 1062.136
w. are equal because they are not different 1062.59
w. are foolish: God made 'em to match men 581.13
w. are like dreams—never the way you would like to have them 1062.115
w. are like riddles; they please us no longer once we know them 1062.119
w. are like the arts, forced unto none 1062.39
w. are most fascinating between thirty-five and forty 1062.38
w. are one and all a set of vultures 1062.114
w. are silver dishes into which we put golden apples 892.23
w. are to admire, not understand 1062.29
w. attached, men cured by w.'s favors 581.31
w. can be vivacious; men, rocklike 581.57
w. can change name and nation 564.49
w.: can't live with or without them 1062.4
w. consider consequences in love, seldom in resentment 1062.27
w., crabs seem to be coming when going 247.4
w. differ as heaven and hell 581.60
w. discovered pants during World War II 338.13
w. don't mock the tears men shed unless they themselves are responsible for them 1062.34
w. dress well where they undress often 267.9
w., easy meat for commerce of fashion 338.4
w., elephants never forget an injury 1062.124
w. enjoy sick talk of one another 1062.52
w. fear endangering men's approval 49.2
w. hate revolutionists and like docile men 819.33
w. have a very positive moral sense 1062.1
w. have contempt for woman 1062.105
w. have no sense of the abstract 1062.62
w. have simple tastes 1062.96
w. have their own egos to keep up 1062.142
w. in power, no wind can upset them 1062.49
w. in the old China did not choose 742.5
w., invariably deceivers, inconstant and lecherous 581.62
w. kissing resemble fighters shaking hands 1062.95
w., like Cape Hatteras, are enormously dangerous and hence enormously fascinating 581.39
w., like flames, have a destroying power 1062.30
w., like princes, find few real friends 1062.88
w. like silent men; think they listen 581.1
w. like to be a man's last romance 581.68
w. like w. fine 1062.89
w. looked like great sea snails 45.15
w. love flattery from high opinion of themselves 349.19
w. made such swell friends 365.54
w. make new experience an ornament 321.38
w. marry to be in hub of things 564.10
w., men do not respond to their troubles 366.5
w. must continue to provide cheap labor 1065.37
w. never confess sincerely 1062.61
w. never reason and thus are seldom wrong 1062.66
w. not so young as they are painted 192.1
w. rarely look into themselves 1062.122
w., secret conspiracy of hearts and pheromones 1062.111
w. see without any wish to act 683.5
w. singly do a good deal of

harm 1062.26
w. speak because they wish to 581.28
w. strongest when armed with their weaknesses 1062.36
w., supreme realists of the race 783.5
w. take too little pains to please men 581.47
w. think it their business to spend money 581.52
w. upset everything 581.53
w. use intelligence to prop up intuition 1062.37
w. want mediocre men 581.38
w. who write as w., engaged in politics of sex 1062.110
w. wish to be loved simply for themselves 1062.3
w. won't or can't do otherwise than lie 1062.17
w. would make less failures in business 581.65
w. would rather be right than reasonable 1062.101
women's: w. bodies shaped to bear children 670.34
w. hearts are like old china 552.8
w. words, light as doomed autumn leaves 1062.109
wonder: philosophy begins and ends in w. 694.43
there are always moments of w. 1063.2
w. is foundation of all philosophy 694.24
w. is the basis of worship 1063.1
w. is the seed of our science 1063.3
wonderful: we think we're w., doesn't mean we are 431.29
wonders: we carry with us the w. we seek without 858.5
wood: w. ten years in water will never become a crocodile 118.1
woodland: w. in color is awesome as a forest fire 995.2
woods: how much we are the w. we wander in 858.30
word: always swayed by power of the w. 1064.3
best way to keep w. is not to give it 743.8
break w. if you do worse to keep it 743.4
honest man's w. good as his bond 425.1
if people have no w. for something, either it doesn't matter or it matters too much 1064.18
man is seldom better than his w. 119.1
man's w. believed to extent of wealth 1000.10
no w. was ever as effective as a pause 898.30
one can add a w., never withdraw one 923.23
soon the w. reappeared in an illumination 1064.33
suit action to w., the w. to action 901.18
the w. is most imprecise of signs 1064.17
to persuade, trust w., not argument 690.3
when thing itself missing, must supply w. 1064.36
who filches from me a good w. 1064.27
w. and stone cannot be called back 507.5
w. carries far, deals destruction 1064.9
w. is dead when it is said, some say 1064.11
w. isn't same with one writer as another 1064.40
w. preserves contact 923.42
w. spoken in due season, how good is it 979.1
words: acts and w. are wee part of a life 818.4
comprehending much in few w. 98.1
culture is perishing in an avalanche of w. 210.16
false w. infect the soul with evil 558.37
gold does more with men than w. 99.2
gumming together long strips of w. 1064.38
hard w. bruise the heart of a child 123.35
how forcible are right w. 822.1
in good writing w. and things are one 1069.38
it's strange that w. are so inadequate 1064.12
less disputes in world if w. taken for signs of ideas, not for things themselves 1064.30
lofty w. cannot construct an alliance 247.5
man determines what is said, not w. 923.62
man does not live by w. alone 1064.48
meanings receive dignity from w. 1064.39
men are ready to suffer anything but w. 206.13
men of few w. are the best men 98.8
men's w. hardly signify their thoughts 349.17
most moving moments find us without w. 898.15
nothing less free than row of four-letter w. 363.46
oaths are but w., and w. but wind 643.2
only w. can give us a sense of purpose 1064.21
our thoughts are unclear until put into w. 1064.6
perfumed and gallant w. make ears belch 349.1
pleasant w. are the food of love 923.45
proper w. in proper places make style 942.20
saddest w. are: it might have been 507.9
shortness is a merit in w. 1064.15
soft w. like roses put in muskets 440.14
some things not totally expressible in w. 492.6
things diminished when expressed in w. 1064.32
those for whom w. have lost their value 443.25
those who run to long w. are mainly the unskillful 1064.16
thought flies, w. go on foot 1069.57
thought itself needs w. 1064.5
to teacher of languages, world a place of w. 524.9
w. without thoughts never to heaven go 723.31
we find w. for things already overcome 1064.37
we leave school filled only with w. 279.23
we must translate w. into facts 1064.22
where w. abound sense is rarely found 1064.42
w. are drowned in visual soup 967.26
w. are healers of the sick temper 758.1
w. are pegs to hang ideas on 1064.4
w. are the great foes of reality 1064.10
w. are the small change of thought 1064.44
w. are the weak support of indifference 551.28
w. are thread to string our experiences 1064.23
w. are wise men's counters, fools' money 1064.20
w. calculated to catch everyone may catch no one 474.6
w. can sting but silence breaks the heart 898.13
w. change us, socialize or unsocialize us 1064.45
w. fall on picture like birds of prey 1064.43
w. half reveal, conceal the soul within 1064.50
w. have no language for secrets of love 551.87
w. have users, but users have w. 1064.24
w. have weight, sound and appearance 1064.34
w. may be deeds 1064.1
w. obscure if they do not aid vision 1064.25
w. pay no debts 222.11
w. should be intense pleasure 1064.51
w. stand for ideas in mind of user 1064.31
w. the happy say are paltry melody 898.3
w. were usually ejected in lumps 923.5
worst sickness: w. that to be kind must lie 519.1
you can stroke people with w. 1064.14
work: all w. is empty save when there is love 1065.33
any w. looks wonderful except what I do 868.3
artists regard w. as play and play as w. 1065.60
blessed is he who has found his w. 1037.4
cessation of w. not accompanied by cessation of expenses 813.1
day's w. is still to do 1065.30
efficient laborer will not crowd his day with w. 1066.5
every man's w. is a portrait of himself 53.18
greatest reward is to have w. acclaimed 207.36
happiness is sweet exhalation of w. 1065.36
hard, continuous and varied w. and living 404.1
he that can w. is king of something 1065.16
he who considers his w. beneath him will be above doing it well 1065.18
I do my intellectual w. inside myself 880.20
if you w. by the job, hours are scourges 1066.6
if you want w. well done, select busy man 10.8
in w., reward added makes pleasure greater 680.5
insists on getting some useful w. done 1065.13
it is the punishment of man

to hate his w. 1065.64
it's necessary to w., even from despair 1065.6
life's best prize is chance to w. hard 1065.61
love, children, w.: sources of contact 504.20
man unable to find w. is saddest sight 1009.1
man's w. is supplement to himself 1065.9
many could make life seem longer with w. 1065.51
meaning has been drained from w. 1065.4
men must w. and women must weep 539.65
men rightly occupied derive amusement from w. 1037.10
minds give way unless we mix w. with play 703.5
much w. merely a way to make money 602.40
no fine w. without toil and doubt 1065.10
nothing seen, heard will reach mind concentrated on w. 1065.58
only thing that a man can do eight hours a day is w. 1065.29
people w. greater part of their time 1065.34
prosperity takes w. away from us 750.9
rightly done task is world's w. 1065.73
those who w. much do not w. hard 1065.68
to crush a man give him useless w. 1065.21
too much w., energy kill a man 312.5
to w. is better than to renounce 10.2
to w., live, die hard and go to hell 416.10
what is w.? what is not? perplexes wise 1065.11
when w. is a pleasure, life is a joy 1065.35
who invented w. and bound free spirit down 1065.48
who pays beforehand has w. ill done 680.6
who will not w. according to his faculty 1065.17
w. expands to fill time available 1065.56
w. is not the curse, but drudgery is 1065.8
w. is prayer, also stink 1065.44
w. spares us evils: boredom, vice, need 1065.70
w. was defined as what men did 1065.65
w. well done invests doer with a certain haughtiness 1065.24
worked: when they were on their uppers, she w. 624.3
worker: democracy has given the w. more dignity 233.31
workhouses: even w. have their aristocracy 780.3
working: it isn't w. that's hard 231.10
workman: bad w. never gets a good tool 463.3
bad w. quarrels with the man who calls him that 463.1
no pleasure subtler than being a good w. 1065.53
no w. may both work well and hastily 411.2
workmanship: instinct of w. will take care of honesty 201.23
works: all w. conceived in solitude 915.24
every man is son of his own w. 867.2
faith without w. is dead 330.5
my nature is subdued to what it w. in 1065.63
my w. are my children 53.87
world: an entire w. becoming just like us 683.6
as if some lesser god had made the w. 457.8
a w. created by and for women 1062.144
childish w. pleased with each new revolution or constitution 819.9
easy to divide your outlook on the w. 689.1
exaggerating our power to remake the w. 309.1
feet in own country, but eyes survey w. 193.3
few persons with high aim and great powers could rule w. 442.3
foolishness excommunicates the w. 354.12
had we but w. enough, and time 857.9
he taught his people and the w. 511.3
in remaking w. we violate kinship of nature 294.4
in the morning we carry the w. like Atlas; at night it crushes us flat 540.2
invented w. must live at the same time as world we live in 436.30
in youth, one believes w. began with him 1071.26
it is a folly to try to improve the w. 790.22
knowledge of the w. acquired in w. 321.6
living in a w. made by man, for man 1067.2
living in the w. of absolute good and evil 390.14
look on w., read truth in her fair page 998.13
many come into, go out of w., ignorant 447.24
maybe each human being lives in unique w. 915.12
mind creates the w. about us 590.8
mind has transformed the w. 590.20
more we get out of w., the less we leave 177.9
most incomprehensible thing about the w. is that it is comprehensible 1067.9
my country is w.; countrymen, mankind 100.6
no better deliverance from w. than art 53.57
nonexistence of w. as possible as existence 1067.19
not certain the w. will remember me 804.20
once w. has used us ill, it continues with less ceremony, as men do a whore 549.7
real w. is not easy to live in 784.7
roam abroad in w. and take its enjoyments 992.42
see a w. in a grain of sand 623.6
there is the w. to live in 100.3
the w. and the men in it are greater than we 869.8
the w. does not live in country clubs 1067.12
this is hard w. where mistakes paid for in full 299.13
this w. cannot explain its difficulties without assistance of another 414.1
this w. is still a miracle 1067.6
this w. was formed to infuriate us 1067.28
to him who looks on the w. rationally 1067.17
to say "no" when the w. wants to hear "yes" 119.13
truly comic, invented w. 436.30
visible w. only an atom in nature 1017.12
we do not make w. of our own 487.6
we milk cow of the w. 1067.30
what's wrong with this w. is, it's not finished yet 1067.11
when w. clowns, something else than comic 1042.81
w. a comedy if men think; tragedy, if feel 1067.29
w. a volume larger than libraries in it 1067.16
w. born anew for him who takes it rightly 729.18
w. credits what is done, is cold to all that might have been 717.6
w. ends not with a bang but a whimper 1067.10
w. exists in your eyes—your conception 1067.13
w. full of nothing but beasts of prey 26.1
w. goes on because some men believe in it 1067.22
w. grows bigger as the light leaves it 217.4
w. is a bride, never bound to anyone 1067.14
w. is a bundle of hay 1067.5
w. is a fine place, worth fighting for 1067.18
w. is a great volume, man the index 1067.7
w. is a neighborhood before a brotherhood 1067.20
w. is an old woman 1026.4
w. is a thing we must either laugh at or be angry at 1067.24
w. is full of simpletons and madmen 559.7
w. is gambling-table; all lose in long run 1067.3
w. is hard to love, but we must love it 1067.8
w. is his who has money to go over it 992.19
w. is right, but you have to be kicked about a little to convince you 321.50
w. is sick for lack of the elemental 177.2
w. is so full of a number of things 1067.26
w. is too much with us 104.37
w. is white no longer 1054.1
w. owes onward impulses to men ill at ease 741.6
w. saved by disinterested men in it 1021.4
w., terrible in mass, pitiable in units 1067.15
world's: w. curriculum doesn't include Latin and Greek 279.53
worldly: be wisely w.; be not w. wise 917.6
worlds: so many w. are at our disposal 53.111

so many w., so much to do 717.5
w. on w. rolling from creation to decay 990.15
worm: engineers, physicists, cannot create a w. 966.15
fate of w. shows danger of early rising 73.1
w., your clan will pay me back 221.100
worries: fine w., at their best after mellowed 43.6
freedom from w., surcease from strain, are illusions 533.15
w. go down better with soup than without 43.17
worry: in war, never w. about doing the right thing 1042.98
rather w. without need 755.2
worship: all men w. money 602.61
no liberty on earth if men w. tyrant above 797.40
so long as men w. them, Caesars and Napoleons will rise, make them miserable 1002.15
where it is a duty to w. the sun 1068.7
wonder is the basis of w. 1063.1
worst: the w. of being poor 625.3
there is so much good in the w. of us 206.11
w. is not so long can say "this the w." 17.54
worth: beauty dies of beauty, w. dies of w. 975.58
everything is w. what purchaser will pay 1026.18
man's w. no greater than w. of ambitions 33.1
men understand w. of blessings when lost 1026.17
outside show poor substitute for inner w. 45.1
slow rises w. by poverty depressed 718.38
so much is a man w. as he esteems himself 869.10
those who do well what is not w. doing at all 972.34
worthy: difficult to make man miserable while he feels w. and claims kindred to God 869.6
wound: history of soldier's w. beguiles its pain 946.47
search not a w. too deep 960.4
wounded: w. deer leaps highest 946.9
wounds: we unbind old w. to prove our past bravery 653.71
w. cannot be cured without searching 476.3
w. heal and become scars; but scars grow 476.13
wrath: background of w. lies in every man 39.8
be swift to hear, slow to w. 167.3
let not the sun go down upon your w. 39.6
tigers of w. are wiser than horses of instruction 39.7
wretched: where two, one cannot be w., other not 1011.10
w. are fortunate: they yearn for happiness 238.19
w. reflect either too much or too little 1011.28
wretchedness: hardly possible to exaggerate man's w. 1011.32
wrinkles: when grace is joined with w. 653.51
within I find not w. but unspent youth 653.24
w.: service stripes in campaign of life 326.2
write: anyone who attempts to w. satirically 630.39
bad book as hard to w. as good book 93.43
better to be able neither to read, w. than to be able to do nothing else 279.37
difficulty of literature is not to w., but to w. what you mean 1069.125
every time you w. you've got to w. 1069.118
having imagination, it takes longer to w. 1069.1
i never think at all when i w. 1069.87
it is the glory, merit of some men to w. well, and of others not to w. at all 1069.75
man may w. at any time 1069.67
man who can w. great works is still a man 401.40
multitude w.; why no work of worth 1069.22
nobody can w. life of a man but friends 81.6
no man can w. unless a humanitarian 1069.43
no one can w. about anything that happened to him after he was twelve 1069.120
some speak well and w. badly 923.47
the best you w. will be best you are 1069.129
to w. clear style, be clear in thoughts 942.9
who can't w. grammerly better shut up shop 398.11
who does not expect a million readers should not w. a line 1069.55
who would w. and can't w. can review 207.32
you can't teach people to w. well 1069.136
you w. because you've got something to say 1069.45
writer: a w. doesn't write for his readers, does he? 1069.58
developed w. reminds us of no one 1069.84
duty of w. to shock 1069.66
every great w. is a w. of history 1069.79
every great w. must create the taste by which he is to be relished 1069.149
good w. is not per se good book critic 207.6
great w. finds style in his soul 942.7
if you would be a w., write 1069.40
in Australia one explains what a w. is 1069.30
thought flies and words go on foot; therein lies all the drama of a w. 1069.57
tragic w. must believe in man 987.8
unless a w. is extremely old when he dies 221.10
until a true w. comes along 1069.72
when we convert a w. into a symbol 1069.73
word isn't the same with one w. as another 1064.40
your business as a w. is not to illustrate virtue 1069.137
w. does not resign himself to loneliness 1069.91
w. for the schoolmasters of ever afterward 1069.44
w. is Faust of today; seems semi-mad 1069.104
w. is man alone with English language 1069.65
w. is more concerned to know than to judge 1069.90
w. is simple-minded, a storyteller 1069.20
w. must never be unfaithful to readers 1069.10
w. needs experience, observation, imagination 1069.42
w. needs no audience other than the few 1069.133
w. ought to know thoroughly one man at least 1069.26
w. who loses self-doubt should stop 1069.27
writer's: sin is the w. element 1069.92
way to get anything out of a w. brains 1069.135
w. greed is appalling 1069.14
w. life in relation to his work 1069.51
w. life seethes within but not without 1069.18
writers: clear w. do not seem so deep as they are 1069.78
don't listen to w. talking about writing 1069.59
every country has w. she deserves 1069.127
fame is promised w. who can offer successive generations a renewed substance 1069.52
humorous w. are responsive to hopeless, uncouth concatenations of life 436.25
subjunctive brings all w. to shame 398.10
w. are not just people who sit down and write 1069.35
w. begin their existence imitatively 451.10
w. cannot truthfully be comic 1069.128
w., dissatisfied with books they could buy 1069.15
w., fascinating because there are so many kinds 1069.119
w. wish not to be studied but read 93.45
writes: man tormented by his bad actions is type that most often w. about himself 405.11
mediocre mind thinks it w. divinely 1069.74
who w. to himself w. to eternal public 1069.37
writing: admiration of fine w. is in proportion to its real difficulty and apparent ease 1069.28
book w. makes horse racing look solid 1069.124
does anybody learn w.? 1069.12
good w. is product of someone's neurosis 1069.126
heard knocking on bedroom door after finished w. of *Macbeth*? 201.18
incurable itch for w. besets many 1069.70
in good w. words and things become one 1069.38
in w., whatever conveys

meaning is justified 1069.106
last thing one settles in w. a book 1069.103
no w. is more apt to miscarry than humour 1069.3
people won't realize w. is craft 1069.110
secret of good w. is sound judgment 1069.63
take away w., you take away glory 386.2
there is no royal path to good w. 1069.140
to start w. about your life is to stop living it 62.8
true ease in w. comes from art not chance 1069.109
when w. is good, everything is symbolic 1069.98
w., at its best, is a lonely life 1069.61
w. comes more easily with something to say 1069.8
w. has laws, just as painting does 1069.21
w. humor not as dangerous as performing it 434.1
w. is a mode of being 1069.85
w. is an undertaking for the modest 1069.97
w. is a vocation of unhappiness 1069.121
w. lonely substitute for conversation 1069.9
w. maketh an exact man 1069.13
w. of oneself one should show no mercy 62.2
w. rapidly does not result in w. well 1069.114
w., something writer dreads or likes 1069.131
w., the desire to carve words on a tombstone 1069.145
w. the last page of a book—sublimity 1069.116
you don't get creative w. like that anymore 18.4
you end by w. so as not to die 1069.48
you should not read about w. while w. 1069.105
written: so much already w. about everything 522.60
what is w. without effort is in general read without pleasure 1069.69
wrong: a possibility of several things going w. 17.10
better to suffer w. than do it 476.8
forgetting a w. is mild revenge 476.9
habit of not thinking a thing w. 790.26
he who is w. fights against himself 299.15
if everyone is w., everyone is right 299.8
if one does w., best to do it pursuing power 1070.8
man owning he has been in the w. is wiser to-day than he was yesterday 299.31
men look for w. even in the righteous 259.10
nobly w. more manly than meanly right 635.4
no peace from acquiescence in w. 46.6
terrible to speak well and be w. 763.15
they ne'er pardon who have done the w. 359.4
those fond of setting things to rights have no objection to seeing them w. 790.12
those who are absent are always w. 2.5
to do a great right, do a little w. 822.18
to go beyond is as w. as to fall short 312.2
truth forever on scaffold, w. on throne 998.77
we are conscious someone w. when w. concerns us 299.28
we condemn w. when it costs us nothing 822.9
we go right enough if we go w. together 983.2
what is divine purpose in putting us into conditions in which so many go w. 307.21
w. enmeshes him from whom it begins 1070.15
w. is deep, clear, and absolute 477.16
w. is that against my constitution 822.7
w. is w., no matter who does, says it 678.12
w. must not win by technicalities 528.1
you cannot do w. without suffering w. 1070.6
you will never find an Englishman in the w. 289.30
wrongdoer: for a w. to be undetected is difficult 1070.7
w. cannot do wrong without hidden will of all 1070.10
w. wrongs himself 1070.2
wronged: since I w. you, I have never liked you 476.19
wrongs: everyone suffers w. which have no remedy 476.10
he that w. his friend w. himself more 476.21
wrote: only a blockhead ever w. except for money 1069.68

Y

Yankee: The Y. is one who, if he once gets his teeth set on a thing 34.24
year: drop last y. into silent limbo of past 631.1
moments make the y. 996.13
y. is going, let him go 631.5
year's: changing y. plan proclaims mortality to man 854.25
y. end is neither an end nor a beginning 631.2
years: count man's y. when nothing else to count 653.23
men spoke grammatically for thousands of y. 398.9
our y. glide silently away 653.48
passing y. steal one thing after another 226.5
y. between fifty and seventy hardest 586.6
y. following y. steal something every day 978.51
y. like great black oxen tread world 978.78
yellowed: y. like a dried apricot at the end 916.15
yes: to say y. you must sweat, roll up sleeves 504.1
y. is the password to utopia 504.3
yesterday: mortgaged to y., we cannot use today 676.12
we are but of y. 990.4
y. is not ours to recover 368.18
yesterday's: today is y. pupil 729.14
yesterdays: all our y. are summarized in our now 729.3
yield: y. to all and you will soon have nothing to y. 46.1
you: y. are, when all is done, just what y. are 444.10
young: advice of elders to y. unreal 19.13
a family in which the y. are thwarted 1071.51
all things are made y. with y. desires 854.44
animals disarmed by caresses to their y. 670.26
crab instructs y.: walk straight ahead 310.2
denunciation of y. necessary to old 653.90
errors of y. men are ruin of business 299.1
for the y. things move so fast 117.25
growing old is dying y. 653.66
if we're not foolish y., we're foolish old 354.4
love, with the y., is heartless 551.37
no y. man believes he shall ever die 1071.30
one must, when y., consider old age 1072.11
pay attention to y., make them good 1071.58
the y. demand sincerity 901.11
the y. fancy their follies are mistaken by the old for happiness 1072.5
the y. have nothing to say 1072.3
the y. man reveres men of genius 376.12
those who love the y. best stay y. longest 1071.19
to remain y. one must change 117.6
when a man notices he is no longer y. 586.15
while y., idea of death, failure, intolerable 1071.13
wish to teach sad y. generation the courage of their confusions 1001.2
women are not so y. as they are painted 192.1
y. and full of stupendous illusions 34.3
y. can shock and keep old up to date 1072.22
y. climber up of knees 123.34
y. faithful to individuals; old, to types 556.2
y. know everything 1072.30
y. man must let his ideas grow 443.19
y. man never feels that he is mortal 1071.41
y. man: so strong, mad, certain, and lost 1071.62
y. man who has not wept is savage 1072.20
y. men fitter to invent than to judge 1071.3
y. men regard elders as senile 1071.1
y. men want to be faithful, and are not 472.16
y. people get mental arteriosclerosis 1071.34
y. people thoughtless as a rule 1071.31
y. people, unbridled, now just want 1071.46
y. permanently in state like intoxication 1071.2
y. suffer from cautiousness of the old 1072.29

y. think old fools, old know y. are fools 1072.4
y. today given education, not upbringing 279.20
y. venerate and despise without nuances 1071.49
younger: happier when poorer, but were also y. 1071.42
to decry y. generation dates a man 374.16
young men: y. get their likes and dislikes from Mencken 656.9
youngster: y. who does not know what he is good at 1.6
yourself: be y. and think for y. 880.10
for impenetrable shield, stand inside y. 31.8
respect y. if you wish others to do so 869.4
you live and die according to what goes on in y. 858.25
youth: affected y. is seeking a face of his own 1071.57
age looks with anger on temerity of y. 1072.10
age not as qualified to instruct as y. 1072.27
allowances made for illusions of y. 1072.25
American y. attributes importance to arriving at driver's-license age 34.47
Americans try to perpetuate y. 34.57
better waste y. than do nothing with it 1071.11
every industrial society has a y. problem 737.2
give me back my y. again 1071.27
how beautiful is y. 1071.43
if we have y., it is easy to be nice 186.18
immature is the love and hatred of the y. 1071.48
impetuous y. longs only for the dazzling 1072.19
in early y. we are like children in a theatre 1071.56
in y., one believes world began with him 1071.26
in y. we clothe ourselves in rainbows 1071.16
it is an illusion that y. is happy 1071.44
life is thorny; y. is vain 39.11
life should begin with age, end with y. 1072.28
man laments y. more than imprudences 653.97
may return to birthplace, but not y. 676.7
must not take faults of y. into old age 653.37
nature, in denying us perennial y. 571.14
not possible for civilization to flow backward while there is y. in the world 1071.38
now y. are fallen from their fear 1072.13
our y. we can have but today 1071.6
recovering the spirit of y., one's indignation would be for what one has become 162.3
riotous y., growing age will correct 1071.36
sign of passing y.: birth of fellowship 571.21
time is the rider that breaks y. 978.31
tragedy of y. is that the young are thrown with adults they do not respect 1071.45
unwept, y. drops its petals one by one 606.20
we are a people afraid of its y. 1071.28
with a smile we should instruct our y. 965.27
within I find not wrinkles but unspent y. 653.24
y. believes it will get away with anything 1072.2
y. blows through sky, does not ask why 1071.5
y. even in sorrows has own brilliancy 1071.33
y. forgives itself nothing 1072.23
y. gets together materials to build a bridge to the moon 254.7
y. immortal; only elderly grow old 1072.17
y. is a blunder; old age a regret 540.5
y. is a fever of the mind 1071.40
y. is first victim of war 1042.3
y. is full of pleasance; age, of care 1072.21
y. is season of hope in the sense that our elders are hopeful about us 1071.15
y. is the time to flash across the world 1071.59
y. is to be regarded with respect 1071.10
y. measures right by world opinion 1072.12
y. of America is their oldest tradition 34.86
y. of an art is its most interesting period 53.19
y. of a nation are trustees of posterity 1071.14
y. smiles without reason 1071.60
y. thinks that all must heed its prayer 1071.39
y. want to defy at not too heavy cost 1071.12
y. wasted on bare period of my desires 1071.35
y. without fire is followed by old age without experience 1072.6
youth's: alas, that y. manuscript should close 1071.50
y. the season made for joys 1071.22
youths: excesses of our y. are drafts on old age 1071.9
Z
zeal: have z. to better thyself, then neighbour 460.4
too much z. offends where indirection works 690.5
z. will do more than knowledge 1073.2
z. without knowledge is fire without light 1073.1
zest: what hunger is to food, z. is to life 513.7
z. is the secret of all beauty 513.2

Index of Categories

Ability 1
EXCELLENCE 311
TALENT 962
VOCATIONS 1037

Absence 2
PARTING 673

Abstinence
SELF-DENIAL 865

The Absurd 3
ABSURDITY 4
ALIENATION 30
EXISTENTIALISM 317
MEANING 573

Absurdity 4
THE ABSURD 3
RIDICULE 820

Accident
CHANCE 116

Accomplishment
ABILITY 1
ACHIEVEMENT 6

Accusation 5
CRITICISM 206
JUDGING OTHERS 515
SLANDER 905

Achievement 6
AMBITION 33
ASPIRATION 55
SUCCESS 945

Acquaintances 7
COMPANY 152
FRIENDSHIP 365

Acquisition 8
GREED 403
MONEY 602
POSSESSION 716
PROPERTY 746

Action 9
ACTIVITY 10
DEEDS 227
INVOLVEMENT 504
THEORY 974

Activity 10
ACTION 9
COMPULSIVENESS 163
HASTE 411
IDLENESS 446
INVOLVEMENT 504
LEISURE 533
RESTLESSNESS 812

Actors 11
AUDIENCE 59
COMEDIANS 144
THEATER 972

Adaptation
ADJUSTMENT 12

Adjustment 12
CONFORMITY 171
NORMALITY 637

Administration 13
EXECUTIVES 315

Admiration 14
APPROVAL 49
FOLLOWING 353
HONORS 426
POPULARITY 712
RESPECT 808
WORSHIP 1068

Adolescence
YOUTH 1071

Adultery
INFIDELITY 472

Advantage 15
COMPARISON 153
COMPENSATION 154
LOSERS 549

Adventure 16
DANGER 216
EXCITEMENT 313

Adversity 17
COMPARISON 153
COMPENSATION 154
COMPLAINT 157
CONSOLATIONS 180
DEFEAT 228
DIFFICULTY 245
ENDURANCE 287
FAILURE 329
LOSERS 549
LOSS 550
PROSPERITY AND ADVERSITY 751
SUFFERING 946

Advertising 18
BUSINESS AND COMMERCE 104
BUYING AND SELLING 105
PROPAGANDA 745
PUBLICITY 760

Advice 19

Aesthetics 20
ART AND ARTISTS 53
BEAUTY 72
CRITICISM, PROFESSIONAL 207
MUSIC 614
POETRY AND POETS 708
WRITING AND WRITERS 1069

Affectation
APPEARANCE 45
PRETENSION 732

Affection 21
AFFINITY 22
EMOTIONS 284
FRIENDSHIP 365
LOVE 551

Affinity 22
ASSOCIATION 57

African-Americans 23
BLACKS 85

Afterlife
HEAVEN 414
HELL 416
IMMORTALITY 454

Afterthought 24

Age
ERA 298
MIDDLE AGE 586
OLD AGE 653
YOUTH 1071

Agents 25
BUSINESS AND COMMERCE 104
BUYING AND SELLING 105

Aggravation
IRRITATIONS 508

Aggression 26
COMPETITION 155
FORCE 357
SELF-ASSERTION 859
VIOLENCE 1032
WAR 1042

Agnosticism
DOUBT, RELIGIOUS 265
SKEPTICISM 904
UNBELIEF 1004

Agreement 27
APPEASEMENT 46
ARGUMENT 51
COMPROMISE 162
CONCILIATION 167
DISCORD 252
QUARRELING 772
TREATIES 994

Agriculture
FARMS AND FARMING 337

Aid
ASSISTANCE 56

Aim
ENDS 286

Aim *(cont.)*
PURPOSE 771

Airplanes 28
TRANSPORTATION 991

Air Pollution 29

Alienation 30
THE ABSURD 3
DEADNESS, SPIRITUAL 219
ENNUI 290
ESCAPE 300
INDIFFERENCE 466
SOLITUDE 915

Aloofness 31
COLDNESS 142
TOGETHERNESS 983

Alternation 32

Altruism
HUMANITARIANISM 433

Ambition 33
ACHIEVEMENT 6
ASPIRATION 55
ENTERPRISE 291
SUCCESS 945

Ambivalence
CONFLICT, INNER 170

America and Americans 34
CALIFORNIA 106
CANADA 107
HOLLYWOOD 421
NEW ENGLAND 628
NEW YORK 632
WASHINGTON, D.C. 1044

Amusement
ENTERTAINMENT 292
HUMOR 436
LAUGHTER 526

Analogy 35
LANGUAGE 524

Anarchy 36
GOVERNMENT 395
SOCIETY 913

Ancestry 37
BIRTH 83
EVOLUTION 308

Angels 38
HEAVEN 414

Anger 39
CURSING 212
INDIGNATION 467
TEMPER, BAD 968

Anglo-Saxons 40

Animals 41
BIRDS 82
FISH 347
INSECTS 481
INSTINCT 486

Answer
INQUIRY 480

Anticipation
EXPECTATION 318
WAITING 1040

Antiquity 42
CLASSICS 136
GREECE, ANCIENT 402
HISTORY AND HISTORIANS 419
PAST 676
TRADITION 986

Ants
INSECTS 481

Anxiety 43
FEAR 343
INSECURITY 482
SELF-DOUBT 868

Apathy
DEADNESS, SPIRITUAL 219
INDIFFERENCE 466

Apology 44
REGRET 792

Appearance 45
ARTIFICIALITY 54
COSMETICS 192
DRESS 267
FASHION 338
HAIR 407
IDENTITY 444
PRETENSION 732
ROLE-PLAYING 825

Appeasement 46
AGREEMENT 27
COMPROMISE 162
CONCILIATION 167
TREATIES 994

Appetite
DESIRES 238
GREED 403
HUNGER 437
INTEMPERANCE 494
TEMPERANCE 970

Appreciation 47
APPRECIATION, LACK OF 48
APPROVAL 49
GRATITUDE 399
PRAISE 722
VALUE 1026

Appreciation, Lack of 48
APPRECIATION 47
INGRATITUDE 475

Appropriateness
SUITABILITY 949

Approval 49
ADMIRATION 14
APPRECIATION 47
INGRATIATION 474
POPULARITY 712
PRAISE 722

April
SEASONS 854

Aptitude
ABILITY 1
GENIUS 376
TALENT 962

Architecture 50
ART AND ARTISTS 53
DESIGN 237
HOUSES 430

Argument 51
DISCORD 252
DISSENT 258
OPINION 656
PERSUASION 690
QUARRELING 772
REASON 785

Aristocracy 52
CLASS 135
MIDDLE CLASS 587
THE PEOPLE 682
RANK 780
SOCIETY 913

Arithmetic
MATHEMATICS 570

Arms
DEFENSE 229
THE MILITARY 588
NUCLEAR POWER 641
WAR 1042
WEAPONS 1049

Army
THE MILITARY 588

Art and Artists 53
AESTHETICS 20
ARCHITECTURE 50
CREATION AND CREATIVITY 201
DESIGN 237
MUSIC 614
PAINTING 666
THEATER 972
WRITING AND WRITERS 1069

Artificiality 54
APPEARANCE 45
AUTHENTICITY 60
PRETENSION 732
SUPERFICIALITY 951

Asceticism
SELF-DENIAL 865

Aspiration 55
ACHIEVEMENT 6
AMBITION 33
SUCCESS 945

Assertion
SELF-ASSERTION 859

Assistance 56
CHARITY 120
DEPENDENCE 235
GIFTS AND GIVING 384
HUMANITARIANISM 433
SERVICE 887
USEFULNESS 1023

Association 57
AFFINITY 22
COMPANY 152
FAMILIARITY 333
REPUTATION 804

Assurance
CERTAINTY 115
SELF-CONFIDENCE 860

Astronomy
THE HEAVENS 415
SCIENCE 849

Atheism
UNBELIEF 1004

Atom
NUCLEAR POWER 641

Attitude 58
PERSPECTIVE 689

Audacity
BOLDNESS 92

Audience 59
ACTORS 11
OBSERVATION 650
THEATER 972

Authenticity 60
ARTIFICIALITY 54

Authority 61
LEADERSHIP 531
OBEDIENCE 644
POWER 719
RULERS 831

Authors
WRITING AND WRITERS 1069

Autobiography 62
BIOGRAPHY 81

Automation 63
TECHNOLOGY 966

Automobiles 64
TRANSPORTATION 991

Autonomy
SELF-DETERMINATION 867
SELF-SUFFICIENCY 880

Autumn
SEASONS 854

Avarice
GREED 403

Awareness
CONSCIOUSNESS 175
SENSIBILITY 883

Babies 65
CHILDREN 123

Bachelors 66

Background 67
ENVIRONMENT 294

Bad
EVIL 307
WICKEDNESS 1055
WRONGDOING 1070

Bad Temper
TEMPER, BAD 968

Banality 68
BORES 95

Banking 69
BUSINESS AND COMMERCE 104

Barbarism 70
CIVILIZATION 133

Baseball 71
SPORTS 929

Bashfulness
TIMIDITY 980

Bathing
CLEANLINESS 137

Beauty 72
CHARM 121
COSMETICS 192
GRACE 396
UGLINESS 1003

Bed 73
MORNING 605
NIGHT 633
SLEEP 906

Bees
INSECTS 481

Beggars 74
GIFTS AND GIVING 384
POVERTY 718

Beginning 75
BEGINNING AND ENDING 76
ENDING 285

Beginning and Ending 76
BEGINNING 75
ENDING 285

Behavior 77
CUSTOM 213
MANNERS 563
MORALITY 604

Being
EXISTENCE 316

Belief 78
CREDULITY 202
DOUBT, RELIGIOUS 265
FAITH 330
SKEPTICISM 904
SUPERSTITION 954
UNBELIEF 1004
UNCERTAINTY 1005

Benevolence
HUMANITARIANISM 433
KINDNESS 519

Betrayal 79
TREASON 993

Bible 80

Bigotry
DOGMATISM 264
FANATICISM 335
INTOLERANCE 500
PREJUDICES 726

Biography 81
AUTOBIOGRAPHY 62
BOOKS AND READING 93
WRITING AND WRITERS 1069

Birds 82

Birth 83
ANCESTRY 37
BEGINNING 75
DEATH 221
LIFE 539

Birth Control 84
POPULATION 713
REPRODUCTION 802

Blacks 85
AFRICAN-AMERICAN 23
MINORITIES 591
RACIAL PREJUDICE 775
WHITES 1054

Blame
CRITICISM 206
GUILT 405
REPROOF 803
SCAPEGOAT 847

Blasphemy
ICONOCLASM 441
IRREVERENCE 506
SWEARING 957

Blindness, Physical 86
SENSES 882
SIGHT 897

Blindness, Spiritual 87
INSENSITIVITY 483
PERCEPTION 683
UNDERSTANDING 1007
VISION 1035

Blunder 88
ERROR 299

Blushing
SHAME 893

Boasting 89
CONCEIT 166

Boats
SHIPS AND BOATS 895

Body 90
HEALTH 413
MIND AND BODY 589

Body and Soul
MIND AND BODY 589

Bohemians 91
CONFORMITY 171
INDIVIDUALISM 468

Boldness 92
AGGRESSION 26
COURAGE 195
SELF-ASSERTION 859
TIMIDITY 980

Bomb, Atom
NUCLEAR POWER 641

Books and Reading 93
AUTOBIOGRAPHY 62
BIOGRAPHY 81
CLASSICS 136
DICTIONARIES 244
FICTION 344
LIBRARIES 538
LITERATURE 545
WORDS 1064
WRITING AND WRITERS 1069

Boredom 94
BORES 95
DULLNESS 270
ENNUI 290

Bores 95
BANALITY 68
BOREDOM 94
DULLNESS 270

Borrowing and Lending 96
DEBT 222
OBLIGATION 647

Bourgeoisie
MIDDLE CLASS 587

Boys 97
CHILDREN 123
SONS 916
YOUTH 1071

Bravery
COURAGE 195

Breeding
ANCESTRY 37
GOOD BREEDING 391
REPRODUCTION 802

Brevity 98
SPEAKING 923

Bribery 99
CORRUPTION 191
TEMPTATION 971

Broad-mindedness
TOLERANCE 984

Brotherhood 100
COMMUNITY 151
INTERNATIONAL RELATIONS 498
NEIGHBORS 626
UNITY 1016

Brothers
FAMILY 334

Budget 101
DEBT, NATIONAL 223

Budget *(cont.)*
ECONOMICS 277
TAXES 964

Bugs
INSECTS 481

Bureaucracy 102
STATISTICS 932

Burial 103
DEATH 221
FUNERALS 367
MOURNING 610

Business and Commerce 104
ADVERTISING 18
AGENTS 25
BANKING 69
BUYING AND SELLING 105
CAPITALISM 108
ECONOMICS 277
EXECUTIVES 315
INSURANCE 489
INVESTMENT 503
PROFITEERING 738

Busyness
ACTIVITY 10

Buying and Selling 105
ACQUISITION 8
ADVERTISING 18
AGENTS 25
BUSINESS AND COMMERCE 104
CAPITALISM 108
PROPERTY 746

Calamity
ADVERSITY 17

California 106

Calmness
COMPOSURE 160
TRANQUILITY 989

Calumny
SLANDER 905

Canada 107

Candor
FRANKNESS 362

Capitalism 108
BUSINESS AND COMMERCE 104
BUYING AND SELLING 105
POSSESSION 716
PROFITEERING 738
PROPERTY 746

Capital Punishment
PUNISHMENT, CAPITAL 767

Captivity 109
PRISON 735
SERVITUDE 889

Card-Playing
GAMBLING 369

Carefulness
CAUTIOUSNESS 112
PREPAREDNESS 728
PRUDENCE 755

Catholicism
CHRISTIANITY 125

Cats
ANIMALS 41

Cause and Effect 110
CHANCE 116
CONSEQUENCES 176
DESTINY 240
RETRIBUTION 815

Causes 111
IDEOLOGY 445
MASS MOVEMENTS 568
PARTISANSHIP 674

Cautiousness 112
PRUDENCE 755

Celebrity
FAME 332

Celibacy
CHASTITY 122
MONASTICISM 601

Censorship 113
PRESS, FREEDOM OF THE 731
RIGHTS 823

Censure
CRITICISM 206
REPROOF 803

Ceremony 114
COURTESY 197
MANNERS 563
PROPRIETY 749

Certainty 115
DOGMATISM 264
SECURITY 856
UNCERTAINTY 1005

Chance 116
CIRCUMSTANCE 129
FATE 340
FORTUNE 360

Change 117
CHANGELESSNESS 118
CONSISTENCY 179
FLEXIBILITY 350
INCONSISTENCY 464
INNOVATION 479
NOVELTY 640
OPEN-MINDEDNESS 654
PROGRESS 741
REPETITION 800
TRANSIENCE 990

Changelessness 118
CHANGE 117

Chaos
DISORDER 257

Character 119
IDENTITY 444
INTEGRITY 491
PERSONALITY 687

Charity 120
GIFTS AND GIVING 384
HUMANITARIANISM 433
KINDNESS 519
LOVE 551
TOLERANCE 984

Charm 121

Chastity 122
MONASTICISM 601
PURITY 770
SELF-DENIAL 865

Cheerfulness
GOOD NATURE 392

Children 123
BABIES 65
BOYS 97
DAUGHTERS 218
FAMILY 334
GIRLS 385
PARENTHOOD 670
SONS 916

Choice 124
PREFERENCE 725
WILL 1056

Christ
JESUS 511

Christianity 125
BIBLE 80
CHURCH 126
CLERGY 138
FAITH 330
JESUS 511
MARTYRS AND MARTYRDOM 565
MISSIONARIES 596
MONASTICISM 601
PURITANS AND PURITANISM 769
RELIGION 797
SABBATH 835
SACRAMENT 836
SAINTS AND SAINTHOOD 840
SALVATION 841

Christmas
HOLIDAYS 420

Church 126
CHRISTIANITY 125
CHURCH AND STATE 127
CHURCHGOING 128
CLERGY 138
MARTYRS AND MARTYRDOM 565
MISSIONARIES 596
MONASTICISM 601
PREACHING AND PREACHERS 724
RELIGION 797
SACRAMENT 836

Church *(cont.)*
SAINTS AND SAINTHOOD 840

Church and State 127
CHURCH 126
STATE 930

Churchgoing 128
CHURCH 126
PREACHING AND PREACHERS 724

Cinema
MOVIES 611

Circumstance 129
CHANCE 116
EVENTS 305
NECESSITY 624

Circus 130

Cities 131
THE COUNTRY 194
LONDON 546
NEW YORK 632
PARIS 671
SUBURBS 944
VENICE 1029
WASHINGTON, D.C. 1044

Citizens 132
GOVERNMENT 395
STATE 930
VOTING 1038

Civilization 133
BARBARISM 70
CULTURE 210
PROGRESS 741
SOCIETY 913

Civil Rights
RIGHTS 823

Clarity 134

Class 135
ARISTOCRACY 52
DEMOCRACY 233
EQUALITY 297
MIDDLE CLASS 587
THE PEOPLE 682
RANK 780
SNOBBERY 910
SOCIETY 913
STATUS 933

Classics 136
ANTIQUITY 42
BOOKS AND READING 93
TRADITION 986

Cleanliness 137
DIRTINESS 248
HEALTH 413

Clergy 138
CHRISTIANITY 125
CHURCH 126
MISSIONARIES 596
MONASTICISM 601
PREACHING AND PREACHERS 724

Cleverness 139
CRAFTINESS 200
INTELLIGENCE 493
SUBTLETY 943
WIT 1061

Climate 140
SUN 950
WEATHER 1050

Cliques
SNOBBERY 910

Clothing
DRESS 267
FASHION 338

Coffee 141

Coldness 142
ALOOFNESS 31

Colonialism
IMPERIALISM 458

Color 143

Comedians 144
COMEDY 145
ENTERTAINMENT 292
HUMOR 436

Comedy 145
COMEDIANS 144
ENTERTAINMENT 292
HUMOR 436
SATIRE 844
THEATER 972
TRAGEDY 987
WIT 1061

Command
AUTHORITY 61
LEADERSHIP 531

Commerce
BUSINESS AND COMMERCE 104
BUYING AND SELLING 105
PROFITEERING 738

Commitment 146
CAUSES 111
INVOLVEMENT 504

Committees 147
MEETINGS 579

Common Man
THE PEOPLE 682

Common Sense 148
PRACTICALITY 720
PRUDENCE 755

Communication 149
CLARITY 134
CONVERSATION 188
OBSCURANTISM 648
SPEAKING 923
WRITING AND WRITERS 1069

Communications
MEDIA 576

Communism 150
GOVERNMENT 395

Communism *(cont.)*
SHARING 894
SOCIALISM 912

Community 151
BROTHERHOOD 100
TOGETHERNESS 983
UNITY 1016

Company 152
ACQUAINTANCES 7
ASSOCIATION 57
FRIENDSHIP 365
HOSPITALITY 428
INTERESTINGNESS 496
RELATIONSHIPS, HUMAN 794
SOCIETY, POLITE 914
TOGETHERNESS 983

Comparison 153
ADVANTAGE 15
ADVERSITY 17
COMPENSATION 154
CONSOLATIONS 180
CONTRAST 187
RELATIVENESS 795

Compassion
MERCY 583
PITY 698

Compensation 154
ADVANTAGE 15
COMPARISON 153
CONSOLATIONS 180
PROSPERITY AND ADVERSITY 751

Competition 155
AGGRESSION 26
AMBITION 33

Complacency 156
CONCEIT 166
PRIDE 733
SMUGNESS 909

Complaint 157

Completion
ENDING 285

Compliance 158
PERSUASION 690

Compliments 159
FLATTERY 349

Composers
MUSIC 614

Composure 160
TRANQUILITY 989

Comprehension 161
UNDERSTANDING 1007

Compromise 162
AGREEMENT 27
APPEASEMENT 46
CONCILIATION 167
TREATIES 994

Compulsiveness 163
ACTIVITY 10
NEUROSIS 627

Compulsiveness *(cont.)*
OBSESSION 651

Computers 164

Concealment 165
CRAFTINESS 200
HYPOCRISY 440

Conceit 166
BOASTING 89
COMPLACENCY 156
HUMILITY 435
PRIDE 733
SELF-LOVE 876
VANITY 1027

Concentration
SINGLE-MINDEDNESS 903

Conciliation 167
APPEASEMENT 46
COMPROMISE 162
TREATIES 994

Condolence
SYMPATHY 960

Conduct
BEHAVIOR 77

Confession 168

Confidence
CERTAINTY 115
OVERCONFIDENCE 664
SECRETS 855
SELF-CONFIDENCE 860

Confidences 169
SECRETS 855

Conflict, Inner 170
INTERESTS, DIVIDED 497
PERVERSENESS 691

Conformity 171
ADJUSTMENT 12
BOHEMIANS 91
INDIVIDUALISM 468
NORMALITY 637
STATUS 933
STEREOTYPES 935

Confusion
DISORDER 257

Congress 172
GOVERNMENT 395
POLITICS AND POLITICIANS 711
PUBLIC OFFICE 761

Conquest 173
SUCCESS 945
WAR 1042

Conscience 174
GUILT 405
MORALITY 604
RIGHT 822
WRONGDOING 1070

Consciousness 175
SENSIBILITY 883
UNCONSCIOUSNESS 1006

Consequences 176
CAUSE AND EFFECT 110
FATE 340
IRREVOCABLENESS 507
RETRIBUTION 815

Conservation 177
AIR POLLUTION 29
ENVIRONMENT 294
TREES 995

Conservatism 178
LIBERALISM 536
POLITICAL PARTIES 710
RADICALISM 776

Consistency 179
CHANGE 117
INCONSISTENCY 464

Consolations 180
ADVERSITY 17
COMPENSATION 154
REMEDIES 798

Constancy and Inconstancy 181
INTEGRITY 491
INFIDELITY 472
LOYALTY 556

Constitutions 182
GOVERNMENT 395

Consumers
BUYING AND SELLING 105

Contemplation 183
PRAYER 723
SELF-KNOWLEDGE 875
SPIRITUALITY 927

Contemporaneousness 184
ERA 298
GENERATIONS 374
MODERNITY 599

Contempt 185
SOUR GRAPES 920

Contentment 186
COMPLACENCY 156
DISCONTENT 251
HAPPINESS 409
PLAIN LIVING 701
SATISFACTION 845
TRANQUILITY 989

Contradiction
INCONSISTENCY 464

Contrast 187
COMPARISON 153

Controversy
ARGUMENT 51
DISCORD 252
QUARRELING 772

Convalescence
SICKNESS 896

Conversation 188
COMMUNICATION 149
LISTENING 543
SPEAKING 923

Cooks and Cooking 189
EATING 274
FOOD 355

Coolness
COLDNESS 142
COMPOSURE 160

Cooperation 190
UNITY 1016

Coquetry
FLIRTATION 351

Corruption 191
BRIBERY 99
EVIL 307
SIN 900
STEALING 934
TEMPTATION 971
WICKEDNESS 1055

Cosmetics 192
FACE 326
PERFUME 685

Cosmopolitanism 193
INTERNATIONAL RELATIONS 498
SOPHISTICATION 917

Cost
VALUE 1026

Counsel
ADVICE 19

The Country 194
CITIES 131
FARMS AND FARMING 337
FLOWERS 352
GARDENING 371
SUBURBS 944

Courage 195
BOLDNESS 92
COWARDICE 199
DESPAIR 239
FEAR 343
STRENGTH 940
TIMIDITY 980

Court, Royal 196
KINGS 520
ROYALTY 829

Court of Law
JUSTICE 517
LAW AND LAWYERS 528

Courtesy 197
CEREMONY 114
GENTLEMAN 378
GOOD BREEDING 391
MANNERS 563
PROPRIETY 749
RUDENESS 830

Courtship 198
FLIRTATION 351
LOVE 551
MARRIAGE 564
ROMANCE 826
SEDUCTION 857

Cowardice 199
COURAGE 195
ESCAPE 300
EVASION 304
FEAR 343
TIMIDITY 980

Craftiness 200
CLEVERNESS 139
CONCEALMENT 165
SUBTLETY 943

Creation and Creativity 201
ART AND ARTISTS 53
DESTRUCTION 241
INSPIRATION 485
POETRY AND POETS 708
SELF-EXPRESSION 872
WRITING AND WRITERS 1069

Credulity 202
BELIEF 78
NAÏVETÉ 618
SURPRISE 955
WONDER 1063

Creeds 203
DOGMATISM 264
FAITH 330
IDEOLOGY 445
RELIGION 797

Crime 204
EVIL 307
ILLEGALITY 448
KILLING 518
SIN 900
STEALING 934
VICE 1030
WRONGDOING 1070

Crises 205
ADVERSITY 17

Criticism 206
ACCUSATION 5
CRITICISM, PROFESSIONAL 207
FAULTS 342
JUDGING OTHERS 515
REPROOF 803
SELF-CRITICISM 863

Criticism, Professional 207
AESTHETICS 20

Crowds 208
MOB 597
POPULATION 713

Cruelty 209
SADISM 838
UNKINDNESS 1018

Culture 210
CIVILIZATION 133
INSTITUTIONS 487
SOCIETY 913

Cures
REMEDIES 798

Curiosity 211
INQUIRY 480

Cursing 212
SWEARING 957

Custom 213
BEHAVIOR 77
HABIT 406
TRADITION 986

Dancing 215

Danger 216
ADVENTURE 16
BOLDNESS 92
COURAGE 195
EXCITEMENT 313
THREAT 976

Darkness 217
NIGHT 633

Daughters 218
GIRLS 385
PARENTHOOD 670

Dawn
MORNING 605

Daydreams
FANTASY 336

Deadness, Spiritual 219
ALIENATION 30
INDIFFERENCE 466
INVOLVEMENT 504

Deafness 220

Death 221
BIRTH 83
BURIAL 103
ETERNITY 302
FUNERALS 367
IMMORTALITY 454
LIFE 539
LIFE AND DEATH 541
MORTALITY 606
MOURNING 610
PUNISHMENT, CAPITAL 767
SUICIDE 948

Debate
ARGUMENT 51

Debauchery
PROFLIGACY 739

Debt 222
BORROWING AND LENDING 96
BUDGET 101
DEBT, NATIONAL 223
OBLIGATION 647

Debt, National 223
BUDGET 101

Decadence
CORRUPTION 191
DECLINE 226
LUXURY 557

Deceit
DECEPTION 224

Decency
PROPRIETY 749

Deception 224
CONCEALMENT 165
FALSEHOOD 331
HYPOCRISY 440
SELF-DECEPTION 864

Decision 225
AFTERTHOUGHT 24
INDECISION 465
RESOLUTION 807

Decline 226
FAILURE 329
OLD AGE 653

Deeds 227
ACTION 9
CONSEQUENCES 176
GOLDEN RULE 388
GOODNESS 393
HUMANITARIANISM 433
SERVICE 887
SERVICES 888
WRONGDOING 1070

Defeat 228
ADVERSITY 17
CONQUEST 173
FAILURE 329

Defense 229
SECURITY 856
SURVIVAL 956

Deference
RESPECT 808

Definition 230
CLARITY 134
DICTIONARIES 244
WORDS 1064

Delay 231
INDECISION 465
PREMATURENESS 727
PUNCTUALITY 765
SLOWNESS 907
TIMELINESS 979

Demagoguery 232
MASS MOVEMENTS 568
POLITICS AND POLITICIANS 711
PUBLIC SPEAKING 763

Democracy 233
CLASS 135
EQUALITY 297
FREEDOM 363
GOVERNMENT 395
LIBERTY 537
MINORITIES 591
SOCIETY 913
VOTING 1038

Democrats
POLITICAL PARTIES 710

Dentists 234

Dependence 235
ASSISTANCE 56
SELF-SUFFICIENCY 880

Deprivation 236
LOSS 550
NEED 625
POVERTY 718

Design 237
ART AND ARTISTS 53

Desires 238
FRUSTRATION 366
PASSION 675
SATISFACTION 845

Despair 239
COURAGE 195
DISCOURAGEMENT 253
HOPE 427

Despotism
TYRANNY 1002

Destiny 240
FATE 340
FORTUNE 360
NECESSITY 624

Destruction 241
ICONOCLASM 441
VIOLENCE 1032

Development
GROWTH AND DEVELOPMENT 404
MATURITY 571

Devil 242
GOD 387
HELL 416

Devotion
WORSHIP 1068

Diagnosis 243
REMEDIES 798

Dictatorship
TYRANNY 1002

Dictionaries 244
DEFINITION 230
WORDS 1064

Difficulty 245
ADVERSITY 17
COMPLAINT 157
EFFORT 281
FACILITY 327
METHOD 585
PERSEVERANCE 686

Dignity 246

Diligence
EFFORT 281

Diplomats and Diplomacy 247
INTERNATIONAL RELATIONS 498
TREATIES 994

Dirtiness 248
CLEANLINESS 137

Disadvantage
ADVANTAGE 15
LOSERS 549

Disagreement
AGREEMENT 27
DISSENT 258
OPPOSITION 658

Disappointment 249
DISILLUSIONMENT 254
EXPECTATION 318
SOUR GRAPES 920

Disaster
ADVERSITY 17

Disciples
FOLLOWING 353

Discipline 250
INDULGENCE 470
PUNISHMENT 766
SELF-CONTROL 862
TRAINING 988

Discontent 251
CONTENTMENT 186
UNHAPPINESS 1011

Discord 252
AGREEMENT 27
ARGUMENT 51
DISSENT 258
FIGHTING 345
OPPOSITION 658
QUARRELING 772
WAR 1042

Discouragement 253
DESPAIR 239

Discovery
INNOVATION 479

Discretion
PRUDENCE 755

Dishonesty
CORRUPTION 191
DECEPTION 224
FALSEHOOD 331
STEALING 934

Disillusionment 254
DISAPPOINTMENT 249

Dislike 255
ENEMIES 288
ESTRANGEMENT 301
HATRED 412
MISANTHROPY 594

Disobedience 256
OBEDIENCE 644
REBELLION 786

Disorder 257
ORDER 661

Disposition
GOOD NATURE 392
TEMPER, BAD 968
TEMPERAMENT 969

Dispute
ARGUMENT 51
QUARRELING 772

Dissent 258
ARGUMENT 51

Dissent *(cont.)*
DISCORD 252
DISOBEDIENCE 256
FREE SPEECH 364
OPPOSITION 658
PRESS, FREEDOM OF THE 731
PROTEST 753
QUARRELING 772
REBELLION 786
REVOLUTION 819
VIOLENCE 1032

Distrust 259
BETRAYAL 79
TRUST 997

Diversity 260
INDIVIDUALITY 469
UNIQUENESS 1014
UNITY 1016

Divided Interests
CONFLICT, INNER 170
INTERESTS, DIVIDED 497

Divine Revelation
REVELATION, DIVINE 816

Divinity 261
GOD 387
HUMANISM 432

Divorce 262
MARRIAGE 564

Doctors 263
DENTISTS 234
MEDICINE 577
PSYCHIATRY 757

Doctrine
THEOLOGY 973

Dogmatism 264
CERTAINTY 115
CREEDS 203
FANATICISM 335
IDEOLOGY 445
INTOLERANCE 500
NARROWNESS 620
PREJUDICES 726
SELF-RIGHTEOUSNESS 879

Dogs
ANIMALS 41

Doubt
DOUBT, RELIGIOUS 265
SKEPTICISM 904
UNCERTAINTY 1005

Doubt, Religious 265
FAITH 330
SKEPTICISM 904
UNBELIEF 1004
UNCERTAINTY 1005

Drama
THEATER 972

Dreams 266
IDEALISM 442
ILLUSION 449

Dreams *(cont.)*
FANTASY 336
SLEEP 906

Dress 267
APPEARANCE 45
FASHION 338
NUDITY 642

Drinking 268

Drudgery
WORK 1065

Drugs 269

Drunkenness
DRINKING 268

Dullness 270
BOREDOM 94
BORES 95
IGNORANCE 447
STUPIDITY 941

Duty 271
OBLIGATION 647
RESPONSIBILITY 810

Earnestness
SERIOUSNESS 886

Earth 272
CONSERVATION 177
THE HEAVENS 415
NATURE 623
WORLD 1067

Ease
FACILITY 327
LEISURE 533

East and West 273
INTERNATIONAL RELATIONS 498

Easter
HOLIDAYS 420

Eating 274
COOKS AND COOKING 189
FOOD 355
GREED 403
HUNGER 437
OBESITY 645
TIPPING 981
VEGETARIANISM 1028

Eavesdropping 275

Eccentricity 276
INDIVIDUALITY 469
ORIGINALITY 662

Economics 277
BUDGET 101
BUSINESS AND COMMERCE 104
TAXES 964

Economy
ECONOMICS 277
THRIFT 977

Ecstasy 278
HAPPINESS 409

Ecstasy *(cont.)*
MYSTICISM 616

Editors and Editing
PUBLISHING 764

Education 279
KNOWLEDGE 522
LEARNING 532
MATHEMATICS 570
SCHOLARS AND SCHOLARSHIP 848
TEACHING 965
TRAINING 988

Effect
CAUSE AND EFFECT 110

Efficiency 280
METHOD 585

Effort 281
DIFFICULTY 245
ENTERPRISE 291
PERSEVERANCE 686
WORK 1065

Egotism
SELF-IMPORTANCE 873

Elections
VOTING 1038

Elegance 282
FASHION 338
STYLE 942
TASTE 963

Eloquence 283
PERSUASION 690
PUBLIC SPEAKING 763
SPEAKING 923

Embarrassment
SHAME 893

Eminence
FAME 332
GLORY 386
SUCCESS 945

Emotions 284
AFFECTION 21
CONFLICT, INNER 170
HATRED 412
LOVE 551
PASSION 675
SENSIBILITY 883
TEMPERAMENT 969

Empathy
SYMPATHY 960
UNDERSTANDING OTHERS 1008

Emulation
IMITATION 451

Endeavor
EFFORT 281

Ending 285
BEGINNING 75
BEGINNING AND ENDING 76
ENDS 286

Ending *(cont.)*
MEANS AND ENDS 574

Ends 286
ENDING 285
MEANS AND ENDS 574
MOTIVES 608
PURPOSE 771

Endurance 287
PATIENCE 677
PERSEVERANCE 686
RESIGNATION 806
STOICISM 937
SURVIVAL 956

Enemies 288
ESTRANGEMENT 301
HATRED 412
INJURY 476
PACIFISM 665
REVENGE 817

Energy
EFFORT 281
VITALITY 1036

England and Englishmen 289
LONDON 546

English
ENGLAND AND ENGLISHMEN 289
LANGUAGE 524

Enjoyment
PLEASURE 704

Ennui 290
ALIENATION 30
BOREDOM 94

Enough
SUFFICIENCY 947

Enterprise 291
AMBITION 33
EFFORT 281
OPPORTUNITY 657
SELF-SUFFICIENCY 880

Entertainment 292
CIRCUS 130
COMEDIANS 144
COMEDY 145
MEDIA 576
MUSIC 614
PLAY 703
THEATER 972

Enthusiasm 293
FANATICISM 335
JOIE DE VIVRE 513
SPONTANEITY 928
VITALITY 1036
ZEAL 1073

Environment 294
BACKGROUND 67
CONSERVATION 177
GARBAGE 370

Envy 295
MALICE 561

Epigrams 296
Maxims 572
Quotations 773

Epoch
Era 298

Equality 297
Class 135
Democracy 233
Inequality 471
Rights 823

Era 298
Contemporaneousness 184
Generations 374
Modernity 599
Nuclear Power 641
Past 676
Twentieth Century 1001

Error 299
Blunder 88
Falsehood 331
Imperfection 457
Inconsistency 464
Perfection 684
Truth and Falsehood 999

Escape 300
Cowardice 199
Evasion 304
Fear 343
Illusion 449

Establishment
Institutions 487

Esteem
Praise 722
Respect 808
Self-Esteem 871

Estrangement 301
Dislike 255
Love, Loss of 552

Eternity 302
Immortality 454
Time 978
Transience 990

Ethics
Morality 604

Etiquette
Manners 563

Europe 303

Evasion 304
Escape 300
Realism 783

Events 305
Circumstance 129

Evidence 306
Portent 715
Proof 744

Evil 307
Corruption 191
Crime 204

Evil *(cont.)*
The Good 389
Good and Evil 390
Goodness 393
Sin 900
Wickedness 1055
Wrongdoing 1070

Evolution 308
Ancestry 37
Progress 741

Exaggeration 309

Example 310

Excellence 311
Ability 1
Genius 376
Merit 584
Superiority 952
Talent 962
Vocations 1037

Excess 312
Exaggeration 309
Extravagance 324
Greed 403
Indulgence 470
Intemperance 494
Luxury 557
Moderation 598
Sufficiency 947
Temperance 970

Excitement 313
Adventure 16
Danger 216

Excuses 314
Explanation 322
Faults 342
Rationalization 782

Executives 315
Administration 13

Exile
Homeland 423

Existence 316
Existentialism 317
Identity 444
Life 539

Existentialism 317
The Absurd 3
Existence 316

Expectation 318
Disappointment 249
Future 368
Hope 427
Waiting 1040

Expediency 319
Means and Ends 574

Expendability 320
Unimportance 1012

Experience 321
Involvement 504
Learning 532
Life 539
Sophistication 917

Experts
Specialists 924

Explanation 322
Excuses 314
Rationalization 782

Exploitation 323
Losers 549

Extravagance 324
Excess 312
Luxury 557
Moderation 598
Thrift 977

Extremism
Fanaticism 335

Eyes 325
Face 326
Senses 882
Sight 897
Spectacles 925

Face 326
Communication 149
Cosmetics 192
Eyes 325
Senses 882

Facility 327
Difficulty 245

Facts 328
Reality 784
Statistics 932
Theory 974

Failure 329
Adversity 17
Decline 226
Defeat 228
Losers 549
Loss 550
Success 945

Faith 330
Belief 78
Creeds 203
Doubt, Religious 265
Skepticism 904
Unbelief 1004

Faithfulness
Constancy and Inconstancy 181
Infidelity 472

Fall
Seasons 854

Falling
Failure 329

Falsehood 331
Deception 224
Lying 558
Self-Deception 864
Truth and Falsehood 999
Truth 998
Truthfulness 1000

Fame 332
Following 353
Glory 386

Fame *(cont.)*
Heroes and Heroism 418
Honors 426
Merit 584
Obscurity 649
Reputation 804
Worship 1068

Familiarity 333
Intimacy 499
The Mundane 612

Family 334
Ancestry 37
Babies 65
Children 123
Daughters 218
Home 422
Marriage 564
Parenthood 670
Relatives 796
Sons 916

Fanaticism 335
Dogmatism 264
Enthusiasm 293
Intolerance 500
Prejudices 726
Zeal 1073

Fantasy 336
Dreams 266
Ghosts 383
Illusion 449
Imagination 450
Reverie 818

Farms and Farming 337

Fashion 338
Appearance 45
Dress 267
Elegance 282
Hair 407
Novelty 640

Fastidiousness 339

Fate 340
Chance 116
Destiny 240
Fortune 360
Necessity 624
Providence 754
Stoicism 937

Fathers
Parenthood 670

Fatigue 341

Fatness
Obesity 645

Faults 342
Confession 168
Criticism 206
Excuses 314
Folly 354
Imperfection 457
Limitations 542
Perfection 684
Reproof 803
Weakness 1047

Favors
Services 888

Fear 343
Anxiety 43
Courage 195
Cowardice 199
Escape 300
Evasion 304
Timidity 980

February
Seasons 854

Feelings
Emotions 284

Fellowship
Company 152

Fiction 344
Storytelling 938
Writing and Writers 1069

Fighting 345
Discord 252
Quarreling 772
War 1042

Finishing
Ending 285

Fire 346

Fish 347
Fishing 348

Fishing 348
Fish 347

Flag
Patriotism 678

Flattery 349
Compliments 159

Flexibility 350
Change 117
Obstinacy 652
Open-Mindedness 654
Opinion 656

Flies
Insects 481

Flight
Airplanes 28
Escape 300

Flirtation 351
Courtship 198
Love 551
Promiscuity 742
Seduction 857

Flowers 352

Fog
Weather 1050

Following 353
Admiration 14
Leadership 531
Mass Movements 568
Worship 1068

Folly 354
Faults 342

Folly *(cont.)*
Fools 356
Rashness 781
Stupidity 941

Food 355
Cooks and Cooking 189
Eating 274
Hunger 437
Vegetarianism 1028

Fools 356
Folly 354
Rashness 781
Stupidity 941

Force 357
Aggression 26
Compliance 158
Gentleness 379
Pacifism 665
Power 719
Repression 801
Strength 940
Violence 1032

Foreigners and Foreignness 358

Foreign Relations
International Relations 498

Forgiveness 359
Mercy 583

Form
Order 661

Fortune 360
Advantage 15
Chance 116
Losers 549
Prosperity and Adversity 751
Wealth 1048

France and Frenchmen 361
Paris 671

Frankness 362
Honesty 425
Sincerity 901
Truthfulness 1000

Fraud
Deception 224

Freedom 363
Captivity 109
Free Speech 363
Liberty 537
Rights 823
Self-Sufficiency 880
Servitude 889

Freedom of the Press
Press, Freedom of the 731

Free Speech 364
Dissent 258
Freedom 364
Liberty 537

Free Speech *(cont.)*
Newspapers 630
Press, Freedom of the 731
Publishing 764

Free Will
Freedom 363
Self-Determination 867

Friendliness
Company 152

Friendship 365
Acquaintances 7
Association 57
Company 152
Confidences 169
Constancy and Inconstancy 181
Estrangement 301
Intimacy 499
Loneliness 547
Promiscuity 742
Relationships, Human 794
Solitude 915

Frugality
Plain Living 701
Thrift 977

Frustration 366
Desires 238
Hope 427
Impotence 459
Unfulfillment 1010

Fulfillment
Involvement 504
Potential 717
Unfulfillment 1010

Funerals 367
Burial 103
Death 221
Mourning 610

Future 368
Destiny 240
Expectation 318
Past 676
Present 729

Gambling 369

Games
Gambling 369
Play 703
Sports 929

Garbage 370

Gardening 371

Gaucherie 372
Grace 396

Generalization 373

Generations 374
Contemporaneousness 184
Era 298

Generosity 375
Assistance 56
Gifts and Giving 384
Humanitarianism 433
Largeness 525
Services 888
Unselfishness 1021

Genius 376
Excellence 311
Genius vs. Talent 377
Greatness 401
Superiority 952

Genius vs. Talent 377
Genius 376

Gentility
Good Breeding 391
Respectability 809

Gentleman 378
Courtesy 197
Good Breeding 391
Manners 563

Gentleness 379
Force 357
Kindness 519

Geography 380
Climate 140

Germany and Germans 381

Germs 382

Ghosts 383
Illusion 449
Fantasy 336
Supernatural 953

Gifts and Giving 384
Beggars 74
Generosity 375
Humanitarianism 433
Kindness 519
Misers 595
Obligation 647
Receiving 787
Services 888
Sharing 894
Stinginess 936

Girls 385
Youth 1071

Giving
Gifts and Giving 384

Glasses
Spectacles 925

Glory 386
Fame 332
Honors 426
Praise 722
Reputation 804

Gluttony
Eating 274
Greed 403

Goals
Ends 286
Purpose 771

God 387
DEVIL 242
DIVINITY 261
PROVIDENCE 754
RELIGION 797
REVELATION, DIVINE 816
THEOLOGY 973
THE UNKNOWN 1019

Golden Age
ERA 298

Golden Rule 388
DEEDS 227

Golf
SPORTS 929

The Good 389
EVIL 307
GOOD AND EVIL 390
GOODNESS 393
RIGHT 822

Good and Evil 390
EVIL 307
THE GOOD 389
GOODNESS 393

Good Breeding 391
COURTESY 197
GENTLEMAN 378
MANNERS 563
PROPRIETY 749

Good Nature 392
TEMPER, BAD 968

Goodness 393
CORRUPTION 191
DEEDS 227
EVIL 307
THE GOOD 389
GOOD AND EVIL 390
HUMANITARIANISM 433
MORALITY 604
PIETY 697
RIGHT 822
VIRTUE 1033

Gossip 394
MEDDLING 575
PETTINESS 693
RUMORS 833
SCANDAL 846
SLANDER 905

Government 395
ANARCHY 36
BUDGET 101
BUREAUCRACY 102
CAPITALISM 108
CITIZENS 132
COMMUNISM 150
CONGRESS 172
DEMOCRACY 233
KINGS 520
THE PEOPLE 682
PRESIDENCY 730
RULERS 831
SOCIALISM 912
SOCIETY 913
STATE 930

Government *(cont.)*
STATESMEN AND STATESMANSHIP 931
TAXES 964
TOTALITARIANISM 985
VOTING 1038

Grace 396
GAUCHERIE 372

Graffiti 397

Grammar 398
LANGUAGE 524
WORDS 1064

Gratitude 399
APPRECIATION 47
INGRATITUDE 475
OBLIGATION 647

Great and Small 400
GREATNESS 401
OBSCURITY 649
SMALLNESS 908
UNIMPORTANCE 1012

Greatness 401
GREAT AND SMALL 400
HEROES AND HEROISM 418
LARGENESS 525
OBSCURITY 649
UNIMPORTANCE 1012

Greece, Ancient 402
ANTIQUITY 42

Greed 403
ACQUISITION 8
EXCESS 312
MISERS 595

Grief
SORROW 918

Group
COMPANY 152
CROWDS 208
MOB 597

Growth and Development 404
IMMATURITY 452
LEARNING 532
MATURITY 571
OPEN-MINDEDNESS 654
POTENTIAL 717
TRAINING 988

Guests
HOSPITALITY 428

Guilt 405
CONSCIENCE 174
SCAPEGOAT 847
SHAME 893

Habit 406
CUSTOM 213
ROUTINE 828

Hair 407

Handshake 408

Happiness 409
CONTENTMENT 186
ECSTASY 278
PLEASURE 704
PROSPERITY 750
UNHAPPINESS 1011

Harm
INJURY 476

Harmony 410
ORDER 661
PROPORTION 748

Haste 411
ACTIVITY 10
IMPATIENCE 456
SLOWNESS 907
SPEED 926

Hatred 412
DISLIKE 255
ENEMIES 288
LOVE 551
LOVE AND HATE 554
MISANTHROPY 594

Haves and Have Nots
ADVANTAGE 15
LOSERS 549
UNHAPPINESS 1011

Health 413
BODY 90
CLEANLINESS 137
MEDICINE 577
MIND AND BODY 589
PHYSICAL FITNESS 696
SANITY 842
SICKNESS 896

Heart
EMOTIONS 284

Heaven 414
ANGELS 38
HELL 416

The Heavens 415
EARTH 272
MOON 603
SPACE 921
SUN 950
UNIVERSE 1017

Hedonism
PLEASURE 704
PLEASURE-SEEKING 706

Hell 416
DEVIL 242
HEAVEN 414

Helping
ASSISTANCE 56
CHARITY 120
GIFTS AND GIVING 384
HUMANITARIANISM 433

Heredity 417
PARENTHOOD 670
REPRODUCTION 802

Heresy
DISSENT 258

Heroes and Heroism 418
FAME 332
GLORY 386
GREATNESS 401

Hesitation
DELAY 231
INDECISION 465

Hiding
CONCEALMENT 165

History and Historians 419
ERA 298
PAST 676
TRADITION 986

Holidays 420
THE NEW YEAR 631
PARADES 667

Hollywood 421
MOVIES 611

Home 422
FAMILY 334
HOMELAND 423
HOSPITALITY 428
HOUSES 430

Homeland 423
PATRIOTISM 678

Homosexuality 424

Honesty 425
FALSEHOOD 331
FRANKNESS 362
INTEGRITY 491
SINCERITY 901
TRUTHFULNESS 1000

Honor
INTEGRITY 491

Honors 426
FAME 332
GLORY 386

Hope 427
DESPAIR 239
EXPECTATION 318
WAITING 1040

Horsemanship
RIDING 821

Horse-Racing
SPORTS 929

Hospitality 428
FOREIGNERS AND FOREIGNNESS 358

Hospitals
SICKNESS 896

Hotels 429

Houses 430
ARCHITECTURE 50
HOME 422
PROPERTY 746

Human Nature 431
INSTINCT 486
MANKIND 562

Humanism 432
Divinity 261

Humanitarianism 433
Assistance 56
Beggars 74
Charity 120
Deeds 227
Gifts and Giving 384
Goodness 393
Misanthropy 594
Reform 790
Service 887
Unselfishness 1021

Humiliation 434
Ridicule 820
Shame 893

Humility 435
Conceit 166
Modesty 600
Pride 733

Humor 436
Comedians 144
Comedy 145
Laughter 526
Puns 768
Ridicule 820
Sense and Nonsense 881
Seriousness 886
Wit 1061

Hunger 437
Eating 274

Hunting 438

Hurry
Haste 411
Speed 926

Hypochondria
Sickness 896

Hypocrisy 440
Deception 224
Personality, Dual 688
Sincerity 901

Iconoclasm 441
Destruction 241
Irreverence 506
Revolution 819
Tradition 986

Idealism 442
Disillusionment 254
Ideology 445
Reform 790
Utopia 1025

Ideas 443
Opinion 656
Thought 975

Identity 444
Appearance 45
Character 119
Existence 316
Individuality 469
Mirrors 593
Names 619

Identity *(cont.)*
Personality, Dual 688
Self 858
Self-Knowledge 875

Ideology 445
Causes 111
Creeds 203
Dogmatism 264
Ideas 443
Mass Movements 568

Idleness 446
Activity 10
Laziness 530
Leisure 533
Rest 811
Retirement 813

Idolatry
Worship 1068

Ignorance 447
Dullness 270
Knowledge 522
Naïveté 618
Stupidity 941

Illegality 448
Crime 204
Sin 900

Illness
Sickness 896

Illusion 449
Dreams 266
Escape 300
Ghosts 383
Myth 617
Fantasy 336
Reality 784

Imagination 450
Mind 590
Fantasy 336
Reverie 818

Imitation 451
Plagiarism 700
Pretension 732

Immaturity 452
Growth and Development 404
Maturity 571

Immigration 453

Immorality
Evil 307
Morality 604
Vice 1030
Wickedness 1055
Wrongdoing 1070

Immortality 454
Eternity 302
Mortality 606

Impartiality 455
Justice 517
Partisanship 674

Impatience 456
Haste 411

Impatience *(cont.)*
Patience 677
Restlessness 812
Waiting 1040

Imperfection 457
Error 299
Faults 342
Limitations 542
Perfection 684

Imperialism 458
Tyranny 1002

Impermanence
Change 117
Transience 990

Impiety
Iconoclasm 441
Irreverence 506

Importance
Self-Importance 873

Impotence 459
Frustration 366
Power 719
Weakness 1047

Improvement 460
Potential 717
Reform 790
Resolution 807

Improvisation
Spontaneity 928

Impulsiveness 461
Spontaneity 928
Whim 1053

Inadequacy 462
Incompetence 463
Limitations 542

Incompetence 463
Inadequacy 462

Incompletion
Ending 285

Inconsistency 464
Change 117
Consistency 179
Perverseness 691

Inconstancy
Constancy and Inconstancy 181
Infidelity 472

Indecision 465
Decision 225
Delay 231
Purpose 771
Uncertainty 1005

Independence
Freedom 363
Liberty 537
Self-Sufficiency 880

Indifference 466
Alienation 30
Deadness, Spiritual 219

Indignation 467
Anger 39

Indiscriminateness
Promiscuity 742

Individualism 468
Bohemians 91
Conformity 171
Identity 444
Individuality 469

Individuality 469
Diversity 260
Eccentricity 276
Identity 444
Individualism 468
Originality 662
Self 858
Uniqueness 1014

Indulgence 470
Discipline 250
Excess 312
Leniency 534

Inequality 471
Equality 297

Infidelity 472
Constancy and Inconstancy 181
Promiscuity 742

Influence 473

Ingratiation 474
Approval 49
Popularity 712

Ingratitude 475
Gratitude 399
Obligation 647

Inheritance
Wills and Inheritance 1058

Initiative
Enterprise 291

Injury 476
Enemies 288
Injustice 477
Insult 488
Pacifism 665
Recompense 789
Revenge 817
Self-Destruction 866
Suffering 946

Injustice 477
Injury 476
Justice 517
Leniency 534
Reform 790

Innocence 478
Naïveté 618
Purity 770
Simplicity 899

Innovation 479
Change 117
Invention 502
Novelty 640

Inquiry 480
  Curiosity 211
Insanity
  Madness 559
Insects 481
Insecurity 482
  Anxiety 43
  Security 856
  Self-Doubt 868
  Uncertainty 1005
Insensitivity 483
  Blindness, Spiritual 87
  Sensibility 883
Insight
  Intuition 501
  Understanding 1007
  Understanding Others 1008
Insignificance
  Unimportance 1012
Insincerity 484
  Hypocrisy 440
  Pretension 732
  Sincerity 901
Insomnia
  Bed 73
Inspiration 485
  Creation and Creativity 201
Instinct 486
  Human Nature 431
Institutions 487
  Bureaucracy 102
Insult 488
  Injury 476
  Rudeness 830
Insurance 489
The Intangible 490
  Spirituality 927
Integrity 491
  Character 119
  Constancy and Inconstancy 181
  Honesty 425
  Loyalty 556
  Morality 604
  Nobility 635
  Principle 734
  Sincerity 901
  Strength 940
  Virtue 1033
Intellectuals and Intellectualism 492
  Intelligence 493
  Mind 590
Intelligence 493
  Cleverness 139
  Mind 590
  Reason 785
Intelligence (*cont.*)
  Stupidity 941
  Understanding 1007
  Wisdom 1060
Intemperance 494
  Drinking 268
  Excess 312
  Profligacy 739
  Temperance 970
Intention
  Purpose 771
Interest 495
  Selfishness 874
Interestingness 496
Interests, Divided 497
  Conflict, Inner 170
International Relations 498
  Brotherhood 100
  Cosmopolitanism 193
  Diplomats and Diplomacy 247
  East and West 273
  Imperialism 458
  Nationalism 622
  Treaties 994
  United Nations 1015
Intimacy 499
  Association 57
  Familiarity 333
  Togetherness 983
Intimidation
  Fear 343
  Force 357
  Threat 976
Intolerance 500
  Dogmatism 264
  Fanaticism 335
  Narrowness 620
  Prejudices 726
  Racial Prejudice 775
  Tolerance 984
Introspection
  Psychoanalysis 758
  Self-Knowledge 875
Intuition 501
  Emotions 284
  Perception 683
  Sensibility 883
Invention 502
  Creation and Creativity 201
  Innovation 479
  Technology 966
Investment 503
  Business and Commerce 104
Involvement 504
  Activity 10
  Commitment 146
  Deadness, Spiritual 219
Involvement (*cont.*)
  Experience 321
  Joie De Vivre 513
Ireland and Irishmen 505
Irony
  Humor 436
Irrationality
  Unreason 1020
Irreverence 506
  Iconoclasm 441
  Worship 1068
Irrevocableness 507
  Consequences 176
  Fate 340
  Necessity 624
  Past 676
  Resignation 806
Irritations 508
Isolation
  Alienation 30
  Aloofness 31
  Solitude 915
Italy and Italians 509
  Venice 1029
Itch
  Scratching 852
January
  Seasons 854
Jealousy 510
  Envy 295
Jesus 511
Jews 512
Joie De Vivre 513
  Enthusiasm 293
  Involvement 504
  Pleasure 704
  Vitality 1036
Jokes
  Humor 436
  Wit 1061
Journalism
  News 629
  Newspapers 630
Joy
  Ecstasy 278
  Happiness 409
  Pleasure 704
Judges 514
  Justice 517
  Law and Lawyers 528
Judging Others 515
  Criticism 206
  Others 663
Judgment 516
  Impartiality 455
Justice 517
  Impartiality 455
  Injustice 477
Justice (*cont.*)
  Judges 514
  Leniency 534
Juvenile Delinquency
  Crime 204
Killing 518
  Violence 1032
  War 1042
Kindness 519
  Charity 120
  Gentleness 379
  Gifts and Giving 384
  Unkindness 1018
Kings 520
  Court, Royal 196
  Government 395
  Royalty 829
  Rulers 831
Kissing 521
Knowledge 522
  Ignorance 447
  Learning 532
  Scholars and Scholarship 848
  Understanding 1007
  The Unknown 1019
Labor
  Unions 1013
  Work 1065
Labor Day
  Holidays 420
Lack
  Deprivation 236
  Need 625
Land
  Farms and Farming 337
  Property 746
Lady 523
Language 524
  Analogy 35
  Clarity 134
  Definition 230
  Grammar 398
  Speaking 923
  Style 942
  Words 1064
  Writing and Writers 1069
Largeness 525
  Generosity 375
  Greatness 401
  Smallness 908
Laughter 526
  Entertainment 292
  Humor 436
  Laughter and Tears 527
  Ridicule 820
  Weeping 1052
  Wit 1061

Laughter and Tears 527
LAUGHTER 526
WEEPING 1052

Law and Lawyers 528
INJUSTICE 477
JUDGES 514
JUSTICE 517
LAW AND ORDER 529
LENIENCY 534

Law and Order 529
LAW AND LAWYERS 528
ORDER 661
POLICE 709

Laziness 530
IDLENESS 446

Leadership 531
AUTHORITY 61
EXECUTIVES 315
FOLLOWING 353
OBEDIENCE 644
RULERS 831

Learning 532
EDUCATION 279
EXPERIENCE 321
GROWTH AND DEVELOPMENT 404
KNOWLEDGE 522
PRACTICE 721
SCHOLARS AND SCHOLARSHIP 848

Legacy
WILLS AND INHERITANCE 1058

Leisure 533
ACTIVITY 10
IDLENESS 446
PLAY 703
REST 811
RETIREMENT 813

Lending
BORROWING AND LENDING 96

Leniency 534
INDULGENCE 470
INJUSTICE 477
JUSTICE 517
MERCY 583
PUNISHMENT 766
SEVERITY 890

Letters 535

Liberalism 536
CONSERVATISM 178
POLITICAL PARTIES 710
RADICALISM 776

Liberality
GENEROSITY 375

Libertinism
PROFLIGACY 739

Liberty 537
CAPTIVITY 109
DEMOCRACY 233
FREEDOM 363

Liberty *(cont.)*
RIGHTS 823
SERVITUDE 889

Libraries 538
BOOKS AND READING 93

Lies
FALSEHOOD 331

Life 539
THE ABSURD 3
BIRTH 83
DEATH 221
EXISTENCE 316
INVOLVEMENT 504
LIFE, STAGES OF 540
LIFE AND DEATH 541
LONGEVITY 548
MEANING 573
MORTALITY 606
TRANSIENCE 990
THE UNKNOWN 1019
WORLD 1067

Life, Stages of 540
LIFE 539
MATURITY 571
OLD AGE 653
YOUTH 1071
YOUTH AND AGE 1072

Life and Death 541
DEATH 221
LIFE 539

Liking
AFFECTION 21
AFFINITY 22
PREFERENCE 725

Limitations 542
FAULTS 342
IMMATURITY 452
IMPERFECTION 457
INADEQUACY 462
WEAKNESS 1047

Liquor
DRINKING 268

Listening 543
CONVERSATION 188
EAVESDROPPING 275
SPEAKING 923

Literalness 544

Literature 545
BOOKS AND READING 93
WRITING AND WRITERS 1069

Loan
BORROWING AND LENDING 96
DEBT 222

Logic
REASON 785

London 546
ENGLAND AND ENGLISHMEN 289

Loneliness 547
SOLITUDE 915

Longevity 548
OLD AGE 653

Losers 549
ADVANTAGE 15
ADVERSITY 17
FAILURE 329

Loss 550
ADVERSITY 17
DEPRIVATION 236
FAILURE 329
LOVE, LOSS OF 552
NOSTALGIA 639

Love 551
AFFECTION 21
AFFINITY 22
CHARITY 120
CONSTANCY AND INCONSTANCY 181
COURTSHIP 198
EMOTIONS 284
FLIRTATION 351
INTIMACY 499
JEALOUSY 510
KISSING 521
LOVE, LOSS OF 552
LOVE, UNREQUITED 553
LOVE AND HATE 554
LOVERS 555
PASSION 675
ROMANCE 826
SEDUCTION 857
SEX 892

Love, Loss of 552
ESTRANGEMENT 301
INFIDELITY 472
LOSS 550
LOVE, UNREQUITED 553
REJECTION 793

Love, Unrequited 553
REJECTION 793

Love and Hate 554
HATRED 412
LOVE 551

Lovers 555
LOVE 551
LOVE, LOSS OF 552
LOVE, UNREQUITED 553
LOVE AND HATE 554

Lower Class
THE PEOPLE 682

Loyalty 556
CONSTANCY AND INCONSTANCY 181
INTEGRITY 491

Luck
FORTUNE 360

Luxury 557
EXCESS 312
EXTRAVAGANCE 324
PROSPERITY 750

Lying 558
DECEPTION 224
SELF-DECEPTION 864
TRUTH AND FALSEHOOD 999
TRUTH 998
TRUTHFULNESS 1000

Machines
TECHNOLOGY 966

Madness 559
NEUROSIS 627
SANITY 842

Mailmen 560

Malice 561
ENVY 295
SLANDER 905

Man, Ages of
LIFE, STAGES OF 540

Management
ADMINISTRATION 13
EXECUTIVES 315

Mankind 562
HUMAN NATURE 431
LIFE 539

Manners 563
CEREMONY 114
COURTESY 197
CUSTOM 213
GENTLEMAN 378
GOOD BREEDING 391
HANDSHAKE 408
PROPRIETY 749
SOCIETY, POLITE 914
TACT 961

March
SEASONS 854

Marriage 564
BACHELORS 66
CHILDREN 123
COURTSHIP 198
DIVORCE 262
FAMILY 334
INFIDELITY 472
INTIMACY 499
PARENTHOOD 670
SEX 892
WEDDINGS 1051

Martyrs and Martyrdom 565
CHRISTIANITY 125
RELIGION 797
SACRIFICE 837
SAINTS AND SAINTHOOD 840
SCAPEGOAT 847

Masculinity and Femininity 566
MEN AND WOMEN 581

Masks
APPEARANCE 45
CONCEALMENT 165
PERSONALITY, DUAL 688
PRETENSION 732

The Masses
THE PEOPLE 682
Masochism 567
SELF-DESTRUCTION 866
Mass Movements 568
CAUSES 111
DEMAGOGUERY 232
FOLLOWING 353
IDEOLOGY 445
REVOLUTION 819
Materialism 569
OBJECTS 646
SPIRITUALITY 927
Mathematics 570
Maturity 571
GROWTH AND DEVELOPMENT 404
IMMATURITY 452
MIDDLE AGE 586
OLD AGE 653
YOUTH 1071
Maxims 572
EPIGRAMS 296
QUOTATIONS 773
May
SEASONS 854
Meaning 573
THE ABSURD 3
SYMBOLS AND SYMBOLISM 959
WORDS 1064
Meanness
PETTINESS 693
STINGINESS 936
Means and Ends 574
EXPEDIENCY 319
METHOD 585
Meddling 575
GOSSIP 394
Media 576
ENTERTAINMENT 292
FREE SPEECH 364
MOVIES 611
NEWSPAPERS 630
PRESS, FREEDOM OF THE 731
PUBLISHING 764
TELEVISION 967
Medicine 577
DIAGNOSIS 243
DOCTORS 263
HEALTH 413
PSYCHIATRY 757
REMEDIES 798
SICKNESS 896
Mediocrity 578
EXCELLENCE 311
Meditation
CONTEMPLATION 183
REVERIE 818
THOUGHT 975
Meekness
HUMILITY 435
TIMIDITY 980
Meetings 579
COMMITTEES 147
Memory 580
NOSTALGIA 639
Men and Women 581
MASCULINITY AND FEMININITY 566
MEN 582
WOMEN 1062
Mental Health
MADNESS 559
SANITY 842
Men 582
BACHELORS 66
GENTLEMAN 378
MASCULINITY AND FEMININITY 566
MEN AND WOMEN 581
WOMEN 1062
Mercy 583
FORGIVENESS 359
LENIENCY 534
PITY 698
Merit 584
EXCELLENCE 311
FAME 332
PRAISE 722
REPUTATION 804
SUPERIORITY 952
Method 585
EFFICIENCY 280
MEANS AND ENDS 574
ORDER 661
PATIENCE 677
PLANS 702
PRACTICE 721
PROBLEMS 737
RULES 832
SINGLE-MINDEDNESS 903
STRATEGY 939
Middle Age 586
LIFE, STAGES OF 540
MATURITY 571
OLD AGE 653
YOUTH 1071
Middle Class 587
ARISTOCRACY 52
CLASS 135
THE PEOPLE 682
RANK 780
SOCIETY 913
STATUS 933
The Military 588
STRATEGY 939
WAR 1042
WEAPONS 1049
Mind and Body 589
BODY 90
HEALTH 413
MIND 590
Mind and Body *(cont.)*
SENSES 882
SOUL 919
SPIRITUALITY 927
Mind 590
IMAGINATION 450
INTELLECTUALS AND INTELLECTUALISM 492
INTELLIGENCE 493
MIND AND BODY 589
REVERIE 818
THOUGHT 975
UNCONSCIOUSNESS 1006
UNDERSTANDING 1007
Minorities 591
BLACKS 85
RACIAL PREJUDICE 775
Miracles 592
SUPERNATURAL 953
Mirrors 593
IDENTITY 444
Misanthropy 594
DISLIKE 255
HATRED 412
HUMANITARIANISM 433
Misers 595
GREED 403
STINGINESS 936
Misery
SUFFERING 946
UNHAPPINESS 1011
Misfortune
ADVERSITY 17
FORTUNE 360
Missionaries 596
SALVATION 841
Mistakes
BLUNDER 88
ERROR 299
Mistrust
DISTRUST 259
Mob 597
CROWDS 208
THE PEOPLE 682
Model
EXAMPLE 310
Moderation 598
EXCESS 312
INTEMPERANCE 494
PROPORTION 748
PRUDENCE 755
SUFFICIENCY 947
TEMPERANCE 970
Modernity 599
CONTEMPORANEOUSNESS 184
Modesty 600
HUMILITY 435
Monasticism 601
CHASTITY 122
Monasticism *(cont.)*
CLERGY 138
CONTEMPLATION 183
SAINTS AND SAINTHOOD 840
SELF-DENIAL 865
SPIRITUALITY 927
Money 602
ACQUISITION 8
BANKING 69
BUSINESS AND COMMERCE 104
INVESTMENT 503
PAYMENT 680
PROSPERITY 750
THRIFT 977
WEALTH 1048
WILLS AND INHERITANCE 1058
Moods
EMOTIONS 284
TEMPERAMENT 969
Moon 603
THE HEAVENS 415
SPACE 921
Morality 604
BEHAVIOR 77
CONSCIENCE 174
GOODNESS 393
INTEGRITY 491
VIRTUE 1033
Morning 605
BED 73
NIGHT 633
SLEEP 906
Mortality 606
DEATH 221
IMMORTALITY 454
TRANSIENCE 990
Mothers 607
PARENTHOOD 670
Motives 608
ENDS 286
PURPOSE 771
Mountains 609
Mourning 610
BURIAL 103
FUNERALS 367
SORROW 918
WEEPING 1052
Movies 611
HOLLYWOOD 421
MEDIA 576
The Mundane 612
FAMILIARITY 333
TRIFLES 996
UNIMPORTANCE 1012
Murder
KILLING 518
Museums 613

Music 614
Musical Instruments 615
Opera 655
Singing 902

Musical Instruments 615
Music 614

Mysticism 616
Ecstasy 278
Spirituality 927

Myth 617
Illusion 449

Naïveté 618
Credulity 202
Ignorance 447
Innocence 478

Names 619
Identity 444

Narcissism
Self-Love 876

Narrowness 620
Fanaticism 335
Intolerance 500
Open-Mindedness 654
Prejudices 726
Single-Mindedness 903

Nation 621
Immigration 453
Nationalism 622
Patriotism 678
State 930

Nationalism 622
International Relations 498
Nation 621
Patriotism 678

Nature 623
Conservation 177
Earth 272
Evolution 308
Flowers 352
The Heavens 415
Human Nature 431
Insects 481
Instinct 486
Moon 603
Mountains 609
Rivers 824
Sea 853
Seasons 854
Snow 911
Sun 950
Trees 995
Water 1046
Weather 1050
Wind 1059

Nakedness
Nudity 642

Necessity 624
Circumstance 129
Destiny 240
Fate 340

Necessity *(cont.)*
Fortune 360
Need 625

Need 625
Deprivation 236
Necessity 624
Poverty 718

Negotiation
Treaties 994

Negroes
Blacks 85

Neighbors 626

Nervousness
Anxiety 43
Fear 343
Neurosis 627

Neurosis 627
Anxiety 43
Compulsiveness 163
Madness 559
Obsession 651
Psychiatry 757
Psychoanalysis 758
Sanity 842
Self-Destruction 866

Neutrality
Impartiality 455
International Relations 498

New England 628

Newness
Innovation 479
Novelty 640

News 629
Newspapers 630

Newspapers 630
Free Speech 364
Media 576
News 629
Press, Freedom of the 731
Publishing 764

The New Year 631

New York 632
Cities 131

Nicknames
Names 619

Night 633
Darkness 217
Morning 605
Sleep 906

Nihilism 634

Nobility 635
Integrity 491
Superiority 952

Noise 636

Nonconformity
Bohemians 91
Dissent 258

Nonconformity *(cont.)*
Individualism 468
Individuality 469

Nonsense
Sense and Nonsense 881

Nonviolence
Pacifism 665

Normality 637
Conformity 171

Nose
Face 326

North and South 638

Nostalgia 639
Loss 550
Memory 580
Past 676

Novels
Fiction 344

Novelty 640
Change 117
Fashion 338
Innovation 479
Invention 502

November
Seasons 854

Nuclear Power 641
Survival 956
Technology 966
Weapons 1049

Nudity 642
Propriety 749
Prudery 756
Shame 893

Oaths 643
Promises 743

Obedience 644
Authority 61
Disobedience 256
Following 353
Leadership 531

Obesity 645

Objectivity
Impartiality 455

Objects 646
Materialism 569

Obligation 647
Debt 222
Duty 271
Gifts and Giving 384
Gratitude 399
Ingratitude 475
Receiving 787

Obscurantism 648
Communication 149

Obscurity 649
Great and Small 400
Smallness 908
Unimportance 1012

Observation 650
Audience 59
Deadness, Spiritual 219
Indifference 466
Perception 683
Sight 897

Obsession 651
Compulsiveness 163
Neurosis 627

Obstinacy 652
Dogmatism 264
Flexibility 350

Ocean
Sea 853

October
Seasons 854

Offense
Injury 476

Old Age 653
Decline 226
Generations 374
Life, Stages of 540
Longevity 548
Maturity 571
Middle Age 586
Retirement 813
Youth and Age 1072

Open-Mindedness 654
Change 117
Flexibility 350
Growth and Development 404
Narrowness 620
Sincerity 901

Opera 655
Singing 902

Opinion 656
Argument 51
Discord 252
Flexibility 350
Ideas 443
Minorities 591
Public Opinion 762

Opportunity 657
Potential 717

Opposites
Contrast 187

Opposition 658
Discord 252
Dissent 258
Protest 753
Rebellion 786
Revolution 819
Violence 1032

Oppression
Servitude 889
Tyranny 1002

Optimism 659
Optimism and Pessimism 660
Pessimism 692

Optimism and Pessimism 660
OPTIMISM 659
PESSIMISM 692

Oratory
PUBLIC SPEAKING 763

Order 661
DISORDER 257
HARMONY 410
LAW AND ORDER 529
METHOD 585
PLANS 702
ROUTINE 828

Originality 662
ECCENTRICITY 276
INDIVIDUALISM 468
INDIVIDUALITY 469
UNIQUENESS 1014

Others 663
JUDGING OTHERS 515
RELATIONSHIPS, HUMAN 794
UNDERSTANDING OTHERS 1008

Overconfidence 664
SELF-CONFIDENCE 860

Overpopulation
BIRTH CONTROL 84
POPULATION 713

Ownership
POSSESSION 716
PROPERTY 746

Pacifism 665
FORCE 357
INJURY 476
PEACE 681

Pain
SUFFERING 946

Painting 666
ART AND ARTISTS 53
COLOR 143

Parades 667

Paradoxes 668

Parasites 669

Pardon
FORGIVENESS 359

Parenthood 670
BABIES 65
BOYS 97
CHILDREN 123
DAUGHTERS 218
FAMILY 334
GIRLS 385
HEREDITY 417
SONS 916
TRAINING 988

Paris 671
FRANCE AND FRENCHMEN 361

Parties 672

Parting 673
ABSENCE 2

Partisanship 674
CAUSES 111
FANATICISM 335
IMPARTIALITY 455
POLITICAL PARTIES 710

Party, Political
POLITICAL PARTIES 710

Passion 675
DESIRES 238
EMOTIONS 284
LOVE 551

Passivity
DEADNESS, SPIRITUAL 219
DEPENDENCE 235
IMPOTENCE 459
INDIFFERENCE 466
OBSERVATION 650

Past 676
ANTIQUITY 42
ERA 298
FUTURE 368
HISTORY AND HISTORIANS 419
IRREVOCABLENESS 507
NOSTALGIA 639
PRESENT 729
TRADITION 986

Patience 677
IMPATIENCE 456
METHOD 585
WAITING 1040

Patients
DOCTORS 263

Patriotism 678
HOMELAND 423
NATIONALISM 622

Patronage 679

Payment 680
OBLIGATION 647
RECOMPENSE 789

Peace 681
CONCILIATION 167
CONQUEST 173
DEFEAT 228
PACIFISM 665
TRANQUILITY 989
WAR 1042

Pedantry
KNOWLEDGE 522
SCHOLARS AND SCHOLARSHIP 848

The People 682
ARISTOCRACY 52
CLASS 135
CROWDS 208
DEMOCRACY 233
MIDDLE CLASS 587
MOB 597
SOCIETY 913

Perception 683
BLINDNESS, SPIRITUAL 87
EYES 325
INTUITION 501
PERSPECTIVE 689
SENSES 882
SENSIBILITY 883
SIGHT 897
UNDERSTANDING 1007
VISION 1035

Perfection 684
ERROR 299
FAULTS 342
IMPERFECTION 457

Perfume 685
COSMETICS 192

Permanence
CHANGELESSNESS 118

Perseverance 686
EFFORT 281
ENDURANCE 287
METHOD 585

Personality 687
CHARACTER 119
PERSONALITY, DUAL 688
TEMPERAMENT 969

Personality, Dual 688
HYPOCRISY 440
IDENTITY 444
PERSONALITY 687

Perspective 689
ATTITUDE 58
FAMILIARITY 333
PERCEPTION 683
RELATIVENESS 795

Persuasion 690
ARGUMENT 51
COMPLIANCE 158
ELOQUENCE 283
PROPAGANDA 745

Perverseness 691
CONFLICT, INNER 170
SELF-DESTRUCTION 866

Pessimism 692
OPTIMISM 659
OPTIMISM AND PESSIMISM 660

Pettiness 693
LARGENESS 525
MEDIOCRITY 578
TRIFLES 996
UNIMPORTANCE 1012

Philanthropy
HUMANITARIANISM 433

Philosophers and Philosophy 694
EXISTENTIALISM 317
HUMANISM 432
MEANING 573
NIHILISM 634
REASON 785
SKEPTICISM 904

Philosophers and Philosophy *(cont.)*
STOICISM 937
THEORY 974
THOUGHT 975
THE UNKNOWN 1019

Photography 695

Physical Fitness 696
SPORTS 929
WALKING 1041

Physicians
DOCTORS 263

Physics
SCIENCE 849

Piety 697
GOODNESS 393
IRREVERENCE 506
PRAYER 723

Pity 698
MERCY 583
SELF-PITY 877
SYMPATHY 960
UNDERSTANDING OTHERS 1008

Place 699
TRAVEL 992

Plagiarism 700
IMITATION 451

Plain Dealing
FRANKNESS 362
HONESTY 425
SINCERITY 901

Plain Living 701
CONTENTMENT 186
THRIFT 977

Plans 702
METHOD 585
ORDER 661
STRATEGY 939

Plants
FARMS AND FARMING 337
FLOWERS 352
GARDENING 371
NATURE 623
TREES 995

Play 703
LEISURE 533
SPORTS 929

Plays
THEATER 972

Pleasure 704
HAPPINESS 409
JOIE DE VIVRE 513
PLEASURE AND PAIN 705
PLEASURE-SEEKING 706
PROFLIGACY 739

Pleasure and Pain 705
PLEASURE 704
SUFFERING 946

Pleasure-Seeking 706
  Pleasure 704
  Profligacy 739

Plumbers 707
  Sewers 891

Poetry and Poets 708
  Creation and Creativity 201
  Language 524
  Writing and Writers 1069

Police 709
  Law and Order 529

Politeness
  Courtesy 197
  Manners 563

Political Parties 710
  Conservatism 178
  Liberalism 536
  Partisanship 674
  Politics and Politicians 711
  Radicalism 776

Politics and Politicians 711
  Citizens 132
  Congress 172
  Demagoguery 232
  Government 395
  International Relations 498
  Nation 621
  Political Parties 710
  Presidency 730
  Public Office 761
  State 930
  Statesmen and Statesmanship 931
  Voting 1038

Poor
  Poverty 718

Popularity 712
  Approval 49
  Ingratiation 474

Population 713
  Birth Control 84
  Crowds 208
  Reproduction 802

Pornography 714

Portent 715
  Evidence 306
  Prudence 755

Position
  Rank 780

Possession 716
  Acquisition 8
  Capitalism 108
  Property 746

Possibilities
  Opportunity 657
  Potential 717

Postponement
  Delay 231

Potential 717
  Opportunity 657
  Unfulfillment 1010

Poverty 718
  Adversity 17
  Beggars 74
  Deprivation 236
  Hunger 437
  Money 602
  Need 625
  Property 746
  Unemployment 1009
  Wealth 1048

Power 719
  Authority 61
  Impotence 459
  Strength 940
  Tyranny 1002

Powerlessness
  Impotence 459

Practicality 720
  Common Sense 148
  Expediency 319
  Prudence 755
  Reason 785
  Usefulness 1023

Practice 721
  Learning 532
  Method 585

Praise 722
  Appreciation 47
  Approval 49
  Merit 584

Prayer 723
  Contemplation 183
  Worship 1068

Preaching and Preachers 724
  Churchgoing 128
  Clergy 138

Prediction
  Future 368
  Portent 715
  Prophecies 747
  Vision 1035

Preference 725
  Choice 124
  Taste 963

Prejudice, Racial
  Racial Prejudice 775

Prejudices 726
  Dogmatism 264
  Intolerance 500
  Narrowness 620

Prematureness 727
  Delay 231
  Timeliness 979

Preparedness 728
  Vision 1035

Present 729
  Future 368
  Past 676

Presidency 730
  Government 395
  Public Office 761

Press, Freedom of the 731
  Censorship 113
  Dissent 258
  Free Speech 364
  Newspapers 630
  Publishing 764
  Rights 823

Pretense
  Concealment 165
  Deception 224
  Hypocrisy 440
  Imagination 450
  Pretension 732

Pretension 732
  Appearance 45
  Artificiality 54
  Imitation 451
  Insincerity 484
  Pride 733
  Role-Playing 825
  Vanity 1027

Pride 733
  Boasting 89
  Complacency 156
  Conceit 166
  Humility 435
  Self-Esteem 871
  Self-Importance 873
  Self-Love 876
  Snobbery 910
  Vanity 1027

Priests
  Clergy 138

Principle 734
  Integrity 491
  Right 822

Printing
  Publishing 764

Prison 735
  Captivity 109

Privacy 736
  Publicity 760
  Solitude 915

Privilege
  Advantage 15

Problems 737
  Method 585

Procrastination
  Delay 231

Profanity
  Swearing 957

Professions
  Vocations 1037

Profiteering 738
  Business and Commerce 104
  Buying and Selling 105

Profligacy 739
  Intemperance 494
  Pleasure-Seeking 706

Profundity 740
  Seriousness 886
  Superficiality 951
  Wisdom 1060

Progress 741
  Evolution 308

Promiscuity 742
  Infidelity 472
  Seduction 857
  Sex 892

Promises 743
  Oaths 643

Promptness
  Timeliness 979

Proof 744
  Evidence 306
  Reason 785

Propaganda 745
  Advertising 18
  Publicity 760

Property 746
  Acquisition 8
  Capitalism 108
  Houses 430
  Money 602
  Possession 716
  Poverty 718
  Wealth 1048

Prophecies 747

Proportion 748
  Extravagance 324
  Harmony 410
  Moderation 598

Propriety 749
  Ceremony 114
  Courtesy 197
  Good Breeding 391
  Manners 563
  Nudity 642
  Prudery 756
  Respectability 809

Prosperity 750
  Adversity 17
  Luxury 557
  Prosperity and Adversity 751
  Success 945
  Wealth 1048

Prosperity and Adversity 751
  Adversity 17
  Fortune 360
  Prosperity 750

Prostitution 752

Protest 753
DISSENT 258
OPPOSITION 658
REBELLION 786

Protestantism
CHRISTIANITY 125

Proverbs
MAXIMS 572

Providence 754
DESTINY 240
FATE 340
GOD 387
SELF-SUFFICIENCY 880

Prudence 755
CAUTIOUSNESS 112
COMMON SENSE 148
FOLLY 354
MODERATION 598
PRACTICALITY 720
PROPORTION 748
RASHNESS 781
WISDOM 1060

Prudery 756
NUDITY 642
PROPRIETY 749
PURITANS AND PURITANISM 769

Prying
MEDDLING 575

Psychiatry 757
NEUROSIS 627
PSYCHOANALYSIS 758
PSYCHOLOGY 759

Psychoanalysis 758
ANXIETY 43
NEUROSIS 627
PSYCHIATRY 757
PSYCHOLOGY 759
SELF-KNOWLEDGE 875

Psychology 759
MIND 590
NEUROSIS 627
PSYCHIATRY 757
PSYCHOANALYSIS 758

The Public
THE PEOPLE 682

Public Office 760
CONGRESS 172
GOVERNMENT 395
POLITICS AND POLITICIANS 711
PRESIDENCY 730
PUBLIC OPINION 762

Public Opinion 761
OPINION 656

Public Relations
ADVERTISING 18
PROPAGANDA 745
PUBLICITY 760

Public Speaking 762
DEMAGOGUERY 232
ELOQUENCE 283

Public Speaking *(cont.)*
SPEAKING 923

Publicity 763
ADVERTISING 18
PRIVACY 736
PROPAGANDA 745

Public Life
FAME 332
PUBLIC OFFICE 761

Publishing 764
FREE SPEECH 364
NEWSPAPERS 630
PRESS, FREEDOM OF THE 731

Punctuality 765
DELAY 231

Punctuation
STYLE 942

Punishment 766
DISCIPLINE 250
PRISON 735
PUNISHMENT, CAPITAL 767
RETRIBUTION 815
SEVERITY 890

Punishment, Capital 767
PUNISHMENT 766

Puns 768
WIT 1061

Puritans and Puritanism 769
PRUDERY 756

Purity 770
ASSOCIATION 57
INNOCENCE 478

Purpose 771
DECISION 225
ENDS 286
INDECISION 465
MOTIVES 608
RESOLUTION 807
SELF-DETERMINATION 867
WILL 1056
WILLINGNESS 1057

Quarreling 772
ARGUMENT 51
DISCORD 252
FIGHTING 345

Questions
INQUIRY 480

Quickness
HASTE 411
SPEED 926

Quotations 773
EPIGRAMS 296
MAXIMS 572

Race 774
ANGLO-SAXONS 40
BLACKS 85
RACIAL PREJUDICE 775
WHITES 1054

Racial Prejudice 775
BLACKS 85
RACE 774
WHITES 1054

Radicalism 776
CONSERVATISM 178
LIBERALISM 536
POLITICAL PARTIES 710

Radio 777

Rain 778
RAINBOWS 778
SEASONS 854
WEATHER 1050

Rainbows 779
RAIN 778

Rank 780
ARISTOCRACY 52
CLASS 135
OBSCURITY 649
PARASITES 669
SNOBBERY 910
STATUS 933
UNIMPORTANCE 1012

Rashness 781
CAUTIOUSNESS 112
FOLLY 354
PRUDENCE 755

Rationalization 782
EXCUSES 314
EXPLANATION 322

Reading
BOOKS AND READING 93

Realism 783
EVASION 304
PRACTICALITY 720
REALITY 784

Reality 784
FACTS 328
ILLUSION 449
REALISM 783

Reason 785
ARGUMENT 51
INTELLIGENCE 493
PROOF 744
THEORY 974
THOUGHT 975
UNREASON 1020

Rebellion 786
DISOBEDIENCE 256
DISSENT 258
OPPOSITION 658
REVOLUTION 819
VIOLENCE 1032

Receiving 787
GIFTS AND GIVING 384
GRATITUDE 399
INGRATITUDE 475
OBLIGATION 647
RECOMPENSE 789

Reciprocity 788

Recklessness
BOLDNESS 92
DANGER 216
RASHNESS 781

Recognition
APPRECIATION 47

Recompense 789
INJURY 476
PAYMENT 680
REVENGE 817

Reform 790
HUMANITARIANISM 433
IDEALISM 442
IMPROVEMENT 460
INJUSTICE 477
UTOPIA 1025

Refusal 791
REQUEST 805

Regret 792
APOLOGY 44

Rejection 793
LOVE, LOSS OF 552
LOVE, UNREQUITED 553

Relationships, Human 794
INTIMACY 499
OTHERS 663
UNDERSTANDING OTHERS 1008

Relativeness 795
COMPARISON 153

Relatives 796
FAMILY 334
RELATIONSHIPS, HUMAN 794

Religion 797
BELIEF 78
BIBLE 80
CHRISTIANITY 125
CHURCH 126
CHURCH AND STATE 127
CHURCHGOING 128
CLERGY 138
DOGMATISM 264
DOUBT, RELIGIOUS 265
FAITH 330
MARTYRS AND MARTYRDOM 565
MISSIONARIES 596
MONASTICISM 601
MYSTICISM 616
PIETY 697
PRAYER 723
PREACHING AND PREACHERS 724
PURITANS AND PURITANISM 769
REVELATION, DIVINE 816
SABBATH 835
SAINTS AND SAINTHOOD 840
SALVATION 841
SCIENCE AND RELIGION 850
THEOLOGY 973
WORSHIP 1068

Remedies 798
CONSOLATIONS 180
DIAGNOSIS 243
MEDICINE 577

Reminiscences
MEMORY 580

Renunciation 799
RESIGNATION 806

Repayment
RECOMPENSE 789

Repetition 800

Representative Assembly
CONGRESS 172

Repression 801
CAPTIVITY 109
FORCE 357
TYRANNY 1002

Reproach
REPROOF 803

Reproduction 802
BIRTH CONTROL 84
HEREDITY 417
POPULATION 713

Reproof 803
CRITICISM 206
FAULTS 342
JUDGING OTHERS 515

Republicans
POLITICAL PARTIES 710

Reputation 804
ASSOCIATION 57
MERIT 584
SLANDER 905

Request 805
REFUSAL 791

Reserve
ALOOFNESS 31
COLDNESS 142

Resignation 806
ENDURANCE 287
IRREVOCABLENESS 507
NECESSITY 624
RENUNCIATION 799
STOICISM 937

Resistance
OPPOSITION 658
REBELLION 786

Resolution 807
DECISION 225
PURPOSE 771
SELF-DETERMINATION 867
WILL 1056

Respect 808
ADMIRATION 14
HONORS 426
WORSHIP 1068

Respectability 809
PROPRIETY 749

Responsibility 810
DUTY 271

Rest 811
IDLENESS 446
LEISURE 533
RETIREMENT 813

Restlessness 812
ACTIVITY 10
IMPATIENCE 456
WAITING 1040

Restraint
MODERATION 598
SUFFICIENCY 947

Retirement 813
IDLENESS 446
LEISURE 533
REST 811

Retreat 814
ESCAPE 300

Retribution 815
CAUSE AND EFFECT 110
CONSEQUENCES 176
PUNISHMENT 766
RECOMPENSE 789
REVENGE 817

Revelation
REVELATION, DIVINE 816
SELF-REVELATION 878

Revelation, Divine 816
GOD 387

Revenge 817
INJURY 476
RECOMPENSE 789
RETRIBUTION 815

Reverence
RESPECT 808
WORSHIP 1068

Reverie 818
IMAGINATION 450
FANTASY 336
THOUGHT 975

Reviews
CRITICISM, PROFESSIONAL 207

Revolution 819
DISSENT 258
ICONOCLASM 441
MASS MOVEMENTS 568
OPPOSITION 658
REBELLION 786
REPRESSION 801
TYRANNY 1002
VIOLENCE 1032

Riches
WEALTH 1048

Ridicule 820
ABSURDITY 4
HUMILIATION 434
HUMOR 436
LAUGHTER 526
SHAME 893

Riding 821

Right 822
CONSCIENCE 174
DEEDS 227
ERROR 299
EXPEDIENCY 319
GOODNESS 393
PRINCIPLE 734
VIRTUE 1033
WRONGDOING 1070

Rights 823
EQUALITY 297
FREE SPEECH 364
LIBERTY 537
PRESS, FREEDOM OF THE 731

Rising
BED 73
MORNING 605

Ritual
CEREMONY 114

Rivalry
COMPETITION 155

Rivers 824
SEA 853
WATER 1046

Robbery
STEALING 934

Role-Playing 825
APPEARANCE 45
PRETENSION 732

Romance 826
COURTSHIP 198
ROMANTICISM 827

Romanticism 827

Routine 828
HABIT 406
ORDER 661

Royalty 829
COURT, ROYAL 196
KINGS 520

Rudeness 830
COURTESY 197
INSULT 488
TACT 961

Ruins
ANTIQUITY 42

Rulers 831
AUTHORITY 61
GOVERNMENT 395
KINGS 520
LEADERSHIP 531
PRESIDENCY 730

Rules 832
METHOD 585

Rumors 833
GOSSIP 394
SCANDAL 846

Russia and Russians 834

Sabbath 835

Sacrament 836
SYMBOLS AND SYMBOLISM 959

Sacrifice 837
MARTYRS AND MARTYRDOM 565
SERVICES 888

Sadism 838
MASOCHISM 567
CRUELTY 209

Sadness
UNHAPPINESS 1011

Safety
SECURITY 856

Sailing 839
SHIPS AND BOATS 895

Saints and Sainthood 840
MARTYRS AND MARTYRDOM 565
SPIRITUALITY 927

Salvation 841
MISSIONARIES 596
SIN 900

Sanity 842
HEALTH 413
MADNESS 559
NEUROSIS 627

Sarcasm 843
WIT 1061

Satire 844
WIT 1061

Satisfaction 845
CONTENTMENT 186
DESIRES 238
SUFFICIENCY 947

Savagery
BARBARISM 70

Scandal 846
GOSSIP 394
RUMORS 833

Scapegoat 847
GUILT 405
MARTYRS AND MARTYRDOM 565

Scholars and Scholarship 848
EDUCATION 279
KNOWLEDGE 522
LEARNING 532
SPECIALISTS 924
TEACHING 965

Science 849
NUCLEAR POWER 641
SCIENCE AND RELIGION 850
SPACE 921
TECHNOLOGY 966
THEORY 974

Science and Religion 850
- Religion 797
- Science 849

Scorn
- Contempt 185

Scotsmen 851

Scratching 852

Sea 853
- Fish 347
- Rivers 824
- Sailing 839
- Ships and Boats 895
- Water 1046

Seasons 854
- Rain 778
- Snow 911
- Weather 1050

Secrets 855
- Confidences 169

Sect
- Partisanship 674

Security 856
- Certainty 115
- Defense 229
- Insecurity 482

Seduction 857
- Courtship 198
- Flirtation 351
- Love 551
- Promiscuity 742
- Sex 892

Seeing
- Sight 897

Segregation
- Racial Prejudice 775

Self 858
- Appearance 45
- Identity 444
- Individuality 469
- Mirrors 593

Self-Assertion 859
- Boldness 92

Self-Confidence 860
- Overconfidence 664
- Self-Doubt 868

Self-Consciousness 861
- Shame 893

Self-Control 862
- Discipline 250

Self-Criticism 863
- Self-Doubt 868
- Self-Hatred 872

Self-Deception 864
- Self-Love 876
- Vanity 1027

Self-Denial 865
- Chastity 122
- Monasticism 601

Self-Destruction 866
- Perverseness 691
- Self-Hatred 872
- Suicide 948

Self-Determination 867
- Identity 444
- Purpose 771
- Resolution 807
- Self-Sufficiency 880
- Will 1056

Self-Doubt 868
- Anxiety 43
- Insecurity 482
- Self-Confidence 860
- Self-Criticism 863
- Self-Esteem 871

Self-Esteem 869
- Pride 733
- Self-Doubt 868
- Self-Hatred 872
- Self-Love 876

Self-Expression 870
- Creation and Creativity 201

Self-Government 871
- Self-Control 862

Self-Hatred 872
- Self-Criticism 863
- Self-Destruction 866
- Self-Doubt 868
- Self-Esteem 871

Self-Importance 873
- Conceit 166
- Self-Love 876
- Vanity 1027

Self-Improvement
- Improvement 460

Self-Indulgence
- Indulgence 470

Self-Interest
- Interest 495
- Selfishness 874
- Self-Love 876

Selfishness 874
- Interest 495
- Self-Love 876
- Stinginess 936

Self-Knowledge 875
- Contemplation 183
- Identity 444
- Psychoanalysis 758
- Self 858

Selflessness
- Humility 435
- Service 887
- Unselfishness 1021

Self-Love 876
- Conceit 166
- Pride 733
- Self-Deception 864
- Self-Esteem 871
- Selfishness 874

Self-Love *(cont.)*
- Vanity 1027

Pity 877
- Pity 698

Self-Preservation
- Defense 229
- Survival 956

Self-Reliance
- Self-Determination 867
- Self-Sufficiency 880

Self-Respect
- Self-Esteem 871
- Self-Love 876

Self-Revelation 878
- Confidences 169

Self-Righteousness 879
- Dogmatism 264
- Fanaticism 335

Self-Sacrifice
- Sacrifice 837

Self-Seeking
- Interest 495
- Selfishness 874
- Self-Love 876

Self-Sufficiency 880
- Dependence 235
- Enterprise 291
- Self-Determination 867

Selling
- Buying and Selling 105

Sense and Nonsense 881

Senses 882
- Deafness 220
- Eyes 325
- Face 326
- Mind and Body 589
- Perception 683
- Sensuality 884
- Sight 897

Sensibility 883
- Consciousness 175
- Emotions 284
- Insensitivity 483
- Intuition 501
- Perception 683

Sensitivity
- Sensibility 883

Sensuality 884
- Senses 882

Sentimentality 885

Separation
- Parting 673

Serenity
- Tranquility 989

Seriousness 886
- Profundity 740

Sermons
- Preaching and Preachers 724

Service 887
- Assistance 56
- Deeds 227
- Humanitarianism 433
- Usefulness 1023

Services 888
- Deeds 227
- Gifts and Giving 384
- Humanitarianism 433
- Sacrifice 837

Servitude 889
- Captivity 109
- Liberty 537
- Tyranny 1002

Severity 890
- Leniency 534
- Punishment 766

Sewers 891
- Plumbers 707

Sex 892
- Chastity 122
- Flirtation 351
- Homosexuality 424
- Kissing 521
- Love 551
- Masculinity and Femininity 566
- Pornography 714
- Promiscuity 742
- Prostitution 752
- Seduction 857
- Sensuality 884

Shame 893
- Guilt 405
- Humiliation 434
- Ridicule 820
- Self-Consciousness 861

Sharing 894
- Gifts and Giving 384

Ships and Boats 895
- Sailing 839

Shyness
- Timidity 980

Sickness 896
- Germs 382
- Health 413
- Medicine 577

Sight 897
- Blindness, Physical 86
- Eyes 325
- Perception 683
- Senses 882
- Vision 1035

Signs
- Evidence 306
- Portent 715

Silence 898
Speaking 923

Simplicity 899
Innocence 478
Plain Living 701

Sin 900
Evil 307
Illegality 448
Salvation 841
Temptation 971
Wickedness 1055
Wrongdoing 1070

Sincerity 901
Frankness 362
Honesty 425
Hypocrisy 440
Insincerity 484
Integrity 491
Truthfulness 1000

Singing 902
Music 614
Opera 655

Single-Mindedness 903
Narrowness 620

Skepticism 904
Doubt, Religious 265
Unbelief 1004

Skill
Ability 1

Slander 905
Accusation 5
Gossip 394
Reputation 804
Scandal 846

Slang
Language 524

Slavery
Servitude 889

Sleep 906
Bed 73
Dreams 266
Morning 605
Night 633

Slowness 907
Delay 231
Haste 411
Speed 926

Slyness
Craftiness 200

Smallness 908
Great and Small 400
Largeness 525
Obscurity 649
Pettiness 693
Trifles 996
Unimportance 1012

Smelling
Senses 882

Smiling
Laughter 526

Smoking
Tobacco 982

Smugness 909
Complacency 156

Snobbery 910
Class 135
Preference 725
Pride 733
Rank 780
Society, Polite 914

Snow 911
Seasons 854

Socialism 912
Communism 150
Government 395

Social Work
Humanitarianism 433

Society 913
Anarchy 36
Aristocracy 52
Civilization 133
Class 135
Government 395
Institutions 487
Middle Class 587
The People 682
State 930

Society, Polite 914
Company 152
Manners 563
Parties 672
Snobbery 910

Solace
Consolations 180
Sympathy 960

Soldiers
The Military 588

Solemnity
Seriousness 886

Solitude 915
Alienation 30
Aloofness 31
Loneliness 547
Privacy 736

Sons 916
Boys 97
Parenthood 670

Sophistication 917
Cosmopolitanism 193
Experience 321

Sorrow 918
Mourning 610
Suffering 946
Unhappiness 1011
Weeping 1052

Soul 919
Spirituality 927

Sound
Music 614
Noise 636
Senses 882

Sour Grapes 920
Contempt 185
Disappointment 249

South
North and South 638

Space 921
The Heavens 415
Moon 603
Universe 1017

Spain and Spaniards 922

Speaking 923
Brevity 98
Clarity 134
Communication 149
Conversation 188
Eloquence 283
Language 524
Listening 543
Public Speaking 763
Silence 898
Tact 961
Words 1064

Specialists 924
Scholars and Scholarship 848
Vocations 1037

Spectacles 925

Spectators
Audience 59
Observation 650

Speech
Conversation 188
Free Speech 364
Public Speaking 763
Speaking 923

Speed 926
Haste 411
Slowness 907

Spirit
Mind 590
Spirituality 927

Spirituality 927
Contemplation 183
The Intangible 490
Materialism 569
Mind and Body 589
Monasticism 601
Mysticism 616
Saints and Sainthood 840

Spontaneity 928
Enthusiasm 293
Impulsiveness 461
Vitality 1036
Whim 1053

Sports 929
Fishing 348
Hunting 438
Physical Fitness 696
Play 703
Riding 821
Walking 1041

Spring
Seasons 854

Stars
The Heavens 415

Starting
Beginning 75

State 930
Church and State 127
Citizens 132
Government 395
Nation 621
Society 913

Statesmen and Statesmanship 931
Diplomats and Diplomacy 247
Politics and Politicians 711

Statistics 932

Status 933
Conformity 171
Rank 780

Stealing 934
Corruption 191
Crime 204

Stereotypes 935
Conformity 171

Stinginess 936
Gifts and Giving 384
Misers 595

Stock Market
Investment 503

Stoicism 937
Endurance 287
Resignation 806

Storytelling 938
Fiction 344
Writing and Writers 1069

Strangers
Foreigners and Foreignness 358

Strategy 939
Method 585

Strength 940
Courage 195
Weakness 1047

Strife
Discord 252

Strikes
Unions 1013

Stubbornness
Obstinacy 652

Study
Learning 532

Stupidity 941
Dullness 270
Folly 354
Fools 356

Stupidity *(cont.)*
IGNORANCE 447
INTELLIGENCE 493

Style 942
ELEGANCE 282
GRAMMAR 398
WRITING AND WRITERS 1069

Subtlety 943
CLEVERNESS 139
CRAFTINESS 200

Suburbs 944
CITIES 131
THE COUNTRY 194

Success 945
ACHIEVEMENT 6
AMBITION 33
CONQUEST 173
FAILURE 329
PROSPERITY 750

Suffering 946
ADVERSITY 17
INJURY 476
PLEASURE 704
PLEASURE AND PAIN 705
SELF-PITY 877
SORROW 918
UNHAPPINESS 1011
WEEPING 1052

Sufficiency 947
EXCESS 312
MODERATION 598
SATISFACTION 845

Suicide 948
SELF-DESTRUCTION 866

Suitability 949
TIMELINESS 979

Summer
SEASONS 854

Sun 950
CLIMATE 140
THE HEAVENS 415

Superficiality 951
ARTIFICIALITY 54
PROFUNDITY 740

Superiority 952
EXCELLENCE 311
MERIT 584
NOBILITY 635

Supernatural 953
GHOSTS 383
MIRACLES 592

Superstition 954
BELIEF 78

Surfeit
EXCESS 312

Surprise 955
CREDULITY 202
WONDER 1063

Survival 956
DEFENSE 229
ENDURANCE 287
NUCLEAR POWER 641
WEAPONS 1049

Suspicion
DISTRUST 259

Swearing 957
CURSING 212
OATHS 643

Switzerland and the Swiss 958

Symbols and Symbolism 959
MEANING 573
SACRAMENT 836

Sympathy 960
CONFIDENCES 169
PITY 698
UNDERSTANDING OTHERS 1008

Tact 961
RUDENESS 830

Talent 962
ABILITY 1
EXCELLENCE 311
GENIUS VS. TALENT 377

Talking
SPEAKING 923

Taste 963
ELEGANCE 282
PREFERENCE 725

Taxes 964
BUDGET 101
ECONOMICS 277

Teaching 965
EDUCATION 279
LEARNING 532

Technology 966
INVENTION 502
NUCLEAR POWER 641
SCIENCE 849
TWENTIETH CENTURY 1001

Teen-agers
YOUTH 1071

Television 967

Temper, Bad 968
ANGER 39
GOOD NATURE 392
TEMPERAMENT 969

Temperament 969
EMOTIONS 284
GOOD NATURE 392
PERSONALITY 687
TEMPER, BAD 968

Temperance 970
DRINKING 268
INTEMPERANCE 494
MODERATION 598

Temptation 971
BRIBERY 99
CORRUPTION 191
SIN 900

Thanks
GRATITUDE 399

Thanksgiving Day
HOLIDAYS 420

Theater 972
ACTORS 11
COMEDIANS 144
COMEDY 145
DANCING 215
MOVIES 611
OPERA 655
TRAGEDY 987

Theft
STEALING 934

Theology 973
GOD 387
RELIGION 797

Theory 974
ACTION 9
FACTS 328
PHILOSOPHERS AND PHILOSOPHY 694
SCIENCE 849

Thief
STEALING 934

Things
OBJECTS 646

Thinking
THOUGHT 975

Thought 975
AFTERTHOUGHT 24
IDEAS 443
INTELLECTUALS AND INTELLECTUALISM 492
INTELLIGENCE 493
MIND 590
PHILOSOPHERS AND PHILOSOPHY 694
REASON 785
REVERIE 818

Threat 976
DANGER 216

Thrift 977
EXTRAVAGANCE 324

Time 978
ETERNITY 302
LIFE, STAGES OF 540
TRANSIENCE 990

Timeliness 979
DELAY 231
PREMATURENESS 727
PUNCTUALITY 765
SUITABILITY 949

The Times
ERA 298

Timidity 980
BOLDNESS 92

Timidity *(cont.)*
CAUTIOUSNESS 112
EVASION 304
FEAR 343
HUMILITY 435

Tipping 981

Tiredness
FATIGUE 341

Titles
NAMES 619

Tobacco 982

Today
PRESENT 729

Togetherness 983
ALOOFNESS 31
COMMUNITY 151
COMPANY 152
INTIMACY 499

Tolerance 984
CHARITY 120
INTOLERANCE 500
KINDNESS 519

Totalitarianism 985
GOVERNMENT 395
TYRANNY 1002

Touch
SENSES 882

Tourism
TRAVEL 992

Trade
BUSINESS AND COMMERCE 104
VOCATIONS 1037

Tradition 986
ANTIQUITY 42
CLASSICS 136
CUSTOM 213
ICONOCLASM 441
PAST 676

Tragedy 987
COMEDY 145
THEATER 972

Training 988
DISCIPLINE 250
EDUCATION 279
GROWTH AND DEVELOPMENT 404

Traitors
TREASON 993

Tranquility 989
COMPOSURE 160
CONTENTMENT 186
PEACE 681

Transience 990
CHANGE 117
ETERNITY 302
MORTALITY 606
TIME 978

Translation
LANGUAGE 524

Transportation 991
AIRPLANES 28
AUTOMOBILES 64

Travel 992
AIRPLANES 28
AUTOMOBILES 64
HOTELS 429
PLACE 699
SAILING 839
TRANSPORTATION 991

Treason 993
BETRAYAL 79

Treaties 994
APPEASEMENT 46
COMPROMISE 162
CONCILIATION 167
INTERNATIONAL RELATIONS 498

Trees 995

Trickery
CRAFTINESS 200
DECEPTION 224
STRATEGY 939

Trifles 996
GREAT AND SMALL 400
THE MUNDANE 612
PETTINESS 693
SMALLNESS 908
UNIMPORTANCE 1012

Triviality
BANALITY 68
TRIFLES 996

Trouble
ADVERSITY 17

Trust 997
BETRAYAL 79
DISTRUST 259

Truth 998
ERROR 299
FALSEHOOD 331
PARADOXES 668
TRUTH AND FALSEHOOD 999
TRUTHFULNESS 1000

Truth and Falsehood 999
TRUTHFULNESS 1000
ERROR 299
FALSEHOOD 331
TRUTH 998

Truthfulness 1000
FALSEHOOD 331
FRANKNESS 362
HONESTY 425
SINCERITY 901
TRUTH 998
TRUTH AND FALSEHOOD 999

Trying
EFFORT 281

Turn
ALTERNATION 32

Twentieth Century 1001
THE ABSURD 3
ERA 298
NUCLEAR POWER 641
TECHNOLOGY 966
WORLD 1067

Tyranny 1002
FORCE 357
IMPERIALISM 458
POWER 719
REPRESSION 801
REVOLUTION 819
SERVITUDE 889
TOTALITARIANISM 985

Ugliness 1003
BEAUTY 72

Unbelief 1004
BELIEF 78
DOUBT, RELIGIOUS 265
FAITH 330
RELIGION 797
SKEPTICISM 904

Uncertainty 1005
CERTAINTY 115
INDECISION 465
INSECURITY 482
SKEPTICISM 904

Unconsciousness 1006
CONSCIOUSNESS 175
MIND 590
UNREASON 1020

Understanding 1007
INTELLIGENCE 493
INTUITION 501
KNOWLEDGE 522
MIND 590
PERCEPTION 683
SENSIBILITY 883
SYMPATHY 960
UNDERSTANDING OTHERS 1008
THE UNKNOWN 1019
WISDOM 1060

Understanding Others 1008
BACKGROUND 67
OTHERS 663
PERCEPTION 683
PITY 698
SYMPATHY 960
UNDERSTANDING 1007

Unemployment 1009

Unfairness
INJUSTICE 477

Unfulfillment 1010
FRUSTRATION 366
POTENTIAL 717

Unhappiness 1011
DISCONTENT 251
HAPPINESS 409
SORROW 918
SOUR GRAPES 920
SUFFERING 946

Unhappiness *(cont.)*
WEEPING 1052

Unimportance 1012
EXPENDABILITY 320
GREAT AND SMALL 400
INDIVIDUALITY 469
THE MUNDANE 612
OBSCURITY 649
PETTINESS 693
SMALLNESS 908
TRIFLES 996

Unions 1013
WORKERS 1066

Uniqueness 1014
DIVERSITY 260
INDIVIDUALITY 469
ORIGINALITY 662

United Nations 1015
INTERNATIONAL RELATIONS 498

Unity 1016
BROTHERHOOD 100
COMMUNITY 151
COOPERATION 190
DIVERSITY 260

Universe 1017
THE HEAVENS 415
SPACE 921
WORLD 1067

Unkindness 1018
CRUELTY 209
KINDNESS 519

The Unknown 1019
KNOWLEDGE 522
UNDERSTANDING 1007

Unreason 1020
REASON 785
UNCONSCIOUSNESS 1006

Unselfishness 1021
GENEROSITY 375
HUMANITARIANISM 433
SELFISHNESS 874
SERVICE 887

Unwillingness 1022
WILLINGNESS 1057

Usefulness 1023
PRACTICALITY 720
SERVICE 887
USELESSNESS 1024

Uselessness 1024
USEFULNESS 1023

Utility
USEFULNESS 1023

Utopia 1025
IDEALISM 442
REFORM 790

Valor
COURAGE 195

Value 1026
APPRECIATION 47

Vanity 1027
CONCEIT 166
PRETENSION 732
PRIDE 733
SELF-DECEPTION 864
SELF-ESTEEM 871
SELF-IMPORTANCE 873
SELF-LOVE 876

Vegetarianism 1028
FOOD 355

Vengeance
RETRIBUTION 815
REVENGE 817

Venice 1029
ITALY AND ITALIANS 509

Vice 1030
CRIME 204
SIN 900
VIRTUE 1033
VIRTUE AND VICE 1034
WICKEDNESS 1055
WRONGDOING 1070

Victory
CONQUEST 173

Viewpoint
ATTITUDE 58
PERSPECTIVE 689

Vice-Presidency 1031
PRESIDENCY 730

Violence 1032
AGGRESSION 26
FORCE 357
KILLING 518
REBELLION 786
WAR 1042

Virtue 1033
GOODNESS 393
INTEGRITY 491
MORALITY 604
RIGHT 822
VICE 1030
VIRTUE AND VICE 1034

Virtue and Vice 1034
VICE 1030
VIRTUE 1033

Vision 1035
PERCEPTION 683
SIGHT 897

Visiting
HOSPITALITY 428

Vitality 1036
ENTHUSIASM 293
JOIE DE VIVRE 513
SPONTANEITY 928

Vocations 1037
ABILITY 1
EXCELLENCE 311
TRAINING 988
WORK 1065

Voting 1038
CITIZENS 132
DEMOCRACY 233
GOVERNMENT 395
POLITICS AND POLITICIANS 711

Vows
PROMISES 743

Vulgarity 1039

Waiting 1040
EXPECTATION 318
HOPE 427
IMPATIENCE 456
PATIENCE 677

Walking 1041
PHYSICAL FITNESS 696
SPORTS 929

Wandering
RESTLESSNESS 812
TRAVEL 992

Wants
DESIRES 238
NEED 625

War 1042
CONQUEST 173
DEFEAT 228
DEFENSE 229
DISCORD 252
FIGHTING 345
KILLING 518
THE MILITARY 588
NUCLEAR POWER 641
PACIFISM 665
PEACE 681
STRATEGY 939
VIOLENCE 1032
WAR, CIVIL 1043
WEAPONS 1049

War, Civil 1043
WAR 1042

Washington, D.C. 1044

Wastefulness 1045
EXTRAVAGANCE 324

Water 1046
RAIN 778
RIVERS 824
SEA 853

Weakness 1047
FAULTS 342
IMPOTENCE 459
LIMITATIONS 542
STRENGTH 940
TIMIDITY 980

Wealth 1048
ACQUISITION 8
GREED 403
LUXURY 557
MONEY 602
POVERTY 718
PROPERTY 746
PROSPERITY 750

Weapons 1049
DEFENSE 229
NUCLEAR POWER 641
SURVIVAL 956
WAR 1042

Weather 1050
CLIMATE 140
RAIN 778
SEASONS 854
SNOW 911
SUN 950
WIND 1059

Weddings 1051
MARRIAGE 564

Weeping 1052
LAUGHTER 526
LAUGHTER AND TEARS 527
MOURNING 610
SORROW 918
SUFFERING 946
UNHAPPINESS 1011

West
EAST AND WEST 273

Whim 1053
IMPULSIVENESS 461
SPONTANEITY 928

Whites 1054
BLACKS 85
RACIAL PREJUDICE 775

Wickedness 1055
CORRUPTION 191
EVIL 307
SIN 900
TEMPTATION 971
VICE 1030
WRONGDOING 1070

Will 1056
CHOICE 124
PURPOSE 771
RESOLUTION 807
SELF-DETERMINATION 867
WILLINGNESS 1057

Willingness 1057
PURPOSE 771
UNWILLINGNESS 1022
WILL 1056

Wills and Inheritance 1058
WEALTH 1048

Wind 1059
SEASONS 854

Wine
DRINKING 268

Winners
ADVANTAGE 15
SUCCESS 945

Winter
SEASONS 854

Wisdom 1060
INTELLIGENCE 493
KNOWLEDGE 522
PROFUNDITY 740
PRUDENCE 755
UNDERSTANDING 1007

Wishes
DESIRES 238

Wit 1061
CLEVERNESS 139
COMEDY 145
HUMOR 436
LAUGHTER 526
PUNS 768
SARCASM 843
SATIRE 844

Women 1062
CHARM 121
COSMETICS 192
DRESS 267
FASHION 338
MASCULINITY AND FEMININITY 566
MEN AND WOMEN 581
MIRRORS 593
PERFUME 685

Wonder 1063
SURPRISE 955

Words 1064
BOOKS AND READING 93
CLARITY 134
DEFINITION 230
DICTIONARIES 244
GRAMMAR 398
LANGUAGE 524
LITERALNESS 544
MEANING 573
SPEAKING 923
WRITING AND WRITERS 1069

Work 1065
EFFORT 281
INCOMPETENCE 463
PAYMENT 680
REST 811
RETIREMENT 813
SPECIALISTS 924
UNEMPLOYMENT 1009
UNIONS 1013
VOCATIONS 1037
WORKERS 1066

Workers 1066
EXECUTIVES 315
UNEMPLOYMENT 1009
UNIONS 1013
WORK 1065

World 1067
EARTH 272
LIFE 539
TWENTIETH CENTURY 1001
UNIVERSE 1017

Worldliness
SOPHISTICATION 917

Worry
ANXIETY 43

Worship 1068
ADMIRATION 14
FOLLOWING 353
ICONOCLASM 441
IRREVERENCE 506
PRAYER 723
RELIGION 797

Worth
VALUE 1026

Writing and Writers 1069
AUTOBIOGRAPHY 62
BIOGRAPHY 81
BOOKS AND READING 93
CLARITY 134
CREATION AND CREATIVITY 201
FICTION 344
GRAMMAR 398
LANGUAGE 524
LITERATURE 545
POETRY AND POETS 708
STORYTELLING 938
STYLE 942
WORDS 1064

Wrong
ERROR 299
INJURY 476
INJUSTICE 477
WRONGDOING 1070

Wrongdoing 1070
CONSCIENCE 174
CORRUPTION 191
CRIME 204
DEEDS 227
EVIL 307
RETRIBUTION 815
SIN 900
VICE 1030
WICKEDNESS 1055

Yankees
AMERICA AND AMERICANS 34

Youth 1071
BOYS 97
CHILDREN 123
GIRLS 385
LIFE, STAGES OF 540
YOUTH AND AGE 1072

Youth and Age 1072
LIFE, STAGES OF 540
OLD AGE 653
YOUTH 1071

Zeal 1073
ENTHUSIASM 293
FANATICISM 335

Zen
RELIGION 798